ISBN 978-0-260-08717-1
PIBN 10926951

THE

AMERICAN AND ENGLISH

ENCYCLOPÆDIA

OF

LAW.

COMPILED UNDER THE EDITORIAL SUPERVISION OF

JOHN HOUSTON MERRILL,

Late Editor of the American and English Railroad Cases and the American and English Corporation Cases.

VOLUME XVIII.

NORTHPORT, LONG ISLAND, N. Y.:
EDWARD THOMPSON COMPANY, LAW PUBLISHERS.
1892.

MADE BY THE
WERNER PRINTING & LITHO. CO.
AKRON, OHIO.

PARTIAL LIST OF CONTRIBUTORS, VOL. XVIII.

Party Wall, ...	ELMER G. SAMMIS, of the New York City Bar.
Patent Law, ...	MARK WILKS COLLET, of the Philadelphia Bar.
Payment, ...	EVERETT W. PATTISON, of the St. Louis Bar.
Pedigree, ...	THOMAS J. MICHIE, of the Editorial Staff Am. & Eng. Encyc. of Law.
Penalties, ...	D. M. MICKEY, of the Editorial Staff Am. & Eng. Encyc. of Law.
Pensions, ...	D. M. MICKEY, of the Editorial Staff Am. & Eng. Encyc. of Law.
Perpetuities, ...	PHILIP H. GOEPP, of the Editorial Staff Am. & Eng. Encyc. of Law.
Perpetuities (Accumulations), . .	J. CLAUDE BEDFORD, of the Philadelphia Bar.
Personal Property, ...	JOHN H. INGHAM, of the Philadelphia Bar.
Pews in Churches, ...	THOMAS J. MICHIE, of the Editorial Staff Am. & Eng. Encyc. of Law.
Pilots, ...	D. M. MICKEY, of the Editorial Staff Am. & Eng. Encyc. of Law.
Pleading, ...	GEORGE WHARTON PEPPER, of the Philadelphia Bar.
Pledge, ...	GEORGE F. WARREN, of the New York City Bar.
Police Power, ...	H. DENT MINOR, of the Editorial Staff Am. & Eng. Encyc. of Law.
Poor and Poor Laws, ...	D. M. MICKEY, of the Editorial Staff Am. & Eng. Encyc. of Law.
Poor Debtor, ...	WILLIAM M. McINNES, of the Boston Bar.
Postal Laws, ...	H. DENT MINOR, of the Editorial Staff Am. & Eng. Encyc. of Law.
Powers, ...	EVERETT W. PATTISON, of the St. Louis Bar.
Words and Phrases, ...	THOMAS J. MICHIE, of the Editorial Staff Am. & Eng. Encyc. of Law.

TABLE OF TITLES AND DEFINITIONS.

See index for numerous sub-titles and definitions contained in the notes.

THE

AMERICAN AND ENGLISH

ENCYCLOPÆDIA OF LAW.

PART PAYMENTS.—See FRAUDS, STATUTE OF, vol. 8, p. 736; LIMITATIONS OF ACTIONS, vol. 13, p. 748; PAYMENT.

PART PERFORMANCE.—See FRAUDS, STATUTE OF, vol. 8, p. 738.

PARTY.—A person concerned or having or taking part in any affair, matter, transaction, or proceeding, considered individually; also a side or part, composed of one or more individuals.[1]—BURRILL.

1. Where a deed is executed by the attorney of the grantor, or officer or agent of a corporation, lawfully authorized, he is the party executing the same who may make the acknowledgment. Lovett *v.* Steam Sawmill Assoc., 6 Paige (N. Y.) 54.

A statute enacting that the holder of any negotiable note or bill may institute one suit against the whole or any number of the parties liable to such holder, but shall not institute more than one suit on such note or bill, should be construed as embracing all the makers as one party, all the endorsers as another, etc.; and, therefore, a suit and judgment upon such joint note or bill against one maker, or one endorsee, etc., will constitute a bar to any other suit against any other maker or endorser, etc. Archer *v.* Heiman, 21 Ind. 29.

A statute declaring every contract for the sale of lands void, unless subscribed by the party by whom such sale is to be made, or by the agent of such party lawfully authorized, requires signatures of all the vendors, when more than one unite in the contract of sale. Snyder *v.* Neefus, 53 Barb. (N. Y.) 63.

In article 10 of the treaty between the United States and Great Britain, August 9, 1842 (8 St. at Large, 576), providing that, on extradition, the expense of apprehension and delivery shall be borne by the "party who makes the requisition, and receives the fugitive," the word "party" refers to the contracting parties to the treaty, and has no reference to any question which may arise between the government which receives the fugitive and its officers or citizens. People *v.* Board of Supervisors, 8 N. Y. Supp. 752.

A Kentucky statute provides that in case of schism or division of the church, each *party* is to have the use of the church and appurtenances a part of the time in proportion to its members. *Held*, that where a number of members of a church congregation, although they constituted a majority thereof, dissolved their connection with the church of which they were members, and with the entire ecclesiastical body of which it is a member, and united with another and distant religious organization, they cannot be regarded as a "party" within the meaning of the statute. McKinney *v.* Griggs, 5

PARTY AGGRIEVED.—(See also AGGRIEVED, vol. 1, p. 449; APPEAL, vol. 1, p. 616; PERSON; NEW TRIAL and other titles under which the term is likely to occur.) The expression "party aggrieved" is not a technical expression; the words are ordinary English words, which are to have the ordinary meaning put upon them.[1]

Bush (Ky.) 401; s. c., 96, Am. Dec. 360.

Party or Privy.—Though a covenant that the covenanter has not done, permitted, or suffered anything preventing him from conveying, is not broken by his having assented to what he could not prevent, yet if the words "or been party or privy to" were added, there would be a breach in such a case (Hobson *v.* Middleton, 6 B. & C. 295; 9 D. & R. 249. Vh. Elph. 490; Dart, 885, 886; Sug. V. & P. 603, 604). Vh. Clifford *v.* Hoare, 43 L. J. D. P. 225; L. R., 9 C. P. 362; PERMIT.

Party Read as Person.—"Signed by the party to be charged therewith," §§ 4, 17, St. of Frauds;—"Party" there is not to be construed *party* as to a deed, but person in general (Sug. V. & P. 129, citing 3 Atk. 503).

"Party" read "Person" in Barlow *v.* Osborne, 6 H. L. Ca. 556.

See also *Re* Quartz Hill Gold Min. Co., 21 Ch. D 642; East London Waterworks Company *v.* Vestry of St. Matthew Bethnal Green, 17 Q. B. D. 484.

Boards for the equalization of taxes are not judicial tribunals and a nomenclature used in acts relating to them, though sometimes such as is used in reference to proceedings in courts is not there used in its technical legal sense. For instance, the word "party" as used in the Arkansas act, is used in its popular sense of "person" and not in its technical sense "party to a suit." Prairie Co. *v.* Matthews, 46 Ark, 383. See also Pulaski Co. Equalization Board Cases, 49 Ark. 518. See also PERSON.

1. Robinson *v.* Currey, 7 Q. B. Div. 470.

Section 1294 Code of Civil Procedure of New York, gives the right of appeal to the "party aggrieved." It was held, in Watts Campbell Co. *v.* Yuengling, 3 N. Y. Supp. 868, that, where judgment was rendered by request of defendant's attorney, defendant is not aggrieved, within the meaning of the statute.

The statute authorizing "the party aggrieved" to prosecute an action to set aside a judgment obtained by means of the fraud of the "prevailing party," held, not to authorize one not a party to the action in which such judgment was recovered, although he was directly interested in the results, to maintain such statutory action. Stewart *v.* Duncan, 40 Minn. 410.

An Indiana act provides that every telegraph company having lines within the State, etc., shall receive, dispatch, and transmit the same, with impartiality, in the order in which they are received, and that any person contravening the act shall be liable to the party aggrieved, to the penalty of $100. *Held*, that the act was penal in its nature and must be construed strictly, and that the sender alone is the party aggrieved within the meaning of the statute. Hadley *v.* Western Union Tel. Co., 115 Ind. 191; s. c., 21 Am. & Eng. Corp. Cas. 72.

A Minnesota statute provides that "a party aggrieved" may appeal from an order appointing an administrator. "This does not include a mere debtor of the estate. It refers to one, who as heir, devisee, legatee, or creditor, has what may be called a legal interest in the assets of the estate and their due administration." *In Re* Hardy, 35 Minn. 193.

In proceedings to vacate an assessment for a street improvement, it appeared that the partitioner purchased the land assessed after the work had been commenced and before the assessment had been laid. The land was conveyed to him, subject to any assessment to be made for the work, and the payment of the assessment was made to the principal consideration for the conveyance. *Held*, that it could not be said, as matter of law, that the petitioner was not a "party aggrieved" within the meaning of the statute; that to effect that result it is necessary that it should affirmatively appear that the legal owner cannot in any respect be injured by the assessment; that the conveyance imposed no liability upon the grantee beyond the payment of any legal assess-

PARTY-WALLS.—(See also EASEMENTS, vol. 6, p. 139; LATERAL AND SUBJACENT SUPPORT, vol. 12, p. 933.)

I. **DEFINITION.**—A party-wall, in the ordinary meaning of the term, is a wall between two adjoining owners, built at common expense and used for common advantage.[1] The term, however, may be used in four different senses: *First*, a wall of which the two adjoining owners are tenants in common;[2] *second*, a wall divided longitudinally into two strips, one belonging to each of the neighboring owners;[3] *third*, a wall which belongs entirely to one of the adjoining owners, but is subject to an easement or right in the other to have it maintained as a dividing wall between the two tenements;[4] *fourth*, a wall divided longitudinally into two

ment that might be made. Matter of Pennie, 108 N. Y. 365.

1. Abb. L. Dict. 252; Hiatt *v.* Morris, 10 Ohio St. 523; Koeing *v.* Haddix, 21 Ill. App. 53; Hammann *v.* Jordan, 9 N. Y. Supp. 423.

One of two adjoining owners of land in a city, who erects a wall over the boundary line under the ordinances of the city respecting party-walls, cannot claim the benefit of such wall as a party-wall, unless it be built of the width prescribed by the ordinance, and also be solid and free from any openings. Traute *v.* White (N. J.), 19 Atl. Rep. 196.

A dividing wall between two buildings in the city of Philadelphia owned by different parties, the foundation of which rest partly upon the ground of each is a party-wall. It is immaterial that the foundation is not equally laid upon the lot of each party, and that the wall itself, above the foundation, is wholly within the lot of one of the adjoining owners. Western Nat. Banks App. 102 Pa. St. 171; Gordon *v.* Milne, 10 Phila. (Pa.) 15. *Compare* Beaver *v.* Nutter, 10 Phila. (Pa.) 345.

2. Montgomery *v.* Masonic Hall, 70 Ga. 38; Brown *v.* Werner, 40 Md. 15; Orman *v.* Day, 5 Fla. 392; Sherred *v.* Cisco, 4 Sandf. (N. Y.) 480; Regina *v.* Copp, 17 Ont. Reps. (Can.) 738; Cubitt *v.* Porter, 8 Barn. & C. 257; Wiltshire *v.* Sidford, 8 Barn. & C. 259; Watson *v.* Gray, 14 Ch. Div. 192; Jones *v.* Read, 10 Is. R. C. L. 315; Standard Band of B. S. A. *v.* Stokes, 9 Ch. D. 68; 47 L. J. Ch. 554; 38 L. T. 672; 26 W. R. 492.

3. **In this case the owners are not tenants in common, even if the wall was erected at their joint expense;** Matts *v.* Hawkins, 5 Taunt. 20; **but where there has been a common user of the wall erected at the common expense, that, in the absence of any other evidence, is sufficient evidence for a jury to find that the wall is held by the two parties as tenants in common;** Cubitt *v.* Porter, 8 Barn. & C. 257; Standard Bank *v.* Stokes, 29 Ch. D. 68.

4. Rogers *v.* Sinsheimer. 50 N. Y. 646.

The term is so used in the English Metropolitan Building Act. 18 & 19 V. ch. 122, § 3; Knight *v.* Pursell, 1 Ch. 1 D. 412. **Such a wall may be a party-wall for some part of its height, and above that height the separate property of one of the adjoining owners;** Weston *v.* Arnold, 43 L. J. Ch. 123; 8 Ch. 1084; **and in same way such a wall may be**

moieties, each moiety being subject to a cross-easement in favor of the owner of the other moiety.[1]

II. **How Created.**—(*a*) Party Wall Agreements.—A wall may become a party wall by contract express or implied, by prescription or by statute.[2]

laterally a party-wall or such distance as it is used by both owners and no further; Knight *v.* Pursell, 11 Ch. D. 412.

1. "Land covered by a party wall remains the several property of the owner of each half, but the title of each owner is qualified by the easement to which the other is entitled of supporting his building by means of the half of the wall belonging to his neighbor." Ingals *v.* Plamondon *et al.* 75 Ill. 118. Gibson *v.* Holden, 115 Ill. 199; Wilcox *v.* Danforth, 5 Ill. App. 378; Nash *v.* Kemp, 49 How. (N. Y.) Pr. 522; Sherred *v.* Cisco, 4 Sandf. (N. Y.) 480; Partridge *v.* Gilbert, 15 N. Y. 601; Hendricks *v.* Stark, 37 N. Y. 106; s. c. 93 Am. Dec. 549; Brooks *v.* Curtis, 50 N. Y. 639; s. c. 10 Am. Rep. 545; Bloch *v.* Isham, 28 Ind. 37, s. c. 92 Am. Dec. 287; Hoffman *v.* Kuhn, 57 Miss. 746; 34 Am. Reps. 491; Burton *v.* Moffit, 3 Or. 29; Graves *v.* Smith, (Ala.) 6 So. Rep. 308; Sanders *v.* Martin, 2 Lea (Tenn.) 213; s. c. 31 Am. Rep. 598; Andrae *v.* Haseltine, 58 Wis. 395; s. c. 46 Am. Rep. 635. For a reference to the English cases see 5 Fisher Dig. 990 & seq.

Part Only May be Party Wall.—A deed conveyed to M. certain premises, extending to the west line of the west wall of a brick building upon the premises; so that it included the whole of the west wall; with the reservation that the owners of the ground on both sides should have the mutual use of the present partition wall. At that time there was a small one-story brick building on the lot adjoining on the west. Subsequently M.'s grantors conveyed this other lot to P., who tore down this small building, and erected one much higher, and extending further along on M.'s wall. *Held*, that the reservation in the deed to M. extended *only* to such portions of the west wall as were then used as a partition between the buildings, and that P. had no right to the mutual use of any other, or greater part of this west wall. Price *v.* McConnell, 27 Ill. 255. See also, Weston *v.* Arnold, 8 L. R. Ch. 1084; 43 L. J. Ch. 123; 22 W. R. 284.

Not an Incumbrance.—It is true that the erection of a party-wall creates a community of interest between neighboring proprietors, but there is no just sense in which the reciprocal easement for its preservation can be deemed a legal incumbrance upon the property. The benefit thus secured to each is not converted into a burden by the mere fact that it is mutual and not exclusive. Hendrick *v.* Stark, 37 N. Y. 106; s. c. 93 Am. Dec. 549; Butterworth *v.* Crawford, 3 Daly (N. Y.) 57; Mohr *v.* Parmelee, 43 N. Y. Super. Ct. 320 (*Compare* Giles *v.* Dugro, 1 Duer 331); Bertram *v.* Curtis, 31 Iowa 46; Weld *v.* Nichols, 17 Pick. (Mass.) 538.

A Party Wall a Dead or Solid Wall.—Windows.—Without an agreement between the owners of property allowing them, windows have no proper place in a party wall. This is evident from the uses and objects of party walls, with which use windows are inconsistent. St. John *v.* Sweeney, 59 How. Pr. (N. Y.) 175; Van Syckel *v.* Tryon, 6 Phila. (Pa.) 401; Rondet *v.* Bedell, 1 Phila. (Pa.) 366; Milne's App. 81 Pa. St. 54; Vollmer's App. 61 Pa. St. 118; Sullivan *v.* Grafford, 35 Iowa 531; Danenhauer *v.* Devine, 61 Tex. 480; Graves *v.* Smith, (Ala.) 6 So. Rep. 308; Weston *v.* Arnold, L. R. 8 Ch. App. 1084 s. c., 7 Eng. Rep. 572. *Compare* Pierce *v.* Lemon, 2 Houst. (Del.) 519. See Hart *v.* Kucher, 5 Serg. & R. (Pa.) 1.

Flues in Wall.—Where one owner of a party wall desired to close a flue in said wall which was necessary to the beneficial use of the other party, *Held*, that as the easement was apparent at the time the party seeking to close the flue obtained her interest in the wall, she could not interfere with the use of the flue by the other party. Ingalls *v.* Plamondon, 75 Ill. 118.

2. List *v.* Hornbrook, 2 W. Va. 340; Quinn *v.* Morse, 130 Mass. 317.

Party Wall Erected by Tenants.—When a party wall was erected by tenants for years, *Held*, that though the wall might be a party wall as between the tenants and adjoining owner, it would not bind the reversioner nor his grantee. Webster *v.* Stevens, 5 Duer (N. Y.) 553.

The owners of adjoining lots, especially in large cities, frequently enter into an agreement, which may or may not be under seal, whereby it is agreed that in the erection of a building either party may place the wall of his building so that it will stand partly on each lot, and that the other party will, when he uses the wall, contribute, proportionately to the cost of erection. An agreement so made constitutes the wall, when erected and used by the adjoining owners, a party-wall.[1]

1. The interest of the licensee in this wall, after it has been built, cannot be annulled by any revocation on the part of either the licensor or his grantee with notice. Wickenham *v.* Orr, 9 Iowa (1 With.) 253.

"Plaintiff and defendant, owning adjoining lots, entered into a parol agreement to jointly build a party wall, and in pursuance thereof built a portion of the wall, when defendant refused to proceed further. Whereupon the plaintiff, who had prepared materials and planned a building in reliance upon the performance of the agreement, proceeded to complete the wall after due notice to the defendant. *Held*, that the parol contract having been partly executed, the parties were estopped from denying the existence of the easement thereby created. Rindge *v.* Baker, 57 N. Y. 209, s. c. 15 Am. Reps. 475.

B. and M. agreed orally that B. who was about to erect a house should put the division wall one-half on the lot of each. The line was not defined but B. began to build on a supposed line. Subsequently a written agreement was entered into by the parties, embodying the terms of the oral agreement. When M. came to build it was found that the foundation was four inches too far over on his land. M. cut off the four inches causing injury to B. *Held*, that M. was liable for the damage because he had allowed B. to go on in good faith. Miller *v.* Brown, 33 Ohio St. 547.

Constructions of Party Wall Agreements.—If one agreed to build a party wall, resting half upon his own land and half upon the land of an adjoining land owner, furnishing the material and labor therefor, and such adjoining land owner agreed that, upon its completion, he would pay one-half of the cost thereof, and should own a joint interest therein, and have the right to use it whenever he desired to build upon his own land; and as the land of the adjoining owner did not extend as far north as the wall, it was agreed that the party erecting it should convey to him the small strip of land lying northward of where his land terminated, such contract was absolute and not conditional; the covenants therein were independent, and the breach of one did not relieve from the obligation of another. Therefore, a conveyance by the party building the wall was not a condition precedent to the enforcement of his claim against the adjoining owner for his proportion of the cost thereof. Ensign *v.* Sharp, 72 Ga. 708.

Where plaintiff purchased a lot of defendant, and agreed to erect a building thereon, and it was further agreed between them that when the defendant erected a building upon the adjoining lot he would construct, in connection with the plaintiff's building, a stairway to the second story, one-half of which should be on the ground of each party, and plaintiff, accordingly, built his wall 20 inches from the line, and defendant not only used the wall so built for the purpose of the stairway, but built into it in such a way as to support his own building, and in a way not demanded for the support of the stairway, then the wall became a party wall, and plaintiff was entitled to recover one-half the value thereof at the time defendant so used it, with interest at six per cent. Molony *v.* Dixon, 65 Iowa, 136 s. c., 54 Am. Rep. 1.

When Liability Accrues.—The plaintiff's lot was vacant. The defendant's lot was occupied by a building one story high, which was of brick on all sides except the one next the plaintiff's lot. On that side it was of wood, and rested by permission, on the plaintiff's land. The plaintiff's purpose was to erect a building on his own land which should be four stories high. In doing this, it would be necessary to remove the wooden side of the defendant's building, so as to make room for the partition wall located one-half on each lot. The parties thereupon agreed that either might build the wall, and that the other might at any time use as much of it as might choose "for the erection of any building" paying to the party erecting the wall the appraised value of so much of it as he shall then use. . . . The plain interpretation of the contract is that the defendant incurs no liability to pay for the value of the wall until he makes some use of it in the future erection of some building, or of some addition to the old one. Shaw *v.* Hitchcock, 19 Mass. 254.

Adjoining owners agreed that one should build a foundation partly on the land of each and that the other should pay for the portion on his premises when he should rebuild his house or sell. *Held*, that the executors of the party who built had no cause of action against the other party until rebuilt or sold and that the addition of a few feet to the front extending to the pavement was not "rebuilding." Elliston *v.* Morrison, 3 Tenn. Ch. 280.

The law will imply that payment is to be made within a reasonable time where no time is fixed for payment in an agreement to contribute toward the erection of a party wall. Rawson *v.* Bell, 46 Ga. 19.

Where it was agreed that "whenever B. or his assigns use said wall by erecting a building on the lot adjoining on the said A.'s, B. or his heirs or assigns putting the joists of their building in said wall, then said A. or his heirs or assigns is to receive one-half of the actual cost of the building of said wall from B. or his heirs or assigns." *Held*, that the use of the wall was the thing contracted for and that the wall having been used as a party wall it was immaterial that the joists of the building were not inserted in the wall. Greenwald *v.* Kappes, 31 Ind. 216.

Under an agreement that one party should pay for a party wall when used, the amount to be determined by appraisers, *Held*, that the plaintiff could not recover until such appraisment or the defendant had done something to prevent and that the demand for payment did not entitle the plaintiff to interest though defendant was using the wall. Thorndyke *v.* Wells Memorial Assoc. (Mass.) 16 N. E. Rep. 747.

It was agreed between owners of adjoining lots that T. should pay for one-half of a party wall when he should "make use" of it. When T. built, the building inspectors required him to line up to the party wall thus obliging him to build a new wall. The party wall, however, supported and added strength to T's wall. *Held*, that T. was liable under the agreement since he did "make use" of it. Kingsland *v.* Tucker, 44 Hun (N. Y.) 91.

A simple contract between adjoining owners recited that one of them had erected a wall on the line intended as a partition wall, and stipulated that whenever the other, his grantees, heirs or assigns, or other persons owning or controlling his lot, should desire to build in connection with said wall, they should first pay the builder one-half of its value. *Held*, that the builder had no title to the half of the wall on the other lot, the contract being a mere license, with an agreement to pay for use, and therefore he, and not his grantee, was entitled to the payment of half the value, when the owners of the adjoining lot desired to build. Behrens *v.* Hoxie, 26 Ill. App. 417.

Under an agreement between the owners of adjoining lots providing that one may build a party-wall resting one-half on each lot, and that the other should have the right of joining thereto on paying one-half its value, the one by whom the wall is built may be enjoined from placing therein doors or other openings, though there is neither allegation nor proof that the other ever intends to use the wall. Harber *v.* Evans (Mo.) 14 S. W. 750.

In an action in the New York city court, where adjoining owners agreed that one might build the wall and that the other might have the use of it on paying one-half its value, it was held that the mutual covenants furnished a sufficient consideration for the promise to pay, though the interest of the promisor in the land was small. Scott *v.* McMillan, 4 N. Y. Supp. 434.

In Kingsland *v.* Tucker, 115 N. Y. 574, it was adjudged that the construction of an independent wall, which touched a party-wall at several points, but which was of sufficient strength to stand alone and fulfilled all the requirements of a wall, was not such a use of a party-wall as was contemplated by an agreement between adjoining owners that one should use the party-wall built by the other for the support of the beams of a house then standing on the lot, but whenever he should make use of the wall in the erection of a new building he should pay for one-half of its value.

Enforcement.—Where there is an

(*b*) Implied Grant.—When one owning adjoining lots erects a wall partly on each lot and then conveys to others, the wall so erected becomes party-wall by implication of law and the different owners have mutual easements of support in that portion of the wall standing on the other's land. [1]

agreement between the owners of adjoining lots, and one of them covenants with the other that he will build a wall, for a certain distance, half on one lot, and half on the other, and upon his failure so to do, the other party enters on the ground, and begins to extend the wall to the point agreed, the latter will not be restrained by injunction.

But where the distance to which the wall is to be extended is a disputed point, and the proper construction of the covenant is an open question, and the extension will render necessary the cutting away of part of the building, thus causing a permanent injury thereto, a temporary injunction will be issued, to continue in force until the question of right can be settled. Rector etc. *v*. Keech, 5 Bosw. (N. Y.) 691.

1. If a person erects two buildings on adjoining lots of his own, with a party wall between them, and subsequently conveys to different persons, each has an easement in the party wall standing on the land of the other for the support of his house. The party disturbing the other in the enjoyment of that easement, even though he do it for the purpose of improving his own lot, and with the greatest diligence, is responsible for damages occasioned to the other by such disturbance. And if he employ another person in the work, both employer and employed are liable for the trespass. The building injured being in possession of a tenant for a term of years, it was held, that the owner could recover only the injury to the building, and nothing for interruption of use and occupation. Eno *v*. Del Vecchio, 6 Duer (N. Y.) 17. Partridge *v*. Gilbert, 15 N. Y. 601, s. c., 69 Am. Dec. 632; Webster *v*. Stevens, 5 Duer (N. Y.) 553; Rogers *v*. Sinsheimer, 50 N. Y. 646; Henry *v*. Koch, 80 Ky. 391; s. c., 44 Am. Rep. 484; Doyle *v*. Ritter, 6 Phila. (Pa.) 577; Goldsmith *v*. Starring, 5 Mackey (D. C.) 582; Richards *v*. Rose, 9 Exch. 218; Murly *v*. McDermott, 8 Ad. & E. 138; Watson *v*. Gray, L. R. 14 Ch. Div. 192.

"Two houses and two lots were originally owned by one Stranahan. He had erected the two houses thereon, and made the wall in question a party wall between them. By two deeds, both dated and recorded at the same time, he conveyed the easterly lot to the grantor of the plaintiff and the westerly lot to the grantor of the defendant, by a description which is claimed by the plaintiff to have so located the line of division as to throw the whole of the wall and two inches of land on the westerly side thereof within the boundaries of the plaintiff's lot. Assuming that the plaintiff is right in his construction of the description, yet the wall being a party wall and at the time of the conveyance serving as a support for the beams of the house erected on the lot now of the defendant, the premises now owned by the plaintiff were charged with the servitude of having the beams of that house supported by the wall in question, and of having the wall stand and serve as an exterior wall for the defendant's house, so long at least as the building should endure. . . . Consequently, on the severance of the two properties, the grantee of the westerly lot acquired an easement corresponding with the servitude to which the easterly lot was subject." Rogers *v*. Sinsheimer, 50 N. Y. 646.

Where the use of a wall was not such as would give a subsequent grantee notice of its use as a party-wall and it is shown that he did not have notice of any right to use. *Held*, that when an adjoining owner erected a brick building in the place of a frame shop of a light and temporary character he could not use the division wall as a party wall without making compensation. Heimbach's Appeal (Pa.) 7 Atl. Rep. 737.

Where the owner of adjoining lots, on each of which was a building with a common wall between them, mortgaged one of the lots, describing the division line as running "partly through the centre of a party-wall," it was held that on the foreclosure and sale of the mortgaged lot the common wall became a party-wall. Heartt *v*. Kruger, 56 Super. Ct. 382.

The owner of two adjoining city lots built a house upon each lot, each separated from the other by a brick wall,

(*c*) PRESCRIPTION.—The continuous use of a wall, by adjoining owners, as a party-wall for the prescriptive period, raises the presumption of a contract between the parties.[1]

(*d*) STATUTES.—In some of the states of the Union there are statutory regulations upon the subject of party-walls.[2]

one-half of which was on each lot, and subsequently conveyed the lots to different persons, each deed describing the boundary line between the houses as "a line running longitudinally through the centre of the partition wall between the houses"; and such wall stood unchanged as the partition wall between the houses for fifty years. *Held*, that the wall was a party-wall. Everett *v.* Edwards, 149 Mass. 588.

And so where A. and B. owned adjacent houses, and the wall was a common wall, and the common grantor of both had conveyed each house by a description which made the dividing line of the lots pass through the centre of the wall, though there was no reference to the wall, it was held that there was an implied grant of the party wall, putting on each the burden and privilege of a party wall. Carlton *v.* Blake, (Mass.) 25 N. E. Rep. 83.

1. An old wall from long *user*, in the absence of evidence, may be deemed a party-wall, presumptively, either from an agreement to that effect, or from its being built upon the line of the two lots for that purpose by the respective owners. Schile *v.* Brokhahns, 80 N. Y. 614; Eno *v.* Del Vecchio, 4 Duer (N. Y.) 53.

A and B owned adjoining houses, the party wall of which was supported by an arch, enclosing a passage-way; B pulled down his house and part of the arch on his estate, in consequesce of which the partition wall fell. In an action of trespass on the case by A against B, there was evidence that A had previously made alterations in his house, and had inserted props under the arch after B's house had been taken down, but that the party wall was not weakened thereby, and it did not appear that A ever assented to the breaking of the arch. *Held*, that the right of support or easement in the ground of B set up by A, was of such a character that it must have originated in a grant, either actual or presumed, as matter of law, from the facts shown by the evidence in the case.

Held, also, that the uninterrupted enjoyment and use of the alley and alley walls for the period shown by the evidence, raised the presumption of mutual grants for such enjoyment for the time the two houses should be capable of safe and beneficial occupation, and that B had no authority or right to interfere with the alley or walls, without the consent of A, unless he could do so without injury to his possession. Dawling *v.* Hennings, 20 Md. 179; Brown *v.* Werner, 40 Md. 15; McLaughlin *v.* Cecconi, 141 Mass. 252, S. C. 5, N. E. Rep. 261: Orman *v.* Day, 5 Fla. 385, Sanders *v.* Marton, 2 Lea (Tenn.) 213; S. C. 31 Am. Rep. 599; Cubitt *v.* Porter, 8 Barn & C. 257; Wiltshire *v.* Sidford, 8 Barn & C. 257; Brown *v.* Windsor, 1 Cromp. & J. 20.

2. In Iowa, South Carolina, Mississippi, Louisiana, and the District of Columbia, one who in a city or town erects a brick building (in Louisiana a stone building) may set half the partition wall on the adjoining lot.

In Iowa and Louisiana, one so erecting a wall cannot compel contribution, but if the adjoining owner uses the wall when he builds, he must pay for one-half of it; and this he must do in South Carolina and Mississippi.

So in Iowa and Louisiana, if the person first building places the wall wholly on his own land, the other who uses it must pay half the value of the strip, and, this being done, they own the wall in common. Under the statutes of these two states a partition wall is presumed to be a wall in common.

Under the Mississippi statute, a party-wall paid for by both cannot be removed by either without the consent of the other. For a general reference to the statutes bearing upon this subject see Stimson's American Statute Law, p. 325. O'Daniel *v.* Bakers' Union, 4 Houst. (Del.) 488; Zugenbuhler *v.* Gilliam, 3 Iowa 391; Thomson *v.* Curtis, 28 Iowa 229; Bertram *v.* Curtis, 31 Iowa 46; Molony *v.* Dixon, 65 Iowa 136, S. C. 54 Am. Rep. 1; Graihle *v.* Honn, 1 La. Ann. 140; Florence *v.* Maillot, 22 La. Ann. 114; Irwin *v.* Peterson, 25 La. Ann. 300; Irwin *v.* Morse, 130 Mass. 317; Ingles *v.* Bringhurst, 1 Dall. (Tex.) 341; Beaver *v.* Nutter, 10

III. **When a Party-Wall Ceases to be Such.**—A wall ceases to be a party-wall with the state of things which created it and there is no obligation upon either of the adjoining owners to continue the use of a wall as a party-wall after such a change of circumstances, or to unite in the construction of a new wall after the destruction of the old one.[1]

Phila. (Pa.) 345; Evens *v.* Jayne, 23 Pa. St. 34; Bell *v.* Bronson, 17 Pa. St. 363; Roberts *v.* Bye, 30 Pa. St. 375, S. C. 71 Am. Dec. 710; Child *v.* Napheys, 112 Pa. St. 504: Miller *v.* Elliott, 5 Cranch C. C. (U. S.) 543.

In such a case it was held that the building regulations of the District of Columbia, adopted in 1791, were to be construed strictly as imposing a burden in invitum on the land and did not authorize the making of windows in a party-wall. Corcoran *v.* Nailor, 6 Mackey (D. C.) 580.

The Prov. St. of 1692–3 (5 W. & M.) c. 13, §2, providing that any one building on his own land in Boston might set half his partition wall on his neighbor's land, and that the neighbor, when he should build, should pay for half of so much of the wall as he should build against, has never been in force in this Commonwealth. Wilkins *v.* Jenett, 139 Mass. 29.

Municipal Ordinances. — Power to pass ordinances to authorize the erection of party-walls has been held to include the power to authorize their erection upon the application of either owner, and without the consent of the other. Hunt *v.* Ambruster, 14 N. J. Eq. 208.

A municipal ordinance relating to party-walls has no application to internal walls dividing a building into separate shops and a conviction under such an ordinance for an alleged offence in the construction of internal walls will be quashed. Regina *v.* Copp, 17 Ont. Reps. (Can.) 738. See also, Marshall *v.* Smith, 8 L. R. C. P. 416; 42 L. J. M. C. 108; 28 L. T. 538.

1. The owners of adjoining buildings, connected by a party-wall resting partly upon the soil of each, are neither joint owners or tenants in common of the wall. Each is possessed in severalty of his own soil up to the dividing line, and of that portion of the wall which rests upon it; but the soil of each, with the wall belonging to him, is burdened with an easement or servitude in favor of the other, to the end that it may afford a support to the wall and building of such other. Each therefore, is bound to permit his portion of the wall to stand, and to do no act to impair or endanger the strength of his neighbor's portion so long as the object for which it was erected, to wit, the common support of the two buildings, can be subserved; and each will consequently be liable to the other for any damage sustained by a disregard of this obligation. But the obligation ceases with the purpose for which it was assumed, namely, the support of the houses of which the wall forms a part. If these houses, or either of them, are destroyed without fault upon the part of the owner, he is not bound to rebuild in exactly the same style and in exactly the same spot because his neighbor demands it. That this is true where the wall itself is swept away with the house, is settled by authority. It must be equally so where the wall alone remains. A wall is but a portion of a house, and the one is valueless without the other. To hold that as long as the wall stands the owner whose home has been destroyed is compelled to lose the use of his lot or to replace the destroyed with another of exactly the same pattern, is to sacrifice the greater to the less, and to impose in perpetuity a servitude which was assumed only for a specific purpose. . . . . We think the obligation is only that so long as the houses stand the owner of neither shall do anything to impair the property of the other, and either shall be at liberty to impair the property of the other, and either shall be at liberty to repair and keep in order the common wall; but when without the fault of either the houses are destroyed, the easement is at an end, and each becomes the owner in severalty of his own soil and of so much of the wall as stands upon it, with a perfect right to tear it down or dispose of it in any way he sees proper." Hoffman *v.* Kuhn, 57 Miss. 746 S. C. 34 Am. Reps. 491.

Sherred *v.* Cisco, 4 Sandf. Sup. Ct. (N. Y.) 480; Partridge *v.* Gilbert, 15 N. Y. 601; Antomarchi's Ex. *v.* Russell, 63 Ala. 356; s. c., 35 Am. Rep. 40.

IV. Rights, Duties and Liabilities of Adjoining Owners.—(*a*) General Statement.—In general each must so deal with the party-wall as not to impair any right which the other may have.[1]

It was held by the New York Court of Appeals in Heartt *v.* Cruger, 24 N. E. Rep. 841, where an owner of two adjoining city lots erected buildings thereon, with a party-wall between, and afterwards conveyed both lots to another, receiving back a mortgage upon one of them, in which the dividing line was described as running through the center of a party-wall, and where the defendant acquired title to this lot through a conveyance upon foreclosure of this mortgage, and mesne conveyances, and both buildings were afterwards destroyed by fire, so that only the foundation remained, that defendant's easement terminated with the destruction of the buildings.

By deed in fee, a grantee had the privilege of putting the wall for the third story of his house on the top of the adjoining wall of the grantor. Held, that the grantor and those claiming under him could not recover of the grantee the land on which the party wall stood, though all the building of the grantor, except this party-wall, had been burnt down. Brondage *v.* Warner, 2 Hill (N. Y.) 145.

Wall Destroyed Before One Party Had Built.—Adjoining owners agreed that one who was about to build should place the wall of his building one half on the land of the other, who should have the right to use it when he built on his lot. The wall was built as agreed but destroyed by fire before the other party built. Subsequently both built at the same time, erecting a new wall which was used as a party-wall. *Held*, that the one who built the first wall was not bound to rebuild it after its destruction, the original agreement would not apply to the second wall, and that both should bear the expense of building the second wall. Huck *v.* Flentye, 80 Ill. 258.

Where One Owner Desired to Change.—A and B built houses at the same time, and built a partition wall on the division line at joint expense, without any agreement as to its maintenance. After a peaceful occupancy of twenty-one years, A's grantee notified B's grantee, that he was about to pull down half the partition wall, in order to erect a better building, and against the objections of the latter, the former pulled down the half on his land, using due care, notwithstanding which the other's building fell. *Held*, that there was no cause of action. Hieatt *v.* Morris, 10 Ohio St. 523.

1. O'Daniel *v.* Bakers' Union, 4 Houst. (Del.) 488; Montgomery *v.* Masonic Hall, 70 Ga. 38; Moody *v.* McClelland, 39 Ala. 45; s. c., 84 Am. Dec. 770; Dowling *v.* Hennings, 20 Md. 179; s. c., 83 Am. Dec. 545; Hoffman *v.* Kuhn, 57 Miss. 746; Eno *v.* Del Vecchio, 4 Duer (N. Y.) 53; s. c., 6 Duer 17; Sherred *v.* Cisco, 4 Sand. Sup. Ct. (N. Y.) 480; Earl *v.* Beadleston, 42 N. Y. Superior Ct. 294; Webster *v.* Stevens, 5 Duer (N. Y.) 553; Sanders *v.* Martin, 2 Lea (Tenn.) 213; s. c., 31 Am. Rep. 598; Brown *v.* Windsor, 1 Cromp. & J. 20.

Plaintiff sold one-half his wall to one F to be used as a party wall, and F, in constructing his building entered into an agreement with a bank to erect a party wall on the other side of F's building. The bank constructed a very heavy vault and failed to put proper foundations under it, by reason of which the bank building settled, and the walls pressing against the building of F caused his building to press against and injure the building of the plaintiff. *Held*, in an action against the bank, that plaintiff, though he may have known in what manner the bank was constructing the foundations, did not in selling one half his wall to F, assume all risks of defective construction by the bank. Feige *v.* First Nat. Bank (Mich.) 24 N. W. Rep. 772.

Windows.—A contract for the erection of a party-wall which provides that the person on whose land it is to be partly built shall not "have the right to obstruct the light for any window" which the other party "shall build into said wall," gives such other party, by implication, the right to build windows in such wall. Grimley *v.* Davidson (Ill.) 24 N. E. 439.

Excavation—Support.—Under N. Y. Laws 1882, ch. 410, § 474, relating to excavations for building purposes in New York city, the duty of one making an excavation to preserve a wall from injury does not cease with the completion of the excavation. There must be also a support so that the wall

(*b*) ERECTION AND USE.—In the construction of a party-wall the one who builds it is under a duty to erect it in a proper and skillful manner, and if he fails to do so, he is liable for the resulting damage.[1]

"The use of a party-wall in its full unrestricted sence, embráces not only the use of the interior face or side of the wall, but also such use of it as is necessary to form a complete and perfect junction, in an ordinary good mechanical manner, between it and the other exterior walls of the house."[2]

(*c*) ALTERATION.—Either party is at liberty to make any change in a party-wall, by underpinning or increasing its height, that he sees fit, provided that, in so doing, he does not interfere with or impair the rights of the other owner. The party making the change is liable for any damage which may result therefrom.[3]

will "remain as stable as before." A contrary construction of the statute would be unreasonable. Bernheimer *v.* Kilpatrick, 53 Hun (N. Y.) 316.

The statute providing that one digging to a depth of more than 10 feet below the curb-line shall protect "party or other walls standing upon or near the boundary lines" does not require him to protect foundations of a stoop standing wholly on the land of the adjoining owner. Berry *v.* Todd, 14 Daly 450.

1. Gorham *v.* Gross, 125 Mass. 232; Glover *v.* Mersman, 4 Mo. App. 90.

One building a party-wall is bound to construct it of sufficient strength to sustain the one of which it forms a part and another of similar size and character. Gilbert *v.* Woodruff, 40 Iowa 320; Cutter *v.* Williams, 3 Allen (Mass.) 196.

2. Fettretch *v.* Leamy, 9 Bosw. (N. Y.) 511; Nash *v.* Kemp, 49 How. Pr. (N. Y.) 522.

"The land lying in front of a party-wall, between that and the line of the street, is to be exclusively enjoyed by its owners, freed from any burden of easement growing out of a simple party wall agreement, and is to be occupied by the adjoining owners according to the boundary lines of their lots for the construction of their fronts. Nash *v.* Kemp, 49 How. Pr. (N. Y.) 522.

Burton *v.* Moffitt, 3 Or. 29; Jamison *v.* Duncan, 12 La. Ann. 785; Marion *v.* Johnson, 23 La. Ann. 597; Moore *v.* Rayner. 58 Md. 411.

3. "The fairer view and the one generally adopted in legislative provisions on the subject, in this and other countries, is to treat a party-wall as a structure for the common benefit and convenience of both of the tenements which it separates, and to permit either party to make any use of it which he may require, either by deepening the foundations or increasing the height, so far as it can be done without injury to the other." The party making such change is obligated to observe care not to occasion injury to the adjoining owner, but the authorities generally seem to hold that in so far as he can use the party wall in the improvement of his own property, without injury to such wall or the adjoining property there is no good reason why he may not be permitted to do so." Field *v.* Leiter, 118 Ill. 17; Graves *v.* Smith (Ala.) 6 So. Rep. 308; Montgomery *v.* Masonic Hall, 70 Ga. 38; Phillips *v.* Bordman, 4 Allen (Mass.) 147; Quinn *v.* Morse, 130 Mass. 317; Matthews *v.* Dixey (Mass.) 22 N. E. Rep. 61; Everett *v.* Edwards (Mass.) 22 N. E. Rep. 52; Dowling *v.* Hennings, 20 Md. 179; s. c., 83 Am. Dec. 545; Brooks *v.* Curtis, 50 N. Y. 639; s. c., 10 Am. Rep. 545; Eno *v.* Del Vecchio, 4 Duer (N. Y.) 53; Schile *v.* Brokhahus, 80 N. Y. 614; Keller *v.* Abrahams, 13 Daly (N. Y.) 188; McGittigan *v.* Evans, 8 Phila. (Pa.) 264; Western Banks App. 102 Pa. St. 171; Sanders *v.* Martin, 2 Lea (Tenn.) 213; s. c., 31 Am. Rep. 598; Danenhauser *v.* Devine, 51 Tex. 480; Andrae *v.* Haseltine, 58 Wis. 395; s. c., 49 Am. Rep. 635; Bradbee *v.* Christ's Hospital, 4 Man. & G. 761; Major *v.* Park Lane Co., L. R., 2 Eq. 453. *Compare* McLaughlin *v.* Cecconi, 141 Mass. 252; Hieatt *v.* Morris, 10 Ohio St. 523; s. c., 78 Am. Dec. 280.

Where two adjoining houses are supported by a party-wall owned in common, and partly on the land of each owner, and which has been used as such for over twenty years, and one owner, without the consent of the other, removes the wall while it is suitable for the purposes for which it was erected, and erects a store on his lot, and a new party-wall, he will be liable to the other owner for any loss of rent, and the expense of repairs rendered necessary by such removal. Potter *v.* White, 6 Bosw. (N. Y.). 644; Schile *v.* Brokhahns, 80 N. Y. 614.

Tearing Down and Repairing.—If a party desiring to erect a building find the adjoining wall too weak to support the building which he is about to erect, he may tear down such wall and replace it with a stronger one. In so doing he must take great care to prevent any more damage than is absolutely necessary. Gettwerth *v.* Hedden, 30 La. Ann. pt. 1, 30; Cubitt *v.* Porter, 2 M. & R. 267; 8 B. & C. 257; Standard Bank of B. S. A. 9 Ch. D. 68; 47 L. J. Ch. 554; 38 L. T. 172; 26 W. R. 492; Fluger *v.* Hocken, 1 F. & F. 142.

The owner of the weak wall cannot under the circumstances mentioned above be compelled to replace the wall with a stronger one at his own expense Ferguson *v.* Fallons, 2 Phila. (Pa.) 168.

The principle that the builder of a new house may take down a party-wall that is insufficient for his purposes, and rebuild it at his own expense, is no invasion of the absolute right of property. Evens *v.* Jayne, 23 Penn. State R. (11 Harris,) 34.

The right granted to one co-proprietor of a wall in common by Civil Code La. art. 682, to demolish the old wall when found insufficient to bear the additional height and weight of a proposed new structure, and to build a new and thicker wall, adequate to support the new building as well as that of the neighbor, at his own expense, and taking the additional thickness from his own estate, is an absolute right, and the previous consent of the neighbor is unnecessary.

The right to build the new and thicker wall includes the right to demolish the old wall, to establish a sufficient foundation for the new one, to disturb the neighbors enjoyment, and to enter upon his property to the extent necessary for the principal right.

When one proprietor exercises the right granted by Civil Code La. article 682, his neighbor is bound to bear, without indemnity, the imconvenience and injury consequent thereon, so far as they are inseparable from the exercise of the right.

He is bound, at his peril, to replace the neighbor, at the end of the work, in a position every way equal to that which he occupied at its beginning, and to furnish him a new wall, fit and adequate to support his building, and for all shortcomings is liable to his neighbor in damages.—Heine *v.* Merrick (La.) 5 So. Rep. 760.

One owner of a party-wall may build it to a greater height to support an addition to his building, doing no injury to his co-owner; and the mere fact that in carrying up the wall he violates a building act will not render him liable to such co-owner.. Everett *v.* Edwards, 149 Mass. 588.

The owner of land on the north side of a city street conveyed two adjoining lots to different persons, each deed providing that the center of the easterly and westerly partition walls of the houses . . . first erected on the said land shall be placed on the division lines between the granted premises and the adjoining lots, and that the one who first built such a wall should be paid by the other, upon his using it, one half its cost. The grantee of the westerly lot erected a house on the front part thereof, with such a wall on the division line between the two, and built a wooden fence on the rest of the line. Subsequently, the grantee of the other lot proceeded to build a higher and deeper house thereon, conforming in all respects to a building act in force in the city, and for that purpose to carry up such wall and to extend it to the rear, necessarily displacing a part of the fence. *Held*, that such additions could rightfully be made without payment being first made of one-half the cost of the existing wall, if no injury was done thereto, and that a bill in equity to prevent their being made could not be maintained. Matthews *v.* Dixey, 149 Mass. 595.

So in Louisiana, one of the co-owners may demolish the old wall, if he finds it insufficient to support a contemplated new structure, and may rebuild on a wider foundation, and this he may do without the consent of the owner. Heine *v.* Merrick, 41 La. Ann. 194.

So under an agreement that the party-wall shall be used free of expense in the erection of a building, while conferring by implication a right to raise the height of the wall, does not authorize

(*d*) REPAIR.—Either owner may repair a party-wall, and after giving due notice of his intention to the adjoining owner he is not liable for any damage resulting from such repairs if they be made with dispatch and without negligence.[1]

(*e*) CONTRIBUTION.—There is no obligation to contribute to the original cost of erecting a party-wall in the absence of an agreement to do so,[2] but the law will sometimes imply an agree-

the insertion of windows or openings therein to the violation of a cross-easement of the adjoining owner. Graves *v.* Smith, 87 Ala. 450.

Where a wall between adjoining houses has for more than 21 years been used by their respective owners, it will be regarded as a party-wall, whether equally on the lot of each or not and one owner will not be liable in trespass for using it on rebuilding or for tearing it down, and replacing it when condemned by the building inspector. —McVey *v.* Durkin (Pa.) 20 Atl. Rep. 541.

It was held in Berry *v.* Todd, 14 Daly (N. Y.) 450, that while an owner of a party-wall might increase its thickness, length, or heighth within the limits of his own lot, he was liable for injury produced to his neighbor's premises.

A building owner who pulls down a party-wall under the authority of the Metropolitan Building Act, 1855, 18 & 19 Vict. c. 122, is not bound to protect by a boarding or otherwise the rooms of the adjoining owner which are left exposed to the weather during the time that the wall is being pulled down and rebuilt. Thompson *v.* Hill, 5 L. R. C. P. 564; 32 L. J. C. p. 264; 22 L. T. 820; 18 W. R. 1076.

See also Bryer *v.* Willis, 23 L. T. 463; 19 W. R. 102; Rex *v.* Hungerford Market Company, 2 N. & M. 340; Knight *v.* Pursell, 11 Ch. D. 412; 48 L. J. Ch. 395; 40 L. T. 391; 27 W. R. 817.

Changed Character of Adjoining House. —One party purchased a dwelling house with provision in the deed that division wall should be a party-wall, but with the understanding that the adjoining house was to be a private residence. Subsequently the adjoining house was altered into a family hotel and in making such alterations the owner raised the party-wall. Application for injunction was made to restrain any addition to the wall for the purposes intended. *Held*, that though the wall might be raised for the purpose of improving the adjoining house as a private residence, it could not be done to change the character of the house, because the other house was purchased subject to the party-wall easement with the understanding that it should be a party-wall between first class residences only. Musgrave *v.* Sherwood, 60 How. Pr. (N. Y.) 339.

Contribution not Condition Precedent. —Payment by the party seeking to enlarge the wall of his share of the costs of the original wall is not a condition precedent to the exercise of his rights therein.—Matthews *v.* Dixey (Mass.) 22 N. E. Rep 61.

Lineal Extensions.—Where one owner built a party-wall some distance back from the street line and it so remained for fifty years after the adjoining owner had built upon his lot. *Held*, that the first builder could not extend the party-wall to the street line without the consent of the adjoining owner. Duncan *v.* Hunbest, 2 Brewst. (Pa.) 362.

See Matthews *v.* Dixey (Mass.) 22 N. E. Rep. 61.

1. Moore *v.* Rayner, 58 Md. 411; Hoffman *v.* Kuhn, 57 Miss. 746; Crashaw *v.* Sumner, 56 Mo. 517; Patridge *v.* Gilbert, 15 N. Y. 601; s. c., 69 Am. Dec. 632; Schile *v.* Brokhahns, 80 N. Y. 614; Sherred *v.* Cisco, 4 Sandf. (N. Y.) 480; Eno *v.* Del Vecchio, 4 Duer (N. Y.) 53; s. c., 6 Id. 17; Sanders *v.* Martin, 2 Lea (Tenn.) 213; s. c., 31 Am. Rep. 598.

2. Preiss *v.* Parker, 67 Ala. 500; Antomarchi *v.* Russell, 63 Ala. 356; s. c., 35 Am. Reps. 40; Orman *v.* Day, 5 Fla. 385; McCord *v.* Herrick, 18 Ill. App. 423; Wilkins *v.* Jewett, 139 Mass. 29; Sherred *v.* Cisco, 4 Sandf. (N. Y.) 480; Sanders *v.* Martin, 2 Lea (Tenn.) 213; s. c., 31 Am. Rep. 598.

Where a party has built a house wholly upon his own lot and his neighbor subsequently erected a house on the adjoining lot and made use of the wall of the adjoining house. *Held*, that the builder of the second house was under no duty to contribute to the cost of erection of the wall so used in the absence of damage arising from

ment from the acts of a party.[1]

Express agreements to contribute to the cost of erection are, of course, binding upon the parties to such agreements,[2] but the

such use. Abrahams *v.* Krantler, 24 Mo. 68; s. c., 66 Am. Dec. 698; Bisquay *v.* Jennelot, 10 Ala. 245; s. c., 44 Am. Dec. 483.

1. Where one party erected a house with the wall party upon the land of the adjoining owner who had reason to know that the wall was being erected and that the party building it expected contribution toward its cost when used by the other party. *Held*, that the jury might properly imply an agreement to contribute from the failure of the owner of the vacant lot to disclaim any liability. Day *v.* Caton, 119 Mass. 513. See also Huck *v.* Flentye, 80 Ill. 258.

Statutes.—In these States where there are statutes providing that one who builds may erect his wall one-half upon the adjoining lot, no express agreement to contribute is necessary. See Lugenbuhler *v.* Gilliam, 3 Clark (Ia.) 391; Bertram *v.* Curtis, 31 Iowa 46; Pew *v.* Buchanan (Iowa) 34 N. W. Rep. 453; Thomson *v.* Curtis, 28 Iowa 229; Davis *v.* Grailhe, 14 La. Ann. 338; Costa *v.* Whitehead, 20 La. Ann. 341; Auch *v.* Labouisse, 20 La. Ann. 553; Marion *v.* Johnson, 23 La. Ann. 597; Irwin *v.* Peterson, 25 La. Ann. 300; Damaker *v.* Riley, 14 Pa. St. 435; Roberts *v.* Bye, 30 Pa. St. 375; s. c., 72 Am. Dec. 710; Beaver *v.* Nutter, 10 Pa. St. 345; Heimbach's Appeal (Pa.) 7 Atl. Rep. 737.

One who takes with Actual Notice of Agreement.—Where owners of adjoining premises made an agreement under seal for themselves, but not acknowledged and recorded, whereby one was to build a party wall, and the other, when he should use it in the construction of his building, was to pay half the cost of such wall, the effect of such agreement was to create cross-easements as to each owner, and a purchaser of the estate with notice, would take it burdened with the liability to pay one-half the cost of the wall whenever he should avail himself of its benefits.

One purchasing under a quit-claim deed, would not, without actual notice, be bound by such agreement. Sharp *v.* Cheatham, 88 Mo. 498; Keating *v.* Korfhage, 88 Mo. 524; Wickersham *v.* Orr, 9 Iowa 253.

Basis on which Contribution is to be Made.—The party seeking contribution for use of a party wall can recover one-half of the original cost of building only, not one-half of the present value. Florence *v.* Maillot, 22 La. Ann. 114; Auch *v.* Labonisse, 20 La. Ann. 553.

Additions Made Use of by Adjoining Owner.—Where one owner of a party wall had made additions thereto by underpinning and adding to height and subsequently these additions were made use of by the adjoining owner. *Held*, that the adjoining owner was under a duty to contribute one-half of the value of the additions used at the time they were used. Sanders *v.* Martin, 2 Lea (Tenn.) 213; s. c., 31 Am. Rep. 598.

Where defendant was sued for one-half the value of a wali which he had made use of as a party wall. *Held*, that he had no interest to question plaintiff's title further than to ascertain whether the claim could safely be paid to him. Irwin *v.* Peterson, 25 La. Ann. 300.

2. Ringe *v.* Baker, 57 N. Y. 209; s. c., 15 Am. Rep. 475; Musson's Appeal, 70 Pa. St. 26; Ensign *v.* Sharp, 72 Ga. 707; McCourt *v.* McCabe, 46 Wis. 596.

Where a Party Sells before Fulfilling Contract to Contribute.—A party contracted with an adjoining owner to pay for one-half of as much of a party-wall as he should use when he built upon his lot. Before building, however, he sold his lot to a third person thus putting it out of his power to fulfill his contract. *Held*, that he was liable in damages to the first party for not building and paying for a part of the wall within a reasonable time. Rawson *v.* Bell, 46 Ga. 19.

Parol Contracts.—An action may be maintained on an oral agreement between adjoining owners, that one shall erect a party wall and the other pay half the expense, if the wall is built before any revocation. But if the one agreeing to build receives from the other a notice of sale of his lot before commencing to build, this is a revocation of the license, and the action will not lie. Rice *v.* Roberts, 24 Wis. 461.

A parol contract to contribute toward the expense of erecting a party wall is binding on the parties to the

authorities conflict on the point as to whether an agreement to contribute made under seal is a covenant running with the land or a mere personal contract.[1]

The expense of making repairs, however, must be borne by both parties, provided such repairs are not in the nature of altera-

contract only. Joy *v.* Boston Penny Savings Bank, 115 Mass. 60; Jenkins *v.* Spooner, 5 Cush. (Mass.) 419; s. c., 52 Am. Dec. 739.

1. **Covenant Running with the Land.**—GRAY J., says: "The defendant having made use of the wall so built, cannot deny the plaintiff's right therein, and is bound to compensate her for such use, either according to the covenant in the deed from his grantors to the plaintiff, or according to the value of the wall. Richardson *v.* Toby, 121 Mass. 457. See also Savage *v.* Mason, 3 Cush. (Mass.) 500; Weld *v.* Nichols, 17 Pick. (Mass.) 538; Bronson *v.* Coffin, 108 Mass. 175; Maine *v.* Cumston, 98 Mass. 317; Rothe *v.* Ullman, 104 Ill. (Dis. in 115 Ill. 119); Platt *v.* Egleston, 20 Ohio St. 414; Thomson *v.* Curtis, 28 Iowa 229; Brown *v.* Pentz, 1 Abb. (N. Y.) App. Dec. 227 (Dis. in Scott *v.* McMillan, 76 N. Y. 141).

Party Wall Agreement Mentioned in Deed.—Where the deed of a party mentioned a party-wall agreement with adjoining owner. *Held*, that the grantee in the deed became liable to contribute under the covenant in the same manner as one assuming a mortgage, that the covenant became united with and formed part of the consideration for which the land was parted with. Stewart *v.* Aldrich, 15 N. Y. Sup. Ct. 241; Christie *v.* Mitchinson, 36 L. T., 621.

Agreement that Whole Wall Shall Remain Property of Builder Until Contribution by the Other Party.—Cases, therefore, where parties are, by the deed under which they take title, given one-half of a wall as a party-wall *when* or *upon condition* of making payment, and cases in which the owner of one lot has licensed the owner of the adjoining lot to build a wall for himself, resting one-half of it on each lot, and reserving the privilege of thereafter purchasing one-half the wall as a party-wall, are not analogous. In all such cases the title to the whole wall may be regarded as appurtenant to the lot of the builder, and so passing, by every conveyance of it, until a severance of the half by the payment of the purchase money. The sale of the half of the wall does not occur, nor the title to it pass, in those cases, until the payment is made; and so necessarily it is, constructively, a sale by the assignee of so much of the wall. His right to the purchase money is not because he is the assignee of a covenant running with the land, but because he is the vendor of so much of the wall. Gibson *v.* Holden, 115 Ill. 199. See also Tomblin *v.* Fish, 18 Ill. App. 439; Standish *v.* Lawrence, 111 Mass. 111.

Covenant a Personal Contract Only.—Cole *v.* Hughes, 54 N. Y. 444, s. c., 13 Am. Rep. 611; Hart *v.* Lyon, 90 N. Y. 663, Scott *v.* McMillan, 76 N. Y. 141; Gibson *v.* Holden, 115 Ill. 199; s. c., 56 Am. Rep. 146; affg. s. c., 16 Ill. App. 411; Behrens *v.* Hixie, 26 Ill. App. 417, Eckleman *v.* Miller, 57 Ind. 88; Bloch *v.* Isham, 28 Ind. 37; s. c., 92 Am. Dec. 287; Kells *v.* Helm, 56 Miss. 700.

L, the plaintiff, owned a lot in fee; C held a contract for the adjoining lot; L erected a building upon his lot, and, by agreement with C, placed half of the partition wall on C's lot; and when C built upon his lot, he, and those deriving title under him, were to pay L half the cost of the wall. C sold his interest to W, who obtained a deed from the owner of the fee. W then conveyed the lot to B, the defendant, allowing him a deduction of $100 from the purchase money, on account of the liability to L for half the wall. The deed to B contained this clause: "The above conveyance is executed subject to the wall now standing on the north line of said lot, the party of the second part assuming all the liability under or by reason of any contract now existing in respect to said wall. B erected a building on his lot, using the partition wall. *Held*, that this was not an agreement, in terms, to pay L, or to pay for the wall or any part of it, but was simply an undertaking to assume W's liability. The parties thereby intended only to limit W's covenant, and to save him harmless from all personal liability. *Held*, also, that the assignment from C of the contract for

tions made for the benefit of one party only.[1]

V. Remedies.—See note 2.

a deed, under which W obtained his title, imposed no personal liability upon him. *ib.*

Held, also, that the deduction from the purchase money was not an admission of W's liability, but merely indicated that the parties were in doubt, and that B took the risk, for that consideration. Lester *v.* Barron, 40 Barb. (N. Y.) 297.

1. List *v.* Hornbrook, 2 W. Va. 340; Campbell *v.* Mesier, 4 Johns. Ch. (N. Y.) 335; s. c., 8 Am. Dec. 570.

A was lessee for ninety-nine years of premises in the city of London, the whole of which were underlet by him for improved rents to persons who took each an interest in his portion of them greater than that of a tenant from year to year. *Held*, that A, was, nevertheless, liable, as an "adjoining owner," to contribute to the expense of repairing or rebuilding a party wall by his neighbor, under the metropolitan building act, 18 and 19 Vict., c. 122. Hunt *v.* Harris, 19 C. B. (N. S.) 13.

Where one of the proprietors of a dangerous party wall neglected to join in making repairs. *Held*, that he could not recover for any inconvenience occasioned by the other party making such repairs with due care and dispatch. Crawshaw *v.* Sumner, 56 Mo. 517; Partridge *v.* Gilbert, 15 N. Y. 601; s. c., 69 Am. Dec. 632.

Landlord and Tenant.—The tenant of a house covenanted in his lease to pay a reasonable share and proportion of supporting, repairing and amending all party-walls, and to pay all taxes, duties, assessments, and impositions, parliamentary and parochial, "it being the intention of the parties that the landlord should receive the clear yearly rent of £60 in net money, without any deduction whatever." During the lease the proprietor of the adjoining house built a party-wall between that house and the house demised under the statute. *Held*, that the tenant (not the landlord) was bound to pay the moiety of the expense of the party wall. Barrett *v.* Bedford (Duke), 8 T. R. 602.

A tenant under covenant to repair could not maintain an action under the statute, against his landlord, for a moiety of the expense of re-building a party-wall, which, being out of repair, the tenant pulled down and rebuilt at the joint expense of himself and the occupier of the adjoining house, to whom he had given the notice required by the statute, in his landlord's name, but without his authority. Pizey *v.* Rogers, R. & M. 357.

2. **Injunction.**—An injunction will be granted to restrain the owner of one-half of an ancient solid party-wall, long used for the support of buildings erected on each side of it, from cutting away a portion of its face, and erecting a new wall upon his own land at a distance of two inches from that portion of the ancient wall which is left standing, and connected with it by occasional projecting bricks and ties. Phillips *v.* Bordman, 4 Allen (Mass.) 147.

Remedy for Obstruction.—If one of two tenants in common of a party-wall excludes the other from the use of it by placing an obstruction on it, the only remedy of the excluded tenant is to remove the obstruction. Watson *v.* Gray, 14 Ch. D. 192; 49 L. J., ch. 243; 42 L. T. 294; 28 W. R. 438; 44 J. P. 537; Cubitt *v.* Porter, 2 M. & R. 267; 8 B. &. C. 257.

Choice of Remedies.—A proceeding at law, which set out a contract and sought to enforce it, for the purpose of recovering one-half of the cost of building the party-wall, was practically as effectual as a bill for the specific execution of the contract. Under it the plaintiff obtained a judgment for money due to him, while the defendant is protected in his right to the conveyance of the land he purchased. Ensign *v.* Sharp, 72 Ga. 708. See also Rindge *v.* Baker, 57 N. Y. 209; s. c., 15 Am. Rep. 475.

Damages.—Loss of profits, consequent upon such a trespass (in this case want of due care during alteration) are properly allowed as an item of damages, provided they are such as might naturally be expected to follow from the wrongful act, and are certain, both in their nature and in respect to their cause.

Where a business has been partially interrupted, because of the trespass, it is competent to prove upon the question of damages the amount of business previously done, and how much less the business was during the months when the injury occurred than during the corresponding months of the pre-

VI. **Practice and Procedure.**—See note 1.

PASS.—(See Tickets and Fares.)—1. In speaking of conveyances or sales, that is said to pass which is transferred from one party to the other, by force of the instrument or contract. Thus the title is said to pass by delivery of the deed; appurtenances are said to pass by a conveyance of a lot and buildings; and, by another form of the expression, the deed, the delivery, etc., is said to pass the lands or the goods.[2]

vious year, and the profits upon the business; and where the evidence is sufficient to show that the falling off of business was in consequence of the wrongful acts of the defendant, the loss of profits thus established is a proper item of damages. Schile *v.* Brokhahns, 80 N. Y. 614.

1. **Proper Parties.**—An administrator may properly bring an action on a party-wall agreement. Burlock *v.* Peck, 2 Duer (N. Y.) 90.

If a party-wall be used by devisees, an action for contribution must be brought against them and not against personal representatives. Keteltas *v.* Penfold, 4 E. D. Smith (N. Y.) 122.

In an action by one joint owner of a party-wall to compel the removal of an addition made by his co-owner, the mortgagees of defendant's lot are properly allowed to become parties defendant, as they are interested in resisting plaintiff's claim. Everett *v.* Edwards (Mass.) 22 N. E. Rep. 52.

Where a contractor was to obtain one-half of his compensation for building a party-wall from the adjoining owner, the legal title to the wall being in the builder. *Held*, that the builder was a trustee of the contractor, and if the builder sold with notice to the purchaser of the agreement, the purchaser becomes substituted as trustee and the contractor must bring his action in the name of the substituted trustee, but if the builder sold without notice to the purchaser, then the contractor must sue the builder for money had and received. Roberts *v.* Bye, 30 Pa. St. 375; s. c., 72 Am. Dec. 710.

Form of Action.—On a count for money laid out and expended, the plaintiff cannot recover one-half the value of a party-wall used by the defendant, but only one-half the money actually expended. Peck *v.* Day, 1 N. Y. Leg. Obs. 312.

An action on the case is the proper remedy by one tenant in common of a party-wall against his co-tenant, for an injury to the wall and the house of the plaintiff of which it forms a part, caused by the negligence and want of skill on the part of his co-tenant in making an excavation on his own land. Moody *v.* McClelland, 39 Ala. 45.

Trespass does not lie by one part owner or tenant in common against the other. Cubitt *v.* Porter, 2 M. & R. 267; 8 B. & C. 257; Wiltshire *v.* Sidford, 1 N. & R. 403.

Statute of Limitations.—The right to recover for a share of the money expended in building a party wall may be barred by the statute of limitations. List *v.* Hornbrook, 2 W. Va. 340.

Nature of Right to Contribution.—The right to recover under a covenant of contribution is a chose in action. McDonnell *v.* Culver, 8 Hun (N. Y.) 155.

The right to recover on a covenant of contribution is subject to attachment and execution. Davids *v.* Harris, 9 Pa. St. 501.

Sufficiency of Proof.—In order to recover a portion of the cost of a party-wall, an agreement to contribute must be proved, and it is not sufficient to allege that the agreement is not in the plaintiff's possession and therefore he cannot state its terms. An agreement must be shown by some proper averment that it contains provisions giving title to relief. McCord *v.* Herrick, 18 Ill. App. 423.

2. Abb. L. Dict. See generally Sales; Assignment, vol. 1, p 826; Conveyances, vol. 4, 123.

Rev. Stats. of Mo., § 2199, provides if the testator shall "by will pass any real estate to his wife, such devise shall be in lieu of dower." *Held*, that the word "pass" in the statute means devise and nothing else. Young *v.* Boardman, 97 Mo. 181. See also Gant *v.* Henley, 64 Mo. 162.

The mere endorsement and delivery of a bill of lading by way of pledge for a loan, does not "*pass* the property in the goods," in the sense of a statute,

2. Likewise a bill or resolution pending before a deliberative or legislative body is said to pass, or to be passed, when all the requisites to effect assent have been finally and formally given. A bill has passed the House or the Senate when the majority of either has voted for it, and this has been duly attested by the presiding officer. It may be said to have passed when both houses have voted for it, though it has not received executive approval, if the connection shows this is excluded; but generally, "to pass," or "passed," applied to a law, includes approval of the Crown, President, or Governor.[1]

3. When the offenses of forgery or counterfeiting are under discussion, to pass is to circulate, put forth, or utter the counterfeit or forged coin or instrument.[2]

PASS BOOKS.—(See ACCOUNT STATED, vol. 1, p. 124.)—A book used by merchants with their customers, in which an entry of goods sold and delivered to a customer is made. It is kept by the buyer, and sent to the merchant whenever he wishes to purchase any article. It ought to be a counterpart of the merchant's books, as far as regards the customer's account.[3]

PASSENGERS. — See CARRIERS OF PASSENGERS; SLEEPING CARS; TICKETS AND FARES.

PASSPORT.—(See also SEA LETTER).—1. A paper containing a permission from the neutral state to the captain or master of a ship or vessel to proceed on the voyage proposed. It usually contains his name and residence; the name, property, description, tonnage, and destination of the ship; the nature and quantity of the cargo; the place from whence it comes, and its destination,

which provides that every endorsee of a bill of lading, "to whom the property in the goods therein mentioned shall *pass*," shall have transferred to him all the rights of suit, and be subject to the same liabilities in respect of such goods, as if the contract contained in the bill of lading had been made with himself. Sewell *v.* Burdock, 10 App. Cas. 74.

1. Abb. L. Dict.

An act of the legislature is passed, only when it has gone through all the forms made necessary by the constitution to give it force and validity, as a binding rule of conduct for the citizen. Whether it receives the signature of the governor, or remains in his hands unreturned for ten days, or being vetoed, is carried by two-thirds of both houses, its passage is dated from the time it ceased to be a mere proposition or bill, and passed into a law. Whartman *v.* Philadelphia, 33 Pa. St. 208. See also Chumasero *v.* Potts, 2 Mont. 285.

2. Abb. L. Dict. See also COUNTERFEITING, vol. 4, p. 333.

"Now Passed."—An indictment alleged that an offence was committed on a certain day of September "now passed," it was held, that the time was not stated with sufficient certainty; as this does not in terms or by reference state any year. Commonwealth *v.* Flynn, 3 Cush. (Mass.) 525.

3. Bouvier's L. Dict. See generally ACCOUNT AND ACCOUNT STATED, vol. 1, p. 108, 110.

Among bankers, the term pass-book is given to a small book made up from time to time from the banker's ledger and forwarded to the customer; this is not considered as a statement of account between the parties; yet when the customer neglects for a long time to make any objection to the correctness of the entries he will be bound by them. Bouvier's L. Dict. See also ACCOUNT STATED, vol. 1, p. 117, n.; GIFTS, vol. 8, pp. 1345, 1349, n.

with such other matters as the practice of the place requires.[1]

2. A document granted in time of war to protect persons or property from the general operation of hostilities.[2]

3. In most countries of Continental Europe passports are given to travelers. These are intended to protect them on their journey from all molestation while they are obedient to the laws. The Secretary of State may issue, or cause to be issued in foreign countries by such diplomatic or consular officers of the United States, and under such rules as the President may prescribe, passports, but only to citizens of the United States.[3]

PATENT AMBIGUITY.—See AMBIGUITY, vol. 1, p. 527.

PATENT FOR LAND.—See PUBLIC LANDS.

1. Bouvier's L. Dict.

Passport and Sea-letter (Distinguished).—The former is a permission from a neutral state, to a master of a ship, to proceed on the voyage proposed, and usually contains his name and residence, the name, description and destination of the ship, with such other matters as the practice of the place requires. The sea-letter specifies the nature and quantity of the cargo, the place from whence it comes, and its destination. Sleght *v.* Hartshorne, 2 Johns. (N. Y.) 543. See also SEA-LETTER.

2. Bouv. L. D.; Wheat. Int. Law 475; 1 Kent 161.

3. Bouvier's L. Dict. See 1 Kent 162, 182; Urtetiqui *v.* D'Arbel, 9 Pet. (U. S.) 692.

"A passport, or sea-letter, is a well-known document in the usage of maritime commerce, and is defined to be a permission from a neutral state to the master of a ship to proceed on his proposed voyage, usually containing his name and residence, and the name, property, tonnage and destination of the ship. Although it evidences the permission of the State to navigate the seas, yet it does not, therefore, follow, that it must issue directly from the supreme power of the State; and some authority ought to be shown to support such a position. This erroneous notion, probably, arises from the practice of our own country, which is different from all other nations. Previous to the year 1793, no other documents were furnished to the merchant vessels of the United States but the certificate of registry and clearance; but the depredations upon our commerce having commenced with the European war which broke out in that year, a form of sea-letter was devised, and to give it greater effect, was signed by the President. On the 28th of November, 1795, a treaty was made with Algiers, by which a passport was to protect our vessels from capture by Algerian cruisers. By the act of the 1st of June, 1796, ch. 339, Congress authorized the Secretary of State to prepare a form, which, when approved by the President, should be the form of passport. Neither the treaty nor the law required the President's signature, but the form prepared was signed by the President, as the sea-letter had been. But this, our peculiar practice, forms no rule of conduct obligatory on others; and will not authorize us to give a more restricted meaning to the term used in a treaty than the general usage of nations will warrant. The word passport, thus used, is taken from the same word, signifying a permission given to individuals to remove from one place to another, and the documents are analogous. Vattel states, that, 'like every other act of supreme cognizance, all safe-conducts or passports flow from the sovereign authority; but the prince may delegate to his officers the power of furnishing them, and with this they are invested, either by express commission, or in consequence of the nature of their function. A general of an army, from the nature of his post, can grant them; and as they are derived, though mediately, from the same prince, all his generals are bound to respect them.' So also Blackstone speaks of the offense of violating passports or safe-conducts granted by the king or his ambassadors." The Amiable Isabella, 6 Wheat. (U. S.) 15.

PATENT LAW—See also DEDICATION, vol. 5, p. 395; INFRINGEMENT, vol. 10, p. 726; INVENTION, vol. 11, p. 780; LICENSE IN PATENT LAW, vol. 13, p. 557.

I. **Property Right in an Unpatented Invention.**—An unpatented invention vests in the discoverer an inchoate right to its exclusive use.[1] This right can be the subject of assignment[2] and other contracts and will be protected against those who, in breach of confidence, undertake to convert it to their own use or to betray it.[3] It can be made absolute by patenting it.[4] This right, however, does not extend to giving the inventor any rights against the public or those who, in good faith, acquire a knowledge of the invention.[5]

II. **Constitutional Provisions.**—Authority is given by the constitution to promote the progress of science and the useful arts, by securing to inventors for limited time the exclusive right to their discoveries.[6]

III. **Power of Congress Over the Grant of Patents.**—The constitution vests in Congress alone the right to grant patents for inventions.[7] This power may be exercised, as it usually is, by general laws; or Congress, in its discretion, may grant patents to inventors outside of the general law,[8] subject only to the limitation, that the grant must be to the inventor, or his legal representa-

1. Gayler *v.* Wilder, 10 How. (U. S.) 477; Evans *v.* Weiss, 2 Wash. (U. S.) 342; Jones *v.* Sewall, 6 Fish. Pat. Cas. 343.

2. Gayler *v.* Wilder, 10 How. (U. S.) 477; Clum *v.* Brewer, 2 Curt. (U. S.) 506; Wright *v.* Randel, 19 Blatchf. (U. S.) 495; s. c., 21 Pat. Off. Gaz. 493; s. c., 8 Fed. Rep. 591.

It makes no difference that the machine was imperfect at the time of sale, if the inventor agrees to perfect and patent it. Rathbone *v.* Orr, 5 McLean (U. S.) 131. Nor does it matter that it was made after rejection by an appeal from the Commissioner of patents. Gay *v.* Cornell, 1 Blatchf. (U. S.) 506. Even if no letters patent could be obtained. Hammond *v.* Mason etc. Organ Co., 92 U. S. 724; s. c., 5 Pat. Off. Gaz. 31.

3. Peabody *v.* Norfolk, 98 Mass. 452; Solomon *v.* Hertz, 35 Pat. Off. Gaz. 1109.

Equity will take jurisdiction to enjoin a breach of trust or contract similar to its protection of trade secrets. Peabody *v.* Norfolk, 98 Mass. 452. See also Injunctions, vol. 10, p. 949.

4. Gayler *v.* Wilder, 10 How. (U. S.) 477.

5. Peabody *v.* Norfolk, 98 Mass. 452; Marsh *v.* Nichols, 128 U. S. 605.

The courts are without jurisdiction to issue an injunction against an infringer of an unpatented invention. Rein *v.* Clayton, 37 Fed. Rep. 354. Disapproving a decision to the contrary in Butler *v.* Ball, 28 Fed. Rep. 754, where an injunction issued while the application for the patent was pending.

Several circuit courts have declared that the inventor has no right of property in the invention until patented. Sargent *v.* Seagrave, 2 Curt. (U. S.) 553; *Ex parte* Robinson, 4 Fish. Pat. Cas. 186; s. c., 2 Biss. (U. S.) 309; Wheaton *v.* Peters, 8 Pet. (U. S.) 591.

The supreme court has said the same thing but with the qualification: "No right of property . . . on which he can maintain suit." Brown *v.* Duchesne, 19 How. (U. S.) 183. Or "No exclusive right." Gayler *v.* Wilder, 10 How. (U. S.) 477.

6. Const. U. S., art. 1, § 8.

"Secure" does not mean the protection of an acknowledged legal right, but the creation of a new one. Wheaton *v.* Peters, 8 Pet. (U. S.) 591.

However, the "securing" is sufficiently the securing of a right to make it unlawful for the *United States* to appropriate it without compensation. James *v.* Campbell, 104 U. S. 356; United States *v.* Palmer, 128 U. S. 271.

7. Const. U. S., art. 1, §§ 6–8.

8. Blanchard *v.* Sprague, 3 Sumn. (U. S.) 535; s. c., 2 Story (U. S.) 164;

tives, and must not take away a right of property in existing patents.[1]

IV. Patent Office—1. Establishment.—The *United States* Patent Office is an office in the Department of the Interior, and is the place where all records, books, drawings, specifications and other papers relating to patents shall be safely kept and preserved. It must contain a library of such scientific works and periodicals, both American and foreign, as may aid the officers in the discharge of their duties. Various statutes provide for the distribution of copies of specifications and drawings of patents, for lithographing drawings and for reports.[2]

2. Officers.—The officers of the Patent Office are a Commissioner, an Assistant Commissioner, three Examiners-in-Chief and Examiners.[3] All officers of the Patent Office are incapable of acquiring or taking patents, except by descent, while employed in the office.[4]

3. Duties of Commissioner.—The Commissioner of Patents, under the direction of the Secretary of the Interior, superintends and performs all duties respecting the granting and issue of patents directed by law.[5]

Bloomer *v.* Stolley, 5 McLean (U. S.) 158.

1. McClurg *v.* Kingsland, 1 How. (U. S.) 202; s. c., 2 Robb Pat. Cas. 145.

The power of Congress to grant an extended or new term is plenary, and may be exercised by it in any way which may seem advantageous to it. Jordan *v.* Dobson, 4 Fish. Pat. Cas. 232; Blanchard *v.* Haynes, 6 West. L. J. 82; Blanchard's Gun Stock etc. Factory *v.* Warner, 1 Blatchf. (U. S.) 258; Bloomer *v.* Stolley, 5 McLean (U. S.) 158; Evans *v.* Robinson, 1 Carolina Law Rep. 209.

A patent may be granted by Congress for an invention which was in public use and enjoyed by the community at the time of the passage of the act granting the patent. Blanchard *v.* Sprague, 2 Story (U. S.) 164; s. c., 3 Sumn. (U. S.) 535; s. c., 1 Robb Pat. Cas. 724; Evans *v.* Jordan, 1 Brock (U. S.) 248; s. c., 9 Cranch (U. S.) 199; s. c., 1 Robb Pat. Cas. 20; Jordan *v.* Dobson, 4 Fish. Pat. Cas. 232; Blanchard's Gun-Stock etc. Factory *v.* Warner, 1 Blatchf. (U. S.) 258; Yuengling *v.* Schile, 12 Fed. Rep. 97; Bloomer *v.* McQuervan, 14 How. (U. S.) 539; McClurg *v.* Kingsland, 1 How. (U. S.) 202; s. c., 2 Robb Pat. Cas. 105; United States *v.* Burns, 12 Wall. (U. S.) 252; Cammeyer *v.* Newton, 94 U. S. 234; McKeever *v.* United States, 23 Pat. Off. Gaz. 1527.

2. U. S. Rev. Stat., §§ 475–496.

3. U. S. Rev. Stat., § 476. The succeeding paragraphs of the statute define the duties of the Commissioner.

Residence.—The official residence of the Commissioner of Patents is Washington, D. C. Butterworth *v.* Hill, 114 U. S. 128.

4. U. S. Rev. Stat., § 480.

Inventions by Patent Office Employees.—A person, however, who makes an invention before he comes into the government's employ, does not forfeit his right. He cannot take out a patent while he is an employee, but can so soon as his employment ceases, and no change in his *status* is caused by the fact of his employment. Page *v.* Holmes etc. Tel. Co., 17 Pat. Off. Gaz. 737; s. c., 1 Fed. Rep. 304; s. c., 5 Bann. & Ard. Pat. Cas. 165.

After the expiration of employment, a patent may be taken out even though the invention was made during the employment. And it may also be carried back to its actual date. Foote *v.* Frost, 3 Bann. & Ard. Pat. Cas. 607; s. c., 14 Pat. Off. Gaz. 860.

5. U. S. Rev. Stat., § 481. And has charge of all books, records, papers, models, machines and other things belonging to the Patent Office. Other statutory powers named in the immediately following sections are the classification of models, etc., and returning models in rejected cases.

4. Qualification and Duties of Examiners-in-Chief.—The Examiners-in-Chief must be persons of competent legal knowledge and scientific ability. Their duties are, on the written petition of the appellant, to revise and determine upon the validity of the adverse decisions of examiners upon applications for patents, and in interference cases.[1]

5. Practice of Patent Office.—The Commissioner of Patents, subject to the approval of the Secretary of the Interior, may, from time to time, establish regulations not inconsistent with law for the conduct of proceedings in the office.[2]

6. Caveats—(*a*) WHO MAY FILE.—Any citizen of the *United States*, or any alien who has resided in the *United States* one year next preceding the filing, and who has made oath of his intention to become a citizen, who makes any new invention or discovery, and desires further time to mature it, may file a caveat.[3] This contains a description of the device with its distinguishing features and a prayer for protection of the caveator's right until he shall have matured his invention.[4]

(*b*) DUTIES OF PATENT OFFICE.—Upon receipt of a caveat, it is filed in the confidential archives of the Patent Office and preserved in secrecy, and is operative for one year from its filing.[5]

(*c*) PURPOSE OF CAVEAT.—A caveat protects the inventor from the granting of any patent for an interfering application without his knowledge,[6] and gives the caveator, who has exercised due diligence in reducing his invention to practice, the right to carry back his invention to the date of the filing of the caveat.[7]

1. U. S. Rev. Stat., § 482. When required by the Commissioner, they shall hear and report upon claims for extensions and perform such other duties as he may assign to them.

2. U. S. Rev. Stat., § 483.

Authority of These Rules.—"Congress, in creating the Patent Office, has, by express legislation, given that office the power to enact rules for its conduct. Those rules, if within the powers of the office, are as authoritative as the laws of Congress itself within the limitation of its powers. United States *v.* Thacher, 7 Pat. Off. Gaz. 603.

3. U. S. Rev. Stat., § 4902.

4. U. S. Rev. Stat., § 4902.

5. U. S. Rev. Stat., § 4902. "And if application is made within one year by any other person for a patent with which such caveat would in any manner interfere, the Commissioner shall deposit the description, specification, drawings and model of such application in like manner in the confidential archives of the office, and give notice thereof, by mail, to the person by whom the caveat was filed. If such person desires to avail himself of his caveat, he shall file his description, specifications, drawings and model within three months from the time of placing the notice in the post-office in Washington, with the usual time required for transmitting it to the caveator added thereto; which time shall be endorsed on the notice.

6. Bell *v.* Daniels, 1 Fish. Pat. Cas. 372; s. c., 1 Bond (U. S.) 212; Allen *v.* Hunter, 6 McLean (U. S.) 303; American etc. Pavement Co. *v.* Elizabeth, 6 Fish. Pat. Cas. 424; Hildreth *v.* Heath, Cranch Pat. Dec. 96; s. c., vol. 2, Pat. Off. Rep. of 1847, p. 804.

A patent for the same invention as that described in the caveat granted during the pendency of the caveat is not void. Cochrane *v.* Waterman, Cranch Pat. Dec. 121.

The proper practice where a caveat is accidentally overlooked, and a patent granted to another during its pendency, is to grant a patent to the caveator. Phelps *v.* Brown, 1 Fish. Pat. Cas. 479; s. c., 4 Blatchf. (U. S.) 362.

7. American etc. Pavement Co. *v.*

7. **Petition.**—An inventor must make application in writing to Commissioner of Patents for a patent for his invention.[1]

8. **Model.**—In all cases which admit of representation by a model, a model of convenient size to exhibit the parts of the device,[2] and, when the invention is of a composition of matter, specimens of the ingredients and of the composition in sufficient quantity for experiment,[3] shall be furnished by the applicant if required by the Commissioner.[4]

9. **Oath**—*Contents.*—The applicant must make an oath, that he does verily believe himself to be the original and first inventor of the invention for which he solicits a patent, that he does not believe the same was ever before known or used, and shall state of what country he is a citizen.[5]

Officer to Administer.—In the *United States,* any officer authorized by law to administer oaths. When the applicant resides in a foreign country any minister, chargé d'affaires, consul, or commer-

Elizabeth, 6 Fish. Pat. Cas. 424; Phelps *v.* Brown, 1 Fish. Pat. Cas. 479; s. c., 4 Blatchf. (U. S.) 362; Allen *v.* Hunter, 6 McLean (U. S.) 303; Hoe *v.* Kahler, 12 Fed. Rep. 111.

It is not necessary for an applicant who desires to carry his invention back of the date of its perfection and reduction to practice, to have a caveat filed in order to be able to anticipate one who has in the meantime perfected his invention, or even obtained a patent. Hildreth *v.* Heath, Cranch Pat. Dec. 96; s. c., vol. 2, Pat. Off. Rep. of 1847, p. 804.

Caveat Not a Substitute for Diligence in Reduction to Practice.—A caveat will not protect an imperfect invention in perfecting which, due diligence has not been employed, against one who has subsequently made the same invention and reduced it to practice in a practical machine. Johnson *v.* Root, 1 Fish. Pat. Cas. 351. Nor against an intervening public use. Bell *v.* Daniels, 1 Fish. Pat. Cas. 372; s. c., 1 Bond (U. S.) 212.

Caveat Not an Admission that the Invention is Imperfect.—A caveat is not conclusive evidence that the invention is imperfect. A person may choose to file a caveat while he is going on and making improvements upon an invention which he has already completed so that it is of practical utility. Johnson *v.* Root, 1 Fish. Pat. Cas. 351.

Caveat by Sole Inventor Does Not Estop Him from Declaring Invention Joint.—A caveat in the name of a sole inventor does not estop him and others who have in fact made the invention, from carrying back the date of the joint invention to the date of the caveator's filing. Hoe *v.* Kahler, 12 Fed. Rep. 111.

1. U. S. Rev. Stat., § 4888; Hogg *v.* Emerson, 6 How. (U. S.) 437.

2. U. S. Rev. Stat., § 4891.

3. U. S. Rev. Stat., § 4890. But the fact that such was not in reality furnished when required, does not invalidate the patent. Tarr *v.* Folsom, 1 Holmes (U. S.) 313; s. c., 5 Pat. Off. Gaz. 92; s. c., 1 Bann. & Ard. Pat. Cas. 24; Badische etc. Fabrik *v.* Cochrane, 16 Blatchf. (U. S.) 155; s. c., 4 Bann. & Ard. Pat. Cas. 215.

4. U. S. Rev. Stat., §§ 4890, 4891.

5. U. S. Rev. Stat., § 4892.

The omission to take an oath does not affect the validity of the patent. Whittemore *v.* Cutter, 1 Gall. (U. S.) 429; s. c., 1 Robb Pat. Cas. 28; Crompton *v.* Belknap Mills, 3 Fish. Pat. Cas. 536; Dyer *v.* Rich, 1 Met. (Mass.) 180.

A recital in the patent that necessary oath was taken, is conclusive. Seymour *v.* Osborne, 11 Wall. (U. S.) 516; De Florez *v.* Reynolds, 14 Blatchf. (U. S.) 505; s.c., 3 Bann. & Ard. Pat. Cas. 292.

But a broadening of the application after the death of the patentee without a new oath by the administrator renders the patent void. Eagle Mfg. Co. *v.* West etc. Mfg. Co., 18 Blatchf. (U. S.) 218; s. c., 2 Fed. Rep. 774; s. c., 5 Bann. & Ard. Pat. Cas. 475; s. c., 17 Pat. Off. Gaz. 1504. The jurat need not be dated. French *v.* Rogers, 1 Fish. Pat. Cas. 133.

A change of words in a claim not broadening the invention but making it

cial agent holding commission under the *United States*, or notary public of the country.[1]

. *By Whom Taken.*—The oath is taken by the inventor if living,[2] otherwise by his administrator or executor.[3]

10. Specification—(*a*) GENERALLY.—The specification must contain a complete description,[4] but the drawings and models, if there are any, are to be taken into consideration in determining whether the specification is sufficiently clear,[5] though the scientific principles on which the device operates need not be known to the inventor or set forth in the specification.[6]

(*b*) SPECIAL RULES RELATING TO COMPOSITION OF MATTER.—The names of the ingredients, and, where the invention cannot be used to advantage without naming them, the proportions[7] must be stated.

(*c*) SPECIAL RULES RELATING TO COMBINATION.—In a combination the devices of which it is composed must be named, their mode of operation given and the new result pointed out.[8]

(*d*) CLEARNESS.—An inventor must file in the Patent Office a written description of his invention and the manner and process

clearer, does not require a new oath. Brush Electric Co. *v.* Julien Electric Co., 41 Fed. Rep. 679.

1. U. S. Rev. Stat., § 4892. Seymour *v.* Osborne, 11 Wall. (U. S.) 516.

2. U. S. Rev. Stat., § 4892.

3. U. S. Rev. Stat., § 4896.

4. Brooks *v.* Jenkins, 3 McLean (U. S.) 432; Dixon *v.* Moyer, 4 Wash. (U. S.) 68; s. c., 1 Robb Pat. Cas. 324; Head *v.* Stephens, 19 Wend. (N. Y.) 411; Wheeler *v.* Clipper Mower etc. Co., 6 Fish. Pat. Cas. 1; s. c., 10 Blatchf. (U. S.) 181; s. c., 2 Pat. Off. Gaz. 442.

A specification is not sufficiently clear which requires experiment and the solution of a problem before the device can be constructed. Webster Loom Co. *v.* Higgins, 105 U. S. 580; s. c., 16 Pat. Off. Gaz. 675.

5. Singer *v.* Walmsley, 1 Fish. Pat. Cas. 558; Earl *v.* Sawyer, 4 Mason (U. S.) 1; s. c., 1 Robb Pat. Cas. 491; Hogg *v.* Emerson, 6 How. (U. S.) 437; Burrall *v.* Jewett, 2 Paige (N. Y.) 134; Washburne *v.* Gould, 3 Story (U. S.) 122; s. c., 2 Robb Pat. Cas. 206; Holt *v.* Kendall, 26 Fed. Rep. 622.

But where a portion of the invention is not described at all in the specification, the fact that it is shown in the drawings is not sufficient. Gunn *v.* Savage, 30 Fed. Rep. 366.

6. Cahill *v.* Beckford, 1 Holmes (U. S.) 48; Andrews *v.* Cross, 19 Blatchf. (U. S.) 294; s. c., 8 Fed. Rep. 269.

A patentee is not confined to technical terms. Hovey *v.* Stephens, 3 Woodb. & M. (U. S.) 17; s. c., 2 Robb Pat. Cas. 567.

A patent which is available for one use named by the inventor, is not invalid because it is not applicable to another use. Phillips *v.* Risser, 26 Fed. Rep. 308.

Specification has reference both to the technical "specification" and "claim." Wilson *v.* Coon, 18 Blatchf. (U. S.) 532; s. c., 2 Fed. Rep. 611; s. c., 14 Pat. Off. Gaz. 482; Badische etc. Fabrik *v.* Higgin, 15 Blatchf. (U. S.) 290; s. c., 3 Bann. & Ard. Pat. Cas. 462; s. c., 14 Pat. Off. Gaz. 414.

7. Wood *v.* Underhill, 5 How. (U. S.) 1; s. c., 2 Robb Pat. Cas. 588; Jenkins *v.* Walker, 1 Holmes (U. S.) 120; s. c., 5 Fish. Pat. Cas. 347; s. c., 1 Pat. Off. Gaz. 359; Tyler *v.* Boston, 7 Wall. (U. S.) 327.

A general rule for proportions is sufficient. Wood *v.* Underhill, 5 How. (U. S.) 1; s. c., 2 Robb Pat. Cas. 588; Goodyear *v.* Wait, 3 Fish. Pat. Cas. 242; s. c., 5 Blatchf. (U. S.) 468; Francis *v.* Mellon, 5 Fish. Pat. Cas. 153; s. c., 1 Pat. Off. Gaz. 48.

Where the amount of an article in a compound can be varied without affecting the result except in degree, the direction to use "a small quantity" is sufficient. Brooker *v.* Dows, 3 Bann. & Ard. Pat. Cas. 518; s. c., 15 Pat. Off. Gaz. 570.

8. Seymour *v.* Osborne, 3 Fish. Pat.

of making, constructing, compounding and using it, in such full, clear, concise and exact terms as to enable any one skilled in the art or science to which it appertains or with which it is most nearly connected to make, construct, compound and use the same.[1]

Cas. 555; Parks *v.* Booth, 102 U. S. 96; s. c., 17 Pat. Off. Gaz. 1089.

1. U. S. Rev. Stat., § 4888. Lowell *v.* Lewis, 1 Mason (U. S.) 182; s. c., 1 Robb Pat. Cas. 131; Wintermute *v.* Redington, 1 Fish. Pat. Cas. 239; Brooks *v.* Jenkins, 3 McLean (U. S.) 432; Page *v.* Terry, 1 Fish. Pat. Cas. 298; Seymour *v.* Osborne, 3 Fish. Pat. Cas. 555; Teese *v.* Phelps, 1 McAll. (U. S.) 48; Westlake *v.* Cartter, 6 Fish. Pat. Cas. 519; s. c., 4 Pat. Off. Gaz. 636; Smith *v.* Prior, 2 Sawy. (U. S.) 461; s. c., 6 Fish. Pat. Cas. 469; Mitchell *v.* Tilghman, 4 Fish. Pat. Cas. 299; Magic Ruffle Co. *v.* Douglas, 2 Fish. Pat. Cas. 330; Page *v.* Ferry, 1 Fish. Pat. Cas. 298; Singer *v.* Walmsley, 1 Fish. Pat. Cas. 558; Hovey *v.* Stephens, 3 Woodb. & M. (U. S.) 17; s. c., 2 Robb Pat. Cas. 567; Gray *v.* James, 1 Pet. (C. C.) 394; s. c., 1 Robb Pat. Cas. 120; Judson *v.* Moore, 1 Bond (U. S.) 285; s. c., 1 Fish. Pat. Cas. 544; Wayne *v.* Holmes, 2 Fish. Pat. Cas. 20; s. c., 1 Bond (U. S.) 27; Winans *v.* Schenectady etc. R. Co., 2 Blatchf. (U. S.) 279; Grant *v.* Reymond, 6 Pet. (U. S.) 218; s. c., 1 Robb Pat. Cas. 604; Downton *v.* Yaeger Milling Co., 1 McCrary (U. S.) 26; s. c., 1 Fed. Rep. 199; s. c., 17 Pat. Off. Gaz. 106; Schneider *v.* Thill, 5 Bann. & Ard. Pat. Cas. 565.

A specification is sufficiently clear if expressed in terms intelligible to persons skilled in the art to which it belongs. Webster Loom Co. *v.* Higgins, 105 U. S. 580; s. c., 21 Pat. Off. Gaz. 2031; Stillwell etc. Mfg. Co. *v.* Cincinnati Gas etc. Co., 1 Bann. & Ard. Pat. Cas. 610; s. c., 7 Pat. Off. Gaz. 829; Shive *v.* Keystone Standard Watch Co., 41 Fed. Rep. 434; Pullman Palace Car Co. *v.* Wagner Palace Car Co., 38 Fed. Rep. 416; Libbey *v.* Mt. Washington Gas Co., 26 Fed. Rep. 757.

Thus where a patent is for a new manufacture, the law does not require that all its constituent parts be described. The description is sufficient, if it enables those who use it and deal in it to recognize it. Badische etc. Fabrik *v.* Higgin, 15 Blatchf. (U. S.) 290; s. c., 3 Bann. & Ard. Pat. Cas. 462; s. c., 14 Pat. Off. Gaz. 414.

Nor describe well known mechanical elements, sizes, proportional parts or absolute precision as to details. Brooks *v.* Jenkins, 3 McLean (U. S.) 432; Dorsey etc. Rake Co. *v.* Marsh, 6 Fish. Pat. Cas. 387; s. c., 9 Phila. (Pa.) 395.

But they must be able to practice it without experiment. Lockwood *v.* Faber, 27 Fed. Rep. 63.

Nor what is within the knowledge of any workman who may be employed to put up the apparatus or construct the machine. Page *v.* Ferry, 1 Fish. Pat. Cas. 298; Monce *v.* Adams, 12 Blatchf. (U. S.) 7; s. c., 7 Pat. Off. Gaz. 177; s. c., 1 Bann. & Ard. Pat. Cas. 126; Pearce *v.* Mulford, 102 U. S. 112; s. c., 18 Pat. Off. Gaz. 1223; Kneass *v.* Schuylkill Bank, 4 Wash. (U. S.) 9; s. c., 1 Robb Pat. Cas. 303; Mowry *v.* Whitney, 5 Fish. Pat. Cas. 513; Hancock Inspirator Co. *v.* Lally, 27 Fed. Rep. 88.

And the specification is sufficient if the invention can be constructed from it by the exercise of the mechanic's skill and judgment. Judson *v.* Moore, 1 Fish. Pat. Cas. 544; s. c., 1 Bond (U. S.) 285; Swift *v.* Whisen, 3 Fish. Pat. Cas. 343; s. c., 2 Bond (U. S.) 115; Mowry *v.* Whitney, 5 Fish. Pat. Cas. 513; Am Ende *v.* Seabury, 36 Fed. Rep. 593.

Even if it omit to describe a part which any workman would supply. Union Paper Bag Co. *v.* Nixon, 6 Fish. Pat. Cas. 402; s. c., 4 Pat. Off. Gaz. 31; Stillwell etc. Mfg. Co. *v.* Cincinnati Gas etc. Co., 1 Bann. & Ard. Pat. Cas. 610; s. c., 7 Pat. Off. Gaz. 829.

Processes.—A chemical process must be sufficiently clear to be intelligible to a chemist. Am Ende *v.* Seabury, 36 Fed. Rep. 593; s. c., 47 Pat. Off. Gaz. 1354.

Things That a Patentee Need Not Specify.—The kind of power to be employed or the means of applying it. Carr *v.* Rice, 1 Fish. Pat. Cas. 198; Lippincott *v.* Kelly, 1 West. L. J. 513; Waterbury Brass Co. *v.* Miller, 9 Blatchf. (U. S.) 77; s. c., 5 Fish. Pat. Cas. 48.

The material of which the parts of a machine are made. Bailey Washing etc. Mach. Co. *v.* Lincoln, 4 Fish. Pat. Cas. 379; Brooks *v.* Bicknell, 3 McLean (U. S.) 250; s. c., 2 Robb Pat. Cas. 118; Aiken *v.* Bemis, 3 Woodb. & M. (U. S.) 348; s. c., 2 Robb Pat. Cas. 644.

Persons to whom a patent specification must be clear and intelligible are

He must state the best mode that he knows.[1]

11. Claim—(*a*) CLAIM AND SPECIFICATION.—Where the claims are not ambiguous, they are to be taken to show the extent of the patent;[2] but where there is an ambiguity, reference to the specification may be made to remove the ambiguity.[3]

12. Drawing.—Where a drawing is essential, the applicant shall furnish one copy thereof and another, furnished by the Patent Office, shall be attached to the patent as part of the specification.[4]

practical workmen of ordinary skill in the particular business. Page *v.* Ferry, 1 Fish. Pat. Cas. 298; Smith *v.* O'Connor, 6 Fish. Pat. Cas. 469; s. c., 4 Pat. Off. Gaz. 633; Mabie *v.* Hasken, 2 Cliff. (U. S.) 507; Lippincott *v.* Kelly, 1 West. L. J. 513; Brooks *v.* Bicknell, 3 McLean (U. S.) 250; s. c., 2 Robb Pat. Cas. 118; Many *v.* Sizer, 1 Fish. Pat. Cas. 17; Mowry *v.* Whitney, 3 Fish. Pat. Cas. 157; Forbes *v.* Bardow Store Co., 2 Cliff. (U. S.) 379.

Acquainted with the state of the art. Tompkins *v.* Gage, 2 Fish. Pat. Cas. 577; s. c., 5 Blatchf. (U. S.) 268; Treadwell *v.* Parrott, 3 Fish. Pat. Cas. 124; s. c., 5 Blatchf. (U. S.) 370.

Defects of Clearness Which Have Been Held Insufficient to Invalidate a Patent.—Stating a fixed rule but stating that the rule can be departed from to some extent. Tilghman *v.* Werk, 1 Bond (U. S.) 511; s. c., 2 Fish. Pat. Cas. 229. Where the specification is referred to as embracing the substantial form of the invention. Brown *v.* Guild, 23 Wall. (U. S.) 181; s. c., 6 Pat. Off. Gaz. 392; s. c., 7 Pat. Off. Gaz. 739. Exaggerated eulogies, where the device is correctly described. Aultman *v.* Holley, 11 Blatchf. (U. S.) 317; s. c., 6 Fish. Pat. Cas. 534; s. c., 5 Pat. Off. Gaz. 3; Eames *v.* Cook, 2 Fish. Pat. Cas. 146.

Or any remote and extreme defect. Blanchard Gun Stock etc. Factory *v.* Warner, 1 Blatchf. (U. S.) 258; Swift *v.* Whisen, 2 Bond (U. S.) 115; s. c., 3 Fish. Pat. Cas. 343.

Defects Which Have Been Stated to Invalidate.—Statements tending to deceive, in regard to the actual construction of the thing claimed. Aultman *v.* Holley, 6 Fish. Pat. Cas. 534; s. c., 11 Blatchf. (U. S.) 317; s. c., 5 Pat. Off. Gaz. 3.

1. U. S. Rev. Stat., § 4888.

Magic Ruffle Co. *v.* Douglas, 2 Fish. Pat. Cas. 330; Page *v.* Ferry, 1 Fish. Pat. Cas. 298.

He need not state all the modes of carrying out his invention, if he states the best mode and adds that there are other modes which he considers protected by his patent. Carver *v.* Braintree Mfg. Co., 2 Story (U. S.) 432; s. c., 2 Robb Pat. Cas. 141; Dibble *v.* Augur, 7 Blatchf. (U. S.) 86; Blanchard *v.* Eldridge, 1 Wall. Jr. (C. C.) 337; 2 Robb Pat. Cas. 737; 2 Whart. Dig. 358.

Even if he does not describe the best way, his intention to do so is sufficient. Magic Ruffle Co. *v.* Douglas, 2 Fish. Pat. Cas. 330.

2. Hazelden *v.* Ogden, 3 Fish. Pat. Cas. 378; Blades *v.* Rand, 27 Fed. Rep. 93; Roemer *v.* Peddie, 27 Fed. Rep. 702.

A claim in letters patent cannot be enlarged beyond a fair construction of its terms. Haines *v.* McLaughlin, 135 U. S. 584; Day *v.* Fair Haven R. Co., 132 U. S. 98.

Peculiarities of construction will not be construed to be a distinctive portion of a claim in order to sustain their validity where neither the specifications nor claims suggest that such peculiarities are a distinctive feature of the invention. Bradley etc. Mfg. Co. *v.* Parker Co., 25 Fed. Rep. 907; Roemer *v.* Newmann, 26 Fed. Rep. 102; Western Electric Co. *v.* Ansonia Brass etc. Co., 114 U. S. 447.

3. Forbes *v.* Barstow Stove Co., 2 Cliff. (U. S.) 379; Morris *v.* Barrett, 1 Fish. Pat. Cas. 461; s. c., 1 Bond (U. S.) 254; Judson *v.* Moore, 1 Fish. Pat. Cas. 544; s. c., 1 Bond (U. S.) 285; Pitts *v.* Edmonds, 2 Fish. Pat. Cas. 52; s. c., 1 Biss. (U. S.) 168; Union Sugar Refinery *v.* Matthiesen, 3 Cliff. (U. S.) 639; s. c., 2 Fish. Pat. Cas. 600; Vogeley *v.* Noel, 18 Fed. Rep. 827.

Especially to the immediately associated parts of the specification. La Rue *v.* Western Electric Co., 28 Fed. Rep. 88.

But a claim repugnant to the specification, renders the patent void for ambiguity. Smith *v.* Murray, 27 Fed. Rep. 69.

4. U. S. Rev. Stats., § 4889.

The drawing is a portion of the patent.[1]

13. Examination.—After the filing of an application and the payment of the fees,[2] the Commissioner of Patents shall cause an examination to be made.[3]

14. Rejection and Amendment.—The Commissioner shall notify the applicant whenever any claim for a patent is rejected, and if, after such notice, the applicant persists in his claim for a patent, with or without altering[4] his specifications, the Commissioner shall order a re-examination.[5]

15. Delay in Patent Office.—A delay of more than two years after filing an application before preparing it for examination, or a failure to prosecute the application within two years after any action therein, causes the application to be abandoned[6] unless the delay be satisfactorily explained.[7] The application must have the final fee paid within six months of the time it was passed and

Filing drawings is not a condition precedent. French *v.* Rogers, 1 Fish. Pat. Cas. 133.

The drawings need not be working drawings, nor is it necessary that a machine made in accordance with them would work. American Hide etc. Co. *v.* American Tool etc. Co., 1 Holmes (U. S.) 503; s. c., 4 Fish. Pat. Cas. 284.

Nor need references be incorporated in the specification; if they are written on the drawings it is enough. Emerson *v.* Hogg, 2 Blatchf. (U. S.) 1; or even without references, where the nature of the machine can be understood without them. Brooks *v.* Bicknell, 3 McLean (U. S.) 250; s. c., 2 Robb Pat. Cas. 118; Washburne *v.* Gould, 3 Story (U. S.) 122; s. c., 2 Robb Pat. Cas. 206.

1. Emerson *v.* Hogg, 2 Blatchf. (U. S.) 1; Washburne *v.* Gould, 3 Story (U. S.)122; s. c., 2 Robb Pat. Cas. 206.

2. Each original application, except for design, $15. In design cases, appiication for three and one-half years, $10; seven years, $15; fourteen years, $30. Application for reissue, $30. U. S. Rev. Stats., § 4934.

3. U. S. Rev. Stats., § 4893.

It is not incumbent upon the Commissioner to have the examination made by any particular officer. Hall *v.* Commissioner, 2 McArthur Pat. Cas. 90; s. c., 7 Pat. Off. Gaz. 559.

4. The specificaton is always open to amendment until the matter is finally disposed of by granting of patent or otherwise. Singer *v.* Brannsdorf, 7 Blatchf. (U. S.) 521; Godfrey *v.* Eames, 1 Wall. (U. S. 317.

Amendments can be made independently of the suggestion of the Commissioner. Godfrey *v.* Eames, 1 Wall. (U. S.) 317.

The question whether new matter can be introduced into the specification depends upon whether such matter can be found in any part of the application. Singer *v.* Brannsdorf, 7 Blatchf. (U. S.) 521; Chicago etc. R. Co. *v.* Sayles, 97 U. S. 554.

But a portion of the invention, if divisible, can be removed from the original to a separate application. Suffolk Mfg. Co. *v.* Hayden, 4 Fish. Pat. Cas. 86.

An inventor may enlarge his claims from time to time by amendment to embrace all that was specified at the start. Railway etc. Mfg. Co. *v.* North Hudson R. Co., 24 Fed. Rep. 793.

5. U. S. Rev. Stats., § 4903. He must give the applicant briefly the reasons for such rejection, together with such information and references as may be useful in judging of the propriety of renewing his application or of altering his specification. U. S. Rev. Stats., § 4903.

6. U. S. Rev. Stats., § 4894.

It is the application, not the invention, that is abandoned, and the inventor may file a new application. Lindsay *v.* Steen, 10 Fed. Rep. 907; s. c., 21 Pat. Off. Gaz. 1613.

For abandonment of invention, see DEDICATION, vol. 5, p. 395.

7. U. S. Rev. Stats., § 4894. The judgment of the Commissioner on this question is conclusive. McMillan *v.* Barclay, 4 Brews. (Pa.) 275; s.c., 5 Fish. Pat. Cas. 189.

A mental disorder, incapacitating the inventor from business, is a sufficient ex-

allowed, in order to be issued;[1] but upon failure to do so, a second application may be filed within two years from the allowance of the first application[2] by any one interested.[3]

16. Testimony for Use in Patent Office.—Affidavits and depositions are taken under the rules established by the Commissioner of Patents, and before any officer authorized by law to take depositions to be used in the *United States* or State courts.[4] Subpœnas will be issued by the clerk of a *United States* court in the district to compel the attendance of witnesses,[5] obedience to which and giving testimony can be enforced in the same manner as in case of a subpœna to testify at court.[6]

17. Interference—(*a*) WHEN IT ARISES.—Whenever an application is made for a patent, which, in the opinion of the Commissioner,[7] would interfere with any pending application,[8] or with any unexpired patent,[9] he shall direct the primary examiner to proceed to determine the priority of invention.[10]

cuse for delay. Ballard *v.* Pittsburg, 12 Fed. Rep. 783.

1. U. S. Rev. Stats., § 4897.

2. U. S. Rev. Stats., § 4897. No person shall be held responsible in damages for the manufacture or use of any article or thing for which a patent was ordered to issue under such renewed application prior to the grant of a patent. And upon the hearing of a renewed applicaton preferred under this section, abandonment will be considered as a question of fact.

This does not prevent the defendants in a suit on a renewed patent, from setting up the defense of abandonment. United States etc. Rifle Co. *v.* Whitney Arms Co., 14 Blatchf. (U. S.) 94; s. c., 2 Bann. & Ard. Pat. Cas. 493; Marsh *v.* Commissioners, 3 Biss. (U. S.) 321; Woodbury etc. Planing Mach. Co. *v.* Keith, 101 U. S. 479; s. c., 17 Pat. Off. Gaz. 1031.

3. U. S. Rev. Stats., § 4897.

4. U. S. Rev. Stats., § 4905.

5. U. S. Rev. Stats., § 4906. The subpœna may direct the witness to be present at any time and at any place within forty miles of where it is served, and they are entitled to the same fees that are allowed witnesses at the *United States* courts. U. S. Rev. Stats., § 4907.

6. U. S. Rev. Stats., § 4908. But to bring him into contempt, his fees for coming and going, and one day's attendance must have been paid or tendered, or be compelled to disclose a secret invention.

7. The Commissioner is free to exercise his discretion in obtaining information of the interfering patents. Potter *v.* Dixon, 5 Blatchf. (U. S.) 160; s. c., 2 Fish. Pat. Cas. 381.

8. An interference can only be declared where an applicant claims that for which a prior application has been filed; not where a prior application is generic to the second and does not claim the species of the second. *Ex parte* Platts, 15 Pat. Off. Gaz. 827.

See Pentlarge *v.* New York Bung etc. Co., 20 Fed. Rep. 314.

9. An interference cannot be declared between a reissue broadening the application and a patent filed after the grant of the surrendered patent. *Ex parte* Mayall, 11 Pat. Off. Gaz. 1107.

10. U. S. Rev. Stats., § 4904.

Priority of invention is the only question that can be heard or determined on an interference. United States *v.* Thacher, 7 Pat. Off. Gaz. 603; Union Paper Bag Co. *v.* Crane, 1 Bann. & Ard. Pat. Cas. 494; s. c., 1 Holmes (U. S.) 429; s. c., 6 Pat. Off. Gaz. 801.

A decision in an interference case does not make the matter *res adjudicata.* Union Paper Bag Co. *v.* Crane, 1 Holmes (U. S.) 429; s. c., 1 Bann. & Ard. Pat. Cas. 494; s. c., 6 Pat. Off. Gaz. 801. Wire Book Sewing Mach. Co. *v.* Stevenson, 11 Fed. Rep. 155.

It has been held in a State court that so long as a decision remains unreversed it is such. Peck *v.* Collins, 70 N. Y. 376.

Nor does a statement made in any other proceeding in the Patent Office, estop an applicant. Crocker's Case, 2 A. L. T. 129; Union Paper Bag Co. *v.* Crane, 1 Holmes (U. S.) 429; s. c., 1 Bann.

(*b*) Practice in Interference Cases.—The Commissioner shall give notice of an interference to the parties,[1] and the proceedings are regulated by such rules as may be adopted.[2]

(*c*) Effect of Decision in Interference Cases.—As to the question of priority between the parties, the decision, if acquiesced in, is conclusive;[3] it is not an estoppel in any other circumstance.[4]

18. Appeal—(*a*) In Patent Office and Supreme Court, District of Columbia.—An applicant for a patent, any of whose claims have been twice rejected, and every party to an interference may appeal to the board of Examiners-in-Chief,[5] from them to the Commissioner in person,[6] and from them to the supreme court of the *District of Columbia* sitting in banc, except in interference cases.[7]

(*b*) Practice on Appeal.—An appellant must give notice to the Commissioner and file in the Patent Office his reasons for appeal.[8] The appellant lays before the court certified copies of all the papers in the case, and the Commissioner furnishes the

& Ard. Pat. Cas. 494; s. c., 6 Pat. Off. Gaz. 801.

1. U. S. Rev. Stats., § 4904.

2. The rules of the Patent Office, so long as they are not abrogated, are as binding as the law itself. Arnold *v.* Bishop, Cranch Pat. Dec. 103.

Various decisions on minor points of practice are found in Perry *v.* Cornell, Cranch Pat. Dec. 132; Smith *v.* Flickinger, Cranch Pat. Dec. 116; Arnold *v.* Bishop, Cranch Pat. Dec. 103.

3. Shuter *v.* Davis, 16 Fed. Rep. 564; s. c., 24 Pat. Off. Gaz. 303; Holliday *v.* Pickhardt, 12 Fed. Rep. 147; s. c., 22 Pat. Off. Gaz. 420; Hanford *v.* Westcott, 16 Pat. Off. Gaz. 1181; Peck etc. Co. *v.* Lindsay, 2 Fed. Rep. 688; Greenwood *v.* Bracher, 1 Fed. Rep. 857.

This does not mean that the parties may not litigate the matter over again in the circuit court. Hubel *v.* Tucker, 24 Fed. Rep. 701; Celluloid Mfg. Co. *v.* Chrolithian Collar etc. Co., 24 Fed. Rep. 275.

4. To a party whose patent, after issue, was put into intererfence with an applicant who was declared the prior inventor. Perry *v.* Starrett, 5 Bann. & Ard. Pat. Cas. 485; s. c., 14 Pat. Off. Gaz. 599.

To a purchaser of a machine from the defeated party from setting up a prior invention in another. Peck etc. Co. *v.* Lindsay, 5 Bann. & Ard. Pat. Cas. 390; s. c., 2 Fed. Rep. 688; s. c., 18 Pat. Off. Gaz. 63.

In an action against third parties they can defend by setting up an invention by a claimant defeated in an interference proceeding. Perry *v.* Perry, 14 Pat. Off. Gaz. 599.

5. U. S. Rev. Stats., § 4909.

If, in an interference proceeding, the Examiners-in-Chief award priority to one party and remand his case to the primary examiner to determine whether he has abandoned his invention, the other party cannot appeal. Bigelow *v.* Thatcher, 2 McArthur (U. S.) 29.

6. U. S. Rev. Stats., § 4910.

7. U. S. Rev. Stats., § 4911.

The appeal is from a refusal to grant a patent. Pomeroy *v.* Commissioner, Cranch Pat. Dec. 112.

The refusal may take the form of a decision that the applicant is not the original and first inventor. Commissioner *v.* Whitely, 4 Wall. (U. S.) 522.

Or that the applicant is not such a person as is entitled to the reissue for which he applies. Commissioner *v.* Whitely, 4 Wall. (U. S.) 522.

An applicant whose patent has been refused may appeal, in spite of being improperly put into interference by the Commissioner. *Ex parte* Platts, 15 Pat. Off. Gaz. 827.

No Appeal in Interference Case to Secretary of Interior.—The action of the Commissioner of Patents in granting or refusing a patent is a judicial act, and therefore is not reviewable by the Secretary of the Interior. Butterworth *v.* Hoe, 112 U. S. 50.

8. U. S. Rev. Stats., § 4912. The rea-

grounds of his decision, touching the reasons of appeal.[1] The court, on petition, hears and determines the appeal, and revises the decision appealed from in a summary way on the evidence produced before the Commissioner.[2] The revision shall be confined to the points set forth in the reasons for appeal.[3] A certificate of the proceedings and decision shall be returned to the Patent Office and shall govern the further proceedings in the case.[4]

(*c*) BILL IN EQUITY TO COMPEL ISSUE OF PATENT.—The applicant for a patent, who has been refused by the Commissioner[5] or the supreme court of the *District of Columbia*, may exhibit a bill in equity against any opposing party;[6] or, where there is no opposing party, against the Commissioner.[7] This proceeding is

sons for appeal must be in writing and filed within such time as the Commissioner may appoint.

1. U. S. Rev. Stats., § 4913. The court gives notice to the Commissioner of the time and place of hearing the appeal, and the Commissioner notifies the parties interested. The Commissioner and examiner can be examined under oath. See Perry *v.* Cornell, Cranch Pat. Dec. 132.

2. U. S. Rev. Stats., § 4914.

3. U. S. Rev. Stats., § 4914; Arnold *v.* Bishop, Cranch Pat. Dec. 103; Smith *v.* Flickinger, Cranch Pat. Dec. 116; *Ex parte* Conklin, 1 McArthur (U. S.) 375.

4. U. S. Rev. Stats., § 4914.

But no opinion or decision of the court in any such case shall preclude any person interested from the right to contest the validity of such patent in any court wherein the same may be called into question.

5. Where the Commissioner withholds the patent by virtue of his supervisory authority, the remedy is by bill against the Commissioner, not by appeal to the supreme court of the *District of Columbia*, or by *mandamus*. Hull *v.* Commissioner, 2 McArthur (U. S.) 90; s. c., 7 Pat. Off. Gaz. 559; rehearing, 2 McArthur (U. S.) 125; s. c., 8 Pat. Off. Gaz. 46.

In Interference Cases.—A question of priority of invention between two parties to an interference can be tried by bill, by party defeated before the Commissioner, against the party prevailing before him. Union Paper Bag Mach. Co. *v.* Crane, 1 Holmes (U. S.) 429; Whipple *v.* Miner, 15 Fed. Rep. 117; s. c., 23 Pat. Off. Gaz. 2236.

6. Whipple *v.* Miner, 15 Fed. Rep. 117; s. c., 23 Pat. Off. Gaz. 2236; Prentiss *v.* Ellsworth, 27 Pat. Off. Gaz. 623; 2 Whart. Dig. 365; Union Paper Bag Mach. Co. *v.* Crane, 1 Holmes (U. S.) 429.

Costs.—Where there are opposing parties, the costs are taxed as in other cases. Butler *v.* Shaw, 21 Fed. Rep. 321.

Parties.—Where there is an opposing party, the Commissioner is not a necessary party. Graham *v.* Teter, 25 Fed. Rep. 555.

7. U. S. Rev. Stats., § 4915. A copy of the bill must be served on the Commissioner, and all expenses of both sides when the bill is brought against the Commissioner, paid by the applicant, whether the patent is granted or not.

The court will examine into the novelty of the alleged invention. *Ex parte* Greely, 1 Holmes (U. S.) 284; s. c., 6 Fish. Pat. Cas. 574; s. c., 4 Pat. Off. Gaz. 612; *Ex parte* Arkell, 4 Bann. & Ard. Pat Cas. 80; s. c., 15 Blatchf. (U. S.) 437.

The applicant must have exhausted all his remedies by appeal before bringing the suit. Kirk *v.* Commissioner, 5 Mackey (U. S.) 229.

And the rejection must have been on the merits. Butterworth *v.* Hoe, 112 U. S. 50; s. c., 29 Pat. Off. Gaz. 618.

And must bring his action in the *District of Columbia*, which is the legal residence of the Commissioner of Patents. Butterworth *v.* Hill, 114 U. S. 133; s. c., 31 Pat. Off. Gaz. 1043; *overruling* Vermont etc. Mach. Co. *v.* Marble, 22 Blatchf. (U. S.) 128; s. c., 20 Fed. Rep. 117; s. c., 27 Pat. Off. Gaz. 622. *Compare* Prentiss *v.* Ellsworth, 27 Pat. Off. Gaz. 623.

The Secretary of the Interior is not a necessary party to a bill of this kind.

original rather than appellate,[1] and does not suspend the action of the Patent Office.[2]

19. Issue of Patents.—Patents are issued under the seal of the Patent Office, and shall be signed by the Secretary of the Interior, countersigned by the Commissioner of Patents,[3] and recorded in the Patent Office.[4]

20. Disclaimer.—(*a*) WHAT CAN BE DISCLAIMED.—A disclaimer can only be filed when the invention that remains after the filing of the disclaimer is a material part of the thing patented[5]. It cannot be used to reform the description in the specification,[6] or change the invention.[7]

(*b*) DISCLAIMER GENERALLY.—Whenever, through inadvert-

against the Commissioner. Kirk *v.* Commissioner, 5 Mackey (U. S.) 229; s. c., 37 Pat. Off. Gaz. 451.

Laches.—The court may inquire into any delay in the prosecution of application in suing to obtain the patent. Gandy *v.* Marble, 122 U. S. 432; s. c., 39 Pat. Off. Gaz. 1423.

1. Whipple *v.* Miner, 15 Fed. Rep. 117; s. c., 23 Pat. Off. Gaz. 2236.

New Evidence.—New evidence may be introduced. *Ex parte* Squire, 3 Bann. & Ard. Pat. Cas. 133; s. c., 12 Pat. Off. Gaz. 1025.

The suit may be decided on any issue. Butler *v.* Shaw, 21 Fed. Rep. 321.

2. Whipple *v.* Miner, 15 Fed. Rep. 117; s. c., 23 Pat. Off. Gaz. 2236.

Parties Plaintiff.—Ordinarily the applicant. U. S. Rev. Stats., § 4915.

Where an assignment has been made it would seem that the assignees are the proper parties. Runstetler *v.* Atkinson, 23 Pat. Off. Gaz. 940.

3. A patent issued without the signature of the Secretary of the Interior is void, and a subsequent signing will not make it valid from its issue, and it cannot be signed by a secretary whose term of office has expired. Marsh *v.* Nichols, 15 Fed. Rep. 914; s. c., 24 Pat. Off. Gaz. 901.

And any alteration made in the patent after his signature, must be communicated to him and receive his sanction. Woodworth *v.* Hall, 1 Woodb. & M. (U. S.) 389; s. c., 2 Robb Pat. Cas. 517.

It may now be countersigned by the Assistant Secretary. 25 Stats. at Large, ch. 15, p. 40.

4. U. S. Rev. Stats., § 4883.

5. U. S. Rev. Stats., § 4917; Root *v.* Welch Mfg. Co., 17 Blatchf. (U. S.) 478; s. c., 5 Bann. & Ard. Pat. Cas. 189; s. c., 4 Fed. Rep. 423; Vance *v.* Campbell, 1 Black (U. S.) 427; Hall *v.* Wiles, 2 Blatchf. (U. S.) 194.

It can be used to disclaim one or more of a number of claims, leaving the remainder to stand. McCormick *v.* Seymour, 3 Blatchf. (U. S.) 209; Tuck *v.* Bramhill, 6 Blatchf. (U. S.) 95; s. c., 3 Fish. Pat. Cas. 400; Taylor *v.* Archer, 8 Blatchf. (U. S.) 315; s. c., 4 Fish. Pat. Cas. 449.

Or a claim in a re-issue unlawfully broadened from the original patent. Tyler *v.* Galloway, 12 Fed. Rep. 567; s. c., 22 Pat. Off. Gaz. 2072.

Or part of a claim. Schillinger *v.* Gunther, 17 Blatchf. (U. S.) 66; s. c., 4 Bann. & Ard. Pat. Cas. 479; s. c., 16 Pat. Off. Gaz. 905.

The claim disclaimed may be invalid for various reasons; the right to disclaim is not limited to a claim invalid from want of novelty in the subject matter. O'Reilly *v.* Morse, 15 How. (U. S.) 62.

A disclaimer cannot be used to disclaim one of the elements of a combination. Vance *v.* Campbell, 1 Black (U. S.) 427.

6. Hailes *v.* Albany Stove Co., 16 Fed. Rep. 240.

A patentee can eliminate a portion of his specification describing an invention disclaimed. Schillinger *v.* Gunther, 17 Blatchf. (U. S.) 66; s. c., 4 Bann. & Ard. Pat. Cas. 479; s. c., 16 Pat. Off. Gaz. 905.

For instance, he may limit his invention to "a rubber eraser having the soft finished erasive surface produced by tumbling the eraser." Lockwood *v.* Hooper, 25 Fed. Rep. 910.

7. It cannot enlarge the scope of a patent. White *v.* Gleason etc. Mfg. Co., 24 Pat. Off. Gaz. 205.

Nor change the patent from a patent for a product to one for a process. Grant *v.* Walter, 38 Fed. Rep. 594.

ence, accident or mistake,[1] and without any fraudulent or deceptive intention, a patentee has claimed more than that of which he is the first inventor or discoverer,[2] a disclaimer can be made to such portions as are not desired to be claimed or held by virtue of the patent or assignment.[3]

(*c*) BY WHOM MADE.—A disclaimer can be made by the inventor,[4] assignee[5] or legal representative,[6] and the extent of the interest of the person disclaiming should be stated in the disclaimer.[7]

(*d*) TIME WITHIN WHICH DISCLAIMER MUST BE MADE.—A disclaimer may be made at any time, even after suit is brought,[8] provided the delay has not been unreasonable.[9] An unreasonable delay, however, cuts off all rights of action.[10]

1. It is immaterial whether the mistake be one of law or of fact. Wyeth *v.* Stone, 1 Story (U. S.) 273; s. c., 2 Robb Pat. Cas. 23.

2. The purpose of the disclaimer is to eliminate all claims for inventions not new with the patentee, and all claims for things which were not inventions with them. Walker on Patents, § 197; United States Cartridge Co. *v.* Union etc. Cartridge Co., 112 U. S. 642.

3. U. S. Rev. Stat. § 4917. Hartes *v.* Albany Stove Co., 123 U. S. 588.

It applied to patents granted before its adoption. Hotchkiss *v.* Oliver, 5 Den. (N. Y.) 314.

The provision applies to re-issues. Tyler *v.* Galloway, 12 Fed. Rep. 567; s. c., 22 Pat. Off. Gaz. 2072.

And to extensions. Brooks *v.* Jenkins, 3 McLean (U. S.) 432.

4. U. S. Rev. Stat. § 4917. Silsby *v.* Foote, 14 How. (U. S.) 218.

5. Wyeth *v.* Stone, 1 Story (U. S.) 273; s. c., 2 Robb Pat. Cas. 23.

An assignee must join with the inventor; otherwise he will not receive the benefit of the disclaimer. This is so, even though he be an assignee subsequent to the grant or issuance of the patent. Wyeth *v.* Stone, 1 Story (U. S.) 273; s. c., 2 Robb Pat. Cas. 23; Rice *v.* Garnhardt, 34 Wis. 453; Myers *v.* Frame, 8 Blatchf. (U. S.) 446; s. c., 4 Fish. Pat Cas. 493.

6. Brooks *v.* Jenkins, 3 McLean (U. S.) 432.

7. U. S. Rev. Stats., § 4917. Brooks *v.* Jenkins, 3 McLean (U. S.) 432.

But a statement merely that the disclaimer is the patentee, is sufficient. Silsby *v.* Foote, 14 How. (U. S.) 221.

8. Smith *v.* Nichols, 1 Holmes (U. S.) 172; s. c., 6 Fish. Pat. Cas. 61; s. c., 2 Pat. Off. Gaz. 649; Silsby *v.* Foote, 20 How. (U. S.) 378; Seymour *v.* McCormick, 19 How. (U. S.) 96; Tuck *v.* Bramhill, 6 Blatchf. (U. S.) 95; Gage *v.* Herring, 14 Blatchf. (U. S.) 293; s. c., 23 Pat. Off. Gaz. 2119; Hill *v.* Biddle, 27 Fed. Rep. 561.

9. U. S. Rev. Stats., §§ 4917, 4922; McCormick *v.* Seymour, 3 Blatchf. (U. S.) 209.

What is an unreasonable delay, has been held to be a question of law. Singer *v.* Walmsley, 1 Fish. Pat. Cas. 558; Seymour *v.* McCormick, 19 How. (U. S.) 96.

And a mixed question of law and fact. Brooks *v.* Jenkins, 3 McLean (U. S.) 432; Washburne *v.* Gould, 3 Story (U. S.) 122; s. c., 2 Robb Pat. Cas. 206; Lippincott *v.* Kelly, 1 West. L. J. 513.

Delay is counted from the time that knowledge is brought to the patentee that he was not the first inventor. Singer *v.* Walmsley, 1 Fish. Pat. Cas. 558.

A claim which has been held valid by a circuit court need not be disclaimed until declared invalid by the highest court. O'Reilly *v.* Morse, 15 How. (U. S.) 62.

Nor until the court has passed on the claims. Stutz *v.* Armstrong, 20 Fed. Rep. 843; Seymour *v.* McCormick, 19 How. (U. S.) 96; Patter *v.* Whitney, 3 Fish. Pat. Cas. 77; Tuck *v.* Bramhill, 6 Blatchf. (U. S.) 95.

A patentee, some of whose claims were declared invalid just as the patent was about to expire, may recover on the valid claims. Kittle *v.* Hall, 30 Fed. Rep. 239.

Or has expired. Yale Lock Mfg. Co. *v.* Sargent, 117 U. S. 553.

10. Brooks *v.* Jenkins, 3 McLean (U.

(*e*) EFFECT OF DISCLAIMER.—The effect of a disclaimer on a patent is to place it in the position of never having contained the matter disclaimed.[1] No costs are recoverable unless proper disclaimer has been filed before the commencement of the suit.[2]

21. Reissue—(*a*) WHEN PATENT CAN BE SURRENDERED.—When a patent is inoperative[3] or invalid[4] by reason of a defective or insufficient specification,[5] or by reason of the patentee claiming

S.) 432; Hall *v.* Wiles, 2 Blatchf. (U. S.) 194; Winans *v.* New York etc. R. Co., 1 Fish. Pat. Cas. 213.

1. Dunbar *v.* Myers, 94 U. S. 187; s. c., 11 Pat. Off. Gaz. 35.

It only affects those by whom it is made. Wyeth *v.* Stone, 1 Story (U. S.) 273.

2. U. S. Rev. Stats., § 4922. Reed *v.* Cutter, 1 Story (U. S.) 591; Burdett *v.* Estey, 5 Bann. & Ard. Pat. Cas. 308; Proctor *v.* Bull, 16 Fed. Rep. 791; Smith *v.* Nichols, 21 Wall. (U. S.) 117.

But a defendant will not be permitted to attack claims not in suit, to avoid costs. American Bell Teleph. Co. *v.* Spencer, 8 Fed. Rep. 512.

3. Giant Powder Co. *v.* California etc. Power Co., 4 Fed. Rep. 720.

Inoperative does not mean "not fully available" to the owner of the patent. Burr *v.* Duryee, 1 Wall. (U. S.) 531; Whitely *v.* Swayne, 4 Fish. Pat. Cas. 117; Poage *v.* McGowan, 15 Fed. Rep. 398.

A want of proper description is a good cause to reissue a patent. Sewing Mach. Co. *v.* Frame, 24 Fed. Rep. 596.

That it is "not fully valid and available," however, will authorize a reissue. Gold & Stock Tel. Co. *v.* Wiley, 17 Fed. Rep. 234. "Not fully operative" is not enough. Hartshorn *v.* Eagle Shade Roller Co., 18 Fed. Rep. 90.

The defect, to cure which a reissue is taken, need not completely vitiate the original. Stimpson *v.* Westchester R. Co., 4 How. (U. S.) 380.

4. Union Paper Collar Co. *v.* Van Dusen, 23 Wall. (U. S.) 530; s. c., 7 Pat. Off. Gaz. 919.

Vogler *v.* Semple, 7 Biss. (U. S.) 382; s. c., 2 Bann. & Ard. Pat. Cas. 556; s. c., 11 Pat. Off. Gaz. 923.

A patent invalid because too broad, may be corrected by reissue. Matthews *v.* Flower, 25 Fed. Rep. 830.

Mistakes That May be Corrected by Reissue.—Mis-statement of date of prior foreign patent. Buerk *v.* Valentine, 9 Blatchf. (U. S.) 479; s. c., 5 Fish. Pat. Cas. 366; s. c., 2 Pat. Off. Gaz. 295.

Clerical Errors.—Clerical errors may or may not be altered in other ways. French *v.* Rogers, 1 Fish. Pat. Cas. 133; Morris *v.* Huntington, 1 Paine (U. S.) 348; s. c., 1 Robb Pat. Cas. 448; Grant *v.* Raymond, 6 Pet. (U. S.) 218; s. c., 1 Robb Pat. Cas. 604; Woodworth *v.* Hall, 1 Woodb. & M. (U. S.) 248; s. c., 2 Robb Pat. Cas. 495; Goodyear Dental etc. Co. *v.* Weatherbee, 2 Cliff. (U. S.) 555; s. c., 3 Fish. Pat. Cas. 87.

A mistake in fixing the date of a patent so that it did not conform to the term of a foreign patent, may be corrected by a reissue. Buerk *v.* Valentine, 9 Blatchf. (U. S.) 479; s. c., 5 Fish. Pat. Cas. 366; s. c., 2 Pat. Office Gaz. 295.

5. The patent need not be void; it is enough that the specification is defective or doubtful in some particulars. Woodworth *v.* Hall, 1 Woodb. & M. (U. S.) 248; s. c., 2 Robb Pat. Cas. 495; Parham *v.* American Button etc. Mach. Co., 4 Fish. Pat. Cas. 468.

But the specification must be defective. Coon *v.* Wilson, 113 U. S. 268.

What Word "Specification" Includes.—Specification includes claim; consequently a claim which does not describe fully the extent of the invention may enable the patent to be surrendered and reissued, and the claim enlarged or altered to cover the invention. Carver *v.* Braintree Mfg. Co., 2 Story (U. S.) 432; s. c., 2 Robb Pat. Cas. 141; Goodyear *v.* Providence Rubber Co., 2 Fish. Pat. Cas. 499; Morey *v.* Lockwood, 8 Wall (U. S.) 230; Worswick Mfg. Co. *v.* Steiger, 17 Fed. Rep. 531; Battin *v.* Taggert, 17 How. (U. S.) 74; Crompton *v.* Belknap Mills, 3 Fish. Pat. Cas. 536; French *v.* Rogers, 1 Fish. Pat. Cas. 133.

No Right to Reissue.—Where the specification is neither defective nor insufficient, there exists no right to reissue. Coon *v.* Wilson, 113 U. S. 268; Brewster *v.* Shuler, 37 Fed. Rep. 785; Mahn *v.* Harwood, 112 U. S. 354; Dunham *v.* Dennison Mfg. Co., 40 Fed. Rep. 667.

A reissue of an original patent in two reissues is not void because one of the

more than he had the right to claim,[1] if the error has arisen by inadvertence, accident or mistake,[2] and without any fraudulent or deceptive[3] intention, the patent may be surrendered and a reissue taken.[4] The provisions for reissue apply as well to a former re-issue[5] or to an extended[6] as to an original patent.

(*b*) SURRENDER.—A surrender of a patent for the purpose of reissue is made by the party having the legal title thereto;[7] though

reissues is identical with the original. International Terra Cotta Lumber Co. *v.* Maurer, 44 Fed. Rep. 618.

1. Gould *v.* Ballard, 3 Bann. & Ard. Pat. Cas. 324; Chicago Fruit House Co. *v.* Busch, 2 Biss. (U. S.) 472; Albright *v.* Celluloid etc. Trimming Co., 2 Bann. & Ard. Pat. Cas. 629; s. c., 12 Pat. Off. Gaz. 227; Carver *v.* Braintree Mfg. Co., 2 Story (U. S.) 432; s. c., 2 Robb Pat. Cas. 141; Coburn *v.* Schroeder, 19 Blatchf. (U. S.) 377; s. c., 8 Fed. Rep. 519; s. c., 20 Pat. Off. Gaz. 1524.

Even where the original patent is too broad, and, hence, invalid, the mistake may be corrected by a reissue. Mathews *v.* Flower, 25 Fed. Rep. 830.

2. Mistake not an error of judgment. Swain etc. Mfg. Co. *v.* Ladd, 102 U. S. 409; s. c., 19 Pat. Off. Gaz. 62; Jones *v.* Barker, 11 Fed. Rep. 597; s. c., 22 Pat. Off. Gaz. 771.

How or when mistake is discovered, is unimportant. Poppenhusen *v.* Falke, 5 Blatchf. (U. S.) 493; s. c., 2 Fish. Pat. Cas. 181; Buffum *v.* Oakland Mfg. Co., 4 Bann. & Ard. Pat. Cas. 599.

The right to reissue exists in cases of defective description, or error arising from inadvertence or mistake. Knight *v.* Baltimore Co., 1 Taney (U. S.) 106.

The *United States* statute conferring jurisdiction on the Commissioner of Patents to re-issue any patent invalid by reason of a defective or insufficient specification arising from inadvertence, accident, or mistake, and without any fraudulent or deceptive intention, authorizes the insertion of new claims founded on the original invention, as exhibited by the specifications or drawings where the claimant uses due diligence in applying for the correction; but the laches of the patentee may estop him. Combined Patents Can Co. *v.* Lloyd, 11 Fed. Rep. 149.

Where by an application for a reissue of a patent it is thought merely to enlarge a claim, a clear mistake and inadvertence must be shown and a speedy application for its correction, without reasonable delay, must be made. Wooster *v.* Handy, 21 Fed. Rep. 51. *Distinguished* in Wooster *v.* Thornton, 26 Fed. Rep. 275.

3. A fraud, especially corrupt collusion between the Commissioner and applicant, invalidates the reissued patent. Swift *v.* Whisen, 3 Fish. Pat. Cas. 343; s. c., 2 Bond (U. S.) 115; House *v.* Young, 3 Fish. Pat. Cas. 335; Conklin *v.* Stafford, 1 McArthur (U. S.) 375.

The evidence must be clear. Jordan *v.* Dobson, 4 Fish. Pat. Cas. 398.

4. U. S. Rev. Stats. § 4916.

5. Selden *v.* Stockwell etc. Gas Burner Co., 9 Fed. Rep. 390; 19 Blatchf. (U. S.) 444; s. c., 20 Pat. Off. Gaz. 1377; Morse *v.* Bain, 9 West. L. J. 106.

Invalid Reissue Can be Reissued.—Even an invalid reissue can be reissued. American etc. Boring Co. *v.* Sullivan Mach. Co., 14 Blatchf. (U. S.) 119; s. c., 2 Bann. & Ard. Pat. Cas. 522; American etc. Boring Co. *v.* Sheldon, 17 Blatchf. (U. S.) 208; s. c., 4 Bann. & Ard. Pat. Cas. 551.

The rule is that a substitute (a reissue) having all the qualities of an original, the right to amend it is equal with the right to amend the original. French *v.* Rogers, 1 Fish. Pat. Cas. 133.

A reissue which has been unlawfully broadened may be re-issued with the original claims and specification. This precludes the idea that the original patent was invalid. Celluloid Mfg. Co. *v.* Zylonite Brush Co., 27 Fed. Rep. 291; Giant Powder Co. *v.* Safety Nitro Powder Co., 19 Fed. Rep. 509; Hubel *v.* Dick, 28 Fed. Rep. 132; Sawyer Spindle Co. *v.* Eureka Spindle Co., 33 Fed. Rep. 836.

A claim which is too broad may be disclaimed, as in an original patent. Torrant *v.* Duluth Lumber Co., 30 Fed. Rep. 830.

6. Gibson *v.* Harris, 1 Blatchf. (U. S.) 167; Wilson *v.* Rousseau, 4 How. (U. S.) 646; s. c., 2 Robb Pat. Cas. 373; Hussey *v.* Bradley, 5 Blatchf. (U. S.) 134; s. c., 2 Fish. Pat. Cas. 362.

7. "Patentee, or, in case of his death or of an assignment of the whole or any undivided part of the original patent

a reissue granted after a surrender by another and its ratification by the legal owner is valid as to third parties.[1] The surrender takes effect at the date of issue of the reissued patent.[2] It may be

then to his executors, administrators or assigns." U. S. Rev. Stats., § 4916; Potter *v.* Holland, 4 Blatchf. (U. S.) 206; s. c., 1 Fish. Pat. Cas. 327; Smith *v.* Mercer, 5 Pa. L. J. 529.

A patent may be surrendered by an assignee whose title has passed through mesne assignments. Swift *v.* Whisen, 2 Bond (U. S.) 115; s. c., 3 Fish. Pat. Cas. 343.

Need Not Join Grantee.—A grantee of an exclusive territory is not such an assignee as must join in the surrender. Meyer *v.* Bailey, 2 Bann. & Ard. Pat. Cas. 73; s. c., 8 Pat. Off. Gaz. 437; Smith *v.* Mercer, 5 Pa. L. J. 529.

The grantee apparently may elect to hold either under the old patent or the reissue. Potter *v.* Holland, 4 Blatchf. (U. S.) 206; s. c., 1 Fish. Pat. Cas. 327; Woodworth *v.* Stone, 3 Story (U. S.) 749; s. c., 2 Robb Pat. Cas. 296; Washburne *v.* Gould, 3 Story (U. S.) 122; s. c., 2 Robb Pat. Cas. 206; McBurney *v.* Goodyear, 11 Cush. (Mass.) 569.

Licensee.—A licensee who has no legal title in the patent. Potter *v.* Holland, 4 Blatchf. (U. S.) 206; s. c., 1 Fish. Pat. Cas. 327; Forbes *v.* Barstow Stove Co., 2 Cliff. (U. S.) 379.

Patentee.—After having assigned his patent, a patentee. Swift *v.* Whisen, 3 Fish. Pat. Cas. 343; s. c., 2 Bond (U. S.) 115.

Assignees of an undivided moiety must join; if not, the reissued patent will be invalid unless the non-joining owner ratifies. Potter *v.* Holland, 4 Blatchf. (U. S.) 206; s. c., 1 Fish. Pat. Cas. 382.

Executors and Administrators.—An executor may surrender the patent and obtain the reissue. Carew *v.* Boston Elastic Fabric Co., 1 Holmes (U. S.) 45; s. c., 3 Cliff. (U. S.) 356; s. c., 5 Fish. Pat. Cas. 90; s. c., 1 Pat. Off. Gaz. 91.

Or an administrator. Woodworth *v.* Hall, 1 Woodb. & M. (U. S.) 248; s. c., 2 Robb Pat. Cas. 495.

Any one of the several personal representatives may surrender and receive a valid grant of a reissue to himself in his fiduciary capacity. Goodyear Rubber Co. *v.* Providence Rubber Co., 2 Cliff. (U. S.) 351; s. c., 2 Fish. Pat. Cas. 499.

Reissue, an Evidence of Title.—The grant of a reissue is evidence that the grantee had the title to the patent. Northwestern Fire Extinguisher Co. *v.* Philadelphia Fire Extinguisher Co., 1 Bann. & Ard. Pat. Cas. 177; s. c., 6 Pat. Off. Gaz. 34; Woodworth *v.* Hall, 1 Woodb. & M. (U. S.) 248; Goodyear *v.* Hullihen, 2 Hughes (U. S.) 492; s. c., 3 Fish. Pat. Cas. 251.

A recital of a prior assignment of a patent is at least *prima facie* evidence thereof. Middletown Co. *v.* Judd, 3 Fish. Pat. Cas. 141; Hoffheins *v.* Brandt, 3 Fish. Pat. Cas. 218.

Verbal Errors.—A verbal error in the reissue will not invalidate. Bignall *v.* Harvey, 18 Blatchf. (U. S.) 352; s. c., 5 Bann. & Ard. Pat. Cas. 636; s. c., 4 Fed. Rep. 334; s. c., 18 Pat. Off. Gaz. 1275; Woodworth *v.* Stone, 3 Story (U. S.) 749; s. c., 2 Robb Pat. Cas. 296.

1. Wing *v.* Warren, 5 Fish. Pat. Cas. 548; s. c., 2 Pat. Off. Gaz. 342; Dental Vulcanite Co. *v.* Weatherbee, 2 Cliff. (U. S.) 555; Woodworth *v.* Stone, 3 Story (U. S.) 749; s. c., 2 Robb Pat. Cas. 296; Meyer *v.* Bailey, 2 Bann. & Ard. Pat. Cas. 73; s. c., 8 Pat. Off. Gaz. 437; Campbell *v.* James, 17 Blatchf. (U. S.) 43; s. c., 4 Bann. & Ard. Pat. Cas. 456; s. c., 18 Pat. Off. Gaz. 979.

A patentee cannot, however, affect the interest of his assignee by surrendering his patent. Barnes *v.* Morgan, 3 Hun (N. Y.) 703.

2. U. S. Rev. Stats., § 4916.

Prior to the issuing of the new patent, what is called a surrender in the case, is, in general, nothing more than a preliminary offer to that effect, as the necessary means of obtaining a reissue; and even when not so intended at the outset, it may be subsequently so treated by the Commissioner, at the request of the party applying for the reissue. Forbes *v.* Barstow Stove Co., 2 Cliff. (U. S.) 379.

If a reissue is invalid for want of authority to make it a surrender, it is ineffective for want of authority to receive it; and the patent stands as if there had been no surrender. French *v.* Rogers, 1 Fish. Pat. Cas. 133; Woodworth *v.* Hall, 1 Woodb. & M. (U. S.) 389; s. c., 2 Robb Pat. Cas. 517; Woodworth *v.* Edwards, 3 Woodb. & M. (U. S.) 120; s. c., 2 Robb Pat. Cas. 610.

Where, however, the title to an invention is in dispute upon the application for a reissue and adjudged against the applicant, the effect of such de-

and may be made in any manner that the rules of the Patent Office may prescribe.[1]

(*c*) ACTION OF COMMISSIONER IN GRANTING REISSUE; HOW FAR REVIEWABLE IN COURT.—The action of the Commissioner in granting a reissue is reviewable only when, upon an inspection of the patents, it can be determined as a matter of law that the inventions described in the original and reissued patents are different;[2] he otherwise has no authority to act or exceed his au-

cision is as fatal to his original patent as to the reissue. Peck *v.* Collins, 103 U. S. 660; s. c., 19 Pat. Off. Gaz. 1137.

Rights of Action.—All rights of action under the original patent expire with the surrender and reissue. Jones *v.* Barker, 11 Fed. Rep. 597; United States Stamping Co. *v.* King, 7 Fed. Rep. 860; Mers *v.* Conover, 11 Pat. Off. Gaz. 4; Fry *v.* Quinlan, 13 Blatchf. (U. S.) 205; Reedy *v.* Scott, 23 Wall. (U. S.) 352; s. c., 7 Pat. Off. Gaz. 463; Burrell *v.* Hackley, 35 Fed. Rep. 833.

But a patentee may sue for an unlawful use of a machine bought before a reissue. Bliss *v.* Brooklyn, 8 Blatchf. (U. S.) 533; s. c., 4 Fish. Pat. Cas. 596; Carr *v.* Rice, 1 Fish. Pat. Cas. 327.

1. Dental Vulcanite Co. *v.* Weatherbee, 2 Cliff. (U. S.) 555; s. c., 3 Fish. Pat. Cas. 87.

And when the applicant has done all he can to make the surrender effective, he has a right to consider his application properly before the Commissioner. Commissioner *v.* Whitely, 4 Wall. (U. S.) 522.

2. Seymour *v.* Osborne, 3 Fish. Pat. Cas. 555; Graham *v.* Mason, 5 Fish. Pat. Cas. 1; s. c., 4 Cliff. (U. S.) 88; La Baw *v.* Hawkins, 1 Bann. & Ard. Pat. Cas. 428; s. c., 6 Pat. Off. Gaz. 724; Milligan etc. Glue Co. *v.* Upton, 97 U. S. 3; Metropolitan Washing Mach. Co. *v.* Providence Tool Co., 1 Holmes (U. S.) 161; Wells *v.* Gill, 6 Fish. Pat. Cas. 89; s. c., 2 Pat. Off. Gaz. 590; Nicholson Pavement Co. *v.* Elizabeth, 6 Fish. Pat. Cas. 424; s. c., 3 Pat. Off. Gaz. 522; Giant Powder Co. *v.* Safety Nitro Powder Co., 19 Fed. Rep. 509; Seckels *v.* Evans, 2 Cliff. (U. S.) 203; Stephens *v.* Pritchard, 4 Cliff. (U. S.) 417; Derring *v.* Nelson, 14 Blatchf. (U. S.) 293; s. c., 3 Bann. & Ard. Pat. Cas. 55; s. c., 12 Pat. Off. Gaz. 753; Tucker *v.* Tucker Mfg. Co., 4 Cliff. (U. S.) 397; s. c., 2 Bann. & Ard. Pat. Cas. 40; s. c., 10 Pat. Off. Gaz. 464; Chicago Fruit House *v.* Busch, 2 Biss. (U. S.) 472; s. c., 4 Fish. Pat. Cas. 395; Carew *v.* Fabric Co., 3 Cliff. (U. S.) 356; s. c., 5 Fish. Pat. Cas. 90; s. c., 1 Pat. Off. Gaz. 91; Heald *v.* Rice, 104 U. S. 737; s. c., 21 Pat. Off. Gaz. 1443; Ball *v.* Langles, 102 U. S. 128; Manufacturing Co. *v.* Du Brul, 2 Bann. & Ard. Pat. Cas. 618; s. c., 12 Pat. Off. Gaz. 351.

Consequently when the original patent is not in evidence, the court cannot declare the reissued patent void for being for a different invention. Doherty *v.* Haynes, 1 Bann. & Ard. Pat. Cas. 289; s. c., 4 Cliff. (U. S.) 291; s. c., 6 Pat. Off. Gaz. 118.

All matters of fact connected with the surrender and reissue of the patent are closed by the action of the Commissioner in granting a reissue. Seymour *v.* Osborne, 3 Fish. Pat. Cas. 555; Jordan *v.* Dobson, 4 Fish. Pat. Cas. 232; Stimpson *v.* West Chester R., 4 How. (U. S.) 380; s. c., 2 Robb Pat. Cas. 335; Colt *v.* Young, 2 Blatchf. (U. S.) 471; Forbes *v.* Barstow Stove Co., 2 Cliff. (U. S.) 379; French *v.* Rogers, 1 Fish. Pat. Cas. 133; Thomas *v.* Shoe Mach. Co., 3 Bann. & Ard. Pat. Cas. 357; s. c., 16 Pat. Off. Gaz. 541; Combined Patents Can Co. *v.* Lloyd, 11 Fed. Rep. 149; Selden *v.* Stockwell etc. Gas Burner Co., 19 Blatchf. (U. S.) 544; s. c., 9 Fed. Rep. 390; s. c., 20 Pat. Off. Gaz. 1377; Parham *v.* American Button etc. Mach. Co., 4 Fish Pat. Cas. 468; Gage *v.* Herring, 23 Pat. Off. Gaz. 2179; s. c., 107 U. S. 640; Smith *v.* Merriam, 6 Fed. Rep. 713; s. c., 19 Pat. Off. Gaz. 601; Asmus *v.* Alden, 27 Fed. Rep. 684; Searls *v.* Worden, 11 Fed. Rep. 501; s. c., 21 Pat. Off. Gaz. 1955; Herring *v.* Nelson, 14 Blatchf. (U. S.) 293; s. c., 12 Pat. Off. Gaz. 753; 3 Bann. & Ard. Pat. Cas. 55.

As a rule the question whether the reissue was made to cure a fault arising from accident or mistake, is decided conclusively by the Commissioner. Asmus *v.* Alden, 27 Fed. Rep. 684.

And *prima facie* the Commissioner has discharged his duty faithfully and correctly, and therefore the reissued

thority.[1]

(*d*) What Can be Included in a Reissue.—A reissue must be for the same invention as was contained in the original patent,[2]

patent is for the same invention as the original patent, and that the surrender was on account of an inadvertence or mistake. Allen *v.* Blunt, 2 Woodb. & M. (U. S.) 121; s. c., 2 Robb Pat. Cas. 530; Allen *v.* Blunt, 3 Story (U. S.) 742; s. c., 2 Robb Pat. Cas. 285; Philadelphia etc. R. *v.* Stimpson, 14 Pet. (U. S.) 448; s. c., 2 Robb Pat. Cas. 46; Smith *v.* Mercer, 5 Pa. L. J. 529; Hussey *v.* Bradley, 5 Blatchf. (U. S.) 134; s. c., 2 Fish. Pat. Cas. 362; Crompton *v.* Belknap Mills, 3 Fish. Pat. Cas. 536; Birdsell *v.* McDonald, 1 Bann. & Ard. Pat. Cas. 165; s. c., 6 Pat. Off. Gaz. 682; Woodworth *v.* Edwards, 3 Woodb. & M. (U. S.) 120; Hussey *v.* McCormick, 1 Biss. (U. S.) 300; s. c., 1 Fish. Pat. Cas. 509; Hussey *v.* Bradley, 5 Blatchf. (U. S.) 134; s. c., 2 Fish. Pat. Cas. 362; Morris *v.* Royer, 3 Fish. Pat. Cas. 176; Middletown Co. *v.* Judd, 3 Fish. Pat. Cas. 141; Goodyear *v.* Berry, 3 Fish. Pat. Cas. 439, s. c., 2 Bond (U. S.) 189; Knight *v.* Baltimore etc. R. Co., 1 Taney (U. S.) 106; s. c., 3 Fish. Pat. Cas. 1; Manufacturing Co. *v.* Du Brul, 2 Bann. & Ard. Pat. Cas. 618; s. c., 12 Pat. Off. Gaz. 351.

And many other cases where the principle is thoroughly established. And that it has not been extended beyond the original invention. Bantz *v.* Elsar, 1 Bann. & Ard. Pat. Cas. 351; s. c., 6 Pat. Off. Gaz. 117.

1. Giant Powder Co. *v.* California etc. Powder Works, 4 Fed. Rep. 720; s. c., 18 Pat. Off. Gaz. 1339; Flower *v.* Rayner, 5 Fed. Rep. 793; s. c., 19 Pat. Off. Gaz. 425.

The action of the Commissioner is now conclusive as to the existence of fraud in making the application. Giant Powder Co. *v.* Safety etc. Powder Co., 10 Sawy. (U. S.) 23; s. c., 19 Fed. Rep. 509; s. c., 27 Pat. Off. Gaz. 99; Seymour *v.* Osborne, 11 Wall. (U. S.) 516; La Baw *v.* Hawkins, 2 Bann. & Ard. Pat. Cas. 428; s. c., 6 Pat. Off. Gaz. 724; Johnsen *v.* Beard, 2 Bann. & Ard. Pat. Cas. 50; s. c., 8 Pat. Off. Gaz. 435; Schullinger *v.* Cranford, 4 Mackey (U. S.) 450; Corn Planter Patent, 23 Wall. (U. S.) 181; s. c., 6 Pat. Off. Gaz. 392.

2. U. S. Rev. Stats., § 4916; Seymour *v.* Osborne, 3 Fish. Pat. Cas. 555; Sickels *v.* Evans, 2 Cliff. (U. S.) 203; s. c., 2 Fish. Pat. Cas. 417; Battin *v.* Taggart, 1 Fish. Pat. Cas. 139; Cahardt *v.* Austin, 2 Fish. Pat. Cas. 543; Sickles *v.* Falls Co., 4 Blatchf. (U. S.) 508; s. c., 2 Fish. Pat. Cas. 202; Goodyear *v.* Berry, 2 Bond (U. S.) 189; s. c., 3 Fish. Pat. Cas. 439; American Wood Paper Co. *v.* Fibre Disintegrating Co., 3 Fish. Pat. Cas. 362; American Wood Paper Co. *v.* Heft, 3 Fish. Pat. Cas. 316; Dunham *v.* Dennison Mfg. Co., 40 Fed. Rep. 667; Hubel *v.* Dick, 24 Blatchf. (U. S.) 139; s. c., 28 Fed. Rep. 656; Combined Patents Can Co. *v.* Lloyd, 11 Fed. Rep. 149; Flower *v.* Rayner, 19 Pat. Off. Gaz. 425; Cummings *v.* Newton, 4 Bann. & Ard. Pat. Cas. 159; s. c., 16 Pat. Off. Gaz. 720; Neacy *v.* Allis, 22 Pat. Off. Gaz. 1621; M'Kay *v.* Stowe, 17 Fed. Rep. 517; United States etc. Felting Co. *v.* Haven, 3 Dill. (U. S.) 131; s. c., 2 Bann. & Ard. Pat. Cas. 164; s. c., 9 Pat. Off. Gaz. 253; Goodyear *v.* Providence Rubber Co., 2 Fish. Pat. Cas. 499; Reed *v.* Chase, 25 Fed. Rep. 94; Haines *v.* Peck, 26 Fed. Rep. 625; Flower *v.* Detroit, 127 U. S. 563; National Pump Cylinder Co. *v.* Simmons Hardware Co., 18 Fed. Rep. 324; Globe Nail Co. *v.* United States etc. Nail Co., 19 Fed. Rep. 819; Philadelphia Novelty Mfg. Co. *v.* Rouss, 39 Fed. Rep. 273.

The original patent consisted of two features: First, in the collars of parchment-paper or paper prepared with animal sizing. Second, in coating one or both sides of the collar with a thin varnish of bleached shellac to give smoothness, strength and stiffness, and to repel moisture; the reissue describes a paper, other than as above described, and did not require the collars to be coated with shellac. *Held*, this was a different invention. Union Paper Collar Co. *v.* Van Dusen, 23 Wall. (U. S.) 530; s. c., 7 Pat. Off. Gaz. 919.

The original patent for one of its elements had the use of a hot, fat liquid; the reissue included both hot and cold. *Held*, not the same invention. Russell *v.* Dodge, 93 U. S. 460; s. c., 11 Pat. Off. Gaz. 151.

The original patent had the canceling device in a letter-canceling and post-marking contrivance, restricted to a tube containing a piece of wood or other material; the reissue claimed a stamp without the peculiar mechan-

and cannot contain new or extraneous matter;[1] although, without

isms. James *v.* Campbell, 104 U. S. 356.

The reasonable inference in the original specification of Green's patent was that an air-tight connection was made between the tube and the earth. *Held*, that a description of means of making such air-tight connection did not describe a different invention. Eames *v.* Andrews, 122 U. S. 40.

The courts will treat a reissue favorably, where the patentee is clearly seeking, by apt words, to cover his invention, and nothing more. Crandal *v.* Parker Carriage Goods Co., 20 Fed. Rep. 851.

Parol testimony of what the invention actually consisted of cannot be used to correct a defect for the purpose of obtaining a reissue. Union Paper Collar Co. *v.* Van Dusen, 23 Wall. (U. S.) 530; s. c., 7 Pat. Off. Gaz. 919; Averill Paint Co. *v.* National Paint Co., 22 Pat. Off. Gaz. 585; Farr *v.* Webb, 10 Blatchf. (U. S.) 96; s. c., 5 Fish. Pat. Cas. 593; s. c., 2 Pat. Off. Gaz. 568; Sarven *v.* Hall, 9 Blatchf. (U. S.) 524.

Nor will a mere inadvertence to insert a portion of the invention in the original specification, be considered a sufficient excuse. Atwater Mfg. Co. *v.* Beecher Mfg. Co., 8 Fed. Rep. 608.

But apparently a proof of what was in a lost or dilapidated model may be received. Meyer *v.* Goodyear etc. Glove Mfg. Co., 22 Pat. Off. Gaz. 681; Aultman *v.* Holley, 11 Blatchf. (U. S.) 317; s. c., 6 Fish. Pat. Cas. 534; s. c., 5 Pat. Off. Gaz. 3; Royer *v.* Russell, 7 Fed. Rep. 696; s. c., 20 Pat. Off. Gaz. 1819.

A liberal construction of the original patent will be made to avoid declaring a reissue void for being not for the same invention as the original. Milligan Glue Co. *v.* Upton, 97 U. S. 3; s. c., 6 Pat. Off. Gaz. 837; Yale Lock Mfg. Co. *v.* New Haven Sav. Bank, 32 Fed. Rep. 167.

1. Giant Powder Co. *v.* California etc. Powder Co., 4 Fed. Rep. 720; s. c., 18 Pat. Off. Gaz. 1339; Flower *v.* Rayner, 5 Fed. Rep. 793; s. c., 19 Pat. Off. Gaz. 425; Wells *v.* Gill, 6 Fish. Pat. Cas. 89; s. c., 2 Pat. Off. Gaz. 590; Heald *v.* Rice, 21 Pat. Off. Gaz. 1447; Fay *v.* Preble, 14 Fed. Rep. 652; Averill Chemical Paint Co. *v.* National etc. Paint Co, 22 Pat. Off. Gaz. 585; Schultz *v.* Ostrander, 27 Fed. Rep. 245; Parker etc. Co. *v.* Yale Lock Co., 18 Fed. Rep. 43; Vacuum Oil Co. *v.* Buffalo Lubricating Co., 20 Fed. Rep. 850; Yale Lock Mfg. Co. *v.* James, 20 Fed. Rep. 903; Reed *v.* Chase, 25 Fed. Rep. 94; Columbia Rubber Co. *v.* Klous, 33 Fed. Rep. 275; Andrews *v.* Hovey, 26 Pat. Off. Gaz. 1011; Schillinger *v.* Cranford, 4 Mackey (U. S.) 450; s. c., 37 Pat. Off. Gaz. 49; Farmers' etc. Mfg. Co. *v.* Challenge Corn Planter Co., 23 Fed. Rep. 42; s. c., 30 Pat. Off. Gaz. 661; Hayes *v.* Seton, 20 Blatchf. (U. S.) 484; s. c., 12 Fed. Rep. 120; Streit *v.* Lauter, 11 Fed. Rep. 309; Hart *v.* Thayer, 20 Blatchf. (U. S.) 315; s. c., 21 Pat. Off. Gaz. 791; s. c., 10 Fed. Rep. 746; Curtis *v.* Branch, 4 Bann. & Ard. Pat. Cas. 189; s. c., 15 Pat. Off. Gaz. 919; Kerosene Lamp Heater Co. *v.* Littell, 3 Bann. & Ard. Pat. Cas. 312; s. c., 13 Pat. Off. Gaz. 1009; Russell *v.* Dodge, 93 U. S. 460; Stevens *v.* Pritchard, 4 Cliff. (U. S.) 417; s. c., 2 Bann. & Ard. Pat. Cas. 390; Cahart *v.* Austin, 2 Cliff. (U. S.) 528; s. c., 2 Fish. Pat. Cas. 468; Knight *v.* Baltimore etc. R. Co., 1 Taney (U. S.) 106; s. c., 3 Fish. Pat. Cas. 1; Dyson *v.* Danforth, 4 Fish. Pat. Cas. 133; Steam Gage etc. Co. *v.* Miller, 11 Fed. Rep. 718; New York Bung etc. Co. *v.* Hoffman, 20 Blatchf. (U. S.) 3; Wicks *v.* Stephens, 2 Woods (U. S.) 310; s. c., 2 Bann. & Ard. Pat. Cas. 318; United States Felting Co. *v.* Haven, 9 Pat. Off. Gaz. 253; Swaine etc. Mfg. Co. *v.* Ladd, 2 Bann. & Ard. Pat. Cas. 488; s. c., 11 Pat. Off. Gaz. 153; Matthews *v.* Iron Clad Mfg. Co., 124 U. S. 349; s. c., 42 Pat. Off. Gaz. 827; Matthews *v.* Boston Mach. Co., 105 U. S. 54; s. c., 21 Pat. Off. Gaz. 1349; Window Screen Co. *v.* Boughton, 1 Bann. & Ard. Pat. Cas. 327; Ives *v.* Sargent, 119 U. S. 652; s. c., 38 Pat. Off. Gaz. 781; Gong etc. Mfg. Co. *v.* Clark, 3 Bann. & Ard. Pat. Cas. 211; Thomas *v.* Shoe Mach. Co., 3 Bann. & Ard. Pat. Cas. 557; s. c., 16 Pat. Off. Gaz. 541; Vogler *v.* Semple, 7 Biss. (U. S.) 382; s. c., 11 Pat. Off. Gaz. 923; Doane etc. Mfg. Co. *v.* Smith, 15 Fed. Rep. 459; s. c., 24 Pat. Off. Gaz. 302; American etc. Drill Co. *v.* Sullivan Mach. Co., 22 Batchf. (U. S.) 298; s. c., 21 Fed. Rep. 74; s. c., 28 Pat. Off. Gaz. 8111; Parker etc. Co. *v.* Yale Clock Co., 123 U. S. 89; Cammeyer *v.* Newton, 4 Bann. & Ard. Pat. Cas. 159; s. c., 16 Pat. Off. Gaz. 720; Campbell *v.* James, 104 U. S. 356; s. c., 2 Pat. Off. Gaz. 337; Gosling *v.* Roberts, 106 U. S.

considering other doctrines limiting the practical extent of this,[1] the invention may be gathered from anything contained in the specifications, drawing or model,[2] and expressed in different

39; s. c., 22 Pat. Off. Gaz. 1785; Moffitt *v.* Rogers, 106 U. S. 423; s. c., 23 Pat. Off. Gaz. 270; Wing *v.* Anthony, 106 U. S. 142; Warring *v.* Johnson, 19 Blatchf. (U. S.) 38; s. c., 6 Fed. Rep. 500.

Hopkins etc. Mfg. Co. *v.* Corbin, 103 U. S. 786; Ball *v.* Langles, 102 U. S. 128; Garneau *v.* Dozier, 102 U. S. 230; Jones *v.* McMurray, 2 Hughes (U. S.) 527; s. c., 3 Bann. & Ard. Pat. Cas. 130; Atwater Mfg. Co. *v.* Beecher Mfg. Co., 8 Fed. Rep. 608.

The later rulings of the supreme court as to what may be included in a reissued patent, seem to rule that it must appear affirmatively from the comparison of the two patents, that the reissue embraces no invention which was not intended to be secured by the original patent. Flower *v.* Detroit, 127 U. S. 563; s. c., 43 Pat. Off. Gaz. 1348; Hoskin *v.* Fisher, 125 U. S. 217; s. c., 43 Pat. Off. Gaz. 509; Parker etc. Co. *v.* Yale Clock Co., 123 U. S. 87; s. c., 41 Pat. Off. Gaz. 811.

New Matter—Definition of.—New matter is anything not embraced in, or necessarily flowing from the invention as originally described, which affects the substance of the invention and might have been the subject of a new patent. Dederick *v.* Cassell, 9 Fed. Rep. 306; s. c., 20 Pat. Off. Gaz. 1233; Christman *v.* Rumsey, 17 Blatchf. (U. S.) 148; s. c., 4 Bann. & Ard. Pat. Cas. 506, s. c., 17 Pat. Off. Gaz. 903; Thomas *v.* Shoe Mach. Co., 3 Bann. & Ard. Pat. Cas. 138; 16 Pat. Off. Gaz. 541; Purviance *v.* Yerrington, 2 Bann. & Ard. Pat. Cas. 237; s. c., 9 Pat. Off. Gaz. 689; Siebert etc. Oil Cup Co. *v.* Harper etc. Lubricator Co., 4 Fed. Rep. 328:

1. See cases cited in subsequent notes.

2. Sickles *v.* Evans, 2 Cliff. (U. S.) 203; s. c., 2 Fish. Pat. Cas. 417; Seymour *v.* Osborne, 3 Fish. Pat. Cas. 555; Cabart *v.* Austin, 2 Cliff. (U. S.) 543; s. c., 2 Fish. Pat. Cas. 543; Knight *v.* Baltimore etc. R. Co., 1 Taney (U. S.) 106, s. c., 2 Fish. Pat. Cas. 1; Hoffheins *v.* Brandt, 3 Fish. Pat. Cas. 218; Sarven *v.* Hall, 9 Blatchf. (U. S.) 524; s. c., 5 Fish. Pat. Cas. 415; s. c., 1 Pat. Off. Gaz. 437, Kirby *v.* Dodge etc. Mfg. Co., 10 Blatchf. (U. S.) 307; s. c., 6 Fish. Pat. Cas. 307; s. c., 3 Pat. Off. Gaz. 181; Adjustable Window Screen Co. *v.* Boughton, 1 Bann. & Ard. Pat. Cas. 327; Flint *v.* Roberts, 4 Bann. & Ard. Pat. Cas. 168; Atwood *v.* Portland Co., 10 Fed. Rep. 283; s. c., 5 Bann. & Ard. Pat. Cas. 533; Holmes etc. Tel. Co. *v.* Domestic Teleph. Co., 42 Fed. Rep. 220; Dederick *v.* Cassell, 9 Fed. Rep. 306; Hendy *v.* Golden State etc. Iron Works, 8 Sawyer (U. S.) 468; s. c., 17 Fed. Rep. 515; Bussey *v.* Wagner, 2 Bann. & Ard. Pat. Cas. 229; s. c., 9 Pat. Off. Gaz. 300; Whittlesey *v.* Ames, 9 Biss. (U. S.) 225; s. c., 13 Fed. Rep. 893; s. c., 5 Bann. & Ard. Pat. Cas. 96; s. c., 18 Pat. Off. Gaz. 357; Calkins *v.* Bertrand, 6 Biss. (U. S.) 494; s. c., 2 Bann. & Ard. Pat. Cas. 215; s. c., 9 Pat. Off. Gaz. 795; Meyer *v.* Goodyear etc. Glove Mfg. Co., 11 Fed. Rep. 891; s. c., 22 Pat. Off. Gaz. 681; Reissner *v.* Anness, 3 Bann. & Ard. Pat. Cas. 176; s. c., 13 Pat. Off. Gaz. 870; Barker *v.* Shoots, 18 Fed. Rep. 647; Peoria Target Co. *v.* Cleveland Target Co., 43 Fed. Rep. 922; Eachus *v.* Broomall, 115 U. S. 429.

So where the drawings and description show that the matter embraced in the reissue was not in the original patent, the reissue is invalid. Covell *v.* Pratt, 18 Blatchf. (U. S.) 126; s. c., 18 Pat. Off. Gaz. 301; s. c., 5 Bann. & Ard. Pat. Cas. 380; s. c., 2 Fed. Rep. 359.

What was suggested or indicated in the original specification, drawing or Patent Office model, is not to be considered as a part of the invention intended to have been covered by the original patent, unless it can be seen from a comparison of the two patents, that the invention which the original patent was intended to cover, embraced the things thus suggested or indicated in the original specification, etc., and unless the original specification indicated that those things were embraced in the invention intended to have been secured in the original patent. Parker etc. Co. *v.* Yale Clock Co., 123 U. S. 87.

Model.—Under this ruling the office model is not sufficient. Flower *v.* Detroit, 127 U. S. 562; s. c., 43 Pat. Off. Gaz. 1348; Parker etc. Co. *v.* Yale Clock Co., 21 Blatchf. (U. S.) 485; s. c., 18 Fed. Rep. 45; probably overruling Hendy *v.* Golden State etc. Iron Works,

terms or language from that which is used in the original patent.[1]

8 Sawy. (U. S.) 468; s. c., 17 Fed. Rep. 515; Reissner v. Anness, 3 Bann. & Ard. Pat. Cas. 176; s. c., 13 Pat. Off. Gaz. 870; Meyer v. Goodyear etc. Glove Mfg. Co., 20 Blatchf. (U. S.) 91; s. c., 11 Fed. Rep. 891.

Drawing.—But if the invention attempted to be covered appears in the drawing, it is sufficient. Meyer v. Goodyear etc. Glove Mfg. Co., 20 Blatchf. (U. S.) 91; s. c., 22 Pat. Off. Gaz. 681; s. c., 11 Fed. Rep. 891.

1. French v. Rogers, 1 Fish. Pat. Cas. 133; Tarr v. Folsom, 1 Holmes (U. S.) 313; s. c., 1 Bann. & Ard. Pat. Cas. 24; s. c., 5 Pat. Off. Gaz. 92; Wells v. Jaques, 1 Bann. & Ard. Pat. Cas. 60; Wonson v. Peterson, 3 Bann. & Ard. Pat. Cas. 249; Carew v. Boston etc. Fabric Co., 1 Holmes (U. S.) 45; s. c., 5 Fish. Pat. Cas. 90; s. c., 1 Pat. Off. Gaz. 91; Crompton v. Belknap Mills, 3 Fish. Pat. Cas. 536; Blake v. Stafford, 6 Blatchf. (U. S.) 195; Tucker v. Tucker Mfg. Co., 4 Cliff. (U. S.) 397; s. c., 3 Fish. Pat. Cas. 294; Morse v. Bain, 9 West. L. J. 106; Stevens v. Pritchard, 10 Pat. Off. Gaz. 505; Lorrilard Co. v. McDowell, 11 Pat. Off. Gaz. 640; Bridge v. Brown, 1 Holmes (U. S.) 53; Searls v. Van Nest, 3 Bann. & Ard. Pat. Cas. 121; s. c., 13 Pat. Off. Gaz. 772; Atlantic etc. Powder Co. v. Rand, 16 Blatchf. (U. S.) 250; s. c., 16 Pat. Off. Gaz. 87; s. c., 4 Bann. & Ard. Pat. Cas. 263; St. Louis Stamping Co. v. Quimby, 4 Bann. & Ard. Pat. Cas. 192; s. c., 16 Pat. Off. Gaz. 135; Thomas v. Shoe Mach. Co., 3 Bann. & Ard. Pat. Cas. 557; s. c., 16 Pat. Off. Gaz. 541; Christman v. Rumsey, 17 Blatchf. (U. S.) 148; s. c., 4 Bann. & Ard. Pat. Cas. 506; s. c., 17 Pat. Off. Gaz. 903; Stephenson v. Second Ave. R. Co., 5 Bann. & Ard. Pat. Cas. 116; s. c., 1 Fed. Rep. 416; Tyler v. Welch, 18 Blatchf. (U. S.) 209; s. c., 3 Fed. Rep. 636; Wisner v. Dodds, 5 Bann. & Ard. Pat. Cas. 447; s. c., 2 Fed. Rep. 781; McCreary v. Pennsylvania Canal Co., 5 Fed. Rep. 367; Marks v. Fox, 18 Blatchf. (U. S.) 502; s. c., 6 Fed. Rep. 727; Loercher v. Crandal, 11 Fed. Rep. 872; s. c., 21 Pat. Off. Gaz. 863; Strobridge v. Landers, 11 Fed. Rep. 880; s. c. 21 Pat. Off. Gaz. 1027; Searls v. Worden, 11 Fed. Rep. 501; s. c., 21 Pat. Off. Gaz. 1955; Putnam v. Keystone Bottle Stopper Co., 38 Fed. Rep. 234; Union Paper Bag Mach. Co. v. Waterbury, 39 Fed. Rep. 389; Pope Mfg. Co. v. Gormully etc. Mfg. Co., 34 Fed. Rep. 896; Walker v. Terre Haute, 44 Fed. Rep. 70; Hubel v. Waldie, 35 Fed. Rep. 414; Turner etc. Mfg. Co. v. Dover Stamping Co., 111 U. S. 319; National Spring Co. v. Union etc. Spring Co., 12 Blatchf. (U. S.) 80; Black v. Thorne, 12 Blatchf. (U. S.) 20.

Illustrations of Changes Which May or May Not be Made in the Specifications.—From an imperfect description of one kind of machine to which an invention may be applied to another kind of machine. Aultman v. Holley, 5 Pat. Off. Gaz. 3; s. c., 11 Blatchf. (U. S.) 317; De Florez v. Raynolds, 14 Blatchf. (U. S.) 505; s. c., 3 Bann. & Ard. Pat. Cas. 292; Patten v. Stewart, 7 Fed. Rep. 215; Mfg. Co. v. Thomas, 5 Fish. Pat. Cas. 148; St. Louis Stamping Co. v. Quimby, 4 Bann. & Ard. Pat. Cas. 192; s. c., 16 Pat. Off. Gaz. 135.

An inserted assertion that the invention belongs to a certain class and accomplishes a certain result, does not invalidate. Reed v. Chase, 25 Fed. Rep. 94; Patten v. Stewart, 18 Blatchf. (U. S.) 561; s. c., 7 Fed. Rep. 215; s. c., 19 Pat. Off. Gaz. 997; Doane etc. Mfg. Co. v. Smith, 15 Fed. Rep. 459; s. c., 24 Pat. Off. Gaz. 302; Schillinger v. Gunther, 15 Blatchf. (U. S.) 303; s. c., 3 Bann. & Ard. Pat. Cas. 491; s. c., 14 Pat. Off. Gaz. 713.

Changes Allowable.—Changes of form where form is not essential. Putnam v. Hutchinson, 12 Fed. Rep. 131; Abbe v. Clark, 3 Bann. & Ard. Pat. Cas. 211; s. c., 13 Pat. Off. Gaz. 274; Decker v. Grote, 10 Blatchf. (U. S.) 331; s. c., 6 Fish. Pat. Cas. 424; s. c., 3 Pat. Off. Gaz. 522.

Otherwise where the change, though slight, is a substantial one producing a new result. Kirby v. Dodge etc. Mfg. Co., 10 Blatchf. (U. S.) 307; s. c., 6 Fish. Pat. Cas. 156; s. c., 3 Pat. Off. Gaz. 181.

Changing the relative importance of various matters. Broadnax v. Central Stock Yard etc. Co., 4 Fed. Rep. 214; s. c., 5 Bann. & Ard. Pat. Cas. 609; Poppenhausen v. Falke, 4 Blatchf. (U. S.) 493; s. c., 2 Fish. Pat. Cas. 181; Robertson v. Secombe Mfg. Co., 10 Blatchf. (U. S.) 481; s. c., 6 Fish. Pat. Cas. 268, s. c., 3 Pat. Off. Gaz. 412; American etc. Pavement Co. v. Elizabeth, 6 Fish. Pat. Cas. 424; s. c., 3 Pat. Off. Gaz. 522.

Or the drawing in immaterial par-

(*e*) COMBINATION, PROCESS, PRODUCT, MACHINE.—A patentee cannot reissue a patent for a combination of fewer elements than he describes and claims as constituting his invention in his original specification.[1] A patent for one of the various subjects of

ticulars. Pearl *v.* Appleton Co., 3 Fed. Rep. 153; s. c., 5 Bann. & Ard. Pat. Cas. 533.

Or stating new results. Putnam *v.* Yerrington, 2 Bann. & Ard. Pat. Cas. 237; s. c., 9 Pat. Off. Gaz. 689.

A new drawing may embrace matter described in the specifications. Union Paper Bag Co. *v.* Nixon, 6 Fish. Pat. Cas. 402; Hank's Case, 2 A. L. T. 129.

A material change in the drawing not warranted by the specification, must not be made. Flower *v.* Detroit, 127 U. S. 563.

Adding expositions of the prior state of the art. Kearney *v.* Lehigh Valley R. Co., 32 Fed. Rep. 320; Adee *v.* Peck, 42 Fed. Rep. 497; Turner etc. Mfg. Co. *v.* Dover Stamping Co., 111 U. S. 319; Robertson *v.* Secombe Mfg. Co., 10 Blatchf. (U. S.) 481; s. c., 6 Fish. Pat. Cas. 268; s. c., 3 Pat. Off. Gaz. 412; Yale Lock Mfg. Co. *v.* Scoville Mfg. Co., 18 Blatchf. (U. S.) 248; s. c., 3 Fed. Rep. 288.

Introduction of the word "preferably" in describing certain mechanical details. Timken *v.* Olin, 37 Fed. Rep. 205.

Correcting the spelling of patentee's name. Bignall *v.* Harvey, 18 Blatchf. (U. S.) 353; s. c., 4 Fed. Rep. 334; s. c., 18 Pat. Off. Gaz. 1275.

But having described certain modifications of a device, and stated that the invention can be modified "in various other equivalent ways, such as would suggest themselves to any intelligent mechanic," other modifications were introduced and called new inventions. *Held*, that the reissue was void. Philadelphia Novelty Mfg. Co. *v.* Rouse, 39 Fed. Rep. 273. *Compare* Broadnax *v.* Central Stock Yard Co., 4 Fed. Rep. 214; s. c., 5 Bann. & Ard. Pat. Cas. 609; Dunbar *v.* White, 4 Woods (U. S.) 116; s. c., 15 Fed. Rep. 747; s. c., 23 Pat. Off. Gaz. 1446.

Omitting ambiguous or substituting clear words and phrases not forbidden. Atlantic etc. Powder Co. *v.* Goodyear, 3 Bann. & Ard. Pat. Cas. 161; s. c., 13 Pat. Off. Gaz. 45; Draper *v.* Potomska Mills, 3 Bann. & Ard. Pat. Cas. 214; s. c., 13 Pat. Off. Gaz. 276.

A change in the wording of a claim by which an invention originally claimed as a new manufacture, may be claimed in the reissue as a new combination. Middletown Tool Co. *v.* Judd, 3 Fish. Pat. Cas. 141.

Latest Rule of Supreme Court Criticising What May be Contained in a Reissued Patent.—Those cases in which this court has held reissues to be invalid, were cases where, by the reissued patent, the scope of the original was so enlarged as to cover and claim as a new invention that which was either not in the original specification as a part of the invention described, or, if described, was, by not being claimed, virtually abandoned and dedicated to public use. Andrews *v.* Hovey, 123 U. S. 267.

Even where the invention is broader than supposed by the patentee it may be covered by the reissue. Tuttle *v.* Loomis, 24 Fed. Rep. 789; s. c., 30 Pat. Off. Gaz. 344; Jenkins *v.* Stetson, 32 Fed. Rep. 398; Odell *v.* Stout, 22 Fed. Rep. 159; Loring *v.* Hall, 15 Pat. Off. Gaz. 471.

1. Gill *v.* Wells, 22 Wall. (U. S.) 1; Washburn etc. Mfg. Co. *v.* Fuchs, 16 Fed. Rep. 661; Matthews *v.* Boston Mach. Co., 105 U. S. 54; s. c., 21 Pat. Off. Gaz. 1349; Johnson *v.* Flushing etc. R. Co., 22 Pat. Off. Gaz. 329; Turrell *v.* Bradford, 23 Pat. Off. Gaz. 1623; Gage *v.* Herring, 23 Pat. Off. Gaz. 2119; s. c., 107 U. S. 641; Yale Lock Mfg. Co. *v.* James, 125 U. S. 447; Brewster *v.* Shuler, 37 Fed. Rep. 785; Jenkins *v.* Stetson, 32 Fed. Rep. 398; Neacy *v.* Allis, 13 Fed. Rep. 874; s. c., 22 Pat. Off. Gaz. 1621; Cammeyer *v.* Newton, 4 Bann. & Ard. Pat. Cas. 159; Redmond *v.* Parham, 16 Pat. Off. Gaz. 359; Hale *v.* Stimpson, 2 Fish. Pat. Cas. 565.

Where the original patent does not suggest that a part is a distinct invention, the patent cannot be reissued to cover that part. Blackman *v.* Hibbler, 17 Blatchf. (U. S.) 333; s. c., 4 Bann. & Ard. Pat. Cas. 641; s. c., 17 Pat. Off. Gaz. 107.

Combined in a Peculiar Manner.—A claim for a combination of parts combined in a certain way cannot be reissued without restriction. McMurray

invention, which describes another as the invention of patentee, may, however, be reissued to embrace the other also.[1]

v. Mallory, 111 U. S. 97; s. c., 27 Pat. Off. Gaz. 915.

Substitution of Element.—A substitution of another element for the one originally contained, and not being an equivalent therefor, is not allowable. Blackman *v.* Hibler, 17 Blatchf. (U. S.) 333; s. c., 4 Bann. & Ard. Pat. Cas. 641; s. c., 17 Pat. Off. Gaz. 107; National Spring Co. *v.* Union Car Spring Co., 12 Blatchf. (U. S.) 80; Decker *v.* Grote, 10 Blatchf. (U. S.) 331; s. c., 6 Fish. Pat. Cas. 143; Gallahue *v.* Butterfield, 10 Blatchf. (U. S.) 236; s. c., 6 Fish. Pat. Cas. 203; s. c., 2 Pat. Off. Gaz. 648.

Under this doctrine a patent for a combination in which one or more of the elements was described and treated as a separate invention, the reissue may claim the various elements thus described. Wheeler *v.* Clipper Mower etc. Co., 10 Blatchf. (U. S.) 181; s. c., 6 Fish. Pat. Cas. 1; s. c., 2 Pat. Off. Gaz. 442; Battin *v.* Taggert, 17 How. (U. S.) 74; Wheeler *v* McCormick, 11 Blatchf. (U. S.) 334; s. c., 6 Fish. Pat. Cas. 551; s. c., 4 Pat. Off. Gaz. 692; Bantz *v.* Frantz, 105 U. S. 160; s. c., 21 Pat. Off. Gaz. 2037; Gallahue *v.* Butterfield, 10 Blatchf. (U. S.) 232; s. c., 6 Fish. Pat. Cas. 203; s. c., 2 Pat. Off. Gaz. 645; Jordon *v.* Dobson, 4 Fish. Pat. Cas. 232; Chicago Fruit House *v.* Busch, 2 Biss. (U. S.) 472; s. c., 4 Fish. Pat. Cas. 395; Jenkins *v.* Stetson, 32 Fed. Rep. 398; Dunbar *v.* White, 4 Woods (U. S.) 116; s. c., 15 Fed. Rep. 747; s. c., 23 Pat. Off. Gaz. 1446.

And this doctrine permits a subcombination which is shown by the specifications or drawings, to have been part of the original invention, to be claimed in a reissue. Kerosene Lamp Heater Co. *v.* Littell, 3 Bann. & Ard. Pat. Cas. 312; s. c., 13 Pat. Off. Gaz. 1009; Christman *v.* Rumsey, 17 Blatchf. (U. S.) 148; s. c., 4 Bann. & Ard. Pat. Cas. 506; s. c., 17 Pat. Off. Gaz. 903; Dederick *v.* Cassell, 9 Fed. Rep. 306; s. c., 20 Pat. Off. Gaz. 1233; Turrell *v.* Spaeth, 3 Bann. & Ard. Pat. Cas. 458.

An omission in a combination of a merely incidental feature of the invention, included by accident in the original patent, does not invalidate the reissue. Adee *v.* Peck, 42 Fed. Rep. 497; McWilliams Mfg. Co. *v.* Blundell, 22 Pat. Off. Gaz. 177; Woodward *v.* Dinsmore, 4 Fish. Pat. Cas. 163.

1. Process.—A patent for a process may be reissued for a process and product. Tucker *v.* Dana, 7 Fed. Rep. 213; Merrill *v.* Yeomans, 1 Holmes (U. S.) 331; s. c., 1 Bann. & Ard. Pat. Cas. 47; s. c., 5 Pat. Off. Gaz. 267.

Limitation.—But not where the product is not set forth as an invention of the patentee. Atlantic etc. Powder Co. *v.* California etc. Powder Works, 98 U. S. 126; s. c., 15 Pat. Off. Gaz. 289.

Product.—A patent for an article in a certain form, cannot be reissued to claim the article without limitation of form. Vacuum Oil Co. *v.* Buffalo etc. Oil Co., 22 Blatchf. (U. S.) 266; s. c., 20 Fed. Rep. 850; s. c., 28 Pat. Off. Gaz. 1101. Or an article made by a certain process, to the same made by any process. Cochrane *v.* Badische etc. Fabrik, 111 U. S. 203; s. c., 27 Pat. Off. Gaz. 813. Or for all purposes. Francis *v.* Mellon, 5 Fish. Pat. Cas. 153; s. c., 1 Pat. Off. Gaz. 48.

But the product and process may be both claimed if both were described. Badische etc. Fabrik *v.* Hamilton Mfg. Co., 3 Bann. & Ard. Pat. Cas. 235; s. c., 13 Pat. Off. Gaz. 273; Badische etc. Fabrik *v.* Higgin, 15 Blatchf. (U. S.) 290; s. c., 3 Bann. & Ard. Pat. Cas. 462; s. c., 14 Pat. Off. Gaz. 414; Holmes *v.* Dunham etc. Mfg. Co., 20 Blatchf. (U. S.) 123; s. c., 9 Fed. Rep. 757. But not otherwise. Averill etc. Paint Co. *v.* National etc. Paint Co., 20 Blatchf. (U. S.) 42; s. c., 9 Fed. Rep. 462; s. c., 22 Pat. Off. Gaz. 585.

Machine and Process.—A process and a machine for applying the process are not necessarily one and the same invention. They are generally distinct and different. James *v.* Campbell, 104 U. S. 356; s. c., 21 Pat. Off. Gaz. 337; Giant Powder Co. *v.* California Powder Works, 28 U. S. 136.

And the question whether a patent describing both and claiming one, can be reissued to cover both, depends upon the fact whether the two are one and the same invention. Wing *v.* Anthony, 106 U. S. 142; Clark *v.* Kennedy Mfg. Co., 14 Blatchf. (U. S.) 79; s. c., 2 Bann. & Ard. Pat. Cas. 479; s. c., 11 Pat. Off. Gaz. 68; Campbell *v.*

(*f*) ESTOPPEL—(1) *By Matters in the Application for a Patent.*—A claim cannot be incorporated in a reissued patent which embraces matter disclaimed in the original application.[1]

(2) *By Abandonment.*—Where the purpose of the reissue is to enlarge the claim, the application must be made within a reasonable time after the granting of the patent.[2]

James, 104 U. S. 356; s. c., 21 Pat. Off. Gaz. 337; Eachus *v.* Broomall, 115 U. S. 429; s. c., 33 Pat. Off. Gaz. 1265; Brainard *v.* Cramme, 20 Blatchf. (U. S.) 530; s. c., 12 Fed. Rep. 621; New *v.* Warren, 22 Pat. Off. Gaz. 587.

1. Streit *v.* Lanter, 11 Fed. Rep. 309; Leggett *v.* Avery, 101 U. S. 256; s. c., 17 Pat. Off. Gaz. 445; Putnam *v.* Tinkham, 4 Fed. Rep. 411; Putnam *v.* Hutchinson, 12 Fed. Rep. 127; Edgarton *v.* Furst etc. Mfg. Co., 10 Biss. (U. S.) 402; s. c., 9 Fed. Rep. 450; s. c., 21 Pat. Off. Gaz. 251; Beecher Mfg. Co. *v.* Atwater Mfg. Co., 114 U. S. 523; Fink *v.* Doty, 13 Pat. Off. Gaz. 322; Wicks *v.* Stevens, 2 Wood (U. S.) 310; s. c., 2 Bann. & Ard. Pat. Cas. 310.

These cases apparently overruled Kells *v.* McKenzie, 9 Fed. Rep. 284; s. c., 20 Pat. Off. Gaz. 1663.

Acquiescence in rejection by the Patent Office disclaims the matter rejected, which cannot afterwards be incorporated in a reissue. Boland *v.* Thompson, 26 Fed. Rep. 633; Arnheim *v.* Finster, 26 Fed. Rep. 277; Dobson *v.* Lees, 30 Fed. Rep. 625.

It is sufficient to prevent the incorporation of a matter in a reissue that the original patent in its specification shows that it was not intended to employ it. James *v.* Campbell, 104 U. S. 356; s. c., 21 Pat. Off. Gaz. 337; Edgarton *v.* Furst etc. Mfg. Co., 10 Biss. (U. S.) 402; s. c., 9 Fed. Rep. 450; s. c., 21 Pat. Off. Gaz. 261; Doane etc. Mfg. Co. *v.* Smith, 15 Fed. Rep. 459.

Daniels *v.* Chesterman, 13 Pat. Off. Gaz. 4; Eames *v.* Andrews, 122 U. S. 40; Yale Lock Mfg. Co. *v.* James, 22 Blatchf. (U. S.) 294; s. c., 20 Fed. Rep. 903; Sheppard *v.* Carrigan, 116 U. S. 593; s. c., 34 Pat. Off. Gaz. 1119; Toepfer *v.* Goetz, 31 Fed. Rep. 913; s. c., 41 Pat. Off. Gaz. 933; Lee *v.* Walsh, 15 Pat. Off. Gaz. 563; Prietz *v.* Bransford, 31 Fed. Rep. 458; Putnam *v.* Hutchinson, 11 Biss. (U. S.) 233; s. c., 12 Fed. Rep. 127; *Ex parte* Hatchman, 3 Mackey (U. S.) 288; s. c., 26 Pat. Off. Gaz. 738; Blades *v.* Rand, 27 Fed. Rep. 93; Ives *v.* Sargent, 119 U. S. 652; Hartshorn *v.* Saginaw Barrel Co., 119 U. S. 664; Dobson *v.* Lees, 30 Fed. Rep. 633.

This admission cannot be contradicted or withdrawn by the patentee. Moffitt *v.* Rogers, 18 Fed. Rep. 147; Crawford *v.* Heysinger, 123 U. S. 589; s. c., 42 Pat. Off. Gaz. 197.

Various Limitations Have Been Made to This Doctrine.—Yale Lock Mfg. Co. *v.* Norwich Nat. Bank, 19 Blatchf. (U. S.) 123; s. c., 6 Fed. Rep. 377; Morey *v.* Lockwood, 8 Wall. (U. S.) 230; Shoe Tip Co. *v.* Protector Co., 2 Bann. & Ard. Pat. Cas. 561; Lee *v.* Walsh, 15 Pat. Off. Gaz. 563; Stutz *v.* Armstrong, 20 Fed. Rep. 843.

Application was made May 9th, 1874, containing a broad claim, the application was rejected and new applications claiming combinations of mechanism were filed; this application pending from March 12th, 1875, to September 25th, 1877, date when original patent was issued; shortly after the applicant reissued with a claim similar to the broad claim in his first application. Reissue held invalid. Yale Lock Mfg. Co. *v.* Berkshire Nat. Bank, 135 U. S. 342.

Cancellation of Claim from Misunderstanding Official Action.—Where, however, the action of the Patent Office did not require an abandonment of part of the invention as claimed in the original application, cancellation of the claims for such part on a misapprehension of the action does not estop the patentee from reissuing to cover this part. Hutchinson *v.* Everett, 33 Fed. Rep. 502; Yale Lock Mfg. Co. *v.* New Haven Sav. Bank, 32 Fed. Rep. 167.

2. Miller *v.* Bridgeport Brass Co., 104 U. S. 350; s. c., 21 Pat. Off. Gaz. 201; Matthews *v.* Boston Mach. Co., 105 U. S. 54; Heald *v.* Rice, 104 U. S. 737; Bantz *v.* Frantz, 105 U. S. 160; s. c., 21 Pat. Off. Gaz. 2037; Johnson *v.* Flushing etc. Co., 105 U. S. 539; s. c., 22 Pat. Off. Gaz. 329; Moffit *v.* Rogers, 106 U. S. 423; s. c., 23 Pat. Off. Gaz. 270; Gage *v.* Herring, 107 U. S. 640; s. c., 23 Pat. Off. Gaz. 2119; Ives *v.* Sargent, 17 Fed. Rep. 447; Shirley *v.* Mayer, 25

(*g*) REASONABLE TIME APPLYING FOR REISSUE.—What is a reasonable time within which to apply for a reissue in which the claims are broadened, is a question to be decided upon the facts of every case.[1] From analogy[2] the space of two years has been suggested in several cases, but cases where a less time has been held to be excessive and a greater time excusable, have been decided.[3]

Fed. Rep. 38, Worden *v.* Searls, 121 U. S. 14, Dryfoos *v.* Wiese, 19 Fed. Rep. 315; Rayer etc. Mach. Co. *v.* American Printing Co., 19 Fed. Rep. 428, American etc. Boring Co. *v.* Sheldon, 25 Fed. Rep. 768; Reed *v.* Chase, 25 Fed. Rep. 94; Asmus *v.* Alden, 27 Fed. Rep. 684, Schultz *v.* Ostrander, 27 Fed. Rep. 295; Hoe *v.* Knap, 27 Fed. Rep. 204; Curran *v.* St. Louis Refrigerator etc. Co., 29 Fed. Rep. 320; Electric Gas Lighting Co. *v.* Tillotson, 21 Fed. Rep. 568; Electric etc. Lighting Co. *v.* Smith etc. Electric Co., 23 Fed. Rep. 195; Electric Gas Lighting Co. *v.* Boston Electric Co., 29 Fed. Rep. 455, Consolidated Oil Well Packer Co. *v.* Galey, 38 Fed. Rep. 918; Wollensak *v.* Reiher, 115 U. S. 96; Mahn *v.* Harwood, 112 U. S. 354; Ives *v.* Sargent, 119 U. S. 652; Gage *v.* Kellogg, 23 Fed. Rep. 891; Wooster *v.* Handy, 21 Fed. Rep. 51; Scrivner *v.* Oakland Gas Co., 22 Fed. Rep. 98; Holt *v.* Keeler, 13 Fed. Rep. 464.

There must be "a clear mistake inadvertently committed in the wording of the claims" to authorize a reissue broadening the claims. Haber *v.* Nelson Mfg. Co., 38 Fed. Rep. 830, Mahn *v.* Harwood, 112 U. S. 354; Dunham *v.* Dennison Mfg. Co., 40 Fed. Rep. 667.

But where a feature incorporated into the claim is evidently "an incidental and preferable feature of the invention" it is, as such, a mistake, and the specification may be amended to omit it as an element. Adee *v.* Peck, 42 Fed. Rep. 497.

"The claim of a specific device or combination, and an omission to claim other devices or combinations apparent on the face of the patent, are in law a dedication to the public of that which is not claimed. . . . This legal effect of the patent cannot be revoked unless the patentee surrenders it, and proves that the specification was framed by real accident, inadvertence or mistake, and this should be done with all due diligence and speed. . . Now we do not deny that a claim may be enlarged in a reissued patent; but this may only be done when an actual mistake has occurred . . . such as a court of chancery, in cases within its ordinary jurisdiction would correct." Miller *v.* Bridgeport Brass Co., 104 U. S. 350; s. c., 21 Pat. Off. Gaz. 201.

Sub-combinations.—This rule applies to claims for sub-combinations which can only be introduced into a reissue when the application claiming them is made within a reasonable time and no intervening rights have accrued. Hubel *v.* Dick, 28 Fed. Rep. 132; Stiles *v.* Rice, 29 Fed. Rep. 445.

This rule, of course, does not apply where the reissue merely describes the device more specifically. Hicks *v.* Otto, 19 Fed. Rep. 749.

The Comparison Is Between the Original and the Last Reissue.—In order to take advantage of a prior reissue to show that there had been no delay in applying to broaden the claim, this reissue must be put in evidence; otherwise the comparison will be made with the original patent, and the time between its issue and the application for the reissue considered in determining plaintiff's laches. Hoskin *v.* Fisher, 125 U. S. 217.

Original Letters Patent When Suit Is on Reissued Letters Patent.—Where the plaintiff fails to introduce into evidence the original letters patent, they may be introduced by the defendant. Parker etc. Co. *v.* Yale Clock Co., 18 Fed. Rep. 43.

1 Mahn *v.* Harwood, 112 U. S. 354, Robinson on Patents, vol. 3, p. 405; Western Union Tel. Co. *v.* Baltimore etc Co., 25 Fed. Rep. 30; Stutz *v.* Armstrong, 20 Fed. Rep. 843.

2. The time allowed for public use of an invention before application for a patent. U. S. Rev. Stat., § 4886. Asmus *v.* Alden, 27 Fed. Rep. 684; Robinson on Patents, vol. 3. p. 406.

An excuse for a delay of over two years must be clearly shown. Ives *v.* Sargent, 119 U. S. 652, s. c., 38 Pat. Off. Gaz. 181.

3. Robinson on Patents, vol. 3. p. 406.

Enlarged Claims Over Two Years—Reissue Invalid.—Enlarged claims de-

(*h*) PARTIAL INVALIDITY.—The fact that some of the claims of a reissue are invalid for any cause does not make the reissue invalid.[1] They may be disclaimed as in an original patent.[2]

(*i*) REISSUED PATENT.—The reissued patent extends only for the remainder of the term of the original,[3] which may, if there are several separate and distinct parts, be reissued in several separate parts.[4] The various requisites to the grant of an original patent

clared invalid when reissue is granted over two years after the date of original. Three and six years. American Co. *v.* Sheldon, 17 Blatchf. (U. S.) 208; over ten years and intervening rights. Hudnut *v.* Lafayette Hominy Mills, 26 Fed. Rep. 636; two years and two months reissue invalid. Phillips *v.* Risser, 26 Fed. Rep. 308. Other spaces of time. Tubular Rivet Co. *v.* Copeland, 26 Fed. Rep. 706; Gage *v.* Kellogg, 26 Fed. Rep. 242; Hubel *v.* Dick, 28 Fed. Rep. 656; Tuttle *v.* Loomis, 24 Fed. Rep. 789; Curran *v.* St. Louis Refrigerator etc. Co., 29 Fed. Rep. 320; Schickle etc. Iron Co. *v.* South St. Louis etc. Co., 29 Fed. Rep. 866; Wollensak *v.* Sargent, 33 Fed. Rep. 840; Philadelphia Novelty Mfg. Co. *v.* Rouss, 39 Fed. Rep. 273.

Enlarged Claims Under Two Years Reissue Invalid.—One year, nine months, ten days and intervening rights, and the fact that the inadvertence, accident or mistake was readily discernible. Arnham *v.* Finster, 24 Fed. Rep. 276; s. c., 26 Fed. Rep. 277.

Enlarged Claims, Reissue Valid.—An application filed within two months was held sufficiently diligent. Russell *v.* Laughlin, 26 Fed. Rep. 699; McArthur *v.* Brooklyn etc. Supply Co., 19 Fed. Rep. 263.

An application filed within less than a month of two years after the grant of the original was held valid, there being no intervening rights. Stutz *v.* Armstrong, 20 Fed. Rep. 843.

Fourteen months and the patent previously sustained. Hammerschlay Mfg. Co. *v.* Spaulding, 35 Fed. Rep. 67.

Question of Law.—What is a reasonable time is a question of law, and can be determined by the courts by comparing the original and reissued patents and the records of the Patent Office when presented for record. Western Union Tel. Co. *v.* Baltimore etc. Tel. Co., 25 Fed. Rep. 30.

Good Excuse for Laches.—Sickness of patentee at time of grant of patent, and his closely following death after he had noticed the defect, and where his administrator had used due diligence. Peoria Target Co. *v.* Cleveland Target Co., 43 Fed. Rep. 922.

What Are Not Good Excuses for Lack of Diligence in Applying for Reissue.—Where the patentee was a foreigner not familiar with the English language, and applied immediately on becoming cognizant of the defect. Boland *v.* Thompson, 26 Fed. Rep. 633.

Ignorance of the law on the part of the patentee. Haines *v.* Peck, 26 Fed. Rep. 625.

1. Gage *v.* Herring, 107 U. S. 641; s. c., 23 Pat. Off. Gaz. 2119; Dunham *v.* Dennison Mfg. Co., 40 Fed. Rep. 667; Tyler *v.* Galloway, 12 Fed. Rep. 567; s. c., 22 Pat. Off. Gaz. 2072; Reed *v.* Chase, 25 Fed. Rep. 94; s. c., 33 Pat. Off. Gaz. 996; American etc. Boring Co. *v.* Sheldon, 25 Fed. Rep. 768; s. c., 33 Pat. Off. Gaz. 1598; Reay *v.* Raynor, 22 Blatchf. (U. S.) 13; s. c., 19 Fed. Rep. 308; Dryfoos *v.* Wise, 22 Blatchf. (U. S.) 19; s. c., 19 Fed. Rep. 315; s. c., 26 Pat. Off. Gaz. 639; Havemeyer *v.* Randall, 21 Fed. Rep. 404; Hayes *v.* Bickelhoupt, 22 Blatchf. (U. S.) 463; s. c., 21 Fed. Rep. 566; Word *v.* Packer, 17 Fed. Rep. 650; Cote *v.* Moffitt, 15 Fed. Rep. 345; Starrett *v.* Athol Mach. Co., 14 Fed. Rep. 910; s. c., 23 Pat. Off. Gaz. 1729; Schillinger *v.* Greenway Brewing Co., 17 Fed. Rep. 244; s. c., 24 Pat. Off. Gaz. 495.

2. O'Reilly *v.* Morse, 15 How. (U. S.) 62; Yale Lock Mfg. Co. *v.* Sargent, 117 U. S. 553; Schillinger *v.* Gunther, 17 Blatchf. (U. S.) 69; Tyler *v.* Galloway, 12 Fed. Rep. 567.

3. Woodworth *v.* Stone, 3 Story, (U. S.) 749; s. c., 2 Robb Pat. Cas. 296; Whitely *v.* Fisher, 4 Fish. Pat. Cas. 248; House *v.* Young, 3 Fish. Pat. Cas. 335; Stanley *v.* Whipple, 2 McLean (U. S.) 35; Shaw *v.* Cooper, 7 Pet. (U. S.) 292; s. c., 1 Robb Pat. Cas. 643; Grant *v.* Raymond, 6 Pet. (U. S.) 218; s. c., 1 Robb Pat. Cas. 604; Whitely *v.* Fisher, 4 Fish. Pat. Cas. 248.

4. Selden *v.* Stockwell etc. Gas

attach to a reissue,[1] which has all the attributes of an original patent.[2]

V. Novelty — 1. Definition of Patentable Novelty. — Patentable novelty is something new invented;[3] a thing which did not exist before, differing from all other things in its structure, movement or effect, by reason of the introduction of some new mechanical combination or principle,[4] a substantial difference in principle

Burner Co., 19 Blatchf. (U. S.) 544; s. c., 9 Fed. Rep. 390; s. c., 20 Pat. Off. Gaz. 1377; Woodworth *v.* Hall, 1 Woodb. & M. (U. S.) 248; s. c., 2 Robb Pat. Cas. 495.

1. See Whiteley *v.* Fisher, 4 Fish. Pat. Cas. 248; Woodworth *v.* Hall, 1 Woodb. & M. (U. S.) 248; s. c., 2 Robb Pat. Cas. 495; Hartshorn *v.* Eagle Shade Roller Co., 18 Fed. Rep. 90; Burr *v.* Duryee, 2 Fish. Pat. Cas. 275; Wisner *v.* Grant, 7 Fed. Rep. 922; Carroll *v.* Morse, 9 Pat. Off. Gaz. 483; Carleton *v.* Bokee, 17 Wall. (U. S.) 463; Sergeant *v.* Burge, 10 Pat. Off. Gaz. 285; Jones *v.* McMurry, 2 Hughes (U. S.) 527; s. c., 3 Bann. & Ard. Pat. Cas. 130; Frinck *v.* Doty, 14 Pat. Off. Gaz. 157; Shaw *v.* Colwell Lead Co., 11 Fed. Rep. 711; s. c., 20 Blatchf. (U. S.) 417; Newton *v.* Mfg. Co., 119 U. S. 373; s. c., 38 Pat. Off. Gaz. 104.

2. French *v.* Rogers, 1 Fish. Pat. Cas. 133; Morse *v.* Baine, 9 West L. J. 106.

3. See INVENTION, vol. 11, p. 780.

Articles may be new in the commercial sense when they are not new in the sense of the Patent Law. New articles of commerce are not patentable as new articles of manufacture, unless it appears in the given case that the production of the new article involved the exercise of invention or discovery beyond what was necessary to construct the apparatus for its manufacture or production. Union Paper Collar Co. *v.* Van Dusen, 23 Wall. (U. S.) 530.

The novelty required by the Patent Law does not refer to the materials out of which the article is made, to the form or workmanship of the parts, or the use of one known equivalent for another. Forbush *v.* Cook, 2 Fish. Pat. Cas. 668; Union Paper Collar Co. *v.* Van Deuzen, 10 Blatchf. (U. S.) 109.

4. Hotchkiss *v.* Greenwood, 4 McLean (U. S.) 456; Aff'g 11 How. (U. S.) 248.

Meaning of Word Principle with Reference to Novelty.—The word principle does not mean new mechanical power, but consists in the mode of applying or contriving mechanical powers to produce a certain result. Smith *v.* Pearce, 2 McLean (U. S.) 176; s. c., 2 Robb Pat. Cas. 13; Dunbar *v.* Marden, 13 N. H. 311.

It is not a new principle in the abstract sense but a new combination or mode. Hotchkiss *v.* Greenwood, 4 McLean (U. S.) 456.

To be new in the sense of the Patent Law, there must be a discovery of new principles, or the employment of old ones in a new proportion, in a new process or to a new purpose. Holden *v.* Curtis, 2 N. H. 61. See Bell *v.* Daniels, 1 Bond (U. S.) 212; s. c., 1 Fish. Pat. Cas. 372.

A new application of a principle by new mechanical contrivances and apparatus, by means of which a new and beneficial result is produced in the use of an article to which it has thus been applied, is patentable. Silsby *v.* Foote, 1 Blatchf. (U. S.) 445; Aff'g 14 How. (U. S.) 218; Mowry *v.* Whitney, 5 Fish. Pet. Cas. 515.

Novelty in principle may consist in a new and valuable mode of applying an old power; effecting it, not merely by a new instrument or form of the machine, but by something giving a new or greater advantage. Hovey *v.* Stephens, 1 Woodb. & M. (U. S.) 290.

When the mechanism in two machines is substantially different from anything before known in its mode of operation, it is new. Lowell *v.* Lewis, 1 Mason (U. S.) 182; s. c., 1 Robb Pat. Cas. 132; Blanchard *v.* Puttman, 2 Bond (U. S.) 84; s. c., 3 Fish. Pat. Cas. 186; Whipple *v.* Baldwin Mfg. Co., 4 Fish. Pat. Cas. 29.

Equivalents.—The doctrine of equivalents must be critically considered. Sayles *v.* Chicago etc. R. Co., 1 Biss. (U. S.) 468; s. c., 2 Fish. Pat. Cas. 523; Blake *v.* Rawson, 1 Holmes (U. S.) 200; s. c., 6 Fish. Pat. Cas. 74; s. c., 3 Pat. Off. Gaz. 122.

Change of Form.—Change of form is immaterial where it does not contrib-

and application,[1] or a new mode of operation produced.[2]

ute to a new result; otherwise where it does. Adams *v.* Edwards, 1 Fish. Pat. Cas. 1.

1. Smith *v.* Pearce, 2 McLean (U. S.) 176; s. c., 2 Robb Pat. Cas. 13.

Examples.—Williams Mfg. Co. *v.* Franklin, 41 Fed. Rep. 393; Hiller *v.* Levy, 41 Fed. Rep. 627; Timken *v.* Olin, 37 Fed. Rep. 205; Ingham *v.* Pierce, 31 Fed. Rep. 822; Gandy *v.* Main Belting Co., 28 Fed. Rep. 573; Boston Electric Co. *v.* Fuller, 29 Fed. Rep. 515.

2. Forbush *v.* Cook, 2 Fish. Pat. Cas. 668; Eames *v.* Cook, 2 Fish. Pat. Cas. 146; Suffolk Mfg. Co. *v.* Hayden, 4 Fish. Pat. Cas. 86; Stainthrop *v.* Humiston, 4 Fish. Pat. Cas. 107; Cook *v.* Earnest, 5 Fish. Pat. Cas. 396; s. c., 2 Pat. Off. Gaz. 89; Waterbury Brass Co. *v.* Miller, 9 Blatchf. (U. S.) 77; s. c., 5 Fish. Pat. Cas. 48; Dukes *v.* Bauerle, 41 Fed. Rep. 778; Pullman Palace Car Co. *v.* Wagner Palace Car Co., 38 Fed. Rep. 416.

Whether a device is new depends upon whether it is the same kind of instrument as another, or whether it acts in the same way and produces the same result in substance. Colt *v.* Massachusetts Arms Co., 1 Fish. Pat. Cas. 108; Washburn *v.* Gould, 3 Story (U. S.) 122; s. c., 2 Robb Pat. Cas. 209; Smith *v.* Higgins, 1 Fish. Pat. Cas. 537; Fisk *v.* Church, 5 Fish. Pat. Cas. 540; s. c., 1 Pat. Off. Gaz. 634; Bray *v.* Hartshorn, 1 Cliff. (U. S.) 538; Robert *v.* Schuyler, 12 Blatchf. (U. S.) 444; s. c., 2 Bann. & Ard. Pat. Cas. 5; Blake *v.* Robertson, 94 U. S. 728; s. c., 11 Pat. Off. Gaz. 887; Butch *v.* Boyer, 8 Phila. (Pa.) 57; Dalton *v.* Jennings, 93 U. S. 271; Chase *v.* Sabin, 1 Holmes (U. S.) 395; s. c., 1 Bann. & Ard. Pat. Cas. 399; s. c., 6 Pat. Off. Gaz. 728; Dane *v.* Chicago Mfg. Co., 6 Fish. Pat. Cas. 130; s. c., 3 Biss. (U. S.) 374; Tufts *v.* Boston Mfg. Co., 1 Holmes (U. S.) 459; s. c., 1 Bann. & Ard. Pat. Cas. 633; s. c., 8 Pat. Off. Gaz. 239; Decker *v.* Silverbrand, 8 Pat. Off. Gaz. 944; Mfg. Co. *v.* Walworth, 9 Pat. Off. Gaz. 746; Lyman Ventilating etc. Co. *v.* Chamberlain, 2 Bann. & Ard. Pat. Cas. 433; s. c., 10 Pat. Off. Gaz. 588; Boomer *v.* United Power Press Co., 13 Blatchf. (U. S.) 107; s. c., 2 Bann. & Ard. Pat. Cas. 107; Fuller *v.* Yentzer, 11 Pat. Off. Gaz. 597; s. c., 1 Bann. & Ard. Pat. Cas. 520; Plastic Slate Roofing Co. *v.* Moore, 1 Holmes (U. S.) 167; United Nickel Co. *v.* Keith, 1 Holmes (U. S.) 328; s. c., 1 Bann. & Ard. Pat. Cas. 44; s. c., 54 Pat. Off. Gaz. 272; Carr *v.* Rice, 1 Fish. Pat. Cas. 198; Howes *v.* Nute, 4 Cliff. (U. S.) 173; s. c., 4 Fish. Pat. Cas. 263; Platt *v.* United States Button etc. Mfg. Co., 5 Fish. Pat. Cas. 265; s. c., 9 Blatchf. (U. S.) 342; s. c., 1 Pat. Off. Gaz. 524; Rumford Chemical Works *v.* Lauer, 10 Blatchf. (U. S.) 122; s. c., 5 Fish. Pat. Cas. 615; s. c., 3 Pat. Off. Gaz. 249; Singer *v.* Braunsdorf, 7 Blatchf. (U. S.) 521; Wilcox *v.* Komp, 7 Blatchf. (U. S.) 126; Springer *v.* Stanton, 2 Pat. Off. Gaz. 2; Studebaker etc. Mfg. Co. *v.* Illinois Iron etc. Co., 42 Fed. Rep. 52; Sackett *v.* Smith, 42 Fed. Rep. 846; National etc. R. Co. *v.* Sioux City etc. R. Co., 42 Fed. Rep. 679; Cleveland Fence Co. *v.* Indianapolis Fence Co., 42 Fed. Rep. 911; Smith *v.* Pittsburg Gas Co., 42 Fed. Rep. 145; Holmes etc. Tel. Co. *v.* Domestic Tel. Co., 42 Fed. Rep. 220; Williams *v.* Barnard, 41 Fed. Rep. 358; Wollensak *v.* Sargent, 41 Fed. Rep. 53; Uhlmann *v.* Bartholomae etc. Brewing Co., 41 Fed. Rep. 132; Consolidated Roller Mill Co. *v.* Coombs, 39 Fed. 25; Norton *v.* Cary, 39 Fed. Rep. 544; Peninsular Novelty Co. *v.* American Shoe Tip Co., 39 Fed. Rep. 791; McDonald *v.* McLean, 38 Fed. Rep. 328; Facer *v.* Midvale Steel Works, 38 Fed. Rep. 231; Whitman Saddle Co. *v.* Smith, 38 Fed. Rep. 414; Hake *v.* Brown, 37 Fed. Rep. 783; Sawyer Spindle Co. *v.* Buttrick, 37 Fed. Rep. 794; Fonduer *v.* Chambers, 37 Fed. Rep. 333; Joel *v.* Gesrwein, 36 Fed. Rep. 592; Stegner *v.* Blake, 36 Fed. Rep. 183; Marvin *v.* Gotschall, 36 Fed. Rep. 314; National Hat Pouncing Mach. Co. *v.* Brown, 36 Fed. Rep. 317; Hill *v.* Sawyer, 31 Fed. Rep. 282; Howe Mach. Co. *v.* National Needle Co., 134 U. S. 388; Day *v.* Fair Haven R. Co., 132 U. S. 98.

To render an article new in the sense of the patent law, it must be more or less efficacious or possess new properties by a combination with other ingredients. Milligan etc. Glue Co. *v.* Upton, 97 U. S. 3; Consolidated Brewing Apparatus Co. *v.* Clausen etc. Brewing Co., 39 Fed. Rep. 277; Fawcett *v.* Rubber etc. Harness Trimming Co., 38 Fed. Rep. 739; Am Ende *v.* Seabury, 36 Fed. Rep. 593; Marchand *v.* Emken,

2. Presumption of Novelty—Novelty Essential to Patentability.—Novelty is presumed on the grant of a patent,[1] and the patent is *prima facie* evidence thereof.[2] Novelty is essential to patentability.[3]

3. Intrinsic Evidence of Novelty.—A new effect, or a materially different effect, or as good an effect more cheaply attained, have been held evidence of the novelty of the device.[4] The production of the same result by two devices,[5] except where the result

132 U. S. 195; Steam Gauge etc. Co. *v.* Kennedy, 41 Fed. Rep. 18; United States Bung Mfg. Co. *v.* Independent Bung Co., 31 Fed. Rep. 76; Adams *v.* Bridgewater Iron Co., 26 Fed. Rep. 324; Western Electric Co. *v.* Ansonia Brass etc. Co, 114 U. S. 447; Van Deusen *v.* Nellis, 18 Fed. Rep. 596.

Extreme Cases.—A process of making whiskey, consisting in the utilization of the small particles of sugar, starch and yeast contained in the slop, in the subsequent operations of whiskey-making, by straining the slop of the chaff and other large particles, and cooling it quickly to prevent the accumulation of acid. The slop in a sweet condition, is added to the liquid in the mash tub at the end of the mashing. *Held*, that though the utilization of the slop from which the fine particles were lost, and the use of the straining and cooling apparatus were old, yet the utilization of the particles being new, the process is a novel one. Frankfort Co. *v.* Mill Creek Co., 37 Fed. Rep. 533.

The only change an increase in heat. Cary *v.* Lovell Mfg Co., 31 Fed. Rep. 344.

Only change increase of time in rubbing off the coating. Lockwood *v.* Hooper, 25 Fed. Rep. 910.

1. Swift *v.* Whisen, 2 Bond (U. S.) 84.

This presumption can only be rebutted on clear proof. Donoughe *v.* Hubbard, 27 Fed. Rep. 742; Cohansey Glass Mfg. Co. *v.* Wharton, 28 Fed. Rep. 189; Butler *v.* Bainbridge, 29 Fed. Rep. 142.

2. Matthews *v.* Skates, 1 Fish. Pat. Cas. 602; Winans *v.* New York etc. R. Co., 1 Fish. Pat. Cas. 213; Hussey *v.* Bradley, 5 Blatchf. (U. S.) 134; s. c., 2 Fish. Pat. Cas. 362; Serrill *v.* Collins, 1 Fish. Pat. Cas. 289; Middletown Tool Co. *v.* Judd, 3 Fish. Pat. Cas. 141; Ransom *v.* Mayor etc. of N. Y., 1 Fish. Pat. Cas. 252; Poppenhausen *v.* N. Y. Gutta Percha Comb Co., 2 Fish. Pat. Cas. 62; Haselden *v.* Ogden, 3 Fish. Pat. Cas. 378; Waterbury Brass Co. *v.* New York etc. Brass Co., 3 Fish. Pat. Cas. 43; Judson *v.* Moore, 1 Bond (U. S.) 285; Goodyear *v.* Beverly Rubber Co., 1 Cliff. (U. S.) 348; Carter *v.* Baker, 1 Sawyer (U. S.) 512; s. c., 4 Fish. Pat. Cas. 404; Huber *v.* Nelson Mfg. Co., 38 Fed. Rep. 830; Frankfort Whiskey Process Co. *v.* Mill Creek Distilling Co., 37 Fed. Rep. 533.

3. Blanchard *v.* Putnam, 2 Bond (U. S.) 84; Rice *v.* Heald, 13 Pac. Law J. 33; Matthews *v.* Skates, 1 Fish. Pat. Cas. 602; Packing Co. Cases, 105 U. S. 566; Bruff *v.* Ives, 14 Blatchf. (U. S. 198; s. c., 2 Bann. & Ard. Pat. Cas. 595; s. c., 11 Pat. Off. Gaz. 924. This point is so well established that authorities which, if exhaustively cited, would embrace almost all cases involving infringement of patents, that further citation is thought unnecessary.

4. Waterbury etc. Brass Co. *v.* New York etc. Brass Co., 3 Fish. Pat. Cas. 43; Suffolk Mfg. Co. *v.* Hayden, 4 Fish. Pat. Cas. 86; Forbush *v.* Cook, 2 Fish. Pat. Cas. 668; Eames *v.* Cook, 2 Fish. Pat. Cas. 146; Roberts *v.* Dickey, 4 Brews. (U. S.) 260; s. c., 4 Fish. Pat. Cas. 532; s. c., 1 Pat. Off. Gaz. 4; Masury *v.* Anderson, 11 Blatchf. (U. S.) 162; s. c., 4 Pat. Off. Gaz. 55; s. c., 6 Fish. Pat. Cas 457; Child *v.* Boston Iron Works, 6 Fish. Pat. Cas. 606; s. c., 1 Holmes (U. S.) 303; s. c., 5 Pat. Off. Gaz. 61; International Tooth Crown Co. *v.* Richmond, 30 Fed. Rep. 775.

5. Eames *v.* Cook, 2 Fish. Pat. Cas. 146; Buerk *v.* Valentine, 5 Fish. Pat. Cas. 366; s. c., 9 Blatchf. (U. S.) 479; Whittemore *v.* Cutter, 1 Gall. (U. S.) 478; s. c., 1 Robb Pat. Cas. 40; Colt *v.* Massachusetts Arms Co., 1 Fish. Pat. Cas. 108; Platt *v.* United States Button etc. Mfg. Co., 5 Fish. Pat. Cas. 265; s. c., 9 Blatchf. (U. S.) 342; s. c., 1 Pat. Off. Gaz. 524; Rumford Chemical Works *v.* Lauer, 5 Fish. Pat. Cas. 615; s. c., 10 Blatchf. (U. S.) 122; s. c., 3

is produced by the same mode of operation,[1] is no criterion to determine that the devices are the same.

4. Date of an Invention—(*a*) AS BETWEEN RIVAL INVENTORS.—Where the question of the date of an invention is between two rival inventors, or the date of the invention of the patentee is to be fixed, the date of the invention is the time at which a complete and intelligible embodiment, by which those skilled in the art could understand it, is made[2]

Pat. Off. Gaz. 249; Singer *v.* Braunsdorf, 7 Blatchf. (U. S.) 521; Wilcox *v.* Komp, 7 Blatchf. (U. S.) 126; Springer *v.* Stanton, 2 Pat. Off. Gaz. 2.

If the same results are produced by combinations of machinery operating in a substantially different manner, the machines are different. Whittemore *v.* Cutter, 1 Gall. (U. S.) 478; s. c., 1 Robb Pat. Cas. 40.

1. Whittemore *v.* Cutter, 1 Gail. (U. S.) 51; s. c., 1 Robb Pat. Cas. 40; Odiorne *v.* Winkley, 2 Gall. (U. S.) 21; s. c., 1 Robb Pat. Cas. 52.

2. Webster Loom Co. *v.* Higgins, 105 U. S. 580; s. c., 21 Pat. Off. Gaz. 2031; Draper *v.* Potomska Mills, 3 Bann. & Ard. Pat. Cas. 214; Reeves *v.* Keystone Bridge Co., 1 Pat. Off. Gaz. 466; Matthews *v.* Skates, 1 Fish. Pat. Cas. 602; Brodie *v.* Ophir Min. Co., 5 Sawy. (U. S.) 608; s. c., 4 Fish. Pat. Cas. 137; Reed *v.* Cutter, 1 Story (U. S.) 590; s. c., 2 Robb Pat. Cas. 81; Williames *v.* Barnard, 41 Fed. Rep. 358.

In the race of diligence between two inventors, he who first reduces the invention to a fixed, positive and practical form, is entitled to a priority of right to a patent. Therefore, Reed *v.* Cutter, 1 Story (U. S.) 590; Parkhurst *v.* Kinsman, 1 Blatchf. (U. S.) 488; Foot *v.* Silsby, 2 Blatchf. (U. S.) 260; Rich *v.* Lippincott, 2 Fish. Pat. Cas. 1; White *v.* Allen, 2 Cliff. (U. S.) 224; Ellithorpe *v.* Robertson, 2 Fish. Pat. Cas. 183; s. c., 4 Blatchf. (U. S.) 307; Whitely *v.* Swayne, 4 Fish. Pat. Cas. 117; Seymour *v.* Osborne, 3 Fish. Pat. Cas. 555.

The inventor who first perfects a machine and makes it capable of useful operation, is entitled to the patent. Agawam Co. *v.* Jordan, 7 Wall. (U. S.) 583; Albright *v.* Celluloid etc. Harness Trimming Co., 2 Bann. & Ard. Pat. Cas. 629; Pennsylvania Diamond Drill Co. *v.* Simpson, 37 Pat. Off. Gaz. 219. Fourteen years. Pickering *v.* Miller, 25 Pat. Off. Gaz. 189; s. c., 16 Fed. Rep. 540.

He is the first inventor who, being the original discoverer, has first perfected and adapted the invention to actual use. Whitely *v.* Swayne, 7 Wall. (U. S.) 685. Quoting Curtis on Patents, §§ 43, 37 (3rd ed.), "who first perfected and adapted the same" (his invention) "to use." Seymour *v.* Osborne, 11 Wall. (U. S.) 516.

Various Statements of Date of Invention.—The date of an invention is the date of the discovery of the principle involved and the attempt to embody it in some machine; not the date of the perfecting of the instrument. Colt *v.* Massachusetts Arms Co., 1 Fish. Pat. Cas. 108; National etc. Oil Co. *v.* Arctic Oil Co., 4 Fish. Pat. Cas. 514; s. c., 8 Blatchf. (U. S.) 416.

The period when he strikes out the plan which he afterwards patents. Adams *v.* Edwards, 1 Fish. Pat. Cas. 1. Or first perfected the intellectual production, or the idea or conception of the thing patented, so that, without more inventive power, further trial or experiment, he could have successfully applied it in practice. Ransom *v.* New York, 1 Fish. Pat. Cas. 252; Stimpson *v.* Woodman, 3 Fish. Pat. Cas. 98.

When the inventor's experiments have reached such a stage of maturity that he has a clear and definite idea of application of principle and has reduced his idea to a distinct form. Matthews *v.* Skates, 1 Fish. Pat. Cas. 602; Brodie *v.* Ophir etc. Min. Co., 5 Sawy. (U. S.) 608.

The date of an invention may be prior to the time the invention is embodied in a form capable of being patented. Colt *v.* Massachusetts Arms Co., 1 Fish. Pat. Cas. 108; National Oil Co. *v.* Arctic Oil Co., 4 Fish. Pat. Cas. 514; s. c., 8 Blatchf. (U. S.) 416; Adams *v.* Edwards, 1 Fish. Pat. Cas. 1; Ransom *v.* New York, 1 Fish. Pat. Cas. 252; Stimpson *v.* Woodman, 10 Wall. (U. S.) 117.

Priority of invention is not scientific precedence. French *v.* Rogers,

in the United States.[1]

5. **Diligence.**—The first of two or more rival inventors is entitled to the patent, provided he uses reasonable diligence in perfecting and adapting his invention.[2] After the perfecting of his invention and its application to practical use, no delay in applying for the patent,[3] unless others are injured by his laches,[4] will deprive him of his right to the patent.

6. **Anticipation**—(*a*) BY INVENTION OF THIRD PARTIES.—Patented inventions can only be anticipated by inventions of third parties, when these have been reduced to a practical form,[5]

1 Fish. Pat. Cas. 133. Nor priority of speculations of a philosopher or a mechanic. Bedford *v.* Hunt, 1 Mason (U. S.) 302. Nor the mere suggestion of an idea of application of a principle to practical purposes. Foote *v.* Silsby, 1 Blatchf. (U. S.) 445. Nor the mere prior conception of an invention however perfect the plan may have been, and although the inventor actually described the plan to another. White *v.* Allen, 2 Fish. Pat. Cas. 440; s. c., 2 Cliff. (U. S.) 224; Parkhurst *v.* Kinsman, 1 Blatchf. (U. S.) 488.

Nor do illustrative drawings of conceived ideas constitute an invention, unless followed up by reasonable observance of the requirements of the patent laws; they have no effect upon subsequently granted patent to another. Reeves *v.* Keystone Bridge Co., 5 Fish. Pat. Cas. 456; Drill Co. *v.* Simpson, 37 Pat. Off. Gaz. 219; Ellithorp *v.* Robertson, 4 Blatchf. (U. S.) 307; Electric etc. Signal Co. *v.* Hall etc. Signal Co., 6 Fed. Rep. 603; Pennsylvania etc. Drill Co. *v.* Simpson, 29 Fed. Rep. 288. Even when an antedated drawing exhibits a perfect machine in all its parts. Detroit Lubricator Mfg. Co. *v.* Renchard, 9 Fed. Rep. 293. But *compare* Webster Loom Co. *v.* Higgins, 105 U. S. 580; s. c., 21 Pat. Off. Gaz. 2031.

1. Brush Electric Co. *v.* Julien Electric Co., 41 Fed. Rep. 679; Electrical Accumulator Co. *v.* Julien Electric Co., 38 Fed. Rep. 117.

2. White *v.* Allen, 2 Fish. Pat. Cas. 440; s. c., 2 Cliff. (U. S.) 224; Reed *v.* Cutter, 1 Story (U. S.) 590; s. c., 2 Robb Pat. Cas. 81; Singer *v.* Walmsley, 1 Fish. Pat. Cas. 558; Cox *v.* Griggs, 1 Biss. (U. S.) 362; s. c., 2 Fish. Pat. Cas. 174; Whitney *v.* Emmet, 1 Baldw. (U. S.) 303; s. c., 1 Robb Pat. Cas. 567; National etc. Oil Co. *v.* Arctic Oil Co., 8 Blatchf. (U. S.) 416; s. c., 4 Fish. Pat. Cas. 514; Kneeland *v.* Sheriff, 5 Bann. & Ard. Pat. Cas. 482; s. c., 2 Fed. Rep. 901; s. c., 18 Pat. Off. Gaz. 242; Agawan Co. *v.* Jordan, 7 Wall. (U. S.) 583; Gates *v.* Benson, 3 A. L. T. 113; Hubell *v.* Dick, 24 Blatchf. (U. S.) 139; s. c., 28 Fed. Rep. 132.

Inventors have the right to take a reasonable time in which to experiment and test the invention. Kendall *v.* Winsor, 21 How. (U. S.) 322; McCormick Harvester Mach. Co. *v.* Minneapolis Harvester Works, 42 Fed. Rep. 152.

But between two inventors, one just as early as the other in their conception and equally meritorious, the one who first gets the patent is to be favored. Cox *v.* Griggs, 2 Fish. Pat. Cas. 174; s. c., 1 Biss. (U. S.) 362; Seibert etc. Oil Cup Co. *v.* Phillips Lubricator Co., 10 Fed. Rep. 677; Eagle Mfg. Co. *v.* Miller, 41 Fed. Rep. 351.

3. Allen *v.* Blunt, 2 Woodb. & M. (U. S.) 121; s. c., 2 Robb. Pat. Cas. 530; Hubel *v.* Dick, 20 Fed. Rep. 132.

4. Where an unreasonable delay is allowed to occur between the perfection of an invention and the application, and in the meanwhile other parties have independently invented the device and put it to use, a patent granted is void. New York *v.* Ransom, 23 How. (U. S.) 487.

5. Cahoon *v.* Ring, 1 Cliff. (U. S.) 592; s. c., 1 Fish. Pat. Cas. 397; Hildreth *v.* Heath, Cranch Pat. Dec. 96.

Drawings not sufficient. Ellithorp *v.* Robertson, Law's Dig. 428, § 48; Reeves *v.* Keystone Bridge Co., 5 Fish. Pat. Cas. 456; s. c., 1 Pat. Off. Gaz. 466; Carleton *v.* Atwood, 2 A. L. T. R. 129.

Use as Evidence of Reduction to Practice.—Putting into use is evidence of reduction to practice. Coffin *v.* Ogden, 7 Blatchf. (U. S.) 61.

Making a machine and applying it to actual use without patenting it is a complete invention. Stephenson *v.*

Brooklyn etc. R. Co. 19 Blachf. (U. S.) 473; s. c., 14 Fed. Rep. 457.

One or two successful applications are sufficient. Miller *v.* Foree, 9 Fed. Rep. 603; s. c., 21 Pat. Off. Gaz. 947.

Insufficient Use.—If a process is practiced once as an experiment and then abandoned, it will not be an obstacle to the right of a subsequent inventor. Piper *v.* Brown, 1 Holmes (U. S.) 20.

What is Experiment Only.—In most cases a sufficient use of the alleged prior invention must be shown to prove that it will accomplish what is claimed; otherwise it rests in the region of mere experiment. Chicago etc. R. Co. *v.* Sayles, 97 U. S. 554.

The party alleged to have made the prior invention, must have proceeded so far as to have entitled himself to a patent. Allen *v.* Hunter, 6 McLean (U. S.) 303.

Contra, Hildreth *v.* Heath, 1 Cranch Pat. Dec. 95.

If a person understood his invention and applied it successfully in one or two instances, it is a sufficient reduction to practice to defeat the claim of a subsequent inventor. Miller *v.* Foree, 21 Pat. Off. Gaz. 947; s. c., 9 Fed. Rep. 603; Rich *v.* Lippincott, 2 Fish. Pat. Cas. 1.

If the machine was complete, capable of working and known to at least five persons, was put into use, tested and successful, it will invalidate a subsequent patent. Coffin *v.* Ogden, 18 Wall. (U. S.) 120.

Extent of Use Necessary.—Where the invention has been put into greater or less use, or extent of diffusion of knowledge, it is not criterion whether it invalidates a subsequent patent. Rich *v.* Lippincott, 2 Fish. Pat. Cas. 1; Spring *v.* Packard, 1 Bann. & Ard. Pat. Cas. 531.

The prior machine must be perfect and capable of being used; it is not necessary that it should have been used. Parker *v.* Ferguson, 1 Blatchf. (U. S.) 407; Pitts *v.* Wemple, 2 Fish. Pat. Cas. 10: s. c., 1 Biss. (U. S.) 87.

The use of a successful invention which needed no change of mechanism, may be entirely discontinued without its ceasing to anticipate a subsequent invention. Shoup *v.* Henrici, 2 Bann. & Ard. Pat. Cas. 249; Waterman *v.* Thompson, 2 Fish. Pat. Cas. 461; McNish *v.* Everson, 2 Fed. Rep. 899.

Success of Use.—The prior invention need not be worked with any greater skill and success than to demonstrate its usefulness. Waterman *v.* Thomson, 2 Fish. Pat. Cas. 461; Pitts *v.* Wemple, 1 Biss. (U. S.) 87; Northwestern Fire Extinguisher Co. *v.* Philadelphia Fire Extinguisher Co., 1 Bann. & Ard. Pat. Cas. 177.

Reduction into Practice Does Not Mean Necessarily Putting Into Use.—"Reduction to practice" does not necessarily mean bringing the invention into use. Heath *v.* Hildreth, 1 Cranch Pat. Dec. 96; Perry *v.* Cornell, 1 Cranch Pat. Dec. 132; Coffin *v.* Ogden, 3 Fish. Pat. Cas. 640; s. c., 7 Blatchf. (U. S.) 61.

But putting the invention into a form ready for practical use. Coffin *v.* Ogden, 3 Fish. Pat. Cas. 640; s. c., 7 Blatchf. (U. S.) 61; Heath *v.* Hildreth, 1 Cranch Pat. Dec. 96.

But it need not be carried to a point where there cannot be any subsequent improvement, and any practical utility, however small, is sufficient to show the invention completed. Johnson *v.* Root, 1 Fish. Pat. Cas. 351.

A completed invention signifies that the invention should be of some practical utility; it need not be of a high degree. Johnson *v.* Root, 1 Fish. Pat. Cas. 351.

A perfected invention is one that is brought to such a condition as to be capable of practical use. Hayden *v.* Suffolk Mfg. Co., 4 Fish. Pat. Cas. 86; aff'g 3 Wall. (U. S.) 315.

A written description of a machine, although illustrated by drawings, which has not been given to the public, does not constitute an invention within the meaning of the Patent Laws. Evidence that such a description was made does show, of itself, a prior invention. Such a description has not the same effect as a printed publication. It lacks the essential quality of such a publication, for even though deposited in the Patent Office, it is not designed for general circulation, nor is it made accessible to the public generally, being so deposited for the special purpose of being examined and passed upon by the Patent Office, and not that it may thereby become known to the public. Although it may incidentally become known, the deposit of it is not a publication of it within the meaning of the statutes of the law. Moreover, although the description may be so full and precise as to enable any one skilled in the art to which it appertains to construct what it describes, it does not attain the proportions or character of a complete invention until it is embodied in a form capable of useful operation.

are beyond the stage of mere experiment,[1] and are of such a character that the patented device can be constructed from them without the exercise of invention.[2]

(*b*) EXPERIMENT.—Where the inventor has never attained a knowledge such as will enable him to put his idea into successful practice, although he has made trials and experiments to accomplish it,[3] or has not reduced his idea to practice and embodied it

Northwestern Fire Fxtinguisher Co. *v.* Philadelphia Fire Extinguisher Co., 6 Pat. Off. Gaz. 34; Lyman Ventilating etc. Co. *v.* Lalor, 12 Blatchf. (U. S.) 303; s. c., 1 Bann. & Ard. Pat. Cas. 403.

1. Where an inventor has perfected his invention and obtained patent therefor the patent cannot be invalidated by showing that crude and unsuccessful experiments were made by others previous to his invention. La Baw *v.* Hawkins, 1 Bann. & Ard. Pat. Cas. 428; Aultman *v.* Holley, 11 Blatchf. (U. S.) 317; s. c., 6 Fish. Pat. Cas. 534; s. c., 5 Pat. Off. Gaz. 3; Albright *v.* Celluloid etc. Harness Trimming Co., 2 Bann. & Ard. Pat. Cas. 629; s. c., 12 Pat. Off. Gaz. 227; Uhlmann *v.* Bartholomae etc. Brewing Co., 41 Fed. Rep. 132; Ansonia Brass etc. Co. *v.* Electrical Supply Co., 32 Fed. Rep. 81.

An article which was made merely as a curiosity and not for the trade will not defeat a subsequent invention. Lamb *v.* Hamblen, 11 Fed. Rep. 722.

2. Crandal *v.* Watters, 20 Blatchf. (U. S.) 97; Crandal *v.* Parker Carriage etc. Co., 28 Pat. Off. Gaz. 369.

Process and Product.—Where an article is patented, a prior publication relied upon to anticipate it, need not describe the process by which it is made, if it describes the article. Cohn *v.* United States Corset Co., 93 U. S. 366.

Where alleged prior invention was shown to be very near the realization of the invention, but could not, at a period long subsequent make a machine embodying the invention, *held*, that it was not sufficient to defeat a patent even though witnesses testified it was successful. Dolbear *v.* American Bell Telephone Co., 126 U. S. 1; Taylor *v.* Wood, 1 Bann. & Ard. Pat. Cas. 270.

Where prior inventors approach very near the discovery of patentee but do not discover the principle feature of his invention, and are not able to give any directions by which same can be successfully prepared and applied, the patent is not anticipated. Cahill *v.* Brown, 3 Bann. & Ard. Pat. Cas. 580.

3. United Nickel Co. *v.* Anthes, 1 Holmes (U. S.) 155; s. c., 5 Fish. Pat. Cas. 517; s. c., 1 Pat. Off. Gaz. 578; New York *v.* Ransom, 23 How. (U. S.) 487; Wayne *v.* Holmes, 1 Bond (U. S.) 27; Hubbell's Case, 5 Ct. of Cl. 1; Stickels *v.* Borden, 3 Blatchf. (U. S.) 535; Smith *v.* Allen, 2 Fish. Pat. Cas. 572; Many *v.* Jagger, 1 Blatchf. (U. S.) 372; Seymour *v.* McCormick, 19 How. (U. S.) 96; Smith *v.* Fay, 6 Fish. Pat. Cas. 446; Latta *v.* Shawk, 1 Fish. Pat. Cas. 465; Doughty *v.* Day, 9 Blatchf. (U. S.) 262; Ellithorp *v.* Robertson, 4 Blatchf. (U. S.) 307; Stainthorp *v.* Humiston, 4 Fish. Pat. Cas. 107; Ball *v.* Murry, 10 Pa. St. 14; Wilcox *v.* Komp, 7 Blatchf. (U. S.) 126.

Two Meanings of "Experiment."—An experiment may be a trial either of an incomplete mechanical structure to ascertain what changes or additions may be necessary to make it accomplish the design of its projector, or of a completed machine to test its efficiency. In the first case, abandonment having taken place, no effect is caused on subsequent invention; but if the experiment, in second case, shows the capacity of machine to effect the inventor's object, he has the merit of producing complete invention. Northwestern Fire Extinguisher Co. *v.* Philadelphia Fire Extinguisher Co., 1 Bann. & Ard. Pat. Cas. 177.

What Amounts to an Abandoned Experiment.—Where an inventor for some reason breaks up his invention, and while not wholly intending to abandon it, yet uncertain whether he will resume the subject, it shows not an unconditional abandoment but an entire uncertainty during the suspension, whether or not the invention will be given to the public, there being no application for a patent; another, who invents the same thing, perfects it, reduces it to practice, patents and consigns it to public use will be regarded as the first inventor. White *v.* Allen, 2 Fish. Pat. Cas. 440; s. c., 2 Cliff. (U. S.) 224; Gallahue *v.* Butterfield, 10 Blatchf. (U. S.) 232; s. c., 6 Fish. Pat.

in some distinct form,[1] he has not progressed beyond an experiment. The idea must be embodied.[2]

Cas. 203; s. c., 2 Pat. Off. Gaz. 645; Adams etc. Mfg. Co. *v.* Rathbone, 26 Fed. Rep. 262; Hutchinson *v.* Everett, 26 Fed. Rep. 531.

A man made and tested several devices, but after testing them, took them to pieces and laid them away. *Held*, an abandoned experiment. Fay *v.* Allen, 24 Fed. Rep. 804.

Extreme Case.—Half a dozen articles were made and the manufacture was abandoned. *Held*, their manufacture was an abandoned experiment. Hicks *v.* Otto, 29 Pat. Off. Gaz. 365; s. c., 19 Fed. Rep. 749.

Abandoned Experiment.—If an alleged prior invention was only an abandoned experiment, never perfected, it cannot affect a subsequent patent. Corn Planter Patent, Brown *v.* Guild, 23 Wall. (U. S.) 161; Adams *v.* Jones, 1 Fish. Pat. Cas. 527; Gottfried *v.* Phillip Best Brewing Co., 5 Bann. & Ard. Pat. Cas. 4; Woodward *v.* Dinsmore, 4 Fish. Pat. Cas. 163; United Nickel Co. *v.* Authes, 1 Holmes (U. S.) 135; s. c., Pat. Office Gaz. 578.

If alleged prior machine is abandoned as useless after experimental trials, presumption will be that it is not identical with subsequent invention of proved merit. Wayne *v.* Holmes, 1 Bond (U. S.) 27.

A single machine abandoned many years before, will not invalidate a patent. Blake *v.* Rawson, 1 Holmes (U. S.) 200; s. c., 3 Pat. Off. Gaz. 122; Taylor *v.* Wood, 12 Blatchf. (U. S.) 110; s. c., 1 Bann. & Ard. Pat. Cas. 270.

If suggestions came to the inventor from prior experiments, and he is the first who reduced these suggestions to practice, he is entitled to his invention. Roberts *v.* Dickey, 1 Pat. Off. Gaz. 4.

1. Parkhurst *v.* Kinsman, 1 Blatchf. (U. S.) 488.

2. Richardson *v.* Noys, 2 Bann. & Ard. Pat. Cas. 398; s. c., 10 Pat. Off. Gaz. 507.

Where a patent has been granted for improvements which, after a full and fair trial, resulted in unsuccessfull experiments and have finally been abandoned, and another person takes up the subject of the improvements and is successful, he is entitled to the merit of them as an original inventor. Whitely *v.* Swayne, 7 Wall. (U. S.) 685.

Although prior unsuccessful experiments involved the same idea or principle as subsequent patent, the latter will not be invalidated. United Nickel Co. *v.* Authes, 5 Fish. Pat. Cas. 517; s. c., 1 Holmes 135; Roberts *v.* Dickey, 3 Brews. (Pa.) 260; American Bell Teleph. Co. *v.* People's Teleph. Co., 25 Fed. Rep. 725.

Model Insufficient.—The mere making a model of an invention, held not to constitute invention, as against a patent subsequently granted to another for the same thing. Stillwell etc. Mfg. Co. *v.* Cincinnati Gas etc. Co., 1 Bann. & Ard. Pat. Cas. 610.

Same rule obtains, although the model was capable of operation for the purpose of experiments. Cahoon *v.* Ring, 1 Cliff. (U. S.) 592.

Especially where the model was one filed in the Patent Office and recalled by the applicant because it did not represent his invention "truly." Decker *v.* Grote, 10 Blatchf. (U. S.) 331; s. c., 6 Fish. Pat. Cas. 143; s. c., 3 Pat. Off. Gaz. 65.

Use of Knowledge Obtained from an Abandoned Experiment—When It Makes Subsequent Patent Void.—If the knowledge derived from a prior abandoned experiment is sufficiently clear and definite to enable an inventor to construct the improvement which is the subject of his invention, the patent is void; otherwise, where an original inventor of an improvement, though having knowledge of such an experiment, who is entitled to the benefit of all unsubstantial changes and improvements, notwithstanding such modifications may run into and include forms of mechanism shown in the abandoned experiment. Union Paper Bag etc. Co. *v.* P. & W. Co., 15 Blatchf. (U. S.) 160; s. c., 3 Bann. & Ard. Pat. Cas. 403; s. c., 15 Pat. Off. Gaz. 423.

The following have been held to be experiments only: A single machine abandoned directly, and apparently impracticable. Blake *v.* Rawson, 6 Fish. Pat. Cas. 74; s. c., 3 Pat. Off. Gaz. 122, Taylor *v.* Wood, 12 Blatchf. (U. S.) 110; s. c., 1 Bann. & Ard. Pat. Cas. 270; s. c., 8 Pat. Off. Gaz. 90; Tatum *v.* Gregory, 41 Fed. Rep. 142.

A device not showing an important element. Roberts *v.* Dicky, 4 Brews. (Pa.) 260; s. c., 20 Fish. Pat. Cas. 532;

(*c*) CONCEALED INVENTION.—A patent is not invalidated by a concealed invention,[1] or by one accidentally made and never communicated.[2]

(*d*) BY PUBLICATION.—A patent is anticipated by a publication,[3]

s. c., 1 Pat. Off. Gaz. 4; Hitchcock *v.* Tremaine, 9 Blatchf. (U. S.) 550; s. c., 5 Fish. Pat. Cas. 537; s. c., 1 Pat. Off. Gaz. 633.

A similar product made by a somewhat similar process, but apparently not successful and not continued. Smith *v.* Glendale etc. Fabric Co., 1 Holmes (U. S.) 340; s. c., 5 Pat. Off. Gaz. 429.

Cases where alleged anticipating device declared experiment through the non-success of the result. Smith *v.* Goodyear Dental etc. Co., 93 U. S. 487; s. c., 11 Pat. Off. Gaz. 246.

1. Whitney *v.* Emmett, 1 Baldw. (U. S.) 303; s. c., 1 Robb Pat. Cas. 567; Rowley *v.* Mason, 2 A. L. T. 106; Judson *v.* Bradford, 3 Bann. & Ard. Pat. Cas. 539; s. c., 16 Pat. Off. Gaz. 171; Sayles *v.* Chicago etc. R. Co., 2 Fish. Pat. Cas. 523; s. c., 1 Biss. (U. S.) 468; Stainthrop *v.* Humiston, 4 Fish. Pat. Cas. 107; Piper *v.* Brown, 4 Fish. Pat. Cas. 175; Zinsser *v.* Kremer, 39 Fed. Rep. 111.

Especially is this the case where an invention is afterward forgotten. Gayler *v.* Wilder, 10 How. (U. S.) 477; Hall *v.* Bird, 3 Fish. Pat. Cas. 595; s. c., 6 Blatchf. (U. S.) 438; Bullock Printing Press Co. *v.* Jones, 3 Bann. & Ard. Pat. Cas. 195.

And where only a single specimen of the invention was in existence. Cahoon *v.* Ring, 1 Fish. Pat. Cas. 397.

That a device had been kept secret some time does not prevent it from being afterwards patented. Ayling *v.* Hall, 2 Cliff. (U. S.) 494.

2. New York *v.* Ransom, 23 How. (U. S.) 322.

3. Publication means put into general circulation. Cotter *v.* Stimson, 20 Fed. Rep. 906.

If an invention has been described in a public work anterior to the supposed discovery, the patent is void. Evans *v.* Eaton, 3 Wheat. (U. S.) 454; s. c., 1 Robb Pat. Cas. 68; Winans *v.* Schenectady etc. R. Co., 2 Blatchf. (U. S.) 279; Evans *v.* Hettick, 3 Wash. (U. S.) 408.

A specification of a prior foreign patent is a prior publication. Sewall *v.* Jones, 91 U. S. 171.

Status of Publication.—"Under the provisions of law, if the publication in the English work preceded the discovery by Heaton, the defense was made out. Under the law the publication is put upon the same footing with a patent taken out at the time of the publication. The sole question is, therefore, did Heaton make his invention before the date of the English publication?" Webb *v.* Quintard, 9 Blatchf. (U. S.) 352; s. c., 5 Fish. Pat. Cas. 276.

When a Printed Description Becomes a "Publication."—A printed description of an invention is not deemed published until after it has been left some time in a place accessible to the public. Coburn *v.* Schroeder, 22 Pat. Off. Gaz. 1538; s. c., 11 Fed. Rep. 425.

What Does Not Amount to a Publication.—A description of an invention contained in an application for a patent which was rejected because it lacks the essential quality of a publication, in that it is not accessible to the public generally or designed for general circulation. Northwestern Fire Extinguisher Co *v.* Philadelphia Fire Extinguisher Co., 1 Bann. & Ard. Pat. Cas. 177; s. c., 6 Pat. Off. Gaz. 34.

Business circulars sent only to persons engaged or supposed to be engaged in the trade. New Process Fermentation Co *v.* Koch, 21 Fed. Rep. 580; Parsons *v.* Colgate, 15 Fed. Rep. 600.

A book, of which there was no evidence other than that furnished by the copy, that the work was ever on sale or circulation. Cottier *v.* Stimson, 20 Fed. Rep. 906.

A book offered as an anticipatory publication must be proved to be put in circulation or offered to the public before the patentee's invention, by other evidence than the date on the title page. Reeves *v.* Keystone Bridge Co., 5 Fish. Pat. Cas. 458; s. c., 9 Phila. (Pa.) 368; s. c., 1 Pat. Off. Gaz. 466.

A written description of a machine, although illustrated by drawings, which has not been given to the public, does not constitute an invention within the meaning of the Patent Laws, so as to defeat a subsequent patent to an inde-

which clearly sets forth the invention it is intended to describe.[1]

pendent inventor, even though it be deposited in the Patent Office as part of an application for a patent. Lyman Ventilating etc. Co. *v.* Lalor, 1 Bann. & Ard. Pat. Cas. 403.

A mere rejected application showing that the device described was ever practically made and used, does not anticipate a patent. Barker *v.* Stowe, 3 Bann. & Ard. Pat. Cas. 337.

When the inventor's idea is perfected by a practical adaption of it in the form of mechanism, a rejected specification with the drawings, must be considered in connection with it, in ascertaining the date of invention, design of inventor, and the principle intended function and mode of operation of his mechanism. Northwestern Fire Extinguisher Co. *v.* Philadelphia Fire Extinguisher Co., 1 Bann. & Ard. Pat. Cas. 177.

A prior application for a patent without evidence to show that the described device was ever constructed, is not sufficient to defeat subsequent patent. Adams *v.* Howard, 26 Pat. Off. Gaz. 825.

An English provisional specification is not a bar to a patent, only as a printed specification describing the invention. The patent constitutes no objection. Cohn *v.* United States Corset Co., 12 Blatchf. (U. S.) 225.

A provisional specification which is not shown to take effect as a publication prior to the date showing the invention, does not anticipate a patent. Ireson *v.* Pierce, 39 Fed. Rep. 795; Smith *v.* Goodyear Dental etc. Co., 93 U. S. 486; s. c., 11 Pat. Off. Gaz. 246.

1. A description in a prior publication, in order to defeat a patent, must contain and exhibit a substantial representation of the patented improvement in such full, clear and exact terms as to enable any person skilled in the art or science to which it appertains to make, construct and practice the invention patented. It must be an account of a complete and operative invention, capable of being put into practical operation. Seymour *v.* Osborne, 11 Wall. (U. S.) 516; Cohn *v.* United States Corset Co., 93 U. S. 366; Electrical Accumulation Co. *v.* Julien Electric Co., 38 Fed. Rep. 117; Adams *v.* Bellaire Stamping Co., 28 Fed. Rep. 360; Downton *v.* Yaeger Milling Co., 108 U. S. 466.

If the thing patented is described, the steps necessarily antecedent need not be. Cohn *v.* United States Corset Co., 93 U. S. 366.

"Inventions patented here cannot be superseded by the mere introduction of a foreign patent or publication, although of prior date, unless the descriptions and drawings contain and exhibit a substantial representation of the patented improvement in such full, clear and exact terms as to enable anyone skilled in the art or science to which it appertains, without resorting to experiments, to make, construct and practice the invention as he would be enabled to do from a prior patent for the same invention." Cahill *v.* Brown, 15 Pat. Off. Gaz. 697; s. c., 3 Bann. & Ard. Pat. Cas. 580, *citing* Betts *v.* Menzies, 7 L. T., N. S. 110.

Where the alleged prior publication remotely suggested the device, but did not construct it so that the public could manufacture and put it to the use designed without further invention. McComb *v.* Ernest, 1 Woods (U. S.) 195; Howe *v.* Williams, 2 Cliff. (U. S.) 245; Carr *v.* Rice, 1 Fish. Pat. Cas. 198.

Scientific Speculation Insufficient.—A publication showing only suggestions and speculations of scientific men who had never tested the practicability of the device. Jensen *v.* Keasbey, 24 Fed. Rep. 144; Hays *v.* Sulsor, 1 Bond (U. S.) 279; s. c., 1 Fish. Pat. Cas. 532.

Incompleteness and Indefiniteness Fatal.—Statements in a prior publication not full and definite enough to enable those skilled in the art to put the invention into practice. Hord *v.* Boston Car Spring Co., 21 Fed. Rep. 67; Cohn *v.* United States Corset Co., 93 U. S. 366; Downton *v.* Yaeger Milling Co., 108 U. S. 466.

When the published description does not give the public a practical knowledge of the invention. Roberts *v.* Dickey, 4 Brew. (Pa.) 260.

Where the invention cannot be made and used merely by use of the publication without the aid of anything not known. Begnall *v.* Harvey, 18 Blatchf. (U. S.) 353; Carr *v.* Rice, 1 Fish. Pat. Cas. 198; Goff *v.* Stafford, 14 Pat. Off. Gaz. 748.

Burden to Show Sufficiency on Defendant.—The defendant has to make out the sufficiency of the description. Cohn *v.* United States Corset Co., 12 Blatchf. (U. S.) 225.

(*e*) KNOWLEDGE OF PRIOR DEVICE OR DESCRIPTION.—A patent is void, even though the inventor had no knowledge of the prior device or description anticipating it;[1] even when an invention is abandoned it becomes public property and cannot be resumed by an inventor.[2]

(*f*) MUST BE PRIOR TO DATE OF INVENTION.—To invalidate a patent the anticipating device or description must be prior to the patentee's invention, not merely prior to his application for a patent.[3]

7. Novelty with Reference to Foreign Inventions.—A patentee must be the inventor with reference to foreign countries, as well as to this;[4] that is, he must be an original inventor, and not an

Completeness of Publication Question of Fact.—Whether a publication offered in evidence describes the invention claimed in the patent, is a question of fact. Adams *v.* Bellaire Stamping Co., 28 Fed. Rep. 360.

1. Evans *v.* Eaton, 3 Wheat. (U. S.) 454; s. c., 1 Robb Pat. Cas. 68; Winans *v.* Schenectady R. Co., 2 Blatchf. (U. S.) 279; Evans *v.* Hettick, 3 Wash. (U. S.) 408, s. c., 1 Robb Pat. Cas. 166; Sewall *v.* Jones, 91 U. S. 171; s. c., 9 Pat. Off. Gaz. 47.

See Reed *v.* Cutter, 1 Story (U. S.) 590; s. c., 2 Robb Pat. Cas. 81.

Presumed to Know Prior Inventions or Patents.—A patentee is presumed to have knowledge of previous inventions. Foote *v.* Silsby, 2 Blatchf. (U. S.) 260; Woodcock *v.* Parker, 1 Gall. (U. S.) 438.

Also presumed to know of a preceding patent. Odiorne *v.* Winkley, 2 Gall. (U. S.) 51.

Foreign Patent.—When an invention has been patented in a foreign country, or described in a public work the alleged inventor here is presumed to have been acquainted with that invention as it was known in the foreign country. Swift *v.* Whisen, 2 Bond (U. S.) 115.

2. Colt *v.* Massachusetts Arms Co., 1 Fish. Pat. Cas. 108; Whipple *v.* Baldwin Mfg. Co., 4 Fish. Pat. Cas. 29; White *v.* Allen, 2 Cliff. (U. S.) 224; s. c., 2 Fish. Pat. Cas. 440; Northwestern Fire Extinguisher Co. *v.* Philadelphia Fire Extinguisher Co., 1 Bann. & Ard. Pat. Cas. 177; Shoup *v.* Henrici, 2 Bann. & Ard. Pat. Cas. 249; s. c., 4 Pat. Off. Gaz. 1162.

Lost Art.—A rediscovered "lost art" has been placed on a different footing. Gayler *v.* Wilder, 10 How. (U. S.) 477.

3. Dixon *v.* Moyer, 4 Wash. (U. S.) 68; Smith *v.* Goodyear Dental etc. Co., 93 U. S. 486; Reeves *v.* Keystone Bridge Co., 5 Fish. Pat. Cas. 462; s. c., 1 Pat. Off. Gaz. 466; Byerly *v.* Cleveland Linseed Oil Works, 31 Fed. Rep. 73; Draper *v.* Potomska Mills, 3 Bann. & Ard. Pat. Cas. 215; Bates *v.* Coe, 98 U. S. 34; Consolidated Bunging Apparatus *v.* Woerle, 29 Fed. Rep. 449.

And, consequently, where an invention is shown to be made before the sealing of an English patent, the invention is not anticipated by it. Railway Registering Mfg. Co. *v.* Broadway etc. R. Co., 26 Fed. Rep. 522.

He can show the date of his invention. Parker *v.* Hulme, 1 Fish. Pat. Cas. 44; Judson *v.* Cope, 1 Bond (U. S.) 327; s. c., 1 Fish. Pat. Cas. 615.

A description in a printed publication cannot invalidate a patent unless prior to the invention. It is not enough that it was prior to the application for letters patent. Bartholomew *v.* Sawyer, 1 Fish. Pat. Cas. 516; s. c., 4 Blatchf. (U. S.) 347; Howe *v.* Morton, 1 Fish Pat. Cas. 586; Cochrane *v.* Deener, 94 U. S. 780; Reeves *v.* Keystone Bridge Co., 5 Fish. Pat. Cas. 458; s. c., 9 Phila. (Pa.) 368; s. c., 1 Pat. Off. Gaz. 466.

English Specifications.—American patentee made his invention before the filing of English specification. *Held*, that his patent was not invalidated. Lorrilard *v.* Dohan, 9 Fed. Rep. 509; s. c., 20 Pat. Off. Gaz. 1587; De Florez *v.* Raynolds, 17 Blatchf. (U. S.) 436; s. c., 17 Pat. Off. Gaz. 503.

The specification or other description must be published before the date of invention of American patentee, provided the latter believed himself, at the time of his application for letters patent, to be the first inventor. Elizabeth *v.* American Pavement Co., 97 U. S. 126.

4. Sewall *v.* Jones, 91. U. S. 171.

importer of the invention.[1]

8. Novelty with Reference to Combinations.—The novelty in combinations consists in the embodiment and adaptation of mechanical appliances which are old.[2]

VI. Public Use.—Where an invention has been in public use or on sale in the United States for more than two years prior to the application for a patent, the patent granted is void.[3] It is immaterial whether the use or sale has or has not been with the consent of the inventor.[4] The test whether a transaction is or is not a public sale or use, is whether the use or sale has been in

1. Thompson *v.* Haight, 1 U. S. L. J. 582.

Proof of prior use in a foreign country will not supersede a patent granted here unless the alleged invention was patented in some foreign country. Proof of such foreign manufacture and use, if known to the applicant for the patent, may be evidence to show he was not the inventor of the alleged new improvement; but it is not sufficient to supersede the patent if he did not borrow his supposed invention from that source, unless the foreign inventor obtained a patent for his improvement or the same was described in some printed publication. Roemer *v.* Simon, 95 U. S. 214; Doyle *v.* Spaulding, 19 Fed. Rep. 744; Illingworth *v.* Spaulding, 9 Fed. Rep. 611.

2. Crandal *v.* Walters, 9 Fed. Rep. 659; Aron *v.* Manhattan R. Co., 132 U. S. 84; Proctor *v.* Bennis, 36 C. D. 740; May *v.* Fond du Lac Co., 27 Fed. Rep. 691.

Novelty in Combinations.—When a patent is for a combination, it is immaterial whether the patentee is the inventor of any of the elements of ingredients. They may all be old, and yet if the patentee was the first to combine them for the particular purpose, he is entitled to be protected in that improvement. Silsby *v.* Foote, 20 How. (U. S.) 378; O'Reilly *v.* Morse, 15 How. (U. S.) 62; Pennock *v.* Dialogue, 4 Wash. (U. S.) 538; s. c., 2 Pet. (U. S.) 1; s. c., 1 Robb Pat. Cas. 466; Ryan *v.* Goodwin, 3 Sumn. (U. S.) 514; s. c., 1 Robb Pat. Cas. 725; Sessions *v.* Romadka, 28 Pat. Off. Gaz. 721.

The theory of a combination is that all the parts are old and the invention consists in the new combination. Union Sugar Refinery Co. *v.* Mathiesen, 2 Fish. Pat. Cas. 600; s. c., 3 Cliff. (U. S.) 639. The test of novelty as applied to a combination seems to be, whether the application of the powers of nature by such means and appliances as the patentee claims to have invented, is new. Bell *v.* Daniels, 1 Fish. Pat. Cas. 372; s. c., 1 Bond (U. S.) 212.

Therefore, where the combination is new, the elements may have been in the most common and extensive use. Ryan *v.* Goodwin, 3 Sumn. (U. S.) 514; s. c., 1 Robb Pat. Cas. 725.

A Substitute or an Improvement.—If a device is a substitute for one element of a combination, and not merely an improvement on it, then a machine containing this substitute and the other old elements is a new and different machine from a machine containing the combination of old elements known before the invention, and not merely an improvement upon such machine containing such combination of old elements. Potter *v.* Holland, 1 Fish. Pat. Cas. 382; s. c., 4 Blatchf. (U. S.) 238.

Although Part of the Apparatus Might Have Been Applied to a Similar Purpose.—A combination is new although part of the apparatus might have been applied to similar purposes in other and different machines. Pitts *v.* Whitman, 2 Story (U. S.) 609; s. c., 2 Robb Pat. Cas. 189.

But the novelty of a combination cannot be supported by the evidence of the novelty of a part. Batten *v.* Clayton, 2 Whart. Dig. 363.

3. U. S. Rev. Stats., § 4886. Lockwood *v.* Cleveland, 18 Fed. Rep. 37; Hutchinson *v.* Everett, 26 Fed. Rep. 531; Cross *v.* Union etc. Fastening Co., 29 Fed. Rep. 293.

A foreign use is not contemplated by the statute. Worswick Mfg. Co. *v.* Steiger, 17 Fed. Rep. 250.

4. Andrews *v.* Hovey, 123 U. S. 267.

The circuit court decisions on this question are collected and analyzed in the motion for rehearing. Andrews *v.* Hovey, 123 U. S. 267.

the ordinary transactions of life in the ordinary course of business,[1]

1. A machine which, whether entirely satisfactory or not, has been used in the ordinary course of business for twenty or thirty years, and is patented precisely as it is used, cannot properly be called an experimental machine. Perkins *v.* Nashua Card etc. Co., 5 Bann. & Ard. Pat. Cas. 395, Campbell *v.* Mayor, 44 Pat. Off. Gaz. 1085.

Even when the patentee expresses himself doubtful of the durability of the device, and claims a desire to test it, a use of a permanent nature in the ordinary course of business for over two years will invalidate the patent. Root *v.* Third Ave. R. Co., 37 Fed. Rep. 673.

What Is Public Use.—Public use is: (1) where an inventor allows his invention to be used by other persons, either with or without compensation, or where it is put on sale without his consent for such use. Elizabeth *v.* American etc. Pavement Co., 97 U. S. 126.

(2) Where an inventor in the general course of business sells his invention even by a conditional sale. Henry *v.* Francestown Soapstone Co., 5 Bann. & Ard. Pat. Cas. 108; Plimpton *v.* Winslow, 23 Pat. Off. Gaz. 1731.

Number of Persons Using, Unimportant.—Whether use is public or not, does not depend upon the number of persons to whom the use is known. Egbert *v.* Lippmann, 104 U. S. 333.

Also Number of Articles Made.—Nor upon the number of articles made; one is sufficient, though a greater number may tend to strengthen the proof. Egbert *v.* Lippmann, 104 U. S. 333; Consolidated Fruit Jar Co. *v.* Wright, 12 Blatchf. (U. S.) 149; s. c., 6 Pat. Off. Gaz. 327; s. c., 1 Bann. & Ard. Pat. Cas. 320; Henry *v.* Francestown Soapstone Co., 5 Bann. & Ard. Pat. Cas. 108.

And Time.—A device was used two and one half months only, then laid aside. *Held*, an anticipation of the patent when the use was not for the purpose of testing the device, but was a public and practical one with as much success as was reasonable to expect at that early stage of a particular art. Brush *v.* Condit, 28 Pat. Off. Gaz. 451; 20 Fed. Rep. 824.

Where a device did such practical work as might reasonably be expected in the state of the art at that time, and was put in ordinary, though not constant use, for a short time, in the presence of employees of a factory, and though but one device was made and was soon laid aside, it was held a perfected invention, and not an abandoned experiment, and the use was held to be public. Brush *v.* Condit, 20 Fed. Rep. 826; 28 Pat. Off. Gaz. 451.

Use of Machine in Factory; Workmen Not Pledged to Secrecy.—Use of machine in a factory where the workmen are not pledged to secrecy, is a public use, even though chance visitors are excluded. Perkins *v.* Nashua Card etc. Co., 5 Bann. & Ard. Pat. Cas. 395.

When an inventor puts his incompiete or experimental device upon the market and sells it as a manufacture more than two years before he applies for his patent, he gives the device to the public in the condition or stage of development in which he sells it; and his patent cannot cover what he has thus given away. Lyman *v.* Maypole, 28 Pat. Off. Gaz. 810; s. c., 19 Fed. Rep. 735.

A machine and a process were used for a series of years without a change in either. *Held*, not an experimental use. Manning *v.* Cape Ann etc. Glue Co., 108 U. S. 462.

An inventor allowed two persons the use of his invention without any injunction of secrecy or other condition. *Held*, a public use. Manning *v.* Cape Ann etc. Glue Co., 108 U. S. 462.

A use of an invention where it cannot be seen by the public eye, if allowed by the inventor to be used in a complete condition, not as a test, and without any obligation of secrecy is a public use. This is an extreme case. A man made a pair of corset steels; they were given to a female friend, and in their use were hidden in the corset. Egbert *v.* Lippman, 104 U. S. 333; s. c., 21 Pat. Off. Gaz. 75.

Double Purpose of Profit and Experiment.—A patent is void if, more than two years before the application for it was filed, the patentee sold the patented article for the double purpose of seeing whether they would sell and of realizing from the proceeds. Consolidated Fruit Jar Co. *v.* Wright, 12 Blatchf. (U. S.) 149.

Offering a device for sale whether any sales were made or not, two years prior to the application, invalidates the patent. Plimpton *v.* Winslow, 23 Pat. Off. Gaz. 1731.

or to test the invention.[1]

VII. Utility—1. General Principles.—That the invention be useful is essential to the validity of a patent.[2] The term "useful" is employed in contradistinction to what is injurious to the moral health or good order of society,[3] or what is merely

Partial Success of Machine.—Though the machine embodying an invention was not a success as a whole, if used or especially if sold over two years prior to the application, the patent is void. Newark Machine Co. *v.* Hargett, 28 Fed. Rep. 567.

1. Where the inventor uses his machine for the *bona fide* intent of testing its qualities, although he makes no alterations. Elizabeth *v.* American etc. Pavement Co., 97 U. S. 126.

Where a use for profit was incidental and subordinate to the experimental use. Jennings *v.* Pierce, 15 Blatchf. (U. S.) 42; s. c., 3 Bann. & Ard. Pat. Cas. 361.

Where the use is an experiment, although the public derived an incidental advantage. Elizabeth *v.* American etc. Pavement Co., 97 U. S. 126.

Where the use prior to the period of two years was by way of trial and resulted in a change of the machine. Pitts *v.* Hall, 2 Blatchf. (U. S.) 229.

Where a machine is imperfect and requires continuous experiments to remedy the defects of its organization. Sprague *v.* Smith etc. Mfg. Co., 12 Fed. Rep. 721; Eastern Paper Bag Co. *v.* Standard Paper Bag Co., 30 Fed. Rep. 63.

Where a machine is put up and used on the premises of another, and the use enures to the benefit of the owner of the establishment, but is used under surveillance of inventor for the purpose of enabling him to test the machine. Elizabeth *v.* American etc. Pavement Co. 97 U. S. 126.

Distinction Between Public Use and Use in Public.—There is an obvious distinction between a public use or a use by the public, and an experimental use in public. Locomotive Truck Co. *v.* R. Co., 1 Bann. & Ard. Pat. Cas. 470.

A Use In Public of a Device Which Cannot be Tested Privately.—If a thing cannot be tested in private, a public use may be deemed experimental. Campbell *v.* New York, 20 Pat. Off. Gaz. 1817; s. c., 9 Fed. Rep. 500.

Sale of Imperfect Invention.—Sale of imperfect invention does not invalidate the patent. American Hide etc. Co. *v.* American Tool etc. Co., 1 Holmes (U. S.) 503; Henry *v.* Francestown Soapstone Co., 5 Bann. & Ard. Pat. Cas. 108.

The test, whether an article is perfect or imperfect, is whether it is or is not the invention—that is, "whether it embodies the whole of it." Draper *v.* Wattles, 3 Bann. & Ard. Pat. Cas. 619.

When Machine Is Altered.—If a machine as originally constructed is subsequently altered so as to make a machine substantially different in its construction and mode of operation, the time begins to run from the completion of the last machine. Haskell *v.* Shoe Mach. Co., 3 Bann. & Ard. Pat. Cas. 553.

Distinction Between Completed Invention and Completed Machine.—The distinction between the invention and the machine which embodies it must be preserved. The invention may be perfect, and the machine which embodies the invention may be an imperfect machine. American Hide etc. Co. *v.* American Tool etc. Co., 1 Holmes (U. S.) 503; s. c., 4 Fish. Pat. Cas. 284.

2. U. S. Rev. Stats., § 4886; Page *v.* Ferry, 1 Fish. Pat. Cas. 299; Lowell *v.* Lewis, 1 Robb Pat. Cas. 131; Wintermute *v.* Redington, 1 Fish. Pat. Cas. 239; Winans *v.* Schenectady etc. R. Co., 2 Blatchf. (U. S.) 279; Vance *v.* Campbell, 1 Fish. Pat. Cas. 483; Shannon *v.* Bruner, 33 Fed. Rep. 289.

An invention which exposes the operator to great bodily harm cannot be regarded as useful. Mitchell *v.* Tilghman, 19 Wall. (U. S.) 287. Or is simply dangerous. Converse *v.* Cannon, 2 Woods (U. S.) 7; s. c., 9 Pat. Off. Gaz. 105; Hoffheins *v.* Brandt, 3 Fish. Pat. Cas. 218.

An improvement, which, in effecting a subsidiary end (as arresting the sparks of a locomotive), is destructive of the ends of the principal machine, is not useful. Wilton *v.* R. Co., 2 Whart. Dig 360.

But it must be of some use or benefit. Cox *v.* Griggs, 2 Fish. Pat. Cas. 174; Wintermute *v.* Redington, 1 Fish. Pat. Cas. 239. It must not be "utterly worthless." Vance *v.* Campbell, 1 Fish. Pat. Cas. 483; s. c., 1 Black (U. S.) 427.

3. Bedford *v.* Hunt, 1 Mason (U. S.)

frivolous.[1]

2. Degree of Utility Requisite.—The amount of utility in an invention is unimportant, provided it is useful to some degree;[2] consequently, the fact that a device is not superior to other devices,[3] or is capable of improvement,[4] or has even been driven out of the market by later inventions,[5] is unimportant.

302; s. c., 1 Robb Pat. Cas. 148; Westlake *v.* Cartter, 6 Fish. Pat. Cas. 519; s. c., 4 Pat. Off. Gaz. 636.

1. Lowell *v.* Lewis, 1 Robb Pat. Cas. 131; Winans *v.* Schenectady etc. R. Co., 2 Blatchf. (U. S.) 279.

An invention must not be for a frivolous object, "like the invention of an improvement in playing cards." Adams *v.* Edwards, 1 Fish. Pat. Cas. 1; Wintermute *v.* Redington, 1 Fish. Pat. Cas. 239. Or only applicable to gambling purposes. Nat. Automatic Device Co. *v.* Lloyd, 40 Fed. Rep. 89.

Utility a Question of Fact.—Utility of an invention is a question of fact usually depending upon the actual experiment. Tilghman *v.* Mitchell, 4 Fish. Pat. Cas. 599. And the court will not declare a patent invalid for want of utility, except on the strongest proof. Kearney *v.* Lehigh Valley R. Co., 32 Fed. Rep. 320.

Evidence of Utility.—Where an invention supersedes all others, it is very strong evidence that some useful result was obtained. Smith *v.* O'Connor, 6 Fish. Pat. Cas. 469.

"In face of the proofs, the denial of the utility of the invented process is remarkable. The evidence shows the invention or process to have been pre-eminently useful. It has gone into very extended use throughout the entire oil regions and its use has immensely increased the production of oil." Roberts *v.* Schreiber, 5 Bann. & Ard. Pat. Cas. 491.

The remarkable increase of demand for brushes of that class, together with substantial imitation of it by the infringer, are conclusive evidence of the utility of the invention. Megrave *v.* Carroll, 5 Bann. & Ard. Pat. Cas. 325.

Any invention which increases the salability of an article may be said to contain the elements of utility. Newbury *v.* Fowler, 28 Fed. Rep. 454.

2. Doherty *v.* Haines, 1 Bann. & Ard. Pat. Cas. 289; Gibbs *v.* Hoefner, 19 Fed. Rep. 323; Curtis on Patents, § 106; Adams *v.* Loft, 4 Bann. & Ard. Pat. Cas. 494; Fryer *v.* Mutual L. Ins. Co., 30 Fed. Rep. 787. The utility need not be general; it may be limited to a few cases. Bedford *v.* Hunt, 1 Mason (U. S.) 304; s. c., 1 Robb Pat. Cas. 148.

3. An invention, to be useful, need not supersede by general utility all other inventions now in practice to accomplish the same purpose. Bedford *v.* Hunt, 1 Mason (U. S.) 302; s. c., 1 Robb Pat. Cas. 148; Shaw *v.* Colwell Lead Co., 20 Blatchf. (U. S.) 417. Nor be better than anything invented before, or that shall come after. Hoffheins *v.* Brandt, 3 Fish. Pat. Cas. 218. Even if it does not accomplish its object as well as other articles intended for the same purpose, the patent is not void. Wilson *v.* Hentges, 26 Minn. 288; Bell *v.* Daniels, 1 Fish. Pat. Cas. 372; s. c., 1 Bond (U. S.) 212. That it does not accomplish its object as well as another affects the value of the patent and not its validity. Bell *v.* Daniels, 1 Fish. Pat. Cas. 372; s. c., 1 Bond (U. S.) 212.

In ascertaining usefulness, it is not important that it should be more valuable than other modes of accomplishing the same results; but it must be a practical method of doing the thing designated, in which its utility may more or less consist. Roberts *v.* Ward, 4 McLean (U. S.) 565. It is not necessary that it should be the best thing of its kind. Winans *v.* Schenectady etc. R. Co., 2 Blatchf. (U. S.) 279.

4. Wheeler *v.* Clipper Mower etc. Co., 10 Blatchf. (U. S.) 181; s. c., 6 Fish. Pat. Cas. 1; s. c., 2 Pat. Off. Gaz. 443; National Hat Pouncing Mach. Co. *v.* Thom. 25 Fed. Rep. 497.

5. Cook *v.* Earnest, 2 Pat. Off. Gaz. 89; s. c., 5 Fish. Pat. Cas. 396; National Hat Pouncing Mach. Co. *v.* Thom, 25 Fed. Rep. 497.

Simplicity of Invention Not a Bar.—An invention may be simple and not import the exercise of very high mechanical or scientific talent. Wayne *v.* Holmes, 2 Fish. Pat. Cas. 20; s. c., 1 Bond (U. S.) 27. Lack of utility is not to be inferred from simplicity. Bell *v.* Daniels, 1 Fish. Pat. Cas. 372; s. c., 1 Bond (U. S.) 212.

A billiard table having the broad side rails beveled or inclined inwards

3. Presumption of Utility.—A presumption of utility arises from the grant of a patent,[1] and from the use by the infringer.[2]

VIII. Dates of Applications for Patents.—The date of an application is the date of its filing in the Patent Office.[3] Any changes in the specifications, even to the extent of filing an entirely new one, where the substance of the invention as originally claimed is sought,[4] are referred back to the original date of filing. This ruling applies also to a second application filed as a continuation of the first,[5] but not to a case where it is not so intended.[6]

so as to give the player opportunity to get his leg under the table, and so constructed as to be cheaper than the curved or ogee form, has sufficient utility to support a patent. Collender *v.* Griffith, 2 Fed. Rep. 206.

1. Parker *v.* Stiles, 5 McLean (U. S.) 44; Mesker *v.* Thuener, 42 Fed. Rep. 329; Huber *v.* Nelson Mfg. Co., 38 Fed. Rep. 830.

The presumption of utility must be rebutted by proof. Kirk *v.* Du Bois, 33 Fed. Rep. 252.

Conclusiveness of the Presumption.—But that it is not conclusive, the invention may be shown to be useless. Lee *v.* Blandy, 2 Fish. Pat. Cas. 89; s. c., 1 Bond (U. S.) 361. Presumption of utility arises from oath of applicant for the patent that it is useful. Hays *v.* Sulsor, 1 Fish. Pat. Cas. 532; s. c., 1 Bond (U. S.) 279. Presumption of utility can only be overcome by clear proof, that the device is utterly worthless. 2 Fish. Pat. Cas. 229; s. c., 1 Bond (U. S.) 511. And if the device is useful even in a small degree, it is not usual for the court to reverse the decision of the Patent Office. Doherty *v.* Haynes, 1 Bann. & Ard. Pat. Cas. 289.

2. The fact that the defendants were contesting a patent is evidence that the invention is useful. Smith *v.* O'Connor, 6 Fish. Pat. Cas. 469; s. c., 2 Sawy. (U. S.) 461; 4 Pat. Off. Gaz. 633; Megraw *v.* Campbell, 4 Bann. & Ard. Pat. Cas. 325; Niles Tool Works *v.* Betts Machine Co., 27 Fed. Rep. 301; Kearney *v.* Lehigh Valley R. Co., 32 Fed. Rep. 320.

And this evidence has been held conclusive. Hays *v.* Sulsor, 1 Fish. Pat. Cas. 532; s. c., 1 Bond (U. S.) 279; Vance *v.* Campbell, 1 Fish. Pat. Cas. 483; Hancock Inspirator Co. *v.* Jenks, 21 Fed. Rep. 911; La Rue *v.* Western Electric Co., 31 Fed. Rep. 80.

3. Birdsall *v.* McDonald, 1 Bann. & Ard. Pat. Cas. 165; s. c., 6 Pat. Off. Gaz. 682; Henry *v.* Francestown Soapstone Co., 2 Fed. Rep. 78; s. c., 17 Pat. Off. Gaz. 569.

Neither filing the model nor writing the paper commonly called the specification, gives the date of the application from which the two years are to be reckoned. "Application," in this connection, includes the paper as some written paper and its presentation to the Commissioner. Henry *v.* Francestown Soapstone Co., 2 Fed. Rep. 78; s. c., 17 Pat. Off. Gaz. 569; Draper *v.* Wattles, 16 Pat. Off. Gaz. 629.

4. Sewall *v.* Jones, 91 U. S. 171; s. c., 9 Pat. Off. Gaz. 47.

5. Godfrey *v* Eames 1 Wall. (U. S.) 317; Smith *v.* O'Connor, 2 Sawy. (U. S.) 461; s. c., 6 Fish. Pat. Cas. 469; s. c., 4 Pat. Off. Gaz. 633; Smith *v.* Goodyear Dental etc. Co., 93 U. S. 486; s. c., 11 Pat. Off. Gaz. 246; Howes *v.* McNeal, 15 Blatchf. (U. S.) 103; s. c., 3 Bann. & Ard. Pat. Cas. 376; s. c., 15 Pat. Off. Gaz. 608; Blandy *v.* Griffith, 3 Fish. Pat. Cas. 609; Howe *v.* Newton, 2 Fish Pat. Cas 531; Goodyear Dental etc. Co *v.* Willis, 1 Flipp. (U. S.) 385; s. c., 1 Bann. & Ard. Pat. Cas. 560; Weston *v.* White, 13 Blatchf. (U. S.) 364; s. c., 2 Bann. & Ard. Pat. Cas. 321; Colgate *v* Western Union Tel. Co., 15 Blatchf. (U. S.) 365; s. c., 4 Bann. & Ard. Pat. Cas. 37; s. c., 14 Pat. Off Gaz. 943; Graham *v.* Geneva etc. Mfg. Co., 11 Fed. Rep. 779.

This rule is modified by § 32 of act of 1870, so that where an application is abandoned by failure to prosecute within two years, a new application filed does not relate back to the date of the prior application, but only to the date of its own filing. Lindsay *v.* Stein, 21 Pat. Off. Gaz. 1613; s. c., 10 Fed. Rep. 907.

6. United States Rifle Co. *v.* Whitney Arms Co., 14 Blatchf. (U. S.) 94;

IX. Power of States Over Patent Rights.—The right of the inventor to use or sell the patented subject-matter is not enlarged by the grant of the patent; and the use and sale of that subject matter can be as lawfully forbidden by the States subsequent to as before the grant of the patent.[1] As a general rule the States have no right to restrain or restrict the use or sale of a patented invention,[2] but can regulate the sale of patented articles in the same manner as other articles not patented.[3]

s. c., 2 Bann. & Ard. Pat. Cas. 493; s. c., 11 Pat. Off. Gaz. 373; Rich *v.* Lippincott, 2 Fish. Pat. Cas. 1.

Whether a new application is a continuance of an old one, is a question of fact. Berin *v.* East Hampton Bell Co., 9 Blatchf. (U. S.) 50; s. c., 5 Fish. Pat. Cas. 23; Weston *v.* White, 13 Blatchf. (U. S.) 364; s. c., 2 Bann. & Ard. Pat. Cas. 321; Rich *v.* Lippincott, 2 Fish. Pat. Cas. 1.

Filing New Application for Rejected Matter.—A second application embracing a claim in a prior application which claim had been rejected and was canceled from the first application after the filing of the second (both applications going to issue), is a continuation of the first application. Graham *v.* McCormick, 20 Biss. (U. S.) 39; s. c., 5 Bann. & Ard. Pat. Cas. 244; s. c., 11 Fed. Rep. 859; s. c., 21 Pat. Off. Gaz. 1533.

But not where the action of the applicant would show intention to abandon the matter contained in the original claim. Pelton *v.* Waters, 1 Bann. & Ard. Pat. Cas. 599; s. c., 7 Pat. Off. Gaz. 425.

1. Patterson *v.* Kentucky, 197 U. S. 501; Webber *v.* Virginia, 103 U. S. 344; Jordan *v.* Overseers of Dayton, 4 Ohio 295; *In re* Brosnahan, 18 Fed. Rep. 62.

There remains in the patentee, as in every other citizen, the power to manage his property or give direction to his laborers at his pleasure, subject only to the paramount claims of society, which require that his enjoyment may be modified by the exigencies of the society to which he belongs, and regulated by the laws which render it subservient to the general welfare, if held subject to State control. Jordan *v.* Overseers of Dayton, 4 Ohio 295; Patterson *v.* Kentucky, 97 U. S. 501; *In re* Brosnahan, 18 Fed. Rep. 62.

2. *Ex parte* Robinson, 2 Biss. (U. S.) 309; s. c., 4 Fish. Pat. Cas. 186; Helm *v.* First Nat. Bank, 43 Ind. 167; Hollida *v.* Hunt, 70 Ill. 109; Crittenden *v.* White, 9 Chic. L. N. 110.

While this power is not expressly prohibited to the States, it is so impliedly. Helm *v.* First Nat. Bank, 43 Ind. 167.

3. Webber *v.* Virginia, 103 U. S. 344; Patterson *v.* Kentucky, 97 U. S. 501; Jordan *v.* Overseers of Dayton, 4 Ohio 294; Thompson *v.* Staats, 15 Wend. (N. Y.) 395; *In re* Brosnahan, 18 Fed. Rep. 62; United States *v.* American Bell Telephone Co., 29 Fed. Rep. 43; May *v.* Buchanan Co., 29 Fed. Rep. 473.

A license which does not impose any discrimination between articles manufactured under a patent and those not so manufactured, is legally imposed. Webber *v.* Virginia, 103 U. S. 344; People *v.* Russell, 49 Mich. 617.

A State has the right to prohibit a dangerous manufacture or the sale of a dangerous product, even if thereby it destroys the availability of a patent. Patterson *v.* Kentucky, 97 U. S. 501.

Or to prevent the use of a patent which is calculated to produce immorality. Vannini *v.* Paine, 1 Harr. (Del.) 65.

A State may regulate the sale of a patented thing and may not regulate the sale of the patent covering that thing. A patentee has two kinds of rights in his invention. He has a right both to make, use and sell specimens of his invention, and to prevent all other persons from doing either of these acts. The first of these is entirely independent of the patent laws; the second exists by virtue of these laws alone. Walker on Patents, 2nd ed. § 155.

Marking Notes Given for Patent Rights.—State statutes compelling, under penalty, a distinguishing mark to be placed on notes given for patent rights, have been declared invalid as in conflict with the constitution of the United States. *Ohio*, State *v.* Peck, 25 Ohio St. 26.

Indiana, Helm *v.* Bank, 43 Ind. 167;

X. Subjects of Invention—1. Art or Process—(*a*) Definition.—An art is a mode of treatment of certain materials to produce a given result; an act or series of acts to be performed upon the subject-matter to be transformed and reduced to a different state or thing.[1] In the sense of the patent law, it is synonymous with "process" or "method"[2] when used to represent the means of producing a beneficial result.

(*b*) Novelty of Mechanical Means Not Necessary.—The mechanical means by which the result is accomplished may be

Fry *v.* State, 63 Ind. 552; Hereth *v.* Bank, 34 Ind. 380; Machine Co. *v.* Butler, 53 Ind. 454; Castle *v.* Hutchinson, 25 Fed. Rep. 394.

Illinois, Hollida *v.* Hunt, 70 Ill. 109; s. c., 22 Am. Rep. 63.

Wisconsin, State *v.* Lockwood, 43 Wis. 403.

Pennsylvania, Bowen *v.* Kemmun, 2 Pearson (Pa.) 250.

Maine, Haskcall *v.* Whitmore, 19 Me. 102.

Kentucky, Patterson *v.* Commonwealth, 11 Bush (Ky.) 311; s. c., 21 Am. Rep. 20.

Nebraska, Welch *v.* Phelps, 25 Pat. Off. Gaz. 981.

In *Pennsylvania* such statutes have been upheld. Haskell *v.* Jones, 86 Pa. St. 173; Shires *v.* Commonwealth, 120 Pa. St. 368.

Statutes of Limitation.—State statutes cannot limit the time within which actions for the infringement of letters patent may be brought in the United States. Collins *v.* Peebles, 2 Fish. Pat. Cas. 541; Parker *v.* Hollock, 2 Fish. Pat. Cas. 543; Anthony *v.* Carroll, 2 Bann. & Ard. Pat. Cas. 195; s. c., 9 Pat. Off. Gaz. 199; Wood *v.* Cleveland Rolling Mill, 4 Fish. Pat. Cas. 550; Sayles *v.* Dubuque R. Co., 5 Dill. (U. S.) 561; s. c., 3 Bann. & Ard. Pat. Cas. 219; Stephens *v.* Kansas Pac. R. Co., 5 Dill. (U. S.) 486; Wetherill *v.* New Jersey Zinc Co., 1 Bann. & Ard. Pat. Cas. 485; Sayles *v.* Louisville etc. R. Co., 9 Fed. Rep. 512; Adams *v.* Bellaire Stamping Co., 25 Fed. Rep. 270; May *v.* Logan Co., 127 Fed. Rep. 692; May *v.* Buchanan Co., 30 Fed. Rep. 257; May *v.* Cass Co., 30 Fed. Rep. 762; May *v.* Ralls Co., 31 Fed. Rep. 473. *Contra*, Parker *v.* Hawk, 2 Fish. Pat. Cas. 58; Rich *v.* Ricketts, 7 Blatchf. (U. S.) 230; Hayden *v.* Oriental Mills, 15 Fed. Rep. 605; Royer *v.* Coupe, 29 Fed. Rep. 362.

1. Cochrane *v.* Deener, 94 U. S. 780; Smith *v.* Frazer, 5 Fish. Pat. Cas. 548; s. c., 2 Pat. Off. Gaz. 175.

A combination of arrangements and processes to work out a new and useful result is an art. Roberts *v.* Dickey, 4 Fish. Pat. Cas. 532; s. c., 4 Brews. (Pa.) 260; s. c., 1 Pat. Off. Gaz. 4.

2. Piper *v.* Brown, 4 Fish. Pat. Cas. 175.

For examples of process, see Tilghman *v.* Norse, 5 Fish. Pat. Cas. 323; s. c., 9 Blatchf. (U. S.) 421; s. c., 1 Pat. Off. Gaz. 574; Piper *v.* Brown, 4 Fish. Pat. Cas. 165; American Bell Telephone Co. *v.* Spencer, 20 Pat. Off. Gaz. 299; s. c., 8 Fed. Rep. 509; American Bell Telephone Co. *v.* Dolbear, 23 Pat. Off. Gaz. 535; s. c., 15 Fed. Rep. 448; The Telephone Cases, 126 U. S. 1.

"Process" or "method," when used to represent the means of producing a beneficial result, are, in law, synonymous with art, provided the means are not effected by mechanism or mechanical combinations. Piper *v.* Brown, 4 Fish. Pat. Cas. 175.

A combination of arrangements and processes to work out a new and useful result, is a new and useful art. Roberts *v.* Dickey, 4 Fish. Pat. Cas. 632; s. c., 4 Brews. (U. S.) 260; s. c., 1 Pat. Off. Gaz. 4, 1000.

A patent for an art must be practicable and referable to something which may prove to be useful. Evans *v.* Eaton, 1 Pet. (C. C.) 322; s. c., 3 Wheat. (U. S.) 454; s. c., 1 Robb Pat. Cas. 68, 243.

A process may be patentable irrespective of the particular form of the instrumentalities used. Cochrane *v.* Deener, 94 U. S. 780.

A new application of some property in nature never before known or in use, by which a new and useful result is produced, is the subject of a patent, independently of any peculiar or new arrangement of machinery. Foot *v.* Silsby, 2 Blatchf. (U. S.) 260; aff'g 20 How. (U. S.) 378.

old,[1] provided the result has not been accomplished by them before.

(*c*) NOT AN ART.—An art must be "useful."[2] It must be something more than the function or abstract effect of a machine,[3] or mere way of making an article[4] or mechanical operation.[5]

The elements of a process may be old, but when combined for the purpose of putting a new idea to practical use, they constitute a new and useful process. Andrews *v.* Cannon, 13 Blatchf. (U. S.) 307; s. c., 2 Bann. & Ard. Pat. Cas. 277; Cochrane *v.* Deener, 94 U. S. 780.

An inventor may use any means, new or old, in the application of the new property to produce the new and useful result to the exclusion of all other means. Foote *v.* Silsby, 2 Blatchf. (U. S.) 260: s. c., 10 How. (U. S.) 378; Dolbear *v.* American Bell Telephone Co., 126 U. S. 1.

Distinction Between an Art or Process and a Principle of Nature.—" In this art —or what is the same thing under the Patent Law, this process, this way of transmitting speech—electricity is employed, but electricity left to itself will not do what is wanted. The art consists in so controlling the force as to make it accomplish the purpose. It had long been believed that if the vibrations of air caused by the voice in speaking could be reproduced at a distance by means of electricity, the speech itself would be reproduced and understood. How to do it was the question. Bell discovered that it could be done by gradually changing the intensity of an electric current so as to make it correspond to the changes in the density of the air caused by the sound of the voice. This was his art." Dolbear *v.* American Bell Telephone Co., 126 U. S. 1.

Distinction Between a Machine and a Process.—A machine is a thing. A process is a mode of acting. The one is visible to the eye. The other a conception of the mind seen only by its effects when being executed or performed. Tilghman *v.* Proctor, 102 U. S. 708.

A patentee who has invented an effective means for giving circular direction to a feed mechanism is entitled to a patent for the means, but not for giving such a direction to his mechanism, nor for the process of operating his mechanism for giving such direction. Dryfoos *v.* Weise, 26 Pat. Off. Gaz. 639.

1. Corning *v.* Burden, 15 How. (U. S.) 252; Mowry *v.* Whitney, 14 Wall. (U. S.) 620; Tilghman *v.* Proctor, 19 Pat. Off. Gaz. 859; s. c., 102 U. S. 707.

2. Smith *v.* Downing, 1 Fish. Pat. Cas. 64; French *v.* Rogers, 1 Fish. Pat. Cas. 133.

3. Cochrane *v.* Deener, 94 U. S. 78.

4. McKay *v.* Jackman, 22 Pat. Off. Gaz. 85; s. c., 12 Fed. Rep. 615.

5. McKay *v.* Jackman, 23 Pat. Off. Gaz. 85; s. c., 12 Fed. Rep. 615; New *v.* Warren, 22 Pat. Off. Gaz. 589.

A process *eo nomine*, is not made the subject of a patent in any act of congress. It is included in the term "useful art." An art may require one or more processes or machines in order to produce a certain result or manufacture. Where the result is produced by chemical action, or by the operation or application of some element or power of nature, or of one substance to another, such modes or methods are called processes. It is when the term process is used to represent the means or method of producing a result, that it is patentable; and it will include all methods or means which are not effected by mechanism or mechanical combinations; but where the term "process" represents the function of a machine, or the effect produced by it on the material subjected to the action of the machine, it is not patentable, since a man cannot have a patent for the function or abstract effect of a machine, but only for the machine which produces it. Corning *v.* Burden, 15 How. (U. S.) 252.

A mere mechanical operation is not patentable as a process and is not within the protection of the Patent Law, when taken apart from the means of performing it. McKay *v.* Jackman, 22 Pat. Off. Gaz. 85; New *v.* Warren, 22 Pat. Off. Gaz. 589.

A mere process for making an article is not of itself a patentable invention. Mackay *v.* Jackman, 12 Fed. Rep. 615.

A person cannot patent a result, but only the means or art by which the result is effected. New Process Fermentation Co. *v.* Maus, 20 Fed. Rep. 725.

2. Machine—(*a*) DEFINITION.—A machine, whether a new organism of mechanism to produce a new effect,[1] or a new combination of devices,[2] is patentable as a machine.[3] The meaning of the word machine has been liberally construed and held to cover a device which is incapable of use except in connection with other mechanisms.[4]

3. Composition of Matter.—A manufacture has been generally held to be synonymous with product,[5] though it has been con-

Reversed, but on the ground that a means was patented. New Process Fermentation Co. *v.* Maus, 122 U. S. 413. *Compare* also Consolidated Bunging Apparatus Co. *v.* Clausen Brewing Co. 39 Fed. Rep. 277; New Process Fermentation Co. *v.* Koch, 21 Fed. Rep. 580.

1. Woodcock *v.* Parker, 1 Gall. (U. S.) 438; s. c., 1 Robb. Pat. Cas. 37; Geiger *v.* Cook, 3 W. & S. (Pa.) 266; Sanford *v.* Merrimack Hat Co., 4 Cliff. (U. S.) 404; s. c., 10 Pat. Off. Gaz. 466; Renwick *v.* Pond, 10 Blatchf. (U. S.) 39; s. c., 5 Fish. Pat. Cas. 569; s. c., 2 Pat. Off. Gaz. 392; Black *v.* Thorne, 10 Blatchf. (U. S.) 66; s. c., 2 Pat. Off. Gaz. 388; Hammerschlag *v.* Scamoni, 7 Fed. Rep. 584; s. c., 20 Pat. Off. Gaz. 75; Bailey etc. Washing Mach. Co. *v.* Lincoln, 4 Fish. Pat. Gaz. 379.

Definition.—A concrete thing consisting of parts or of certain devices or combination of devices. Burr *v.* Duryee, 1 Wall. (U. S.) 531. See Hatch *v.* Moffitt, 15 Fed. Rep. 252.

2. Wintermute *v.* Redington, 1 Fish. Pat. Cas. 239; Williams *v.* Rome etc. R. Co., 15 Blatchf. (U. S.) 200; s. c., 3 Bann. & Ard. Pat. Cas. 413; s. c., 15 Pat. Off. Gaz. 563; Sanford *v.* Merrimack Hat Co., 4 Cliff. (U. S.) 404; s. c., 10 Pat. Off. Gaz. 466; Edgarton *v.* Furst etc. Mfg. Co., 10 Biss. (U. S.) 402; s. c., 9 Fed. Rep. 450; s. c., 21 Pat. Off. Gaz. 261; Hill *v.* Sawyer, 31 Fed. Rep. 282; Burgess *v.* Chapman, 44 Fed. Rep. 427; Holliday *v.* Rheem, 18 Pa. St. 368; Union Paper Bag Mach. Co. *v.* Murphy, 97 U. S. 120.

A patent for a combination does not cover the parts separately. Treadwell *v.* Bladen, 4 Wash. (U. S.) 703; s. c., 1 Robb Pat. Cas. 531; Case *v.* Brown, 2 Wall. (U. S.) 320; Roberts *v.* Harnden, 2 Cliff. (U. S.) 500; Metropolitan Washing Mach. Co. *v.* Providence Tool Co., 20 Wall. (U. S.) 342; McCormick *v.* Talcott, 20 How. (U. S.) 402; Eddy *v.* Dennis, 95 U. S. 560; Schumacher *v.* Cornell, 96 U. S. 249; Goss *v.* Cameron, 14 Fed. Rep. 576; Matterson *v.* Caine, 8 Sawy. (U. S.) 488.

The principle is well established and is implied in almost every case in infringement of combination.

3. U. S. Rev. Stats. § 4886.

It has been held to cover a hotel register constructed to receive advertisements about its margin. Hawes *v.* Washburne, 5 Pat. Off. Gaz. 491; Hawes *v.* Cook, 5 Pat. Off. Gaz. 493.

Probably the coupon book held patentable belongs to this class of inventions. Munson v. Mayor etc. of N. Y., 18 Blatchf. (U. S.) 237; s. c., 5 Bann. & Ard. Pat. Cas. 486; s. c., 3 Fed. Rep. 338.

But not a balloon with a banner having an advertisement attached thereto. *Ex parte* Gould, 1 McArthur (U. S.) 410; s. c., 5 Pat. Off. Gaz. 121.

A machine need not be automatic. Coupe *v.* Weatherhead, 16 Fed. Rep. 673; s. c., 23 Pat. Off. Gaz. 1927.

4. Wheeler *v.* Clipper Mower etc. Co., 10 Blatchf. (U. S.) 181; s. c., 6 Fish. Pat. Cas. 1; s. c., 2 Pat. Off. Gaz. 442.

An added element or substantial change of the element, to a machine, makes a new machine. Bliss *v.* Brooklyn, 10 Blatchf. (U.S.) 521; s. c., 6 Fish. Pat. Cas. 289; s. c., 3 Pat. Off. Gaz. 269; Rheem *v.* Holliday, 16 Pa. St. 347; Hale *v.* Stimpson, 2 Fish. Pat. Cas. 565; Sharp *v.* Tift, 18 Blatchf. (U. S.) 132; s. c., 5 Bann. & Ard. Pat. Cas. 399; s. c., 2 Fed. Rep. 687; s. c., 17 Pat. Off. Gaz. 1282.

5. American Wood Paper Co. *v.* Fibre Disintegrating Co., 23 Wall. (U. S.) 566; Goodyear *v.* Providence Rubber Co., 2 Fish. Pat. Cas. 499; s. c., 2 Cliff. (U. S.) 351; Goodyear *v.* Railroad, 2 Wall., Jr. (C. C.) 356; s. c., 1 Fish. Pat. Cas. 626; Goodyear *v.* Wait, 9 Blatchf. (U. S.) 77; United Nickel Co. *v.* Pendleton, 15 Fed. Rep. 739; Simpson *v.* Davis, 20 Blatchf. (U. S.) 413; 12 Fed. Rep. 144.

strued to mean the process of manufacturing.[1] It is patentable in the sense of product only when it is new in itself,[2] not merely when it is produced by a new process,[3] or new machinery.[4] A composition of matter has been held to be a mechanical or chemical combination of ingredients.[5]

4. Improvement.—An improvement is defined as something in aid of the old mode which makes the old mode better.[6] It is patentable[7]

A new form of an old manufacture may be a new manufacture. Duff *v.* Calkins, 25 Pat. Off. Gaz. 601.

But a new feature perceived in an old substance does not make it a new manufacture. Ansonia Co. *v.* Supply Co., 32 Fed. Rep. 81; s. c., 42 Pat. Off. Gaz. 1168.

1. Merrill *v.* Yeomans, 94 U. S. 568; s. c., 11 Pat. Off. Gaz. 970.

2. Goodyear *v.* Providence Rubber Co., 2 Cliff. (U. S.) 351; s. c., 2 Fish. Pat. Cas. 499; Goodyear *v.* Railroad, 2 Wall. Jr. (C. C.) 356; s. c., 1 Fish. Pat. Cas. 626; Anaiin Fabrik *v.* Hamilton, 3 Bann. & Ard. Pat. Cas. 235; s. c., 13 Pat. Off. Gaz. 273; Draper *v.* Hudson, 6 Fish. Pat. Cas. 327; s. c., 3 Pat. Off. Gaz. 354; Young *v.* Lippman, 9 Blatchf. (U. S.) 277; s. c., 5 Fish. Pat. Cas. 230; s. c., 2 Pat. Off. Gaz. 249; Woodward *v.* Morrison, 1 Holmes (U. S.) 124; s. c., 5 Fish. Pat. Cas. 357; United Nickel Co. *v.* Pendleton, 21 Blatchf. (U. S.) 226; s. c., 24 Pat. Off. Gaz. 704.

3. American Wood Paper Co. *v.* Fibre Disintegrating Co., 23 Wall. (U. S.) 566; McCloskey *v.* Du Bois, 19 Blatchf. (U. S.) 205; s. c., 8 Fed. Rep. 710; s. c., 19 Pat. Off. Gaz. 1286; McKloskey *v.* Du Bois, 20 Blatchf. (U. S.) 371; s. c., 9 Fed. Rep. 38; Badische etc. Fabrik *v.* Hamilton Mfg. Co., 3 Bann. & Ard. Pat. Cas. 235; s. c., 13 Pat. Off. Gaz. 273; Rex *v.* Else, 1 Web. Pat. Cas. (Eng.) 76; Wooster *v.* Calhoun, 11 Blatchf. (U. S.) 215; s. c., 6 Fish. Pat. Cas. 514. *Compare* Anilin *v.* Cochrane, 16 Blatchf. (U. S.) 155; Anilin *v.* Higgin, 15 Blatchf. (U. S.) 290; Lamb *v.* Hamblen, 11 Fed. Rep. 722; which, however, are probably overruled by Cochrane *v.* Badische etc. Co., 111 U. S. 293; s. c., 27 Pat. Off. Gaz. 813.

4. Draper *v.* Hudson, 1 Holmes (U. S.) 208; s. c., 6 Fish. Pat. Cas. 327; s. c., 3 Pat. Off. Gaz. 354; Wooster *v.* Calhoun, 11 Blatchf. (U. S.) 215; s. c., 6 Fish. Pat. Cas. 514.

5. Tyler *v.* Boston, 7 Wall. (U. S.) 327; Goodyear *v.* Berry, 2 Bond (U. S.) 189; Cahill *v.* Brown, 3 Bann. & Ard. Pat. Cas. 580; Bowker *v.* Dows, 3 Bann. & Ard. Pat. Cas. 518; s. c., 15 Pat. Off. Gaz. 510; Jenkins *v.* Walker, 1 Holmes (U. S.) 120; Root *v.* Hyndman, 6 Fish. Pat. Cas. 439; s. c., 4 Pat. Off. Gaz. 29; Rumford Chemical Works *v.* Lauer, 10 Blatchf. (U. S.) 122; Woodward *v.* Morrison, 1 Holmes (U. S.) 124; s. c., 2 Pat. Off. Gaz. 120.

It is sometimes used synonymously with composition, compound and manufacture. Klein *v.* Russell, 19 Wall. (U. S.) 433; Goodyear *v.* Railroad, 2 Wall., Jr. (C. C.) 356; s. c., 1 Fish. Pat. Cas. 626.

6. Potter *v.* Holland, 4 Blatchf. (U. S.) 238; s. c., 1 Fish. Pat. Cas. 382; Kirby *v.* Dodge etc. Mfg. Co., 10 Blatchf. (U. S.) 307; s. c., 3 Pat. Off. Gaz. 181; s. c., 6 Fish. Pat. Cas. 156; Foxwell *v.* Bostick, 12 W. R. 723.

An improvement has essential reference to a subject matter to be improved. It is not original, but embraces and either adds to or alters the original. Bray *v.* Hartshorn, 1 Cliff. (U. S.) 538; Turrill *v.* Illinois etc. R. Co., 3 Biss. (U. S.) 66; s. c., 3 Fish. Pat. Cas. 330; Evans *v.* Eaton, 3 Wash. (U. S.) 443; s. c., 1 Robb Pat. Cas. 193; Page *v.* Ferry, 1 Fish. Pat. Cas. 298; Aspinwall Mfg. Co. *v.* Gill, 32 Fed. Rep. 697; s. c., 40 Pat. Off. Gaz. 1133.

Improvement has been defined as synonymous with "invention" in Reese's Appeal, 22 W. N. C. (Pa.) 501. This decision is opposed to the authority of the United States courts and those of other States.

7. An improvement can be patented to the inventor of an invention which is the basis of the improvement. O'Reilly *v.* Morse, 15 How. (U. S.) 62; Smith *v.* Ely, 5 McLean (U. S.) 76; Eagle Mfg. Co. *v.* Bradley, 35 Fed. Rep. 295.

All the improver can patent is his improvement. Colt *v.* Massachusetts Arms Co., 1 Fish. Pat. Cas. 108; Larabee *v.* Cortlan, 1 Taney (U. S.) 180;

when the change amounts to an invention.[1]

XI. Actions Concerning Patents—1. Jurisdiction of State Courts.—(*a*) Contractual.—The State courts have exclusive jurisdiction over questions arising out of contracts made concerning patent rights,[2] or inventions,[3] where there is no other source of Federal jurisdiction involved.[4]

(*b*) Torts.—State courts have jurisdiction over questions arising out of torts not involving the infringement or validity of the patent.[5]

2. Jurisdiction of United States Courts.—The State courts have no jurisdiction where any question affecting the validity or in-

s. c., 3 Fish. Pat. Cas. 5; Conover *v.* Roach, 4 Fish. Pat. Cas. 12; Leach *v.* Dresser, 69 Me. 129; Carsteadt *v.* United States Corset Co., 13 Blatchf. (U. S.) 371; s. c., 2 Bann. & Ard. Pat. Cas. 331; s. c., 10 Pat. Off. Gaz. 3; Plimpton *v.* Winslow, 3 Fed. Rep. 333.

But he patents it with reference to all machines. Burke *v.* Partridge, 58 N. H. 349.

1. Hall *v.* Wiles, 2 Blatchf. (U. S.) 194; Buck *v.* Hermance, 1 Blatchf. (U. S.) 398; Smith *v.* Pearce, 2 McLean (U. S.) 176; s. c., 2 Robb Pat. Cas. 13; Williams *v.* Barker, 2 Fed. Rep. 649; s. c., 18 Pat. Off. Gaz. 242; Sinclair *v.* Backus, 4 Fed. Rep. 539; s. c., 5 Bann. & Ard. Pat. Cas. 81; s. c., 17 Pat. Off. Gaz. 1503.

2. Goodyear *v.* Day, 1 Blatchf. (U. S.) 565; Blanchard *v.* Sprague, 1 Cliff. (U. S.) 288; Wilson *v.* Sandford, 10 How. (U. S.) 99; Goodyear *v.* Union India Rubber Co., 4 Blatchf. (U. S.) 63; Magic Ruffle Co. *v.* Elm City Co., 13 Blatchf. (U. S.) 151; s. c., 8 Pat. Off. Gaz. 773; s. c., 2 Bann. & Ard. Pat. Cas. 152; Billings *v.* Ames, 32 Mo. 265; Albright *v.* Teas, 106 U. S. 613; s. c., 23 Pat. Off. Gaz. 829; Hartell *v.* Tilghman, 99 U. S. 547; Adams *v.* Meyrose, 7 Fed. Rep. 208; s. c., 2 McCrary (U. S.) 360; Ingalls *v.* Tice, 14 Fed. Rep. 352; Smith *v.* Standard Mach. Co., 22 Pat. Off. Gaz. 587.

3. Nesmith *v.* Calvert, 1 Woodb. & M. (U. S.) 34; s. c., 2 Robb Pat. Cas. 311; Hammer *v.* Barnes, 26 How. Pr. (N. Y.) 174; Brooks *v.* Stolley, 3 McLean (U. S.) 523; s. c., 2 Robb Pat. Cas. 281.

4. Fraudulent representations in the sale of a patent and to inquire whether the patent was for the purpose represented. Hunt *v.* Hoover, 24 Iowa 231.

Controversies of the following character, where no other sources of Federal jurisdiction existed, have been specifically decided not to be within the jurisdiction of the United States courts: A suit thereby to recover royalty on a license. Hartell *v.* Tilghman, 99 U. S. 547; Ingalls *v.* Tice, 14 Fed. Rep. 352; Albright *v.* Teas, 106 U. S. 613; s. c., 23 Pat. Off. Gaz. 829.

A bill in equity to cancel the license, on account of the alleged invalidity of the patent, the subject matter of the license. Meserole *v.* Union Paper Collar Co., 3 Fish. Pat. Cas. 483; s. c., 6 Blatchf. (U. S.) 356.

Bill in equity by a licensee to enjoin a patentee from violating his agreement not to use the invented device in a certain manner. Hill *v.* Whitcomb, 1 Holmes (U. S.) 317; s. c., 1 Bann. & Ard. Pat. Cas. 34; s. c., 5 Pat. Off. Gaz. 430.

Bill for specific performance of a contract to assign a patent. Burr *v.* Gregory, 2 Paine (U. S.) 426; Perry *v.* Littlefield, 17 Blatchf. (U. S.) 272; s. c., 4 Bann. & Ard. Pat. Cas. 624.

A creditor's bill to reach a patent award by the debtor. Ryan *v.* Lee, 10 Fed. Rep. 917.

A bill to determine the meaning of a license or to ascertain whether defendant has done an act upon which a right to a reduction of royalty arises. Florence Sewing Machine Co. *v.* Singer Mfg. Co., 4 Fish. Pat. Cas. 329; s. c., 8 Blatchf. (U. S.) 113.

Whether the jurisdiction is in the circuit or State courts is not necessarily determined by the pleadings. Where it appears at trial that there is no federal question involved, the circuit court may dismiss a bill containing sufficient allegations to authorize the court to take cognizance. Blanchard *v.* Sprague, 1 Cliff. (U. S.) 288.

5. Fraudulent representations in the sale of a patent and to inquire whether the patent was for the purpose represented. Hunt *v.* Hoover, 24 Iowa 231.

fringement of letters patent[1] is directly concerned.[2]

(*a*) GENERALLY; PARTIES.—The plaintiff in an action for infringement must be the one who holds the legal title,[3] either as patentee,[4] mortgagee,[5]

1. Parsons *v.* Barnard, 7 Johns. (N. Y.) 144; Dudley *v.* Mayhew, 3 N. Y. 9; Tomlinson *v.* Battel, 4 Abb. Pr. (N. Y.) 266; Slemmer's Appeal, 58 Pa. St. 155; Kendal *v.* Winsor, 6 R. I. 453.

The defendant cannot agree for a valuable consideration, to waive an objection to want of jurisdiction. Dudley *v.* Mayhew, 3 N. Y. 9.

Nor will State courts enjoin United States courts while proceeding in an infringement suit. Kendall *v.* Winsor, 6 R. I. 453.

2. They may decide upon the validity of a patent where the question arises collaterally. Slemmer's Appeal, 58 Pa. St. 155; Rich *v.* Atwater, 16 Conn. 409; Lindsay *v.* Roraback, 4 Jones Eq. (N. Car.) 124; Sherman *v.* Champlain Transp. Co., 31 Vt. 162.

3. Gayer *v.* Wilder, 10 How. (U. S.) 477; Suydam *v.* Day, 2 Blatchf. (U. S.) 20; Sanford *v.* Messer, 5 Fish. Pat. Cas. 411; s. c., 1 Holmes (U. S.) 149; s. c., 2 Pat. Off. Gaz. 470; Blanchard *v.* Eldridge, 1 Wall. Jr. (C. C.) 337; s. c., 2 Robb Pat. Cas. 737; Graham *v.* McCormick, 20 Biss. (U. S.) 39; s. c., 11 Fed. Rep. 859; s. c., 5 Bann. & Ard. Pat. Cas. 244; s. c., 21 Pat. Off. Gaz. 1533; Graham *v.* Geneva etc. Mfg. Co., 11 Fed. Rep. 138; s. c., 21 Pat. Off. Gaz. 1536; North *v.* Kershaw, 4 Blatchf. (U. S.) 70; Sargent *v.* Yale Lock Mfg. Co., 17 Blatchf. (U. S.) 249; s. c., 4 Bann. & Ard. Pat. Cas. 579; s. c., 17 Pat. Off. Gaz. 105; Loercher *v.* Crandall, 11 Fed. Rep. 872; s. c., 21 Pat. Off. Gaz. 863; Goldsmith *v.* American Paper Collar Co., 18 Blatchf. (U. S.) 82; s. c., 5 Bann. & Ard. Pat. Cas. 300; s. c., 18 Pat. Off. Gaz. 192; Elm City Co. *v.* Wooster, 6 Fish. Pat. Cas. 452; s. c., 4 Pat. Off. Gaz. 83; Yale Lock Mfg. Co. *v.* Sargent, 117 U. S. 536.

A trustee may maintain a bill in his own name, and in the absence of objection without joining *cestui que trust.* Campbell *v.* James, 17 Blatchf. (U. S.) 42; s. c., 4 Bann. & Ard. Pat. Cas. 456; s. c., 18 Pat. Off. Gaz. 979. *Compare* Northwestern Fire Extinguisher Co. *v.* Philadelphia Fire Extinguisher Co., 1 Bann. & Ard. Pat. Cas. 177; s. c., 6 Pat. Off. Gaz. 34. And a married woman by herself where the State laws permit her to own property as a *feme sole.* Lorrilard *v.* Standard Oil Co., 5 Bann. & Ard. Pat. Cas. 432; s. c., 2 Fed. Rep. 902; s. c., 17 Pat. Off. Gaz. 902; Fetter *v.* Newhall, 17 Fed. Rep. 841; s. c., 25 Pat. Off. Gaz. 502.

All the joint owners of the patent should join. Ambler *v.* Chouteau, 3 Cent. L. J. 333.

But not one who merely has an interest in the profits. Goodyear *v.* New Jersey etc. R. Co., 1 Fish. Pat. Cas. 626; s. c., 1 Wall Jr. (C. C.) 356.

4. Hussey *v.* Whiteley, 2 Fish. Pat. Cas. 120; s. c., 1 Bond (U. S.) 407; Still *v.* Reading, 9 Fed. Rep. 40; s. c., 20 Pat. Off. Gaz. 1025.

A patentee who has parted with his title to the patent, can maintain an action at law for damages for past infringement occurring during the time he owned the patent. Moore *v.* Marsh, 7 Wall. (U. S.) 515.

5. Waterman *v.* McKenzie, 54 Pat. Off. Gaz. 1562.

A person who has no legal title, but only a collateral interest, need not be made a party. Goodyear *v.* New Jersey etc. R. Co., 1 Fish. Pat. Cas. 626; s. c., 2 Wall. Jr. (C. C.) 356; Morse *v.* O'Reilly, 6 Pa. L. J. 501; Graham *v.* Geneva etc. Mfg. Co., 11 Fed. Rep. 138; 21 Pat. Off. Gaz. 1536; Hodge *v.* North Missouri R. Co., 1 Dill. (U. S.) 104; s. c., 4 Fish. Pat. Cas. 161.

Licensees. — Consequently licensees cannot in their own name sue strangers who infringe. Littlefield *v.* Perry, 21 Wall. (U. S.) 205; Hill *v.* Whitcomb, 1 Holmes (U. S.) 317; s. c., 1 Bann. & Ard. Pat. Cas. 34; s. c., 5 Pat. Off. Gaz. 430; Nelson *v.* McMann, 16 Blatchf. (U. S.) 139; s. c., 4 Bann. & Ard. Pat. Cas. 203; s. c., 16 Pat. Off. Gaz. 761; Union Paper Bag Co. *v.* Nixon, 105 U. S. 766; s. c., 21 Pat. Off. Gaz. 1275; Hayward *v.* Andrews, 106 U. S. 672; s. c., 23 Pat. Off. Gaz. 533; Wilson *v.* Chickering, 14 Fed. Rep. 917; s. c., 23 Pat. Off. Gaz. 1730; Gamewell Fire Alarm Tel. Co. *v.* Brooklyn, 14 Fed. Rep. 255; s. c., 22 Pat. Off. Gaz. 1978; Ingalls *v.* Tice, 14 Fed. Rep. 352; Ingalls *v.* Tice, 22 Pat. Off. Gaz, 2160; Suydam *v.* Day, 2

grantee,[1] or assignee,[2] though there are instances when licensees[3]

Blatchf. (U. S.) 20; Gayler *v.* Wilder, 10 How. (U. S.) 477; Waterman *v.* McKenzie, 54 Pat. Off. Gaz. 1562; Cottle *v.* Kerementz, 25 Fed. Rep. 494. *Compare* Brammer *v.* Jones, 3 Fish. Pat. Cas. 340; s. c., 2 Bond (U. S.) 100.

But they can sue in their own names their licensor for infringement. Littlefield *v.* Perry, 21 Wall. (U. S.) 205; s. c., 1 Pat. Off. Gaz. 964; Perry *v.* Littlefield, 17 Blatchf. (U. S.) 272; s. c., 2 Fed. Rep. 464; s. c., 4 Bann. & Ard. Pat. Cas. 624; s. c., 18 Pat. Off. Gaz. 571; Stanley Rule etc. Co. *v.* Bailey, 14 Blatchf. (U. S.) 510; s. c., 3 Bann. & Ard. Pat. Cas. 297.

And against strangers in the name of the licensor (at law). Goodyear *v.* McBurney, 3 Blatchf. (U. S.) 32; Goodyear *v.* Bishop, 4 Blatchf. (U. S.) 438; s. c., 2 Fish. Pat. Cas. 96.

And where they have authority to bring suit in the name of the licensor or his assigns they need not obtain his consent for every suit. Bassett *v.* Malone, 11 Fed. Rep. 801.

The patentee may claim indemnity for costs. Goodyear *v.* Bishop, 4 Blatchf. (U. S.) 438; s. c., 2 Fish. Pat. Cas. 96.

He cannot consent to a dismissal of the suit. Goodyear *v.* Bishop, 4 Blatchf. (U. S.) 438; s. c., 2 Fish. Pat. Cas. 96.

The administrator of a licensee having a personal license only, cannot sue in his grantor's name, for damages for infringement. Oliver *v.* Rumford Chemical Works, 109 U. S. 75.

Equitable and Legal Owner.—In an equity suit, an equitable owner and one holding the legal title should be joined. Stimpson *v.* Rogers, 4 Blatchf. (U. S.) 333; Aiken *v.* Dolan, 3 Fish. Pat. Cas. 197; Dibble *v.* Augur, 7 Blatch. (U. S.) 86.

But at law the legal owner only. Park *v.* Little, 3 Wash. (U. S.) 196; s. c., 1 Robb Pat. Cas. 17; Blanchard *v.* Eldridge, 1 Wall. Jr. (C. C.) 337; s. c., 2 Robb Pat. Cas. 737.

1. Chambers *v.* Smith, 5 Fish. Pat. Cas. 12; s. c., 7 Phila. (Pa.) 575; Olcott *v.* Hawkins, 2 Am. L. J. N. S. 317; Wilson *v.* Rousseau, 4 How. (U. S.) 646.

Grantee and patentee may join. Woodworth *v.* Wilson, 4 How. (U. S.) 712; s. c., 2 Robb Pat. Cas. 473; Ogle *v.* Edge, 4 Wash. (U. S.) 584; s. c., 1 Robb Pat. Cas. 516; Bach *v.* Cobb, 9 L. R. 545.

A grantee who had reserved for himself by the patentee certain rights in part of territory granted, need not join the patentee in suing for an infringement in a State not subject to the reservation. Hobbie *v.* Smith, 27 Fed. Rep. 656.

2. Henry *v.* Francestown etc. Stove Co., 2 Bann. & Ard. Pat. Cas. 221; s. c., 9 Pat. Off. Gaz. 408; Hamilton *v.* Rollins, 5 Dill. (U. S.) 495; s. c., 3 Bann. & Ard. Pat. Cas. 157; Jenkins *v.* Greenwald, 1 Bond (U. S.) 126; s. c., 2 Fish. Pat. Cas. 37, Shaw *v.* Colwell Lead Co., 11 Fed. Rep. 711; Campbell *v.* James, 2 Fed. Rep. 338; s. c., 5 Bann. & Ard. Pat. Cas. 354; s. c., 18 Blatchf. (U. S.) 921; s. c., 18 Pat. Off. Gaz. 1111; Herbert *v.* Adams, 4 Mason (U. S.) 15; s. c., 1 Robb Pat. Cas. 505; Suydam *v.* Day, 2 Blatchf. (U. S.) 20; Tyler *v.* Tuel, 6 Cranch (U. S.) 324; s. c., 1 Robb Pat. Cas. 14.

Assignees as tenants in common may join. Stein *v.* Goddard, 1 McAll. (U. S.) 82. See Whittemore *v.* Cutter, 1 Gall. (U. S.) 429; s. c., 1 Robb Pat. Cas. 28.

Assignor and assignee may join in a bill in equity where infringement occurred before assignment. Anthony *v.* Carroll, 9 Pat. Off. Gaz. 199; s. c., 2 Bann & Ard. Pat. Cas. 195.

And in a suit against a former licensee whose license has been forfeited, the assignor who granted the license is a necessary party. Woodworth *v.* Cook, 2 Blatchf. (U. S.) 151.

An assignee of a patent with the assignment of the right to damages for past infringement may maintain an action at law in his own name. Spring *v.* Domestic Sewing Mach. Co., 13 Fed. Rep. 446; s. c., 22 Pat. Off. Gaz. 1445.

3. Goodyear *v.* Railroad, 1 Fish. Pat. Cas. 626; s. c., 2 Wall. Jr. (C. C.) 356; Goodyear *v.* Allyn, 3 Fish. Pat. Cas. 374; s. c., 6 Blatchf. (U. S.) 33; Dorsey etc. Rake Co. *v.* Bradley Mfg. Co., 12 Blatchf. (U. S.) 202; s. c., 1 Bann. & Ard. Pat. Cas. 330.

But ordinarily a licensee has not such an interest as compells his joining. Potter *v.* Wilson, 2 Fish. Pat. Cas. 102; Grover etc. Sewing Mach. Co. *v.* Sloat, 2 Fish. Pat. Cas. 112; Nellis *v.* Pennock Mfg. Co., 13 Fed. Rep. 451; s. c., 22 Pat. Off. Gaz. 1131.

and others[1] are proper parties to be joined, especially in equity.

(*b*) ACTION AT LAW; DECLARATION.—The proper legal action for the infringement of a patent is an action on the case.[2] The declaration must show title in plaintiff,[3] a lawful issue and delivery of the patent,[4] the nature of the invention[5] and aver an infringement by the defendant;[6] and if the patent has been extended, such extension must be averred.[7]

But an exclusive licensee should be. Hammond *v.* Hunt, 4 Bann. & Ard. Pat. Cas. 111.

And in certain cases should be the sole party. Herman *v.* Herman, 29 Fed. Rep. 92.

1. **Personal Representatives.**—Until an assignment is made, all suits must be brought in the name of the personal representative of the deceased owner. Hodge *v.* North Missouri R. Co., 1 Dill. (U. S.) 104; s. c., 4 Fish. Pat. Cas. 161; Northwestern Fire Extinguisher Co. *v.* Philadelphia Fire Extinguisher Co., 1 Bann & Ard. Pat. Cas. 177; s. c., 6 Pat. Off. Gaz. 34.

But where the equitable interest passed out of the patentee during his lifetime, the administrator is trustee for the equitable owner, and the heirs are not necessary parties. Northwestern Fire Extinguisher Co. *v.* Philadelphia Fire Extinguisher Co., 1 Bann. & Ard. Pat. Cas. 177; s. c., 6 Pat. Off. Gaz. 34.

A foreign administrator can sue without taking out letters of administration in the State where suit is brought. Smith *v.* Mercer, 5 Pa. L. J., 529; Goodyear *v.* Hullihen, 2 Hughes (U. S.) 492; s. c., 3 Fish. Pat. Cas. 251.

The executor in whom the legal title is only necessary. Goodyear *v.* Providence Rubber Co., 2 Fish. Pat. Cas. 499.

A holder of the equitable title to a patent may maintain a bill in equity against a party having the legal title. Ruggles *v.* Eddy, 10 Blatchf. (U. S.) 52; s. c., 5 Fish. Pat. Cas. 583.

Joint Owners.—In equity one joint owner of a patent cannot sue the other. Clum *v.* Brewer, 2 Curt. (U. S.) 506.

Apparently otherwise at law. Pitts *v.* Hall, 3 Blatchf. (U. S.) 201.

Partners.—One partner cannot file a bill without joining his co-partners for infringement of a firm patent. Ambler *v.* Chouteau, 3 Cent. L. J. 333.

2. U. S. Rev. Stat., § 4919; Stein *v.* Goddard, McAll. (U. S.) 82; Byam *v.* Ballard, 1 Curt. (U. S.) 100.

3. Gray *v.* James, 1 Pet. (C. C.) 476; s. c., 1 Robb Pat. Cas. 140.

4. Cutting *v.* Myers, 4 Wash. (U. S.) 220; s. c., 1 Robb Pat. Cas. 159.

It is enough to set forth the grant in substance. Wilder *v.* McCormick, 2 Blatchf. (U. S.) 31.

But a variance is fatal if the grant is professed to be set forth according to its tenor. Tryon *v.* White, Pet. (C. C.) 96.

Novelty and Utility.—The novelty and utility of the invention must be set up. Wilder *v.* McCormick, 2 Blatchf. (U. S.) 31.

5. Peterson *v.* Wooden, 3 McLean (U. S.) 248; s. c., 1 Robb Pat. Cas. 116.

Either the letters patent can be annexed to the declaration or a profert made. Pitts *v.* Whitman, 2 Story (U. S.) 609; s. c., 2 Robb Pat. Cas. 189; Wilder *v.* McCormick, 2 Blatchf. (U. S.) 31.

6. Cutting *v.* Myers, 4 Wash. (U. S.) 220; s. c., 1 Robb Pat. Cas. 159; Seymour *v.* Osborne, 11 Wall. (U. S.) 516.

The plaintiff is confined to the times within which he declares the infringement to have taken place. Eastman *v.* Bodfish, 1 Story (U. S.) 528; s. c., 2 Robb Pat. Cas. 72.

Distinct infringements of one patent may be set up in one count. Wilder *v.* McCormick, 2 Blatchf. (U. S.) 31.

And infringements of a generic patent and an improvement when both are held by the same party, must be brought together. Case *v.* Redfield, 4 McLean (U. S.) 526; s. c., 2 Robb Pat. Cas. 741.

7. Phelps *v.* Comstock, 4 McLean (U. S.) 353.

Where plaintiff wishes to recover under both original and extended patents, he must file distinct and independent counts for each patent. Eastman *v.* Bodfish, 1 Story (U. S.) 528; s. c., 2 Robb Pat. Cas. 72.

(*c*) SUIT IN EQUITY.—(1) *Foundation.*—The jurisdiction of a court of equity in patent cases to grant an injunction is founded on the irreparable injury which would otherwise be caused the complainant, and the desire of the court to prevent a multiplicity of suits.[1] This power has been confirmed by statute.[2]

(2) *When Court of Equity Will Take Jurisdiction.*—A court of equity will take jurisdiction in an action for the infringement of a patent only when the patent has not expired prior to the commencement of the action,[3] and will not expire before equitable relief could be obtained,[4] unless there is some other equity out-

Defects Cured By Verdict.—A breach too general in not setting up the number of machines used by defendant. Gray *v.* James, Pet. (C. C.) 476; s. c., 1 Robb Pat. Cas. 140.

Any uncertainty in the title where there is sufficient certainty to enable the court to give judgment. Gray *v.* James, 1 Pet. (C. C.) 476; s. c., 1 Robb Pat. Cas. 140; Cutting *v.* Myers, 4 Wash. (U. S.) 220; s. c., 1 Robb Pat. Cas. 159.

1. Foster's Federal Practice, § 216; Daniel Chan. Prac. (5 Am. ed.) 1642–1648; Brooks *v.* Miller, 28 Fed. Rep. 615; Brick *v.* Staten Island R. Co., 25 Fed. Rep. 553.

This power is of ancient use in equity. Foster's Fed. Prac., § 216; Hogg *v.* Kirby, 8 Ves. (Eng.) 215; Wilkins *v.* Aikin, 17 Ves. (Eng.) 427.

2. "The several courts vested with jurisdiction of cases arising under the patent laws shall have power to grant injunctions according to the course and principles of a court of equity, to prevent the violation of any right secured by patent, upon such terms as the court may deem reasonable." U. S. Rev. Stats., § 4921; prior Stat. July 4, 1836, § 16; 5 Stat. at Large 123.

Right of Patentee to Injunction.—The right of a patentee to enjoin an infringement is incontestable. Birdsell *v.* Shalioll, 112 U. S. 487; Bragg *v.* Stockton, 27 Fed. Rep. 509.

3. Root *v.* Lake Shore etc. R. Co., 105 U. S. 211; s. c., 21 Pat. Off. Gaz. 1112; Roemer *v.* Neumann, 26 Fed. Rep. 332; Lord *v.* Whitehead etc. Mach. Co., 24 Fed. Rep. 801; Vaughan *v.* East Tennessee etc. R. Co., 1 Flipp. (U. S.) 621; Sayles *v.* Richmond etc. R. Co., 3 Hughes (U. S.) 172; s. c., 4 Bann. & Ard. Pat. Cas. 239; s. c., 16 Pat. Off. Gaz. 43.

And the same rule holds where all the necessary parties to the action are not brought in until after the expiration of the patent. Hewitt *v.* Pennsylvania Steel Co., 24 Fed. Rep. 367.

The principle is that, as the jurisdiction of equity rests on the prevention of an irreparable injury arising from the infringement and the prevention of a multiplicity of suits, there is an adequate remedy at law when the patent has expired.

4. Gottfried *v.* Moerlein, 14 Fed. Rep. 170; Burdell *v.* Comstock, 15 Fed. Rep. 395; Davis *v.* Smith, 19 Fed. Rep. 823; Betts *v.* Gallais, 10 L. R. Eq. (Eng.) 392; American Cable R. Co. *v.* Chicago City R. Co., 41 Fed. Rep. 522; Mershon *v.* J. F. Pease Furnace Co., 24 Fed. Rep. 741; McMillin *v.* St. Louis etc. Transp. Co., 18 Fed. Rep. 260.

Where there is time for equitable relief to be obtained, the court will take jurisdiction. Lake Shore etc. R. Co. *v.* National etc. Shoe Co., 110 U. S. 229; s. c., 26 Pat. Off. Gaz. 915. The patent expired four months after the bill was filed, and a shorter time in Consolidated Safety Valve Co. *v.* Crosby etc. Valve Co., 113 U. S. 157.

The circuit courts have entertained suits where the patent will expire in three weeks after bill filed. Adams *v.* Bridgewater Iron Co., 26 Fed. Rep. 324; s. c., 34 Pat. Off. Gaz. 1045; Kittle *v.* De Graff, 30 Fed. Rep. 689. And six weeks. Dick *v.* Struthers, 25 Fed. Rep. 103. See also Singer Mfg. Co. *v.* Wilson Sewing Mach. Co., 38 Fed. Rep. 586; New York Sugar Co. *v.* Peoria Sugar Co., 21 Fed. Rep. 878; Kittle *v.* Rogers, 33 Fed. Rep. 49.

And an amended bill to cover a reissue, has been allowed to be filed, although the patent alleged to be infringed by the first bill had expired. Reay *v.* Raynor, 19 Fed. Rep. 308, 311.

The right to come into equity when the patent is about to expire, exists where "the court of equity could, by the exercise of its jurisdiction in the ordinary course of procedure, give to

side of mere infringement to be adjusted between the parties.[1]

the plaintiff the most moderate relief which he prays or would be entitled to, on his allegations." Marshon *v.* J. F. Pease Furnace Co., 24 Fed. Rep. 741.

Where the relief could have been obtained, the failure to obtain or ask for it does not oust the jurisdiction of equity. Toledo Mower etc. Co. *v.* Johnston Harvester Co., 24 Fed. Rep. 739; Adams *v.* Bridgewater Iron Co., 26 Eed. Rep. 324.

In such cases the court will retain the suit to administer any relief found necessary. Gottfried *v.* Moerlein, 14 Fed. Rep. 170. *Compare*, however, American Cable R. Co. *v.* Chicago City R. Co., 41 Fed. Rep. 522; Avery *v.* Wilson, 20 Fed. Rep. 856.

It does not exist where the coming into a court of equity appears to be a pretense to avoid coming into a court of law. Mershon *v.* J. F. Pease Furnace Co., 24 Fed. Rep. 741; Adams *v.* Bridgewater Iron Co., 26 Fed. Rep. 324.

For instance, where a suit was brought five days prior to the expiration of patent, and an injunction was asked for, which could not be obtained and was not desired for the purpose of giving jurisdiction. Burdell *v.* Comstock, 15 Fed. Rep. 395. Or where, although the patent expired fourteen days after the commencement of the suit, no injunction *pendente lite* had been asked for, and the patent would have expired before return day of the process and before the complainant would have been entitled to a default. American Cable R. Co. *v.* Chicago City R. Co., 41 Fed. Rep. 522.

An assignee of the right of damages, cannot sue in equity merely because he cannot sue in his own name at law. Haywood *v.* Andrews, 106 U. S. 672.

1. While the general rule is, that where an injunction could not be granted, equity will not take jurisdiction, grounds of equitable relief may arise other than in this, as where the title of the complainant is equitable merely, or equitable interposition is necessary on account of the impediments which prevent a resort to remedies purely legal; and such an equity may arise out of and inhere in the nature of the account itself, springing from special and peculiar circumstances which disable the patentee from a recovery at law altogether, or render his remedy in a legal tribunal difficult, inadequate and incomplete; and as such cases cannot be defined more exactly, each must rest upon its own particular circumstances, as furnishing a clear and satisfactory ground of exception from the general rule. Root *v.* Lake Shore etc. R. Co., 105 U. S. 211; s. c., 21 Pat. Off. Gaz. 1112. A bill will not be merely for an account. Root *v.* Lake Shore etc. R. Co., 105 U. S. 211; s. c., 21 Pat. Off. Gaz. 1112; Vaughan *v.* East Tennessee etc. R. Co., 1 Fish. (U. S.) 621; s. c., 11 Pat. Off. Gaz. 789; s. c., 2 Bann. & Ard. Pat. Cas. 537; Davis *v.* Smith, 19 Fed. Rep. 823. An intricate account will not give jurisdiction. Lord *v.* Whitehead, etc. Machine Co., 24 Fed. Rep. 801; Roemer *v.* Neumann, 26 Fed. Rep. 332. But where a discovery and an account were both prayed for, and the account was such as could not readily be taken before a jury, equity will take jurisdiction. Vaughan *v.* East Tenn. etc. R. Co., 1 Flipp. (U. S.) 621; s. c., 11 Pat. Off. Gaz. 789; s. c., 2 Bann. & Ard. Pat. Cas. 537; McKay *v.* Smith, 24 Fed. Rep. 295. See Kirk *v.* DuBois, 28 Fed. Rep. 460. But the mere fact that the defendants were concealing the facts necessary to obtain an account. Lord *v.* Whitehead Mach. Co., 24 Fed. Rep. 891.

Where the defendants were advised of the claim that their manufacture was an infringement, and a suit was pending for such infringement, they were enjoined after the expiration of the patent from selling the infringing articles made during its term. New York Belting etc. Co. *v.* Macgowan, 28 Fed. Rep. 14. And the fact that the defendants had ceased their infringement at the request of the complainant, does not prevent an injunction from going out. Facer *v.* Midvale Steel Works, 38 Fed. Rep. 231.

In the cases prior to Root *v.* Lake Shore etc. R. Co., 105 U. S. 211, s. c., 21 Pat. Off. Gaz. 1112, it was frequently stated that the infringer was a trustee *de son tort* of the profits he had made, and that an action in equity to compel him to account could be had on that ground only. Nevins *v.* Johnson, 3 Blatchf. (U. S.) 80; Howes *v.* Nute, 4 Cliff (U. S.) 173; s. c., 4 Fish. Pat. Cas. 263; Gordon *v.* Anthony, 16 Pat. Off. Gaz. 1135; s. c., 16 Blatchf. (U. S.) 234; s. c., 4 Bann. & Ard. Pat. Cas. 246; McComb *v.* Beard, 3 Pat. Off. Gaz. 33; s. c., 6 Fish. Pat. Cas. 254; s. c., 10

(*d*) BILL IN EQUITY.—(1) *Certainty.*—The bill to enjoin the infringement of a patent must contain an allegation that the complainant, or the person through whom he claims, was the inventor or discoverer of the thing or process patented;[1] but it need not trace the title beyond averring that it is in himself;[2] it should state the number and date of the letters patent, but need not allege the character of the improvement except in general terms,[3] and is only obliged to charge infringement generally.[4] He must set out that the defendant is an inhabitant of the district in which suit is brought,[5] except where the jurisdiction depends upon the diversity of citizenship.[6]

(2) *Multifariousness.*—The subject-matter of a bill is not made multifarious by joining two patents which are infringed by one device of the respondent;[7] nor by joining a prayer for an adjudi-

Blatchf. (U. S.) 550; Sayles *v.* Dubuque etc. R. Co., 5 Dill. (U. S.) 561; s. c., 3 Bann. & Ard. Pat. Cas. 219; Stephens *v.* Kansas Pacific R. Co., 5 Dill. (U. S.) 486; Perry *v.* Corning, 6 Blatchf. (U. S.) 134; Dibble *v.* Augur, 7 Blatchf. (U. S.) 86.

1. Foster's Fed. Prac., § 377; Sullivan *v.* Redfield; 1 Paine (U. S.) 441.

2. Nourse *v.* Allen, 4 Blatchf. (U. S.) 376; s. c., 3 Fish. Pat. Cas. 63; Clement Mfg. Co. *v.* Upton etc. Co., 40 Fed. Rep. 471; Edison Electric Light Co. *v.* Consolidated Electric Light Co., 25 Fed. Rep. 719.

3. Haven *v.* Brown, 6 Fish. Pat. Cas. 413; Turrell *v.* Cammerer, 3 Fish. Pat. Cas. 462; Poppenhausen *v.* Falke, 2 Fish. Pat. Cas. 181; s. c., 5 Blatchf. (U. S.) 493.

Where a profert is made, the title of the device need only be recited. McMillin *v.* St. Louis etc. Transp. Co., 18 Fed. Rep. 260; Foster's Fed. Prac., § 77. For form of profert, see Wilder *v.* McCormick, 2 Blatchf. (U. S.) 31.

A bill identifying an invention only by its title, without the specifications being annexed, does not show sufficient certainty as to what the invention is. Wise *v.* Grand Ave. R. Co., 33 Fed. Rep. 277.

4. Turrell *v.* Cammerer, 3 Fish. Pat. Cas. 462; Poppenhausen *v.* Falke, 5 Blatchf. (U. S.) 493; s. c., 2 Fish. Pat. Cas. 181; McMillin *v.* St. Louis etc. Transp. Co., 18 Fed. Rep. 260.

The bill need not specify the claims infringed, even though the defendant is only infringing some of the them. Thatcher Heating Co. *v.* Carbon Stove Co., 4 Bann. & Ard. Pat. Cas. 68; s. c., 15 Pat. Off. Gaz. 1051.

5. Foster's Fed. Prac., § 77.

6. Foster's Fed. Prac., § 77.

7. Gamewell etc. Tel. Co. *v.* Chillicothe, 7 Fed. Rep. 351; Kelleher *v.* Darling, 3 Bann. & Ard. Pat. Cas. 438; s. c., 4 Cliff. (U. S.) 424; s. c., 14 Pat. Off. Gaz. 673; Nellis *v.* Pennock Mfg. Co., 13 Fed. Rep. 451; s. c., 22 Pat. Off. Gaz. 1131; Seymour *v.* Osborne, 3 Fish. Pat. Cas. 555; Nourse *v.* Allen, 4 Blatchf. (U. S.) 376; s. c., 3 Fish. Pat. Cas. 63; Horman Pat. Mfg. Co. *v.* Brooklyn City R. Co., 15 Blatchf. (U. S.) 444; s. c., 4 Bann. & Ard. Pat. Cas. 86; Gillespie *v.* Cummings, 3 Sawy. (U. S.) 259; s. c., 1 Bann. & Ard. Pat. Cas. 587; Case *v.* Redfield, 4 McLean (U. S.) 526. But complainant must aver that the defendant's device infringes all his patents. Nellis *v.* McLenahan, 6 Fish. Pat. Cas. 286.

Where two assignments, each assigning a patent, embrace the territory in which there is an infringement of both, in a single device, one bill may be exhibited. Gillespie *v.* Cummings, 3 Sawy. (U. S.) 259; s. c., 1 Bann. & Ard. Pat. Cas. 587.

Not Where Patents Are Distinct.—But one bill cannot be exhibited for the infringement of distinct patents, covering inventions not capable of being used together. Hayes *v.* Dayton, 18 Blatchf. (U. S.) 420; s. c., 8 Fed. Rep. 702; s. c., 18 Pat. Off. Gaz. 1406; Hayes *v.* Bickelhoupt, 19 Pat. Off. Gaz. 177; Pope Mfg. Co. *v.* Marqua, 15 Fed. Rep. 400; Barney *v.* Peck, 16 Fed. Rep. 413; s. c. 24 Pat. Off. Gaz. 101. Nor where the patents, though infringed by one machine, are capable of a separate use. Consolidated Electric Light Co. *v.*

cation concerning conflicting patents to a bill for infringement in the use of one of the patents.[1]

(*e*) MOTION FOR PRELIMINARY INJUNCTION.—(1) *General Principles.*—The issue of a preliminary injunction is always a matter of discretion and depends upon the peculiar circumstances of each case and the comparative expense and inconvenience to which the parties will be subjected in case of granting the injunction on the one hand,[2] or withholding it on the other.[3]

Brush etc. Electric Light Co., 20 Fed. Rep. 502.

The bill must allege and the proofs show that the inventions are capable of conjoint use and can be used together. Lilliendahl *v.* Detwiler, 18 Fed. Rep. 176; Griffith *v.* Segar, 29 Fed. Rep. 707.

Where several patents are closely connected and used on one machine, the court will sometimes consolidate suits brought on; separate ones at the motion of the defendant. Deering *v.* Winona Harvester Works, 24 Fed. Rep. 90.

1. Leach *v.* Chandler, 18 Fed. Rep. 262.

Averments That Are Proper in a Bill. Prior litigation. Doughty *v.* West, 2 Fish. Pat. 553; Blandy *v.* Griffith, 3 Fish. Pat. Cas. 609; Stain Gauge etc. Co., *v.* McRoberts, 26 Fed. Rep. 705. Public acquiescence and use. Gutta Percha Co. *v.* Goodyear Rubber Co., 3 Sawy. (U.S.) 543. History of invention. Lantern Co. *v.* McRoberts, 26 Fed. Rep. 858. That defendant is acting without authority. Still *v.* Reading, 9 Fed. Rep. 20; s. c., 20 Pat. Off. Gaz. 1025.

Necessary Averments.—In a bill seeking an injunction after the expiration of a patent, a statement that the defendant is using machines made during the life of a patent or a fear of such use. American etc. Boring Co. *v.* Rutland Marble Co., 18 Blatchf. (U. S.) 146; s. c., 2 Fed. Rep. 355; s. c., 5 Bann. & Ard. Pat. Cas. 354.

An excuse for delay when a patent has been surrendered for reissue more than two years after issue. Wollensak *v.* Reiher, 115 U. S. 96. Or in a suit to compel the granting of a patent, a delay of two years between the actions in the Patent Office. Gandy *v.* Marble, 122 U. S. 432.

Unnecessary Averments.—That the patentee marked the articles made or vended under the patent as required by the Patent Law. Goodyear *v.* Allyn, 6 Blatchf. (U. S.) 33; s. c., 3 Fish. Pat. Cas. 374. A statement where a corporation is located or doing business. National Hay Rake Co. *v.* Harbert, 2 W. N. C. (Pa.) 100. The specific ground on which a patent was reissued. Spaeth *v.* Barney, 22 Fed. Rep. 828.

In a suit against a licensee that the licensor has kept his covenants in the license. Stanley etc. Co. *v.* Bailey, 14 Blatchf. (U. S.) 510; s. c., 3 Bann. & Ard. Pat. Cas. 297.

2. Parker *v.* Sears, 1 Fish. Pat. Cas. 93; Earth Closet Co. *v.* Fenner, 5 Fish. Pat. Cas. 15; Potter *v.* Davis Sewing Machine Co., 3 Fish. Pat. Cas. 472; Goodyear *v.* Rust, 3 Fish. Pat. Cas. 456; s. c., 6 Blatchf. (U. S.) 229; Potter *v.* Crowell, 3 Fish. Pat. Cas. 112; s. c., 1 Abb. (U. S.) 89; Irwin *v.* Dane, 4 Fish. Pat. Cas. 359; s. c., 2 Biss. (U. S.) 442; Smith *v.* Mercer, 5 Pa. Leg. J. 529; s. c., 4 West L. J. 49; Hussey *v.* Whiteley, 2 Fish. Pat. Cas. 120; s. c., 1 Bond (U. S.) 407; Potter *v.* Muller, 2 Fish. Pat. Cas. 465; Potter *v.* Schenck, 1 Biss. (U. S.) 515; s. c., 3 Fish. Pat. Cas. 82; Hodge *v.* Hudson River R. Co., 6 Blatchf. (U. S.) 165; s. c., 3 Fish. Pat. Cas. 410; Poppenhausen *v.* New York etc. Comb Co., 2 Fish. Pat. Cas. 74; s. c., 4 Blatchf. (U. S.) 184; Root *v.* Mt. Adams etc. R. Co., 40 Fed. Rep. 760.

3. Hockholtzer *v.* Eager, 2 Sawy. (U. S.) 361; Bliss *v.* Brooklyn, 4 Fish. Pat. Cas. 596; s. c., 8 Blatchf. (U. S.) 533; Forbush *v.* Bradford, 1 Fish. Pat. Cas. 317; Morris *v.* Lowell Mfg. Co., 3 Fish. Pat. Cas. 67; New York Grape Sugar Co. *v.* American Grape Sugar Co., 10 Fed. Rep. 835; Hall *v.* Speer, 6 Pitts. Leg. J. 403; Howe *v.* Newton, 2 Fish. Pat. Cas. 531; Brooks *v.* Bicknell, 3 McLean (U. S.) 250; Irwin *v.* Dane, 4 Fish. Pat. Cas. 359; s. c., 2 Biss. (U. S.) 442.

Where the Patent Had Previously Been Sustained.—A preliminary injunction on a patent for a portion of a large machine intended to print a daily paper refused where the removal of the

(2) *Title and Prior Adjudication.*—The title of the complainant must be clear[1] and ordinarily the patent declared valid by an adjudication.[2]

part covered by the patent, though possible, was yet very difficult, and the injunction would do no especial good to the complainants. Hoe *v.* Boston etc. Advertiser Corp., 14 Fed. Rep. 914; s. c., 23 Pat. Off. Gaz. 1124. See also Consolidated Roller Mill Co. *v.* Richmond City Mill Works, 40 Fed. Rep. 474; Root *v.* Mt. Adams etc R. Co., 40 Fed. Rep. 760; Eagle Mfg. Co. *v.* Chamberlain Plow Co., 36 Fed. Rep. 905; Eastern Paper Bag Co. *v.* Nixon, 35 Fed. Rep. 752.

Consequential damages resulting from groundless fears not a reason for refusing an injunction. Rumford Chemical Works *v.* Vice, 14 Blatchf. (U. S.) 179; s. c., 11 Pat. Off. Gaz. 600.

Nor will an injunction be refused where it merely prohibits the sale of articles which are manufactured elsewhere. Potter *v.* Fuller, 2 Fish. Pat. Cas. 251.

A preliminary injunction will not be granted when another to the same effect is in force in a different suit. Gold and Stock Tel. Co. *v.* Pearce, 19 Fed. Rep. 419.

1. Potter *v.* Whitney, 1 Low. (U. S.) 87; Forbush *v.* Bradford, 1 Fish. Pat. Cas. 317; Woodworth *v.* Rogers, 3 Woodb. & M. (U. S.) 135; s. c., 2 Robb Pat. Cas. 625; Standard Paint Co. *v.* Reynolds, 43 Fed. Rep. 304; Herman *v.* Hermann, 29 Fed. Rep. 92.

The validity of the patent should be clear. Sullivan *v.* Redfield, 1 Paine (U. S.) 441; s. c., 1 Robb Pat. Cas. 477; Arnheim *v.* Fruster, 24 Fed. Rep. 276. Also design patent. Osborn *v.* Judd, 29 Fed. Rep. 76.

2. Sickels *v.* Tileston, 4 Blatchf. (U. S.) 109; Parker *v.* Brant, 1 Fish. Pat. Cas. 58; Orr *v.* Badger, 7 L. R. 465; Poppenhusen *v.* New York etc. Comb Co., 2 Fish. Pat. Cas. 74; s. c., 4 Blatchf. (U. S.) 184; Potter *v.* Muller, 2 Fish. Pat. Cas. 631; Potter *v.* Stevens, 2 Fish. Pat. Cas. 163; Potter *v.* Fuller, 2 Fish. Pat. Cas. 251; Orr *v.* Littlefield, 1 Woodb. & B. M. (U. S.) 13; s. c., 2 Robb Pat. Cas. 323; Potter *v.* Whitney, 3 Fish. Pat. Cas. 77; s. c., 1 Low. (U. S.) 87; Putnam *v.* Wetherbee, 1 Holmes (U. S.) 497; s. c., 8 Pat. Off. Gaz. 320; s. c., 2 Bann. & Ard. Pat. Cas. 78; Goodyear *v.* Hullihen, 3 Fish. Pat. Cas. 251; s. c., 2 Hughes (U. S.) 492; Jones *v.* Merrill, 8 Pat. Off. Gaz. 401; Thompson *v.* Mendelsohn, 5 Fish. Pat. Cas. 187; Robertson *v.* Hill, 6 Fish. Pat. Cas. 465; s. c., 4 Pat. Off. Gaz. 132; American Shoe etc. Co. *v.* National Shoe etc. Co., 2 Bann. & Ard. Pat. Cas. 551; s. c. 11 Pat. Off. Gaz. 740; United States Felting Co. *v.* Asbestos Felting Co., 10 Pat. Off. Gaz. 828; Bailey Wringing Mach. Co. *v.* Adams, 3 Bann. & Ard. Pat. Cas. 96; Atlantic Giant Powder Co. *v.* Goodyear, 3 Bann. & Ard. Pat. Cas. 161; Green *v.* French, 4 Bann. & Ard. Pat. Cas. 169; Bradley etc. Mfg. Co. *v.* Chas. Parke Co., 17 Fed. Rep. 240; Barr Co. *v.* New York etc. Sprinkler Co., 32 Fed. Rep. 79; Baldwin *v.* Conway etc. Co., 32 Fed. Rep. 795, Cary *v.* Domestic Spring Bed Co., 26 Fed Rep. 38; Cary *v.* Domestic Spring Bed Co., 27 Fed. Rep. 299; American Bell Teleph. Co. *v.* National Improved Teleph. Co., 27 Fed. Rep. 663; Hurlburt *v.* Carter, 39 Fed. Rep. 802; Raymond *v.* Boston Woven Hose Co., 39 Fed. Rep. 365; Stuart *v.* Thorman, 37 Fed. Rep. 90; Upton *v.* Wayland, 36 Fed. Rep. 691; Schneider *v.* Missouri Glass Co., 36 Fed. Rep. 582.

While the favorable judgment (or an equivalent acquiesence) is not absolutely necessary where the validity of the patent has not been assailed. (New York Grape Sugar Co. *v.* American Grape Sugar Co., 10 Fed. Rep. 835; Potter *v.* Whitney, 1 Low. (U. S.) 87; Sickels *v.* Mitchell, 3 Blatchf. (U. S.) 548; North *v.* Kershaw, 4 Blatchf. (U. S.) 70), yet ordinarily when the patent is new and its validity assailed by sufficient evidence to create a doubt in the mind of the court, the injunction will be refused. Foster's Fed. Practice 312, § 216 and cases cited in note 10.

The fact of a patent having been adjudged invalid in another court, while it had been adjudged valid after a long contest in the same court as that in which the preliminary injunction is sought, will not prevent the allowance of a preliminary injunction. Atlantic Giant Powder Co. *v.* Goodyear, 3 Bann & Ard. Pat. Cas. 161; s. c., 13 Pat. Off. Gaz. 45.

The adjudication which will warrant the grant of a preliminary injunction may be a judgment in a trial at law,[1] or a final decree in equity,[2] which latter is held more persuasive evidence.[3] A judgment by agreement, which is not collusive, is equally persuasive.[4]

(3) *Favorable Decision in Interference.*—A decision in an interference between the parties to the suit, favorable to the plaintiff in the suit, is such an adjudication of plaintiff's right between the parties that a preliminary injunction will ordinarily issue against the respondent.[5]

1. Sickels *v.* Tileston, 4 Blatchf. (U. S.) 109; Parker *v.* Brandt, 1 Fish. Pat. Cas. 58; Sargent *v.* Seagrave, 2 Curt. (U. S.) 553; Wells *v.* Gill, 6 Fish. Pat. Cas. 89; s. c., 2 Pat. Off. Gaz. 490.

2. Pierpont *v.* Fowle, 2 Woodb. & M. (U. S.) 23; American etc. Purifier Co. *v.* Christian, 3 Bann. & Ard. Pat. Cas. 42; United Nickel Co. *v.* Manhattan Brass Co., 4 Bann. & Ard. Pat. Cas. 173; 16 Blatchf. (U. S.) 68; Steam Gauge etc. Co. *v.* Miller, 8 Fed. Rep. 314; Blaisdell *v.* Puffer, 4 Bann. & Ard. Pat. Cas. 500; Blaisdell *v.* Dows, 4 Bann. & Ard. Pat. Cas. 499; Odorless Excavating Co. *v.* Lauman, 12 Fed. Rep. 788; Coburn *v.* Clarke, 24 Pat. Off. Gaz. 899; Potter *v.* Fuller, 2 Fish. Pat. Cas. 251.

3. Goodyear *v.* Muller, 3 Fish. Pat. Cas. 420;

Special Circumstances Connected with Adjudication which are Persuasive to Granting a Preliminary Injunction.—The wealth of the former defendant and his interest in defeating the patent, and the fact of present defendant being connected with former defendant. Colgate *v.* Gold and Stock Tel. Co., 4 Bann. & Ard. Pat. Cas. 559.

The defendant was interested in the result of a former suit. Robertson *v.* Hill, 6 Fish. Pat. Cas. 468; s. c., 4 Pat. Off. Gaz. 132; Robinson *v.* Randolph, 4 Bann. & Ard. Pat. Cas. 163; United States etc. Felting Co. *v.* Asbestos Felting Co., 10 Pat. Off. Gaz. 828; Birdsall *v.* Hagerstown etc. Mfg. Co., 1 Bann. & Ard. Pat. Cas. 426; s. c., 6 Pat. Off. Gaz. 604.

4. Orr *v.* Littlefield, 1 Woodb. & M. (U. S.) 13; s. c., 2 Robb. Pat. Cas. 323; Grover Sewing Mach. Co. *v.* Williams, 2 Fish. Pat. Cas. 133; Potter *v.* Fuller, 2 Fish. Pat. Cas. 251; McWilliams Mfg. Co. *v.* Blundell, 11 Fed. Rep. 419; s. c., 22 Pat. Off. Gaz. 177.

Compare Hayes *v.* Leton, 5 Fed. Rep. 521; Warner *v.* Bassett, 7 Fed. Rep. 468.

Where defendant in prior action the same as in the one to be decided, a preliminary injunction is granted almost as a matter of course. Poppenhusen *v.* New York etc. Comb Co., 2 Fish. Pat. Cas. 74; s. c., 4 Blatchf. (U. S.) 184; Clark *v.* Johnson, 4 Bann. & Ard. Pat. Cas. 403; s. c., 16 Blatchf. (U. S.) 495; s. c., 17 Pat. Off. Gaz. 1401.

And an adjudication of the patent by the supreme court carries overwhelming weight. American etc. Purifier Co. *v.* Christian, 2 Bann. & Ard. Pat. Cas. 42; s. c., 4 Dill. (U. S.) 448; America etc. Purifier Co. *v.* Atlantic Milling Co., 3 Bann. & Ard. Pat. Cas. 168.

A decision affirming the validity of a patent will be followed in all cases except where evidence is brought forth which, if produced in the former case, would have lead to a different result therein. Ladd *v.* Cameron, 25 Fed. Rep. 37; Carey *v.* Domestic Spring Bed Co., 26 Fed. Rep. 38.

But when the evidence is doubtful where there have been a number of adjudications, the injunction will be granted. Seibert etc. Oil Cup Co. *v.* Michigan Lubricator Co., 34 Fed. Rep. 33.

A writ of error taken to a former decision favorable to the patent does not destroy its authority to induce the court to grant a preliminary injunction. Forbush *v.* Bradford, 1 Fish. Pat. Cas. 317; Wells *v.* Gill, 6 Fish. Pat. Cas. 89; s. c., 2 Pat. Off. Gaz. 590; Morris *v.* Lowell Mfg. Co., 3 Fish. Pat. Cas. 67; Day *v.* Hartshorn, 3 Fish. Pat. Cas. 32.

An extension of a patent, which was granted in the face of resistance on the ground of lack of novelty, greatly strengthens the presumption of validity of the patent. Cook *v.* Ernest, 5 Fish. Pat. Cas. 396; s. c., 2 Pat. Off. Gaz. 89.

5. Smith *v.* Halkyard, 16 Fed. Rep.

(4) *Adjudications Not Warranting Preliminary Injunction.*—A preliminary injunction will not be granted because of a decision favorable to the patent on a motion for an attachment,[1] or on a motion for a preliminary injunction,[2] where the judgment or decree was collusive.[3] The prior adjudication must have determined the point involved satisfactorily.[4]

414; s. c., 23 Pat. Off. Gaz. 1833; Holliday *v.* Pickhardt, 12 Fed. Rep. 147; s. c., 22 Pat. Off. Gaz. 420; Pentlarge *v.* Beeston, 14 Blatchf. (U. S.) 352; s. c., 3 Bann. & Ard. Pat. Cas. 142; Hanford *v.* Westcott, 16 Pat. Off. Gaz. 1181; Barr Co. *v.* New York etc. Sprinkler Co., 32 Fed. Rep. 856.

A preliminary injunction will in such cases be granted even when a patent is recent. Greenwood *v.* Bracher, 17 Pat. Off. Gaz. 115; s. c., 5 Bann. & Ard. Pat. Cas. 302; s. c., 1 Fed. Rep. 856.

While a defendant who has been defeated in an interference with the complainant, is not estopped from setting up lack of novelty to defeat the invention, yet if he had knowledge of the condition of the art at the time of his application, a want of novelty in the invention must be clearly apparent, or a preliminary injunction will be granted. Smith *v.* Halkyard, 16 Fed. Rep. 414; s. c., 23 Pat. Off. Gaz. 1833; Greenwood *v.* Bracher, 1 Fed. Rep. 856; s. c., 5 Bann. & Ard. Pat. Cas. 302; s. c., 17 Pat. Off. Gaz. 1151.

Compare, however, Thompson *v.* American Bank Note Co., 35 Fed. Rep. 203; Minneapolis Harvester Works *v.* McCormick Harvesting Mach. Co., 28 Fed. Rep. 565.

Where the defeated party to an interference had acquiesced in the judgment awarding priority to the opposite party, had disclaimed the matter in interference and taken out a more limited patent, these facts should have great weight in favor of granting a preliminary injunction where a defense of lack of novelty is set up. Reck etc. Co. *v.* Lindsay, 18 Pat. Off. Gaz. 63.

This doctrine does not hold where the decision in the interference has not been acquiesced in by the defeated party. Minneapolis Harvester Works *v.* McCormick Harvesting Mach Co., 28 Fed. Rep. 565.

Between Whom Binding.—The adjudication in an interference is only binding between the parties and privies. Barr Co. *v.* New York etc. Sprinkler Co., 32 Fed. Rep. 79.

The action of the Patent Office in granting a reissue, after an exhaustive discussion and examination of the art in which opposing interests were represented, will induce the court to grant a preliminary injunction. Consolidated Bunging Co. *v.* Schoenhofen Brewing Co., 28 Fed. Rep. 428.

1. Sargeant Mfg. Co. *v.* Woodruff, 5 Biss. (U. S.) 444.

2. Warner *v.* Bassett, 19 Blatchf. (U. S.) 145; s. c., 7 Fed. Rep. 468.

Contra, Ladd *v.* Cameron, 25 Fed. Rep. 37.

3. Kirby Bung Mfg. Co. *v.* White, 5 Bann. & Ard. Pat. Cas. 263; s. c., 1 McCrary (U. S.) 155; s. c., 17 Pat. Off. Gaz. 974; s. c., 1 Fed. Rep. 604.

Consequently a decree entered by agreement in favor of the complainant after a decision in the suit declaring the patent invalid, will have very little weight. Spring *v.* Domestic Sewing Mach. Co., 4 Bann. & Ard. Pat. Cas. 427; s. c., 16 Pat. Off. Gaz. 721.

4. Steam Gauge etc. Co. *v.* Miller, 11 Fed. Rep. 718. See Coburne *v.* Clark, 24 Pat. Off. Gaz. 899.

Ordinarily, the considerations which would induce a court to disregard a prior decision, must be such as would justify setting aside a verdict. Parker *v.* Brant, 1 Fish. Pat. Cas. 58; Thayer *v.* Wales, 5 Fish. Pat. Cas. 130; s. c., 9 Blatchf. (U. S.) 170; American etc. Pavement Co. *v.* Elizabeth, 4 Fish. Pat. Cas. 189; Tilghman *v.* Mitchell, 4 Fish. Pat. Cas. 615.

Where the evidence is different, the court will not be bound by a decision in another circuit. Edgarton *v.* Furst etc. Mfg. Co., 9 Fed. Rep. 450; s. c., 10 Biss. (U. S.) 402; s. c., 21 Pat. Off. Gaz. 261; U. S. Stamping Co. *v.* King, 17 Blatchf. (U. S.) 55; s. c., 4 Bann. & Ard. Pat. Cas. 469; s. c., 7 Fed. Rep. 860; s. c., 17 Pat. Off. Gaz. 1399; Bailey etc. Wringing Mach. Co. *v.* Adams, 3 Bann. & Ard. Pat. Cas. 96; Albany Steam Trap Co. *v.* Felthousen, 26 Fed. Rep. 313; Lockwood *v.* Faber, 27 Fed. Rep. 63. And small weight will be given where verdicts have been obtained on inconsistent and contradictory

(5) *Plaintiff's Laches.*—An unreasonable delay to prosecute an infringer after having acquired information of the infringement, will induce the court to refuse a preliminary injunction.[1]

(6) *Willingness of Defendant to Accept License.*—Where the defendant will agree to pay a reasonable license fee and accept a license, the court may be especially induced where plaintiff sells licenses to refuse a preliminary injunction.[2] This does not hold

claims. Parker *v.* Sears, 1 Fish. Pat. Cas. 93. Or different construction of the patent. Mowry *v.* Grand St. R. Co., 10 Blatchf. (U. S.) 89; s. c., 5 Fish. Pat. Cas. 587. Or where the results of previous trials were conflicting. Allen *v.* Sprague, 1 Blatchf. (U. S.) 567; Batten *v.* Silliman, 3 Wall. Jr. (C. C.) 124; Grover etc. Sewing Mach. Co. *v.* Williams, 2 Fish. Pat. Cas. 133; Eastern Paper Bag Co. *v.* Nixon, 35 Fed. Rep. 752.

New Defense or Evidence.—Or where a new point of defense is made, or new evidence produced. Lockwood *v.* Faber, 27 Fed. Rep. 33; Ladd *v.* Cameron, 25 Fed. Rep. 37; Bailey etc. Wringing Mach. Co. *v.* Adams, 3 Bann. & Ard. Pat. Cas. 96.

1. Parker *v.* Sears, 1 Fish. Pat. Cas. 93; Jones *v.* Merrill, 8 Pat. Off. Gaz. 401; Cooper *v.* Mathews, 5 Pa. L. J. 38; s. c., 8 L. R. 413; North *v.* Kershaw, 4 Blatchf. (U. S.) 70; Whitney *v.* Rolestone, Mach. Wks., 8 Pat. Off. Gaz. 908; s. c., 2 Bann. & Ard. Pat. Cas. 170; Goodyear *v.* Housinger, 3 Fish. Pat. Cas. 147; s. c., 2 Biss. (U. S.) 1; Morris *v.* Lowell Mfg. Co., 3 Fish. Pat. Cas. 67; Hockholzer *v.* Eager, 2 Sawy. (U. S.) 361; Sloat *v.* Plympton, 2 Whart. Dig. 365; Sperry *v.* Ribbans, 3 Bann. & Ard. Pat. Cas. 260; Ballow Shoe Mach. Co. *v.* Dizer, 5 Bann. & Ard. Pat. Cas. 540; Tillinghast *v.* Hicks, 13 Fed. Rep. 388; s. c., 23 Pat. Off. Gaz. 739; Ladd *v.* Cameron, 25 Fed. Rep. 37; Hurlburt *v.* Carter, 39 Fed. Rep. 802.

Especially where the plaintiff has acquiesced with the understanding that the compensation shall be fixed by agreement, and the defendant is willing to pay what the court will allow. Smith *v.* Sharp's Rifle Mfg. Co., 3 Blatchf. (U. S.) 545.

A delay of three months is not unreasonable. Union Paper Bag etc. Co. *v.* Binney, 5 Fish. Pat. Cas. 166.

He must, however, either know that that is an infringement or have means of knowing. Wortendyke *v.* White, 2 Bann. & Ard. Pat. Cas. 23.

Mere forbearance to sue without affirmative encouragement to continue the infringement, does not induce the court to refuse. Collignon *v.* Hayes, 8 Fed. Rep. 912; s. c., 20 Pat. Off. Gaz. 447.

Where the defendants had been accustomed to make and repair pieces of a machine for plaintiff and manufacture them for others, with plaintiff's knowledge, preliminary injunction refused. Amazeen Mach. Co. *v.* Knight, 39 Fed. Rep. 612.

Delay During Pendency of Other Suits.—Where a plaintiff has proceeded to bring suits against other infringers whereby the validity of the patent might be determined, a delay to bring suit against a particular defendant, after knowledge of an infringement by him, is not laches. Green *v.* French, 4 Bann. & Ard. Pat. Cas. 169; s. c., 16 Pat. Off. Gaz. 215; Van Hook *v.* Pendleton, 1 Blatchf. (U. S.) 187; McWilliams Mfg. Co. *v.* Blundell, 11 Fed. Rep. 419; s. c., 22 Pat. Off. Gaz. 177; Rumford Chemical Works *v.* Vice, 14 Blatchf. (U. S.) 179; s. c., 11 Pat. Off. Gaz. 600.

For length of time not laches, see Brick *v.* Staten Island R. Co., 25 Fed. Rep. 553.

An injunction may be withheld until the complainant explains his apparent laches. Sykes *v.* Manhattan Elevator etc. Co., 6 Blatchf. (U. S.) 496.

2. Hodge *v.* Hudson River R. Co., 6 Blatchf. (U. S.) 85; s. c., 3 Fish. Pat. Cas. 410; Colgate *v.* Gold & Stock Tel. Co., 16 Blatchf. (U. S.) 583; s. c., 4 Bann. & Ard. Pat. Cas. 415; s. c., 16 Pat. Off. Gaz. 583; Blake *v.* Greenwood Cemetery, 14 Blatchf. (U. S.) 342; s. c., 3 Bann. & Ard. Pat. Cas. 112; s. c., 13 Pat. Off. Gaz. 1046.

Especially in cases where there are other considerations this is a make weight. Howe *v.* Newton, 2 Fish. Pat. Cas. 531; Forbush *v.* Bradford, 1 Fish. Pat. Cas. 317; Potter *v.* Schenck, 1 Biss. (U. S.) 515; s. c., 3 Fish. Pat. Cas. 82; Morris *v.* Lowell Mfg. Co., 3 Fish. Pat. Cas. 67; Livingston *v.* Jones, 2 Fish. Pat. Cas. 207; s. c., 3 Wall. Jr. (C. C.) 330; Batten *v.* Silliman, 3 Wall. Jr. (C.

where the plaintiff is able and willing to supply the market demand.[1]

(7) *Ability of Defendant to Respond in Damages.*—The ability[2] or inability[3] of the defendant to pay the profits or damages that may be adjudged or decreed, is a consideration, though not a controlling one,[4] with the court.

(8) *Contractual Relation Between the Parties.*—A contractual relation existing between the parties by which the patent has been treated as valid, will induce the court to grant a preliminary injunction.[5]

(9) *Infringement Not Clear.*—Where the infringement of complainant's patent by defendant's device is not clear, the injunction will be refused.[6] What is sufficient evidence of infringement is

C.) 124; McMillan *v.* Conrad, 16 Fed. Rep. 128; Hoe *v.* Boston etc. Advertiser Corp., 14 Fed. Rep. 914; s. c., 23 Pat. Off. Gaz. 1124; National Hat Pouncing Mach. Co. *v.* Hedden, 29 Fed. Rep. 147.

1. Baldwin *v.* Shultz, 9 Blatchf. (U. S.) 494; s. c., 5 Fish. Pat. Cas. 75; s. c., 2 Pat. Off. Gaz. 315.

2. Morris *v.* Lowell Mfg. Co., 3 Fish. Pat. Cas. 67; Guidet *v.* Palmer, 6 Fish. Pat. Cas. 82; s. c., 10 Blatchf. (U. S.) 217; Pullman *v.* Baltimore etc. R. Co., 4 Hughes (U. S.) 236; s. c., 5 Fed. Rep. 72; s. c., 19 Pat. Off. Gaz. 224; Dorsey etc. Rake Co. *v.* Bradey Mfg. Co., 1 Bann. & Ard. Pat. Cas. 330; s. c., 12 Blatchf. (U. S.) 202; Tillinghast *v.* Hicks, 13 Fed. Rep. 388; s. c., 23 Pat. Off. Gaz. 139; National Hat Pouncing Mach. Co. *v.* Hedden, 29 Fed. Rep. 147; Celluloid Mfg. Co. *v.* Eastman Dry Plate etc. Co., 42 Fed. Rep. 159; Johnson *v.* Aldrich, 40 Fed. Rep. 675; Hurlbart *v.* Carter, 39 Fed. Rep. 802.

3. Brooks *v.* Bicknell, 3 McLean (U. S.) 250; s. c., 2 Robb Pat. Cas. 118; Goodyear *v.* Muller, 3 Fish. Pat. Cas. 420.

4. But in a clear case the defendant cannot insist on being allowed to continue his infringement, although able to pay the damages, even when the inconvenience caused by the grant of the injunction is very great. Sickels *v.* Mitchell, 3 Blatchf. (U. S.) 548.

The fact that defendant is manufacturing under a patent, will in some cases prevent the granting of a preliminary injunction. Celluloid Co. *v.* Eastman Dry Plate etc. Co., 42 Fed. Rep. 159.

But it must be set up in the answer. Zinn *v.* Weiss, 7 Fed. Rep. 914.

And that he is not using his alleged infringing article in the manner in which the plaintiff uses the patented article. Celluloid Mfg. Co. *v.* Eastman Dry Plate etc. Co., 42 Fed. Rep. 159.

Risk caused to the public by stopping the use of a device. Root *v.* R. Co., 40 Fed. Rep. 760.

5. Burr *v.* Kimbark, 28 Fed. Rep. 574; Steam Gauge etc. Co. *v.* Ham Mfg. Co., 28 Fed. Rep. 618; American Paper Barrel Co. *v.* Laraway, 28 Fed. Rep. 141; Hat Sweat Mfg. Co. *v.* Porter, 34 Fed. Rep. 745; Goddard *v.* Wilde, 17 Fed. Rep. 845; Goodyear *v.* Congress Rubber Co., 3 Blatchf. (U. S.) 449.

Limitation.—But not where complainant does not come in with clean hands. Crowell *v.* Parmenter, 3 Bann. & Ard. Pat. Cas. 480; s. c., 18 Pat. Off. Gaz. 360.

6. High on Inj. 606; Parker *v.* Sears, 1 Fish. Pat. Cas. 93; Dodge *v.* Caid, 2 Fish. Pat. Cas. 116; Jones *v.* Osgood, 3 Fish. Pat. Cas. 591; s. c., 6 Blatchf. (U. S.) 435; Grover etc. Sewing Mach. Co. *v.* Williams, 2 Bish. Pat. Cas. 133; American Pavement Co. *v.* Elizabeth, 4 Fish. Pat. Cas. 189; Marks *v.* Corr, 11 Fed. Rep. 900; s. c., 23 Pat. Off. Gaz. 94; Cross *v.* Livermore, 9 Fed. Rep. 607; s. c., 21 Pat. Off. Gaz. 139; Ballow Shoe Mach. Co. *v.* Dizer, 5 Bann. & Ard. Pat. Cas. 540; Pullman *v.* Baltimore etc. R. Co., 5 Fed. Rep. 72; s. c., 19 Pat. Off. Gaz. 224; s. c., 4 Hughes (U. S.) 236; Zinssler *v.* Cooledge, 17 Fed. Rep. 538; Fraim *v.* Sharon Valley etc. Iron Co., 27 Fed. Rep. 457; Hammerschlag Mfg. Co. *v.* Judd, 28 Fed. Rep. 621; American Fire Hose Mfg. Co. *v.* Calahan Co., 41 Fed. Rep. 50; Judson L. Thompson Mfg. Co. *v.* Hatheway, 41 Fed. Rep. 519; Russel *v.* Hyde, 39 Fed. Rep. 614; Morss *v.* Knapp, 39 Fed. Rep. 608; Thompson *v.* Rand Avery Supply Co., 30 Fed. Rep. 112;

stated in the note.[1]

(10) *Public Acquiescence.*—An exclusive possession of some duration[2] will influence the court to grant a preliminary injunction. This possession should be open and notorious,[3] and

Norton Door Check etc. Co. *v.* Hall, 37 Fed. Rep. 691; Carey *v.* Miller, 34 Fed. Rep. 392; Steam Gauge etc. Co. *v.* St. Louis etc. Supply Co., 25 Fed. Rep. 491.

A lack of clearness of infringement may arise from a dubious construction of the patent. Dickerson *v.* De la Verne Refrigerating Co., 35 Fed. Rep. 143.

1. Evidence of infringement held sufficient to induce the court to grant a preliminary injunction.

An admission of past infringement, even when coupled with the declaration that the defendants did not intend to continue the use of the infringing device. Celluloid Mfg. Co. *v.* Arlington Mfg. Co., 34 Fed. Rep. 324; Jenkins *v.* Greenwald, 2 Fish. Pat. Cas. 37; Goodyear *v.* Berry, 3 Fish. Pat. Cas. 439; s. c., 2 Bond (U. S.) 189; Potter *v.* Crowell, 3 Fish. Pat. Cas. 112; Rumford Chemical Works *v.* Vice, 14 Blatchf. (U. S.) 179; s. c., 11 Pat. Off. Gaz. 600; White *v.* Heath, 10 Fed. Rep. 291; s. c., 22 Pat. Off. Gaz. 500; American Bell Teleph. Co. *v.* Ghegan, 23 Pat. Off. Gaz. 537.

The fact that the patent under which the defendants are working, on its face shows that its working involves an infringement of the complainant's patent. Goodyear *v.* Evans, 6 Blatchf. (U. S.) 121; s. c., 3 Fish. Pat. Cas. 390.

Evidence of infringement held sufficient in following cases: Boston Electric Co. *v.* Holtzer etc. Electric Co., 41 Fed. Rep. 390; Stuart *v.* Thornton, 37 Fed. Rep. 90; Maltby *v.* Graham, 35 Fed. Rep. 206.

The question of infringement arises anew in each particular case independently of prior adjudication. Hammerschlag Mfg. Co. *v.* Judd, 28 Fed. Rep. 621.

2. Sullivan *v.* Redfield, 1 Paine (U. S.) 441; s. c., 1 Robb. Pat. Cas. 477; Hockholzer *v.* Eager, 2 Sawy. (U. S.) 361; Isaac *v.* Cooper, 4 Wash. (U. S.) 259; s. c., 1 Robb Pat. Cas. 332; Jappan *v.* National Bank Note Co., 2 Fish. Pat. Cas. 195; s. c., Blatchf. 4 (U. S.) 509; Goodyear *v.* Railroad, 1 Fish. Pat. Cas. 626; s. c., 2 Wall. Jr. (C. C.) 356; Washburn *v.* Gould, 3 Story (U. S.) 122; s. c., 2 Robb Pat. Cas. 206; Ogle *v.* Edge, 4 Wash. (U. S.) 584; s. c., 1 Robb Pat. Cas. 516; Sargent *v.* Carter, 1 Fish. Pat. Cas. 277; Woodworth *v.* Sherman, 3 Story (U. S.) 171; s. c., 2 Robb Pat. Cas. 257; Morse etc. Pen Co. *v.* Esterbrook etc. Pen Co., 3 Fish. Pat. Cas. 515; Hovey *v.* Stephens, 1 Woodb. & M. (U. S.) 290; s. c., 2 Robb Pat. Cas. 479; Cook *v.* Earnest, 5 Fish. Pat. Cas. 396; s. c., 2 Pat. Off. Gaz. 89; Brooks *v.* Bicknell, 3 McLean (U. S.) 250; s. c., 2 Robb Pat. Cas. 118; Gibson *v.* Betts, 1 Blatchf. (U. S.) 163; Woodworth *v.* Rogers, 3 Woodb. & M. (U. S.) 135; s. c., 2 Robb Pat. Cas. 625; Hussey *v.* Whitely, 2 Fish. Pat. Cas. 120; s. c., 1 Bond (U. S.) 407; Potter *v.* Muller, 2 Fish. Pat. Cas. 465; Miller *v.* Androscoggin Pulp Co., 5 Fish. Pat. Cas. 340 s. c., 1 Holmes (U. S.) 142; s. c., 1 Pat. Off. Gaz. 409; Parker *v.* Brandt 1 Fish. Pat. Cas. 58; Sargent *v.* Seagrave, 2 Curt. (U. S.) 553; White *v.* Heath, 10 Fed. Rep. 291; s. c., 22 Pat. Off. Gaz. 500; Bar Co. *v.* New York etc. Sprinkler Co., 32 Fed. Rep. 79; Tillinghast *v.* Hicks, 13 Fed. Rep. 388; s. c., 23 Pat. Off. Gaz. 739; White *v.* Surdam, 41 Fed. Rep. 790; Schneider *v.* Missouri Glass Co., 36 Fed. Rep. 582.

Where exclusive possession for a term of years alleged, the reason for the grant of the preliminary injunction is the presumption of the validity of the patent arising from the acquiescence of the public in that right, which would not exist unless the right was well founded. This public acquiescence has weight according to the degree of utility of the invention, and the number of persons whose trade or business is affected by it. Foster *v.* Moore, 1 Curt. (U. S.) 279; Sargent *v.* Seagrave, 2 Curt. (U. S.) 553.

Accordingly, the shortness of the time after the grant, where articles have been sold publicly and separately, and have been so sold and used without dispute, is immaterial. Orr *v.* Littlefield, 1 Woodb. & M. (U. S.) 13; s. c., 2 Robb Pat. Cas. 323.

3. Potter *v.* Whitney, 3 Fish. Pat. Cas. 77; s. c., 1 Low (U. S.) 87; Grover etc. Sewing Mach. Co. *v* Williams, 2 Fish. Pat. Cas. 133.

An exclusive use or sale of the inven-

attended with circumstances indicating that there would not have been this acquiescence if any fair doubt had existed as to the validity of the patent.[1] A lack of public acquiescence, where the device is certainly new and useful, will not prevent the grant of a preliminary injunction.[2]

(11) *Former Construction Followed.*—The construction given in the prior adjudication of the patent will be followed in deciding upon a contest over a preliminary injunction.[3]

(12) *Power of Court to Impose Conditions.*—A preliminary injunction may be refused upon condition that the defendant give a bond with proper security,[4] or will keep an account,[5] or the injunction may be granted on condition that the complainant file a bond to indemnify the defendant for his losses, if he fail at final hearing,[6]

tion prior to the application for a patent, if open and under a claim of right, may raise a presumption in favor of the patent. Tappan *v.* National Bank Note Co., 2 Fish. Pat. Cas. 195; s. c., 4 Blatchf. (U. S.) 509; Sargent *v.* Seagrave, 2 Curt. (U. S.) 553.

The use of an invention for several years along with other patented inventions in a patented lamp, is not an acquiescence of the public. Upton *v.* Wayland, 36 Fed. Rep. 691.

1. Guidet *v.* Palmer, 6 Fish. Pat. Cas. 82; s. c., 10 Blatchf. (U. S.) 217.

Estoppel.—An acquiescence in and assertion of the validity of the patent by officers of a company who were formerly in the employ of the plaintiff, will act as an inducement to a grant of a preliminary injunction against the company. Steam Gauge etc. Lantern Co. *v.* Ham. Mfg. Co., 28 Fed. Rep. 618.

Where the bill does not aver that the patentee has ever sold or used his improvement, the preliminary injunction will not be granted. Isaac *v.* Cooper, 4 Wash. (U. S.) 259; s. c., 1 Robb Pat. Cas. 332.

A large number of licenses had been taken, some voluntarily and some in settlement of litigation, and the invention had been thoroughly investigated in the Patent Office, and there had been a *quasi* adjudication. *Held*, sufficient public acquiescence to justify preliminary injunction in face of affidavits denying novelty. Hat Sweat Mfg. Co. *v.* Davis Mach. Co., 32 Fed. Rep. 974.

An unsuccessful attempt to interrupt a possession strengthens the presumption. It shows that persons who have found it to their interest to question the right have questioned it, but finally submitted. Such submission is the most persuasive kind of acquiescence. Sargent *v.* Seagrave, 2 Curt. (U. S.) 553; Cook *v.* Earnest, 5 Fish. Pat. Cas. 396; s. c., 2 Pat. Off. Gaz. 89.

A preliminary injunction will not be granted where the defendant has been in possession and use of the invention for a long period adverse to the title of complainant under color of right. Hall *v.* Spier, 6 Pittsb. L. J. 403; Isaac *v.* Cooper, 4 Wash. (U. S.) 259; s. c., 1 Robb Pat. Cas. 332. See *infra* this title, *Laches.*

Where the art is very complex, less weight will be given to prior acquiescence. Warner *v.* Bassett, 7 Fed. Rep. 468.

An acquiscence of less than a year is insufficient where the patent is of doubtful construction. Johnston Ruffler Co. *v.* Avery Mach. Co., 28 Fed. Rep. 193.

2. Hussey Mfg. Co. *v.* Deering, 20 Fed. Rep. 795.

3. Mallory Mfg. Co. *v.* Hicok, 20 Fed. Rep. 116; Hammerschlag Mfg. Co. *v.* Judd, 28 Fed. Rep. 621.

A patent will be presumed to be valid only to the extent it has been adjudicated so. Carey *v.* Miller, 34 Fed. Rep. 392.

4. Dorsey etc. Rake Co. *v.* Marsh, 6 Fish. Pat. Cas. 387; s. c., 9 Phila. (Pa.) 395; Morris *v.* Shelburne, 4 Fish. Pat. Cas. 377; s. c., 8 Blatchf. (U. S.) 266; Steam Gauge etc. Co. *v.* St. Louis etc. Supply Co., 25 Fed. Rep. 491.

5. Wilder *v.* Gaylor, 1 Blatchf. (U. S.) 511.

6. Brammer *v.* Jones, 2 Bond (U. S.) 100; s. c., 3 Fish. Pat. Cas. 340; Shelly *v.* Brannon, 4 Fish. Pat. Cas. 198; s. c.,

or other conditions.[1]

(*f*) Provision in Decree for Dissolving Injunction.—The decree for an injunction may provide for its dissolution on the defendant's giving bond and security for accounting.[2]

XII. Defenses to Action for Infringement.—1. Statutory.—(*a*) As to Specification.—It is provided by statute that the defendant may defend by setting up that, for the purpose of deceiving the public, the description and specification filed by the patentee in the Patent Office was made to contain less than the whole truth relative to his invention or discovery; or more than was necessary to produce the desired effect.[3]

2 Biss. (U. S.) 315; Allis *v.* Stowell, 15 Fed. Rep. 242; Tobey Furniture Co. *v.* Colby, 35 Fed. Rep. 592.

Especially where the injunction leads to serious injury in suspending works. Orr *v.* Littlefield, 1 Woodb. & M. (U. S.) 13; s. c., 2 Robb. Pat. Cas. 332; Morse *v.* O'Reilly, 6 W. L. J. 102.

The defendant, however, has no *right* to demand that a bond shall be substituted for the injunction. Sickels *v.* Mitchell, 3 Blatchf. (U. S.) 548; Tracy *v.* Torrey, 2 Blatchf. (U. S.) 275; Tilghman *v.* Mitchell, 4 Fish. Pat. Cas. 615; s. c., 9 Blatchf. (U. S.) 18; Gibson *v.* Van Dresar, 1 Blatchf. (U. S.) 532; Conover *v.* Mers, 3 Fish. Pat. Cas. 386; Ely *v.* Monson etc. Mfg. Co., 4 Fish. Pat. Cas. 64; Consolidated Fruit Jar Co. *v.* Whitney, 1 Bann. & Ard. Pat. Cas. 356; Hodge *v.* Hudson River R. Co., 6 Blatchf. (U. S.) 165.

A bond can only be required in a case in which, if it is not given, the injunction must issue. American Co. *v.* Atlantic Co., 4 Dill. (U. S.) 100; s. c., 3 Bann. & Ard. Pat. Cas. 168.

However, it is for the court to say whether the rights of the complainant are so clear that they ought to be protected by an injunction, or not so clear so that they can be sufficiently protected by bond and security. Ely *v.* Monson Mfg. Co., 4 Fish. Pat. Cas. 64; Kirby Bung Mfg. Co. *v.* White, 1 McCrary (U. S.) 155; s. c., 1 Fed. Rep. 604; s. c., 5 Bann. & Ard. Pat. Cas. 263; s. c., 17 Pat. Off. Gaz. 974.

1. Woodworth *v.* Rogers, 3 Woodb. & M. (U. S.) 135; s. c., 2 Robb Pat. Cas. 625; Orr *v.* Merrill, 1 Woodb. & M. (U. S.) 376; s. c., 2 Robb Pat. Cas. 331; Serrell *v.* Collins, 4 Blatchf. (U. S.) 61; Orr *v.* Littlefield, 1 Woodb. & M. (U. S.) 13; s. c., 2 Robb Pat. Cas. 331; Rogers *v.* Abbott, 4 Wash. (U. S.) 514; s. c., 1 Robb Pat. Cas. 405; Wise *v.* Grand Ave. R. Co., 33 Fed. Rep. 277.

2. Brooks *v.* Bicknell, 3 McLean (U. S.) 250; s. c., 2 Robb Pat. Cas. 118; Foster *v.* Moore, 1 Curt. (U. S.) 279; Gilbert etc. Mfg. Co. *v.* Bussing 12 Blatchf. (U. S.) 426; s. c., 8 Pat. Off. Gaz. 144; s. c., 1 Bann. & Ard. Pat. Cas. 621; Howe *v.* Morton, 1 Fish. Pat. Cas. 586; Jones *v.* Merrell, 8 Pat. Off. Gaz. 401; Annunciator Co. *v.* Hills, 3 Fish. Pat. Cas. 134; American etc. Pavement Co. *v.* Elizabeth, 4 Fish. Pat. Cas. 189; Goodyear *v.* Housinger, 3 Fish. Pat. Cas. 147; s. c., 2 Biss. (U. S.) 1; Sykes *v.* Manhattan Elevator etc. Co., 6 Blatchf. (U. S.) 496; American etc. Purifier Co. *v.* Christian, 4 Dill. (U. S.) 448; s. c., 3 Bann. & Ard. Pat. Cas. 42; Irwin *v.* McRobets, 4 Bann. & Ard. Pat. Cas. 411; s. c., 16 Pat. Off. Gaz. 853; Greenwood *v.* Bracher, 5 Bann. & Ard. Pat. Cas. 302; s. c., 1 Fed. Rep. 856; s. c., 17 Pat. Off. Gaz. 1151.

3. U. S. Rev. Stats. § 4920.

See *supra Specification*, *supra Clearness*, *supra Specification and Claim*.

The fraudulent attempt is essential to this defense. Lowell *v.* Lewis, 1 Mason (U. S.) 182; s. c., 1 Robb Pat. Cas. 131.

Containing Too Much.—The fact that the specification contains too much does not make it *prima facie* fraudulent. Hotchkiss *v.* Oliver, 5 Den. (U. S.) 314.

Matters Concealed.—The matters not disclosed must appear to have been concealed to deceive the public. Park *v.* Little, 3 Wash. (U. S.) 196; s. c., 1 Robb Pat. Cas. 17; Gray *v.* James, 1 Pet. (C. C.) 394; s. c., 1 Robb Pat. Cas. 120; Durden *v.* Corning, 2 Fish. Pat. Cas. 477; Whittemore *v.* Cutter, 1 Gall. (U. S.) 429; s. c., 1 Robb Pat.

(*b*) PRIOR PATENT OR DESCRIPTION.—That the invention had been patented,[1] or described in some printed publication[2] prior to his supposed invention or discovery thereof.[3]

(*c*) PUBLIC USE.—Public use or sale of the patented device two years prior to the date of the application for a patent.[4]

(*d*) SURREPTITIOUSLY OBTAINING A PATENT.—That he had surreptitiously or unjustly obtained the patent for what was, in fact, invented by another,[5] who was using reasonable diligence[6] in

Cas. 28; Grant *v.* Raymond, 6 Pet. (U. S.) 218.

Tetley *v.* Easton, 1 Macrory (Eng.) 48; Walton *v.* Bateman, 1 Web. Pat. Cas. (Eng.) 613; Neilson *v.* Harford, 1 Web. Pat. Cas. (Eng.) 295; Lewis *v.* Marling, 1 Web. Pat. Cas. (Eng.) 493; s. c., 1 Abb. Pat. Cas. 421; Bovill *v.* Moore, 1 Davies Pat. Cas. (Eng.) 361; s. c., 1 Abb. Pat. Cas. (Eng.) 231.

A fraudulent intention may be shown by circumstantial evidence. Gray *v.* James, 1 Pet. (C. C.) 394; s. c., 1 Robb Pat. Cas. 120; Dyson *v.* Danforth, 4 Fish. Pat. Cas. 133.

Material defects in the specification etc., *held* may be such evidence. Whittemore *v.* Cutter, 1 Gall. (U. S.) 429; s. c., 1 Robb Pat. Cas. 28; Gray *v.* James, 1 Pet. (C. C.) 394; s.c., 1 Robb Pat. Cas. 120; Rentgen *v.* Kanowrs, 1 Wash. (U. S.) 168; s. c., 1 Robb Pat. Cas. 1.

1. See *supra, Anticipation by Patent et seq.*

2. See *supra, Anticipation by Publication.*

The defenses in notes one and two cannot be made in a suit in equity by plea. Carnrick *v.* McKesson, 19 Blatchf. (U. S.) 369; Zinn *v.* Weiss, 7 Fed. Rep. 914.

3. U. S. Rev. Stats., § 4920.

This defense requires a description of the invention (as to what amounts to a description see *Publication*, *supra*) that it shall be contained in a work of public character, and that the work be made accessible to the public before the discovery of the patentee. Reeves *v.* Keystone Bridge Co., 5 Fish. Pat. Cas. 456; s. c., 1 Pat. Off. Gaz. 466.

The construction of the description is a matter of law; the identity or diversity of the thing described is a question of fact. Tyler *v.* Boston, 7 Wall. (U. S.) 327; Bischoff *v.* Wethered, 9 Wall. (U. S.) 812; Stevens *v.* Pierpont, 42 Conn. 360; Waterbury Brass Co. *v.* New York etc. Brass Co., 6 Fish. Pat. Cas. 43; Jackson *v.* Allen, 120 Mass. 64; Tucker *v.* Spaulding, 5 Fish. Pat. Cas. 297; s. c., 1 Deady (U. S.) 649; s. c., 1 Pat. Off. Gaz. 144; Kidd *v.* Spence, 4 Fish. Pat. Cas. 37; Tillotson *v.* Ramsay, 51 Vt. 309; Teese *v.* Phelps, 1 McAll. (U. S.) 17; Sickles *v.* Borden, 3 Blatchf. (U. S.) 535; Turrill *v.* Michigan etc. R. Co., 1 Wall. (U. S.) 491; Serrell *v.* Collins, 1 Fish. Pat. Cas. 289.

What is identity is a question of law. Latta *v.* Shawk, 1 Bond (U. S.) 259; s. c., 1 Fish. Pat. Cas. 465.

This is a different defense from prior use. Meyers *v.* Bushby, 32 Fed. Rep. 670.

This defense cannot be made by plea in equity. Walker on Patents, (2nd ed.), § 600.

May be given under general issue with notice or special plea at law. Walker on Patents (2nd ed.), § 447.

It is a different defense from that of public use or sale within the United States for two years prior to the application for the patent. Meyers *v.* Bushby, 32 Fed. Rep. 670.

A prior publication renders an English patent void. Also Chemical Electric etc. Light Co. *v.* Howard, 148 Mass. 352.

4. See *supra* this title, *Public Use.*

This defense applies only to a use within the United States. Hurlburt *v.* Schillinger, 130 U. S. 456.

For a clause held sufficient compliance with the statute with reference to this defense. See Anderson *v.* Miller, 129 U. S. 70.

With reference to this defense where several divisional applications arise out of a single original, the date of the applications is to be considered as the date of all the applications. Frankfort Whiskey Process Co. *v.* Mill Creek Distilling Co., 37 Fed. Rep. 533.

5. See *supra*, *Date of Invention.*

A foreign inventor cannot claim his invention as of a date prior to his foreign patent or of a printed publication. Electrical Accumulator Co. *v.* Julien Electric Co., 38 Fed. Rep. 117.

6. See *supra*, *Diligence.*

adapting and perfecting the same.[1]

(*e*) ABANDONMENT.—That the invention has been abandoned.[2]

(*f*) LACK OF UTILITY.—That the invention is not useful.[3]

2. Notice of Special Defenses.—Where the defendant intends to employ any of these defenses, he must give notice[4] to the plaintiff[5] in writing[6] thirty days before trial.[7] At law this may be

1. U. S. Rev. Stats., § 4920. This defense is distinct from prior public use, and a notice of a witness for this defense will not permit him to testify in for the other or *vice versa*. Meyers *v.* Busby, 32 Fed. Rep. 670.

This defense is not complete unless all the above mentioned elements are present. Agawam Co. *v.* Jordan, 7 Wall. (U. S.) 583; Reed *v.* Cutter (U. S.) 590; s. c., 2 Robb Pat. Cas. 81; Singer *v.* Walmesley, 1 Fis. Pat. Cas. 558; Dixon *v.* Moyer, 4 Wash. (U. S.) 68; s. c., 1 Robb Pat. Cas. 324.

A case stated where the elements are present to make a good defense. Phelps *v.* Brown, 1 Fish. Pat. Cas. 479; s. c., 4 Blatchf. (U. S.) 362.

2. See DEDICATION OR ABANDONMENT OF AN INVENTION, vol. 5, p. 420.

This defense is distinct from that of "two years' public use prior to application for a patent." Jones *v.* Sewall, 3 Cliff. (U. S.) 563; s. c., 6 Fish. Pat. Cas. 343; s. c., 3 Pat. Off. Gaz. 630.

Abandonment can be either actual or constructive, and may be interposed at law by general issue with or without special notice. Walker on Patents, (2nd ed.), § 449, in equity by answer. Walker on Patents, (2nd. ed.), § 602; Root *v.* Ball, 4 McLean (U. S.) 177.

Abandonment is a question of fact. Kendall *v.* Windsor, 21 How. (U. S.) 322; American Hide etc. Co. *v.* American Tool etc. Co.; 1 Holmes, (U. S.) 503; s. c., 4 Fish. Pat. Cas. 284.

A plea of abandonment is not sustained by showing that the proceedings of the Patent Office were such as would render void the claim said to be infringed. Hutchinson *v.* Everett, 33 Fed. Rep. 502.

3. See UTILITY.

Whether an invention is useful is a question of fact. Wintermute *v.* Redington, 1 Fish. Pat. Cas. 239; Langdon *v.* De Groot, 1 Paine (U. S.) 203; s. c., 1 Robb Pat. Cas. 433.

Can be made at law under general issue with notice or by special plea. Walker on Patents (2nd ed.), § 448. And must be set up in answer in equity. Walker on Patents (2nd ed.), § 601; McKesson *v.* Carnrick, 19 Blatchf. (U. S.) 158.

4. Most of these defenses could, without the statute, be given in evidence under the general issue. Wilder *v.* Gaylor, 1 Blatchf. (U. S.) 599; Stephenson *v.* Magowan, 31 Fed. Rep. 824; s. c., 42 Pat. Off. Gaz, 1063; Odiorne *v.* Denney, 3 Bann. & Ard. Pat. Cas. 287; s. c., 13 Pat. Off. Gaz. 965; Roemer *v.* Simon, 95 U. S. 214; s. c., 12 Pat. Off. Gaz. 796; Pickering *v.* Phillips, 4 Cliff. (U. S.) 383; s. c., 2 Bann. & Ard. Pat. 417; s. c., 10 Pat. Off. Gaz. 420; Bates *v.* Coe, 98 U. S. 31; s. c., 15 Pat. Off. Gaz. 337; Seymour *v.* Osborne, 11 Wall. (U. S.) 516; Root *v.* Ball, 4 McLean (U. S.) 177. But the statute makes the notice obligatory. Kneass *v.* Schuylkill Bank, 4 Wash. (U. S.) 9; s. c., 1 Robb Pat. Cas. 303; Kelleher *v.* Darling, 4 Cliff. (U. S.) 424; s. c., 3 Bann. & Ard. Pat. Cas. 328; s. c., 14 Pat. Off. Gaz. 673; O'Reilly *v.* Morse, 15 How. (U. S.) 62; Parker *v.* Haworth, 4 McLean (U. S.) 370; Root *v.* Ball, 4 McLean (U. S.) 177.

The object being that the plaintiff should not be surprised. Philadelphia etc. R. Co. *v.* Stimpson, 14 Pet. (U. S.) 448; s. c., 2 Robb Pat. Cas. 46; Silsby *v.* Foote, 14 How. (U. S.) 218.

Exception.—Where public use is the only defense, and that public use is by plaintiff himself, notice need not be given. American Hide etc. Co. *v.* American Tool etc. Co., 1 Holmes (U. S.) 503.

5. Or his attorney. U. S. Rev. Stat., § 4920; Teese *v.* Huntington, 23 How. (U. S.) 2.

6. U. S. Rev. Stat., § 4920; New York Pharmical Co. *v.* Tilden, 21 Blatchf. (U. S.) 191; s. c., 14 Fed. Rep. 740; s. c., 23 Pat. Off. Gaz. 272; Teese *v.* Huntington, 23 How. (U. S.) 2; Hudson *v.* Bradford, 1 Bann. & Ard. Pat. Cas. 539; s. c., 16 Pat. Off. Gaz. 171.

7. U. S. Rev. Stat., § 4920; Teese *v.* Huntington, 23 How. (U. S.) 2; Westlake *v.* Cartter, 6 Fish. Pat. Cas.

done either by a special notice[1] under the general issue or, where permitted, by the practice by special pleading.[2] In equity, notice must be given in the answer.[3]

(*a*) WHERE PRIOR INVENTION OR KNOWLEDGE OR PUBLIC USE IS ALLEGED.—In notices as to proof of prior invention, knowledge or use of the thing patented, the defendant shall state the names of the patentees,[4] the date of their patents and when

518; s. c., 4 Pat. Off. Gaz. 636. A defective notice may be supplemented by a second, if in time and form. Teese *v.* Huntington, 23 How. (U. S.) 2.

1. Teese *v.* Huntington, 23 How. (U. S.) 2.

2. Evans *v.* Eaton, 3 Wheat. (U. S.) 454; s. c., 1 Robb Pat. Cas. 68; Grant *v.* Raymond, 6 Pet. (U. S.) 218; s. c., 1 Robb Pat. Cas. 604; Read *v.* Miller, 2 Biss. (U. S.) 12; s. c., 3 Fish. Pat. Cas. 310; Phillips *v.* Comstock, 4 McLean (U. S.) 525; s. c., 2 Robb Pat. Cas. 724; Day *v.* New England Car Spring Co., 3 Blatchf. (U. S.) 179; Wilder *v.* Gayler, 1 Blatchf. (U. S.) 597; Cottier *v.* Stimson, 20 Fed. Rep. 906.

It was held that the statutory notice could not be given in an answer under the Oregon Code. Cottier *v.* Stimson, 20 Fed. Rep. 906.

The plea must be filed thirty days before trial. Phillips *v.* Comstock, 4 McLean (U. S.) 528.

And the plea and notice must not raise same defense. Latta *v.* Shawk, 1 Bond (U. S.) 259; s. c., 1 Fish. Pat. Cas. 465; Read *v.* Miller, 2 Biss. (U. S.) 12.

A special plea and the general issue with notice may be joined. Cottier *v.* Stimpson, 9 Sawy. (U. S.) 435.

3. Pickering *v.* Phillips, 2 Bann. & Ard. Pat. Cas. 417; s. c., 4 Cliff. (U. S.) 383; Agawam Co. *v.* Jordan, 7 Wall. (U. S.) 583; Cook *v.* Howard, 4 Fish. Pat. Cas. 269; Seymour *v.* Osborne, 3 Fish. Pat. Cas. 555; Collender *v.* Griffith, 11 Blatchf. (U. S.) 212; Decker *v.* Grote, 10 Blatchf. (U. S.) 331; s. c., 6 Fish. Pat. Cas. 143; s. c., 3 Pat. Off. Gaz. 65; O'Reilly *v.* Morse, 15 How. (U. S.) 62; Geier *v.* Goetinger, 1 Bann. & Ard. Pat. Cas. 553; s. c., 7 Pat. Off. Gaz. 563; Pitts *v.* Edmonds, 2 Fish. Pat. Cas. 52; s. c., 1 Biss. (U. S.) 168; Jordan *v.* Dobson, 4 Fish. Pat. Cas. 232; Forbes *v.* Barstow Stove Co., 12 Cliff. (U. S.) 379; Orr *v.* Merrill, 1 Woodb. & M. (U. S.) 376; s. c., 2 Robb Pat. Cas. 331; Eureka Co. *v.* Bailey Co., 11 Wall. (U. S.) 488; Union Paper Bag Co. *v.* Pueltz etc. Co., 15 Blatchf. (U. S.) 160; s. c., 3 Bann. & Ard. Pat. Cas. 403; s. c., 15 Pat. Off. Gaz. 423; Kelleher *v.* Darling, 4 Cliff. (U. S.) 424; s. c., 3 Bann. & Ard. Pat. Cas. 438; s. c., 14 Pat. Off. Gaz. 673; Bates *v.* Coe, 98 U. S. 31; s. c., 15 Pat. Off. Gaz. 337; Parks *v.* Booth, 102 U. S. 96; s. c., 17 Pat. Off. Gaz. 1089; Graham *v.* Barber, 5 Pat. Off. Gaz. 149; Middleton Tool Co. *v.* Judd, 3 Fish. Pat. Cas. 141; Wyeth *v.* Stone, 1 Story (U. S.) 273; s. c., 2 Robb Pat. Cas. 23; Williams *v.* Boston etc. R. Co., 17 Blatchf. (U. S.) 21; s. c., 4 Bann. & Ard. Pat. Cas. 441; s. c., 16 Pat. Off. Gaz. 906; Marks *v.* Fox, 18 Blatchf. (U. S.) 502; s. c., 6 Fed. Rep. 727; Wonson *v.* Peterson, 13 Bann. & Ard. Pat. Cas. 548; Odiorne *v.* Denney, 3 Bann. & Ard. Pat. Cas. 287; Earle *v.* Dexter, 1 Holmes (U. S.) 412; Pitts *v.* Edmonds, 1 Biss. (U. S.) 168.

The special defense must be set up specifically and exactly. Agawam Co. *v.* Jordan, 7 Wall. (U. S.) 583; Bates *v.* Coe, 98 U. S. 31; s. c., 15 Pat. Off. Gaz. 337.

The answer must be amended to include the name, etc., of a witness introduced to show prior use, if objection to the introduction of the witness is made before the examiner. Kiesele *v.* Haas, 32 Fed. Rep. 794.

Evidence introduced collaterally to establish facts relative to matters already in evidence need not be set up in the answer. Atlantic Works *v.* Brady, 107 U. S. 192; s. c., 23 Pat. Off. Gaz. 1330.

The answer must state the same things as are required to be set up by the notice of special matter. Agawam Co. *v.* Jordan, 7 Wall. (U. S.) 583; Bates *v.* Coe, 98 U. S. 34; Woodbury etc. Planing Mach. Co. *v.* Keith, 101 U. S. 493.

4. It is sufficient to specify the patents and allege that the invention is contained in them. Webster Loom Co. *v.* Higgins, 105 U. S. 1580; s. c., 21 Pat. Off. Gaz. 2031.

Publication.—A publication pleaded as anticipation must have designated the page or heading. Foote *v.* Silsby,

granted,[1] and the names and residences[2] of the persons alleged to have invented or to have had knowledge of the thing patented,[3] and where it was used.[4]

Where Objection Is to be Taken.—Objection to evidence for lack of notice must be taken at trial or before the examiner,[5] or else notice will be regarded waived.

3. Not Statutory—(*a*) STATUTE NOT ALL EMBRACING.—Naming certain defenses does not prevent the patentee from making others.[6] The defenses ordinarily enumerated are the following:[7]

1 Blatchf. (U. S.) 445; s. c., 1 Fish. Pat. Cas. 268.

1. The provision that the patent shall not be antedated would seem to, and as practice has done away with two dates of grant and date.

2. Orr *v.* Merrill, 1 Woodb. & M. (U. S.) 376; Lyon *v.* Donaldson, 34 Fed. Rep. 789.

3. The names of the persons who invented or have had knowledge, not of the witnesses who were expected to prove the prior invention or knowledge. Woodbury Planing Machine Co. *v.* Keith, 101 U. S. 479; s. c., 17 Pat. Off. Gaz. 1031; Wilton *v.* Railroads, 1 Wall. Jr. (C. C.) 196; Many *v.* Jagger, 1 Blatchf. (U. S.) 376; Roemer *v.* Simon, 95 U. S. 218; s. c., 12 Pat. Off. Gaz. 796; Allis *v.* Buckstaff, 22 Pat. Off. Gaz. 1705; Sutro *v.* Moll, 19 Blatchf. (U. S.) 89; s. c., 8 Fed. Rep. 909.

See Judson *v.* Cope, 1 Bond (U. S.) 327; s. c., 1 Fish. Pat. Cas. 615.

4. A notice that a certain machine was used in New York City, N. Y., held sufficient, where the names of witnesses and their residence were given, the court saying, "We do not think that the party giving notice is bound to be so specific as to relieve the other from all inquiry, or effort to investigate the facts. If he fairly puts his adversary in the way that he may ascertain all that is necessary to his defense or answer, it is all that is required." Wise *v.* Allis, 9 Wall. (U. S.) 737; Wilton *v.* Railroads, 1 Wall. Jr. (C. C.) 192.

But a notice which merely states the county where a thing was used, is not sufficiently explicit. Hays *v.* Sulsor, 1 Bond (U. S.) 279; s. c., 1 Fish. Pat. Cas. 532.

And the actual place must be designated or it cannot be proved. Dixon *v.* Moyer, 4 Wash. (U. S.) 68; s. c., 1 Robb Pat. Cas. 324; Searles *v.* Bouton, 20 Blatchf. (U. S.) 426; s. c., 12 Fed. Rep. 140; s. c., 21 Pat. Off. Gaz. 1784.

A failure to state where the article relied on as an anticipation was used, is fatal to the introduction of the testimony. Silsby *v.* Foote, 14 How. (U. S.) 218; Roemer *v.* Simon, 95 U. S. 214; Searles *v.* Bouton, 12 Fed. Rep. 140; s. c., 21 Pat. Off. Gaz. 1784.

The time of the use need not be stated, nor is the defendant bound by such statement when made. Phillips *v.* Page, 24 How. (U. S.) 164; Evans *v.* Kremer, 1 Pet. (C. C.) 215; s. c., 1 Robb Pat. Cas. 66.

It is not proper pleading to aver that *part* of the invented device was in use. Williams *v.* Empire Transp. Co., 3 Bann. & Ard. Pat. Cas. 533.

5. Blanchard *v.* Putnam, 8 Wall. (U. S.) 420; Roemer *v.* Simon, 95 U. S. 214; s. c., 12 Pat. Off. Gaz. 796; Graham *v.* Mason, 5 Fish. Pat. Cas. 6; Brown *v.* Hall, 3 Fish. Pat. Cas. 531; s. c., 6 Blatchf. (U. S.) 401; Phillips *v.* Page, 24 How. (U. S.) 168; Webster Loom Co. *v.* Higgins, 105 U. S. 580; s. c., 21 Pat. Off. Gaz. 2031; Woodbury etc. Planing Mach. Co. *v.* Keith, 101 U. S. 479; s. c., 17 Pat. Off. Gaz. 1031; Kiesele *v.* Haas, 32 Fed. Rep. 794; Barker *v.* Shoots, 20 Blatchf. (U. S.) 178; s. c., 18 Fed. Rep. 647; American Whip Co. *v.* Lombard, 4 Cliff. (U. S.) 495; Gibbs *v.* Ellethorp, 1 McArthur Pat. Cas. 702; Evans *v.* Hettick, 7 Wheat. (U. S.) 453. Court below. 3 Wash. (U. S.) 408.

6. Whittemore *v.* Cutter, 1 Gall. (U. S) 429; s. c., 1 Robb Pat. Cas. 28; Kneass *v.* Schuylkill Bank, 4 Wash. (U. S.) 9; s. c., 1 Robb Pat. Cas. 303; Grant *v.* Raymond, 6 Pet. (U. S.) 218; s. c., 1 Robb Pat. Cas. 604; Gardner *v.* Hertz, 118 U. S. 190; s. c., 35 Pat. Off. Gaz. 999.

7. Walker on Patents (2nd ed.), § 440.

The defenses are very analytically considered. They are here grouped more compactly.

See *Issue of Patents* and other sections on Patent Office, *supra*. Marsh *v.* Nichols, 128 U. S. 605.

(*b*) DEFENSES IN RELATION TO THE GRANT OF THE PATENT, OR THE APPLICATION.—That the patent was in some manner defective in the grant,[1] or the specification or other parts of the application.[2] These defenses can be taken by demurrer sometimes where profert is made,[3] or by plea[4] or answer.[5]

(*c*) LICENSE OR RELEASE; ESTOPPEL.—A license in force to use, make or sell the patented invention,[6] or a release by the

1. See *Specification, Clearness, Specifications, supra.* Kneass *v.* Schuylkill Bank, 4 Wash. (U. S.) 106.

How Set Up.—This defense must in a suit in equity be set up in the answer. Jennings *v.* Pierce, 15 Blatchf. (U. S.) 42; s. c., 3 Bann. & Ard. Pat. Cas. 361; Goodyear *v.* Providence Rubber Co., 2 Cliff. (U. S.) 351; s. c., 2 Fish. Pat. Cas. 499. *Compare* Kneass *v.* Schuylkill Bank, 4 Wash. (U. S.) 106.

The defectiveness of the specification so far as it concerns the ability to make from it is a question of fact. Brooks *v.* Jenkins, 3 McLean (U. S.) 432; Hawkes *v.* Remington, 111 Mass. 171; Wood *v.* Underhill, 5 How. (U. S.) 1; s. c., 2 Robb Pat. Cas. 588; Howes *v.* Nute, 4 Cliff. (U. S.) 173; s. c., 4 Fish. Pat. Cas. 263.

Whether the invention itself is described with reasonable certainty, is a question of law. Lowell *v.* Lewis, 1 Mason (U. S.) 187; s. c., 1 Robb Pat. Cas. 131; Wilton *v.* R. Co., 2 Whart. Dig. 359; Wayne *v.* Holmes, 1 Bond (U. S.) 27; s. c., 2 Fish. Pat. Cas. 20; Hogg *v.* Emerson, 6 How. (U. S.) 437.

2. See *Specification; Clearness*, etc., *ante;* Robinson on Patents, § 970; O'Reilly *v.* Morse, 15 How. (U. S.) 62; Carlton *v.* Bokee, 17 Wall. (U. S.) 472.

3. Where the claims are not distinct, if there is a profert of the patent, the defense can be made a demurrer. Walker on Patents, § 608.

4. Where the specification is at fault by special plea at law. Walker on Pat. (2nd ed.), § 454. It cannot be made by plea in equity. Walker on Patents (2nd ed.), § 605; Goodyear *v.* Providence Rubber Co., 2 Cliff. (U. S.) 351.

5. Walker on Pat. (2nd ed.), §§ 607, 608; Blandy *v.* Griffith, 3 Fish. Pat. Cas. 609.

6. See LICENSE, vol. 13, p. 514.

This defense should be pleaded specially at law. Mini *v.* Adams, 3 Wall. Jr. (C. C.) 20.

Where a license to run a machine contained a restriction against selling material operated upon by such machine to be carried out of a specified territory and resold as an article of merchandise, the restriction being both an invention by the licensee and a condition of the grant—*held*, that under no circumstances could such material, with the privity or consent of the licensee, be sold out of the territory as an article of merchandise, or, with his privity or consent, be sold within the territory to be carried out and resold as such article of merchandise. Further, that a provisional injunction would be granted against such licensee to restrain his use of the machine, if applied for during his violation of such restriction; but such injunction was refused where it appeared that the licensee had violated the restriction under a misapprehension of his rights, and had discontinued the violation. Wilson *v.* Sherman, 1 Blatchf. (U. S.) 536. See also Burr *v.* Duryee, 2 Fish. Pat. Cas. 275.

Or the injunction may be granted unless the licensee will conform to the conditions of the license. Brooks *v.* Stolley, 3 McLean (U. S.) 523; s. c., 2 Robb Pat. Cas. 281.

Where the license has been forfeited, the further working by the former licensee will be enjoined as an infringement. Woodworth *v.* Cook, 2 Blatchf. (U. S.) 151; Day *v.* Hartshorn, 3 Fish. Pat. Cas. 32; Cohn *v.* National Rubber Co., 5 Bann. & Ard. Pat. Cas. 568; s. c., 15 Pat. Off. Gaz. 829; Goodyear *v.* Congress Rubber Co., 3 Blatchf. (U. S.) 449; Armstrong *v.* Hanlenback, 3 N. Y. Leg. Obs. 43.

A suit in equity, however, cannot be maintained to forfeit the license for condition broken. Morse *v.* O'Reilly, 6 Pa. L. J. 501; Brooks *v.* Stolley, 3 McLean (U. S.) 523; s. c., 2 Robb Pat. Cas. 281.

A license may be proved by oral testimony where there has been no written agreement. Black *v.* Hubbard, 3 Bann. & Ard. Pat. Cas. 39; s. c., 12 Pat. Off. Gaz. 842.

At law this defense should be raised

patentee or plaintiff,[1] or an estoppel[2] to bring suit, can be set up as a defense.

(*d*) EXPIRATION OR REPEAL OF PATENTS.—The expiration or repeal of the patent prior to the infringement is a good defense in law[3] and before the bringing of suit to a suit in equity.[4]

(1) *Prior Foreign Patents to Inventor.*—Unless the invention has been in public use in the United States for more than two years prior to the application for a patent,[5] a prior[6] foreign pat-

by special plea, but may probably be raised by general issue. In equity by plea or answer. Walker on Patents, (2nd ed.), §§ 465, 618.

1. Bendell *v.* Denig, 92 U. S. 721, Bailey *v.* Bussing, 28 Conn. 461.

This defense should at law be pleaded specially, but may be proved under general issue. In equity by plea. Walker on Patents (2nd ed.), §§ 465, 619; Daniels' Chancery Practice, § 669.

2. Parkhurst *v.* Kinsman, 1 Blatchf. (U. S.) 488; Concord *v.* Norton, 16 Fed. Rep. 477; Dickerson *v.* Colgrove, 100 U. S. 578; Morgan *v* Chicago etc. R. Co., 96 U. S. 716; Barnard *v.* Campbell, 55 N. Y. 456; Rice *v.* Barrett, 116 Mass. 312, Bronson *v.* Campbell, 12 Wall. (U. S.) 681.

But mere laches is not an estoppel in a suit at law. Concord *v.* Norton, 16 Fed. Rep. 477. Nor is taking out several patents an estoppel to show that the invention was joint. Barrett *v.* Hall, 1 Mason (U. S.) 477; s. c., 1 Robb Pat. Cas. 207. See similarly Allen *v.* Blunt, 2 Woodb. & M. (U. S.) 121; s. c., 2 Robb Pat. Cas. 530.

Great laches of complainant is an estoppel to a suit in equity. Piatt *v.* Vattier, 9 Pet. (U. S.) 405; Wyeth *v.* Stone, 1 Story (U. S.) 273; Wallensak *v.* Reiher, 115 U. S. 101; Kittle *v.* Hall, 29 Fed. Rep. 508.

A delay of two years has been held sufficient to estop complainant in an action in equity. Sperry *v.* Ribbans, 3 Bann. & Ard. Pat. Cas. 260.

But a delay to enforce a right after the defendant has been notified, and *continues* notwithstanding *to infringe* will not estop a party. Concord *v.* Norton, 16 Fed. Rep. 477.

Striking out a portion of an application at the request of the Patent Office on the allegation that it was a duplication of the part allowed, does not estop the inventor from setting up the claim to a construction covered by the part stricken out. Ewart Mfg. Co. *v.* Bridgeport etc. Iron Co., 31 Fed. Rep. 149.

Generally it is an estoppel only where there is a duty on party alleged to be estopped which is violated. Pickard *v.* Sears, 6 Ad. & El. (Eng.) 469; Young *v.* Grote, 4 Bing. (Eng.) 253; Bank of U. S. *v.* Lee, 13 Pet. (U. S.) 107; Reay *v.* Raynor, 19 Fed. Rep. 308; s. c., 22 Blatchf. (U. S.) 13; s. c., 26 Pat. Off. Gaz. 1111; New York Grape Sugar Co. *v.* Buffalo Grape Sugar Co., 21 Blatchf. (U. S.) 519; s. c., 18 Fed. Rep. 638; s. c., 25 Pat. Off. Gaz. 1076; Bassett *v.* Bradley, 148 Conn. 224; Drexel *v.* Berney, 16 Fed. Rep. 522; s. c., 21 Blatchf. (U. S.) 348; Concord *v.* Norton, 16 Fed. Rep. 477.

This defense is raised by special plea at law, or plea in equity. Walker on Patents (2nd ed.), §§ 470, 661.

In this country equitable estoppel is a defense at law. Concord *v.* Norton, 16 Fed. Rep. 477.

An admission is not an estoppel if not acted upon. Gear *v.* Grosvenor, 1 Holmes (U. S.) 215; s. c., 6 Fish. Pat. Cas. 314; s. c., 3 Pat. Off. Gaz. 380; Commercial Mfg. Co. *v.* Fairbank Canning Co., 27 Pat. Off. Gaz. 78; s. c., 36 Pat. Off. Gaz. 1473.

3. See *Duration of Right*, *supra*. There is no precedent to show what the pleading should be where the patent has been repeated. See Walker on Patents, § 461. Where it has expired, the plea at law is a special one. Walker on Patents (2nd ed.) 462.

In equity the defense of repeal can be made by plea or answer. The defense that the patent has expired by demurrer, if sufficient, appears on the record by answer otherwise. Walker on Patents §§ 614, 615.

4. See *Jurisdiction of Equity*, *supra*.

5. U. S. Rev. Stats., § 4887. American Hide etc. Co. *v.* American Tool Co., 1 Holmes (U. S.) 503; s. c., 4 Fish. Pat. Cas. 284; Henry *v.* Providence Tool Co., 3 Bann. & Ard. Pat. Cas. 501; s. c., 14 Pat. Off. Gaz. 855; Vogeley *v.* Noel, 18 Fed. Rep. 827.

6. French *v.* Rogers, 1 Fish. Pat.

ent granted to the inventor[1] does not debar him from obtaining a patent or make the patent granted invalid.[2]

(2) *Limitation of Term Because of Prior Foreign Patent.*—A patent granted on an invention previously patented to the applicant in a foreign country is limited to expire with the foreign patent; and, where there are more than one, with the patent having the shortest term.[3] In computing the term of the foreign patents, the original term and such extensions as are granted, of course, are to be included,[4] and the term of the American patent is

Cas. 133; *In re* Cushman, 1 McArthur Pat. Cas. 577.

The priority is that of the grant, not of the application. Bate Refrigerating Co. *v.* Gillett, 13 Fed. Rep. 553; Gramme Electrical Co. *v.* Arnoux etc. Electric Co., 25 Pat. Off. Gaz. 193; s. c., 21 Blatchf. (U. S.) 450; Globe Mail Co. *v.* Superior Mail Co., 27 Fed. Rep. 450.

Under the old statutes of March 3, 1839, and July 4, 1836, it was different. French *v.* Rogers, 1 Fish. Pat. Cas. 133.

A patent which was granted after the date of the sealing of the provisional specification, but before the sealing of the complete specification, does not come within the rule. Emerson *v.* Lippert, 31 Fed. Rep. 911. See Brooks *v.* Norcross, 2 Fish. Pat. Cas. 61; Howe *v.* Morton, 13 L. Rep. (U. S.) 70; American etc. Boring Co. *v.* Sheldon, 17 Blatchf. (U. S.) 303; s. c., 4 Bann. & Ard. Pat. Cas. 603; Schoerken *v.* Swift etc. Co., 19 Blatchf. (U. S.) 209. Which declare that a secret patent does not limit a subsequent United States patent granted before the foreign patent was published. *Compare* Gramme Electrical Co. *v.* Arnoux etc. Electric Co., 21 Blatchf. (U. S.) 450; s. c., 25 Pat. Off. Gaz. 193.

Sealing.—The date of the sealing of the foreign patent, being subsequent, though the application for and date of the foreign patent was prior, *held*, that the American patent was not limited. Gold & Stock Tel. Co. *v.* Commercial Tel. Co., 23 Blatchf. (U. S.) 199.

The sealing of a British patent is the equivalent of publication. Guarantee Co. *v.* Sellers, 41 Pat. Off. Gaz. 1165.

1. A foreign inventor is within the statute, even if his foreign patent is invalid. Cornely *v.* Marckwald, 17 Fed. Rep. 83; s. c., 24 Pat. Off. Gaz. 498; Electric Light Co. *v.* Electric Lighting Co., 43 Pat. Off. Gaz. 1456.

2. The statute refers to a patent granted to the inventor. A prior patent obtained inimicably after the invention by the American patentee or applicant, does not affect his patent. Kendrick *v.* Emmons, 2 Bann. & Ard. Pat. Cas. 208; s. c., 9 Pat. Off. Gaz. 201.

3. U. S. Rev. Stats. 4887; Edison Electric Light Co. *v.* Westinghouse, 40 Fed. Rep. 666.

The American patent cannot run longer than seventeen years. U. S. Rev. Stats. § 4887; Weston *v.* White, 13 Blatchf. (U. S.) 364; s. c., 2 Bann. & Ard. Pat. Cas. 321; s. c., 9 Pat. Off. Gaz. 1196.

This provision does not extend to patents granted prior to 1870. Goff *v.* Stafford, 3 Bann. & Ard. Pat. Cas. 610; s. c., 14 Pat. Off. Gaz. 748; De Florez *v.* Raynolds, 8 Fed. Rep. 434; Badische etc. Fabrik *v.* Hamilton Mfg. Co., 3 Bann. & Ard. Pat. Cas. 235; s, c., 13 Pat. Off. Gaz. 273.

For decision on the prior statutes, see Smith *v.* Ely, 5 McLean (U. S.) 76; O'Reilly *v.* Morse, 15 How. (U. S.) 62; Weston *v.* White, 2 Bann. & Ard. Pat. Cas. 321; s. c., 13 Blatchf. (U. S.) 364; Nathan *v.* New York etc. R. Co., 2 Fed. Rep. 225; s, c., 5 Bann. & Ard. Pat. Cas. 280; Telghman *v.* Proctor, 102 U. S. 707; s. c., 19 Pat. Off. Gaz. 859; American etc. Boring Co. *v.* Sheldon, 17 Blatchf. (U. S.) 303; s. c., 4 Bann. & Ard. Pat. Cas. 603.

Guaranty Trust Co. *v.* Sellers, 41 Pat. Off. Gaz. 1165. "An inventor taking out a patent in the first instance in this country, is entitled to seventeen years' protection; but, if he has previously obtained letters patent in one or more foreign countries, then, while not deprived of his right to a patent here, the term to which the law in such case limits his protection is a period not extending beyond the date of the expiration of that one of the foreign patent first expiring." United States *v.* Marble, 22 Pat. Off. Gaz. 1365.

4. Bate Refrigerator Co. *v.* Hammond, 129 U. S. 151; s. c., 46 Pat. Off.

not shortened by a termination of the foreign patent at a time previous to the length of the grant by any default of the owner of the foreign patent.[1] The American patent, where the existence of the foreign patent is known to the Patent Office, is limited on its face to the term of the foreign patent;[2] but a failure to so limit it, neither invalidates the patent nor lengthens its term.[3] The foreign patent must be substantially identical with the American in order to limit the duration of the latter.[4]

(*e*) THAT THE SUBJECT MATTER IS UNPATENTABLE.—The subject matter of the patent is not such as the laws authorize a patent to be granted for.[5]

(*f*) LACK OF INVENTION.—That the contrivance of the patentee did not involve the exercise of the inventive faculty.[6] This defense can be made sometimes on demurrer,[7] on the plea at

Gaz. 689; Consolidated Rolling Mill Co. *v.* Walker, 43 Fed. Rep. 575.

By this ruling the rulings in Reissner *v.* Sharp, 16 Blatchf. (U. S.) 383; s. c., 4 Bann. & Ard. Pat. Cas. 366; s. c., 16 Pat. Off. Gaz. 355; Henry *v.* Providence Tool Co., 3 Bann. & Ard. Pat. Cas. 301; s. c., 14 Pat. Off. Gaz. 855; Bate Refrigerating Co. *v.* Gillett, 13 Fed. Rep. 553; s. c., 22 Pat. Off. Gaz. 1205; Gramme Electrical Co. *v.* Arnaux etc. Electric Co., 17 Fed. Rep. 838; s. c., 25 Pat. Off. Gaz. 1129, are overruled. See Huber *v.* Nelson Mfg. Co., 38 Fed. Rep. 830; s. c., 46 Pat. Off. Gaz. 1732, which has itself been overruled.

1. Pohl *v.* Brewing Co., 134 U. S., 381; s. c., 51 Pat. Off. Gaz. 156; Electric Light Co. *v.* Electric Lamp Co., 42 Fed. Rep. 327; s. c., 52 Pat. Off. Gaz. 1570; Holmes Electric Protective Co. *v.* Metropolitan Burglar Alarm Co., 22 Blatchf. (U. S.) 471; Paillard *v.* Bruno, 29 Fed. Rep. 864; s. c., 38 Pat. Off. Gaz. 900. Overruling, Haber *v.* Mfg. Co., 38 Fed. Rep. 830; s. c., 46 Pat. Off. Gaz. 1732. See Badische etc. Fabrik *v.* Hamilton Co., 3 Bann. & Ard. Pat. Cas. 235; s. c., 13 Pat. Off. Gaz. 273.

This doctrine extends to a case where the patentee of a foreign patent, having the right to successive prolongations, fails to secure them by neglect, it being held that this did not invalidate the American patent. Consolidated Roller Mill Co. *v.* Walker, 43 Fed. Rep. 575.

2. Opinion Sec. Int., 21 Pat. Off. Gaz. 1197.

The Patent Office can require the applicant to state whether he has any prior patent in foreign countries. United States *v.* Marble, 22 Pat. Off. Gaz. 1365; *Ex parte* Bland, 15 Pat. Off. Gaz. 828.

3. Bate Refrigerating Co. *v.* Gillett, 129 U. S. 151; s. c., 46 Pat. Off. Gaz. 689; Canan *v.* Pound Mfg. Co., 23 Blatchf. (U. S.) 173; s. c., 23 Fed. Rep. 185; s. c., 31 Pat. Off. Gaz. 119; American Paper Barrel Co. *v.* Laraway, 28 Fed. Rep. 141; s. c., 37 Pat. Off. Gaz. 674; New American File Co. *v.* Nicholson File Co., 8 Fed. Rep. 816; Siemens *v.* Sellers, 23 Pat. Off. Gaz. 2234. Overruling Paillard *v.* Gautschi, 20 Pat. Off. Gaz. 1893.

4. Siemens *v.* Sellers, 16 Fed. Rep. 856; s. c., 23 Pat. Off. Gaz. 2234; Clark *v.* Wilson, 28 Fed. Rep. 95; Commercial Mfg. Co. *v.* Fairbank Canning Co., 36 Pat. Off. Gaz. 1473; s. c., 27 Fed. Rep. 78.

Where the differences between the thing shown and described in the two patents are merely differences of degree, the two patents are subtantially the same. Commercial Mfg. Co. *v.* Fairbank Canning Co., 27 Fed. Rep. 78.

5. 3 Rob. on Pat., §§ 962, 968.

See *supra*, *Art Machine Manufacture*, *Composition of Matter*.

This defense may be set up at the hearing. Guidet *v.* Barber, 5 Pat. Off. Gaz. 149; Hendy *v.* Iron Works, 127 U. S. 370; s. c., 43 Pat. Off. Gaz. 1117.

Or can be made on demurrer. Walker on Patents, § 598.

Or made under a general denial ot patentable novelty in the answers. Guidet *v.* Barber, 5 Pat. Off. Gaz. 149.

6. See article, "*Invention.*"

7. Robinson on Patents, § 959. This must be where it will clearly appear, on inspection, by the application of judicial

law,[1] or in the answer in equity,[2] or set up at hearing.[3]

(*g*) PATENT DIFFERENT FROM APPLICATION.—That the invention claimed in the patent is substantially different from any invention described, suggested or indicated in the original application.[4]

(*h*) REISSUE INVALID.—That the reissue patent is invalid on account of its being reissued illegally.[5]

(*i*) UNLAWFUL EXTENSION.—That the patent had been unlawfully extended.[6]

(*j*) UNLAWFUL AMENDMENT BY REPRESENTATIVE.—That the representative of the inventor subsequently unlawfully amended the application without making a new oath.[7]

(*k*) LACK OF TITLE IN PLAINTIFF TO BRING SUIT.—That the plaintiff is not the owner of the letters patent sued[8] on or is not the sole owner; [9] that he is not the inventor[10] or the sole inventor; [11] or of two claiming to be joint inventors that they are not such inventors.[12]

knowledge, that there is no invention. Eclipse Mfg. Co. *v.* Adkins, 36 Fed. Rep. 554; West *v.* Rae, 33 Fed. Rep. 45; Blessing *v.* John Trageser etc. Copper Works, 34 Fed. Rep. 753.

1. Walker on Patents (2nd ed.), § 446. But cannot be set up on pleas in equity. Walker on Patents (2nd ed.), § 594.

2. It is not necessary to state the facts intended to be proved in its support. Walker on Patents, § 599; Vana *v.* Campbell, 1 Black (U. S.) 430.

3. Slawson *v.* Grand St. etc. R. Co., 17 Blatchf. (U. S.) 512; s. c., 5 Bann. & Ard. Pat. Cas. 210; s. c., 4 Fed. Rep. 531; s. c., 24 Pat. Off. Gaz. 99; Gardner *v.* Hertz, 118 U. S. 1180; s. c., 35 Pat. Off. Gaz. 999; Mahn *v.* Harwood, 112 U. S. 354; s. c., 30 Pat. Off. Gaz. 657.

4. Walker on Patents (2nd ed.), §§ 440, 450, 603; Chicago etc. R. Co. *v.* Sayles, 97 U. S. 563; Kittle *v.* Hall, 29 Fed. Rep. 508; Eagleton Mfg. Co. *v.* West etc. Mfg. Co., 111 U. S. 490; Woodbury etc. Planing Mach. Co. *v.* Keith, 101 U. S. 479; Lindsay *v.* Stein, 10 Fed. Rep. 913; United States etc. Rifle Co. *v.* Whitney Arms Co., 14 Blatchf. (U. S.) 98; s. c., 2 Bann. & Ard. Pat. Cas. 293; s. c., 11 Pat. Off. Gaz. 373; Bevin *v.* East Hampton Bell Co., 9 Blatchf. (U. S.) 50; s. c., 5 Fish. Pat. Cas. 23.

But a liberal construction is to be adopted in considering this question. Brush Electric Co. *v.* Julien Electric Co., 41 Fed. Rep. 679; Electrical Accumulator Co. *v.* Julien Electric Co., 38 Fed. Rep. 117.

5. See *Reissue.*

At law this defense is made by special plea. Walker on Patents, §§ 457, 458, 459.

In equity where both the original and reissued patents are incorporated in the bill, this defense can be made by demurrer, otherwise by answer, though the broadening of claims after delay may be taken advantage of at the hearing. Walker on Patents (2nd ed.), §§ 610, 611 and 612; International Terra Cotta Lumber Co. *v.* Maurer, 44 Fed. Rep. 618.

6. See ***Extension of Patent, infra.***

Raised by special plea at law in equity by demurrer when sufficient facts appear on the record; otherwise by answer. Walker on Patents 2nd. Ed. §§ 525, 613.

7. This defense may be made with special notice, or setting it up in the answer. Eagleton Mfg. Co. *v.* West Bradley etc. Mfg. Co., 111 U. S. 490; s. c., 27 Pat. Off. Gaz. 1237.

8. See ***Parties Plaintiff, supra.***

Walker on Pat. 2nd. Ed. § 617; Providence Rubber Co. *v.* Goodyear, 9 Wall. (U. S.) 788; Dueber Watch Case Mfg. Co. *v.* Faley's Watch Case Co., 45 Fed. Rep. 697.

9. See ***Parties Plaintiff, supra.***

10. See ***Invention, Diligence, supra.***

The manner of setting up this defense is same as above.

11. See *Joint Inventors. Sole Inventors.*

12. See *Joint Inventors. Sole Inventors.*

The defenses of notes four and five

(*l*) NON-INFRINGEMENT.—The non-infringement of the device by the defendant is a good defense.[1]

(*m*) LIMITATIONS.—That the cause of action is barred by a statute of limitation.[2]

4. Defenses to Costs and Damages.—As a defense to plaintiff's claim for costs, defendants may aver an undue delay to enter a disclaimer;[3] and the recovery of damages, that the goods were not marked patented in accordance with the law, and that no notice had been given of the fact of infringement[4]

5. Estoppel of Defendant to Set Up Certain Defenses.—An assignor, when sued by his assignee, is estopped from setting up the invalidity of the patent[5] or his lack of title at the time of the assign-

must be made at law under special plea. Walker on Patents (2nd ed.), § 452. In equity they may be raised by a plea or in the answer. Walker on Patents, § 605. Adams *v.* Howard, 22 Blatchf. (U. S.) 47.

1. See article *Infringement, supra.* Whittemore *v.* Cutter, 1 Gallis (U. S.) 424; s. c., 1 Robb Pat. Cas. 28.

How Made.—This defense must be clearly set up in the answer. Jordan *v.* Wallace, 5 Fish. Pat. Cas. 185; Theberath *v.* Rubber etc. Trimming Co., 5 Bann. & Ard. Pat. Cas. 585; Sharp *v.* Reissner, 20 Blatchf. (U. S.) 10.

Is admissible under general issue at law. Blanchard *v.* Puttman, 3 Fish. Pat. Cas. 186; Dunbar *v.* Myers, 94 U. S. 198; Eachus *v.* Broomall, 115 U. S. 434; Grier *v.* Wilt, 120 U. S. 412. And cannot be set up in special plea. Hubbell *v.* DeLand, 11 Biss. (U. S.) 382; s. c., 14 Fed. Rep. 471; s. c., 22 Pat. Off. Gaz. 1883.

2. Whether the State statutes apply is doubtful. See *Limitation, supra.* Also McGinnis *v.* Erie Co., 45 Fed. Rep. 91; May *v.* Buchanan Co., 29 Fed. Rep. 469; May *v.* Cass Co., 30 Fed. Rep. 762; May *v.* Ralls Co., 31 Fed. Rep. 473.

Prior to July 8, 1870, no U. S. statute of limitations applied to patent cases. Wood *v.* Cleveland Rolling Mill Co., 4 Fish. Pat. Cas. 550.

This statute (Stats. at Large, vol. 16, § 55) provided that all actions for the infringement of patents be brought within six years from the expiration of the patent, was not re-enacted by the Revised Statutes. Robinson on Pat., § 980; May *v.* Logan Co., 30 Fed. Rep. 250; s. c., 41 Pat. Off. Gaz. 1387.

The rights of action accruing under patents that expired during that time were subject to the rule. Hayden *v.* Oriental Mills, 22 Fed. Rep. 103. See on this subject, Sayles *v.* Richmond etc. R. Co., 3 Hughes (U. S.) 172; s. c., 4 Bann. & Ard. Pat. Cas. 239; s. c., 16 Pat. Off. Gaz. 43; Vaughan *v.* East Tennessee R. Co., 1 Flipp. (U. S.) 621; s. c., 2 Bann. & Ard. Pat. Cas. 537; s. c., 11 Pat. Off. Gaz. 789; Hayward *v.* St. Louis, 3 McCrary (U. S.) 614; s. c., 11 Fed. Rep. 427.

This defense must be especially pleaded or it will be disregarded. Neale *v.* Walker, 1 Cranch (C. C.) 57; 1 Chitty on Pleading 498; Walker on Patents (2nd ed.), § 471.

Several pleas covering different times may be filed. Hayden *v.* Oriental Mills, 22 Fed. Rep. 103.

In equity this defense is made under demurrer, where the bill states the time within which the infringement was committed; otherwise by plea or answer. Walker on Pat. (2nd ed.), § 622; Adams *v.* Bridgewater Iron Co., 6 Fed. Rep. 179.

3. See *Disclaimer, supra.*

This defense must be made in an action at law by special plea; in equity by answer or plea. Walker on Patents, §§ 456, 609. In answer only. Worden *v.* Searls, 21 Fed. Rep. 574.

4. See *Failure to Mark Patented Article, infra;* U. S. Rev. Stats., § 4900; Goodyear *v.* Allyn, 6 Blatchf. (U. S.) 33.

See *Marking Article Patented, infra.*

Should be made at law by special plea. Walker on Pat. (2nd ed.), 463.

In equity by plea or in the answer. Walker on Pat. (2nd ed.), § 616. In answer only. Sessions *v.* Romadka, 21 Fed. Rep. 124.

5. Time Tel. Co. *v.* Heimner, 19 Fed. Rep. 322; Curran *v.* Burdsall, 20 Fed. Rep. 835; Rumsey *v.* Buck, 20

ment;[1] nor can one who has acknowledged in some agreement, for value, complainant's rights, afterwards dispute them.[2]

XIII. **Plea in Equity.**—The plea must present a single point going to a complete defense.[3] Setting it down for argument is

Fed. Rep. 697; Burdsall *v.* Curran, 31 Fed. Rep. 918; Parkhurst *v.* Kinsman, 1 Blatchf. (U. S.) 488; Newell *v.* West, 13 Blatchf. (U. S.) 114; Underwood *v.* Warren, 21 Fed. Rep. 573; Parker *v.* Mckee, 24 Fed. Rep. 808; s. c., 32 Pat. Off. Gaz. 137; Alabastine Co. *v.* Payne, 27 Fed. Rep. 559; American Barrel Co. *v.* Laraway, 28 Fed. Rep. 141; Burdsall *v.* Curran, 31 Fed. Rep. 918; Adee *v.* Thomas, 41 Fed. Rep. 343.

An assignor cannot acquire a prior patent against his assignee. Curran *v.* Burdsall, 20 Fed. Rep. 835.

See, however, King *v.* Gedney, 20 Law. Rep. (U. S.) 631.

1. Newell *v.* West, 13 Blatchf. (U. S.) 114; s. c., 2 Bann. & Ard. Pat. Cas. 113; s. c., 8 Pat. Off. Gaz. 598; Herbert *v.* Adams, 4 Mason (U. S.) 15. See, however, Kearney *v.* Lehigh Valley R. Co., 27 Fed. Rep. 699.

For examples of other estoppels preventing defenses to patents, see Carroll *v.* Gambrill, 1 McArthur Pat. Cas. 581; Downton *v.* Yeager Milling Co., 1 McCrary (U. S.) 26; s. c., 1 Fed. Rep. 199; s. c., 5 Bann. & Ard. Pat. Cas. 112; s. c., 17 Pat. Off. Gaz. 906; Time Tel.. Co. *v.* Carey, 22 Blatchf. (U. S.) 34; s. c., 19 Fed. Rep. 322; s. c., 26 Pat. Off. Gaz. 826.

But the fact that the defendants have adopted the complainant's device bodily, and have used and sold it in preference to prior structures, does not estop them from questioning its patentability. Simmonds *v.* Morrison, 44 Fed. Rep. 757.

2. Baltimore Car Wheel Co. *v.* North Baltimore etc. R. Co., 21 Fed. Rep. 47; Eclipse Windmill Co. *v.* May, 17 Fed. Rep. 344; Washburn etc. Mfg. Co. *v.* Cincinnati etc Co., 22 Fed. Rep. 712; Pope Mfg. Co. *v.* Owsley, 27 Fed. Rep. 100; Morse Arms Co. *v.* United States, 16 Ct. of Cl. 296; Clark *v.* Amoskeag Mfg. Co., 62 N. H. 612.

An estoppel of a licensee does not arise when the licensee stands out from under his license. Brown *v.* Lapham, 23 Blatchf. (U. S.) 475; s. c., 27 Fed. Rep. 77; s. c., 37 Pat. Off. Gaz. 676.

Or where the complainant elects to treat licensee as infringer. Baltimore Car Wheel Co. *v.* North Baltimore etc. R. Co., 21 Fed. Rep. 47.

A grantee of a patent is not estopped from denying its validity out of his territory. Hobbie *v.* Smith, 27 Fed. Rep. 656.

3. Reissner *v.* Anness, 3 Bann. & Ard. Pat. Cas. 148; s. c., 12 Pat. Off. Gaz. 842; White *v.* Lee, 4 Fed. Rep. 916; Graham *v.* Mason, 4 Cliff. (U. S.) 88; s. c., 5 Fish. Pat. Cas. 1; Giant Powder Co. *v.* Safety Nitro Powder Co., 10 Sawy. (U. S.) 23; s. c., 19 Fed. Rep. 509; s. c., 27 Pat. Off. Gaz. 99; Secombe *v.* Campbell, 18 Blatchf. (U. S.) 108.

A plea is intended to dispose of the case on a single issue; it will not be allowed where it will cause the case to be tried piece meal. Giant Powder Co. *v.* Safety Nitro Powder Co., 19 Fed. Rep. 509.

Where the plea is double the respondent may elect which ground he will stand on. Reissner *v.* Anness, 3 Bann. & Ard. Pat. Cas. 148; s. c., 12 Pat. Off. Gaz. 842. And permission may sometimes be obtained to plead double. Winne *v.* Snow, 19 Fed. Rep. 507.

Defenses Which May be Set Up by Plea.—Non-joinder of necessary party. Hammond *v.* Hunt, 4 Bann. & Ard. Pat. Cas. 111; Wallace *v.* Holmes, 9 Blatchf. (U. S.) 65; s. c., 5 Fish. Pat. Cas. 37; s. c., 1 Pat. Off. Gaz. 117; Goodyear *v.* Toby, 6 Blatchf. (U. S.) 130. That the complainant alleged to be a corporation is not incorporated. Goodyear Dental etc. Co. *v.* Wetherbee, 3 Cliff. (U. S.) 555; s. c., 3 Fish. Pat. Cas. 87. *Lis pendens*. Wheeler *v.* McCormick, 8 Blatchf. (U. S.) 267; 4 Fish. Pat. Cas. 483. That reissue is void as not for same invention as original. Hubbell *v.* DeLand, 12 Pat. Off. Gaz. 1883.

That the plaintiff is only a licensee. Cottle *v.* Krementz, 25 Fed. Rep. 494.

To the jurisdiction of equity that the patent has expired. Edison Electric Light Co. *v.* United States Electric Light Co., 35 Fed. Rep. 134. That the defendants had settled the damages. Burdell *v.* Denig, 15 Fed. Rep. 347. That defendant is suing on a patent which has been surrendered for reissue. Burrell *v.* Hackley, 35 Fed. Rep. 833.

an admission of the facts alleged[1] and a waiver of irregularities.[2] When a plea is overruled the defendant is permitted to answer[3] and sometimes the plea is allowed to remain as the answer or part of the answer.[4]

XVI. Demurrer.—A demurrer, at law or in equity, is to take advantage of defects appearing upon record.[5]

Defenses Which Cannot be Set Up in a Plea.—Infringement. Korn *v.* Wilbusch, 33 Fed. Rep. 50; Matthews *v.* Lalance Mfg. Co., 18 Blatchf. (U. S.) 84; s. c., 5 Bann. & Ard. Pat. Cas. 319; s. c., 2 Fed. Rep. 232; s. c., 17 Pat. Off. Gaz. 1284.

Where the determination of the issues sought to be raised by the plea, required the patents specified in the bill to be examined and passed on by the court, the defendant will be ordered to answer. White *v.* Lee, 4 Fed. Rep. 916. Every plea should have certificate and affidavit of counsel; but this is waived by demurrer and argument to the merits. Goodyear *v.* Toby, 6 Blatchf. (U. S.) 130.

1. Wheeler *v.* McCormick, 8 Blatchf. (U. S.) 267; s. c., 4 Fish. Pat. Cas. 433; Birdseye *v.* Heilner, 26 Fed. Rep. 147.

2. Goodyear *v.* Toby, 6 Blatchf. (U. S.) 130. But a replication filed where the plea is bad in substance does not prevent it from being overruled. Matthews *v.* Lalance etc. Mfg. Co., 18 Blatchf. (U. S.) 84; s. c., 2 Fed. Rep. 232; s. c., 17 Pat. Off. Gaz. 1284; s. c., 5 Bann. & Ard. Pat. Cas. 319.

Right to Begin and Close.—If a replication is filed, complainant has right to begin and close. Reissner *v.* Anness, 3 Bann. & Ard. Pat. Cas. 176; s. c., 13 Pat. Off. Gaz. 870.

3. Wooster *v.* Blake, 7 Fed. Rep. 816; s. c., 20 Pat. Off. Gaz. 158.

The matter litigated by a plea cannot generally be raised again by an answer. Hubbell *v.* DeLand, 11 Bliss. (U. S.) 383.

But the court may permit an answer to be filed upon terms raising the same point. Matthews *v.* Lalance etc. Mfg. Co., 18 Blatchf. (U. S.) 84.

Exception as to Plea in Confession and Avoidance—A plea confessing and avoiding, where the matter in avoidance is decided against the plea, being overruled, and the main facts of the bill admitted by the plea, warrants a a decree for complainant Lilienthal *v.* Washburn, 8 Fed. Rep. 707.

4. Albright *v.* Empire Trans. Co., 14 Pat. Off. Gaz. 523.

Where a defendant makes a plea part of his answer, he will not be compelled more or otherwise than if he had filed a regular plea. Adams *v.* Bridgewater Iron Co., 6 Fed. Rep. 179.

5. Laches of complainant can be raised by demurrer. McLaughlin *v.* People's R. Co., 21 Fed. Rep. 574.

Where, in an equity suit, the defendant desires to avail himself of the defense that the patent is too near its expiration to warrant an injunction. New York Grape Sugar Co. *v.* Peoria Grape Sugar Co., 21 Fed. Rep. 878. Or that two patents do not interfere with each other. Morris *v.* Kempshall Mfg. Co., 20 Fed. Rep. 121. Or that plaintiff had not alleged that defendant had not derived right from a licensee who had power to give such right. Still *v.* Reading, 4 Woods (U. S.) 345; s. c., 9 Fed. Rep. 40; s. c., 20 Pat. Off. Gaz. 1025. Or that a license was not averred to be properly revoked. White *v.* Lee, 3 Fed. Rep. 222; Bloomer *v.* Gilpin, 4 Fish. Pat. Cas. 50.

Where profert is made an objection to, it may be taken by demurrer. Bogart *v.* Hinds, 25 Fed. Rep. 484; s. c., 33 Pat. Off. Gaz. 1268.

A demurrer to a bill joining in one action a corporation and its assignee, alleging that the causes of action against the corporation and its assignee are distinct is bad. Gordon *v.* St. Paul Harvester Works, 23 Fed. Rep. 147.

Questions of Pleading.—Questions of pleading must be raised by demurrer. Pellam *v.* Edelmeyer, 21 Blatchf. (U. S.) 188; Gillespie *v.* Cummings, 3 Sawy. (U. S.) 259; Hodge *v.* North Missouri R. Co., 1 Dill. (U. S.) 104; Case *v.* Redfield, 4 McLean (U. S.) 526; Phillips *v.* Comstock, 4 McLean (U. S.) 525; Wilder *v.* McCormick, 2 Blatchf. (U. S.) 31; Peterson *v.* Wooden, 3 McLean (U. S.) 248; Stanley *v.* Whipple, 2 McLean (U. S.) 35; Dobson *v.* Campbell, 1 Sumn. (U. S.) 319; Tryon *v.* White, 1 Pet. (C. C.) 96; Evans *v.* Kremer, 1 Pet. (C. C.) 215; Evans *v.* Eaton, 1 Pet. (C. C.) 322.

XV. Answer—1. Responsively and as Defense.—All the material allegations of the bill must be answered;[1] but if the answer responds to the bill the defendant is in no default by refusing to answer any part thereof to which he is not specially interrogated;[2] and all allegations of defense, which cannot be made at hearing, made.[3]

A bill which alleges both joint and several infringement by the defendants, is demurrable. Putnam *v.* Hollender, 19 Blatchf. (U. S.) 48. Or to a bill bad for multifariousness. Hayes *v.* Dayton, 18 Blatchf. (U. S.) 420.

A demurrer can be filed to a replication where the latter sets up a new defense. Burdell *v.* Denig, 15 Fed. Rep. 397.

A demurrer to a bill entitled to the circuit court act, in chancery sitting, is bad. Sterrick *v.* Pugsley, 1 Flipp. (U. S.) 350.

A demurrer to a bill which did not allege the location of complainants and which was not sworn to, has been overruled. National Hay Rake Co. *v.* Harber, 2 W. N. C. (Pa.) 100.

Waiver of Right to Demur.—Putting in an answer to the whole bill is a waiver of the right to demur. Adams *v.* Howard, 20 Blatchf. (U. S.) 38; s. c., 9 Fed. Rep. 347; s. c., 21 Pat. Off. Gaz. 364.

To What Demurrer Must Apply.—A demurrer must apply only to the pleading which is bad or it will be overruled. 2 Curt. (U. S.) 97.

A demurrer may, where there are special grounds for action, be sustained in part and overruled in part. International Co. *v.* Maurer, 44 Fed. Rep. 618.

But a demurrer should not be filed to a mere surplusage. Stirratt *v.* Excelsior Mfg. Co., 44 Fed. Rep. 142.

A demurrer to a bill for infringement on the ground that there was no invention in the devise patented, will not be sustained unless the case is a very clear one. Blessing *v.* John Trageser Steam Copper Works, 34 Fed. Rep. 753; Standard Oil Co. *v.* Southern Pac. R. Co., 42 Fed. Rep. 295. See *Judicial Knowledge, infra*,

But where by judicial knowledge, upon an inspection of the device, the court can see there is no invention, it will sustain a demurrer and dismiss the bill. West *v.* Rae, 33 Fed. Rep. 45.

A demurrer will not lie to a "notice" under the statute of special defenses. Henry *v.* United States, 22 Ct. of Cl. 75.

1. Perry *v.* Corning, 6 Blatchf. (U. S.) 134; Jordan *v.* Wallace, 5 Fish. Pat. Cas. 185; Agawam Co. *v.* Jordan, 7 Wall. (U. S.) 583.

Irresponsive Sworn Answer Not Evidence for Defendant.—An answer under oath which is irresponsive to the bill, is not evidence for the defendant. Sargent *v.* Larned, 2 Curt. (U. S.) 340.

The answer must be on "knowledge, information and belief," not on knowledge only, if all three are required. Parks *v.* Bryan, 1 Story (U. S.) 296.

A corporation cannot be compelled to answer under oath, but can be made to answer fully where oath is waived. Colgate *v.* Campagnie Francaise du Telegraphe, 23 Fed. Rep. 82.

The answer must be by the party and not by the attorney. Wooster *v.* Muser, 20 Fed. Rep. 162. And be sworn to, unless the oath is waived, by all the parties professing to answer. Washing Machine Co. *v.* Young, 1 Bann. & Ard. Pat. Cas. 362.

2. Brooks *v.* Bicknell, 3 McLean (U. S.) 250; s. c., 2 Robb Pat. Cas. 118.

If the bill requires an answer under oath to certain interrogatories, the rest of the answer is not evidence of facts averred therein. Wren *v.* Spencer etc. Mfg. Co., 5 Bann. & Ard. Pat. Cas. 61; s. c., 18 Pat. Off. Gaz. 857.

Separate answers may, if defendant so desires, be filed to each patent sued on. Kelleher *v.* Darling, 4 Cliff. (U. S.) 424; s. c., 3 Bann. & Ard. Pat. Cas. 438; s. c., 14 Pat. Off. Gaz. 673.

3. Goodyear *v.* Providence Rubber Co., 2 Fish. Pat. Cas. 499; s. c., 2 Cliff. (U. S.) 351; Yale etc. Mfg. Co. *v.* North, 3 Fish. Pat. Cas. 279; s. c., 5 Blatchf. (U. S.) 455; Howes *v.* Nute, 4 Cliff. (U. S.) 173; s. c., 4 Fish. Pat. Cas. 263; Russell Mfg. Co. *v.* Mallory, 10 Blatchf. (U. S.) 140; s. c., 5 Fish. Pat. Cas. 632; s. c., 2 Pat. Off. Gaz. 495; Jennings *v.* Pierce, 15 Blatchf. (U. S.) 42; s. c., 3 Bann. & Ard. Pat. Cas. 361; Wonson *v.* Peterson, 3 Bann. & Ard. Pat. Cas. 259; s. c., 13 Pat. Off. Gaz. 548; Bragg *v.* Stockton, 27 Fed. Rep. 509.

Clearness of Defense.—The defense must be set up clearly. Puetz *v.*

2. Exceptions and Replications.—Where a defect in the answer is a proper subject for amendment, the objection should be taken by exception,[1] and a replication filed where the matters pleaded in defendant's answer or plea are to be put in issue.[2]

3. Amendment of Answer.—Defects in answer must be cured by amendments;[3] and an amendment which presents a new defense or makes more than a formal alteration in the bill[4] must show that the matter of the proposed amendment could not have been introduced into the answer sooner by using reasonable diligence.[5]

Bransford, 31 Fed. Rep. 458; Day *v.* Combination Rubber Co., 2 Fed. Rep. 570; s. c., 5 Bann. & Ard. Pat. Cas. 385; s. c., 17 Pat. Off. Gaz. 1347; Jordan *v.* Wallace, 1 Leg. Gaz. Rep. (Pa.) 354; Fisher *v.* Hayes, 19 Blatchf. (U. S.) 26; s. c., 6 Fed. Rep. 76; s. c., 20 Pat. Off. Gaz. 239.

A matter which does not constitute a bar, but which will be considered in determining the relief to be granted, is proper to be set up in the answer. Sun Vapor Street Light Co. *v.* Cedar Rapid, 39 Fed. Rep. 698.

Apparently where a sufficient defense has been set up once, a new defense cannot be made. Consolidated Electric Light Co. *v.* Brush etc. Electric Light Co., 22 Blatchf. (U. S.) 206.

1. Foster's Federal Practice, § 153, and cases there cited. Graham *v.* Mason, 4 Cliff. (U. S.) 88; s. c., 5 Fish. Pat. Cas. 1; Steam Gauge etc. Co. *v.* McRoberts, 26 Fed. Rep. 765; Stirratt *v.* Excelsior Mfg. Co., 44 Fed. Rep. 142.

A failure to except and to move to take answer of files, or to have bill taken *pro confesso*, admits the answer to be sufficient. Morris *v.* Kemphall Mfg. Co., 20 Fed. Rep. 121.

In certain cases, exceptions will not be permitted to be filed without leave. Allis *v.* Stowell, 10 Biss. (U. S.) 57.

2. Foster's Fed. Practice, §§ 156, 157, 158, 159.

Complainant cannot file a replication after trying his case on bill and answer. Bullinger *v.* Mackey, 14 Blatchf. (U. S.) 355.

Complainant may be allowed to file a replication *nunc pro tunc* on sufficient excuse. Robinson *v.* Randolph, 4 Bann. & Ard. Pat. Cas. 163.

A replication cannot make out a different case. Burdell *v.* Denig, 15 Fed. Rep. 397. But a replication containing a general traverse and special matter may be good for the general traverse, and the special matter be disregarded. Wren *v.* Spencer etc. Mfg. Co., 5 Bann. & Ard. Pat. Cas. 61; s. c., 18 Pat. Off. Gaz. 857. But a replication may be special and in avoidance. Goodyear *v.* McBurney, 3 Blatchf. (U. S.) 32.

The want of a replication cannot be objected to, after parties have proceeded to take testimony on the merits. Fischer *v.* Wilson, 16 Blatchf. (U. S.) 220; s. c., 4 Bann. & Ard. Pat. Cas. 228; s. c., 16 Pat. Off. Gaz. 455.

If a replication is sufficient other matter will be treated as surplusage merely. Wren *v.* Spencer etc. Mfg. Co., 5 Bann. & Ard. Pat. Cas. 61; s. c., 18 Pat. Off. Gaz. 857.

Form of Plea.—See Wheeler *v.* McCormick, 8 Blatchf. (U. S.) 267.

Effect of Decree on Plea.—See Keller *v.* Stolsenbach, 20 Fed. Rep. 47; s. c., 27 Pat. Off. Gaz. 209.

Replication to a Plea.—A replication to a plea admits its sufficiency both in form and substance. Bean *v.* Clark, 40 Pat. Off. Gaz. 1154; Birdseye *v.* Heilner, 26 Fed. Rep. 147; s. c., 34 Pat. Off. Gaz. 139 2.

Replication to Answer.—A replication to an answer is a waiver to defects therein or to its insufficiency. Wooster *v.* Muser, 20 Fed. Rep. 162.

3. Doughty *v.* West, 2 Fish. Pat. Cas. 553; Dental Vulcanite Co. *v.* Wetherbee, 3 Fish. Pat. Cas. 87; s. c., 2 Cliff. (U. S.) 555; Babcock etc. Co. *v.* Pioneer Iron Works, 34 Fed. Rep. 338.

Leave to amend in other than formal matters, is in the discretion of the court. Pentlarge *v.* Beeston, 4 Bann. & Ard. Pat. Cas. 23. And will sometimes only be granted on terms. Underwood *v.* Gerber, 37 Fed. Rep. 796.

4. Brown *v.* Hall, 6 Blatchf. (U. S.) 401; s. c., 3 Fish. Pat. Cas. 531; Roberts *v.* Ryer, 6 Fish. Pat. Cas. 293; s. c., 11 Blatchf. (U. S.) 11; s. c., 3 Pat. Off. Gaz. 550.

5. India Rubber Comb Co. *v.* Phelps, 8 Blatchf. (U. S.) 85; s. c., 4 Fish. Pat.

Especially a fact admitted generally will not be allowed to be denied by an amendment,[1] nor a new defense dependent wholly on parol evidence be permitted to be set up.[2]

XVI. Motions.—Where suits are brought which, in reality, all embrace the same cause of action, the court will, on motion, consolidate them:[3] or where the pleadings contain scandal or impertinence, the court will, on motion or exception, cause the same to be stricken out.[4]

Cas. 315; Rumford Chemical Works *v.* Hecker, 2 Bann. & Ard. Pat. Cas. 351; Hitchcock *v.* Tremaine, 9 Blatchf. (U. S.) 550; s. c., 5 Fish. Pat. Cas. 537; s. c., 1 Pat. Off. Gas. 633; Richardson *v.* Croft, 11 Fed. Rep. 800; s. c., 20 Pat. Off. Gaz. 372; Ruggles *v.* Eddy, 11 Blatchf. (U. S.) 524; s. c., 5 Fish. Pat. Cas. 583; Snow *v.* Tapley, 3 Bann. & Ard. Pat. Cas. 228; s. c., 13 Pat. Off. Gaz. 548; Roberts *v.* Ryer, 6 Fish. Pat. Cas. 293; s. c., 11 Blatchf. (U. S.) 11; s. c., 3 Pat. Off. Gaz. 550.

Instead of amending, defendant is sometimes permitted to file a supplemental answer. Morehead *v.* Jones, 3 Wall. Jr. (C. C.) 306.

Costs on Amendment.—Upon an amendment of the answer, a portion of the costs may be placed on the defendant. Morehead *v.* Jones, 3 Wall. Jr. (C. C.) 306; Roberts *v.* Buck, 1 Holmes (U. S.) 224; s. c., 6 Fish. Pat. Cas. 325; s. c., 3 Pat. Off. Gaz. 268.

Effect of Amendment on Admissibility of Testimony.—An amendment to an answer will not make testimony admissible which was taken under objection before the answer was amended. Roberts *v.* Buck, 1 Holmes (U. S.) 224; s. c., 6 Fish. Pat. Cas. 325; s. c., 3 Pat. Off. Gaz. 268.

Element of Surprise to Plaintiff.—If the answer contains a general averment, and the amendment is to particularize this averment, and the plaintiff will not be taken by surprise, the defendant may be allowed to amend even at final hearing. Brown *v.* Hall, 6 Blatchf. (U. S.) 401; s. c., 3 Fish. Pat. Cas. 531; Roberts *v.* Ryer, 11 Blatchf. 11; s. c., 3 Pat. Off. Gaz. 55; s. c., 6 Fish. Pat. Cas. 293.

1. Pentlarge *v.* Beeston, 15 Blatchf. (U. S.) 347; s. c., 4 Bann. & Ard. Pat. Cas. 23; Morehead *v.* Jones, 3 Wall. Jr. (C. C.) 306; Ruggles *v.* Eddy, 11 Blatchf. (U. S.) 524; s. c., 5 Fish. Pat. Cas. 581; Webster Loom Co. *v.* Higgins, 13 Blatchf. (U. S.) 349; s. c., 16 Pat. Off. Gaz. 665.

2. India Rubber Comb Co. *v.* Phelps, 8 Blatchf. (U. S.) 85; s. c., 4 Fish. Pat. Cas. 315. Nor of any allegation where there is doubt if evidence can be procured to sustain it. Hicks *v.* Otto, 17 Fed. Rep. 539.

An assignee of a patent can amend his bill by introducing a claim for damages by a prior infringement. New York Grape Sugar Co. *v.* Buffalo Grape Sugar Co., 20 Fed. Rep. 505. Nor can an amendment be made which would virtually make a new suit. Goodyear *v.* Bourn, 3 Blatchf. (U. S.) 266.

Time When Amendment Can Be Made.—There is no fixed time within which amendments must be made; they can be made even after final hearing. Brown *v.* Hall, 6 Blatchf. (U. S.) 401; s. c., 3 Fish. Pat. Cas. 531.

Effect of Amendment.—An amendment does not, of itself, permit the admission of testimony which, though admissible under the amendment, would not be admissible under the original answer. Roberts *v.* Blake, 3 Pat. Off. Gaz. 268. But see Roberts *v.* Ryer, 11 Blatchf. (U. S.) 11; Roberts *v.* Buck, 1 Holmes (U. S.) 224.

3. Different suits brought for infringement of different patents which are all embraced in a single structure made by defendant. Deering *v.* Winona Harvester Works, 24 Fed. Rep. 90.

4. Miller *v.* Buchanan, 5 Fed. Rep. 366.

Admission of Manufacturer to Defend Suit.—A manufacturer will be admitted to defend in a suit brought against a purchaser of his manufactured device on petition. Curran *v.* St. Charles Car Co., 32 Fed. Rep. 835.

A motion to extend time of taking testimony, will not be granted where there has been great laches on part of party applying. Dederick *v.* Farquehar, 39 Fed. Rep. 346; Streat *v.* Steinam, 38 Fed. Rep. 548.

XVII. EVIDENCE—1. Answer as Evidence.—The sworn answer, responsive to the bill, is evidence as in other equity cases,[1] and an answer not under oath is evidence[2] against the defendant as an admission, and the averments in avoidance must be proved.[3]

2. Presumption—(*a*) RELATING TO PATENTS.—The patent is *prima facie* evidence that it is valid, as it is presumed that the Commissioner has performed his duty,[4] and that the patentee is the inventor.[5] A patent to two or more as joint inventors involves a

1. Woodworth *v.* Hall, 1 Woodb. & M. (U. S.) 248; s. c., 2 Robb. Pat. Cas. 495; Hovey *v.* Stevens, 1 Woodb. & M. (U. S.) 290; s. c., 2 Robb Pat. Cas. 479.

But the denial of infringement must be positive. Goodyear *v.* Berry, 2 Bond (U. S.) 189; s. c., 3 Fish. Pat. Cas. 439; Poppenhusen *v.* New York etc. Comb Co., 4 Blatchf. (U. S.) 185; s. c., 2 Fisher Pat. Cas. 74.

If the denial of novelty in the answer is positive and under oath it requires more than the testimony of one witness to establish infringement. Hovey *v.* Stevens, 1 Woodb. (U. S.) 290.

2. Smith *v.* Potter, 3 Wis. 432.

3. Hoffheins *v.* Brandt, 3 Fisher. Pat. Cas. 218.

Admissions in Answer.—An admission in the answer is not waived by taking testimony on the subject. Jones *v.* Morehead, 1 Wall. (U. S.) 155.

And a disclaimer of desire to contest the patent, is an admission warranting a decree in sustaining the validity of the patent and finding infringement. Globe Nail Co. *v.* Superior Nail Co, 27 Fed. Rep. 454.

4. Potter *v.* Holland, 1 Fish. Pat. Cas. 382; s. c., 4 Blatchf. (U S.) 238; Magic Ruffle Co. *v.* Douglass, 2 Fish. Pat. Cas. 330; s. c., 5 Blatchf. (U. S.) 134; Lowell *v.* Lewis, 1 Mason (U. S.) 182; s. c., 1 Robb Pat. Cas. 121; Cox *v.* Griggs, 2 Fish. Pat. Cas. 174; s. c., 1 Biss. (U. S.) 362; Clark Patent etc. Co. *v.* Copeland, 2 Fish. Pat. Cas. 221; Poppenhusen *v.* New York etc. Comb Co., 2 Fish. Pat. Cas. 62; Waterman *v.* Thompson, 2 Fish. Pat. Cas. 461; Allen *v.* Hunter, 6 McLean (U. S.) 303; Alden *v.* Dewy, 1 Story (U. S.) 336; s. c., 2 Robb Pat. Cas. 17; Brooks *v.* Jenkins, 3 McLean (U. S.) 432; Heinrich *v.* Luther, 6 McLean (U. S.) 345; Wayne *v.* Holmes, 1 Bond (U. S.) 27; Woodworth *v.* Rogers, 3 Woodb. & M. (U. S.) 135; Hudson *v.* Draper, 4 Cliff. (U. S.) 178; s. c., 4 Fish. Pat. Cas. 253; Waterbury etc. Brass. Co. *v.* New York etc. Brass Co., 3 Fish. Pat. Cas. 43; Sands *v.* Wardwell, 3 Cliff. (U. S.) 277; Heating Co. *v.* Drummond, 3 Bann. & Ard. Pat. Cas. 138; Union Stone Co. *v.* Allen, 14 Fed. Rep. 353; Tilghman *v.* Werk, 1 Bond. (U. S.) 511; s. c., 2 Fish. Pat. Cas. 229; American Bell Teleph. Co. *v.* Globe Teleph. Co, 31 Fed. Rep. 729; Byerly *v.* Cleveland Linseed Oil Works, 31 Fed. Rep. 73; Good *v.* Baily, 33 Fed. Rep. 42; s. c., 41 Pat. Off. Gaz. 935; Osborne *v.* Glazier, 31 Fed. Rep. 402; American Box Mach. Co. *v.* Day, 32 Fed. Rep. 585; Bostock *v.* Goodrich, 21 Fed. Rep. 316; McMillin *v.* Vicksburg Anchor Line, 22 Fed. Rep. 169; Celluloid Mfg. Co. *v.* Chrolithion Collar etc. Co., 23 Fed. Rep. 397; Adams etc. Mfg. Co. *v.* Rathbone, 26 Fed. Rep. 262; American Box Mach. Co. *v.* Day, 32 Fed. Rep. 585; Konold *v.* Klein, 3 Bann. & Ard. Pat. Cas. 226; Wayne *v.* Holmes, 1 Bond (U. S.) 27; s. c., 2 Fish. Pat. Cas. 20; McClure *v.* Jeffrey, 8 Ind. 74; McBride *v.* Grand De Tour Plow Co., 40 Fed. Rep. 162; Mesker *v.* Thaener, 42 Fed. Rep. 329.

The presumption of validity has been held to arise also from the oath of the inventor filed with the application. *In re* Wagner, 1 MacArthur Pat. Cas. 510.

5. Serrell *v.* Collins, 1 Fish. Pat. Cas. 289; Conover *v.* Rapp, 4 Fish. Pat. Cas. 57; Forbes *v.* Barstow Stove Co., 2 Cliff. (U. S.) 379; Roberts *v.* Harnden, 2 Cliff. (U. S.) 500; Goodyear Dental etc. Co. *v.* Gardner, 4 Fish. Pat. Cas. 224; s. c., 2 Cliff. (U. S.) 408; Knight *v.* Baltimore etc. R. Co., 1 Taney (U. S.) 106; s. c., 3 Fish. Pat. Cas. 1; Sherman *v.* Champlain Transp. Co., 31 Vt. 162; Ayling *v.* Hull, 2 Cliff. (U. S.) 494; Whipple *v.* Baldwin etc. Mfg. Co., 4 Fish. Pat. Cas. 29; Bierce *v.* Stocking, 77 Mass. 174; Brooks *v.* Jenkins, 4 McLean (U. S.) 432; Ashcroft *v.* Cutter, 6 Blatchf. (U. S.) 511; Parham *v.* American Button etc. Mach. Co., 4 Fish. Pat. Cas. 468; Earle *v.*

presumption that they were such.[1] A patent is presumed to correspond with the application,[2] and there is a slight presumption that a person having a subsequent patent is not an infringer.[3]

(*b*) PRESUMPTION OF NON-INFRINGEMENT.—The presumption of innocence raises the presumption of non-infringement by the defendant.[4]

Sawyer, 4 Mason (U. S.) 1; s. c., 1 Robb Pat. Cas. 491; Whitney *v.* Emmett, 1 Baldw. (U. S.) 303; s. c., 1 Robb Pat. Cas. 567; Brodie *v.* Ophir etc. Min. Co., 5 Taney (U. S.) 608; Masury *v.* Tiemann, 8 Blatchf. (U. S.) 426; s. c., 4 Fish. Pat. Cas. 524; Tompkins *v.* Gage, 2 Fish. Pat. Cas. 577; Konold *v.* Klein, 3 Bann. & Ard. Pat. Cas. 26; Sands *v.* Wardwell, 3 Cliff. (U. S.) 277; Green *v.* French, 11 Fed. Rep. 591; s. c., 21 Pat. Off. Gaz. 1351; Magic Ruffle Co. *v.* Douglas, 2 Fish. Pat. Cas. 330; Sewall *v.* Jones, 91 U. S. 171; s. c., 9 Pat. Off. Gaz. 47; Crouch *v.* Spear, 1 Bann. & Ard. Pat. Cas. 145; s. c., 6 Pat. Off. Gaz. 187; Hawes *v.* Antisdel, 2 Bann. & Ard. Pat. Cas. 10; s. c., 8 Pat. Off. Gaz. 685; Taylor *v.* Wood, 12 Blatchf. (U. S.) 110; s. c., 1 Bann. & Ard. Pat. Cas. 270; s. c., 8 Pat. Off. Gaz. 90; Patterson *v.* Duff, 20 Fed. Rep. 641; Rogers *v.* Beecher, 3 Fed. Rep. 639; Eclypse Mfg. Co. *v.* Adkins, 44 Fed. Rep. 280.

This Presumption Strengthened by Extension.—Cook *v.* Ernest, 5 Fish. Pat. Cas. 396; s. c., 2 Pat. Off. Gaz. 89.

Date of Presumption of Novelty.—Presumption of novelty relates back to time of invention. Klein *v.* Russell, 19 Wall. (U. S.) 433.

Rebuttal of Presumption.—To overthrow the presumption arising from the patent, the proof must be clear. Magic Ruffle Co. *v.* Douglas, 2 Fish. Pat. Cas. 330; Crouch *v.* Spear, 1 Bann. & Ard. Pat. Cas. 145; s. c., 6 Pat. Off. Gaz. 187; Rogers *v.* Beeche, 3 Fed. Rep. 639; Miller *v.* Smith, 5 Fed. Rep. 359; s. c., 18 Pat. Off. Gaz. 1047; Stilwell etc. Mfg. Co. *v.* Cincinnati Gas Light etc. Co., 1 Bann. & Ard. Pat. Cas. 610; s. c., 7 Pat. Off. Gaz. 829.

1. Worden *v.* Fisher, 11 Fed. Rep. 505; s. c., 21 Pat. Off. Gaz. 1957; Godfried *v.* Brewing Co., 5 Bann & Ard. Pat. Cas. 4; s. c., 17 Pat. Off. Gaz. 675; Hotchkiss *v.* Greenwood, 4 McLean (U. S.) 456; Consolidated Bunging Apparatus *v.* Woerle, 29 Fed. Rep. 449; s. c., 38 Pat. Off. Gaz. 1015.

Similarly of a patent to a sole inventor. Puetz *v.* Bransford, 31 Fed. Rep. 458; s. c., 39 Pat. Off. Gaz. 1083. A foreign patent to the American patentee jointly with another, does not shift the burden of proof. Hoe *v.* Cottrell, 17 Blatchf. (U. S.) 546; s. c., 1 Fed. Rep. 597; s. c., 5 Bann. & Ard. Pat. Cas. 256; s. c., 18 Pat. Off. Gaz. 59.

2. Webster Loom Co. *v.* Higgins, 105 U. S. 580; s. c., 21 Pat. Off. Gaz. 2031.

Presumption of Title.—There is a presumption that the owner of the patent has not parted with any of his rights. Watson *v.* Smith, 7 Fed. Rep. 350; s. c., 20 Pat. Off. Gaz. 300.

3. Coming *v.* Burden, 15 How. (U. S.) 252; American Pin Co. *v.* Oakville Co., 3 Blatchf. (U. S.) 190; Stearns *v.* Barrett, 1 Mason (U. S.) 153; s. c., 1 Robb Pat. Cas. 97; Smith *v.* Woodruff, 1 McArthur (U. S.) 459; s. c., 6 Fish. Pat. Cas. 476; s. c., 4 Pat. Off. Gaz. 635; Westlake *v.* Carter, 6 Fish. Pat. Cas. 519; s. c., 4 Pat. Off. Gaz. 636; Trader *v.* Missmore, 1 Bann. & Ard. Pat. Cas. 639; s. c., 7 Pat. Off. Gaz. 385; New York Rubber Co. *v.* Chaskel, 9 Pat. Off. Gaz. 923.

Other Presumptions Arising Out of Patent.—That the date of application was the date of grant. Worley *v.* Loker Tobacco Co., 104 U. S. 340; s. c., 21 Pat. Off. Gaz. 559.

That the patent unlimited on its face is not to be limited by a prior foreign patent to same inventor. American etc. Boring Co. *v.* Sheldon, 17 Blatchf. (U. S.) 303; s. c., 4 Bann. & Ard. Pat. Cas. 603.

4. Union Sugar Refinery *v.* Mathieson, 3 Cliff. (U. S.) 639; s. c., 2 Fish. Pat. Cas. 600; Bell *v.* Daniels, 1 Bond (U. S.) 212; s. c., 1 Fish. Pat. Cas. 372; Forbes *v.* Barstow Stove Co., 2 Cliff. (U. S.) 379; Hudson *v.* Draper, 4 Fish. Pat. Cas. 256; s. c., 4 Cliff. (U. S.) 178; Francis *v.* Mellor, 5 Fish. Pat. Cas. 153; s. c., 1 Pat. Off. Gaz. 48; Price *v.* Kelley, 20 Pat. Off. Gaz. 1452; Lehigh Valley R. Co. *v.* Mellon, 104 U. S. 112; s. c., 20 Pat. Off. Gaz. 1891; Dixon *v.* Moyer, 1 Robb Pat. Cas. 324; s. c., 4 Wash. (U. S.) 68; Roger *v.* Chicago

3. Judicial Notice.—The court will take notice of scientific matters of common knowledge.[1]

Mfg. Co., 20 Fed. Rep. 853; Mallory Mfg. Co. *v.* Hickok, 25 Fed. Rep. 827; American etc. Purifier Co. *v.* Atlantic Milling Co., 4 Dill. (U. S.) 100; s. c., 4 Bann. & Ard. Pat. Cas. 148; s. c., 15 Pat. Off. Gaz. 467; Hayden *v.* Suffolk Mfg. Co., 4 Fish. Pat. Cas. 86.

Where the evidence of infringement is not clear it is insufficient. Hill *v.* Holyoke Envelope Co., 30 Fed. Rep. 623; Reay *v.* Rau, 15 Fed. Rep. 749.

What is held sufficient evidence of infringement. Kiesele *v.* Haas, 32 Fed. Rep. 794; Dryfoos *v.* Friedman, 21 Blatchf. 563; s. c., 18 Fed. Rep. 824; Peterson *v.* Simpkins, 25 Fed. Rep. 486; Spring *v.* Domestic Sewing Mach. Co., 9 Fed. Rep. 505; Woven Wire Mattress Co. *v.* Wire Bed Co., 8 Fed. Rep. 87; Fischer *v.* Hayes, 6 Fed. Rep. 86; Fischer *v.* O'Shaughnessey, 6 Fed. Rep. 92; Gear *v.* Fitch, 3 Bann. & Ard. Pat. Cas. 573; s. c., 16 Pat. Off. Gaz. 1231; Union Paper Bag Mach. Co. *v.* Binney, 5 Fish. Pat. Cas. 166; Eastman *v.* Bodfish, 1 Story (U. S.) 528; Colleng *v.* Jackson, 45 Fed. Rep. 639; Schneider *v.* Missouri Glass Co., 36 Fed. Rep. 582.

Burden of Proof When Shifted.—The burden of proof is shifted to the complainant to establish a prior invention, when an invention prior to the date of application. Thayer *v.* Hart, 22 Blatchf. (U. S.) 229.

Burden of proof is on defendant to show non-infringement when the court was satisfied that the devices were the same. National Hat Pouncing Mach. Co. *v.* Thom, 25 Fed. Rep. 496.

Other Miscellaneous Presumptions.—That mechanics who take out a patent or build a machine are conversant with the state of the art. Crompton *v.* Knowles, 7 Fed. Rep. 204; James *v.* Campbell, 104 U. S. 356.

1. That iron and steel may be successfully welded without a flux. Needham *v.* Washburn, 7 Pat. Off. Gaz. 749. The existence of the common forms of ice cream freezers. Brown *v.* Piper, 91 U. S. 37; s. c., 10 Pat. Off. Gaz. 417. The ordinary construction of sewer traps. McKloskey *v.* Dubois, 8 Fed. Rep. 710; s. c., 19 Blatchf. (U. S.) 205; s. c., 19 Pat. Off. Gaz. 1286. Marking out soles on leather so that they would fit with each other and save material. Walker *v.* Rawson, 4 Bann. & Ard. Pat. Cas. 128. The use of water to remove obstructions in sinking piles. Knapp *v.* Benedict, 26 Fed. Rep. 627. See also Terhune *v.* Phillips, 99 U. S. 592; Quirolo *v.* Ardito, 17 Blatchf. (U. S.) 400; Snow *v.* Taylor, 14 Pat. Off. Gaz. 861; Anson *v.* Woodbury, 12 Pat. Off. Gaz. 1; King *v.* Gallun, 109 U. S. 99; s. c., 25 Pat. Off. Gaz. 980; Slawson *v.* Grand St. etc. R. Co., 107 U. S. 649; s. c., 24 Pat. Off. Gaz. 99; Torrent etc. Lumber Co. *v.* Rodgers, 112 U. S. 659; s. c., 30 Pat. Off. Gaz. 449; Phillips *v.* Detroit, 111 U. S. 604; Reed *v.* Lawrence, 29 Fed. Rep. 915.

The court will consider scientific facts of general knowledge when the bill is demurred to for want of novelty in the patent. New York Belting Co. *v.* New Jersey Car Spring etc. Co., 30 Fed. Rep. 785.

It will take judicial notice of things in common use in such case. West *v.* Rae, 38 Fed. Rep. 45.

And may declare the patent invalid. Fougeres *v.* Murbarger, 44 Fed. Rep. 292; Nicodemus *v.* Frazier, 19 Fed. Rep. 260.

But will not do so in a doubtful case. Standard Oil Co. *v.* Southern Pac. R. Co., 42 Fed. Rep. 295.

Where an article required some time to get on the market, the court will presume that in due course of business it took some time to produce the articles before they were found on the market. Wen *v.* Morden, 21 Fed. Rep. 243.

That the file wrapper is frequently altered in the Patent Office. Hoe *v.* Kahlter, 23 Blatchf. (U. S.) 354.

Of What the Court Will Not Take Judicial Notice.—The Model of an invention. Everett *v.* Thatcher, 3 Bann. & Ard. Pat. Cas. 435.

Of matters of science, not strictly of common knowledge. Kaolatype Engraving Co. *v.* Hoke, 30 Fed. Rep. 444. Of Facts of which experts differ. St. Louis Gas Light etc. Co. *v.* American F. Ins. Co., 33 Mo. App. 348. See also Finger *v.* Kingston (Supreme Ct.), 9 N. Y. Supp. 175.

Of What It Will Take Judicial Notice.—Of the meaning of the word "whisky." Frese *v.* State, 23 Fla. 267.

Of the existence and construction of grain elevators at a certain date. Richards *v.* Michigan etc. R. Co., 40 Fed. Rep. 165.

4. Documentary Evidence—(*a*) CERTIFIED COPIES.—Certified copies of patents and other papers in the Patent Office are evidence in the same manner as the original should be.[1]

(*b*) OTHER DOCUMENTS.—In the case of other documents the ordinary rules of evidence are applied.[2]

(*c*) FILE WRAPPER AND CONTENTS.—The file wrapper and its contents containing the correspondence between the Patent Office and the applicant may be put in evidence as part of the *res gestæ* and used to aid in the construction of the patent and for other purposes.[3]

Of the shape, size and construction of uncommon wagon axles. Studebaker etc. Mfg. Co. *v.* Illinois Iron etc. Co., 42 Fed. Rep. 52.

1. U. S. Rev. Stats., §§ 882, 883, 884; Foster's Fed. Practice, § 268 and cases there cited; Peck *v.* Farrington, 9 Wend. (N. Y.) 44.

A certified copy of a restored drawing is evidence. Emerson *v.* Hogg, 2 Blatchf. (U. S.) 1.

Also a certified copy of an assignment. Brooks *v.* Jenkins, 3 McLean (U. S.) 432.

A certified copy of a surrendered and cancelled patent, is competent evidence to prove prior invention. Delano *v.* Scott, 1 Gilp. (U. S.) 489; s. c., 1 Robb Pat. Cas. 700.

Specifications.—See Davis *v.* Gray, 17 Ohio St. 330. See Marsh *v.* Nichols, 128 U. S. 608; Tinker *v.* Wilbur etc. Mfg. Co., 1 Fed. Rep. 138; s. c., 5 Bann. & Ard. Pat. Cas. 92.

As to foreign patents, see Schoerken *v.* Swift etc. Mfg. Co., 19 Blatchf. (U. S.) 209; s. c., 7 Fed. Rep. 469; s. c., 19 Pat. Off. Gaz. 493; 1 Peck *v.* Farrington, 9 Wend. (N. Y.) 44; *Ex parte* Trotter, 32 Pat. Off. Gaz. 1603.

As to disclaimers, see Foote *v.* Silsby, 1 Blatchf. (U. S.) 445.

2. **Minute Books of Corporation.**—Pennock *v.* Dialogue, 4 Wash. (U. S.) 538; s. c., 2 Pet. (U. S.) 1; s. c., 1 Robb. Pat. Cas. 466, 542. A French patent certified by a "Directeur de la Conservatoire National des Arts et Metiers de la France," under seal of Minister of Agriculture and Commerce, and Minister of Foreign Affairs, is admissible under the statute. Schoerken *v.* Swift etc. Mfg. Co., 19 Blatchf. (U. S.) 209; s. c., 7 Fed. Rep. 469; s. c., 19 Pat. Off. Gaz. 1493.

Receipts.—Burdell *v.* Dewy, 92 U. S. 716.

Sealed instruments consideration. Day *v.* Hartshorn, 3 Fish. Pat. Cas. 32.

Admissions.—Evidence produced by a party at the preliminary injunction motion, is evidence for the other party as admission of the party. Western Union Tel. Co. *v.* Baltimore etc. R. Co., 26 Fed. Rep. 55.

Amending a subsequent patent by defendant to avoid the patent sued on, is an admission of the validity of that patent. Sugar Apparatus Mfg. Co. *v.* Yaryan Mfg. Co., 43 Fed. Rep. 140.

An exhibit filed in a case in pencil, will not be compelled to be changed to an ink one, on motion of opposing party. Tutman *v.* Watson Mfg. Co., 44 Fed. Rep. 429.

A prior pending application is evidence on the question of priority of invention. Westinghouse *v.* Chartiers Valley Gas Co., 43 Fed. Rep. 582.

3. Allen *v.* Blunt, 2 Woodb. & M. (U. S.) 121; s. c., 2 Robb Pat. Cas. 530; Pike *v.* Potter, 3 Fish. Pat. Cas. 55; Goodyear Dental etc. Co. *v.* Davis, 102 U. S. 222; s. c., 19 Pat. Off. Gaz. 543; Pettibone *v.* Derringer, 4 Wash. (U. S.) 215; s. c., 1 Robb Pat. Cas. 152; Sulter *v.* Robinson, 119 U. S. 630; s. c., 38 Pat. Off. Gaz. 230.

We do not mean to be understood as asserting that any correspondence between an applicant and the Commissioner of Patents can be allowed to enlarge, diminish or vary the language of a patent afterwards issued. Undoubtedly a patent like any other written instrument, is to be interpreted by its own terms; but when a patent bears on its face a particular construction, inasmuch as the specification and claim are in the words of the patentee, it is reasonable to hold that such a construction may be confirmed by what the patentee said when he was making his application. The understanding of a party to a contract has always been regarded as of some importance in its interpretation. Goodyear Dental etc. Co.

5. Exhibits—(*a*) PRIOR DEVICES.—Devices prior to the patentee's invention may be introduced into evidence and are relevant with reference to the question of novelty of the complainant's patent,[1] or of public use.[2]

(*b*) MODEL OF THE INVENTION.—A model of the invention is evidence to determine whether it involves patentable novelty[3] and infringement.[4]

6. Expert Evidence—(*a*) RELEVANCY.—Expert evidence in patent cases is relevant to determine the meaning of the terms of the art,[5] the identity or dissimilarity of mechanical structures,[6] or of principle.[7]

(*b*) IRRELEVANCY.—Expert evidence is not relevant to determine a question of law,[8] to determine a question of fact,[9] or on a

v. Davis, 102 U. S. 222; s. c., 19 Pat. Off. Gaz. 543.

Not Evidence.—The report of the examiner and the decision of the Commissioner upon the question of an extension is not evidence of the invalidity of the original patent. McMahon *v.* Tyng, 14 Allen (Mass.) 167.

When a patent to a third party is set up to prove prior use, the file wrapper is not evidence to prove that the invention was made when the oath was taken. It is *res inter alios*. Howes *v.* McNeal, 4 Fed. Rep. 151; s. c., 5 Bann. & Ard. Pat. Cas. 77; s. c., 17 Pat. Off. Gaz. 799.

1. Judson *v.* Cope, 1 Bond (U. S.) 327; s. c., 1 Fish. Pat. Cas. 615; Miller *v.* Smith, 5 Fed. Rep. 359; Singer *v.* Walmsley, 1 Fish. Pat. Cas. 558.

2. Carter *v.* Baker, 1 Sawy. (U. S.) 512; s. c., 4 Fish. Pat. Cas. 404.

3. Everett *v.* Thatcher, 3 Bann. & Ard. Pat. Cas. 435; s. c., 2 Flipp. (U. S.) 234; s. c., 16 Pat. Off. Gaz. 1046: Morris *v.* Barrett, 1 Bond (U. S.) 254.

A certified copy of the Patent Office model is not conclusive evidence of the character of the model. Johnsen *v.* Beard, 2 Bann. & Ard. Pat. Cas. 50; s. c., 8 Pat. Off. Gaz. 435.

4. Evans *v.* Hettick, 3 Wash. (U. S.) 408; s. c., 1 Robb Pat. Cas. 417; Seymour *v.* Osborne, 1 Wall. (U. S.) 516; Smith *v.* Pearce, 2 McLean (U. S.) 176.

But exhibits should be properly explained. Miller *v.* Smith, 5 Fed. Rep. 359; s. c., 18 Pat. Off. Gaz. 1047.

5. Corning *v.* Burden, 15 How. (U. S.) 252; Jackson *v* Allen, 120 Mass. 64; Winans *v.* New York etc. R. Co., 1 Fish. Pat. Cas. 213; Day *v.* Stellman, 1 Fish. Pat. Cas. 487; Ely *v.* Monson etc. Mfg. Co., 4 Fish. Pat. Cas. 64; Cahoon *v.* Ring, 1 Cliff. (U. S.) 592; s. c., 1 Fish. Pat. Cas. 397; Many *v.* Sizer, 1 Fish. Pat. Cas. 17; Ingels *v.* Mast, 6 Fish. Pat. Cas. 415. And generally a knowledge of the art. Johnson *v.* Root, 1 Fish. Pat. Cas. 551.

The consideration of the patent application in the Patent Office is expert testimony. Westlake *v.* Cartter, 6 Fish. Pat. Cas. 519.

6. Corning *v.* Burden, 15 How. (U. S.) 252; Barrett *v.* Hall, 1 Mason (U. S.) 447.

7. Barrett *v.* Hall, 1 Mason (U. S.) 447; s. c., 1 Robb Pat. Cas. 207; Conover *v.* Rapp, 4 Fish. Pat. Cas. 57; Tillotson *v.* Ramsay, 51 Vt. 309; Tucker *v.* Spaulding, 13 Wall. (U. S.) 453; s. c., 1 Pat. Off. Gaz. 144.

The admission of expert evidence is in the discretion of the court; it is not error to refuse to admit it. 3 Rob. on Pat., § 10, 14.

See Pullman *v.* Baltimore etc. R. Co., 4 Hughes (U. S.) 236; s. c., 5 Fed. Rep. 72; s. c., 19 Pat. Off. Gaz. 224.

8. Ely *v.* Munson etc. Mfg. Co., 4 Fish. Pat. Cas. 64; Corning *v.* Burden, 15 How. (U. S.) 252; Waterbury Brass Co. *v.* New York etc. Brass Co., 3 Fish, Pat. Cas. 43; Tompkins *v.* Butterfield, 33 Pat. Off. Gaz. 758.

9. McMahon *v.* Tyng, 14 Allen (Mass.) 167.

Weight of Expert Evidence.—Its weight is to be considered by the jury. Barrett *v.* Hall, 1 Mason (U. S.) 467; Carter *v.* Baker, 1 Sawy. (U. S.) 512; St. Louis Gaslight Co. *v.* American F. Ins. Co., 33 Mo. App. 348; May *v.* Fond du Lac Co., 27 Fed. Rep. 691.

And the reasons given by the expert for his opinion are to be taken into consideration. Jordan *v.* Dobson, 2 Abb. (U. S.) 398; Seymour *v.* Marsh, 9 Phila (Pa.) 380; Parham *v.* American

mere matter of speculation.[1]

7. Evidence of the State of the Art.—Evidence, whether of exhibits[2]

Buttonhole Mach. Co., 4 Fish. Pat. Cas. 468; Johnson *v.* Root, 1 Fish. Pat. Cas. 351; United States Annunciator etc. Co. *v.* Sanderson, 3 Blatchf. (U. S.) 184; Béné *v.* Jeantet, 129 U. S. 685.

1. Judson *v.* Cape, 1 Bond (U. S.) 327; s. c., 1 Fish. Pat. Cas. 615.

The credibility of an expert witness is a question of fact to be taken in con sideration with other things. Johnson *v.* Root, 1 Fish. Pat. Cas. 351; Bierce *v.* Stocking, 11 Gray (Mass.) 171; Tucker *v.* Spaulding, 13 Wall. (U. S.) 453; s. c., 1 Pat. Off. Gaz. 144; May *v.* Fond Du Lac, 27 Fed. Rep. 691; Carter *v.* Baker, 1 Sawy. (U. S.) 512; United States Annunciator etc. Co. *v.* Sanderson, 3 Blatchf. (U. S.) 184; Many cases could be cited; the principle is well established.

Various criticisms of expert testimony in patent cases which may be of value, are given in the following cases: Winans *v.* New York etc. R. Co., 1 Fish. Pat. Cas. 213; Conover *v.* Rapp, 4 Fish. Pat. Cas. 57; Tilghman *v.* Mitchel, 4 Fish. Pat. Cas. 599; King *v.* Leoisville Cement Co., 6 Fish. Pat. Cas. 336; s. c, 4 Pat. Off. Gaz. 181; Sargent *v.* Carter, 1 Fish. Pat. Cas. 277; United States Annunciator etc. Co. *v.* Sanderson, 3 Blatchf. (U. S.) 184; Barrett *v.* Hall, 1 Mason (U. S.) 447; Adams *v.* Jones, 1 Fish. Pat. Cas. 527; Cox *v.* Grigg, 1 Biss. (U. S.) 362 s. c., 2 Fish. Pat. Cas. 174; Hoffheins *v.* Brandt, 3 Fish. Pat. Cas. 18; Middlings Purifier Co. *v.* Christian, 4 Dill. (U. S.) 448; Steam Gauge and Lantern Co. *v.* Hame Mfg. Co., 28 Fed. Rep. 618

What Is a Mechanical Expert.—An expert is one skilled in the art or science to which his opinion or judgment appertains. Page *v.* Ferry, 1 Fish. Pat. Cas. 298.

Artisans skilled in the trade to which the patented improvement belongs. Allen *v.* Blunt, 3 Story (U. S.) 742; Page *v.* Ferry, 1 Fish. Pat. Cas. 298.

Persons conversant with scientific mechanics are competent though not artisans. Allen *v.* Blunt, 3 Story (U. S.) 742.

The president of a manufacturing company who has taken out patents and is familiar with the art, is a competent expert. Sugar Apparatus Mfg. Co. *v.* Yaryan Mfg. Co., 43 Fed. Rep. 140.

An expert only can give opinion evidence. Toohey *v.* Harding, 4 Hughes (U. S.) 253.

Admissions by Experts.—The admission of an expert against the interest of the calling party is conclusive if uncontradicted. Wells *v.* Jaques, 1 Bann. & Ard. Pat. Cas. 60.

Expert Not Indispensable.—An expert need not be called to show an infringemenf where the case is clear. Bostock *v.* Goodrich, 21 Fed. Rep. 316; Hayes *v.* Bickelhoupt, 23 Fed. Rep. 183; Doyle *v.* Spaulding, 19 Fed. Rep. 744.

And will not prevail over facts. Tilghman *v.* Werk, 1 Bond (U. S.) 511; s. c., 2 Fish. Pat. Cas. 229; Hudson *v.* Draper, 4 Cliff. (U. S.) 178; s. c., 4 Fish. Pat. Cas. 256; Seymour *v.* Marsh, 6 Fish. Pat. Cas. 118; s. c., 2 Pat. Off. Gaz. 675.

The court may call an expert of its own independent of those summoned by the parties. Analine Fabrik *v.* Levinstein, L. R., Ch. D. (Eng.) 156; King *v.* Louisville Cement Co., 6 Fish. Pat. Cas. 336. Or examine for itself. La Baw *v.* Hawkins, 1 Bann. & Ard. Pat. Cas. 428; s. c., 6 Pat. Off. Gaz. 724.

Contradictory expert evidence is of small value. Pullman *v.* Baltimore etc. R. Co., 4 Hughes (U. S.) 236; s. c., 5 Fed. Rep. 72; s. c., 19 Pat. Off. Gaz. 224.

A decree may be given for complainant merely on the expert testimony, if it is supported by models, etc. Tsheppe *v.* Bernheim, 42 Fed. Rep. 59.

2. Stevenson *v.* Macgowan, 30 Fed. Rep. 824; American Clay Bird *v.* Ligowiski Clay Pigeon Co., 30 Fed. Rep. 466; Geier *v.* Goetinger, 1 Bann. & Ard. Pat. Cas. 553; s. c., 7 Pat. Off. Gaz. 563.

Patents.—Eachus *v.* Broomall, 115 U. S. 429.

But a scientific work cannot be offered in evidence to show the state of the art. Westlake *v.* Cartter, 6 Fish. Pat. Cas. 519. Nor can memoranda; but these last may be used to refresh the memory of a witness. Jones *v.* Wetherill, 1 MacArthur's Pat. Cas. 404.

A Patent Office examiner is com-

or oral,[1] is admissible to show the state of the art[2] at the time of the invention. This evidence, provided it does not go to establish a lack of novelty in the complainant's patent, need not be given notice of beforehand.[3]

8. Evidence of Prior Use or Lack of Novelty.—The best evidence of prior use or of an existence of a patented device prior to the time of the invention by the patentee, is the production of the device itself and its proper identification.[4] The testimony of witnesses who have seen the device is much less satisfactory,[5] and

petent to prove what documents are in Patent Office. Sone *v.* Palmer, 28 Mo. 539.

1. Zane *v.* Loffe, 2 Fed. Rep. 229.

An expert called to show identity between the complainant's invention and defendant's device, cannot be requested not to go into the state of the art. American Linoleum Mfg. Co. *v.* Union Linoleum Co., 44 Fed. Rep. 755.

2. Dunbar *v.* Meyers, 94 U. S. 187; s. c., 11 Pat. Off. Gaz. 35; Zane *v.* Loffe, 2 Fed. Rep. 229: Nashua Lock Co. *v.* Norwich Lock Mfg. Co., 32 Fed. Rep. 87; Ausable Horse Nail Co. *v.* Essex Horse Nail Co., 32 Fed. Rep. 94.

3. Zane *v.* Loffe, 2 Fed. Rep. 229; Grier *v.* Wilt, 120 U. S. 412; Eachus *v.* Bromall, 115 U. S. 429; Vance *v.* Campbell, 1 Fish. Pat. Cas. 483; Brown *v.* Piper, 91 U. S. 37; Westlake *v.* Cartter, 6 Fish. Pat. Cas. 519; s. c., 4 Pat. Off. Gaz. 636; Delong *v.* Bickford, 13 Fed. Rep. 32; American Saddle Co. *v.* Hogg, 1 Holmes (U. S.) 133: Philadelphia etc. R. Co. *v.* Dubois, 12 Wall. (U. S.) 47.

4. Hawes *v.* Antisdel, 2 Bann. & Ard. Pat. Cas. 10; s. c., 8 Pat. Off. Gaz. 685; Buchan *v* McKesson, 18 Blatchf. (U. S.) 485; s. c., 7 Fed. Rep. 100; s. c., 19 Pat. Off. Gaz. 222.

The non-production of an alleged prior machine works against those refusing to produce it. Bailey etc. Wringing Machine Co. *v.* Lincoln, 4 Fish. Pat. Cas. 379.

Evidence.—Priority of invention is made out where a sample of the prior device is produced and identified by several witnesses whose character for veracity plaintiffs have failed to substantially affect. Miller *v.* Foree, 33 Pat. Off. Gaz. 1497; Pennock *v.* Dialogue, 4 Wash. (U. S.) 538.

Negative Testimony.—Negative Testimony of the non-existence of a device, is entitled, as a rule, to less weight than to positive testimony of the existence of such a device. Hawes *v.* Antisdel, 2 Bann. & Ard. Pat. Cas. 10; s. c., 8 Pat. Off. Gaz. 685; Cornell *v.* Hyatt, 1 McArthur Pat. Cas. 423. But an exception exists where the witnesses testifying would have been likely to have known of the prior use had it existed. American Ballastlog Co. *v.* Cotter, 11 Fed. Rep. 728; s. c., 21 Pat. Off. Gaz. 1030; Shirley *v.* Sanderson, 8 Fed. Rep. 905.

5. Hawes *v.* Antisdel, 2 Bann. & Ard. Pat. Cas. 10; s. c., 8 Pat. Off. Gaz. 688; Sinclair *v.* Backus, 4 Fed. Rep. 539; s. c., 5 Bann. & Ard. Pat. Cas. 81; s. c., 17 Pat. Off. Gaz. 1503; Green *v.* French, 11 Fed. Rep. 591; s. c., 21 Pat. Off. Gaz. 1351; Woven Wire Mattress Co. *v.* Wire Bed Co., 8 Fed. Rep. 87; Zane *v.* Peck, 9 Fed. Rep. 101; Washburne etc. Mfg. Co. *v.* Harsh, 10 Biss. (U. S.) 68; s. c., 4 Fed. Rep. 900; s. c., 19 Fed. Rep. 173; Greenwood *v.* Bracher, 1 Fed. Rep. 856; Sayles *v.* Chicago etc. R. Co., 1 Biss. (U. S.) 468; s. c., 2 Fish. Pat. Cas. 523; Wing *v.* Richardson, 2 Cliff. (U. S.) 449; Stephens *v.* Salisbury, 1 McArthur Pat. Cas. 379; Richardson *v.* Hicks, 1 McArthur Pat. Cas. 335; Zinner *v.* Kremer, 39 Fed. Rep. 111. But where the oral evidence of witness speaking largely from memory, is coupled with corroborative circumstances, the presumption of novelty will be overcome. Doubleday *v.* Beatty, 11 Fed. Rep. 729; Simmonds *v.* Morrison, 44 Fed. Rep. 757.

A circumstantial account of a series of experiments ending successfully corroborated, will overcome presumption of patent. Electrical Accumulator Co. *v.* Julien Electric Co., 38 Fed. Rep. 117.

And generally the circumstances throwing doubt on the testimony of a witness will also be considered. Atlantic etc. Powder Co. *v.* Dittmar Powder Co., 17 Blatchf. (U. S.) 531; s. c., 5 Bann. & Ard. Pat. Cas. 222; s. c., 17 Pat. Off. Gaz. 969; Milmann *v.* Bartholomae etc. Brewing Co., 41 Fed. Rep. 132.

in all cases the testimony must clearly establish the facts set forth.[1]

9. **Privilege.**—While the ordinary privileges attach to a patent suit,[2] no extra privileges can be given a party by the rules of the Patent Office.[3]

XVIII. **Practice—1. Generally.**—Practice in equity in patent cases is substantially governed by the ordinary equity rules[4] and

An inventor's testimony tending to invalidate his patent will be looked on with a great deal of suspicion. Sinclair *v.* Backus, 4 Fed. Rep. 539; s. c., 5 Bann. & Ard. Pat. Cas. 81; s. c., 17 Pat. Off. Gaz. 1503.

A long space of time between the date of observation of the device and the date of testimony tends to discredit the evidence. Wing *v.* Richardson, 2 Cliff. (U. S.) 449; s. c., 2 Fish. Pat. Cas. 535; Sayles *v.* Chicago etc. R. Co., 1 Biss. (U. S.) 468; Ely *v.* Monson etc. Mfg. Co., 4 Fish. Pat. Cas. 64; Sickles *v.* Gloucester Mfg. Co., 3 Wall. Jr. (C. C.) 196; Parker *v.* Hulme, 7 West 417; Tatum *v.* Gregory, 41 Fed. Rep. 142; Electrical Accumulator Co. *v.* Julien Electric Co., 38 Fed. Rep. 117.

1. Wood *v.* Union Iron Works, 4 Fish. Pat. Cas. 550; Parham *v.* American Button etc. Mach. Co., 4 Fish. Pat. Cas. 468; Sayles *v.* Chicago etc. R. Co., 4 Fish. Pat. Cas. 584; Crouch *v.* Speir, 1 Bann. & Ard. Pat. Cas. 145; s. c., 6 Pat. Off. Gaz. 187; Bostock *v.* Goodrich, 21 Fed. Rep. 316; Thayer *v.* Hart, 22 Blatchf. (U. S.) 229; s. c., 20 Fed. Rep. 693; s. c., 28 Pat. Off. Gaz. 542; United States Stamping Co. *v.* Jewett, 18 Blatchf. (U. S.) 469; Wilson *v.* Coon, 18 Blatchf. (U. S.) 532; s. c., 6 Fed. Rep. 611; s. c., 19 Pat. Off. Gaz. 482; Miller *v.* Smith, 5 Fed. Rep. 359; Carter *v.* Carter, 1 MacArthur Pat. Cas. 388. Both the existence of the anticipation and its similarity to the invented device must be clearly shown. Cottier *v.* Stimson, 20 Fed. Rep. 906.

2. Privilege of counsel. Edison Electric Light Co. *v.* United States Electric Lighting Co., 44 Fed. Rep. 294.

Which privilege, however, is waived by putting in evidence, any communication relating to a transaction, so far as that transaction is concerned. Western Union Tel. Co. *v.* Baltimore etc. Tel. Co., 26 Fed. Rep. 55; Edison Electric Light Co. *v.* United States Electric Lighting Co., 45 Fed. Rep. 55. Or from betraying his business secrets. Roberts *v.* Walley, 14 Fed. Rep. 167.

A defendant can be compelled to state whether he has in his possession, the machine alleged to be an improvement before a *prima facie* case is made out. Delamater *v.* Reinhardt, 43 Fed. Rep. 76.

3. Edison Electric Light Co. *v.* United States Electric Lighting Co., 44 Fed. Rep. 294.

The applicant for a patent can be compelled to bring in all papers which may be the best evidence, relating to an application for patent by *subpœna duces tecum*. Edison Electric Light Co. *v.* United States Electric Lighting Co., 44 Fed. Rep. 294.

4. A circuit court was an authority to rescind a rule adopted by the supreme court for the government of its practice in chancery. Jenkins *v.* Greenwald, 1 Bond (U. S.) 126.

Exceptions to the rule in English chancery practice are equally binding with the rules. Brooks *v.* Bicknell, 3 McLean (U. S.) 250; s. c., 2 Robb Pat. Cas. 118.

Appearance and answer is a waiver of an irregularity in serving the subpœna. Goodyear *v.* Chaffee, 3 Blatchf. (U. S.) 268.

Equitable and Legal Title.—The court will protect the real owners against those who are only nominal owners. Campbell *v.* James, 2 Fed. Rep. 338; s. c., 18 Blatchf. (U. S.) 42; s. c., 5 Bann. & Ard. Pat. Cas. 354; s. c., 18 Pat. Off. Gaz. 1111; Dean *v.* Mason, 20 How. (U. S.) 198.

Retention of Suit.—See Lockwood *v.* Cutter Tower Co., 11 Fed. Rep. 724; Miller *v.* Liggett etc. Tobacco Co., 7 Fed. Rep. 91.

Issue at Law.—Watt *v.* Starke, 101 U. S. 247; s. c., 17 Pat. Off. Gaz. 1093.

When Infringement Must be Shown.—An infringement prior to the filing of the bill must be shown. Slessinger *v.* Buckingham, 8 Sawy. (U. S.) 469.

Leave to dismiss will not be granted where an answer has been filed, setting up an affirmative defense and proofs have been taken. Electrical Ac-

doctrines.[1]

2. Cross-Bills.—A cross-bill is filed where the defendant desires to obtain some affirmative relief or a discovery from the complainant.[2]

3. Bill of Revivor.—A bill of revivor is employed in patent as in other equity causes to substitute his representatives for a deceased

cumulator Co. *v.* Brush Electric Co., 44 Fed. Rep. 602.

Leave to Take Additional Testimony.—To obtain leave to introduce testimony after the time for taking it is past, the character of the testimony must be clearly disclosed. Streat *v.* Streinam, 38 Fed. Rep. 548.

But the court may grant leave to take further testimony even when the case is before it for final hearing. Frazer *v.* Gates etc. Iron Works, 22 Fed. Rep. 439.

A court may take notice that the patent is void even upon a motion made to increase the damages already awarded. Welling *v.* Le Baw, 35 Fed. Rep. 302.

1. Permission to Introduce New Evidence.—The court can admit evidence after the time for taking it has expired, and can set terms on its admission. Goodyear *v.* Beverly Rubber Co., 1 Cliff. (U. S.) 348; Stainthorp *v.* Humiston, 4 Fish. Pat. Cas. 107; Knapp *v.* Shaw, 15 Fed. Rep. 115; s. c., 23 Pat. Off. Gaz. 2236. But will do so only when it appears likely the desired testimony will be secured. Hicks *v.* Otto, 17 Fed. Rep. 539.

Divided Court.—Where court is divided on a question of infringement, decree will go for defendant. California Art Stone Paving Co. *v.* Moliter, 119 U. S. 401; s. c., 38 Pat. Off. Gaz. 329.

Waivers.—See Jenkins *v.* Greenwald, 1 Bond (U. S.) 126; s. c., 2 Fish. Pat. Cas. 37.

Parol Agreements of Counsel.—See American Saddle Co. *v.* Hogg, 1 Holmes (U. S.) 13; s. c., 6 Fish. Pat. Cas. 67; s. c., 2 Pat. Off. Gaz. 595.

What may be awarded under prayer for general relief. Emerson *v.* Simm, 6 Fish. Pat. Cas. 281; s. c., 3 Pat. Off. Gaz. 293.

Defects in the Return.—Where the defect appears on the face of the return, a motion to quash the service or abate the writ is the proper mode of bringing the matter to the attention of the court. Objections not appearing on the face of the return are sometimes taken by motion to dismiss or set aside the service; but the better practice is by plea in abatement. United States *v.* American Bell Teleph. Co., 29 Fed. Rep. 17.

Decree Pro Confesso.—Decree *pro confesso* is made by the court. Thomson *v.* Wooster, 114 U. S. 104.

And after a decree *pro confesso* the defendant cannot assail the patent. Dobson *v.* Hartford Carpet Co., 114 U. S. 439.

2. A cross bill must be filed by leave of court after due notice to complainant, and no order of publication can be obtained on a cross bill against a non-resident complainant. Webster Loom Co. *v.* Short, 10 Pat. Off. Gaz. 1019. But a cross bill may be filed in a suit in which the complainant is a non-resident. Birdsell *v.* Hagerstown etc. Mfg. Co., 11 Pat. Off. Gaz. 641. In such case a substituted service on the solicitor may be made. Johnson Railway Signal Co. *v.* Union Switch etc. Co., 43 Fed. Rep. 331.

The respondent is not prevented from filing a cross bill because he has previously filed a bill in a State court for the same purpose, and a new party may be brought in. Prime *v.* Brandon Mfg. Co., 14 Blatchf. (U. S.) 371; s. c., 3 Bann. & Ard. Pat. Cas. 191.

A cross bill may be filed by a manufacturer against whom a suit is brought to prevent the complainant from bringing suit against his customers. Birdsell *v.* Hagerstown etc. Mfg. Co., 11 Pat. Off. Gaz. 641.

A cross bill by an assignor, in a suit by his assignee against him for infringement of the assigned patent, claiming a right to a trade mark designating the system assigned and used by the assignee, is distinct matter and must be stricken out. Johnson Railroad Signal Co. *v.* Union Switch etc. Co., 43 Fed. Rep. 337.

A cross bill cannot be filed by defendant to prevent the complainant from infringing defendant's patent. McCormick Harvester Machine Co. *v.* Deering, 47 Pat. Off. Gaz. 1222. Nor to compel an assignment of part of the patent. Puetz *v.* Bransford, 32 Fed. Rep. 318.

Leave to file a cross bill is not an adjudication of the right under the cross

party.[1]

4. Stare Decisis.—A decision on the same state of facts will generally be followed by a court of co-ordinate jurisdiction;[2] but not where the record presents a different state of facts.[3]

bill. Brush Electric Co. *v.* Brush-Swan Electric Light Co., 43 Fed. Rep. 701.

1. After the death of an infringer, a bill of revivor will lie to prevent the abatement of the suit. Smith *v.* Baker, 1 Bann. & Ard. Pat. Cas. 117; s. c., 5 Pat. Off. Gaz. 496; Atterbury *v.* Gill, 2 Flipp. (U. S.) 239; s. c., 3 Bann. & Ard. Pat. Cas. 174; s. c., 13 Pat. Off. Gaz. 276; Kirk *v.* Du Bois, 28 Fed. Rep. 460.

But a bill of revivor will not lie to bring in the other representatives of a deceased member of a firm against which there is a suit for infringement; unless it is alleged that the complainant cannot get satisfaction out of the survivor. Troy Iron etc. Factory *v.* Winslow, 11 Blatchf. (U. S.) 513. And the interest of the person to be brought in must have been acquired by the death of a party and not merely by an assignment which was followed by the death of the party. Metal Stamping Co. *v.* Cravdall, 18 Pat. Off. Gaz. 1531.

A bill of revivor may be used to revive a suit as to part of the relief asked. Hohorst *v.* Howard, 37 Fed. Rep. 97.

2. Putnam *v.* Ferrington, 2 Bann. & Ard. Pat. Cas. 237; s. c., 9 Pat. Off. Gaz. 689; Washburn *v.* Gould, 3 Story (U. S.) 122; s. c., 2 Robb Pat. Cas. 206; Goodyear *v.* Providence Rubber Co., 2 Cliff. (U. S.) 351; s. c., 2. Fish. Pat. Cas. 499; American Wood Paper Co. *v.* Fiber Disintegrating Co., 3 Fish. Pat. Cas. 363; Goodyear *v.* Berry, 3 Fish. Pat. Cas. 443; Tilghman *v.* Werk, 1 Bond (U. S.) 511; s. c., 2 Fish. Pat. Cas. 229; Tilghman *v* Mitchell, 4 Fish. Pat. Cas. 624; Goodyear Dental etc. Co. *v.* Root, 6 Pat. Off. Gaz. 154; Goodyear *v.* Willis, 1 Flipp. (U. S.) 385; s. c., 1 Bann. & Ard. Pat. Cas. 568; s. c., 7 Pat. Off. Gaz. 41; Hammerschlag *v.* Garrett, 9 Fed. Rep. 43; American Ballast Log Co. *v.* Cotter, 11 Fed. Rep. 728; s. c., 31 Pat. Off. Gaz. 1030; Strobridge *v.* Landers, 11 Fed Rep. 880; s. c., 21 Pat. Off. Gaz. 1027; Searls *v.* Worden, 11 Fed. Rep. 501; s. c., 21 Pat. Off. Gaz. 1955; McCloskey *v.* Hamill, 15 Fed. Rep. 750; s. c., 23 Pat. Off. Gaz. 2122; Richardson *v.* Lockwood, 4 Cliff. (U. S.) 128; Jones *v.* Wetherill, 1 McArthur Pat. Cas. 409.

Ruling by Superior Judge.—A ruling by an official superior in the same circuit is binding on the court. May *v.* Fond du Lac Co., 27 Fed. Rep. 691.

And generally a decision in the same circuit is binding. Holliday *v.* Matheson, 23 Blatchf. (U. S.) 239; s. c., 24 Fed. Rep. 185; s. c., 31 Pat. Off. Gaz. 1444; Field *v.* Ireland, 28 Pat. Off. Gaz. 284; s. c., 19 Fed. Rep. 835; Hayes *v.* Dayton, 20 Fed. Rep. 690.

The prior adjudicated case must have been decided on an actual contest. Schillinger *v.* Crawford, 37 Pat. Off. Gaz. 1349.

A verdict in law does not affect a subsequent suit between other parties; but a dismissal of a prior suit for the same subject matter may be pleaded in bar in a chancery suit. Allen *v.* Blunt, 2 Woodb. & M. 121; s. c., 2 Robb Pat. Cas. 530; Heysinger *v.* Rouss, 40 Fed. Rep. 584. *Compare* Dubois *v.* Philadelphia etc. R. Co., 5 Fish. Pat. Cas. 208.

This proceeds upon the principle that, while the decision of the courts of one circuit are not binding on those of another, the necessity for uniformity of the law requires that the courts of one circuit follow those of another with reference to the validity of a patent. Worswick Mfg. Co. *v.* Philadelphia, 30 Fed. Rep. 625.

A patent was granted to an alleged invention; after its grant, it was put in interference with an application, and the applicant declared a prior invention and a patent awarded to him. The patentee under the first patent sued the patentee under the second, and it was held that the first patentee had upon him the burden of proof. Wire Book Sewing Mach. Co. *v.* Stevenson, 11 Fed. Rep. 155.

3. McCloskey *v.* Hamill, 15 Fed. Rep. 750; s. c., 23 Pat. Off. Gaz. 2122; Mfg. Co. *v.* Walworth, 9 Pat. Off. Gaz. 746; Allen *v.* Blunt, 2 Woodb. & M. (U. S.) 121; s. c., 2 Robb Pat. Cas. 530; Tinsser *v.* Krueger, 45 Fed. Rep. 572; Reed *v.* Lawrence, 29 Fed. Rep. 915; Lockwood *v.* Tabeb, 27 Fed. Rep. 63; United Nickel Co. *v.* California Electrical Works, 25 Fed. Rep. 475.

5. Res Judicata and Lis Pendens.—A decree[1] or judgment[2] deciding that a device is an infringement of a patent,[3] or that the patent is valid or invalid,[4] is binding between the parties and their privies,[5] and on parties who contribute to the expense of suit in which the decision was made.[6] A pendency of suit in a State court will not bar a proceeding for the same cause of action between the same parties in a federal court.[7]

This is especially so in injunction suits. Many *v.* Sizer, 1 Fish. Pat. Cas. 31; Cornell *v.* Little John, 2 Bann. & Ard. Pat. Cas. 324; s. c., 9 Pat. Off. Gaz. 837; Potter *v.* Whitney, 3 Fish. Pat. Cas. 77; s. c., Low. (U. S.) 87; s. c., Sargent Mfg. Co. *v.* Woodruff, 5 Biss. (U. S.) 444.

The decree should state that the court followed the ruling of another court out of comity. Rumford Chemical Works *v.* Hecker, 2 Bann. & Ard. Pat. Cas. 386; s. c., 11 Pat. Off. Gaz. 330.

The doctrine of *stare decisis* does not apply to prior decisions of the Commissioner of Patents, although entitled to weight. Gloucester Isinglass etc. Co. *v.* Brooks, 19 Fed. Rep. 426.

1. Barker *v.* Stowe, 11 Fed. Rep. 303; United Nickel Co. *v.* Worthington, 23 Pat. Off. Gaz. 939.

A decree dismissing a suit for want of prosecution is not an estoppel. American etc. Boring Co. *v.* Sheldon, 17 Blatchf. (U. S.) 208; s. c., 4 Bann. & Ard. Pat. Cas. 551.

Nor for failure of defendant to appear and argue a demurrer. Wollensak *v.* Sargent, 33 Fed. Rep. 840.

Nor an interlocutor decree. Gilbert etc. Co. *v.* Bussing, 12 Blatchf. (U. S.) 426; s. c., 1 Bann. & Ard. Pat. Cas. 621; s. c., 8 Pat. Off. Gaz. 144.

Nor does a decree decide a point not argued. Celluloid Mfg. Co. *v.* Tower, 26 Fed. Rep. 451; Keller *v.* Stolzenbach, 27 Pat. Off. Gaz. 209; s. c., 20 Fed. Rep. 47. But a decree by consent is. Tomkinson *v.* Willetts Mfg. Co., 23 Fed. Rep. 895.

2. Wells *v.* Jaques, 5 Pat. Off. Gaz. 364.

But to estop a party in an action at law the nature of the infringement, must be shown by the record, or by extrinsic evidence. Russell *v.* Place, 94 U. S. 606; s. c., 12 Pat. Off. Gaz. 53.

3. A decree is not conclusive when the alleged infringing device litigated is different. Clarke *v.* Johnson, 16 Blatchf. (U. S.) 495; s. c., 4 Bann. & Ard. Pat. Cas. 407; s. c., 17 Pat. Off. Gaz. 1401.

4. American etc. Boring Co. *v.* Sheldon, 17 Blatchf. (U. S.) 208; s. c., 4 Bann. & Ard. Pat. Cas. 551; Day *v.* Combination Rubber Co., 2 Fed. Rep. 570; s. c., 5 Bann. & Ard. Pat. Cas. 385; s. c., 17 Pat. Off. Gaz. 1347.

A licensee who took a license prior to the beginning of the suit, is not concluded by a decree enjoining his licensor. Ingersoll *v.* Jewett, 16 Blatchf. (U. S.) 378.

After a decree has been satisfied against a vendor, a vendee is not liable. Perrigo *v.* Spaulding, 13 Blatchf. (U. S.) 389; s. c., 2 Bann. & Ard. Pat. Cas. 348; s. c., 12 Pat. Off. Gaz. 352; Gilbert etc. Mfg. Co. *v.* Bussing, 12 Blatchf. (U. S.) 426; s. c., 1 Bann. & Ard. Pat. Cas. 621; s. c., 8 Pat. Off. Gaz. 144.

But a decree against one of several joint infringers is not a bar to a decree against the other joint infringers. Union Nickel Co. *v.* Worthington, 23 Pat. Off. Gaz. 939.

5. United States etc. Felting Co. *v.* Asbestos Felting Co., 18 Blatchf. (U. S.) 312; s. c., 4 Fed. Rep. 813; s. c., 5 Bann. & Ard. Pat. Cas. 624; s. c., 19 Pat. Off. Gaz. 362; Miller *v.* Liggett etc. Tobacco Co., 7 Fed. Rep. 91; s. c., 19 Pat. Off. Gaz. 1138; United States etc. Packing Co. *v.* Tripp, 31 Fed. Rep. 350; Gloucester Isinglass Co. *v.* Le Page, 30 Fed. Rep. 370; American Bell Teleph. Co. *v.* National Improved Teleph. Co., 27 Fed. Rep, 663.

A decree that a patent is invalid, does not prevent the same or a different plaintiff from prosecuting a suit against another defendant. Consolidated Roller-Mill Co *v.* George T. Smith Middlings Purifier Co., 40 Fed. Rep. 305.

6. Birdsell *v.* Hagerstown etc. Mfg. Co., 1 Bann. & Ard. Pat. Cas. 426; s. c., 6 Pat. Off. Gaz. 604; Robertson *v.* Hill, 6 Fish. Pat. 465; Miller *v.* Liggett etc. Tobacco Co., 7 Fed. Red. 91; American Bell Teleph. Co. *v.* National Improved Teleph. Co., 27 Fed. Rep. 663; United States etc. Felting Co. *v.* Asbestos Felting Co., 4 Fed. Rep. 813.

7. Washburn etc. Mfg. Co. *v.* Scutt & Co., 22 Fed. Rep. 710.

6. Trial at Law.—A patentee may recover a verdict against one of several defendants.[1] The court is bound to give instructions only as to the matters arising in the case.[2] The relations of the judge and jury are the same as in any other civil case.[3]

7. Final Injunction; When Granted.—A final injunction is granted whenever there is no especial equity[4] to prevent it on the side of

1. Reutgen *v.* Kanowrs, 1 Wash. (U. S.) 168; s. c., 1 Robb Pat. Cas. 1.

2. Pitts *v.* Whitman, 2 Story (U. S.) 609; s. c., 2 Robb Pat. Cas. 189; Allen *v.* Blunt, 2 Woodb. & M. (U. S.) 121; s. c., 2 Robb Pat. Cas. 530.

3. Cahoon *v.* Ring, 1 Cliff. (U. S.) 592; Conover *v.* Roach, 4 Fish. Pat. Cas. 12.

As to testimony, Johnson *v.* Root, 1 Fish. Pat. Cas. 351; Union Sugar Refining Co. *v.* Matthiesen, 3 Cliff. (U. S.) 639; s. c., 2 Fish. Pat. Cas. 600.

Nonsuit.—As to power to give peremptory nonsuit. Silsby *v.* Foote, 14 How. (U. S.) 218.

Jury.—A defective notice will not permit motion for withdrawal of juror, and vacancy can be filed in a panel after beginning of trial, if the objecting party is not thereby injured. Silsby *v.* Foote, 14 How. (U. S.) 218. A jury having disagreed, the case must go over for a new venire. Wilson *v.* Barnum, 1 Wall. Jr. (C. C.) 347; s. c., 2 Fish. Pat. Cas. 635.

Verdict.—A special verdict may be rendered which will be sufficient, although not in the terms of the issue if the court can clearly collect the point in issue out of it. Stearns *v.* Barrett, 1 Mason (U. S.) 153; s. c., 1 Robb Pat. Cas. 97. A verdict of a jury is entitled to less regard in patent than in other civil cases. Roberts *v.* Schuyler, 12 Blatchf. (U. S.) 444; s. c., 2 Bann. & Ard. Pat. Cas. 5.

Power to Direct Verdict.—See Roger *v.* Shultz Belting Co., 29 Fed. Rep. 281.

4. Potter *v.* Mack, 3 Fish. Pat. Cas. 428; Rumford Chemical Works *v.* Hecker, 2 Bann. & Ard. Pat. Cas. 386; s. c., 11 Pat. Off. Gaz. 330; Sanders *v.* Logan, 2 Fish. Pat. Cas. 167; Lowell Mfg. Co. *v.* Hartford Carpet Co., 2 Fish. Pat. Cas. 472.

If an estoppel exists. Merriam *v.* Smith, 11 Fed. Rep. 588. Or if the suit is merely for collection purposes. Blanchard *v.* Sprague, 1 Cliff. (U. S.) 288. Or if complainant assigns his patent, pending the suit. Boomer *v.* United Power Press Co., 13 Blatchf. (U. S.) 107; s. c., 2 Bann. & Ard. Pat. Cas. 107; Wheeler *v.* McCormick, 11 Blatchf. (U. S.) 334; s. c., 6 Fish. Pat. Cas. 551; s. c., 4 Pat. Off. Gaz. 692.

Laches.—This may be changed if the defendant is guilty of laches. Salt Co. *v.* Barry, 2 W. N. C. (Pa.) 100; Brush Electric Light Co. *v.* Ball Electric Light Co., 43 Fed. Rep 899.

A long acquiescence may prevent the grant of an injunction. Kittle *v.* Hall, 29 Fed. Rep. 508; Kittle *v.* DeGraaf, 30 Fed. Rep. 689; McLaughlin *v.* People's R. Co., 21 Fed. Rep. 574; United Nickel Co. *v.* New Home Sewing Mach. Co., 21 Blatchf. (U. S.) 415; s. c., 17 Fed. Rep. 528. But it is no estoppel where the inventor did not know that others were investing under the supposition that the field was clear. Sprague *v.* Adriance, 3 Bann. & Ard. Pat. Cas. 124; s. c., 14 Pat. Off. Gaz. 308; Green *v.* Barney, 19 Fed. Rep. 420; Green *v.* French, 4 Bann. & Ard. Pat. Cas. 169; American etc. Purifier Co. *v.* Christian, 4 Dill. (U. S.) 448; s. c., 3 Bann. & Ard. Pat. Cas. 42; Child *v.* Boston etc. Iron Works, 19 Fed. Rep. 258; Adams *v.* Howard, 22 Blatchf. (U. S.) 47; s. c., 19 Fed. Rep. 317; s. c., 26. Pat. Off. Gaz. 825.

But where the complainant has acquiesced for many years the injunction may be withheld until the coming in of the master's report. Waite *v.* Chichester Chair Co., 45 Fed. Rep. 258.

Especially if laches is coupled with acquiescence in the acts of the defendant. Amazeen Mach. Co. *v.* Knight, 39 Fed. Rep. 612; Raymond *v.* Boston Woven Hose Co., 39 Fed. Rep. 365; s. c., 48 Pat. Off. Gaz. 1776; Upton *v.* Wayland, 36 Fed. Rep. 691.

Profits Denied on Account of Laches. Entire good faith on part of defendant and inexcusable laches on part of complainant; complainants then may be refused account of profits. Keller *v.* Stotzenback, 28 Fed. Rep. 81; s. c., 37 Pat. Off. Gaz. 564. Or even be a bar to any relief in equity. New York Grape Sugar Co. *v.* Buffalo Grape Sugar Co., 24 Fed. Rep. 604; s. c., 32 Pat. Off. Gaz. 1356.

Various Reasons Which Have Prevented

the defendant, and the title of the complainant is clear.[1] It may, and ordinarily will, be granted without any trial at law.[2] It may be suspended if thereby an oppression of the defendant can be avoided without injury to complainant.[3]

Courts from Granting Injunctions.—Unfair treatment of licensee by defendant. Seibert etc. Oil Cup Co. *v.* Detroit Lubricator Co. 34 Fed. Rep. 216.

Where an infringement was not wilful, and was stopped in good faith. North American Iron Works *v.* Fiske; 30 Fed. Rep. 622; Odell *v.* Stout, 22 Fed. Rep. 159; s. c., 29 Pat. Off. Gaz. 862; Proctor *v.* Bayley, 42 Ch. Div. L. R. (Eng.) 390. Combined with other circumstances the fact that final decree will soon be rendered. Pope Mfg. Co. *v.* Johnson, 40 Fed. Rep. 584.

A final injunction will not be refused because the defendant was insane when he infringed. Avery *v.* Wilson, 20 Fed. Rep. 856.

1. Potter *v.* Mack, 3 Fish. Pat. Cas. 428; Merriam *v.* Smith, 11 Fed. Rep. 588; Motte *v.* Bennett, 2 Fish. Pat. Cas. 642; Goodyear *v.* Berry, 2 Bond (U. S.) 189; s. c., 3 Fish. Pat. Cas. 439; Robinson on Patents, § 1220; Gear *v.* Holmes, 6 Fish. Pat. Cas. 595.

An injunction will not be refused because the defendant no longer infringes. Bullock Press Co. *v.* Jones, 3 Bann. & Ard. Pat. Cas. 195; s. c. 13 Pat. Off. Gaz. 124. Even where the use has been merely experimental. Albright *v.* Celluloid &c. Trimming Co., 2 Bann. & Ard. Pat. Cas. 629; s. c., 12 Pat. Off. Gaz. 227. See Rumford Chemical Works *v.* Lauer, 10 Blatchf. (U. S.) 122; s. c., 5 Fish. Pat. Cas. 615; s. c., 3 Pat. Off. Gaz. 349.

Granted Against.—It may be granted against a mere salesman. Maltby *v.* Bobo, 14 Blatchf. (U. S.) 53; s. c., 2 Bann. & Ard. Pat. Cas. 459. Or one who has the exclusive right to use the class of articles to which the invention appertains. Colgate *v.* International etc. Tel. Co., 17 Blatchf. (U. S.) 308; s. c., 4 Bann. & Ard. Pat. Cas. 609. Or a carrier who refuses to disclose the names of parties delivering articles to him for transportation. American Cotton Tel. Co. *v.* McCready, 17 Blatchf. (U. S.) 355; s. c., 4 Bann. & Ard. Pat. Cas. 588; s. c., 17 Pat. Off. Gaz. 565.

Against the officers of a corporation. American Bell Teleph. Co. *v.* Globe Teleph. Co., 31 Fed. Rep. 729; Boston Woolen Hose Co. *v.* Star Rubber Co., 40 Fed. Rep. 167; Howard *v.* St. Paul Plow Works, 35 Fed. Rep. 743; s. c., 45 Pat. Off. Gaz. 1067.

A licensee exceeding his license. Covell *v.* Bostwick, 39 Fed. Rep. 421; Union Nickel Co *v.* California Electric Works, 11 Sawy. (U. S.) 250; Tappan *v.* Tiffany etc. Car Co., 39 Fed. Rep. 420. But see Chase *v.* Cox, 41 Fed. Rep. 475.

An injunction may restrain the use after the expiration of articles made during the life of the patent. American etc. Boring Co. *v.* Sheldon, 18 Blatchf. (U. S.) 50; s. c., 5 Bann. & Ard. Pat. Cas. 292; s. c., 1 Fed. Rep. 870; American etc. Boring Co. *v.* Rutland Marble Co., 2 Fed. Rep. 356; s. c., 18 Blatchf. (U. S.) 147; s. c., 5 Bann. & Ard. Pat. Cas. 346. Or where the defendant has ceased to infringe. Facer *v.* Midvale Steel Works, 38 Fed. Rep. 231. But will not where the defendant is a corporation and has disposed of the business in which the patented device was used and has not used it since. Kane *v.* Huggins Cracker etc. Co., 44 Fed. Rep. 287. See DISSOLUTION OF INJUNCTION.

Equity, having jurisdiction over defendant's person, may act to restrain him from a use and construction of the infringing device beyond the jurisdiction of the court. Boyd *v.* McAlpin, 3 McLean (U. S.) 427; s. c., 2 Robb Pat. Cas. 277; Wilson *v.* Sherman, 1 Blatchf. (U. S.) 536; Thompson *v.* Mendelsohn, 5 Fish. Pat. Cas. 187; Wheeler *v.* McCormick, 8 Blatchf. (U. S.) 267. But an infringement prior to the filing of the bill must be shown. Slessinger *v.* Buckingham, 8 Sawy. (U. S.) 469.

2. Buchanan *v.* Howland, 2 Fish. Pat. Cas. 341; s. c., 5 Blatchf. (U. S.) 151; Doughty *v.* West, 2 Fish. Pat. Cas. 553; Hoffheins *v.* Brandt, 3 Fish. Pat. Cas. 218; Wise *v.* Grand Ave. R. Co., 33 Fed. Rep. 277; McCoy *v.* Nelson, 121 U. S. 487.

3. Potter *v.* Mack, 3 Fish. Pat. Cas. 428; Mowry *v.* Whitney, 5 Fish. Pat. Cas. 496; Barnard *v.* Gibson, 7 How. (U. S.) 650; Bliss *v.* Brooklyn, 4 Fish. Pat. Cas. 597; McElroy *v.* Kansas City, 21 Fed. Rep. 257; Ballard *v.* Pitts-

Other Relief by Decree.—The court may by decree order the infringing articles to be delivered up to be destroyed,[1] or grant other equitable relief.[2]

burg, 12 Fed. Rep. 783; Munson *v.* Mayor etc. of N. Y., 19 Fed. Rep. 313; Roller Mill Co. *v.* Coombs, 39 Fed. Rep. 803; s. c. 48 Pat. Off. Gaz. 973. But it is not a matter of right even if the defendant will give bond and the patent is about to expire. Brown *v.* Deere, 6 Fed. Rep. 487; s. c., 19 Pat. Off. Gaz. 1217.

An injunction will not be suspended until the final decree to permit the defendant to have time to change his machine, unless there is a probability of his being able to do so in such a manner as will evade the patent. Brown *v.* Deere, 6 Fed. Rep. 487; s. c., 19 Pat. Off. Gaz. 1217.

An injunction will be granted although the plaintiff has withdrawn the patented device from a State on account of alleged oppressive legislative exactments. American Bell Telephone Co. *v.* Cushman Telephone Co., 36 Fed. Rep. 488; s. c., 45 Pat. Off. Gaz. 1193.

Expiration of Patent Before Decree.—Where a patent expires before final hearing, the injunction will not be granted. Bliss *v.* Brooklyn, 8 Blatchf. (U. S.) 533; Tilghman *v.* Mitchell, 9 Blatchf. (U. S.) 18; s. c., 4 Fish. Pat. Cas. 615.

A case where the injury to plaintiff consists only in the failure to pay the price of his license, will not warrant an injunction. Sanders *v.* Logan, 2 Fish. Pat. Cas. 167.

Where the plaintiff is not a manufacturer the injunction may be refused upon his receiving proper compensation. Dorsey etc. Rake Co. *v.* Marsh, 6 Fish. Pat. Cas. 387.

The principle being that, where the injury to the defendant was greater than the advantage to complainant, the injunction should be refused. McCrary *v.* Pennsylvania Canal Co., 5 Fed. Rep. 567. All of these cases are in third circuit, which, as stated by JUDGE BROWN in Consolidated Roller Mill Co. *v.* Coombs, 39 Fed. Rep. 803, seems to have a different rule of decision from that obtaining in other circuits and was refused to be followed.

An injunction has been denied on the ground that the patentee did not put his patent into use or allow others to use it on equitable terms. Hoe *v.* Knap, 27 Fed. Rep. 204.

That a patentee is compelled to put his invention into use is denied by Consolidated Roller Mill Co. *v.* Combs, 39 Fed. Rep. 803.

The right of the plaintiff to his injunction is stated to be based on the fact that the chancellor cannot in the decree give the complainant less than his full right and cannot bargain with him what he may or may not choose to do. Penn *v.* Bibby, L. R., 3 Eq. (Eng.) 308. See Birdsell *v.* Shaliol, 112 U. S. 485.

The ordinary practice is for an injunction, *as a matter of course*, to follow a decree in favor of the complainant on the merits. Rumford Chemical Works *v.* Hecker, 11 Pat. Off. Gaz. 330.

An injunction will not ordinarily be continued as to articles manufactured during the life of the patent. Westinghouse *v.* Carpenter, 43 Fed. Rep. 894. *Contra*, Crosby *v.* Gas Light Co., 1 Web. Pat. Cas. (Eng.) 119; American etc. Boring Co. *v.* Sheldon, 18 Blatchf. (U. S.) 52; s. c., 2 Fed. Rep. 353; Mower etc. Co. *v.* Johnston Harvester Co., 24 Fed. Rep. 739; New York Belting etc. Co. *v.* Macgowan, 27 Fed. Rep. 111.

But not as to articles made from elements made before the expiration, when the elements were old and the combination the only thing patentable. Johnson *v.* Brooklyn etc. R. Co., 37 Fed. Rep. 147.

Liability of Complainant on Bond.—Where the complainant has given bond to obtain an injunction, he is liable on failure for damages for loss of sales, depreciation of goods on hand, etc. Toby Furniture Co. *v.* Colby, 35 Fed. Rep. 392.

1. Birdsell *v.* Shaliol, 112 U. S. 487; Needham *v.* Oxley, 8 L. T., N. S. (Eng.) 604; Frearson *v.* Loe, 9 Ch. Div. (Eng.) 67; Betts *v.* De Vitre, 34 L. J., Ch. (Eng.) 289; American Bell Teleph. Co. *v.* Kitsell, 35 Fed. Rep. 521; Emperor *v.* Day, 2 Giff. (U. S.) 628.

But this relief should not be granted when there is no reason to believe that the defendant will act in bad faith in regard to the matter. American Bell Teleph. Co. *v.* Kitsell, 35 Fed. Rep. 521.

2. See INFRINGEMENT, vol. 10, pp. 754, 762 *et seq.*

8. New Trial and Arrest of Judgment.—New trial is granted where a material[1] error has been committed,[2] or the verdict is against the weight of the evidence;[3] or the new evidence, which could not have been obtained at the time of the trial[4] and which is not merely cumulative,[5] can be and is presented by the losing party.

9. Re-hearing.—The granting of a rehearing is governed by substantially the same rules as govern the granting of a new trial,[6]

1. Allen *v.* Blunt, 2 Woodb. & M. (U. S.) 121; s. c., 2 Robb Pat. Cas. 530; Cowing *v.* Rumsey, 8 Blatchf. (U. S.) 36; s. c., 4 Fish. Pat. Cas. 275.

2. The error must have been excepted to at the time. Allen *v.* Blunt, 2 Woodb. & M. (U. S.) 121; s. c., 2 Robb Pat. Cas. 130; Silsby *v.* Foote, 14 How. (U. S.) 218; Keyes *v.* Grant, 118 U. S. 25.

3. Wilson *v.* James, 3 Blatchf. (U. S.) 227; Aikens *v.* Bemis, 3 Woodb. & M. (U. S.) 348; s. c., 2 Robb Pat. Cas. 644; Bray *v.* Hartshorn, 1 Cliff. (U. S.) 538; Roberts *v.* Schuyler, 12 Blatchf. (U. S.) 444; s. c., 2 Bann. & Ard. Pat. Cas. 5.

A court will rarely set aside a verdict on account of the amount of damages. Alden *v.* Dewey, 1 Story (U. S.) 336; s. c., 2 Robb Pat. Cas. 17; Whitney *v.* Emmett, 1 Baldw. (U. S.) 303; s. c., 1 Robb Pat. Cas. 567; Stimpson *v.* Railroads, 1 Wall. Jr. (C. C.) 164, s. c., 2 Robb Pat. Cas. 593.

Sometimes a party may be given the choice to remit part of the damages or the other party will get a new trial. Johnson *v.* Root, 2 Cliff. (U. S.) 108; s. c., 2 Fish. Pat. Cas. 291; Cowing *v.* Rumsey, 8 Blatchf. (U. S.) 36; s. c., 4 Fish. Pat. Cas. 275.

4. Washburn *v.* Gould, 3 Story (U. S.) 122; s. c., 1 Robb Pat. Cas. 689.

5. Ames *v.* Howard, 1 Sumn. (U. S.) 482; s. c., 1 Robb Pat. Cas. 689; Aikens *v.* Bemis, 3 Woodb. & M. (U. S.) 348; s. c., 2 Robb Pat. Cas. 644.

A motion for a new trial in an issue sent for trial to a court of law, will not be noticed in the suit in equity. Watt *v.* Starke, 101 U. S. 247; s. c., 17 Pat. Off. Gaz. 1093.

6. Ready Roofing Co. *v.* Taylor, 15 Blatchf. (U. S.) 95; s. c., 3 Bann. & Ard. Pat. Cas. 368; Electrical Accumulator Co. *v.* Julien Electric Co., 39 Fed. Rep. 490.

Newly Discovered Evidence.—It must be shown that the evidence is such as would cause the court to come to another decision. Buerk *v.* Imhauser, 14 Blatchf. (U. S.) 19; s. c., 2 Bann. & Ard. Pat. Cas. 452; s. c., 10 Pat. Off. Gaz. 907; Adair *v.* Thayer, 7 Fed. Rep. 920; s. c., 20 Pat. Off. Gaz. 523; Allis *v.* Stowell, 5 Bann. & Ard. Pat. Cas. 458; s. c., 18 Pat. Off. Gaz. 465; Craig *v.* Smith, 100 U. S. 226; s. c., 17 Pat. Off. Gaz. 145; Hake *v.* Brown, 44 Fed. Rep. 283; Starling *v.* St. Paul Plow Works, 32 Fed. Rep. 290; Reed *v.* Lawrence, 32 Fed. Rep. 228.

It must be shown that it was not in the possession of the party at the time of the hearing and that due diligence had been exercised. Reeves *v.* Keystone Bridge Co., 2 Bann. & Ard. Pat. Cas. 256; s. c., 9 Pat. Off. Gaz. 885; Munson *v.* New York, 22 Pat. Off. Gaz. 586; Yerrington *v.* Putnam, 2 Bann. & Ard. Pat. Cas. 601; Barker *v.* Stowe, 4 Bann. & Ard. Pat. Cas. 485; s. c., 16 Pat. Off. Gaz. 807; Gillett *v.* Bate Refrigerating Co., 12 Fed. Rep. 108; Page *v.* Holmes etc. Tel. Co., 18 Blatchf. (U. S.) 118 s. c., 5 Bann. & Ard. Pat. Cas. 439; s. c., 2 Fed. Rep. 330; Ingersoll *v.* Benham, 14 Blatchf. (U. S.) 362; s. c., 3 Bann. & Ard. Pat. Cas. 439; Allis *v.* Stowell, 5 Bann. & Ard. Pat. Cas. 458; s. c., 18 Pat. Off. Gaz. 465; Witters *v.* Sowles, 32 Fed. Rep. 765; Burdsall *v.* Curran, 31 Fed. Rep. 918; Albany Steam Trap Co. *v.* Felthousen, 26 Fed. Rep. 318; Hoe *v.* Kahler, 23 Blatchf. (U. S.) 354; s. c., 25 Fed. Rep. 271; s. c., 34 Pat. Off. Gaz. 127.

New evidence not introduced on account of the incompetence of the former solicitor, is no reason to grant a rehearing. De Florez *v.* Raynolds, 16 Blatchf. (U. S.) 397; s. c., 4 Bann. & Ard. Pat. Cas. 431; Railway Reg. Mfg. Co. *v.* North Hudson R. Co., 26 Fed. Rep. 411.

Lack of expert testimony will not induce the court to grant a rehearing. Hitchcock *v.* Tremaine, 9 Blatchf. (U. S.) 550; s. c., 5 Fish. Pat. Cas. 537; s. c., 1 Pat. Off. Gaz. 633.

Merely cumulative new evidence will not induce the court to grant a

excepting the fact that a decree for an injunction, being interlocutory,[1] makes it subject to revision until the making of a final decree,[2] and that the equitable doctrines are applied.[3]

rehearing. Pfanschmidt *v.* Kelly Mercantile Co., 32 Fed. Rep. 667; Witters *v.* Sowles, 32 Fed. Rep. 765.

1. Reeves *v.* Keystone Bridge Co., 2 Bann. & Ard. Pat. Cas. 256; s. c., 9 Pat. Off. Gaz. 885; Schneider *v.* Thill, 5 Bann. & Ard. Pat. Cas. 565.

An interlocutory decree may be opened and the bill dismissed on account of the complainant having an adequate remedy at law. Spring *v.* Domestic Sewing Mach. Co., 13 Fed. Rep. 446; s. c., 22 Pat. Off. Gaz. 1445.

2. Magie Ruffle Co. *v.* Elm City Co., 14 Blatchf. (U. S.) 109; s. c., 2 Bann. & Ard. Pat. Cas. 506; s. c., 11 Pat. Off. Gaz. 501; Coburn *v.* Schroeder, 11 Fed. Rep. 425; s. c., 22 Pat. Off. Gaz. 1538; Willimantic Linen Co. *v.* Clark Thread Co., 32 Pat. Off. Gaz. 1356; s. c., 24 Fed. Rep. 799; Wooster *v.* Handy, 22 Blatchf. (U. S.) 307; s. c., 21 Fed. Rep. 31; s. c., 28 Pat. Off. Gaz. 629; Steam Stone Cutter Co. *v.* Sheldon, 22 Blatchf. (U. S.) 484; s. c., 21 Fed. Rep. 875.

Defendant who, subsequent to decree, discovers that the patent sued on is limited by a foreign patent to patentee, may have decree amended to limit the injunction to the life of the American patent as limited by the foreign patent. DeFlorez *v.* Raynolds, 17 Blatchf. (U. S.) 436; s. c., 8 Fed. Rep. 434; s. c., 17 Pat. Off. Gaz. 503.

3. **Laches** will prevent a party from obtaining a rehearing. Andrews *v.* Denslow, 14 Blatchf. (U. S.) 182; s. c., 2 Bann. & Ard. Pat. Cas. 587; Doubleday *v.* Sherman, 6 Blatchf. (U. S.) 513; Willimantic Linen Co. *v.* Clark Thread Co., 24 Fed. Rep. 799; s. c., 32 Pat. Off. Gaz. 1356.

But the laches must be considerable. Hake *v.* Brown, 44 Fed. Rep. 283.

Fraud.—A collusive decree will be stricken out. Barker *v.* Todd, 15 Fed. Rep. 265; s. c., 23 Pat. Off. Gaz. 438.

Where the court is not satisfied with the conclusion reached, it may grant a re-hearing with leave to take additional proof. Rumford Chemical Works *v.* Lauer, 10 Blatchf. (U. S.) 122; s. c., 5 Fish. Pat. Cas. 615; s. c., 3 Pat. Off. Gaz. 349.

The court will very rarely grant a re-hearing when no new facts are brought forward. Gage *v.* Kellogg, 26 Fed. Rep. 242; s. c., 36 Pat. Off. Gaz. 238; Tufts *v.* Tufts, 3 Woodb. & M. (U. S.) 429; Rogers *v.* Reissner, 34 Fed. Rep. 270; Giant Powder Co. *v.* California etc. Powder Co., 5 Fed. Rep. 197.

Practice in Amendment of Decree.—In decrees or decretal orders a mere clerical correction, especially where the decree has not been enrolled, will be made on motion. Witters *v.* Sowles, 32 Fed. Rep. 130; Union Sugar Refinery *v.* Mathiesson, 3 Cliff. (U. S.) 146, 597.

Practice on Motion for Re-hearing.—After an interlocutery decree has been entered, application for re-hearing on account of new evidence must be by petition for leave to file supplemental bill or answer and for re-hearing when supplemental bill or answer may be ready for hearing. Reeves *v.* Keystone Bridge Co., 2 Bann. & Ard. Pat. Cas. 256; s. c., 9 Pat. Off. Gaz. 885; Hop Bitters Mfg. Co. *v.* Warner, 28 Fed. Rep. 577.

Or to file a petition in the court where the decision was had, and obtain from the court an order upon the other party to show cause on the following rule day or on some other day mentioned, why its prayer should not be granted. The other party can then answer the petition, and upon the petition and answer, the application can be heard. Giant Powder Co. *v.* California etc. Powder Co., 5 Fed. Rep. 197.

Practice Petition.—The petition must be signed by counsel and the affidavit cannot be made before an officer who is also attorney for petitioner; it must, if re-hearing is sought on the ground of new evidence, state the nature of the evidence; that it was not in possession of the party until after the hearing; that diligence was used to discover it; when it was discovered and the circumstances of its discovery. Allis *v.* Stowell, 5 Bann. & Ard. Pat. Cas. 458; s. c., 18 Pat. Off. Gaz. 465.

Terms.—A decree made on re-hearing may make terms under circumstances which would otherwise cause great oppression on a party. Campbell *v.* New York, 35 Fed. Rep. 504.

Where a re-hearing pending an accounting is granted, the testimony al-

10. Proceedings on Accounting.—The proceedings in the master's office are substantially the same as in other cases of reference on an accounting.[1]

ready taken before the master will be retained for use in a subsequent accounting if such be ordered. American etc. Boring Co. *v.* Sheldon, 23 Blatchf. (U. S.) 286.

Who Can Move to Amend Decree.—A stranger to the decree, even if his rights would be affected by the decree, cannot move to have it amended. *In re* Iowa etc. Wire Co., 5 Bann. & Ard. Pat. Cas. 279; Washburn etc. Mfg. Co. *v.* Colwell etc. Fence Co., 1 Fed. Rep. 225; Page *v.* Holmes Telegraph Co., 18 Blatchf. (U. S.) 118; s. c., 2 Fed. Rep. 320; s. c., 5 Bann. & Ard. Pat. Cas. 439.

1. The following has been stated to be the proper practice on an accounting in a patent suit by JUDGES NELSON and LOWELL: "The master appoints a day for proceeding with the reference, and gives notice, by mail or otherwise, to the parties or their solicitors. We think the solicitor should be notified; though probably under rule seventy-five, notice to the party is good notice. If the defendant does not appear the master proceeds *ex parte*, and makes out the profits and damages, if he can, from the evidence produced by the plaintiff. If it appears that an account of profits is necessary to a just decision of the cause, and is desired by the plaintiff, he makes an order that the defendant furnish an account by a certain day, and adjourns the hearing to that day. The defendant should be served personally with a notice of this adjournment; and of the order to produce his account, if it is intended to move for an attachment in case he fails to appear. The service may be made by any disinterested party and need not be by the marshal. If the defendant then fails to appear he will be in contempt." Kerosene Lamp Heater Co. *v.* Fisher, 1 Fed. Rep. 91; s. c., 5 Bann. & Ard. Pat. Cas. 78.

The court will not, however, instruct the master in advance as to the course he is to pursue. Fisher *v.* Consolidated Amador Mine, 25 Fed. Rep. 201; Wooster *v.* Gumbirnner, 20 Fed. Rep. 167.

Nor review each alleged error by special motion. Lull *v.* Clark, 22 Blatchf. (U. S.) 209; s. c., 20 Fed. Rep. 454.

Exceptions. — Exceptions should be taken on the spot to a ruling of the master, in overruling or sustaining objections to admission of testimony. Troy Iron etc. Factory *v.* Corning, 6 Blatchf. (U. S.) 328; s. c., 3 Fish. Pat. Cas. 497; American etc. Pavement Co. *v.* Elizabeth, 1 Bann. & Ard. Pat. Cas. 463; s. c., 6 Pat. Off. Gaz. 764.

The objections to testimony should state the ground of the objection. Brown *v.* Hall, 6 Blatchf. (U. S.) 401; s. c., 3 Fish. Pat. Cas. 531.

And the objection should be made at the time of alleged error and afterwards reduced to writing and filed with the master. Fisher *v.* Hayes, 16 Fed. Rep. 469; s. c., 24 Pat. Off. Gaz, 304.

And unless objections similar to the exceptions taken were made to the draught report, such exceptions will be overruled.

Form of Exception.—Exception should point out the error alleged to have been committed, and the evidence. Turrill *v.* Illinois Cent. R. Co., 3 Biss. (U. S.) 72; Cutting *v.* Florida etc. R. etc. Co., 43 Fed. Rep. 743.

When No Exceptions Can be Taken.—Where the master's report is based upon an inspection as well as upon the evidence, the findings of fact will not be reversed. Piper *v.* Brown, 6 Fish. Pat. Cas. 240; s. c., 1 Holmes (U. S.) 196; s. c., 3 Pat. Off. Gaz. 97.

Or a master's report upon conflicting evidence. Welling *v.* LeBaw, 34 Fed. Rep. 40.

See as to case where interrogatories were adjusted by master. Union Sugar Refinery *v.* Matthiesson, 3 Cliff. (U. S.) 146.

No exception can be taken to a report on account of error in the interlocutory decree. Williams *v.* Leonard, 9 Blatchf. (U. S.) 476; s. c., 5 Fish. Pat. Cas. 381; Turrell *v.* Speath, 2 Bann. & Ard. Pat. Cas. 185; s. c., 8 Pat. Off. Gaz. 986.

Re-committal of Report.—A re-committal of report will be made where a mistake has been made in it. McKay *v.* Jackman, 17 Fed. Rep. 641; s. c., 24 Pat. Off. Gaz. 1177.

Or the master has failed to clearly state his conclusions. Webster Loom Co. *v.* Higgins, 43 Fed. Rep. 673.

But it will not be re-committed merely to allow a party to remedy a neglect. Fisher *v.* Hayes, 16 Fed. Rep. 469; s. c.,

11. Costs.—The general rule is to give costs to the prevailing party.[1] The exceptions are few and rest on strong grounds.[2] They are generally where the award of them would be against equity and good conscience.[3] It is, however, a purely statu-

24 Pat. Off. Gaz. 304; Garretson *v.* Clark, 15 Blatchf. (U. S.) 70; s. c., 3 Bann. & Ard. Pat. Cas. 352; s. c., 14 Pat. Off. Gaz. 485.

But see Webster Loom Co. *v.* Higgins, 43 Fed. Rep. 673; Porter Needle Co. *v.* National Needle Co., 22 Fed. Rep. 829.

Nor will it be re-committed where the mistake can be corrected by the facts appearing in the case aside from the evidence before the master. Witters *v.* Sowles, 43 Fed. Rep. 405.

Opening the Report.—A report will not be opened to admit new testimony when it is evident that all important testimony is in. Morss *v.* Union Form Co., 39 Fed. Rep. 468.

What Questions Are Not at Issue Before the Master—The validity of the patent. Skinner *v.* Vulcan Iron Works, 39 Fed. Rep. 870; Thomson *v.* Wooster, 114 U. S. 104.

Adjudications made by the court upon motion of a party, directing a rule for the computation of profits, are not open to review by exceptions to report. Webster Loom Co. *v.* Higgins, 39 Fed. Rep. 462.

Reporting the Evidence.—Where, at a hearing before a master, the evidence is not in writing, no order can be made on the master to report the evidence. Hammacher *v.* Wilson, 32 Fed. Rep. 796. See also Loud *v.* Stone, 28 Fed. Rep. 749.

1. Hovey *v.* Stevens, 3 Woodb. & M. (U. S.) 17; s. c., 2 Robb. Pat. Cas. 567; Urner *v.* Kayton, 17 Fed. Rep. 845; Calkins *v.* Bertrand, 10 Biss. U. S. 445; s. c., 8 Fed. Rep. 755; Merchant *v.* Lewis, 1 Bond (U. S.) 172; Green *v.* Barney, 19 Fed. Rep. 420; McKay *v.* Jackman, 17 Fed. Rep. 641.

Reference.—The cost of a reference to a master where the decree is for nominal damages only are taxed against complainant. Garretson *v.* Clark, 111 U. S. 120; Everest *v.* Buffalo Lubricating etc. Co., 30 Fed. Rep. 848; Moffitt *v.* Cavanagh, 27 Fed. Rep. 511; Dobson *v.* Hartford Carpet Co., 114 U. S. 439.

The complainant pays the master's fee, and then, if he recovers, has it taxed. Macdonald *v.* Shepard, 10 Fed. Rep. 919; *contra*, Urner *v.* Kayton, 17 Fed. Rep. 539; s. c., 24 Pat. Off. Gaz. 1178.

2. Hovey *v.* Stevens, 3 Woodb. & M. (U. S.) 7; s. c., 2 Robb Pat. Cas. 567; Elfelt *v.* Steinhart, 6 Sawy. (U. S.) 480; s. c., 5 Bann. & Ard. Pat. Cas. 596; s. c., 11 Fed. Rep. 896; Yale Mfg. Co. *v.* North, 5 Blatchf. (U. S.) 455; s. c., 3 Fish. Pat. Cas. 279; Hake *v.* Brown, 37 Fed. Rep. 783.

They may sometimes be divided. Fiske *v.* West etc. Mfg. Co., 19 Pat. Off. Gaz. 545; Garretson *v.* Clark, 16 Pat. Off. Gaz. 806; Brooks *v.* Byam, 2 Story (U. S.) 525.

3. For instance, where defendant has been induced by complainant to believe that his machine did not infringe the patent. Sarven *v.* Hall, 11 Blatchf. (U. S.) 295; s. c., 6 Fish. Pat. Cas. 495; s. c., 4 Pat. Off. Gaz. 666.

Or where the defendants who have prevailed, have made a profit by reason of the existence of the patent. Hussey *v.* Bradley, 5 Blatchf. (U. S.) 134; s. c., 2 Fish. Pat. Cas. 362.

Where defendant has prevailed on answer on a defense that should have clearly been raised by demurrer. Brooks *v.* Byam, 2 Story (U. S.) 525.

An offer having been made by defendant to pay over the profits. Ford *v.* Kurtz, 12 Fed. Rep. 789.

But not where a general offer to pay royalty has been made and refused. Allen *v.* Deacon, 21 Fed. Rep. 122.

Where complainant has been defeated on the most of his claim. Albany Steam Trap. Co. *v.* Felthousen, 20 Fed. Rep. 633; Fay *v.* Allen, 24 Fed. Rep. 804; Schimd *v.* Scovill Mfg. Co., 37 Fed. Rep. 345; Hayes *v.* Bickelhoupt, 21 Fed. Rep. 567; Adams *v.* Howard, 22 Blatchf. (U. S.) 47; s. c., 19 Fed. Rep. 317; s. c., 26 Pat Off. Gaz. 825.

But lack of disclaimer in reissue which has had its claims unduly broadened, does not hinder the costs from going to complainant where he has the decree. The plaintiff was the original inventor of the things claimed but had abandoned them. Mundy *v.* Lidgerwood Mfg. Co., 20 Fed. Rep. 191; Yale Lock Mfg. Co. *v.* Sargent, 117 U. S. 537.

Prevailing Only on a Side Issue.—

tory right.[1] Security for costs can be demanded in some cases.[2]

Where complainant has been defeated on the main issue and succeeded only on an issue of trivial importance, costs will be refused. Marks etc. Chair Co. *v.* Wilson, 43 Fed. Rep. 302; Railway Mfg. Co. *v.* R. Co., 34 Pat. Off. Gaz. 921; Wooster *v.* Handy, 23 Blatchf. (U. S.) 113; s. c., 23 Fed. Rep. 49; Wooster *v.* Hill, 22 Fed. Rep. 830.

But where defendant fails to defend a branch of the case, costs will go against him on this branch. Chicopee Folding Box Co. *v.* Rogers, 32 Fed. Rep. 695.

Reference to Master.—Where the costs on a reference to a master had been augmented by the production of irrelevant testimony by the prevailing party. Troy Iron etc. Factory *v.* Cornning, 6 Fish. Pat. Cas. 85; s. c., 10 Blatchf. (U. S.) 223.

Where rehearing is had to let plaintiff give in evidence he should have given in originally. Fay *v.* Allen, 30 Fed. Rep. 446.

Costs on Dismissal.—See Ryan *v.* Gould, 41 Pat. Off. Gaz. 1392.

1. Hathaway *v.* Roach, 2 Woodb. & M. (U. S.) 63.

But courts of equity may allow costs other than those prescribed in the statute. Spaulding *v.* Tucker, 4 Fish. Pat. Cas. 633.

2. As a general rule, security will not be required. Woodworth *v.* Sherman, 3 Story (U. S.) 171; s. c., 2 Robb Pat. Cas. 257.

For cases in which security has been required, see Orr *v.* Littlefield, 1 Woodb. & M. (U. S.) 13; s. c., 2 Robb Pat. Cas. 323.

The rule to enter security must be taken at the proper time. Bliss *v.* Brooklyn, 10 Blatchf. (U. S.) 217.

When Costs Are Given.—Although costs are usually only given when the cause is decided, yet a court may grant them with reference to matters completely settled before that time. Avery *v.* Wilson, 20 Fed. Rep. 856.

What May be Taxed.—Telegrams in the progress of the suit. Hussey *v.* Bradley, 5 Blatchf. (U. S.) 210.

Postage on the transmission and return of a commission. Prouty *v.* Draper, 2 Story (U. S.) 199.

Copies of assignments. Hathaway *v.* Roach, 2 Woodb. & M. (U. S.) 53.

Procuring models of the invention by defendant. Hathaway *v.* Roach, 2 Woodb. & M. (U. S.) 63.

Witnesses.—Where the testimony of witnesses is taken under a deposition by consent, a reasonable sum as costs for procuring the attendance of witnesses may be allowed. Hathaway *v.* Roach, 2 Woodb. & M. (U. S.) 63.

Fees of witnesses who actually attend before the plaintiff becomes nonsuit, though not examined. Hathaway *v.* Roach, 2 Woodb. & M. (U. S.) 63.

Not to be Taxed—Witnesses.—A witness attending merely by request of a party. Woodruff *v.* Barney, 1 Bond (U. S.) 528; s. c., 2 Fish. Pat. Cas. 244; Spaulding *v.* Tucker, 4 Fish. Pat. Cas. 633.

Mileage of witnesses who have come twice in the same term. Hathaway *v.* Roach, 2 Woodb. & M. (U. S.) 63.

Mileage for officers of defendant corporation. American etc. Drill Co. *v.* Sullivan Mach. Co., 32 Fed. Rep. 552.

A deposition cannot be taxed where it is dispensed with by the party taking it and the party called as a witness. Hathaway *v.* Roach, 2 Woodb. & M. (U. S.) 63.

A party is not entitled to counsel fees for witnesses before a master. Strauss *v.* Meyer, 22 Fed. Rep. 467.

Witnesses before a master whose testimony was afterwards abandoned or given up, or stricken out or rejected by the master and the striking out or rejection sustained by the court. Troy Iron Factory *v.* Corning, 7 Blatchf. (U. S.) 16.

General Treatise.—For a general treatise on taxable costs, see Wooster *v.* Handy, 23 Blatchf. (U. S.) 113; s. c., 23 Fed. Rep. 49.

What May Not be Taxed.—Models not referred to in the patent. Woodruff *v.* Barney, 1 Bond (U. S.) 528; s. c., 2 Fish. Pat. Cas. 244; Hussey *v.* Bradley, 5 Blatchf. (U. S.) 210; Parker *v.* Bigler, 1 Fish. Pat. Cas. 285.

Model of the infringing machine. Cornelly *v.* Markwald, 24 Fed. Rep. 187.

Mileage.—To marshal serving a rule to plead on defendant. Parker *v.* Bigler, 1 Fish. Pat. Cas. 285.

Or for over one hundred miles when the subpœna is served in another district, though the marshal really travels further. Parker *v.* Bigler, 1 Fish. Pat. Cas. 285.

12. Bills of Review.—Bills of review follow, in patent cases, the same rules as regulate them in other equity proceedings.[1]

13. Attachment for Contempt.—Where a violation of an injunction is plain and proved to the satisfaction of the court,[2] the

No mileage of officers of a corporation testifying on its behalf. American etc. Drill Co. *v.* Sullivan Mach. Co., 32 Fed. Rep. 552.

Copies and Printing.—Copies of pleadings or proofs. Hussey *v.* Bradley, 5 Blatchf. (U. S.) 210.

Printing record is not an item of cost where it is done voluntarily. Spaulding *v.* Tucker, 4 Fish. Pat. Cas. 633.

Where ordered by court the expense may be equally divided. Brooks *v.* Byam, 2 Story (U. S.) 525.

Of a copy of patent procured by defendant. Hathaway *v.* Roach, 2 Woodb. & M. (U. S.) 63.

Time of Taxing Costs—Costs are almost invariably taxed after the judgment is rendered and entered by direction of the court *nunc pro tunc* as part of the original judgment. They may be taxed and entered on the record after a transcript has been sent to the supreme court. Sizer *v.* Many, 16 How. (U. S.) 98.

By Whom Taxed.—Costs are taxed with a few exceptions by the clerk. He cannot, however, fix the master's fee. Doughty *v.* West etc. Mfg. Co., 4 Fish. Pat. Cas. 318.

See, for a complicated taxation with reference to master's fee, American etc. Drill Co. *v.* Sullivan Mach. Co., 32 Fed. Rep. 552.

1. See Foster's Fed. Practice, §§ 353, 354, 355, 356, 357.

Where the bill of review is filed on account of a matter of fact, leave of court to file it must be first obtained; where filed on account of newly discovered evidence, the evidence must be more than merely cumulative, and must have been discovered within a reasonable time before the filing of the bill. Blandy *v.* Griffith, 6 Fish. Pat. Cas. 434.

There must have been an effort to obtain the evidence for the first trial, and where there has been a decree against a party who failed to take any evidence while he could have obtained such by using proper diligence. Irwin *v.* Meyrose, 2 McCrary (U. S.) 244.

A decree by consent cannot be set aside by a bill of review. *In re* Pentlarge, 17 Blatchf. (U. S.) 306; s. c., 4 Bann. & Ard. Pat. Cas. 607. See, however, Thompson *v.* Wooster, 114 U. S. 104; s. c., 31 Pat. Off. Gaz. 913.

Evidence in a Proceeding Before a Master—Where Taken.—May be taken abroad. Bate Refrigerating Co. *v.* Gillette, 28 Fed. Rep. 673.

Suspension of Accounting.—Accounting will not be suspended pending an appeal of a case on the same patent decided in another circuit adversely to complainant. Celluloid Mfg. Co. *v.* Comstock etc. Co., 27 Fed. Rep. 358.

How Damages Are to be Paid When Several Are Interested in Patent.—Where several parties are entitled to a share of the damages, they are paid in proportion to their respective interests. Campbell *v.* James, 18 Blatchf. (U. S.) 92; s. c. 5 Bann. & Ard. Pat. Cas. 354; s. c., 2 Fed. Rep. 338; s. c., 18 Pat. Off. Gaz. 1261; Herring *v.* Gas Consumers Assoc, 9 Fed. Rep. 556; s. c., 21 Pat. Off. Gaz. 203.

But the defendant may be allowed to pay the gross amount into court. Campbell *v.* James, 18 Blatchf. (U. S.) 92; s. c., 5 Bann. &. Ard. Pat. Cas. 354; s. c., 2 Fed. Rep. 338; s. c., 18 Pat. Off. Gaz. 1111; Timken *v.* Olin, 41 Fed. Rep. 169.

2. Birdsell *v.* Hagerstown etc. Mfg. Co., 1 Hughes (U. S.) 59; s. c., 2 Bann. & Ard. Pat. Cas. 519; s. c., 11 Pat. Off. Gaz. 420; Wetherill *v.* New Jersey Zinc Co., 1 Bann. & Ard. Pat. Cas. 105; s. c., 5 Pat. Off. Gaz. 460; Atlantic etc. Giant Powder Co. *v.* Dittmar etc. Powder Mfg. Co., 9 Fed. Rep. 316; s. c., 20 Pat. Off. Gaz. 1380; Pennsylvania Diamond Drill Co. *v.* Simpson, 39 Fed. Rep. 284; s. c., 48 Pat. Off. Gaz. 676.

A mere sending of a machine from the maker to an agent is not enough. McKay *v.* Scott etc. Mach. Co., 20 Pat. Off. Gaz. 372.

Or an advertisement that a party makes a machine. Allis *v.* Stowell, 9 Pat. Off. Gaz. 727.

But fitting up a factory to make the infringing articles is. Goodyear *v.* Mullee, 5 Blatchf. (U. S.) 429; s. c., 3 Fish. Pat. Cas. 209.

Or combining to aid others to infringe. Bate Refrigerating Co. *v.* Gillett, 30 Fed. Rep. 683.

invention practiced, if changed from that which was enjoined, being merely colorably so,[1] and the terms[2] of the injunction and fact of its service[3] being clear, the defendant will be attached for contempt,[4] and punished in the like manner as in other contempts.[5]

Or partially making the device and sending it to others to be finished. Knowles *v.* Peck, 42 Conn. 386.

The contempt is the violation of the *injunction*, not the continuation of the infringement of the patent, and the injunction, if. wrong, should be rectified by the court on motion of the defendant. Hamilton *v.* Simons, 5 Biss. (U. S.) 77; Sickels *v.* Borden, 4 Blatchf. (U. S.) 14; Craig *v.* Fisher, 2 Sawy. (U. S.) 345.

1. Liddle *v.* Cory, 7 Blatchf. (U. S.) 1; Putnam *v.* Hollander, 11 Fed. Rep. 75; Bate Refrigerating Co. *v.* Eastman, 11 Fed. Rep. 902; Burk *v.* Imhauser, 2 Bann. & Ard. Pat. Cas. 465; s. c., 11 Pat. Off. Gaz. 112; Onderdonk *v.* Fanning, 2 Fed. Rep. 568; s. c., 5 Bann. & Ard. Pat. Cas. 562; California Art Stone Co. *v.* Molitio, 119 U. S. 451; s. c., 38 Pat. Off. Gaz. 329; Western etc. Mfg. Co. *v.* Rosenstock, 30 Fed. Rep. 67.

A real difference from the article enjoined will not subject the maker to an action for contempt; the remedy is a second suit for infringement, even if the article is within the patent. Michaels *v.* Roessler, 38 Fed. Rep. 742.

2. Whipple *v.* Hutchinson, 4 Blatchf. (U. S.) 190; Goodyear *v.* Mullee, 5 Blatchf. (U. S.) 429; s. c., 3 Fish. Pat. Cas. 209.

3. Whipple *v.* Hutchinson, 4 Blatchf. (U. S.) 190; Phillips *v.* Detroit, 2 Flipp. (U. S.) 92; s. c., 3 Bann. & Ard. Pat. Cas. 100; s. c., 16 Pat. Off. Gaz. 627.

4. Wetherell *v.* New Jersey Zinc Co., 1 Bann. & Ard. Pat. Cas. 105; s. c., 5 Pat. Off. Gaz. 460. See Wellesly *v.* Earl of Mornington, 11 Beav. (Eng.) 180.

A defendant neglecting to notify his agents of the injunction, is responsible for their acts. Mundy *v.* Ridgewood Mfg. Co., 34 Fed. Rep. 541.

The party in contempt must be a party to the suit. A corporation which purchases the business of another party who subsequently were enjoined, will not be in contempt for not obeying the injunction. Bate Refrigerating Co. *v.* Gillett, 30 Fed. Rep. 685.

A party may be punished for contempt or may be proceeded against by injunction where he violates the injunction in another circuit. Roemer *v.* Neumann, 23 Fed. Rep. 447.

5. Where the violation is not wilful, defendant will be merely required to pay the profits as damages and costs. Ready Roofing Co. *v.* Taylor, 15 Blatchf. (U. S.) 95; s. c., 3 Bann. & Ard. Pat. Cas. 368; Matthews *v.* Spangenberg, 23 Pat. Off. Gaz. 1624.

Counsel fees of complainant may be exacted. Doubleday *v.* Sherman, 8 Blatchf. (U. S.) 45; s. c., 4 Fish. Pat. Cas. 253; Schillinger *v.* Gunther, 14 Blatchf. (U. S.) 152; s. c., 2 Bann. & Ard. Pat. Cas. 544; s. c., 11 Pat. Off. Gaz. 831; Phillips *v.* Detroit, 2 Flipp. (U. S.) 92; s. c., 3 Bann. & Ard. Pat. Cas. 150; s. c., 16 Pat. Off. Gaz. 627; Searls *v.* Worden, 13 Fed. Rep. 716.

An order imposing a fine may be made. Fisher *v.* Hayes, 19 Blatchf. (U. S.) 13; s. c., 6 Fed. Rep. 63; s. c., 20 Pat. Off. Gaz. 601.

He may committed. Goodyear *v.* Mullee, 5 Blatchf. (U. S.) 463; s. c., 3 Fish. Pat. Cas. 260; Fischer *v.* Hayes, 20 Pat. Off. Gaz. 672.

Mitigating Circumstances.—Mitigating circumstances showing that the violation of an injunction was not wilful but unintentional, will lighten the penalty. Matthews *v.* Spangenberg, 15 Fed. Rep. 813; Barb Steel Wire Co. *v.* Southern Barbed Wire Co., 30 Fed. Rep. 615; s. c., 40 Pat. Off. Gaz. 578; Morss *v.* Domestic Sewing Mach. Co., 38 Fed. Rep. 482.

The advice of counsel is no excuse for a contempt. Bate Refrigerating Co. *v.* Gillett, 30 Fed. Rep. 683; Barr *v.* Kimbark, 29 Fed. Rep. 428; s. c., 40 Pat. Off. Gaz. 246; Goodyear *v.* Mullee, 5 Blatchf. (U. S.) 429; s. c., 3 Fish. Pat. Cas. 209; Morss *v.* Domestic Sewing Mach. Co., 38 Fed. Rep. 482.

Nor a mistake. Barb. Steel Wire Co. *v.* Southern Co., 30 Fed. Rep. 615; s. c., 40 Pat. Off. Gaz. 578.

Practice on Contempt.—The court can order an inspection of the device alleged to be made in contempt of the decree and refer the matter to a master to determine the facts. The contempt

XIX. Extension of Patent.[1]—An extension of patents was formerly allowed upon the application of the patentee[2] or his administrator[3] to the Commissioner of Patents,[4] and a setting forth of facts showing the value conferred upon the public by the invention and the inadequacy of the return to the patentee.[5] No ex-

is a criminal offence, and the fine or other penalty is a criminal judgment, which cannot be altered after the expiration of the term. The punishment for a contempt may be imposed by an order in the suit in which the injunction was granted, though it is not irregular to entitle the proceedings as "The People" *v.*———, or same "on relation of"———.the fine may be made payable to the party injured by the contempt, and the party in contempt ordered to pay expenses caused by his contempt; he may be committed; there cannot be an imprisonment and fine, but the party may be fined and committed until the fine be paid; and the court may make several orders in the case without exhausting its powers. It need not be averred in the order adjudging contempt that the injunction violated was lawful, nor the offense recited. Fischer *v.* Hayes, 6 Fed. Rep. 63.

1. While this subject of patent law is practically dead, yet it would leave the article incomplete to omit all reference; so the notes consist merely of a list of cases bearing on the text but not set forth at length.

2. Woodworth *v.* Sherman, 3 Story (U. S.) 171; s. c., 2 Robb Pat. Cas. 257; Brooks *v.* Bicknell, 4 McLean (U. S.) 64; Crompton *v.* Belknap Mills, 3 Fish. Pat. Cas. 536; Potter *v.* Braunsdorf, 7 Blatchf. (U. S.) 97.

3. Brooks *v.* Bicknell, 3 McLean (U. S.) 250; s. c., 2 Robb Pat. Cas. 118; Brooks *v.* Jenkins, 3 McLean (U. S.) 432; Washburn *v.* Gould, 3 Story (U. S.) 122; s. c., 2 Robb P. Cas. 206, Wilson *v.* Rousseau, 4 How. (U. S.) 646; s. c., 2 Robb Pat. Cas. 373; Woodworth *v.* Sherman, 3 Story (U. S.) 171; s. c., 2 Robb Pat. Cas. 257; Kellberg's Appeal, 86 Pa. St. 129.

4. U. S. Rev. Stats., § 4924.

Practice.—See U. S. Rev. Stats., §§ 4924, 4925; Brooks *v.* Bicknell, 3 McLean (U. S.) 250; s. c., 2 Robb Pat. Cas. 118; Gear *v.* Grosvenor, 6 Fish. Pat. Cas. 314; s. c., 1 Holmes (U. S.) 215; s. c., 3 Pat. Off. Gaz. 380; Johnson *v.* McCullough, 4 Fish. Pat. Cas. 170.

Practice in deciding whether to grant extension. See U. S. Rev. Stats., §§ 4926, 4927.

As to How Far the Decision of Commissioner Is Conclusive.—Dorsey etc. Rake Co. *v.* Marsh, 6 Fish. Pat. Cas. 387; s. c., 9 Phila. (Pa.) 395; Clum *v.* Brewer, 2 Curt. (U. S.) 506; Colt *v.* Young, 2 Blatchf. (U. S.) 471; Brooks *v.* Bicknell, 3 McLean (U. S.) 250; s. c., 2 Robb Pat. Cas. 118; Jordan *v.* Dobson, 4 Fish. Pat. Cas. 232; s. c., 2 Abb. (U. S.) 398; Goodyear *v.* Providence Rubber Co., 2 Fish. Pat. Cas. 499; s. c., 2 Cliff. (U. S.) 351; Gear *v.* Grosvenor, 1 Holmes (U. S.) 215; s. c., 6 Fish. Pat. Cas. 314; s. c., 3 Pat. Off. Gaz. 380; Crompton *v.* Belknap Mills, 3 Fish. Pat. Cas. 536; Eureka Co. *v.* Bartley Co., 11 Wall. (U. S.) 488; Mowry *v.* Whitney, 8 Fish. Pat. Cas. 157; Mowry *v.* Whitney, 4 Fish. Pat. Cas. 307; Mowry *v.* Whitney, 5 Fish. Pat. Cas. 496; Mowry *v.* Whitney, 14 Wall. (U. S.) 620; American Wood Paper Co. *v.* Glens Falls Paper Co., 8 Blatchf. (U. S.) 518; s. c., 4 Fish Pat. Cas. 324; Tilghman *v.* Mitchell, 9 Blatchf. (U. S.) 18; s. c., 4 Fish. Pat. Cas. 499.

Is Not Conclusive.—Brooks *v.* Bicknell, 3 McLean (U. S.) 250; s. c., 2 Robb Pat. Cas. 118; Wilson *v.* Rousseau, 4 How. (U. S.) 646.

What is a decision. See American Wood Paper Co. *v.* Glens Falls Paper Co., 8 Blatchf. (U. S.) 513; s. c., 4 Fish. Pat. Cas. 561.

Foreign patent will not prevent an extension. Tilghman *v.* Mitchell, 9 Blatchf. (U. S.) 18; s. c., 4 Fish. Pat. Cas. 615; New American File Co. *v.* Nicholson File Co., 8 Fed. Rep. 816; s. c., 20 Pat. Off. Gaz. 524.

5. That the patentee, without neglect or fault on his part, has failed to obtain from the use and sale of his invention or discovery a reasonable remuneration for the time, ingenuity and expense bestowed upon it, and the introduction of it into use, and that it is just and proper, having due regard to the public interest, that the term of the patent should be extended. U. S. Rev. Stats. 4929.

tension is now granted except by Congress.[1]

The extended patent and original term are considered as two distinct terms,[2] but the rights of assignees and grantees to use the thing patented of the original term have been, by statute,[3] extended into the extended term.[4]

XX. Special Actions Relating to Patents—1. Bills to Restrain Suits Against the Customers of a Manufacturer.—On the ground of preventing a multiplicity of suits, equity will sometimes enjoin the prosecution of suits against customers of a manufacturer where the proceedings against them are vexatious, and a suit is pending against the manufacturer.[5]

1. See *Rights Given by Act of Congress, supra.*

A special act procured by fraud is binding on the courts, and the only remedy is to obtain a repeal of the patent. Gibson *v.* Gifford, 1 Blatchf. (U. S.) 529.

And the form of an extension under a special act may be the same as that in general use. Agawam Co. *v.* Jordan, 7 Wall. (U. S.) 583.

A special act extending the patent is effected by the statute saving the rights of persons having the lawful right to use the thing patented into the extended term. Bloomer *v.* McQuewan, 14 How. (U. S.) 539; Bloomer *v.* Millinger, 1 Wall. (U. S.) 340; Blanchard *v.* Whitney, 3 Blatchf. (U. S.) 307.

Compare Bloomer *v.* Stolley, 5 McLean (U. S.) 158; Gibson *v.* Gifford, 1 Blatchf. (U. S.) 529.

2. Sayles *v.* Louisville etc. R. Co., 9 Fed. Rep. 512; Potter *v.* Empire Sewing Mach. Co., 3 Fish. Pat. Cas. 474.

3. U. S. Rev. Stats., § 4928.

4. It only means that one having a machine lawfully in use during the original term may continue lawfully to use it in the same manner during the extension. Wilson *v.* Rousseau, 4 How. (U. S.) 646; Woodworth *v.* Sherman, 3 Story (U. S.) 171; Wilson *v.* Turner, 4 How. (U. S.) 712; Blanchard *v.* Whitney, 3 Blatchf. (U. S.) 307, Bloomer *v.* Millinger, 1 Wall. (U. S.) 340; Wooster *v.* Seidenberg, 13 Blatchf. (U. S.) 88; s. c., 2 Bann. & Ard. Pat. Cas. 91; Day *v.* Union India Rubber Co., 3 Blatchf. (U. S.) 488; Union Mfg. Co. *v.* Lounsbury, 41 N. Y. 363; Mitchell *v.* Hawley, 1 Holmes (U. S.) 42; Mitchell *v.* Hawley, 16 Wall. (U. S.) 544; s. c., 3 Pat. Off. Gaz. 241; Chaffee *v.* Boston Belting Co., 22 How. (U. S.) 217; Eunson *v.* Dodge, 18 Wall. (U. S.) 414; s. c., 5 Pat. Off. Gaz. 95; Woodworth *v.* Curtis, 2 Woodb. & M. (U. S.) 424; s. c., 2 Robb Pat. Cas. 603; Woodworth *v.* Cook, 2 Blatchf. (U. S.) 151; Wetherill *v.* Passaic Zinc Co., 6 Fish. Pat. Cas. 50; s. c., 2 Pat. Off. Gaz. 471; Wilson *v.* Simpson, 9 How. (U. S.) 109; Farrington *v.* Water Commissioners, 4 Fish. Pat. Cas. 216; Aiken *v.* Manchester Print Works, 2 Cliff. (U. S.) 435; Bloomer *v.* McQuewan, 14 How. (U. S.) 539; Bloomer *v.* Stolley, McLean (U. S.) 158.

Where several rights besides using are given, the assignee may continue to use, but the other rights fall. Wood *v.* Michigan etc. R. Co., 2 Biss. (U. S.) 65; s. c., 3 Fish. Pat. Cas. 464; Hodge *v.* Hudson River R. Co., 6 Blatchf. (U. S.) 85; s. c., 3 Fish. Pat. Cas. 410.

5. Kelley *v.* Ypsilanti Dress Stay Mfg. Co., 44 Fed. Rep. 19; Allis *v.* Stowell. 16 Fed. Rep. 783; Rumford Chemical Works *v.* Hecker, 11 Blatchf. (U. S.) 552; s. c., 5 Pat. Off. Gaz. 644; Booth *v.* Seevers, 19 Pat. Off. Gaz. 1140; Birdsell *v* Hagerstown Agricultural Mfg. Co., 1 Hughes (U. S.) 64; Ide *v.* Ball Engine Co., 31 Fed. Rep. 901; National Cash Register Co. *v.* Boston Cash Indicator Co., 41 Fed. Rep. 51.

But a complainant will not be compelled to elect between several using purchasers. Celluloid Mfg. Co. *v.* Goodyear etc. Dental Co., 13 Blatchf. (U. S.) 375; s. c., 2 Bann. & Ard. Pat. Cas. 334; s. c., 10 Pat. Off. Gaz. 14.

The application must be made before proceedings have advanced far in the other suits. Rumford Chemical Works *v.* Hecker, 11 Blatchf. (U. S.) 552; s. c., 5 Pat. Off. Gaz. 644.

The articles claimed to infringe must be the same both in the cases against the purchasers and the case against the manufacturer. Allis *v.* Stowell, 16 Fed. Rep. 783.

2. Bills to Enjoin Libel of Patent Right.—A court of equity will not enjoin a libel in relation to matters connected with patent rights,[1] but a false and malicious statement published and used for the wilful purpose of inflicting an injury, authorizes the court to protect the injured party by an injunction.[2]

3. Fraudulent Marking of an Article "Patented."—The United States statutes give a *qui tam* action[3] against the offender for fraudulently marking articles in three cases.

(*a*) IMITATING THE NAME OF PATENTEE.—1. Where one marks upon anything made, used or sold by him, the name or any imitation of the name of any person who has obtained a patent therefor without the consent of such patentee, or his assigns or legal representatives.[4]

In some cases the court has refused to act except in cases in the district where application to stay proceedings was made. Chemical Works *v.* Hecker, 11 Blatchf. (U. S.) 552; s. c., 5 Pat. Off. Gaz. 644; Asbestos Felting Co. *v.* United States etc. Felting Co., 13 Blatchf. (U. S.) 453. But where the suit is not vexatious the court will not restrain. Tuttle *v.* Matthews, 28 Fed. Rep. 98.

1. Palmer *v.* Travers, 20 Fed. Rep. 501; Francis *v.* Flinn, 118 U. S. 385; Kidd *v.* Horry, 28 Fed. Rep. 773; Baltimore Car Wheel Co. *v.* Bemis, 29 Fed. Rep. 95; International Tooth Crown Co. *v.* Carmichael, 54 Pat. Off. Gaz. 1116; Kelley *v.* Ypsilanti Dress Stay Mfg. Co., 44 Fed. Rep. 19; Whitehead *v.* Kitson, 119 Mass. 484.

Especially where the purpose is merely to save persons from incurring liability by purchasing an infringing article. Chase *v.* Tuttle, 27 Fed. Rep. 110; Boston Diatite Co. *v.* Florence Mfg. Co., 114 Mass. 69.

Ide *v.* Ball Engine Co., 31 Fed. Rep. 901.

A court will not enjoin the publication of an injunction decree. Westinghouse Air Brake Co. *v.* Carpenter, 32 Fed. Rep. 545.

2. Ide *v.* Ball Engine Co., 31 Fed. Rep. 901; Emack *v.* Kane, 34 Fed. Rep. 46; Hovey *v.* Rubber etc. Pencil Co., 57 N. Y. 119; Snow *v.* Judson, 38 Barb. (N. Y.) 210; Croft *v.* Richardson, 59 How. Pr. (N. Y.) 356; Wren *v.* Weild, 42 B. Div. (Eng.) 730; Kelley *v.* Ypsilanti Dress Stay Mfg. Co., 44 Fed. Rep. 19; Bell *v.* Singer Mfg. Co., 65 Ga. 452.

In *England* the rule prior to the Patent act was that allegations must not only assert the statement to be untrue, but that it was without reasonable and probable cause. Halsey *v.* Brotherhood, 15 Ch. Div. L. R. (Eng.) 514; Challender *v.* Royle, 38 Ch. Div., L. R. (Eng.) 425; Wren *v.* Weild, 42 B. (Eng.) 730; Prudential Assoc. Co. *v.* Knott, 10 Ch. App. (Eng.) 143. Later English rulings, see Colley *v.* Hart, 44 Ch. Div., (Eng.) 579.

Practice.—Ordinarily, a bill praying relief both for infringement and against the publication of slanderous circulars concerning the patent is multifarious. Fougeres *v.* Murbarger, 44 Fed. Rep. 292.

Jurisdiction.—The action is in the federal courts only. Dudley *v.* Mayhew, 3 N. Y. 9; Middlebrook *v.* Broadbent, 47 N. Y. 443; Childs *v.* Tuttle, 54 Hun (N. Y.) 57.

3. One-half of said penalty to the person who shall sue for the same, and the other to the use of the United States, to be recovered by suit in any district court of the United States within whose jurisdiction such offense may have been committed. U. S. Rev. Stats., § 4901.

4. U. S. Rev. Stats., § 4901.

Practice.—The action cannot be prosecuted in the name of the United States alone; it should be in the name of the informer. If the United States be joined it should be "suing as well on account of the United States as of himself." United States *v.* Morris, 2 Bond (U. S.) 23; s. c., 3 Fish. Pat. Cas. 72; Winne *v.* Snow, 19 Fed. Rep. 507.

Place to Bring Suit.—Suit must be brought in the place where the offense was committed. Hat Sweat Mfg. Co. *v.* Davis Sewing Mach. Co., 31 Fed. Rep. 294.

Amount recoverable is just $100 for each offense. Stimpson *v.* Pond, 2 Curt. (U. S.) 502.

(*b*) FRAUDULENTLY PIRATING THE NAME OF ANOTHER'S PATENT.—2. Where one placed the word "patent" or similar words on a patented article with intent to imitate or counterfeit the mark or device of the patentee without the license or consent of such patentee, or his assigns or legal representatives.[1]

(*c*) FRAUDULENTLY MARKING AN UNPATENTED ARTICLE.—3. The constituents of the third action are: (1) That the defendant has placed the word "patent," or any word purporting that the same is patented;[2] (2) that he has done so on an unpatented article;[3] (3) and that he has done so for the purpose of deceiving the public,[4]

Special damage cannot be pleaded. Winne *v.* Snow, 19 Fed. Rep. 507.

Respondent Superior.—An employer who orders goods to be marked patented is responsible for the acts of his employees in so marking them. Kass *v.* Hawlowetz, 33 Pat. Off. Gaz. 1135; Nichols *v.* Newell, 1 Fish. Pat. Cas. 647.

Limitation.—Action must be brought within five years. Stimpson *v.* Pond, 2 Curt. (U. S.) 502.

Certainty in pleading to a common extent after the analogy of the State practice in civil actions, is sufficient. Fish *v.* Manning, 31 Fed. Rep. 340; Hat Sweat Mfg. Co. *v.* Davis Sewing Mach. Co., 31 Fed. Rep. 294.

1. U. S. Rev. Stat., § 4901.

The essentials to maintain an action under this clause are: the placing the word patented, the fact that the article is patented, that the patent belongs to another, that there be an attempt to imitate or counterfeit it, and that there be no consent from a party authorized or who could be deemed authorized to give such consent. French *v.* Foley, 11 Fed. Rep. 804.

Expired Patent.—It has been held on a bill in equity that while, after the expiration of a patent, the public have the right to use the patent, yet no one can represent that the goods are made by the patentee. Frost *v.* Rends Kopf, 42 Fed. Rep. 408.

2. If the word patent is put on in any way or in any part of the article it answers the statute. Nichols *v.* Newell, 1 Fish. Pat. Cas. 647.

But the use of the phrase "patent applied for" is not a violation of the statute; it does not make it appear that the article is patented. Schewbel *v.* Bothe, 40 Fed. Rep. 478.

3. A fraud with reference to an article actually patented is not under the contemplation of this clause of the act. French *v.* Foley, 11 Fed. Rep. 804; Wilson *v.* Singer Mfg. Co., 9 Biss. (U. S.) 173; s. c., 4 Bann. & Ard. Pat. Cas. 637; s. c., 12 Fed. Rep. 298.

Where defendant justifies under a patent, the court will construe the patent, and will determine whether the defendant's device is made under the patent. Hawlowetz *v.* Kass, 25 Fed. Rep. 765; s. c., 33 Pat. Off. Gaz. 1499; Tompkins *v.* Butterfield, 33 Pat. Off. Gaz. 758; s. c., 25 Fed. Rep. 556.

However, the jury were directed to find whether a new or different arrangement of parts from the arrangement of same parts in the patent, served any new or additional use that is valuable on the market. Duval *v.* Banker, 45 Pat. Off. Gaz. 591.

4. Nichols *v.* Newell, 1 Fish. Pat. 647; Oliphant *v.* Salem Flouring Mills Co., 5 Sawy. (U. S.) 128; s. c., 3 Bann. & Ard. Pat. Cas. 256; Walker *v.* Hawxhurst, 5 Blatchf. (U. S.) 494; Kass *v.* Hawlowetz, 33 Pat. Off. Gaz. 1135.

"For the purpose of deceiving the public" means "the purpose of making the public believe that the article is covered by a patent." Tomkins *v.* Butterfield, 33 Pat. Off. Gaz. 758; s. c., 25 Fed. Rep. 556.

There need not be more shown than a reckless disregard of the question whether there be a patent or not, to sustain this portion of the charge. Tompkins *v.* Butterfield, 33 Pat. Off. Gaz. 758.

The question whether the false marks were put on for the purpose of deceiving the public is a question of fact; although the presumption is that, if the article was unpatented, they were put on for the purpose of deception. Oliphant *v.* Salem Flouring Mills, 5 Sawy. (U. S.) 128; s. c., 3 Bann. &. Ard. Pat. Cas. 256.

But putting on a hose supporters the date of a patent for grain ties is not

all of which must be proved;[1] whether the plaintiff's evidence must convince the jury beyond a reasonable doubt,[2] or whether by a reasonable preponderance of evidence[3] is contradictorily decided.

XXI. Marking Article "Patented" by Patentee.—It is the duty of all patentees and their assignees and legal representatives to notify the public by marking the article made that it is patented,[4] in default of which damages cannot be recovered,[5] unless it be proved that the defendant was notified of the infringement and continued to infringe after notice.[6]

evidence of intent to deceive; the device is not clearly outside the patent. Frost *v.* Rindskopf, 42 Fed. Rep. 418; but the conduct of the defendant may be gone into by either side both during and before the act, to show the intent. Nichols *v.* Newell, 1 Fish. Pat. Cas. 647.

But putting on a structure the word patented *with the date of the patent*, after the patent has expired will negative the idea of fraud. Wilson *v.* Singer Mfg. Co., 11 Biss. (U. S.) 298; s c., 12 Fed. Rep. 57.

Respondant Superior.—A label which calls for a patent not applying to the articles on which it was placed, it having been put on them by an employee afterwards a director, it was held that the defendants were not affected by his knowledge if they had no actual knowledg themselves. Lawrence *v.* Holmes, 45 Fed. Rep. 357.

1. Nichols *v.* Newell, 1 Fish. Pat. Cas. 647.

2. Tompkins *v.* Butterfield, 33 Pat. Off. Gaz. 758.

3. Hawlowetz *v.* Kass, 33 Pat. Off. Gaz. 1499.

Deverall *v.* Banker, 45 Pat. Off. Gaz. 591.

These cases are both in the second circuit and establish the rule there In that circuit also the courts have refused to treat the action as a semi-criminal one, or to compel the plaintiff to prove his case with the same particularity, and exactness as a trial of an indictment. Hawlowetz *v.* Kass, 33 Pat. Off. Gaz. 1495; s. c., 25 Fed. Rep. 765; Kass *v.* Hawlowetz, 33 Pat. Off. Gaz. 1135; Fish *v.* Manning, 31 Fed. Rep. 340.

4. U. S. Rev. Stats., § 4900.

The statute refers only to a patenter; it has no application to an infringer. Herring *v.* Gage, 15 Blatchf. (U. S.) 124; s. c., 3 Bann. & Ard. Pat. Cas. 396. Nor any one else. Goodyear *v.* Allyn, 6 Blatchf. (U. S.) 33; s. c., 37 Fish. Pat. Cas. 374.

The statute provides that this marking shall be done "either by fixing (on the article) the word 'patented' together with the day and year the patent was granted; or when, from the character of the article, this cannot be done, by fixing to it, or to the package wherein one or more of them is inclosed, a label containing the like notice. Where the article can be stamped at a trifling cost, it must be stamped." Putnam *v.* Sudhoff, 1 Bann. & Ard. Pat. Cas. 198.

Presumption as to Marking.—The presumption is that the article was properly marked or the notice otherwise properly attached. Schofield *v.* Dunlop, 42 Fed. Rep. 323; Providence Rubber Co. *v.* Goodyear, 9 Wall. (U. S.) 788; Goodyear *v.* Allyn, 6 Blatchf. (U. S.) 33; s. c., 3 Fish. Pat. Cas. 374; Herring *v.* Gage, 15 Blatchf. (U. S.) 129; Walker on Patents (2nd ed.), § 463.

5. U. S. Rev. Stats, § 4900; McComb *v.* Brodie, 1 Wood (U. S.) 153; s. c., 5 Fish. Pat. Cas. 384; s. c., 2 Pat. Off. Gaz. 117.

This does not affect the right to an injunction. Goodyear *v.* Allyn, 6 Blatchf. (U. S.) 33; s. c., 3 Fish. Pat. Cas. 374.

6. U. S. Rev. Stats., § 4900.

The burden to prove (where there has been no "marking") notice and infringement after notice, is on the complainant. Goodyear *v.* Allyn, 6 Blatchf. (U. S.) 33. But the defendant must first prove that there has been no notice by marking. Schofield *v.* Dunlop, 42 Fed. Rep. 323.

The notice may be verbal or written. New York Pharmical Assoc. *v.* Tilden, 14 Fed. Rep. 740.

There is no trade-mark in the word patented, nor can the patentee claim

XXII. Repeal of Patent—1. By Act of Owner of Interfering Patent.—A party interested in a patent or in the working of an invention under patent[1] may, by bill in equity[2] against the owners of an interfering patent, have the patent declared invalid.[3] The decree may declare either of the patents invalid,[4] and other relief may be asked in the bill.[5] A decree, however, relative to the priority of the two patents should be made, unless the court dismiss the bill for lack of interference.[6] The decree affects the interests of the parties to the suit only.[7]

2. Repeal of Patent by the United States.—Patents can be repealed in a proceeding by bill in equity[8] by the United States

the exclusive right to use the word patented on articles manufactured under an expired patent. Fairbanks *v.* Jacobus, 14 Blatchf. (U. S.) 339; s. c., 3 Bann. & Ard. Pat. Cas. 108.

A party, however, need not notify the infringer of his infringement before he brings his action. Royer *v.* Coupe, 29 Fed. Rep. 358.

1. U. S. Rev. Stats., § 4918, Gay *v.* Cornell, 1 Blatchf. (U. S.) 506; Gold & Silver Ore etc. Co. *v.* United States Ore etc. Co., 6 Blaatchf. (U. S.) 307; s. c., 3 Fish. Pat. Cas. 489.

The complainant must have obtained or be interested in a patent, not merely claim to be the inventor of an invention patented to another. Hoeltge *v.* Hoeller, 2 Bond (U. S.) 386; Mason *v.* Rowley, 3 Am. L. T., N. S. 8.

2. Liggett etc. Tobacco Co. *v.* Miller, 1 McCrary (U. S.) 31; s. c., 1 Fed. Rep. 203; s. c., 5 Bann. & Ard. Pat. Cas. 237; s. c., 17 Pat. Off. Gaz. 798.

3. U. S. Rev. Stats., § 4918.

The interfering patent may be older or younger than the patent owned by complainant. Sturges *v.* Van Hagen, 6 Fish. Pat. Cas. 572.

But it must be an interfering patent. Garratt *v.* Seibert, 98 U. S. 75, s. c., 15 Pat. Off. Gaz. 383; Putnam *v.* Hutchinson, 12 Fed. Rep. 131; Gilmore *v.* Golay, 3 Fish. Pat. Cas. 522.

But the interference may be either or the whole of the part or of part. Gold & Silver Ore etc. Co. *v.* United States Ore etc. Co., 6 Blatchf. (U. S.) 307; s. c., 3 Fish. Pat. Cas. 489.

4. But not both; the question brought to issue is only that of priority. Pentlarge *v.* Pentlarge, 19 Fed. Rep. 817, Lockwood *v.* Cleveland, 20 Fed. Rep. 164; Sawyer *v.* Massey, 25 Fed. Rep. 144; American Clay Bird Co. *v.* Ligowski Clay Pigeon Co., 31 Fed. Rep. 466; Electric Accumulator Co. *v.* Brush Electric Co., 44 Fed. Rep 602; Foster *v.* Lindsay, 3 Dill. (U. S.) 126, s. c., 2 Bann. & Ard. Pat. Cas. 172, Foster *v.* Lindsay, 1 Bann. & Ard. Cas. 605; s. c., 7 Pat. Off. Gaz. 514.

Method of Attacking Complainant's Patent.—A proper method of making the defense that the patent of complainant is invalid, is by cross-bill as the relief sought is affirmative; but, as the statute gives the court the power on notice to adverse parties and other due proceedings had according to equity, the relief may be had without filing cross-bill. American Clay Bird Co. *v.* Ligowski Clay Pigeon Co., 31 Fed. Rep. 466. But see Lockwood *v.* Cleveland, 6 Fed. Rep. 721.

Method of Raising Issue Whether There Is an Interference in Fact.—May be raised by demurrer. Morris *v.* Kempshall Mfg. Co., 20 Fed. Rep. 121.

5. Potter *v.* Dixon, 5 Blatchf. (U. S.) 160; s. c., 2 Fish. Pat. Cas. 381, American Clay Bird Co. *v.* Ligowski Clay Pigeon Co., 31 Fed. Rep. 466.

6. Tyler *v.* Hyde, 2 Blatchf. (U. S.) 308.

7. U. S. Rev. Stats., § 4918.

8. United States *v.* American Bell Teleph. Co., 128 U. S. 315; s. c., 45 Pat. Off. Gaz. 1311; Mowry *v.* Whitney, 14 Wall. (U. S.) 434; United States *v.* Gunning, 18 Fed. Rep. 511.

The jurisdiction of a court of equity to repeal a patent is based on the general powers of a court of equity to annul and set aside contracts as instruments obtained by fraud, to correct mistakes made in them and to give all other appropriate relief against documents of that character, such as requiring their delivering up their cancellation or their correction in order to make them conform to the intention of the parties. United States *v.* American Bell Teleph. Co., 128 U. S. 315; s. c., 45 Pat. Off. Gaz. 1311.

Scire facias is not a proper remedy

against the holder of the patent where the patent has been fraudulently obtained.[1]

XXIII. Property in Patents—(See also License).—**1. Generally.**—A patent right has always been considered as property.[2] The right consists of the right to prevent the use, sale or making of a certain invention by others than the patentee.[3]

2. Kind of Property.—A patent right is personal property,[4] and after the death of the owner of the patent it vests in the personal representatives of the decedent.[5]

in America. United States *v.* American Bell Teleph. Co., 128 U. S. 1311, s. c., 45 Pat. Off. Gaz. 1311. Nor can the attorney general proceed under his own name by information. Atty. Gen. *v.* Hecker, 2 Bann. & Ard. Pat. Cas. 298; s. c., 32 Fed. Rep. 618.

There is no jurisdiction in equity after the patent has expired to repeal the patent. Providence Rubber Co. *v.* Goodyear, 9 Wall. (U. S.) 811.

Nor will a patent be repealed where it is merely alleged that the application had been rejected and the applicant denied a patent by the appellate tribunal, and the patent afterwards granted, possibly otherwise, where the bill to repeal alleged that the same matter was presented in the second application. United States *v.* Colgate, 32 Fed. Rep. 624. Nor in a case where the suit is in reality in the interest of a private party and the United States is indemnified from loss. United States *v.* Frazer, 22 Fed. Rep. 106.

1. United States *v.* American Bell Teleph. Co., 128 U. S. 315; s. c., 45 Pat. Off. Gaz. 1311; United States *v.* American Teleph. Co., 39 Fed. Rep. 716; s. c., 49 Pat. Off. Gaz. 284, Mahn *v.* Harwood, 112 U. S. 354. Overruling and reversing United States *v.* American Bell Teleph. Co., 32 Fed. Rep. 591. See also same case again before the same court in 30 Fed. Rep. 523.

2. McKeever *v.* United States, 14 Ct. of Cl. 396, Hockett *v.* State, 105 Ind. 257; Wilson *v.* Rousseau, 4 How. (U. S.) 646; Patterson *v.* Kentucky, 97 U. S. 506; Webber *v.* Virginia, 103 U. S. 347; Hammond *v.* Mason, 92 U. S. 728; Hendrie *v.* Sayles, 98 U. S. 546; Doughty *v.* West, 6 Blatchf. (U. S.) 429; s. c., 3 Fish. Pat. Cas. 580; Sloat *v.* Patten, 1 Fish. Pat. Cas. 154.

3. Jordan *v.* Overseers of Dayton, 4 Ohio 309; Tod *v.* Wick, 36 Ohio St. 384; Hawks *v.* Swett, 4 Hun (N. Y.) 150; Patterson *v.* Commonwealth, 11 Bush (Ky.) 315; Celluloid Mfg. Co. *v.* Goodyear Dental etc. Co., 2 Bann & Ard. Pat. Cas. 334; *In re* Brosnahan, 18 Fed. Rep. 64; Bloomer *v.* McQuewan, 14 How. (U. S.) 539; Patterson *v.* Kentucky, 97 U. S. 503; McKeever *v.* United States, 14 Ct. of Cl. 396; Boyd *v.* Brown, 3 McLean (U. S.) 295; Dewitt *v.* Elmira etc. Mfg. Co., 5 Hun (N. Y.) 301.

Consequently an authorization by a municipality to its officers to advertise for the lowest bids on a patented article, must mean that the lowest bidder authorized to employ the article is intended. Greaton *v.* Griffin, 4 Abb. Pr. N. S. (N. Y.) 310.

The rights conferred by each patent are separate; no patent gives a right to use improvements and no improvement the right to use the original. Gray *v.* James, Pet. (C. C.) 394.

4. Shaw Relief Valve Co. *v.* New Bedford, 19 Fed. Rep. 753; s. c., 28 Pat. Off. Gaz. 283, Bradley *v.* Dull, 19 Fed. Rep. 913; s. c., 27 Pat. Off. Gaz. 625; Vose *v.* Singer, 4 Allen (Mass.) 230, Holden *v.* Curtis, 2 N. H. 61.

A patent right has been treated as a chose in action and as analagous to a share of stock. Hull Patent Estate, § 13 etc.; Williams on Personal Property, pp. 98, 244.

5. Shaw Relief Valve Co. *v.* New Bedford, 19 Fed. Rep. 757; s. c., 28 Pat. Off. Gaz. 283; Bradley *v.* Dull, 19 Fed. Rep. 913, s. c., 27 Pat. Off. Gaz. 675; Peoria Target Co. *v.* Cleveland Target Co., 43 Fed. Rep. 922; Hodge *v.* Nroth Missouri R. Co., 1 Dill. (U. S.) 104; s. c., 4 Fish. Pat. Cas. 161.

An executor can maintain suit on a patent in the same manner as if he were trustee. Providence Rubber Co. *v.* Goodyear, 9 Wall. (U. S.) 788.

The right to take out a patent passes to the personal representatives of a decedent. Stimpson *v.* Rogers, 4 Blatchf. (U. S.) 333; Rice *v.* Burt, 16 Pat. Off. Gaz. 1050.

3. Joint Owners.—Joint owners of a patent right are owners in common thereof,[1] and in the absence of any specific agreement,[2] are not partners.[3] They are not liable to each other for an individual use of the patented invention.[4] A conveyance of a joint owner's portion may be made[5] and a license granted by one under which the licensee will not be liable to the others.[6] How far the joint owners are accountable to each other for profits made is undecided.[7]

The executor takes the patent in trust for the next of kin, as the grant of personal property to a man and his heirs means to him and the next of kin according to the statute of distribution. Shaw Relief Valve Co. *v.* New Bedford, 19 Fed. Rep. 753; Pelham *v.* Edelmeyer, 25 Pat. Off. Gaz. 292.

Contra, that they are not personal assets but a franchise to be held in trust for the heirs. Goodyear *v.* Hullihen, 2 Hughes (U. S.) 492; s. c., 3 Fish. Pat. Cas. 257.

Where a devise has been made in the will which would include the patent, the personal representative takes it in trust for devisee. Stimpson *v.* Rogers, 4 Blatchf. (U. S.) 333.

1. Dunham *v.* Indianapolis etc. R. Co., 7 Biss. (U. S.) 223; s. c., 2 Bann. & Ard. Pat. Cas. 327; Whitney *v.* Graves, 3 Bann. & Ard. Pat. Cas. 222; s. c., 13 Pat. Off. Gaz. 455; Vose *v.* Singer, 4 Allen (Mass.) 226; Duke *v.* Graham, 19 Fed. Rep. 647.

2. Pitts *v.* Hull, 3 Blatchf. (U. S.) 201.

They can enter into partnership and stipulate that one shall have sole control of the business. Kinsman *v.* Parkhurst, 18 How. (U. S.) 289.

But a mere agreement to account to each other does not make them partners. Fraser *v.* Gales, 20 Reporter 427.

3. Pitts *v.* Hall, 3 Blatchf. (U. S.) 201.

A right restricted to a partnership and not extending to assigns does not pass to corporations organized by the co-partners. Lock *v.* Lane etc. Co., 35 Fed. Rep. 289.

4. Vose *v.* Singer, 4 Allen (Mass.) 226; DeWitt *v.* Elmira etc. Mfg. Co., 66 N. Y. 459; Parkhurst *v.* Kinsman, 9 N. J. Eq. 600; Dunham *v.* Indianapolis etc. R. Co., 7 Biss. (U. S.) 223; s. c., 2 Bann. & Ard. Pat. Cas. 327; Whiting *v.* Graves, 3 Bann. & Ard. Pat. Cas. 222.

5. May *v.* Chaffee, 2 Dill. (U. S.) 385; s. c., 5 Fish. Pat. Cas. 160.

But can sell only his own share. Pitts *v.* Hall, 3 Blatchf. (U. S.) 201.

6. Dunham *v.* Indianapolis etc. R. Co., 7 Biss. (U. S.) 223; s. c., Bann. & Ard. Pat. Cas. 327; DeWitt *v.* Elmira etc. Mfg. Co., 66 N. Y. 459; Clum *v.* Brewer, 2 Curt. (U. S.) 506; Mathers *v.* Gran, L. R., 1 Ch. App. 29.

7. "The exact mutual rights of part owners of a patent have never yet been authoritatively settled. If one part owner derives a profit from a patent, either by getting the royalties from its use, or purchase money for sale of rights, it would seem that he should be accountable to the other part owners for their portion of such profit. And probably a bill for an account would be sustained therefor." Aspinwall Mfg. Co. *v.* Gill, 32 Fed. Rep. 697; Gates *v.* Fraser, 9 Ill. App. 628.

An agreement to divide license fees will compel accounting. Gates *v.* Fraser, 9 Ill. App. 624.

Or where inventor agreed to take patent for benefit of himself and tenant in common. Blakeney *v.* Goode, 30 Ohio St. 350; Marston *v.* Swett, 66 N. Y. 206.

An agreement between joint owners to account for the sales of the right to use a machine, does not compel them to account for profits on sales of machines to those having the right to use, or for profits of manufacture. Hubenthal *v.* Kennedy, 76 Iowa 707.

Estoppel of Joint Inventors.—A joint patentee cannot set up the invalidity of the patent against his co-owner. Stearns *v.* Barrett, 1 Pick. (Mass.) 443.

Where two joint inventors apply for a patent and one of them subsequently obtains it, the other has a joint interest in the invention and patent. Vetter *v.* Leutzinger, 31 Iowa 182.

Trust Doctrine Between Joint Owners.—An issue of a patent to one of two joint owners of a patent enures to both. Vetter *v.* Leutzinger, 31 Iowa 182.

4. **Assignment.**—(1) DEFINITION.—An assignment is a conveyance of the whole interest in a patent or any undivided part of such whole interest, in every portion of the United States.[1]

(2) DEFINITION OF GRANT.—A grant is a conveyance of the exclusive right under the patent to make and use, and to grant to others the right to make and use, the thing patented within and throughout some specified part or portion of the United States.[2]

(3) RIGHTS AND LIABILITIES OF TERRITORIAL GRANTEE.—A territorial grantee has a right to sell within his territory articles to be used outside of it in the territory of the patentee or of a grantee subsequent in time to him.[3] A purchase from him will not protect a purchaser who buys the goods in the territory for the purpose of selling them outside.[4]

(4) REQUISITES OF ASSIGNMENT.—Any patent or an interest therein[5]

1. Potter *v.* Holland, 4 Blatchf. (U. S.) 206; s. c., 1 Fish. Pat. Cas. 327; Gaylor *v.* Wilder, 10 How. (U. S.) 477; Blanchard *v.* Eldridge, 1 Wall. Jr. (C. C.) 337; s. c., 2 Robb Pat. Cas. 737; Pitts *v.* Jameson, 15 Barb. (N. Y.) 310; Buss *v.* Patney, 38 N. H. 44; Meyer *v.* Bailey, 2 Bann. & Ard. Pat. Cas. 73; s. c., 8 Pat. Off. Gaz. 437; Tyler *v.* Tuel, 6 Cranch (U. S.) 324.

Other cases do not strictly carry out this definition, but what are now called grants are also called assignments. Baldwin *v.* Libbey, 1 Cliff. (U. S.) 150; Farrington *v.* Gregory, 4 Fish. Pat. Cas. 221.

But a grant carrying the above rights, is an assignment regardless of its form of words. Nellis *v.* Pennock Mfg. Co., 13 Fed. Rep. 451; s. c., 22 Pat. Off. Gaz. 1131.

2. Potter *v.* Holland, 4 Blatchf. (U. S.) 206; s. c., 1 Fish. Pat. Cas. 327; Whittemore *v.* Cutter, 1 Gall. (U. S.) 429.

Contents of Instrument Prevails.—The fact that the form of an assignment or grant was adopted to serve ulterior ends, does not make the instrument less an assignment or grant. Siebert etc. Oil Cup Co. *v.* Beggs, 32 Fed. Rep. 790.

Anything less than these is only a license. Theberath *v.* Celluloid Mfg. Co., 3 Fed. Rep. 143; Hill *v.* Whitcomb, 1 Holmes (U. S.) 317; s. c., 1 Bann. & Ard. Pat. Cas. 34, s. c., 5 Pat. Off. Gaz. 430; Still *v.* Reading, 4 Wood (U. S.) 345, s. c., 9 Fed. Rep. 40; s. c., 20 Pat. Off. Gaz. 1025; Gamewell Fire Alarm Tel. Co. *v.* Brooklyn, 14 Fed. Rep. 255; Stanley Rule etc. Co. *v.* Bailey, 14 Blatchf. (U. S.) 510; Farrington *v.* Gregory, 4 Fish. Pat. Cas. 221; Glover *v.* Messer, 5 Fish. Pat. Cas. 411; Hatfield *v.* Smith, 44 Fed. Rep. 355; Dorsey etc. Rake Co. *v.* Bradley Mfg. Co., 12 Blatchf. (U. S.) 202.

3. Adams *v.* Burke, 17 Wall. (U. S.) 453; Washing Mach. Co. *v.* Earle, 3 Wall. (C. C.) 320; Simpson *v.* Wilson, 4 How. (U. S.) 709.

And it is unimportant whether the vendor knows that the goods are to be used outside or not. Hobbie *v.* Smith, 27 Fed. Rep. 656; Hobbie *v.* Jennison, 40 Fed. Rep. 887; *Contra*, Washburne etc. Co. *v.* Southern Wine Co., 37 Fed. Rep. 428; Hatch *v.* Hall, 30 Fed. Rep. 613.

The patentee cannot, however, sell for use in a territory for which he has made a grant. Ferrel *v.* Smith, 29 La. Ann. 811.

4. Standard Folding Bed Co. *v.* Keeler, 37 Fed. Rep. 693; Standard Folding Bed Co. *v.* Keeler, 41 Fed. Rep. 51, Hatch *v.* Adams, 22 Fed. Rep. 434; Hatch *v.* Hall, 22 Fed. Rep. 434; Hatch *v.* Adams, 30 Fed. Rep. 613; American Paper Barrel Co. *v.* Laraway, 28 Fed. Rep. 141, Union Paper Bag Co. *v.* Nixon, 1 Flipp. (U. S.) 491; s. c., 2 Bann. & Ard. Pat. Cas. 244; s. c., 9 Pat. Off. Gaz. 691.

5. The assignment of a patent is regulated by the statute, which must be followed strictly. Gayler *v.* Wilder, 10 How. (U. S.) 477.

But as patents are now granted to the patentee and his legal representa-

shall be assignable in law by an instrument in writing,[1] and the patentee, or his assigns or legal representatives may, in like manner, grant and convey an exclusive right under his patent to the whole or any specified part of the United States.

(5) FORMAL REQUISITES OF ASSIGNMENT OR GRANT.—Any instrument containing operative words showing an intention to assign[2] and a sufficiently clear designation of the subject matter

tives, they are assignable as other chattels by force of the grant. Blanchard *v.* Eldredge, 1 Wall. Jr. (C. C.) 337; s. c., 2 Robb Pat. Cas. 737.

States have no right to restrict sale of patents or determine the form of the assignment. Hollida *v.* Hunt, 70 Ill. 109; Crittenden *v.* White, 23 Minn. 29, Cranson *v.* Smith, 37 Mich. 309; Patterson *v.* Commonwealth, 11 Bush (Ky.) 311.

In *Indiana* a statute providing that the patentee must file a copy of the patent right in the county where any sale took place, was passed upon, but a decision of its validity not given. Hankey *v.* Downey, 116 Ind. 118; New *v.* Walker, 108 Ind. 365.

1. Horne *v.* Chatham, 64 Tex. 36; Campbell *v.* James, 18 Blatchf. (U. S.) 92; s. c., 18 Pat. Off. Gaz. 1111; s. c., 2 Fed. Rep. 338.

The various rights of selling, using and making under the patent, cannot be assigned separately. Gayler *v.* Wilder, 10 How. (U. S.) 477; Suydam *v.* Day, 2 Blatchf. (U. S.) 20; Sanford *v.* Messer, 1 Holmes (U. S.) 149; s. c., 5 Fish. Pat. Cas. 411; s. c., 2 Pat. Off. Gaz. 470.

A single claim under a patent may be assigned. Pope Mfg. Co. *v.* Gormully etc. Co., 34 Fed. Rep. 893.

An agreement which is not an assignment or grant, need not be in writing. Blakeney *v.* Goode, 30 Ohio St. 350; Springfield *v.* Drake, 58 N. H. 19.

Nor need the assignment of a right to canvass for and sell a patented machine. Springfield *v.* Drake, 58 N. H. 19.

Nor an agreement to assign an interest in a contemplated invention. Burr *v.* De La Vergue, 102 N. Y. 415.

Assignment by Written Instrument.—The instrument of conveyance must be in writing. Baldwin *v.* Sibley, 1 Cliff. (U. S.) 150; Jordan *v.* Dobson, 4 Fish. Pat. Cas. 232; s. c., 2 Abb. (U. S.) 398; s. c., 7 Phila. (Pa.) 533, Davy *v.* Morgan, 56 Barb. (N. Y.) 218; Gibson *v.* Cook, 2 Blatchf. (U. S.) 144; Case *v.* Redfield, 4 McLean (U. S.) 526; Black *v.* Stone, 33 Ala. 327; McKeman *v.* Hite, 6 Ind. 428; Moore *v.* Bare, 11 Iowa 198; Stone *v.* Palmer, 28 Mo. 839; Holden *v.* Curtis, 2 N. H. 61; Boyd *v.* McAlpin, 3 McLean (U. S.) 427; Galpin *v.* Atwater, 29 Conn. 93.

Seal.—But need not be under seal. Godfried *v.* Miller, 104 U. S. 521; s. c., 21 Pat. Off. Gaz. 711.

Verbal Assignment.—A verbal assignment, however, gives an equitable right. Burke *v.* Partridge, 58 N. H. 349.

Acknowledgment.—An acknowledgment before a notary public dispenses with the necessity of proving the signature of the assignor. New York Pharmical Association *v.* Tilden, 14 Fed. Rep. 740; s. c., 23 Pat. Off. Gaz. 272.

U. S. Rev. Stats., § 4898 provides: "Every patent or any interest therein shall be assignable in law by an instrument in writing; and the patentee or his assigns or legal representatives may, in like manner, grant and convey an exclusive right under his patent to the whole or any specified part of the United States. An assignment, grant or conveyance shall be void as against any subsequent purchaser or mortgagee for a valuable consideration, without notice, until it is recorded in the Patent Office within three months of the date thereof."

This section is confined to assignments after the grant of the patent. Wright *v.* Randel, 19 Blatchf. (U. S.) 495; s. c., 8 Fed. Rep. 591.

2. Campbell *v.* James, 18 Blatchf. (U. S.) 92; s. c., 2 Fed. Rep. 338; s. c., 5 Bann. & Ard. Pat. Cas. 354; s. c., 18 Pat. Off. Gaz. 1111.

Where it is ambiguous from the words whether or not an instrument is intended as an assignment, the intention of the parties may be considered. Kearney *v.* Lehigh Valley R. Co., 27 Fed. Rep. 699.

to be assigned[1] and the parties to the contract,[2] is sufficient. It is to be construed, as in any other contract,[3] by the whole agreement,[4] and under the ordinary rules governing the interpretation of written contracts.[5]

(6) ASSIGNOR.—The instrument of assignment follows the ordinary rules governing the contract[6] and the State laws where the contract is made,[7] as to the rights of agents,[8] corpora-

1. Harmon *v.* Bird, 22 Wend. (N. Y.) 113; Myers *v.* Turner, 17 Ill. 179; Hill *v.* Thuermer, 13 Ind. 351; Washburne etc. Mfg. Co. *v.* Haish, 4 Fed. Rep. 910; s. c., 19 Pat. Off. Gaz. 173; Nellis *v.* Pennock Mfg Co., 13 Fed. Rep. 451; s. c., 22 Pat. Off. Gaz. 1131; Campbell *v.* James, 18 Blatchf. (U. S.) 92, s. c., 5 Bann. & Ard. Pat. Cas. 354; s. c., 2 Fed. Rep. 338, s. c., 18 Pat. Off. Gaz. 1111.

2. Where the parties can be ascertained it is sufficient. Fisk *v.* Hollander, 4 McArthur (D. C.) 355.

3. Washburne *v.* Gould, 3 Story (U. S.) 122; s. c., 2 Robb Pat. Cas. 206; Morse *v.* O'Reilly, 6 Pa. L. J. (Pa.) 501; Philadelphia R. Co. *v.* Trimble, 10 Wall. (U. S.) 367; Eureka Co. *v.* Bailey Co., 1 Wall. (U. S.) 488; Perry *v.* Corning, 1 Blatchf. (U. S.) 195; Hope Iron Works *v.* Holden, 58 Me. 146; Taylor *v.* Collins, 102 Mass. 248; Seibert etc. Oil Cup Co. *v.* Phillips Lubricator Co., 10 Fed. Rep. 677; Seibert Co. *v.* Beggs, 32 Fed. Rep. 790; Wilson *v.* Chickering, 14 Fed. Rep. 917.

Intention of Parties.—It should be construed to carry out the intention of the parties. American etc. Pavement Co. *v.* Jenkins, 14 Wall. (U. S.) 452; s. c., 1 Pat. Off. Gaz. 465; Hall *v.* Speer, 6 Pitts. L. J. 403; Perry *v.* Corning, 7 Blatchf. (U. S.) 195; Wetherill *v.* Passaic Zinc Co., 6 Fish. Pat. Cas. 50; s. c., 2 Pat. Off. Gaz. 471.

Law of the Land.—Assignments will not be construed in conflict with the law of the land unless the intention is clearly indicated by the terms of the agreement. Wilson *v.* Rousseau, 4 How. (U. S.) 646.

4. Goodyear *v.* Cary, 4 Blatchf. (U. S.) 271; Baldwin *v.* Sibley, 1 Cliff. (U. S.) 150; Washburne *v.* Gould, 3 Story (U. S.) 122; s. c., 2 Robb Pat. Cas. 256.

5. Words are supposed to be used in their common sense. Goodyear *v.* Cary, 4 Blatchf. (U. S.) 271.

And no other meaning is to be given them unless it appears that some other or different meaning was intended. Goodyear *v.* Cary, 4 Blatchf. (U. S.) 271; Woodworth *v.* Sherman, 3 Story (U. S.) 171, s. c., 2 Robb Pat. Cas. 257; Troy Iron etc. Factory *v.* Corning, 14 How. (U. S.) 193.

What May Be Referred to in Interpreting an Assignment.—The circumstances under which the agreement was made. Read *v.* Bowman, 2 Wall. (U. S.) 591; Troy Iron etc. Factory *v.* Corning, 14 How. (U. S.) 193; Wetherill *v.* Passaic Zinc Co., 6 Fish. Pat. Cas. 50; s. c., 2 Pat. Off. Gaz. 471; Steam Cutter Co. *v.* Sheldon, 10 Blatchf. (U. S.) 1.

The specification where the assignment refers to it. Read *v.* Bowman, 2 Wall. (U. S.) 591.

A subsequent confirmatory instrument. R. Co. *v.* Trimble, 10 Wall. (U. S.) 367.

Doubt is to be resolved against grantor. Smith *v.* Selden, 1 Blatchf. (U. S.) 475; May *v.* Chaffee, 2 Dill. (U. S.) 385; s. c., 5 Fish. Pat. Cas. 160.

Oral Testimony as Effecting Interpretation.—Declarations written or oral as to the meaning of the contract or motives for making it, cannot vary the sense of the written contract. Wetherill *v.* Passaic Zinc Co., 6 Fish. Pat. Cas. 50; s. c.. 2 Pat. Off. Gaz. 471.

The date of delivery may be shown to be different from the date of the instrument. Dyer *v.* Rich, 1 Met. (Mass.) 180.

Also what was the consideration. Wheeler *v.* Billings, 38 N. Y. 263.

6. Kinsman *v.* Parkhurst, 18 How. (U. S.) 289; Wilson *v.* Rousseau, 4 How. (U. S.) 646; s. c., 2 Robb Pat. Cas. 372.

Several territorial grantees may unite in a single instrument as assignors. Ladd *v.* Mills, 22 Blatchf. (U. S.) 242; s. c., 20 Fed. Rep. 792.

7. Fetter *v.* Newhall, 21 Blatchf. (U. S.) 445; s. c., 17 Fed. Rep. 841.

8. **Agent.**—Contracts may be executed

tions,[1] married women[2] and others.[3]

(7) EXECUTION AND PROOF OF ASSIGNMENT.—The manner of executing and proving an assignment follows the State practice.[4]

(8) CONDITION.—A condition in an assignment does not reduce it to a license;[5] if the condition is precedent, the assignee takes no title until performance,[6] otherwise where the condition is subsequent.[7]

(9) COVENANTS.[8]

by the agent of a corporation, but the agent should, in the body of the contract, name the corporation as the contracting party and sign as its agent or officer. Gottfried *v.* Miller, 104 U. S. 521; s. c., 21 Pat. Off. Gaz. 711; Bellas *v.* Hays, 5. S. & R. (Pa.) 427. And where the assignment is executed by the agent, there must be proof of the agent's authority. Sone *v.* Palmer, 28 Mo. 539. And the authority must be under seal to authorize an assignment under seal. Bellas *v.* Hays, 5 S. & R. (Pa.) 427; Stetson *v.* Patten, 2 Me. 358.

Administrator and Executor.—Donoughe *v.* Hubbard, 27 Fed. Rep. 742; Bradley *v.* Dull, 19 Fed. Rep. 913; s. c., 27 Pat. Off. Gaz. 625; Northwestern Fire Extinguisher Co. *v.* Philadelphia Fire Extinguisher Co., 1 Bann. & Ard. Pat. Cas. 177; s. c., 6 Pat. Off. Gaz. 34.

The State laws cannot limit the authority of the administrator to *assign.* Brooks *v.* Jenkins, 3 McLean (U. S.) 432; Goodyear *v.* Hullihen, 2 Hughes (U. S.) 492; s. c., 3 Fish. Pat. Cas. 251.

1. Where the assignment was made by an officer having authority, or was ratified, it is a good execution. Eureka Co. *v.* Bailey Co., 11 Wall. (U. S.) 488. See as to what is a good execution for corporation. Campbell *v.* James, 17 Blatchf. (U. S.) 42; s. c., 18 Pat. Off. Gaz. 979; Gottfried *v.* Miller, 104 U. S. 321; s. c., 21 Pat. Off. Gaz. 711.

2. In *New York* where the property of a married woman is distinctly her own, she may, by her sole deed, assign her interest in a patent. Fetter *v.* Newhall, 21 Blatchf. (U. S.) 445; s. c., 17 Fed. Rep. 841, s. c., 28 Pat. Off. Gaz. 502.

3. **Administrators**—An administrator may assign. Brooks *v.* Jenkins, 3 McLean (U. S.) 432. And an assignment by one administrator gives a perfect title generally. Donoughe *v.* Hubbard, 27 Fed. Rep. 742; Bradley *v.* Dull, 19 Fed. Rep. 913; s. c., 27 Pat. Off. Gaz. 625; Wintermute *v.* Redington, 1 Fish. Pat. Cas. 239.

Infants.—An infant must assign by guardian. Fetter *v.* Newhall, 21 Blatchf. (U. S.) 445; s. c., 17 Fed. Rep. 841; s. c., 25 Pat. Off. Gaz. 502.

4. Houghton *v.* Jones, 1 Wall (U. S.) 703; Fetter *v.* Newhall, 21 Blatchf. (U. S.) 445; s. c., 17 Fed. Rep. 841; s. c., 25 Pat. Off. Gaz. 502.

5. Littlefield *v.* Perry, 21 Wall. (U. S.) 205; s. c., 7 Pat. Off. Gaz. 964; Ritter *v.* Serrell, 2 Blatchf. (U. S.) 379; Dorsey etc. Rake Co. *v.* Bradley Mfg. Co., 12 Blatchf. (U. S.) 202; s. c., 1 Bann. & Ard. Pat. Cas. 330.

6. Pitts *v.* Hall, 3 Blatchf. (U. S.) Philadelphia etc. R. Co. *v.* Trimble, 10 Wall. (U.S.) 367.

Where a contract shows that arbitrage is to be a condition precedent to a right to sue upon the contract, the plaintiff must make all reasonable efforts for an arbitration before he can sue. Perkins *v.* United States Electric Light Co., 21 Blatchf. (U. S.) 308; s. c., 16 Fed. Rep. 513; s. c., 24 Pat. Off. Gaz. 204. But suit can be brought if arbitration fails. Humaston *v.* American Tel. Co., 20 Wall. (U. S.) 20.

7. Stanley Rule etc. Co. *v.* Bailey, 14 Blatchf. (U. S.) 510; s. c., 3 Bann. & Ard. Pat. Cas. 297.

Where there is a condition of reassignment the court will decree a retransfer upon breach of condition. Andrews *v.* Fielding, 20 Fed. Rep. 123.

A condition in a patent assignment cannot be apportioned. Tinkham *v.* Erie R. Co., 53 Barb. (N. Y.) 393.

8. **Prosecution of Infringers.**—A covenant that all unlicensed persons should be prosecuted was reasonably fulfilled by taking action that resulted in stopping all infringements. Foster *v.* Goldschmidt, 21 Fed. Rep. 70. Nor does this covenant apply where the parties prosecuted are declared not to be infringers. Covell *v.* Bostwick, 39 Fed. Rep. 421. See Brewster *v.* Tuthill Spring Co., 34 Fed. Rep. 769.

A covenant to proscute infringers is not a warrantee that the vendee shall en-

(10) Implied Warrantee.—The vendor impliedly warrants the validity of the patent[1] and the title.[2]

5. Assignment of Unpatented Invention.—An assignment of an unpatented invention gives only an equitable title to the letters patent when issued,[3] except where the assignment contains matter showing that it was intended to operate upon the legal title to the letters patent, when the right to the monopoly and the property it created is by the operation of the assignment vested in the assignee.[4] An assignment of an unpatented inven-

joy privilege against persons not claiming rights under vendor, or estop him from showing that his patent is invalid in mitigation of damages. Jackson *v.* Allen, 120 Mass. 64. Nor that the patentee shall have the benefit of the invention as fully as patentee holds it. McKenzie *v.* Bailie, 4 Cin. L. B. 1 (Ohio) 209. See also Implied Warranty. vol. 10, p. 85.

1. Faulks *v.* Kamp, 17 Blatchf. (U. S.) 432; s. c., 5 Bann. & Ard. Pat. Cas. 73; s. c., 3 Fed. Rep. 898; s. c., 17 Pat. Off. Gaz. 851; Dickinson *v.* Hall, 14 Pick. (Mass.) 217; Rowe *v.* Blanchard, 18 Wis. 441; Shepherd *v.* Jenkins, 73 Mo. 510.

Hence a void patent is not a good consideration for a promissory note. Dickinson *v.* Hull, 14 Pick. (Mass.) 217; Bliss *v.* Negus, 8 Mass. 46; Cross *v.* Huntley, 13 Wend. (N. Y.) 385; Gieger *v.* Cook, 3 W. & S. (Pa.) 266; Bellas *v.* Hays, 5 S. & R. (Pa.) 427; Bierce *v.* Stocking, 11 Gray (Mass.) 174; Head *v.* Stephens, 19 Wend. (N. Y.) 411; Higgins *v.* Strong, 4 Blackf. (Ind.) 182; McClure *v.* Jeffrey, 8 Ind. 79; Rowe *v.* Blanchard, 18 Wis. 441; First Bank *v.* Peck, 8 Kan. 660; Turner *v.* Johnson, 2 Cranch (C. C.) 287; Nye *v.* Raymond, 16 Ill. 153; Jolliffe *v.* Collins, 21 Mo. 338; Springfield *v.* Drake, 58 N. H. 19; Lester *v.* Palmer, 4 Allen (Mass.) 145. See *Failure of Consideration, infra.*

2. Faulks *v.* Kamp, 17 Blatchf. (U. S.) 432; s. c., 3 Fed. Rep. 898; s. c., 5 Bann. & Ard. Pat. Cas. 85; s. c., 17 Pat. Off. Gaz. 851; Onderdonk *v.* Fanning, 5 Bann. & Ard. Pat. Cas. 85; s. c., 4 Fed. Rep. 148; Curran *v.* Birdsall, 20 Fed. Rep. 148; Curran *v.* Birdsall, 20 Fed. Rep. 885; s. c., 27 Pat. Off. Gaz. 1319.

3. Wright *v.* Randel, 8 Fed. Rep. 591; s. c., 19 Blatchf. (U. S.) 495; s. c., 21 Pat. Off. Gaz. 493; Clenn *v.* Brewer, 2 Curt. (U. S.) 506; Hammond *v.* Hunt, 4 Bann. & Ard. Pat. Cas. 111; Littlefield *v.* Perry, 21 Wall. (U. S.) 205; s. c., 7 Pat. Off. Gaz. 964; Woodworth *v.* Sherman, 3 Story (U. S.) 171; s. c., 2 Robb Pat. Cas. 257; Troy Iron etc. Co. *v.* Corning, 14 How. (U. S.) 192; Gayler *v.* Wilder, 10 How. (U. S.) 477; Aspinwall Mfg. Co. *v.* Gill, 40 Pat. Off. Gaz. 1133; United States Stamping Co. *v.* Jewett, 18 Blatchf. (U. S.) 469; s. c., 18 Pat. Off. Gaz. 1529; s. c., 7 Fed. Rep. 869; Hammond *v.* Pratt, 16 Pat. Off. Gaz. 124.

The legal title vests only when the patent issues. Pontiac Knit Boot Co. *v.* Merino Shoe Co., 31 Fed. Rep. 286.

Circumstances held not to be an equitable transfer of a subsequently granted patent. Dueber Watch Case Co. *v.* Dalzell, 38 Fed. Rep. 597, Fuller etc. Co. *v.* Bartlett, 68 Wis. 73.

4. Gayler *v.* Wilder, 10 How. (U. S.) 477; Rathbone *v.* Orr, 5 McLean (U. S.) 131; Rich *v.* Lippincott, 2 Fish. Pat. Cas. 1; Herbert *v.* Adams, 4 Mason (U. S.) 15; s. c., 1 Robb Pat. Cas. 50; United States Stamping Co. *v.* Jewett, 18 Blatchf. (U. S.) 469; s. c., 7 Fed. Rep. 869; s. c., 18 Pat. Off. Gaz. 1529; Clenn *v.* Brewer, 2 Curt. (U. S.) 506; Hendrie *v.* Sayles, 98 U. S. 546; Emmons *v.* Sladdin, 2 Bann. & Ard. Pat. Cas. 199; s. c., 9 Pat. Off. Gaz. 352.

The ultimate assignee at the date of the issue of the patent, if the assignments show that they intend to operate upon the legal title to letters patent, is the legal owner of them. Selden *v.* Stockwell etc. Gas Burner Co., 9 Fed. Rep. 390, s. c., 19 Blatchf. (U. S.) 544, s. c., 20 Pat. Off. Gaz. 1377; Consolidated Electric Light Co. *v.* Edison Electric Light Co., 33 Pat. Off. Gaz. 1597, s. c., 23 Blatchf. (U. S.) 412; s. c., 25 Fed. Rep. 719; Consolidated Electric Light Co. *v.* McKeesport Light Co., 34 Fed. Rep. 335; s. c., 44 Pat. Off. Gaz. 110.

When Assignment Can be Made.—An assignment can be made whenever there is any right in the assignor; it does not matter that the device is not complete.

tion gives a right to all patents that may be issued thereon.[1]

6. Recording Contracts.—(1) WHAT MAY BE RECORDED.—A conveyance assigning the entire patent right, an undivided part thereof, or of an exclusive right under the patent, within any specified part or portion of the United States, may be recorded properly in the Patent Office.[2] There is no authority to record an agreement for future assignment of any of these interests,[3] or for the conveyance of any different interest.[4]

Rathbone *v.* Orr, 5 McLean (U. S.) 131; Maurice *v.* Devol, 23 W. Va. 247.

Nor that it is made after a rejection of the application. Gay *v.* Cornell, 1 Blatchf. (U. S.) 506.

Or even when the inventions are yet in embryo in the inventor's mind. Nesmith *v.* Calvert, 1 Woodb. & M. (U. S.) 34; s. c., 2 Robb Pat. Cas. 311; Aspinwall Mfg. Co. *v.* Gill, 32 Fed. Rep. 697.

Or even a general sale of the inventive power of a man's mind. Hapgood *v.* Hewitt, 11 Fed. Rep. 422; s. c., 21 Pat. Off. Gaz. 1786; Continental Co. *v.* Empire Co., 8 Blatchf. (U. S.) 295; s. c., 4 Fish. Pat. Cas. 428; Green *v.* Willard Barrel Co., 1 Mo. App. 202; Appleton *v.* Bacon, 2 Black (U. S.) 699; Dueber Watch Case Co. *v.* Dalzel, 38 Fed. Rep. 597.

Or which may be made relating to a certain manufacture. Reese's Appeal, 122 Pa. St. 392.

An assignment of the invention is not a putting of it on sale, and does not make a patent granted on an application filed over two years subsequent to such assignment, void. United States Electric Lighting Co. *v.* Consolidated Electric Light Co., 33 Fed. Rep. 869.

1. Puetz *v.* Bransford, 31 Fed. Rep. 458.

An assignment of all right, title and interest in an improvement of a machine already patented, conveys no interest in the original patent. Leach *v.* Dresser, 69 Me. 129.

A right given under an invention not patented will protect the user of it from suit by assignees of patent rights of the vendor of the right under the unpatented invention. Hammond *v.* Mason etc. Organ Co., 6 Fish. Pat. Cas. 599.

What Amounts to an Assignment of an Unpatented Invention.—An irrevocable power of attorney. Hartshorn *v.* Day, 19 How. (U. S.) 211.

Employee Hired to Invent.—An employee may be hired to invent, in which case an equitable title is in the employer for the invention. Joliet Mfg. Co. *v.* Dice, 109 Ill. 649; Continental Windmill Co. *v.* Empire Windmill Co., 8 Blatchf. (U. S.) 295; s. c., 4 Fish. Pat. Cas. 428.

But no such right exists in the absence of such an agreement. Hapgood *v.* Hewitt, 119 U. S. 226; s. c., 37 Pat. Off. Gaz. 1247; McWilliams Mfg. Co. *v.* Blundell, 11 Fed. Rep. 419; s. c., 22 Pat. Off. Gaz. 177; Green *v.* Willard Barrel Co., 1 Mo. App. 202. Nor after the expiration of agreement. Appleton *v.* Bacon, 2 Black (U. S.) 699.

A contract for the sale of an unpatented invention may be proved by parol. Lockwood *v.* Lockwood, 33 Iowa 509; Burr *v.* De La Vergne, 102 N. Y. 415.

Estoppel.—An assignement of an interest in a patent does not by itself give any interest in a patent for another invention. Warren *v.* Cole, 15 Mich. 265; United Nickel Co. *v.* American Nickel Plating Works, 4 Bann. & Ard. Pat. Cas. 74.

2. Brooks *v.* Byam, 2 Story (U. S.) 525; s. c., 2 Robb Pat. Cas. 161; Blanchard *v.* Eldridge, 1 Wall. Jr. (C. C.) 337; s. c., 2 Robb Pat. Cas. 737; Stevens *v.* Head, 9 Vt. 174; Gibson *v.* Cook, 2 Blatchf. (U. S.) 144; Case *v.* Redfield, 4 McLean (U. S.) 526; Black *v.* Stone, 33 Ala. 327; McKernan *v.* Hite, 6 Ind. 428; Moore *v.* Bare, 11 Iowa 198; Sone *v.* Palmer, 28 Mo. 539; Holden *v.* Curtis, 2 N. H. 61.

3. New York Paper Bag Mach. Co. *v.* Union Paper Bag Mach. Co., 32 Fed. Rep. 783; Wright *v.* Randel, 19 Blatchf. (U. S.) 495; s. c., 8 Fed. Rep. 591; s. c., 21 Pat. Off. Gaz. 493.

4. Chambers *v.* Smith, 5 Fish. Pat. Cas. 12; s. c., 7 Phila. (Pa.) 575; Farrington *v.* Gregory, 4 Fish. Pat. Cas. 221; Buss *v.* Putney, 38 N. H. 44; Consolidated Fruit Jar Co. *v.* Whitney, 2 Bann. & Ard. Pat. Cas. 30; Gear *v.* Fitch, 16 Pat. Off. Gaz. 1231; s. c., 3 Bann. & Ard. Pat. Cas. 573; Brooks *v.*

(2) EFFECT OF RECORDING.—The recording of an assignment is not requisite to its validity;[1] and an unrecorded assignment is binding on the parties thereto[2] and on others having notice thereof,[3] or mere trespassers.[4] To protect the assignee from subsequent purchasers without notice, it must be recorded within three months of its date.[5] When so recorded it is a complete

Byam, 2 Story (U. S.) 525; Stevens *v.* Head. 9 Vt. 174.

1. Pitts *v.* Whitman, 2 Story (U. S.) 609; Peck *v.* Bacon, 18 Conn. 377.

The contrary doctrine obtains in *Indiana.* Higgins *v.* Strong, 4 Blackf. (Ind.) 182; Mullikin *v.* Latchem, 7 Blackf. (Ind.) 136.

2. Holden *v.* Curtis, 2 N. H. 61; Black *v.* Stone, 33 Ala. 327; Moore *v.* Bare, 11 Iowa 198; Continental Windmill Co. *v.* Empire Windmill Co., 8 Blatchf. (U. S.) 296; Horne *v.* Chatham, 64 Tex. 36.

Assignees Without Consideration.—And against subsequent assignees without consideration. Saxton *v.* Aultman, 15 Ohio St. 471.

3. Perry *v.* Corning, 7 Blatchf. (U. S.) 195. Continental Windmill Co. *v.* Empire Windmill Co., 8 Blatchf. (U. S.) 295; s. c., 4 Fish. Pat. Cas. 428; Peck *v.* Bacon, 18 Conn. 377; Holden *v.* Curtis, 5 N. H. 61; Sone *v.* Palmer, 28 Mo. 539; Moore *v.* Bare, 11 Iowa 198; McKernan *v.* Hite, 6 Ind. 428; Hapgood *v.* Rosenstock, 23 Fed. Rep. 86.

What Is Notice of a Prior Contract.—A notice of a prior interest. Wright *v.* Randel, 19 Blatchf. (U. S.) 495; s. c., 8 Fed. Rep. 591; s. c., 21 Pat. Off. Gaz. 493.

Where the assignee is a corporation of which the patentee is director and manager, it has notice through him of any unrecorded assignment. Continental Windmill Co. *v.* Empire Windmill Co., 8 Blatchf. (U. S.) 295; s. c., 4 Fish. Pat. Cas. 428; Steam Cutter Co. *v.* Sheldon, 10 Blatchf. (U. S.) 1.

Where an assignment of a right under a patent refers to the invention as being in use by a certain party. Prine *v.* Brandon Mfg. Co., 16 Blatchf. (U. S.) 453; s. c., 4 Bann. & Ard. Pat. Cas. 379.

The record of an assignment as administrator is notice of an assignment of same invention by same person as executor of same decedent. Newell *v.* West, 13 Blatchf. (U. S.) 114; s. c., 2 Bann. & Ard. Pat. Cas. 113; s. c., 8 Pat. Off. Gaz. 598; s. c., 9 Pat. Off. Gaz. 1110.

And in general anything that puts a person on inquiry. Hawley *v.* Mitchell, 4 Fish. Pat. Cas. 388; Sheldon Axle Co. *v.* Standard Axle Works, 37 Fed. Rep. 789; Dueber Watch Case Co. *v.* Dalzel, 38 Fed. Rep. 597.

Duty to See What Right, etc., Assignor Has Where It Is Not Stated in Assignment.—And where an assignment merely conveys the right, title and interest of the assignor, it does not cut off a previous unrecorded assignment where there is anything on which the subsequent assignment can operate. Turnbull *v.* Weir Plough Co., 6 Biss. (U. S.) 225; s. c., 1 Bann. & Ard. Pat. Cas. 544; s. c., 7 Pat. Off. Gaz. 173; Ashcroft *v.* Walworth, 5 Fish. Pat. Cas. 528; s. c., 1 Holmes (U. S.) 152; s. c., 2 Pat. Off. Gaz. 546; Hamilton *v.* Kingsbury, 17 Blatchf. (U. S.) 460; s. c., 4 Fed. Rep. 428; s. c., 5 Bann. & Ard. Pat. Cas. 157; s. c., 17 Pat. Off. Gaz. 847; Turnbull *v.* Weir Plough Co., 9 Biss. (U. S.) 334; s. c., 14 Fed. Rep. 108; s. c., 5 Bann. & Ard. Pat. Cas. 288; s. c., 23 Pat. Off. Gaz. 91.

The assignee takes subject to whatever limitations affect the title of his assignor. Pennington *v.* Hunt, 20 Fed. Rep. 195.

4. Pitts *v.* Whitman, 2 Story (U. S.) 609; s. c., 2 Robb Pat. Cas. 189; Sone *v.* Palmer, 28 Mo. 539; Hall *v.* Speer, 6 Pitts. L. J. (Pa.) 403; Olcott *v.* Hawkins, 2 Am. L. J. 317; Brooks *v.* Byam, 2 Story (U. S.) 525; s. c., 2 Robb Pat. Cas. 161; Boyd *v.* McAlpin, 3 McLean (U. S.) 427; s. c., 2 Robb Pat. Cas. 277; Case *v.* Redfield, 4 McLean (U. S.) 526; McKernan *v.* Hite, 6 Ind. 428; Louden *v.* Birt, 4 Ind. 566.

It has been held by some circuits and in some State courts that the assignment must be recorded before bringing suit against an infringer. Wyeth *v.* Stone, 1 Story (U. S.) 273; s. c., 2 Robb Pat. Cas. 23.

5. Gibson *v.* Cook, 2 Blatchf. (U. S.) 144; Case *v.* Redfield, 4 McLean (U. S.) 526; Black *v.* Stone, 33 Ala. 327; McKernan *v.* Hite, 6 Ind. 428; Moore *v.* Bare, 11 Iowa 198; Sone *v.* Palmer,

protection to the assignee and his assignees.[1]

7. Agency.—An agency in relation to patent rights is, as any other agency, revocable,[2] except where coupled with an interest.[3]

8. Other Contracts Respecting Patent Rights.—Contracts between owners of patents concerning the manner in which the patent rights of each shall be employed, and the articles to be made under them,[4] and options to purchase within a certain time,[5] and other agreements,[6] have been held valid.

28 Mo. 539; Holden *v.* Curtis, 2 N. H. 61; Campbell *v.* James, 18 Blatchf. (U. S.) 72; s. c., 2 Fed. Rep. 338; s. c., 5 Bann. & Ard. Pat. Cas. 354; s. c., 18 Pat. Off. Gaz. 1111.

1. A *bona fide* purchaser, whose assignment is duly recorded, will not be affected by any parol contract between the parties to a prior assignment as to what it should cover. Campbell *v.* James, 18 Blatchf. (U. S.) 92; s. c., 2 Fed. Rep. 338; s. c., 5 Bann. & Ard. Pat. Cas. 354; s. c., 18 Pat. Off. Gaz. 1111.

He is completely protected. Aspinwall Mfg. Co. *v.* Gill, 32 Fed. Rep. 697.

The record of an instrument not required to be recorded by the statute, will not affect the rights of subsequent assignees by its recording. Wright *v.* Randel, 19 Blatchf. (U. S.) 495; s. c., 8 Fed. Rep. 591; s. c., 21 Pat. Off. Rep. 493; New York Paper Bag Mach. Co. *v.* Union Paper Bag Mach. Co., 32 Fed. Rep. 783.

Chambers *v.* Smith, 5 Fish. Pat. Cas. 12; s. c., 7 Phila. (Pa.) 575.

See License, vol. 13, p. 514.

Nor can a subsequent *bona fide* assignee, who took title after the lapse of more than three months after the date of a prior assignment be affected by a mutual mistake in a prior conveyance, which mistake cannot be corrected after that time to the disadvantage of the subsequent purchaser. Gibson *v.* Cook, 2 Blatchf. (U. S.) 144; Woodworth *v.* Cook, 2 Blatchf. (U. S.) 151.

Racine Seeder Co. *v.* Joliet Wirecheck Rower Co., 27 Fed. Rep. 367.

2. Burdell *v.* Denig, 2 Fish. Pat. Cas. 588.

3. Day *v.* Candee, 3 Fish. Pat. Cas. 9; Burdell *v.* Denig, 2 Fish. Pat. Cas. 588.. See Assignors.

4. Star Salt Castor Co. *v.* Crossman, 4 Cliff. (U. S.) 568; Seibert etc. Oil Cup Co. *v.* William Powell Co., 38 Fed. Rep. 600.

An agreement of this kind is not binding on a purchaser of a machine from either party. Pratt *v.* Marean, 25 Ill. App. 516.

Such a contract does not necessarily give an exclusive license to either party. Seibert etc. Oil Cup Co. *v.* William Powell Co., 38 Fed. Rep. 600. See Woodworth *v.* Cook, 2 Blatchf. (U. S.) 151; McBurney *v.* Goodyear, 11 Cush. (Mass.) 569; Howe *v.* Wooldredge, 12 Allen (Mass.) 18.

5. An option to purchase and an agreement not to sell during the option, does not give a license to manufacture during that time. Iowa Barb Steel Wire Co. *v.* Southern Barbed Wire Co., 30 Fed. Rep. 615.

6. To extend time for payment of royalties. Brush-Swan Electric Light Co. *v.* Brush Electric Co., 41 Fed. Rep. 163. Or privies. Iowa Barb Steel Wire Co. *v.* Southern Barbed Wire Co., 30 Fed. Rep. 615.

Agreements relating to the exclusive right to manufacture for a patented device. Gally *v.* Cotts etc. Fire Arms Co., 30 Fed. Rep. 118; Houghton *v.* Rowley, 9 Phila. (Pa.) 288.

Agreements Giving an Equitable Right.—An assignee of a patent agreed to share the profits with the patentee, his assignor. At the instance of said assignor an extension of the patent was granted. *Held*, that the assignee had the benefit of the extended term, although his assignor had an equitable interest in it. Sayles *v.* Dubuque etc. R. Co., 5 Dill. (U. S.) 551.

Sale of Right to Royalties.—A contract may be made selling the right to royalties under a contract. United States *v.* Burns, 12 Wall. (U. S.) 246.

Equitable Doctrines as Applied to Patent Contracts—Estoppel.—An admission that a third party had power to grant rights under a patent by the true owner will estop him from prosecuting any one who, on account of this admission, has obtained rights for a valuable consideration from such third party. Gear *v.* Grosvenor, 1 Holmes (U. S.) 215. See *supra*, this title,

9. Royalty.—An agreement to account and pay royalties may form part of the consideration of an assignment without reducing it to a license.[1] An acceptance of an assignment makes the assignee liable for any sale under the invention assigned,[2] and is an implied agreement to manufacture under the patent.[3] In general the rules governing actions on contracts of assignments govern actions for royalties.[4]

Estoppel of Defendant to Set Up Certain Defenses.

Resulting Trusts.—One who obtains the legal title of patent with knowledge of an equitable title in another, holds it in trust for the true owner. Whiting *v.* Graves, 23 Pat. Off. Gaz. 940; Pontiac Knit Boot Co. *v.* Merino Shoe Co., 31 Fed. Rep. 286.

1. Littlefield *v.* Perry, 21 Wall. (U. S.) 205; s. c., 7 Pat. Off. Gaz. 964.

A contract to pay royalties for the use of an unpatented invention begins, unless otherwise designated, when the patent issues. Travis *v.* Minneapolis Sweeper Co., 41 Minn. 176.

2. As a general thing, royalty is due wherever the party manufacturing under it has enjoyed the benefits of the patent. Covell *v.* Bostwick, 39 Fed. Rep. 421; Jones *v.* Burnham, 67 Me. 93; National Rubber Co. *v.* Boston Rubber Shoe Co., 41 Fed. Rep. 48; Rogers *v.* Reissner, 30 Fed. Rep. 525; Marston *v.* Sweet, 66 N. Y. 206; Marston *v.* Swett, 82 N. Y. 526; Hyatt *v.* Dale Tile Mfg. Co., 106 N. Y. 651; Paper Stock Disinfecting Co. *v.* Boston Disinfecting Co., 147 Mass. 318; Wilder *v.* Adams, 16 Gray (Mass.) 478; Wilder *v.* Stearns, 48 N. Y. 656; Johnson *v.* Willimantic Co., 33 Conn. 436.

Where an assignee agrees to pay the patentee a certain sum "for each and every one of said machines sold or caused to be sold by him," *held* that this covered any transfer or settlement by which the right to use a machine passed. Rodgers *v.* Torrant, 43 Mich. 113.

Where an assignment is made of an invention and a patent to be granted thereon any article made embracing the "invention" will require a royalty. Milligan *v.* Lalance etc. Mfg. Co., 21 Fed. Rep. 570.

An assignor is entitled to royalty on machines which were sold by one adjudged an infringer of the patent at the suit of the assignee, when the purchasers from the infringer have paid the assignee for the right to use. Porter *v.* Standard Measuring Machine Co., 142 Mass. 191.

Where articles finished or unfinished made under the patent were turned over to the successor of the defendant, this is a sale, and royalty is due. Marsh *v.* Dodge, 6 Thomp. & C. (N. Y.) 568; s. c., 4 Hun (N. Y.) 278.

Where articles substantially the same as those described are made, royalty is due on them. Wilder *v.* Adams, 16 Gray (Mass.) 478.

Where one properly authorized licensee purchases from another properly authorized licensee, and sells again, only one royalty is collectible. Howe *v.* Wooldredge, 12 Allen (Mass.) 18.

Cessation of Royalty.—Royalty ceases on termination of contract. Garver *v.* Bement, 69 Mich. 149.

But where the contractor attempts to put an end to the license which is not acquiesced in by the contractee, the contractee is liable for royalty on articles made after as well as articles made before the notice of termination. Union Mfg. Co. *v.* Lounsbury, 41 N. Y. 363; Wilde *v.* Smith, 8 Daly (N. Y.) 196.

Manufacture and shipment are presumptive evidence of sale. Marsh *v.* Dodge, 5 Lans. (N. Y.) 541; Smith *v.* Standard Laundry Mach. Co., 11 Daly (N. Y.) 154.

An acceptance of royalty is an acceptance of a transfer. Bloomer *v.* Gilpin, 4 Fish. Pat. Cas. 50.

A royalty may be recovered on a *quantum meruit* where an implied contract is made to use a patented invention and pay for the use. Deane *v.* Hodge, 35 Minn. 146.

3. Wilson *v.* Marlow, 66 Ill. 385.

But not to manufacture to a certain extent unless expressly stipulated. Hornbostel *v.* Kinney, 110 N. Y. 94; Babcock *v.* Northern Pac. R. Co., 26 Fed. Rep. 756. See Washburne etc. Co. *v.* Southern Wire Co., 37 Fed. Rep. 428.

4. **Lack of Consideration.**—Lack of novelty in an invention is not a good

10. Actions on Contracts.—(1) SPECIFIC PERFORMANCE.—Equity will enforce the specific performance of a contract of sale of a patent right.[1] The ordinary equitable doctrines are enforced,[2] and an account and other equitable remedies are employed,[3] even

defense by an assignee to royalties due, when there has been no eviction. Patterson's Appeal, 99 Pa. St. 521; Shaw *v.* Soule, 20 Fed. Rep. 790. See also LICENSE, vol. 13, p. 514.

But a decree of a United States court declaring the patent void, is a good defense to royalties accruing subsequently thereto. Hawks *v.* Swett, 4 Hun (N. Y.) 146; Marston *v.* Swett, 4 Hun (N. Y.) 153. See *supra*, this title, *Defenses to an action for Infringement.*

Invalidity of patent where the party owing royalties has received the benefit of a patent is no defense to royalties. McKay *v.* Smith, 39 Fed. Rep. 556; Covell *v.* Bostwick, 39 Fed. Rep. 421; Hyatt *v.* Ingalls, 49 N. Y. Super. Ct. 375; Patterson's Appeal, 99 Pa. St. 521; Angier *v.* Eaton etc. Co., 98 Pa. St. 594; Jones *v.* Burnham, 67 Me. 93; Hall Mfg. Co. *v.* American etc. Supply Co., 48 Mich. 331; Birdsall *v.* Perego, 5 Blatchf. (U. S.) 251; Clark *v.* Amoskeag Mfg. Co., 62 N. H. 612; Washburne etc. Mfg. Co. *v.* Wilson, 48 N. Y. Super. Ct. 159; Eureka Co. *v.* Baily Co., 11 Wall. (U. S.) 488; Marsh *v.* Harris Mfg. Co., 63 Wis. 176; Evory *v.* Candee, 17 Blatchf. (U. S.) 200; s. c., 4 Bann. & Ard. Pat. Cas. 540; Milligan *v.* Lalance etc. Co., 21 Fed. Rep. 570; s. c., 29 Pat. Off. Gaz. 367; White *v.* Lee, 14 Fed. Rep. 789; s. c., 23 Pat. Off. Gaz. 1631.

A failure to prevent others from manufacturing unless some stipulation to that effect is contained in the agreement, is not a defense to actions for royalty. National Rubber Co. *v.* Boston Rubber Shoe Co., 41 Fed. Rep. 48.

1. Adams *v.* Messinger, 147 Mass. 185; Somerby *v.* Buntin, 118 Mass. 279; Hapgood *v.* Rosenstock, 23 Blatchf. (U. S.) 95; Satterthwaite *v.* Marshall, 4 Del. Ch. 337; Fuller etc. Co. *v.* Bartlett, 68 Wis. 73; Pontiac Knit Boot Co. *v.* Merino Shoe Co., 31 Fed. Rep. 286; Annin *v.* Wren, 51 Hun (N. Y.) 352; Berolzheimer *v.* Strauss, 19 Jones & S. (N. Y.) 96; Goodyear *v.* Day, 6 Duer (N. Y.) 154; Newell *v.* West, 13 Blatchf. (U. S.) 114; s. c., 2 Bann. & Ard. Pat. Cas. 113; Hartshorn *v.* Day, 19 How. (U. S.) 211; Day *v.* Candee, 1 Fish. Pat. Cas. 9; Aikin *v.* Dolan, 3 Fish. Pat. Cas. 197; Emmons *v.* Sladdin, 2 Bann. & Ard. Pat. Cas. 199; s. c., 9 Pat. Off. Gaz. 352; Woodworth *v.* Sherman, 3 Story (U. S.) 171; s. c., 2 Robb Pat.Cas. 257.

An agreement to assign future inventions may be enforced. Reese's Appeal, 122 Pa. St. 392; Somerby *v.* Buntin, 118 Mass. 279; Nesmith *v.* Calvert, 1 Woodb. & M. (U. S.) 34; s. c., 2 Robb Pat. Cas. 311.

Oral Agreement.—The agreement may be merely oral. Searle *v.* Hill, 73 Iowa 367; Sombery *v.* Buntin, 118 Mass. 279; Burr *v.* De La Verne, 102 N. Y. 415.

Implied Agreement.—Or even only implied. Fuller etc. Co. *v.* Bartlett, 68 Wis. 73; Fire Extinguisher Mfg. Co. *v.* Graham, 16 Fed. Rep. 543.

2. Specific performance will not be enforced where there is an adequate remedy at law and complainant has not been free from fault. Brewster *v.* Tuthill Spring Co., 34 Fed. Rep. 769.

Nor the transfer of a void patent. Kennedy *v.* Hazleton, 33 Fed. Rep. 293; s. c., 46 Pat. Off. Gaz. 973; Kennedy *v.* Hazleton, 128 U. S. 667.

Nor where the contract which the complainant was suing to enforce was unconscionable or against public policy. Pope Mfg. Co. *v.* Gormully, 34 Fed. Rep. 877.

Nor where complainant was in fault. Ohio etc. Fence Co. *v.* Washburne etc. Co., 26 Fed. Rep. 703; s. c., 35 Pat. Off. Gaz. 1337; Foster *v.* Goldschmidt, 22 Blatchf. (U. S.) 289; s. c., 21 Fed. Rep. 70; s. c., 28 Pat. Off. Gaz. 915; Werden *v.* Graham, 107 Ill. 169; Brewster *v.* Tuthill Spring Co., 34 Fed. Rep. 769. Werden *v.* Graham, 107 Ill. 169.

Nor in detriment of the accrued rights of innocent third parties. Whitney *v.* Burr, 115 Ill. 289.

Laches.—Nor where the complainant has been guilty of laches. New York Paper Bag Mach. Co. *v.* Union Paper Bag Mach. Co., 32 Fed. Rep. 783; Werden *v.* Graham, 107 Ill. 169.

Nor where the court could not give suitable relief by the decree. Wollensak *v.* Briggs, 20 Ill. App. 50; s. c., 37 Pat. Off. Gaz. 339.

3. **Conveyance Upon Conditional Agree-**

where for some cause specific performance may not be decreed.[1]

(2) RESCISSION OF CONTRACT.—A statement by the vendor which is only a matter of opinion,[2] or a mere matter of law,[3] or which is immaterial,[4] or is not relied on by the vendee,[5] is not ground for rescinding the contract; but a false representation of a material fact [6] will justify the rescission; but the right to rescind must be exercised within a reasonable time.[7]

11. Defenses to Actions Growing Out of Contracts.—(1) WANT OF CONSIDERATION.—Where the patent is invalid,[8] or no such

ment.—Where an agreement is made to convey a patent upon the happening of certain contingencies, specific performance may be decreed on proof that these contingencies had happened. Andrews *v.* Fielding, 20 Fed. Rep. 123.

1. An owner of a patent may be enjoined from selling to any one else a patent he has agreed to sell to complainant, where the court is unwilling to decree the specific performance of the contract. Singer Sewing Mach. Mfg. Co. *v.* Union Button-Hole etc. Co., 1 Holmes (U. S.) 253; s. c., 6 Fish. Pat. Cas. 480; s. c., 4 Pat. Off. Gaz. 553; Goddard *v.* Wilde, 17 Fed. Rep. 845; Adams *v.* Nessinger, 147 Mass. 185; Brush-Swan Electric Light Co. *v.* Brush Electric Co., 41 Fed. Rep. 163.

2. London *v.* Birt, 4 Ind. 568; Fowler *v.* Swift, 3 Ind. 188; Neidefer *v.* Chastain, 71 Ind. 363; Gatling *v.* Newell, 12 Ind. 118; Miller *v.* Young, 33 Ill. 354.

3. Rawson *v.* Harger, 48 Iowa 269; West *v.* Morrison, 2 Bibb (Ky.) 376.

Compare, however, Rose *v.* Hurley, 39 Ind. 77.

4. Neidefer *v.* Chastain, 71 Ind. 363.

A false representation of the price at which the patentee was accustomed to sell the machine will not vitiate the contract. Williams *v.* Hicks, 2 Vt. 36.

5. Percival *v.* Hager, 40 Iowa 286; Hess *v.* Young, 59 Ind. 379.

Other Circumstances Held Not Grounds For Rescission.—Excess of price over value of patent. Bierce *v.* Stocking, 11 Gray (Mass.) 174; Percival *v.* Harger, 40 Iowa 286; Cowan *v.* Mitchell, 11 Heisk. (Tenn.) 87.

6. Pierce *v.* Wilson, 34 Ala. 596; Hall *v.* Orvis, 35 Iowa 366; Page *v.* Dickerson, 28 Wis. 694; Neil *v.* Cummings, 75 Ill. 170.

A false representation that a man has a patent right such as he has not. Bull *v.* Pratt, 1 Conn. 342; Brown *v.* Wright, 17 Ark. 9; McKee *v.* Eaton, 26 Kan. 226; David *v.* Park, 103 Mass. 501.

It does not matter that the purchaser might have discovered the fraud by searching the records at the Patent Office. McKee *v.* Eaton, 26 Kan. 226.

A false representation that a patented article is salable. Hull *v.* Fields, 76 Va. 594.

A false representation of the amount derived annually from a royalty on a patent. Crosland *v.* Hall, 33 N. J. Eq. 111.

A false representation as to what is covered by the patent. Rose *v.* Hurley, 39 Ind. 77.

This representation may be made by showing a machine containing improvements not embraced in patent assigned, which improvements were afterward patented. Cowan *v.* Mitchell, 11 Heisk. (Tenn.) 87.

7. Rawson *v.* Harger, 48 Iowa 269; Kingsley *v.* Wallis, 14 Me. 57; Pierce *v.* Wilson, 34 Ala. 596.

The assignee alone can have the contract rescinded. Edmunds *v.* Hildreth, 16 Ill. 214.

8. Dickinson *v.* Hall, 14 Pick. (Mass.) 217; Lester *v.* Palmer, 4 Allen (Mass.) 145; Bliss *v.* Negus, 8 Mass. 46; Bierce *v.* Stocking, 11 Gray (Mass.) 174; Geiger *v.* Cook, 3 W. & S. (Pa.) 266; Bellas *v.* Hays, 5 S. & R. (Pa.) 427; Elmer *v.* Pennell, 40 Me. 430; Green *v.* Stuart, 7 Baxt. (Tenn.) 418; Cross *v.* Huntley, 13 Wend. (N. Y.) 385; Kernsdle *v.* Hunt, 4 Blackf. (Ind.) 27; McClure *v.* Jeffrey, 8 Ind. 79; Nye *v.* Raymond, 16 Ill. 153; Jolliffe *v.* Collins, 21 Mo. App. 338; Rowe *v.* Blanchard, 18 Wis. 441; Rice *v.* Garnhart, 34 Wis. 453; Marston *v.* Swett, 82 N. Y. 526.

This is not a defense even *pro tanto*, where several patents are conveyed by quit claim deed, and one turns out void. Gilmore *v.* Aiken, 118 Mass. 94.

patent had been granted,[1] or the vendor had no title,[2] or the invention was utterly useless,[3] there is a failure of consideration for the contract,[4] which is a complete defense[5] to an action brought on the contract or on anything connected with it.

(2) BREACH OF WARRANTEE.—If a warrantee is given a breach of warrantee is a defense.[6]

It can only be set up as disputed in the contract. Ball *v.* Murry, 10 Pa. St. 111.

It cannot be set up as a defense to a suit on an instrument under seal. Bellas *v.* Hays, 5 S. & R. (Pa.) 421; Wilder *v.* Adams, 2 Woodb. & M. (U. S.) 329.

1. McDowell *v.* Meredith, 4 Whart. (Pa.) 311; Nye *v.* Raymond, 16 Ill. 153; Shepherd *v.* Jenkins, 73 Mo. 510.

This defense can be made on a bond given for such a patent. Brown *v.* Wright, 17 Ark. 9.

But a delay in obtaining a patent is no defense to an action for purchase money to be paid therefor. Reid *v.* Bowman, 2 Wall. (U. S.) 591.

2. Stevens *v.* Head, 9 Vt. 174; Buss *v.* Putney, 38 N. H. 44; Holden *v.* Curtis, 2 N. H. 61.

3. Clough *v.* Patrick, 37 Vt. 421; Cragin *v.* Fowler, 34 Vt. 326; Williams *v.* Hicks, 2 Vt. 36; Scott *v.* Sweet, 2 Greene (Iowa) 224; Bliss *v.* Negus, 8 Mass. 46; Lester *v.* Palmer, 4 Allen (Mass.) 145; Rowe *v.* Blanchard, 18 Wis. 441; Geeger *v.* Cook, 3 W. & S. (Pa.) 266; McDoughall *v.* Fogg, 2 Bosw. (N. Y.) 387.

As to evidence see Wilson *v.* Hentges, 26 Minn. 288; Bierce *v.* Stocking, 11 Gray (Mass.) 174.

Limitation.—This doctrine does not refer to a case where the invention was rendered worthless by subsequent improvements. Harmon *v.* Bird, 22 Wend. (N. Y.) 113.

Nor where the risk of success was taken by the assignee and the patented process employed. Palmer's Appeal, 96 Pa. St. 106.

Nor where the lack of utility is only with reference to certain uses. Midkiff *v.* Boggess, 75 Ind. 210.

Nor where merely it cannot be used profitably. Nash *v.* Lull, 102 Mass. 60; Howe *v.* Richards, 102 Mass. 64, n.; Neidefer *v.* Chastain, 71 Ind. 363.

If the patent be of any value, the patentee is entitled to recover. Vaughan *v.* Porter, 16 Vt. 260. And also where the assignee has in his turn assigned for a valuable consideration. Thomas *v.* Quintard, 5 Duer (N. Y.) 80.

4. The fact that the patent granted cannot be used without infringing other patents is a good defense. Davis *v.* Gray, 17 Ohio 330; Orr *v.* Burwell, 15 Ala. 378.

But not where the prior patent which was infringed has been declared void. Shaw *v.* Soule, 20 Fed. Rep. 790.

Vague Description.—A patent which describes a machine in such a manner that it cannot be determined what the invention consists in, is not a good consideration for a note. Cross *v.* Huntly, 13 Wend. (N. Y.) 385.

5. It must be shown as a matter of defense that the patent lacks novelty or utility. Case *v.* Morey, 1 N. H. 347; Myers *v.* Turner, 17 Ill. 179; Hardesty *v.* Smith, 3 Ind. 39.

It has been held, that in the absence of a decision of a United States court, a State court cannot allow the defendant to show the invalidity of the patent. Elmer *v.* Pennel, 40 Me. 430.

That the vendor had no title must be shown as matter of defense. Buss *v.* Putney, 38 N. H. 44; Holden *v.* Curtis, 2 N. H. 61; Stevens *v.* Head, 9 Vt. 174.

A defendant is not estopped in an action on a bond given for purchase of a patent to show non-existence of patent, invalidity or lack of title in assignor. Nye *v.* Raymond, 16 Ill. 153.

Contra, the vendor must show a title in himself and tender a conveyance according to the contract unless such tender is dispensed with before recovery. Edwards *v.* Richards, Wright (Ohio) 596; Bellas *v.* Hays, 5 S. & R. (Pa.) 427.

6. Vaughan *v.* Porter, 16 Vt. 266; Jolliffe *v.* Collins, 21 Mo. 338, Van Ostrand *v.* Reed, 1 Wend. (N. Y.) 424; Orr *v.* Burwell, 15 Ala. 378; Case *v.* Morey, 1 N. H. 347; Myers *v.* Turner, 17 Ill. 179; Hardesty *v.* Smith, 3 Ind. 39; Jackson *v.* Allen, 120 Mass. 64; Croninger *v.* Paige, 48 Wis. 229; Hiatt *v.* Twomey, 1 Dev. & B. Eq. (N. Car.) 315; Darst *v.* Brockway, 11

(3) Fraud.—Fraud on the part of one of the contracting parties is a good defense.[1]

(4) Defense Pro Tanto.—A misrepresentation of the utility of a patented invention, where the device is not entirely useless,[2] a breach of contract by the assignor,[3] and other matters showing a partial failure of consideration, may be set up in mitigation of the plaintiff's claim.[4]

(5) Duty of Vendee to Return Patent.—When a contract is rescinded[5] or failure of consideration set up on a defense,[6] the vendee should tender back the patent right or show it is worthless. This does not apply to cases where an action is brought for fraud in a sale of a patent right.[7]

12. Actions Arising Out of Fraud in Contract.—Where an assignment has been procured by fraud, an action of deceit lies,[8] or the purchaser may recover back the price paid.[9]

Ohio St. 462; Cansler *v.* Eaton, 2 Jones (N. Car.) 499; Wright *v.* Wilson, 11 Rich. (S. Car.) 144.

Recovery can be had where a process has been warranted to produce a certain effect and does not do it. Hawes *v.* Twogood, 12 Iowa 582.

A warrantee not contaned in the original assignment cannot be proved unless it is averred to be fraudulent: McClure *v.* Jeffrey, 8 Ind. 79; Jolliffe *v.* Collins, 21 Mo. 338; Van Ostrand *v.* Reed, 1 Wend. (N. Y.) 432; Rose *v.* Hurley, 39 Ind. 77.

But defendant must have relied upon a misrepresentation to render it a warrantee and a defense. Saxton *v.* Dodge, 57 Barb. (N. Y.) 84.

1. Turner *v.* Johnsen, 2 Cranch (C. C.) 287; McDowell *v.* Meredith, 4 Whart. (Pa.) 311; Nye *v.* Raymond, 16 Ill. 153.

2. Mullikin *v.* Latchem, 7 Blackf. (Ind.) 136; Hardesty *v.* Smith, 3 Ind. 39.

3. Pitts *v.* Jameson, 15 Barb. (N. Y.) 310; Moore *v.* Bare, 11 Iowa 198.

4. But a purchaser of the right, title and interest of a party in an unpatented invention is not entitled to a reduction for the money expended by him in procuring a patent, or in obtaining the interest of the true inventor. Vetter *v.* Lentzinger, 31 Iowa 182.

5. Pierce *v.* Wilson, 34 Ala. 596.

6. Mullikin *v.* Latchem, 7 Blackf. (Ind.) 136; Hardesty *v.* Smith, 3 Ind. 39; Burns *v.* Barnes, 58 Ind. 436.

7. Hess *v.* Young, 59 Ind. 379.

Where, however, equity is resorted to to compel a rescission of a contract, the complainant must tender a return of the patent, or value, if sold. Edmunds *v.* Myers, 16 Ill. 207; Edmunds *v.* Hildreth, 16 Ill. 214.

8. Warren *v.* Cole, 15 Mich. 265.

Fraudulent representations known to be such at the time or recklessly made without knowledge, will enable the vendee, if injured, to bring action for deceit. Jolliffe *v.* Collins, 21 Mo. 338; Somers *v.* Richards, 46 Vt. 170; Newell *v.* Gatling, 7 Ind. 147; Gatling *v.* Newell, 9 Ind. 572; Gatling *v.* Newell, 12 Ind. 118; Bull *v.* Pratt, 1 Conn. 342.

In an action for deceit the vendor may show the true state of facts, although they are different from that set up in the assignment. Swazey *v.* Herr, 11 Pa. St. 278.

9. Foss *v.* Richardson, 15 Gray (Mass.) 303; Hiatt *v.* Twomey, 1 Dev. & B. Eq. (N. Car.) 315; Cansler *v.* Eaton, 2 Jones Eq. (N. Car.) 499; McKenzie *v.* Bailie, 4 Cin. L. B. (Ohio) 209; Stevens *v.* Head, 9 Vt. 174; Darst *v.* Brockway, 11 Ohio St. 642; McDowell *v.* Meredith, 4 Whart. (Pa.) 311; Dickinson *v.* Hall, 14 Pick. (Mass.) 217.

Where an assignment implies that a patent has been issued, the assignor may recover back his money if such is not the fact. Shepherd *v.* Jenkins, 73 Mo. App. 510. Or if the inventor sells his patent by the exhibition of a device supposed to be the one patented, but afterwards discovered to differ materially from it. Burrall *v.* Jewett, 2 Paige (N. Y.) 134. But the mere invalidity of the patent, in absence of fraud, will not warrant the recovery of the purchase money. Hiatt *v.* Twomey, 1 Dev. & B. Eq. (N. Car.) 315.

13. Claims Arising Out of Patented Invention Prior to the Assignment.—Unless otherwise provided in the instrument,[1] claims arising out of the use, sale or making of the patented invention at any time prior to the assignment, do not pass to the assignee.[2] These claims may be the subject of a separate conveyance,[3] or the right to sue for them remains in the assignor.[4]

14. Jurisdiction of Equity for Fraud and Mistake.—Equity will decree the reformation or cancellation of an instrument containing a contract concerning a patent right, on the gronnd of mutual mistake,[5] or compel the surrender and cancellation of an instrument tainted with fraud.[6]

15. Jurisdiction of Equity to Enforce Discovery or Enjoin Violation of Agreement.—Equity will enforce a discovery of the number of patented articles made,[7] and will enjoin the violation of an agreement[8] concerning patent property where there is not an ade-

A false representation that the goods made in accordance with patent are equal to the quality of goods made in the usual way. Nelson *v.* Wood, 62 Ala. 175.

1. An assignment of "all the right, title, interest, claims and demands" which the assignor has "in, to, by, under and through" specified letters patent, carries damages for past infringements.. May *v.* Logan Co., 30 Fed. Rep. 250; May *v.* Saginaw Co., 32 Fed. Rep. 629. See Campbell *v.* James, 18 Blatchf. (U. S.) 92.

2. Merriam *v.* Smith, 11 Fed. Rep. 588; New York Grape Sugar Co. *v.* Buffalo Grape Sugar Co., 21 Blatchf. (U. S.) 519; s. c., 18 Fed. Rep. 638; s. c., 25 Pat. Off. Gaz. 1076; Moore *v.* Marsh, 7 Wall. (U. S.) 515; Emerson *v.* Hubbard, 34 Fed. Rep. 327; May *v.* Juneau Co., 30 Fed. Rep. 241; Knowlton Platform etc. Co. *v.* Cook, 70 Me. 143.

A mere intention to do so is not sufficient; the instrument of conveyance must show the intention. Emerson *v.* Hubbard, 34 Fed. Rep. 327.

3. Hamilton *v.* Rollins, 5 Dill. (U. S.) 495; s. c., 3 Bann. & Ard. Pat. Cas. 157; Shaw *v.* Colwell Lead Co., 20 Blatchf. (U. S.) 417; s. c., 11 Fed. Rep. 711; May *v.* Logan Co., 30 Fed. Rep. 250; s. c., 41 Pat. Off. Gaz. 1387.

An assignment of this kind conveys no interest in the patent right. Tilghman *v.* Proctor, 125 U. S. 136. Campbell *v.* James, 18 Blatchf. (U. S.) 92; s. c., 2 Fed. Rep. 338; s. c., 18 Pat. Off. Gaz. 1111.

The assignee of claims for past infringement takes subject to equities. New York Grape Sugar Co. *v.* Buffalo Grape Sugar Co., 18 Fed. Rep. 638; s. c., 25 Pat. Off. Gaz. 1076; s. c., 21 Blatchf. (U. S.) 519.

4. Spring *v.* Domestic Sewing Mach. Co., 13 Fed. Rep. 446.

Such a claim passes to an administrator. May *v.* Juneau Co., 30 Fed. Rep. 241; s. c., 41 Pat. Off. Gaz. 578.

5. Burrall *v.* Jewett, 2 Paige (N. Y.) 134; Foss *v.* Richardson, 15 Gray (Mass.) 303; Black *v.* Stone, 33 Ala. 327.

A request for the alteration desired to be made, or a reason for the omission of such request must be shown by the complainant. Black *v.* Stone, 33 Ala. 327.

A mistake collateral to the instrument is not ground for cancellation or reformation. Overshiner *v.* Wisehart, 59 Ind. 135.

6. For undue influence. Colburn *v.* Van Velzer, 11 Fed. Rep. 795.

Where a negotiable instrument is given for a void patent the court will compel its surrender and cancellation. Darst *v.* Brockway, 11 Ohio 462; Bellas *v.* Hays, 5 S. & R. (Pa.) 427. But not a non-negotiable instrument. Cansler *v.* Eaton, 2 Jones Eq. (N. Car.) 499.

An assignment of right, title and interest in an improvement does not carry extensions. Johnson *v.* Sewing Mach. Co., 27 Fed. Rep. 689.

7. Hobbie *v.* Owsley, 27 Fed. Rep. 100; Pope Mfg. Co. *v.* Jennison, 40 Fed. Rep. 887.

And an account. McKay *v.* Smith, 29 Fed. Rep. 265.

8. Wilson *v.* Sherman, 1 Blatchf. (U. S.) 536.

quate remedy at law.[1]

Equity will order the conveyance of a property to a party having the equitable right by a party having the legal title.[2]

16. Execution on a Patent Right.—A patent right may be taken in execution on a bill in the nature of a creditor's bill praying that the owner may be compelled to assign his rights in the court in which the judgment is obtained.[3] In some States other proceedings have been upheld by which the patent right has been subjected to execution.

17. Insolvency and Bankruptcy.—A patent right does not pass by the mere assignment under a State insolvent law,[4] but does under a bankrupt act.[5]

1. McKay *v.* Smith, 29 Fed. Rep. 295.

To enjoin the breach of a mutual agreement by holders of patent rights as to the way in which they shall manufacture. Star Salt Castor Co. *v.* Crossman, 4 Cliff. (U. S.) 568.

Where a plaintiff is suing for royalties, he will not be enjoined from so doing on account of a breach of his agreement with defendant, but will be enjoined, pending his suit, from determining the contract. An adequate remedy at law existing in one case but not in the other. Baker Mfg. Co. *v.* Washburne etc. Mfg. Co., 5 McCrary (U. S.) 504; s. c., 18 Fed. Rep. 172.

But equity will not enjoin at the suit of complainant guilty of fraudulent concealment to the disadvantage of the defendant. Washburne etc. Mfg. Co. *v.* Scutt, 22 Fed. Rep. 710; Washburne etc. Mfg. Co. *v.* Cincinnati Barbed Wire Fence Co., 22 Fed. Rep. 712.

2. Emmons *v.* Sladdin, 2 Bann. & Ard. Pat. Cas. 199; s. c., 9 Pat. Off. Gaz. 352.

A court will decree the conveyance of the right to royalties by the holder of the legal title, to the holder of the equitable right. Rogers *v.* Riessner, 30 Fed. Rep. 525.

The court will decree the conveyance where the trust is a constructive one. Fire Extinguisher Mfg. Co. *v.* Graham, 16 Fed. Rep. 543.

3. Barnes *v.* Morgan, 3 Hun (N. Y.) 703; Pacific Bank *v.* Robinson, 57 Cal. 520; s. c., 20 Pat. Off. Gaz. 1314; Murray *v.* Ager, 20 Pat. Off. Gaz. 1311; s. c., 1 Mackey (D. C.) 87; Ager *v.* Murray, 105 U. S. 126; s. c., 21 Pat. Off. Gaz. 1197; Clan Ranald *v.* Wyckhoff, 41 N. Y. Super. Ct. 527; Carver *v.* Peck, 131 Mass. 291; Gillett *v.* Bate, 86 N. Y. 87; Edmeston *v.* Lyde, 1 Paige (N. Y.) 637; Brinkerhoff *v.* Brown, 4 Johns. Ch. (N. Y.) 671; McDermutt *v.* Strong, 4 Johns. Ch. (N. Y.) 687; Spader *v.* Davis, 5 Johns. Ch. (N. Y.) 280; Hadden *v.* Spader, 20 Johns. Ch. (N. Y.) 554.

Where the owner of the patent is insolvent, he may be compelled by an insolvent court or court of equity to assign his rights to a receiver or trustee. Petition of Keech, 14 R. I. 571.

Ordinarily the owner of the patent must be compelled to assign in the regular manner. Ashcroft *v.* Walworth, 1 Holmes (U. S.) 152; s. c., 5 Fish. Pat. Cas. 528; s. c., 2 Pat. Off. Gaz. 546.

In *Pennsylvania* apparently the patent right cannot be reached by equitable process.

Rutter's Appeal (Pa. 1887), 8 Atl. Rep. 170; Bakewell *v.* Keller, 11 W. N. C. (Pa.) 300.

In some jurisdictions it can be reached by a creditor's bill in the usual form. Gorrell *v.* Dickson, 26 Fed. Rep. 454; Gillett *v.* Bate, 86 N. Y. 87.

And a federal court can take jurisdiction in a creditor's bill where the State court could not grant relief. Gorrell *v.* Dickson, 26 Fed. Rep. 454.

Generally a patent right cannot be subjected to any of the usual methods of execution. It has been held that it could not be thus seized in Carver *v.* Peck, 131 Mass. 291; Pacific Bank *v.* Robinson, 57 Cal. 520; Stevens *v.* Gladding, 17 How. (U. S.) 447; Stevens *v.* Cady, 14 How. (U. S.) 528.

4. Ashcroft *v.* Walworth, 1 Holmes (U. S.) 152; s. c., 5 Fish. Pat. Cas. 528; s. c., 2 Pat. Off. Gaz. 546; Gordon *v.* Anthony, 16 Blatchf. (U. S.) 234; s. c., 4 Bann. & Ard. Pat. Cas. 248; s. c., 16 Pat. Off. Gaz. 1135; Petition of Keach, 14 R. I. 571.

5. Prime *v.* Brandon Mfg. Co., 16 Blatchf. (U. S.) 453; s. c., 4 Bann & Ard. Pat. Cas. 379.

18. Jurisdiction in Suits Over Patent Property.—In cases where the validity or infringement of patent rights are not involved,[1] the jurisdiction in suits on contracts relating to patent rights or for the redress of wrongs connected therewith, is in the courts of the States,[2] unless the courts of the United States obtain jurisdiction by diverse citizenship.

An assignment by a bankruptcy court need not be recorded in Patent Office. Prime *v.* Brandon Mfg. Co., 16 Blatchf. (U. S.) 453; s. c., 4 Bann. & Ard. Pat. Cas. 379.

But it will not override prior agreements. Frane *v.* Galis, 20 Reporter 427.

1. Dudley *v.* Mayhew, 3 N. Y. 9; Parkhurst *v.* Kinsman, 6 N. J. Eq. 600; Kempton *v.* Bray, 99 Mass. 350; Tomlinsion *v.* Buttel, 4 Abb. Pr. (N. Y.) 266, Gibson *v.* Woodworth, 8 Paige (N. Y.) 132; Parsons *v.* Barnard, 7 Johns. (N. Y.) 144; Stone *v.* Edwards, 35 Tex. 556; Elmer *v.* Pennel, 40 Me. 430; Albright *v.* Teas, 106 U. S. 613.

Nor can it acquire jurisdiction suing in the form of an action to recover upon a *quantum valebat* for use of the patented invention. Battin *v.* Kear, 2 Phila. (Pa.) 301; De Witt *v.* Elmira etc. Mfg. Co., 66 N. Y. 459.

Has Not Equitable Jurisdiction.— A State court cannot enjoin the collection of a decree of a United States court. Kendall *v.* Winsor, 6 R. I. 453.

Nor to restrain a party from an alleged illegal act when that party justifies under a patent. Hovey *v.* Rubber Tip Pencil Co., 33 N. Y. Super. Ct. 522.

Nor to consider a set-off consisting of a claim for infringement of a patent. Smith *v.* McClelland, 11 Bush (Ky.) 523.

But a State court may incidentally in the course of a controversy, inquire into the validity, etc., of a patent. Burrall *v.* Jewett, 2 Paige (N. Y.) 134; Sherman *v.* Champlain Transp. Co., 31 Vt. 162; Lindsay *v.* Roraback, 4 Jones' Eq. (N. Car.) 124; Middlebrook *v.* Broadbent, 47 N. Y. 443; Saxton *v.* Dodge, 57 Barb. (N. Y.) 84; Beebe *v.* Mackenzie, 47 N. Y. 662; Rich *v.* Atwater, 16 Conn. 409; Nash *v.* Lull, 102 Mass. 60; McKenzie *v.* Bailie, 3 Cin. L. B. (Ohio) 209; Slemmer's Appeal, 58 Pa. St. 155; Keith *v.* Hobbs, 69 Mo. 84.

2. Rice *v.* Garnhart, 34 Wis. 453; Street *v.* Silver, Bright. (Pa.) 96; Hunt *v.* Hoover, 24 Iowa 231; Warren *v.* Cole, 15 Mich. 265; David *v.* Park, 103 Mass. 501; Billings *v.* Ames, 32 Mo. 265; Lockwood *v.* Lockwood, 33 Iowa 509; McDougall *v.* Fogg, 2 Bosw. (N. Y.) 387; Bloomer *v.* McQuewan, 14 How. (U. S.) 539; Chaffee *v.* Boston Belting Co., 22 How. (U. S.) 217; Kelly *v.* Porter, 8 Sawy. (U. S.) 482; s. c., 17 Fed. Rep. 519.

And as well in actions in equity as in law. To rescind a contract. Lindsay *v.* Roraback, 4 Jones' Eq. (N. Car.) 124; Page *v.* Dickerson, 28 Wis. 694; Consolidated Fruit Jar Co. *v.* Whitney, 2 Bann. & Ard. Pat. Cas. 30.

To compel an account of royalties. Adams' Appeal, 113 Pa. St. 449.

For specific performance of a contract. Binney *v.* Annan, 107 Mass. 94; Brooks *v.* Stolley, 3 McLean (U. S.) 523; s. c., 2 Robb Pat. Cas. 28; Perry *v.* Littlefield, 17 Blatchf. (U. S.) 272; s. c., 17 Pat. Off. Gaz. 51; Fuller etc. Co. *v.* Bartlett, 68 Wis. 73.

Jurisdiction of Equity Over Assignments on the Ground of Fraud or Mistake.—Where an assignment agreement has been entered into by fraud. Colburn *v.* Van Velzer, 11 Fed. Rep. 795; Secombe *v.* Campbell, 18 Blatchf. (U. S.) 108.

A negotiable instrument given for a void patent will be compelled to be given up and cancelled. Darst *v.* Brockway, 11 Ohio 462; Bellas *v.* Hays, 5 S. & R. (Pa.) 427.

Otherwise in the case of a non-negotiable instrument where there was no actual fraud in the sale. Cansler *v.* Eaton, 2 Jones (N. Car.) 499. Or a mutual mistake made.

Burrall *v.* Jewett, 2 Paige (N. Y.) 134; Black *v.* Stoul, 33 Ala. 327; Foss *v.* Richardson, 15 Gray (Mass.) 303; Gay *v.* Cornell, 1 Blatchf. (U. S.) 506. The instrument may be cancelled or reformed.

Bona Fide Purchaser.—A plea of *bona fide* purchaser for "good and valuable consideration," when interposed in a case where equity would otherwise grant a reformation and profits, must set forth the consideration. Secombe *v.* Campbell, 18 Blatchf. (U. S.) 108.

Authorities for Patent Law.—Curtis on Patents, once the only authorized

PATERNITY.—See BASTARDY, vol. 2, p. 129; CHILD, vol. 3, p. 229; ILLEGITIMATE CHILDREN, vol. 9, p. 930; PARENT AND CHILD.

PATRIMONY.—Property received from one's father, or ancestors, whence patrimonial.[1]

PATRONAGE; PATRONIZE.—See note 2.

PAUPER.—See POOR and POOR LAWS.

PAWN, PAWNBROKER.—See BAILMENT, vol. 2, p. 40; PLEDGE AND COLLATERAL SECURITY.

PAY; PAYABLE; PAID—(See also PAYMENT).—"Pay." To pay is defined by lexicographers to discharge a debt, to deliver a creditor the value of a debt, either in money or in goods, to his acceptance, by which the debt is discharged.[3]

text-book, is now somewhat antiquated. The second edition of Walker on Patents of 1889 presents a clear, terse view of the law, coming down to April 30th, 1889. Robinson on Patents, 1890, a scholarly work containing a full citation of cases, coming down, by means of an appendix in the last volume, to 1890, is the latest work on the subject. Simonds' (present Commissioner of Patents) Digest is extremely full in all cases of practical value to the practitioner. Bumps on Patents, Trademark and Copyright, coming down to October, 1883, is practically a complete compilation of patent cases to that time. In Special Departments Duryee's Assignment of Patent Rights has much value. Fenton, Law of Patents for Designs, coming down to January, 1889 is the unquestioned, and unquestionable authority on its subject. Hall's Patent Estate is of value. Among older digests may be mentioned Preble's Patent Case Index.

1. And. L. Dict.

"Patrimony" is not necessarily restricted to property derived directly from a father. (Green *v.* Giles, 5 Ir. Ch. Rep. 25.)

2. The female inmates of a house of ill-fame cannot be said to "patronize" the house. Raymond *v.* People, 9 Bradw. (Ill.) 344.

The court said: "The primary meaning of the word 'patronize' is to act as patron toward. . . The patrons of the house, within the meaning of the law, are those who go there in the character of purchasers to be accommodated and entertained in the way of a bawdy-house. . . But the patrons of a house are not those who are occupied in the house, in and about the premises of the house."

To state "that a loose woman is under the *patronage* of a man named, is a technical statement that she is supported by him for the purpose of sexual indulgence. More *v.* Bennet, 48 N. Y. 472, 475.

3. Beals *v.* Home Ins. Co., 36 N. Y. 522; Aff'g 36 Barb. (N. Y.) 614.

To pay is to discharge an obligation by a performance according to its terms or requirements. Tolman *v.* Manufacturers' Ins. Co, 1 Cush. (Mass.) 76.

Pay is a fixed and direct amount given by law to persons in the military service, in consideration of and as compensation for their personal service. Sherburne *v.* United States, 16 Ct. of Cl. 496.

Though the word "pay" has sometimes a wide sense which includes payment in other things than money (Anderson's L. Dict., "Payment"; Foley *v.* Mason, 6 M. & D. 37), yet, where an agent's authority was to "pay bills," it was held that he exceeded it by making payment in merchandise. Claflin *v.* Continental Jersey Works (Ga. 1890), 11 S. E. Rep. 723.

Payable.—Where there is a gift to a remainderman on attaining twenty-one or marrying, but to go over in case of his death before his share becomes "payable," this word will generally be read as "vested." Emperor *v.* Rolfe, 1 Ves. Sen. 208.

Payable in Currency.—See MONEY.

"Payable in trade" (as used in a dealer's written contract to pay a specified sum for services rendered "payable in trade"), means payable in such articles as the promisor deals in. Dudley *v.* Vose, 114 Mass. 34.

Payable as Convenient.—A written contract containing a provision that a certain sum shall be payable as convenient, cannot be construed so that it shall not be payable at all, but only as an extension of credit. Black *v.* Bachelder, 120 Mass. 171.

Payable in one or two years is not an uncommon form of expression in memoranda of agreements and other writings, and is always understood to mean at the expiration of one and two years respectively. Allentown School Dist. *v.* Derr, 115 Pa. St. 439. See also DUE, vol. 6, p. 36; DEBT, vol. 5, p. 165.

Paid.—A testamentary direction that all legacies are to be "*paid*" free of legacy duty, will be read as including the idea of satisfaction, transfer or delivery; so that chattels, stock or shares, the subject of a specific legacy, will, like payment of a pecuniary legacy, have to be delivered or transferred free of duty to the legatee. Ansley *v.* Cotton, 16 L. J. Ch. 55; *Re* Johnston, Cockerell *v.* Essex, 26 Ch. D. 538.

A testamentary direction that debts are to be "paid" (whether legacies are also mentioned or not) prevents the presumption that a legacy to a creditor is in satisfaction of his claim. *Re* Huish, 43 Ch. D. 260; disapproving Edmunds *v.* Low, 3 K. & J. 318; s. c., 26 L. J. Ch. 432.

Articles of a company which empower the declaration of dividends "to be paid" to members, do not authorize the issue of bonds for dividends. Wood *v.* Odessa Water W. Co., 42 Ch. D. 636, 628; Hoole *v.* Great Western Ry., 3 Ch. 262.

A bill of sale "truly sets forth its consideration," within the English bills of sales act of 1882, if the money therein stated to be "paid" did not actually pass in cash, but was a sum owing by the grantor to the grantee for unpaid purchase money of the chattels therein comprised. *Ex parte* Bolland, 21 Ch. D. 543.

In a charter-party agreeing to pay the highest sum proved to have been paid, "paid" may be read as meaning "contracted to be paid." Gether *v.* Capper, 15 C. B. 701.

A Minnesota tax law provides that judgments and sales for delinquent taxes shall be void upon proof at any time that such tax shall have been paid or (that) such property was exempt. The word "paid" is here used in a comprehensive sense, embracing the meaning of the words "satisfied by payment, redemption or sale," which were used in a previous section. The court says: "This is within the proper signification of the word itself; among the primary definitions are, to satisfy, to discharge one's obligations to." Forrest *v.* Henry, 33 Minn. 434.

Where a statute required a payment of rates before the person could become a voter in a burrough, it was held that from the words "unless he shall have paid" it was to be inferred that the voter must pay himself and payment for him by another would not satisfy the statute. Reg. *v.* Bridgnorth, 10 A. & E. 68; s. c., 37 E. C. L. 46.

A Connecticut statute provided that all damages done by dogs to sheep, in any town, should be *paid* by such town. Held, where the selectmen gave to a person, whose sheep had been injured by dogs, an order on the town treasurer, which was given and received in satisfaction of the claim, that it was "payment" within the meaning of the statute. Wilton *v.* Weston, 48 Conn. 325.

Paid up Policies.—See INSURANCE, vol. 11, p. 306.

To be Paid.—This phrase in an agreement *inter partes* creates a covenant to pay. Bower *v.* Hodges, 13 C. B. 765.

In a will it is generally synonymous with PAYABLE. See further 1 Jarman on Wills 837. In Martineau *v.* Rogers, 25 L. J. Ch. 398; s. c., 8 D. G. M. & G. 328, a testator bequeathed legacies to two nephews and a niece by name, if they respectively survived him and attained twenty-one, when the nephews' legacies were "to be paid." In case of the death of either of the nephews or of the niece leaving issue, such issue to take the parent's legacy as the parent should by will appoint. But in case of the death of either of the nephews or the niece before his or her legacy became payable, the legacy to go to the survivors. During the minorities of the legatees the trustees were to apply the income of the legacies for their maintenance and education. The legacy of the niece and any share she might acquire by the death of her brothers, or either of them, was to be settled for her separate use. *Held*, that upon the whole context, the word "paid" must be construed as "vested" or "payable," and that the executory gift to the issue would take effect in the event of the parent dying after attaining twenty-one.

PAYMENT—(See also ACCORD AND SATISFACTION, vol. 1, p. 94; DEBTOR AND CREDITOR, vol. 5, p. 179; DEBTS OF DECEDENTS, vol. 5, p. 206; DEMAND, vol. 5, p. 522; FRAUDS, STATUTE OF, vol. 8, p. 657; INTEREST, vol. 11, p. 379; MISTAKE, vol. 15, p. 625; NOVATION, vol. 16, p. 862; TENDER; UNITED STATES).

I. DEFINITION.—Payment is the discharge in money of a sum due.[1]

1. Bouvier's Law Dict.

This is the definition of "payment" in its most restricted sense. In its most general acceptation, it is the fulfillment of a promise, the performance of an agreement, the accomplishment of every obligation, whether it consists in giving or in doing. It is a not technical term, and has been imported into law proceedings from the exchange, and not from law treatises. To prove payment, the party pleading it must show the payment of money or something accepted in its stead. Bouv. Law Dict., 2 Greenl. Evid. (13th ed.), § 516; 5 Masse, Droit Commerciel 229.

Abbott says (Law Dict.): "To pay, as usually understood, means to deliver money. This is, however, not necessarily involved. The word does, however, imply a delivery of value, and that it is the value called for by the engagement to be discharged. For when that engagement calls for something else than a simple delivery of value, *performance* is the proper term; and when something else than what is called for is delivered and accepted, this is a *compromise* or a *discharge*, and *pay* does not apply."

Payment is a transfer of money from one person, the payor, to another, the payee. Rap. & Lawr. Law Dict.

The act of discharging a debt, duty, or obligation by delivering the value for which it calls; also the money or other value delivered. Abbott's Law Dict.

Delivery by a debtor to his creditor of the amount due—as a plea, money, or its equivalent in value. Anderson's Law Dict.

" 'Payment' is not a technical word: it has been imported into law proceedings from the exchange and not from law treatises. It does not necessarily

II. **What Constitutes Payment—1. In General.**—Payment is a mode of extinguishing obligations. It is an act calling for the exercise of will, of consent. To constitute a payment, money or some other valuable thing must be delivered by the debtor to the creditor for the purpose of extinguishing the debt, and the creditor must receive it for the same purpose.[1]

mean payment in satisfaction and discharge, but may be used in a popular sense." Dwarris on Statutes, (2nd ed.) 675, *citing* Maillard *v.* Argyle, 6 M. & G. 40.

"Payment" properly means the full satisfaction of a debt by money, not by an exchange or compromise, or an accord and satisfaction. Manice *v.* Hudson River R. Co., 3 Duer (N. Y.) 426, 441.

To pay is to discharge a debt, to deliver a creditor the value of a debt, either in money or in goods, to his acceptance, by which the debt is discharged. Beals *v.* Home Ins. Co., 36 N. Y. 522, 527; Tolman *v.* Manufacturers Ins. Co., 1 Cush. (Mass.) 73.

The word "pay" implies an indebtedness. Lent *v.* Hodgman, 15 Barb. (N. Y.) 274, 278.

Payment is not merely the delivery of a sum of money, but the performance of an obligation; it is an act calling for the exercise of the will of consent, without which it has not the characteristics of that mode of extinguishing obligations. Germon *v.* McCan, 23 La. Ann. 84.

"To pay is to discharge an obligation by a performance according to its terms or requirements. If the obligation be for money the payment is made in money; if for merchandise or labor, a delivery of the merchandise or a performance of the labor is payment; or if for the erection of a building, performance according to the terms of the contract is payment." Tolman *v.* Manufacturers Ins. Co., 1 Cush. (Mass.) 73, 76. See also, Beals *v.* Home Ins. Co., 36 N. Y. 527.

"Payment, in its largest sense, is the actual accomplishment of the thing that the party obliges himself *to give* or *to do*, whatever they may be; although, in our acceptation, it is ordinarily confined to money engagements, and it is therefore the natural manner in which obligations are extinguished. When the obligation is *to give something*, the payment is accomplished when the property in the thing is to be given is actually transferred to the creditor, and, of course, in order to constitute the transaction a payment, there must be both a delivery by the debtor and an acceptance by the creditor, with the purpose, on the part of the former, to part from, and of the latter to accept of the immediate ownership of the thing passed from the one to the other. In a payment we ordinarily look to the act of the party making it; but yet its legal import is an act in which the debtor *tenders* and the creditor *accepts* that which is offered. '*Ut itaque solutio fieri posset, necessario requisitur set untrinsque tam præstant is quam accipientis voluntas concurrat*,' is the definition given in the Roman law, and may be safely adopted as a correct definition of a common law payment." Thompson *v.* Kellogg, 23 Mo. 285.

In the above case the creditor's agent presented a draft to the debtor and demanded payment. Therefore the debtor uncovered a large quantity of dimes and half dimes lying on the table, and told the agent there was the money for him. The agent went up to the table, put his hand on the money and in running his hand over it mixed the coin together somewhat, and said: "I suppose I shall have to take it, and I will go to my office to get bags for it." While he was gone the sheriff levied on the coin as the property of the debtor. In an action to determine the question whether the draft had been paid the court instructed the jury that if the agent received the coin "in immediate satisfaction of the draft" it constituted a payment. And the jury having formed that it was not so received, the supreme court refused to disturb the verdict.

1. Bloodworth *v.* Jacobs, 2 La. Ann. 24; Kingston Bank *v.* Gay, 19 Barb. (N. Y.) 459; Cushing *v.* Wyman, 44 Me. 121; Caine *v.* Coulson, 1 H. & C. 746; s. c., 32 L. J. Exch. 97.

Payment means satisfaction by money not by an exchange or compromise, or an accord and satisfaction. Manice *v.* Hudson River R. Co., 3 Duer (N. Y.) 426, 441.

"Payment, in a legal sense, is the

discharge of a contract or obligation in money or its equivalent, and it is usually made with the assent of both parties to the contract. The word is not used in statutes or by text-writers in the bad sense of revenge or punishment. No creditor is permitted by the laws to seize his debtor's property and to declare at his own pleasure that he will take it in satisfaction of his demand. If he so takes it he is a trespasser, and liable in damages." Brady *v.* Wasson, 6 Heisk. (Tenn.) 131.

"As to the mode of payment it may be by any lawful method agreed upon between the parties and fully executed. The meaning and intention of the parties when it can be distinctly known is to have effect, unless that intention contravenes some well established principle of law." Dodge *v.* Swazey, 35 Me. 535.

Says PEARSON, J.: "Payment must be made either in money or in money's worth; but to amount to a payment, the thing must be done, the money must be paid, or the thing taken as money must be passed so as presently to become the property of the other party. A promise or undertaking to pay, either in money or other thing, is not payment. The contract is executory; whereas payment is executed, a thing done." Rhodes *v.* Chesson, Busb. L. (N. Car.) 336.

Says MR. DANIEL: "By payment is meant the discharge of a contract to pay money by giving to the party entitled to receive it the amount agreed to be paid by one of the parties who entered into the agreement. Payment is not a contract. It is the discharge of a contract, in which the party of the first part has a right to demand payment," and the party of the second part has a right to make payment. 2 Dan. Neg. Instr. (3d ed.), § 1221.

See also, Moran *v.* Abbey, 63 Cal. 56.

It is not a payment until the money has actually reached the hands of the party for whom it is intended, or his authorized agent. Remsen *v.* Wheeler, 105 N. Y. 573.

The agent of the debtor took money to the attorney of the creditor for the purpose of paying the debt. A dispute arose as to the correct amount tendered, and the money was handed to a bystander to count, said bystander being an officer who, at the time, held a writ of attachment against the creditor. The officer counted it, found the amount and then attached it as the property of the creditor. The attorney of the creditor refused to consider the transaction a payment. But it was held to constitute a payment, even though it was shown that there was connivance between the agent of defendant and the party who attached the money. Root *v.* Ross, 29 Vt. 488.

Money paid to a person to whom it properly belongs, though under a mistake as to the right under which it accrues to him, extinguishes the debt, and he cannot again enforce payment in his lawful right. Hemphill *v.* Moody, 64 Ala. 468.

Where A, having in his hands money belonging to B, agreed to apply it for the benefit of C, a creditor of B, the latter having neither authorized nor assented to the agreement, such arrangement would not operate as a payment of A's debt to B. Bowman *v.* Ainslie, 1 Idaho N. S. 644.

A creditor cannot pay himself with the debtor's money without the debtor's consent, express or implied. If the debtor delivers him money for a purpose which negatives the idea of payment, the creditor must use it for the purpose for which it was given him. Detroit etc. R. Co. *v.* Smith, 50 Mich. 112.

The distinction is sometimes made between payment in law and payment in fact. Payment in fact is said to be an actual payment from the payor to the payee; payment in law a transaction equivalent to actual payment. Rap. & Lawr. Law Dict.

"In any transaction having in view the payment of an obligation, it is required that it shall be actually paid in order to discharge it, or that something shall be received by the creditor from the debtor under an express agreement that it shall operate as payment." People *v.* Cromwell, 102 N. Y. 477, 485.

Where money was forwarded by the debtor to the creditor, but the creditor refused to receive it and informed the debtor that the money was subject to his order, this was not a payment. Kingston Bank *v.* Gay, 19 Barb. (N. Y.) 459.

Where one of two joint makers paid the note, but by agreement between him and the payee the payment was kept a secret, and only half the amount was indorsed on the note, and an attempt was made to collect the balance of the co-maker, this constituted an extinguishment of the note, and the only liability of the co-maker was for contribution. Davis *v.* Stevens, 10 N. H. 186.

A, an agent of B, held funds of his principal to the full amount of bills drawn upon him by B, which the latter had delivered to his creditors. The creditors without B's knowledge, made a composition with A, and gave him up the bills upon receiving from him 10*s*. in the pound. B afterwards became bankrupt, and his assignee brought an action against A for the difference between the amount of the bills and the composition, but it was held that the assignee could not recover, since, as B was benefited to the full amount of the bills, as between him and A. the composition was a payment. Stonehouse *v*. Read, 5 Dowl. & Ry. Co, 3 B. & C. 669.

A cross demand cannot be treated as a payment, except by agreement to that effect between the parties. Wharton *v*. King, 69 Ala. 365; McCurdy *v*. Middleton, 82 Ala. 131, Rowland *v*. Blakesley, 2 G. & Dav. 734; 1 Q. B. 403, 6 Jur. 732; Livingston *v*. Whiting, 19 L. J., Q. B. 528; 15 Q. B. 722; Smith *v*. Winter, 12 C. B. 487; 21 L. J., C. P. 158.

Where A held B's note, and B, in making out an account current between himself and A, charged A with the note, and afterwards gave him credit for it, this did not constitute a payment of the note. Bettison *v*. Jennings, 11 Ark. 116. See Matossy *v*. Frosh, 9 Tex. 610.

Where one who is liable on a bill of exchange is a depositor in the bank holding the bill, and has a balance there to his credit, the bank cannot be compelled to appropriate such balance toward payment of the bill. Citizen's Bank *v*. Carson, 32 Mo. 191.

A draft upon a debtor having been indorsed and sent for collection to the bank where the debtor kept his account and where the debtor had funds sufficient to meet the draft, the bank, at the debtor's direction, charged up the amount of the draft to the debtor's account, and then drew its own check for the same amount payable to the creditor, but before the check was paid the bank closed its doors. *Held*, that the draft was paid. Welge *v*. Batty, 11 Ill. App. 461.

A, being the holder of a note payable at a certain bank, in which he was a depositor, sent it at maturity to that bank for payment, the bank, supposing the maker to be in funds, credited the amount of the note to A, but on discovering their mistake the next day, sent notices to the indorsers of non-payment. *Held*, that the note had not been paid. Troy City Bank *v*. Grant, Hill & D. Supp. (N. Y.) 119. See also, Dewey *v*. Bowers, 4 Ired. (N. Car.) 538.

Where a bank writes upon a check the word "good," or any similar word or words which indicate a statement that the drawer has funds in the bank applicable to the payment of the check, and that it will so apply them, this amounts to a payment as to the drawer and will discharge him. First National Bank *v*. Whitman, 94 U. S. 343; Meads *v*. Merchants' Bank, 25 N. Y. 143; s. c., 82 Am. Dec. 331; First Nat. Bank *v*. Leach, 52 N. Y. 350, s. c., 11 Am. Rep. 708.

The maker of a note payable at a certain bank, before maturity thereof, gave to the bank the check of a third person drawn on itself for the amount of the note. The check was by the bank placed with the note, and on the day of its maturity it was entered on the books of the bank as paid, and the account of the third person charged with the amount of the check. *Held*, that the note was paid, though the third person's account was at the time overdrawn. Pratt *v*. Foote, 10 N Y. 599. See s. c., 9 N. Y. 463.

A bank, which was not accustomed to receive for collection checks drawn upon itself, received a check drawn by one of its depositors in favor of another depositor, credited it in the pass book of the payee, placed it on the file of paid and cancelled checks where it was not the custom to place checks received for collection, and credited the payee and charged the drawer with it in the books of the bank. It was *held* that this constituted a payment of the check which could not be retracted upon discovery that it was an overdraft, and the drawer was insolvent. City Nat. Bank *v*. Burns, 68 Ala. 267; s. c., 44 Am. Rep. 138.

This decision is placed on the ground that the evidence clearly shows that the check was not taken for collection. For the mere receipt of a check and entering it in the depositor's bank book does not ordinarily constitute a payment of it, though it is drawn on the bank where it is deposited. Morse on Banking 320. In the opinion of BRICKELL, C. J., in the above case, two decisions are referred to as maintaining this view: Boyd *v*. Emerson, 2 Ad. & El. 184; Kilsby *v*. Williams, 5 B & Ald. 815. But the court holds that in the case before it the check was not taken for collection, and that it falls within the principal of Bolton *v.* Richard, 6 T. R. 139, where it was held that when a bank credits a depositor with the amount of a check drawn upon it by another customer and there is no want of good faith on the part of the depositor, the act of crediting is equivalent to a payment in money. This is the view taken by the Supreme Court of the United States in First Nat. Bank *v.* Burkhardt, 100 U. S. 686, and the other cases cited in the opinion. *Compare* Watervliet Bank *v.* White, 1 Den. (N. Y.) 608; McLemore *v.* Hawkins, 46 Miss. 716; Nightingale *v.* City Bank, 26 Up. Can. C. P. 74.

A bank in Nashville discounted a note for the benefit of a bank in Knoxville, the same being indorsed by defendant, and by the Knoxville bank. The banks were regular correspondents of each other and settled their accounts monthly. At the maturity of the note the Nashville bank sent it to the Knoxville bank with instructions to collect and credit. The latter bank entered the amount on its books to the credit the former. At that time the Knoxville bank had money sufficient to pay the note, but no money was actually paid, and the bank was then insolvent. Two days afterward it closed its doors. *Held*, that this constituted a payment, and that defendant was not liable. First Nat. Bank. *v.* McClung, 7 Lea (Tenn.) 492; s. c., 40 Am. Rep. 66. *Compare* Warwick *v.* Rogers, 5 Man. & G. 340; s. c., 6 Scott (N. R.) 1; Prince *v.* Oriental Bank, L. R., 3 App. 325; s. c., 24 Moak's Rep. 221.

It was the course of business between a banker and his customer that when claims against the customer were sent to the banker, he should pay them out of the customer's deposits, if he had any, and charge them in the account. A particular claim against the customer was sent the banker for collection, to pay which and others the depositor placed money with the banker with directions to use it in paying those claims. Before the money was so applied the banker failed. It was held that the customer was still liable on the claims. Moore *v.* Meyer, 57 Ala. 20.

In October the creditor authorized the debtor to pay in at certain bankers the amount of the debt. Owing to a mistake it was not then paid; but on Friday, the 9th of December, the debtor, who kept an account at the same bank, transferred the sum to the credit of the creditor. The latter being at a distance did not receive notice of the transfer till the following Sunday, and on Saturday the bankers failed. *Held*, that this was a good payment. Eyles *v.* Ellis, 4 Bing. 112; 12 Moore 306. *Compare* Brown *v.* Kewley, 2 Bos. & Pul. 518.

A purchased goods of B and agreed to pay for them by bill at three months. A gave B a check on his bankers, who were also the bankers of B, requiring them to pay B on demand in a bill at three months. B paid the check in at the bankers, but instead of taking a bill from them the amount was transferred on the books of the bank from A's account to B's, with the knowledge of both. The bankers failed before the check became due. *Held*, that B could not recover from A the value of the goods. Bolton *v.* Richard, 6 T. R. 139; 1 Esp. 100. See Smith *v.* Ferrard, 7 B. & C. 19; 9 Dow. & Ry. 803: and *compare* Pedder *v.* Watt, 2 Chit. 619.

Where plaintiff's attorney wrote to the defendant to remit the balance of the account due plaintiff, with costs, and defendant remitted by post a banker's bill payable at sight for the account, without costs, and the attorney wrote refusing to accept the bill unless the costs were also remitted, but kept the bill, though he did not cash it, the payment was held to be good, as it was the duty of the attorney to return the banker's bill if he did not choose to receive it in payment. Caine *v.* Coulson, 32 L. J., Exch. 97; s. c., 1 H. & C. 764; s. c., 11 W. R. 239.

A judgment debtor sent money by his son to the clerk of the court to be paid to the judgment creditor. The clerk deposited the money in bank in his own name with a memorandum showing for whom it was intended. A few months afterwards the debtor inquired of the creditor if he had been paid, and the latter replied: "No, but the money is deposited in the bank for me." The clerk subsequently died, and the creditor not having applied for the money, the administrator paid it back to the son of the debtor. *Held*, that there was no acceptance of the money, and the debt was still due. Moore *v.* Tate, 22 Gratt. (Va.) 351.

B offered to sell a promissory note owned by him for $500. V, who was the holder of a note executed by B for $488, proposed to purchase the note held by B for the price asked, and having requested to see it, the note was handed to him by B. V laid down upon the table B's $488 note, and $12 in cash, and retained the note belonging to B. B objected to this proceeding, but afterwards took the money and note from the table, to prevent their being lost. *Held*, that his act under the circumstances did not constitute an acceptance of payment. Van Cleave *v.* Beach, 110 Ind. 269.

Where the debtor offers to the creditor a certain sum in payment of a debt, the amount of which is open and unliquidated, and accompanies his offer with the condition that the money, if taken at all, must be received *in full* or in *satisfaction* of the debt, and the creditor receives it, this operates as a payment, even though the creditor, when receiving the money, declares that he will only take it in part satisfaction of the debt, as far as it will extend. McDaniels *v.* Lapham, 21 Vt. 222; McDaniels *v.* Bank of Rutland, 29 Vt. 230; s. c., 70 Am. Dec. 406; Cole *v.* Champlain Transp. Co., 26 Vt. 87; Calkins *v.* State, 13 Wis. 395; Day *v.* Murdock, 1 Munf. (Va.) 460.

See also, *infra*, *Part Payment*.

Compare King *v.* Phillips, 94 N. Car. 555; Thomas *v.* Cross, 7 Exch. 728; 21 L. J. Exch. 251.

A payment to a sheriff by the purchaser of land at execution sale of the amount of his bid is none the less a valid payment by reason of the fact that the purchaser at the time gives the sheriff notice not to pay over a certain portion of the money. Spraker *v.* Cook, 16 N. Y. 567.

Where property of the testator is delivered to a specialty creditor, this will be treated as a payment of the debt, though it was delivered to him as residuary legatee. Stephenson *v.* Axson, 1 Bailey Eq. (S. Car.) 274.

Defendant had been accustomed to paying his indebtedness to the plaintiff by depositing money to his credit at any one of several banks, the indebtedness not being considered as discharged till plaintiff received notice of the deposit. It was agreed that a particular debt should be paid by depositing the sum due at a certain bank. *Held*, that the bank thus designated became the plaintiff's agent, and the debt was overcharged by making the deposit, though no notice thereof was given to plaintiff. Exchange Bank *v.* Cookman, 1 W. Va. 69.

Where items were originally charged to a wife, but were embraced in an account rendered by the creditor against the husband in the usual course of dealing between them, the balance being in the husband's favor, this constitutes a payment of such items. Florance *v.* Michell, 5 La. Ann. 17.

If it is agreed between the parties to a note that payment may be made in a particular manner, a performance of the agreement by the maker before action brought, will be a defense to a suit on the note. Gilson *v.* Gilson, 16 Vt. 464.

Where contemporaneously with the execution of a written obligation to pay money there is an oral agreement that the obligation is to be discharged by the doing of something other than the payment of money, this agreement when performed operates as a completed discharge of the obligation. Patrick *v.* Petty, 83 Ala. 420.

Where contemporaneously with the execution of a promissory note it is orally agreed that, if the maker marries the payee, the latter will dismiss a pending suit for bastardy and breach of promise, and the note shall be deemed satisfied, the maker may set up the performance of this agreement as a payment and a defense to an action on the note. But such defense may be avoided by proof that the agreement of the maker was not merely to marry plaintiff, but also to take care of and treat her as a husband should his wife, and that, though he had married her, he had treated her in a manner so cruel and inhuman as to drive her from his home, so that she was compelled to obtain a divorce. Tucker *v.* Tucker, 113 Ind. 272.

Where it was agreed at the time of giving the note that the maker should pay the interest and such part of the principal as he could by orders drawn on him by the payee, and by paying the premiums due from the payee to an insurance company, evidence that the agreement was performed by the maker is admissible under a plea of payment. Jones *v.* Snow, 64 Cal. 456.

Where the agreement is performed in part, and full performance prevented by the act of the payee, this would constitute payment *pro tanto*. Thus, where, at the time of executing the note, it was agreed between the parties that if the payee lived through the year 1884, and the maker boarded and cared for her during said year, the note was to be discharged, and the payee died in September, 1884, this constituted a payment of the note *pro tanto.* Patrick *v.* Petty, 83 Ala. 420.

An agreement to credit on a note the value of work done does not constitute a payment *pro tanto.* Cook *v.* Cook, 24 S. Car. 204; Weeks *v.* Elliott, 33 Me. 488.

But if the work is done under such agreement it constitutes a payment. Moore *v.* Stadden, Wright (Ohio) 88.

Where suit is pending on a promissory note against maker and indorser, a payment by the indorser is such a payment as will bar a further prosecution of the suit against the maker even for the indorser's benefit. Griffin *v.* Hampton, 21 Ga. 198.

Same principle applies to payment of judgment. Boggs *v.* Lancaster Bank, 7 W. & S. (Pa.) 331; Davis *v.* Barkley, 1 Bailey (S. Car.) 141. *Compare* Low *v.* Blodgett, 21 N. H. 121.

The payee of a promissory note agreed with the maker to take it up from an indorsee who was the holder, and in settlement to deliver it to the maker. After it was thus taken up, there was a balance due from the payee to the maker which exceeded the amount of the note. *Held*, that these facts constituted a payment of the note. Peabody *v.* Peters, 5 Pick. (Mass.) 1.

Defendant being indebted to a bank was authorized by the latter to discharge such indebtedness by taking up certain notes and certificates of the bank, which had been guaranteed by defendant, and the bank offered to receive them at par in payment of such debt. *Held*, that the production and lender to the bank of such notes and certificates constituted a complete discharge of the defendant's indebtedness, notwithstanding the fact that such notes and certificates were illegally issued, and the bank was not liable on them. Leavitt *v.* Beers, Hill & D. Supp. (N. Y.) 221.

The indorser of a protested draft held by a bank procured his note to be discounted by the bank with a view to paying the bill, but having given no direction as to the application of the proceeds, the amount was placed to his credit on the books of the bank, and some time afterwards applied by the cashier to the note which was therefore cancelled and delivered up to the maker. *Held*, that the note was extinguished and no action could be maintained on it. Shaw *v.* Branch Bank, 16 Ala. 708.

If the laws of the place where a vessel touches require that the physician's bill for attendance upon a seaman shall be paid by the vessel before she can leave port, and the amount is paid by the master, this is a payment *pro tanto* of the seaman's wages, and does not constitute merely a set-off. Pray *v.* Stinson, 21 Me. 402.

Where the payee of a joint and several promissory note assigns the same to one of the makers, this amounts to a payment; and the note cannot be revived by an assignment by such maker after maturity. Gordon *v.* Wonsey, 21 Cal. 77.

One who was in debt to a bank made a payment on account in the bank to one of the clerks. On a subsequent day the debtor agreed to lend the clerk the amount so paid, and the clerk took the money and used it, the amount never having been credited to the debtor on the books of the bank. *Held*, that the debt was extinguished *pro tanto.* Rhodes *v.* Hinckley, 6 Cal. 283.

A mortgagor placed in the bank at which the secured note was made payable the money necessary to meet the note, with instructions to the bank to retain the money until proper authority was given to cancel the mortgage and the title to the land for which the note was given should appear perfect. The title proving defective, the mortgagee set about remedying the difficulty. Before this was accomplished the note was transferred to a third person, who filed a bill for foreclosure, and it was held that the payment, being only conditional, was not a bar to the foreclosure. Coburn *v.* Hough, 32 Ill. 344.

Where the debtor makes an absolute deed of land to the creditor, this constitutes a payment to the extent of the value of the land. So also does a mortgage of land, after foreclosure. 2 Greenl. Evid. (13th ed.), § 524; Fales *v.* Reynolds, 14 Me. 89. See Hogan *v.* Hall, 1 Strobh. Eq. (S. Car.) 323.

While the foreclosure of a mortgage is not in a strict sense a payment, yet the value of the land enures by way of payment. Briggs *v.* Richmond, 10 Pick. (Mass.) 391; s. c., 20 Am. Dec. 526; Case *v.* Boughton, 11 Wend. (N. Y.) 106.

Where chattels are mortgaged to secure a debt, a taking and retaining the chattels, or selling them without a foreclosure, will operate as a payment of the mortgage debt. Landon *v.* White, 101 Ind. 249. See Hunt *v.* Nevers, 15 Pick. (Mass.) 500; s. c., 26 Am. Dec. 616; Wright *v.* Storrs, 32 N. Y. 691; Dismukes *v.* Wright, 3 Dev. & B. L. (N. Car.) 78.

Where a mortagee who holds two mortgages, one covering real estate and the other personalty, to secure the same debt, forecloses the personal mortgage, takes possession of the property and converts it to his own use, this operates as a payment of the debt and a satisfaction of the realty mortgage, if the value of the personalty exceeds the debt secured. Androscoggin Sav. Bank *v.* McKenney, 78 Me. 442.

Where a negotiable promissory note was transferred before due as collateral security, and was afterwards paid to the payee, who transmitted the money to the holder, and the holder, in ignorance of the fact that the money was the proceeds of the collateral note, applied it to the payment of the note secured thereby, but not to the collateral itself, this was a discharge of the collateral note. Coleman *v.* Jenkins, 78 Ga. 605.

A, being the holder of B's note, employed an agent to collect the same. B also appointed the same agent to collect certain rents and notes and apply the proceeds to the payment of the note to A. The agent collected for B a sum greater than the amount of B's note to A, but made no credit or endorsement of payment on the note, simply crediting B on his books with the money received. *Held*, that the note was not paid. Phillips *v.* Mayer, 7 Cal. 81. *Compare* Grandy *v.* Abbott, 92 N. Car. 33, 38; Smith *v.* Lamberts, 7 Gratt. (Va.) 138.

An agreement between an agent of an insurance company, having authority to receive premiums, and a party insured, that the agent shall become responsible to the company for the premium and the insured become his personal debtor therefor, constitutes a payment of the premium as between the insured and the company. Sheldon *v.* Connecticut Mut. L. Ins. Co., 25 Conn. 207; s. c., 65 Am. Dec. 565; Bouton *v.* American Mut. L. Ins. Co., 25 Conn. 542. See Home Ins. Co. *v.* Gilman, 112 Ind. 7.

But the mere acquittance or release to the agent of his personal debt to the debtor, will not constitute a payment to the principal. Bostick *v.* Hardy, 30 Ga. 836; Smith *v.* Morrill, 39 Kan. 665.

Where a party who is indebted to an insurance broker hands to the broker a policy of insurance that the latter may adjust the loss, and upon adjusting it the broker debits the insurance company and credits the insured, this constitutes a payment of the policy, unless the insured dissents at the time. Bethune *v.* Neilson, 2 Cai. (N. Y.) 139.

Plaintiff, the owner of a note executed by A, placed it in the hands of an attorney for collection. It was then agreed between A and the attorney that the latter should borrow for A from B a sum of money sufficient to pay the note, which was done, A executing a deed of trust to secure B, the lender of the money, and A's note was delivered up to him by the attorney upon the receipt of the money from B. *Held*, that as soon as the money was thus received by the attorney it operated *eo instanti* as an extinguishment of the note. Grandy *v.* Abbott, 92 N. Car. 33.

The owner of certain State bonds, redeemable at the treasury, deposited them with the State treasurer, who afterward, without the owner's authority, took from the treasury money to the amount of the bonds and converted the same to his own use, cancelling the bonds. He credited himself with the amount as for money paid in the redemption of bonds, and in a settlement with the State was allowed credit for the amount. *Held*, that as against the owner of the bonds this did not constitute a payment. Bassett *v.* State, 26 Ohio St. 543.

Where a collector receives for taxes a negotiable order drawn by the selectmen on the town treasurer, this does not, of itself, constitute a payment of the order. Willey *v.* Greenfield, 30 Me. 452.

The purchaser of a lot from his father-in-law signed his own father's name, to the notes given for the purchase money, and had the lot conveyed to his father. Afterward, in the settlement of the father-in-law's estate, these notes were taken by the son and his wife as part of her distributive share. *Held*, that this constituted a payment of the notes. Scheerer *v.* Scheerer, 109 Ill. 11.

W, a district school teacher, received for a month's salary an order of the district committee on the treasurer, which he transferred, indorsed in blank, to a third person, who in good faith paid him the money on it. This had been the usual mode of monthly payment for two years. *Held*, to operate as a payment to W as against a creditor of his who garnisheed the treasurer before the order was presented, and before the treasurer had received notice of the transfer. Seymour *v.* Over River School District, 53 Conn. 502.

A brakeman took out a policy of insurance, the premium of which was to be paid by instalments, and gave to the insurance company a written order on the railway company by which he was employed to pay such instalments out of his wages as they fell due, which order was delivered to the railway company by the insurance company, in accordance with an existing custom in such cases. The railway company neglected to pay one of the instalments, but the insurance company failed to notify the brakeman of that fact, and within the period covered by such instalment he was killed. *Held*, that the instalment must be regarded as paid. Lyon *v.* Traveler's Ins. Co., 55 Mich. 141; s. c., 54 Am. Rep. 354.

A debt may be paid by a third person becoming responsible to the creditor with the concurrence of the debtor. Logan *v.* Williamson, 3 Ark. 216.

An agrement between maker and payee that the note shall be deemed to be paid by being allowed in discharge of a mortgage from the payee to a third person, does not extinguish the note, unless the assent of such third person is shown. Hewes *v.* Hanscom, 10 Gray (Mass.) 336.

The holder of a note brought an action thereon against the maker. At the trial, the plaintiff, against the protest of defendant, credited on the note the amount of an account which he owed defendant, took judgment for the balance, and defendant afterward paid the judgment. *Held*, that this did not constitute a payment of the account due defendant. Keith *v.* Smith, 1 Swan (Tenn.) 92.

Plaintiff employed a traveling agent to sell goods, and fixed the minimum prices to be charged therefor. Defendants, who knew the limitations as to prices, bought goods of the agent upon an agreement with him that they should settle for the goods at prices less than the minimum. The agent then sent to plaintiff an order for the goods, with the minimum prices affixed thereto. Plaintiff, in ignorance of the agreement between his agent and defendants, shipped the goods together with a bill thereof showing the minimum prices, and charged the goods to defendants at those prices. Defendants received the goods and made no objection to the bill, but they settled with the agent at the prices agreed upon between them, and the agent reported to plaintiff that he had received the full sum charged by plaintiff for the goods. Thereupon plaintiff charged the agent and credited the defendants with the amount of the bill, but there has been no final settlement between plaintiff and his agent. In a suit to recover of defendants the difference between the amount paid to the agent and the face of the bills rendered, *held*, that the bills had not been paid and plaintiff was entitled to recover. Rogers *v.* Holden, 142 Mass. 196.

H owing to P for a set of tombstones, made an agreement with S that S should pay P for the stones upon their delivery, H to credit S with the sum upon a demand which he held against him. P was indebted to B upon a past due promissory note, and agreed with B that B should receive payment of S for the stones and apply the amount on the note, S consenting thereto. P thereupon delivered the stones to B with notice to S of that fact. *Held*, that the transaction amounted to a payment *in praesenti* of the amount upon P's note to B. Butts *v.* Perkins, 41 Barb. (N. Y.) 509.

A draft indorsed by defendant for the accommodation of the drawer, and subsequently by plaintiff for the same purpose was discounted at the instance of the drawer, and not being paid by him was taken up by the plaintiff, due notice being given to defendant as first indorser. Subsequently, in order to reimburse the plaintiff, a note was made by plaintiff and indorsed by the defendant, discounted by a bank and the proceeds remitted to the plaintiff. Plaintiff's clerk without his knowledge credited the amount on the books of plaintiff to the drawer of the draft, which act was disaffirmed by plaintiff upon its coming to his knowledge. The note was not paid by defendant, but was taken up by plaintiff. *Held*, that the discount of the note and the receipt by plaintiff of the proceeds was not an extinguishment of the liability of defendant as first indorser of the draft. Oliphant *v.* Church, 19 Pa. St. 318.

Plaintiff obtained from defendant an advance of £15,000 upon the security of goods then in transit to M V, consigned to S, and of six bills of exchange drawn by plaintiff upon S against the shipment and accepted by S. Two of the bills were duly paid. Two of the remaining four having been dishonored, defendants at M V proposed to realize on the goods at once, whereupon plaintiff delivered them a cheque for £2,500 with the request not to sell but to hold the £2,500 as collateral security for S's acceptance, to be returned to plaintiff when all the bills were paid. S having failed to pay the remaining bills, defendants proceeded against him at M V, under which proceedings the goods were sold by judicial arrangement, and the bills were cancelled and delivered up to S, without plaintiff's knowledge or consent. The sale of the goods did not produce sufficient, even with the £2,500, to pay all the dishonored bills. Plaintiff brought his action to recover back the £2,500. *Held*, that while plaintiff might have an accounting against defendants for what they realized or might have realized by means of the securities but for their own acts and negligence, that is, for the real value of the cancelled bills, yet the transaction above recited did not constitute a payment of the bills, and he was not entitled to recover the £2,500. Yglesias *v.* Mercantile Bank, L. R. 3 C. P. Div. 46; s. c., affirmed on appeal, L. R., 3 C. P. Div. 330; s. c., 30 Moak's Rep. 46, 198.

S was trustee of funds belonging to defendant, and also cashier of a bank. He placed in such bank certain sums to his credit as trustee, and gave defendant permission to draw on the bank at pleasure. Defendant accordingly drew cheques repeatedly on the bank, which were always paid up to the time of the death of S. After his death defendant drew two more cheques, the aggregate amount of which was less than the sum standing to the credit of S, as trustee, on the books of the bank. These cheques were paid by the cashier who succeeded S, who did so with the intention of charging them against the balance to the credit of S, as trustee. They were never actually so charged, and the bank soon became insolvent and went into the hands of a receiver, who brought an action to recover the amounts so paid defendant on her two cheques. *Held*, that, in equity, the money to the credit of S as trustee belonged to the defendant, and the acts of S amounted, in an indirect way, to a payment thereof to her, and the receiver could not recover it back. Bank of Slatesville *v.* Waddell, 100 N. Car. 338.

The maker of a promissory note was one of the distributees of the estate of the holder thereof. She agreed with the administrator that before the final settlement of the estate, the amount due on the note should be deducted from her share of the estate in payment of said note. The estate had never been settled, no account had been rendered, and it had never been ascertained what the maker's distributive share would amount to. *Held*, that this was a mere executory agreement, and not sufficient to establish a payment. Taylor *v.* Lewis, 146 Mass. 222.

Compare Gardiner *v.* Callender, 12 Pick. (Mass.) 374.

Where a testator was indebted to the person named as his executor, and by the will leaves certain property to the executor in payment of the debt, the executor cannot, after proving the will, assert his right to take other assets of the estate in payment of his debt, though the property mentioned in the will proves to be of less value than the amount of the debt. Syme *v.* Badger, 92 N. Car. 706.

Where a clerk in a bank stole money from the drawer of a fellow clerk and delivered it to the cashier, who accepted it in satisfaction of a debt due from the former to the bank, such transaction did not constitute a payment of the clerk's debt. State Bank *v.* Welles, 3 Pick. (Mass.) 394.

Where a payment is made in a manner not contemplated by the contract, the payee may adopt and ratify it. But if he has a right to elect whether he will ratify or disaffirm it, he must ratify it or disaffirm it as an entirety. Williams *v.* Jones, 77 Ala. 294.

Whether the transaction amounts to a payment is a question of fact for the jury. Binford *v.* Adams, 104 Ind. 41; Monticello *v.* Grant, 104 Ind. 168.

As to what constitutes payment of a debt due by or to an executor or administrator to or by the decedent, see *infra*, *Presumption of Payment.*

As to distinction between payment and facts constituting a set-off, see Dodge *v.* Swazy, 35 Me. 535.

payment or for the purpose of extinguishing the debt due him.[1]

1. School Town of Monticello *v.* Grant, 104 Ind. 168.

Unless prohibited by statute it is competent for the owner and contractor to agree upon the method and time of payment of moneys due or to become due upon a building contract; and when payment is made in accordance with such agreement, it is binding upon all parties, unless impeached for fraud or collusion. Crane *v.* Genin, 60 N. Y. 127; Payne *v.* Wilson, 74 N. Y. 348; Gibson *v.* Lenane, 94 N. Y. 183.

The following cases illustrate the doctrine of what constitutes a payment:

United States.—Gill *v.* Packard, 4 Woods (U. S.) 271; Shortridge *v.* Macon, 1 Abb. (U. S.) 58; Levy *v.* Bank of U. S., 4 Dall. (U. S.) 234; Orchard *v.* Hughes, 1 Wall. (U. S.) 73; Gwathney *v.* McLean, 3 McLean (U. S.) 371.

Alabama.—Franklin *v.* McGuire, 10 Ala. 557; Wilkinson *v.* Bradley, 54 Ala. 677; White *v.* Toles, 7 Ala. 569; McPherson *v.* Foust (Ala. 1890), 8 So. Rep. 193; Merchants' etc. Bank *v.* Coleman, 81 Ala. 170; Steiner *v.* Ballard, 42 Ala. 153; Sledge *v.* Tubb, 11 Ala. 383.

California.—Wright *v.* Mix. 76 Cal. 465.

Connecticut.—Marvin *v.* Keeler, 5 Conn. 271; Norton *v.* Plumb, 14 Conn. 512; Stamford Bank *v.* Benedict, 15 Conn. 437; Dutles *v.* DeForrest, 19 Conn. 190; Woodruff etc. Works *v.* Stetson, 31 Conn. 51; Meeker *v.* Meeker, 16 Conn. 403.

Georgia.—Rice *v.* Georgia Nat. Bank, 64 Ga. 173; Jones *v.* Grantham, 80 Ga. 472.

Illinois.—Bodley *v.* Anderson, 2 Ill. App. 450; Miller *v.* Montgomery, 31 Ill. 350.

Indiana.—Foy *v.* Reddick, 31 Ind. 414; Hyatt *v.* Clements, 65 Ind. 12; Monticello *v.* Grant, 104 Ind. 168; McClure *v.* Andrews, 68 Ind. 97; Dakin *v.* Anderson, 18 Ind. 52.

Kentucky.—Watson *v.* Cresap, 1 B. Mon. (Ky.) 195; s. c., 36 Am. Dec. 572; Railey *v.* Jones, 7 J. J. Marsh (Ky.) 303; Nelson *v.* Cartmel, 6 Dana (Ky.) 7; Anderson *v.* Mason, 6 Dana (Ky.) 217.

Louisiana.—Mouton *v.* Noble, 1 La. Ann. 194; Bowers *v.* Hale, 14 La. Ann. 421.

Maine.—Woodman *v.* Woodman, 3 Me. 350; Ingalls *v.* Fiske, 34 Me. 232; Stackpole *v.* Keay, 45 Me. 297; Herrick *v.* Bean, 20 Me. 51.

Maryland.—Cheston *v.* Page, 4 Har. & J. (Md.) 466.

Massachusetts.—Young *v.* Adams, 6 Mass. 182; George *v.* Cushing, 17 Pick. (Mass.) 448; Capen *v.* Alden, 5 Met. (Mass.) 268; Leland *v.* Loring, 10 Met. (Mass.) 122; Taylor *v.* Wilson, 11 Met. (Mass.) 44; s. c., 45 Am. Dec. 180; Hall *v.* Holden, 116 Mass. 172; Merriam *v.* Bacon, 5 Met. (Mass.) 95; Reed *v.* Parsons, 11 Cush. (Mass.) 255.

Michigan.—Pennsylvania etc. Co. *v.* Brady, 14 Mich. 360; Iron Cliffs Co. *v.* Gingrass, 42 Mich. 30; Pease *v.* Warren, 29 Mich. 9; Ryan *v.* O'Neil, 49 Mich. 281.

Minnesota.—Fogarty *v.* Wilson, 30 Minn. 289; Nutting *v.* McCutcheon, 5 Minn. 382.

Mississippi.—Knight *v.* Yarborough, 7 Smed. & M. (Miss.) 179; Dunlap *v.* Petrie, 35 Miss. 322.

Missouri.—Coy *v.* Dewitt, 19 Mo. 322.

Nebraska.—Hughes *v.* Kellogg, 3 Neb. 186.

New Hampshire.—Grafton Bank *v.* Hunt, 4 N. H. 488.

New Jersey.—Clark *v.* Mershon, 2 N. J. L. 70.

New York.—Hodge *v.* Hoppock, 75 N. Y. 491; Concord Granite Co. *v.* French, 12 Daly (N. Y.) 228; Dinkel *v.* Wehle, 63 How. Pr. (N. Y.) 298; Catlin *v.* Munn, 37 Hun (N. Y.) 23; Chemung Canal Bank *v.* Chemung Co., 5 Den. (N. Y.) 517; Davis *v.* Spencer, 24 N. Y. 386; White *v.* Howard, 1 Sandf. (N. Y.) 81; Cowperthwaite *v.* Sheffield, 1 Sandf. (N. Y.) 416; s. c., 3 N. Y. 243; Read *v.* Mutual Safety Ins. Co. 3 Sandf. (N. Y.) 54.

North Carolina.—Hardgrave *v.* Dusenberry, 2 Hawks (N. Car.) 326; Shortridge *v.* Macon, Phill. L. (N. Car.) 392.

Oregon.—Hindman *v.* Edgar (Oregon 1888), 17 Pac. Rep. 862.

Pennsylvania.—Ormsby Coal Co. *v.* Bestwick (Pa. 1889), 18 Atl. Rep. 538; Bailey *v.* Pittsburg etc. Gas etc. Co., 69 Pa. St. 334; Fullerton *v.* Mobley (Pa. 1888), 15 Atl. Rep. 856; Curcier *v.* Pennock, 14 S. & R. (Pa.) 51; Levy *v.* Bank of U. S., 1 Binn. (Pa.) 27; Pearl *v.* Clark, 2 Pa. St. 350.

2. By Levy of Execution.—The levy of execution on lands does not constitute a payment of the judgment debt, nor does the seizure of goods and chattels under execution.[1]

Part payment to an officer holding an execution or distress warrant is a discharge *pro tanto*, and the plaintiff must look to the officer.[2]

3. Payment or Purchase.—Where a note or bill is taken up, or a debt paid by a stranger, the question arises whether the transaction amounts to a purchase or a payment. The general rule is, that the demand of a creditor which is paid with the money of a third person, without any agreement that the security shall be

Rhode Island.—Quidnick Co. *v.* Chafee, 13 R. I. 438.

South Carolina.—Seabrook *v.* Hammond, 5 Rich. (S. Car.) 160; Miller *v.* Kerr, 1 Bailey (S. Car.) 4.

Tennessee.—Wharton *v.* Lavender, 14 Lea (Tenn.) 178.

Texas.—Chalmers *v.* Harris, 22 Tex. 265; Luter *v.* Hunter, 30 Tex. 688; Canfield *v.* Hunter, 30 Tex. 712; Culbreath *v.* Hunter, 30 Tex. 713; Levison *v.* Norris, 30 Tex. 713; Levison *v.* Krohne, 30 Tex. 714.

Vermont.—Chellis *v.* Woods, 11 Vt. 466; Heartt *v.* Johnson, 13 Vt. 89; McIntyre *v.* Corss, 18 Vt. 451; Tracy *v.* Pearl, 20 Vt. 162; Smith *v.* Day, 23 Vt. 656; Farmers' Bank *v.* Burchard, 33 Vt. 346; Robinson *v.* Hurlburt, 34 Vt. 115; Newell *v.* Keith, 11 Vt. 214; Putnam *v.* Russell, 17 Vt. 54; s. c., 42 Am. Dec. 478.

Virginia.—Harpers *v.* Patton, 1 Leigh (Va.) 306; Laidley *v.* Merrifield, 7 Leigh (Va.) 346; Pindall *v.* Northwestern Bank, 7 Leigh (Va.) 617.

Wisconsin.—Eastman *v.* Porter, 14 Wis. 39; Gray *v.* Herman, 75 Wis. 453.

1. Trapnall *v.* Richardson, 13 Ark. 543; s. c., 58 Am. Dec. 338; Dugan *v.* Fowler, 14 Ark. 132; Cowles *v.* Bacon, 21 Conn. 451; s. c., 56 Am. Dec. 371; Gregory *v.* Stark, 4 Ill. 611; Nelson *v.* Rockwell, 14 Ill. 375; Williams *v.* Gartrell, 4 Green (Iowa) 287; Sasscer *v.* Walker, 5 Gill. & J. (Md.) 102; s. c., 25 Am. Dec. 272; Dehority *v.* Paxson, 115 Ind. 124; Spafford *v.* Beach, 2 Dougl. (Mich.) 150; Smith *v.* Walker, 10 Smed. & M. (Miss.) 584; Peale *v.* Bolton, 24 Miss. 630; Green *v.* Burke. 23 Wend. (N. Y.) 490; Lytle *v.* Mehaffy, 8 Watts (Pa.) 267; Campbell's Appeal, 32 Pa. St. 88.

But in the following cases a levy is held to be *prima facie* a satisfaction of the judgment: Mickles *v.* Haskin, 11 Wend. (N. Y.) 125; Maginac *v.* Thompson, 15 How. (U. S.) 281; Freeman *v.* Smith, 7 Ind. 582; Alexander *v.* Polk, 39 Miss. 737; Wade *v.* Watt, 41 Miss. 248; Peay *v.* Fleming, 2 Hill Eq. (S. Car.) 96; Pigg *v.* Sparrow, 3 Hayw. (Tenn.) 144; Warrensburg *v.* Simpson, 22 Mo. App. 695; Richey *v.* Merritt, 108 Ind. 347.

But it is held by some courts that while a levy on real property of sufficient value to discharge the execution is not a satisfaction, yet it is otherwise where personal property is levied on. Hogshead *v.* Carruth, 5 Yerg. (Tenn.) 227; Carroll *v.* Fields, 6 Yerg. (Tenn.) 305.

The plaintiff cannot abandon an execution against the will of the debtor. Trapnall *v.* Richardson, 13 Ark. 543; s. c., 58 Am. Dec. 338.

Where an attachment has been levied on property, and the record does not show any disposition of the levy, the presumption is that the debt was satisfied. Benson *v.* Benson, 24 Miss. 625.

The return of an execution satisfied raises a presumption that the money was received by the plaintiff. Boyd *v.* Foot, 5 Bosw. (N. Y.) 110.

Under the Alabama statute where an execution has been sued out within a year and a day and has been returned *nulla bona*, an *alias* execution may be sued out at any time within 10 years from the return of the original. *Held*, that this does not raise a presumption of payment, nor does it cast upon the plaintiff the burden of proving the judgment unsatisfied, either in a *scire facias* to revive the judgment or in an action of debt. Collins *v.* Boyd, 14 Ala. 505.

2. White *v.* Mandeville, 72 Ga. 705.

assigned or kept on foot for the benefit of such third person, is absolutely extinguished.[1]

1. Sheldon on Subrogation, §§ 3, 28; Thorner *v.* Smith, 2 L. M. & P. 43; 15 Jur. 469; 20 L. J., C. P. 71; Simpson *v.* Eggerton, 10 Exch. 845; Dooley *v.* Virginia F. & M. Ins. Co., 3 Hughes (U. S.) 221; Stockly *v.* Horsey, 4 Houst. (Del.) 603; Day *v.* Humphrey, 79 Ill. 452; Johnson *v.* Glover, 121 Ill. 283; Pearce *v.* Bryant Coal Co., 121 Ill. 590; Binford *v.* Adams, 104 Ind. 41; Montgomery *v.* Vickery, 110 Ind. 211; Bunch *v.* Grave, 111 Ind. 351; Dougherty *v.* Deeney, 45 Iowa 443; Newport Bridge Co. *v.* Douglass, 12 Bush (Ky.) 673; Brice *v.* Watkins, 30 La. Ann., pt. 1, 21; Moody *v.* Moody, 68 Maine 155; Tuckerman *v.* Sleeper, 9 Cush. (Mass.) 177; American Bank *v.* Jenness, 2 Met. (Mass.) 288; Hoysradt *v.* Holland, 50 N. H. 433; Eastman *v.* Plummer, 32 N. H. 238; New Jersey Midland R. Co. *v.* Wortendyke, 27 N. J. Eq. 658; Sanford *v.* McLean, 3 Paige (N. Y.) 117; s. c., 23 Am. Dec. 773; Banta *v.* Gavow, 1 Sandf. Ch. (N. Y.) 383; Wilkes *v.* Harper, 1 N. Y. 586; Lancey *v.* Clark, 64 N. Y. 209; s. c., 21 Am. Rep. 604; Gadsden *v.* Brown, Spears Eq. (S. Car.) 41; Campbell *v.* Sloan, 21 S. Car. 301; Douglass *v.* Fagg, 8 Leigh (Va.) 588; Cravatte *v.* Esterly, 26 Wis. 675. *Compare* St. Louis Min. Co. *v.* Sandoval Min. Co., 116 Ill. 170; Haven *v.* Grand Junction R. & Depot Co., 109 Mass. 88; Granite Nat. Bank *v.* Fitch, 145 Mass. 567; Hartshorn *v.* Brace, 25 Barb. (N. Y.) 126; Crounse *v.* Fitch, 23 How. Pr. (N. Y.) 350; s. c., 14 Abb. Pr. (N. Y.) 346; Brown *v.* Rich, 40 Barb. (N. Y.) 28; Smith *v.* Miller, 25 N. Y. 619.

Where one not a party to the contract pays a debt, it is an extinguishment of the demand, whether made with the assent of the debtor or not. Harrison *v.* Hicks, 1 Port. (Ala.) 423; s. c., 27 Am. Dec. 638.

And this rule obtains where a third person pays a partnership note for one member of the firm. In such case the person paying the note cannot recover on it against the firm. Childress *v.* Stone, Ga. Dec., pt. 2, 157.

"There is an important difference between the payment of a note and the purchase of it from the owner. Payment is the discharge of a debt. The purchase of a note is a contract of sale." ELLIOTT, J., in Binford *v.* Adams, 104 Ind. 43; *citing* 2 Dan. Neg. Inst. (3rd ed.), § 1221.

In this section Mr. Daniel says that a sale is different from a payment. A sale "is a contract which does not extinguish a bill or note, but continues it in circulation as a valid security against all parties. And it is necessary to constitute a transaction a sale that both parties should then 'expressly or impliedly agree, the one to sell, and the other to purchase, the paper." Section 1221, and cases cited in note.

A's wife conveyed to B an undivided half of a lot owned by her, and he therefore purchased the other undivided half, erected some buildings thereon and deeded the whole to A's wife. In order to put up the buildings some money was borrowed, for which notes were given signed by A's wife and B, which notes A afterwards took up. *Held*, that this constituted a payment and not a purchase, and that B's estate was not liable thereon. Washington *v.* Bedford, 10 Lea (Tenn.) 243.

In a Missouri case the owner of a promissory note placed it in bank for collection, with no authority to the officers of the bank to sell it. By an arrangement between the maker of the note and a defendant, the latter agreed to take up the note and hold it for a few months for the maker's accommodation, and defendant accordingly went to the bank and handed his cheque to the latter, who thereupon erased the owner's name which was indorsed thereon, and handed the note to the defendant. *Held*, that this constituted a payment. Wolff *v.* Walter, 56 Mo. 292. To same effect, Burr *v.* Smith, 21 Barb. (N. Y.) 262; Kennedy *v.* Chapin, 67 Md. 454. *Compare* Swope *v.* Leffingwell, 72 Mo. 348; Dodge *v.* Freedman's Sav. etc. Co., 93 U. S. 379.

Three notes were secured by a single mortgage. The maker being unable to meet the first, got a third party to take it up with the agreement that he was to hold it till certain claims were collected, and if the claims were not collected in three years the note was to be paid by a sale under the mortgage. This was *held* not to work an extinguishment of the note, though the payee, after its transfer, gave the maker a written acknowledgment of its payment. Ramsey *v.* Daniels, 1 Mackey (D. C.) 16.

The payee of a note presented it at maturity to the maker, who gave him a letter to a third party which he, the payee, did not read, and upon presentation of which the third party gave to the payee the amount of the note, and the payee wrote a receipt for the same on the note and surrendered it to the party who paid him the money. *Held*, that this was a payment of the note, and an action would not lie on the note in the name of the payee, though for the benefit of the third party, against the maker. Blundell *v.* Vaughan, 12 Smed. & M. (Miss.) 625.

During the pendency of a suit by a bank against the maker and accommodation indorser of a note, a friend of the maker, at the maker's request, procured the notes from the plaintiff's attorney, paying him the whole amount due thereon, upon the assurance of the attorney that he had full authority from the bank to make the transfer. This was held to be a sale and not a payment of the note, and the transferrer had the same rights against the accommodation indorser as the bank had before the purchase. Warner *v.* Chappell, 32 Barb. (N. Y.) 309. See also Concord Granite Co. *v.* French, 65 How. Pr. (N. Y.) 317.

A furnished the money to enable a mortgagor to take up one of several notes owned by B. The mortgagor informed B at the time the money was paid that it was A's money, and directed B not to cancel the note, as A was going to hold it. B, however, did not understand that he had sold the note to A. *Held*, that a payment must be presumed, not a purchase. Collins *v.* Adams, 53 Vt. 433.

The payee of a joint and several note, at the request of the principal maker, for whose accommodation it had been executed by the others, sent it to a bank for collection. Plaintiff, at the request of said principal maker, and upon the understanding that the note should be transferred to him, delivered to the bank the amount of the note, and the note was thereupon delivered to him. The bank forwarded the money to the payee, who received it, not knowing but that it was a payment, but after learning the facts, nevertheless, retained the money. Plaintiff brought suit on the note, and was held entitled to recover, the court, FINDE, J., saying: "Whatever may be true as to the want of authority to sell the note in the bank which received it for collection, it is quite certain that the transaction between the plaintiff and the collecting agent was a sale, or an entirely void proceeding. It could not be transformed into a payment in hostility to the expressed intentions of both parties who acted in the transfer. There was a sale, or an attempt at a sale which utterly failed, but never a payment; and an erroneous supposition by Peters, the payee, as to the fact which produced the money, traceable to his ignorance of the truth, cannot alter the nature of that truth. The note, then, being unpaid, is due from the makers to some one, and must be payable to Peters or the plaintiff. The only concern of the defendants, if the rights of the sureties have not been infringed, is to know to which of two parties they may safely pay the debt. . . . Their sole defense is that the bank had no authority to sell, and so plaintiff got no title. Undoubtedly Peters might have repudiated the act of his agent when he learned what it was. The moment he became possessed of that knowledge, he was bound in common honesty to return the money paid him by mistake, or retain it as it was given to his agent. The law will not endure that he shall keep the product of the agent's act and yet repudiate his authority." Coykendall *v.* Constable, 99 N. Y. 309.

On the insolvency of a banking company, W, one of the principal shareholders, gave securities to another bank to cover advances to be made by the latter bank for the payment of the public creditors of the insolvent bank. The creditors in question were paid out of such advances, and the debts so paid were assigned to R as a trustee for W, the deed of assignment reciting the facts, and that R had agreed to pay the amount of the bills on having an assignment to him of the debts. *Held*, that this was not a payment. McIntyre *v.* Miller, 13 M. & W. 725.

Where A borrowed money on his bond through his attorney, who acted as agent for him in his pecuniary affairs, and payment being demanded, the attorney, without A's knowledge, obtained from his bankers an advance by depositing the bond in question with them, and then stated in a letter

A note paid in fact is not upheld as a subsisting debt by a legal fiction of equitable assignment, when there is no ground of justice to support the fiction.[1]

III. **Medium of Payment—1. In Money.**—Where nothing is said as to the terms of payment an absolute payment in cash is always implied.[2]

to the obligee in the bond that he had laid down the money to prevent her any inconvenience, this was not a payment of the bond, and an action might be maintained thereon by the bankers in the name of the obligee against A. Lucas *v.* Wilkinson, 26 L. J. Exch. 13; 1 H. & N. 420.

Whether the transaction is of such a character as to constitute a payment or a sale is generally a question of fact for the jury. Moran *v.* Abbey, 63 Cal. 56; Balohradsky *v.* Carlisle, 14 Ill. App. 289; Binford *v.* Adams, 104 Ind. 41; Dougherty *v.* Deeney, 45 Iowa 443; Jones *v.* Bobbitt, 90 N. Car 391; Wilcoxson *v.* Logan, 91 N. Car. 449.

The rule is different where the stranger is compelled to pay the debt for the protection of his own property. Weiss *v.* Guerineau, 109 Ind. 438; Harbach *v.* Colvin, 73 Iowa 638.

Where a partner voluntarily pays a firm debt out of his individual means, he does not thereby become a creditor of the firm for the amount so paid. Lyons *v.* Murray, 95 Mo. 23; s. c., 6 Am. St. Rep. 17.

Where an agent receives a note for collection he may, in Michigan, pay the amount to his principal and then sue on it in his own name. Coy *v.* Stiner, 53 Mich. 42.

The maker of a promissory note given for the purchase of land procured the transfer to himself of a judgment against the payee, and then, upon the surrender of his note by the payee, entered satisfaction of the judgment. Afterwards he delivered the note to the assignor and real owner of the judgment, whose agent he had been in the transaction. *Held*, that these facts showed only an exchange of the note for the judgment, and did not operate as a payment of the note, and that an assignee thereof could recover against the maker. Flournoy *v.* Harper, 81 Ala. 494.

The party assigning or consenting to the assignment of a note or bill would still be held thereon. Aetna Life Ins. Co. *v.* Corn, 89 Ill. 170; Baker *v.* Seeley, 17 How. Pr. (N. Y.) 297.

As to keeping judgment alive for benefit of surety who has paid it, see Chandler *v.* Higgins, 109 Ill. 602.

1. Rolfe *v.* Wooster, 58 N. H. 526.

2. Benjamin *v.* Sales (1st Am. ed.), §§ 706, 712; Means *v.* Harrison, 114 Ill. 248. *Compare* Foley *v.* Mason, 6 Md. 37.

Where silver is by the act of Congress made legal tender in amounts not exceeding $5, a payment in silver of costs to a clerk of court is good, though the fee bill is $15.50 it not appearing that more than $5 of such costs was due any one person. Harnmann *v.* Mink, 99 Ind. 279.

Where rent is reserved in "lawful silver money of the United States, each dollar weighing 17 dwt., 6 grs. at least," a payment in gold coin is good. Morris *v.* Bancroft, 9 Phila. (Pa.) 277.

Where the contract on a sale of land was for payment in gold, the receipt of the purchase money in currency together with a delivery of the deed, is a waiver of the requirement as to payment in gold. Leffermann *v.* Renshaw, 45 Md. 119.

A payment in currency under a contract to pay in gold will discharge the indebtedness to the amount of the gold value of the currency at the date of payment. Hittson *v.* Davenport, 4 Colo. 169.

The word "dollars" in a promissory note means dollars in lawful money of the United States, and an agent for collection has no authority to receive depreciated currency in payment. Stoughton *v.* Hill, 3 Wood (U. S) 404.

An agreement to pay $5,000 in lawful silver money of the United States may be extinguished by the payment of that amount in silver half-dollar coins. Parrish *v.* Kohler, 11 Phila. (Pa.) 346.

In payments between individuals, treasury notes and gold coin are to be considered as equivalent. Riddlesbarger *v.* McDaniel, 38 Mo. 138.

2. **Bank bills** are deemed money and pass as such, unless objected to on that ground; and, if accepted, they constitute a payment.[1]

According to Comyns, payment by merchants must be made in money or by bill. Com. Dig. Merchant (F); Bouv. Law Dict. Payment.

The creditor is not bound to receive a cheque in payment. Beauchamp *v.* Archer, 58 Cal. 431; s. c., 41 Am. Rep. 266.

The clerk of a court has no power to receive payment of a judgment in anything but legal tender, without authority from the owner of the judgment. Prather *v.* State Bank, 3 Ind. 356; Bone *v.* Torry, 16 Ark. 83. See Woodson *v.* Bank of Gallipolis, 4 B. Mon. (Ky.) 203.

Where certain notes were payable in "cost notes," and it appeared from the wording of the instruments that a payment was intended more beneficial to the maker than money, the question of the manner of payment was properly left to the jury. Ward *v.* Lattimer, 2 Tex. 245.

"Specie" means gold and silver of the country where used; "currency" means paper money, or notes current in the community as money. Trebilcock *v.* Wilson, 12 Wall. (U. S.) 687.

The term "lawful money" in a bond has been held to mean such currency as shall be lawful at the place and time when payment is actually made. O'Neil *v.* McKewn, 1 S. Car. 147.

The debtor sent to the creditor a sum in gold with instructions to sell at a specified premium and apply the proceeds to the debt. The market value never reached the premium named by the debtor. The creditor retained the gold for two years without further instructions, and then credited the debtor with its market value at that time, which was below the value at the time the gold was received. *Held*, that he was not liable for the value at the time of its receipt. Patterson *v.* Currier, 106 Mass. 410.

Where $3,000, due for freight, is payable at Hull, in England, the pound sterling is to be reckoned at its value at the time and place of payment. Jelison *v.* Lee, 1 Woodb. & M. (U. S.) 368. See also Stanwood *v.* Flagg, 98 Mass. 124. And see generally, on the question of the obligation to pay in money, the additional cases of McElderry *v.* Jones, 67 Ala. 203; Blackwell *v.* The Auditor, 1 Ill. (Breese) 152; Berry *v.* Nall, 54 Ala. 446; Ballard *v.* Wall, 2 La. Ann. 404; Atkinson *v.* Lanier, 69 Ga. 460; Missoula Co. *v.* McCormick, 4 Mont. 115; Crutcher *v.* Sterling, 1 Idaho, N. S. 306.

1. 2 Greenl. Evid. (13th ed.), § 522; Wright *v.* Read, 3 T R. 554; Owenson *v.* Morse, 7 T. R. 64; Jones *v.* Ryde, 5 Taunt. 488; Snow *v.* Perry, 9 Pick. (Mass.) 539 (and cases cited in note 1 on page 542); Young *v.* Adams, 6 Mass. 182; Phillips *v.* Blake, 1 Met. (Mass.) 156; Muton *v.* Old Colony Ins. Co., 2 Met. (Mass.) 1, 5; Bayard *v.* Shunk, 1 W. & S. (Pa.) 92; s. c., 37 Am. Dec. 441; Lowry *v.* Murrell, 2 Port. (Ala.) 280; Corbitt *v.* Bank of Smyrna, 2 Harr. (Del.) 236; s. c., 30 Am. Dec. 635; Edmunds *v.* Digges, 1 Gratt. (Va.) 359 (dissenting opinion, p. 549); s. c., 42 Am. Dec. 561; Scruggs *v.* Gass, 8 Yerg. (Tenn.) 175; s. c., 29 Am. Dec. 114; Williams *v.* Roser, 7 Mo. 556. See Warren *v.* Mains, 7 Johns. (N. Y.) 476.

But if the bank was at the time insolvent, and had stopped payment, the acceptance of its bills does not constitute a satisfaction of the debt, though at the time and place of the payment the bills were in full credit, and both parties were ignorant of the bank's insolvency. Jefferson *v.* Holland, 1 Del. Ch. 116; Lightbody *v.* Ontario Bank, 11 Wend. (N. Y.) 9; s. c., on error, 13 Wend. (N. Y.) 101; s. c., 27 Am. Dec. 179; Thomas *v.* Todd, 6 Hill (N. Y.) 340; Honore *v.* Colmesnil, 1 J. J. Marsh. (Ky.) 523; Frontier Bank *v.* Morse, 22 Me. 88; s. c., 38 Am. Dec. 284; Fogg *v.* Sawyer, 9 N. H. 365; Westfall *v.* Braley, 10 Ohio St. 188; s. c., 75 Am. Dec. 509; Wainwright *v.* Webster, 11 Vt. 576; s. c., 34 Am. Dec. 707; Townsend *v.* Bank of Racine, 7 Wis. 185. See Magee *v.* Carmack, 13 Ill. 289; Bayard *v.* Schunk, 1 W. & S. (Pa.) 92; s. c., 37 Am. Dec. 441; Scruggs *v.* Gass, 8 Yerg. (Tenn.) 75; s. c., 29 Am. Dec. 114. And *compare* Lowry *v.* Murrell, 2 Port. (Ala.) 280; Ware *v.* Street, 2 Head (Tenn.) 609; s. c., 75 Am. Dec. 755.

In the payment and receipt of bank bills there is an implied contract on the part of the payer that they are current and would pass readily in mercantile and business transactions as money. Kottwitz *v.* Bagby, 16 Tex. 656.

Current notes mean notes which are current at their face value. If they are depreciated they cease to be "current" wherever the depreciation exists.[1]

3. Confederate notes are to be regarded as a currency imposed upon the community by irresistible force and are considered by the courts as currency issued by a foreign government temporarily occupying by force a part of the territory of the United States.[2] If voluntarily received by the creditor during the pendency of the war at their nominal value, confederate notes constituted a valid payment.[3]

As between a bank and a debtor to the bank, its notes are cash. Northampton Bank *v.* Ballie, 8 W. & S. 311; s. c, 42 Am. Dec. 297.

Where the maker of a note sent bank bills to the payee, with directions to the bearer to see the amount indorsed on the note or take a receipt, and the payee gave a receipt promising to indorse the payment on the note or return the bills when called for, this constituted an amount, though before the maker knew of the receipt the bank failed. Snow *v.* Perry, 9 Pick. (Mass.) 539.

The fact that a note is made payable at a certain bank does not render the notes of such bank receivable in payment. Bull *v.* Harrell, 7 How. (Miss.) 9. And see McDougal *v.* Holmes, 1 Ohio 376.

1. Williams *v.* Mosley, 2 Fla. 304. And the creditor cannot be compelled to take such. Howe *v.* Wade, 4 McLean (U. S.) 317; Magee *v.* Carmack, 13 Ill. 289; Bragdon *v.* Goulam, 1 T. B. Mon. (Ky.) 115.

Compare Ridenow *v.* McClurkin, 6 Blatchf. (Ind.) 411.

And where an obligation is payable in the "current money" of any particular State, this means gold and silver. Moore *v.* Morris, 20 Ill. 255; Cockrill *v.* Kirkpatrick, 9 Mo. 697; Searcy *v.* Vance, Mart. & Y. (Tenn.) 225.

Compare Deming *v.* Marsh, Kirby (Conn.) 424.

A note payable in "*Mississippi* currency" is payable in gold and silver, in the absence of proof that notes of the banks of that State were intended. Ballard *v.* Wall, 2 La. Ann. 404. And see, as involving a like question in relation to "Illinois currency," Hulbert *v.* Carver, 40 Barb. (N. Y.) 245.

In 1860 a bank issued a certificate showing a deposit of $480 "in current notes of the different banks of the State of North Carolina, which sum is payable in like current notes." The certificate was held until 1868, at which time the State bank notes had by depreciation become uncurrent. *Held*, that the bank was liable for the amount in United States currency. Fort *v.* Bank of Cape Fear, Phil. (N. Car.) 417.

Compare Wilson *v.* Keeling, 1 Wash. (Va.) 194.

If a note payable in current bank notes fell due at a time and place during the late war when and where no such notes were in circulation, the amount due is to be measured by a gold standard. Jones *v.* Kincaid, 5 Lea (Tenn.) 677.

An agreement that payment of a note should be made in a currency which afterwards depreciated, does not constitute a defense to an action on the note, but reduces the right of recovery to the value of the sum in the depreciated currency at maturity. Powe *v.* Powe, 42 Ala. 113.

And credits in currency, indorsed as such on a note payable in specie, are payments only to the extent of the value in specie of such currency at the time of payment. Walkup *v.* Houston, 65 N. Car. 501.

Where paper was made payable in "current bank notes," if there were at the time the paper matured bank notes in circulation current as money and used in business transactions in the liquidation of debts, the debtor had the right to pay in such bank notes, though as compared with gold they were greatly depreciated in value. Moore *v.* Gooch, 6 Heisk. (Tenn.) 104.

Compare Western etc. R. Co. *v.* Taylor, 6 Heisk. (Tenn.) 408.

2. Thorington *v.* Smith, 8 Wall. (U. S.) 1. See Wilmington etc. R. Co. *v.* King, 91 U. S. 3.

3. Berry *v.* Bellows, 30 Ark. 198; Hester *v.* Watkins, 54 Ala. 44; King *v.* King, 37 Ga. 205; Caruthers *v.* Corbin, 38 Ga. 75; Green *v.* Jones, 38 Ga. 347; Luzenburg *v.* Cleveland, 19 La. Ann.

473; Mercer *v.* Wiggins, 74 N. Car. 48; Flintt *v.* Nelson, 15 Rich. (S. Car.) 9; Hyatt *v.* McBurney, 18 S. Car. 199; Jones *v.* Thomas, 5 Coldw. (Tenn.) 465; Thorington *v.* Smith, 8 Wall. (U. S.) 1. *Compare* Wright *v.* Overall, 2 Coldw. (Tenn.) 336; Blalock *v.* Phillips, 38 Ga. 216; Strauss *v.* Bloom, 18 La. Ann. 48; Emmerson *v.* Mallett, Phil. Eq. (N. Car.) 234; Glenn *v.* Case, 25 Ark. 616; Draughan *v.* White, 21 La. Ann. 175; Cuyler *v.* Ferrill, 1 Abb. (U. S.) 169; Ransom *v.* Alexander, 31 Tex. 443.

If an administrator receives confederate money in payment of debts owing the estate, he must, if he is a creditor of the estate, apply the same currency to the discharge of his own debt. Dickie *v.* Dickie, 80 Ala. 57.

Where the agent of the payee of a note received payment in Confederate notes and delivered up the note to the maker, the debt was thereby extinguished. Reed *v.* Nelson, 33 Tex. 471.

Compare Clark *v.* Thomas, 4 Heisk. (Tenn.) 419; Neely *v.* Woodward, 7 Heisk. (Tenn.) 495.

Payments by debtors in the Confederate States to the agents or trustees of creditors in the loyal States, in any currency other than legal currency of the United States would not extinguish the debts so sought to be paid. Fretz *v.* Stover, 22 Wall. (U. S.) 198; Taylor *v.* Thomas, 22 Wall. (U. S.) 479.

A note was given before the war, for money belonging to citizens of New York to a citizen of North Carolina, who acted as the agent of the New York parties, and was, in 1863, surrendered by such agent to a Confederate receiver, who accepted in payment thereof Confederate money. *Held*, that such payment was no defense to a suit by the payee to the use of the beneficial owner. Justice *v.* Hamilton, 67 N. Car. 111.

In the absence of instructions to the contrary a circuit clerk was justified in receiving confederate money in payment of a judgment at a time when that was the chief circulating medium. Douglas *v.* Neil, 7 Heisk. (Tenn.) 437; Binford *v.* Memphis Bulletin Co., 10 Heisk. (Tenn.) 355.

A clerk of a court, administrator, or other person sustaining a fiduciary relation, taking Confederate notes in payment in good faith will not be held to account for more than their value. Burford *v.* Memphis Bulletin Co., 9 Heisk. (Tenn.) 691; Morris *v.* Morris, 9 Heisk. (Tenn.) 814; Pilson *v.* Bushong, 29 Gratt. (Va.) 229. See Jones *v.* Jones, 49 Tex. 683.

The rule established in *Tennessee* in actions to recover the value of Confederate notes is to estimate the same in U. S. treasury notes, and not in gold. Lustsr *v.* Maloney, 6 Baxt. (Tenn.) 374.

Where payments of principal and interest on a promissory note, executed in New Orleans in 1862, were made in United States money, and where no claim was made before suit brought that the term "dollars" was to be construed as meaning "Confederate dollars," judgment will be rendered for the amount due to be paid in lawful money. Cook *v.* Lillo, 103 U. S. 792.

And see generally on the question of payments in Confederate money, Pieggar *v.* Twohig, 37 Tex. 225; Vander Hoven *v.* Nette, 32 Tex. 184; Pettis *v.* Campbell, 47 Ga. 596; Matthews *v.* Thompson, 2 Heisk. (Tenn.) 588; Opie *v.* Castleman, 32 Fed. Rep. 511; Clark *v.* Bernstein, 49 Ala. 596; Coleman *v.* Wingfield, 4 Heisk. (Tenn.) 133; Blackwell *v.* Tucker, 7 S. Car. 387; Bond *v.* Perkins, 4 Heisk. (Tenn.) 364; Cokrell *v.* Wiley, 4 Heisk. (Tenn.) 472; Darby *v.* Stribling, 24 S. Car. 422; Davis *v.* Mississippi Cent. R. Co., 46 Miss. 552; Harshaw *v.* Dobson, 67 N. Car. 203; Sirrine *v.* Griffin, 40 Ga. 169; Sharp *v.* Harrison, 10 Heisk. (Tenn.) 573; Wintz *v.* Weakes, 10 Heisk. (Tenn.) 593; Dillon *v.* Smith, 10 Heisk. (Tenn.) 595; Henderson *v.* McGhee, 6 Heisk. (Tenn.) 55; Kelley *v.* Story, 6 Heisk. (Tenn.) 202; Pryor *v.* Bank of Tennessee, 6 Heisk. (Tenn.) 442; Pointer *v.* Smith, 7 Heisk. (Tenn.) 137; Wilburn *v.* McCollom, 7 Heisk. (Tenn.) 267; Alderson *v.* Clear, 7 Heisk. (Tenn.) 667; Smith *v.* Smith, 101 N. Car. 461; Ellis *v.* Smith, 42 Ala. 349; Wood *v.* Cooper, 2 Heisk. (Tenn.) 441; Hill *v.* Erwin, 60 Ala. 341; Ritchie *v.* Sweet, 32 Tex 333; s. c., 5 Am. Rep. 245; Ponder *v.* Scott, 44 Ala. 241; Vance *v.* Cooper, 22 La. Ann. 508; Washington *v.* Burnett, 4 W. Va. 84; Robinson *v.* International L. Assur. Soc. 42 N. Y. 54; s. c., 1 Am. Rep. 400; Hall *v.* Craige, 65 N. Car. 51; Cross *v.* Sells, 1 Heisk. (Tenn.) 83; Cable *v.* Harden, 67 N. Car. 472; Bryan *v.* Heck, 67 N. Car. 322; Gilkeson *v.* Smith, 15 W. Va. 44; Ewart *v.* Saunders, 25 Gratt. (Va.) 203; Trustees of Howard College *v.* Turner, 71 Ala. 429; s. c., 46 Am. Rep. 326.

4. Illegal Currency.—A payment in an illegal or void currency is a nullity.[1]

Counterfeit money, though supposed to be genuine by both parties and accepted by the creditor, are no payment, if the creditor offer to return them without unnecessary delay after discovering their worthlessness.[2]

5. An account against a stranger to the transaction may be received in payment if such is the agreement between the parties; and whether such was the agreement is a question for the jury.[3]

6. Payment by Note, Bill or Cheque—(*a*) GENERAL RULE.—A cheque, draft or promissory note of a debtor or of a third party, if not itself paid, does not constitute a payment, unless received by the creditor under an express agreement to accept it as an absolute payment.[4]

1. Richards *v.* Stogsdell, 21 Ind. 74.

2. 2 Greenl. Evid. (13th ed.), § 522; Baker *v.* Bonesteel, 2 Hilt. (N. Y.) 397; Thomas *v.* Todd, 6 Hill (N. Y.) 340; Markle *v.* Hatfield, 2 Johns. (N. Y.) 455; s. c., 3 Am. Dec. 446; Atwood *v.* Cornwall, 28 Mich. 336; s. c., 15 Am. Rep. 219; Eagle Bank *v.* Smith, 5 Conn. 71; s. c., 13 Am. Dec. 37; Leake *v.* Brown, 43 Ill. 372; Ramsdale *v.* Horton, 3 Pa. St. 330; Young *v.* Anams, 6 Mass. 182; Hargrave *v.* Dusenbury, 2 Hawks (N. Car.) 326; Anderson *v.* Hawkins, 3 Hawks (N. Car.) 568; Semmes *v.* Wilson; 5 Cranch (C. C.) 285. See Corn Exchange Bank *v.* National Bank, 78 Pa. St. 233.

But any unnecessary delay in notifying the debtor will deprive the creditor of his right to treat the debt as still existing. Atwood *v.* Cornwall, 28 Mich. 336; s. c., 15 Am. Rep. 219; Wingate *v.* Neidlinger, 50 Ind. 520; Lawrenceburg Nat. Bank *v.* Stevenson, 51 Ind. 594.

What is a reasonable time within which to return the note must depend upon the situation of the parties and the circumstances of each case. Simms *v.* Clark, 11 Ill. 137; Burrill *v.* Watertown Bank, 51 Barb. (N. Y.) 105.

In one case two months was held to be too long a delay in returning the bills. Thomas *v.* Todd, 6 Hill (N. Y.) 340. In another, a neglect for fifteen days to return them was held to prevent the payee from recovering. Gloucester Bank *v.* Salem Bank, 17 Mass. 42. In another case three years. Crucier *v.* Pennock, 14 S. & R. (Pa.) 51. *Compare* Prather *v.* State Bank, 3 Ind. 356.

It is a question of fact for the jury. Magee *v.* Carmack, 13 Ill. 289; Union Nat. Bank *v.* Baldenwick, 45 Ill. 376.

If the party paying the counterfeit bills states, upon being notified that they are not genuine, that he will not take them back, this dispenses with an immediate offer to return them. Simms *v.* Clark, 11 Ill. 137.

But a *bona fide* payment made to a bank in notes purporting to be issued by said bank is good, though the notes prove to be counterfeit. Bank of U. S. *v.* Bank of Georgia, 10 Wheat. (U. S.) 333.

Where goods are delivered under an agreement to take a specific parcel of copper money in payment, the delivery of such parcel is a good payment though it was, in fact, counterfeit. Alexander *v.* Owen, 1 T. R. 225.

3. Willard *v.* Germer, 1 Sandf. (N. Y.) 50.

And if the creditor agrees to take a claim of his debtor against a third party as payment *in presenti*, it is virtually a purchase of his debtor's claim, and an agreement to accept it as payment *pro tanto* of his own claim. Hayden *v.* Johnson, 26 Vt. 768.

A held certain notes against B, and B held a note against A for a less amount, payable in instalments. A, without the assent of B, indorsed the amount of the instalments as they fell due on his note to B, as the notes he held against B, which were not then payable. *Held*, that this did not constitute a payment of his note to B. Greenough *v.* Walker, 5 Mass. 214.

4. Story *v.* Sales (4th ed.), § 219; 2 Greenl. Evid. (13th ed.) § 521; Benjamin on Sales (1 Am. ed.), § 729; 2 Benj. on Sales (4 Am. ed.), 939, 940; Owernon *v.* Morse, 7 T. R. 64; Burden *v.* Halton, 4 Bing. 454; Shipton *v.* Casson, 8 Dow. & R. 130; 5 B. &

C. 178; Sayer *v.* Wagstaff, 5 Beav. 415; 13 L. J., Ch. 161; 3 Jur. 1083; Belshaw *v.* Bush, 14 Eng. L. & Eq. 269; *In re* London etc. Bank, 34 Beav. 332; 34 L. J., Ch. 418; Bottomly *v.* Nuttall, 5 C. B., N. S. 122; 28 L. J., C. P. 110; Peter *v.* Beverly, 10 Pet. (U. S.) 532; Bank of U. S. *v.* Daniel, 12 Pet. (U. S.) 32; Gallagher *v.* Roberts, 2 Wash. (U. S.) 191; Parker *v.* United States, Pet. (C. C.) 266; Allen *v.* King, 4 McLean (U. S.) 128; Wallace *v.* Agry, 2 Mason (U. S.) 336; Sheeley *v.* Mandeville, 6 Cranch (U. S.) 253; The Kimball, 3 Wall. (U. S.) 37; Bank of St. Mary's *v.* St. John, 25 Ala. 566; Abercrombie *v.* Mosely, 9 Port. Ala. 145; Crockett *v.* Trotter, 1 Stew. & P. (Ala.) 446; Fickling *v.* Brewer, 38 Ala. 685; Mooring *v.* Mobile M. Ins. Co., 27 Ala. 254; Marshall *v.* Marshall, 42 Ala. 149; Graves *v.* Shulman, 59 Ala. 406; Keel *v.* Larkin, 72 Ala. 493; Lee *v.* Green, 83 Ala. 491; Lane *v.* Jones, 79 Ala. 156; Pope *v.* Tunstall, 2 Ark. 209; Costar *v.* Davies, 8 Ark. 213; s. c., 46 Am. Dec. 311; Viser *v.* Bertrand, 14 Ark. 267; Brugman *v.* McGuire, 32 Ark. 733; Caldwell *v.* Hall, 49 Ark. 508; s. c., 4 Am. St. Rep. 64; Griffith *v.* Grogan, 12 Cal. 317; Crary *v.* Bowers, 20 Cal. 85; Welch *v.* Ailington, 23 Cal. 322; Anderson *v.* Henshaw, 2 Day (Conn.) 272; Davidson *v.* Bridgeport, 8 Conn. 472; Bill *v.* Porter, 9 Conn. 23; Bonnell *v.* Chamberlin, 26 Conn. 487; May *v.* Gamble, 14 Fla. 467; Salomon *v.* Pioneer Cooperative Co., 21 Fla. 374; s. c., 58 Am. Rep. 667; Mims *v.* McDowell, 4 Ga. 182; Butts *v.* Cuthbertson, 6 Ga. 166; Hatcher *v.* Corner, 75 Ga. 728; Ryan *v.* Dunlap, 17 Ill. 40; s. c., 63 Am. Dec. 334; Rayburn *v.* Day, 27 Ill. 46; Strong *v.* King, 35 Ill. 1; s. c., 85 Am. Dec. 336; Archibald *v.* Argall, 53 Ill. 307; Wilhelm *v.* Schmidt, 84 Ill. 183; Jewett *v.* Pleak, 43 Ind. 368; Hardin *v.* Branner, 25 Iowa 364; McLaren *v.* Hall, 26 Iowa 297; Hunt *v.* Higman, 70 Iowa 406 (Iowa cases cited); Cunningham *v.* McGowan, 71 Iowa 461; Kermeyer *v.* Newby, 14 Kan. 164; Harlan *v.* Wingate, 2 J. J. Marsh. (Ky.) 138; Sneed *v.* Wiester, 2 A. K. Marsh. (Ky.) 277; Comstock *v.* Smith, 23 Me. 202; Newall *v.* Hussey, 18 Me. 249; Wolgamot *v.* Bruner, 4 Har. & Mc. H. (Md.) 89; Morgan *v.* Bitzenberger, 3 Gill. (Md.) 350; Harness *v.* Chesapeake etc. Canal Co., 1 Md. Ch. 248; Banorgee *v.* Hovey, 5 Mass. 11; s. c., 4 Am. Dec. 17; where the authorities are cited; Watkins *v.* Hill, 8 Pick. (Mass) 522; Pomroy *v.* Rice, 16 Pick. (Mass.) 22; Gardner *v.* Gorham, 1 Dougl. (Mich.) 507; Keough *v.* McNitt, 6 Minn. 513; Slocumb *v.* Holmes, 1 How. (Miss.) 139; Wakefield *v.* Spencer, 8 Minn. 376; Bacon *v.* Ventress, 32 Miss. 158; Berteaux *v.* Dillon, 20 Mo. App. 603; Selby *v.* McCallough, 26 Mo. App. 66; Wear *v.* Lee, 26 Mo. App. 99; Cave *v.* Hall, 5 Mo. 59; Steamboat Charlotte *v.* Lumm, 9 Mo. 64; Appleton *v.* Kennon, 19 Mo. 637; Howard *v.* Jones, 33 Mo. 583; Block *v.* Dorman, 51 Mo. 31; Wadlington *v.* Covert, 51 Miss. 631; Smith *v.* Smith, 27 N. H. 244; Coburn *v.* Odell, 30 N. H. 540; Barnet *v.* Smith, 30 N. H. 257; s. c., 64 Am. Dec. 290; Gilman *v.* Stevens, 63 N. H. 342; Coxe *v.* Hankinson, 1 N. J. L. 85; Ayres *v.* Van Lieu, 5 N. J. L. 765; Park *v.* Miller, 27 N. J. L. 338; Fry *v.* Patterson, 49 N. J. L. 612; Middlesex *v.* Thomas, 20 N. J. Eq. 39; Swain *v.* Frazier, 35 N. J. Eq. 326; Johnson *v.* Weed, 9 Johns. (N. Y.) 310; s. c., 6 Am. Dec. 279; Booth *v.* Smith, 3 Wend. (N. Y.) 66; Porter *v.* Talcott, 1 Cow. (N. Y.) 359; Raymond *v.* Merchant, 3 Cow. (N. Y.) 147; Smith *v.* Applegate, 1 Daly (N. Y.) 91; Van Steenburg *v.* Hoffman, 15 Barb. (N. Y.) 28; Crane *v.* McDonald, 45 Barb. (N. Y.) 354; Vail *v.* Foster, 4 (N. Y.) 312; Noel *v.* Murray, 13 N. Y. 167; (cheque) Cromwell *v.* Lovett, 1 Hall (N. Y.) 56; People *v.* Baker. 20 Wend. (N. Y.) 602; Tamner *v.* Bank of Fox Lake, 23 How. Pr. (N. Y.) 399; Burkhalter *v.* Second Nat. Bank, 42 N. Y. 538; s. c., 40 How. Pr. (N. Y.) 324; Smitherman *v.* *v.* Kidd, 1 Ired. Eq. (N. Car.) 86; Merrick *v.* Boury, 4 Ohio St. 60; McGinn *v.* Holmes, 2 Watts. (Pa.) 121; McIntyre *v.* Kennedy, 29 Pa. St. 448; Kilpatrick *v.* Home Bldg. & Loan Assoc., 119 Pa. St. 30; Wilbur *v.* Jernegan, 11 R. I. 113; Dogan *v.* Ashbey, 1 Rich. (S. Car.) 36; in which the earlier South Carolina cases are cited; Watson *v.* Owens, 1 Rich. (S. Car.) 111; Barrelli *v.* Brown, 1 McCord (S. Car.) 449; s. c., 10 Am. Dec. 683; Costelo *v.* Cave, 2 Hill (S. Car.) 528; s. c., 27 Am. Dec. 404; Hill *v.* Riley, 21 S. Car. 602; Bermingham *v.* Forsythe, 26 S. Car. 358; Kennall *v.* Muncey, Peck (Tenn.) 273; McGuire *v.* Bidwell, 64 Tex. 43; Torrey *v.* Baxter, 13 Vt. 452; McGuire *v.* Gadsby, 3 Call. (Va.) 234; Moses *v.* Trice, 21 Gratt.

(Va.) 556; s. c., 5 Am. Rep. 609; Blair *v.* Wilson, 28 Gratt. (Va.) 165; Hornbrooks *v.* Lucas, 24 W. Va. 493 (where the West Virginia decisions are fully cited); s. c., 49 Am. Rep. 277; Lindsey *v.* McClelland, 18 Wis. 481; s. c., 86 Am. Dec. 786; Matteson *v.* Ellsworth, 33 Wis. 488. *Compare* Woodville *v.* Reed, 26 Md. 179; Cornwall *v.* Gould, 4 Pick. (Mass.) 444; Huse *v.* Alexander, 2 Met. (Mass.) 157; Spooner *v.* Rowland, 4 Allen (Mass.) 485; Van Ostrandt *v.* Reed, 1 Wend. (N. Y.) 424.

Some courts hold that the mere taking of a note does not even raise a presumption of payment. Marshall *v.* Marshall, 42 Ala. 149; Doebling *v.* Loos, 45 Mo. 150; Graham *v.* Sykes, 15 La. Ann. 49; Devlin *v.* Chamberlin, 6 Minn. 468; Randlet *v.* Herren, 20 N. H. 102; Whitney *v.* Goin, 20 N. H. 354.

While others hold that it is not necessary to prove an express agreement. White *v.* Jones, 38 Ill. 159; Hotchin *v.* Secor, 8 Mich. 494.

But in *Pennsylvania*, it is held that the taking of a cheque of a third party raises the presumption of a conditional payment only. McIntyre *v.* Kennedy, 29 Pa. St. 448. *Compare* Plankinhorn *v.* Cave, 2 Yeates (Pa.) 370.

The fact that the note given is secured by mortgage does not affect the question. Blunt *v.* Walker, 11 Wis. 334; s. c., 78 Am. Dec. 709.

The taking of a new note with personal security does not of itself operate as a satisfaction of a mortgage. McDonald *v.* Hulse, 16 Mo. 503.

A debtor gave his creditor the check of a third party for the amount of the debt, which was payable to bearer, and not indorsed. The creditor kept it 26 days before presenting it, and when presented the bank had failed, and payment was refused. The drawer had no funds in the bank at the time he drew the cheque, but the president testified that it would have been paid if it had been presented before suspension. There was no agreement that the cheque should be received as payment. Upon its dishonor, the cheque was returned to the debtor and by him to the drawer, who promised to pay the amount to the debtor. *Held*, not to be a payment. Mordis *v.* Kennedy, 23 Kan. 408; s. c., 33 Am. Rep. 169.

It is held by the English courts that the acceptance by the creditor of a cheque in his favor drawn by the debtor operates as a payment unless the cheque is dishonored. Pearce *v.* Davis, 1 M. & Rob. 365; Bridges *v.* Garrett, 5 L. R., C. P. 451; 39 L. J., C. P. 251; *reversing*, s. c., 4 L. R., C. P. 580; Boswell *v.* Smith, 6 Car. & P. 60.

But to operate as payment the cheque must be absolute, and contain no condition. If it states in the body thereof that it is given for a balance of account, it is not payment. Hough *v.* May, 4 Ad. & El. 954; 6 Nev. & M. 535.

The question whether the note was received as absolute payment is one for the jury. Goldshede *v.* Cottrell, 2 Mees. & W. 20; Lyman *v.* Bank of U. S., 12 How. (U. S.) 225; Myatts *v.* Bell, 41 Ala. 222; Melledge *v.* Boston Iron Co., 5 Cush. (Mass.) 158, 170; s. c., 51 Am. Dec. 59; Casey *v.* Weaver, 141 Mass. 280; Corner *v.* Pratt, 138 Mass. 446; Johnson *v.* Weed, 9 Johns. (N. Y.) 310; s. c., 6 Am. Dec. 279; Coburn *v.* Odell, 30 N. H. 540, 557; Johnson *v.* Cleaves, 15 N. H. 332; Crabtree *v.* Rowand, 33 Ill. 421; White *v.* Jones, 38 Ill. 159; Bonnell *v.* Chamberlin, 26 Conn. 487; Susquehanna Fertilizer Co. *v.* White, 66 Md. 444; s. c., 59 Am. Rep. 186; Salomon *v.* Pioneer Co-operative Co., 20 Fla. 374; s. c., 58 Am. Rep. 667; Bullen *v.* McGilcuddy, 2 Dana (Ky.) 91; Gardner *v.* Gorham, 1 Dougl. (Mich.) 507; Keerl *v.* Bridgers, 10 Smed. & M. (Miss.) 612; Seltzer *v.* Coleman, 32 Pa. St. 493; Horner *v.* Hower, 49 Pa. St. 475; Brown *v.* Scott, 51 Pa. St. 357; Union Bank *v.* Smizer, 1 Sneed (Tenn.) 501.

As to what is evidence of the agreement. Van Eps *v.* Dillage, 6 Barb. (N. Y.) 244; Roberts *v.* Fisher, 53 Barb. (N. Y.) 69; s. c., 43 N. Y. 159; s. c., 3 Am. Rep. 680.

The surrender of the old note will not raise a presumption that the new note was taken as absolute payment; especially if the creditor would thereby lose some security which he held for the debt. Hess *v.* Dille, 23 W. Va. 90; Olcott *v.* Rathbone, 5 Wend. (N. Y.) 490; Winsted Bank *v.* Webb, 39 N. Y. 325; s. c., 100 Am. Dec. 435; Welch *v.* Allington, 23 Cal. 322; Moses *v.* Trice, 21 Gratt. (Va.) 556; s. c., 8 Am. Rep. 609; Wade *v.* Thrasher, 10 Smed. & M. (Miss.) 358. *Compare* 2 Parsons on Notes and

Bills (2nd ed.) 203; Dennis *v.* Williams, 40 Ala. 633; Anderson *v.* Henshaw, 2 Day (Conn.) 272; Woodbridge *v.* Skinner, 15 Conn. 306; Livingston *v.* Radcliff, 6 Barb. (N. Y.) 201; Waydell *v.* Luer, 3 Den. (N. Y.) 410; Arnold *v.* Camp, 12 Johns. (N. Y.) 409; s. c., 7 Am. Dec. 328; Neff *v.* Clute, 12 Barb. (N. Y.) 466.

Where the new note is that of a third person not previously bound for the debt the taking thereof and the surrendering of the old note will, *prima facie*, discharge the old note and release the maker from personal liability thereon. But where the debt is a lien on land of which the maker of the new note has become the purchaser and assumed the debts as a part of the consideration therefor, the taking of the new note and surrender of the old will not extinguish the lien nor be regarded as a payment of the debt, will release the maker from his personal liability on the old note. Hess *v.* Dille, 23 W. Va. 90.

Where the accommodation indorser of a note gave a new note to the holder for the amount of the original note, but left the latter in the hands of the holder as security, this did not constitute a payment of the original note. East River Bank *v.* Butterworth, 45 Barb. (N. Y.) 476.

Receipt of a note for a part of the debt and cash for the balance is *prima facie* payment of the debt. Phelan *v.* Crosby, 2 Gill. (Md.) 462.

Where a debtor offered to his creditor to give to him in payment of his account, either the note of a third person at once or the cash at an early day, and the creditor said he would take the note, which was thereupon delivered to him, and he credited it to the debtor, this discharged the debt. St. John *v.* Purdy, 1 Sandf. (N. Y.) 9.

If it affirmatively appears that the note was neither given nor received in payment, the fact that the creditor credited the note to the debtor in his books will not alter the rights of the parties. Follett *v.* Steele, 16 Vt. 30.

M. & Co. were the legal depositaries of the moneys belonging to Westchester county applicable to the payments of its county bonds, and funds sufficient to pay the interest coupons on said bonds had been deposited with them by the county treasurer. The Port Chester Savings bank held certain coupons which it presented to M. & Co. The latter asked how the bank desired payment, and upon its requesting a draft for the amount, M. & Co. delivered to it their sight draft on a New York bank, took up the coupons, immediately charged them to the account of the county treasurer as paid, and afterwards delivered them up to him. At the time of the transaction M. & Co. were insolvent, but had on hand money sufficient to pay the coupons, and would have paid them but for the election of the bank to take a draft. The draft was never paid, and before its return to the bank M. & Co. failed. *Held*, that the authority of M. & Co. was limited to payment, and the bank having accepted the draft in lieu of money, did so upon its own responsibility, and as against the county, the transaction constituted a payment. (Indig *v.* National City Bank, 80 N. Y. 100, and Turner *v.* Bank of Fox Lake, 3 Keyes (N. Y.) 425, distinguished.) People *v.* Cromwell, 102 N. Y. 477; reversing s. c., 38 Hun (N. Y.) 384.

A receipt stating that the note was "payment in full to date," is not conclusive. Howard *v.* Jones, 33 Mo. 583; Johnson *v.* Weed, 9 Johns. (N. Y.) 310; s. c., 6 Am. Dec. 279; Elwood *v.* Deifendorf, 5 Barb. (N. Y.) 398; Muldon *v.* Whitlock, 1 Cow. (N. Y.) 290; s. c., 13 Am. Dec. 533; Glenn *v.* Smith, 2 Gill. & J. (Md.) 493; s. c., 20 Am. Dec. 452; Berry *v.* Griffin, 10 Md. 27; s. c., 69 Am. Dec. 123; Mosely *v.* Floyd, 31 Ga. 564; Swain *v.* Frazier, 35 N. J. Eq. 326; Butts *v.* Dean, 2 Met. (Mass.) 76; s. c., 35 Am. Dec. 389; Feamster *v.* Withrow, 12 W. Va. 611. *Compare* Bonnell *v.* Chamberlain, 26 Conn. 487; Dogan *v.* Ashby, 1 Rich. (S. Car.) 36; Day *v.* Thompson, 65 Ala. 269; Wheeler *v.* Schroeder, 4 R. I. 383; *In re* Hurst, 1 Flip. (U. S.) 462.

Where a note of a third party is given to a creditor, and it is specially stated in the receipt that the amount when collected is to be credited on a certain note held by the creditor, this does not constitute an absolute payment. Holmes *v.* Lykins, 50 Mo. 399.

Plaintiff received in payment of a debt due from defendant an order on the latter's agent. Upon presentation of the order the agent gave his cheque, which plaintiff accepted and executed a receipt in full. *Held*, that the cheque having been dishonored, defendant was still liable. Ocean Co. *v.* Ophelia, 11 La. Ann. 28.

(*b*) THIRD PARTY.—The rule is the same whether the debtor gives his own note or that of a third party.[1] If the note of a

But it has been held that such a receipt is *prima facie* evidence that the note was taken in payment. Palmer *v.* Priest, 1 Sprague (U. S.) 512; Davenport *v.* Schram, 9 Wis. 119; Stephens *v.* Thompson, 28 Vt. 77.

Where a collecting agent, upon presenting a draft, received from the drawee his cheque on a local bank for the amount and surrendered the draft, which was thereupon by the payee stamped "paid," this is not such a payment as to discharge the drawer if payment of the cheque is refused on due presentment. Turner *v.* Bank of Fox Lake, 4 Abb. App. Dec. (N. Y.) 434.

The surrendering of the note and tearing off the maker's name upon receiving a cheque for the amount is not conclusive that the cheque was taken in payment. Heartt *v.* Rhodes, 66 Ill. 351.

Where one holding an account for wages against a steamboat took the note of the owner, indorsed by a third party as security, and bearing a higher rate of interest than the account bore, these facts, with other circumstances tending to show a purpose to take the note in extinguishment of the debt, were held to destroy his lien on the boat. Risher *v.* The Frolic, 1 Wood (U. S.) 92.

The fact that the note of a third party was taken by the creditor and entered upon his books as a payment of the debt, is not conclusive that it was taken as absolute payment. Brigham *v.* Lally, 130 Mas. 485.

The burden of proof is on the party asserting the payment. 2 Pars. on Contr. 756; Susquehanna Fertilizer Co. *v.* White, 66 Md. 444; s. c., 59 Am. Rep. 186; Geib *v.* Reynolds, 35 Minn. 331; Randlet *v.* Herren, 20 N. H. 102; Whitney *v.* Goin, 20 N. H. 354; Hutchinson *v.* Swartsweller, 31 N. J. Eq. 205; Tyner *v.* Stoops, 11 Ind. 22; s. c., 71 Am. Dec. 341; Sneed *v.* Wiester, 2 A. K. Marsh. (Ky.) 277; Nightingale *v.* Chafee, 11 R. I. 609; s. c., 23 Am. Rep. 531; Feamster *v.* Withrow, 12 W. Va. 611. *Compare* Smith *v.* Bissell, 2 Greene (Iowa) 379; Burrow *v.* Cook, 17 Iowa 436.

In *New York* the giving and receiving of a promissory note is *prima facie* evidence of a settlement of all demands between the parties. Lake *v.* Tysen, 6 N. Y. 461.

1. Brown *v.* Olmstead, 50 Cal. 162; Tobey *v.* Barber, 5 Johns. (N. Y.) 68; s. c., 4 Am. Dec. 326; Ely *v.* James, 123 Mass. 36; Appleton *v.* Kennon, 19 Mo. 637; Commiskey *v.* McPike, 20 Mo. App. 82; Fleig *v.* Sleet, 43 Ohio St. 53; s. c., 54 Am. Rep. 800; Spear *v.* Atkinson, 1 Ired. (N. Car.) 262; Kilpatrick *v.* Home Bldg. & Loan Assoc., 119 Pa. St. 30. *Compare* Wright *v.* Temple, 13 La. Ann. 413.

The fact that the creditor did not require his debtor to indorse the third party's note is *prima facie* evidence that he agreed to take it in payment. Breed *v.* Cook, 15 Johns. (N. Y.) 241; Whitbeck *v.* Van Ness, 11 Johns. (N. Y.) 409; s. c., 6 Am. Dec. 383; where the English and American cases are reviewed; Union Bank *v.* Smiser, 1 Sneed (Tenn.) 501.

The reverse of this is the settled doctrine of the Pennsylvania courts. Hunter *v.* Moul, 98 Pa. St. 13; s. c., 42 Am. Rep. 610, where the Pennsylvania cases are cited. See Hunt *v.* Higman, 70 Iowa 406; Susquehanna Fertilizer Co. *v.* White, 66 Md. 444; s. c., 59 Am. Rep. 186.

A debtor offered to his creditor the note of a third party in payment only, and not as collateral. The creditor afterward obtained the note from the clerk of the debtor, who was unauthorized to deliver it. *Held*, that this constituted a payment, and the creditor will not be permitted to show that he did not intend to take it in payment, and did not give the debtor so to understand. Burlington Gas light Co. *v.* Greene, 22 Iowa 508.

Where the debtor assigns to the creditor the note of a third party, not due, on account of the debt, and the creditor take judgment by confession for his whole claim, it will be presumed that the agreement was that he should take the note as collateral security. Caldwell *v.* Fifield, 24 N. J. L. 150.

Where the creditor directs the money to be remitted by post office money order or by check, and the debtor sent the check of his private bankers, as he had been accustomed to do, and received from his creditor a receipt therefor, this was held to be a payment, though the bankers failed before the check was presented. McLeish *v.* Howard, 3 Up. Can. App. Rep. 503.

Where the creditor takes the individual note of one of two joint debtors, the other is not discharged, in the absence of an express agreement to that effect. Bowers *v.* Still, 49 Pa. St. 65; Schollenberger *v.* Sheldonridge, 49 Pa. St. 83; Nightingale *v.* Chafee, 11 R. I. 609; s. c., 23 Am. Rep. 531.

Taking a bill from a new firm does not *per se* discharge the old firm. Spenceley *v.* Greenwood, 1 F. & F. 297.

After the dissolution of a partnership the liquidating partner, without the knowledge of his co-partner, gave the firm note to a creditor of the partnership, under an agreement that it should extinguish the debt. *Held*, to constitute a payment, though both parties erroneously supposed that the other partner would be bound by the new note. Fowler *v.* Richardson, 3 Sneed (Tenn.) 508.

Where a partnership is dissolved and one of the partners takes the assets and assumes the obligations of the firm, a new note given by the remaining partner and his wife, for the purpose of extending an old one is not a payment of the firm debt. Van Staden *v.* Kline, 64 Iowa 180. See also Fry *v.* Patterson, 49 N. J. L. 612.

Where the creditor of a firm accepts a new note executed by a part only of the members of the firm, and gives up the old note, while this fact does not raise a legal presumption that the debt is extinguished, and the remaining partners discharged from liability, yet it is entitled to great weight with the jury. Powell *v.* Charless, 34 Mo. 485; Lindley on Partn. 454.

In *Vermont* it is held to be a satisfaction of the debt. Stephens *v.* Thompson, 28 Vt. 77. But in *England* it has been held that an agreement to accept the liability of a portion of the partners in lieu of the whole is without consideration. Lodge *v.* Dicas, 3 B. & Ald. 611; David *v.* Ellice, 5 B. & C. 196. But *compare* Thompson *v.* Percival, 2 B. & Ad. 969; Hart *v.* Alexander, 2 Mees. & W. 484.

Where the surviving partners gave a promissory note for an account due by the firm, it does not constitute a payment unless agreed to be received as such. Thompson *v.* Briggs, 28 N. H. 40; Leach *v.* Church, 15 Ohio St. 169. And such a note will not discharge dormant partners not known to the creditor. Nichols *v.* Cheairs, 4 Sneed (Tenn.) 229.

After the dissolution of a firm, one of the partners adjusted a note against the firm by giving some money and a note of a third party in part payment, and his own individual note for the the balance, upon receipt of which the creditor gave up the firm note. *Held*, that the firm note was extinguished, and no action could be maintained against the other partners therein. Waydell *v.* Luer, 3 Den. (N. Y.) 410. *Compare* Murray *v.* Gouverneur, 2 Johns. Cas. (N. Y.) 438; s. c., 1 Am. Dec. 177.

One of several makers of a note makes an arrangement with his co-makers by which provision is made for the payment of the note, and means are put into his hands for that purpose. Thereupon he takes up the note, paying a part of the amount in cash and giving his own note for the balance, which is accepted by the holder and the original note given up. *Held*, that the original note was paid, and the makers thereof discharged. Livingston *v.* Radcliff, 6 Barb. (N. Y.) 201. *Compare* Van Ep *v.* Dillaye, 6 Barb. (N. Y.) 244.

Where a firm agreed to settle their account by note, and after the dissolution a partnership note was given by the remaining partner, such note is not a payment, if the other partner repudiates his obligation thereon. Goodspeed *v.* South Bend Chilled Plow Co., 45 Mich. 237.

A bank, holder of a note, accepted in renewal thereof a new note signed by one new maker, and from which two of the former makers were dropped. Upon obtaining knowledge that one of the signatures to the new note was forged, the bank brought suit thereon, obtained judgment against one of the parties, issued execution and obtained a part of the money. *Held*, that these facts amounted to a payment and discharge of the first note. Bank of Commonwealth *v.* Ray, 7 J. J. Marsh. (Ky.) 272.

Where before maturity of a note a part of the debt is paid and a new note is executed for the residue by the debtor, with an express agreement that the old note should be surrendered, this operates as a payment of the old note. Whether such would be the effect if the transaction had taken place after the maturity of the first note,

third party is expressly accepted as payment, it will discharge even a judgment debt.[1]

(*c*) WHERE THERE IS EVIDENCE OF A COURSE OF DEALING between the parties in which cheques are uniformly accepted as cash, such evidence tends to rebut the presumption of a conditional payment, and raises a question of fact which should be submitted to the jury.[2]

seems to be doubted. Bantz *v.* Basnett, 12 W. Va. 772.

A creditor, by taking the note of an agent for the debt of the principal with knowledge of the latter's liability, discharges the principal. Ames Packing etc. Co. *v.* Tucker, 8 Mo. App. 95.

Where the creditor of a corporation received from the president part cash and the balance in a note at 30 days, made by a firm of which the president was a member, and gave a receipt for the entire amount of the debt, this does not constitute a payment unless it was so expressly agreed at the time, although the president was at the time largely indebted to the company, and was subsequently credited by the company on account as having paid the whole sum due to the creditor, the corporation not having been actually prejudiced by the transaction. Higby *v.* New York etc. R. Co., 3 Bosw. (N. Y.) 497; s. c., 7 Abb. Pr. (N. Y.) 259.

Defendants were owners of a ship, of which A was ship's husband. Plaintiff furnished supplies for the ship, charging them to the "ship and owners," there being no evidence that he knew who the owners were. A gave plaintiff his note for the amount, taking from him a receipt in full, and defendants, not knowing how A had settled with plaintiff, settled with A as if he had paid plaintiff. A became insolvent and the note was not paid. It was *held* that the note did not constitute a payment, and defendants were liable for the supplies furnished. Johnson *v.* Cleaves, 15 N. H. 332. See also Muldon *v.* Whitlock, 1 Cow. (N. Y.) 290; s. c., 13 Am. Dec. 533.

Where the note of a third party is taken before maturity in payment of a debt, the knowledge on the part of the creditor that the debtor was insolvent, and that the maker of the note was also her creditor, would constitute no defense to a suit on the note by the endorsee. Flower *v.* Noble, 38 La. Ann. 938.

Where the debtor, at the request of the creditor, executes his negotiable note to a third person in settlement of the debt, this is *prima facie* a payment of the original debt. Ralston *v.* Wood, 15 Ill. 159; s. c., 58 Am. Dec. 604; Smalley *v.* Edey, 19 Ill. 207; Leake *v.* Brown, 43 Ill. 372. And where the debtor executes a written promise to pay money to "A or B" in settlement of a debt due from the promisor to A, this is a payment of the debt to A. Parker *v.* Osgood, 4 Gray (Mass.) 456.

As to the effect of taking a note indorsed by a third party for a sum less than the debt, see *infra*, *Partial Payments*. See also Winslow *v.* Hardin, 3 Dana (Ky.) 543.

1. Witherby *v.* Mann, 11 Johns. (N. Y.) 518; New York State Bank *v.* Fletcher, 5 Wend. (N. Y.) 85; Dogan *v.* Ashbey, 1 Rich. (S. Car.) 36; Day *v.* Stickney, 14 Allen (Mass.) 255. See also, Howe *v.* Buffalo etc. R. Co., 38 Barb. (N. Y.) 124. And *compare* Morriss *v.* Harvey, 75 Va. 726. So if the note is the joint note of the debtor and a third party. Clark *v.* Pinney, 6 Cow. (N. Y.) 298.

2. Briggs *v.* Holmes, 118 Pa. St. 283; s. c., 4 Am. St. Rep. 597. To like effect, Benneson *v.* Thayer, 23 Ill. 374.

Just before the maturity of a negotiable note payable to A. H. D & Co. the makers applied to A. H. D. to permit them to draw a draft on D. & E., a firm in which A. H. D. was a partner, for the amount of the note, said draft to be payable in 90 days. D, for the firm of D. & E. agrees that this may be done for the accommodation of the makers of the note, the latter proposing to take up the note with the draft, and to pay the draft at its maturity. Accordingly the draft was drawn payable in 90 days. The makers of the note and drawer of the draft had the draft discounted by the bank which held the note for collection. Thereupon the bank surrendered the note to the makers, and sent the amount thereof to A. H. D. & Co., the owners of the note. The makers of the note, immediately upon its surrender to them, sent it to D. & E., the firm upon which the

(*d*) A CHEQUE given in payment and afterward paid becomes a valid payment as of the date of its receipt.[1]

(*e*) WORTHLESS CHEQUE OR NOTE.—Payment by a worthless cheque or note is no payment.[2]

draft was drawn. The drawers of the draft failed to pay it at maturity, according to their promise, and it was paid by the drawees, D. & E. Thereupon A. H. D. & Co., the payees of the note, paid to D. & E. the full amount of the draft, D. & E. re-transferring the note to A. H. D. & Co. *Held*, that this was not a payment of the note, but an extension of it for 90 days, and its payment might be enforced by A. H. D. & Co. Hopkins *v.* Detwiler, 25 W. Va. 734.

1. Hunter *v.* Wetsell, 17 Hun (N. Y.) 135; s. c., 84 N. Y. 549; s. c., 38 Am. Rep. 544. See also, same case, 57 N. Y. 375; 15 Am. Rep. 508. See also, on the question of the effect of a check as payment, Henry *v.* Conley, 48 Ark. 267; Comptoir D'Escompte de Paris *v.* Dresbach, 78 Cal. 15; Phillips *v.* Bullard, 58 Ga. 256; Mullins *v.* Brown, 32 Kan. 312; Borne *v.* First Nat. Bank, 123 Ind. 78; United States *v.* Thompson, 33 Md. 575; Good *v.* Singleton, 39 Minn. 340; Overman *v.* Hoboken City Bank, 30 N. J. L. 61; Johnson *v.* Bank of North America, 5 Robt. (N. Y.) 554; Smith *v.* Miller, 6 Robt. (N. Y.) 413; Kelty *v.* Second Nat. Bank, 52 Barb. (N. Y.) 328; Syracuse etc. R. Co. *v.* Collins, 3 Lans. (N. Y.) 29; Smith *v.* Miller, 43 N. Y. 171; Gloversville Bank *v.* Wells, 79 N. Y. 498; Bernheimer *v.* Herrman, 44 Hun (N. Y.) 110; Flynn *v.* Woolsey (Supreme Ct.), 10 N. Y. Supp. 875; Olcott *v.* Erwin (Supreme Ct.), 9 N. Y. Supp. 71; Tiddy *v.* Harris, 101 N. Car. 589; Holmes *v.* Briggs, 131 Pa. St. 233, 25 W. N. C. (Pa.) 255; Washington Nat. Gas Co. *v.* Johnson, 123 Pa. St. 576; Lingenfelter *v.* Williams (Pa. 1887), 9 Atl. Rep. 653; Larue *v.* Cloud, 22 Gratt. (Va.) 513; La Fayette Co. Monument Corp. *v.* Magoon, 73 Wis. 627.

2. Peoria etc. R. Co. *v.* Buckley, 114 Ill. 337; Taylor *v.* Thompson, 61 N. H. 156; Walker *v.* Tatum, Ga. Dec., pt. 2, 161; Wright *v.* Lawton, 37 Conn. 167; Warriner *v.* People, 74 Ill. 346; Kephart *v.* Butcher, 17 Iowa 240; Vallier *v.* Ditson, 74 Me. 553; Dennie *v.* Hart, 2 Pick. (Mass.) 204; Holmes *v.* First Nat. River Bank, 126 Mass. 353; People *v.* Howell, 4 Johns. (N. Y.) 296; Central City Bank *v.* Dana, 32 Barb. (N. Y.) 296; Syracuse etc. R. Co. *v.* Collins, 3 Lans. (N. Y.) 29; Patton *v.* Ash, 7 S. & R. (Pa.) 116; Emerine *v.* O'Brien, 36 Ohio St. 491. See also McLaughlin *v.* Blount, 61 Ga. 168.

Though the party paying was at the time ignorant that it was worthless. Offut *v.* Bank of Kentucky, 1 Bush (Ky.) 166; Semmes *v.* Wilson, 5 Cranch (C. C.) 285; Roberts *v.* Fisher, 43 N. Y. 159; s. c., 3 Am. Rep. 680. *Compare* Murdock *v.* Coleman, 1 La. Ann. 410.

Though the note of a third party be expressly accepted as payment, yet if the maker thereof was insolvent at the time, and this fact was unknown to both parties, there is no payment. Roberts *v.* Fisher, 43 N. Y. 159; s. c., 3 Am. Rep. 680.

Where defendant, by a charter party agreed that the freight should be paid partly in cash and partly by approved bill, and the owner, without apprising the defendant, took a bill from his agent, the consignee, which was dishonored, this did not discharge the defendant. Taylor *v.* Briggs, M. & M. 28.

But where the note of a third person is given and accepted as payment, without fraud on the part of the debtor, it will extinguish the debt, though it turn out afterwards that at the time the maker of the note was an absconding insolvent, which fact was unknown to the parties. Heidenheimer *v.* Lyon, 3 E. D. Smith (N. Y.) 54; Long *v.* Spruill, 7 Jones (N. Car.) 96. *Compare* Galoupeau *v.* Ketchum, 3 E. D. Smith (N. Y.) 175.

Otherwise if such acceptance is induced by fraudulent misrepresentations on the part of the debtor. Hoopes *v.* Strasburger, 37 Ind. 390; s. c., 11 Am. Rep. 538.

Where the signature of the maker was forged, the note cannot be regarded as payment, though the payee supposed it to be genuine. Goodrich *v.* Tracy, 43 Vt. 314; s. c., 5 Am. Rep. 281.

Where the note of a third party given in payment was void because

(*f*) NOTE NEGOTIATED.—If the note is negotiable, and has been actually negotiated by the creditor, and has passed beyond his control so that it cannot be produced on the trial for the

given for a gambling consideration, an action may be maintained for the value of the goods sold without having attempted to collect the note from the maker. Beard *v.* Brandon, 2 Nott. & M. (S. Car.) 102. So where the note is void for usury. Meshke *v.* Van Doren, 16 Wis. 319; Lee *v.* Peckham, 17 Wis. 383.

If the note of a third person given in payment of a pre-existing debt is non-enforcible by reason of an agreement between the maker thereof and the debtor, the creditor may recover on the original consideration. Torrey *v.* Baxter, 13 Vt. 452.

And if the debtor appropriates the fund out of which a cheque given by himself or his agent is to be paid, and thereby causes it to be dishonored, he cannot claim that the receipt of such cheque by the creditor constituted a payment. Atkinson *v.* Minot, 75 Me. 189. See also, Thayer *v.* Peck, 93 Ill. 357; Loughnan *v.* Barry, 5 Ir. Rep., C. L. 538.

Where the debtor offers in payment of his debt cash or a cheque on his banker, and the creditor chooses the latter, the debt is not discharged if the cheque is dishonored on due presentation, though the banker fails with a large account on his books to the credit of the debtor. Everett *v.* Collins, 2 Camp. 515.

The holder of a cheque, payment of which had been refused for want of funds, passed it to his vendor, stating, in answer to inquiries, that there was nothing wrong about it. *Held*, that the suppression of the facts constituted a fraud on the vendor, and his receipt of the cheque did not extinguish the debt. Martin *v.* Pennock, 2 Pa. St. 376.

Where the creditor receives notes of a third party guaranteed by the debtor, he cannot maintain an action on the original indebtedness because of false representations of the debtor as to the solvency of the maker, if he has taken no proper steps to rescind the contract, and has not tendered back the notes. Williams *v.* Ketchum, 21 Wis. 432.

A sold to B a patent right, and received therefor B's note, void, because the fact that it was for a patent right was not written on its face, as the law requires. *Held*, that the note should not be deemed payment; that the original debt remained in force as though no note had been given. Graham's Estate, 14 Phila. (Pa.) 280.

If the drawer of a cheque has neither funds nor credit in the bank in which the cheque is drawn, its acceptance by the creditor does not constitute a payment, no matter whether the act of the debtor was fraudulent or *bona fide*. And there is no difference in effect whether the cheque is drawn by the debtor or a third person. Fleig *v.* Sleet, 43 Ohio St. 53; s. c., 54 Am. Rep. 800. See also, Tobey *v.* Barber, 5 Johns. (N. Y.) 68; s. c., 4 Am. Dec. 326; Comiskey *v.* McPike, 20 Mo. App. 82.

A collecting agent, upon presenting a draft, receives a cheque on a local bank and surrenders the draft to the drawee, who thereupon marks it "paid." Upon presenting the cheque payment is refused. *Held*, not to constitute a payment. Turner *v.* Bank of Fox Lake, 4 Abb. App. Dec. (N. Y.) 434; affirming 23 How. Pr. (N. Y.) 399. To the same effect, Jorbitt *v.* Goundry, 29 Barb. (N. Y.) 509.

In an *Illinois* case the following facts were relied on to prove payment: The debtor called on the cashier of a bank and made an agreement with him to answer his cheque for $8,000. The understanding was that the money was not to be drawn from the bank on the cheque, but when the debtor's cheque on the bank should be presented, the cashier was to tell the holder that it was good. After this arrangement, the debtor drew a cheque for $8,000 in favor of the agent of the creditor on the bank in question, and when the agent presented it at the bank he was informed that it was good, though, as a matter of fact, the debtor had no funds in said bank. The agent did not ask for payment of the cheque, but immediately made a new loan to the debtor of the exact amount of the debt at a lower rate of interest. *Held*, that the original debt was not paid. Woodburn *v.* Woodburn, 115 Ill. 427.

purpose of being cancelled, the creditor cannot sue on the original cause of action.[1]

(*g*) THERE CAN BE NO RECOVERY ON THE ORIGINAL CAUSE OF ACTION without producing the note at the trial for cancellation.[2]

1. Hughes *v.* Wheeler, 8 Cow. (N. Y.) 77; Elwood *v.* Diefendorf, 5 Barb. (N. Y.) 398, 408 (in which the preceding decisions are cited); Wallace *v.* Agry, 4 Mason (U. S.) 336, 343; McCrary *v.* Carrington, 35 Ala. 698; Alcock *v.* Hopkins, 6 Cush. (Mass.) 484; Leake *v.* Brown, 43 Ill. 372; Salomon *v.* Pioneer Co-operative Co., 21 Fla. 374; s. c., 58 Am. Rep. 667; Sutliff *v.* Atwood, 15 Ohio St. 186.

But if the note is produced and offered to be delivered up, the creditor may sue on the original debt. Zerrano *v.* Wilson, 8 Cush. (Mass.) 426; Derickson *v.* Whitney, 6 Gray (Mass.) 248; Whitton *v.* Mayo, 114 Mass. 179; Ward *v.* Bourne, 56 Me. 161; Torrey *v.* Baxter, 13 Vt. 452; Winsted Bank *v.* Webb, 39 N. Y. 325; s. c., 100 Am. Dec. 435. *Compare* Lanata *v.* Bayhi, 31 La. Ann. 229.

Where the creditor takes a note in payment, which he indorses and gets discounted at a bank, the original debt is not extinguished if the creditor is obliged to take up the note at its maturity. Kean *v.* Dufresne, 3 S. & R. (Pa.) 233.

Where a negotiable promissory note taken for a pre-existing debt, but without any agreement that it shall constitute a payment, is assigned, indorsed in blank, together with other property of the party so taking it, to an assignee for the benefit of his creditor, this will not prevent an action in the name of the assignor on the original debt. Lyman *v.* Bank of U. S., 12 How. (U. S.) 225.

Whether a provisional payment has been converted into an absolute payment by the subsequent conduct of the holder must be determined from all the circumstances of the case. Hamilton *v.* Cunningham, 2 Brock. (U. S.) 350.

If the creditor receives a cheque, and, instead of having it cashed, procures it to be certified, this will discharge the debtor. First Nat. Bank *v.* Leach, 52 N. Y. 350; s. c., 11 Am. Rep. 708.

2. Miller *v.* Lumsden, 16 Ill. 161; Reyburn *v.* Day, 27 Ill. 46; Schepflin *v.* Dessar, 20 Mo. App. 569; Bertiaux *v.* Dillon, 20 Mo. App. 603; Brewster *v.* Bours, 8 Cal. 501; Street *v.* Hall, 29 Vt. 165. *Compare* Lee *v.* Fontaine, 10 Ala. 755; s. c., 44 Am. Dec. 505; Trotter *v.* Crockett, 2 Port. (Ala.) 401; Holmes *v.* DeCamp, 1 Johns. (N. Y.) 34; s. c., 3 Am. Dec. 293; Sweet *v.* Titus, 67 Barb. (N. Y.) 327; Dixon *v.* Dixon, 31 Vt. 450; s. c., 76 Am. Dec. 129. See Meyer *v.* Huneke, 65 Barb. (N. Y.) 304.

What will excuse the production of the note, see Miller *v.* Lumsden, 16 Ill. 161; Morrison *v.* Welty, 18 Md. 169; Matthews *v.* Dare, 20 Md. 248; Hays *v.* McClurg, 4 Watts (Pa.) 452; Widders *v.* Gorton, 26 L. J., C. P. 165; 1 C. B., N. S. 576.

The creditor has his choice to sue on the note or the original cause of action. Holmes *v.* De Camp, 1 Johns. (N. Y.) 34; s. c., 3 Am. Dec. 293; Angel *v.* Felton, 8 Johns. (N. Y.) 149; Smith *v.* Lockwood, 10 Johns. (N. Y.) 366; Burdick *v.* Green, 15 Johns. (N. Y.) 247.

Where the creditor receives a note and indorses and delivers it to a third party, and the indorsee recovers judgment against the maker, which judgment is unsatisfied, he cannot recover on the original consideration, though he produces the note to be canceled, unless he shows that the judgment is satisfied, or that the title to the note is again in him. Teaz *v.* Chrystie, 2 E. D. Smith (N. Y.) 621.

But it is held in *Massachusetts* that, where a party had received two promissory notes, under an agreement to release a demand when they should be paid at maturity, caused one to be discounted and took it up after protest for non-payment, and prosecuted the other to judgment, but received nothing on either, he was not debarred from suing on the original cause of action upon tendering in court the discounted note and an assignment of the judgment. Lord *v.* Bigelow, 124 Mass. 185.

Where a note is taken in payment and is lost, but not destroyed, it will discharge the debt, even though the creditor offers to indemnify the debtor

(*k*) RIGHT OF ACTION SUSPENDED.—The taking of a note for a debt, whether such note is negotiable or not, operates to suspend the right of the creditor to sue on the original cause of action until after the maturity of the note.[1]

against any claim on the note. Woodford *v.* Whiteley, M. & M. 517.

1. Story on Sales (4th ed.), §§ 219, 237. And see cases cited under last head. Higgins *v.* Wortell, 18 Cal. 330; Smith *v.* Owens, 21 Cal. 11; Brown *v.* Cronise, 21 Cal. 386; Hornbrooks *v.* Lucas, 24 W. Va. 493; s. c., 49 Am. Rep. 277; Happy *v.* Mosher, 48 N. Y. 313; Stuart *v.* Cawse, 5 C. B., N. S. 737; 5 Jur., N. S. 650; 28 L. J., C. P. 193.

The right to sue for rent is suspended by the taking of a note therefor; such a debt does not differ in this respect from a simple contract debt. Hornbrooks *v.* Lucas, 24 W. Va. 493; s. c., 49 Am. Rep. 277. See Lewis *v.* Lozee, 3 Wend. (N. Y.) 79.

And it may constitute a payment if the creditor has so acted in reference to it that its value to the debtor has been destroyed. McCrary *v.* Carrington, 35 Ala. 698; Thomason *v.* Cooper, 57 Ala. 560; Brown *v.* Cronise, 21 Cal. 386; Cochran *v.* Wheeler, 7 N. H. 202; s. c., 26 Am. Dec. 732; Kenniston *v.* Avery, 16 N. H. 117; Whitcher *v.* Dexter, 61 N. H. 91; Shipman *v.* Cook, 16 N. J. Eq. 251; Middlesex *v.* Thomas, 20 N. J. Eq. 39; Copper *v.* Powell, Anth. (N. Y.) 68; Mehlberg *v.* Tisher, 24 Wis. 607.

If the creditor neglects to enforce the note until rights have sprung up in favor of third parties, the note will be held to constitute a payment. Lear *v.* Friedlander, 45 Miss. 559.

If the agreement is that the note is to constitute a payment if it proves collectible, the creditor is bound to use ordinary means and diligence to collect. *Re* Onimette, 1 Sawy (U. S.) 47.

A, the maker of a note, sent to the holder, as payment, cash for a part and the note of a third party, indorsed by A, for the balance. This note the holder delivered to his attorney, who lost it before its maturity, but did not inform A of the loss until its maturity, four months afterward. The attorney then wrote A that the creditor refused to receive the note of the third party, and demanded payment of the original note. *Held*, that the original note was extinguished. Swett *v.* Southworth, 125 Mass. 417.

A creditor took from his debtor an order on a third person for a sum which the debtor stated would be due in a few days. Whereupon the creditor took from the person on whom the order was drawn his notes for the amount of the order, payable in six and nine months. *Held*, that he thereby made the debt his own, and that he could not, in case the notes were not paid, look to his original debtor. Southwick *v.* Sax, 9 Wend. (N. Y.) 122.

In another case in the same State it was held that a draft drawn on a third person by the debtor in favor of the creditor, under an agreement that it shall be in full satisfaction of the debt when paid, is a *prima facie* payment of the original debt. And to rebut the presumption in an action in the original debt, the creditor must show diligence to obtain payment and notice of non-payment, or he must show an excuse for non-presentment and produce the bill at the trial to be canceled. Dayton *v.* Trull, 23 Wend. (N. Y.) 345.

So, too, if the creditor has received a cheque from the debtor, he cannot return it and sue on the original cause of action, without having first demanded payment of the cheque unless he can show that no injury has resulted to the debtor from his failure to present the cheque. Bradford *v.* Fox, 39 Barb. (N. Y.) 203. See same case, 38 N. Y. 289; Syracuse etc. Co. *v.* Collins, 1 Abb. N. Cas. (N. Y.) 47; Stevens *v.* Park, 73 Ill. 387.

Where a second note is taken in payment of a prior note, the holder must use due diligence to collect it before he can bring his action on the first note; and such diligence must be shown on the trial. Gordon *v.* Price, 10 Ired. (N. Car.) 385.

Compare Martin *v.* Pennock, 2 Pa. St. 376.

Where a note of a third person, void because given for a gambling consideration, is given in payment of goods sold, the creditor may sue for the value of the goods without waiting to proceed against the maker. Beard *v.* Brandon, 2 Nott & M. (S. Car.) 102.

A creditor who takes from his debtor's agent on account of the debt the

(*i*) THE INDIANA COURTS have adopted the following rules:

1. That taking a promissory note not governed by the law merchant, by the creditor from his debtor for an existing debt, is not a payment of the debt, unless it is is agreed to be by the parties, and the onus of proving such agreement would lie upon the debtor.

2. That taking a bill of exchange or a promissory note governed by the law merchant, by the creditor from his debtor for an existing debt, is a payment of the debt, unless it is otherwise agreed by the parties, and the onus of proving such agreement would lie upon the creditor.

And these rules are held to apply whether the paper is that of the debtor or of some third party.[1]

cheque of the agent, is bound to present it for payment within a reasonable time, and if he fails to do so, and by reason of the delay the position of the debtor is altered for the worse, the debt is extinguished, though the debtor was not a party to the cheque. Hopkins *v*. Ware, 38 L. J. Exch. 147; 4 L. R. Exch. 268; 20 L. T., N. S. 147.

Where a precedent liability has been suspended or released by the acceptance of a note indorsed by one liable on the former demand, plaintiff cannot recover on the primary liability without showing the same state of facts as would enable him to recover on the indorsement. Bradford *v*. Haggerty, 11 Ala. 698.

See also Phoenix Ins. Co. *v*. Allen, 11 Mich. 501; s. c., 83 Am. Dec. 756; Stam *v*. Kerr, 31 Miss. 199.

At the request of the holder of a promissory note, a new note was made and indorsed by the same parties as on the old note, which new note was sent to the holder with a request that he retain the old note. No notice was taken of this request, nor were the indorsers notified of the non-payment of the new note. *Held*, that the indorsers were discharged. Sage *v*. Walker, 12 Mich 425.

The reception of a draft as conditional payment suspends the plaintiff's original right of action till the draft is properly presented for payment and payment is refused. Phœnix Ins. Co. *v*. Allen, 11 Mich. 501; s. c., 83 Am. Dec. 756.

Plaintiff, being a creditor of defendant, received from him an order on M for the amount, which plaintiff testified was not to be considered payment unless paid, while defendant testified that he did not remember any such understanding. Plaintiff sent the order to M by a boy with instructions to bring it back if it was not paid. M put it in his pocket, and claimed that he would apply it on an indebtedness of plaintiff to him. *Held*, that plaintiff was bound to account for the order, and that there was evidence to go to the jury that he accepted it in payment. Knott *v*. Whitfield, 99 N. Car. 76.

The maker of a note gave to the payee an order on a third party which, when collected, was to be applied on the note. The payee surrendered the order to the person on whom it was drawn, receiving from him his own note on time for the amount. *Held*, that the first note was paid *pro tanto*. Tuttle *v*. Chapman, 10 Iowa, 437.

Plaintiff, the holder of a note of which A was the maker, drew an order on A for a certain sum in favor of B, which order was accepted by A and the amount thereof indorsed upon the note. A failed to pay the order, but as it did not appear that it had ever been returned to plaintiff, it was held to be a payment *pro tanto* of the note. Shaw *v*. Gookin, 7 N. H. 16.

Where the creditor gives a receipt for an order containing the words "to credit it when paid," the original debt will remain due in full until the order is paid. Smith *v*. Wood, 1 N. J. Eq. 74.

If a note is accepted as absolute payment of a bond secured by mortgage, and the mortgagor guaranties its payment, the non-payment of the note will not restore the obligation, but the mortgagor will be responsible on his personal guaranty. Shipman *v*. Cook, 16 N. J. Eq, 251.

See Torrey *v*. Baxter, 13 Vt. 452.

1. Smith *v*. Bettger, 68 Ind. 254; s. c., 34 Am. Rep. 256.

The reason given by the court for the above rules is that "when the debt-

(*k*) IN MASSACHUSETTS AND MAINE the doctrine was early established that the taking of a negotiable security is *prima facie* evidence of an absolute payment, where there is no express agreement to the contrary; and this rule has been followed in some of the other States.[1]

or gives a promissory note not governed by the law-merchant for an existing debt, he cannot be subjected to the payment of the debt twice, for the payment of either the original debt or the note is a discharge of both; but when the debtor gives a bill of exchange or a promissory note governed by the law-merchant, and it should pass into the hands of an innocent holder, he might be compelled to pay it, either as maker or indorser, notwithstanding he had previously paid the creditor the original debt."

This is followed in Nixon *v.* Beard, 111 Ind. 137, and Johnson *v.* Moore, 112 Ind. 91.

See also Thornton *v.* Williams, 14 Ind. 518; Gaskin *v.* Wells, 15 Ind. 253; Alford *v.* Baker, 53 Ind. 279.

And *compare* Olvey *v.* Jackson, 106 Ind. 286; Reider *v.* Nay, 95 Ind. 164.

1. Bark Chusan, 2 Story (U. S.) 455; Kimball *v.* The Anna Kimball, 2 Cliff. (U. S.) 4; Goodenow *v.* Tyler, 7 Mass. 36; s. c., 5 Am. Dec. 22; Johnson *v.* Johnson, 11 Mass. 359; Reed *v.* Upton, 10 Pick. (Mass.) 522; s. c., 20 Am. Dec. 545; Butts *v.* Dean, 2 Met. (Mass.) 76; s. c., 35 Am. Dec. 389; Ilsley *v.* Jewett, 2 Met. (Mass.) 168; Tracy *v.* Lincoln, 145 Mass. 357; Varner *v.* Nobleborough, 2 Me. 121; s. c., 11 Am. Dec. 48; Gilmore *v.* Bussey, 12 Me. 418; Milliken *v.* Whitehouse, 49 Me. 527; Paine *v.* Dwinel, 53 Me. 52; s. c., 87 Am. Dec. 533; Bunker *v.* Barron, 79 Me. 62. In the last two cases the prior decisions are *cited* and reviewed. See also Snow *v.* Foster, 79 Me. 558; Bigelow *v.* Capen, 145 Mass. 270; Granite Nat. Bank *v.* Fitch, 145 Mass. 567. And *compare* Canfield *v.* Ives, 18 Pick. (Mass.) 253.

The same rule obtains in *Vermont.* Hutchins *v.* Olcutt, 4 Vt. 549; s. c., 24 Am. Dec. 634; Torrey *v.* Baxter, 13 Vt. 452; Dickinson *v.* King, 28 Vt. 378; Collamer *v.* Langdon, 29 Vt. 32; Arnold *v.* Sprague, 34 Vt. 402. And in *Louisiana.* Hunt *v.* Boyd, 2 La. 109. And in *Alabama.* Maynard *v.* Johnson, 4 Ala. 116. And *Arkansas.* Camp *v.* Gullett, 7 Ark. 524; Costar *v.* Davies, 8 Ark. 213; s. c., 46 Am. Dec. 311. And so it would seem in *Illinois.* Smalley *v.* Edey, 19 Ill. 207.

In *Rhode Island* it is held that the mere taking of a draft or negotiable promissory note from the debtor, on account of a pre-existing debt, does not extinguish the debt. But if the paper is actually negotiated, this fact raises a *prima facie* presumption that the parties intended it to be a discharge of the debt. This presumption may, however, be rebutted, and the fact that a lien would not be given up, or a security for the debt lost or abandoned, raises a counterpresumption which rebuts that arising from the negotiation of the note. Sweet *v.* James, 2 R. I. 270. See also Wheeler *v.* Schroeder, 4 R. I. 383; Nightingale *v.* Chafee, 11 R. I. 609; s. c., 23 Am. Rep. 531; Dickenson *v.* King, 28 Vt. 378.

In *South Carolina* it is held that the legal presumption from the giving of a note is that all precedent indebtedness of the maker is covered by it. Morse *v.* Ellerbe, 4 Rich. (S. Car.) 600.

As to rule in *Pennsylvania*, see Plankenhorn *v.* Cave, 2 Yeates (Pa.) 370.

The giving of a new note for a former one extinguishes the former. Cornwall *v.* Gould, 4 Pick. (Mass.) 444; Huse *v.* Alexander, 2 Met. (Mass.) 157.

And if given for only a part of the debt, it extinguishes the debt *pro tanto.* Ilsley *v.* Jewett, 2 Met. (Mass.) 68; Scott *v.* Ray, 18 Pick. (Mass.) 360.

The rule applies where a note is given for an amount due on execution. Day *v.* Stickney, 14 Allen (Mass.) 255.

If the payee of a note at maturity takes another note signed by persons, some of whom are not parties to the first note, and retains the first note, no presumption arises that the second note was taken in payment of the first. Woods *v.* Woods, 127 Mass. 141.

A promissory note of the debtor, or that of a third person with the debtor's guaranty, given in settlement of a pre-existing account, is, in *Vermont*, a payment of such account, unless the note is unproductive without the fault of the creditor. If the note is non-enforcible by reason of a contract between the

But the cases are numerous in which this presumption is held to be overcome by the facts and circumstances surrounding the transaction of giving the note. And, as a general rule, and in the absence of express agreement, such presumption will be overcome if it would deprive the creditor of the benefit of a security.[1]

maker thereof and the debtor, the creditor may resort to his original demand. Torrey *v.* Baxter, 13 Vt. 452.

1. Bunker *v.* Barron, 79 Me. 62, *citing* decisions in *Maine*, *Massachusetts* and *Vermont;* Parham Sewing Machine Co. *v.* Brock, 113 Mass. 194; Cotton *v.* Atlas Nat. Bank, 145 Mass. 43. See also Hutchinson *v.* Woodwell, 107 Pa. St. 509.

The presumption may be rebutted by proof of concealment, misapprehension or unfairness in giving the new security. Palmer *v.* Elliott, 1 Cliff. (U. S.) 63; Wait *v.* Brewster, 31 Vt. 516.

Where it appears that the note was not the obligation of all the parties who were liable for the original debt, or if the note was given by a third party, the presumption may be rebutted by slight circumstances. Hudson *v.* Bradley, 2 Cliff. (U. S.) 130.

Where A sells goods to B, who is the agent of an undisclosed principal, C, and takes the note of B in ignorance that he is the agent of C, the presumption that the note was taken in payment is rebutted, and A may resort to C for payment. Lovell *v.* Williams, 125 Mass. 439.

If it appears that the creditor had other and better security than the note, it will not be presumed that he intended to abandon such security and rely upon the note. Mehan *v.* Thompson, 71 Me. 492.

If not intended as payment it will not operate as such. Page *v.* Hubbard, 1 Sprague (U. S.) 335; Vancleef *v.* Therasson, 3 Pick. (Mass.) 12; Watkins *v.* Hill, 8 Pick. (Mass.) 522; Jones *v.* Kennedy, 11 Pick. (Mass.) 125; Thacher *v.* Dinsmore, 5 Mass. 299; s. c., 4 Am. Dec. 61; Greenwood *v.* Curtis, 6 Mass. 358; s. c., 4 Am. Dec. 145; Johnson *v.* Johnson, 11 Mass. 359; Emerson *v.* Providence Hat Mfg. Co., 12 Mass. 237; s. c., 7 Am. Dec. 66; Melledge *v.* Boston Iron Co., 5 Cush. (Mass.) 158; s. c., 51 Am. Dec. 59; Appleton *v.* Parker, 15 Gray (Mass.) 173.

If the note is that of a third person, it is taken at the risk of the creditor, unless there is fraud or an express agreement to the contray. Wiseman *v.* Lyman, 7 Mass. 286

A creditor receiving from his debtor a draft for collection with directions to pass the proceeds, when paid, to the debtor's credit, negotiated it and passed the proceeds to the credit of the debtor. He was afterwards obliged to pay the same as indorsee. *Held*, that the debt had not been satisfied *pro tanto*. Goodnow *v.* Howe, 20 Me. 164; s. c., 37 Am. Dec. 46.

So if a note signed by the treasurer of a town is taken in payment under a misapprehension caused by the treasurer himself, it will not be considered a payment. Atkinson *v.* Minot, 75 Me. 189.

The presumption will not be enforced against a seaman who receives from the owners of a vessel their negotiable note for his wages. Neither the claim for wages nor the lien against the vessel will be extinguished thereby, unless it is distinctly stated to the seaman at the time he receives the note that such will be its effect, and the note is accompanied by some additional security or advantage to him as a consideration for his relinquishment of the lien. The Betsy & Rhoda, Dav. (U. S.) 112.

But in order to rebut the presumption, it is not sufficient to show that the note was taken by the creditor under a misapprehension of the rights of the parties, or ignorance of what effect taking the note would have on his rights. To have such effect the misapprehension must arise out of a want of full knowledge of the facts. Fowler *v.* Ludwig, 34 Me. 455. See Hedge *v.* McQuaid, 11 Cush. (Mass.) 352.

Where a trader gave to a merchant bond with surety to secure a present indebtedness and future indebtedness "for goods and cash," this is sufficient to authorize the finding of a jury that notes given from time to time by the trader to the merchant were not intended as payment for goods and cash. Shumway *v.* Reed, 34 Me. 560; s. c., 56 Am. Dec. 679.

Even an order for the payment of the money, when given and received in payment, extinguishes the original claim. Govern *v.* Littlefield, 13 Allen (Mass.) 127.

Where a debtor executes a conditional

acceptance of an order drawn on him by the creditor in favor of a third party, such order does not operate as a payment, especially if it be afterward surrendered to the debtor by such third party unpaid. Bassett *v.* Sanborn, 9 Cush. (Mass.) 58.

If the new note is avoided on the ground of usury, it does not constitute a payment. Thurston *v.* Percival, 1 Pick. (Mass.) 415; Stebbins *v.* Smith, 4 Pick. (Mass.) 97, 100; Ramsdell *v.* Soule, 12 Pick. (Mass.) 126; Johnson *v.* Johnson, 11 Mass. 359, 363.

Where a negotiable note is given for an instalment due on a mortgage note, it discharges the mortgage *pro tanto.* Fowler *v.* Bush, 21 Pick. (Mass.) 230.

Yet the question is one for the jury. Brown *v.* Scott, 51 Pa. St, 357.

Where there are several promisors, all equally liable for goods purchased, a negotiable promissory note given by one discharges the debt as to all. French *v.* Price, 24 Pick. (Mass.) 13. See also Washburn *v.* Pond, 2 Allen (Mass.) 474.

The presumption does not apply to a non-negotiable note. Bartlett *v.* Mayo, 33 Me. 518; Jose *v.* Baker, 37 Me. 465.

Where the new note is given in another State, in which a promissory note is not presumed to be accepted in payment, it is a question for the jury whether crediting the new note on the books of the holder is evidence of its acceptance in payment. Connecticut Trust Co. *v.* Melendy, 119 Mass. 449.

A having built certain houses under contract with B, for which there was a balance still due him, and for which he had a mechanic's lien on the houses and lot, was indebted to the firm of H & T on account. H & T requested payment of the debt, and A, replying that he had no money, a member of the firm said to him: "You get C's note for thirty days and we will take that." A accordingly requested C to give a note payable to H & T at thirty days for $500. C said that he had no dealings with H & T, but would make a negotiable note payable to the order of A, which was done. This note A indorsed and delivered to H & T. A never gave C credit for the amount of this note, and, in a written statement of credits subsequently rendered, did not include it, but gave C the following receipt: "Received of C five hundred dollars on house account." Before the note matured C failed and the same was not paid. *Held*, that the presumption that the note was taken in payment was rebutted, and that the note was not a payment. Quimby *v.* Durgin, 148 Mass. 104.

In *Illinois* a distinction is made between a debt growing out of an account and one arising from a loan of money, it being held that in the former case the giving of a promissory note is *prima facie* payment; but the giving of a note for money borrowed is in no sense a payment or evidence of payment. Hoodless *v.* Reid, 112 Ill. 105.

The following cases in addition to those cited above, will be found to illustrate the doctrine of payment by note:

Alabama.—Fickling *v.* Brewer, 38 Ala. 685.

Arkansas.—Malpas *v.* Lowestine, 46 Ark. 552; Newman *v.* Henry, 29 Ark. 496; Real Estate Bank *v.* Rawdon, 5 Ark. 558; Akin *v.* Peters, 45 Ark. 313; Pendergrass *v.* Hellman, 50 Ark. 261.

Connecticut.—Bartsch *v.* Atwater, 1 Conn. 409; Stebbins *v.* Kellogg, 5 Conn. 265.

Georgia.—Groverstein *v.* Brewer, 76 Ga. 763; Mosely *v.* Floyd, 31 Ga. 564; Pritchard *v.* Smith, 77 Ga. 463.

Illinois.—Cheltenham Stone & Gravel Co. *v.* Gates Iron Works, 23 Ill. App. 635; Chisholm *v.* Williams, 128 Ill. 115; Petefish *v.* Watkins, 124 Ill. 384; Pope *v.* Dodson, 58 Ill. 361.

Indiana.—Dick *v.* Flanagan (Ind.), 23 N. E. Rep. 765; Nixon *v.* Beard, 111 Ind. 137; Godfrey *v.* Crisler, 121 Ind. 203; Hill *v.* Sleeper, 58 Ind. 221; Weston *v.* Wiley, 78 Ind. 54.

Iowa.—Bank of Monroe *v.* Gifford, 79 Iowa 300; Upton *v.* Paxton, 72 Iowa 295; Burlington Gas Light Co. *v.* Greene, 28 Iowa 289; Quigley *v.* Duffey, 52 Iowa 610.

Kansas.—Bradley *v.* Harwi, 43 Kan. 314.

Kentucky.—Jarmen *v.* Davis, 4 T. B. Mon. (Ky.) 115; Greenwade *v.* Greenwade, 3 Dana (Ky.) 495; Proctor *v.* Mather, 3 B. Mon. (Ky.) 353.

Louisiana.—Whitla *v.* Taylor, 6 La. Ann. 480.

Massachusetts.—Quimby *v.* Durgin, 148 Mass. 104; United States *v.* Rousmaniere, 2 Mason (U. S.) 373; Leonard *v.* First Congregational Soc., 2 Cush. (Mass.) 462; Amos *v.* Bennett, 125 Mass. 120; Green *v.* Russell, 132 Mass. 536.

Maine.—Richmond *v.* Toothaker, 69 Me. 451; Bangor *v.* Warren, 34 Me. 324; Parkhurst *v.* Jackson, 36 Me. 404; Paine *v.* Dwinel, 53 Me. 52; s. c.,

(*l*) GOODS SOLD AT THE TIME.—Where the note of a third person is taken in payment for goods sold at the time, and not for a precedent debt, it is taken at the risk of the vendor.[1]

87 Am. Dec. 533; Greenleaf *v.* Hill, 31 Me. 562; Sandy River Bank *v.* Miller, 82 Me. 137; Titcomb *v.* McAllister, 81 Me. 399; 17 Atl. Rep. 315.

Michigan.—Tiffany *v.* Glasgow (Mich. 1890), 46 N. W. Rep. 231; Mason *v.* Warner, 43 Mich. 439; Robertson *v.* First Nat. Bank, 41 Mich. 356.

Mississippi.—Guion *v.* Doherty, 43 Miss. 538.

Missouri.—O'Bryan *v.* Jones, 38 Mo. App. 90; Matson *v.* Walther, 23 Mo. App. 263; Wiles *v.* Robinson, 80 Mo. 47.

Maryland.—Hall *v.* Richardson, 16 Md. 396; s. c., 77 Am. Dec. 303.

Nebraska.—Pasewalk *v.* Bollman (Neb. 1890), 45 N. W. Rep. 780.

New York.—Cumming *v.* Hackley, 8 Johns. (N. Y.) 202; Graham *v.* Negus (Supreme Ct.), 8 N. Y. Supp. 679; Highland Bank *v.* Dubois, 5 Den. (N. Y.) 558; Geller *v.* Seixas, 4 Abb. Pr. (N. Y.) 103; Glenn *v.* Burrows, 37 Hun (N. Y.) 602; Fuller *v.* Negus (Supreme Ct.), 8 N. Y. Supp. 681; Downer *v.* Carpenter, 1 Hun (N. Y.) 591; Central City Bank *v.* Dana, 32 Barb. (N. Y.) 296; Auburn City Nat. Bank *v.* Hunsiker, 72 N. Y. 252; Averill *v.* Loucks, 6 Barb. (N. Y.) 470; Parsons *v.* Gaylord, 3 Johns. (N. Y.) 463; Lewis *v.* Lozee, 3 Wend. (N. Y.) 79; Fisher *v.* Marvin, 47 Barb. (N. Y.) 159; Dias *v.* Wanamaker, 1 Sandf. (N. Y.) 469.

New Jersey.—Corrigan *v.* Trenton Falls Co., 7 N. J. Eq. 489; Fry *v.* Patterson, 49 N. J. L. 612; Sayre *v.* Sayre, 3 N. J. L. 587.

New Hampshire.—Wright *v.* Buck, 62 N. H. 656; Exeter Bank *v.* Gordon, 8 N. H. 66.

Ohio.—Bank of Cadiz *v.* Slemmons, 34 Ohio St. 142; s. c., 32 Am. Rep. 364; McKee *v.* Hamilton, 33 Ohio St. 7; Shinkle *v.* First Nat. Bank, 22 Ohio St. 516.

Pennsylvania.—Kemmerer's Appeal, 102 Pa. St. 558; Cake *v.* First Nat. Bank, 86 Pa. St. 303; Van Haagen Soap Mfg. Co.'s Assigned Estate, 8 Pa. Co. Ct. Rep. 84; Appeal of Kimberly (Pa. 1886), 7 Atl. Rep. 75; McCord *v.* Durant, 134 Pa. St. 184.

South Carolina.—Adger *v.* Pringle, 11 S. Car. 527; *Ex parte* Williams, 17 S. Car. 396; Quackenbush *v.* Miller, 4 Strobh. (S. Car.) 235; Prescott *v.* Hubbell, 1 McCord (S. Car.) 94; Barrelli *v.* Brown, 1 McCord (S. Car.) 449.

Texas.—Bell *v.* Boyd, 76 Tex. 133.

Utah.—Heath *v.* White, 3 Utah 474.

Vermont.—Hatch *v.* Barnum, 23 Vt. 133; s. c., 56 Am. Dec. 59; Surdam *v.* Lyman, 36 Vt. 733; Curtis *v.* Ingham, 2 Vt. 290; Ormsby *v.* Fifield, 38 Vt. 143; Keyes *v.* Carpenter, 3 Vt. 209; Hadley *v.* Bordo (Vt. 1890), 19 Atl. Rep. 476; Ricker *v.* Adams, 59 Vt. 154.

West Virginia.—Hoge *v.* Vintroux, 21 W. Va. 1; Dryden *v.* Stephens, 19 W. Va. 1.

Wisconsin.—First Nat. Bank *v.* Case, 63 Wis. 504.

United States.—Lyman *v.* United States Bank, 12 How. (U. S.) 225; Baker *v.* Draper, 1 Cliff. (U. S.) 420; Benedict *v.* Maynard, 4 McLean (U. S.) 569; *Re* Clap, 2 Low. (U. S.) 226, 230; *Re* Hurst, 1 Flip. (U. S.) 462.

And the following, payment by bill of exchange or draft: Loth *v.* Mothner (Ark. 1890), 13 S. W. Rep. 594; Webster *v.* Howe Machine Co., 54 Conn. 394; Weaver *v.* Nixon, 69 Ga. 699; Scattergood *v.* Findlay, 20 Ga. 425; Alexander *v.* Byers, 19 Ind. 301; Hodgen *v.* Latham, 33 Ill. 344; Belleville Sav. Bank *v.* Bornman, 124 Ill. 200; 10 N. E. Rep. 552; Graham *v.* Sykes, 15 La. Ann. 49; Smith *v.* Atlas Cordage Co., 41 La. Ann. 1; Descadillas *v.* Harris, 8 Me. 298; Varner *v.* Nobleborough, 2 Me. 121; 11 Am. Dec. 48; Wallace *v.* Agry, 4 Mason (U. S.) 343; Wadlington *v.* Covert, 51 Miss. 631; Hammond *v.* Christie, 5 Robt. (N. Y.) 160; Hall *v.* Stevens, 116 N. Y. 201; 22 N. E. Rep. 374; Wise *v.* Chase, 3 Robt. (N. Y.) 35; Bright *v.* Judson, 47 Barb. (N. Y. 29; Ligon *v.* Dunn, 6 Ired. (N. Car.) 133; Riddlesburg Coal & Iron Co's Appeal, 114 Pa. St. 58; Connelly *v.* McKean, 64 Pa. St. 113; Alder *v.* Buckley, 1 Swan (Tenn.) 69; Rugeley *v.* Smalley, 12 Tex. 238; Churchill *v.* Bowman, 39 Vt. 518; Thornton *v.* Spotswood, 1 Wash. (Va.) 142; Hopkins *v.* Detwiler, 25 W. Va. 734; Fairfax *v.* Fairfax, 2 Cranch C. C. 25; Olyphant *v.* St. Louis, Ore etc. Co., 28 Fed. Rep. 729.

1. 2 Benjamin on Sales (4th Am. ed.)

938; Whitbeck *v.* Van Ness, 11 Johns. (N. Y.) 409; s. c., 6 Am. Dec. 383. Explaining Johnson *v.* Weed, 9 Johns. 310; 6 Am. Dec. 279. And reviewing the English and the prior New York decisions. Bulen *v.* Burroughs, 53 Mich. 464. And see Muldon *v.* Whitlock, 1 Cow. (N. Y.) 290; s. c., 13 Am. Dec. 533; Rew *v.* Barker, 3 Cow. (N. Y.) 272; Noel *v.* Murray, 1 Duer (N. Y.) 385: Ferdon *v.* Jones, 2 E. D. Smith (N. Y.) 106; Bach *v.* Levy, 101 N. Y. 511; Davis *v.* Maltz, 57 Mich. 496; Paine *v.* Smith, 33 Minn. 495; Ellis *v.* Wild, 6 Mass. 321; Salem Bank *v.* Gloucester Bank, 17 Mass. 1; s. c., 9 Am. Dec. 111; Perkins *v.* Cady, 111 Mass. 318. *Compare* Owenson *v.* Morse, 7 T. R. 64.

Unless the vendor is induced by fraud to take the notes. Wilson *v.* Foree, 6 Johns. (N. Y.) 110; s. c., 5 Am. Dec. 195; Whitbeck *v.* Van Ness, 11 Johns. (N. Y.) 409; s. c., 6 Am. Dec. 383; Pierce *v.* Drake, 15 Johns. (N. Y.) 475; Allen *v.* Bantel, 2 Th. & C. (N. Y.) 342; Susquehanna Fertilizer Co. *v.* White, 66 Md. 444; s. c., 59 Am. Rep. 186; Bridge *v.* Batchelder, 9 Allen (Mass.) 394; Farr *v.* Stevens, 26 Vt. 299; Wemet *v.* Missisquoi Lime Co., 46 Vt. 458. Also cases above cited. And see Slocomb *v.* Lurty, 1 Hempst. (U. S.) 431; Johnson *v.* Mechanics' etc. Bank, 25 Ga. 643.

But if the seller has been induced by fraud to take the note, he cannot recover for the goods sold without offering to return the note, unless he shows that it is absolutely worthless. Estabrook *v.* Swett, 116 Mass. 303.

A gave to B in payment of corn purchased from the latter the cheque of C on a bank in which C had no funds. The bank suspended before B presented the cheque, which he thereupon returned to A, and it was by A returned to C, who agreed to pay A the amount thereof. A continued to have dealings with C until the latter failed, but never obtained payment of the cheque. It was held that A was still liable to B for the corn. Mordis *v.* Kennedy, 23 Kan. 408; s. c., 36 Am. Rep. 169.

Where the purchaser agreed to pay for merchandise in government vouchers, which he delivered to the seller and took a receipt therefor expressed to be "in payment of said bill," this constituted a payment, though the government afterwards refused to redeem the vouchers in full. Wise *v.* Chase, 44 N. Y. 337.

Where notes of a third party are given in payment for property sold, with an agreement that if they are not collected the purchaser shall make up the deficiency, this constitutes a conditional payment only. Dodge *v.* Stanton, 12 Mich. 408.

One of the owners of a vessel, acting as ship's husband, gave his note for supplies furnished the vessel, and took a receipt in full. The note not being paid, *held*, that the debt was not extinguished and all the owners were liable. Schemerhorn *v.* Loines, 7 Johns. (N. Y.) 311; Johnson *v.* Cleaves, 15 N. H. 332. See also King *v.* Lowry, 20 Barb. (N. Y.) 532. *Compare* Ames Packing etc. Co. *v.* Tucker, 8 Mo. App. 95.

Where a bill of exchange is given in payment of goods sold, the liability of the purchaser upon the original consideration is extinguished, and he is liable only as indorser. The insolvency of the acceptor at the maturity of the bill, together with the fact that the purchaser had previously given the seller notice that he should resist payment of the bill on the ground that the goods were defective does not vary the rule. Francia *v.* Del Banco, 2 Duer (N. Y.) 133; Soffe *v.* Gallagher, 3 E. D. Smith (N. Y.) 507. See also Sellars *v.* Johnson, 65 N. Car. 104.

In general when the obligation of a third party is received from the debtor by the creditor at the time when the debt is contracted, the presumption is that it was taken in payment. Youngs *v.* Stahelin, 34 N. Y. 258; Torry *v.* Hadley, 27 Barb. (N. Y.) 192. See Darnall *v.* Morehouse, 36 How. Pr. (N. Y.) 511; Cole *v.* Sackett, 1 Hill (N. Y.) 516.

As to the difference in effect between note of the purchaser and that of a third person, see Gunn *v.* Bolckow, 44 L. J. Ch. 732; 10 L. R., Ch. 491; 32 L. T., N. S. 781.

Where an act of incorporation required payments to be made in money, the giving of a promissory note does not constitute such payment. Leighty *v.* Susquehanna etc. Turnpike Co., 14 S. & R. (Pa.) 434.

The purchaser of a horse agreed to give the vendor in payment a good and collectible note of a third person responsible for the price. He after-

(*m*) WHERE A SURETY pays the debt of his principal by giving his note therefor, this is such a payment as entitles him to contribution from his co-sureties.[1]

(*n*) EXECUTOR, ETC.—A promissory note given by an executor or administrator for the debt of the decedent does not constitute a payment, though it may suspend the right of action on the original debt until the maturity of the note.[2]

(*o*) CERTIFICATE OF DEPOSIT.—In the absence of a special agreement to that effect, the transfer and receipt of a bank certificate of deposit does not operate as absolute payment.[3]

(*p*) AN ORDER on a third party for the payment of money, which has neither been paid nor accepted by the party on whom it is drawn, does not constitute a payment of a precedent debt.[4]

wards sent the vendor the note of one P, and the vendor laid it away, remarking that he did not know P. At the maturity of the note P was insolvent, and the purchaser was held liable for the price of the horse. Torry *v.* Hadley, 27 Barb. (N. Y.) 192.

A note given in another State for goods sold there must be governed by the law of that State as to whether or not it constitutes a payment. Pecker *v.* Kennison, 46 N. H. 488.

1. Stubbins *v.* Mitchell, 82 Ky. 536.

2. Schouler's Exec. & Adm., § 441; Taylor *v.* Perry, 48 Ala. 240.

3. Huse *v.* McDaniel, 33 Iowa 406.

A debtor offered to the creditor a certificate of deposit issued to and indorsed by the foreman. The creditor declined to receive it, through want of confidence in the bank, until the debtor declared himself to be good for it, and promised to pay it in case the bank did not. The next day the bank failed, and the creditor deposited the certificate in court in a suit on the original debt. *Held*, that the certificate was not taken in payment, and the above facts constituted no defense. Leake *v.* Brown, 43 Ill. 372.

An agreement for a loan having been made, the lender offered, and the borrower received, instead of cash, but without any express agreement as to whose should be the risk, a certificate of deposit, post-dated. Before maturity of the certificate, the bank by which it was issued failed. *Held*, that the fair inference, from all the attendant circumstances, was that the borrower received the certificate, not as payment, but as a collateral means of obtaining the cash in the mode most convenient to the lender; and that the lender should bear the loss. This was so held, notwithstanding the fact that the lender, after transferring the certificate, settled his account with the bank, giving the bank credit for the amount of the certificate; and the further fact that complainant made an attempt to get the certificate cashed before its maturity. Burrows *v.* Bangs, 34 Mich. 304.

Where the creditor accepts certificates of indebtedness in place of cash, in payment of a claim against the government, he cannot afterwards recover the difference in value between the certificates and money. Gibbons *v.* United States, 2 Ct. of Cl. 421.

4. Haines *v.* Pearce, 41 Md. 221; McNeil *v.* McCamly, 6 Tex. 163; Rogers *v.* Shelburne, 42 Vt. 550. *Compare* Farwell *v.* Salpaugh, 32 Iowa 582.

An order for money constitutes a payment if accepted as such in the absence of fraud. Harrison *v.* Hicks, 1 Port. (Ala.) 423; s. c., 27 Am. Dec. 638.

Where the debtor gave the creditor an order on a third party which was to be considered a payment in case the order was accepted, and the party on whom it was drawn refused acceptance, the debt was not extinguished, even though the debtor was not notified of the non-acceptance of the order. Geiser *v.* Kershner, 4 Gill & J. (Md.) 305; s. c., 23 Am. Dec. 566. See also Briggs *v.* Parsons, 39 Mich. 400.

In *Vermont* the delivery by the debtor and acceptance by the creditor of a town order operates as a satisfaction of the debt, and the remedy is only on the order. Dalrymple *v.* Whitingham, 26 Vt. 345.

So in *Maine* unless the order was

7. The giving of a higher security constitutes a payment of a simple contract debt, unless it is otherwise agreed at the time.[1]

utterly worthless through want of authority. Hussey *v.* Sibley, 66 Me. 192; s. c., 22 Am. Rep. 557.

If a city warrant is to operate as an extinguishment of a judgment debt only when paid, the creditor must return it, or offer to return it, before he can proceed by execution. New Orleans *v.* Smith, 24 La. Ann. 405.

But the party receiving the order may by his actions preclude himself from recovering on the original debt. Sherwin *v.* Colburn, 25 Vt. 613.

Where a party rendering services agreed to accept in part payment an order on a third party, who accepted the order and was in good credit at the time, but subsequently failed, this constituted a payment for the services. Besley *v.* Dumas, 6 Ill. App. 291.

An agreement to take it in payment may be inferred from the circumstances. Haines *v.* Pearce, 41 Md. 221; Carpenter *v.* Murpheree, 49 Ala. 84; Knox *v.* Gerhauser, 3 Mont. 267.

As to agent's authority to receive note or cheque in payment, see *infra*, "*To Whom Payment is going to be Made.*"

Where the owner of a building at the request of the original contractor, and before any one has attempted to create a mechanic's lien, assumes a legal obligation to pay sub-contractors or material-men for labor or material used in the erection of the building, as by accepting orders drawn on him by the contractor in favor of such parties, this constitutes a valid payment upon the contract to the extent of the obligation assumed. Garrison *v.* Mooney, 9 Daly (N. Y.) 218; Gibson *v.* Lenane, 94 N. Y. 183.

An order payable at sight drawn by the duly authorized agent of an insurance company upon its secretary for a loss under a policy issued by the company, and received by the assured in full satisfaction thereof, will operate as a payment even before its presentation to the secretary. Spooner *v.* Rowland, 4 Allen (Mass.) 485.

See also as to the effect of an order as payment, Alabama etc. R. Co. *v.* Sanford, 36 Ala. 703; McWilliams *v.* Phillips, 71 Ala. 80; Burgen *v.* Dwinal, 11 Ark. 314; Preston *v.* Jones, 3 Ill. App. 632; Porter *v.* Walker, 1 Iowa 456; Palmeteer *v.* Gatewood, 4 J. J. Marsh. (Ky.) 503; Chapman *v.* Coffin, 14 Gray (Mass.) 454; Waite *v.* Vose, 62 Me. 184; Olson *v.* Cremer, 43 Minn. 232; Rice *v.* Dudley, 34 Mo. App. 383; Lupton *v.* Freeman (Mich. 1890), 46 N. W. Rep. 1042; Knox *v.* Gerhauser, 3 Mont. 267; Hoar *v.* Clute, 15 Johns. (N. Y.) 224; Missen *v.* Tucker, 1 Jones (N. Car.) 176; Commercial Bank *v.* Bobo, 9 Rich. (S. Car.) 31; Graves *v.* Allen, 66 Tex. 589; Goodrich *v.* Barney, 2 Vt. 422; Finney *v.* Edwards, 75 Va. 44; Schierl *v.* Baumel, 75 Wis. 69.

1. 2 Greenl. Evid. (—ed.), § 519; Lee *v.* Green, 83 Ala. 491; Gardner *v.* Hust, 2 Rich. (S. Car.) 608; Chalmers *v.* Turnipseed, 21 S. Car. 126; Howell *v.* Webb, 2 Ark. 360; Rowe *v.* Collier, 25 Tex. Supp. 252. *Compare* Stamper *v.* Johnson, 3 Tex. 1; Cumming *v.* Hackley, 8 Johns. (N. Y.) 202; Bailey *v.* Wright, 3 McCord. (S. Car.) 484.

Where the bond of a third person is received in part payment of a preceding debt, it constitutes payment though the obligor was insolvent at the time. Muir *v.* Geiger, 1 Cranch (C. C.) 323.

It is held in *Dakota* that the giving of a security, either by mortgage or trust deed, is not payment of an antecedent debt evidenced by note. Star Wagon Co. *v.* Matthiessen, 3 Dak. 233.

The same is held by the *Michigan* courts. Brown *v.* Dunckel, 46 Mich. 29.

As to view of *South Carolina* courts on this point, see Chewning *v.* Proctor, 2 McCord Eq. (S. Car.) 11. Of courts of New York, Coonley *v.* Coonley, Hill & D. Supp. (N. Y.) 312. And of Massachusetts, Dodge *v.* Emerson, 131 Mass. 467.

A note under seal given for an account extinguishes the account. Mills *v.* Starr, 2 Baily (S. Car.) 359; Robertson *v.* Branch, 3 Sneed (Tenn.) 506.

The sealed note of two partners extinguishes a note of the firm for which it is given. Chalmers *v.* Turnipseed, 21 S. Car. 126.

To same effect Averill *v.* Loucks, 6 Barb. (N. Y.) 19.

But the receipt of an obligation of equal dignity does not extinguish the debt. Bowers *v.* State, 7 Har. & J. (Md.) 32; Clopper *v.* Union Bank, 7 Har. & J. (Md.) 92; s. c., 16 Am. Dec. 294; Hart *v.* Boller, 15 S. & R. (Pa.) 162; s. c.,

8. **Payment in specific articles** is as good as though made in cash, if such was the agreement of the parties when the debt was contracted,[1] and the creditor may receive property in payment of his debt, though such was not the original agreement.[2]

16 Am. Dec. 536; Bailey *v.* Wright, 3 McCord (S. Car.) 484.

A security is not extinguished merely by the creditor's in acceptance of a new one from other parties, for the same debt. Potter *v.* McCoy, 26 Pa. St. 458; Covington *v.* Clark, 5 J. J. Marsh. (Ky.) 59. See also Hamilton *v.* Callender, 1 Dall. (U. S.) 420.

Where insurance policies are lodged with the creditor as collateral security, they do not operate as a payment until the money is actually received upon them, though under a submission to arbitration an award has been made that a certain sum is due on them. Scott *v.* Lifford, 9 East 347; 1 Camp. 346.

Where a note is given for public securities, payments thereon made in public securities are to be applied according to their value at the time the payments are made. Thatcher *v.* Prentiss, 2 Root (Conn.) 20.

1. Butman *v.* Howell, 144 Mass. 66; Tinsley *v.* Ryon, 9 Tex. 405.

When a sale is for cash, and securities which are void or prove to be void, are taken in payment, the creditor may sue and recover on the original cause of action. School Town of Monticello *v.* Grant, 104 Ind. 168.

It was agreed between the vendor and vendee of land that the cotton grown thereon should be forwarded to the vendor to be by him sold and the proceeds applied to the payment of the purchase money. *Held*, that as fast as any moneys arising from the sale of the cotton came into the hands of the vendor, the indebtedness was *pro tanto* reduced, and as to that part could only be revived with the consent of the vendee. Williams *v.* Whiting, 92 N. Car. 683.

Where the debt is to be paid in specific articles, it may be discharged by the payment of money. Sessions *v.* Ainsworth, 1 Root (Conn.) 181; Jones *v.* Dimmock, 2 Mich. N. P. 87.

And, ordinarily, the debtor has the election either to pay the price or deliver the articles. Cleveland etc. R. Co. *v.* Kelley, 5 Ohio St. 180.

But it seems the election must be exercised by the debtor at or before maturity of the debt; after that, the creditor's right to demand money is absolute. Church *v.* Feterow, 2 P. & W. (Pa.) 301.

Where notes were payable in grain, to be delivered at the maker's mill at maturity at a fixed price, and the maker set apart a sufficient quantity of grain to meet the notes, the property in the grain was charged and the notes were paid. Zinn *v.* Rowley, 4 Pa. St. 169.

2. Ralston *v.* Wood, 15 Ill. 159; s. c., 58 Am. Dec. 604; Smith *v.* Hobleman, 12 Neb. 502; Smith *v.* Whitfield, 67 Tex. 124; Phillips *v.* Afalo, 4 Man. & G. 846; 12 L. J., C. P. 49; Breton *v.* Cope, Peake, 31.

"Originally payment was the performance of a promise to pay money at the time and in the manner required by the terms of the contract. But it has been extended to include the delivery of money in satisfaction of a debt after a default has been made in payment according to the terms of the contract. If wood is delivered and received as a payment of money due on a note, it is only by virtue of a subsequent and independent agreement to that effect, and there is an accord and satisfaction. And the agreement by which the acceptance of the wood operates as a satisfaction of the contract, and the delivery and receipt of the wood under this agreement, are substantive facts which should be set forth in the answer." Ulsch *v.* Muller, 143 Mass. 379.

If a bank discounts a bill of exchange for the drawer an acceptance of a conveyance of property from the drawer in discharge of his liability while the paper is still the property of the bank, constitutes a payment of the bill. Williams *v.* Jones, 77 Ala. 294.

If a judgment creditor agrees to accept a specific article in satisfaction of the judgment, and the article is delivered to him and accepted, the judgment is thereby extinguished. Brown *v.* Feeter, 7 Wend. (N. Y.) 301. See Fowler *v.* Moller, 10 Bosw. (N. Y.) 374.

The maker of a past due note delivered to the holder thereof a quantity of corn to be shipped to Galveston. The

Where there is an agreement to pay for services rendered a certain sum "payable in trade," this means payable in such articles as the promisor deals in.[1]

IV. By Whom Payment May be Made—1. In General.—The payor or obligor or debtor, or any one of several joint payors, obligors or debtors, or any one in his behalf and at his request or with his consent, may make payment.[2]

2. By a Third Party.—One person cannot, without authority, pay the debt of another and charge the amount against the party for whose benefit the payment was made.[3]

holder shipped a part of the corn but the rest rotted in the pens, though there were then frequent opportunities for shipping to Galveston. *Held*, that a finding of the jury that the corn was a payment on the note to the extent of its market value at the time would not be disturbed. Copes *v.* Perkins, 6 Tex. 150.

Where the debtor delivered to the creditor a mare to sell and apply the proceeds to the payment of the debt, and the creditor exchanged the mare for other property, this constituted a payment of the debt, notwithstanding a dispute as to the amount to be applied. Strong *v.* Kennedy, 40 Mich. 327.

Where there was a written agreement to pay $572, when a certain note was paid, a delivery of personal property and acceptance thereof in satisfaction of the note, accompanied by a surrender and cancellation of the note, is such a payment as makes the $572 payable. Bacon *v.* Lamb, 4 Colo. 578.

Where the debtor places property in the hands of the creditor it is not to be considered as payment in full, unless such appears to be the intention of the parties. Perit *v.* Pittfield, 5 Rawle (Pa.) 166. *Compare* Kelly *v.* Kelly, 6 Rand. (Va.) 176; s. c., 18 Am. Dec. 710.

If the creditor accept a deed of land in payment of the debt, the debt is extinguished, though the title to the land be defective. Miller *v.* Young, 2 Cranch (C. C.) 53; Hays *v.* Smith, 4 Ill. 427.

Where a debt is payable in lumber, lime and rock, the quantities, time and place to be fixed by the payee, an unqualified refusal by the payor to deliver any lumber thereon avoids the necessity of any formal demand by the creditor fixing quantity, time or place. Ritchie *v.* Huntington, 7 Kan. 249.

Where a debtor gave his creditor authority to take certain goods passing by delivery, and sell them, and out of the proceeds to retain the amount of his debt, the creditor thereby acquired a lien, as against the administrator of the debtor, to the extent of his claim. Gurnell *v.* Gardner, 4 Giff. 626; 9 L. T., N. S. 367; 12 W. R. 67.

1. Dudley *v.* Vose, 114 Mass. 34.

Where a note is to be paid in specific articles at "factory prices," this is construed to mean the prices at which such goods are sold at factories, unless it is shown that there is a different technical sense universally established by the custom of trade. Whipple *v.* Levett, 2 Mason (U. S.) 89.

2. Beaumont *v.* Greathead, 2 C. B. 454; 3 D. & L. 631; 15 L. J., C. P. 130; Moran *v.* Abbey, 63 Cal. 56.

In the absence of proof to the contrary, it will be presumed that payment was made by the party bound, and not by another. Ames *v.* Merchants' Ins. Co., 2 La. Ann. 594.

3. McGee *v.* San Jose, 68 Cal. 91.

The payment of a debt by a person not legally liable for it is a satisfaction of the debt, if so received by the creditor. Martin *v.* Quinn, 37 Cal. 55; Burr *v.* Smith, 21 Barb. (N. Y.) 262; Welby *v.* Drake, 1 Car. & P. 557.

But it must be deliberately intended to operate as a payment. Kemp *v.* Balls, 10 Exch. 607; Gernon *v.* McCan, 23 La. Ann. 84; Breck *v.* Blanchard, 22 N. H. 303; Merryman *v.* Slate, 6 Har. & J. (Md.) 423; Whiting *v.* Independent Mut. Ins. Co., 15 Md. 297.

A payment by a third party to a constable on behalf of the judgment debtor is good. Cain *v.* Bryant, 12 Heisk. (Tenn.) 45.

Any third person, who demands no subrogation, may tender to a creditor, either in his own name or that of the debtor, the amount of a debt due by the latter, in whatever species of property the debt is payable, and compel

V. To Whom Payment May be Made—1. In General.—That a payment may operate as an extinguishment of a debt, it must be made to the creditor or to a person authorized by him to receive it.[1]

the creditor to accept the payment in that property. State *v.* Pilsbury, 29 La. Ann. 787.

A voluntary payment by a stranger cannot be set up as a defense to an action by the original creditor. Lucas *v.* Wilkinson, 1 H. & N. 420; Kemp *v.* Balls, 10 Exch. 607; 24 L. J. Exch. 47; Muller *v.* Eno, 14 N. Y. 605.

Payment by a stranger for a debtor and on his account, and after wards ratified by him, is a good payment. Belshaer *v.* Bush, 11 C.B. 191; 22 L. T., C. P. 24.

But payment by a stranger without the authority, prior or subsequent, of the debtor, is not. James *v.* Broadhurst, 9 C. B. 173; James *v.* Isaacs, 12 C. B. 791; 2 L. J., C. P. 73; Cook *v.* Lister, 13 C. B., N. S. 543; Goodwin *v.* Cremer, 18 Q. B. 757.

And such ratification will be good, though not made until after the commencement of an action, as by plea of payment. Belshaer *v.* Bush, 11 C. B. 191; 22 L. J., C. P. 24; Simpson *v.* Egginton, 10 Exch. 845.

But if the creditor, before any ratification by the debtor, cancels the payment by returning the money to the stranger, the debtor cannot afterwards ratify the payment. Walter *v.* James, 6 L. R. Exch. 124; 24 L. T., N. S. 188; 40 L. J. Exch. 104; 19 W. R. 472.

Where, after a note has become due, a stranger calls upon the holder and pays the amount, declines to have it canceled and takes it away with him, nothing being said about buying it, this will be held a payment and satisfaction of the note, so as to prevent a suit being brought thereon by a person receiving it from the stranger. Burr *v.* Smith, 21 Barb. (N. Y.) 262.

Though a bank is not liable in notes and certificates illegally issued by it, yet if at its request a third party who is indebted to it takes up such notes and certificates in payment of his indebtedness to the bank, such fact constitutes a payment of the third party's debt. Leavitt *v.* Beers, Hill & D. Supp. (N. Y.) 221.

A voluntary payment by a stranger of another's debt gives the payor no right of action against the debtor in his own name. Brown *v.* Chesterville, 63 Me. 241; Wilkes *v.* Harper, 1 N. Y. 586.

Where A delivers to B, who is a creditor of C, certain chattels which B accepts in satisfaction of C's indebtedness to him, C not being a party to the transaction, this satisfies both the debt of C to B and any liability of B to A for the price of the chattels; and A, after delivering the goods and inducing B to accept them in payment, is estopped from alleging the contract to be within the Statute of Frauds, upon the ground that the agreement was a parol promise to pay the debt of another. Fowler *v.* Moller, 10 Bosw. (N. Y.) 374.

1. 2 Benj. on Sales (4 Am. ed.) 952; Artley *v.* Morrison, 73 Iowa 132; Robinson *v.* Weeks, 6 How. Pr. (N. Y.) 161; Wilson *v.* Rogers, 1 Wyoming Ter. 51.

Where a note and mortgage are executed to a trustee, and the same are left in his possession, payment of interest to the trustee will bind the beneficiary. Thomassen *v.* Van Wyngoorden, 65 Iowa 687.

Where the obligor pays to the obligee the amount of a bond which has been assigned, without notice thereof to the obligor, the bond is discharged. Preston *v.* Grayson Co., 30 Gratt. (Va.) 496.

Payments made to a *de facto* administrator are valid. Chicago etc. R. Co. *v.* Gould, 64 Iowa 343.

A payment made to a guardian authorized to receive payment is valid. Wuesthoff *v.* Germania L. Ins. Co., 107 N. Y. 580.

Where the widow was sole legatee for life, and the estate was not in debt, and no administration pending, a payment to the widow is good. Hannah *v.* Lankford, 43 Ala. 163.

Payment made by an administrator to the husband of a distributee, without her knowledge and consent, is no more than unauthorized payment to a stranger, unless it can be traced to her hands or to her use. Jones *v.* Commercial Bank, 78 Ky. 413.

If payment is made to a stranger to

the transaction, the creditor may afterwards ratify it and then becomes a valid payment. Hoinire *v.* Rodgers, 74 Iowa 395; Strayhorn *v.* Webb, 2 Jones (N. Car.) 199; s. c., 64 Am. Dec. 580.

A ratification of a wrongful payment must be an entirety. Williams *v.* Jones, 77 Ala. 294.

The authority of the person to whom payment is made to receive it may be inferred from circumstances or from the course of dealing of the parties. Sax *v.* Drake, 69 Iowa 760.

If a mortgagor makes payment to the person to whom the administrator of the mortgagee says the mortgage and notes belong, he is protected thereby. Reynolds *v.* Smith, 57 Mich. 194.

Payment to the son of the agent authorized to receive payment is not binding on the creditor, if he does not actually receive the money. Lewis *v.* Ingersoll, 3 Abb. App. Dec. (N. Y.) 55.

The collection of other securities or the interest, or a part of the principal debt, are insufficient to raise an implied authority to receive payment. Smith *v.* Kidd, 68 N. Y. 130; s. c., 23 Am. Rep. 157; Cox *v.* Cutter, 28 N. J. Eq. 13; Garrels *v.* Morton, 26 Ill. App. 433.

Where the creditor has authorized the debtor to send to a third person the money due, the debtor must notify the creditor that he has so sent it. And it is not sufficient that he writes a letter to the creditor, if the creditor never in fact receives it, and therefore loses the benefit of the payment. Holland *v.* Tyns, 56 Ga. 56.

A sold to B certain chattels upon which C had a lien, and B, in order to get possession of the chattels, was compelled to pay C's claim. *Held*, that this constituted a payment to A of the purchase-money *pro tanto*. Partridge *v.* Dartmouth College, 5 N. H. 286.

A payment to a person simulating the creditor, will not bar a recovery on the debt by the real creditor. People *v.* Smith, 43 Ill. 219; s. c., 92 Am. Dec. 109.

Where an insurance company in one of the Confederate States, during the pendency of the war, paid the amount due the insured for a loss to a quartermaster of the government, such payment being made by virtue of a military order of the commander of the Federal forces, this constituted a valid payment, and a defense to an action by the assured on the policy. Slocomb *v.* Merchants' Mut. Ins. Co., 24 La. Ann. 291.

A compulsory payment of a debt to a receiver under the sequestration acts of the Confederate government is no defense to a suit by the creditor. Shortridge *v.* Macon, Chase Dec. (U. S.) 136.

The fact that the note is made payable at the recorder's office, does not confer authority on the recorder to receive payment. Aguilar *v.* Bourgeois, 12 La. Ann. 122.

And the same rule applies where the note is made payable at the office of a mercantile firm. Rowland *v.* Levy, 14 La. Ann. 219.

A justice of the peace in whose hands notes have been placed for suit may receive payment; and a payment to him will bar a subsequent suit on the notes. Johnson *v.* Hall, 5 Ga. 384.

Under the code of Ohio, where an execution has been issued by a justice of the peace against a judgment debtor, any person indebted to him may pay to the constable his debt, or so much thereof as is necessary to satisfy the judgment, and the constable's reciept is a sufficient discharge of the amount so paid. Hallanon *v.* Crow, 15 Ohio St. 176.

And see, under *Wisconsin* statute, Dunbar *v.* Harnesberger, 12 Wis. 373.

Payment of a debt due the school fund to a school commissioner who had been removed from office, and whose removal was known to the debtor, is not an extinguishment of the debt. Jameson *v.* Conway, 10 Ill. 227.

Where the plaintiff is only a nominal one, and not the real party in interest, a payment of the judgment to him is not a satisfaction thereof. Triplett *v.* Scott, 12 Ill. 137.

A savings bank required that every depositor should sign the by-laws and agree to conform to them. Among the by-laws was one providing that the bank would not be responsible for loss sustained by payments made on presentation of the pass-book, when the depositor had not given notice of its having been lost or stolen, and that it would not be answerable for the consequences of any mistake as to identity of the person presenting it. A depositor received a pass-book containing the by-laws, but she was unable to read and signed them by her mark. She having died, the book was presented to the

2. After Assignment.—A payment of any debt, not evidenced by paper negotiable by the law-merchant, made by the debtor to the original creditor, after an assignment thereof by the latter, when made in good faith without notice, actual or constructive, of the assignment, is valid.[1]

3. To the Holder of a Bill or Note.—The holder of a note who presents the same for payment is presumed to be the legal owner thereof.[2]

bank by one who fraudulently personated her, and the deposit was paid, the bank having received no notice of the loss of the book. *Held*, that her executor could not recover from the bank the amount of the deposit. Donlan *v.* Provident Institution, 127 Mass. 183; s. c., 34 Am. Rep. 358.

And see further on the general subject: United States *v.* Keehler, 9 Wall. (U. S.) 83; Cheney *v.* Libby, 134 U. S. 68; Wilcox *v.* Carr, 37 Fed. Rep. 130; Berrel *v.* Davis, 44 Mo. 407; Crowell *v.* Simpson, 7 Jones L. (N. Car.) 285; De St. Romes *v.* Levee Steam Cotton Press, 20 La. Ann. 381; Smith *v.* Atlas Cordage Co., 41 La. Ann. 1; Rush *v.* Fister, 23 Ill. App. 348; Loomis *v.* Downs, 26 Ill. App. 257; Frey *v.* Thompson, 20 Nev. 253; Baughan *v.* Brown, 122 Ind. 115; Walker *v.* Newton, 53 Wis. 336; Cavanaugh *v.* Buehler, 120 Pa. St. 441; Seiberling *v.* Demaree, 27 Neb. 854; Crane *v.* Gruenewald, 120 N. Y. 274; Tummonds *v.* Moody (Supreme Ct.) 3 N. Y. Supp. 714; Dean *v.* International Tile Co., 47 Hun (N. Y.) 319.

1. Van Keuren *v.* Corkins, 66 N. Y. 79; Preston *v.* Grayson Co., 30 Gratt. (Va.) 496.

But if the debt is evidenced by a non-negotiable instrument, as a bond, and the instrument is not produced when the payment is made, such payment is made at the risk of the debtor; and if it turns out that the instrument has been assigned and is held at the time of payment by another party, the payment is not a valid one. Clarke *v.* Iglestrom, 51 How. Pr. (N. Y.) 407; Mobley *v.* Ryan, 14 Ill. 51; 56 Am. Dec. 488; Capps *v.* Gorham, 14 Ill. 198.

If the note is non-negotiable, but the maker has notice that it has been assigned, a payment to the original payee is at the maker's risk; *a fortiori*, if suit has been brought on it by one claiming to be assignee. Hickok *v.* Labussier, 1 Morr. (Iowa) 115; Holden *v.* Kirby, 21 Wis. 149.

Even if paid on garnishee process. Gillan *v.* Huber, 4 Greene (Iowa) 155.

2. Stoddard *v.* Burton, 41 Iowa 582; Holly *v.* Holly, 94 N. Car. 670.

If the payee pays a holder whom he knows has no right to receive payment, this will not extinguish the note. Netterville *v.* Stevens, 2 How. (Miss.) 642.

The maker of a note has a right to pay it to the holder where it is properly indorsed by the payee, even though paid before maturity; the element of good faith does not enter into the case. Loomis *v.* Downs, 26 Ill. App. 257.

The holder of a note payable to himself or bearer has the legal title thereto, though it was taken by way of division in payment of a note given to him and another person for property which they jointly owned; and the maker cannot discharge the debt by paying the other person and taking his receipt against the note in the holder's hand. Enochs *v.* Therrell, 61 Miss. 178.

Payment of a bill of exchange or a negotiable promissory note by the acceptor or maker to one who is *bona fide* in possession of the instrument, though without indorsement, is a good payment. Edwards *v.* Parks, 1 Winst. Eq. No. 2 (N. Car.) 49.

A payment to the payee or indorsee of a draft or note who had not possession of it, but who gave a receipt in full and agreed to get the paper and surrender it, is not a payment, and will not protect the maker or drawer against a suit by a *bona fide* holder thereof. Wilcox *v.* Aultman, 64 Ga. 544; s. c., 37 Am. Rep. 92; Howard *v.* Rice, 54 Ga. 52; Best *v.* Crall, 23 Kan. 482; s. c., 33 Am. Rep. 185; Wheeler *v.* Guild, 20 Pick. (Mass.) 545; s. c., 32 Am. Dec. 231; Brayley *v.* Ellis, 71 Iowa 155; Osborn *v.* Baird, 45 Wis. 189; s. c., 30 Am. Rep. 710; Gosling *v.* Griffin, 85 Tenn. 737. *Compare* Allein *v.* Agricultural Bank, 3 Smed. & M. (Miss.) 48.

But if the paper is non-negotiable a

4. Lost or Stolen Bills or Notes.—Where a note payable to bearer, or indorsed in blank, is lost or stolen, a payment by the maker to the holder is good, and even gross negligence on the part of the maker, if unattended with *mala fides*, will not invalidate the payment.[1]

5. To an Agent.—Where a payment is made to an agent of the creditor, there must be some evidence of his authority to receive payment.[2] The delivery of a note to the agent of the holder for

different rule prevails. Johnston *v.* Allen, 22 Fla. 224; Heath *v.* Powers, 9 Mo. 774.

See Murray *v.* Gibson, 2 La. Ann. 311; Johnston *v.* Lewis, 1 A. K. Marsh. (Ky.) 401; Gibson *v.* Pew, 3 J. J. Marsh. (Ky.) 222; Bartholomew *v.* Hendrix, 5 Blackf. (Ind.) 572.

A payment to a mere custodian of a note, when the debtor knows that the money represented by the note belongs to another, will not discharge the debt. Lochenmeyer *v.* Fogarty, 112 Ill. 572.

But a payment to the real owner of a note is good, though the note is at the time held by another, if the payee had no notice of that fact. Richardson *v.* Farnsworth, 1 Stew. (Ala.) 55.

And payment in good faith to the holder of a note indorsed in blank is good. Davis *v.* Lusitanian Portuguese Ben. Association, 20 La. Ann. 24.

1. Story on Prom. Notes (7th ed.), § 382; Edwards on Bills (3rd ed.), §§ 434–438; Goodman *v.* Harvey, 4 Ad. & Ell. 870; Uther *v.* Rich, 10 Ad. & Ell. 748; Hall *v.* Wilson, 16 Barb. (N. Y.) 548; Magee *v.* Badger, 30 Barb. (N. Y.) 247; Ellsworth *v.* Fogg, 35 Vt. 355.

Compare 2 Pars. Bills and Notes, 212–215; Byles on Bills 271; Crooks *v.* Jadis, 5 B. & Ad. 909; Gill *v.* Cubitt, 3 B. & C. 466.

In a New York case it is held that the maker is protected in paying a lost note even to a stranger who produces no evidence of his title other than possession after maturity. Cothran *v.* Collins, 29 How. Pr. (N. Y.) 113.

2. 2 Greenl. Evid. (13th ed.) § 578; Abbott's Trial Evid. 276 (5); 800 (4).

The authority may be presumed from the authority to sell. Henry *v.* Marvin, 4 E. D. Smith (N. Y.) 71.

A payment by the maker to an agent of the payee, before a transfer by the payee, may be a good payment. Renard *v.* Turner, 42 Ala. 117.

The fact that the holder of the note receives money as the agent of the maker does not constitute a payment of the note, unless the maker assents to such application of the money. McGill *v.* Ott, 10 Lea (Tenn.) 147.

A payment to a duly authorized agent of the holder is good, though the agent has not possession of the note at the time. Dunn *v.* Hornbeck, 7 Hun (N. Y.) 629; s. c., affirmed, 72 N. Y. 80. See Jones on Mortg., § 964.

A payment to the party's attorney is in general sufficient. Jackson *v.* Rome, 78 Ga. 343; Yates *v.* Freckleton, 2 Dougl. 623; Hudson *v.* Johnson, 1 Wash. (Va.) 10. But not to the clerk of the attorney. Yates *v.* Freckleton, 2 Dougl. 623; Perry *v.* Turner, 1 Dowe Pr. Cas. 300; 2 C. & J. 89; 2 Tyr. 128.

Payment of a judgment to the attorney by whom it was obtained is good, though made more than a year after the judgment was received. Powell *v.* Litte, 1 W. Bl. 8; Branch *v.* Burnley, 1 Call (Va.) 147; Langdon *v.* Potter, 13 Mass. 319; Lewis *v.* Gamaje, 1 Pick. (Mass.) 347; Jackson *v.* Bartlett, 8 Johns. (N. Y.) 361; Kellog *v.* Gilbert, 10 Johns. (N. Y.) 220; s. c., 6 Am. Dec. 335.

The facts that an attorney was employed to draw up a bond and mortgage, and that the money was advanced thereon by his client through such attorney, and that the attorney collected the interest, will not raise the inference that he is authorized to collect the principal, where the securities are not in his custody. Smith *v.* Kidd, 68 N. Y. 130; s. c., 23 Am. Rep. 157. The same rule applied to brokers. Stiger *v.* Bent, 111 Ill. 328.

While the authority of an agent to receive payment may be inferred from his having made the loan and retained the securities, this inference fails when the notes are withdrawn from his custody. Garrels *v.* Morton, 26 Ill. App. 433. To same effect, Lane *v.* Duchac, 75 Wis. 646; Roberts *v.* Matthews, 1 Vern. 150; Westenholm *v.* Davies,

Freem. Ch. R. 298; Curtis *v.* Drought, 1 Molloy, 487.

A mortgagor at the time of making payment to the agent of the mortgagee inquired of him for the papers, whereupon search was made for them, but they were not found. The mortgagor then suggested that they might be at the recorder's office, to which the agent replied that they probably were. The mortgagee was insolvent and had assigned the mortgage. *Held*, that there was no presumption that the mortgagor knew of the assignment. Foster *v.* Beals, 21 N. Y. 247.

The burden of proof is on the debtor to show that the securities were in the custody of the agent at the time of payment. Williams *v.* Walker, 2 Sandf. Ch. (N. Y.) 325; Smith *v.* Kidd, 68 N. Y. 130; s. c., 23 Am. Rep. 157; Garrels *v.* Morton, 26 Ill. App. 433.

A receipt given in the name of a firm, but in the form used by agents, puts the person making the payment on inquiry as to the authority of the party to whom payment is made. Chase *v.* Buhl Iron Works, 55 Mich. 139.

Payment to the clerk of a merchant is not valid unless it is within the scope of his employment to collect bills, and his mere statement that he has such authority is not sufficient, though the bill is made out on one of the merchant's bill heads.

"The usual employment of a clerk in a retail store is to sell goods to customers or purchasers, and it is implied from such employment that he has authority to receive pay for them on such sale. But there is no implication from such employment that he has authority, after goods are delivered and taken from the store, to present bills and collect money due to his employers, because it is not in the scope of the usual employment of such clerks." Hirshfield *v.* Waldron, 54 Mich. 649.

One Cox sold defendant an engine for plaintiffs, being their agent to sell. Another agent took notes from the defendant for the price of the engine, made payable to plaintiffs. These notes were indorsed by Cox. Defendant sent to Cox some carloads of shingles to sell and pay the notes off, but the notes were never paid. *Held*, not to constitute a payment. Hooks *v.* Frick, 75 Ga. 715.

If a clerk is authorized to receive payment over the counter only, a payment made to him elsewhere is not good. Kaye *v.* Brett, 5 Exch. 269; Jackson *v.* Jacob, 5 Scott 79.

Plaintiff placed goods in the warehouse of E. & Co. for sale, and two parcels were sold the defendant, who resided at a distance. After defendant had paid plaintiff for one parcel, he received a letter from one T, a clerk of E & Co., inclosing an invoice of the other parcel, and requesting payment, stating that E & Co. were authorized to receive the money for the plaintiff. The letter purported to be signed by E & Co. per per. of the plaintiff. Defendant remitted the amount in accordance with the request, but T intercepted the letter at the office of E & Co. and appropriated the money. T had authority from the plaintiff to receive payments over the counter only. *Held*, that not to constitute payment for the parcel. Kage *v.* Brett, 5 Exch. 296; 19 L. J. Exch. 346.

Payment to a person found in a merchant's counting house, ostensibly intrusted with the conduct of the business there, is a good payment to the merchant, though it turn out that the person was never employed by the merchant. Barrett *v.* Deere, M. & M. 200.

A factor made purchases for his principal, and the latter made him payments on account. The vendor wrote to the factor pressing him for payment, and the letter came into the hands of the principal, who transmitted it to the factor and with a knowledge of its contents paid the factor the balance of the purchase money. *Held*, that he was liable over to the vendor for the balance so paid. Powell *v.* Nelson, 15 East 65.

A payment to a broker is good, where the name of the principal is not disclosed, though the purchaser knew that the broker was selling for some principal. But to be valid it is necessary that the mode of payment should not vary from the terms of the original contract. Campbell *v.* Hassell, 1 Stark 233; Thornton *v.* Meux, M. & M. 43. See Drakeford *v.* Piercy, 7 B. & S. 515; 14 L. T., N. S. 443.

A purchased goods of B through a broker, and paid the broker for them partly by an advance on his general account with the broker before the delivery of the goods, and partly by cash on a settlement of accounts after delivery. The broker became bankrupt before paying over the money to B, and the latter brought an action

collection will authorize such agent to receive the money when due, and to deliver the note to the maker on payment.[1] The

against A to recover such part of the purchase money as had not been paid to the broker in cash. *Held*, that it was a question for the jury, depending upon the custom of the trade, whether payment to a broker in advance was a good payment as against the principal. Catteral *v.* Hindle, 2 L. R., C. P. 368.

Where goods are bought by a broker, the effect of a payment to the broker would seem to depend upon the time when it was made. If the principal is called upon for payment by the vendor at the time the payment is due, it is no defense that the principal had previously made payment to the broker; otherwise, if the day of payment is allowed to pass without a demand on the principal by the vendor. Kymer *v.* Suwercropp, Camp. 109. *Compare* Smyth *v.* Anderson, 7 C. B. 39; 18 L. J., C. P. 114; Armstrong *v.* Stokes, 7 L. R., Q. B. 598, 607; 41 L. J., Q. B. 253, 258.

If the broker does not mention his principal, the latter is liable to the vendor, though the broker becomes insolvent and is indebted to his principal. Waring *v.* Favenck, 1 Camp. 85.

An auctioneer has a right to collect the money due on his sales, and may maintain an action for it. Harlow *v.* Sparr, 15 Mo. 184.

A, being in the employ of B, and authorized to collect money for him, but without authority to deposit the money so collected, did deposit such money in a bank and took certificates of deposit in the name of "B by A." A afterward drew the money so deposited, and re-delivered the certificate to the bank. Thereafter B ascertained the fact that such deposits had been made, and brought suit to recover the amount thereof. *Held*, that he was entitled to recover. Honig *v.* Pacific Bank, 73 Cal. 464.

Money was deposited by the treasurer of a committee in a bank in his name as such treasurer. The bank paid it out to another party upon the order of the committee. *Held*, that the payment was a valid one. Jay *v.* Concord Sav. Bank, 60 N. H. 277.

A payment to an attorney after notice of substitution is not valid. Weist *v.* Lee, 3 Yeates (Pa.) 47. Or of revocation. Parker *v.* Downing, 13 Mass. 465.

Where a creditor has once authorized payment to an agent, he cannot revoke that authority after the debtor has, pursuant to the authority, given such a pledge to pay to the agent as would be binding in a court of law. Hodgson *v.* Anderson, 5 D. & R. 735; 3 B. & B. 842. See Pooley *v.* Godwin, 4 Ad. & El. 64; 5 N. & M. 466.

The authority of the agent to collect the debt is revoked by the death of the creditor. Lochenmeyer *v.* Fogarty, 112 Ill. 572; Cassiday *v.* McKenzie, 4 W. & S. (Pa.) 282; s. c., 39 Am. Dec. 76; Wallace *v.* Cook, 5 Esp. 117.

1. Whelan *v.* Reilley, 61 Mo. 565; Yazel *v.* Palmer, 81 Ill. 82; Padfield *v.* Green, 85 Ill. 529; Johnson *v.* Glover, 121 Ill. 283; Haines *v.* Pohlman, 25 N. J. Eq. 179; Camp *v.* Wiggins, 72 Iowa 643; Thomassen *v.* Van Wyngaarden, 65 Iowa 687. *Compare* Taylor *v.* Vingert, 33 Leg. Int., C. P. 238; Brown *v.* Taylor, 32 Gratt. (Va.) 135.

He is not authorized to receive payment before it is due. Smith *v.* Kidd, 68 N. Y. 130; s. c., 23 Am. Rep. 157. *Compare* Merritt *v.* Cole, 9 Hun (N. Y.) 98.

Possession of the securities by the agent indispensable evidence of his authority to collect. Jones on Mortg., § 964.

The burden of proof is on the debtor to show that the note was in the agent's possession when the payment was made. Stiger *v.* Bent, 111 Ill. 328. To same effect, Eaton *v.* Knowles, 61 Mich. 625.

An authority to receive the whole of a debt implies a power to receive part. Whelan *v.* Reilley, 61 Mo. 565. But an authority to receive interest is not an authority to receive the principal. Ritch *v.* Smith, 60 How. Pr. (N. Y.) 157; Cox *v.* Cutter, 28 N. J. Eq. 13.

Defendant executed to plaintiff a note payable in ten days at a certain bank. Two days afterwards he paid the bank the amount of the note and took a receipt therefor, the note not being there. Three days after the payment, the bank sent him notice of the time and place of payment, in which notice it was stated that notes in the hands of the bank might be paid at any time before due. Two days after the sending of this notice

general rule is that the agent is authorized to receive payment only in cash.[1]

plaintiff left the note with the bank for collection, and the next day, and before the maturity of the note, the bank suspended payment, and the money was never paid over to plaintiff. *Held*, that the payment was good, on the ground that it was a payment to plaintiff's agent, and that such agent expressly authorized its payment before maturity. Osborn *v.* Baird, 45 Wis. 189; s. c., 30 Am. Rep. 710.

And the general rule is that where the payee of a note leaves it with a bank for collection, the bank becomes his agent to receive the money, and payment at the bank discharges the maker, though the bank fail to remit the amount to the payee. Smith *v.* Essex Co. Bank, 22 Barb. (N. Y.) 627.

1. Williams *v.* Evans, 1 L. R., Q. B. 352; 35 L. J., Q. B. 111.

An authority to collect is not an authority to commute the debt. 1 Pars. Cent. 42. Nor to release it upon a composition, nor to pledge it, nor to obtain a judgment on it for the agent's own use. Padfield *v.* Green, 85 Ill. 529; Eaton *v.* Knowles, 61 Mich. 625; Kingston *v.* Kincaid, · Wash. (U. S.) 448. Nor to take payment by a release of the agent's own debt to the debtor. Smith *v.* Morrill, 39 Kan. 665; Bostick *v.* Hardy, 30 Ga. 836; Maynard *v.* Cleveland, 76 Ga. 52; Chase *v.* Buhl Iron Works, 55 Mich. 139; Parsons *v.* Webb, 8 Me. 38; s. c., 22 Am. Dec. 220; Williams *v.* Johnston, 92 N. Car. 532; s. c., 53 Am. Rep. 428; Underwood *v.* Nicholls, 17 C. B. 239; 25 L. J., C. P. 79.

Nor to take a note or other commercial paper for it. And if the debtor pays the debt by giving his note payable to the agent, which note the agent sells before maturity, and the maker pays, this does not prevent a recovery by the principal. Lochenmeyer *v.* Fogarty, 112 Ill. 572. To same effect, Harbach *v.* Colvin, 73 Iowa 638; British etc. Mortgage Corp. *v.* Tibbals, 63 Iowa 468. *Compare* Mulcrone *v.* American Lumber Co., 55 Mich. 622; Anderson *v.* Hillies, 12 C. B. 499; 16 Jur. 819; 21 L. J., C. P. 150.

An auctioneer to whom commissions are due may allow a purchaser at the auction sale credit on his purchase for the auctioneer's individual debt to such purchaser, not to exceed the amount of his commission. Harlow *v.* Sparr, 15 Mo. 184.

An agent who is authorized to collect a note cannot receive in payment anything but money; and if the agent receive from the debtor other notes or claims on third parties, they will not constitute a payment unless actually collected by the agent. Mudgett *v.* Day, 12 Col. 139; Locke *v.* Mackinson, 14 La. Ann. 361; Spence *v.* Rose, 28 W. Va. 333; Anderson *v.* Boyd, 64 Tex. 108. Nor can an agent accept in full payment any less than the amount due. Rohr *v.* Anderson, 51 Md. 205; Chalfants *v.* Martin, 25 W. Va. 394.

Where an attorney receives notes or evidences of debt in payment of claims placed in his hands for collection, the claims are not thereby paid. And if the attorney proceeds to collect such notes and evidences of debt, the money arising therefrom is at the risk of the debtor, so long as it remains in the hands of the attorney. Kenny *v.* Hazeltine, 6 Humph. (Tenn.) 62.

An agent authorized to collect a debt, received from the debtor his note payable to the creditor. The agent indorsed it as the creditor's agent, and sold it to a third person, to whom it was paid by the debtor. The creditor never received the money. *Held*, no authority of the agent to indorse being shown, the debt was not discharged. David *v.* Neven, 10 La. Ann. 642.

If the owner of goods allows the broker through whom he sells them to sell as principal, the purchaser will be discharged by a payment to the broker in any way which would have been sufficient had he been the real owner. Coates *v.* Lewes, 1 Camp. 444.

And if the principal has, in the course of dealing, allowed his broker to take payment for goods sold by drawing bills upon the purchaser in his own name, without mention of the principal, a payment thus made is good, though the broker fail before the money is actually paid to the principal. Townsend *v.* Inglis, Holt 278.

Where the agent is a bank of deposit, it may receive its own certificates of deposit as money, and the

6. Joint Payees.—Payment to one of several joint payees extinguishes the debt.[1]

VI. How Payment Is to be Made—1. General Rule.—The general rule is that payment must be made to the creditor or his agent personally; but a payment made in any manner requested or agreed to by the creditor will discharge the debtor, though the money never reach the creditor's hands.[2]

2. Debtor Not Bound to Pay in Any Other Than the Usual Mode.—The debtor is under no obligation to follow the mode prescribed by the creditor, but may pay directly to the creditor or his

principal will be bound thereby and the debtor discharged, even though the bank soon after becomes insolvent, and never remits to its principal. British etc. Mortgage Co. *v.* Tibballs, 63 Iowa 468. *Compare* Francis *v.* Evans, 69 Wis. 115.

1. Lyman *v.* Gedney, 114 Ill. 388; s. c., 55 Am. Rep. 871; Morrow *v.* Starke, 4 J. J. Marsh. (Ky.) 367; Henry *v.* Mt. Pleasant, 70 Mo. 500.

So of payment to one of several partners, trustees or executors. Porter *v.* Taylor, 6 M. & S. 156; Carr *v.* Reed, 3 Atk. 695; Stone *v.* Marsh. Ry. & M. 364; Bryant *v.* Smith, 10 Cush. (Mass.) 169.

2. 2 Greenl. Evid., (13th ed.), § 519; Benjamin on Sales (1 Am. ed.), § 710; 2 Benj. Sales, (4th Am. ed.), p. 923; Gurney *v.* Howe, 9 Gray (Mass.) 404; s. c., 69 Am. Dec. 299.

Thus if the creditor direct the money to be transmitted by post, and it is lost or stolen, the payment is nevertheless good. Warwicke *v.* Noakes, Peake 67; Kington *v.* Kington, 11 Mees. & W. 233; 12 L. J. Exch. 248; Wakefield *v.* Lithgow, 3 Mass. 249.

But the letter must be delivered at the general post, or a receiving house appointed by that office, and not to a bell-man in the street. Hawkins *v.* Rutt, Peake 186.

The burden is on the debtor, however, to show that the creditor authorized this mode of remittance, either by express assent or direction, or a usage and course of dealing from which such assent or direction may be fairly inferred. Gurney *v.* Howe, 9 Gray (Mass.) 404; s. c., 69 Am. Dec. 299; Crane *v.* Pratt, 12 Gray (Mass.) 348; Yon *v.* Blanchard, 75 Ga. 519; Gordon *v.* Strange, 1 Exch. 477.

In the absence of any evidence of usage and custom to remit by mail, or of special authority from the creditor to so remit, a remittance in that manner is at the debtor's risk, and is not a discharge of the debt unless received. A remittance in a single previous instance, not objected to by the creditor, will not establish such a custom; nor will a letter of the creditor requesting a remittance, but specifying no mode, prove such authority. Burr *v.* Sickles, 17 Ark. 428; s. c., 65 Am. Dec. 437; Morton *v.* Morris, 31 Ga. 378; Boyd *v.* Reed, 6 Heisk. (Tenn.) 631. *Compare* Townsend *v.* Henry, 9 Rich. (S. Car.) 318.

Defendants were commission merchants in Massachusetts, and had in their hands produce belonging to the plaintiffs, who were residents of Vermont, to sell for the plaintiffs. Plaintiffs gave defendants a special order to remit a part of the proceeds to them in a particular way. *Held*, that this did not authorize the defendants to remit the balance of the proceeds in the same way, and such a remittance of the balance was at the risk of defendants. Dodge *v.* Smith, 34 Vt. 178.

If the creditor authorizes the debtor to remit to him by mail under certain specified precautionary observances, and the debtor remits without observing such precautions, it is no excuse that their observance was impossible. Williams *v.* Carpenter, 36 Ala. 9; s. c., 76 Am. Dec. 316.

Where the debtor, in answer to a letter demanding payment, sent a postoffice order in which the creditor was described by a wrong Christian name, this was not a payment, though the creditor kept the order without cashing it, and was informed at the postoffice that he might receive the money at any time by signing the name actually used in the order. Gordon *v.* Strange, 11 Jur. 1019; 1 Exch. 477.

duly authorized agent.[1]

3. Applying Bank Deposit.—A banker may apply a deposit of his customer to the payment of the customer's note held by the bank at its maturity, without any request or direction to that effect by the customer.[2]

VII. When Payment Must be Made—1. At Exact Time Agreed Upon.--Payment must be made at the exact time agreed on. At common law, if a condition for the payment of money at a day certain was broken by a failure to pay on that day, the debt could not be discharged by a subsequent payment, unless accepted in satisfaction.[3] The only relief was in equity.[4]

2. When no time is fixed for the payment, it must be made within a reasonable time[5]

1. Meyer *v.* Hehner, 96 Ill. 400. In this case the creditor gave a power of attorney to one to receive payment of a debt, and afterwards wrote to the debtor requesting him, instead of making payment to the attorney, to purchase an interest-bearing certificate of deposit which he would take in payment. The attorney who held the note, collected a part thereof from the debtor, and credited it on the note. *Held*, that the payment was good. The debtor was under no legal obligation to procure a certificate of deposit instead of paying the money to the attorney.

2. Knapp *v.* Cowell, 77 Iowa 528.

So, too, a payment may be made by means of a credit on a mutual account, where such is the agreement between the parties. Livingston *v.* Whitney, 19 L. J., Q. B. 528; s. c., 15 Q. B. 722.

See Wharton *v.* King, 69 Ala. 365; McCurdy *v.* Middleton, 82 Ala. 131; Thomas *v.* Thomas, 62 Miss. 531; Sutton *v.* Page, 3 C. B. 204; Callendar *v.* Howard, 10 C. B. 290; Ashby *v.* James, 11 Mees. & W. 542; Scholey *v.* Walton, 12 Mees. & W. 510; Smith *v.* Page, 15 Mees. & W. 683; Owens *v.* Denton, 1 Cr. M. & R. 711; McKellar *v.* Wallace, 8 Moo. P. C. 378; Sturdy *v.* Arnaut, 3 T. R. 599; Worthington *v.* Grinesditch, 7 Q. B. 479; Livingston *v.* Whiting, 15 Q. B. 722; Clark *v.* Alexander, 8 Scott (N. R.) 147.

Or it is so provided by statutes, as in the case of a bankrupt. U. S. Rev. Stat., § 5073.

3. Smith *v.* Trousdale, 3 El. & B. 83; Thompson *v.* Hunt, 3 Leving. 368; Hume *v.* Peploe, 8 East 167; Poole *v.* Tumbridge, 2 Mees. & W. 223; Kington *v.* Kington, 11 Mees. & W. 233; Wheeler *v.* Walker, 2 Conn. 196; s. c., 7 Am. Dec. 264; Walker *v.* Wheeler, 2 Conn. 299; Parsons *v.* Welles, 17 Mass. 419; Howe *v.* Lewis, 14 Pick. (Mass.) 329.

See *infra*, this title, *Pleading Payment.*

And this applies to a covenant for payment of rent. Green's Case, 1 Leon. 262; Pennant's Case, 3 Co. 64.

And to the debt due under a mortgage. Doton *v.* Russell, 17 Conn. 146; Parsons *v.* Welles, 17 Mass. 419; Maynard *v.* Hunt, 5 Pick. (Mass.) 240; Howe *v.* Lewis, 14 Pick. (Mass.) 329.

When payment is to be made within a certain time after a day named, that day is to be excluded in computing the time. Campbell *v.* International L. Assur. Soc., 4 Bosw. (N. Y.) 298.

4. Whittington *v.* Roberts, 4 T. B. Mon. (Ky.) 173; Atkins *v.* Chilson, 11 Met. (Mass.) 112; Sanborn *v.* Woodman, 5 Cush. (Mass.) 36; Walker *v.* Wheeler, 2 Conn. 196, 299; Carpenter *v.* Wescott, 4 R. I. 225; Ragan *v.* Walker, 1 Wis. 527.

The later cases hold that the defense of payment may be raised at law. Atkins *v.* Chilson, 11 Met. (Mass.) 112.

5. Bank of Columbia *v.* Hagner, 1 Pet. (U. S.) 455; Brown *v.* Brown, 103 Ind. 23.

Where a vendee agrees to execute notes in payment for goods sold, they must be executed within a reasonable time, or the whole sum becomes due forthwith. Hays *v.* Weatherman, 14 Ind. 341.

Two years and three months held not to be a reasonable time to make payment in case of sale of lands. Fowler *v.* Sutherland, 68 Cal. 414.

If by inference of law the money is to be paid in a reasonable time, the

or on demand.[1]

3. As Depending Upon Performance.—Where the time fixed for payment is to happen, or may happen, before the time fixed for performance, the right to payment does not depend upon performance.[2]

4. For Goods Sold.—In an ordinary contract of sale, where it is not expressly stipulated that credit shall be given, or the time of payment is not agreed upon, the buyer is bound to pay as soon as the vendor is ready to deliver.[3]

debtor has no election to make it payable at different times and in different years. O'Donnell *v.* Leeman, 43 Me. 158; s. c., 69 Am. Dec. 54.

Where a contract provided that a sum should be "payable as convenient," this cannot be construed so that it snall not be payable at all, but only as an extension of credit. Black *v.* Bachelder, 120 Mass. 171.

1. Bank of Columbia *v.* Hagner, 1 Pet. (U. S.) 455; Payne *v.* Mattox, 1 Bibb (Ky.) 164; Slack *v.* Price, 1 Bibb (Ky.) 272; Colburn *v.* First Baptist Church, 60 Mich. 198; Dorland *v.* Dorland, 66 Cal. 189.

A promissory note which states no time of payment is payable on demand, even though the interest is made payable annually. Converse *v.* Johnson, 146 Mass. 20.

A debt acknowledged to be due, without mentioning any time of payment, is payable immediately. Payne *v.* Mattox, 1 Bibb (Ky.) 164.

On an award or a covenant to pay money, without any day fixed, no demand is necessary, and the money is due forthwith. Slack *v.* Price, 1 Bibb (Ky.) 272; Kendall *v.* Talbott, 1 A. K. Marsh. (Ky.) 321.

But if it is expressly agreed, or established by custom, that payment is to be made only after demand or notice, a reasonable time after demand or notice is allowed for the debtor to bring the money. Benj. on Sales (1 Am. ed.), § 709, *citing* Brighty *v.* Norton, 32 L. J., Q. B. 38; s. c., 3 Best & S. 305; Jones *v.* Wilson, 32 L. J., Q. B. 33, 382; s. c., 4 Best & S. 442, 455; Massey *v.* Sladen, L. R., 4 Exch. 14; Loughborough *v.* Nevin, 74 Cal. 250.

In the case of Toms *v.* Wilson, *cited* by Mr. Benjamin, plaintiff being indebted to the defendant, executed to the latter a bill of sale of his household furniture, whereby he agreed to pay the debt "immediately upon demand thereof in writing," and in case of failure to so pay, defendants were authorized to take possession of and sell the furniture. Defendants placed in the hands of a sheriff's officer a written demand of payment, who delivered it to plaintiff at his house, and upon his failure to make immediate payment, seized the furniture. It was held that the seizure was premature. Says COCKBURN, C. J.: "By the terms of the bill of sale plaintiff was under an obligation to pay this money *immediately upon demand* in writing, and, if he did not, then the defendants were entitled to take possession of and sell the goods. Here such a demand was made. The deed must receive a reasonable construction, and it could not have meant that the plaintiff was bound to pay the money in the very next instant of time after the demand, but he must have a reasonable time to get it from some convenient place. For instance, he might require time to get it from his desk, or to go across the street, or to his bankers for it." 4 Best & Smith 453.

And BLACKBURN, J., said: "By a reasonable time must be understood time enough to ascertain the will of the creditor, or of a person authorized by him to receive the money."

The demand in this case having been made by an agent of the creditors, it was further held that the debtor must have a reasonable opportunity to inquire into the authority of the person making the demand.

2. 1 Whart. on Contr., § 582; Petty *v.* Church of Christ, 95 Ind. 278.

3. Benj. on Sales (1 Am. ed.), §§ 706, 707; Endsley *v.* Johns, 120 Ill. 469; s. c., 60 Am. Rep. 572; Wright *v.* Wabash etc. R. Co., 120 Ill. 541; Lentz *v.* Flint etc. R. Co., 53 Mich. 444; Hill *v.* Gayle, 1 Ala. 275; Falls *v.* Garther, 9 Port. (Ala.) 605; Robbins *v.* Harrison, 31 Ala. 160; Robinson *v.* Marney, 5 Blackf. (Ind.) 329; Kirby *v.* Stude-

5. Of Note Before Maturity.—Payments made by the maker of a negotiable promissory note before its maturity are made at his risk.[1]

6. A payment made on Sunday is good if the creditor retains the money.[2]

VIII. Where Payment Must be Made—1. The General Rule is that the payee must, if no specific place of payment is designated or agreed upon, seek out the creditor and pay him.[3]

baker, 15 Ind. 45; Terwilliger *v.* Murphy, 104 Ind. 32; Hundley *v.* Buckner, 6 Smed. & M. (Miss.) 70; Peabody *v.* Maguire, 79 Me. 572; Genin *v.* Tompkins, 12 Barb. (N. Y.) 265; Cook *v.* Ferral, 13 Wend. (N. Y.) 285; McCombs *v.* McKennan, 2 W. & S. (Pa.) 216; s. c., 37 Am. Dec. 505; Fitzpatrick *v.* Fain, 3 Coldw. (Tenn.) 15; Bliss *v.* Arnold, 8 Vt. 252; s. c., 30 Am. Dec. 467; Fay *v.* Fay, 43 N. J. Eq. 438.

The buyer has no right to delay till a demand is made, nor till the vendor actually offers to deliver; nor till he sends or carries the articles purchased to the purchaser. Benj. on Sales (1 Am. ed.), § 707.

In *Vermont*, a sale for cash by a commission merchant is held to mean that the money is to be paid on delivery of the property. Bliss *v.* Arnold, 8 Vt. 252; s. c., 30 Am. Dec. 467.

1. Ebersole *v.* Redding, 22 Ind. 232; Jefferson *v.* Fox, 1 Morr. (Iowa) 48.

But this applies only to negotiable paper. Merritt *v.* Cole, 9 Hun (N. Y.) 98.

And has no application to paper made payable "on or before" a certain day. Stoddard *v.* Burton, 41 Iowa 582.

The fact that an attorney has authority to receive payment of a note, does not authorize him to accept payment before the note is due. Smith *v.* Kidd, 68 N. Y. 130; s. c., 23 Am. Rep. 157. *Compare* Merritt *v.* Cole, 9 Hun (N. Y.) 98.

One J, in order to obtain a loan from M, procured S to execute to M his promissory note. Thereupon J and his wife executed to S their joint promissory note for the same amount, which latter note was secured by a mortgage on the wife's land. The joint note and mortgage, indorsed by S, were delivered to M, together with S's note to M, both payable in bank, and both given solely to procure said loan. Certain payments made to M by J were indorsed on the individual note of S, but not on the joint note of J and his wife. Afterward M surrendered to S the note executed by him, retaining only the joint note secured by the mortgage. This note he indorsed, and sold it and the mortgage for value before maturity to one who had no knowledge of the payments and who procured judgment on the note and foreclosure of the mortgage. J being insolvent and the mortgaged property having been sold to satisfy the judgment, J's wife brought an action against M to recover the amount of the payments which he had failed to credit on the joint note. *Held*, that she was entitled to recover. Moorman *v.* Shockney, 95 Ind. 88.

2. Johnson *v.* Willis, 7 Gray (Mass.) 164. See also Sunday.

3. King *v.* Finch, 60 Ind. 420; Gale *v.* Corey, 112 Ind. 39; McKinder *v.* Littlejohn, 4 Ired. (N. Car.) 198; Sanders *v.* Norton, 4 T. B. Mon. (Ky.) 464.

The maker of a note payable at an Ypsilanti bank deposited money with his own bankers in Ann Arbor, requesting them to get the note from Ypsilanti and pay it. The Ann Arbor bankers wrote to Ypsilanti for the note, which was sent to them indorsed "for collection." They did not, however, remit the money, and upon their failure shortly afterwards, the note was found among their collection paper, uncanceled. *Held*, that the note was not paid. It was the maker's "duty to see that the note was paid at maturity, and instead of paying it himself he intrusted the money to his own bankers, who never applied it. . . . We can see no plausible ground for holding the note paid." Sutherland *v.* First Nat. Bank, 31 Mich. 230.

Where payment was to be made in grain on a day fixed, but no place of delivery was designated, the parties may subsequently agree on a place, and this agreement will be binding, though the original contract was in writing and the place was fixed by parol. Miles *v.* Roberts, 34 N. H. 245.

2. Notes and other securities made payable at a particular bank are payable absolutely, and it is not necessary for the owner to present them at the place where they are made payable in order to hold the maker. And though the maker deposit funds with the bank to meet such paper, and it would have been paid had the holder presented it at such bank at maturity, the maker is still liable, notwithstanding the funds are lost through a subsequent failure of the bank.[1]

1. Adams *v.* Hackensack Imp. Commission, 44 N. J. L. 638; s. c., 43 Am. Rep. 406.

Mr. JUSTICE STORY states the reverse of this to be the law, both in England and in this country. That is, while the maker is not discharged by the mere failure of the holder to present the note at the designated place, yet, "if by such omission or neglect of presentment and demand, he has sustained any loss or injury, as if the bill or note were payable at a bank and the acceptor or maker had funds there at the time, which have been lost by the failure of the bank, then, and in such case, the acceptor or maker will be exonerated from liability to the extent of the loss or injury so sustained." Story on Prom. Notes, §§ 227, 228. Mr. Parsons and Mr. Daniels announce the same rule and *cite* Story as their authority. 1 Pars. Contr. 273; 1 Dan. Neg. Inst. (3rd ed.), § 643.

But in the case cited, and which has been recently decided by New Jersey courts, it is insisted that Mr. Story's view of the law is not correct, and that it is not supported by the authorities which he cites. The doctrine as announced in the text is there maintained in a well reasoned opinion. Adams *v.* Hackensack Imp. Commission, 44 N. J. L. 638; s. c., 43 Am. Rep. 406.

In Bank of U. S. *v.* Smith, 11 Wheat. (U. S.) 172, the Federal Supreme Court declines to pass upon the question, as it did not necessarily arise in that case. In Wallace *v.* McConnell, 13 Pet. (U. S.) 136, the question was whether, in suing on a note made payable at a particular place, it was necessary to aver a demand at that place. The American cases are reviewed at length, and the conclusion is reached that such an allegation is not necessary; that it is matter of defense on the part of the defendant to show that he was in attendance to pay or had the money there to pay, but that plaintiff was not there to receive it; "which defense *generally* will be in bar of damages only, and not in bar of the debt;" and it is said further in that case, though it is merely a *dictum*, that should the maker "not find his note or bill at the bank he can deposit his money to meet the note when presented, and should he be afterwards prosecuted he would be exonerated from all costs and damages upon proving such tender and deposit."

In a recent case in *New York*, the rule is declared to be as stated in the text, the court of appeals holding that if the bank fails with sufficient funds of the maker in its hands to pay the note, the maker is still liable. Indig *v.* Nat. City Bank, 80 N. Y. 100.

The courts of *Iowa* and of *South Carolina* have followed the rule laid down by Story. Lazier *v.* Horan, 55 Iowa 75; s. c., 39 Am. Rep. 167; Bank of Charleston *v.* Zorn, 14 S. Car. 444; s. c., 37 Am. Rep. 733.

But in a later case decided by the Supreme Court of Iowa, SEEVERS, J., says: "We do not feel disposed to extend the rule" of Lazier *v.* Horan, and intimates an approval of the case cited above from *New Jersey* (Adams *v.* Hackensack Imp. Commission, 44 N. J. L. 638); Callanan *v.* Williams, 71 Iowa 363; where it is held that if the note is payable at the office of one not a banker, the deposit of money by the maker at such office is not a payment, unless the money actually reaches the payee of the note.

If the note is made payable at a particular place, the maker is not in default until it is deposited at such place, where it is attempted to enforce a forfeiture on account of the nonpayment. Robinson *v.* Cheney, 17 Neb. 673; Ballard *v.* Cheney, 19 Neb. 58.

Where the note is payable at the office of one not a banker, and who is not the holder of the note, a deposit of the amount at such place is not a payment Callanan *v.* Williams, 71 Iowa 363.

Where it is agreed between the parties that a note may be paid at a certain store, and a part of the amount is left

IX. Evidence of Payment—1. Receipt of Payment.[1]—A receipt is only *prima facie* evidence of payment.[2]

2. Book entries made by the payor in his own account books are not evidence in his favor, unless brought to the knowledge of the creditor,[3] unless admissible on grounds common to all book entries.[4]

at the store by the maker, which act is ratified by the holder with full knowledge of all the circumstances, this will constitute a payment *pro tanto*, though the creditor never actually receives the money. Ingalls *v.* Fiske, 34 Me. 232.

1. See, for a full exposition of the law relative to receipts, RECEIPTS.

2. 1 Greenl. Evid. (13th ed.), § 305; 2 Greenl. Evid. (13th ed.), § 517; Whart. Evid., §§ 1064, 1130, 1365; Skaife *v.* Jackson, 5 Dowl. & Ry. 290; Field *v.* Bevil, 12 Ala. 608; Shropshire *v.* Long, 68 Iowa 537; St. Louis, Ft. Scott etc. R. Co. *v.* Davis, 35 Kan. 464; Nicholson *v.* Frazier, 4 Harr. (Del.) 206; McAllister *v.* Engle, 52 Mich. 56; Foster *v.* Beals, 21 N. Y. 247; Lambert *v.* Seely, 17 How. Pr. (N. Y.) 432; Megargel *v.* Megargel, 105 Pa. St. 475.

And a receipt is inadmissible as against a stranger to the transaction. Ferris *v.* Boxell, 34 Minn. 262; Ranney *v.* Hardy, 43 Ohio St. 157; Megargel *v.* Megargel, 105 Pa. St. 475.

Parol evidence of the payment is admissible, though a receipt was given; and it is not necessary to account for the absence of the receipt. 1 Whart. Evid., § 77; Southwick *v.* Hayden, 7 Cow. (N. Y.) 334.

Marking a note or bill "paid" by the officers of a bank in which it had been deposited for collection, or the marking of it canceled, or erasing the name of the maker, are not conclusive evidence of its actual payment; and it may be shown that these acts were done through mistake.

Irving Bank *v.* Wetherald, 34 Barb. (N. Y.) 323; s. c., affirmed, 36 N. Y. 335. Prince *v.* Oriental Bank Corporation, L. R., 3 App. 325; s. c., 24 Moak's Rep. 221; Warwick *v.* Rogers, 5 Man. & G. 340.

A bank was accustomed, before sending out for collection cheques on other banks, to stamp them on their face as paid. *Held*, that such stamp does not necessarily cancel the cheque, but it may be shown that the cheque is not in fact paid. Scott *v.* Betts, Hill & D. Supp. (N. Y.) 363.

The acknowledgment contained in a deed of the payment of the consideration money, is, in the absence of any evidence that it has not been in fact paid, sufficient evidence of its payment; Wood *v.* Chapin, 13 N. Y. 509; s. c., 67 Am. Dec. 62.

As to effect where the instrument is silent as to the payment of the consideration, see Solary *v.* Stultz, 22 Fla. 263. Such recitals may be rebutted by parol. Cravens *v.* Dewey, 13 Cal. 40.

3. Abbott's Trial Evid. 322, 809; Clark *v.* Wells, 5 Gray (Mass.) 69; Maine *v.* Harper, 4 Allen (Mass.) 115; Meyer *v.* Reichardt, 112 Mass. 108; Germania F. Ins. Co. *v.* Stone, 21 Fla. 555; Bonnett *v.* Glattfeldt, 120 Ill. 166; Brannin *v.* Foree, 12 B. Mon. (Ky.) 506; Hess's Appeal, 112 Pa. St. 168; Manion Blacksmith and Wrecking Co. *v.* Carreras, 19 Mo. App. 162; Whitehouse *v.* Bank of Cooperstown, 48 N. Y. 239; Himes *v.* Barnitz, 8 Watts (Pa.) 39; Hess's Appeal, 112 Pa. St. 168.

But where the creditor is a witness in his own behalf the entries in his books may be read in evidence. Bonnett *v.* Glattfeldt, 120 Ill. 166.

In an action by a mine foreman to recover from the owners money advanced by him to pay for labor, the time-account of the laborers whom he has paid, and the receipts given him by such laborers, are admissible. Martin *v.* Victor, Mill & Min. Co., 19 Nev. 180.

4. See article on BOOKS AS EVIDENCE, vol. 2, p. 467; 1 Greenl. Evid., §§ 117, 118; 1 Smith's Lead Cs. (7th am. ed.) 552. *Compare* Veith *v.* Haage, 8 Iowa, 163; Young *v.* Jones, 8 Iowa 219. The entries must be made by the party himself in the course of his business, or by the person whose duty it was to make them. Tate on Evid., 276; Pitman *v.* Maddox, 2 Salk. 690; Ld. Raym. 732; Glynn *v.* Bank, 2 Ves. 40; Lefebure *v.* Worden, 2 Ves. 54; Merrill *v.* Ithaca etc. R. Co., 16 Wend. (N. Y.) 586; 30 Am. Dec. s. c., 130; Sterret *v.* Bull, 1 Binn. (Pa.) 234. *Compare* Cummings *v.* Nichols, 13 N. H. 420; s. c., 38 Am. Dec. 501.

Entries in the creditor's books, showing payment in full of an account due him, are *prima facie* evidence against him.[1]

3. **The burden of proving** payment is on the party pleading it;[2] but may be proved by circumstances.[3]

The form in which the account is kept or the entries made is not of essential importance. Smith *v.* Smith, 4 Harr. (Del.) 532; Hall *v.* Field, 4 Harr. (Del.) 533, note; Taylor *v.* Tucker, 1 Ga. 231, where the entries were made on scraps of paper (*compare* Barber *v.* Bennett, 58 Vt. 476;) s. c., 56 Am. Rep. 565; Hall *v.* Glidden, 39 Me. 445; Landis *v.* Turner, 14 Cal. 573, where they were made on a slate; Rowland *v.* Burton, 2 Harr. (Del.) 288, when a notched stick was used; Miller *v.* Shay, 145 Mass. 162, where the entries were mere marks in a memorandum book. But a pocket memorandum book has been excluded. Richardson *v.* Emery, 23 N. H. 220; Thayer *v.* Deen, 2 Hill (S. Car.) 677. And any mode other than regular books is not looked upon with favor. Jones *v.* Jones, 21 N. H. 19; Hall *v.* Glidden, 39 Me. 445; Faxon *v.* Hollis, 13 Mass. 428; Matties *v.* Robinson, 8 Met.(Mass.) 269; s. c., 41 Am. Dec. 505.

There must have been a course of dealing between the parties. Corning *v.* Ashley, 4 Den. (N. Y.) 354.

1. Guest *v.* Burlington Opera House Co., 74 Iowa 457. See Beaver *v.* Taylor, 1 Wall. (U. S.) 637; Reynolds *v.* Sumner (Ill. 1888), 14 N. E. Rep. 661. And compare Libbey *v.* Brown, 78 Me. 492; Oberg *v.* Breen, 50 N. J. L. 145.

But where both the creditor and the person to whom the payments are credited testify that the account was not paid, and the action is against another party, the question of payment should be left to the jury. Guest *v.* Burlington Opera House Co., 74 Iowa 457.

2. 2 Greenl. Evid., § 516; Shulman *v.* Brantley, 50 Ala. 81; Adams *v.* Field, 25 Mich. 16; Atwood *v.* Cornwall, 25 Mich. 142; Star Wagon Co. *v.* Matthiessen, 3 Dak. 233; Van Buskirk *v.* Chandler, 18 Neb. 584; Tootle *v.* Maben, 21 Neb. 617; Baldwin *v.* Clock, 78 Mich. 201; Bell's Appeal, 122 Pa. St. 486; Wingett's Appeal, 122 Pa. St. 486; Snodgrass *v.* Caldwell (Ala. 1890), 7 So. Rep. 834; Stokes *v.* Taylor (N. Car. 1887), 12 S. E. Rep. 510; Hutchins *v.* Hamilton, 34 Tex. 290; Irvin *v.* Gernon, 18 La. Ann. 288; Winter *v.* Simonton, 3 Cranch (C. C.) 104; Edmonds *v.* Edmonds, 1 Ala. 401; McLendon *v.* Hamblin, 34 Ala. 86; Caulfield *v.* Sanders, 17 Cal. 569; Powel *v.* Swan, 5 Dana (Ky.) 1; Witherell *v.* Swan, 32 Me. 247; Yarnell *v.* Anderson, 14 Mo. 619; Buzzell *v.* Snell, 25 N. H. 474; Smith *v.* Burnet, 17 N. J. Eq. 40; McKinney *v.* Slack, 19 N. J. Eq. 164; Lovelock *v.* Gregg (Colo. 1890), 23 Pac. Rep. 86; Gutterman *v.* Schroeder, 40 Kan. 507; Doolittle *v.* Gavigan, 74 Mich. 11; Zachary *v.* Phillips, 101 N. Car. 571; Hussey *v.* Culver (Supreme Ct.), 6 N. Y. Supp. 466; Rogers *v.* Priest, 74 Wis. 538.

Where the purchase money of land was payable in instalments and the legal title is retained by the vendor, the burden of proof is on the purchaser to show payment. McCurdy *v.* Middleton, 82 Ala. 131.

The fact that since the date of the note sued on the payee has received from the maker checks to an amount sufficient to extinguish the note, does not of itself establish the payment of the particular note, nor does it shift the burden of proof. Smith's Appeal, 52 Mich. 415.

3. Declarations of the creditor, or of his agent, that the debt is discharged are *prima facie* evidence of payment. State Bank *v.* Wilson, 1 Dev. L. (N. Car.) 484. And an admission of payment in full is competent, though the specific payments as shown by the other evidence are less than the debt. Henderson *v.* Moore, 5 Cranch (U. S.) 11. Evidence that the money was sent by mail is admissible, and if strengthened by corroborating circumstances becomes *prima facie* evidence of payment. Waydell *v.* Velie, 1 Bradf. (N. Y.) 277.

Where plaintiff had, some eighteen months before suit brought, received from the defendant accounts and claims for the purpose of collecting them and applying the proceeds on the note sued on, evidence of this fact is relevant on a plea of payment. Cuthbert *v.* Newell, 7 Ala. 457.

In a suit against a maker of a note he offered in evidence to show payment a check on a bank, signed by his wife, in favor of the plaintiff and indorsed by the latter. *Held*, to be admissible, and, in the absence of proof of any other transaction to which the check could be applied, to be evidence of payment of the note. Murphy *v.* Breck, 33 Pa. St. 235. To same effect, Mountford *v.* Harper, 16 Mees. & W. 825; 16 L. J. Exch. 182.

The fact that the creditor having no money, called upon the debtor and came away with money in his possession which he said he got from the debtor, is evidence of payment. Whisler *v.* Drake, 35 Iowa 103. But evidence that the debtor borrowed money for the ostensible purpose of paying is not admissible. Reed *v.* Pierson, 3 N. J. L. 681. *Compare* Burlen *v.* Hubbell, 1 Thomp. & C. (N. Y.) 235.

An indorsement on a note or bond made by the payee or obligee without the privity of the maker or obligor, is inadmissible as evidenee of payment in favor of the party making it, unless it be shown that it was made at a time when it would be against the interest of the party making it. Roseboom *v.* Billington, 17 Johns. (N. Y.) 182. And see Walker *v.* Wykoff, 14 Ala. 560; Marshall *v.* Daniels, 18 N. H. 364. *Compare* Morris *v.* Morris, 5 Mich. 171.

Where a testator had promised a certain sum to one named as a legatee, and an additional sum as interest, the fact that the legacy was of a sum equal to the principal is not evidence to prove satisfaction thereof. Parker *v.* Coburn, 10 Allen (Mass.) 82. See Strong *v.* Williams, 12 Mass. 390; s. c., 7 Am. Dec. 81.

A party holding three notes credited a partial payment on the first note. He afterwards received a sum amounting to the exact balance due on that note, and it appeared that the note was delivered to the maker. The holder subsequently received a further sum more than sufficient to pay the second note, which he applied to the payment of that note, crediting the surplus on the third note. *Held*, that the evidence was sufficient to show that the first note had been fully paid. Lindsay *v.* McCormick, 82 Va. 479.

A check drawn by the defendant in favor of the creditor *or bearer*, with the bank's canceling mark upon it and produced by the debtor, is no evidence of a payment. Lowe *v.* McClerg, 3 Cranch (C. C.) 254.

A party indebted to his step-mother, repeatedly offered to pay her the debt and she refused to receive it, declaring that she never intended to collect it from him, as he had made the money for her, and that if not paid in her lifetime it was to be his. The debt was not paid in her lifetime. *Held*, that the above facts constituted evidence only of an unexecuted intention to discharge the debt, and that the debt was not in fact extinguished. McGuire *v.* Adams, 8 Pa.St. 286.

Defendants were sued as obligors in a bond and pleaded payment. In support of the plea they introduced evidence tending to show that one of them placed in the hands of a third person money sufficient to pay the debt, and the latter informed plaintiff that he had the money to pay off the bond; that plaintiff refused to receive the money, saying that he owed the other obligor more money, though he did not state that the debt was settled. *Held*, that this was not sufficient to prove payment. Green *v.* Buckner, 6 Leigh (Va.) 82.

Where real estate was sold and notes secured by mortgage given for the purchase money, and the property transferred and laid off in lots and a portion resold, bonds and notes being taken for the latter sales; and where a suit for foreclosure was brought and payment set up as a defense, it was proper, the principal owner of the property being dead, to permit the introduction in evidence of a letter from the father of the deceased owner to the plaintiff, inclosing a receipt from plaintiff's attorney to the deceased for a sum of money in excess of the mortgage debt, said sum having been paid at the request of the plaintiff, the letter connecting the payment with the mortgage, and being admitted with other evidence in relation to the transactions of the parties. Cook *v.* Woodruff, 97 Ind. 134.

The final settlement of a guardian showing a sum due the ward, together with an order of the court approving the settlement and discharging the guardian, does not constitute evidence of the payment of the money to the ward. Naugle *v.* State, 101 Ind. 284.

Where an indorsement on a note was shown, and a separate receipt of a different date but of a like amount signed by plaintiff's agent, this is not

X. Presumption of Payment—1. From Circumstances.—A presumption of payment may arise from the circumstances of the case, in the absence of positive evidence either way, and such presumption is a question for the jury.[1] The presumption is not

necessarily proof of two different payments. Doty *v.* Janes, 28 Wis. 319.

The mother of Mrs. H and defendant, who were her only children, at some period before her death gave to Mrs. H a considerable amount of property with the understanding that she would thereafter make her home with Mrs. H. After some time had elapsed, she became dissatisfied, and changed her home to defendant's home. About a year after the change, defendant and her mother had an accounting, though it does not appear whether the same was in full, and thereupon defendant executed to her mother a note and mortgage. The mother continued to live with defendant until her death. During that time she employed an attorney to draw her will, and instructed him that defendant was then paying the note by boarding her, the testatrix, and that at her death the note was to be given up and the mortgage canceled. The will was drawn as instructed and duly executed, but Mrs. H afterwards, to use her own language, *compelled* her mother to destroy it. *Held*, that this was evidence sufficient to establish a part payment of the note. Hughes *v.* Walker, 14 Oregon 481.

In the following cases the evidence was held to be sufficient to prove payment: Kuder *v.* Twidale, 20 Neb. 390; Hammond *v.* Jewett, 22 Neb. 363.

For various questions relating to the competency and weight of evidence of payment in particular cases, see Pickle *v.* People's Nat. Bank, 88 Tenn. 380; Melvin *v.* Stevens, 84 N. Car. 78; Mason *v.* Marshall, 39 Kan. 424; Oldham *v.* Henderson, 4 Mo. 295; Appeal of Schuey, 130 Pa. St. 16; Applegate *v.*.Baxley, 93 Ind. 147; Baughan *v.* Brown, 122 Ind. 115; Pryor *v.* Wood, 31 Pa. St. 142; Maddox *v.* Bramlett (Ga. 1889), 11 S. E. Rep. 128; McNail *v.* Welch, 26 Ill. App. 482; McRae *v.* McDonald, 57 Ala. 423; Amos *v.* Flournoy, 80 Ga. 771; Block *v.* Cross, 36 Miss. 549; Amis *v.* Merchants' Ins. Co., 2 La. Ann. 594; Doolittle *v.* Gavagan, 74 Mich. 11; Crain *v.* Barnes, 1 Md. Ch. 151; Crowe *v.* Colbeth, 63 Wis. 643; Daniels *v.* Moses, 12 S. Car. 130; Cushman *v.* Hall, 28 Vt. 656; Dews *v.* Pickard, R. M. Charlt. (Ga.) 479; Carson *v.* Lineburger, 70 N. Car. 173; Swan *v.* Brewster, 1 N. Y. Supp. 584; Succession of Moreira, 16 La. Ann. 368; Tolliaferro *v.* Ives, 51 Ill. 247; Elston *v.* Kennicott, 52 Ill. 272; Stevens *v.* Gainesville Nat. Bank, 62 Tex. 499; Smith *v.* Smith, 6 N. Y. Supp. 90; Smith *v.* Camp (Ga. 1889), 10 S. E. Rep. 539; Griffin *v.* Petty, 101 N. Car. 380; Green *v.* Buckner, 6 Leigh (Va.) 82; Grimmell *v.* Warner, 21 Iowa 11; Just *v.* Porter, 64 Mich. 565; Woods *v.* Hamilton, 39 Kan. 69; Bradley *v.* Long, 2 Strobh. (S. Car.) 160; Brown *v.* Cahalin, 3 Oregon 45; Brown *v.* Sadler, 16 La. Ann. 206; Broward *v.* Doggett, 2 Fla. 49; Scott *v.* Scott, 36 Ga. 484; Rogers *v.* Priest, 74 Wis. 538; King *v.* Bush, 36 Ill. 142; Koltze *v.* Messenbrink, 74 Iowa 242; Reed *v.* Rice, 25 Vt. 171; Holladay *v.* Littlepage, 2 Munf. (Va.) 316; Hussey *v.* Culver (Supreme Ct.), 6 N. Y. Supp. 466; Holcomb *v.* Campbell, 118 N. Y. 46; Goldsmid *v.* Lewis Co. Bank, 7 Barb. (N. Y.) 427; Filer *v.* Peebles, 8 N. H. 226; Flick *v.* Fridley, 83 Va. 777; Meyer *v.* Reichardt, 112 Mass. 108; Watts *v.* Shewell, 31 Ohio St. 331; Fuller *v.* Smith, 5 Jones Eq. (N. Car.) 192; Carr *v.* Beck, 51 Pa. St. 269; Church *v.* Fagin, 43 Mo. 123; Smith *v.* Camp, 84 Ga. 117; McCurdy *v.* Middleton (Ala. 1890), 7 So. Rep. 655; Lindsey *v.* Le Mars Bank, 79 Iowa 607; Joiner *v.* Enos, 23 Ill. App. 224; Selser's Assigned Estate, 7 Pa. Co. Ct. Rep. 417; Grant *v.* Gooch, 105 N. Car. 278; Gray *v.* Herman, 75 Wis. 453; Allison *v.* McClun, 40 Kan. 525; Gafford *v.* American Mortgage etc. Co., 77 Iowa 736; McNail *v.* Welch, 26 Ill. App. 482; Smith *v.* Smith, 6 N. Y. Supp. 90; Leith *v.* Carter, 83 Va. 889; Perkins *v.* Hawkins, 9 Gratt. (Va.) 649; Lovelock *v.* Gregg (Colo. 1890), 23 Pac. Rep. 86.

1. 2 Greenl. Evid. (13th ed.), § 527; 2 Whart. Evid., §§ 1362, 1363; Abbott's Trial Evid., 809, 810; Williams *v.* Peal, 4 Dev. & B. (N. Car.) 471; Smith *v.* Nevin, 31 Pa. St. 238; Shaw *v.* Bowie, 3 Brev. (S. Car.) 409; Stephens

v. Stephens, 1 McCord (S. Car.) 87.

Where notes were turned over to the creditor by the debtor, his receipt and retention of them for three or four years, whether they were collected or collectible or not, raises the presumption that they were taken in payment. Hapgood Plow Co. *v.* Martin, 16 Neb. 27. See, to same effect, Day *v.* Clarke, 1 A. K. Marsh. (Ky.) 521.

Slight proofs of payment do not raise a presumption of payment, except where there is such confidential relation between the parties as will call into exercise that artificial presumption which courts resort to in such cases to aid and help out defective proof. Vaughan *v.* Lewellyn, 94 N. Car. 472. See Atkins *v.* Withers, 94 N. Car. 581.

The debtor may show as presumptive evidence of payment that after the time when the debt became due the creditor gave to him an obligation or security for the payment of money. De Freest *v.* Bloomingdale, 5 Den. (N. Y.) 304; Duguid *v.* Ogilvie, 3 E. D. Smith (N. Y.) 527; s. c., 1 Abb. Pr. (N. Y.) 145; Chewsing *v.* Proctor, 2 McCord (S. Car.) 11, 15; Callaway *v.* Hearn, 1 Houst. (Del.) 607.

But no presumption of payment arises from the fact that the debtor, in enumerating his debts, made no mention of the one in question. Abercrombie *v.* Sheldon, 8 Allen (Mass.) 532.

Nor, except as bearing on a presumption arising from lapse of time, can it be shown that the debtor was in the habit of paying his debts promptly. Abercrombie *v.* Sheldon, 8 Allen (Mass.) 532. Or was solvent or wealthy. Church *v.* Fagin, 43 Mo. 123; Veazie *v.* Hosmer, 11 Gray (Mass.) 396; Hilton *v.* Scarborough, 5 Gray (Mass.) 422. See Beach *v.* Allen, 7 Hun (N. Y.) 441. And *compare* Orr *v.* Jackson, 1 Ill. App. 439.

The payment of a subsequent debt or instalment of a debt, raises some presumption that prior debts have been paid. Mathews *v.* Light, 40 Me. 394; Attleborough *v.* Middleborough, 10 Pick (Mass.) 378; Patterson *v.* O'Hara, 2 E. D. Smith (N. Y.) 58; Decker *v.* Livingston, 15 Johns. (N. Y.) 479. *Compare* Sennett *v.* Johnson, 9 Pa. St. 335; Ham *v.* Barret, 28 Mo. 388; Bougher *v.* Kimball, 30 Mo. 193.

Where it is shown that the debtor has paid interest after the day of payment, this raises a strong presumption that the debt has not been paid. 3 Phil. Evid. 485.

Where testator had given a bond for certain services rendered, the fact that he names the obligee in the bond as one of his legatees does not raise the presumption that the legacy was intended as a payment of the bond, unless it is shown that the legacy was given in consideration of the same services. Strong *v.* Williams, 12 Mass. 391; s. c., 7 Am. Dec. 81.

The signature of the maker of a promissory note was torn off, but it still remained in the possession of the payee. *Held*, not to raise a presumption of payment. Powell *v.* Swan, 5 Dana (Ky.) 1.

An indorsement on a note of part payment is presumptive evidence of such payment. Morris *v.* Morris, 5 Mich. 171. Though it is made with pencil. Greenough *v.* Taylor, 17 Ill. 602. *Compare* Walker *v.* Wykoff, 14 Ala. 560; Marshall *v.* Daniels, 18 N. H. 364; Roseboom *v.* Billington, 17 Johns. (N. Y.) 182.

In an action against the payee of a note, the note being offered in evidence by the plaintiff, sundry indorsements of payments appeared thereon, which were not shown to be in the handwriting of the payee. *Held*, that these indorsements were *prima facie* made by the plaintiff, and were presumptive evidence that the payments had been made. Brown *v.* Gooden, 16 Ind. 444.

Where the same person is administrator of the estates of a debtor and creditor, and a decree is rendered against him as administrator of the former in favor of himself as administrator of the latter, which is void for want of jurisdiction in the court to make it, there is no presumption in his favor or in favor of a surety on his bond that he has paid or transferred the funds from the debtor to the creditor estate. Eatman *v.* Eastman, 82 Ala. 223.

A performed work under three contracts with the State. Under the first he had been largely overpaid, while on the other two there were amounts still due, amounting in the aggregate to less than the overpayment on the first contract. *Held*, that such overpayment will be presumed to have been applied by the creditor in payment of the other

conclusive, and may be rebutted by circumstances.[1]

2. Payment or Loan.—The mere delivery of money by one party to another, unexplained, is presumptive evidence of payment of an antecedent debt, and not of a loan.[2]

obligations as they accrued. Says DANFORTH, J.: "The money received by the claimants in overpayment on one contract must be deemed to have been money in their hands for the use of the State, the State entitled to its application, and the claimants be presumed to have applied it in payment of the other obligation the moment it accrued. The existence of means of payment in the hands of the creditor, and the lapse of time, are conclusive evidence of the pre-existing fact of an actual discharge of the accruing debt, or are of themselves facts which require a court of equity to adjudge such application to have been made. Equity requires that one demand should extinguish the other by deducting the less from the greater. Belden *v.* State, 103 N. Y. 1.

Where a broker renders accounts to his principal in which no mention is made of a claim for which the principal, jointly with others, was liable, the presumption is raised that the joint debt had been paid, which presumption is subject to explanation. Smith *v.* Tucker, 2 E. D. Smith (N. Y.) 193.

Where one party had paid a note at a bank as surety for another, and afterwards two different settlements were had between the parties, it will be presumed that the note was included in one or the other of the settlements. Ward *v.* Grayson, 9 Dana (Ky.) 280.

To same effect as to book account, Bushee *v*, Allen, 31 Vt. 631.

The following additional cases may be referred to as raising questions of presumption of payment under particular circumstances: M'Rae *v.* Boast, 3 Rand. (Va.) 481; Morrison *v.* Collins (Pa.), 17 Atl. Rep. 753; Mechanics' Bank *v.* Wright, 53 Mo. 153; Merrick *v.* Hulbert, 17 Ill. App. 90; *Re* Oakley, 2 Edw. Ch. (N. Y.) 478; Norvell *v.* Little, 79 Va. 141; Neal *v.* Brainerd, 24 Me. 115; Tunstall *v.* Withers, 76 Va. 892; Turner *v.* Turner, 79 Cal. 565; Tyler *v.* Heidorn. 46 Barb. (N.Y.) 439; Reynolds *v.* Richards, 14 Pa. St. 205; Calwell *v.* Prindle, 19 W. Va. 604; Rodman *v.* Hoops, 1 Dall. (U. S.) 85; Mills *v.* Hyde, 19 Vt. 59; s. c., 46 Am. Dec. 177; Morrison *v.* Collins, 127 Pa. St. 28; Scott *v.* Isaacs, 85 Va. 712; Clark *v.* Bogardus, 2 Edw. Ch. (N. Y.) 387.

As to force of circumstances in connection with the lapse of time, see *infra*, this title, ***Payment or Loan.***

1. 2 Whart. Evid., § 1364; Foulk *v.* Brown, 2 Watts (Pa.) 209; Strohm's Appeal, 23 Pa. St. 351; Bushee *v.* Allen, 3 Vt. 631.

As by showing the debtor's poverty. Farmers' Bank *v.* Leonard, 4 Harr. (Del.) 536. Circumstances making it inconvenient to pay or receive the debt. McClellan *v.* Crofton, 6 Me. 307; Crooker *v.* Crooker, 49 Me. 416; Eustace *v.* Gaskins, 1 Wash. (Va.) 188.

2. 1 Greenl. Evid. (13 ed.), § 38; Sayles *v.* Olmstead, 66 Barb. (N. Y.) 590; Duguid *v.* Ogilvie, 3 E. D. Smith (N. Y.) 527; Poucher *v.* Scott, 98 N. Y. 422; Hansen *v.* Kirtley, 11 Iowa 565; Rohrbracker *v.* Schilling, 12 La. Ann. 17; Fletcher *v.* Manning, 12 Mees. & W. 571; 13 L. J. Exch. 150.

Where the debtor draws a check in favor of his creditor, and the creditor receives the money thereon, the presumption is that it was in payment of the debt. Masser *v.* Bowen, 29 Pa. St. 128; s. c., 72 Am. Dec. 619.

Where a father who is indebted to his children conveys to them property of a greater value than the amount of the indebtedness, the debt will, in the absence of proof of a contrary intention, be presumed to have been paid thereby. Kelley *v.* Kelley, 6 Rand. (Va.) 176; s. c., 18 Am. Dec. 710.

Compare Perit *v.* Pittfield, 5 Rawle (Pa.) 166.

While the mere delivery of money by the payer to the holder of a note is presumptive evidence of payment, this presumption may be rebutted by circumstances. Dougherty *v.* Deeney, 45 Iowa 443.

The payee of a check is not presumed to have received payment where it is not shown to have been indorsed. The question of payment is for the jury. Smith's Appeal, 52 Mich. 415.

A testator, some three months prior to his death, gave his check for $100 to defendant, who drew the money there-

3. From Possession of Instrument by Debtor.—A bill of exchange, promissory note, or order for the payment of money, found in the hands of the drawee or maker, is presumptive evidence of its payment.[1]

on. It appeared that the testator was a snug business man, substantially out of debt, and not a borrower of money. Defendant gave no proof that he had rendered any services to testator, or sold him any property for the $100, and at that time he owed interest in excess of that amount on his mortgage to the testator, and when told by the executor that he found the claim of $100 due from him to the estate, defendant made no reply. *Held*, that while resting upon the cheque alone the legal presumption would be that it was given in payment of a debt, the circumstances justified the finding that it was a loan. Stimson *v.* Vroman, 99 N. Y. 74.

1. 1 Greenl. Evid. (13th ed.), §§ 38, 527; Hill *v.* Gayle, 1 Ala. 275; Lipscomb *v.* DeLemos, 68 Ala. 592; Fedens *v.* Schumers, 112 Ill. 263; Callahan *v.* First Nat. Bank, 78 Ky. 604; s. c., 39 Am. Rep. 262; Levy *v.* Merrill, 52 How. Pr. (N. Y.) 360; Skannel *v.* Taylor, 12 La. Ann. 773; Succession of Penny, 14 La. Ann. 190; Chandler *v.* Davis, 47 N. H. 462; Blount *v.* Starkey, 1 Tayl. (N. Car.) 110; Close *v.* Fields, 2 Tex. 232; s. c., 9 Tex. 422; s. c., 13 Tex. 623; Hillyard *v.* Crabtree, 11 Tex. 264; s. c., 62 Am. Dec. 475; Hays *v.* Samuels, 55 Tex. 560.

A due bill found among the papers of a deceased administrator, signed by him individually and payable to one of the distributees of the estate, is not admissible against the payee as showing a settlement between her and the administrator on account of her distributive interest in the estate, in the absence of evidence tending to show that the payee ever had possession of it or agreed to accept it. Hart *v.* Kendall, 82 Ala. 144.

The surrender of a note is *prima facie* evidence of its payment. Smith *v.* Harper, 5 Cal. 329.

So the production of a note secured by mortgage, on the hearing of a bill to foreclose, raises the presumption that it has not been paid, and is still the property of the plaintiff. Stiger *v.* Bent, 111 Ill. 328. *Compare* Thorp *v.* Feltz, 6 B. Mon. (Ky.) 6.

The possession by the drawer of a canceled bank cheque, who testifies that on the day of its date he made and delivered it to the drawer in payment of a debt, is *prima facie* evidence of the payment of the amount named in the cheque. Peavy *v.* Hovey, 16 Neb. 416.

The cancellation of a cheque upon a bank, and its retention by the bank, is evidence of its payment. Conway *v.* Case, 22 Ill. 127.

The fact that the payee of a note delivered it to the maker is not conclusive evidence of payment of the note, but is subject to explanation. Fellows *v.* Kress, 5 Blackf. (Ind.) 536.

As to what circumstances are sufficient to rebut the presumption, see Sutphen *v.* Cushman, 35 Ill. 186.

Evidence is admissible that another note of the same tenor has been substituted for the one in the maker's possession. Potts *v.* Coleman, 67 Ala. 221.

Mere possession of a policy of insurance, without anything more, is not evidence that the premium has been paid. Millick *v.* Peterson, 2 Wash. (U. S.) 31.

Possession by one of two joint makers raises the presumption. Chandler *v.* Davis, 47 N. H. 462.

An indorsement upon a promissory note to the effect that it was endorsed by the payee to the surety for value received, together with the possession of the note by the surety, raises the presumption, in the absence of controverting evidence, that the surety had paid the note and was its owner. Waldrip *v.* Black, 74 Cal. 409.

Where a written instrument is for an expressed consideration, but is silent as to whether or not the consideration has been paid, the presumption of law is that it was paid at the time of delivery of the instrument; but this presumption is subject to be rebutted. Solary *v.* Stultz, 22 Fla. 263.

Where a sheriff brought suit on his deputy's bond, alleging it to be lost, and the deputy denied any indebtedness, and exhibited the bond in answer, the mere possession of the bond, unaccounted for was held insufficient to prove an extinguishment thereof, there being evidence tending to show that

4. Same Party Debtor and Creditor.—Where the same party is a debtor in his individual capacity and a creditor in a representative capacity the presumption of payment will vary according to the circumstances.[1]

5. From Lapse of Time.—After twenty years a presumption of payment arises as to every instrument, whether under seal or otherwise,[2] and a jury may infer payment from circumstances,

at the last settlement between the parties there was a balance due from the deputy, and the bond was not given up. Graves *v.* Wood, 3 B. Mon. (Ky.) 34.

And see further on this head: Porter *v.* Nelson, 121 Pa. St. 628; Carroll *v.* Bowie, 7 Gill. (Md.) 34; Bracken *v.* Miller, 4 W. & S. (Pa.) 102; Turner *v.* Turner, 80 Cal. 141.

1. Winship *v.* Bass, 12 Mass. 199, 205. "When an administrator becomes a purchaser of real estate sold by himself as such, he occupies antagonistic relations — of purchaser claiming an adverse right, and of administrator representing the heirs as to the collection and distribution of the purchase money. Having the right to receive payment as administrator, and being under obligation to pay as such purchaser, presumed payment arises when the purchase money matures, so far as to render him chargeable therewith in the settlement of his administrator's accounts, but not for the purpose of entitling him to a conveyance of title. So long as he continues administrator, and the purchase money is unaccounted for, there is no payment such as is required by the statute, to authorize the court to order a conveyance of title. When the purchase money becomes due, the heirs have the right to elect whether they will treat it as paid and charge the administrator, or as unpaid, and resort to the law to enforce its payment." Ligon *v.* Ligon, 84 Ala. 555.

Where an administrator is a creditor of the estate, his debt will be presumed to have been paid whenever he receives assets which he can lawfully apply to the payment of debts. And if he receives Confederate currency in payment of debts due the estate, he must apply the same currency in discharge of his own debt. Dickie *v.* Dickie, 80 Ala. 57; compare Trimble *v.* Fariss, 78 Ala. 260.

Where an executor recovers judgment against a debtor of the estate, and the latter becomes administrator *de bonis non* after the death of the executor, the judgment will be considered as paid and extinguished, and the amount thereof as assets in the hands of the administrator. Lane *v.* Westmoreland, 79 Ala. 372; Donnan *v.* Watts, 22 S. Car. 430.

Where one and the same person is creditor in one representative capacity and debtor in another, and it becomes his legal duty to appropriate funds received in the latter capacity to claims held in the former, it will be presumed that such appropriation was made. Ruffin *v.* Harrison, 81 N. Car. 208; s. c., 86 N. Car. 190.

2. 2 Bouv. Law Dict.; Perry on Trusts, § 869; 3 Phil. Evid. 485; 2 Whart. Evid. § 1360; Colsell *v.* Budd 1 Camp. 2; Dunlop *v.* Ball, 2 Cranch (U. S.) 180; Higginson *v.* Mein, 4 Cranch (U. S.) 420; Kingsland *v.* Roberts, 2 Paige (N. Y.) 193; Jackson *v.* Hotchkiss, 6 Cow. (N. Y.) 401; Tilghman *v.* Fisher, 9 Watts. (Pa.) 441; Cope *v.* Humphreys, 14 S. & R. (Pa.) 15; Lash *v.* Von Neida, 109 Pa. St. 207; Peters' Appeal, 106 Pa. St. 340; King *v.* Coulter, 2 Grant's Cas. (Pa.) 77; Blake *v.* Quash, 3 McCord (S. Car.) 340; Sartor *v.* Beaty, 25 S. Car. 293; McKinlay *v.* Gaddy, 26 S. Car. 573; Moore *v.* Pogne, 1 Duv. (Ky.) 327; Davenport *v.* Labaure, 5 La. Ann. 140; Copley *v.* Edwards, 5 La. Ann. 647; Wooten *v.* Harrison, 9 La. Ann. 234.

O'Brien *v.* Coulter, 2 Blackf. (Ind.) 421; Fleming *v.* Emory, 5 Harr. (Del.) 46; Clark *v.* Clemen, 33 N. H. 563; Milledge *v.* Gardner, 33 Ga. 397; Barned *v.* Barned. 21 N. J. Eq. 245; Atkinson *v.* Dance, 9 Yerg. (Tenn.) 424; s. c., 30 Am. Dec. 422; Young *v.* Price, 2 Munf. (Va.) 534; Wells *v.* Washington, 6 Munf. (Va.) 534; Sweetser *v.* Lowell, 33 Me. 446. And the rule applies not only to ordinary bonds and specialties. Cottle *v.* Payne, 3 Day (Conn.) 289; Durham *v.* Greenly, 2 Harr. (Del.) 124; Bartlett *v.* Bartlett, 9 N. H. 398; Shepherd's Appeal, 2 Grant. Cas. (Pa.) 402; Levy *v.* Hampton, 1 McCord (S. Car.) 145; Haskell *v.* Keen,

2 Nott & M. (S. Car.) 160; Tinsley *v.* Anderson, 3 Call (Va.) 329. But also to a recognizance entered into in court. Ankeny *v.* Penrose, 18 Pa. St. 190. The presumption applies to a contract for the purchase of land.. McCormick *v.* Evans, 33 Ill. 327; Morrison *v.* Funk, 23 Pa. St. 421. And to money due for taxes. Dalton *v.* Bethleham, 20 N. H. 505; Colebrook *v.* Stewartson, 28 N. H. 75; Andover *v.* Merrimack, 37 N. H. 437. And to money due a legatee. Hayes *v.* Whitall, 13 N. J. Eq. 241; Okeson's Appeal, 2 Grant's Cas. (Pa.) 303. *Compare* Strohm's Appeal, 23 Pa. St. 351.

A church claimed two legacies, as to the right to which there was some doubt. Upon the church executing a bond payable in three years, secured by mortgage, and which was delivered as an indemnity to the executors, the latter paid over the amount of the legacies. Twenty-six years afterward the residuary legatee sought to enforce the mortgage. *Held*, that his right was barred by lapse of time, though the church had in fact no right to the legacies. Newcomb *v.* St. Peter's Church, 2 Sandf. Ch. (N. Y.) 636.

Payment presumed after thirty years. O'Brien *v.* Holland, 3 Blackf. (Ind.) 490; Frane *v.* Kenny, 2 A. K. Marsh. (Ky.) 145; s. c., 12 Am. Dec. 367; irrespective of probabilities in fact. Downs *v.* Sooy, 28 N. J. Eq. 55. See Arden *v.* Arden, 1 Johns. Ch. (N. Y.) 313.

The twenty year presumption applies in *Missouri* to bonds executed prior to 1835, and to judgments, the common law presumption not being affected by the statute. Smith *v.* Benton, 15 Mo. 371; Clemens *v.* Wilkinson, 10 Mo. 97.

The common law presumption of payment applies only to cases where twenty years have elapsed after the right of action accrued. Updike *v.* Lane, 78 Va. 132. *Compare* Didlake *v.* Robb, 1 Woods (U. S.) 680.

The presumption of payment of a mortgage debt arising from possession and lapse of time was formerly resorted to for want of a statute of limitation. Lewis *v.* Schwenn, 93 Mo. 26. And courts of equity act in analogy to the statute of limitations. Therefore, if a bill be filed to foreclose a mortgage after the lapse of so great a time that complainant could not maintain an action at law for the recovery of the mortgaged premises, a court of equity will presume payment and satisfaction of the mortgage debt. McDonald *v.* Sims, 3 Ga. 383; Field *v.* Wilson, 6 B. Mon. (Ky.) 497; Martin *v.* Bowker, 19 Vt. 526.

But the presumption is not available to the owner of the equity of redemption to defeat a foreclosure, if the mortgagor has made payments upon the bond secured by the mortgage within twenty years before the commencement of foreclosure proceedings. New York L. Ins. & Trust Co. *v.* Covert, 3 Abb. App. Dec. (N. Y.) 350.

The presumption applies to rent reserved in a lease. Lyon *v.* Odell, 65 N. Y. 28. But a non-payment for more than twenty years does not raise the presumption that the covenant to pay rent has been released and discharged. Lynn *v.* Odell, 65 N. Y. 28.

When a note is payable on demand, a failure to present it for any time short of the statute of limitations will not raise a presumption that it has been paid. Smith's Appeal, 52 Mich. 415. See also Aultman *v.* Connor, 25 Ill. App. 654.

A presumption of payment does not arise from the fact that no interest has been paid for nineteen years. Boon *v.* Pierpont, 28 N. J. Eq. 7.

A bill for an accounting will not be sustained after a lapse of more than twenty years from the date of the transactions out of which the account arose, especially if no good cause is shown for the delay. Ellison *v.* Moffatt, 1 Johns. Ch. (N. Y.) 46; Kingsland *v.* Roberts, 2 Paige (N. Y.) 193.

Presumption of payment from lapse of time is as applicable to a case where payment in a specific mode is pleaded, as where it is pleaded generally. Manning *v.* Meredith, 69 Iowa 430.

Where the debt is payable by instalments and secured by a penal bond, the presumption applies to each instalment as it falls due. State *v.* Lobb, 3 Harr. (Del.) 421.

And the lapse of fourteen years after the payment of the last instalment upon a bond and mortgage may, in connection with other circumstances, raise the presumption that the bond has been paid. Bander *v.* Snyder, 5 Barb. (N. Y.) 63.

The presumption is available only as a shield, and can only be set up to defeat a right of action; it cannot be used for affirmative, aggressive action. Thus where complainant seeks to compel a conveyance of land upon an allegation that he has paid the purchase

though the lapse of time be shorter.[1] And the same rule

money, he cannot avail himself of this presumption to prove the payment. Morey *v.* Farmers' Loan and Trust Co., 14 N. Y. 302. As to distinction between presumption and limitation, see *infra*, this title, *Presumption of Payment.*

It seems that the presumption is always one for the jury. Lyon *v.* Guild, 5 Heisk. (Tenn.) 175; McBride *v.* Moore, Wright (Ohio) 542. *Compare* Winstanley *v.* Savage, 2 McCord Eq. (S. Car.) 435. And its effect is to shift the burden of proof. McQueen *v.* Fletcher, 4 Rich. Eq. (S. Car.) 152.

But from mere lapse of time short of the twenty years, without other circumstances, a jury is not at liberty to presume payment. Smithpeter *v.* Ison, 4 Rich. (S. Car.) 203; s. c., 53 Am. Dec. 732; Farrington *v.* King, 1 Bradf. (N. Y.) 182; Rogers *v.* Burns, 27 Pa. St. 525; Thomas *v.* Hunnicutt, 54 Ga. 337; Grafton Bank *v.* Doe, 19 Vt. 463; s. c., 47 Am. Dec. 697.

The revised statute of North Carolina of 1835 provided that presumption of payment or satisfaction on all judgments, contracts and agreements should arise within ten years after the right of action, or the same should accrue, under the same rules, regulations and restrictions as now exist at law in such cases. Rev. Stat. (1835) Ch. 65, § 18, p. 375.

This statute has received the construction of the supreme court of that State in Pearsall *v.* Houston, 3 Jones (N. Car.) 346; Spruill *v.* Davenport, 5 Ired. L. (N. Car.) 663; Johnson *v.* England, 4 Dev. & B. (N. Car.) 70; Campbell *v.* Brown, 86 N. Car. 376; s. c., 41 Am. Rep. 464; Lane *v.* Richardson, 79 N. Car. 159; Rogers *v.* Clements, 92 N. Car. 81; s. c., 98 N. Car. 180; Mull *v.* Walker, 100 N. Car. 46; Headen *v.* Womack, 88 N. Car. 468; Perry *v.* Jackson, 88 N. Car. 103; Houck *v.* Adams, 98 N. Car. 519.

But the revisions of 1875 and 1883 do not contain any similar provision, the statute of limitations alone applies.

And the courts of that State have held that the presumption of payment from lapse of time as to a bond executed in another State is governed by the law of North Carolina, and not that of the State in which the bond was executed Haws *v.* Cragie, 4 Jones (N. Car.) 394.

1. 3 Phil. Evid. 675; Rector *v.* Morehouse, 17 Ark. 131; Hughes *v.* Hughes, 54 Pa. St. 240; Brubaker *v.* Taylor, 76 Pa. St. 83; Peters' Appeal, 106 Pa. St. 340; Hess *v.* Frankinfield, 106 Pa. St. 440; Garnier *v.* Renner, 51 Ind. 372; Bander *v.* Snyder, 5 Barb. (N. Y.) 63; Baker *v.* Stonebraker, 36 Mo. 338; Perkins *v.* Kent, 1 Root (Conn.) 312; Milledge *v.* Gardner, 33 Ga. 397; Matthews *v.* Smith, 2 Dev. & B. (N. Car.) 287; Smithpeter *v.* Ison, 4 Rich. (S. Car.) 203; s. c., 53 Am. Dec. 732; Blanton *v.* Stephenson, 1 A. K. Marsh (Ky.) 570; Bailey *v.* Gould, Walker (Mich.) 478; Thompson *v.* Thompson, 2 Head, (Tenn.) 405; Gould *v.* White, 26 N. H. 178; Sadler *v.* Kennedy, 11 W. Va. 187; Criss *v.* Criss, 28 W. Va. 388.

The question is always one for the jury. Lyon *v.* Guild, 5 Heisk. (Tenn.) 175; Waters *v.* Waters, 1 Metc. (Ky.) 519.

"The presumption of payment from lapse of time is founded upon the rational ground that a person naturally desires to possess and enjoy his own, and that an unexplained neglect to enforce an alleged right for a long period casts suspicion upon the existence of the right itself. This presumption may be fortified or rebutted by circumstances. Bean *v.* Tonnele, 94 N. Y. 381; s. c., 46 Am. Rep. 153.

Slight circumstances may go to the jury when sixteen years have elapsed. Blackburn *v.* Squib, Peck (Tenn.) 60.

And, if unexplained, the lapse of sixteen years raises the presumption of payment of a judgment. Kilpatrick *v.* Brashear, 10 Heisk. (Tenn.) 372. *Compare* Cannon *v.* Mathias, 10 Heisk. (Tenn.) 575.

The fact that a plaintiff, during the period when he might have enforced his demand by suit, was in indigent circumstances and needed the use of his means, is a circumstance tending to fortify the presumption that the demand has been paid or otherwise satisfied. Bean *v.* Tonnele, 94 N. Y. 381; s. c., 46 Am. Rep. 153, and cases cited; *In re* Neilley, 95 N. Y. 382; Hughes *v.* Hughes, 54 Pa. St. 240; Phillips *v.* Adams, 78 Ala. 225. *Compare* Orr *v.* Jason, 1 Ill. App. 439.

So also the fact that defendant had failed during the time and made a compromise with his creditors would tend to rebut such presumption. Walker *v.* Russell, 73 Iowa 340; Woodbury *v.*

applies to a judgment.[1] But the presumption operates as a payment only in favor of the party entitled to the benefit thereof,

Taylor, 3 Jones (N. Car.) 504. *Compare* Biddle *v.* Girard Nat. Bank, 109 Pa. St. 349; Veazie *v.* Hosmer, 11 Gray (Mass.) 396.

The character of the creditor for promptness in the collection of debts would constitute a circumstance in aid of the presumption of payment after the lapse of eight years. Leiper *v.* Erwin, 5 Yerg. (Tenn.) 97; Orr *v.* Jason, 1 Ill. App. 439. *Compare* Abercrombie *v.* Sheldon, 8 Allen (Mass.) 532.

Where the plaintiff lived in the neighborhood of the debtor, against whom he had a judgment, for thirteen years after its rendition, and after the first year made no effort to collect it, finally moving away without making any effort to collect it, and the debtor during all the time had ample property to satisfy the judgment, these facts will raise the presumption that the debt has been paid. Husky *v.* Maples, 2 Coldw. (Tenn.) 25; s. c., 88 Am. Dec. 588.

Mere lapse of time less than that fixed by the statute of limitations, together with the pecuniary ability of the defendant to pay, do not raise a presumption of payment. Daby *v.* Ericsson, 45 N. Y. 786.

After the lapse of nineteen years, slight circumstances will warrant the inference of payment. Briggs' Appeal, 93 Pa. St. 485.

A delay of seven or eight years in bringing suit on a sealed instrument, is slight evidence of payment, varying according to circumstances. Where it is submitted to a jury to infer payment from circumstances, the weight to be given in delay or promptness in bringing suit is for them to determine. Lee *v.* Newell, 107 Pa. St. 283.

So the lapse of fourteen years may be considered by the jury, though the payee is in possession of the note. Walker *v.* Emerson, 20 Tex. 706; s. c., 73 Am. Dec. 207. *Compare* Hendricks *v.* Wallis, 7 Iowa 224.

The transcript of the judgment of a justice of the peace was filed in the common pleas more than nineteen years after it was rendered, and there was nothing to show whether or not execution had ever issued on it, nor was the justice called nor the docket produced. *Held*, that the jury were at liberty to infer payment from the lapse of time and other circumstances. Diamond *v.* Tobias, 12 Pa. St. 312.

The records of judgments which have been rendered against the debtor during the twenty years, and which have been satisfied, are admissible in aid of the presumption of payment. Levers *v.* Van Buskirk, 4 Pa. St. 309.

Plaintiff was employed as a servant at a certain sum per week, to be paid weekly. After remaining in her situation for over three years, she left the service, and about four years afterward brought an action for her wages against the executor of her employer. It was shown that it was not usual for domestic servants to give receipts for their wages. *Held*, that no legal presumption that the claim was paid was raised by the lapse of time, though taken in connection with the proof as to receipts. Snediker *v.* Everingham, 27 N. J. L. 143.

Where the full period of twenty years has not elapsed, the circumstances relied on to raise the presumption of payment of a sealed instrument must be such as to produce a conviction that payment has been made. Bradley *v.* Jennings, 15 Rich. (S. Car.) 34.

The fact that the time in which a right of entry on land is barred, or the right to bring an action of ejectment, has been reduced to less than twenty years by statute, does not operate to reduce the time in which the presumption arises of payment of a debt secured by mortgage. Criss *v.* Criss, 28 W. Va. 388.

1. Burton *v.* Cannon, 5 Harr. (Del.) 13; Campbell *v.* Carey, 5 Harr. (Del.) 427; Moore *v.* Smith, 81 Pa. St. 182; Biddle *v.* Girard Nat. Bank, 109 Pa. St. 349; Hess *v.* Frankenfield, 106 Pa. St. 440; Kennedy *v.* Denoon, 3 Brev. (S. Car.) 476; McDaniel *v.* Goodall, 2 Coldw. (Tenn.) 391.

The presumption begins to run from the date of entry of the judgment. Cloud *v.* Temple, 5 Houst. (Del.) 587.

But mere lapse of time less than the twenty years will not suffice. Thayer *v.* Mowry, 36 Me. 287; Fister *v.* Hunter, 4 Rich. Eq. (S. Car.) 16; McMahan *v.* Crabtree, 30 Ala. 470.

The same rule prevails in equity. Edwards *v.* Giboney, 51 Mo. 129; Bird *v.* Inslee, 23 N. J. Eq. 363; Miner *v.* Beekman, 14 Abb. Pr., N. S. (N. Y.) 1.

and does not necessarily satisfy the debt as to all the debtors.[1]

6. Rebutting Presumption.--The presumption may always be re-

1. New York L. Ins. & Trust Co. *v.* Covert, 29 Barb. (N. Y.) 435. *Compare* Pearsall *v.* Houston, 3 Jones (N. Car.) 346.

Presumption of payment has been held not to arise in the following cases:

From lapse of time against the government. United States *v.* Williams, 4 McLean (U. S.) 567.

From a forbearance to sue for nine months; under any circumstance or in any court. Holmes *v.* The Lodemia, Crabbe (U. S.) 434.

Where the evidence shows an acknowledgment of the claimant's right within the period of limitation. Arline *v.* Miller, 22 Ga. 330

From lapse of time less than twenty years. Forsyth *v.* Ripley, 2 Greene (Iowa) 181.

From the mere lapse of five years since the maturity of a pomissory note. Nash *v.* Gibson, 16 Iowa 305.

From mere lapse of time, short of twenty years, of an amount due upon a covenant. Stockton *v.* Johnson, 6 B. Mon. (Ky.) 408.

Of a judgment, till after a year and a day from its recovery; and if within that time a judgment creditor of an insolvent estate files a petition in the probate court against the administrator, praying that he might be required to give new security, the petition need not aver that the petitioner's judgment has not been paid. Meyer *v.* Dorrance, 32 Miss. 263.

From lapse of time, that taxes were paid, where a referee has expressly found the fact that they were not paid either in money or labor. Haverhill *v.* Orange, 47 N. H. 273.

From the non-payment of rent from twenty to twenty-four years, where circumstances excuse the delay in demanding the rent; nor will a release or conveyance extinguishing the rent, be presumed. Cole *v.* Patterson, 25 Wend. (N. Y.) 457.

From delay by a British creditor to sue, which occurred during the doubts in relation to confiscation attendant upon the American Revolution. McMair *v.* Ragland, 1 Dev. Eq. (N. Car.) 533.

From the lapse of ten years, if, during a portion of that period, it appears that the debtor was insolvent. Woodbury *v.* Taylor, 3 Jones L. (N. Car.) 504.

From the lapse of seven years, after a legacy is demandable. Strohm's Appeal, 23 Pa. St. 351.

From lapse of time of a bond on which interest has been regularly paid. Nixon *v.* Bynum, 1 Bailey (S. Car.) 148.

Of a judgment from lapse of time; unless the lapse of twenty years is complete. Foster *v.* Hunter, 4 Rich. Eq. (S. Car.) 16; Thayer *v.* Mowry, 36 Me. 287.

For additional cases raising questions of the presumption of payment from lapse of time, see Stockton *v.* Johnson, 6 B. Mon. (Ky.) 409; Anderson *v.* Smith, 3 Metc. (Ky.) 491; Helm *v.* Jones, 3 Dana (Ky.) 86; Potter *v.* Titcomb, 7 Me. 302; West *v.* Brison, 99 Mo. 684; Doe *v.* Gildart, 5 How. (Miss.) 606; Owen *v.* Calhoun (Supreme Ct.), 8 N. Y. Supp. 447; Macauley *v.* Palmer (Supreme Ct.), 6 N. Y. Supp. 402; Clark *v.* Hopkins, 7 Johns. (N. Y.) 556; Ingraham *v.* Baldwin, 9 N. Y. 45; Lammer *v.* Stoddard, 103 N. Y. 672; Phillips *v.* Prevost, 4 Johns. Ch. (N. Y.) 205; Livingston *v.* Livingston, 4 Johns. Ch. (N. Y.) 294; s. c., 8 Am. Dec. 562; Walker *v.* Wright, 2 Jones (N. Car.) 155; Giles *v.* Baremore, 5 Johns. Ch. (N. Y.) 545; Kerlee *v.* Corpening, 97 N. Car. 330; Hall *v.* Gibbs, 87 N. Car. 4; Holman's Appeal, 24 Pa. St. 174; Drysdale's Appeal, 14 Pa. St. 531; Brubaker *v.* Taylor, 76 Pa. St. 83; Connelly *v.* McKean, 64 Pa. St. 113; Birkey *v.* McMakin, 64 Pa. St. 343; Mertz's Appeal (Pa. 1886), 7 Atl. Rep. 187; Bentley's Appeal, 99 Pa. St. 500; Sartor *v.* Beaty, 25 S. Car. 293; Shaw *v.* Barksdale, 25 S. Car. 204; Wightman *v.* Butler, 2 Spears (S. Car.) 357; Brewton *v.* Cannon, 1 Bay (S. Car.) 482; Agnew *v.* Renwick, 27 S. Car. 562; Yarnell *v.* Moore, 3 Coldw. (Tenn.) 173; Winston *v.* Street, 2 Patt. & H. (Va.) 169; Barbour *v.* Duncanson, 77 Va. 76; Dwight *v.* Eastman (Vt.), 20 Atl. Rep. 594; Smith *v.* Niagara F. Ins. Co., 60 Vt. 682; Sparhawk *v.* Buell, 9 Vt. 41; Delaney *v.* Brunette, 62 Wis. 615; Hopkirk *v.* Page, 2 Brock. (U. S) 20; Kirkpatrick *v.* Laugphier, 1 Cranch (C. C.) 85; Miller *v.* Evans, 2 Cranch (C. C.) 72; McCormick *v.* Eliot, 43

butted or overcome by showing the facts and circumstances.[1]

Fed. Rep. 469; Denniston *v.* M'Keen, 2 McLean (U. S.) 253.

1. Daggett *v.* Tallman, 8 Conn. 168; Herndon *v.* Bartlett, 7 Mon. (Ky.) 449; Knight *v.* Macomber, 55 Me. 132; Abbott *v.* Godfrey, 1 Mich. 178; Lewis *v.* Schwenn, 93 Mo. 26; Morris *v.* Wadsworth, 17 Wend. (N. Y.) 103, Cole *v.* Patterson, 25 Wend. (N. Y.) 457; Jackson *v.* Hotchkiss, 6 Cow. (N. Y.) 401; McKinder *v.* Littlejohn, 1 Ired. L. (N. Car.) 66; Buil *v.* Buil, 2 Ired. L. (N. Car.) 87; White *v.* Beaman, 96 N. Car. 122; Lash *v.* Von Neida, 109 Pa. St. 207; Biddle *v.* Girard Nat. Bank, 109 Pa. St. 349; McNair *v.* Ingraham, 21 S. Car. 70; Dickson *v.* Goudin, 26 S. Car. 391.

Even though the time elapsed is thirty years. Arden *v.* Arden, 1 Johns. Ch. (N. Y.) 313. *Compare* Downs *v.* Soov, 28 N. J. Eq. 55.

The presumption may be rebutted and overcome by proof of any facts and circumstances, the legitimate tendency of which is to render it more probable than otherwise that payment has not in fact been made. Grantham *v.* Canaan, 38 N. H. 268; McKinder *v.* Littlejohn, 1 Ired. L. (N. Car.) 66; Wood *v.* Deen, 1 Ired. L. (N. Car.) 230.

Where the surety on a sealed note had said that the payee had promised not to push him during his, the surety's lifetime, this would rebut the presumption. Fisher *v.* Phillips, 4 Baxt. (Tenn.) 243.

It may be rebutted by express admissions within twenty years: By payment of interest or part of principle; by proof of the obligor's inability to pay; by the suspension of collection by stay-law or war, and even by proof of the near relationship of the parties. Updike *v.* Lane, 78 Va. 132; Cole *v.* Ballard, 78 Va. 139; Criss *v.* Criss, 28 W. Wa. 388; Lyon *v.* Adde, 63 Barb. (N. Y.) 89. *Ex parte* acts of the creditors cannot be shown to rebut the presumption. Colvin *v.* Phillips, 25 S. Car. 228. *Compare* Dabney *v.* Dabney, 2 Rob. (Va.) 622; s. c., 40 Am. Dec. 761.

The presumption may be rebutted after the lapse of the twenty years. Strickland *v.* Bridges, 21 S. Car. 21. See McQueen *v.* Fletcher, 4 Rich. Eq. (S. Car.) 161.

But there is a distinction between the force of admissions made on a debt not yet presumed to be paid, and on one where the presumption of payment is complete. Roberts *v.* Smith, 21 S. Car. 455.

And the facts and circumstances relied on to rebut the presumption must have occurred within twenty years before suit brought. Gregory *v.* Commonwealth, 121 Pa. St. 611; s. c., 6 Am. St. Rep. 804.

After the presumption of payment is complete, it can only be rebutted by such proof as would take an action upon a promissory note out of the statute of limitations. The rebuttal of the presumption by a part payment is not upon the theory of a new promise, but of an admission by which the old debt is acknowledged to be unpaid. Dickson *v.* Gourdin, 26 S. Car. 391.

The recogniton of a debt by a personal representative may rebut the presumption of payment, though it would not revive a demand barred by limitation. Tucker *v.* Baker, 94 N. Car. 162; Richardson *v.* Peterson, 2 Harr. (Del.) 366. *Compare* Blake *v.* Quash, 3 McCord (S. Car.) 340.

Same rule applies to a recognition by a principal as affecting a surety. McKeethan *v.* Atkinson, 1 Jones L. (N. Car.) 421.

So, too, a payment by an assignee in bankruptcy with the assent of the obligor. Hamlin *v.* Hamlin, 3 Jones Eq. (N. Car.) 191.

If there is positive proof of non-payment, mere lapse of time is no bar to the action. Evarts *v.* Mason, 11 Vt. 122.

The regular payment of interest will rebut the presumption. Nixon *v.* Bynum, 1 Bailey (S. Car.) 148.

But before credits on a bond can have any force to rebut the presumption of payment, it must be shown that they were made before the presumption of payment had ripened. Lash *v.* Von Neida, 109 Pa. St. 207.

Presumption of the payment of a judgment may be rebutted by showing that three executions have been returned *nulla bona;* that the defendant, when payment had been demanded, had replied that he had no property and could not pay; that about the time when the original suit was commenced he commenced to put his property, real and personal, out of his hands, and claimed not to be the owner of any property since, and had during all the time had the reputation of being insolvent. Knight *v.* Macomber, 55 Me. 132.

As to rebutting presumption of payment of a judgment under the *New York* statute, see Waddell *v.* Elmendorf, 10 N. Y. 170.

In calculating the period necessary to raise the presumption, such time must be excluded, if any, in which for any reason the creditor has no legal right or power to bring an action for the debt. Criss *v.* Criss, 28 W. Va. 388.

If during the twenty years the creditor becomes an alien enemy, the time during which such disability continues is to be deducted from the time elapsed. Bailey *v.* Jackson, 16 Johns. (N. Y.) 210; s. c., 8 Am. Dec. 309. And see Brewton *v.* Cannon, 1 Bay (S. Car.) 482.

The presumption is rebutted by the fact that the debtor had removed to another State and resided therein during the time which had elapsed. Boardman *v.* De Forrest, 5 Conn. 1; Mann *v.* Manning, 12 Smed. & M. (Miss.) 615. *Compare* Kline *v.* Kline, 20 Pa. St. 503.

While the presumption of payment of a mortgage debt, arising from the possession of the mortgaged premises by the mortgagor, or his assigns, for more than twenty years after the maturity of the debt may be rebutted, the proof to rebut the presumption should always be ample and explicit. Where the holder of the mortgage permitted his mother, who was the mortgagor, and his sister, to whom the mother had conveyed the equity, to occupy the premises, and he testified without contradiction that the debt had not been paid, and that he permitted the occupancy because of the relationship, this is sufficient to rebut the presumption. Philbrook *v.* Clark, 77 Me. 176.

To same effect, Brown *v.* Hardcastle, 63 Md. 484; Baent *v.* Kennicutt, 57 Mich. 268; Peters' Appeal, 106 Pa. St. 340.

Where a trust is recognized by the trustee as continuing, the presumption of payment which would otherwise arise after the lapse of twenty years, is thereby rebutted; and an informal settlement in the probate court, wherein the trustee charged himself with assets and claimed credit for disbursements, is such a recognition of the trust. Prior cases cited. Werborn *v.* Austin, 82 Ala. 498.

A bill to enforce a vendor's lien was filed more than twenty years after the last instalment of purchase money became due, the land having been sold under a probate decree, and the administrator himself being the purchaser and defendant in the lien suit. *Held*, that the presumption of payment would not be overcome by evidence, that defendant advanced or paid to the complainants different amounts of money on their respective interests in said estate, taking their receipts for the same, and now claims that such payments were payments on the purchase money of the land; nor is the allegation that defendant "has never denied, but always admitted, that the purchase money of said land is due and unpaid" sufficient to overcome such presumption, where the bill is demurred to. Solomon *v.* Solomon, 81 Ala. 505; s. c., 83 Ala. 394.

Where the creditor endeavors to rebut the presumption by showing the insolvency of the debtor during the twenty years, he may show that the debtor lived at a great distance from him, as tending to prove that, though the debtor may have had property for a short time, yet the creditor had no opportunity of knowing that fact and of getting satisfaction out of that property. McKinder *v.* Littlejohn, 4 Ired. L. (N. Car.) 198.

But the mere poverty of the debtor is not sufficient to rebut the presumption. Rogers *v.* Judd, 5 Vt. 236; s. c., 26 Am. Dec. 301.

Where insolvency of the obligor is relied on to rebut the presumption, such a state of insolvency must be shown during the entire time as to prove that he did not pay because he could not. Grant *v.* Burgwyn, 84 N. Car. 560.

Payment by the principal in a bond will rebut the presumption as to the surety. McKeethan *v.* Atkinson, 1 Jones (N. Car.) 421.

And see the following cases raising questions of the rebuttal of the presumption of payment under particular circumstances: Werborn *v.* Austin, 82 Ala. 498; Girard *v.* Futterer, 84 Ala. 323; Farmers' Bank *v.* Leonard, 4 Harr. (Del.) 536; Walker *v.* Russell, 73 Iowa 340; Wood *v.* Egan, 39 La. Ann. 684; Mann *v.* Manning, 12 Smed. & M. (Miss.) 615; Boardman *v.* De Forrest, 5 Conn. 1;

7. Distinction Between Presumption of Payment and Statute of Limitations.—The statute of limitations creates a legal bar to the action; lapse of time merely raises a presumption of payment which may be rebutted.[1]

XI. Waiver by Payment.—Payment of the contract price will not of itself constitute a waiver of the right to recover for defects in the article paid for, even though the party paying was aware of the defects. The right to recover must depend on all the circumstances of the case.[2]

XII. Voluntary Payment—1. Cannot be Recovered Back.—A voluntary payment of money under a claim of right cannot, in general, be recovered back. To warrant such recovery there must be compulsion, actual, present, potential, and the demand

Wiltsie *v.* Wiltsie (Supreme Ct.), 1 N. Y. Supp. 559; Dorgeloh *v.* Bassford, 50 N. Y. Super. Ct. 450; Alston *v.* Hawkins, 105 N. Car. 3; Lowe *v.* Sowell, 4 Jones (N. Car.) 135; Hinsaman *v.* Hinsaman, 7 Jones (N. Car.) 510; Wiley *v.* Lineberry, 89 N. Car. 15; Wilfong *v.* Cline, 1 Jones (N. Car.) 499; Williams *v.* Alexander, 6 Jones (N. Car.) 137; Rowland *v.* Windley, 86 N. Car. 36; Alston *v.* Hawkins, 105 N. Car. 3; Cartwright *v.* Kerman, 105 N. Car. 1; Levers *v.* Van Buskirk, 7 W. & S. (Pa.) 70; Eby *v.* Eby, 5 Pa. St. 435; Kirkpatrick *v.* Laugphier, 1 Cranch (C. C.) 85; Cremer's Estate, 5 W. & S. (Pa.) 331; Kitchen *v.* Deardoff, 2 Pa. St. 481; Bissell *v.* Jaudon, 16 Ohio St. 498; Martin *v.* Bowker, 19 Vt. 526; Sellers *v.* Holman, 20 Pa. St. 321; Gregory *v.* Commonwealth, 121 Pa. St. 611; Van Looh *v.* Smith, 103 Pa. St. 238; Breneman's Appeal, 120 Pa. St. 641; Runner's Appeal, 121 Pa. St. 649; Wilson *v.* Wilson, 29 S. Car. 260; North *v.* Drayton, Harp. Eq. (S. Car.) 34; Palmer *v.* Dubois, 1 Mill Const. (S. Car.) 178; Boyce *v.* Lake, 17 S. Car. 481; s. c., 43 Am. Rep. 618; Duncan *v.* Rawls, 16 Tex. 478; Dabney *v.* Dabney, 2 Rob. (Va.) 622; s. c., 40 Am. Dec. 761; Eustace *v.* Gaskins, 1 Wash. (Va.) 188; McLellan *v.* Crofton, 6 Me. 307; Bowie *v.* Westmoreland Poor School Soc., 75 Va. 300; McCleary *v.* Grantham, 29 W. Va. 301.

1. Reed *v.* Reed, 46 Pa. St. 239; Bell's Appeal, 122 Pa. St. 486; Biddle *v.* Girard Nat. Bank, 109 Pa. St. 349; Shubrick *v.* Adams, 20 S. Car. 49; Dickson *v.* Gourdin, 26 S. Car. 391; Colvin *v.* Phillips, 25 S. Car. 228; Tucker *v.* Baker, 94 N. Car. 162; Threadgill *v.* West, 13 Ired. L. (N. Car.) 310; Alston *v.* Hawkins, 105 N. Car. 3; Currie *v.* Clark, 101 N. Car. 329; Mason *v.* Spurlock, 4 Baxt. (Tenn.) 554; Hale *v.* Pack, 10 W. Va. 145. See also Roberts *v.* Johns, 24 S. Car. 580; Roberts *v.* Smith, 21 S. Car 455.

The presumption of payment is applicable as well to cases in which a bar is prescribed by the statute of limitations as to other cases. Wright *v.* Mars, 22 S. Car. 585.

"The latter (statute of limitations) is a prohibition of the action; the former (presumption) *prima facie* obliterates the debt." 2 Whart. Evid., § 1361.

After the lapse of time an artificial presumption of law is raised, as a fact to be passed on by the jury. It is not a presumption of law, such as arises from an adverse occupancy of land, from which a grant is presumed, and which is not allowed to be controverted; but of fact, open to disproof in showing that no payment had been made, or such facts as in law are held sufficient to remove the presumption by explaining the inaction of the creditor. Long *v.* Clegg, 94 N. Car. 763.

The presumption of payment from lapse of time is an artificial and arbitrary rule of law, and is not, like the statute of limitations, a bar to an action on the original contract, and a new promise is not, therefore, necessary to enable the creditor to sue on the original cause of action. An admission rebuts the presumption, even though accompanied by a refusal to pay. Gregory *v.* Commonwealth, 121 Pa. St. 611; s. c., 6 Am. St. Rep. 804.

2. Flannery *v.* Rohrmayer, 46 Conn. 558; s. c., 33 Am. Rep. 36.

must be illegal. In the absence of such compulsion, a mere protest is not sufficient. The element of coercion is essential to the right.[1]

But it is held in *Vermont* that where an article, manufactured in accordance with a special contract, is accepted and retained by the vendee, there being no warranty and the defects, if any, patent and obvious, a payment of the contract price is a waiver of the defects. Gibson *v.* Bingham, 43 Vt. 410; s. c., 5 Am. Rep. 289. See *infra*, this title, *Part Payments.*

1. Union Pac. R. Co. *v.* Dodge Co., 98 U. S. 541; Keener *v.* Bank of U. S., 2 Pa. St. 237; Hospital *v.* Philadelphia Co., 24 Pa. St. 229; Taylor *v.* Board of Health, 31 Pa. St. 73; s. c., 72 Am. Dec. 724; McCrickart *v.* Pittsburgh, 88 Pa. St. 133; Harvey *v.* Girard Nat. Bank, 119 Pa. St. 212; Vick *v.* Shinn, 49 Ark. 70; s. c., 4 Am. St. Rep. 26; Raisler *v.* Mayor etc. of Athens, 66 Ala. 194; Forbes *v.* Appleton, 5 Cush. (Mass.) 115; Carew *v.* Rutherford, 106 Mass. 1; s. c., 8 Am. Rep. 287, where the question is fully considered and many cases are cited and reviewed. Mayor etc. of Baltimore *v.* Hussey, 67 Md. 112; Eaton *v.* *v.* Eaton, 35 N. J. L. 290; Wabaunsee Co. *v.* Walker, 8 Kan. 431; Kansas Pac. R. Co. *v.* Wyandotte Co., 16 Kan. 587; Flower *v.* Lance, 59 N. Y. 603; Patterson *v.* Cox, 25 Ind. 261; Woodburn *v.* Stout, 28 Ind. 77; Maxwell *v.* San Luis Obispe Co., 71 Cal. 466; McMillan *v.* Richards, 9 Cal. 365, 417; s. c., 70 Am. Dec. 655; Wills *v.* Austin, 53 Cal. 152; Gibson *v.* Bingham, 43 Vt. 410; s. c., 5 Am. Rep. 289; Andrews *v.* Hancock, 1 Bond & Bing. 37.

The rule applies to a payment by one municipal corporation to another, as well as to a payment between individuals. Macon Co. *v.* Jackson Co., 75 N. Car. 240.

The agents of a line of ocean steamers affording the only safe means of shipment between San Francisco and New York, refused to receive silver and gold for transportation and issue bills of lading for the same unless the shipper furnished stamps for the bills under the acts of 1857 and 1858. A shipper furnished the stamps but under protest, denying the company's right to exact them, and claiming that the acts were unconstitutional. *Held*, that the payment for the stamps was voluntary, and this was not a case showing such coercion as to render the payment compulsory. Brumagim *v.* Tillinghast, 18 Cal. 265. And the same ruling was applied to stamps purchased for passage tickets. Garrison *v.* Tillinghast, 18 Cal. 404.

Where a corporation paid under protest a passenger tax, imposed by a statute which was afterwards by the Supreme Court of the United States declared to be unconstitutional, and the tax was paid to avoid penalties which could have been collected only by a judicial proceeding, the payment was voluntary, and could not be recovered back. Oceanic Steam Nav. Co. *v.* Tappan, 16 Blatchf. (U. S.) 296.

Where the master of a military transport, appointed by the owner, is removed by the military authorities and another put by them in his place, and the owner is required to pay the wages of this latter, which he does without protest, he cannot recover such payment. White *v.* United States, 11 Ct. of Cl. 578.

A lease provided that lessee should keep the premises in repair, except in case of fire, but should they be rendered unfit for tenancy by fire, a just proportionate abatement of rent should be made. The premises were rendered untenantable by fire, but the lessor insisted on the full rent, and the lessee paid it under protest. *Held*, that no part of it could be recovered back.

"The fact that the plaintiff in this case," says the court, "might have been under embarrassment as to the amount of rent which he would withhold, or which he might properly claim to rebate, does not affect the principle. It was his right to litigate that question with his lessor, and his election to pay the full amount rather than resist the payment of any portion of it, makes the payment a voluntary one." Regan *v.* Baldwin, 126 Mass. 485; s. c., 30 Am. Rep. 689. To same effect, Emmons *v.* Scudder, 115 Mass. 367.

Where a contractor for the erection of a building pays to a sub-contractor, in settlement of claims against the latter, an amount in excess of the price agreed to be paid him, no liens having been established against the building, such payment is voluntary, and cannot be recovered back. Morley *v.* Carlson, 27 Mo. App. 5.

In Carew *v.* Rutherford (106 Mass. 1; 8 Am. Rep. 277;), it is held that a conspiracy against a mechanic, who is under the necessity of employing workmen to carry on his business, to obtain a sum of money from him which he is under no legal liability to pay, by inducing his workmen to leave him, and by deterring others from entering his employment, or by threatening to do these acts, so that he is induced to pay the money demanded, under a reasonable apprehension that he cannot carry on his business without yielding to the illegal demand, is an illegal conspiracy; the acts done under it are illegal, and the money thus obtained may be recovered back.

A certain railroad company paid to defendant, an insurance company, a premium upon a policy of insurance; whereupon the defendant paid plaintiff, as an insurance broker, full commissions thereon. Eight days afterwards the policy was canceled, and the defendant paid back to the railway company the amount of the premium, less the earned premium and the commission paid plaintiff, and then demanded from plaintiff that he return to defendant the amount of his commission, claiming that such was the agreement made with him before the issuance of the policy. Plaintiff repaid the amount of the commission under protest, and asserting that he waived no rights thereby, and brought his action to recover the amount so repaid. *Held*, that the payment was voluntary, and plaintiff was not entitled to recover. Devereux *v.* Rochester German Ins. Co., 98 N. Car. 6.

Where a void execution is levied on property, and the party pays the amount of the execution to save his property, he may recover it back. But such is not the rule where the execution is merely erroneous and amendable. Bobb *v.* Dillon, 20 Mo. App. 309. *Compare* Gould *v.* McFall, 118 Pa. St. 455; s. c., 4 Am. St. Rep. 606; Lord *v.* Waterhouse, 1 Root (Conn.) 430.

Plaintiff was arrested for violation of an invalid city ordinance. He pleaded not guilty, but made no objection to the validity of the ordinance. He was found guilty and fined, and paid the fine while under arrest, but without protest, believing that the judgment imposing the fine was a valid one. *Held*, that the payment was voluntary. Bailey *v.* Paullina, 69 Iowa 463.

Where under threats of prosecution one voluntarily pays a bill of costs to an officer, no compulsion or mistake of fact being shown, nor any fraudulent or wrongful purpose toward the plaintiff on the part of the clerk, such payment cannot be recovered back. Thompson *v.* Doty, 72 Ind. 336.

Plaintiff's financial circumstances were such that he was compelled to mortgage his real estate in order to raise money. A judgment against him, for which he had appealed, was a lien on the property, and he was unable to negotiate the loan without paying off the judgment, and thus removing the lien. *Held*, that payment of the judgment under such circumstances was a voluntary one. Hipp *v.* Crenshaw, 64 Iowa 404.

Under an execution against A the sheriff levied upon a lot of gold, silver and copper coins belonging to B. While this money was in the hands of the sheriff, B substituted therefor certain bank bills, under an understanding that the property thus substituted should be considered the property levied on instead of the coin. *Held*, not to constitute a voluntary payment nor a waiver by B of his right to recover the money. St. Louis etc. R. Co. *v.* Castello, 28 Mo. 379.

In an action to enforce a mechanic's lien on real estate, there was a recovery by plaintiff therein, and it was adjudged that a certain prior mortgage on the real estate was junior and subordinate to such lien. The property was sold under the decree and purchased by the judgment plaintiff. The mortgagee filed a bill to review the judgment, wherein he was defeated, and appealed. The year given by statute for the redemption of the land sold under the mechanic's lien, judgment being about to expire, and the mortgagor being insolvent, the mortgagee paid the redemption money to the clerk of the court for the purchaser at the judgment sale, and the latter received it from the clerk. At the time of paying the money to the clerk, the mortgagee notified the purchaser of his purpose to prosecute an appeal in the case brought to review the judgment, and filed with the clerk a written protest, reserving therein the right to recover the redemption money if the judgment appealed from should be reversed. After the year for redemption had expired, the judgment refusing the mortgagee the right of review was reversed, and the mechanic's lien judgment was afterwards declared void as to the mortgagee. The mortgagee thereupon foreclosed his mortgage, and purchased the property at the foreclosure sale. Upon demand for a return of the redemption money, the original plaintiff refused to pay back the same, and the mortgagee brought an action to recover the money so paid. *Held*, that the payment was a voluntary one, and the money could not be recovered back. Connecticut Mut. L. Ins. Co. *v.* Stewart, 95 Ind. 588.

Defendant, as executrix of her husband, of whom she was the principal legatee, presented the will for probate, upon which there was a contest.

Pending the litigation, defendant transferred to plaintiff all her right, title and interest in the estate, the instrument of transfer providing that plaintiff might continue the proceedings for probate. Defendant had agreed with her attorney to pay him a specified sum, in addition to the counsel fee and costs allowed him by the surrogate; and it was the express understanding that out of the purchase money received from plaintiff she was to pay her attorney and extinguish his claim. The attorney proceeded with the litigation to a decree which charged the cost of the proponent upon the estate. Plaintiff, who had become temporary administrator of the estate, paid the amount of the costs to the attorney, and sued to recover the same back from the defendant. *Held*, that the payment was not a voluntary one; that while, as against defendant, plaintiff could have prevented the collection of the costs out of the estate, as against the attorney he could not; and as the payment was necessary to relieve the estate of the lien, it was compulsory. Dodge *v.* Zimmer, 110 N. Y. 43.

A purchased for $15,000 certain premises upon which she held mortgages to the amount of $11,400, it being agreed that she should give a mortgage for the purchase price, the amount of her mortgages being first deducted. The mortgages were satisfied and delivered up on her receipt of the deed, but the mortgage which was presented for her signature was for the full amount of the purchase price, without any deduction for the mortgages surrendered. This mortgage so presented to her she executed, supposing it to be for the balance of the price only, and it was immediately assigned by the mortgagee. She afterwards conveyed the premises to B, subject to the mortgage, and B, with full knowledge of the facts, paid $1,050 specifically as one year's interest on the mortgage. *Held*, that while the surrender by A of her mortgages operated as a payment *pro tanto* of the mortgage executed by her, even as against a *bona fide* purchaser, and though B was not estopped, by his payment of the sum specifically as interest due, from disputing the validity of the mortgage as to the full amount, yet as his payment was a voluntary one on a disputed claim, he could not recover it back, nor could he have the excess over the interest actually due applied on the principal of the mortgage debt. Bennett *v.* Bates, 94 N. Y. 354. And see on the general subject, Abercrombie *v.* Skinner, 42 Ala. 633; Kaufman *v.* Dickensheets, 30 Ind. 258; s. c., 90 Am. Dec. 694; Meyer *v.* Clark, 2 Daly (N. Y.) 497; Shelley *v.* Lash, 14 Minn. 498; Beecher *v.* Buckingham, 18 Conn. 110; s. c., 44 Am. Dec. 580; Montgomery *v.* Gibbs, 40 Iowa 652; Chicago etc R. Co. *v.* Chicago etc. Coal Co., 79 Ill. 121; Puckett *v.* Roquemore, 55 Ga. 235; Ligonier *v.* Ackerman, 46 Ind. 552; s. c., 15 Am. Rep. 323; Irwin *v.* Thomas, 12 Kan. 93; Juneau *v.* Stunkle, 40 Kan. 756; Potomac Coal Co. *v.* Cumberland etc. R. Co., 38 Md. 226; Tompkins *v.* Hollister, 60 Mich. 485; Hope *v.* Evans, 1 Smed. & M. Ch. (Miss.) 195; Sheldon *v.* South School District, 24 Conn. 88; Cummins *v.* White, 4 Blackf. (Ind.) 356; Gerecke *v.* Campbell, 24 Neb. 306; Randall *v.* Lyon Co. (Nev. 1887), 14 Pac. Rep. 583; Newell *v.* March, 8 Ired. (N. Car.) 441; Gilpatrick *v.* Sayward, 5 Me. 465; Rawson *v.* Porter, 9 Me. 119; Association *v.* Ellslen, 6 Phila. (Pa.) 6; Speise *v.* McCoy, 6 W. & S. (Pa.) 485; s. c., 40 Am. Dec. 579; Eaton *v.* Eaton, 35 N. J. L. 290; Mayor etc. of N. Y. *v.* Erben, 10 Bosw. (N. Y.) 189; 24 How. Pr. (N. Y.) 358; Jackson *v.* Ferguson, 7 La. Ann. 723; Buffington *v.* Dink

2. Under Duress or by Fraud.—Yet to render a payment voluntary, in the proper sense of the word, the parties must stand upon equal terms. There must be no duress operating upon the one; there must be no oppressiom or fraud practiced by the other.[1]

grave, 4 La. Ann. 550; Edgar *v.* Shields, 1 Grant Cas. (Pa.) 361; Wyman *v.* Farnsworth, 3 Barb. (N. Y.) 369; Abell *v.* Douglas, 4 Den. (N. Y.) 305; Tyler *v.* Smith, 18 B. Mon. (Ky.) 793; Baltimore etc. R. Co. *v.* Faunce, 6 Gill (Md.) 68; Waite *v.* Leggett, 8 Cow. (N. Y.) 195; s. c., 18 Am. Dec. 441; Commercial Bank *v.* Reed, 11 Ohio 498; Lake *v.* Artisans' Bank, 3 Abb. App. Dec. (N. Y.) 10; Schlaefer *v.* Heiberger (Supreme Ct.), 4 N. Y. Supp. 74; Gwynn *v.* Gwynn (S. Car. 1889), 10 S. E. Rep. 221; Gillett *v.* Brewster (Vt. 1890), 20 Atl. Rep. 105; Comstock *v.* Tupper, 50 Vt. 596; Moffitt *v.* Carr, 1 Black (U. S.) 273; White *v.* United States, 11 Ct. of Cl. 578; The Nicanor, 40 Fed. Rep. 361.

1. Morgan *v.* Palmer, 4 D. & R. 283; Moses *v.* McFarlan, 2 Burr. 1005; Arnold *v.* Georgia etc. R. Co., 50 Ga. 304; Beckwith *v.* Frisbie, 32 Vt. 559. See also cases cited under preceding head.

A mere apprehension of legal proceedings does not make the payment a compulsory one. Ligonier *v.* Ackerman, 46 Ind. 552; s. c., 15 Am. Rep. 323.

Duress of goods does not exist because a mortgagee of chattels threatens to take possession and sell in pursuance of the power contained in the mortgage, unless the mortgagor pays an amount in excess of what is due. Vick *v.* Shinn, 49 Ark. 70; s. c., 4 Am. St. Rep. 26.

Coercion or duress, to render a payment involuntary, must consist of some actual or threatened exercise of power possessed, or believed to be possessed, by the party exacting or receiving the payment, over the person or property of another, from which that other has no immediate means of relief than by making payment. Radich *v.* Hutchins, 95 U. S. 210. Or the payment must have been made to release the person or property of the party from detention, or to prevent a seizure of either one by one having apparent authority to seize it without resorting to an action. Waubaunsee Co. *v.* Walker, 8 Kan. 431; Devlin *v.* United States, 12 Ct. of Cl. 266; Wolfe *v.* Marshall, 52 Mo. 167.

Where one having in his possession the property of another upon which he claims a lien, refuses to deliver it up to the owner without payment of the lien, and the owner thereupon pays the amount under protest in order to get possession of his property, such payment is not a voluntary one, and may be recovered back. Briggs *v.* Boyd, 56 N. Y. 289.

Where an officer of the United States was induced to pay a balance claimed by the suspension of his official functions and compensation, and his apprehension of being tried by a court martial, this was not such duress as would make the payment an involuntary one. Hall *v.* United States, 9 Ct. of Cl. 270. Neither is the mere fear of a criminal prosecution. St. Louis etc. R. Co. *v.* Thomas, 85 Ill. 464; Comstock *v.* Tupper, 50 Vt. 596.

A member of a stock board, against whom a claim is made by another member under the rules of the board for a deficiency arising from a sale of stock, and who, upon being cited to appear before the arbitration committee, pays the claim with full knowledge of all the facts, cannot recover it back. Quincy *v.* White, 63 N. Y. 370.

The mere fact that one will be sued for a demand is not such compulsion as will warrant his paying under protest, and a payment so made cannot be recovered back. Muscatine *v.* Keokuk etc. Packet Co., 45 Iowa 185.

Money may be recovered back which is obtained by abuse of legal process. Cadaval *v.* Collins, 4 Ad. & El. 858; s. c., 6 Nev. & Man. 324; Cocke *v.* Porter, 2 Humph. (Tenn.) 15; De Bow *v.* United States, 11 Ct. of Cl. 672.

Thus where the goods of a party have been attached by one who knows that he has no cause of action, and for the purpose of extorting money, a payment to free the goods from the attachment is not voluntary, and the money may be recovered back. Chandler *v.* Sanger, 114 Mass. 364; s. c., 19 Am. Rep. 367. To same effect, Spaids *v.* Barrett, 57 Ill. 289; s. c., 11 Am. Rep. 10; Nicodemus *v.* East Saginaw, 25 Mich. 456; Adams

3. Protest.—In such case the payment must be made under protest, in order to entitle the party to reclaim it.[1]

v. Reeves, 68 N. Car. 134; s. c., 12 Am. Rep. 627.

An obligor, offering to pay his bond in Confederate money, said to the obligee that he dare not refuse to accept Confederate notes, and that if he did he would be imprisoned as disloyal. This was held not to be enough, standing alone, to constitute such duress as would avoid the payment. Simmons *v.* Trumbo, 9 W. Va. 358.

A when not in custody nor threatened with illegal arrest, but being indebted to B for the amount of two notes forged by A and transferred to B, agreed that A's wagon, then in B's possession, should be sold at auction, and that B should in consideration thereof surrender the notes to A. The wagon was sold, B becoming the purchaser, and thereupon the notes were surrendered to A, who destroyed them. In an action by A against B to recover the value of the wagon, it was held that he was not entitled to recover. Kissock *v.* House, 23 Hun (N. Y.) 35.

But where the money was paid under threat of defendant to have plaintiff's son arrested and prosecuted for burglary and larceny, and was not given to compound a felony, it may be recovered back. Schultz *v.* Culbertson, 49 Wis. 122. See also Heckman *v.* Swartz, 50 Wis. 267.

Where an agreement to make the payment is made under duress, a subsequent payment in accordance with such agreement is not involuntary, where no legal steps are taken to resist the enforcement of the agreement. Mayor etc. of Savannah *v.* Feeley, 66 Ga. 31.

And see generally on the subject of the recovery back of money alleged to have been paid by reason of duress or of fraud, *In re* Walter (Ala. 1890), 7 So. Rep. 400; Durr *v.* Howard, 6 Ark. 461; People *v.* Vischer, 9 Cal. 365; Jefferson Co. *v.* Hawkins, 23 Fla. 223; Ingalls *v.* Miller (Ind.), 22 N. E. Rep. 995; Lyman *v.* Lauderbaugh, 75 Iowa 484; Wabaunsee Co. *v.* Walker, 8 Kan. 431; Wolfe *v.* Marshall, 52 Mo. 167; First Nat. Bank *v.* Watkins, 21 Mich. 483; Elston *v.* Chicago, 40 Ill. 514; s. c., 89 Am. Dec. 361; Storer *v.* Mitchell, 45 Ill. 213; Mayor etc. of Baltimore *v.* Lefferman, 4 Gill (Md.) 425; s. c., 45 Am. Dec. 145; Claflin *v.* McDonough, 33 Mo. 412; s. c., 84 Am. Dec. 54; Irving *v.* St. Louis, 33 Mo. 575; Hayes *v.* Huffstater, 65 Barb. (N. Y.) 531; Quincey *v.* White, 63 N. Y. 370; Arnold *v.* Crane, 8 Johns. (N. Y.) 79; Anderson *v.* Lewis, 31 Tex. 675; McCartney *v.* Wade, 2 Heisk. (Tenn.) 369; Wilkerson *v.* Bishop, 7 Coldw. (Tenn.) 24; Wood *v.* Willis, 32 Tex. 670; Buford *v.* Lonergan (Utah 1889), 22 Pac. Rep. 164; Maxwell *v.* Griswold, 10 How. (U. S.) 242; Tutt *v.* Ide, 3 Blatchf. (U. S.) 249; Schlesinger *v.* United States, 1 Ct. of Cl. 16; Harmony *v.* Bingham, 12 N. Y. 99; s. c., 62 Am. Dec. 142; White *v.* Heylman, 34 Pa. St. 142; Beckwith *v.* Frisbie, 32 Vt. 559; De Bow *v.* United States, 11 Ct. of Cl. 672; Devlin *v.* United States, 12 Ct. of Cl. 266; Corkle *v.* Maxwell, 3 Blatchf. (U. S.) 413.

1. Town of Ligonier *v.* Ackerman, 46 Ind. 552; s. c., 15 Am. Rep. 323; White *v.* United States, 11 Ct. of Cl. 578.

And the protest must state the grounds of illegality. Meek *v.* McClure, 49 Cal. 624.

But if a public officer who illegally demands money of a person and exacts the payment thereof by coercion, has notice of the facts which render the demand illegal, a protest is unnecessary. Meek *v.* McClure, 49 Cal. 624.

A protest alone, however, cannot change what would otherwise in law be a voluntary payment into an involuntary one. Detroit *v.* Martin, 34 Mich. 170; s. c., 22 Am. Rep. 572. See also cases cited *supra*.

Where the statute requires the protest to be in writing, an oral statement to the clerk of a city treasurer that the payment is made under protest is not sufficient, though the clerk acting upon instructions to make a note of all protests, wrote upon the receipt that the tax was paid under protest, and also made a memorandum to that effect on the treasurer's books. Knowles *v.* Boston, 129 Mass. 551.

But it is no objection that it was written across the face of the tax-bill, nor that after presentation to the collector it was not left with him but was taken away by the tax-payer. Bor-

4. Of Taxes.—A voluntary payment of an illegal tax cannot be recovered back; and if there is no mode of collecting the tax except by an ordinary proceeding at law or in equity, a payment will be considered voluntary, though made under protest.[1]

land *v.* Boston, 132 Mass. 89; s. c., 42 Am. Rep. 424.

See generally as to the effect of a protest, McMillan *v.* Richards, 9 Cal. 365; Kansas Pac. R. Co. *v.* Wyandotte Co., 16 Kan. 587; Wabaunsee Co. *v.* Walker, 8 Kan. 431; Forbes *v.* Appleton, 5 Cush. (Mass.) 115; Benson *v.* Monroe, 7 Cush. (Mass.) 125; Cook *v.* Boston, 9 Allen (Mass.) 393; Awalt *v.* Eutaw, etc. Assoc., 34 Md. 435; Williams *v.* Colby, 44 Vt. 40; Detroit *v.* Martin, 34 Mich. 170; Copas *v.* Anglo-American Provision Co., 73 Mich. 541; McCabe *v.* Shaver, 69 Mich 25.

1. Wills *v.* Austin, 53 Cal. 152; Merrill *v.* Austin, 53 Cal. 379; Goddard *v.* Seymour, 30 Conn. 394; Garrigan *v.* Knight, 47 Iowa 525; Morris *v.* Mayor etc. of Baltimore, 5 Gill (Md.) 248; Marietta *v.* Shlocomb, 6 Ohio St. 471; Drake *v.* Shurtliff, 24 Hun (N. Y.) 422.

An assessment for a municipal improvement, if voluntarily paid, cannot be recovered back, though the payment was made under protest, and the law authorizing the assessment was subsequently adjudged unconstitutional. Peebles *v.* Pittsburg, 101 Pa. St. 304; s. c., 47 Am. Rep. 714 (cases reviewed); Rogers *v.* Greenbush, 58 Me. 390; s. c., 4 Am. Rep. 292; Detroit *v.* Martin, 34 Mich. 170; s. c., 22 Am. Rep. 512, and note p. 519; Wabaunsee Co. *v.* Walker, 8 Kan. 431; Bucknell *v.* Story, 46 Cal. 589; s. c., 13 Am. Rep. 220; Ligonier *v.* Ackerman, 46 Ind. 552; s. c., 15 Am. Rep. 323. In this last case there is a very full citation and review of the authorities. First Nat. Bank *v.* Mayor etc. of Americus, 68 Ga. 119; s. c., 45 Am. Rep. 476.

Compare Parcher *v.* Marathon Co., 52 Wis. 388; s. c., 38 Am. Rep, 745; Peyser *v* Mayor, etc. of N. Y., 70 N. Y. 497; s. c., 26 Am. Rep. 624; Jersey City *v.* Riker, 38 N. J. L. 225; s. c., 20 Am. Rep. 386; Louisville *v.* Anderson, 79 Ky. 334; s. c., 42 Am. Rep. 220.

Unless there is a statute specially authorizing such recovery. Durham *v.* Montgomery Co., 95 Ind. 182.

If property is assessed for street improvements to a stranger, and the true owner, with knowledge of the facts, but under a misapprehension of, or in ignorance of, the law, pays the tax under protest and to prevent a threatened sale by the tax collector, such payment is voluntary and cannot be recovered back. Bucknell *v.* Story, 46 Cal. 589; s c., 13 Am. Rep. 220.

Land having been sold to a city for unpaid taxes, the owner made a written proposition to the city government, with a view to avoid any unnecessary dispute, to pay the tax if the city would remit the interest and penalty and release all claim to the land, the payment to be without any prejudice to any right of such owner in the premises, or to their assertion in the courts. The proposition was accepted and acted upon, the collector's receipt for the taxes stating that "the above amount is paid under protest." *Held*, that the payment was a voluntary one, and the money could not be recovered back though the land was not subject to taxation. Galveston City Co. *v.* Galveston, 56 Tex. 486.

Where the money was paid for taxes or as redemption money on lands, the entry of which had been suspended by the Land Department for failure of the local land officers to account for the entrance money to the United States, it cannot be recovered back pending such suspension. Whether it can be after the entry is finally canceled, *quære.* Foster *v.* Pierce Co., 15 Neb. 48.

A tax paid cannot be recovered back on the ground of the unconstitutionality of the statute under which it was levied, where there was no compulsion except the threat of selling the land. Detroit *v.* Martin, 34 Mich. 170; s. c., 22 Am. Rep. 512; San Francisco etc. R. Co. *v.* Dinwiddie, 8 Sawyer (U. S.) 312.

The owner of a city lot tendered to the treasurer of the county the taxes due thereon. The lot had also been assessed by the city for a street improvement, which assessment had been certified to the county auditor, and placed upon the duplicate for collection, as other taxes, but was void for want of authority to make it. The county treasurer refused to receive the taxes legally due, unless the owner would

5. Officer Threatening to Execute Warrant.—But if the officer demanding the tax or assessment have in his possession at the time a warrant which is in the nature of an execution running against the property, and the party can save himself in no other way than by paying the illegal demand, he may then pay it under protest, and recover it back upon showing that the demand was illegal.[1]

also pay the assessment, and upon his declining to do so, the lot was returned delinquent and was about to be sold at tax sale. To prevent such sale, the owner paid the assessment under protest, and also the taxes. It was held that such payment was not voluntary, and could be recovered back. Stephen *v.* Daniels, 27 Ohio St. 527.

Where, by an official survey made by a city engineer, certain property was included within the corporate limits, and the owner, without protest, paid the municipal tax thereon, he cannot recover the amount, though on a resurvey by a subsequent engineer the property was found to be outside the city limits. Jackson *v.* Atlanta, 61 Ga. 228.

Compare Indianapolis *v.* McAvoy, 86 Ind. 587.

And it is held by the court of appeals of Kentucky that though the illegal taxes were voluntarily paid, yet if it were paid under a mistake of both law and fact, it may be recovered back. (*Citing* cases from Kentucky, Connecticut and Alabama). Louisville *v.* Anderson, 79 Ky. 334; s. c., 42 Am. Rep. 220.

In *Indiana* there is a statutory provision for the refunding of taxes, wrongfully assessed. (1 Rev. Stat. 1876 310, 311, §§ 84, 85; 1881, § 5813). To bring a case within the statute, however, it is not enough to show that the taxes were irregularly assessed; it must be made to appear that they were not legally or equitably owing. Carroll Co. *v.* Graham, 98 Ind. 279.

See also Indianapolis *v.* McAvoy, 86 Ind. 587; Durham *v.* Montgomery Co. 95 Ind. 182.

In *Iowa* it is held that where a tax is not merely informal and irregular, but is illegal and void as being levied on property not liable to taxation, and the owner of the property makes payment under protest, the better rule is that he may recover it back. Winzer *v.* Burlington, 68 Iowa 279 (where cases are to some extent compared); Thomas *v.* Burlington, 69 Iowa 140.

But these cases are decided more upon the wording of the statute than upon the rule as it exists independently of statutory provisions, § 870 of the Iowa Code providing for the refunding of taxes found to have been erroneously or illegally exacted or paid. See Isbell *v.* Crawford Co., 40 Iowa 102 and earlier decisions.

Where water commissioners collected an excessive rate from a manufacturing corporation, under threats that if it were not paid the water would be turned off, thus closing the factory and throwing a large number of hands out of employment, it was held that the payment was not a voluntary one, that the excess could be recovered back. Westlake *v.* St. Louis, 77 Mo. 47; s. c. 46 Am. Rep. 4.

A town having passed an ordinance requiring a license for selling liquors, the legality of which was questioned, an agreement was entered into between the town trustees and the liquor dealers, that if the latter would pay the license fee, such fee should be refunded in case the town should fail to recover judgment in certain cases then pending in the courts to test the legality of the ordinance. Plaintiff paid the license fee, and the ordinance was subsequently adjudged invalid. *Held*, that this was not a voluntary payment, but one made under contract, and plaintiff was entitled to recover. Columbia City *v.* Anthes, 84 Ind. 31; s. c., 43 Am. Rep. 80.

See also Edinburg *v.* Hackney, 54 Ind. 83.

A payment to the treasurer of San Francisco to purchase a license as a passenger broker cannot be recovered back. Garrison *v.* Tillinghast, 18 Cal. 408.

And see, on the general subject, Carr *v.* Stewart, 58 Ind. 581; Mearkle *v.* Hennepin Co. (Minn. 1890), 47 N. W. Rep. 165; Smyth *v.* Mayor etc. of N. Y., 11 N. Y. Supp. 583; Vanderbeck *v.* Rochester (N. Y. 1890), 25 N. E. Rep. 408.

1. Union Pac. R. Co. *v.* Dodge Co., 98

6. A mere threat to sell realty for an illegal and void tax will not render the payment voluntary, since such a sale will not cast a cloud on the title.[1]

7. Payment to Common Carrier.—A payment made to a common carrier of a sum of money illegally charged for freight, upon a refusal by the carrier to transport the goods unless the illegal freight is paid, is not voluntary but compulsory.[2]

U. S. 541; Kansas Pac. R. Co. *v.* Wyandotte Co., 16 Kan. 587; Preston *v.* Boston, 12 Pick. (Mass.) 14; Wright *v.* Boston, 9 Cush. (Mass.) 241; Boston etc. Glass Co. *v.* Boston, 4 Met. (Mass.) 189; Borough of Allentown *v.* Saeger, 20 Pa. St. 421; Bruecher *v.* Village of Port Chester, 101 N. Y. 240; Tuttle *v.* Everett, 51 Mass. 27; s. c., 24 Am. Rep. 622; Maguire *v.* State Sav. Assoc., 62 Mo. 344; Kimball *v.* Corn Exchange Nat. Bank, 1 Ill. Abb. 209; Chicago *v.* Fidelity Sav. Bank, 11 Ill. App. 165; Western Union Tel. Co. *v.* Mayer, 28 Ohio St. 521; O'Brien *v.* Colusa Co., 67 Cal. 503; Grimley *v.* Santa Clara Co., 68 Cal. 575; Bates *v.* York Co. 15 Neb. 284; Foster *v.* Pierce Co., 15 Neb. 48; Welton *v.* Merrick Co., 16 Neb. 83.

So if the officer hold legal process purporting to authorize the arrest or seizure of property to enforce a collection of any kind. Atwell *v.* Zeluff, 26 Mich. 118; McKee *v.* Campbell, 27 Mich. 497; Post *v.* Clark, 35 Conn. 339.

It is not necessary to show that the distress was actually made. It is sufficient that the circumstances lead to the conclusion that such distress is impending and will certainly be made if the tax is not paid. Howard *v.* Augusta, 74 Me. 79.

Payment made under protest of an illegal tax, on demand by the sheriff, to prevent levy and sale, is not a voluntary payment, though there is no present threat of levy. Parcher *v.* Marathon Co., 52 Wis. 388; s. c. 38 Am. Rep. 745.

In order to recover from the collector in such cases, suit must be brought promptly before he is obliged to pay over the money. Hardesty *v.* Fleming, 57 Tex. 395.

Where the tax is paid under a threat of the city collector to shut up the payor's shop, it is not voluntary, and may be recovered back from the collector, but not from the city. Vicksburgh *v.* Butler, 56 Miss. 72.

1. 2 Dill. Mun. Corp. (3d ed.) § 942; Bucknall *v.* Story, 46 Cal. 589; s. c., 13 Am. Rep. 220; Rogers *v.* Greenbush, 58 Me. 390; s. c., 4 Am. Rep. 292; Murphey *v.* Mayor etc. of Wilmington (Md., 1880), 10 Atl. Rep. 765; Detroit *v.* Martin, 34 Mich. 170; s. c., 22 Am. Rep. 512.

A tax deed which is void on its face is not a cloud upon title, and a mere threat by a tax-collector to sell property and make such a deed will not render the payment of a tax voluntary. Wills *v.* Austin, 53 Cal. 152; Sears *v.* Marshall Co., 59 Iowa 603; Shane *v.* St. Paul, 26 Minn. 543.

Plaintiff refused payment of a personal tax on the ground of non-residence, whereupon proceedings were instituted, which resulted in an order on him by the county judge to pay the tax, and enjoining him from disposing of his property. Plaintiff accordingly paid the tax, and sued the assessors to recover the amount. *Held*, that the payment was voluntary. Drake *v.* Shurtliff, 24 Hun (N. Y.) 422.

2. 2 Greenl. Evid. § 121; Mobile etc. R. Co. *v.* Steiner, 61 Ala. 560; Chicago etc. R. Co. *v.* Chicago etc. Coal Co., 79 Ill. 121; Lafayette etc. R. Co. *v.* Pattison, 41 Ind. 312; McGregor *v.* Erie R. Co., 35 N. J. L. 89; West Virginia Transp. Co. *v.* Sweetzer, 25 W. Va. 434.

Compare Potomac Coal Co. *v.* Cumberland etc. R. Co., 38 Md. 226.

A carrier exacted from a shipper illegal and unauthorized rates, and the shipper was required to pay the same in order to procure the transportation of his property, the failure to transport which would, by reason of the character of his business, have occasioned the shipper great loss. The shipper paid the illegal charges, complaining and objecting thereto. *Held*, that such payment was not voluntary, and may be recovered back. Peters *v.* Railroad Co., 42 Ohio St. 275; s. c., 51 Am. Rep. 814.

In the case of Parker *v.* Great West-

8. Made in Ignorance of Law.—Money voluntarily paid to another under a mistake of law but with a knowledge of all the facts, cannot be recovered back.[1] But it seems to be settled that when money is paid on a judgment which is afterwards reversed, the

ern R. Co. (7 Man. & Gr. 253), which was a case involving this question, decided in 1844, TINDAL, C. J., says: "We are of opinion that the payments were not voluntary. They were made in order to induce the company to do that which they were bound to do without them, and for the refusal to do which an action on the case might have been maintained. . . . The case very much resembles that of —— *v.* Piggott, mentioned by LORD KENYON, in Cartwright *v.* Rowley, 2 Esp. N. P. C. 723. That was an action brought to recover back money paid to the steward of a manor for producing at a trial some deeds and court rolls, for which he had charged extravagantly. The objection was taken that the money had been voluntarily paid, and so could not be recovered back again; but, it appearing that the party could not do without the deeds so that the money was paid through necessity and the urgency of the case, it was held to be recoverable. We think the principle upon which that decision proceeded is a sound one, and strictly applicable in the present case, and that the defendants cannot, by the assistance of that rule of law on which they relied, retain the money that they have improperly received."

This decision is referred to with approval by MR. JUSTICE MATTHEWS, in Swift etc. Co. *v.* United States (111 U. S. 29). See also Feamley *v.* Morley, 5 B. & C. 25; Parker *v.* R. Co., 6 Exch. 702.

In the *Illinois* case cited above, the court says: "It can hardly be said the enhanced charges were voluntarily paid by the appellees. It was a case of life and death with them, as they had no other means of conveying their coals to the markets offered by the Illinois Central, and were bound to accede to any terms the appellants might impose. They were under a sort of moral duress, by submitting to which appellants have recovered money from them which in equity and good conscience they ought not to retain." Chicago etc. R. Co. *v.* Chicago etc. Coal Co., 79 Ill. 128.

Nor does it affect the right to recover that the payments were made periodically. Peters *v.* Railroad Co., 42 Ohio St. 275; s. c., 51 Am. Rep. 814; Swift etc. Co. *v.* United States, 111 U. S. 22.

A navigation company which was bound to keep in repair certain dams failed to do so, and when an owner of logs refused to pay tolls threatened that unless he paid them a certain dam should be cut, the effect of which would have been the practical ruin of his business. A payment made by him under these circumstances was not voluntary, and he could recover back the tolls thus extorted. Lehigh Coal etc. Co. *v.* Brown, 100 Pa. St. 338.

1. Bilbie *v.* Lumley, 2 East 469; Stevens *v.* Lynch, 12 East 38; Lowrie *v.* Bourdieu, Doug. 467; Livermore *v.* Peru, 55 Me. 469; Clarke *v.* Dutcher, 9 Cow. (N. Y.) 674; Norton *v.* Marden, 15 Me. 45; s. c., 32 Am. Dec. 132; Milwaukee etc. R. Co. *v.* Soutter, 13 Wall. (U. S.) 517; Bank of U. S. *v.* Daniel, 12 Pet. (U. S.) 32; Champlin *v.* Laytin, 18 Wend. (N. Y.) 407; s. c., 31 Am. Dec. 382; Elliot *v.* Swartwout, 10 Pet. (U. S.) 137; Brisbane *v.* Dacres, 5 Taunt. 144; Wilson *v.* Bryan, 6 Yerg. (Tenn.) 485; Hubbard *v.* Martin, 8 Yerg. (Tenn.) 498; Jones *v.* Watkins, 1 Stew. (Ala.) 81; Milnes *v.* Duncan, 6 B. & C. 671; Mowatt *v.* Wright, 1 Wend. (N. Y.) 355; s. c., 19 Am. Dec. 508; Lammot *v.* Bowly, 6 Har. & J. (Md.) 500; Erkens *v.* Nicolin, 39 Minn. 461; Real Estate Sav. Institution *v.* Linder, 74 Pa. St. 371; Irvine *v.* Hanlin, 10 S. & R. (Pa.) 219; Deysher *v.* Triebel, 64 Pa. St. 383; Natcher *v* Natcher, 47 Pa. St. 496; Snelson *v.* State, 16 Ind. 29; Rector *v.* Collins, 46 Ark. 167; s. c., 55 Am. Rep. 571; Downs *v.* Donnely, 5 Ind. 496; Supervisors of Onondaga *v.* Briggs, 2 Den. (N. Y.) 26; New York etc. R. Co. *v.* Marsh, 12 N. Y. 308; Hunt *v.* Rousmanier, 2 Mason (U. S.) 342; s. c., 3 Mason (U. S.) 294; s. c., on appeal, 8 Wheat. (U. S.) 174. See also Hunt *v.* Rhodes, 1 Pet. (U. S.) 1; Northrop *v.* Graves, 19 Conn. 548; s. c., 50 Am. Dec. 264; Haigh *v.* United States Building etc. Assoc., 19 W. Va. 792; West Virginia Transp. Co. *v.* Sweetzer, 25 W. Va. 434.

There is some confusion among the decisions as to the limitations of the rule. Champlin *v.* Laytin, 18 Wend. (N. Y.) 407; s. c., 31 Am. Dec. 382; Haven *v.* Foster, 9 Pick. (Mass.) 112; s. c., 19 Am. Dec. 353; Claflin *v.* Godfry, 21 Pick. (Mass.) 14.

Though it has sometimes been doubted whether ignorance of law will prevent the recovery of money voluntarily paid, where there is full knowledge as to the facts. See Champlin *v.* Laytin, 6 Paige (N. Y.) 189; s. c., 18 Wend. (N. Y.) 407; s. c., 31 Am. Dec. 382; Clarke *v.* Dutcher, 9 Cow. (N. Y.) 674; Bize *v.* Dickason, 1 T. R. 285; Farmen *v.* Arundel, 2 W. Blacks. 825; Brigham *v.* Brigham, 1 Ves. Sr. 126; Cliflion *v.* Cockburn, 3 Ml. & Ky. 76; Northrop *v.* Graves, 19 Conn. 548; s. c., 50 Am. Dec. 264; Stedwell *v.* Anderson, 21 Conn. 139; Culbreath *v.* Culbreath, 7 Ga. 64; s. c., 50 Am. Dec. 375; Underwood *v.* Brockman, 4 Dana (Ky.) 309; s. c., 29 Am. Dec. 407; Ray *v.* Bank of Kentucky, 3 B. Mon. (Ky.) 510; s. c., 39 Am. Dec. 479; Lammot *v.* Bowley, 6 Har. & J. (Md.) 500; Haven *v.* Fister, 9 Pick. (Mass.) 112, 129; s. c., 19 Am. Dec. 353.

Yet the weight of authority is in accordance with the statement of the text. Bilbie *v.* Lumley, 2 East 469; Stevens *v.* Lynch, 12 East 38; Millins *v.* Duncan, 6 B. & C. 671; Brumston *v.* Robins, 4 Bing. 11; Bank of United States *v.* Daniel, 12 Pet. (U. S.) 32; Jones *v.* Watkins, 1 Stew. (Ala.) 81; Wheaton *v.* Wheaton, 9 Conn. 96; Pinkham *v.* Gear, 3 N. H. 163; Peterborough *v.* Lancaster, 14 N. H. 382; Clarke *v.* Dutcher, 9 Cow. (N. Y.) 674; Mowatt *v.* Wright, 1 Wend. (N. Y.) 355; s. c., 19 Am. Dec. 508; Real Estate Sav. Institution *v.* Linder, 74 Pa. St. 371; Gould *v.* McFall, 118 Pa. St. 455; s. c., 4 Am. St. Rep. 606; Mayor of Richmond *v.* Judah, 5 Leigh (Va.) 305; West Virginia Transp. Co. *v.* Sweetzer, 25 W. Va. 434; Beard *v.* Beard, 25 W. Va. 486; s. c., 52 Am. Rep. 219.

In Bilbie *v.* Lumley (2 East 469) in which it was sought to recover back money paid under a policy of insurance, on the ground that a certain letter had not been disclosed at the time the assurance was effected which fact was known to the underwriter at the time the loss was adjusted, plaintiff's counsel was asked by LORD ELLENBOROUGH whether he could state any case where a party paying money voluntarily, with full knowledge of the facts of the case, could recover it back on account of his ignorance of the law; adding: "Every man must be taken to be cognizant of the law; otherwise there is no saying to what extent ignorance might not be carried."

And this is the view taken in Brisbane *v.* Dacres, 5 Taunt. 143; Gomery *v.* Bond, 3 M. & S. 378; East India Co. *v.* Tritton, 3 B. & C. 280; Baumston *v.* Robins, 4 Bing. 11; Platt *v.* Bromage, 24 L. J., N. S. Exch. 63; McCarthy *v.* Decaix, 2 R. & Myln. 614.

A payment voluntary made in gold coin before the decision of the United States Supreme Court declaring the legal tender act constitutional cannot be recovered back after such decision, if made without any misapprehension or mistake of fact. Doll *v.* Earle, 65 Barb. (N. Y.) 298.

While ordinarily a payment made under a mutual mistake of law cannot be recovered back, yet where goods are in possession of an officer, who has no authority to retain them, yet exacts from the owner a fee as a condition of restoring them, the payment of such fee is not voluntary, though both parties believed it to be legal. De Bow *v.* United States, 11 Ct. of Cl. 672.

Where two parties claimed the same land under a will, and with knowledge of all the facts and without any fraud or imposition, collected and voluntarily divided the rents and profits, neither can subsequently recover from the other the rents so voluntarily paid or allowed to be paid. White *v.* Rowland, 67 Ga. 546; s. c., 44 Am. Rep. 731.

It is held in *Minnesota* that money paid under mistake of law cannot be recovered back where the transaction is unaffected by any fraud, trust, confidence or the like, but both parties acted in good faith, knew all the facts and had equal means of knowing them. Erkens *v.* Nicolin, 39 Minn. 461.

Where the members of a mutual fire insurance company pay money to a receiver upon an assessment which turns out to be invalid, the money so paid cannot be recovered back. Wilde *v.* Baker, 14 Allen (Mass.) 349.

A party in ignorance of the law that distances must yield to natural boundaries called for in a deed, paid money for a quit-claim deed of property, which, under this rule, already belonged to him. *Held*, that the money could not be recovered back. Erkens *v.* Nicolin, 39 Minn. 461.

But it is held in Illinois that where

money so paid may be recovered back.[1] If part of the money is paid voluntarily after suit is brought and a decree is rendered for the balance, which decree is finally set aside, there can be no recovery for the money paid.[2] Money paid under a mistake of a foreign law may be recovered back on the ground that such a mistake is one of fact.[3]

9. Under Mistake of Fact.—Money paid under a mistake of a

the defendant in an action of contract has paid interest, erroneously deeming himself liable to pay it, the court, in assessing the amount due on the contract, will deduct such payments. Hall *v.* Jackson Co., 5 Ill. App. 609.

Defendant without fraudulent intent, made certain representaions to plaintiff as to a patent. whereby plaintiff was induced to pay defendant a fixed sum for the privilege of operating under said patent. It was not claimed that there was any misrepresenation as to the actual contents of the patent and specifications, but the misrepresentations were as to the legal validity thereof as against certain other patents. *Held*, that the money so paid could not be recovered back, (cases reviewed). Schwazenbach *v.* Odorless Excavating Apparatus Co., 65 Md. 34; s. c., 57 Am. Rep. 301.

If after a suit has been brought to recover a sum of money, but before any judgment or decree has been rendered requiring it to be paid, defendant voluntarily pays the money, he cannot recover it back, even though the judgment which is afterwards rendered against him for the amount is reversed on writ of error. Brisbane *v.* Dacres, 5 Taunt. 152; Brown *v.* McKinnally, 1 Esp. 279; Humbt *v.* Richardson, 9 Benj. 644; Milnes *v.* Duncan, 6 B. & C. 679; Forbes *v.* Appleton, 5 Cush. (Mass.) 155; Benson *v.* Monroe, 7 Cush. (Mass.) 125; s. c., 54 Am. Dec. 716; Beard *v.* Beard, 25 W. Va. 486; s. c., 52 Am. Rep. 219.

And see on the subject of the recovery back of money paid in ignorance of law: Patterson *v.* Cox, 25 Ind. 261; Peterborough *v.* Lancaster, 14 N. H. 382; Vinal *v.* Continental Const. & Imp. Co. (Supreme Ct.), 6 N. Y. Supp. 595; 53 Hun (N. Y.) 247; Silliman *v.* Wing, 7 Hill (N. Y.) 159; Supervisors of Onondaga *v.* Briggs, 2 Den. (N. Y.) 26; Ege *v.* Koontze, 3 Pa. St. 109; Robinson *v.* City Council of Charleston, 2 Rich. (S. Car.) 317; Natcher *v.* Natcher, 47 Pa. St. 496; Valley R. Co. *v.* Lake Erie Iron Co., 46 Ohio St. 44; Real Estate Sav. Institution *v.* Linder, 74 Pa. St. 371.

1. Homer *v.* Barrett, 2 Root (Conn.) 156; Sturges *v.* Allis, 10 Wend. (N. Y.) 354; Duncan *v.* Kirkpatrick, 13 S. & R. (Pa.) 292; Duncan *v.* Ware, 5 Stew. & P. (Ala.) 119; Green *v.* Stone, 1 Har. & J. (Md.) 405; Clark *v.* Pinney, 6 Cow. (N. Y.) 297; Dennett *v.* Nevers, 7 Me. 399; Raun *v.* Reynolds, 18 Cal. 275; McDonald *v.* Napier, 14 Ga. 89; Stevens *v.* Fitch, 11 Met. (Mass.) 248; Maghee *v.* Kellogg, 24 Wend. (N. Y.) 32; Bank of U. S. *v.* Bank of Washington, 6 Pet. (U. S.) 8; Paulding *v.* Watson, 26 Ala. 205; Williams *v.* Simmons, 22 Ala. 425.

But money paid upon lawful process of execution cannot be recovered back though not justly or lawfully due by defendant in the execution to the plaintiff. Federal Ins. Co. *v.* Robinson, 82 Pa. St. 357; Rapalje *v.* Emory, 2 Dall. (Pa.) 51.

In Gould *v.* McFall, 118 Pa. St. 455; s. c., 4 Am. St. Rep. 606, a judgment was rendered against the defendants and an execution placed in the hands of the sheriff and the judgment, costs and interest were paid by one of the defendants. The judgment was reversed on appeal, but it was held that the money had been paid voluntarily and could not be recovered.

The court say: "And the general principle appears to be that money voluntarily paid upon a claim of right cannot be recovered back however unfounded such a claim may afterwards turn out to be."

See also Bond *v.* Coats, 16 Ind. 202; Gooding *v.* Morgan, 37 Me. 419; Jefferson Co. *v.* Hawkins, 23 Fla. 223. *Compare* Logan *v.* Sumter, 28 Ga. 242.

2. Beard *v.* Beard, 25 W. Va. 486; s. c., 652 Am. Rep. 219.

3. Vinal *v.* Continental Const. & Imp. Co. (Supreme Ct.), 6 N. Y. Supp. 595; Bently *v.* Whittemore, 18 N. J. Eq. 336; King *v.* Doolittle, 1 Head (Tenn.) 77; Haven *v.* Foster, 9 Pick. (Mass.) 122; s. c., 19 Am. Dec. 353; Sawyer *v* Hammatt, 15 Me. 43.

material fact may be recovered back.[1] But it must appear that

1. Davis *v.* Krum, 12 Mo. App. 279; Grimes *v.* Blake, 16 Ind. 160; Goodspeed *v.* Fuller, 46 Me. 141; s. c., 71 Am. Dec. 572; Glen *v.* Shannon, 12 S. Car. 570; Newell *v.* Smith, 53 Conn. 72; Wolfe *v.* Beaird, 123 Ill. 585; Wheadon *v.* Olds, 20 Wend. (N. Y.) 174; Baldwin *v.* Foss, 17 Iowa 389; Canal Bank *v.* Bank of Albany, 1 Hill (N. Y.) 287; McLean Co. Bank *v.* Mitchell, 88 Ill. 52; Stempel *v.* Thomas, 89 Ill. 147; Higgins *v.* Mendenhall, 51 Iowa 135; Van Saten *v.* Standard Oil Co., 17 Hun (N. Y.) 140; Clark *v.* Sylvester (Me. 1888), 13 Atl. Rep. 404; Lane *v.* Pere Marquette etc. Co., 62 Mich. 63; Buffalo *v.* O'Malley, 61 Wis. 255; Townsend *v.* Crowdy, 8 C. B. N., S. 477; Billingslea *v.* Ware, 32 Ala. 415; Guild *v.* Baldridge, 2 Swan (Tenn.) 295; Southwick *v.* First Nat. Bank, 20 Hun (N. Y.) 349; Neitzey *v.* District of Columbia, 17 Ct. of Cl. 111; United States *v.* Onondaga Co. Sav. Bank, 39 Fed. Rep. 259; Vinal *v.* Continental Const. & Imp. Co., 53 Hun (N. Y.) 247; Johnson *v.* Leffingwell, 74 Iowa 114; Lake *v.* Artisans' Bank, 3 Abb. App. Dec. (N. Y.) 10; Sharkey *v.* Mansfield, 90 N. Y. 228; s. c., 43 Am. Rep. 161; Wood *v.* Armory, 105 N. Y. 278; Fraker *v.* Little, 24 Kan. 598; s. c., 36 Am. Rep. 262; Du Souchet *v.* Dutcher, 113 Ind. 249; Baldwin *v.* Foss, 71 Iowa 389. (Iowa cases cited.) *Compare* Montgomery's Appeal, 92 Pa St. 202; s. c., 37 Am. Rep. 670; Glenn *v.* Shannon, 12 S. Car. 570. But it has been held that in order to recover back money paid for a valid consideration it must be shown that the defendant was in some way responsible for the mistake. Manzy *v.* Hardy, 13 Neb. 33.

When money has been paid under a mutual mistake or by the mistake of one party and fraudulently received by the other, an action to recover the same will lie, but is barred by the statute of limitations in five years. Higgins *v.* Mendenhall, 51 Iowa 135, overruling Higgins *v.* Mendenhall, 42 Iowa 675; McGinnis *v.* Hunt, 47 Iowa 668.

Money paid under a mistake of fact may be recovered, notwithstanding a negligent failure to use the means of knowledge open to plaintiff. Disapproving Layfayette etc. R. Co. *v.* Pattison, 41 Ind. 312; Indianapolis *v.* McAvoy, 86 Ind. 587, and cases cited; Lyle *v.* Shinnebarger, 17 Mo. App. 66; Dobson *v.* Winner, 26 Mo. App. 329; Lawrence *v.* American Nat. Bank, 54 N. Y. 432; Mayer *v.* Mayor etc. of N. Y., 63 N. Y. 455; Alston *v.* Richardson, 51 Tex. 1. *Compare* Neal *v.* Read, 7 Baxt. (Tenn.) 333; Union Sav. Assoc. *v.* Kehlor, 7 Mo. App. 158.

Where the debtor trusts the creditor to make the calculation of interest on notes, and the creditor after making it assures the debtor that it is correct, and the statement is accepted and interest paid accordingly, the debtor may, upon discovering that the calculation was erroneous, recover the excess paid. Worley *v.* Moore, 97 Ind. 15. To same effect, Hanson *v.* Jones, 20 Mo. App. 595.

In a *Michigan* case, where the trial court instructed that unless the payment was made under a *gross* mistake of fact, the money could not be recovered back, the supreme court held that the charge was as favorable, if not more so, as the defendant could reasonably ask. Lane *v.* Pere Marquette Boom Co., 62 Mich. 63.

The facts in the above case were as follows: The plaintiff made a written contract with defendant to drive his logs to L at an agreed price per thousand feet. A weekly statement was to be made by the owners of the mills to which the logs were delivered, which was to be made up from statements of the scaler, and the final settlement was to be made on the woods' scale. Plaintiff's scaler, at his request, rendered to the boom company a statement of the woods scale, and plaintiff paid defendant upon the basis of such statement. After the logs were manufactured, plaintiff discovered that a gross error had been made in the measurement, whereby he had largely overpaid defendant, and brought suit to recover the excess paid by him. The court below charged the jury that if the discrepancy in the quantity of logs, as shown by the woods scale and those delivered, was caused by the difference in judgment of the different scalers on account of defects in the quality of the logs, or the circumstances under which the scale was made, then the plaintiff would be bound by the woods scale, and that the woods scale must control, unless clearly and positively impeached by showing a gross mistake. *Held*, no error.

Where one by mistake pays taxes on

another's land, he may recover the amount so paid from the true owner. Goodnow *v.* Litchfield, 63 Iowa 282; Goodnow *v.* Oakley, 68 Iowa 25; Union R. & T. Co. *v.* Skinner, 9 Mo. App. 189. *Compare* Carr *v.* Stewart, 58 Ind. 581.

But when the title to the land is in controversy, and one of the parties, whose title is afterward adjudged invalid, pays the taxes, he cannot recover the amount so paid from the other. Garrigan *v.* Knight, 47 Iowa 525. *Compare* Goodnow *v.* Moulton, 51 Iowa 555; Montgomery County *v.* Severson, 68 Iowa 451.

Money paid upon a parol contract sale of goods, under a mutual mistaken belief that a certain inventory thereof made by a third party stated their true cash value, may be recovered back. Sheffield *v.* Hamlin, 26 Hun (N. Y.) 237.

If one after an investigation becomes satisfied that a claim is correct and pays it, he cannot recover the money back on the ground that it was paid under a mistake of fact, though he afterward discovers the claim to be baseless. McArthur *v.* Luce, 43 Mich. 435; s. c., 38 Am. Rep. 204; Wheeler *v.* Hathaway, 58 Mich. 77. See Reisenleiter *v.* Lutherische Kirche, 29 Mo. App. 291.

Where a clerk of a court certified the same bill of costs for the same services three times, and the county board relying upon the certificates, made to the sheriff treble payments, the money so paid could be recovered. Holmes *v.* Lucas Co., 53 Iowa 211.

A government officer who has been paid money to which he is not entitled, through a mistake of the accounting officers, may be compelled to refund it. McElrath *v.* United States, 12 Ct. of Cl. 201.

In *Massachusetts* an indorser was held entitled to recover money which he had paid to take up the note, he having relied upon the certificate of a notary as to its dishonor, and it afterwards appearing that the demand upon the maker was insufficient to charge the indorser. Talbot *v.* National Bank, 129 Mass. 67; s. c., 37 Am. Rep. 302.

A party who has paid money on an indorsement which he recognized as genuine, but which he afterwards discovered to be a forgery, cannot recover it back. Lewis *v.* White's Bank, 27 Hun (N. Y.) 396.

If an executor or administrator carelessly, negligently and voluntarily pays legacies or distributive shares before the estate is settled, and afterwards finds he has overpaid the legatee or distributee, he cannot recover the sum so paid unless he can show reasonable diligence on his part in ascertaining the condition of the estate, and special circumstances that reasonably misled him in making the payments. Lyle *v.* Siler, 103 N. Car. 26.

Where the money is paid for a valid consideration, it cannot be recovered on the ground that it has been paid under a mistake of fact, unless it is shown that the party receiving it is in some way responsible for the mistake. Manzy *v.* Hardy, 13 Neb. 36.

Where an agreement had been made whereby the creditors were to receive fifty per cent. of their claims against the debtor, and one of the creditors received the full amount of his claim on account of the debtor supposing it to be twice as large as it really was, which mistake was known to the creditor, an action will lie to recover back the amount overpaid. Trecy *v.* Jefts, 149 Mass. 211.

Money paid under a mistake as to the law of another State, may be recovered back on the ground that such a mistake is one of fact. Vinal *v.* Continental Const. & Imp. Co., 53 Hun (N. Y.) 247.

Where A, believing that he owed certain money to B, by arrangement paid it to C, a creditor of B, who received it in good faith from A, the latter cannot recover it back from C, who in consequence may have lost or waived remedy against the debtor B. Guild *v.* Baldridge, 2 Swan (Tenn.) 295.

Where a mistake had been made in deducting the amount of duty which the parties to a sale of goods thought would be the proper amount, the amount deducted being 25 cents per pound, while the legal rate was only 20 cents per pound, it was held that it was a mistake of fact and not one of law, and a recovery of the excess was allowed. Renard *v.* Fiedler, 3 Duer (N. Y.) 318.

Money paid by the agents of the government in excess of their authority may be recovered back by the government. United States *v.* City Bank, 6 McLean (U. S.) 130. But see United States *v.* Union Bank, 10 Ben. (U. S.) 408.

Money paid by one bank to a New

York bank to be credited to another bank in excess of the amount due the latter bank from the first, may be recovered back and the proceeds could be taken wherever found, unless they had passed into the hands of an innocent holder. First Nat. Bank *v.* Mastin Bank, 2 McCrary (U. S.) 438.

Under a contract to purchase milk at a certain price per gallon with the understanding that the cans in which the milk was delivered contained eight gallons, when in fact they contained much less, an action will lie to recover the money paid over the true amount due. Devine *v.* Edwards, 101 Ill. 138.

In Boyce *v.* Wilson, 32 Md. 122, the parties entered into an agreement for the purchase of property, and the agreement expressed the consideration as $90,322, which sum was paid. But it was afterwards found that there had been a mistake in an arithmetical computation of $9,072. An action at law was brought to recover this amount, and it was held, 1st, that the terms of the agreement could not be varied by parol evidence; 2nd, that the mistake was not such a one as a court of law could correct, as the payment was just as the contract provided for; 3rd, that the contract would have to be reformed in equity.

In Piscataquis *v.* Kingsbury, 73 Me. 326, an execution was taken out against a town, and property not belonging to the town was sold at a sheriff's sale. It was held that the purchase could recover the money paid because there was mistake of fact.

A mistake by a county clerk in making out an execution is a mistake of fact. Piscataquis *v.* Kingsbury, 73 Me. 326.

In Moore *v.* Moore, 127 Mass. 22, an executor paid money under a mistake or misapprehension of the meaning of the testator's will. It was held that an action would not lie against the person who received the money, believing it to be his own, in favor of him who was entitled to it under the will.

When both parties were mistaken as to the title to certain premises, it was held that an action would lie to recover the rents and profits from the person who supposed he had the right to receive them. Shaw *v.* Mussey, 48 Me. 247.

A demand for the money paid by mistake of the payor, when the payee knew it was paid by mistake is not necessary before bringing suit for its recovery. Sharkey *v.* Mansfield, 90 N. Y. 227; s. c., 43 Am. Rep. 161.

Money overpaid on a mortgage on account of ignorance of the amount due, reliance having been placed upon the statements of the creditor may be recovered back. Byrnes *v.* Martin, 67 Mich. 399.

When a son forged two mortgages on his father's land and the second mortgagee took the money to be paid, by him and paid up the first mortgage, he cannot after the discovery of the forgery maintain an action against the first mortgagee for the money so paid. Walker *v.* Conant, 69 Mich. 321.

Under the Kentucky statute providing that where by mistake one creditor of a decedent is paid more than his proportion of the assets the amount overpaid may be recovered back by the personal representatives, where a widow who is the executrix of her deceased husband pays his debts from the proceeds of an insurance policy which belong to her, on the supposition that the estate was solvent and would pay her back, which turns out to be insolvent, the creditors receiving such insurance money will be compelled to pay it back pro rata. Moore *v.* Morris, (Ky. 1889), 11 S. W. Rep. 780.

When by mutual mistake in settling an account one of the parties receives and cashes a check overpaying the amount due him, an action of tort will not lie against him for converting the check to his own use. Richardson *v.* Stevens (Supreme Ct.), 6 N. Y. Supp. 361.

Computation of Interest.—A common mistake of fact for which money may be usually recovered, arises in computing interest. Major *v.* Tardos, 14 La. Ann. 10; Worley *v.* Moore, 97 Ind. 15; Boon *v.* Miller, 16 Mo. 457.

When a mortgage deed called for 4½£ per cent. interest, but the deed being lost only 4£ per cent. was collected, it was held that the difference could be recovered in a proper action. Gregory *v.* Philkington, 39 Eng. L. & Eq. 316.

Where a mortgagor paid interest twice by mistake, it was held that an action would not lie to recover the overpayment as long as a larger sum was due from him on the mortgage, and that he would have the benefit of the payment when the bond and mortgage would be foreclosed. Jackson *v.* McKnight, 17 Hun (N. Y.) 2.

the money paid was not equitably due.[1] And when money has been paid under a mistake of fact which the payor had the means of knowing, it has been held that it could not be recovered back.[2] However, this doctrine has been seriously questioned by many courts, and may still be regarded as unsettled.[3] So also when money is paid under a *bona fide* forgetfulness of facts which disentitled the defendant to receive it, an action will lie to recover it back.[4] Where money is paid when a mistake is in question,

When interest was paid upon a note designedly made without interest, by reason of a mistake of fact, it was allowed to be recovered back. Hathaway *v.* Hagan, 59 Vt. 75.

And see on the question of a mistake of fact, as giving the right to recover back money which otherwise might be deemed to have been paid voluntarily, Rutherford *v.* McIvor, 21 Ala. 750; Banks *v.* Marshall, 23 Cal. 223; Vernon *v.* West School District, 38 Conn. 112; Brown *v.* College Corner etc. Gravel Road Co., 56 Ind. 110; Lewellen *v.* Garrett, 58 Ind. 442; Stuart *v.* Sears, 119 Mass. 143; Welch *v.* Goodwin, 123 Mass. 71; Millett *v.* Holt, 60 Me. 169; Worthington *v.* New York Cent. R. Co., 6 Lans. (N. Y.) 257; Mc Goren *v.* Avery, 37 Mich. 120; Foster *v.* Kirby, 31 Mo. 496; Koontz *v.* Central Nat. Bank, 51 Mo. 275; West *v.* Houston, 4 Harr. (Del.) 170; Mutual Life Ins. Co. *v.* Wager, 27 Barb. (N. Y.) 354; Duncan *v.* Berline, 60 N. Y. 151; Mayer *v.* Mayor, etc., of N. Y.,63 N. Y. 455; Lawrence *v.* American Nat. Bank, 54 N. Y. 432; Ransom *v.* Masten (Supreme Ct.), 4 N. Y. Supp. 781; Emerson *v.* Loveland (Supreme.Ct.),9 N. Y. Supp. 768; Brummitt *v.* McGuire (N. Car. 1890), 12 S. E. Rep. 191; Ormsby Coal Co. *v.* Bestwick (Pa. 1889), 18 Atl. Rep. 538; Gilliam *v.* Alford, 69 Tex. 267; Citizens Nat. Bank *v.* Manoni, 76 Va. 802.

1. Foster *v.* Kirby, 31 Mo. 496; Genn *v.* Shannon, 12 S. Car. 570.

2. Union Savings Assoc. *v.* Kehlor, 7 Mo. App. 158; Neal *v.* Reed, 7 Baxter (Tenn.) 333; Gooding *v.* Morgan, 37 Me. 419; Wood *v.* Patterson, 4 Md. Ch. Dec. 335; Warner *v.* Daniels, 1 Woodb. & M. (U. S.) 90.

Where an agreement was made between a mortgagor and mortgagee that a mortgage not yet due should be discharged for the payment of $500, a part of which was paid at the time, it was held that the mortgagor could not avoid his contract on learning that at the time the bargain was made there was due on the mortgage only $400, as he had the means of ascertaining the correct amount due which he failed to use. Scott *v.* Frink, 53 Barb. (N. Y.) 533.

3. Townsend *v.* Crowdy, 8 C. B. S. N. C. 477; Alston *v.* Richardson, 51 Tex.1; Kelley *v.* Solari, 9 M. & W. 54; Lyle *v.* Shinnebarger, 17 Mo. App. 66; Bell *v.* Gardiner, 4 M. & G. 11; Milnes *v.* Duncan, 6 B. & C. 671; Brown *v.* College Corner etc. Gravel Road Co., 56 Ind. 110; Stanley Rule & Level Co. *v.* Bailey, 45 Conn. 464; Devine *v.* Edwards, 87 Ill. 177; Koontz *v.* Central Nat. Bank, 51 Mo. 275; Marriott *v.* Hampton, 2 Sm. Lead. Cas. 403, notes; National Bank of Commerce *v.* National Mechanics,Banking Assoc., 55 N. Y. 211; Lawrence *v.* American Nat. Bank, 54 N. Y. 435; Fraker *v.* Little, 24 Kan. 598; s. c., 36 Am. Rep. 262; Morrison *v.* Collier, 79 Ind. 417.

In Kelley *v.* Solari, 9 M. & W. 54, Parke, B, says: "The position that a person so paying is precluded from recovering by laches in not availing himself of the means of knowledge in his power seems from the cases cited to have been founded on the doctrine of Mr. Justice Bayley, in the case of Milnes *v.* Duncan, and with all due respect to that authority, I do not think it can be sustained in point of law. If it is paid under the impression of the truth of a fact which is untrue, it may, generally speaking, be recoved back, however careless the party paying may have been in omitting to use diligence to inquire into the fact."

In Walker *v.* Conant, 65 Mich 194, it was held that the payment of money negligently by the payor did not preclude its recovery unless the condition of the party receiving it had been changed so as to make it inequitable to allow a recovery.

4. Kelley *v.* Solari, 9 M. & W. 54; Lucus *v.* Worswick, 1 M. & Rob. 293.

with the intention of waiving inquiry, no action will lie for an overpayment.[1]

XIII. Part Payment—1. Effect Generally—(*a*) Does Not Extinguish the Debt.—The payment of a part of a liquidated demand or debt will not extinguish the debt, even though such be the agreement of the parties at the time of payment.[2] But this applies only to liquidated demands arising from contract or of record,[3]

1. Windbiel *v.* Carroll, 16 Hun (N. Y.) 101; Frambers *v.* Risk, 2 Ill. App. 499.

In Windbiel *v.* Carroll, 16 Hun (N. Y.) 101, a purchaser of real estate assumed a mortgage which had been placed thereon by the vendor. In settling with the holder of the mortgage he claimed that a payment had been made by the mortgagor which had not been indorsed, but at the time was unable to produce the receipt. He paid the whole amount claimed, and said that he would bring an action to recover the overpayment. In that action he produced the receipt, but it was held that the money was not paid under a mistake of fact and could not be recovered.

In Frambers *v.* Risk, 2 Ill. App. 499, a purchaser of a certain number of hogs at an agreed price per hundred weight, disputed the weight which at Tolona was 15,120 pounds and at Chicago 10,750 pounds but having paid the price as claimed by the vendor, could not recover the deficiency in weight.

2. 2 Chit. Contr. 1101; Fitch *v.* Sutton, 5 East, 230; Cumber *v.* Wane, 1 Strange 426; Cavaness *v.* Ross, 33 Ark. 572; Warren *v.* Skinner, 20 Conn. 559; Curtiss *v.* Martin, 20 Ill. 557; Speer *v.* Cobb, 22 Ill. 528; Markel *v.* Spilter, 28 Ind. 488; McLean *v.* Equitable L. Assur. Soc., 100 Ind. 127; s. c. 50 Am. Rep. 779; Rea *v.* Owens, 37 Iowa, 262; St. Louis etc. R. Co. *v.* Davis, 35 Kan. 464; Nelson *v.* Weeks, 111 Mass. 223; Grinnell *v.* Spink, 128 Mass. 25; Helling *v.* United Order of Honor, 29 Mo. App. 309; Whiting *v.* Plumas Co., 64 Cal. 65; Albert *v.* Citizens' Bank, 5 La. Ann. 721; White *v.* Jordan, 27 Me. 370; Jones *v.* Rickets, 7 Ind. 108; Price *v.* Cannon, 3 Mo. 453; Bunge *v.* Koop, 48 N. Y. 225; s. c., 8 Am. Rep. 546; Hawley *v.* Foote, 19 Wend. (N. Y.) 516; Muldon *v.* Whitlock, 1 Cow. (N. Y.) 306; s. c., 13 Am. Dec. 533; Cole *v.* Sackett, 1 Hill (N. Y.) 517; Wheeler *v.* Wheeler, 11 Vt. 60. *Compare* Berrian *v.* Mayor etc. of N. Y., 4 Robt. (N. Y.) 538; Emrie *v.* Gilbert, Wright (Ohio) 764; Keen *v.* Vaughan, 48 Pa. St. 477; Milliken *v.* Brown, 1 Rawle (Pa.) 391.

"The ground upon which this rule of law, which is not particularly favored by the courts, rests, is that such an agreement is without consideration. The receipt of less than the whole debt, if due, is no benefit to the creditor in a legal sense, for he was entitled to it; its payment could not legally prejudice or injure the debtor, for he owed the sum paid and it was his duty to pay it. But where there is any additional consideration, however small, courts will uphold such agreements. As, if the debt is not due, though it has but a day in which to mature, the receipt of a sum less than the whole debt will be held to be valid; and so if the sum is to be paid in commercial paper." Wells *v.* Morrison, 91 Ind. 51; Fletcher *v.* Wurgler, 97 Ind. 223; Longworth *v.* Higham, 89 Ind. 352; Curtiss *v.* Martin, 20 Ill. 557; Wheeler *v.* Wheeler, 11 Vt. 60; Jamison *v.* Ludlow, 3 La. Ann. 492.

It has been said that "the history of judicial decisions upon the subject has shown a constant effort to escape from its absurdity and injustice." Harper *v.* Graham, 20 Ohio, 105, 115.

In an action of debt on a note for $55, the evidence showed that there was a dispute between the parties as to the amount due, and they finally fixed upon the sum of $40, which was paid. It was thereupon agreed that the suit was settled and to be dismissed at plaintiff's costs. *Held*, that the effect of this evidence was to show that all over $40 had been previously paid and that it was not an agreement to take a less sum in satisfaction of a greater. Stepp *v.* Cole, 1 Ind. 146.

3. Wilkinson *v.* Byers, 1 Ad. & El. 106; Longridge *v.* Dorville, 5 B. & A. 117; Atlee *v.* Backhouse, 3 Mees. & W. 651; Sibree *v.* Tripp, 15 Mees. & W.

and to cases where the payment is of money merely.[1] Payment of a less sum is a satisfaction of a larger sum, if the payment is made at a different time or place from that required by the contract;[2] or if the payment is made by a third party;[3] or if

23; Huntington Co. *v.* State, 109 Ind. 596; Donohue *v.* Woodbury, 6 Cush. (Mass.) 150; Lamb *v.* Goodwin, 10 Ired. (N. Car.) 320; Mathis *v.* Bryson, 4 Jones (N. Car.) 508; McDaniels *v.* Lapham, 21 Vt. 223.

To make a receipt of a part a discharge of the whole, there must be a new consideration or a voluntary compromise of a disputable and disputed demand, by which each party yields something, or an accord and satisfaction by which a new contract is substituted, or a submission to arbitration. Baldwin *v.* United States, 15 Ct. of Cl. 297.

If a party holding a note payable on a contingency and receives in lieu thereof a note for a smaller sum payable absolutely, it constitutes a payment. Winslow *v.* Hardin, 3 Dana (Ky.) 543. See Jenness *v.* Lane, 26 Me. 475.

The rule does not apply to a claim founded upon a statutory proceeding assessing a tax in aid of a railroad corporation. Huntington Co. *v.* State, 109 Ind. 596.

Plaintiff, having a claim against the county, presented it to the board of supervisors for allowance, by which body it was allowed in part and rejected in part. Plaintiff, with knowledge of the action of the board, accepted payment of the part allowed. *Held*, that this was a satisfaction of the entire claim. (*Citing* Wapello Co. *v.* Sinnaman, 1 G. Greene (Iowa) 413) Brick *v.* Plymouth Co., 63 Iowa 462; Perry *v.* Cheboygan, 55 Mich. 250. To same effect, Johnson *v.* United States, 2 Ct. of Cl. 169; King *v.* New Orleans, 14 La. Ann. 389; Hancock Co. *v.* Binford, 70 Ind. 208.

If he had accepted payment without knowledge of the action of the board it seems the effect would have been different. Fulton *v.* Monona Co., 47 Iowa 622.

1. Cumber *v.* Wane, 1 Strange 426; Pinnel's Case, 5 Co. 117; Thompson *v.* Percival, 5 B. & Ad. 925; Gavin *v.* Annan, 2 Cal. 494; Bateman *v.* Daniels, 5 Blackf. (Ind.) 71: Arnold *v.* Bailey, 24 S. Car. 493: Gaffney *v.* Chapman, 4 Robt. (N. Y.) 275; Boyd *v.* Hitchcock, 20 Johns. (N. Y.) 76; LePage *v.* McCrea, 1 Wend. (N. Y.) 164; s. c., 19 Am. Dec. 469.

Taking a check or receipt for a smaller sum than the amount due on promissory notes "in payment and satisfaction of the notes," is not necessarily an attempt to discharge a larger sum by payment of a smaller, the notes being salable like any other personal property. Rockwell *v.* Taylor, 41 Conn. 55.

It is held in *South Carolina* that a sealed note can be extinguished by the acceptance in place thereof of an unsealed note for a smaller sum. Bolt *v.* Dawkins, 16 S. Car. 198.

The receipt by a creditor of a less sum of money and of the promissory note of a third person for a portion of the balance, in full of a demand, is an extinguishment of original indebtedness. Conkling *v.* King, 10 N. Y. 440. See Booth *v.* Smith, 3 Wend. (N. Y.) 66.

2. Smith *v.* Brown, 3 Hawks (N. Car.) 580; Arnold *v.* Park, 8 Bush (Ky.) 3; Jones *v.* Perkins, 29 Miss. 139, 141; s. c., 64 Am. Dec. 136.

If the debt is not due, though it has but a day to mature, the receipt of a less sum will be a satisfaction. Fletcher *v.* Wurgler, 97 Ind. 223.

The fact that the settlement was made a few days before payment of the debt could have been legally demanded and enforced by suit, is of no consequence, where it appears that the payment before maturity was not the consideration, either in whole or part, for such settlement. McLean *v.* Equitable Life Assur. Soc., 100 Ind. 127; s. c., 50 Am. Rep. 779.

3. Henderson *v.* Stobart, 5 Exch. 99; Welby *v.* Drake, 1 Car. & P. 557; Laboyteaux *v.* Swigart, 103 Ind. 596; Steele *v.* Atkinson, 14 S. Car. 154; s. c., 37 Am. Rep. 728.

If a debtor gives and the creditor receives, in full satisfaction of the debt, a note indorsed by a third person for a less sum than the amount of the debt, it is a full payment. And a subsequent promise to pay the balance is not binding. (Cases reveiwed.) Varney *v.* Conery, 77 Me. 527; New York State Bank *v.* Fletcher, 5 Wend. (N. Y.) 85;

there were an additional consideration;[1] or if the agreement is under seal;[2] or made by way of composition with creditors.[3]

(*b*) AS AN ADMISSION.—A part payment without more is an admission of some liability.[4]

Smith *v.* Ballou, 1 R. I. 496; Brooks *v.* White, 2 Met. (Mass.) 283; s. c., 37 Am. Dec. 95. *Compare* Kellogg *v.* Richards, 14 Wend. (N. Y.) 116.

Where a creditor receives a part of his debt in cash, and the note of a third person for a portion of the balance, it being agreed that the debt is thus ratified, this constitutes a payment in full. Conkling *v.* King, 10 Barb. (N. Y.) 372; s. c., 10 N. Y. 440. See Booth *v.* Smith, 3 Wend. (N. Y.) 66.

1. Steinman *v.* Magnus, 1 East. 390; 2 Camp. 124; Bradley *v.* Gregory, 2 Camp. 383; Boothby *v.* Sowden, 3 Camp. 175; Wood *v.* Roberts, 2 Stark 417; Andrew *v.* Booghay, Dyer 756; Sibree *v.* Tripp, 15 Mees. & W. 23; Jones *v.* Bullitt, 2 Litt. (Ky.) 49; Musgrove *v.* Gibbs, 1 Dall. (U. S.) 216; Smalley *v.* Mores, 65 Iowa 386; Bateman *v.* Daniels, 5 Blackf. (Ind.) 71; Brooks *v.* White, 2 Met. (Mass.) 283; s. c., 37 Am. Dec. 95; Miller *v.* Holbrook, 1 Wend. (N. Y.) 317; McKenzie *v.* Culbreth, 66 N. Car. 534.

But if the payment of a less sum of money is accompanied with a gift or transfer of any other thing, however slight, it constitutes a good satisfaction. Thus it is said in *Pennel's Case* (3 Co. 238): "Payment of a lesser sum on the day, in satisfaction of a greater, cannot be any satisfaction for the whole, because it appears to the judges that by no possibility a lesser sum can be a satisfaction to the plaintiff for a greater sum; but the gift of a hawk, horse, robe, etc., in satisfaction, is good, for it shall be intended that a horse, hawk or robe, etc., might be more beneficial to the plaintiff than the money, in respect of some circumstances, or otherwise the plaintiff would not have accepted it in satisfaction."

See also Fletcher *v.* Wurgler, 97 Ind. 223.

Where a party paid $100 and a cow in full satisfaction of a judgment against him for $200, the value of the cow being $40, this extinguished the judgment, and an execution thereon for $60 interest and costs was held insufficient to support a levy and sale thereunder. Neal *v.* Handley, 116 Ill. 418; s. c., 56 Am. Rep. 784.

Payment of a smaller sum with an agreement to abandon a defense and pay costs, may be pleaded as a satisfaction of a larger demand, whether liquidated or unliquidated. Cooper *v.* Parker, 15 C. B. 822; 3 C. L. R. 823; 24 L. J., C. P. 68; 1 Jur., N. S. 281.

A note payable by instalments provided that a less sum would be accepted in full payment if each instalment were paid punctually. *Held*, that the large sum was in the nature of a penalty, and that the payment of the less sum extinguished the note, though all the instalments had not been punctually paid. Longworth *v.* Askrew, 15 Ohio St. 370.

But the reservation of a right to have full payment of a sum actually due on an existing contract, should there be a failure to pay a smaller sum on a day certain, cannot be treated as a penalty. Thompson *v.* Hudson, 4 L. R., H. L. Cas. 1; 38 L. J., Ch. 431.

2. Williams *v.* Carrington, 1 Hilt. (N. Y.) 515; Corbett *v.* Lucas, 4 McCord (S. Car.) 323; Arnold *v.* Bailey, 24 S. Car. 493; Rohr *v.* Anderson, 51 Md. 205.

3. Reay *v.* White, 3 Tyrw. 596; 1 C. & M. 748; Garrard *v.* Woolner, 8 Bing. 258; Reay *v.* Richardson, 2 C. M. & R. 422; Wilks *v.* Slaughter, 49 Ark. 235; Cutter *v.* Reynolds, 8 B. Mon. (Ky.) 596; McKenzie *v.* Culbreth, 66 N. Car. 534.

The acceptance in writing of the terms of an assignment for the benefit of creditors, accompanied by a receipt of a portion of the proceeds of the assigned estate, is a sufficient consideration to support the agreement to accept in full, and neither the acceptance nor the receipt need be under seal. Arnold *v.* Bailey, 24 S. Car. 493.

4. St. Louis, etc. R. Co. *v.* Tiernan, 37 Kan. 606, 629.

A judgment debtor who makes a part payment on the judgment, and thus secures a postponement of levy of execution, thereby waives his right to a review of the judgment. Smith *v.* O'Brien, 146 Mass. 294.

As to effect of part payment as a waiver of damages, see Button *v.* Russell, 55 Mich. 478; and of fraud, Hal-

(*c*) CREDITOR NOT BOUND TO ACCEPT.—The creditor is not bound to receive payment of part of the amount due.[1]

(*d*) DOES NOT MAKE ACCOUNT MUTUAL.—A part payment on an account does not have the effect of rendering the account a mutual one.[2]

2. Effect on Statute of Limitations.—See LIMITATION OF ACTIONS, vol. 13, p. 748, *et seq.*

3. Computing Interest on Partial Payments.—The rule is that payments are to be applied, first, to the extinguishment of the interest due, and, second, towards payment of the principal.[3]

Shoemaker *v.* Benedict, 11 N. Y. 176; s. c., 62 Am. Dec. 95; Winchell *v.* Hicks, 18 N. Y. 558; Mostyn *v.* Mostyn, 5 L. R., Ch. 457; 22 L. T., N. S. 461; 39 L. J., Ch. 780.

A part payment cannot, however, give vitality to a void debt. Miner *v.* Lorman, 56 Mich. 212; Gill *v.* Appanoose Co., 68 Iowa 20.

Compare St. Louis etc. R. Co. *v.* Tiernan, 37 Kan. 606.

Nor change what was originally a mere moral obligation into a legal debt. Mostyn *v.* Mostyn, 39 L. J. Ch. 780; 22 L. T., N. S. 461; 5 L. R. Ch. 457; 18 W. R. 657.

But when the vendee of a machine, after discovering its defects, is induced to make payments on it by a promise of the vendor that he will make it fulfill the warranty, such payments will not affect the defense of the vendee, if the promise is not complied with. Hayner *v.* Churchill, 29 Mo. App. 676.

Where an indorser has been released from liability by the neglect of the holder to notify him of the dishonor of the paper, a partial payment, made with full knowledge of such release, will bind him to the payment of the whole. Margetson *v.* Aitkin, 3 C. & P. 388; Dixon *v.* Elliot, 5 C. & P. 437; Harvey *v.* Troupe, 23 Miss. 538; Shaw *v.* McNeill, 95 N. Car. 535.

The mere fact that a widow paid all of her deceased husband's debts but one, would not tend to establish an obligation on her part to pay that one. Briswalter *v.* Palomares, 66 Cal. 259.

1. Jennings *v.* Shriver, 5 Black. (Ind.) 37.

2. Norton *v.* Larco, 30 Cal. 127, 134; s. c., 89 Am. Dec. 70; Rocca *v.* Klein, 74 Cal. 526.

3. Monroe *v.* Fohl, 72 Cal. 568; Hart *v.* Dorman, 2 Fla. 445; s. c., 50 Am. Dec. 285; McFadden *v.* Fortier, 20 Ill. 509; Estebene *v.* Estebene, 5 La. Ann. 738; Union Bank *v.* Lobdell, 10 La. Ann. 130; Eyle *v.* Roman Catholic Church, 36 La. Ann. 310; Frazier *v.* Hyland, 1 Har. & J. (Md.) 98; Morgan *v.* Michigan etc. R. Co., 57 Mich. 430; Lash *v.* Edgerton, 13 Minn. 210; Bond *v.* Jones, 8 Smed. M. (Miss.) 368; Peebles *v.* Gee, 1 Dev. (N. Car.) 341; Hammer *v.* Nevill, Wright (Ohio) 169; Spires *v.* Hamot, 8 W. & S. (Pa.) 17; De Bruhl *v.* Neuffer, 1 Strobh. (S. Car.) 426; Genin *v.* Ingersoll, 11 W. Va. 549; Hearn *v.* Cutberth, 10 Tex. 216.

The fact of part payment is merely evidence of a promise to pay the balance. Parsons *v.* Clark, 59 Mich. 414; Haldane *v.* Sweet, 55 Mich. 196; Heylin *v.* Hastings, 1 Salk. 29; s. c., 12 Mod. Rep. 223.

The rule as laid down by the supreme court of *Massachusetts* is as follows: "Compute the interest on the principal sum from the time when the interest commenced to the first time when a payment was made, which exceeds, either alone or in conjunction with the preceding payments, if any, the interest at that time due; add that interest to the principal, and from the sum subtract the payment made at that time, together with the preceding payments, if any, and the remainder forms a new principal, on which compute and subtract the interest, as upon the first principal, and proceed in this manner to the time of the judgment." Dean *v.* Williams, 17 Mass. 417.

This rule is approved and followed in Ferry *v.* Ferry, 2 Cush. (Mass.) 92, and Downer *v.* Whittier, 144 Mass. 448, and substantially adopted by the Supreme Court of *Missouri.* Riney *v.* Hill, 14 Mo. 500; s. c., 55 Am. Dec. 119; State *v.* Donegan, 94 Mo. 66; State *v.* Shaw, 1 Mo. App. 511. See Cruce *v.* Cruce, 81 Mo. 676, 689.

If payment is made before the principal is due, it will be applied first to the extinguishment of the accrued interest,

XIV. Application of Payments--1. By Debtor--(*a*) Right to Direct in First Instance.--The debtor may, at or before the time of payment, prescribe the application of such payment and it is the duty of the creditor to so apply it.[1]

and the residue to that part of the principal which first becomes due; but if nothing is due it is to be applied ratably to principal and interest, so as to extinguish a part of the principal and the interest which has accrued on the part so extinguished. Jencks *v.* Alexander, 11 Paige (N. Y.) 619; Miami Exporting Co. *v.* Bank of U. S., 5 Ohio 260; Mills *v.* Saunders, 4 Neb. 190; McCormick *v.* Mitchell, 57 Ind. 248. See Starr *v.* Richmond, 30 Ill. 276; s. c., 83 Am. Dec. 189; McElrath *v.* Duprey, 2 La. Ann. 520.

Where interest on a note is paid in advance for a stipulated time, and the principal is paid before the expiration of that time, the excess of interest is to be appled as so much paid on the principal. Freeman's Bank *v.* Rollins, 13 Me. 202.

Where one of two obligors in a joint and several bond became bankrupt, dividends paid on his estate are, as to the co-obligor, to be considered as ordinary payments on account, and are to be applied first to the payment of interest due at the date of the dividend, and the surplus, if any, in reduction of the principal. Bower *v.* Marris, 1 Craig & Ph. 351.

Where accrued interest itself bears interest, payments will be applied: First, to the interest on the interest; secondly, to the interest on the principal; thirdly, to the principal. Anketel *v.* Converse, 17 Ohio St. 11; s. c., 91 Am. Dec. 115.

Where several sales were made simultaneously by the same vendor to the same vendee at various prices, the purchase money to be paid in equal instalments in one, two and three years, bearing the same interest, after maturity of the last instalment the whole debt is to be treated as one, and payments made generally must be applied first to all accrued interest on the entire debt and the surplus to the entire principal. Smith *v.* Nettles, 9 La. Ann. 455. To same effect. Genin *v.* Ingersoll, 11 W. Va. 549.

Where some of the makers of a joint and several note make payments of their shares of the principal and interest due from them at the time thereof, such payments must be applied to the *pro rata* of principal as well as interest due by the makers so paying. Donaldson *v.* Cothran, 60 Ga. 603.

As to what is sufficient part payment under the Statute of Frauds, see Statute of Frauds, vol. 8, p. 659.

1. 3 Phil. Evid. (Hill & Cowen's Notes) *441; 1 Amer. Lead. Cas. *276 (3rd ed. 288); Mayor etc. of Alexandria *v.* Patten, 4 Cranch (U. S.) 317; Tayler *v.* Sandiford, 7 Wheat (U. S.) 13; Leef *v.* Goodwin, Taney Dec. (U. S.) 460; Sherwood *v.* Haight, 26 Conn. 432; Pickering *v.* Day, 2 Del. Ch. 333; s. c., on appeal, 3 Houst. (Del.) 474; s. c., 95 Am. Dec. 291; Semmes *v.* Boykin, 27 Ga. 47; Whitaker *v.* Groover, 54 Ga. 174; Coleman *v.* Slade, 75 Ga. 61; Hatcher *v.* Conner, 75 Ga. 728; Jackson *v.* Bailey, 12 Ill. 159; Forelander *v.* Hicks, 6 Ind. 448; King *v.* Andrews, 30 Ind. 429; Trentman *v.* Fletcher, 100 Ind. 105; Ross *v.* Crane, 74 Iowa 375; Irwin *v.* Paulett, 1 Kan. 418; Nuttall *v.* Brannin, 5 Bush (Ky.) 11; McDaniel *v.* Barnes, 5 Bush (Ky.) 183; Bloodworthn *v.* Jacobs, 2 La. Ann. 24; Adams *v.* Bank of Louisiana, 3 La. Ann. 351; Robson *v.* McKoin, 18 La. Ann. 544; Treadwell *v.* Moore, 34 Me. 112; Mitchell *v.* Dall, 2 Har. & G. (Md.) 159; s. c., 4 Gill & J. (Md.) 461; Calvert *v.* Carter, 18 Md. 73; Dickey *v.* Permanent Land Co., 63 Md. 170; Gilchrist *v.* Ward, 4 Mass. 692; Hall *v.* Marston, 17 Mass. 575; Bonaffe *v.* Woodberry, 12 Pick. (Mass.) 463; Hussey *v.* Manufacturers' etc. Bank, 10 Pick. (Mass.) 415; Reed *v.* Boardman, 20 Pick. (Mass.) 441; Solomon *v.* Dreschler, 4 Minn. 278; Brady *v.* Hill, 1 Mo. 317; s. c., 13 Am. Dec. 503; Gartner *v.* Kemfer, 58 Mo. 570; Poulson *v.* Collier, 18 Mo. App. 583; Bean *v.* Brown, 54 N. H. 395; Martin *v.* Draher, 5 Watts (Pa.) 544; Black *v.* Shooler, 2 McCord (S. Car.) 293; McDonald *v.* Pickett, 2 Bailey (S. Car.) 617; McKee *v.* Stroup, 1 Rice (S. Car.) 291; Bell *v.* Bell, 20 S. Car. 34; Willis *v.* McIntyre, 70 Tex. 34; Lapham *v.* Kelley, 35 Vt. 195; Jones *v.* Williams, 39 Wis. 300; Champenois *v.* Fort, 45 Miss. 356.

The rule of the text applies only to payments voluntarily made, and not to those made by process of law. Black-

(*b*) CREDITOR MUST ACCEPT DEBTOR'S APPROPRIATION.—If the creditor receives money with a direction from the debtor to appropriate it to a particular debt, it must go to that debt, no matter what the creditor may say at the time: and an appropriation once made by the debtor cannot be changed by the creditor without the debtor's consent.[1]

stone Bank *v.* Hill, 10 Pick. (Mass.) 129.

By the terms of a mortgage all the notes became due and payable upon default as to those first falling due. Those first falling due were indorsed; and upon default of payment of these, the mortgage was foreclosed. It was held that the debtor could not insist that the notes first maturing should be paid from the proceeds, but that the creditor had the right to make the application. Nichols *v.* Knowles, 3 McCrary (U. S.) 477; s. c., 17 Fed. Rep. 494.

Where an officer has served two successive terms, with different sets of sureties for each term, he may appropriate funds collected during his second term, to discharge a deficit of his first term if the county treasurer receives the money in good faith. State *v.* Smith, 26 Mo. 226; s. c., 72 Am. Dec. 204. See Draffen *v.* Boonville, 8 Mo. 395; St. Joseph *v.* Merlatt, 26 Mo. 233; s. c., 72 Am. Dec. 207; Seymour *v.* Van Slyck, 8 Wend. (N. Y.) 403.

In the following additional cases the rule governing the debtor's right to apply payments is discussed: Greer *v.* Turner, 47 Ark. 17; Whipple *v.* Crocker, 6 Ill. App. 133; Sankey *v.* Cook, 78 Iowa 419; Kahler *v.* Hanson, 53 Iowa 698; Fowke *v.* Bowie, 4 Har. & J. (Md.) 566; Shelden *v.* Bennett, 44 Mich. 634; Vaughan *v.* Powell, 65 Miss. 401; Lauten *v.* Rowan, 59 N. H. 215; Boyd *v.* Webster, 59 N. H. 89; Long *v.* Miller, 93 N. Car. 233; Moorehead *v.* West Branch Bank, 3 W. & S. (Pa.) 550; Bray *v.* Crain, 59 Tex. 649; Roakes *v.* Bailey, 55 Vt. 542; Webster *v.* Mitchell, 22 Fed. Rep. 869.

1. Wharton on Cont. 923; Benj. on Sales 746; Levystein *v.* Whitman, 59 Ala. 345; Reed *v.* Boardman, 20 Pick. (Mass.) 443; Smuller *v.* Union Canal Co., 37 Pa. St. 68; Godfrey *v.* Warner, Hill & D. Supp. (N. Y.) 32; Eylar *v.* Read, 60 Tex. 387; Runyon *v.* Latham, 5 Ired. L. (N. Car.) 551; Stewart *v.* Hopkins, 30 Ohio St. 502.

And if the creditor fails to so apply it, he cannot complain if he is compelled to make the application, even though he thereby loses the debt to which he attempted to apply it, by reason of its becoming barred by limitation. Eylar *v.* Reed, 60 Tex. 387.

Where A, being indebted to B both on mortgage and open account, sent B money with instructions to apply it to the mortgage note, and B failed so to do, he is liable to A's assignee in bankruptcy for the amount, and in a suit by said assignee for the amount B cannot plead the account as a set-off. Libby *v.* Hopkins, 104 U. S. 303.

And the debtor is not estopped to insist on the appropriation designated by him, though he accept a receipt showing a different appropriation by the creditor. Eylar *v.* Read, 60 Tex. 387. See Starkweather *v.* Kittle, 17 Wend. (N. Y.) 20 (per Bronson, J.).

It matters not that the creditor refuses to accept the application made by the debtor at the time of payment. If he receives the money he is bound by the appropriation made. Anonymous, Cro. Eliz. 68; Pinnell's Case, 5 Coke 117; Colt *v.* Nettleville, 2 P. Wms. 304; Thomas *v.* Cross, 7 Exch. 728; Randall *v.* Parramore, 1 Fla. 410; Bayley *v.* Wynkoff, 5 Ill. 449; Jackson *v.* Bailey, 12 Ill. 161; Bosley *v.* Porter, 4 J. J. Marsh. (Ky.) 621; Hussey *v.* Manufacturers' etc. Bank, 10 Pick. (Mass.) 415; Reed *v.* Boardman, 20 Pick. (Mass.) 441; Caldwell *v.* Wentworth, 14 N. H. 431; Long *v.* Miller, 93 N. Car. 233; Martin *v.* Draher, 5 Watts (Pa.) 544; Boutwell *v.* Mason, 12 Vt. 608; Black *v.* Shooler, 2 McCord (S. Car.) 293; McDonald *v.* Pickett, 2 Bailey (S. Car.) 617.

While a creditor is not bound to receive payment on an account not due, yet if he does receive it he is bound to apply it in accordance with the directions of the debtor. Thus, if a part of a debt not due is secured by guaranty, and the guarantor and debtor send money to the creditor with directions to apply the same to their account, the creditor is not at liberty to apply it to a part of the account which is due and

(*c*) WHEN DEBTOR MUST MAKE APPLICATION.—The application must be made by the debtor at the time of the payment; otherwise the right of election devolves on the creditor.[1]

(*d*) HOW SHOWN.—The application by the debtor can be shown

not covered by the guaranty. Wethereli *v.* Joy, 40 Me. 325.

A being indebted to B and C, drew on B in favor of C, which draft B accepted upon receiving a mortgage from C conditioned that C would see that funds were provided to meet the drafts when they matured. Under an agreement between A and C, the former shipped produce to B, the proceeds to be applied to the payment of the drafts, and afterwards by letter directed B to dispose of the produce as he should see proper. B applied the proceeds first to the extinguishment of A's debt to him, and the balance to the payment of the drafts. In a proceeding to foreclose the mortgage it was held that the whole of the proceeds should have been applied to the payment of the drafts, and that the direction to dispose of the produce as he thought proper did not authorize B to use the proceeds as he pleased. Sproule *v.* Samuel, 5 Ill. 135.

A bank discounted a note for B, a town treasurer, the proceeds to be used in his official capacity, which note was indorsed by P. The day before this note matured, a personal note of B to the bank matured, and the president of the bank directed the cashier to apply the balance of B's account to the personal note. Three days afterwards, P presented B's cheque to the bank, in which he directed the balance of his account to be applied to the official note. This the cashier refused to do, and brought suit on the official note. *Held*, that neither B nor P could insist that B's balance should be applied on the note sued on. National Mahaiwe Bank *v.* Peck, 127 Mass. 298; s. c., 34 Am. Rep. 368.

A creditor cannot compel application of a payment to a debt barred by limitation by merely expressing his wish to that effect to the debtor. There must be an express assent by the debtor, or it must be shown that the debtor did not object to the positive statement by the creditor that he should make such application. Sitterly *v.* Gregg, 22 Hun (N. Y.) 258.

Where interest is due on the debt, the debtor may, without the consent of the creditor, apply a payment to the reduction of the principal, without first paying off the interest. Pindall *v.* Bank of Marietta, 10 Leigh (Va.) 484; Miller *v.* Trevilian, 2 Rob. (Va.) 1. *Compare* Johnson *v.* Robbins, 20 La. Ann. 569. And see Steele *v.* Taylor, 4 Dana (Ky.) 445.

Where money is placed in the hands of an agent to pay two notes held by the same party, and such fact is known to the holder, he will not be allowed by means of an attachment suit on one of the notes to appropriate the whole to the payment of such note. Jones *v.* Perkins, 29 Miss. 139; s. c., 64 Am. Dec. 136.

A debtor intrusted money to an agent to compromise certain claims held by a creditor. The debtor deposited the money thus intrusted to him, together with money of his own, with the creditor in the agent's own name. Afterwards the creditor caused the money deposited to be attached, and refused to return the agent's own money unless he would apply that belonging to the debtor to one of the claims for which there was no security. This the agent did under protest, and without the knowledge of the debtor. *Held*, that the debtor was not thereby deprived of his right to apply the money to either of the claims he saw fit. Dennis *v.* M'Laurin, 31 Miss. 606.

If the debtor directs the appropriation, a court of equity has no power to change the appropriation. Selfridge *v.* Northampton Bank, 8 W. & S. (Pa.) 320.

1. Aderholt *v.* Embry, 78 Ala. 185; McCurdy *v.* Middleton, 82 Ala. 131; Long *v.* Miller, 93 N. Car. 233; Reynolds *v.* McFarlane, 1 Overt. (Tenn.) 488. *Compare* Wittkowsky *v.* Reid, 82 N. Car. 116.

And the burden is on the debtor to show that he directed the application. Thatcher *v.* Massey, 26 S. Car. 155; Harrison *v.* Dayries, 23 La. Ann. 216;

Where cotton is shipped by a debtor to a creditor holding two demands, the direction as to the application must be made at the time of shipment by verbal declaration, or by an account rendered showing the application, or by any acts which manifest his intention.[1]

2. By Creditor—(*a*) ON FAILURE OF DEBTOR TO DIRECT APPLICATION.—If the debtor fails to make the application when he might, the creditor may apply it as he pleases.[2]

and not at the time of sale. Frost *v.* Weathersbee, 23 S. Car. 354.

1. Am. Lead. Cas. (3d ed.) 290; Waters *v.* Tompkins, 2 Cr. Mees. & R. 723; 1 Tyr. & G. 137; Peters *v.* Anderson, 5 Taunt. 596; Newmarch *v.* Clay, 14 East 239; Cross *v.* Johnson, 30 Ark. 396; Howland *v.* Rencle, 7 Blackf. (Ind.) 236; Adams Express Co. *v.* Black, 62 Ind. 128; Poulson *v.* Collier, 18 Mo. App. 583; Mitchell *v.* Dall, 2 Har. & G. (Md.) 159; Terhune *v.* Colton, 12 N. J. Eq. 233, 312; Stone *v.* Seymour, 15 Wend. (N. Y.) 19, 24; 22 Wend. (N. Y.) 554; Wittkowsky *v.* Reid, 82 N. Car. 116; Moorehead *v.* West Branch Bank, 5 W. & S. (Pa.) 542; Stewart *v.* Keith, 12 Pa. St. 238; Hill *v.* Gregory, Wythe (Va.) 13; Champenois *v.* Fort, 45 Miss. 356.

If the debtor at the time of making the payment makes an entry in his books, showing a specific appropriation, and at the same time shows the entry to the creditor, this is such an appropriation by the debtor as would be binding on the creditor. Frazer *v.* Bunn, 8 Car. & P. 704.

The receipt may show the application. Stewart *v.* Keith, 12 Pa. St. 238.

But the intention of the debtor, uncommunicated to the creditor, to apply the payment to a particular debt, cannot affect the creditor's right to make the application. Munger App. Payt. 28; Long *v.* Miller, 93 N. Car. 233; Brice *v.* Hamilton, 12 S. Car. 32.

It is not necessary that the intention should be manifested by a writing. Ilsley *v.* Jewett, 2 Met. (Mass.) 168.

The expression of a wish by the debtor is sufficient. Hansen *v.* Rounsavel, 74 Ill. 238. Or the declarations of the bearer of the money at the time of delivering it to the creditor. Gay *v.* Gay, 5 Allen (Mass.) 157.

The same rules apply to a payment in property as to a payment in money. Smith *v.* Vaughan, 78 Ala. 201.

Where a debtor receives without objection an account current from his creditor, which imputes payments made by him to the less onerous part of his debt, he is held by his silence to ratify such imputation. McLear *v.* Hunsicker, 30 La. Ann., pt. 2, 1225.

If from the very nature of the transaction it appears to be the intention of the debtor that the money shall be appropriated to a particular debt, the creditor cannot make another and different appropriation of it. Phillips *v.* McGuire, 73 Ga. 517; Holley *v.* Hardeman, 76 Ga. 328.

The facts in the latter case were as follows: H & G held a note and mortgage to secure the same executed by A. They subsequently purchased two promissory notes made by A, of which fact A was ignorant. A sent H & G certain cotton to sell and pay upon the indebtedness which he owed them. H & G applied the proceeds of the cotton to the payment of the two notes purchased by them, and proceeded to foreclose the mortgage. It was held that the note secured by the mortgage was paid by the proceeds of the cotton. Holley *v.* Hardeman, 76 Ga. 328.

To same effect, Marx *v.* Schwartz, 14 Oregon 177. *Compare* Stewart *v.* Hopkins, 30 Ohio St. 502.

Where the payment was precisely the amount of one debt and not of another, it may properly be inferred that the debtor intended it should be appropriated to the former. Robert *v.* Garnie, 3 Cai. Cas. (N. Y.) 14; Seymour *v.* Van Slyck, 8 Wend. (N. Y.) 403; Davis *v.* Fargo, Clarke Ch. (N. Y.) 470.

The question whether there has been an appropriation is one for the jury. Walker *v.* Butler, 6 El. & Bl. 506; 25 L. J., Q. B. 377; 2 Jur. N. S. 687.

2. 1 Amer. Lead Cas. *276; Mayor etc. of Alexandria *v.* Patten, 4 Cranch (U. S.) 316; United States *v.* Bradbury, Dav. (U. S.) 146; Bobe *v.* Stickney, 36 Ala. 482; Johnson *v.* Thomas, 77 Ala. 367; Marshall *v.* Sloan, 26 Ark. 513; Bell *v.* Radcliff, 32 Ark. 645; Blinn *v.* Chester, 5 Day (Conn.) 166; Pickering *v.* Day, 2 Del. Ch. 333; s. c., on appeal, 4 Houst. 474; s. c., 95 Am. Dec. 291; Randall *v.* Parramore, 1 Fla. 409; Hargroves *v.* Cooke, 15 Ga. 321; Johnson *v.* Johnson, 30 Ga. 857; Holmes *v.*

(*b*) MUST BE TO DEBT DUE.--The application by the creditor

Pratt, 34 Ga. 557; Perry *v.* Bozeman, 67 Ga. 643; Howland *v.* Rench, 7 Blackf. (Ind.) 236; Fargo *v.* Buell, 1 Iowa, 292; Brewer *v.* Knapp, 1 Pick. (Mass.) 332; Blackstone Bank *v.* Hill, 10 Pick. (Mass.) 129; Crisler *v.* McCoy, 33 Miss. 445; Brady *v.* Hill, 1 Mo. 315; S.C., 13 Am. Dec. 503; Middleton *v.* Frame, 21 Mo. 412; Waterman *v.* Younger, 49 Mo. 413; Sawyer *v.* Tappan, 14 N. H. 352; Sickle *v.* Ayres, 6 N. J. Eq. 29; Bird *v.* Davis, 14 N. J. Eq. 467; Seymour *v.* Marvin, 11 Barb. (N. Y.) 80; California Bank *v.* Webb, 48 N. Y. Super. Ct. 175; Wittkowski *v.* Reid, 84 N. Car. 21; Logan *v.* Mason, 6 W. & S. (Pa.) 9; Watt *v.* Hoch, 25 Pa. St. 411; Smith *v.* Screven, 1 McCord (S. Car.) 368; Ayer *v.* Hawkins, 19 Vt. 26; Howard *v.* McCall, 21 Gratt. (Va.) 205; Stone *v.* Talbot, 4 Wis. 442; Campbell *v.* Hodgson, Gow. 74; Hall *v.* Wood, 14 East 243, *n.*; Peters *v.* Anderson, 5 Taunt. 596; 1 Marsh 238. *Compare* Lamprell *v.* Billericay Union, 3 Exch. 283; 18 L. J. Exch. 283; Thompson *v.* Hudson, 6 L. R., Ch. 320; 40 L. J., Ch. 28.

The rule is subject to the condition that there are no circumstances which would render the exercise of the discretion by the creditor unreasonable, or which would enable him to work injustice to the debtor. Arnold *v.* Johnson, 2 Ill. 196; Ayer *v.* Hawkins, 19 Vt. 26; Taylor *v.* Coleman, 20 Tex. 772.

He is not bound to apply the payment to the oldest claim. Maguire *v.* Filley, 9 Mo. App. 586.

If the creditor holds several notes of the same debtor, he may apply a payment to a part only of the notes, and is not bound to apply it to all *pro rata.* Blackman *v.* Leonard, 15 La. Ann. 59. And it has been held that he must apply the whole on one note, and not *pro rata*, where the sum received is less than the amount due on either note. Wheeler *v.* House, 27 Vt. 735. *Compare* Taylor *v.* Foster, 132 Mass. 30. But a surety on one of the notes may insist upon a *pro rata* appropriation to such note. Blackstone Bank *v.* Hill, 10 Pick. (Mass.) 129. *Compare* Clark *v.* Smith, 13 S. Car. 585.

Where the creditor holds a debt due to himself, and another from the same debtor due to himself and a third party, he must apply all payments ratably on the two debts. Colby *v.* Copp, 35 N. H. 434.

A purchased and from B, which was encumbered by a mortgage from B to C, as agent of D. C also held a debt in his own right against B. A paid money to C on B's account, not knowing of the latter's indebtedness to C individually, and made no express appropriation of the payment. *Held*, that C could not apply the payment to the individual indebtedness, but would be held to appropriate it to reduce the encumbrance on the land. Poindexter *v.* LaRoche, 7 Smed. & M. (Miss.) 699.

Where the creditor credits the money on an open account, it will be held that he intended to apply the payment to the earliest items of the account, even though those are the only ones secured. Van Rensselaer *v.* Roberts, 5 Den. (N. Y.) 470; Crompton *v.* Pratt, 105 Mass. 255. And notwithstanding they were barred by limitation. Hill *v.* Robbins, 22 Mich. 475.

The creditor may make the application to any valid demand, whether the debtor acknowledge his liability thereon or not. McLendon *v.* Frost, 57 Ga. 448; Lee *v.* Early, 44 Md. 80. But it is for the creditor to prove the existence and validity of such demand. Mann *v.* Mayor, 6 Rob. (La.) 475. See Trundle *v.* Williams, 4 Gill (Md.) 313.

Where A, who is indebted to B, and also to B and C jointly, makes a shipment to B to apply the proceeds on the individual debt, and there is a surplus after extinguishing this debt, B may retain such surplus and apply it on the joint debt, but not on his own part of the joint debt to the exclusion of C. Cole *v.* Trull, 9 Pick. (Mass.) 325.

Where an attorney has in his hands the claims of several creditors against the same debtor, all of which are due, and the debtor makes a payment to the attorney without designating the debt to which he wishes it applied, the attorney may apply it to such of the debts as he sees fit. Carpenter *v.* Goin, 19 N. H. 479. Or the several creditors may direct its application. Taylor *v.* Jones, 1 Ind. 17.

If the owner of any one of the notes has in fact received no part of such payment, the maker cannot, in an action brought on such note, insist that any part of such payment shall be appro-

must be made to a debt that is due in preference to one not due.[1]

(*c*) MAY MAKE APPLICATION MOST FAVORABLE TO HIMSELF.—The creditor may make the application which is most to his own interest, and is not bound to make that which is most beneficial to the debtor.[2]

(*d*) TO UNSECURED DEBT.—The creditor has the right to make the application to an unsecured debt, rather than to one which is secured, and to a debt of the debtor individually rather than to one he owes jointly with others; and neither a surety nor a co-

priated to the note sued on. Taylor *v.* Jones, 1 Ind. 17.

1. Byrnes *v.* Claffey, 69 Cal. 120; Bobe *v.* Stickney, 36 Ala. 482; McCurdy *v.* Middleton, 82 Ala. 131; Heard *v.* Pulaski, 80 Ala. 502; Bacon *v.* Brown, 1 Bibb (Ky.) 334; s. c., 4 Am. Dec. 640; Heintz *v.* Cahn, 29 Ill. 308; Richardson *v.* Coddington, 49 Mich. 1; Cloney *v.* Richardson, 34 Mo. 370; Hammersly *v.* Knowlys, 2 Esp. 666; Dawe *v.* Holdsworth, Peake 64. And it cannot be made to a debt arising subsequently to the payment, unless the debtor assent thereto. Law *v.* Sutherland, 5 Gratt. (Va.) 357.

Where an officer who has served two successive terms, with different sureties for each term, makes a payment which the county treasurer in good faith applies to a deficit arising during the first term, such application is good, though the money was derived from collections made during his second term. State *v.* Smith, 26 Mo. 226; s. c., 72 Am. Dec. 204. See Draffen *v.* Boonville, 8 Mo, 395; Speck *v.* Commonwealth, 3 W. & S. (Pa.) 324; Helen *v.* Commonwealth, 79 Ky. 67. And *compare* Myers *v.* United States, 1 McLean (U. S.) 493.

2. Shortridge *v.* Pardee, 2 Mo. App. 363; Niagara Bank *v.* Rosevel, 9 Cow. (N. Y.) 409; Willis *v.* McIntyre, 70 Tex. 34.

Provided the rights of third parties have not intervened before he exercises the right. If such rights have intervened, the right of the creditor to appropriate the payment as his own interests may dictate is gone as against such third persons. Harrison *v.* Johnson, 27 Ala. 445; Pattison *v.* Hull, 9 Cow. (N. Y.) 747; Berghans *v.* Alter, 9 Watts (Pa.) 386; Harker *v.* Conrad, 12 S. & R. (Pa.) 301; s. c., 14 Am. Dec. 691; Crompton *v.* Pratt, 105 Mass. 257; Willis *v.* McIntyre, 70 Tex. 34.

Even though the party whose right is affected holds under a conveyance fraudulent as to creditors. Miller *v.* Miller, 23 Me. 24; s. c., 39 Am. Dec. 597.

The provision of the civil law that the creditor must make the application which is most for the debtor's interest has not been adopted as a part of the common law. Logan *v.* Mason, 6 W. & S. (Pa.) 9. See Spiller *v.* Creditors, 16 La. Ann. 292; Miller *v.* Trabue, 16 La. Ann. 375. But some courts follow the rule of the civil law. Those where one debt bears interest and the other does not, payments made generally by the debtor have been applied to the interest bearing debt, in preference to the other. Bussey *v.* Gant, 10 Humph. (Tenn.) 238; Blanton *v.* Rice, 5 T. B. Mon. (Ky.) 253; Gass *v.* Stinson, 3 Sumn. (U. S.) 98. See also Scott *v.* Fisher, 4 T. B. Mon. (Ky.) 387.

The holder of two notes made by the same person brought an action on one of them. After the second note became due sufficient money was received from the maker to pay the note in suit, but no specific appropriation of it was made by the debtor. *Held*, that the creditor had the right to apply it to the note not in suit. Allen *v.* Kimball, 23 Pick. (Mass.) 473. See also Washington Bank *v.* Prescott, 20 Pick. (Mass.) 339.

The creditor may appropriate the payment to the discharge of a prior and purely equitable debt, and sue at law for a subsequent legal demand. Bosanquet *v.* Wray, 6 Taunt. 599; 2 Marsh. 319.

Where there are several notes secured by the same deed of trust, the holder may apply the entire proceeds of sale to those last maturing, and will not thereby be precluded from recovering against a surety on the note first falling due. Mathews *v.* Switzler, 46 Mo. 301. As to the application which the law will make in such cases, see *infra*.

debtor can compel the creditor to make the appropriation otherwise.[1]

(*e*) TO DEBT NOT LEGALLY ENFORCEABLE.—If the debtor fails to make the appropriation the creditor may apply the money in payment of a demand which could not be enforced at law in preference to one which could be.[2]

1. Driver *v.* Fortner, 5 Port. (Ala. 9; Soluble Pac. Guano Co. *v.* Harris, 78 Ga. 20; Hanson *v.* Manley, 72 Iowa, 48; Burks *v.* Albert, 4 J. J. Marsh. (Ky.) 97; s. c., 20 Am. Dec. 209; Capron *v.* Strout, 11 Nev. 304; Paterson Sav. Institution *v.* Brush, 29 N. J. Eq. 119; Wilson *v.* Allen, 11 Oreg. 154; Pelzer *v.* Steadman, 22 S. Car. 279. See Donally *v.* Wilson, 5 Leigh (Va.) 329.

The rule applies whether the security on one of the debts is personal or otherwise. Harding *v.* Tifft, 75 N. Y. 461; Poulson *v.* Collier, 18 Mo. App. 583; Gaetz *v.* Piel, 26 Mo. App. 634; Kirby *v.* Marlborough, 2 M. & Sel. 18.

Where both debts are secured, the creditor may apply it to either. Brown *v.* Davenport, 76 Ga. 799.

Payments made generally to the creditor on the account of a person for whom a guaranty is given, may be applied by the creditor in liquidation of a balance existing against him before the execution of the guaranty; and the guarantor cannot insist upon their being applied in exoneration of his liability, though at the time he executed the guaranty he had no notice of the balance. Kirby *v.* Marlborough, 2 M. & Selw. 18.

Where the party making the payment is indebted both on a judgment and a simple contract debt, the creditor may apply the payment in liquidation of either. Chitty *v.* Naish, 2 Dowl. Pr. Cas. 511. See also Brazier *v.* Bryant, 2 Dowl. Pr. Cas. 477.

Where A held for collection a claim against B individually on book account and also on note and mortgage, and at the same time held claims against a firm of which B was a member, and B paid A a sum in excess of the book account to be applied on his individual indebtedness, without further direction, A was bound to apply the whole amount to the individual indebtedness of B then existing, and could not divert any part thereof to the firm indebtedness, or to debts thereafter contracted by B. Miles *v.* Ogden, 54 Wis. 573.

A was a creditor of a firm and also of the surviving member thereof individually. The surviving partner made a payment out of the firm assets without designating on which debt it should apply. It was held that the application must be made by the creditor to the firm debt. Wiesenfeld *v.* Byrd, 17 S. Car. 106. To same effect, Thompson *v.* Brown, Mood. & M. 40.

And generally if the creditor have an account against a firm, and also one against an individual member thereof, a payment by the individual must be appropriated to his individual account, unless his consent to the appropriation to the firm account be shown. Johnson *v.* Boone, 2 Harr. (Del.) 172. See Sneed *v.* Weister, 2 A. K. Marsh. (Ky.) 277; Schuylkill Co. *v.* Commonwealth, 36 Pa. St. 524. And *compare* Van Rensselaer *v.* Roberts, 5 Den. (N. Y.) 470; Brown *v.* Brabham, 3 Ohio 277; Smith *v.* Wigley, 3 M. & Scott 174.

Where a firm indebted to B on running account took in a new member, and continued to run up an account with B, payments made by the new firm could not be applied by B to the indebtedness of the old firm. St. Louis Type Foundry Co. *v.* Wisdom, 4 Lea (Tenn.) 695.

2. Philpott *v.* Jones, 2 Ad. & El. 41; Crookshank *v.* Rose, 5 Car. & P. 19. Treadwell *v.* Moore, 34 Me. 112; Reid *v.* Duncan, 1 La. Am. 265. See Livermore *v.* Rand, 26 N. H. 85. And *compare* Adams *v.* Mahnken, 41 N. J. Eq. 332; Kidder *v.* Morris, 18 N. H. 532; Bancroft *v.* Dumas, 21 Vt. 456; Burland *v.* Nash, 2 Fest. & Fin. 687. And see *infra* under 5. As to a debt barred by limitations, Armistead *v.* Brooke, 18 Ark. 521; Mills *v.* Fowkes, 7 Scott 444; 5 Bing. N. C., 3 Jur. 406.

Compare Nash *v.* Hodgson, 5 De. G. M. & G. 474; 25 L. J., Ch. 186.

It seems that the payment cannot be distributed to several notes so as to take them all out of the statute. Ayer *v.* Hawkins, 19 Vt. 26.

But *compare* Jackson *v.* Burke, 1 Dill. (U. S.) 311. It may be applied

(*f*) WHEN CREDITOR MAY MAKE APPLICATION.—As to this authorities differ; it need not be made immediately.[1] But some

so as to prevent the bar of the statute. Williams *v.* Griffith, 5 Mees. & W. 300. So the payment may be applied to a debt within the Statute of Frauds. Haynes *v.* Nice, 100 Mass. 327; s. c., 1 Am. Rep. 109.

But the following cases hold with more or less positiveness that the creditor cannot apply it to a demand which is positively unlawful; as, for instance, a claim for usurious interest. Phillips *v.* Moses, 65 Me. 70; Rohan *v.* Hanson, 11 Cush. (Mass.) 44; McCausland *v.* Ralston, 12 Nev. 195; s. c., 28 Am. Rep. 781; Greene *v.* Tyler, 39 Pa. St. 361; Pickett *v.* Merchants' Nat. Bank, 32 Ark. 346.

And in a *Louisiana* case, where B held the note of a third party secured by mortgage as collateral for an open account due from A, and the mortgage notes were paid, it was held that B could not, by crediting the payment on another account due from A, prevent prescription as to such other account. In this case the debtor had himself indicated the application. Walmsley *v.* Morse, 34 La. Ann. 262.

On this point the court of appeals of Virginia says: "There is this well recognized exception to the rule, that the creditor may apply where the debtor does not, that the creditor has no right to apply the money paid to him to the satisfaction of what does not, nor ever did, constitute any legal or equitable demand against the party making the payment." Turner *v.* Turner, 80 Va. 379. And this was a case where the defense of usury was interposed. The language used by the court is quoted from Chitty (Contract, 11, 14). The same view is taken by the Supreme Court of Texas in a case involving a usurious contract. (Stanley *v.* Westrop, 16 Tex. 200), and by the Wisconsin courts (Gill *v.* Rice, 13 Wis. 549).

A creditor held two notes against the same debtor, one usurious and the other not. The debtor having made a payment greater than the usurious note without any specific application, the creditor applied it to discharge the usurious note, and credited the excess on the other note. In an action on the latter note, it was held that defendant could not set up the usury in the paid note as a defense, but that it might be pleaded as a set-off. Rackley *v.* Pearce, 1 Ga. 241.

The creditor may apply the payment on a bill of exchange which is void for want of a stamp. Biggs *v.* Dwight, 5 Man. & Ry. 308.

An attorney had an account against a municipal corporation, and money had been paid him on general account. The attorney applied the payment in discharge of two bills for business done, in respect of which he had no sufficient retainer, and in part discharge of a third bill for extra costs incurred by him in his capacity of town clerk. The appropriation was sustained by the court, though he could not have recovered on the first two bills. Arnold *v.* Poole, 4 Man. & Gr. 860; 2 Dowl., N. S. 574; 5 Scott N. R. 741; 7 Jur. 653.

Where the debtor is indebted on two accounts, one illegal because for spirituous liquors sold in quantities not amounting to 20*s.* at a time, and the other legal, being for board and lodging, the creditor may apply payments made generally to the account for the liquors. Cruickshanks *v.* Rose, 1 M. & Rob. 100.

Where the debtor makes payments generally upon a running account, part of the items of which were made before, and part after, his discharge in bankruptcy, of which proceeding the creditor had no notice, the creditor may apply the payments to the items first due. Hill *v.* Robbins, 22 Mich. 475.

1. Mayor etc. of Alexandria *v.* Patten, 4 Cranch (U. S.) 317; Brady *v.* Hill, 1 Mo. 315; s. c., 13 Am. Dec. 503; Heilbron *v.* Bissel, 1 Bailey Eq. (S. Car.) 430.

Compare Hill *v.* Southerland, 1 Wash. (Va.) 128; Logan *v.* Mason, 6 W. & S. (Pa.) 9.

Says COLTMAN, J., in Mills *v.* Fowkes, (5 Bing., N. C. 455): "The creditor is not imited in point of time." p. 464.

The creditor may make the application "not only at the instant of payment, but up to the very last moment." City Discount Co. *v.* McLean, 9 L. R., C. P. 692. "At the time of payment or at any subsequent time." Howard *v.* McCall, 21. Gratt. (Va.) 205; Plummer *v.* Erskine, 58 Me. 59.

Some cases hold that it should be

authorities hold that it may be done at any time before trial, or even at the trial;[1] others that it must be done before suit is commenced.[2]

(*g*) APPLICATION, HOW SHOWN.—An application by the creditor may be shown by circumstances. It is not necessary that he should notify the debtor what application he has made.[3]

made within a reasonable time. Allen *v.* Culver, 3 Den. (N. Y.) 284; Pattison *v.* Hull, 9 Cow. (N. Y.) 749; Harker *v.* Conrad, 12 S. & R. (Pa.) 301; s. c., 14 Am. Dec. 691; Briggs *v.* Williams, 2 Vt. 283.

The application cannot be made by the creditor after a controversy has arisen between the parties in reference thereto. United States *v.* Kirkpatrick, 9 Wheat. (U. S.) 920; Applegate *v.* Koons, 74 Ind. 247. Nor, it seems, can either party then make such application. Lazarus *v.* Friedheim, 51 Ark. 371.

See Robinson *v.* Doolittle, 12 Vt. 246, 249; Milliken *v.* Tuffts, 31 Me. 497; Fairchild *v.* Holly, 10 Conn. 176, 184. See also Gass *v.* Stinson, 2 Sumn. (U. S.) 98.

1. Bosanquet *v.* Wray, 6 Taunt. 597; Philpot *v.* Jones (per TAUNTON, J.), 2 Ad. & Ell. 41; Johnson *v.* Thomas, 77 Ala. 367; Haynes *v.* Waite, 14 Cal. 446; Larrabee *v.* Lumbert, 32 Me. 98.

In *South Carolina* it has has been held that it may be made at any time before judgment or verdict. Brice *v.* Hamilton, 12 S. Car. 32. And in *New York* an application was allowed to be made even after judgment. Marsh *v.* Oneida Central Bank, 34 Barb. (N. Y.) 298.

2. Shortridge *v.* Pardee, 2 Mo. App. 363; Poulson *v.* Collier, 18 Mo. App. 583, 607; Moss *v.* Adams, 4 Ired. Eq. (N. Car.) 42, 51; Callahan *v.* Boazman, 21 Ala. 246; Richards *v.* Columbia, 55 N. H. 96; Whetmore *v.* Murdock, 3 Woodb & M. (U. S.) 390; Simson *v.* Ingham, 2 B. & Cres. 65.

Where one who owes two debts to the same creditor pays a sum of money in gross, without directing its application, and the creditor omits to apply it to either debt, the debtor may, when sued on one of the debts, apply the payment in discharge of the debt sued on, though the creditor has delayed action on both debts, it not being shown that both were extended by reason of such payment. Dent *v.* State Bank, 12 Ala, 275.

The institution of suit is of itself a sufficient appropriation. Haynes *v.* Waite, 14 Cal. 446; Starrett *v.* Barber, 20 Me. 457; Peters *v.* Anderson, 5 Taunt. 596.

3. Johnson *v.* Thomas, 77 Ala. 367; Jones *v.* United States, 7 How. (U. S.) 681; Truscott *v.* King, 6 N. Y. 147.

The entries made by the creditor in his own books are competent evidence of the application. Van Rensselaer *v.* Roberts, 5 Den. (N. Y.) 470. But this is not conclusive till it has been communicated to the debtor. Seymour *v.* Marion, 11 Barb. (N. Y.) 80; Allen *v.* Culver, 3 Den. (N. Y.) 284. See Dulles *v.* De Forest, 19 Conn. 190.

It may be manifested by the institution of suit on the debt to which the appropriation was not made. Peters *v.* Anderson, 5 Taunt. 596; Haynes *v.* Waite, 14 Cal. 446; Starrett *v.* Barber, 20 Me. 457.

Where the creditor holds two notes against the same debtor, and a payment is made sufficient to extinguish one of them, bringing suit upon one is an election to appropriate such payment to the other. Starrett *v.* Barber, 20 Me. 457. See also Haynes *v.* Waite, 14 Cal. 446.

A landlord who had business transactions with his tenant charged the latter on his ledger rent as it fell due monthly, and also cash advances made him from time to time. The landlord received from time to time the proceeds of the sale of iron belonging to the tenant, and credited such proceeds generally on the account. Finally the landlord distrained for rent, and it was held that his action in distraining constituted an election to appropriate the moneys received to the items of the account outside of the rent. Garrett's Appeal, 100 Pa. St. 597.

A being indebted to B and to B & Co., paid to B a sum less than the aggregate of the two debts, and took from him a receipt in full signed B & Co., B at the time voluntarily promising to receive the part payment as a satisfaction of both demands. *Held*, that the receipt indicated an application of the payment first to the firm

3. Money Realized from Mortgage, etc.—The proceeds of property on which there is a mortgage or other lien cannot be applied to a debt other than that secured by the mortgage or lien without the consent of both parties.[1]

4. Application Once Made, Conclusive.—If the application is once

account, and that B might recover from A the unpaid balance of his individual account. Otto *v.* Klauber, 23 Wis. 471.

The following additional cases illustrate the rule governing the creditor's right to apply payments made by the debtor, where the debtor has not himself made the application:

Alabama.—Driver *v.* Fortner, 5 Port. (Ala.) 9.

Arkansas.—Gates *v.* Burkett, 44 Ark. 90; Lazarus *v.* Friedheim, 51 Ark. 371.

California.—Byrnes *v.* Claffey, 69 Cal. 120; Molaskey *v.* Peery, 76 Cal. 84.

Connecticut.—Lewis *v.* Hartford Silk Mfg. Co., 56 Conn. 215.

Delaware.—McCartney *v.* Buck, (Del. 1887), 12 Atl. Rep. 717.

Georgia.—Pritchard *v.* Comer, 71 Ga. 18; Simmons *v.* Cates, 56 Ga. 609; Greer *v.* Burnam, 71 Ga. 31; Holley *v.* Hardeman, 76 Ga. 328; Cox *v.* Wall (Ga. 1890), 11 S. E. Rep. 137.

Illinois.—Scheik *v.* Trustees of Schools, 24 Ill. App. 369; Plain *v.* Roth, 107 Ill. 588.

Indiana.—Applegate *v.* Koons, 74 Ind. 247.

Iowa.—Blair Town Lot and Land Co. *v.* Hillis, 76 Iowa 246.

Kentucky.—Burks *v.* Albert, 4 J. J. Marsh. (Ky.) 97; s. c., 20 Am. Dec. 209; Darling *v.* Brown, (Ky. 1888) 7 S. W. Rep. 565.

Louisiana.—Standifer *v.* Covington, 35 La. Ann. 896; Walmsley *v.* Morse, 34 La. Ann. 262.

Maine.—Lambert *v.* Winslow, 48 Me. 196.

Massachusetts.—Barrett *v.* Lewis, 2 Pick. (Mass.) 123; Cole *v.* Trull, 9 Pick. (Mass.) 325.

Michigan.—Wood *v.* Callaghan, 61 Mich. 402; Blair *v.* Carpenter, 75 Mich. 167.

Missouri.—Beck *v.* Haas, 31 Mo. App. 180.

New Hampshire.—Livermore *v.* Rand, 26 N. H. 85.

New Jersey.—Keyser *v.* Burd, 43 N. J. Eq. 697; Adams *v.* Mahnken, 41 N. J. Eq. 332.

New York.—Long Island Bank *v.* Townsend, Hill & D. Supp. (N. Y.) 204; Jones *v.* Benedict, 83 N. Y. 79; Calfornia Bank *v.* Webb, 94 N. Y. 467; White Sewing Machine Co. *v.* Fargo (Supreme Ct.), 3 N. Y. Supp. 494.

North Carolina.—State Bank *v.* Armstrong, 4 Dev. L. (N. Car.) 519; State Bank *v.* Locke, 4 Dev. L. (N. Car.) 529; Wittakowski *v.* Reid, 84 N. Car. 21.

Pennsylvania.—Wagner's Appeal, 103 Pa. St. 185; Schuylkill Co. *v.* Commonwealth, 36 Pa. St. 524.

South Carolina.—Thatcher *v.* Massey, 20 S. Car. 542; Ellis *v.* Mason (S. Car. 1889), 10 S. E. Rep. 1069.

Tennessee.—Harding *v.* Wormley, 8 Baxt. (Tenn.) 578.

Vermont.—Cass *v.* McDonald, 39 Vt. 65.

Virginia.—Donally *v.* Wilson, 5 Leigh (Va.) 329.

Wisconsin.—Mendel *v.* Paepke, 69 Wis. 527; North Wisconsin Lumber Co. *v.* American Express Co. 73 Wis., 656.

Sanborn *v.* Stark, 31 Fed. Rep. 18; Phillips *v.* Bossard, 35 Fed. Rep. 99; L'Hommedieu *v.* The H. L. Dayton, 38 Fed. Rep. 926.

1. Askers *v.* Steiner, 76 Ala. 218; Taylor *v.* Cockrell, 80 Ala. 236; Streckland *v.* Harde, 82 Ala. 412, and cases there cited; Caldwell *v.* Hall, 49 Ark. 508; s. c., 4 Am. St. Rep. 64; Marzion *v.* Pioche, 8 Cal. 522; Merrimack Bank *v.* Brown, 12 N. H. 320; Avera *v.* McNeil, 77 N. Car. 50; Hicks *v.* Bingham, 11 Mass. 390; Parker *v.* Mercer, 6 How. (Miss.) 320; s. c., 38 Am. Dec. 438.

Compare Whilden *v.* Pearce, 27 S. Car. 44; White *v.* Beem, 80 Ind. 239.

A principal cannot require his factor to apply the proceeds of cotton, on which the latter has a lien for advances to another debt, after having surrendered personal property to him under a mortgage of the same given to secure the debt. Baldwin *v.* Flesh, 59 Miss. 61.

made by either party, it is conclusive, and both parties are bound thereby.[1]

5. Right Confined to Original Parties.—The right to make the application is strictly confined to the debtor and creditor, and no third person can insist on any appropriation which has not been made by either party.[2]

1. 1 Am. Lead Cas. (3rd ed.) 288; Bank of North America *v.* Meredith, 2 Wash. (U. S.) 47; Mayor, etc. of Alexandria *v.* Patten, 4 Cranch (U. S.) 317; Miller *v.* Montgomery, 31 Ill. 350; Coon's Appeal, 52 Conn. 186; Codman *v.* Armstrong, 28 Me. 91; Poulson *v.* Collier, 18 Mo. App. 583; Brown *v.* Burns, 6 Me. 535; Dorsey *v.* Wayman, 6 Gill (Md.) 59; Bank of Muskingum *v.* Carpenter, 7 Ohio 21; s. c., 28 Am. Dec. 616; Tooke *v.* Bonds, 29 Tex. 419; Hill *v.* Southerland, 1 Wash. (Va.) 128.

Though the application was made to a debt which could not have been enforced. Mueller *v.* Wiebracht, 47 Mo. 468.

If the debtor has directed the payment to be applied to satisfy an illegal claim, he cannot afterwards change the application without the consent of the creditor. Hubbell *v.* Flint, 15 Gray (Mass.) 550; Richardson *v.* Woodbury, 12 Cush. (Mass.) 279; Caldwell *v.* Wentworth, 14 N. H. 431; Reid *v.* Duncan, 1 La. Ann. 265.

Where debits and credits have been made absolutely, both parties consenting, credits cannot afterwards be shifted for the purpose of confining payments to unsecured liabilities. McMaster *v.* Merrick, 41 Mich. 505.

An application by the creditor becomes irrevocable when he has exercised his right of election and communicated the fact to the debtor. 2 Whart. Contr., § 932; 1 Addison Contr., § 350; 2 Parsons Contr. (6th ed.) 630; Johnson *v.* Thomas, 77 Ala. 367; Seymour *v.* Marvin, 11 Barb. (N. Y.) 80; Allen *v.* Culver, 3 Den. (N. Y.) 284. *Compare* Dulles *v.* DeForrest, 19 Conn. 190.

Where neither the debtor nor creditor makes a special appropriation of the payments at the time they are made, but they are entered as general credits on the general account, the creditor is without right to make a special application thereafter to any special part of the account, to serve his interests as may subsequently be developed. Lane *v.* Jones, 79 Ala. 156. See Jones *v.* United States, 7 How. (U. S.) 681.

But the application may be changed with the consent of both parties. Rundlett *v.* Small, 25 Me. 29. Unless the rights of third parties would be affected by such change. Thayer *v.* Denton, 4 Mich. 192; Smith *v.* Wood, 1 N. J. Eq. 74; Chancellor *v.* Schott, 23 Pa. St. 68.

In a suit to foreclose a mortgage, which the defendant alleged had been paid, the plaintiff proved an agreement to change the appropriation of the payments, previously agreed to be applied on the mortgage debt, to another debt. *Held*, that the defendant might then prove that the agreement to change the appropriation was made after he had applied for the benefit of the insolvent laws, and therefore invalid. Richmond Iron Works *v.* Woodruff, 8 Gray (Mass.) 447.

Where the consignor of goods appropriates the proceeds in discharge of a particular antecedent debt, he may change such appropriation at any time before the goods actually come into possession of the party whose debt they were to discharge, unless notice has been given him of the prior appropriation. Hankey *v.* Hunter, Peak's Add. Cas. 107.

If A receive money belonging to B, through the agent of the latter, and at the time of receiving the money both B and his agent are his debtors, and A has no reason to believe that the money was to be applied to B's account, and therefore appropriates it to the credit of the agent, B cannot recover it back. Dwinel *v.* Sawyer, 53 Me. 24.

2. Gordon *v.* Hobart, 2 Story (U. S.) 243; Cole *v.* Withers, 33 Gratt. (Va.) 186.

A bank was the holder of several notes by the same maker, some indorsed by its cashier and some by others. It was agreed between the cashier and the other indorsers that he would do what was best for all, and that the loss should be shared by all. Money having been realized

6. **By the Court.**—(*a*) WHERE NEITHER PARTY MAKES THE APPLICATION the general rule is that the court will direct the appropriation according to the justice and equity of the case.[1]

on a mortgage given to secure all the notes, the cashier had no right, either as against the bank or the other indorsers, to apply it first to the notes on which he was indorser. Bridenbecker *v.* Lowell, 32 Barb. (N. Y.) 9.

Neither a surety nor a guarantor can insist that an appropriation shall be made for his benefit. Blanton *v.* Rice, 5 Mon. (Ky.) 253; Poulson *v.* Collier, 18 Mo. App. 583; Goetz *v.* Piel, 26 Mo. App. 634; Harding *v.* Tifft, 75 N. Y. 461; Kirby *v.* Marlborough, 2 Maule & Sel. 18; Williams *v.* Rawlinson, 10 Moore, 362; 3 Bing. 71; Ry. & M. 233.

Compare Marryatts *v.* White, 2 Stark 101.

1. Postmaster General *v.* Norvell, Gilp. (U. S.) 106; Cremer *v.* Higginson, 1 Mason (U. S.) 323; United States *v.* Kirkpatrick, 9 Wheat. (U. S.) 720; Callahan *v.* Boazman, 21 Ala. 246; Selleck *v.* Sugar Hollow Turnpike Co., 13 Conn. 453; Pickering *v.* Day, 2 Del. Ch. 333; s. c., on appeal, 3 Houst. 474; s. c., 95 Am. Dec. 291.

Randall *v.* Parramore, 1 Fla. 409; McFarland *v.* Lewis, 3 Ill. 344; Bayley *v.* Wynkoop, 10 Ill. 549; Dehmer *v.* Helmbacher etc. Mills., 7 Ill. App. 47; Starrett *v.* Barber, 20 Me. 457; Gwin *v.* Whitaker, 1 Har. & J. (Md.) 754; Youmans *v.* Heartt, 34 Mich. 397; Benny *v.* Rhodes, 18 Mo. 147; s. c., 59 Am. Dec. 293; Young *v.* Woodward, 44 N. H. 250; White *v.* Trumbull, 15 N. J. L. 314; s. c., 29 Am. Dec. 687; Oliver *v.* Phelps, 20 N. J. L. 180; Harker *v.* Conrad, 12 S. & R. (Pa.) 301; s. c., 14 Am. Dec. 691; Carson *v.* Hill, 1 McMull (S. Car.) 76; Proctor *v.* Marshall, 18 Tex. 63; Briggs *v.* Williams, 2 Vt. 283; Robinson *v.* Doolittle, 12 Vt. 246; Rosseau *v.* Cull, 14 Vt. 83; Pierce *v.* Knight, 3, Vt. 701; Smith *v.* Loyd, 11 Leigh (Va.) 512; s. c., 37 Am. Dec. 621; Margarity *v.* Shipman, 82 Va. 784.

The law does not apply money until it has passed from the debtor. Phillips *v.* Mayer, 7 Cal. 81.

It is frequently held that the application which the law will make is that which is most favorable to the debtor. See 1 Story Eq. Jur., § 459 d; Johnson *v.* Robbins, 20 La. Ann. 569.

Compare Nelsom *v.* D'Armond, 13 La. Ann. 294.

To the words in the text the court of appeals of Virginia adds: "And so that it may be most beneficial to both parties." And the court says further: "As the direction of the debtor would have controlled the application in the first place, the court did not err, in the absence of any application by the creditor, in applying them in the manner most beneficial to the debtor, to the debt bearing the highest rate of interest." Magarity *v.* Shipman, 82 Va. 784.

See also Hamer *v.* Kirkwood, 25 Miss. 95; Byrne *v.* Grayson, 15 La. Ann. 457; Slaughter *v.* Milling, 15 La. Ann. 526; Milliken *v.* Tufts, 31 Me. 497, 500; Bussey *v.* Gant, 10 Humph. (Tenn.) 242; Gass *v.* Stinson, 3 Sumn. (U. S.) 99.

Where some of the items of an account bear interest and others do not, payments will be appropriated to the former in the order in which they fall due. Scott *v.* Cleveland, 33 Miss. 447.

Where, however, there is an express agreement between the parties, or a course of business from which an agreement would be implied, that the appropriation shall be made in a manner most beneficial to the creditor, the court will make the application accordingly. Gwin *v.* McLean, 62 Miss. 121.

If only one demand is shown to exist, the law will apply the payment to that demand. McDonnell *v.* Branch Bank, 20 Ala. 313.

Where a creditor holds several notes against the same debtor, on part of which a third person is surety, the surety may insist upon a payment being applied ratably to the notes on which he is liable. Blackstone Bank *v.* Hill, 10 Pick. (Mass.) 129.

Where the rights of securities alone are to be considered, the court will determine the application on equitable principles. Campbell *v.* Vedder, 1 Abb. App. Dec. (N. Y.) 295.

Where a mortgage is given to secure two promissory notes and a draft, on two of which the mortgagor was the principal debtor, and on the remaining one only a surety, the proceeds

(*b*) COURT WILL NOT DISTURB APPLICATION MADE BY PARTIES.—The law never makes an application of payment when the parties have already done so.[1] And this rule obtains even where the parties have applied the money to the payment of an account current which is not recoverable in an action at law.[2]

(*c*) RULES GOVERNING APPLICATION.—But in making such appropriation the court is to be governed by certain general and established rules, and is not at liberty to adopt its own notions of what may be just and equitable in each particular case.[3]

of the mortgage sale will be applied *pro rata* on the different obligations, unless the mortgage contains a specific direction as to the application. Orleans Co. Nat. Bank *v.* Moore, 21 N. Y. St. Rep. 609; 3 L. Rep., Ann. 302.

A party agreed to sell to a railroad company certain land for $300, and the right of way through his remaining land for $1,225, and also agreed to remove certain buildings, for which the company was to pay him $2,275. He removed the buildings and the company paid him $2,012, and built its road. *Held*, that the court properly applied the payment made to the amount due for removing the buildings. Hempfield R. Co. *v.* Thornburg, 1 W. Va. 261.

1. Watt *v.* Hoch, 25 Pa. St. 411.

2. Dickey *v.* Permanent Land Co., 63 Md. 170; Feldman *v.* Gamble, 26 N. J. Eq. 494.

While a party who has paid money as the consideration of an illegal sale may recover it back, yet if the court should apply it to the payment of other lawful debts, this would be, in effect, to make a new contract for the parties against their wishes and intentions, and different from that which the law raises from the circumstance that the money may be recovered back. Tomlinson Carriage Co. *v.* Kinsella, 31 Conn. 272.

The same rule is applied where the payment has been made on a usurious contract. Feldman *v.* Gamble, 26 N. J. Eq. 494; Treadwell *v.* Moore, 34 Me. 112; Reid *v.* Duncan, 1 La. Ann. 265. *Compare* Crane *v.* Goodwin, 77 Ga. 362; Cobb *v.* Morgan, 83 N. Car. 211.

So when part of a creditor's claim was for liquors sold by him in violation of a statute, which part was for that reason uncollectible, if the debtor made payments specifically on those items, the court will not afterwards change the application to items which were for groceries and other goods, the sale of which was fully sanctioned by law. Caldwell *v.* Wentworth, 14 N. H. 431; Richardson *v.* Woodbury, 12 Cush. (Mass.) 279; Hubbell *v.* Flint, 15 Gray (Mass.) 550; Tomlinson Carriage Co. *v.* Kinsella, 31 Conn. 268.

Says APPLETON, J., in Treadwell *v.* Moore, 34 Maine 112: "It is urged that these payments may be treated as unappropriated, if they have been applied to illegal claims. But such is not the law. The money is none the less appropriated, though in violation of law, and though the party paying may repent of such appropriation of his funds, and by suit recover them back."

And he says further: "No case can be found where the law by its own vigor has withdrawn a payment deliberately made to the discharge of a claim, however illegal, and appropriated it in payment of some legal claim existing against the individual making the payment. No such principle as applicable to the appropriation of payments is recognized."

The rule obtains where a corporation has directed the application of a payment made by it to a contract which is *ultra vires*. Williamson *v.* New Jersey S. R. Co., 28 N. J. Eq. 277.

The principle holds good whether the application is made by the debtor himself at the time of the payment, or by the creditor under a previous agreement with the debtor that it should be so applied. Dickey *v.* Permanent Land Co., 63 Md. 170.

The application will ordinarily be made to a note due absolutely to the creditor, rather than to one held by him as collateral security only. Bank of Portland *v.* Brown, 22 Me. 295.

3. Bobe *v.* Stickney, 36 Ala. 482; Miller *v.* Miller, 23 Me. 22; s. c., 39 Am. Dec. 97; Hersey *v.* Bennett, 28 Minn. 86; s. c., 41 Am. Rep. 271.

(*d*) TO OLDEST CHARGES.—It may be said, generally, that the law will appropriate the credit to the payment of the oldest charges.[1]

Where several notes are secured by the same mortgage, and all the notes are due at the time the money is realized under it, it will be applied to them all ratably. Parker *v.* Mercer, 6 How. (Miss.) 320; s. c., 38 Am. Dec. 438. See Bank of U. S. *v.* Singer, 13 Ohio 240; Newton *v.* Nunnally, 4 Ga. 356; Stamford Bank *v.* Benedict, 15 Conn. 438.

Where the money is realized on execution or is paid by an assignee in bankruptcy or insolvency, or under an assignment for the benefit of creditors, it must be applied ratably to all the debts. Bardwell *v.* Lydall, 7 Bing. 489; Blackstone Bank *v.* Hill, 10 Pick. (Mass.) 129; Commercial Bank *v.* Cunningham, 24 Pick. (Mass.) 270; s. c., 35 Am. Dec. 322; Scott *v.* Ray, 18 Pick. (Mass.) 360. *Compare* Bank of Portland *v.* Brown, 22 Me. 295.

If it is possible to ascertain the understanding of the parties, the appropriation will be made in accordance therewith. Emery *v.* Tichout, 13 Vt. 15; Chitty *v.* Naish, 2 Dowl. Pr. Cas. 511.

The court will ordinarily apply the payment to the debt which first becomes due. Allen *v.* Brown, 39 Iowa 330; Hanson *v.* Manley, 72 Iowa 48; Marks *v.* Robinson, 82 Ala. 69; Thompson *v.* Phelan, 22 N. H. 339; Parks *v.* Ingram, 22 N. H. 283; s. c., 55 Am. Dec. 153.

And this rule is applicable to a case where a seaman served under two masters on the same voyage. Payments made by the second master will be first applied to wages accruing under the former master. Smith *v.* Oakes, 141 Mass. 451; s. c., 55 Am. Rep. 487. And to cases of mechanics' liens. Sexton *v.* Weaver, 141 Mass. 273.

1. Toulmin *v.* Copeland, 2 Cl. & Fin. 681; McKenzie *v.* Nevins, 22 Me. 138; s. c., 38 Am. Dec. 291; Millikin *v.* Tufts, 31 Me. 497; Allstan *v.* Contee, 4 Har. & J. (Md.) 351; Bloom *v.* Kern, 30 La. Ann. 1263; Allen *v.* Culver, 3 Den. (N. Y.) 284; St. Albans *v.* Failey, 46 Vt. 448; Langdon *v.* Bowen, 46 Vt. 512; Genin *v.* Ingersoll, 11 W. Va. 549. *Compare* Shaw *v.* Pratt, 22 Pick. (Mass.) 305; Killorin *v.* Bacon, 57 Ga. 497.

Even though there has been a change in the membership of the debtor firm. Allen *v.* Brown, 39 Iowa 330.

And though some of the earlier items are secured, and the later ones are not. Worthley *v.* Emerson, 116 Mass. 374.

The payment will be applied to a prior legal, in preference to a subsequent equitable, demand. Goddard *v.* Hodges, 1 Cr. & Mees. 33; 3 Tyr. 259.

If securities are pledged as collateral for any balance of indebtedness which then does or may thereafter exist, the proceeds of a sale of the collateral will, in the absence of any application by the parties, be applied to the earliest items of the account.. Thompson *v.* St. Nicholas Nat. Bank, 113 N. Y. 325.

Where by an account between an agent and his principal the agent charges himself with a balance, and continues to receive moneys for the principal, subsequent payments are not necessarily to be first applied to the extinction of the balance, especially if the subsequent receipts correspond in amount with the subseqent payments. Lysaght *v.* Walker, 5 Bligh, N. S. 1.

The rule applies where there are dealings with a firm, followed by dealings with an individual member of the firm. Laing *v.* Campbell, 36 Beav. 3.

A firm being indebted to their banker in the sum of £979, the banker transferred his business, with the consent of the firm, to the Midland Bank. The firm account with the Midland Bank commenced with the debit of £979, and continued open for some time, during which the firm paid in money amounting in the aggregate to more than £979, the pass-book being regularly sent to the firm, by whom no objection was made. *Held*, that the debt of £979 was extinguished. Beale *v.* Caddick, 2 Hurl. & N. 326; 26 L. J. Exch. 356. See also Bodenham *v.* Purchas, 2 B. & Ald. 39.

Where a county collector owes sums for the last official year and also for a preceding one, and after the close of his last year pays to his successor a sum of money less than his entire indebtedness, and there is nothing to show whence the money was derived or

(*e*) TO DEBT DUE.—And they will be applied to a debt which is due in preference to one which is not due.[1]

(*f*) TO LEGAL DEBT.—The application will be made to such debts as the debtor was legally bound to pay, and not to such as he was not bound to pay.[2]

whether it was received by him during either of his official years, and no application is made by the parties, the law will, in the absence of any equity in favor of third parties requiring a different application, apply the payment to the oldest debt. Frost *v.* Mixsell, 38 N. J. Eq. 586.

Where a collector has served successive terms, the presumption is that payments made during any one year are designed to extinquish the liabilities of that year; but if the payments are made before the officer is chargeable with the revenue of the year in which they are made, they will, in the absence of all proof of intention, and it not appearing from what source the money so paid was derived, be applied to the oldest item of indebtedness. Draffen *v.* Boonville, 8 Mo. 395.

See Boody *v.* United States, 1 Woodb. & M. (U. S.) 150; Pickering *v.* Day, 2 Del. Ch. 333; s. c., on appeal, 4 Houst. (Del.) 474; s. c., 95 Am. Dec. 291; Helm *v.* Commonwealth, 79 Ky. 67.

Where it is agreed that debts due to a former partnership shall, upon the formation of a new firm between a partner of the old firm and a third party, be transferred to the new firm as a part of the capital of the new firm as against the debts from the old firm; payments made by customers of the old firm without appropriation must be applied in payment of the debts of the old firm. Toulmin *v.* Copeland, 2 Cl. & Fin. 681; West 164.

Payments made by A, after the dissolution of a firm of which he was a member, to a firm creditor, must be applied to the payment of firm debts, though T became personally indebted to the same creditor subsequently to the dissolution of the firm. Smith *v.* Wigley, 3 M. & S. 174.

1. Harrison *v.* Johnston, 27 Ala. 445; Bobe *v.* Stickney, 36 Ala. 482; Heintz *v.* Cohn, 29 Ill. 308; Bacon *v.* Brown, 1 Bibb (Ky.) 334; s. c., 4 Am. Dec. 640; Effinger *v.* Henderson, 33 Miss. 449; Cloney *v.* Richardson, 34 Mo. 370; Hunter *v.* Osterhondt, 11 Barb. (N. Y.) 33; Seymour *v.* Sexton, 10 Watts (Pa.) 255; Whetmore *v.* Murdock, 3 Woodb. & M. (U. S.) 390.

Payments made generally on account for work done on several contracts, some of which have not been completed, must be applied in the first place to extinguish the amounts due on those contracts which have been completed, before any application is made to those not completed. McDowell *v.* Blackstone Canal Co., 5 Mason (U. S.) 11.

A merchant agreed to accept bills drawn by his correspondent to the amount of two-thirds the value of an intended shipment. The vessel and cargo having been lost, the consignees were authorized by all parties in interest to settle with the insurance company for two-thirds of the claim. The consignors having drawn in excess of the amount agreed upon, and the insurance money being consequently insufficient to pay all the drafts, they were ordered to be paid in full, in the order in which they were presented, until the fund was exhausted. Cabada *v.* De Jongh, 10 Phila. (Pa.) 422.

Moneys paid upon an outstanding account cannot be applied to debts subsequently contracted. Hill *v.* Morrison, 46 N. J. L. 488.

Where several notes payable in merchandise fall due on the first days of three successive years, merchandise delivered in the course of each year should be applied in satisfaction of the note falling due the first day of the succeeding year. Anderson *v.* Mason, 6 Dana. (Ky.) 217.

2. Wright *v.* Laing, 4 Dowl. & R. 783; 3 B. & Cr. 165; *Ex parte* Randleson, 2 Deac. & Chit. 534; Kean *v.* Branden, 12 La. Ann. 20; Hilton *v.* Burley, 2 N. H. 193; Dunbar *v.* Garrity, 58 N. H. 575; Storer *v.* Haskell, 50 Vt. 341.

Compare Fletcher *v.* Gillan, 62 Miss. 8; Thurlow *v.* Gilmore, 40 Me. 378.

Where a debt is usurious, and no application has been specially made by either party to the payment of interest, the court will apply the payment to the principal. Turner *v.* Turner, 80

(*g*) PRINCIPAL AND INTEREST.—Where a payment is made upon an interest bearing debt, it will be first applied to extinguish the interest due and afterwards to the principal.[1]

(*h*) RUNNING OPEN ACCOUNT.—Where there is a running open account between the parties, and no appropriation made by either, the law will apply the payments according to priority of time, the first item on the credit side going to discharge or reduce the first item on the debit side.[2]

Va. 379; Burrows *v.* Cook, 17 Iowa 436; Parchman *v.* McKinney, 12 Smed. & M. (Miss.) 631; Stanley *v.* Westrop, 16 Tex. 200; Bank of Cadiz *v.* Slemmons, 34 Ohio St. 142; s. c., 32 Am. Rep. 364; Moore *v.* Holland, 16 S. Car. 15.

And legal interest; Bartholomew *v.* Yaw, 9 Paige (N. Y.) 165.

If one debt becomes barred by the statute of limitations after the payment has been made, the law will apply it to that debt. Robinson *v.* Allison, 36 Ala. 525.

Where the payor was indebted in four different demands, only one of which was lawful, payments made by him will be applied to the single valid debt, irrespective of its order in the account. Backman *v.* Wright, 27 Vt. 187; s. c., 65 Am. Dec. 187.

If an account is made up partly of legal and partly of illegal sales payments made generally are to be applied to the charges for the legal sales. Solomon *v.* Dreschler, 4 Minn. 278; Hall *v.* Clement, 41 N. H. 166. But if at any time the aggregate payments exceed the amount due for legal sales, the excess will be applied to the charges for illegal sales; it will not be presumed that payments were made in advance to apply on future legal sales. Hall *v.* Clement, 41 N. H. 166.

1. See *supra*, this title, *Part Payments;* People *v.* New York Co., 5 Cow. (N. Y.) 331; Eberlin *v.* Palmer, (Supreme Ct.), 10 N. Y. Supp. 660; Steele *v.* Taylor, 4 Dana (Ky.) 445; Anderson *v.* Perkins (Mont. 1890), 25 Pac. Rep. 92.

The rule applies even though no part of the principal is due. But if neither is due, the payment is applied to the extinguishment of principal and interest ratably. Jencks *v.* Alexander, 11 Paige (N. Y.) 619.

In *Michigan*, the rule for computing interest is the Massachusetts, and not the Connecticut, rule; that is, partial payments, instead of being applied directly to the discharge of the principal, are first applied to the payment of the interest then due. Wallace *v.* Glaser, (Mich. 1890), 46 N. W. Rep. 227.

Monthly payments by a debtor, in excess of interest payable on the debt, will be applied to the principal of the debt, and will not be treated as compensation for extensions of time, though they were so denominated by the parties when made. Bateman *v.* Blake, 81 Mich. 227.

Interest paid on a note in excess of the rate allowed by law will not be applied in payment of the principal until the maker so requests. Peterborough Sav. Bank *v.* Hodgdon, 62 N. H. 300.

2. 3 Phil. Evid. (Hill & Cowen's notes) *442; Devaynes *v.* Noble (Clayton's Case), 1 Mer. 572; Pemberton *v.* Oakes, 4 Russ. 154; Bodenham *v.* Purchas, 2 B. & Ald. 39; Field *v.* Farr, 5 Bing. 13, where it is said that the rule laid down in Clayton's Case has received the sanction of every court in Westminster Hall.

United States *v.* Kirkpatrick, 9 Wheat. (U. S.) 720; Leef *v.* Goodwin, Taney Dec. (U. S.) 460; Postmaster General *v.* Furber, 4 Mason (U.S.) 332; Harrison *v.* Johnston, 27 Ala. 445; Wendt *v.* Ross, 33 Cal. 650; Fairchild *v.* Holly, 10 Conn. 175; Sanford *v.* Clark, 29 Conn. 457; Pickering *v.* Day, 2 Del. Ch. 333; s. c., on appeal, 4 Houst. (Del.) 474; s. c., 95 Am. Dec. 291; Horne *v.* Planters' Bank, 32 Ga. 1; Sprague *v.* Hazenwinkle, 53 Ill. 419.

McKenzie *v.* Nevins, 22 Me. 138; s. c., 38 Am. Dec. 291; Hammett *v.* Dudley, 62 Md. 154; Hersey *v.* Bennett, 28 Minn. 86; s. c., 41 Am. Rep. 271; Goetz *v.* Piel, 26 Mo. App. 634; Warren *v.* Maloney, 29 Mo. App. 101; Dows *v.* Morewood, 10 Barb. (N. Y.) 183; Berrian *v.* Mayor etc. of N. Y., 4 Robt. (N. Y.) 538; Wheeler *v.* Cropsey, 5 How. Pr. (N. Y.) 288; McKee *v.* Commonwealth, 2 Grant's Cas. (Pa.) 23;

Pierce *v.* Sweet, 33 Pa. St. 151; Souder *v.* Schechterly, 91 Pa. St. 83; Willis *v.* McIntyre, 70 Tex. 34; Shedd *v.* Wilson, 27 Vt. 478; Thompson *v.* Davenport, 1 Wash. (Va.) 125.

This rule may be varied by the circumstances of the case. Wilson *v.* Hirst, 1 Nev. & M. 746.

A general payment must be applied to that part of the account which is due at the time. Effinger *v.* Henderson, 33 Miss. 449.

The rule does not apply to cases where an appropriation has been made by the party entitled to make it, nor to cases in which, in the absence of such appropriation, the law makes it upon the relation of the parties to do justice between them. Upham *v.* Lefavour, 11 Met. (Mass.) 174.

Nor to cases where it can be gathered from the dealings of the parties that they intended the rule should not apply. City Discount Co. *v.* M'Lean, 9 L. R., C. P. 692; 43 L. J., C. P. 344; 30 L. T., N. S. § 883; Dulles *v.* De Forrest, 19 Conn. 190.

The rule will be applied though the earlier items of the account are barred by the statute of limitations, and the later ones are not. Fletcher *v.* Gillan, 62 Miss. 8.

So, too, though the earlier items accrued during the infancy of the debtor. Thurlow *v.* Gilmore, 40 Me 378.

Where, in the course of trade dealings between A and B, the accounts between them are periodically made up in such a manner as to show that sums paid to the credit of A have, at the termination of each periodical account, been allowed for, so as to diminish A's indebtedness on that account, the parties have applied the rule of Clayton's Case for themselves. *Ex parte* Smith, 25 W. R. 760.

The rule will be applied, though one item is better secured than another. Hersey *v.* Bennett, 28 Minn. 86; s. c., 41 Am. Rep. 271; Cushing *v.* Wyman, 44 Me. 121; Truscott *v.* King, 6 N. Y. 147.

See also Berghans *v.* Alter, 9 Watts (Pa.) 386 and next head, "Appropriation to Secure Debts."

Where a husband has a general account with a merchant for supplies furnished and goods sold and delivered, some of which are chargeable against the wife's separate estate, payments made by the husband must be credited on the account generally, without regard to the question whether a part of the money was derived from the wife's estate Lee *v.* Fannenbaum, 62 Ala. 401, Lewis *v.* Dillard, 66 Ala. 1. See also May *v.* Taylor, 62 Miss. 500.

And the same principle applies where a sole debtor takes a partner, and the account continues to run with the firm. Lake *v.* Gaines, 75 Ala. 143.

Where a partnership is dissolved and one or more of the partners continue the business, and a creditor of the firm continues the credit, and blends together his accounts with the old firm and the new, payments made by the new firm with specific application will be appropriated to the debts of the old firm. Hooper *v.* Keay, 1 L. R., Q. B. Div. 178; 34 L. T., N. S. 574; 24 W. R. 485.

The creditor of a firm took partnership notes in settlement, and after the dissolution of the firm opened a running account with the continuing partner, by whose consent the amount paid by the creditor to take up the firm-notes upon their dishonor was charged in such account. The continuing partner made general payments after the amount of the notes was so charged. *Held*, that such payments must be applied to the earliest items of the account, and if they were sufficient to extinguish the notes and all earlier items in the account, the notes must be considered as paid. Allcott *v.* Strong, 9 Cush. (Mass.) 323.

To same effect, Laing *v.* Campbell, 36 Beav. 3.

A factor agreed to make advances to a firm to be paid at a future day, and took the firm's mortgage to secure the same. Other debts to the factor for advances not secured were afterwards contracted by the firm. Payments made on the general account before the mortgage debt became due, without any special application, were held properly carried into the general account of debts assumed and advances made, leaving the balance at the foot of the account to constitute the mortgage debt. Williams *v.* Vance, 9 S. Car. 344; s. c., 30 Am. Rep. 26.

But where services were rendered upon a special promise of the party requesting them to pay for them in cash, payments will be applied to such services, though the debtor had an account against the person rendering the services. Sanford *v.* Clark, 29 Conn. 457.

The rule obtains even in cases where

(*i*) TO UNSECURED DEBTS.—Where the debtor is indebted on several accounts, some of which are secured and others not, and makes payments, of which neither the debtor nor the creditor has made any application, the court will apply them first to the debts which are not secured, or of which the security is the most precarious.[1]

the goods were sold on condition that they should not become the property of the purchaser till paid for. Crompton *v.* Pratt, 105 Mass. 255.

A bought goods under such a contract, to be paid for by instalments. Subsequently he bought other goods from time to time on like terms. He made payments from time to time for which he took general receipts, but never paid the entire amount due. It was held that the successive purchases were several contracts, and that the payments should be applied to the earliest items, and whenever enough was paid to amount to the price of the goods embraced in any one purchase, the title to such goods vested in A. Sweet *v.* Boyce, 134 Mass. 381.

The rule of the text has been applied even to cases where the creditor had the right of appropriation. Morgan *v.* Tarbell, 28 Vt. 498.

1. 1 Am. Lead Cas. (3rd ed.) 292, 296; Field *v.* Holland, 6 Cranch (U. S.) 8; Gordon *v.* Hobart, 2 Story (U. S.) 243; The Antarctic, 1 Sprague (U. S.) 206; Williams *v.* Rawlinson, 10 Moore 362; 3 Bing. 71, Ry. & Mood. 233; Johnson's Appeal, 37 Pa. St. 268; McCurdy *v.* Middleton, 82 Ala. 131; Chester *v.* Wheelright, 15 Conn. 562; Bowen *v.* Fridley, 8 Ill. App. 595; Bosley *v.* Porter, 4 J. J. Marsh. (Ky.) 621; Burks *v.* Albert, 4 J. J. Marsh. (Ky.) 97; s. c., 20 Am. Dec. 209; Thiac *v.* Jumonville, 32 La. Ann. 142; Gwinn *v.* Whitaker, 1 Har. & J. (Md.) 754; Dedham Bank *v.* Chickering, 4 Pick. (Mass.) 314; Wood *v.* Callaghan, 61 Mich. 402; Hersey *v.* Bennet, 28 Minn. 86; s. c., 41 Am. Rep. 271; Poulson *v.* Collier, 18 Mo. App. 583; Goetz *v.* Piel, 26 Mo. App. 634; Planters' Bank *v.* Stockman, 1 Freem. Ch. (Miss.) 502; Baine *v.* Williams, 10 Smed. & M. (Miss.) 113; Hilton *v.* Burley, 2 N. H. 193; Smith *v.* Wood, 1 N. J. Eq. 74; Leeds *v.* Gifford, 41 N. J. Eq. 464; Pattison *v.* Hull, 9 Cow. (N. Y.) 747; Thomas *v.* Kelsey, 30 Barb. (N. Y.) 268; Trullinger *v.* Kofoed, 7 Oregon 228; s. c., 33 Am. Rep. 708; Pierce *v.* Sweet, 33 Pa. St. 151; McQuaide *v.* Stewart, 48 Pa. St. 198; Garrett's Appeal, 100 Pa. St. 597; Sager *v.* Warley, Rice Eq. (S. Car.) 26; Heilbron *v.* Bissell, 1 Bailey Eq. (S. Car.) 430; Gregory *v.* Forrester, 1 McCord Eq. (S. Car.) 318; Jones *v.* Kilgore, 2 Rich. Eq. (S. Car.) 63; Briggs *v.* Williams, 2 Vt. 283; Langdon *v.* Bowen, 46 Vt. 512. See Casey *v.* Weaver, 141 Mass. 280; and *compare* New Orleans Ins. Co. *v.* Tio, 15 La Ann. 174; McTarish *v.* Carroll, 1 Md. Ch. 160; Dorsey *v.* Garraway, 2 Har. & J. (Md.) 402; s. c., 3 Am. Dec. 557; Hollister *v.* Davis, 54 Pa. St. 508; Worthley *v.* Emerson, 116 Mass. 374; Neal *v.* Allison, 50 Miss. 175; Windsor *v.* Kennedy, 52 Miss. 164; Moore *v.* Kiff, 78 Pa. St. 96; Schuelenburg *v.* Martin, 1 McCrary (U. S.) 348; Ross *v.* McLauchlan, 7 Gratt. (Va.) 86.

It would seem that the law in *England* is that the money is to be first applied to the secured debt. Kinnaird *v.* Webster, L. R., 10 Ch. Div. 139. *Compare* Taylor *v.* Kymer, 3 B. & Ad. 320.

A mortgage was given to secure a note upon which there was a surety, and afterwards another mortgage on other property was executed by the same mortgagor to the same mortgagee to secure said note, and also another note given by the mortgagor to the same person. The latter mortgage was foreclosed first, and it was held that the proceeds should be applied *pro rata* to both notes.

Graham *v.* Jones, 24 S. Car. 241. See Orleans Co., Nat. Bank *v.* Morse, 3 L. Rep., Ann. 302; 21 N. Y. St. Rep. 609.

Where real and personal property were sold in one transaction, and one note given for the purchase-money, payments made by the grantee with any specific appropriation will be appropriated by the court to discharge the price of the personalty, and a vendor's lien will be decreed against the realty for the balance due. Mc-

Cauley *v.* Holtz, 62 Ind. 205. See White *v.* Blakemore, 8 Lea (Tenn.) 49.

A material man had an account against a vessel, some of the items of which were maritime and others not. *Held*, that payments made on general account should be first applied to the items which were not maritime. The D. B. Steelman, 5 Hughes (U. S.) 210.

A having a legal claim on B on drafts accepted by B, and having also possession of a mortgage executed by B to a third person, of which he might compel an assignment in equity, B paid money to A on account, without prejudice to his claim on any securities.[1] It was held that the payment must be applied to the bills. Birch *v.* Tebbutt, 2 Stark 74.

A being indebted to B to the amount of $10,000 gave him a mortgage to secure $3,000 thereof. A subsequently made several payments to B, none of which were specifically applied by either party. A creditor of A then levied on his equity of redemption in the mortgaged land and bid it in at $1. B subsequently filed a bill for foreclosure of the mortgage, when the purchaser of the equity of redemption claimed that the payments made should be applied to the mortgage debt. *Held*, that such application would not be made, but that the payments would be applied to the unsecured part of the debt. Chester *v.* Wheelright, 15 Conn. 562.

A executed two notes to B who indorsed and delivered them to C. At the maturity of the first note C sued both A and B, obtaining judgment against A's administrators, but being nonsuited as to B. A having died insolvent, C had the amount of his judgment and the remaining note both allowed against his estate, and received a dividend of 72 per cent. on the whole demand. *Held*, that this dividend should be credited *pro rata* on judgment and the note, and that it was not proper to appropriate it first to the satisfaction of the judgment, and the balance only on the note. Stamps *v.* Brown, Walk. Ch. (Miss.) 526.

So, where the payment is made by one who is under a several, as well as a joint liability to the creditor, the law will apply it to the several liability, unless there are circumstances showing that a different appropriation was intended, or that such appropriation would be inequitable. Lee *v.* Fontaine, 10 Ala. 755; s. c., 44 Am. Dec. 505; Livermore *v.* Claridge, 33 Me. 428.

Where the debtor is indebted on his own account and also as to surety for another, a payment made without any designation by him will be applied to his own debt. Newman *v.* Meek, 1 Smed. & M., Ch. (Miss.) 331.

If the money paid were derived from the fund from which the joint liability was to be met, the rule would be different. Livermore *v.* Claridge, 33 Me. 428; Brander *v.* Phillips, 16 Pet. (U. S.) 121.

Thus where a farm lease is signed by two as lessees, grain raised on the farm and delivered to the lessor cannot be applied to the individual debt of one lessee, leaving the rent unpaid, without the consent of both, no matter whether they are co-tenants, or one is surety for the other. Kahler *v.* Hanson, 53 Iowa 698.

Where several claims against the same party are placed in an officer's hands for collection, money collected by him should be first applied to those claims whose security is most precarious. Ramsour *v.* Thomas, 10 Ired. L. (N. Car.) 165; State *v.* Thomas, 11 Ired. (N. Car.) 251.

Where an assignment is made for the benefit of such creditors as become parties thereto and release their claims, a creditor who has several claims against the debtor must apply any dividends received *pro rata* to all the claims, whether secured or unsecured. Commercial Bank *v.* Cunningham, 24 Pick. (Mass.) 270; s. c., 35 Am. Dec. 322; Scott *v.* Ray, 18 Pick. (Mass.) 360.

The following additional cases illustrate the rules governing courts in applying payments, where neither the debtor nor the creditor has exercised the right to make the application:

Alabama.—Robinson *v.* Allison, 36 Ala. 525; Bradley *v.* Murray, 66 Ala. 269; Moses *v.* Noble, 85 Ala. 407.

Arkansas.—Byers *v.* Fowler, 14 Ark. 86; Kline *v.* Ragland, 47 Ark. 111; Lazarus *v.* Friedheim, 51 Ark. 371; Rogers *v.* Yarnell, 51 Ark. 198.

California.—Duncan *v.* Thomas, 81 Cal. 56.

Colorado.—Mackey *v.* Fullerton, 7 Colo. 556.

Connecticut.—Selleck *v.* Sugar Hollow Turnpike Co., 13 Conn. 453; Fairchild *v.* Holly, 10 Conn. 175; Welch

XV. Tender.—See TENDER.

XVI. Payment Into Court.—See TENDER.

XVII. Pleading Payment—1. Payment is an affirmative defense, and must be pleaded and established by the defendant.[1] But pay-

v. Wadsworth, 30 Conn. 149; s. c., 79 Am. Dec. 239; Tomlinson Carriage Co. *v.* Kinsella, 31 Conn. 268.

Georgia.—Price *v.* Cutts, 29 Ga. 142; s. c., 74 Am. Dec. 52; Mercer *v.* Tift, 79 Ga. 174; Lawton *v.* Blitch, 83 Ga. 663.

Illinois.—Bowen *v.* Fridley, 8 Ill. App. 595; Dehner *v.* Helmbacher Forge etc. Mills, 7 Ill. App. 47; M'Farland *v.* Lewis, 3 Ill. 344; Stanwood *v.* Smith, 3 Ill. App. 647.

Iowa.—Blair Town Lot & Land Co. *v.* Hillis, 76 Iowa 246.

Kentucky.—Lansdale *v.* Mitchell, 14 B. Mon. (Ky.) 281; Apperson *v.* Exchange Bank (Ky. 1888), 10 S. W. Rep. 801.

Louisiana.—Moore *v.* Gray, 22 La. Ann. 289; Duncan *v.* Helm, 22 La. Ann. 418; Byrne *v.* Grayson, 15 La. Ann. 457.

Maine. — Bangor Boom Corp. *v.* Whiting, 29 Me. 123; Starrett *v.* Barber, 20 Me. 457; Cushing *v.* Wyman, 44 Me. 121.

Maryland.—Suter *v.* Ives, 47 Md. 520; Frazier *v.* Lanahan, 71 Md. 131.

Massachusetts.—Stanwood *v.* Owen, 14 Gray (Mass.) 195; Shaw *v.* Pratt, 22 Pick. (Mass.) 305.

Minnesota.—Scheffer *v.* Tozier, 25 Minn. 478; Jefferson *v.* Church of St. Matthew, 41 Minn. 392.

Mississippi.—Miller *v.* Leflore, 32 Miss. 634; Clark *v.* Clark, 58 Miss. 68; Windsor *v.* Kennedy, 52 Miss. 164; Cage *v.* Iler, 5 Smed. & M. (Miss.) 410; s. c., 43 Am. Dec. 521.

Missouri.—St. Joseph *v.* Merlatt, 26 Mo. 233; s. c., 72 Am. Dec. 207.

Nebraska.—Ashby *v.* Washburn, 23 Neb. 571.

New Hampshire.—Bancroft *v.* Holton, 59 N. H. 141; Price *v.* Dearborn, 34 N. H. 481.

New Jersey.—Ayers *v.* Staley (N. J. 1889), 18 Atl. Rep. 1046; Oliver *v.* Phelps, 20 N. J. L. 180; White *v.* Trumbull, 15 N. J. L. 314; s. c., 29 Am. Dec. 687.

New York. — Righter *v.* Stall, 3 Sandf. Ch. (N. Y.) 608; Griswold *v.* Onondaga Co. Sav. Bank, 93 N. Y. 301; Camp *v.* Smith, 1 N. Y. Supp. 375; Thompson *v.* St. Nicholas Nat. Bank, 113 N. Y. 325; Truscott *v.* King, 6 N. Y. 147; National Park Bank *v.* Seaboard Bank, 114 N. Y. 28.

North Carolina.—Johnson *v.* Johnson, 5 Jones Eq. (N. Car.) 167.

Oregon. — State *v.* Chadwick, 10 Oregon 423.

Pennsylvania. — Chancellor *v.* Schott, 23 Pa. St. 68; Pardee *v.* Markle, 111 Pa. St. 548; s. c., 56 Am. Rep. 299; Johnson's Appeal, 37 Pa. St. 268; Smith *v.* Brooke, 49 Pa. St. 147; Bell's Appeal (Pa. 1887), 8 Atl. Rep. 927; Appeal of Pennsylvania Co. etc. (Pa. 1886), 7 Atl. Rep. 70.

South Carolina.—Ordinary *v.* McCollum, 3 Strobh. (S. Car.) 494; Smith *v.* Macon, 1 Hill Eq. (S. Car.) 339; Carson *v.* Hill, 1 McMull. (S. Car.) 76; Huger *v.* Boucquet, 1 Bay (S. Car.) 497.

Texas.—Tucker *v.* Brackett, 25 Tex. Supp. 199; Lazarus *v.* Henrietta Nat. Bank, 72 Tex. 354.

Vermont.—Rosseau *v.* Cull, 14 Vt. 83; Robinson *v.* Doolittle, 12 Vt. 246; Backman *v.* Wright, 27 Vt. 187; s. c., 65 Am. Dec. 187.

Virginia.—Ross *v.* McLauchlan, 7 Gratt. (Va.) 86; Pitzer *v.* Logan, 85 Va. 374.

West Virginia.—Buster *v.* Holland, 27 W. Va. 510.

Wisconsin.—Robbins *v.* Lincoln, 12 Wis. 1; Fay *v.* Lovejoy, 20 Wis. 403.

United States.—McNamara *v.* Condon, 2 MacArthur (D. C.) 365; The Antarctic, 1 Sprague (U. S.) 206; Schulenburg *v.* Martin, 1 McCrary (U. S.) 348; The D. B. Steelman, 5 Hughes (U. S.) 210; Postmaster-General *v.* Norvell, Gilp. (U. S.) 106; Bennett *v.* McGillan, 28 Fed. Rep. 411; The Martha, 29 Fed. Rep. 708; Mack *v.* Adler, 22 Fed. Rep. 570.

1. 2 Greenl. Evid. (10th ed.), § 516; Wolffe *v.* Nail, 62 Ala. 24; Lerche *v.* Brasher, 104 N. Y. 157; Clark *v.* Mullen, 16 Neb. 481; Savage *v.* Aiken, 21 Neb. 605; Tootle *v.* Maben, 21 Neb. 617.

Payment should be pleaded by confession and avoidance. Goodchild *v.* Pledge, 1 Mees. & W. 363; 5 Dowl. Pr. Cas. 89; 2 Gale 7.

Though plaintiff in his pleading

ment can be pleaded only where there has been a performance at the time and place fixed by the contract; if payment is made after the day, accord and satisfaction must be pleaded.[1]

2. General Averrment Sufficient.—The general rule is that a plea of payment is good which alleges payment generally, without stating the amount paid, the date of payment or the person to whom made.[2]

3. General Issue.—When the petition states the facts constituting the plaintiff's claim, a general denial does not raise the issue

negative payment, the negative averment is to be taken as true until the defendant disproves it. Wolffe *v.* Nall, 62 Ala. 24.

Where plaintiff in an action on a contract under seal, alleged that defendant had not paid the sum therein agreed upon, and defendant pleaded *non est factum*, and payment, it was held that issue as to payment could be joined on these pleadings alone, although the affirmative was asserted by the defendant. McCart *v.* Regester, 68 Md. 429.

Defendant, in order to avail himself of a presumption of payment, must aver a payment. Stanley *v.* McKinzer, 7 Lea (Tenn.) 454.

As to sufficiency of allegation of non-payment, see Palmer *v.* Uncas Min. Co., 70 Cal. 614; Scroufe *v.* Clay, 71 Cal. 123.

As to sufficient plea of presumption, of payment from lapse of time, see Pemberton *v.* Simmons, 100 N. Car. 316.

A plea of payment should conclude to the country; and, where payment is pleaded, plaintiff may, without the formal addition of the *similiter*, proceed to trial as though the issue had been formally joined. Kinsley *v.* Monongalia Co., 31 W. Va. 464.

1. Hume *v.* Peploe, 8 East 167; Poole *v.* Tumbridge, 2 Mees. & W. 223; Kington *v.* Kington, 11 Mees & W. 233.

A plea that defendant paid, or was ready and offered to pay, when requested, is a good plea. Chew *v.* Wooley, 7 Johns. (N. Y.) 401.

2. Cranor *v.* Winters, 75 Ind. 301; Epperson *v.* Hostetter, 95 Ind. 583; Johnson *v.* Breedlove, 104 Ind. 521; Holmes *v.* Deplaigne, 23 La. Ann. 238. But see O'Neal *v.* Phillips, 83 Ga. 556, where it was held, in an action on a note, that a plea of payment which failed to state the time of payment was demurrable; and Baer *v.* Christian, 83 Ga. 322, holding that the objection was not available under a general demurrer, which did not point out the omission.

Payment, where pleaded, means payment in anything that was receivable in payment. Bush *v.* Sproat, 43 Ark. 416.

An averment in an answer that defendant, before the commencement of the action, paid the sum then demanded to plaintiff's agent, is not a good plea of payment, as the whole sum sued for may not have been demanded at that time. Toledo Agricultural Works *v.* Work, 70 Ind. 253.

Under a plea of payment generally it cannot be shown that goods were delivered and accepted under an agreement that the price of the goods should be taken as payment of the debt. Ulsch *v.* Muller, 143 Mass. 379 (*citing*. Grinnell *v.* Spink, 128 Mass. 251). See Wheaton *v.* Nelson, 11 Gray (Mass.) 15.

One cannot, under a plea of payment, avail himself of a counter-claim. Wagener *v.* Mars, 20 S. Car. 533.

Under a general allegation of payment, a particular agreement may be shown that certain accounts should be received as payment. Sullivan *v.* Sullivan, 20 S. Car. 509.

Where payment by giving a note and due bill is pleaded, there should be an averment that the same were accepted by the plaintiff in satisfaction. Blunt *v.* Williams, 27 Ark. 374.

But the notes need not be described. Wardlaw *v.* McConnell, 46 Ga. 273.

Plea of part payment is a good plea *pro tanto*. 2 Chitty Plead. *20, *445, *446; Solary *v.* Stultz, 22 Fla. 263. But not a good plea in bar to the entire cause of action. Indianapolis etc. R. Co. *v.* Hyde, 122 Ind. 188.

And under a plea of payment, part payment may be shown. Keyes *v.* Fuller, 9 Ill. App. 528.

of payment.[1]

PAYMENT INTO COURT.—See TENDER.

PEACE.—JUSTICE OF THE PEACE, vol. 12, p. 392; BREACH OF THE PEACE, vol. 2, p. 513.

1. The tranquillity enjoyed by a political society, internally by the good order which reigns among its members, externally by the good understanding it has with other nations.[2]

2. The quiet orderly behavior of individuals towards one another and towards the government, which is said to be broken by acts of a certain kind.[3]

PECULATION.—The unlawful appropriation by a custodian of public funds, of the moneys, securities, or goods intrusted to his care; embezzlement of the public funds.[4]

PECUNIARY.—(See also MONEY). See note 5.

1. Steves *v.* Thompson, 5 Kan. 305; St. Louis etc. R. Co. *v.* Grove, 39 Kan. 731; Farnham *v.* Murch, 36 Minn. 328; Potter *v.* Gates (Supreme Ct.), 9 N. Y. Supp. 87.

But this rule does not apply when the fact of non-payment is alleged in the complaint as a necessary and material fact to constitute a cause of action. (Cases cited.) Knapp *v.* Roche, 94 N. Y. 329.

2. Bouvier's L. Dict.

"Ten days after peace is made" means ten days after peace, irrespective of the ratification of the treaty of peace. Chapman *v.* Wacaser, 64 N. Car. 532.

3. Corvallis *v.* Carlile, 10 Oregon 139; 45 Am. Rep. 136. *Citing* Abbott's & Burrill's Law Dicts.

A charter authority to make ordinances "to secure the health, *peace* and improvement" of a city does not warrant an ordinance enjoining the closing of stores on Sunday, that act being forbidden by the general law. Corvallis *v.* Carlile, 10 Oregon 139; 45 Am. Rep. 134.

Peace, Articles of the.—Where a person says that his life is endangered through the hostility of some one, he may exhibit articles of the peace (being a formal statement of the danger) to the court or a magistrate, who will thereupon require the party informed against to give security to keep the peace.

Bouvier's L. Dict. See also BREACH OF THE PEACE, vol. 2, p. 515.

Bill of Peace.—See BILL OF PEACE, vol. 2, p. 253.

Peace, Time of.—When the courts of justice be open, and the judges and ministers of the same may by law protect men from wrong and violence, and distribute justice to all, it is said to be time of peace. Skeen *v.* Monkeimer, 21 Ind. 3.

4. And. L. Dict.; Abb. L. Dict.

It was one of the purposes of the New York act, 1875, ch. 19, as the word peculation in the title indicates, and perhaps its primary purpose, to afford additional security against the betrayal of official trusts, by imposing severe punishment for embezzlement or other frauds when committed by public officers in mis-applying public property, than was provided by existing laws. Bork *v.* People, 91 N. Y. 16.

5. Where a statute provides that a divorce may be had from a husband who, without cause, grossly or wantonly and cruelly refuses or neglects to provide suitable maintenance for his wife, he being of "sufficient pecuniary ability" to make such provision, it was held, that the reference is to the possession of means in property to provide the necessary maintenance, not to capacity for acquiring such means by labor. Farnsworth *v.* Farnsworth, 58 Vt. 555; Hammond *v.* Hammond, 15 R. I. 40.

Where damages were sought by a parent for the negligent killing of a child, it was held that the trial court did not err in charging that in measuring the damages by a "pecuniary recompense," the word "pecuniary" is not to be construed in a strict sense. The words "pecuniary recompense," in characterizing the nature of the compensation are not to be construed to limit the recovery to the present loss of money, but prospective advantages of a pecuniary nature are embraced in the phrase. Mayor etc. of Vicksburg *v.* McLain (Miss.) 6 So. Rep. 774.

Pecuniary Consideration.—An *English* statute (17 Geo. III, ch. 26) requires the grant of an annuity to be registered, but § 8 of the same chapter exempts from such registration "any voluntary annuity granted without regard to pecuniary consideration." A "pecuniary consideration," within the meaning of this statute, has been held not to comprise the case of grantee of an annuity giving up his business to the grantor. Crespigny *v.* Wittenoon, 4 T. R. 790; Hutton *v.* Lewis, 5 T. R. 639. Nor is the assignment of a leasehold interest a "pecuniary consideration." James *v.* James, 2 B. & B. 702. Nor a transfer of stock. Cumberland *v.* Kelly, 3 B. & A. 602. But bank notes, Wright *v.* Reed, 3 T. R. 554; Cowsins *v.* Thompson, 6 T. R. 335; Morris *v.* Wall, 1 B. & P. 208. Checks. Pool *v.* Cabanes, 8 T. R. 328. And bills of exchange, or promissory notes, were held to be "pecuniary considerations" within the section. And under a similar statute (53 Geo. III, ch. 141) it was held that the surrender of a life interest in a sum of money, and of a contingent interest in the *corpus* was not a "pecuniary consideration." Evatt *v.* Hunt, 2 El. & B. 374; Blake *v.* Attersoll, 2 B. & C. 875.

A verbal promise to pay a debt in full is a "pecuniary consideration" within the meaning of *Massachusetts* Stat. 1848, ch. 304, § 9, which declares any certificate of discharge in insolvency to be void, if the assent thereto of any creditor is procured by any pecuniary consideration. Phelps *v.* Thomas, 6 Gray (Mass.) 327. See also Estudillo *v.* Meyerstein, 72 Cal. 317.

Pecuniary Interest. — Wagers upon the result of an election give to one party a *pecuniary interest* in the election of a person to office, and to another the same interest in such person's defeat, consequently, such wagers are against public policy, and therefore invalid. Stoddard *v.* Martin, 1 R. I.; 19 Am. Dec. 643.

See also GAMBLING CONTRACTS, vol. 8, p. 992.

Pecuniary Legacies. — "If you find simply the word 'legacy' used, and a direction to apportion property amongst the legatees, there—unless there be something apparent on the face of the will which shows that the testator has not used the word in its ordinary legal signification—it will include annuitants. The expression, pecuniary legatees', in itself, I do not think, would go further than this—it would exclude specific legatees, that is, 'legatees of mere chattels, but it would have no effect in excluding *prima facie* annuitants from taking the same benefit as they would have taken if the word had been 'legatees' instead of 'pecuniary legatees,'" per WOOD, V. C., GASKIN *v.* Rogers, L. R., 2 Eq. 291; in which case, however, annuitants were excluded, by a context, from participating in a residue given to persons "taking pecuniary legacies." See also ANNUITIES, vol. 1, p. 594; LEGACIES, vol. 13, p. 15, note.

Pecuniary Loss.—A pecuniary loss is of money or of something by which money or a thing of money value, may be acquired. Green *v.* Hudson River R. Co., 32 Barb. (N. Y.) 33; Tilley *v.* Hudson River R. Co., 29 N. Y. 274.

"Pecuniary obligation," as that term is applied to a forged instrument in a statutory definition of forgery, means "every instrument having money for its object, and every obligation for the breach of which a civil action for damages may be lawfully brought." The alleged forged instrument in this case was a telegram, dispatched in the name of one McK., at San Antonio, to one E., at Austin, announcing the death of one L., and asking a remittance of money "for her remains." *Held*, that the instrument comes within the statute and is the subject of forgery. Dooley *v.* State, 21 Tex. App. 549. See also OBLIGATION.

Pecuniary Provision.—(Such as under *Maine* Rev. Stat., ch. 103, § 8, will bar dower.) Does not apply to a provision in an agreement for alimony specifically dividing personal property of the parties. Davis *v.* Davis, 61 Me. 395.

Pecuniary Profit.—A corporation for educational purposes, as an academy, is not one for "pecuniary profit," merely because fees are charged for tuition. A corporation for pecuniary profit is one organized "for the pecuniary profit of its stockholders or members." Female Academy *v.* Sullivan, 116 Ill. 376; 56 Am. Rep. 782.

PEDIGREE.—(See also AGE, vol. 1, p. 327; DEATH, vol. 5, p. 140; FAMILY, vol. 7, p. 803; LEGITIMACY, vol. 13, p. 224; MARRIAGE, vol. 14, p. 519.)

I. **DEFINITION.**—Pedigree is the lineage, descent or succession of families.[1] The principal legal question which arises upon the consideration of this term is the admissibility of hearsay or secondary evidence in proof of the facts which are embraced in the general term pedigree. And, in this relation, the term embraces not only descent and relationship, but also the facts of birth, marriage and death, and the times when these events happened.[2]

1. Anderson's L. Dict.

Bouvier's definition of the term is as follows: A succession of degrees from the origin: it is the state of the family as far as regards the relationship of the different members, their births, marriages, and deaths. This term is applied to persons or families who trace their origin or descent. Bouv. Law Dict. (3rd ed.).

2. 1 Greenl. on Ev. (14th ed.), § 104; 1 Whart. on Ev. (3rd ed.), § 208; Swink *v.* French, 11 Lea (Tenn.) 80; American L. Ins. Co. *v.* Rosenagle, 77 Pa. St. 506; Kelly *v.* McGuire, 15 Ark. 604.

What Facts Are Included in the Term Pedigree.—Mr. Abbott enumerates the facts which constitute pedigree, within the rule admitting hearsay evidence in proof of pedigree, as follows:

Birth.—North Brookfield *v.* Warren, 16 Gray (Mass.) 174; American L. Ins. Co. *v.* Rosenagle, 77 Pa. St. 507, 516.

Living or Survival.—Johnson *v.* Pembroke, 11 East 504.

Marriage.—Caujolle *v.* Ferrie, 23 N. Y. 90.

Issue or Want of Issue.—People *v.* Fulton's F. Ins. Co., 25 Wend. (N. Y.) 208.

Death.—Nasons *v.* Fuller, 45 Vt. 29.

The times either definite (Roe *v.* Randall, 7 East 290), are relative (Bridger *v.* Hewitt, 2 Fost. & F. 35) of these facts.

Relative Age or Seniority.—Johnson *v.* Pembroke, 11 East 504.

Name.—Monkton *v.* Attorney-General, 2 Russ. & M. 158.

Relationship Generally. — Doe *v.* Randall, 2 Mo. & P. 20, 26; Vowles *v* Young, 13 Ves. 147.

The Degree of Relationship.—Webb *v.* Richardson, 42 Vt. 465. And see Chapman *v.* Chapman, 2 Conn. 350.

The Place of Residence When Proved for Purpose of Identification.—Cuddy *v.* Brown, 78 Ill. 415; Shields *v.* Boucher, 1 De G. & Sm. 40; Doe *v.* Randal, 2 Mo. & P. 20.

At this limit the rule stops. It does not admit hearsay evidence as to a specified fact, however closely connected with these facts of family history, if one which, in its nature is susceptible of being proved by witnesses speaking from their own knowledge, even although all such witnesses are dead. Abbott's Trial Ev., p. 91.

"Still, the hearsay evidence must, it seems, be confined to such facts as are immediately connected with the question of pedigree; and declarations as to independent facts, from which a date of genealogical event may be inferred, will probably be rejected. It is not easy to express this limitation of the rule in intelligible language, but the following cases will explain its purport: In a question of legitimacy, turning upon the time of birth, a declaration by the deceased sister of the alleged bastard's mother, stating that she had suckled the child, was tendered in evidence; and being coupled with the

II. **Proof.**—Questions of pedigree form an exception to the general rule excluding hearsay evidence, and 'all the authorities agree that, with certain qualifications, which will be considered hereafter, pedigree and the facts that constitute it are open to proof by hearsay.[1] This exception is owing to the obvious difficulty, and in many cases impossibility, of obtaining better evidence in such cases; as it often happens that facts must be proved which occurred many years before the trial, and which were known to but few people, so that to enforce the ordinary rules of evidence would in many instances lead to a manifest failure of justice.[2] And, moreover, as will be seen, the hearsay evidence is confined to the declarations of relations as to facts of family history; and, therefore, "the law resorts to hearsay evidence in cases of pedigree upon the ground of the interest of the

proof of the time when her own child was born, it tended to fix the alleged bastard's birth at a period subsequent to its parent's marriage. Mr. Baron Gurney admitted this evidence; but Lord Cottonham expressed an opinion that he was wrong in so doing. Isaac *v.* Gompertz, cited in Hubb. Ev. of Suc. 650. In another case (Vin. Ab. Ev. T. b. 91, probably referred to, as Spadwell *v.*———, by Lawrence, J., in the Berkeley Peer., 4 Camp. 410), where the question turned on the relative seniority of three sons, born at a birth, declarations by his father that he had christened them Stephanus, Fortunatus, and Achaicus, according to the order of the names in St. Paul's First Epistle to the Corinthians (ch. 16, v. 17), for the purpose of distinguishing their seniority, as also declarations by an aunt, who was present at the confinement, and who, with a similar object, had tied strings around the arms of the second and third child, was admitted. The distinction between these two cases is clear. In the former, the fact of suckling the child had no direct bearing on its age or legitimacy, but was only a species of circumstantial evidence from which these facts might be inferred; whereas in the latter, the christening and the tying strings around the arms of the children were intended from the first to afford the means of ascertaining their relative seniority." Taylor on Ev. Text Book Series, § 582.

1. Greenl. on Ev. (14th ed.), § 103; 1 Whart. on Ev. (3d ed.), § 201; 1 Taylor (Text Book Series), § 635. And see hereon Crease *v.* Barrett, 1 C., M. & R. 928; Vowles *v.* Young, 13 Ves. Jr. 140; Crouch *v.* Hooper, 16 Beav. 182; Hubbard *v.* Lees, L. R., 1 Ex. 255; Cuddy *v.* Brown, 78 Ill. 415; Crispin *v.* Doglioni, 32 L. J., P. & M. 109; Monkton *v.* Attorney General, 2 R. & M. 147; Davis *v.* Wood, 1 Wheat. (U. S.) 6; Banert *v.* Day, 3 Wash. (U. S.) 243; Dupont *v.* Davis, 30 Wis. 178; Chirac *v.* Reinecker, 2 Pet. (U. S.) 621; Ellicott *v.* Pearl, 10 Pet. (U. S.) 412; Jewell *v.* Jewell, 17 Pet. (U. S.) 213; 1 How. (U. S.) 219; Blackburn *v.* Crawford, 3 Wall. (U. S.) 175; Secrist *v.* Green, 3 Wall. (U. S.) 744; Denoyer *v.* Ryan, 24 Fed. Rep. 77; Gaines *v.* New Orleans, 6 Wall. (U. S.) 642; Dussert *v.* Roe, 1 Wall. Jr. (C. C.) 39; Mooers *v.* Bunker, 29 N. H. 420; Webb *v.* Richardson, 42 Vt. 465; Mason *v.* Fuller, 45 Vt. 29; North Brookfield *v.* Warren, 16 Gray (Mass.) 174; Chapman *v.* Chapman, 2 Conn. 347; Jackson *v.* Cooley, 8 Johns. (N. Y.) 128; Jackson *v.* Browner, 18 Johns. (N. Y.) 37; Douglass *v.* Sanderson, 2 Dall. (U. S.) 116; Winder *v.* Little, 1 Yeates (Pa.) 152; Watson *v.* Brewster, 1 Pa. St. 381; American L. Ins. Co. *v.* Rosenagle, 77 Pa. St. 507; Shuman *v.* Shuman, 27 Pa. St. 90; State *v.* Grennwell, 4 Gill & J. (Md.) 407; Jones *v.* Jones, 36 Md. 447; Stumpff *v.* Osterhage, 111 Ill. 82; Van Vickle *v.* Gibson, 40 Md. Ch. 170; Morgan *v.* Purnell, 4 Hawks (N. Car.) 95; Cowan *v.* Hite, 2 A. K. Marsh. (Ky.) 238; Saunders *v.* Fuller, 4 Humph. (Tenn.) 516; Eaton *v.* Tallmadge, 24 Wis. 217; Anderson *v.* Parker, 6 Cal. 197; Lovat Peerage Case, 10 App. Cas. 763.

2. 1 Taylor on Ev. (Text Book Series), § 635; Higman *v.* Ridgeway, 10 East 120; Jackson *v.* Browner, 18

declarants in the person from whom the descent is made out, and their consequent interest in knowing the connections of the family."[1]

1. Qualifications—(*a*) RELATIONSHIP.—It is essential to the admissibility of declarations as to pedigree that they should have been made by relations of the family in question.[2] There is some conflict of opinion as to what constitutes such a relationship as will entitle the declarant's statements to be admitted. One authority thus states the principle: "The rule of admission is therefore restricted to the declarations of deceased persons who were related by blood or marriage to the person, and therefore interested in the succession in question.' This view probably has the support of the weight of authority in the *United States.*[3] In certain instances there has been a lax, or perhaps a mistaken,

Johns. (N. Y.) 37; Johnson *v.* Lawson, 2 Bing. 86; Chapman *v.* Chapman, 2 Conn. 348.

And such evidence will not be rejected, because living witnesses might have been called to prove the very facts to which it relates. 1 Taylor, § 577; Ph. on Ev. 212;; Pearson *v.* Pearson, 46 Cal. 633.

1. 1 Greenl. on Ev. (14th ed.) 103.

2. "The law resorts to hearsay of relations upon the principle of interest in the person from whom the descent is to be made out; and it is not necessary that evidence of consanguinity should have the correctness required as to other facts. If a person says another is his relative or next of kin, it is not necessary to state how the consanguinity exists. It is sufficient that he says A is his relation, without stating the particular degree, which perhaps he could not tell if asked. But it is evidence, from the interest of the person in knowing the connections of the family; therefore the opinion of the neighborhood of what passed among the acquaintances will not do." Per LORD ERSKINE, Vowles *v.* Young, 13 Ves. 147. See also Blackburn *v.* Crawford, 7 U. S. 175; Goodwright *v.* Moss, Cowp. 591, 594; as expounded by Lord Eldon, in Whitelock *v.* Baker, 13 Ves. 514; Johnson *v.* Lawson, 2 Bing. 86; Monkton *v.* Attorney-General, 2 Russ. & My. 147, 156; Crease *v.* Barrett, 1 Cr. M. & R. 919, 928; Casey *v.* O'Shaunessy, 7 Jur. 1140; Jackson *v.* Browner, 6 Johns. (N. Y.) 37; Conn. Mut. Life Ins. Co. *v.* Schwenk, 98 U. S. 593; Gregory *v.* Baugh, 4 Rand. 611; Jewell *v.* Jewell, 1 How. (U. S.) 231; Speed *v.* Brooks, 7 J. J. Marsh. (Ky.) 119; 17 Pet. (U. S.) 213; Kaywood *v.* Barnett, 3 Dev. & B. (N. Car.) 91; Greenwood *v.* Spiller, 3 Ill. 501; Jackson *v.* Browner, 18 Johns. (N. Y.) 37; Chapman *v.* Chapman, 2 Conn. 347; Caines *v.* Crandall, 10 Iowa 376; Henderson *v.* Cargill, 31 Miss. 418; Waldron *v.* Tuttle, 4 N. H. 371; Murray *v.* Milner, L. R., 12 Ch. Div. 845; Cuddy *v.* Brown, 78 Ill. 415; Jones *v.* Jones, 36 Md. 447; Caines *v.* Crandall, 10 Iowa 377; Emerson *v.* White, 29 N. H. 482; Kelley *v.* McGuire, 15 Ark. 555.

The declarations of a mother, in disparagement of the legitimacy of her child, have been received in a question of succession. Hargrave *v.* Hargrave, 2 C. & K. 701. See also Haddock *v.* Boston etc. R. Co., 3 Allen (Mass.) 298; Goodright *v.* Moss, Cowp. 591.

3. Greenleaf on Evidence, § 103; De-Haven *v.* DeHaven, 77 Ind. 236.

C died intestate and B claimed title as his nephew, and sought to introduce the declaration of E, who was a sister of his mother, asserting the marriage of his mother with the brother of C. It was held that such a declaration was not admissible, as it was not shown that E was "by blood or marriage related" to the family of the intestate C, whose succession was in question. Blackburn *v.* Crawford, 3 Wall. (U. S.) 175. See also Connecticut Mut. L. Ins. Co. *v.* Schwenk, 98 U. S. 593.

In Kelley *v.* McGuire, 15 Ark. 555, the declaration of a father affirming the legitimacy of his children were held to be admissible.

In Northport *v.* Hale, 76 Me. 306, the declaration of intestate's sister that the claimant was the natural son

application of this rule.[1] The *English* rule is somewhat stricter, requiring "the declarations to be made by a declarant shown to be legitimately related by blood to the person to whom they relate, or by the husband or wife of such person."[2] It is necessary that the declarant's relationship to the family should be shown by some proof *dehors* the declarations.[3] Slight evidence, however, will be sufficient, it being only necessary to establish a *prima facie* case, since the relationship of the declarant with the family might be as difficult to prove as the other fact in contro-

of the intestate was held to be admissible.

Declaration of deceased servants and intimate acquaintances are refused. Johnson *v.* Lawson, 9 Moore 183.

1. Mr. Wharton, in speaking of the *English* rule, declares that its strictness is owing to the fact that in England, where families adhere to one spot from generation to generation, and where in that spot there is, as a general rule an ample supply of blood relations from whom family traditions can be drawn, it may be equitable enough that, as the declarations of such blood relations are attainable, they must, as being more likely to be accurate, exclude declarations from persons more remote; but, he adds, that in this country the rule should be relaxed in proportion to the degree in which, from the scattering of families in new settlements, such declarations of blood relations become unattainable. 1 Whart. on Ev. (3rd ed.), § 216. And this view is supported in Carter *v.* Montgomery, 2 Tenn. Ch. 228. See also Banert *v.* Day, 3 Wash. (U. S.) 243; Boudereau *v.* Montgomery, 4 Wash. (U. S.) 186; Jackson *v.* Cooley, 8 Johns. (N. Y.) 128; Pegram *v.* Isabell, 2 Hen. & M. (Va.) 193; Walkup *v.* Pratt, 5 Har. & J. (Md.) 51.

2. Stephen's Dig. of Evidence, article 31; Shrewsbury Peerage Case, 7 H. L. 26; Fred Albin's Case, L. R., 1 H. of L. Sc. 182; Hitchings *v.* Hurdley, L. R., 2 P. & N. 248; Smith *v.* Tebbett. L. R., 1 P. & N. 354.

Bastards.—So under the English rule it has been held more than once, that a bastard's declarations as to the pedigree of his putative family, or, conversely, the declarations of a member of the family, as to a bastard, are not admissible. This is a logical outcome of the strictness of the rule, as a bastard has no family. Doe *v.* Barton, 2 M. & Rob. 28; Doe *v.* Davies, 10 P. B. 314; Crispin *v.* Doglioni, 3 Sw. & Tr. 44.

But in this country the declarations of a deceased father, that a son is illegitimate, have been received on the issue of legitimacy. Tyler *v.* Flanders, 57 N. H. 618; Barnum *v.* Barnum, 42 Md. 251. And if the doctrine above was ever the law, it would seem, that it has lost its force in the United States, at least to the mother's family, in view of the statutes which almost all of the States have passed, modifying the common law status of a bastard, so as to make his mother's family his. See BASTARDY, vol. 2, p. 129.

3. 1 Whart. on Ev. (3rd ed.), § 218; 1 Taylor on Ev., § 640; Rex *v.* All Saints, 7 B. & C. 789; Davies *v.* Morgan, 1 C. & J. 591; Atty. Gen. *v.* Kohler, 9 H. L. 660; Dike *v.* Williams, 2 Sw. & Tr. 491; Banbury Peerage Case, 2 Selw. N. P. 764; Doe *v.* Randall, 2 M. & P. 24; Blackburn *v.* Crawford, 3 Wall. (U. S.) 175; Monkton *v.* Atty. Gen., 2 Russ. & Myl. 156, 157; The Berkley Peerage, 4 Camp. 419; Plant *v.* Taylor, 7 H. & N. 211; Northport *v.* Hale, 76 Me. 306; Thompson *v.* Wolf, 8 Oregon 455; Green *v.* Norment, 5 Mackey (D. C.) 80. See also Emerson *v.* White, 29 N. H. 482; Chapman *v.* Chapman, 2 Conn. 347.

Relationship Between Two Supposed Branches of a Family.—If the question be whether any or what relationship subsists between the two supposed branches of the same family, it is only necessary to establish the connection of the declarant with either branch. 1 Taylor Ev. (Text Book Series), § 640, *citing* Monkton *v.* Att. Gen., 2 Russ. & M. (Eng.) 157; Smith *v.* Tibbitt, 1 L. R. P., & D. 354.

Or the proposition may be put in this manner: Where, in a pedigree case, the object is to connect A with C, after proving that B, a deceased person, is related to A, it is competent to give in evidence declarations by B in which he claimed relationship with C. Monkton *v.* Att. Gen., 2 Russ. & M. (Eng.)

157. See also Att. Gen. *v.* Kohler, 9 H. L. Cas. (Eng.) 653. And Setler *v.* Gehr, 105 Pa. St. 577, where the authorities upon this question are exhaustively discussed.

Monkton v. Atty. Gen. Distinguished.—In Blackburn *v.* Crawford, 70 U. S. 175, the claimants sought to establish the marriage of their mother, Elizabeth Taylor, with Thomas B. Crawford, the brother of the intestate, David Crawford, and to do this introduced the declaration of Sarah Evans, to the effect that there had been such a marriage. It was shown *aliunde* that Sarah Evans was a sister of claimant's mother, and that she had been several years deceased. The court distinguished the case from that of Monkton *v.* Atty. Gen., 2 Russ. & M. 156, saying: "It is insisted by the defendants in error, upon the authority of Monkton *v.* Atty. Gen., 2 Russ. & M. 156, that it was sufficient to show the relationship of the declarant to Elizabeth Taylor. As we understand that case, it has no application to the point under consideration. None of the writers on the law of evidence have given it so wide a scope. Hubback thus states the principle which it decides: 'It is sufficient that the declarant be connected by extrinsic evidence with one branch of the family touching which his declaration is tendered.' LORD BROUGHAM himself said in that case: 'I entirely agree that, in order to admit hearsay evidence in pedigree, you must, by evidence *dehors* the declarations, connect the persons making them with the family. To say that you cannot prove the declarations of A, who is proved to be a relation by blood of B, touching the relationship of B with C, unless you have first connected him with C, is a proposition which has no warrant, either in the principle upon which hearsay is let in, or in the decided cases.' If it had been proved by independent testimony that Sarah Evans was related by blood to any branch of the family of David Crawford, and her declarations had been offered to prove the relationship of another person claiming, or claimed to belong also to that family, this case would be in point. But the declaration of Sarah Evans, offerred to prove that her sister was connected by marriage with a member of that family, was neither within the principle nor the language of that authority."

Admissibility of Intestate's Declarations as to His Own Family.—While this rule has not been controverted where it was sought to set up some right derived through the declarant and to establish that right by his own statements as to the pedigree of the family of which he claimed to be a member, *e. g.*, where a claimant seeks to establish his right to the estate of a decedent, and, in order to do that, seeks to introduce the declarations of his (the claimant's) father that the decedent was his brother, it is necessary that he should first make some proof from other sources that the declarant is what he claims to be, *i. e.*, a member of the family in question. But when the case is reversed and the plaintiff is seeking to reach the estate of the declarant by evidence of what he (the declarant) said with reference to his family and kindred, the rule is more questionable.

In Wise *v.* Winn, 59 Miss. 590, one Charles Wise, who had lived in Mississippi for forty years and whose antecedents were entirely unknown, died intestate. His supposed heirs at law proved that they were the children of one Thomas Wise of A, Va.; that their father had a younger brother Charles, who left that State forty years previously; nothing had been heard of him since; they then sought to introduce the testimony of two witnesses to the effect that Charles Wise, whose estate was in question, had told them that he had a brother Thomas, who lived in A, Va., and that he himself had lived there. The court held that these declarations were admissible, saying: "It is quite clear that I cannot establish my right to share in the estate of A, by proof alone of the fact that my father declared in his lifetime that A was his brother, but may I not do so by showing that A himself so declared? Upon this question we find a singular dearth of authorities. In Adie *v.* Commonwealth, 25 Gratt. (Va.) 712, a case strikingly like this in all its features, testimony of this character seems to have been admitted without objection, and so also in Cuddy *v.* Brown, 78 Ill. 415. In Moffit *v.* Witherspoon, 10 Ired. (N. Car.) 185, persons who claimed to be the nephews and nieces of Mrs. Donahoe, in an ejectment suit brought after her death to recover certain real estate belonging to her during her life, were permitted to prove that she had declared, many years before her death, that the mother of the plaintiff's was her only sister, and no other proof of

versy.[1] Nor is it necessary that the degree of relationship existing between the declarant and the person in question should be made out. It is enough if some relationship is shown;[2] and it is for the judge to decide whether the relationship is established.[3]

The declarant being otherwise properly qualified, it is no objection to his declaration "that it is hearsay upon hearsay," provided that all the declarations are within the family,[4] and even general repute in the family, proved by the testimony of a surviving member is considered as falling within the rule.[5] Where one has been connected with a family by marriage, which connection is severed by death, his declarations subsequently made are admissible.[6]

(*b*) DECLARANT MUST BE DEAD.—All the authorities agree that the relation whose declarations are sought to be introduced must be dead.[7] Yet, such declarations, if the declarant be deceased,

heirship than this seems to have been offered. In Shields *v.* Boucler, 1 DeG. & Sm. 40, SIR KNIGHT BRUCE expressed the strong conviction that in a controversy purely genealogical declarations made by a deceased person, as to where he or his family came from, of what place his father was designated, and what occupation he followed, would be admissible, and might be most material evidence for the purpose of identifying and individualizing the person and family under discussion.

Independently of these or of any authorities, we think *ex necessitate rei* and as a matter of common sense, that declarations such as were offered here and under the circumstances here existing, should always be received in evidence."

1. 1 Wharton on Evidence (3rd ed.), § 218; Fulkerson *v.* Holmes, 117 U. S. 397; Vowles *v.* Young, 13 Ves. 147; Monkton *v.* Atty. Gen., 2 Russ. & M. 157.

2. Best Pr. Ev. 498, N. C.

1 Taylor's Ev., § 640, *citing* Vowles *v.* Young, 13 Ves. 147.

3. Best Pr. Ev. (Am. ed.) 498, N. C. Setler *v.* Gehr, 105 Pa. St. 577; 51 Am. Rep. 214.

Even where the question is the same with that on which the jury are to pass. Doe *v.* Davies, 10 Q. B. 323.

4. Taylor on Evidence (Text Book Series), § 639; Doe *v.* Randall, 2 M. & P. 20; Monkton *v.* Atty. Gen., 2 Russ. & M. 165; Elliott *v.* Piersol, 1 Pet. (U. S.) 328; Davies *v.* Lowndes, 6 Man. & Gr. 525; Strickland *v.* Poole, 1 Dall. (U. S.) 14.

5. 1 Greenleaf on Evidence (14 ed.), § 103; 1 Taylor on Evidence (Text Book Series), § 639; Doe *v.* Griffin, 15 East 293; American etc. Co. *v.* Rosenagle, 77 Pa. St. 516; Setler *v.* Gehr, 150 Pa. St. 577; Barnum *v.* Barnum, 42 Md. 251; Jewell *v.* Jewell, 1 How. (U. S.) 219; Webb *v.* Richardson, 42 Vt. 465; Van Syckel *v.* Gibson, 40 Mich. 170; Eaton *v.* Tallmage, 24 Wis. 217. See also Copes *v.* Pearce, 7 Gill (Md.) 247; Clements *v.* Hunt, 1 Jones (N. Car.) 400; Proctor *v.* Bigelow, 38 Mich. 282; Watson *v.* Brewster, 1 Pa. St. 385.

Reputation in the family is equally admissible with direct statements by deceased members. Morgan *v.* Purnell, 4 Hawks (N. Car.) 95.

Thus a witness may state his own age. Pearce *v.* Kyzer, 16 Lea (Tenn.) 521; 57 Am. Rep. 240; State *v.* Cain, 9 W. Va. 559, 570; Cheever *v.* Congdon, 34 Mich. 96; Morrison *v.* Emsley, 53 Mich. 564; Commonwealth *v.* Stevenson, 142 Mass. 466.

6. Vowles *v.* Young, 13 Ves. 140; Doe *v.* Harvey, Ry. & M. 297. Unless, it would seem, it should appear that the information detailed was received since the severance of his connection with the family. 1 Wharton's Evidence 217.

In Vowles *v.* Young, 13 Ves. 140, the court presumed that the knowledge must have been obtained while the declarant was a member of the family in question. 1 Taylor's Evidence (Text Book Series), § 574.

7. 1 Whart., § 215; 1 Taylor, § 641; 1 Greenl., § 103; Pendrill *v.* Pendrill, 2 Str. 924; Butler *v.* Mountgarrett, 7 H. L. Cas. 633; Stegall *v.* Stegall, 2

are not excluded by the fact that living members of the same family can be examined on the same point.[1]

(*c*) LIS MOTA—INTEREST.—The declarations must be *ante litem motam*.[2] Though it seems that a declaration made with the express purpose of preventing disputes will be admissible.[3]

Brock. (U. S.) 256; White *v.* Strather, 11 Ala. 720; Greenleaf *v.* Dubuque R. Co., 30 Iowa 301; Mooers *v.* Bunker, 29 N. H. 420; Robinson *v.* Blakeley. 4 Rich. (S. Car.) 586. See also Covert *v.* Hertzog, 4 Pa. St. 145; Car skadden *v.* Poorman, 10 Watts (Pa.) 82.

In an Irish case, where, in order to establish a Scotch marriage, a relative of the supposed husband had been asked at the trial what she had heard on the subject from members of the family, her answer was held by the court of error to have been rightly rejected on the ground that the question had not been limited to statements made by deceased relatives. Butler *v.* Mountgarrett, 6 Ir., L. R., N. S. 77; 7 H. L. Cas. 633.

1. 1 Whart. § 215; 2 Taylor on Ev. 577; Ph. on Ev. 212; Pearson *v.* Pearson, 46 Cal. 633.

2. 1 Taylor's Ev., § 577; Caujolle *v.* Ferrie, 26 Barb. (N. Y.) 127; Elliot *v.* Pearl, 10 Pet. (U. S.) 412; Morgan *v.* Pernell, 4 Hawks (N. Car.) 95; Butler *v.* Mountgarrett, 7 H. L. Cas. 633; Barnet *v.* Day, 3 Wash. (U. S.) 243; Gee *v.* Ward, 7 E. & B. 509. See also De Haven *v.* De Haven, 77 Ind. 237.

The phrase *ante litem motam* is, it seems, to be translated "before the arising of actual controversy" on the point covered by the declaration. By Roman law *lis mota* was the beginning of the trial. The common law apparently includes in the phrase the controversy which culminates in such actual litigation, but, *semble*, it does not include the mere existence of the state of facts which render such controversy a thing naturally to be apprehended. 1 Greenl. Ev., § 104, note, 131–134; 1 Whart., §§ 193, 213.

It is the beginning of the dispute involving the very point in question, not that of the state of facts from which the dispute sprang nor that of resulting litigation, which terminates the competency. Shedden *v.* Patrick, 2 S. W. & T. R. 170.

But it is not necessary that a suit should havebeen actually instituted. If the controversy preliminary to it is begun, the declaration will be inadmissible. Butler *v.* Mountgarrett, 7 H. L. Cas. 633.

"In the cases cited above it is sometimes said that such declarations must be *ante litem motam;* and so has it been expressly ruled in the English courts of last resort. Yet, especially in view of the recent statutes admitting parties as witnesses, it is hard to see why the suspicion of concoction, imputable to declarations *post litem motam*, should not be left to the determination of the jury. There are some pedigree cases so old, that if declarations of deceased persons concerning them be received at all, such declarations must be *post litem motam*, nor is it always possible to determine where the suspicion in question begins.

A dispute about legitimacy, for instance, often agitates and divides a family as effectively before suit brought as afterwards; and if conflicts of this class should exclude evidence in any case, it should exclude it in all cases.

Nor should it be forgotten that even where the declaration is *ante litem motam*, the person who undertakes to recollect and repeat it does so *post litem motam*, and the evidence takes shape, therefore, under the influences which are declared fatal to its reception. The better view is to apply the test *ante litem motam* leniently, even if under the new statutes it still exists; for the reason that while it may shut out much reliable evidence, it does not shut out much that is unreliable; and to increase the scrutiny to which, on the question of credibility, we should subject the declarations of deceased relatives, declarations which in many cases are steeped in family pride, and in few cases are made free from the prejudices of family contention, if not litigation." 1 Whart., § 213.

3. 1 Whart., § 214; Berkeley Peerage Cas., 4 Camp. 401. In which case it was held that an entry made in a book, by a father, for the express purpose of establishing the legitimacy of his son, if the same should ever come in question, was admissible.

And the fact that the declarations are in direct support of the declarant's title will not exclude them.[1] Nor will the mere fact that the declarant was in the same situation touching the matter in contest with the party relying on the declaration, render such evidence incompetent.[2] But the declarations must not be made obviously in the declarant's own interest.[3] Declarations made for the purpose of evidence would, of course, be incompetent.[4]

(*d*) PEDIGREE IN ISSUE.—It has been said "that such declarations are admissible only in cases in which the pedigree to which they relate is in issue, and not to those in which it is only relevant to the issue;[5]" but this rule has been weakened by some of the decisions of the courts in the *United States*, and some authorities have declared it to have absolutely no force in this country, nor has it escaped animadversion even in *England*.[6]

2. Forms of Hearsay—(*a*) ORAL DECLARATIONS.—Oral declarations of deceased relations are clearly admissible with the qualifications as stated in the preceding sections.[7]

1. Doe *v.* Davies, 10 Q. B. 325.

2. 1 Whart., § 214; Monkton *v.* Attorney-Gen'l, 2 Russ. & M. 160; Powell's Evidence (4th ed.) 165; Mosely *v.* Davies, 11 Price 162; Harwood *v.* Sims, Wightw. 117; Deacle *v.* Hancock, 13 Price, 236, 237; Freeman *v.* Phillips, 4 M. & S. 486, 491; Davies *v.* Morgan, 1 C. & J. 593; Nicholls *v.* Parker, 14 East 331; Doe *v.* Faiver, R. & M. 141, 142. See also Shedden *v.* Attorney-Gen'l, 2 Sw. & T. 170. Overruling Walker *v.* Beauchamp, 6 C. & P. 552; Reilly *v.* Fitzgerald, 1 Drury Chan. 120–140; Davies *v.* Lowndes, 7 Scott N. R. 198; 6 M. & Gr. 517. And see Butler *v.* Mountgarrett, 7 H. L. Cas. 633; Elliot *v.* Peirsol, 1 Pet. (U. S.) 328.

3. 1 Whart., § 207. See also Best's Ev., § 498.

Thus the statement by a deceased person who has been twice married, tending to invalidate his first and thus establish his second marriage has been rejected. Grant *v.* Taylor, 7 H. & M. 211; DeHaven *v.* DeHaven, 77 Ind. 238.

4. Chapman *v.* Chapman, 2 Conn. 747.

5. Stephen Dig. of Evidence, art. 31; Whittuck *v.* Walters, 4 C. & P. 375; 1 Greenleaf's Evidence, § 103, note b; 1 Taylor on Evidence 645; Shields *v.* Boucher, 1 De G. & Sm. 40; Smith *v.* Smith, L. R., 10 Eq. 273; 1 L. R., Irish 206; Figg *v.* Wederburn, 6 Jur. 218; Haynes *v.* Guthrie, 139 B. D. 818; R. *v.* Erith, 8 East 539. See also Londonderry *v.* Andover, 28 Vt. 416; Union *v.* Plainfield, 39 Conn. 563; Independence *v.* Pompton, 9 N. J. L. 209; Wilmington *v.* Burlington, 4 Pick. (Mass.) 174; Adams *v.* Swansea, 116 Mass. 591.

6. 1 Whart. Ev., 206. In Brookfield *v.* Warren, 16 Gray (Mass.) 174, the court said: "Some of the authorities seem to limit the competency of this species of proof to cases where the main subject of inquiry relates to pedigree, and where the existence of birth, marriage and death and the times when these events happened are put directly in issue; but upon principle we can see no reason for such a limitation. If this evidence is admissible to prove such facts at all it is equally so in all cases whenever they become legitimate subjects of judicial inquiry and investigation. Mr. Taylor has this to say of the rule: 'As Mr. Phillips justly observes, there appears to be no foundation for any distinction between cases where a matter of pedigree is the direct subject of inquiry and other cases where it occurs incidentally.'" Taylor on Evidence, § 581, *citing* 1 Ph. on Evidence, 215, note 5. See also Wilson *v.* Brownlee, 24 Ark. 586; Abbott's Trial Evidence 90, where the learned author denies that the rule has any force in the United States, *citing* North Brookfield *v.* Warren, 16 Gray (Mass.) 174; Prim *v.* Stewart, 7 Tex. 178.

7. 1 Taylor on Evidence, § 583; Crouch *v.* Hooper, 16 Beav. 184, 189; Webb *v.* Haycock, 19 Beav. 342; Clement *v.* Hunt, 1 Jones (N. Car.) L. 400.

(*b*) FAMILY CONDUCT.—Family conduct, such as the tacit recognition of relationship, and the disposition and devolution of property, is admissible evidence from which the opinion and belief of the family may be inferred. Thus it was said, "if the father is proved to have brought up the party as his legitimate son, this amounts to a daily assertion that the son is legitimate."[1]

(*c*) FAMILY RECORDS—ENTRIES IN BIBLES—CORRESPONDENCE, ETC.—Entries made by a parent or by a relation in Bibles,[2] prayer-books,[3] missals,[4] almanacs,[5] or indeed in any other book, document, or paper,[6] are all admissible to show facts

Such declarations are seldom entitled to any great weight; for not only are they generally sought to be established by connections of the family or other persons interested in the result of the litigation, but they are often recorded or remembered for the first time after the contest has arisen. In these cases the court necessarily runs considerable risk of being deceived by deliberate falsehood, for it is obviously difficult, not to say impossible, to convict a witness of perjury, in narrating what he alleges that he heard in a conversation with a deceased person. And, even assuming that the sincerity of the witness cannot reasonably be doubted, it often happens that little reliance can be placed on the accuracy of his testimony; for men without deliberately intending to falsify facts, are extremely prone to believe what they wish, and to confound what they believe with what they have heard, and ascribe to memory what is merely the result of imagination. 1 Taylor on Evidence, § 583; *citing* Romely M. R., in Crouch *v.* Hooper, 16 Beav. 184, 189. See also as to the weight of such oral declarations the opinion of Langdale, M. R., in Johnston *v.* Todd, 5 Beav. 599.

1. Mansfield, C. J., in Berkeley Peerage Case, 4 Camp. 413; 1 Greenl. Ev., § 106; 1 Taylor Ev., § 649; Morris *v.* Davies, 5 Cl. & Fin. 163, 241; Banbury Peer., 1 Sim. & St. 153; Rex *v.* Mansfield, 1 Q. B. 444; Townshend Peer., 10 Cl. & Fin. 289; Atchly *v.* Sprigg, 33 L. J., Ch. 345; Hargrave *v.* Hargrave, 2 C. & Kir. 701.

The declarations of a person, since deceased, that he was going to visit his relatives at such a place have been held admissible to show that the family had relatives there. Rishton *v.* Nesbitt, 2 Moo. & R. 554.

Where it is shown that two persons recognized one another as brothers so long ago that living witnesses acquainted with their ancestors cannot be found, it may be presumed that their parents were married. Green *v.* Norment, 5 Mackey (D. C.) 80.

Again if the question be whether a person from whom the claimant traces his descent was the son of a particular testator, the fact that all members of the family appear to have been mentioned in the will, but that no notice is taken of such a person, is strong evidence to show that he was not the son, or, at least, that he had died without issue before the date of the will. 1 Taylor Ev., § 584; Tracy Peer., 10 Cl. & Fin. 100; Robinson *v.* Attorney-Gen'l, 10 Cl. & Fin. 498–500.

And where the object be to prove that a man left no children the production of his will of which no notice is taken of his family, and by which his property is bequeathed to strangers or collateral relations, is cogent evidence of having died childless. Hungate *v.* Gascoyne, 2 Ph. 25; De Ross Peer., 2 Cowp. 540.

The fact that the son took the name of a person with whom his mother, at the time of his birth, lived in a state of adultery, which name he and his descendants ever after retained, constitutes "a very strong family recognition of his illegitimacy." Goodright *v.* Saul, 4 T. R. 356.

So a marked difference in the treatment of the bastard and the legitimate children is a fact for consideration. Murray *v.* Milner, 12 Ch. D. 845.

2. Berkeley Peer. Cases, 4 Camp. 401; Lewis *v.* Marshall, 5 Pet. (U. S.) 470, 476; Watson *v.* Brewster, 1 Pa. St. 381.

3. Leigh Peer. Cases, Pr. Min. 310.

4. Slane Peer. Cases, 5 Cl. & Fin. 41.

5. Herbert *v.* Tuckal, T. Ray 84.

6. Jackson *v.* Cooley, 8 Johns. (N. Y.) 128, 131; Douglas *v.* Saunderson, 2 Dall. (U. S.) 116; Carskadden *v.*

which constitute pedigree.[1] Entries in a family Bible or Testament will be admissible, even without proof that they have been made by a relative; for as the book is the ordinary register of families, and is usually accessible to all its members, the presumption is that the whole family, more or less, have adopted the entries contained in it and have thereby given them authenticity.[2] This presumption, however, will not prevail in favor of any entry in any other book, however religious its character may be, but proof must be given either that the entry was made by some member of the family, or that it was acknowledged by a relative as a correct family memorial.[3] The correspondence of deceased members of the family[4] will be received on proof of the handwriting,[5] as will the recitals of any marriage settlements[6] and other family deeds,[7] descriptions in wills[8] and the like.

In regard to recitals of pedigree in bills and answers in chancery, a distinction has been taken between those facts which are

Poorman, 10 Watts (Pa.) 82; Collins *v.* Grantham, 12 Ind. 440; Clara *v.* Ewell, 2 Cranch (C. C.) 288.

1. 1 Taylor on Evidence, § 585. See also cases cited above and in this section.

2. Berkeley Peer. Cases, 4 Camp. 421; Monkton *v.* Attorney-General, 2 Russ. & M. 162; Hubbard *v.* Lees, 1 L. R., Exch. 255; 4 H. & C. 418.

3. 1 Taylor on Evidence, § 585; Tracy Peer. Cases, 10 Cl. & Fin. 100; Crawford & Lindsay Peer. Cases, 2 H. L. 558, 560; Hood *v.* Beauchamp, 8 Sim. 26; Carkshadden *v.* Poorman, 10 Watts (Pa.) 82.

4. Huntington Peer., Atty. Gen. Rep. 357; Kidney *v.* Cockbury, 2 Russ. & M. 168; Leigh Peer. Pr. Min., pt. 2, p. 140; Hastings Peer. Pr. Min. 196. See also Butler *v.* Ganett, 6 Ir. L. R., N. S. 77; 7 H. L. 633.

5. 1 Taylor's Ev., § 586; Marshmont Peer. Pr. Min. 345, 353. See also Arith Peer. Pr. Min. 105. But see Hubbard *v.* Lees, - L. R., 1 Ex. 265.

6. Neal *v.* Wilding, 2 Str. 1151; De Ross Peer., 2 Coop. 541, 542; Chandos Peer. Pr. Min. 27; Stafford Peer. Pr. Min. 110; Zouch Peer. Pr. Min. 276; Lisle Peer. Pr. Min. 116; Van Bury Peer. Pr. Min. 6, 117; Baux Peer. Pr. Min. 44; Huntley Peer. Pr. Min. 15; Roscommon Peer. Pr. Min. 36.

7. Smith *v.* Tibbot, 1 L. R., P. & D. 354; Schaeff *v.* Keener, 64 Pa. St. 376.

So recitals of descent and descriptions of parties in deeds or other than family instruments will be received, provided the deeds come from the proper custody and are proved, or may from age, be presumed to have been executed by some member of the family to which the statements referred. 1 Taylor Ev. 586 and cases cited; but the execution of the deed by a relation is an indispensable requisite; and, therefore, where an indenture of assignment which recited that the assignee was a son of certain parties, was executed alone by the assignor, who was not a member of the family, it was rejected. Slaney *v.* Wade, 1 Myl. & Cr. 338. See also Fort *v.* Clark, 1 Russ. 601; Jackson *v.* Cooley, 8 Johns. (N. Y.) 128; Jackson *v.* Russell, 4 Wend. (N. Y.) 543; Keller *v.* Nutz, 5 S. & R. (Pa.) 251.

A deed sixty years old, admissible as an ancient deed, contained recitals to the effect that a former owner of the land died intestate, and that the grantor was his only son and heir. *Held*, that the recitals were admissible on the question of pedigree. Fulkerson *v.* Holmes, 117 U. S. 389.

8. 1 Taylor Ev., § 586; Vullieny *v.* Huskisson, 3 Y. & C. Exr. 82; De Ross Peer., 2 Coop. 540; Russell *v.* Jackson, 22 Wend. (N. Y.) 277; Pearson *v.* Pearson, 46 Cal. 677; Blackburn *v.* Crawford, 70 U. S. 175.

Even a canceled will, which did not appear to have been acted upon, has been admitted on proof that it was found among the papers of a descendant of the testator, who seemed to have kept it as containing statements relative to the family. Doe *v.* Pembrook, 11 East 504.

not in dispute and those which are in controversy, the former being admitted, the latter excluded.[1]

(*d*) INSCRIPTIONS.—Inscriptions on tomb-stones,[2] coffin-plates,[3] mural monuments,[4] family portraits,[5] engravings on rings,[6] hatchments,[7] charts of pedigree,[8] and the like, are also admissible. Those which are proved to have been made by or under the direction of a deceased relative are admitted as his declarations, but if they have been publicly exhibited, and may therefore be supposed to have been well known to the family, their publicity supplies any defect of proof that they were declarations of deceased members of the family, and they are admitted on the ground of tacit and common assent.[9] Mural and other funeral inscriptions are provable by copies or other secondary evidence. Their value as evidence depends much on the authority under which they are set up, and on the distance of time between their erection and the events which they commemorate.[10]

1. 1 Greenleaf's Evidence, § 104; 1 Ph. Evidence, §§ 119 220, and authorities there cited. 1 Taylor's Evidence, § 586; De Roos Peer., 2 Cowp. 543, 544; Goodright *v.* Moss, 2 Cowp. 591.

Ex parte affidavits made several years before to prove pedigree by official requirement, and prior to any *lis mota*, are admissible. Hurst *v.* Jones, 1 Wall. Jr. (C. C.) 373.

Similar recitals in old bills in equity are, it seems from the English cases, always inadmissible, as these last are regarded as mere flourishes by the draughtsmen. Boileau *v.* Rutland, 2 Exch. 678, per PARKE, B., *citing* Barder Peer. Cas., 2 Selden N. P., 756 (10th ed.) These cases appear to overrule Taylor *v.* Cole, 7 T. R. 9 n.

2. 1 Taylor's Evidence, § 587; 1 Greenleaf's Evidence, § 105; Monkton *v.* Attorney-Gen'l, 2 Russ. & Myl. 163; Goodright *v.* Moss, 2 Cowp. 594.

3. Chandos Peer., Pr. Min. 10; Rokeby Peer., Pr. Min. 4; Lovat Peer., Pr. Min. 77.

4. Slaney *v.* Wade, 1 Myl. & Cr. 338; De Roos Peer., 2 Cowp. 544, 545.

5. Camoyes Peer., 6 Cl. & Fin. 801.

6. Vowles *v.* Young, 13 Ves. 144.

7. Hungate *v.* Gascoigne, 2 Cowp. 414.

8. Monkton *v.* Attorney-Gen'l, 2 Russ. & Myl. 163; Goodright *v.* Moss, 2 Cowp. 594; North Brookfield *v.* Warren, 16 Gray (Mass.) 174.

9. 1 Taylor's Evidence, § 587; 1 Greenleaf's Evidence, § 105; Monkton *v.* Attorney-Gen'l, 2 Russ. & Myl. 163; Davies *v.* Loundes, 7 Scott N. R. 163. See also Vowles *v.* Young, 13 Ves. 155; North Brookfield *v.* Warren, 16 Gray (Mass.) 174; Eastman *v.* Martin, 19 N. H. 152; Haslam *v.* Cron, 19 W. R. 968.

10. 1 Greenleaf's Evidence, § 105; 1 Taylor's Evidence, § 585; 1 Phillips Evidence, § 222.

Armorial Bearings.—An ancient pedigree purporting to have been collected from history as well as from other sources was held admissible, at least to show the relationship of persons described by the framer as living, and therefore to be presumed as known to him. Davies *v.* Lowndes, 7 Scott, N. R. 141. Armorial bearings proved to have existed while the heralds had the power to punish usurpations possess an official weight and credit. But this authority is thought to no longer exist in *England*, and of course has never existed in this country; and, at present, they amount to no more than family declarations. Greenleaf on Ev., § 105, n. 1.

They are admissible in cases of pedigree; not only as tending to prove that the person who assumed them was of the family to which they of right belonged, but as illustrating the particular branch from which the descent was claimed, or as showing, by the impalings or quarterings, the nature of the blazonry, or the shape of the shield, what families were allied by marriage, or what members of the family were descended from an illegitimate stock, or were maidens, widows, or heiresses. Taylor on Evidence, § 657.

PEDIS POSSESSIO.—A foothold; an actual possession. To constitute adverse possession, there must be *pedis possessio*, or a substantial inclosure.[1]

PEDDLER.—See HAWKERS AND PEDDLERS, vol. 9. p. 307.

PEER.—An equal in rank or condition, as in 'trial by one's peers."[2] Judgment of his peers means "trial *per pais*," that is, by a jury.[3]

PENAL.—That which involves suffering: hence more largely, that which pertains to punishment; to inflict loss by way of restraint or sanction.

Penal is used as a synonym of criminal in secondary senses of that word. Penal and criminal offense, penal and criminal code, and penal and criminal justice are equivalent expressions. In many connections the two words are not interchangeable; as in the expressions criminal or penal action, criminal conduct, penal bill or bond.[4]

1. Bouvier's L. Dict. See also ADVERSE POSSESSION, vol. 1, p. 252. See generally LIMITATION OF ACTIONS, vol. 13, p. 639.

2. And. L. Dict.

3. Fetter *v.* Wilt, 46 Pa. St. 460, Craig *v.* Kline, 65 Pa. St. 399.

4. Abb. L. Dict.

Penal Action.—See PENALTIES AND PENAL ACTIONS.

Penal Bill—Penal Bond.—Vol. 2, p. 448. See BONDS, vol. 2, pp. 462, 467 a; OBLIGATIONS.

Penal Clause.—That particular portion or subdivision of a statute which declares the consequences in the nature of punishment or losses which are to follow a violation of previous provisions. Abbott's L. Dict. See also STATUTES.

"Penal Institutions of the State."—Where a statute prohibited the employment of the convicts in "the penal institutions of the State" in certain trades and at certain labor, it was held that "penal institutions of the State" did not include a penitentiary erected, maintained and operated by a county. Bronk *v.* Riley (Supreme Ct.), 2 N. Y. Supp. 266.

Penal Statutes.—CRIMINAL LAW, vol. 4, p. 641; PENALTIES AND PENAL ACTIONS. See STATUTES.

The constitution of *Michigan* declares that "all fines assessed and collected in the several counties and townships for any breach of the penal laws," shall be exclusively applied to the support of libraries. In Fennel *v.* Common Council of Bay City, 36 Mich. 190, the court by CAMPBELL, J., said: "We have heretofore on more than one occasion intimated that the penal laws referred to in the State constitution were the laws of the State. The term law, as defined by the elementary writers, emanates from the sovereignty and not from its creatures. The legislative power of the State is vested in the State legislature, and their enactments are the only instruments that can in any proper sense be called laws. In the decisions of this court referring to the class of provisions now before us, the distinction has been very expressly indicated. It is claimed, however, that certain of these fines may be regarded as imposed under the laws of the State, and the cases in 17 Mich. 390, and 18 Mich. 445, are cited for that purpose. Those cases, however, are very different. There the city charter, which was itself a State law, authorized the police court, which had no jurisdiction whatever, to impose any penalties in the cases in question but those defined by the law itself, to deal with those particular cases and punish them as the statute directed. The authority was distinctly statutory, and the penalties were neither imposed nor governed by the ordinances. The only important question involved was, whether special provision could be made for punishing unlawful acts in a single city; and that was decided to be lawful."

PENALTIES; PENAL AND QUI TAM ACTIONS—(See BONDS, vol. 2, p. 467 *a*; CONTEMPT, vol. 3, p. 795; COPYRIGHT, vol. 4, p. 162; DAMAGES, vol. 5, p. 24; EXTORTION, vol. 7, p. 595; FORFEITURE, vol. 8, p. 443; FREIGHT, vol. 8, p. 938; HABEAS CORPUS, vol. 9, p. 183: INDICTMENT, vol. 10, p. 458; INFORMERS, vol. 10, p. 711; LIQUIDATED DAMAGES, vol. 13, p. 848; LOTTERIES, vol. 13, p. 1182; MANUFACTURING CORPORATIONS, vol. 14, p. 284; MARRIAGE, vol. 14, p. 538; MUNICIPAL SECURITIES, vol. 15, p. 1314; ORDINANCES; POOR AND POOR LAWS; SHIPPING).

I. **DEFINITION—1. Penalty.**—The term penalty involves the idea of punishment.[1] A penalty is in the nature of a punishment for the non-performance of an act, or for the performance of an unlawful act.[2] It may be defined as the punishment which a law inflicts for its violation. It is commonly, but not exclusively, a pecuniary punishment.[3] It may embrace the idea of a forfeiture as well as of a fine.[4] It is used frequently as meaning a fine.[5]

1. FIELD, J., in United States *v.* Chouteau, 102 U. S. 611.

2. SEARLES, C., in San Luis Obispo *v.* Hendricks, 71 Cal. 245.

3. Hunt *v.* Hunt, 28 Eng. L. & Eq. 396; Lancaster *v.* Richardson, 4 Lans. (N. Y.) 136; United States *v.* Mathews, 23 Fed. Rep. 74. See also United States *v.* Ulrici, 3 Dill. (U. S.) 532.

4. Gosselink *v.* Campbell, 4 Iowa 300, wherein WOODWARD, J., says: "The terms, fine, forfeiture, and penalty, are often used loosely and even confusedly. But when a discrimination is made, the word 'penalty' is found to be generic in its character, including both fine and forfeiture. A fine is a pecuniary penalty, and is commonly (perhaps always) to be collected by suit in some form. A 'forfeiture' is a penalty by which one loses his rights and interest in his property."

5. People *v.* Nedron, 122 Ill. 363, wherein MAGRUDER, J., says: "Although this amendment uses the words 'fines' and 'forfeitures,' and does not make use of the word 'penalties,' yet there can be no doubt that the expression 'fines or forfeitures' is broad enough to cover and include the 'penalties' referred to in the 15th section of the Pharmacy act;" and then, after giving Bouvier's definitions, says: "From these definitions it would appear that the word 'fine' and the word 'penalty' are often used interchangeably to designate the same thing. They both mean 'pecuniary punishment,' and may, in many cases, be regarded as equivalents of each other. One of Webster's definitions of 'forfeiture' is: 'a fine or mulct;' and he refers to the words 'fine, mulct, amercement, penalty,' as being synonyms of the word 'forfeiture.'"

"The term penalty is used very loosely in statutes in some cases, and might without much strain of its ordinary meaning be held to embrace all the consequences visited by law upon the heads of those who violate police regulations." COOLEY, J., in Grover *v.* Huckins, 26 Mich. 482.

2. Penal and Qui Tam Actions.—A penal action is an action for the recovery of a penalty imposed by a statute.[1] A *qui tam* action is similar to a penal action, except that the *qui tam* action, or, as it is sometimes called, the popular action, is brought by the informer, to whom, under the statute inflicting the penalty, a part of the penalty goes, while the penal action is brought by a public officer, and the penalty goes to the king or State.[2]

II. **Penal Statutes—1. Rules of Interpretation.**—A penal statute is a statute imposing a penalty for doing that which the statute prohibits, or for omitting to do that which the statute requires.[3]

The interpretation of these statutes is governed by the rules applied to the interpretation of statutes generally,[4] and by the further rule that they are strictly construed when their penal provisions are invoked against one charged with their violation.[5]

1. 3 Stephen's Com. 535; Bouvier's Law Dict.

2. Bouvier's Law Dict. and authorities there cited.

3. Mitchell *v.* Hotchkiss, 48 Conn. 19; 40 Am. Rep. 146, defining a penal statute as one inflicting a penalty for the violation of some of its provisions, and citing Bouvier's Law Dict.

4. See Interpretation, vol. 11, p. 507; Statutes.

5. See the following cases for illustrations of the rules of interpretation as applied to penal statutes:

Steelman *v.* Bolton, 2 N. J. L. 303; Bradwell *v.* Conger, 2 N. J. L. 195; Adams *v.* Scull, 3 N. J. L. 311; Scudder *v.* Bloomfield, 3 N. J. L. 506; Sayre *v.* Sayre, 3 N. J. L. 587; Allaire *v.* Howell Works Co., 14 N. J. L. 21; Edwards *v.* Hill, 11 Ill. 22; Gilbert *v.* Bone, 79 Ill. 343; Worth *v.* Peck, 7 Pa. St. 268; United States *v.* Starr, Hempst. (U. S.) 469; Commonwealth *v.* Martin 17 Mass. 359; Hall *v.* State, 20 Ohio 7; Seaving *v.* Brinkerhoff, 5 Johns. Ch. (N. Y.) 329; Van Rensslaer *v.* Onondaga Co., 1 Cow. (N. Y.) 443; Andrews *v.* United States, 2 Story (U. S.) 202; State *v.* Solomon, 3 Hill (S. Car.) 96; Van Valkenburgh *v.* Torrey, 7 Cow. (N. Y.) 252; United States *v.* Ramsay, Hempst. (U. S.) 481; United States *v.* Ragsdale, Hempst. (U. S.) 497; Western Union Tel. Co. *v.* Harding, 103 Ind. 505; 10 Am. & Eng. Corp. Cas. 617; Johnson *v.* State, 63 Miss. 228; Commonwealth *v.* Kentston, 5 Pick. (Mass.) 420; State *v.* Upchurch, 9 Ired. (N. Car.) 454; Gibson *v.* State, 38 Ga. 571; Reed *v.* Davis, 8 Pick. (Mass.) 514; Lair *v.* Killmer, 25 N. J. L. 522; Warner *v.* Commonwealth, 1 Pa. St. 154; 44 Am. Dec. 114; State *v.* Whetstone, 13 La. Ann. 376; United States *v.* Wiltberger, 5 Wheat. (U. S.) 76; Strong *v.* Stebbins, 5 Cow. (N. Y.) 210; Gunter *v.* Leckey, 30 Ala. 591; Randolph *v.* State, 9 Tex. 521; Carpenter *v.* People, 8 Barb. (N. Y.) 603; Leonard *v.* Bosworth, 4 Conn. 421; State *v.* Fox, 15 Vt. 22; Fairbanks *v.* Antrim, 2 N. H. 105; Henderson *v.* Sherbourne, 2 M. & W. 236; Bay City etc. R. Co. *v.* Austin, 21 Mich. 390; Allen *v.* Stevens, 29 N. J. L. 509; Cole *v.* Groves, 134 Mass. 471; Palmer *v.* York Bank, 18 Me. 166; Marston *v.* Tryon, 108 Pa. St. 270; Merchants' Bank *v.* Bliss, 13 Abb. Pr. (N. Y.) 225; Bayard *v.* Smith, 17 Wend. (N. Y.) 88; Titusville's Appeal, 108 Pa. St. 609; Cumberland etc. Canal Co. *v.* Hitchings, 57 Me. 146; Read *v.* Stewart, 129 Mass. 407; Reed *v.* Northfield, 13 Pick. (Mass.) 96; 23 Am. Dec. 662; Breiting *v.* Lindauer, 37 Mich. 217; Cotheal *v.* Brower, 5 N. Y. 562; Verona Cent. Cheese Co. *v.* Murtaugh, 50 N. Y. 314; Leonard *v.* Bosworth, 4 Conn. 421; Hines *v.* Wilmington etc. R. Co., 95 N. Car. 434; Phillips *v.* Meade, 75 Ill. 334; Jones *v.* Estie, 2 Johns. (N. Y.) 379; Chicago etc. R. Co. *v.* People, 67 Ill. 11; 16 Am. Rep. 599; Ohio etc. R. Co. *v.* Lackey, 78 Ill. 57.

A statute affixing a penalty of "not less than $10" was constructed not to include the costs. Taylor *v.* State, 35 Wis. 298.

A statute imposing a penalty on the sale of cord-wood, at a certain penalty per cord, was construed not to apply to a sale of any amount less than a cord. Pray *v.* Burbank, 12 N. H. 277.

The third section of a statute gave

2. Rights of Action Under.—Where a right of action at common law exists, the remedy given by a statute imposing a penalty for the violation of such right is a cumulative remedy, unless the right of action at common law is taken away in terms, or by necessary implication.[1] It is difficult to say with precision to

an action to recover the penalty imposed by the preceding section. Only one penalty was imposed by the second section, but others were imposed by the first. *Held*, that the word "section" should be construed "sections" and apply to both preceding sections. Ellis *v.* Whitlock, 10 Mo. 71.

Section 1196, Gen. St. *South Carolina*, providing that "the rates of storage of cotton shall not exceed twelve and one-half cents per week for each bale of cotton, and the charges for weighing cotton shall not exceed ten cents for each bale," and imposing certain penalties on any person violating the statute, prohibits only the making not the paying of a charge higher than that authorized. Holman *v.* Frost, 26 S. Car. 290.

1. In Caswell *v.* Worth, 5 El. & Bl. 848, an action on the case for negligence, it was said by COLERIDGE, J.: "The statute makes the omission of a certain act irregular, and subjects the parties omitting it to penalties. But there can be no doubt that a party receiving bodily injury through such omission has the right of suing at common law."

Couch *v.* Steel, 3 El. & Bl. 402, was an action against a ship owner by a seaman, who charged that his illness was due to defendant's failure to provide medicines, as required by the statute. It was declared that though the statute imposed a penalty, recoverable by a common informer, as the specific punishment for the shipowner's breach of duty to the public, a seaman sustaining a private injury from the breach of such statutory duty was entitled to maintain an action to recover damages. The court said: "As far as the public wrong is concerned, there is no remedy but that prescribed by act of Parliament. There is, however, beyond the public wrong, a special and particular damage sustained by the plaintiff by reason of the breach of duty by the defendant, for which he has no remedy unless an action on the case at his suit be maintainable; and the question is whether the penalty annexed to the offense concludes the plaintiff who has sustained a special and particular damage, as well as the public, though no part of the penalty is payable to him;" and that "No authority has been cited to us, nor are we aware of any, in which it has been held that, in such a case as the present, the common law right to maintain an action in respect of a special damage resulting from the breach of a public duty (whether such duty exists at common law or is created by statute) is taken away by reason of a penalty, recoverable by a common informer, being annexed as a punishment for the non-performance of the public duty." The court reviewed the authorities and distinguished the case of Stevens *v.* Jeacocke, 11 Q. B. 731, where no duty was imposed on the defendant by the statute, he having been prohibited only under a penalty from exercising the right of fishing to the extent possessed by him at the common law, and where he was not bound to perform any particular duty created by the act, but to forbear to do that which, but for the act, he might have done. Underhill *v.* Ellicombe, M'Clel. & Y. 450 was also distinguished, wherein it was held that where highway rates were payable by the provisions of a statute which prescribed a particular mode for their recovery, that mode only could be pursued; and Bishop of Rochester *v.* Bridges, 1 B. & Ad. 847, wherein it was held that, a statute having prescribed a particular mode for the recovery of an equivalent for land tax redeemed, no other mode could be adopted for enforcing the payment of the equivalent; and said that in the case at bar "if the statute had prescribed a particular mode by which a person sustaining actual damage by reason of a breach of the duty imposed by statute was to recover compensation, undoubtedly that mode only could be adopted;" but that the statute relied on in the case at bar made no provision for compensation to a person sustaining special damage by reason of a breach of the duty prescribed by the act, and that the act

what extent individuals may invoke a penal statute or municipal ordinance as the foundation of a right of action for an injury charged to its violation. The authorities are not in harmony, and sometimes it is not easy to define their exact scope. The difference between giving a remedy and creating a right seems sometimes to be lost sight of to the confusion of the subject. Again, some of the opinions advert to a distinction between a public statute, general in its nature and application, and a municipal ordinance: and, further, attempts have been made to distinguish again between ordinances which impose duties and obligations analogous to and in line with duties and obligations imposed by or within the general scope of public statutes, and those which, on their face, apply to matters local in their nature and more particularly have the character of police regulations of limited application.[1] An extra-territorial effect will not be given

contained no words taking away the right which the injured party would have had at common law to maintain an action for special damage arising from a breach of public duty. Rowning *v.* Goodchild, 2 W. & Bl. 906, was also adverted to, wherein an action upon the case was held to be maintainable against a deputy postmaster for a breach of duty in not delivering a post letter as required by the statute, though he was by the same statute liable to a penalty for detaining letters. In that case, the court was of opinion that though the duty was created by statute, the action lay at common law. In that case, as in the case at bar, the penalty was recoverable by a common informer, and not by the party grieved. In summing up, the court said: "Upon principle, then, as well as upon authority, as far as we have been able to find any upon the point, we think the second count is maintainable, and that the plaintiff's right, by the common law, to maintain an action on the case for special damage sustained by the breach of a public duty is not taken away by reason of the statute which creates the duty imposing a penalty recoverable by a common informer for neglect to perform it, though no actual damage be sustained by anyone."

In Aldrich *v.* Howard, 7 R. I. 199, the action was in case against one whose failure to comply with a municipal building act specially injured the plaintiff, and it was held that the action lay. The pecuniary penalties fixed by the act were divided between the city and the State, and, therefore, were in punishment of the public offense only. Here the court said: "The statute does not, as in some of the cases cited, in creating the offense, notice also the private injury, and, through the penalties, give the private recompense. Had it done so, there would have been some reason for confining the party injured to the statute compensation, however inadequate it might seem to be. As it is, the party specially injured has no redress unless by the equity of the old statute of Westminster 2d—designed to afford a remedy for every wrong not redressed by any of the formed actions of the common law, if an action of the case can afford it. We have no doubt that when a statute makes the doing or omitting any act illegal, and subjects the offending parties to penalties for the public wrong only, a party specially injured by the illegal act or omission has the right of suing therefor at the common law."

In Almy *v.* Harris, 5 Johns. (N. Y.) 175, the common law right of action was denied on the ground that in the circumstances it had never existed, and that plaintiff's only rights were under the statute imposing the penalty. The principle underlying the foregoing cases was recognized.

See also Wheaton *v.* Hibbard, 20 Johns. (N. Y.) 290; 11 Am. Dec. 284; Porter *v.* Mount, 41 Barb. (N. Y.) 561; Lowe *v.* Peers, 4 Burr. 2225; Atkinson *v.* Newcastle etc. Waterworks Co., L. R., 2 Exch. Div. 441; Blamires *v.* Lancashire etc. R. Co., L. R., 8 Ex. 283; Steam Navigation Co. *v.* Morrison, 13 C. B., N. S. 581, 594.

1. In Flynn *v.* Canton Co., 40 Md. 312; Taylor *v.* Lake Shore etc. R.

Co., 45 Mich. 74; Hartford *v.* Talcott, 48 Conn. 525; Heeney *v.* Sprague, 11 R. I. 456, it was held that the violator of a municipal ordinance, requiring the removal of ice and snow from the sidewalk in front of his premises, under penalty of a fine, was not liable to an individual injured because of the neglect of duty. To the same effect are Van Dyke *v.* Cincinnati, 1 Disney (Ohio) 532, and Kirby *v.* Boston Market Assoc., 14 Gray (Mass.) 249.

In the *Michigan* case, COOLEY, J., remarked in the opinion affirming the judgment below: "It is said on behalf of the plaintiff that the obligation to keep the sidewalks free from snow and ice is imposed as a duty to all persons who may have occasion to use the walks in passing and repassing, and that the neglect to do so, in consequence of which any one lawfully using the walk is injured, is a neglect of duty to him, and entitles him on well recognized principles to maintain an action. Couch *v.* Steel, 3 El. & Bl. 402; Aldrich *v.* Howard, 7 R. I. 214. To maintain this proposition it is necessary to make it appear that the duty imposed was a duty to individuals rather than a duty to the whole public of the city; for, if it was only a public duty it cannot be pretended that a private action can be maintained for a breach thereof. A breach of public duty must be punished in some form of public prosecution, and not by way of individual recovery of damages. Nevertheless, the burden that individuals are required to bear for the public protection or benefit may in part be imposed for the protection or benefit of some particular individual or class of individuals also, and then there may be an individual right of action as well as a public prosecution of a breach of the duty which causes individual injury. Atkinson *v.* Waterworks Co., L. R., 6 Exch. 404. The nature of the duty and the benefits to be accomplished through its performance must generally determine whether it is a duty to the public in part or exclusively, or whether individuals may claim that it is a duty imposed wholly or in part for their especial benefit. In this case the duty was to keep the sidewalks free from obstructions. It will not be claimed that this was not a duty to the whole public of the city, and the disputed question is whether it is also a duty to each individual making use of the walks."

In the *Maryland* case, attempt was made to confine the liability to cases in which the neglected duty is prescribed for the benefit of particular persons, or of a particular class of persons, or in consideration of some emolument or privilege conferred, or provision made, for its performance, and to show that it does not extend to a duty imposed without consideration, and for the benefit of the public at large—the only liability for the neglect of such a duty being the penalty prescribed.

In the *Rhode Island* case the court adopted the reasoning of the *Maryland* court, deemed it to be supported by Hickok *v.* Plattsburg, 16 N. Y. 161; Eastman *v.* Meredith, 36 N. H. 284; Bigelow *v.* Randolph, 14 Gray (Mass.) 541; Aldrich *v.* Tripp, 11 R. I. 141, and observed: "But even supposing the liability is not subject to any such qualification, then, inasmuch as the neglected duty was not enjoined by statute but by a municipal ordinance, the question arises whether in this respect an ordinance is as effectual as a statute. There are many things forbidden by ordinance which are nuisances or torts, and actionable as such at common law. The question does not relate to them. The defendant has not done anything injurious to others which she was forbidden to do; she has simply left undone something beneficial to others which she was required to do under a penalty in case of default. The thing required was not obligatory upon her at common law. It was a duty newly created by ordinance, which, but for the ordinance, she might have omitted with entire impunity. The question is, whether a person neglecting such a duty is subject not only to the penalty prescribed, but also to a civil action in favor of any person specially injured by the neglect. . . . And further, if the liability exists under the ordinance in question, it exists, *pari ratione*, under every ordinance prescribing a similar duty. To hold that it exists is therefore to recognize, outside the legislature, a legislative power as between individuals, which, though indirectly exercised, is, nevertheless, in a high degree, delicate and important. This we ought not to do, unless upon principle or precedent our duty to do it is clear, for we do not suppose that the creation of new civil liabilities between individuals was any part of the

to penal statutes, whether the penalty provided for is given to the public or to individuals; nor have the principles of interstate comity any application.[1]

III. The Action—1. Form.—At common law, the action of debt is the appropriate action for the recovery of a statutory penalty, upon the ground of an implied promise, which the law annexes to the liability.[2] With the abolition of the action of debt in

object for which the power to enact ordinances was granted."

In Philadelphia etc. R. Co. *v.* Ervin, 89 Pa. St. 71, it appeared that an ordinance of the city of Philadelphia required that a cap-log be placed on the sides and ends of every wharf, and, through the company's neglect of such ordinance, the plaintiff suffered damage by his horse backing off the company's wharf. The court would allow no recovery. In its opinion the court observes: "There are indeed cases where such ordinances have been received in evidence in common-law actions for negligence, but they are generally such as enter into the case itself or enforce a common-law duty. Such are ordinances regulating the speed of railroad trains when passing through towns or cities. Here the ordinance may, and usually does, enter in the question of negligence, for the rate of speed to be anticipated has much to do with the care to be exercised by those crossing the tracks. So, on the other hand, those in charge of trains are not only subject to the common-law duty of passing through towns slowly and cautiously, but they must know that persons depending upon the observance of the municipal regulations will not take all that care which would be required in the open country. The case in hand, however, involved no such duties. Whether the defendant should or should not have had cap-logs upon its wharves was a matter which addressed itself to the judgment of those having its affairs in hand. The omission of these caps did not, *per se*, involve the company in any responsibility beyond the penalty of the ordinance. Neither could the plaintiff have placed any dependence upon the observance of such ordinance, for he knew that if it applied at all to the defendant's wharves it had not been observed; he knew that he must depend for the preservation of his property upon his own care and skill, and, these failing, he then had his common-law remedy for compensation."

The foregoing cases cannot be reconciled easily with Bott *v.* Pratt, 33 Minn. 323; 53 Am. Rep. 47. Here, the city ordinance made it unlawful to leave a team unfastened in a public street, and the action was brought by the owner of the team injured by defendant's team, which, in violation of the ordinance, had been left standing unfastened. There was no evidence showing the particular circumstances causing defendant's horses to take fright and run away, so that the action rested on the violation of the ordinance.

See on this subject a note appended to the foregoing case in 53 Am. Rep. 52.

In Salisbury *v.* Herchenroder, 106 Mass. 458, the action was one of tort for injuries done to a building during an extraordinary gale by a sign which defendant, in violation of a city ordinance, had maintained suspended over a street. The court, in affirming the judgment for plaintiff, said: "But the defendant's sign was suspended over the street in violation of a public ordinance of the city of Boston, by which he was subject to a penalty. He placed and kept it there illegally, and this illegal act of his has contributed to the plaintiff's injury. The gale would not of itself afford the injury if the defendant had not wrongfully placed this substance in its way."

As to the effect of the breach of a statute or ordinance on the question of negligence, see also NEGLIGENCE, vol. 16, pp. 420, 451.

1. Blaine *v.* Curtis, 59 Vt. 120; 59 Am. Rep. 702. See Ogden *v.* Folliot, 3 T. R. 736; Scovill *v.* Canfield, 14 Johns. (N. Y.) 338; First Nat. Bank *v.* Price, 33 Md. 47; Derrickson *v.* Smith, 27 N. J. L., 166; Barnes *v.* Whitaker, 22 Ill. 606; Sherman *v.* Gassett, 9 Ill. 521; Henry *v.* Sargent, 13 N. H. 321; 41 Am. Dec. 146; Slack *v.* Gibbs, 14 Vt. 357.

2. 3 Bl. Com. 158; Chitty Pl. 128,

many of the States of the Union, the penal action in some jurisdictions is in form *ex contractu* (and it would seem that upon principle this should be so) while in certain other jurisdictions it is in form *ex delicto*.[1] It is said that a statutory penalty may be recovered by indictment or information, where this mode of procedure is not excluded by the statute.[2]

2. When Maintainable.—At common law the action for a penalty must be brought while the statute is in force, because the repeal of the statute takes away the right of action.[3]

IV. Rights of Informers.[4]—It is a general rule that a common informer cannot sue for a penalty without express statutory

404; 4 Minor's Inst. 498; 2 Greenl. on Ev., § 279; Vaughan *v.* Thompson, 15 Ill. 39; Portland Dry Dock etc. Co. *v.* Portland, 12 B. Mon. (Ky.) 77; Strange *v.* Powell, 15 Ala. 453; Commonwealth *v.* Davenger, 10 Phila. (Pa.) 478.

1. Chicago *v.* Enright, 27 Ill. App. 559; Partridge *v.* Snyder, 78 Ill. 522; Ewbanks *v.* Ashley, 36 Ill. 177; Hoyer *v.* Mascoutah, 59 Ill. 137; Graubner *v.* Jacksonville, 50 Ill. 87; Carle *v.* People, 12 Ill. 285; Jacksonville *v.* Block, 36 Ill. 507; Israel *v.* Jacksonville, 2 Ill. 290; United States *v.* Lyman, 1 Mason (U. S.) 481; United States *v.* Willard, 5 Ben. (U. S.) 220; *In re* Rosey, 6 Ben. (U. S.) 507; Cato *v.* Gill, 1 N. J. L. 11; Miller *v.* Stoy, 5 N. J. L. 476; Indianapolis etc. R. Co. *v.* People, 91 Ill. 452; Katzenstein *v.* Raleigh etc. R. Co., 84 N. Car. 688; 6 Am. & Eng. R. Cas. 469. See also Debt, vol. 5, p. 165.

In McCoun *v.* New York Cent. etc. R. Co., 50 N. Y. 176, it was held that an action to recover a statutory penalty did not "arise on contract" within § 129 of the Code.

As in *Wisconsin*, Graham *v.* R. Co., 49 Wis. 532; Smith *v.* R. Co., 49 Wis. 443; Graham *v.* R. Co., 53 Wis. 473; and *Iowa*, Koons *v.* Chicago etc. R. Co., 23 Iowa 493; Herriman *v.* Burlington etc. R. Co., 57 Iowa 187; 9 Am. & Eng. R. Cas. 339; Heiserman *v.* Burlington etc. Co., 63 Iowa 732; 16 Am. & Eng. R. Cas. 46.

2. State *v.* Helgen, 1 Speer (S. Car.) 310; State *v.* Meyer, 1 Speer (S. Car.) 305; State *v.* Maze, 6 Humph. (Tenn.) 17; Hodgman *v.* People, 4 Den. (N. Y.) 235; State *v.* Corwin, 4 Mo. 609; United States *v.* Howard, 17 Fed. Rep. 638; State *v.* Wabash etc. R. Co., 89 Mo. 562.

3. State *v.* Tombigbee Bank, 1 Stew (Ala.) 347; Cummings *v.* Chandler, 26 Me. 453; Eaton *v.* Graham, 11 Ill. 619; Coles *v.* Madison Co., 1 Ill. 154. See Commonwealth *v.* Welch, 2 Dana (Ky.) 330; Taylor *v.* Rushing, 2 Stew. (Ala.) 160; Sumner *v.* Cummings, 23 Vt. 427; Rankin *v.* Beaird, 1 Ill. 123; Allen *v.* Farrow, 2 Bailey (S. Car.) 584; Mix *v.* Illinois Cent. R. Co., 116 Ill. 502; Union Pac. R. Co. *v.* Proctor, 12 Colo. 194; Denver etc. R. Co. *v.* Crawford, 11 Colo. 598; State *v.* Mason, 108 Ind. 48; Western Union Tel. Co. *v.* Brown, 108 Ind. 538.

Statutes in some instances have abrogated this rule, as in *Indiana*, where it is held that although there is no vested right in a penalty, and it will be lost where the statute conferring it is repealed, yet in *Indiana*, to recover an accrued penalty for delaying a telegram is, by special provision of the statute, saved to the person injured by the delay, notwithstanding the repeal of the statute prescribing it. Western Union Tel. Co. *v.* Brown, 108 Ind. 538; 14 Am. & Eng. Corp. Cas. 139.

And in *Missouri*, where the Rev. Stat., § 3151 declares that penalties incurred before the repeal of the statute providing for them shall not be affected by the repeal, it was held that the *Missouri* act of 1885, amending act of 1881, providing for a penalty in the case of railroads failing to maintain stations at crossings, did not affect the right to recover penalties incurred before the passage of the act of 1885. State *v.* Kansas City etc. R. Co., 32 Fed. Rep. 722.

And in *Kentucky*, the statute has abrogated the rule of the common law. Commonwealth *v.* Sherman, 85 Ky. 686.

4. See Informers, vol. 10, p. 711.

authority.[1] No special formula is requisite to confer the right to sue. It is enough if it be seen that the intent was to confer the right.[2]

When a penal statute provides that the penalty may be recovered by indictment or civil action, and one moiety goes to the State and the other to him who prosecutes or sues for the same, and an indictment is found by the grand jury, it must appear of record that some person complained or sued for the same, in order to entitle him to the penalty; otherwise the whole penalty goes to the State.[3] So when the penalty is given to the informer and others, he and the others may join in an action therefor, or he may sue in his own name, declaring specially *qui tam*, that the interest of those who have the right may appear of record.[4] An informer in a *qui tam* action brought under the statute does not acquire a vested right to the penalty until after judgment.[5] So the right of an informer to his share of the proceeds of a forfeiture does not vest until the money is ready for distribution; and, therefore, where money has been paid into court to abide the final decree of the court, the amount of the informer's share must be determined by the laws in force at the time of such final decree.[6]

V. Parties.—Where a statute does not in terms declare in whose name a suit shall be conducted for the recovery of a penalty for its violation, the suit must be in the name of

1. Colburn *v.* Swett, 1 Met. (Mass.) 232; Drew *v.* Hilliker, 56 Vt. 641; Nye *v.* Lamphere, 2 Gray (Mass.) 297; Barnard *v.* Gostling, 2 East 569. See United States *v.* Griswold, 5 Sawy. (U. S.) 25.

In Vandeventer *v.* Van Cort, 2 N. J. L. 155; Megargell *v.* Hazleton Coal Co., 8 W. & S. (Pa.) 342, it was held, that at common law, a common informer could bring an action in his own name.

2. Drew *v.* Hilliker, 56 Vt. 641. In many cases the formula "who may prosecute" or "who prosecutes" has been held sufficient to show the legislative intent to confer the right. Drew *v.* Hilliker, 56 Vt. 641.

In Nye *v.* Lamphere, 2 Gray (Mass.) 295, it was held, that giving the forfeiture, or a part of it, "to any person who shall prosecute therefor," gave authority to a common informer to sue.

3. State *v.* Smith, 49 N. H. 155; 6 Am. Rep. 480; Commonwealth *v.* Frost, 5 Mass. 53; Commonwealth *v.* Davenger, 10 Phila. (Pa.) 478.

A witness, sworn in support of an indictment founded on a statute, which, in case of conviction, gives one-half the penalty to the informer, is not to be considered the informer, from the mere fact that he is the only witness in the case. Williamson *v.* State, 16 Ala. 431.

No exertions of a party to procure condemnation of a vessel, under a supposition that he is entitled to part of the penalty as informer, can make him an informer, unless he actually gave the information which led to the seizure. Brewster *v.* Gelston, 1 Paine (U. S.) 426.

4. Butler *v.* College of Physicians & Surgeons, Cro. Car. 256; Vandenter *v.* Van Court, 2 N. J. L. 155.

5. Bank of St. Mary's *v.* State, 12 Ga. 475; Chicago etc. R. Co. *v.* Adler, 56 Ill. 344.

6. About Twenty-five Thousand Gallons of Distilled Spirits, 1 Ben. (U. S.) 307.

In a case of forfeiture under the internal revenue laws the right of the informer becomes fixed on the receipt by the marshal of the money, and a subsequent circular of the Secretary of the Treasury can have no effect to reduce the amount to which under the then existing regulation the informer was entitled. United States *v.* Twenty

the people.[1] If the party injured is authorized to sue for a penalty, any one of several parties jointly injured by the offense may sue and recover the penalty.[2] If a private person is authorized to sue in his own name only where certain officers, upon notice of the offense, fail to sue, a defendant sued for such penalty, is not entitled to move to dismiss the action on the mere ground that it was brought without authority from the nominal plaintiffs and without notice to them.[3]

In a *qui tam* action, a common informer may, upon express statutory authority, sue in his own name as well as on behalf of the people.[4] The party who first commences a *qui tam* action to recover a penalty given by statute, acquires an interest in the penalty which cannot be divested by a subsequent suit brought by any other common informer, though the latter suit be first prosecuted to judgment.[5] Where a statute prohibits an act under a penalty and gives one moiety to the public and another to the informer, the State may prosecute for the whole, unless the informer has commenced a *qui tam* action.[6]

A joint action may be maintained against two or more persons jointly concerned in doing an act. The number of penalties re-

Five Thousand Segars, 5 Blatchf. (U. S.) 500. Eight Barrels of Distilled Spirits, 1 Ben. (U. S.) 472.

1. People *v.* Young, 72 Ill. 411. See Caroon *v.* Rogers, 6 Jones (N. Car.) 240.

Illinois Rev. Stat. (ch. *Marriages*), § 10, providing that the clerk shall forfeit "to the use of the father," a penalty for wrongfully issuing a marriage license to a minor, enables the father to sue for the penalty in his own name. Adams *v.* Cutright, 53 Ill. 361.

An action to recover the penalty for violating the statute of *Maine* respecting innholders, etc., may be brought in the name of the town where the offense is committed. Wiscasset *v.* Trundy, 12 Me. 204.

Where a statute imposed a penalty of $20 for every offense against it, "one half to the complainant and the other half to the county treasurer, for the benefit of the poor fund of the county," and did not say who should sue and bring the action for the penalty—*held*, that a person bringing the action could not recover without showing some authority for suing. Seward *v.* Beach, 29 Barb. (N. Y.) 239.

2. Phillips *v.* Bevans, 23 N. J. L. 373.

A penal action cannot be maintained by several persons jointly as common informers, unless the statute imposing the penalty expressly authorizes such a proceeding. Commonwealth *v.* Winchester, 3 Pa. L. J. Rep. 34.

3. New York City & Co. *v.* Purdy, 13 Abb. Pr. (N. Y.) 434; 36 Barb. (N. Y.) 266. See Pomroy *v.* Sperry, 16 How. Pr. (N. Y.) 211.

4. Chicago etc. R. Co. *v.* Howard, 38 Ill. 414; Nye *v.* Lamphere, 2 Gray (Mass.) 295; Myers *v.* Van Alstyne, 10 Wend. (N. Y.) 97; Cloud *v.* Hewitt, 3 Cranch (C. C.) 199. See Lynch *v.* The Economy, 27 Wis. 69; Vandeventer *v.* Van Court, 2 N. J. L. 155.

Where an act of Assembly directs a penalty to be recovered by any person suing for the same, the sum when recovered, to be paid, one half to the person suing, the other to the treasurer or county commissioners, a common informer may sue in his own name. Megargell *v.* Hazelton Coal Co., 8 W. & S. (Pa.) 342.

The person claiming the penalty, and not the State, is the proper plaintiff in an action for the penalty imposed on railroads by § 1967 of the *North Carolina* Code. Middleton *v.* Wilmington etc. R. Co., 95 N. Car. 167.

5. Beadleston *v.* Sprague, 6 Johns. (N. Y.) 101; Pike *v.* Madbury, 12 N. H. 262.

6. State *v.* Bishop, 7 Conn. 181; Commonwealth *v.* Howard, 13 Mass. 222; Rex *v.* Hyman, 7 T. R. 536.

coverable depends upon the language and provisions of the statute creating them. If the offense is single and cannot be separated, but one penalty is recoverable.[1] An offense is in its nature single or entire when the statute contemplates one offense, in the commission of which two classes of offenders may be engaged. But where the offense is in its nature several, and where every person concerned may be separately guilty of it, there each offender is separately liable to the penalty, because the offense of each is distinct from the offense of the others, and each is punishable for his own offense.[2] A claim for penalties incurred by every person concerned may be included in the same action.[3] See CRIMINAL PROCEDURE, vol. 4. pp. 755, 756.

Where the imposition of but one penalty is authorized, and instead of one action a number of actions are brought simultaneously, they will be quashed on motion.[4] Where the penalty is specific and does not rest in computation, the parties injured must join in a single action; more than one action is not maintainable.[5]

VI. PLEADINGS.—In an action upon a penalty the statute imposing it and the section thereof must be pleaded with certainty.[6]

1. Warren *v.* Doolittle, 5 Cow. (N. Y.) 678; Palmer *v.* Conly, 4 Den. (N. Y.) 374; 2 N. Y. 182; Curtis *v.* Hurlburt, 2 Conn. 309; Kempton *v.* Sullivan Sav. Inst., 53 N. H. 581; Burnham *v.* Webster, 5 Mass. 266.

In Ingersoll *v.* Skinner, 1 Den. (N. Y.) 540, it was held, that a single action for the penalty may be sustained against several, who join in selling liquors without license, and although several concur in the commission of the act, only one penalty could be recovered, either in one or several actions.

Missouri act of 1881, requiring railroad companies to maintain depots at crossings, gave a penalty of $25 for each day's delay after a certain date. *Held*, that for a delay of 1,338 days, a penalty for each day was recoverable. State *v.* Kansas City etc. R. Co., 32 Fed. Rep. 722.

In an action on the statute prohibiting the cutting and carrying away of trees from the lands of the State, under a penalty of $25 for each tree cut, the plaintiff may allege, in a single count, that the defendant is indebted in a sum equal to 20 penalties, and may recover any amount of penalties that he can prove the defendant has incurred, though the same be less than 20. People *v.* M'Fadden, 13 Wend. (N. Y.) 396.

But a second offense, which subjects to an accumulated penalty, must be of the same nature as the first, and after a legal conviction. Scott *v.* Turner, 1 Root (Conn.) 163.

2. Rex *v.* Clarke, Cowp. 610; Curtis *v.* Hurlburt, 2 Conn. 309.

3. Bartolett *v.* Achey, 38 Pa. St. 273; Gibson *v.* Gault, 33 Pa. St. 44. See Hill *v.* Davis, 4 Mass. 137.

Where two or more persons were concerned in drawing a bush-seine in a river, in violation of a statute, it was held that this was a several offense, and each person concerned in it was separately liable to the penalty imposed by the act. Curtis *v.* Hurlburt, 2 Conn. 309.

4. Clark *v.* Lisbon, 19 N. H. 286.

5. Edwards *v.* Hill, 11 Ill. 22.

6. Fish *v.* Manning, 31 Fed. Rep. 340; People *v.* Brooks, 4 Den. (N. Y.) 469; McKay *v.* Woodle, 6 Ired. (N. Car.) 352; Kirkpatrick *v.* Stewart, 19 Ark. 695; People *v.* Grand Rapids etc. Plank Road Co., 64 Mich. 618. And where an action is brought for more than one penalty, each particular offense must be set out with certainty. Hill *v.* Herbert, 3 N. J. L. 483.

It is not fatal to a complaint that while it follows the language of the statute as to a forfeiture, it adopts the future tense. State *v.* Adams, 78 Me. 486.

But where a statute is merely remedial, giving an additional remedy for a wrong at common law, the statute

Every essential fact constituting a statutory offense must be distinctly alleged.[1] The declaration or complaint must conclude "against the form of the statute."[2] But it need not allege to whom the prescribed penalty is to go.[3]

VII. Evidence.—In proceedings to recover a penalty for a violation of a penal statute, the burden of proof is on the prose-

need not be declared upon. McKay v. Woodle, 6 Ired. (N. Car.) 352.

1. Whitecraft v. Vanderver, 12 Ill. 235; Chew v. Thompson, 9 N. J. L. 249; Duck v. Harrisburg, 7 Watts (Pa.) 181; Fairbanks v. Antrim, 2 N. H. 105; Kempton v. Sullivan Sav. Inst., 53 N. H. 581; Abney v. Austin, 6 Ill. App. 49; Morrell v. Fuller, 8 Johns. (N. Y.) 218; State v. Androscoggin R. Co., 76 Me. 411; Duffy v. Averitt, 5 Ired. (N. Car.) 455; Allaire v. Howell Works Co., 14 N. J. L. 22; Western Union Tel. Co. v. Wilson, 108 Ind. 308; 16 Am. & Eng. Corp Cas. 257.

See CRIMINAL PROCEDURE, vol. 4, p. 741.

In an action for a penalty for altering an inspector's marks on barrels of flour it is necessary to set out the marks in the manner of the alteration. Cloud v. Hewitt, 3 Cranch (C. C.) 199; Reagh v. Spann, 3 Stew. (Ala.) 100.

So in an action against a constable for the penalty given by statute of *Maine* of 1821, ch. 92, § 9, for serving a justice's execution and taking fees before he had given bond, it is necessary that the amount of the debt should be set forth, that it may appear that the precept was within his authority to serve. Barter v. Martin, 5 Me. 76.

Where the declaration alleged, by way of recital, that "whereas the said defendant having," etc., it was held bad. Harrington v. M'Farland, Cam. & N. (N. Car.) 408.

Every circumstance in the description of the offense, contained in the clause of the statute which creates it and gives the penalty, must be so set forth as to bring the defendant within the statute. Ellis v. Hull, 2 Aik. (Vt.) 41; Greer v. Bumpass, Mart. & Y. (Tenn.) 94.

In an action against a bank, to recover the penalty provided by *Massachusetts* Rev. St., ch. 36, § 29, for delaying payment of its bills it is not necessary to set out copies of the bills in the declaration. Suffolk Bank v. Lowell Bank, 8 Allen (Mass.) 355.

In an action to recover a statutory penalty for failure to transmit a telegram, the complaint need not aver non-payment of the penalty. Western Union Tel. Co. v. Young, 93 Ind. 118.

2. Sears v. United States, 1 Gall. (U. S.) 257; Cross v. United States, 1 Gall. (U. S.) 26; Nichols v. Squire, 5 Pick. (Mass.) 168; United States v. Babson, Ware (U. S.) 450; Haskell v. Moody, 9 Pick. (Mass.) 162; Smith v. United States, 1 Gall. (U. S.) 261; Hobbs v. Staples, 19 Me. 219; Peabody v. Hayt, 10 Mass. 36; Penley v. Whitney, 48 Me. 351; Reed v. Northfield, 13 Pick. (Mass.) 94; 23 Am. Dec. 662; Scroter v. Harrington, 1 Hawks (N. Car.) 192; Crawford v. New Jersey etc. Co., 28 N. J. L. 479; Doyle v. Baltimore Co., 12 Gill & J. (Md.) 484; Lee v. Clarke, 2 East 333; Wells v. Iggueden, 5 D. & R. 13; Lee v. Nelms, 57 Ga. 253; Smith v. Moore, 6 Me. 274. *Compare* Barkhamsted v. Parsons, 3 Conn. 1; Levy v. Gowdy, 2 Allen (Mass.) 320; Fowler v. Tuttle, 24 N. H. 9; Crain v. State, 2 Yerg. (Tenn.) 390; People v. Bartow, 6 Cow. (N. Y.) 290.

See also INDICTMENT, vol. 10, p. 515.

If a declaration of a statute penalty concludes against the form of the statutes, when it is founded on a single statute, it is good on error. Kenrick v. United States, 1 Gall. (U. S.) 268.

A declaration for a penalty imposed by a village ordinance need not conclude *contra forman statuti.* Winooski v. Gokey, 49 Vt. 282.

In action under *Massachusetts* Stat. 1819, ch. 37, imposing a penalty on keepers of livery stables giving credit to undergraduates in any college in the commonwealth, the declaration must aver that rules have been established and an officer appointed, etc. Soper v. Harvard College, 1 Pick. (Mass.) 177.

3. State v. Thrasher, 79 Me. 17; Sears v. United States, 1 Gall. (U. S.) 257; Scroter v. Harrington, 1 Hawks (N. Car.) 192.

It is said in 4 Minor's Inst. 631, that, "In debt on statute at the suit of a party aggrieved, or by an informer

cution.[1] It is sometimes necessary, contrary to the usual rule of evidence, not only to prove an affirmative, but to prove a negative.[2]

An action for money had and received, brought on a statute against usury by a person not a party to the usury, is a penal action and full proof is required as in actions of a criminal nature, and a mere preponderance of testimony is not sufficient to warrant a recovery.[3] But an action of debt *qui tam* to recover a penalty given by statute, is not a criminal prosecution, and in order to authorize a verdict for the plaintiff, the jury need not be convinced that the case against the defendant is proved beyond a reasonable doubt.[4] So it is not necessary that the proof should be co-extensive with the charge. If part of the injury charged, or one of several injuries laid in the same court, is proved, the plaintiff will be entitled to recover *pro tanto,* provided that part

when the whole penalty by the statute accrues to him, the commencement is the same as in debt on a contract; but when a part of the penalty only is given to the informer, and the commonwealth or the overseers of the poor are entitled to the residue, the commencement and the other parts of the declaration usually state that the plaintiff sues *tam pro republica quam pro se ipso.* The date of the statute, supposing it to be a public one, need not, and had better not, be stated; but the offense or act charged must appear to be within the provisions of the statute, and all the circumstances necessary to support the action must be stated. Morever, where the act or omission on which the suit is founded is not an offense at common law, it is necessary in all cases to conclude 'against the form of the statute,' or 'statutes;'" *citing* 1 Chit. Pl. 404, *et seq;* Com. Dig. Pleader (C. 76); Com. Dig. action upon statute (E. 1); 3 Rob. Pr. (2d ed.) 612, *et seq.* See also DEBT, vol. 5, p. 165; PLEADING.

1. The Pope Catlin, 31 Fed. Rep. 408; Chaffee *v.* United States, 18 Wall. (U. S.) 516; White *v.* Comstock, 6 Vt. 405.

In an action for the penalty prescribed by laws *New York,* 1883, ch. 183, § 19, for violations of the preceding sections of the chapter which prohibit the manufacture, possession, and sale of products from "animal fat, or animal or vegetable oils, not produced from unadulterated milk or cream," "designed to take the place of natural butter or cheese," the burden of showing that the product was manufactured or in process of manufacture at the time of the passage of the act, so as to be exempted as provided in section 21, is on defendants. People *v.* Briggs, 114 N. Y. 56.

In an action to recover a penalty for falsely, corruptly, etc., certifying to a greater number of days' attendance as a witness than the defendant actually attended, it is sufficient to prove that the certificate was false; it is for the defendant to show that the act was not corrupt, etc. Chesley *v.* Brown, 11 Me. 143.

To maintain an action for a penalty for leaving open a swinging gate across a private or by-road, the plaintiff must prove that the way in question is a private road, laid out or made such in the manner prescribed by statute. Allen *v.* Stevens, 29 N. J. L. 509.

2. White *v.* Comstock, 6 Vt. 405. See Bell *v.* Wallace, 81 Ala. 422. In prosecutions for a penalty given by statute, if it contains negative matter, the negative must be alleged and proved—unless such matter be particularly within the knowledge of the other party. Hopper *v.* State, 19 Ark. 143.

Where a statute, giving a penal action, contains, either in the same section or a subsequent one, a proviso or exception which forms no part of the plaintiff's title, but is mere matter of excuse or justification to the defendant, the plaintiff need not negative it; but the defendant, to take advantage of it, must plead it. Teel *v.* Fonda, 4 Johns. (N. Y.) 304.

3. White *v.* Comstock, 6 Vt. 405.

4. Hitchcock *v.* Munger, 15 N. H. 97.

which is proved affords *per se* a sufficient cause of action.[1]

VIII. Compounding Penalties.—Actions *qui tam* cannot be compromised without leave of court, upon suggestion of matter which entitles the defendant to indulgence. If they are otherwise compromised, the defendant is left still liable to the penalty.[2] It is within the discretion of the court, under the statute of *New York*, to allow the plaintiffs to compound on such terms as they deem proper. And, as a general rule, the court will require, as one of the terms of leave to compound, that the people's moiety of the penalty be paid; but under special circumstances leave to discontinue will be granted on the payment of costs only.[3]

Where an action is brought to recover a penalty for violation of a statute, and any person is authorized to prosecute therefor in the name of a certain officer in case the proper persons refuse to bring such action, the officer in whose name the action is brought has no power to consent to its discontinuance without the consent of the person by whom it was commenced.[4] But it has been held that in an action commenced by a city treasurer against one who had incurred a penalty under a statute which gave "one-half for the use of the city, and the other half for the use of the person furnishing the necessary evidence in the case," a nonsuit might be entered by agreement of the plaintiff and the defendant against the objection of the person who furnished the evidence.[5]

IX. Verdict and Judgment.—Where the statute fails to direct whether the amount of the penalty prescribed shall be fixed by the court or by the jury, the amount of the penalty is for the jury.[6] If a statute gives double the value of goods by way of penalty to be recovered in an action, the jury may find the value of the goods by their verdict, and the court may then double the

1. Hyde *v.* Morgan, 14 Conn. 104.

2. Rayham *v.* Rounesville, 9 Pick. (Mass.) 44; Burley *v.* Burley, 6 N. H. 200; Caswell *v.* Allen, 10 Johns. (N. Y.) 118; Middleton *v.* Wilmington, etc. R. Co., 95 N. Car. 167.

Where a judgment was recovered in the name of the wardens of the poor, by a relator, for a penalty, to one-half of which he is by law entitled, he may release one-half of the judgment, that being his own share, but he cannot release the other half, which belongs to the wardens. Wardens *v.* Cope, 2 Ired. (N. Car.) 44.

3. Bradway *v.* Le Worthy, 9 Johns. (N. Y.) 251; Haskins *v.* Newcomb, 2 Johns. (N. Y.) 405.

4. Record *v.* Messenger, 8 Hun (N. Y.) 283; United States *v.* Griswold, 30 Fed. Rep. 762.

It was held in the confiscation cases, 7 Wall. (U. S.) 454, that an informer in prosecutions under the confiscation acts of Congress, Aug. 6 1861, had no vested interest in the subject-matter of the suit, and that the Attorney-General might move to dismiss an appeal to this court without regard to the interest of such informer.

5. Wheeler *v.* Goulding, 3 Gray (Mass.) 539. The parties to a *qui tam* action may lawfully agree, the plaintiff to discontinue the suit, and the defendant to pay the costs; for discontinuing is not compounding or compromising a popular action, within the "act to redress disorders by common informers;" nor is payment of costs by the defendant a composition. Haskins *v.* Newcomb, 2 Johns. (N. Y.) 405.

6. McDaniel *v.* Gates City Gas Light Co., 79 Ga. 58.

amount in entering the judgment.[1] But if, in such a case, the jury find a verdict for a specific sum, it is to be considered as the double value unless the contrary appears.[2]

In a *qui tam* action judgment should be in favor of the informer for the uses expressed in the statute.[3] If one-half is to be paid to the informer and the other half into the treasury of the town, the judgment should be that he recover the penalty, one-half to his own use, the other half to be paid into the treasury of the town.[4] A verdict in an action *qui tam* to recover a number of penalties should specify the particular offenses for which the verdict was rendered.[5] And where a statute directs that a penalty shall be appropriated in a certain way, a judgment that appropriates it differently is erroneous.[6]

1. Dygert *v.* Schenck, 23 Wend. (N. Y.) 446.

2. Cross *v.* United States, 1 Gall. (U. S.) 26.

3. Doss *v.* State, 6 Tex. 433.

4. Bradley *v.* Baldwin, 5 Conn. 288.

In an admiralty seizure cause, the court cannot award a proportion of the proceeds of the property condemned to informers, unless the case be within some statute provision; but it will allow compensation for expenses incurred in securing and preserving the property. *Ex parte* Cahoone, 2 Mason (U. S.) 85. In this case STORY, J., reasoned substantially as follows: The present claim is not for any expenses incurred or labor performed by the petitioners in seizing, preserving or securing the property which has been condemned to the United States. In such cases the court would know how to deal with the claim, for, as incidental to its general jurisdiction over seizures, it would, on the admiralty side, entertain petitions for compensation. But here the whole claim rests merely on the ground that the petitioners were the first informers, through whose instrumentality the forfeiture to the United States has been successfully asserted. In certain cases, as we all know, the laws with a view to encourage information of breaches of the revenue system, have given a certain portion of the penalties and forfeitures annexed to such breaches, to informers. Where such provision has been made, the path is plain, and the court will sedulously guard the rights of those who thus become entitled to the bounty. There is no pretence that any such provision exists in the present case; and if the court are to grant compensation here, it must grant it in every other case, where the government desires information material to enforce a forfeiture. Strictly speaking, it is the duty of every citizen to give all his aid, as well by communicating information as otherwise, to the government, to enable it to suppress violations of the laws and to punish the offenders, and to enforce forfeitures *in rem.* This is more especially the duty of revenue officers, like the petitioners, who are placed as a watch to guard the public against frauds committed in the course of navigation and commerce; and this duty has been peremptorily pressed upon them in many cases by the express injunctions of statutes. Now I am not aware that any court are at liberty to grant rewards in cases where the party has performed a public duty, unless there be some positive regulation which provides for such cases. It is not sufficient that the services be meritorious and acceptable, nor even that it goes beyond the limits of mere official duty; much less that it is strict conformity with such duty. To found a title for compensation, there must be either some direct extraordinary assistance or service, or expense, which the law recognizes as a just charge *in rem.* independent of any notion of official duty, or some positive statutable enactment in point. Otherwise the party must be left, as Sir William Scott has declared on another occasion, to the general reward of all good citizens and good officers, the fair estimation of his countrymen and the consciousness of his own right conduct.

5. Westbrook *v.* Van Auken, 5 N. J. L. 478; Bloodgood *v.* Vanderveer, 3 N. J. L. 486.

6. Werfel *v.* Commonwealth, 5 Binn. (Pa.) 65.

PENCIL.—See WRITING.

PENDING.—(See also LIS PENDENS, vol. 8, p. 868; FORMER SUIT PENDING, vol. 8, p. 549). See note 1.

PENETRATION.—See ASSAULT, vol. 1, p. 805; note; RAPE; SEDUCTION.

PENITENTIARY.—See PRISON.

PENSIONS.—(See also ASSIGNMENT, vol. 1, p. 829; CONSTITUTIONAL LAW, vol. 3, p. 706; EXTORTION, vol. 7, p. 593).

1. "Pending" implies that the cause is in court. Thomas *v.* Hopkins, 2 Browne (Pa.) 146.

Where a statute provided that a "pending" action should not abate by the death of either party, it was held that "'pending' action means nothing more 'than remaining undecided,' an action may without doubt be considered as pending from the commencement." Clindenin *v.* Allen, 4 N. H. 386.

Under the Oregon Code, § 2544, which provides that any person wishing to contest an election shall give notice in writing to the person whose election he intends to contest, within thirty days from the time said person shall claim to have been elected, it was held, that a contested election case is not "pending" until notice to the person whose election it is intended to contest has been filed, though "proceedings are instituted" before the service of such notice. Whitney *v.* Blackburn, 17 Oregon, 564.

Although judgment has been recovered in an action, the action is "pending" as long as such judgment remains unsatisfied. Wegman *v.* Childs, 41 N. Y. 159; Howell *v.* Bowers, 2 Cr. M. & R. 626; Mitchell Furniture Co. *v.* Sampson, 40 Fed. Rep. 805; Redfield *v.* Wickham, 13 App. Cas. 467.

"Pending" applies to a judgment on which successive *fieri facias venditionis* have been issued, but not fully satisfied. Ulsafer *v.* Stewart, 77 Pa. St. 170.

Examples of Cases Pending at the Time Various Statutes Took Effect.—The issue of a citation for dissolution of a voidable marriage, though only issued seven days before the statute of 5 & 6 Wm. IV, ch. 54 received the royal assent, constituted a suit "depending" at the passing of the act. Sherwood *v.* Ray, 1 Moore, P. C. 353; 1 Curt. 173.

A petition for a highway as soon as filed with the clerk of the proper office, is pending. Wentworth *v.* Farmington, 48 N. H. 207.

A case that had been heard by a justice of the peace and appealed but not entered on the docket of the county court at the time of the passage of No. 40, Stats. of *Vermont* 1878, relating to the apportionment of costs, is not exempt from the operation of that statute under the exception therein of cases "pending" in county court. Tilden *v.* Johnson, 52 Vt. 628.

Pending Action.—An action for infringement of a patent is not after judgment a "pending action," although an appeal from the judgment is pending, within the meaning of § 18 (10) *English* Patent Acts of 1883, which provides that the foregoing provisions of the same section shall not apply as long as any action for infringement or other legal proceeding in relation to a patent is pending. Cropper *v.* Smith, 28 Ch. Div. 148.

Depending for Settlement.—Where an estate, represented insolvent, has turned out to be solvent, and the administration account has been presented to the court of probate, and accepted, the estate is no longer to be regarded as "depending for settlement" within the meaning of the 58th section of the *Connecticut* "act for the settlement of estates," which provides

I. **Definition.**—A pension is a stated and certain allowance granted by the government to an individual, or those who represent him, for valuable services performed by him for the country.[1]

II. **Nature and History of Pension Laws.**—In *England* pensions are given to soldiers and sailors or those dependent upon them[2], officers of the courts,[3] political officers,[4] colonial governors,[5] and persons in the diplomatic service.[6]

In the *United States* the English system of awarding pensions to others than soldiers and sailors has not been adopted. Pensions may be awarded under the *United States* statutes to soldiers and sailors, or their widows and orphans, and to the widows and children of deceased members of the life-saving service. Certain of the States have adopted statutes allowing pensions to persons disabled in military service.[7]

The foundation for the system of pension legislation in force in the United States was laid during the War of the Revolution.[8]

that no suit shall be brought against the administrator while the estate is in settlement. Bacon *v.* Thorp, 27 Conn. 251.

Examination of a Poor Debtor.—The examination of a debtor, who has applied to take the oath for the relief of poor debtors, is "pending" within the meaning of the *Massachusetts* Pub. Stats. 162, § 49, so that the creditor may file charges of fraud against him, until the announcement of the decision of the magistrate, although the hearing of evidence and arguments has closed, and the magistrate has continued the cause for the purpose of considering the questions of law and fact involved therein. Andrews *v.* Cassidy, 142 Mass. 96.

1. Bouvier's Law Dict.

2. 7 Geo. IV, ch. 16, § 10; 28 and 29 Vict., ch. 73.

The statute 35 and 36 Vict., ch. 67, § 5, provides that the admiralty may, under regulations to be from time to time made by them, provide wholly or in part for the education and maintenance of sons and daughters of deceased or distressed commissioned officers, royal navy and marines.

Sergeants, etc., having served in the local militia twenty years are given a pension. E. 52 Geo. III, 38, § 93.

3. 42 and 43 Vict., ch. 78, §§ 15–21.

4. 32 and 33 Vict., ch. 60; 22 Vict., ch. 26, § 12.

5. 28 and 29 Vict., ch. 110; 35 and 36 Vict., ch. 29.

6. 32 and 33 Vict., ch. 43.

7. See §§ 1, 3, March, 1865; §§ 5, 6, June, 1866, and act of March 1, 1879; *South Carolina* Act of Dec. 24, 1887.

In *Louisiana* there is a statute giving pensions to the veterans of the War of 1812 and their widows. La. Act No. 70, 1883, p. 125; La. Act No. 61, 1876, p. 103.

In *North Carolina* every person who may have been disabled by wrongs in the militia service of the State or rendered incapable thereby of procuring subsistence for themselves and families, and the widows and orphans of such officers who may have died are given a pension, providing such officers or persons were not engaged in the late civil war. Code of North Car. 1883, vol. 2, § 3472.

A pension of $10 a month is given to a soldier from *Tennessee* in the Army of the Confederate States who lost his eyes while engaged in battle in the war between the States. Code of Tenn. 1884, § 2132, p. 375.

8. Congress by resolution of August 26, 1776, provided that every commissioned and non-commissioned officer, and private soldier in the army, who was so disabled in the service of the State in the war then existing with the mother country, as to be rendered incapable "afterward of getting a livelihood" should receive, during life, or the continuance of such disability, one-half his monthly pay after his pay as a soldier should cease. The same provision was made for commanders, commissioned officers, marines and seamen on ships of war and armed vessels of the United

The policy thus outlined has been pursued in statutes passed by Congress from time to time since the Revolution. In the acts regulating the military establishment of the United States, provision was made for pensioning officers and soldiers wounded or disabled while in the line of duty. The acts authorizing the raising of additional military forces during the War of 1812, the Mexican War, and the War of the Rebellion, placed such forces on the same footing, in respect to pensions and bounty lands, as the Regular Army. By act of Congress, approved July 14, 1862, general provision was made for the payment of pensions to invalids in the War of the Rebellion, or to the widows and orphans, or mothers and minor sisters of such as might die or be killed in the line of duty. Since the close of this war, many different pension acts have been passed by Congress, and so much of the statutory regulations of pensions as are still in force, and come within the scope of this title, are set out elsewhere herein.

III. The Pension Office is the office through which applications for pensions are made. The Department of the Interior has general supervisory and appellate powers over the Pension Office. The Commissioner of Pensions is required to perform, under the direction of the Secretary of the Interior, such duties as may be prescribed by the President. He is required by statute to furnish to each claimant or applicant instructions and the forms to be used in establishing pension claims. And it is also made his duty to determine all applications for pensions and construe and interpret all questions which may arise as to the construction of the several acts of Congress relating to pensions, subject only to the direction of the Secretary of the Interior, to whom appeal may be made.[1] The Interior Department is a special tribunal of judicial or *quasi*-judicial powers, appointed by law to ascertain and determine all the facts, and to adjudicate and allow a pension to the party entitled, and its decision is held, by some cases, to be final and conclusive.[2]

States, who should be so disabled as to be incapable of obtaining a livelihood. Two years later the provisions of this resolution were extended to all persons who were disabled in the service of the United Colonies or States of America before the passage of the above resolution; and by the resolution of April 23rd, 1782, all such sick or wounded soldiers as were reported unfit for duty, either in the field or garrison, were entitled to a discharge upon application for the same, and also to receive as a pension five dollars per month in lieu of all pay and emoluments. Sundry acts were subsequently passed, altering, modifying, or repealing the last named act, and they in turn submitted to like processes, and finally by Act of April 10, 1806, all former laws were repealed, and general provision was made for the payment of pensions to invalids of the Revolution.

1. Stokely *v.* De Camp, 2 Grant (Pa.) 17.

2. United States *v.* Scott, 25 Fed. Rep. 470. See United States *v.* Germaine, 9 Otto 508.

In Daly *v.* United States, 17 Ct. of Cl. 144, the court, by DRAKE, C. J., said: "Without laboring through the pension laws to show the fact, nothing can be clearer, or better known to everybody having ordinary knowledge of those laws, than that the whole matter of ascertaining, determining and certifying who is lawfully entitled

IV. Who Entitled to Pension.—It may be said generally that commissioned and non-commissioned officers of the army (including regulars, volunteers, rangers and militia) and navy, including the navy proper, sea-fencibles, flotilla service, marine corps and revenue cutters when co-operating with the navy; musicians, privates, marines, seaman, ordinary seamen and all others, in whatsoever capacity they may have served, who were regularly enlisted or drafted, or who volunteered, and who, while in the line of duty, were disabled by wounds or sickness from subsequently procuring a livelihood, are entitled to pensions under the present laws.[1] The heirs or legal representatives of any

to the gratuity authorized to be bestowed on account of military service is confided to certain executive officers, and nowhere to the judiciary. No right to a pension is fixed until those officers declare it so. If they decide against the right, there is no appeal against that decision, except to Gongress."

In United States *v.* Moore, 95 U. S. 760–764, the court said: "The construction given to a statute by those charged with the duty of executing it is always entitled to the most respectful consideration, and ought not to be overruled without cogent reasons. Edwards *v.* Darby, 12 Wheat. (U. S.) 210; United States *v.* Bank, 6 Pet. (U. S.) 29; United States *v.* Macdaniel, 7 Pet. (U. S.) 1. The officers concerned are usually able men, and masters of the subject. Not unfrequently they are the draftsmen of the laws they are afterwards called upon to interpret." See Bowen *v.* United States, 14 Ct. Cl. 162.

In United States *v.* Purdy, 38 Fed. Rep. 902, SAGE, J., in charging the jury said: "Something has been read to you from the opinions of the Secretary of the Interior as to the construction of that section. Now his opinion, while it may be used in argument to the court, is not an authority on the construction of the law, because the constitution vests that power in the judiciary alone. So that the construction of the Secretary of the Interior does not fix the meaning of the law; and while it is correct in some respects it is clearly wrong in others."

In Alexander *v.* United States, 4 Ct. Cl. 218, it is held that the certificate of the Commissioner of Pensions is *prima facie* evidence of title to a pension and of all the facts that make the title.

1. **Who Entitled to Pensions.**—The following persons are entitled to pensions under the present laws:

First. Any officer of the army, including regulars, volunteers and militia, or any officer in the navy, or marine corps, or any enlisted man, however employed, in the military or naval service of the United States, or in its marine corps, whether regularly mustered, or not, disabled by reason of any wound or injury received, or disease contracted while in the service of the United States and in the line of duty.

Second. Any master serving on a gunboat, or any pilot, engineer, sailor, or other person not regularly mustered, serving upon any gunboat or war-vessel of the United States, disabled by any wound or injury received, or otherwise incapacitated, while in the line of duty, for procuring his subsistence by manual labor.

Third. Any person not an enlisted soldier in the army, serving for the time being as a member of the militia of any State, under orders of an officer of the United States, or who volunteered for the time being to serve with any regularly organized military or naval force of the United States, or who otherwise volunteered and rendered service in any engagement with rebels or Indians, disabled in consequence of wounds or injury received in the line of duty in such temporary service. But no claim of a State militiaman, or non-enlisted person, on account of disability from wounds or injury received in battle with rebels or Indians, while temporarily rendering service, shall be valid unless prosecuted to a successful issue prior to the fourth day of July, 1874.

Fourth. Any acting assistant or

officer are by statute entitled to receive the arrears of pay due such officer and the pension, if any, authorized by law for the grade into which he was mustered.[1] Under this statute the widow is entitled to such pension without regard to the pension which her

contract surgeon disabled by any wound or injury received by disease contracted in the line of duty while actually performing the duties of assistant surgeon or acting assistant surgeon with any military force in the field, or *in transitu*, or in hospital.

Fifth. Any provost-marshal deputy provost-marshal, or enrolling officer, disabled by reason of any wound or injury, received in the discharge of his duty, to procure a subsistence by manual labor. U. S. Rev. St., § 4693. See Pension Laws 1890, p. 5.

If any person embraced within the provisions of the above section has died since the fourth day of March, eighteen hundred and sixty-one, or hereafter dies by reason of any wound, injury, or disease, which, under the conditions and limitations of such sections, would have entitled him to an invalid pension had he been disabled, his widow, or if there be no widow, or in case of her death, without payment to her of any part of the pension hereinafter mentioned, his child or children, under sixteen years of age, shall be entitled to receive the same pension as the husband or father would have been entitled to had he been totally disabled, to commence from the death of the husband or father, to continue to the widow during her widowhood, and unto his child or children until they severally attain the age of sixteen years, and no longer; and, if the widow remarry, the child or children shall be entitled from the date of remarriage. U. S. Rev. St., § 4702. See Pension Laws of 1890, p. 10.

Pensions to the Survivors of the War of 1812.—The widows and children under the age of sixteen years of the officers, non-commissioned officers, musicians and privates of the regulars, militia and volunteers of the War of 1812, and the various Indian wars since 1790, who remained at the date of their death in the service of the United States, or who received an honorable discharge, and have died, or shall hereafter die of injury received or disease contracted in the service and in the line of duty, are entitled to receive one-half the monthly pay to which the deceased was entitled at the time he received the injury or contracted the disease which resulted in his death. But no half-pay pension shall exceed one-half of the pay of a lieutenant colonel, and such half-pay pension shall be varied after the 25th day of July, 1866, in accordance with the provisions of sec. 4, 712 of the present statutes. U. S. Rev. Stat., § 4732.

Pensions to Regulars and Volunteers of the Mexican War.—Any officer, noncommissioned officer, musician or private, whether of the regular army or volunteer, disabled by reason of injury received or disease contracted while in the line of duty in actual service in the war with Mexico, or in going to or returning from the same, who has received an honorable discharge, is given a pension proportionate to his disability, not exceeding for total disability one-half of the pay of his rank on the date on which he received the wound or contracted the disease which resulted in such disability. In case the officer or other person referred to has died after the passage of the statute by reason of injury received or disease contracted in the war, his widow is entitled to receive the same pension as the husband would have been entitled to had he been totally disabled. See United States Rev. Stat., §§ 4730 and 4731.

1. St. June 3, 1884, ch. 63, §§ 2 and 3.

The pension due at the death of a widow, under the act of June 19, 1840, goes to her children and not to her creditors, although payable to the executor or administrator. Shireley *v.* Walker, 31 Me. 541; Froud *v.* Perkins, 9 N. H. 101.

The pension due to a widow under statute June 4, 1836, and statute March 3, 1837, and disposed of by her by will becomes a part of her estate and goes to her executor and not to her children, although certificate was issued after her decease. Foot *v.* Knowles, 4 Metc. (Mass.) 386. *Compare* Slade *v.* Slade, 11 Cush. (Mass.) 466; Garland *v.* Thompson, 29 N. H. 396.

The provision that the accrued pen-

husband was receiving.[1] A claim upon the United States for a pension due a decedent must, however, be prosecuted by the administrator, not by the heirs, as it is personal estate.[2]

The widow of a soldier of the Revolution, having remarried since his death, is entitled, under the act of August 23, 1842, to the pension given by the act of July 7, 1838, as well during the period of her coverture as during her widowhood occasioned by the death of her second husband, provided she be a widow at the time she makes her application.[3] But a deserted wife, who remarries, thinking her first husband dead and continues in her new relation after discovering her husband to be alive, is precluded from claiming a pension, her husband having, meanwhile, entered and died in the service of the United States.[4]

Under the earlier statutes, an adopted child is not entitled to a pension. But an illegitimate child, which, by intermarriage of the parents, and acknowledged as their child, becomes legitimized by the law of the State in which the parents reside, is entitled to a pension if the father dies in the naval service and the mother marries again.[5] So the grandchildren of a deceased pensioner are construed to be included in the word "children," and are entitled *per stirpes* to a distributive share of the pension.[6]

Under a statute providing that if a soldier has died entitled to a pension, leaving neither the widow nor minor children, his mother or father, or orphan brothers and sisters, not dependent on him at the time of his death, shall be entitled to the pension, a mother is dependent upon her son, though having some money of her own invested, and she is not bound to use the capital for her support. She is dependent upon the son within the meaning of the

sion shall not be considered as part of the assets of the estate, was held to apply to the latter act of January 25, 1879, providing for "arrears of pensions." The issuing of a certificate for arrears of pension does not create a debt against the government, but survives to the administrator. Bonnelly *v.* United States, 17 Ct. of Cl. 105.

Under the term "accrued pension," it has been held that the executor of a deceased widow cannot be compelled to apply unexpended pension money left by her to the payment of her debts, she leaving children under sixteen years of age surviving her. Hodge *v.* Leaning, 2 Dem. (N. Y.) 553.

1. Burnett *v.* United States, 116 U. S. 158; 20 Ct. Cl. 190.

2. Chamberlin *v.* United States, 17 Ct. of Cl. 631.

3. Koucher *v.* United States, 1 Ct. of Cl. 207.

For construction of § 2 of U. S. St., Feb. 3, 1853, providing that widows of soldiers of the Revolutionary war, married subsequently to January, 1800, shall be entitled to a pension "in the same manner" as those who were married before that date, see United States *v.* Alexander, 12 Wall. (U. S.) 177; reversing, s. c., 4 Ct. Cl. 218.

4. United States *v.* Hays, 20 Fed. Rep. 17.

Under the *South Carolina* act of Dec. 24, 1887, providing for a pension to a widow of a confederate soldier "while she remains unmarried," a soldier's widow who, after his death, has married again, and subsequently becomes a second time a widow, does not remain the widow of the first husband, so as to be entitled to a pension as such. State, Foucee *v.* Verner (S. Car.), 9 S. E. Rep. 113.

5. United States *v.* Skam, 5 Cr. C. C. 367.

6. Walton *v* Cotton, 19 How. (U. S.) 355.

statute, and though she still keeps her money at interest, using the income for her support as far as it will go. But if the mother has made a contract with a third person for her support during life she is not entitled to any pension from the date of such contract.[1]

Under a statute providing "that any person who is now receiving or shall hereafter receive a pension under a special act shall be entitled to receive, in addition thereto, a pension under the general law, unless the special act expressly states that the pension granted thereby is in addition to the pension which said person is entitled to receive under the general law," a double pension will be refused.[2]

So one who voluntarily surrenders his pension under a special act in order to receive a larger pension to which he becomes entitled on the passage of a general act, thereby surrenders his right to the former. He cannot have both.[3]

V. Proof Required to Sustain Pension Claims—False Evidence.— Before the name of any person is placed upon the pension roll the pension laws require that proof of the right to the pension shall be furnished by the applicant,[4] and certain penalties are imposed for false evidence, however produced.[5] The mere fact that there were false statements in an application for a pension, even if they were intentionally false, is not sufficient to invalidate the pension. It must appear further that they were material and necessary in

1. United States *v.* Purdy, 38 Fed. Rep. 902.

2. United States *v.* Teller, 107 U. S. 64.

Where a pension is provided for a widow for the services of her husband as an officer in the navy of the United States, by a special act of Congress, and a general act, passed the same day, provides a pension for widows of officers who have died in the naval service, such widow, having elected to take under the general law, and having taken under the same although under protest by receiving the same, did not prejudice her claim under the resolution of the same date, and cannot take under the special act. Decatur *v.* Paulding, 14 Pet. (U. S.) 497.

3. United States *v.* Burnett, 17 Otto (U. S.) 64.

4. United States Rev. Stat., § 4731, Pension Laws, 1890, p. 21.

As soon as practicable after the receipt of the claim for a pension, application is made by the Pension Office, in army cases, to the Adjutant General and the Surgeon General of the army, for a report of the applicant's service, and evidence in regard to the disability alleged, which may appear upon the rolls and other records in the possession of these officers. In navy cases application for such evidence is made to the proper bureau of the Navy Department. When the records of the War or Navy Departments do not furnish satisfactory evidence that the disability, on account of which the claim is made, originated in the service of the United States and in the line of duty, the claimant is required to furnish such evidence in accordance with the instructions given by the Commissioner of Pensions, compliance with which must be full and definite, and if the disability results in a wound or other injury, the nature and location of the wound or injury, time when, place where, and the manner in which it was received, whether in battle or otherwise, should be shown by the affidavit of some one who was a commissioned officer and had personal knowledge of the facts. Black's Army and Navy Pension Laws of the United States, p. 78; Pension Laws, 1890, p. 110.

5. United States Rev. Stat., § 4746.

Indictment.—In an indictment for presenting for payment a false and fraudulent claim for pension moneys, it is not sufficient to allege the offense in the words of the statute. The facts

order to procure the pension.[1] But it is an offense to transmit to the Commissioner of Pensions an affidavit which is false in the facts which it professes to narrate, though sworn to by a person who really existed, the person transmitting it knowing that it is false.[2] An indictment for making a false deposition with intent to enable another to obtain payment of a fraudulent pension claim need not allege that it was ever attempted to use the deposition, or that the claim had been presented.[3] Nor is it ground for quashing an indictment under the statute for aiding and procuring one to make a false affidavit for the purpose of procuring a pension, that the affidavit was in fact made before a proper officer, as the statute applies also to the offense of using a genuine instrument containing false statements, knowing them to be false with intent to defraud the United States.[4]

When the Commissioner of Pensions prescribes a regulation that "all evidence in a claim for pension other than the declaration may be verified before an officer duly authorized to administer oaths for general purposes," such a regulation is proper and a justice of the peace is an officer duly authorized to administer oaths within the purview of such regulation.[5]

VI. Payment of Pensions.—The several agents for the payments of pensions are required to prepare a quarterly voucher for every person whose pension is payable at his agency and transmit the same by mail directed to the address of the pensioner named in such voucher, who, on or after the time fixed by the statute, may execute and return the same to the agency at which it was prepared, and at which the pension of such person is due and payable. Upon the receipt of such voucher, properly executed, and the identity of the person being established, and proved in the manner prescribed by the Secretary of the Interior, the agent for the payment of pensions immediately draws his check on the proper assistant treasurer, or designated depositary of the United States, for the amount due such pensioner, payable to his order, and transmits the same by mail directed to the address of the pensioner entitled thereto.[6] If the pensioner dies before payment, but after the certificate is issued, the issuing of the certificate does not create a debt against the government which survives to the administrator of the pensioner.[7] If the vouchers are signed and the drafts issued in

constituting the offense should be set out with such certainty as to apprise the defendant of what is intended to be proved against him, to the end that he may prepare his defense and plead the judgment as a bar to any subsequent prosecution for the same offense. United States *v.* Goggin, 1 Fed. Rep. 49; 9 Biss. (U. S.) 269.

1. United States *v.* Purdy, 38 Fed. Rep. 902.

2. United States *v.* Statts, 8 How. (U. S.) 41.

3. United States *v.* Rhodes, 30 Fed. Rep. 439.

4. United States *v.* Gowdy, 37 Fed. Rep. 332.

5. United States *v.* Boggs, 31 Fed. Rep. 337.

6. U. S. Rev. Stat., § 4764. See also Pension Laws, 1890.

7. Donnelly *v.* United States, 17 Ct. of Cl. 105.

the usual course of business, the officials of the Pension Office are not guilty of negligence in failing to discover the death of the applicant prior to the issuing of the vouchers.[1] So where pension drafts are paid with a forged indorsement of the name of the applicant having notice on the back that the "payee's indorsement of this check must correspond to the signature on the voucher for which the check is given," the government can, on discovering the fraud, afterwards recover the amount from one who in good faith cashed the drafts and indorsed them to the United States without returning the draft to him.[2]

The navy pensions are paid from the navy fund of which the Secretary of the Navy is trustee.[3] Where the claimant applies to him for the pension[4] and he refuses to pay on the ground that he is not an "enlisted officer," it is held that the jurisdiction of the Secretary of the Navy is conclusive.[5] So *mandamus* will not lie to compel the Secretary of the Navy to pay money out of the fund where his discretion may be exercised.[6]

The Secretary of the Interior is authorized to strike from the pension roll the name of any person whenever it appears by proof satisfactory that such name was put upon such roll through false or fraudulent representations.[7] This authority extends to all persons, and may be exercised upon the evidence of an *ex parte* report of special agents, notwithstanding the first part of the section relates wholly to soldiers of the War of 1812.[8]

VII. Attorney's Fees.—Provision is made in pension laws for limiting the compensation of agents or attorneys for their service in procuring pensions.[9] In order that this provision be not inoperative, a penalty is provided for receiving greater fees than those prescribed.[10] The legal fee in a claim for a pension, or for a bounty land warrant under the statute passed July 4th, 1884, is

1. United States *v.* Onondaga Co. Sav. Bk., 39 Fed. Rep. 259.
2. United States *v.* Onondaga Co. Sav. Bk., 39 Fed. Rep. 259.
3. United States Rev. Stat., §§ 4753 and 4758.
4. Rev. St., § 4756.
5. Davidson *v.* United States, 20 Ct. of Cl. 298.
6. Decatur *v.* Paulding, 14 Pet. (U. S.) 497; United States *v.* Black, 12 U. S. 40.
7. Rev. Stat., § 4739. See Pension Laws, 1890, p. 21.
8. Harrison *v.* United States, 20 Ct. of Cl. 122, *citing* United States *v.* Moore, 95 U. S. 763; United States *v.* Pugh, 99 U. S. 265; Hahn *v.* United States, 107 U. S. 402.
9. Rev. Stat. (U. S.), § 5485; United States *v.* Brown, 40 Fed. Rep. 457.
10. United States *v.* Marks, 2 Abb. (U. S.) 531.

Statute.—An agent or attorney or any other person instrumental in procuring any claim for pension or bounty land, who shall directly or indirectly contract for, demand, or receive or retain any greater compensation for his services than is provided in the title pertaining to pensions, or who shall wrongfully withhold from the pensioner or claimant the whole or any part of the pension or claim allowed to such pensioner or claimant or the land warrant issued to any such claim, shall be guilty of a high misdemeanor, and upon conviction thereof, shall for every such offense be fined not exceeding five hundred dollars, or imprisonment at hard labor not exceeding two years, or both at the discretion of the court. United States Rev. Stat., § 5485.

Enforcement of Statute.—The Federal statute limiting the fee recovera-

twenty-five dollars on contract; otherwise ten dollars payable in both cases by the United States pension agent upon the allowance of the claim.[1]

It is a violation of the statute which forbids any agent or attorney, or other person instrumental in prosecuting any claim for pension, directly or indirectly to contract for, demand, receive, or retain any greater compensation for his services than the legal fee. Any scheme or contrivance by which, under the guise of a loan, a mortgage, or a gift, or other dealing, the claim agent retains more than the legal fee, is a violation of the statute.[2] So evidence will be admitted to show that trickery was practiced to evade the statute,[3] but fraud or extortion is not, however, a necessary element in the offense.[4]

The statute does not, however, prohibit a charge in excess of the statutory fee for services in causing the removal of a charge for desertion,[5] nor does it forbid reimbursement for money advanced for the expenses incurred.[6] See EXTORTION, vol. 7, p. 593.

No claim agent or other person is entitled to receive any compensation for services in making application for arrears of pensions.[7] No more than the lawful fee can be recovered even upon a *quantum meruit*;[8] and if more has been paid it may be recovered[9] even though paid voluntarily and understandingly,[10] and no action can be maintained, even upon the promise of a third per-

ble for obtaining a pension is a beneficent one, and should be enforced by the courts for the protection of the soldier and his family, in such a manner as to accomplish the object intended. Hall *v.* Kimmer, 61 Mich. 269, 1 Am. St. Rep. 575.

Indictment.—An indictment following the language of section 5485, Rev. Stat. U. S., charging the accused with receiving an excessive fee for his services "in prosecuting a pension claim," sufficiently charges him with receiving the same "in a pension case;" the language setting forth the elements necessary to constitute the crime, and apprises the accused with reasonable certainty of the accusation against him. United States *v.* Wilson, 29 Fed. Rep. 286.

The indictment need not state how the accused was instrumental and what he did in procuring the pension. It is also unnecessary to state that the defendant "wilfully and wrongfully" did the act charged. United States *v.* Koch, 21 Fed. Rep. 873.

1. U. S. Rev. Stat. 5485.

The limitation as to pension fees, in U. S. Rev. Stat., § 5485, and Supp., § 602, does not apply to a claim under § 4718 for reimbursement out of an accrued pension by one who bore the expenses of the last sickness and burial of a pensioner, nor to the attorney of such claimant. United States *v.* Nicewonger, 20 Fed. Rep. 438.

2. United States *v.* Brown, 40 Fed. Rep. 457; United States *v.* Moyers, 15 Fed. Rep. 411.

3. United States *v.* Koch, 21 Fed. Rep. 73. See also United States *v.* Moyers, 15 Fed. Rep. 411; United States *v.* Rickman, 12 Fed. Rep. 486.

4. The offense of taking more than the statutory allowance is complete under U. S. Rev. Stats., § 5485, when more is demanded. United States *v.* Moore, 8 Fed. Rep. 686.

5. United States *v.* Snow, 2 Flipp. C. C. 1.

6. See Morgan *v.* Davis, 47 Vt. 610; Crane *v.* Linnues, 77 Me. 59; United States *v.* Hewitt, 11 Fed. Rep. 243.

7. United States Rev. St., § 4711. See St. Jan. 25, 1879, Ch. 23, § 4.

8. Morgan *v.* Davis, 47 Vt. 610.

9. Smith *v.* White, 17 Me. 332; 40 Am. Rep. 356; Hall *v.* Kimmer, 61 Mich. 269.

10. Ladd *v.* Barton, 64 N. H. 613.

son, for more than the statutory fee.[1]

VIII. Detaining Pension.—Under the constitutional authority "to raise and support armies," Congress is authorized to enact statutes making it an offense punishable in the national courts to detain from a military pensioner any portion of a sum collected in his behalf as his pension.[2] It is competent for Congress to protect the fund both before and after it reaches the hands of the pensioners; and to this end may declare the embezzlement, by a guardian, of money which came to his hands as pension money for his wards, to be a crime against the United States, and as such, punishable in the United States courts.[3] These statutory provisions are not confined to withholding pensions authorized by the statute under which they were granted. Withholding any pension is indictable.[4]

Any pledge, mortgage, sale, assignment, or transfer of any right, claim or interest in any pension which may be granted is void; and any person who so pledges or receives as a pledge, mortgage, sale, assignment or transfer of any right, claim or interest in the pension or pension certificate which may be granted, or who holds the same as collateral security for any debt or promise, is guilty of a misdemeanor and liable to a penalty under the statute.[5] Under this statute a verbal promise by a pension

1. Wolcott *v.* Frissel, 134 Mass. 1.

2. United States *v.* Fairchilds, 1 Abb. (U. S.) 74; United States *v.* Marks, 2 Abb. (U. S.) 531.

3. United States *v.* Hall, 8 Otto (U. S.) 343.

4. United States *v.* Chaffee, 4 Ben. (U. S.) 330.

Compare United States *v.* Marks, 2 Abb. (U. S.) 531.

5. By the construction of the act of July 29, 1848, and of other acts of Congress, a widow to whom a pension has been granted for the services of her husband cannot pledge the certificate by anticipation to an agent employed to obtain the pension to secure to him a compensation for his services. Such a pledge, no matter to whom made, or for what purpose, is wholly void. Payne *v.* Woodhull, 4 Duer (N. Y.) 169.

An agreement between a widow of a soldier of the Revolution entitled to a pension under the act of Congress of 1848, ch. 120, and an agent, that the latter was to receive a certain part of the pension money for his services in obtaining it, is void, and money received under such an agreement can be recovered by the pensioner in an action of assumpsit. Powell *v.* Jennings, 3 Jones (N. Car.) 547.

But an instrument executed by H reciting that he is a pensioner of the United States, and is entitled to an addition to his pension under the act of June, 1832, and that J has undertaken, at his request and on his behalf to protect his claim to such increased pension, and promising and agreeing in consideration thereof that, in case J shall obtain such additional allowance or increase of pension, he shall receive for his services in obtaining same, one-third of the amount of such increase, etc., is held not to be a transfer. Jukur *v.* Hooker, 19 Barb. (N. Y.) 435.

Proof of Violation.—In order to convict under the U. S. Rev. St., § 4745, imposing a penalty for wrongfully withholding a pension, it must be shown by the evidence—

1st. That the person from whom it is alleged that the whole or any part of a pension is wrongfully withheld is a pensioner of the United States.

2nd. That the amount alleged to be wrongfully withheld is the whole or part of a pension or claim allowed and due such pensioner or claimant.

3rd. That the person charged with wrongfully withholding was an agent or an attorney of the pensioner, instrumental in prosecuting the pensioner's claim for pension, or, if not an agent

claimant to pay a debt out of his pension money is not a "pledge;"[1] nor is a gift by a pensioner to his wife of a check, received in settlement of a pension, such a transfer as the statute declares void, though the money be still in "course of transmission" and so exempt from execution.[2] The enactment as to "wrongfully withholding," is not limited to pension agents;[3] although not carried into the Revised Statutes, it is still in force as to the prohibition of the retention by claim agents of soldiers' discharges.[4]

IX. Exemption of Pension Money.—It is provided that "No sum of money due or to become due to any pensioner shall be liable to attachment, levy, or seizure by or under any legal or equitable process whatever, whether the same remains with the pension office, or with any officer or agent thereof, or is in course of transmission to the pensioner entitled thereto, but shall inure wholly to the benefit of such pensioner.[5] The object of this statute is to insure the actual reception of the pension by the person entitled to it,[6] and the protection extends so long as the money remains in the Pension Office or its agencies, or is in course of transmission to the pensioner. When the money is actually in the posession of the pensioner the protection is gone.[7] It is not, therefore, exempt after the pensioner deposits the same to his

or an attorney, was a person through whose instrumentality the claim was prosecuted.

4th. That the whole or part of the pension claim allowed and due such pensioner or claimant, was wrongfully withheld from the pensioner or claimant, by such agent or attorney or other person instrumental in procuring the claim for pension. United States *v.* Howard, 7 Biss. (U. S.) 56.

A person indicted for wrongfully withholding a pension cannot be allowed to show that the person to whom the Pension Office has allowed the pension as due was not entitled to it. United States *v.* Schindler, 18 Blatchf. (U. S.) 227.

Nor is parol evidence that the person from whom the defendant withholds the money is a pensioner of the United States admissible on an indictment under such statute. Nor are the entries in the local pension agent's book copied from the pensioner's certificate admissible to prove the fact; nor can it be shown by parol that the checks received were for pensions. United States *v.* Scott, 25 Fed. Rep. 470.

1. Crane *v.* Linneus, 77 Me. 59.

2. Rev. Stat. U. S., § 4747; Farmer *v.* Turner, 64 Iowa 691.

3. Rev. Stat. 5485; United States *v.* Chandler, 18 Blatchf. (U. S.) 227; 10 Fed. Rep. 547.

4. United States *v.* Webster, 21 Fed. Rep. 187.

5. U. S. Rev. Stat., § 4747.

6. Friend *v.* Garcelon, 77 Me. 25; 52 Am. Rep. 739.

7. Sims *v.* Walshal (Ky.), 7 S. W. Rep. 537; Robbin *v.* Walker, 82 Ky. 60; Roselle *v.* Rhodes, 116 Pa. St. 129; Crane *v.* Linneus, 17 Me. 59; Friend *v.* Garcelon, 77 Me. 25; Triplett *v.* Graham, 58 Iowa 135.

In Jardain *v.* Fairton Saving Fund Assoc., 44 N. J. L. 376, the same conclusion was reached, where it is said by the court: "The fund is not placed in the hands of a pensioner as a trust, but it is to enure wholly to his benefit. When it comes to him in hand or personal control, it is his money as effectually and for all purposes as the proceeds of his work or labor would be, and whether he expends it in new contracts, or it be taken to pay the consideration due from him for those of the past, it equally enures to his benefit." In Spelman *v.* Aldrich, 126 Mass. 113, it was held that "even if, by the laws of the United States, the pension was exempt from attachment while it remained in the form of a pension check,

credit in the bank,[1] or where the attorney, with the consent of the pensioner, deposits the money due him to the credit of the pensioner's wife,[2] nor when the pensioner sells the pension draft to the bank, and is credited in a general account with the proceeds, and portions of the same are from time to time checked out by him.[3]

This exemption is extended still further by statutes in some of the States. Thus, in *Iowa* it is provided that "All money received by any person resident of the State as a pension from the United States government, whether the same shall be in the actual possession of such pensioner or deposited, loaned, or invested by him, shall be exempted from execution, or attachment, or seizure by or under any legal process whatever, whether such pensioner shall be the head of a family or not." The homestead of any such pensioner, whether the head of a family or not, purchased and paid for with any such pension money, or the proceeds from an accumulation of such pension money, is also exempted.[4] See EXECUTIONS, vol. 7, p. 141.

the exemption ceased after the money was drawn upon the check."

Rev. St. U. S., § 4747, does not protect pension money which has actually been received by a pensioner from the government, and by him placed in the hands of a third person for safe-keeping. Rozelle *v.* Rhodes (Pa.), 9 Atl. Rep. 160.

1. Jardain *v.* Fairton Sav. Fund Assoc., 44 N. J. L. 376; Webb *v.* Holt, 57 Iowa 712; Cranz *v.* White, 27 Kan. 319; Martin *v.* Hurlburt, 60 Vt. 364.

And in *Vermont* a credit to a United States pensioner arising from the deposit of a pension check, or the money derived therefrom, is not exempt from trustee process under R. L. Vermont, § 1076, which exempts credits due for the sale of exempted property. Martin *v.* Hurlburt & Rutland Sav. Bank (Vt.), 14 Atl. Rep. 649.

2. Spellman *v.* Aldrich, 126 Mass. 113.

3. Cranz *v.* White, 27 Kan. 319; 41 Am. Rep. 408.

Pension Money Received and Invested.—Land purchased in her own name by a wife, to whom her husband gave a check for pension money, which she collected and invested in the real estate, is exempt from seizure for his debts, under U. S. Rev. Stat., § 4747, providing that pension money "shall enure wholly to the benefit of such pensioner." Holmes *v.* Taladay, 125 Pa. St. 133.

But in *Kentucky*, land in which a pensioner has invested his pension money, is not exempt from seizure for his debts. *Overruling* Eckert *v.* McKee, 9 Bush (Ky.) 355; Robin *v.* Walker, 82 Ky. 60. See EXECUTIONS, vol. 7, p. 141.

Where a check for pension money has been received by a pensioner, and the money obtained thereon given to his sons, who purchased land therewith, it is held that such land is not exempt from execution upon the judgment against the pensioner, obtained prior to the gift.

And where lands conveyed to a wife are paid for by a third person with the proceeds of the check made payable to the husband for pension money and indorsed by him, the transaction is a voluntary conveyance and the land is liable for the husband's debts. Johnson *v.* Elkins (Ky.), 13 S. W. Rep. 448.

4. Act 20 Gen. Assembly Iowa, ch. 23, § 1; Diamond *v.* Palmer (Iowa), 44 N. W. Rep. 819.

It exempts in the widow's hands, all personal property "which in his hands, as the head of the family, would be exempt from execution." Perkins *v.* Hinckley, 71 Iowa 499. But these laws have no application to the money of a pensioner who dies before their enactment. Baugh *v.* Barrett, 69 Iowa 495.

In *New York*, under a section of the code providing that a pension granted by the United States for military services is exempt from seizure for nonpayment of taxes or any other legal

PENT ROAD.—See note 1.

PEOPLE—(See also STATE; SOVEREIGN).—The entire body of the inhabitants of a state or nation, taken collectively, in their capacity of sovereign.[2]

proceeding, it was held that money deposited in the savings bank on interest was exempt from execution. Stockwell *v.* National Bank of Malone, 36 Hun (N. Y.) 583; Burgett *v.* Fanchett, 35 Hun (N. Y.) 647.

So the home of an ex-soldier of the United States, purchased with the proceeds of a pension, is exempt from execution for his debts, under Code Civ. Proc. of N. Y., § 1393, exempting pensions granted by the United States for military services. Yates County National Bank *v.* Carpenter (N. Y.), 23 N. E. Rep. 1108.

After the death of the pensioner, the pension goes to his widow and cannot be taken by the creditors of his estate. Hodge *v.* Learning, 2 Dem. (N. Y.) 553. The pension money, however, is not exempted, after the pensioner's death, from liability for his debts in favor of his descendants, other than a family for whom the pensioner provided. *Re* Wians, 5 Dem. (N. Y.) 138.

In *West Virginia*, land held for the use of the wife of a pensioner, bought with the proceeds of pension drafts, was held not liable for the payment of a judgment against the pensioner. Hisson *v.* Johnson, 27 W. Va. 644.

Accrued Pension.—Under an apparent misapprehension of the meaning of the term "accrued pension," it has been held that the executor of a deceased widow pensioner cannot be compelled to apply unexpected pension money, left by her, to the payment of her debts, she leaving children under sixteen years of age surviving her. Hodge *v.* Leaning, 2 Dem. (N. Y.) 553.

Exemption from Taxation.—In *Oregon*, pensions receivable from the United States are exempt from taxation. Oregon Rev. St., § 1038, p. 658.

1. Trespass *quare clausum* was brought for tearing down and destroying gates erected by the plaintiff on a highway running through his land. The road in question was laid out and established "as a pent road." The court, by KELLOG, J., said: "The plaintiff had a right to erect gates and bars on his own land unless this right was taken away by reason of the laying out and opening of a highway as a pent road over it. All pent roads are public highways, though called in the early statutes "private roads,"—that is to say; they may be used by all,—but they are not open highways. A road could not be a pent road if it was not shut up or closed at its terminal points; and the term "pent" (penned, shut up, confined, or closed,) is employed to distinguish such a road from an open road. To say that a pent road is an open road would be confounding the signification of the terms." And it was held that plaintiff should recover. Wolcott *v.* Whitcomb, 40 Vt. 41.

2. The simple word "people" is sometimes applied to a nation or a foreign power. United States *v.* Quincy, 6 Pet. (U. S.) 467.

The *United States* government proceeds directly from the people; is "ordained and established" in the name of the people. It is emphatically and truly a government of the people. In form and substance it emanates from them. Its powers are granted by them, and are to be exercised directly on them, and for their benefit. M'Culloch *v.* Maryland, 4 Wheat. (U. S.) 403, 404.

Under our system, the "people," who, in *England*, are called "subjects," constitute the sovereign. United States *v.* Lee, 106 U. S. 208.

Marine Insurance.—In a marine insurance, "people" means the people of all nations in their respective collective capacities, and not bodies of insurgents acting in opposition to their rulers. It means the governing power of the country; therefore if a corn vessel is seized and detained by a hungry mob, or a party of rebels, that is not a detention by "the people." Nesbitt *v.* Lushington, 4 T. R. 783. See also Rotch *v.* Edie, 6 T. R. 413; 1 Maude & P. 487.

See generally MARINE INSURANCE, vol. 9, pp. 375, 378.

Process.—When the constitution of a State directs that process shall run in the name of the State, a process in the name of the "people" will be held deficient, notwithstanding the form be

When the term "the people" is made use of in constitutional law or discussions, it is often the case that those only are intended who have a share in the government through being clothed with elective franchise. Thus, the people elect delegates to a constitutional convention, and determine by their votes whether the completed work of the convention shall or shall not be adopted; the people choose the officers under the constitution, and so on. For these and similiar purposes the electors, though constituting but a minority of the whole body of the cummunity, nevertheless act for all, and, as being for the time the representatives of sovereignty, they are considered and spoken of as the sovereign people. But in all the enumerations and guaranties of rights the whole people are intended, because the rights of all are equal, and are meant to be equally protected.[1]

PER—(See also PUR).—A Latin preposition meaning by, through. The word frequently introduces both Latin and English phrases having a technical meaning. For example of which see note 2.

statutory. Manville *v.* Battle Mountain etc. Co., 17 Fed. Rep. 126; Perkins *v.* State, 60 Ala. 9.

1. Cooley Const. 267; Blair *v.* Ridgely, 41 Mo. 176; Koehler *v.* Hill, 60 Iowa 568; Commonwealth *v.* Mellet, (Ky. 1889) 5 Ry. & Corp. L. J. 226.

The words "the people" must be determined by the connection. In some cases they refer to the qualified voters, in others to the State in its sovereign capacity. Black *v.* Trower, 79 Va. 126.

2. Curtiss *v.* Howell, 39 N. Y. 213.

Per Agreement.—The addition of the words "per agreement" to a bill of particulars for services, does not preclude from recovering the value of the services specified, although no agreement for the payment of a specified sum is proven. Robinson *v.* Weil, 45 N. Y. 810.

Per Capita.—When descendants take as individuals and not by right of representation (*per stirpes*) they are said to take *per capita*. Bouv. L. Dict. See also STATUTES OF DISTRIBUTION.

Per Curiam.—A phrase occasionally used in the reports, and meaning that the presiding judge or judges spoke to this or that effect. Brown's L. Dict.

Per Fraudem.—By fraud; as, a replication alleging fraud as to matter pleaded in discharge. And. L. Dict. See also PLEADING; FRAUD; vol. 8, p. 635.

Per Infortunium.—By misadventure. This phrase is used to distinguish that class of homicides in which a man in doing a lawful act, and without intent to hurt, kills another by mere misadventure. Abb. L. Dict. See also, HOMICIDE, vol. 9, p. 529.

Per Minas.—By threats. When a man is compelled to enter into a contract by threats or menaces, either for fear of loss of life or mayhem, he may avoid it afterwards. See also DURESS, vol. 6, p. 64; THREATS.

Per My et Per Tout.—This phrase is applied to joint tenants who are said to be seised *per my et per tout;* that is, by the half or moiety and by all; that is, they each have the entire possession as well of every parcel or piece of the land as of the whole, considered in the aggregate. Brown's L. Dict. See also, JOINT TENANTS, vol. 11, p. 1057.

Per Proc—Per Procuration.—By procuration; by letter of attorney. The expression "per procuration;" does not necessarily mean that the act is done under procuration; all that it means is this: "I am an agent, not acting on any authority of my own in the case, but authorized by my principal to enter into this contract." Smith *v.* M'Guire, 27 L. J. Ex. 468; 3 H. & N. 554.

A signature of a bill of exchange or promissory note, "by procuration, operates as notice that the agent has but a limited authority to sign, and the principal is only bound by such

PERAMBULATION—(See also PROCESSIONING).—A perambulation, or, as it might more correctly be called, a circumambulation, is the custom of going round the boundaries of a manor or parish, with witnesses, to determine and preserve recollection of its extent, and to see that no encroachments have been made upon it, and that the landmarks have not been taken away.[1]

PERCEPTION.—Taking into possession: thus perception of crops or profits is reducing them into possession.[2]

PERCH.—See note 3.

signature if the agent, in so signing, was acting within the actual limits of his authority." §§ 25, 89; English Bills of Ex. Act, 1882, codifying Stagg *v.* Elliott, 12 C. B., N. S. 373. See also AGENCY, vol. 1, p. 331; POWER OF ATTORNEY; POWERS.

Per Quod. — By which; whereby. In common-law pleading, introduces a conclusion of law upon facts previously stated. The rule that special damage must be particularly charged, is termed "laying the action with a *per quod.* And. L. Dict. See also PLEADING.

Per Quod Consortium Amisit. — By which he lost her company. This phrase was used in declarations in Latin in actions of trespass by a husband for an injury to his wife, introducing an averment of the loss of her society and assistance, for which he sought to recover special damage. Abb. L. Dict. See also HUSBAND AND WIFE, vol. 9, p. 789.

Per Quod Servitium Amisit. — By which he lost her (or his) service. This phrase was used in declarations in Latin in actions of trespass by a master for an injury to his servant, introducing an averment of the loss of service sustained by him, for which damages are sought. The phrase was also used as descriptive of this particular class of actions. The proceeding was the usual remedy of a father for the seduction of his daughter, on the theory of a loss by him of her services. To sustain such an action, some evidence, however slight, must be given of the relation of master and servant, and of a loss of service, or other special damage. See also SEDUCTION; MASTER AND SERVANT, vol. 14, p. 788.

Per Sample.—Declaration stated that defendant bargained for and bought of plaintiff a quantity of E. I. rice, according to the conditions of sale of the E. I. Company to be put up at the next E. I. Company's sale by the proprietors, if required, at a certain price there mentioned. The proof was, that, besides these conditions, the rice was sold per sample. This is no variance, the word "per sample" not being a description of the commodity sold, but a collateral engagement that it shall be of a particular quality. Parker *v.* Palmer, 4 B. & Ald. 387. See also IMPLIED WARRANTY, vol. 10, p. 165; SALES.

Per Se.—By itself; in itself considered. As an act of negligence *per se;* fraud *per se;* a nuisance *per se;* a thing *malum per se.* And. L. Dict.

Per Stirpes. — By roots; by the stocks; according to representation. Opposed, *per capita,* which see And. L. Dict.

Per Verba De Praesenti: By words in the present tense. *Per verba de futuro*: by words in the future tense. These two phrases are applied to different modes of contracting marriage; words importing a present assent to the marriage being deemed sufficient evidence of the contract at common law, while words importing an assent to a future marriage must be followed by consummation, to establish a valid marriage, even by the canon law; and did not even then meet the requirement of the common law. Abb. L. Dict. See also MARRIAGE, vol. 14, pp. 470, 512.

Per Year, in a contract, is equivalent to the word annually. Curtis *v.* Howell, 39 N. Y. 211.

1. Greenville *v.* Mason, 57 N. H. 392, *quoting* Hone's Year Book, p. 589.

2. Abb. L. Dict.

3. **Perch.** — A contract to build a church at so much per perch, will be construed to mean the statute perch of twenty-five feet, in the absence of any evidence upon its face

PERFECT; PERFECTING.—See note 1.

PERFORM; PERFORMANCE—(See also CONTRACTS, vol. 3, p. 823; PART PERFORMANCE; RESCISSION; SATISFACTION; SPECIFIC PERFORMANCE; TENDER).—Performance is, as the term implies, such a thorough fulfillment of a duty as puts an end to obligations by leaving nothing more to be done.[2]

PERILS OF THE SEA.—See MARINE INSURANCE, vol. 14, p. 375, note; SHIPPING; BILL OF LADING, vol. 2, p. 233.

PERIOD.—A stated and recurring interval of time; a round or series of years, by which time is measured. When used to designate an act to be done or to be begun, though its completion may take an uncertain time, it must mean the day when the thing commences, as the exportation of goods.[3]

that it was made with reference to some custom. Harris *v.* Rutledge, 19 Iowa 388.

1. The word "perfect" implies either moral, physical or mechanical perfection. Mallan *v.* Radloff 17 C. B., N. S. 601.

A perfect "machine" may mean a "perfected" invention; not a machine perfectly constructed, but so constructed as to embody all the essential elements of the invention, in a form that would make them practical and operative, so as to accomplish the result. American Hide etc. Co. *v.* American Tool etc. Co., 4 Fish. Pat. Cas. 298, 299. See generally, INVENTION, vol. 11, p. 780; PATENTS.

Where the vendor, selling goods which he knows to be designed by the vendee for a particular use, warrants them to be "perfect," this must be construed to mean that they are perfect for the use intended; and parol evidence of the vendor's knowledge of the intended use is admissible to explain such a warranty in writing. Roe *v.* Batcheldor, 41 Wis. 360.

A turnpike corporation by its charter, has authority to take gravel from the neighboring lands for "perfecting" the road. "Perfecting," as here used, is equivalent to finishing or completing, and the privilege does not extend to repairing the road. Whitenack *v.* Tunison, 16 N. J. L. 77.

Perfect Obligation.—A perfect external "obligation" confers the right of compulsion; a perfect "right" the right to compel those who refuse to fulfill the corresponding obligation. Aycock *v.* Martin, 37 Ga. 128; Vattel, Law of Nations, § 17. See also OBLIGATION, vol. 17, p. 2.

Perfect Title.—A perfect "title" means a title which is good in law and equity. Warner *v.* Middlesex Mut. Assur. Co., 21 Conn. 449. See also VENDOR AND PURCHASER.

2. Hare on Contracts, 269.

Performed is synonymous with fulfill. Ætna Ins. Co. *v.* Kittles, 81 Ind. 97.

Performed (in Statute of Frauds).—*Ex vi termini* must mean the complete performance or consummation of the work. Boydell *v.* Drummond, 11 East 156. See also FRAUDS, STATUTE OF, vol. 8, p. 685.

Performance and Satisfaction (Distinguished).—The distinction between "performance" and "satisfaction" is, that the former is the performance in specie of the agreement; the latter is, where the contracting party has done something in lieu of the thing contracted for. Johnson *v.* Collins, 20 Ala. 435.

3. People *v.* Leask, 67 N. Y. 528; Sampson *v.* Peaslee, 20 How. 579.

Maryland Acts 1867, ch. 367, authorized the board of police commissioners of Baltimore to order all drinking saloons to be closed "temporarily" whenever in their judgment public peace required it, and made it a misdemeanor to disobey such order "during such period as said board shall forbid." The board issued an order that drinking saloons "be so temporarily closed until further notice." *Held*, that the legislature had in no way exceeded its authority in conferring such

PERIODICAL—(See also PERIOD).—Recurring, made or to be made, after the lapse of a specified or regular interval of time; as, periodical allowances of money, payments of interest or of principal and interest.[1]

PERISHABLE GOODS.—See PERISHABLE PROPERTY.

PERISHABLE PROPERTY.—See CARRIERS OF GOODS, vol. 2, p. 853; LEGACIES AND DEVISES, vol. 13, p. 201; SHERIFFS SALES; SUPPLEMENTARY PROCEEDINGS.

PERJURY.—(See also AFFIDAVITS, vol. 1. p. 307; FALSE SWEARING, vol. 7, p. 793; OATH).

I. DEFINITION.—Perjury is an assertion, upon an oath duly administered in a judicial proceeding, before a competent court, of the truth of some matter of fact, material to the question depending in that proceeding, which assertion the asserter does not believe to be true when he makes it, or on which he knows himself to be ignorant.[2]

power upon the board of police commissioners, yet such board was authorized by the statute to close the drinking saloons only for a short and definite interval, and consequently the order to close them "until further notice" was void, and no indictment could be founded thereon. State *v.* Strauss, 49 Md. 288. See also PERIODICAL.

1. Anderson's L. Dict.

"Periodical payments," apportionable under the *English* Apportionment Act, 1870 (33 & 34 Vict., ch. 35, § 2), "must be payments occurring periodically, that is, at fixed times, from some antecedent obligation, and not at variable periods at the discretion of individuals." Jones *v.* Ogle, 42 L. J., Ch. 337; 8 Ch. 192. Therefore it was held that in that case that profits in a private trading partnership were not within the phrase.

A "periodical work," within the *English* Copyright Act, 1842 (5 & 6 Vict., ch. 45), is "a work that comes out from time to time and is miscellaneous in its articles." Brown *v.* Cooke, 16 L. J., C. H. 142. But a newspaper was held not a "periodical" within §§ 18, 19 of that act. Cox *v.* Land and Water Journal Co., L. R., 9 Eq. 324. But in Walter *v.* Howe, 17 Ch. D. 708; Cox *v.* Land etc. Co., it was not followed, and the "Times" newspaper was held to be a "periodical work" within the sections. See also NEWSPAPERS.

As to customs' duties on periodicals, see REVENUE LAWS.

2. This is Mr. Stephen's definition of perjury as it appears in his Digest of

the Criminal Law. He further adds: "In this definition, the word 'oath' includes every affirmation which any class of persons are by law permitted to make in place of an oath.

"The expression 'duly administered' means administered in a form binding on his conscience, to a witness legally called before them, by any court, judge, justice, officer, commissioner, arbitrator, or other person who, by the law for the time being in force, or by consent of the parties, has authority to hear, receive, and examine evidence.

"The fact that a person takes an oath in any particular form is a binding admission that he regards it as binding on his conscience; *citing* Ides *v.* Hoare, 2 B. & B. 232.

"The expression of 'judicial proceeding' means a proceeding which takes place in or under the authority of any court of justice, or which relates in any way to the administration of justice, or which legally ascertains any right or liability.

"The word 'fact' includes the fact that the witness holds any opinion or belief; *citing* Reg. *v.* Schlesinger, 10 Q. B. 670.

"The word 'material' means of such a nature as to affect in any way, directly or indirectly, the probability of anything to be determined by the proceeding, or the credit of any witness, and a fact may be material although evidence of its existence was improperly admitted." See Reg. *v.* Gibbon, L. & C. 109.

The following is Hawkins' definition: "Perjury, by the common law, seemeth to be a willful false oath, by one who, being lawfully required to depose the truth in any proceeding in a course of justice, swears absolutely in a matter of some consequence to the point in question, whether he be believed or not."1 Hawk. P. C. (Curw. ed.) 429.

Coke's definition is as follows: "Perjury is a crime committed when a lawful oath is ministered by any that hath authority, to any person, in any judicial proceeding, who sweareth absolutely and falsely in a matter material to the issue or cause in question, by their own act, or by the subornation of others." 3 Inst. 164. Blackstone's definition is the same in substance as Coke's. 4 Bl. Com. 137. The definitions in Russell on Crimes (2 Russ. Crimes 596) and in Bacon's Abridgment (title, Perjury) are similar. In Scotch law Hume defines perjury as the "judicial affirmation of falsehood upon oath." 1 Hume Crim. Law, (2d ed.) 360. Bishop's definition is thus: "Perjury is the willful giving, under oath, in a judicial proceeding or course of justice, of false testimony material to the issue or point of inquiry. 2 Bishop's Crim. Law, § 1015.

Greenleaf's definition (3 Greenleaf on Evidence, § 188) is as follows: "The crime, as described in the common law, is committed when a lawful oath is administered, in some judicial proceedings or due course of justice, to a person who swears willfully, absolutely and falsely, in a matter material to the issue or point in question."

See also Commonwealth *v.* Powell, 2 Metc. (Ky.) 10; Cothran *v.* State, 39 Miss. 541; Hood *v.* State, 44 Ala. 86.

In the Appendix to Stephen's Digest of Criminal Law is a curious and interesting note on the historical features of the law of perjury-features little understood. Mr. Stephen says that there are a few references to the offense in the laws of the Anglo-Saxon kings, but that these are very vague and general: the kind of offense now known as perjury differing wholly from the perjury there mentioned. Perjury in those times appeared to have been not so much a lie told about a specific matter of fact in the witness box, as a false oath taken in a case in which the matter at issue was decided by the oaths of the persons interested and their compurgators. At that time and for several centuries afterward the only perjury of which the common law took notice was the perjury of jurors, and this was punished not as a substantial offense, but as an incidental result of the process called "attaint," the main object of which was to set aside a false verdict in certain kinds of actions. The punishment of jurors, if their verdict was set aside on the ground of perjury was very severe. Mr. Stephen thinks that the Year Books contain no reference to the offense of perjury. There is no such title in Broke's Abridgment. There is one case in Fitzherbert. Perjury was regarded as a spiritual offense, of course. The first statutory reference to perjury was in the statute 3 Hen. VII, ch. 1, which established, or, at all events, greatly strengthened and extended the power of the court of Star Chamber. By the statute 32 Hen. VIII, ch. 9, § 3, temporary penalties were first imposed

II. Essential Elements of Perjury.—1. The Oath, Its Requisites and Form.—To constitute a valid oath, for the falsity of which perjury will lie, there must be an unequivocal and present act in some form in the presence of an officer authorized to administer oaths, by which the affiant consciously takes upon himself the obligation of an oath.[1] The form of the oath is immaterial, though it should be solemnly administered in such a way as to bind the conscience of him who takes it and to accord with his religious belief.

upon the offense of subornation of perjury; perjury itself, however, being left unpunished. Then followed 5 Eliz., ch. 9, which punished subornation of perjury and also perjury. This account of the state of the law in the sixteenth century is supported by Devonport *v.* Sympson, Cro. Eliz. 520. The law as it now exists in England is fully recognized in many acts of Parliament in many cases, and is in daily use; but it rests, Mr. Stephen says, simply upon a usurpation of the court of Star Chamber under the statute 3 Hen. VII, ch. 1.

1. Coke defines an oath as "an affirmation or denial by any Christian of anything lawful and honest, before one or more that have authority to give the same, for advancement of truth and right, calling Almighty God to witness that his testimony is true." This definition does not accord fully with the modern view of the subject. Bishop (2 Criminal Law, § 1018) amends it thus: "An oath is a solemn asseveration of the truth of a thing, made by a person under the sanction of his religion, appealing to the Supreme Being, in the presence of one having the civil authority to administer it."

See O'Reiley *v.* People, 86 N. Y. 154; State *v.* Keene, 26 Me. 33.

Where, on the trial of an indictment for perjury, the evidence showed a verbal statement before a commissioner, charging B with violating the revenue law, and the commissioner reduced his statement to writing, beginning with the words, M, "being duly sworn," etc., and ending with the jurat, and on being told, "If you swear to this statement, put your mark here," defendant made his mark, it was held, that this was an oath. United States *v.* Mallard, 40 Fed. Rep. 151.

On the trial of an indictment for making a false affidavit, it was held that the want of signature was immaterial, the signature being no part of the declaration, but merely authenticating it. Commwealth *v.* Carel, 105 Mass. 582.

The English authorities usually speak of a corporal oath, meaning simply an oath taken on the Bible and by touching it. It has never been held necessary, however, that the indictment should aver this, it being enough to aver that the witness was sworn upon the Holy Gospels to speak the truth, etc. Atcheson *v.* Everitt, 1 Cowp. 383; 1 Chitty's Crim. Law 616. In State *v.* Farrow, 10 Rich. (S. Car.) 165 and Dodge *v.* State, 23 N. J. L. 455, it was held sufficient to allege that the accused was "duly sworn," without alleging the mode of administering the oath and from Rex *v.* MacArthur, Peake 155, it would seem that if the indictment stated that the accused was sworn on the Gospels, and the proof was that he was sworn otherwise, the variance would be fatal. But see Rex *v.* Rowley, R. & M., N. P. 302, to the point that proof that the witness was sworn generally would support the allegation. It has been held that the words, "corporal oath" and "solemn oath" are synonymous, and that an oath taken with the uplifted hand was described properly by either term. Jackson *v.* State, 1 Ind. 184; State *v.* Norris, 9 N. H. 96. Even though the statute prescribes the form of the oath, a departure in form merely and not in substance is immaterial. State *v.* Dayton, 23 N. J. L. 49; s. c., 53 Am. Dec. 270, Sharp *v.* Wilhite, 2 Humph. (Tenn.) 434; State *v.* Owen, 72 N. Car. 605; State *v.* Pile, 5 Ala. 72; Faith *v.* State, 32 Tex. 373. And see also Tuttle *v.* People, 36 N. Y. 431; State *v.* Keene, 26 Me. 33; State *v.* Whisenhurst, 2 Hawks (N. Car.) 458; Reg. *v.* Southwood, 1 F. & F. 356. Johnson *v.* State, 76 Ga. 790; United States *v.* Baer, 18 Blatchf. (U. S.) 493; Commonwealth *v.* Smith, 11 Allen (Mass.) 252; State *v.* Gates, 17 N. H. 373; State *v.* Green, 24 Ark. 591. And where a

An oath taken voluntarily without the authority of court or statute is extra-judicial and may not be made the foundation of an indictment for perjury.[1] A promissory or official oath, *i. e.*, one taken in qualifying for office, cannot, though false, be the subject of an indictment for perjury.[2] There may be perjury, though the oath is taken without the compulsion of a subpœna,[3] or where an incompetent witness is erroneously sworn,[4] or where a witness in testifying waived a constitutional immunity as to giving testimony against himself.[5]

The effect of an affirmation is the same as regards perjury as that of an oath, the affirmation being designed by statute to meet the conscientious scruples of Quakers, Moravians, and such sects as deem it wrong to take an oath.

2. Court, Tribunal, or Officer Administering Oath.—To constitute perjury the oath must have been administered by a tribunal or officer having authority or jurisdiction in the premises.[6] If the oath was taken before a court, there must have been jurisdiction of the subject matter of the proceeding; otherwise, the oath is extra-judicial.[7]

witness takes an oath without objecting to the manner in which it is offered and swears falsely he is guilty of perjury. State *v.* Whisenhurst, 2 Hawks (N. Car.) 458.

If, however, the substance of the statute is not followed there is no perjury. Ashburn *v.* State, 15 Ga. 246.

So where the sworn disclosure in trustee process is required by the statute to be in writing, an indictment for perjury will not lie if the disclosure is oral. State *v.* Trask, 42 Vt. 152.

Though the testimony taken at an examining trial should be reduced to writing, as directed by the Texas Code of Procedure, yet perjury may be assigned upon oral testimony taken, but not reduced to writing in such trial. Covey *v.* State, 23 Tex. App. 388.

1. People *v.* Travis, 1 Buffalo N. Y. Super. Ct. 545; United States *v.* Babcock, 4 McLean (U. S.) 115; State *v.* McCarthy, 41 Minn. 59. And see Pegram *v.* Styron, 1 Bailey (S. Car.) 595; Van Steenbergh *v.* Kortz, 10 Johns. (N. Y.) 167; Lamden *v.* State, 5 Humph. (Tenn.) 83.

2. United States *v.* Glover, 4 Cranch (C. C.) 190.

In *Missouri*, under the constitution, a violation of the oath of office by a member of the legislature is perjury.

3. Commonwealth *v.* Knight, 12 Mass. 274; s. c., 7 Am. Dec. 72.

4. State *v.* Molier, 1 Dev. (N. Car.) 263; Sharp *v.* Wilhite, 2 Humph. (Tenn.) 434; Haley *v.* McPhearson, 3 Humph. (Tenn.) 104; People *v.* Bowe, 34 Hun (N. Y.) 528; Patrick *v.* Smoke. 3 Strobh. (S. Car.) 147; Chamberlain *v.* People, 23 N. Y. 85; s. c., 80 Am. Dec. 255; Montgomery *v.* State, 10 Ohio 220; Shaffer *v.* Kintzer, 1 Binn. (Pa.) 542; s. c., 2 Am. Dec. 488; Van Steenbergh, *v.* Kortz, 10 Johns. (N. Y.) 167; Rex *v.* Dummer, 1 Salk. 374.

5. Mackin *v.* People, 115 Ill. 312; s. c., 56 Am. Rep. 167; Mattingly *v.* State, 8 Tex. App. 345; State *v.* Maxwell, 28 La. Ann. 361.

6. Rex *v.* Wood, 2 Russ. Crimes (3d. Eng. ed.) 632; McGragor *v.* State, 1 Ind. 232; State *v.* McCroskey, 3 McCord (S. Car.) 308; Rex *v.* Hanks, 3 Car. & P. 419; Morrell *v.* People, 32 Ill. 499; Commonwealth *v.* Hughes, 5 Allen (Mass.) 499; State *v.* Jenkins, 26 S. Car. 121; Renew *v.* State, 79 Ga. 162; State *v.* Wimberly (La. 1888), 4 S. E. Rep. 161; Territory *v.* Anderson (Idaho 1889), 21 Pac. Rep. 417; Lavender *v.* State (Ga. 1890), 11 S. E. Rep. 861; Anderson *v.* State, 24 Tex. App. 715; State *v.* Wilson, 87 Tenn. 693.

7. State *v.* Alexander, 4 Hawks (N. Car.) 182; State *v.* Hayward, 1 Nott & M. (S. Car.) 546; State *v.* M'Croskey, 3 McCord (S. Car.) 308; State *v.* Wyatt, 2 Hayw. (N. Car.) 56; Commonwealth *v.* White, 8 Pick. (Mass.) 453; State *v.* Furlong, 26 Me. 69; Jackson *v.* Humphrey, 1 Johns. (N. Y.) 498; Boling *v.* Luther, 2 Tayl. (N. Car.)

It is essential that the oath should have been administered by a person authorized by law to administer an oath.[1]

An oath administered by the clerk of a court in open court, and under the direction of the court, is an oath administered by the court.[2] But while this is so and while all presumptions are in favor of the authority of the officer administering the oath, even where it is not administered in the presence of the court, it may be shown by the defendant, upon the trial of the indictment for perjury, that the officer was not an officer *de jure*.[3]

3. Nature of Proceeding Wherein Oath Is Administered.—(*a*) IN GENERAL.—In regard to the character of the proceeding in which the oath is taken, it may be stated, as the general principle, that wherever an oath is required in the regular administration of justice or of civil government under the general laws of the land, the crime of perjury may be committed.[4]

202; Weston *v.* Lumley, 33 Ind. 486; Pankey *v.* People, 2 Ill. 80; Montgomery *v.* State, 10 Ohio 220; State *v.* Lavalley, 9 Mo. 824.

1. Morrell *v.* People, 32 Ill. 499; McGragor *v.* State, 1 Ind. 232; State *v.* Dayton, 23 N. J. L. 49; s. c., 53 Am. Dec. 270; Biggerstaff *v.* Commonwealth, 11 Bush (Ky.) 169.

2. Rowland *v.* Thompson, 65 N. Car. 110; State *v.* Knight, 84 N. Car. 793; Stephens *v.* State, 1 Swan (Tenn.) 157; Oaks *v.* Rodgers, 48 Cal. 197; Staight *v.* State, 39 Ohio St. 498.

3. It was held in the leading case of Rex *v.* Vereist, 3 Camp. 432, where the person administering the oath had been an officer *de facto* for twenty years, that case has been followed repeatedly in *England* and in the *United States*. Reg. *v.* Roberts, 14 Cox (C. C.) 101; R. *v.* Newton, 1 C. & K. 469; State *v.* Hayward, 1 Nott & M. (S. Car.) 546; Muir *v.* State, 8 Blackf. (Ind.) 154; State *v.* Hascall, 6 N. H. 352; Biggerstaff *v.* Commonwealth, 11 Bush (Ky.) 169; Lambert *v.* People, 76 N. Y. 220.

A non-judicial oath taken before a person unauthorized to administer it cannot be made the subject of an assignment of perjury, where the oath was administered by a judge of election who had not qualified by taking the prescribed oath of office. Biggerstaff *v.* Commonwealth, 11 Bush (Ky.) 199. Or by a township assessor before he was authorized to enter upon the duties of his office. State *v.* Phippen, 62 Iowa 54. See also State *v.* Cannon, 79 Mo. 343. Or by a township assessor outside of his territorial jurisdiction, Van Dusen *v.* People, 78 Ill. 645. Or by a notary public, who, at the time of administering the oath, was a resident of State other than that in which he was acting. Lambert *v.* People, 76 N. Y. 220. Or by a justice of the peace in a case where he had no authority by law to administer an oath as in a cororner's inquest. State *v.* Knight, 84 N. Car. 789. Or by a justice acting under a *prima facie* void appointment. People *v.* Albertson, 8 How. Pr. (N. Y.) 363. Or by a deputy clerk of a circuit court in swearing to an answer in chancery, where a formal appointment as deputy in writing according to the requirements of the statute had not been made. Muir *v.* State, 8 Blackf. (Ind.) 154.

4. 3 Greenleaf on Ev., § 190. State *v.* Hayward, 1 Nott & M. (S. Car.) 546; State *v.* Wyatt, 2 Hayw. (N. Car.) 56; Commonwealth *v.* White, 8 Pick. (Mass.) 453; State *v.* Furlong, 26 Me. 69; Boling *v.* Luther, N. Car. Term. R. 202; Pankey *v.* People, 2 Ill. 80; Montgomery *v.* State, 10 Ohio 220; Clark *v.* Ellis, 2 Blackf. (Ind.) 8; Weston *v.* Lumley, 33 Ind. 486.

One may commit perjury in a judicial proceeding by falsely swearing to an answer in chancery. Reg. *v.* Yates, C. & M. 132. Though not where the bill does not call for an answer under oath. Silver *v.* State, 17 Ohio 365. Nor where the answer denies a promise absolutely void under the statute of frauds. Rex *v.* Benesech, Peake's Add. Cas. 93; Reg *v.* Dunston, R. & M. 109. Nor where the general manager of a corporation, not himself made a respondent in the bill, answers in a matter not affecting the issue or strengthening the answer. Beecher *v.* Anderson, 45 Mich. 543.

A party filing a bill for an injunction, and making an affidavit of matters material to it, is indictable for perjury committed in that affidavit, though no motion was ever made for the injunction. Rex *v.* White, M. & M. 271.

Falsely swearing as to one's qualification to go bail for another is perjury. Commonwealth *v.* Hughes, 5 Allen (Mass.) 499; Stratton *v.* People, 20 Hun (N. Y.) 288; Commonwealth *v.* Rutland, 119 Mass. 317.

But falsely swearing to an affidavit accompanying exceptions to the sufficiency of bail is not perjury, in the absence of any law requiring such exceptions to be sworn to. Linn *v.* Commonwealth, 96 Pa. St. 285.

Perjury may be assigned on an oath administered by a justice of the peace in a matter submitted to arbitration by a rule of court with consent of the parties. State *v.* Stephenson, 4 M'Cord (S. Car.) 165. But not in case of a parol submission to arbitrators not made a rule of court. Mahan *v.* Berry, 5 Mo. 21.

An order of reference filed *nunc pro tunc* will not relate back so as to give an extra judicial oath, the effect of one legally administered. Bonner *v.* McPhail, 31 Barb. (N. Y.) 106.

In an arbitration under *Ohio* Rev. St., §§ 5601, 5613, an oath administered by a notary public is extra judicial, as the statute requires the oaths in such proceedings to be administered by a judge or justice of the peace. State *v.* Jackson, 36 Ohio St. 281.

Perjury may be assigned on the oath taken by a juror on his *voir dire.* Hilliard *v.* State, 14 Lea (Tenn.) 648; State *v.* Wall, 9 Yerg. (Tenn.) 347. On an affidavit to procure a search warrant, charging a felony though no particular person. Carpenter *v.* State, 4 How. (Miss.) 163; s. c., 34 Am. Dec. 116. On the oath to a complaint made to commence a prosecution. Langboro *v.* State, 9 Tex. App. 283; Pennaman *v.* State, 58 Ga. 336; Hoch *v.* People, 3 Mich. 552.

But not on the oath to a complaint under the statutory requirement jurisdiction. Johnson *v.* State, 58 Ga. 397. On the oath to a false statement of material matter in an affidavit to procure a writ of *habeas corpus.* White *v.* State, 1 Smed. & M. (Miss.) 149.

To swear falsely before a grand jury is perjury. State *v.* Offutt, 4 Blackf. (Ind.) 335; Pipes *v.* State, 26 Tex. App. 318; People *v.* Greenwell, 5 Utah 112. And see Commonwealth *v.* Parker, 2 Cush. (Mass.) 212. But not if the answer is to an immaterial question put in the course of a general inquisitorial investigation by the grand jury directed to no particular end. Banks *v.* State, 78 Ala. 14. To swear falsely to an affidavit made to obtain a *certiorari* is perjury. Pratt *v.* Price, 11 Wend. (N. Y.) 127.

To swear falsely to a material point in an affidavit used in a motion for the continuance of a cause is perjury. State *v.* Johnson, 7 Blackf. (Ind.) 49; State *v.* Flagg, 27 Ind. 24; State *v.* Shupe, 16 Iowa 36; s. c., 85 Am. Dec. 485. Or to an affidavit of merits. McDonnell *v.* Olwell, 17 Ill. 375. To an affidavit amounting to a plea of *non est factum* to a note in proceedings before a justice of the peace. State *v.* Roberts, 11 Humph. (Tenn.) 539.

It seems that taking a false oath before a court martial is perjury at common law. Reg. *v.* Heane, 9 Cox C. C. 433.

An affidavit not connected with a judicial proceeding, though capable of being used in a motion during the pendency of a suit, cannot be made the subject of an assignment of perjury. People *v.* Fox, 25 Mich. 492.

In *Ex parte* McCarthy, 29 Cal. 395, it was adjudged that perjury might be committed in the course of a legislative investigation. It has been held perjury to swear falsely in procuring a marriage license. Reg. *v.* Barnes, 10 Cox C. C. 539; Call *v.* State, 20 Ohio St. 330; Warwick *v.* State, 25 Ohio St. 21. Perjury may be assigned on false swearing in depositions taken for foreign use. Commonwealth *v.* Smith, 11 Allen (Mass.) 243; Stewart *v.* State, 22 Ohio St. 477. And see generally relative to the various proceedings in relation to which perjury may be committed, Reg. *v.* Greenland, L. R., 1 C. C. 65; Reg. *v.* Tomlinson, L. R., 1 C. C. 49; 10 Cox C. C. 332; Reg *v.* Proud, L. R., 1 C. C. 71; 10 Cox C. C. 121; 10 Cox C. C. 455; Reg. *v.* Berry, Bell C. C. 46; 8 Cox C. C. 121; People *v.* Travis, 4 Parker Cr. (N. Y.) 213; Harris *v.* People, 6 Thomp. & C. (N. Y.) 206; 4 Hun (N. Y.) 1.

It was held by a divided court in an early *Connecticut* case that a false oath before an ecclesiastical council, in a course of discipline, would support an

False swearing elsewhere than in the course of a judicial proceeding may constitute a punishable common law offense, though not perjury; as, for example, the making of a false affidavit.[1]

(*b*) STATUTORY PROCEEDINGS.—Whether the oath be taken in a judicial proceeding before a court of common law, or acting under a statute, it is equally an oath taken in a judicial proceeding.[2]

indictment for perjury. Chapman *v.* Gillett, 2 Conn. 40. But it is doubtful whether this would be accepted as law to-day in the States of the Union.

Under the *South Carolina* statute, providing that whoever shall willfully and knowingly swear falsely in taking any oath required by law, it is not essential that the proceeding be a judicial proceeding. State *v.* Byrd, 28 S. Car. 18.

In Cordway *v.* State, 25 Tex. App. 405, it was held that where one accused of two murders was brought back for one of them under extradition proceedings, and indicted and tried for the other, false swearing on the trial constituted perjury.

In O'Bryan *v.* State, 27 Tex. App. 339, it was held that a public school teacher was guilty of perjury in falsely swearing to a statement required by law on procuring pay for his services.

In People *v.* McCaffrey, 75 Mich. 115, it was adjudged that perjury might be assigned upon the oath to a bill in a divorce suit.

1. Rex *v.* De Beauvoir, 7 Car. &. P. 17; *Ex parte* Overton, 2 Rose 257; Rex *v.* O'Brian, 2 Strange 1144. And see Musgrave *v.* Medex, 19 Ves. 652; O'Mealy *v.* Newell, 8 East. 364; Calliand *v.* Vaughan, 1 B. & P. 210.

It was held in the English case of Reg. *v.* Chapman, 1 Den. C. C. 432, that to take a false oath before a surrogate to induce the granting of a marriage certificate was a misdemeanor, though not perjury. As a Texas county clerk, while having authority to administer oaths, is not required, upon an application for a marriage license, to take an affidavit as to the age of the parties, the making of a false affidavit upon that subject will support an assignment for false swearing, but not for perjury. Davidson *v.* State, 22 Tex. App. 372; Steber *v.* State, 23 Tex. App. 176. So it was held in the English case of Reg. *v.* Hodgkins, L. R., 1 C. C. 212, that to make a false affidavit under the Bills of Sale acts to procure the registry of a bill of sale was a common law misdemeanor, though not perjury.

But in Tuttle *v.* People, 36 N. Y. 431, it was adjudged to be perjury falsely to swear that the affiant was a subscribing witness to a deed.

See for a general exposition of this subject, FALSE SWEARING, vol. 7, p. 793.

2. Reg. *v.* Castro, 9 L. R., Q. B. 350.

It is perjury to swear falsely before a county board of equalization, if the defendant be a resident of the county or has not been taxed elsewhere, in case he has become a resident since the beginning of the tax year. State *v.* Wood, 110 Ind. 82.

False swearing in a matter legitimately before the metropolitan fire marshal in New York is perjury. Harris *v.* People, 4 Hun (N. Y.) 1.

So is false swearing in proceedings before a board of fence viewers under the Massachusetts statute. Jones *v.* Daniels, 15 Gray (Mass.) 438.

In *California*, to appear before a notary public to acknowledge a deed, and falsely to represent one's self under oath to be the grantor named therein, is perjury. *Ex parte* Carpenter, 64 Cal. 267.

It is perjury to omit property from a schedule in insolvency, and it is none the less perjury because the insolvent act of California makes such omission a misdemeanor. People *v.* Platt, 67 Cal. 21.

False taking of the poor debtor's oath before a magistrate authorized to administer it is perjury. Arden *v.* State, 11 Conn. 408; Commonwealth *v.* Calvert, 1 Va. Car. 181.

So is a false return by a teacher as to the number of scholars taught made so as to enable him to get compensation which he could not legally receive for having taught a number of days in excess of the regular term. Vance *v.* State, 62 Miss. 137. False swearing before a local marine board in a mattter lawfully before them in pursuance of 17 & 17 Vict., ch. 104, and 25 &

(*c*) PROCEEDINGS in FEDERAL COURTS.—Where the perjury is in the course of a proceeding under the United States statute, there is no offense punishable under the State law. Nor has the rule, under which certain offenses may constitute offenses against both State and Federal law in certain instances, any application.[1]

26 Vict., ch. 63, has been adjudged to be perjury. Reg. *v.* Tomlinson, 1 L. R. C. C. 49.

And, under Mass. St. 1887, ch. 214, § 60, requiring a statement from a claimant under an insurance policy, a false oath subscribed thereto is perjury. Avery *v.* Ward, 150 Mass. 160.

If the record of a cause is erroneous, no perjury can be assigned for false testimony given in the course of the trial. Rex *v.* Cohen, 1 Stark 511.

One who swears falsely in a proceeding void on its face, cannot be convicted of perjury. Collins *v.* State, 78 Ala. 433.

Perjury is not committed in swearing falsely to an account to prepare it for a set-off in a trial before a justice of the peace. Waggoner *v.* Richmond, Wright (Ohio) 173. Nor where one is authorized by statute to prove an account by his own oath, if sworn to "within twelve months after the first article therein shall become due," and the oath is not taken within the twelve months. Warner *v.* Fowler, 8 Md. 25. Nor in a proceeding for the violation of a void municipal ordinance. Buell *v.* State, 45 Ark. 336. Nor on a trial before a justice, subsequent to a default, where, there having been no continuance, the justice had taken off the default without authority. State *v.* Hall, 49 Me. 412. Nor in a hearing where the judge amended the title of the cause by inserting the name of the husband of a female party who had married during the pendency of the action. Reg. *v.* Pearce, 9 Cox C. C. 258. Nor in bankruptcy proceedings where there was no good petitioning creditor's debt to support the feat. Reg. *v.* Ewington, 2 M. C. C. 223; Car. & M. 319. But the failure to enter a plea to an information does not render a subsequent trial so far void that false swearing thereon cannot be perjury. State *v.* Lewis, 10 Kan. 157.

In Anderson *v.* State, 24 Tex. App. 705, in a case where a complaint before a justice upon which an information was based was not sworn to, it was held that the common law rule as to jurisdiction did not prevail in *Texas.*

Perjury may be assigned in *Ohio* upon an oath and deposition taken before a proper officer in *Ohio*, in a suit for divorce pending in *Indiana*, although the petitioner was never a resident of Indiana, as required by the divorce law thereof. Stewart *v.* State, 22 Ohio St. 477.

Perjury cannot be assigned on the oath of an applicant for naturalization as to his residence, inasmuch as the statute prohibits the taking of the oath by the applicant himself in order to prove his residence. State *v.* Helle, 2 Hill (S. Car.) 290; United States *v.* Grottkan, 30 Fed. Rep. 672.

1. It goes without saying that perjury committed in a Federal court in a proceeding authorized by a Federal statute, is punishable, not as a common law offense, but as an offense against the Federal law. Anonymous, 1 Wash. (U. S.) 84.

Where the perjury is committed in a state court in naturalization proceedings under the Federal statute, there is a diversity of opinion as to the jurisdiction of the State court over the indictment for perjury. In Rump *v.* Commonwealth, 20 Pa. St. 475, it was held that the State court had jurisdiction; and so in State *v.* Whittemore, 50 N. H. 245; s. c., 9 Am. Dec. 196. To the contrary is People *v.* Sweetman, 3 Park. Cr. (N. Y.) 358. In United States *v.* Jones, 14 Blatchf. (U. S.) 90, the jurisdiction seems to be taken for granted.

See, in support of the proposition of the text, *Ex parte* Bridges, 2 Wood (U. S.) 428; People *v.* Kelly, 38 Cal. 145; State *v.* Pike, 15 N. H. 83; State *v.* Adams, 4 Blackf. (Ind.) 147; Houston *v.* Moore, 5 Wheat. (U. S.) 1; State *v.* Shelley, 11 Lea (Tenn.) 594; 1 Kent Comm. 398; 3 Story Comm. 623.

Section 5392 of U. S. Rev. Stat. declares that, "every person who, having taken an oath before a competent tribunal, officer or person, in any case in which a law of the United States authorizes an oath to be administered, that he will testify, declare, depose, or certify truly, or that any written testimony, declaration, deposition or certificate by him subscribed is true, willfully and contrary to such oath states or subscribes any material matter which he does not believe to be true, is guilty of perjury, and shall be punished by a fine of not more than two thousand dollars, and by imprisonment, at hard labor, not more than five years; and shall, moreover, thereafter be incapable of giving testimony in any court of the United States until such time as the judgment against him is reversed."

This section and the section following, relating to subornation of perjury, where incorporated in the United States Revised Statutes to take the place of the numerous provisions of Federal law, which fixed the pains and penalties of perjury anew every time a statutory oath before a judicial or administrative officer was required.

Prosecutions for false swearing may be maintained in the United States courts, where false affidavits have been made before officers authorized generally to administer oaths for the purpose of supporting claims against the United States, although the particular statute under which the claims are made is silent on the subject. 2 Attorney General Opinions 700.

When a circuit court clerk swore falsely to his emolument return and account for services rendered, it was held that the words "declaration" and "certificate" were used in their popular sense, and not technically; that they signified any statement of material matters of fact sworn to and subscribed by the party charged, and that an indictment would lie. United States *v.* Ambrose, 108 U. S. 336.

Under the statute an indictment for perjury may be founded on a false oath in swearing before a justice of the peace to an affidavit to support a pension claim. United States *v.* Boggs, 31 Fed. Rep. 337. See also United States *v.* Bailey, 9 Pet. (U. S.) 238; United States *v.* Winchester, 2 McLean (U. S.) 135.

Where one swears falsely in making return of his income, although the Income Tax act did not provide for a compulsory disclosure under oath. United States *v.* Smith, 1 Sawy. (U. S.) 277. For an intentional omission of property from bankruptcy schedules. United States *v.* Nihols, 4 McLean (U. S.) 23. For false testimony as to the credibility of a witness; or that one has never been in prison, the fact being otherwise. United States *v.* Lansberg, 21 Blatchf. (U. S.) 169. For false statements made in justifying as bail. United States *v.* Volz, 14 Blatchf. (U. S.) 15. For perjury committed on an examination before a United States commissioner under a statute. *Ex parte* Bridges, 2 Wood (U. S.) 428.

So when the Secretary of War has authority to prescribe what facts shall be stated in affidavits by drafted men claiming exemption from military service, false swearing is perjury. United States *v.* Sonachall, 4 Biss. (U. S.) 425.

And likewise the Treasury Department may require an affidavit as to the qualification of the sureties on a match stamp bond, upon which perjury may be assigned. Ralph *v.* United States, 1 Biss. (U. S.) 88.

Perjury may be committed by falsely swearing before a legal deputy of a collector of customs acting under the law. United States *v.* Barton, Gilp. (U. S.) 439.

If, however, the officer administering the oath is without authority in the premises, there is no perjury. United States *v.* Babcock, 4 McLean (U. S.) 113; United States *v.* Howard, 37 Fed. Rep. 666; United States *v.* Deeming, 4 McLean (U. S.) 3; United States *v.* Curtis, 107 U. S. 671. In the latter case a national bank officer verified his report before a notary public, who, under the statute in force at the time, was without authority to administer such an oath. A witness's false oath as to the distance traveled is not perjury, where such an oath is not required by law or a rule of court, but only by the usage of a ministerial officer. United States *v.* Howard, 37 Fed. Rep. 666.

As to perjury under U. S. acts, March 1, 1823, and March 3, 1825, to prevent false swearing touching public money, see United States *v.* Bailey, 9 Pet. (U. S.) 238; United States *v.* Moore, 7 Low. (U. S.) 232. Under United States act 1813, ch. 34, relating to bounties to the owners of vessels in certain circumstances, see United States *v.* Kendrick, 2 Mason (U. S.) 69; United States *v.* Nickerson, 1 Sprague (U. S.) 232. As to perjury in connection with proceedings in the Land Office, see United States *v.* Shinn, 14 Fed. Rep. 447; Babcock *v.* United States, 34 Fed. Rep. 873. And see United States *v.* Stanley, 6 McLean

4. Materiality of the False Statement.—The statement alleged to be false must be material to the subject then under consideration, otherwise it does not amount to the offense of perjury.[1]

(U. S.) 409; United States *v.* Dickey, Morr. (Iowa) 412.

1. 1 Hawkins P. C., ch. 69, § 8; 2 Archbold's Crim. Pr. 1727; 3 Co. Inst. 167; 3 Greenleaf on Evidence, § 195; 2 Bishop's Crim. Law, § 1030; Rex *v.* Griepe, 1 Ld. Raym. 256.

Hawkins says, that it is clear that if the subject matter is wholly foreign to the purpose, tending neither to extenuate nor increase either the damages or the guilt, nor likely to induce the jury to give a more easy credit to the substantial part of the evidence, an indictment will not lie. See Commonwealth *v.* Knight, 12 Mass. 274; Studdard *v.* Linville, 3 Hawks (N. Car.) 474; State *v.* Kennerly, 10 Rich. (S. Car.) 152; United States *v.* Shinn, 14 Fed. Rep. 447.

Though Coke's definition of a perjury includes the doctrine of materiality, it is thought that Coke was in error and not supported by the ancient authorities; though upon the passage of Coke containing the definition, cases were decided, as appeared from 1 Hawkins P. C. 433, 435 which introduced a doubt whether perjury could be committed by a fact which, though relevant to the issue, was not essential to its determination, and the doctrine became so well recognized as a part of the law that an averment of the materiality of the matter on which perjury is assigned forms a necessary part of every indictment, though of late the judges have given so wide an interpretation to the word "material" that the rule has ceased to do much harm. See Stephen's Dig. Cr. Law App., p. 375.

The proposition of the text is supported by State *v.* Lawson, 98 N. Car. 759; Commonwealth *v.* Farley, Thatcher Cr. Cas. (Mass.) 654; Miller *v.* State, 15 Fla. 577; People *v.* Perrazo, 64 Cal. 106; State *v.* Bailey, 34 Mo. 350; State *v.* Hattaway, 2 Nott & M. (S. Car.) 118; s. c., 10 Am. Dec. 580; Hinch *v.* State, 2 Mo. 158; Gibson *v.* State, 44 Ala. 17; Hood *v.* State, 44 Ala. 87; Lawrence *v.* State, 2 Tex. App. 479; Nelson *v.* State, 32 Ark. 192; Bullock *v.* Koon, 4 Wend. (N. Y.) 531; Hembree *v.* State, 52 Ga. 242; Commonwealth *v.* Grant, 116 Mass. 17; State *v.* Gibson, 26 La. Ann. 71; State *v.* Trask, 42 Vt. 152; State *v.* Aikens, 32 Iowa 303; Nelson *v.* State, 47 Miss. 621; Galloway *v.* State, 29 Ind. 442; State *v.* Hobbs, 40 N. H. 239; Wood *v.* People, 59 N. Y. 117; State *v.* Trask, 42 Vt. 152.

It is sometimes said that the false statement in addition to being material, must be of a nature to prejudice some person or State (see authorities cited in 2 Bishop's Crim. Law, § 1031). In regard to which Mr. Bishop says that the proposition is merely formal and of no practical consequence. See also Pollard *v.* People, 69 Ill. 148, where it is stated that it is the act of false swearing in respect to a matter material to the point of inquiry that constitutes the crime of perjury and not the injury which it may have done to individuals.

Instances of material evidence for false swearing in regard to which perjury will lie are as follows: Denial of previous expressions of hostility toward the defendant on a trial for carrying a concealed weapon, and knowledge of such carrying. Williams *v.* State, 68 Ala. 551. False testimony that a girl was a big girl 13 years previous, and that the witness had then picked cotton with her, on the trial of one for making a false affidavit in order to secure a marriage license. Davidson *v.* State, 22 Tex. App. 372. False swearing on the part of the witness that he did not know his son went to school, when such knowledge was material to an issue in a civil suit. Floyd *v.* State, 30 Ala. 511. The particulars of the offer, where the person accused of perjury testified on a murder trial that the deceased offered him at a certain time and place named, a sum of money to slay the defendant in the murder trial. Anderson *v.* People, 117 Ill. 265. False statements as to the acts of either of three who were jointly concerned in an assault. State *v.* Norris, 9 N. H. 96.

Evidence tending to induce the jury to give greater credit to a substantial fact in controversy is material in the sense that it may support an indictment for perjury. Reg. *v.* Tyson, 11 Cox C. C. 1. So false testimony by a party to an action concerning his name, and which resulted in the striking out of the cause. Reg. *v.* Mul-

But if it tend even circumstantially to the proof of the issue, it

lany, 10 Cox C. C. 97. And false testimony concerning the signature to a delivery note for certain goods. Reg. *v.* Naylor, 11 Cox C. C. 13. See also State *v.* Schultz, 57 Ind. 19.

When the Senate is engaged in investigating charges of bribery made against its own members under a resolution reciting such charges and providing for their investigation, there is a material issue before it within the meaning of the statute against perjury. *Ex parte* McCarthy, 29 Cal. 395.

N sued T in trespass for entering upon his lands, cutting down trees and throwing down fences. A witness testified to the particular injury charged, and also to an injury inflicted on the plaintiff's stock, denying that he, the witness, had any interest in the stock. *Held*, that all these statements were so material that a charge of perjury could be founded on either of them, if the witness knowingly swore falsely. Salmons *v.* Tait, 31 Ga. 676.

Where it was proved that a forgery had been committed in a note, and that at the same time, and in the same ink, and by the same hand, an interlineation had been made in a warrant, and it was proved and admitted on a trial against B for forgery, that either A or B had committed the forgery, *held*, that the oath of B, denying that the interlineation made in the warrant was in his handwriting was material to the issue, and that if he swore falsely in that respect, it was perjury. Smith *v.* Deaver, 6 Jones (N. Car.) 563.

Upon the trial of C for perjury committed in an affidavit, proof was given that the signature to the affidavit was in his handwriting, and there was no other proof that he was the person who made the affidavit. The prisoner was then called and swore that the affidavit was used before the taxing master; that C was then present, and that it was publicly mentioned, so that everybody present must have heard it, that the affidavit was C's. *Held*, that the matters sworn were material upon the trial of C. Reg. *v.* Alsop, 11 Cox C. C. 264.

For additional instances of material evidence, see Hicks *v.* State, 86 Ala. 30; United States *v.* Brown (Utah), 21 Pac. Rep. 461; Gandy *v.* State, 23 Neb. 436; Commonwealth *v.* Edison (Ky. 1888), 9 S. W. Rep. 161; State *v.* Murphy, 101 N. Car. 697; Sanders *v.* People, 124 Ill. 218.

Immaterial matters which will not sustain an indictment for perjury are swearing that the defendant made a promissory note, but not one containing the words "value received," the latter words not being material in a note. People *v.* McDermott, 8 Cal. 288. An allegation of something not required to be alleged in an application for an attachment, or for a writ of *habeas corpus*. Gibson *v.* State, 44 Ala. 17; Hood *v.* State, 44 Ala. 81. A statement before a grand jury that a certain person had not "unlawfully" sold or given liquor to the witness, such statement being a matter of opinion and not of fact. State *v.* Henderson, 90 Ind. 406. An oath by a laboring man, a householder and head of a family, in a proceeding by garnishment to subject his wages, not exceeding $50 per month due him from his employer, to the lien of an execution; that he did not sign a writing purporting to be signed by him, waiving all exemptions, including his claim as a laborer, inasmuch as the exemption to laborers, under Va. Code 1873, ch. 184, § 3, cannot be waived so as to give a lien by *fi. fa.* thereon. Crump *v.* Commonwealth, 75 Va. 922). A false statement by a party in qualifiying for bail as to the location of a certain number of tons of hay which he owned, and misstatements as to the total value of the witness's property are immaterial, so long as he does not mislead as to his ability to discharge the obligation he is assuming. The material point of inquiry not being whether he is worth a certain sum, but whether the penalty of the bail bond with interests and costs can be made out of it on execution. Pollard *v.* People, 69 Ill. 148. A statement on the trial of a husband for an assault on his wife, that the witness had seen the wife committing adultery is too irrelevant to sustain an assignment of perjury. Reg. *v.* Tate, 12 Cox C. C. (Eng.) 7. Contradictory statements as to the dates when defendant on a trial for the larceny of bacon had attempted to sell it to the witness. Rhodes *v.* Commonwealth, 78 Va. 692. See also Jennings *v.* State (Miss. 1890), 7 So. Rep. 462.

will be deemed material.[1]

And it may thus be material, though not of itself sufficient to maintain the issue.[2]

If it tend in any way to lessen or aggravate the damages, it is material.[3]

All questions put to a witness on cross-examination for the purpose of testing his credit may be deemed material, whether they have a tendency to prove the issue or not.[4]

5. Intent or Want of Knowledge.—While it may be stated generally that in perjury, as in other crimes, a guilty intent must appear, it is difficult to define the precise extent to which a specific intent must be shown.[5]

1. 2 Archbold's Crim. Pr., 1727; 3 Greenleaf Ev., § 195.

As where, in an action for trespass by sheep, a witness proved that he saw thirty or forty sheep in the close, and he knew they were the defendant's by their being marked in a particular way, describing it, whereas the defendant never marked his sheep in that way; this was holden to be material, for the reason assigned by him made his account more credible. 1 Hawkins P. C., ch. 69, § 8. See also Robinson *v.* State, 18 Fla. 898; Wood *v.* People, 59 N. Y. 117; Commonwealth *v.* Grant, 116 Mass. 17; Mackin *v.* People, 115 Ill. 312; s. c., 56 Am. Rep. 167.

2. Rex *v.* Rhodes, Ld. Raym. 887; 2 Archbold's Cr. Pr. 1729; Rex *v.* Overton, C. & M. 655; State *v.* Hattaway, 2 Nott & M. (S. Car.) 118; s. c., 10 Am. Dec. 580.

3. 1 Hawkins P. C., ch. 69, § 8; 2 Archbold's Cr. Pr. 1729; Stephens *v.* State, 1 Swan (Tenn.) 157; State *v.* Norris, 9 N. H. 96. See also State *v.* Keenan, 8 Rich. (S. Car.) 456.

4. This is undeniably the English rule. 2 Archbold's Cr. Pr. 1730; Rex *v.* Greepe, 2 Salk. (Eng.) 513; Rex *v.* Overton, C. & M. 655; Reg. *v.* Gibbon, Leigh & C. 109; Reg. *v.* Lavey, 3 C. & K. (Eng.) 26; Reg. *v.* Phillpotts, 2 Den. C. C. 302; Reg. *v.* Murray, 1 F. & F. 80. See also Reg. *v.* Mullany, L. & C. 593; Reg. *v.* Worley, 3 Cox C. C. 535.

The rule was asserted to the full extent to which the English cases carry it, in United States *v.* Landsberg, 23 Fed. Rep. 585, BENEDICT, J., *citing* the English cases on the Massachusetts case of Commonwealth *v.* Bonner, 97 Mass. 587, where it was held material to ask a witness on cross-examination if he had been in a house of correction for any crime. In the Massachusetts case, however, the question of perjury was not raised, the court saying merely, on the objection to the question, that, though the witness was the defendant in a criminal prosecution, if he availed himself of his privilege to become a witness, he subjected himself to the liabilities incident to that position, and was not exempted from cross-examination and impeachment as a witness.

In People *v.* Courtney, 31 Hun (N. Y.) 199, the general term of the Supreme Court of New York, DAVIS, P. J., delivering the opinion, followed United States *v.* Landsberg, *cited* above; and the decision was affirmed by the court of appeals in People *v.* Courtney, 94 N. Y. 490. To the same effect are Washington *v.* State, 22 Tex. App. 26; Williams *v.* State, 28 Tex. App. 301; Studdard *v.* Linville, 3 Hawks (N. Car.) 474.

An assignment of perjury may be founded on testimony material to the issue, and a denial of having made a different statement previously. People *v.* Barry, 63 Cal. 62. And this, although such different statement was made on the trial of another cause, wherein it was immaterial, the reason being that the answer affects the witness's credibility. State *v.* Mooney, 65 Mo. 494.

5. Perhaps no modern definition has improved upon that of Hawkins, who says: "It seemeth that no one ought to be found guilty (of perjury) without clear proof that the false oath alleged against him was taken with some degree of deliberation; for if, upon the whole circumstances of the case, it shall appear probable that it was owing rather to weakness than to perverseness of the party, as where it was occasioned by surprise or inadvertency, or a mistake of the true state of the question, it cannot but be hard to make it amount to voluntary and corrupt perjury." 1 Hawkins P. C. 429, § 2.

That there must be willfullness and corruptness is settled by the cases. See Wyld *v.* Cookman, Cro. Eliz. 492; Rex. *v.* Richards, 7 D. & R. 665; United States *v.* Babcock, 4 McLean (U. S.) 114; State *v.* Carland, 3 Dev. (N. Car.) 114; State *v.* Hascall, 6 N. H. 352; Green *v.* State, 41 Ala. 419; Cothran *v.* State, 39 Miss. 541; Green *v.* State, 41 Ala. 419; State *v.* Perry, 42 Tex. 238; Miller *v.* State, 15 Fla. 577; Bell *v.* Seneff, 83 Ill. 122; Miller *v.* State, 15 Fla. 577; Schaller *v.* State, 14 Mo. 502.

It is no defense that defendant was induced to testify falsely by threats against his life, made out of court, and some time before the trial. Bain *v.* State (Miss. 1890), 7 So. Rep. 408.

The perjury cannot be assigned upon a mere mistake. See Reg. *v.* Muscot, 10 Mod. 192; Rex *v.* De Beauvoir, 7 Car. & P. 17; Reg. *v.* Moreau, 11 Q. B. 1028; Scott *v.* Cook, 1 Duv. (Ky.) 314; Cook's Case, 1 Rob. (Va.) 729; State *v.* Lea, 3 Ala. 602; Thomas *v.* State, 71 Ga. 252. As, for example, where a party makes a true statement to his legal adviser, by whom the statement is reduced to writing, and swears to it on the representation of his adviser that the writing corresponds with the oral statement, there is no perjury though such correspondence does not exist. United States *v.* Stanley, 6 McLean (U. S.) 409. And see United States *v.* Conner, 3 McLean (U. S.) 573; Jesse *v.* State, 20 Ga. 156. So if the testimony was honestly given under legal advice there is no perjury. Hood *v.* State, 44 Ala. 81. Otherwise, however, if the matter involved no question of law. Barnett *v.* State, 89 Ala. 165. And so if a misstatement is given rashly, but without a corrupt intent. United States *v.* Atkins, 1 Sprague (U. S.) 558. And see United States *v.* Moore, 7 Low. (U. S.) 232, in which latter case, LOWELL, J., said: "There must be some fact falsely stated with knowledge of its falsity before there can be perjury." See also Johnson *v.* People, 94 Ill. 505.

In People *v.* Wiley, 2 Park. Cr. (N. Y.) 19, it was stated that it was no defense that the witness was intoxicated when he testified. But in Lytle *v.* State, 31 Ohio St. 196, it was held that this was a circumstance for the jury.

Where intoxication was relied on as a defense, it was held that a charge giving the provisions of Pen. Code Tex., art. 189, providing that a "false statement made through inadvertence or under agitation or by mistake is not perjury," was sufficient, without calling special attention to defendant's intoxicated condition. Sisk *v.* State, 28 Tex. App. 432.

In United States *v.* Shellmire, Baldw. (U. S.) 370, BALDWIN, J, said: "That a reckless disregard of truth by one who did not believe that he was swearing to an untruth, did not constitute perjury." The court said: "His negligence or carelessness in coming to that belief or conclusion of mind, without taking proper pains to enable him to ascertain the truth of the facts to which he swears, does not make his oath corrupt, and perjury cannot be willful where the oath is according to the belief and conviction of the witness as to its truth." Mr. Bishop thinks the doctrine best supported to be that the intent must be specific to swear untruly. 1 Bishop Crim. Law 320; 2 id. 1048.

In State *v.* Gates, 17 N. H. 373, it was held that to swear to that of which the witness knew he had no knowledge was perjury; and in State *v.* Knox, Phil. (N. Car.) 312, it was added by READE, J., "although he believes it to be true, and although it turns out to be true." In Martin *v.* Miller, 4 Mo. 47; s. c., 28 Am. Dec. 342, it was held that a retraction in a subsequent stage of a trial, of testimony willfully and corruptly given, made the offense none the less perjury. But it is a well recognized principle that to prevent the retraction from being inoperative, the testimony must have been willfully and corruptly false in the first instance. See Rex *v.* Carr, 1 Sid. 418; 2 Russell on Crimes 666; Rex *v.* Jones, 1 Peake's Cas. 38; Rex *v.* Dowlin, 1 Peake's Cas. 170; Rex *v.* Rowley, Ry. & M. 299.

Mr. Greenleaf (3 Greenleaf on Evidence, § 200) asserts that, "The allegation that the oath was willfully and corruptly false may also be supported by evidence that the prisoner swore rashly to a matter which he never saw nor knew; as, where he swore posi-

III. The Indictment—1. In General.—The facts constituting the offense must be averred directly, positively, and with certainty, not by way of inference or argument;[1] and should be set forth with such particularity and certainty as to give the accused reasonable notice of what he is to defend himself against.[2]

If the indictment names the cause and court in which the perjury was committed, avers the jurisdiction competent to administer the oath, the materiality of the matter sworn to, and the corrupt intent, sets out the facts sworn to and negatives their truth, it is sufficient.[3]

tively to the value of goods of which he knew nothing, though his valuation was correct;" and *cites* as authority, Co. Inst. 166; People *v.* McKinney, 3 Park Cr. (N. Y.) 510; "or, where he swears falsely to a matter, the truth of which, though he believed, yet he had no probable cause for believing, and might with little trouble have ascertained the fact;" and *cites* Commonwealth *v.* Cornish, 6 Binn. (Pa.) 249. In Commonwealth *v.* Brady, 5 Gray (Mass.) 78, it was said that a false swearing "to the best of the opinion of the witness" to a statement which is not true, which the witness has no reasonable cause to believe to be true, but which he does believe to be true, is not perjury.

In State *v.* Cruikshank, 6 Blackf. (Ind.) 62, the court said: "Where a man swears that a thing is so, or that he believes it to be so, when, in truth, he does not believe it to be so, the oath is false though the fact really be as stated."

In *Virginia*, an indictment against an insolvent debtor for perjury, in swearing to a schedule which did not discover certain debts owing to him, was held bad on demurrer for not averring that he well knew and remembered that the omitted debts were then justly due and owing to him. Cook's Case, 1 Rob. (Va.) 729.

When the affidavit, upon which the perjury is founded, merely states the belief of the affiant, that a larceny has been committed, the assignment of the perjury must negative the words of the affidavit, and it is not sufficient to allege generally that the persons charged had not committed the larceny; it is necessary, when the defendant only states his belief, to aver that the fact was otherwise, and that the defendant knew the contrary of what he swore. State *v.* Lea, 3 Ala. 602.

An averment, that the defendant "well knew" the falsity of the facts to which he testified, instead of an averment simply negativing his oath, is good. State *v.* Lindenburg, 13 Tex. 27.

The willful and corrupt intent cannot be presumed from the fact that there is a material conflict between the testimonies of the parties to a suit as to the term of a contract. Bell *v.* Senneff, 83 Ill. 122.

When a coroner deposed as to making an inquisition, when in fact there was no inquest because the coroner's jury did not view the deceased, it was held not necessarily willful and corrupt false swearing. Dempsey *v.* People, 20 Hun (N. Y.) 261.

If perjury is assigned on the affidavit of one who could not read, his understanding of its statements must be proved. Hernandez *v.* State, 18 Tex. App. 134; s. c., 51 Am. Dec. 295.

An indictment for perjury cannot be maintained where the supposed perjury depends upon the construction of a deed. State *v.* Wolverton, 8 Blackf. (Ind.) 452. See also Rex *v.* Crispigmy, 1 Esp. R. 280; Rex *v.* Pepys, Peake 138.

1. State *v.* Powell, 28 Tex. 626.

2. Stofer *v.* State, 3 W. Va. 692.

An indictment for perjury, charging that the defendant, in securing registration, swore falsely that he had not been "convicted of an infamous crime," was held too indefinite in not specifying the crime. State *v.* Bixler, 62 Md. 354.

For an indictment held too indefinite in alleging merely that the defendant swore falsely in respect to his schedule in taking the bankrupt's oath, see United States *v.* Morgan, 1 Morr. (Iowa) 341. But *compare* United States *v.* Chapman, 3 McLean (U. S.) 390; United States *v.* Deming, 4 McLean (U. S.) 3; People *v.* Phelps, 5 Wend. (N. Y.) 9.

3. State *v.* Huckeby, 87 Mo. 414; Cox

2. Averments as to the Oath.—It must be distinctly averred that the defendant was sworn.[1] It is sufficient to allege that he was "duly sworn."[2] Only the substance of the false oath need be set out.[3]

3. Averments as to Jurisdiction.—While it must appear with certainty, from the indictment, that the person administering the oath had jurisdiction or authority to do so,[4]

v. State, 13 Tex. App. 479. *Compare* State *v.* Stillman, 7 Coldw. (Tenn.) 341.

It is not necessary that the prisoner be charged, *in haec verba*, with having committed perjury. Massie *v.* State, 5 Tex. App. 81.

It is not necessary to set forth the record of the proceeding wherein the oath was administered. Burk *v.* State, 81 Ind. 128; State *v.* Roberson, 98 N. Car. 751. Though if the record is set forth, it must be set forth correctly. State *v.* Ammons, 3 Murph. (N. Car.) 123. The pleadings need not be set forth. State *v.* Hoyle, 6 Ired. (N. Car.) 1. Nor the interrogatories on the answers to which the perjury is assigned. State *v.* Bishop, 1 D. Chip. (Vt.) 124.

The issue joined in the proceeding wherein the perjury was committed need not be described specifically. Covey *v.* State, 23 Tex. App. 388; People *v.* Grimshaw, 33 Hun (N. Y.) 505.

Where the indictment distinctly charges that the false oath was taken in a judicial proceeding, and in a matter material to the issue, and where the proceeding and the issue are plainly indicated, any mere vagueness or incompleteness of description must be excepted to before trial, and is not cause for arresting the judgment. Pennaman *v.* State, 58 Ga. 336.

The question whether the indictment contains a charge of perjury should not be entertained on motion to quash, but the prisoner should be put to his demurrer. Commonwealth *v.* Litton, 6 Gratt. (Va.) 691.

And see, generally, Barnett *v.* State, 89 Ala. 165; Hicks *v.* State, 86 Ala. 30; People *v.* Ah Bean, 77 Cal. 12; Territory *v.* Anderson (Idaho, 1889), 21 Pac. Rep. 417; State *v.* Smith, 40 Kan. 631; Commonwealth *v.* Jarboe (Ky. 1889), 12 S. W. Rep. 138; State *v.* Corson, 59 Me. 137; State *v.* Murphy, 101 N. Car. 697; State *v.* Ah Lee, 18 Oregon 540; Cover *v.* Commonwealth (Pa. 1887), 8 Atl. Rep. 196; Menasco *v.* State (Tex. 1889), 11 S. W. Rep. 898; State *v.* Collins (Vt. 1890), 19 Atl. Rep. 368.

1. United States *v.* McConaughy, 33 Fed. Rep. 168; State *v.* Hamilton, 65 Mo. 667; Reg. *v.* Goodfellow, C. & M. 569.

"Made and subscribed in open court wickedly, falsely, willfully, corruptly, and knowingly, the following false and corrupt oath, which is in substance as follows," then setting out the affidavit, is not a sufficient allegation that the party was sworn. State *v.* Divoll, 44 N. H. 140.

2. Dodge *v.* State, 24 N. J. L. 455; Tuttle *v.* People, 36 N. Y. 431; State *v.* Farow, 10 Rich. (S. Car.) 165; Jackson *v.* State, 15 Tex. App. 579; Rex *v.* M'Arthur, Peake (Eng.) 155.

In an indictment for perjury against a person voting at an election, an averment that he was sworn "by and before the board" of inspectors, is a sufficient averment that the oath was administered by the board. Campbell *v.* People, 8 Wend. (N. Y.) 636.

3. People *v.* Warner, 5 Wend. (N. Y.) 271; State *v.* Neal, 42 Mo. 119.

For perjury committed in taking an extra judicial oath, the deposition must be so far set out that the court may judge whether or not it is of the nature contemplated by the statute. Reg. *v.* Nott, 4 Q. B. 768; 9 Cox C. C. 301. *Compare* State *v.* Umdenstock, 43 Tex. 554; Coppach *v.* State, 36 Ind. 513.

It is not necessary that it should appear whether the false testimony of the witness was given in answer to a specific question put to him, or in the course of his own relation of the facts; for, in either case, he is equally required by law to depose the truth. Commonwealth *v.* Knight, 12 Mass. 274.

4. State *v.* Plummer, 50 Me. 217; State *v.* Nickerson, 46 Iowa 447; State *v.* McCone, 59 Vt. 117; State *v.* Owen, 73 Mo. 440; State *v.* Lamont, 2 Wis. 437; Anderson *v.* State, 18 Tex. App. 17; State *v.* Chamberlain, 30 Vt. 559; State *v.* Simons, 30 Vt. 620; Reg. *v.* Overton, 4 Q. B. 83; Reg. *v.* Bishop, 1 C. & M. 302.

it is not necessary to set forth the facts giving the authority or jurisdiction.[1]

The style of the court, however, before which the perjury is alleged to have been committed, must be legally set forth[2] and also the name and official title of the officer administering the oath.[3]

1. Halleck *v.* State, 11 Ohio 400; State *v.* Belew, 79 Mo. 584; State *v.* Marshall, 47 Mo. 378; People *v.* Phelps, 5 Wend. (N. Y.) 9; People *v.* Tredway, 3 Barb. (N. Y.) 470; State *v.* Newton, 1 Greene (Iowa) 160; s. c., 48 Am. Dec. 367; Bradberry *v.* State, 7 Tex. App. 375; Stewart *v.* State, 6 Tex. App. 184; State *v.* Peters, 42 Tex. 7; Powers *v.* State, 17 Tex. App. 428; State *v.* Ellison, 8 Blackf. (Ind.) 225; Lavey *v.* Reg., 17 Q. B. 496; 5 Cox C. C. 259; Reg. *v.* Lawlor, 6 Cox C. C. 187; Reg. *v.* Dunning, 1 L. R., C. C. 290; 11 Cox C. C. 651.

But see, as to United States commissioners, United States *v.* Wilcox, 4 Blatchf. (U. S.) 391; and, as to a bill in equity, People *v.* Gaige, 26 Mich. 30.

As to perjury committed under the English Insolvent Debtors act it was held, that the jurisdiction of the court sufficiently appeared, though there was no express allegation that the defendant had resided for six calendar months before the filing of the petition within the district of the county court, as required by 11 & 12 Vict., ch. 102, § 6. Walker *v.* Reg., 8 El. & Bl. 439.

It being averred that an issue was duly joined before a justice in his court, and came on to be tried before him in due form of law, and that he had competent authority to administer the oath, it is not necessary to aver further that the land mentioned in the suit was within the county. Without such averment the jurisdiction sufficiently appears. Commonwealth *v.* Knight, 12 Mass. 274; s. c., 7 Am. Dec. 72.

2. State *v.* Street, 1 Murph. (N. Car.) 156; s. c., 30 Am. Dec. 682; State *v.* Harlis, 33 La. Ann. 1172. *Compare* Reg. *v.* Child, 5 Cox C. C. 197.

3. United States *v.* Wilcox, 4 Blatchf. (U. S.) 391; Kerr *v.* People, 42 Ill. 307; State *v.* Harlis, 33 La. Ann. 1172.

If the draughtsman is in doubt, whether the oath was administered by the judge or the clerk, or the deputy clerk, he should set out the offense in three counts. An indictment in one count alleging the oath was administered by the three, is bad on motion in arrest. Hitesman *v.* State, 48 Ind. 473; State *v.* Oppenheimer, 41 Tex. 82.

That designating the court without naming the officer is sufficient. See State *v.* Spencer, 6 Oregon 152.

An indictment for perjury before a grand jury need not allege its jurisdiction over the subject matter. State *v.* Keel, 54 Mo. 183.

The foreman's name need not be alleged. St. Clair *v.* State, 11 Tex. App. 297. Nor need it be alleged that he had authority to administer an oath. State *v.* Green, 24 Ark. 591.

For perjury committed in a criminal trial the indictment need not allege that the judicial proceeding was pending on an indictment found by a grand jury. State *v.* Grover, 38 La. Ann. 567. Nor whether the proceeding was by indictment or information. State *v.* Wise, 3 Lea (Tenn.) 38. But see *contra* Steinston *v.* State, 6 Yerg. (Tenn.) 531.

An indictment for perjury in taking a false oath before a regimental court of inquiry should set forth the number of officers of which such court consisted, their respective rank and the subject of the inquiry before such court. Conner *v.* Commonwealth, 2 Va. Cas. 30.

In an indictment for perjury committed in *scire facias* proceedings it is not sufficient to allege that it was in a proceeding in a court of justice. State *v.* Hanson, 39 Me. 337.

In Commonwealth *v.* Alden, 14 Mass. 388, it was held that an indictment for perjury in taking the poor prisoner's oath need not aver that it was committed within prison limits, the statute not requiring the oath to be administered within such limits.

In an indictment for perjury committed in a justice's court, the charging it to have been committed "on the trial of the cause or issue," was held not bad for ambiguity. State *v.* Bishop, 1 D. Chip. (Vt.) 120.

An indictment for perjury committed in an affidavit to hold to bail, need not allege the pendency of an action, as such affidavit may be sworn to before the issuing of the writ of summons in the action. King *v.* Reg., 5

4. Averments as to Falsity and Corrupt Intent.—It is essential to allege that the defendant willfully, corruptly, and falsely testified as charged.[1]

The matter falsely sworn to must be expressly contradicted,[2] and the omission to charge directly that the facts sworn to were false renders the indictment fatally defective.[3]

Cox C. C. 161; 14 Q. B. 31. And see, generally, State *v.* Ayer, 40 Kan. 43; State *v.* Roberson, 98 N. Car. 751; State *v.* Green, 100 N. Car. 419; State *v.* Byrd, 28 S. Car. 18; Covey *v.* State, 23 Tex. App. 388; People *v.* Greenwell, 5 Utah 112; United States *v.* Boggs, 31 Fed. Rep. 337.

1. State *v.* Morse, 90 Mo. 91; State *v.* Davis, 84 N. Car. 787; States *v.* Webb, 41 Tex. 67; Allen *v.* State, 42 Tex. 12; Smith *v.* State, 1 Tex. App. 620; Thomas' Case, 2 Rob. (Va.) 795; Perdue *v.* Commonwealth, 96 Pa. St. 311; Rex *v.* Richards, 7 D. & R. 655; s. c., *nom.*, Rex *v.* Stevens, 5 B. & C. 346; Reg. *v.* Bent, 2 C. & K. 179; 1 Den. C. C. 157; R. *v.* Harris, 1 D. & R. 578; 5 B. & A. 926.

A charge that one "deposed and gave in evidence to the jury willfully and corruptly" amounts to a charge that he swore willfully and corruptly. State *v.* Bobbitt, 70 N. Car. 81.

An indictment for perjury need not negative that the false statement was made, as in the provision of Tex. Penal Code, art. 189, "through inadvertence, or under agitation, or by mistake." Brown *v.* State, 9 Tex. App. 171.

The word "willful" is not necessary in an indictment for perjury at common law. Rex *v.* Cox, 1 Leach C. C. 71. Otherwise in an indictment for perjury in 5 Eliz., ch. 9, ib. It is necessary also in *Missouri.* State *v.* Day, 100 Mo. 242. And under the federal statute. United States *v.* Edwards, 43 Fed. Rep. 67.

2. Gibson *v.* State, 44 Ala. 17.

A traverse so worded as to negative an immaterial part of the false testimony, *e. g.*, the time of an act but not the act itself renders the assignment defective. Martinez *v.* State, 7 Tex. App. 394. *Compare* Dilcher *v.* State, 39 Ohio St. 130.

Where an indictment for perjury, in swearing to a false return of the condition of a bank, charged generally that the return was false, it was held that the county attorney was not bound to specify in what particulars he expected to prove the return false. Commonwealth *v.* Dunham, Thach. Cr. Cas. (Mass.) 519.

3. People *v.* Clements, 42 Hun (N. Y.) 353.

An indictment charged defendant with perjury in verifying a bank report. Statements contained in the report were set forth, and the indictment averred that defendant well knew that these statements were not true. *Held*, equivalent to an allegation that the statements were false. People *v.* Clements, 107 N. Y. 205.

An indictment for perjury in an investigation before a grand jury need not allege the guilt or innocence of the person under investigation, nor the facts in regard to his offense. State *v.* Schill, 27 Iowa 263.

An indictment which charges that the prisoner "feloniously, corruptly, knowingly, willfully, and maliciously swore," omitting the word "falsely," but concluding, "and so the defendant, in manner and form aforesaid, did commit willful and corrupt perjury," is bad. Reg. *v.* Oxley, 3 C. & K. 317.

An indictment is bad under Iowa statute, which does not use, in charging falsity and corrupt intent, the exact language of the act. State *v.* Morse, 1 Greene (Iowa) 503.

An indictment alleging that defendant "willfully, corruptly, and feloniously" made a false affidavit, was held good notwithstanding omission of the statutory word "falsely." State *v.* Anderson, 103 Ind. 170.

An indictment charging that the defendant swore "willflully, knowingly, maliciously and falsely" was held to be sufficient without the use of the word "corruptly." State *v.* Bixler, 62 Me. 345.

An indictment for perjury in a declaration of intention to become a citizen need not set forth the declaration. United States *v.* Walsh, 22 Fed. Rep. 644.

In pleading perjury in taking the poor debtor's oath, the particular false statements should be set forth. Willington *v.* Stearns, 1 Pick. (Mass.) 497.

An averment that the defendant knew the falsity of the matter testified to by him is not requisite, except where the perjury is assigned upon the statement by the accused of his belief, or denial of his belief, of the alleged false matter.[1]

5. Averments as to Materiality.—The indictment must show that the testimony on which the perjury is assigned was material to the issue.[2]

This may be done by a general averment of materiality, or by the setting forth of facts sufficient to show the materiality.[3]

An indictment for perjury in swearing to a plea to a suit on three different notes should negative the statement as to each note, and set out the truth in regard thereto, instead of averring in general that each and all the statements contained in the plea are false. Gabrielsky *v.* State, 13 Tex. App. 428.

1. State *v.* Raymond, 20 Iowa 582. *Compare* Johnson *v.* People, 94 Ill. 505.

In an indictment for perjury by a person making affidavit that he believes A has committed a larceny specified in the affidavit, it is not sufficient merely to negative the larceny, but it must be further averred that the affiant knew the fact to be otherwise. State *v.* Lea, 3 Ala. 602; State *v.* Carland, 3 Dev. (N. Car.) 114; Juaraqui *v.* State, 28 Tex. 625.

Not only the truth of the oath, but also the information and belief, must be negatived in an indictment for perjury committed in verifyng an affidavit wherein averments are made upon information, knowledge and belief. Lambert *v.* People, 76 N. Y. 220, reversing 14 Hun (N. Y.) 512. See also Williams *v.* State, 7 Humph. (Tenn.) 47.

In *Virginia*, an indictment against an insolvent debtor for perjury in swearing to a schedule which did not state certain debts owing to him, was *held* bad on demurrer for not averring that he well "knew and remembered" that the omitted debts were then justly due and owing to him. Cook's Case, 1 Rob. (Va.) 729.

It was held by the New York Supreme Court, in People *v.* Williams, 2 N. Y. Supp. 382, that an indictment alleging that the defendant wickedly, falsely, feloniously, etc., testified to certain matters specified, though not in full compliance with Code Crim. Proc. N. Y., § 291, requiring it to contain proper allegations of the falsity of the matter on which perjury is assigned, should be sustained.

An indictment for perjury, which alleges that the defendant, at a certain time, testified to certain matters, "whereas he did know" they were false, sufficiently states that he knew their falsity at the time that he testified to them. State *v.* Wood, 17 Iowa 18; State *v.* Lindenburg, 13 Tex. 27.

2. Weathers *v.* State, 2 Blackf. (Ind.) 278; State *v.* Flagg, 25 Ind. 243; People *v.* Collier, 1 Mich. 137; s. c., 48 Am. Dec. 699; State *v.* Hobbs, 40 N. H. 229; State *v.* Beard, 25 N. J. L. 384; State *v.* Hayward, 1 Nott & M. (S. Car.) 546; Pickering's Case, 8 Gratt. (Va.) 628; State *v.* Thrift, 30 Ind. 211; State *v.* Chandler, 42 Vt. 446; Hembree *v.* State, 52 Ga. 242; State *v.* Trask, 42 Vt. 152; Wood *v.* People, 59 N. Y. 117; Commonwealth *v.* Knight, 12 Mass. 274; s. c., 7 Am. Dec. 72; State *v.* Holden, 48 Mo. 93.

3. Mr. Bishop says that "Where the false testimony was delivered in a trial, the former is the common method and the better practically. Even a few of the cases seem to require it to the exclusion of the latter. Where the perjury was in an affidavit, the latter is perhaps the more common method." 2 Bishop's Crim. Proc., § 921.

See cases cited in last note, and also Partain *v.* State, 22 Tex. App. 100; United States *v.* McHenry, 6 Blatchf. (U. S.) 503; Gandy *v.* State, 23 Neb. 436; Sisk *v.* State, 28 Tex. App. 432; Reg. *v.* Harvey, 8 Cox C. C. 99; State *v.* Nees, 47 Ark. 553; Lea *v.* State, 64 Miss. 278; Washington *v.* State, 22 Tex. App. 26.

Where, upon an indictment for perjury, on a trial for felony, it neither appeared that the matter sworn was material, nor was it alleged to be so, *held*, that if the original indictment had been set out, and the materiality could plainly have been collected, it would have been sufficient without any

6. Averments as to Time and Place.—The rules governing allegations of time and place are those applicable to indictments

special averment, but that one or the other was absolutely necessary. Rex *v.* Dunn, 1 D. & R. 10.

If the indictment shows on its face that the alleged false testimony was material to the issue, an express averment that it was material is unnecessary.

State *v.* Hall, 7 Blackf. (Ind.) 25; State *v.* Johnson, 7 Blackf. (Ind.) 49; Hendricks *v.* State, 26 Ind. 493; Galloway *v.* State, 29 Ind. 442; State *v.* Biebusch, 32 Mo. 276; Lamden *v.* State, 5 Humph. (Tenn.) 83; Reg. *v.* Harvey, 8 Cox C. C. 99; State *v.* Marshall, 47 Mo. 378. So, if facts are stated from which the materiality results as a legal conclusion. State *v.* Nees, 47 Ark. 553.

An indictment for perjury on an arson trial, stating that defendant falsely swore that he saw defendant in the arson case take shavings and light them beside the house which was burned, was held sufficiently to state the materiality of the issue. State *v.* Cave, 81 Mo. 450.

On the other hand, some cases hold that the materiality should appear, not by setting forth the circumstances in detail, as by describing at length the proceedings in the former trial, but by a general allegation that the particular question became material. State *v.* Davis, 69 N. Car. 495; Washington *v.* State, 22 Tex. App. 26, where it is held that the facts showing the materiality of the false statements to the issue need not be stated in the indictment. See also State *v.* Maxwell, 28 La. Ann. 361; State *v.* Trask, 42 Vt. 152.

No false testimony can be included in an assignment of perjury, unless its materiality is alleged. Donohoe *v.* State, 14 Tex. App. 638.

An indictment for perjury for false swearing before a grand jury, which fails to allege that the matter sworn to was material in the investigation before the grand jury, is fatally defective. State *v.* McCormick, 52 Ind. 169.

Where the indictment for perjury contains an express averment of the materiality of the oath, the indictment is sufficient, unless it affirmatively appears from the other averments that it was immaterial. People *v.* Brilliant, 58 Cal. 214; Commonwealth *v.* Farley, Thatch. Cr. Cas. (Mass.) 654.

In an indictment for perjury, an express averment that a question was material lets in evidence to prove that it was so. Reg. *v.* Bennet, 3 C. & K. 124; 5 Cox C. C. 207.

Where the affidavit, on which an indictment for perjury is predicated, was that required as a prerequisite to a marriage license, and the indictment so stated, it need not be averred in terms that the affidavit was "material matter." The fact is sufficiently evident. People *v.* Kelly, 59 Cal. 372.

It is sufficient to charge generally that the false oath was material to the trial of the issue upon which it was taken. State *v.* Mumford, 1 Div. (N. Car.) 519; s. c., 17 Am. Dec. 573; Williams *v.* State, 68 Ala. 551.

On the other hand some cases hold that the other method of charging the materiality is necessary; *i. e.*, that the substance of the matter in respect to which perjury was committed and the effect of the testimony must be set out. See State *v.* Witham, 6 Oregon 366; State *v.* Groves, Busbee (N. Car.) 402; also State *v.* Bowles where it is held that the facts necessary to show that the matter sworn to was material must be distinctly averred, and that a statement of them as a part of the matter is not sufficient.

An indictment is sufficient which avers that upon a certain trial it was a material question whether certain chattels were sold in part payment of one debt or of a certain other debt, and that the defendant falsely swore that they were sold in payment of the debt first named. Commonwealth *v.* Johns, 6 Gray (Mass.) 274.

So where it is averred that each and every part of the testimony tending to establish an alibi on a criminal trial became and was material to such defense. Commonwealth *v.* Flynn, 3 Cush. (Mass.) 525.

See also Lawson *v.* State, 3 Lea (Tenn.) 309; Woods *v.* State, 14 Lea (Tenn.) 460; Reg. *v.* Gardner, 8 C. & P. 737.

See also Reg. *v.* Scott, 13 Cox C. C. 594; Reg. *v.* Bennett, 3 C. & K. 124.

It is not necessary to set forth so much of the proceedings of the former trial as will show the materiality of the question on which the perjury is as-

generally.[1]

7. Counts and Assignments; Miscellaneous Matters; Precedents of Indictments.—One good assignment of perjury will support a general verdict of guilty, although other assignments in the indictment are defective or are not sustained by the proof.[2]

signed; it is sufficient to allege generally that the particular question became material. Rex *v.* Dowlin, 5 T. R. 311.

So held where it was assigned upon a statement made by the accused before a grand jury, upon an investigation of a charge of embezzlement against a banker, that he had deposited with the banker a package containing $525 in county orders in the name of his wife. In such case the indictment need not describe the county orders. Kimmel *v.* People, 92 Ill. 457. See also Pollard *v.* People, 69 Ill. 148.

For examples of indictments held bad for want of sufficient averments of materiality, see State *v.* Tappan, 58 N. H. 152; State *v.* Mace, 76 Me. 64; Commonwealth *v.* Byron, 14 Gray (Mass.) 31; Rex *v.* Nicholl, 1 B. & Ad. 21; Reg. *v.* Goodfellow, C. & M. 569; Reg. *v.* Bartholomew, 1 C. & K. 366; Reg. *v.* Cutts, 4 Cox C. C. 435; State *v.* Shanks, 66 Mo. 560; *In re* Rothaker 11 Abb. N. Cas. (N. Y.) 122; Davis *v.* State, 79 Ala. 20; State *v.* Wood, 11 Ind. 82; Maddox *v.* State, 28 Tex. App. 533; State *v.* McCone, 59 Vt. 117.

1. Rhodes *v.* Commonwealth, 78 Va. 692; Rex *v.* Aylett, 1 T. R. 63. These are sometimes material and necessary to be laid with precision and sometimes not. Rex *v.* Aylett, 1 T. R. 63. A day certain must be named. State *v.* Offutt, 4 Blackf. (Ind.) 355. *Contra*, People *v.* Hoag, 2 Park. Cr. (N. Y.) 9. And see Keaton *v.* People, 32 Mich. 484. An allegation referring only to a certain term of court is insufficient. State *v.* Fenlason, 79 Me. 117. And where the perjury is charged as of the wrong term of court the variance is fatal. State *v.* Lewis, 93 N. Car. 581.

Where a day was not stated upon which trial took place and on which the defendant was sworn the court arrested judgment. United States *v.* Bowman, 2 Wash. (U. S.) 328.

That an indictment stated the time when the offense was committed thus: "At the April term of the H. circuit court, in the year 1867," was held sufficiently certain under the Indiana Code (2 Gav. & H. 402, § 56). State *v.* Thrift, 30 Ind. 211.

An indictment not rendered bad by alleging matter on account of which the perjury was committed to have occurred at a time subsequent to the perjury itself. Richey *v.* Commonwealth, 81 Ky. 524.

It is not a sufficiently precise allegation upon which to found an indictment for perjury, that the prisoner swore that a certain event did not happen within two fixed dates, his attention not having been called to the particular day upon which the transaction was alleged to have taken place. Reg. *v.* Stolady, 1 F. & F. 518.

Allegations that the false swearing was committed before the board of commissioners of said county, and in a proceeding then and there had, are sufficiently definite, where the county and the day and year have been previously mentioned, so that the meaning of the words of reference is plain. State *v.* Schultz, 57 Ind. 19.

Where the examination of a debtor on supplementary proceedings was mainly as to property which had previously belonged to him at different times, an indictment for perjury, alleging that he was then and there owner of a certain amount of property, is too indefinite as to time. State *v.* Cunningham, 116 Ind. 209.

2. Commonwealth *v.* Johns, 6 Gray (Mass.) 274; State *v.* Blaisdell, 59 N. H. 328; Harris *v.* People, 64 N. Y. 148; s. c., 6 Thomp. & C. (N. Y.) 206, 401; Commonwealth *v.* McLaughlin, 122 Mass. 449; State *v.* Hascall, 6 N. H. 352; State *v.* Bordeaux, 93 N. Car. 560. All the several particulars in which the prisoner swore falsely may be embraced in one count. State *v.* Bishop, 1 D. Chip. (Vt.) 120.

Where an indictment contains, in the same count, several assignments of perjury, some of which are good and others are defective in form or not sustained by proof upon the trial, and the court upon its attention being specifically called thereto, refuses to withdraw from the consideration of the jury the defective or unsustained assignments, and exception is taken,

A defect in one count cannot be supplied by intendment from another.[1]

the error is fatal, and a conviction will be reversed. Wood *v.* People, 59 N. Y. 117.

If an indictment contains several assignments of perjury, on one of which no evidence is given on the part of the prosecution, the defendant cannot go into proof to show that the evidence charged by that assignment of perjury to be false, was in reality true. Rex *v.* Hemp, 5 C. & P. 468.

1. Rex *v.* Richards, 7 D. & R. 655; s. c., *Nomine* Rex *v.* Stevens, 5 B. & C. 346.

Variance and Amendment.—An indictment for perjury, alleged as committed on the trial of an issue in a cause, with averments of materiality to such issue, is sustained, although it appears that there were several issues in the cause. Reg. *v.* Smith, 1 F. & F. 98.

A variance between the form of oath proved and that stated in the indictment is immaterial. Reg. *v.* Southwood, 1 F. & F. 356.

Where an indictment alleged that the prisoner was sworn and examined in behalf of J. B., and the proof was that he was sworn and examined in a cause wherein the said J. B. was a party, it was held that the variance was not fatal. People *v.* Burroughs, 1 Park. Cr. (N. Y.) 211.

Where the averment was that the perjury was committed on a trial for setting fire to a certain barn, and the proof was that the offense was setting fire to a stack of barley, an amendment was permitted under 14 & 15 Vict., ch. 100, § 1.

Where the charge was falsely swearing as to the possession of a certain deed to Mary Holt, and the proof was that the prisoner had a deed to Polly Holt and knew that Polly Holt was known as Mary Holt, the variance was held immaterial. Commonwealth *v.* Terry, 114 Mass. 263.

In an indictment for perjury, assigned on the testimony contained in a deposition, it was alleged that the oath was administered by the commissioner on a day specified, he "then being a justice of the peace, and duly authorized to administer said oath;" and that the commissioner was appointed by the court at a term thereof subsequent to the day specified as that on which the oath was administered. *Held*, that the latter allegation was not descriptive, and might be rejected as surplusage. State *v.* Langley, 34 N. H. 529.

U. S. Rev. St., § 5392, defines perjury to be to willfully "state" or "subscribe" what is false, etc. An indictment against a director of a bank charged that he falsely stated that he was *bona fide* owner of stock standing in his name, etc. The instrument produced in evidence purported to be "subscribed," by defendant. *Held*, that it might be shown that a false statement was made; that the question of variance could not be raised because the word "subscribe" alone was used in the instrument aforesaid. United States *v.* Neale, 14 Fed. Rep. 767.

Where the indictment charged that the prisoner swore to having seen A at the house of B on Oct. 30, proof that he swore to having seen A at the house of B on Oct. 29 was held to raise a material variance. State *v.* Ah Sam, 7 Oregon, 477.

So where the charge was that the defendant swore that two persons were together at a certain place "on or about March 1, 1880," and the evidence failed to show that defendant testified to their being together at the place named on or about the date alleged. Roberts *v.* People, 99 Ill. 275.

Where the charge was perjury committed before A and the verdict was "guilty before A and T," the variance was held fatal. State *v.* Mayson, 3 Brev. (S. Car.) 284.

A charge of swearing falsely that $20 was unlawfully received as interest for a loan of $400 is not sustained by proof that the sum lent was $380 and a note given for $400 and interest. State *v.* Tappan, 21 N. H. 56.

An indictment against "John G. T." for perjury in making an affidavit signed by him is sustained by an affidavit signed "Jonh G. T." Tardy *v.* State, 4 Blackf. (Ind.) 152.

An allegation in an indictment for perjury, that A and four others committed an assault on B, is not proved by the production of a record which sets forth a bill of indictment charging A and five others with an assault on B. State *v.* Harvell, 4 Jones (N. Car.) 55.

The indictment set forth that "a warrant for debt due on account for rent" was sued out by the defendant. The warrant given in evidence was not for rent, but for other things. *Held*, that this was a material variance. Commonwealth *v.* Hickman, 2 Va. Cas. 323.

In State *v.* Frisby, 90 Mo. 530, it was held a fatal variance where the matter sworn to was alleged to have taken place on a certain day of the year 1882, while the indictment recited the year 1883. So where the person connected with the matter in question was charged to have been named John and it appeared that his name was Jeremiah. Gandy *v* State, 27 Neb. 707. But where the information charged the affidavit on which the perjury was assigned to have been made by James R. Shea, and the record entry made by the officer before whom the affidavit was made stated that the affidavit was made by R. Shea, but the affidavit itself showed the mistake in the record entry, it was held that there was no material variance. Stefani *v.* State, 124 Ind. 3.

If an indictment undertakes to set out continuously the substance and effect of what the defendant swore when examined as a witness, it is necessary to prove that in substance and effect he swore the whole of that which is thus set out, though the indictment contains several distinct assignments of perjury. Rex *v.* Leefe, 2 Camp. 134.

On a charge of perjury alleged to have been committed before commissioners to examine witnesses in a chancery suit, the indictment stated that the four commissioners were commanded to examine the witnesses. Their commission was put in, and by it the commissioners, or any three or two of them, were commanded to examine the witnesses. *Held*, a fatal variance, and not amendable under 9 Geo. IV, ch. 15; Reg. *v.* Hewins, 9 C. & P. 786.

As to the power of a judge to amend an inaccurate description of a statute referred to in the indictment, see Reg. *v.* Westley, 5 Jur., N. S. 1362; Bell C. C. 193.

It is immaterial that the oath upon which the perjury is assigned contains more than is specified in the assignment. State *v.* Wakefield, 9 Mo. App. 326.

Affidavits. — The indictment must charge that the affidavit was made by the accused, otherwise it cannot be introduced as evidence. Copeland *v.* State, 23 Miss. 257.

An indictment which does not purport to set out a copy of the affidavit or of any part of it, nor its tenor, in whole or in part, but only the substance, is fatally defective. Coppack *v.* State, 36 Ind. 513; State *v.* Umdenstock, 43 Tex. 554.

An indictment for swearing to an account was held defective for not setting out the account with the oath attached and negativing each of the items. Rohrer *v.* State, 13 Tex. App. 163.

In order to a conviction for perjury under N. J. Rev., p. 740, the indictment must allege that the affidavit was necessary and proper to be made, and for a lawful purpose. State *v.* Union Co. Quarter Sessions, 45 N. J. L. 523.

An indictment for perjury, assigned on an affidavit sworn before the court, need not state, nor is it necessary to prove, that the affidavit was filed of record, or exhibited to the court, or in any manner used by the party. Rex *v.* Crossley, 7 T. R. 315.

In an indictment for making a false affidavit, it is sufficient to state that the defendant came before A and took his corporal oath (A having power to administer an oath), without setting out the nature of A's authority. Rex *v.* Callanan, 6 B. & C. 102; 9 D. & R. 97.

Where perjury is assigned upon several parts of an affidavit, those parts may be set out in the indictment as if continuous, although they are in fact separated by the introduction of other matter. Rex *v.* Callanan, 6 B. & C. 102; 9 D. & R. 97.

Where perjury is assigned upon several parts of an affidavit, those parts may be set out in the indictment as if continuous, although they are in fact separated by the introduction of other matter. Rex *v.* Callanan, 6 B. & C. 102; 9 D. & R. 97.

An indictment may be supported against a marksman for swearing falsely in an affidavit, though it would not be receivable in the court it was sworn in, because the jurat did not state that it had been read over to the party swearing it; but the person administering the oath must prove that the party swearing it in fact understood its contents, and the perjury is complete at the time of the swearing of the affidavit; and whether it is receivable in the court or not is immaterial, if the reason why it is not receivable is that some formal regulation is not complied with. Rex *v.* Hailey, 1 C. & P. 258; R. & M. 94.

A person cannot be convicted of perjury on an affidavit, if it refers to a former affidavit, which the prosecutor is not in a condition to prove. Rex *v.* Hailey, 1 C. & P. 258; R. & M. 94.

Swearing in One's Vote at an election.—An indictment is not defective because it does not state the names nor number of the inspectors of election before whom the vote was taken; nor because it does not state that the inspectors in the ward, before whom the vote was taken, were acting for such ward; nor because it does not describe the manner nor form in which the vote was administered, averring that the defendant "was duly sworn and did take his corporal oath" being sufficient; nor because it does not state in terms that the place where the inspectors were convened was legally appointed for holding the election, averring that an election was held at ——— pursuant to the laws, etc., before a board of inspectors legally constituted, etc., being sufficient.

But where, in such an indictment, the allegation of the false oath was that the prisoner swore he had not previously voted at that election; and the assignment of the perjury was that he had voted previously at said election, specifying the place; but without stating that he had so voted before a board of officers duly constituted and authorized according to law, or that any lawful election had been appointed, it was held that this assignment was too general and uncertain, under the rule requiring assignments of perjury to be by special averment negativing the oath; and that a conviction upon the indictment must be reversed. Burns *v.* People, 59 Barb. (N. Y.) 531. See State *v.* Houston, 103 N. Car. 383.

Juror.—As to requisites of an indictment for perjury committed by a juror on his *voir dire*, see State *v.* Moffat, 7 Humph. (Tenn.) 250; Stoekley's Case, 10 Leigh (Va.) 678.

Forms of Indictments.—See, for forms and precedents of indictments, the following cases collected in Bishop's Directions and Forms, § 871, note:

Alabama.—State *v.* Lea, 3 Ala. 603; Gibson *v.* State, 44 Ala. 17, 21; Hood *v.* State, 44 Ala. 81; Johnson *v.* State, 46 Ala. 212; Jacobs *v.* State, 61 Ala. 448.

Arkansas.—State *v.* Green, 24 Ark. 591; State *v.* Kirkpatrick, 32 Ark. 117; Nelson *v.* State, 32 Ark. 192.

California.—People *v.* Brilliant, 58 Cal. 214.

Connecticut.—Arden *v.* State, 11 Conn. 408.

Florida.—Humphreys *v.* State, 17 Fla. 381, 383; Dennis *v.* State, 17 Fla. 389, 390.

Georgia.—Hembree *v.* State, 52 Ga. 242; Pennaman *v.* State, 58 Ga. 336.

Illinois.—Morrell *v.* People, 32 Ill. 499; Kimmel *v.* People, 92 Ill. 457.

Indiana.—Weathers *v.* State, 2 Blackf. (Ind.) 278; Galloway *v.* State, 29 Ind. 442; State *v.* Walls, 54 Ind. 407; State *v.* Schultz, 57 Ind. 19; State *v.* Howard, 63 Ind. 502.

Iowa.—United States *v.* Morgan, Morr. (Iowa) 341; United States *v.* Dickey, Morr. (Iowa) 412; State *v.* Schill, 27 Iowa 263; State *v.* Kinley, 43 Iowa 294; State *v.* Nickerson, 46 Iowa 447.

Kentucky.—Commonwealth *v.* Powell, 2 Metc. (Ky.) 10.

Louisiana.—State *v.* Gibson, 26 La. Ann. 71.

Maine.—State *v.* Corson, 59 Me. 137.

Maryland.—Deckard *v.* State, 38 Md. 186, 188.

Massachusetts.—Commonwealth *v.* Knight, 12 Mass. 274; s. c., 7 Am. Dec. 72; Commonwealth *v.* Warden, 11 Met. (Mass.) 406; Commonwealth *v.* Flynn, 3 Cush. (Mass.) 525; Commonwealth *v.* Johns, 7 Gray (Mass.) 274; Commonwealth *v.* Carel, 105 Mass. 682; Commonwealth *v.* Kimball, 108 Mass. 473; Commonwealth *v.* Terry, 114 Mass. 263; Commonwealth *v.* Grant, 116 Mass. 17; Commonwealth *v.* Butland, 119 Mass. 317, 318; Commonwealth *v.* McLaughlin, 122 Mass. 449; Commonwealth *v.* Sargent, 129 Mass. 115.

Michigan.—People *v.* Fox, 25 Mich. 492.

Mississippi.—Cothran *v.* State, 39 Miss. 541.

Missouri.—State *v.* Bailey, 34 Mo. 350; State *v.* Marshall, 47 Mo. 378; State *v.* Keel, 54 Mo. 183; State *v.* Foulks, 57 Mo. 461; State *v.* Hamilton, 65 Mo. 667; State *v.* Wakefield, 9 Mo. App. 326.

New Hampshire.—State *v.* Hascall, 6 N. H. 352; State *v.* Bailey, 31 N. H. 521.

New York.—People *v.* Phelps, 5 Wend. (N. Y.) 9; Campbell *v.* People,

IV. THE EVIDENCE.—1. Number of Witnesses; Corroborative Evidence Required.—A charge of perjury must be substantiated by the oath of two witnesses, or of one witness supported by corroborating and independent circumstances equivalent in weight to the testimony of a single witness, as the unsupported evidence of one witness would be simply one oath against another.[1]

8 Wend. (N. Y.) 636; Eighmy *v.* People, 79 N. Y. 546; Burns *v.* People, 5 Lans. (N. Y.) 189; People *v.* Burroughs, 1 Park. Cr. (N. Y.) 211; Smith *v.* People, 1 Park. Cr. (N. Y.) 317; People *v.* Sweetman, 3 Park. Cr. (N. Y.) 358; People *v.* McKinney, 3 Park. Cr. (N. Y.) 510.

North Carolina.—State *v.* Ammons, 3 Murph. (N. Car.) 123; State *v.* Mumford, 1 Dev. (N. Car.) 519; s. c., 17 Am. Dec. 573; State *v.* Carland, 3 Dev. (N. Car.) 114; State *v.* Bobbitt, 70 N. Car. 81; State *v.* Colbert, 75 N. Car. 368; State *v.* Davis, 84 N. Car. 787.

Ohio.—Crusen *v.* State, 10 Ohio St. 258; State *v.* Jackson, 36 Ohio St. 281.

Pennsylvania.—Perdue *v.* Commonwealth, 96 Pa. St. 311.

South Carolina.—State *v.* Haywood, 1 Nott & M. (S. Car.) 546; State *v.* McCroskey, 3 McCord (S. Car.) 308.

Tennessee.—State *v.* Steele, 1 Yerg. (Tenn.) 394; Lamden *v.* State, 5 Humph. (Tenn.) 83; State *v.* Bowlus, 3 Heisk. (Tenn.) 29; State *v.* Wise, 3 Lea (Tenn.) 38; Lawson *v.* State, 3 Lea (Tenn.) 309.

Texas.—State *v.* Lindenburg, 13 Tex. 27; State *v.* Powell, 28 Tex. 626; State *v.* Webb, 41 Tex. 67, 68; State *v.* Smith, 43 Tex. 655; Massie *v.* State, 5 Tex. App. 81; Martinez *v.* State, 7 Tex. App. 394; Rohrer *v.* State, 13 Tex. App. 163, 166; Gabrielsky *v.* State, 13 Tex. App. 428; Cox *v.* State, 13 Tex. App. 479.

Vermont.—State *v.* Chamberlain, 30 Vt. 559.

Virginia.—Conner *v.* Commonwealth, 2 Va. Cas. 30; Commonwealth *v.* Hickman, 2 Va. Cas. 323; Stockley's Case, 10 Leigh (Va.) 678; Thomas' Case, 2 Rob. (Va.) 795; Roach's Case, 1 Gratt. (Va.) 561: Pickering's Case, 8 Gratt. (Va.) 628.

West Virginia.—Stofer *v.* State, 3 W. Va. 689.

See also Archbold's Cr. Prac. & Pl., § 592.

Tax Laws.—As to the sufficiency and requisites of indictments for perjury committed in proceedings connected with assessments of taxes, see State *v.* Foulks, 57 Mo. 461; State *v.* Smith, 43 Tex. 655; State *v.* Blackstone, 74 Ind. 592; State *v.* Peters, 57 Vt. 86; State *v.* Reynolds, 108 Ind. 353; State *v.* Cunningham, 66 Iowa 94.

As to sufficiency of indictments in particular cases, see Commonwealth *v.* Sargent, 129 Mass. 115; De Bernie *v.* State, 19 Ala. 23; Commonwealth *v.* Warden, 11 Met. (Mass.) 406; Smith *v.* People, 1 Park. Cr. (N. Y.) 317; State *v.* Sleeper, 37 Vt. 122; State *v.* Flagg, 25 Ind. 369; State *v.* Gallimore, 2 Ired. (N. Car.) 372; McMurray *v.* State, 6 Ala. 324; West *v.* State, 8 Tex. App. 119; Mattingly *v.* State, 8 Tex. App. 345; Brown *v.* State, 47 Ala. 47; State *v.* Walls, 54 Ind. 407; Flint *v.* People, 35 Mich. 491; Wood *v.* People, 3 Thomp. & C. (N. Y.) 506; s. c., 1 Hun (N. Y.) 381; Rex. *v.* Browne, 3 C. & P. 572; Reg. *v.* Pearson, 8 C. & P. 119; Reg. *v.* Chapman, 2 C. & K. 846; 1 Den. C. C. 432; Rex *v.* Foster, R. & R., C. C. 152; Reg. *v.* Burraston, 4 Jur. 697; Reg. *v.* Webster, Bell C. C. 154; 8 Cox C. C. 187; Reg. *v.* Whitehouse, 3 Cox C. C. 86; Reg. *v.* Schlisinger, 10 Q. B. 670; 2 Cox C. C. 200; Reg. *v.* Verrier, 4 P. & D. 161; 12 A. & E. 317; Reg. *v.* London, 12 Cox C. C. 50; Reg. *v.* Parker, 1 L. R., C. C. 225; 18 W. R. 353; Reg. *v.* Parker, C. & M. 639; Ryals *v.* Reg., 11 Q. B. 781; 3 Cox C. C. 254; Stefani *v.* State, 124 Ind. 3; Kerfoot *v.* Commonwealth (Ky. 1889), 12 S. W. Rep. 189; People *v.* Naylor, 82 Cal. 607; United States *v.* Cuddy, 39 Fed. Rep. 696.

1. Rex *v.* Lee, 3 Russ. C. &. M. 78; Champney's Case, 2 Lewin C. C. 258; Reg. *v.* Braithwaite, 8 Cox C. C. 254; 1 F. & F. 638; Reg. *v.* Boulter, 3 C. & K. 236; 2 Den. C. C. 396; 5 Cox C. C. 543; People *v.* Stone, 32 Hun (N. Y.) 41; McClerkin *v.* State, 20 Fla. 879; Gartman *v.* State, 16 Tex. App. 215; State *v.* Heed, 57 Mo. 252; People *v.* Davis, 61 Cal. 536; Williams *v.* Commonwealth, 91 Pa. St. 493.

The circumstances corroborating the testimony of a single witness must relate to a material matter adduced by the

The testimony of a single witness, however, is sufficient to prove that the defendant swore as alleged in the indictment,[1] as it is not necessary to prove by two witnesses every fact which goes to make out the assignment of perjury.[2]

Proving merely that the defendant has testified at different times to irreconcilable facts is not enough. By further independent evidence one or the other statement must be shown to be false.[3]

But the direct oath of one witness together with the declarations of the prisoner, contradictory of the oath on which perjury is assigned, is sufficient to convict.[4]

State in support of the charge, and must produce a deep conviction in the minds of the court and jury. Hernandez *v.* State, 18 Tex. App. 134; s. c., 51 Am. Rep. 295; State *v.* Bine, 43 Tex. 532.

The rule that the testimony of a single witness is not sufficient to sustain an indictment for perjury is not a mere technical rule, but a rule founded on substantial justice; and evidence confirmatory of that one witness in some slight particulars only is not sufficient to warrant a conviction. Reg. *v.* Yates, C. & M. 132.

The corroborative evidence need not be such as to equal the positive and direct oath of a witness if it be enough to give a clear preponderance to the proof on the part of the State. Crusen *v.* State, 10 Ohio St. 258.

Where there are several assignments of perjury in the indictment, the testimony of a single witness as to one assignment is not corroborated by testimony of another witness as to another assignment; but with respect to the matter of each assignment the testimony of a single witness must be corroborated. Williams *v.* Commonwealth, 91 Pa. St. 493.

A witness cannot corroborate himself by showing that he brought suit on notes falsely sworn by defendant to be accommodation notes. Gabrielsky *v.* State, 13 Tex. App. 428.

1. Commonwealth *v.* Pollard, 12 Met. (Mass.) 225; State *v.* Hayward, 1 Nott & M. (S. Car.) 546; State *v.* Wood, 17 Iowa 18; 2 Hawk. P. C., ch. 46, § 10; Roscoe Crim. Ev. (2d. ed.) 770; 1 McNally on Ev. 37; 3 Greenleaf on Ev., § 198. There is a statement to the contrary in a report, two lines in length only, of State *v.* Howard, 4 McCord (S. Car.) 159, but it would seem that this should be entitled to no weight.

2. Reg. *v.* Roberts, 2 C. & K. 607, where A, to prove an alibi for B, had sworn that B was not out of his sight between the hours of 8 a. m. and 9 a. m. on a certain day, and on this perjury was assigned. Proof by one witness that between those hours A was at one place on foot, and by another witness that between those hours B was walking at another place six miles off—*held*, to be sufficient proof of the assignment of perjury.

3. Freeman *v.* State, 19 Fla. 552; State *v.* Williams, 30 Mo. 364; Peterson *v.* State, 74 Ala. 34; Reg. *v.* Wheatland, 8 C. & P. 238; Reg. *v.* Hughes, 1 C. & K. 519.

But where a defendant, by a subsequent deposition, expressly contradicts and falsifies a former one made by him, and in such subsequent deposition expressly admits and alleges that such former one was intentionally false at the time it was made, or in such subsequent deposition testifies to such other facts and circumstances as to render the corrupt motive apparent and negative the probability of mistake in regard to the first, he may be properly convicted upon an indictment charging the first deposition to be false, without any other proof than that of the two depositions. People *v.* Burden, 9 Barb. (N. Y.) 467.

On an indictment for perjury in swearing falsely to a deposition, the deponent having afterwards testified on the stand that the facts stated therein were not true, the prisoner is not estopped from showing, in his defense, the truth of the facts stated in the deposition. State *v.* J. B., 1 Tyler (Vt.) 269.

4. State *v.* Molier, 1 Dev. (N. Car.) 263; Rex *v.* Knill, 5 B. & A. 929, n.

As where, in addition to the evidence of one witness, there is proof of an account, or a letter written by the defendant contradicting his statement on oath. Rex *v.* Mayhew, 6 C. & P. 315.

On a trial for perjury committed in a certain trial, evidence that defendant made a contradictory sworn statement before the grand jury is not to be considered as corroborative of the witness who testifies to what the defendant swore at the trial. A conviction cannot be had on the strength of these former statements, unless their truth is substantiated by other evidence. Peterson *v.* State, 74 Ala. 34.

In one case, the contradictory statement of the prisoner—a policeman—in making a sworn complaint, together with two different declarations at different times to different persons to the same effect, as to what he swore to in the complaint, and his admissions on the trial of the complaint showing a corrupt motive for his testimony there was held sufficient to convict. Reg. *v.* Hook, Dears. & B. C. C. 606; 8 Cox C. C. 5.

The prisoner's manner and testimony may be sufficient to justify conviction on the testimony of one other witness where he testifies in his own behalf. State *v.* Miller, 24 W. Va. 802.

To convict of perjury, under the act of March 1, 1823, in making false entries at the custom-house in regard to the cost of imported goods, documentary evidence and the correspondence of the accused are sufficient without living witnesses; and such evidence is the best.

The cases in which a living witness to the *corpus delicti* of the defendant, in a prosecution for perjury, may be dispensed with are: 1st. All such where a person charged with a perjury by false swearing to a fact directly disproved by documentary or written testimony springing from himself, with circumstances showing the corrupt intent.

2nd. In cases where the perjury charged is contradicted by a public record, proved to have been well known to the defendant when he took the oath, the oath only being proved to have been taken. 3rd. In cases where the party is charged with taking an oath contrary to what he must necessarily have known to be the truth, and the false swearing can be proved by his own letters relating to the fact sworn to, or by other written testimony existing and being found in the possession of the defendant, and which has been treated by him as containing the evidence of the fact recited in it. United States *v.* Wood, 14 Pet. (U. S.) 430.

The history of this relaxation of the sternness of the old rule is thus stated by Mr. JUSTICE WAYNE, in delivering the opinion of the court in United States *v.* Wood, 14 Pet. (U. S.) 440, 441: "At first two witnesses were required to convict in a case of perjury; both swearing directly adversely from the defendant's oath. Contemporaneously with this requisition, the larger number of witnesses on one side or the other prevailed. Then a single witness, corroborated by other witnesses, swearing to circumstances bearing directly upon the imputed *corpus delicti* of a defendant, was deemed sufficient. Next, as in the case of Rex *v.* Knill, 5 B. & A. 929, n., with a long interval between it and the preceding, a witness who gave proof only of the contradictory oaths of the defendant on two occasions, one being an examination before the House of Lords, and the other an examination before the House of Commons, was held to be sufficient; though this principle had been acted on as early as 1764, by JUSTICE YATES, as may be seen in the note to the case of Rex *v.* Harris, 5 B. & Ald. 937, and was acquiesced in by LORD MANSFIELD, and JUSTICES WILMOT and ASTON. We are aware that, in a note to Rex *v.* Mayhew, 6 C. & P. 315, a doubt is implied concerning the case decided by JUSTICE YATES; but it has the stamp of authenticity from its having been referred to in a case happening ten years afterwards before JUSTICE CHAMBRE, as will appear by the note in 5 B. & Ald. 937. Afterwards, a single witness, with the defendant's bill of costs (not sworn to) in lieu of a second witness, delivered by the defendant to the prosecutor, was held sufficient to contradict his oath; and in that case LORD DENMAN says: 'A letter written by the defendant contradicting his statement on oath, would be sufficient to make it unnecessary to have a second witness,' 6 C. & P. 315. We thus see that this rule, in its proper application, has been expanded beyond its literal terms, as cases have occurred in which proofs have been offered equivalent to the end intended to be accomplished by the rule."

For instances of evidence held to be sufficiently corroborative to take the case to the jury, or to support a conviction, see Reg. *v.* Gardiner, 8 C. & P. 737; Reg. *v.* Webster, 1 F. & F.

2. Miscellaneous Matters of Evidence.—If made in court any one present can testify to the oath as in other proceedings.[1]

The person by whom the oath was administered may testify to the fact that he was an acting magistrate, and his testimony, in connection with the original certificate of the administration of the oath, is sufficient to show the administration of the oath, without producing a copy of the record.[2] To call him as a witness, however, is not absolutely necessary.[3]

Proof that the officer has acted as such is sufficient *prima facie* proof of his authority without putting in evidence his commission or other facts giving jurisdiction.[4]

Where depositions have been made out of court, the *jurat*, with proof as to the signature of the notary or other officer and the affiant, is sufficient *prima facie* proof of the taking of the oath.[5]

The place of administering the oath is also sufficiently shown

515; Reg. *v.* Hare, 13 Cox C. C. 174.

For instances where the evidence was held not to be sufficiently corroborative to support a conviction, see Reg. *v.* Parker, C. & M. 639; Reg. *v.* Owen, 6 Cox C. C. 105; Reg. *v.* Boulter, 3 C. & K. 236; 5 Cox C. C. 543.

Where one is indicted for falsely swearing that he had not sold liquor unlawfully, proof of one sale is not corroborative evidence of another sale. Lea *v.* State, 64 Miss. 278.

And see also on the general question of the quantity of evidence necessary to sustain a conviction, Flemister *v.* State, 81 Ga. 768; State *v.* Aikens, 32 Iowa 403; Wells *v.* Commonwealth (Ky. 1887), 6 S. W. Rep. 150; Lea *v.* State, 64 Miss. 278; State *v.* Day, 100 Mo. 242; Gandy *v.* State, 23 Neb. 436; State *v.* Swaim, 97 N. Car. 462; Smith *v.* State, 22 Tex. App. 196; Washington *v.* State, 22 Tex. App. 26; Parker *v.* State, 25 Tex. App. 743; Maines *v.* State, 26 Tex. App. 14; Kitchen *v.* State (Tex. 1890), 14 S. W. Rep. 392; United States *v.* Mayer, Deady (U. S.) 127.

1. Bish. Crim. Proc., § 933, *citing* Rex *v.* Canning, 19 Howell St. Tr. 283, 323; Keator *v.* People, 32 Mich. 484; Reg. *v.* Tew, Dears. 429; 29 Eng. L. & Eq. 537; Rex *v.* Rowley, R. & M., N. P. 299; Rex *v.* McArthur, Peake, § 155; Rex *v.* Brady, 1 Leach (4th ed.) 327.

2. State *v.* Harcall, 6 N. H. 352.

3. Rex *v.* Browning, 3 Cox C. C. 437.

4. State *v.* Gregory, 2 Murph. (N. Car.) 69; Keator *v.* People, 32 Mich. 484; Lambert *v.* People, 6 Abb. N. Cas. (N. Y.) 181.

5. Rex *v.* Spencer, 1 C. & P. 260; R. & M. 97; Rex *v.* Morris, 1 Leach 50; Rex *v.* Benson, 2 Camp. 508; Rex *v.* Morris, 2 Burr. 1189; Rex *v.* Howard, 1 Moody & R. 187; Commonwealth *v.* Warden, 11 Met. (Mass.) 406, 409.

If the affidavit were actually used by the prisoner in the cause in which it was taken, proof of this fact will supersede the necessity of proving his handwriting. Rex *v.* James, 1 Show. 397; Carth. 220. Carthew's report of this case was denied in Crook *v.* Dowling, 3 Doug. 75, it not appearing that the affidavit, of which a copy only was offered, had been used by the prisoner. And see Rex *v.* Bowen, McClel. & Yo. 383; 3 Greenl. Ev., § 192.

Where the notary testified that he knew nothing of the transaction, except from seeing his signature, and other witnesses testified that the jurat was filled out in the absence of the prisoner, it was held that there must be an acquittal in the absence of evidence, independent of the jurat, as to the taking of the oath. Case *v.* People, 76 N. Y. 242, reversing 14 Hun (N. Y.) 503.

The prosecution need not prove that the notary signing the jurat resided in the State, or that he had taken the oath of office; but evidence to the contrary is admissible in behalf of the prisoner. Lambert *v.* People, 14 Hun (N. Y.) 512; s. c., 6 Abb. N. Cas. (N. Y.) 181.

by its mention in the *jurat*, in the absence of proof to the contrary.[1]

1. Rex *v.* Spencer, Ryan & Moody, N. P. 97; 1 Car. & P. 260. And see Reg. *v.* Turner, 2 C. & K. 732; Rex *v.* Emden, 9 East 437; Van Dusen *v.* People, 78 Ill. 645.

Proof that the defendant was "sworn and examined as a witness," supports an averment that he was sworn on the Holy Gospel, that being the ordinary mode of swearing. Rex *v.* Rowley, R. & M. 302. But see Rex *v.* M'Carther, Peake 155.

It being affirmatively shown that an oath was administered, the presumption is that it was rightfully done. State *v.* Mace, 86 N. Car. 668. And where a witness testifies that the defendant swore, it cannot be contended that there was no evidence of an oath having been taken in the proceeding on which the charge of perjury is based. State *v.* Glisson, 93 N. Car. 506.

The testimony of the person by whom the oath was administered is admissible to show that he was an acting magistrate. His testimony is also sufficient, in connection with the original certificate of the administration of the oath, to show that the oath was administered by him to the respondent without the production of a copy of the record. State *v.* Hascall, 6 N. H. 352.

To prove that the oath was administered as indicated by the clerk's jurat, evidence is admissible of a general practice in court to administer an oath to petitioners for certain writs in certain cases. Commonwealth *v.* Kimball, 108 Mass. 473.

But it was held error to instruct the jury that they must find that the defendant was sworn before giving the testimony complained of; but that "it being the uniform rule and custom in the courts to administer oaths to witnesses before they testify, you will be justified in finding that the defendant was sworn on less evidence than would be necessary to establish a fact of a different character, not occurring according to any fixed rule or custom." A court has no right to assume the existence of a rule or custom not proved or admitted of record. Hitesman *v.* State, 48 Ind. 473.

To prove the making of a false declaration under the English Pawnbrokers' Act (39 & 40 Geo. III, ch. 99), it is not absolutely necessary to call the magistrate before whom it was made or some one present at the time. Reg. *v.* Browning, 3 Cox C. C. 437.

B was indicted for perjury committed in an affidavit alleged to have been made by him in order to obtain a marriage license. The evidence showed that some person went to the vicar-general's office, and gave certain instructions, in accordance with which an affidavit was filled up by one of the clerks, which, after having been read over to the applicant, was signed by him. B's father proved that the signature to the affidavit was in his son's handwriting. The custom of the vicar-general's office was for the clerk who filled up the affidavit to go with the applicant, and get him to swear to it before a surrogate. Neither the clerk in the vicar-general's office nor the surrogate could identify B as having sworn to the affidavit, and, although the clergyman who married B recognized him as being the person who was married under the license granted on the strength of the affidavit signed by him, yet he did not receive it from him on the day of the marriage, but he received it on the previous day from the verger of his church. *Held*, that further proof of the identity of the person who swore to the affidavit with the person who signed it was necessary, before B could be convicted of perjury assigned on a false statement contained in it. Reg. *v.* Barnes, 10 Cox C. C. 539.

An office copy of a bill in chancery, which a witness examined with the original, but which office copy contained abbreviations, such as "pnl. este." for the words "personal estate" in the original bill, is not such an examined copy as will be evidence to support an allegation of a bill in chancery on an indictment for perjury, committed in an affidavit in that suit in chancery. Reg. *v.* Christian, C. & M. 388.

An indictment against a deponent for perjury, committed in giving a deposition taken in *perpetuam*, concluded with the following words: "As by his answers to said interrogatories written in said deposition remaining, will, among other things, appear." *Held*, that, upon the rejection of the deposition, parol evidence was inadmissible to prove the testimony of the deponent. Commonwealth *v.* Stone, Thach. Cr. Cas. (Mass.) 604.

On an indictment for perjury, setting forth, with proper innuendoes, a copy of a deposition before a magistrate, written in the English language, and signed by the defendant, he may be convicted on proof of a verbal deposition in the Welsh language of which the written deposition, signed by him, is the substance. Reg. *v.* Thomas, 2 C. & K. 806.

Corrupt Intent.—On a trial for perjury, evidence is admissible to show that the motives which actuated the prisoner, at the time of committing the alleged offense, were corrupt; as, for instance, to show that, when he swore to a complaint against the prosecutor, ostensibly to procure sureties of the peace, his object was, in fact, to coerce that person to settle a civil suit. State *v.* Hascall, 6 N. H. 352.

To show that perjury was willful and corrupt, evidence may be given of expressions of malice used by the party towards the person against whom he gave the false evidence. Rex *v.* Munton, 3 C. & P. 498.

Where a person is indicted for having made a false declaration as to a fire having taken place at his house, evidence may be given, that, with the declaration, he sent a certificate, which stated the fire to have occurred, and that the signatures to that certificate were all forgeries, as this evidence may go to show that the declaration was willfully false. Reg. *v.* Boynes, 1 C. & K. 65.

Where the assignment of perjury, was, that the defendant had falsely sworn that A had struck him, when in fact another assailant struck the blow, evidence is competent in order to disprove a corrupt motive that the defendant on recovering from the unconsciousness caused by the blow, had given the same account of the transaction as in his testimony on the trial of the case in which perjury was charged. State *v.* Curtis, 12 Ired. (N. Car.) 270.

Where defendant is charged with swearing falsely as to the non-existence of a partnership, it is competent to show that he was legally advised that such partnership did not exist. State *v.* McKinney, 42 Iowa 205.

Where the issue on a trial of an indictment for perjury was whether the defendant swore willfully, absolutely, knowingly and falsely, in swearing that he did not make and deliver a promissory note to the prosecutor, nor authorize any one else to make the note for him, and it was in evidence that the defendant could not read or write, and that the note was written and signed by a third party, though at the request of defendant, and read to him, it was error in the court to refuse to permit the defendant to prove that "it was the understanding of the parties to the paper which was executed that the same was not intended as a note, but simply as a memorandum of an agreement to submit a controversy to arbitration." Flemister *v.* State, 48 Ga. 170.

On a trial for perjury, alleged to have been committed at the hearing of a complaint for burning a ship, the district attorney introduced evidence that a reward was offered by the owner of the ship, and by citizens of the town where the ship was burned, for the detection of the incendiary, and was known to this defendant, and contended that it was this reward which induced the commission of the alleged perjury. *Held*, that evidence was then admissible for the defendant; that he came from his residence in another State to give such evidence on that hearing, reluctantly, and at the earnest solicitation of the insurers of the ship. Commonwealth *v.* Brady, 7 Gray (Mass.) 320.

Competency of Witnesses.—Where perjury was alleged to have been committed before a grand jury it is not illegal for the jurors before whom the false testimony was given to testify before the grand jury which finds the indictment for perjury, although they were not required to do so by judicial order.

For the obligation of secrecy imposed on a grand jury is due and owing to the public, and not to a witness appearing before them, and therefore its violation cannot be an occasion of offense to him. The rule is designed not for the protection of witnesses but for that of grand jurors, and in furtherance of public justice. People *v.* Young, 31 Cal. 564. See also State *v.* Broughton, 7 Ired. (N. Car.) 96; s. c., 45 Am. Dec. 507.

It seems that this would not be permitted at common law. See Rex *v.* Hughes, 1 C. & K. 519.

But a person may be indicted for perjury who gives false evidence before a grand jury when examined as a witness before them upon a bill of indictment; and another witness on the same indictment who is in the grand jury-room while such person is under examination, is competent to prove that such witness swore before the grand jury, and so is a police-officer, who was stationed within the grand jury-room door, to receive the different bills at the door, and take them to the foreman of the grand jury; these persons not being sworn to secrecy, although the grand jury is. Reg. *v.* Hughes, 1 C. & K. 519.

On an indictment for perjury alleged to have been committed at the *quarter sessions*, the chairman at the quarter sessions ought not to be called upon to give evidence as to what the defendant swore at the quarter sessions. Reg. *v.* Gazard, 8 C. & P. 595.

Summons—Proving Commencement of Judicial Proceedings.—In an indictment for perjury before justices of the peace, there must be formal proof of the commencement of the proceedings by production of the summons, information or the like. Reg. *v.* Hurrell, 3 F. & F. 271.

A summons was granted upon an information, and upon the hearing of the summons at the Westminster police court, the perjury assigned was committed. The production of the information without the summons on the perjury trial was held insufficient. Rex *v.* Whybrow, 8 Cox C. C. 438. But *compare* Reg. *v.* Scott, 2 L. R., Q. B. Div. 415; 13 Cox C. C. 594; Reg. *v.* Smith, 1 L. R., C. C. 110; 11 Cox C. C. 10.

In perjury, the affidavit of service of notice or application for leave to issue execution against a shareholder in a joint stock company is insufficient evidence, not having the notice annexed to it. Reg. *v.* Hudson, 1 F. & F. 56.

A defendant was indicted for perjury, alleged to have been committed by him on the hearing before justices of a summons charging him with being the father of an illegitimate child. *Held*, that, to support the indictment, it was necessary to give evidence of the charge made by the mother, either by production of the original order made thereon, or by giving secondary evidence of the summons after notice to the defendant to produce it; and that, in the absence of such notice, it was not sufficient to produce the minutes of the proceedings by the clerk to the justices, those minutes being of no greater authority than the notes of a short-hand writer. Reg. *v.* Newall, 6 Cox C. C. 21.

Records.—In an indictment for perjury on a trial at *nisi prius*, it was held that the *postea* must be produced by the plaintiff. Respublica *v.* Gross, 2 Yeates (Pa.) 479; and that the *postea* alone was sufficient evidence to prove that there was a trial, on an indictment for perjury committed on the trial of a former cause. Anonymous, Bull. N. P. 243.

Where no *postea* was drawn up, owing to the fact that a rule for a new trial was pending, the *nisi prius* record with the minute of the verdict indorsed upon it, was deemed to afford sufficient proof of the trial at *nisi prius*. Rex *v.* Browne, 3 C. & P. 572: M. & M. 315.

It is not necessary to produce a copy of the second of the same court in the cause in which the perjury was committed. The court is presumed to know its own record. United States *v.* Erskine, 4 Cranch C. C. 299.

On a trial for perjury in an action growing out of a written contract, it is necessary to produce the record or papers of the suit and the contract. M'Murry *v.* State, 6 Ala. 324.

The record of the court at which perjury is charged to have been committed, is not excluded in consequence of the day of holding being misrecited in the indictment, especially if under a *videlicet*. State *v.* Clark, 2 Tyler (Vt.) 277.

An allegation in an indictment for perjury, that judgment was entered up in an action, is proved by the production of the book from the judgment office in which the *incipitur* is entered. Reg. *v.* Gordon, C. & M. 410.

If, in an indictment for perjury against C D, it is averred that a cause was depending between A B and C D, a notice of set-off entitled in a cause A B *v.* C D, and signed by the attorney of C D, is not sufficient evidence to support the allegation. Rex *v.* Stoveld, 6 C. & P. 489.

An allegation, that, "on, etc., at, etc., a certain indictment was preferred at the quarter sessions of the peace then and there holden in and for the county of W, against the defendant and one T E, which indictment was then and there found a true bill," is not supported by the production of the original indictment with the words "true bill" indorsed on it, it being necessary that a regular record should be drawn up and proved, either by its production or an examined copy of it. Porter *v.* Cooper, 6 C. P. 354.

See also, Rex *v.* Ward, 6 C. & P. 366; Reg. *v.* Dodsworth, 8 C. & P. 218; 2 Jur. 131; Reg. *v.* Newman, 3 C.

& K. 240; 2 Den. C. C. 390; 16 Jur. 111; 5 Cox C. C. 547.

Proving the Testimony on Which the Perjury Is Assigned.—It is necessary to prove only so much of the testimony of the witness as relates to the particular fact on which the perjury is assigned. United States *v.* Erskine, 4 Cranch (C. C.) 299; Rex *v.* Rowley, R. & M. 299.

One older English case held that the whole of the defendant's testimony had to be proved. Rex *v.* Jones, Peake 37; and another that such was the rule except where the matter arose upon cross-examination of the defendant. Rex *v.* Dowlin, Peake 170.

The whole of that set out in the indictment as sworn to by the accused must be substantially proved. State *v.* Frisby, 90 Mo. 530.

The exact words used by the prisoner need not be proved, provided the substance of his testimony is given. Taylor *v.* State, 48 Ala. 157.

Although the perjury is alleged to have been committed on an examination before a committing magistrate, parol evidence may be introduced to show what the accused swore to before the magistrate. People *v.* Curtis, 50 Cal. 95.

The notes of evidence taken by a judge on a trial are not admissible in evidence to prove what was said on that trial. When, therefore, on a trial for perjury, alleged to have been committed by the defendant as a witness on a trial of felony before a queen's counsel assisting the judges, his notes of the evidence given on that occasion were tendered (on proof of his handwriting) —*held*, that such notes were not admissible. Reg. *v.* Child, 5 Cox C. C. 197. *Compare* Reg. *v.* Morgan, 6 Cox C. C. 107.

The assessor's memorandum book containing pencil notes of property handed in by the defendant is not competent evidence to prove that the property therein was that returned by the defendant; that it was all that was returned by him, or that he swore to it as a correct list, on a trial for perjury in swearing to a false list of property. People *v.* Quinn, 18 Cal. 122.

Proof as to the Falsity of the Testimony.—In *Iowa*, where the defendant in a civil action pleads in bar the statute of limitations, the plaintiff may call him as a witness to remove the bar, and is bound by his evidence. Nevertheless one swearing falsely under such circumstances may be indicted for perjury, and evidence (inadmissible for that purpose in the civil action) may be introduced to show that he swore falsely. State *v.* Voght, 27 Iowa 117.

On a charge of perjury in swearing that the defendant owned land in a certain town worth $5,000, the grantee in a deed to a defendant of the land may be admitted as a witness to prove that the defendant paid him nothing for the land. A charge that the defendant falsely swore to the possession of personal property at G, in the county of E, and commonwealth of M, is supported by proof of his swearing to a written statement as to property at G, in county of E, without mentioning the commonwealth of M. Commonwealth *v.* Butland, 119 Mass. 317.

On a charge of perjury in swearing to an alibi, evidence showing the falsity of the alibi is admissible; but declarations of the defendant on the former trial made before that took place and tending to show his guilt, but not made in the presence of the one accused of perjury, are inadmissible. Brown *v.* State, 57 Miss. 424.

An indictment for perjury by testifying, upon the trial of a complaint for an assault upon this defendant, that the person complained of did not assault him on a day named, whereas, in fact, as this indictment alleged, he did so assault him on that day, is not supported by evidence that this defendant testified as alleged, and that he was so assaulted either on the day named or the day before. Commonwealth *v.* Monahan, 9 Gray (Mass.) 119.

On trial of a person for perjury, in having sworn that he witnessed the sale of certain property—*held*, that he might prove that the sale took place on a different day from the one he had sworn to, although this would contradict another witness without having laid the basis therefor. State *v.* Faulk, 30 La. Ann., pt. 2, 831.

Where prosecution, for the purpose of showing the falsity of testimony given for the defense in a hearing before magistrates, attempted to introduce in evidence a conviction by the magistrates in the face of the testimony on which perjury was assigned, such conviction was held irrelevant. Reg. *v.* Goodfellow, C. & M. 569.

Hearsay evidence as to indebtedness of the accused is inadmissible to show falsity of defendant's deposition in qualifying as bail. Pollard *v.* People, 69 Ill. 148.

On a trial for perjury in testifying, on a former trial of a third person for murder, that a confession of defendant therein offered in evidence by the prosecution, had been obtained by intimidation, evidence of the attorneys for such third person that, about an hour after his purported confession, they visited him in jail, found him greatly agitated, and that he told them that the county attorney had threatened him that he would be hung if he did not confess, and also evidence tending to show that the purported confession was false in fact, other parties having committed the murder, is admissible, where defendant's testimony as to the intimidation, though positively denied by the prosecution, was corroborated by circumstances. Parker *v.* State, 25 Tex. App. 743.

F was indicted for perjury, committed by deposing to an affidavit in a cause wherein he was the plaintiff, and E the defendant, that he owed him £50. *Held*, that, in support of this indictment, evidence was not admissible; that the cause of F against E was, after the making of the affidavit, referred by consent, and an award made that E owed nothing to F. Reg. *v.* Moreau, 11 Q. B. 1028; 12 Jur. 626; 17 L. J., Q. B. 187.

If A is indicted for perjury, in swearing that he did not enter into a verbal agreement with B and C for them to become joint dealers and copartners in the trade or business of druggists, and it appears that, in fact, B was a druggist, keeping a shop with which A had nothing to do, but that A and C, being sworn brokers, could not trade, and therefore made speculations in drugs in B's name with his consent, he agreeing to divide profits and losses with A and C, this will not support the indictment, as this is not the sort of partnership denied by A upon oath. Rex *v.* Tucker, 2 C. & P. 500.

Secondary Evidence.—Where perjury is assigned upon a written instrument, subsequently lost, secondary evidence is admissible. Reg. *v.* Milnes, 2 F. & F. 10.

A solicitor was indicted for having sworn that there was no draft of a certain statutory declaration made by a client. No notice to produce the draft had been given to the solicitor, and upon his trial it was proved to have been last seen in his possession. Secondary evidence having been given of its contents—*held*, that, in the absence of such notice, secondary evidence was inadmissible. Reg. *v.* Elworthy, 1 L. R., C. C. 103; 10 Cox C. C. 579. On the other hand, where the witness swearing to the words spoken by way of oath by the prisoner when he administered the same, said that he held a paper in his hand at the same time when he administered the oath, from which it was supposed that he read the words—*held*, that parol evidence of what he in fact said was sufficient without giving him notice to produce such paper. Rex *v.* Moore, 6 East 419.

Documents.—An allegation that the defendant made his warrant of attorney directed to R. W. and F. B., "then and still being attorneys," is proved by putting in the warant of attorney. Rex *v.* Cooke, 7 C. & P. 559.

An indictment for making a false declaration under 5 & 6 Wm. IV, ch. 62, § 18, cannot be sustained when the deed or written instrument of which the declaration is confirmatory is not duly proved. Reg. *v.* Cox, 4 F. & F. 42.

Where a written paper is referred to, the place and time of subscribing it by the accused being involved in the alleged perjury, as set forth in the indictment, such paper is proper evidence at the trial. Osburn *v.* State, 7 Ohio 212.

In an indictment for perjury, it was alleged that A made his will, and thereby appointed B his executor, the production of the probate is the proper proof of this allegation; but if it had been necessary to prove that A had devised real estates, the original will must have been produced. and one of the attesting witnesses called. Reg. *v.* Turner, 2 C. & K. 732.

In an indictment for perjury, it was averred that a suit was instituted in the prerogative court by C against B, to dispute the validity of a codicil to a will. *Held*, that the production of the original allegations of both parties in the suit, signed by their advocates, and proof of their advocate's signatures, and that they acted as advocates in that court, such allegations being produced from the registrar of the court, was sufficient proof of the averment, and that the caveat need not be produced. Reg. *v.* Turner, 2 C. & K. 732.

Character.—Good character is evidence, but not strong, in favor of the defendant. Schaller *v.* State, 14 Mo. 502. See also Rex *v.* Hemp, 5 C. & P. 468.

Dying declarations are not admissible in evidence on a perjury trial. Rex *v.* Mead, 4 D. & R. 120; 2 B. & C. 605.

V. Subornation of Perjury.—Subornation of perjury is procuring a person to commit a perjury, which he actually commits in consequence of such procurement.[1] As to the requisites of the indictment and proof, nothing especial need be said beyond the statements already made in foregoing sections of this title.[2]

Admissions and Declarations.—On the trial of an indictment for perjury on the crown side of the assizes, where it appeared that the attorneys on both sides had agreed that the formal proofs should be dispensed with, and that part of the prosecutor's case should be admitted, the judge would not allow this admission. Reg. *v.* Thornhill, 8 C. & P. 574.

A judge will not allow a criminal case upon the crown side of the assizes to be tried on admissions, unless they are made at the trial by the defendant or his counsel. Reg. *v.* Thornhill, 8 C. & P. 574.

And see further as bearing upon miscellaneous questions of evidence raised on trials for perjury, Barnett *v.* State, 89 Ala. 165; Gordon *v.* State, 48 N. J. L. 611; Lambert *v.* People, 6 Abb. N. Cas. (N. Y.) 181; State *v.* Green, 100 N. Car. 547; Davidson *v.* State 22 Tex. App. 372; Maines *v.* State, 23 Tex. App. 568; Brown *v.* State, 24 Tex. App. 170; Littlefield *v.* State, 24 Tex. App. 167; Anderson *v.* State, 24 Tex. App. 705; Woodson *v.* State, 24 Tex. App. 153; Cordway *v.* State, 25 Tex. App. 405; Kitchen *v.* State, 26 Tex. App. 165; Kitchen *v.* State (Tex. 1890), 14 S. W. Rep. 392; Brookin *v.* State, 27 Tex. App. 701; Partain *v.* State, 22 Tex. App. 100; Hill *v.* State, 22 Tex. App. 579; Washington *v.* State, 23 Tex. App. 336.

1. Hawkins P. C., ch. 87, § 10. This also is the definition given by Mr. Stephen in his Digest of the Criminal Law, p. 93.

It was said by WILDE, J., in Commonwealth *v.* Douglass, 5 Met. (Mass.) 241, that "To constitute subornation of perjury, the party charged must have procured the commission of the perjury by inciting, instigating, or persuading the guilty party to commit the crime. The calling of a witness to testify with the knowledge or belief that he will voluntarily testify falsely is certainly not sufficient to constitute the crime of subornation of perjury."

HOAR, J., in Commonwealth *v.* Smith, 11 Allen (Mass.) 243, said: "The crime of subornation of perjury is clearly in its nature that of an accessory before the fact to the perjury."

WOOD, J., in United States *v.* Dennee, 3 Wood (U. S.) 39, said: "The crime of subornation of perjury has several indispensable ingredients which must be charged in the indictment or it will be fatally defective. (1) The testimony of the witness suborned must be false. (2) It must be given willfully and corruptly by the witness knowing it to be false. (3) The suborner must know or believe that the testimony of the witness given or about to be given will be false. (4) He must know or believe that the witness will willfully and corruptly testify to facts which he knows to be false." See also Watson *v.* State, 5 Tex. App. 11.

Mr. Bishop says (2 Bish. Crim. Proc., § 1019): "It is a separate offense [from perjury] only in name; being in fact a particular sort of perjury, or in one form or another accessorial thereto. It is so even when made punishable by statute."

The attempt to suborn a witness to commit perjury, though unsuccessful, is a statutory offense in many of the States, and in former times the attempt itself was deemed to be subornation of perjury. 1 Hawkins, P. C. 435, §§ 9 and 10.

2. See cases cited in preceding note, and State *v.* Simons, 30 Vt. 620; Stewart *v.* State, 22 Ohio St. 477; United States *v.* Wilcox, 4 Blatchf. (U. S.) 393; State *v.* Leach, 27 Vt. 317; State *v.* Holding, 1 McCord (S. Car.) 31; State *v.* Joaquin, 69 Me. 218; People *v.* Thomas, 63 Cal. 482; Elkin *v.* People, 28 N. Y. 177; Stratton *v.* People, 81 N. Y. 629; People *v.* Brown, 74 Cal. 306; Coyne *v.* People, 124 Ill. 17; Babcock *v.* United States, 34 Fed Rep. 873; United States *v.* Thomson, 31 Fed. Rep. 331. See also, on precedents of indictments, Archbold's Cr. Pl. Pr. 606; Bishop on Directions and Forms, §§ 967, 968, and the following authorities cited therein, namely: 2 Chitty Crim. Law 475–484; 4 Went. Pl. 234, 250; Rex *v.* Hawkins, Trem. P. C. 167; Rex *v.* Margerum, Trem.

PERMANENT.—See note 1. See also COUNTY SEAT, vol. 4, p. 404.

P. C. 168; Rex *v.* Tasborough, Trem. P. C. 169; Rex *v.* Hickley, Trem. P. C. 171; Rex *v.* Hilton, Trem. P. C. 174; Rex *v.* Braddon, 9 Howell St. Tr. 1127.

1. **Permanently Locate.** — Numerous subscription papers were circulated, and large sums were subscribed aggregating several thousand dollars, by the citizens of a town, on condition, as expressed upon the subscription papers, "that the Baptist Educational Society should locate permanently, a literary and theological seminary in the village of Hamilton." And, accordingly, the seminary was located in the village; but afterwards the society desired to remove the seminary to another site. The court, by GRIDLEY, J., said: "What, then, is the true interpretation of the word "permanent," as used by the contracting parties in this agreement? Does it mean that the seminary was to be located at Hamilton while the trustees chose to keep it there, and no longer? Did the contracting parties contemplate that the board would have the power and right to remove the institution in one year, or in ten years, if they saw fit? If this be the true construction of the agreement, then the word "permanent" is without significancy, and adds nothing to the meaning of the sentence; for if the contributors of the $6,000 had merely stipulated for the location of the institution at Hamilton, Hamilton would have continued to be the location, in the contemplation of all parties, until some good reason should arise, sufficient in the judgment of the trustees to justify a removal. The parties therefore meant something more than this. I acknowledge that the word "permanent" does not always embrace the idea of absolute perpetuity, as when an individual is said to have selected a particular place as his permanent, in opposition to a temporary residence. But when the citizens of a certain locality give large sums of money, on condition that an institution of learning shall be permanently located there, the word has a different meaning. When such a stipulation is incorporated into an agreement, it means that the place agreed on shall be the site of the institution as long as the institution endures. Those who part with their funds on the faith of such an agreement, look to the enduring benefits to be derived from such an institution, by themselves, their successors, and the citizens of the entire locality, while the institution shall continue to dispense its varied blessings." Hascall *v.* Madison University, etc., 8 Barb. (N. Y) 186.

See however, Texas etc. R. Co. *v.* Marshall, 136 U. S. 393. In which case it was held, where a city had donated a large sum in the city bonds to a railroad, and the company, in consideration of the donation, had agreed "to permanently establish its eastern terminus and State offices at the city of Marshall," that the word permanent, "does not mean forever, or lasting forever, or existing forever," and therefore, the company, having established its terminus and offices in the city in accordance with its agreement, did not break the condition by removing such offices, and changing its terminus after the lapse of eight years. The court, by MILLER, J., said:

"It appears to us, that the contract on the part of the railroad company is satisfied and performed when it establishes and keeps a depot, and sets in operation car works and machine shops, and keeps them going for eight years, and until the interests of the railroad company and the public demand the removal of some or all of these subjects of the contract to some other place. This was the establishment at that point of the things contracted for in the agreement. It was the fair meaning of the words "permanent establishment," as there was no intention at the time of removing or abandoning them." See also Mead *v.* Ballard, 7 Wall. (U. S.) 290; ESTABLISH, vol. 6, p. 875 note.

Permanently Affect and Injure.—The issue to be determined was whether the erection of a certain dam "has seriously and permanently affected and injured the meadow of the complainants lying above it." It was held, that an injury may be permanent in the sense of the term used in the issue without continuing forever. Basset *v.* Johnson, 2 N. J. Eq. 155.

"**Permanent Abode.**" — See ELECTIONS, vol. 6, p. 275, note 3.

PERMIT; PERMISSIVE—(See also ALLOW, vol. I, p. 492).—Permit is more positive than "allow" or "suffer," and denotes decided assent.[1]

PERPETRATION.—See note 2.

PERPETUATION OF TESTIMONY.—See BILL TO PERPETUATE TESTIMONY, vol. 2, p. 277; BILL TO TAKE TESTIMONY DE BENE ESSE, vol, 2, p. 285; DEPOSITIONS, vol. 5, p, 581; WITNESSES.

Permanent Employment. — "Permanent employment" is nothing more than an employment for an indefinite time which may be severed by either party. Thus, in Lord *v.* Goldberg, 81 Cal. 596, where the defendants employed the plaintiff as salesman, promising, "that they would give him permanent employment so long as he would use his best efforts to extend their business," it was held, that the employment was to be "permanent;" "but that only meant that it was to continue indefinitely and until one or the other of the parties should wish, for some good reason, to sever the relation." So in Perry *v.* Wheeler 12 Bush (Ky.) 541, the plaintiff was elected "permanent" rector of a church, and was afterwards, as he claimed, wrongfully dismissed. The court said: "He was certainly elected permanent rector, but we do not understand the term permanent, as used in this case, to mean that the parties were to be bound together by ties to be dissolved only by mutual consent, or for sufficient legal or ecclesiastical reasons. . . . We understand that the plaintiff was called as rector of the church for an indefinite period, and that it was intended that he should continue to hold the place until one or the other contracting parties should desire to terminate the connection.

And in Elderton *v.* Emmens, 4 C. B. 479, plaintiff claimed that he was employed as "permanent" attorney and solicitor for defendants, but it was held, that the word "permanent," as used in the resolution of appointment, denoted nothing more than a general employment as contradistinguished from an occasional and special employment.

Permanent Trespass.—A trespass consisting of trespasses of one and the same kind, committed on several days, which are in their nature capable of renewal or continuation, and are actually renewed or continued from day to day, so that the particular injury done on each particular day cannot be distinguished from what was done on another day. In declaring for such trespasses, they may be laid with a *continuando*. Bouv. L. Dict. See also TRESPASS.

1. Chicago *v.* Stearns, 105 Ill. 558. "Permit" implies consent given or leave granted. Loosey *v.* Orser, 4 Bosw. (N. Y.) 391, 404.

"Permit" may mean "suffer." *Ex parte* Eyston, 7 Ch. D. 145; Territory *v.* Stone, 2 Dak. 155. "Permit" has been defined to mean "allow by not prohibiting." As in a city ordinance that "no person shall permit swine to go upon any sidewalk," etc., means "allow by not prohibiting." Commonwealth *v.* Curtis, 9 Allen (Mass.) 266. See also Commercial Wharf Co. *v.* Winsor, 146 Mass. 539; Cowley *v.* People, 83 N. Y. 471.

One who has engaged not to permit a ditch to be dug on his land, is liable, if it is made by one to whom he has sold the premises without a restriction; such a sale permits the work. Bennet *v.* Kennedy, 7 Wend. (N. Y.) 163.

Every definition of "suffer" and "permit" includes knowledge of what is to be done under the sufferance and permission, and intention that what is done is what was to be done. Gregory *v.* United States, 17 Blatchf. (U. S.) 325.

A licensed person cannot be convicted of "permitting" drunkenness under the 13th section of the *English* Licensing Act, 1872, by reason of getting drunk on his own premises. Warden *v.* Tye, 2 C. P. D. 74.

Permissive Waste. — That kind of waste which is a matter of omission only; as by suffering a house to fall for want of necessary reparations. Burrill Law Dict. See also WASTE.

2. An *Indiana* statute provides that if a homicide is committed "in the perpetration" of burglary and certain other of the higher felonies, it shall be murder. In Bissot *v.* State, 53 Ind. 413, the defendant, having burglariously entered a house, while still in, the house was fired upon by a watchman, and returning the fire, killed the watchman, defendant's counsel con-

PERPETUITIES (The rule against) and TRUSTS FOR ACCUMULATION. (See also CHARITIES, vol. 3, p. 122; CONFLICT OF LAWS, vol. 3, p. 499; EQUITABLE CONVERSION, vol. 6, p. 664; ESTATES, vol, 6. p. 875; LEGACIES AND DEVISES, vol. 13, p. 7; REMAINDERS; TRUSTS; WILLS.)

I. **THE COMMON LAW RULE—1. Exposition**—(*a*) ORIGIN.—In the beginning of the common law there could be no question of re-

tended that as the act of burglary had been completed by the entrance of the house, that the homicide could not be said to have been committed "in the perpetration" of the burglary; but the court, by BIDDLE, J., said: "In our opinion, when the homicide is committed within the *res gestæ* of the felony charged, it is committed "in the perpetration" of, or attempt to perpetrate felony, within the meaning of the statute." And we think, according to this view, that the evidence in this case fairly warrants that the homicide alleged was committed "in the perpetration" of the burglary.

moteness in the vesting of future interests, since, by the necessity of livery of seisin in all conveyances, every interest granted was a vested one. Freehold estates could be granted with a view to future possession only as remainders. A rule, grounded on the same principle, prevented the granting of incorporeal hereditaments, as well as remainders and reversions, *in futuro.*[1]

In such reversionary interests as after estates with special limitations (such as the old fee simple conditional), the same principle prevented the question of remoteness. And this seems to have applied equally to estates on condition properly so called, though the interest was not reversionary, but a purely contractual right.[2] After the statute *De Donis* changed the "fee simple conditional" into a fee tail, and the courts had sanctioned fines and common recoveries, all estates limited to vest in posession after estates tail could be destroyed by the tenant in tail. There was therefore less reason for a question of remoteness to arise here. The statute *Quia Emptores,* in enacting that in conveyances in fee, the whole estate of the grantor shall pass, and the grantee shall hold of the grantor's lord, abolished all qualified fees, and with them all possibilities of reverter.[3]

Thus far no necessity of considering remoteness in conveyances existed, in theory at least. Inasmuch, however, as in practice, the vesting in possession of remainders and reversions after estates tail (after other conditional fees they had ceased to exist) were, for all purposes, uncertain in their devolution, and in so far a drag on commerce in land, the question might have arisen here, had not the method of barring estates tail and thereby destroying all remainders and reversions limited after them, removed the whole cause.[4] Contingent remainders were a late fruit of the common law. But here the same reason as in estates tail prevented the urgency for a rule against remoteness; the tenant for life could easily destroy such remainders.[5]

Whatever may be the foundation of the cases in the doctrine of a possibility on a possibility,[6] or of the rule forbidding limiting

1. See note, Gray's Rule against Perpetuities, § 123. See also § 10, *citing* Wms. Real Property (13th ed.), 265–267, 40 Edw. III, 9 c.

See Marsden's note at the end of ch. 1.

2. See *infra,* this title, *Scope; Reversionary Interest; Contractual Rights.*

3. Estates for life or in tail were, of course, not affected. An estate in fee, with right of entry for condition broken, not being a reversionary interest, was also unaffected. The right of entry is contractual, and the entry a substitution of the original feoffor in the feoffee's place.

See Gray's Rule against Perp., §§ 14, 20–51. See Marsden's Perp. 71, 72; Pollock's Land Law, 213–215. See, however, Challis on Real Property, 168.

4. Gray, § 19, *citing* Digby's Hist. Law Real Prop., ch. 5, § 2; 2 Bl. Com. 348–364; Wms. Real Prop., ch. 2; Marsden on Perp. 37; Butler's note to Fearne on Cont. Rem. 561.

5. Gray, § 10, § 134, *citing* Williams on Seisin 190–191; Wms. Real Prop. (13th ed.), 265–267. See 40 Edw. III, 9 b.

6. This doctrine is commonly ascribed to Chief Justice Popham, in the Rector of Chedington's Case, 1 Co. 153 a. 156 b. It is denied in Blamford *v.* Blamford, 3 Bulst. 98; 1 Roll. R. 318,

an estate to the issue of an unborn person[1] which is found in various guises, there is no doubt that they were successive attempts to supply in the executory estates of the common law the remedy which the Rule against Perpetuities afforded against remote executory devises and conditional limitations.[2]

It is a mistake, however, to hold that the Rule against Perpetuities arose in application to interests outside of the common law. It had, it is true, no reference to common law estates in real property. But its origin can be traced directly as a restriction on executory interests at common law in chattels real.[3]

The urgency began when an executory devise of a term after a devise for life was held good,—an estate which the first taker could not destroy.[4] The Rule obtained in the Duke of Norfolk's case[5] for the first time its character as an inhibition, not against certain

321, and in The Duke of Norfolk's Case, 3 Cha. Cas. 1, 29. See Gray on Perp., §§ 125–132, 288; Fearne on Cont. Rem., Butler's note to p. 561.

1. Sir Edward Sugden, in Cole *v.* Sewall, calls the doctrine against possibilities "obsolete," but credits to it the origin of the second rule. 4 Dr. & W. 28–32. See Nicholls *v.* Sheffield, 2 Bro. C. C. 215. Prof. Gray discusses both theories very thoroughly. Gray on Perp., § 287. He denies existence to any doctrine other than as a rule against remoteness, based on the rule against perpetuities, supporting himself by Mogg *v.* Mogg, 1 Mer. 654; and Cattlin *v.* Brown, 11 Hare 372, 375. He argues that the Rule against Perpetuities applies to remainders, a question on which the authorities are closely divided. See Gray on Perp. §§ 296–299, *citing* 1 Jarm. Wills (4th ed.) 255–258, 260–263; 2 Jarm. Wills 845; 60 L. T. 247; 69 L. T. 360; Theob. Wills (22 ed.) 424–429; Tud. L. C. in Real Prop. (3d ed.), 470–475; 1 Hayes, Conv. (5th ed.) 494, 495; Wood *v.* Griffin, 4 N. H. 230, 235. So Lewis' Perp., ch. 16.

Against the view are, besides Wms. Real Prop. (13th ed.), 274–277; 8 Jur., pt. 2, 20, 283; 69 L. T. 336; Sugd. Pow. (8th ed.) 393–394; Fearne Cont. Rem. 501; 3 Dav. Prec. Conv. (3d ed.) 270, 336–338; Third Rep. Real Prop. Comm. 29–31; notably Challis on Real Prop., who denies its application to the old common law limitations, 152 *et. seq.*, 207. See Marsden on Perp., ch. 8, who seems to follow Cattlin *v.* Brown, 11 Hare, 372, 375.

Both of these doctrines, that forbidding remainders to the issue of unborn persons, and the rule against a possibility on a possibility, have been unexpectedly revived in two modern English cases, that of Whitby *v.* Mitchell, 42 Ch. D. 494; aff. 44 Ch. D. 85; and *In re* Frost, 43 Ch. D. 246, 251. 262. See for a discussion of them, *infra*, this title, *Scope*.

2. See Gray on Perp. §§ 191–199.

3. Only if an extreme distinction be allowed, can terms of years be excluded from common law estates, as argued by Challis' Real Property 47. Although not protected by the law until the statute 21 Hen. VII, ch. 15, in a collusive recovery, they were yet as much a part of the common law as estates by the custom of the manor. See Co. Litt. 46 a., Harg., n. 2. And Marsden (Perp., ch. 1.), while he is right in calling the Rule "an invention of the chancellors" (see *In re* Ridley, 11 Ch. D. 645, 649), is wrong in so far as he ascribes to it the purpose of governing the interests created by the Statute of Uses, since that statute did not affect leaseholds. Nor was the Rule intended primarily for the executory devises permitted by the statute against wills, since leaseholds were devisable before the statute. See, for a thorough discussion of the question, Gray on Perp., §§ 148–158, 160–169, 296–298, 300–302, 312, 315, 316, 319, 321, 323. See Statute of Uses, 27 Hen. VIII, ch. 10; Statute of Wills, 32 Hen. VIII, ch. 1.

For cases of devises of terms directly, not in trust, see the text, *infra*, under *Scope*.

4. Manning's Case, 8 Co., 94 c; Lampet's Case, 10 Co. 46 b.

5. See 3 Ch. Cas. 1; Pollesf. 223, entirely overturning the effect of Child *v.* Baylie (Cro. Jac. 459; Palm. 48, 333),

kinds of contingencies (such as an indefinite failure of issue), but purely against remoteness of limitation, as measured by lives in being.

The extension of the period by the addition, first of a minority,[1] then of a term of twenty years in gross[2] together with the period of gestation, after lives in being, resulted from a misconceived analogy with the period, during which at common law, after the statute *De Donis*, the alienation of remainders could be restrained.[3] The confusion, which has often been pointed out,[4] was of the vesting of estates with the restraint of their alienation. The Rule, being worded against the vesting of estates, enlarged the period of suspension of alienation beyond the intended limits.

The importance of distinguishing these often confused terms appears in the *New York* statutes and the cases which interpret it. Throughout the *United States* this confusion has materially altered and complicated the application of the Rule. The Rule has thus been shown to have been developed in the determination of the limits within which executory estates in personalty might be created. How far it was subsequently applied to other interests will be considered separately under another subdivision.[5]

(*b*) STATEMENT.—Future limitations are void unless they must vest if at all within lives in being at the creation of the limitation and twenty-one years thereafter.[6]

which in forbidding "perpetuities" referred only to peculiar contingencies, not at all to remoteness of time.

1. Lloyd *v.* Carew, Prec. Ch. 72, 106; Taylor *v.* Biddall, 2 Mod. 289; Stephens *v.* Stephens, Cas. temp. Talb. 228.

2. Caddell *v.* Palmer, 1 Cl. & F. 372.

3. The extension was established by Lloyd *v.* Carew, Prec. Ch. 72, where it is noteworthy that the decree of the chancellor and the opinions of the chief justice and other judges was overruled by a lay body.

4. See Gray on Perp., §§ 178, 186–188, who quotes Treby, C. J., in Scattergood *v.* Edge, 12 Mod. 278; Lord Brougham, in Tollemache *v.* Coventry, 2 Cl. & F. 611, 624, and Phipps *v.* Ackers, 9 Cl. & F. 583, 598, and most emphatically in Dungannon, 12 Cl. & F. 546, 629, 680, where he says: "I have a strong opinion . . . that it (the Rule) arises out of an accidental circumstance, out of a confusion, I may say, a misapprehension in confounding together the nature of the estate with the remedy at law by fine and recovery, which could not be applied till a certain life came to twenty-one years."

See also Cole *v.* Sewell, 2 H. L. C. 186, 233; Sugd. Law of Property, 315, 316, all these collected in Gray's Perp., § 186, n. 6.

5. See *infra*, this title, *Rights Affected by the Rule*.

6. The definitions by Sanders and Lewis of a perpetuity have been approved by the English courts. The first is "a future limitation, restraining the owner of the estate from aliening the fee simple of the property, discharged of such future use or estate, before the event is determined, or the period arrived, when such future use or estate is to arrive." Sanders on Uses and Trusts, vol. 1., p. 204. See Marsden, ch. 1, p. 1; London etc. R. Co. *v.* Gomm, 20 Ch. D. 562; 51 L. J., Ch. 193, 530.

That of Lewis is "a future limitation whether executory or by way of remainder, and of either real or personal property, which is not to vest until after the expiration of, or which will not necessarily vest within, the period fixed and prescribed by law for the creation of future estates and interests; and which is not destructible by the persons for the time being entitled to the property subject to the future limitation, except with the concurrence of the individual interested under that limitation." See Lewis on Perp., p.

(*c*) PURPOSE.—In the application of the Rule it is all-important to observe, first, that the Rule is not exclusively directed against absolute restraint or suspension of alienation. If it were, there would be no reason why, wherever the several persons in whom the whole estate or ownership lies, are in being and determined (though their relative interests are uncertain), the Rule should apply, since alienation is not prevented or suspended; as when the class to which the undetermined beneficiaries belong is ascertained, and therefore a conveyance by the whole class would pass the entire interest;[1] or why conditional limitations which are releasable should be too remote,[2]—or a trust estate with full power of investment in the trustees.[3]

Secondly, the Rule is directed against and is intended to prevent the practice of rendering uncertain the value of the ownership of property by a creation of remote contingent interests therein.[4]

(*d*) PERIOD.—The full period allowed by the common law Rule against Perpetuities for the creation of limitations in prop-

164, Marsden on Perp., Ch. 1, p. 1. Lewis' definition was approved in the same case, 20 Ch. D. 562.

Gray's definition of the Rule is undoubtedly the most authoritative one in existence: "No interest subject to a condition precedent is good unless the condition must be fulfilled, if at all, within twenty-one years after some life in being at the creation of the interest." Gray's Rule against Perp., § 201. "Lives" might have been clearer than "some life." The common law rule never restricted the choice of the lives in being. Gray does not mean "one life." See § 216.

The definition of Powell, J., in Scatterwood *v.* Edge, 12 Mod. 278, quoted in many decisions in the several States, has been the direct source of most of the misconceptions. It is that "every executory devise is a perpetuity as far as it goes—that is to say, an estate unalienable, though all mankind join in the conveyance." Scatterwood *v.* Edge, 1 Salk. 229. It will be noticed, *infra*, this title, *Purpose*.

No definition should be framed having a reference to restraint of alienation. The whole purpose of the Rule is thereby changed. See, *infra*, this title, *Purpose; The New York Statute*. See Coggins' Appeal, 124 Pa. St. 27.

1. Gray's Perp., §§ 268, 277; Edmondson's Est., L. R., 5 Eq. 389; Hobbs *v.* Parsons, 2 Sm. & G. 212; Courtier *v.* Oram, 21 Beav. 91; Garland *v.* Brown, 10 L. T. 292. See *infra*, this title, *Limitations to Classes*.

2. Grey *v.* Montague, 2 Eden. 205; Johnson's Trusts, L. R., 2 Eq. 716; Brown & Silbey's Contract, 3 Ch. D. 156; Brattle Sq. Church *v.* Grant, 3 Gray (Mass.) 142; Soc. for Theol. Ed. *v.* Attorney-Gen'l, 135 Mass. 285.

3. See 4 Kent's Com. 283 (12th ed.).

See, *contra*, cases which have been overruled, Gilbertson *v.* Richards, 4 H. & N. 277, 5 H. & N. 453; Birmingham Canal Co. *v.* Cartwright, 11 Ch. D. 421; Arner *v.* Lloyd, 4 H. & N. 277. See for thorough discussion, Gray on Perp., ch. 7.

4. The error of mistaking this purpose has been corrected in *England*. See London & S. W. R. Co. *v.* Gomm, 20 Ch. D. 562; Courtier *v.* Oram, 21 Beav. 91; Garland *v.* Brown, 10 L. T., N. S. 292. But in the *United States* it has greatly affected the application of the Rule, and in some States (see Todhunter *v.* D. M. I. & M. A. Co., 58 Iowa 205) changed its actual statutory definition. In *New York* the rule (Rev. Stats. pt. 2, ch. 4, tit. 4) is: "Every future estate shall be void in its creation, which shall suspend the absolute power of alienation for a longer period. . . . Such power of alienation is suspended when there are no persons in being by whom an absolute fee in possession can be conveyed." The same definition is found in *Michigan* (2 Comp. Laws 1871, ch. 147), §§ 14–21, 23, 24, 36–40; *Wisconsin* (2 Rev. St. (1858), ch. 83, §§ 14–21, 23, 24, 36–40); *Minnesota* (Gen. Sts. (1866), ch. 45, §§ 14–21, 23, 24,

erty is any number of lives[1] in being and twenty-one years after the death of the survivor. The term of twenty-one years may be taken in gross.[2] This may be increased by the period of

36–40). See *infra*, this title, *Independent System of New York, etc.*

1. This was definitely settled in Caddell *v.* Palmer, 1 Cl. & F. Here twenty-eight lives were taken, some of whom had no interest under the will which was sustained. See also Thelusson *v.* Woodford, 4 Ves. 227. Marsden on Perp., p. 32. Nor is it necessary that the "lives" be named. A class description was employed in both of the cases just cited. No limit except that of lives whose determination can be readily proved has ever been judicially declared. Gray on Perp., § 218; Thelusson *v.* Woodford, 4 Ves. 278; 11 Ves. 134, 136, 146; Harg. Thel. Act, § 18; Real Pro perty Commissioners' Report, pp. 37, 39.

United States.—It is in this part of the Rule, the number and choice of the lives which may be taken to determine the period, that radical and arbitrary changes have been made in the *United States* by statute.

In *Alabama*, "lands may be conveyed to the wife and children, or children only, severally, successively and jointly; and to the heirs of the body of the survivor, if they come of age, and in default thereof over; but conveyances to other than the wife and children, or children only, cannot extend beyond three lives in being at the date of the conveyance and ten years thereafter. 1 *Alabama* Rev. Code of 1876, § 2188.

In *Mississippi* "a conveyance, or a devise of lands" may be made "to a succession of donees then living, not exceeding two; and to the heirs of the body of the remainderman, and in default thereof, to the right heirs of the donor in fee simple." *Mississippi* Rev. Code of 1871, § 2286. See Cannon *v.* Barry, 59 Miss. 289.

The *New York* statute restricts the suspension of the absolute power of alienation to two lives in being. 1 *New York* Rev. Sts. 722, § 15.

Michigan and *Minnesota* have the same limit as *New York. Michigan* Sts. 1882, § 5527, *et seq.; Minnesota* Gen. Sts. 1891, § 3973–3295.

In *Wisconsin* the act of 1887 enlarged this period, adding twenty-one years. See Sanford & Berryman Ann. Sts., *Wisconsin* 2038–2063. See *infra*, this title, *Independent System of New York, etc.*

In *Connecticut* and *Ohio* no estate may be given to any persons but such as are in being or to their immediate descendants. *Connecticut* Gen. Sts., ch. 63, art. 1, § 27; *Ohio* Stats. 1880, 4200. See next note.

2. As has been shown, this period had its origin in a false analogy to infancy in remainders at common law. It may now be taken as a period of years preceded or not by a number of lives. Cadell *v.* Palmer, 1 Cl. & F. 372; Barnitz *v.* Casey, 7 Cr. 456; Pleasants *v.* Pleasants, 2 Call 319, 331. Here, again, statutory restrictions exist in the *United States*, which in some States revert to the original conception of the minority period.

In *Indiana, New York, Michigan, Wisconsin* and *Minnesota* the only extension of the period permitted is that "a contingent remainder in fee may be created on a prior remainder in fee, to take effect in the event that the persons to whom the first remainder is limited shall die under the age of twenty-one years, or upon any other contingency, by which the estate of such persons may be determined before they attain their full age."

Indiana Rev. Sts. (1876), ch. 82, § 40. See 1 *New York* Rev. Sts. 722, § 15; *Michigan* Sts. 1882, § 5527; *Minnesota* Gen. Sts. 1891, § 3913–3925; Sanford & Berryman, Ann. Sts. *Wisconsin*, § 2038–2063.

By the *Connecticut* and *Ohio* provisions, limitations of estates, after those to persons in being are confined to "their immediate issue or descendants."

Connecticut Gen. Sts. (1875), tit. 18, ch. 6, pt. 1, § 3, p. 352; *Ohio* Rev. Sts. (1880), § 4200.

In *Ohio* the immediate descendants have been construed to mean grandchildren when the children are dead. Turley *v.* Turley, 11 Ohio St. 173; McArthur *v.* Scott, 113 U. S. 340, 383; Stevenson *v.* Evans, 10 Ohio St. 307; Brasher *v.* Marsh, 15 Ohio St. 103. The *Connecticut* statute applies to personalty, that of *Ohio* does not. Gray's Perp., §§ 739, 740; Alfred *v.* Marks, 49 Conn. 473; Gibson *v.* McNeely, 11 Ohio St. 131.

gestation, but only in the actual case of gestation.[1] As a "life in being" includes for the purpose of the Rule a child *en ventre sa mere*, there may be two periods of gestation.[2] And a case involving three periods of gestation has been raised, though not decided.[3]

The period is reckoned to begin at the creation of the limitations, which, in conveyances, is the date of the execution of the instrument, in wills is the death of the testator. Where the limitation is subject to the exercise of a power, the creation of the limitation is, for the purposes of the Rule, referred to the creation of the power.[4] That in wills the period runs from the testator's death, is almost universally held, even where the wording of statutes seems hostile to that meaning.[5]

(*e*) SCOPE.—Just what kinds of interests and rights come within the restraining effect of the Rule against Perpetuities, is a question about which eminent authorities differ fundamentally, even as regards so important a class as common law estates in realty.[6] Before entering on a categorical account, it is necessary to premise that the Rule does not apply to vested interests. Were the line between vested and contingent interests clearly drawn at the question of certainty of ultimate devolution to a person (or his heirs), it would not be necessary to mention the Rule in this connection. But the fact that "vested rights" have been allowed by the courts to encroach on what would seem to fall naturally under contingent rights, has led to confusion and disagreement in the distinction and in the application of the Rule. Strictly speaking, rules of construction of vested or contingent interests do not fall within the present article, since the Rule against Perpetuities is

1. Marsden on Perp., p. 35; Cadell *v.* Palmer, 1 Cl. & F. 372.

2. Marsden on Perp., p. 35; Gulliver *v.* Nickett, 1 Wils. 105; Long *v.* Blackall, 7 T. R. 100; Thelusson *v.* Woodford, 11 Ves. 112, 143.

3. Gray mentions such a case, which is constructed by supposing in addition to the period in womb of one of the "lives in being and of the person whose minority forms part of the period, that of the last devisee."

See Gray on Perp., § 222; Smith *v.* Farr, 3 Y. & C. 328; Lewis on Perp., Addenda, 726.

4. See *infra*, this title, *Powers*.

5. Marsden's Perp. 34; Gray on Perp., § 231, *citing* Vanderplank *v.* King, 3 Hare 1, 17; Faulkner *v.* Daniel, 3 Hare 199, 216; Williams *v.* Teale, 6 Hare 239, 251; Cattlin *v.* Brown, 11 Hare 372, 382; Dungannon *v.* Smith, 12 Cl. & F. 546; Peard *v.* Kekewich, 15 Beav. 166; Southern *v.* Wollaston, 16 Beav. 166, 276; Monypenny *v.* Dering, 2 De G. M. & G. 145, 170; Hale *v.* Hale, 3 Ch. D. 643, 645; Hosea *v.* Jacobs, 98 Mass. 65, 67.

1 Jarm. on Wills (4th ed.) 254; Lewis Perp. Suppl. 53, 57; 4 Kent Com. (12th ed.) 283, n. 1.

See *contra*, Harris *v.* Davis, 1 Coll. 416; Andrew *v.* Andrew, 1 Coll. 690; Attorney General *v.* Gill, 2 P. Wms 369, 370; Gash *v.* Grosvenor, 5 Mad. 337, 341.

In *New York* there has been some difference: Lang *v.* Ropke, 5 Sandf., (N. Y.) 363; Lang *v.* Wilbraham, 2 Duer (N. Y.) 171; Griffen *v.* Ford, 1 Bosw. (N. Y.) 123. See *contra*, Odell *v.* Youngs, 64 How. Pr. (N. Y.) 56.

In *Ohio*, where the statute (2 Rev. Sts. 1880) § 4200 reads, "At the time of making such deed or will," "the time when the will takes effect by the death of the testator" is denoted. McArthur *v.* Scott, 113 U. S. 340.

6. Against the application of the

not a rule of construction.[1] But a brief definition, necessary to a clear understanding of the limits of the Rule, is elsewhere given.[2] The argument against the inclusion of common law interests is based largely on historical reasons, which have been already touched upon.[3] In *England* a statute[4] which enacts that every contingent remainder "which would have been valid as a springing or shifting use, or executory devise, or other limitation, had it not had a sufficient estate to support it as a contingent remainder," shall be protected from destruction (by determination of the previous estate), subjects these remainders to the Rule against Perpetuities.[5]

In regard to remainders not included in the act (those created before Aug. 2nd, 1877, and those which do not conform to the rules governing other executory interests), it would seem from recent decisions that the old rule against a possibility on a possibility, which forbids limitations of remainders to the issue of persons unborn, is in force in *England* as an independent rule, distinct from the Rule against Perpetuities.[6]

But whether another rule of limitation applies separately to contingent remainders or not, it seems to be settled in *England* that the Rule against Perpetuities does govern them.[7] In the *United States* the application of the Rule against Perpetuities to

Rule to common law limitations are: Williams' Real Prop. (13th ed.) App. F.; Challis' Real Prop., 159–162.

See also Law Quarterly, October 1890. On the opposite side are: Lewis' Perp. 592–621; Sanders' Uses and Trusts 197; Real Prop. Commissioners, 3. Rep. 29, 36; Marsden's Perp. and Accum. 4, 40; Gray's Perp., §§ 283–316. See *infra*, this title, *Rights Affected by the Rule*.

1. See *infra*, this title, *Application;* Gray on Perp., § 629, etc.; Marsden on Perp., ch. 13.

2. See *infra*, this title, *Rights Affected by the Rule; Vested and Contingent Remainders.*

3. See *supra*, this title, *Origin.*

4. 40 and 41 Vict. ch., 33.

5. See Challis' Real Prop. 95, 112, 161.

6. The cases referred to are the decisions of Mr. Justice Kay in Whitby *v.* Mitchell, 42 Ch. D. 494, affirmed by the court of appeal in 44 Ch. D. 58, and *In re* Frost, 42 Ch. D. 246, 251. A remainder whose limitation was clearly valid within the Rule against Perpetuities, was held void because limited to the unborn issue of unborn persons.

In the last-mentioned case the doctrine of a possibility on a possibility was reaffirmed, as the basis of the former rule. See an article in the Law Quarterly of October 1890, on Remoteness and Perpetuity, by J. Savill Vaizey, vigorously attacking the decision of Whitby *v.* Mitchell (42 Ch. D. 494), reducing the judicial authority for the independent rule to naught, and other authority to two private opinions, showing that there are many authorities, judicial and other, against the doctrine, and that, historically, there is no reason, nor practically any convenience in the independent rule. The only authorities in favor are Fearne Cont. Rem. 251; Williams' Real Prop. (6th ed.) 248, 451, 452. Against it are: Real Prop. Commrs. 3d Rep. 41; Lewis' Perp. 420; 1 Jarman on Wills (4th ed.) 258, note; 179, 211, 213; Marsden, Perp. 175, 150; Gray's Perp. 139. The cases of Marlborough *v.* Godolphin, 1 Eden 415, 416; Cadell *v.* Palmer, 1 Cl. & F. 372, are, too, almost diametrically opposed.

7. Mr. Justice Kay, whose decision in Whitby *v.* Mitchell (42 Ch. D. 494), is the single judicial authority for the independent rule forbidding limitations of remainders to issue of unborn persons, has himself declared, in a subsequent case, (*In re* Frost, 43 Cl. D. 246), that the Rule against Perpetuities does apply to contingent remainders. To the same purpose are: Cattlin *v.* Brown, 11 Hare

future interests in property is in no wise affected by the question of their origin, whether in the common law, in courts of equity, or in statutes.[1]

In this connection it is proper to mention that the Rule never applies to interests which are destructible by a present owner. Thus a limitation after an estate tail is not too remote. And the distinction must not be confused in this aspect of the Rule between destructible, and releasable or alienable interests. Where a present owner can destroy succeeding limitations, he is regarded, for the purpose of the Rule, as absolute owner, and, accordingly, the subsequent limitations as no interests; the Rule disregards them entirely.[2] But the mere fact that an interest is releasable, and the whole ownership is therefore not inalienable, does not remove the reason for the application, as has been shown above.[3]

The common law right of entry which remained in the grantor of an estate on condition, was certainly an interest in property (though not a reversionary right) and not a mere remedy for a contractual right. Nevertheless it may be considered certain, that in the *United States* such a right of entry does not come within the operation of the Rule or statutes against Perpetuities. In *England* such a right when attached to a grant in fee, must comply with the Rule against Perpetuities.[4] Quite distinct from this is the right to enter and hold until the arrears of rent are dis-

372, 374; Knapping *v.* Tomlinson, 34 L. J., Ch. 3, 6. See also Spencer *v.* Duke of Marlborough, 3 Bro. P. C. (Toml. ed.) 232, 246; Hay *v.* Earl of Coventry, 3 T. R., 83; and Brudenwell *v.* Elwes, 1 East 442,—cases which are all discussed in Law Quarterly, October, 1890, 415–418. The main reliance of the opposite side is a remark of Mr. Sugden's in Cole *v.* Sewall, 4 D. & W. 1.

Writers in favor of the Rule against Perpetuities as applying to contingent remainders, are: Fearne, Cont. Rem. 502; 2 Preston Ab. 148, 166, 168; 1 Jarman, Wills (4th Ed.), 279; Lewis, Perp. 408–426; Marsden's Perp. 166; Gray's Perp. 139. *Contra*, are Williams' Real Prop.; Challis' Real Prop.; Real Prop. Commissioners, 3d Rep.

1. See the statutory rule in *New York*, *Michigan*, *Wisconsin* and *Minnesota*.

In *New York* the statute (11 Rev. Sts. 722, 1) reads at § 16: "A contingent remainder in fee may be created on a prior remainder in fee, to take effect in the event that the persons to whom the first remainder is limited, shall die under the age of twenty-one years, or upon any other contingency, by which the estate of such persons may be determined before they attain their full age." See also § 20 as to a contingent remainder created on a term of years. *Michigan* Stats. 1882, §§ 5527, *et seq; Minnesota* Gen. Sts. 1891, §§ 3973–3995. *Wisconsin*, Sayborn and Berryman, Ann. Stats., §§ 2038–2063.

The same provision is found in the *Indiana* Rev. Sts. 1876, ch. 82, § 40.

For *Pennsylvania* and *Massachusetts* (where the common law rule obtains), see Coggins' Appeal, 23 W. N. C. (Pa.) 206; Odell *v.* Odell, 92 Mass. 1; Blake *v.* Dexter, 66 Mass. 559; Brattle Sq. Church *v.* Grant, 69 Mass. 142; Smith *v.* Harrington, 86 Mass. 566; Fosdick *v.* Fosdick, 88 Mass. 41; Otis *v.* McLellan, 95 Mass. 339; Smith's Appeal, 88 Pa. St. 492.

2. See Gray on Perp. §§ 203, 443, *citing* Lewis' Perp. 664, 665; Ferrand *v.* Wilson, 4 Hare 344, 374; Turvin *v.* Newcome, 3 K. & J. 16, 19. See *infra*, this title *Reversionary Interests*. For a discussion of conditional fees simple in *South Carolina* and in *Pennsylvania*, see Gray on Perp. § 455, p. 14–20.

3. See *Supra*, this title, *Purpose*.

4. This, together with the other rights here mentioned, will be discussed at length in their respective places below. Gray treats this question thoroughly in §§ 299–311. English cases enforcing

charged,[1] or a right of entry attached to a lease for years.[2] The province of the Rule is confined to rights in property; it does not include personal obligations as such. The boundary of this province touches on one side on rights which are merely remedies for the enforcement of an obligation, such as distraint and entry; on another side are rights which are vested. A discussion of both distinctions will be found further on.[3] There is no reason why incorporeal hereditaments, as easements, should not be governed by the Rule. But in the absence of decisions, it remains debatable with the authorities.[4]

The Rule against Perpetuities applies to Chattels Real and Personal. It was almost exclusively in connection with the former that the Rule was evolved. While the rules of limitation of the common law forbidding the creation *in futuro* of freehold estates in realty never applied here, yet there were other peculiar restrictions on the alienation of personalty, whose removal made a rule against remoteness necessary.[5] To-day the only remaining

the Rule are: *In re* Macleay, L. R., 20 Eq. 186; Dunn *v.* Flood, 25 Ch. D. 629. See Marsden's Perp. 4, 5. But *contra*, Challis' Real Prop. 152–154.

In the *United States* the absence of mention of the Rule in many cases is the strongest reason for not applying it. See French *v.* Old South Soc., 106 Mass. 479; Tobey *v.* Moore, 130 Mass. 448; Brattle Sq. Church *v.*Grant, 3 Gray (Mass.) 142, 148; Hunt *v.* Wright, 47 N. H. 396; Lawe *v.* Hyde, 39 Wis. 345. See also Giles *v.* Boston Society, 10 Allen (Mass.) 335; Gray on Perp., § 311.

1. Being a mere remedy, not a right in property, it cannot be too remote. See Marsden's Perp., 7, 15, 248; Gray's Rule against Perp., § 303; Lewis' Perp. 618, 619. This would apply in the case of a rent-charge. See Gilbertson *v.* Richards, 4 H. & N. 277. Otherwise in a case as explained in the next note.

2. The right of entry is excluded from the Rule for an entirely different reason from that of the last note—*i. e.*, that the right is a vested interest, incident to the reversion. See Gray on Perp., § 303; Marsden on Perp. 7; but see Roe d. Hunter *v.* Galliers, 2 T. R. 133, 140.

3. See *infra*, this title, *Rights Affected by the Rule, Remainders; Contractual Rights.* See Gray's Perp., §§ 329, 330, 273 a, 316, *citing* Walsh *v.* Secretary of State for India, 10 H. L. C. 367; Challis' Real Prop., 150, 341, 351, 353; Marsden's Perp. 25, 26; Aspden *v.* Leddon, 1 Ex. D. 496; Morgan *v.* Davey, 1 Cab. & El. 114. As to a rent charge, with right of distraint, see Gilbertson *v.* Richards, 4 H. & N. 277. That a covenant for perpetual renewal cannot be too remote is seen in London, S. W. R. & Co. *v.* Gorum, 20 Ch. D. 562, and Challis' Real Prop. 151. But *contra*, see Morrison *v.* Rossignol, 5 Cal. 64. See also Syms *v.* Mayor, 18 Jones & Sp. (N. Y.) 286. See Gray on Perp., § 230.

As to an equitable right in property enforceable by the obligee by a decree for specific performance, see London S. W. R. *v.* Gomm, 20 Ch. D. 562.

For the distinction between the creation of an obligation and the transfer of an obligation when created, see Gray on Perp. § 329, n. 2.

4. The discussion is, of course, confined to the creation of easements *in futuro* since the common law rule of limitation forbids the granting *in futuro* of an existing incorporeal hereditament, just as a similar rule forbids the granting of a remainder or a reversion. Challis' Real Prop. 87, 88, 1 Prest. Est. 217, 219; Gray's Rule against Perp., § 17.

Mr. Gray argues with the majority of authorities for the operation of the Rule with a possible exception of rents, considered as obligations. He cites Lewis' Perp. ch. 29; Gilbert's Rents 59, 60; Fearne Cont. Rem. 529, Butler's note; Gilbert's Uses 175 n.; 1 Sand. Uses 203–205. *Contra*, Marsden's, Perp. 20. See London S. W. R. Co. *v.* Gomm, 20 Ch. D. 562, 585. See also Gilbertson *v.* Richards, 4 H. & N. 277.

5. The cases in which the validity (or indestructibility) of an executory

restriction is that which forbids a gift (*inter vivos*) of a future interest in personalty.[1] It is probable that even at the common law a leasehold may be granted (as it may be devised) after the gift to another for life.[2] At any rate it can be done by way of trust.

Chattels personal, it is safe to say, may also be bequeathed over after a bequest for life, both in *England* and the *United States.*[3] Finally, personal property may be limited by deed to vest *in futuro* in every jurisdiction except *North Carolina.*[4] In several of the *United States*, where statutes against perpetuities refer to real estate only, the question arises whether the statute abrogates the common law rule entirely, leaving the alienation of personal property free from all restraint in regard to remoteness.[5]

That the Rule applies to equitable estates there is no doubt. Whether equitable interests can be contingent remainders, with the character of legal contingent remainders, is important in a discussion of perpetuities, since a future interest limited after a life-estate to one in being, must, as a legal remainder, vest immediately on the determination of the preceding estate, and cannot, therefore, be too remote, while, as a conditional limitation, it may be too remote.[6] The same difference which exists between the law of *England* and that of the *United States* in regard to right of entry for breach of condition in a conveyance in fee, would, by analogy, exclude resulting trusts in the *United States* from the sphere of the Rule. The question has, however, never been expressly decided.[7]

devise of a term after a devise for life was established, are the famous Manning's Case (8 Co. 94 b) and Lampet's Case (10 Co. 46 b). The development of executory estates in personalty, as it is closely interwoven with the history of the Rule against Perpetuities, is described very clearly by Professor Gray in his chapter on Origin and History.

1. Delivery is necessary for the gift of personal property. Ward *v.* Turner, 2 Ves. Jr. 431, 442.

2. Wright *v.* Cartwright, 1 Burr. 282. See Gray's Rule against Perp., §§ 71–76.

3. The authorities are discussed in Gray on Perp., §§ 77–86. A single decision to the contrary in the *United States* is Homer *v.* Shelton, 2 Met. (Mass.) 194, which leaves the state of the law in *Massachusetts* on the question somewhat doubtful.

4. Hunt *v.* Davis, 3 Dev. & B. (N. Car.) 42; Harrell *v.* Davis, 8 Jones (N. Car.) 359; Gray on Perp. § 91.

5. The States in which the question can arise are *Michigan*, *Wisconsin*, *Minnesota* and *Ohio.*

In Dodge *v.* Williams, 46 Wis. 71, the English rule was distinctly held to be abrogated. The point was, however, not deemed to be necessary to the decision. The correctness of the position was doubted in De Wolf *v.* Lawson, 61 Wis. 474. But it seems to be the settled law. See Ford *v.* Ford, 70 Wis. 19.

See also Toms *v.* Williams, 41 Mich. 572. In Williamson *v.* Hall, 10 Am. Law Reg., N. S. 466, it was held that personal property may be limited over by way of executory bequest after the determination of a life estate in like manner and to the same extent as real estate.

6. See Marsden's Perp. 169, Abbiss *v.* Burney, 17 Ch. D. 211; Hopkins *v.* Hopkins, West 606. See also Roe *v.* Briggs, 16 East 406, 413. See Gray on Perp. §§ 325, 326; Blasgrove *v.* Hancock, 16 Sim. 371; Bull *v.* Pritchard, 5 Hare 567. The most general view is, no doubt, the construction of all equitable remainders, so-called, as executory limitations.

7. See Gray on Perp. § 327. See

Charitable trusts, which are commonly supposed to be an exception to the rule, are so only in a limited sense. They will be discussed separately at the end of this article.[1]

(*f*) APPLICATION.—In its application the Rule appears strikingly as designed, not to construe and carry into effect the implied intentions of the testator, but as a device to curtail the final disposition of property, in so far as the owner is tempted to cause an abeyance of the ultimate ownership, to the disadvantage of general interchange.[2] It would be inconsistent with its purpose as a restraint on the right of disposition, to import it into the intentions of the testator. These must, therefore, be first determined, and then the Rule applied.[3]

Easterbrooke *v.* Tillinghast, 5 Gray (Mass.) 17; Daniel *v.* Jackoway, Freem. Ch. (Miss.) 59.

1. In so far as they may not be created beyond the period of the Rule, they are not an exception.

See *infra*, this title, *Charitable Trusts.*

2. It cannot be said that the Rule exists for the benefit of the ultimate remainderman, since he cannot claim more than the testator chooses to give him.

3. Important cases on this point are Dungannon *v.* Smith, 12 Cl. & F. 546; Speakman *v.* Speakman, 8 Hare 180; Catlin *v.* Brown, 11 Hare 372, and others. See Gray's Rule Against Perp.; ch. 19; Marsden's, Perp. ch. 4. But, *contra*, Buchanan *v.* Schulderman, 11 Oregon 150.

This principle, of the application of the Rule to the instruments creating the limitations, is far from being free from exceptions. Chief among them is the doctrine of *cy pres*, which may, however, be considered as an independent rule of limitation at common law. For the latter view, see Challis on Real Prop. 91, 159, 160; Fearne Cont. Rem. 2, 265. For a discussion of the cases Humbertson *v.* Humbertson (1 P. W. 331) and Moneypenny *v.* Dering (16 M. & W. 418, 428), see Marsden's Perp. 269. See also Sugden on Powers, (8th ed.) 498. The definition given by Gray's Perp., § 643, where he begins a lengthy consideration of the doctrine, is, "When land is devised to an unborn person for life, remainder to his children in tail, either successively or as tenants in common with cross-remainders, the unborn person takes an estate tail, and when land is devised to an unborn person for life, remainder to his sons in tail male, either successively or as tenants in common with cross-remainders, the unborn person takes an estate tail male."

As regards its application to a perpetual series of life estates, see Marsden on Perp. 273; Gray on Perp. § 652.

But the principle that the Rule against Perpetuities is not applied in the construction of a limitation, does not forbid its consideration when the terms of the limitation are in themselves ambiguous. Where a limitation is not necessarily hostile to the Rule, there is no reason why the Rule should be presumed not to have existed in the mind of the testator. Marsden Perp. 208; Gosling *v.* Gosling, 5 Jur., N. S. 910.

See Gray on Perp. § 633, *citing:* Thelusson *v.* Woodford, 4 Ves. 227, 312; Peaks *v.* Moseley, 5 Ap. Cases 714, 719; Butler *v.* Butler, 3 Barb. Ch. (N. Y.) 304, 310; Post *v.* Hover, 33 N. Y. 593; Du Bois *v.* Ray, 35 N. Y. 162; Wolf's Estate, 9 W. N. C. (Pa.) 260; Hancock *v.* Butler, 21 Tex. 804, 806.

In *New York*, where the arbitrary period fixed by statute, together with the narrow wording of the purpose of the Rule, has greatly increased the difficulty of sustaining wills, the courts have established a policy of construction almost diametrically opposed to the common rule. In Tiers *v.* Tiers, 98 N. Y. 568, it was said: "It is quite evident that the ulterior, contingent limitation is quite separable from the primary trust, and merely incidental; its only purpose being to provide for a contingency which may never arise; and the failure of that provision would not affect the general scheme of the testatrix. In such cases the rule is quite well settled that an ulterior limitation, though invalid, will not be al-

The essential requirement is that the limitation be such that it cannot possibly take effect beyond the prescribed period. But a limitation is not void merely because it will not certainly take effect within the period, since a valid limitation might be one which must take effect either within the period or not at all.[1] When the period of limitation is in itself too remote, but the nature of the interest is such that the limitation cannot fall beyond the period, the Rule, it seems, is liberally applied.[2] And, in general, facts, existing at the time of the creation of the limitation, which, if allowed to measure the period, will bring it within the Rule, will be taken into account.

But such a fact as that a woman is past the age of child-bearing, will, it seems, not be considered where the possibility of her having children after the creation of the limitation would render void the limitation.[3] Of course events subsequent to the operation of the instrument creating the limitations, can never cure a limitation originally invalid.[4]

Where a limitation of property is made in the exercise of a power, the period within which the limitation must fall is reckoned from the date of the instrument creating the power. But an exception to the principle under discussion appears in so far as the creation of a power is not void merely because its terms permit an exercise creating a limitation which is void for remoteness.[5]

Further, the Rule is construed in a practical spirit so far as technical expression is concerned. Thus a bequest of the rents of property to a person and his heirs forever, is a devise of the fee simple, to which the Rule does not apply. The same is true of the income of personalty or of a trust to pay the income of rents.[6]

lowed to invalidate the primary disposition of the will, but will be cut off in the case of a trust, which is not an entirety, as well as in the case of a limitation of a legal estate."

See Harrison *v.* Harrison, 36 N. Y. 543; Henderson *v.* Henderson, 113 N. Y. 15. The application of the Rule in *New York*, which is quite separate from that of the common rule, will be specially considered *infra*, this title *Independent System of New York, etc.*

1. See Challis' Real Property 146.

2. Marsden's, Perp. 24, mentioning an example of a limitation of leaseholds having twenty years to run to the first son of A, a bachelor, who attains twenty-one years, has doubts of the validity, where there is no express proviso confining the limitation to the period. See Miles *v.* Harford, 12 Ch. D. 691.

3. Lee *v.* Audley, 2 Ves. 365; *In re* Sayer's Trusts, L. J., Ch. 350; Marsden's Perp. 68; Gray's Perp., §§ 215, 215 a. *Contra*, Cooper *v.* Laroche, 17 Ch. D. 368; Challis' Real Prop. 155.

4. Challis' Real Prop. 155.

Instances of this are numerous. Some will be found *infra*, this title. *Limitations to Classes.* Such are bequests to the children of a person in being who shall attain the age of twenty-five. If no child were living at the age of twenty-five at the testator's death, the bequest would be inevitably bad. The limitation is valid where by the existence of such a child, the class is ascertained when the instrument which creates the limitation goes into effect.

See Picken *v.* Matthews, 10 Ch. D. 264; 48 L. J., Ch. 150; Marsden's Perp. 68.

5. See *infra*, this title, *Powers;* Gray's Perp., ch. 15; Marsden's Perp. 234.

See Collins *v.* Foley, 3 Md. 158.

6. Marsden'sPerp. 26; Doe *v.* Goldin

2. Rights Affected by the Rule—(*a*) REMAINDERS—(1) *Vested.*—Vested interests are not subject to the Rule against Perpetuities; those only being affected which, contingent at their creation, may become vested at a future time.[1] The distinction of such interests as come within the Rule by reason of their contingent character, from those which do not, is a question with which a discussion of the Rule has, strictly speaking, nothing to do. But a clear view of the working of the Rule involves necessarily an exact knowledge of the rights and interests within its sphere. This can be gained of contingent interests only by a distinct separation from those which are not contingent.

The term "vested" is not confined to common law estates in realty; it applies also to equitable interests, and interests in personalty. It is convenient, however, to frame a definition applicable to legal estates, and to construe other interests by analogy, as if they were legal. A remainder is said to be vested in a person, when that person has an indefeasible right of enjoyment immediately upon the determination of the preceding particular estate, whenever this may occur; provided only the remainder be not itself determined by its own limitation.[2] Where there is an estate to A for life, remainder to B for life, the chance that B

v. Lakeman, 2 B. & Ad. 30; Adamson *v.* Armitage, 19 Ves. 415,418.

1. Where a vested interest comes into possession after a particular interest which may be determined by a contingency at a time beyond the period of the Rule against Perpetuities, though on principle the Rule does not apply, yet the vested interest has been held void for remoteness. Such a case was, that of Donohue *v.* McNichol, 61 Pa. 73, where the testatrix devised after the death of her son's lawful issue, unborn, at her death, all her estate to her lawful heirs, their heirs and assigns forever. The result of the decision was, however, the same as if the devise had been sustained. That a remainder after a lease for nine hundred and ninety-nine years is not void for remoteness, was expressly decided in Todhunter *v.* D. M. I. & M. R. Co., 58 Iowa 205.

The Rule, there considered, is statutory, being worded after the *New York* statute: "Every disposition of property is void which suspends the absolute power of controlling the same for a longer period than . . *Iowa* Code, § 1920. See, to the same effect, Toms *v.* Williams, 41 Mich. 552, 572.

There is no theoretical reason why, where a particular estate is determinable by a contingency before its natural limit, the succeeding vested remainder should be void, merely because its actual coming into possession is thereby accelerated. Gray points out the abuse which may undoubtedly be made of such limitations, and suggests the prohibition, by legislation, of long lease-holds, such as exist in *Alabama* (Rev. Code (1876), § 2190). Gray's Rule Against Perpetuities, § 210; Gray's Restraints on Alienation, § 103. For a discussion of vested interests after contingent interests, void for remoteness, see *infra*, this title, *Effect of Limitations Void for Remoteness on Prior and Subsequent Limitations.*

In *New York*, where the Rule is quite distinct from the common rule, vested interests may, it seems, be void in so far as there is an undue "suspension of the absolute power of alienation." See Henderson *v.* Henderson, 46 Hun. (N. Y.) 509; reversed 113 N Y. 1. See *infra*, this title, *Statutory Provisions in the United States.*

2. The important elements are: certainty of the contingency, on which the interest is limited to come into possession, and certainty of the person who will enjoy the possession. See Fearne Cont. Rem, 1, 2. Other definitions, materially to the same effect, are those of Gray's Rule against Perp., § 101; 4 Kent's Com. (12th ed.) 203, note 1. See 6 Alb. L. J. 361.

The fact that the preceding estate is such that it must be certain to deter-

may die before A does not affect the certainty of his right of enjoyment of an estate for life.[1]

But there is a class of so-called vested remainders which are contingent in character not only as regards the actual enjoyment, but also as regards the right of enjoyment. They are favored with the name "vested" only by reason of the absence of the condition in the words which create them; a divesting clause being added after what, alone, would give a vested remainder.[2] It must be remembered that the Rule against Perpetuities is practical in its working; that it attacks all future interests contingent as to the right of enjoyment beyond a certain period, and that it does not spare interests which hide their contingency under the guise of a term arbitrarily applied. The word "vested," when it is applied to future interests which are subject to be divested, exists solely for purposes entirely foreign to the question of remoteness. In such cases interests are said to vest at a period before the time when they might be divested, in order to carry out the intention of the testator as to transmission, or as to the enjoyment of intermediate income. It is submitted then, that within the meaning of the Rule against Perpetuities, this notion of a contingent vested

mine is, of necessity, not emphasized in a definition of vested legal interests. At common law every particular estate carved out of a fee is, in theory, certain of being determined. And so a remainder after an estate tail is strictly a vested remainder; for, says Fearne (Cont. Rem. 2, 192), "though it is entirely uncertain when it will happen, it is considered certain to happen some time or other." For practical purposes every particular estate "may, when applied in analogy to estates other than those of common law, be considered to mean an interest certain to be determined. For a remainder after the only estate which is not certain, an estate tail, is not affected by the Rule against Perpetuities, for a separate reason: because it is a destructible interest. See, *supra*, this title, *Origin*.

The definition of a leading *Massachusetts* case, emphasizes expressly this requisite in the particular estate, that it must "determine by an event that must unavoidably happen by the efflux of time." Blanchard *v.* Blanchard, 1 Allen (Mass.) 227. See Doe, Lessee of Poor *v.* Considine, 6. Wall. (U. S.) 476.

1. The only cases which, differing from the accepted doctrine, hold to a strict construction of "contingent" interests are two decisions of the Supreme Court of *New Hampshire*. They stand absolutely alone on this point. They are: Hall *v.* Nute, 38 N. H. 422, and Hayes *v.* Tabor, 41 N. H. 521.

The term "vested" is not equivalent to descendible, because vested remainders are frequently to a person for life, and descendible estate may be contingent.

2. The law having once for all disregarded natural distinctions in conditions precedent and subsequent, calls interests vested which may never come into possession at all. Hence no other than an arbitrary limitation of the term "vested" can be possible. Thus a remainder to a person after a life estate, but if he should die before the termination of the life estate, to another person and his heirs, would still be a vested estate.

The common case where the wording of the limitation determines whether it is vested or contingent is an estate to one for life, remainder to such of his children as shall be living at his death, where it is contingent, or an estate to one for life, remainder to his children, but if any child dies before the termination of the life estate, his share to go to the survivors,—where the remainder is vested. See Gray on Perp. § 108, n. 2; Coggins' Appeal, 124 Pa. 34; De Lassus *v.* Gatewood, 71 Mo. 371.

In Henderson *v.* Henderson, 46 Hun (N. Y.) 509, *reversed* in 113 N. Y. 1, after a clause, "I

interest does not exist.[1] But when the question arises of the application of the Rule to such interests the distinction does become important. The general rule seems to be, where a remainder is such that it must vest within the legal period, but by a subsequent clause it is liable to be divested at a time beyond the legal period, the latter clause is void, and the remainder vests absolutely by the first clause.[2]

It is essential to the conception of the term, that the definition do not omit the person in whom the estate vests. The omission of a fixed person in the idea of "vesting" leads to a definition which is found in many decisions in the *United States*, viz: a remainder is vested at any time, if there is, at that time, a person who would come into possession if the preceding particular estate should then be determined.[3]

While this specious definition is found in many decisions, its actual effect in changing the common distinction is confined to

do hereby give, etc., to each of my said children the share or portion of my estate," to be partitioned within a period of five years after the testator's death, there is a subsequent clause: "Provided, that if any of my children shall die leaving issue, then the child or children (who shall be living at the time of such partition) of such deceased child of mine, shall take and have the share or portion which the parent would have taken if living." The court held that "the interest in the realty, which vested in the testator's children upon his death, was liable to be divested, under the provisions of the will, by death before partition completed." See Gray's Perp., § 108; Blanchard *v.* Blanchard, 1 Allen (Mass.) 223; Jeefers *v.* Lampson, 10 Ohio St. 1023; Doe *v.* Considine, 6 Wall. (U. S.) 473.

For cases where the wording gives a contingent limitation, see Mergenthaler's Estate, 15 W. N. C. (Pa.) 441; Thompson *v.* Ludington, 104 Mass. 193; Alverson *v.* Randall, 13 R. I. 71; Bouknight *v.* Brown, 16 S. Car. 155; Stephen *v.* Evans, 30 Ind. 39; Peoria *v.* Darst, 101 Ill. 606; De Lassus *v.* Gatewood, 71 Mo. 371.

1. See Coggins' Appeal, 23 W. N. C. (Pa.) 206. See also Henderson *v.* Henderson, 46 Hun (N.Y.) 509; 113 N.Y. 1.

2. See *infra*, this title, *Limitations to Classes;* Coggins' Appeal, 23 W. N. C. (Pa.) 206; M'Arthur *v.* Scott, 113 U. S. 340; Gray on Perp. §§ 278, 641.

This has, at first sight, a strong resemblance to a transgression of the doctrine which forbids importing the Rule against Perpetuities into the construction of a gift. But there is no reason why the vesting and divesting clauses should necessarily be construed as a whole. Where separately considered, the original gift is absolute, and the second clause, modifying or divesting it, is void for remoteness, the natural effect is that the first clause receives its full effect. But the view is not arrived at by a construction which seeks to save the original gift from the operation of the Rule against Perpetuities. See Marsden's Perp. 43; 278; Wynne *v.* Wynne, 2 Man. & Gr. 8, 14; Ring *v.* Hardwick, 2 B. 352; Carver *v.* Bowles, 2 Russ. & M. 301; Gray's Rule against Perp., § 372 with note.

See also Coggins' Appeal, 23 W. N. C. (Pa.) 206.

See *contra*, Henderson *v.* Henderson, 46 Hun (N. Y.) 509, reversed, however, in 113 N. Y. 1.

See *infra*, this title, *Limitations to Classes.*

Quite distinct from this is, of course, the law which rejects on the ground of repugnancy, a direction to pay at a future time, when the gift has been previously given absolutely. See Marsden's Perp., ch. 16, 206; Gray's Rule against Perp., ch. 4.

3. The definition in the *New York* Rev. Stat. seems in one sentence to adopt this view, but the second sentence is: "They (future estates) are contingent, whilst the person to whom, or the event upon which they are limited to take effect, remains uncertain."

Chancellor Kent, in his Commentaries, is the undesigning author of much

very few jurisdictions.[1] It no longer exists in *New York* as the test of vested remainders.[2]

Future interests, other than remainders, are construed as to their vested or contingent character, as if they were legal remainders.[3] That a limitation of personal property over after a life estate is vested, there can be no doubt.[4] It is necessary to remember that an estate which is contingent on its creation, may be such that it must become vested within the period of the Rule.[5]

of this misapprehension where, dilating on the distinction, he says: "The present capacity of taking effect in possession—if the possession were to become vacant—distinguishes a vested from a contingent remainder." 4 Kent's Com. 282.

1. The test of Chancellor Kent, quoted in the last note, is found in very many American decisions. In most of them, however, it does not effect a change from the common view, that there must be more than a certainty of the happening of the event—*i. e.*, an ascertained person who would take at any point of time if the event had happened then. There must be the certainty of the coming into possession of an ascertained person (or those to whom his interest descends), provided the remainder have not then been destroyed by a condition subsequent.

The *Massachusetts* Supreme Court recognized this test in the case of Blanchard *v.* Blanchard (1 Allen 227), when they said, "Where a remainder is limited to take effect in possession, if ever, immediately upon the determination of a particular estate, which estate is to determine by an event that must unavoidably happen by the efflux of time, the remainder vests in interest as soon as the remainderman is *in esse* and ascertained, provided nothing but his own death before the determination of the particular estate will prevent such remainder from vesting in possession."

Doe, Lessee of Poor *v.* Considine, 6 Wall. (U. S.) 476. The U. S. Supreme Court quotes both definitions, that of Kent and of the *Massachusetts* Supreme Court, as if they were reconcilable. In the same way the case of Jeefers *v.* Lampson (10 Ohio St. 101) is not an exception to the true definition. In Croxall *v.* Shererd, 5 Wall. (U. S) 288, the U. S. Supreme Court undoubtedly falls into the error of testing the vesting by a supposed present contingency.

In *Illinois*, in the case of Smith *v.* West, 103 Ill. 332, the decision is undoubtedly wrong, in so far as it construes a vested remainder in a conveyance to a woman of a life estate, remainder to the children of her body, or such as may be living at her death, or the descendants of any one that may be then deceased.

Equally erroneous is the decision of the Supreme Court of *Alabama* in holding, in Kumpe *v.* Coons, 63 Ala. 448, under a devise of lands to a married woman for life, "and after her death to her children then living," that the children take a vested remainder.

2. It is significant that while both of the decisions last mentioned in the preceding note are based on early definitions in *New York*, later cases in that State have entirely changed the original interpretation of the statutory distinction.

The *New York* Statutes (1 *New York* Rev. Stat. 722, § 13) read: "Future estates are either vested or contingent. They are vested when there is a person in being who would have an immediate right to the possession of the lands upon the ceasing of the intermediate or precedent estate. They are contingent, whilst the person to whom, or the event upon which they are limited to take effect, remains uncertain." The doctrine in Moore *v.* Littel, 41 N. Y. 66, which held that a remainder to the heirs of a person living, at his death, was vested, has been rejected in such late cases as Henessy *v.* Patterson, 85 N. Y. 103; Purdy *v.* Hoyt, 92 N. Y. 447; and especially the late case of Dana *v.* Murray, 26 N. E. Rep. 21 (1890). See also Leonard *v.* Burr, 18 N. Y. 96–107; Radley *v.* Kuhn, 97 N. Y. 26–34.

3. Gray on Perp. §§ 116, 117, 205; *citing* Routledge *v.* Dorril 2 Ves. Jr. 357; Evans *v.* Walker, 3 Ch. D. 211; Loring *v.* Blake, 98 Mass. 253; Bowditch *v.* Andrew, 8 Allen (Mass.) 339.

4. Loring *v.* Blake, 98 Mass. 253.

5. Gray on Perp., § 206; Goodier *v.*

(2) *Contingent.*—Contingent remainders are subject to the Rule against Perpetuities.[1]

(*b*) REVERSIONARY INTERESTS.—Possibilities of reverter, as they are called, must be separated from the right of entry after condition broken, the former being a reversionary interest coming into possession after the natural determination of a qualified or determinable fee,[2] the latter a contractual right.[3] Whether possibilities of reverter exist in *England*, since the statute *Quia Emptores*, is uncertain.[4] That they do exist in the *United States* where that statute is not in force, there is no doubt.[5]

In none of the cases in which possibilities of reverter have been recognized, has the question of remoteness been discussed. It is therefore, impossible to say how the question would be treated by the courts to-day. It must be remembered, that the Rule against Perpetuities cannot be reconciled with the feudal theory of common law estates. It acts, regardless of nice conceits based upon the fiction of a seisin, as a practical rule looking only to actual contingency: whether, or not, a future estate is certain ever to

Johnson, 18 Ch. D. 441; Marsden's Perp. 180.

1. See *supra*, this title, *Scope*. Lewis, Perp., 592, 621; Sanders' Uses & Trusts 197; Real Prop. Commissioners, 3 Rep. 29, 36; Marsden's Perp. 440; Gray on Perp. §§ 283, 316. See Law Quarterly, October 1890. *Contra*, Williams' Real Prop. (13th ed.) App.; Challis' Real Prop. 159, 162.

In the *United States* the decisions are unanimous. See list of cases *supra*, this title, *Scope*. In *England* the latest decisions are of great importance in finally settling the law there. Whitby *v.* Mitchell, 42 Ch. D. 494, affirmed in 44 Ch. D. 85. *In re* Frost, 43 Ch. D. 246, 251, 26.

For the statutes especially including contingent remainders, see *supra*, this title, *Scope*.

2. This is often called a "fee simple conditional," though that name was confined, before the statute *De Donis*, to that estate which became by the statute an estate tail. The risk of confusion with an estate on condition, with right of entry for breach, which is mentioned in the text, is a further reason against the term, "fee simple conditional."

3. See *supra*, this title, *Scope; Contractual Right.*

4. Mr. Gray argues clearly that the statute *Quia Emptores*, in ending tenure between the grantor of an estate in fee simple and the grantee, made impossible determinable fees and possibilities of reverter (Gray's Rule against Perp., §§ 31–36). He sustains his position with such authorities as: 1 Sand. Uses (5th ed.) 208; Leake's Land Law 36, note d; Marsden's Perp. 71, 72; Pollock's Land Law, 213–215; and with such decisions as that of Sir George Jessel in Collier *v.* Walters, L. R., 17 Eq. 252, and that of *In re* Machu, 21 Ch. D. 838.

But there are not wanting *dicta* in English case, assuming the validity of qualified fees, notably Pool *v.* Needham, Yelv. 149. See Gray on Perp., § 33. See especially, for this view, Challis' Real Property, Ch. 17.

5. That they exist in *Pennsylvania* there is no doubt. See Sheetz *v.* Fitzwater, 5 Pa. St. 126; Pennsylvania R. Co. *v.* Parke, 42 Pa. St. 31; Henderson *v.* Hunter, 59 Pa. St. 336; First Methodist Church *v.* Old Columbia Co., 14 W. N. C. (Pa.) 229.

In *South Carolina*, estates in fee simple conditional, in its strict sense, exist (Jones *v.* Portell, Harp. (S. Car.) 92). In *Pennsylvania* and in *South Carolina* the statute *Quia Emptores* is not in force, and there is therefore no reason on principle against the validity of possibilities of reverter. In other States the same reason should exclude them as in *England*. In Leonard *v.* Burr, 18 N. Y. 96, however they are expressly decided to be valid,—"the only weighty case reported on either side of the Atlantic," says Mr. Gray, § 41, "since the passage of the statute of *Quia*

come into possession. It has no regard for mere nomenclature. The use of such a term as "vested" cannot protect an estate, where there is an actual uncertainty of its coming into possession. So a remainder after an estate tail, whether it is called vested or contingent, is removed from the operation of the Rule only because it may be destroyed by the tenant in tail. As to all reversionary interests, there is no reason why the Rule should not be strictly applied. Rights of entry, it must be remembered, are not an exception here, since they are not reversionary rights. The subject of escheat is, by its nature, an exception, and the only exception to the operation of the Rule on reversionary interests.

(*c*) EASEMENTS.—It is difficult to discern a reason for omitting easements and other rights, less than ownership, in land of others, from the sphere of the Rule against Perpetuities. In addition to the reason affecting reversionary interests, is the circumstance that easements can at common law be transferred *in futuro.* Nevertheless the balance of authority has hitherto excluded them, together with other similar interests in land (less than ownership) created by contract.[1]

(*d*) EXECUTORY LIMITATIONS.—It is to the class of interests created by the Statutes of Uses and of Wills that the Rule against Perpetuities applies with especial fitness (although it cannot, correctly, be said to have been invented exclusively with a view to their legal limitation). The special reason for their subjection to the Rule is their independence of the rules of limitation at the common law. Thus, there is no bar in a limitation by way of use, to the creation of a fee upon a fee—what is commonly called a shifting use; nor to the creation of an estate in fee to begin *in futuro* by way of a springing use. The same freedom exists in limitations by will, which are then termed executory devises[2] Without the Rule against Perpetuities, these limitations could be created to take effect in an indefinitely remote future upon any number of successive contingencies.[3]

Emptores, in which the validity of a possibilty of reverter has been clearly adjudicated." In a few other cases (discussed by Mr. Gray in § 40) there was, at least, an implication of their validity. See Wood *v.* Cheshire, 32 N. H. 421; Jamaica Pond Aqueduct Co. *v.* Chandler, 9 Allen (Mass.) 159; State *v.* Brown, 7 Dutch. (N. J.) 13; Foy *v.* Mayor etc. of Baltimore, 4 Gill (Md.) 394; Daniells *v.* Wilson, 27 Wis. 492.

1. See Marsden's Perpetuities, 13, 20; London etc. R. Co. *v.* Gomm, 51 L. J., Ch. 630. See, however, Gray's Rule against Perp., §§ 314–316; Lewis' Perp., ch. 29; Gilbert's Rents, 59–60; Fearne's C. R. 529; Butler's note; Gilbert's Uses (Sugd. ed.), 195, note; Sand. Uses (5th ed.) 203–205. See also Rowbotham *v.* Wilson, 8 H. L. C. 362; Low *v.* Innes, 10 Jur., N. S. 1037; Gale on Easements (5th ed.) 85. See *infra*, this title, *Contractual Rights.*

2. The generic term "executory limitation" is, perhaps, the best. The term "conditional limitation" covers all cases of shifting uses and shifting devises since a fee cannot be determined by a fixed period. But the term "conditional limitation" fails of being generic, in so far as a remainder can be limited by way of use or devise after an estate for years. See Challis' Real Prop. 140; Gray's Perp., §§ 54, 58–60.

3. Mr. Gray discusses at length the question whether the Rule against Perpetuities is the sole restraint on

(*e*) EQUITABLE ESTATES; TRUSTS.—Although equitable interests do not owe their origin to the Statutes of Uses and of Wills, yet they are universally agreed to come within the operation of the Rule against Perpetuities. The fact that equitable remainders (as they are called, with perhaps little fitness) need not, like legal remainders, be supported by a preceding particular estate of freehold, and need not, therefore, vest at the expiration of the preceding limitations (the legal estate being, of course, throughout in trustees), deprives them of the excuse which, it is claimed, removes legal remainders from rules against remoteness.[1]

There is a class of equitable future interests which are closely analogous to possibilities of reverter after a qualified fee. It is the class of resulting trusts to the creator of a trust for a specified object, when the object of the trust has ceased to exist. Both of these classes of future contingent interests, together with a class of contractual rights (rights of entry for breach of a condition),[2] have, in the *United States*, never been held to be affected by the Rule against Perpetuities. But as the question of remoteness has never been raised in their connection, it cannot be said to be settled by the decisions.[3]

Such a resulting trust must not be confounded with a resulting trust to the heirs or next of kin, where, the legal interest being in trustees, there is an equitable limitation which is void for remoteness. This has nothing to do with the Rule against Perpetuities; it is simply the case of property undisposed of by will.[4] Except where the *New York* statute has been adopted,[5] it is wrong to

the creation of future estates in land, either by way of use or by will. He inquires whether: (1) A future freehold can be raised by a bargain and sale; (2) Whether a contingent use is good, although preceded by an estate for years; and (3) Whether a bargain and sale to a person not *in esse* is good. He answers all three questions in the affirmative, and concludes that the Rule against Perpetuities is the only restraint on the creation of future estates in land. Gray on Perp., §§ 56–66.

1. The case of Hopkins *v.* Hopkins, (West 600), decided by Lord Hardwicke, applied the rules of legal remainders strictly to equitable remainders. But a recent decision in chancery, based on Hopkins *v.* Hopkins, was reversed by the court of appeals, which held that equitable remainders should not be excepted from the operation of the Rule against Perpetuities. Abbiss *v.* Burney, 50 L. J. Ch. 348; Marsden's Perp. 168; Gray's Perp., § 326. Recent decisions seem to remove even legal remainders from the number of exceptions to the Rule. See Whitby *v.* Mitchell, 42 Ch. D. 494; 44 Ch. D. 85; *In re* Frost, 43 Ch. D. 246, 251. Whatever doubt there may be here, has certainly disappeared as to equitable remainders.

2. See, *infra*, this title, *Contractual Rights.*

3. The American cases on the subject are Easterbrooke *v.* Tillinghast, 5 Gray (Mass.) 17, and Daniel *v.* Jackoway, Freem. Ch. (Miss.) 59. The former was the case of a devise in special trust to apply the income and profits of the devised property to the support of the gospel and the maintenance of a pastor in a church "as long as the members of the church should maintain the visibility of a church" in a certain faith and practice.

4. See Tregonwell *v.* Sydenham, 3 Dow. 194. See Marsden's Perp. 291; Gray's Perp., § 414. The distinction in the two classes is clear in that in the second class there is no future contingency whatever, but a present vesting in place of a void limitation.

5. See *infra*, this title, *Independent*

say that a trust is void if it may extend beyond a period of lives in being and twenty-one years thereafter. In devises and bequests in trusts the Rule is applied to the equitable interests (as to the remoteness of their vesting) precisely as to future interests under other forms of disposition. If under the trust, any equitable estate may vest beyond the period, it is void; and there is, in so far, a resulting trust to the heir or next of kin. If every equitable interest is thus too remote and void, the whole trust is void, since there is no object. Where the equitable interests are vested, an entirely distinct rule against restraint of alienation gives the *cestui que trust* the right to call on the trustee for the legal title. The Rule against Perpetuities operates against vested interests.[1] Where, however, the trust itself is executory and may not be executed within the period, it is, of course, void for remoteness.

Charitable trusts will be discussed under a separate section of this title.[2]

(*f*) CONTRACTUAL RIGHTS.—Rights created by contract are governed by the Rule against Perpetuities only in so far as they involve rights in specific property. This is illustrated very clearly in the distinction at English law between the right of entry of the grantor of an estate on condition, and the right to enter and hold until the arrears of rent are discharged. The former is properly an interest in property (though not a reversionary one),[3] and is, therefore, in *England*, subject to the Rule.[4] The latter is merely a remedy to enforce a contractual right, and cannot, therefore, be too remote.[5] It is well to notice in connection, a second distinction involving a third right of entry—*i. e.*, that which is attached to a lease for years. The reason why this last right is not void for

System of New York, Michigan, Wisconsin and Minnesota; the Statutes of California, Idaho and Dakota; the Statute of Indiana where the statute is discussed in reference to trusts.

1. In several *Maryland* cases, the courts have fallen into this error; notably in Barnum *v.* Barnum, 26 Md. 119. See the same cases reported in 90 Am. Dec. 88, with the note appended, which fails, however, to state the true principle, although it refers to Mr. Gray's book. See also Deford *v.* Deford, 36 Md. 168; Goldsborough *v.* Martin, 41 Md. 488; Slade *v.* Patten, 68 Me. 382. See Gray on Perp., §§ 234, 236, 475-124, 509.
See Cresson *v.* Ferree, 70 Pa. St. 446; Tait *v.* Swinstead, 26 Beav. 525; Peters *v.* Lewes etc. R. Co., 18 Ch. D. 429; *Re* Cotton's Trusts, 19 Ch. D. 624, 629. See also Blackstone *v.* Davis, 21 Pick. (Mass.) 43; Sparhawk *v.* Cloon, 125 Mass. 262; Daniels *v* Eldredge, 125 Mass. 350.

2. See *infra*, this title, *Charitable Trusts*.

3. Such a right of entry differs from the possibility of reverter after a qualified fee in that it is simply a right of the feoffor to substitute himself for the feoffee. It is therefore not affected by the statute *Quia Emptores*. See Gray's Perp., §§ 30, 31; Co. Lit. 202.

4. The question of the application of the Rule here is treated fully by Gray on Perp., in §§ 290-311. English cases enforcing the Rule are: *In re* Macleay, L. R. 20 Eq. 186; Dunn *v.* Flood, 25 Ch. D. 629. See Marsden's Perp. 4, 5; *contra*, Challis' Real Prop. 152-154.

5. See Marsden's Perp., 7, 15, 248; Gray, on Perp. § 303; Lewis, on Perp., 618, 619. See Gilbertson *v.* Richards, 4 H. & N. 277; where the right to a rent charge to

remoteness, is because it is a vested interest, being incident to the reversion.[1]

While it is quite clear that the spirit of the Rule embraces all interests in property which may by possibility arise beyond the stated period, without regard to the manner in which they have been created, the whole array of cases involving interests created by contract, in which the question of remoteness did arise, or ought naturally to have been considered, present an almost unbroken line of decisions against the application of the Rule against Perpetuities. It is doubtful whether, in the *United States*, any interest in land, created by contract, short of a contract for the transfer of ownership, would, under any conditions, be held to be remote. In *England*, a recent case has been decided that a covenant by the purchaser of the fee, giving the vendor and his assigns forever a right of pre-emption, is void for remoteness.[2] There can be but little doubt that this case is a beginning of a universal extension of the Rule. The classes of cases of interests in property arising under contract, which are legitimately excepted from the operation of the Rule against Perpetuities may be grouped as follows:

1. Where the right which may arise is merely a remedy for the enforcement of the right which is the principal subject of the contract; as a power of sale in a mortgage, or a right of entry or of distress to secure a rent-charge.[3]

2. Where the right which may arise is incident to the reversion, and is, therefore, vested in character, as a right of entry reserved to the lessor.[4]

3. A covenant or contract, which is merely restrictive as to use of the land, is not obnoxious to the Rule against Perpetuities, though it may, in equity, be enforceable against successive owners.[5]

4. Finally the same reasons which make exceptions to the Rule in wills and conveyances apply in cases of contract, such as

arise on certain conditions was held not within the Rule.

1. See Gray on Perp., § 303; Marsden on Perp., 7. But see Roe d. Hunter *v.* Galliers, 2 T. R. 133, 140.

2. London & S. W. R. *v.* Gomm, 20 Ch. D. 562; 51 L. J., Ch. 530. This case expressly overrules Birmingham Canal Co. *v.* Cartwright, 11 Ch. D. 421; 48 L. J., Ch. 552,—relating to a covenant giving to a purchaser, his heirs and assigns, the refusal of certain mines under adjoining lands, whenever these adjoining lands should be sold.

In Hope *v.* Mayor and Corporation of Gloucester, 7 D. M. & G. 647; 25 L. J., Ch. 145; see Marsden's Perp. 10, a covenant is a deed of conveyance, for a new lease, to be made at the request of any of the heirs of a person named in the deed of conveyance, on the expiration of a term in the lands, then subsisting, was held void for remoteness.

3. See Marsden's Perpetuities 12, 248; Sugden on Powers (8th. ed.) 16; Gilbertson *v.* Richards, 4 H. & N. 277; Lewis on Perp. 561.

4. See Marsden on Perp. 15, 248; Daniel *v.* Stepney, L. R. 7 Ex. 327. But see Roe d. Hunter *v.* Galliers, 2 T. R. 133, 140.

5. See the recent case of MacKenzie *v.* Childers, L. R. 43; Ch. D. 265. See also Marsden's Perp. 16; and the leading case on such covenant in *England*, Tulk *v.* Moxhay, 18 L. J., Ch. 83.

conditions which are void as being repugnant to the estate granted, or an undue restraint upon trade.[1]

Almost all other classes of interests in property which may arise under a covenant or contract, for whose exception no valid reason is discernible, have, in the *United States*, been upheld either without the question of remoteness being raised, or the Rule against Perpetuities has been held expressly inapplicable.[2]

(*g*) POWERS.—It has been said in the introductory review, that there is an exception to the rule which requires that, in obedience to the Rule against Perpetuities, every future interest must not only vest, if at all, within the required period, but must, at its creation, be certain to vest, if at all, within lives in being and twenty-one years thereafter. This exception is an interest granted in the exercise of a power. But it is necessary to distinguish carefully the precise limits of this exception. In the first place, it is well settled that the remoteness of an appointment under a power is measured from the time of the creation of the power, not from the time of its exercise.[3]

1. See Marsden on Perp., 8, as to contract not to aliene. Co. Lit. 206 b; Butler's note Co. Lit. 379 b; McLean *v.* McKay, L. R., 5 P. C. 327, 334; Hawley *v.* Northampton, 8 Mass. 3; Theol. Ed. Soc. *v.* Attorney Genl., 135 Mass. 285; Pratt *v.* Alger, 136 Mass. 550; Brandenburg *v.* Thorndike, 139 Mass. 102.

2. Thus in *Massachusetts* a line of cases hold that the Rule is not applicable to conditions in a conveyance in fee for the breach of which a right of entry is reserved to the grantor (or devisor) and his heirs. See Toby *v.* Moore, 130 Mass. 448; Gray *v.* Blanchard, 25 Mass. 284; Austin *v.* Cambridgeport Parish, 38 Mass. 215; Brattle Sq. Church *v.* Grant, 69 Mass. 142; French *v.* Old South Soc., 106 Mass. 479.

3. This seems clear enough; and yet slips of far-reaching importance have been made by eminent authorities in the application of it.

In Smith's Appeal, 88 Pa. St. 492, there was an exercise by will of a power of appointment of the principal, in which the testatrix had a life interest. The appointment was made to the children of the testatrix for their lives, remainders over "to such persons and for such estates as they might by will limit and appoint, and in default of appointment to the person or persons that would take under them if they had died intestate owning the same."

The children of the testatrix had all been born in the lifetime of the creator of the power. The court held the appointments after the death of the children (and also the life-estate to the children as inseparable from the remainders) void, because while the children were actually in being in the lifetime of the creator of the power, there might have been children born after his decease. This was undoubtedly wrong, as Mr. Gray has ably shown. (Rule against Perpetuities, §§ 523–525;) and, indeed, has been admitted, *obiter*, in several recent cases by the same court. See Coggins' Appeal, 124 Pa. St. 10; Lawrence's Estate, 136 Pa. St. 336; Mifflin's Appeal, 22 W. N. C. (Pa.) 199. The case is a very interesting illustration of the way in which the principle under consideration should be applied, and, indeed, how it should not be applied. While the time of vesting of an interest created by an appointment in the exercise of a power should be measured from the time of the creation of the power, this must be done only after it has been clearly seen what the appointment was in fact, with regard to the time at which and the circumstances under which it was made. The words of the appointment must never be read literally into the original instrument, where such words might have a different effect in the two instruments, because what was certain under the later instrument might have been uncertain under the original instrument. Thus, in the instrument creating the power, the word "children" would

But in the second place it is equally well settled, and this is the exception indicated: that a power is not void, because by the terms of its creation an appointment under the exercise of the power would be possible by which an interest might be limited to vest beyond the legal period counted from the time of the creation of the power.[1] There is no uncertainty as to this principle, but there seems to be some confusion as to the application of the former.[2]

It follows, naturally, that a power is void *ab initio*, if it may by any possibility be exercised beyond the limits of the period of the Rule. The only exception is one which exists equally as to the vesting of all interests, viz: a power is valid though it may be executed beyond the period of the Rule, provided it must become destructible within the period. This occurs in the common case where powers of sale are attached to a settlement for life-estates, with an equitable remainder in fee, and the owner of the equitable fee may call for a conveyance.[3]

Where, however, the power is general and is not confined to exercise by will, it can never be obnoxious to the Rule against Perpetuities. This follows directly from the principle that the Rule has nothing to do with destructible interests. The donee of the power in such a case is treated precisely as absolute owner in

have quite a different meaning than it could possibly have at the death of the testatrix, when the same word related to ascertained persons, without any possibility of enlargement. Mr. Gray words the principle thus: "No appointment made under a power is good unless at the time of the creation it was certain that if the appointment was ever made, the appointee's interest would vest, if at all, within twenty-one years after lives then in being." Rule against Perpetuities, § 515.

In Lawrence's Estate, 136 Pa. St. 355, it was held—directly overruling Smith's Appeal, 88 Pa. St. 492, —that where the donee of a power to devise, who was in being at the creation of the power, appoints by will in trust for life tenants to take at his death, with remainder over, such appointment for life will be good. As to the separability of a valid from an invalid portion of an appointment, see also Sugden on Powers 394, 683; Lewis on Perpetuities 496, *citing* Bristow *v.* Warde, 2 Ves. Jr. 336; Butcher *v.* Butcher, 9 Ves. 382. See also Davenport *v.* Harris, 3 Gr. 168; Mifflin's Appeal, 121 Pa. St. 205.

1. Lewis on Perp. 487. The direct and specific object of the power according to its terms, is not to create a perpetuity; and, as the exercise of it is necessarily according to a certain discretion or latitude of choice in the donee, the security which the law provides against the violation of the law of remoteness, is in the failure of any disposition which results from the abuse of that discretion. This is quoted in Lawrence's Estate, 136 Pa. St. 364. See Marsden's Perp. 237.

English authorities on this point are: Routledge *v.* Darril, 2 Ves. Jr. 357; Attenborough *v.* Attenborough, 1 K. & J. 296, 300; 1 Jarm. on Wills (4th ed.) 290. See Gray's Rule against Perps., §§ 510–513.

2. See the discussion in the note above, under the first principle.

3. In Cresson *v.* Ferree, 70 Pa. St. 446, there was a trust of equal shares of the testator's estate to distinct trustees, for the separate use of each of his daughters for life; and after the death of a daughter to go according to the intestate laws, the trustees to have power at discretion to sell and convey his real estate, and invest the proceeds for the uses before provided. It was held that the power of sale was limited to the continuance of the trusts, and was, therefore, not obnoxious to the Rule against Perpetuities. Upon the death of the daughters, the trusts respective-

fee.[1] But where a general power can be exercised by will only, the Rule, according to the best authorities, applies.[2]

3. Effect of Limitations Void for Remoteness Upon Subsequent and Prior Limitations.—It is a question of much uncertainty which of the two conflicting rules is supreme: a vested interest is never too remote, although preceded by other interests which are too remote;[3] or, a limitation ulterior to or dependent or expectant upon a previous limitation that is too remote, cannot take effect.[4] The better reason seems to favor the former, while the weight of *English* authority seems to favor the latter rule.[5]

It would seem as if the basis of the English decision were an unwarranted imputation of opinion to the testator (or settlor), that because certain prior limitations were once for all invalid on account of remoteness, therefore, to allow subsequent limitations to take effect were contrary to his intention.[6]

As to the effect of limitations void for remoteness on prior limitations, it is only necessary to consider whether such prior limitation is first determinable by the succeeding void limitations; or, second, whether it is itself a limited estate. In the first case, the prior interest is treated as if the subsequent void limita-

ly ceased, and the shares became executed in their children, who thereupon became entitled to a conveyance from the trustee. See Tait *v.* Swinstead, 26 Beav. 525; Gray's Rule against Perps., §§ 475–509, *citing* Ware *v.* Polhill, 11 Ves. 257; Crawford *v.* Lundy, 23 Grant 244; Peters *v.* Lewes etc. R. Co., 18 Ch. D. 429; *Re* Cotton's Trusts, 19 Ch. D. 624, 629. See, however, Barnum *v.* Barnum, 26 Md. 119.

1. In Mifflin's Appeal, 121 Pa. St. 205, the Supreme Court of *Pennsylvania* emphasizes this distinction clearly. Lawrence's Estate, 136 Pa. St. 355; Bray *v.* Bree, 2 Cl. & F. 453; Sugden on Powers 394, 683; Lewis on Perp. 483; Gray on Perp. § 477; Hillyard *v.* Miller, 10 Pa. St. 334; Wollaston *v.* King, L. R., 8 Eq. 165; Morgan *v.* Gronow, L. R., 16 Eq. 1; Bray *v.* Hammersley, 3 Sim. 513.

2. See authorities cited in the preceding note. See Beardsley *v.* Hotchkiss, 96 N. Y. 201; Crooke *v.* Kings Co., 97 N. Y. 421.

3. See Gray's Rule against Perp., § 251. Of course there must be included with vested interests, so far as this Rule is concerned, such interests as must become vested within the limits fixed by the Rule against Perpetuities.

A common example of such a vested interest is a remainder to a person (in being) for life, limited on the indefinite failure of issue of a prior remainderman, whose estate is void because limited on indefinite failure of issue of the first remainderman.

4. Marsden's Perpetuities 288.

5. The cases are, Beard *v.* Wetscott, 5 B. & Ald. 801; Moneypenny *v.* Dering, 2 De G., M. & G. 145; Thatcher's Trusts, 26 Beav. 365; Burley *v.* Evelyn, 16 Sim. 290. The basis of the English theory is the intention of the testator, which did not foresee or expect a subsequent limitation to succeed in the place of a prior limitation.

6. Such a subsequent limitation might be a life estate to a person in being limited on a contingency which might happen beyond the period; but in its nature must happen, if at all, within a life in being. Or it might be a vested remainder in fee to a person in being, where the enjoyment was postponed to a contingency beyond the period of the Rule. See the discussion in Gray, on Perp., § 251, *et seq.*

It is very important to distinguish alternative limitations from a subsequent limitation in which a lapse of the prior limitation was not provided for. In Cruikshank *v.* Chase (N. Y.), 21 N. E. Rep. 64, it was held that a residuary clause giving a fund to certain uses in the event that a devise should be adjudged or prove invalid, does not suspend the vesting of the fund until the invalidity of the devise is determined by the final judgment of a court, but it vests at the instant of the

tions had never been created.[1] In the second case, the property after the expiration of the prior interest follows the rules of the devolution of property not disposed of by will.[2]

4. Limitations to Classes.—In an *English* case[3] the substance of the law as to the application of the Rule against Perpetuities to limitations to classes was tersely and clearly stated: "The vice of remoteness affects the class as a whole, if it may affect an unascertained number of its members." In other words, though as to certain individuals a limitation would, if independent, be valid, yet if these individuals are members of a class, of whom some may not be ascertained within the period of the Rule, the whole limitation falls. The common example is to such of the grandchildren of the testator as may attain the age of twenty-five. Though some grandchildren may be alive at the death of the testator, their shares fall if there may be children born afterwards.

In such cases it must first be settled when the limitations to the grandchildren are to vest. Then if they are held to vest at the age of twenty-five, they are void. If, however, they vest at the death of the life-tenant, subject to be divested at the latter period, only the divesting clause fails; the limitations vest absolutely at the death of the life-tenant.[4]

testator's death. See Longhead d. Hopkins *v.* Phelps, 2 W. Bl. 703. See Marsden's Perp. 74, *et seq.*

1. See Gray on Perp. § 247; Brattle Sq. Church *v.* Grant, 3 Gray (Mass.) 142.

Separable Limitations.—It was in regard to the separability of a preceding life-estate from a void remainder, that the decision in Smith's Appeal, 88 Pa. St. 492, was expressly overruled in Lawrence's Estate, 136 Pa. St. 354. The rule as given by Lewis on Perp., p. 496, is "Where, under a power, interests are given by way of particular estate and remainder (including analogous gifts of personal estate), and the particular estate is limited to a valid object of the power, but the remainder is too remote, the appointment will not be wholly void but only the gift in remainder. In such case the interests in respect of which there is an excess of the power, being distinct and separable from the valid portion of the appointment, there is no reason for involving the primary limitations in the remoteness of the remainder." *Citing* Adams *v.* Adams, Cowp. 651; Bristow *v.* Warde, 2 Ves. Jr. 336; Routledge *v.* Dorrill, 2 Ves. Jr. 357; Brudenell *v.* Elwes, 1 East 442; Butcher *v.* Butcher, 9 Ves. 382. See also Davenport *v.* Harris, 3 Grant's Cas. (Pa.) 158.

See *supra*, this title, *Powers.*

2. Gray on Perp., § 248 note; Tongue *v.* Nutwell, 13 Md. 415; Deford *v.* Deford, 36 Md. 168; Van Kleeck *v.* Reformed Dutch Church, 20 Wend. (N. Y.) 457; Greene *v.* Dennis, 6 Conn. 292. See Hayden *v.* Houghton, 5 Pick. (Mass.) 528; Massey's Appeal, 88 Pa. St. 470. But see Caldwell *v.* Willis, 57 Miss. 555.

3. Pearks *v.* Moseley, 5 Up. Ca. 714, 723; 50 L. J., Ch. 57. See Marsden's Perp., ch. 5, where the definition of a class in that case is quoted: "A gift is said to be to a class of persons, when it is to all those who shall come within a certain category or description defined by a general or collective formula, and who if they take at all, are to take one divisible subject in certain proportionate shares."

4. In Coggins' Appeal, 124 Pa. St. 27, there was a bequest to children for lives, "and upon the decease of either of my said children, and successively of each of them, then as respects one equal fourth part of the *corpus* or principal of my residuary estate to and for the only proper use of his or her child, to all of his or her children, if more than one, who shall have attained, or shall attain, the age of twenty-five years, and the issue of any such who shall have died under that age, in equal shares; so, however, that

The class is said to "close" when one member reaches the required age. As to one or more of such members, who are born within the lifetime of the testator, it is certain that if they take at all, they must do so within the required period. And after such an event, all are excluded who are not *in esse*. The minimum share of such member may then be said to be fixed. But since their shares may be increased by the failure of others to reach the required age, the precise share which each takes may not be ascertained within the period. The whole gift to the class, therefore, fails.[1] It may happen, however, that at the death of the testator, there may be one or more members who have attained the required age. The class is then closed, and though there are others *in esse*, the period of ascertainment must fall within the period of the rule.[2]

It is important to notice that though there may be a common description of persons, yet if the gift to each is not affected by the gift to any other, there is no limitation to a class.[3] There is a class of cases of which the following may serve as a type: A devise to A for life, remainder to his children for life, the share of each child to go to its children in fee.[4] Here, though the

the issue of any such deceased child, if more than one person, shall take equally among them such share only as their parent would have taken, if living; but if either of my said children shall die without leaving a child, or issue of a child, him or her surviving, then . . . "

By a codicil the testator directed distribution among grandchildren *per capita* instead of *per stirpes*. There were left surviving four children and eleven grandchildren, of whom ten were living at the adjudication, most of them over twenty-five. No grandchild had been born since the testator's death. It was held that the vesting was suspended until the attainment of the age of twenty-five years, even though the limitation over was only to take effect in case of the devisee's death under that age in that issue. The attainment of a certain age formed part of the original description. As a grandchild might be born within one year before the death of a life-tenant, the gift to the whole class of grandchildren was void. As to the vesting was *cited* Schott's Estate, 78 Pa. St. 40; M'Arthur *v.* Scott, 113 U. S. 340; Leaming *v.* Sharatt, 2 Hare 14; Bagley *v.* Bishop, 6 Ves. 9; Redfield on Wills, § 37; Gray on Perp., §§ 278, 641; Randall on Perp. 85, and especially Davenport *v.* Harris, 3 Grant's Cas. (Pa.) 164; Liebert's Appeal, 13 Pa. St. 501; also Bull *v.* Pritchard, 1 Russ. 213; Hunter *v.* Judd, 4 Sim. 555; Judd *v.* Judd, 3 Sim. 525; Ring *v.* Hardwicke, 2 Beav. 352; Pickford *v.* Brown, 2 Kay & J. 426; Vawdry *v.* Geddes, 1 Russ. & M. 203.

It was strongly urged as a reason for the shares vesting at the death of the surviving life-tenant that there was a limitation over on the death of any one of testator's children "dying without issue."

1. The leading case on this principle is Leake *v.* Robinson, 2 Mer. 263; Andrews *v.* Pattington, 3 Br. C. C. 404; Porter *v.* Fox, 6 Sim. 483; Blagrove *v.* Hancock, 16 Sim. 371; Dodd *v.* Wake, 3 Sim. 615; Newman *v.* Newman, 10 Sim. 51; Vawdry *v.* Geddes, 1 Russ. & M. 203; Williams on Real Property 305; Perry on Trusts 6 § 381; Lewis on Perp. 456; Hillyard *v.* Miller, 10 Pa. St. 334; Smith's Appeal, 88 Pa. St. 492, *cited* in Coggins' Appeal, 124 Pa. St. 30. The case of the Estate of Williamson, 12 Phila. (Pa.) 64, seems to have disregarded the principle. See Gray on Perp., § 375 a. See Dulaney *v.* Middleton (Md. 1890), 19 Atl. Rep. 146. See also Goldtree *v.* Thompson, 79 Cal. 613.

2. Gray on Perp., § 379, *citing* Picken *v.* Matthews, 10 Ch. D. 264.

3. See Gray on Perp., § 389, *citing* Storrs *v.* Benbow, 2 Myl. & K. 46; Boughton *v.* James, 1 Coll. 26.

4. Lowry *v.* Muldrow, 8 Rich. Eq.

remainder to the children for life is to a class, the remainders in fee are separate and independent limitations, to persons of whom the existence of one does not affect the share of another. The remainders to the children of those of the children of A who were alive at the time of the testator's death are therefore valid while the remainders to children of A's children not born in the testator's lifetime are void.[1]

5. Charitable Trusts.—In considering the effect of the Rule against Perpetuities upon charitable trusts, the fact must be remembered that the Rule has to do with the time of the vesting of an estate, and in no wise affects its continuance after it has once vested. A striking characteristic of charitable trusts is that they continue forever. They are perpetuities, using the word "perpetuity" in its natural sense. In the Rule against Perpetuities, the word "perpetuity" has a peculiar technical signification, denoting the period of time beyond which a future interest cannot vest. It would have been more fortunate had the rule been styled the "Rule against Remoteness."

Charitable trusts usually commence *in præsenti*, and on this account the question of remoteness seldom arises; they may, however, begin in some future time, in which case they are not exempt from the operation of the Rule against Perpetuities.

A charitable trust differs from others in that it has no definite *cestui que trust*. There is no determinate person or persons possessing such positive right to the property given in trust as would enable him to transfer his interest by deed. It is no objection to a devise for a charity that it is so vague and indefinite that no particular person may have such an interest as will give him a right to demand its execution, if there be a trustee named clothed with discretionary power to carry out the general objects of the power.[2]

Although the uncertainty of individual object is a characteristic of charity, yet there have been cases where the personal or individual certainty has not been fatal to it. In these cases the persons who are the *cestuis que trustent* are so limited or extended in number as to constitute a definite class.[3]

(S. Car.) 241. See Gray on Perp., § 389. Here all the children of A were alive at the death of the testator. The limitations to their children were held valid.

1. See other cases discussed by Gray on Perp. §§ 389-398; *Re* Michael's Trust, 46 L. J., Ch. 651; Greenwood *v.* Roberts, 15 Beav. 92; Hill *v.* Simonds, 125 Mass. 535; and the following, in which the principle was disregarded: Sears *v.* Russell, 8 Gray (Mass.) 86; Lovering *v.* Lovering, 129 Mass. 67; Smith's Appeal, 88 Pa. St. 492, the statement of which has been given *supra*, this title, *Powers*.

The same principle would seem to govern limitations to a series of persons, the question of one taking being unaffected by the existence of the others. See Gray's Perp., ch. 11, §§ 396-398, discussing Goldsborough *v.* Martin, 41 Md. 488; Caldwell *v.* Willis, 55 Miss. 555.

2. Zeisweiss *v.* James 63 Pa. St. 465; Whitman *v.* Lex, 17 S. & R. (Pa.) 88; Mayor etc. of Philadelphia *v.* Elliott, 3 Rawle (Pa.) 170; Burke *v.* Roper, 79 Ala. 142. See Holland *v.* Alcock, 108 N. Y. 312, 330.

3. The following gifts have been held to be charitable: A bequest of a sum

Generally speaking, the Rule against Perpetuities does not extend to charitable trusts.[1]

of money to assist the donor's "poor relations." Attorney General *v.* Bucknall, 2 Atk. 328; Mahon *v.* Savage, 1 Sch. & Lef. 111. In such cases "the testator's design was to give to them as objects of charity, and not merely as relations." If, however, he intended that an immediate distribution should be made, there will be no charity, and the property will be divided among the testator's next of kin who are poor. Mahon *v.* Savage, 1 Sch. & Lef. 111; Brunsden *v.* Woolredge, Amb. 507; Widmore *v.* Woodroffe, Amb. 636; Green *v.* Howard, 1 Bro. C. C. 31; Carr *v.* Bedford, 2 Ch. Rep. 146; Smith *v.* Harrington, 4 Allen (Mass.) 566; McNeilledge *v.* Galbraith, 8 S. & R. (Pa.) 43; McNeilledge *v.* Barclay, 11 S. & R. (Pa.) 103. Where the gift to poor relations is charitable, the persons entitled must be absolutely poor, and need not necessarily be the next of kin. Gray on Rule against Perpetuities, § 683, and note; Attorney General *v.* Northumberland, L. R., 7 Ch. D. 745; Swasey *v.* American Bible Society, 57 Me. 523; Gillam *v.* Taylor, L. R. 16 Eq. 581. A gift to the minister of a church forever, and one to the master of a certain school, have been held good. Attorney General *v.* Dublin, 38 N. H. 459. Cheeseman *v.* Partridge, 1 Atk. 436. See also, Vanderbolgen *v.* Yates, 3 Barb. Ch. (N. Y.) 242; King *v.* Parker, 9 Cush. (Mass.) 71. In Wright *v.* Linn, 9 Pa. St. 433, land was conveyed to trustees and their successors, to erect a schoolhouse for the perpetual use of the parties to the deed and the inhabitants residing nearer to that school than to any other, and such other persons as the inhabitants might see fit to admit. *Held* a good charity. The court in this case decided that permanency is not essential to constitute a charitable gift.

1. In Philadelphia *v.* Girard, 45 Pa. St. 9 Lowrie, C. J., said: "Perpetuities are grants of property, wherein the vesting of an estate or interest is unlawfully postponed. (Saunders on Uses and Trusts 196); and they are called perpetuities, not because the grant, as written, would actually make them perpetual, but because they transgress the limits which the law has set in restraint of grants that tend to a perpetual suspense of the title, or of its vesting; or, as is sometimes, with less accuracy, expressed, to a perpetual prevention of alienation. According to this definition, a present gift to a charity is never a perpetuity, though intended to be inalienable (24 How. 495); and no vested grant is a perpetuity."

In Perrin *v.* Carey, 24 How. (U. S.) 465, the testator devised certain real and personal property to the city of Cincinnati and its successors, in trust forever, for the purpose of building, establishing and maintaining, as far as practicable, two colleges for the education of boys and girls. The court in its opinion said:

"Charities had their origin in the great command 'to love thy neighbor as thyself.' But when the Emperor Constantine permitted his subjects to bequeath their property to the church, it was soon abused; so much so, that afterwards, when it became too common to give land to religious uses, consistently with the free circulation of property, the supreme authority of every nation in Europe, where Christianity prevailed, found it necessary to limit such devises by Statutes of Mortmain.

"In *France*, by the ancient constitutions of that kingdom, churches, communities, chapters, colleges, convents, etc., were not permitted to acquire or hold immovable property. Dumoulin sur, 1st art., 51 de la Cou., Paris. This incapacity after a long time was relaxed, and they were allowed to hold by license of the king.

"In *Spain*, the communities mentioned before could neither acquire nor hold property, unless by authority of the sovereign; but in *England* corporations had the capacity to take property by the common law. (Co. Litt. 99.) They were incapable of purchasing without the king's license, by a succession of statutes from Magna Charta (9 Henry III to 9 Geo. II). They are known as the Statutes of Mortmain; that is, as it was the privilege of any one, before such statutes restrained it, to leave his property of every kind by testament to whom he pleased, and for such purposes, charitable or otherwise, as he chose; and the will was, in every particular, administered according to the testator's intentions, sometimes by the courts of common law, and at others by a court in chan-

The question of remoteness may arise in any of the three following cases: First, a gift to a charity, then over to an individual. Second, a gift to an individual, and then over to a charity. Third, a gift to a charity, then over to another charity. In such case there may or may not be a change of trustees. In the first and second cases, where the gift is to a charity, followed by a gift to an individual, and where the gift is to an individual followed by a gift to a charity, the Rule against Perpetuities applies, and if the

cery, as may be seen from the cases in Duke, and other writers upon charities.

"Alienation in mortmain, in its primary signification, is an alienation of lands or tenements to any corporation, aggregate, ecclesiastical, or temporal, the consequence of which, in former times was, that by allowing lands to become vested in objects endued with perpetuity of duration, the lands were deprived of escheats and other feudal profits, and the general policy of the common law, which favored the free circulation of property, was frustrated, athough it is true that at the common law the power of purchasing lands was incident to every corporation. The effect of these statutes deprived every corporation in *England*, spiritual or secular, from acquiring, either by purchase or gift, real property of any description, without a general license from the crown enabling it to hold lands in mortmain, or a special license in reference to any particular acquisition. These restraints were subsequently relaxed in many particulars, including gifts to a corporation for the purposes of education. From an early day the courts in *England* held that devises to corporations, which generally cannot take lands under a will, were good when made in favor of charities, and that such gifts, from the purposes to which they were to be applied, and the ownership to which they are subjected, have had the protection of courts of equity to prevent any alienation of them on the part of the person or body interested with the offices of giving them effect; and that in all such cases land has been decreed by courts of equity to be practically inalienable, or that a perpetuity of them exists in corporations when they are charitable gifts." Hillam's Cas, Duke 80, 375; Mayor of Bristol *v.* Whitton (1633), Duke 81, 377; Mayor of Reading *v.* Lane (1601), Duke 81, 361; Lewis on Perpetuity 684; 1 Macnaghten and S. Gordon 460; Christ's Hospital *v.* Granger, 1 Mac. & G. 460; Griffin *v.* Graham, 1 Hawks (N. Car.) 130; Franklin *v.* Armfield, 2 Sneed (Tenn.) 305; Paschal *v.* Acklin, 27 Tex. 173; Wood *v.* Humphreys, 12 Gratt. (Va.) 333; Clark's Trusts, 24 W. R. 233; Russell *v.* Allen, 107 U. S. 163; *In re* Dutton, 4 Ex. D. 54; Yeap Cheap Neo *v.* Ong Cheng Neo, 6 L. R., P. C. 381; Miller *v.* Chittenden, 2 Iowa 362; Gass *v.* Wilhite, 2 Dana (Ky.) 183.

In Odell *v.* Odell, 10 Allen (Mass.) 6, Gray, J., said: "The rule of public policy which forbids estates to be indefinitely inalienable in the hands of individuals does not apply to charities. These, being established for objects of public, general and lasting benefits are allowed by the law to be as permanent as any human institution can be, and courts will readily infer an intention in the donor that they should be perpetual." 1 Spence on Eq. 588; Mayor etc. of Bristol *v.* Whitson, Dwight's Charity Cases 171; Magdalen College *v.* Atty. Gen., 6 H. L. Cas. 202; Perrin *v.* Carey, 24 How. (U. S.) 465; King *v.* Parker, 9 Cush. (Mass.) 82; Dexter *v.* Gardener, 7 Allen (Mass.) 246; Chamberlayne *v.* Brockett, 8 L. R., Ch. App. 206; Atty. Gen. *v.* Greenhill, 9 Jur., N. S. 1307; Jones *v.* Habersham, 107 U. S. 174; Grissom *v.* Hill, 17 Ark. 483; State *v.* Griffith, 2 Del. Ch. 392; White *v.* Fisk, 22 Conn. 31; Williams *v.* Williams, 8 N. Y. 525; Trustees *v.* Kellogg, 16 N. Y. 83; Levy *v.* Levy, 33 N. Y. 97; Adams *v.* Perry, 43 N. Y. 487; Holmes *v.* Mead, 52 N. Y. 332; Banks *v.* Phelan, 4 Barb. (N.Y.) 80; Rose *v* Rose, 4 Abb. App. Dec. (N. Y.) 108; King *v.* Rundle, 15 Barb. (N. Y.) 139; Wilson *v.* Lynt, 30 Barb. (N.Y.) 124; Andrew *v.* New York Bib. Soc., 4 Sandf. (N. Y.) 156; State *v.* Gerhard, 2 Ired. Eq. (N. Car.) 210; Hillyard *v.* Miller, 10 Pa. St. 326; Philadelphia *v.* Girard, 45 Pa. St. 26; White *v.* Hale, 2 Coldw. (Tenn.) 77; Yard's App. 64 Pa. St. 95. See Bascombe *v.* Albert-

event or contingency upon which the gift over is to take effect does not come within the time allowed by the Rule, it is void.[1]

In the third case, where the gift over is from one charity to another, the Rule against Perpetuities does not apply, thus forming an exception.[2]

Where a gift to a charity is not present and absolute, but dependent upon the happening of some future event or contingency, and such an event or contingency may not happen till after the time allowed by the Rule, the gift is void for remoteness.[3]

son, 34 N. Y. 598; Beekman v. Bonson, 23 N. Y. 308; Andrews v. Andrews, 110 Ill. 230; Richmond v. Davis, 103 Ind. 449; Webster v. Morris, 66 Wis. 366.

1. Company of Pewterers v. Christ's Hospital, 1 Vern. 161; Atty. General v. Gill, 2 P. Wms. 369; Wells v. Heath, 10 Gray (Mass.) 25; Atty. General v. Hall, W. Kel. 13; Commissioners of Donations v. De Clifford, 1 Dru. & War. 254; Brattle Sq. Ch. v. Grant, 3 Gray (Mass). 142; Smith v. Townsend, 32 Pa. St. 434; Johnson's Trusts, L. R., 2 Eq. 716; Leonard v. Burr, 18 N. Y. 96; Marsden's Perp. 307; Gray Perp., §§ 593–596; Society for Promoting Theological Education v. Attorney General, 135 Mass. 285.

2. Christ's Hospital v. Granger (16 Sim. 83; 1 Mc N. & G. 460; 1 H. & Tw. 533) is the leading case on this subject. In it there was a gift to the corporation of the city of Reading upon certain charitable trusts, with a proviso annexed, that if the corporation neglected for one year to apply the trust funds in the proper manner, the property should be transferred to the corporation of the city of London, upon trust for the benefit of Christ's Hospital.

The city of Reading having violated the proviso, it was held that the city of London was entitled to a transfer.

It will be noted that there is no time fixed within which the proviso must take effect. It might occur within the time allowed by the Rule against Perpetuities, or at some time in the indefinite future, and there was even a possibility, if not a probability, of its never coming to pass. The court held, however, that "the property was neither more nor less alienable," by reason of the proviso, and consequently the validity of the proviso was not affected by the Rule against Perpetuities. Mr. Gray, in his work on perpetuities, §§ 598 *et seq.*, states that the decision in Christ's Hospital v. Granger (16 Sim. 83) has stood for a long time, and will probably be followed in the future. Yet in those jurisdictions where the question has not been finally settled, "the correctness of the decision deserves careful consideration. As an original question it seems hard to support the case."

In commenting on the reasons given by the court for its decision, he remarks: "But here, with submission to so great an authority, is the common confusion between perpetuity in the sense of inalienability and perpetuity in the sense of remoteness. Property dedicated to a charity is inalienable necessarily; but there is no need of allowing a gift to charity to commence in the remote future. The prevention of property from inalienability is simply an incident of the Rule against Perpetuities, not its object. The true object of the Rule is to restrain the creation of future conditional interests. If a remote gift to a charity after a gift to another charity is good, because they are by nature inalienable, then a gift to a charity after a gift to an individual should be good; the individual can alienate the whole of his present interest, and the remote interest is no more and no less inalienable than when limited after another charity. Yet after a gift to an individual a gift to a charity may be unquestionably bad for remoteness."

Approving the decision, see Odell v. Odell, 10 Allen (Mass.) 1; Jones v. Habersham, 107 U. S. 174; Marsden's Perp. 306; 1 Jarman on Wills 291; Theobald on Wills 424; Storr's Agricultural School v. Whitney (Conn.), 8 Atl. Rep. 141.

3. Gray on Perp., § 605; Tudor's L. C. in Real Prop. (3rd. ed.) 580; 1 Jarman on Wills (4th ed.) 245; Carbery v

Where, however, the evident intent of the testator or settlor is to have the gift take effect immediately, it will be construed as a present absolute interest, not subject to a condition precedent for its vesting, and consequently not subject to the Rule against Perpetuities. If the testator or settlor has annexed to the gift directions as to the method of executing the charitable purpose, and for any reason his directions cannot be followed, the court will carry out the general intent *cy pres.* A gift to an unincorporated society or association will be upheld, where the formation of the corporation is not a condition precedent. The courts are inclined to hold the property for a reasonable time, until the body can be incorporated, but will not wait indefinitely.[1]

Cox, 3 Ir. Ch. 231; Sims *v.* Quinlan, 16 Ir. Ch. 191; Cherry *v.* Mott, 1 Myl. & Cr. 123; Attorney General *v.* Whitchurch, 3 Ves. Jr. 141; Corbyn *v.* French, 4 Vesey 418; De Themmines *v.* Bonneval, 5 Russ. 288; Clark *v.* Taylor, 1 Drew 642; Attorney General *v.* Jolly, 2 Stroh. Eq. 379; Jocelyn *v.* Nott, 44 Conn. 55; Chamberlayne *v.* Brockett, L. R., 8 Ch. 206; *In re* Wood's Estate, 55 Hun (N. Y.) 204.

1. Gray on Perp., § 607, Attorney General *v.* Bishop of Chester, 1 Bro. C. C. 444; Henshaw *v.* Aikinson, 3 Mad. 306; Chamberlayne *v.* Brockett, L. R., 8 Ch. 206, 211; Sinnett *v.* Herbert, L. R., 7 Ch. 232; Attorney General *v.* Bowyer, 3 Vesey Jr. 714; Martin *v.* Margham, 14 Sim. 230; Attorney General *v.* Craven, 21 Beav. 392; Attorney General *v.* Downing, Ambl. 550. "Where a testator directed funds to be provided for certain charity schools, by accumulating his property, but fixed no time for the continuance of the accumulations, which must necessarily have exceeded the legal period, the direction to accumulate was held to be void and consequently the ulterior dispositions of the will to fail; but as the testator had shown an intention to devote his property to charitable purposes, it was directed that his intention be carried into effect, *cy pres*, by means of a scheme to be settled by the master. The VICE-CHANCELLOR said: "Although the particular mode in which the testator meant the benefits to be doled out to the objects of his bounty cannot take effect, yet, as there is, confessedly, a devotion of his personal estate to charitable purposes, my opinion is that his next of kin have no claim at all to his property. I conceive that, if a testator has expressed his intention that his personal estate shall be, in substance, applied for charitable purposes, the particular mode which he may have pointed out for effecting those purposes has nothing to do with the question whether the devotion for charitable purposes shall take place or not; and that, whatever the difficulty may be, the court, if it is compelled to yield to circumstances, will carry the charitable intentions into effect through the medium of some other scheme." Martin *v.* Margham, 14 Sim. 230. See also, Attorney General *v.* Ironmongers' Company, 2 Myl. & Keen 576; Moggridge *v.* Thackwell, 7 Vesey 36; Philadelphia *v.* Girard, 45 Pa. St. 1.

Russell *v.* Allen, 5 Dill. (U. S.) 235; 107 U. S. 163; Jones *v.* Habersham, 107 U. S. 174, 190, 191; Inglis *v.* Sailors' Snug Harbor, 3 Pet. (U. S.) 99; Ould *v.* Washington Hospital, 95 U. S. 303; Williams *v.* First Presbyterian Soc., 1 Ohio St. 478; Trustees McIntire School *v.* Zanesville, 9 Ohio 203; Swasey *v.* American Bible Society, 57 Me. 523; Cumming *v.* Reid Memorial Church, 64 Ga. 105; Schmidt *v.* Hess, 60 Mo. 591; Odell *v.* Odell, 10 Allen (Mass.) 1; *In re* Taylor Orphan Asylum, 36 Wis. 534; Dodge *v.* Williams, 46 Wis. 70; Gould *v.* Taylor Orphan Asylum, 46 Wis. 106; Field *v.* Drew Theological Seminary, 41 Fed. Rep. 371. See also Burr *v.* Smith, 7 Vt. 241; Milne *v.* Milne, 17 La. 46; Cromie *v.* Louisville Orphan's Home Soc., 3 Bush (Ky.) 365; Sanderson *v.* White, 18 Pick. (Mass.) 328; Henser *v.* Harris, 42 Ill. 425.

The fact that a religious society, to whose trustees land is conveyed for religious purposes, had not been incorporated when the deed was delivered, does not invalidate the trust. Fadness *v.* Braunborg, 73 Wis. 257.

Maryland, act 1888, ch. 249, provides that no devise of real property for any

The laws of the different States do not agree on the subject of the application of the doctrine of *cy pres* to charitable gifts to unincorporated associations. Some States, as *New York, Michigan, Minnesota*, etc., repudiate the doctrine entirely; others, as *Virginia, North Carolina*, etc., refuse to recognize the doctrine, yet support charitable gifts to corporations not in existence, or not capable of taking at the time of the gift; while others accept it. Following is a reference to the decisions in the different States:

New York.—The doctrine of *cy pres* does not exist. A devise to an unincorporated charitable association is void, and is not made valid by the incorporation of such association after the death of the testator. So, also, a subsequent amendment of its charter imparts no vitality to a devise to a corporation not authorized to take at the time of such death.[1]

charitable use shall be void for any uncertainty as to the beneficiaries, where the will making the same shall contain directions for the formation of a corporation to take it. Chase *v.* Stockett, 19 Atl. Rep. 761. See, prior to the act, State *v.* Warren, 28 Md. 338.

See also Peckham *v.* Newton, 15 R. I. 321; Women's Union Missionary Society *v.* Mead (Ill.), 23 N. E. Rep. 603.

1. White *v.* Howard, 46 N. Y. 144; Leonard *v.* Burr, 18 N. Y. 107; Bascom *v.* Albertson, 34 N. Y. 384.

In Downing *v.* Marshall, 23 N. Y. 366, the will attempted to devise real estate, used as a manufacturing establishment, to an executor in trust, to continue the factory in operation for two lives in being, and upon the death of the survivor of them, to sell the same; the income of the property and the proceeds after the conversion, to be distributed to one unincorporated association and three corporations for religious and charitable purposes. *Held*, that the provision failed as a trust to receive and apply the rents and profits of real estate, because the lives on which the trust depended, were those of persons having no interest in its performance, while the statute (1 *New York* Rev. Stat., p. 278, § 55, subd. 3) requires it to be dependent on the life of the beneficiary. That the provision was void both as to real and personal estate, so far as respects the unincorporated association. Leslie *v.* Marshall, 31 Barb. (N. Y.) 560; Sherwood *v.* American Bible Society, 1 Keyes (N. Y.) 561; Wetmore *v.* Parker, 57 N. Y. 450; Yates *v.* Yates, 9 Barb. (N. Y.) 343; Owens *v.* Missionary Society, 14 N. Y. 406; Beekman *v.* People, 23 N. Y. 312; McCaughal *v.* Ryan, 27 Barb. (N. Y.) 395. 398, 409; Jackson *v.* Staats, 11 Johns. (N. Y.) 337; Jackson *v.* Mervill, 6 Johns. (N. Y.) 185. See also Williams *v.* Williams, 8 N. Y. 525; Phelps *v.* Phelps, 28 Barb. (N. Y.) 121; Rose *v.* Rose, 4 Abb. App. Dec. (N.Y.) 108; Beekman *v.* Bonsor, 23 N. Y. 298; Phelps *v.* Pond, 23 N. Y. 69; Burrill *v.* Boardman, 43 N. Y. 254; Marx *v.* McGlynn, 88 N. Y. 357; Mapes *v.* American Home Missionary Soc., 33 Hun (N. Y.) 360; Shipman *v.* Rollins, 33 Hun (N. Y.) 89; Carpenter *v.* Historical Society, 1 Dem. (N. Y.) 606, 2 Dem. (N Y.) 574; Holmes *v.* Mead, 52 N. Y. 332; McKeon *v.* Kearney, 57 How. Pr. (N. Y.) 349; First Presby. Society *v.* Bowen, 21 Hun (N. Y.) 389; Wilson *v.* Lynt, 30 Barb. 124; Levy *v.* Levy, 33 N. Y. 97; Kilpatrick *v.* Johnson, 15 N. Y. 327; Matter of Starr, 2 Dem. 141.

In a charitable bequest to a corporation whose organization is to be procured by the executors and trustees within two lives in being named in the will, the period prescribed by the *New York* statute against perpetuities, does not offend against the statute because the executors and trustees might omit to procure the incorporation within the two lives.

The period of two lives not having elapsed, the will cannot be declared void, though the corporation created may not answer the description, as a

If there is a condition, express or implied, that the non-existent corporation shall come into being within the time allowed for the vesting of future estates, the gift is good.[1]

Pennsylvania.—Charitable gifts to corporations not *in esse* are valid.[2]

If a gift be made to a charity, but the trustee is a corporation forbidden by law to hold the legal title, the court will appoint a trustee who is capable of taking and will use the corporation to distribute the charity among those entitled to it.[3]

new corporation may still be created. Tilden *v.* Green, 2 N. Y. Supp. 584.

1. Gray on Rule against Perpetuities, § 609. F, by his will devised certain real estate to his widow for life, and directed the executors to sell sufficient of his other real estate to provide a fund to be invested so as to produce a specified annuity to be paid her during life, etc. and after the widow's death he authorized the executors to sell the residue of the real estate, add the proceeds to the amount invested, and after paying therefrom certain items specified, he directed that the balance be "then" divided into eight parts, four of which he gave to certain religious associations not then incorporated, the language of the will showing that the testator was aware of this fact and contemplated a future incorporation after the death; but before the death of the widow the said associations were duly incorporated. The court held that the legacies so given did not vest until the death of the widow and the creation of the fund provided for; and as the beneficiaries named were then capable of taking, that the bequests were valid. Shipman *v.* Rollins, 78 N. Y. 311; Burrill *v.* Boardman, 43 N. Y. 254. See Cruikshank *v.* Home for the Friendless, 113 N. Y. 337.

2. Evangelical Association's Appeal, 35 Pa. St. 316; Zimmerman *v.* Anders, 6 W. & S. (Pa.) 218; Witman *v.* Lex, 17 S. & R. (Pa.) 88; Miller *v.* Porter, 53 Pa. St. 292.

See also Zeisweiss *v.* James, 63 Pa. St. 465, where the testator directed that upon the death of the devisees for life the real estate should go to "The Infidel Society in Philadelphia, hereafter to be incorporated, and to be held and disposed of by them for the purpose of building a hall for the free discussion of religion, politics, etc.," and it was held that the remainder limited to a corporation thereafter to be created was void, because there was no devisee competent to take at the time, and the possibility that there might be such a corporation during the particular estate for life, was too remote. The court seemed to think that the purposes of the association mentioned in the will were not charitable and were such that the association could not obtain a charter under the general laws of *Pennsylvania.* The court, however, recognized the principle "that if the purpose for which the devise over was made, be a valid charitable use, which can be enforced and administered in a court of equity, it will not be allowed to fail for want of a trustee."

3. "In the present case, it was agreed that Catharine Moore, by her will dated April 9, 1863, and proved and filed on February 3, 1864, devised, *inter alia,* an undivided moiety of two yearly ground rents of $45 unto The Domestic and Foreign Missionary Committee of the Protestant Episcopal Church in the United States of America, and that there was not, and is not now, any such committee; but there was and is a corporation called The Domestic and Foreign Missionary Society of the Protestant Episcopal Church in the United States of America, which was chartered by the State of New York on May 13, 1846, the object or work of which is the support of missionaries or religious teachers of the Protestant Episcopal Church in the United States of America, within the United States and Foreign Countries. In consequence of the Act of April 26, 1855, § 5, prohibiting corporations not incorporated under the laws of this State, from acquiring and holding any real estate within this commonwealth, directly or by any trustee, unless authorized to hold such property by the laws of this commonwealth, an application was

A contingent gift to a now existing charity, taking effect at a time beyond the period allowed by the Rule against Perpetuities, is void ; but where there is a separation of the gift from the estate of the testator, and the beneficiary is in being and is made trustee for its own benefit, and only the ultimate application of the gift is deferred, then it will be upheld.[1]

made to this court for the appointment of a trusteee to hold a moiety of said ground rents, with authority to extinguish the same.

Here we have a good charitable use, but a trustee who is forbidden to take. This court has sustained the charitable use, raised up a trustee to support it, and thus the will of the testatrix has been carried out. This is done, not in violation of the law, but in obedience to it. The trustee will collect the income, and use the organization of the Missionary Society to distribute it to the persons whom the testatrix intended to benefit. When the rent is redeemed, the money will be applied by the trustee to the same uses and by the same agency. It will no longer be real estate, but movable personal property." Frazier *v.* Rector etc. of St. Luke's Church, 48 Leg. Int. (Pa.) 276.

1. "Here there was a separation of the gift from the estate of the testator; the beneficiary was in being, and the gift, though its application for the purposes ultimately intended was deferred, was immediate, and the beneficiary was itself the trustee. It is an established rule that if a testator leaves a legacy, absolutely as regards his estate, but restricts the mode of the legatee's enjoyment of it to certain objects for the benefit of the legatee, upon failure of such objects the absolute gift prevails. This proposition, which was declared by Lord Cappenham in Lassence *v.* Tierney (1 Mac. & Gord. 551), was adopted by the House of Lords in Kellett *v.* Kellett (Law Rep., 3 H. L. 160), and has been followed in numerous subsequent cases. It was applied in Philadelphia *v.* Girard, 9 Wright (Pa.) 9, where it was held that where a vested estate for a lawful purpose is distinctly given, and there are annexed to it unlawful conditions, limitations, powers, trusts or restraints, the unlawful conditions, etc., and the estate limited thereon are alone void, and the principal or vested estate remains. It is said by Mr. Gray: 'If the court can see an intention to make an unconditional gift to charity (and the court is very keen-sighted to discover this intention), then the gift will be regarded as immediate, not subject to any condition precedent and therefore not within the Rule against Perpetuities. And where there is an unconditional gift to charity, the gift will be regarded as immediate and good, although the particular mode of carrying out the charity which the donor has indicated is too remote. Consequently, in such a case, if a direction for accumulation is too remote, the only result is that the income is immediately distributable in charity; the heirs or next of kin are not let in.'

"A gift to a charity after a prior provision for accumulation for its benefit, which would otherwise transgress the rule, was held good in Odell *v.* Odell, 10 Allen (Mass.) 1;" Penrose, J., in Franklin's Estate, 27 W. N. C. (Pa.) 545.

A testator who died domiciled in *Georgia*, created a trust for accumulation, valid under the laws of *Georgia*, but void according to the laws of *Pennsylvania.* After disposing of five-sixths of the annual income of his estate in trust, to pay annuities to his widow and children for life, he devised the remaining one-sixth, to be reinvested and to accumulate for the benefit of his children's children; and on failure of issue, or if such issue all died before attaining the age of twenty-one, without having issue, then over to trustees to establish a hospital for incurables in Philadelphia County. "The rule certainly applies as to matters of mere local or State policy, resulting from custom or legislative enactment, as distinguished from public policy founded on some immutable principle of right and wrong, and universally recognized by all civilized nations and countries.

"Our act of April 18, 1853, regulating trusts for accumulation, was not intended to have any extra-territorial operation. It was designed only to regulate the holding of property under

In *Michigan*,[1] *Minnesota*,[2] *Indiana*,[3] *Alabama*,[4] and *Tennessee*,[5] the doctrine of *cy pres* is not recognized.

In *Virginia*,[6] *West Virginia*,[7] *Connecticut*,[8] *North Carolina*,[9] and *Iowa*,[10] the courts do not admit the doctrine of *cy-pres*; but yet support charitable gifts to corporations not in existence, or not having the necessary powers at the time of gift.

II. Statutory Provisions in the United States.—The law in the United States on the subject of remoteness is far from harmonious, the statutory enactments ranging from declarations or modifications of the common law to an entirely new system, which obtains in *New York*, *Michigan*, *Wisconsin*, *Minnesota* and in a less radical form in *California*.

our laws and in our own State, and a trust intending to take effect in another State falls neither within its letter nor spirit." "It is well settled that statutes relating to gifts to charities are local in their action, and that they do not affect a gift of personal estate in aid of a foreign charity." Lawrence *v.* Kitteridge, 21 Conn. 577; Chamberlain *v.* Chamberlain, 43 N. Y. 433; Draper *v.* College, 57 How. Pr. (N. Y.) 269; School Directors *v.* James, 5 Wend. (N. Y.) 571.

In Hillyard *v.* Miller, 10 Pa. St. 326, the court by Gibson, C. J., said: "Trusts for accumulation beyond the period allowed for the vesting of an executory limitation are absolutely void, although the fund thus to be created is directed to be ultimately applied to the formation and support of a charity.

But though, as it is said, trusts for accumulation have no immediate connection with the doctrine of perpetuities, they may sometimes fall within the rule against them."

Act 7th July, 1885, P. L. (*Pennsylvania*) 259, provides, "That in the disposition of property by will made or to be made for any religious, charitable, literary, educational or scientific use or purpose, if the same shall be void for uncertainty or the object of the trust be not ascertainable, or has ceased to exist, or by an unlawful perpetuity, such property shall go to the heirs at law and next of kin of the decedent, as in the case of persons who have died or may die intestate."

1. Methodist Church *v.* Clark, 41 Mich. 730.

2. Little *v.* Millford, 31 Minn. 173.

3. Grimes *v.* Harmon, 35 Ind. 198.

4. Caster *v.* Balfour, 9 Ala. 814, 830. See Williams *v.* Pearson, 38 Ala. 299.

5. Green *v.* Allen, 5 Humph. (Tenn.) 170; White *v.* Hale, 2 Coldw. (Tenn.) 77; Dickson *v.* Montgomery, 1 Swan (Tenn.) 348.

6. Gallego *v.* Attorney General, 3 Leigh (Va.) 450; Janey *v.* Latane, 4 Leigh (Va.) 327; Seaburn *v.* Seaburn, 15 Gratt. (Va.) 423; Kelly *v.* Love, 20 Gratt. (Va.) 124; Wheeler *v.* Smith, 9 How. (U. S.) 55; Kain *v.* Gibboney, 101 U. S. 362. But see Literary Fund *v.* Dawson, 10 Leigh (Va.) 147; 1 Rob. 421; Kinnaird *v.* Miller, 25 Gratt. (Va.) 107.

7. Carpenter *v.* Miller, 3 W. Va. 174; Mong *v.* Roush, 29 W. Va. 119. See University *v.* Tucker, 31 W. Va. 621.

8. *Connecticut* Gen. Sts. (Rev. 1875), tit. 18, ch. 6, pt. 1, § 3; White *v.* Fisk, 22 Conn. 31; Jocelyn *v.* Nott, 44 Conn. 55; Hughes *v.* Daly, 49 Conn. 34; Fairfield *v.* Lawson, 50 Conn. 501; Coit *v.* Comstock, 51 Conn. 352. But see Treat's Appeal, 30 Conn. 113; Adye *v.* Smith, 44 Conn. 60; White *v.* Howard, 38 Conn. 342.

9. Holland *v.* Peck, 2 Ired. Eq. (N. Car.) 255; White *v.* University, 4 Ired. Eq. (N. Car.) 19; Bridges *v.* Pleasants, 4 Ired. Eq. (N. Car.) 26; McAuley *v.* Wilson, 1 Dev. Eq. (N. Car.) 276. See Miller *v.* Atkinson, 63 N. Car. 537; Griffin *v.* Graham, 1 Hawks (N. Car.) 96.

10. Miller *v.* Chittenden, 2 Iowa 315; 4 Iowa 252. See Johnson *v.* Mayne, 4 Iowa 180; Byers *v.* McCartney, 62 Iowa 339.

1. Statutes which but slightly modify the common law rule exist in the following States: *Georgia*,[1] *Iowa*,[2] *Kentucky*.[3]

2. Decided modifications of the common law doctrine have been made in the States of *Connecticut*,[4] *Ohio*,[5] and *Alabama*,[6]

1. *Georgia* Rev. Code, art. 49, § 2: "Limitations of estate may extend through any number of lives in being at the time when the limitations commence, and twenty-one years. A limitation beyond that period the law terms a perpetuity, and forbids its creation. When an attempt is made to create a perpetuity, the law gives effect to the limitations not too remote, declaring the others void, and thereby vests the fee in the last taker under the legal limitations." See Jones *v.* Haversham, 107 U. S. 174.

2. *Iowa* Code of 1873, § 2267: "Every disposition of property is void which suspends the absolute power of controlling the same for a longer period than during the lives of persons then in being and for twenty-one years thereafter." See Todhunter *v.* R. Co., 58 Iowa 205. See Gray on Perp. 435.

3. *Kentucky* Gen. Sts. (1873), ch. 63, art. 1, § 27: "The absolute power of alienation shall not be suspended by any limitation or condition whatever for a longer period than during the continuance of a life or lives in being at the creation of the estate, and twenty-one years and ten months thereafter."

See the recent case of Davis *v.* Buford (Ky.), 3 S.W. Rep. 4.. See Moore *v.* Howe, 4 Mon. (Ky.) 199.

Common Law Rule.—Recent cases in States where the English rule is unchanged by statute are: In *Massachusetts*, Doring *v.* Lovering, 147 Mass. 530; in *Pennsylvania*, Lawrence's Estate, 136 Pa. St. 366; in *New Jersey*, Stout *v.* Stout, 44 N. J. Eq. 479; Randolph *v.* Randolph, 3 Cent. Rep. 106; in *Virginia*, Woodruff *v.* Pleasant, 81 Va. 37; in *Tennessee*, Brown *v.* Brown, 6 S. W. Rep. 869; in *Maryland*, Collins *v.* Foley, 63 Md. 158.

Louisiana —The articles of the *Louisiana* Code as to the validity of contingent gifts are: Rev. Code, 1870, art. 542, 1482, 1698, 1699, 1534. See Gray on Perp., §§ 766–772. See also Succession of Strauss, 38 La. Ann. 55.

4. *Connecticut* Gen. St. (1875), tit. 18, ch. 6, pt. 1, § 3, p. 352: "No estate in fee simple, fee tail or any less estate, shall be given, by deed or will, to any persons but such as are, at the time of making such deed or will, in being, or to their immediate issue or descendants." See the recent cases of Farnam *v.* Farnam, 1 N. E. Rep. 312; also Rand *v.* Butler, 48 Conn. 293; Bronson *v.* Stowe, 57 Conn. 147; Anthony *v.* Anthony, 55 Conn. 256. See also Alfred *v.* Marks, 49 Conn. 473.

In Anthony *v.* Anthony, 55 Conn. 256, a provision by which the testator left $4,000 to be divided equally among the widow's legal heirs after death, was held void under the *Connecticut* statute, since the legacy could not obviously vest until the death of the widow.

By the same will, the income of the residuary estate was left to trustees for the benefit of the testator's two sons, "and their families," during the lives of the sons; upon the death of either leaving "no heirs," over. The word "heirs" was held to mean children; the provision was sustained.

5. *Ohio* Rev. Sts. (1880), § 4200: "No estate in fee simple, fee tail, or any lesser estate, in lands or tenements, lying within this State, shall be given or granted by deed or will, to any person or persons but such as are in being, or to the immediate issue or descendants of such as are in being at the time of making such deed or will." The word "immediate descendants" is construed more liberally in *Ohio* than in *Connecticut.* See M'Arthur *v.* Scott, 113 U. S. 340.

There the devise of their parent's share to the children of any grandchild deceased before the time of divison, was held valid as to those great-grandchildren whose parent, a grandchild of the testator, was living at the time of his death, because they would be immediate issue of a person in being at that time; likewise such devise was held valid as to any great-grandchildren whose parent, though born after the testator's death, had died before their grandparent, a child of the testator, because they were, if not immediate issue, certainly immediate descendants of that child, who was in being at that time.

See also Stevenson *v.* Evans, 10 Ohio St. 307; Turley *v.* Turley, 11 Ohio St. 173.

6. *Alabama* Rev. Code of 1876, §

and also in the State of *Mississippi*[1] and the Territory of *Arizona*.[2]

3. *Statutes Enacting an Independent Rule.*—The statutory provisions of *New York, Michigan, Wisconsin, and Minnesota;* the Statutes of *California* and *Idaho*; the Statutes of *Michigan, Wisconsin* and *Minnesota*, on the subject of perpetuities, are copied from that of *New York*, except that the clauses relating to personalty are omitted.[3] It is to be observed also that the act of

2188: Land may be conveyed to the wife and children or children only, generally, successively and jointly; and to the heirs of the body of the survivor if they come of age, and in default thereof over, but conveyances to other than the wife and children or children only, cannot extend beyond the lives in being at the date of the conveyance, and ten years thereafter. The statute, § 2190, forbids the creation of leasehold estates for more than twenty years.

1. *Mississippi* Rev. Code of 1871, § 2286: "Estates in fee tail are prohibited, and every estate which shall be created an estate in fee tail, shall be an estate in fee simple, provided, that any person may make a conveyance or a devise of lands to a succession of donees then living, not exceeding two; and to the heirs of the body of the remainderman, and in default thereof, to the right heirs of the donor in fee simple." See Cannon *v.* Burg, 59 Wis. 289.

2. In *Arizona*, any person may by deed convey real estate to his legitimate child or children, and natural child or children, or his child or children by adoption, and their issue during their natural lives, whether born or begotten before or after the conveyance; and in such conveyance may inhibit the alienation of such estate during the natural lives of such children and issue. *Arizona* Comp. Laws 1877, 2287.

3. The statute is here given in full, except the clauses relating to accumulations, which will be found *infra*, this title, under *Accumulations*.

1. *New York* Rev. Stat. 722, § 14: "Every future estate shall be void in its creation which shall suspend the absolute power, of alienation for a longer period than is prescribed in this article. Such power of alienation is suspended, when there are no persons in being, by whom an absolute fee in possession can be conveyed.

"§ 15. The absolute power of alienation shall not be suspended by any limitation or condition whatever, for a longer period than during the continuance of not more than two lives in being at the creation of the estate, except in the single case mentioned in the next section.

"§ 16. A contingent remainder in fee may be created on a prior remainder in fee, to take effect in the event that the persons to whom the first remainder is limited, shall die under the age of twenty-one years, or upon any other contingency, by which the estate of such persons may be determined before they attain their full age.

"§ 17. Successive estates for life shall not be limited, unless to persons in being at the creation thereof; and where a remainder shall be limited on more than two successive estates for life, all the life estates subsequent to those of the two persons first entitled thereto, shall be void, and upon the death of those persons the remainder shall take effect, in the same manner as if no other life estates had been created.

"§ 18. No remainder shall be created upon an estate for the life of any other person or persons than the grantee or devisee of such estate, unless such remainder be in fee; nor shall a remainder be created upon such an estate in a term for years, unless it be for the whole residue of such term.

"§ 19. When a remainder shall be created upon any such life-estate, and more than two persons shall be named, as the persons during whose lives the life-estate shall continue, the remainder shall take effect upon the death of the persons first, in the same manner as if no other lives had been introduced.

"§ 20. A contingent remainder shall not be created on a term of years unless the nature of the contingency on which it is limited be such that the remainder must vest in interest, during the continuance of not more than two lives in being at the creation of such re-

1887 has extended the period in *Wisconsin* to two lives and twenty-one years thereafter.[1]

The interpretation by the *New York* courts has been adopted in these Western States. The discussion of the *New York* statute, in so far as it relates to real estate, applies, therefore, equally in all these States.

At the outset it must be observed that the *New York* system is, in its tenor and purpose, entirely distinct from the *English* rule; that therefore few of the principles which determine the operation of the English rule have any bearing on the *New York* rule. This latter is not primarily a rule fixing the period within which future limitations must vest. Its operation is not restricted to future contingent interests. Its purpose is to prevent "the suspension of the absolute power of alienation" of real estate, and of the "absolute ownership of personal property" beyond a certain period, no matter in what manner this suspension may be attempted. Such suspension of the absolute power of alienation is, in the opening clause of the statute, said to exist

mainder, or upon the termination thereof.

"§ 21. No estate for life shall be limited as a remainder on a term of years, except to a person in being at the creation of such estate.

"§ 23. All the provisions contained in this article relative to future estates shall be construed to apply to limitations of chattels real, as well as of freehold estates, so that the absolute ownership of a term of years shall not be suspended for a longer period than the absolute power of alienation can be suspended in respect to a fee.

"§ 24. Subject to the rules established in the preceding sections of this article, a freehold estate, as well as a chattel real, may be created to commence at a future day; an estate for life may be created in a term of years, and a remainder limited thereon; a remainder of a freehold or chattel real, either contingent or vested, may be created expectant on the determination of a term of years; and a fee may be limited on a fee, upon a contingency, which, if it should occur, must happen within the period prescribed in this article. . . ."

New York Rev. St. 773:

"§ 1. The absolute ownership of personal property shall not be suspended by any limitation or condition whatever, for a longer period than during the continuance and until the termination of not more than two lives in being at the date of the instrument containing such limitation or condition; or if such instrument be a will, for not more than two lives in being at the death of the testator."

"§ 2. In all other respects, limitations of future or contingent interests in personal property shall be subject to the rules prescribed in the first chapter of this act in relation to future estates in lands."

1. The statutes of *Michigan*, *Wisconsin* and *Minnesota* have copied the foregoing statutes of *New York*, except the last two paragraphs relating to personal property. *Michigan* Sts. 1882, §§ 5527 *et seq.*; *Minnesota* Gen. Sts. 1891, §§ 3973–3995; *Wisconsin*, Sanborn and Berryman's Anno. Sts, §§ 2038–2063.

In *Wisconsin*, however, the act of 1887 has enlarged the period by adding twenty-one years. This act (S. & B. Annot. Sts. § 2039) reads as follows: "The absolute power of alienation shall not be suspended by any limitation or condition whatever for a longer period than during the continuance of two lives in being at the creation of the estates and twenty-one years thereafter, except when real estate is given, granted or devised to literary or charitable corporations, which shall have been organized under the laws of this State, for their sole use and benefit, and except also in the single case mentioned in the next section." The section is the same as § 16 of the *New York* statutes relating to contingent remainders.

"when there are no persons in being by whom an absolute fee in possession can be conveyed.[1]

Thus, while the evil sought to be corrected is probably the same, the conception and operation of the common law rule and of the statutory rule are almost diametrically opposed. In both, the aim is certainty of title of property, and its unrestricted marketability. The common law rule works indirectly by a general provision as to the creation of future contingent interests. The *New York* statute strikes directly at the suspension of the power of alienation; but it defines this suspension in terms so large that in themselves they permit a large class of limitations prohibited by the English rule, and, on the other hand, prohibit present vested interests which the latter does not touch.

Secondly, the period within which the suspension of the power of alienation is prohibited by the second clause of the statute,[2] is narrowed to an arbitrary term of "two lives in being" without any succeeding absolute number of years. The result of this is to defeat a common class of dispositions such as that by which life estates are given by a testator to his children, and the survivors or survivor of these (where there are more than two) with a contingent remainder over to their descendants.

Furthermore, besides causing a large amount of litigation, this provision has compelled the court to adopt or extend ingeniously principles relating to the construction of wills and limitations of interests, in order to save them from being invalidated. The general character of the interpretation will be examined below.

It is pre-eminently necessary, in order to understand the effect of the statute, to notice its relation to other statutes, with which it forms a system of law of interests in property.

Of these the most important are: The statute which defines the classes of future interests;[3] that which defines the distinction between vested and contingent remainders, with its effect as interpreted, in abolishing the rule in Shelley's Case;[4] the statute which makes contingent remainders alienable;[5] the statute which defines valid trusts in real property;[6] that which

1. 1 *New York* Rev. Sts. 722, § 14.

2. 1 *New York* Rev. Sts. 722, § 15.

3. 1 *New York* Rev. Sts. 722, §§ 7–13; §§ 2429–2528; §§ 91–96.

4. 1 *New York* Rev. Sts. 722, § 13. See, as to the construction, *supra*, this title, *Remainders, Vested and Contingent*. The statute is, "Future estates are either vested or contingent. They are vested, when there is a person in being who would have an immediate right to the possession of the lands, upon the ceasing of the intermediate or precedent estate. They are contingent, whilst the person to whom, or the event upon which, they are limited to take effect, remains uncertain."

See Moore *v.* Littel, 41 N. Y. 66; House *v.* Jackson, 50 N. Y. 161; also, Hennessy *v.* Patterson, 85 N. Y. 91; and Purdy *v.* Hoyt, 92 N. Y. 446. See Gray on Perp., § 107.

5. 1 *New York* Rev. Sts. 722, § 11: "Where a future estate is dependent on a precedent estate it may be termed a remainder, and may be created and transferred by that name."

6. 1 *New York* Rev. Sts. 727, §§ 45–68; § 60, with close bearing upon the statute against the suspension of the

prohibits alienation in trusts, either by trustee or *cestui que trust;* the statute which declares that every estate granted or devised to two or more persons in their own right, shall be a tenancy in common, unless expressly declared to be a joint tenancy;[1] finally the statute defining the word "issue" in the phrase "dying without issue."[2] Of these, some are fundamental to the rule against suspension of the power of alienation, defining its terms; others modify its effect.

Most striking among the judicial devices for the purposes of sustaining testamentary dispositions is the construction, which, in pursuance of the statute, discovers separate limitations in tenancies in common even where there is an admitted joint tenancy, and where the devise is made expressly *in solido,* provided there is no actually expressed joint tenancy, and provided the intentions of the testator can thereby be fulfilled,[3] the incident of survivorship being preserved by tenancy in common with cross-remainders.[4]

This policy of construction of separable limitations is applied to the preservation of trusts,[5] and a void limitation is rejected whenever it may be separated without disappointing the

power of alienation, says: "Every express trust, valid, as such, in its creation, except as herein otherwise provided, shall vest the whole estate in the trustees, in law and in equity, subject only to the execution of the trust. The persons for whose benefit the trust is created shall take no estate or interest in the lands, but may enforce the performance of the trust in equity."

1. 1 *New York* Rev. Sts. 727, §§ 43–44.

2. 1 *New York* Rev. Sts. 723, § 22. "Where a remainder shall be limited to take effect on the death of any person without heirs, or heirs of his body, or without issue, the words "heirs" or "issue" shall be construed to mean heirs or issue living at the death of the person named as ancestor."

3. In Hillyer *v.* Vandewater, 121 N. Y. 681, a residuary estate was devised "*in solido*" to executors in trust to divide the net income equally among the three daughters of the testatrix, and at the end of ten years to distribute the principal among them in the same proportion. It was held that there were three several trusts for each daughter, respectively, the estates vesting in the daughters at the death of the testatrix. See Lorillard *v.* Coster, 5 Paige (N. Y.) 172; 24 Wend. (N. Y.) 265; Savage *v.* Burnham, 17 N. Y. 561; Everitt *v.* Everitt, 29 N. Y. 39; McKinstry *v.* Sanders, 2 Thomp. & C. (N. Y.) 181; 58 N. Y. 662; Grebel *v.* Wolff, 113 N. Y. 405; Smith *v.* Edwards, 88 N. Y. 405; *In re* Verplanck, 91 N. Y. 439.

4. In Purdy *v.* Hayt, 92 N. Y. 457, after two life-estates in tenancy in common with cross-remainders, it was held that a third life estate was void as to the share of the first person dying, but valid as to the share of the second. The court admitted that the rule was settled that the mere possibility of an unlawful suspension invalidates a limitation, regardless of subsequent events. Hawley *v.* James, 16 Wend. (N. Y.) 121; Gilman *v.* Reddington, 24 N. Y. 9; Manice *v.* Manice, 43 N. Y. 303. It admitted, also, that, during the life of the person dying, there was an uncertainty as to each share, whether the limitation over would offend against the statute. But it held that the uncertainty was of a different kind from that prohibited, it being certain that of the limitations over of two equal shares, one would be valid, and the only question was which that was. See, to the same effect, the recent case of Dana *v.* Murray, (N. Y. 1891) 26 N. E. Rep. 21. See also Greene *v.* Greene, 54 Hun (N. Y.) 93.

5. Where the trust as a whole depends on more than two lives, but the property is divided into shares, each of which depends on only two lives or less, it is valid. Wells *v.* Wells, 88 N. Y. 323. A devise in trust for three children in equal shares, the share of

general intent of the testator.[1] Other principles of construc-

the one first dying to go to his heirs, if he has any, otherwise to be divided into two parts to be held in trust and to vest on the death of either of the others, is valid, as each share depends on only two lives. (The suspension here referred to is that prohibited by § 17, relating to successive life-estates.) Moore *v.* Hegeman, 72 N. Y. 376, 383; Everitt *v.* Everitt, 39 N. Y. 29; Stevenson *v.* Lesley, 20 N. Y. 512. See Parks *v.* Parks, 9 Paige (N. Y.) 107; Bulkley *v.* Peyster, 26 Wend. (N. Y.) 21. When the share of any beneficiary vests, the trust then ceases *pro tanto.* Savage *v.* Burnham, 17 N. Y. 571; Ford *v.* Ford, 70 Wis. 19.

1. Savage *v.* Burnham, 17 N. Y. 571; Ford *v.* Ford, 70 Wis. 19; Woodgate *v.* Fleet, 64 N. Y. 566, 576; Harrison *v.* Harrison, 36 N. Y. 303, 384. See Van Schuyver *v.* Mulford, 59 N. Y. 426; Knox *v.* Jones, 47 N. Y. 389; Post *v.* Hover, 33 N. Y. 593; Amory *v.* Lord, 9 N. Y. 403. A devise in trust to pay over one-third of the estate to the trustee himself gives him an absolute fee, and does not suspend the power of alienation as to such part. But if the residue is made to wait the death of more than two lives, the devise is void as to such residue. McSorley *v.* Wilson, 4 Sandf. Ch. (N. Y.) 515. A limitation to take on one of two alternatives, one of which is valid, will be sustained. Schettler *v.* Smith, 41 N. Y. 328.

See Darling *v.* Rogers, 22 Wend. (N. Y.) 483; Holmes *v.* Mead, 52 N. Y. 333. See generally, Sanborn & Berryman's notes in their Annotated Statutes of *Wisconsin*, §§ 2038–2063. Knox *v.* Jones, 47 N. Y. 389, shows how the whole trust is sometimes void if there is an equitable limitation of interests beyond the statutory period. There the first two life-interests are not permitted to stand. See also Boynton *v.* Hoyt, 1 Den. (N. Y.) 53; Gott *v.* Cook, 2 Paige (N. Y.) 521; Schettler *v.* Smith, 41 N. Y. 328; Wood *v.* Wood, 5 Paige (N. Y.) 596; VanVechten *v.* VanVechten, 8 Paige (N. Y.) 104.

In Cane *v.* Gott, 24 Wend. (N. Y.) 641, it was said in regard to the principle that a will or any other instrument passing an estate may be void in part, and yet good for the residue: "There is no rule of law which calls for greater latitude and even ingenuity in enlarging and extending it." Darling *v.* Rogers, 22 Wend. (N. Y.) 483. See, however, Coster *v.* Lorillard, 14 Wend. (N. Y.) 265; Hawley *v.* James, 16 Wend. (N. Y.) 61; Root *v.* Stuyvesant, 18 Wend. (N. Y.) 257.

See the recent case of Palms *v.* Palms, 68 Mich. 365. In that case a testator left his property in trust, one-half of the income to be paid to his son for life, and one-half to his daughter. Upon the death of either of his children, one-half of the estate to go to their issue. Upon the death of either child without issue, his or her share of the income to go to the survivor, and the principal of the estate to the survivor's issue upon his or her death.

The tenth clause of the will, the only one which involved the question of remoteness, was: "The share of any grandchild, who may be a minor upon the death of his father (he being my son), or of his mother (she being my daughter) shall remain a part of said trust estate, and under the management of said trustees until such child shall be of age. . . . " The trusts were held not invalid, either as to the personalty or as to the land. The principal ground of the decision was that the remote possibility of the death of all the children of the son before his death, and the marriage of the daughter and her death, leaving issue minors—this possibility should be eliminated, and, if it occurred, be held void. It does not seem that the improbability of the occurrence of any contingency should have any effect on the application to a limitation of the Rule against Perpetuities. Such a position is a novelty in the treatment of a rule, the purpose of which requires that it should be applied without any regard to degrees of probability. See *supra*, this title, *Application.*

Whether the clause in question contained a provision which might be separated from the other provisions of the trusts, is another question, which must be decided, not on grounds of probability of occurrence, but of the independence of the provision. The court rested for this point on Woodgate *v.* Fleet, 64 N. Y. 573; Harrison *v.* Harrison, 36 N. Y 543; Savage *v.* Burnham, 17 N. Y. 561; Manice *v.* Manice, 43 N. Y. 303; De Kay *v.* Irving, 5 Den. (N. Y.) 646; Knox *v.* Jones, 47 N. Y. 389; Tiers *v.*

tion will be noticed in a categorical discussion of the statute.[1]

It is first necessary to inquire precisely when the absolute power of alienation is suspended by a series of limitations. The statute declares that it exists when there are no persons in being by whom an absolute fee in possession can be conveyed.[2] It is clear that in itself, this permits all dispositions of succeeding life estates however numerous, with contingent limitations over which may not vest until beyond even the period of the English rule, provided the limitations are to persons in being. In other words, if the contingency is one not of person, but of the event, it does not work a suspension of the power of alienation. And there may be even a contingency as to the person who takes, whose ascertainment may fall beyond any fixed period, provided the class to which the person must belong, consists of persons who are all in being at the creation of the limitation.[3]

Without doubt the most fertile source of the suspension which the statute prohibits, is the class of express trusts which are by another statute made inalienable either by trustee or *cestui que trust*.[4] In fact, it is an accurate summary of the whole to say

Tiers, 98 N. Y. 568; Toms *v.* Williams, 41 Mich. 567.

But it does not appear that any of these cases sustain the separate rejection of a limitation by which the devolution not of a distinct fraction, but of the whole of the trust property is directed.

1. A rule of construction which has an important bearing, where successive life interests are devised, is that which holds that a devise to designated persons and the survivors or survivor of them, refers to the death of the testator, and designates the persons then surviving as the takers.

Moore *v.* Lyons, 25 Wend. (N. Y.) 119; Stevenson *v.* Lesley, 70 N. Y. 512–515; Van Cott *v.* Prentice, 104 N. Y. 56.

2. 1 *New York* Rev. Sts. 723, § 14.

3. See Beardsley *v.* Hotchkiss, 96 N. Y. 201.

Since by the statute (1 *New York* Rev. Sts. 725, § 35) contingent remainders are alienable, where in a share given to each of several children, all the other children had a contingent remainder, there was no suspension of the power of alienation. See Miller *v.* Emans, 19 N. Y. 384; Moore *v.* Littel, 41 N. Y. 66; Woodgate *v.* Fleet, 44 N. Y. 1; Ham *v.* Van Orden, 84 N. Y. 257; Mott *v.* Ackerman, 92 N. Y. 539, 549. See also Case *v.* Green, 78 Mich. 540. It was there held that a lease to a man and wife on condition, and after death to a son, who was "in being," on the same conditions, did not suspend the power of alienation for more than two lives in being, as there was no time when persons in being could not convey an absolute title. It may be questioned, however, whether the limitation over did not violate the clause as to successive life estates. 1 *New York* Rev. Sts. 723, § 17.

4. But the mere creation of a trust does not, *ipso facto*, suspend alienation. See Sanborn & Berryman's Annotated Statutes of *Wisconsin*, §§ 2038–2061. There is no suspension unless a sale by the trustees would be in contravention of the trust. Where the trustee is empowered to sell there is no suspension, though the exercise of the power may be postponed by the non-action of the trustee, or on account of a discretion given him. Robert *v.* Corning, 89 N. Y., 225, 235. See, however, Amory *v.* Lord, 9 N. Y. 403, 417.

A trust does not render the estate inalienable where it is for the payment of a sum in gross (1 *New York* Rev. Sts. 730, § 63), the interests of the *cestuis que trustent* being assignable.

Only a trust to receive rents and profits of land, and apply them to the use of a person generally, or a trust to accumulate rents and profits generally,

that, leaving out of consideration the clause against successive life estates,[1] there are but two modes in which the absolute power of alienation can be suspended, viz: by an express trust or power in trust, of such a character that the land cannot be alienated during its continuance, or by a contingent limitation.[2] The sharp contrast of this statutory rule with the common law rule is seen in the case of dispositions in trust, where suspension of the power of alienation is caused as well by vested as by contingent remainders.[3]

The provision of the period of two lives[4] is construed literally as to the person whose life forms part of the stipulated term.[5]

Section sixteen of the statute permits the single exception to the invalidity of limitations suspending the power of alienation beyond the period of two lives, *i. e.*, "there may be a contingent remainder in fee, created on a prior remainder in fee determinable by the contingency that the prior remaindermen die under twenty-one years."[6] This has not been interpreted with entire uniformity.[7]

for the benefit of one or more minors, renders the estate inalienable. If the sum required to make payment is provided in any other way, the trustee is not guilty of any violation of the trust in uniting with the *cestui que trust* in a conveyance of the land. Radley *v.* Kuhn, 97 N. Y. 32.

A denominational trust in favor of an unincorporated religious society does not, in *Wisconsin*, suspend the power of alienation. DeWolf *v.* Lawson, 61 Wis. 469. See Ford *v.* Ford, 20 Wis. 19; Fadness *v.* Braunborg, 41 N. W. Rep. 84. See *Wisconsin* Stats., §§ 2086 and 2091.

1. 1 *New York* Rev. Sts. 723, § 17.

2. Radley *v.* Kuhn, 97 N. Y. 34. For Western cases on the general subject, see Thatcher *v.* St. Andrew's Church, 37 Mich. 270; Church of Newark *v.* Clark, 41 Mich. 740; Paton *v.* Langley, 50 Mich. 428, 433.

3. It has been held that a remainder vested in a person after the expiration of a trust estate, the trustee being given power to convey to him, cannot be aliened, as the remainderman would still be entitled to conveyance.

See Hawley *v.* James, 16 Wend. (N. Y.) 121, 122; Ford *v.* Ford, 70 Wis. 19, 61.

4. 1 *New York* Rev. Sts. 723, § 16.

5. A devise to the wife of the testator in trust to pay over the income to the sons during their lives was held to be bounded by the life of the trustee, and therefore good. Hunter *v.* Hunter, 31 Barb. (N. Y.) 334.

But an absolute term is prohibited. If the estate is to be kept in bulk until a beneficiary attains a certain age, though several other beneficiaries may die in the meantime without causing a vesting or division, the devise is void as founded on a term. If the vesting of an estate depends alone upon some person reaching a certain age, and not also upon his death before that age, the limitation is void, being founded not on life, but on an absolute term. Field *v.* Field, 4 Sandf. Ch. (N. Y.) 528.

6. 1 *New York* Rev. Sts. 723, § 16.

7. According to Hawley *v.* James, 16 Wend. (N. Y.) 123, the section authorizes a limitation such as the following: An estate to A for life, remainder to his children (however numerous) in fee; but in case such children shall die under twenty-one, then to B in fee.

According to Manice *v.* Manice, 43 N. Y. 303, 374, a remainder in fee after the termination of two lives may be limited to an unborn person (with a trust to accumulate during his minority) if in being when the lives terminate, and if he shall die under age, a contingent remainder may be limited to a second unborn person.

See also, Temple *v.* Hawley, 1 Sandf. Ch. (N. Y.) 153. 178.

In Radley *v.* Kuhn, 97 N. Y. 36, the court, in treating the prior determinable remainder as a vested remainder liable to be divested, said: "In such

In regard to the following section,[1] which forbids more than two successive life estates, the third and all subsequent ones being void and the remainder taking effect after the second life estate, it is clear that it does not apply the main rule to a special class of limitations. It is an entirely distinct provision and a far more serious restraint on freedom of disposition. By the definition of the opening clause of the statute, successive life estates, however numerous, would not tend towards a suspension provided they are granted to persons "in being."[2]

Sections eighteen and nineteen apply the principle of section seventeen to an estate for the life or lives of another or others.[3]

Personal Property.—The remaining sections relating to real property do not require interpretation.

As regards personal property, the statutes of *Wisconsin*, *Michigan* and *Minnesota*,[4] omit those sections of the *New York* statute applying to it. Accordingly the Rule against Perpetuities has been held to be abolished in *Wisconsin* in so far as

cases the suspension is not caused by the provision that the infant shall take when he arrives at twenty-one. The suspension is caused wholly by the contingent limitation over in case he dies before twenty-one."

Personalty.—It is important to notice that this section does not hold good as to personal property.

Manice *v.* Manice, 43 N. Y. 381, 383. The above distinction made by the court in Radley *v.* Kuhn, 97 N. Y. 36, has less value in itself than as an illustration of the principle of Boraston's Case (2 Co. R. 19), which is applied to such limitations as, to A for life, and if he should die leaving any lawful children, to them when they arrive at the age of twenty-one years. Manice *v.* Manice, 43 N. Y. 381. Radley *v.* Kuhn, 91 N. Y. 36. See Toms *v.* Williams, 41 Mich. 572.

1. 1 *New York* Rev. Sts. 723, § 17. The clause seems to disregard the fact that successive life estates are vested remainders, unless it is remembered that the power of alienation is suspended whenever immediate possession cannot, even if expectant interests can be conveyed.

If only a conditional fee can be conveyed subject to be defeated by some person who cannot now give and release his interest, alienation is suspended. Hawley *v.* James, 16 Wend. (N. Y.) 176.

2. In Purdy *v.* Hayt, 92 N. Y. 446, however, it was decided that the section refers only to vested, not to contingent remainders, and executes the remainders in possession only in favor of such ascertained person as, except for the void life estate, would, under the will or deed, be entitled to immediate possession. Where the gift in remainder is upon a contingency which has not happened at the time of the death of the second life tenant, it does not apply, and the gift is invalid.

Confined thus to successive life estates, where there are two persons in being at the creation of the limitations with a vested remainder, it is difficult to see what connection the clause has with the suspension of the power of alienation, and, of course, still less, with the common law rule. It becomes simply a statutory inhibition that no remainder shall be created to await the determination of more than two successive life estates. See Knox *v.* Jones, 47 N. Y. 397; Smith *v.* Edwards, 88 N. Y. 104.

3. 1 *New York* Rev. Sts. 723, §§ 18, 19. It was held in Gilman *v.* Reddington, 24 N. Y. 9, that § 18 does not invalidate a trust such as to apply the rents and profits to the use of the testator's youngest children and their unborn issue during the lives of his two youngest children, though it is possible that two or more successive generations may enjoy the estate during such lives.

4. *Michigan* Sts. 1882, § 5527, *et seq.* *Wisconsin*, Sanborn & Berryman's Ann. Sts., §§ 2038–2063; *Minnesota* Gen. Sts. 1891, §§ 3973–3995.

it relates to personalty.[1] In *Michigan* it is now settled that there are two rules regulating the disposition of property—the statute applying to real property, and the common law, applying to the creation of future interests in personalty.[2]

There are conflicting decisions in *New York* as to whether the statute against the suspension of the power of alienation applies equally to all kinds of property, personal and real, or whether the rules of real property are not impressed upon personal property, except as to future contingent limitations.[3] The greater weight of authority seems to lie on the side of the former position, by which the statute applies equally to realty and personalty.[4]

The *California*, *Idaho* and *Dakota* statutes are modelled as to expression after the *New York* statute. But the period in them differs from the *New York* period in the very important respect of being limited simply to lives in being, without any numerical restriction.[5]

1. Dodge *v.* Williams, 46 Wis. 70; DeWolf *v.* Lawson, 61 Wis. 469; Ford *v.* Ford, 80 Mich. 42.

2. See Palms *v.* Palms 68 Mich. 365. See also Toms *v.* Williams, 41 Mich. 572. As to equitable conversion, see Wells *v.* Wells, 88 N. Y. 323, 331; Kane *v.* Gott, 24 Wend. (N. Y.) 641, 659; Dodge *v.* Williams, 46 Wis. 70; Chandler's Appeal, 34 Wis. 505; Lent *v.* Howard, 89 N. Y. 169; Gould *v.* Orphan Asylum, 46 Wis. 106; Scott *v.* West, 63 Wis. 529 558; Webster *v.* Morris, 66 Wis. 366, 399.

A will creating trusts, suspending the power of alienation longer than two lives, which would in *Michigan* be in violation of the statute, is not void where the immediate and absolute sale of all of the testator's estate in *Michigan* is directed, and it is to be converted into lands in another State where the trusts are declared. Ford *v.* Ford, 80 Mich. 42.

3. Kane *v.* Gott, 24 Wend. (N.Y.) 641; Grant *v.* Schoonhoven, 1 Sandf. Ch. (N. Y.) 336.

4. In Campbell *v.* Foster, 35 N. Y. 371, the following from the opinion of the majority in Graff *v.* Bonnett, 31 N. Y." It has been held in several cases that the statute which provides that limitations of future or contingent interests in personal property shall be subject to the statutory rules prescribed in relation to future estates in land, was in effect, a legislative application of the same principles and policy to both classes of property; and that, even if the provisions were not sufficiently comprehensive absolutely to require as a peremptory injunction of statute law, their application in all their length and breadth, and in the same degree to both classes of property, the argument to be derived from the general similarity of the legislative enactments in regard to both classes of property, from the similar if not equal mischiefs to be remedied and from the general policy of the law, would authorize a court of equity, in the exercise of its acknowledged powers, to apply the same rule of construction to both." See 1 *New York* Rev. Sts. 730, § 63; 1 *New York* Rev. Sts. 778, § 2; Hallett *v.* Thompson, 5 Paige (N. Y.) 553; Gott *v.* Cook, 7 Paige (N. Y.) 531; Clute *v.* Bool, 8 Paige (N. Y.) 83; Hone *v.* Van Schaack, 7 Paige (N. Y.) 222; Degraw *v.* Clason, 11 Paige (N. Y.) 136. The question seems to have been settled by the recent case of Cruikshank *v.* Chase, (N. Y. 1889), 21 N. E. Rep. 64.

5. See Civil Code, Cal., § 716.

In Goldtree *v.* Thompson, 79 Cal. 613, it was held that a bequest of personal property in trust to divide and pay the income to testator's nephews and nieces during their respective lives, and, after their death in trust for their children who shall attain the age of twenty-one years or marry, is not void. The birth of a child to one of testator's nephews, after the death of testator, which child died single and minor during its father's lifetime, was held not to affect the validity of the bequest.

The *Indiana* statute is an unsuccessful attempt at improvement on the *New York* rule.[1]

III. **Trusts for Accumulation—1. Definition.**—A trust for accumulation is where an estate is given to trustees to hold in trust until the happening of a certain event or contingency, or until the expiration of a fixed period of time; the trustees are to receive and invest, either in whole or in part, the interest and income of the personal property and the rents and profits of the real estate; when the certain event or contingency has occurred, or the period of time elapsed, they are to deliver up the fund thus accumulated to the person or persons entitled to the same under the provisions of the will or instrument creating the trust.

The principles of the common law and their modifications by statute affect trusts for accumulation principally in respect of their duration. They limit the time within which such a trust may continue.

The time allowed by the common law for the continuance of trusts for accumulation was discovered to be injurious to the general welfare, and to give to the owner of property too great a power over its future disposition.

By the Thelluson Act in *England*, the Revised Statutes in *New York*, the Act of 1853 in *Pennsylvania*, and statutory provisions in other States, the common law period has been limited.

Consequently a consideration of the subject of trusts for accumulation has to do principally with the restrictions placed by the common law and statutes upon the time during which such trusts may continue.

See *Idaho* Rev. Sts. 1887, tit. 5, ch. 1, §§ 2839–2839. See Civil Code (1883) 202.

1. *Indiana* Rev. Sts. (1876), ch. 82, § 40: "The absolute power of aliening lands shall not be suspended by any limitation or condition whatever, contained in any grant, conveyance or devise, for a longer period than during the existence of a life, or any number of lives, in being at the creation of the estate conveyed, granted, devised, and therein specified, with the exception that a contingent remainder in fee may be created on a prior remainder in fee, to take effect, in the event that the person or persons to whom the first remainder is limited, shall die under the age of twenty-one years, or upon any other contingency, by which the estate of such person or persons may be determined before they attain their full age." *Indiana* Rev. Sts. (1876), ch. 82, § 41: "Where a remainder for life shall be limited on any other than a life or lives in being at the creation of such estate, and the life estate subsequent to those persons entitled to take life-estates according to the provisions of the last preceding section shall be void; and upon the death of these persons entitled to take the remainder, shall take effect in the same manner as if such void estate had not been created." It is impossible to make sense of these provisions.

Estates for Years.—A defect in the Rule against Perpetuities, so far as its ultimate purpose is concerned, is the possibility of the creation of long terms with remainders thereafter. In *Alabama*, a statute forbids the creation of leasehold estates for more than twenty years. *Alabama* Rev. Code (1876), § 2190. See this subject in Gray on Perp., § 210. See Todhunter *v.* D. M. I. & M. R. Co., 58 Iowa 205.

Actual Perpetuities.—In many States there are constitutional prohibitions of perpetuities in the strict sense; with these, however, the Rule against Perpetuities has no connection.

In Bates *v.* Bates, 134 Mass. 110, a testatrix provided for the sale of her real estate, in order to constitute a per-

2. **At the Common Law.**—At the common law, the period during which one could direct the income or profit of an estate to be accumulated, was governed by the Rule against Perpetuities, which limited the time within which a future interest might vest—*i. e.*, a life or lives in being and twenty-one years and nine months thereafter. Thus the same principle of law determined the two questions: How long can one defer the enjoyment of property by a direction to accumulate its income? and how long can one control the vesting of a future interest in property? That which was too remote for the one was too remote for the other, and the same results followed the remoteness of a direction to accumulate as attended the remoteness of an executory devise or bequest.

It is a well settled rule that a trust for accumulation must be confined within the limits fixed by the Rule against Perpetuities, and that if it may possibly extend beyond that time it is wholly void *ab initio.* If the period fixed for the determination of the trust is a condition precedent to the gift of the accumulated fund, and that period may possibly not happen till after the time fixed by the rule, both the direction to accumulate and the gift of the accumulated fund are void absolutely. There is no power vested in the court by which it can lessen the time for accumulation, provided for in the will or settlement, and thus bring the direction to accumulate within the Rule against Perpetuities. It was the intention of the testator or settlor, that the gift should take effect at a certain time or on a certain event.[1]

manent fund for beautifying a monument and keeping it in order. The court held that "funds cannot be established indefinitely alienable in the hands of those to whom they are intrusted and their successors, the income of which is to be perpetually devoted to uses which are not, legally speaking, charitable." See also *In re* Bailey, 24 Abb. N. Cas. (N. Y.) 206; Penny *v.* Croul, 76 Mich. 471; Cottman *v.* Grace, 112 N.Y. 299; Hale *v.* Hale, 125 Ill. 399; Goesele *v.* Bimeler, 14 How. (U. S.) 589.

If, however, the testatrix in Bates *v.* Bates (134 Mass. 110) had devised the property on condition that the devisee should beautify the monument and keep it in repair, it seems that the condition would not have been void for remoteness. See Giles *v.* Boston Society, 10 Allen (Mass.) 355.

1. Curtis *v.* Lukin, 5 Beav. 147; Boughton *v.* Boughton, 1 H. L. Ca. 406; Boughton *v.* James, 1 Coll. 26; Vawdry *v.* Geddes, 1 Russ. & M. 203; Southampton *v.* Hertford, 2 V. & B. 54; Scarisbrick *v.* Skelmersdale, 17 Sim. 187; Marshall *v.* Holloway, 2 Swanst. 432; Turvin *v.* Newcome, 3 K. & J. 16; Smith *v.* Cunninghame, 13 L. R., Ir. 480; Palmer *v.* Holford, 4 Russ. 403; Thorndike *v.* Loring, 15 Gray (Mass.) 391; Armory *v.* Lord, 5 Seld. (N. Y.) 403; Gray on Rule against Perpetuities, § 674; 1 Jarm. on Wills 573; 1 Perry on Trusts 393; Craig *v.* Craig, 3 Barb. Ch. (N. Y.) 76; Hooper *v.* Hooper, 9 Cush. (Mass.) 122; Matthews *v.* Keble, L. R., 1 Eq. 467; Killam *v.* Allen, 52 Barb. (N. Y.) 605; Dutch Reformed Church *v.* Brandon, 52 Barb. (N. Y.) 228; White *v.* Howard, 52 Barb. (N. Y.) 294; Fosdick *v.* Fosdick, 6 Allen (Mass.) 43; Hillyard *v.* Miller, 10 Pa. St. 326; Hargrave's Thellușon act, § 74; Lewis on Perpetuities 593; Studholme *v.* Hodgson, 3 P. Wms. 305; Green *v.* Ekins, 2 Atk. 473; Mole *v.* Mole, 1 Dick. 310; Hopkins *v.* Hopkins, 1 Atk. 581; 1 Vesey St. 268; West 606; Lade *v.* Holford, 1 W. Bl. 428; Phipps *v.* Kelynge, 2 V. & B. 57 note b; Harrison *v.* Harrison, 4 Vesey 286; Perry *v.* Phelips, 4 Vesey 108; Sir John Webb's Will, 4 Vesey 287; Shaftsbury *v.* Sir John

Webb, 7 Vesey 480 (1802;) 6 Mad. 100 (1821); 3 Myl. & K. 599 (1834).

Thelluson *v.* Woodford, 4 Vesey 227. A devise of real estate of the annual value of near 5000l, and other estates directed to be purchased with the residue of the personal estate, amounting to above 600,000l. to trustees and their heirs, etc., upon trust during the lives of the testator's sons, A, B and C, and of his grandson, D, and of such other sons as A now has or may have and of such issue as D may have and of such issue as any other sons of A may have and of such sons as B and C may have and of such issue as such sons may have as shall be living at his decease or born in due time afterwards and during the life of the survivor, to receive the rents and profits and from time to time to invest the same and the produce of timber, etc., in other purchases of real estate; and after the death of the survivor of the said several persons, that the said estate shall be divided into three lots, and that one lot shall be conveyed to the eldest male lineal descendant then living of A, in tail male; remainder to the second, etc., and all and every other male lineal descendant or descendants then living, who shall be incapable of taking as heir in tail male of any of the persons to whom a prior estate is limited, of A, successively in tail male; remainder in equal moieties to the eldest and every other male lineal descendant or descendants then living of B and C, as tenants in common in tail male in the same manner, with cross-remainders; or, if but one such male lineal descendant, to him in tail male; remainder to the trustees, their heirs, etc.

The other two lots were directed to be conveyed to the male descendants of B and C, respectively, in the same manner and with similar limitations to the male descendants of their brothers, and to the trustees in fee; and it was directed that the trustees should stand seised upon the failure of male lineal descendents of A, B and C as aforesaid upon trust to sell and pay the produce to his majesty, his heirs and successors, to the use of the sinking fund; the accumulation, till the purchases or sales can take place, to go to the same purpose, with a direction that all the persons becoming entitled shall use the surname of the testator only. The trusts of the will were established.

In a note to the report of this remarkable case on page 227, it is stated: "This case is memorable in the history of the English law from the importance of the questions and the amount of property under adjudication, and from the revelation it affords of the unnatural meanness and ostentation of the testator, depriving his immediate descendants of their just share of his fortune, not to found any noble charity, but that it might accumulate in the hands of trustees, for the miserable satisfaction of enjoying in anticipation the wealth and aggrandizement of a distant posterity, who should bear his name. . . . The testator's object was to protract the power of alienation by taking in lives of persons who were mere nominees without any corresponding interest. The property was thus tied up from alienation and enjoyment for three generations. Shortly after executing this extraordinary will, on the 21st of July, 1797, Mr. Thelluson died. The money which the will sought to accumulate was estimated at £600,000. Mr. Morgan, the actuary, calculated the accumulation, limiting it to seventy-five years, the shortest probable period at which the fortune might be alienated, at £27,182,000. . . .

"After the judgment of the court, establishing the trusts, Lord Loughborough, to prevent such a morbid grasp of property in the future, introduced and carried a bill with the unanimous consent of both branches of the legislature, 39 and 40 Geo. III, ch. 98, restraining dispositions by way of accumulation to the life of the settlor, or twenty-one years after his decease, or the minority of any party living at the time of his decease."

This act has been styled the "Thelluson Act."

Bacon *v.* Proctor, T. & R. 31; Martin *v.* Margham, 14 Sim. 230; Attorney General *v.* The Bishop of Chester, 1 Bro. C. C. 444; The Attorney General *v.* Ironmongers' Company, 2 Myers & Keen 576; Moggridge *v.* Hackwell, 7 Vesey 36; Phipps *v.* Kelynge, 2 V. & B. 57, note; Lord Southampton *v.* Hertford, 2 V. & B. 57; Tregonwell *v.* Sydenham, 3 Dow. 213; Saunders *v.* Vantier, 1 Cr. & Ph. 240; s. c., 4 Beavan 115; Josselyn *v.* Josselyn, 9 Sim. 63; Thorndike *v.* Loring, 15 Gray 391; Perry on Trusts 396.

Where a vested estate for a lawful purpose is distinctly given, and there

3. Present Vested Interest.—Before considering the statutory limitations of the common law it will be well to state that where there exists a vested indefeasible right to the possession of the accumulations or the principal on the part of the person to whom the accumulated income is to be paid, the direction to accumulate is an illegal restraint on alienation and therefore void. The person entitled has a right to put an end to accumulation at any time. For this reason it matters not whether the direction to accumulate violates the Rule against Perpetuities or any of the statutory provisions limiting the time during which a trust for accumulation may continue.[1]

are annexed to it unlawful conditions, limitations, powers, trusts or restraints, the unlawful conditions, etc., and the estate limited thereon only are void, while the principal or vested estate remains. Philadelphia *v.* Girard, 45 Pa. St. 1.

When a legacy is directed to accumulate for a certain period, or where the payment is postponed, the legatee, if he has an absolute, indefeasible interest, is not bound to wait until the expiration of that period, but may require payment the moment he is competent to give a valid discharge.

Saunders *v.* Vantier, 4 Beav. 115; Josselyn *v.* Josselyn, 9 Sim. 63; Rocke *v.* Rocke, 9 Beavan 66; Jackson *v.* Marjoribanks, 12 Sim. 92; Curtis *v* Lukin, 5 Beavan, 155; Magrath *v.* Morehead, L. R. 12 Eq. 491.

1. Thelluson Act, 39 & 40 Geo. III (1800): Whereas it is expedient that all dispositions of real or personal estates whereby the profits and produce thereof are directed to be accumulated, and the beneficial enjoyment thereof is postponed, should be made subject to the restrictions hereinafter contained; may it therefore please your Majesty that it may be enacted: and be it enacted by the king's most excellent Majesty, by and with the advice and consent of the Lords Spiritual and Temporal, and Commons, in Parliament assembled, and by the authority of the same, That no person or persons shall, after the passing of this act, by any deed or deeds, surrender or surrenders, will, codicil or otherwise howsoever, settle or dispose of any real or personal property, so and in such manner that the rents, issues, profits or produce thereof shall be wholly or partially accumulated, for any longer term than the life or lives of any such grantor or grantors, settlor or settlors; or the term of twenty-one years from the death of any such grantor, settlor, devisor or testator; or during the minority or respective minorities of any person or persons who shall be living, or *en ventre sa mere* at the time of the death of such grantor, devisor or testator; or during the minority or respective minorities only of any person or persons who, under the uses or trusts of the deed, surrender, will or other assurances directing such accumulations, would, for the time being, if of full age, be entitled unto the rents, issues and profits, or the interest, dividends or annual produce so directed to be accumulated: and in every case where any accumulations shall be directed otherwise than as aforesaid, such direction shall be null and void, and the rents, issues, profits and produce of such property so directed to be accumulated, shall, so long as the same shall be directed to be accumulated contrary to the provisions of this Act, go to and be received by such person or persons as would have been entitled thereto if such accumulation had not been directed.

II. Provided always, and be it enacted, That nothing in this Act contained shall extend to any provision for payment of debts of any grantor, settlor, or devisor, or other person or persons, or any provision for raising portions for any child or children of any grantor, settlor or devisor, or any child or children of any person taking any interest under any such conveyance, settlement or devise, or to any direction touching the produce of timber or wood upon any lands or tenements; but that all such provisions and directions shall and may be made and given as if this act had not passed.

III. Provided also, and be it enacted, That nothing in this act contained

4. The Thelluson Act, England.—The first modification of the common law occurred in 1800, when the Thelluson Act of '39 and '40 George III, was passed. It provides four periods during which accumulations may continue. First, during the life or lives of any grantor or grantors, settlor or settlors. Second, during the term of twenty-one years from the death of any such grantor, settlor, devisor or testator. Third, during the minority or respective minorities of any person or persons who shall be living or *en ventre sa mere* at the time of the death of such grantor, devisor or testator. Fourth, during the minority or respective minorities only of any person or persons who, under the uses or trusts of the deed, surrender, will or other assurances directing such accumulations, would, for the time being, if of full age, be entitled unto the rents, issues, profits, or the interest, dividends, or annual produce so directed to be accumulated.

The second section of the act exempts from its operation any provision for payment of debts of any grantor, settlor or devisor, or other person or persons; or any provisions for raising portions for any child or children of any grantor, settlor or devisor, or any child or children of any person taking any interest under any such conveyance, settlement or devise, or to any direction touching the produce of timber or wood upon any lands or tenements. The full text of the act is to be found in the notes.

a. FIRST PERIOD.—The first period is "the life or lives of any such grantor or grantors, settlor or settlors. This provision is applicable only to trusts for accumulation created by deed.

The Thelluson Act receives the same construction in the case of a trust for accumulation created by deed as it receives in the case of a similar trust created by will.[1]

b. SECOND PERIOD.—The period of twenty-one years provided for in the second clause, "the term of twenty-one years from the death of any such grantor, settlor, devisor, or testator," is exclusive of the day of the death of said grantor, etc.[2]

shall extend to any disposition respecting hereditable property within that part of Great Britain, called *Scotland*.

IV. Provided also, and be it enacted, That the restrictions in this act contained shall take effect and be in force with respect to wills and testaments made and executed before the passing of this act, in such cases only where the devisor or testator shall be living, and of sound and disposing mind, after the expiration of twelve calendar months from the passing of this act.

1. *In re* Lady Rosslyn's Trust, 16 Sim. 39.

So also does the *Pennsylvania* Act of April 18, 1853. The terms of this Act relating to accumulations, apply to an estate held under a deed just as they would if held upon the same terms under a will. In either case directions for accumulation are void so far as they are in conflict with the Act, and it can make no difference whether such accumulations, where the property passed by deed, accrued within the lifetime of the grantor or after his decease. Carson *v.* Rutter, 12 W. N. C. (Pa.) 161; Gray on Perpetuities, § 696; Heywood *v.* Heywood, 29 Beav. 9; Harg. Thel. Act, § 89.

2. In Gorst *v.* Lowndes, 11 Sim. 434, a testator directed the income of his property to be accumulated for the term of twenty-one years from his death. The testator died on the fifth of January, 1820. *Held*, that in the computation of the term, the day of his

Where a testator directs the accumulation of a fund to commence at a time subsequent to his decease, the accumulation becomes void at the expiration of twenty-one years from his decease, although at that period there has been on the whole less than twenty-one years of accumulations.[1]

c. THIRD PERIOD.—The third period is "during the minority or respective minorities of any person or persons who shall be living or *en ventre sa mere* at the time of the death of such grantor, devisor or testator."[2]

d. FOURTH PERIOD—The fourth and last period allows accumulation "during the minority or respective minorities only of any person or persons who, under the trusts of the deed, surrender, will or other assurances directing such accumulations, would, for the time being, if of full age, be entitled unto the rents, issues and profits, or the interest, dividends or annual produce so directed to be accumulated."

This provision does not permit accumulation during a minority and any time to elapse between the death of the testator and the commencement of the minority.[3]

death was to be excluded; and consequently, that the dividends on stock which became due on the fifth of January, 1841, were subject to the trust for accumulation. Lester *v.* Garland, 15 Vesey 248.

Even at common law, the day of the death was excluded. Toder *v.* Sansom, 1 Brown, P. C. 648.

1. A testator gave annuities to A and B, respectively, charged on money in the funds; and he directed that when either died, the annuity should accumulate until the death of the survivor. A died some time after the testator. B being still living. *Held*, that the accumulation must cease at the expiration of twenty-one years from the death of the testator, and not twenty-one years from the decease of A. Webb *v.* Webb, 2 Beav. 493.

In Attorney General *v.* Poulden, 3 Hare 555, a sum of money was directed to be invested in stock and taken in the name of trustees, who were to pay thereout annuities to various persons. The trustees were to hold the said stock and dividends thereof, subject to the annuities upon trust, as to so much of the dividends as from time to time should fall in by the determination of the annuities, until one-half of the dividends should have so fallen in, to invest the same and the resulting income thereof, in order to increase the capital of said fund by accumulation; and so soon as one-half of the dividends should have so fallen in, to apply such moiety of the dividends, and also such further parts of the same as should from time to time fall in by the determination of the annuities, respectively, and the whole of the dividends, when all the annuities should have ceased to certain charitable uses. The money was invested according to the will. The death of some of the annuitants afterwards released a part of the dividends, and the sums so fallen in were accumulated. In an information to establish the charity, held, that although the accumulation of the dividends had not begun till the death of the annuitants, many years after the death of the testator, yet, by the statute 40 Geo. III, ch. 98, the accumulation must cease at the expiration of twenty-one years from his death.

See also Nettleton *v.* Stephenson, 3 De G. & S. 366; Shaw *v.* Rhodes, 1 N. Y. & Cr. 154.

2. Harg. Thel. Act, §§ 93, *et seq.*

3. In Ellis *v.* Maxwell, 3 Beav. 587, 595, the testator directed the accumulation of the whole of his personal estate for the benefit of his grandchildren.

Master of the Rolls: "Mrs. Maxwell admits the accumulation to be good for twenty-one years; she has scarcely suggested that it may not be good during the minority of Henry William Maxwell Lyte, who was *en ventre sa mere* at the time of the testator's death; but she insists that it can be good no longer; whilst the younger grandchildren insist that they are persons, who under the uses created by the testator, will, upon the attaining the age of twenty-one years, be entitled to the annual produce of the whole fund.

"The difficulty of attributing a distinct and efficient meaning to all the words of this act has frequently been acknowledged. If the accumulation is permitted only during the minority of a person entitled under the uses of the will, and no time is to be allowed, either before the minority commences or after it has ceased, it does not seem that anything is added to the permission to accumulate during the minority of a person living at the death of the testator. But taking the words as they are, they do not appear to permit accumulation during a minority and any time to elapse between the death of the testator and the commencement of the minority, or in favor of any person who would not for the time being, if of full age, be entitled to the annual produce of the fund; and accordingly, in the case of Longdon *v.* Simson (12 Vesey 295), where an accumulation was intended to be made till unborn children attained twenty-one, Sir William Grant decreed an accumulation for twenty-one years only; and in Haley *v.* Bannister (4 Maddock 277), Sir John Leach, V. C., expressed his opinion to be, that the statute prevents an accumulation during the minority of an unborn child. These cases prevent me from considering, that upon the construction of the act, the accumulation would be lawful during the minority of any grandchild born after the death of the testator. Moreover, upon the construction of this will, it will have to be considered whether the younger grandchildren attaining twenty-one will be entitled to the annual produce of the fund, although it may be lawful for the trustees to make an allowance for their maintenance and education out of it, after they have attained twenty-one." Griffiths *v.* Vere, 9 Vesey 127.

Jarman on Wills, *305, *et seq.*, commenting on the above cases, states: "By the words, 'during the minority of an unborn child,' the V. C. must, it is conceived, have meant 'until an unborn child should come of age,' which was the case before him; his decision in this view could only be that the whole of such period could not be taken, not that the part commencing with the birth of the child could not be taken alone. . . . The case, like Longdon *v.* Simson (22 Ves. 295), and Haley *v.* Bannister (4 Madd. 277), involved an accumulation not only during the minority of an unborn person, but also until he should be born; and though it has been said (Bryan *v.* Collins, 16 Beav. 17) that, as in Haley *v.* Bannister, Sir J. Leach held, that the statute referred only to the minority or successive minorities of persons in existence at the time the will came into effect, and that the same point was affirmed and extended in Ellis *v.* Maxwell, yet it is clear that the point was not touched by the actual decision in either of those cases, which fell under the ordinary rule that only one of the periods allowed by the statute can be taken. The construction put upon the statute by the *dicta* cited above virtually strikes out of the act the clause in question, and seems to place in some peril the accumulating trusts ordinarily introduced into provisions for the maintenance during minority of persons unborn at the testator's decease, which direct the unapplied surplus income from time to time to be added to the principal. Such trusts, however, are distinguishable from the bequest in Haley *v.* Bannister (4 Madd. 277), in this, that they extend only to the unapplied surplus, and not to the entire income (but the act expressly includes partial accumulations), and, therefore, approach more closely to the principle of the rule of law, which accumulates the income of minors after providing for maintenance;' though they differ from that rule in regard to the ultimate destination of the accumulated fund, which the law gives to the minor himself, but which the express trust commonly attaches to the principal fund; though even this difference is considerably narrowed, where the trustees possess (as they commonly do, and always ought to do) a power of applying the accumulated fund at any subsequent period of minority, which clause would certainly afford a strong argument for taking the trusts in question out of the principle of Haley *v.* Bannister, if (the doctrine sometimes deduced from) that case can be supported. Indeed, considering the extreme inconvenience of holding the ordinary accumulating maintenance trusts in favor of unborn persons to be invalid, the courts would

e. TWO PERIODS CANNOT BE USED.—The testator or settlor cannot direct the accumulation of the income of a fund for two or more of the periods provided for in the act. He is limited to one period.[1]

f. WHERE THE TIME FOR ACCUMULATION EXCEEDS THE PERIOD OF THE RULE AGAINST PERPETUITIES.—Where the time during which the accumulation is to continue exceeds that allowed by the Rule against Perpetuities, not only the direction to accumulate, but the gift over is void.[2]

no doubt struggle to avoid such a conclusion."

1. In Wilson *v.* Wilson, 1 Simons N. R. 288, the will directed the interest and dividends of the trust funds to be accumulated during two successive periods, namely, during the term of twenty-one years from the death of the testator, and after the expiration of that term, during the minority or respective minorities of any person or persons who, for the time being, should be entitled to the then expectant vested interest in the trust funds. The court said, "that the ordinary grammatical construction of the act restricts the accumulation to one only of the allowed periods; that there is nothing on the face of the act showing that the ordinary construction of the words is not to be adopted, and that such a construction leads to no absurdity or inconsistency. I am, therefore, of opinion that the direction to accumulate during the minority of the son, and the subsequent gift of the fund so accumulated, are void; and therefore, that the annual produce during such minority is undisposed of, and goes to the next of kin." Ellis *v.* Maxwell, 3 Beav. 587; Perry on Trusts, § 395; Rosslyn's Trust, 16 Sim. 391.

2. A testator directed his trustees to accumulate the income of certain property for twenty-eight (28) years after his death and then transfer the accumulated fund "unto all and every the child and children of my said son Charles Thomas Hudson, who shall be living at the end and expiration of the term of twenty-eight years, to be computed from my decease," and in case there be no child or children, then over. It was held that the direction to accumulate and gift over were void absolutely. Palmer *v.* Holford, 4 Russ. 403.

The fact that there is a possibility of the gift taking effect without violating the Rule against Perpetuities, is not sufficient to prevent its being declared void. Palmer *v.* Holford, 4 Russ. 403. Griffiths *v.* Vere, 9 Vesey 127.

"If the arrival of the period fixed for, or needed for, the determination of a trust for accumulation is a condition precedent to the gift of the accumulated fund, and if this period may possibly fall beyond the limits of the Rule against Perpetuities, then the gift of the accumulated fund is void and the provision for the accumulation is bad altogether. The courts cannot cut the trust down to the legitimate extent by substituting a shorter time or a speedier event than the settlor or testator directs. And the persons entitled to the property and the income which the law releases from the accumulation are those who would have been entitled to them had the direction to accumulate and the gift of the accumulated fund both been omitted from the will. In this case the gift is made subject to the illegal direction to accumulate, and, in fact, out of the accumulated fund itself; the direction to accumulate cannot be separate from the gift, without destroying the substantial form of the gift itself; consequently, since the form of the gift is of the substance of it, the gift itself fails with the void trust for accumulation." Mr. William C. Scott's Essay on "Trust for Accumulation," § 51; Marshall *v.* Holloway, 2 Swanston 432.

A testator directed a settlement of certain estates to be made, so far as the rules of law and equity would allow, to certain uses—as to part, it was to be settled to the use of trustees for 2000 years, in his W estate, in trust to pay any child of his body, or the issue of such child (who, under the limitations of the will, should be entitled to the possession of the rents of his W estate, and who, having attained twenty-one, should be under the age of twenty-five) an annual sum of 800l., till he should have attained twenty-one or die under that age; and to accumulate the sur-

g. WHERE THE TIME EXCEEDS THE PERIOD OF THE ACT, AND IS WITHIN THE PERIOD OF THE RULE.—Where there is a direction to accumulate for a period longer than that allowed by the act, yet within the Rule against Perpetuities, the direction is good for the time specified in the act, but void as to the excess.[1]

h. VOID DIRECTIONS TO ACCUMULATE.—The Thelluson Act provides that "in every case where any accumulation shall be directed otherwise than as aforesaid, such direction shall be null and void, and the rents, issues, profits and produce of such property so directed to be accumulated, shall, so long as the same shall be directed to be accumulated contrary to the provisions of this act, go to and be received by such person or persons as would have been entitled thereto if such accumulation had not been directed." A similar provision is to be found in the *Pennsylvania* Act of 1853.

If the above provision had not been placed in the act, the income, so illegally directed to be accumulated, would have been enjoyed by the same persons as provided for in the act. In other words, the act, in this particular, is merely declaratory of existing law. The void direction to accumulate is considered as if it were not.

The question as to who is entitled to the income, interest and profits of the estate so directed to be accumulated, depends upon the further questions whether there is a present gift in possession or whether the possession of a vested interest, or the vesting of a contingent interest, is postponed until the expiration of the period for accumulation.

plus, as well during the minority or respective minorities of every person so for the time being entitled, as during such time as any child of his body so being entitled as aforesaid, should be under the age of twenty-five, and at the end of every period of accumulation, to apply the accumulated fund towards payment of his debts. The attempt was to create a trust for accumulation, which may endure during the minorities of issue down to the remotest generation. The scheme was for one continuous, unbroken accumulation of the rents for successive minorities, and it was held void. Scarisbrick *v.* Skelmersdale, 17 Sim. 187; Vawdry *v.* Geddes, 1 R. & M. 203; Armory *v.* Lord, 5 Seld. (N. Y.) 403; Southampton *v.* Hertford, 2 V. & B. 54; Boughton *v.* Boughton, 1 H. L. Ca. 406; Curtis *v.* Lukin, 5 Beav. 147; Turvin *v.* Newcome, 3 K. & J. 16; Perry on Trusts, § 396; Hargrave's Thelluson Act, §§ 74 *et seq.;* Curran *v.* Philadelphia Trust Co., 39 Leg. Int. (Pa.) 158; McKee's Appeal, 96 Pa. St. 277; Odell *v.* Odell, 10 Allen (Mass.) 1; Carson's Appeal, 99 Pa. St. 325.

Trusts for accumulation beyond the period allowed for the vesting of an executory limitation are absolutely void, although the fund thus to be created is directed to be ultimately applied to the foundation and support of a charity Where land is devised which is void as tending to create a perpetuity, the heir is entitled to recover. Hillyard *v.* Miller, 10 Pa. St. 326.

The subsequent grant by the legislature of a charter to execute such a trust, though in pursuance of the will of the testator, would not aid the devise or divest the estate of the heir. Hillyard *v.* Miller, 10 Pa. St. 326.

1. A transferred stock to trustees, and, by a deed, directed them to accumulate the dividends during the joint lives of M and N, that direction was held to be good for so much only of the joint lives as expired between the date of the deed and A's death. *In re* Lady Rosslyn's Trust, 16 Sim. 391.

Griffiths *v.* Vere, 9 Vesey 127;

If there is a present gift in possession, so that the legatee or devisee has a present vested interest, the income, released by the act from accumulation, goes to the person or persons entitled to the present vested interest.[1]

Where there is no present vested interest the following rules apply:

(1) *Personal Property.*—Where the fund out of which the income is to be derived is personal property, and is not part of the residuary estate, the income released by the act vests in the residuary legatee, and if there be no residuary legatee, then to the next of kin.[2]

(2) *Real Property.*—If there is a direction to accumulate the income and profits of real estate, which is not part of the residue, the released income vests in the heir entitled at common law, thus following the general rule as to void devises; but if the will is governed by the Wills Act,[3] it goes to the residuary devisee.[4]

Thelluson *v.* Woodford, 4 Vesey 343; Mr. Hovenden's note (6); Longdon *v.* Simson, 12 Vesey 295; Palmer *v.* Halford, 4 Russ. 403; Freke *v.* Lord, Carbery L. R., 16 Eq. 461.

1. Coombe *v.* Hughes, 34 Beav. 127; Trickey *v.* Trickey, 3 Myl. & K. 560, 565; Ogilvie *v.* Kirk, Session of Dundee, 8 D. 1229; Maxwell *v.* Maxwell, 4 R. 962; Chulow's Trust, 1 J. & H. 639; Smyth *v.* Kinlock, 7 R. 1176; MacKenzie *v.* MacKenzie, 4 R. 962; Stille's Appeal, 4 W. N. C. (Pa.) 42; Matter of Sergeant, 11 Phila. (Pa.) 8; Washington's Estate, 75 Pa. St. 102; Philadelphia *v.* Girard, 45 Pa. St. 9; Carson's Appeal, 99 Pa. St. 325; Furness Minor's Estate, 14 W. N. C. (Pa.) 391; Penrose's Appeal, 102 Pa. St. 448; Potter's Estate, 36 Leg. Int. (Pa.) 461.

2. Webb *v.* Webb, 2 Beav. 493; Ellis *v.* Maxwell, 3 Beav. 587; Drakeley's Trust, 19 Beav. 395; Attorney General *v.* Poulden, 3 Hare 555; Jones *v.* Maggs, 9 Hare 605; Haley *v.* Bannister, 4 Mad. 275; Crawley *v.* Crawley, 7 Sim. 427; O'Neill *v.* Lucas, 2 Keen 313; Thouron's Estate, 11 W. N. C. (Pa.) 285; Thouron's Appeal, 18 W. N. C. (Pa.) 56; Sergeant's Estate, 32 Leg. Int. (Pa.) 29; McKee's Appeal, 96 Pa. St. 277.

"The accumulations raised by a null and void part of a will are necessarily undisposed of by that part, and must come within the operation of the residuary clause, except when by that clause itself such accumulations are directed to be made." Sergeant's Estate, 32 Leg. Int. (Pa.) 29. See also Weatherall *v.* Thornburgh, 8 Ch. D. 261; Oddie *v.* Brown, 4 De G. & J. 179; Matthews *v.* Keble, L. R., 3 Ch. 691; Burt *v.* Sturt, 10 Hare 415; Browne *v.* Buckton, 2 Sim., N. S. 91; Elborne *v.* Goode, 14 Sim. 165; Pursell *v.* Elder, 4 Macq. 992.

3. 1 Vict., ch. 26, § 25.

4. Eyre *v.* Marsden, 2 Keen 564; Nettleton *v.* Stephenson, 3 De G. & Sm. 366; Edwards *v.* Tuck, 3 De G. M. & G. 40; *In re* Drakeley's Trust, 4 De G. J. & S. 565, 572; Sewell *v.* Denny, 10 Beav. 315; Barrington *v.* Liddell, 10 Hare 429; Wildes *v.* Davies, 1 Sm. & G. 475: Morgan *v.* Morgan, 4 De G. & Sim. 175; Talbot *v.* Jevers, 20 L. J., Eq. 255; Halford *v.* Stains, 16 Sim. 488; Macdonald *v.* Bryce, 2 Keen 276.

"Unless a contrary intention shall appear by the will, such real estate or interest therein as shall be comprised or intended to be comprised in any devise in such will contained, which shall fail or be void by reason of the death of the devisee in the lifetime of the testator, or by reason of such devise being contrary to law, or otherwise incapable of taking effect, shall be included in the residuary devise, if any, contained in such will."

Act of 4 June 1879, § 2, P. L. 88, *Pennsylvania*. This act has no application to lapsed shares of the residuary devise. Everman *v.* Everman, 15 W. N. C. (Pa.) 417, in which the court said: "The act of June 4, 1879, P. L. 88, makes the law respecting the devolution of a lapsed devise the same as it is in the case of a lapsed bequest. No

(3) *Residue.*—If the income of the residue is directed to be accumulated, the nature of the property, whether real or personal, determines the devolution of the income released by the act. The income of personalty going to the next of kin, and of realty to the heir.[1]

If the residue be partly real and partly personal the income of the realty goes to the heir or residuary devisee; and of the personalty to the next of kin or residuary legatee.[2]

Where the estate the income of which is to be accumulated, is personalty, the income of the accumulated income goes to the residuary legatee or next of kin; but where it is realty, to the residuary devisee or heir at law.[3]

doubt the act was passed in consequence of the decisions in Yarr *v.* Murray (86 Pa. St. 113), and Massey's Appeal (88 Pa. St. 471), in the first of which it was held that a lapsed devise descends to the heir-at-law, and in the second, that a lapsed bequest falls into the residue and goes to the residuary legatee. Having in view the old law, the mischief, and the remedy, we are of opinion that the act of 1879 was intended to apply only to lapsed specific devises in the body of the will, and that, as to lapsed shares in the residue, no change was intended or effected. Where there is a bequest or devise of the residue to two persons, without words indicating that the survivor shall take the whole, the intent is clear that one of them shall not have the whole, but a moiety only. The case is within the exception mentioned in the statute; the lapsed share cannot go to the survivor, because that intention does not appear by the will. If the residue of an estate, either real or personal, is given to persons by name and not in a class, each is entitled to a share and no more; and if there should happen to be a lapsed share of the residue, it goes to the next of kin, if it consists of personalty, and to the heir if realty. This was held in two cases, Williams *v.* Neff, and Neff's Appeal (52 Pa. St. 326), arising out of the same will; and the reason is there cannot be a residue of a residue. The act of 1879 is a copy of the English Wills Act of 1st Victoria (1837), and there it was held before the statute, in Barber *v.* Barber (3 Mylne *v.* Craig, 688); and since, in Spencer *v.* Wilson (16 Law Rep., Eq. 501), that a lapsed share of a residuary devise goes to the heir and not to the surviving residuary devisees. And so it was held in Sohier *v.* Inches, 12 Gray (Mass). 385." See also *Pennsylvania* Act 7th July, 1885, P. L. 259.

1. Wildes *v.* Davies, 1 Sm. & G. 475; Browne *v.* Buckton, 2 Sim., N. S. 91; Wilson *v.* Wilson, 1 Sim., N. S. 288; Halford *v.* Stains, 16 Sim. 488; Eyre *v.* Marsden, 2 Keen 564; Simmons *v.* Pitt, 8 L. R., Ch., App. 978; Talbot *v.* Jevers, 20 L. R., Eq. 255; Matthews *v.* Keble, 4 L. R., Eq. 467; 3 L. R., Ch. App. 691; Green *v.* Gascoyne, 4 D. J. & S. 565; Oddie *v.* Brown, 4 De G. & J. 179; Morgan *v.* Morgan, 4 De G. & Sm. 164; Weatherall *v.* Thornburgh, 8 Ch. D. 261; Macdonald *v.* Bryce, 2 Keen 276; Pursell *v.* Elder, 4 Macq. 992; Keith *v.* Keith, 19 D. 1040; Lord *v.* Colvin, 23 D. 111; Pride *v.* Fooks, 2 Beav. 430; Edwards *v.* Tuck, 3 De G. M. & G. 40; Mitcheson's Estate, 15 Phila. (Pa.) 523; 11 W. N. C. (Pa.) 547; Grim's Estate, 15 Phila. (Pa.) 603; 12 W. N. C. (Pa.) 354; 42 Leg. Int. (Pa.) 464; Grim's Appeal, 17 W. N. C. (Pa.) 3; Mellon's Estate, 41 Leg. Int. (Pa.) 54; Gowen's Appeal, 41 Leg. Int. (Pa.) 429.

2. Gray on Rule against Perpetuities, § 705; Eyre *v.* Marsden, 2 Keen 564; Ralph *v.* Carrick, 5 Ch. D. 984, 997, 998. See Talbot *v.* Jevers, L. R., 20 Eq. 255.

3. Eyre *v.* Marsden, 2 Keen 577; Marsden on Perpetuities 342; 1 Jarman on Wills (4th ed.) 312. Gray on Perpetuities § 706, says: "The accumulations of the income of realty (unless ordered to be invested in realty) would seem, in spite of their origin, to be personalty, and their income therefore also to go to the residuary legatees or next of kin." Mr. Jarman's editors say: "The accumulations of rents and profits seem to preserve their character of realty, so that

i. EXEMPTIONS FROM THE OPERATION OF THE ACT.—The second section of the act exempts three classes of provisions from its operation:

(1) *Payment of Debts.*—First. "Any provision for payment of debts of any grantor, settlor or devisor, or other person or persons." Accumulation for payment of the debts of the testator does not contravene the Rule against Perpetuities, and is, therefore, good, though its duration be unlimited.[1]

the heir is entitled to the income of such accumulations." Eyre *v.* Marsden (2 Keen 577) cited by them for this, is not a very satisfactory authority on the point. It was there held that when the purposes, which for the conversion of land was ordered partly failed, the proceeds of the land were to be considered as realty, and that the income beyond the lawful period of accumulation went to the heir. The language of the decision appears to carry to the heir also the income of the accumulations lawfully made; but no reason is given for this, and the attention of the court does not seem to have been directed to the point."

1. It was contended that the plaintiff was entitled as heir at law, because there was a trust for certain accumulations which looked to an indefinite period, and no interest was given to any person till after the accumulation was determined.

Held, "that the testator's intention was simply to provide a fund for some special debts and charges, and then that the persons entitled should take. He had no intention of suspending the beneficial interest in the meantime till the debts and charges should be paid. All the authorities show that where an estate is given to trustees to pay debts, and then to a person designated, the person designated takes at once subject to the debts. This case is not open to objection on account of the accumulation directed by will. There is no accumulation for purpose of suspension. The act of 39 and 40, Geo. III, does not apply; and if it did, there is an express exception in the case of debts and portions. Under these circumstances it is quite clear that it is the enjoyment and not the property that is tied up, and the estate vests in the same manner as if the testator had created a term for payment of his debts." Bacon *v.* Proctor, T. & R. 40.

A testator devised his real estate in strict settlement, subject to a term of 2000 years, limited to trustees for raising £500 a year, and accumulating it as a sinking fund for payment of his mortgage debts etc., to a considerable amount.

Contended (*a*), That the trust for raising and accumulating a sinking fund for payment of the mortgages is void for remoteness or as tending to a perpetuity.

Held, "With regard to the term and the trust for accumulation, First, that the debts for the payment of which the accumulation is directed, are mortgages either existing at the testator's death or made pursuant to his will; charges on the estate of an amount ascertained or to be ascertained in the execution of valid trusts.

"Secondly, That the amount compared with the rents of the property comprised in the term is so great, that the accumulation of rent, managed as the testator has directed, would not be sufficient to pay the mortgages till after the lapse of very many years, too long, if considered as an absolute term, for accumulation.

Thirdly, That the mode in which the testator has limited the estate, subject to the term, is not liable to any objection. The first tenant in tail attaining twenty-one years of age may acquire absolute dominion over the estate, subject to the mortgages.

"Fourthly, That on that event taking place, the trustees of the term will become trustees for the owner of the estate, who may deal with the term and with the estate at his own discretion, subject only to the mortgages. Without consent of the owner of the estate, the trust for accumulation cannot continue beyond the time during which the law permits a suspension of full power over the estate.

"The period during which the attainment of full power over the estate is suspended is permitted by law, and the accumulation, except at the will of the

(2) *Raising Portions.*—Second. "Any provision for raising portions for any child or children of any grantor, settlor or devisor, or any child or children of any person taking any interest under any such conveyance, settlement or devise." A portion cannot consist of the whole of the testator's estate, or of the bulk of it, in a residue.[1]

(3) *Produce of Timber or Wood.*—Third. "Any direction touching the produce of timber or wood upon any lands or tenements."[2]

j. THE ACT OF SCOTLAND.—The third section of the Thelluson

owner, can continue only during that lawful suspension; and considering this case to be within the exceptions of the statute, it does not appear that I can hold the term and the trust for accumulation to be void for remoteness."

"I think this a very improvident and indiscreet mode of raising money for the payment of debts, but it does not appear to me to be unlawful. The inconvenience of it may, perhaps, be mitigated, by the exercise of the discretionary power of the trustees, to apply any portion of the accumulated fund in satisfaction of mortgages, before the accumulated fund is sufficient to pay all, or by the exercise of the power which the mortgagees have to enforce payment of their mortgages or foreclose the estate without regard to the trust for accumulation." Bateman *v.* Hotchkiss, 10 Beav. 426.

In the above case, the testator died in June, 1843, at which time his debts were stated to amount to £72,000 and they had been since increased. The personal estate not specifically bequeathed was wholly inadequate to pay the testator's debts. See Carter *v.* Barnardiston, 1 P. Wms. 505; 2 Swanst. 439. See Powys *v.* Mansfield, 6 Sim. 528; 3 Myl. & Cr. 359.

The act of *Pennsylvania* does not, as the Thelluson act, allow accumulation for the purpose of the payment of debts or to provide for raising portions for children. Lutz's Estate, 27 W. N. C. (Pa.) 403. See also Varlo *v.* Faden, 27 Beav. 255, 264; Barrington *v.* Liddell, 2 De G. M. & G. 480, 498.

1. Eyre *v.* Marsden, 2 Keen 564, 573; Wildes *v.* Davies, 1 Sm. & G. 475; Shaw *v.* Rhodes, 1 Myl. & Cr. 135, 159; Edwards *v.* Tuck, 3 De G. M. & G. 40; Browne *v.* Buckton, 2 Sim., N. S. 91; Matthews *v.* Keble, L. R., 3 Ch. 691.

It is doubtful whether a gift of a specific sum to be accumulated for children is a portion. Gray on Rule against Perpetuities, § 711, and cases cited; Marsden on Perpetuities, 345; Kindersley V. C. in Watt *v.* Wood, 1 Dr. & Sm. 56, 60, said, "portions" is a word, "a precise definition of which no judge has ventured to give."

If the portions are for a class of children, those entitled must be children of persons who receive an interest under the will.

Burt *v.* Sturt, 10 Ha. 415; Eyre *v.* Marsden, 2 Keen 564. Such interest of the parent may be any interest under the will, and need not be in the accumulated property. Evans *v.* Hellier, 5 Cl. & F. 114.

Browne *v.* Buckton, 2 Sim., N. S. 91; Barrington *v.* Liddell, 2 De G. M. & G. 480; Morgan *v.* Morgan, 4 De G. & Sm. 164; Marsden on Perp. 346; Gray on Perp., § 711.

The whole gift is made void by the fact that some of the parents take no interest under the will or settlement. Eyre *v.* Marsden, 2 Keen 564.

A trust to accumulate for portions of children of a person who never has children will continue until his death, at which time the accumulations, instead of going to the persons provided for in the will or settlement, if the person died without children, will go to such person or persons as would have been entitled to the same if there had been no direction to accumulate. *In re* Clulow's Trust, 1 J. & H. 639; 28 L. J., Ch. 696.

The children must be legitimate. Shaw *v.* Rhodes, 1 Myl. & Cr. 135, 159.

The portions included within the exception include not only those created by the deed or will directing the accumulation, but also those created by any instrument prior thereto. Beech *v.* Lord St. Vincent, 3 De G. & S. 678; Barrington *v.* Liddell, 10 Hare 429; Middleton *v.* Losh, 1 Sm. & G. 61.

2. Harg. Thel., Act §§ 163, *et seq.* Marsden on Perp. 346, 347.

Act is as follows: "Provided also, and be it enacted, That nothing in this act contained shall extend to any disposition respecting heritable property within that part of Great Britain called *Scotland.*' By the Statute of 11 and 12 Vict., ch. 36, § 41 (1848), this provision of the act was repealed, and it was declared that the act "shall, in future, apply to heritable property in *Scotland.*"[1]

k. TIME OF TAKING EFFECT.—The fourth section of the Thelluson act reads as follows: "Provided also, and be it enacted, That the restrictions in this act contained shall take effect, and be in force with respect to wills and testaments made and executed before the passing of this act, in such cases only where the devisor or testator shall be living, and of sound and disposing mind, after the expiration of twelve calendar months from the passing of this act."[2]

5. Trusts for Accumulation in Pennsylvania.—The *Pennsylvania* statute on the subject is given in full in the note.[3]

The Act of April 18th, 1853, provides that no person or persons shall, after the passage thereof, by any deed, will or otherwise, settle or dispose of any real or personal property, so and in such manner that the rents, issues and profits thereof shall be wholly or partially accumulated for any longer term than the life or lives of any such grantor or grantors, settlor or settlors, or testator, and the term of twenty-one years from the death of any such grantor or testator; that is to say, only after such decease, during the minority or respective minorities, with allowance for the period of gestation, of any person or persons who, under the uses and trusts of the deed, will or other assurance directing accumulation, would, for the time being, if of full age, be entitled

1. Ogilvie *v.* Kirk, Session of Dundee, 8 D. 1229; Keith *v.* Keith, 19 D. 1040; McLarty *v.* McLaverty, 2 Macph. 489. The Thelluson act does not extend to *Ireland.*

2. Harg. Thel. act, §§ 171-173. See the following cases, on the question of costs in suits involving the application of the Thelluson act: Barrett *v.* Buck, 12 Jur. 771; Ralph *v.* Carrick, 5 Ch. D. 984; Eyre *v.* Marsden, 4 Myl. & Cr. 231; Elborne *v.* Goode, 14 Sim. 165; Green *v.* Gascoyne, 4 De G. J. & S. 565.

3. "No person or persons shall, after the passing of this act, by any deed, will, or otherwise, settle or dispose of any real or personal property, so and in such manner that the rents, issues, interests or profits thereof shall be wholly or partially accumulated for any longer term than the life or lives of any such grantor or grantors, settlor or settlors, or testator, and the term of twenty-one years from the death of any such grantor, settlor or testator; that is to say, only after such decease, during the minority or respective minorities, with allowance for the period of gestation of any person or persons who, under the uses and trusts of the deed, will, or other assurance directing such accumulation, would, for the time being, if of full age, be entitled unto the rents, issues, interests and profits so directed to accumulate. And in every case where any accumulation shall be directed otherwise than as aforesaid, such direction shall be null and void, in so far as it shall exceed the limits of this act; and the rents, issues, interests and profits so directed to be accumulated, contrary to the provisions of this act, shall go to and be received by such person or persons as would have been entitled thereto; if such accumulation had not been directed: Provided, That any donation, bequest or devise for any

to the rents, issues, interests and profits so directed to accumulate. All other accumulations are in express terms rendered void, except those mentioned in the first proviso, and the rents or profits so appropriated pass to the person or persons who would have been entitled thereto, if such accumulation had not been directed.[1]

literary, scientific, charitable or religious purpose, shall not come within the prohibition of this section; which shall take effect and be in force, as well in respect to wills heretofore made by persons yet living and of competent mind, as in respect to wills hereafter to be made: And provided, That notwithstanding any direction to accumulate rents, issues, interests and profits, for the benefit of any minor or minors, it shall be lawful for the proper court as aforesaid, on the application of the guardian, where there shall be no other means for maintenance or education, to decree an adequate allowance for such purpose, but in such manner as to make an equal distribution among those having equal rights or expectancies, whether at the time being minors or of lawful age." Act of April 18, 1853, § 9; 2 Brightly's Purd. Dig. (1885) 1460, pl. 9.

1. A testator allowed an annual sum out of the income of his estate for the use of a minor child, and directed "the balance of such income to be invested and to accumulate during the minority of my said daughter, for the benefit of my estate," and that after she attained full age the income of his estate "shall be paid to my said daughter, etc." *Held*, that under the act of April 18th, 1853, the direction for accumulation during minority was void, and the accumulations went to the daughter.

"According to the act, accumulations are allowed only in favor of one class of persons, who are to be possessed of two qualifications: (1) They must be minors. (2) They must be such persons who, if not minors when the deed or will goes into effect, will be entitled to take the rents and profits from which the accumulations are to arise.

"If these accumulations go not to the minor, and it be conceded that such minor must, in order to satisfy the terms of the statute, be a beneficiary, it follows that the benefit may be so small as virtually to amount to nothing. In order to avoid a perversion of the statute such as above stated, it is necessary to construe the act in such a manner as to permit the accumulation during the period of minority of any minor selected for that purpose, whether it be the beneficiary or any one else. In other words, this is the period allowed in which the estate may be permitted to accumulate, and when the period of majority arrives this aggregate estate may be distributed according to the directions of the deed or will creating it, without any regard whatever to the person during whose minority it was accumulated.

"But, under this reading of the act, it must be conceded that cases may arise in which the person, during whose minority the accumulations accrue, may not be the one who, if of full age, would be entitled to the rents, issues and profits so directed to accumulate, which would be in conflict with the statute. In the English act there are four distinct cases or periods in which or during which accumulations are allowed: (1) During the life of the grantor or settlor; (2) Twenty-one years from the death of the grantor, settlor or testator; (3) During the minority or respective minorities of any person or persons who shall be living, or *en ventre sa mere* at the time of the death of said grantor, etc.; and (4) during the minority or respective minorities only of any person or persons who, under the uses and trusts of the deed, surrender, will or other assurance directing such accumulations, would for the time being, if of full age, be entitled unto the rents, issues, profits, etc., directed to be accumulated.

"The act of April 18th, 1853, is almost a literal transcript of the British statute (39 and 40 Geo. III, ch. 98) omitting the second and third clauses thereof. Therefore, it becomes certain that, with the exceptions stated in the first proviso, the legislature intended that there should be no accumulations of the estate of decedents, except in favor of those minors who should be beneficiaries under the deed or will by which the trust should be raised. And it is a singular interpretation of the act, which, whilst it must admit of the starting of accumulations with the minority of one, who, if of full age,

The terms of the Act of April 18th, 1853, relating to accumulations, apply to an estate held under a deed just as they would if held upon the same terms under a will. In either case directions for accumulation are void, so far as they are in conflict with the act, and it can make no difference whether such accumulations, where the property passed by deed, accrued within the lifetime of the grantor or after his decease.[1]

A trust for accumulation may be inferred as well as expressed by language of testator's will.

A direction to hold surplus income to cover deficiencies in annuities during future years constitutes a trust for accumulation, and is void within the statute.

A direction to appropriate the surplus income to the improvement and repair of the real estate belonging to the trust, will not prevent the trust from being void under the statute, as a direction to accumulate.[2]

It seems that a devise in trust for the maintenance and support of a minor and at majority to pay her the whole income for life,

would be entitled to the rents, issues and profits directed to be accumulated, nevertheless insists that such person may not be so entitled when such rents, issues and profits have been accumulated.

In Washington's Estate, (Pa.) 13 Atl. Rep. 212, the court by Gordon, J., said: "It is not conceivable that the framers of this statute intended a construction so contradictory."

Schwartz's Appeal, (Pa.) 13 Atl. Rep. 212. A bequest to testator's daughter, providing for the accumulation of interest during the life of her husband, the principal and interest to go to her children after her death, vests an absolute title in her after the lapse of twenty-one years from the testator's death. Brubaker's Appeal (Pa.), 15 Atl. Rep. 708.

1. Carson *v.* Rutter, 12 W. N. C. Pa. 161.

A executed an indenture whereby he assigned and transferred certain personalty to trustees in trust to apply so much of the income thereof as they thought fit to the maintenance of his daughter until she should attain the age of twenty-one years, those portions of the income not so applied he directed the trustees to invest. Upon his daughter attaining majority he directed the trustees to pay over to her the whole income of the estate, including the income of the accumulations, for her life, and after her death directed said estate, including said accumulations, to be held in trust for his daughter's appointees by will, and in default of such appointment, for her issue. The daughter, having attained majority, filed a bill in equity against the trustees, praying that all accumulations during her minority be paid to her absolutely. *Held*, that under the Act of April 18, 1853, § 9, the capitalization of the accumulations in the manner directed by A was void, and that the complainant was entitled to such accumulations absolutely. Washington's Estate, 75 Pa. St. 102; Stille's Estate, 4 W. N.C.(Pa.)42; 8 Phila. Pa. 182; McKee's Appeal, 96 Pa. St. 277.

2. The testator devised his estate in trust and directed that from the income arising, annuities be paid to his children for life, with a further provision that if in any one year there should not be enough to pay the annuities, the deficiency should be made up from any surplus of former years that may be in the hands of the trustees, and that after payment of the annuities in full the surplus may be applied by the trustees in the alteration or repair of the trust estate.

As the surplus income was held as a trust to accumulate and, not being limited to an existing minority or for the benefit of a minor it transgresses the Act of April 18, 1853, and the surplus income passes, therefore, either to the residuary devisee or under the intestate law. Mitcheson's Estate, 11 W. N. C.(Pa.)547.

entitles the *cestui que trust* to the surplus income arising during the operation of the trust.[1]

A testamentary direction to pay debts or incumbrances out of income, transgresses the Act of April 18, 1853, and is invalid.

A trust for payment of debts is not affected by the Rule against Perpetuities, since it is terminable at any time by the creditors intended to be benefited.[2]

Where there is a provision that the fund with its accumulations shall go to the children of minor grandchildren dying in their minority, the grandchildren are nevertheless entitled to a proper allowance out of the fund, and the rights of subsequent takers are subordinate to this provision.[3]

"A residuary devise, being in trust for a charitable use and purpose, comes within the proviso of the ninth section of the Act of April 18th, 1853, and therefore is not within the prohibitory clause of the section forbidding accumulations after the death of the testator, for a term longer than therein specified."[4]

1. A testator gave all the residue of his estate to his executors in trust to invest the same in certain securities, and to pay the income thereof to his granddaughter if she should attain the age of twenty-one years, with a devise over in case of her decease before attaining that age; and during her majority a liberal allowance for her maintenance.

Should his granddaughter arrive at the age of twenty-one years, she was to have power of disposition of one-half of the residuary estate.

It cannot be doubted, under the decisions with reference to trusts for accumulations since the act of April 18th, 1853, that the *cestui que trust*, upon attaining her majority, became entitled to the surplus income which had been until then accumulated.

Washington's Estate, 75 Pa. St. 102; Stilles' Appeal, 4 W. N. C. (Pa.) 42; Howell's Estate, 5 W. N. C. (Pa.) 430.

2. Penrose, J., said: "Nearly twenty years ago Chief Justice Paxson, then sitting in the orphans' court of Philadelphia, called attention to the fact that the provision of the Thellusson Act permitting the application of income, during the restricted period, to the payment of debts, had been omitted from the act of 1853 (Washington's Estate, 8 Phila., (Pa.) 182); and in 1882, in Carson's Appeal (99 Pa. St. 329), the supreme court, while concurring in his opinion that the omission was unwise, attached much importance to the failure of the legislature to correct the defects of the original act, after they had been pointed out by the courts." Lutz's Estate, 27 W. N. C. (Pa.) 403.

3. "It is far from clear that the act, of April 18, 1853, contemplated an accumulation through a succession of minorities; certainly a trust for this purpose, which might last for more than twenty-one years after the expiration of a life or lives in being at the death of the testator, would trangress not only the act of assembly, but would be void as creating a perpetuity.

"The act provides that 'notwithstanding any direction to accumulate for the benefit of any minor or minors, it shall be lawful for the proper court, where there shall be no other means, to decree an adequate allowance for such purpose;' and, accordingly, in Washington's Estate (75 Pa. St. 102), it was held, though the minor's interest in the *corpus* was but for life, that an allowance out of the accumulations was properly made." Furness, Minor Estate, 14 W. N. C. (Pa.) 391; McKee's Appeal, 96 Pa. St. 277.

4. Biddle's Appeal, 99 Pa. St. 525. A testator by his will, after bequeathing certain legacies, devised and bequeathed all the residue of his estate to his executors in trust to let and demise the real estate, to collect the rents and profits, to sell and convey the real estate, and, out of the income of his estate, to pay certain annuities and a legacy; he then further directed his executors, that after the decease of the annuitants, and of the legatee before attaining majority, to convey and assign all the residue of his estate, real

A specific bequest of the *corpus* of a legacy carries with it to the legatee the right to all accumulations of the income made for his benefit in a direction of the will contrary to the Act of April 18th, 1853.[1]

6. Trusts for Accumulation in New York.—*New York.* The provisions of the Revised Statutes relating to the accumulation of rents and profits of real estate, and of interest and income of personal estate, are given in full in the note.[2]

and personal, together with accumulations which might be in their hands after the death of the said annuitants and legatee, to a charity. Postponements of enjoyments of vested remainders, by charities, are respected where similar directions as against individuals would not be.

The income of the estate was more than sufficient to pay the said annuities and the legacy, but the court held that the charity was not entitled to enjoy the benefits of the devise until after the decease of all of the said annuitants, although the accumulations might last longer than permitted, in case of individuals, by the act of April 18th, 1853. Hillyard *v.* Miller, 10 Pa St. 326; Philadelphia *v.* Girard, 45 Pa. St. 1; Harbin *v.* Masterman, L. R., 12 Eq. 559.

1. A testatrix devised and bequeathed one-fifth part of her residuary estate to trustees for the benefit of two granddaughters, the income of which was to be accumulated until their majority or marriage, and then the portions with the accumulations to be held as a trust fund for their separate use for life, the income to be paid annually, with remainder to their children. *Held*, that although the direction to accumulate was void under the act of April 18, 1853, yet as it clearly appeared that the testatrix did not intend to die intestate as to any portion of her estate, the bequest of the *corpus* of the legacy carried with it to the legatees the right to the accumulations of the income.

Striking the direction to accumulate out of the present will, there remains the gift of the income to the granddaughter, from the death of the testatrix, and as they would have been entitled to said income as it accrued, if the invalidity of the trust for accumulation had been judicially determined at the death of the testatrix, so now they are entitled to it in its accumulated form.

The accumulations were claimed by the next of kin, who were dismissed in the orphan court and the report of the auditor was confirmed. Dwight, J., saying, "The act of 1853 says that the unlawful accumulations shall go to and be received by such person or persons as would have been entitled thereto, if such accumulation had not been directed." The act itself does not determine specifically the individual recipients. It merely designates them as "those who would have been entitled" to the accruing products, in case the will had been silent respecting their destination. Stilles' Appeal, 4 W. N. C. (Pa.) 42; 1 W. N. C. (Pa.) 249.

2. Rev. Sts., pt. 2, ch. 1, tit. 2.

"§ 37. An accumulation of rents and profits of real estate for the benefit of one or more persons, may be directed by any will or deed, sufficient to pass real estate as follows:

"1. If such accumulation be directed to commence on the creation of the estate, out of which the rents and profits are to arise, it must be made for the benefit of one or more minors then in being, and terminate at the expiration of their minority.

"2. If such accumulation be directed to commence at any time subsequent to the creation of the estate out of which the rents and profits are to arise, it shall commence within the time in this article permitted for the vesting of future estates, and during the minority of the persons for whose benefit it is directed, and shall terminate at the expiration of such minority.

"§ 38. If, in either of the cases mentioned in the last section, the direction for such accumulation shall be for a longer term than during the minority of the persons intended to be benefited thereby, it shall be void as respects the time beyond such minority. And all directions for the accumulation of the rents and profits of real estate, except such as are herein allowed, shall be void.

"§ 39. Where such rents and profits

A trust to accumulate is valid if it be limited to two lives in being, and if it is for the benefit of one or more minors in being, and will terminate at or before the expiration of such minority.[1]

To render a trust for an accumulation of the rents and profits, or income, of an estate valid, the accumulation must be for the sole benefit of a minor or minors, and must be payable to him or them at the expiration of the minority.[2] A direction to accumulate may be implied, and comes within the statute.[3] It is void, if made for an absolute term, no matter how short.[4]

are directed to be accumulated for the benefit of infants entitled to the expectant estate, and such infants shall be destitute of other sufficient means of support and education, the chancellor upon the application of their guardian, may direct a suitable sum out of such rents and profits to be applied to their maintenance and education.

"§ 40. When, in consequence of a valid limitation of an expectant estate, there shall be a suspense of the power of alienation, or of the ownership, during the continuance of which the rents and profits shall be undisposed of, and no valid direction for their accumulation is given, such rents and profits shall belong to the persons presumptively entitled to the next eventual estate." Rev. Sts., pt. 2, ch. 4, tit. 4.

§ 3. "An accumulation of the interest money, the produce of stock or other income or profit arising from personal property, may be directed by any instrument sufficient in law to pass such personal property as follows:

"1. If the accumulation be directed to commence from the date of the instrument, or from the death of the person executing the same, such accumulation must be directed to be made for the benefit of one or more minors then in being, or in being at such death, and to terminate at the expiration of their minority.

"2. If the accumulation be directed to commence at any period subsequent to the date of the instrument, or subsequent to the death of the person executing such instrument, it must be directed to commence within the time allowed in the first section of this title, for the suspension of the absolute ownership of personal property, and at some time during the minority of the persons for whose benefit it is intended, and must terminate at the expiration of their minority.

"§ 4. All directions for the accumulation of the interest, income or profit of personal property, other than such as are herein allowed, shall be void; but a direction for an accumulation, in either of the cases specified in the last section, for a longer term than the minority of the persons intended to be benefited thereby, shall be void only as respects the time beyond such minority.

"§ 5. When any minor, for whose benefit a valid accumulation of the interest or income of personal property shall have been directed, shall be destitute of other sufficient means of support or of education, the chancellor, upon the application of such minor or his guardian, may cause a suitable sum to be taken from the moneys accumulated or directed to be accumulated, and to be applied to the support or education of such minor."

1. Thompson *v.* Clendenning, 1 Sand. Ch. (N. Y.) 387; Mason *v.* Mason, 2 Sand. Ch. (N. Y.) 432; Kane *v.* Gott, 24 Wend. (N. Y.) 641; Vail *v.* Vail, 7 Barb. (N. Y.) 226; Cromwell *v.* Cromwell, 2 Edw. (N. Y.) Ch. 495; Savage *v.* Burnham, 17 N. Y. 561; Merserole *v.* Merserole, 1 Hun (N. Y.) 66; Hunter *v.* Hunter, 17 Barb. (N. Y.) 25.

If the estate limited to the infant is contingent, an accumulation of the income during his minority cannot be said to be for his benefit. Manice *v.* Manice, 43 N. Y. 303.

2. Hawley *v.* James, 5 Paige (N.Y.) 318; Pray *v.* Hegeman, 92 N. Y. 508.

3. Vail *v.* Vail, 4 Paige (N.Y.) 317; Hawley *v.* James, 5 Paige (N.Y.) 318; Haxtun *v.* Corse, 2 Barb. Ch. (N. Y.) 506.

4. Hone *v.* Van Schaick, 20 Wend. (N. Y.) 564; Tucker *v.* Tucker, 5 N. Y. 408. Mr. Justice Bronson, in Hawley *v.* James, 5 Paige (N. Y.) 318, said: "The question is, not whether the trust probably will, but whether it can transgress the statute rule." "The statute has given lives as the measure, and nothing else.

A trust for accumulation which is not for the benefit of a minor solely and during his minority, and when the period of accumulation ceases, the accumulated fund is not released from further restraint and paid over to the person for whose benefit the accumulation is directed, is void.[1]

An accumulation for the benefit of an unborn child, to commence after his birth and to terminate with his minority, is lawful, provided, in case of real estate, that the accumulation shall commence within the time allowed by law for the vesting of future estates; and in case of personal property, within the time allowed for the suspension of absolute ownership.[2]

Life must in some form enter into the limitation. No absolute term, however moderate, or however short, can be maintained; and no uncertain term, the utmost limit of which is not bounded by lives, can be sustained."

In same case the CHIEF JUSTICE concluded: "The trust term is void, 1. Because it is an estate limited to determine upon thirteen lives, as well as upon minorities, and may postpone the power of alienation for a longer period than is allowed by law. 2. That if it should be considered properly, a term for twenty years and ten days, determinable upon thirteen minorities, it is still void because the power of alienation may be suspended for more than two lives of the thirteen individuals upon which it depends; and 3. Because the trust term is not limited to depend upon one or two specified lives in being within the true construction of the 15th section; the only measure for the suspension of the power of alienation since the adoption of the Revised Statutes, being a life or lives."

1. Pray *v.* Hegeman, 92 N. Y. 508. Where there was a direction for accumulation during a minority, accompanied with a gift of the income of the accumulated fund after the expiration of the minority, to the minor for life, and of the principal upon his death, to other persons, it was held void.

A direction for accumulation for the benefit of minors and adults was held void in Kilpatrick *v.* Johnson (15 N. Y. 326); and in Boynton *v.* Hoyt (1 Den. (N.Y.) 54) a direction to accumulate rents and profits of land for the benefit of the testator's wife and minor children was held void.

See also Vail *v.* Vail, 4 Paige (N.Y.) 331; Lang *v.* Ropke, 5 Sandf. (N. Y.) 363; Hawley *v.* James, 16 Wend (N.Y.) 62; Manice *v.* Manice, 43 N. Y. 377; Harris *v.* Clarke, 7 N. Y. 242; Riggs *v.* Cragg, 89 N. Y. 486.

A direction that testator's interest in a business concern be continued, and the profits paid to his executors until the majority of the youngest child, then to be divided between the wife and children, and providing that the "fee" of the business should pass to his residuary estate, violates 3 *New York* Rev. St., p. 2256, §§ 3, 4, prohibiting accumulations unless for the benefit of one or more minors and to terminate at the conclusion of the minority, and is therefore invalid as to the accumulation attempted, because not wholly for the benefit of minors, but the principal will nevertheless pass to the residuary estate. *In re* Sand's Will, 3 Amer. Dig. (1889) 4003.

2. In Manice *v.* Manice, 43 N.Y. 303, the court by Rapallo, J., said: "Neither do the provisions authorizing accumulations require that the minor for whose benefit the accumulation is to be made should be in being at the death of the testator, unless the accumulation is to commence at his (testator's) death. If it is to commence at a subsequent period, the beneficiary must be in being at the time of the commencement of the accumulation, otherwise it cannot be said to commence during the minority of the person for whose benefit it is directed. An accumulation for the benefit of an unborn child, to commence after the birth of the child, and to terminate with his minority, is lawful, provided that it is also to commence within the time permitted for the vesting of future estates; that is to say, on the expiration of two lives in being; of an unborn child, but an accumulation for the benefit to commence before his birth is not permitted under any circumstances, and this was the objection

A trust for accumulation for the benefit of a number of minors *in esse*, and the interest of each one is to vest when he arrives at the age of twenty-one, is good, If, however, the direction be that the accumulation continue till the youngest of a number of minors *in esse* arrives at full age, and the accumulated fund is then to be divided, such direction is void for the excess beyond minority, and the interest of each beneficiary vests when he arrives at full age.[1]

It has been held that where several minors take as tenants in common, and distributively and not jointly, with the right of survivorship, a trust to accumulate until the youngest arrives at age, is valid.[2] But where the accumulation is for their joint benefit and that of the survivor, it is void.[3]

Where a direction to accumulate is illegal and it can be separated from the gift, which in other respects is good, without destroying the substantial form of the latter, such direction to accumulate will be declared void and the gift good.[4] If, however, the part which is good cannot be separated from that which is bad, the whole must be rejected.[5]

The rents, profits, or income released by reason of a void or illegal direction to accumulate go to the heir, next of kin or residuary devisee or legatee.[6]

7. Trusts for Accumulation in Other States.—The provisions of the *New York* statutes on the subject of the accumulation of the rents and profits of real estate, have been closely followed by

to the validity of the accumulations in the cases of Haxtun *v.* Corse (2 Barb. Ch. (N. Y.) 518), and Kilpatrick *v.* Johnson (15 N. Y. 322).

1. In Savage *v.* Burnham, 17 N. Y. 561, a testator devised his estate, real and personal, upon these trusts: 1. To sell the real estate after the death of his widow; 2. That she should, during her life receive and take to her own use one-third part of the clear yearly rents and profits of the real estate; the residue of the rents and profits, until the sale of the real estate, to be deemed part of the personal estate and subject to the same dispositions; which were, 3. To apply the income to the maintenance and education of six sons and four daughters, named in the will, in equal shares, until the sons should attain the age of twenty-one years, and the daughters attain that age or be married, respectively; 4. To pay or transfer the principal in equal shares to the sons and daughters; the shares of the sons to become vested at twenty-one, and then to be paid or transferred; the shares of the daughters to be vested in the trustees, the income to be paid to them after twenty-one or marriage during life. *Held*, a valid trust as to the real estate within the statute.

See also Simpson *v.* English, 1 Hun (N. Y.) 559; Bolton *v.* Jacks, 6 Robt. (N. Y.) 166; Gilman *v.* Reddington, 24 N. Y. 9.

2. Everitt *v.* Everitt, 29 N. Y. 39.

3. Thompson *v.* Clendenning, 1 Sandf. Ch. (N. Y.) 387; Scott *v.* Monell, 1 Redf. (N. Y.) 431.

4. Westerfield *v.* Westerfield, 1 Bradf. (N. Y.) 137; Haxtun *v.* Corse, 2 Barb. Ch. (N. Y.) 506; Kilpatrick *v.* Johnson, 15 N. Y. 322; Gilman *v.* Reddington, 24 N. Y. 7; Savage *v.* Burnham, 17 N. Y. 561; Hawley *v.* James, 5 Paige (N. Y.) 318; Dodge *v.* Pond, 23 N. Y. 69; Killam *v.* Allen, 52 Barb. (N. Y.) 605.

5. Smith *v.* Edwards, 23 Hun (N. Y.) 223.

6. Field *v.* Field, 4 Sandf. Ch. (N. Y.) 528; Thorn *v.* Coles, 3 Edw. Ch. (N. Y.) 330; Van Vetchen *v.* Van Vetchen, 8 Paige (N. Y.) 104; McGrath *v.* Van Stavoren, 8 Daly (N. Y.) 454; Yates *v.* Yates, 9 Barb. (N. Y.) 324; Dodge *v.* Pond, 23 N. Y. 69;

similar statutes in some of the other States, as for instance, *Wisconsin*,[1] *Michigan*[2] and *Minnesota*.[3] The construction of the Statutes in the later States have followed the decisions under the Revised Statutes of *New York*.[4] No one of these three States has made any statutory provision for the accumulation of the interest and income of personal property.[5]

On the other hand, *Indiana* has followed the *New York* statutes, relating to the accumulation of the income and interest of personal property, but has not adopted those relating to accumulation of the rents and profits of real estate.[6]

California: "All directions for the accumulation of property, except such as are allowed by this title, are void. An accumulation of the income of property for the benefit of one or more persons, may be directed by any will or transfer in writing sufficient to pass the property out of which the accumulation is to arise, as follows: 1. If such accumulation is directed to commence on the creation of the interest out of which the income is to arise, it must be made for the benefit of one or more minors then in being, and terminate at the expiration of their minority; or 2, if such accumulation is directed to commence at any time subsequent to the creation of the interest and of which the income is to arise, it must commence within the time in this title permitted for the vesting of future interests, and during the minority of the beneficiaries, and terminate at the expiration of such minority.[7]

"If in either of the cases mentioned in the last section the direction for an accumulation is for a longer term than during the minority of the beneficiaries, the direction only, whether separable or not from other provisions of the instrument, is void as respects the time beyond such minority."[8]

When a minor for whose benefit an accumulation has been directed, is destitute of other sufficient means of support and education, the proper court, upon application, may direct a suitable sum to be applied thereto out of the fund.[9]

Vail *v.* Vail, 4 Paige (N. Y.) 317; Hull *v.* Hull, 24 N. Y. 647; Rice *v.* Barrest, 102 N. Y. 161.

1. 2 *Wisconsin* Rev. Sts. (1858), ch. 83, §§ 37-40; De Wolf *v.* Lawson, 61 Wis. 469; Scott *v.* West, 63 Wis. 529.

2. 2 *Michigan* Comp. Laws (1871), ch. 147, §§ 37-40; Toms *v.* Williams, 41 Mich. 552; Palms *v.* Palms, 36 N. W. Rep. 419.

3. *Minnesota* Gen. Sts. (1866), ch. 45., §§ 37-40.

4. Scott *v.* West, 63 Wis. 529.

5. De Wolf *v.* Lawson, 61 Wis. 469; Scott *v.* West, 63 Wis. 529; Toms *v.* Williams, 41 Mich. 552.

6. *Indiana* Revised Statutes (1881), §§ 6058-6059. See Dyson *v.* Repp, 29 Ind. 482.

7. Civil Code, §§ 723, 724.

8. Civil Code, § 725.

9. Civil Code, § 726.

Where there is a bequest in trust to divide and pay the income to testator's nephews and nieces during their respective lives, and after their deaths in trust for their children who shall attain the age of twenty-one years or marry, as no accumulation is provided for by such a bequest until after the death of the parties entitled to the income, which accumulation is for the benefit of their children during their minority, the provision is valid within § 724 of the Civil

Alabama: "No trust of estates for the purpose of accumulation only, can have any force or effect for a longer term than ten years, unless when, for the benefit of a minor, in being at the date of the conveyance, or if by will, at the death of the testator; in which case, the trust may extend to the termination of the minority."[1] This statute has been taken from the Thelluson Act.

PERSON; PERSONAL—See note 2.

Code, restricting accumulations of income to provisions for the benefit of minors in being at the creation of the fund, and requiring such accumulation to terminate with the minority of the beneficiary. Goldtree *v.* Thompson, 79 Cal. 613.

1. Revised Code (1886), § 1835. In construing this provision of the Code, the decisions under both the Thelluson Act and the *Pennsylvania* statute of 1853, would apply.

It is difficult to express the benefit and assistance which the writers feel they have gained from Mr. Gray's masterly Treatise on the Rule against Perpetuities.

Other text books which they have consulted, are: Marsden on Perpetuities; Lewis on Perpetuities; Challis on Real Property; Mr. Wm. C. Scott's Treatise on Trusts for Accumulations, published in the American edition of Lewis on Trusts; Fearne on Contingent Remainders.

2. **Person.**—The person consists of both soul and body; and the phrase, the removal of such person, in a law relating to residence, means the removal of the soul and body in life, and not the withdrawal of the former from the latter merely. Tute *v.* James, 46 Vt. 60.

An *Iowa* statute gives a right of action to any one who shall be injured "in person." It was held that the words "in person" are equivalent to "in body," and an action will not lie under the statute for an injury to the feelings. Calloway *v.* Laydon, 47 Iowa 458.

Massachusetts Stat. 1842, ch. 89, § 1, providing that the action of trespass on the case for injuries to the person shall survive, extends only to injuries of a physical character; such torts as slander, breach of promise to marry, etc., are not embraced. Smith *v.* Sherman, 4 Cush. (Mass.) 408. But see Delamater *v.* Russell, 4 How. Pr. (N. Y.) 234, where it was held that an action for crim. con. was an action for an "injury to the person."

Where a woman, four or five months pregnant, fell on a defective highway, and was delivered of the child, which survived but a few minutes, it was held that the child was not a "person" within the statute giving a cause of action for negligent death to the administrator. Districh *v.* Northampton, 138 Mass. 14.

Person includes an Indian as used in *United States Habeas Corpus* act. United States *v.* Crook, 5 Dill. (U. S.) 459. And in the Intercourse acts. United States *v.* Shaw-mux, 2 Sawy. (U. S.) 364.

As used in *New York* Code of Pro., § 497, means one or more, and should be read "person or persons." People *v.* Croton Aqueduct Board, 5 Abb. Pr. (N. Y.) 316. See also Chaput *v.* Robert, 14 Ont. App. 361. But see Denny *v.* Smith, 18 N. Y. 567.

The word "person" ordinarily includes both sexes. Brown *v.* Hemphill, 74 Ga. 795; Opinion of the Justices, 136 Mass. 580. See also Benney *v.* Globe Nat. Bank, 150 Mass. 581, where it was held to include married as well as single women. Matter of Hall, 50 Conn. 131.

Women are comprised in, and entitled to vote under, the phrase "every person of full age," § 22, Towns Improvement (Ireland) act, 1854. R. *v.* Crosthwaite, 17 Ir. C. L. Rep. 157.

In Billings *v.* State, 107 Ind. 54, it was held that the estate of a decedent was a person within the meaning of a statute, which forbids the forging of another's name with intent to defraud any "person."

A statute declaring the owner of a dog liable to any person injured by it, for the damage, includes injuries to property. "Person" should be understood as here used in its broad sense of "anybody," and not in distinction from property. Brewer *v.* Crosby, 11 Gray (Mass.) 29. See generally ANIMALS, vol. 1, p. 571.

The term "any person" in a statute prohibiting removal of soil, will include the owners of the soil, if it appears consonant to the purpose entertained by the legislature in passing the act. Commonwealth *v.* Tewksbury, 11 Met. (Mass.) 55.

A Partnership.—In Oak Ridge Coal Co. *v.* Rogers, 108 Pa. St. 147, it was held that a partnership association, limited, organized under the *Pennsylvania* act of June 2, 1874, which, by its agent, trespasses upon the land of another, is liable in an action to recover damages for such trespass under the provisions of the act of May 8, 1876, authorizing such an action against "any person or corporation," and that such an association was a *quasi* corporation, and as such was included in the designation "any person."

A Judge.—Person, as used in *Georgia* Code, § 4579, making it criminal for any person whatever to pursue his ordinary calling on the Lord's Day, applies to a judge holding court. Bass *v.* Irvin, 49 Ga. 436.

As used in the *Illinois* Rev. Stat. of 1874, ch. 62, § 1, regulating garnishments, person must be taken in a restricted sense, and does not apply to an executor, guardian, sheriff, clerk of court, receiver, trustee of insolvents, assignee in bankruptcy, municipal corporation, or common carrier. Michigan etc. R. Co. *v.* Chicago etc. R. Co., 1 Ill. App. 399.

Natural and Artificial Person (Distinguished).—The plain and broad distinction between a natural and an artificial person is, that whilst the former may do any act which he is not prohibited by law from doing, the latter can do none which the charter giving it existence does not expressly, or by fair inference, to enable it to perform its functions, authorize it to do; and when it transcends the limits within which it is confined by its charter, its acts are wholly void. Smith *v.* Alabama L. Ins. etc. Co., 4 Ala. 568.

Artificial person is a body politic deriving its existence and powers from legislation. United States *v.* Fox, 94 U. S. 315. See generally CORPORATION, vol. 4, p. 184, and kindred titles.

Person Interested.—See INTERESTED, vol. 11, p. 442.

As to Whether "Person" Includes a State or the United States, or a Foreign Country. — The decisions upon this question are not easily reconciled, but the better opinion seems to be that the word "person" does not in its ordinary or legal signification, embrace a State or government. Blair *v.* Worley, 2 Ill. 177; Alabama Certificates, 12 Op. Atty. Gen. 176; Taxation of State Railroads, 12 Op. Atty. Gen. 217; Matter of Fox's Will, 52 N. Y. 535; aff'd. 94 U. S. 315.

In that case the decedent has devised his realty, situate in New York, to the United States. *The New York* Statute of Wills provides that a devise of land may be made "to any person capable by law of holding real estate." It was held that the United States was not a "person" within the meaning of the statute, and could not take under the devise. The court, by FIELD, J., said: "The term 'person,' as here used applies to natural persons and also to artificial persons—bodies politic, deriving their existence and power from legislation—but cannot be so extended as to include within its meaning the Federal Government. It would require an express definition to that effect to give it a sense thus extended."

But in Indiana *v.* Warren, 2 Hill (N. Y.) 33, it was held that a State was a corporation and might be a party to a promissory note within the meaning of the Statute of *Anne*, which provides that "all notes in writing made and signed by any person," etc.

It was held that a State is a person within the meaning of a *Texas* statute forbidding the fraudulent alteration of a public record "with intent that any person may be defrauded." Martin *v.* State, 24 Tex. 61.

A *Kansas* act to prevent trespass makes it an offense for anyone to cut down, etc., any trees, etc., growing on the land of any other "person." *Held*, that the *United States* is a "person" within the meaning of the act. State *v.* Herold, 9 Kan. 134.

New York Co. Civ. Pro., § 3268, provides that a defendant may require security for costs from a plaintiff who is "a person residing without the State." *Held*, that a foreign country is a "person." Republic of Honduras *v.* Soto, 112 N. Y. 310.

As to Whether "Person" Includes a Corporation.—For a discussion of this question and for a collection of the cases, see FRANCHISES, vol. 8, p. 625. As is there stated, the word "person" is a generic term and *prima facie*, in a public statute, includes artificial as well as natural persons, unless it appears from the context that the word was used in a more limited sense.

Van Horne *v.* State, 5 Ark. 349; Douglass *v.* Pacific Mail etc. Co., 4 Cal. 304; South Western R. Co. *v.* Paulk, 24 Ga. 356; McIntire *v.* State, 10 Ill. 48; North Western Mo. R. Co. *v.* Akers, 4 Kan. 435; La Farge *v.* Exchange Ins. Co., 22 N. Y. 352; Field *v.* New York Cent. R. Co., 29 Barb. (N. Y.) 176; Carey *v.* Marston, 56 Barb. (N. Y.) 27; United States Tel. Co. *v.* Western Union Tel. Co., 56 Barb. (N. Y.) 46; M'Queen *v.* Middletown Mfg. Co., 16 Johns. (N. Y.) 5; St. Michael's *v.* Connolly, Bright. (Pa.) 21; Baltimore etc. R. Co. *v.* Gallahue, 12 Gratt. (Va.) 655; Miller *v.* Commonwealth, 27 Gratt. (Va.) 110; *Re* Oregon etc. Co., 13 Nat. Bankr. Reg. 199; Pharmaceutical Soc. *v.* London etc. Assoc., 5 App. Cas. 857.

In the leading English case upon this word, Pharmaceutical Soc. *v.* London etc. Assoc., 5 App. Cas. (Eng.) 857, Ld. Blackburn, said: "The word 'person' may very well include both a natural person (a human being) and an artificial person (a corporation). I think that in an act of Parliament, unless there be something to the contrary, probably (I would not like to pledge myself to that) it ought to be held to include both. I have equally no doubt in common talk, in the language of men (not speaking technically), a 'person' does not include a corporation. . . . It is plain that in common speech 'person' would mean a natural person. In technical language it may include the other, but which meaning it has in any particular act, must depend upon the context subject matter. I do not think that the presumption that it includes an artificial person— a corporation—(if the presumption does arise) —is at all strong."

A corporation has been held to be a "person" within the meaning of statutes applying to the following matters:

To Usury.—Thornton *v.* Bank of Washington, 3 Pet. (U. S.) 36; Commercial Bank *v.* Nolan, 7 How. (Miss.) 508; Grand Gulf Bank *v.* Archer, 8 Smed. & M. (Miss.) 151.

To Limitation of Actions.—People *v.* Trinity Church, 22 N. Y. 44; Thompson *v.* Tioga R. Co., 36 Barb. (N. Y.) 79; Alcott *v.* Tioga R. Co., 20 N. Y. 210; North Missouri R. Co. *v.* Akers, 4 Kan. 453.

To Taxation.—Louisville etc. R. Co. *v.* Commonwealth, 1 Bush (Ky.) 250; People *v.* Commissioners of Taxes, 23 N. Y. 242; British etc. L. Ins. Co. *v.* Commissioners of Taxes, 31 N. Y. 32. See also People *v.* M'Lean, 80 N. Y. 259. But see School Directors *v.* Carlisle Bank, 8 Watts (Pa.) 289; Savings Fund *v.* Yard, 8 Pa. St. 359; Fox's Appeal, 112 Pa. St. 351.

Attachments.—Planters' etc. Bank *v.* Andrews, 8 Port. (Ala.) 404; South Carolina R. Co. *v.* McDonald, 5 Ga. 531; Bray *v.* Wallingford, 20 Conn. 418; Flagg *v.* Platt, 32 Conn. 216; Knox *v.* Protection Ins. Co., 9 Conn. 430; 25 Am. Dec. 33; Union Bank *v.* United States Bank, 4 Humph. (Tenn.) 369; Libby *v.* Hodgdon, 9 N. H. 394; Martin *v.* Branch Bank, 14 La. 415; United States Bank *v.* Merchants' Bank, 1 Rob. (Va.) 573. But see M'Queen *v.* Middleton Mfg. Co., 16 Johns. (N. Y.) 5; Mayor etc. of Baltimore *v.* Root, 8 Md. 95.

To Qualifying a Person to Testify in His Own Behalf. — Within the meaning of *New York* act qualifying a party to testify in his own behalf when the other party is a "living person," it was held that a corporation was included within the phrase "living person." La Farge *v.* Exchange F. Ins. Co., 22 N. Y. 352; Field *v.* New York Cent. R. Co., 29 Barb. (N. Y.) 176; Johnson *v.* McIntosh, 31 Barb. (N. Y.) 267; Wallace *v.* Mayor etc. of New York, 2 Hilt. (N. Y.) 440.

United States Statutes — 14th Amendment.—The word "person," as used in the 14th amendment prohibiting the States from denying to any "person" the equal protection of the laws, includes a corporation. Pembina etc. Min. Co. *v.* Pennsylvania, 125 U. S. 180; Santa Clara Co. *v.* Southern Pac. R. Co., 118 U. S. 394; 24 Am. & Eng. R. Cas. 523; Minneapolis etc. R. Co. *v.* Beckwith, 129 U. S. 26.

And so a corporation was held to be included in the word "person" in the Civil Rights act of Congress of April 20, 1871. Northwestern Fertilizing Co. *v.* Hyde Park, 3 Biss. (U. S.) 480.

The United States Crimes act of the 26th of March, 1804, ch. 393, § 2, provides, that if any person shall on the high seas willfully and corruptly cast away, etc., any ship or vessel of which he is the owner in part or in whole, with design to prejudice "any person or persons" who have underwritten the said vessel, he shall be deemed guilty of felony. The term "person or persons" extends to corporations and bodies politic as well as to natural persons. United States *v.* Amedy, 11 Wheat. (U. S.) 392.

To Miscellaneous Matters.—In a statute against trespassers it was held that "person" included a railroad company and that the act rendered such a company liable as a trespasser. Bartee *v.* Houston etc. R. Co., 36 Tex. 648.

In People *v.* May, 27 Barb. (N. Y.) 238, it was held that "person" includes a corporation within the meaning of an act which gave the right of appeal from an order made by a commissioner of highways, for laying out a highway.

Within the meaning of a clause in a treaty against confiscation and prosecution directed against any "person," a corporation is to be deemed a "person." Society for Propagation of the Gospel *v.* New Haven, 8 Wheat. (U. 464.

And in the following cases "person," as used in various statutes, was held to include a corporation. Union Steamship Co. *v.* Melbourne Harbor Comms., 9 App. Cas. 365; People *v.* Riverside, 66 Cal. 288; Ricker *v.* American Loan etc. Co., 140 Mass. 346; Dickie *v.* Boston etc. R. Co., 131 Mass. 516; Greene Foundation *v.* Boston, 12 Cush. (Mass.) 59; Turnbull *v.* Prentiss Lumber Co., 55 Mich. 393; Billings *v.* State, 107 Ind. 546; Stewart *v.* Waterloo Turn Verein, 71 Iowa 226; 60 Am. Rep. 786; Wales *v.* Muscatine, 4 Iowa 302; Norris *v.* State, 25 Ohio St. 217; Springfield *v.* Walker, 42 Ohio St. 543; First Nat. Bank *v.* Loyhed, 28 Minn. 396; Forest *v.* Henry, 33 Minn. 434; Fagan *v.* Boyle Ice Mach. Co., 65 Tex. 331; Chippeway Valley etc. R. Co. *v.* Chicago etc. R. Co., 75 Wis. 253.

"Person" held not to include a corporation. Where a statute creates an offense against any "private person," it does not apply to a municipal corporation. Coates *v.* People, 22 N. Y. 245.

In a statute providing for proceedings against a defendant abroad, it has been held that "person" does not apply to a corporation. Valoney *v.* Sydney, 2 Nova Scotia Dec.

A corporation is not a person within the English Mortmain act. 9 Ges. II, ch. 36, §. 1; Walker *v.* Richardson, 2 M. & W. 882.

It has been held that a corporation is not a person within an *English* statute giving the penalties imposed for certain offenses to "the person or persons who shall inform and sue for the same." Guardians of St. Leonard *v.* Franklin, 3 C. P. Div. 377; 30 Moak Rep. 287.

And for other cases holding that, in particular statutes, "person" does not include a corporation. See School Directors *v.* Carlisle Bank, 8 Watts (Pa.) 289; Savings Fund *v.* Goeth, 8 Pa. St. 359; Fox's Appeal, 112 Pa. St. 351; Pharmaceutical Soc. *v.* London etc. Assoc., 5 App. Cas. 857; Ingate *v.* Loyd, 4 C. B., N. S. 704; McQueen *v.* Middleton Mfg. Co., 16 Johns. (N. Y.) 5; Mayor etc. of Baltimore *v.* Rost, 8 Md. 95.

Personal Action.—A personal action is one brought for damages or other redress for breach of contract, or for injuries of every other description; the specific recovery of lands, tenements and hereditaments only excepted. Boyd *v.* Cronan, 71 Me. 287, *citing*, Bouvier's L. Dict. And in that case trespass *quare clausum fregit* was held to be such an action.

Personal actions are such whereby a man claims a debt or personal duty, or damage in lieu thereof. Reeves *v.* Brown, 2 Penn. L. J. 200.

A *Massachusetts* Stat. permits all controversies which may be "the subject of a personal action at law or of a suit in equity," to be submitted to arbitration. In Osborn *v.* Fall River, 140 Mass. 508, plaintiff claimed that the proceedings by which he was entitled to assert his claim for damages, when the city, exercising a lawful authority, changed the grade of the street near his premises, might properly be termed a personal action. The court by DEVENS, J. said: "Personal actions are those which are brought for the recovery of a debt, or damages for a breach of contract, or for a specified personal chattel, or for satisfaction in damages because of some injury to the person or personal or real property," *citing*, Chit. Pl. (16th Am. ed.) 142. "They are divided by the statute into three classes—actions of contract, of tort, and of replevin. Within neither can be included the right which the plaintiff had to proceed for damages, if injury was occasioned to his premises by change of the grade of the streets upon which his estate abutted."

As used in a *Wisconsin* statute designating the manner in which a mechanic's lien may be enforced against a debtor, it was held not to mean "the ordinary action *in personam* for the recovery of a sum of money, or damages against the debtor." Dewey *v.* Fifield, 2 Wis. 73; Dean *v.* Wheeler, 2 Wis. 224; Wright *v.* Allen, 26 Wis. 661.

Personal Annuities. — See LEGACIES AND DEVISES, vol. 13, p. 15.

Personal Goods. — The term "personal goods," as used in the Crimes Act of Congress of 1790, ch. 36, § 16, which provides that if any one shall steal, etc., the "personal goods" of another, within the exclusive jurisdiction of the United States, he shall be subject to punishment, does not include choses in action. United States *v.* Davis, 5 Mason (U. S.) 356.

It does include bank-notes, money and coin. United States *v.* Murray, 1 Cranch (C. C.) 141; United States *v.* Moulton, 5 Mason (U. S.) 537, 540.

Under a statute designating "personal goods" as a subject of larceny, dogs untaxed are not included. State *v.* Doe, 79 Ind. 9; 41 Am. Rep. 599. See generally ANIMALS, vol. 1. p. 571.

As to the effect of the term on margin of a bill of lading, see The Elvira Harbeck, 2 Blatchf. (U. S.) 336.

In re Butler (38 ch. D. 290), COTTON, L. J., in discussing the meaning to be attached to the words "personal goods," as used by Coke, in Co. Litt. 185 b, said that the words did not mean all personal property whatsoever; but only "that property which passes by hand, and property which marriage passed from the wife to the husband."

"**Personal Judgment.**"—As used in a *Minnesota* statute, providing for service of summons in an action to foreclose a mortgage, *held* to mean a money judgment for the mortgage debt. Bardwell *v.* Anderson (Minn. 1890), 46 N. W. Rep. 315.

Personal Representative.—The words "personal representative" must, in the absence of other controlling words, be taken to mean person claiming as executor or administrator. Wyndam's Trusts, L. R., 1 Eq. Cas. 293.

An executor (though he has not taken probate) of a surviving trustee, is such trustee's "personal representative" within §§ 25, 13 and 14 Vict., ch. 60; *Re* Ellis, 24 Bea. 426.

The executor or administrator, except in special cases, represents the deceased only as to the personal estate, and, hence, is denominated the "personal representative," while the heir at law, though not technically so denominated, is equally the representative as to the real estate. Card *v.* Card, 39 N. Y. 317.

The words "representative" or "legal representative," or "personal representative" primarily mean executors and administrators, and in order to put any other meaning on them, you must find in the context some special reason for so doing. Stockdale *v.* Nicholson, L. R., 4 Eq. Cas. 367.

So the term does not include the widow. Hagen *v.* Keen, 3 Dill. (U. S.) 124. Nor the heirs or devisees of land. Anderson *v.* Austin, 34 Barb. (N. Y.) 319. Nor does it include an agent. Jones *v.* Tainter, 15 Minn. 512; Atkinson *v.* Duffy, 16 Minn. 45.

But it may be shown by the context to mean descendants of children of testatrix. Rainford *v.* Nose, 59 L. T. 359. Or next of kin. Davies *v.* Davies, 55 Conn. 319; *Re* Stroud, W. N. (74) 180; *Re* Gryll's Trusts, L. R., Eq. 589. Or when used in a deed, those who succeed the grantee in the title of the lands. Woodruff *v.* Woodruff, 1 L. R. Ann. 380. See also LEGAL, vol. 3, p. 221.

See generally EXECUTORS AND ADMINISTRATORS, vol. 7, p. 165.

Personal Services.—Under a statute giving lumbermen a lien on lumber cut and hauled by them for their "personal services," it has been held that there is no lien for labor performed by their servants and teams. Hale *v.* Brown, 59 N. H. 551; 47 Am. Rep. 224. See also Coburn *v.* Kerswell, 35 Me. 126; McCrillis *v.* Wilson, 34 Me. 286. See also LOGS AND LUMBER, vol. 13, p. 1040.

Personal Securities.—The power to invest in "personal securities" embraces power to purchase a bill of exchange. Gee *v.* Alabama L. Ins. etc. Co., 13 Ala. 581. See generally INVESTMENTS, vol. 11, p. 815.

Personal Tax.—A personal tax is the burden imposed by a government upon its own citizens for the benefits which that government affords by its protection and its laws. State *v.* Ross, 23 N. J. L. 521. See generally TAXATION.

Personal Transaction.—As to what is a "personal transaction" within the meaning of § 829, *New York* Co. Civ. Pro., which declares: "Upon the trial of an action, . . . a party or person interested in the event . . . shall not be examined as a witness in his own behalf or interest, . . . against . . . a person deriving

PERSONAL ANNUITIES.—See LEGACIES AND DEVISES, vol. 13, p. 15.

PERSON AGGRIEVED—(See also AGGRIEVED, vol. 1, p. 449; AGGRIEVED PERSON, vol. 1, p. 450; NEW TRIAL; PARTY AGGRIEVED; PARTIES TO ACTIONS).—See note 1.

PERSONAL INJURIES.—See COMPARATIVE NEGLIGENCE, vol. 3, p. 367; CONTRIBUTORY NEGLIGENCE, vol. 4, p. 15; DAMAGES, vol. 5, pp. 40, 68; DEATH, vol. 5, p. 125; FELLOW SERVANTS, vol. 7, p. 821; LIVERY STABLE KEEPERS, vol 13, p. 942; MASTER AND SERVANT, vol. 14, p. 740; NEGLIGENCE, vol. 16, p. 386; and cross-references under that title.

PERSONAL LIBERTY.—See CONSTITUTIONAL LAW, vol. 3, pp. 726, 729; EXTRADITION, vol. 7, p. 603; HABEAS CORPUS, vol. 9, p. 161; IMPRISONMENT, vol. 10, p. 197; IMPRISONMENT FOR DEBT, vol. 10, p. 212; LIBERTY, vol. 13, p. 505; POLICE POWER.

PERSONAL PROPERTY—(See for cross-references the notes to this article).

I. **DEFINITION AND NATURE OF PERSONAL PROPERTY.**—Personal property embraces all objects and rights which are capable of ownership, except freehold estates in land, and incorporeal hereditaments issuing thereout, or exercisable within the same.[2] The words are co-extensive with "chattels," which are divided into .

his title or interest from, through or under a deceased person, by assignment or otherwise, concerning a personal transaction or communication between the witness and the deceased person." See Doolittle *v.* Stone (Supreme Ct.), 8 N. Y. Supp. 605; Van Gelder *v.* Van Gelder, 81 N. Y. 128 *In re* Page, 6 Alb. L. J. 126; Howell *v.* Taylor, 11 Hun (N. Y.) 214. For a general treatment of this and of corresponding provisions in other States, see WITNESS.

1. See the following additional cases upon this subject: Woodward *v.* Spear, 10 Vt. 420; Hemmenway *v.* Corey, 16 Vt. 225; O'Rourke *v.* Elsbree, 11 R. I. 430; Pierce *v.* Gould, 143 Mass 234; Chicago etc. R. Co. *v.* People, 24 Ill. App. 562; Martin *v.* Gage, 147 Mass. 204; Dexter *v.* Codman, 148 Mass. 421, Morrow *v.* Wood, 56 Ala. 1; Masterson *v.* Gibson, 56 Ala 57; Porter *v.* United States, 2 Paine (U. S.) 315; Grove's Case, L. R., 4 Q. B. 715; *Re* Woods, 11 Ch. Div. 56; *Re* Tucker, 12 Ch. Div. 308; *Re* White, 14 Ch. Div. 71; Rex *v.* Justices, 3 B. & Ad. 938; Johnson *v.* Mayor etc. of Crogdon, 16 Q. B. Div. 708; *In re* Payne, 18 Q. B. Div. 154.

2. Brantly's Pers. Prop. 5.

1. Chattels real or interests which are annexed to or concern real estate; and

2. Chattels personal, which include every species of property lacking the two characteristics of real estate; viz, immobility as to place, and indeterminate duration as to time, and such as is not amended to real estate.[1] The latter are again subdivided into:

a. Corporeal things or "choses in possession," which include all things which, being themselves capable of motion or of being moved, may be perceived by the senses—seen, touched, taken possession of—in short, live stock or dead, manufactured goods or raw material, everything capable of touch and not fixed to the soil.[2]

b. Incorporeal—Choses in Actions.—Things incorporeal, a man has not the occupation but merely a bare right to occupy the thing in question, the possession whereof may, however, be recovered by a suit or action in law; whence the thing so recoverable is called a thing or chose in action.[3]

II. **KINDS OF PERSONAL PROPERTY.**—There are certain kinds of personal property which are more closely allied than others to real property and are subject to some of the rules governing the latter. These are 1. Heir-looms, which are such personal chattels as descend to the heir along with the inheritance.[4]

2. Title deeds, keys, etc., also go to the one who is entitled to the land.[5]

3. Growing crops which, upon the death of the person who planted them, pass to his executor and not to his heir, and are ordinarily treated as personalty.[6]

4. Emblements which are the right of a tenant to the profit of his crop after termination of his estate.[7]

5. Fixtures are those personal chattels which a temporary occupier has annexed to the land, and which he or his representatives may afterwards sever and remove against the will of the owner or successor to the freehold.[8]

6. Among other special kinds of personal property, tame animals may be held by an absolute property, and animals *feræ naturæ* by a qualified right.[9]

7. Property in ships is governed by peculiar laws of registry, etc.[10]

1. Schouler's Pers. Prop. 22, 51.
2. Goodeve's Pers. Prop. 8.
3. 2 Bl. Com. 396. See CHATTELS, vol. 3, p. 163; CHOSES IN ACTION, vol. 3, p. 235.
4. See HEIRLOOMS, vol. 9, p. 357.
5. See KEY, vol. 12, p. 518; TITLE.
6. See CROPS, vol. 4, p. 887. On a sale of real estate to pay debts of an intestate, wood cut and corded on the land and crops growing when the petition is filed do not pass. Barrett *v.* Choen (Ind.), 20 N. E. Rep. 145.
7. See EMBLEMENTS.
8. See FIXTURES, vol. 8, p. 41.
9. See ANIMALS, vol. 1, p. 571.
10. See SHIPPING.

8. Money is a species of personal property of unusual significance.[1]

Of special kinds of incorporeal chattels may be mentioned, 1. Negotiable paper;[2] 2. Insurance policies and annuities;[3] 3. Patents, copyrights, and trade mark;[4] 4. Seats in exchanges;[5] 5. Debts and demands, including the law of guaranty and suretyship;[6] 6. Shares of stock;[7] 7. Good will, names, etc.[8]

III. **Manner of Ownership.**—Personal property, like real, may belong either to one owner or to several holding the relation of

1. Joint tenants or tenants in common;[9] 2. Partners;[10] 3. Part owners of ships;[11] 4. Members of corporations and joint stock companies.[12] It is subject also to peculiar laws respecting married persons,[13] infants,[14] and aliens.[15]

IV. **Time of Enjoyment.**—The doctrine of interests or estates in expectancy has come at last to be applied with much the same force to personal as to real property, and interests for life or years may be created in various ways, followed by an expectant estate in the nature of a remainder or reversion.[16] This is frequently accomplished by means of trusts and settlements;[17] the rule against perpetuities also applies to personal property.[18]

V. **Title to Personal Property** may be acquired by—

1. **Occupancy.**—Occupancy or the taking of possession with the intent to appropriate them, of things which before be-

1. Schouler's Pers. Prop. 395. See MONEY, 15, p. 701.

2. See BILLS AND NOTES, vol. 2, p. 313; CHECKS, vol. 3, p. 211; NEGOTIABLE INSTRUMENTS, vol. 16, p. 478.

3. See INSURANCE, vol. 11, p. 278; ANNUITIES, vol. 1, p. 592.

4. See PATENT LAW, vol. 18, p. 20; COPYRIGHT, vol. 4, p. 147; TRADE MARK.

5. See STOCK EXCHANGE.

6. See DEBTS, vol. 5, p. 163; DEBTOR AND CREDITOR, vol. 5, p. 179; JUDGMENT, vol. 12, p. 58; PLEDGE; SURETYSHIP; GUARANTY, vol. 9, p. 67.

7. Tregear *v.* Etiwanda Water Co., 76 Cal. 537. See PLEDGE; STOCK.

8. See GOOD-WILL, vol. 8, p. 1366; NAMES, vol. 16, p. 112; TRADE MARK.

9. See JOINT TENANTS, vol. 11, p. 1057. Personal property willed to several legatees to be divided among them, will vest in them without partition or judicial distribution; and it is competent for them to hold it in common so long as they may agree, subject to the payment of debts of the estate and of any provisions of the will charged upon it. Baskin *v.* Hays, 12 N. Y. Supp. 632.

10. See PARTNERSHIP.

11. See SHIPPING.

12. See CORPORATIONS, vol. 4, p. 184; JOINT STOCK COMPANIES, vol. 11, p. 1036.

13. See HUSBAND AND WIFE, vol. 9, p. 789; MARRIED WOMEN, vol. 14, p 589.

14. See INFANTS, vol. 10, p. 613.

15. See ALIEN, vol. 1, p. 456.

16. Schouler's Pers. Prop. 151 See Wilmoth *v.* Wilmoth (W. Va.), 12 S. E. Rep. 731.

A life estate in personal property gives the donee a right to consume such articles as cannot be enjoyed without consuming them, and to wear out such as are necessarily destroyed by use. Walker *v.* Pritchard, 121 Ill. 221. See REMAINDER; REVERSION; ESTATES, vol. 6, p. 875.

17. See TRUSTS; SETTLEMENTS; MARRIAGE SETTLEMENTS, vol. 14, p. 538. But in such settlements the rules derived from and applicable to inheritable tenures do not apply, as, for example, where the word "heirs" is *held* in a real conveyance a word of limitation. Pillot *v.* Landon, 46 N. J. Eq. 310.

18. See PERPETUITIES.

longed to nobody or of things abandoned or lost by unknown owners.[1]

2. Possession.—Title by possession comprises two elements; (a) a physical condition—that corporeal relation to the thing which makes it possible for one to dispose of and control it; (b) a will directed to the thing; viz, the intention to possess it as owner of the *animus domini.*[2]

3. Accession and Confusion.—Accession, where the original owner of a corporeal substance that receives an addition by natural or artificial means not changing it into a new species, is entitled to the chattels in its improved condition; and confusion, which arises where the like chattels of several persons are so mixed as to be undistinguishable.[3]

4. Gift.—Title may arise by gift accompanied by delivery of possession.[4]

5. Deed.—Title may arise by deed, the important condition of which supplies the want of delivery and of actual consideration.[5]

6. Sale.—Title may also arise by sale, the common method of alienation.[6]

7. Devolution on Death.—Title also arises by the devolution of property by will or intestacy on the death of the owner.[7]

VI. Incidents Connected with Personal Property.—Various matters that affect the possession or ownership of personal property which are treated under their proper titles and need only be mentioned here are · 1. Bankruptcy, insolvency and assignments;[8]

1. 2 Bl. Com. 258. See Occupancy. The owner of personal property can be divested of his title only by his own act; and the fact that the purchaser had no notice of such title does not alter the rule. Velsian *v* Lewis, 15 Oregon 539.

2. Brantly's Pers. Prop 220. See Possession. Possession of personal property is *prima facie* title thereto. Crawford *v.* Kimbrough, 76 Ga. 299. But if the custody and possession of such property is shown to be equally consistent with an outstanding ownership in a third person as with a title in the one having possession, no presumption of ownership arises solely from such possession. Lowery *v.* Erskine, 113 N. Y. 52. The delivery of the possession of inclosed land carries with it the possession of personal property thereon. Lerraris *v.* Kyle, 19 Nev. 435.

Scraping off snow from the surface of the ice in a public pond and driving stakes to indicate where the line of scraping is, gives a person no title or ght o possession to the ice included within the stakes, and no action will lie against another for cutting and removing such ice. People's Ice Co. *v.* Davenport, 149 Mass. 322. See Ice and Ice Companies, vol. 9. p. 852

3. See Accession, vol. 1, p. 50.

4. See Gift, vol. 8, p. 1308.

5. See Deed, vol. 5, p. 423. See *Re* Patrick (1891), 1 Ch. Div. 82, which appears to overrule some earlier decisions.

6. See Sale.

7. See Wills; Statutes of Distribution; Legacies and Devises, vol. 13, p. 7. Rents accruing on devised real estate during the year in which the testator died are a part of the personal property and do not go to the devisee. Parker *v.* Chestnutt, 80 Ga. 12.

8. See Bankruptcy, vol. 2, p. 67; Insolvency, vol. 11, p. 167; Assignment, vol. 1, p. 826; Assignment for Benefit of Creditors, vol. 1, p. 845

2. Arbitration;[1] 3. Mortgage;[2] 4. Bailment and pledge;[3] 5. Lien;[4] 6. Insurance;[5] 7. Interest;[6] 8. Fraud;[7] 9. Taxation.[8]

VII. Actions Concerning and Offenses Against Personal Property.—For the treatment of the various actions connected with personal property, reference may be had to the titles of the different personal actions;[9] offenses connected with personal property are matters properly relating to criminal law.[10] As connected with these matters, see also DAMAGES,[11] LIMITATION OF ACTIONS.

VIII. Conflict of Laws.—The variation of the law governing personal property in different States and countries is treated elsewhere.[12]

PERSONATION.—See FALSE PERSONATION, vol. 7, p. 695.

PERSUADE.—See note 13.

PERTAINING.—See note 14.

PERVERSE VERDICT.—When a jury choose not to take the law from the judge, but will act on their own erroneous view of the law. In such cases, however honest the intentions of the jury may be, their verdict is perverse.[15]

PETITION.—An instrument in writing or printing, containing a prayer from the person presenting it, called the petitioner, to the body or person to whom it is presented, for the redress of some wrong or the grant of some favor which the latter has a right to give.[16]

1. See ARBITRATION AND AWARD, vol. 1, p. 646.

2. See MORTGAGES, vol. 15, p. 725; CHATTEL MORTGAGES, vol. 3, p. 175.

3. See BAILMENT, vol. 2, p. 40; PLEDGE.

4. See LIEN, vol. 13, p. 574.

5. See INSURANCE, vol. 11, p. 278.

6. See INTEREST, vol. 11, p. 379.

7. See FRAUD, vol. 8, p. 635.

8. See TAXATION.

9. See ASSUMPSIT, vol. 1, p. 882; DEBT, vol. 5, p. 163; DETINUE, vol. 5, p. 651; TRESPASS; TROVER; REPLEVIN; CONVERSION, vol. 4, p. 104, etc.

10. See CRIMINAL LAW, vol. 4, p. 641; LARCENY, vol. 12, p. 760; EMBEZZLEMENT, vol. 6, p. 450; BURGLARY, vol. 2, p. 659; ROBBERY, RECEIVING STOLEN PROPERTY, etc.

11. Recovering judgment for damages for injuries causing a total loss of personal property does not give the defendant a title to the property. Dow *v.* King, 52 Ark. 282.

12. See CONFLICT OF LAWS, vol. 3, p. 567.

13. To "inveigle, persuade, or entice" a child into involuntary servitude, necessarily implies assent yielded as the result of the persuading or enticing, by whomsoever the influence is brought to bear, whether by parents, uncles, or others. United States *v.* Aucarola, 17 Blatchf. (U. S.) 423, 430.

14. In a statute giving the right of suffrage to women at elections "pertaining" to school matters, it was held, that an election for the choosing of any school officers, or school employes, would be an election "pertaining to school matters," and that the choosing or selecting of any other officers is not an "election pertaining to school matters," within the meaning of the act. Brown *v.* Phillips, 71 Wis. 239.

15. Saunders *v.* Davies, 14 Eng. L. & Eq. 532. See also VERDICT.

16. Bouv. Law Dict. followed in Eustis *v.* Holmes, 48 Miss. 36.

In Equity. — Interlocutory applications, when made *viva voce* to the court, are called motions; when they are made in writing, they are called petitions. There does not appear to be any very distinct line of demarkation between the cases in which they should be made by motion and those in which

PETROLEUM.—See OIL.

PETTIFOGGING.—See note 1.

PEWS—(See also CEMETERIES, vol. 3, p. 49; RELIGIOUS SOCIETIES.)

they should be made by petition; but, as a general rule, where any long or intricate statement of facts is required, the application should be made by petition; while, in other cases, a motion will be sufficient. 2 Dan. Ch. Pr. 1587.

A petition is the proper course to obtain a reversal of an interlocutory decree, wrongfully made, the cause yet pending. It cannot be done on motion, or bill of review. Wilcox *v.* McLain, 2 Hayw. (N. Car.) 175. *Cited* in 2 Dan. Ch. Pr. 1587.

It would seem that ordinarily proceedings in equity, in States where the equity and common law jurisdictions are still distinct, cannot be instituted by petition, the proper method being by bill filed.

In Receiver of State Bank *v* First Nat. Bank, 34 N. J. Eq. 457, which was a suit by the receiver of an insolvent bank to recover moneys of the bank received by one of its creditors, subsequently to his appointment, the court by VAN FLEET V. C. said: "But if my judgment was for the petitioner on all points, I think it is clear, according to the established practice of the court, that the court could give the petitioner no relief on the present record. He is here by petition, and not by bill. So far as I am aware, no instance exists in which relief of the character sought, and on a case similar to that exhibited here, has been awarded on a petition. It is undoubtedly true that there are cases in which a suitor may institute a suit or proceedings in this court by petition, but I think the use of such process, for such a purpose, must be held to be limited to those instances in which the legislature has expressly authorized its use, or where its use has the sanction of long established practice. Suits for divorce may be commenced by petition, and so may a suit to procure an adjudication of insolvency against a corporation, and proceedings for the sale of lands limited over may be begun in the same manner. And by the long established practice of the court, infants may have guardians assigned for them, and orders for maintenance made, under proceedings instituted by petition and without bill. *Ex parte* Salter, 3 Br. C. C. 500; *Ex parte* Mountfort, 15 Ves. 445; *In re* Bostwick, 4 Johns. Ch. (N. Y.) 100. Except in these and a few other instances, I think the use of a petition as the initial process in an equity suit or proceeding is without precedent, and contrary to the uniform course of practice. It is ordinarily used for interlocutory purposes."

In Codwise *v.* Gelston, 10 Johns. (N. Y.) 521, the court, by KENT, CH. J., said: "It may be difficult to draw a precise line between cases in which a party may be relieved upon petition, and in which he must apply more formally by bill. Petitions are generally for things which are matters of course, or upon some collateral matter which has reference to a suit in court. . . . The mode of application depends very much upon the discretion of the court."

See generally, EQUITY PLEADING, vol. 6, p. 724.

Distinguished from Motion.—A petition, in common phrase is a request in writing; and, in legal language describes an application to a court in writing, in contradistinction to a motion which may be made *viva voce.* Shaft *v.* Phoenix etc. Ins. Co., 67 N. Y. 547; 23 Am. Rep. 138; Bergen *v.* Jones, 4 Met. (Mass.) 371.

In Code Practice.—A petition is, under code practice, the first pleading filed by a plaintiff wherein he states the facts of his case as they actually occurred. Anderson's L. Dict., *citing* Atchinson etc. R. Co. *v.* Rice, 36 Kan. 599; Taylor *v.* Miles (Oregon, 1890), 25 Pac. Rep. 143. See generally, PLEADING.

1. In an action of libel, it was said, that the designation "pettifogging shys-

I. **Definition.**—The word "pew" is said to be derived from "puye" and to signify a seat inclosed in a church.[1]

II. **Rights of Pew Holders—1. Nature of the Right.**—In considering pew holder's distinctive rights as the owner of a pew, care must be taken not to confuse them with any rights which he may have as a member of the religious society, which latter will be fully treated under another title.[2]

A pew holder has a right to the exclusive occupation and use of his pew upon those occasions for which pews are designed to be used.[3] This right to use and occupation is by some writers termed an easement.[4]

ter" must mean an unscrupulous practitioner who disgraces his profession by doing mean work, and resorts to sharp practice to do it." Bailey *v.* Kalamazoo Pub. Co., 40 Mich. 256.

1. Brumfitt *v.* Roberts, L. R., 5 C. P. 224.

Pews constitute a subject of peculiar ownership. They are defined to be inclosed seats in churches, and it is said that according to modern use and idea they were not known till long after the Reformation, and that inclosed pews were not in general use before the middle of the seventeenth century, being for a long time confined to the family of the patron. Hook's Church Dict., tit. Pews, quoted in O'Hear *v.* De Goesbriand, 33 Vt. 593; 80 Am. Dec. 652.

2. See Religious Societies.

3. Gay *v.* Baker, 17 Mass. 435; 9 Am. Dec. 159; Kimball *v.* Second Parish, 24 Pick. (Mass.) 349; First Baptist Society *v.* Grant, 59 Me. 245; Kellog *v.* Dickinson, 18 Vt. 266; O'Hear *v.* Goesbriand, 33 Vt. 892; 80 Am. Dec. 652.

A pewholder's right is only a right to occupy his pew during public worship; and, when the meeting house is in such ruinous condition that it cannot be and is not occupied for public worship, he can recover only nominal damages for injury to his pew. Howe *v.* Stevens, 47 Vt. 262.

Where a meeting house is conveyed to trustees for the use of a certain church and society, for a place of public religious worship for such church and society, and for no other use, intent or purpose whatsoever, and in the deeds of the pews in such house, which are given to an individual, the provisions of the conveyance of the house are referred to and recognized, the pew owner has a right to the sole use of his pews on all occasions when the house is occupied, though it be opened for purposes different from those mentioned in the conveyance thereof; and he has a right to exclude all others from his pew, on such occasions, by fastening the pew doors, or otherwise, in such manner as not to interrupt or annoy those who may occupy other pews; and any person who enters such pew knowing the facts, is a trespasser, and liable to an action by the owner. But *quaere* as to the right of pew holders, generally, to the exclusive occupation of their pews when the church is used for other purposes than religious services. For the court by Shaw, C. J., said: "This case hardly raises any question as to the general rights of the holders of pews in meeting-houses, as the meeting-house in question, and the land on which it stands, are held under an indenture of four parts, very elaborately drawn, the general tenor of which is, that the premises shall be held and improved for the use of a Baptist meeting-house, for public worship only." Jackson *v.* Rounseville, 5 Met. (Mass.) 132.

4. Washburne on Easem. 515; Union House *v.* Rowell, 66 Me. 402; First Baptist Society *v.* Grant, 59 Me. 251.

But it may be doubted whether the right of a pew holder to his pew is an easement unless it is appurtenant to some dominant tenement. Rights of Pew Holders by J. A. Seddon, 15 Cent. L. J. 101; Beach on Priv. Corp. 81.

In O'Hear *v.* De Goesbriand, 33 Vt. 606; 80 Am. Dec. 652, the court by Kellogg, J., said: "In *England* the right of property in a pew is a mere easement or incorporeal right, and hence the English doctrine that case only will lie for the disturbance of the occupant. . . . But in this country the owner of the pew has an exclusive

It is a qualified interest, subject to the rights of the religious society owning the land and building,[1] and is necessarily limited in point of time, for if the house be burnt or destroyed by time, the right is gone.[2]

It is now settled that, in the absence of statutory provisions,[3]

right to its possession and enjoyment for the purpose of public worship, not as an easement, but by virtue of an individual right of property derived, in theory at least, from the proprietors of the edifice or freehold, and hence trespass *quare clausum* lies for a violation of the owner's right of possession." See also Show *v.* Beveridge, 3 Hill (N. Y.) 26; 38 Am. Dec. 616.

1. First Baptist Society *v.* Grand, 59 Me. 251; Abernethey *v.* Society of the Church of the Puritans, 3 Daly (N. Y.) 1; Freligh *v.* Platt, 5 Cow. (N. Y.) 494; Erwin *v.* Hurd, 13 Abb. N. Cas. (N. Y.) 96; Kimball *v.* Second Parish, 24 Pick. (Mass.) 349; Daniel *v.* Wood, 1 Pick. (Mass.) 104; 11 Am. Dec. 151; Church *v.* Wells, 24 Pa. St. 249; Sohier *v.* Trinity Church, 109 Mass. 21.

Pews are held by very peculiar titles. They constitute a qualified and usufructuary right, being a right to occupy under certain restrictions. Sohier *v.* Trinity Church, 109 Mass. 21.

"The right to a pew is property of a peculiar nature, derivative and dependent. It is an exclusive right to occupy a particular portion of a house of public worship, under certain restrictions." SHAW, C. J., in Attorney General *v.* Federal St. Meeting-house, 3 Gray (Mass.) 45.

2. Abernethey *v.* Society of the Church of the Puritans, 3 Daly (N. Y.) 1; Freligh *v.* Platt, 5 Cow. (N. Y.) 494; Voorhees *v.* Presbyterian Church, 17 Barb. (N. Y.) 108.

In England.—In *England* no separate seats were allowed in the church, except in a few instances, prior to the Reformation, and the body of the church was common to all the parishioners. But after the Reformation, the ordinary or bishop granted the right to particular seats to individual parishioners, and this grant was called a "faculty." See Burns Ecc. L., tit. Church, ch. 7; Hook's Church Dict., tit. Pews; First Presb. Church *v.* Andruss, 21 N. J. L. 329, n. And the right to a pew in a church, in *England*, can only exist by faculty or by prescription; Morgan *v.* Curtis, 3 M. & R. 389; and in an action for disturbance in the enjoyment of the right, the plaintiff must prove a prescriptive right, or a faculty, and should claim it in his declaration as appurtenant to a messuage in the parish. Mainwaring *v.* Giles, 5 Barn. & Ald. 356; Stocks *v.* Booth, 1 T. R. 432; Brumfitt *v.* Roberts, L. R., 5 C. P. 232; for the grant of a pew in *England* to any person, without regard to a messuage or inhabitancy within the parish, is void by the general law. Brumfitt *v.* Roberts, L. R., 5 C. P. 232; Ridout *v.* Harris, 17 U. C. C. P. 88. Non-parishioners have no right to a pew or sitting, except by prescription. Byerley *v.* Windus, 7 Dowl. & Ry. 564; 5 Barn. & C. 1 Every parishioner has, however, a right to be seated, though not in a pew. *In re* Cathedral Church, 8 L. T., N. S. 861.

The interest which a pew holder has in his pew is held by the English cases to be of an incorporeal nature only. It is in the nature of an easement, a right or privilege in the lands of another; and the holder of a pew or seat is not deemed the owner of so much of the site of a church as is comprised within the area of such pew or seat. Mainwaring *v.* Giles, 5 Barn. & Ald. 356; Gully *v.* Bishop of Exeter, 4 Bing. 294; Brumfitt *v.* Roberts, L. R., 5 C. P. 232. It appears to be the right to enter and occupy the pew during the celebration of divine services, and not the right to be there at all times, or any other time than when the church is open for church purposes. Brumfitt *v.* Roberts, L. R., 5 C. P. 232; Ridout *v.* Harris, 17 U. C. C. P. 88. That a corporation may hold a pew, see Reg. *v.* Mayor etc. of Warwick, 8 Q. B. 926, 10 Jur. 962. See also note in O'Hear *v.* De Goesbriand, 33 Vt. 593; 80 Am. Dec. 662.

3. Pews in churches are in some States declared by statute to be real, and in others, personal estate. In the absence of such statute, they partake of the nature of realty, although the ownership is that of an exclusive easement for special purposes since the general property in the house usually belongs to the parish or corporation that erected it. 1 Washb. on Real Property 9.

the pew holder's interest is to be considered as realty,[1] and subject to the incidents of other real estate.[2]

By *Massachusetts* Stat. 1855 ch. 122, pews in all houses of public worship were made personal property.

In *Vermont*, pews are declared by statute to be real property. See O'Hear *v.* De Goesbriand, 33 Vt. 573; 80 Am. 9 Dec. 633.

1. O'Hear *v.* De Goesbriand, 33 Vt. 602; 80 Am. Dec 652; Barnard *v.* Whipple, 29 Vt. 401; 7 Am. Dec. 422; Kellogg *v.* Dickinson, 18 Vt. 266; Howe *v.* Stevens, 47 Vt. 259; Baptist Church *v.* Bigelow, 16 Wend. (N. Y.) 28; Voorhees *v.* Presbyterian Church, 17 Barb. (N. Y.) 104; First Baptist Church *v.* Witherell, 3 Paige (N. Y.) 302; 24 Am. Dec. 223; St. Paul Church *v.* Ford, 34 Barb. (N. Y.) 16; McNabb *v.* Pond, 4 Bradf. (N. Y.) 1; Shaw *v.* Beveridge, 3 Hill (N. Y.) 26; 38 Am. Dec. 616; Third Presb. Church *v.* Andruss, 21 N. J. L. 325; Price *v.* Lyon, 14 Conn. 279; Bates *v.* Sparrell, 10 Mass. 324; Jackson *v.* Rounseville, 5 Met. (Mass.) 132; Attorney General *v.* Federal St. Meeting-house, 3 Gray. (Mass.) 37; Succession of Gamble, 23 La. Ann. 9. See also Johnson *v.* Corbett, 11 Paige (N. Y.) 276.

In Boston.—Pews in Boston have always been held to be personal estate. Attorney General *v.* Federal St. Meeting-house, 3 Gray. (Mass.) 45; and by *Massachusetts* Stat. 1855, ch. 122, pews in all houses of worship throughout the State were made personal property.

In Pennsylvania.—In *Pennsylvania*, however, it appears that the pew holder's estate, in a case of intestacy at least, is considered personal property, the pew going to the personal representative and not to the heirs. In the case of Church *v.* Wells, 24 Pa. St. 251, the court held, that although the exclusive right to a particular pew is a sort of interest in real estate, yet as property, it is so conditional and impermanent that it cannot be called real estate, but must necessarily pass to the personal representative.

Maryland.—In *Maryland* the point does not seem to have been decided. In Hatchinson *v.* Tilden, 4 Har. & M. (Md.) 279, the plaintiff was a candidate for sheriff. The constitution of *Maryland* required as a qualification that he should be possessed of property within the State to the value of £1,000. The plaintiff, not having the requisite property, offered to introduce evidence of his right to a pew in a church as heir-at-law to his father, alleging that the pew was real property. The court rejected the evidence without argument.

In Stoddert *v.* Port Tobacco Parish, 2 Gill & J. (Md.) 227, an action of assumpsit for the price of a pew, the defendant prayed the court to instruct the jury that the auctioneer, who sold the pew, being one of the vestry who were the vendors, could not make such a memorandum as would satisfy the requisitions of the Statute of Frauds in relation to the sale of real estate. The court refused the prayer, and was sustained by the appellate court, who seemingly assumed that property in a pew was real estate.

New York.—In Heeney *v.* St. Peter's Church, 2 Edw. Ch. (N. Y.) 608, and *In re* Brick Presb. Church, 3 Edw. Ch. (N. Y.) 155, it was said, *citing* Freligh *v.* Platt, 5 Cow. (N. Y.) 494, that a pew right was not real estate, but an examination of Freligh *v.* Platt, 5 Cow. (N. Y.) 494, will show that such was not the decision of the court in that case, and the *New York* cases just cited in support of the text proposition would seem decisive.

2. **Statute of Frauds.**—A contract for the sale of a pew is within the Statute of Frauds. Hodges *v.* Green, 28 Vt. 358; Barnard *v.* Whipple, 29 Vt. 401; 7 Am. Dec. 422; Livingston *v.* Trinity Church, 45 N. J. L. 237; Price *v.* Lyon, 14 Conn. 279. *Compare* Stoddert *v.* Port Tobacco Parish, 2 Gill & J. (Md.) 227.

Although the interest acquired in a pew in a church is a limited and qualified interest, it is notwithstanding an interest in real estate, and requires a writing to support it if the interest extends beyond a lease for a year. First Baptist Church *v.* Bigelow, 16 Wend. (N. Y.) 28.

Tenancy in Common.—Two or more persons may be tenants in common of a pew, and hold it subject to all rules governing a tenancy in common of real estate. St. Paul's Church *v.* Ford, 34 Barb. (N. Y.) 16.

Real Actions.—That the real actions lie for an injury to a pew right see *infra*, this title, *Pew Holder's Remedies*.

Goes to the Heir.—Property in a pew passes to the heir in case of intestacy,

But it must be borne in mind that his right is incorporeal, giving him no legal interest in the church edifice, the materials of which it is composed, or the land upon which it stands.[1]

There is a close analogy between a pew right and the right of burial in a public burying ground or cemetery.[2]

2. How Acquired.—It is said that an individual right to the occupation of a particular pew cannot arise from an occupation alone; that the right can only be acquired by a faculty, which is personal to the grantee; or by prescription, which will not arise from a possession unless it be annexed to a tenement; or by grant, which, as it creates an incorporeal interest in lands must be by deed or writing. This last mode is practically the only method by which a pew right is acquired in the *United States.*[3]

and not to the personal representative. M'Nabb *v.* Pond, 4 Bradf. (N. Y.) 7.

Husband Cannot Convey Directly to His Wife.—As a pew is real estate, it could not at common law be conveyed directly by a husband to his wife. Voorhes *v.* Presb. Church, 17 Barb. (N. Y.) 103.

1. Abernethy *v.* Society of the Church of the Puritans, 3 Daly (N. Y.) 7; *In re* Reformed Dutch Church, 16 Barb. (N. Y.) 237; Gay *v.* Baker, 17 Mass. 435; 9 Am. Dec. 159.

A pew-holder has no right beyond that of using the pew as a seat in the church edifice. He has no exclusive right in the soil below the pew, or in the timber or materials of which the house or any of its parts is composed, and when this use is destroyed, his right, if any remains to him, is a right of indemnity or compensation for injury. Cooper *v.* First Presb. Church, 32 Barb. (N. Y.) 234.

But it would seem that the pew holder has some interest in the church edifice apart from his pew. In Revere *v.* Gannett, 1 Pick. (Mass.) 169 it was held that, where a society had built a meeting-house and sold pews to individuals, that an execution against the corporation could not be extended to the pulpit. The court said: "The meeting-house corporation had sold the pews to individuals; the purchasers must be supposed to take with the pews that which renders them valuable. The sellers can have no right to take away the windows of the meeting-house, or the wall, or the pulpit, or the singers' loft. The proprietors of pews are entitled to various privileges, such as passing through the aisles, being addressed from the pulpit, etc. There is no property in the pulpit distinct from the right of enjoying the house for public worship. The levy on the pulpit is, therefore, void."

2. Kincaid's Appeal, 66 Pa. St. 411; Price *v.* M. E. Church, 4 Ohio 541; Sohier *v.* Trinity Church, 109 Mass. 21; Craig *v.* First Presb. Church, 88 Pa. St. 51; 32 Am. Rep. 417; Perkins *v.* Lawrence, 138 Mass. 362; CEMETERIES, vol. 3, p. 49.

3. New Jersey *v.* Trinity Church, 45 N. J. L. 230; 1 Am. & Eng. Corp. Cases 280.

The plaintiff placed a loose bench in a church and by the consent of the society it remained there and he occupied it for a term of ten or twelve years. Then by order of the trustees it was removed. Plaintiff brought trespass, and it was held that his use and occupation of the bench did not constitute him a pew holder in the church, and that he could not maintain the action. Niebuhr *v.* Piersdorff, 24 Wis. 316.

Conditions.—A condition, prescribed by a by-law, in the deeds of pews by an incorporated religious society, that the grantee shall forfeit the pew to the society if he shall leave the meeting-house without first offering it to them for a certain price, is valid. The court said: "The doctrine, that conditions against alienation in a conveyance in fee simple are void, has never been held to be applicable to conveyances of pews for the reason stated by Chief Justice Shaw in Attorney Gen'l *v.* Federal Street Meeting-house, 3 Gray (Mass.) 1, 47; viz: "It is competent for such a society to make such reasonable by-laws and regulations, respecting the sale and purchase of pews as they think their interests as a religious society may require. And it is usual for such societies to make such regulations in regard to

3. As Against the Religious Society.—The qualified right of the pewholder is subject to the paramount rights of the religious society to remodel and alter the internal structure of the building, to remove the place of worship to another house, to sell the church property and rebuild elsewhere, and to change the forms of the pews or to destroy them entirely for the purpose of repairs,[1] and

the sale of their pews and express them in the deeds they issue, as to prevent an indiscriminate sale of pews, and they retain some right to elect and determine whom they will associate with, or rather who may associate with them. Otherwise, if it were free to anybody to purchase pews without restraint, a number of people of another denomination, finding pews low, might purchase them, and become a majority, and thus turn the proper congregation out of their own house." French *v.* Old South Society, 106 Mass. 479; Crocker *v.* Old South Society, 106 Mass. 489.

As to conditions providing that a pew shall revert for non-payment of assessments, see *infra*, this title, *Assessments and Taxes Levied by the Religious Society.*

1. **The Paramount Right of the Society.**—Sohier *v.* Trinity Church, 109 Mass. 21; Van Houten *v.* First Reformed Dutch Church, 17 N. J. Eq. 130; Kimball *v.* Second Parish, 24 Pick. (Mass.) 349; Gay *v.* Baker, 17 Mass. 435; 9 Am. Dec. 159; Kellogg *v.* Dickinson, 18 Vt. 263; Cooper *v.* First Presb. Church, 32 Barb. (N. Y.) 222; Church *v.* Wells, 24 Pa. St. 249; Jones *v.* Towne, 58 N. H. 462; Colby *v.* Northfield etc. Society, 63 N. H. 64; Price *v.* M. E. Church, 4 Ohio 541; Solomon *v.* Congregation of B'nai Jeshurun, 49 How. Pr. (N. Y.) 264; White *v.* First M. E. Society, 3 Lans. (N. Y.) 477; Presb. Church *v.* Andruss, 21 N. J. L. 325.

The grant of a pew in a church edifice in perpetuity does not give to the pew-owner an absolute right of property as in a grant of land in fee. He has a limited usufructuary right only. He must be presumed from the very nature of the subject-matter, to have taken the grant under all the conditions and limitations incident to such property. If the edifice becomes useless by dilapidation, or is destroyed by fire or any other casualty, the right of the pew-owner is gone; so, if from age, decay or other injury, the house has to be rebuilt in the same place, or from some necessary cause the location must be changed, or the old edifice sold and a new one erected on another spot, the pew owner has no claim, either in law or equity. Sharswood, J., in Kincaid's Appeal, 66 Pa. St. 422.

In Fisher *v.* Glover, 4 N. H. 181, it was held that a religious society owning a meeting-house might remove it to another place about a mile distant, and that the owner of the pew could not maintain an action for a disturbance of his right to the use of the pew. The court by Richardson, C. J., said: "Meeting-houses belong to the society which erects them; but it is usual to grant to individuals the exclusive use of pews, and these grants give to those individuals certain rights, which are to be protected. The rights thus acquired, are, however, limited, and are in our opinion subject to the right of the society to have the meeting-house in such place as will best accommodate the whole. A reservation of this right is implied in the grant of a pew in a house of public worship. The convenience of individuals must in such case be subject to the general convenience of the whole, and whoever purchases a pew purchases it subject to this right of the society."

The property in a pew in a meeting-house is not an absolute, but a qualified property; it is an exclusive right to occupy a certain part of the meeting-house, for the purpose of attending upon public worship, and for no other purpose, and is necessarily subject to the right in the parish to take down and rebuild the meeting-house, and make such alterations as the good of the society may require. This restriction upon the property of the plaintiff grows out of the nature of the property and the purposes to which it is applied. He cannot convert it to any other use, for, having acquired it as part of a house for public worship, he can do nothing which may interfere with, or impair the use of the building for the purpose, or which may injure other holders of pews in the right enjoyment of their property. Daniel *v.* Wood, 1 Pick. (Mass.) 103; 11 Am. Dec. 151.

in doing these things the society are in the exercise of their legal rights and commit no tort.[1] Nor can the pew holder prevent the society from changing the mode of worship.[2]

Whether the pew holder is entitled to compensation, when the religious society, by the exercise of its paramount rights, as specified above, deprives him of the use of his pew, is a question which has been much discussed; and in some States has been settled by statute.[3] Apart from any statutory regulations the better doctrine, and the one supported by the weight of authority, is that if the society exercises its rights from necessity, as, for example, demolishing an utterly ruinous building, the pew holder can have no claim for compensation; but, if from motives of mere convenience or ornament the parish should destroy a pew or disturb the owner in the use of it, he would be entitled to a reasonable compensation, and much more so if the act were a wanton one.[4]

"The several pew-holders had an easement in and not a title to the freehold. Each pew holder has a property in his pew and the right to its exclusive possession. But this right was subject to the paramount rights of the parish. The parish was the legal owner of the house and the land on which it stood. It had the control of the house; the right to determine at what hours on the Sabbath and at other times it should be open for public worship; to select the pastor; to contract with him as to the terms of his settlement; to determine who should be admitted to the pulpit in his absence, and to see that the house should be kept in a proper condition for its public use. The pew holder has certain privileges by reason of his ownership—such as passing through the aisles, being addressed from the pulpit, etc. His property is not absolute but qualified. He may own a pew and yet not be a member of the parish corporation. The corporation may own the land and building thereon, while the pew holder has only a qualified property in his pew." First Baptist Society *v.* Grant, 59 Me. 250.

1. Kimball *v.* Second Parish, 24 Pick. (Mass.) 349; Daniel *v.* Wood, 1 Pick. (Mass.) 103; 11 Am. Dec. 151; and see cases in preceding note.

2. Solomon *v.* Congregation, B'nai Jeshurun, 49 How. Pr. (N. Y.) 263. See also First Baptist Church *v.* Witherell, 3 Paige (N. Y.) 296; 24 Am. Dec. 223. *Compare* RELIGIOUS SOCIETIES.

3. See *Massachusetts* Stat. referred to in Sohier *v.* Trinity Church, 109 Mass. 21.

But the *Massachusetts* statute of 1817, ch. 189, has been held to have been only declaratory of the common law. Daniel *v.* Wood, 1 Pick. (Mass.) 102; 11 Am. Dec. 151. See also Kimball *v.* Second Parish, 24 Pick. (Mass.) 347; Cooper *v.* First Presb. Church, 32 Barb. (N. Y.) 228; Gay *v.* Baker, 17 (Mass.) 438; 9 Am. Dec. 159.

In Colby *v.* Northfield etc. Society, 63 N. H. 64, it was held that Gen. Laws of *New Hampshire*, ch. 154, §§ 12, 13, did not change the common law right of a pew holder which is "a modified ownership, subject to the superior title included in the ownership of the house;" but only prescribe the way in which the paramount right of the society may be enjoyed and enforced.

4. **Compensation.**—Kellogg *v.* Dickinson, 18 Vt. 266; Vorhees *v.* Presbyterian Church, 17 Barb. (N. Y.) 109; Kincaid's Appeal, 66 Pa. St 422; Cooper *v.* First Presb. Church, 32 Barb. (N. Y.) 227; Howard *v.* First Parish, 7 Pick. (Mass.) 137; Jones *v.* Towne, 58 N. H. 464; 42 Am. Rep. 602; Wentworth *v.* First Parish, 3 Pick. (Mass.) 344; Kimball *v.* Second Parish, 24 Pick. (Mass.) 347; White *v.* First M. E. Society, 3 Lans. (N. Y.) 477.

A grantee of a pew takes a limited estate, an usufructuary interest, subject to the general right of the owners of the church. If the church edifice becomes useless by dilapidation, or is destroyed by fire or casualty, or has to

The rights of the pew holder in his pew, though in some respects subordinate, are distinct from those of the society in the land and church edifice.[1]

be rebuilt as to its interior, the right of the pew holder is gone; though he has a remedy in damages where his pew is destroyed for convenience only, or where the trustees have been guilty of a wanton and malicious abuse of power. Voorhees *v.* Presbyterian Church, 17 Barb. (N. Y.) 103; Bronson *v.* St. Peter's Church, 7 N. Y. Leg. Obs. 361.

If a parish abandon its meeting-house as a place of public worship, although it continue to be fit for that purpose, and erect a new one on a different site, it does not thereby subject itself to any liability to the proprietor of a pew in the old meeting-house, it not appearing that the parish acted wantonly or with any intention to injure him. The court by Wilde, J., said: "In Gay *v.* Baker, 17 Mass. 435, 9 Am. Dec. 159, it is said that when, by altering or enlarging a meeting-house, the pews are destroyed, it is incumbent on the parish making such alteration or enlargement to provide an indemnity for the pew holders on just and equitable principles. But the parish are not required to provide any indemnity for the pew holders, when it becomes necessary to take down an old meeting-house, which is unfit for use as a place of public worship, unless such indemnity is provided for by statute as was decided in Wenthworth *v.* First Parish, 3 Pick. (Mass.) 346. And in no case can be found any intimation that a parish or religious society would subject themselves to any liability to the pew holders, in consequence of abandoning their meeting-house as a place of public worship, although the pews may thereby be rendered useless.

The law is the same if public worship should be wholly discontinued, either in the meeting-house or elsewhere, by reason of the inability of the parish to maintain public worship, and to pay the necessary expenses of repairing the meeting-house, whether this inability be caused by the reduction of the number of parishioners or otherwise." Fassett *v.* First Parish, 19 Pick. (Mass.) 363.

In Abernethy *v.* Society of the Church of Puritans, 3 Daly (N. Y.) 1, it was held, that a pew holder was not entitled, as compensation for the loss of his pew right, to a part of the proceeds of the sale of the church edifice at the expiration of the lease of the land upon which it stood.

In Gorton *v.* Hadsell, 9 Cush. (Mass.) 508, it was held, that unless a meeting-house, at the time it was torn down by vote of the proprietors, was so old and ruinous as to render its entire demolition necessary, a pew-holder was entitled to compensation.

"But it may be asked what remedy is there for a minority of pew holders, if the majority shall determine to demolish the building, and thus destroy the pew? We answer none, if the act is necessary or proper; if, on the other hand, there should be a wanton or malicious abuse of power, the laws will give a remedy to the extent of the injury received." Wentworth *v.* First Parish, 3 Pick. (Mass.) 344.

Where the edifice was reasonably capable of further use as a church, the interest of the pew owners would no doubt be a subject to be considered by this court. But if overruling considerations existed rendering it expedient upon the whole matter that a sale should take place, the interests of the owners of pews would necessarily be destroyed. Wheaton *v.* Gates, 18 N. Y. 395.

1. Shaw *v.* Beveridge, 3 Hill (N. Y.) 26; 38 Am. Dec. 616; O'Hear *v.* De Goesbriand, 33 Vt. 593; 80 Am. Dec. 652; Howe *v.* Stevens, 47 Vt. 262.

So where one conveyed to the trustees of a church, certain premises "for church purposes," upon the condition that if the seats of any church erected upon the said premises should be rented or sold, the premises should revert to the grantor, it was held, that a sale of the premises was not a breach of the condition not to sell or rent the pews. The court, by Miller, J., said: "The fee of the land and the use of the pews are placed on a different footing. The former may be transferred, because such transfer is not forbidden and is not inconsistent with either the purpose or the condition of the conveyance. If the pews are disposed of, the condition is violated, the grant becomes void, and the land reverts as provided. The interest in the pew is separate from the fee, and the owner of the former may maintain an action against a trespasser

4. As Against a Stranger.—As a pew holder has no legal interest in the church edifice or land, he cannot maintain an action for a wrongful entry or trespass upon the premises, unless such entry or trespass is accompanied by an injury to his individual right to the use and occupation of his pew, as by the destruction of the pew, and though a stranger may have obtained possession of the house so far as to oust the religious society, yet the pewholder's right to the exclusive possession of his pew is so distinct from the ownership and possession of the building by the society that he may maintain an action for any invasion of his individual right after such ouster; but if the religious society has abandoned the building, he could only recover nominal damages.[1]

III. Remedies.—As in *England*, the right of property is considered a mere easement, an incorporeal right;[2] the only remedy for an injury to a pew right is an action on the case.[3] While there is some confusion in the decisions, and it has been held that this remedy is likewise available in the *United States*,[4] the best considered cases seem to establish that a pew owner's right in a pew is so far in the nature of an interest in real estate as to render necessary the use of the real actions to protect his rights, and he may therefore maintain trespass *quare clausum fregit*, ejectment or writ of entry, according to circumstances, for an ouster or disturbance of his right of possession.[5]

or any person who infringes upon his rights, and they may be leased and held distinct from the fee." Woodworth *v.* Payne, 74 N. Y. 200.

1. Howe *v.* Stevens, 47 Vt. 262.

If neither claimant to a pew has any legal title thereto, the one in possession will not be disturbed. Montgomery *v.* Johnson, 9 How. Pr. (N. Y.) 232. And being in possession, although without title, he is justified in defending the possession by force against the entry of any person having no title. Brett *v.* Mullerkey, 7 Ir., C. P. 120.

2. Shaw *v.* Beveridge, 3 Hill (N. Y.) 26; 38 Am. Dec. 616; O'Hear *v.* De Goesbriand, 33 Vt. 606; 80 Am. Dec. 652.

3. Shaw *v.* Beveridge, 3 Hill (N. Y.) 26; 38 Am. Dec. 616; Mainwaring *v.* Giles, 5 Barn. & Ald. 356.

And this action cannot be maintained unless the right be claimed as appurtenant to a messuage in the parish, and be so averred in the declaration. Mainwaring *v.* Giles, 5 Barn. & Ald. 356; Bryan *v.* Whistler, 8 Barn. & C. 294; 2 Moo. & R. 332; Brumfitt *v.* Roberts, L. R., 5 P. C. 232. Trespass will not lie for entering into a pew. Stocks *v.* Booth, 1 T. R. 432. Nor is ejectment maintainable. Ridout *v.* Harris, 17 U. C. C. P. 88.

4. **Trespass on the Case.**—A pewholder's appropriate remedy for a mere disturbance in the enjoyment of his right not amounting to the destruction of the pew, is trespass on the case. The court by Redfield, C. J., said: "In all such cases the appropriate remedy for a disturbance in the enjoyment of the right is trespass on the case. That, indeed, is the only remedy for the disturbance of the enjoyment of such rights ordinarily. The right to occupy a pew is such that in some cases it is held that trespass or ejectment will lie. But not for a mere disturbance in the use, such as is proved in the present case." Perrin *v.* Granger, 33 Vt. 104. See also Kellogg *v.* Dickinson, 18 Vt. 266.

Compare also cases cited under succeeding note.

5. Shaw *v.* Beveridge, 3 Hill (N. Y.) 26; 38 Am. Dec. 616; O'Hear *v.* De Goesbriand, 33 Vt. 606; 80 Am. Dec. 652; First Baptist Church *v.* Witherell, 3 Paige (N. Y.) 302; 24 Am. Dec. 223; Howe *v.* Stevens, 47 Vt. 262; Gay *v.* Baker, 17 Mass. 438; 9 Am. Dec. 159; Wentworth *v.* First Parish, 3

But when the disturbance or ouster is by the religious society, in the exercise of its superior rights, the plaintiff's remedy, if he has any, is an action on the case for damages,[1] and a court of equity will refuse to grant an injunction upon the application of a pew holder restraining the religious society from tearing down, remodeling, or rebuilding the church edifice, or from selling the premises, when the society shall deem it expedient and proper.[2]

IV. Assessments and Taxes Levied by the Religious Society.— The validity of assessments made by a religious society upon the pews in its church edifice, for the purpose of meeting the expenses of the society, must be determined in each instance by the charter and by-laws of the society, and the deed or contract by which the owner holds his pew.[3]

Pick. (Mass.) 346. As we have no ecclesiastical courts in this country, and as the right to a pew, or a seat in a church, is unquestioned here, and the property therein is considered as partaking of the character of real estate, there can be no valid objection to sustaining an action of trespass *vi et armis*, if the owner is disturbed in his possession. This action is rightly brought to recover for the injury of which the plaintiff complains, if there exists no other objections to his recovery, inasmuch as he proved that he was owner of the pew in question. Gay *v.* Baker, 17 Mass. 435; 9 Am. Dec. 159.

In an action of trespass for breaking and entering the plaintiff's pew, the court by Shaw, C. J., said: "The first question discussed was, whether an action of trespass *quare clausum fregit* will lie in such case. So long as pews are considered in point of law as real estate, as they are in this commonwealth, except in the city of Boston, we can perceive no reason why the actual form of action, given by the common law, to redress a wrong done to the right of possession of real estate, is not the legal and proper remedy. We are of opinion that the charge, in that particular, was correct." Jackson *v.* Rounseville, 5 Met. (Mass.) 132.

1. Daniel *v.* Wood, 1 Pick. (Mass.) 104; 11 Am. Dec. 151.

See also Kimball *v.* Second Parish, 24 Pick. (Mass.) 351.

The pew holder cannot maintain either trespass or ejectment against the trustees, but the action must be to recover damages by way of indemnity for the loss of his pew. Cooper *v.* First Presb. Church, 32 Barb. (N. Y.) 230; Voorhees *v.* Presb Church, 8 Barb. (N. Y.) 152.

2. Van Houten *v.* First Reformed Dutch Church, 17 N. J. Eq. 131; Cooper *v.* First Presb. Church, 32 Barb. (N. Y.) 232.

See also Heeney *v.* St. Peter's Church, 2 Edw. Ch. (N. Y.) 608; *In re* Buik Presb. Church, 3 Edw. Ch. (N. Y.) 155.

3. If the power of a religious society to assess a tax upon the pews in their church is derived from and limited by the deeds of the society to the pew owner, a tax assessed in part for purposes not specifically named in the deeds is invalid. First Methodist Episcopal Society *v.* Brayton, 9 Allen (Mass.) 248. See generally Mussey *v.* Bulfinch Street Soc., 1 Cush. (Mass.) 148; Bailey *v.* Power St. M. E. Church, 6 R. I. 491.

The pews of a church were, by vote of the congregation, sold at auction, free of rent, for the purpose of raising money to complete the building. A purchased a pew, of which he remained in possession several years, without any lease or other agreement as to the pew or rent. In assumpsit, by the trustees, against him, to recover his proportion of the assessments laid by the corporation on the pews, in order to defray the salary of the minister, held, that A was not liable to any implied assumpsit; and that the trustees having no power to levy assessments *in personam*, A was not liable personally, unless some contract or promise to pay was shown. First Presb. Congregation *v.* Quackenbush, 10 Johns. (N. Y.) 217; see also St. Paul's Church *v.* Ford, 34 Barb. (N. Y.) 16.

Forfeiture of Pews for Non-Payment

V. **Executions and Attachments.**—In *Massachusetts* certain decisions have construed a statute authorizing executions against the interest of a pew holder in pews.[1]

PHARMACY.—See Drugs, vol. 6, p. 33; Druggist, vol. 6, p. 31.

PHOTOGRAPHS.

I. **Copyright in Photographs.**—A photograph, under U. S. Rev. Stat., § 4952, may be the subject of a copyright. It was otherwise under the Act of 1831.[2] The constitutionality of the statute was at one time doubted, but the question is now set at rest.[3]

of Assessments.—Deeds of pews from a religious society to individuals not unusually contain a condition that the pew shall revert to the society upon a failure to pay rent or assessments, as the forfeiture depends upon the validity of the assessment. The following cases are appended determining the propriety and legality of particular assessments upon different states of facts: First Parish *v.* Dow, 3 Allen (Mass.) 369; Perrin *v.* Granger, 30 Vt. 395; 33 Vt. 101; Mayberry *v.* Mead, 80 Me. 27.

1. **Executions and Attachments on Pews.**—An attachment of a pew upon mesne process was held valid though the officer did not enter the church or come within sight of the pew, he not being able to obtain the key of the church. Perrin *v.* Leverett, 13 Mass. 128.

Massachusetts statute of 1822, ch. 93, § 7, directed that notice in writing of an attachment of a pew should be given by the officer making such attachment to the clerk of the parish or religious society in whose house the pew is situated. It was held that where a person owned more than one pew within a church, that an attested copy of the writ without any copy of the officer's return to show which pew the officer had attached was an insufficient notice under the statute. Sargent *v.* Peirce, 2 Met. (Mass.) 80. And see same case for a construction of statutes providing for the record of executions levied on pews.

2. Wood *v.* Abbott, 5 Blatchf. (U. S.) 325, on the ground that under the act of 1831 a photograph was not a print, cut or engraving.

3. Burrow-Giles Lith. Co. *v.* Sarony, 111 U. S. 53; Thornton *v.* Schreiber, 124 U. S. 612. The circuit court thought the question an open one in the same case, 17 Fed. Rep. 591, as did the *United States* district court for the *Pennsylvania* district in Schreiber *v.* Thornton, 17 Fed. Rep. 603. In 17 Fed. Rep. 596, *et seq.*, is a learned discussion of the question whether a photograph deserves copyright protection at all, and lengthy extracts are made from a translation of a discussion of the subject in Pouillet's Propriete Litteraire et Artistique, where a French statute is reviewed.

In Falk *v.* Howell, 37 Fed. Rep. 202, it was adjudged that a copyright of a photograph artistically designed to illustrate a musical composition was infringed by stamping an imitation in raised figures on leathern chair bottoms and backs.

In Nottage *v.* Jackson, 11 Q. B. Div. 627, it was adjudged that within the English Copyright Act of 1882, the author of a photograph was the person who took the negative, and not the concern which employed him. This case recognizes the fact that authorship and originality of intellectual creation have a right to protection.

It was held in Thornton *v.* Schreiber, 124 U. S. 612, that the penalty provided for by U. S. Rev. St., § 4965, of one dollar for each sheet of a copyrighted plate "found in the possession" of the defendant, was not recoverable from one who was only the employe of the

II. **Photographs as Evidence.**—As evidence, photographs are admissible on questions of identity and comparison of handwriting, and as secondary evidence where the primary and better evidence is not obtainable. In fact, it may be said generally that they are never admitted but as secondary evidence. As the art of photography is of comparatively recent date, the Daguerrean process being no later than 1839, the principles governing the admissibility of photographs have been laid down and examined of late years in several jurisdictions, and though the utterances of the courts are not altogether harmonious, the consensus of opinion is as above stated. For the introduction of photographs in evidence a foundation must be laid, as in other cases where secondary evidence is offered, and it is said that the judgment of the trial court as to the sufficiency of such foundation is conclusive, and not open to examination on the appeal.[1]

proprietor of the establishment owning such sheets, and who had possession only as such employe; that the statute conferred no right of action to recover damages as such, but limited the remedy to the forfeiture of the plates and sheets, and for the further forfeiture of one dollar for each sheet found in the possession of the defendant; and that the words of the statute "found in his possession" did not refer to the finding of the jury, but to the finding in the possession of the defendant.

1. **Identity of Persons.**—In Udderzook *v.* Com., 76 Pa. St. 340, decided in 1874, the question of the admissibility of photographs on the question of identity appears to have come before the *Pennsylvania* Supreme court for the first time. Here a photograph was offered on a trial for murder to show that the person murdered and one A were one and the same person. The court said: "It is evident that the competency of the evidence in such a case depends on the reliability of the photograph as a work of art, and this, in the case before us, in which no proof was made by experts of this reliability, must depend upon the judicial cognizance we may take of photographs as an established means of producing a correct likeness. The Daguerrean process was first given to the world in 1839. It was soon followed by photography, of which we have had nearly a generation's experience. It has become a customary and a common mode of taking and preserving views as well as the liknesses of persons, and has obtained universal assent to the correctness of its delineations. We know that its principles are derived from science; that the images on the plate, made by the rays of light through the camera, are dependent on the same general laws which produce the images of outward forms upon the retina through the lenses of the eye. The process has become one in general use, so common that we cannot refuse to take judicial cognizance of it as a proper means of producing correct likenesses."

In a still later case, Cowley *v.* People, 83 N. Y. 464; 38 Am. Rep. 464, decided in 1881, the court said: "We know not of a rule, applicable to all cases, ever having been declared, that they (photographs) are not competent. Nor do we see, in the nature of things, a reason for a rule that they are never competent. We do not fail to notice, and we may notice judicially, that all civilized communities rely upon photographic pictures for taking and presenting resemblances of persons and animals, of scenery and all natural objects, of buildings and other artificial objects. It is of frequent occurrence, that fugitives from justice are arrested on the identification given by them. . . . So the signs of the portrait and the photograph, if authenticated by other testimony, may give truthful representations. When shown by such testimony to be correct resemblances of a person, we see not why they may not be shown to the triers of the facts, not as conclusive, but as aids in determining the matter in issue, still being open, like other proofs of identity or similar matter, to rebuttal or doubt."

In this case the photographs were offered to show the change in the appearance of a boy towards whom the defendant was charged with cruelty.

To the same effect on the question of of identity are Luke *v.* Calhoun Co., 52 Ala. 118, and Ruloff *v.* People, 45 N. Y. 213. In each of these cases there was other evidence of identity. In the latter case the court said that "photographs were competent, though slight, evidence in addition to the other and more reliable testimony." See also Beavers *v.* State, 58 Ind. 530.

In Washington L. Ins. Co. *v.* Schaible, 9 Phila. (Pa.) 36, in an action on a life insurance policy, where the assured died of consumption, and the defence to an action was a breach of warranty, a photograph of the deceased taken shortly before her death, and testified as being a good likeness, was admitted in evidence, and the supreme court on appeal held that this was not error.

It is said in Taylor on Evidence, § 1613, note, that photography affords an easy mode of establishing the identity of the person against whom it is sought to show a previous conviction, and Bemish *v.* Bemish, Ir., 10 C. L. 413, and Reg. *v.* Tolson, F. & F. 103, are cited.

Identity of Things.—And in the cases aforesaid the photographs were offered on the question of the identity of persons. They have been admitted also to identify things; as, for example, premises. Church *v.* Milwaukee, 31 Wis. 512. To show a defect in a highway. Blair *v.* Pelham, 118 Mass. 421; Cozzens *v.* Higgins, 33 How. Pr. (N. Y.) 439; Reg *v.* United Kingdom, etc. Co., 3 F. & F. 73. See also Locke *v.* Sioux City, etc. R. Co., 46 Iowa 112; Dyson *v.* New York R. etc. Co., 57 Conn. 9; County Com'rs. *v.* Wise (Md. 1889), 18 Atl. Rep. 31; Shaw *v.* Sttae, 83 Ga. 92; Randall *v.* Chase, 133 Mass. 210.

In Hollenbeck *v.* Rowley, 8 Allen (Mass.) 473, a photographic view of premises, the boundaries of which were in dispute, was held to have been properly rejected because offered simply as a "chalk representation," without being verified by the oath of the photographer.

In Blair *v.* Pelham, 118 Mass. 420, the court, by Gray, C. J., said that the photograph must be verified by proof that it was a true representation of the subject, and that whether it was sufficiently verified was a preliminary question of fact to be decided by the judge presiding at the trial, and not open to exception.

The People's Passenger R. Co. *v.* Green, 56 Md. 84; 6 Am. & Eng. R. Cas., 168, it was held, in an action against a street railway company to recover for personal injuries, that a photograph of another car than that in which the accident happened was inadmissible, notwithstanding an offer to show that it was an exact representation of the car upon which the accident happened.

Handwriting.—In Marcy *v.* Barnes, 16 Gray (Mass.) 161; 77 Am. Dec. 495, on the issue of the genuineness of a signature, magnified photographic copies of the signature, and of admitted genuine signatures of the same person were held admissible when accompanied by competent preliminary proof that the copies were accurate in all respects, except as to size and coloring. The courts say that this "is not dissimilar to examination with a magnifying glass," and affords an additional and useful means of making comparisons between admitted signatures and one which is alleged to be only an imitation.

In matter of Foster's Will, 34 Mich. 21, where a will having been proved by the subscribing witnesses, the contestants proposed to furnish the jury with photographic copies, which the trial court declined to permit, the appellate court refused to reverse, apparently, on the ground stated in the text of this article, that the question was for the trial court and a matter within its discretion.

It is said in 1 Wharton on Evidence § 676, that "in cases involving delicate questions of identity of hands, a photograph should not be relied on without investigating the refractive power of the lens, the angle at which the original was inclined to the sensitive plane, the accuracy of the focusing, and the skill of the operator;" and The Taylor Will Case, 10 Abb. Pr., N. S. (N. Y.) 300, is cited. This was a case before the New York surrogate in 1871, and is hardly in line with the current of authority. It is said here that photographic copies of a signature are not admissible to aid an expert as a basis of opinion as to the genuineness of the original signature, and that the opinions of those acquainted with the handwriting in question formed from an examination of photographic copies of the signature are entitled to but little weight. Dr. Wharton thinks otherwise, and says (2 Wharton on Evidence, § 720): "Photographers who have been accustomed to scrutinize handwriting in reference to forgeries, and have been in the habit of using photographic copies for this purpose, may be examined as experts in questions of forgery, even though their opinion is founded partly on photographic copies, which they have themselves made, and which have been put in evidence;" and cites in support of this opinion, Marcy *v.* Barnes, 16 Gray (Mass.) 161; 77 Am. Dec. 405.

In Tome *v.* Parkersburg R. Co., 39 Md. 36; 17 Am. Rep. 540, however, a reversal was had on the ground of error on the part of the trial court in admitting photographic copies of signatures, accompanied by the evidence of a photographer as an expert in handwriting on the question of comparison. The court here said that the photographer's testimony was offered to establish the forgery of the certificates in controversy by comparing them with copies (obtained by photographic processes, either magnified or of the natural size) of certain signatures assumed or admitted to be genuine, and pointing out the differences between the supposed genuine and the disputed signatures. The court said: "As a general rule, in proportion as the *media* of evidence are multiplied, the chances of error or mistake are increased. Photographers do not always produce exact fac-similes of the objects delineated, and however indebted we may be to that beautiful science for much that is useful as well as ornamental, it is at least a mimetic art, which furnishes only secondary impressions of the original, that vary according to the lights or shadows which prevail whilst being taken." This case, decided in 1873, would seem to be opposed to the weight of authority, and it may perhaps be questioned whether in view of the great advances made in the photographic art since then, the same view of the question would obtain to-day.

A comparison of a signature in dispute with photographic copies of other writings, for the purpose of getting an opinion from an expert as to the character of the signature as real or feigned, where the originals from which the copies are made are not brought before the jury and cannot be shown to other witnesses, should not be permitted, at least where there is no proof as to the manner and exactness of the photographic method used. Hynes *v.* McDermott, 82 N. Y. 413; 37 Am. Rep. 538.

In Eborn *v.* Zimpleman, 47 Tex. 503; 26 Am. Rep. 315, photographic copies were held to have been properly rejected on the issue of a comparison of handwritings, solely on the ground that no proper foundation was laid for their introduction as secondary evidence.

In Luco *v.* U. S., 23 How. (U. S.) 515, the court examined photographs on the question of forgery of signatures. In Duffin *v.* People, 107 Ill. 113, 47 Am. Rep. 431, they were held admissible. In the famous English Tichborne Case, photographs of letters and documents were used in facilitating the comparison of handwriting, for the purpose of identifying the writer.

Records.—Photographs have been admitted in evidence to present accurate copies of public records which could not be withdrawn from the files. In *re* Stephens, L. R., 9 C. P. 187, Coleridge, C. J. said, on refusing an application for leave to take certain documents from the file 2, that, if the identification of handwriting should become necessary, "that difficulty might be got over by taking photographic copies—a thing which is by no means uncommon at the present day."

In Leathers *v.* Salvor Wrecking Co., 2 Woods (U. S.) 682, it was held that photographic copies of documents on file in one of the executive departments of the government were admissible in evidence on authentication of their genuineness in the usual manner by proof of the handwriting. So in Daly *v.* Maguire, 6 Blatchf. (U. S.) 137, an action for an infringement of the copyright of a play, where a printed programme of a theatrical performance and newspaper slips had been annexed to a deposition on file, an application for leave to take them from the files and annex them to a commission to be sent away was granted on condition that their place should be supplied under the direction of the clerk by photographic fac-similes. And see Luco *v.* U. S., 23 How. (U. S.) 515.

And see on the general subject, Taylor Will Cases, 10 Abb. Pr. (N. Y.) 300.

In U. S. *v.* Messman, 1 Cent. L. J. 121, in the U. S. Dist. Court, 1874, Blatchford, J., held that a photographic copy of a pay-roll was not admissible from which to prove its forgery, when the original was procurable.

III. **Miscellaneous.**—A photographer, who had taken a negative likeness of a lady to supply her with copies for money, was restrained from selling or exhibiting copies, both on the ground that there was an implied contract not to use the negative for such purposes, and also on the ground that such sale or exhibition was a breach of confidence.[1] It has been held under a statute exempting from execution in the hands of mechanics engaged in the pursuit of their trades and occupations, one set of mechanic's tools, such as are usual and necessary to the pursuit of the trade, that a photographer was not a mechanic, and that his photographic implements were not exempt. It may be doubted, however, whether this decision would be followed in all jurisdictions and under (possibly) varying statutes.[2]

PHYSICAL; PHYSICALLY.—(See also FORCE, vol. 8, p. 99.) See note 3.

PHYSICIANS AND SURGEONS—(See also BOARD OF HEALTH, vol. 2, p. 429; COUNTIES, vol. 4, p. 367; CORONER, vol. 4, p. 179; DENTIST, vol. 5, p. 557; HEALTH, vol. 9, p. 318; HOSPITAL, vol. 9, p. 771; MALPRACTICE, vol. 14, p. 76; MEDICAL JURISPRUDENCE, vol. 15, p. 205).

I. **Definition**—**Physician.**—A person who has received the degree of Doctor of Medicine from an incorporated institution. One lawfully engaged in the practice of medicine.[4]

1. Pollard *v.* Photographic Company, L. R., 40 Ch. Div. 345. This decision was followed by the Supreme court of *Minnesota* in Moore *v.* Rugg, 44 Minn. 28, an action for damages.

2. Story *v.* Walker, 11 Lea (Tenn.) 515; 47 Am. Rep. 305.

3. The term "physically incapacitated," as used in *Alabama* Code, which provides, that when either party at the time of the marriage was "physically incapacitated" from entering into the marriage state, the other may have a divorce, is equivalent to "impotent." Anonymous, 89 Ala. 291.

See generally MARRIAGE, vol. 14, pp. 492, 536.

4. Bouv. Law Dict.

Limited to No Particular School.—As used in statutes regulating the practice of medicine, providing for the organization of medical societies, etc., it has been held that the word physician is not limited to any particular school of practitioners. Raynor *v.* State, 62 Wis. 289; White *v.* Carroll, 42 N. Y. 161; Corsi *v.* Maretzek, 4 E. D. Smith (N. Y.) 1.

Family Physician.—In Price *v.* Phœnix Mut. L. Ins. Co., 17 Minn. 497, 10 Am. Rep. 166, it was said that the phrase "family physician" is in common use, "and has not so far as we are aware, any technical signification;" and, as used in an insurance policy, requiring the name, etc. of a family physician of the party insured signified the physician who usually attends and is consulted by the members of the family in the capacity of a physician. "We employ the word 'usually' both because we do not deem it necessary, to constitute a person a family physician, as the phrase is used in this instance, that he should invariably attend and be consulted by the members of the family in the capacity of a physician, and because we do not deem it necessary that he should attend and be consulted as such physician by each and all of the members of the family."

The term "family physician" means

Surgeon.—"A surgeon, formerly, was a mere operator, who joined his practice to that of a barber. But the business of a surgeon is, properly speaking, with external ailments and injuries of the limbs."[1]

II. **Statutory Regulations**—*License.*—Statutes regulating the practice of medicine, and requiring that the practitioner should be registered or licensed, have been enacted by many of the States; and the constitutionality of these enactments as a valid exercise of the police power of the State has been almost invariably upheld by the courts.[2]

one who is accustomed to attend members of a family in the capacity of a physician, not one who has only occasionally so attended them. Reid *v.* Piedmont etc. L. Ins. Co., 58 Mo. 421.

Medical Attendant.—A physician who merely makes a casual prescription for a friend, when meeting him in the street, cannot be called his medical attendant. That term means a person to whom the care of a sick person has been intrusted. Edington *v.* Mutual L. Ins. Co., 5 Hun (N. Y.) 1.

Graduate in Medicine.—The words "suitable graduate in medicine," as used in the county government act *California*, § 25, subd. 5, providing that the board of supervisors shall appoint some suitable graduate in medicine to attend the indigent sick, etc., mean a person legally licensed to practice medicine under the laws of the State, and do not exclude all but college graduates. People *v.* Eichelroth, 78 Cal. 141.

1. (Per Best, C. J., in Allison *v.* Hayden, 4 Bing. 621). But "with a view to the recovery of a patient in a case of that description, he may, perhaps, prescribe and dispense medicine." Allison *v.* Haydon, 4 Bing. 621. See also Apothecaries Co. *v.* Lotinga, 2 Moo. & R. 499.

"In strictness, to act as a surgeon something must be done by the hand" (per Knight-Bruce, L. J., in *Ex parte* Crabb, *Re* Palmer, 25 L. J., Bank. 49).

A contract by a physician with the board of supervisors "to perform the duties of physician" for the paupers of a county, held, to embrace the usual cases of surgery as well as the administration of medicine. Wetherell *v.* Marion Co., 28 Iowa 22.

An agreement by a physician with a board of supervisors to give the paupers of the county "medical" treatment construed to include services in surgical cases. Clinton Co. *v.* Ramsey, 20 Ill. App. 577.

2. Eastman *v.* State, 109 Ind. 278; State *v.* Hibbard, 3 Ohio 63; State *v.* Gazley, 5 Ohio 21; Hewitt *v.* Charier, 16 Pick. (Mass.) 353; State *v.* Fleischer, 41 Minn. 69; Orr *v.* Meek, 111 Ind. 40; *Ex parte* McNulty, 77 Cal. 164; State *v.* Creditor (Kan. 1870), 24 Pac. Rep. 346; Williams *v.* People, 121 Ill. 84; Dent *v.* State, 129 U. S. 114; 25 W. Va. 1; State *v.* Green, 112 Ind. 462; Harding *v.* People, 10 Colo. 387; Logan *v.* State, 5 Tex. App. 306; Sheldon *v.* Clark, 1 Johns. (N. Y.) 513; Alcott *v.* Barber, 1 Wend. (N. Y.) 526; Timmerman *v.* Morrison, 14 Johns. (N. Y.) 369; Thompson *v.* Staats, 15 Wend. (N. Y.) 595; Bailey *v.* Mogg, 4 Den. (N. Y.) 60; Finch *v.* Gridley, 25 Wend. (N. Y.) 469; Antle *v.* State, 6 Tex. App. 202; Musser *v.* Chase, 29 Ohio St. 577; Wert *v.* Clutter, 37 Ohio St. 347; Bibber *v.* Simpson, 59 Me. 181; Thompson *v.* Hazen, 25 Me. 104; State *v.* Gregory, 83 Mo. 123; 53 Am. Rep. 565.

See, however, State *v.* Pennoyer (N. H. 1889), 18 Atl. Rep. 878, where it was held that the general laws of *New Hampshire*, ch. 132, §§ 1, 2, 6 and 8, requiring that all physicians, except those who had practiced their profession for five years at the same place, shall obtain a license and pay therefor, are unconstitutional, as discriminating in favor of one class of citizens to the detriment of another.

In construing section 6 of the *Nevada* Act, which provides that it shall not apply "to those who have practiced medicine or surgery in this State for a period of ten years next preceding the passage of this act" (Stat. 1875, 47): *Held*, that there is some reason for requiring ten years' practice in this State as a qualification for the continued practice of medicine or surgery; but there is no sort of reason for requiring that practice to have extended over the particular ten years immediately preceding the enactment of the law.

These statutes differ widely in the general qualifications which they require of the practitioner before he may become licensed or registered, and differ also as to the manner of obtaining a license or registering, and as to the officials from whom or before whom such license shall be obtained, or such registry made. And it would be impossible to treat the law of the various States connectedly upon this subject; but a collection of the decisions upon the several points involved will be found in the notes.[1]

and to this extent the law is unconstitutional, because in violation of the fourteenth amendment to the Federal Constitution; but omitting the words "next preceding the passage of this act," leaves a good and perfect statute. By Beatty, J., *Ex parte* Spinney, 10 Nev. 323.

In Brown *v.* People, 11 Colo. 109, the *Colorado* statute was held to be constitutional notwithstanding that there was no provision that each school of medicine named in the act should be equally represented on the State board of medical examiners.

1. To Whom Applicable.—One who administers medicine and receives money for his services without registration falls within the *Arkansas* Act regulating the practice of medicine. Richardson *v.* State, 47 Ark. 562.

The professional services of a medical clairvoyant are medical services within the meaning of Revised Statutes of *Maine*, Ch. 13, § 3. Bibber *v.* Simpson, 59 Me. 181.

Several of the States have provisions in their statutes that the regulations therein provided shall not apply to practitioners who have practiced continuously for a certain number of years; and this has been held not to confer special privileges on such practitioners, but to be simply a qualification for practicing medicine. Willlams *v.* People, 121 Ill. 84. See also People *v.* Phippin, 70 Mich. 6; Wert *v.* Clutter, 37 Ohio St. 347; *Ex parte* Spinney, 10 Nev. 323; Underwood *v.* Scott, 43 Kan. 714.

A physician lawfully licensed to practise medicine anywhere in the State, cannot be compelled by the authorities of Savannah to take out a license before practicing in that city. Savannah *v.* Charlton, 36 Ga. 460.

The *New York* Law of 1874, ch. 436, making it a misdemeanor for any person to practice medicine or surgery who is not authorized to do so by license or diploma from some chartered college, etc., does not apply to one who undertakes to cure diseases by manipulating the patient's body by rubbing, kneading, and pressing it; and such person, though unauthorized to practice medicine is entitled to recover his fees. Smith *v.* Lane, 24 Hun (N. Y.) 632.

The *Missouri* statute, preventing one who "practices medicine, or surgery" from recovering compensation for his professional services unless he has complied with its terms, applies to one who, as a physician, gives electric treatment. Davidson *v.* Bohlman, 37 Mo. App. 576.

Qualification.—In People *v.* Fulder, (Supreme Ct.), 4 N. Y. Supp. 946, it was held that a person who had received a medical education in Germany, but not a full diploma, such as was given by universities at which he had studied, upon the completion of the course, and who had passed an examination for a commission as a medical officer in the New York volunteers, had not satisfied § 356 of the Penal Code, which forbids any one to practice medicine without first having obtained a license from some chartered school, State board of medical examiners, or medical society.

A physician having a diploma of another State, is not authorized to register by a detached certificate of the secretary of a Pennsylvania medical college that he had "examined the diploma, and believed it to be genuine, and legally issued to the doctor whose name it bears." Bauer's Appeal (Pa. 1886), 3 Cent. Rep. 157.

Under *Nebraska* Laws 1881, 282–286, providing that no person shall be entitled to registration as a physician or to practise medicine "unless he or she shall be possessed of one of the qualifications named in this section," held, that no one could practice without possessing one of those qualifications, even though he had an M. D. degree from a regular college. Doge *v.* State, 17 Neb. 140.

A board of censors of a medical society may not refuse a license to an applicant on the sole ground that he is not worthy of public confidence. Gage *v.* Censors, 63 N. H. 92; 56 Am. Rep. 492.

Laws 21st Gen. Assem. *Iowa*, ch. 104, regulating the practice of medicine, provides, *inter alia*, that if any applicant for a certificate "has been in continuous practice for a period of not less than five years," such fact constitutes a *prima facie* qualification. *Held*, that under section 7 of said act, providing that the examining board may "refuse a certificate to any person who has been convicted of felony, . . or may revoke certificates for like cause, or for palpable evidence of incompetency," the board could refuse a certificate for palpable evidence of incompetency, despite the established fact of prior practice for the statutory time. State *v.* Mosher, 78 Iowa 321.

A medical practitioner's certificate of qualification, under the *Texas* Act of 1873 must, on his change of domicile to another county, be furnished to the district clerk thereof for record. Hilliard *v.* State, 7 Tex. App. 69.

Under the *Michigan* Act, No. 167 Pub. Acts 1883, any graduate of any legally authorized medical college, having registered, etc., and physicians who have practiced continuously for five years before the act, may practice medicine. People *v.* Phippin, 70 Mich. 6.

Where a State board, authorized by statute to determine what colleges are reputable, has prescribed a rule that "it will recognize as reputable only such colleges as require" a certain requisite for graduation, it has exercised its judicial power, and so long as the rule is in force, only the ministerial act remains to be done. Illinois State Board *v.* People, 20 Ill. App. 457.

Revocation.—The *Illinois* statute provides that the State board of health may revoke a physician's license "for unprofessional or dishonorable conduct." It was held in People *v* McCoy, 125 Ill. 289, that a charge against a practitioner for making representations, which were calculated to deceive and defraud the public, that he could cure certain diseases, would be, if true, sufficient ground for such revocation; but that such a charge was not sufficiently sustained by evidence of advertisements reciting the high professional attainments of the physician. Under a similar statute in *Minnesota* it was held to be unprofessional conduct where a physician published advertisements containing false statements as to his ability to cure diseases, knowing them to be false when he made them and intending thereby to impose upon and deceive the public. State *v.* State Board Medical Examiners, 34 Minn. 391. Upon the construction of the *Minnesota* statute it was held that the revocation of such certificates was not an exercise of judicial power, and hence might be vested in the State board of medical examiners. State *v.* State Board Medical Examiners, 34 Minn. 387. See also Wilkins *v.* State, 113 Ind. 514.

The court of common pleas has no jurisdiction to strike from the register, names of veterinary surgeons whose names were not registered within the time prescribed by Act *Pennsylvania* April 11, 1889, and cannot pass upon the constitutionality of that act. The remedy provided in the quarter sessions for violations of the act is exclusive, under Act March 31, 1860. Veterinary Surgeons' Case, 8 Pa. Co. Ct. Rep. 185.

While the *Indiana* Act of April 11, 1885, declares that a license procured by fraud shall be void, no provision is made for any judicial proceeding to have it so adjudged, and as a license to practice medicine is not a franchise, an information in the nature of a *quo warranto* cannot be brought by the prosecuting attorney against the licensee to annul the license. And the court expressed the opinion that, until such a license was judicially declared to be void, it would protect the licensee from prosecution for practicing her profession, and enable her to recover compensation for her services. State *v.* Green, 112 Ind. 462.

Prosecutions for Practicing Without a License.—Where a statute makes it a misdemeanor for one to practice medicine "without having first obtained a license or diploma, or certificate of qualification, or, not being a regular graduate of a medical college of this State, having had his diploma recorded," a conviction cannot be had against a person having a diploma of a regular medical college of another State and who has had it recorded in the county in which he is practicing. Brooks *v.* State, 88 Ala. 123.

An *Iowa* statute exempts from its penal provisions physicians who have practiced five years, "provided such physicians shall furnish the State board

. . . satisfactory evidence of such practice, and shall procure a proper certificate;" but a defendant cannot avail himself of this exception unless he has a proper certificate showing that he has practiced five years, even though he may be able to prove at the trial that he has practiced for such a length of time. State *v.* Mosher, 44 Iowa 321.

Where a person prefixed "doctor" to his name, and advertised that he would effect a complete cure of the opium habit, and issued a number of letters addressed to him as doctor, from former patients, testifying to the success of his treatment, it was held that he clearly held himself out as a practising physician. Benham *v.* State, 116 Ind. 112.

A diploma issued by a regularly incorporated college constitutes a *prima facie* defense to a prosecution for practising medicine contrary to law. *Wisconsin* Laws of 1881, ch. 256, § 1. See Raynor *v.* State, 62 Wis. 289; Wendel *v.* State, 62 Wis. 300.

A parchment, purporting to be a diploma to practise medicine, is not evidence *per se* that the college issuing it is a regularly constituted medical institution. Hill *v.* Boddie, 2 Stew. & P. (Ala.) 56.

A charge that "a person who was attending a single case could not be adjudged guilty of practising medicine, though he held and filed no certificate as required by law," was held, properly refused, and that proof of a single act, in connection with other circumstances, might suffice to warant a conviction,—as, for instance, that he held himself out to the community as a physician. Antle *v.* State, 6 Tex. App. 202.

The Complaint.—The rules as to the sufficiency or insufficiency of a complaint or indictment against an unqualified practitioner, are the same as those which govern indictments and complaints under other penal statutes. See also for cases bearing on this question, People *v.* Phippin, 70 Mich. 6; Denton *v.* State, 21 Neb. 445; Benham *v.* State, 116 Ind. 112; State *v.* Fussell, 45 Ark. 65; State *v.* Goldman, 44 Tex. 104; State *v.* Roberts, 33 Mo. App. 524; State *v.* Hale, 15 Mo. 607; Sheldon *v.* Clark, 1 Johns. (N. Y.) 513; Antle *v.* State, 6 Tex. App. 202.

Miscellaneous.—The fact that the defendant, in an action under the *New York* Code, practiced medicine before the enactment of the law of 1874, which formed the basis of section 356 of the Code, does not restrict the power of the statute to compel the taking out of a license in order to justify his practice. People *v.* Fulda (Supreme Ct.), 4 N. Y. Supp. 946.

It has been held, under the statutes of some of the States, that it is necessary for a physician to be registered or licensed in each county in which he practises. Ege *v.* Com. (Pa. 1887), 9 Atl. Rep. 471; 20 W. N. C. 73; Orr *v.* Meek, 111 Ind. 40. But see Martino *v.* Kirk, 55 Hun (N. Y.) 474.

The *California* statute of April 3, 1876, as amended April 3, 1878, provides that a person who has not procured a medical certificate may render medical attention in cases of emergency. It was held that a case of emergency, within the statute, is one in which the ordinary and qualified practitioners are not readily obtainable, and does not include a case where a sick person has been given up as incurable by the physicians of the schools. People *v.* Lee-Wah, 71 Cal. 80.

Where a physician did his best to register and did register as soon as he could, but was delayed by the neglect of the clerk, he may recover fees for services rendered during such delay. Parish *v.* Foss, 75 Ga. 439.

To make a defense for the sale of opium by a practising physician complete, defendant must show that he comes within the provisions of the act "to prevent the practice of medicine and surgery by unqualified persons." State *v.* Ching Gang, 16 Nev. 62.

Itinerants.—Code *West Virginia*, ch. 150, § 14, prohibits an itinerant physician from practising medicine; an itinerant vendor of drugs, etc., intended for the treatment of disease, from selling such drugs; or any one, by any drug, nostrum, ointment, or appliance of any kind, from treating diseases—without first paying a special tax. *Held*, that an indictment under this statute might charge in one count that the defendant was an itinerant physician, and an itinerant vendor of drugs, and that he, as such physician and vendor of drugs, sold drugs, etc., and practiced medicine without paying the special tax. State *v.* Ragland, 31 W. Va. 453.

A corporation organized under a statute permitting the incorporation of societies for the purpose of establishing "literary and scientific institutions," has not the power to issue medical di-

Where the question of license or qualification of a physician arises collaterally in a civil action between party and party, or between the doctor and the one who employs him, then the license or due qualification under a statute to practice will be presumed, and the burden of proof thrown upon him who denies such qualification or license.[1] But in case of a prosecution on behalf of the public, the rule is otherwise, and in such cases license or due qualification under statute is not presumed, and it rests with the defendant to prove it.[2]

III. **Right to Compensation.**—A physician's right to compensation depends upon contract, express or implied.[3] The services of a physician being valuable, the law will imply a contract to pay a reasonable consideration therefor by any one receiving the benefit of such services.[4] This implied contract is in the first instance usually with the patient, or where one stands in such a rela-

plomas; and a person holding a diploma issued by such a corporation cannot obtain a *mandamus* addressed to the board of medical examiners in Vermont, who are authorized by the statutes of that State to license physicians, commanding the board to license the holder of the certificate. Townshend *v.* Gray, (Vt. 1890), 19 Atl. Rep. 635.

Where a statute confers power to grant a certificate to an applicant for leave to practise medicine, upon a board of medical examiners, or board of health, etc., it has been held that the power conferred is a discretionary one, and that a *mandamus* will not lie to compel such a board to grant a certificate. State *v.* Gregory, 83 Mo. 123; 53 Am. Rep. 565; State *v.* State Medical etc. Board, 32 Minn. 324; 50 Am. Rep. 575.

1. Chicago *v.* Wood, 24 Ill. App. 42; Williams *v.* People, 20 Ill. App. 92; McPherson *v.* Cheadell, 24 Wend. (N. Y.) 15; Thompson *v.* Sayre, 1 Den. (N. Y.) 175; Pearce *v.* Whale, 5 Barn. & C. 38.

The reason for this rule is that when the positive law commands an act to be done the law will presume that it has been done, and therefore one relying on the omission of such an act must make some proof of it, though it be a negative. Williams *v.* People, 20 Ill. App. 92; see also Chicago etc. R. Co. *v.* Smith, 21 Ill. App. 202; see, however, Westmoreland *v.* Bragg, 2 Hill (S. Car.) 414; Dow *v.* Haley, 30 N.J. L. 354; Adams *v.* Stewart, 5 Harr. (Del.) 144.

Assumpsit on a note, payable to F, or bearer, and transferred after due to plaintiff; plea, the general issue. The note was given for medical service rendered by F, and the defense was, that F was not a licensed physician. Neither the plaintiff nor F had notice of the nature of the defense before the trial. *Held*, that the *onus* was on defendant to show that F had no license. Barton *v.* Sutherland, 6 Rich. (S. Car.) 57.

2. Apothecaries Co. *v.* Bentley, Ry. & Moo. 159; Sheldon *v.* Clark, 1 Johns. (N. Y.) 513; Sherwood *v.* Mitchell, 4 Den. (N. Y.) 435; Smith *v.* Joyce, 12 Barb. (N. Y.) 21; Brown *v.* Young, 2 B. Mon. (Ky.) 26; Redding *v.* Com. 3 B. Mon. (Ky.) 339; State *v.* Crowell, 25 Me. 171; Williams *v.* People, 20 Ill. App. 92; Raynor *v.* State, 62 Wis. 299; Benham *v.* State, 116 Ind. 112; 1 Greenlf., § 79.

3. Smith *v.* Chambers, 2 Ph. 221; 11 Jur. 359.

4. *In re* Scott, 1 Redf. (N. Y.) 234; Baxter *v.* Gray, 4 Scott, N. R. 274; Garrey *v.* Stadler, 67 Wis. 512; 58 Am. Rep. 877; Gibbon *v.* Budd, 2 H. & C. 92.

Thus, where a physician was summoned to attend his aunt upon matters of business, but while with her rendered valuable medical attendance which she accepted, it was held that he was entitled to recover for such services. Succession of Dickey, 41 La. Ann. 1010.

In Forbes *v.* Chichester (Supreme Ct.), 8 N. Y. Supp. 747, it was held that the demand of a physician against the estate of a decedent must be proved strictly, and that no promise could be implied in favor of the plain-

tion with the patient as to be liable for necessaries furnished him, as the relation of parent and child, husband and wife, guardian and ward, the implied promise is by such person.[1]

But a promise of a third person to pay for medical services rendered another may be inferred, as in any other case, where the circumstances are strong enough.[2]

tiff where it appears that he did not render any service.

So, it has been held, that where a physician is called in consultation by an attending physician, he may recover his fee from the patient, although there may have been an engagement between the attending physician and the patient that the former should pay the consultation fee. Shelton *v.* Johnson, 40 Iowa 84; Garrey *v.* Stadler, 67 Wis. 512; 58 Am. Rep. 877.

1. Cooper *v.* Phillips, 4 C. & P. 581.

Where the wife of the defendant, being afflicted with a dangerous disease, was carried by him to a distance from his residence, and left under the care of the plaintiff as a surgeon, and after the lapse of some weeks the plaintiff performed an operation on her for the cure of the disease, soon after which she died—*held*, in an action by the plaintiff against the defendant to recover compensation for his services, that the performance of the operation was within the scope of the plaintiff's authority, if, in his judgment, it was necessary or expedient; and that it was not incumbent on him to prove that it was necessary or proper under the circumstances; or that, before he performed it, he gave notice to the defendant; or that it would have been dangerous to the wife to wait until notice could be given to the defendant. M'Clallen *v.* Adams, 19 Pick. (Mass.) 333; 31 Am. Rep. 140.

Liability of a County for Services to Paupers.—There is no implied promise by a county to pay for services rendered by a physician or surgeon to the poor if there has been no judicial ascertainment that the person cared for is a pauper. Lee Co. *v.* Lackie, 30 Ark. 764; Prewett *v.* Mississippi Co., 38 Ark. 213; Cantrell *v.* Clark Co., 47 Ark. 40.

The presumption is rather that the physician looks to his patient for pay or bestows his services in charity. Cantrell *v.* Clark Co., 47 Ark. 240; Blakesley *v.* Directors of the Poor, 102 Pa. St. 274.

The rule under the *Pennsylvania* statute is that the directors of the poor, etc., are answerable to the physician for services rendered in a case of emergency to any persons who are chargeable upon the county or who become so immediately afterwards. Westmoreland etc. Poor Directors *v.* Donnelly (Pa. 1886), 7 Atl. Rep. 204. See also Directors of the House of Employment *v.* Murray, 32 Pa. St. 178; Directors of Poor House etc. *v.* Worthington, 38 Pa. St. 160.

See also Pottawatomie Co. *v.* Monall, 19 Kan. 141; Hunter *v.* Jasper Co., 40 Iowa 568; Rouse *v.* Peoria Co., 7 Ill. 99; Kellogg *v.* St. George, 28 Me. 255; Childs *v.* Phillips, 45 Me. 408.

See also POOR AND POOR LAWS.

It is no part of the duty of a physician employed under contract by a county to treat its poor to make a *post mortem* examination of the body of a dead pauper, and when he does so at the request of the coroner he is entitled to compensation. Lang *v.* Perry Co., 121 Ind. 133.

Rule of Evidence.—The *Mississippi* court has gone so far as to authorize a physician to recover in an action against his patients, by establishing upon a trial the facts of his habit of keeping correct books of accounts, and that the account sued upon had been correctly copied from his books. Hazlett *v.* Leggett, 6 Smed. & M. (Miss.) 632. But with this exception, physicians must be held, like others, to the customary rules of evidence, and proof that the plaintiff, a physician, practised in the family of the defendant and was seen going and returning from defendant's house, coupled with proof that the items as charged were according to the customary rates, does not create a legal presumption of indebtedness by the defendant. Simmons *v.* Means, 8 Smed. & M. (Miss.) 397.

2. Thus, where a person called at the office of a physician and left his business card, having written on it, "call on Mrs. D., No. —— —— St.," with the clerk, requesting him to tell the physician to call at once, it was held that he became liable to pay for the physician's attendance upon Mrs. D. Bradley *v.* Dodge, 45 How. Pr. (N. Y.) 57. And see Clark *v.* Waterman, 7 Vt. 76; 29 Am. Dec. 150.

When a justice of the peace, acting as coroner, requests a physician to make an examination of the body over which an inquest is being held, and he makes an examination, and the justice so certifies to the county commissioners, the physician will be entitled to an allowance. Stevens *v.* Harrison Co., 46 Ind. 541.

In an action to set aside a will, two physicians were appointed by the court to examine and report whether the widow of the testator were pregnant. *Held*, that, having been appointed by the court, they were *quasi* officers of the court, and were entitled to be paid out of the estate, without awaiting the termination or event of the litigation. Rollwagen *v.* Powell, 8 Hun (N. Y.) 210.

No Promise Implied.—Where a person was sent for a physician, and not finding the one sent for, spoke to another, and on the arrival of the latter, before any service was performed, in his presence, the manner of his employment, and the nature of the service to be performed, were explained to the patient. *Held*, in an action by the physician against the messenger, that the latter was not liable. Smith *v.* Riddick, 5 Jones (N. Car.) 342.

Where A, the plantation physician of a planter, found a surgical operation necessary on one of the negroes, and requested the overseer to send for B, another physician, who came and performed the operation without any assistance from A, held, that B could not maintain an action against A to recover for his services. Guerard *v.* Jenkins, 1 Strobh. (S. Car.) 171.

A physician cannot recover of a brother of an insane person for medical attendance, etc., rendered the latter, at the request of such brother, unless there was an employment under such circumstances as to show an intention on the part of such brother to pay for the services, and so understood by him and the physician. Smith *v.* Watson, 14 Vt. 332. See also Boyd *v.* Sappington, 4 Watts (Pa.) 247.

Where defendants were liable by a bond for the support of a patient, who had called in a physician without the consent of the defendants, no implication arises that the defendants will be answerable for the physician's services. Shaw *v.* Graves, 79 Me. 166.

Authority of Railway Officers and Employes to Bind the Company by Contracts for Medical Services.—*Generally.* It is a matter of frequent occurrence for railway officials and even subordinate employes, as conductors and station agents, to engage physicians and nurses to attend upon employes and passengers injured in railway accidents. The bills for services so rendered are often disputed on the ground that the officer or servant contracting for them acted *ultra vires*. The cases passing upon the authority of different railway agents in this respect will be reviewed in this note. Primarily, where a physician attends upon persons injured in a railway accident, the liability of the railroad company for such services must depend upon the contract. Ellis *v.* Central Pac. R. Co, 5 Nev. 255. The physician's services must have been rendered upon the credit of the company. Thus, where a person was injured, and a physician having been called in, the agent of the company during the treatment requested the physician to continue the treatment, and promised on the company's behalf to pay the bill, it was held that the company was nevertheless not liable unless the jury believed that the services were rendered on the company's credit. Northern Cent. R. Co. *v.* Prentiss, 11 Md. 119.

Superintendent.—By the weight of authority it is held that the general superintendent of a railway company may, in the exercise of his powers as such, bind the company for the payment of expenses, for nursing and medical attendance necessary to cure an injured employe. Toledo etc. R. Co. *v.* Rodrigues, 47 Ill. 188; Toledo etc. R. Co. *v.* Prince, 50 Ill. 26; Indianapolis etc. R. Co. *v.* Morris, 67 Ill. 295; Cairo etc. R. Co. *v.* Mahoney, 82 Ill. 73; 25 Am. Rep. 299. Thus where a laborer on a railroad is injured while in the service of the railroad company, a telegram from the general superintendent directing one of his subordinates to employ a physician and do all he can to save the injured limb and make the sufferer comfortable, is authority for a contract binding the company to pay for the board and care of the injured party while recovering from the injury. Atchison etc. R. Co. *v.* Reecher, 24 Kan. 228, 1 Am. & Eng. R. Cas. 343.

In Cincinnati etc. R. Co. *v.* Davis

(Ind.), 43 Am. & Eng. R. Cas. 459, it was held that the general superintendent of a railroad company has authority to employ a surgeon to give attention to persons injured by the trains of the company.

In the case of Marquette etc. R. Co. *v.* Taft, 28 Mich. 289, however, a laborer in the service of the company was struck and injured by one of its trains, and the yardmaster and the superintendent employed a surgeon, and the court divided on the question of the company's liability, Graves and Campbell, JJ., denying its liability, and Cooley, J., and Christiancy, C. J., affirming that it was liable to the surgeon. The case of Brown *v.* Missouri, etc. R. Co., 67 Mo. 122, was an action for drugs to a woman who had been hurt by one of the company's trains. They were furnished upon orders given by a division superintendent. The court said: "No proof was offered as to the duties of such officer, and the courts cannot take judicial notice of them." For want of such proof the judgment was reversed. In Union Pac. R. Co. *v.* Beatty, 35 Kan. 265; 26 Am. & Eng. R. R. Cas. 84, it appeared that a railway passenger train was derailed, and some of the passengers were injured by inevitable accident. The court held that no obligation rested upon the company to furnish medical care and attention to the injured passengers; and it cannot be made liable for such care and attention by the contract of the division superintendent unless authority was given him to make it liable. It was also said that where a division superintendent employs a physician to attend upon passengers so injured, and the company denies his authority and contests its liability under the employment, it is error to instruct the jury that the division superintendent is presumed to have such authority until the contrary appears. The decision in this case appears to go upon the ground that the considerations which will authorize such a contract to secure the speedy cure of employes who have been disabled and the early resumption of their duties, are wanting in case of passengers who have been injured by unavoidable accident.

In Stephenson *v.* New York etc. R. Co., 2 Duer (N. Y.) 341, it was held that the superintendent of a railroad company who stated that his office gave him general supervisory control over the whole line of the road, everything connected with the running of the road being under his supervision and control, and that he paid money to drivers, conductors, and other persons employed by him as superintendent, but had no power over the treasurer, has no authority to bind the company by the employment of a physician or surgeon to attend upon a child who had been run over by a car and severely injured.

General Manager or Agent.—In *England* it is held that the general manager of a railroad company has, as incidental to his employment, authority to bind the company to pay for surgical attendance bestowed at his request on a servant of the company injured by an accident. Walker *v.* Great Western R. Co., L. R., 2 Exch. 228. In this case Chief Baron Kelley, in the course of the argument, inquired: "Must a board be convened before a man who has both his legs broken can have medical assistance?" And in the case of Atlantic etc. R. Co. *v.* Reisner, 18 Kan. 458, without proof of the duties and powers of the general agent, the company was held liable upon his contract with a hotel keeper for board and attendance to a brakeman, injured while working for the company. It was said: "In the case of a general agency, the principal holds out the agent to the public as having unlimited authority as to all his business. When the witness testified that Hyde was the general agent of the road at Atchison, he thereby gave evidence that the railroad company held out to the public such person as its agent in all its business and employment. In other words, the general agent of the company is virtually the corporation itself. . . . General manager and general agent are synonymous terms." And in Louisville etc. R. Co. *v.* McVay, 98 Ind. 391; 22 Am. & Eng. R. Cas. 382, it is held that the courts will presume from the ordinary meaning of the term, "general manager" that such an officer has the general direction and control of the affairs of the corporation, and authority to bind it by contracts for nursing, etc., of persons injured on the line of the railway.

Station Agent.—In Cox *v.* Midland Counties R. Co., 3 Welsby, H. & G. 268, the station master of the railroad company at Birmingham, who acted there as chief officer of the passenger and other departments, employed a surgeon to perform a surgical operation upon a passenger injured by a train of the railway company, and the company contested its liability for the service on the ground that its servants had no authority to bind them by contracts of that description, and the court held that there was no liability against the company therefor, because the power to enter into the contracts was not incident either to the employment of the station master or of the superintendent of the road.

The case of Tucker *v.* St. Louis etc. R. Co., 54 Mo. 177, was an action by a physician against the company to recover for surgical and medical treatment of a brakeman injured while on duty. He was employed by the section agent and the conductor of the train. It was held that he could not recover. After stating that there was no evidence that they had any authority to employ the physician on the corporation's account, the court said: "It is only shown that they were agents of defendant in conducting its railroad business, which of itself could certainly give them no authority to employ physicians, for the defendant, to attend to and treat persons accidentally injured on the road." And in *Illinois* it is said that where a surgeon has been employed by the station agent of a railway company, to attend an employe injured while in the service of the company, although he may not have express authority to do so, yet slight acts of ratification by the company will authorize a jury in finding the employment was the act of the company. Cairo etc. R. Co. *v.* Mahoney, 82 Ill. 73; 25 Am. Rep. 299.

Conductor.—It has been held that, where an injury to an employe is done at a point distant from the chief offices of the company, and there is urgent necessity for the employment of a surgeon to render professional services to an injured employe, the conductor, if he is the highest agent of the company on the ground, has authority to bind the corporation by the employment of a surgeon to render the services required by the emergency. Terre Haute etc. R. Co. *v.* McMurray, 98 Ind. 358; 22 Am. & Eng. R. Cas. 371. But the authority existing in such cases is exceptional. The conductor has no general authority to employ a surgeon. It grows out of the present emergency, and the absence, and consequent inability to act, of the railway's managing agent; its existence cannot extend beyond the causes from which it sprang. St. Louis etc. R. Co. *v.* Hoover (Ark. 1890), 13 S. W. Rep. 107; Tucker *v.* St. Louis etc. R. Co., 54 Mo. 177; Terre Haute etc. R. Co. *v.* McMurray, 98 Ind. 358; 22 Am. & Eng. R. Cas. 371; and see Indianapolis etc. R. Co. *v.* Morris, 67 Ill. 295.

Company's Physician.—The fact that a physician in the service of a railroad company is authorized to buy medicines on the credit of the company, does not imply a power to bind the company by a contract for board, lodging, attendance and nursing of a person injured on the company's road. Mayberry *v.* Chicago etc. R. Co., 75 Mo. 492; 11 Am. & Eng. R. Cas. 29; and see Brown *v.* Missouri etc. R. Co., 67 Mo. 122.

Bigham *v.* Chicago etc. R. Co., 79 Iowa 534, was an action against a railroad company for services, as nurse, rendered one of defendant's employes; an agent of defendant testified that, in pursuance of his authority, he employed a physician to attend such employe, and authorized him to employ two nurses. Plaintiff and his brother testified that the physician, by letter, employed the plaintiff as nurse, which letter had been lost; and the physician testified that plaintiff had rendered the services alleged, but that he could not remember whether it was at his request or whether he wrote the letter testified to by plaintiff. The court held that the evidence was sufficient to support a finding that plaintiff was employed by the physician, by virtue of authority conferred upon him by defendant's agent.

President of Company.—The plaintiff, a physician, was, at the instance and request of certain parties wounded by a railroad accident, attending them when the president of the railroad company (though not in the presence of the physician) told the wounded persons to employ whatever physician they chose, and the company would pay the bills. This was conveyed to the plaintiff; but he testified that he attended the wounded until their recovery, in pursuance of the original calling. *Held*, in an action against the company upon contract for services performed, that there was no mutuality of contract by consent between them, and no liability attached to the railroad company for the services performed by the plaintiff to the persons who employed him. Canney

The express contract to pay for a physician's services, as well as the implied contract, may be made with a patient or with a

v. South Pac. Coast R. Co., 63 Cal. 501; 12 Am. & Eng. R. Cas. 310.

Roadmaster.—Courts cannot judicially know, or presume, without further proof of the duties and powers of a "roadmaster" than what the term indicates, that such an employe has authority to bind the corporation by a contract with a third party for nursing a person injured upon the line of the railway. But such a contract of the roadmaster may be ratified by the general manager. Louisville etc. R Co. *v.* McVay, 98 Ind. 391; 22 Am. & Eng. R. Cas. 382.

Engineer.—In an action by a physician against a railroad company, for professional services rendered to an employe of the company who had sustained an injury on its cars, evidence that the engineer of the train on which the injury happened, telegraphed to a station agent to have a doctor at the station when the train arrived, does not show an employment of plaintiff by the company, in the absence of evidence of the authority of the engineer to bind the company. Cooper *v.* New York Cent. etc. R. Co., 6 Hun (N. Y.) 276.

Yardmaster.—The case of Marquette etc. R. Co. *v.* Taft, 28 Mich. 289, was an action by a surgeon against the company for services rendered an employe who was injured while on duty. He was employed by the superintendent and the yardmaster who had charge of the business and men in the yard where the employe was engaged when injured and who had the right to employ men for all purposes they were required for in the yard, and to discharge them. While the court divided as to the authority of the superintendent, the judges all agreed that, under the evidence, the yardmaster had no authority to bind the company by the employment of the surgeon.

Attorney.—The attorney for a railroad company has no authority as such to employ a physician on its behalf. St. Louis etc. R. Co. *v.* Hoover, 53 Ark. 377.

The sub-inspector of railway police has implied power to employ surgical aid for an injured employe. Langan *v.* Great Western R. Co., 30 L. T., N. S. 173.

Ratification of Unauthorized Employment.—Where an employe of a railway company has received injury, while in the discharge of his duty, and the station agent, in his capacity as such, assumes certain liabilities in his behalf, for nurse and medical attendance, and writes a letter to the general superintendent, stating the facts, it is presumed that the general superintendent received such notice, and in the absence of any instructions to the contrary, consented on the part of the railroad company, to assume the liabilities of the station agent for all reasonable charges in this behalf. Toledo etc. R. Co. *v.* Rodrigues, 47 Ill. 188. And where a railroad station agent engages a surgeon to attend an employe injured in the service of the company, although such act is unauthorized, yet the company will be liable, if, upon due notice given to the superintendent, the act is not repudiated. To avoid responsibility in such case the superintendent should have dissented from the action of the station agent, and directed him to apprise the surgeon of such dissent. Toledo etc. R. Co. *v.* Prince, 50 Ill. 26.

Where the conductor of the defendant railway company brought a brakeman, who had received a serious injury whilst in defendant's service, to the plaintiff's house, to be cared for, and immediately after telegraphed to the officers of the company the facts, and they never notified the plaintiff of their intention that the company should not be responsible, held, in an action by the plaintiff against the company, that the company was liable to pay the plaintiff what his services were reasonably worth. Indianapolis etc. R. Co. *v.* Morris, 67 Ill. 295.

And if a conductor places a man who has been injured by the train of which he has charge, in the care of a physician, and the company immediately thereafter acquires full knowledge of all the facts and circumstances of the physician's employment and permits him to go on and render services after it acquired such knowledge, it thereby becomes liable for the services rendered, it being its duty to notify the physician if it repudiates his employment. Terre Haute etc. R. Co. *v.* Stockwell, 118 Ind. 98; 37 Am. & Eng. R. Cas. 278.

The company is bound by the ratification by the general manager of a contract for medical services made by the roadmaster. Louisville etc. R. Co. *v.*

third party.[1] When the contract is express it may be conditional, and the physician will not be entitled to recover until he shows that the condition has been performed. Thus, where a person professes to cure certain diseases within a specified time, he cannot recover from a person whom he induced to employ him upon such profession of his skill, unless he cures the patient within such time.[2]

Where the contract is not express, a physician is entitled to recover a reasonable compensation for his services; and it has been held that, in order to show the value of his services, he may testify to the nature of the disease and his mode of treatment; that such evidence cannot be excluded upon the ground that it is a confidential communication,[3] and that it is immaterial what his income from his profession averages.[4] So, as bearing upon the value of his services, he may show that his professional standing is high.[5] And the defendant may prove that for similar services upon a former occasion the plaintiff charged a less sum than that which he demands in his complaint, and that no contract was entered into as to the fee for which suit is brought.[6]

McVay, 98 Ind. 391, 22 Am. & Eng. R. Cas. 382.

1. In White *v.* Mastin, 38 Ala. 147, it was held that there was nothing in the relation between physician and patient which would prevent the former from discontinuing his services upon the account of the latter upon the intervention of a third party who promised to pay for such services, even though the patient does not consent to such an arrangement. White *v.* Mastin, 38 Ala. 147.

The physician of the State penitentiary, which was leased to an individual. was appointed by the inspectors, removable by them only, and his salary was to be paid by the lessee. The lessee refused to permit the physician to enter the penitentiary, and thereupon the latter brought an action against the former for his salary. *Held*, that he was entitled to recover, although he did not perform the duties. Jones *v.* Graham, 21 Ala. 654.

2. Hupe *v.* Phelps, 2 Stark. 480; Smith *v.* Hyde, 19 Vt. 54; Mock *v.* Kelly, 3 Ala. 387.

So where a drunkard had contracted with a physician to cure him, and, after taking the medicines prescribed, abstained from intoxicating liquors for six months and told his friends that he had lost his appetite for such liquors, but that he thought that by taking cider and wine he would acquire the habit again, it was held, that this was a cure, even though the party returned to his habits of drunkenness. Fisk *v.* Townsend, 7 Yerg. (Tenn.) 146.

3. Kendall *v.* Gray, 2 Hilt. (N. Y.) 300; Dutchess of Kingston's Case, 11 Harr. 243; 1 Greenleaf Evidence, 248; Morgan *v.* Hallen, 8 Ad. & E. 489.

A person who is elected a city physician by the city council, and whose compensation is not fixed by law, is entitled to recover from the city what his services are reasonably worth. Tucker *v.* Mayor etc. of Virginia City, 4 Nev. 20.

4. Marion Co. *v.* Chambers, 75 Ind. 409.

5. Lange *v.* Kearney (Supreme Ct.), 4 N. Y. Supp. 14.

6. Sidener *v.* Fetter, 19 Ind. 310.

In a suit for services rendered by a physician, the defendant may show that the physician had promised him not to attend small-pox patients while in attendance upon defendant, and the physician had broken this promise, and that defendant had contracted small-pox while the physician was attending him. Piper *v.* Menifee, 12 B. Mon. (Ky.) 465; 54 Am. Dec. 547.

It is not competent for one not a physician to give his opinion in evidence as to the value of services rendered by a physician. Mock *v.* Kelly, 3 Ala. 387. And it has been held that the physician is the proper judge as to the necessity of frequent visits; and in the absence of proof to the contrary,

When a physician is employed to attend upon a sick person, his employment continues while the sickness lasts, and the relation of physician and patient continues, unless it is put an end to by the assent of the parties, or is revoked by the express dismissal of the physician ; and the physician is entitled to recovery for attendance during such time.[1]

A physician may also recover for services necessarily rendered by his assistant or even his students, in attendance upon his patients.[2]

In *England* it was held that a physician had no remedy at law for his services, but that his employment was wholly honorary.[3] This rule, however, has never had place in this country.[4]

It is expressly enacted, by statutes, regulating the practice of medicine that, unless the practitioner has complied with their provisions, he shall not be entitled to recover compensation for his services.[5]

And, even where there is no express provision that the contract for remuneration for services rendered by an unlicensed physician shall be void, still if a statute imposes a penalty upon a physician for practicing without having obtained a license, or without

the court will presume that the physician's visits were necessary. Todd *v.* Myres, 40 Cal. 357.

In Czarnowski *v.* Zeyer, 35 La. Ann. 796, it is said that a physician in charging for his services may properly consider his patient's ability to pay. See also Lange *v.* Kearney (Supreme Ct.), 4 N. Y. Supp. 15.

If a surgeon, in a bill to his patient, leaves a blank for his charge for attendances, and the patient pays a sum on account, the former is bound by the bill, and cannot recover more than the sum paid into court by the latter. Tuson *v.* Batting, 3 Esp. 192. See also Kendall *v.* Grey, 2 Hilt. (N. Y.) 300; Danziger *v.* Hoyt, 46 Hun (N. Y.) 270.

Specific Account.—Charges upon a physician's bill, for "visits and medicines," are sufficiently specific, although the quality and quantity of the medicines are not designated; it not appearing that they varied from the usual mode adopted by physicians in making charges. Bassett *v.* Spofford, 11 N. H. 167.

Whether a physician's account is sufficiently specific, rests with the court. Schmidt *v.* Quin, 1 Mill Const. (S. Car.) 418.

In *South Carolina*, a physician must give a specific bill of the medicine and attendance for which he brings an action; his charges may be too general to sustain his action. Hughes *v.* Hampton, Treadw. Const. (S. Car.) 745.

1. Potter *v.* Virgil, 67 Barb. (N. Y.) 578; Terre Haute R. Co. *v.* Stockwell, 118 Ind. 98; Dale *v.* Donaldson Lumber Co., 48 Ark. 188; Bradley *v.* Dodge, 45 How. Pr. (N. Y.) 57. See also MALPRACTICE, vol. 14, p. 79.

2. People *v.* Monroe, 4 Wend. (N. Y.) 200; Jay Co. *v.* Brewington, 74 Ind. 7.

3. Parsons on Contracts, vol. 2, p. 56; Chorley *v.* Balcott, 4 T. R. 317; Lipscombe *v.* Holmes, 2 Camp. 441; Poucher *v.* Norman, 3 B. & C. 745; Allison *v.* Hayden, 1 Mo. & P. 591; 4 Bing. 619.

4. Parsons on Contracts, vol. 2, p. 56; Judah *v.* McMamee, 3 Blackf. (Ind.) 269; Mooney *v.* Lloyd, 5 S. & R. (Pa.) 412; 1 Dane's Abridgment and Digest 619; Hewitt *v.* Wilcox, 1 Met. (Mass.) 154; Todd *v.* Myres, 40 Cal. 355.

5. Coyle *v.* Campbell, 10 Ga. 570; Dow *v.* Haley, 30 N. J. L. 354; Orr *v.* Meek, 111 Ind. 40; Puckett *v.* Alexander, 102 N. Car. 95.

And, when the patient makes an unlicensed physician an express promise to pay for services which he has rendered, the promise cannot be enforced for want of a valuable consideration. Puckett *v.* Alexander, 102 N. Car. 95.

having any other qualification required, the courts will imply a prohibition, and a recovery cannot be had for his services.[1]

1. Fox *v.* Dixon (Supreme Ct.), 12 N. Y. Supp. 267; Oscanyan *v.* Winchester etc. Arms Co., 103 U. S. 261; Harrison *v.* Jones, 80 Ala. 412; O'Donnell *v.* Sweeny, 5 Ala. 468; 39 Am. Dec. 336, in which it was said: "It would, indeed, be a strange anomaly if a contract made in violation of a statute and prohibited by a penalty could be enforced in the courts of the same country, whose laws are thus trampled on and set in defiance." See also Renfro *v.* Loyd, 64 Ala. 94. See, however, Finch *v.* Gridley, 25 Wend. (N. Y.) 469.

Under *California* St. 1875-76, p. 792, § 13, and St. 1877-78, p. 918, § 7, making it a misdemeanor for a person to practice medicine without having first procured a certificate from a medical board, a physician cannot recover for services rendered before the issuance of his certificate by the board, though he made application therefor before his employment began; Civil Code *California*, § 1667, making that unlawful which is "contrary to the policy of express law, though not expressly prohibited." Gardner *v.* Tatum, 81 Cal. 370.

Where a physician is disqualified to practice by a statute which is afterwards repealed, he cannot, after such repeal, recover for services rendered while the statute was in operation. Warren *v.* Saxby, 12 Vt. 146; Nichols *v.* Poulson, 6 Ohio 305; Bailey *v.* Mogg, 4 Den. (N. Y.) 60; Puckett *v.* Alexander, 102 N. Car. 95. But see Hewitt *v.* Wilcox, 1 Met. (Mass.) 154.

Where a statute prohibits an unqualified person from collecting his fees for medical or surgical attendance, he will be barred, though, before suit is brought, but after the services rendered, he has become qualified. Thompson *v.* Hazen, 25 Me. 104.

But even where the law would afford an unqualified practitioner no remedy for the collection of his charges, yet in a suit by him for injuries received, which deprived him of his capacity to attend to his business, the loss sustained thereby is an element of damages. Holmes *v.* Halde, 74 Me. 28; McNamara *v.* Clintonville, 62 Wis. 207; 51 Am. Rep. 722.

A physician, who obtains a temporary license from year to year, from a member of the board of physicians of that State, may charge for his professional services rendered during the time he is so licensed, provided a license has never been refused him by that board. Wragg *v.* Strickland, 36 Ga. 559.

Recovery for Medicines Furnished by an Unqualified Practitioner.—"The statute in question forbids any one from practicing medicine for reward, or compensation, without having the qualifications prescribed therein. The object of this law, doubtless, was to prevent unauthorized and unqualified persons from practicing medicine in any of its branches. The right to practice the calling of a physician is, by this statute, taken from certain unqualified persons, and the statute should not be so construed as to give a person the privilege of exercising a right which is in violation of any of its provisions. To hold that a person who furnished medicine, as a physician, could recover compensation for the medicine so furnished or prescribed, would, in our judgment, render the statute nugatory, and any other unauthorized person might prescribe for a patient and simply charge for his medicine, and thus defeat the very object of the law. The practice of medicine may be said to consist in three things: First, in judging the nature, character and symptoms of the disease; second, in determining the proper remedy for the disease; third, in giving or prescribing the application of the remedy to the disease. If the person who makes a diagnosis of a case also gives the the medicine to the patient, he is, in our judgment, practicing medicine within the provisions of the statute in question; and if unauthorized to practice, or is acting in violation of the provisions of the statute, he is not entitled to compensation for the medicine which he furnished at the time, as a physician; and the instructions of the court which said to the jury that the plaintiff below could recover for the medicine furnished, though he might not have been entitled to practice medicine, was erroneous; and for this reason the judgment of the court below should be reversed." Underwood *v.* Scott, 43 Kan. 717. See also Alcott *v.* Barber, 1 Wend. (N. Y.) 526; Thompson *v.* Staats, 15 Wend. (N. Y.)

Where a physician brings suit to recover the value of his services, defendant may plead as a bar to such recovery the incompetence and want of skill of the physician.[1] This rule is a very ancient one and is equally applicable to all professions, whose followers profess to possess technical skill.[2]

But a physician's title to remuneration does not depend upon whether or not he has effected a cure, if he has used due care and diligence.[3]

595; Smith *v.* Tracy, 2 Hall (N. Y.) 465.

In Holland *v.* Adams, 21 Ala. 680, it was held, that a note given in consideration of services rendered by the payee as a physician, when he has not obtained a license, was made void by statute; yet if he sells drugs and medicines apart from his professional business as a physician, he may recover for them, if they constitute a part of the consideration for the note.

Christian Science.—Under the *Maine* statute, which provides that no person, who has not received a medical degree in any public medical institution in the United States, or a license from a Maine medical association, shall recover compensation for his services, unless prior to such service he has obtained a certificate of good moral character from the municipal officers of the town where he then resided, it was held, that one who practiced the healing art according to the principles and practice of the Christian Scientists, and has obtained the said certificate of good moral character, and who uses no medicines but depends altogether upon Christian science, may recover for his services. Wheeler *v.* Sawyer (Me. 1888), 15 Atl. Rep. 67.

1. Eastman *v.* State, 109 Ind. 278; Ely *v.* Wilbur, 49 N. J. L. 685; 60 Am. Rep. 668.

It is a good defense to an action by an apothecary, that he treated the patient ignorantly or improperly. Kannen *v.* M'Mullen, Peake 59.

A physician cannot recover a claim for professional services, unless he possesses the requisite skill. Longolf *v.* Pfromer, 2 Phila. (Pa.) 17.

One sued for physician's services may show that they were of no value and that the medicine prescribed was worthless. Jonas *v.* King, 81 Ala. 285.

A surgeon is entitled to compensation for an operation not performed with the highest degree of skill, and which might have been performed more skillfully by others, provided the operation was beneficial to the patient. Alder *v.* Buckley, 1 Swan (Tenn.) 69.

Where suit was brought on a physician's account for services and medicine, it might be pleaded that he did not do his work skillfully, or a plea of recoupment might be filed, springing out of the contract; but a plea of setoff, based on a tort in giving defendant too large a dose of medicine, which injured him to the amount of two hundred dollars, was not proper as matter of defense; nor does it matter whether the defendant was insolvent or not.

To state in a plea of set-off that an overdose of ipecac damaged a man $200, without stating wherein and how, is too loose, and does not set out the defense plainly and distinctly. McKleroy *v.* Sewell, 39 Ga. 657.

As to what care, skill and diligence is required of a physician, see MALPRACTICE, vol. 14, p. 76.

2. Bunham's Case, 8 Coke's Rep. 107; College of Physicians *v.* Levy, 1 Ld. Raym. 472; Ely *v.* Wilbur, 49 N. J. L. 685; 60 Am. Rep. 668; § 3 Wait's Act & Def. 595; Patten *v.* Wiggin, 2 Am. L. Reg., N. S. 403; Briggs *v.* Taylor, 28 Vt. 180; Tefft *v.* Wilcox, 6 Kan. 46; McNevins *v.* Lane, 40 Ill. 209.

3. Hupe *v.* Phelps, 2 Stark. 480; Gallaher *v.* Thompson, Wright (Ohio) 466.

So in Ely *v.* Wilbur, 49 N. J. L. 685; 60 Am. Rep. 668, it was held that though the physician was perhaps mistaken in his diagnosis of the case, yet he was entitled to compensation.

A continuous running account between the same parties is an entire thing, not susceptible of division, the aggregate of all the items being the amount due; and therefore a recovery of a part by suit will bar an action for the residue. The rule applies to a physician's account, who, having sued for and recovered a part, cannot main-

PICTURES.—See note 1.

tain an action for the residue of the account. Oliver *v.* Holt, 11 Ala. 574; 46 Am. Rep. 228.

In a suit brought for medical services, evidence tending to show that the services had been rendered gratuitously is no legal bar to the recovery; however distinct such evidence is, it should be submitted to the jury. Huston *v.* Barstow, 19 Pa. St. 169.

1. It was held in Gibson *v.* Cranage, 3 Mich. 49, that where one agrees with an artist for a portrait that need not be taken or paid for if unsatisfactory, the customer need not pay for it if unsatisfactory to him, even though artists or third persons might think that it ought to be satisfactory.

Artist's Proofs.—A very recent suit in the Westminster (English) county court raises the question of what are "artists proofs." Plaintiff's, picture-dealers, claimed the sum of eight guineas as the price of an artist's proof of a celebrated picture, for which plaintiffs had paid two thousand guineas. The defense was that the plaintiffs had printed a thousand impressions, and that the defendant was informed that only a few copies would be printed. Expert testimony was taken. The court decided that the engraving could not be called an artist's proof if there were a thousand impressions, and gave judgment for the defendant. London Law. Times, cited in Albany Law Journal, May 31, 1890.

Property in Pictures.—The courts recognize the right of property in pictures to the extent that, in the absence of publication by the owner, a publication or copies by others will be restrained. Prince Albert & Strange, 1 McN. & G. 25; Turner *v.* Robinson, 10 Ir. Ch. 121, 510.

This principle was recognized in Oertel *v.* Wood, 40 How. Pr. (N. Y.) 10, a special term case, where, however, the right to the injunction was denied because of the voluntary publication by the plaintiffs and owners of the picture.

A person lending prints or photographs to another, who, with his consent, takes and sells copies, cannot only sue in detinue for the originals, but also for the copies, and can likewise sustain an injunction to prevent the sale of any copies remaining, and this quite apart from copyright, and although there has been a publication. Mayall *v.* Higby, 10 W. R. 631; 6 L. T., N. S. 362.

A, the proprietor and publisher of a magazine, agreed to purchase from him the right to engrave photographs to illustrate a series of articles in the magazine. A afterwards commenced publishing these articles in a separate form, illustrated by engravings from the same photographs. *Held*, that he had no authority for so doing. Strahan *v.* Graham, 16 L. T., N. S. 87.

Copyright.—The copyright laws protect pictures and paintings.

A painting only seven by four inches in size, from a design made by the president of a corporation from a woodcut, and painted by a painter employed by the corporation, may be copyrighted by such corporation. That the painting is susceptible of being lithographed and used as an advertising label will not affect the copyright.

Schumacher *v.* Schwencke, 25 Fed. Rep. 466.

But if the court find that the picture is intended to be printed on labels, it is not the subject of copyright, as act of Congress June 18th, 1874, § 3, provides that no print label designed to be used for any article of manufacture can be copyrighted, but authorizing them to be registered as trade marks.

Schumacher *v.* Wagram, 35 Fed. Rep. 210, under the English statute.

When there are designs which form part of a book in which copyright exists, such copyright extends to the designs as well as to the letter press. Bogue *v.* Houlston, 21 L. J. Ch. 470; 16 Jur. 372.

An illustrated catalogue is a subject of copyright as a book and the engravings are protected. Maple *v.* Junior Army and Navy Stores, 21 L. R., Ch. D. 369; and this, even though it contain no such letter press as could be the subject of copyright. It makes no difference that it is given away as an advertisement. Maple *v.* Junior Army and Navy Stores, 21 L. R., Ch. D. 369; overruling Cobbett *v.* Woodword, L. R. 14, Eq. 407.

The word manuscript in § 9 of the copyright act does not include picture, and hence the consent of the author or proprietor in writing signed in the presence of two credible witnesses is not necessary in order to obtain the

PIER.—See note 1.

PILFER.—To pilfer means to steal, in its plain and popular sense.[2]

PILOTS.—See NAVIGATION; SHIPPING.

right to reproduce or chromo a picture. Title may pass together with the right to make copies by oral contract, provided it be obtained fairly and understandingly and for a valuable consideration. Parton *v.* Prang, 3 Cliff. (U. S.) 527.

The object of the act 25 & 26 Vict., ch. 68, is that enough should be stated in the register of copyright to identify the picture, etc., and whether the description of the subject-matter is sufficient for this purpose is a question of fact for the tribunal. *Ex parte* Beal, 9 B. & S. 395; 3 L. R., Q. B. 387.

But where the proprietor of the copyright of a print cannot show a title derived from the author and designer, an alien, neither he nor the author are entitled to a copyright. Yuengling *v.* Schile, 20 Blatchf. (U. S.) 452.

Where one assigns the copyright of a painting for the purpose of producing an engraving of a certain size, the right of producing copies in other ways or by engravings of other sizes remains in the assignor, subject to assignment by him to a third person. Lucas *v.* Cook, L. R., 13 Ch. Div. 872.

It is not an infringement merely to make a plate from a copy of a copyrighted picture, without printing or publishing copies of such picture. Harper *v.* Shoppell, 26 Fed. Rep. 519.

A made a copy of a print invented by B in colors, and of large dimensions, and exhibited it as a diorama. A court of equity refused to restrain the exhibition until the right had been established by law. Martin *v.* Wright, 6 Sim. 297.

A person having a copyright in a print or an engraving may maintain an action against a person for selling pirated copies of it, though such person has no knowledge that the prints are piracies. Gambart *v.* Sumner, 5 H. & N. 5; 29 L. J. Exch. 98.

Where the engraver took off several proof impressions and afterwards attempted to sell them, held that the Stat. 17 Geo. III, ch. 57, applied to impressions of engravings pirated from other engravings and not prints taken from a lawful plate. Murray *v.* Heath, 1 B. & Ad. 804.

Paintings as Fixtures.—It was held in D'Eyncourt *v.* Gregory, L. R., 3 Eq. 382, that a portrait in oil screwed to blocks inserted in the brick work of a wall so as to become part of the wall by taking the place of paper or paneling, even though it could be removed easily and its place supplied by other material, was a fixture.

1. **"Pier."**—A structure erected for ferry purposes, which was simply a ferry rack and bridge—held, not to be a pier within *New York* L. 1857, ch. 763, which provides that piers shall not be built at less than one hundred feet apart. Stevens *v.* Rhinelander, 5 Robt. (N. Y.) 285.

2. So defined in Beckett *v.* Sterrett, 4 Blackf. (Ind.) 500, a slander case.

I. **Definition.**—A pilot is defined to be first an officer serving on board of a ship during the course of a voyage and having charge of the helm and the ship's route; and secondly, an officer authorized by law who is taken on board at a particular place for the purpose of conducting a ship through a river, road, or channel, or from or into a port.[1]

Pilotage is the service and also the compensation for the service of steering a vessel through particular waters rendered by a person specially acquainted with them and appointed so to do.[2]

II. **Legislative Control.**—Article 1, § 8, of the Constitution of the *United States*, confers upon Congress the power to regulate pilots and pilotage.[3] But this does not deprive the States of their power to legislate upon the subject.[4] Congress recognizes the concurrent power of the States.[5] So State laws are valid when they do not conflict with the regulations prescribed by the Federal Government.[6] And in the absence of Federal

1. See People *v.* Francisco, 4 Park. Cr. (N. Y.) 139; 2 Bouv. L. Dict. 337; 10 Abb. Pr. (N. Y.) 30; 18 How. Pr. (N. Y.) 475.

The pilot is an officer of the ship when on board in the exercise of his duty; but when the captain is on board he is master, and the orders of the pilot are considered the master's. U. S. *v.* Forbes, 1 Crabbe (U. S.) 558.

In Cooley *v.* Board of Wardens, 12 How. (U. S.) 299, it is held that a pilot of a vessel in that part of the voyage which is his pilotage ground, is the temporary master, charged with the safety of the vessel and cargo, and of the lives of those on board, and intrusted with the command of the crew.

The office of pilot is not a public one; it is a private profession, trade or calling. Low *v.* Comrs., R. M. Charlt. (Ga.) 302.

2. 2 Abb. L. Dict. 278; Pothier Des Avaries 147.

3. Cooley *v.* Board of Port Wardens, 12 How. (U. S.) 299; The Clymene, 9 Fed. Rep. 166; The Abercorn, 26 Fed. Rep. 877; The Glencarne, 7 Sawy. (U. S.) 202; 7 Fed. Rep. 604; The Alcalde, 30 Fed. Rep. 133; The Panama, 1 Deady (U. S.) 31.

4. Com. of Pilotage *v.* Steamboat Cuba, 28 Ala. 185; Stillwell *v.* Raynor, 1 Daly (N. Y.) 47; The Chase, 14 Fed. Rep. 854; Cooley *v.* Board of Wardens, 12 How. (U. S.) 299. The States retain the power to legislate upon the subject of pilotage within their own territories, and over their own citizens, unless such legislation interferes with some act of Congress. Low *v.* Comrs., R. M. Charlt. (Ga.) 302. The law of *Indiana*, "regulating the licensing of pilots at the Falls of the Ohio," etc., is valid, at least so far as commercial intercourse may be carried on between the parts of said State named in said act, by citizens of said State. 1 G. & H. 473; Barnaby *v.* State, 21 Ind. 450.

State pilotage laws are enacted in virtue of an original power of a State, not by force of a grant of power from the national government. They need not be uniform throughout an entire State, nor are they objectionable on the ground that powers they grant to local Boards are powers which should not be delegated. The Chase, 14 Fed. Rep. 854.

5. Edwards *v.* Str. Panama, 1 Oregon 418. See the William Law, 14 Fed. Rep. 792; The Alcalde, 30 Fed. Rep. 133.

6. Cooley *v.* Board of Port Wardens, 12 How. (U. S.) 299; Edwards *v.* Str. Panama, 1 Oregon 418; Cribb *v.* State, 9 Fla. 409; The Alameda *v.* Neal, 32 Fed. Rep. 331; Wilson *v.* McNamee, 102 U. S. 572; Steamship Co. *v.* Joliffe, 2 Wall. (U. S.) 450; Low *v.* Comrs., R. M. Charlt. (Ga.) 302; Cisco *v.* Roberts, 6 Bosw. (N. Y.) 494; Freeman *v.* The Undaunted, 37 Fed. Rep. 662; The Panama, Deady (U. S.) 27; *Ex parte* McNiel, 13 Wall. (U. S.) 236; The South Cambria, 27 Fed. Rep. 526.

A State pilot act, which discriminates in favor of "coasters within the State" or vessels of that and the two adjoining States, conflicts with the

legislation, the States have a right to exercise such rights on the neighboring seas as are essential to the protection of their own domain,[1] although Congress authorizes the States to enact pilotage laws for territory within their own jurisdiction, yet such laws are liable to be controlled by subsequent Congressional legislation.[2] The power of Congress to regulate commerce is exclusive when exercised.[3] The States have concurrent power with Congress to pass pilotage laws until Congress shall take exclusive control of the subject by the enactment of a general and uniform law, and such acts as Congress shall make are of paramount authority, and all State laws in collision must yield.[4]

The object of the Constitution in creating a national control of pilotage was to prevent conflicts between the laws of neighboring States, and discriminations favorable or adverse to commerce with particular foreign nations.[5]

III. Construction of Statutes.—The statutes regulating pilots are reasonably construed.[6] So an act does not operate to legislate out of office pilots licensed under previous statutes whose terms of office had not expired when the act went into operation.[7]

Federal statute § 4237 R. S. and is void. Spraigue v. Thompson, 118 U. S. 90.

1. Cisco v. Roberts, 36 N. Y. 292. See The Charles A. Sparks, 16 Fed. Rep. 480.

2. Cisco v. Roberts, 6 Bosw. (N. Y.) 494.

3. Mitchell v. Steelman, 8 Cal. 363.

4. The South Cambria, 27 Fed. Rep. 526; Cooley v. Board of Wardens, 12 How. (U. S.) 299; *Ex parte* McNiel, 13 Wall. (U. S.) 236, 241. See The William Law 14 Fed. Rep. 794; The Chase, 14 Fed. Rep. 856; The Glenearne, 7 Sawy. (U. S.) 200; 7 Fed. Rep. 606; License Cases, 5 How. (U. S.) 580; Gibbons v. Ogden, 9 Wheat. (U. S.) 207; Henderson v. Spofford, 59 N. Y. 131; Ogden v. Saunders, 12 Wheat. (U. S.) 213.

5. Cooley v. Board of Port Wardens, 12 How. (U. S.) 317.

6. See *infra*, this title, *Obligations to Take a Pilot.*

The word "States," in the act of Congress of March 2, 1837, regulating the employment of pilots on water forming the boundary between two "States," is construed to include a Territory of the United States. The Abercorn, 26 Fed. Rep. 877; Neil v. Wilson, 14 Oregon 410; Edward v. The Panama, 1 Oregon 418; The Ullock, 19 Fed. Rep. 207. See Watson v. Brooks, 13 Fed. Rep. 540. *Compare* New Orleans v. Winter, 1 Wheat. (U. S.) 91.

So under the act of 1789, conferring on the States power to regulate pilotage in the ports of a State, the "Delaware Breakwater" is construed to be a port of Delaware. The William Law, 14 Fed. Rep. 792.

Where a statute directs that the license of a pilot shall be revoked by the commissioners "if he shall be found not sufficiently skilled, or shall become incapable of acting, or shall be negligent, or misbehave in his duty toward the commissioners, the word "negligent" applies to the discharge of his duties as a pilot, and a neglect in not boarding a vessel when he ought to do so will authorize the suspension of a pilot. Low v. Comrs., R. M. Charlt. (Ga.) 302.

And the words "regularly employed" in a statute (*Massachusetts* St. 1873, ch. 284, § 1) exempting a vessel "regularly employed in the coasting trade" from compulsory pilotage, include the case of a vessel actually and legally so employed at the time the services of a pilot are tendered, even though the vessel is sailing under a register, and is not continuously so employed. Wilson v. Gray, 127 Mass. 98.

"Wanting a Pilot"—The words "wanting a pilot," 6 Geo. IV., ch. 125, § 72, are not to be confined to such vessels as are, by the act, bound to take a pilot, but apply to any vessel, the master or owner of which thinks fit to require one. Lucy v. Ingram, 6 M. & W. 302.

7. Flynn v. Abbott, 16 Cal. 358.

IV. **Licensing Pilots.**—In some States pilots are licensed by a board of commissioners appointed by the governor.[1] In others the governor alone appoints them.[2] But where an act of Congress provides for the licensing of pilots, such act takes place of any State law, and a license protects the holder against penalties inflicted by a State law for not obtaining a license under its provisions.[3] So State laws that conflict with the act of Congress providing that a master of a vessel may employ a person to act as pilot in waters dividing two States, who is licensed by either State are unconstitutional.[4]

A pilot who is not licensed according to the requirements of the act of Congress is not entitled to recover his fees, although he be licensed by the State board of pilot commissioners and has complied with their regulations. The regulations of such a board of commissioners are valid and continue in force only so far as they are consistent with the acts of Congress.[5] So a pilot under State jurisdiction must be legally licensed in order to recover for tender of services.[6]

"Navigating Within."—"The words 'navigating within,' in the Merchant Shipping Act, 1854, § 379, mean 'being within;' and, therefore, a vessel belonging to the port of London, not carrying passengers and coming from the west, is not bound to employ a licensed pilot when she is within the limits of the port of London." 1 Maude & P. 278, *citing* The Stettin, Br. & L. 199. In that case Dr. Lushington said: "Though I do not deny that the word 'navigating' alone is a doubtful expression, yet, coupled with the word 'within,' it appears to me to negative voyages beyond the limits, and to be confined to those within the limits." General Steam Nav. Co. *v.* British & Colonial Steam Nav. Co., L. R., 3 Ex. 330.

"Pilotage Dues."—The 10s. 6d. per day to which a licensed pilot, taken, without his consent, to sea or beyond the limits of his pilotage district, in any ship, is entitled by 17 & 18 Vict., ch. 104 (Merchant Shipping Act, 1854), § 357, are not "pilotage dues" for which the ship-brokers are liable under § 363. Morteo *v.* Julian, 4 C. P. D. 216; 48 L. J., M. C. 126.

1. Palmer *v.* Woodbury, 14 Cal. 43.

A license to be valid must be signed by all the commissioners, or it must appear from the minutes of the board that the matter was acted upon and the license granted at a meeting of the commissioners when all of them were present, or such license must contain a direct recital or averment of such meeting and action in reference to such license. The California, 1 Sawy. (U. S.) 596.

2. Barnaby *v.* State, 21 Ind. 450.

3. Dryden *v.* Commonwealth, 16 B. Mon. (Ky.) 598; United States *ex rel.* Spink, 19 Fed. Rep. 631.

4. Cribb *v.* State, 9 Fla. 409.

The State of *Oregon* and the Territory of *Washington* have equal powers over the subject of the regulation of pilots and pilotage on the Columbia river, and may appoint pilots for the river, and prescribe their duties and compensation as to any and all vessels bound in or out of the same, whether the business or commerce in which they are engaged pertains to *Oregon* or *Washington*, and neither can require that the legislation of the other shall conform to its own in any respect. The Alcalde, 30 Fed. Rep. 133; Neil *v.* Wilson, 14 Oregon 410.

And this applies to employing pilots upon a navigable river within two adjoining States, although it is not a separating boundary. The Clymene, 9 Fed. Rep. 164; 12 Fed. Rep. 346; Flannigen *v.* Washington Ins. Co., 7 Pa. St. 306; The Ullock, 19 Fed. Rep. 211; The Abercorn, 26 Fed. Rep. 877.

5. Cisco *v.* Roberts, 6 Bosw. (N. Y.) 494.

6. Under *Massachusetts* Pub. St. Ch. 70, § 17, providing that no person shall exercise the office of pilot until he has given bond with two sureties in the sum

V. Powers of Pilot Commissioners.—The pilot commissioners have discretion to appoint from among persons possessing certain qualifications as to length of service, etc., prescribed by the statute, but no power to appoint one who has not those qualifications.[1] They may prohibit the use of steam vessels for purposes of pilotage.[2] They may rightfully employ counsel to acquaint its members with the proper mode of proceeding in hearing a charge against a pilot, especially when the pilot under the charge appears by attorneys, and interposes a variety of technical objections, and the board is composed of men selected according to statute for their practical knowledge of navigation.[3] But they cannot contract with the licensed pilots to restrict the number, without regard to what may be necessary for the business of the port.[4]

A board of pilot commissioners are not bound by the technical rules in their proceedings which govern courts of justice; and where, on an appeal from an order of such board revoking the license of a pilot, the authority of the board is not questioned, nor the sufficiency of the cause for revocation, their action will not be set aside because they did not meet on the day the pilot was notified they would consider the charges filed against him, where it appears that he was present and had ample opportunity to make his defense when such charges were considered.[5] So the court will not reverse the action of the commissioners because the pilot was refused the aid of counsel in cross-examining witnesses and in arguing his case.[6]

VI. Obligations To Take A Pilot.—Vessels are required by statute to take a licensed pilot.[7] These statutes, in some of

of $1,000 held, that a person acting as pilot under a bond reciting that the two sureties are bound in the sum of $500 each could not recover of the owner of a vessel compulsory pilotage fees. Dolliver *v.* Parks, 136 Mass. 499.

1. Palmer *v.* Woodbury, 14 Cal. 43.

2. People *v.* Board of Comrs., 23 Hun (N. Y.) 603.

3. Snow *v.* Reed, 14 Oregon 342.

4. Wright *v.* St. Simon's Pilotage Comrs., 69 Ga. 247.

The *Louisiana* pilot laws do not inhibit a partnership or association of pilots to further their common interests. It is not opposed to public policy though they are State officers. Levine *v.* Michel, 35 La. Ann. 1121.

So in Jones *v.* Fell, 5 Fla. 510, it is held that an agreement amongst pilots for an association in their business is not illegal.

5. Snow *v.* Reid, 14 Oregon 342.

6. State *v.* Courtenay, 23 S. Car. 180.

7. The China, 7 Wall. (U. S.) 53; Camp *v.* The Ship Marcellus, 1 Cliff. (U. S.) 483; People *v.* Sperry, 50 Barb. (N. Y.) 170; Chapman *v.* Jackson, 9 Rich. (S. Car.) 209; The Agricola, 2 Rob. Adm. 10; The Johanna Stoll, Lush. 295; The Edith Godden, 25 Fed. Rep. 511.

A ship which stands in need of a salvage service is not bound to accept the offer of pilotage if her need is for something more which pilotage can supply. Flanders *v.* Tripp, 2 Low. (U. S.) 15.

The employment of a pilot is not compulsory on a vessel being towed from one dock to another in the port of Hull, as the vessel is neither passing "into or out" of the port, nor "bound to or from" the port within the Hull pilot act. The Maria, Law Rep., 1 Adm. & Ecc. 358.

Vessels under tow are not required to take a pilot in *Oregon.* The Glaramara, 10 Fed. Rep. 678.

Coasting Trade.—Vessels regularly

the States, have been construed so as to make the taking of a pilot or the payment of pilotage optional.[1]

Where a license is required for a particular harbor, and no such licensed pilot seasonably offers his services, the master may employ any other person to pilot his vessel in, and such person may do so without incurring any penalty.[2]

VII. Tender of Service.—Pilotage must be paid to the first pilot offering service.[3] This rule relating to the tender of

employed in the coasting trade are exempt from compulsory pilotage. Chase *v.* Philadelphia etc. R. Co., 135 Mass. 347; Spraigue *v.* Thompson, 118 U. S. 90; Hunt *v.* Card, 14 Pick. (Mass.) 135.

England. — The legislature imposes the obligation on foreign ships inward-bound to take a pilot at a convenient station beyond three miles from the British shore. The Annapolis and The Johanna Stoll, Lush. 295; 4 L. T., N. S. 417; Dublin Port and Docks Board *v.* Shannon, 7 Ir. R., C. L. 116; The Lloyd's or The Sea Queen, B. & L. 359; 9 L. T., N. S. 236; Davidson *v.* Mekibben, 6 Moore 387; 3 B. & B. 112. *Compare* The Stettin, 31 L. J. Adm. 208; 6 L. T., N. S. 613.

The exemption given by St. 6 Geo. IV., ch. 125, § 59, from the necessity of employing licensed pilots, to masters piloting their own ships on the voyages there specified, without the aid of an unlicensed pilot, is continued by the Merchant Shipping Act 1854 (17 and 18 Vict., ch. 104), § 353; and this exemption applies as well to ships carrying as to ships not carrying passengers, and is not affected by the exemption given in § 379 of the same act to ships on particular voyages, and not carrying passengers. Regina *v.* Stanton, 8 Ellis & B. 445.

Coasting Vessels Are Exempted.—The only reason why coasting vessels are exempted from the obligation of taking a pilot, is, that from their frequent egress and ingress to the particular port, their masters must be presumed to be perfectly acquainted with the locality. The Agricola, 2 Rob. Adm. Rep. 10; 7 Jur. 157.

It is not compulsory on a passenger ship to take a licensed pilot on board when she is not carrying passengers, and the owners are responsible for the negligence of the pilot, where they were not compellable to put him in charge of their vessel. The Lion. 2 L. R., P. C. 525; 6 Moore P. C. C., N. S. 163; 38 L. J., Adm. 51; 17 W. R. 993; 21 L. T., N. S. 41; affirming 2 L. R., Adm. 102; 37 L. J., Adm. 39; 18 L. T., N. S. 803; 17 W. R. 577; The Wesley, Lush. 268; The Earl of Auckland, Lush. 387; 15 Moore P. C. C. 304; The Hanna, 36 L. J. Adm. 1; 15 W. R. 263.

1. The *Pennsylvania* Pilot Act of 29th March, 1803, which "obliges" vessels going out of or coming into the port of Philadelphia to receive a pilot, under a "penalty," and "forfeiture" of half-pilotage, which the act makes a lien upon the ship, and recoverable in the admiralty, not being, as is decided, compulsory, but optional, the ship need not take a pilot, if it prefers to pay the penalty or forfeiture. Smith *v.* The Creole, 2 Wall. Jr. (C. C.) 485.

In *Massachusetts* vessels are not bound in any case, to employ a pilot, whether going in or coming out of a harbor, but when inward bound, and a pilot seasonably offers his services, and is ready to enter upon the duty, the ship must pay pilotage fees, even if his services are refused. Camp *v.* Ship Marcellus, 1 Cliff. (U. S.) 481. See also Hunt *v.* Carlisle, 1 Gray (Mass.) 257; Martin *v.* Hilton, 9 Met. (Mass.) 371; Hunt *v.* Mickey, 12 Met. (Mass.) 346; Com. *v.* Ricketson, 5 Met. (Mass.) 412.

2. Com. *v.* Ricketson, 5 Met. (Mass.) 412.

3. Camp *v.* Ship Marcellus, 1 Cliff. (U. S.) 481; Com. *v.* Ricketson, 5 Met. (Mass.) 412; Gerrish *v.* Johnson, 1 Jones (N. Car.) 335; The China, 7 Wall. (U. S.) 53; Hunt *v.* Carlisle, 1 Gray (Mass.) 257; Steamship Co. *v.* Joliffe, 2 Wall. (U. S.) 450; People *v.* Sperry, 50 Barb. (N. Y.) 170; The Alameda *v.* Neal, 32 Fed. Rep. 331; The Alenza, 14 Fed. Rep. 174; The Francisco *v.* Garquilo, 14 Fed. Rep. 495; Wilson *v.* McNamee, 102 U. S. 572; Beckwith *v.* Baldwin, 12 Ala. 720; The Edith Godden, 25 Fed. Rep. 511; The Traveller, 6 Ben. (U. S.) 280; The Lord Clive, 12 Fed. Rep. 81; Affg. 10 Fed. Rep. 135. *Compare* Neil *v.* Wil-

service applies to vessels "bound to or from a port."[1] A pilot may recover pilotage, although his services were tendered to, and refused by, the master of the vessel when she was without the jurisdiction of the State.[2]

A pilot who fails to be on hand at high water when he should be, to tow a vessel to sea, cannot recover pilotage fees if the vessel goes off without him.[3]

1. What Constitutes Valid Tender.—A State statute may require pilot commissioners to declare by rule what shall constitute a valid offer of pilot service on pilot grounds by signal addressed to the eye, and they may, under such statute, prescribe the distance from the vessel within which such signal must be made.[4] It is a sufficient offer of a pilot's services, in the night, to the master of a vessel bound into a harbor, if the pilot approaches such vessel and hails her, and makes all the tender which the time and circumstances permit, and his hail is heard on board, though it is not answered. It is not necessary, in such case, that there should be an actual offer to the master, and that he should have actual knowledge of such offer.[5]

2. Sufficient Authority for Tender of Service.—The pilot must be licensed. Some State statutes provide that any person not licensed that attempts to pilot a vessel shall be punished by fine

son, 14 Oregon 410; The Abercorn, 26 Fed. Rep. 877; Sprague *v.* Thompson, 118 U. S. 90; Winslow *v.* Prince, 6 Cush. (Mass.) 368.

1. Wright *v.* Lake, 75 Ga. 219; Cisco *v.* Roberts, 36 N. Y. 292. *Compare* Neissner *v.* Stein, 72 Ga. 234.

The pilotage acts are founded on public necessity, for the security of commerce and the protection of life; and it is not apparent why an outward-bound vessel should not have the protection of a skillful and experienced pilot, as well as one inward bound. Wright *v.* Lake, 75 Ga. 219.

Steamboats have a right to tow vessels through Hellgate, without being subject to the law relating to pilotage, being excepted from its operation by § 10 of the act of 1847. Francisco *v.* People, 4 Park. Cr. (N. Y.) 139. See The Glaramara, 8 Sawy. (U. S.) 22.

2. Wilson *v.* McNamee, 102 U. S. 572. See The Whistler, 8 Sawy. (U. S.) 232.

A pilot of the harbor of Boston who offers his services to the master of an inward-bound vessel subject to the pilotage laws, outside of the line prescribed by *Massachusetts* Rev. Stats., ch. 32, § 24, is entitled to pilotage fees, although the vessel in tacking has already been inside the line beyond which she need not take a pilot. Hunt *v.* Carlisle, 1 Gray (Mass.) 257.

Hellgate pilots cannot make legal tender of services as far east as Block Island. The S. & B. Small, 8 Ben. (U. S.) 523.

3. The Ocean Express, 22 Fed. Rep. 176.

A pilot who, under a State statute, was entitled to take a vessel out of port, having brought her in, by appointment with the master, went to a designated place to go on board, but the vessel did not appear as promised, and went to sea without the pilot. *Held*, that the pilot had a right of action which was enforceable by a libel in admiralty. The Francisco Garguilo, 14 Fed. Rep. 495.

4. The Ullock, 19 Fed. Rep. 207.

5. Com. *v.* Ricketson, 5 Met. (Mass.) 412.

A pilot left his pilot-boat anchored two and a half miles from the channel, and came with a small boat, showing no light, until within from one to three hundred feet of a steamer, and no flash-light until the steamer had passed and left him abaft the beam, so that such flash was not seen by any of the officers of the steamer. The pilot's hail was not heard by those on the steamer. *Held*, that there was no such speaking

and imprisonment,[1] and also that one employing an unlicensed pilot shall-be punished by fine.[2]

The exhibition of a warrant to act as pilot entitles the person showing it to be treated, and requires the ship to receive him, as *prima facie* a pilot.[3]

3. Refusing Service.—Refusing the first pilot offering service incurs the penalty of paying to him full fees in some States,[4] in others, half pilotage.[5] And the subsequent repeal of the statute

as would entitle him to pilotage. The Mascotte, 39 Fed. Rep. 871.

1. The China, 7 Wall. (U. S.) 53. See Com. *v.* Ricketson, 5 Met. (Mass.) 412.

Where a Boston pilot seasonably offers his services to the master of a vessel bound into Boston harbor, and the master does not accept the services, but employs a person who is not authorized as a pilot for said harbor to pilot his vessel in, the master thereby incurs no penalty; but such person, by undertaking to pilot the vessel in, incurs the penalty imposed by the *Massachusetts* Rev. Sts., ch. 32, § 23. Com. *v.* Ricketson, 5 Met. (Mass.) 412.

The *South Carolina* act of 1878, prescribing a system of pilotage, makes the penalties applicable to masters bringing their own vessels into port without a pilot, as well as to pilots presuming to act without a license. The words "no person" are sufficiently comprehensive to make this apparent. State *v.* Penny, 19 S. Car. 218.

2. The China, 7 Wall. (U. S.) 53.

3. Edwards *v.* Str. Panama, 1 Oregon 418; The Alcalde, 30 Fed. Rep. 133.

Under the pilot act of the Territory of *Washington* of Jan. 26th, 1863, a pilot on tendering his service must exhibit his warrant unless prevented by the wrongful act of the master. It is not the duty of the master to demand the production of the warrant, but he must allow the pilot a reasonable opportunity to exhibit it. The Eldridge, Deady 176.

In England.—The master of a ship was not liable to the penalty imposed by 6 Geo. IV, ch. 125, § 58, for refusing to employ a pilot, unless the pilot produced his license as required by § 66, although it was demanded. Hammond *v.* Blake, 10 B. & C. 424; 5 M. & R. 361.

4. Com. *v.* Rickeston, 5 Met. (Mass.) 412; Hunt *v.* Carlisle, 1 Gray (Mass.) 257; Beckwith *v.* Baldwin, 12 Ala. 720; Martin *v.* Hilton, 9 Met. (Mass.) 371; Gerrish *v.* Johnson, 1 Jones (N. Car.) 335. See Comrs. *v.* Low, R. M. Charlt. (Ga.) 298.

Where a pilot tenders his services to a vessel over one hundred and twenty tons' burden, bound in, over the bar of Ocracocke, before she gets to the bar, the commander is bound to pay the usual rates of pilotage, though he refuses to receive such pilot on board his vessel, and though the weather is fair, and though it is in the month of August, and though the defendant is fully competent to bring in his vessel with safety. Gerrish *v.* Johnson, 1 Jones (N. Car.) 335.

5. The Alameda *v.* Neal, 32 Fed. Rep. 331; Steamship Co. *v.* Joliffe, 2 Wall. (U. S.) 450; The Australia, 36 Fed. Rep. 332; The Georgia D. Loud, 8 Ben. (U. S.) 392; The Charles A. Sparks, 16 Fed. Rep. 480; The William Law, 14 Fed. Rep. 792.

Compare The Belle Hooper, 28 Fed. Rep. 928.

"The object of the regulations established by the statute was to create a body of hardy and skillful seamen, thoroughly acquainted with the harbor, to pilot vessels seeking to enter or depart from the port, and thus give security to life and property exposed to the dangers of a difficult navigation. This object would be in a great degree defeated if the selection of a pilot were left to the option of the master of the vessel, or the exertions of the pilot to reach the vessel, in order to tender his services, were without any remuneration. The experience of all commercial States has shown the necessity, in order to create and maintain an efficient class of pilots, of providing compensation, not only when the services tendered are accepted by the master of the vessel, but also when they are declined. If the services are accepted, a contract is created between the master or owner of the vessel and the pilot, the terms of which, it is true, are fixed by the statute, but the transaction is not less a contract on that account. If the services tendered are declined, the half fees allowed are by way of compensation for the exertions and labor made by the pilot

does not affect a judgment rendered in an action brought to recover the claim for half pilotage, or the jurisdiction of the *United States* Supreme court to review the judgment on writ of error.[1]

VIII. Powers and Duties of Pilots—1. Generally.—The duty of the pilot is to attend to the navigation of the ship, and of the master and crew to keep a good look-out.[2] And in giving directions for the navigation of a steam vessel, of which he is in charge, it is his province to determine the rate of speed at which he should proceed.[3] He is obliged to use ordinary skill and care,[4] and it is his duty, and not that of the master, to determine where and whether or not the ship shall be brought up.[5] His authority over the boat and cargo is, under ordinary circumstances, limited to the mere duty of transportation and preservation; but under circumstances of great emergency—as in the case of wreck and imminent danger of an entire loss—he has authority to dispose of the boat and cargo, from the very nature and necessity of the case.[6]

2. Local Customs.—No special custom as to the power and authority of pilots of vessels prevailing at the port of shipment, different from the general custom, would be binding on persons residing elsewhere in the absence of any proof that they had notice of such special custom.[7]

and the expenses and risks incurred by him in placing himself in a position to render the services, which, in the majority of cases, would be required."

Steamship Co. *v.* Joliffe, 2 Wall. (U. S.) 456; The Alameda *v.* Neal, 32 Fed. Rep. 331.

The *Pennsylvania* Pilot Act of March 29th, 1803, which "obliges" vessels going out of or coming into the port of Philadelphia to receive a pilot under a "penalty," and "forfeiture" of half pilotage, which the act makes a lien upon the ship, and recoverable in the admiralty, not being, as is decided, compulsory, but optional, the ship need not take a pilot, if it prefers to pay the penalty or forfeiture. Hence, there being a direct privity between the pilot and the ship, the latter is liable in admiralty for damage caused by his acts. Smith *v.* The Creole, 2 Wall. Jr. (C. C.) 485.

England.—By the Liverpool Pilot Act, 5 Geo. IV., ch. 73, § 37, in case the master of any ship outward bound shall proceed to sea, and shall refuse to take on board a pilot, he shall pay the pilot who shall first offer his service, at a certain rate as if the pilot had piloted the vessel. See The Hankow, 4 L. R., P. Div. 197; 48 L. J., P. Div. 29; The Vesta, 7 L. R., P. Div. 240; 51 L. J., P. Div. 25; The Cachapool, 7 L. R., P. Div. 217; 46 L. T., N. S. 171.

1. Steamship Co. *v.* Joliffe, 2 Wall. (U. S.) 450.

2. The Iona, 1 L. R., P. C. 426; 16 L. T., N. S. 158. See Oakley *v.* Speedy, 40 L. T., N. S. 881.

The pilot is an officer of the ship when on board in the exercise of his duty; but when the captain is on board he is master, and the orders of the pilot are considered the master's. U. S. *v.* Forbes, Crabbe (U. S.) 558.

When a steam-tug is engaged to tow a vessel which is in charge of a pilot, the tug is bound to obey the orders of the pilot, and the pilot is bound to give the tug proper directions and to superintend her navigation. The Energy, 3 L. R., Adm. 48; 39 L. J., Adm. 25.

3. The Calabar, 2 L. R., P. C. 238; 19 L. T., N. S. 268. See The James A. Garfield, 21 Fed. Rep. 474.

4. St Louis etc. Packet Co. *v.* Keokuk etc. Bridge Co., 31 Fed. Rep. 755.

5. The Lochlibo, 3 Rob. Adm. 310.

6. Marlatt *v.* Clary, 20 Ark. 251.

7. Marlatt *v.* Clary, 20 Ark. 251.

IX. Liability of Pilots.—A vessel having a pilot by compulsion of law on board, and damage is caused solely through his misconduct, he will be liable.[1] But a pilot is not chargeable for the damage resulting from a collision for which he was in no way in fault.[2] So when a pilot, in piloting a vessel, has used his best skill and judgment, he is not liable for her loss, although the result shows that his best judgment was wrong.[3]

X. Immunity of Owners.—The rule that the wrong-doing vessel is exempted from liability when the pilot in charge is employed by compulsion of law, and alone in fault, is now well settled in English jurisprudence.[4] But this exemption applies only where the pilot is actually in charge of the vessel and solely in fault.[5] If there be anything which concurred with the fault of the pilot

1. Marshall *v.* Moran, The Ocean Wave, 23 L. T., N. S. 218; The City of Cambridge, 30 L. T., N. S. 439; 22 W. R. 578. See The Energy, 3 L. R., Adm. 48; 39 L. J., Adm. 25; Sideracude *v.* Mapes, 3 Fed. Rep. 873; The China, 7 Wall. (U. S.) 53.

In a cause of collision occasioned by a vessel under compulsory pilotage, where no contributory negligence on the part of the master and crew is proved, the pilot in charge is solely responsible, and the owners are exempt from the consequences of his neglect or default. The Calabar, 2 L. R., P. C. 238; 19 L. T., N. S. 768.

Owners are not exonerated from responsibility for the default of a pilot whom they have selected and placed in charge, when there was no obligation imposed on them to take such pilot and put him in charge. The Lion, 37 L. J., Adm. 39; 2 L. R., Adm. 102; 18 L. T., N. S. 803; affirmed on appeal, 38 L. J., Adm. 51; 21 L. T., N. S. 41; The Woburn Abbey, 38 L. J., Adm. 28.

2. The Governor Newell, 31 Fed. Rep. 362; The Sinquasi, 5 L. R., P. Div. 241; 50 L.J., P. Div. 5; The Rikon, 10 L. R., P. Div. 65; 54 L. J., P. Div. 56.

The association of branch pilots of the port of New Orleans, when without fault itself, is not liable for damages to a vessel sustained from the negligence, want of skill, or fault of a member of the association while engaged in piloting her. Mason *v.* Ervine, 27 Fed. Rep. 459.

3. Mason *v.* Ervine, 27 Fed. Rep. 459. See Comfort *v.* The Wallace, 32 Fed. Rep. 972.

A pilot is not an insurer. Where one piloting a tug with a schooner in tow, and pursuing the customary course near the mid-channel of East River off Nineteenth Street, ran the schooner against a newly discovered rock, twelve feet below low-water mark it was held that he was not liable for the consequent damage. The James A. Garfield, 21 Fed. Rep. 474.

4. The Johanna Stoll, Lush. 295; 30 L. J., Adm. 201; The Agricola, 2 Rob. Adm. 10; The Batavier, 2 Rob. Adm. 407. See General Steam Navigation Co. *v.* British Colonial Navigation Co., 38 L. J. Exch. 97; The City of Cambridge, 39 L. T., N. S. 439; The Daisy, 37 L. T., N. S. 137; The Princeton, 3 L. R., Adm. Div. 90; 47 L. J., Adm. 33; The Rigborg's Minde, 8 L. R., P. Div. 132; 52 L. J., P. Div. 74; The Guy Mannering, 7 L. R., P. Div. 132; 51 L. J., P. Div. 57; The Clan Gordon, 7 L. R. P., Div. 190; The Vesta, 7 L. R. P. Div. 240; The Proctor, 1 W. Rob. 45; Pollock *v.* M'Alpin, 7 Moore P. C. C. 427; Stuart *v.* Iremonger, 4 Moore P. C. C. 11; Lucy *v.* Ingram, 6 M. & W. 302; McIntosh *v.* Slade, 6 B. & C. 657; 9 D. & R. 738. See Conservators of the River Thames *v.* Hall, L. R., 3 C. P. 415; 37 L. J., C. P. 163. See The Hibernian, 21 W. R. 276; 42 L. J., Adm. 8. *Compare* The Druid, 1 W. Rob. 399; The Neptune, 1 Dod, 467; The Attorney General *v.* Case, 3 Price 303; Carruthers *v.* Sydebotham, 4 M. & S. 77; The Guolamo, 3 Hagg. 169; The Baron Holberg, 3 Hagg. 244.

5. The General De Caen, 1 Swab. 10; The Diana, 1 W. Rob. 135; The Proctor, 1 W. Rob. 60; The Christiana, 7 Moore P. C. 171; The Minna, L. R., Adm. 97; The Iona, L. R., 1 P. C. 426; The Carrier Dove, B. & L. 113; 2 Moore P. C. C., N. S. 261. See Schwalbe, 4 L. T., N. S. 160; Lush. 239.

in producing the accident, the exemption does not apply, and the vessel's master and owners are liable.[1]

In this country, the fact that the law compels the master to take a pilot, does not exonerate the vessel from liability for damages, which were entirely the result of his gross mis-management.[2] If there be any fault on the part of the pilot, the owner has the same remedies against him as against other delinquents on board, and if the remedy of the damaged vessel was confined to the culpable pilot, it would frequently be a mere delusion. He would often be unable to respond by payment—especially if the amount recovered were large.[3]

In the absence of the master the pilot has, while on board, the exclusive management and control of the vessel; but if the master is present, the power of the pilot does not so far supersede the authority of the master that the latter may not, in case of obvious and certain disability, or gross ignorance, and palpable and imminently dangerous mistake, disobey his orders, and interfere for the protection of the ship and the lives of those on board.[4]

XI. Compensation.—The rates of port pilots are regulated by statute.[5] Compensation thus allowed is not a tax, impost or toll in the sense of the constitution of *California*.[6] There is no settled rule, either as to sea-going or inland vessels, requiring them to employ two licensed pilots or forbidding the master from acting as one of two pilots, which can preclude a master from recovering for services rendered in the capacity of pilot.[7] Off-shore pilotage, or compensation for services rendered beyond pilot

1. The Velasquez, 1 L. R., P. C. 494; 16 W. R. 89; Netherlands Steamboat Co. *v.* Styles, 9 Moore P. C. C. 286. See Spaight *v.* Ted Castle, 6 L. R. App. Cas. 217; 44 L. T., N. S. 589; The Mary, 5 L. R., P. Div. 14; 48 L. J., P. Div. 66.

2. The China, 7 Wall. (U. S.) 53; Smith *v.* The Creole, 2 Wall. Jr. (C. C.) 485; The E. M. Norton, 15 Fed. Rep. 686; Bussy *v.* Donaldson, 4 Dall. (U. S.) 206; Williamson *v.* Price, 4 Mart., N. S. (La.) 399; Denison *v.* Seymour, 9 Wend. (N. Y.) 1. See Snell *v.* Rich, 1 Johns. (N. Y.) 305.

Where a collision between American vessels occurs in an English port, the rights of the parties depend upon the provisions of the British statutes and the master or owner of the vessel causing the injury is not answerable for damages occasioned by the fault of the pilot. Smith *v.* Condrey, 1 How. (U. S.) 29.

3. The China, 7 Wall. (U. S.) 53.

In Yates *v.* Brown, 8 Pick. (Mass.) 22, Parker, C. J., said: "It is more convenient that such owner should seek his remedy against the pilot, whom he has selected for this service, than that the injured party should; and it is more conformable to the general spirit of the law; for although the pilot holds his commission under the executive authority of the commonwealth, yet in many respects he is the servant of the owner who employs him, and in regard to the time of sailing is undoubtedly under the direction of the owner. The master, in such case, would not be liable, for he is answerable only in respect of his authority over the vessel, which authority is entirely superseded by that of the pilot, when the vessel is under sail within pilot ground."

4. Camp *v.* The Ship Marcellus, 1 Cliff. (U. S.) 481; The Argo, 1 Swab. 112; The Christiana, 7 Moore P. C. 172.

5. The Alameda, 31 Fed. Rep. 366; The Wisconsin, 30 Fed. Rep. 846.

6. Harrison *v.* Green, 18 Cal. 94.

7. Bissell *v.* Mepham, 1 Woolw. (U. S.) 225.

Compare The Nevada, 7 Ben. (U. S.) 386.

grounds cannot be recovered.[1] So where a pilot voluntarily leaves the boat in consequence of being told by the captain that wages would be stopped while the boat remained at that point, he will have no action either for damages or for wages, beyond the time during which he actually served, he not having put defendant in default.[2]

A pilot running unusual risk in serving a vessel in distress is entitled to extraordinary compensation in the nature of salvage.[3] But whenever they are permitted to become salvors, public policy requires that they should first be held strictly to the discharge of their duty as pilots.[4]

XII. Lien for Services—1. Generally.—A pilot has a lien for services rendered to a foreign vessel coming in and going out of port.[5] So a contract between a pilot and a boat making short and regular trips gives the pilot a maritime lien.[6] To make pilotage a lien on the ship itself, or on the owners, the contract must have been made by some person in the employment of the owner duly authorized to make the contract, such as the master or the *quasi*-master. But mere wrongdoers or usurpers of the command of the ship, not acknowledged or appointed by the owner, cannot create a charge on the ship or personally bind the owner by contract, whether it be beneficial to them or not.[7]

The master of the vessel can have no lien for services as pilot.[8] But a pilot's lien for wages is not impaired by the fact that when the vessel was in port he acted as master.[9]

2. Proffered Service.—A pilot who has proffered his services to a vessel, which have been refused, and who is entitled to fees

1. The Alaska, 3 Ben. (U. S.) 391.

2. Patterson *v.* Haslep, 19 La. Ann. 178.

3. The Grid, 21 Fed. Rep. 423; Love *v.* Hinckley, 1 Abb. Adm. 436; The Wisconsin, 30 Fed. Rep. 846. See Hope *v.* Dido, 2 Paine (U. S.) 243; The Susan, 1 Sprague (U. S.) 499; Hobart *v.* Drogan, 10 Pet. (U. S.) 108; Flanders *v.* Tripp, 2 Low. (U. S.) 15; The C. D. Bryant, 19 Fed. Rep. 603.

A pilot in a smooth sea boarded a barque in a thick fog while she lay aground in Columbia River at low tide, and next flood sailed her over into deep water, and after drifting out to sea in the night brought her into Portland the next morning. She had some slight bruises from contact with the fluke of the anchor in the sand. *Held*, that the service involved no "extraordinary danger or risk," within *Oregon* Sess. Laws, 1882, p. 15, § 27, entitling him to salvage above pilot's compensation. The C. D. Bryant, 19 Fed. Rep. 603.

The libellants piloted a vessel partially crippled, but not in immediate peril, nor unnavigable, through the Sandy Hook channel, and claimed extra fees, as for a vessel in distress, on the ground of usage of the port. *Held*, 1. That the proofs in the cause did not authorize the court to say, that the term distress was by the usage of the port applicable to the condition of the vessel in question. Love *v.* Hinckley, 1 Abb. Adm. 436.

4. Hope *v.* The Dido, 2 Paine (U. S.) 243; Lea *v.* Ship Alexander, 2 Paine (U. S.) 466.

5. The Pirate, 32 Fed. Rep. 486.

6. The Mary Elizabeth, 24 Fed. Rep. 397.

7. The Anne, 1 Mason (U. S.) 508.

8. The Æolian, 1 Biss. (U. S.) 321.

9. Logan *v.* The Æolian, 1 Bond (U. S.) 267.

One who is engaged and ships as pilot of a vessel, whereon another stands as registered master, has a lien on the boat for his wages, although he may be in entire charge of her navigation. The Atlas, 42 Fed. Rep. 793.

therefor by a statute of a State, has no lien upon the vessel for such fees, unless lien is in terms given by the statute.[1] But the right to enforce such claims by libel *in rem* has been repeatedly sustained, even where the State statute did not in express terms make the vessel liable.[2]

3. Waiver of Lien.—A pilot does not waive his lien by taking promissory notes for his claim for services.[3]

XIII. Injury to Pilot by Negligence of Crew.—There is no implied contract between the owners of a ship and a pilot whom they are compelled to employ, that the pilot shall take upon himself the risk of injury from the negligence of the ship-owners' servants; and an action will lie by the pilot against the ship-owners for injuries caused to him, while acting as pilot on board their vessel, by the negligence of their servants.[4]

XIV. Suspension of Pilots.—1. Generally.—Pilot commissioners may suspend for dereliction of duty not specified in the statute as cause for removal.[5] But the negligence of a pilot which is punishable by suspension is not a crime, and proceedings to suspend him are not criminal.[6]

When the term of his suspension expires, he can resume the duties of his office, and they cannot as a further punishment revoke his license. They cannot retry him and inflict an additional punishment upon him for an offense for which he has been already punished by suspension from office.[7]

2. When Certiorari Granted.—A writ of *certiorari* will not be granted to a suspended pilot, until he has exhausted the remedy of an appeal for a rehearing by the board of pilot commissioners, given him by statute.[8]

XV. Pleading.—Suits for pilotage on the high seas and on waters navigable from the sea, as far as the tide ebbs and flows, are within the *United States* courts' maritime jurisdiction.[9] This jurisdiction extends to an action brought by a pilot to recover half pilotage awarded by a State statute to the first pilot who tenders his services to a vessel, even though the State statute has not been adopted by the *United States*, provided that no act of

1. The Robert J. Mercer, 1 Sprague (U. S.) 284. See The America, 1 Low. (U. S.) 176.

2. The Edith Godden, 25 Fed. Rep. 511; The Glenearne, 7 Fed. Rep. 604; The Lord Clive, 10 Fed. Rep. 135; The Kalmer, 10 Ben. (U. S.) 242.

3. The Argo, 7 Ben. (U. S.) 304.

4. Smith *v.* Steele, 10 L. R., Q. B. 125; 23 W. R. 388.

5. State *v.* Comrs. of Pilotage, 23 S. Car. 175; State *v.* Courtenay, 23 S. Car. 180.

6. Low *v.* Comrs., R. M. Charlt. (Ga.) 302.

Proceedings against pilots for dereliction of duty, under *Georgia* Code, §§ 1504–1542, are in the nature of criminal proceedings, and a judgment for the defendant cannot be reviewed. St. Simons Pilotage Comrs. *v.* Tabbot, 72 Ga. 89.

7. State *v.* Nerney, 29 N. J. L. 189.

8. People *v.* Board of Comrs., 37 Barb. (N. Y.) 126.

9. Hobart *v.* Drogan, 10 Pet. (U. S.) 108; The Anne, 1 Mason (U. S.) 508; The Wave *v.* Hye, 2 Paine (U. S.) 131; The Wave, Blatchf. & H. (U. S.) 235; Gottfried *v.* Miller, 104 U. S. 521; *Ex parte* McNiel, 13 Wall. (U. S.) 236; The Alzena, 14 Fed. Rep. 174;

Congress has been found adverse to it.[1] It is no objection to the jurisdiction of the admiralty court in suits for pilotage that a fixed compensation has been established under the authority of Congress by the State laws. The only effect of the adoption of the State laws by the act of Congress, was to leave the jurisdiction concurrent in the State courts, and to limit the recovery, in case of a suit brought in admiralty, to the precise sum to which the party would have been entitled under the State laws adopted by Congress if he has sued in the State courts.[2]

XVI. Evidence—1. Generally.—The evidence must show a refusal to accept the services of a pilot, or the pilot's libel against the vessel for the value of the services which were not rendered will be dismissed.[3] The pilot must also show a tender of service and that no pilot was employed. Slight circumstances will, however, be sufficient to warrant the inference that no pilot was employed.[4]

2. Burden of Proof.—Where, by the mismanagement of a vessel which is proceeding to sea, damage is done, the owners will not be exonerated, unless they show that the damage was occasioned exclusively by the fault of the pilot,[5] and that pilotage was compulsory.[6]

When the defense of compulsory pilotage is relied upon, the onus of proving negligence on the part of the defendant or his servants causing or contributing to the collision, is on the plaintiff.[7]

The Edith Godden, 25 Fed. Rep. 511; The William Law, 14 Fed. Rep. 795.

1. The Alzena, 14 Fed. Rep. 174; *Ex parte* McNeil, 13 Wall. (U. S.) 236; The California, 1 Sawyer (U. S.) 463; Bantá *v.* McNeil, 5 Ben. (U. S.) 74.

2. Hobart *v.* Drogan, 10 Pet. (U. S.) 108. *Compare* The Wave *v.* Hyer, 2 Paine (U. S.) 131.

Justice Courts.—Under the *Georgia* statute vesting the commissioners of pilotage with power to regulate pilots a justice court may exercise jurisdiction over a demand for pilotage when the sum does not exceed $30. Taylor *v.* Thomas, Dudley (Ga.) 59.

3. The Harriet *v.* Jackson, 32 Fed. Rep. 110; The Talisman, 23 Fed. Rep. 111.

Where the pilot's services are alleged to have been refused and the refusal is denied, the burden is on the pilot to prove the refusal. The Thomas Turral, 6 Ben. (U. S.) 404.

4. The Nellie Husted, 9 Ben. (U. S.) 42.

Such inference may be drawn from the fact that when the libellant presented his bill, the master of the ship said it was all right, no evidence being offered to show that a pilot was employed. The Nellie Husted, 9 Ben. (U. S.) 42.

5. Rodrigues *v.* Melhuish, 10 Exch. 110; The Velasquez, 4 Moore P. C. C., N. S. 426.

If a licensed pilot is on board a vessel, in order to exempt the owner from liability for damage occasioned by collision, the *onus probandi* lies upon the owner to establish that the collision was occasioned solely by the negligence of the pilot, and it is the duty of the owner relying upon such a defense to call the pilot as a witness. The Carrier Dove, 2 Moore P. C. C., N. S. 261.

6. The Peerless, 30 L. J., Adm. 89; Lush. 103.

7. The Dawz, 37 L. T., N. S. 137. In order to entitle the owner of a ship having, by compulsion of law, a pilot on board, to the benefit of the exemption from liability for damage by default of the pilot, it is not enough to prove that there was fault or negligence on the pilot's part, but the owner must show that there was no default on the part of the master and crew, which might have in any degree been con-

When a ship is under the compulsory charge of a licensed pilot the owners are not responsible for damage occasioned by his fault or incapacity, although they must meet and rebut any relevant allegation of negligence on their own part.[1] And the question in such actions is not whether he possessed proper skill, but whether in the present case he exercised it.[2]

3. Admissions.—An admission, in defendant's special plea, that plaintiff was defendant's servant, precludes defendant from insisting that the proof on the point was meagre and somewhat conflicting.[3]

PIMP.—One who provides gratification for the lust of others; a procurer; a panderer.[4]

PIN MONEY.—See HUSBAND AND WIFE, vol. 9, p. 847.

PIPE LINES.—See CORPORATIONS, vol. 4, p. 184; EMINENT DOMAIN, vol. 6, p. 509; FRANCHISES, vol. 8, p. 584; GAS COMPANIES, vol. 8, p. 1268; NATURAL GAS COMPANIES, vol. 16, p. 222; WATER COMPANIES.

I. **DEFINITION.**—In their common legal significance pipe lines are a connecting series of pipes for the transportation of oil, gas, or water. The right to lay and maintain them may exist in corporations created for a public use, sometimes called *quasi* public corporations,[5] or it may be acquired by private persons or corporations by grant from private owners.[6] The former is the more common and will alone be considered.

II. **RIGHT TO LAY.**—The purpose for which pipe lines are ordinarily laid are generally admitted to the distinction of a "public use." A legislature has the right, therefore, to confer the power of eminent domain on corporations for such purposes authorizing an appropriation of private property by condemnation.[7] The right to use the public streets of a city for laying pipes must be

ducive to the damage. The Iona, 1 L. R., P. C. 426; 16 L. T., N. S. 158.

1. Clyde Navigation Co. *v.* Barclay, 1 L. R., App. Cas. 790. See The Meteor, 9 Ir. R. Eq. 567.

2. Slade *v.* State, 2 Ind. 33.

3. Somerset etc. R. Co. *v.* Galbraith, 109 Pa. St. 32.

4. Webster's Dict. followed in People *v.* Gastro, 75 Mich. 127. See also Fahnestock *v.* State, 102 Ind. 156.

5. As to the distinction between public, *quasi* public and private corporations, see FRANCHISES, vol. 8, p. 588, *et seq.*; CORPORATIONS, vol. 4, p. 186.

6. See Tide-water Pipe Co. *v.* Berry, 33 Am. & E. Corp. Cases 64.

7. Confusion on this point and on the distinction of kinds of corporations arises frequently from disregard of the fact that there is no connection or correspondence between the terms "public corporation" and "public use;" that the actual benefit of a public use may be confined to a particular portion of the commonwealth; that the determination of what is a public use rests in a wide discretion of the legislature (subject to a very limited review by the courts). Thus even private individuals have been authorized to take private property for such purposes as constructing wharves, establishing ferries, etc. See GAS COMPANIES, vol.

exercised under the authority of the legislature.[1] Without ex-

8, pp. 1269, 1270. See also EMINENT DOMAIN, vol. 6, p. 509, with cases cited. Bloomfield etc. Natural Gas Co. *v.* Richardson, 63 Barb. (N. Y.) 437; Beekman *v.* R. Co., 3 Paige (N. Y.) 45; Buffalo etc. R. Co. *v.* Brainard, 5 Seld. (N. Y.) 109; Williams *v.* Mutual Gas Co., 52 Mich. 499; 4 Am. & E. Corp. Cases 66; New Orleans Gaslight Co. *v.* Louisiana Light etc. Mfg. Co., 115 U. S. 516; 10 Am. & E. Corp. Cas. 639.

Gas Companies.—In Bloomfield etc. Nat. Gas Co. *v.* Richardson, 63 Barb. (N. Y.) 437, the business of a gas company was expressly declared to be a public use.

The cases which seem to go the other way relate to companies which were not authorized to take private property, not already appropriated to public uses.

In Com. *v.* Gas Light Co., 12 Allen (Mass.) 75, it was held that no public duty was imposed upon the gas company; that it could not, therefore, be exempted from taxation on the same principle as turnpike, railroad, canal and other like corporations, established for the convenience and accommodation of the public. (*Massachusetts* St. 1849, ch. 234; Gen. Sts., ch. 61, § 16.)

In McCune *v.* Norwich City Gas Co., 30 Conn. 521, it was held that in the absence of any contract, express or implied, and where the charter of the company contains no provision on the subject, a gas company is under no more obligation to continue to supply its customers, than the venders of any other article. See also N. Y. Central etc. R. Co. *v.* Met. Gas Light Co., 63 N. Y. 326.

In all these cases, the companies had no power to appropriate private property by condemnation. But the opinions seem to represent a theory contrary to the general one.

Natural Gas Companies.—See NATURAL GAS COMPANIES, vol. 16, p. 222.

In *Pennsylvania* the Natural Gas Act of May 29th, 1885, P. L. 29, declares the transportation and supply of natural gas to be a public use, and provides by general law for the incorporation and regulation of natural gas companies. In the preamble, it was declared that natural gas had become a prime necessity for use as a fuel and otherwise in the development of trade. By the tenth section "any and all corporations that is or are now, or shall thereafter be, engaged in such business shall have the right of eminent domain for the laying of pipe-lines for the transportation and distribution of natural gas." Provisions follow for the assessment of damages.

See Carother's Appeal, 118 Pa. St. 468. See also McDevitt *v.* People's Natural Gas Co. (Pa.), 7 Atl. Rep. 588. See article of W. W. Thornton, Esq. on "Some Natural Gas Cases," in 30 Cent. L. J. 497. See Appeal of Pittsburgh, 115 Pa. St. 4.

In Johnson's Appeal (Pa.), 7 Atl. Rep. 167 the same act was sustained by the Supreme court of *Pennsylvania* in these words: "It is a serious objection to set up against the act of May 29th. 1885, in view of the present consumption of gas, that its use is not a public one, and that, therefore, those corporations which are engaged in its transportation may not be vested with the right of eminent domains. Well might this objection be urged against the vesting of this power in those companies which have been incorporated for the purpose of supplying our towns and villages with water, in which the public interest is found, not in the transportation, but in the use of that fluid after it has, by these agencies been transported. Nor would it seem to us as of the slightest materiality that the water thus produced had been drawn from a single spring, well or basin. Just so with natural gas. It has become a public necessity; but, as it cannot be used except it be piped to the manufactories and residences of the people, it follows that, as the piping of it is necessary to its use, the means so used for its transportation must be of prime importance to the public, and directly affect its welfare." See Sterling's Appeal, 111 Pa. St. 35.

1. See Gas Light & Coke Co. *v.* Avondale, 43 Ohio St. 257.

Oil Companies.—In Columbia Conduit Co. *v.* Com., 90 Pa. St. 307, it was held that an oil pipe line is a transportation company within the meaning of § 4, Act of April 24th, 1874. See West Virginia Transportation Co. *v.* Volcanic Oil etc. Co., 5 W. Va. 382; Jones *v.* Tanner, 27 Pitts. L. J. 79.

For the general system for the assessment of damages provided by the act of

press authority, the municipality cannot grant the exclusive right of its streets for such purposes.[1]

III. Nature of Property in Pipe Lines—Taxation.—A corporation which is invested with a franchise to lay pipes for the purpose of transporting oil, gas or water, acquires property therein of two kinds: 1st. An incorporeal hereditament or easement in the land through which its pipes are laid.[2] 2nd. A property in the pipes, which is assessed differently in different States; in some as fixtures in the lands through which the pipes are laid by

1885, see Carothers' Appeal, 118 Pa. St. 468.

See Gas Companies, vol. 8, p. 1276, with cases cited; Jersey City Gas Co. *v.* Dwight. 29 N. J. Eq. 242; State *v.* Cincinnati Gas Co., 18 Ohio St. 262; Milhan *v.* Sharp, 15 Barb. (N. Y.) 210; Norwich Gas Light Co. *v.* Norwich City Gas Co., 25 Conn. 19; Smith *v.* Met. Gas Co., 12 How. Pr. (N. Y.) 187; People *v.* Bowen, 30 Barb. (N. Y.) 24. See Commissioners *v.* Northern Liberties G. Co., 12 Pa. St. 318. See also Brookly *v.* Jourdon, 71 App. (N. C.) 23; State *v.* Cincinnati G. Co., 18 Ohio St. 262; Jersey City G. Co. *v.* Dwight, 29 N. J. Eq. 242. Apparently *contra* is People *v.* Mutual Gas Light Co., 38 Mich. 154.

County Highways.—See Gas Companies, vol. 8, p. 1277. According to Boston *v.* Richardson, 13 Allen (Mass.) 160, the right of a town without express authority from the legislature to lay gas pipes in the highways, is not clear. Bloomfield Gas Co. *v.* Calkins, 62 N. Y. 386; Kelsey *v.* King, 32 Barb. (N. Y.) 410; Mills on Em. Dom. § 55; Bloomfield etc. Nat. Gas Light Co. *v.* Richardson, 63 Barb. (N. Y.) 437.

1. See Gas Companies, vol. 8, p. 1277, note 1, and cases cited; also pp. 1278–80. See also Indianapolis *v.* Indianapolis Gas Co., 66 Ind. 396; Richmond Gas Light Co. *v.* Middletown, 59 N. Y. 226; Norwich Gas Light Co. *v.* Norwich City Gas Co., 25 Conn. 19. See also 24 Central L. J. 502; Waddington *v.* Allegheny Heating Co., 6 Pa. Co. Ct. Rep. 96; Sewickley *v.* Ohio Valley Gas Co., 6 Pa. Co. Ct. Rep. 99.

Pipes in Highways.—It is not clear how far the appropriation of land for the use of a highway authorizes its use for other purposes without compensation to the owner of the fee; but, notwithstanding the *Massachusetts* doctrine, it seems that, at least in the country, a highway cannot be used for the laying of pipes without the consent of, or compensation to, the owner of the land. See Bloomfield and Rochester Nat. Gaslight Co. *v.* Calkins, 62 N. Y. 386. See also Eminent Domain, vol. 6, pp. 552, 557. *Compare* Boston *v.* Richardson, 13 Allen (Mass.) 160.

2. See Providence Gas Co. *v.* Thurber, 2 R. I. 15; 55 Am. Dec. 622, where the nature of the company's right was likened to that of a railroad company to build and occupy their road, or a canal company their canal, under the provisions in their charter, which grant the power to take the land, upon rendering compensation to the owners; *citing* Binney's Case, 2 Bland (Md.) 145. See also Boston Water Power Co. *v.* Boston, 29 Met. (Mass.) 202.

In Queen *v.* Cambridge Gas Co., 35 Eng. C. L. 333, the company were held ratable as occupants of the land in the different parishes, by their apparatus, pipes, etc., under the statute of 43 Eliz., ch. 2. See People *v.* Mutual Gas Light Co. of Detroit, 38 Mich. 154. See also Gas Companies, vol. 8, p. 1281; Bloomfield etc. Nat. Gas Light Co. *v.* Calkins, 62 N. Y. 386. See also Jersey City Gas Co. *v.* Dwight, 29 N. J. Eq. 242; Rome G. L. Co. *v.* Meyerhardt, 61 Ga. 287.

In *England*, it has been held that the word "hereditaments" comprehends land in general, and that a gas light company was ratable for ground occupied by the pipes and other apparatus. Rex *v.* Shrewsbury, 2 B. & A. 216.

But in Chelsea Water Works *v.* Bowley, 17 Q. B. 358, a company which was empowered to lay pipes in the roads, street, etc., and did lay pipes accordingly, was held not liable to the land tax for the land occupied by the pipes. Lord Campbell, C. J., said: "The right question, where exercised, appears to us to be in the

virtue of the easement therein;[1] in others as real estate appurtenant to the main plant;[2] in others as personal property;[3] and,

nature of an easement and neither land nor hereditaments . . . . the mere power to lay the pipes in land cannot be considered land or "hereditaments." But this decision seems to have special reference to the Land Tax Act, 38 Geo. III, ch. 3, which in speaking of lands and hereditaments contemplated "property to be let by a landlord to a tenant, and property the land tax of which might be redeemed." Its scope was "to throw the tax as a charge upon the landlord," the tenant, having paid the tax, being authorized to deduct it out of the rent. The decision in regard to the interest of the company in the land was based on the fact that they were not tenants of the land and that there was no rent from which they could deduct the amount of the assessment when they had paid it.

Lord Campbell, further says: "The 'land' . . . has various meanings, it may . . . mean the ground on which the chattel is deposited in the exercise of an easement, although in other acts of Parliament, it means a legal interest in the soil." The latter meaning was construed by the court to hold for this case. See Rex *v.* Corporation of Bath, 14 East 609; Rex *v.* Brighton Gas Light Co., 5 B. & C. 466; Rex *v.* Chelsea Water Works Co., 5 B. & Ad. 156.

1. The question was thoroughly discussed in Providence Gas Co. *v.* Thurber, 2 R. I. 15; 55 Am. Dec. 622. After referring to the definitions of a fixture in Farrar *v.* Stackpole, 6 Me. 157; Voorhis *v.* Freeman, 2 W. & S. (Pa.) 116; Pyle *v.* Pennock, 2 W. & S. (Pa.) 116; Gale *v.* Ward, 14 Mass. 352; Swift *v.* Thompson, 9 Conn. 67, and Walker *v.* Sherman, 20 Wend. (N. Y.) 638, the court enounce the rule: "That a personal chattel does not become a fixture so as to be a part of the real estate, unless it be so affixed to the freehold as to be incapable of severance from it without violence and injury to the freehold, and if it be so annexed, it is a fixture, whether the annexation be for use, for ornament, or from mere caprice."

But a farther test, the court find, is whether the pipes had been laid in the land by parol license; or whether the owner had granted by deed the right in fee to lay the pipes through his land. In the latter case, they would be fixtures, because the annexation would be under legal title. See Ashmun *v.* Williams, 8 Pick. (Mass.) 402, Marcy *v.* Darling, 8 Pick. (Mass.) 283, Aldrich *v.* Parsons, 6 N. H. 555 The court conclude that the pipes being annexed to the freehold, and the gas company having an easement in fee, the pipes are fixtures, and rightfully assessed as real estate.

In Tidewater Pipe Co. *v.* Berry (N. J. 1889), 33 Am. & E. Corp. Cases it was held that § 3 of the Act of 1866, Revision, p. 1150, defining the term "real estate," applied to a pipeline laid by a foreign corporation, under a right acquired by a deed of grant under seal, that the reservation by the grantor of power to revoke the grant for violation of the terms of the grant did not detract from the grantee's estate, that the reservation was in the nature of a right of re-entry for condition broken.

2. In Appeal of the Des Moines Water Company, 48 Iowa 324, the land, machinery and water-mains were all held to be real estate, and appurtenant to the water-works or main structure, though the whole length of the mains were not laid upon the lots owned by appellant, and extended into other townships. The court argued that the mains acquired their real estate character by being appurtenant to the water-works, and, in a conveyance of the works, would pass as incident to the principal thing, without any conveyance of the land where they were located. Hence no assessment was required except in the place where the water-works and lots were situated. See also Capital City Gas Light Co. *v.* Charter Oak Ins. Co., 51 Iowa 31.

3. In *New York*, however, it has been decided that the mains of a gas company running under the streets of the city, not being erected upon or affixed to the company's land, cannot be regarded as real estate under the statute [1 *New York* Rev. Sts. 388; par. 3 and 1 *New York* Rev. St. (5th ed.) 905, par. 3], for purposes of taxation. People *v.* Board of Assessors, 39 N. Y. 81.

In Borrell *v.* Mayor etc., 2 Sandf. (N. Y.) 552, it had been held, under

finally, as "machinery" by statutory provision in the State of *Massachusetts.*[1]

PIRACY (**a Crime**).—(See also INTERNATIONAL LAW, vol. 11, p. 431.)—Piracy is robbery, or a forcible depredation on the high seas, without lawful authority, and done *animo furandi*, and in the spirit and intention of universal hostility. It is the same offense on sea as robbery is on land.[2]

Congress, under the power conferred by the Constitution (art. 1, § 8), "to define and punish piracies and felonies committed on the high seas, and offenses against the law of nations," has legislated against the crime of piracy as defined by the law of nations,[3] and, in addition, has made certain acts piracy which would not be piracy under international law.[4]

PIRACY (**a Tort**).—The plagiarism of a work protected by a copyright. (See COPYRIGHT, vol. 4, p. 147).

the same statute, that incorporeal hereditaments were not subject to taxation as land or real estate. See, however, Smith *v.* Mayor etc., 68 N. Y. 552. It is difficult to understand by what theory such a classification is arrived at, nor, indeed, do the courts attempt to reconcile the statutory provisions for purposes of taxation with the common law. See People *v.* Board of Assessors, 39 N. Y. 81 See FIXTURES, vol. 8 p. 41.

1. In *Massachusetts* gas pipes are regarded as "machinery" under the statute of 1864, ch. 208, par. 1, which classes real estate and machinery together for the purpose of assessment of certain corporations. The fact that machinery here is equivalent to real estate is shown by a separate provision for the assessment of personal estate of such corporations. See *Massachusetts* Rev. Sts., ch. 7, par. 4, 9, 10; and also by the manner in which such machinery is assessed, it being laid in the town or other place where such machinery may be situated or employed. *Massachusetts* Rev. Sts., ch. 7, par. 10. See Com. *v.* Lowell Gas Light Co., 12 Allen (Mass.) 75; Boston Water Power Co. *v.* Boston, 9 Met. (Mass.) 199.

California.—See *California* Civil Code, §§ 657–663.

2. 1 Kent Com 183. U. S *v.* Palmer, 3 Wheat. (U. S.) 610; U. S. *v.* Smith, 5 Wheat. (U. S.) 153; U S. *v.* Furlong, 5 Wheat. (U. S.) 184; U. S. *v.* Jones, 3 Wash. (U. S.) 209. And see for analogous definitions, 3 Inst. 113, 1 Russ. Crimes (3d Eng. ed.) 94; Rex *v.* Dawson, 13 Howell's St. Tr. 454; Bishop's Cr. Law (7th ed.), § 1058.

3. U. S. acts March 3, 1819 (3 Sts. at Large, ch. 77, § 5), May 15, 1820 (3 Sts. at Large, ch. 113, § 2), U. S. Rev. St. § 5368.

4. U. S. Rev. Sts. §§ 5369–5376. Under the earlier act of April 30, 1790 (1 Sts. at Large, 113), defining statutory piracies, it was held that robbery committed on a foreign vessel by one not a citizen of the United States was not piracy. U. S. *v.* Palmer, 3 Wheat. (U. S.) 610. But in U. S. *v.* Klintock, 5 Wheat. (U. S.) 144, it was held that the act of 1790 extended to any person on any vessel acknowledging the authority of no acknowledged power cruising piratically and committing piracy on other vessels, and so U. S. *v.* Holmes, 5 Wheat. (U. S.) 412. In U. S. *v.* The Malek Adhel, a case arising under the act of 1819, it was held that any piratical aggression subjected the vessel to forfeiture, although not made *causa lucri*, and that it made no difference that the owner was innocent and that the vessel was armed for a lawful purpose and started for a lawful voyage, but that the owner's innocence saved his cargo from forfeiture. The robbery contemplated by the act of 1790 was robbery as defined by the common law. U. S. *v.* Palmer, 3 Wheat. (U. S.) 610, personal violence was not an indispensable requisite of the crime, if the intent, *animo furandi* appeared. U. S. *v.* Tully, 1 Gall. (U. S.) 247

It was held in the Marianna Flora, 11 Wheat. (U. S.) 1, that an attack on a vessel of the United States by an armed vessel, upon a mistaken supposition that she was a piratical cruiser, but without felonious intent, was not a piratical aggression.

An American citizen, fitting out a

PIRATE—(See also PIRACY).—One who roves the sea in an armed vessel without any commission from any sovereign State, on his own authority, and for the purpose of seizing by force and appropriating to himself, without discrimination, every vessel he may meet.[1]

A sea-robber, who, to enrich himself, by subtlety or open force, setteth upon merchants and others trading by sea, despoiling them of their loading, and sometimes bereaving them of life and sinking their ships.[2]

PISTOL CARTRIDGES.—See note 3.

PLACE is a very indefinite term. It is applied to any locality, limited by boundaries, however large or however small. It may be used to designate a country, State, county, town, or a very small portion of a town. The extent of the locality designated by it, must, generally, be determined by the connection in which it is used.[4]

vessel in an American port, really to cruise against a power at peace with the United States is not protected, by a commission from a power belligerent as to the power against which he undertakes to cruise, from offenses committed by him against the United States. U. S. *v.* Furlong, 5 Wheat. (U. S.), 184.

That one of two powers at war with another has not been recognized by the United States is not ground for treating the cruisers of such unrecognized power as piratical. The Josefa Segunda, 5 Wheat. (U. S.) 338; though it is otherwise if seisures are made *animo furandi* and not *jure belli.* U. S. *v.* Klintock, 5 Wheat. (U. S.) 144; and see on the general subject of what constitutes piracy the additional cases of The Antelope, 10 Wheat. (U. S.) 66; Harmony *v.* U. S., 2 How. (U. S.) 210; U. S. *v.* Howard, 3 Wash. (U. S.) 340; U. S. *v.* Gibert, 2 Sumn. (U. S.) 19; U. S. *v.* Hutchings, 2 Wheel. Cr. Cas. (U. S.) 543; Adams *v.* People, 1 N. Y. 173.

Jurisdiction.—In U. S. *v.* Ross, 1 Gall. (U. S.) 624, it was held that the U. S. circuit court had jurisdiction, under the act of 1790, of an indictment for an act of piracy committed on board an American vessel lying in open roadstead, adjacent to a foreign territory, and within half a mile of the shore. And see on the general question of jurisdiction, U. S. *v.* Furlong, 5 Wheat. (U. S.) 184; Talbot *v.* Janson, 3 Dall. (U. S.) 133.

Robbery on a ferry-boat plying in waters within the criminal jurisdiction of the State courts, *e. g.*, on the Potomac river, between Washington and Alexandria, is not piracy cognizable by a Federal court.

Indictment.—The use of the technical word "piratically" is essential to a charge of piracy. Hawk. Pl. Cr. book 1, ch. 37, § 15; 1 Chitty Crim. Law 244.

Evidence.—In a proceding *in rem* for a piratical aggression a previous conviction of the person need neither be alleged nor proved. The Palmyra, 12 Wheat. (U. S.) 1, on the trial of an indictment the national character of the vessel may be found on satisfactory evidence without production of the certificate of registry or other documents, and without proof of their having been on board. U. S. *v.* Furlong, 5 Wheat. (U. S.) 184.

1. Nelson, J., in Warburton's Trial of the officers and crew of the Savannah 370; Davison *v.* Seal-skins, 2 Paine (U. S.) 324.

2. Bouvier's Law Dict. and authorities there cited.

3. In an *Alabama* statute, requiring a dealer in "pistol cartridges," pistols, etc., to obtain a license, the term "pistol cartridges" will include cartridges primarily designed for rifles, if they are also adaptable to pistols. Union, etc, Co. *v.* Teague, 83 Ala. 475.

4. Law *v.* Fairfield, 46 Vt. 432. See also Clapp *v.* Burlington, 42 Vt. 582; State *v.* Hart, 31 N. J. L. 439; State *v.* Haight, 31 N. J. L. 414.

Place in the Sense of Sell.—A principal wrote to his agent that he proposed to "place" his goods at a certain price. *Held*, that this gave the agent no authority to warrant that his principal would not sell for a less price. Anderson *v.* Bruner, 112 Mass. 14.

Parties to a contract for "placing" mortgages may mean selling or realizing upon them. Bailey *v.* Joy, 132 Mass. 356.

An agreement "to place" shares in a company is not equivalent to an agreement to take them, and the contractor is thereby liable, not as a contributory, but only in damages for breach of contract. Gorrissen's Case, 8 Ch. 507.

Miscellaneous.—"Place" often denotes a specific place within a city or town at which a person dwells or transacts business; as, in the expressions, "place of business," "usual place of business," "usual place of abode," etc., found in statutes fixing the venue of transitory actions, referring to trustee process, taxation of partnership property, and in provisions for serving writs, notices, etc. Palmer *v.* Kelleher, 111 Mass. 321-322.

The word place is associated with objects which are in their nature fixed and territorial. U. S. *v.* Bevans, 3 Wheat. (U. S.) 336, 390.

Under Revenue Laws.—In the provisions of the internal revenue law, restricting the carrying on of a manufacture to the place designated in the license, the word place is not used as an equivalent for town, city, or county, so as to allow a manufacturer under one license to carry on several distinct factories in the same town. On the other hand, he is not obliged to take out two licenses because he uses two sets of apparatus, if they are used upon premises so connected as to form, in common understanding, one place of manufacture. Salt Co. *v.* Wilkinson, 8 Blatchf. (U. S.) 30.

Intoxicating Liquors.—Within the meaning of a statute which prohibited the sale of liquor in any "building or place" within four hundred feet of a building occupied by a public school, it was held, that "place" is intended to cover the case where there is no building but where a tent, booth, excavation in the ground, or something similar, is used for the purpose of selling liquor. Com. *v.* Jones, 142 Mass. 573. See also INTOXICATING LIQUORS, vol. 11, p. 567.

English Betting Houses' Act.—Section 3 of the English Betting Houses Act (16 & 17 Vict. ch. 119), creates a prohibition against keeping or using any "house, office, room, or place" for betting; and, within that section, a large umbrella temporarily fixed into the ground by means of its spiked, telescopic handle, so as to form a tent, is a "place." Bows *v.* Fenwick, 43 L. J., M. C. 107; L. R., 9 C. P. 339, 22 W. R. 804; so is a wooden box on which the betting man stands, and which temporarily rests on a spot in "the ring" of a race-course. Galloway *v.* Maries, 8 Q. B. D. 275; so is an inclosed yard or ground, whether roofed over or not, and however large its dimensions. Shaw *v.* Morley, L. R., 3 Ex. 137; Eastwood *v.* Miller, L. R., 9 Q. B. 440; Haigh *v.* Sheffield, L. R., 10 Q. B. 102. But such a "place" must, during its use, be an "ascertained" place, and the habitual standing, or using a table, under a tree in Hyde Park does not make it a place for betting. Per Bramwell, B., Mellor, J, and Piggott, B., in Doggett *v.* Catterns, 19 C. B., N. S. 765; for a person using the shelter of a tree in public property like Hyde Park, has no right to use it for betting. Per Pollock, C. B., Channel, B., and Blackburn, J., in Doggett *v.* Catterns, 19 C. B., N. S. 765, and see the judgment of Lush, J., in Eastwood *v.* Miller, L. R., 9 Q. B. 440. Habitual user, indeed, has in the Betting Act no value either way; for whilst Doggett *v.* Catterns shows that such a user will not convert a mere standing into a "place," neither, on the other hand, is habitual user of the essence of a "place." Haigh *v.* Sheffield, L. R., 10 Q. B. 102. It comes almost to this, that any piece of ground appropriated, by its owner or occupier for the time being, for the purposes of betting is a "place" within the statute. Galloway *v.* Maries, 51 L. J., M. C. 56. But the ground must be so appropriated, and must be an ascertained place; and therefore betting *ambulando*, in an inclosed field where races are going on, is not within the statute. Snow *v.* Hill, 14 Q. B. D. 588. See further Henretty *v.* Hart, 13 Sess. Ca. 10.

Any Place.—In *Ireland* it has been held that a cart moving along the street was within the phrase "Any place" as used in § 116, P. H. Act, 1875, so as to justify the seizure of diseased meat therein. Daly *v.* Webb, Ir. Rep., 4 C. L. 309. This seems a strong order. See, however, Young *v.* Gattridge, L. R., 4 Q. B. 166.

Place of Abode.—"Place of abode" usually means the place of residence. "In Johnson's Dictionary, 'abode' is defined to be 'habitation, dwelling, place of residence,' and 'residence' is defined to be 'place of abode, dwelling.' A man's residence, where he lives with his family and sleeps at night, is always his place of abode in the full sense of that expression." Per Campbell, C. J., R. *v.* Hammond, 17 Q. B. 772.

"Place of abode" occurs frequently in the Forms provided by the Acts for the Registration of Voters (6 Vict. ch. 18; 41 & 42 Vict. ch. 26). What is a person's place of abode within the meaning of these acts is "rather a question of fact than of law." Per Erle C. J.; Courtis *v.* Blight, 31 L. J., C. P. 48; 5 L. T. 450. See also Sheldon *v.* Fletcher, 5 C. B. 17.

In a notice of action a solicitor's "place of abode" is sufficiently given by his business address. Roberts *v.* Williams, 5 L. J., M. C. 23; 2 Cr., M. & R. 561.

Place of Burial.—See BURIAL, vol. 2, p. 698.

Place of Business.—Where a turnpike corporation had a toll-house in one county where it kept an agent to collect the tolls and sell tickets, and where its treasurer sometimes paid its employes, it was held, that this was 'an established or usual place of business," in the meaning of the *Massachusetts* statute allowing actions to be brought in the county where a corporation has "an established or usual place of business." And this, though the corporation had an office in another county where its business was chiefly transacted. Rhodes *v.* Salem etc. Corporation, 98 Mass. 95. See also FOREIGN CORPORATIONS, vol. 8, p. 346, *et seq.*

A *California* statute required executors, etc., to publish a notice to the creditors requiring them to present their claims to the executor, etc., "at the place of his residence or business," to be specified in the notice. *Held*, that the words "place of his business" are to be construed to include the place where the administrator transacts the business of the estate, though he may be engaged in transacting some other kind of business elsewhere. Pollinger *v.* Manning, 79 Cal. 7.

Under the statutory provision in *New York*, that in case no newspaper is published in the town where the business of the corporation is carried on, the annual report shall be published "in some newspaper published nearest the place" of business, the town is the "place" of business, and publication in the newspaper published nearer to a point in the town than any other newspaper is to to the same point, is sufficient, although some other newspaper may be published nearer to some other point in the town. Cameron *v.* Seaman, 69 N. Y. 396.

Within the meaning of a statute requiring certain dealers to have their weights and measures sealed in the town in which they had their usual "place of business," "the place of business" of a provision dealer who had a shop in one town, but conducted most of his business by driving a cart through a route in another town, and selling from the cart to his customers at their houses, was held to be the town where the shop was and not where the route lies. Palmer *v.* Kelleher, 111 Mass. 320.

"A place of business" must be understood to be a place actually occupied either continually or at regular periods, by a person or his clerks or those in his employment. If business is transacted at a place occasionally, but not at stated periods, it cannot be termed "a place of business." Stephenson *v.* Primrose, 8 Port. (Ala.) 155; 33 Am. Dec. 287.

That is not the "place of business" of an indorser, within the rules relative to serving notice, which has no public notoriety as such, no open or public business carried on at it by the party, but only occasional employment by him there, two or three times a week, in a house occupied by another person, he being only engaged in setting up his old business. Bank of Columbia *v.* Lawrence, 1 Pet. (U. S.) 578.

The "place of business" contemplated by the act giving permission to one to bear arms" on his or her own premises, or at his or her own place of business," has reference to some particular locality, appropriated exclusively to a local business, such as the farm, store, shop, or dwelling place. It does not authorize the carrying of concealed deadly weapons in the woods while hunting stock. Baird *v.* State, 38 Tex. 599. See also CONCEALED WEAPONS, vol. 3, p. 408.

Where an insurance company had their head office in H and transacted business by agents in K where they re-

PLACER CLAIM.—See MINES AND MINING CLAIMS, vol. 15, p. 523.

PLAIN.—See note 1.

PLANK ROAD.—See TURNPIKES.

PLANT.—The fixtures and tools necessary to carry on any trade or mechanical business.[2]

PLANTATION, strictly speaking, denotes a place planted, but the word, as ordinarily used, is nearly synonymous with farm, and includes all the land forming the parcel or parcels under culture as one farm, or even what is worked by one set of hands.[3]

ceived applications for insurances which they forwarded to the head office from which all policies issued ready for delivery, and the premiums were collected in K, it was held that they had a "place of business" in K within the meaning of the Assessment Act. Kingston *v.* Canada Life Assur. Co., 9 Can. L. T. (Occl. N.) 445.

Place of Manufacture.—The "place of manufacture," at which "liquors and wines," under former *North Carolina* revenue acts, and "wines" under the present act, may be sold without license or tax, is confined to the distillery, or to places so near as to be used in the business of distilling. State *v.* Whissenhunt, 98 N. Car. 682.

Place of Trust or Profit.—It was held that a person employed mainly to guard a public building at night to prevent its destruction or injury by fire, does not hold a "place of trust and profit" within the meaning of the *North Carolina* constitution, which provides that no person who holds a "place of trust and profit" under the *United States* shall be eligible for a State office. Doyle *v.* Raleigh, 89 N. Car. 136. See generally, PUBLIC OFFICERS.

Place of Worship.—"A place of worship" is constituted by the congregating of numerous worshippers thereat. State *v.* Swink, 4 Dev. & B. (N. Car.) 359.

The reading of the Bible at stated times by the teacher of a public school to the pupils converts the school-house into a "place of worship" within the meaning of the constitution of *Wisconsin*, which declares that "no man shall be compelled to . . . erect or support any place of worship." State *v.* District Board, 76 Wis. 177. See generally DISTURBING MEETINGS, vol. 5, p. 721.

1. **Plain Statement.**—The plain statement required by the *New York* Code is one that may be readily understood, not merely by lawyers, but by all who are sufficiently acquainted with the language in which it is written. Mann *v.* Morewood, 5 Sandf. (N. Y.) 564.

As used in *North Carolina* Code, the term is not predicable of a statement that omits any of the facts necessary to the plaintiff's recovery. Comrs. *v.* Pender, 79 N. Car. 574.

Plain Type.—As used in a statute requiring inn-keepers to post up copies of the hotel law, means large or ordinary sized type and not very small type. Porter *v.* Gilkey, 57 Mo. 255.

2. Webster's Dict. followed in Liberty etc. Co. *v.* Barnes, 77 Ga. 748, where it was held that the stock of goods in a promiscuous country store could not be termed part of the "plant" of a saw mill, though such store was attached to the mill.

In Yarmouth *v.* France, 19 Q. B. D. 647, it was held that a horse was part of the "plant" used in the business of a wharfinger.

Plant and Good Will.—A legacy of "plant and good will" has been held to pass the house of business held by a lease. Blake *v.* Shaw, 8 W. R. 410.

3. Attorney Gen'l *v.* Judges, 38 Cal. 291; Stowe *v.* Davis, 10 Ired. (N. Car.) 431.

"A plantation is a large estate, cultivated chiefly by negroes, either slaves or free, who live in a distinct community, on the estate, under the control of the proprietor or master." Webster's Dict. followed in Robson *v.* Du Bose, 79 Ga. 721, where it was held that it was essential in order to constitute a plantation that the estate should be under the control of one proprietor and, that an estate which had been under the control of one owner, but which after his death, had been divided by his executors into smaller

Plantation had formerly a meaning, which is now obsolete. By the word "plant" was then intended, when applied to a tract of land, to settle or to establish; and a plantation, the derivative of planting, denoted sometimes a colony and sometimes a farm or cultivated estate.[1]

PLASTERING.—See note 2.

PLAT.—A plat is a subdivision of lands into lots, streets and alleys, marked upon the earth and represented upon paper.[3]

PLATE.—The term "plate" is not commonly understood to embrace articles of ordinary use, whatever may be the material, but only the more pretentious articles which are displayed on the tables of the wealthy or ostentatious, and which are to be considered rather as articles of luxury than as household furniture.[4]

PLAY.—See GAMING, vol. 8, p. 1033.

tracts and rented to different tenants, was no longer a plantation.

The devise of a "plantation" will, it seems, pass also the stock, implements, utensils, etc., upon it. Lushington *v.* Sewell, 1 Sim. 435, cited Wms. Exrs. 1206.

Plantation Supplies.—A *Mississippi* statute gave a lien "for an advance of money, purchase of supplies, etc., or other things necessary for the cultivation of a farm or plantation." What the act means by "other things necessary for the cultivation of a farm or plantation" must depend upon the usage and customs of agricultural pursuits, taking into account the system of agriculture. But where the farmer has in good faith, taken up the goods on the faith of the lien, and it is questioned whether this or that article falls within the statute, there should be evidence that the things were not needed for farm purposes, or that they are of such a nature in themselves as to be unfit for that purpose. When a planter is indebted to laborers for wages, and pays them off in goods obtained from a merchant, such purchase will be protected by the lien, whether the goods be of the class embraced in the provisions of the statute or not. It would be the same as advancing the money to pay the hands. Herman *v.* Perkins, 52 Miss. 813. See generally, CROPS, vol. 4, p. 902.

Plantation Stock.—Cotton seed does not pass by a devise of "plantation stock." Purnell *v.* Dudley, 4 Jones Eq. (N. Car.) 203.

1. East Haven *v.* Hemingway, 7 Conn. 201; Com. *v.* Roxbury, 9 Gray (Mass.) 485.

In the early colonial history of *Massachusetts*, the terms "plantation," "town," and "township" seem to have been used almost indiscriminately to indicate a cluster or body of persons dwelling near each other, upon whom, when they became designated by a name, certain powers were conferred by general orders and laws, such as to manage their own prudential concerns, to elect deputies, and the like, which in effect made them municipal corporations. Com. *v.* Roxbury, 9 Gray (Mass.) 451, 485.

2. **Plastering.**—As commonly understood, includes the work of "lathing." INTENT, vol. 11, p. 370. See also Higgins *v.* Lee, 16 Ill. 502; Walls *v.* Bailey, 49 N. Y. 464.

3. McDaniel *v.* Mace, 47 Iowa 510. See also Wilhite *v.* Barr, 67 Mo. 284; LOT, vol. 13, p. 1162.

4. Hanover F. Ins. Co. *v.* Mannasson, 29 Mich. 317, and in that case it was held that silver forks, tea and table spoons, were not included in the term "plate" so as to be excluded from a policy of insurance by a clause excluding, "money, bullion, jewels, plate, and watches," unless particularly specified.

In Wills.—"Plate," will not pass plated articles where the testator is possessed of solid silver ones. Holden *v.* Ramsbottom, 4 Giff. 205.

In Field *v.* Peckett, 30 L. J. Ch. 813; 29 Bea. 573, it was held that "plate and china" would carry snuff boxes of gold, silver and china. See further Domvile *v.* Taylor, 32 Bea. 604.

PLEADING.—See ACTION, vol. 1, p. 178; ASSUMPSIT, vol. 1, p. 882; CONVERSION, vol. 4, p. 104; DEBT, vol. 5, p. 163; DECLARATION, vol. 5, p. 349; DEMURRER, vol. 5, p. 549; DETINUE, vol. 5, p. 651; EQUITY PLEADING, vol. 6, p. 724; PARTIES TO ACTIONS; REPLEVIN; TRESPASS; TRESPASS ON THE CASE; TROVER, and the various titles and subtitles in the following analysis:

I. **PLEADING IN GENERAL** [1]—**1. Definition.**—Pleading is the stating in a logical and legal form the facts which constitute the plaintiff's cause of action or the defendant's ground of defense; it is the formal mode of alleging that on the record which constitutes the support or the defense of the party in evidence.[2] The alternate statements of claim and of defense are called the pleadings.[3] The law of pleading deals both with the matter which the pleadings must contain and with the form in which that matter must be set forth. It is, as appears from the definition, a part of the law of procedure, and, as such, is a branch of remedial law.

2. Theory of Pleading at Common Law.—The law of pleading has for its foundation this proposition, that every dispute between man and man, no matter how complicated its nature is, may, nevertheless, be resolved into its elements and be shown to spring from a single point of fact or law as to which the parties are at variance. The object of a system of pleading is to unearth this disputed point from the mass of unimportant details which usually surround it, and to present it to the court for decision.

3. Pleading at Common Law Contrasted with Continental Systems.—The method adopted by the common law for attaining this end differs in many essential particulars from the general course of all other judicatures. Under systems other than the English, the parties are allowed to make their statements at large, and with no view to the extrication of the precise question in controversy. The different statements are then examined with care, in order that undisputed and irrelevant matter may be sifted out. This examination, in the case of some judicatures, is made privately by each of the parties for himself, as a necessary preliminary to the adjustment of his evidence. In others, the point for decision is selected by the court, or its officer, in advance of the trial. By the common law, however, the parties are obliged so to plead as

1. This article deals with pleading at common law only. For pleading in equity, see EQUITY PLEADINGS, vol. 6, p. 724.
2. Bouvier's Law Dict.
3. Pleading may be defined with reference to the object which the system contemplates, as the entering upon the record of alternate allegations of claim and defense by plaintiff and defendant, which allegations are so developed as to arrive ultimately at a material point

to evolve some disputed question by the effect of their own alternate allegations, and to agree upon this question so evolved as the point for decision in the cause.[1]

4. The Issue.—This specific point or matter affirmed on the one side and denied on the other is called the issue—the *exitus*, or outcome of the pleadings.[2] The issue may be a question either of fact or of law. If the parties are agreed as to the facts, and are at variance only as to the law applicable to them, the issue is decided by the court alone. If the facts are disputed, the parties have recourse to some one of the various modes of trial which are known to the common law.

5. Modes of Trial.—These modes of trial are seven in number: The trial by the record, by certificate, by witnesses, by inspection, by wager of battle, by wager of law, and by jury. The first is the appropriate form of trial when the existence of a record is affirmed on one side and denied on the other, upon an issue of *nul tiel record*.[3] The trial by certificate is of rare occurrence in modern times, being almost entirely confined to the issue of *ne unques accouple en loial matrimonie*.[4] This form of issue can arise only in dower; it

of fact or law affirmed by one party and denied by the other.

Obviously each of the pleadings must contain the elements of a good syllogism. Usually the major premise consists of the statement of a legal principle; the minor contains the matters of fact in the particular case, and "the conclusion is the legal inference resulting from the law and fact together, as they appear in the premises." See Gould, Princ. Plead. (5th ed.), § 8.

1. Abridged from Stephen on Pleading (Heard, 9th Am. ed.), 125, *et seq; q. v.*, for a discussion of this peculiarity of English law.

2. Stephen on Plead. 24. Coke defines the issue as follows: "Issue—*exitus*—a single, certain and material point issuing out of the allegations or pleas of the plaintiff and defendant, consisting regularly upon an affirmative and negative, to be tried by twelve men." Bract. 268 a. This definition applies only to issues of fact, and, among issues of fact, to such only as were triable by a jury. It is therefore defective. A similar objection applies to the definition by HEATH, C. J.: "That point of matter depending in suit, whereon the parties join, and put their cause to the trial of the jury." Heath's Maxims, ch. 4. SIR M. HALE, followed by MR. JUSTICE BLACKSTONE, says: "When in the course of pleading they come to a point which is affirmed on one side and denied on the other, they are then said to be at issue." Hale's Analysis, § L; 3 Blackst. Com. 313. "An issue is, when both the parties join upon somewhat that they refer unto a trial, to make an end of the plea" (*i. e.*, suit). Finch's Law, bk. 4, ch. 35, p. 396, ed. 1759.

3. Co. Litt., 117, b; Br. Trials, pl. 40. This issue is the proper one when the question is as to what has judicially taken place in a superior court of record. When the court is one not of record the issue should be upon the fact of whether or not the proceeding took place. Dyson *v.* Wood, 3 B. & C. 449; Steph. Pl., 102 (note). By the Rules of Court of Hilary Term, 4 Wm. IV, a party pleading the judgment of another court must state in the margin of the plea, its date, and the number of the roll, or the plaintiff will be at liberty to sign judgment; and on certificate of its being falsely stated, judgment may also be signed. A similar regulation had already been made in regard to judgments of the same court. 1 Tidd 363; Steph. Pl., 102 (note).

4. BLACKSTONE (bk. 3, 333) mentions six cases in which this form of trial was proper: (1). When the question is, whether A was with the king and his army out of the realm, the trial by the certificate of the mareschall of the host is appropriate. (2). If, to avoid out-

is not allowed in personal actions.[1] The trial by witnesses is, at the common law, applicable only to a very few issues; but it is the only form of trial which is known to the civil law.[2] It is the proper form of trial when, to a widow's writ of dower, the tenant pleads that the husband is alive.[3]

The trial by inspection or examination occurred when the judges, upon the testimony of their own sense, were able to decide the point in dispute.[4] This mode of trial seems to have been incidentally swept away in *England* in the demolition of real actions.[5] The wager of battle was an appeal to arms, and proceeded upon the theory that Heaven would give the victory to him who had the right.[6] It was confined, as far as civil actions are concerned, to issue joined in a writ of right, "the last and most solemn decision of real property."[7] It was abolished by statute.[8] Wager of law was a method of deciding the issue by permitting the defendant to swear to the truth of his defense. He

lawry, the allegation is that the defendant was beyond the seas imprisoned in a foreign town under English dominion (*e. g.*, Calais, Bordeaux), the fact may be proved by the certificate of the captain or mayor. (3). Customs of London are proved by the certificate of mayor and aldermen. (4). To determine whether or not A is a citizen of London, recourse is had to the sheriff's certificate. (5). Matters of ecclesiastical jurisdiction are tried by the bishop's certificate, as marriage, excommunication, general (but not special) bastardy. General bastardy is where the child is a bastard by both the canon and the common law (as where there is no subsequent intermarriage of parents); special bastardy is where the child is a bastard by the common law and not by the canon—as where the parents subsequently intermarry. It was deemed improper in the latter case that the bishop's certificate should be admitted to prove a fact which was regarded differently in the two jurisdictions. (6). Matters of custom and practice of courts are proved, in general, by the certificate of the proper officer.

1. 11 Hen. IV, 78, *cited* in Bac. Ab. Bastardy. Jones' case, Comb. 473; Machell *v.* Garrett, 3 Salk. 64; 12 Mod. 276; Vin., tit. Baron and Feme (D. b) 39.

2. Blackst., bk. 3, 336.

3. Finch (Law, 423) declares that this is the only instance of its use at the common law. LORD COKE (1 Inst. 6) mentions a few other cases, and remarks that the affirmative must be proved in all cases by two witnesses at least.

4. As, for example, in a suit to reverse a fine because the cognizor was a minor, where a writ issued to the sheriff commanding him to constrain the party to appear that the justices might determine by the view of his body whether he was of full age or not. If they were in doubt, proofs were taken; the infant was examined on his *voire dire*, or his mother or god-father was sworn. Blackst., bk. 3, 332. See also 9 Rep. 31 and 2 Roll. Abr. 573. The words of the writ, whence the trial derived its name were: "*Ut per aspectum corporis sui constare poterit justiciariis nostris, si praedictus A, sit plene aetatis necne.*"

5. Steph. Pl. 77 (note).

6. Blackst. bk. 3, 337. For a learned and exhaustive account of the wager of law and wager of battle, see the essays on these subjects in "Superstition and Force," by Henry C. Lea, Philadelphia. See also "The Older Modes of Trial" by Prof. J. B. Thayer, Harvard Law Rev., vol. 5, p. 45. This article contains an account of the obsolete trial by Ordeal.

7. Blackst., bk. 3, 338, *q. v.*, for a detailed account of the trial.

8. 59 Geo. III, ch. 46. This statute was passed in consequence of the defendant's having waged his battle in Ashford *v.* Thornton, 1 B. & Ald. 405. It is said in the Mirror (ch. 3, § 23) that wager of battle is allowable on the authority of the single combat between David and Goliath. Pope Nicholas I, however, in all seriousness, decides that this reasoning is fallacious. Decret.,

brought eleven compurgators with him into court who swore that they believed that he spoke the truth; and the oaths of the twelve were as conclusive against the plaintiff as a verdict would have been.[1] This method of trial also has been abolished in *England* by statute.[2] The seventh, and by far the most important mode of trial, is the trial by jury, called also the trial *per pais*, or by the country. It is on account of the peculiar characteristics of the trial by jury that the system of pleading at common law is what it is; and many of the rules which have been criticised as most technical and artificial, prove to be both logical and sound when considered in relation to the tribunal for whose guidance they were framed.[3] Trial by jury is, with the exception of the trial by the record, the only form of trial in use in the *United States*.[4]

6. **Historical Sketch of the Development of Common Law Pleading**—*a*. FROM EARLIEST TIMES TO REIGN OF EDWARD I.—Pleading in the earliest times of which there are records was an oral altercation conducted in open court by the parties or their counsel.[5] This practice prevailed not only in *England* but in all the early *European* judicatures.[6] Prior to the reign of Edward I, English pleading

pt. 2, caus. 2, qu. 5 ch. 22; Blackst., bk. 3, 338.

1. See Blackst., bk. 3, 343.

2. 3 & 4 W. IV, ch. 42, § 13. The right to wage law in debt on a simple contract was insisted on as late as the case of Rex *v.* Williams, 2 B. & C. 538. The defendant waged his law and applied to the court to fix the number of compurgators. This the court declined to do, not wishing to revive the obsolete trial, but left the defendant to the advice of his counsel, intimating that the plaintiff would be heard if he chose to object to the number selected. The defendant prepared to bring eleven compurgators, but the plaintiff abandoned the action. See Bary *v.* Robinson, 1 Bos. & Pul. New Rep. 297; Blackst., bk. 3. 341 (Chitty's notes).

3. "I consider the system of special pleading which prevails in the laws of *England* to be founded upon and to be adapted to, the peculiar mode of trial established in this country—the trial by jury—and that its object is to bring the case, before trial, to a simple, and as far as practicable, a single question of fact; whereby, not only the duties of the jury may be more easily and conveniently discharged, but the expense to be incurred by the suitors may be rendered as small as possible. And experience has abundantly proved that both these objects are better attained, where the issues and matter of fact to be tried are narrowed and brought to a point, by the previous proceedings and pleadings on the record, than where the matter is left at large to be established by proof, either by the plaintiff in the maintenance of his action or by the defendant in resisting the claim made upon him." Per LORD TENTERDEN in Selby *v.* Bardons, 3 B. & Ad. 16.

4. See Gould Prin. of Plead. 312, n. 3, to the effect that while certain facts are provable by certificate (*e. g.*, the fact of marriage), yet it does not appear that the issue upon such fact ever concludes to the certificate. In the State of *Connecticut*, any issue in fact in a civil case may, by the agreement of both parties, be tried by the court. When this is done the agreement must be suggested in the conclusion of the plea which tenders issue in the following way: "Of this the said C D by agreement puts himself upon the court;" or, "this the said A B, by agreement, prays may be inquired of by the court." See also JURY AND JURY TRIAL, vol. 12, p. 318; TRIAL.

5. Steph. Plead. (9th Am. ed.) 23; 3 Reeves 61, n. (*b*).

6. Thus it appears from Muratori, as cited in note 7 of appendix to Steph. Plead. (9th Am. ed.), that the pleadings among the Lombards were not submitted to the court in writing, but were delivered orally in the presence of the

seems to have been in a crude and inartificial state.[1] The fundamental object seems to have been to require each party so to state his case as to enable the adversary to judge of its nature and frame his answer thereto.[2] This system, which tended to the extrication of the point in dispute, was early known as proceeding to issue,[3] but before the reign above referred to there is no record of any definite rule or regulation which controlled the allegations of the pleaders.[4] The work of Bracton, while professing in one of its parts[5] to deal with pleading in detail, is applicable rather to the civil than to the common law on that subject,[6] and does not necessitate a modification of the foregoing statement. It seems clear, however, that this work is a witness to the increasing attention which the courts were paying to procedure, and it makes it possible to understand the marked development which took place after the reign of Edward I.

b. FROM EDWARD I TO HENRY VI.[7]—From this time the books contain evidence that the judges began to formulate and enforce rules of statement which embodied principles of long standing not before put into exact language, as well as those then announced for the first time.[8] To arrive at an issue became "not only the constant effect, but the professed aim and object of plead-

judge. Murat. Script. Rer. Ital., vol. 1. To the same effect is Stephen's citation from Heineccius (lib., tit. 4, § 156.), with regard to pleading among the German tribes in general.

As to the employment of pleaders or advocates, a practice which dates from early times, see Steph. Plead. (9th Am. ed.) App., note (8).

1. Steph. Plead. (9th Am. ed.) App., note (35).

2. 3 Reeves 61, n. (*a*).

3. Glanville (lib. 6, ch. 43) leads us to the inference that the system was in effect in the reign of Henry II. And see 3 Reeves 61, n. (*b*). The term "issue" occurs in the very beginning of the Year Books (Year Book 1, Edw. II, f. 14), and it there appears to be a term in common use.

4. Steph. Plead. (9th Am. ed.) App , note (35), *citing* Glan., lib. 12, ch. 14. Thus in the reign of John there are examples of pleas which neither traverse nor confess and avoid, and of others which but a few years later would have been held bad for duplicity. "In the same reign," says Mr. Stephen (Steph. Plead., 9th Am. ed., App. note 34) "the fault of argumentativeness appears to have been common."

5. De Exceptionibus, Bract. 400 a.

6. See for a full discussion of this subject, note (35) of App. to Steph. Plead. (9th Am. ed.). Thus Bracton uses terms derived from the civil law which have no exact English equivalent, and he gives precedents which are themselves defective in point of form—judged by the later standard—as containing neither a denial nor a confession.

Authorities.—The authorities for the state of pleading prior to the reign of Edward I are Glanville's treatise (time of Henry II), Bracton's Work (time of Henry III), and the Placitorum Abbreviatio which contains extracts from the records from the time of Richard I.

7. This reign is taken as an epoch in accordance with the view of Mr. Stephen, who considers himself justified in dating the scientific development of the system from this time on account of the imperfection which preceded and the relative perfection which immediately followed it.

8. Steph. Plead. (9th Am. ed.) 123. These rules, it is instructive to notice, were rules of court, "judge-made law," not statutory enactments; and it has been a feature of the history of pleading that jurists in all ages have considered it safer to leave the regulation of the pleadings to the judges than to impose upon them the restrictions of a statute. *Compare* the Hilary Rules, 4 Wm. IV, the Orders of Court of 1883, and such

ing."[1] The requisites of a good issue were investigated and determined upon, and rules were enforced tending to attain materiality and singleness in the issue, and certainty and consistency in statement.[2] During the reign of Edward III, the process of development continued, and, especially during the latter years of that king the pleadings were much more polished; without running, however, into uncertainty, prolixity or obscurity.[3] This seems to confirm the view[4] that during this reign it became the practice to draw up the declaration and pleas out of court. The putting of the pleadings into writing prepared the way for the refinement and subtlety which characterized this branch of the law in later times, though at first it operated only to bring the matter

provisions as are contained in the *Delaware* Rev. Stat. See *infra*, p. 481.

1. Steph. Plead. (9th Am. ed) 128.

2. In the Year Book, 3 Edw. II 59, is found the distinction between issues in law and issues in fact, and the very terms themselves; and in Year Book 21 Edw. IV 35, is found a definition of issue—*i. e.*, "*Exitus idem est quod finis sive determinatio placiti.*"

Growth of Technicality.—"In the reign of Edward II," says Mr. Reeves (vol. 3, p. 62, note), "pleading was already beginning to be perverted by niceties and formalities which had no practical utility. Thus, for instance, the objection as to negative pregnant, as when a man pleaded that a house was not burnt by his negligence, he was met by the stupid quibble that this might mean that the house was not burnt at all; and so, in the senseless jargon of the age, it was "a negative pregnant with an affirmative," and "ambiguous" and so-forth (Year Book, 7 Edw. II 213, 226; 28 Hen. VI 7), an objection which, in after ages, delighted the souls of pedantic lawyers of the Coke school (Slade Drake Hob. 231), but was as far removed from plain sense as it is possible to conceive." But it would seem that the doctrine of negatives pregnant is not necessarily a quibble. In the case suggested by Mr. Reeves, it is well to remember that such a plea would have been sustained at the trial by proof, either that the defendant did not in fact burn or that he had used reasonable care. Granted that duplicity in the issue was objectionable, the doctrine of negatives pregnant was a necessity. It was a single averment pregnant with duplicity.

3. Sir Matthew Hale, Hist. Com. Law 173.

4. See Gilbert's Origin of the King's Bench, *passim*.

Mr. Reeves is loth to admit that such a change was introduced at this time, and he cites in confirmation the reports for the reign which state the cases in the same manner as when the allegations were confessedly oral. His valuable note on the characteristics of oral pleading is here given in full: "It is most important to bear in mind that during this age, as the pleading was only oral, upon any objection taken at the bar by reason of demurrer, the other party could at once discuss it, and, if he saw any ground for it, demand his pleading; and it was only if both parties insisted on the point—one on his pleading and the other on his objection—that they remained in judgment, as it was called, and even then, before judgment, either party could withdraw his pleading (Bellewe's Cases, temp. Rich. II, fol. 131). It was only when the parties remained in judgment that the demurrer was entered (Keilway 81). It is evident, therefore, that the rules of pleading might well, under such a system, be safely enforced, for the judgment could never be given upon the pleading unless it was really material. The author, following Gilbert, supposes that the ancient practice was changed in this reign, but it appears by the case from Bellewe's Reports that it was not so; and all through the Year Books of this and ensuing reigns there is no trace of any alteration in the practice, but pleading went on orally at the bar, either party amending upon any objection made, if he elected so to do at the time, and if ever pleadings were put into writing it could only have been when the parties either 'remained in judgment' on demurrer, or, on the other hand, when they had 'pleaded to issue,' and, of course, the record was made up for *nisi prius.*

"It would indeed have been idle to re-

before the court with precision.[1] In this reign the French, which had been theretofore used in the pleadings, was displaced by English, and they have ever since been conducted in the mother tongue.[2] At this time, too, the first of the several statutes of jeofails was enacted.[3]

c. FROM HENRY VI TO 4 & 5 ANNE.—It was, however, during the latter part of the reign of Henry VI and the reign of Edward IV that the science of pleading attained its full proportions. It became, in the words of Littleton, "one of the most honorable, laudable and profitable things in the law to have the science of well-pleading in actions, real and personal."[4] A large part of the time of the judges was devoted to the scrutinizing of the form of pleadings, and the result of this was that the reigns of these kings saw the science of pleading established upon the basis which endured until our own times. The forms then determined upon became the precedents for future ages, "and the rules and maxims of pleading now settled have governed ever since in our courts."[5] Change and development marked the years that followed, and important statutes, such as 27 Eliz.[6] modified the law, but no radical change occurred until the reign of Queen Anne, when the permission to plead several pleas revolutionized the entire system.

d. FROM 4 & 5 ANNE TO THE HILARY RULES.—From what has already been said it is clear that the essence of the system of pleading is the extrication of a single and material issue. Any measure which tended to negative the theory that every transaction can, for the purposes of judicial investigation, be reduced to a single disputed point was a measure calculated to overturn the system of pleading and not to develop it. Such a measure was the statute of 4 Anne, ch. 16 which permitted the defendant to plead as many several matters as he saw fit, the leave of the court

duce the pleadings to writing until they were finally settled, either on a demurrer or on issue of fact, the pleading being undoubtedly oral, in the first instance, all through the Year Books, up to the reign of Henry VIII. But no doubt when the parties had agreed as to their pleadings, the prothonotaries entered then [them] of record, and to that end required each party to present his pleading in writing." 3 Reeves 292, n. (*a*).

1. See 3 Reeves 293.

2. 36 Edw. III, St. 1, ch. 15. Latin, however, continued to be used for enrolment until 4 Geo. II, ch. 26.

3. 14 Edw. III, ch. 6. The others are 9 Hen. V, ch. 4: 4 Hen. VI, ch. 3; 8 Hen. VI, ch. 12, 15; 32 Hen. VIII, ch. 30; 18 Eliz., ch. 14; 21 Jac. 1, ch. 13; 16 & 17 Car. II, ch. 8; 4 & 5 Anne, ch. 16; 9 Anne, ch. 20; 5 Geo. I, ch. 13; 3 Black. Com. 407. Their cumulative effect is that neither after verdict, nor judgment by confession, *nil dicit*, or *non sum informatus* can the judgment be arrested or reversed for any defect in form. Steph. Plead. (9th Am. ed.) 149.

4. "*Et sache mon fils, que est un des plus honorables laudables et profitables choses en nostre ley, de aver le science du bien pleader en actions reals et personels; et pur ceo, jco toy counsaile especialement de metter ton courage et cure de ceo apprender.*" Litt. Ten., § 534.

5. 3 Reeves 578. It follows, therefore, that the student of pleading must pursue his investigations with especial reference to the cases determined during this and the subsequent periods.

6. 27 Eliz. ch. 5, § 1. Defects in form to be taken advantage of only on special demurrer.

being first had and obtained, and thus to create as many issues in a given suit as there were pleas filed.[1] From the passage of this act the history of pleading becomes the record of efforts on the part of the courts to adapt the old rules and principles to the new condition of things—efforts which, although temporarily successful, made the ultimate remodeling of the system a necessity. The multiplication of counts and pleas came, in process of time, to be an unmixed evil. Instances of records which contained from ten to fifteen counts and special pleas were by no means rare, and it frequently happened that all of these related to the same substantial defense. The cost of litigation was thus enormously increased, if regard be had only to the expense of drawing up papers. But there was a feature even worse than this, namely the fact that the intricate combination of counts and pleas often presented the case to judge and jury in a state of great complexity, and thus the system was productive of confusion and of mistake in the administration of justice. The scope of the general issues, on the other hand, had been greatly extended and it had gradually become the practice to give in evidence under the general issue, matters which operated by confession and avoidance. Nothing being admitted upon the record in such a case, it became necessary for each party to prepare himself for the proof of every fact which might conceivably bear upon his case, and as the cost of preparing proof was the most considerable of all legal costs, so the expense of a law suit was in this way increased as well as in that already referred to.[2] Such a state of things called loudly for a revision, and in *England* this revision came in the shape of the Hilary Rules of 4 William IV.

1. "This act was really the deathblow to the doctrine of pleading as theretofore in use; and while, it is true, its subtleties and refinements lingered for a long time, and possibly continue to linger even in the present day, yet the symmetry of the system was marred, and the mode of trial, so efficient when the issues were simple and single, necessarily underwent considerable variation when the defendant in any action or suit was authorized with leave of the court to plead as many several matters thereto as he should think necessary for his defense. The practice of demanding the opinion of the judge, who superintended the trial upon the points of law which arose, the finding of the facts at large by means of a special verdict, the demurring to the evidence, some or perhaps all of which were in use before the statute of Anne, increased very much; while the habit which was permitted in many jurisdictions of giving the special matter in evidence under the general issue, or some general plea, and the enlargement of the action for money had and received almost into the proportions of a bill in equity, were indicative of a desire in escaping from the trammels of the old law to reach the real merits of the controversy which ran the risk of being lost, either from the inelastic character of the forms of the legal instrument made use of, or from the incompetency of the instrument to perform the work intrusted to it. These are all protests against the logic by which it is sought to hang the solution of a complicated controversy upon single issues of law or fact." George W. Biddle: "An Inquiry into the Proper Mode of Trial," Philadelphia, 1885, p. 12.

2. This criticism on the state of pleading is substantially a condensation of a part of the report of the common law commissioners on which the Hilary Rules were founded. See appendix to Steph. Plead. (9th Am. ed.).

e. FROM HILARY RULES TO RULES OF 1883.—These rules sought to remedy the evils above referred to principally by restricting the scope of the general issue,[1] and by regulating the use of counts and pleas. Their tendency was, therefore, towards a restoration and purification of the common law system. It was in no sense a measure hostile to the science of pleading, but rather a step in the development of it.[2] They received interpretation at the hands of various judges of consummate ability and profound learning,[3] and this branch of the law was by them placed upon a reasonable, logical and scientific basis. Changes were of course introduced from time to time, and one of the most notable of these was the abolition of special demurrer and the substitution of a motion to strike out or amend any pleading which was "so framed as to prejudice, embarrass or deláy the fair trial of the action."[4] By the Common Law Procedure act of 1854, the courts were authorized to entertain equitable pleas.

f. RULES OF 1883.—These rules,[5] like those which they superseded, are intended to accomplish three principal objects: to make each party acquainted with the intended case of his opponent, and thus to prevent surprise at the trial; to save the expense of collecting unnecessary evidence, and to bring legal defenses more prominently forward on the face of the record.[6] To accomplish this result they take ground far more radical than that of the Hilary Rules, for they have the practical effect of doing away with the general issue in the plea.[7] It is to be noted, however, that in the reply, or in any subsequent pleading, the general form of traverse is permissible, excepting to a counter-claim alleged in the plea, in which case the reply must be as specific as the defense.[8] With a view to dispensing with unnecessary proofs,

1. "The views taken by different persons are surprisingly dissimilar, one set of opinions pointing to the restriction of the general issue, and another to its wider application, and to a corresponding extinguishment of special pleading. It will be found, however, on reference to the written communications addressed to us, that there is a decided preponderance of authority in favor of the former course." Report of Commissioners, App. Steph. Plead. (9th Am. ed.).

2. It follows that only an imperfect view of the science of common law pleading is obtained if the attention is confined to the state of the law before the Hilary Rules. For this reason in treating of the general issues and their scope, this article seeks to present the condition of the system as well after as before the Rules. Subsequent changes of the law in the *United States* in so far as they abolish instead of revising the system, are hereinafter touched upon, but not treated at length. But see *infra*, this title, *Pleading Under Codes*.

3. Notably by BARON PARKE in a long line of decisions.

4. 15 & 16 Vict., ch. 76, §§ 50–52.

5. The rules were principally contained in Order 19 of the Rules of the Supreme Court, 1883, and went into operation on October 24th of that year.

6. Abridged from Taylor Evid. (8th Eng. ed.), § 299, *citing* the remarks of LORD ABINGER in Isaac V. Farrar, 1 M. & W. 65, in relation to the object of the Hilary Rules.

7. See Taylor Evid. (8th Eng. ed.), § 302.

8. The rules in substance provide for a statement of claim, for a statement of defense, set-off or counter-claim, for a reply (if any), and finally, for a joinder of issue on one side or the other. Conditions precedent are to be distinctly

the rules provide that in any pleading, not being a petition or summons, all allegations of fact not denied, or stated to be not admitted, shall be taken to be admitted.[1] In short, the policy of the Hilary Rules is indorsed, and reform of the system of pleading is thought to be best attained by still further restricting the operation of general traverses as distinguished from the American plan of sacrificing special pleading to them.

II. **Pleading in the United States.**—A system of pleading has been prescribed for each of the States of the Union by the respective legislatures, and the science of pleading at common law nowhere exists in its completeness on this side of the Atlantic. When the laws of the several States are examined, they exhibit all manner of legislative experiments and devices for preparing a cause for trial. In some jurisdictions the system adopted closely resembles that which was developed at the common law. In others, the resemblance may still be traced, but it is more faint; while in others (and this class includes a majority of the jurisdictions), the legislatures have declared their independence of the common law, and have established a system that is radically different. The division of the subject of pleading in the *United States* thus suggested is, therefore, into Common Law Pleading Modified, and Code Pleading.

1. Classification of States.—A further classification of the States may be made by noting in each case the presence or absence of one or both of the following elements: (1) The survival of a distinction between forms of action; and (2) the existence of a right to plead pleas other than the general issue or an answer. Thus, four possible combinations are obtained, and each combination will be found represented by one State or more.

(1) Where there exists more than one form of civil action, and where special pleas are (to some extent) permitted. This class most

specified by either party. It is not sufficient for the statement of defense to deny the grounds of claim generally, but each party must deal specifically with each disputed allegation of fact, and either party must raise in his pleading all matter which shows that the action (or counter-claim) is not maintainable, or that the transaction is void or voidable by the common law or by statute, and all matter of defense or reply which would otherwise be apt to operate as surprise or to raise new issues—as fraud, the bar of the statute, release, payment, performance, and the Statute of Frauds. New assignment is abolished, and its object is accomplished by amendment or reply. Subject to the preceding, the plaintiff in the reply and each party subsequently, may join issue generally on the pleading adversely alleged, and such joinder operates as a denial of all material facts. But although this course may be adopted, yet each party may at his option traverse generally or specially or confess and avoid. For the rest, brevity is enjoined, and pleaders are forbidden to insert in their pleadings, mere matters of evidence. See Taylor Evid. (8th Eng. ed.) § 299, *et seq.;* Harris *v.* Gamble, L. R., 7 Ch. D. 877; Rutter *v.* Tregent, L. R., 12 Ch. D. 758; Earp *v.* Henderson, L. R., 3 Ch. Div. 254; Hall *v.* Eve, L. R., 4 Ch. Div. 341; Heap *v.* Marris, L. R., 2 Q. B. D. 630; Philipps *v.* Philipps, L. R., 4 Q. B. D. 127. For plea of "Not Guilty by Statute," see Taylor Evid. (8th Eng. ed.), § 311 *et seq.*

1. Tildesley *v.* Harper, 48 L. J., Ch. 495.

closely resembles the ancient system, although many of the distinctive features of that system have passed away. It includes *Maine, New Hampshire, Vermont, Rhode Island, New Jersey, Delaware, Maryland, Virginia, West Virginia, Florida, Alabama, Tennessee, Mississippi,* and the Territory of *New Mexico.*

(2) Where there exists more than one form of civil action, but where special pleas are not permitted. This class is represented by *Massachusetts* and *Pennsylvania.*[1]

(3) Where only one form of civil action exists but where special pleas are permitted. This class includes *Georgia* and *Texas.*

(4) Where only one form of civil action exists and where special pleas are not permitted. This class comprises *New York, Connecticut, North Carolina, South Carolina, Ohio, Indiana, Kentucky, Missouri, Wisconsin, Iowa, Minnesota, Arkansas, Kansas, Nebraska, Colorado, Oregon, California,* and the Territories of *Arizona* and *Utah.*

The systems in force in the first three groups exhibit common law pleading modified. The system adopted by the States in the last group is the system treated separately in this article as PLEADING UNDER CODES.[2]

2. Common Law Pleading Modified.—*a.* SEVERAL ACTIONS AND SPECIAL PLEAS.—Where there exists more than one form of civil action, and where special pleas are to some extent permitted.[3]

Maine.[4] The various actions exist in *Maine,* but the distinction between trespass and case has been abolished. "The general issue may be pleaded in all cases, and a brief statement of special matter of defense, or a special plea, or double pleas in bar, may be filed. The plaintiff may join a general issue and may file a counter brief statement. The defendant may file a general demurrer to the declaration; and at any subsequent stage of the pleadings either party may demur, but no motion in arrest of judgment in a civil action can be entertained. Where the declaration contains a good count, and also bad ones, and no written objection is made before the case goes to the jury, a general verdict cannot be set aside on writ of error.

New Hampshire.[5] The various forms of action are in existence, and the pleadings retain their ancient names. Certainty to common intent only is required, and will render all pleadings sufficient.

1. This State might be placed in the first group, since the defendant in assumpsit may plead payment, set-off or the bar of the statute. But set-off is not a common law plea, and payment and the statute are such stereotyped forms that they scarcely come within the spirit of the division.

2. See *infra,* this title, *Pleading Under Codes.*

3. The States follow in the order suggested in the text. The paragraph devoted to each State is a summary of the laws relating to pleading as set forth in the Revised Statutes of the respective States. The annual or biennial laws subsequent to the revision have in each case been examined to January 1st, 1891.

4. *Maine* Revised Statutes, 1881, tit. 9, § 1, *et seq.*

5. *New Hampshire* General Laws, 1878, pp. 509, 528, 576.

No special plea is required in a civil action,[1] but any defense, including set-off, may, as a rule, be proved under the general issue, upon a brief statement thereof being filed in such time as the court may order. The defendant may, however, plead specially if he so desire, and it is provided[2] that in actions against tenants any defense which may bring the title of the premises in question must be specially pleaded. Evidence of it is not admissible under the general issue. When the defendant in any case pleads one or more special pleas, the plaintiff may file as many several replications as the case requires. It is further provided that wherever to an action on a bill of exchange, draft or promissory note, a total want or failure of consideration would be a defense, the defendant may, upon filing a brief statement thereof with his plea, prove a partial want or failure of consideration in reduction of the damages.

Vermont.[3] The distinction between the forms of action survives, and the pleadings retain their names as at common law. The defendant may plead the general issue in all cases, with notice of special matter. In default of such notice, no evidence of special matter will be received. Defects in form can be reached only on special demurrer; and no writ, declaration, return, process, judgment, or other proceeding in civil causes shall be abated, arrested, quashed, or reversed for any defect or want of form.

The party against whom matter is specially pleaded in confession and avoidance, in answer to matter by him antecedently alleged, may, by a general form of denial, traverse and put in issue all the material facts so pleaded. It is further provided that in actions upon written instruments between the original parties, a defendant may, by plea or notice, set up a partial failure of consideration, and judgment shall be rendered for the sum found due. Defenses arising in a suit after its commencement may be pleaded as of right at the next term of the court, or, by leave of the court, at a subsequent time.[4]

Rhode Island.[5] In this State the distinction between the various forms of action is retained. The defendant in any action, and the plaintiff in replevin, may, with the leave of the court, plead as many matters as he shall think necessary to his defense; and, with like leave, the plaintiff may file as many replications to the

1. Except a plea of title to real estate to actions in police and justice courts, ch. 227, § 3.

2. Ch. 250, § 11.

3. *Vermont* Revised Laws, 1880, § 906, *et seq.*

4. Section 691 of the Revised Laws provides that the pleadings shall be in the English language. Accordingly the supreme court decided that a declaration in assumpsit was demurrable, which stated the amount of a note in this way :—"$226.17"—on the ground that the dollar mark was no part of the English language within the meaning of the statute. Clark *v.* Stoughton, 18 Vt. 50; 44 Am. Dec. 361. See also State *v.* Clark, 44 Vt. 637, where the court, after argument, decides that there is no duplicity in a complaint which charges that an act was done "on the 4th day of November, 1871" without specifying whether the era is or is not the Christian era.

5. *Rhode Island*, Public Statutes, 1882, pp. 578, *et seq.*

plea or pleas as he deems proper. It is provided that in actions for libel or slander, truth may be proved under the general issue, upon the filing, with the plea, of a written notice that such is the defense. And a plea of payment is declared to be a bar to an action of debt on a bond, even if the payment was not made strictly according to the defeasance with respect to time and place.

New Jersey.[1] In this State the declaration retains its name, and pleadings subsequent to the plea are permitted when necessary. An affidavit is required to be filed with every demurrer or plea, to the effect that no delay is intended, and that the defendant has a just and legal defense to the action.[2] Under this section it has been decided that in a suit on a contract against joint promisors the affidavit of one is a compliance with the statute.[3] So also a dilatory plea must be supported by affidavit.

Several pleas are permitted to the defendant, and a similar latitude is extended to the plaintiff in replevin, but the plaintiff may require a specification of the defenses to be set up under the general issue; and the defendant may plead the general issue and give notice of special matter.[4] If the defendant adopts the latter course, the plaintiff, under his reply, is confined to matters of evidence in denial, unless he too gives notice of special matter of avoidance. And the plaintiff, with leave of court, may "reply double" to the plea or subsequent pleading; and the defendant, with leave of court, may plead several pleas to the replication, etc.[5] Express color is declared unnecessary; likewise the special traverse; but the use of a special traverse has been subsequently approved.[6] Pleadings *puis darrein continuance* are pleadable by permission of the court.

It is further provided that no pleading shall be deemed insufficient for any defect which theretofore could have been objected to only on special demurrer.[7] Where there are issues in fact as well as issues in law the latter shall be determined first.

Delaware.[8] In this State the legislature left the modification of the rules of pleading in the hands of the judges, with the proviso that no rule adopted by them shall have the effect of depriving any person of the power of pleading the general issue, and of giving the special matter in evidence, "in any case where such power is, or shall be given by act of the General Assembly." This stat-

1. *New Jersey* Statutes revised to 1886.
2. Municipal Corporations are excepted from this rule. Act February 20th, 1886.
3. Slack *v.* Reeder, 30 N. J. L. 348.
4. *Compare* the rule in *Pennsylvania.*
5. Act of 1885.
6. McWilliams *v.* King, 32 N. J. L. 21. See *infra*, p. 548.
7. Act of 1855, this would seem to have reinstated the old general demurrer, its operation being restricted to matters of substance. But, by the act of 1882 upon demand the party demurring is compellable to furnish specifications of the grounds of demurrer.
8. *Delaware* Revised Statutes of 1874, ch. 106.

ute can scarcely be said to modify the common law on the subject of pleading.

The pleadings retain their ancient names—declaration, plea, replication, rejoinder, surrejoinder, etc.[1]

The distinction between trespass and case has been abolished. There have been some slight modifications of the Revised Statutes of 1874, as, for example, the provision that when a demurrer is overruled the party demurring may plead over without withdrawing the demurrer.[2]

Maryland.[3] The various forms of action remain in existence. The common law rules of statement are re-enacted—forbidding surplusage, argumentativeness, statement of inferences and matters of evidence or law. But formal defects, apart from these actual vices, are immaterial; although the ancient precedents may be followed by the pleader in lieu of those provided by the act. Formal commencements and conclusions and formal statements of time and place are abolished and profert is declared unnecessary—oyer being granted without it in proper cases. Special demurrers are abolished and general demurrers operate only on insufficiency in substance. Upon the overruling of a demurrer the party may plead over, without withdrawing and upon appeal or writ of error the issue of law shall be determined as if it stood alone. Several pleas are permitted at all stages subsequent to the declaration, but consistency is required and departure forbidden. *Non est factum* must be verified by affidavit, except where special permission is obtained from the court by an heir, executor or administrator. A subsequent statute permits a plea setting up an equitable defense, as well in replevin as in other actions, and provides for the striking out of the same wherever it cannot be dealt with by a court of law so as to do justice between the parties.[4]

Virginia.[5] Technical informalities are declared to be no ground for demurrer and a general form of demurrer is prescribed, designed to reach defects in substance only. Protestation is declared to be unnecessary, and oyer (as in *Maryland*) is demandable without profert in cases where it is proper. The defendant may, without leave of court, plead as many several matters, "whether of law or fact," as he thinks necessary; but in no pleading are prayers for judgment, allegations of *actionem non, precludi non*, or the like, to be required. All special traverses "or traverses

1. See Act 14th March, 1883.

2. Act of 14th March, 1883.

It is believed that in *Delaware* the system of pleading resembles the common law system more closely than that in force in any other State. The writer has been informed that a question growing out of the use of a special traverse occupied the attention of the court during the current year (1891). The case is not yet reported. It has been decided in Collins *v.* Bilderback, 5 Harr. (Del.) 133, that in actions *ex delicto* matters in justification may be given in evidence under the general issue.

3. *Maryland* Public General Laws, 1888, p. 1092 *et seq.*

4. See Laws of 1888, p. 906.

5. *Virginia*, Code, 1887, §§ 32, 36, *et seq.*

with an inducement of affirmative matter" are to conclude to the country, but the opposite party may plead to the inducement where the traverse is immaterial.[1] The Supreme Court of appeals is authorized to prepare a system of practice and pleading.[2]

West Virginia.[3] In this State the provisons are strikingly similar to those in *Virginia*, especially in regard to technical informalities, protestation, *precludi non* and *actionem non*, profert and oyer, special traverse, demurrer and several pleas. It is further provided that no plea inconsistent with *non est factum* shall be pleaded therewith without leave of court. To any special plea the plaintiff may put in as many special replications as he may deem necessary.

Florida.[4] The various forms of action remain in existence. Demurrers for formal defects are prohibited, but demurrers for defects in substance are permitted, provided that the objectionable feature is stated in the margin. The defendant may traverse the declaration generally, or he may use a specific traverse whether or not its denial falls within the scope of the general form. He may also plead specially a release, set-off payment and the bar of the statute in actions *ex contractu*, and in actions *ex delicto* a license, *son assault demesne*, or a right of way. Among the enumerated causes of action, to those corresponding to counts in general assumpsit the plea "never indebted" is sanctioned. *Non assumpsit* (or, in the words of the statute "that he did not promise as alleged,") is permitted to declarations on contracts other than bills and notes. A plea equivalent to *non est factum* is given where the defense is a denial of the deed. An equitable defense by way of plea is permitted, similar to that which exists in *Maryland.* The plaintiff may join issue upon the defendant's plea or pleas; or he may traverse in his replication the release, right of way, etc.; or he may plead in confession and avoidance to the set-off alleging that it did not accrue within six years; or that the assault alleged by the defendant occurred in endeavoring to remove the defendant gently from the plaintiff's land. Or the plaintiff, in proper cases, may new-assign. Express color is declared unnecessary. The provisions in regard to technical informalities, *actionem non, precludi non*, profert and oyer and special traverse are similar to those in *Virginia.* By a subsequent act[5] a party whose demurrer has been overruled has the right upon writ of error or appeal to have the action of the court reviewed whether he has pleaded over or amended or not.[6]

Alabama.[7] The various forms of action exist in this State, but all actions on contracts, whether express or implied, simple or under

1. See Mayor of Orford *v.* Richardson, *infra*, p. 550 note (3).
2. § 3112.
3. *West Virginia*, Code, 1887, p. 750 *et seq.*
4. *Florida*, Digest, 1881, § 41, *et seq.*
5. Act of March 5th, 1883, Laws of *Florida*, 1883, p. 53.
6. *Compare* provision of *Maryland* code.
7. *Alabama*, Code, 1886, §§ 2664 *et seq.*

seal, may be united in the same action; and counts in trespass and case may be joined when they relate to the same subject-matter. The declaration is known as the complaint. Demurrers are allowed only for errors in substance, which the party demurring must specify; and if a demurrer is overruled, the party demurring may plead over and, on appeal, assign the action of the court as error, unless, indeed, he has subsequently had the benefit sought by the demurrer upon the trial of other equivalent issues. Pleas are sufficient if a material issue can be taken on them. The defendant may plead more pleas than one, and if he does not rely solely on a denial of the plaintiff's cause of action, must plead specially the matter of defense. It is further provided that in all actions for defamation, or for injuries to the person, or to real or personal property, the general issue shall be not guilty which shall put in issue all the material allegations of the complaint. In all other actions, the general issue is an averment that the allegations of the complaint are untrue, and, except as may be otherwise provided, puts in issue only the truth of such allegations. Pleas of tender are sanctioned, and also pleas of recoupment and set-off, except in the case of negotiable paper. Pleas since the last continuance do not operate as a waiver of prior pleas. The plaintiff may file one or more replications—either by way of traverse or in confession and avoidance, and subsequent pleadings are governed by the same principles as those already mentioned.

Tennessee.[1] All contracts may be sued for in the same form of action, and wrongs and injuries to person or property where money damages are demanded may be redressed by "an action on the facts of the case." The same rule holds in penal actions. Counts in tort and contract may be joined. Replevin, detinue, ejectment, forcible entry and detainer may be brought. Surplusage is to be avoided, and double, prolix and frivolous pleadings may be stricken out; but any pleading is declared to be sufficient if it is good in substance and is certain to common intent. The defendant may plead in abatement, or he may demur or answer by pleading as many pleas as he has real grounds of defense. A plea since the last continuance is not a waiver of prior pleas. Demurrers are allowed only for substantial defects, but all demurrers must state the objection relied on. If overruled, the action of the court may be reviewed on error even after pleading over. A plea equivalent to the general issue is permitted in all cases; but notice of the real defense is required even where, before the code, the matter could have been proved under the general issue. If, however, he so desires, the defendant may plead specially either in confession and avoidance or by way of set-off or tender. To a plea containing new matter the plaintiff may demur or reply, either by way of traverse or by confession and avoidance. For

1. *Tennessee*, Code, 1884, §§ 3440 *et seq*, and 3592 *et seq*.

cause shown he may have more than one replication; and it is a general principle that matter not denied by a subsequent pleading is to be taken as admitted.

Mississippi.[1] The distinction between the various forms of action survives, but formal objections to the pleadings are not to be taken. The declaration shall contain a statement of the facts in ordinary and concise language, and to it the defendant may demur specially, or he may plead several pleas in abatement or several in bar. The following pleas in bar may in proper cases be pleaded as of course—either singly or two or more together: The general issue, denial of the debt or contract sued on, tender in whole or in part, statute of limitations, set-off, *plene administravit*, infancy, payment, accord and satisfaction, release, not guilty, a denial of plaintiff's property in the thing injured, leave and license, duress, *son assault demesne*, performance, justification in libel, slander and other actions, and any other pleas which by law are allowed to be pleaded together. But under the plea of not guilty in libel, slander, assault and battery and false imprisonment, the defendant may give in evidence matter in mitigation of damages, notwithstanding he may have pleaded a justification. If, however, the defendant desire to prove affirmative matter under the general issue (in cases where by law such matter is admissible under that plea), he must give notice to the plaintiff of such matter. And it is to be noted that, upon condition of giving notice of special matter to his adversary, the defendant in all cases may plead the general issue. In answer to the plea, the plaintiff may, by leave of court, file several replications, surrejoinders, etc.; and at each subsequent stage the defendant may plead as many several matters as are necessary to his defense, upon affidavit to that effect. Express color and special traverses are not necessary in any case; nor is formal defense required in a plea, and allegations of *actionem non* and *precludi non* are unnecessary.

Territory of New Mexico.[2] The distinction between the forms of action exists, and it is prescribed by statute that pleadings shall be according to the forms and rules of the common law. Permission is, however, extended to both parties to plead as many matters as they think proper; and pleas of set-off and counter-claim are sanctioned. When formal objections are sustained, liberty to amend is granted freely.

b. SEVERAL ACTIONS AND NO SPECIAL PLEAS.—Where there exists more than one form of civil action, but where special pleas are not permitted.

Massachusetts.[3] There are three divisions of personal actions —contract, including assumpsit, covenant and debt, except for penalties; tort, including trespass, case, trover, and all actions for penalties; and, finally, replevin. Declarations in these ac-

1. *Mississippi* Revised Code, 1880, §§ 1536, *et seq.*
2. *New Mexico* Compiled Laws, 1884, §§ 1907, *et seq.*
3. *Massachusetts* Public Statutes, 1882, pp. 964, *et seq.*

tions need contain no merely formal averments, but certainty and conciseness are encouraged. One count only need be inserted for each cause of action, but any number of breaches may be assigned. To raise an issue in law, the answer should contain a statement that the defendant demurs to the whole or to a part of the declaration, the causes being specially assigned. Any defense to a real, personal or mixed action which formerly might have been made by plea in abatement, may now be made by answer. But a defense on the merits must be made by a plea of the general issue in real and mixed actions and by answer in personal actions. Special pleas are abolished. The answer must set forth the defense specifically, and, if it contains new matter, the same shall be deemed to be denied, although the court on motion may compel the plaintiff to reply to it specifically. The plaintiff may demur to the answer, but in no case will the court on demurrer consider defects only in form.

A subsequent statute [1] provides that interest, whether arising as damages for the detention of money or otherwise, may be declared on, in addition to the forms of pleading now authorized by law, by including in any count which is followed by an account annexed, or bill of particulars, the words "and interest," and setting forth as an item in the account annexed or bill of particulars the times and amounts for and upon which interest is claimed, and the amount of interest so claimed.

Pennsylvania.[2] The distinction between the actions of trespass, trover, and case is abolished and a single action, known as the action of trespass, is substituted for them. Similarly, debt, covenant, and assumpsit are reduced to a single form of action, denominated the action of assumpsit. Replevin is not affected by the act, nor is detinue, which is seldom resorted to in this State.[3] Special pleading is in terms abolished, and not guilty is the prescribed plea in trespass, and *non assumpsit* in assumpsit. In the latter action, however, it is provided that the defendant, in addition to the general issue, may plead payment, set-off, and the bar of the statute, but no other pleas. Permission is by the act extended to the various courts to make rules regulating notice of special matter of defense; and in Philadelphia county the rules of court require, in effect, that such notice must be given in all cases where, before the act, it would have been necessary to plead specially.

1. Act of June 11th, 1890, Acts and Resolves 356.

2. Act 25th June, 1887, P. L. 271; Purdon's Dig. p. 2369.

3. **Real and Mixed Actions.**—In *Pennsylvania* the real actions of dower and partition are in existence and the latter is resorted to with comparative frequency. In dower there is strictly no general issue, but it is the custom in this State to plead *ne unques seisie que dower* with notice to the demandant of special matter. In partition the general issue is *non tenent insimul.* See Coleman's Appeal, 62 Pa. St. 273. The mixed action of ejectment is, as modified by *Pennsylvania* statutes, a most convenient mode of trying title. It is made a substitute for a bill for specific performance by permitting a re-

c. ONE FORM OF ACTION AND SPECIAL PLEAS.—*Georgia.*[1] Distinctions between real, personal and mixed actions are abolished. A civil action is defined to be one founded on private right arising either from contract or tort, and such an action may be brought against the person or property, or both. But it is provided that no other evidence shall be admissible under the general issue except such as disproves the plaintiff's cause of action; all other matters in satisfaction or avoidance must be specially pleaded. Demurrers at law appear to be unaffected by the code.[2] But the Supreme Court has repudiated the "English practice" of holding that a "demurrer roves through the whole record," and of giving judgment against the party first in default.[3]

By a recent act it is provided that in actions of tort, where the defendant acted under authority of law, he may plead that defense by way of justification, and shall be entitled to the privileges of one holding the affirmative of the issue. But the right to begin and conclude is not given by the plea, unless it is filed before the plaintiff opens his evidence.[4]

Texas.[5] The forms of action are reduced to one—the civil suit—and the distinction between suits at law and in equity is abolished. In all civil suits the pleadings are by petition and answer, which pleadings must consist of a statement, in logical and legal form, of the facts constituting the plaintiff's cause of action or the defendant's ground of defense. The defendant's answer includes all manner of defenses, whether of law or fact, in abatement or in bar. It may amount to a general denial, or it may set up new facts by way of avoidance or estoppel.[6] These may be pleaded together, or in several special pleas. Special matter is deemed to be denied without the formality of a replication. The following defenses must be specially pleaded: Bank-

covery on an equitable title. The only plea in ejectment is not guilty.

Affidavit of Defense. — In *Pennsylvania*, independently of the pleadings, strictly so called, the defendant in assumpsit is required to file an "affidavit of defense," which is an allegation under oath that he has a just defense to the whole or part of the plaintiff's claim with a specific statement of its nature and character. If the defendant omits to file such an affidavit within the time prescribed, the plaintiff may have judgment for want of it. If, when it is filed, the plaintiff thinks it insufficient in substance, he may take a rule for judgment for want of a sufficient affidavit, and the court hears argument upon the rule as upon demurrer. Leave to file a supplemental affidavit is granted in proper cases, but generally, if the court is of opinion that the defense disclosed is insufficient the plaintiff will have judgment. If the court are satisfied with the affidavit, the rule is discharged and the parties go to trial.

1. *Georgia*, Code, 1882, §§ 3250, *et seq.* and 3448, *et seq.*
2. Note to p. 873 of the code.
3. Winn *v.* Lee, 5 Ga. 218.
4. Act of December 24th, 1888, (Georgia Laws of 1888, p. 35).
5. *Texas* Revised Statutes, 1887, §§ 1187, *et seq.*
6. Rule 7, 47 Tex. 617. See Welden *v.* Texas etc. Meat Co., 65 Tex. 487.

ruptcy,[1] want or failure of consideration,[2] estoppel,[3] former judgment,[4] fraud or mistake,[5] illegality,[6] infancy,[7] limitation,[8] *lis pendens*,[9] payment [10] and tender,[11] suretyship and discharge,[12] and usury.[13]

d. CODE PLEADING—ONE FORM OF ACTION AND NO SPECIAL PLEAS.—Where only one form of civil action exists and where special pleas are not permitted.[14]

The State of *New York* was the first to take strong ground against the system of pleading at common law, and as early as 1848 adopted a code which in terms provided for the abolition of the then existing forms of actions and pleading in cases at common law. This enactment was superseded in 1876 by the Code of Civil Procedure, which has been the model after which the legislatures of the States in the fourth group have fashioned their respective codes.

New York.[15] In *New York* actions are divided into two classes, civil and criminal. A criminal action is prosecuted by the people of the State, as a party, against a person charged with a public offense, for the punishment thereof. Every other action is a civil action, which is of one form only, as all distinctions between actions at law and suits in equity, and the forms of those actions and suits, have been abolished. In the civil action, the first pleading on the part of the plaintiff is the complaint, which must contain an introduction,[16] a plain and concise statement of the facts

1. Coffee *v.* Ball, 49 Tex. 16; Jackson *v.* Elliott, 49 Tex. 62; Miller *v.* Clements, 54 Tex. 35.

2. Rev. Stat., art. 272. See Ladd *v.* Pleasants, 39 Tex. 415.

3. Texas Banking etc. Co. *v.* Hutchins, 53 Tex. 61.

4. Philipowski *v.* Spencer, 63 Tex. 604.

5. Loper *v.* Robinson, 54 Tex. 510.

6. Turner *v.* Gibson, 2 App. C. C. (Tex.), § 714.

7. Moke *v.* Fellman, 17 Tex. 367; 69 Am. Dec. 656.

8. Rev. Stat. 3220.

9. Langham *v.* Thomason, 5 Tex. 127.

10. Pettigrew *v.* Dix, 33 Tex. 277.

11. Tooke *v.* Bonds, 29 Tex. 419.

12. Babcock *v.* Milmo Nat. Bank, 1 App. C. C. (Tex.), § 818.

13. Moseley *v.* Smith, 21 Tex. 441.

14. See also *infra*, this title, *Pleading Under Codes.*

"Since the enactment of the Code, and the abolition of forms of actions, every action is an action upon the case in the sense that it is founded upon the particular facts set forth in the complaint. No set form of words is now essential to the statement of any cause of action or defense. The pleader may choose his own language and state his case in his own way, if in so doing he confines himself to facts which are pertinent and material. Under the code, that pleading is best which states clearly in the fewest words the facts from which flow all the legal conclusions necessary to the support of the pleader's case. Skill in pleading is still an essential qualification of a sucessful lawyer, and a proper pleading is as important now as formerly; but the code regards the substance rather than the form of a pleading, and mere technical defects, by which neither party could be prejudiced, have ceased to be important." Baylies' Code Pleading (Rochester, 1890), Preface.

15. See *New York* Rev. Stat. Codes and Laws, 1890, C. F. Birdseye, title, "Actions," "Pleadings." The provisions of the *New York* code are given at some length because they represent with substantial accuracy the system of pleading in all the "Code States." *Connecticut*, as being a representative disciple of New York, is treated separately.

16. Merrill *v.* Grinnell, 10 How. Pr.

constituting the cause of action,[1] and a demand of the judgment to which the plaintiff supposes himself entitled.[2] The defendant may either demur or answer. He may adopt the former course if one or more of the following objections appear upon the face of the complaint: (1) Lack of jurisdiction of the person or subject matter;[3] (2) lack of legal capacity in the plaintiff to sue;[4] (3) the pendency of another action;[5] (4) misjoinder of parties plaintiff or a defect in parties defendant;[6] (5) improper joinder of causes of action;[7] (6) the failure of the complaint to state facts sufficient to constitute a cause of action.[8] The demurrer must specify the grounds of objection, and it may be pointed at the whole complaint or to one or more separate causes of action stated therein; and in the latter case the defendant may answer the portions not demurred to. The answer, which may be to the whole or a part of the complaint, must contain a specific denial of each material allegation of the complaint controverted by the defendant,[9] or a statement of new matter constituting a defense,[10] or a statement of counter-claim, which, as being a cause of action arising out of the contract or transaction set forth in the complaint as

(N. Y.) 31; Dorman *v.* Kellam, 4 Abb. Pr. (N. Y.) 202; Murray *v.* Church, 1 Hun (N. Y.) 49; Stanley *v.* Chappell, 8 Cow. (N. Y.) 235; Murray *v.* Church, 3 Thomp. & C. (N. Y.) 145; Bonesteel *v.* Garlinghouse, 60 Barb. (N. Y.) 338; Beers *v.* Shannon, 73 N. Y. 292; Litchfield *v.* Flint, 104 N. Y. 543; Bannow *v.* McGrane, 45 N. Y. Super. 517; Cordier *v.* Thompson, 8 Daly (N. Y.) 172. See also note in 18 Abb. N. Cas. (N. Y.) 201.

1. Murray *v.* Church, 3 Thomp. & C. (N. Y.) 145; Degraw *v.* Elmore, 50 N. Y. 1; Sheridan *v.* Jackson, 72 N. Y. 170; Bowery Nat. Bank *v.* Duryear, 56 How. Pr. (N. Y.) 42; Mann *v.* Morewood, 5 Sandf. (N. Y.) 557; Woolley *v.* Newcombe, 9 Daly (N. Y.) 75; Longprey *v.* Yates, 31 Hun (N. Y.) 433; Blank *v.* Hartshorn, 37 Hun (N. Y.) 101; Reubens *v.* Ludgate Hill S. S. Co., 21 Abb. N. Cas. (N. Y.) 467.

2. Waters *v.* Crawford, 2 Thomp. & C. (N. Y.) 602; Hopkins *v.* Lane, 2 Hun (N. Y.) 38; Linden *v.* Hepburn, 3 Sandf. (N. Y.) 668; Durant *v.* Gardner, 10 Abb. Pr. (N. Y.) 445; Swart *v.* Boughton, 35 Hun (N. Y.) 285.

3. Wheelock *v.* Lee, 74 N. Y. 495; Gilbert *v.* York, 111 N. Y. 544.

4. People *v.* Metropolitan Teleph. Co., 31 Hun (N. Y.) 599; Van Zandt *v.* Van Zandt, 17 Civ. Pro. Rep. (N. Y.) 448.

5. Allen *v.* Malcolm, 12 Abb. Pr., N. S. (N. Y.) 335; Newton *v.* Keech, 9 Hun (N. Y.) 361.

6. Fourth Nat. Bank *v.* Scott, 31 Hun (N. Y.) 304; Anderton *v.* Wolf, 41 Hun (N. Y.) 572.

7. Walker *v.* Spencer, 45 N. Y. Super. Ct. 71; Taylor *v.* Metropolitan etc. R. Co., 50 N. Y. Super. Ct. 311.

8. Kœnig *v.* Nott, 8 Abb. Pr. (N. Y.) 384; Groesbeeck *v.* Dunscomb, 41 How. Pr. (N. Y.) 302; Freeman *v.* Dutcher, 15 Abb. N. Cas. (N. Y.) 432; Phoenix Bank *v.* Donnell, 40 N. Y. 410; People *v.* Crooks, 53 N. Y. 648; Gray *v.* Green, 41 Hun (N. Y.) 527.

9. Meehan *v.* Harlem Sav. Bank, 5 Hun (N. Y.) 439; Boomer *v.* Koon, 6 Hun (N. Y.) 645; Saltsman *v.* Shults, 14 Hun (N. Y.) 256; Crane *v.* Crane, 43 Hun (N. Y.) 309; Weaver *v.* Barden, 49 N. Y. 286; People *v.* Fields, 58 N. Y. 491; Jones *v.* Ludlum, 74 N. Y. 61; Blair *v.* Bartlett, 75 N. Y. 150; 31 Am. Rep. 455; Baylis *v.* Stimson, 110 N. Y. 621; Powers *v.* Rome etc. R. Co., 5 Thomp. & C. (N. Y.) 449; Goodwin *v.* Hirsch, 37 N. Y. Super. Ct. 503; Sherman *v.* Boehm, 15 Abb. N. Cas. (N. Y.) 260.

10. Weaver *v.* Barden, 49 N. Y. 286; Dubois *v.* Hermance, 56 N. Y. 673; Evans *v.* Williams, 60 Barb. (N. Y.) 346; Pacific Mail Steamship Co. *v.* Irwin, 67 Barb. (N. Y.) 277; Wehle *v.* Butler, 43 How. Pr. (N. Y.) 5; Humbert *v.* Abeel, 7 Civ. Pro. (N. Y.) 417.

the foundation of the plaintiff's claim, or connected with the subject of the action;[1] or as being (in the case of an action on a contract) any other cause of action on contract existing at the commencement of the action,[2] must operate to defeat or diminish the plaintiff's recovery. If the counter-claim, when established, entitles the defendant to an affirmative judgment, judgment is rendered for him accordingly.[3] The answer may disclose as many defenses or counter-claims as the defendant has, whether their nature be legal or equitable.

The plaintiff may demur to the answer for insufficiency in law; or, where the answer sets up a counter-claim, he may reply by a specific denial of the material allegations which he desires to controvert, or by a statement of one or more distinct avoidances of the same defense or counter-claim.[4] When the defendant, in his counter-claim, demands an affirmative judgment, the plaintiff may demur specially to the counter-claim if, upon the face of it, it appears (1) that the court lacks jurisdiction of the subject matter,[5] or (2) that the defendant lacks legal capacity to recover, or (3) that another action is pending,[6] or (4) that the counter-claim is not of the nature above set forth, or (5) that the counter-claim is insufficient in substance.[7]

Material allegations in the pleadings are, for the purposes of the action, admitted by failure to deny; but new matter in an answer to which a reply is not required, or new matter in a reply, is to be deemed controverted by the adverse party, by traverse or avoidance, as the case requires.[8]

It is sufficient if things be stated according to their legal effect. Thus, in an action for libel or slander, it is sufficient if the plaintiff avers that the defamatory matter was published or spoken concerning him.[9] Of course if the allegation is controverted, the plaintiff must establish it on the trial. And in such an action the defendant may prove mitigating circumstances, notwithstanding he has pleaded or attempted to prove a justification. Where the cause of action, defense or counter-claim is founded upon an instrument for the payment of money only, the party may set forth a copy of the instrument and state that a specified sum is due

1. Wilder *v.* Boynton, 63 Barb. (N. Y.) 547; Chamboret *v.* Cagney, 41 How. Pr. (N. Y.) 125; Webster *v.* Cole, 17 Hun (N. Y.) 510; Pendergast *v.* Greenfield, 40 Hun (N.Y.) 496.

2. Hunt *v.* Chapman, 51 N. Y. 555; Tallman *v.* Bresler, 65 Barb. (N. Y.) 369; Waring *v.* O'Neill, 15 Hun (N. Y.) 105; Van Dyck *v.* McQuade, 57 How. Pr. (N. Y.) 62.

3. Trust Co. *v.* R. Co., 18 Abb. N. Cas. (N. Y.) 377.

4. Dillon *v.* Sixth Ave. R. Co., 46 N. Y. Super. 21; Del Valle *v.* Navarro, 21 Abb. N. Cas. (N. Y.) 143.

5. Cragin *v.* Lovell, 88 N. Y. 258.

6. Ansorge *v.* Kaiser, 22 Abb. N. Cas. (N. Y.) 306.

7. Armour *v.* Leslie, 39 N. Y. Super. Ct. 353; Safford *v.* Snedeker, 67 How. Pr. (N. Y.) 264.

8. Fry *v.* Bennett, 5 Sandf. (N. Y.) 54; Spies *v.* Roberts, 50 N. Y. Super. Ct. 305; Dambman *v.* Schulting, 4 Hun (N. Y.) 50.

9. No extrinsic fact need be stated for the purpose of showing the application of the defamatory matter to the plaintiff. See Bennett *v.* Matthews, 64 Barb. (N. Y.) 410; Bassil *v.* Elmore,

him thereon from his adversary, which he accordingly claims; and such an allegation is equivalent to setting forth the instrument according to its legal effect.[1] Motions of various kinds are freely allowed, their object being to supplement the work of the demurrer, to enable the court to control the cause as it progresses, and, generally, to accomplish ends which, at the common law, could be attained only in a more formal way.[2]

Connecticut.[3] In *Connecticut* there is but one form of civil action. The complaint supersedes the common law declaration, and an answer is the only plea in bar. General demurrers are abolished, and dilatory pleas, as such, are confined to a single specified form which includes an objection to the jurisdiction of the court with a defense by way of abatement. All other defenses must be set up on answer or demurrer. The answer may partake of the nature of a specific traverse, denying a given allegation in the complaint and admitting the others, or it may be general in its form. If the defense consists of matter in confession and avoidance, the answer must amount in effect, to a plea of that nature; for evidence in excuse or discharge will not be admitted when the record discloses an answer in the nature of a traverse. The same principle applies to the "reply"—which may be general or specific—under which the plaintiff will be confined to evidence in denial, unless he has set out the special matter. Further pleadings are permitted by leave of court; and the plaintiff may demur to the reply.

Motions to expunge are heard when a pleading is scandalous, impertinent, prolix or uncertain.

Judgment on demurrer is that the party plead over, and costs are in the discretion of the court.

III. **Pleading Under Codes—1. Code Pleading as a System.**—There are but two forms of action known to the codes, the crimi-

65 Barb. (N. Y.) 627; Fleischmann *v.* Bennett, 87 N. Y. 231; Hatfield *v.* Lasher, 57 How. Pr. (N. Y.) 258; Cook *v.* Rief, 52 N. Y. Super. Ct. 302.

1. Peyser *v.* McCormack, 7 Hun (N. Y.) 300; Ranney *v.* Smith, 6 How. Pr. (N. Y.) 420; Chappell *v.* Bissell, 10 How. Pr. (N. Y.) 274; Marshall *v.* Rockwood, 12 How. Pr. (N. Y.) 452; Butchers' etc. Bank *v.* Jacobson, 24 How. Pr. (N. Y.) 204; Gunning *v.* Appleton, 58 How. Pr. (N. Y.) 471; Cook *v.* Rief, 52 N. Y. Super. Ct. 302.

2. The following are instances of such motions—Motion to strike out sham answer; Code of Civ. Pro., § 538; Bailey *v.* Lane, 21 How. (N. Y.) 475; People *v.* McCumber, 18 N. Y. 315; 72 Am. Dec. 515; Fettretch *v.* McKay, 47 N. Y. 426; Miln *v.* Vose, 4 Sandf. (N. Y.) 660.

Motion for judgment on frivolous pleading; Code of Civ. Pro., § 537; Strong *v.* Sproul, 53 N. Y. 497; Sixpenny Sav. Bank *v.* Sloan, 2 Abb. Pr. (N. Y.) 414.

Motion to strike out irrelevant or scandalous matter; Code of Civ. Pro., § 545; Seward *v.* Miller, 6 How. Pr. (N. Y.) 312; Fasnacht *v.* Stehn, 53 Barb. (N. Y.) 650; Struver *v.* Ocean Ins. Co., 9 Abb. Pr. (N. Y.) 23.

Motion to compel party to make pleading more definite. Code of Civ. Pro., § 546. Wall *v.* Bulger, 46 Hun (N. Y.) 346; People *v.* Ryder, 12 N. Y. 433; Olcott *v.* Carroll, 39 N. Y. 436; Brooks *v.* Hanchett, 36 Hun (N. Y.) 70.

3. *Connecticut* Revised Statutes, 1888, §§ 872–1029, *passim.* The provisions of the *New York* and *Connecticut*

nal and the civil action.[1] A criminal action is prosecuted by the people of the State as a party against a person charged with a public offense for the punishment thereof.[2] Every other action is a civil action.[3] The distinction between actions at law and suits in equity, and the forms of those actions and suits, have been abolished.[4] But where the defense is based upon equitable grounds it is often proper to set forth the facts at greater length than would be necessary in a case which involved common law principles only.[5] The codes regard the substance and not the form of a pleading, and mere technical defects by which neither party could be prejudiced have ceased to be important.[6] But the system of code pleading does not ignore form, and an ideal pleading under the code, just as at common law, is single, material, true, unambiguous, consistent and certain to common intent as to time, place, person and quantity.[7] The common law provided a sanction for the rule prescribing these requisites, and the smallest breach as well as the greatest was punished on demurrer by an adverse judgment. The codes seek to distinguish between material and immaterial breaches, by disregarding the latter and providing redress for the former by remedial motions.[8] The common law in early times aimed at and attained singleness in the issue and succeeded in narrowing the controversy in each case down to a single disputed point of fact or law.[9] But the statute of 3 & 4 Anne marred the system by permitting the defendant to raise as many issues as he had defenses.[10] Thereafter the common law rule prescribing singleness was limited in its application to the internal structure of each issue: each issue must be single, but there might be many issues. The codes, on the other hand, abandoned the theory of singleness in both its broader and narrower sense, for, by substituting the answer for the plea, they have in effect abolished the issue. The codes, however, discourage duplicity, using that term in a limited sense, by forbidding the joinder in one statement of matters giving rise to several causes of action. This is discountenanced both where the statement seeks for a single recovery on a double

Codes are given as representatives of the system of code pleading. The other States mentioned as belonging to the group of "Code States" follow *New York* as closely as does *Connecticut.*

1. N. Y. Code Civ. Proc., § 3335.

2. N. Y. Code Civ. Proc., § 3336.

3. N. Y. Code Civ. Proc., § 3337. The word "action" as used in the New Revision of the Statutes of New York, when applied to judicial proceedings, signifies an ordinary prosecution, in a court of justice, by a party against another party, for the enforcement or protection of a right, the redress or prevention of a wrong, or the punishment of a public offense. N. Y. Code Civ. Proc., § 3333.

4. N. Y. Code Civ. Proc., § 3339.

5. Peck *v.* Newton, 46 Barb. (N. Y.) 173; Onderdonk *v.* Mott, 34 Barb. (N. Y.) 106.

6. Preface to Baylies on Code Pleading.

7. Boyce *v.* Brown, 7 Barb. (N. Y.) 80.

8. See *infra*, this title, *Sanction of Rules of Pleading.*

9. See *infra*, this title, *Singleness.*

10. See *infra*, this title, *Several Pleas.*

ground, and where it seeks distinct recoveries on each cause of action.[1]

Code pleading is indeed a new system; but the materials of the older structure are freely used. And whenever they are used, they are taken bodily from one system into the other, it being assumed in every case that the practitioner under the new order of things is familiar with the theory and practice under the old.[2]

If any single comprehensive statement can be made of the nature and character of code pleading, it is the statement that code pleading is the system produced by amalgamating pleading at law and pleading in equity, with the consequent loss of the inconsistent features of both systems. The petition or complaint is the offspring of declaration and bill, having each parent in it; while the answer under the codes combines the informality of the answer in equity with the conciseness of the plea at law. The verification of an allegation by oath, a requisite common to the pleading under most codes, is a feature unknown to the common law,[3] but familiar enough in equity. The demurrer under the code, resembling the common law general demurrer in its scope, is distinctly analogous to the demurrer in equity in that the defendant, if his demurrer is overruled, may answer to the merits. If a demurrer is sustained, the party in fault may, in the discretion of the court, plead anew or amend.[4] Amendments are allowed with great liberality under the codes, and in some cases a pleader may even amend within a prescribed time without obtaining leave of court.[5]

The whole system of code pleading is the protest of an era of practical business-like methods against the refinement and subtleties of an earlier age. If the pleader could be trained under the old system in accuracy of thought and expression and then made to practice under the new, code pleading would be found to be an ideal system. But it is clear that, as a system, code pleading has

1. Bliss, Code Plead. (2nd. ed.), § 290. Of course a complaint or petition may contain as many causes of action as the plaintiff may be able to declare on; but the codes require a separate and distinct *statement* in the complaint of each cause of action. See *infra*, this title, *Complaint*.

2. "It is assumed that the student of the Code is familiar with the common law and equity systems of pleading. If not he is groping in the dark, and much that is offered will escape his apprehension. This knowledge is deemed essential, not only because well educated lawyers must know the history of our jurisprudence, must live through, as it were, and measure every step of its marvelous progress, but because the foundation idea of pleading has not changed." Bliss, Code Plead. (2d. ed.), § 141. This statement made by one strongly inclined to favor the code system, answers the possible criticism that the statement in the text is made. in a controversial spirit.

3. Save in the case of a plea in abatement.

4. N. Y. Code Civ. Proc., § 497.

In fine, it should seem that the system of pleading under the codes is a logical, not to say inevitable, result of the abolition of the distinction between law and equity. In this, as in most cases, it appears that reformers must be prepared to take extreme measures or else they must let the common law system stand. There is no middle point at which they can consistently stop.

5. See *infra*, p. 505.

not the educational value which belongs to pleading at common law, and it may be doubted whether the average practitioner with no other training than that which the letter of the code supplies, is competent to do the system justice.

2. The Consecutive Pleadings—*a.* THE COMPLAINT.—The first pleading on the part of the plaintiff is the complaint, or, as it is sometimes called, the petition. It supersedes the declaration, the count and the bill in equity.

(1) *Essentials of the Complaint.*—The codes agree in requiring the complaint to consist of three principal parts: (1) The title of the cause, with the name of the county in which the action is brought and the names of parties plaintiff and defendant. (2) A plain and concise statement of the facts constituting each cause of action without unnecessary repetition. (3) A demand of the judgment or relief to which the plaintiff supposes himself entitled.

(*a*) *The Title.*—As in *New York*, the action may be brought in one county and tried in another, the title must, if the action is brought in the supreme court of that State, specify the name of the county which the plaintiff designates as the place of trial.[1] The full names of plaintiff and defendant should be given in the form of a title to the cause, and, according to the practice in some jurisdictions, they should be described in the body of the complaint. In an action against partners the full names of all the partners should be stated, except in those jurisdictions, as *Ohio* and *Iowa*, where the firm is treated like a corporation to the extent that partners may be sued by the firm name.[2] If the defendant's name is unknown, the plaintiff may give him a fictitious name, and amend when the true name is discovered.[3] Where such permission is not given by the code, the complaint will be subject to objection only on the ground of misnomer.

(*b*) *The Statement*—(See DECLARATION).—The plain and concise statement of facts constituting the cause of action is obviously nothing more nor less than an informal declaration, all fictions being excluded[4] and formal commencements and conclusions being abolished. But the substance remains unchanged, and the distinction between the inducement and the gist is as well marked as

1. N. Y. Code Civ. Proc., § 481.

2. See Bliss Code Plead. (2nd ed.), § 145.

Misnomer.—In *England* the plea in abatement for misnomer was abolished by 3 & 4 Wm. IV, ch. 42, § 11. Under the codes it should seem that a motion to correct the names would be the appropriate mode of proceeding. In some jurisdictions it has been held under the codes that misnomer is still pleadable in abatement. See Linton *v.* Steamboat Roberts, 46 Ind. 478. See, for a discussion of the subject, Bliss Code Plead. (2nd ed.), § 427.

3. In *Iowa* the plaintiff, instead of giving the defendant a fictitious name, describes him as accurately as possible. Code 1873, § 2557.

4. *E. g.*, the alleged *finding* in trover and the *promise* in general assumpsit. Where the plaintiff, being entitled so to do, desires to waive the tort and sue in contract, it is good practice, since the fictitious promise has been abolished, to state explicitly the fact of his choice or

ever. The common law rules in regard to pleading title and authority still obtain, and must be observed with greatest care.[1]

(*c*) *Several Causes of Action.*—The codes permit the joinder of certain causes of action in the same complaint. The provisions of the New York code on this subject have been adopted, with but slight modification, in the other code States, and are therefore given here: "The plaintiff may unite, in the same complaint, two or more causes of action, whether they are such as were formerly denominated legal or equitable,[2] or both, where they are brought to recover as follows: (1) Upon contract, express or implied.[3] (2) For personal injuries, except libel, slander, criminal conversation, or seduction.[4] (3) For libel or slander. (4) For injuries to real property.[5] (5) Real property in ejectment, with or without damages for the withholding thereof. (6) For injuries to personal property.[6] (7) Chattels, with or without damages for the taking or detention thereof. (8) Upon claims against a trustee, by virtue of a contract or by operation of law.[7] (9) Upon claims arising out of the same transaction, or transactions connected with the same subject of action, and not included within one of the foregoing subdivisions.[8] But it must appear, on the face of the complaint, that all the causes of action so united belong to one of the foregoing subdivisions; that they are consistent with each other; and, except as otherwise prescribed by law, that

to indicate it in the prayer for relief. See Corry *v.* Gaynor, 21 Ohio St. 277; Gillett *v.* Treganza, 13 Wis. 472.

1. See *infra*, this title, *Pleading Title.*

2. The codes of *Iowa*, *Kentucky* and *Arkansas* provide that proceedings in a civil action may be either ordinary or equitable. The plaintiff in these States may bring equitable proceedings wherever the chancellor before the code had jurisdiction, and *must* do so where that jurisdiction was exclusive. Bullitt's Code, Ky., §§ 5, 61; Gantt's Dig. Ark., 1874, §§ 4453, 4454; Iowa Code of 1873, §§ 2507, 2508. In *Iowa* the union, *inter sese*, is permitted of all causes of action that are legal, and, *inter sese*, of all that are equitable. The *Indiana* classification has reference to the similarity or dissimilarity of the objects of the action.

3. Mappier *v.* Mortinier, 11 Abb., N. S. (N. Y.) 455; Booth *v.* Farmers' Bank, 65 Barb. (N. Y.) 457; Keep *v.* Kauffman, 56 N. Y. 332; Walters *v.* Continental Ins. Co., 5 Hun (N. Y.) 343.

4. Anderson *v.* Hill, 53 Barb. (N. Y.) 238; Howe *v.* Peckham, 10 Barb. (N. Y.) 656; McIntosh *v.* McIntosh, 12 Barb. (N. Y.) 289; Henry *v.* Henry, 17 Abb. (N. Y.) 411.

5. Watts *v.* Hilton, 3 Hun (N. Y.) 606. The codes of *California* and *Nevada* place injuries to person and injuries to character in distinct classes.

6. Rodgers *v.* Rodgers, 11 Barb. (N. Y.) 595; Cleveland *v.* Barrows, 59 Barb. (N. Y.) 364.

7. Petrie *v.* Petrie, 7 Lans. (N. Y.) 90; Sortore *v.* Scott, 6 Lans. (N. Y.) 271; Bonnell *v.* Wheeler, 1 Hun (N. Y.) 332. The *Missouri* code substitutes "party in some representative capacity" for "trustee."

8. Tradesmen's Bank *v.* McFeeley, 6 Barb. (N. Y.) 522; Austin *v.* Monroe, 4 Lans. (N. Y.) 67; Schnitzer *v.* Cohen, 7 Hun (N. Y.) 665. The codes of *Kentucky*, *Arkansas*, *California* and *Nevada* omit this class.

The Colorado Classification.—The *Colorado* Code recognizes but three classes: (1) Actions may be united for recovery of real property with damages, rents, profits, etc. (2) Actions for recovery of personal property, with damages, etc. (3) All actions for damages, whether for breach of contract or for injuries to person, property or character. Colo. Code Civ. Proc., § 70.

they affect all the parties to the action:[1] and it must appear upon the face of the complaint that they do not require different places of trial."[2]

(1) *Causes of Action to be Separately Stated.*—Where the complaint sets forth two or more causes of action, the statement of the facts constituting each cause of action must be separate and numbered.[3]

(*d*) *Complaint for Libel and Slander.*—It is a general rule, under the codes, that the plaintiff in an action for libel or slander need not state any extrinsic fact to show the application to him of the defamatory matter; but if the application is controverted, the plaintiff must prove it at the trial.[4]

(*e*) *The Prayer for Relief or Demand of Judgment.*—The complaint must conclude with a demand of the judgment to which the plaintiff supposes himself entitled.[5] Since the court has power to grant any relief consistent with the case made, it should seem to be surplusage to insert, in addition to the specific demand, the familiar general prayer for relief.[6] It is to be noted that if more kinds of relief than one are prayed for, they should be consistent.[7]

(*f*) *Verification.*—The rules in regard to the verification of pleadings by oath differ in the several States. In *New York* the pleadings may or may not be sworn to. But when a pleading is verified, each subsequent pleading, except a demurrer, must also be verified. In *Missouri* and in *Indiana* no verification is required. No dilatory defense can be pleaded unless it is verified.[8]

b. THE DEMURRER.—The only pleading on the part of the defendant is the demurrer or answer. The object of the demurrer is, as at common law, to bring down judicial disapproval upon some defect in the adversary's pleading. But the grounds of demurrer under the codes are enumerated and defined, and the scope of the demurrer is therefore greatly diminished.

(1) *Grounds of Demurrer.*—It is in general the rule that the defendant may demur to the complaint when one or more of the following objections appear upon the face of it: (1) That the court has not jurisdiction of the person of the defendant.[9] (2) That the court has not jurisdiction of the subject of the action.[10]

1. Hubbell *v.* Lerch, 58 N. Y. 237; Slisbee *v.* Smith, 60 Barb. (N. Y.) 372; Haines *v.* Hollister, 64 N. Y. 1; Schnitzer *v.* Cohen, 7 Hun (N. Y.) 665.

2. N. Y. Code Civ. Proc., § 484.

Misjoinder.—An offense against the rules laid down in this section is known as *misjoinder*. Misjoinder is a defect in the substance of the pleading as distinguished from the so-called *duplicity* under the codes—which consists in a failure to state causes of action *separately*, and is accordingly a merely formal defect.

3. N. Y. Code Civ. Proc., § 483. An offense against this section is called duplicity, as is pointed out in the preceding note.

4. See N. Y. Code Civ. Proc., § 535.

5. N. Y. Code Civ. Proc., § 481.

6. Which in olden times was said to be, in point of efficacy, second only to the Lord's Prayer.

7. See Bliss Code Plead. (2nd ed.), § 164.

8. See N. Y. Code Civ. Proc., § 513.

9. Nones *v.* Ins. Co., 5 How. (N. Y.) 96; s. c., 8 Barb. (N. Y.) 541.

10. Hotchkiss *v.* Elting, 36 Barb. (N. Y.) 38.

(3) That the plaintiff has not legal capacity to sue.[1] (4) That there is another action pending between the same parties, for the same cause.[2] (5) That there is a misjoinder of parties plaintiff.[3] (6) That there is a defect of parties plaintiff or defendant.[4] (7) That the causes of action have been improperly united.[5] (8) That the complaint does not state facts sufficient to constitute a cause of action.[6]

(2) *General Rules.*—The demurrer must in all cases be *special*—that is, it must specify the ground of objection.[7] The defendant may demur to the whole complaint, or he may demur to one or more causes of action and answer the rest.[8]

(3) *Demurrer to Reply.*—The defendant may demur to the reply, or to a separate traverse to or avoidance of a defense or counter-claim contained in the reply, upon the ground that, upon the face of the pleading, it appears to be insufficient in law.[9]

(4) *Demurrer to Answer.*—On the other hand, the plaintiff may demur for insufficiency in law apparent upon the face of an answer setting forth a defense by way of new matter or counter-claim.[10] The *New York* code gives the following grounds of demurrer in the latter case:[11] (1) That the court has not jurisdiction of the subject thereof. (2) That the defendant has not legal capacity to recover upon the same. (3) That there is another action pending between the same parties for the same cause. (4) That the counter-claim is not one recognized by the code. (5) That the counter-claim does not state facts sufficient to constitute a cause of action.[12] A demurrer taken on any of these grounds must specify the objection with particularity.

It is a general rule that the demurrer does not go to the relief prayed for, but only to the statement of the facts.[13] If the demurrer is overruled, the party demurring should ask leave to withdraw

1. Phoenix Bank *v.* Donnell, 40 N. Y. 410; Kennedy *v.* Cotton, 28 Barb. (N. Y.) 59; Wright *v.* Wright, 54 N. Y. 437.

2. Burrows *v.* Leonard, 20 How. (N. Y.) 143; Auburn Bank *v.* Miller, 5 How. (N. Y.) 51.

3. People *v.* Crooks, 53 N. Y. 648; Simar *v.* Canaday, 53 N. Y. 298.

4. Groesbeck *v.* Dunscomb, 41 How. (N. Y.) 302; Moore *v.* Hegeman, 6 Hun (N. Y.) 290.

5. Anderson *v.* Hill, 53 Barb. (N. Y.) 238; Blossom *v.* Barrett, 37 N. Y. 434.

6. Allen *v.* Malcolm, 12 Abb. N. S. (N. Y.) 335; Mackey *v.* Auer, 8 Hun (N. Y.) 180.

The eight grounds of demurrer given in the text are taken from the *New York* Code Civ. Proc., § 488. The *California* Code adds another ground "that the complaint is ambiguous, unintelligible or uncertain." The *Iowa* Code permits a demurrer when the claim appears upon its face to be barred by the statute; but it does not authorize a demurrer for misjoinder of causes of action. The bar of the statute is recognized as a ground of demurrer by the *Oregon* Code.

7. N. Y. Code Civ. Proc., § 490.

8. Nicholl *v.* Fash, 59 Barb. (N. Y.) 275; Matthews *v.* Beach, 8 N. Y. 173.

9. See Thomas *v.* Bank, 38 N. Y. Supr. Ct. 466.

10. N. Y. Code Civ. Proc., § 494. See Armour *v.* Leslie, 39 N. Y. Supr. Ct. 353; Murphy *v.* Allerton, 7 Hun (N. Y.) 650.

11. N. Y. Code Civ. Proc., § 495.

12. See in general Armour *v.* Leslie, 39 N. Y. Super. Ct. 353; Graham *v.* Dunnigan, 4 Abb. (N. Y.) 426.

13. Kemp *v.* Mitchell, 29 Ind. 163; Conner *v.* Board of Education, 10

his demurrer and to answer or reply as the case may be.[1] Leave to plead to the merits, and the filing of such a plea, is usually treated as a withdrawal.[2] If he desires to avail himself of an error in the overruling of the demurrer, the party demurring should allow judgment to be entered. If he answers, he is taken to waive all objection to the ruling, except on the ground of lack of jurisdiction or of the absence of a valid cause of action.[3]

c. THE ANSWER.—The answer of the defendant combines in itself the functions of the plea at common law, the answer in equity, and the statutory defense of set-off. It may take the form of a general or specific traverse, or it may set up new matter, operating as a defense by way of confession and avoidance, or by way of counter-claim on which the defendant demands an affirmative judgment.

(1) *By Way of Traverse or Denial.*—The answer must contain a general or specific denial of each material allegation controverted by the defendant,[4] or of any knowledge or information thereof sufficient to form a belief.[5] The effect of the denial, no matter what its scope, is to put the case at issue. Each material allegation of the complaint not controverted by the answer, and each material allegation of new matter in the answer not controverted by the reply,[6] must, for the purposes of the action, be taken as true.[7] Where a part of the plaintiff's claim is expressly or impliedly admitted by the defendant, judgment may be entered for the part so admitted.[8]

(2) *By Way of Avoidance.*—See *infra,* this title, PLEAS IN CONFESSION AND AVOIDANCE.

(3) *By Way of Counter-claim.*—The counter-claim must tend in some way to diminish or defeat the plaintiff's recovery,[9] and must be between the same parties. An answer by way of counter-claim should be tested as if it were a complaint by defendant against plaintiff.[10] If the counter-claim is for less than the plain-

Minn. 439; Hammond *v.* Cockle, 2 Hun (N. Y.) 495.

1. Bliss Code Plead. (2d. ed.), § 417.

2. Pickering *v.* Telegraph Co., 47 Mo. 457.

3. See Fisher *v.* Scholte, 30 Iowa, 221; Township *v.* Hackman, 48 Mo. 243. For the general principles governing demurrers, see DEMURRER vol. 5, p. 542 and EQUITY PLEADINGS, vol. 6, p. 724.

4. Mack *v.* Burt, 5 Hun (N. Y.) 28; Walsh *v.* Mehrbeck, 5 Hun (N. Y.) 448; Weaver *v.* Barden, 49 N. Y. 286; Allis *v.* Leonard, 46 N. Y. 688; Miller *v.* Ins. Co., 1 Abb., N. C. (N. Y.) 470; Goodwin *v.* Hirsch, 37 N. Y. Supr. Ct. 503; Greenfield *v.* Mass. Mutual Ins. Co., 47 N. Y. 430.

5. Meehan *v.* Savings Bank, 5 Hun (N. Y.) 439; Lloyd *v.* Burns, 38 N. Y. Supr. Ct. 423; People *v.* Fields, 58 N. Y. 491.

6. That is, where a reply is required. An allegation of new matter in an answer to which a reply is not required or of new matter in a reply, is to be deemed controverted by the adverse party by traverse or avoidance, as the case requires. N. Y. Code Civ. Proc., § 522.

7. N. Y. Code Civ. Proc., § 522.

8. See N. Y. Code Civ. Proc., § 511.

9. Nat. Fire Ins. Co. *v.* McKay, 21 N. Y. 191; Waddell *v.* Darling, 51 N. Y. 327; Caryl *v.* Williams, 7 Lans. (N. Y.) 416.

10. Vassear *v.* Livingston, 13 N. Y. 248.

Counter Claim.—The counter claim

tiff's demand, the plaintiff has judgment for the difference; but if the counter-claim equals or exceeds the demand in the complaint, judgment must be for the defendant.[1]

(4) *Several Defenses.*—While before the codes the defendant was required to plead a separate plea for each defense that he had, under the codes he can set up all defenses that he may have in his single answer. This permission extends to the case in which the defendant has several counter-claims.[2] The several defenses must be separately stated, and they must refer to the cause of action which they are intended to answer.

(5) *Partial Defenses.*—Provided its character is distinctly stated, a partial defense is permitted.[3] It is generally provided by the codes that this class of defenses includes matters which tend to mitigate damages in actions for breach of promise to marry, for injuries to the person, and for injuries to property.[4]

d. THE REPLY.—Where the answer contains a counter-claim, the plaintiff, if he does not demur, may reply to the counter-claim. The reply must contain a general or specific denial of each material allegation of the counter-claim controverted by the plaintiff, or of any knowledge or information thereof sufficient to form a belief; and it may set forth in ordinary and concise language, without repetition, new matter not inconsistent with the complaint constituting a defense to the counter-claim.[5] If the answer contains new matter constituting a defense by way of avoidance, the court may in its discretion, upon the application of the defendant, direct the plaintiff to reply to the new matter, and the principles governing in such a case, whether or not the plaintiff complies, are similar to those which control in the case of the counter-claim.[6]

3. Rules of Form Prescribed by the Code—*a.* CERTAINTY OF PLACE, TIME AND VALUE.[7]—Pleadings must have certainty of time, place and value wherever these are material.[8]

(1) *Place.*—Although the formal statement of a venue is unnecessary and, when fictitious, is even prohibited, yet the distinction between local and transitory actions survives under the codes, and, in the former case, the pleadings must specify the county which gives the court jurisdiction.[9] So, where there is an agreement to receive and pay at a particular place, an averment of readiness to receive and pay at that place is necessary to a com-

of the codes embraces both the preexisting cross-demands of recoupment and set-off. See *infra*, this title, *Set-off.*

1. See N. Y. Code Civ. Proc., § 503.

2. Benedict *v.* Seymour, 6 How. (N. Y.) 297; Hicks *v.* Sheppard, 4 Lans. (N. Y.) 335.

3. Huger *v.* Tibbets, 2 Abb., N. S. (N. Y.) 97; Bennett *v.* Matthews, 64 Barb. (N. Y.) 410.

4. See N. Y. Code Civ. Proc., § 508.

5. N. Y. Code Civ. Proc., § 514.

6. Hubbell *v.* Fowler, 1 Abb. N. S. (N. Y.) 1.

7. See *infra*, this title, pp. 567-570.

8. Baylies' Code Plead. 32. See Code of Missouri Rev. Stat., 1879, § 3537.

9. Bliss Code Plead. (2nd ed.), § 284.

plaint for non-delivery.[1] And in general, where an action is brought in a county court, the complaint must allege that the defendant is a resident of the county.[2]

(2) *Time.*—It may be laid down as a general rule that time, as an element of definite description, must always be stated.[3] But, just as at the common law, the pleader is held to a strict proof only when time is material.[4]

(3) *Value.*—Allegations of value usually relate only to the amount of damages, and are therefore not traversable.[5] But value has been held material in actions for goods sold or for services.[6]

(4) *Subordinate Rules of Certainty.*—These rules, as formulated by Stephen and summarized in subsequent pages,[7] apply to pleading under the codes. Matters of evidence should not be pleaded, nor matters necessarily implied or presumed by the law, nor matters of which the court will take judicial knowledge. Less certainty is required where the facts lie more in the knowledge of the other party, and no greater certainty is insisted upon than the nature of the thing pleaded will conveniently admit. Less particularity is required in stating matter of inducement; and with respect to acts valid at common law, but regulated as to the mode of performance by statute, it is sufficient to use such certainty of allegation as was sufficient before the statute.[8]

b. PLEADING TITLE.—The rules governing the pleading of title and authority under the codes remain as at common law, except in so far as the statutes of each State prescribe a particular form of statement of title to real estate.[9]

c. CONSISTENCY.—At common law a pleading must be consistent with itself and also with the other pleadings of the same party.[10] This rule applied alike to the pleadings of plaintiff and defendant. The codes recognize the same rule, but from force of circumstances it affects the plaintiff only. The complaint and the reply must be both internally and mutually consistent. As the answer, however, is the defendant's only pleading, the latter requisite cannot apply; and the former has no application, because the answer gives the defendant all his common law rights, and at common

1. Clark *v.* Dales, 20 Barb. (N. Y.) 42.

2. Judge *v.* Hall, 5 Lans. (N. Y.) 69; Gilbert *v.* York, 41 Hun (N. Y.) 594.

3. See People *v.* Ryder, 12 N. Y. 433; Opinion of MARVIN, J.

4. Thus if it is sought to charge the indorser of a bill or note, or the drawer of a bill of exchange it is necessary so to allege and prove the date of demand and notice as to charge the defendant.

5. Woodruff *v.* Cook, 25 Barb. (N. Y.) 505.

6. See Gregory *v.* Wright, 11 Abb. (N. Y.) 417.

7. See *infra*, pp. 568, 569.

8. See in general, Bliss Code Plead., § 308, *et seq.*

9. See this subject discussed *infra*, this title, *Pleading Title.* For the formulæ required by the various State laws, see Bliss Code Plead. (2nd ed.), § 223, *et seq.*

10. See *infra*, this title, *Consistency.* A pleading inconsistent with itself was said to be insensible or repugnant; while a pleading inconsistent with

law, after the Statute of 3 & 4 Anne, the defendant could set up several inconsistent defenses.[1]

If several causes of action are united in a complaint they must be consistent with each other.[2]

d. MATERIALITY.—The rule that pleadings should state all facts pertinent and material is a rule of substance as well as of form, and as such is enforced as well by the codes as by the common law.[3] To attempt the application of this rule to every class of cases would require one to traverse the entire domain of the law, since, in order to ascertain what, in a given case, is a material allegation, it is first necessary to determine the principle of substantive law which relates to it.[4] But it is a rule of unfailing application, and the rule is susceptible of no more definite statement, that when substantive law determines a given fact to be essential to the existence of a right or of a wrong, then the pleader who seeks to enforce that right or to redress that wrong must state the fact in question in his pleading.[5]

e. SINGLENESS.—It is a rule of the common law that pleadings must not be double.[6] This rule forbade the joining in the declaration of two or more causes of action in support of a single demand, and the statement in any pleading subsequent to the declaration of more answers than one to the pleading opposed to it. The law also prohibited the filing of more pleas than one to a single declaration, but a new liberty was granted by the statute of 3 & 4 Anne, which enacted that the defendant might, with leave of court, plead as many several pleas as he had defenses.[7] Under the codes, the plaintiff is entitled to embody in his complaint as many causes of action as he may have, and a similar permission in regard to defenses is extended to the defendant when he comes to frame his answer. But each cause of action,

the last antecedent pleading of the same party was said to constitute a *departure*. A departure was a vice fatal on both general and special demurrer.

1. See, however, *infra*, p. 565 and note (2).

Old Rule in New York.—The *New York* Code of Civ. Procedure originally required the various defenses and counter claims to be consistent with each other, § 507. But this section was amended in 1879 and the restrictive clause was omitted. See Bruce *v.* Burr, 67 N. Y. 237. The newer rule holds in *North Carolina*, *Colorado* and *Ohio*. See Reed *v.* Reed, 93 N. C. 517; Hummel *v.* Moore, 15 Fed. Rep. 380; Bank *v.* Closson, 29 Ohio St. 78.

2. N. Y. Code of Civ. Proc., § 484. Nebenzahl *v.* Townsend, 61 How. (N. Y.) 353; Springstead *v.* Lawson, 23 How. (N. Y.) 302; Sweet *v.* Ingerson, 12 How. 331.

3. See *infra*, this title, *Materiality*.

4. Writers on pleading indulge in elaborate dissertations on such questions as "In actions on contract; when should the complaint show privity?" Bliss Code Plead., § 234, *et seq*. This seems out of place—so do all discussions of the consideration of contracts, etc.

5. This statement answers such questions as "When should *malice* be alleged?" (Discussed by Bliss, Code Plead., § 287, *et seq.*). It should be alleged when material. When is it material? For the answer to this question, see (not Pleading) but Libel, Slander, Malicious Prosecution—or whatever title the action falls under.

6. See *infra*, this title, *Singleness*.

7. See *supra*, this title, From 4 &

and each defense must be the subject of a separate and distinct statement. The pleader who fails thus to distinguish between and keep separate the different grounds of action and of defense, and who confuses them in one statement, is said to be guilty of the vice of *duplicity.* Duplicity in this sense differs from multifariousness in equity. Multifariousness is a fault in substance, and consists in the improper union in one bill of distinct and independent matters, and the consequent confounding of them.[1] It is analogous to *misjoinder* under the codes, although this latter vice is sometimes erroneously called duplicity.[2]

f. DIRECTNESS.—Hypothetical and alternative pleading is prohibited as well by the codes as by the common law.[3]

g. EXCEPTIONS, PROVISOS AND CONDITIONS PRECEDENT—It is a general rule that a pleader should not anticipate possible defenses. If he does, his adversary may treat the allegation as a nullity and plead as if it had not been made.[4] The common law rule as to exceptions and provisos holds under the codes to the effect that an exception in a statute must be negatived in pleading, but that a proviso need not be. This is not inconsistent with the rule above laid down; so far from its being anticipation to negative an exception, such a course is essential to the making out of a *prima facie* case.[5]

h. MISCELLANEOUS RULES.—Things should be pleaded according to their legal effect.[6] Pleadings should state facts and not conclusions of law.[7] And, in general, it may be said that surplusage is to be avoided, and that conciseness is recommended.[8] But the rules regarding the observance of precedents have no place under the codes. As there are no formal commencements and conclusions, and no formulæ of any kind, the rules of the common law relative to these matters have been abrogated.[9]

4. Sanction of Rules of Pleading.—The codes enforce the rules governing the form and substance of pleadings by means of the

5 Anne to the Hilary Rules; and *infra*, this title, *Singleness.*

1. See Story's Eq. Plead., § 271.

2. See Rev. Stat. of *Missouri*, 1879, § 21.

3. Lewis *v.* Kendall, 6 How. (N. Y.) 59; Goodman *v.* Robb, 41 Hun (N. Y.) 605; McMurray *v.* Gifford, 5 How. 14. See *infra*, this title.

4. See this subject discussed, *infra* this title.

5. See this subject discussed, *infra* this title, *Exceptions and Provisos.*

6. *Infra* this title. Thayer *v.* Gile, 42 Hun (N. Y.) 268.

7. *Infra* this title. Swart *v.* Boughton, 35 Hun (N. Y.) 281.

8. See Baylie's Code Plead. 34. These rules, however binding they were at the common law, have but a feeble sanction under the code. Experience would seem to prove that, with the bar as a whole, pleadings will never be drawn with scrupulous nicety unless adverse judgments or heavy costs of amendment are made penalties for carelessness.

9. In his work on code pleading, Mr. Bliss disclaims all intention of giving an appendix of precedents, for, under the code system, he thinks there can be none. Mr. Baylies, in his work, published some ten years later, meets the increasing demand for forms by printing a collection of them in an appendix. He protests that they are not precedents, but their presence reminds us that the evolution of the common law precedent was not very different. How long will it be, with the constant change

demurrer,[1] and by *motions*, which are applications for peremptory orders to remedy the objectionable feature.[2]

a. LACK OF CERTAINTY.—Where one or more denials or allegations contained in a pleading are so indefinite or uncertain that the precise meaning or application thereof is not apparent,[3] the court may require the pleading to be made definite and certain by amendment.[4] The uncertainty and indefiniteness contemplated by this provision are of course only such as appear on the face of the pleading.[5]

b. IRRELEVANT, REDUNDANT AND SCANDALOUS MATTER.—Irrelevant, redundant or scandalous matter contained in a pleading may be stricken out, upon the motion of a person aggrieved thereby.[6] A pleading is irrelevant which has no substantial relation to the controversy between the parties to the action.[7] Redundancy is a needless repetition of material averments;[8] and the rule governing the exercise of the court's discretion in this matter has been said to be that unless it is clear that no evidence can properly be received under the allegations objected to, they will be retained until the trial.[9] And matter, though clearly redundant, will not be stricken out if it tends neither to incumber the record nor seriously to prejudice the opposite party.[10]

c. FRIVOLOUS PLEADINGS.—If a demurrer, answer or reply is frivolous, the party prejudiced thereby may, upon notice, apply to the court for judgment thereupon, and judgment may be given accordingly.[11] A frivolous pleading is one that is trifling, trivial or nugatory; and it may also be said that answers, whether by way of traverse or by way of confession and avoidance, will be treated as frivolous if they are manifestly imperfect, irrelevant,

of language, before Mr. Baylies' "Forms" will be referred to as quaint and cumbersome "precedents?"

1. The subject of the demurrer is treated at length, *supra*, this title, *Demurrer*.

2. N. Y. Code Civ. Proc, § 768.

3. N. Y. Code Civ. Proc., § 546. The code uses the word "apparent" as cited in the text; it obviously means "evident."

Counterclaim.—A counterclaim may be made on motion more definite and certain as well as a complaint. Fettretch *v.* McKay, 47 N. Y. 426; 11 Abb., N. S. (N. Y.) 453.

4. N. Y. Code Civ. Proc., § 546.

5. Brown *v.* So. Mich. R. Co., 6 Abb. (N. Y.) 237.

6. N. Y. Code Civ. Proc., § 545. It is further provided in *New York* that where scandalous matter is thus stricken out, the attorney whose name is subscribed to the pleading may be directed to pay the costs of the motion, and his failure to pay them may be punished as a contempt of the court.

7. Seward *v.* Miller, 6 How. (N. Y.) 313; Fasnacht *v.* Stehn, 53 Barb. (N. Y.) 650; Straver *v.* Ins. Co., 9 Abb. (N. Y.) 23. See Bank *v.* Kitching, 11 Abb. (N. Y.) 435; Fabricotti *v.* Launitz, 1 C. R., N. S. (N. Y.) 121; Doran *v.* Dinsmore, 33 Barb. (N. Y.) 86; Jeffras *v.* McK. & S. Co., 2 Hun (N. Y.) 351; Aubrey *v.* Fiske, 36 N. Y. 47.

8. Bowman *v.* Sheldon, 5 Sand. (N. Y.) 657.

9. Follett *v.* Jewett, 11 N. Y. Leg. Obs. 193.

10. Clark *v.* Harwood, 8 How. (N.Y.) 470; Pacific Mail S. S. Co. *v.* Irwin, 67 Barb. (N. Y.) 277; 4 Hun (N. Y.) 671.

11. See *New York* Code Civ. Proc., § 537. This practice prevails in all the code States, although all the codes do not make specific provision for it.

evasive, and tend to no valid issue.[1] But a pleading to be treated as frivolous must be manifestly defective in these respects, or in some one of them. Its character must not be doubtful. It must be so clearly and palpably bad as to require no argument or illustration to show its character—one which would be pronounced frivolous and indicative of bad faith in the pleader on bare inspection.[2] Thus, a demurrer is frivolous when it is taken for a cause not named in the statute;[3] but a defective counter-claim cannot be treated as frivolous, although it may be demurred to or may be made the subject of a motion to make more certain.[4] It is to be noted in general that when relevant and irrelevant matters are mingled in a pleading, so that they cannot be separated, the whole will be stricken out.[5]

d. SHAM PLEADING.—A sham pleading is one that is false in fact although it may be good in form. Such a pleading may be stricken out by the court upon motion.[6] But the party making the motion must not himself be in default; if his own pleading is defective, the attention of the court is called to it by his motion, just as if at common law he had demurred.[7] Although the codes do not all contain a provision for such a motion, yet, as the right to move to strike out existed at common law, there is no reason to suppose that it has been lost.[8] There is some conflict of decision among the States as to the scope of the term "sham." It has been held that an answer might be treated as sham, no matter whether it operated by way of denial or whether it set up new matter.[9] But the better opinion is, that a pleading can never be treated as sham unless new facts are pleaded which upon their face constitute a good defense.[10] There is also a difference of judicial opinion as to the extent of the inquiry into the truth of the pleading which the courts will tolerate. In *Indiana*, the pleading will not be stricken out unless it contradicts the record or the court's judicial knowledge.[11] A different rule obtains in *New York*, but even there the court is unwilling to hear affidavits and counter-affidavits concerning the *bona fides* of the defense.[12]

1. See Strong *v.* Sproul, 53 N. Y. 497; Mutual Co. *v.* Mayor, 49 How. (N. Y.) 227; Griffin *v.* Todd, 48 How. (N. Y.) 15; Rice *v.* Ehele, 55 N. Y. 518; Munger *v.* Shannon, 61 N. Y. 251; Samuels *v.* Mail Assoc., 52 N. Y. 625.

2. See remarks of ALLEN, J., in Strong *v.* Sproul, 53 N. Y. 497. See also Boylston *v.* Crews, 2 S. C. (N. S.) 422; Cottrill *v.* Cramer, 40 Wis. 555; Youngs *v.* Kent, 46 N. Y. 672.

3. Kenworthy *v.* Williams, 5 Ind. 375.

4. Fettretch *v.* McKay, 47 N. Y. 426.

5. Clough *v.* Murray, 19 Abb. Pr. (N. Y.) 97.

6. N. Y. Code Civ. Proc., § 538.

7. See Bliss Code Plead. (2nd ed.), § 422.

8. See 1 Chitty Plead. 441, *et seq.* But it should seem that the motion was overruled wherever the defendant made an affidavit of the truth of his plea or a general affidavit of merits. Tucker *v.* Ladd, 4 Cow. (N. Y.) 47.

9. Bliss Code Plead. (2nd ed.) § 422.

10. Bank *v.* Smith, 15 How. Pr. (N. Y.) 329; Claflin *v.* Jaraslauski, 64 Barb. (N. Y.) 463; Thompson *v.* R. R. Co., 45 N. Y. 468.

11. Brown *v.* Lewis, 10 Ind. 232; Boggess *v.* Davis, 34 Ind. 82; Mooney *v.* Musser, 34 Ind. 373.

12. See Bliss Code Plead. (2nd ed.), § 422.

5. Remedy for Defects—*a.* BY AIDER—(1) *Aider by Pleading Over.*—This doctrine remains as at the common law, and is looked upon with favor by the codes.[1]

(2) *Aider by Verdict*—See VERDICT.

b. BY AMENDMENT.—The codes of all the States either provide for or imply the right of the pleader to amend his pleading after demurrer without leave of court; and they also permit an amendment without leave at any time before the adverse party has filed a responsive pleading.[2] Substantial amendments of the complaint are in the sound discretion of the court, and no definite rule can be laid down. If there is any assignable limit to the right to amend the complaint, it is the requirement that the cause of action shall remain unchanged.[3] The defendant's answer is not subject to the same limitation, for the substitution of a new defense does not prejudice the merits of the plaintiff's case.[4] It is an unfailing rule, however, that the defendant in applying for leave to amend must base his application on some substantial ground, and he must disclose the amendment which he desires to make.[5] The permission to amend, in all cases where permission is required, being within the court's discretion, that permission will be refused wherever it would be unconscionable to grant it. Thus the courts were slow to permit the defense of usury to be set up by amendment when usury worked a forfeiture of the principal.[6] So also the statute of limitations cannot be set up by amendment, unless that defense can, under the circumstances, be shown to appeal to the conscience of the court.[7]

IV. General Divisions of Pleading—1. The Declaration.[8]—See DECLARATION, vol. 5, p. 349.

a. IN VARIOUS ACTIONS—See each action under its own title.

b. PARTS AND REQUISITES—See DECLARATION, vol. 5, p. 349.

c. PARTIES PLAINTIFF AND DEFENDANT—See PARTIES TO ACTIONS.

1. The doctrine is that defects in form are waived by failure to demur.

For a summary of American statutes in aid of defective pleading, see Bliss Code Plead (2nd ed.), § 440.

2. Bliss Code Plead. (2nd ed.), § 428.

3. This rule, which obtained at common law, seems to have survived the codes. See Steffy *v.* Carpenter, 37 Pa. St. 41; Milliken *v.* Whitehouse, 49 Me. 527; Lottman *v.* Barnett, 62 Mo. 159. Thus in an action for overflowing the plaintiff's land the court refused to sanction such an amendment as would, under the statute, charge the defendant for appropriating the land to his own use. Newton *v.* Allis, 12 Wis. 378.

4. Bowman *v.* DePeyster, 2 Daly (N. Y.) 203. The same liberality in favor of the defendant prevailed at common law. Waters *v.* Borell, 1 Wils. 223.

5. Allen *v.* Ransom, 44 Mo. 263. If the defendant had full knowledge of the defense and merely neglected to plead it, no amendment will be permitted; and it is well settled that when the answer admits a fact, an amendment denying it will not be sanctioned. See Clark *v.* Spencer, 14 Kan. 398; Harrison's Adm. *v.* Hastings, 28 Mo. 346.

6. Dole *v.* Northrop, 19 Wis. 249. For the rule in *New York* which is in some respects different, see Barnett *v.* Meyers, 17 Sup. Ct., N. Y. 109 and cases there cited.

7. Cooke *v.* Spears, 2 Cal. 409.

8. In addition to the definition given

2. Courses Open to the Defendant.—Having appeared,[1] the defendant must decide what course to adopt in order to meet the plaintiff's claim.

a. IMPARLANCE.—In ancient times the defendant, before being compelled to plead, was entitled to an allowance of time to talk or confer with the plaintiff, with a view to bringing the suit to an amicable termination. This allowance, which was granted upon the defendant's prayer, was known as *licentia loquendi*, or imparlance. The term in its most general sense is an allowance to either party of time to answer his adversary.[2] Imparlances are of three kinds—general, special, and more special.[3] On general imparlance the defendant reserves to himself no exceptions, and so waives all right to question the jurisdiction of the court or to take advantage of any other ground for dilatory plea; he can plead only to the action.[4] General imparlances are always from one term to another.[5] A special imparlance reserves to the defendant the right to set up a defense by plea in abatement.[6] The right to

in the article DECLARATION, vol. 5, p. 349, it will be well to cite Chitty's "A declaration is a specification in a methodical and legal form of the circumstances which constitute the plaintiff's cause of action which necessarily consists of the statement of a legal right recognized in courts of law and not merely in a court of equity, and of an injury to such right remediable at law by action as distinguished from the remedy by bill in equity." 1 Chitty Plead. (16 Am. ed.) 264. See also Bac. Ab. Pleas B, Com. Dig. Pleader, ch. 7; Co. Litt. 17 a, 303 a; Heath's Maxims 1, 2; Smith *v.* Fowle, 12 Wend (N. Y.) 10; Cheetham *v.* Tillotson, 5 Johns. (N. Y) 435.

1. For the manner of compelling the defendant to appear see ACTION, vol. 1 p. 178. Appearance is either in person or by attorney, but was in ancient times, in either case, an actual appearance in open court. This fact is demonstrated by the following passage in Glanville (temp. Hen. II):—"*Utroque litigantum, apparante in curia petens ipse loquelam suam et clameum ostendat, in hunc modum: Peto versus istum, etc.*" Clam. lib. 2, ch. 3. "*Utroque presente in curia, is qui petit jus suum in haec verba versus adversarium suum proponat—Peto,* etc. *Audito autem clameo,* etc. Clan. lib. 4, ch. 6. For evidence from Bracton to the same effect, see Appendix to Stephen on Pleading (Heard) (9th ed.) *12, where it is also stated "that it was probably the statute of Westminster 2 (13 Ed. 1, ch. 10) which first gave the general liberty to all persons of suing and defending by attorney; and that before that statute, a special warrant from the crown for that purpose was required. It seems, however, that this is only to be understood of appearance by attorney, and not to the contract [*sic*] of the suit by attorney after appearance once made. For it is clear that long prior to the 13 Ed. 1, and even in the time of Glanville, a party might, upon appearance first made by himself in person, appoint a *responsalis* (whose office, though in some respects different, was in substance the same as that of an attorney) to represent him during the progress of the cause, '*ad lucrandum vel perdendum pro eo,*' and it is not said by Glanville that this required a warrant from the crown." See also Beecher's Case, 3 Rep. 58b acc. Appearance in modern times takes the form of an entry in the docket or record made on behalf of the party by his attorney. In the case of those under disability who are incapable of appointing an attorney (as an infant, an idiot or a married woman sued alone) the appearance and pleadings do not purport to be by attorney but take a peculiar form, for which see 1 Tidd's Practice (8th ed.) 87, 88, 94.

2. Gould Plead. (5th ed.) 21, Com. Dig. Pleader D. 1, 1 Tidd 417.

3. 3 Blackst. Com. 301.

4. Gould Plead. (5th ed.) 21.

5. Gould Plead. (5th ed.) 21.

6. The saving clause is in these words. "Saving to himself all advantages and exceptions as well to the writ as to the

except does not, however, extend to the jurisdiction of the court.[1] To enable the defendant to raise the question of jurisdiction, he must pray for a more special imparlance, which reserves "all advantages and exceptions whatsoever."[2] Special and more special imparlances may extend only to a future day in the same term in which they are granted.[3]

b. DEFENSE—(See also DEFENSE, vol. 5, p. 515).—Defense, in its technical sense, signifies resistance or denial. It does not necessarily involve the conception of an admission coupled with justification or excuse.[4] It is the defendant's statement at large that he has an answer to the action, which statement he subsequently develops and renders specific in the body of his plea.[5]

(1) *Half Defense.*—This form of defense is appropriate when the defendant is about to resort to a plea to the jurisdiction of the court or to the competency of the plaintiff to sue.[6]

(2) *Full Defense.*—This is adapted to all other pleas than those above referred to—the theory of the law as to them being, that

declaration aforesaid." 2 Chitt. Plead. (16th Am. ed.) 407.

1. Gould Plead. (5th ed.) 22.

2. 2 Chitt. Pl. (16th Am. ed.) 408. It is to be noted that a defendant, after imparlance of any kind, can never plead a tender with a *touts temps prist:* for it would be a contradiction to allow a pleader time to put in a defense the essence of which is that he has been at all times ready to pay. See 1 Tidd Prac. 418. In this case and generally whenever the defendant after imparlance pleads what he has waived, the plaintiff is entitled to treat the plea as a nullity and to sign judgment against him as for want of a plea. Or, as in such case the record shows upon its face that the plea is ill-pleaded, the plaintiff may demur, or he may move to have the plea set aside; or in his replication he may specially reply the imparlance by way of estoppel. 1 Tidd Prac. 419; Buddle *v.* Wilson, 6 T. R. 369; Brewster *v.* Copper, 1 Wils. 261; 1 Black. R. 51; Onslow *v.* Smith, 2 Bos. & Pul. 384; Lloyd *v.* Williams, 2 M. & S. 484. If the plaintiff does not take advantage of his opportunity and answers the plea without objection, the plea will stand as if it had been pleaded without an imparlance. Gould Plead. (5th ed.) 24; Dacres *v.* Duncomb, 1 Vent. 236.

The object attained by the prayer for imparlance is in modern times reached by settled rules of court in the various jurisdictions, or (as in *New York*) to some extent by codes and acts of the legislature. In these cases a time is fixed within which the defendant must appear and plead, and in default of either the one or the other the plaintiff is entitled to sign judgment against him.

3. Gould Plead. (5th ed.) 21; Com. Dig. *Pleader*, D. 1; 1 Tidd Prac. 417.

4. Gould Plead. (5th ed.) 17, where in support of this statement the author cites the ancient form of "full defense:" "And the said C D by E F, his attorney, comes and defends the wrong and injury when and where it shall behoove him, and the damages and whatsoever else he ought to defend." See also 1 Chitty Plead. (16th Am. ed.) 444. *Compare* defense to a writ of entry. "Defense" in § 149 of the *New York* code is confined in its signification to the statement of new matter in the answer, and does not refer to the mere denials of averments in the complaint. See Note z[1] to 1 Chitty Plead. (16th. Am. ed.) 444; Houghton *v.* Townsend, 8 How. Pr. (N. Y.) 441; Ross *v.* Longmuir, 24 How. Pr. (N. Y.) 49; Bush *v.* Prosser, 11 N. Y. 347. See also Hubler *v.* Pullen, 9 Ind. 273.

5. Omission of defense was formerly ground for giving judgment against the defendant, even where the body of the plea was good in substance. Co. Litt. 127*b*; Hampson *v.* Bill, 3 Lev. 240; Bac. Abr. Pleas, D.; Alexander *v.* Mawman, Willes 41. Otherwise in *scire facias.* 1 Chitty Plead. (16 Am. ed.) 444; North *v.* Hoyle, 3 Lev. 182.

6. Gould Plead. (5th ed.) 18; Co. Litt. 127

Half defense is set out in this way:

the defendant waives his right to except to the jurisdiction when he defends "when and where it shall behoove him," and that he admits the plaintiff's competency to sue by defending "the damages and whatsoever else he ought to defend."[1]

c. PROFERT AND OYER.—At the common law, when a party who presumably had control[2] of a deed, pleaded it and made title under it,[3] he must needs make profert of it by averring in his pleading that he "brings here into court the said writing obliga-

"And the said C D by E F, his attorney, comes and defends the force and injury." Bac. Abr. Pleas, D.; 2 Chitty Plead. (16th Am. ed.) 409.

1. Gould Plead. (5th ed.) 18. Com. Dig. *Abatement* 1, 16,—— where it is implied that full defense is improper with any kind of dilatory plea. Conversely, half defense is taken to be a waiver of all right to take exception to points other than jurisdiction and competency to sue; therefore when it is joined to any other form of plea it is inconsistent with it and repugnant to it, and is therefore vicious.

The subtleties and nice distinctions which once obscured the subject of defense have long since come to be looked upon as obsolete law. In *England*, Reg. Gen. Hil. Term, 4 Wm. IV, Reg. 10, ordered that no formal defense shall be required in a plea; and it is believed to be nowhere necessary in this country.

2. Exceptions to the rule requiring profert of deeds under which title is made occur where there is an actual or presumptive inability on the part of a pleader to produce the document. "Thus" says Gould, Plead. (5th ed.) 415 "one who claims title, accruing by operation of law under a deed to another may plead the deed without profert: As where, in a writ of dower, the demandant pleads a grant to her deceased husband, of the subject in which she demands dower." See also Co. Litt. 225; Bac. Abr. Pleas, I., 12 (1); Com. Dig. Pleader, O. 9.

But in the case of a tenant by curtesy, although his is a legal estate for life, profert must be made of deeds to which the wife was a party: for "he is presumed," says the same author, "to have possession of her muniments of title, and may retain them, during his life," *citing* Co. Litt. 226 a; Bac. Abr. Pleas, etc., I. 12 (1); 10 Co. 94; Com. Dig. Pleader, O. 9.

Profert is, for the reason stated above, dispensed with when the deed is in the power or possession of the adverse party. Barbour *v.* Archer, 3 Bibb (Ky.) 8; Francis *v.* Hazlerig, 1 A. K. Marsh. (Ky.) 93. Or has been destoyed. Powers *v.* Ware, 2 Pick. (Mass.) 451. Either by the adverse party or by time or accident. Paddock *v.* Higgins, 2 Root (Conn.) 316, 482; Kelley *v.* Riggs, 2 Root (Conn.) 13; Respublica *v.* Coates, 1 Yeates (Pa.) 2. Formerly, however, the remedy in case of loss by accident was only in equity. And see Hendy *v.* Stephenson, 10 East 55, and Metcalf *v.* Standeford, 1 Bibb (Ky.) 618; Branch *v.* Riley, 1 Root (Conn.) 541.

So also, profert is not required of a deed pleaded by a stranger to it. Com. Dig. Pleader, O. 8; Huntington *v.* Mildmay, Cro. Jac. 217; Reynell *v.* Long, Carthew 316; Stockman *v.* Hampton, Cro. Car. 441; Birney *v.* Haim, 2 Litt. (Ky.) 262.

But the fact that the deed, upon which an action of covenant is brought, was, for the benefit of the parties, delivered to a third person at the time of execution, will not excuse the want of profert in the declaration. So held in *New York* before the code. Wheeler *v.* Miller, 2 Den. (N. Y.) 172. But oyer cannot be demanded of an instrument in the possession of neither party but equally accessible to both. Rockhill *v.* Hanna, 4 McLean (U. S.) 200. Nor is profert essential when a specialty has been pleaded with profert and remains in another court. Moore *v.* Paul, 2 Bibb (Ky.) 330; Smith *v.* Lloyd, 16 Gratt. (Va.) 295.

3. Where the deed (as in covenant broken) is the foundation of the action, the declaration must make profert. Austin *v.* Dills, 1 Tyler (Vt.) 308. In many cases, however, a deed may be given in evidence to make title without pleading it, and in such a case no profert need be made. Gould Plead. (5th ed.) 412. This occurs where by the common law the obligaton relied

tory."[1] Profert is required of no other instruments than deeds,[2] except in the case of suits brought by executors or administrators,

upon exists independently of the instrument in question, the latter being mere evidence of it. Thus, no writing of any kind is necessary to a lease, or to a conveyance by livery of seisin in fee, in tail, or for life, even where the conveyance was actually made by deed. Co. Litt. 121 b, 9 a (n. 1). Duppa *v.* Mayo, 1 Saund. 276 (n. 1). See Gould Plead. (5th ed.) 178. But if the deed be pleaded unnecessarily (as where an interest might pass without deed) profert must nevertheless be made. Bac. Abr. Pleas. I. 12 (1). But some rights and interests at common law could not pass except by deed. Such rights are said to lie in grant, and the most familiar instance of them is in the case of the incorporeal heriditaments. Where the pleader relies upon any such right he must plead the deed, and must, of course, make profert of it where it is the foundation of his action. See likewise, Brown *v.* Copp, 5 N. H. 223. If, however, the deed is pleaded and no title is made under it there is no obligation to make profert. For example, in case for the stoppage of an easement or an action for the disturbance of a right of way, the deed which creates the right need not be pleaded with profert because the action is founded, not upon the deed, but upon the tort. The gist of the action is the wrong done; the statement of right is mere matter of inducement. See 1 Chitty Plead. (16th Am. ed.) 476. See also 2 Chitty Plead. (16th Am. ed.) 174 (n. z); Gould Plead. (5th ed.) 414. It seems that in case a party is entitled to inspect original papers referred to in general terms, he may obtain a view of them on motion but no profert need be made. Cecil *v.* Dynes, 2 Ind. 226. And in *Michigan* profert is not required where the declaration sets forth the written contract in full. Regents *v.* Detroit etc. Soc., 12 Mich. 138.

1. See Gould Plead. (5th ed.) 408; Steph Plead. (Heard, 9th ed.) 66, 437; Com. Dig. Pleader, O. 1. Patten *v.* Heustis, 26 N. J. L. 293; 3 Black. Com. App. 22; Bender *v.* Sampson, 11 Mass. 42. See Powers *v.* Ware, 2 Pick. (Mass.) 451.

2. Gould Plead. (5th ed.) 411, Mason *v.* Buckmaster, 1 Ill. 27; Magee *v.* Fisher, 8 Ala. 320. See Gatton *v.* Dimmitt, 27 Ill. 400. Under the modern commercial law, it is the custom to count upon negotiable paper as an instrument, and accordingly, in many jurisdictions, the court, on prayer, will order a copy to be delivered to the defendant before requiring him to plead. In some jurisdictions, as in *Pennsylvania*, the declaration is required by act of legislature to have annexed to it a copy of the instrument sued upon. It seems, however, that in order to avail himself by plea of matter contained in the instrument, the defendant must demand oyer. Gould Plead. (5th ed.) 411; Bac. Abr. Pleas & ch. 1, 12 (2). See Comerford *v.* Cobb, 2 Fla. 418. In *Kentucky*, it seems that oyer is demandable of any written instrument. Anderson *v.* Barry, 2 J. J. Marsh. (Ky.) 265. Except, it appears, an injunction bond. Carson *v.* Pearl, 4 J. J. Marsh. (Ky.) 92. In *Georgia*, profert is required of the note or instrument on which the action is founded, whatever be its nature. In *Tennessee*, the plaintiff must make profert of the notes declared on. Anderson *v.* Allison, 2 Head (Tenn.) 122. It is said in Co. Litt. 225 that oyer is not demandable of records, since these are kept in public offices where all men have an equal opportunity to consult them. Hall *v.* State, 9 Ala. 827; Butler *v.* State, 5 Gill & J. (Md.) 511; Gould Plead. (5th ed.) 412. And moreover the court will take judicial notice of them. Guild *v.* Richardson, 6 Pick. (Mass.) 364. See McNutt *v.* Lancaster, 9 Smed. & M. (Miss.) 570.

But in *Connecticut* oyer must be given, when required, of the record of the superior court. Williams *v.* Perry, 2 Root (Conn.) 462. And for the rule in *Massachusetts*, see Commonwealth *v.* Roby, 12 Pick. (Mass.) 496; Guild *v.* Richardson, 6 Pick., (Mass.) 364, and Slayton *v.* Chester, 4 Mass. 478.

In *Maryland*, where a record of the same or of another court is pleaded, it was a fatal defect on special demurrer to omit the *prout patet per recordum*. Shafer *v.* Stonebraker, 4 Gill & J. (Md.) 345. The *prout*, however, does not amount to a profert, but it is sufficient, even on special demurrer. Clapp *v.* Gilman, 2 Blackf. (Ind.) 45. The writ being part of the record, profert of it is unnecessary. Renner *v.*

when profert of the letters testamentary or of the letters of administration is essential.[1] The effect of profert is to enable the court to inspect the instrument and to entitle the adverse party to oyer of it. To crave oyer meant, in ancient practice, to pray to hear the document in question read; and the effect of the reading was to make the document part of the record.[2] In modern times the term usually signifies the demand by one of the parties for a copy of the instrument pleaded against him.[3] When one who is entitled to oyer demands it, he need not answer until it is granted, but a failure to demand it is, as in other cases, a waiver of the right.[4] Oyer is demandable whenever profert is necessarily made.[5] If profert is wrongly omitted, the proper course for the adverse party is not to demand oyer but to demur.[6]

Reed, 3 Ark. 339; Commonwealth *v.* Roby, 12 Pick. (Mass.) 496.

1. Steph. Plead. (Heard 9th ed.) 66; Gould Plead. (5th ed.) 412; Com. Dig. Pleader, O. 3; Brown *v.* Jones, 10 Gill & J. (Md.) 334. See Beach *v.* Pears, 1 N. J. L. 288; Thatcher *v.* Lyman, 5 Mass. 260; Judge of Probate *v.* Merrill, 6 N. H. 256. Omission of profert was, at the common law, a fault in substance cognizable on general demurrer. Com. Dig. Pleader, O. 17; Cutts *v.* Bennet, Cro. Jac. 412; 3 Bulstr. 223; Hob. 83; Edwards *v.* Stapleton, Cro. Eliz. 551. Although this is questioned in Lee and Cureton's case, 1 Leon. 300, and denied in Salisbury *v.* Williams, 2 Salk. 47. By 16 and 17 Car. 2, ch. 8, the omission is cured by verdict; and by 4 and 5 Anne, ch. 16, is cognizable only on special demurrer. Bac. Abr. Pleas, etc., I, 12 (1).

2. Commissioners *v.* Gains, Treadw. Const. (S. Car.) 459; Tucker *v.* State, 11 Md. 322; Rantin *v.* Robertson, 2 Strobh. (S. Car.) 366.

3. Bac. Abr. Pleas, etc., I, 12 (1, 2); Steph. Plead. (Heard, 9th ed.) 87.

4. Gould Plead. (5th ed.) 418; Smith *v.* Alworth, 18 Johns. (N. Y.) 445; Pollard *v.* Yoder, 2 A. K. Marsh. (Ky.) 264; Baily *v.* Wallen, 1 Overt. (Tenn.) 198; Adams *v.* Macy, 1 Bibb (Ky.) 328; Gist *v.* Steele, 1 Bibb (Ky.) 571; Palmer *v.* McGinnis, Hard. (Ky.) 513. The proper mode of obtaining oyer is by prayer entered on the record, to which the opposite party may counter plead. But when the papers are on file, a statement in the demurrer that oyer is craved (there being no objection) is sufficient Thatcher *v.* Lyman, 5 Mass. 260; Judge of Probate *v.* Merrill, 6 N. H. 256. A prayer not entered on the record is insufficient. Williams *v.* Bryan, 5 Coldw. (Tenn.) 105. Oyer can be craved only once in the same suit. Taylor *v.* Bank of Kentucky, 2 J. J. Marsh. (Ky.) 264.

5. Steph. Plead. (Heard, 9th ed.) 67; Van Renssalaer *v.* Saunders, 2 How. Pr. (N. Y.) 250; Bettle *v.* Wilson, 14 Ohio 257.

6. Metcalf *v.* Standeford, 1 Bibb (Ky.) 618. But see Anderson *v.* Barry, 2 J. J. Marsh. (Ky.) 265; Briggs *v.* Greenlee, Minor (Ala.) 123.

In *Alabama,* the omission of profert is not available on general demurrer. Mallory *v.* Matlock, 7 Ala. 757. See Hall *v.* Williams, 8 Me. 434; Hanna *v.* Yocum, 17 Ill. 387. If profert where necessary, is omitted, the defect must be taken advantage of before verdict. Francis *v.* Hazlerig, 1 A. K. Marsh. (Ky.) 93; Tucker *v.* Real Estate Bank, 4 Ark. 429.

It has already been said that a party is not entitled to oyer where there is no profert; but if he nevertheless demands it, and his adversary grants it, he may make use of it. Story *v.* Kimball, 6 Vt. 541; S. P. Campbell *v.* Strong, Hempst. (U. S.) 265.

If profert is made of the writing declared on and oyer is not craved, the instrument is taken to be as stated in the declaration. Pollard *v.* Yoder, 2 A. K. Marsh. (Ky.) 264; Wriston *v.* Lacy, 7 J. J. Marsh. (Ky.) 219. Profert of a bond includes profert of the condition. United States *v.* Spalding, 2 Mason (U. S.) 478. But oyer of a bond does not include oyer of the condition; nor *e converso.* United States *v.* Sawyer, 1 Gall. (U. S.) 86. Nor oyer of a note, oyer of the indorsements. Tuggle *v.* Adams, 3 A. K. Marsh. (Ky.) 429. See McLain *v.* Onstott, 3 Ark. 478. But the omission to crave oyer of the

Profert unnecessarily made does not entitle to oyer.[1] It is not error to award oyer when it is not properly demandable; otherwise, of a refusal of it when a party is entitled to it.[2]

d. DEMURRER—(See also DEMURRER, vol. 5, p. 549)—(1) *Definition.*[3]—If the defendant thinks the declaration insufficient in substance or in form, or if at any subsequent stage either party conceives the preceding pleading to be faulty in these respects, his course is to demur, and thus to submit to the court the question of the sufficiency of the pleading.[4] A demurrer is therefore

condition is amendable. Alabama University *v.* Winston, 5 Stew. & P. (Ala.) 17. Where (in a jurisdiction where profert of writings not under seal is made) there were two counts in a declaration on two notes, profert of both notes at the conclusion of the last count was held sufficient. Hynson *v.* Ruddell, 11 Ark. 33. And see Estill *v.* Jenkins, 4 Dana (Ky.) 75. Oyer of a deed set forth in one count does not apply the deed to other counts. Hughes *v.* Moore, 7 Cranch (U. S.) 176.

1. But if oyer is craved when the party is not entitled to it, and the prayer is granted, the deed becomes part of the record. Deming *v.* Bullitt, 1 Blackf. (Ind.) 241; Russell *v.* Drummond, 6 Ind. 216.

2. Longavil *v.* Isleworth, 2 Salk. 498; 2 Lill. Abr. 338; 1 Chitty Plead. (16th Am. ed.) 417; Lawes' Plead. 99; Erskine *v.* Townsend, 2 Mass. 494; 3 Am. Dec. 71; Gould Plead. (5th ed.) 420; State *v.* Hicks, 2 Blackf. (Ind.) 336; 20 Am. Dec. 118.

When a party entitled to oyer demands and obtains it, he may or may not make use of it. Matter heard upon oyer becomes part of the record and the party may at his option demur or plead according to the nature of the facts disclosed. Thus if upon oyer it appears that there is only a partial statement of the deed, the pleader may demur. Hobson *v.* McArthur, 3 McLean (U. S.) 241; Duval *v.* Malone, 14 Gratt. (Va.) 24; Bogardus *v.* Trial, 2 Ill. 63; Martin *v.* Bank of Tenn., 2 Coldw. (Tenn.) 332. So if profert is made of an original and a copy is offered on oyer the defendant may demur. Wellford *v.* Miller, 1 Cranch (C.C.) 485; Jones *v.* Simmons, 4 Humph. (Tenn.) 314; Moore *v.* Fenwick, Gilm. (Va.) 214; McCormick *v.* Kenyon, 13 Mo. 131. In Brooks *v.* Brooks, 6 N. J. L. 404, it is said that the time to object to an insufficient compliance with demand for oyer is at the trial. 3 Black. Comm. 299; Gould Plead. (5th ed.) 418. But a writing proffered is not part of the record unless oyer is craved. Adams *v.* Macey, 1 Bibb (Ky.) 328; Palmer *v.* McGinnis, Hard. (Ky.) 513; Gist *v.* Steele, 1 Bibb (Ky.) 157. But if the party avails himself of oyer and sets out the deed of his adversary, he must recite it *verbatim.* If he misquotes, his opponent may sign judgment against him, since his plea is then bad in part and (therefore) bad altogether. Or the adversary may make the error of the citation appear upon the record by praying to have the true deed enrolled; having done which, he may demur. Wallace *v.* Duchess of Cumberland, 4 T. R. 370; Jerens *v.* Harridge, 1 Saund. 9 b (n. 1) 316, 317; Abney *v.* White, Carth. 301; Simmons *v.* Parmenter, 1 Wils. 97; Rudisill *v.* Sill, 4 Blackf. (Ind.) 282; 1 Chitty Plead. (16th Am. ed.) 418; Gould Plead. (5th ed.) 420; United States *v.* Sawyer, 1 Gall. (U. S.) 86. There is no profert and no oyer under the New York code, but that instrument provides for the production of papers on motion in all the cases (it should seem) in which a bill of discovery would lie in Chancery. Code 388. See note (xi) Gould Plead. (5th ed.) 408.

3. The statements contained under this head should be taken in connection with the matter contained in the special article on demurrers. The two are intended to be complementary.

4. Demurrer cometh of the Latin word *demorari,* to abide; and therefore he which demurreth in law is said he that abideth in law: *Moratur* or *demoratur in lege.* Whensoever the learned counsel of a party is of opinion that the count or plea of the adverse party is insufficient in law, then he demurreth or abideth in law, and referreth the same to the judgment of the court. Co. Litt. 71 b.

an excuse for not pleading,[1] and may be defined to be a statement by a party that his adversary, on his own showing, has no legal right to succeed. The office of a demurrer is to call the attention of the court to a positive or negative defect in the pleading at which it is pointed, which defect vitiates the pleading in law. A positive defect occurs when the pleading contains matter which it ought not to contain.[2] A negative defect occurs when the pleading does not contain matter which it ought to contain,[3] or when the matter is not set forth with the fullness or formality required by law.[4] The first and third of these defects, viz, excess of matter and breaches of the laws of statement, are defects in form only. The second, deficiency of matter, is a fault in substance. Defects in substance are cognizable on general or special demurrer. Defects in form are cognizable on special demurrer only. Therefore every special demurrer includes a general one.[5] It is a general demurrer and something more.

(2) *General Demurrer.*—A general demurrer is an exception in general terms to the sufficiency of a pleading; it does not point out the particular imperfection. When pleading was oral and objections were taken *ore tenus*, a general demurrer answered every purpose, for it was always clear to court and counsel which point was objected to. Accordingly, at common law, a special demurrer, or one which specifies the particular imperfection, was unnecessary.[6] But when it became the practice to reduce the pleadings to writing, the party whose pleading was objected to by general demurrer went into court not knowing what he was to argue. This mischief was remedied by the statute of 27 Elizabeth, ch. 5,[7] which provided in substance that, upon joinder in demurrer,

1. Haiton *v.* Jeffries, 10 Mod. 280. It is in accordance with this principle that the rule is laid down that a party cannot demur and plead at the same time. In early times, however, the principle does not seem to have been recognized, and a demurrer together with a plea was sometimes permitted.

2. As for example where the plea contains not one answer to the declaration, but two—duplicity.

3. As in the case of a declaration in assumpsit which omits to allege a consideration.

4. As where the form of statement in a pleading is argumentative.

5. State *v.* Peck, 60 Me. 498.

6. It is often said that at common law a special demurrer was necessary in cases of duplicity. So says Chitty, Plead. (16th Am. ed.) 694, *citing* as an authority Powdick *v.* Lyon, 11 East 565. But in that case there is nothing to sustain the assertion. There was no question of duplicity, and the decision turned on the familiar principle that where the demurrer to a declaration is too large judgment will be given for the plaintiff.

7. The provisions of this statute are as follows: Forasmuch as excessive charges and expenses, and great delay and hindrance of justice hath grown in actions and suits between the subjects of this realm, by reason that upon some small mistaking or want of form in pleading, judgments are often reversed by writs of error, and oftentimes upon demurrers in law given otherwise than the matter in law, and very right of the cause doth require, whereby the parties are constrained either utterly to lose their rights, or else, after long time and great trouble and expense, to renew again their suits; for remedy whereof, be it enacted by the Queen's most excellent majesty, the lords spiritual and temporal, and the commons, in this present parliament assembled, and by the authority

judgment should be given on the merits without regard to any defects in form, except those which the party demurring specially set down. "The chief difficulty which arose in the construction of this statute," says Chitty,[1] "was the distinguishing between what was matter of form and matter of substance; and many defects which are now deemed mere form were holden not to be aided by this statute, such as the omission of the words *vi et armis, contra pacem,* etc." Accordingly, the 4 & 5 Anne, ch. 16,[2] was enacted to emphasize the principles of the earlier statute, and it specified with greater particularity what were those matters of form which a general demurrer was insufficient to reach. These statutes, however, have been construed as not applying to pleas in abatement,[3] and the form of such a plea, as well as its sub-

of the same, that from henceforth, after demurrer joined and entered in any action or suit in any court of record within this realm, the judges shall proceed and give judgment according as the very right and cause of the matter in law shall appear unto them, without regarding any imperfection, defect or want of form in any writ, return, plaint, declaration, or other pleading, process, or course of proceeding whatsoever, except those only which the party demurring shall specially and particularly set down and express together with his demurrer; and that no judgment to be given shall be reversed by any writ of error, for any such imperfection, defect or want of form as is aforesaid, except such only as is before excepted.

1. 1 Chitty Plead. (16th Am. ed.) 695.

2. The provisions of this statute are as follows: For the amendment of the law in several particulars, and for the easier, speedier, and better advancement of justice, be it enacted by the Queen's most excellent majesty, by and with the consent of the lords spiritual and temporal, and commons, in this present parliament assembled, and by the authority of the same, that from and after the first day of Trinity term, which shall be in the year of our Lord one thousand seven hundred and six, where any demurrer shall be joined, and entered in any action or suit in any court of record within this realm, the judges shall proceed and give judgment, according as the very right of the cause and matter in law shall appear unto them, without regarding any imperfection, omission or defect in any writ, return, plaint, declaration, or other pleading, process or course of proceeding whatsoever, except those only which the party demurring shall specially and particularly set down and express, together with his demurrer, as causes of the same, notwithstanding that such imperfection, omission or defect might have heretofore been taken to be matter of substance, and not aided by the statute made in the twenty-seventh year of Queen Elizabeth, entitled, "An act for the furtherance of justice in case of demurrer and pleadings," so as sufficient matter appear in the said pleadings, upon which the court may give judgment according to the very right of the cause; and therefore from and after the said first day of Trinity term, no advantage or exception shall be taken of or for an immaterial traverse; or of or for the default of entering pledges upon any bill or declaration; or of or for the default of alleging the bringing into court any bond, bill, indenture or other deed whatsoever mentioned in the declaration or other pleading; or of or for the default of alleging of the bringing into court letters testamentary, or letters of administration; or of or for the omission of *vi et armis et contra pacem,* or either of them; or of or for the want of averment of *hoc paratus est verificare,* or *hoc paratus est verificare per recordum;* or of or for not alleging *prout patet per recordum,* but the court shall give judgment according to the very right of the cause, as aforesaid, without regarding any such imperfections, omissions and defects, or any other matter of like nature, except the same shall be specially and particularly set down and shown for cause of demurrer.

3. Walden *v.* Holman, 2 Ld. Ray. 1015. Plaintiff declared against the defendant by the name of John, who

stance, will be scrutinized by the court on general demurrer.[1] For a merely formal defect, it is, even in this case, advisable to demur specially.[2]

(3) *Special Demurrer.*—The origin and nature of special demurrers having been already pointed out, it remains to state that they have in practice supplanted general demurrers throughout the *United States;*[3] but they have been abolished in *England* by statute, and a motion to strike out has been substituted.[4]

(4) *Effect of Demurrer in Opening Record*[5]—(*a*) *General Principles.*—Upon demurrer the court will examine the whole record and give judgment for him who upon the whole appears to be entitled to it.[6] This is subject to an exception in the case of a demurrer to a plea in abatement, where the court, if the decision is adverse to the plea, will give judgment of *respondeat ouster* without regard to defects in the declaration.[7] And while it is true that a demurrer opens the record to the inspection of the court, yet where, by the filing of several pleas, as many records have been constituted as there are pleas, a demurrer will open only that record in which it occurs. An admission in one line of pleading is not available on a demurrer occurring in another line.[8]

pleaded in abatement that he was baptized by the name of Benjamin, *absque hoc quod idem Johannes* was ever known by the name of John. Upon general demurrer a *respondeat ouster* was awarded, LORD HOLT declaring that the statute of Elizabeth meant only that matters of form in pleas which go to the action shall be helped on general demurrer. Pleas in abatement remain as before the statute in this respect, and this one was clearly informal, for the *quod idem* confesses the defendant's name to be John, whereas he subsequently states that he was never known by that name. In short, the plea was repugnant.

1. Lloyd *v.* Williams, 2 M. & Sel. 485; Hoppin *v.* Jenckes, 9 R. I. 102.

2. Hixon *v.* Binns, 3 T. R. 186.

3. This statement applies both to those States in which technical demurrers exist, and to those in which defenses by way of demurrer are set up in an answer. In most cases the practice acts or codes specify the grounds which will sustain objections akin to demurrers, and these grounds must be set out specifically.

4. 15 & 16 Vict., ch. 76, § 50, *et seq.* The text of the statute is as follows: Either party may object by demurrer to the pleading of the opposite party, on the ground that such pleading does not set forth sufficient ground of action, defense or reply, as the case may be; and, where issue is joined on such demurrer, the court shall proceed and give judgment according as the very right of the cause and matter in law shall appear unto them, without regarding any imperfection, omission, defect in or lack of form; and no judgment shall be arrested, stayed or reversed for any such imperfection, omission, defect in or lack of form.

No pleading shall be deemed insufficient for any defect which could heretofore only be objected to by special demurrer.

If any pleading be so framed as to prejudice, embarrass or delay the fair trial of the action, the opposite party may apply to the court or a judge to strike out or amend such pleading, and the court or any judge shall make such order respecting the same, and also respecting the costs of the application, as such court or judge shall see fit.

5. See DEMURRER, vol. 5, p. 549.

6. Steph. Plead. (9th Am. ed.) 143.

7. In Hastrop *v.* Hastings, 1 Salk. 212, there was a demurrer to a plea in abatement. Upon argument, counsel for the defendant sought to insist upon divers faults in the declaration, but the court would not listen to him; for it was said *per curiam* that on demurrer to plea in abatement, the plea only will be scrutinized, and accordingly a *respondeat ouster* was awarded.

8. In Davies *v.* Penton, 6 B. & C.

(*b*) *Where Plaintiff Mistakes Cause of Action.*—An important modification of the rule that a demurrer opens the whole record occurs in the case in which a plaintiff with a good cause of action nevertheless rests his case on the wrong ground. The principle is that a plaintiff must recover, if at all, on the ground of action set forth in his declaration without assistance from matter disclosed by the defendant's plea.[1]

(*c*) *Discontinuance.*—Another modification of the general rule occurs where upon the whole record the right appears to be with the plaintiff, but where he, by being guilty of a discontinuance, is not in a position to demand judgment. A discontinuance takes place when the plaintiff neglects to take advantage of an opportunity of signing judgment. Thus, where a plea begins as an answer to a part of the claim only, and is in fact only a partial answer, the plaintiff should sign judgment as by *nil dicit* for the part unanswered.[2] Or he should resign his claim by entering a

216, an action was brought upon articles of agreement whereby the defendant agreed to sell to the plaintiff the stock and good will of his business as an apothecary, covenanting that he would not himself carry on said business within five miles of the establishment. As part of the consideration for the sale, the plaintiff agreed to pay and discharge two bills of exchange. Breach, that the defendant did carry on the said business within five miles. Plea (1), that the plaintiff did not pay the bills of exchange, (2) a set-off. To plea (1), a demurrer; to plea (2), replication of bankruptcy. Upon this state of the record it appeared to the court that plea (1) was bad (presumably for duplicity); but CHITTY for the defendant argued that inasmuch as the plaintiff in his replication had confessed himself a bankrupt, the court upon demurrer should notice this fact as being disclosed by the record and should declare that the plaintiff's declaration was bad, since, being a bankrupt, he had no right to sue. But the court were of opinion that upon demurrer they could consider only that line of pleadings in which the demurrer occurred — the declaration and the first plea. LITTLEDALE, J., touched the heart of the matter when he said: "We must treat the count, plea and replication, and the count, plea and demurrer as distinct records and give judgment upon each without reference to the other." In other words, the court upon demurrer will indeed consider the whole record, but the whole of that record only in which the demurrer occurs. Matter cannot be imported from one branch into another to support a failing case. Judgment was accordingly given for the plaintiff.

1. In Marsh *v.* Bulteel (5 B. & Ald. 507) the action was covenant upon a deed whereby the parties agreed to submit certain differences to the award of arbitrators. The first count set forth the defendant's covenant to abide by the award and not to hinder the arbitrators from performing the award. It then set forth the making of the award wherein they directed the defendant to pay to the plaintiff certain sums of money. Breach, that the defendant did not pay those sums. The defendant pleaded that before the award was made he revoked the authority of the arbitrators by deed, of which they had notice. Demurrer to the plea. The court was of opinion that the defendant was entitled to judgment, upon the ground that the plea was a good answer to the breach alleged, and ABBOTT, C., J. remarked, "It never has been held that a plaintiff who seeks to recover damages for one ground of action stated in his count is entitled to recover in respect of another, disclosed by the defendant's plea. I am of opinion that a plaintiff can recover only in respect of the ground of action stated in his declaration." See Steph. Plead. (9th Am. ed.) 144, and Head *v.* Baldrey, 6 A. & E. 468.

2. 1 Chitty Plead. (16th Am. ed.) 549. There is an important distinction between a plea which professes to be a complete answer but which is not, and

nolle prosequi thereto.[1] But if he adopts neither course, there occurs a chasm or *hiatus* in the proceedings which has the effect of discontinuing the whole action.[2] And if there are several defendants, a discontinuance as to one is a discontinuance as to all.[3] The plaintiff by a discontinuance is put out of court, and not being in court he is incapable of demanding judgment on the demurrer.[4] A discontinuance is cured after verdict by the statute of jeofails;[5] and after judgment by *nil dicit*, confession or *non sum informatus* by 4 Ann., ch. 16.[6]

(5) *Judgment on Demurrer.*—See JUDGMENT, vol. 12, page 58.

e. PLEA AND SUBSEQUENT PLEADINGS—(1) *Protestation.*—As a result of the principle that a party was deemed to admit such matters as he neither traversed nor confessed and avoided, the use of a protestation was sanctioned by the courts. This has the effect of preventing an adverse allegation of fact, which stands confessed by the pleadings, from operating as an estoppel in another suit between the same parties. It is said to be the exclusion of a conclusion,[7] and is, in strictness, no part of the pleadings; it rather has the effect of suspending the operation of the rules of pleading. It has no effect upon the record as far as the principal case is concerned, for the purposes of which the matters covered by the protestation are deemed to be admitted.[8] Hence a superfluous or repugnant protestation does not injure the plead-

one which professes to be, and in fact is, only a partial answer. It is only in the latter case that judgment can be signed for the part unanswered: in the former case the plaintiff should demur. Steph. Plead. (9th Am. ed.) 216.

1. 1 Chitty Plead. (16th Am. ed.) 550.

2. Steph. Plead. (9th Am. ed.) 215.

3. Bro. Abr. *Discontinuance de Process*, pl. 22; Green *v.* Chernock, Cro. Eliz. 762.

4. One of the leading cases on the subject of discontinuance is Tippet *v.* May, 1 B. & P. 411. In that case, to a declaration in assumpsit against three, two of the defendants pleaded a debt of record by way of set-off, but took no notice of the third. The plaintiffs replied *nul tiel record*, and gave a day for the production of the record, but entered no suggestion on the roll respecting the third. To this the defendants demurred generally. MARSHALL, Sergt., made a learned argument in support of the demurrer, and the court gave him judgment, on the ground that there had been a discontinuance as to one defendant, and therefore a discontinuance as to all. Although the defendants' plea was bad the court declared, *per* EYRE, C. J., that the plaintiffs having been guilty of a discontinuance, were not in a position to take advantage of that fact; or as ROOKE, J., put it, "the plaintiffs not being in court, cannot call upon the court to give them judgment." See Gilb. Hist., C. P. 155–158; 1 Rol. Abr., fo. 487–488; Com. Dig. Pleader (Wm. III); Bro. Abr. *Discontinuance de Process*, pl. 22; Green *v.* Charnock, 1 Cro. Eliz. 762; Paston *v.* Lusher, Yelv. 155.

5. 32 Hen. VIII, ch. 30,

6. See Steph. Plead. (9th Am. ed.) 216, note (d).

7. Co. Litt. 124 b, 126. Gould Plead. (16th ed.)

8. The following is the form of a protestation: Replication, *precludi non:* because protesting that the defendant *did not give notice to the plaintiffs in manner and form* as the defendant has above in her plea in that behalf alleged. The effect of this is to admit for the purposes of the pending action that notice was given, but to protest against this admission being used against the plaintiffs on any other occasion. Gould Plead. (5th ed.) 549.

ing with which it is connected, even on special demurrer.[1] When the pleading is shown to be false, the protestation is deprived of its force, and it will not, therefore, avail the party protesting if the issue be found against him.[2]

(2) *Puis Darrein Continuance.*—When the defendant, at the common law, within the time prescribed, pleads the single plea allowed him, he is as a rule confined in his defense to the matter contained in that plea. He cannot withdraw the plea filed and substitute another as the cause progresses.[3]

But if any matter of defense arises after issue joined, whether in fact or in law,[4] the defendant is at liberty to plead it.[5] Such a plea does not seek to bar the original cause of action, but tends to impugn the right of further maintenance of the suit.[6] Pleas

1. Com. Dig. Pleader, n.; Gould Plead. (5th ed.) 384.

2. Co. Lit. 124 b, 126 a; Gould Plead. (5th ed.) 384. The latter author considers that this restriction of the effect of a protestation (or *protestando*, as it is sometimes called) occurs only when the facts protested might have been directly traversed.

The Hilary Rules, 4 Wm. IV, declare that "no protestation shall hereafter be made in pleadings, but either party shall be entitled to the same advantage in that or other action, as if a protestation had been made." See also Steph. Plead. (9th Am. ed.) 218 and note.

3. Gould Plead. (5th ed.) 1. This is upon the presumption that the rights of the parties remain throughout the proceedings as they were at the commencement of it.

4. Com. Dig. Abatement, I, 24; Stoner *v.* Gibson, Hob. 81; Sparkes *v.* Crofts, 1 Ld. Rayd. 266; 1 Chitty Plead. (16th Am. ed.) 689.

5. Feagin *v.* Pearson, 42 Ala. 332; Brownfield *v.* Braddee, 9 Watts (Pa) 149. The plea derives its name from the ancient practice of adjourning or continuing the proceedings from day to day, or from term to term. In such a case matter arising while the parties were out of court was pleaded as having happened "*puis darrein continuance*" or "*post ultimam continuationem.*" Steph. Plead. (9th Am. ed.) 64. See Rundle *v.* Little, 6 Q. B. 174; Burns *v.* Hindman, 7 Ala. 531; Canfield *v.* Eleventh School Dist. 19 Conn. 529; Allen *v.* Newberry, 8 Iowa 65; Semmes *v.* Naylor, 12 Gill & J. (Md.) 358; Longworth *v.* Flagg, 10 Ohio St. 300; Bank of U. S. *v.* Merchants' Bank, 7 Gill (Md.) 415; Jackson *v.* Ramsay, 3 Cow. (N. Y.) 75; 15 Am. Dec. 242; Hart *v.* Meeker, 1 Sandf. (N. Y.) 623; Elms *v.* Beers, 3 McCord (S. Car.) 1. But see Johns *v.* Bolton, 12 Pa. St. 339; State *v.* Moses, 20 S. Car. 465; Cutter *v.* Folsom, 17 N. H. 139. A plea *puis darrein continuance* will be permitted even after the cause has been remanded from the court of appeals. McGowan *v.* Hoy, 4 J. J. Marsh. (Ky.) 223; Gardner *v.* Way, 8 Gray (Mass.) 189.

6. Yeaton *v.* Lynn, 5 Pet. (U. S.) 224; Lockington *v.* Smith, Pet. (C. C.) 466; McDougald *v.* Rutherford, 30 Ala. 253; Rowell *v.* Hayden, 40 Me. 582; Andrews *v.* Hooper, 13 Mass. 472; Hendrickson *v.* Hutchinson, 29 N. J. L. 180; Cobb *v.* Curtiss, 8 Johns. (N. Y.) 470.

What Defenses Should be So Pleaded.—The following matters have been taken advantage of by plea *puis darrein continuance*: *Release.* Wisheart *v.* Legro, 33 N. H. 177; Kimball *v.* Wilson, 3 N. H. 96; 14 Am. Dec. 342; Bul. N. P. 309; Wade *v.* Emerson, 17 Mo 267; 1 Chitty Plead. (16th Am. ed.) 689. But the rule is otherwise in ejectment. Doe *v.* Brewer, 4 M. & Sel. 300; Doe *v.* Franklin, 7 Taunt. 9.

In an action where the release is no defense (as where it is given by a nominal plaintiff) the plea will be stricken out, and the release be ordered to be canceled. Hickey *v.* Burt, 7 Taunt. 48; 1 Chitty Plead. (16th Am. ed.) 689, n. (p); Innell *v.* Newman, 4 B. & Ald. 419. "But unless a very strong case of fraud be made out, the court will not control the legal power of a co-plaintiff to execute a release." 1 Chitty Plead. (16th Am. ed.) 689 n. (p.), *citing*

of this kind are either in abatement or in bar.[1] But in no case can the plea be used if the party suffers another continuance to intervene.[2] Nor is the plea permitted after judgment on demurrer or after verdict on issue in fact.[3] But a plea setting out matter which occurred before issue joined or plea filed, is not a plea *puis darrein continuance*, although the matter arose pending the suit.[4] But the filing of the plea, where it is proper, waives all prior pleas.[5] The form of pleas *puis darrein continuance* is closely scrutinized.[6] Great certainty is required, and a plea is bad which omits to state the date of the last continuance.[7] Where one of several defendants pleads new matter as to himself alone, the plaintiff may enter a *nolle prosequi* as to that defendant and pro-

Jones *v.* Herbert, 7 Taunt. 431; Johnson *v.* Holdsworth, 4 Dowl. 63; Hubert *v.* Piggott, 2 Dowl. 392; Chitty's Arch. Pr. (7th ed.) 299.

Bankruptcy of Plaintiff. Kinnaird *v.* Tarrant, 15 East 622; Biggs *v.* Cox, 4 B. & C. 920; 1 Chitty Plead. (16th Am. ed.) 690. But see Tanner *v.* Roberts, 1 Mo. 416. *Of defendant.* Lewis *v.* Shattuck, 4 Gray (Mass.) 572; 1 Chitty Plead. (16th Am. ed.) 690. Otherwise when offered after three years' delay. Sanford *v.* Sinclair, 3 Den. (N. Y.) 269.

Outlawry of Plaintiff. 1 Chitty Plead. (16th Am. ed.) 690.

Award on reference after issue. Storey *v.* Bloxam, 2 Esp. 504.

Payment. Herod *v.* Snyder, 61 Ind. 453.

Revocation of Authority, as when plaintiff's letters of administration have been revoked. Bul. N. P. 309.

Acquisition of Authority, as where one who is sued as executor *de son tort* defends on the ground of a subsequent grant of letters. Vaughan *v.* Browne, 2 Stra. 1106.

Accord and Satisfaction. Good *v.* Davis, Hempst. (U. S.) 16; 1 Chitty Plead. (16th Am. ed.) 690, n. (y); *citing* Watkinson *v.* Inglesby, 5 Johns. (N. Y.) 392; Bowne *v.* Joy, 9 Johns. (N. Y.) 221; Yeaton *v.* Lynn, 5 Pet. (U. S.) 231; Commercial Bank *v.* Love, 19 Wend. (N. Y.) 98.

1. Com. Dig. Abatement, 1 Chitty Plead. (16th Am. ed.) 690.

2. 3 Black. Com. 316; Gould Plead. (5th ed.) 346.

3. 3 Black. Com. 317; Gould Plead. (5th ed.) 347; Otis *v.* Currier, 17 N. H. 463.

4. Sadler *v.* Fisher, 3 Ala. 200; Clark *v.* Fox, 9 Dana (Ky.) 193. And see Moore *v.* Moore, 1 N. J. L. 363, to the effect that while in the old cases the plea of *actio non* referred to the time of plea pleaded, it now refers to the commencement of the suit.

5. Simonton *v.* Younge, 1 Strobh. (S. Car.) 17; Webb *v.* Steele, 13 N. H. 230; Culver *v.* Barney, 14 Wend. (N. Y.) 161; Lincoln *v.* Kreall, 26 Vt. 304. Spafford *v.* Woodruff, 2 McLean (U. S.) 191; Morse *v.* Small, 73 Me. 465; Scott *v.* Brokaw, 6 Blackf. (Ind.) 241; Den *v.* Sanderson, 18 N. J. L. 426; Sadler *v.* Fisher, 3 Ala. 200; Good *v.* Davis, Hempst. (U. S.) 16; Lacy *v.* Rockett, 11 Ala. 1002; Burton *v.* Hynson, 7 Ark. 502; Prather *v.* Ruddell, 8 Blackf. (Ind.) 393; McKeen *v.* Parker, 51 Me. 389; Waldo *v.* Mitchell, 24 N. H. 229; Adams *v.* Filer, 7 Wis. 306; 73 Am. Dec. 410. But a plea *puis darrein continuance*, when treated, not as a substitute, but as a supplemental plea, does not act as a waiver of former pleas. Thatcher *v.* Rockwell, 4 Colo. 375. Nor does it operate as a waiver after being stricken from the files. Dinet *v.* Pfirshing, 86 Ill. 83. And for the general effect of *puis darrein continuance* upon prior pleas, see Waterbury *v.* McMillan, 46 Miss. 635.

A plea *puis darrein continuance* of a discharge under the act abolishing imprisonment for debt, in *New York*, in certain cases, was not a waiver of a plea in bar before put in; and the plaintiff could not confess the plea and take judgment, but must proceed and try the former issues. Rayner *v.* Dyett, 2 Wend. (N. Y.) 300.

6. Gibson *v.* Bourland, 13 Ill. App. 352; Henry *v.* Porter, 29 Ala. 619.

7. Augusta *v.* Moulton, 75 Me. 551; Ross *v.* Nesbit, 7 Ill. 252; Vicary *v.* Moore, 2 Watts (Pa.) 451; 27 Am. Dec. 323.

ceed to trial as to the others.[1] A plea *puis darrein continuance* cannot be filed after verdict.[2]

(3) *Dilatory Plea.*—A dilatory plea is one in which the defendant seeks to delay the plaintiff's remedy by showing that there is an objection to the action founded on principles of remedial as distinguished from substantive law.[3] Such a plea therefore leaves untouched the question of the merits of the plaintiff's case, and relies solely upon the alleged breach by the plaintiff of some one of those well-defined rules of law which circumscribe the jurisdiction of courts, which limit the right of persons to sue and be sued, and which regulate the conduct of a suit from its beginning to its end. Dilatory pleas are accordingly divided into three classes: (1) Pleas to the jurisdiction of the court; (2) Pleas in abatement to the disability of one of the parties; (3) Pleas in abatement of the writ or declaration. The last two classes are pleas in abatement, and have the conclusion *quod billa cassetur.*

1. Beekman *v.* Peck, 5 Hill (N. Y.) 513. See also Wheelock *v.* Rice, 1 Dougl. (Mich.) 267.

2. Palmer *v.* Hutchins, 1 Cow. (N. Y.) 42. Nor can a judgment be pleaded which was obtained after the pleadings in the action were made up. Grier *v.* Comb, 1 Tayl. (N. Car.) 138. Other authorities on the use of this plea are Stockdale *v.* Young, 3 Strobh. (S. Car.) 501; Bowne *v.* Joy, 9 Johns. (N. Y.) 221; Leavitt *v.* School District No. 19, 78 Me. 574; White *v.* Judge, 47 Mich. 645.

It is as matter of discretion with the court to permit a defendant to plead *puis darrein continuance* matters which arose prior to the last continuance. Hosteter *v.* Kaufman, 11 S. & R. (Pa.) 146; Cummings *v.* Smith, 50 Me. 568; 79 Am. Dec. 629; Thomas *v.* Van Doren, 6 Mo. 201; Rangely *v.* Webster, 11 N. H. 299; Stevens *v.* Thompson, 15 N. H. 410; Morgan *v.* Dyer, 10 Johns. (N. Y.) 161; Lyon *v.* Marclay, 1 Watts (Pa.) 271; Nettles *v.* Swezea, 2 Mo. 100.

For the practice under the *Colorado* Code, see Whitsett *v.* Clayton, 5 Colo. 476.

It has been held that a modern practice act permitting the filing of additional pleas at any time before final judgment does not operate to abolish the common law rule governing pleas *puis darrein continuance.* Straight *v.* Hanchett, 23 Ill. App. 584. And in that State the plea may be filed at any time before trial. Robinson *v.* Burkell, 3 Ill. 278.

3. The following definitions of a dilatory plea have been given: One which goes to defeat the particular action brought, merely, and which does not answer as to the general right of the plaintiff. *Bouvier.*

One that resists the plaintiff's present right of recovery by interposing some temporary objection, as that the court has no jurisdiction, that the plaintiff lacks capacity to sue. *Anderson.*

Dilatory pleas are "such as tend merely to delay, or put off the suit." *Blackstone* (3 Com. 301).

Dilatory pleas are such as delay the plaintiff's remedy, by questioning, not the cause of action, but the propriety of the suit or the mode in which the remedy is sought. *Gould* (Pleading, 4th ed. 29). The definition given in the text is suggested because the definitions of BOUVIER and ANDERSON are unscientific, because BLACKSTONE's is incorrect, and because GOULD'S (although far better than the others) does not emphasize the principle which, it is submitted, constitutes the true distinction between dilatory pleas and pleas in bar—to-wit, that the former rely upon a defense deducible from remedial law, while the latter derive their significance from the appropriate principles of substantive law. That this is the substantial difference between them is further suggested by the character of those defenses which are pleadable either in abatement or in bar. They all have a double aspect, the one being the disability of the plaintiff to sue, the other being some circumstance

Pleas to the jurisdiction are not technically pleas in abatement. They have their proper conclusion *respondere non debet* or *si curia cognoscere velit.*[1]

(*a*) *Pleas to the Jurisdiction.*—The plea to the jurisdiction of the court stands first in the order of pleadings open to the defendant.[2] A difference between such a plea and a plea in abatement has already been noted.[3] Two other distinctions are of importance: it must be pleaded in person and, before the Hilary Rules, only half defense should be made.[4] A plea to the juris-

which constitutes an answer on the merits. Thus "alien enemy" is pleadable either in abatement or in bar. Harman *v.* Kingston, 3 Campb. 152. An alien enemy has no standing to sue—a dilatory defense. An alien enemy is so regarded by the law that no legal liability to him can exist during the war (1 Blackst. Com. 371) —a defense on the merits. So also of outlawry for felony. 1 Chitty Plead. (16th Am. ed.) 463. And of attainder. Co. Litt. 128 b; Facquire *v.* Kynaston, 2 Ld. Ray. 1249. *Compare* the rule that property in a stranger may be pleaded in replevin either in abatement or in bar. Presgrave *v.* Saunders, 1 Salk. 5. This is obviously a defense upon the merits. And it is also a dilatory defense in consequence of the rule peculiar to replevin that mere possession is not sufficient to sustain the action. Wilson *v.* Gray, 8 Watts (Pa.) 34.

1. See Steph. Plead. (9th Am. ed.) App. note (20); Moseley *v.* Hunter, 3 Ired. (N. Car.) 543.

2. The weight of authority has long designated the following order of pleading:

(1) To the jurisdiction of the court.
(2) To the disability of the person.
  (a) Of the plaintiff.
  (b) Of the defendant.
(3) To the count or declaration.
(4) To the writ.
  (a) To the form of the writ.
    1. Matter apparent on its face.
    2. Matter dehor.
  (b) To the action of the writ.
(5) To the action itself in bar thereof.

See 1 Chitty Plead. (16th Am. ed.) 456. "This, it is said, is the natural order of pleading, because each subsequent plea admits that there is no foundation for the former, and precludes the defendant from afterwards availing himself of the matter." Thus if the defendant plead in abatement of the writ he admits the plaintiff's right to sue. But pleading over does not give jurisdiction to a court which is totally without it. The lack of jurisdiction in such cases may be ground for nonsuit at the trial. Trevor *v.* Wall, 1 T. R. 151 (of an inferior court). But see Storm *v.* Worland, 19 Ind. 203. Or it may be given in evidence under the general issue. King *v.* Johnson, 6 East 583; Parker *v.* Elding, 1 East 352. It can in general be taken advantage of at any stage of the cause. Black *v.* Black, 34 Pa. St. 354. But although lack of jurisdiction may be taken advantage of by motion, etc., later in the proceeding, yet, as far as a technical plea to the jurisdiction is concerned, the defendant loses his right by failing to plead it in due time. See Peters *v.* Finney, 12 Smed. & M. (Miss.) 449. And see also Bliss *v.* Burnes, McCahon (Kan.) 91; and Girty *v.* Logan, 6 Bush (Ky.) 8. In *Arkansas* it was held that such a plea could be filed after calling for a bill of particulars. Watkins *v.* Brown, 5 Ark. 197. If issue in law is taken by demurrer on any plea of the first four orders the judgment, if adverse to the plea, will be *respondeat ouster* only; and therefore the defendant may in turn run through the entire series; being defeated on one issue, he resorts to another. But as soon as an issue in fact on a dilatory plea arises, the judgment rendered is final, and the defendant is not at liberty in that case, to resort to any other kind of plea. Steph. Plead. (9th Am. ed.) 431.

3. See *Supra*, this title, *Dilatory Plea.*

4. 1 Chitty Plead. (16th Am. ed.) 457. The effect of a plea in abatement is, indeed, to abate the writ; but this is incidental merely. But see Ingalls *v.* Richardson, 3 Met. (Mass.) 340; Osgood *v.* Thurston, 23 Pick. (Mass.) 110.

diction, like a plea in abatement, should be verified by affidavit.[1] This plea is the proper method of excepting to the jurisdiction in all cases. Thus it is appropriate when a local action has been brought in the wrong forum.[2] But the real defendant in ejectment, having agreed to enter into the consent rule and plead the general issue, can plead to the jurisdiction only by leave of court.[3] Pleas of personal privilege are in reality pleas to the jurisdiction,[4] as in the case of an attorney, or a university scholar sued out the proper court.[5]

A plea to the jurisdiction must show facts sufficient to take the case out of the jurisdiction, and must show in addition that there is some other court which has jurisdiction.[6] For if there be no other place of trial that fact gives the court jurisdiction.[7] Otherwise of a court the jurisdiction of which is definitely circumscribed by statute.[8] If the plaintiff thinks the plea informal or substantially insufficient he should demur. If the decision is adverse to the plea a *respondeat ouster* is awarded.[9]

(*b*) *Pleas to the Disability of the Parties.*—See ABATEMENT, vol. 1, p. 6.

(*c*) *Pleas in Abatement of the Writ or Declaration.*—See ABATEMENT, vol. 1, p. 6.

(4) *Pleas to the Action*—(*a*) **Traverse.**—A traverse is a denial of one or more allegations in the pleading, adversely alleged.[10] Traverses are of three kinds:[11] *specific*, *general* and *special*.

1. 1 Chitty Plead. (16th Am. ed.) 462.

2. That the cause of action accrued in a jurisdiction into which *breve domini regis non currit.* Gilb. Hist. C. P. 191; Lampley *v.* Thomas, 1 Wils. 206; Grant *v.* Bagge, 3 East 128; Doe *dem* Morton *v.* Roe, 10 East 523; Goodright *v.* Sheuffil, 2 Ld. Ray. 1418; Barker *v.* Wish, 1 Salk. 56.

3. 1 Chitty Plead. (16th Am. ed.) 460; Williams *dem* Johnson *v.* Keene, 1 Bl. 197; Hatch *v.* Cannon, 3 Wils. 51.

4. 1 Chitty Plead. (16th Am. ed.) 460. They conclude, "whether the court ought to have further conusance of the suit." Wilkes *v.* Williams, 8 T. R. 631.

5. 1 Chitty Plead. (16th Am. ed.) 460; *citing* also King *v.* Coit, 4 Day (Conn.) 129.

6. Heilman *v.* Martin, 2 Ark. 158; Fields *v.* Walker, 23 Ala. 155; Rea *v.* Hayden, 3 Mass. 24; Lawrence *v.* Smith, 5 Mass. 362; Jones *v.* Winchester, 6 N. H. 497; Dumoussay *v.* Delevit, 3 Har. & M. (Md.) 151. And see Teasdale *v.* The Rambler, Bee Adm. 9.

7. Rex *v.* Johnson, 6 East 587 n.; Mostyn *v.* Fabrigas, Cowp. 172, 1 S. L. C. 1027; Davis *v.* Stringer, Carth. 335; R. Co. *v.* Tapster, 1 G. & D. 657.

8. In the case of courts of a limited jurisdiction it is often said that the plea to the jurisdiction is a plea in bar. Smith *v.* McCleod, 1 Cranch (C. C.) 43.

9. Vin. Abr. Courts, Jurisdiction, n. a; Com. Dig. Abatement, I, 14; 1 Chitty Plead. (16th Am. ed.) 462.

For form of demurrer see R. Co. *v.* Tapster, 1 G. & D. 657.

In *Illinois* it was held that a demurrer should not be filed to a defective plea to the jurisdiction. It should be set down for hearing, when its sufficiency will be considered. Lester *v.* Stevens, 29 Ill. 155.

10. "There is no distinction between traverses and denials; they are the same in substance. Lambert *v.* Strooth-er, Willes 224. Any pleading by which the truth of the opponent's allegation is disputed is termed a pleading by way of traverse or denial." 1 Chitty Plead. (16th Am. ed.) 632.

11. Chitty classes the traverse which denies a specific fact under the head of general traverses. This would seem to be a contradiction in terms. See 1 Chitty Plead. (16th Am. ed.) 632.

1. *Specific Traverse.*—This form of denial is used when a pleader desires to deny a particular fact pleaded by his adversary. Such a traverse should be used to deny only those facts which are not covered by the broader denial of the general issue, for it is a rule that a plea which amounts to the general issue should be so pleaded.[1]

2. *General Traverse*—This is of two forms, the general issue in the plea, and the replication *de injuria* in the replication. The effect of such a traverse is to deny all or almost all of the material allegations in the pleading to which it is opposed.

a. General Issue—aa. Its Form in the Several Actions.—This traverse has a form which varies with each action, but in any given action it is always the same. In debt on a simple contract it is *nil debet;*[2] in debt on a specialty it is *non est factum;*[3] in detinue it is *non detinet;*[4] in trover, trespass and trespass on the case it is not guilty;[5] in replevin it is *non cepit;*[6] and in assumpsit it is *non-assumpsit.*[7] The scope of the denial of each of these

1. Steph. Plead. (9th Am. ed.) 418. Thus where trespass was brought for entering plaintiff's garden, a specific traverse to the effect that the plaintiff had no garden was held bad on demurrer. Year Book, 10 Hen. VI, 16; Doct. Pl. 42, *citing* 22 Hen. VI 37. This principle of course applies to pleas which purport to confess and avoid, but which in reality amount to traverses. The application of the rule to them will be considered under the head general issue.

General Requisites.—For the general requisites of such traverses see *infra*, these titles, *Requisites of Pleading in General, Materiality, Singleness, Certainty, Directness, Consistency, Technical Requisites.*

2. For this the Hilary Rules substituted the plea never indebted of which the following is the form: "And the said defendant by —— his attorney, says that he never was indebted in manner and form as in the declaration alleged, and of this he puts himself upon the country."

3. The same form is used as a plea to the action of covenant, but in that case it seems to partake of the nature of a specific traverse rather than of the general issue—its regularity of form being explained by reference to the stereotyped form of that action. Thus in covenant *non est factum* denies the existence of a debt only indirectly; its direct effect is to deny the deed. Hence Chitty, Tidd and others deny that there exists any general issue in covenant broken. See Tidd 593; 1 Chitty Plead. (16th Am. ed.) 482; and the American editor's note. Gould Plead. (5th ed.) 284.

4. "And the said defendant, by —— his attorney, says that he does not detain the said goods and chattels [or as the case may be] in the said declaration specified, or any part thereof, in manner and form as the said plaintiff hath above complained. And of this the said defendant puts himself upon the country."

5. "And the said defendant, by ——, his attorney, says, that he is not guilty of the said trespasses [or "the premises" if the action be case] above laid to his charge, or any part thereof in manner and form as the said plaintiff hath above complained, and of this the said defendant puts himself upon the country."

6. "And the said defendant, by ——, his attorney, says that he did not take the said goods and chattels [or as the case may be] in the said declaration mentioned, or any of them, in manner and form as the said plaintiff hath above complained. And of this the said defendant puts himself upon the country."

7. "And the said defendant, by ——, his attorney, says, that he did not undertake or promise in manner and form as the said plaintiff hath above complained. And of this the said defendant puts himself upon the country."

Two other forms of general issue

forms determines the issue (as is obviously the case with all traverses), and the issue determines the relevancy of evidence. It is therefore of the greatest importance to examine the scope of each general issue both at the common law and also as modified and restricted by the Hilary Rules.[1]

bb. Scope in the Several Actions.[2]—*(a) Debt on Simple Contract*—(See also DEBT (Action of), vol. 5, p. 165)—*At the Common Law.*—*Nil debet*, being in the present tense, operates as a denial that the defendant owes the debt at the time of the pleading.[3] It is applicable, therefore, to any case in which the defense consists of the denial of an existing debt. Hence, matter in confession and avoidance, which tends to admit the debt and excuse payment can be given in evidence under the traverse.[4] But the statute of limitations must be pleaded.[5]

After Hilary Rules.[6]—The form never indebted[7] being substi-

may be mentioned. That in Formedon "simply denies the gift in tail to have been made in manner and form as alleged." Steph. Plead. (9th Am. ed.) 162 (note); Dowland *v.* Slade, 5 East 289. In *quare impedit* the general issue is adapted only to the case in which the defendant denies that he obstructed the presentation. Steph. Plead. (9th Am. ed.) 162 (note).

1. The Hilary Rules not being in force in the *United States*, the scope of the general issues, where special pleading survives, is determined (subject to local modifications) by the state of the law before those rules, and it is accordingly under that head that the American authorities are cited.

2. The "action of account" is omitted from the list, as in it there is no general issue, nor is it noticed by the Hilary Rules. See 1 Chitty Plead. (16 Am. ed.) 516. The defendant may plead infancy, or that he was not bailiff or receiver, or that he has accounted or a release, or the bar of the statute. But matters in excuse, as distinguished from discharge, must be pleaded before the auditors. Godfrey *v.* Saunders, 3 Wils. 78.

3. Fidler *v.* Hershey, 90 Pa. St. 363. For an able sketch of the differentiation of the pleas of *nil debet* and *non* assumpsit and of the development of the law relating to them, see opinion of Selden, J., in McKyring *v.* Bull, 16 N. Y. 298, 69 Am. Dec. 696.

4. Steph. Plead. (9th Am. ed.) 162; 1 Chitty Plead. (7th Am. ed.) 517. Among the defenses permitted under *nil debet* are payment and release. Fidler *v.* Hershey, 90 Pa. St. 363; Linds *v.* Gardner, 1 Cranch (U. S.) 343. It was the practice to plead a tender specially, and the same was true of a set-off. Wager of law had to be pleaded; but this form of trial was abolished by 3 and 4 Wm. IV, ch. 42, § 13. See *supra*, this title, *Modes of Trial.*

5. 1 Chitty Plead. (7th Am. ed.) 517. It was at one time suggested that the statute could be set up under *nil debet* and in penal actions this was permitted (per LAWRENCE, J., in 2 East 336), but the better practice both in debt and assumpsit was as is stated above.

6. "The plea of *nil debet* shall not be allowed in any action. In actions of debt on simple contract, other than on bills of exchange and promissory notes, the defendant may plead, that 'he was never indebted in manner and form as in the declaration alleged,' and such plea shall have the same operation as the plea of *non assumpsit in indebitatus assumpsit;* and all matters in confession and avoidance shall be pleaded specially, as above directed in actions of assumpsit.

In other actions of debt, in which the plea of *nil debet* has been hitherto allowed, including those on bills of exchange and promissory notes, the defendant shall deny specially some particular matter of fact alleged in the declaration, or plead specially in confession and avoidance." Gen. Reg. Hil. T., 4 Wm. IV.

7. The plea must follow the language prescribed by the rule. Pleas "that the defendant never did owe" and "that the defendant never did

tuted for *nil debet*, the issue was in consequence greatly restricted. The operation of this plea was expressly identical with *non-assumpsit* in *indebitatus assumpsit* as modified by the Rules.[1] The form of the count determines whether the ground of the action is the obligation created by the delivery of the goods or the implied promise to pay for them.[2]

(*b*) *Debt on Specialty and Covenant—At Common Law.—Non est factum* denies that the deed mentioned in the declaration is the deed of the defendant.[3] Under this plea the defendant can prove that he never executed the deed in point of fact, or that it is void in law,[4] as distinguished from being merely voidable. Matter which makes the deed voidable must be specially pleaded.[5]

promise" are bad on special demurrer. Smedeley *v.* Joyce, 2 Cr. M. & R. 721; King *v.* Myers, 5. Dowl. 686.

In Gardner *v.* Alexander, 3 Dowl. 146, an application was made to the court in an action for goods bargained and sold, for leave to plead special conditions with regard to the shipping and delivery of the goods. The motion was refused, the court declaring that evidence of the special contract might be given under the general issue.

Broomfield *v.* Smith, 1 M. & W. 542, was an action of debt for goods sold and delivered. Under the plea of *nunquam indebitatus* the court held that the defendant could prove that the goods had been sold on a credit which had not yet expired. The theory upon which this case proceeds is that as the action was based upon a promise implied by law, and as the law will not imply a promise before it is necessary (*i. e.*, until the money comes due) the defendant at any time before that period can obviously deny that an obligation exists. Where, however, the obligation sued upon arises (as where the count is in debt) upon the delivery of the goods, the defendant must plead specially.

When the defense is that no debt has arisen, obviously *nunquam indebitatus* is the proper plea. Where the circumstances are such that the law (if it may be so said) does not think it worth while to imply a promise, a case of this kind arises. Thus in Bussey *v.* Barnett, 9 M. & W. 312, it was held that under the plea of *nunquam indebitatus* in an action for goods sold and delivered, it was permissible for the defendant to prove a cash payment upon delivery of the goods. "In this case," said LORD ABINGER, "the goods were not delivered upon a contract out of which a debt arose; there was no promise to pay, but immediate payment."

1. 1 Chitty Plead. (16th Am. ed.) 511. Therefore the decisions here cited are applicable to that plea, *q. v. infra.*

2. See Smith *v.* Webb, 16 Ill. 105. An illustration of the distinction occurs in the case of goods sold on credit, the defense being that the credit has not yet expired. Here there exists a debt from the fact of the delivery, although it is *solvendum in futuro.* But there is no implied promise to pay until the money is due, and therefore, if the action is based on the promise, the general issue is proper. This distinction was overlooked in Edmunds *v.* Harris, 2 Ad. & El. 414, but was subsequently recognized in Broomfield *v.* Smith, 1 M. & W. 542.

3. Steph. Plead. (9th Am.ed.) 162. See *supra*, p. 522 note (3).

4. As, for example, where the obligor or covenantor was at the time of execution a *feme covert* or a lunatic. Com. Dig. Pleader, Steph. Plead. (9th Am. ed.) 162; Yates *v.* Boen, 2 Stra. 7104. Or where the bond has been altered or spoliated. Pigot's case, 11 Rep. 26 b.

5. Collins *v.* Blantern, 2 Wils. 347. In this case the bond appeared to have been given to compound a felony. See able opinion by WILMOT, C. J.

For the distinction between void and voidable, see Steph. Plead. (9th Am. ed.) 162, note, *citing* Whelpdale's case, 2 Reps. 119 a; 2 Inst. 483; Darby *v.* Boucher, 1 Salk. 279; Thompson *v.* Leech, 2 Salk. 675; Zouch *v.* Parsons, 3 Burr, 1805; Lord Bernard *v.* Saul, 1 Stra. 498; Gibbs *v.* Merril, 3 Taunt. 307; Baylis *v.* Dinely, 3 M. & W. 477; Keane *v.* Boycott, 2 H. Bl. 515; Edwards *v.* Brown, 1 Tyr. Rep. 281; Col-

So also illegality arising from the prohibition of an act of Parliament or other statute must be pleaded: evidence of it is inadmissible under *non est factum*.[1]

After Hilary Rules.—The provision of the Rules is as follows: "In debt on specialty[2] or covenant, the plea of *non est factum* shall operate as a denial of the execution of the deed, in point of fact only, and all other defenses shall be specially pleaded, including matters which make the deed absolutely void, as well as those which make it voidable." It was of some importance before the Rules to distinguish between the case in which the deed was the foundation and that in which it was only the inducement to the action, for in the latter case *nil debet* was a good plea.[3] But

ton *v.* Goodridge, 2 W. Bl. 1108; Ferguson *v.* Spring, 1 Ad. & El. 576; Mazzinghi *v.* Stephenson, 1 Campt. 291; Harmer *v.* Rowe, 2 Chit. Rep. 334. In some States it is held that *non est factum* puts in issue only the fact of execution. People *v.* Rowland, 5 Barb. (N. Y.) 449; Utter *v.* Vance, 7 Blackf. (Ind.) 514; Chambers *v.* Games, 2 Greene (Iowa) 320. This coincides with the restriction imposed by the Hilary Rules. See also DEBT (ACTION OF) vol. 5, p. 175.

1. Steph. Plead. (9th Am. ed.) 162, note. Whelpdale's case, 5 Reps. 109 a; Mestayer *v.* Biggs, 4 Tyr. 471; Massey *v.* Nanney, 3 Bing. N. C. 480.

Where a deed is only inducement to the action and matter of fact is its foundation *nil debet* is a good plea. 1 Chitty Plead. (16th Am. ed.) 511 n.; United States *v.* Cumpton, 3 McLean (U. S.) 163; Love *v.* Kidwell, 4 Blackf. (Ind.) 535; Crigler *v.* Quarles, 10 Mo. 324; Hyatt *v.* Robinson, 15 Ohio 372; Matthews *v.* Redwine, 23 Miss. 233; Boynton *v.* Reynolds, 3 Mo. 79; Gates *v.* Wheeler, 2 Hill (N. Y.) 232; Bullis *v.* Giddens, 8 Johns. (N. Y.) 82; King *v.* Ramsay, 13 Ill. 619; Trimble *v.* State, 4 Blackf. (Ind.) 435.

2. **Debt on Records.**—To debt on a record where the defendant wishes to deny the existence of the record, *nul tiel record* is the proper plea. See DEBT (ACTION OF), vol. 5, p. 165. At common law, a plea of payment to an action on a record was bad, as payment is a matter *in pais*. The plea was sanctioned by 4 Ann. ch. 16, § 12, in cases where payment has been in fact co-extensive with the judgment. It is, by that act, a complete defense or none at all. Peploe *v.* Galliers, 4 Moore 165; 1 Chitty Plead. (16th Am. ed.) 512. But the act does not authorize a plea of accord and satisfaction. See, however, Crawford *v.* Ellison, 1 Brev. (S. Car.) 378; and Kershaw *v.* Robinson, 1 Brev. (S. Car.) 380; and *nil debet* is an insufficient plea where the record is the foundation of the action.

Debt on a Judgment.—To debt on judgment of a sister State *nil debet* is a bad plea. Mills *v.* Duryee, 7 Cranch (U. S.) 481; St. Albans *v.* Bush, 4 Vt. 58; 23 Am. Dec. 246; Newcomb *v.* Peck, 17 Vt. 302; 44 Am. Dec. 340; Clarke *v.* Day, 2 Leigh. (Va.) 172; Spencer *v.* Brockway, 1 Ohio 260, 13 Am. Dec. 615; Goodrich *v.* Jenkins, 6 Ohio 43; Gulick *v.* Loder, 13 N. J. L. 68; Larming *v.* Shute, 2 South. 778; Chipps *v.* Yancey, 1 Ill. 19.

A contrary doctrine may be derived from the following decisions: Clark *v.* Mann, 33 Me. 268; Thurber *v.* Blackburne, 1 N. H. 242; Judkins *v.* Union Mut. F. Ins. Co., 37 N. H. 470; Wright *v.* Boynton, 37 N. H. 9; 72 Am. Dec. 319; Hall *v.* Williams, 6 Pick. (Mass.) 247, 17 Am. Dec. 356; M'Rae *v.* Mattoon, 13 Pick. (Mass.) 53; Curtis *v.* Gibbe, 2 N. J. L. 290; Starbuck *v* Murray, 5 Wend. (N. Y.) 148; 21 Am. Dec. 172.

But to debt on a foreign judgment *nil debet* is a good plea. Williams *v.* Preston, 3 J. J. Marsh. (Ky.) 600; 20 Am. Dec. 179.

For other authorities relating to debt on judgments, see DEBT (ACTION OF) vol. 5, p. 174.

Debt on Statutes.—In this action *nil debet* is the proper plea, although not guilty has been sustained. Burnham *v.* Webster, 5 Mass. 270; Stilson *v.* Tobey, 2 Mass. 521. Bac. Abr. Plus I.; Com. Dig. *Pleader* 2, § 11, 17. See Jones *v.* Williams, 4 M. & W. 375; Earl Spencer *v.* Swannell, 3 M. & W. 154; Faulkner *v.* Chevell, Ad. & El. 213.

3. See *supra*, p. 508 note (3).

under the above provisions the defendant must plead specially every defense except the denial of the fact of execution.[1]

(c) *Detinue*—(See also DETINUE, vol. 5, p. 651)—*At Common Law.*—*Non detinet* operates as a denial of the detainer and is also applicable to the case where the defendant wishes to deny the plaintiff's property. For as the declaration charges a detainer of the plaintiff's goods the defendant is obviously discharged from liability where the goods withheld are not the goods of the plaintiff.[2] But a pledge of the goods must be pleaded specially,[3] and the same rule applies to all liens.[4] Evidence of a gift from the plaintiff is, however, admissible under *non detinet.*[5] The allegation of bailment or finding is formal merely, and cannot be traversed.[6]

After Hilary Rules.[7]—The language of the Rules, clear enough in itself, was strictly construed by the courts.[8] The proper plea by which to deny the plaintiff's property in the goods is the specific traverse "not possessed," and under it the defendant may give in evidence any matter which tends to negative the plaintiff's title to maintain the action.[9] But it seems that a lien must be specially pleaded.[10] To this effect are the authorities cited in

1. 1 Chitty Plead. (16th Am. ed.) 511; Grand Chute *v.* Winegar, 15 Wall. (U. S.) 355.

2. Chitty Plead. (7th Am. ed.) 525.

3. Co. Litt. 283 a. See opinion of BARON PARKE. Richards *v.* Frankum, 6 M. & W. 420.

4. Philips *v.* Robinson, 4 Bing. 106, opinion of GASELEE, J.

5. Co. Litt. 283 a.

6. Chitty Plead. (7th Am. ed.) 525; Gledstane *v.* Hewitt, 1 C. & J. 565.

By Executors or Administrators.—The defendant may, in addition to the usual defenses, deny the representative character of the plaintiff. This, if not specifically denied, is admitted. The rule is the same in assumpsit. M'Kimm *v.* Riddle, 2 Dall. (Pa.) 100; Champlin *v.* Tilley, 3 Day (Conn.) 303. But where it is part of the plaintiff's case to prove his representative character, as where he sues in trover when he has never had actual possession, then a defect in the letters, etc., will be fatal on *non detinet.* 1 Chitty Plead. (16th Am. ed.) 517; Hunt *v.* Stevens, 3 Taunt. 113.

Against Executors or Administrators.—In addition to the other defenses, the defendant may avail himself of the plea *ne unques executor* or *administrator;* or that he has no assets. See ADMINISTRATOR AND EXECUTOR, vol. 7, p. 165.

Against Heir or Devisee.—Here the defendant may avail himself of all defenses which would have been valid against the ancestor or devisor, and may in addition deny either the representative character or that he took anything by descent or devise. Com. Dig. Pleader 2 E. 3. Or a devisee may plead that the debt did not accrue during the life of the devisor. 1 Chitty Plead. (17th Am. ed.) 518. Or the defendant may plead in abatement the non-joinder of other heirs who (by statute) took from the ancestor. St. Mary's Church *v.* Wallace, 10 N. J. L. 311.

7. "The plea of *non detinet* shall operate as a denial of the detention of the goods by the defendant, but not of the plaintiff's property therein; and no other defense than such denial shall be admissible under that plea." Gen. Reg. Hil. T, 4 Wm. IV.

8. Richards *v.* Frankum, 6 M. & W. 420, where it was held that evidence of the assignment of the note in suit did not support the plea of the general issue.

9. Mason *v.* Farnell, 12 M. & W. 674.

10. Mason *v.* Farnell, 12 M. & W. 674. See Richards *v.* Frankum, 6 M. & W. 420.

In the former case PARKE, B., in delivering the judgment of the court, says: "There is no doubt that in the action of trover the court of common pleas, in Owen *v.* Knight, 4 New Cases 54, 5 Scott 307, have decided that, under the plea of not possessed, the defendant may give in evidence a lien, on the ground that this plea denies the plain-

the note, but as a lien operates directly to defeat the plaintiff's right to sue and only indirectly to deny the detainer, it would seem proper to give such a defense in evidence under "not possessed." And this view is sustained by respectable authority.[1] The bailment or finding alleged in the declaration is not traversable.[2]

(*d*) *Trover—At Common Law.*—The general issue in trover is exceedingly extensive in its scope, and it has long been the practice to plead specially only in the case of the statute of limitations or of a release.[3] Thus, bankruptcy of the plaintiff, where it was a defense,[4] could be given in evidence under not guilty. But it seems that a defendant can, if he so desires, plead specially anything which admits the property and the conversion and avoids

tiff's right to the immediate possession of the goods, as well as his property in them; and in the case of White *v.* Teal, 12 Ad. & E. 106, 4 P. & D. 43, the court of Queen's Bench held on similar grounds that such a defense was not admissible under not guilty. It is proper to abide by the authority of these decisions, in the action of trover, though, no doubt, plausible reasons may be assigned for saying that the proper plea on which such defense as a lien or the like may be made, is the plea of not guilty, by which the conversion is denied; but we are of opinion that, in the action of detinue, this plea of not possessed cannot have the same effect. In this form of action we are not embarrassed with the difficulty which exists in the action of trover founded on conversion, which is always a wrongful act and cannot, therefore, be confessed and avoided. The detainer, which alone is in issue under *non detinet*, may be lawful or unlawful, and therefore it may be denied altogether or may be admitted and justified as a lawful act; and this we find supported by the older authorities." . . . "The plea of not possessed we think, on these authorities—Co. Litt. 283 a; Isack *v.* Clarke, 1 Roll. R. 126; 2 Buist. 306, puts only the property of the plaintiff in issue; and if, therefore, the plaintiff has such a property as will enable him to maintain detinue, it is enough."

It seems clear, however, that the view of the learned judge is erroneous. A detainer, like a conversion, must be a wrongful act, and, as such, cannot be justified. Its essence is the fact that the defendant holds adversely, as was decided, subsequently to Mason *v.* Farnell, in Clements *v.* Flight, 16 M. & W. 42. It is, on principle, as impossible to confess a detainer and then justify it, as it is to confess and justify a conversion. See *infra*, p. 527 note (2). An examination of the authorities reveals the fact that so-called pleas in confession and excuse in detinue either amount to the general issue or disclose matter in discharge.

1. BARON PARKE himself admitted evidence of a lien under "not possessed," in Lane *v.* Tewson, 1 Gale & Dav. 584, and his action was sustained in the Queen's Bench.

2. 1 Chitty Plead. (17th Am. ed.) 516; Walker *v.* Jones, 2 Cr. & M. 672.

Nature of a Detainer.—If detainer means detention in fact, then *tender* is a good plea in detinue. If, however, it means a wrongful withholding, tender would be bad as amounting to the general issue—for its effect is to deny that the holding is wrongful. After a period of doubt on this point the latter view was sustained in Clements *v.* Flight, 8 Law Times. 166; 16 M. & W. 42. This was an action of detinue for papers and scrip certificates left by way of pledge for money advanced. The defendant pleaded a tender, to which the plaintiff demurred, and the court gave him judgment on the ground that since a detainer means not only a holding of the goods, but a wrongful withholding of them, a plea of tender is nothing more than an argumentative *non detinet*.

3. 1 Chitty Plead. (7th Am. ed.) 536. In Hawley *v.* Peacock, 2 Campb. 558, there is a *dictum* of LORD ELLENBOROUGH to the effect that a release in trover must be specially pleaded. The language used is not entirely clear; but the statement, if such is its import, is not law. See 1 Chitty Plead. (7th Am. ed.) 536 n. (g).

4. See Parker *v.* Norton, 6 T. R. 695.

the latter.[1] If trover be brought upon the possession of an intestate, the defendant cannot, under not guilty, give in evidence a will and an executor; he should plead specially.[2] But if it be brought upon the possession of the administrator, the defendant may set up his defense under the general issue. And if an executor brings trover upon his testator's possession, not guilty pleaded admits that the plaintiff is executor, and absolves him from proving his representative capacity.[3] If the executor declares for property of which he has had actual possession, of course he need not show title in himself to make a *prima facie* case. But if he declares upon his constructive possession as executor, and omits to name himself as executor, he must prove his executorship, for not guilty does not admit it.[4]

After Hilary Rules.—The Hilary Rules, treating trover as an action on the case, subjected it to this general regulation: That "in all actions on the case, the plea of not guilty shall operate as a denial only of the breach of duty or wrongful act alleged to have been committed by the defendant, and no other defense than such denial shall be admissible under that plea. All other pleas in demurrer." Examples of the precedents referred to may be found in the following: Ward *v.* Blunt, Cro. Eliz. 147; Warner *v.* Wainsford, Hob. 127; Aylesworth *v.* Harrison, Winch. 20; Rex *v.* Rotham, 1 Freem. 39; Whittlesey *v.* Wolcott, 2 Day (Conn.) 431. Such sweeping statements as those in Kennedy *v.* Strong may be commended as introducing a desirable practice; but they must be admitted to be opposed to the principles of scientific pleading. Matter in discharge ought to be pleaded, although it is equally clear that so-called matter of excuse ought not. Considerations of form dictate the former observation, and a due regard for principles of substantive law the latter: it is idle to set out on the record, in the form of a plea in excuse, matter which is either a denial in fact or no answer at all. This is illustrated by the decision of LORD HOLT in Kenicot *v.* Bogan, Yelv. 199, which (with deference to so eminent an authority) is clearly erroneous. See 2nd App. Steph. Plead. (9th Am. ed.).

1. 1 Chitty Plead. (7th Am. ed.) 536; Com. Dig. Pleader, E. 14. It is obviously incorrect to speak, as Chitty does, of justifying a conversion: the conversion, *ex vi termini*, must be unjustifiable. This is pointed out in the note to Yelverton 174 (a), where the true rule is laid down—viz., that there cannot be in trover any special plea in excuse, but only in discharge. Thus a release may be pleaded; so may accord, arbitrament and award. Former recovery (whether in trover or in a concurrent remedy), the bar of the statute, bankruptcy and outlawry. And see Markham's case, 3 Leon. 205. But see Kennedy *v.* Strong, 10 Johns. (N. Y.) 291. In that case the defendant pleaded that he sold the goods in question on commission, and that he was discharged under the Insolvent Debtor's act. The court on special demurrer decided that the plea was double, and that it was also bad as amounting to the general issue. "Though the old books contain numerous precedents of special pleas in trover, they are deservedly discountenanced in modern times, as leading to unnecessary expense and troublesome prolixity. The defendant could avail himself, under the general issue, of the matter pleaded; and though a special plea in trover was admitted in the late case of Webb *v.* Fox, 7 T. R. 391, yet LORD KENYON, who censured the plea, said it would have been bad on special demurrer." Examples of the precedents referred to may be found in the following: Ward *v.* Blunt, Cro. Eliz. 147; Warner *v.* Wainsford, Hob. 127; Aylesworth *v.* Harrison, Winch. 20; Rex *v.* Rotham, 1 Freem. 39; Whittlesey *v.* Wolcott, 2 Day (Conn.) 431. Such sweeping statements as those in Kennedy *v.* Strong may be commended as introducing a desirable practice; but they must be admitted to be opposed to the principles of scientific pleading. Matter in discharge ought to be pleaded, although it is equally clear that so-called matter of excuse ought not. Considerations of form dictate the former observation, and a due regard for principles of substantive law the latter: it is idle to set out on the record, in the form of a plea in excuse, matter which is either a denial in fact or no answer at all. This is illustrated by the decision of LORD HOLT in Kenicot *v.* Bogan, Yelv. 199, which (with deference to so eminent an authority) is clearly erroneous. See 2nd App. Steph. Plead. (9th Am. ed.).

2. 2 Saunders Plead. (5th Am. ed.) 1142.

3. For here he must necessarily describe himself as executor, and make profert of the letters testamentary, and these averments are admitted by not guilty. Thynne *v.* Protheroe, 2 M. & S. 553; Hunt *v.* Stevens, 2 Taunt. 113.

4. See Blainfield *v.* March, 7 Mod. 141.

denial shall take issue on some particular matter of fact alleged in the declaration."[1] Hence, not guilty denies only the conversion.[2] Conversion means a wrongful conversion and not the so-called "conversion in fact."[3] If the defendant wished to deny the plaintiff's property he must use the specific traverse not possessed; by pleading not guilty he admitted the plaintiff's property as part of the inducement.[4] Accordingly, it was decided that a lien, as being in effect a denial of the plaintiff's possession, must be given in evidence under not possessed.[5] And it was held that where the plaintiff's goods in the possession of X were sold under an execution against X, the defendant might prove under not

1. Gen. Reg. Hil. T. 4 Wm. IV. 1.

2. White *v.* Teale, 12 Ad. & El. 106.

3. Chitty (1 Chitty Plead., 16th Am. ed. 530) says that the plea puts in issue a conversion in fact and not merely a wrongful conversion, and he bases his statement on Stancliffe *v.* Hardwicke, 2 Cr. M. & R. 1. But this case was overruled in Whitmore *v.* Green, 13 M. & W. 107 (per PARKE B.), and it was also repudiated in Kynaston *v.* Crouch, 14 M. & W. 266. The law was finally settled, as stated in the text, in the case of Young *v.* Cooper, 6 Exch. Reps. 259. In that case trover was brought by the assignees of a bankrupt. The defendant pleaded that he had recovered a judgment against the bankrupt and that the goods had been taken and sold by the sheriff in execution thereon in part satisfaction of the debt. Verification. There was a special demurrer, and upon it the court gave judgment for the plaintiff. In support of the demurrer it was argued that as a conversion is a tortious act, it therefore cannot be justified; so that either this plea was no defense at all or it was an argumentative denial of the conversion; *citing* Agar *v.* Lisle, Hob. 187; Ascue *v.* Sanderson. Cro. Eliz, 433, and Hartford *v.* Jones, 1 Ld. Raym. 393. This being the state of the law before the Hilary Rules, it was further argued that those Rules did not alter the effect of the plea of not guilty. It still operated as a denial of the conversion, which, however, must as ever be a tortious act and not, for example, a mere refusal to deliver up goods—*citing* the amended view of the law set forth in the exchequer since the decision in Stancliffe *v.* Hardwick, 2 C. M. & R. See Whitmore *v.* Green, 13 M. &. W. 107. The court agreed with this argument, BARON PARKE saying, "I think that the plea is bad. We must abide by our amended view of the law which we adopted since the case of Stancliffe *v.* Hardwick. We have, since that decision, come to the conclusion that the term "conversion" used in the rule in question, means a wrongful conversion. The rule says that the plea of not guilty shall operate as a denial of the conversion only, and not of the plaintiff's title. It then goes on to direct that all matters in confession and avoidance shall be specially pleaded, *i. e.*, such matters as can be properly pleaded as such. But according to the preceding view of this rule, the present plea does not set up such a defense. The plea, therefore, cannot be supported, and the plaintiffs are entitled to judgment."

A plea denying the plaintiff's property means property as against the defendant. Nicolls *v.* Bastard, 2 C. M. & R. 659.

4. In White *v.* Teale 9 L. J. Reps., Q. B. 377. The action was trover and the plea not guilty. The defendant on the trial offered to prove that the goods in question were deposited as security for an unpaid board bill. LORD DENMAN refused the evidence and the court of Queen's Bench sustained him. The ground of the decision was that since the Hilary Rules the plea of not guilty denies the conversion but admits the property. Since a lien is inconsistent with the allegation of property, it must be given in evidence under "not possessed." To permit the proof of it under not guilty would be to allow a defendant to contradict in his evidence what he had admitted in his pleadings.

5. In Owen *v.* Knight, 4 Bing. N. C. 54, the action was trover for the conversion of a lease. The defendant pleaded that the plaintiff was not possessed, and

possessed that the plaintiff acquiesced in the sale.[1] Not guilty and not possessed seem to cover all defenses except matter in *discharge*. Such matter should be pleaded in confession and avoidance as before the rules.[2]

(*e*) *Trespass—At Common Law.*—Under the general issue, no matter whether the injury complained of relates to person or property, the defendant can give in evidence matter which operates as a direct denial of the doing of the act alleged.[3] So also when the act in question was in fact done, but the defendant wishes to prove that he was a passive agent in the hands of a superior power, he can offer evidence of such a defense under the general issue.[4] But if the defendant is *prima facie* a trespasser

upon the trial proved that the indenture had been deposited to secure an advance of money. The verdict having been found for the defendant, the court refused a new trial on the ground that a lien, which is inconsistent, necessarily, with the plaintiff's right of immediate possession, might well be given in evidence upon the specific traverse "not possessed."

It would follow logically from this decision that not possessed is the only plea under which a lien can be given in evidence; for a plea in confession in avoidance setting up a lien would amount to an argumentative traverse. The very point arose in Dorrington *v.* Carter, 1 Exch. 566, where trover was brought for goods and chattels. Plea that the defendant had a lien upon them to secure the payment of certain charges due him by the plaintiff; concluding with a verification. Upon special demurrer it was held that the plea was bad as amounting to an argumentative denial of the plaintiff's right of possession at the time of the conversion. The plea in setting forth a lien states that which is inconsistent with the plaintiff's lawful possession. See Jackson *v.* Cummins, 5 M. & W. 349, *cited* by Professor Ames in note to Dorrington *v.* Carter. Cases on Pleading, p. 63.

1. Pickard *v.* Sears, 6 A. & E. 469.

2. The statements on this point made by Chitty (1 Chitty Plead., 16th Am. ed. 532) must be modified as has been seen *supra*, p. 529 n. 3), in view of the overruling of Stancliffe *v.* Hardwicke, 2 C. M. & R. 1, on which case he relies for such propositions as that a defendant must plead specially where there has been a "conversion in fact," but the defendant insists that the conversion is lawful. Chitty cites Weeding *v.* Aldrich, 9 A. & E. 861. This case also received a quietus in Young *v.* Cooper, 6 Exch. 259 (*supra*, p. 529 note 3).

3. 1 Chitty Plead. (7th Am. ed.) 538; Weathrell *v.* Howard, 10 Moore, 502; Pearcy *v.* Walter, 6 C. & P. 232; Fuller *v.* Rounceville, 29 N. H. 554.

4. Gibbons *v.* Pepper, 1 Ld. Raym. 387. And no one can be compelled to justify who is not *prima facie* a trespasser. Bodkin *v.* Powell, Cowp. 478; Rawson *v.* Morse, 4 Pick. (Mass.) 127; 1 Chitty Plead. (17th Am. ed.) 535.

Gibbons *v.* Pepper, 1 Ld. Raym. 387, was an action for trespass for assault and battery. The defendant pleaded that he rode upon a horse on the king's highway, and that the horse, being affrighted, ran away with him, and that although he shouted to the plaintiff to get out of the way, yet the plaintiff did not get out of the way and the horse ran over the plaintiff against the will of the defendant. Verification. To this plea the plaintiff demurred, on the ground that in this case the defendant justified a battery which was no battery, of which opinion was the whole court; "for if I ride upon a horse and J S whips the horse, so that he runs away with me and runs over any other person, he who whips the horse is guilty of the battery and not me [*sic*]. But if I by spurring was the cause of such accident then I am guilty. In the same manner if A takes the hand of B and with it strikes C, A is the trespasser and not B. And, *per curiam*, the defendant might have given this justification in evidence upon the general issue pleaded. And therefore judgment was given for the plaintiff."

With this case it is instructive to contrast Hall *v.* Fearnley, 3 Q. B

he must plead his justification specially.[1] And this rule applies even where the defense is inevitable accident.[2] So also *son assault demesne*,[3] moderate correction,[4] *molliter manus imposuit* to preserve the peace,[5] and a justification that the act was done in defense of property,[6] must be specially pleaded. And a defendant must plead a justification under civil process,[7] or as an individual acting under authority of law:[8] and where his justification is an arrest for reasonable and probable cause, or for a breach of peace, the reasons for suspecting the plaintiff must be set out, and also the fact that the breach of peace was continuing.[9] But no one is bound to justify who is not *prima facie* a trespasser.[10] Therefore a plea in confession and avoidance which fails to show that

919, in which it was decided that where A in walking near the curbstone, is knocked into the culvert and run over by a cab, it is proper to set up the defense of inevitable accident by means of a plea in confession and avoidance. The distinction between these cases seems to be that in Gibbons *v.* Pepper, where the defendant found himself in the power of a superior agency, there was not even a *prima facie* trespass, but in Hall *v.* Fearnley, although in fact the defendant might have been powerless to prevent the accident, there is nothing in the nature of the case to show this, and the defense is essentially a matter of excuse, and must be so pleaded. This distinction, however, seems to the writer to be fallacious. The defendant in Gibbons *v.* Pepper was *prima facie* a trespasser, *for the act complained of in the declaration was done*, and it is matter of excuse to show that he was powerless to prevent it; and this excuse might be nullified by proof that the defendant was a poor rider and had ventured out on a horse which he knew he could not control.

1. Knapp *v.* Salsbury, 2 Campbell 505. This was an action of trespass for running against the plaintiff's chaise with a cart. Under the plea of not guilty the defendant attempted to prove that the plaintiff was guilty of contributory negligence. The evidence was rejected, LORD ELLENBOROUGH remarking, "These facts ought to have been pleaded specially. The only thing to be tried under the plea of not guilty is whether the defendant's cart struck the plaintiff's chaise." Suppose the defendant in Gibbons *v.* Pepper had pleaded not guilty and had attempted to prove before LORD ELLENBOROUGH that his horse was unmanageable, is it to be supposed that his lordship would have admitted the evidence?

See also Milman *v.* Dolwell, 2 Camp 378; Boss *v.* Litton, 5 C. & P. 408; Pearcy *v.* Walter, 6 C. & P. 232.

2. Hall *v.* Fearnley, 3. Q. B. 919; Cotterill *v.* Starkey, 8 C. & P. 691.

3. Gregory *v.* Hill, 8 T. R. 299.

4. Hannen *v.* Edes, 15 Mass. 347.

5. Weaver *v.* Bush, 8 T. R. 78. As to substance of pleas, see Gates *v.* Lounsbury, 20 Johns. (N. Y.) 427; Shain *v.* Markham, 4 J. J. Marsh. (Ky.) 578; 20 Am. Dec. 233.

6. 1 Chitty Plead. (17th Am. ed.) 536 and note; Baldwin *v.* Hayden, 6 Conn. 453; Hyatt *v.* Wood, 3 Johns. (N. Y.) 239; Sampson *v.* Henry, 11 Pick. (Mass.) 379; Robinson *v.* Hawkins, 4 T. B. Mon. (Ky.) 134; Ford *v.* Logan, 2 A. K. Marsh. (Ky.) 325; McIlroy *v.* Cockran, 2 A. K. Marsh. (Ky.) 271.

7. Whether of superior, inferior or foreign courts. 1 Chitty Plead. (16th Am. ed.) 536. See Barker *v.* Braham, 3 Wils. 370.

8. Smith *v.* Edge, 6 T. R. 562.

9. Baynes *v.* Brewster, 1 G. & D. 669. For distinction between right of private individual to interfere to prevent breach of peace and right of constable under similar circumstances, see Allen *v.* Wright, 8 C. & P. 522; Matthew *v.* Biddulph, 3 M. & G. 390; Beckwith *v.* Philby, 6 B. & C. 637; Samuel *v.* Payne, Dougl. 359; White *v.* Taylor, 4 Esp. 80; Coke *v.* Nethercote, 6 C. & P. 723; Hobbs *v.* Branscombe, 3 Camp. 420; Cowper *v.* Henley, 2 Esp. 540; Bac. Abr. Trespass, D. 3.

10. Bodkin *v.* Powell, Cowp. 478.

the defendant was guilty of even an appearance of wrong is bad as amounting to the general issue.[1] This distinction is often a fine one, but it is founded on sound principles and it is of great importance. Thus, a distress or seizure for tolls,[2] stallage at a fair, etc.,[3] under a by-law,[4] or for damage-feasant by the occupier,[5] or by a commoner,[6] were required to be pleaded specially.[7] So also of a justification under a rent-charge,[8] or in respect of any easement or incorporeal right.[9]

In trespass *quare clausum fregit* under not guilty the defendant can give in evidence title in himself or in another whose authority he pleads. Nevertheless, the special plea, *liberum tenementum*, that the *locus in quo* was the defendant's freehold, has received the sanction of the courts from the earliest times.[10] It is a plea somewhat anomalous in its nature, as in some cases it would seem to amount to the general issue; and, on principle, it seems to be defective in substance.[11] It was probably permitted in order to relieve the defendant from the hardship which would otherwise

1. In the Earl of Manchester *v.* Vale (1 Saunders 27) trespass was brought for breaking the plaintiff's close and the grass there with feet in walking, treading down, and with cattle eating up, with a *continuando*, etc. The defendant pleaded in bar that one, J S had a right of common in the place where, etc., for all his commonable cattle, levant and couchant, and further says that the said J S appointed the defendant to take care of said cattle. He then averred that J S caused divers commonable cattle to be placed in said close, which at the time when, etc., were in the place where, etc.; whereupon the defendant as servant entered into the said close to see after the cattle, and in so entering trod down the grass, which is the same trespass, etc. Upon demurrer the plea was adjudged bad, because it did not state that the defendant put the cattle in the close. He only stated that they *were there*, but as they were not his own cattle he was not responsible if he did not put them there and therefore his plea amounted to not guilty. SAUNDERS, of counsel with plaintiff, adds a note to the effect that there was another fault in the plea, because it was not averred that the cattle were levant and couchant; but this was not moved.

Contrast with this case Wise *v.* Hodsoll (11 A. & E. 816) where a plea in trespass was distinguished from that in the Earl of Manchester *v.* Vale.

2. Bennington *v.* Taylor, Lutw. 1519.
3. Bodle *v.* Wilkins, 3 Lev. 224.
4. Kirk *v.* Nowill, 1, T. R. 119.
5. 1 Saund. 221.
6. Cope *v.* Marshall, 2 Wils. 51.
7. 1 Chitty Plead. (16th Am. ed.) 537.
8. 1 Chitty Plead. (16th Am. ed.) 537.
9. Per LD. LOUGHBOROUGH, 1 H. B. 352. Thus common of pasture. 1 Saund. 25. Common of fishery, Com. Dig. Piscary. Of turbary, 6 T. R. 748. And a right of way—whether public or private, whether by grant, will, prescription, custom, or necessity. 1 Chitty Plead. 16th Am. ed.) 537, 538.
10. See Gould Plead. (5th ed.) 327. Called also the "common bar." See *infra*, p. 576, note 1.
11. See Welles, 222, and 1 Saund. 299 c (n. 6).

Liberum Tenementum.—This plea is extensively used when the plaintiff does not describe his close by the abuttals or by name in the declaration. Its use was chiefly to drive the plaintiff to a new-assignment. See *infra*, this title, *Ambiguity*. But it is also adapted to the case in which the freehold is alleged to be in a third person, whose authority the defendant claims. In such a case the plaintiff is put to his election as to whether he will traverse the title or the authority—since he cannot deny both; and as the one not denied will be admitted, the defendant thereby gains an advantage. Thus *liberum tenementum*, or a still more special plea of title, is used by the defendant when he wishes the plaintiff to state his title still more specially on the record. As to the rule that pleas of title must give color, see *infra*, p. 556. As to pleading title in general, see *infra*, p. 570.

have resulted where the plaintiff did not describe his close in the declaration.[1]

After Hilary Rules.[2]—The rules made no change in the law in regard to trespass to persons and injuries to personal property. In actions of trespass *de bonis asportatis* they provided that the general issue should no longer put the plaintiff's property in issue. If the defendant claim the goods he must deny the plaintiff's property or possession, or plead the facts specially, and therefore under not guilty he could not show property in himself as assignee of a bankrupt or otherwise.[3]

In trespass *quare clausum fregit* the proper plea by which to deny the plaintiff's possession is the traverse that the close is not the close of the plaintiff. This operates as a denial of the plaintiff's title to the same extent that he would have been required to prove it under the general issue before the rules.[4] But "a mere trespasser cannot," says Chitty, "by the very act of trespass, immediately and without acquiescence, give himself what the law understands by possession against the person whom he ejects, and drive him to produce his title, if he can without delay reinstate

1. See Gould Plead. (5th ed.) 328. For a full discussion of *liberum tenementum* in this connection, see *infra*, p. 576, note 1.

2. The Reg. Gen. Hil. T., 4 W. IV, so far as they relate to trespass, are as folfows:

"In actions of trespass *quare clausum fregit*, the plea of not guilty shall operate as a denial that the defendant committed the trespass alleged in the place mentioned, but not as a denial of the plaintiff's possession, or right of possession of that place, which, if intended to he denied, must be traversed specially.

"In actions of trespass *de bonis asportatis*, the plea of not guilty shall operate as a denial of the defendant having committed the trespass alleged, by taking or damaging the goods mentioned, but not of the plaintiff's property therein."

3. Chitty Plead. (16th Am. ed.) 537.

4. 1 Chitty Plead. (16th Am. ed.) 538. At the common law, the plea of not guilty to an action of trespass *quare clausum fregit* entitled the defendant to give in evidence title in himself or in another by whose command he entered. The reason for this was that the proof falsified the declaration, inasmuch as it showed that the defendant did not break the *plaintiff's* close, as the declaration set forth. Argent *v.* Durrant (8 T. R. 403). But the Hilary Rules restricted the scope of the general issue in trespass q. c. f. by enacting that the plea of not guilty should "operate as a denial that the defendant committed the trespass alleged in the place mentioned, but not as a denial of the plaintiff's possession or right of possession of that place, which, if intended to be denied, must be traversed specially. Thus in Jones *v.* Chapman (18 Law Journal Reps., Exchequer 456), which was an action of trespass for breaking and entering the plaintiff's dwelling house, the defendant pleaded that the house was not at the time when, etc., the dwelling house of the plaintiff *modo et forma.* At the trial BARON PARKE instructed the jury to find for the defendant if they were satisfied that one H M was entitled to the possession of the dwelling house at the time when and that the defendant had committed the alleged trespass under his authority. The jury found for the defendant and an exception to the above direction was argued in the Exchequer Chamber, where a majority of the judges upheld BARON PARKE's ruling. This case, therefore, decides that the traverse "not possessed" puts in issue the actual possession of the plaintiff and also his right of possession—in which construction of the Hilary Rules it differs from the decision of the Queen's Bench in Whittington *v.* Boxall, 5 Q. B. Reps. 139. 12 Law J. Reps., N. S., Q. B. 318; The decision in Jones *v.* Chapman seems to be correct on principle, although

himself in his former possession."[1] The strict rule in regard to pleading specially all matters of justification and excuse is, of course, applicable after as well as before the rules. In actions founded on loss of service it seems that not guilty does not put in issue the fact of service. If the defendant wishes to deny the relation he should use a specific traverse.[2]

(*f*) *Trespass on the Case.*—At common law, the general issue not guilty is in form a traverse or denial of the facts which form the subject of complaint. On principle, the evidence admissible under it should be confined to matters of defense which rest in denial. But by a gradual relaxation of the practice similiar to that which occurred in assumpsit, evidence came to be received not only of matters in denial, but of defenses by way of confession and avoidance.[3] There is, therefore, an essential difference between actions of trespass and on the case. The former are *stricti juris*, and accordingly a former recovery, release or satisfaction cannot be given in evidence under the general issue, but must be specially pleaded. But the latter are founded on the mere justice and conscience of the plaintiff's case and are in the nature of a bill in equity and in effect are so, and therefore a former recovery, release or satisfaction need not be pleaded, but may be given in evidence;[4] for whatever *in equity and conscience* would preclude the plaintiff from recovering may be given in evidence under the general issue.[5]

On the general issue the plaintiff is put to the proof of his whole case, and the defendant may give in evidence any justification or excuse of it.[6] Thus a license, which in trespass must

Coleridge, J., and Wightman, J., delivered dissenting opinions. The former thought that a distinct specific traverse was necessary in order to deny the plaintiff's right of possession, while the latter held that a plea in confession and avoidance was the proper method of defending by showing right of possession either in the defendant or in a third person.

1. Chitty Plead. (16th Am. ed.) 538. See Browne *v.* Dawson, 12 A. & E. 628.

Where the plaintiff declared for an injury to a messuage and the defendant traversed the plaintiff's possession, proof of possession of two rooms only was held sufficient to maintain the plaintiff's case. Fenn *v.* Grafton, 2 Bing. N. C. 617. But a defendant's plea of possession in himself would not be sustained by such evidence. Monks *v.* Dykes, 4 M. & W. 567; Bond *v.* Downton, 2 A. & E. 26.

2. Torrence *v.* Gibbons, 5 Q. B. Rep. 297. This was an action of trespass for debauching the plaintiff's daughter, "who, during all the time aforesaid was, and still is, the servant of the plaintiff; whereby she became pregnant," etc. Plea, that the daughter was not the servant of the plaintiff, *modo et forma.* Upon demurrer the court gave judgment for the defendant on the ground that not guilty would have been inappropriate as a plea, for it did not deny the right of the plaintiff to bring the action—which was here the basis of the defendant's case. But see Holloway *v.* Abell, 7 C. & P. 528; and Foreman *v.* Dawes, Car. & M. 127.

3. Steph. Plead. (9th Am. ed.) 162, note.

4. Per Duncan, J., in Greenwalt *v.* Horner, 6 S. & R. (Pa.) 76.

5. Per Lord Mansfield, in Bird *v.* Randall, 3 Burr 1353.

6. Birch *v.* Wilson, 2 Mod. 276; Bradley *v.* Wyndham, 1 Wils. 44; Brown *v.* Best, 1 Wils. 175. See also Barber *v.* Dixon, 1 Wils. 45.

be pleaded, may in case be given in evidence under not guilty.[1] And where case was brought for obstructing ancient lights the defendant under not guilty was permitted to prove a custom to build ancient foundations to any height.[2] To this general rule an exception is to be noted in actions for defamation ; in such cases truth must be pleaded specially.[3] It is probably the only defense which does not amount to the general issue. But the circumstance that proof of a certain fact *tends to prove the truth* of the imputation will not render such evidence inadmissible under not guilty, if the purpose of the offer is to rebut malice and to mitigate damages, and not to set up a complete defense to the action.[4] The defense that the alleged libel was a privileged communication can be set up under not guilty.[5] And where the occasion imposes on the plaintiff the duty of proving malice in fact, evidence to rebut it is properly admissible under the general issue.[6]

After Hilary Rules.[7]—As the rule declares with entire distinctness that not guilty shall operate as a denial only of the wrongful

1. Chitty Plead., 1st Eng. ed. 478.

2. Newton *v.* Creswick, 3 Mod. 166. So where case was brought for obstructing the plaintiff's right of way it was deemed proper for the defendant under not guilty to give in evidence an agreement between his predecessor in title and the plaintiff, which authorized the closing of the road in such a contingencey as had actually happened. Greenwalt *v.* Horner, 6 S. & R. (Pa.) 70.

3. **Libel and Slander.**—Broad as is the scope of not guilty in case, it is yet a general rule that *truth* must be pleaded specially. The defendant is not permitted on the general issue to go into evidence as to the truth of the imputation, because it is said the proof of it does not contradict or repel any matter which the plaintiff is bound to prove. Folkard's Starkie on Sl. and Lib. (4th Eng. ed.) § 4476. This explanation seems insufficient: upon the same principle many matters of justification should be excluded which are always admitted under not guilty. The true explanation is that the rule is a piece of judge-made law, deliberately framed to prevent surprise upon the plaintiff. That this is the case appears from the following extract from the opinion of the Chief Justice in Underwood *v.* Parks, 2 Stra. 1200: "At a meeting of all the judges, upon a case that arose in the common pleas, a large majority of them had determined not to allow it, for the future, but it should be pleaded, whereby the plaintiff might be prepared to defend himself, as well as to prove the speaking of the words." See also Huson *v.* Dale, 19 Mich. 28; 2 Am. Rep. 66. As to the plea of truth generally, see Underwood *v.* Parks, 2 Stra. 1200; Manning *v.* Clement, 7 Bing. 367; Andrews *v.* Vanduzer, 11 Johns. (N. Y.) 38; Van Ankin *v.* Westfall, 14 Johns. (N. Y.) 233; Kelley *v.* Dillon, 5 Ind. 426; Douge *v.* Pearce, 13 Ala. 127; Kay *v.* Fredrigal, 3 Pa. St. 221; Taylor *v.* Robinson, 29 Me. 323; Bodwell *v.* Swan, 3 Pick. (Mass.) 376; Updegrove *v.* Zimmerman, 13 Pa. St. 619; Treat *v.* Browning, 4 Conn. 408; 10 Am. Dec. 156; Sheahan *v.* Collins, 20 Ill. 325; 71 Am. Dec. 271; Harper *v.* Harper, 10 Bush (Ky.) 447; Storey *v.* Early, 86 Ill. 461; Swift *v.* Dickerman, 31 Conn. 285.

4. Huson *v.* Dale, 19 Mich. 16. See in this case a thoughtful opinion by Christiancy, J., classifying the authorities on this subject, and crisicising those decisions (and there are several) which lay down a rule different from the statement in the text.

5. Lillie *v.* Price, 5 A. & E. 645; Lucan *v.* Smith, 1 H. & N. 481; Hoare *v.* Silverlock, 9 C. B. 20; Hounsfield *v.* Drury, 11 A. & E. 98.

6. Hackett *v.* Brown, 2 Heisk. (Tenn.) 264; 2 Greenl. Ev., § 421.

7. Rule 4 Reg. Gen. Hil. T., 4 Wm. IV, contains the following provisions: In actions on the case, the plea of not

act and not of any matter contained in the inducement, the chief difficulty which presented itself was to distinguish in a given case between the inducement and the gist.[1] When it is determined in a given case what is inducement and what is gist then almost

guilty shall operate as a denial only of the breach of duty or wrongful act alleged to have been committed by the defendant, and not of the facts stated in the inducement; and no other defense than such denial shall be admissible under that plea; all other pleas in denial shall take issue on some particular matter of fact alleged in the declaration.

Ex. gr. In an action on the case for a nuisance to the occupation of a house, by carrying on an offensive trade, the plea of not guilty will operate as a denial, only that the defendant carried on the alleged trade in such a way as to be a nuisance to the occupation of the house; and will not operate as a denial of the plaintiff's occupation of the house.

In an action on the case for obstructing a right of way, such plea will operate as a denial of the obstruction only, and not of the plaintiff's right of way; and in actions for converting the plaintiff's goods, the conversion only, and not the plaintiff's title to the goods.

In an action of slander of the plaintiff in his office, profession or trade, the plea of not guilty will operate to the same extent precisely as at present, in denial of speaking the words, of speaking them maliciously, and in the sense imputed, and with reference to the plaintiff's office, profession or trade; but it will not operate as a denial of the fact of the plaintiff's holding the office, or of being of the profession or trade alleged.

In actions for an escape it will operate as a denial of the neglect or default of the sheriff or his officers, but not of the debt, judgment or preliminary proceedings.

In this form of action against a carrier, the plea of not guilty will operate as a denial of the loss or damage, but not of the receipt of the goods by the defendant as a carrier for hire, or of the purpose for which they were received.

All matters in confession and avoidance shall be pleaded specially, as in actions of *assumpsit.*

1. By *inducement* is here meant the statement of the plaintiff's right, and by *gist*, the statement of the defendant's wrong. The following are the most important cases on the question of the scope of the general issue:

Injuries to the Person—In Thomas *v.* Morgan (2 C. M. & R. 496) the declaration was in case for wrongfully and injuriously keeping divers ferocious dogs. The plea was not guilty, which was held not to be an admission of the *scienter*, as the latter was no mere inducement, but a part of the cause of action. The plaintiff was therefore non-suited on account of his failure to prove it.

In Bridge *v.* The Grand Junction Rwy. Co., 3 M. & W. 244, a plaintiff who had been injured in a railway accident, brought an action on the case to recover damages for injuries sustained by him through the alleged negligence of the defendant. Plea, that the train in which the plaintiff was riding was not the train of the defendant, and that it collided with the defendant's train as well through the negligence of the other company as through the negligence of the defendant. Verification.

Upon special demurrer the court gave judgment for the plaintiff both because the plea was bad in substance and because in point of form it amounted to no more than a simple negation of the negligence which would make the defendant liable, and therefore amounted to the general issue. See Dakin *v.* Brown, 8 C. B. 62.

Where case was brought for malicious prosecution, the defendant pleaded not guilty, and, secondly, a long special plea in denial of the absence of reasonable and probable cause. The court made absolute a rule to strike out the whole of the second plea, for as the injury complained of was not merely in the indicting, nor in the indictments being wrongful, but in maliciously indicting and in doing so without reasonable or probable cause, the plea of not guilty was declared to be sufficient. Cotton *v.* Brown, 3 A. & E. 312. See Rowe *v.* Ames, 6 M. & W. 747.

Since case for malicious prosecution cannot be maintained until the former suit is terminated, it is obvious that an averrment of the discontinuance of such suit is a material allegation, which if the defendant desires to controvert, he must specifically deny. Not guilty puts in issue merely the malicious arrest without probable cause. Watkins *v.* Lee, 5 M. & W. 270. See also Atkinson *v.* Raleigh, 3 Q. B. 79; Haddrick *v.* Heslop, 12 Q. B. 267.

Libel and Slander.—(For these subjects before Hilary Rules, see *supra*, p. 535 n. 3). In case for libel or slander the general issue is appropriate where the defendant wishes to deny the speaking or publishing of the words in fact, or where he denies that they were spoken of the plaintiff, or denies that there is special damage (where special damage is necessary to sustain the action), or claims that the occasion warranted the publication. 1 Chitty Plead. (16th Am. ed.) 519. Thus in Lillie *v.* Price, 5 A. & E. 645, Lord Denman decided that a privileged communication could be given in evidence under not guilty in an action on the case for libel. But see Goodwin *v.* Daniels, 7 Allen (Mass.) 61; Bradley *v.* Heath, 12 Pick. (Mass.) 163; 22 Am. Dec. 418; Jackson *v.* Stetson, 15 Mass. 50. See also Buddington *v.* Davis, 6 How. Pr. (N. Y.) 401.

But it is a general rule that *truth* must be specially pleaded. See *supra*, p. 535 n. 3. And if the meaning of the words is alleged by *innuendo*, not guilty denies that they had the meaning attributed to them. 1 Chitty Plead. (16th Am. ed.) 521. But if the meaning of the words is made matter of inducement, then, under the rule, the meaning must be specifically traversed. McGregor *v.* Gregory, 2 Dowl., N. S. 779.

Injuries to Personal Property and Breach of Duty.—In Lewis *v.* Alcock, 3 M. & W. 188, case was brought against a sheriff for a false return. The declaration alleged that the writ was delivered to him; that there were goods of the debtor within his bailiwick, and that it became his duty to seize them. It then averred that he did not use due diligence to make the levy, and that he returned *nulla bona*. Upon not guilty pleaded, the defendant sought to prove that he had desisted from levying on account of a bill of sale given by the debtor to a third person. The plaintiff contended that the defendant's ownership of the goods was not put in issue by the plea, but was admitted by it. Of that opinion was the court, BARON PARKE declaring that the failure to use due diligence and the return *nulla bona* were the only two propositions in issue. See Wright *v.* Lainson, 2 M. & W. 739.

In Taverner *v.* Little, 5 Bing. N. C. 678, which was an action, on the case after the Hilary Rules, the plaintiff averred that the defendant carelessly and negligently drove his cart into the plaintiff's chaise, etc. Plea, not guilty. It was held that the defendant's possession of the cart was a matter of inducement which was admitted by the plea of the general issue, and the defendant was not allowed upon the trial to give in evidence the fact that before the accident he had lent his cart to someone else, who was driving when the accident occurred.

In Perring *v.* Harris (2 M. & R. 5) the action was case against an overseer of the poor for wrongfully and maliciously omitting the plaintiff's name from the tax list whereby she was prevented from obtaining a license. Plea that the plaintiff was not entitled to be assessed, etc. It was held that as the special damage went to the very essence of the plaintiff's right of action, the latter was absolved from proving it by the defendant's plea.

In Crouch *v.* The London etc. R. Co. (7 Exch. 705) case was brought against a common carrier for failure to deliver a certain package, the bailment of which to the defendant was averred in the declaration. Plea, that the defendants gave notice that they would not carry any package containing several packages collected from different parties and addressed to and intended for several different parties, although inclosed in one package and addressed to one party, unless contents were declared, etc. Averment, that the package in question was of this nature and that its contents were not declared. Verification. Upon special demurrer the court held that the plea denied argumentatively that the package was delivered to and received by the defendants as common carriers, and gave judgment for the plaintiff.

See also Elwall *v.* Grand Junction etc. R. Co. M. & W. 669.

In Spenser *v.* Dawson (1 M. & R. 552) BARON PARK held that not guilty pleaded after the Hilary Rules to an action on the case for deceit in the warranty of a horse, put in issue the whole declaration except the bargain and sale. This being mere matter of inducement must be specifically traversed.

Injuries to Real Property and Ease-

all difficulty is at an end: for from the rule that not guilty denies only the wrongful act or gist, it inevitably follows that not guilty admits the inducement to be true. Accordingly no evidence which tends to dispute the statements constituting the inducement will be received under the general issue. To admit such evidence would be to permit the defendant to contradict at the trial what he had admitted in his pleadings.[1]

(*g*) *Replevin.*—The so-called general issue *non cepit* denies the taking alleged and also the taking in the place mentioned in the declaration.[2] It admits the plaintiff's property in the chattels, and evidence to dispute his property will not be admitted under it.[3] And where *non cepit* is pleaded and a seizure is proved the court will direct a verdict for the plaintiff even where he fails to prove any property in the chattels or that he was possessed at the time of the seizure.[4] If the defendant wishes to dispute the plaintiff's property he may plead property in himself or in a stranger.[5] For replevin differs from the other personal actions

ments.—That section of the Hilary Rules which declares that the general issue in case shall operate as a denial only of the wrongful act alleged, and not of facts stated in the inducement, came up for construction in Frankum *v.* the Earl of Falmouth (2 A. & E. 452). The declaration was for wrongfully diverting the water supply of the plaintiff's mill, and the plea was not guilty. The plaintiff proved the fact of diversion, but failed to show that the mill was an ancient one, or that the water had been used for twenty years. Upon this state of facts it was argued by the plaintiff that he had proved his case, since the title was a mere matter of inducement, and as such must be taken to be admitted on not guilty. The court gave him judgment, LORD DENMAN declaring that the word "wrongfully" contained in the declaration did not put the title in issue, but merely imported a reference to the inducement. In other words, if the defense was that the act was not wrongful, it ought to have been so pleaded.

In Norton *v.* Scholefield (9 M. & W. 665) case was brought for erecting a cesspool so near the well and pump of the plaintiff as to contaminate his water and render it unfit for use. The court refused leave to plead a special plea, denying the contamination of the water. "Not guilty," said BARON PARKE, "puts in issue both the act complained of and its consequences." And BARON ALDERSON remarked, "by the general issue the defendant says 'I am not guilty of erecting a building which is a nuisance.'"

1. Taverner *v.* Little, 5 Bing. N. C. 678.

2. Johnson *v.* Wollyer, 1 Stra. 507; 1 Saund. 347; Walton *v.* Kersop, 2 Wils. 355; Smith *v.* Snyder, 15 Wend. (N. Y.) 325. But under this plea the defendant cannot have a return of the cattle. If he desire such return he should plead a taking in another place, and traverse the place laid in the declaration, and then, in order to have the return, should avow or make cognizance, stating his justification. 1 Chitty Plead. (16th Am. ed.) 533. And if the defendant thus pleads *cepit in alio loco* with an avowry or cognizance for a return the plaintiff can take issue only on the traverse of the place and cannot reply to the avowry or cognizance. See 1 Saund. 347, note (1), and 1 Chitty Plead. (16th Am. ed.) 617.

Non detinet is also used as a plea in replevin. It admits the property and denies the detainer. See Cobbey on Replev. § 738.

3. Of course *non cepit* may be accompanied by a second plea, denying the plaintiff's property. Simpson *v.* McFarland, 18 Pick. (Mass.) 427; 29 Am. Dec. 602. For several pleas are permitted the defendant in replevin. Martin *v.* Ray, 1 Blackf. (Ind.) 291; Sprague *v.* Kneeland, 12 Wend. (N. Y.) 161. The rule was different in Virginia. Vaiden *v.* Bell, 3 Rand. (Va.) 448.

4. Dover *v.* Rawlings, 2 M. & Rob. 544, per TINDAL, C. J.

5. Gilb. on Replev. 127, *et seq.*; Marsh *v.* Pier, 4 Rawle (Pa.) 273; 26 Am. Dec. 131. And this may be pleaded either in abatement or in bar. Indeed

in that the plaintiff must prove either a general or a special property in the chattels; bare possession is not sufficient.[1] And if the defendant pleads property in himself he does not confess the caption.[2] Nor does the plea of property admit the plaintiff's right to sue.[3] Under a plea of property in himself the defendant can give in evidence a lien upon the goods for work done upon them.[4]

If, however, the defendant as landlord wishes to admit the property and the taking and to justify the latter he makes *avowry*,[5] and admits the taking by way of distress for rent in arrear. If the plaintiff desires to deny that rent is in arrear he uses the traverse *rien en arrere*.[6] This plea has been sometimes called a

four cases of property out of the plaintiff have arisen as follows: (1) Property in the defendant. This may be pleaded in abatement or in bar. Presgrave *v.* Saunders, 1 Salk. 5. (2) Property in a stranger. This likewise may be pleaded either in abatement or in bar. Gilb. on Replev. 127. (3) Property in defendent and plaintiff. The same rule applies. Wilson *v.* Gray, 8 Watts (Pa.) 36. In these three cases the defendant is entitled to a return. The reason for this in the first two cases is obvious, in the third it must be remembered that the interests of plaintiff and defendant are equal, but the defendant has been wrongfully deprived of possession. He should, therefore, have a return. (4) Property in the plaintiff and a stranger. Here the defense is dilatory only and must be pleaded in abatement. Gilb. on Replev., 128. See Wilson *v.* Gray, 8 Watts (Pa.) 35.

1. Co. Litt. 145.

2. Gilb. on Replev. 127. Marsh *v.* Pier, 4 Rawle (Pa.) 283, where it is said that this must be especially true in Pennsylvania where replevin may be maintained by the plaintiff to recover the possession of goods and chattels to which he is entitled as owner in all cases, as well as where the defendant came by the possession of them lawfully and withholds them from the plaintiff unlawfully, as where he got them tortiously. Accordingly the burden of proof still lies upon the plaintiff in replevin notwithstanding the plea of property. Clemson *v.* Davidson, 5 Binn. (Pa.) 399.

3. Seibert *v.* McHenry, 6 Watts (Pa.) 301. In this case a husband and wife sued jointly to recover property belonging to the wife before marriage, and taken afterwards. It was held that as the property vested upon marriage in the husband alone he only was the proper plaintiff, and that the misjoinder of the wife could be taken advantage of under the plea of property.

4. Matthias *v.* Sellers, 86 Pa. St. 492; 27 Am. Rep. 723.

5. The justification in the defendant's own right is called an avowry; when he justifies under the authority of another, it is called a cognizance.

6. **Rien en Arrere.**—In the action of replevin where the defendant avows or makes cognizance, his pleading amounts to a statement of substantive right to take the goods in question and partakes of the nature of a declaration. Hence the third pleading in the series is rather a plea than a replication, and, indeed, exchanges the latter name for the former. Thus, where the plaintiff brings replevin and the defendant avows the taking for rent in arrear, he takes it upon himself to deduce the title to the rent in question with all the particularity that he would be compelled to observe were he declaring for rents in arrear in a suit upon the indenture of lease. Of course the defense may be that the goods have never been taken—or that they have not been taken as the goods of the plaintiff—and then the proper plea is *non cepit*, or property. But when the defense is by way of avowry (as in the above example) for rents in arrear, the plaintiff is said to "plead to the avowry," and if he wishes to deny, as is usually the case, that rent is in arrear, he does so by means of the plea of *riens en arrere*. This plea, although the third in the series, may be called a second general issue—so great is its importance and so common its use. The case of Hill *v.* Wright, 2 Esp. 669, is an authority to the effect that *rien en arrere* merely denies according to its tenor that rent is in arrear, while it ad-

general issue,[1] a term which shows how strong is the analogy between the avowry and a new declaration.[2]

(*h*) *Assumpsit—At Common Law.*—The scope of the general issue *non-assumpsit* depended originally upon the nature of the contract upon which recovery was sought. In the action of *special assumpsit,* which is assumpsit founded upon an *express* promise, the defendant was compelled to conform to the language and principle of the general issue and was permitted, under it, to contest only the fact of the promise, or to show that the promise was void in law by reason of some illegality.[3] In the action of *general assumpsit,* which is assumpsit founded upon an *implied* promise, inasmuch as the plaintiff's case rested upon proof of such circumstances as would give rise to the implication of a promise, it was thought reasonable that the defendant should be at liberty to prove all facts which tended to exclude such implication.[4] Among such facts were release and performance.[5] It was found impossible in practice to prevent the latter more liberal view from being applied to the case of express promises; and this was done step by step at the sacrifice of principle and precedent. Thus special defenses, such as *infancy* and *coverture,* can be given in evidence under the general issue.[6] So also the defense that the defendant was *non compos* at the time of making the promise.[7] Or that the defendant was drunk.[8] And the same is true of all matters in discharge,[9] and of objections to the considera-

mits the title of the defendant together with the lease as stated in the avowry. Accordingly where the plaintiff in this case filed this plea, it was held that he could not give in evidence the fact that the rent was reserved half-yearly and not quarterly, as stated by the defendant.

1. The term "general issue" has but little of its true meaning left. It was originally so called because, says BLACKSTONE, by importing an absolute and general denial of what is alleged in the indictment or declaration it amounts at once to an issue. But *non cepit* is in meaning and effect rather in the nature of a specific traverse. The same is true of *rien en arrere. Non est factum* in covenant has at common law the narrow office of denying the execution of the deed—or, rather, of denying execution in fact or of asserting absolute invalidity in law. *Non assumpsit* could never, consistently with the meaning of the words, be a true general issue in an action which seeks damages for *breach* of a contract, for the breach is not in terms denied by it. Not guilty in trespass answers to the definition more nearly than the others.

2. The rule that a plea amounting to the general issue should be so pleaded applies to *rien en arrere.* Horn *v.* Lewin, 2 Salk. 583.

Non Tenure.—If the plaintiff desires to deny the tenancy he pleads non tenure. See Cobbey on Replev., § 734.

3. Fits *v.* Freestone, 1 Mod. 310; Abbot *v.* Chapman, 2 Lev. 81. See 1 Chitty Plead. (1st Eng. ed.) 471.

4. This summary of the development of non-assumpsit is based upon MR. SERGEANT STEPHEN'S. See Steph. Plead. (9th Am. ed.) 162, note.

5 Steph. Plead. (9th Am. ed.) 162, note.

6. Wailing *v.* Toll, 9 Johns. (N. Y.) 141; Vasse *v.* Smith, 6 Cranch (U. S.) 231; Stansbury *v.* Marks, 4 Dall. (Pa.) 130.

7. Webster *v.* Woodford, 3 Day (Conn.) 90; Mitchell *v.* Kingman, 5 Pick. (Mass.) 431.

8. Especially where the defendant caused plaintiff to become drunk. Duncan *v.* McCullough, 4 S. & R. (Pa.) 438; Rutherford *v.* Ruff, 4 Desaus. (S. Car.) 364.

9. Edson *v.* Weston, 7 Cow. (N. Y.) 278; Smart *v.* Bough, 3 J. J. Marsh. (Ky.) 363; Wilt *v.* Ogden, 13 John. (N. Y.) 56; Craig *v.* Whips, 1 Dana (Ky.)

tion.[1] And so, in general, of any matter which shows that the plaintiff never had any cause of action.[2]

After Hilary Rules.[3]—The Hilary Rules emphasize the division of actions of assumpsit into *general* and *special;* and their effect is to restore the law in some measure to its condition before the liberality of the practice in regard to the general issue in general assumpsit had crept into the domain of special assumpsit as well. But a great restriction was put upon the use of the general issue by forbidding the defendant to plead it in actions upon bills of exchange and promissory notes. In such cases every traverse must be specific.

In actions on implied contracts *non-assumpsit* puts in issue the matters of fact out of which the contract or promise is said to arise.[4] Thus where goods are sold on credit the defendant under

375; Baylies *v.* Fettyplace, 7 Mass. 325. So of *payment.* Drake *v.* Drake, 11 Johns. (N. Y.) 531; Britton *v.* Bishop, 11 Vt. 70. And *former recovery.* Carvill *v.* Garrigues, 5 Pa. St. 152; Offutt *v.* Offutt, 2 Har. & G. (Md.) 178. *Release.* Dawson *v.* Tibbs, 4 Yeates (Pa.) 349; Offut *v.* Offut, 2 Har. & G. (Md.) 178.

1. Craig *v.* Missouri, 4 Pet. (U. S.) 436; Hilton *v.* Burley, 2 N. H. 193; Talbert *v.* Cason, 1 Brev. (S. C.) 298.

2. Sill *v.* Rood, 15 Johns. (N. Y.) 230; Taft *v.* Montague, 14 Mass. 282; 7 Am. Dec. 215; Edson *v.* Weston, 7 Cow. (N. Y.) 278; Young *v.* Black, 7 Cranch (U. S.) 565; 1 Chitty Plead. (16th Am. ed.) 493. And cases *cited* in note (r[2]).

3. The Reg. Gen. Hil. T. 4 W. IV, contain the following provision:

"In all actions of assumpsit, except on bills of exchange and promissory notes, the plea of *non-assumpsit* shall operate only as a denial in fact, of the express contract or promise alleged, or of the matters of fact from which the contract or promise alleged may be implied by law. Ex. gr. In an action on warranty the plea will operate as a denial of the fact of the warranty having been given upon the alleged consideration, but not of the breach; and in an action on a policy of insurance, of the subscription to the alleged policy, by the defendant, but not of the interest, of the commencement of the risk, of the loss, or of the alleged compliance with warranties.

"In actions against carriers and other bailees, for not delivering, or not keeping goods safe, or not returning them on request, and in actions against agents for not accounting, the plea will operate as a denial of any express contract to the effect alleged in the declaration, and of such bailment or employment as would raise a promise in law, to the effect alleged, but not of the breach.

"In an action of *indebitatus assumpsit*, for goods sold and delivered, the plea of *non assumpsit* will operate as a denial of the sale and delivery in point of fact; in the like action for money had and received, it will operate as a denial both of the receipt of the money and the existence of those facts which make such receipt by the defendant a receipt to the use of the plaintiff.

"In all actions upon bills of exchange and promissory notes the plea of *non-assumpsit* shall be inadmissible. In such actions, therefore, a plea in denial must traverse some matter of fact, ex. gr. the drawing, or making, or indorsing, or accepting, or presenting, or notice of dishonor of, the bill or note.

"In every species of assumpsit, all matters in confession and avoidance, including not only those by way of discharge, but those that show the transaction to be either void or voidable in point of law, on the ground of fraud, or otherwise, shall be specially pleaded; ex. gr. infancy, coverture, release, payment, performance, illegality of consideration, either by statute or by common law; drawing, indorsing, accepting, etc., bills or notes, by way of accommodation, set-off, mutual credit, unseaworthiness, misrepresentation, concealment, deviation, and various other defenses must be pleaded."

4. Martin *v.* Smith, 4 Bing. N. C. 439; per TINDAL, C. J.

this plea can prove that it has not yet expired.[1] So the defendant can show that he refused to accept the goods because a special condition had not been complied with.[2] And where the defendant was sued for the price of a machine he was permitted to prove that it was sold subject to the condition that no charge would be made if it failed to work, and that upon trial it proved useless.[3] In *indebitatus assumpsit* for work and labor and materials the defendant under *non-assumpsit* may show that the work done or materials provided were not such as to render him liable to pay for them under his contract.[4] So in an action for work the defendant may prove that it was not done in a workmanlike manner.[5] Where the suit is for money paid, *non-assumpsit* puts in issue the payment at the express or implied request of the defendant.[6] If it was applied for an illegal purpose, or if the contract was void at common law or by statute the defense must be specially pleaded.[7] *Non-assumpsit* to an action of money had and received denies the receipt of the money or that it was received to the plaintiff's use.[8] The general issue pleaded to an action on an account stated raises the question both of the statement of the account and of whether or not the defendant is in-

1. Broomfield *v.* Smith, 1 M. & W. 542. If the money is not payable the law will not yet raise the implied promise to pay it. The rule was at first thought to be the other way. Edmunds *v.* Harris, 2 A. & E. 414.

2. Alexander *v.* Gardner, 1 Bing. N. C. 671.

3. Grounsell *v.* Lamb, 1 M. & W. 352.

In Hayselden *v.* Staff, 5 A. & E. 153, *indebitatus assumpsit* was brought for the value of work done and materials furnished at the request of defendant. Plea, that the work had been done and the materials provided in order to prevent a certain chimney from smoking, under an agreement between plaintiff and defendant that neither materials nor work should be paid for unless the attempt was successful. Averment that the attempt was not successful. Verification. Upon special demurrer the Court of King's Bench, per LORD DENMAN, decided that the plea was bad. "The allegation in the declaration is that the defendant is indebted for work, labor and materials; and that, being so indebted, he promised to pay on request. The plea does not confess that the defendant was indebted at all; it admits that work was done and materials were found and provided; but, instead of confessing that any debt was created by that, and showing anything to avoid it, it says that no money was to be paid unless the chimney was cured of smoking, which was not done; and which is really saying, in the most distinct terms, that no debt ever arose, and therefore falls completely within the meaning of what may be termed an argumentative denial of that debt."

4. 1 Chitty Plead. (16th Am. ed.) 495, quoting PARKE B. in Cousins *v.* Paddon, 2 C. M. & R. 547.

5. Cousins *v.* Paddon, 2 C. M. & R. 547; Chapel *v.* Hickes, 2 C. & M. 214.

6. 1 Chitty Plead. (16th Am. ed.) 496.

7. This is in strict accordance with the letter and spirit of the rules, which provide that all matters shall be specially pleaded which show the transaction to be either void or voidable in point of law, on the ground of fraud or otherwise.

8. This latter point is well illustrated by the case of Solly *v.* Neish, 2 C. M. & R. 355. The defendant pleaded that goods owned jointly by plaintiff and X were, by plaintiff's connivance, held by X as his sole property. Not knowing of the plaintiff's interest, defendant advanced money to X on the security of the goods and subsequently sold them in order to repay himself by virtue of a power lodged with him for that purpose. It was held that these facts constituted a denial of the receipt of the money to the sole use of the plaintiff, and the plea was declared to be there-

debted thereon.[1] Thus where the account stated was in fact incorrect that defense could be set up under *non-assumpsit* as it negatived the defendant's indebtedness.[2] Under the general issue in assumpsit for use and occupation the defendant can prove the existence of a nuisance which rendered the premises unin-habitable.[3] And he can show that he held under a lease and was evicted by the plaintiff before the time named in the lease for the payment of rent.[4] He can also show that the premises were mortgaged and that he paid the rent to the mortgagee as it fell due in compliance with a notice from the latter.[5] But as to rent falling due before the notice the defense operates as an excuse and should be specially pleaded.[6]

In special assumpsit, the general issue is appropriate whenever the defendant desires to deny that the contract stated in the declaration was the contract which he in fact made. Thus, where a defeasance is by law attached to a contract, it is a misdescription to declare upon it as an unqualified contract, and the variance will be fatal on *non-assumpsit.*[7] If a declaration against a common carrier sets out a contract to carry safely, the defendant should plead non-assumpsit if the contract in fact contained a provision for such a contingency as that on which he relies for his defense.[8] But if the defendant relies upon a condition *collateral* to the contract, or one which operates as a mere *defeasance of his liability,* then he cannot deny the contract but must plead in confession and avoidance.[9] But if the defense is that the contract alleged

fore bad as amounting to the general issue.

1. 1 Chitty Plead. (16th ed.) 497.

2. Thomas *v.* Hawkes, 8 M. & W. 140. See French *v.* French, 2 M. & G. 644; Clarke *v.* Webb, 1 C. M. & R. 29; Smith *v.* Winter, 12 C. B. 487; Wilson *v.* Wilson, 14 C. B. 616.

3. Smith *v.* Marrable, 2 Dowl., N. S. 810.

4. Prentice *v.* Elliott 5 M. & W. 606.

5. Waddilove *v.* Barnett, 2 Bing. N. C. 538. After notice by the mortgagee, the defendant was in by permission and sufferance of the *mortgagee.* This evidence tended to support the denial that he was in by permission of the *mortgagor.*

6. For until the notice the defendant *was* in by permission of the mortgagor. The notice has no retroactive effect.

7. Metzner *v.* Bolton, 9 Exch. 518. In this case the declaration set forth a contract between plaintiff and defendant by which the latter agreed to employ the former for one whole year. Breach, that the defendant had wrongfully dismissed the plaintiff within a year. Plea, *non-assumpsit.* At the trial the plaintiff admitted on cross examination the usage of trade to put an end to any yearly hiring on three months' notice, and the defendant contended that under these circumstances there was a misdescription of the contract in the declaration and a variance upon *non-assumpsit.* A verdict having been found for the plaintiff, a rule to set it aside for the above reason, was made absolute upon the ground that since this defeasance was attached by law to the contract as made, it should have been set forth in the declaration; for had it been set up as a defense in confession and avoidance, it would have been demurrable as qualifying the contract and as amounting to the general issue. "A contract with a defeasance," said the court," "is not the same as a contract without one, consequently the variance is fatal."

8. Brind *v.* Dale, 2 M. & W. 775.

9. Smart *v.* Hyde, 8 M. & W. 723. There are probably no cases more difficult to analyze with a view to finding a justification for the decisions than that class of which Brind *v.* Dale, 2 M. &

W. 775, and Smart *v.* Hyde, 8 M. & W. 723, are the representatives. The question in these cases is as to the propriety of pleading in confession and avoidance or of pleading the general issue—the decision of the question turning upon whether the defendant does or does not desire to set up a defense which will in effect *qualify* the declaration as the plaintiff has set it forth. If, for example, a plaintiff states a contract and the defense is that the contract as made is different in its essence from the contract as stated, obviously *non assumpsit* is the proper plea, for that denies that any such contract as the one set forth has been entered into. Therefore in Brind *v.* Dale (2 M. & W. 775) where in assumpsit the plaintiff set out a bailment of a trunk to a carrier and averred the promise by the carrier to convey the trunk in safety to a given place and assigned as a breach the failure of the carrier to deliver the chattel at that place, it was obviously improper for the defendant to plead in confession and avoidance where his defense was that the contract as made contained a stipulation that the plaintiff would watch and protect the goods in transit, from theft or loss, which stipulation the plaintiff had not performed. Counsel for the plaintiff put the case very clearly when he said: "The defendant is in this dilemma—either the plea amounts to the general issue, or it is no answer to the action." As BARON PARKE remarked: "The effect of the agreement is to protect the carrier from theft or loss; that qualifies the contract."

In Smart *v.* Hyde (8 M. & W. 723) the facts were these: The action was assumpsit, the plaintiff averring that in consideration that the plaintiff would buy of the defendant a mare at a certain price, the defendant promised the plaintiff that the mare was sound. Breach, that the mare was not sound. The defendant pleaded, *inter alia*, that before the promise he sent the mare to a certain bazar, there to be sold under certain rules, which were to the effect that all warranties of soundness should be deemed to expire at noon on the day after the sale, unless in the meantime a notice of breach of warranty was delivered at the office of the proprietor. The plea further set forth that the plaintiff had notice of these terms, that the sale and the promise were subject to them, that the same were agreed to by the parties, and that although the time limited by the rules for notice of breach had elapsed before suit commenced, yet no such notice had been delivered. Verification. To this the plaintiff filed a special demurrer assigning for causes that the plea amounted to the general issue, and that whereas the plaintiff had declared on an absolute and unqualified undertaking that the mare was sound, the defendant had attempted to qualify said promise by limiting the time for the duration of the warranty. Judgment was given for the defendant. BARON PARKE and BARON ALDERSON delivering opinions in which BARONS GURNEY and ROLFE concurred. BARON PARKE declared that the plea was not a denial of the warranty, but a mere condition annexed to it. He added. "If the matter relating to notice had been by way of proviso upon the warranty, it might perhaps have been necessary to state it in the declaration; but upon that point I give no opinion. It is enough to say that every word of this plea is consistent with the contract stated in the declaration."

Side by side with these cases may be placed Lyall *v.* Higgins (4 Q. B. 528). The action was assumpsit by the employer of a collecting clerk against the defendant, who had agreed to be security to the amount of £250 for the faithful performance by the clerk of his duties as collector and accountant. The declaration alleged that the plaintiff had employed the clerk upon the faith of the defendant's promise to be answerable for all default, and it averred that the clerk had made default which the defendant upon demand had refused to make good. The defendant pleaded that before the making of the promise the plaintiff was already under contract to employ the clerk, and that the defendant made no promise such as that mentioned in the declaration until after the plaintiff and the clerk had entered into their binding agreement. Verification. Upon special demurrer to this plea the court decided that it amounted to an argumentative denial of the consideration, and that it was therefore bad. "The matter," said LORD DENMAN, "might have been given in evidence under *non-assumpsit*. It is not a confession, but adds something to the statement in the dec-

in the declaration was not *made* by the plaintiff, a clear case for the use of *non-assumpsit* arises. Where, for example, the plaintiff alleged that he caused a policy of insurance to be effected on certain cotton, and that in consideration that the plaintiff had paid the premiums the defendants had agreed to make good all losses, but had failed so to do, it was held to amount to the general issue for the defendant to plead that the policy was not caused to be made by or on behalf of the plaintiff.[1] On the other hand, *non-assumpsit* takes issue on the making of the contract *in fact*, and is not appropriate where the defense is that an agreement by parol should have been in writing.[2] And where the defendant was sued for breach of a contract to buy the copyright of an opera, *non-assumpsit* was held to admit that the plaintiff was the author.[3] And while *non-assumpsit* denies the contract, it does not deny the *breach*. Thus, in an action for breach of warranty of soundness on the sale of a horse, the defendant, under the general issue, sought to prove that the horse was sound at the time of the sale, and that the plaintiff had himself subsequently done the injury. The evidence was excluded on the ground that the question of soundness was not in issue.[4]

While the Hilary Rules forbid the use of the general issue in actions on bills of exchange and promissory notes, yet the prohibition is confined to cases where the action is *only* on the note: if it is necessary to the plaintiff's case to prove any promise other than that contained in the instrument, the general issue will be appropriate.[5]

laration, which makes a different contract."

In view of these decisions it seems impossible to support the judgment of the court of common pleas in Sieveking *v.* Dutton, 3 C. B. 331. There the declaration alleged an absolute contract on the part of the defendant to receive wool without any condition as to quality, or any specific description. In assumpsit for non-acceptance the defendant pleaded that the sale was made with a warranty that the bulk was equal to sample, and averred that the goods tendered were not equal to sample. Verification. The court overruled a special demurrer to this plea, but assigned no satisfactory reason for so doing, although SERGEANT DOWLING argued ably in support of the demurrer.

1. Sutherland *v.* Pratt, 2 Dowl., N. S. 813. See 1 Chitty Plead. (16th Am. ed.) 499.

2. De Pinna *v.* Polhill, 8 C. & P. 78; Barnett *v.* Glossop, 3 Dowl. Pr. Cas. 625.

3. De Pinna *v.* Polhill, 8 C. & P. 78. In this case assumpsit was brought for breach of a contract to buy the poetry and music of a certain opera. Plea, *non-assumpsit.* It being admitted on cross examination that some of the opera was written by a third person, the defendant relied on this admission to support his plea. The court decided that the authorship and right to sell were not in issue; the defendant should have traversed the averment in the declaration that the plaintiff was author, and that he had the right. It was further urged that the property was such as could pass by deed only, and here the contract was not under seal. But the court held that objections to the form of the contract could not be raised: the question was—was there a contract in fact?

4. Smith *v.* Parsons, 8 C. & P. 199.

5. The rule is to be read thus: "In all actions on bills of exchange and promissory notes *simpliciter*, without any other matter." Per PARKE B., Timmis *v.* Platt, 2 M. & W. 720. In this case the suit was brought by an executor on a note given to the testator, and the declaration alleged a promise

b. Replication de Injuria.[1]—As the defendant by the general issue is permitted to deny in a general way the allegations in the declaration, so to the plaintiff is extended a similar privilege when he seeks to traverse the plea. There is this important difference, however, between the general issue and the *replication de injuria* —that while the defendant is always at liberty to plead the former, subject to the strict rules as to the scope of the evidence he can introduce, the plaintiff is permitted to use *de injuria* only in certain actions and under certain conditions. Originally it was confined to the actions of trespass and trespass on the case,[2] but its use in replevin was subsequently sanctioned,[3] then it was permitted in assumpsit,[4] and finally in debt.[5] It is a traverse which is adapted to answer matter of excuse disclosed by the plea, and will be improper where the plea operates by way of denial.[6] And the rule is the same even if the plea purports to be a plea in confession and avoidance by way of excuse, if it does in fact amount to a traverse or denial.[7] In addition to the restriction that *de injuria* is proper only in certain actions and in answer to pleas in excuse, it is a well settled rule that this traverse will be improper wherever it is taken to a plea containing matter of record,[8] matter

to the plaintiff as executor. It was held that *non-assumpsit* as to the alleged express promise was a good plea.

1. The full name of the traverse is the replication *de injuria sua propria absque tali causa—that the defendant of his own wrong and without any such cause* [*excuse*] *as is in his plea alleged* did the wrong complained of in the declaration

2. Steph. Plead. (9th Am. ed.) 164; Finch Law 398; Jones *v.* Kitchen, 1 B. & P. 76.

3. Selby *v.* Bardons, 3 B. & Ald. 2 (1832).

4. Isaac *v.* Farrar, 1 M. & W. 65 (1836), where LORD ABINGER says: "This form, though most commonly used in actions of trespass, or trespass on the case for injury, is not inappropriate to an action of trespass on the case for a breach of promise, where the plea admits a breach and contains only matter of excuse for having committed that breach. The defendant's breach of promise may be considered a wrong done, and the matter included under the general traverse *absque tali causa*, and thereby denied, as matter of excuse alleged for the breach—quoting LORD ELLENBOROUGH in Barnes *v.* Hunt, 11 East 455. But see Coffin *v.* Bassett, 2 Pick. (Mass.) 357.

5. In Salter *v.* Purchell, 1 Q. B. 197, *de injuria* was used in debt, but the case was decided against the plaintiff on another ground and the propriety of its use was not settled. In Cowper *v.* Garbett, 13 M. & W. 33, however, the use of this replication in debt was distinctly sanctioned.

6. Crogate's Case, 8 Reps. 66 (2nd Resolution); Doct. Plead. 115; Bro. Abr. *De son Tort Demesne;* Com. Dig. Pleader F. 18, *et seq.*

7. Fisher *v.* Wood, 1 Dowl., N. S. 54. This was assumpsit by the drawer against the acceptor of a bill of exchange. The defendant pleaded that he wrote his name on the paper in the form of an acceptance and that he agreed that the defendant should draw thereon a bill of exchange payable at two months; but that the defendant, in violation of his agreement, made it payable in one month. Replication *de injuria*. Special demurrer. PARKE, B.: "The plea is a denial of the contract. It is like the case of a man giving an authority to his agent to accept one kind of bill, who, instead of doing so, accepts another. You had better amend." See also Whittaker *v.* Mason, 2 Bing. N. C. 359; Cleworth *v.* Pickford, 9 M. & W. 314; Schild *v.* Kilpin, 8 M. & W. 673. But see Allen *v.* Crofoot, 7 Cow. (N. Y.) 46.

8. For the obvious reason that to permit the replication in such a case would lead to the wrong kind of trial and

of title or interest in land,[1] or an authority derived mediately or immediately from the plaintiff.[2] This includes title by lease, license or gift from the plaintiff, or lease from his lessee.[3]

It is often said that *de injuria* will be improper wherever it puts in issue an authority given by law.[4] This statement is incorrect: all authority is traversable by *de injuria* except authority under a record or from the plaintiff.[5] *De injuria* puts in issue only the existence of the cause or excuse alleged in the plea and not the character of it.[6] As *de injuria* is a traverse the form of which is

would put matter of record "in issue to the common people." Crogate's Case, 8 Reps. 66; Fursdon *v.* Weeks, L. Rev. 65. In such a case the plaintiff should reply *de injuria sua propria* and traverse the issuing of the warrant, which is matter of fact. Crogate's Case 8, Rep. 66.

1. Crogate's Case, 8 Reps. 66 (2nd Resolution); Cockerill *v.* Armstrong, Willes 99. Thus in replevin for goods and chattels *de injuria* was put in to a cognizance which averred that the place where, etc., was a house held by plaintiff of X on a yearly rent; that the rent was unpaid, and that defendant, as bailiff of X, took the chattels by way of distress. On demurrer the court held the replication bad on the ground that where the excuse arises even in part out of the seisin in fee of another, there *de injuria* is not to be received. Jones *v.* Kitchen, 1 B. & P. 76. See also Hyatt *v.* Wood, 4 Johns. (N. Y.) 150; 4 Am. Dec. 258, and cases *cited* on p. 153 (note) of Ames' Cases on Pleading. The reason for the rule seems to be that the trial of title is too weighty a matter to be made a part of an issue wherein the jury must pass on other matters as well. Accordingly the rule does not apply to a case in which title or interest is alleged only as an *inducement* to the defense, as distinguished from the case where the defendant by his plea makes title to a thing in opposition to the plaintiff. Thus, where in trespass for a battery the defendant pleaded that he was seised of the rectory of D in fee, that corn was severed from the nine parts, and that the alleged battery occurred in preventing the plaintiff from taking away defendant's corn, it was held proper to reply *de injuria*, on the ground that the plaintiff claimed nothing in the land or corn, and merely sought damages for the battery. Taylor *v.* Markham, Cro. Jack. 224; Vivian *v.* Jenkins, 3 A. & E. 741; Skeville *v.* Avery, Cro. Car. 138.

2. Crogate's Case, 8 Reps. 66 (3rd Resolution). The reason for this rule follows from the fact that the replication *de injuria* is a general replication permitted as a favor to the plaintiff. Now if the plaintiff *has* authorized the defendant to do the act in question, his case falls; if he has *not*, as the matter lies entirely in his own knowledge, there is no hardship in requiring him to deny it specially. See remarks of TINDAL, C. J., Salter *v.* Purchell, 1 Q. B. 197.

3. BARON PARKE, in Selby *v.* Bardons, 3 B. & Ad. 12. See Solly *v.* Neish, 4 Dowl. P. C. 254; Crisp *v.* Griffiths, C. M. & R. 162; Bowler *v.* Nicholon, 12 A. & E. 341.

4. Crogate's Case, 8 Reps. 66 (3rd Resolution).

5. "As a general proposition it is untrue that authority of law may not be included in the traverse, it being clear that an arrest by a private individual or a peace officer is by an authority from the law, and yet pleas containing such a justification may be denied by a general traverse." Per BARON PARKE, Selly *v.* Bardons, 3 B. & Ad. 13. See Bowler *v.* Nicholson, 12 A. & E. 354; Piggott *v.* Kemp, 1 C. & M. 197.

So when one justifies under an act of Parliament *de injuria* is proper, for the statute, as general law, can never be part of the issue. Chance *v.* Weeden, 2 Salk. 628. But see Allen *v.* Scott, 13 Ill. 80; Stickle *v.* Richmond, 1 Hill (N. Y.) 77.

6. Penn *v.* Ward, 2 C. M. & R. 338. This was an action of trespass for assault and battery. Pleas, first, not guilty; secondly, that the plaintiff was the apprentice of the defendant and conducted himself saucily, wherefore the defendant moderately chastized him, etc. Replication *de injuria* to the latter plea. At the trial the impudent behavior was proved, and thereupon the plaintiff's counsel offered to show that the defendant, in administering the

prescribed by law it would seem that it is no more open to the objection of duplicity when put in as an answer to a double plea than is the general issue when pleaded to a double declaration.[1] The improper use of *de injuria* is ground for special but not for general demurrer.[2]

3. *Special Traverse.*—This form of traverse is of a highly technical character and although anciently it was in frequent use, it is but seldom resorted to in modern times.[3] It consists of three parts, the introduction or *inducement*, the traverse or *absque hoc*, and the conclusion. The inducement usually consists of a statement of new matter amounting to an argumentative denial of the facts adversely alleged. The *absque hoc*[4] is a specific traverse of some allegation in the pleading opposed to it; and the conclusion, like that of all pleadings which contain new matter, is by way of verification. By the Hilary Rules, however, it is provided that this traverse shall conclude to the country.[5] The object of the special traverse and the reason for its use are points in regard to which the authorities differ.[6] One thing is clear from the cases, that the forms sometimes taken by this traverse varied from the normal form just described in several particulars, and that every

correction, had used excessive violence.

The evidence was admitted, and a verdict was given for the plaintiff, but a rule for a new trial was made absolute, on the ground that the excess was not in issue, and that to put it in issue a replication of excess would have been necessary. "The plaintiff puts in issue the cause, not the character, of the chastisement—that is to say, whether or no he misconducted himself as an apprentice." Per ALDERSON, B. On the question raised in this case the authorities are divided. The weight of authority in *England* supports the decision, while in America the cases manifest a tendency to disagree with it. See Hannen *v.* Edes, 15 Mass. 347. And cases *cited* in note 1, p. 173, Ames, Cases on Plead.

1. See *infra*, this title, *Duplicity*.

2. Parker *v.* Riley, 3 M. & W. 230; overruling Fursdon *v.* Weeks, Lev. 65; and Hooker *v.* Nye, 1 C. M. & R. 258. But see, to the contrary, Coffin *v.* Bassett, 2 Pick. (Mass.) 357.

3. Steph. Plead. (9th Am. ed.) 174.

4. *Absque hoc* signifies *without this that*, and is nothing more than a clumsy denial. Mr. SERGEANT STEPHEN calls it a "peculiar and barbarous formula." Steph. Plead. (9th Am. ed.) 168.

5. Gen. Reg. Hil. T., 4 W. IV. And see Steph. Plead. (9th Am. ed.) 181.

6. See Steph. Plead. (9th Am. ed.) 174, *et seq.* That learned author says that the design of the special traverse is to *explain or qualify the denial* instead of putting it in the direct and absolute form. But why explain and qualify? He answers this question by an illustration—an action of covenant brought by the heir for non-payment of rent under a lease from his ancestor, in which the defense is that the lessor had only a life estate. Here, says MR. STEPHEN, the defendant cannot traverse in the common form that the reversion belonged to the heir, for he is estopped from disputing the landlord's title; and, therefore, MR. STEPHEN concludes, the defendant must set out the limited title of the lessor by inducement, and traverse the descent of the reversion *absque hoc*. But it does not appear that a lessor for years is forbidden to traverse the allegation in the declaration that the lessor was seised in fee. Indeed, it is familiar law that he is permitted to show that the lessor had a limited interest which terminated before suit brought. MR. STEPHEN then gives a second illustration—the case in which a lease for fifty years is alleged to have been ratified by the ordinary. The fact is that the lease was ratified by the ordinary when the length of the term was left blank and was subsequently filled in as fifty years. A common traverse of the

variation involved, on strict principle, a breach of some rule of pleading. Some of these abnormal forms were tolerated by the courts for reasons of convenience or from a fondness for elaborate and subtle forms of pleading, while others were uniformly discountenanced. In the normal form of the traverse each part is essential to the validity of the whole.[1] In the first abnormal form, the *absque hoc* is a complete and sufficient answer in itself. Here an inducement is surplusage and cannot be traversed.[2] This form is sanctioned by the courts.[3]

In the second abnormal form the inducement is in itself a complete answer and the *absque hoc* is surplusage.[4] It is in such a

ratification sends the case to the jury, and the question whether such a ratification is valid in law is determined by them under the direction of the judge. But, says MR. STEPHEN, it may be desirable to keep such a case from the jury. The defendant therefore sets out the facts in the inducement, and on demurrer the whole question is decided by the court. But it is to be noted that the plaintiff *need* not demur: he may take issue on the *absque hoc*. The only certain way of accomplishing the desired end is by an *agreement* that the plaintiff should demur. But if the question is reduced to one of amicable agreement, the object could be attained more readily by a case stated or the like. But this latter reason, though possibly unsound on principle, is yet doubtless a valid illustration of the nature of the reasons which induced the courts to permit the use of some of the *abnormal* forms. It is conceived that the *normal* form can be vindicated on the basis of the strictest rules of pleading. See the following note.

1. The inducement is necessary to the validity of the *absque hoc*, and the *absque hoc* is necessary to complete the inducement. This becomes clear when reference is made to the explanation of the use of the normal form suggested by MR. EVANS. Evans on Pleading (2nd ed.), p. 29, *et seq.* That author contends that the special traverse is used where the pleader desires to traverse a point in the opposite party's pleading which is *prima facie immaterial.* The inducement accordingly states facts which show the point to be *material* and the *absque hoc* then traverses it. Thus if to a declaration charging him with a false imprisonment on the 10th of May, the defendant wishes to reply that he is sheriff and arrested the plaintiff under a writ issued, not on the 10th, but on the 15th of May, he would show by his inducement that by reason of the circumstance of the writ the *time* is material, and then by his *absque hoc*, he would deny that he arrested the plaintiff on the 10th of May, as was in the declaration alleged. See Evans on Pleading (2nd ed.) 29. In such a case, of course, Stephen's rule, that the inducement cannot be traversed falls to the ground. Steph. Plead. (9th Am. ed.) 186. He relies upon an anonymous case in 3 Salk. 353, where the inducement amounted to a direct denial, and the *absque hoc* was declared unnecessary. Such an inducement is obviously not traversable, but the abnormal form can furnish no rule for the normal. See the following note: See also Thorn *v.* Shering, Cro. Car. 586.

2. Thorn *v.* Shering, Cro. Car. 586; Trespass q. c. f. The defendant justifies by command of J S. The plaintiff replies a lease at will from J S, who was seised in fee, and traverses the command of J S. The defendant maintains his bar and traverses the lease at will. Upon demurrer it was decided that the traverse of the inducement to the replication was bad; for the *absque hoc* in the replication was a good traverse. The obvious reason for this decision is that the tenancy at will, being material upon the face of the pleadings, could be specifically traversed by the plaintiff, and accordingly the inducement was surplusage. A traverse of the inducement was therefore bad as a matter of course. See also Gerrish *v.* Train, 3 Pick. (Mass.) 124; Prosser *v.* Woodward, 21 Wend. (N. Y.) 205.

3. Thorn *v.* Shering, Cro. Car. 586.

4. Thus in Huish *v.* Philips, Cro. Eliz. 754, there was an averment that the plaintiff was bound in a statute-merchant of £600 to the defendant to

case a double plea and is bad on special demurrer.[1] In the normal form and the first two abnormal forms the inducement necessarily amounts to an indirect denial of the pleading adversely alleged.[2]

In the third abnormal form the *absque hoc* is insufficient and immaterial, and the inducement does not succeed in making it material. In such a case there is no valid traverse. The *absque hoc* may be disregarded and the inducement may be traversed by the adverse party.[3]

(*b*) **Confession and Avoidance.**—If a party does not *demur* to the pleading opposed to him he must *plead.* If he does not plead by way of *traverse,* he must plead by way of *confession and avoidance.*[4] Pleas in confession and avoidance are of two sorts—in

the use of one B, with a defeasance on payment to B on certain days, with an averment that on the days named he was at the appointed place to pay the sums, but that B was not there to receive them. The defendant pleaded that B was at the place where, etc., but that the plaintiff was not. *Absque hoc* that the plaintiff obtulit the said sum at the said day, etc. Upon demurrer it was held that the traverse was good without the *absque hoc*—in other words, that the *absque hoc* was surplusage. This case is analogous to the case in 3 Salk. 353, cited by Stephen. See *supra,* note 1. Here the inducement could not be traversed because it is itself a traverse.

1. Anon., 3 Salk. 353.

2. This circumstance leads STEPHEN to say that the *absque hoc* is required to remedy the defect of argumentativeness in the inducement. On the view here advocated the inducement is required to remedy an apparent defect in the *absque hoc.*

In Fortescue *v.* Holt, 1 Ventr. 213, which was a *sci. fa.* on a judgment as administrator of J S, the defendant pleaded that before administration was granted to the plaintiff, to-wit, etc., administration was granted to J N who is still alive. The plaintiff replied that J N died. Upon demurrer it was decided that the replication was bad for argumentativeness and the court think that the plaintiff should have traversed *absque hoc* that he was alive. But with all due deference it should seem that a special traverse need not have been used at all, and that the plaintiff might have traversed that J N was alive.

3. Mayor of Orford *v.* Richardson, 2 H. Bl. 182. This was an action of trespass for fishing in the plaintiff's free fishery, and also in their several fishery in Orford Haven, Suffolk. Plea, that Orford Haven hath been from time immemorial and is, an arm of the sea, in which every subject of the realm hath liberty to fish. Replication, that the plaintiff corporation is a corporation by prescription and by charter, and has by immemorial custom enjoyed the exclusive liberty, etc., *absque hoc* that in the said arm of the sea every subject has a right of free fishing. Rejoinder that the place in which, etc., hath been immemorially an arm of the sea, in which every subject has a right to fish, traversing the prescriptive right, claimed by the plaintiffs in the replication. Demurrer, on the ground that the defendant had taken a traverse upon a traverse. But the court held that the *absque hoc* in the replication tended to raise an immaterial issue, it being immaterial whether *every* subject had a right to fish, and that the defendant might well disregard the vicious *absque hoc* and deny the traversable matter in the inducement. See Rex *v.* Bolton, 1 Stra. 117; Thrale *v.* Bishop, 1 H. Bl. 376, and Breck *v.* Blanchard, 20 N. H. 323.

4. Steph. Plead. (9th Am. ed.) 137. *Est common erudition que le defendant en son respons et barre doit ou traverser ou confesser et avoider.* Dyer 66, b. And see Reg. Plac. 59; 21 Hen. VI, 12; 5 Hen. VII, 13 a, 14 a, b. Arlett *v.* Ellis, 7 B. & C. 346; McPherson *v.* Daniels, 10 B. & C. 263.

Pleas Amounting to General Issue.—If a plea purports to be in confession and avoidance and yet in fact amounts in substance to the general issue it is bad in form as being an argumentative traverse and will be so held on special

discharge and in *justification* or *excuse*.[1] Both sorts tend to defeat the plaintiff's suit by denying the existence of a cause of action. The former admits that a cause of action once existed, but avers that it has been discharged. The latter denies that a cause of action ever existed; for, while it admits the act charged, it contends that it was lawful.[2]

1. IN DISCHARGE.—The most important pleas of this class are payment, set-off, bar of the statute of limitations, infancy, coverture, tender, release, and bankruptcy.

a. Payment.—The defense of payment may, at common law, be given in evidence under *non-assumpsit* and under *nil debet*.[3] But in debt on specialty or on a record it must be specially pleaded.[4] After the Hilary Rules it was required to be specially pleaded in all cases.[5]

b. Set-off.—At common law, and independently of the statutes of set-off, a defendant is in general entitled to retain, or claim by way of deduction, all just allowances or demands accruing to him, or payments made by him, in respect of the *same* transaction or account which forms the ground of action.[6] But before

demurrer. For this reason and in order to compel the pleaders to hasten to issue it has long been a rule that a plea which amounts to the general issue must be so pleaded. See this subject discussed, *infra* p. 573.

1. Steph. Plead. (9th Am. ed.) 198. Com. Dig. Pleader, 3 M. 12.

2. Steph. Plead. (9th Am. ed.) 198. The division of pleas in confession and avoidance into pleas in discharge and pleas in justification or excuse seems to apply only to the *plea*. In replications and subsequent pleadings no distinction is noted between them. But pleas in confession and avoidance, wherever they occur, are subject to the rules of form given in the text.

The foregoing statement must be modified in the case of *a replication to a plea of set-off*. In such a case the distinction between excuse and discharge seems to exist. For example of such a plea see Davies *v.* Penton, 6 B. & C. 216. The set-off is virtually a new declaration: *e. g.*, several pleas may be pleaded to it.

3. Steph. Plead. (9th Am. ed.) 162, note.

4. See 2 Greenl. Ev., § 516.

5. See Goodchild *v.* Pledge, 1 M. & W. 363. There debt was brought for goods sold and delivered in the sum of £20 for board, lodging and other necessaries, etc. Pleas (1) *nunquam indebitatus;* (2) that before the commencement of the suit and when the said sum of £20 became payable, to-wit, etc., the defendant paid to the plaintiff the said sum according to the contract. Concluding to the country. The latter plea was specially demurred to on the ground that it ought to have concluded with a verification. The defendant argued that the plea was a simple denial of the breach not introducing new matter, and that it therefore properly concluded to the country. He insisted that there never was any suable cause of action, because the moment that the debt accrued, he paid it. BARON PARKE, interrupting counsel, asked, "Is the statement of the breach in debt anything more than a mere form? The moment the goods are delivered, is there not a cause of action throwing the proof of its discharge on the defendant? If the breach is mere form, you cannot traverse it; then your plea is in discharge and ought to conclude with a verification. Suppose *nil debet* pleaded under the old form; would it not be sufficient to prove the debt contracted? *The new general issue, that the defendant never was indebted, that is, at no instant of time, was framed for the express purpose of making all these defenses pleadable by way of discharge.* Leave was given the defendant to amend, ALDERSON, B., remarking, "If this is payment, it is payment of a debt; then it admits a debt; therefore it is in discharge, not in denial."

6. 1 Chitty Plead. (16th Am. ed.) 595.

the statutes of set-off,[1] where there were *cross-demands unconnected with each other*, a defendant could not set up that fact as a legal defense, but was compelled to seek relief in chancery.[2] And this was true even where the plaintiff was indebted in an amount greater than that claimed in the declaration. By the first statute of set-off it was provided that mutual debts between plaintiff and defendant, whether the suit be between them in person or whether either party sues or is sued as executor or administrator of one of the original parties to the contract, may be set against one another; and evidence of such defense may be put in under the general issue, if notice is first given; or the defense may, in proper cases, be pleaded in bar.[3] By the second statute, the question as to whether there could be a set-off of debts of a *different nature* was settled by the declaration that mutual debts could be set against one another, notwithstanding that such debts are deemed in law to be of a different nature. But where either of the debts is in the nature of a penalty it must be pleaded in bar, and the plea must specify the real debt, and judgment will be entered accordingly.[4] The debts must be *mutual debts*, and must be due to each of the parties in the same right or character.[5] The claims to be set-off must be *debts;* so that there can be no set-off in actions *ex delicto*, nor can a tort be set off against a contract. And even in actions *ex contractu* the claims must be for a sum certain or liquidated damages.[6] The debt attempted to be set-off must be due and in arrear at the time the action was commenced and not merely at the time of pleading;[7] and the debt at that time must have been a debt with a *legal* existence, not barred by the statute or satisfied by execution against the person of the debtor.[8]

1. 2 Geo. II, ch. 22, § 13; 8 Geo. II, ch. 24.

2. Collins *v.* Collins, 2 Burr. 820; Baskerville *v.* Brown, 2 Burr. 1230; Green *v.* Farmer, 4 Burr. 2214. For an account of the origin and nature of set-off, see Hayne's Outlines of Equity 158. Although the courts of common law have now such ample powers in relation to set-off, yet there are some few cases in which relief under this head can be had only in chancery. See Bisph. Eq. (4th ed.), § 327. For an account of the principles of the equitable jurisdiction in matters of set-off, see *Ex parte* Stephens, 11 Ves. 27; Freeman *v.* Lomas, 9 Hare 109.

3. 2 Geo. II, ch. 22, § 13.

4. 8 Geo. II, ch. 24, § 4. These statutes are not imperative; the defendant may waive the set-off and bring an independent suit. Brown *v.* Pigeon, 2 Camp. 595; Carpenter *v.* Butterfield, 3 Johns. Cas. (N. Y.) 146. For the rule in *New Jersey*, see Schenck *v.* Schenck, 10 N. J. L. 276. And see Lairy *v.* Chatham, 1 Camp. 252.

5. 1 Chitty Plead. (16th Am. ed.) 598. Thus, a joint debt cannot, in the absence of agreement, be set-off against a separate demand; nor *vice versa.* Grant *v.* Royal Ex. Assur. Co., 5 M. & S. 439; Kinnerly *v.* Hossack, 2 Taunt. 173; Francis *v.* Rand, 7 Conn. 221. But where to the common law powers of a court there are superadded powers akin to those of the chancellor, a defendant sued with another may set-off a debt due by the plaintiff to him. Such was the decision in *Pennsylvania*, even before the grant of equity powers to the courts. Stewart *v.* Coulter, 12 S. & R. (Pa.) 252; 14 Am. Dec. 680.

6. 1 Chitty Plead. (16th Am. ed.) 599.

7. Evans *v.* Prosser, 3 T. R. 186; Rogerson *v.* Ladbroke, 1 Bing. 93; Braithwaite *v.* Coleman, 4 N. & M. 654; 1 Chitty Plead. (16th Am. ed.) 599.

8. Remington *v.* Stevens, 2 Stra. 1271;

But the pendency of an action to recover the debt will not prevent the defendant from setting it off.[1] Nor will the right be defeated by the pendency of a writ of error where the set-off is upon a judgment.[2]

A plea of set-off must contain all the requisites essential to the validity of a plea in bar, and should also show that the debt is one which the defendant is entitled to set off.[3] Such a plea is in the nature of a new declaration; and if two distinct debts are set forth, the plea is treated like a declaration containing different counts.[4]

c. Statute of Limitations.—It is a general rule that the statute of limitations must be specially pleaded.[5] This was the rule as well before as after the Hilary Rules.[6] Where an answer has superseded the plea, this defense must be interposed by answer.[7] In some States it is the law that where the declaration or petition shows upon its face that the claim is barred, a special demurrer

Taylor *v.* Waters, 5 M. & Sel. 103. The theory of this last case is that although charging a defendant in execution does not *extinguish* the debt, it nevertheless bars all proceedings during his life. If, however, suit were brought by a debtor's executors it would seem that the debt due by the testator might be set-off notwithstanding his arrest. See remarks of LORD ELLENBOROUGH, p. 104.

If the plaintiff issues process and so tolls the statute of limitations which otherwise would have barred both claims at the date of the pleading, such action will prevent the statute from running against the defendant's set-off, although he issued no process. Ord *v.* Ruspini, 2 Esp. 570; Catlin *v.* Koulding, 6 T. R. 189.

1. Baskerville *v.* Brown, 2 Burr. 1229; Le Bret *v.* Papillon, 4 East 507.

2. Evans *v.* Prosser, 3 T. R. 188; 1 Chitty Plead. (16th Am. ed.) 600, and cases there *cited*.

3. 1 Chitty Plead. (16th Am. ed.) 602.

4. Therefore if one is good and the other defective a demurrer must not be taken to the whole on pain of being too large. Dowsland *v.* Thompson, 2 Bl. 910.

Set-off in the United States.—The practice acts or codes of the several States provide for the defense of set-off either by plea or answer. The principles outlined in the text underlie all of these statutory provisions. Such changes as have been introduced operate to extend the defense and to enlarge its operations. In *Pennsylvania*, for example, under the act of 1705, it has been decided that the *chancery* doctrine of set-off is in force. Morgan *v.* Bank N. A., 8 S. & R. (Pa.) 73; 11 Am. Dec. 575.

5. Gould *v.* Johnson, 1 Salk. 278; Draper *v.* Glassop, 1 Ld. Raym. 153; Ware *v.* Webb, 32 Me. 41; Cook *v.* Kibbee, 16 Vt. 434; Benoist *v.* Darby, 12 Mo. 196; Petty *v.* Cleveland, 2 Tex. 404. It is sometimes said that under the plea of *nil debet* the bar of the statute could be proved at the common law. And there are authorities for this view. See 1 Salk. 278. *Sed quaere*, 1 Saund. 283, note 2.

6. 1 Chitty Plead. (16th Am. ed.) 506.

7. And where statutes provide that the general issue shall be pleaded and notice of special matter given the bar of the statute must be specified as a ground of defense before the trial. See generally Parker *v.* Kane, 4 Wis. 1; 65 Am. Dec. 283; Peck *v.* Cheney, 4 Wis. 249; Humphrey *v.* Persons, 23 Barb. (N. Y.) 313; Young *v.* Epperson, 14 Tex. 618; Tazewell *v.* Whittle, 13 Gratt. (Va.) 329; Borders *v.* Murphy, 78 Ill. 81; Heath *v.* Page, 48 Pa. St. 130; Gullick *v.* Loder, 2 N. J. Eq. 68. And it is laid down as a general rule in the United States that when the defendant pleads the statute the plaintiff must reply specially and in such a manner as to apprise the defendant of the issue intended to be raised. Jarvis *v.* Pike, 11 Abb. Pr. N. S. (N. Y.) 398; Van Dike *v.* Van Dike, 15 N. J. L. 289; Crosby *v.* Stone, 3 N. J. L. 542; Webster *v.* Newbold, 41 Pa.

may be interposed.[1] But the defendant can never avail himself of the defense of the statute on general demurrer.[2]

d. Infancy.—At the common law, the defense of infancy may be given in evidence under the general issue in assumpsit,[3] but in debt on a specialty[4] in account[5] and in covenant[6] it must be specially pleaded. If the defendant waives his privilege of pleading infancy he cannot rely upon it as a ground of non-suit at the trial.[7] To a plea of infancy the plaintiff may reply that the defendant is of age;[8] or that after becoming of age he ratified the contract;[9] or that the goods were necessaries and suitable to the defendant's situation in life.[10] But evidence of a promise made after the commencement of the action will not support a replication of ratification.[11] Nor will a replication of a new promise after the defendant came of age be supported by proof of part payment.[12] Where, in assumpsit for a farrier's bill, the plaintiff, to a plea of infancy, replied that the shoeing was necessary for the horsès, the replication was adjudged ill, for *non constat* that the horses were necessary for the infant.[13]

By the Hilary Rules it is provided that infancy must in all cases be specially pleaded.

e. Coverture—(See ABATEMENT vol. 1, p. 6).—Where a *feme covert* sues, either alone or with her husband, she having no legal interest in the cause, the defense is one of substance and is available on the general issue, or by plea in bar, or by demurrer, as the case may be.[14] And it is the general rule that where two sue as husband and wife, and the defendant disputes the relation, he should plead in abatement;[15] but in an action on the case by husband and wife for slander of the wife, it was held that a plea denying that the woman was the wife of her co-plaintiff was a good plea in bar[16]

The defendant's coverture is usually pleadable in abatement,[17]

St. 482; 82 Am. Dec. 487. In England it needs no decision to establish such a point, the principles and rules of common law pleading make this course necessary.

1. Hudson *v.* Wheeler, 34 Tex. 356; Moulton *v.* Walsh, 30 Iowa 361; Vore *v.* Woodford, 29 Ohio St. 245; Collins *v.* Mack, 31 Ark. 648.

2. Rivers *v.* Washington, 34 Tex. 267.

3. Seaton *v.* Gilbert, 2 Lev. 144; Darby *v.* Boucher, 1 Salk. 279. But it was *advisable* to plead specially. 1 Chitty Plead. (1st Eng. ed.) 421.

4. Baylis *v.* Dineley, 3 M. & S. 478.

5. Com. Dig. Accompt. E. 5.

6. Com. Dig. Pleader 2, V. 4.

7. Derisley *v.* Custance, 4 T. R. 77.

8. Com. Dig. Pleader 2 W. 22.

9. Coen *v.* Armstrong, 1 M. & S. 724; Borthwick *v.* Carruthers, 1 T. R. 649; Thornton *v.* Illingworth, 2 B. & C. 824.

10. Truman *v.* Hurst, 1 T. R. 40.

11. Thornton *v.* Illingworth, 2 B. & C. 824; Coen *v.* Armstrong, 1 M. & S. 724.

12. Thrupp *v.* Fielder, 2 Esp. 628, per Lord Kenyon.

13. Clowes *v.* Brooke, 2 Stra. 1101.

If to a replication that the goods were necessaries the defendant were to demur, judgment would be given against him upon the familiar principle that facts well pleaded are confessed by demurrer—and here the defendant has admitted that the goods were in fact necessaries. Barber *v.* Vincent, Freeman 531.

14. Caudell *v.* Shaw, 4 T. R. 361; Nelthrop *v.* Anderson, 1 Salk. 114.

15. Bac. Ab. Abt. G.

16. Chantler *v.* Lindsay, 16 M. & W. 82.

17. See ABATEMENT, vol. 1, p. 6.

but in the important case where the wife is sued upon a contract alleged to have been made by her after marriage, her coverture is pleadable in bar.[1]

After the Hilary Rules, coverture was required to be specially pleaded. Before the rules, it could be given in evidence under *non-assumpsit* and *non est factum*.[2]

f. Tender.—The principle of a plea of tender is that the defendant has always been ready at all times to pay upon request, and that on a particular occasion he offered the money.[3] It must always be pleaded specially; it cannot be given in evidence under the general issue in any action.[4] It can be pleaded in general only to a money demand, for which debt or *indebitatus assumpsit* would lie and where the defendant could pay money into court.[5] If the defendant plead a tender without paying the money into court the plaintiff can sign judgment.[6] The plea is applicable only to cases in which the defendant has never been guilty of any breach of his contract.[7] And in assumpsit a tender cannot be pleaded in bar of the damages.[8] It is otherwise in the action of debt.[9] A tender may be pleaded to the whole declaration, though the practice is to plead to a particular count only.[10] The defendant is not permitted, however, to plead *non-assumpsit* or *non est factum* as to the whole and also a tender as to a part.[11] The plea should be tender of a part and *non-assumpsit* as to the part not tendered.[12] The plea should state the amount tendered and the

1. King *v.* Jones, 2 Ld. Raym. 1525; Marshall *v.* Rutton, 8 T. R. 545; Steer *v.* Steer, 14 S. & R. (Pa.) 379.

2. James *v.* Fowks, 12 Mod. 101, and see Moss *v.* Smith, 1 M. & G. 228.

3. Hesketh *v.* Fawcett, 11 M. & W. 356. If the declaration and plea show that the defendant was not *always* ready and willing to pay, such plea will be bad. Thus the acceptor of a bill of exchange who has dishonored it when due, cannot plead a subsequent tender of the amount charges and interest before action brought. Hume *v.* Peploe, 10 East 168. See Giles *v.* Hartis, 2 Salk. 622.

4. 2 Saund. Plead. 1041; 1 Saund. 33, n. 2.

5. Com. Dig. Tender. It was at first thought that a tender could not be pleaded to a count upon a *quantum meruit*. Giles *v.* Hartis, 1 Ld. Raym. 255. But the law is settled the other way. Johnson *v.* Lancaster, 1 Stra. 576; Cox *v.* Brain, 3 Taunt. 95.

6. Anon., 1 Tidd Pr. 612. See Chapman *v.* Hicks, 2 C. M. & R. 633.

7. 2 Saund. Plead. 1042, quoting Lord Ellenborough. Originally the plea of tender was regarded in the light of a dilatory plea and was construed with the same strictness. It was accordingly held that it could not be pleaded after a general imparlance. 1 Saund. 33, n. 2. It subsequently came to be regarded as a fair and honest plea to the merits of the action. Kielwick *v.* Maidman, 1 Burr. 59.

8. For that would preclude the plaintiff from recovering since the action is brought to recover damages. The proper form is to confess the damages due and pray judgment of *further* damages, interest, costs, etc. 2 Saund. Plead. 33, n. 2.

9. For the judgment is to recover the *debt*, and damages for detention, etc., are merely ancillary. The proper form, therefore, is to plead a tender in bar of the damages. See Giles *v.* Hartis, 2 Salk. 623.

10. 2 Saund. Plead. 1042.

11. Dowgall *v.* Bowman, 3 Wils. 145; Maclellan *v.* Howard, 4 T. R. 194; Jenkins *v.* Edwards, 5 T. R. 97; Orgill *v.* Kemshead, 4 Taunt. 459. See *infra*, this title, *Several Pleas*.

12. Archer *v.* Gerrard, 3 M. & W. 63.

precise sum is traversable.[1] The precise date of the tender is immaterial.[2]

2. IN EXCUSE.—While defenses which operate by discharging the defendant's liability may, by reason of their limited number, be enumerated and classified, it is obvious that the number of *excuses* of which a defendant may avail himself has no assignable limit. All pleas in confession and avoidance which are not pleas in discharge are pleas in justification or excuse.

3. REQUISITES.—Pleas in confession and avoidance must confess the truth of the allegation which they propose to answer.[3] It is clear that a pleading which contains no confession of the adverse statement must, if it be an answer at all, operate by way of denial. It therefore becomes an affirmative statement that amounts to a traverse or denial, and is accordingly bad for argumentativeness. Again it is a rule that pleadings in confession and avoidance must *avoid*, and that the avoidance must be co-extensive with the confession.[4] The extent of the confession which is required by the law is expressed in the rule that pleadings in confession and avoidance must give color.[5]

a. Color is an apparent or *prima facie* right,[6] and the meaning of the rule is that a pleading in confession and avoidance must admit in the adverse party at least enough apparent right to require an avoidance to overcome it.[7] Color is of two kinds, *implied* and *express*.

1. Marks *v.* Lahee, 3 Bing. N. C. 408.

2. 2 Saund. Plead. 1042.

3. Steph. Plead. (9th Am. ed.) 199. Formerly such pleas began with a formal confession—*true it is, that*, etc.—but this method of statement has been long since abandoned.

4. Earl of Manchester *v.* Vale, 1 Saund. 27.

5. Hatton *v.* Morse, 3 Salk. 273; Hallet *v.* Byrt, 5 Mod. 252; Holler *v.* Bush, 1 Salk. 394; Steph. Plead. (9th Am. ed.) 202. See Y. B. 40 Edw. III 23. For an analogous principle in the pleadings of the civil law, see Inst. lib. 4, tit. 14.

6. Steph. Plead. (9th Am. ed.) 202. "The plea in avoidance must give color to the plaintiff, that is, must give him credit for having an apparent or *prima facie* right of action, independently of the matter disclosed in the plea to destroy it." 1 Chitty Plead. (16th Am. ed.) 552. As CHITTY points out, there must be a confession, or there will be no room for an avoidance.

7. In case for slander the plaintiff declared that the defendant had falsely and maliciously alleged that the plaintiff had been arrested for debt and that the bailiffs were in his house—concluding with an averment of special damage. Plea, that before the speaking of the words complained of, one J S spoke and published the following words [setting out those complained of] and that the defendant then did speak and publish them as he lawfully might, alleging to those who heard him, that he repeated them as the words of J S. General demurrer and joinder therein. PARKE, B., disposed of the plea in a lucid opinion. "This plea is bad for two reasons. To be a good plea, it must confess and avoid the cause of action stated in the declaration. But this plea either does not confess, or if it confesses, does not avoid, that cause of action." He then proceeds to show that as the declaration contained no averment that the words were spoken as the words of another, it must be taken to mean that an *unqualified assertion* has been made by the defendant. Now, in order that the plea may be a good confession, the defendant must admit that the circumstances of the repetition does not amount to a qualification; but if he does this, he has deprived himself of the material for his

aa. Implied Color.—A plea is said to give implied color when it, to some extent, confesses the plaintiff's right upon the ground on which he himself has based it.[1] Thus in trespass for taking the plaintiff's corn, it is proper for the defendant to plead that the corn was set out for tithe and that he took it as rector; for it is sufficient color that the pleadings show the plaintiff to have been the original owner and entitled as against all the world except the defendant.[2]

bb. Express Color.—Express color, on the other hand, is a fictitious statement of fact injected into the declaration, and is of such a character that if it had been therein set forth the defendant in his plea might have given implied color.[3] It occurs only in trespass,[4] and was devised to facilitate the trial of title to real property. Thus in trespass *quare clausum fregit* the defense may be that J S was seised in fee and demised to the defendant for years. If the defendant pleads not guilty he will be compelled to prove his whole title. If, however, he can place upon the record an allegation of title in J S and the lease to himself, the plaintiff in his replication will be forbidden by the rule against duplicity to traverse more than one of these points. The other, greatly to the defendant's advantage, must be admitted. But the allegation of title in J S and of the lease to defendant would give no color and amount to the general issue. The defendant,

avoidance. If, on the other hand, he maintains that the repetition is a good avoidance, obviously the plea is bad as not giving color. Such is, in brief, BARON PARKE's masterly argument. McPherson *v.* Daniels, 10 B. & C. 263. See Davis *v.* Matthews, 2 Ohio 257.

1. Stephen says that implied color is "a latent quality, naturally inherent in the structure of all regular pleadings in confession and avoidance, and has been called *implied* color, to distinguish it from another kind which is in some instances formally inserted in the pleadings, and is, therefore, known by the name of *express* color." Steph. Plead. (9th Am. ed.) 205. The terms express and implied are perhaps unfortunate, as they do not suggest the true distinction. All color was originally *express*, in the sense that the plea began by the explicit confession "*true it is, that, etc.*," and yet the distinction in question existed then and was as clearly marked as it was subsequently when the formal confession was omitted. It seems that the true distinction consists in this—that in one case the defendant confesses that the plaintiff's claim, *as the plaintiff states it*, gives him an appearance of right; while in the other case the defense leaves the plaintiff *no right at all upon his own showing*, but reads into the declaration a fictitious statement of facts sufficient to give the requisite appearance of right. In short, while it is true that color of the second kind *is* express, that fact is only an incident and not its distinguishing feature. The terms "actual color" and "constructive color" are suggested as far more accurate.

2. Leyfield's Case, 10 Reps. 88. Steph. Plead. (9th Am. ed.) 203. So to trespass for taking the plaintiff's sheep, the defendant may plead that J S was possessed of them and sold them to the defendant in market overt. Such a plea does not exclude the hypothesis that the plaintiff owned the sheep — that J S was a conversioner — and that *but for the sale in market overt* the plaintiff might have followed the sheep into defendant's hands. Comyns *v.* Boyer, Cro. Eliz. 485.

3. "A feigned matter, pleaded by the defendant in an action of trespass, from which the plaintiff seems to have a good cause of action, whereas he has in truth only an appearance or color of cause." Bac. Abr. Trespasses, T. 4.

4. It occurred also in *writ of entry* and *assize*, 3 Reeves 438.

therefore, making use of a fiction, avers that the plaintiff claims by virtue of a charter of demise for the term of his life made to him by J S, whereas nothing passed by that charter, and that the plaintiff had entered under the same. He then avers his own entry under the lease from J S—as he lawfully might, which is the same trespass, etc. In short, the apparent right of the plaintiff is derived from the charter of demise, but the plea shows on its face that the right was only apparent, for the demise for life is not pleaded as a feoffment and does not appear to have been accompanied by livery of seisin.[1] Of course the right assigned must be apparent only; if it amounts to an actual right the defendant loses his case as by confession.[2]

V. Requisites of Pleading in General.—1. Materiality.—As the system of pleading at common law contemplates a decision of the entire case by the decision of a single point, it is plain that this point should be one which touches the merits of the controversy. This principle underlies the rule that all pleadings must contain matter material to the cause and material matter only.[3]

If they contain no material matter they are bad in substance; if they contain matter in excess of what is material they are bad in form. If the excess amounts to a second claim or defense the pleading is bad for duplicity;[4] if the excess falls short of a second claim or answer the plea is vicious as containing surplusage. The plainest case of immateriality occurs when a traverse is taken on a point wholly immaterial.[5] Another instance of the vice is the case in which a traverse is taken upon a point which is material to the question of damages by way of aggravation, but which is im-

1. Leyfield's Case, 10 Reps. 89 b.

2. Radford *v.* Harbyn, Cro. Jac. 122. For a discussion of the subject of color, see Steph. Plead. (9th Am. ed.) 202, *et seq.*

3. 1 Chitty Plead. (16th Am. ed.) 641; Bac. Abr. Pleas, H. 5; Austin *v.* Walker, 26 N. H. 456. See Steph. Plead. (9th Am. ed.) 239, *citing* Anon., 2 Vent. 196, where, to an action upon the promise of an intestate, the administratrix pleaded that *she, the defendant*, did not promise, etc. The plea was of course adjudged bad. See Jones *v.* Powell, 5 B. & C. 647; Hall *v.* Tapper, 3 B. & Ad. 655, and Strong *v.* Smith, 3 Cai. (N. Y.) 163.

It is important to distinguish between *informal* issues and *immaterial* issues. The former arises where a material allegation is traversed in an improper or inartificial manner (Chitty); and this error is aided by verdict in accordance with 32 Hen. VIII, ch. 30. See Gilb. Hist. C. P. 147. The latter occurs where an immaterial allegation is traversed; and this fault is not aided by verdict. 1 Chitty Plead. (16th Am. ed.) 685.

4. See *infra*, this title, *Duplicity*.

5. Steph. Plead. (9th Am. ed.) 241, Bac. Ab. Pleas, etc., H. 5; Com. Dig. Pleader, R. 8, G. 10; Walker *v.* Jones, 2 C. & M. 672; Burroughs *v.* Hodson, 9 A. & E. 499; Spaeth *v.* Hare, 9 M. & W. 326; De Medina *v.* Norman, 9 M. & W. 820; Rudford *v.* Smith, 3 M. & W. 254; Gwynne *v.* Burnell, 6 Bing. (N. C.) 453; Reg. *v.* Dendy, 22 L. J., Q. B. 247. But see Powell *v.* Bradbury, 7 C. B. 201. This case was, however, overruled in Lush *v.* Russell, 5 Exch. 203.

When in trespass for assault and battery, the defendant alleged that he assaulted the plaintiff in aid of bailiffs and at their command, as the plaintiff was attempting a rescue, it was held to be a traverse upon an immaterial point for the plaintiff to reply by denying that the defendant assaulted him by the command of the bailiffs. The defendant had a right to assist the bailiffs without their command, as an attempt

material to the existence of a cause of action.[1] An immaterial issue will also arise where a traverse is so framed that it will make the opposite party prove more than is necessary to sustain his case.[2] So also where a traverse is taken upon a point material to the case but which is alleged prematurely or by way of anticipation.[3] Nor is a traverse permitted to be taken on matter not alleged.[4] But a traverse may be taken on what is necessarily im-

at rescue is a breach of the peace. Bridgwater *v.* Bythway, 3 Lev. 113.

1. Steph. Plead. (9th Am. ed.) 242, *citing* Leech *v.* Widsley, 1 Vent, 54. This case was trespass for chasing a sheep, *per quod* the sheep died. Traverse of the *per quod* held immaterial and vicious.

2. Colborne *v.* Stockdale (1 Strange 493) decides that where, to a suit upon a bond, the defendant pleads that a part of the sum, to wit, £1,500, was won by gaming, the plaintiff is guilty of traversing an immaterial point, if he replies that £1,500 was not won by gaming *modo et forma*. Such a traverse would compel the defendant to prove the sum as alleged, whereas if so much as a single pound had been so won, that fact would vitiate the bond.

So a traverse may compel the opposite party to prove too much by being taken in the *conjunctive* instead of the *disjunctive*. Thus in Goram *v.* Sweeting, 2 Saunders 205, assumpsit was brought upon a policy of insurance, the plaintiff averring that the ship, tackle, apparel, ordnance, munitions, artillery, boat and other furniture were sunk and destroyed, and claiming therefor the amount of the insurance. The defendant pleaded that the above articles arrived in safety, without this that the ship, tackle, etc., *and* other furniture were sunk and destroyed. Upon demurrer judgment was given for the plaintiff on the ground that the traverse compelled the plaintiff to prove an entire loss of all the articles mentioned in order to recover anything; whereas if there had been the loss of a single spar he should have had the right to recover *pro tanto*. The traverse should have been in the disjunctive, instead of in the conjunctive.

In Lane *v.* Alexander (Cro. James 202) the plaintiff in ejectment entitled himself in his replication by copy granted 1st June, 43 Eliz. The defendant, maintaining his bar, traversed *absque hoc* that the queen on the 1st June, in the forty-third year of her reign, granted the land by copy *modo et forma*, etc. On general demurrer judgment was given for the plaintiff on the ground that the traverse was taken upon an immaterial point; the question being, which royal grant was prior, and not the precise date of either grant.

See cases *cited* in note 2, p. 86, Ames' Cases on Pleading, to wit, Y. B., fol. 10, pl. 47; Anon. Leon. 13; Sherman *v.* Brampton, Latch. 92; Rex *v.* Kilderly, 1 Saund. 312; Dring *v.* Respass, 1 Lev. 193; Thomas *v.* Nichols, 3 Lev. 41; Payne *v.* Brigham, 3 Lev. 228; Palmer *v.* Elkins, 2 Stra. 818; Brown *v.* Johnson, 2 Mod. 145; Helliot *v.* Shelby, 2 Ray, 902; Osborne *v.* Rogers, 1 Saund. 267; Thurman *v.* Wild, 11 A. & E. 453; Basan *v.* Arnold, 6 M. & W. 559; De Medina *v.* Norman, 9 M. & W. 820; Tempest *v.* Kilner, 2 C. B. 300; Aldis *v.* Mason, 11 C. B. 140; Caulfield *v.* Sanders, 17 Cal. 569; Thompson *v.* Fellows, 21 N. H. 425; Rogers *v.* Burk, 10 Johns. (N. Y.) 400; Baker *v.* Bailey, 16 Barb. (N. Y.) 54; Salinger *v.* Lusk, 7 How. Pr. (N. Y.) 430; Davison *v.* Powell, 16 How. Pr. (N. Y.) 467; Schaetzel *v.* Germantown etc. Ins. Co., 22 Wis. 412.

3. Thus in Sir Ralph Bovy's Case (1 Ventris 217) debt was brought upon an escape, the plaintiff setting forth in his declaration a voluntary escape. The defendant pleaded that he took the prisoner on fresh pursuit, to which it was demurred because he did not traverse the voluntary escape. But the court held that the allegation in the declaration was premature, and that therefore the defendant had a right to treat it as impertinent matter, and to pass it by as he had done. "It is out of time to set it forth in the declaration; but it should have come in the replication. It is like leaping, as HALE, C. J., said, before one comes to the stile." "As if," said the late Hon. Eli K. Price, in a marginal note to his copy of Stephen on Pleading, "any one would be fool enough to leap when he *did* come to a stile!"

4. Powers *v.* Cooke, 1 Ld. Raym. 63; Trower *v.* Chadwick, 3 Bing. N. C.

plied.[1] And where there are several material allegations the pleader may traverse which he pleases.[2] An allegation of title or estate may be traversed to the extent that it is alleged, although it need not have been alleged to that extent.[3] If a traverse is

334; Bishton *v.* Evans, 2 Cr. M. & R. 12; Worley *v.* Harrison. 3 A. & E. 669; Bird *v.* Holman, 9 M. & W. 761; Talbot *v.* Woodhouse, 3 Lutw. 474; Rex *v.* Jordan, C. T. Hurd. 255; Breck *v.* Blanchard, 20 N. H. 323; 51 Am. Dec. 222. Probably the leading case on this point is Crosse *v.* Hunt, Carthew 99. In debt upon a specialty conditioned that the defendant would marry the plaintiff, the breach assigned was that he had refused to marry her. Plea, that the defendant offered to marry the plaintiff, but she refused; *absque hoc* that he refused to take her before she refused to take him. The court held that the plaintiff did right in putting in a replication which simply denied the offer of the defendant; for the question of priority raised by the plea was idle, frivolous and impertinent: it was a traverse of matter not alleged.

1. Meriton *v.* Briggs, 1 Ld. Raym. 39; Bonner *v.* Walker, Cro. Eliz. 524; Chambers *v.* Jones, 11 East 406; R. R. Co. *v.* Hibblewhite, 6 M. & W. 707; Bowdon *v.* Hall, 4 Q. B. 840.

In Gilbert *v.* Parker, 2 Salk. 629, the defendant in replevin made cognizance that he took the cattle in question damage feasant upon the land of his master, A, who was seised of the *locus in quo.* The plaintiff answered that he was seised of one-third part and put in his cattle, *absque hoc* that A was sole-seised. Upon demurrer the court held that it was necessarily implied in the cognizance that A was sole-seised, and that therefore the plea might well traverse the sole-seisin without being open to the objection of being a traverse taken upon matter not alleged.

2. Steph. Plead. (9th Am. ed.) 243; Com. Dig. Pleader, G. 10; Moore *v.* Pudsey, Hardr. 317; Read's Case, 6 Rep. 24; Helyar's Case, 6 Rep. 24 b; Baker *v.* Blackman, Cro. Jac. 682; Young *v.* Rudd, Carth. 347; Young *v.* Ruddle, Salk. 627; Heydon *v.* Thompson, 1 A. & E. 210; Learmouth *v.* Grandine, 4 M. & W. 658.

Matter of Inducement.—It is often said that a traverse must not be taken on matter of *inducement.* This statement is misleading. It is untrue in so far as it relates to the inducement of a declaration—using that term to designate the statement of the plaintiff's *right* which the defendant is alleged to have infringed. Here the inducement can be traversed. A familiar instance is the denial of the plaintiff's property by "not possessed" after the Hilary Rules. If inducement is taken to mean all the allegations which do not involve the special charge against the defendant (see Wright *v.* Lainson, 2 M. & W. 739; Taverner *v.* Little, 5 Bing. N. C. 678) then the statement is too broad; it must be modified as suggested above. What, then, in the inducement (using it in this second and broader sense), may not be traversed? Nothing, it is submitted, except surplusage and formal matter akin to legal fictions. But the traversing of surplusage is forbidden by the general rule; therefore the statement is to be understood as having only the very limited scope of prohibiting the gainsaying of forms and fictions sanctioned by law. Thus it is said that a common or special bailment in detinue is "mere inducement" (LORD LYNDHURST, Gledstane *v.* Hewitt, 1 C. & J. 565) or "merely surplusage" (POLLOCK, C. B., Clements *v.* Flight, 16th M. & W. 42) *and is therefore not traversable.*

3. Steph. Plead. (9th Am. ed.) 247; Cockerill *v.* Armstrong, Willes 103; Tatem *v.* Perient, Yelv. 195; Wood *v.* Budden, Hob. 119; Smith *v.* Dixon, 7 A. & E. 1; Sutton *v.* Page, 3 C. B. 204; Webb *v.* Rose. 4 H. & N. 111. This rule is well illustrated in Sir Francis Leke's Case, Dyer 365, pl. 32. This was a replevin in which the defendants made cognizance of the taking of the cattle as in the soil and freehold of Sir Francis; to which the plaintiff pleaded that he was seised in his demesne as of fee of and in a close adjoining the said freehold of Sir Francis, and that from time whereof the memory of man runneth not to the contrary, Sir Francis Leke and those whose estate he hath, were used to inclose the same; but by reason of his default the cattle entered and depastured until, etc. The defendants for replication traversed that the plaintiff was seised in his demesne as of

applied to a part only of an allegation which is in its nature indivisible, it tends to raise an immaterial issue and will be bad as being too narrow.[1]

2. Singleness.—In addition to being material, the common law requires that the issue shall be *single*.

a. DUPLICITY.—It is a general rule that pleadings must not be double.[2] The declaration must not set out, in support of a single demand, several distinct matters any one of which would be sufficient to support it.[3] No plea or subsequent pleading should contain more than one complete answer to the pleading opposed

fee. To which there was a demurrer on the ground that the precise estate was not traversable; for if the plaintiff have but a license to put in his cattle, it is sufficient. But the court held that the plaintiff by setting out seisin in fee, had given this advantage to his adversary of traversing the estate as it was alleged, and they accordingly gave judgment for the defendants.

1. Morewood *v.* Wood, 4 T. R. 157; Steph. Plead. (9th Am. ed.) 249; Priddle and Napper's Case, 11 Reps. 10 b; Bradburne *v.* Kennerdale, Carth. 164.

Repleader.—Where the parties have gone to trial on an issue which is necessarily immaterial, and a verdict has been rendered thereon, relief is afforded to the defeated party by the grant of a *repleader*. This may be said to be an act of the court grantable in sound discretion to prevent injustice, and the effect of it is to cleanse the record of the immaterial issue and to compel the parties to plead anew from the point at which the error occurred. Much of the learning on immaterial issues is found in the cases relating to repleaders, which see, *infra*, this title, *Repleader*.

2. Steph. Plead. (9th Am. ed.) 251; Chitty Plead. (16th Am. ed.) 249, etc.; Com. Dig. Pleader C. 33, E. 2, F. 16; Humphreys *v.* Bethily, 2 Vent. 198; Anon., Brookes Abr., Double Plea, pl. Saunders *v.* Crawley, 1 Rolle 112; Gaile *v.* Betts, 3 Salk. 142.

This rule may be said to have had a double significance prior to 3 & 4 Anne, and but a single meaning since that statute. At the common law, a defendant could plead, in consequence of this rule, but a single plea; and also in consequence of this rule, that single plea (and the same was true of every other pleading) must needs contain only one answer or defense to the pleading opposed to it. When the statute above referred to was passed, permitting the defendant to plead several pleas, it destroyed one-half of the common law theory of singleness, and confined the operation of the rule against duplicity to the frame of a given pleading.

The rule, as given, is founded upon a principle which is of the essence of the system of pleading at common law.

3. Steph. Plead. (9th Am. ed.) 251; Currie *v.* Henry, 2 Johns. (N. Y.) 433; Jarman *v.* Windsor, 2 Harr. (Del.) 162; Bryan *v.* Buford, 7 J. J. Marsh. (Ky.) 335; Benner *v.* Elliott, 5 Blackf. (Ind.) 451; Porter *v.* Brackenridge, 2 Blackf. (Ind.) 385; Hand *v.* Taylor, 4 Ind. 409; Welch *v.* Jamison, 2 Miss. 160. And see Phillips *v.* Price, 38 Sel. 182.

Several Counts.—Before the Hilary Rules a declaration might consist of several counts, and the jury might assess entire or distinct damages on all the counts. 1 Chitty Plead. (16th Am. ed.) 424; Onslow *v.* Horne, 3 Wils. 177; Neal *v.* Lewis, 2 Bay (S. Car.) 206; 1 Am. Dec. 640; Peake *v.* Oldham, Cowp. 276; Grant *v.* Astle, Dougl. 722; Cooke *v.* Cox, 3 M. & Sel. 110; Richmond *v.* Whittlesey, 2 Allen (Mass.) 239; Vaughan *v.* Havens, 8 Johns. (N. Y.) 110; Van Rensselaer *v.* Platner, 2 Johns. Cas. (N. Y.) 21; Benson *v.* Swift, 2 Mass. 53; Blanchard *v.* Fiske, 2 N. H. 398. Counts are restatements of the plaintiff's cause of action in various and distinct shapes, and their object is to enable the plaintiff to recover on one statement if his proof fails to support him in the other. They were therefore termed *safety valves* by BARON VAUGHN in Ward *v.* Bell, 2 Dowl. 76. A substantial variation between the counts was required, and redundant counts were stricken out on motion. Lane *v.* Smith, 3 Smith 113; Meeke *v.* Oxlade, 1 New Reps.

to it.[1] But a plea may contain a statement of numerous matters, provided that they together constitute but a single defense.[2] Nor

289; Newly *v.* Mason, 1 D. & R. 508; Cunnack *v.* Gundry, 1 Chit. Rep. 709; Nelson *v.* Griffiths, 2 Bing. 412. The permission to use several counts was granted by the common law; but the practice became more common after 3 & 4 Anne, and was so greatly abused in the century following that statute, that the Hilary Rules remodeled the law on the subject as appears below.

The same count must not contain two promises in respect to the same subject matter, as a promise to pay a specific sum for attending a patient and also a promise to pay a *quantum meruit.* Hart *v.* Longfield, 7 Mod. 148. Where, however, the court can construe the promises as constituting two different (though informal) counts, that course will be adopted and the declaration will be upheld. Galway *v.* Rose, 6 M. & W. 291; Jourdain *v.* Johnson, 2 C. M. & R. 564; Cheetham *v.* Tillotson, 5 Johns. (N. Y.) 435. For full discussion of several counts, see *Declaration* and 1 Chitty Plead. (16th Am. ed.) 424.

1. Steph. Plead. (9th Am. ed.) 251. Thus, where defendant pleaded in abatement ten different outlawries in disability of the plaintiff, it was held that the plea was bad, because *one* outlawry would have sufficed to disable the plaintiff. Trevelian *v.* Seccomb, Carth. 8. The reporter in this case seems to imply that duplicity is generally no objection to a plea in abatement. "This," says MR. STEPHEN (App., note [53]), "is not law." See Bac. Ab. Abatement (P.). For other examples of duplicity, see Smith *v.* Dixon, 7 Ad. & El. 1; Rawlinson *v.* Shand, 5 M. & W. 468; Cheaseley *v.* Barnes, 10 East 73; Watriss *v.* Pierce, 36 N. H. 236; Tebbets *v.* Tilton, 24 N. H. 120; Downer *v.* Rowell, 26 Vt. 397; Hulme *v.* Muggleston, 3 M. & W. 31; Brooks *v.* Stuart, 9 Ad. & El. 854; Faulkner *v.* Chevell, 5 Ad. & El. 213; Butcher *v.* Stewart, 9 M. & W. 405; Stephens *v.* Underwood, 4 Bing. N. C. 655; Deacon *v.* Stodhart, 5 Bing. N. C. 594; Pursford *v.* Peck, 9 M. & W. 196; Tubbs *v.* Caswell, 8 Wend. (N. Y.) 129. Thus, a plea will be double which denies the authority of A to release, *and* the fact that the release was made. Nichols *v.* Arnold, 8 Pick. (Mass.) 172. See McConnell *v.* Stettimus, 7 Ill. 707. So where defendant pleaded to an action on a note that there was a failure of consideration and that the plaintiff took the note by fraud, his plea was held bad for duplicity. Burrass *v.* Hewitt, 4 Ill. 224. It is duplicity for the defendant to deny the plaintiff's seisin and to allege a right of dower in his wife. Wann *v.* M'Goon, 3 Ill. 74. In Stanton *v.* Seymour, 5 McLean 267, it was held to be duplicity for the defendant to set up legal process as justification of the imprisonment charged, and also to deny the fact of the arrest. And see United States *v.* Gurney, 1 Wash. (U. S.) 446; Exum *v.* Sheppard, 2 Murph. (N. Car.) 86; and Star Brick Co. *v.* Ridsdale, 34 N. J. L. 428.

On the other hand, a declaration is not double which counts on a two-instalment note, averring that both are due and that the defendant promised to pay both. Tucker *v.* Randall, 2 Mass. 283. And it is held in Otis *v.* Blake, 6 Mass. 336, not to be duplicity for a plaintiff in an action on an indemnity bond to set forth an attachment on his property and a payment in discharge of the suit. Nor is it duplicity in trespass to plead as to a part and to justify as to the residue. Parker *v.* Parker, 17 Pick. (Mass.) 236. A declaration in ejectment is good though there is only a single count for distinct parcels of land. Hotchkiss *v.* Butler, 18 Conn. 287. Nor is it duplicity to pray judgment for certain sums *and* interest thereon. Starr *v.* Henshaw, 1 Root (Conn.) 242. See also Darrow *v.* Langdon, 20 Conn. 288; Richmond etc. Turnpike Co. *v.* Rife, 2 Ind. 316; Commonwealth *v.* Curtis, 11 Pick. (Mass.) 134; and Sturdivant *v.* Smith, 29 Me. 387.

2. Robinson *v.* Rayley, 1 Burrow 316; Jackson *v.* Rundlet, 1 Woodb. & M. (U. S.) 381; Harker *v.* Brink, 24 N. J. L. 333; Patcher *v.* Sprague, 2 Johns. (N. Y.) 462; Tucker *v.* Ladd, 7 Cow. (N. Y.) 450; Strong *v.* Smith, 3 Cai. (N. Y.) 160; Beckley *v.* Moore, 1 McCord (S. Car.) 464; Potter *v.* Titcomb, 10 Me. 53; Waddams *v.* Burnham, 1 Tyler (Vt.) 233; Bank *v.* Hinton, 1 Dev. (N. Car.) 397; Torrey *v.* Field, 10 Vt. 353; Dent *v.* Coleman, 10 Smed. & M. (Miss.) 83; Calhoun *v.* Wright, 4 Ill. 74; Holland *v.* Kibbe, 16 Ill. 133; Stewardson *v.* White, 3 Har. & M. (Md.) 455.

will matter which is mere surplusage and which is wholly immaterial suffice to make a pleading double.[1] But matter which amounts to a second claim or answer will operate to make a pleading double notwithstanding that it is ill pleaded.[2] And a pleading which contains several answers will be double even if only one is sustainable.[3] The question is not one of substance, but of form. It follows that duplicity is a fault which can be taken advantage of only on special demurrer.[4] A pleader is not bound to demur for duplicity: he may answer both the material parts of the plea.[5]

Robinson *v.* Rayley has often been affirmed in *England.* Webb *v.* Weatherby, 1 Bing. N. C. 502; De Bernhardis *v.* Spalding, Dav. & M. 43; Bennison *v.* Thelwell, 7 M. & W. 512; Palmer *v.* Gooden, 8 M. & W. 890; Brogden *v.* Marriott, 2 Bing. N. C. 473; Rowles *v.* Lusty, 4 Bing. 428.

1. Steph. Plead. (9th Am. ed.) 259. Countess of Northumberlands' Case, 5 Reps. 98 a; Executors of Greenliffe's Case, Dyer. 42 b; Lord *v.* Tyler, 14 Pick. (Mass.) 156; Dunning *v.* Owen, 14 Mass. 157; Perry *v.* Marsh, 25 Ala. 659; Elminger *v.* Drew, 4 McLean (U. S.) 388; Stewardson *v.* White, 3 Har. & M. (Md.) 455. There is a dictum of DODDRIDGE, J., that a plea may be double although only one of the matters is material. Calfe *v.* Nevil, Poph. 186. And see Vaughan *v.* Everts, 40 Vt. 526. But such a view is contrary to the weight of authority.

2. Steph. Plead. (9th Am. ed.) 259; Bac. Ab. Pleas etc. (K. 2); Bleke *v.* Grove, 1 Sid. 175. The reason for these rules is obvious. The pleader's adversary is not permitted to plead to an immaterial point: therefore it is not possible in the first case that two issues will be presented to the jury. The mischief aimed at by the rule against duplicity is removed and the rule falls. But where there are two answers, the mischief *may* result, notwithstanding one is ill pleaded; for there is nothing to prevent the adversary from waiving the defect in form and joining both issues to the jury.

3. Wright *v.* Watts, 3 Q. B. 94, Per Patteson, J.

4. Humphreys *v.* Bethily, 2 Vent. 198; Saunders *v.* Crawley, 1 Rolle 112; Anonymous, 3 Salk. 108; Seymour *v.* Mitchell, 2 Root (Conn.) 145; Smith *v.* Northrup, 1 Root (Conn.) 387; Otis *v.* Blake, 6 Mass. 336; Stewardson *v.* White, 3 Har. & M. (Md.) 455; Martin *v.* Ray, 1 Blackf. (Ind.) 291; Briggs *v.* Grand Trunk R. Co., 54 Me. 375; Carpenter *v.* McClure, 40 Vt. 108; Currie *v.* Henry, 2 Johns. (N. Y.) 433; Bank *v.* Bartlet, Wright (Ohio) 741; Buell *v.* Warner, 33 Vt. 570; Cunningham *v.* Smith, 10 Gratt. (Va.) 255; 60 Am. Dec. 333; Armstrong *v.* Webster, 30 Ill. 333; Franey *v.* True, 26 Ill. 184; Little *v.* Perkins, 3 N. H. 469; Onion *v.* Clark, 18 Vt. 363; Green *v.* Seymour, 12 A. (Vt.) 206; Phillips *v.* Willeson, 2 Brev. (S. Car.) 477.

Therefore, where special demurrers are abolished, and their place is not supplied by a substitute, duplicity ceases to be a vice. It may remain as a blemish to the pleading in theory; but the rule against it is a law without a sanction. See Bryan *v.* Buford, 7 J. J. Marsh. (Ky.) 335; King *v.* Howard, 1 Cush. (Mass.) 137; Coyle *v.* Baltimore etc. R. Co., 11 W. Va. 94.

Except in dilatory pleas duplicity is no objection to a pleading in Alabama. Cannon *v.* Lindsey, 85 Ala. 198; Ewing *v.* Shaw, 83 Ala. 333. In California a demurrer cannot reach two or more causes of action improperly joined in one count. Frazer *v.* Oakdale Lumber etc. Co., 73 Cal. 187.

5. 1 Chitty Plead. (16th Am. ed.) 559. MR. CHITTY cites in support of his assertion that the pleader who does not demur *must* answer both matters, the cases of Bolton *v.* Cannon, 1 Vent. 272; Eyre *v.* Shelley, 6 M. & W. 274; Reynolds *v.* Blackburn, 7 Ad. & El. 161. That the pleader *may* take issue on one of the matters only is decided in Gould *v.* Ray, 13 Wend. (N. Y.) 633.

Effect of Double Plea on Replication de Injuria.—The question has never been satisfactorily settled whether or not *de injuria* will be bad for duplicity when replied to a double plea. The court in some cases appears to assume that the replication *is* double in such a case, but seems to decide that the de-

b. SEVERAL PLEAS.—The common law rule restricting the defendant to a single plea in bar was abrogated by the statute 4 & 5 Anne, ch. 16, § § 4 and 5,[1] which permits the defendant (and the plaintiff's in replevin), with leave of court, to plead as many several matters as he shall think necessary for his defense. The grounds of defense must be substantially different, but it is no objection that they appear mutually contradictory and inconsistent.[2] Thus in trespass not guilty may be pleaded with a justification and accord and satisfaction, and infancy, a release, or the

fendant cannot take advantage of the fault, because his own plea is responsible for it. Thus, in Reynolds *v.* Blackburn, 7 Ad. & El. 161, cited above by Chitty, PATTESON, J., says, "You attempt to set up a plea which you allege to be bad, because, as you contend, the plaintiff has made a bad replication. If your plea is double and there is a general replication, you cannot take advantage of your plea to make the replication bad." And LORD DENMAN adds: "The replication is at least as good as the plea." In other words, they hold that the defendant is *estopped* from finding fault with the replication. But this is not valid reasoning: for, as duplicity is a defect in form only, it is entirely cured by pleading over. Yet the two answers remain *in fact*, and the general replication puts them both in issue. Accordingly, it has been decided in some cases that *de injuria* will be held bad in such a case, as the mischief aimed at by the rule would otherwise be allowed to remain. It is submitted, however, that the decision in Reynolds *v.* Blackburn, 7 Ad. & El. 161 is correct, but that the reason there given is erroneous. *Duplicity is a fault in the frame of the plea, and can never occur where the pleader uses one of the general forms prescribed by the common law.* It is believed that no one ever objected to the general issue because the declaration might have been demurred to for deplicity. Yet the replication *de injuria* is simply a general issue permitted to the plaintiff. The same principles apply in each case; and the explanation offered above is conceived to be correct, although it has not been advanced before.

1. The text of the portion of the statute in question is as follows: "It shall be lawful for any *defendant* or tenant in any action or suit, or for any *plaintiff in replevin*, in any court of *record*, with the *leave of the court*, to plead as many several matters thereto as he shall think necessary for his defense; provided nevertheless, that if any such matter shall, upon a demurrer joined, be judged insufficient, costs shall be given at the discretion of the court; or if a verdict shall be found upon any issue in the said cause for the plaintiff or demandant, costs shall be also given in like manner; unless the judge who tried the said issue shall certify that the defendant or tenant, or plaintiff in replevin, had a probable cause to plead such matter, which upon the issue shall be found against him. Provided also that nothing in this act shall extend to any writ, declaration or suit of appeal of felony, etc., or to any writ, bill, action or information upon *any penal* statute."

2. 1 Chitty Plead. (16th Am. ed.) 588; Tidd's Prac. (9th ed.) 656; Gordan *v.* Peirce, 11 Me. 213; Watriss *v.* Pierce, 36 N. H. 236; Mott *v.* Burnett, 2 E. D. Smith (N. Y.) 52; Kellogg *v.* Baker, 15 Ab. Pr. (N. Y.) 286; Peters *v.* Ulmer, 74 Pa. St. 402.

Under codes of procedure several defenses and counter-claims may be set forth by answer. See *supra*, this title, *Pleading Under Codes*, and the following cases: Otis *v.* Ross, 8 How. Pr. (N. Y.) 193; Willet *v.* Ins. Co., 2 Bosw. (N. Y.) 679; Longworthy *v.* Knapp, 4 Abb. Pr. (N. Y.) 115; Hollenbeck *v.* Clow, 9 How. Pr. (N. Y.) 289; Blake *v.* Eldred, 18 How. Pr. (N. Y.) 240; Boyce *v.* Brown, 7 Barb. (N. Y.) 80.

The same result is accomplished under the less radical practice acts by enlarging the scope of the general issue. See *supra*, this title, *Pleading Under Codes*, and remarks of CHAPMAN, J., in Montague *v.* Boston etc. Iron Works, 97 Mass. 502. See also Wheaton *v.* Nelson, 11 Gray (Mass.) 15; Payson *v.* Macomber, 3 Allen (Mass.) 69; Granite State Bank *v.* Otis, 53 Me. 133.

statute of limitations may be joined with *non-assumpsit.*[1] But the permission to plead several pleas is within the discretion of the court, and if the proposed pleas are clearly repugnant and would create unjust delay the permission will be refused or the rule to plead will be rescinded.[2] The statutory permission applies only to courts of record, and double pleading in a county or other inferior [English] court is bad by the common law.[3]

It is a general rule that one plea cannot be taken advantage of to help or destroy another;[4] nor is one plea evidence for the plaintiff of facts disputed by the defendant in another.[5] It may be said that each plea and subsequent pleading constitutes a distinct record, the declaration being common to all; and it is a rule that a demurrer, in opening the record, opens only that branch which it terminates.[6]

The practice of inserting several counts in the declaration and the permission to plead several pleas having been grievously abused, it became necessary to impose restrictions upon the pleaders, and this was done in England by Reg. 5 of Reg. Gen. Hil. Term, 4 W. IV. This rule in terms prohibits more than one

1. 1 Chitty Plead. (16th Am. ed.) 588; Mott *v.* Burnett, 2 E. D. Smith (N. Y.) 52; Ormsby *v.* Douglas, 5 Duer (N. Y.) 665; Buhler *v.* Wentworth, 17 Barb. (N. Y.) 649.

2. 1 Chitty Plead. (16th Am. ed.) 589; Chitty *v.* Hume, 13 East 255; Gully *v.* Bishop of Exeter, 5 Bing. 42; Hammond *v.* Teague, 6 Bing. 197.

Thus the defendant cannot plead *non-assumpsit* or *non est factum* to the whole declaration and a tender as to part. Maclellan *v.* Howard, 4 T. R. 194; Fox *v.* Chandler, 2 Bl. Rep. 905; Jenkins *v.* Edwards, 5 T. R. 97; Orgill *v.* Kemshead, 4 Taunt. 459; Jackson *v.* Stetson, 15 Mass. 54. Nor can payment at the day and before the day be pleaded together. Thayer *v.* Rogers, 1 Johns. Cas. (N. Y.) 152. Nor can the defendant plead *non-assumpsit* and the stock-jobbing act, or *non-assumpsit* and alien enemy. Shaw *v.* Everett, 1 B. & P. 222; Thyatt *v.* Young, 2 B. & P. 72; Truckenbrodt *v.* Payne, 12 East 206; Shombeck *v.* De la Cour, 10 East 326. See also Dow *v.* Epping, 48 N. H. 75; Merry *v.* Gay, 3 Pick. (Mass.) 388; Union Bank *v.* Ridgeley, 1 Har. & G. (Md.) 324. And see instances *cited* in 1 Chitty Plead. 587.

3. 1 Chitty Plead. (16th Am. ed.) 587; Chitty *v.* Dendy, 1 H. & W. 169.

4. It is "a known rule and never controverted, that one plea cannot be taken in to help or destroy another, but every plea must stand or fall by itself." WILLES, C. J., in Grills *v.* Mannell, Willes 378. See Harrington *v.* Macmorris, 5 Taunt. 228; Robertson *v.* McDougall, 4 Bing. 670. See also Potter *v.* Earnest, 45 Ind. 416, and Ayrault *v.* Chamberlain, 33 Barb. (N. Y.) 229.

5. "It is well settled doctrine in our court, that each plea and pleading stands on its own ground and is not affected by any other plea, and the admissions made in pleading one plea, or found in one set of pleadings, cannot be used as cause of demurrer, or as matter of evidence in issues joined in other pleadings." BELL, J., in Bartlett *v.* Prescott, 41 N. H. 499, *cited* in 1 Chitty Plead. (16th Am. ed.) 589, note (e). See also Davies *v.* Penton, 6 B. & C. 216, and the following New Hampshire cases: Cilley *v.* Jenness, 2 N. H. 89; Chapman *v.* Sloan, 2 N. H. 464; Kimball *v.* Bellows, 13 N. H. 68; Buzzell *v.* Snell, 25 N. H. 480; Bump *v.* Smith, 11 N. H. 48; Nye *v.* Spencer, 41 Me. 272. See also Swett *v.* Patrick, 11 Me. 181; Alderman *v.* French, 1 Pick. (Mass.) 1; 11 Am. Dec. 114; Dodge *v.* McKay, 4 Ala. 346; Moore *v.* Leseur, 18 Ala. 606; Clarke *v.* Holt, 16 Ark. 257; Tommey *v.* Ellis, 41 Ga. 260; Ryan *v.* May, 14 Ill. 49; Hunter *v.* Bilyeu, 39 Ill. 367; Weems *v.* Millard, 2 Har. & G. (Md.) 143.

6. Davies *v.* Penton, 6 B. & C. 216, and cases cited in preceding note.

plea stating the same subject-matter of defense and varying only in statement. Inconsistent pleas might, however, still be pleaded under these rules if they supported grounds of defense that were substantially different.[1]

1. 1 Chitty Plead. (16th Am. ed.) 590; Duere *v.* Triebner, 5 M. & S. 103, where BOSANQUET, J., says: "The word '*inconsistent*' was studiously kept out of the rules, for the subject was discussed, and it was felt that there might be cases in which pleas might be inconsistent with each other, and sustain substantially different defenses. The object had in view was to prevent the *same* defense being pleaded in *different forms.*

The rules relating to counts and pleas are as follows: "Several counts shall not be allowed, unless a distinct subject-matter of complaint is intended to be established in respect of each; nor shall several pleas, or avowries, or recognizances be allowed, unless a distinct ground of answer or defense is intended to be established in respect of each.

Therefore counts founded on one and the same principal matter of complaint, but varied in statement, description, or circumstances only, are not to be allowed: *ex. gr.* counts founded on the same contract, described in one as a contract without a condition, and in another as a contract with a condition, are not to be allowed; for they are founded on the same subject-matter of complaint, and are only variations in the statement of one and the same contract.

So counts for not giving, or delivering, or accepting a bill of exchange in payment, according to the contract of sale, for goods sold and delivered, and for the price of the same goods to be paid in money, are not to be allowed.

So counts for not accepting and paying for goods sold, and for the price of the same goods as bargained and sold, are not to be allowed.

But counts upon a bill of exchange or promissory note, and for the consideration of the bill or note, in goods, money, or otherwise are to be considered as founded on distinct subject-matters of complaint, for the debt and the security are different contracts, and such counts are to be allowed.

Two counts upon the same policy of insurance are not to be allowed.

But a count upon a policy of insurance, and a count for money had and received, to recover back the premium upon a contract implied by law, are to be allowed.

Two counts on the same charter-party are not to be allowed.

But a count for freight upon a charter-party, and for freight *pro rata itineris* upon a contract implied by law, are to be allowed.

Counts upon a demise, and for use and occupation of the same land for the same time, are not to be allowed.

In actions of tort for misfeasance, several counts for the same injury varying the description of it, are not to be allowed.

In the like actions for nonfeasance several counts founded on various statements of the same duty are not to be allowed.

Several counts in trespass, for acts committed at the same time and place, are not to be allowed. Where several debts are alleged in indebitatus assumpsit to be due in respect of several matters, *ex. gr.* for wages, work and labor as a hired servant, work and labor generally, goods sold and delivered, goods bargained and sold, money lent, money paid, money had and received, and the like, the statement of each debt is to be considered as amounting to a several count within the meaning of the rule which forbids the use of several counts, though one promise to pay only is alleged, in consideration of all the debts.

Provided that a count for money due on an account stated may be joined with any other count for a money demand, though it may not be intended to establish a distinct subject-matter of complaint in respect of each of such counts.

The rule which forbids the use of several counts is not to be considered as precluding the plaintiff from alleging more breaches than one, of the same contract, in the same count.

Pleas, avowries, and cognizances, founded on one and the same principal matter, but varied in statement, description, or circumstances only (and pleas in bar in replevin are within the rule) are not to be allowed.

3. Certainty.—The facts set forth in pleading must be alleged with certainty.[1] Certainty is said to be of three sorts: 1st, certain-

Ex. gr. pleas of *solvit ad diem*, and of *solvit post diem*, are both pleas of payment, varied in the circumstances of time only, and are not to be allowed.

But pleas of payment, and of accord and satisfaction, or of release, are distinct, and are not to be allowed.

But pleas of payment and of accord and satisfaction, or of release, are distinct, and are to be allowed.

Pleas of an agreement to accept the security of A B in discharge of the plaintiff's demand, and of an agreement to accept the security of C D for the like purpose, are also distinct, and are to be allowed.

But pleas of an agreement to accept the security of a third person in discharge of the plaintiff's demand, and of the same agreement, describing it to be an agreement to forbear for a time, in consideration of the same security, are not distinct, for they are only variations in the statement of one and the same agreement, whether more or less extensive, in consideration of the same security, and not to be allowed.

In trespass *quare clausam fregit*, pleas of soil and freehold of the defendant, in the *locus in quo*, and of the defendant's right to an easement there, pleas of right and of way, of common of pasture, of common of turbary, and of common of estovers, are distinct, and are to be allowed.

But pleas of right of common at all times of the year, and of such right at particular times, or in a qualified manner, are not to be allowed.

So pleas of a right of way over the *locus in quo*, varying the termini or the purposes, are not to be allowed.

Avowries for distress for rent, and for distress damage feasant, are to be allowed.

But avowries for distress for rent varying the amount of rent reserved, or the times at which the rent is payable, are not to be allowed.

The examples in this and other places specified, are given as some instances only of the application of the rules to which they relate, but the principles contained in the rule are not to be considered as restricted by the examples specified.

Where more than one count, plea, avowry, or cognizance shall have been used, in apparent violation of the preceding rule, the opposite party shall be at liberty to apply to a judge, suggesting that two or more of the counts, pleas, avowries, or cognizances, are founded on the same subject-matter of complaint, or ground of answer or defense, for an order that all the counts, pleas, avowries, or cognizances, be stricken out upon which he shall indorse upon the summons, or state in his order, as the case may be, that he is so satisfied; and shall also specify the counts, pleas, avowries, or cognizances mentioned in such application, which shall be allowed.

Upon the trial, where there is more than one count, plea, avowry, or cognizance upon the record, and the party pleading fails to establish a distinct subject-matter of complaint in respect of each count, or some distinct ground of answer or defense in respect of each plea, avowry, or cognizance, a verdict and judgment shall pass against him upon each count, plea, avowry, or cognizance, which he shall have so failed to establish, and he shall be liable to the other party for all costs occasioned by such count, plea, avowry, or cognizance, including those of the evidence as well as those of the pleadings; and further, in all cases in which an application to a judge has been made under the preceding rule, any count, plea, avowry, or cognizance, allowed as aforesaid, upon the ground that some distinct subject-matter of complaint was *bona fide* intended to be established at the trial, in respect of each count so allowed, if the court or judge before whom the trial is had shall be of opinion that no such distinct subject-matter of complaint was *bona fide* intended to be established in respect of each count so allowed, or no such distinct ground of answer or defense in respect of each plea, avowry, or cognizance so allowed, and shall so certify before final judgment, such party so pleading shall not recover any costs upon the issue or issues upon which he succeeds, arising out of any count. plea, avowry, or cognizances with respect to which the judge shall so certify."

1. Com. Dig. Pleader, ch. 17; Steph. Plead. (9th Am. ed.) 333; 1 Chitty

ty to a common intent; 2dly, to a certain intent in general; 3dly, to a certain intent in every particular.[1] A pleading is *certain to a common intent* when the language used can be made to have more than one meaning only by argument or inference.[2] This is certainty of the lowest degree, but it suffices in a plea in bar.[3] The courts are sharp sighted to discover a reasonable intendment in the construction of a pleading, and in favor of such an intendment even strict grammatical construction will not always be regarded.[4] *Certain intent in general* is said to characterize a pleading when upon the facts which appear, as distinguished from possible or conceivable facts, it can have but a single meaning.[5] Certainty of this degree is required in indictments, declarations, replications, and in returns to writs of mandamus.[6] *Certain intent in every particular* is that which precludes all argument, inference or presumption against the party pleading.[7] It is required in the case of estoppels,[8] and in pleas not favored by the law, such as the plea of alien enemy.[9] Although certainty is required in all pleadings, yet it is not necessary to state that which is merely

Plead. (16th Am. ed.) 256. This term signifies a clear and distinct statement of the facts which constitute the cause of action or ground of defense, so that they may be understood by the party who is to answer them, by the jury who are to ascertain the truth of the allegations, and by the court who are to give judgment. Rex *v.* Horne, Cowp. 682.

1. Co. Litt. 303; Dovaston *v.* Payne, 2 H. Bl. 530. In this case MR. JUSTICE BULLER, after adopting the classification, remarks, "I remember to have heard MR. JUSTICE ASHTON treat these distinctions as a jargon of words without meaning. They have, however, long been made, and ought not altogether to be departed from." See Rex *v.* Lyme Regis, Doug. 149.

2. When words are used which will bear a natural sense and also an artificial one, or one to be made out by argument or inference, the natural sense shall prevail. The term common intent suggests a rule of *construction*, and not of *addition;* common intent cannot add to a sentence words which are omitted. Per BULLER, J., Dovaston *v.* Payne, 2 H. Bl. 530.

3. 1 Chitty Plead. (16th Am. ed.) 257; Rex *v.* Horne, Cowp. 682; Rockfeller *v.* Donnelly, 8 Cow. (N. Y.) 623; Oystead *v.* Shed, 12 Mass. 509; Spencer *v.* Southwick, 9 Johns. (N. Y.) 314; Washburn *v.* Mosely, 22 Me. 160; Long's Case, 5 Rep. 121 a; Colthirst *v.* Bejushin, Plow. 26; Fulmerston *v.* Stewart, Plow. 102; Cooper *v.* Monke, Willes 52; Hamond *v.* Dod, Cro. Car. 5; Poynter *v.* Poynter, Cro. Car. 194; Jacobs *v.* Nelson, 3 Taunt. 423; Innes *v.* Colquhoun, 7 Bing. 265. See Harlow *v.* Wright, Cro. Car. 105.

4. Steph. Plead. (9th Am. ed.) 380, note (c); Spyer *v.* Thelwall, 2 Cr. H. & R. 692; Rex *v.* Wright, 1 A. & E. 448; Debenham *v.* Chambers, 3 M. & W. 128; Dellevene *v.* Percer, 7 M. & W. 439.

5. Spencer *v.* Southwick, 9 Johns. (N. Y.) 317; Fuller *v.* Hampton, 5 Conn. 423. So where codes of procedure give relief against indefiniteness upon motion, it is held that the indefiniteness contemplated by the code is that which appears on the face of the pleading, and not that arising from extrinsic facts. Todd *v.* Minneapolis etc. R. Co., 37 Minn. 358.

6. 1 Chitty Plead. (16th Am. ed.) 258.

7. 1 Chitty Plead. (16th Am. ed.) 258. It is that technical accuracy which is not liable to the most subtle and scrupulous objection, so that it is not merely a rule of construction but of addition; for when this certainty is necessary, the party must not only state the facts of his case in the most precise way, but add to them such facts as show that they are not to be controverted, and, as it were, anticipate the case of his adversary. Lawes Plead. 54.

8. Dovaston *v.* Payne, 2 H. Bl. 530.

9. Casseres *v.* Bell, 8 T. R. 166.

matter of evidence.[1] Nor matter of which the court will take judicial knowledge.[2] Nor matter which is necessarily implied,[3] or which the law will presume.[4] A general mode of pleading is allowed when great prolixity is thereby avoided;[5] and so also when the allegation on the other side must reduce the matter to certainty.[6] And it is a general rule that no greater particularity is required than the nature of the thing pleaded will conveniently admit.[7] Less particularity is required when the facts lie more in the knowledge of the opposite party than of the party pleading,[8] and less particularity is requisite in the statement of matter of inducement and aggravation than in the main allegations.[9] With respect to acts valid at common law but regulated as to the mode of performance by statute, it is sufficient to use such certainty of allegation as was sufficient before the statute.[10]

a. TIME.—Pleadings must allege the time at which traversable facts occurred,[11] but time need not be alleged to matter of inducement or aggravation.[12] And the statement of the time is in general formal merely and cannot be traversed.[13] Otherwise, if it

1. See Steph. Plead. (9th. Am. ed.) 341. This statement and those which immediately follow are taken from this author's list of "subordinate rules tending to limit or restrain the degree of certainty." See also Dowman's Case, 9 Reps. 9 b; Eaton *v.* Southby, Willes 131; Digby *v.* Alexander, 8 Bing. 418.

2. Co. Lit. 303 b; Deybel's Case, 4 B. & Ald. 243.

3. Vynior's Case, 8 Reps. 81, b; Handford *v.* Palmer, 3 Brod. & Bing. 359.

4. Wilson *v.* Hobday, 4 M. & S. 125.

5. Co. Lit. 303 b; Barton *v.* Webb, 8 T. R. 459; Grey *v.* Friar, 15 Q. B. 891.

6. Mints *v.* Bethil, Cro. Eliz. 739. For the application of this rule to the plea of performance and *non damnificatus* in an action on a bond, see Steph. Plead. (9th ed.) 858, *et seq.*

7. Bac. Ab. Pleas. etc. B. 5, 5, Wimbish *v.* Talbois, Plow. 54; Smith *v.* London etc. R. Co., 7 C. B. 782. Thus in trespass for breaking the plaintiff's close with beasts, and eating his peas, a declaration not showing the quantity of peas eaten was held sufficient, because, as it was quaintly observed, "nobody can measure the peas that beasts can eat." Bac. Ab. Pleas, etc., B. 5. 5.

8. Com. Dig. Pleader, C. 26; Robert Bradshaw's Case, 9 Reps. 60 b; Rider *v.* Smith, 3 T. R. 766; Derisley *v.* Custance, 4 T. R. 77; A. G. *v.* Meller, Hard. 459; Denham *v.* Stephenson, 1 Salk. 355; Gale *v.* Read, 8 East 80. In this last case the defendant had covenanted not to carry on the business of rope making except under certain conditions, and was sued for breach of covenant. The declaration was held sufficient, although it did not specify the persons for whom it was alleged defendant made the rope. They were best known to defendant himself.

9. Co. Litt. 303 a; Bishop of Salisbury's Case, 10 Reps. 59 b; Com. Dig. Pleader, C. 31, C. 43, E. 10, E. 18; Wetherell *v.* Clerkson, 12 Mod. 597; Chamberlain *v.* Greenfield, 3 Wils. 292; Alsope *v.* Sytwell, Yelv. 17; Riggs *v.* Bullingham, Cro. Eliz. 715.

10. This is the last of the propositions laid down by MR. STEPHEN. He cites as an illustration the familiar case of a declaration in debt for rent on a demise for more than three years. In this case it is not necessary to aver that the lease was in writing, although the Statute of Frauds requires that it shall be. This rule is sometimes expressed by saying that the presumption is that the statute has been complied with: if it has not been, the defendant must plead the statute in bar. See generally Anon., 2 Salk. 519; Birch *v.* Bellamy, 12 Mod. 540; Chalie *v.* Belshaw, 6 Bing. 529.

11. Steph. Plead. (9th Am. ed.) 291; Com. Dig. Pleader, C. 19; Halsey *v.* Carpenter. Cro. Jac. 359; Denison *v.* Richardson, 14 East 291; Ring *v.* Roxborough, 2 Tyr. 473.

12. Rex *v.* Holland, 5 T. R. 607.

13. Co. Lit. 283 a; Coke *v.* Birt, 5 Taunt. 765. But it is generally the rule

forms a material point in the merits of the case.[1] The omission of the formal allegation of time is cured by pleading over, on general demurrer, or by verdict.[2] In real and mixed actions only the reign of the sovereign was required to be stated, and not the day month and year.[3]

b. PLACE.—The place at which traversable facts occurred must be alleged with certainty.[4] The place thus stated is called the *visne* or *venue*, and the allegation of the place is called *laying the venue*. In local actions the venue must be alleged truly.[5] In transitory actions the allegation is merely formal and may be laid with a videlicet.[6]

(1) *Venue.*—See VENUE.

(2) *Videlicet.*—See VENUE.

c. QUALITY, QUANTITY AND VALUE.—Pleadings must specify quality, quantity and value.[7] This rule applies both in actions for injuries to goods and to chattels,[8] and in actions brought for the recovery of real estate.[9] It does not apply in debt and *indebitatus assumpsit*.[10] But the allegations of quantity and value need not in general be proved as laid,[11] but a verdict cannot be obtained for a larger quantity or value than is alleged.[12] Allegations of quality must be strictly proved.[13]

d. PLEADING TITLE.—Pleadings must show title.[14] The meaning of this rule is that the title necessary to support the party's case must be alleged, and alleged with certainty and particularity.[15] And the title alleged must be proved as laid, even if it be set forth to an extent greater than is necessary.[16] Where a party

that the statement of time in such cases should be laid under a videlicet. Otherwise the pleader is liable to be held to proof of the time alleged. But it scarcely needed a decision to establish the rule that a videlicet cannot make that immaterial which is in law material. See Steph. Plead. (9th Am. ed.) 292, note (v) and cases there cited.

1. Nightingale *v.* Wilcoxon, 10 B. & C. 215; Edge *v.* Strafford, 1 Cromp. & J. 391;

2. Steph. Plead. (9th Am. ed.) 295, *citing* Higgins *v.* Highfield, 13 East 407.

3. Com. Dig. Pleader, C. 19.

4. Steph. Plead. (9th Am. ed.) 279; Co. Litt. 125 a. The importance of this rule in early times is obvious if regard be had to the fact that the jurors were witnesses, and that the sheriff depended upon the allegations on the record for information as to the execution of the venire. See Ilderton *v.* Ilderton, 2 H. Bl. 145; and Gilb. Hist. C. P. 84.

5. Steph. Plead. (9th Am. ed.) 283.

6. Vin. Ab., Trial M. f.; Co. Lit. 282 a. See App. to Steph. Plead. (9th Am. ed.), note (60), and Mostyn *v.* Fabrigas, Cowp. 176. This subject is fully discussed in the articles, JURY, VENUE, VIDELICET, ACTIONS.

7. Steph. Plead. (9th Am. ed.) 296.

8. Steph. Plead. (9th Am. ed.) 296.

9. Harpur's Case, 11 Reps. 25 b; Knight *v.* Symns, Carth. 204; Andrews *v.* Whitehead, 13 East 102.

10. Steph. Plead. (9th Am. ed.) 299.

11. Crispin *v.* Williamson, 8 Taunt. 107. Here, also, the practice is to lay the allegation under a videlicet. For a case in which the allegation may be material, see Rubery *v.* Stevens, 4 B. & Ad. 241.

12. Steph. Plead. (9th Am. ed.) 299.

13. Steph. Plead. (9th Am. ed.) 300.

14. Steph. Plead. (9th Am. ed.) 303. See this subject lucidly treated by that learned author.

15. For the forms appropriate to the different estates and tenures, see 2 Chitty Plead.

16. Cudlip *v.* Rundle, Carth. 202; Sir Francis Leke's Case, Dyer, 365, pl. 32.

makes a fee simple title in himself or in another whose authority he claims, it is sufficient to aver that he was seised in his demesne as of fee;[1] but in pleading a particular estate its commencement must be shown.[2] A party who claims under a conveyance must state its nature,[3] and one who claims as heir must state his pedigree and show how he is heir.[4] With regard to the *amount* of title which must be shown, it is in general sufficient in personal actions to allege a title of mere possession.[5] But in replevin the plaintiff must show a general or special property in the chattels.[6] It is often sufficient to plead a general freehold title.[7] In alleging title in an adversary it is not in general necessary to allege it more precisely than is sufficient to show a liability in the party charged.[8] Accordingly, in such a case, it is not necessary to state the commencement of a particular estate,[9] nor to supplement the allegation of heirship by showing *how* the adversary is heir.[10]

e. EXCEPTIONS AND PROVISOS.—Where the plaintiff declares upon a statute or upon an instrument, and the statute or instrument contains a saving clause on which the defendant intends to rely, the question arises whether the plaintiff must notice the clause in his declaration and aver that his adversary is not within the exception, or whether he can omit all mention of it and leave it as a defense to be pleaded by the defendant. The rule is that when a *prima facie* cause of action is disclosed by the statute or instrument notwithstanding the clause, the plaintiff may disregard it.[11] This is the case when the exception occurs in a statute or clause subsequent to the statute or general clause on which the plaintiff relies.[12] If, on the other hand, it appears on the face of the statute or instrument that there is not a shadow of right in the plaintiff unless he negatives the exception, he must in his declaration show that his adversary is not within it.[13] Thus if a statute

1. For there would be no end to the chain if the pleader were required to trace the estate back to its *creation*.

2. Co. Lit. 203 b; Scilly *v.* Dally, 2 Salk. 562; Hendy *v.* Stephenson, 10 East 60. This rule does not apply when the estate is pleaded merely by way of inducement. Com. Dig. Pleader, E. 19, ch. 43; Skevill *v.* Avery, Cro. Car. 138; Lodge *v.* Frye, Cro. Jac. 52.

3. Com. Dig. Pleader E. 23, E. 24.

4. The omission to allege heirship is a fault in substance; the failure to show *how* the pleader is heir is an error in form only. See Heard *v.* Baskerville, Hobart 232.

5. See the separate article on each action—as TRESPASS, TROVER, DETINUE, etc.

6. See *supra*, p. 539.

7. For the plea of *liberum tenementum*, see *infra*, p. 576, n. 1.

8. Steph. Plead. (9th Am. ed.) 321. For although a party is bound to know the particulars of his own title it is otherwise with respect to that of his adversary. Rider *v.* Smith, 3 T. R. 766.

9. Blake *v.* Foster, 8 T. R. 487.

10. Denham *v.* Stephenson, 1 Salk. 355.

11. See opinion in Commonwealth *v.* Hart, 11 Cush. (Mass.) 135.,

12. Spieres *v.* Parker, 1 T. R. 141; Rex *v.* Jarvis, 1 East 643. See Minis *v.* United States, 15 Pet. (U. S.) 445.

13. Plowd. Com. 410; Steph. Plead. (9th Am. ed.) 443.

"If," says LORD TENTERDEN, in Vavasour *v.* Ormrod, 6 B. & C. 430, "an *act of parliament* or a *private instrument*, contain in it, first, a general clause, and afterwards a separate and distinct clause, something which would otherwise be included in it, a party relying upon the general clause, in pleading

creates an offense, and a subsequent section recognizes an exception, the exception need not be noticed by the party prosecuting.[1]

4. Directness.—Pleadings should state *facts* only, not matters of law; and the facts must be alleged with directness, not by way of argument or inference or in ambiguous terms.[2]

a. ARGUMENTATIVENESS.—Although the pleader should avoid the statement of conclusions of *law*, he should be careful to state conclusions of *fact*. And the rule against argumentativeness applies not only to the frame of the pleading taken by itself,[3] but also to the form of the pleading when regarded as an answer to another pleading.[4] It is argumentative to allege that a piece of cloth was found upon measuring to be ten yards long, when the object of the pleader is to state its length. The averment should be that it was ten yards in length and was so found upon measuring.[5] On the other hand, it is argumentative to seek to deny liability to the plaintiff for carrying goods away by alleging that the plaintiff never had any goods.[6] So also it is generally true that two affirmatives do not make a good issue;[7] for unless the second

may set out that clause only, without noticing the separate and distinct clause which operates as an exception. But if the exception itself be incorporated in the general clause, then the party relying upon it must in pleading state it with the exception; and if he state it as containing an absolute unconditional stipulation, without noticing the exception, it will be a variance. This is a middle case. Here the exception is not in express terms introduced into the reservation, but by *reference only* to some subsequent matter in the instrument. The words are 'except as hereinafter mentioned.' The rule here applies *verba relata inesse videntur*. And the clause thereinafter mentioned must be considered as an exception in the general clause, by which the rent is reserved; and then, according to the rule above laid down, the plaintiff ought in his declaration to have stated the reservation and the exception. Not having done so, I am of opinion that the variance is fatal, and that there is no ground for setting aside the nonsuit."

1. "There is a manifest difference between a proviso and an exception. If an exception occurs in the description of the offense in the statute, the exception must be negatived, or the party will not be brought within the description. But, if the exception comes by way of proviso, and does not alter the offense, but merely states what persons are to take advantage of it, then the defense must be specially pleaded, or may be given in evidence under the general issue, according to circumstances." Per BARON ALDERSON, in Simpson *v.* Ready, 12 M. & W. 740.

2. Rex *v.* Horne, Cowp. 683; Baynes *v.* Brewster, 1 G. & D. 674; Randall *v.* Shropshire, 4 Metc. (Ky.) 327; Watriss *v.* Pierce, 36 N. H. 236; Goshen etc. Turnpike Co. *v.* Sears, 7 Conn. 92; Clark *v.* Lineberger, 44 Ind. 223; Hale *v.* Dennie, 4 Pick. (Mass.) 503; Fidler *v.* Delavan, 20 Wend. (N. Y.) 57. See 1 Chitty Plead. (16th Am. ed.) 236, note (g), *citing* statement of LORD DENMAN in Baynes *v.* Brewster, 1 G. & D. 660: "The general propositions necessary to the case of a party should be stated in plain terms, and not left to inference from particular circumstances."

3. Steph. Plead. (9th Am. ed.) 384.

4. Steph. Plead. (9th Am. ed.) 386.

5. Ledesham *v.* Lubram, Cro. Eliz. 870. This case is a good example of the excessive technicality which brought the science of pleading into disfavor. But like all extreme cases it serves the purposes of illustration.

6. Doct. Pl. 4; Dyer, 43 a, cited in Steph. Plead. (9th Am. ed.) 384. In this case the court remarked, "This is an infallible *argument* that the defendant is not guilty, and yet it is no plea." See also Wood *v.* Butts, Cro. Eliz. 260.

7. Steph Plead. (9th Am. ed.) 384.

is inconsistent with the first it constitutes no answer; and if it *is* inconsistent, it operates as a denial only by way of inference.[1] Nor do two negatives make a good issue; as where it is alleged that the defendant requested the plaintiff to deliver a certain paper, but that the plaintiff neglected to deliver the same, and the plaintiff replies that *he did not neglect* instead of averring that *he did deliver*.[2]

The most important branch of this rule is expressed in the formula that a plea which amounts to the general issue should be so pleaded.[3] The theoretical objection to such a special plea is that it is argumentative; the practical objection is that, by postponing the conclusion to the country, it tends to prolixity and delay in the pleadings.[4] It is a rule of general, although not of universal, application: it is said that the court is not bound to enforce it, and may in its discretion allow a special plea which amounts to the general issue, "if it involve such matter of law as might be unfit for the decision of a jury."[5] As the matter lies in the discretion of the court, it was formerly the practice to raise the objection by motion;[6] but subsequently a demurrer was used for the same purpose and seems to have supplanted the motion. There is an important difference between matter which may be

1. Thus where it is alleged that A was seised in fee, and the reply avers that he was seised in tail, it is obviously only by the application to the allegations of a piece of legal reasoning that we discover the second averment to be a denial of the first. Doct. Pl. 349; 5 Hen. VII, 11, 12.

Argumentativeness and the Special Traverse.—"It is this branch of the rule against *argumentativeness* that gave rise to the form of a *special traverse*. Where, for any of the reasons mentioned in a preceding part of this work, it becomes expedient for a party traversing to set forth new affirmative matter, tending to explain or qualify his denial, he is allowed to do so; but as this, standing alone, will render his pleading *argumentative*, he is required to add to his affirmative allegation an express denial, which is held to cure or prevent the argumentativeness." Steph. Plead. (9th Am. ed.) 386. There can be no question that the inducement of a special traverse, standing alone, would be argumentative, and that the effect of the *absque hoc* is to render the traverse valid. But whether it be the *object* of the inducement to explain and qualify the adversary's case, as MR. STEPHEN thinks it is, is a matter discussed, *supra* this title, *Special Traverse*.

2. Martin *v.* Smith. 6 East 555; Steph. Plead. (9th Am. ed.) 386. It may be doubted whether the true explanation of this rule is not the impossibility of proving the allegations. As a negative is not susceptible of proof, the affirmative element must be introduced into the issue by one party or the other.

3. Steph. Plead. (9th Am. ed.) 418; Holler *v.* Bush, Salk. 394; Warnear *v.* Wainsford, Hob. 127; Birch *v.* Wilson, 2 Mod. 227; Brind *v.* Dale, 2 M. & W. 775; Clements *v.* Flight, 16 M. & W. 42. But see Dewes *v.* Manhattan Ins. Co. 34 N. J. L. 244.

4. Warner *v.* Wainsford, Hob. 127. See remarks of MR. STEPHEN (9th Am. ed.) 420. The explanation of the rule should seem to be two-fold—as given above in the text. It is hard to conceive of a case (as MR. STEPHEN does) in which a plea amounts to the general issue without being argumentative—or at least "inferential."

5. Steph. Plead. (9th Am. ed.) 420; Birch *v.* Wilson, 2 Mod. 274; Carr *v.* Hinchlifie, 4 B. & C. 547. Examples of such pleas in the action of trover are numerous; the following are a few of the cases which exhibit them: Ward *v.* Blunt, Cro. Eliz. 147; Warner *v.* Wainsford, Hob. 127; Aylesworth *v.* Harrison, Winch. 20; King *v.* Rotham, 1 Freem. 39; Whittelsey *v.* Wolcott, 2 Day 431.

6. Ward & Blunt's Case, 1 Leon 178.

given in evidence under the general issue and matter which *amounts* to the general issue. Thus in assumpsit a release may, by laxity of practice, be given in evidence under *non assumpsit;* but it is clear that it might be pleaded specially without objection.[1]

b. AMBIGUITY.—It is a branch of the rule in favor of directness that pleadings must not be ambiguous.[2] When a pleading is susceptible of two meanings, the courts will adopt that which is the more unfavorable to the party pleading.[3] Thus, if there be a reasonable doubt as to whether the justification alleged in the plea extends to the particular acts charged in the declaration, the doubt will be resolved in favor of the plaintiff.[4]

The subject of ambiguity may be examined under the several heads of Negative Pregnant, Affirmative Pregnant, Common Bar, and New Assignment.

(1) *Negative Pregnant.*—A negative pregnant is a statement of fact, negative in form, which suggests a material affirmative statement of different significance.[5] Thus where, to a declaration in trespass, the defendant pleaded that he entered by license, it was a negative pregnant for the plaintiff to reply that he did not enter by license. It was ambiguous and doubtful whether the plaintiff meant to deny the license or the entry; he might traverse either

1. See also Dewees *v.* Manhattan Ins. Co., 34 N. J. L. 244.

It is clear that the decision of the question whether or not a plea in a given action amounts to the general issue depends upon the decision of the prior question—what is the scope of the general issue in that particular action? This subject is discussed, *supra,* under the title, *General Issue.*

2. Steph. Plead. (9th Am. ed.) 378.

3. Bac. Max. Reg. 3; Co. Lit. 303 b; Purcell *v.* Bradly, Yelv. 36; Rose *v.* Standen, 2 Mod. 295; Dovaston *v.* Payne, 2 H. Bl. 530; Thornton *v.* Adams, 5 M. & S. 38; Lord Huntingtower *v.* Gardiner, 1 B. & C. 297; Howard *v.* Gosset, 10 Q. B. 359; Fletcher *v.* Pogson, 3 B. & C. 192; Ackroyd *v.* Smith, 10 C. B. 164; Goldham *v.* Edwards, 18 C. B. 389. In this latter case the very important principle was enunciated that there is no distinction in the mode of construing a plea whether it comes before the court on demurrer or on motion for judgment *non obstante veredicto.* It had formerly been thought that ambiguity was aided by pleading over. See Steph. Plead. (9th Am. ed.) 378, note (t).

4. Thus in Goodday *v.* Michell, Cro. Eliz. 441, where trespass was brought for breaking down two gates and three hedges, the defendant pleaded a right of way over the land in question, alleging that the plaintiff wrongfully erected two gates and three hedges to obstruct the right of way, whereupon he, the defendant, broke down those gates and hedges as he lawfully might. Upon demurrer, WALMSLEY, J., remarked that the plaintiff might have erected *four* gates and *six* hedges—one-half of each rightfully and one-half wrongfully—and that the action might be brought to recover for the tearing down of those rightfully erected. Accordingly, as there was nothing to show that the gates and hedges mentioned in the plea were the same as those mentioned in the declaration, the word "*aforesaid*" or its equivalent being omitted, the court unanimously gave judgment against the plea. See also Com. Dig. Pleader, E. 5; Manser's Case, 2 Reps. 3.

5. "A *negative* allegation, involving or admitting of an affirmative implication, or at least, an implication of some kind favorable to the adverse party." Gould Plead. (5th ed.) 295, *citing* Lit. Rep. 65; Com. Dig. Pleader, R. 5; 2 Lill Ab.. 274; Bac. Abr. Pleas, etc., n. 6. It was said by the ancient writers to be a negative pregnant with an affirmative. Mr. Stephen says it is "such a form of negative expression as

separately, but not both together.[1] But if the affirmative statement with which the negative is pregnant is an immaterial statement no ground for exception arises.[2]

The objection to a negative pregnant must be taken on special demurrer, since the various statutes of jeofails.[3] At the common law, a general demurrer was sufficient. By the common law, a negative pregnant was aided by a verdict in which the finding showed for which party judgment ought to be given.[4] But by statute a negative pregnant is aided by a verdict for either of the parties.[5]

(2) *Affirmative Pregnant.*—An affirmative pregnant is an affirmative allegation implying some *negative* in favor of the adverse party.[6] Thus where, to a declaration in assumpsit, the defendant pleads that he did not undertake within *ten* years, it is an affirmative pregnant to reply that the defendant did undertake within *ten* years. For there is here an implication that the defendant did *not* undertake within the statutory period of six years.[7] The same principles apply to affirmatives pregnant as to negatives pregnant, and the pleader's proper course is to demur.[8]

(3) *Common Bar.*[9]—Where in trespass *quare clausum fregit* the plaintiff at the common law declared generally for a trespass in

may imply or carry with it an affirmative." P. 380 (9th Am. ed). See Appendix to Steph. Plead. note (65).

1. Myn *v.* Cole, Cro. Jac. 87. "Therefore the law refuseth double pleading, and negative pregnant, though they be true, because they do inveigle, and not settle the judgment on one point." Per LORD HOBART, Slade *v.* Drake, Hob. 295.

Where A brought an action for negligently keeping a fire whereby his house was burnt, B pleaded that the house was not burnt by defendant's negligence in keeping the fire. The plea was held bad, as having two intendments—a denial of the burning or a denial of the negligence. Y. B. 28 Hen. VI, 7.

2. Gould Plead. (5th ed.) 298. Thus in debt for labor done where the plaintiff alleged that the defendant retained him *in husbandry*, and the defendant pleaded that he did not retain the plaintiff *in husbandry*, it was held that the implication of a different retainer was immaterial and not a technical negative pregnant, for proof of any retainer other than in husbandry would not maintain the declaration, but would be a variance.

3. Bac. Abr. Abatement, etc., B. Pleas, etc., I 6; Gould Plead. (5th ed.) 298.

4. Thus where the defendant pleads a release since the issuing of the writ and the plaintiff traverses that he released since the issuing of the writ, the verdict, if found for the defendant, will entitle him to judgment and will cure the negative; but if found for plaintiff it does not show who is entitled to judgment; for the affirmative implication of *release before the date of the writ* (which, if true, is a complete defense) is still undetermined. See Gould Plead. (5th ed.) 297.

5. 32 Hen. VIII, ch. 30.

6. Gould Plead. (5th ed.) 295.

7. Blackmore *v.* Tidderley, 2 Ld. Raym. 1099; Macfadzen *v.* Olivant, 6 East 387. It is obvious that no proper issue could be joined on such a plea for reasons suggested in the case of a negative pregnant. If the verdict were for the defendant on issue joined, he would indeed have more than defended himself; but if it were for the plaintiff it would still be doubtful whether his cause of action were barred or not. The plaintiff should therefore demur to the plea. *Quaere*, whether he might not treat the allegation of more years than six in the defendant's plea as surplusage and reply that *the defendant did undertake and promise within six years*.

8. Gould Plead. (5th ed.) 299.

9. Common Bar is treated of in this

the township of A, the defendant might plead that the act alleged occurred in B, in the said township (B being a place either real or fictitious), which was the defendant's own freehold. This plea was called the *common bar*, and its effect was to compel the plaintiff to new-assign, and to specify without ambiguity or indefiniteness the place in which the alleged trespass occurred. The law on this point is summarized by Mr. JUSTICE BLACKSTONE in the opinion cited in the note.[1]

place because of its intimate relation with new-assignment—and new-assignment seems to range itself under the head of ambiguity, as it is made necessary by an indefinite or ambiguous declaration. The division-line is by no means clear, and the whole topic might be treated under *certainty*.

1. This lucid opinion is printed by Professor Ames in a note on page 234 of his collection of "Cases on Pleading." Professor Ames there says: "In Martin *v.* Kesterton, 2 Blackst. 1089, on a demurrer to a declaration in trespass *quare clausum fregit*, containing neither the number, names, nor any description of the closes, BLACKSTONE, J., delivered the following opinion: I have looked into this matter with some attention. And I conceive that anciently, upon a writ of *quare clausum fregit*, the plaintiff might (and may still) declare either generally, for breaking his close at A, or might name the close in his count, as for breaking and entering his close called Blackacre in A, or might otherwise certainly describe the same. If he declared generally, and the defendant pleaded the general issue, the plaintiff might give evidence of a trespass in any part of the township of A. Heath Maxims 12. So that for the advantage of the defendant, and to enforce the plaintiff to ascertain the place exactly, a method was devised of permitting the defendant to plead what is called the common bar, that is, to name any place, as Bloomfield (true or false was immaterial), and in A as the place where the supposed trespass happened, and then to allege that such place so named was the defendant's own freehold. And, as the plaintiff could prove no trespass in Bloomfield, this drove him to a new assignment of the *locus in quo*, by naming the place in certain, as a close called Blackacre, to which the defendant was now to plead afresh. And this came to be so much the course that (though it had been held in 9 Edw. IV 23, 24, that if the plaintiff named the place in certain by his count, he could not afterwards vary from it), yet in 15 Edw. IV 23, it was held by Brian and Littleton that it was mere nugation and surplusage for the plaintiff to name the close in his declaration, and that it should not put the defendant out of his usual course of pleading the common bar and giving the close another name; and an amendment (quite contrary to what is now wished) was directed striking the name out of the plaintiff's declaration. AndBrook, abridging this case (Travers III), draws from it this general rule, "That a thing put in declaration, which is not usual, shall not put the other partyout of his common course of pleading." And the same is laid down as law in Hob. 16, 10 Jac. I, "That if the plaintiff in trespass assigns a place,the defendant may plead at another place without traversing the place assigned by the plaintiff,and then the plaintiff may take a new assigment." Catesby, however, 21 Edw. IV 18, held the contrary; that if the plaintiff names the place, the defendant shall answer to the place as laid, and shall not give it another name. At length Fairfax, 22 Edw. IV 17, lays down the rule very clearly, and reconciled the whole by taking this difference: "If the plaintiff gives a name by his writ, the defendant cannot vary from this name. But if the writ be only in general, *quare clausum fregit*, and the plaintiff gives a name in his count, this shall not bind the defendant, but he may give the plaintiff another name, and change the name he has given. But if the name be in the writ and also in the count, then it cannot be varied from." That is, in short, that upon a general writ the plaintiff ought not to declare specially; and if he does the special name is surplusage. And so it was understood, 5 Hen. VII 28; Bro. Trespass 277: "*Hoc patet* that in a general writ of trespass the defendant may give a name, but the plaintiff in his count cannot give it a name."

(4) *New Assignment.*—Whenever the defendant, either by availing himself of the common bar or other intentionally evasive plea, or by a *bona fide* misapprehension of the declaration, has framed a plea in reference to other facts than those which the plaintiff has in mind, the latter must *new-assign*—that is, set forth with greater definiteness and exactness in the replication the cause of action which has already been set forth in the declaration.[1] New assignment, having for its object to set the defendant right in regard to the meaning of the declaration, obviously differs from an ordinary replication in that it does not profess to *reply* to the plea.[2] It is rather a new and more specific declaration. And this is the theory upon which it has been decided that a new assignment does

And as it became a practice to sue out only general *clausum fregits*, and the law was held that upon such general writs the plaintiff either could not at all, or could not to any conclusive effect, count of any close in certain, the mode of declaring generally, pleading the common bar, and making a new assignment, seems to have been universally adopted. See Aston 505, in 11 Eliz., and all Coke's Entries of Cases in the Common Pleas, for in the proceedings by bill in the King's Bench the declarations are all of a place certain. But as this practice was circuitous and full of delay, a rule was made in the Common Pleas about the time of Heath Max. 13 (and he was Chief Justice in Charles the First's time), for the benefit of the plaintiffs, to permit them to declare in certain; which was afterwards engrafted into the code of rules, A. D. 1654, and is clearly only permissive, and not compulsory upon the plaintiff. "The declaration upon an original or bill *quare clausum fregit*, may mention the place certainly, and so prevent the use and necessity of the common bar and new assignment," § 17; but when the plaintiff has so declared, § 19, is peremptory on the defendant, "that the common bar and new assignment be forborne, where the declaration contains the certainty equivalent to a new assignment." And that it was so understood at the time, and immediately after, and appears from the many precedents to be met with in the many books of general declarations, with the common bar and new assignment, subsequent to 1654. As in Lilly 444, 33 Car. 2, Lutw. 1301, 1372, 1385, 1399, 1467, from 36 Car. II to 9 Wm. III. For the practisers could not be induced all at once to depart from their ancient forms, though as the new regulations were evidently calculated for the benefit of the plaintiff, by preventing circuity and delay, the old practice gradually wore out; and the last of these general declarations which I have seen (till the present) is in the Common Pleas 5 Geo. I. Still, however, the law permits the plaintiff to use this circuity and to delay himself, if he be so advised; and therefore the reporter of Elwis and Lomb, H. 2 Ann. in the King's Bench, 6 Mod. 110, is a little mistaken, or has expressed himself ambiguously in one point, by supposing the rule to be compulsory on the plaintiff instead of optional. If we read *may*, instead of *shall*, what he represents the court to have said will be perfectly right. "Now there is a fixed course established in the Common Pleas, that in local actions the plaintiff shall ascertain the place in his declaration, to prevent such general pleas and the prolixity of a new assignment; and the defendant is confined to the place ascertained in the declaration." Salkeld, in reporting the same case, 453, states the manner of declaring to be still optional in the plaintiff. "In trespass *quare clausam fregit* in D. (i. e., without naming the close), if the defendant plead *liberum tenementum*, and issue be joined thereon, it is sufficient for the defendant to show any close that is his freehold. But if the plaintiff gives the close a name, he must prove a freehold in the close named. So adjudged in the Common Pleas, and the judgment affirmed in the King's Bench on a writ of error."

1. See Steph. Plead. (9th Am. ed.) 220 *et seq.*

2. 1 Chitty Plead. (16th Am. ed.) 654. For other authorities on new assignment, see Com. Dig. Pleader, 3 M. 34;

not, by its silence, admit the truth of facts alleged in the plea.[1] As the new assignment is a *restatement* of the declaration, it is obvious that it should disclose no other cause of action than that relied upon in the declaration; if it does the plaintiff is guilty of departure.[2] But if the defendant in his plea answers a part of the declaration and mistakes the rest, the plaintiff may well reply to the part which the defendant has hit and new-assign as to the rest.[3] If the defendant justifies and proves his justification but fails to answer in full matter of aggravation alleged in the declaration the plaintiff cannot obtain damages for the matter unanswered unless he new-assigns.[4] Where the plaintiff in trespass *quare clausum fregit* names his close and supports his allegation by proof, he is not bound to new-assign, although the defendant has a close of the same name in the same parish.[5] New-assignment occurs generally in the action of trespass, but it seems to be allowed in all actions in which the form of the declaration makes the reason for it equally applicable.[6] In cases where it is necessary, successive new-assignments may be made.[7]

Steph. Plead. (9th Am. ed.) 220, *et seq.;* Gould Plead. (5th ed.) 425; Tidd (9th ed.) 690.

1. Norman *v.* Westcombe, 2 M. & W. 360. This was an action of trespass for breaking and entering the plaintiff's house. Plea, a justification by way of entry to distrain goods fraudulently removed by F, the defendant's tenant, and deposited with plaintiff. New assignment that the defendants broke and entered upon an occasion other than that mentioned in the plea. To the new-assignment the defendants pleaded the same defense as before, but on the trial they fail to prove that F was their tenant or that rent was in arrear. It was contended that as these facts were averred in the original plea, they stood admitted on the record by the new-assignment. But the court decided that an assignment had no such operation. "It is not an admission, but is the same as if the plaintiff were to say, "I do not choose, and never intended to go for that trespass, which you have attempted to justify." Per. Lord Abinger, C. B. And see Dand *v.* Kingscote, 6 M. & W. 197; Robertson *v.* Gantlett, 16 M. & W. 289; Brancker *v.* Molyneux, 1 M. & G. 710; Wilmshurst *v.* Bowker, 5 Bing. N. C. 35. It is, in effect, an assertion that the cause of action referred to in the plea is not the cause of action of which the plaintiff complains.

2. In Taylor *v.* Smith, 7 Taunt. 156, trespass was brought for stopping the plaintiff's cattle and cart on the 17th of October. The defendant pleaded not guilty and a sufficient justification, and thereupon the plaintiff replied *de injuria* to the justification and newly assigned acts of trespass on other distinct days. The court, on motion to set aside a verdict in favor of defendant, held that as the only act complained of in the declaration had been adequately answered by the plea there could be no new-assignment.

3. Prettyman *v.* Lawrence. Cro. Eliz. 812.

4. Monprivatt *v.* Smith, 2 Camp. 275. But where the acts alleged in the declaration constitute distinct trespasses and are not mere matter of aggravation, and the defendant pleads not guilty, there the plaintiff can recover damages for all without new-assigning. Bush *v.* Parker, 1 B., N. C. 72.

5. Cocker *v.* Crompton, 1 B. & C. 489. Here the defendant, who had pleaded that the close was his own close soil and freehold, ingeniously argued that he was at liberty to apply all the proof to his own close. But the court were of a contrary opinion. "I am clearly of opinion," said Chief Justice Abbott, "that the plaintiff was not bound to new-assign in this case. In order to compel him to do that, as a name was given to the close in the declaration, the defendant should have given some further description in his plea."

6. Steph. Plead. (9th Am. ed.) 226. See Batt *v.* Bradley, Cro. Jac. 141.

7. Pugh *v.* Griffiths, 7 A. & E. 827.

5. Consistency.—As it is required that neither the effect of a pleading taken alone nor its effect as an answer to a prior plea shall be left to deduction or inference, so it is required that a pleading be consistent with itself and also consistent with the other pleadings of the same party. When a pleading is inconsistent with itself it is said to be *repugnant;* when it is inconsistent with the prior pleading of the same party, the pleader is guilty of *departure.*

a. REPUGNANCY.—Pleadings must not be insensible nor repugnant.[1] If the repugnant allegation can be suppressed so that the pleading will be substantially good without it, then it may be stricken out on motion, and the pleading be allowed to stand.[2] But if the repugnancy is, as it were, *of the essence of the pleading,* the whole will be declared bad on special demurrer.[3] And the pleading will be bad on special demurrer if the excision of the inconsistency would leave the pleading without an allegation of time or other material matter.[4] Such a pleading is, however, in many cases aided by verdict.[5]

b. DEPARTURE.—A departure takes place when, in any pleading, the party deserts the ground that he took in his last antecedent pleading and resorts to another.[6] Such a proceeding, if permitted, would spin out the record and be productive of endless prolixity.[7] A departure may be either from *fact to fact* or

1. Steph. Plead. (9th Am. ed.) 377.

2. The same principle applies to such a pleading as to one which contains immaterial matter. If it is possible to separate the wheat from the chaff, the court will not sacrifice the good with the bad. The maxim "*utile per inutile non vitiatur*" applies to such a case. See *supra,* this title, *Materiality.* See also Gilb. Hist. C. P. 131; Rex *v.* Stevens, 5 East 255; Co. Lit. 303 b.

3. 1 Chitty Plead. (16th Am. ed.) 255; Com. Dig. Pleader, C. 23; Wyat *v.* Ayland, 1 Salk. 324; Nevil *v.* Soper, 1 Salk. 213; Butt's Case, 7 Reps. 25 a; Hutchinson *v.* Jackson, 2 Lut. 1324; Hart *v.* Longfield, 7 Mod. 148; Byass *v.* Wylie, 1 C. M. & R. 686; Sibley *v.* Brown, 4 Pick. (Mass.) 137; Barber *v.* Summers, 5 Blackf. (Ind.) 339.

In Nevil *v.* Soper, 1 Salk. 213, the plaintiff declared for the removal of timber which was to be used for the completion of a house then lately built. The declaration was held to be repugnant; for it is idle to talk of completing a house already built.

So of a count on a promise to pay a *quantum meruit* and also a specific sum for the same service. Hart *v.* Longfield, 7 Mod. 148. So of a plea that, in virtue of a grant out of a term, the defendant became seised of a freehold. Butt's Case, 7 Reps. 25 a.

4. 1 Chitty Plead. (16th Am. ed.) 255; Gilb. Hist. C. P. 131.

5. Gilb. Hist. C. P. 131. And see Denison *v.* Richards, 14 East 291.

6. Steph. Plead. (9th Am. ed.) 410. "A departure in pleading is said to be, when the second plea containeth matter not pursuant to the former, and which fortifieth not the same; and therefore it is called decessus, because he departeth from his former plea." Co. Litt. 304 a. "A departure in pleading is said to be when a man quits or departs from one defense which he has first made and has recourse to another: it is when the second plea does not contain matter pursuant to his first plea, and which does not support and fortify it." MR. SERGEANT WILLIAMS, in 2 Saund. 84, note (11).

7. 2 Saund. 84 a, note (1); Steph. Plead. (9th Am. ed.) 410. And see Dudlow *v.* Watchorn, 16 East 39; Winstone *v.* Linn, 1 B. & C. 460; Richards *v.* Hodges, 2 Saund. 84; Prince *v.* Brunatt, 1 Bing. N. C. 435; Tolputt *v.* Wells, 1 M. & S. 395; Fisher *v.* Pimbley, 11 East. 188; Meyer *v.* Haworth, 8 A. & E. 457; Green *v.* James,

from *law to law:* an illustration of the latter being the case where the declaration is founded on the common law while the replication relies on special custom or statute.[1] But it is no departure to forsake an allegation which is *immaterial*.[2] Nor is matter a departure which explains or fortifies the declaration or plea.[3] A departure obviously cannot occur before the replication, but it may, of course, occur in that or in any subsequent pleading. And it is settled law that a departure, wherever it occurs, is a fault in sub-

6 M. & W. 656; Keay *v.* Goodwin, 16 Mass. 1; Hapgood *v.* Houghton, 8 Pick. (Mass.) 451; Haley *v.* McPherson, 3 Humph. (Tenn.) 104; Andrus *v.* Waring, 20 Johns. (N. Y.) 160; Tarleton *v.* Wells, 2 N. H. 308; McGavock *v.* Whitfield, 45 Miss. 452.

1. 1 Chitty Plead. (16th Am. ed.) 675; Co. Litt. 304 a; Rex *v.* Larwood, Carth. 306.

2. Thus in Gledstane *v.* Hewitt, 1 Cr. & J. 565. 1 Tyr. 450, detinue was brought on bailment of a promissory note to be redelivered on request. The defendant set up a defense by way of pledge, and the replication averred a tender of the amount of the loan. The question was whether the admission of the special bailment in the replication was a departure from the allegation of general bailment in the declaration. It was held to be no departure, as the statement of bailment in detinue is formal merely, and not traversable. See Lee *v.* Rogers, 1 Lev. 110.

So in Legg *v.* Evans and Another, 6 M. & W. 36, a declaration in trover alleged that the plaintiff was lawfully possessed *as of his own property*, The replication disclosed a special property by way of lien. This was held to be no departure: for the property set forth in the replication was sufficient to support the action.

3. Countess of Arran *v.* Crispe, 1 Salk. 221; Dye *v.* Leathersdale, 3 Wils. 20; Bagshawe *v.* Goward, Cro. Jac. 148; Darling *v.* Chapman, 14 Mass. 103. Thus, in Owen *v.* Reynolds, Fortesc. 341, debt was brought on a bond to indemnify the plaintiff from tonnage due to J S. . The defendant pleaded *non damnificatus;* the plaintiff replied that J S distrained for the coals, and the rejoinder averred that nothing was due to J S for tonnage. It was held to be no departure; for if nothing was due there could have been no damage—at least according to the condition of the bond.

In Fisher *v.* Pimbley, 11 East 188, the action was debt on a bond conditioned to perform an award. The defendant pleaded *no award made.* The replication set out an award in part; and the rejoinder set out the entire award—which was upon its face illegal as being contrary to the terms of submission. It was held to be no departure: for the rejoinder did but emphasize the plea that no award was made—no award, that is, which had any proper legal existence. Per LORD ELLENBOROUGH, C. J. *Quaere* of the doctrine of this case. It should seem that the defendant should have pleaded his defense in bar at the first. *Compare* Richards *v.* Hodges, 2 Saund. 83. This was debt on a bond conditioned to save the plaintiff harmless. The plea was that the plaintiff had not been damnified. The replication specified a damnification. The defendant rejoined that he had offered to bear the expense, etc., that the plaintiff refused, and that the damnification was of the plaintiff's own wrong. Yet the court held the rejoinder was a departure, and that the defendant should have pleaded his defense in bar. And this is in accord with the cases of Cossens *v.* Cossens, Willes 25, and Cutler *v.* Southern, 1 Saund. 116. Here the decision is, in effect, that it is departure to deny that damage in fact occurred and then to admit damage in fact but to deny damage in law. So in Fisher *v.* Pimbley it should be a departure to deny an award in fact and subsequently to admit an award in fact and to deny only its legal sufficiency. Fisher *v.* Pimbley is followed, however, in Young *v.* Beck, 1 C. M. & R. 448; Hickes *v.* Crackwell, 3 M. & W. 72; Gisbourne *v.* Hart, 5 M. & W. 50, and in Allen *v.* Watson, 61 Johns. (N. Y.) 205. In this last case, which is strikingly similar to Fisher *v.* Pimbley, SPENCER, C. J., says, "I confess that until I examined the case of *Fisher* and *Pimbley*, my impressions were that the rejoinder was a depart-

stance, cognizable on general demurrer.[1] A demurrer is the only mode of taking advantage of a departure.[2] And if either party, instead of demurring, takes issue on a pleading containing a departure, the court will not arrest the judgment if the verdict is given against him.[3]

6. Technical Requisites.—Law, as a science, has its own terminology, and remedial law, in particular, recognizes and favors certain formal rules which look toward the enforcement of the rights of parties in an orderly way. As a branch of remedial law, the science of pleading comprises a great number of these rules, the wisdom and utility of which have in many cases been recognized from the earliest times to the present day.

a. CONFORMITY TO PRECEDENT.—Pleadings should observe the known and ancient forms of expression as contained in approved precedents.[4] This rule is obviously rather directory than mandatory: it is only in plain cases of willful disregard of legal forms that a pleading faulty in this respect will receive more than a passing condemnation. But in extreme cases the courts will, on demurrer, reject a plea which departs from a well established and useful custom.[5]

ture; but I cannot resist the solid reasoning of the judges in that case, that a void award is no award, and that it is not inconsistent to say that there is no award, and afterwards point out in a subsequent pleading, facts which conclusively show that what is alleged to be an award is not an award" (p. 207). Possibly a different conclusion would have been reached had the court examined Richards *v.* Hodges, 2 Saund. 83. Joy *v.* Simpson, 2 N. H. 179 asserts a doctrine contrary to that of Fisher *v.* Pimbley; but the court relies upon Barlow *v.* Todd, 3 Johns. (N. Y.) 367, which must be considered as superseded by Allen *v.* Watson, 16 Johns. (N. Y.) 205. On the whole, although the doctrine of Richards *v.* Hodges was once well established, that case should now seem to have been overruled.

1. 1 Chitty Plead. (16th Am. ed.) 679; Palmer *v.* Stone, 2 Wils. 96; Tarleton *v.* Wells, 2 N. H. 306. It seems reasonable to hold the plaintiff guilty of an error in substance if he forsakes the ground of recovery taken in his declaration, but it is not so clear that the defendant does a substantial wrong when he shifts his ground of defense. The defendant's fault would seem to be one of form only—if it be a fault at all. See Com. Dig. Pleader, F. 10, and 1 Saund. 117.

2. Keay *v.* Goodwin, 16 Mass. 1; Andrus *v.* Waring, 20 Johns. (N. Y.) 160; Spencer *v.* Southwick, 10 Johns. (N. Y.) 259; Brine *v.* Great Western R. Co., 2 B. & S. 402. But see Reilly *v.* Rucker, 16 Ind. 303, *cited* in 1 Chitty Plead. (16th Am. ed.) 679, note (r^1).

3. 1 Chitty Plead. (16th Am. ed.) 679; Lee *v.* Raynes, Sir T. Raym. 86; 2 Saund. 84 d.

4. Steph. Plead. (9th Am. ed.) 391; Com. Dig. Abatement, G. 7; Buckley *v.* Thomas, Plow. 123; Dally *v.* King, 1 H. Bl. 1; Dowland *v.* Slade, 5 East 272; Rex *v.* Frazer, 6 East 351; Wright *v.* Clements, 3 B. & Ald. 507. "The object of having certain recognized forms of pleading is to prevent the time of the court from being occupied with vain and useless speculations as to the meaning of ambiguous terms." POLLOCK, C. B., in Williams *v.* Jarman, 13 M. & W. 128.

5. Thus in Dyster *v.* Battye, 3 B. & Ald. 448, the defendant, relying on the Statute of Limitations, pleaded that he was *not guilty within six years*. "From the passing of the statute to the present case," said CHIEF JUSTICE ABBOTT, "the invariable form of pleading the statute to an action on the case for a wrong, has been, to allege *that the cause of action did not accrue within six years, etc.*, and it is important to the administration of justice that the usual and established forms of plead-

b. COMMENCEMENTS AND CONCLUSIONS.—For reasons similar to those which have just been noted, it is a rule of the common law that the pleadings shall have their proper formal commencements and conclusions.[1] These are the stereotyped formulas with which the pleadings begin and end.[2] A defect or im-

ing should be observed." A demurrer to the plea was accordingly sustained. *Cf.* the language of LORD COKE: "The order of good pleading is to be observed, which, being inverted, great prejudice may grow to the party tending to the subversion of the law. *Ordine placitandi servato servatur et jus.*" Co. Lit. 303 a.

"It was impossible" says Mr. Reeves (vol. 3, 463), "that a set form of expression should be designed for every matter that might become the subject of a declaration or plea. But many modes and circumstances of properties recurred so often in judicial inquiries as to obtain apt and stated forms of description and allegation, which were established by long usage; the experience of them having shown them preferable to all others. These, therefore, were adhered to by pleaders, and the nicety with which they were conceived is a strong mark of the refinement and curiosity with which this part of our law was cultivated."

1. Steph. Plead. (9th Am. ed.) 393; Co. Lit. 303 b; Com. Dig. Plead. E. 27, 28, 32, 33, F. 4, 5, G. 1; Bower *v.* Cook, 5 Mod. 146.

2. The following summary of commencements and conclusions with the remarks upon each form is taken from Stephen on Pleading (9th Am. ed.) 393, *et seq.* A plea to the jurisdiction has usually no *commencement* of the kind in question. Its *conclusion* is as follows:

—— the said defendant prays judgment, if the court of our lord the king will or ought to have further cognizance of the plea aforesaid; or (in some cases) thus:

—— the said defendant prays judgment if he ought to be compelled to answer to the said plea here in court.

A plea in suspension seems also to be in general pleaded without formal *commencement.* Its *conclusion* is thus:

—— the said defendant, prays that the suit may remain or be respited without day until, etc.

A plea in abatement is also usually pleaded without a formal *commencement* within the meaning of this rule. The *conclusion* is thus:

——In case of plea founded on objection to the frame of the original writ (in real or mixed) on the declaration (in personal) actions:

—— prays judgment of the said writ (or declaration), and that the same may be quashed.

In case of plea founded on the disability of the party:

—— prays judgment, if the said plaintiff ought to be answered to his said declaration.

A plea in bar has this *commencement:*

—— says that the said plaintiff ought not to have or maintain his aforesaid action against him the said defendant, because he says, etc.

This formula is called *actio. non.*

The *conclusion* is:

—— prays judgment if the said plaintiff ought to have or maintain his aforesaid action against him.

A replication to the plea to the jurisdiction has this *commencement:*

—— says, that notwithstanding anything by the said defendant above alleged, the court of our lord the king here ought not to be precluded from having further cognizance of the plea aforesaid, because he says, etc.; or this:

——Says that the said defendant ought to answer to the said plea here in court, because he says, etc.

And this *conclusion:*

——Wherefore he prays judgment, that the court here may take cognizance of the plea aforesaid, and that the said defendant may answer over, etc.

A replication to a plea in suspension should probably have this *commencement:*

—— says that notwithstanding anything by the said defendant above alleged, the suit ought not to stay or be respited because, he says, etc.

And this conclusion:

——Wherefore, he prays judgment if the suit ought to stay or be respited, and that the said defendant may answer over.

A replication to a plea in abatement has this *commencement:* Where the plea was founded on objection to the declaration:

—— says, that his said declaration by reason of anything in the said plea

propriety in respect of these commencements and conclusions is, in general, ground for demurrer.[1] But if the proper judgment is prayed for in the commencement an improper prayer in the conclusion is immaterial.[2] So also a proper prayer in conclusion is sufficient though the commencement be informal.[3]

c. PLEADING ACCORDING TO LEGAL EFFECT.—Things are to be pleaded according to their legal effect.[4] This rule extends to

alleged, ought not to be quashed; because he says, etc.

Where the plea was founded on the disability of the party:

——says that, notwithstanding anything in the said plea alleged, he, the said plaintiff, ought to be answered to his said declaration, because he says, etc.

The *conclusion* in most cases is thus, in the former kind of plea:

——Wherefore, he prays judgment, and the said judgment may be adjudged good, and that the said defendant may answer over, etc.; in the latter:

——Wherefore he prays judgment, and that said defendant may answer over, etc.

A replication to a plea in bar has this *commencement:*

——says, that by reason of anything in the said plea alleged he ought not to be barred from having and maintaining his aforesaid action against him, the said defendant, because he says, etc.

This formula is commonly called *precludi non.*

The *conclusion* was thus; in debt:

——Wherefore he prays judgment and his debt aforesaid, together with his damages by him sustained, by reason of the detention thereof, to be adjudged to him.

In *covenant:*

——Wherefore he prays judgment and his damages by him sustained, by reason of the said breach of covenant, to be adjudged to him.

In *Trespass:*

——Wherefore, he prays judgment, and his damages by him sustained, by reason of the committing of said trespass, to be adjudged to him.

In *trespass on the case;* in assumpsit;

——Wherefore he prays judgment, and his damages by him sustained, by reason of the not performing of the said several promises and undertakings to be adjudged to him.

In trespass on the case—in general;

——Wherefore, he prays judgment, and his damages by him sustained, by reason of the committing of the said several grievances, to be adjudged to him.

And in all *other actions* the replication, in like manner, concluded with a prayer of judgment for damages, or other appropriate redress, according to the nature of the action. With respect to pleadings subsequent to the replication, it will be sufficient to observe in general, that those on the part of the defendant commence and conclude like the plea; those on the part of the plaintiff, like the replication.

While pleadings have thus, in general, their formal *commencements* and *conclusions*, it is to be observed there is an exception to this rule, in the case of all such pleadings as *tender issue.* These, instead of the conclusions with a *prayer of judgment*, as in the above forms, conclude (in the case of the trial by jury) *to the country;* or (if a different mode of trial be proposed) with other appropriate formulæ. Pleadings which tender issue have, however, the formal *commencements*, unless they are pleaded in bar or maintenance of the whole action generally; for in that case the rule of court dispenses with these formulæ altogether.

1. Steph. Plead. (9th Am. ed.) 403; Nowland *v.* Geddes, 1 East 634; Wilson *v.* Kemp, 2 M. & S. 549; Le-Bret *v.* Papillon, 4 East 502; Weeks *v.* Peach, 1 Salk. 179; Powell *v.* Fullerton, 2 B. & P. 420; Com. Dig. Pleader, E. 27. For the doctrine that a bad conclusion nullifies the plea and, in certain cases, operates as a discontinuance, see Bisse *v.* Harcourt, 3 Mod. 282, and Weeks *v.* Peach, 1 Salk. 179.

2. Steph. Plead. (9th Am. ed.) 403.

3. Steph. Plead. (9th Am. ed.) 403.

4. Com. Dig. Pleader, C. 37; Steph. Plead. (9th Am. ed.) 389. Thus the conveyance by a joint tenant to his fellow is pleaded as a *release;* the grant of his estate by tenant for life to reversioner as a *surrender;* a lease for years as a *demise*, etc. See Steph. Plead. (9th Am. ed.) 390.

all instruments in writing and to all contracts, written or oral.[1] In the case of declarations in actions for words an exception occurs, and the words themselves, being the basis of the action, must be set forth.

d. ORDER OF PLEAS—See *supra*, p. 520, n. 2.

e. CONSTRUCTION OF PLEADINGS—See INTERPRETATION.

VI. MOTIONS BASED UPON THE PLEADINGS—1. In Arrest of Judgment—See JUDGMENT.

a. AIDER BY VERDICT—See AMENDMENT; VERDICT.

2. Non Obstante Veredicto—See JUDGMENT; VERDICT.

3. Repleader.—When issue has been joined on an immaterial point the court will award a repleader if that is the only way in which substantial justice can be effected.[2] The effect of a repleader is to cleanse the record of the faulty pleadings and those subsequent to it, and to compel the parties to plead anew.[3] It is said to be an *act of the court*, and, as such, is in the judge's discretion. On repleader each party pays his own costs, because it is a judgment of the court on the pleading.[4] A repleader will not be granted except where the issue *must* be immaterial. If it *may* be material the application will be refused.[5] Nor will a repleader be granted to the party who made the first substantial fault in the pleading.[6] Nor where technically there has been no issue.[7] Nor where the pleading traversed discloses facts fatal to the case of the party pleading it.[8] In such a case if the party in default is plaintiff the judgment will be arrested; if he is defendant, judgment will be given *non obstante veredicto*.[9] As a repleader will be granted only when there is no other means of avoiding injus-

1. Steph. Plead. (9th Am. ed.) 391; Stwud *v.* Lady Gerard, 1 Salk. 8.

2. 2 Saund. 319*b*; Staple *v.* Heydon, 6 Mod. 1; Havens *v.* Bush, 2 Johns. (N. Y.) 388; Gould *v.* Ray, 13 Wend. (N. Y.) 638; Gerrish *v.* Train, 3 Pick. (Mass.) 124; Eaton *v.* Stone, 7 Mass. 312. See in particular Goodburne *v.* Bowman, 9 Bing. 667.

3. Staple *v.* Heydon, 6 Mod. 1. In this case it is said that when a repleader is awarded the amendment must begin when the plea which makes the issue bad begins to be faulty; and therefore if one makes himself a bad title to his declaration, to which there is a bad bar, and thereupon a bad replication, on which there is issue, there the repleader must be awarded and entered on record; and the plaintiff shall declare *de novo*, etc. But if the bar be good or the plea be good, and the replication bad, and issue thereupon, there a repleader will be only as to replication; but if bar and replication be both bad, and a repleader is awarded, it must be as to both.

4. Staple *v.* Heydon, 6 Mod. 1.

5. Thus in trespass for taking and impounding cattle, the defendant pleads title to the place where, averring that he demised the same to W, and took the cattle as distress for rent in arrear. The plaintiff replies that the cattle were not levant and couchant, upon which they go to issue and a verdict is given for the plaintiff. The court refused to order a repleader, for perhaps the defendant chased the cattle upon the land liable to the distress and then levancy and couchancy is material. Kemp *v.* Crews, 1 Ld. Raym. 167. See Clears *v.* Stevens, 8 Taunt. 413.

6. Doogood *v.* Rose, 9 C. B. 132; Taylor *v.* Whitehead, 2 Dougl. 475.

7. This was the case in Staple *v.* Haydon, 6 Mod. 1.

8. Rex *v.* Philips, 1 Stra. 394.

9. Steph. Plead. (5th ed.) 110. See Witts *v.* Polehampton, 3 Salk. 305. It is to be recollected that the motion in

tice, it would seem that if an aggrieved defendant can in all cases have a motion in arrest of judgment and that if an aggrieved plaintiff may move for judgment *non obstante*, there is no room for a motion for a repleader. But there appears to be one case in which the remedy by motion for judgment *non obstante* fails the plaintiff, and that is the case where the defendant has confessed the cause of action, not expressly, but *by silence*. Here judgment *non obstante* will not be granted, while a repleader must be.[1] At common law a repleader, when proper, might be awarded before verdict, but since the statutes which provide that a verdict may cure informal issues a repleader is generally not granted until after verdict.[2] And where there are several pleas on the record one of which raises an immaterial issue, a repleader will not be awarded if material issues are raised by the others.[3]

PLEASURE CARRIAGE.—See CARRIAGE, vol. 2, p. 737; BICYCLE, vol. 2, p. 191.

PLEDGE AND COLLATERAL SECURITY.—See also BAILMENTS, vol. 2, p. 40; BILLS AND NOTES, vol. 2, p. 313; CONDITIONAL SALES, vol. 3, p. 324; MORTGAGE, vol. 15, p. 725; CHATTEL MORTGAGE, vol. 1, p. 175.

arrest of judgment is one which the defendant alone can make. The motion for judgment *non obstante* is usually made by the plaintiff, but is probably open to both parties.

1. Duke of Rutland *v.* Bagshawe, 19 L. J. R., Q. B. 234.

2. Staple *v.* Haydon, 6 Mod. 1. That the statutes of jeofails do not cure *immaterial* issues is seen from Reed *v.* Dawson, 2 Mod. 140, ATKINS, J., dissentiente. In this case "SCROGGS, J., asked, merrily, if debt be brought upon a bond, and the defendant plead that Robin Hood dwelt in a wood, and the plaintiff join issue that he did not, this is an immaterial issue; and shall there not be a repleader in such a case after verdict? *Ad quod non fuit responsum.* The reason given in the text for the difference of practice before and after the statute of jeofails is that assigned by the court in Staple *v.* Heydon, 6 Mod. 1. But as the statute did not affect an immaterial issue it is difficult to see any logic in the explanation. Saunders thinks the word "immaterial" is a mistake of the reporter, 2 Saund. 319, note (6.)

3. Negelen *v.* Mitchell, 1 Dowl., N. S. 110; 1 Chitty Plead. (16th Am. ed.) 687, note (s).

I. **Definition.**—A pledge is a bailment of personal property, as a security for some debt or engagement.[1] Where the thing

1. Story on Bailments, §§ 7, 286; Bouvier's Law Dict.; 2 Kent's Com. 577; Anderson's Law Dict.; Brewster *v.* Hartley, 37 Cal. 15; Markham *v.* Jaudon, 41 N. Y. 241; Mitchell *v.* Roberts, 17 Fed. Rep. 778.

A deposit of personal property as security, with an implied power of sale upon default. Jones on Pledges, § 1; Corbett *v.* Underwood, 83 Ill. 324; Doane *v.* Russell, 3 Gray (Mass.) 382.

A pledge is where the owner of a chattel agrees with another person that it shall be held by the latter as security for the payment of a debt or performance of an obligation. This entitles the pledgee to hold the chattel until payment or performance, and upon failure of payment or performance at the proper time, to sell it; but until he does so, the pledgor may redeem it by payment or performance. Sweet's Law Dict.

Statutory Definition.—In *California*, *Dakota*, and *Idaho*, every contract by which the possession of personal property is transferred as security only, is declared by statute to be a pledge. *California* Civ. Code, § 2986; *Dakota* Civ. Code, § 1757; *Idaho* Rev. St., § 3410. The *Louisiana* Civ. Code, § 3133 declares that "the pledge is a contract by which the debtor gives something to his creditor as a security for his debt." The *Georgia* statute declares a pledge to be a deposit of property with another as security for the payment of a debt. *Georgia* Code, § 2138.

Other Definitions.—Morris Canal etc Co. *v.* Fisher, 9 N. J. Eq. 686; Chamberlain *v.* Martin, 43 Barb. (N. Y.) 610; Parshall *v.* Eggart, 52 Barb. (N. Y.) 374; Belden *v.* Perkins, 78 Ill. 452; Doak *v.* State Bank, 6 Ired. (N. Car.) 309; Surber *v.* McClintic, 10 W. Va. 242; Sonoma Valley Bank *v.* Hill, 59 Cal. 107.

An act of the legislature provided that certificates issued by the commissioner of the New Albany and Vincennes road should be paid from the tolls received, and pledged all money, not otherwise appropriated, arising from said road, for the redemption of said certificates. *Held*, to be not a pledge but only a promise that certificates should be paid. Clendenin *v.* Frazier, 1 Ind. 553.

Pawn.—At common law, the terms "pawn" and "pledge" are synonymous, but in modern usage "pawn" is usually understood to mean a pledge of property to a person engaged in the business of receiving property for money advanced. It is used in this sense in the statutes regulating the business of pawnbrokers. See Revenue Act, July 13, 1866, § 9; 14 U. S. St. L. 116; *Illinois* Act of June 4, 1879, § 1 (1 Starr & C. Rev. St. 1369); Chicago *v.* Hulbert, 118 Ill. 632.

For the distinction between "pledge" and "hypothecation," see Hypothecation, vol. 9, p. 852. While there is a distinction in law between the meanings of these two words yet in popular speech they are synomynous. Stormonth's Dict.

pledged is a chose in action the term "collateral security" is now most commonly applied to the transaction; but this change of name has worked no change in the law.[1] He who delivers a pledge is called the pledgor, he who receives it, the pledgee.[2]

II. **Nature of Pledge—1. In General.**—A pledge has the general characteristics of a lien, but differs from it in that the holder of a pledge has, in addition to the right of possession, the implied

Distinguished from Antichresis.—See also Antichresis, vol. 1, p. 610.

At common law a pledge could only be made of personal property, but by the civil law as recognized in *Louisiana* a pledge of immovable property known as "antichresis," is allowed. By the law of that State, the "antichresis" must be reduced to writing. The creditor acquires the right of reaping the fruit and all other revenues of the immovable given in pledge on condition of deducting the proceeds from the amount of his claim. In the absence of any express contract to the contrary, the creditor is charged with the duty of paying the taxes, and annual charges of the property pledged. He is also bound to repair the pledged estate. The failure of the debtor to make payment at the stipulated time does not vest the creditor with any right of property, and any stipulation in the contract to that effect is null. The debtor cannot before full payment of the debt, claim the enjoyment of the property given in pledge, but the creditor, if he wishes to free himself from the obligations imposed upon him by the contract, may himself compel the debtor to retake possession of the property. Livingston *v.* Story, 11 Pet. (U. S.) 388.

Statutory Pledge.—There may be a statutory pledge, as where a statute authorizing the issue of city bonds to assist a railroad, orders a certain number of shares of the railroad's stock to be forever pledged to the city for the redemption of the bonds. U. S. *v.* New Orleans, 98 U. S. 381.

1. Mitchell *v.* Roberts, 17 Fed. Rep. 778.

The term "collateral security" has in recent years come into general use to designate a pledge of negotiable paper, corporate stocks, or other incorporeal personalty, as distinguished from a pledge of corporeal chattels. Jones on Pledges, § 1.

In a broad sense "collateral security" is one, side by side with, or in addition to, the first, or in addition to the debtor's own obligation. Chambersburg Ins. Co. *v.* Smith, 11 Pa. St. 120.

We find the expression "collateral security" used in some of the late reports in an uncertain way, as though courts were bewildered in distinguishing between the pledge and chattel mortgage, or wished to use some convenient term which did not commit them to a distinction. Fraker *v.* Reeve, 36 Wis. 85; Smithhurst *v.* Edmunds, 14 N. J. Eq. 408; First Nat. Bank *v.* Kelly, 57 N. Y. 34; Leach *v.* Kimball, 34 N. H. 568; Stearns *v.* Marsh, 4 Den. (N. Y.) 227; Wilson *v.* Little, 2 N. Y. 443; Gay *v.* Morse, 34 Cal. 125; Hancock *v.* Franklin Ins. Co., 114 Mass. 155; Belden *v.* Perkins, 78 Ill. 449. But the better view is that "collateral security" embraces, in the broadest sense, both pledge and chattel-mortgage transactions, while more appropriately applied to the former class, and in the stricter phrase to pledges of incorporeal personalty alone. Schouler's Bailments & Carriers, § 164; Story on Bailments and Carriers, § 164; Story on Bailments, § 288, n.

"Collateral," in the commercial sense of the word, is a security given in addition to a principal obligation, and subsidiary thereto; and is used as generally descriptive of all choses in action as distinguished from tangible personal property. Colebrooke on Collateral Security, § 2.

A separate obligation attached to another contract to guaranty its performance. Bouv. Law Dict.

2. Anderson's Law Dict.; Schouler on Bailments, § 165. So the terms "pawner" and "pawnee" are used. Schouler on Bailments, § 165.

power of sale.[1] A pledge is something less than a mortgage.[2]

2. Difference Between Pledge and Mortgage.—A contract of pledge need not be in writing;[3] it depends for its validity on delivery and possession of the subject-matter,[4] and only a special property, not the title,[5] passes, in all of which it differs from a chattel

1. Pothomer *v.* Dawson, Holt 383; McNeil *v.* Tenth Nat. Bank, 46 N. Y. 325; Parker *v.* Brancher, 22 Pick. (Mass.) 40; Walter *v.* Smith, 5 B. & Ald. 439.

3 Parsons on Contract *272.

In a lien by custom there is no power of sale, but in the case of pledge, when the debt has become due and remains unpaid, the creditor after a reasonable time may sell the pledge. Doane *v.* Russell, 3 Gray (Mass.) 382.

Under the circumstances in the following case, only a lien was said to exist. Salinas City Bank *v.* Graves, 79 Cal. 192.

2. Jones *v.* Smith, 2 Ves. Jr. 372; Walter *v.* Smith, 5 B. & Ald. 439; Maughan *v.* Sharp, 17 C. B., N. S. 443; Halliday *v.* Holgate, L. R., 3 Ex. 299; Jones on Pledges, § 3.

In Halliday *v.* Holgate, L. R., 3 Ex. 299, Willes, J., says: "There are three kinds of security; the first, a simple lien; the second, a mortgage passing the property out and out; the third, a security intermediate between a lien and a mortgage, viz: a pledge, where by contract a deposit of goods is made security for a debt, and the right to the property vests in the pledgee so far as is necessary to secure the debt." Rice *v.* Dillingham, 73 Me. 59.

3. Jones on Pledge, § 5; Day *v.* Swift, 48 Me. 368; Arendale *v.* Morgan, 5 Sneed (Tenn.) 703; Sanders *v.* Davis, 13 B. Mon. (Ky.) 432; Camp *v.* Camp, 2 Hill (N. Y.) 628; Bonsey *v.* Amee, 8 Pick. (Mass.) 237.

Under *Louisiana* Code, art. 3158, requiring a contract of pledge of movable property, other than notes, bills, and stocks, to be in writing, to affect third parties, parol evidence is inadmissible to prove a written instrument to be a pledge. De Blois *v.* Reiss, 32 La. Ann. 586.

Registration of Written Contract of Pledge Unnecessary.—First Nat. Bank *v.* Kelly, 57 N. Y. 34; Parshall *v.* Eggert, 54 N. Y. 18; Hubert *v.* Creditors, 1 La. Ann. 443; Griffin *v.* Rogers, 38 Pa. St. 382; Roeder *v.* Green Tree Brewery Co., 33 Mo. App. 69; McCready *v.* Haslock, 3 Tenn. Ch. 13; Thoms *v.* Southard, 2 Dana (Ky.) 475; Shaw *v.* Wilshire, 65 Me. 485; Doak *v.* State Bank, 6 Ired. (N. Car.) 309; Mathews *v.* Rutherford, 7 La. Ann. 225.

Tennessee St. 1831, ch. 90, requiring a writing proved and registered to make a valid sale or mortgage of a slave does not apply to a pledge. Arendale *v.* Morgan, 5 Sneed (Tenn.) 703.

In order to make a pledge effective as to third persons in *Louisiana*, it need not be recorded, if the object thereof, comes into the actual possession of the pledgee before any conflicting lien has attached to it. Helm *v.* Meyer, 30 La. Ann. 943.

A pledge of personal property is not within the statute of *North Carolina*, requiring mortgages of personal property to be recorded. Doak *v.* State Bank, 6 Ired. (N. Car.) 309.

The statute in *South Carolina* requires a pledge contract to be in writing and signed by the parties to be good against third persons. Voorhies' Rev. Civil Code *Louisiana*, art. 3158.

Where the terms of the contract were fully described in the notes secured, this was held to fulfill the statute. Freiburg *v.* Dreyfus, 135 U. S. 478.

4. See *infra*, this title, *Delivery and Possession.*

5. Brownell *v.* Hawkins, 4 Barb. (N. Y.) 491; Lewis *v.* Graham, 4 Abb. Pr. (N. Y.) 106; Brown *v.* Bement, 8 Johns. (N. Y.) 96; Ackley *v.* Finch, 7 Cow. (N. Y.) 290; Campbell *v.* Parker, 9 Bosw. (N. Y.) 322; State *v.* Adams, 76 Mo. 605; Williams *v.* Rorer, 7 Mo. 556; Wood *v.* Dudley, 8 Vt. 435; Heyland *v.* Badger, 35 Cal. 404; Wright *v.* Ross, 36 Cal. 414; Evans *v.* Darlington, 5 Blackf. (Ind.) 320; Eastman *v.* Avery, 23 Me. 248; Shaw *v.* Wilshire, 65 Me. 485; White *v.* Platt, 5 Den. (N. Y.) 269; Garlick *v.* James, 12 Johns. (N. Y.) 146; Bank of British Columbia *v.* Marshall, 11 Fed. Rep. 19; Jones *v.* Baldwin, 12 Pick. (Mass.) 315; Robertson *v.* Wilcox, 36 Conn. 426; Sanders *v.* Davis, 13 B. Mon. (Ky.) 432; Sims *v.* Canfield, 2 Ala. 555; Chamber-

mortgage.[1] In practice, the distinction between pledges and chattel mortgages, as shown by the instruments evidencing them,

lain *v.* Martin, 43 Barb. (N. Y.) 607; Hoskins *v.* Kelly, 1 Abb. Pr., N. S. (N. Y.) 63; Fletcher *v.* Howard, 2 Aik. (Vt.) 115; Lobban *v.* Garnett, 9 Dana (Ky.) 389; Petitt *v.* First Nat. Bank, 4 Bush (Ky.) 334; Hamilton *v.* Wagner, 2 A. K. Marsh. (Ky.) 332; Bates *v.* Wiles, 1 Handy (Ohio) 532; Union Trust Co. *v.* Rigdon, 93 Ill. 458; Barfield *v.* Cole, 4 Sneed (Tenn.) 465; Brewster *v.* Hartley, 37 Cal. 15; Laflin etc. Powder Co. *v.* Burkhardt, 97 U. S. 110; White *v.* Phelps, 14 Minn. 27; *Georgia* Code, 3873, § 2142; Co. Litt. 89 a; Southcole's Case, 4 Rep. 83b; Coggs *v.* Bernard, 2 Ld. Raym. 917; Ratcliff *v.* Davies, Cro. Jac. 244.

Title, as to Third Persons, Passes in a Pledge of Negotiable and Quasi-Negotiable Choses in Action.—Wilson *v.* Little, 2 N. Y. 443; Hasbrouck *v.* Vandervoort, 4 Sandf. (N. Y.) 74; Lewis *v.* Graham, 4 Abb. Pr. (N. Y.) 106; Dewey *v.* Bowman, 8 Cal. 145; Jones on Pledges, § 9; Lewis *v.* Mott, 36 N. Y. 395.

If the transfer be to secure a debt, and the debtor has the right to the restoration of the property on payment of the debt at any time, the transaction is a pledge and not a mortgage, although the legal title passes to the creditor. Parsons on Contracts, vol. 2, p. 113.

A transfer of title is necessary in order that the creditor may have full control of the contract and the means of promptly enforcing it. Gay *v.* Moss, 34 Cal. 125.

The transfer of the legal title like the delivery of possession, constitutes the evidence of the pledgee's right of property in the thing pledged. Brewster *v.* Hartley, 37 Cal. 15.

Although in such case the pledgee receives the apparent legal title, the general property remains in the pledgor. Cross *v.* Eureka Lake etc. Canal Co., 73 Cal. 302; Garlick *v.* James, 12 Johns. (N. Y.) 146; Campbell *v.* Parker, 9 Bosw. (N. Y.) 322; Evans *v.* Darlington, 5 Blackf. (Ind.) 320; Allen *v.* Dykers, 3 Hill (N. Y.) 593; Gilpin *v.* Howell, 5 Pa. St. 41; Morris Canal etc. Co. *v.* Fisher, 9 N. J. Eq. 667; Morris Canal etc. Co. *v.* Lewis, 12 N. J. Eq. 323; Dungan *v.* Mutual Ben. L. Ins. Co., 38 Md. 242; Hasbrouck *v.* Vandervoort, 4 Sandf. (N. Y.) 74; Mechanics' Bldg. etc. Assoc. *v.* Conover, 14 N. J. Eq. 219; Brewster *v.* Hartley, 37 Cal. 15.

For whenever it appears by the terms of the contract that the debtor has a legal right to the restoration of the security, on payment of the debt, he may be said to have the general property in it. This general property is nothing more than the legal right to the restoration of the thing pledged on payment of the debt. Wilson *v.* Little, 2 N. Y. 443.

1. See also CHATTEL MORTAGES, vol. 3 p. 175; Story on Bailments, § 287; Schouler on Bailments and Carriers, § 167; Jones on Pledges, 4.

Parsons on Contracts (7th ed.) vol. 1, p. 611, n; vol. 2, p. 122; vol. 3, p. 289; 4 Kent Com. *138; Cortelyou *v.* Lansing, 2 Cai. Cas. (N. Y.) 200; Barrow *v.* Paxton, 5 Johns. (N. Y.) 258; Lucketts *v.* Townsend 3 Tex. 119; Gleason *v.* Drew, 9 Me. 82; Haven *v.* Low, 2 N. H. 13; Ash *v.* Savage, 5 N. H. 545; Lewis *v.* Stevenson, 2 Hall (N. Y.) 63; McLean *v.* Walker, 10 Johns. (N. Y.) 471; Portland Bank *v.* Stubbs, 6 Mass. 425; Conrad *v.* Atlantic Ins. Co., 1 Pet. (U. S.) 449; Farmers' Turnpike Co. *v.* Coventry, 10 Johns. (N. Y.) 389; Parshall *v.* Eggert, 54 N. Y. 18, *reversing* 52 Barb. (N. Y.) 367; Hanselt *v.* Harrison, 105 U. S. 401; Mitchell *v.* Roberts, 17 Fed. Rep. 776; Stearns *v.* Marsh, 4 Den. (N. Y.) 227; West *v.* Crary, 47 N. Y. 425; Brown *v.* Bement, 8 Johns. (N. Y.) 96; McFarland *v.* Wheeler, 26 Wend. (N. Y.) 467.

The essential difference between a mortgage and a pledge as to matter of right is, that in the one case the title passes, and in the other it does not. But the difference in substance and fact, is that in the case of a pawn the possession of the article must pass out of the pawner; in the case of a mortgage it need not. And in determining whether an agreement is a pledge or a mortgage, regard must be had to these two considerations. Huskins *v.* Patterson, 1 Edm. Sel. Cas. (N. Y.) 201.

An actual or constructive change of possession better comports with the character of a pledge than a mortgage. Schouler on Bailments, § 168; Homes *v.* Crane, 2 Pick. (Mass.) 607; Coty *v.* Barnes, 20 Vt. 78.

is not clear, and the intent of the parties must govern.[1] In cases of doubt a pledge is preferred to a mortgage,[2] but contracts will be construed to indicate that security which will best effectuate the intentions of the parties and subserve the purposes of justice.[3]

1. Brewster *v.* Hartley, 37 Cal. 15; Bank of British Columbia *v.* Marshall, 11 Fed. Rep. 19; Milliken *v.* Dehon, 27 N. Y. 364; Murdock *v.* Columbus Ins. Co., 5 Miss. 152.

While the distinction between these two forms of security is well defined, yet, owing to the haste with which transactions are often made, and to the meagerness or abbreviations of the written papers which accompany them, it is not always easy to determine what character is properly to be attributed to them. Thompson *v.* Dolliver, 132 Mass. 103.

Whether the transaction shall be treated as a mortgage or a pledge must often depend upon the intent of the parties. Ward *v.* Sumner, 5 Pick. (Mass.) 59.

The same terms which will create a pledge, if the possession passes, will often be held to create a mortgage. Conner *v.* Carpenter, 28 Vt. 237.

In regard to the transfer of shares of stock it may be said that when made in the ordinary form of indorsement of a certificate, or by delivery of it with a power of attorney to make a transfer upon the books of the corporation, or by actual transfer upon the books, it is a pledge and not a mortgage. It is immaterial in this respect whether such transfer appear to be absolute, or is expressed to be made as security, though if made in the usual form of a mortgage, with a defeasance, it would doubtless be regarded as a mortgage.

Hasbrouck *v.* Vandervoort, 4 Sandf. (N. Y.) 74; Nabring *v.* Bank of Mobile, 58 Ala. 204; Brewster *v.* Hartley, 37 Cal. 15; Dungan *v.* Mutual Ben. L. Ins. Co., 38 Md. 242; Ede *v.* Johnson, 15 Cal. 53; Smith *v.* Quartz Min. Co., 14 Cal. 242.

But if the original contract was not in reality a security for a loan but an option to resell, it is not a pledge. Melvin *v.* Leamar Ins. Co., 80 Ill. 446; Lauman's Appeal, 68 Pa. St. 88.

2. Schouler on Bailments 168; Jones on Pledges, § 14.

In all cases, then, where personal property is given as security for a debt or engagement, accompanied by a change of possession either actual or constructive, the transaction better comports with the character of a pledge than a mortgage; and where the transaction imports nothing more than giving a security without a sale or change of title of the property, the law favors the conclusion that it was intended as a pledge and not a mortgage. Bank of British Columbia *v.* Marshall, 11 Fed. Rep. 19.

3. Schouler on Bailments, § 168; Jones on Pledges, § 13; Ward *v.* Sumner, 5 Pick. (Mass.) 59; Wright *v.* Bucher, 5 Mo. App. 322; Prescott *v.* Prescott, 41 Vt. 131; Haskins *v.* Patterson, 1 Edm. Sel. Cas. (N. Y.) 120; Gregory *v.* Morris, 96 U. S. 619.

Even though the words, "I pledge and give a lien" are used in the instrument, it may be construed to be a mortgage. Langdon *v.* Buell, 9 Wend. (N. Y.) 80.

Where the words "pledged, hypothecated and mortgaged" were used, still held to be a pledge. Thoms *v.* Southard, 2 Dana (Ky.) 475.

Where a vessel was turned over to a creditor with an instrument acknowledging the debt, containing the words, "I hereby give this guaranty mortgage, etc.," it nevertheless was held to be a pledge. Wilson *v.* Knapp, 70 N. Y. 596.

In ***Missouri***, a mortgage in possession under a defective mortgage given to secure a debt, may still hold against other creditors on the theory of possession under a contract of pledge. Greeley *v.* Reading, 74 Mo. 309; Nash *v.* Norment, 5 Mo. App. 545. But see Pettee *v.* Dustin, 58 N. H. 309.

Though a mortgage of property not yet acquired by the mortgagor is ineffectual against third persons still, if the mortgagee is in possession before any third person gets a lien on it, he may hold the property by way of pledge. Cameron *v.* Marvin, 26 Kan. 612.

In *New Hampshire* a pledge of a stock of goods to be sold in the usual course of trade is good, while a mortgage under the same circumstances would not be unless it provides that the proceeds of all the sales shall be turned over to the mortgagee. Janvrin *v.* Fogg, 49 N. H. 340.

Where there was no proof to ex-

What was in its inception a chattel mortgage may sometimes be subsequently changed by agreement of the parties into a pledge.[1]

3. Difference Between Pledge and Sale.—In a sale there must be an agreed price; an absolute transfer of title and possession need not pass at once, wherein it differs from a pledge.[2] Parol evidence

plain it, "Turned out and delivered to A one white-and-red cow, which he may dispose of in fourteen days to satisfy an execution," was held to be a mortgage. Atwater *v.* Mower, 10 Vt. 75. Similar case in Coty *v.* Barns, 20 Vt. 78.

A mortgagor of chattels making a new and distinct contract with the mortgagee to deliver to him the mortgaged chattels, and also other chattels to be held as securities for payment of the debt which the mortgage was made to secure, and delivering them accordingly, and the mortgagee takes and holds possession of them under such new contract, he thereby becomes pawnee of all the chattels so delivered. Rowley *v.* Rice, 10 Met. (Mass.) 7.

Where a creditor takes a bill of sale of property subject to a mortgage, which he assumes, and agrees to credit the debtor with the proceeds of the property after paying the mortgage, he is a purchaser of the legal title, and not a mere pledgee. Foster *v.* Magill, 119 Ill. 75.

Where a cow was given with a bill of sale as security for a promissory note, to be kept "until all the note is paid," it was held a mortgage. Woodman *v.* Chesley, 39 Me. 45.

Where the instrument stated that the property "was given as collateral security," still held a mortgage. Fraker *v.* Reeve, 36 Wis. 85. Other doubtful cases held mortgages. Rees *v.* Logsdon, 68 Md. 93.

The delivery of a bill of sale, copies of gauger's returns, and a warehouse receipt for whiskey in a United States bonded warehouse, to secure a note, was held a pledge and not a chattel mortgage. Conrad *v.* Fisher, 37 Mo. App. 352.

Where a person, to secure money borrowed to form a partnership, agreed to pledge all his interest in the partnership, he however to remain in possession, and to make an assignment on demand, and afterwards formed a partnership, but with different persons from those at first contemplated, and then died, the transaction was held a pledge, and that the pledgee was entitled to the pledgor's interest in the partnership. Collins' Appeal, 107 Pa. St. 590.

Interest in certain patents were assigned to secure debt, in the agreement that the assignees should retain their interests and claims herein till they shall be fully paid their said indebtedness up to such time as they shall terminate this agreement, which they had the right to do, but they shall, upon payment to them of the said indebtedness, reassign their said interest in said inventions. *Held,* a pledge. Barry *v.* Coville (Supreme Ct.), 7 N. Y. Supp. 36.

Transfer of Bond or Note and Mortgage a Pledge.—Such transfers were at first called mortgages. Henry *v.* Davis, 7 Johns. Ch. (N. Y.) 40; Slee *v.* Manhattan Co., 1 Paige (N. Y.) 48. But it is now regarded as a pledge rather than a mortgage. Kamena *v.* Huelbig, 23 N. J. Eq. 78; Swope *v.* Leffingwell, 72 Mo. 348; Mechanics' Bldg. Assoc. *v.* Ferguson, 29 La. Ann. 548; Fraker *v.* Reeme, 36 Wis. 85.

The intention of the parties will be carried out, however. Wright *v.* Ross, 36 Cal. 414; Dungan *v.* Mutual Ben. L. Ins. Co., 38 Md. 242; and such a transaction may be held a mortgage Wright *v.* Rose, 36 Cal. 414; Dewey *v* Bowman, 8 Cal. 145; Wendell *v.* New Hampshire Bank, 9 N. H. 404.

Where the assignment appears absolute on its face it may be shown to be a pledge. Briggs *v.* Rice, 130 Mass. 50.

1. See CHATTEL MORTAGES, vol. 3, p. 175.

Where a chattel mortgage was given on wheat and afterwards money was loaned on the same wheat as security, it was held that the parties could agree to make the transaction a pledge. Granger's etc. Assoc. *v.* Clark, 84 Cal. 201.

After a mortgage had been adjudged invalid it was held error to admit testimony to show a pledge relationship. Marsh *v.* Wade (Wash.), 20 Pac. Rep. 578.

2. Bank of Rochester *v.* Jones, 4 Den. (N. Y.) 489; 2 Kent's Com. *477,

492; Klimpeter *v.* Harrigan, 21 La. Ann. 196; Fuller *v.* Bean, 34 N. H. 290; Flagg *v.* Mann, 2 Sumn. (U. S.) 486; Eldridge *v.* Kuehl, 27 Iowa 160; Wittowsky *v.* Wasson, 71 N. Car. 451; Clay *v.* Creditors, 4 Mart. (La.) 644; Benjamin on Sales § 1; Bouv. Law Dict.

Some confusion between these transactions has arisen and the cases are here given.

The delivery of personal property by a debtor to his creditor, in order that the latter may "sell the same and apply the proceeds to the payment of a pre-existing debt," is a pledge, and not a sale of the property to the creditor. Harris *v.* Lombard, 60 Miss. 29.

A note of a third person formerly double the amount of the sum borrowed, is transferred "as collateral security" with the condition that in case of default "B is to hold the note as his own property" is deemed a pledge and not a sale. Williamson *v.* Culpepper, 16 Ala. 211.

Where a tenant placed a lot of corn in the hands of the administrator of his landlord, as security for the payment of rent due, held, the legal *status* was that of pledged property; and the mere fact that the pledgor had the right to determine the time when the corn should be sold did not affect the legal character of the contract. Belden *v.* Perkins, 78 Ill. 449.

See also for doubtful cases: Rohrle *v.* Stidger, 50 Cal. 207; Wilkie *v.* Day, 141 Mass. 68; Fairbanks *v.* Sargent, 117 N. Y. 320; Sperry *v.* Clarke, 76 Iowa 503; Barry *v.* Coville, 53 Hun (N. Y.) 620; Beidler *v.* Crane (Ill. 1889), 19 N. E. Rep. 714; Houser *v.* Kemp, 3 Pa. St. 208; Leblanc *v.* Bouchereau, 16 La. Ann. 11; Taggart *v.* Packard, 39 Vt. 628; Morgan *v.* Dod, 3 Colo. 553; Hart *v.* Burton, 7 J. J. Marsh. (Ky.) 322; Hines *v.* Strong, 46 How. Pr. (N. Y.) 97; Partee *v.* Bedford, 51 Miss. 84; Comstock *v.* Smith, 23 Me. 202; Wood *v.* Matthews, 73 Mo. 477; Marshall *v.* Williams, 2 Hayw. (N. Car.) 405; Hyde *v.* Nick, 5 Leigh (Va.) 336; Peck *v.* Merrill, 26 Vt. 686.

A trust deed to personal property accompanied by possession, the owner having the right to redeem, is a pledge. Hudson *v.* Wilkinson, 45 Tex. 444.

Where the complainant *feme covert*, unconditionally assigned a mortgage to the defendant and delivered it to her husband, who delivered it to defendant, and defendant gave a receipt to the husband stating that he received the mortgage as collateral security for debt owed by the husband to him, and there was no evidence of any transaction or understanding relative to said mortgage between said complainant and defendant, or that the transfer was merely as security and conditional, it was held, that upon these facts the court cannot say that the assignment was only meant as security and not as an absolute transfer to defendant. Durfee *v.* McClurg, 6 Mich. 223.

Where stocks and bonds are assigned to a trustee by a written instrument which contains power to sell at discretion, and requires him to dispose of enough to discharge a note due to a third person if the interest thereon is not promptly paid, the transaction does not constitute a pledge. Murdock *v.* Columbus Ins. etc. Co., 59 Miss. 152. The court decided this case on the ground that it was not a mere pledge, but a transfer in trust to a third person other than the creditor, with a power to sell and pay certan debts. It was distinguished from the cases of Nabring *v.* Bank of Mobile, 58 Ala. 204, and Wilson *v.* Little, 2 N. Y. 443, on the ground that the transfer in these cases was made to the creditor, and from Brewster *v.* Hartley, 37 Cal. 15, on the ground that the transferee in that case, although called a trustee, was a mere agent of the creditors, and the delivery of the property to him was the same as a delivery to the creditors.

In Com. *v.* Reading Sav. Bank, 137 Mass. 431, it was held, that an assignment of a mortgage by a savings bank for a price paid was a sale, and not a pledge, even though the transfer was made with the condition attached, that the transferee should re-assign upon repayment to him of the price paid.

In Reeves *v.* Sebern, 16 Iowa 234, it was held that a sale of goods for a certain sum, with a further agreement that if when sold, more than such sum should be realized, the excess, after deducting the expenses of the sale, should be credited to the vendors, was a sale and not a pledge.

See also, Brown *v.* Bank, 41 Ohio St. 445; Pomez *v.* Camors, 36 La. Ann. 464; Milliken *v.* Dehon, 27 N. Y. 364.

A Bill of Sale and Receipted Bills of Parcels.—When intended as security and accompanied by delivery, these are held pledges. Walker *v.* Staples,

may be introduced to show that transfers apparently absolute were intended to be for security only.[1]

III. **CONTRACT OF PLEDGE.—1. In General.**—A pledge is a bailment, the consideration for which is the mutual benefit of both parties; for while the pledgee obtains security for his debt, the pledgor obtains credit or delay, or other indulgence.[2] To consummate the contract there is required mutual assent, free from fraud or duress,[3] by proper parties,[4] in regard to the subject-matter to be pledged[5] and the debt to be secured,[6] together with the delivery and possession of the subject-matter in accordance with the terms of the agreement.[7]

2. Delivery and Possession.—It may be affirmed, in general, that there must always be a delivery, actual or constructive,[8] of the

5 Allen (Mass.) 34; Kimball *v.* Hildreth, 8 Allen (Mass.) 167; Hazard *v.* Loring, 10 Cush. (Mass.) 267; Whitaker *v.* Sumner, 20 Pick. (Mass.) 399; Bright *v.* Nagle, 3 Dana (Ky.) 257; Shaw *v.* Wilshire, 65 Me. 485; Beeman *v.* Lawton, 37 Me. 543; Morgan *v.* Dod, 3 Colo. 551; Thompson *v.* Dolliver, 132 Mass. 103.

But a bill of sale conditional in form is held to be a mortgage. Wood *v.* Dudley, 8 Vt. 430; Homes *v.* Crane, 2 Pick. (Mass.) 607; Barrow *v.* Paxton, 5 Johns. (N. Y.) 258.

So if absolute in form but with a separate defeasance. Brown *v.* Dement, 8 Johns. (N. Y.) 96; Clark *v.* Henry, 2 Cow. (N. Y.) 324; Barfield *v.* Cole, 4 Sneed (Tenn.) 465.

In *Vermont*, even if defeasance is verbal. Blodgett *v.* Blodgett, 48 Vt. 32.

Assignments.—Where there is no evidence to the contrary, assignments of securities by a debtor to his creditor are presumed to be pledges. Leas *v.* James, 10 S. & R. (Pa.) 307; Perit *v.* Pittfield, 5 Rawle (Pa.) 166; Jones *v.* Johnson, 3 W. & S. (Pa.) 276; Eby *v.* Hoopes, 1 Pennypacker (Pa.) 175; Dewey *v.* Bowman, 8 Cal. 145; Jarboe *v.* Templer, 38 Fed. Rep. 213; Rowland *v.* Plummer, 50 Ala. 182; Beidler *v.* Crane (Ill. 1889), 19 N. E. Rep. 714; Rohrle *v.* Stidzer, 50 Cal. 207; Griffin *v.* Rogers. 38 Pa. St. 382.

1. See PAROL EVIDENCE.

2. 2 Parsons on Contracts *110; Schouler on Bailments, § 162; Story on Bailments, § 3; St. Losky *v.* Davidson, 6 Cal. 643; Commercial Bank *v.* Martin, 1 La. Ann. 344; Mead *v.* Bunn, 32 N. Y. 275.

3. Schouler on Bailments, § 179; Mead *v.* Bunn, 32 N. Y. 275.

4. See *infra*, this title, *Parties to the Contract.*

5. See *infra*, this title, *Subject-matter.*

6. See *infra*, this title, *Debt or Engagement Secured.*

7. See *infra*, this title, *Delivery and Possession.*

8. Formal delivery is unnecessary if the property be present so that the pledgee can take possession of it, and he does take possession and either retains it himself or leaves it in the control of a third person. Tibbetts *v.* Flanders, 18 N. H. 284; Combs *v.* Tuchelt, 24 Minn. 423.

Constructive or Symbolic Delivery.—Such delivery is sufficient wherever it would be so in case of a sale of the same property. Jones on Pledges, § 36; Hilliker *v.* Kuhn, 71 Cal. 214; Woods *v.* Bugbey, 29 Cal. 466.

It may be made of all property incapable of manual delivery. So logs in a boom may be effectually delivered by pointing them out to the pledgee. Jewett *v.* Warren, 12 Mass. 300.

Oats in a bin may be constructively delivered. Nevan *v.* Roup, 8 Iowa 207.

Transfer of bill of lading of ship at sea or the key of a warehouse legally transfers possession of the thing so symbolized. Schouler on Bailments, § 189; Story on Bailments, § 297; Bedlam *v.* Tucker, 1 Pick. (Mass.) 386; Ryall *v.* Rolle, 1 Atk. 165; Atkinson *v.* Maling, 2 T. R. 462; Barber *v.* Meyerstein, L. R., 4 H. L. 317.

Chattels in possession of a third person may be delivered by an order to the custodian to hold the goods for the pledgee. Whitaker *v.* Sumner, 20 Pick. (Mass.) 399; Tuxworth *v.* Moore, 9 Pick. (Mass.) 346.

Delivery of savings bank book will carry the deposit. Boynton *v.* Payrow, 67 Me. 587.

Delivery of a bill of lading, of a warehouse receipt or wharfingers receipt will deliver the goods represented by such instruments. Dows *v.* National Exch. Bank, 91 U. S. 618; Michigan Cent. R. Co. *v.* Phillip, 60 Ill. 190; First Nat. Bank *v.* Kelly, 57 N. Y. 34; West Union R. Co. *v.* Wagner, 65 Ill. 197; Cartwright *v.* Wilmerding, 24 N. Y. 521; Burton *v.* Curyea, 40 Ill. 325; Osborn *v.* Koenigheim, 57 Tex. 91; Newcomb *v.* Cabell, 10 Bush (Ky.) 460; First Nat. Bank *v.* Bates, 1 Fed. Rep. 702; Freiburg *v.* Dryfus, 135 U. S. 478; Harris *v.* Bradley, 2 Dill (U. S.) 285; Whitney *v.* Tibbits, 17 Wis. 369; McNeil *v.* Hill, 1 Woolw. (U. S.) 96; Petitt *v.* First Nat. Bank, 4 Bush (Ky.) 334; Hathaway *v.* Haynes, 124 Mass. 311; Conrad *v.* Fisher, 37 Mo. App. 352; Brent *v.* Miller, 81 Ala. 309; Meyerstein *v.* Barber, L. R. 2 C. P. 38. Of railway receipt, Taylor *v.* Turner, 87 Ill. 296.

Mere agreement of the parties is not equivalent to actual or symbolic delivery. Russell *v.* Scudder, 42 Barb. (N. Y.) 31; Caffin *v.* Karwan, 7 La. Ann. 221.

It has been held that delivery of part of the chattels pledged, is constructive delivery of the whole. Martin *v.* Reid, 11 C. B., N. S. 750.

Certain stock of a mining corporation was "pooled." F, who was cashier of the D bank, and also a member of the firm of S, M & F was the chief trustee of the combination. R, one of those who "pooled" the stock, was indebted to S, M & F, and pledged his stock to them as collateral; the certificate, which was indorsed by R, remaining in possession of F as trustee of the "pool." He subsequently pledged it, while still in the "pool," to secure an indebtedness to the bank. *Held*, that both pledges were valid, under Civil Code *Dakota* § 1759, providing that "the lien of a pledge is dependent on possession, and no pledge is valid until the property pledged is delivered to the pledgee or to a pledgeholder." Van Cise *v.* Merchants' Nat. Bank (S. Dak. 1887), 33 N. W. Rep. 897.

One of two joint owners of a chattel both being in possession, may pledge his share to the other joint owner, and he by continuing in possession and control has a valid pledge. Thoms *v.* Southard, 2 Dana (Ky.) 475.

Where certain manufacturers of cloth agreed that one of their workmen should select and hold a certain number of pieces of cloth for the use of their creditors, and this workman, at the requisition of the creditors, selected the pieces and removed them to another room of the factory where he worked and gave notice thereof to one of the manufacturers and to his own attendants, it was held that the creditor had acquired a lien which was valid against an attachment subsequently made on the same goods by another creditor of the manufacturers, and it was not necessary that the goods should be removed from the premises of the manufacturers as long as the special bailee could have legal custody of them, could notify third persons that they were held in pledge and could remove the goods if it should be necessary for the safety of his principal. Sumner *v.* Hamlet, 12 Pick. (Mass.) 76; and see Thorndike *v.* Bath, 114 Mass. 116.

Executory Contracts of Pledge.—Until the delivery of the pledge the transaction rests in an executory contract, however strong may be the engagement to deliver it; and the pledgee acquires no right of property in the thing. Story on Bailment, § 297; Cortelyon *v.* Lansing, 2 Cai. Cas. (N. Y.) 200; Beeman *v.* Lawton, 37 Me. 543; Portland Bank *v.* Stubbs, 6 Mass. 422; Tucker *v.* Buffington, 15 Mass. 477; Gale *v.* Ward, 14 Mass. 352; First Nat. Bank. *v.* Nelson, 38 Ga. 391; Walcott *v.* Keith, 22 N. H. 196; Silverman *v.* McGrath, 10 Ill. App. 413; Propst *v.* Roseman, 4 Jones (N. Car.) 130; Succession of D'Meza, 26 La. Ann. 35; Smyth *v.* Craig, 3 W. & S. (Pa.) 14; Davenport *v.* City Bank, 9 Paige (N. Y.) 12; Casey *v.* Cavaroc, 96 U. S. 467; Williams *v.* Gillespie, 30 W. Va. 586; Gittings *v.* Nelson, 86 Ill. 591.

Though an executory contract of pledge may be good between the parties, Keiser *v.* Topping, 72 Ill. 226; Tuttle *v.* Robinson, 78 Ill. 332, it will not be enforced to the injury of other creditors. City F. Ins. Co. *v.* Olmstead, 33 Conn. 476; Casey *v.* Cavaroc, 96 U. S. 467.

Subsequent Delivery.—A contract of pledge ineffectual for want of delivery may be made valid by subseqent delivery, even against the right of general creditors accruing in the interval between the agreement and delivery pro-

pledge[1] by the pledgor or his agent[2] into the possession of the pledgee,[3] or his agent,[4] in order to pass any right of property in the thing pledged.[5] In many cases it is a matter of law whether

vided, however, that no other special lien has been allowed to attach. Parshall *v.* Eggert, 54 N. Y. 18, *reversing* 52 Barb. (N. Y.) 367; Nelson *v.* Edwards, 40 Barb. (N. Y.) 279.

But if done in contemplation of bankruptcy or insolvency, it is fraudulent and void. Nisbit *v.* Macon Bank etc. Co., 12 Fed. Rep. 686.

Upon an agreement at the time the advance was made to desposit securities, a subsequent delivery of them is enough to make the pledgee a holder for value upon a present advance. Fenby *v.* Pritchard, 2 Sandf. (N. Y.) 151.

1. Where part of a quantity of goods is pledged, that portion must be taken out and separated from the rest. Collins *v.* Buck, 63 Me. 459.

It has been questioned as to whether an undivided share of a chattel can be pledged without giving up possession of the whole. Portland Bank *v.* Stubbs, 6 Mass. 425.

2. Delivery may be by agents as well as by their principals. Schouler on Bailments, § 192; Cartwright *v.* Wilmerding, 24 N. Y. 521.

3. If the property to be pledged is already in the pledgee's possession, no formal delivery is needed. Brown *v.* Warren, 43 N. H. 430; Parsons *v.* Overmire, 22 Ill. 58; Providence Thread Co. *v.* Aldrich, 12 R. I. 77.

The possession of the pledged property may be according to the nature of the subject matter. Wilson *v.* Little, 2 N. Y. 443; Donald *v.* Suckling, 1 L. R., Q. B. 587; Russell *v.* Scudder, 42 Barb. (N. Y.) 31.

4. Brown *v.* Warren, 43 N. H. 430; Tibbetts *v.* Flanders, 18 N. H. 285; McCready *v.* Haslock, 3 Tenn. Ch. 13; Johnson *v.* Smith, 11 Humph. (Tenn.) 396; Weens *v.* Delta Moss Co., 33 La. Ann. 973; Boynton *v.* Payrow, 67 Me. 587; City Bank *v.* Perkins, 29 N. Y. 554; Bank of Chenango *v.* Hyde, 4 Cow. (N. Y.) 567.

Pledgor's employés may be agents for pledgee. Combs *v.* Tuchelt, 24 Minn. 423; Sumner *v.* Hamlet, 12 Pick. (Mass.) 76.

One pledgee may hold for himself and other creditors at the same time. Macomber *v.* Parker, 14 Pick. (Mass.) 497; Danforth *v.* Denny, 25 N. H. 155.

Statutory Pledge-Holders.—In a few States there are statutory provisions enabling the parties to the contract to choose a pledge holder, who, if rewarded cannot exonerate himself and if gratuitous can only do so by giving reasonable notice to his appointors to choose somebody else. If they fail to agree he may deposit the pledge with an impartial third person who may receive reasonable compensation for his services. A pledge holder must enforce the rights of pledges unless authorized to waive them. Jones on Pledges, § 34; *California* Codes and Stats. 1876, §§ 7993, 7998; *Dakota* R. Codes, 1877, §§ 1764, 1769 of Civ. Code; Rev. Civ. Code, *Louisiana*, art. 3162.

Pledgor as Pledgee's Agent.—As to whether the pledgor may be the pledgee's agent to hold where the goods have never left the former's possession, there is some question, but the strongest cases seem to uphold the general rule that delivery is necessary to shut out the rights of third persons. Casey *v.* Cavaroc, 96 U. S. 467; First Nat. Bank *v.* Nelson, 38 Ga. 391; Geddes *v.* Bennett, 6 La. Ann. 516; Schouler on Bailments, § 193.

But see Martin *v.* Reid, 11 C. B., N. S. 750, where a delivery of part of the goods was held to pledge all the goods enumerated in the instrument of pledge. Donger *v.* New Orleans, 32 La. Ann. 1250. Also *dictum* in Johnson *v.* Smith, 11 Humph. (Tenn.) 396.

5. Ceas *v.* Bramley, 18 Hun (N. Y.) 187; Langdon *v.* Buell, 9 Wend. (N. Y.) 80; Parshall *v.* Eggart, 54 N. Y. 18, *reversing* 52 Barb. (N.Y.) 367; Brownell *v.* Hawkins, 4 Barb. (N. Y.) 491; Siedenbach *v.* Riley, 111 N. Y. 560; Taylor *v.* Perkins, 26 Wend. (N. Y.) 124; Bank of Rochester *v.* Jones, 4 Den. (N. Y.) 489; Kimball *v.* Hildreth, 8 Allen (Mass.) 167; Walker *v.* Staples, 5 Allen (Mass.) 34; Homes *v.* Crane, 2 Pick. (Mass.) 607; Bonsey *v.* Amee, 8 Pick. (Mass.) 236; Gale *v.* Ward, 14 Mass. 352; Thompson *v.* Dolliver, 132 Mass. 103; Collins *v.* Buck, 63 Me. 459; Beeman *v.* Lawton, 37 Me. 544; Day *v.* Swift, 48 Me. 368; Eastman *v.* Avery, 23 Me. 248; Walcott *v.* Keith, 22 N. H. 196. Colby *v.* Cressy, 5 N. H. 237; Pinkerton *v.* Manchester R. Co., 42 N.

delivery has taken place;[1] for an actual delivery is not requisite. To keep the pledge good, the property pledged must remain in the possesion or under the control of the pledgee,[2] though a temporary re-delivery for a special purpose to the pledgor, who then holds as pledgee's agent, is not fatal.[3] The lien will not be lost if the pledgor gets control and possession wrongfully and without

H. 424; Haven *v.* Low, 2 N. H. 16; Silverman *v.* McGrath, 10 Ill. App. 413; Corbett *v.* Underwood, 83 Ill. 324; Cooper *v.* Ray, 47 Ill. 53; Keiser *v.* Topping, 72 Ill. 226; Parsons *v.* Overmire, 22 Ill. 58.

Owens *v.* Knisey, 7 Jones (N. Car.) 245; Doak *v.* State Bank, 6 Ired. (N. Car.) 309; Smith *v.* Sasser, 4 Jones (N. Car.) 43; Thompson *v.* Andrews, 8 Jones (N. Car.) 453; Propst *v.* Roseman, 4 Jones (N. Car.) 130; Crisp *v.* Miller, 5 Heisk. (Tenn.) 697; Johnson *v.* Smith, 11 Humph. (Tenn.) 396; Lee *v.* Bradler, 8 Mart. (La.) 20; Hiligsherg *v.* Succession, 1 La. Ann. 340; Faltier *v.* Schroder, 19 La. Ann. 17; Martin *v.* Creditors, 15 La. Ann. 165; Dirigo Tool Co. *v.* Woodruff, 41 N. J. Eq. 336; Beekman *v.* Barber (N. J. 1888), 3 Atl. Rep. 33; Brewster *v.* Hartley, 37 Cal. 15; Hilliker *v.* Kuhn, 71 Cal. 214.

First Nat. Bank *v.* Nelson, 38 Ga. 391; Combs *v.* Tuchelt, 24 Minn. 423; Seymour *v.* Colburn, 43 Wis. 67; Nevan *v.* Roup, 8 Iowa 207; Raper *v.* Harrison, 37 Kan. 243; Fletcher *v.* Howard, 2 Aik. (Vt.) 115.

1. Story on Bailments, § 297; Jones on Pledges, § 23; Silverman *v.* McGrath, 10 Ill. App. 413.

2. Ryall *v.* Rolle, 1 Atk. 165; Citizens' Nat. Bank *v.* Hooper, 47 Md. 88; Wyeth *v.* National M. Bank, 132 Mass. 597; Look *v.* Comstock, 15 Wend. (N. Y.) 244; Fletcher *v.* Howard, 2 Aik. (Vt.) 115; Shaw *v.* Wilshire, 65 Me. 485; First Nat. Bank *v.* Nelson, 38 Ga. 391; Geddes *v.* Bennett, 6 La. Ann. 516; Collins *v.* Buck, 63 Me. 459; Arendale *v.* Morgan, 5 Sneed (Tenn.) 703; Barrett *v.* Cole, 4 Jones (N. Car.) 40; Smith *v.* Sasser, 4 Jones (N. Car.) 43; Day *v.* Swift, 48 Me. 368; Eastman *v.* Avery, 23 Me. 248; Walcott *v.* Keith, 22 N. H. 196; Treadwell *v.* Davis, 34 Cal. 601; Kimball *v.* Hildreth, 8 Allen (Mass.) 167; Bodenhammer *v.* Newsom, 5 Jones (N. Car.) 107; Whitaker *v.* Sumner, 20 Pick. (Mass.) 399; Black *v.* Bogert, 65 N. Y. 601; Homes *v.* Crane, 2 Pick. (Mass.) 607; Jarvis *v.* Rogers, 15 Mass. 389; Sumner *v.* Hamlet, 12 Pick. (Mass.) 76; Bonsey *v.* Amee, 8 Pick. (Mass.) 236; Reeves *v.* Capper, 5 Bing. N. Cas. 136; Grinnell *v.* Cook, 3 Hill (N. Y.) 485; Walker *v.* Staples, 5 Allen (Mass.) 34; Mills *v.* Stewart, 5 Humph. (Tenn.) 308; Roberts *v.* Wyatt, 2 Taunt. 268; Johnson *v.* Stear, 15 C. B. (N. S.) 330; Combs *v.* Tuchelt, 24 Minn. 423.

Actual possession of negotiable paper is requisite to establish the title of a *bona fide* holder as against the equities of third persons. Muller *v.* Pondir, 55 N. Y. 325; *affirming* 6 Lans. (N. Y.) 472.

Redelivery for pledgor's benefit destroys the lien. Walter *v.* Staples, 5 Allen (Mass.) 34; Day *v.* Swift, 48 Me. 368; Colby *v.* Cressy, 5 N. H. 237; Barrett *v.* Cole, 4 Jones (N. Car.) 40; Salinas City Bank *v.* Graves, 79 Cal. 192.

3. Story on Bailm., § 299; Hutton *v.* Arnett, 51 Ill. 198; Hays *v.* Riddle, 1 Sandf. (N. Y.) 248; Citizens' Nat. Bank *v.* Hooper, 47 Md. 88; Cooper *v.* Ray, 47 Ill. 53; Martin *v.* Reid, 11 C. B., N. S. 730; Macomber *v.* Parker, 14 Pick. (Mass.) 497: Thorndike *v.* Bath, 114 Mass. 116; Walker *v.* Staples, 5 Allen (Mass.) 34; Palmtag *v.* Dontrick, 59 Cal. 154; Pier *v.* Bullis, 48 Wis. 429; Skarratt *v.* Vaughan, 2 Taunt. 266; Reves *v.* Capper, 5 Bing. N. Cas. 136.

To the contrary, however, see Bodenhammer *v.* Newson, 5 Jones (N. Car.) 107.

Held not good against third persons. Way *v.* Davidson, 12 Gray (Mass.) 466; Smith *v.* Sasser, 4 Jones (N. Car.) 43; Barrett *v.* Cole, 4 Jones (N. Car.) 107.

The mere fact that the pledgor assists the pledgee, with or without his knowledge or consent, in taking care of the pledged property, after its delivery, does not necessarily affect the pledgee's rights as against the pledgors' creditors. Hilliker *v.* Kuhn, 71 Cal. 214.

A pledgee with power to sell the goods and apply the proceeds on the debt does not forfeit his lien by employing

the pledgee's assent.[1] Pledgor's possession is *prima facie* evidence of fraud but may be rebutted.[2]

IV. Debt or Engagement Secured.—This may be primary or secondary, absolute or conditional,[3] for the payment of money or

the pledgor as agent to make the sale, allowing him to contract for it in his own name, and delivering the goods on his order to the purchaser. Thayer *v.* Dwight, 104 Mass. 254.

Where a pledge is temporarily re-delivered the debtor is estopped by his contract from denying the right of his creditor in the property, and if he disposes of the property pledged he holds the proceeds as a trustee for the pledgor. White *v.* Platt, 5 Den. (N. Y.) 269.

Where the property pledged to a bank was never in the bank's possession, though the money received on the sale of the pledged property was deposited to the pledgor's credit, he not appropriating it to pay the debts secured, and subsequently drawing it out, it was held that the bank had lost its lien. Randall *v.* Pettes, 12 Fla. 517.

Pledgee may redeliver negotiable paper to pledgor for collection and still be protected. Clark *v.* Iselin, 21 Wall. (U. S.) 360; White *v.* Platt, 5 Den. (N. Y.) 269; Whipple *v.* Blackington, 97 Mass. 476; Hurst *v.* Coley, 15 Fed. Rep. 645.

And see Biebinger *v.* Continental Bank, 99 U. S. 143; Casey *v.* Cavaroc, 96 U. S. 467.

So redelivery for collection. Clark *v.* Iselin, 21 Wall. (U. S.) 260.

A banker made advances to leather merchants on hides, for which bills of parcels were given to him, or bills of lading taken to his order, or indorsed to him with power to take possession and sell for his security or reimbursement. He indorsed the bills of lading to the firm to get the hides from the carriers, and gave it the custody upon its express agreement to hold as his agents, and to redeliver the identical hides when tanned. *Held*, that the banker took the title to the hides, and did not divest by his indorsement of release of custody. Moors *v.* Wyman, 146 Mass. 60.

1. Walcott *v.* Keith, 22 N. H. 196; Way *v.* Davidson, 12 Gray (Mass.) 466; Roberts *v.* Wyatt, 2 Taunt. 268; Soule *v.* White, 14 Me. 436; Palmtag *v.* Dontrick, 59 Cal. 154; Coleman *v.* Shelton, 2 McCord, Eq. (S. Car.) 126.

So where pledgor gets possession by theft. Bruley *v.* Rose, 57 Iowa 651.

But if pledgee voluntarily relinquishes the possession, his remedy at law is gone, though he may have been induced to surrender the possession by the misrepresentations of the pledgor. Mills *v.* Stewart, 5 Humph. (Tenn.) 308.

This rule is modified as to collateral security. See *infra*, this title.

2. Possession of a chattel by the pledgor is evidence of fraud, that may be rebutted by showing that he holds as agent of pledgee. Macomber *v.* Parker, 14 Pick. (Mass.) 497. If the circumstances make out a good reason for giving the custody and apparent control to the pledgor there may not even be evidence of fraud; but at most, his possession will only be evidence either that the pledge has been abandoned, or that the transaction is fraudulent. *Ex parte* Ritz, 2 Low. (U. S.) 519.

3. Schouler on Bailments, § 178; Stevens *v.* Bell, 6 Mass. 339. It is of no consequence whether the debt or engagement for which the security was given, is that of the pledgor or some other person; for if there is assent by all the proper parties, it is equally obligatory in each case. Story on Bailment, § 300; Jones on Pledges, § 354; Merchants' Nat. Bank *v.* Hall, 83 N. Y. 338.

The security for a debt, in whose hands soever it may be, is a fund held in trust for the payment of such debt; if in the hands of the creditor, the surety having paid the debt, may call for it to indemnify himself; if in the hands of surety, the creditor may resort to it for the satisfaction of his debt. See Subrogation; New London Bank *v.* Lee, 11 Conn. 111; Brick *v.* Freehold Nat. Banking Co., 37 N. J. L. 307; Stewart *v.* Davis, 18 Ind. 74.

Pledgee was a surety in Jewett *v.* Warren, 12 Mass. 300; Blackwood *v.* Brown, 34 Mich. 4; Gilson *v.* Martin, 49 Vt. 474. He was an indorser in Third Nat. Bank *v.* Boyd, 44 Md. 47.

Statutes in *California* and *Dakota* provide that one who pledges property for the debt of another cannot withdraw it except as a pledgor might; and

for any other lawful performance of an engagement,[1] but it must be founded on a legal consideration.[2] The pledge may be given to secure a present, future,[3] or pre-existing debt,[4] or to cover a present liability together with those to be incurred in the future.[5]

if he receives from his debtor a consideration for the pledge, he cannot withdraw it without his consent. Codes and Stats., 1876, § 7994 of Civ. Code, § 2994; *Dakota* Ter. R. Codes., 1877, § 1765 of Civ. Code.

In *Louisiana* provisions covering the general ground of common law pledges are found. *Louisiana* R. Civil Code, 1870, p. 373, arts. 3136–3141.

1. Story on Bailments, § 300; Vest *v.* Green, 3 Mo. 219.

2. Jones on Pledge, § 354; Schouler on Bailments, § 180.

If the debt be without consideration, or the consideration be an illegal or immoral one, no court will lend its aid to either party to give effect to the contract. Jones on Pledge, § 354. So debts tainted with usury. Causey *v.* Yeates, 8 Humph. (Tenn.) 605; 1 Schouler Pers. Prop., §§ 265, 290. Where one who has purchased securities which have been pledged to secure usurious loan, obtains a further usurious loan from the same lender, giving one note for the total amount, and pledges other property to secure the whole, the property last pledged cannot be retained by the lender as security for the original loan. Beecher *v.* Ackerman, 1 Abb. Pr., N. S. (N. Y.) 141. To supply victuals for a debauch in a brothel. Taylor *v.* Chester, L. R., 4 Q. B. 309. Debts made on Sunday. King *v.* Green, 6 Allen (Mass.) 139.

But the pledgee may keep the possession of the pledge in accordance with the maxim, *in pari delicto potier est conditio possidentis.* Curtis *v.* Leavitt, 15 N. Y. 9. The debtor in order to recover his property must pay the demand against him and sue for the pledge on the general ground of ownership. King *v.* Green, 6 Allen (Mass.) 139; Causey *v.* Yeates, 8 Humph. (Tenn.) 605; Schouler on Bailments, § 92.

A pawnbroker gave the pledgor of an article a memorandum not complying with the law and on its face showing usury. *Held*, in the pledgor's action to recover the value of the pledge, that the defendant might show an oral agreement to charge legal interest only, but that his explanation not corroborated by his book and contradicted by plaintiff, was insufficient to show such an agreement. Roosvelt *v.* Dreyer, 12 Daly (N. Y.) 370.

Where a valid loan is made and an illegal certificate of the debt taken, together with the pledge given as collateral to the certificate, and the debt, the law annexes the pledge to the debt and not to the evidence of the debt and upholds the pledge. Curtis *v.* Leavitt, 15 N. Y. 9.

3. Story on Bailments, § 300; Jones on Pledge, §§ 355, 361; Stearns *v.* Marsh, 4 Den. (N. Y.) 227; Conard *v.* Atlantic Ins. Co., 1 Pet. (U. S.) 386; D'Wolf *v.* Harris, 4 Mason (U. S.) 515; Eichelberger *v.* Murdock, 10 Md. 373; Calkins *v.* Lockwood, 16 Conn. 275; Wolf *v.* Wolf, 12 La. Ann. 529.

4. Story on Bailments, § 300; Schouler on Bailments, § 178.

Where a chattel is pledged for a pre-existing debt, the pledgee is not a holder for value to the extent that it will enable him to retain it as against the true owner from whom it has been obtained by fraud, as he could do if he were a true holder for value. Goodwin *v.* Massachusetts L. & T. Co. (Mass.), 25 N. E. Rep. 100.

5. Badlam *v.* Tucker, 1 Pick. (Mass.) 389; Holbrook *v.* Baker, 5 Me. 309; D'Wolf *v.* Harris, 4 Mason (U.S.) 515; Conard *v.* Atlantic Ins. Co., 1 Pet. (U. S.) 448; Third Nat. Bank *v.* Boyd, 44 Md. 47; Van Blarcom *v.* Broadway Bank, 9 Bosw. (N. Y.) 532.

Whether a person holding personal property in pledge for money loaned, can retain such property as security for advances subsequently made, must depend upon the understanding and agreement of the parties at the time such subsequent advances were made. James' Appeal, 89 Pa. St. 54.

But a contract for future advances will be binding between the parties at least, for any and all advances made prior to the time of third parties acquiring an interest in the collateral pledged. Buchanan *v.* International Bank, 78 Ill. 500.

Where stock is pledged to a bank "as security for the payment of any

A security may be for one or many debts,[1] and is presumed to be for the whole and every part of the debt secured.[2] The agreement of the parties, expressed or implied must determine what debt is to be secured,[3] and property specifically pledged for a par-

demands it may from time to time hold against" a debtor named, the terms include all demands the bank holds against him at the time, as well as those that might arise afterwards. Merchants' Nat. Bank *v.* Hall, 83 N. Y. 338; Douglass *v.* Reynolds, 7 Pet. (U. S.) 113; Agawam Bank *v.* Striver, 18 N. Y. 502.

Where a debtor confessed judgment to his creditor to secure existing liabilities and also what liabilities the creditor would assume in the future, it was held that there was no obligation to assume future liabilities. Therefore, the judgment would not protect debts incurred by the creditor after getting notice of a subsequent judgment against the debtor. McClure *v.* Roman, 52 Pa. St. 458.

Where a negotiable instrument wrongfully acquired by the debtor is given in pledge to secure future advances, the creditor is protected by it for advances made before its maturity, but after maturity being charged constructively with notice of the debtor's wrongful acquirement of it, he can no longer rely on it for security. Texas Banking etc. Co. *v.* Turnley, 61 Tex. 365.

The pledgee of negotiable instruments for future advances or loans before maturity and without notice is a holder for value in the usual course of business. State Sav. Assoc. *v.* Hunt, 17 Kan. 532.

These are binding for any and all advances made thereon prior to notice of claims of third persons. Walker *v.* Kee, 14 S. Car. 142.

In *Tennessee*, however, the holder receives such paper subject to the equities existing at the time of the transfer but not those arising subsequent thereto. Richardson *v.* Rice, 9 Baxt. (Tenn.) 290; 40 Am. Rep. 92.

A note pledged before maturity as security for future advances is good in the creditor's hands for all advances made before he has notice of equities between the original parties, but not for advances made after such notice unless he had already bound himself at the time of taking the security to make advances to a definite amount. Kerr *v.* Cowen, 2 Dev. Eq. (N. Car.) 356.

1. Story on Bailments, § 300; Schouler on Bailments, § 178; Beach *v.* State Bank, 2 Md. 488; Wilcox *v.* Faishaner Bank, 7 Allen (Mass.) 270.

A part of a debt may be secured. Fridley *v.* Bowen, 103 Ill. 633.

A bond and mortgage may be given to a pledgee to hold for his own debt as well as for that of another. Hubbell *v.* Blakeslee, 71 N. Y. 63; Harbeck *v.* Vanderbilt, 20 N. Y. 395; Champney *v.* Coope, 32 N. Y. 543.

The repayment of one debt does not prevent the pledgee's holding the security for the other. Kellogg *v.* Ames, 41 N. Y. 259.

Where a corporation to secure its bonds, deposited bonds and mortgages, all *bona fide* purchasers of the bonds were interested in the whole collateral. Palmor *v.* Yates, 3 Sandf. (N. Y.) 137.

2. Schouler on Bailment, § 187; Baldwin *v.* Bradley, 69 Ill. 32.

3. Jones on Pledges, § 355.

In determining the effect to be given to absolute assignments of securities, the whole transaction between the parties must be taken into account. Boardman *v.* Holmes, 124 Mass. 438; Charles *v.* Coker, 2 S. Car. 122; Hilton *v.* Sims, 45 Ga. 565.

Where a written instrument evidences that a pledge has been made for the loan of a definite sum, parol evidence will not be admitted to show that it was agreed between the parties that the same property should be held in security for such further advances as the pledgee might afterwards make. Hamilton *v.* Wagner, 2 A. K. Marsh. (Ky.) 331.

Parol evidence is admissible to show what debts are secured by a note which on its face states that it is to be used as "collateral security." Garton *v.* Union City Bank, 34 Mich. 279.

In the contract of pledge, the mention of the amount of the debt intended to be secured, required by article 3125 of the Civil Code, is in no sense a formality. It is essential to the contract, and as such not abolished by section 2 of the act of 1855, relative to

ticular loan cannot, in the absence of special agreement, be held by the pledgee for any other.[1]

pledges. Cater *v.* Merrell, 14 La. Ann. 376.

1 Talmadge *v.* Third Nat. Bank, 16 N. Y. Wkly. Dig. 487; Gilliat *v.* Lynch, 2 Leigh (Va.) 493; Jarvis *v.* Rogers, 15 Mass. 389; St. John *v.* O'Connell, 7 Port. (Ala.) 466; Phillips *v.* Thompson, 2 Johns. Ch. (N. Y.) 418; Schiffer *v.* Feagin, 51 Ala. 335; Teutonia Nat. Bank *v.* Loeb, 27 La. Ann. 110; Mayo *v.* Avery, 18 Cal. 309; Robinson *v.* Frost, 14 Barb. (N. Y.) 536; Wooley *v.* Louisville Banking Co., 81 Ky. 527; Loyd *v.* Lynchburg Nat. Bank, 86 Va. 690; Burnap *v.* National Bank, 96 N. Y. 125; Scheppers' Appeal, 125 Pa. St. 598; Bowditch *v.* Green, 3 Met. (Mass.) 360; Ball *v.* Stanley, 5 Yerg. (Tenn.) 199; James' Appeal, 89 Pa. St. 54; Jarvis *v.* Rogers, 15 Mass. 389; Allen *v.* Megguire, 15 Mass. 490; Adams *v.* Sturges, 55 Ill. 468; Neponset Bank *v.* Leland, 5 Met. (Mass.) 259; Post *v.* Tradesmen's Bank, 28 Conn. 420; Watkins *v.* Hill, 8 Pick. (Mass.) 522; Geffcken *v.* Slingerland, 1 Bosw. (N. Y.) 449; Bulkley *v.* Garrett, 60 Pa. St. 333.

When the pledgee tried to apply the surplus above the debt secured to other debts he was compelled to pay it to the general creditors. Talbot *v.* Frere, L. R., 9 Ch. D. 568.

If the evidence of the debt secured on its face makes the debtor liable for interest, the pledged property will also be security for the interest. Swasey *v.* North Car. R. Co., 1 Hughes (U. S.) 17.

A pledgee cannot retain a pledge to secure other debts, or to apply to other objects than those for which it is given. Nor can the government, where one of its revenue officers acts as pledgee, and pays the money into the treasury upon another and different debt than that for which it was deposited. Boughton *v.* U. S., 12 Ct. of Cl. 336; State Nat. Bank *v.* U. S., 10 Ct. of Cl. 519.

Where a party pledged a lot of whisky for the repayment of a sum of money borrowed, with interest, storage, etc., and a few weeks after pledged another lot for a similar loan, and there was no proof that either pledge was dependent on the other, or that when the first pledge was made a future loan was anticipated, or that when the second one was made the first was allued to, held, that each pledge was a security for the loan made at the time, and not both for the first loan. Baldwin *v.* Bradley, 69 Ill. 32.

Where the defendant assigned to the plaintiff a certificate of stock "as security for the payment of any demand" plaintiff "may from time to time have or hold against" her husband, in an action to foreclose the plaintiff's lien upon the stock pledged, it was held that the assignment by its terms included and secured all demands had and held by plaintiff after its execution as well as those existing at that time, and that this was the intent of the parties. Merchants' Nat. Bank *v.* Hall, 83 N. Y. 338; Boardman *v.* Holmes, 124 Mass. 438.

Where a pledgor of stock as security for a specified debt afterward wrote a letter to the pledgee authorizing him "to hold the stock as a general collateral security for all the writer's liabilities to the said bank at present existing, or which may hereafter be incurred by him," it was held that under this authority after payment of the specified debt a surplus from the sale of the stock could be applied *pro rata* to all the general liabilities. Eichelberger *v.* Murdock, 10 Md. 373; Buchanan *v.* International Bank, 78 Ill. 500; Van Blarcom *v.* Broadway Bank, 37 N. Y. 540; Smith *v.* Dennison, 101 Ill. 531.

Where stock was pledged as collateral security for a note with authority to the holder to sell the same "on the non-performance of this promise he giving me credit for any balance of the net proceeds of such sale and paying all sums then due from me to said holder," it was held that on tender of the amount due on the note at its maturity, the holder thereof had no right to retain the stock as security for other debts then due him from the maker. Hathway *v.* Fall River Nat. Bank, 131 Mass. 14.

But where no specific debt is designated, security in the possession of the creditor may be applied to any debts owed him by the debtor. Norton *v.* Plum, 14 Conn. 512; Fairchild *v.* Holly, 10 Conn. 179; U. S. *v.* Kirkpatrick, 9 Wheat. (U. S.) 720.

After a particular debt for which security is given has been paid, the creditor holding it, in order to get a lien on

a. RECITAL OF COLLATERAL SECURITIES IN PRINCIPAL NOTE.—Such a recital does not affect the negotiability of the principal note, as the amount to be paid, the time, and person to whom payment is to be made remain certain,[1] though the agreement in the note as to the disposition of the collateral must be followed.[2]

the property, must issue an attachment against it as any other creditor would have to do. Allen *v.* Megguire, 15 Mass. 490.

Where collateral was pledged generally for the debts of a partnership, it could not be held for a private debt of one of the partners. San Antonio Nat. Bank *v.* Blocker, 77 Tex. 73.

When a note was deposited for the credit of a firm it could not be held as security for a draft accepted by the firm for the accommodation of another and discounted by the pledgee. Loyd *v.* Lynchburg Nat. Bank, 86 Va. 690.

A city pledged its stock in a railroad company as security for its bonds issued in aid of the road, and the bonds provided that the holders might exchange the same for a like amount of the stock, and be substituted as stockholders in the place of the city. *Held*, that the bondholders had a lien upon the whole of the stock, but that one bond could not bind more than one share of stock. Aurora *v.* Cobb, 21 Ind. 492.

General Lien.—When securities are pledged to a banker or broker for the payment of a particular loan or debt, he has no lien upon such securities for a general balance or for the payment of other claims. Story on Agency, § 381; Wyckoff *v.* Anthony, 9 Daly (N. Y.) 417; *In re* Medewe, 26 Beav. 588; Vanderzee *v.* Willis, 3 Bro. C. C. 21; Jarvis *v.* Rogers, 15 Mass. 389; Lane *v.* Bailey, 47 Barb. (N. Y.) 395; Grant *v.* Taylor, 3 Jones & S. (N. Y.) 338; Duncan *v.* Brennan, 83 N. Y. 487; Biebinger *v.* Continental Bank, 99 U. S. 143; Wyeth *v.* National Market Bank, 132 Mass. 597; Woolby *v.* Louisville Banking Co., 81 Ky., 527; Reynes *v.* Dumont, 130 U. S. 354; Masonic Sav. Bank *v.* Bangs, 84 Ky. 135.

Renewals.—The renewal of a note by the same parties is a mere change of evidence of indebtedness, and in the absence of intention in no way affects a pledge made to secure it. Bank of America *v.* McNeil, 10 Bush (Ky.) 54; Pinney *v.* Kimpton, 46 Vt. 83; Mosar *v.* Trice, 21 Gratt. (Va.) 556; 8 Am. Rep 609; Merchants' Bank *v.* Hall, 83 N. Y. 338; Wadsworth *v.* Thompson, 8 Ill. 423; Shrewsbury Sav. Inst. Appeal, 94 Pa. St. 309; Dayton Bank *v.* Merchants' Bank, 37 Ohio St. 208; Union Bank *v.* Slacomb, 34 La. Ann. 927; Jones *v.* Guaranty etc. Co., 101 U. S. 622; Worcester Nat. Bank *v.* Cheeney, 87 Ill. 602; Cherry *v.* Frost, 7 Lea (Tenn.) 1; Cover *v.* Black, 1 Pa. St. 493; Lytle's Appeal, 36 Pa. St. 131; Brinckerhoff *v.* Lansing, 4 Johns. Ch. (N. Y.) 65; Agawam Bank *v.* Strever, 18 N. Y. 338; Patterson *v.* Johnson, 7 Ohio 225; Davis *v.* Maynard, 9 Mass. 242; Watkins *v.* Hill, 8 Pick. (Mass.) 522; Pomeroy *v.* Rice, 16 Pick. (Mass.) 22; Taber *v.* Hamilton, 97 Mass. 489; Reddish *v.* Watson, 6 Ham (Ohio) 510; New Hampshire Savings Bank *v.* Gill, 16 N. H. 578; Collins *v.* Dawley, 4 Colo. 1383. The question of renewal is one of intention. Williams *v.* National Bank, 70 Md. 343.

A note pledged as collateral security for a debt due to the plaintiffs from the pledgor continues valid and effectual until such debt is paid, notwithstanding the evidence of it has been changed from a promissory note to a judgment of a court of record. Fisher *v.* Fisher, 98 Mass. 303.

1. Willoughby *v.* Comstock, 3 Hill (N. Y.) 389; Cook *v.* Satterlee, 6 Cow. (N. Y.) 108; Arnold *v.* Rock River etc. R. Co., 5 Duer (N. Y.) 207; Ocean Nat. Bank *v.* Faut, 50 N. Y. 475; Barning *v.* Markham, 13 Gray (Mass.) 454; Stultze *v.* Silva, 119 Mass. 139; Towne *v.* Rice, 122 Mass. 67; Fancourt *v.* Thorne, 9 Q. B. 312; Bolton *v.* Dugdale, 4 B. & Ad. 619; Wise *v.* Charlton, 4 A. & E. 786.

Even though the note contains an agreement that the maker will pay any deficiency necessary to satisfy the principal note after the sale of the collateral security it does not destroy its negotiability. Arnold *v.* Rock River etc. R. Co., 5 Duer (N. Y.) 207.

2. Williams *v.* U. S. Trust Co., N. Y. L. Journal, July 8, 1891.

V. Pledgor's Title.—When the pledgor is not the owner, a pledge of corporeal property will be held good as between the parties and as to the general public,[1] but the pledgee has no lien against the true owner,[2] unless the latter assents thereto.[3] But

1. Schouler on Bailments, § 181.

The pledgor by the act of pledging impliedly warrants that he is the owner of the property pledged. Story on Bailments, 352; Malrs *v.* Taylor, 40 Pa. St. 446; Goldstein *v.* Hort, 30 Cal. 372.

Where the ownership of any part of it is not in him he is liable to the pledgee in damages if by reason of defective title it is taken from him. Mairs *v.* Taylor, 40 Pa. St. 446; Cass *v.* Higenbotan, 27 Hun (N. Y.) 406. A person pledging to another goods which he does not own and at the same time making delivery of them, is estopped from setting up a title to the goods subsequently acquired during the existence of the pledge, and the pledgee in such case may recover possession of them as against him or anybody possessing the right. Goldstein *v.* Hort, 30 Cal. 372.

Where the pledgor has no title, the pledgee may return the property to the true owner and not be liable to the pledgor for its return. Jones on Pledge, § 52. Cheesman *v.* Exall, 6 Exch. 341; Jarvis *v.* Rogers, 13 Mass. 105.

In Cheesman *v.* Exall, 6 Ex. 341, Pollock, C. B., said: "It may be that a person with whom property is pledged may contract absolutely, and in all events, to deliver back the property to the pledgor; in which case I agree that the former would be answerable in damages for the breach of such contract, though the damages might be nominal only. That, however, is not the ordinary result of the common contract. In that case, the person who pledges impliedly, undertakes that the property pledged is his own; and if it turns out not to be so, the pledgee may restore it to the lawful owner." Parke, B., said: "I think that a person with whom property is pledged may set up the *jus tertii*, unless he has entered into an engagement with the person who pledged it to return the property to him."

But it seems that the pledgee should not be allowed to set up the title of a third person against the pledgor unless such third, person has given him authority so to do or has enforced his own superior right of property. Story on Bailments, § 291; Palmtag *v.* Dontrick, 59 Cal. 154; Biddle *v.* Bond, 6 B. & S. 225; Garth *v.* Howard, 5 C. & P. 346.

In *Louisiana* the debtor can pledge whatever property he has. Where his ownership is liable to be divested or is subject to incumbrances, he can confer only what right he himself has in the property at the time it was pledged; but if he has since acquired it his ownership relates back to the time of the contract and the pledge will be good. *Louisiana* Civil Code, 1870, p. 374, articles, 3142–3150.

The pledgor by the act of pledging impliedly warrants that he has the title to the property pledged and if he has not and the property is taken from the pledgee, he is answerable to the pledgee in damages. Mairs *v.* Taylor, 40 Pa. St. 446.

2. Jones on Pledge, § 55; Duell *v.* Cudlipp, 1 Hilt. (N. Y.) 166; Agnew *v.* Johnson, 22 Pa. St. 471; Taylor *v.* Turner, 87 Ill. 296; Hooper *v.* Ramsbottom, 4 Campb. 121.

Where a bailee of goods for safekeeping pledges them, with intent to convert the proceeds to his own use, the pledgee acquires no title as against the owner, though he dealt *bona fide* with the pledgor. Gottlieb *v.* Hartman, 3 Colo. 53; Hartop *v.* Hoare, 3 Atk. 44.

A common carrier cannot pledge goods put in his possession. Kitchell *v.* Vanadar, 1 Blackf. (Ind.) 355.

Where the terms of a contract of sale leave personal property in the possession of the vendor, it may be pledged by him to another who has done work upon it to secure payment for his services, and the pledgee can hold the same until his claim is satisfied. Dean *v.* Lawham, 7 Oregon 422.

3. Story on Bailm., § 291; Jones on Pledge, § 53; Small *v.* Robinson, 69 Me. 425; Singer Mfg. Co. *v.* Clark, 5 Ex. D. 37.

One person may pledge the property of another provided it be with the express or tacit consent of the owner, but this tacit consent must be inferred from

where the true owner intrusts the property or the *indicia* of title to another's hands so carelessly that, even though an agency for the pledge was not strictly conferred, the owner enabled the wrong of inducing the loan upon its security to be committed, a *bona fide* holder of the same for value will be protected.[1] One having only a partial interest in property may pledge that interest;

circumstances so strong as to leave no doubt of the owner's intention as if he was present at the making of the contract or as if he himself delivered to the creditor the thing pledged. Although the property of another cannot be given in pledge without his consent, yet so long as the owner refrains from claiming it, the debtor who has given it in pledge cannot seek to have it restored until his debt has been entirely discharged. Jones on Pledge, § 53.

Where a debtor directed another to assist in the settlement of the debtor's affairs he did not thereby authorize him to pledge property as security for debts. Sweet *v.* Brown, 5 Pick. (Mass.) 178.

Where a borrowed horse was pledged and the owner said he would see the pledgee "and see what the bill was, and he would either pay it and take the horse, or let the horse go to pay it," it was not a ratification of the pledge, but expressed merely a disposition to do so in the future. Cox *v.* McGuire, 26 Ill. App. 315.

An attorney cannot give in pledge the property of his principal without the consent of the latter or an express power to that effect. Reeves *v.* Smith, 1 La. Ann. 379. Nevertheless, where the power of attorney contains a general authority to mortgage the property of the principal, this power includes that of giving it in pledge. The property of cities and other corporations can only be given in pledge according to the rules and subject to the restrictions prescribed on that head by their respective acts of incorporation. Jones on Pledge, § 53.

One authorized to sell is not authorized to pledge. Delauney *v.* Barker, 2 Stark. 539.

In *California* and *Dakota*, statutes provide that where one has permitted another to assume the apparent ownership of property for the purpose of transferring it, he cannot set up his own title to defeat the pledge of property of a pledgee who has received it in good faith in the ordinary course of business and for value. Codes and Stats. 1876, § 7991; Civ. Code, § 2991. R. Codes, 1877, § 1762 of Civ. Code.

The master of the vessel may, without the consent of its owners, hypothecate a portion of his cargo when this is necessary to enable him to continue the voyage. United Ins. Co. *v.* Scott, 1 Johns. (N. Y.) 106; The Fortitude, 3 Sumn. (U. S.) 228; The Gratitudine, 3 Rob. Adm. 240; Freeman *v.* East India Co., 5 B. & Ald. 617. In doing this he is regarded as acting as an authorized agent, but it must appear in order that his authority may be ratified that the vessel was in a foreign port, that the voyage was unfinished, and that the pledge was indispensable to enable the vessel to complete the voyage. Marziou *v.* Pioche, 8 Cal. 522.

Pledges by Joint Owners.—One joint owner of a chattel, though in possession of it, cannot pledge the interest of the other without his consent, but he may pledge his own interest without the consent of the other, and if the pledgor had the right of possession the pledgee will take the same right of possession as against the other owner. In such case, the latter cannot maintain replevin against the pledgee for the thing pledged, nor can both joint owners jointly maintain the action without paying the debt secured. Frans *v.* Young, 24 Iowa 375.

1. Schouler Bailm., § 182; Calais Steamboat Co. *v.* Scudder, 2 Black (U. S.) 372; Babcock *v.* Lawson, 4 Q. B. Div. 394.

Mere possession of goods by a bailee or agent, gives him no right to pledge them for his own debt. Branson *v.* Heckler, 22 Kan, 424; Agnew *v.* Johnson, 22 Pa. St. 471; Gallaher *v.* Cohen, 1 Browne (Pa.) 43.

A borrower of property is not clothed with such *indicia* of ownership as will affect the owner's rights when such property is pledged. Cox *v.* McGuire, 26 Ill. App. 315.

If a mortgagor while in possession sells or pledges the property to a *bona fide* purchaser or pledgee who is ignorant of the mortgage, and has no

but in this case, however, the possession of the pledgee is only temporary and the pledge must be delivered up when the pledgor's term expires.[1]

VI. Subject-Matter of the Contract—1. In General.—In gen-

cause for suspicion or inquiry, and delivers the possession, the sale or pledge will be good, and the rights of such a purchaser or pledgee are paramount to those of the mortgagee. Lewis *v.* Stevenson, 2 Hall (N. Y.) 63.

Though the vendee in possession of chattels under a conditional sale has not the title between himself and the owner, yet he may pledge the property to one who loans him money *bona fide* without notice, and the latter will acquire a valid and binding lien on the property for the payment of the money loaned, and will be protected against the vendor's claim for the purchase money. Ohio etc. R. Co. *v.* Kerr, 49 Ill. 458; Western Union R. Co. *v.* Wagner, 65 Ill. 197; Mich. Cent. R. Co. *v.* Phillips, 60 Ill. 190; Jennings *v.* Gage, 13 Ill. 611; Brundage *v.* Camp, 21 Ill. 329; Burton *v.* Curyea, 40 Ill. 320.

Under the *Iowa* Code of 1873, § 1922, which requires contracts for the conditional sale of chattels to be recorded in order to be valid against creditors and subsequent purchasers without notice, the pledgee's right to property pledged by a vendee in possession under a conditional sale unrecorded, was held superior to that of the vendor. Pittsburgh Locomotive Car Works *v.* State Nat. Bank, 21 Int. Rev. Rec. 349.

Felony and Fraud.—There is a well settled distinction between the cases of possession of goods acquired by felony and fraud. As to the latter, the consequences are very different so far as respects purchasers from the fraudulent vendee, as in the one case, the title passes and in the other it does not. As between the immediate parties themselves, the vendor and the frandulent vendee, the contract may indeed be avoided by reason of the fraud, and upon demand to have the goods delivered back the vendor will be revested with the title and may recover the goods from the pretended purchaser or any one to whom he may have sold them with knowledge of the fraud. But if the fraudulent vendee has sold them to a *bona fide* purchaser before the vendor has signified his dissent from the contract or interposed to regain the possession, the title of such *bona fide* purchaser cannot be defeated. And the same rule applies where goods so obtained have been pledged for advances. The pledgee who has made the advances without knowledge of the fraud, has a lien upon the goods for reimbursement as against the vendor so defrauded. But if the goods have been stolen and then pledged the pledgee will have no lien upon them as against the owner. Arendale *v.* Morgan, 5 Sneed (Tenn.) 703.

Mowrey *v.* Walsh, 8 Cow. (N. Y.) 238; Hoffman *v.* Carow, 22 Wend. (N. Y.) 285; Jarvis *v.* Rogers, 15 Mass. 389; White *v.* Garden, 10 C. B. 919; Pasherd *v.* Patrick, 5 T. R. 175; Caldwell *v.* Bartlett, 3 Duer (N. Y.) 341; Wood *v.* Yeatman, 15 B. Mon. (Ky.) 270.

But if pledgee has notice of the fraud his right is gone. Merchants etc. Nat. Bank *v.* Masonic Hall, 62 Ga. 271.

1. Story on Bailments, § 295; Jones on Pledge, § 58; Robertson *v.* Wilcox, 36 Conn. 426.

One having a life interest may pledge that. Hoare *v.* Pasher, 2 T. R. 376.

By statute in *California* and *Dakota*, one who has a lien on property can pledge it to the extent of his lien. *California* Codes, Statutes 1876, § 7990; Civ. Code, § 2990; *Dakota* R. Codes, 1877, § 1761 of Civ. Code.

If an agent or broker having a lien on goods for a general balance tortiously pledges them as his own to secure his own debt, his pledgee cannot hold them as against the principal for even the amount of the lien which the agent had upon the goods. McCornbie *v.* Davies, 7 East. 5.

Pledge of a bond, and as incident thereto of collaterals, is not, *per se* a conversion of the collaterals. If the principal bond and the collaterals are redeemed by the obligee of the bond, before maturity and before suit brought, and are in the hands of the obligee ready to be restored upon the payment of the bond, the obligor has no cause for complaint. Shelton *v.* French, 33 Conn. 489.

For sub-pledge see *infra*, this title, *Pledgee's Rights and Liabilities Before Default.*

eral, every kind of personal property in existence and capable of delivery may be pledged.[1]

2. Corporeal Property.—Corporeal personal property of the simpler kind, such as jewelry, wearing apparel and domestic animals were the subject of pawn in the earlier days, and in regard thereto the first principles of the law of pledge were enunciated.[2] Though in later days the list of articles that may be pledged is much increased, yet the general principles of the early law of pledge continue to govern.[3]

3. Incorporeal Property or Collateral Security.—All kinds of choses in action capable of transfer, negotiable, *quasi* negotiable, and non-negotiable, have been held proper subjects of pledge.[4] Delivery and possession are as necessary to the validity of a pledge of this class of security as in the case of corporeal property, but may vary in accordance with the nature of the property to be pledged.[5]

1. Story Bailm., § 290; Schouler Bailm., § 172; Jones on Pledge, § 49.

The owner of the chattel property which is exempt by law from execution and sale for the payment of debts can pledge them in security for his debts, but in case he does so he waives the benefit of the exemption so far as the incumbrance extends or is operative. Frost *v.* Shaw, 3 Ohio St. 270; Jones *v.* Scott, 10 Kan. 33.

Where the consideration for the pledge fails it will be fraudulent for the pledgee to retain the property. Hollingshead *v.* McKenzie, 8 Ga. 457.

Statutory Exemption.—A pension certificate may not be pledged. Act of Congress July 29, 1048; U. S. Rev. Stat., § 4745; Payne *v.* Woodhull, 6 Duer (N. Y.) 169; Moffatt *v.* Van Doren, 4 Bosw. (N. Y.) 609.

National banks cannot loan or discount on the security of their own stock unless it be needful in order to prevent loss of a debt previously contracted in good faith. First Nat. Bank *v.* Lanier, 11 Wall. (U. S.) 369; Brewster *v.* Hartley, 37 Cal. 15.

One cannot pledge a cause of action growing out of a personal wrong. Pindell *v.* Grooms, 18 B. Mon. (Ky.) 501.

Property not yet in existence, not yet acquired, or out of possession cannot be pledged, for there can be no delivery of it. Gittings *v.* Nelson, 86 Ill. 591; Smithhurst *v.* Edmunds, 14 N. J. Eq. 408; Owens *v.* Kinsey, 7 Jones (N. Car.) 245.

But there may be a contract in the nature of an agreement to pledge, which will attach to the chattel as soon as produced. Macomber *v.* Parker, 14 Pick. (Mass.) 497. See Smith *v.* Atkins 18 Vt. 461; Goodenow *v.* Dunn, 21 Me. 86; Ayers *v.* South Australian Banking Co., L. R., 3 P. C. 548.

See also FUTURE-ACQUIRED PROPERTY, vol. 8, p. 987.

2. Coggs *v.* Bernard, 2 Ld. Raym. 917.

3. Schouler Bailm., § 172.

4. Colebrooke Coll. Security, § 1; Schouler Bailm., § 172.

In Wilson *v.* Little, 2 N. Y. 443, the court by Ruggles, C. J., said: "There seems to be no reason why any legal or equitable interest whatever in personal property may not be pledged, provided the interest can be put by actual delivery or by written transfer, into the hands or within the power of the pledgee so as to be made available to him for the satisfaction of the debt."

Coupon bonds can be pledged. Stewart *v.* Lansing, 104 U. S. 505; Morris Canal etc. Co. *v.* Foster, 9 N. J. Eq. 667.

A note given for collection, and the amount of which when collected, is to be credited upon another note, and held as an offset thereto, is merely a collateral security for the payment of the note last named; and is not to be treated as payment of the same, before the amount is actually collected. Holmes *v.* Lykins, 50 Mo. 399.

5. See *infra*, this title, *Delivery and Possession.*

In a pledge of chattels, mere delivery of the chattel is, usually, enough to vest in the pledgee the special prop-

VII. Pledge of Negotiable Securities—1. In General.—The act of pledge of negotiable instruments payable "to order" consists in delivery accompanied by indorsement; or, if indorsed in blank or payable "to bearer," by mere delivery alone.[1]

The delivery of negotiable instruments unindorsed, where indorsement is required, vests in the pledgee a contingent equitable interest only in the instruments pledged or in the proceeds thereof, subject to the prior equities of third persons as against the pledgor.[2] Such securities are practically non-negotiable and subject to defenses.[3]

2. Pledgee a Holder for Value.—The "*bona fide*" pledgee of negotiable instruments, received in the usual course of business before maturity for a valuable consideration without notice is a holder for value and is protected from all equities arising between the original parties either before or after the act of pledge, just as surely as if the transfer were by absolute sale.[4]

erty requisite to sustain the pledge. But incorporeal property, being incapable of manual delivery, cannot be pledged without a written transfer of the title. Debts, negotiable instruments, stocks in incorporated companies, and choses in action generally are pledged in that mode. Such transfer of the title performs the same office that the delivery of possession does in case of a pledge of corporeal property. The transfer of the title to these, like the delivery of possession of chattels, constitutes the evidence of the pledgee's right of property in the thing pledged. Thus the transfer in writing of shares of stock not only does not prove that the transaction is not a pledge, but the stock, unless it is expressly made assignable by the delivery of the certificates, cannot be pledged in any other manner. Brewster *v.* Hartley, 37 Cal. 15; Wilson *v.* Little, 2 N. Y. 443; Russell *v.* Scudder, 42 Barb. (N. Y.) 31.

1. The pledgee of a promissory note payable to the owner's own order and by him indorsed in blank, may sue and recover on the note without the indorsement of the pledgor. Louisiana State Bank *v.* Gaienne, 21 La. Ann. 555.

Negotiable Bonds and Coupons.—Negotiable, municipal or corporation bonds payable to bearer or holder issued under statutory authority pass by delivery and vest the legal title in a *bona fide* pledgee before maturity, and for value. See also Bonds, vol. 2, p. 448.

This is also true of coupons when severed from the bond, they becoming practically promissory notes. See also Coupons, vol. 4, p. 430,

2. Snow *v.* Fourth Nat. Bank, 7 Robt. (N. Y.) 479; Allen *v.* King, 4 McLean (U. S.) 128; White *v.* Phelps, 14 Minn. 21; Hedges *v.* Sealey, 9 Barb. (N. Y.) 214; Dunn *v.* Meserve, 58 N. H. 429.

But in *Georgia*, where one deposited a note payable "to order" without indorsement as collateral security for a debt, it was held that the pledgee stood in the place of a purchaser and was protected against subsequent liens against the pledgor, whether or no the subsequent creditor had notice of this equity or not. Smith *v.* Jennings, 74 Ga. 551.

Where a bill of exchange was deposited as collateral security without proper indorsement, the pledgor becoming bankrupt, equity will compel the pledgor's assignee to make the necessary indorsement to the pledgee. *Ex parte* Rice, 3 M. D. & D. 586.

In *Louisiana*, delivery of negotiable securities unindorsed, is sufficient to constitute a valid act of pledge. Casey *v.* Schneider, 95 U. S. 497; Partee *v.* Corning, 9 La. Ann. 539; Rev. St. La. 1876, § 2904; Stimson Am. Stat.

3. Simpson *v.* Hall, 47 Conn. 417. But the pledgee may sue in his own name. White *v.* Phelps, 14 Minn. 27; Van Riper *v.* Baldwin, 19 Hun (N. Y.) 344.

4. Swift *v.* Tyson, 16 Pet. (U. S.) 1; Bell *v.* Bell, 12 Pa. St. 235; Irwin *v.* Bailey, 8 Biss. (U. S.) 523; Warner *v.* Fourth Nat. Bank, 115 N. Y. 251; Oates

v. National Bank, 100 U. S. 239; Manhattan Co. *v.* Reynolds, 2 Hill (N. Y.) 140; Poughkeepsie Bank *v.* Hasbrouck, 6 N. Y. 230; Nelson *v.* Eaton, 26 N. Y. 410; City Bank *v.* Perkins, 29 N. Y. 554; Nelson *v.* Wellington, 5 Bosw. (N. Y.) 178; Dix *v.* Tully, 14 La. Ann. 460; Smith *v.* Isaacs, 23 La. Ann. 454; Louisiana State Bank *v.* Gaiennie, 21 La. Ann. 555; Gardner *v.* Maxwell, 27 La. Ann. 561; Bealle *v.* Southern Bank, 57 Ga. 274; Bonaud *v.* Genesi, 42 Ga. 639; Exchange Bank *v.* Butner, 60 Ga. 654; Griswold *v.* Davis, 31 Vt. 390; Curtis *v.* Mohr, 18 Wis. 645; Bond *v.* Wiltse, 12 Wis. 682; Jenkins *v.* Schaub, 14 Wis. 1; Cook *v.* Helms, 5 Wis. 107; Lyon *v.* Ewings, 17 Wis. 63; Kinney *v.* Kruse, 28 Wis. 183.

Munn *v.* McDonald, 10 Watts (Pa.) 273; Hunt *v.* Nevers, 15 Pick. (Mass.) 500; Taylor *v.* Wilson, 11 Met. (Mass.) 44; Logan *v.* Smith, 62 Mo. 455; State Sav. Assoc. *v.* Hunt, 17 Kan. 532; Allen *v.* King, 4 McLean (U. S.) 128; Kempner *v.* Comer, 73 Tex. 196.

Worcester Nat. Bank *v.* Cheeney, 87 Ill. 602; Manning *v.* McClure, 36 Ill. 490; Stotts *v.* Byers, 17 Iowa 303.

Lehman *v.* Tallahassee Mfg. Co., 64 Ala. 567; Miller *v.* Pollock, 99 Pa. St. 202; Slotts *v.* Byers, 17 Iowa 303; State Sav. Assoc. *v.* Hurst, 17 Kan. 532; Best *v.* Crall, 23 Kan. 482; Logan *v.* Smith, 62 Mo. 455; Duncombe *v.* New York etc. R. Co., 84 N. Y. 190; Richardson *v.* Crandall, 48 N. Y. 348; Williams *v.* Smith, 2 Hill (N. Y.) 301; Ferdon *v.* Jones, 2 E. D. Smith (N. Y.) 106; Bank of N. Y. *v.* Vanderhorst, 32 N. Y. 553; Farwell *v.* Importer's etc. Nat. Bank, 90 N. Y. 483; Holbrook *v.* Bassett, 5 Bosw. (N. Y.) 147; Brookman *v.* Metcalf, 5 Bosw. (N. Y.) 429; Van Blarculm *v.* Broadway Bank, 37 N. Y. 540; Munn *v.* McDonald, 10 Watts (Pa.) 270; Brown *v.* Warren, 43 N. H. 430; Chicopee Bank *v.* Chapin, 8 Met. (Mass.) 40; Tarbell *v.* Sturtevant, 26 Vt. 513; Bond *v.* Wiltze, 12 Wis. 682; Crosby *v.* Raub, 16 Wis. 645; Lyon *v.* Ewings, 17 Wis. 61; Curtis *v.* Mohr, 18 Wis. 645; Bowman *v.* Van Kuren, 29 Wis. 219; Mechanics Bldg. Assoc. *v.* Ferguson, 29 La. Ann. 549; Hotchkiss *v.* National Banks, 21 Wall. (U. S.) 354; Tiffany *v.* Boatman's Inst. 18 Wall. (U. S.) Michigan Bank *v.* Eldred, 9 Wall. (U. S.) 544; Brookman *v.* Metcalf, 32 N. Y. 591; Belmont Branch Bank *v.* Hoge, 35 N. Y. 65; City Bank *v.* Perkins, 29 N. Y. 564; Peacock *v.* Purcell, 14 C. B., N. S. 728; *In re* European Bank, L. R., 8 Ch. 41; Collins *v.* Martin, 1 B. & P. 648; Palmer *v.* Richards, 15 W. Jur. 41.

The only cases *contra* are in *New Hampshire*; Jenness *v.* Bean, 10 N. H. 266; Williams *v.* Little, 11 N. H. 66; Goss *v.* Emerson, 23 N. H. 38.

"The peculiar doctrine, as expressed in Jenness *v.* Bean, 10 N. H. 266, and Williams *v.* Little, 11 N. H. 66, that negotiable paper, pledged to the holder as collateral security, is not, in the hands of an innocent pledgee, exonerated from defenses or defective title, is not recognized outside of *New Hampshire*, and within this State has been so limited as not to include cases like the one under consideration. In Clement *v.* Leverett, 12 N. H. 317, an agent of the defendants, intrusted by them with bills drawn by him payable to his own order, and by them accepted to enable him to raise money for them, pledged the bills to a *bona fide* holder to secure money borrowed for his own use. It was held that the defendants, having enabled their agent to hold himself out as owner, were bound by the pledge, and liable to the pledgee. Parker, C. J., delivering the opinion, says of Jenness *v.* Bean, and Williams *v.* Little, that the court advanced the doctrine of those cases, because the general ownership or property of the bill or note pledged as collateral security remained in the indorser. 'But,' he remarks, 'there is another principle, of earlier application, and of paramout influence in this case (Clement *v.* Leverett). The defendants intrusted Burley (their agent) with these bills, accepted by them, and thereby enabled him to hold himself out as the owner of them. . . . Assuming that Burley abused the confidence reposed in him, the defendants, who intrusted him with these negotiable evidences of debt against themselves, must bear the loss. . . . The plaintiff is a *bona fide* holder without notice.'" Tucker *v.* New Hampshire Sav. Bank, 58 N. H. 83.

A loan of money made to one insolvent upon securities pledged at the time of the advances, the same being free from fraud even though the pledgee has reason to believe the pledgor insolvent, is a valid transaction. The power to raise money under such circumstances may be of great value to the borrower. Tiffany *v.* Boatman's Inst., 18 Wall. (U. S.) 376; Cook *v.* Tullis, 18 Wall. (U. S.) 340; Wilson *v.* City Bank, 17 Wall. (U. S.) 375; Mays *v.*

VIII. Pledge of Quasi-Negotiable Securities.—1. In General.— The transfer of documents and *indicia* of title, *quasi* negotiable, under blank indorsement as collateral security for the payment of loans and discount of commercial paper is universally recognized.[1] The rules of estoppel *in pais* are invoked for the protection of the pledgee for value without notice of such *quasi*-negotiable instrument.[2]

2. Stock.—*a.* In General.—Whether stock, being intangible and incapable of delivery, could be the subject of pledge, was at first doubted, and though by actual transfer on the books of the company, the legal title vested in the transferee, making the transaction resemble very much a mortgage, still it is well settled that stock may be pledged and that this passing of the legal title is not incompatible with the idea of a pledge as long as the pledgee has a right on payment of the debt secured to demand a re-transfer.[3] Did this transfer always actually take place on the books of the company, the law of the pledge of stock would be comparatively simple. But the fact that the holder of the certificate of stock, accompanied by a power of attorney to transfer, indorsed to him or in blank, is *prima facie* the owner of the stock, and may make himself actually so by demanding a transfer on the books of the company, has led to a practice approximating in essence if not in name to the pledging of the certificate itself in the character of a negotiable instrument, complicated, however, by the fact that it is still but a mere muniment of title, and liable

Fritton, 20 Wall. (U. S.) 414; Clark *v.* Iselin, 21 Wall. (U. S.) 360; Watson *v.* Taylor, 21 Wall. (U. S.) 378; Burnhisel *v.* Firman, 22 Wall. (U. S.) 170; Sawyer *v.* Turpin, 91 U. S. 114; Jerome *v.* McCarter, 94 U. S. 734; Hutton *v.* Critwell, 1 El. & Bl. 15; Bittleston *v.* Cook, 6 El. & Bl. 296; Harris *v.* Rickett, 4 H. & N. 1; Bell *v.* Simpson, 2 H. & N. 410; Hunt *v.* Mortimer, 10 B. & C. 44; Lee *v.* Hart, 11 Exch. 380; Pennell *v.* Reynolds, 11 C. B., N. S. 709.

Where a husband indorsed his wife's name on a note belonging to her and gave it to a partnership of which he was a member and the partnership pledged it, the pledgee did not get a good title, as the note was not properly indorsed nor taken in the usual course of business. Kempner *v.* Comfer, 73 Tex. 196.

A pledgee of notes as security for indorsements afterwards to be made, is a *bona fide* holder for the amount only due on the indorsements against which it was designed to secure him. Williams *v.* Smith, 2 Hill (N. Y.) 301.

Where a pledgee acting in good faith has taken a good title to securities wrongfully pledged, the recovery of the securities through the false representations of the pledgor does not revest the title to the securities in the owner from whom they were originally wrongfully taken by the pledgor. Ringling *v.* Kohn, 4 Mo. App. 59.

The rules of law governing the relations of the parties to negotiable securities pledged as collateral are treated in Bills and Notes, vol. 2, p. 313; Municipal Securities, vol. 15, p. 1204.

1. Schouler Bailm. § 172; Colebrooke's Collateral Security, § 263.

2. Colebrooke's Collateral Security, 342, n. 1.

3. Newton *v.* Fay, 10 Allen (Mass.) 505; Wilson *v.* Little, 2 N. Y. 443; Allen *v.* Dykers, 3 Hill (N. Y.) 593; Vanpell *v.* Woodward, 2 Sandf. Ch. (N. Y.) 143; White *v.* Platt, 5 Den. (N. Y.) 269; Gilpin *v.* Howell, 5 Pa. St. 41; Morris Canal etc. Co. *v.* Fisher, 9 N. J., Eq. 667; Morris Canal etc. Co. *v.* Lewis, 12 N. J. Eq. 323; Murdock *v.* Columbus Ins. Co., 59 Miss. 152; Dayton Nat. Bank *v.* Merchants' Nat. Bank, 37 Ohio St. 208.

to be divested of its negotiable character under certain contingencies.[1]

This confusion between the pledge of the stock itself and the pledge of its certificate has given rise to litigation.

Where no statute intervenes the transfer is governed by the common law,[2] and a mere rule of a corporation unauthorized by statute cannot affect the rights of purchasers and pledgees of its stock;[3] it is the policy of the law to make the transfer of stock as free from restrictions as possible.[4]

b. TITLE OF PLEDGEE BY TRANSFER ON THE BOOKS.—When stock has been pledged by transfer into the pledgee's name on the books of the company, the legal title passes to the pledgee free from all equities except that raised by the pledge contract itself, and even that may not be asserted against a *bona fide* purchaser from him for value without notice.[5]

c. TITLE OF PLEDGEE BY MERE DELIVERY OF CERTIFICATE.—Though the general rule is that to constitute a pledge of stock in addition to the mere delivery of the certificate there should be a transfer on the books of the company or a power of attorney authorizing a transfer, or some assignment or contract in writing by which the holder may assert title and compel a transfer when desired,[6] yet the pledge of stock by mere delivery of the certificate without any power of transfer properly signed, vests in the pledgee an equitable title only subject to the rights of third persons who have acquired them *bona fide*.[7] The pledgee is unable to enforce his security upon default by the ordinary processes of sale; but equity, if the rights of third persons have not intervened, will de-

1. As to the nature of a stock certificate, its approach to negotiability protected by estoppel *in pais*, etc., see STOCK AND STOCKHOLDERS.

2. Cormick *v.* Richards, 3 Lea (Tenn.) 1; Tippecanoe Co. *v.* Reynolds, 44 Ind. 509.

But statutes of doubtful meaning relating to transfers of stock in corporations will not be construed to control the recognized rules of the common law in regard to the mode of transfer. Boston Music Hall Assoc. *v.* Cory, 129 Mass. 435.

3. Carroll *v.* Mullanphy Sav. Bank, 8 Mo. App. 249; Chouteau Spring Co. *v.* Harris, 20 Mo. 382; Moore *v.* Bank of Commerce, 52 Mo. 377; Bank of Attica *v.* Manufacturer's Bank, 20 N. Y. 501; Rosenback *v.* Bank, 53 Barb. (N. Y.) 495; Steamship Dock Co. *v.* Heron, 52 Pa. St. 280.

4. Smith *v.* Crescent City Live Stock etc. Co., 30 La. Ann. 1378; Cormick *v.* Richards, 3 Lea (Tenn.) 1.

5. Wilson *v.* Little, 2 N. Y. 443; Pinkerton *v.* Manchester etc. R. Co., 42 N. H. 424; Weston *v.* Bear River M. Co., 5 Cal. 186; Roberts' Appeal, 85 Pa. St. 84.

As the rule in the text is negatively stated or implied in nearly all cases and statutes cited elsewhere on the question of the transfer of stock, further citations will not be given here.

6 Nisbit *v.* Macon Bank etc. Co., 12 Fed. Rep. 686.

In *Louisiana* stock cannot be pledged unless it be evidenced by certificates, which must be transferred and delivered to the pledgee. Lallande *v.* Ingram, 19 La. Ann. 364.

7. State F. Ins. Co. *v.* Olmstead, 33 Conn. 480; Shropshire Unions R. Co. *v.* Reg., L. R., 7 H. L. 496.

So a subsequent pledgee of the same shares of stock advancing money in good faith without notice of the previous pledge, who has obtained an actual transfer of the shares to his own name on the books of the company will be protected. Platt *v.* Hawkins, 43 Conn. 139; Platt *v.* Birmingham Axle Co., 41 Conn. 255.

cree the performance of the acts necessary to render the security available.[1]

d. TITLE OF PLEDGEE BY TRANSFER OF CERTIFICATE INDORSED IN BLANK—(1) *Between the Parties.*—It is well settled that between the parties to a transfer of stock by delivery of the certificate with a power of attorney indorsed in blank, the title passes without any transfer upon the books of the company,[2] even without filling up the transfer if it has been signed in blank,[3] the by-laws of the corporation to the contrary notwithstanding.[4] Nor

1. Nisbit *v.* Macon Bank etc. Co., 12 Fed. Rep. 686; Johnson *v.* Dexter, 2 McArthur (D. C.) 530; Allen *v.* Dykers, 3 Hill (N. Y.) 593; 7 Hill (N. Y.) 497; Wilson *v.* Little, 2 N. Y. 443; Newton *v.* Fay, 10 Allen (Mass.) 505; *Ex parte* Boulton, 1 De G. & J. 163.

2. Johnston *v.* Laflin, 103 U. S. 800; First Nat. Bank *v.* Lanier, 11 Wall. (U. S.) 369; Cecil Nat. Bank *v.* Watsontown Bank, 105 U. S. 217; *Ex parte* Dobson, 2 Mont. D. & De G. 685; Dickinson *v.* Central Nat. Bank, 129 Mass. 279; Sibley *v.* Quinsigamond Nat. Bank, 133 Mass. 515; Fitchburg Sav. Bank *v.* Torrey, 134 Mass. 239; Cherry *v.* Frost, 7 Lea (Tenn.) 1; Strange *v.* Houston etc. R. Co., 53 Tex. 162; McAllister *v.* Kuhns, 96 U. S. 87; Webster *v.* Upton, 91 U. S. 65; Holbrook *v.* New Jersey Zinc Co., 57 N. Y. 616; Driscoll *v.* West Bradley etc. Mfg. Co., 59 N. Y. 96; McNeil *v.* Tenth Nat. Bank, 46 N. Y. 331; Lutch *v.* Wells, 48 N. Y. 592; New York etc. R. Co. *v.* Schuyler, 34 N. Y. 30; Johnson *v.* Underhill, 52 N. Y. 203; Cushman *v.* Thayer Mfg. Co., 76 N. Y. 365; Cutting *v.* Damerel, 88 N. Y. 410; Kortright *v.* Buffalo Commercial Bank, 20 Wend. (N. Y.) 91; 22 Wend. (N. Y.) 362; Smith *v.* Crescent City Live Stock etc. Co., 30 La. Ann. 1378; Corniack *v.* Richards, 3 Lea (Tenn.) 1; Broadway Bank *v.* McElrath, 13 N. J. Eq. 26; Mount Holly etc. Co. *v.* Ferree, 17 N. J. Eq. 118; Hunterdon Bank *v.* Nassau Bank, 17 N. J. Eq. 496; Rogers *v.* New Jersey Ins. Co., 8 N. J. Eq. 167; Moore *v.* Bank of Commerce, 52 Mo. 377; Carroll *v.* Mullanphy Sav. Bank, 8 Mo. App. 249; *affirmed* 74 Mo. 77; Sargent *v.* Franklin Ins. Co., 8 Pick. (Mass.) 90; Strange *v.* Houston etc. R. Co., 53 Tex. 162; R. Co. *v.* Thomasson, 40 Ga. 411; Dorey's Appeal, 97 Pa. St. 153; Lightner's Appeal, 82 Pa. St. 301; German Union etc. Assoc. *v.* Sendmeyer, 50 Pa. St. 67; Com. *v.* Watmough, 6 Whart. (Pa.) 117; Duke *v.* Cahawba Nav. Co., 10 Ala. 82; Bank of Commerce's Appeal, 73 Pa. St. 59; Pittsburg etc. R. Co. *v.* Clarke, 29 Pa. St. 146; Gilbert *v.* Manchester Mfg. Co., 11 Wend. (N. Y.) 628; Bank of Utica *v.* Smalley, 2 Cow. (N. Y.) 777; People's Bank *v.* Gridley, 91 Ill. 457; Kellogg *v.* Stockwell, 75 Ill. 68; Baldwin *v.* Canfield, 26 Minn. 43; Swift *v.* Smith, 65 Md. 428.

3. Otis *v.* Gardner, 105 Ill. 436; Ross *v.* Southwestern R. Co., 53 Ga. 514; Comeau *v.* Guild Farm Oil Co., 3 Daly (N. Y.) 218; Smith *v.* Crescent City etc. Live Stock etc. Co., 30 La. Ann. 1378.

4. Johnson *v.* Laflin, 5 Dill. (U. S.) 65; 103 U. S. 800; 17 Alb. Law J. 146; Thompson's Nat. Bank Cases 343; First Nat. Bank *v.* Lanier, 11 Wall. (U. S.) 369; Ross *v.* Southwestern R. Co., 53 Ga. 514; R. Co. *v.* Thomasson, 40 Ga. 411; Dickinson *v.* Central Nat. Bank, 129 Mass. 279; Sibley *v.* Quinsigamond Nat. Bank, 133 Mass. 515; Sargent *v.* Franklin Ins. Co., 8 Pick. (Mass.) 90; Fitchburg Sav. Bank *v.* Torrey, 134 Mass. 239; Merchants' Nat. Bank *v.* Richards, 6 Mo. App. 454; Moore *v.* Bank of Commerce, 52 Mo. 377; Carroll *v.* Mullanphy Sav. Bank, 8 Mo. App. 249; Hoppin *v.* Buffum, 9 R. I. 513; Beckwith *v.* Burrough, 13 R. I. 294; German Union etc. Assoc. *v.* Sendmeyer, 50 Pa. St. 67; U. S. *v.* Vaughn, 3 Binn. (Pa.) 394; Leavitt *v.* Fisher, 4 Duer (N. Y.) 1; Munn *v.* Barnum, 24 Barb. (N. Y.) 283; Orr *v.* Bigelow, 20 Barb. (N. Y.) 21; Strange *v.* Houston etc. R. Co., 53 Tex. 162; Kellogg *v.* Stockwell, 75 Ill. 68; Baldwin *v.* Canfield, 26 Minn. 43; Fraser *v.* Charleston, 11 S. Car. 486; Baltimore etc. R. Co. *v.* Sewell, 35 Md. 238; Noyes *v.* Spaulding, 27 Vt. 420; Cornick *v.* Richards, 3 Lea (Tenn.) 1; Bank of America *v.* McNeil, 10 Bush (Ky.) 54.

does it matter as between the parties whether this title is legal or equitable.[1]

(2) *Between the Parties and the Corporation.*—The holder of a certificate of stock indorsed in blank cannot assert a legal title against the corporation without a transfer on the books.[2]

And this is true even where there is no provision in the charter, by-laws or in the stock certificate, requiring such transfer.[3] Where the certificates do set forth the manner of transfer, they constitute the regulations thereof.[4] Until such transfer is made on the company's books, the assignee of shares cannot assert the rights,[5] nor is he subject to the limitations[6] of stockholders. Before actual transfer on the books of the company, the pledgee has a mere equitable interest in the stock;[7] that is, a power coupled with an interest to demand a transfer and the issue of a new certificate, which power can only be revoked by payment of the debt secured.[8]

Possession of the certificate, with authority to transfer, is *prima facie* sufficient to require the corporation issuing the same to extend to the holder the privileges and benefits to which the person

1. Cecil Nat. Bank *v.* Watsontown Bank, 105 U. S. 217; Carroll *v.* Mullanphy Sav. Bank, 8 Mo. App. 249; Merchants' Nat. Bank *v.* Richards, 6 Mo. App. 454; Johnson *v.* Underhill, 52 N. Y. 203; McNeil *v.* Tenth Nat. Bank, 46 N. Y. 325.

In Johnston *v.* Laflin, 103 U. S. 800, the court by Field, J., said: "As between them (the parties) the title to the shares then passed; whether that be deemed a legal or equitable one matters not; the right to the shares then vested in the purchaser."

2. Stockwell *v.* St. Louis Mercantile Co., 9 Mo. App. 133; Becher *v.* Wells Flouring Mill Co., 1 Fed. Rep. 276; Laing *v.* Burley, 101 Ill. 591; Otis *v.* Gardner, 105 Ill. 436; Manning *v.* Quicksilver Min. Co., 24 Hun (N. Y.) 360; Cheever *v.* Meyer, 52 Vt. 66; Bank of Commerce's Appeal, 73 Pa. St. 59; People *v.* Robinson, 64 Cal. 373.

"The by-law which requires transfers of stock to be recorded on the books of a corporation, regulates merely the respective rights of the corporation and the individual stockholders. No one can claim to be a stockholder and to exercise the rights of a corporator, in virtue of sale of stock to him until the corporation has taken cognizance of the sale, and by transfer on its books has substituted the purchaser for the seller. Whether one has acquired the character and rights of a corporator is a question to be determined by the laws of the corporation. Whether the purchaser has acquired a good and perfect title to any property or thing, tangible or intangible, is a question to be solved by the general laws of the State applicable to the sale and transfer of such objects." Smith *v.* Crescent City Live-Stock etc. Co., 30 La. Ann. 1378.

3. Denny *v.* Lyon, 38 Pa. St. 98; Sitgreaves *v.* Farmers' etc. Bank, 49 Pa. St. 359; Bank of Commerce's Appeal, 73 Pa. St. 59.

4. First Nat. Bank *v.* Lanier, 11 Wall. (U. S.) 369; Vansands *v.* Middlesex Co. Bank, 26 Conn. 144; Townsend *v.* McIver, 2 Rich. (S. Car.) 43; Williams *v.* Mechanics' Bank, 5 Blatchf. (U. S.) 59; People's Bank *v.* Gridley, 91 Ill. 457; Bank of Holly Springs *v.* Pinson, 58 Miss. 421.

5. Oxford Turnpike Co. *v.* Bunnel, 6 Conn. 552.

6. Marlborough Mfg. Co. *v.* Smith, 2 Conn. 579; Helm *v.* Swiggett, 12 Ind. 194; Union Bank *v.* Laird, 2 Wheat. (U. S.) 390.

7. Becher *v.* Wells Flouring Mill Co., 1 Fed. Rep. 276; New York etc. R. Co. *v.* Schuyler, 34 N. Y. 30.

8. Leightner's Appeal, 82 Pa. St. 301; Dickinson *v.* Central Nat. Bank, 129 Mass. 279; Rich *v.* Boyce, 39 Md. 314; People *v.* Robinson, 64 Cal. 372; Swift *v.* Smith, 65 Md. 428; Gill *v.* Continental Gas Co., L. R., 7 Ex. 332.

in whose name such certificate was originally issued, was entitled.[1] But application for transfer, without the production of the certificate, is, *per se*, notice to a company, through its officers, that the title to the shares of stock represented thereby may be in a third person, a holder for value without notice.[2] The corporation has no discretionary power outside of statute or charter authority to refuse to make the record of a transfer properly made and in good faith.[3] Those regulations made in accordance with such authority must be reasonable.[4] Upon refusal of the corporation to make the transfer and issue a new certificate, the pledgee may sue at law for the actual value of the stock at the time of such refusal, or may go into equity for specific relief.[5] But a buyer in good faith, from the person in whose name the stock stands on the books, who takes a transfer in conformity to the charter or authorized by-laws, though without holding the certificate permitted to be made by the authorized officer of the corporation, becomes vested with a complete title to the stock, and cuts off all the rights and equities of the holder of the certificate to the stock itself, and the latter's only remedy against the corporation is a suit for the value of the stock,[6] the bank being estopped from

1. Strange *v.* Houston etc. R. Co., 53 Tex. 162.

2. Strange *v.* Houston etc. R. Co., 53 Tex. 162; New York etc. R. Co. *v.* Schuyler, 34 N. Y. 81; Brisbane *v.* Delaware R. Co., 25 Hun (N. Y.) 438; Bayard *v.* Farmers' etc. Bank, 52 Pa. St. 235; Holbrook *v.* New Jersey Zinc Works, 57 N. Y. 616.

3. Weston's Case, L. R., 4 Ch. 20.

4. In Johnson *v.* Laflin, 103 U. S. 800, the court by Field, J., says, the power of corporations "in that respect, however, can only go to the extent of prescribing conditions essential to the protection of the association against fraudulent transfers, or such as may be designed to evade the just responsibility of the stockholder. It is to be exercised reasonably. Under the pretence of prescribing the manner of the transfer, the association cannot clog the transfer with useless restrictions, or make it dependent upon the consent of the directors or other stockholders. It is not necessary, however, to consider what restriction would be within its power, for it had imposed none. The entry of the transaction on the books of the bank, where stock is sold, is required, not for the translation of the title, but for the protection of the parties and others dealing with the bank, and to enable it to know who are its stockholders, entitled to vote at their meetings and receive dividends when declared. It is necessary to protect the seller against subsequent liability as a stockholder, and perhaps also to protect the purchaser against proceedings of the seller's creditors. Purchasers and creditors, in the absence of other knowledge, are only bound to look at the books of the registry of the bank."

5. Case *v.* Citizens Bank, 100 U. S. 446; Johnston *v.* Laflin, 103 U. S. 800; McAllister *v.* Kuhn, 96 U. S. 87; Bank of America *v.* McNeil, 10 Bush (Ky.) 56; Dayton National Bank *v.* Merchants' Nat. Bank, 37 Ohio St. 208; German Union etc. Assoc. *v.* Sandmeyer, 50 Pa. St. 67; Hill *v.* Pine River Bank, 45 N. H. 300; Baltimore etc. R. Co. *v.* Sewall, 35 Md. 239; Fraser *v.* Charleston, 11 S. Car. 486; Bond *v.* Mount Hope Iron Co., 99 Mass. 506; Sargeant *v.* Franklin Ins. Co., 8 Pick. (Mass.) 100; Gray *v.* Portland Bank, 3 Mass. 364; Kortwright *v.* Buffalo Commercial Bank, 20 Wend. (N. Y.) 96; Bank of Attica *v.* Manufacturers' etc. Bank, 20 N. Y. 505; Gill *v.* Continental Gas. Co., L. R., 7 Ex. 332.

6. First Nat. Bank *v.* Lanier, 11 Wall. (U. S.) 369; New York etc. R. Co. *v.* Schuyler, 34 N. Y. 30; Stebbins *v.* Phœnix F. Ins. Co., 3 Paige (N. Y.) 350; Union Bank *v.* Laird, 2 Wheat. (U. S.) 390; Mechanics' Bank *v.* New York etc. R. Co., 13 N. Y.

denying the statement made in the certificate that only on its surrender would the shares of stock be transferred.[1] Nor in such a case need a holder for value give notice to the company that the certificate has been indorsed and delivered to him.[2]

(3) *As to Creditors.*—Whether a transfer of the certificate of stock, accompanied by a power of attorney indorsed in blank, carries the full title against outside equities and attaching creditors is a question concerning which there has been frequent controversy, arising chiefly from the construction of statutes, charters, and by-laws regulating the transfer.

In the absence of an express provision of statute or of the charter of the corporation requiring a transfer on the books to shut out creditors, a certificate indorsed in blank will carry a good title against them.[3] The delivery of the certificate with the power to transfer is a sufficient delivery at common law.[4]

In some States statutes have been passed expressly providing that the transfer in blank shall not be good against creditors.[5]

Most States, however, have by statute provided for the transfer of stock on the books of the corporation, or have allowed it to be transferred on the books in a manner prescribed in the charter or by-laws of the corporation. The courts of the most prominent commercial States, as *New York*, *New Jersey*, *Pennsylvania* and some others, recognizing the importance of making a certificate indorsed in blank as nearly negotiable as possible, have declared that the registry on the books of the company, so pro-

621; Bank of Utica *v.* Smalley, 2 Cow. (N. Y.) 770; Gilbert *v.* Manchester Mfg. Co., 11 Wend. (N.Y.) 627; Upton *v.* Burnham, 3 Biss. (U. S.) 431.

The non-production and surrender of the certificate at the time of the transfer is not fatal to the title of the transferee. It is only essential to the safety of the corporation and may be waived by it at its own peril. New York etc. R. Co. *v.* Schuyler, 34 N. Y. 30.

1. Strange *v.* Houston etc. R. Co., 53 Tex. 162; Holbrook *v.* New Jersey Zinc Co., 57 N. Y. 616; McNeil *v.* Tenth Nat. Bank, 46 N. Y. 331; *In re* Bahia etc. R. Co., L. R., 3 Q. B. 584.

2. Bank *v.* Lanier, 11 Wall. (U. S.) 369.

3. Boston Music Hall Assoc. *v.* Cory, 129 Mass. 435; Sargent *v.* Franklyn Ins. Co., 8 Pick. (Mass.) 90; Fisher *v.* Essex Bank, 5 Gray (Mass.) 373; Dickinson *v.* Central Nat. Bank, 129 Mass. 279; Sayles *v.* Bates, 15 R. I. 342; Scott *v.* Pequonnock Nat. Bank, 15 Fed. Rep. 494; Continental Nat. Bank, *v.* Eliot Nat. Bank, 7 Fed. Rep. 369. *Contra*, Pinkerton *v.* Manchester etc. R. Co., 42 N. H. 424.

4. Scott *v.* Pequonnock Nat. Bank, 15 Fed. Rep. 494.

5. *Alabama* Code, 1876, §§ 2043, 2044; *Dakota* R. Code, 1887, § 398 Civ. Code; *Idaho* R. Laws, 1875, pp. 621, 622, §§ 9, 12; *Iowa* R. Code, 1880, p. 772, § 1078; *Kansas* Laws, 1879, p. 220, § 1090; Topeka Mfg. Co. *v.* Hale, 39 Kan. 23; *Maine* R. Stat. 1871, ch. 46, § 11; Skowhegan Bank *v.* Cutler, 49 Me. 315; *Montana*, R. Stat. 1879, §§ 739, 714; *Nevada*, Comp. Laws, 1873, vol. 2, §§ 3397, 3400; *Washington*, Code 1881, §§ 2429, 2432; *Wisconsin*, R. Stat. 1878, p. 110, § 1751, p. 532, § 1825; *Michigan* Comp. Laws, 1871, ch. 130, § 7; Howell's Annot. Stat. 1882, ch. 191, § 7. Under the earlier statute, Rev. Stat., ch. 55, § 7, p. 211, it was held that a stock certificate indorsed in blank approximated very closely to negotiability, and passed a good title against creditors. Mandlebaum *v.* North America Min. Co., 4 Mich. 465; Walker *v.* Detroit Transit Co., 47 Mich. 338.

In *Colorado*, G. L. 1877, p. 154, § 222;

vided for by statute, charter, or by-law, is for the company's benefit alone, and that a blank transfer to a *bona fide* holder for value is good against everybody but the corporation.[1]

New Mexico, G. L. 1880, pp. 205, 206, §§ 9, 12, p. 214, § 7; *District of Columbia*, Rev. Stat. 1875, p. 70, § 581, it is provided that a blank transfer is good for no purpose except to render the person to whom it is transferred liable for the debts of the company.

In *Massachusetts* it is provided by statute that an unregistered transfer, except for an interval of ten days thereafter, is good only between the parties, unless transferred on the books of the corporation. *Massachusetts* Pub. Stat. 1882, ch. 105, § 24; Act of 1881, ch. 302, § 1.

1. **New York.**—McNeil *v.* Tenth Nat. Bank, 46 N. Y. 325; Smith *v.* American Coal Co., 7 Lans. (N. Y.) 317; New York etc. R. Co. *v.* Schuyler, 34 N. Y. 30; Bank of Utica *v.* Smalley, 2 Cow. (N. Y.) 770; Buffalo Commercial Bank *v.* Kortright, 22 Wend. (N. Y.) 348; 20 Wend. (N. Y.) 91; Holbrook *v.* New Jersey Zinc Co., 57 N. Y. 516; Weaver *v.* Barden, 49 N. Y. 286; Leitch *v.* Wells, 48 N. Y. 585; Hill *v.* Newichawanick Co., 48 How. Pr. (N. Y.) 427; Driscoll *v.* West Bradley Co., 36 N. Y. Super. Ct. 484; 59 N. Y. 96; Commeau *v.* Gill Farm Oil Co., 3 Daly (N. Y.) 218; Manhattan Beach Co. *v.* Harned, 27 Fed. Rep. 484; Fatman *v.* Loback, 1 Duer (N. Y.) 354; Gilbert *v.* Manchester Mfg. Co., 11 Wend. (N.Y.) 628.

Upon a contract to deliver stock, a tender of a certificate with a blank power to transfer is sufficient without an actual transfer as to the name of the purchaser. Orr *v.* Bigelow, 20 Barb. (N. Y.) 21; Munn *v.* Barnum, 24 Barb. (N. Y.) 283; Driscoll *v.* West Bradley Mfg. Co., 36 N. Y. Super. Ct. 488; 59 N. Y. 96.

New Jersey.—Broadway Bank *v.* McElrath, 13 N. J. Eq. 24; Hunterdon *v.* Nassau Bank, 17 N. J. Eq. 496; Rogers *v.* New Jersey Ins. Co., 8 N. J. Eq. 167; Mount Holly etc. Co. *v.* Ferree, 17 N. J. Eq. 117; Prall *v.* Tilt, 28 N. J. Eq. 480.

Pennsylvania.—Finney's Appeal, 59 Pa. St. 398; Com. *v.* Watmough, 6 Whart. (Pa.) 117; U. S. *v.* Vaughan, 3 Binn. (Pa.) 394. And see Early's Appeal, 89 Pa. St. 411; Bank of Commerce's Appeal, 73 Pa. St. 59; Telford etc. Turnpike Co. *v.* Gerhab (Pa. 1888), 13 Atl. Rep. 90; Chambersburg Ins. Co. *v.* Smith, 11 Pa. St. 120.

An assignment of the stock of a corporation to itself as collateral security for a loan divests the title of the assignor so far as to prevent a sale of it under a *fieri facias* against him. Eby *v.* Guest, 94 Pa. St. 160.

Louisiana.—Blouin *v.* Hart, 30 La. Ann. 714; Smith *v.* Crescent City Live Stock etc. Co., 30 La. Ann. 1378; Factors' etc. Ins. Co. *v.* Marine Dry Dock etc. Co., 31 La. Ann. 149; Pitot *v.* Johnson, 33 La. Ann. 1286; New Orleans Banking Assoc. *v.* Wiltz, 10 Fed. Rep. 330; Black *v.* Zachare, 3 How. (U. S.) 483; Crescent Seltzer etc. Mfg. Co. *v.* Deblieux, 40 La. Ann. 155; James *v.* Pike, 23 La. Ann. 478; Allande *v.* Ingram, 19 La. Ann. 364.

Tennessee.—In *Tennessee*, the earlier decisions held that the right of a creditor without notice was superior to that of a holder of an unregistered stock certificate. State Ins. Co. *v.* Sax, 2 Tenn. Ch. 507; Clodfelter *v.* Cox, 1 Sneed (Tenn.) 330. This was based on the English rule that notice is necessary to perfect an assignment of a chose in action. Judson *v.* Cochran, 17 How. (U. S.) 612. But when notice was given to the creditor even without a transfer on the books, the holder of a stock certificate indorsed in blank was protected. State Ins. Co. *v.* Gennett, 2 Tenn. Ch. 100. But the later cases have disregarded the earlier rule and made a holder of a certificate indorsed in blank a possessor of a complete legal title, effectual against the assignment of creditors without any registry upon the books of the corporation and without notice to it of the assignment. Cornick *v.* Richards, 3 Lea (Tenn.) 1; Cherry *v.* Frost, 7 Lea (Tenn.) 1; 21 Am. Law Reg., N. S. 57.

Missouri.—Merchants' Nat. Bank *v.* Richards, 74 Mo. 77; affg. 6 Mo. App. 454; Carroll *v.* Mullanphy Sav. Bank, 8 Mo. App. 249.

Virginia and West Virginia.—The rule in the text is expressly provided for by statute. *Virginia*, Code, 1873, ch. 58, § 29; *West Virginia*, Rev. Stat. 1879, ch. 25, § 37.

The courts of other States have, however, just as strongly held that a statute charter or authorized by-law provision that stock shall only be transferred on the books of the corporation is to show to all the world where the legal title is, and that, therefore, an unregistered transfer is not good against creditors of the assignor.[1]

Other States.—Baldwin *v.* Canfield, 26 Minn. 43; Strange *v.* Houston etc. R. Co., 53 Tex. 162; Thurber *v.* Crump, 86 Ky. 408; Fraser *v.* Charleston, 11 S. Car. 486.

In *Rhode Island* it is unsettled as to whether or not an unregistered transfer of stock certificate gives a holder a good title against attaching creditor. Beckwith *v.* Burrouger, 13 R. I. 294.

In McNeil *v.* Tenth Nat. Bank, 46 N. Y. 325, the court by Rapallo, J., said: "It has been settled, by repeated adjudications, that, as between the parties, the delivery of the certificate, with assignment and power indorsed, passes the entire title, legal and equitable, in the shares, notwithstanding that, by the terms of the charter or by-laws of the corporation, the stock is declared to be transferable only on its books; that such provisions are intended solely for the protection of the corporation, and can be waived or asserted at its pleasure, and that no effect is given to them except for the protection of the corporation; that they do not incapacitate the shareholder from parting with his interest, and that his assignment, not on the the books, passes the entire legal title of the stock, subject only to such liens or claims as the corporation may have upon it, and excepting the right of voting at elections."

In Broadway Bank *v.* McElrath, 13 N. J. Eq. 24, the court by Green, C., said: "The pledge of stocks as collateral security has become a prevalent, and, to the borrower especially, an advantageous mode of effecting loans. In manufacturing companies, especially, where the business of the company is carried on by the stockholder, and where his capital is mainly or exclusively vested in the stock, and employed in the active operations of business, the pledge of stock affords the most ready and advantageous mode of effecting loans for the demands of business. To require a transfer of the stock to the lender as security for the loan, against the right of attaching or execution creditors, will at once destroy the value of the security, or compel the borrower to divest himself of his character as corporator, to forfeit his control of the business of the corporation, of his right to dividends, and of all his other rights as a stockholder in the corporation. Why should the owner of stocks be deprived of the privilege of mortgaging or pledging his stock for the security of a loan, without stripping himself of all his rights of ownership, more than the owner of any other property?"

It is not, therefore, to apprise the world and prevent it from giving false credit to the apparent owner of stock that the transfer thereof is required to be made on the books of the bank in the presence of one of its officers. The great object of requiring transfers to be made in this manner is to prevent all difficulty that otherwise might arise with those who have the direction and management of the corporation, in ascertaining the persons who are to be regarded and treated by them as owners of the stock and corporators. No persons, therefore, are to be regarded by them as such, excepting those in whose name the stock is entered and holden. Com. *v.* Watmough, 6 Whart. (Pa.) 117.

1. **California.**—Parrott *v.* Byers, 40 Cal. 614; Weston *v.* Bear River etc. Min. Co., 5 Cal. 186; 6 Cal. 425; Strout *v.* Natoma Min. Co., 9 Cal. 78; Naglee *v.* Pacific Wharf Co., 20 Cal. 529; People *v.* Elmore, 35 Cal. 653; Winter Belmont Min. Co., 53 Cal. 428. See Thompson *v.* Toland, 48 Cal. 99. In Winter *v.* Belmont Min. Co., 53 Cal. 428, the court said that the only point decided in the case of Sherwood *v.* Meadow Valley Min. Co., 50 Cal. 412, was that a stock certificate was not negotiable in the sense that bills of exchange and other similar instruments were, the point in the text not being considered.

Massachusetts.—Before the passage of the statute in this State affirming specifically the rule in the text (preceding note), when the charter of the corporation and not merely its by-laws, provided that stock should "be transferable only at its banking-house and on its books," it had been held that this mode of transfer must be followed to pass a good title against attaching creditors. Fisher *v.* Essex Bank, 5 Gray (Mass.) 373; Rock *v.* Nichols, 3 Allen (Mass.) 342; Blanchard *v.* Dedham Gas Light Co., 12 Gray (Mass.) 213; but in an earlier case where only the by-laws of the corporation made such provision, it was held that an assignment by deed, accompanied by delivery of the certificates was valid, without such transfers on the books, even against the attaching creditors without notice. Sargent *v.* Essex etc. R. Co., 9 Pick. (Mass.) 202; Sargent *v.* Franklin Ins. Co., 8 Pick. (Mass.) 90; so in a recent case, this distinction between a requirement of the charter and one of the by-laws of a corporation was carried out in the same way. Dickinson *v.* Central Nat. Bank, 129 Mass. 279; see also, Sibley *v.* Quinsigmond Nat. Bank, 133 Mass. 515.

Connecticut.—Before the passage of the statute in *Connecticut*, providing that an unregistered transfer in pledge of a stock certificate, accompanied by a power of attorney indorsed in blank should be effectual only against a pledgor and his executors and administrators, it was held, creditors being at that time highly favored, that stock could only be transferred in accordance with the method provided for in the charter and by-laws of the corporation, and if the stock was made transferable only on the books of the company, an unregistered transfer was not good against creditors. Marlborough Mfg. Co. *v.* Smith, 2 Conn. 579; Northrup *v.* Curtis, 5 Conn. 246; Oxford Turnpike Co. *v.* Bunnel, 6 Conn. 552; Dutton *v.* Connecticut Bank, 13 Conn. 493; Shipman *v.* Aetna Ins. Co., 29 Conn. 245.

Even though there be a written declaration attached to the certificate that the stock was thereby pledged for the debt described. Platt *v.* Hawkins, 43 Conn. 139.

An entry by the clerk of the corporation upon the deed of assignment that it had been received for record, was not sufficient to protect the stock from attachment as the property of the assignor. Northrup *v.* Newton etc. Turnpike Co., 3 Conn. 544.

The rule was relaxed later, so that if the pledgee could give a good reason for his failure to procure the transfer, and that he had done all that was possible for him to do by giving notice of the assignment to the corporation, he was protected against subsequent attachments just as the assignee of any chose in action. Colt *v.* Ives, 31 Conn. 25.

Illinois.—People's Bank *v.* Gridley, 91 Ill. 457; Otis *v.* Gardner, 105 Ill. 436.

New Hampshire.—Pinkerton *v.* Manchester etc. R. Co., 42 N. H. 424; 1 Am. Law Reg., N. S. 596. See also Scripture *v.* Francestown Soapstone Co., 50 N. H. 571.

It sometimes happens that the transfer agent of the corporation is at some distance from the home office of the corporation, transfers not being completed until made at this office. If the pledgee surrenders his certificate to this agent without loss of time, it has been held that he will be protected from an attachment made between that time and the time of actual record on the books. Pinkerton *v.* Manchester etc. R. Co., 42 N. H. 424.

Vermont.—Sabine *v.* Bank of Woodstock, 21 Vt. 353; Cheever *v.* Meyer, 52 Vt. 66.

It is held that the delivery of a certificate with the power of transfer vests the title in the transferee, the object of having the transfer recorded on the books of the corporation acting only as a notice; therefore such transfer, though unrecorded, is good against the party himself and all those who have notice of the fact. Noyes *v.* Spaulding, 27 Vt. 420.

Maine.—Before the present statute. Agricultural Bank *v.* Burr, 24 Me. 256; Fiske *v.* Carr, 20 Me. 301.

Other States.—*In re* Murphy, 51 Wis. 519; Conant *v.* Seneca Co. Bank, 1 Ohio St. 298.

In Fisher *v.* Essex Bank, 5 Gray (Mass.) 373, the court by Shaw, C. J., said: "As a great amount of property is held in the shares of corporations, it is of great importance that the title be easily and certainly ascertained, that the mode of acquiring and alienating it be fixed and known, and that it may at any time be made available, by process of law, for the debts of the owner . . . It is necessary to fix some act and some point of time at which the property changes and vests in the vendee; and it will tend to the security of all parties concerned to make that turning point consist in an act which, while it may be easily proved, does at the same time give notoriety to the transfer. It

In all States courts of law as well as courts of equity hold that a prior assignment of the equitable interest in stock by delivery of the certificate supersedes the rights of attaching creditors who attach the same with a full knowledge of the assignment.[1]

e. TITLE OF PLEDGEE TO STOCK EVIDENCED BY FICTITIOUS, FRAUDULENT OR MISAPPROPRIATED CERTIFICATES—(1) *In General.*—While there is a decided tendency, especially in commercial States, to put certificates of stock on the same footing as negotiable paper,[2] still they are simply *indicia* or muniments of title, and in considering them, it must be remembered that they are merely non-negotiable choses in action, subject to equities existing against the assignor.[3]

would seem to us to be going beyond the rules of just exposition, to hold that a plain provision of statute law, calculated to promote the security of important legal rights of parties in important particulars, should be construed to be a regulation made for the convenience of banks."

The reason of the rule is stated by the court in Colt *v.* Ives, 31 Conn. 25, as follows: "In regard to chattels, there must be a substantial change of possession accompanying and following the sale, or it will, unexplained, be conclusive evidence of fraudulent trust, which will render the sale void as to creditors. . . . And in the case of the purchase of stock in a corporation, there must be such a transfer of it as the legislature in the charter or by statute prescribes; and notice of the assignment of choses in action, and the transfer required by statute of corporate stock, stand in lieu of the taking and retaining of the possession of personal chattels sold, being the only possession the nature of the property admits of."

1. Black *v.* Zacharie, 3 How. (U. S.) 483; Continental Nat. Bank *v.* Eliot Nat. Bank, 7 Fed. Rep. 369; Scripture *v.* Francestown Soapstone Co., 50 N. H. 571.

So a judgment creditor buying stock at an execution sale, which he then knows has been previously transferred by an unrecorded assignment of the debtor, acquires no better title than the debtor himself had. Newberry *v.* Detroit etc. Iron Mfg. Co., 17 Mich. 141; Weston *v.* Bear River Min. Co., 6 Cal. 425.

2. Leavitt *v.* Fisher, 4 Duer (N. Y.) 1; Mount Holly etc. Co. *v.* Ferree, 17 N. J. Eq. 117; Broadway Bank *v.* McElrath, 13 N. J. Eq. 24.

In Prall *v.* Tilt, 28 N. J. Eq. 479, the court by Green, J., said: "By commercial usage, as universally acknowledged by the business community as the law of negotiable paper, and sanctioned by repeated adjudications in our courts, as well as in those of other States, a certificate of stock, accompanied by an irrevocable power of attorney, either filled up or in blank, is, in the hands of a third party, presumptive evidence of ownership in the holder; and where the party in whose hands the certificate is found is a holder for value, without notice of any intervening equity, his title cannot be impeached. The holder of the certificate may fill up the letter of attorney, execute the power, and thus obtain the legal title to the stock, and such power is not limited to the power to whom it was first delivered, but inures to each *bona fide* holder into whose hands the certificate may pass. Under these well recognized principles large amounts of property daily pass from hand to hand; are sold and resold, or hypothecated for loans without an actual transfer on the books of the corporation, and without other evidence of ownership than the possession by the holder of the certificate and power of attorney."

3. Biddle *v.* Bayard, 13 Pa. St. 150; Burton *v.* Peterson, 35 Leg. Int. (Pa.) 144; Winter *v.* Belmont Min. Co., 53 Cal. 428; Atkins *v.* Gamble, 42 Cal. 86; Sherwood *v.* Meadow Valley Min. Co., 50 Cal. 412.

So it was not permitted to be shown that there was a usage among brokers to treat stock certificates as negotiable instruments and the custom of giving blank powers of attorney was declared vicious, though such a custom is perfectly legal. Aull *v.* Colkett, 2 W. N. C. (Pa.) 322; Denny *v.* Lyon, 38 Pa. St. 98.

(2) *Elements Necessary to Make Pledgee Holder for Value and Bona Fide.*—Where the owner of stock has voluntarily let the certificate go from him with a blank power of attorney, to entitle the pledgee, who has received it from an agent, to possess the legal title, it is absolutely essential that he should have paid a valuable consideration for it, and have taken without notice of the relations between the owner and his agent, and in good faith.[1]

Any valuable thing given or change of position on the part of the pledgee will constitute a valuable consideration.[2] On the question whether a precedent debt is a valuable consideration the authorities are divided, as on the same question in regard to negotiable instruments. The Federal courts and those of some States hold that the precedent debt is a good consideration while the *New York* courts and others hold the opposite.[3]

Notice.—Where the pledgee has actual or constructive notice of the invalidity of the certificate or of the agent's lack of power to pledge it, he gets only the right in it that the pledgor has.[4]

In Mechanics' Bank *v.* New York etc. R. Co., 13 N. Y. 599, the court, by Comstock, J., said: "Stocks are not like bank notes, the immediate representative of money, and intended for circulation. The distinction between a bank bill and a share of bank stock is not difficult to appreciate. Nor are they, like notes and bills of exchange, less adapted to circulation, but invented to supply the exigencies of commerce, and governed by the peculiar code of the commercial law. They are not like exchequer bills and government securities, which are made negotiable either for circulation or to find a market; nor are they like corporation bonds, which are issued in negotiable form for sale, and as a means for raising money for corporate uses. The distinction between all these and corporate stocks is marked and striking. They are all in some form the representative of money, and may be satisfied by payment in money at a time specified. Certificates of stock are not securities for money in any sense, much less are they negotiable securities. They are simply the muniment and evidence of the holder's title to a given share in the property and franchises of the corporation of which he is a member."

1. Merchants' Bank *v.* Livingston, 74 N. Y. 223; Crocker *v.* Crocker, 31 N. Y. 507; Porter *v.* Parks, 49 N. Y. 564; Strange *v.* Houston etc. R. Co., 53 Tex. 162.

2. Cherry *v.* Frost, 7 Lea (Tenn.) 1.

Where money was loaned on the strength of a promise of security which was given a few days later, the pledgee was held a *bona fide* holder. Greeff *v.* Dieckerhoff, 5 N. Y. Supp. 16.

Usury.—And taking a stock certificate as collateral for a usurious debt was not considered a *bona fide* holder for value. Ramsdell *v.* Morgan, 16 Wend. (N. Y.) 574; Sands *v.* Church, 6 N. Y. 347; Dean *v.* Howell, Hill & Den. Supp. (N. Y.) 39; Felt *v.* Heye, 23 How. Pr. (N. Y.) 359.

3. Werner *v.* Barden, 49 N. Y. 286; Moodie *v.* Seventh Nat. Bank, 33 Leg. Int. (Pa.) 400; Ashton's Appeal, 73 Pa. St. 153; Dovey's Appeal, 97 Pa. St. 153; Cleveland *v.* State Bank, 16 Ohio St. 236.

An assignment of the certificate partly for a precedent debt and partly for a present consideration, makes the assignee a holder for value to the amount of the present consideration. Gould *v.* Farmer's T. etc. Co., 23 Hun (N. Y.) 322.

Exchange of collaterals is a good consideration for those taken. Cherry *v.* Frost, 7 Lea (Tenn.) 1.

4. Porter *v.* Parks, 49 N. Y. 564.

Where stock was sold on execution and bought by the judgment creditor who knew that the certificate had already been indorsed over to another, he got only the debtor's title. Newberry *v.* Detroit etc. Mfg. Co., 17 Mich. 141.

An agent was given stock to pledge for his principal, the pledgee's name being written in the power of attorney.

(3) *Fictitious Stock Certificates.*—That these certificates are not negotiable is easily seen by the fact that where the capital stock of a corporation is limited in amount by the act of law creating it, and its officers issue stock certificates beyond the authorized amount, these certificates, though precisely like the authorized ones in appearance, still represent no value in themselves, not even to a *bona fide* holder for value. It is true the corporation must respond in damages to the full value of the certificate, but on an entirely different theory from that of the certificate being negotiable. The rule of estoppel prevents the corporation, having given their agent apparent authority to issue stock, from washing its hands of the whole matter, but compels it to make reparation.

The certificate after being given to the pledgee, was returned to the agent who erased the original pledgee's name and pledged it for his own debt. It was held that the second pledgee was chargeable with knowledge that the pledge was unauthorized. Denny *v.* Lyon, 38 Pa. St. 98; but see Sitgreaves *v.* Farmers' etc. Bank, 49 Pa. St. 359.

But on the repledge of stock, the fact that the certificate was in the first pledgee's name and the power of attorney signed by him was not enough to charge the second pledgee with knowledge. Felt *v.* Heye, 23 How. Pr. (N. Y.) 359.

If the assignee of stock holding the certificate by a power of attorney indorsed in blank, pledges it, the pledgee holds the title. Otis *v.* Gardner, 105 Ill. 436.

Where the cashier of a bank gave as collateral for his personal debt, stock of the bank, the pledgee was held to be charged with the duty to investigate, and the pledge being unauthorized he was not a *bona fide* holder. Moores *v.* Citizens Nat. Bank, 15 Fed. Rep. 141.

Where a broker pledging stock for his own debt signed his name with "trustee" after it, it was held to be notice to the pledgee that his authority might be limited. Fowle *v.* Ward, 113 Mass. 548.

Where the power of attorney indorsed in blank gives power to "bargain, sell, and transfer" the securities, it is notice that the holder cannot pledge. Taliaferro *v.* Baltimore etc. Bank, 71 Md. 200.

The pledgee of a certificate of stock, which has printed thereon a by-law which provides that no transfer of the stock shall be made while the owner is indebted to the corporation, takes it with notice. State Sav. Assoc. *v.* Nixon-Jones Printing Co., 25 Mo. App. 642.

A bank lent money to M, H's agent, for H, knowing that the stocks pledged as collateral belonged to H. The bank afterwards claimed the right to hold the collateral as security for further loans made to M. *Held*, that H was entitled to her collateral upon repayment of the amount lent to her; that the bank was chargeable with notice of M's want of authority to borrow more money for himself; and that the fact that H, before bringing suit, had tendered a larger amount than she in fact owed, for the sake of preventing litigation, could not be construed into an admission of her liability for the larger amount. Talmage *v.* Third Nat. Bank, 91 N. Y. 531.

When an officer of a corporation newly issues stock in the name of the pledgee for the officer's own debt, the pledgee is chargeable with notice of whatever could have been found out on inquiry. Farrington *v.* South Boston R. Co., 150 Mass. 406.

Where the pledgee knows that the pledgor is an agent, the authority to pledge cannot be inferred from the possession by the agent of the certificate of stock with an irrevocable power of attorney indorsed in blank. Merchants' Bank *v.* Livingston, 74 N. Y. 223. See Hakes *v.* Myrick, 69 Iowa 189.

A broker who buys stock for another broker knowing that it is for a customer of the latter, is charged with knowledge that it is trust stock and cannot receive it in pledge for the first broker's private debt. Foster *v.* Brown, 104 Mass. 259. If he does not know of the trust, he is unaffected thereby. Dodds *v.* Hill, 2 Hem. Mil. 424; Martin *v.* Sedgwick, 9 Beav. 333.

Therefore the difference between a stock certificate and negotiable paper issued by a corporation is clearly seen, and that a fictitious certificate gives no title to any one.[1]

(4) *Fraudulent or Misappropriated Stock Certificates.*—In discussing the rights of the pledgee of forged, fraudulent, or misappropriated stocks, a distinction must be drawn between the case where the certificate has passed from the owner by his voluntary act, whether induced by fraudulent representations or not, and the case in which the owner has been deprived of his certificate against his will.

In the first case, the pledgee who afterwards receives such stock certificate indorsed in blank, in good faith and for value gets the legal title, for the owner having voluntarily intrusted the *indicia* of his title to another and thus permitted the fraud, is bound to be the loser by it.[2] One who purchases such stock from the

1. New York etc. R. Co. *v.* Schuyler, 34 N. Y. 30; Bridgeport Bank *v.* New York etc R. C., 30 Conn. 231; Leavitt *v.* Fisher, 4 Duer (N. Y.) 1; Fatman *v.* Loback, 1 Duer (N. Y.) 354; Bank of Kentucky *v.* Schuylkill Bank, 1 Pars. (Pa.) 180; Hall *v.* Rose Hill etc. Road Co., 70 Ill. 673; Willis *v.* Fry, 73 Phila. (Pa.) 33; *In re* Bahia etc. R. Co., L. R. 3 Q. B. 584. See also STOCK.

Measure of Damages.—Pledgees of fictitious stock, while they recover damages from the corporation, their stock being liable for any loss caused by the fraud or negligence of the officers of the corporation, receive only the value of the stock less the depreciation. Willis *v.* Fry, 13 Phila. (Pa.) 33.

2. McNeil *v.* Tenth Nat. Bank, 46 N. Y. 325; Wood's Appeal, 92 Pa. St. 379; Moore *v.* Miller, 6 Lans. (N. Y.) 396; Moore *v.* Metropolitan Nat. Bank, 55 N. Y. 41; Saltus *v.* Everett, 20 Wend. (N. Y.) 278; Crocker *v.* Crocker, 31 N. Y. 507; Burton *v.* Peterson, 12 Phila. (Pa.) 397; Burton's Appeal, 93 Pa. St. 214; Pennsylvania R. Co.'s Appeal, 86 Pa. St. 80; Moodie *v.* Seventh Nat. Bank, 33 Leg. Int. (Pa.) 400; West Branch etc. Co.'s Appeal, 81½ Pa. St. 19; Dovey's Appeal, 97 Pa. St. 153; Weaver *v.* Barden, 49 N. Y. 286; State Bank *v.* Cox, 11 Rich. Eq. (S. Car.) 344; Walker *v.* Detroit Transit Co., 47 Mich. 338; Otis *v.* Gardner, 105 Ill. 436; Strange *v.* Houston etc. Co., 53 Tex. 162; Stone *v.* Marye, 14 Nev. 362; Borland *v.* Clark, 26 Kan. 349; Mount Holly etc. Co. *v.* Ferree, 17 N. J. Eq. 117; Stone *v.* Marye, 14 Nev. 362; Thompson *v.* Toland, 48 Cal. 112; Goss *v.* Hampton, 16 Nev. 185; Wing *v.* Holland Trust Co. (Supreme Ct.), 5 N. Y. Supp. 384.

But see Leiper's Appeal, 108 Pa. St. 377.

In Wood's Appeal, 92 Pa. St. 379, the court by Trunkey, J., said: "The rights of a *bona fide* holder as against the true owner of the stock to whom the apparent owner of the stock has either sold or pledged, do not depend on the negotiable character in the certificates, but rest on another principle; 'namely, That one who has conferred upon another by a written transfer all the *indicia* of ownership of property, is estopped to assert title to it as against a third person who has in good faith purchased it for value from the apparent owner.'"

It is sometimes necessary to apply a supplementary maxim that "when one of two innocent parties who are equally innocent of actual fraud must lose, it is the suggestion of common sense as well as equity that the one whose misplaced confidence in an agent or attorney has been the cause of the loss, shall not throw it on the other." Pennsylvania R. Co.'s Appeal, 86 Pa. St. 80; Fatman *v.* Loback, 1 Duer (N. Y.) 554; White *v.* Springfield Bank, 3 Sandf. (N. Y.) 222.

But it should be only supplementary for "the principle upon which these transactions have been, and ought to be, established is this: that when the owner of stock, in the ordinary course of business and in the method common to all mercantile communities, by his own act has armed another, his agent or attorney, with the power to act for him, and when this agent or attorney

pledgee in good faith gets a good title, and a sub-pledgee in good faith can hold it for his advances.[1]

For the purchaser or pledgee is not, without notice, charged with any trusts existing between the original parties.[2] One dealing with the holder of a certificate of stock with a blank power of attorney has a right to believe that he is the owner of it,[3] and the true owner is estopped from denying that his agent has the title.[4]

But in the second case, the owner, unless he may have estopped himself by carelessly indorsing the power of attorney in blank,[5] cannot without his consent be deprived of his title to the stock, and therefore the pledgee gets no title.[6]

If, however, the pledgee has had the stock transferred to his name on the books of the corporation and a new certificate issued, the corporation is estopped from denying the statement made in the certificate that the pledgee is the owner of the stock.[7]

deals with innocent parties, who, without notice or other intervening equity advance money upon the faith of the evidence of title in the possession of the attorney or agent, the owner takes every risk, and is bound by the act of the person whom he sees fit to hold out to the world as his attorney or agent." Burton *v.* Peterson, 35 Leg. Int.(Pa.) 144; Jarvis *v.* Rogers, 13 Mass. 105; Moodie *v.* Seventh Nat. Bank, 3 W. N. C. (Pa.) 118; Persch *v.* Quiggle, 57 Pa. St. 247.

1. McNeil *v.* Tenth Nat. Bank, 46 N. Y. 325; Cushman *v.* Thayer Mfg. Co., 76 N. Y. 365; Bridgeport Bank *v.* New York etc. R. Co., 30 Conn. 231; Holbrok *v.* New Jersey Zinc Co., 57 N. Y. 616; First Nat. Bank *v.* Lanier, 11 Wall. (U. S.) 369; Lowry *v.* Bank of Baltimore, Taney (U. S.) 310; Mount Holly etc. Co. *v.* Ferrell, 17 N. J. Eq. 117; Prall *v.* Tilt, 27 N. J. Eq. 393; Brewster *v.* Sime, 42 Cal. 139; Willis *v.* Philadelphia etc. R. Co., 6 W. N. C. (Pa.) 461; Cherry *v.* Frost, 7 Lea (Tenn.) 1; Cowdry *v.* Vandenburgh, 101 U. S. 572; Honold *v.* Meyer, 31 La. Ann. 585; Stone *v.* Brown, 54 Tex. 330; Kisterbock's Appeal (Pa. 1889), 18 Atl. Rep. 381. See cases in preceding note.

One to whom stocks are indorsed and delivered for safekeeping may vest in a *bona fide* pledgee the right to retain the stocks as security for the loan to the original bailee. Ambrose *v.* Evans, 66 Cal. 74; Arnold *v.* Johnson, 66 Cal. 402.

2. Thompson *v.* Toland, 48 Cal. 99; Jarvis *v.* Rogers, 13 Mass. 105; Savage *v.* Smyth, 48 Ga. 562; Dovey's Appeal, 97 Pa. St. 153; Williams *v.* Fletcher, 129 Ill. 356.

3. Leavitt *v.* Fisher, 4 Duer (N. Y.) 1; Fatman *v.* Lobach, 1 Duer (N. Y.) 354.

4. Burton's Appeal, 93 Pa. St. 214; Zulick *v.* Markham, 6 Daly (N. Y.) 129; Dickinson *v.* Dudley, 17 Hun (N. Y.) 569. See cases in preceding notes.

5. It has been much discussed whether the execution of a blank transfer negligently is enough to estop the owner from claiming his stock, but the best opinion seems to be that it is not. Swan *v.* N. British etc. R. Co., 2 H. & C. 175. But see Pennsylvania R. Co.'s Appeal, 86 Pa. St. 80; Biddle *v.* Bayard, 13 Pa. St. 150; Denny *v.* Lyon, 38 Pa. St. 98; Wright's Appeal, 99 Pa. St. 425; Borland *v.* Clark, 26 Kan. 349; Crull *v.* Colket, 2 W. N. C. (Pa.) 322; Coles *v.* Bank of England, 10 A. & E. 437; Young *v.* Grote, 4 Bing. 252.

6. Western Union Tel. Co. *v.* Davenport, 97 U. S. 369; Pollock *v.* National Bank, 7 N. Y. 274; Pratt *v.* Machinists' Nat. Bank, 123 Mass. 110; Sewall *v.* Boston Water Power Co., 4 Allen (Mass.) 277; Machinists' Nat. Bank *v.* Field, 126 Mass. 345; Bercich *v.* Marye, 9 Nev. 312; Aull *v.* Colkett, 2 W. N. C. (Pa.) 322.

Davis *v.* Bank of England, 2 Bing. 393; Sloman *v.* Bank of England, 14 Sim. 475; Ashby *v.* Blackwell, 2 Eden 299; Bank of England *v.* Parsons, 5 Ves. 665; Taylor *v.* Great Indian etc. R. Co., 4 De G. & J. 559; Swan *v.* N. British etc. Co., 2 H. & C. 175; Hartga *v.* Bank of England, 3 Ves. 55.

7. First Nat. Bank *v.* Lanier, 11

The corporation is still liable to the original owner of the stock, and unless the latter has estopped himself, must issue him new stock or pay him its value.[1] We see therefore that stock certificates are in all cases, except where the owner has voluntarily done some act whereby he has estopped himself, sudject to equities.

In any event the pledgee takes the stock subject to the equities existing between the original owner and the corporation.[2]

(5) *Stock Charged with a Trust.*—Stock held in trust cannot be pledged by the trustee for his own debts.

The question, as far as the pledgee is concerned, is almost entirely whether he had notice of the trust in dealing with the pledgor.

In dealing with a trustee of stock a very strict sense of duty of inquiry is required of the pledgee. While it is true that one lending money on stock which does not in any way indicate that it is held in trust, and without knowledge that there is such a trust, takes a good title,[3] yet where the pledgee, receiving the stock in pledge for the trustee's own debt, has knowledge that the pledgor is a trustee[4] or where anything on the face of the certificates seems to indicate a trust, the pledgee is bound to inquire whether the pledgor is acting within the terms of his authority, and if he does not inquire he takes the stock at his peril. A subsequent *bona fide* holder for value, however, is protected.[5]

Wall. (U. S.) 369; Lowry *v.* Commercial Bank, Camp. 310; Strange *v.* Houston etc. R. Co., 53 Tex. 162; Pratt *v.* Machinists' Nat. Bank, 123 Mass. 110; Salisbury Mills *v.* Townsend, 109 Mass. 115; *In re* Bahia etc. R. Co., L. R., 2 Q. B. 584; Hart *v.* Frontino etc. Co., L. R., 5 Ex. 111.

Even though the corporation has issued certificates for more capital stock than authorized, the pledgee cannot be compelled to surrender them. Machinists' Nat. Bank *v.* Field, 126 Mass. 345.

1. Sewall *v.* Boston Water Power Co., 4 Allen (Mass.) 277; Western Union Tel. Co. *v.* Davenport, 97 U. S. 369; Lowry *v.* Commercial Bank, Taney (U. S.) 310; Pollock *v.* National Bank, 7 N. Y. 274; Pratt *v.* Machinists' Nat. Bank, 123 Mass. 110; Mayor etc. of Baltimore *v.* Ketchum, 57 Md. 23; Chew *v.* Bank of Baltimore, 14 Md. 299; Strange *v.* Houston etc. R. Co., 53 Tex. 162; Ashly *v.* Bluckwell, 2 Eden 299; Sloman *v.* Bank of England, 14 Sim. 475; Midland R. Co. *v.* Taylor, 28 Beav. 287; Davis *v.* Bank of England, 2 Bing. 293.

2. Moore *v.* Metropolitan Nat. Bank, 55 N. Y. 41.

3. Lowry *v.* Commercial etc. Bank, Taney (U. S.) 310; Bayard *v.* Farmers' etc. Bank, 52 Pa. St. 232; Salisbury Mills *v.* Townsend, 109 Mass. 115; Crocker *v.* Crocker, 31 N. Y. 507; Atkinson *v.* Atkinson, 8 Allen (Mass.) 15.

But if the corporation knew that the pledgor was trustee of the stock and for whom he held it in trust, it is chargeable with damage for negligence in recording such a transfer. Western Union Tel. Co. *v.* Davenport, 97 U. S. 369; Loring *v.* Salisbury Mills, 125 Mass. 138; Pratt *v.* Taunton Copper Co., 123 Mass. 110; Salisbury Mills *v.* Townsend, 109 Mass. 115; Maywood *v.* Railroad Bank, 5 S. Car. 379; Willis *v.* Philadelphia etc. R. Co., 6 W. N. C. (Pa.) 461.

4. Loring *v.* Brodie, 134 Mass. 453; Crocker *v.* Crocker, 31 N. Y. 507.

When the certificate shows on its face that it is a trust certificate, the bank is chargeable with knowledge whether the bank officials read the certificate or not. Loring *v.* Brodie, 134 Mass. 453.

5. National City Bank *v.* Jaudon, 8 Blatchf. (U. S.) 430; Duncan *v.* Jaudon, 15 Wall. (U. S.) 165; Germania Nat.

So the fact that the certificate on its face states that the pledgor holds "as trustee" without designation, the person for whom he is trustee is enough to put the pledgee on his guard[1]

Bank *v.* Case, 99 U. S. 628; First Nat. Bank *v.* Stewart, 15 Chic. L. N. 429; Shaw *v.* Spencer, 100 Mass. 382; Sprague *v.* Cocheco Mfg. Co., 10 Blatchf. (U. S.) 173; Simons *v.* South Western R. Bank, 2 Am. L. Reg. 546; Budd *v.* Munroe, 18 Hun (N. Y.) 316; Hann *v.* Hann, 58 N. H. 70; Ashton *v.* Atlantic Bank, 3 Allen (Mass.) 217; Leitch *v.* Wells, 48 N. Y. 585; Winter *v.* Belmont Min. Co., 53 Cal. 428; Goodwin *v.* American Nat. Bank, 48 Conn. 550; Carter *v.* Manufacturers' Nat. Bank, 71 Me. 448; Persch *v.* Consolidated Nat. Bank, 13 Phila. (Pa.) 157; Wood's Appeal, 92 Pa. St. 379; Baldwin *v.* Canfield, 26 Minn. 43; Prall *v.* Tilt, 28 N. J. Eq. 479; Gass *v.* Hampton, 16 Nev. 185; McLeod *v.* Drummond, 17 Ves. 154; Shropshire etc. R. Co. *v.* Reg. L. R., 7 App. 496; Pearson *v.* Scott, L. R., 9 Ch. D. 198.

1. Budd *v.* Munroe, 18 Hun (N. Y.) 316; Baker *v.* Bliss, 39 N. Y. 70; Field *v.* Schreffelin, 7 Johns. Ch. (N. Y.) 150; Pendleton *v.* Fay, 2 Paige (N. Y.) 202; Swan *v.* Produce Bank, 24 Hun (N. Y.) 277; Crocker *v.* Crocker, 31 N. Y. 507; Shaw *v.* Spencer, 100 Mass. 382; Atkinson *v.* Atkinson, 8 Allen (Mass.) 15; Fisher *v.* Brown, 104 Mass. 259; Fowle *v.* Ward, 113 Mass. 548; Ashton *v.* Atlantic Bank, 13 Allen (Mass.) 217; Sturtevant *v.* Jacques, 14 Allen (Mass.) 523; Bayard *v.* Farmers' Bank, 52 Pa. St. 232; Gaston *v.* American etc. Nat. Bank, 29 N. J. Eq. 98; Bank of Metropolis *v.* New England Bank, 6 How. (U. S.) 212; Lowry *v.* Commercial Bank, Camp. 310; Sprague *v.* Cocheco Mfg. Co., 10 Blatchf. (U. S.) 173; Carr *v.* Hilton, 1 Curt. (U. S.) 390; Duncan *v.* Jaudon, 15 Wall. (U. S.) 165; Walsh *v.* Stille, 2 Pars. (Pa.) 17; Maples *v.* Medlin, 1 Murph. (N. Car.) 219; Fish *v.* Kempton, 7 C. B. 687; McLeod *v.* Drummond, 17 Ves. 152; Brandon *v.* Barnett, 1 M. & G. 508.

"The appropriation of corporate stock held in trust, as collateral security for the trustee's own debt, or a debt which he owes jointly with others, is a transaction so far beyond the ordinary scope of a trustee's authority, and out of the common course of business, as to be in itself a suspicious circumstance, imposing upon the creditor the duty of inquiry. This would hardly be controverted in a case where the stock was held by 'A. B., trustee for C. D.' But the effect of the word 'trustee' alone is the same. It means trustee for some one whose name is not disclosed, and there is no greater reason for assuming that a trustee is authorized to pledge for his own debt the property of an unnamed *cestui que trust*, than the property of one whose name is known. In either case, it is highly improbable that the right to do so exists. The apparent difference between the two springs from the erroneous assumption that the word 'trustee' alone has no meaning or legal effect." Shaw *v.* Spencer, 100 Mass. 382.

"One of two innocent parties must suffer, the pledgee or the *cestui que trust;* and it is but just that the loss should fall on the former, who might, by the exercise of reasonable care, have protected himself. In such cases reasonable care is a duty." Gastris *v.* American etc. Nat. Bank, 29 N. J. Eq. 98.

So where a certificate of stock was issued to "the estate of" a deceased person and a trustee of such person tried to pledge, the pledgee is chargeable with the duty to inquire. Ham *v.* Ham, 58 N. H. 70; Pannell *v.* Hurley, 2 Coll. 241. Where the loan secured is illegal, whatever claim the pledgee may have is destroyed. Brewster *v.* Sime, 42 Cal. 139; Albert *v.* Savings Bank, 2 Md. 159; Thompson *v.* Toland, 48 Cal. 99; Winters *v.* Belmont Min. Co., 53 Cal. 428; Gass *v.* Hampton, 16 Nev. 185.

Rule in California, Nevada and Maryland.—In these States it is held that, contrary to the rule in the text, the addition of the word "trustee" in the certificate puts no burden of inquiry on the pledgee. Thompson *v.* Toland, 48 Cal. 99; Winter *v.* Belmont Min. Co., 53 Cal. 428. But see Brewster *v.* Huntley, 37 Cal. 15; Albert *v.* Savings Bank, 1 Md. Ch. 407; Gass *v.* Hampton, 16 Nev. 185.

In Brewster *v.* Sime, 42 Cal. 139, the court, by Crockett, J., said: "The mere addition of the word "trustee" after the name in the certificate is not, in this State, of itself, nothing more appearing, to be deemed constructive notice of the equities of a

and still more so if the name of the *cestui que trust* appears thereon.[1]

(6) *Stock Pledged by Executor or Administrator.*—An executor or administrator stands on a different footing from that of a trustee, for, while the latter presumptively holds the trust property only to invest for the *cestui que trust*,[2] with no presumptive right to dispose of it,[3] the former sells and transfers stock in the ordinary line of his duty and presumptively has the right so to do. The pledgee who deals with an executor, even though he knows him to be such, is not bound to inquire whether the will of the testator gives the executor power to dispose of or pledge stock nor for what purpose it is done, for if letters testamentary have been issued[4] the executor is presumed to have that power.[5] The same rule applies to dealings with administrators.[6]

Moreover, one of several executors has the power to pledge alone and the pledgee need not inquire the purpose,[7] while one trustee cannot act alone, and if he does the pledgee must be on his guard.[8] But if the pledgee has knowledge,[9] or

secret owner of the stock. If it is intended that the so called trustee shall not have power to sell or hypothecate the stock, without the express consent of the equitable owner, it is an easy matter to limit his authority by apt words in the certificate. Considerations of public policy and common justice demand that when stock is placed in the name of a trustee under these circumstances, the secret owner shall be bound by the act of his trustee dealing with persons who have no actual notice of the relations between the parties."

1. Duncan *v.* Jaudon, 15 Wall. (U. S.) 165; Jaudon *v.* National City Bank, 8 Blatchf. (U. S.) 430; Magwood *v.* Railroad Bank, 5 S. Car. 379; Bayard *v.* Farmers' etc. Bank, 52 Pa. St. 232.

But a *bona fide* purchaser taking the new certificate issued is protected, and the corporation issuing it will be liable. Magwood *v.* Railroad Bank, 5 S. Car. 379; Bayard *v.* Farmers' etc. Bank, 52 Pa. St. 232.

2. Jaudon *v.* National City Bank, 8 Blatchf. (U. S.) 430; Leitch *v.* Wells, 48 N. Y. 585; Prall *v.* Tilt, 28 N. J. Eq. 479; Bayard *v.* Farmers' etc. Bank, 52 Pa. St. 232; Carter *v.* National Bank, 71 Me. 448.

3. Wood's Appeal, 92 Pa. St. 379.

4. Wood's Appeal, 92 Pa. St. 379; Bayard *v.* Farmers' etc. Bank, 52 Pa. St. 532; Carter *v.* Manufacturers' Nat. Bank, 71 Me. 448; Goodwin *v.* American Nat. Bank, 48 Conn. 550.

The pledgee receiving stock for an execution is not bound to see to the application of the loan given on the stock. Goodwin *v.* American Nat. Bank, 48 Conn. 550; Stinson *v.* Thornton, 56 Ga. 377; Wood *v.* Smith, 92 Pa. St. 379; Leitch *v.* Wells, 48 N. Y. 585.

5. Smith *v.* Ayer, 101 U. S. 320; Prall *v.* Tilt, 28 N. J. Eq. 479; Jaudon *v.* National City Bank, 8 Blatchf. (U. S.) 430; Bayard *v.* Farmers' etc. Bank, 52 Pa. St. 232.

6. Bayard *v.* Farmers' etc. Bank, 52 Pa. St. 232:

The trustee of an insolvent debtor stands on the same ground, as he holds for administration only. Bayard *v.* Farmers' etc. Bank, 52 Pa. St. 232.

A foreign executor or administrator is included in the rule. Hobbs *v.* Western Nat. Bank, 8 W. N. C. (Pa.) 131.

7. Wheeler *v.* Wheeler, 9 Cow. (N. Y.) 34; Woods' Appeal, 92 Pa. St. 379.

8. Ham *v.* Ham, 58 N. H. 70; Cottam *v.* East. etc. R. Co., 1 Johns. & H. 243.

9. Smith *v.* Ayer, 101 U. S. 320; Duncan *v.* Jaudon, 15 Wall. (U. S.) 176; Wood *v.* Ellis, 31 Leg. Int. (Pa.) 140; Woods Appeal, 92 Pa. St. 379; Carter *v.* Manufacturers Nat. Bank, 71 Me. 448; Davis *v.* French, 20 Me. 21; Dey *v.* Dey, 26 N. J. Eq. 182; Nicholls *v.* Peak, 12 N. J. Eq. 69; Williamson *v.* Morton, 2 Md. Ch. 94; Ashton *v.* Atlantic Bank, 3 Allen (Mass.) 217; Ab-

might have,[1] that the executor is misappropriating the stock, he can acquire no title to it, and is liable for the loss sustained.[2] The stock misappropriated with the knowledge of the pledgee may be recovered from him.[3] But by the intervention of the rules of estoppel a sub-pledgee taking in good faith and for value can get a good title.[4]

3. Bills of Lading[5]—*a.* IN GENERAL.—The confusion between the pledging of the bill of lading itself as collateral and the pledging of the goods represented thereby gives rise to the necessity of treating separately this branch of the subject.

In the first place, the bill of lading is a symbol of the goods delivered to the carrier, and the delivery of a bill of lading properly indorsed is delivery of the goods represented thereby,[6] but fur-

bott *v.* Reeves, 49 Pa. St. 494; Pendleton *v.* Fay, 2 Paige (N. Y.) 202.

So where an executrix pledged stock to gain credit for her sons who were in business to the knowledge of the pledgee, the latter got no title. Prall *v.* Hamil, 28 N. J. Eq. 66.

But where the executrix indorsed the certificate to her sons and they got the loan, the pledgee was protected. Prall *v.* Tilt, 28 N. J. Eq. 479.

1. One dealing with an executor is bound to know the source of his authority and the limits of it, and if the executor acts outside the authority given him by law, the pledgee is by law charged with the knowledge of the excess of power used. Webb *v.* Graniteville Mfg. Co., 11 S. Car. 396; Ellis's Appeal, 8 W. N. C. (Pa.) 538.

When an executor borrowed money on a note of the estate for use in a copartnership to which he belonged, the pledgee was held chargeable with notice. Loring *v.* Brodie, 134 Mass. 453; Smitt *v.* Ayers, 181 U. S. 320; Thomasson *v.* Brown, 43 Ind. 203; Prosser *v.* Leatherman, 4 How. (Miss.) 237.

That an executor pledges a stock the certificate of which is made to him as "executor," is not notice to the pledgee of a misappropriation, for the executor has the presumptive right to so pledge. Carter *v.* Manufacturers' Nat. Bank, 71 Me. 448; Pettingill *v.* Pettingill, 60 Me. 412.

Knowledge of the pledgee that there are valid claims upon the securities of the estate does not destroy his lien. Leitch *v.* Wells, 48 N. Y. 585.

But where the loan was made so long after the testator's death that it could not be presumed that the money would be required for the use of the estate, the pledgee is chargeable with knowledge. Miller *v.* Ege, 8 Pa. St. 352; Bellas *v.* McCarty, 10 Watts (Pa.) 13; Lowry *v.* Commercial Bank, Camp. 310; Collinson *v.* Lister, 7 De G. M. & J. 634.

Notice to Corporation.—Corporations are chargeable with notice under the same circumstances as an individual. Collinson *v.* Lister, 7 De G. M. &. G. 633.

2. Lowry *v.* Commercial Bank, Camp. 310; Yerger *v.* Jones, 16 How. (U. S.) 30.

3. Thomasson *v.* Brown, 43 Ind. 203; Smith *v.* Ayer, 101 U. S. 320.

4. Prall *v.* Tilt, 28 N. J. Eq. 480; Wood's Appeal, 92 Pa. St. 379.

So where by statute in *Georgia* administrators are ordered to sell assets publicly and an administrator sold stock privately and the purchaser resold it to a *bona fide* purchaser, the latter got a good title. Nutting *v.* Thomasson, 46 Ga. 34.

5. For the general law on the subject of bills of lading, see BILLS OF LADING, vol. 2, p. 223.

6. Gibson *v.* Stevens, 8 How. (U. S.) 384; Shaw *v.* Merchants' Nat. Bank, 101 U. S. 564; Dows *v.* National Exch. Bank, 91 U. S. 618; Bank of Rochester *v.* Jones, 4 N. Y. 497; Holbrooke *v* Wright, 24 Wend. (N. Y.) 169; Rawles *v.* Deshler; 3 Keyes (N. Y.) 572; Cayuga Co. Nat. Bank *v.* Daniels, 47 N. Y. 631; Farmers' Bank *v.* Logan, 74 N. Y. 568; First Nat. Bank *v.* Kelly, 57 N. Y. 34; Forbes *v.* Boston etc. R. Co., 133 Mass. 154; Hathaway *v.* Haynes, 124 Mass. 311; First Nat. Bank *v.* Dearborn, 115 Mass. 219; First Nat. Bank *v.* Crocker, 111 Mass. 163; Allen *v.* Williams, 12 Pick. (Mass.) 297; De Wolf *v.* Gardner, 12 Cush. (Mass.) 19; Henry

ther than this the bill of lading is the muniment or *indicia* of title to the goods, and becomes, under the rules of estoppel, *quasi* negotiable,[1] and protection is thereby given to a *bona fide* pledgee for value to a certain extent from equities existing between the carrier and the consignor and against those of third persons.

b. ACT OF PLEDGE.—When the bill of lading is drawn to the order of a certain person, it is properly transferred by the indorsement of that person;[2] where it is made in blank[3] or even drawn to order it can be transferred by mere delivery alone if it be the intention of the parties so to transfer it in pledge.[4]

v. Philadelphia etc. Co., 81 Pa. St. 76; Holmes *v.* German etc. Bank, 87 Pa. St. 525; Emery *v.* Irving Nat. Bank, 25 Ohio St. 360; Peters *v.* Elliot, 78 Ill. 326; Michigan Cent. R. Co. *v.* Phillips, 60 Ill. 190; Taylor *v.* Turner, 87 Ill. 296; Security Bank *v.* Luttgen, 29 Minn. 363; First Nat. Bank *v.* Northern R. Co., 58 N. H. 203; Adoue *v.* Seeligson, 54 Tex. 593; Dodge *v.* Meyer, 10 Pac. Coast L. J. 169; McCants *v.* Wells, 4 S. Car. 381.

1. Barnard *v.* Campbell, 56 N. Y. 462; Allen *v.* Williams, 12 Pick. (Mass.) 297; Rowley *v.* Bigelow, 12 Pick. (Mass.) 307; Davenport Nat. Bank *v.* Homeyer, 45 Mo. 145.

"When the right of possession is changed by a sale or pledge of the property itself, the transfer of the bill of lading operates as a change of possession of the property, the carrier in the meantime being the custodian for the real owner or party in interest. While a bill of lading is not a negotiable instrument in the sense in which a bill of exchange or promissory note is negotiable, yet as the representative of a valuable commodity, it is assignable to the party entitled to control the possession of that commodity to the same extent and for the same purposes as the property itself would be if corporeally present; inasmuch, therefore, as these instruments are capable of performing very important functions in commercial transactions, innocent holders thereof for value ought to receive the same protection as if they held possession of the property itself." Stone *v.* Wabash etc. R. Co., 9 Ill. App. 48.

2. Shaw *v.* Merchants' Nat. Bank Co., 101 U. S. 564; The Thames, 14 Wall. (U. S.) 106; Conrad *v.* Atlantic Ins. Co., 1 Pet. (U. S.) 445; Walter *v.* Ross, 2 Wash. 283; Hieskell *v.* Farmers' etc. Bank, 89 Pa. St. 155; Tilden *v.* Minor, 45 Vt. 196; Winslow *v.* Norton, 29 Me. 419; Robinson *v.* Stuart, 68 Me. 61; Western Union R. Co. *v.* Wagner, 65 Ill. 198; Michigan Cent. R. Co. *v.* Phillips, 60 Ill. 198; Skilling *v.* Bollman, 73 Mo. 665; Henderson *v.* Comptoir. L. R., 5 Pr. C. 253; Thompson *v.* Donning, 14 M. & W. 403; Glyn *v.* E. & W. I. Docks Co., L. R., 7 App. 591; Caldwell *v.* Ball, 1 Term 205; Short *v.* Simpson, L. R., 1 C. P. 248; Kreft *v.* Thompson, L. R., 10 Ex. 285; Wright *v.* Campbell, 2 Burr. 2051.

An indorsement without delivery is not sufficient. Buffington *v.* Curtis, 15 Mass. 528.

3. Bank of Rochester *v.* Jones, 4 N. Y. 497; City Bank *v.* Rome R. Co., 44 N. Y. 136; Marine Bank *v.* Wright, 46 Barb. (N. Y.) 45; Merchants' Bank *v.* Union R. etc. Co., 67 N. Y. 373; Becker *v.* Hallgarten, 86 N. Y. 167; Farmers' etc. Bank *v.* Logan, 74 N. Y. 568; Mich. Cent. R. Co. *v.* Phillips, 60 Ill. 190; Ohio etc. R. Co. *v.* Kerr, 49 Ill. 459; Peters *v.* Elliott, 78 Ill. 327; Allen *v.* Williams, 12 Pick. (Mass.) 302; Hathaway *v.* Haines, 124 Mass. 311; De Wolf *v.* Gardner, 12 Cush. (Mass.) 19; Forbes *v.* Boston etc. R. Co., 9 Am. & Eng. R. Cas. 76; First Nat. Bank *v.* Dearborn, 115 Mass. 219; Davenport Nat. Bank *v.* Homeyer, 45 Mo. 145; Lickbarrow *v.* Mason, 1 H. Bl. 360; Meyerstein *v.* Barber, L. R. 4 H. L. 325; Nathan *v.* Giles, 5 Taunt. 558.

4. Gibson *v.* Stevens, 8 How. (U. S.) 381; First Nat. Bank *v.* Crocker, 111 Mass. 163; First Nat. Bank *v.* Dearborn, 115 Mass. 219.

Where the bill of lading designated no conveyance, and contained the words, "this receipt is not transferable," it was still held that the transfer by delivery vested a special property in the transferee. Peters *v.* Elliott, 78 Ill. 321.

c. TITLE OF PLEDGEE—(1) *In General.*—In *England*, and in many of the States of the Union, by statute, bills of lading are made negotiable and placed on the same footing as bills of exchange. In such States there is no doubt that the pledgee, holding for value and in good faith in the usual course of business, gets an indefeasible title to the property represented by the bill of lading.[1] But leaving out of view these statutory enactments, where the bill of lading is regarded strictly as the symbol of the goods, it naturally follows that the pledgee of the bill of lading has no more title in the goods than he would if the goods themselves were delivered: that is, he gets only the title that the assignee had.[2]

The tendency is, however, in commercial States, by the application of the doctrine of estoppel, to make the pledgee of bills of lading holding by proper indorsement for value, in the usual course of business, the legal owner of the goods against the world.[3]

So where one who paid a draft, receiving the bill of lading as security, the title to the goods became vested in him. Tiedeman *v.* Knox, 53 Md. 612.

Shipment of an agricultural product by a consignor to a factor whom he owes, and delivery of the bill of lading to the carrier for transmission, is a pledge, within *Louisiana* Acts 1874, No. 66; and this cannot be affected by the consignors selling the property *in transitu*, and instructing the carrier to destroy the bill, and issue a new one to another consignee. Phelps *v.* Howell, 35 La. Ann. 87.

1. *New York*, 3 Rev. Stat. (7th ed., 1882), p. 2260; *Pennsylvania* Brightley's Pur. Dig. '73, p. 114, § 1; *California* C. & S., '76, § 7127; *Minnesota* L. '78, ch. 124, § 17; *Maryland* R. C. '78, p. 298, art. 35, § 12; *Wisconsin* Rev. Stat. '78, p. 101, § 4194; *Missouri* Rev. Stat. '79, p. 88, § 558.

Unless the statute provides that the bill of lading shall be negotiable in all respects as a bill of exchange, or promissory note, as in *Maryland*, contrary to cases previously decided (Baltimore etc. R. Co. *v.* Wilkens, 14 Md. 11), the mere statement that bills of lading shall be negotiable as are bills of exchange or promissory notes does not make them completely so; for if a bill of lading should be stolen from the owner of the goods the innocent holder thereof would never get a good title to the goods. Shaw *v.* Merchants' Nat. Co., 101 U. S. 557.

2. The Idaho, 93 U. S. 575; Dows *v.* Green, 24 N. Y. 638; Saltus *v.* Everett, 20 Wend. (N. Y.) 269; Farmers' Bank *v.* Logan, 74 N. Y. 568; Covill *v.* Hill, 4 Den. (N. Y.) 323; Barnard *v.* Campbell, 55 N. Y. 462; Davenport Nat. Bank *v.* Homeyer, 45 Mo. 1451; Allen *v.* Williams, 12 Pick. (Mass.) 297; Rowley *v.* Bigelow, 12 Pick. (Mass.) 307; Forbes *v.* Boston etc. R. Co., 133 Mass. 154; Canadian Bank *v.* McCrea, 106 Ill. 281; Burton *v.* Curyea, 40 Ill. 320; Hunt *v.* Mississippi Cent. R. Co., 29 La. Ann. 446; Fellows *v.* Powell, 16 La. Ann. 316; Evansville etc. R. Co. *v.* Erwin, 84 Ind. 457; Burdict *v.* Sewell, 10 Q. B. D. 363; Gurney *v.* Behrend, 3 El. & Bl. 622.

In Pollard *v.* Vinton, the court by Miller, J., said: "In the hands of the holder the bill of lading is evidence of ownership, special or general, of the property mentioned in it and of the right to receive said property at the place of delivery. Its transfer does not preclude, as in the case of negotiable instruments, all inquiry into the transaction in which it originated, because it has come into hands of persons who have innocently paid value for it. The doctrine of *bona fide* purchasers only applies to it in a limited sense."

So where an agent was authorized to ship goods but not in his own name, and the agent took the bill of lading in his own name and pledged it for advances to him, the pledgee got no title to the goods. Moore *v.* Robinson, 62 Ala. 537.

3. Gibson *v.* Stevens, 8 How. (U. S.)

The pledgee's lien covers the carrier's charges for freight, if paid by him, as well as the debt secured.[1]

It is a general rule that an antecedent debt is sufficient to make the pledgee of a bill of lading a holder for value;[2] but in some States this rule does not obtain.[3]

Where duplicate bills of lading are issued for the same property and each bill is pledged to a different person, that pledgee who first receives one of the bills for a valuable consideration in good faith, gets the title to the goods, although the pledgee of the duplicate bill may have given value and acted in good faith.[4]

Though the holder of the bill of lading first negotiated has the title to the goods, he should notify the carrier on the arrival of the goods at their destination, of his title to prevent delivery to a subsequent holder of a duplicate bill.[5]

(2) *Against the Pledgor.*—The pledgee of a bill of lading for advances made, has in the goods constructively in his possession, the title of an ordinary pledgee of corporeal property and likewise subject to be divested by the payment of the debt secured. He has the same rights and liabilities before and after default as does an ordinary pledgee.[6]

384; Farmers' Nat. Bank *v.* Logan, 74 N. Y. 568; Commercial Bank *v.* Pfeiffer, 22 Hun (N. Y.) 327; First Nat. Bank *v.* Kelly, 57 N. Y. 34; Dows *v.* Kidder, 84 N. Y. 121; Smith *v.* Lynes, 5 N. Y. 41; Comer *v.* Coningham, 77 N. Y. 391; Paddon *v.* Taylor, 44 N. Y. 371; Crocker *v.* Crocker, 31 N. Y. 507; Rawles *v.* Deshler, 3 Keyes (N. Y.) 572; Smith *v.* Lynes, 5 N. Y. 41; Saltus *v.* Everett, 20 Wend. (N. Y.) 267; Fleeman *v.* McKean, 25 Barb. (N. Y.) 474; Beavers *v.* Lane, 6 Duer (N. Y.) 238; First Nat. Bank *v.* Crocker, 111 Mass. 163; Forbes *v.* Boston etc. R. Co., 133 Mass. 154; First Nat. Bank *v.* Bayley, 115 Mass. 228; DeWolf *v.* Gardner, 12 Cush. (Mass.) 19; Holmes *v.* German etc. Bank, 87 Pa. St. 525; Holmes *v.* Bailey, 92 Pa. St. 57; Emery *v* Irving Nat. Bank, 25 Ohio St. 360; Glyn *v.* E. & M. Ind. Docks Co., L. R. App. 591; Lee *v.* Bowen, 5 Biss. (U. S.) 154.

The pledgee of a bill of lading if not the absolute owner of the goods, stands in the position of a mortgagee in possession, and is not required to file the papers as a chattel mortgage. First National Bank *v.* Kelly, 57 N. Y. 34.

1. Clark *v.* Dearborn, 103 Mass. 335.

2. Leask *v.* Scott, 2 Q. B. D. 376; Tiedman *v.* Knox, 53 Md. 612; Skilling *v.* Bollman, 6 Mo. App. 76; Halsey *v.* Warden, 25 Can. 128; Peters *v.* Elliott, 78 Ill. 325.

So an agreement for future advances is a good consideration. Stevens *v.* Boston etc. R. Co., 8 Gray (Mass.) 262.

3. Harris *v.* Pratt, 17 N. Y. 249; Loeb *v.* Peters, 63 Ala. 243; Lessassier *v.* Southwestern R. Co., 2 Woods (U. S.) 35.

4. The Thames, 14 Wall. (U. S.) 98; Skilling *v.* Bollman, 6 Mo. App. 76; Barber *v.* Meyerstein, L. R., 4 H. L. 317.

When goods before their arrival at their destination were reshipped and a new bill of lading issued, which was pledged to a *bona fide* holder for value, the holder for value in good faith of the first bill of lading had a better title than did the holder of the second. Hieskell *v.* Farmers' etc. Bank, 89 Pa. St. 155.

Where two of a set of duplicate bills were pledged to the same person for advances, and the third fraudulently to another person, who got actual possession of the goods, all the pledgees acting in good faith and holding for value, the title of the former pledgee was preferred to that of the latter. Barber *v.* Meyerstein, L. R., 4 H. L. 317.

5. Glyn *v.* E. & W. I. Docks Co, L. R. 7 App. 600.

6. Forbes *v.* Boston etc. R. Co., 133 Mass. 154; Stollenwerck *v.* Thatcher, 115 Mass. 224; First National Bank *v.* Northern R. Co., 58 N. H. 203; Western Union R. Co. *v.* Wagner, 65 Ill.

(3) *Against Third Persons.*—The pledgee of the bill of lading received thus in good faith from a third person for value gets a good title against the consignor himself,[1] and against his creditors,[2] and one that cannot be divested by the consignor's right of stoppage *in transitu.*[3]

(4) *Against Carrier*—(*a*) *In General.*—If the goods have been actually delivered to the carrier by the consignor, there is no doubt but that the pledgee has the right to demand delivery of them to him on presentation of the bill of lading, and if the carrier has delivered them to any one else, including even the consignee without good excuse, he is liable to the pledgee in damages.[4]

197; Moore *v.* Robinson, 62 Ala. 537; Lineker *v.* Ayeshford, 1 Cal. 76; Thompson *v.* Downing, 14 M. & W. 403.

The pledgor may pledge the surplus of the value of the goods over and above the amount of the first debt secured. Portalis *v.* Tetley, L. R., 5 Eq. 140.

A bill of lading was pledged to two creditors, and the factor to whom the goods were consigned sent money to one creditor enough to pay both, the pledgor falsely representing that the other creditor had waived payment, the money was applied to other debts owed to the first creditor. *Held*, that the debt was discharged for the debt of the first creditor only. Peters *v.* Pacific Guano Co., 42 La. Ann., 7 So. Rep. 790.

1. Farmers' etc. Bank *v.* Hazeltine, 78 N. Y. 104; The Argentina, L. R., 1 A. & E. 370; Gurney *v.* Behrend, 3 El. & Bl. 622.

So the pledgee is not chargeable with equities existing between the consignor and the consignee, Wait *v.* Greene, 36 N. Y. 556; Western Union R. Co. *v.* Wagner, 65 Ill. 197; Winne *v.* McDonald, 36 N. Y. 233.

One who advances money on the faith of a bill of lading is not bound by oral understanding varying its terms between the original parties of which he had no knowledge. Garden Grove Bank *v.* Humeston R. Co., 67 Iowa 526.

2. Forbes *v.* Boston etc. R. Co., 133 Mass. 154; Hathaway *v.* Haynes, 124 Mass. 311; Petitt *v.* First Nat. Bank, 4 Bush (Ky.) 334.

3. Becker *v.* Hallgarten, 86 N. Y. 167; Dows *v.* Greene, 24 N. Y. 638; Rawles *v.* Deshler, 1 Sheld. (N. Y.) 48; Dows *v.* Rush, 28 Barb. (N. Y.) 157; Loeb *v.* Peters, 63 Ala. 243; Chandler *v.* Fulton, 10 Tex. 2; Walter *v.* Ross, 2 Wash. (U. S.) 283; Audenried *v.* Randall, 3 Cliff. (U. S.) 99; Lee *v.* Kimball, 45 Me. 172; Vertue *v.* Jewell, 4 Camp. 31; Leask *v.* Scott, 2 Q. B. D. 376; Lickbarrow *v.* Mason, 2 T. R. 63; Barber *v.* Meyerstein, L. R. 4 H. L. 317; The Mary Ann Guest, Olc. Adm. 498.

If, however, the debt secured by the pledgee of the bill of lading is less than the value of the goods the consignor's right of stoppage *in transitu* exists as to the surplus over the debt secured. Kemp *v.* Falk, L. R., 7 App. 573; Coventy *v.* Gladstone, L. R., 6 Eq. 44; *In re* Westzinthus, 5 B. & Ad. 817; *Ex parte* Golding, L. R., 13 Ch. D. 624; Spaulding *v.* Reeding, 6 Beav. 376.

4. Southern Express Co. *v.* Dickson, 94 U. S. 549; The Thames, 14 Wall. (U. S.) 98; Hawkins *v.* Hoffman, 6 Hill (N. Y.) 586; Viner *v.* New York etc. R. Co., 50 N. Y. 23; Forbes *v.* Boston etc. R. Co., 133 Mass. 154; Alderman *v.* Eastern R. Co., 115 Mass. 233; Newcomb *v.* Boston etc. R. Co., 115 Mass 230; Wright *v.* North Cent. R. Co., 8 Phila. (Pa.) 19; First Nat. Bank *v.* Northern R. Co., 58 N. H. 203; Winslow *v.* Vermont etc. R. Co., 42 Vt. 700.

Pollard *v.* Vinton, 105 U. S. 7; Robinson *v.* Memphis etc. R. Co., 9 Fed. Rep. 129; The Vaughan, 14 Wall. (U. S.) 258; Merchants' Bank *v.* Union R. etc. Co., 69 N. Y. 373; Newcomb *v.* Boston etc. R. Co., 115 Mass. 230; Forbes *v.* Boston etc. R. Co., 133 Mass. 454; First Nat. Bank *v.* North R. Co., 58 N. H. 203.

McEwen *v.* Jeffersonville R. Co., 33 Ind. 368; Jeffersonville etc. R. Co. *v.* Irish, 46 Ind. 180; Hieskell *v.* Farmers' etc. Bank, 89 Pa. St. 155; People's Nat. Bank *v.* Stewart, 3 Pugs. & Bur. (N. B.) 268; Meyerstein *v.* Barber, L. R., 2 C. P. 38.

The pledgee is under no obligation to give notice to the carrier that he holds the bill of lading, nor is he bound to demand the goods immediately on their arrival. It is no excuse for delivery to the wrong person that the carrier does not know of the pledgee, and cannot send him notice. The carrier under such circumstances must hold the goods until the bill of lading is presented.[1] While the title to the goods of which duplicate bills of lading are issued is in the pledgee of the bill first negotiated for value, still the carrier who has received no notice of prior equities is justified in delivering the goods to the holder of the bill of lading first presented to him, and the one having the title to the goods must seek his remedy against the possessor of the goods.[2]

(*b*) *Carrier's Responsibility for Statements in the Bill of Lading.*—Where the agent of a carrier has signed a bill of lading for goods not in his possession at the time of signing, there is a difference of opinion as to whether or not the carrier is estopped from denying that the goods were delivered, against a *bona fide* holder of the

So where goods are transported by several carriers the last carrier is bound to deliver the goods only to the holder of the bill of lading issued by the first carrier. Forbes *v.* Boston etc. R. Co., 133 Mass. 154.

But if the bill of lading is made payable definitely to the consignee and not to "order or assigns" a delivery by the carrier to the person named in the bill of lading is held valid where a custom to so deliver is shown to exist, and it is held that the pledgee is presumed to have known the custom when he accepted the bill of lading as security. Forbes *v.* Boston etc. R. Co., 133 Mass. 154.

Under ordinary circumstances it is presumed that the consignee is the owner of the goods. Lawrence *v.* Minturn, 17 How. (U. S.) 100; O'Dougherty *v.* Boston etc. R. Co., 1 Thomp. & C. (N. Y.) 477; Sweet *v.* Barney, 23 N. Y. 335.

Amount of Recovery Against Carrier.—Where the carrier is liable for loss of the goods, the pledgee of the bill of lading can recover only the value of the goods less the amount of freight. Forbes *v.* Boston etc. R. Co., 133 Mass. 154.

But where a third person who had agreed to purchase the goods had, in bad faith, obtained them from the carrier by paying the freight and storage, the pledgee in suing for the recovery of the goods is not liable for the freight and storage. Adams *v.* O'Connor, 100 Mass. 515.

If the carrier delivers up goods in obedience to a valid writ from a court having jurisdiction, he is excused for non-delivery to a person holding the bill of lading, provided that person has received immediate notice of the service of the writ.

Stiles *v.* Davis, 1 Black (U. S.) 101; Robinson *v.* Memphis etc. R. Co., 16 Fed. Rep. 59; Rosenfield *v.* Express Co., 1 Wood (U. S.) 131; Blivin *v.* Hudson River Co., 36 N. Y. 403; Kiff *v.* Old Colony etc. R. Co., 117 Mass. 591; Ohio etc. R. Co. *v.* Yohe, 51 Ind. 181; Burton *v.* Wilkinson, 18 Vt. 187.

It is no excuse for non-delivery to the pledgee that the carrier has delivered up the goods on the receipt of a fictitious bill of lading. Marine Bank *v.* Fiske, 71 N. Y. 353.

1. The Thames, 14 Wall. (U. S.) 98; Farmers' etc. Bank *v.* Logan, 74 N. Y. 568; Forbes *v.* Boston etc. R. Co., 133 Mass. 154; Glyn *v.* E. & W. I. Docks Co., L. R., 7 App. 605; Barber *v.* Meyerstein, L. R., 4 H. L. 317.

A delay of four months by the pledgee of the bill of lading in demanding the goods, though in the meantime they had been fraudulently obtained by the consignee, does not excuse the carrier for delivery to the wrong person. Forbes *v.* Boston etc. R. Co., 133 Mass. 154.

2. Glyn *v.* E. & W. India Dock Co., L. R., 7 App. Cas. 591; Sanders *v.* Maclean, L. R., 11 Q. B. D. 327; Meyerstein *v.* Barber, L. R., 4 H. L. 317, overruling earlier case which allowed

bill of lading for value. If the goods after the signing of the bill of lading, come into the carrier's possession and are shipped, the holder of the bill of lading gets a good title to the goods.[1]

If the agent signs for goods which never came into the carrier's possession, the general rule is that the carrier is not bound by the bill and the pledgee of it for value has no recovery against the carrier,[2] though he has a claim against the pledgor.[3]

In *New York*, *Kansas* and *Nebraska*, on the contrary, the rule is followed, that where a bill of lading not fictitious, comes into the hands of a holder for value in good faith the carrier is not permitted to deny that he has received the goods set forth in the bill or to set up fraud on the part of the consignor.[4]

the carrier with notice to deliver the goods to the person he thought entitled.

1. The Idaho, 93 U. S. 575; The L. J. Farwell, 8 Biss. (U. S.) 61; Halliday *v.* Hamilton, 11 Wall. (U. S.) 560; Robinson *v.* Memphis etc. R. Co., 16 Fed. Rep. 57; Rowley *v.* Bigelow, 12 Pick. (Mass.) 314.

Even where the issuing of bills of lading without actual receipt of the goods is made an offense by statute, if the goods are afterwards delivered, the statute will not render it imperative. The Idaho, 93 U. S. 575.

2. See BILL OF LADING, vol. 2, p. 223; Pollard *v.* Vinton, 105 U. S. 7; The Mayflower, 3 Ware (U. S.) 300; Schooner Freeman *v.* Buckingham, 18 How. (U. S.) 182; The Loon, 7 Blatchf. (U. S.) 244; The Lady Franklin, 8 Wall. (U. S.) 325; The Keokuk, 9 Wall. (U. S.) 519; The Joseph Grant, 1 Biss. (U. S.) 193; Backus *v.* The Marengo, 6 McLean (U. S.) 487; King *v.* Shepherd, 3 Story (U. S.) 349; Sears *v.* Wingate, 3 Allen (Mass.) 103; Walter *v.* Brewer, 11 Mass. 99; Robinson *v.* Memphis etc. R. Co., 9 Fed. Rep. 129; Dean *v.* King, 22 Ohio St. 118; Louisiana Nat. Bank *v.* Laveille, 52 Mo. 380; Baltimore etc. R. Co. *v.* Wilkens, 44 Md. 11; Tiedeman *v.* Knox, 53 Md. 612; Hunt *v.* Mississippi R. Co., 29 La. Ann. 446; Stone *v.* Wabash etc. R. Co., 9 Ill. App. 48; Grant *v.* Norway, 10 C. B. 665; Brown *v.* Powell etc. Co., L. R., 10 C. P. 562; Hubbersty *v.* Ward, 8 Exch. 330; Coleman *v.* Riches, 16 C. B. 104; Mackay *v.* Commercial Bank, L. R., 5 P. C. 394; McLean *v.* Fleming, L. R., 2 H. L. 128; Jessel *v.* Bath, L. R., 2 Ex. 267; Erb *v.* Gt. West. R. Co., 42 U. C., Q. B. 90.

The same rule is applicable both to carriers on land and those by water. Robinson *v.* Memphis etc. R. Co., 9 Fed. Rep. 129.

"The taker of the bill of lading assumes the risk not only of the genuineness of the signature, and of the fact that the signer was the master of the vessel, but also of the apparent authority of the master to issue the bill of lading. But the master of a vessel has no more apparent authority to sign bills of lading than he has to sign bills of sale of the ship. He has an apparent authority if the ship be a general one, to sign bills of lading for cargo actually shipped; and he has also authority to sign a bill of sale of the ship when, in case of disaster, his power of sale arises. But the authority in each case arises out of and depends upon a particular state of facts. It is not an unlimited authority in one case more than in the other; and his act in either case does not bind the owner even in favor of an innocent purchaser, if the facts on which his power depended did not exist; and it is incumbent upon those who are about to change their condition upon the faith of his authority to ascertain the existence of all the facts upon which his authority depends." Schooner Freeman *v.* Buckingham, 18 How. (U. S.) 182.

A custom, either general or local, cannot be shown in order to make the carrier liable as he would be on negotiable paper. Robinson *v.* Memphis etc. R. Co., 9 Fed. Rep. 129.

3. Adone *v.* Seeligson, 54 Tex. 593.

4. Armour *v.* Michigan Cent. R. Co., 65 N. Y. 111; Farmers' etc. Bank *v.* Erie R. Co., 72 N. Y. 189; Griswold *v.* Harven, 125 N. Y. 595; Hern *v.* Nichols, 1 Salk. 289; Savings Bank *v.* R. Co., 20 Kan. 529; Wichita Sav. Bank *v.* Atchison etc. R. Co., 20 Kan.

In any case the carrier, when the bill has come into the possession of a *bona fide* holder for value, is estopped to deny the truth of any matter stated in the bill of lading which is or ought to be in his own knowledge or that of his servants.[1]

d. TITLE OF PLEDGEE TO FICTITIOUS BILL OF LADING.—A fictitious bill of lading, or one forged, is void, and the pledgee of it, with or without knowledge of the fraud, gets no security for his advance.[2]

When an agent of a carrier issues a bill of lading for goods never received, the pledgee of such bill for value and in good faith is not protected in the Federal courts and others, but is in *New York.*[3]

e. TITLE OF PLEDGEE TO MISAPPROPRIATED BILLS OF LADING.—The rules that where the owner of property intrusts the *indicia* of title to another, those dealing with the latter as the apparent owner on the strength of such *indicia*, will be protected,[4] and that where one of two innocent parties must suffer from the wrongful acts of a third person, he must suffer who allowed the third person to commit the wrong, are applied to protect the title of a pledgee who for value and in good faith receives a bill of lad-

519; Sioux City etc. R. Co. *v.* First Nat. Bank, 10 Neb. 556.

In Meyer *v.* Peck, 28 N. Y. 590, the court by Denio, J., said: "There is an established distinction in favor of a *bona fide* indorsee, grounded upon the doctrine of estoppel. By signing the bill of lading, acknowledging the receipt of a given quantity of merchandise, the master has enabled the shipper to go into the market and obtain money on the credit of the shipment, and cannot be permitted, as against the person so advancing, to set up his own or the master's want of care at the expense of the indorsee. This results from the qualified negotiability of these instruments."

The carrier is liable to the innocent indorsee of the bill of lading for value for any damage caused by misstatements in the bill. Miller *v.* Hannibal etc. R. Co., 24 Hun (N. Y.) 607.

By statute in *England* the carrier is estopped from denying statements made in the bill of lading when it has come into the hands of an innocent holder for value. 18 & 19 Vict., Ch. 111, § 3.

But even under this statute, the carrier could show that the weight of the goods delivered differed from that stated in the bill of lading. McLean *v.* Fleming, L. R., 2 H. L. 128; Blanchett *v.* Powell's Co., L. R., 9 Ex. 74; Brown *v.* Powell Coal Co., L. R., 10 C. P. 562; Carr *v.* London etc. R. Co., L. R., 10 C. P. 307.

There is a similar statute in *Maryland* R. Code, '78, p. 298, §§ 13, 14, and in some other States.

1. Dows *v.* Perrin, 16 N. Y. 325; Dickerson *v.* Seelye, 12 Barb. (N. Y.) 102; Meyer *v.* Peck, 28 N. Y. 590; Sears *v.* Wingate, 3 Allen (Mass.) 103; Dean *v.* King, 22 Ohio St. 118; Bates *v.* Todd, 1 M. & R. 106; Relyea *v.* New Haven etc. Co., 42 Conn. 579; Bradstreet *v.* Heran, 3 Blatchf. (U. S.) 116.

So a material difference between the actual weight of the goods and that stated in the bill of lading could not be shown by the carrier. Sears *v.* Wingate, 3 Allen (Mass.) 103; Relyea *v.* New York etc. Co., 42 Conn. 579; Bradstreet *v.* Heran, 2 Blatchf. (U. S.) 116.

2. Schooner Freeman *v.* Buckingham, 18 How. (U. S.) 182; Brower *v.* Peabody, 13 N. Y. 121; Bassett *v.* Spofford, 45 N. Y. 587; Saltus *v.* Everett, 20 Wend. (N. Y.) 267; Maybee *v.* Tregent, 47 Mich. 495; Grant *v.* Norway, 10 C. B. 665.

3. See *infra*, this title, *Pledgee's Title Against Carrier.*

4. Comer *v.* Creughan, 77 N. Y. 391; Dows *v.* Kidder, 84 N. Y. 121. See cases *infra*, this title, *Pledgee's Title, in General.*

ing as security for a debt of one who has no authority to pledge.[1] So where an agent, holding the bill of lading, without authority, pledges it,[2] or where the indorsement and transfer of the bill of lading is procured by fraudulent representations, the pledgee who took for value and without notice, is protected against the owner.[3]

But the owner to estop himself must voluntarily intrust the bill of lading to another; therefore, where the bill of lading has been stolen from him, or has been issued by a carrier on stolen goods or to one who has no authority to deliver the goods to the carrier, a pledgee for value in good faith is not protected.[4]

Of course if the pledgee has notice of any prior equities or that the pledge is illegal he is not protected; and, if he has gotten actual possession of the goods, is liable to the owner for their value.[5]

The pledgee is chargeable with notice of anything that may be learned from the face of the bill of lading.[6]

1. Bradstreet *v.* Heran, 2 Blatchf. (U. S.) 116; The J. W. Brown, 1 Biss. (U. S.) 76; Armour *v.* Michigan Cent. R. Co., 65 N. Y. 111; Rawles *v.* Deshler, 3 Keys (N. Y.) 572; Wichita Sav. Bank *v.* Atchison etc. R. Co., 20 Kan. 519; Relyea *v.* New Haven etc. R. Co., 42 Conn. 579; Carr *v.* London R. Co., L. R., 10 C. P. 307; Lickbarrow *v.* Mason, 2 T. R. 63.

2. Henry *v.* Philadelphia, 81 Pa. St. 76.

The statute in *Missouri*, affixing a penalty to the pledge of a bill of lading by an agent or consignee without a written authority of the owner or consignor, does not affect a transfer previously valid. Allen *v.* St. Louis Nat. Bank, 20 U. S. 20.

3. Dows *v.* Greene, 24 N. Y. 638; Kreeft *v.* Thompson, L. R., 10 Ex. 282; Gabarron *v.* Kreeft, L. R., 10. Ex. 274.

4. Shaw *v.* Merchants' Nat. Bank, 101 U. S. 564; Saltus *v.* Everett, 20 Wend. (N. Y.) 267; Bradner *v.* Campbell, 55 N. Y. 456; Farmers' Bank *v.* Logan, 74 N. Y. 568; Michigan State Bank *v.* Gardner, 15 Gray (Mass.) 362; Coggill *v.* Hartford etc. R. Co., 3 Gray (Mass.) 545; Evansville etc. R. Co. *v.* Ervin, 84 Ind. 457; Maybee *v.* Tregent, 47 Mich. 495.

So where the bill of lading was pledged to a *bona fide* holder for value and afterwards the pledgor and general owner by means of a false bill again pledged the same goods, the second pledgee getting actual possession, the first pledgee having done no affirmative act assisting the wrong, was not estopped from demanding the goods from the second pledgee, though the latter took in good faith. Dows *v.* National Exch. Bank, 91 U. S. 618; Marine Bank *v.* Fiske, 71 N. Y. 353; Bank of Rochester *v.* Jones, 4 N. Y. 497; Barnard *v.* Campell, 55 N. Y. 456; Mechanics' etc Bank *v.* Farmers' etc. Nat. Bank, 60 N. Y. 40; Jenkyns *v.* Brown, 14 Q. B. 496.

The second pledgee, when the carrier fraudulently issued a second bill of lading, was allowed to recover from the carrier. Farmers' etc. Bank *v.* Erie R. Co., 72 N. Y. 188.

5. U. S. *v.* State Bank, 96 U. S. 30; Dows *v.* Kidder, 84 N. Y. 121; Caussidiere *v.* Beers, 2 Keyes (N. Y.) 198; Van Alen *v.* Am. Nat. Bank, 52 N. Y. 1; Cobb. *v.* Dows, 10 N. Y. 341; Veil *v.* Mitchell, 4 Wash. (U. S.) 105; Merrill *v.* Bank of Norfolk, 19 Pick. (Mass.) 32; Pennell *v.* Deffell, 4 De G. M. &. G. 372; Frith *v.* Cortland, 2 H. &. M. 417.

So where bills of lading were issued in duplicate a pledgee of the second bill, knowing that the first had previously been pledged, gets no title. Shaw *v.* National Bank, 101 U. S. 564; Guilbert *v.* Guignon, L. R., 8 Ch. 16.

So if a second bill is fraudulently issued on the same goods, the pledgee of the second bill, knowing of the first or the facts, gets no title. Stevens *v.* Boston etc. R. Co., 8 Gray (Mass.) 262.

6. Bank of Rochester *v.* Jones, 4 N. Y. 497; Marine Bank *v.* Fiske, 71 N. Y. 353; Bank of Commerce *v.* Bissell, 72 N. Y. 615; Dows *v.* Perrin, 16 N. Y.

f. PLEDGE BY CONSIGNOR—(1) *In General.*—It is a common occurrence for the consignor of goods consigned to a consignee, to have the bill of lading made to his own order, and on delivering the draft drawn on the consignee for the price of the goods for discount to a bank to deliver also the bill of lading as security for the acceptance of the draft.[1] By so doing the title to the goods is presumed not to pass to the consignee,[2] even if the consignee's name had been written in the bill of lading.[3]

Unless it is expressly stipulated that the bill of lading is given to the pledgee as security for the collection of the draft,[4] it is presumed that the security is for the acceptance of it only.[5] Therefore, if the draft is accepted by the consignee, in the absence of direction to the contrary by the consignor, in which case the direction must be followed,[6] the pledgee may surrender the bill of lading to the consignee.[7]

The consignee of goods has no title to them until he accepts

325; Farmers' Bank *v.* Logan, 74 N. Y. 568; Farmers' etc. Bank *v.* Hazeltine, 78 N. Y. 104; Mechanics' etc. Bank *v.* Farmers' etc. Nat. Bank, 60 N. Y. 40; First Nat. Bank *v.* Shaw, 61 N. Y. 283.

So the indorsement may be restricted. Farmers' Bank *v.* Atkinson, 74 N. Y. 587; Farmers' Bank *v.* Logan, 74 N. Y. 568.

1. Brent *v.* Miller, 81 Ala. 309.

2. Dows *v.* National Exch. Bank, 91 U. S. 618; The Thames, 14 Wall. (U. S.) 107; Alderman *v.* Eastern R. Co., 115 Mass. 233; Security Bank *v.* Suttgen, 29 Minn. 363; Mitchell *v.* Ede, 11 Ad. & E., N. S. 888; Jenkyns *v.* Brown, 14 Q. B. 496; People's Nat. Bank *v.* Stewart, 3 Pugs. &. Bur. (N. B.) 268; Mason *v.* Great West. R. Co., 31 U. C., Q. B. 73; Ogg *v.* Shuter, L. R., 10 C. P. 159.

3. Bank of Rochester *v.* Jones, 4 N. Y. 497; Taylor *v.* Turner, 87 Ill. 296; Michigan Cent. R. Co. *v.* Phillips, 60 Ill. 190; First Nat. Bank *v.* Crocker, 111 Mass. 163; Pratt *v.* Parkman, 24 Pick. (Mass.) 42; Valle *v.* Cerre, 36 Mo. 575; Jenkyns *v.* Brown, 14 Q. B. 496.

4. Schuchardt *v.* Hall, 36 Md. 590; People's Nat. Bank *v.* Stewart, 3 Pugs. & Bur. (N. B.) 268.

5. Dows *v.* National Exch. Bank, 91 U. S. 618.

6. Dows *v.* National Exch. Bank, 91 U. S. 618; Stollenwerck *v.* Thatcher, 115 Mass. 224; Pease *v.* Gloahee, L. R., 1 P. C. 219; Gurney *v.* Behrend, 3 El. & Bl. 622.

Parol evidence is admissible to show an agreement between the consignor and pledgee that the bill of lading should not be delivered to the consignee until the payment of the draft. Security Bank *v.* Luttgen, 29 Minn. 363.

7. National Bank *v.* Merchants' etc. Bank, 91 U. S. 92; Cayuga Co. Nat. Bank *v.* Daniels, 47 N. Y. 631; Marine Bank *v.* Wright, 48 N. Y. 1; Mears *v.* Naples, 4 Houst. (Del.) 62; Lanfear *v.* Blossman, 1 La. Ann. 148; Security Bank *v.* Luttgen, 29 Minn. 363; Schuchardt *v.* Hall, 36 Md. 590; Wis. M. & F. Ins. Co. *v.* Bank of B. N. A., 21 U. C., Q. B. 284; Clark *v.* Bank of Mont., 13 Grant's Ch. (Can.) 211; Goodenough *v.* City Bank, 10 U. C. C. P. 51.

In National Bank *v.* Merchants' Nat. Bank, 91 U. S. 92, the court by Strong, J., said: "We feel justified in saying that, in our opinion, no respectable case can be found in which it has been decided that when a time draft has been drawn against a consignment to order, and has been forwarded to an agent for collection with the bill of lading attached, without any further instructions, the agent is not justified in delivering over the bill of lading on the acceptance of the draft."

There is in *England* a custom to hold the bill of lading until payment of the draft, but it is not encouraged. Coventry *v.* Gladstone, L. R., 4 Eq. 493; Gurney *v.* Behrend, 3 El. & Bl. 622.

the draft drawn on him for their price,[1] even though the bill of lading be in his possession.[2]

(2) *Title of Pledgee When Consignor is Pledgor.*—Any pledgee to whom the bill of lading is given as security by the consignor, gets the legal title to the goods represented thereby, and the right to possession of them, if such is the intention of the parties;[3] but it is presumed that a pledgee to whom the bill of lading of goods delivered to the carrier has been given by the consignor on the discount of a draft drawn on the consignee, as security for the acceptance or payment of the draft, has the right to the full legal title to the goods just as he would were the goods themselves actually delivered to him.[4]

1. Allen *v.* William, 12 Pick. (Mass.) 297.

2. Shepherd *v.* Harrison, L. R., 5 H. L. 116; Bancs. etc. Bank, 8 Ch. D. 160.

3. Bank of Rochester *v.* Jones, 4 N. Y. 497; Becker *v.* Hallgarten, 86 N. Y. 167; City Bank *v.* Rome etc. R. Co., 44 N. Y. 136; Holmes *v.* German etc. Bank, 87 Pa. St. 525; Holmes *v.* Bailey, 92 Pa. St. 57; *contra*, Bissell *v.* Steel, 67 Pa. St. 443; Allen *v.* Williams, 12 Pick. (Mass.) 29; Peters *v.* Elliott, 78 Ill. 321.

Michigan Cent. R. Co. *v.* Phillips, 60 Ill. 190; Petitt *v.* First Nat. Bank, 4 Bush (Ky.) 334; St. Louis Nat. Bank *v.* Ross, 9 Mo. App. 399; Shilling *v.* Bollman, 6 Mo. App. 76; Davenport Nat. Bank *v.* Homeyer, 45 Mo. 145; Dodge *v.* Meyer (Cal.), 10 Pac. C. L. J. 169; Gledden *v.* Lucas, 7 Cal. 26.

The intention may be implied from the surrounding circumstances. Merchants' Bank *v.* Union R. etc. Co., 69 N. Y. 373.

4. Dows *v.* National Exch. Bank, 91 U. S. 618; Merchants Bank *v.* Union R. etc. Co., 69 N. Y. 373; Cayuga Co. Nat. Bank *v.* Daniels, 47 N. Y. 631; Hieskell *v.* Farmers' etc. Bank, 89 Pa. St. 155; Security Bank *v.* Luttgen, 29 Minn. 363; Hathaway *v.* Haynes, 124 Mass. 311; Forbes *v.* Boston etc. R. Co., 133 Mass. 154.

Even though the goods be shipped in a vessel of the consignee, the assignee of the bill of lading has his special property in the goods. Ellershaw *v.* Magniac, 6 Exch. 570; Schotsman *v.* R. Co., L. R., 2 Ch. App. 336; Turner *v.* Liverpool Docks, 6 Exch. 543.

The title of the pledgee is not affected by an agreement between the consignor and consignee that the proceeds of the goods shall be applied to an old debt owed by the consignor to the consignee. Taylor *v.* Turner, 87 Ill. 296.

Where the consignor himself pledged the bill of lading, his right of stoppage *in transitu* still exists against third persons, though it must be exercised subject to the right of the pledgee.

Kemp *v.* Falk, L. R., 7 App. Cas. 573; Spaulding *v.* Reeding, 6 Beav. 376; *In re* Westzenthus, 5 B. & Ad. 817.

The pledgee who, before the draft was accepted, delivered the goods to the consignee for safekeeping by giving him the bill of lading indorsed "in trust for this purpose, and is not to be diverted to any other use until the draft is paid," does not lose his title thereby.

Farmers' etc. Bank *v.* Logan, 74 N. Y. 568; Farmers' etc. Bank *v.* Hazeltine, 78 N. Y. 104; Farmers' etc. Bank *v.* Atkinson, 74 N. Y. 587.

Where creditors of the consignor levied on the goods while in transit it was held that the pledgee of the bill of lading to secure the acceptance of a draft drawn on the consignee had the better title. Skilling *v.* Bollman, 6 Mo. App. 76; Petitt *v.* First Nat. Bank, 4 Bush (Ky.) 334.

The consignee took possession of the goods from the carrier and sold them for an old debt due him from the consignor, knowing that the bill of lading had been given to a bank to secure the acceptance of a discounted draft on him. It was held that he had no right to make such appropriation. Holmes *v.* German etc. Bank, 87 Pa. St. 525; Holmes *v.* Bailey, 92 Pa. St. 57; Allen *v.* Williams, 12 Pick. (Mass.) 297.

Where the pledgee of the bill of lading holding them from the consignor as security for the acceptance of drafts by the consignee, on the acceptance by the latter, delivered at his request the goods to a broker to sell who misappropri-

On the non-acceptance of the draft by the consignee, the consignor has only the right to the surplus money remaining after payment of the draft from the proceeds of the sale of the goods.[1] When the draft is accepted by the consignee the bill of the pledgee is divested thereby[2] and passes to the consignee.[3]

g. REMEDY OF PLEDGEE FOR MISAPPROPRIATION OF GOODS. —The pledgee, having special property in and control of the goods, may, if they have been attached, recover them by an action of replevin,[4] or, against one who has taken the goods, may have damages in an action of trover.[5] If the goods have been taken and sold under legal procedure, he may come in and share the proceeds to the extent of his claim.[6]

4. Warehouse Receipts.—See WAREHOUSE RECEIPTS.

IX. PLEDGE OF NON-NEGOTIABLE SECURITIES.—1. In General.—All kinds of non-negotiable choses in action, except those growing out of transactions intensely personal to the pledgor, can be pledged,[7] but the pledgee, unless the pledgor or owner, by his

ated the proceeds, the pledgee was allowed to recover on the bills of exchange, without being liable for the misappropriation, the broker being considered a trustee for the consignee. Magoun *v.* Sinclair, 66 N. Y. 30.

1. National Bank *v.* Merchants' Bank, 91 U S. 92; Dows *v.* National Exch. Bank, 91 U. S. 618; Brent *v.* Miller, 81 Ala. 309; First Nat. Bank *v.* Bayley, 115 Mass. 228; DeWolf *v.* Gardner, 12 Cush. (Mass.) 19; Lanfear *v.* Blossman, 1 La. Ann. 153.

2. Cayuga Co. Nat. Bank *v.* Daniels, 47 N. Y. 631; Marine Bank *v.* Wright, 48 N. Y. 1; Allen *v.* Williams, 12 Pick. (Mass.) 297; First Nat. Bank *v.* Crocker, 111 Mass. 163; Pettit *v.* First Nat. Bank, 4 Bush (Ky.) 334.

If it is expressly provided that the bill of lading shall not be delivered to the consignee until payment of the draft, the pledgee's title is good until then. Hieskell *v.* Farmers' etc. Bank, 89 Pa. St. 154; Dodge *v.* Meyer, 10 Pac. C. L. J. 169; Jenkyns *v.* Brown, 14 Q. B. 496.

3. Flash *v.* Schwabacker, 32 La. Ann. 356.

4. Peters *v.* Elliott, 78 Ill. 321; Michigan Cent. R. Co. *v.* Phillips, 60 Ill. 190; Alderman *v.* Eastern R. Co., 115 Mass. 233; Stone *v.* Wabash etc. R. Co., 9 Ill. App. 48.

5. Dows *v.* Nat. Exch. Bank, 91 U. S. 618; Burke *v.* Savage, 13 Allen (Mass.) 408; Adams *v.* O'Connor, 100 Mass. 515; Tiedeman *v.* Knox, 53 Md. 612.

He recovers the full value and holds the surplus for the general owner. Adams *v.* O'Connor, 100 Mass. 515; Ullman *v.* Barnard, 7 Gray (Mass.) 554; Harris *v.* Birch, 9 M. & W. 591.

Where the consignee gets the goods and sells them and holds the proceeds for a previous indebtedness, the pledgee of the bill of lading should sue for money had and received. Taylor *v.* Turner, 87 Ill. 296.

When a connecting line, knowing nothing of the bill of lading, delivered the goods to the consignee, the pledgee of the bill of lading was allowed to sue it in conversion for damage. Alderman *v.* Eastern R. Co., 115 Mass. 233.

When a common carrier by water delivered the goods to the wrong person the pledgee of the bill of lading was allowed to libel the vessel. The Thems, 14 Wall. (U. S.) 98.

When a pledgee of the bill of lading asserts ownership of the goods against the consignor, he cannot afterwards change his ground and claim to be a pledgee. Cohen *v.* Haynes, 41 La. Ann. 545.

6. Hathaway *v.* Haynes, 124 Mass. 311.

7. A deposited with a bank, of which he was a customer, as collateral security for his current indebtedness, the note of a third person, secured by mortgage, and, after the note had matured, withdrew it and the mortgage for the purposes of foreclosure and collection, under an agreement to return the proceeds or to replace the note by securities of equal value. At the foreclosure

acts, omissions, or laches, has brought himself within the limits of estoppel, takes such unnegotiable choses in action subject to all the equities *in esse* at the time of the transfer[1] and to all defenses that might be urged against the original parties.[2]

Equities arising subsequent to the time of pledge do not affect the pledgee.[3]

2. Act of Pledge.—Choses in action may be transferred in pledge by mere delivery, except where the terms of the instrument made indorsement necessary, but a written assignment is always to be preferred.[4]

sale A became the purchaser, and, at the request of the bank, deposited with it his deed of the property. He had then paid all his indebtedness to the bank, and his dealings with it were temporarily suspended. Having afterwards become indebted to the bank, he became bankrupt, and the bank brought a bill against his assignee, claiming an equitable lien on the property; but there was no allegation therein of money loaned or debt created on the faith of the deposit of the deed. *Held*, that the deposit created no equitable lien in favor of the bank. Biebinger *v.* Continental Bank, 99 U. S. 143.

1. Cowdry *v.* Vandenbburgh, 101 U. S. 572; Wickham *v.* Moorehouse, 16 Fed. Rep. 324; Judson *v.* Corcoran, 17 How. (U. S.) 612; Ingraham *v.* Disborough, 47 N. Y. 421; Bush *v.* Lathrop, 22 N. Y. 535; Davis *v.* Bechstein, 69 N. Y. 442; Cutts *v.* Guild, 57 N. Y. 229; Chickering *v.* Fullerton, 90 Ill. 520; Irish *v.* Sharp, 89 Ill. 26; Baker *v.* Bishop Hill Colony, 45 Ill. 264; Storey *v.* Dutton; 46 Mich 539; Jasper Co. *v.* Tavis, 76 Mo. 13; Watson *v.* Mid-Wales R. Co., L. R., 2, C. P. 593; Parter *v.* Coleman, L. R, 19 Ch. D. 630.

These equities follow the chose however remotely it may be assigned. Cutts *v.* Guild. 57 N. Y. 229; Union College *v.* Wheeler, 61 N. Y. 114; Combes *v.* Chandler, 33 Ohio St. 178; Ord *v.* White, Beav. 357.

When a deed of land was given to secure a note, and the pledgee transferred the note. the pledgee has only a naked trust in the lands for the security of the note. Briggs *v.* Haunoweld, 35 Mich. 474.

2. Moore *v.* Metropolitan Nat. Bank, 55 N. Y. 41; Davis *v.* Bechstein, 69 N. Y. 442; Combes *v.* Chandler, 33 Ohio St. 178; People *v.* Johnson, 100 Ill. 537; Isett *v.* Lucas, 17 Iowa 507; Burtis *v.* Cook, 16 Iowa 194; Piper *v.* Piper, L. R., 1 Ch. D 90; Graham *v.* Johnson, L. R., 9 Eq. 36; *In re* Agra Bank, L. R., 2 Ch. 39.

Where the instrument evidencing the chose in action was fraudulently executed, that is a good defense for the maker against the pledgee, but that the maker of such instrument knowing what he was doing, was induced to make it by fraudulent representations is not a good defense against an innocent pledgee. George *v.* Tate, 102 U. S. 564; Hartshorn *v.* Day, 19 How. (U. S.) 211; Franchot *v.* Leach, 5 Cow. (N. Y.) 506; Osterhout *v.* Shoemaker, 3 Hill (N. Y.) 513; Belden *v.* Davies, 2 Hall (N. Y.) 433.

3. George *v.* Tate, 102 U. S. 564; Harter *v.* Doleman, L. R., 19 Ch. D. 639.

Equities between the original parties arising out of other transactions do not affect the pledgee's title. Clarke *v.* Roberts, 25 Hun (N. Y.) 86; Isett *v.* Lucas, 17 Iowa 507.

4. Stout *v.* Yaeger etc. Co., 13 Fed. Rep. 802; Williams *v.* Ingersoll, 89 N. Y. 518; Kingman *v.* Perkins, 105 Mass. 111; Thayer *v.* Daniels, 113 Mass. 126; Dix *v.* Cobb, 4 Mass. 508; Jones *v.* Witter, 13 Mass. 304; Norton *v.* Piscataqua Ins. Co., 111 Mass. 532.

To pledge profits of a contract for road building a written assignment is necessary. Dewey *v.* Bowman, 8 Cal. 151; Gay *v.* Moss, 34 Cal. 125.

Deposit Books.—The delivery of a deposit book without an indorsement or assignment, conveys an equitable title to the deposits that is preferred to subsequently attaching creditors. Taft *v.* Bowker, 132 Mass. 277; Kingman *v.* Perkins, 105 Mass. 111; Pierce *v.* Boston Sav. Bank, 129 Mass. 425; Boynton *v.* Payrow, 67 Me. 587.

The delivery of the deposit book to a third person to be given to a creditor

3. Equitable Assignment of Funds.—Such assignments of non-negotiable choses in action, when made in good faith, are upheld against subsequent assignees when, though a formal assignment is not made, it is shown that the pledgor has put it out of his power to collect the chose.[1] A mere promise to pay a debt out of a certain fund, where the debtor can at any time withdraw his promise and defeat the pledgee's recovery will not be upheld.[2]

as security is a good pledge. Boynton *v.* Payrow, 67 Me. 587.

A legal title to deposits was given by a written indorsement on the book as against a delivery of the book without indorsement. Weirick *v.* Mahoning Co. Bank, 16 Ohio St. 296; Combes *v.* Chandler, 33 Ohio St. 178.

Certificates of Deposit.—Certificates of deposit issued by banks are closely allied to negotiable paper in their nature, and pass best by indorsement and delivery. Pardee *v.* Fish, 60 N. Y. 265; Cassiday *v.* First Nat. Bank, 30 Minn. 86; International Bank *v.* German Bank, 71 Mo. 883; Klauber *v.* Biggerstaff, 47 Wis. 551.

Where the certificate is made payable to the depositor "or his order, upon the return of this certificate properly indorsed," the pledgee comes within the statutory rule that allows him to sue in his own name thereon. Beal *v.* Warren, 2 Gray (Mass.) 447; Pease *v.* Rush, 2 Minn. 107; Cassiday *v.* First Nat. Bank, 30 Minn. 86.

Judgments.—To pledge a judgment the evidence thereof should be delivered to the pledgee, who may prosecute the same but in the assignor's name. Heligsberg's Succession, 1 La. Ann. 340.

Where a sum due on a judgment was assigned as collateral, the pledgee agreeing not to collect, was held to be on its face a pledge. Mulford *v.* Miller, 3 Abb. App. Dec. (N. Y.) 330.

Land Certificates.—Land certificates in *Wisconsin* issued by the State are not a proper subject of pledge. Smith *v.* Mariner, 5 Wis. 551; Whitney *v.* State Bank, 7 Wis. 620. But when they are given as security are held as an equitable mortgage. Mowry *v.* Wood, 12 Wis. 413.

In *Texas* a land certificate for land not located is personal property, and may be pledged. Stone *v.* Brown, 54 Tex. 330.

In *Wisconsin*, the rules of estoppel do not protect a *bona fide* holder of a land certificate. Whitney *v.* State Bank, 7 Wis. 520; while in *Texas* they do. Stone *v.* Brown, 54 Tex. 330.

1. Beal *v.* Warren, 2 Gray (Mass.) 447; Risley *v.* Phœnix Bank, 83 N. Y. 318; Morton *v.* Naylor, 1 Hill (N. Y.) 583; Rankin *v.* Alford, L. R., 5 Ch. D. 786; *In re* Mann, L. R., 5 Ch. D. 367. See cases in succeeding notes.

So the pledgor can equitably assign the surplus of a chose already pledged by an equitable assignment. Meyers *v.* United Guar. Co., 7 De G. M. & G. 112.

When the pledgor promised "I hereby undertake that I will, when and as received, pay over to you all dividends coming to me in respect of my proof upon the estate of A," the pledgee for value got a good equitable title to the dividends. *In re* Irving, L. R., 7 Ch. D. 419.

A, the holder of a bond for a conveyance of land, assigned the same to B, as collateral security for money advanced, and afterward B permitted the same bond to be assigned to C as security for debts due from A, and to be placed in C's hands. While there, the assignment to B was stricken out, without his consent, and a further assignment made to C, D, and E, as security for debts due them from A. A paid the purchase-money of the land, and the same was conveyed to C, D, and E, and the bond canceled. After the first assignment to B, A continued in possession of the land, and offered to sell it, with the knowledge and consent of B. Upon a bill in equity filed by B, to set aside the conveyance, and vest the title in himself, it was held, that the assignment to B was an equitable security, upon which he was entitled to be paid the money advanced, but not to have the land conveyed to him, and that A, or his representatives must be made parties to the bill. St. John *v.* Freeman, 1 Carter (Ind.) 84.

2. Trist *v.* Child, 21 Wall. (U. S.) 441; Christmas *v.* Russell, 14 Wall. (U. S.) 69; Rogers *v.* Hosack, 18 Wend. (N. Y.) 319; Williams *v.* Inger-

Equitable assignments of parts of choses in action and funds are allowed and equity, when all the parties are before it, will in one action settle the rights of all concerned.[1] A court of law will not interfere, owing to the multiplicity of actions that would follow.[2]

4. Title of Pledgee Under Estoppel—*a.* IN GENERAL.—Where the person liable on a non-negotiable chose in action has declared on the face of the instrument or by indorsement that he has no defenses[3] or has signed a separate instrument, usually under seal, "that he has no defenses in law or in equity" to the chose, he is forever after estopped from setting up such defense against an action by a *bona fide* pledgee of such chose,[4] or by those who in good faith and for value claim through him.[5]

So where the owner of a non-negotiable chose in action voluntarily intrusts the *indicia* of title, by delivery or indorsement if required, to another, a *bona fide* pledgee for value who took the chose from the pledgor trusting to his apparent ownership, gets a good title against the original owner, who, by his own act, is estopped from setting up his title.[6]

soll, 89 N. Y. 518; Hopkins *v.* Beebe, 26 Pa. St. 85; Hull *v.* Jackson, 20 Pick. (Mass.) 197; Christmas *v.* Griswold, 8 Ohio St. 558; Field *v.* Megaw, L. R., 4 C. P. 660; Malcolm *v.* Scott, 3 Hare 46.

1. Dowell *v.* Cardwell, 4 Sawy. (U. S.) 217; Bradley *v.* Root, 5 Paige (N. Y.) 632; Fairbanks *v.* Sargent, 117 N. Y. 320; National Exch. Bank *v.* McLoon, 73 Me. 498; Philadelphia's Appeal, 86 Pa. St. 76; Superintendent etc. of Public Schools *v.* Heath, 15 N. J. Eq. 22; Claflin *v.* Kimball, 52 Vt. 6; Whitney *v.* Cowan, 55 Miss. 626; Etheridge *v.* Vernoy, 74 N. Car. 800; Daniels *v.* Menihard, 53 Ga. 359; Wellsburg Bank *v.* Kimberlands, 16 W. Va. 555; Wood *v.* Wallace, 24 Ind. 226; Lapping *v.* Duffy, 47 Ind. 51; Christie *v.* Sawyer, 44 N.H. 298; Thompson *v.* Simpson, L. R., 5 Ch. 659; *Ex parte* South, 3 Swanst. 392; *Ex parte* Hall, 10 L. R., 5 Ch. D. 786; Addison *v.* Cox, 8 L. R., 5 Ch. 659.

2. Welch *v.* Mandeville, 1 Wheat. (U. S.) 233; Tripp *v.* Brownell, 12 Cush. (Mass.) 376; Palmer *v.* Merrill, 6 Cush. (Mass.) 282; Bullard *v.* Randall, 1 Gray (Mass.) 605; Gibson *v.* Cooke, 20 Pick. (Mass.) 15; Tierman *v.* Jackson, 5 Vt. 580; Stanbery *v.* Smythe, 13 Ohio St. 495; Creighton *v.* Hyde Park, 6 Ill. App. 273; Robbins *v.* Bacon, 3 Me. 346.

The assignment should be drawn against a particular fund and not generally against the debtor. National Exch. Bank *v.* McLoon, 73 Me. 498.

But not when the municipality is the debtor. Mandeville *v.* Welch, 5 Wheat. (U. S.) 277; Jermyn *v.* Moffitt, 75 Pa. St. 399.

Though the fund is only potentially in existence and its amount undefined, a part of it may be equitably assigned. Wellsburg Bank *v.* Kimberlands, 16 W. Va. 555.

3. Payne *v.* Burnham, 62 N. Y. 69; Smyth *v.* Munroe, 84 N. Y. 354.

4. Weyh *v.* Boylan, 85 N. Y. 394; Ryall *v.* Rowles, W. & T. L. Cas., L. 2, p. 2, 1673.

5. Ashton's Appeal, 73 Pa. St. 153.

6. Cowdrey *v.* Vanderburgh, 101 U. S. 572; Moore *v.* Metropolitan Nat. Bank, 55 N. Y. 41; NcNeil *v.* Tenth Nat. Bank, 46 N. Y. 325; Davis *v.* Bechstein, 69 N. Y. 442; Combes *v.* Chandler, 33 Ohio St. 178; Horn *v.* Cole, 51 N. H. 287; Merchants' Bank *v.* Phœnix etc. Co., L. R., 5 Ch. D. 217; Goodwin *v.* Robarts, L. R., 10 Ex. 76; Herrick *v.* Attwood, 25 Beav. 205; Briggs *v.* Jones, L. R., 10 Eq. 92; Vickers *v.* Hertz, L. R., 2 Sc. App. 113; The Marie Joseph, L. R., 1 Pr. C. 219.

Where the owner of a letter of credit indorses it in blank and hands it to another, who pledges it to a *bona fide* holder for value, the latter gets a good title against the owner. Weirick *v.* Mahoning Co. Bank, 16 Ohio St. 296.

If the pledgee, either by the terms of the instrument or in any other way, has notice of outstanding equities, he is bound by them.[1]

The presumption is that the pledgee is *bona fide*[2] and paid a valuable consideration for the pledge.[3]

b. NOTICE TO DEBTOR.—It is not necessary for the pledgee of a chose in action to notify the debtor of the pledge to protect the pledgee from the debtor's creditors of subsequent assignees of the same collateral,[4] but notice should be given to the debtor to keep him from binding the pledgee by making payments to the pledgor.[5]

So under the same circumstances where the owner indorsed in blank a non-negotiable deposit certificate. International Bank *v.* German Bank, 71 Mo. 183.

If a *cestui que trust* clothes the trustee with the *indicia* of title, he is estopped from denying the title of the *bona fide* pledgee for value. Dillaye *v.* Commercial Bank, 51 N. Y. 345.

The owner cannot set up his own infirmity of title against the pledgee. Clarke *v.* Roberts, 25 Hun (N. Y.) 86.

Though the pledgor had induced the owner to give him the *indicia* of title, as long as the owner did so voluntarily the effect is the same. Kingsford *v.* Merry, 11 Ex. 577.

The presumption of title is in favor of the pledgee. Baldwin *v.* Ely, 9 How. (U. S.) 580.

Where the non-negotiable chose in action was a mere statement of an account of work done, made out by an officer of the city, with no promises to pay, its transfer in pledge gives no title under estoppel to the pledgee. But if the pledgor indorsed it in blank and the pledgee wrote an absolute assignment over it and then transferred it for value to an innocent holder, the latter got a good title against the true owner. Cowdrey *v.* Vanderburgh, 101 U. S. 572.

1. Swan *v.* Produce Bank, 24 Hun (N. Y.) 277; Dewey *v.* Bowman, 8 Cal. 145; Brewster *v.* Galloway, 4 Lea (Tenn.) 558; Heritage *v.* Hedges, 72 Ind. 247.

Where an agent pledged a judgment for his own debt, signing the principal note "as agent and attorney," the pledgee was put upon his guard and chargeable with knowledge of what he could have found out by inquiry. Wickham *v.* Morehouse, 16 Fed. Rep. 324.

2. Stone *v.* Brown, 54 Tex. 330.

3. Belden *v.* Meeker, 47 N. Y. 311; Tallman *v.* Hoey, 89 N. Y. 537.

4. U. S. *v.* Vaughan, 3 Binn. (Pa.) 394; Greentree *v.* Rosenstock, 61 N. Y. 583; Muir *v.* Schenck, 3 Hill (N. Y.) 228; Williams *v.* Ingersoll, 89 N. Y. 518; Freund *v.* Importers' etc. Bank, 76 N. Y. 352; Kingman *v.* Perkins, 105 Mass. 111; Thayer *v.* Daniels, 113 Mass. 129; Richards *v.* Smith, 9 Gray (Mass.) 315; Dix *v.* Cobb, 4 Mass. 508; Martin *v.* Potter, 11 Gray (Mass.) 37; Stevens *v.* Stevens, 1 Ashm. (Pa.) 190.

The pledgee is protected against creditors although the assignment is by bare delivery only. Norton *v.* Piscataqua F. & M. Ins. Co., 111 Mass. 532; Thayer *v.* Daniels, 113 Mass. 129; Taft *v.* Bowker, 132 Mass. 277.

The pledgee of the chose who receives the documents of title without notifying the debtor, is preferred to a subsequent innocent pledgee of the same chose. Muir *v.* Schenck, 3 Hill (N. Y.) 228.

But where the pledgee did not receive the documents of title, although the debtor was notified, the subsequent pledgee who did get the documents and assignment was preferred. Spencer *v.* Clarke, L. R., 9 Ch. D. 137.

In *England*, the rule in the text is now followed. Robinson *v.* Nesbitt, L. R., 3 C. P. 264; Pickering *v.* Ilfrasombe R. Co., L. R., 3 C. P. 235, Kinderley *v.* Jervis, 23 Beav. 1; Beavan *v.* Oxford, 6 De G. M. & G. 492; though formerly of two assignees of the same chose, that one was protected who first notified the debtor. Foster *v.* Blackstone, 1 M. & K. 297; Watts *v.* Porter, 3 E. & B. 743; Loveridge *v.* Cooper, 3 Russ. 60; Deasle *v.* Hall, 3 Russ. 1; Meux *v.* Bell, 1 Hare 73; Mangles *v.* Dixon, McG. Dr. 437.

5. Williams *v.* Ingersoll, 89 N. Y. 518.

Where there has been assigned to the pledgee a potential interest in funds in the hands of a debtor, trustee or third person, which consignment is evidenced by an independent instrument, the pledgee should immediately notify such debtor, trustee or third person of the assignment; for if he does not, a subsequent assignee in good faith of the same interest who does not notify the holder of the fund of his assignment will get a better title to the fund than the first pledgee.[1]

If after being notified of the pledge of the chose, the debtor or a trustee of equitable funds makes any compromise, arrangement or settlement with the assignor or others without the consent of the pledgee, all such transactions are void and form no defense to an action by the pledgee.[2]

5. Rights, Liabilities, and Remedies of Pledgee[3]—*a.* DUTY TO COLLECT.—It is the duty of the pledgee of non-negotiable choses in action to use reasonable care and diligence in their collection.[4] Where it is actually proved that the security is lost by the failure of the pledgee to use due diligence in collection, he will be liable for its face value [5]

b. POWER TO SELL.—The pledgee has no implied power to sell the security before default, but after default he may, on demanding payment, and giving notice of the time and place of sale.[6] If, the pledgee has a power of sale he may or may not, as he pleases

Between an assignee of a chose in action and the debtor, the rights of the parties are determined by the time the debtor had notice, not by the time of the assignment. Miller *v.* Kreiter, 76 Pa. St. 78.

1. Judson *v.* Corcoran, 17 How. (U. S.) 612; Moore *v.* Holcombe, 3 Leigh (Va.) 597; Murray *v.* Lylburn, 2 Johns. Ch. (N. Y.) 442.

Where one equitable title is recorded, a subsequent assignee of the same equitable title is chargeable with notice of the record. Tarbell *v.* West, 86 N. Y. 280; Bentley *v.* Bates, 4 Y. & C. 190.

2. Field *v.* Mayor etc. of New York, 7 N. Y. 179; Littlefield *v.* Story, 3 Johns. (N. Y.) 426; Morris *v.* Cheney, 51 Ill. 451; Carr *v.* Waugh, 28 Ill. 418; Andrews *v.* Becker, 1 Johns. Cas. (N. Y.) 411; Creighton *v.* Hyde Park, 6 Ill. App. 272.

3. The rights and remedies of the pledgee of non-negotiable choses in action are in general those of a pledgee of corporeal property, and here only those peculiar to pledgees of this class of securities will be touched on.

4. Whittaker *v.* Charleston Gas Co., 16 W. Va. 717.

The pledgee of a case should collect the rents. Dewey *v.* Bowman, 8 Cal. 145.

The pledgee of a part interest in a note need not collect it. Smouse *v.* Bail, 1 Grant's Cas. (Pa.) 397.

Where a judgment was assigned as collateral with a power of sale on default, it was held that the contract of pledge being written, and nothing said about collection, the pledgee could not be compelled to levy until his debt was due, even though the judgment debtor failed in the meantime. The pledgor should have enforced the judgment. Bast *v.* First Nat. Bank, 101 U. S. 93.

5. Burrows *v.* Bangs, 34 Mich. 304; Ward *v.* Morgan, 5 Sneed (Tenn.) 79; Reeves *v.* Plough, 41 Ind. 204; Wellsburg Bank *v.* Kimberlands, 16 W. Va. 555; Williams *v.* Price, 1 Sim. & S. 581; Hanna *v.* Holton, 78 Pa. St. 334; Hoffman *v.* Johnson, 1 Bland (Md.) 103.

In the absence of fraud or gross negligence the loss of the chose by failure of the pledgee to enforce payment, does not make the pledgee liable. Runals *v.* Harding, 83 Ill. 75.

6. Robinson *v.* Hurley, 11 Iowa 410; Dewey *v.* Bowman, 8 Cal. 145.

take advantage of it.[1] Where the pledgee wrongfully sells the chose, the pledgor can only regain it by tendering his debt.[2]

c. REMEDY IN EQUITY.—A court of equity will not assist a pledgee of a non-negotiable chose in action in enforcing his security, unless the remedy at law is inadequate.[3]

At common law the pledgee of such a chose was compelled on enforcing it in law to sue under the assignor's name, but now, generally by code or statute, he is allowed to sue in his own name.[4] The pledgee, though he has security may sue on the debt secured.[5]

d. AMOUNT OF RECOVERY.—The pledgee of non-negotiable choses in action is entitled to recover the full face value of the security holding the surplus for the pledgor.[6] His actual recovery is limited to the amount of his debt with interest and proper charges.[7]

1. Robinson *v.* Hurley, 11 Iowa 410.

2. Talty *v.* Freedman's Sav. etc. Co., 93 U. S. 321; Donald *v.* Suckling, L. R., 1 Q. B. 585; Johnson *v.* Stear, 15 C. B., N. S. 330; Halliday *v.* Holgate, L. R., 3 Eq. 299.

3. Thayer *v.* Daniels, 113 Mass. 129. Equity will decree a foreclosure and sale where necessary. Robinson *v.* Hurley, 11 Iowa 410.

The fact that the chose is an equitable interest will not insure the interference of a court of equity. New York Guaranty etc. Co. *v.* Memphis Water Co., 107 U. S. 205.

Where there is no right to have a sale of the security, equity will not order one. Whitteker *v.* Charleston Gas Co., 16 W. Va. 717.

Where an insurance policy was assigned to secure a debt three times its face value and pledgor dying, no administrators of his estate were appointed, and on this account the insurance company refused to pay over the money to the pledgee, equity compelled it to do so. Curtius *v.* Caledonia Ins. Co., L. R., 19 Ch. D. 534; Crossley *v.* Glasgow Ins. Co., L. R., 4 Ch. D. 421.

Where the amount of the mortgage debt was greater than the policy money, equity would not interfere. Webster *v.* British Empire Ins. Co., L. R., 15 Ch. D. 169.

Where the pledgee desires to enforce a judgment obtained on a debt, assigned as security, equity will not compel him to resort first to other securities not shown to be more valuable than the balance of the debt secured over the amount of the judgment. Batesville Inst. *v.* Kauffman, 18 Wall. (U. S.) 151.

A deposit of deeds as collateral security for a debt does not create such a lien on the land as can be foreclosed by law. A bill in equity will lie to compel the contract and subject the land to sale, to apply the proceeds to payment of the debt. English *v.* McElroy, 62 Ga. 413.

4. Welch *v.* Mandeville, 1 Wheat. (U. S.) 236; Whitteker *v.* Charleston Gas Co., 16 W. Va. 717; Brice *v.* Bannister, L. R., 3 Q. B. D. 569; Brown *v.* Bateman, L. R., 6 Q. B. D. 272; Field *v.* Megaw, L. R., 4 Q. B. D. 610.

Where, by assignment, the legal title vests in the pledgee, he can sue in his own name. Creighton *v.* Hyde Park, 6 Ill. App. 274; People *v.* Johnson, 100 Ill. 537.

The assignor of a non-negotiable chose in action surreptitiously having a suit brought in his name dismissed, and the assignee suing again on the same chose, it was held that the first suit was not a bar to the second. Welch *v.* Mandeville, 1 Wheat. (U. S.) 236.

5. Reeves *v.* Plough, 41 Ind. 204; Burrows *v.* Bangs, 34 Mich. 304.

6. Where the security is a life insurance policy in the name of the wife and on the pledgor's death the pledgee collects the face value, the widow of the pledgor is entitled to the surplus over the debt secured. Grenville *v.* Crawford, 13 Ga. 355; King *v.* Van Vleck, 40 Hun (N. Y.) 68.

7. Baldwin *v.* Ely, 9 How. (U. S.) 580; International Bank *v.* German Bank, 71 Mo. 183; Orr *v.* Churchill, 1 H. Bl. 232.

Where the pledgor became insolvent,

e. DUTY TO RETURN COLLATERAL.—On payment or tender[1] of the debt secured the pledgor of a non-negotiable chose in action is entitled to receive back the security, or in lieu thereof the sums collected thereon.[2] There is no presumption that the pledgee took the security in payment instead of as security.[3]

6. Note and Mortgage—*a.* IN GENERAL.—A negotiable note and mortgage may be pledged, and, in that case, the note has all the characteristics of ordinary commercial paper, the pledgee having the mortgage as additional security.[4]

The pledgee of a note and mortgage is as to the note a *bona fide* indorsee for value in the usual course of business, and his position in regard to the mortgage is determined by the rules

the pledgee was allowed to put in a claim for the unpaid portion of his debt.

In re Kit Hill Tunnel Co., L. R., 16 Ch. D. 590. In another case he was allowed to prove his costs in litigation also. *Ex parte* Carr, L. R., 11 Ch. D. 62.

Where a fund was deposited as collateral for the performance of certain contracts, on the breach the pledge was allowed to receive from the fund enough to pay the balance of his debt not liquidated by other securities. Kidd *v.* McCormick, 83 N. Y. 391.

Where a lease was assigned as collateral with the privilege of renewal, the pledgee was allowed to collect the rents, which had been subsequently pledged to another, until his debt was paid. Storey *v.* Dutton, 46 Mich. 539.

Where a policy of insurance was payable to "assigns" the pledgee was required to pay over to the specialty creditors, the surplus recovered by him. Talbot *v.* Frere, L. R., 9 Ch. D. 568; *Ex parte* Bank, L. R., 14 Eq. 507; *In re* Haselpot's Estate, L. R., 13 Eq. 327.

1. Haskins *v.* Kelly, 1 Robt. (N. Y.) 160.

2. White *v.* British Empire Ins. Co., L. R., 7 Eq. 374.

Where an insurance policy was given as security for a bond and mortgage the pledgor was entitled to receive back the policy until the bond is paid, though the mortgage may have been released. Hallis *v.* Ins. Co., 12 Phila. (Pa.) 331.

3. West *v.* Carolina Ins. Co., 31 Ark. 476; Scott *v.* Lifford, Campb. 246.

Where real estate was conveyed as collateral security for the payment of a judgment, it was not a satisfaction. DeClerq *v.* Jackson, 103 Ill. 658.

Where by agreement of the parties, the pledgee in satisfaction of his debt, kept an insurance policy, the pledgor had had no claim for subsequently returned premiums. Merrifield *v.* Baker, 11 Allen (Mass.) 43.

4. Swift *v.* Smith, 102 U. S. 442; Sawyer *v.* Prickett, 19 Wall. (U. S.) 147; Union Nat. Bank *v.* Matthews, 98 U. S. 621; Smith *v.* Burgess, 133 Mass. 511; Stevens *v.* Dedham Sav. Inst., 129 Mass. 547; Foley *v.* Rose, 123 Mass. 557; Strong *v.* Jackson, 123 Mass. 60; Blunt *v.* Morris, 123 Mass. 55; Morris *v.* Bacon, 123 Mass. 58; International Bank *v.* Jenkins, 104 Ill. 143; Zimpleman *v.* Veeder, 98 Ill. 613; Tooke *v.* Newman, 75 Ill. 215; Miller *v.* Larned, 103 Ill. 562; Lowenthal *v.* McCormick, 101 Ill. 143; Worcester Nat. Bank *v.* Cheeney, 87 Ill. 602; Brown *v.* Tyler, 8 Gray (Mass.) 135; Montague *v.* Boston etc. R. Co., 124 Mass. 242; Fletcher *v.* Dickinson, 7 Allen (Mass.) 23; Briggs *v.* Rice, 130 Mass. 50; Wright *v.* Ross, 36 Cal. 414; Bell *v.* Simpson, 75 Mo. 485; Morris *v.* White, 28 La. Ann. 855; Richardson *v.* Mann, 30 La. Ann. 1060; Logan *v.* Smith, 62 Mo. 455; Clasey *v.* Sigg, 51 Iowa 371; Preston *v.* Case, 42 Iowa 549; McCrum *v.* Cosby, 11 Kan. 464; Lewis *v.* Kirk, 28 Kan. 497; Wells *v.* Wells, 53 Vt. 1; George *v.* Woodward, 40 Vt. 672; Whitin *v.* Paul, 13 R. I. 40; Potts *v.* Blackwell, 4 Jones' Eq. (N. Car.) 58; Walker *v.* Kee, 14 S. Car. 142; Gibson *v.* Milne, 1 Nev. 526; Levy *v.* Ford, 41 La. Ann. 873.

After the note and mortgage has once been pledged and redeemed it may be reissued for the same purpose. Levy *v.* Ford, 41 La. Ann. 873.

A debtor may execute and deliver his own note and mortgage in pledge to secure a debt but to make it a good pledge there must be a debt separate from that which is the consideration of

governing the negotiability of a bond when transferred with a negotiable note to a purchaser for value.[1]

The broad rule of the Federal courts, followed by the courts of some States, is that the assignee of a note and mortgage takes the mortgage as he takes the note—free from the objections to which it was liable in the hands of the mortgagee.[2] This has been specifically held in regard to a *bona fide* pledgee for value of the note and mortgage.[3]

The restricted rule, as followed in *Illinois* and some other States, makes the position of a *bona fide* pledgee for value depend on what remedy he follows on default. If he tries to enforce the note he is protected from all prior equities, but if he seeks to recover on the mortgage he does so subject to equities.[4] In all courts, if, for any reason, the pledgee is not a *bona fide* holder of the note, so letting in the equities, the mortgage is held in the same way.[5] A negotiable note and mortgage may be pledged without any written assignment, although properly a written assignment should be made.[6]

the note and mortgage. Harding *v.* Commercial Loan Co., 84 Ill. 251.

But see Atlantic F. & M. Ins. Co. *v.* Boies, 6 Duer (N. Y.) 583.

1. Michigan Bank *v.* Eldred, 9 Wall. (U. S.) 544; Morris *v.* Bacon, 123 Mass. 58; Chicopee Bank *v.* Chapin, 8 Met. (Mass.) 40; Palmer *v.* Yates, 3 Sandf. (N. Y.) 137; Blanchard *v.* Stevens, 3 Cush. (Mass.) 162; Stoddard *v.* Kimball, 6 Cush. (Mass.) 469; Atkinson *v.* Brooks, 26 Vt. 569.

2. See Colebrooke on Collateral Securities, §§ 161-174 and cases cited; Carpenter *v.* Logan, 16 Wall. (U. S.) 271; Preston *v.* Case, 42 Iowa 549; Webb *v.* Haselton, 4 Neb. 308; Gabbert *v.* Schwartz, 69 Ind. 450; Murray *v.* Jones, 50 Ga. 109; Paige *v.* Chapman, 58 N. H. 334; Dutton *v.* Ives, 5 Mich. 515; Judge *v.* Vogel, 38 Mich. 568; Hurt *v.* Wilson, 38 Cal. 263; Ord *v.* McKee, 5 Cal. 516; Duncan *v.* Louisville, 14 Bush (Ky.) 385; Lewis *v.* Kirk, 28 Kan. 497; McCrum *v.* Cosby, 11 Kan. 464; Logan *v.* Smith, 62 Mo. 455; Goodfellow *v.* Stillwell, 73 Mo. 17; Potts *v.* Blackwell, 4 Jones' Eq. (N. Car.) 58; Crane *v.* March, 4 Pick. (Mass.) 131; Taylor *v.* Page, 6 Allen (Mass.) 86; Morris *v.* Bacon, 123 Mass. 58; Walker *v.* Kee, 14 S. Car. 142; Croft *v.* Bunster, 9 Wis. 503; Cornell *v* Hichens, 11 Wis. 368; Pierce *v.* Faunce, 47 Me. 507; Palmer *v.* Yates, 3 Sandf. (N. Y.) 137; Paige *v.* Chapman, 58 N. H. 333; Tucker *v.* New Hampshire Nat. Bank, 58 N. H. 83.

3. Swift *v.* Smith, 102 U. S. 442; Sawyer *v.* Prickett, 19 Wall. (U. S.) 147; Union Nat. Bank *v.* Matthews, 98 U. S. 621; Kenicott *v.* Wayne Co., 16 Wall. (U. S.) 452; George *v.* Woodward, 40 Vt. 672; Lane *v.* Sleeper, 18 N. H. 209; Power *v.* McElvy, 47 Cal. 154.

4. Olds *v.* Cummings, 31 Ill. 188; McIntire *v.* Yates, 104 Ill. 491; Union Cent. L. Ins. Co. *v.* Curtis, 35 Ohio St. 343; Johnsón *v.* Carpenter, 7 Minn. 177; Blumenthal *v.* Jassoy, 29 Minn. 177.

5. Pierce *v.* Kibbee, 51 Vt. 559; Butler *v.* Slocomb, 33 La. Ann. 170; Wanzer *v.* Cary, 76 N. Y. 526.

So where the note and mortgage requiring indorsement for a valid transfer was passed to the pledgee unindorsed the equities were let in on both the note and the mortgage. Smith *v.* Burgess, 133 Mass. 511; Blunt *v.* Norris, 123 Mass. 55; McCrum *v.* Cosby, 11 Kan. 464.

So where they were transferred after the maturity of the note. Foley *v.* Smith, 6 Wall. (U. S.) 493.

6. Crain *v.* Paine, 4 Cush. (Mass.) 483.

Where the note and mortgage is so delivered, the payee of the note may sell it subject to the pledge contract. Proctor *v.* Baldwin, 82 Ind. 370.

A transfer of the note without the mortgage securing it gives the pledgee the benefit of the mortgage security. Logan *v.* Smith, 62 Mo. 455; Morris etc. Co. *v.* Fisher, 9 N. J. Eq. 667;

b. TITLE TO MISAPPROPRIATED SECURITIES.—Where the owner of a note and mortgage has placed them in the hands of another with the proper indorsement and assignment to make them transferable, a subsequent *bona fide* pledgee of the same, for value, though such pledge be unauthorized and a misappropriation by the one thus intrusted with the legal title, the pledgee will be protected.[1] He is, however, chargeable with notice under the same circumstances as would be the holder of ordinary commercial paper.[2]

c. ENFORCEMENT OF SECURITY.—The pledgee of a note and mortgage is, on default, allowed to recover the face value of the security, holding the surplus for those holding equities therein.[3]

Lowenthal *v.* McCormick, 101 Ill. 143.

A transfer of a negotiable note secured by mortgage with an agreement to assign the mortgage when found carries the mortgage with it in the same manner as if a written assignment of the mortgage were made at the same time, and if the written assignment is not executed until after the note has become due this will not affect the rights of the assignee as against the maker of the note. Body *v.* Jewsen, 33 Wis. 402.

1. Morris *v.* Bacon, 123 Mass. 58; Swift *v.* Smith, 102 U. S. 442; Miller *v.* Larned, 103 Ill. 562.

Though the note and mortgage were obtained from the owner by artifice and pledged by the defrauder "without recourse," the pledgee for value without notice of prior equities or assignments is protected. Blunt *v.* Norris, 123 Mass. 55.

A fraudulent release of the mortgage by the mortgagee, does not affect the title of the *bona fide* pledgee. Gibson *v.* Milne, 1 Nev. 526.

The sub-pledgee of a note and mortgage for a debt larger than the original debt secured is a *bona fide* purchaser to the extent of his advances, the original pledgor having to suffer for his misplaced confidence. Briggs *v.* Rice, 130 Mass. 50.

Where a note, showing on its face that it was secured by a mortgage, was transferred in pledge, the pledgee took it subject to equities. Strong *v.* Jackson, 123 Mass. 60,

Though the note and mortgage may be void between the original parties for usury or illegal consideration to a *bona fide* pledgee for value, they will be supported. Taylor *v.* Page, 6 Allen (Mass.) 86. But only to the amount of the debt secured Shaw *v.* Carpenter, 54 Vt. 155.

2. As where the note shows on its face the existence of a trust. Duncan *v.* Jaudon, 15 Wall. (U. S.) 175; Shaw *v.* Spencer, 100 Mass. 382; Sturtevant *v.* Jaques, 14 Allen (Mass.) 523; Monitor Mut. F. Ins. Co. *v.* Buffum, 115 Mass. 345; Fisher *v.* Brown, 104 Mass. 261.

Where the writing is obscured the pledgee must take pains to read it. Smith *v.* Burgess, 133 Mass. 511.

Where a note and mortgage was indorsed over by trustees to their successor and by him pledged without authority, the pledgee, though ignorant of trust, was charged with notice of it. Turner *v.* Hoyle, 95 Mo. 337.

3. Hurst *v.* Coley, 15 Fed. Rep. 645; Gibson *v.* Milne, 1 Nev. 526; McCrum *v.* Cosby, 11 Kan. 464.

So a sub-pledgee of a note and mortgage collects the face value thereof on the same terms. Miller *v.* Larned, 103 Ill. 565; Briggs *v.* Rice, 130 Mass. 50.

In States where the pledgee in enforcing the mortgage pledged with a note is subjected to defenses, a subpledgee of the note and mortgage is restricted in his recovery against the mortgagor purchasers, *bona fide* and for value, to advances made by him to lift the first debt. Lowenthal *v.* McCormick, 101 Ill. 143.

If the pledgee delivers the security to the pledgor to collect and the latter fails to account for or return it, the pledgee may sue the pledgor in trover and recover the amount of his loan. Hurst *v.* Coley, 15 Fed. Rep. 645.

Where note and mortgage was deposited by the mortgagee as security for a debt, any payments made by the mortgagor to the mortgagee are held by the latter as agent of the pledgee.

A sub-pledgee of a note and mortgage who has loaned thereon less than the original debt, although the pledgee's whole interest therein is assigned as security, can actually recover from the mortgagor only the amount of his advances.[1]

Where the pledgee has the power to sell the security he may do so, but absolute good faith is demanded of him.[2]

The pledgee is entitled to foreclose the mortgage, enter and take possession of the premises.[3] He gets in that case an absolute title against every one but the pledgor,[4] and as to him the

Newman *v.* Bank of Greenville, 66 Miss. 323.

Where a note secured by a deed of trust was given as collateral and the note was satisfied, the pledgee could not hold the trust deed as security for the pledgor's indebtedness. Newman *v.* Bank of Greenville, 66 Miss. 323.

Under *Louisiana* Code, art. 3170, authorizing the pledgee of a note to "take measures to recover it," if it be secured by mortgage, he can enforce the collection by executory, as well as by ordinary process; and this without consent of the pledgor. Chaffe *v.* Du Bose, 36 La. Ann. 257.

The pledgee of negotiable corporate bonds secured by mortgage is entitled to a proportionate part of the security. On foreclosure of the mortgage he is allowed to claim the face value of the bonds to determine the proportion that shall come to him, but to receive only the amount of his debt. Lehman *v.* Tahassee Mfg. Co., 64 Ala. 567; Duncomb *v.* New York etc. R. Co., 84 N. Y. 190.

1. Draper *v.* Saxton, 118 Mass. 429. Under the circumstances in the text, where the mortgagor became insolvent the sub-pledgee was allowed to put in a claim for the face of the note and mortgage but to recover only the amount of his advances. *In re* Burrill, L. R., 7 Eq. 379.

Where the pledgee of a note and mortgage given to secure another note sold the latter note and re-pledged the note and mortgage as security therefor, the sub-pledgee holds the note and mortgage in trust for the original pledgor subject to the payment of the note secured, and he has the right to realize on the note and mortgage, without proving his claim against the original pledgor. Williams *v.* Lumpkin, 74 Tex. 601.

2. Zimpleman *v.* Veeder, 98 Ill. 613. Where the note and mortgage were, under a power of sale, sold by the pledgee to the mortgagor for exactly the amount of the debt secured, the pledgor was allowed to foreclose and sell the land crediting the mortgagor with the amount of the loan. Zimpleman *v.* Veeder, 98 Ill. 613.

Where the pledgee himself purchased the note and mortgage at the sale and again resold them for a higher sum, he was chargeable with a sum that would buy them back again, though that exceeded what he received for them. Richardson *v.* Mann, 30 La. Ann. 1060.

A creditor who holds a note secured by mortgage, as collateral security for his debt, has no right to sell such security for less than its value, knowing that the purchaser buys it with intent to cancel it. Fletcher *v.* Dickinson, 7 Allen (Mass.) 23.

The pledgee of a note and mortgage deposited them in a bank, where they were seized by the sheriff and sold on execution against the pledgor. *Held* that the pledgee could purchase without becoming a trustee purchasing at his own sale. Clark *v.* Holland, 72 Iowa 34.

3. Brown *v.* Tyler, 8 Gray (Mass.) 135.

4. Dalton *v.* Smith, 86 N. Y. 176; Stevens *v.* Dedham Sav. Inst., 129 Mass. 547; Montague *v.* Boston etc. Co., 124 Mass. 242.

When the land has remained in the possession of the pledgee and his assigns for twenty years, equity will hesitate to interfere. Ayres *v.* Waite, 10 Cush. (Mass.) 72.

Where, after selling the land, the surplus over the debt secured remains in the pledgee's hands, the Statute of Limitations begins to run against the pledgor from the time the land was turned into money. Brown *v.* Tyler, 8 Gray (Mass.) 135.

pledgee holds the land in pledge in place of the note and mortgage,[1] not as payment of his debt.[2] He should as trustee of the pledgor convert the land into money as soon as possible,[3] or if the pledgor sooner pays the debt secured, turn over to him the property.[4]

7. **Bond and Mortgage.**—A bond and mortgage may be given as collateral security, and a *bona fide* pledgee for value has the same rights and is subject to the same equities as is a purchaser.[5] But the pledgor holds the general property in the bond and mortgage, the pledgee having a special property for his advances.[6]

The *bona fide* pledgee for value of a bond and mortgage is not bound by secret equities between the original parties.[7]

Nor is he bound by a fraudulent release executed by the mortgagee to the mortgagor.[8]

1. Dalton *v.* Smith, 86 N. Y. 176; Hoyt *v.* Martense, 16 N. Y. 231; Slee *v.* Manhattan Co., 1 Paige (N. Y.) 52; Henry *v.* Davis, 7 Johns. Ch. (N. Y.) 40; Montague *v.* Boston etc. R. Co., 124 Mass. 242; Brown *v.* Tyler, 8 Gray (Mass.) 135; Clapp *v.* Shepard, 2 Met. (Mass.) 127; Rice *v.* Dillingham, 73 Me. 59.

2. Stevens *v.* Dedham Sav. Inst., 129 Mass. 547.

3. Brown *v.* Tyler, 8 Gray (Mass.) 135.

4. Dalton *v.* Smith, 86 N. Y. 176; Stevens *v.* Dedham Sav. Inst., 129 Mass. 547; Montague *v.* Boston etc. R. Co., 124 Mass. 242.

5. Campbell *v.* Parker, 9 Bosw. (N. Y.) 322; Haskins *v.* Kelly, 1 Robt. (N. Y.) 160; Carr *v.* Carr, 52 N. Y. 251; Clark *v.* Henry, 2 Cow. (N. Y.) 324; Slee *v.* Manhattan Co., 1 Paige (N. Y.) 48; Rice *v.* Dillingham, 73 Me. 59.

Where a bond and mortgage were executed but never delivered to the mortgagee, they may be pledged by the mortgagor, but they get their validity from that moment, and the pledgee is subject only to equities arising after that time. Schaefer *v.* Reilly, 50 N. Y. 61.

Where a bond and mortgage were issued to secure a contract which was afterwards canceled, the pledgee then assigning it again in pledge to a *bona fide* holder for value, the latter got no title against the mortgagor. Wanzer *v.* Cary, 76 N. Y. 526.

A sub-pledgee of a bond and mortgage not protected by estoppel, is subject to all preceding equities, whether he has notice or not. Bush *v.* Lathrop, 22 N. Y. 535.

When a bond and mortgage was pledged and then sub-pledged the latter transaction being only equitable, and the mortgagor paid the first pledgee's debt and took possession of the bond and mortgage, on a suit by the sub-pledgee to enforce his claim, the mortgagor was allowed to set off first the amount of the debt of the first pledgee, though the sub-pledgee had no actual notice of the first pledge. Kamena *v.* Huelbig, 23 N. J. Eq. 78.

6. O'Dougherty *v.* Remington Paper Co., 81 N. Y. 496.

7. Greene *v.* Warnick, 64 N. Y. 230; Dillage *v.* Commercial Bank, 51 N. Y. 345; First Nat. Bank *v.* Stiles, 22 Hun (N. Y.) 339.

When the wife of one of the parties of a firm loaned her husband a bond and mortgage to be pledged for a firm indebtedness, the pledgee of the bond and mortgage was not bound by the agreement between the parties that the debt should be paid out of the earnings of the firm. Ferdon *v.* Miller, 34 N. J. Eq. 10.

Nor will the pledgee be stopped from foreclosing the mortgage by the fact that his pledgor, the mortgagee, fraudulently induced the mortgagor to make it. Duncan *v.* Gilbert, 29 N. J. L. 521; Jacobsen *v.* Dodd, 32 N. J. Eq. 403.

8. Brown *v.* Blydenburgh, 7 N. Y. 141.

So one who advances money on a bond and mortgage which are not produced is chargeable with notice of whatever may make his assignor's title

A bond and mortgage may be pledged by a regular assignment in writing[1] or by parol agreement with mere delivery alone.[2]

It is customary for the assignee of a bond and mortgage in pledge to get an "estoppel paper" from the mortgagor, stating that he "has no defenses either in law or in equity," and when this is done or the mortgagor has estopped himself by other acts or omissions, the pledgee under the protection of estoppel gets a good title to the bond and mortgage against the world.[3]

After default the pledgee of a bond and mortgage can enforce the security as if he were the absolute owner thereof.[4] He may

defective. Kellogg *v.* Smith, 26 N. Y. 20.

1. Where the assignment is absolute on its face it may be shown by parol evidence to be a pledge. O'Dougherty *v.* Remington Paper Co., 81 N. Y. 496.

2. Prescott *v.* Hull, 17 Johns. (N. Y.) 292; Runyan *v.* Mesereau, 11 Johns. (N. Y.) 534; Jackson *v.* Willard, 4 Johns. (N. Y.) 41; Wilson *v.* Troup, 2 Cow. (N. Y.) 195; Kamena *v.* Huelbig, 23 N. J. Eq. 78; Galway *v.* Fullerton, 17 N. J. Eq. 389.

A mere promise to assign is not enough. Coffin *v.* Kirwan, 7 La. Ann. 221; Sevin *v.* Caillouet, 30 La. Ann. 528.

3. Ashton's Appeal, 73 Pa. St. 153; Woodruff *v.* Morristown Inst., 34 N. J. Eq. 174; Bush *v.* Cushman, 27 N. J. Eq. 131; Diercks *v.* Kennedy, 16 N. J. Eq. 210.

An antecedent in the restrictive States does not make the pledgee a holder for value. Ashton's Appeal, 73 Pa. St. 153; McConnell *v.* Wenrich, 16 Pa. St. 365.

Where the pledgee of a bond and mortgage is protected by an "estoppel paper," collateral agreements of which he has no notice do not affect him. Riggs *v.* Purssell, 89 N. Y. 608.

M executed and delivered to N a bond for $10,000, secured by mortgage on certain realty, with a parol understanding that N should sell the property and apply the proceeds to the payment of three drafts, amounting thereto, which N had accepted for M's accommodation. On the next day N, without the knowledge or consent of M or of the holders of the drafts, assigned and delivered the bond and mortgage to S, the president of a banking company, as collateral security for any sums coming due from N to the company, who took in good faith, unaware of the agreement between M and N and discounted for N commercial paper to that amount. Afterwards the company purchased from M the bond and mortgage absolutely, and surrendered the paper, unaware of the existence of the drafts or of N's want of right of disposal. Including the acceptances, M owed N $15,000 at the time of giving the bond and mortgage, and six months afterwards N credited him with the amount of the bond. In an action by the holders of the unpaid drafts to restrain the company from selling under a foreclosure decree, held, that both M and the holders were estopped from disputing the validity of the title acquired by the company by its assignment from N, and from insisting on an application of the proceeds to the payment of the drafts. First Nat. Bank *v.* Stiles, 22 Hun (N. Y.) 339.

4. See *infra*, this title, *Note and Mortgage;* FORECLOSURE OF MORTGAGES, vol. 8, p. 208.

If he has the power to sell the security he must act in good faith. Campbell *v.* Parker, 9 Bosw. (N. Y.) 322.

In enforcing the security he is not subject to the defense of usury in the debt secured. Stevens *v.* Reeves, 33 N. J. Eq. 427.

While a subsequent mortgagee might, against the holder of a previous mortgage, holding other securities for his debt, compel him to marshal them, a *bona fide* pledgee for value of the first mortgage, cannot be so compelled. Reilly *v.* Mayer, 12 N. J. Eq. 55.

The pledgor, requesting the pledgee to foreclose the mortgage assigned as collateral, on the refusal of the latter, was allowed to do so himself, and to restrain the pledgee from so doing thereafter. Burlingame *v.* Parce, 12 Hun (N. Y.) 149.

pursue all his remedies at once as long as he does not get a double satisfaction.[1]

8. Insurance Policies.—Insurance policies may be pledged with or without a written assignment.[2]

Where the pledgee brought suit to foreclose the security, claiming only the amount of his debt, and obtained a decree making his claim a lien on the land, the pledgor on paying the pledgor's debt was allowed to foreclose the mortgage, the suit by the pledgee not being a bar. O'Dougherty *v.* Remington Paper Co., 81 N. Y. 496.

A payment of the bond and mortgage by the mortgagor to the pledgee, after the debt secured is due, operates to discharge the debt *pro tanto*, against the receiver of the pledgor. Bell *v.* Weir (Supreme Ct.), 8 N. Y. Supp. 661.

Where A pledges mortgage bonds to B, and B assigns them as collateral security for a debt of his own to C, who, foreclosing against A without making B a party, buys in the bonds himself, C is bound to account to B for the bonds or their value, and not merely for the amount paid at the sale. Jeffersonville Bank *v.* Ohio Falls Car etc. Works, 20 Fed. Rep. 65.

The pledgee of a mortgage held by him as security for a debt of the mortgagee, the mortgagor having notice of the transaction, cannot affect the rights of the mortgagee by accepting a conveyance of the mortgaged premises from the mortgagor, and releasing the mortgage. The consent of the mortgagee is necessary to bind him, and if no such consent is given, he may bring an action to set aside the conveyance, and release, and to foreclose the mortgage. Chester *v.* Hill, 66 Cal. 480.

1. Newbold *v.* Newbold, 1 Del. Ch. 310; Thayer *v.* Daniels, 113 Mass. 129.

2. Collins *v.* Dawley, 4 Colo. 138; Stout *v.* Yaeger etc. Co., 13 Fed. Rep. 803; Norwood *v.* Guerdon, 60 Ill. 253.

A mere promise of a policy as collateral is not a good delivery. D'Meza's Succession, 26 La. Ann. 35; especially not against a prior pledgee by delivery. Spencer *v.* Clark, L. R., 9 Ch. D. 137. Though where the policy is made payable to a certain person or his assigns the policy should be indorsed. Merrifield *v.* Baker, 11 Allen (Mass.) 43; Shearman *v.* Niagara F. Ins. Co., 46 N.Y. 526. Where the policy was delivered, the pledgor agreeing to indorse it later but died before doing so, equity allowed the pledgee to recover. Crossley *v.* Glasgow F. Ins. Co., L. R., 4 Ch. D. 421; and see Webster *v.* British Empire Ins. Co., L. R., 15 Ch. D. 169. Delivery alone will at least give an equitable title to the pledgee. West *v.* Carolina Ins. Co., 31 Ark. 476; Soule *v.* Union Bank, 45 Barb. (N. Y.) 111; Latham *v.* Chart. Bank etc., L. R., 17 Eq. 205; Edwards *v.* Martin, L. R., 1 Eq. 121; Bruce *v.* Gardner, L. R., 5 Ch. 32.

Where the pledgee of a policy was notified to hold the surplus for a subsequent pledgee for value, it was a sufficient pledging of the surplus. Myers *v.* Guar. etc. Co., 7 De G. M. & G. 112.

A condition in a policy that it shall not be assigned without the written consent of the insurance company does not prevent such assignment but gives the company the right to declare the policy void at any time thereafter. Merrill *v.* New England Mut. L. Ins. Co., 103 Mass. 245. But it is held that the condition does not effect a pledge of the policy. Ellis *v.* Kreutzingen, 27 Mo. 311.

Where a married woman delivered a policy payable to her, to her husband, indorsed in blank, and he wrote an absolute assignment over it and transferred it as collateral, it was held a good pledge. Norwood *v.* Guerdon, 60 Ill. 253.

The pledgee has a lien on the proceeds of the policy against the company, the insured and all having notice. Wells *v.* Archer, 10 S. & R. (Pa.) 412; Godin *v.* London Ins. Co., 1 Burr. 494.

Where pledgee of a life insurance policy paid premiums thereon, he could not receive credit for the same where he did not show that it was part of the pledge contract that he should pay them. Lambertville Nat. Bank *v.* McCready B. & P. Co. (N. J. 1888), 15 Atl. Rep. 388.

Where a creditor takes out a policy on his debtor's life and charges the premiums as a part of the principal, he is bound to keep the policy alive for the benefit of the debtor. Soule *v.* Union Bank, 45 Barb. (N. Y.) 111.

An equitable lien on the proceeds of a policy may be created by the pay-

X. Rights and Liabilities of Pledgor—1. Right to Sell or Assign His Interest.—The pledgor may sell the property pledged, subject to the lien of the pledgee.[1] In this case, though the actual possession does not pass, the possession of the pledgee after he is notified of the sale, is the possession of the purchaser.[2] If the pledgee, having received notice of the assignment, delivers the

ment of the premiums, when that is done under an agreement with the insured. Aylwyn *v.* Witly, 30 L. J., Ch. 860; *In re* Leslie, L. R., Ch. D. 552.

Where an insurance policy was assigned as collateral security in a fraudulent transaction, the pledgor agreeing to pay the premiums, and on his failure so to do, the pledgee paid them, on a suit by the pledgor to set the whole matter aside for fraud, the pledgee was protected to the extent of his advances. Pennell *v.* Millar, 23 Beav. 172.

A creditor who included in a mortgage a premium for a policy of insurance on the life of the debtor, as additional security for the debt, held, liable under the circumstances of the case for his neglect to effect insurance, as proposed, to the amount of the sum which should have been insured without proof of any express agreement to insure. Soule *v.* Union Bank, 45 Barb. (N. Y.) 111; 30 How. Pr. (N. Y.) 105.

1. Whitaker *v.* Sumner, 20 Pick. (Mass.) 399; Tuxworth *v.* Moore, 9 Pick. (Mass.) 347; Fettyplace *v.* Dutch, 13 Pick. (Mass.) 388; Cooper *v.* Ray, 47 Ill. 53; Sanders *v.* Davis, 13 B. Mon. (Ky.) 432; Bush *v.* Lyons, 9 Cow. (N. Y.) 52; Ratcliffe *v.* Vance, 2 Mill (S. Car.) 239; Franklyn *v.* Neate, 13 M. & W. 481; Goss *v.* Emerson, 23 N. H. 38; Van Blarcom *v.* Broadway Bank, 37 N. Y. 540.

The purchaser acquires only the pledgor's rights and is chargeable with full notice of the contract of pledge. Taggart *v.* Packard, 39 Vt. 628.

The power reserved by the pledgor to sell or pledge at any time upon payment of the debt secured gives him no right to sell it until he has first paid the debt, and if he obtains possession of the property and sells it without the pledgee's consent he is liable for conversion of it. Prescott *v.* Prescott, 41 Vt. 131.

One who has purchased from the general owner goods pledged for advances, with knowledge or notice of the lien of the pledgee, and who receives the goods from the latter with notice of his claim of a lien thereon for a specific amount, takes them with the obligation to pay the lien, and in an action therefor, cannot offset a claim against the pledgor. Carrington *v.* Ward, 71 N. Y. 360; Nottebohm *v.* Maas, 3 Robt. (N. Y.) 249.

The payee of a negotiable note, who has indorsed it in blank, and delivered it in pledge to another, as collateral security for his own debt, may still negotiate it to a third person, who may maintain an action on it, in his own name, as indorsee, if the pawnee's lien be discharged before judgment. Fisher *v.* Bradford, 7 Me. 28.

A bill of exchange already pledged cannot be mortgaged to another by the pledgor to the prejudice of the pledgee, but a surplus remaining after the pledgee's claim is satisfied may be transferred. Sanders *v.* Davis, 13 B. Mon. (Ky.) 432.

Where bonds and stocks are pledged as collateral security, under a contract stipulating that in the event of the reduction of the indebtedness, the pledgor should be entitled to select and withdraw from the securities so pledged an amount equal to the reduction, one to whom the pledgor has sold and transferred a part of such securities can maintain his right to them, as against the pledgee, where it is shown that prior to such transfer the pledgor had paid, or caused to be paid, on such indebtedness, a sum in excess of the value of the securities so transferred.

In such case, the pledgor can sell and transfer, either with or without consideration, the securities which he had the right under the contract to withdraw. First Nat. Bank *v.* Root, 107 Ind. 225.

Where the evidence shows that a person taking a pledge in writing has authority to sell all the articles in a certain building containing the articles in pledge, mixed with others belonging to the pledgor, the sale of all the articles in the building by the pledgor is valid. Clark *v.* Bouvain, 20 La. Ann. 70.

2. Whitaker *v.* Sumner, 20 Pick. (Mass.) 399.

Where one has delivered a chattel,

property to the pledgor or any one else, without the assignee's assent, he is liable; but, for a conversion taking place before the assignment, the assignee has no claim in his own name against the pledgee.[1]

The assignee is at all times entitled to redeem the pledge by paying such sum as would have canceled and discharged the pledgee's claim, and in case the pledgee has sold the property the assignee is entitled to receive the surplus over the debt secured.[2]

The pledgee by the act of delivering up collateral securities to the assignee does not affirm their genuineness; for, on receiving the debt secured he is bound to deliver the property irrespective of its character, to whomsoever the pledgor may direct.[3]

2. Liability of His Interest to Attachment and Execution.—At common law, as the pledgor lacks possession of the property, and as the pledgee cannot be compelled to deliver it up before his debt is due,[4] the pledgor's interest cannot be attached,[5]

with authority conferred on the bailee to sell it and credit the amount on a debt owing by himself to the bailee, the bailor may afterward and before such sale is effected, sell the same chattel to a third party and vest in him a good title. And the sale will convey an immediate and valid title, notwithstanding that, at the time, the possession is in the bailee, and that no formal delivery is made by him to the purchaser. In the sale of personal property, it is not necessary that the vendor should be in possession at the time. And the possession of his agent or bailee after the sale is the possession of the purchaser. Erwin *v.* Arthur, 61 Mo. 386.

1. Duell *v.* Cudlipp, 1 Hilt. (N. Y.) 166.

But where the cause of action for conversion as well as the pledge is assigned, he may sue in his own name or in that of his assignor. McKee *v.* Judd, 12 N. Y. 622.

2. Van Blarcom *v.* Broadway Bank, 37 N. Y. 540; Dupre *v.* Fall, 10 Cal. 430.

Where goods pledged have been disposed of by the pledgee, who, however, substitutes in their place and delivers to a purchaser from the pledgor, upon the order of the latter, other goods of the same kind, quality and value, which are accepted by the purchaser, the latter cannot take advantage of the pledgee; and it is no defense to an action by the pledgee to recover the amount of his lien upon the goods. Carrington *v.* Ward, 71 N. Y. 360.

3. Baker *v.* Arnot, 67 N. Y. 448.

The transaction is not a sale between the pledgee and the purchaser, even though the pledgee receives the money, and in such case the purchaser cannot recover back the money from him if the securities are spurious. Ketchum *v.* Stevens, 19 N. Y. 499.

4. Picquet *v.* Swan, 4 Mason (U. S.) 443.

5. Badlam *v.* Tucker, 1 Pick. (Mass.) 389; Pomeroy *v.* Smith, 17 Pick. (Mass.) 85; Hunt *v.* Holton, 13 Pick. (Mass.) 216; Holbrook *v.* Baker, 5 Me. 309; Soule *v.* White, 14 Me. 436; Thompson *v.* Stevens, 10 Me. 27; Wilkes *v.* Ferris, 5 Johns. (N. Y.) 336; Marsh *v.* Lawrence, 4 Cow. (N. Y.) 461; Stief *v.* Hart, 1 N. Y. 20: Srodes *v.* Caven, 3 Watts (Pa.) 258; Briggs *v.* Walker, 21 N. H. 72; Hudson *v.* Hunt, 5 N. H. 538; Dowler *v.* Cushwa, 27 Md. 354; Scott *v.* Scholey, 8 East 467; Metcalf *v.* Scholey, 5 Bos. & Pull. 461.

As to whether the pledgor's interest in property pledged can be attached except by statute, by paying or tendering to the pledgee the full amount of his lien, there seems to be no direct authority. But attachment has generally been regarded as too doubtful and uncertain to attempt its enforcement. Sargent *v.* Carr, 12 Me. 396; Mechanics' B. & L. Assoc. *v.* Conover, 14 N. J. Eq. 219.

The creditor can get his remedy in a court of equity where he may be allowed to redeem. Badlam *v.* Tucker, 1 Pick. (Mass.) 389; Shirley *v.* Watts, 3 Atk. 200. See Mechanics' B. & L. Assoc. *v.* Conover, 14 N. J. Eq. 219.

nor can it be reached by the trustee or garnishee process.[1] If, however, the pledgee surrenders voluntarily the possession of the pledge on receiving payment of his debt, the property then may be subject to levy.[2]

He is secured either by paying or tendering him his debt, or the property is sold subject to his interest therein, the purchaser standing in place of the pledgor.[3]

The measure of damages for unlawfully levying on pledged property was the value of the property, not the amount of the lien. Soule *v.* White, 14 Me. 436.

1. See GARNISHMENT, vol. 8, p. 1096.

2. Mowe *v.* Stickney, 5 Minn. 397; Meeker *v.* Wilson, 1 Gall. (U. S.) 419; Mechanics' B. & L. Assoc. *v.* Conover, 14 N. J. Eq. 219.

If the maker of a pledged note pay it to the pledgee after it has been levied on by the sheriff with notice of the levy, he is not thereby discharged as to the balance above the debt for which it was pledged. Mower *v.* Stickney, 5 Minn. 397.

3. A sheriff in levying an execution upon the interest of a pledgor may take actual possession of the goods, holding them until he sells them, and after the sale the pledgee is entitled to possession until the purchaser redeems them from the pledge. Bakewell *v.* Ellsworth, 6 Hill (N. Y.) 484; Stief *v.* Hart, 1 N. Y. 20; Cotton *v.* Watkins, 6 Wis. 629.

In *Alabama*, though there is no special statute authorizing it, it seems that the interest of the pledgor may be reached by execution, for it is provided that the sheriff has the right to take property into his possession for the purpose of making a levy on the mortgagor's interest where the property had been previously mortgaged. McConeghy *v.* McCaw, 31 Ala. 447.

In *California*, property capable of manual delivery can be taken on execution, but that incapable of such delivery can only be taken by the process of garnishment and not by execution. Treadwell *v.* Davis, 34 Cal. 601.

In *Louisiana*, it is well settled that the pledge is subject to attachment and to levy of execution in a suit against the pledgor, the pledgee's right however, being respected. Auge *v.* Variol, 31 La. Ann. 865; Horner *v.* Dennis, 34 La. Ann. 389; Pickens *v.* Webster, 31 La. Ann. 870; Flournoy *v.* Milling, 15 La. Ann. 473.

In *Massachusetts*, property can only be taken on execution after it has previously been subject to attachment or the trustee process. Lyon *v.* Coburn, 1 Cush. (Mass.) 278.

A pledgee is entitled to recover from an officer who wrongfully attaches the goods pledged, not merely the amount of the debt secured, but the full value of the property. Pomeroy *v.* Smith, 17 Pick. (Mass.) 85; Treadwell *v.* Davis, 34 Cal. 601.

An attachment of property conveyed by a bill of sale absolute in form and intended as collateral security can only be dissolved on the pledgee's making demand for his interest therein in accordance with statute. Putnam *v.* Rowe, 110 Mass. 28.

Where a debtor agrees to hold property in trust for certain creditors it does not protect it from attachment and execution by general creditors, it being an evasion of the general policy of the law respecting pledges and mortgages. Huntington *v.* Clemence, 103 Mass. 482.

In *New Hampshire*, prior to the act of June 30, 1841, property mortgaged or pledged, could not be attached in any manner, without paying or tendering to the mortgagee the amount of his claim. Briggs *v.* Walker, 21 N. H. 72.

The purchaser of a pledgor's interest at a sheriff's sale takes only that interest which is the right to redeem the pledge on payment of the debt due. Saul *v.* Kruger, 9 How. Pr. (N. Y.) 569.

Property held in pledge may be sold upon execution against the pledgor, but the sale must be subject to the rights and interests of the pledgee. The pledgee has the right to retain possession until his lien is satisfied. Reichenbach *v.* McKean, 95 Pa. St. 432; Srodes *v.* Caven, 3 Watts (Pa.) 258; Baugh *v.* Kirkpatrick, 54 Pa. St. 84; First Nat. Bank *v.* Pettit, 9 Heisk. (Tenn.) 447.

The fact that a creditor procures a transfer of property held in pledge in

But it has been generally provided by statute that the pledgor's interest in the pledged property can be reached by the process of attachment and execution, full protection, however, being given to the pledgee.[1]

3. Right to Redeem.—See *infra*, this title, *Redemption.*

XI. Rights and Liabilities of Pledgee of Corporeal Property Before Default—1. Right to Possession.—From the very nature of the contract of pledge, the pledgee has a right to hold the pledge undisturbed until it is redeemed.[2] Where he has been dispossessed wrongfully he may sue to recover the thing itself or for dam-

another State and thereupon levies an attachment upon it in a suit against the pledgor, is not such a transaction devised to get the property within the jurisdiction of the court as will avoid the attachment. National Bank *v.* Winston, 5 Baxt. (Tenn.) 685.

A pledgee in an action brought by him to recover the property pledged, against a sheriff who had taken the same under an execution against the pledgor, cannot avail himself of a title acquired subsequent to the commencement of the action. Barnhart *v.* Fulkerth, 73 Cal. 526.

1. The right of the pledgor to demand the surplus after the collection of a pledged note is property, and subject of attachment as a demand against the person within the meaning of § 649 C. C. P., and can be levied on "by leaving a certified copy of the warrant and a notice showing the property attached," with the person against whom the demand exists, that is, the pledgee. Warner *v.* Fourth Nat. Bank, 115 N. Y. 251.

2. See *infra*, this title, *Nature of the Contract.* Yeatman *v.* New Orleans Sav. Inst., 95 U. S. 764; Mitchell *v.* Brown, 6 Coldw. (Tenn.) 505; Printup *v.* Johnson, 19 Ga. 73.

So the pledgee has a right to hold collaterals until he is fully paid. *In re* Litchfield Bank, 28 Conn. 575; Kittera's Estate, 17 Pa. St. 416.

Where stock was pledged for an existing debt as well as those to arise in the future, no adverse holding to the pledgee could arise until the pledgee repudiated his claim by giving notice of his intention to sell. Gilmer *v.* Morris, 35 Fed. Rep. 682.

But where a party holds goods merely as security for a debt, with a privilege on the same, he has no right to prevent the seizure of the goods, by another party also claiming a privilege against the owner. The right of the party holding goods in this manner is limited to a judicial proceeding to make his privilege available against the goods. Flournoy *v.* Milling, 15 La. Ann. 473.

A creditor may hold several securities for the same debt, and cannot be compelled to yield up either, until the debt is paid. Thus a bank may take security from one of the parties to a note discounted by it, and also hold the shares of another party pledged for payment thereof. Union Bank *v.* Laird, 2 Wheat. (U. S.) 390; Elder *v.* Rouse, 15 Wend. (N. Y.) 218.

Upon the death of the pledgee his right to hold the pledge passes to his personal representative, who may hold and enforce the pledge in the same manner and to the same extent as the creditor himself might if he were living. Henry *v.* Eddy, 34 Ill. 508.

Substitution or Exchange.—The substitution or exchange of other securities for those deposited as collateral does not affect the rights of the pledgee, as the surrender of the old collateral is a sufficient consideration for the giving of the new and makes the pledgee a holder for value in the usual course of business. Clark *v.* Iselin, 21 Wall. (U. S.) 360; Greenwell *v.* Hayden, 78 Ky. 332; Cherry *v.* Frost, 7 Lea (Tenn.) 1; Sawyer *v.* Turpin, 91 U. S. 114.

Even after pledgee is known to be insolvent, substitution will be upheld if securities of no greater value are received by the pledgee for those surrendered. Cook *v.* Tullis, 18 Wall. (U. S.) 340; Tiffany *v.* Boatmen's Sav. Inst., 18 Wall. (U. S.) 375; Clark *v.* Iselin, 21 Wall. (U. S.) 360; Burnhisel *v.* Firman, 22 Wall. (U. S.) 170; Sawyer *v.* Turpin, 91 U. S. 114; *In re* Swenk, 9 Fed. Rep. 643; Stevens *v.* Blanchard, 3 Cush. (Mass.) 169; Abbott *v.* Pomfert, 1 Bing. N. Cas. 462.

ages at his election.[1] Nor is his remedy confined to an action against the wrongful taker himself, but, after demand for the return of the pledge, he may sue one who has received it from such taker.[2] For the injury or conversion of the property by a stranger either the pledgor or the pledgee may sue, but a recovery by the one will bar a suit by the other for the same cause of action.[3] In an action by the pledgee against a stranger for the conversion of pledged property the rule is, that plaintiff is entitled to recover its full value, being answerable to pledgor for the surplus;[4]

The rule undoubtedly is that the holder of collaterals is bound to employ reasonable care, skill and diligence in regard to them and in regard to rendering them as valuable as possible for the purposes intended, that if they are lost by negligence of the holder he must account for them at their value. It has been held that taking a less security would be evidence of misuse which if not satisfactorily explained would render the holder responsible. Bank of U. S. *v.* Peabody, 20 Pa. St. 454; Muirhead *v.* Kirkpatrick, 21 Pa. St. 237; Sellers *v.* Jones, 22 Pa. St. 423; Girard F. & M. Ins. Co. *v.* Marr, 46 Pa. St. 504.

1. Treadwell *v.* Davis, 34 Cal. 601; Noles *v.* Marable, 50 Ala. 366; Woodruff *v.* Halsey, 8 Pick. (Mass.) 333; Brownell *v.* Hawkins, 4 Barb. (N. Y.) 491; U. S. Express Co. *v.* Meints, 72 Ill. 293; Roeder *v.* Green Tree Brewery Co., 33 Mo. App. 67.

If the pledgee sues one who has converted the pledged property and recovers in damages more than the debt secured he holds the balance in trust for the pledgor. Miles *v.* Walther, 3 Mo. App. 96.

Where the pledgee sues a third person who has connected himself with and derives title for the pledgor, in trover for conversion of the pledged property, he can recover only the amount of his debt secured. Brownell *v.* Hawkins, 4 Barb. (N. Y.) 491.

Bill in Equity.—In Taylor *v.* Turner, 87 Ill. 296, it was held that a bill in equity would not lie by a pledgee against one intrusted with property for the purpose of selling, there being a complete remedy at law by the action money had and received.

But the reverse was held in Coleman *v.* Shelton, 2 McCord (S.Car.) 126.

Redelivery to Pledgor for Temporary Purpose.—When a pledge has been so delivered by the pledgee to the pledgor, the pledgee may on the fulfillment of that purpose, and refusal of pledgor to return, recover the pledge or its value by action. Cooper *v.* Ray, 47 Ill. 53; Hutton *v.* Arnett, 51 Ill. 198; Roberts *v.* Wyatt, 2 Taunt. 268.

So on redelivery of a note for collection. Hurst *v.* Coley, 15 Fed. Rep. 645; or for exchange, even though there was no fraud. Way *v.* Davidson, 12 Gray (Mass.) 465.

In such an action by the pledgee it is no defense that the pledgee wrongfully sold other securities which he held for the same debt. Hays *v.* Riddle, 1 Sandf. (N. Y.) 248.

Where the pledgee redelivered goods to the pledgor for sale the price to be returned to the pledgee, the purchaser who agreed to pay over the price to the pledgee was liable not only for the amount of the debt secured, but also the full price of the goods. Nottebohm *v.* Maas, 3 Robt. (N. Y.) 249.

Where stock, for the transfer of which the owner had delivered a power of attorney in blank authorizing its transfer, but only for a special purpose, which having been accomplished was afterwards transferred again, and held as collateral security for a promissory note of the attorney in fact, indorsed by a third party, and the holder released the indorser for the purpose of making him a witness in a proceeding in equity, for its recovery at the suit of the original owner of the stock, it was held that the stock, even if rightfully held, was released by this act, without the consent of the owner, and could not be held for the purpose of enforcing payment of the note. Denny *v.* Lyon, 38 Pa. St. 98.

2. U. S. Express Co. *v.* Meints, 72 Ill. 293.

3. Green *v.* Clark, 12 N. Y. 343; Chesley *v.* St. Clair, 1 N. H. 189.

4. Thompson *v.* Toland, 48 Cal. 99;

but if against the owner, or one acting in privity with him, then only for plaintiff's special interest therein as pledgee, because this settles the rights of the parties and leaves nothing open for further litigation between them.[1] A pledgee may hold several securities for the same debt, and cannot be compelled to yield up either until the debt is paid.[2]

2. Right to Use and Hold Profits.—The pledgee cannot make use of the thing pledged without the express or implied permission of the pledgor.[3] If the use would be for the benefit of the pledgee the assent of the owner may well be presumed;[4] if to his injury, or perilous, it ought not to be presumed;[5] if the use

Soule *v.* White, 14 Me. 436; Baldwin *v.* Bradley, 69 Ill. 32; Lyle *v.* Barker, 5 Binn. (Pa.) 457; Dean *v.* Lawham, 7 Oregon 423; Adams *v.* O'Connor, 100 Mass. 515; Ullman *v.* Barnard, 7 Gray (Mass.) 554; Benjamin *v.* Stremple, 13 Ill. 466; Treadwell *v.* Davis, 34 Cal. 601; U. S. Express Co. *v.* Meints, 72 Ill. 293; Swire *v.* Leach, 18 C. B., N. S. 479.

When the goods are taken from the possession of the pledgee by an officer acting without statutory authority, the measure of damages is the full value of the goods. Pomeroy *v.* Smith, 17 Pick. (Mass.) 85; Soule *v.* White, 14 Me. 436.

If the pledgor, however, has an interest that is subject to execution, the officer is regarded as the agent of the pledgor, and the amount recovered is only the value of the pledgee's special interest. Treadwell *v.* Davis, 34 Cal. 601.

Where gold coin given in pledge was wrongfully taken from the pledgee, and he brought an action for money had and received to recover it, the damages were limited to the amount of money with interest, and could not be increased by regarding the coin as merchandise. If, however, an action of trover had been brought regarding the coin as merchandise, the measure of damages would be the value of the gold at the time of the conversion. Frothingham *v.* Morse, 45 N. H. 545.

1. Treadwell *v.* Davis, 34 Cal. 601; Ingersoll *v.* Van Bokkelen, 7 Cow. (N. Y.) 670; Hurst *v.* Coley, 15 Fed. Rep. 645; Hays *v.* Riddle, 1 Sandf. (N. Y.) 248; Miles *v.* Walther, 3 Mo. App. 96; Dilworthy *v.* McKelvy, 30 Mo. 149.

If the judgment between the parties should be entered for the full value of the property, this exceeding in amount the debt secured, the pledgee will hold the surplus after satisfying his debt to the use of the pledgor, for the judgment determines not the question of title but only that of possession. Miles *v.* Walther, 3 Mo. App. 96.

Where collateral was re-delivered to the pledgee for collection on a failure by him to account for the proceeds the measure of damages in a suit to recover the same is pledgee's interest in the collaterals, which interest cannot exceed the debt or the value of the collaterals. Hurst *v.* Coley, 15 Fed. Rep. 644.

2. Union Bank *v.* Laird, 2 Wheat. (U. S.) 390; Elder *v.* Rouse, 15 Wend. (N. Y.) 218; Cullum *v.* Emanuel, 1 Ala. 23; Buchanan *v.* Internat. Bank, 78 Ill. 500; Andrews *v.* Scotton, 2 Bland. (Md.) 629.

3. See Story Bailm., §§ 90, 329. Where property is pledged, the pledgee may, with the assent of the pledgor, use it in any way consistent with the general ownership and the ultimate rights of the pledgor. Lawrence *v.* Maxwell, 53 N. Y. 19.

4. Such as exercising horses, milking cows and hunting with dogs for the preservation of their health and habits. Story Bailm., § 329.

But he is answerable for damages caused by such use. Thompson *v.* Patrick, 4 Watts (Pa.) 414.

The *Georgia* Code, 1873, § 2141, provides that pledgee may use the goods pledged provided the use does not impair their real value.

5. Such as wearing of clothes pledged. Story Bailm., § 329. So it was held that a pledged sewing machine could not be used. McArthur *v.* Howett, 72 Ill. 358; nor could a harness. Thompson *v.* Patrick, 4 Watts (Pa.) 414.

There has been some discussion as to whether jewels pledged could be

would be indifferent and other circumstances do not incline either way, the use may be deemed not allowable.[1]

However much the views of the standard text-book writers may vary as to the application of the foregoing principles, it is well settled that the pledgee has a right to collect the rents and profits accruing from the thing pledged, and, where there is expense connected with the keeping of the pledge, it is his duty to make it profitable if possible.[2] When collected he must hold these profits for the benefit of the pledgor, for he will be accountable for them.[3]

3. Right to Incur Expense.—Necessary and proper expenses may be incurred by a pledgee about the thing pledged, for which he must be re-imbursed by the pledgor. These may include the reasonable charges incurred for its keep and preservation, for protecting the title, or for making the security available on maturity.[4]

worn at the pledgees' peril. Sir William Jones, and the court in Coggs *v.* Bernard, 2 Ld. Raym. 909, hold the affirmative, while Judge Story, on the ground that the owner cannot be presumed to wish his property to be so exposed, wisely supports the negative. Story Bailm., § 330.

1. It is held by Judge Story that books pledged may be used as though the use would be indifferent; the owner may be presumed to wish them to be used. But this supposition seems doubtful. Story Bailm., §329; Schouler Bailm., § 211.

2. Story on Bailments, § 331; Schouler on Bailments, § 212; 2 Kent's Com. 578; Coggs *v.* Bernard, 2 Ld. Raym. 909.

So it seems the pledgee of coupon bonds can collect the coupons as they fall due. Androscoggin R. Co. *v.* Auburn Bank, 48 Me. 335. In this case the pledgor, a corporation, pledged its own bonds and itself paid the coupons when presented; therefore the question above did not arise, though the court said it would have been so decided had it arisen.

So the pledgee of stock can collect the dividends. Gaty *v.* Holeday, 8 Mo. App. 118; Hunsaker *v.* Sturgis, 29 Cal. 142; Hagar *v.* Union Nat. Bank, 63 Me. 509.

If the pledgee omits to obtain a transfer upon the books of the corporation, the corporation is justified in paying the dividends to the pledgor, but the latter holds them as trustee of the pledgee and must account for the same. Merchants' Nat. Bank *v.* Richards, 6 Mo. App. 454; Gaty *v.* Holeday, 8 Mo. App. 118; Bell *v.* Lafferty, 1 Penn. (Pa.) 454; Hermann *v.* Maxwell, 47 N. Y. Super. Ct. 347. In the case of Hill *v.* Newichawanick Co., 48 How. Pr. (N. Y.) 427, the dividends pass to the pledgee, not by operation of law, but by the consent of the pledgor.

If the corporation unjustifiably refuses to make a transfer of stock upon its books at the request of the pledgee holding the certificate of stock indorsed in blank, the pledgee may recover of the corporation by suit any dividends accruing upon the stock while he held it in pledge. Merchants' Nat. Bank *v.* Richards, 6 Mo. App. 454.

Where the same stock was continued in pledge to secure a second debt after the first had been discharged, the pledgee had no authority to collect dividends accruing before the second giving in pledge. Fairbanks *v.* Merchants' Bank, 30 Ill. App. 28.

3. Hunasher *v.* Sturgis, 29 Cal. 142; Hauton *v.* Holliday, 2 Murph. (N. Car.) 111; Geron *v.* Geron, 15 Ala. 558; Davenport *v.* Tarlton, 1 A. K. Marsh. (Ky.) 244; Woodard *v.* Fitzpatrick, 9 Dana (Ky.) 117.

So for interest on money deposited as security for an engagement. Gibson *v.* Martin, 49 Vt. 474.

So the assignee of an insurance policy who collects a return premium is accountable to the assignor for the same. Felton *v.* Brooks, 4 Cush. (Mass.) 203; Merrifield *v.* Baker, 9 Allen (Mass.) 29.

4. Schouler Bailm., § 215; Starrett *v.* Barber, 20 Me. 457; Hills *v.* Smith, 28 N. H. 369.

The pledgee, while bound to make

For all such expenses the pledge becomes security; but where the expenses and charges are excessive in amount or are incurred out of the line of the pledgee's duty, without the authorization of the pledgor, the latter is not liable personally nor upon the pledge.[1]

4. Duty to Care for Pledge—*a.* DEGREE OF CARE.—As the contract of pledge is one of mutual benefit to the parties, the pledgee is bound to exercise the degree of care that an ordinarily prudent man would usually bestow on property of a like nature under similar circumstances; and he is liable to the pledgor for loss or injury resulting from failure to use such care.[2] If the pledge be to one whose vocation implies skill or unusual facilities, as a banker, such diligence is required as persons commonly prudent in that class are wont to exercise in such affairs.[3] It is compe-

useful and necessary repairs, cannot make new, expensive and unusal improvements, or such as materially change the mode of cultivating or using the estate. If he does he can recover his outlay, but only the increased value resulting therefrom. When, however, the debtor consents to the outlay, there is as between him and the grantee no reason for complaint. Pickersgill *v.* Brown, 7 La. Ann. 298.

Under an assignment of personal property by a debtor to his creditor to secure existing claims and future liabilities, the creditor will be entitled to the commissions for the management of the property as stipulated, unless they are so extravagant as to afford evidence of fraud toward other creditors. Hendricks *v.* Robinson, 2 Johns. Ch. (N. Y.) 283.

Assessments rightfully paid on pledged stock are allowed against the pledgor. McCalla *v.* Clark, 55 Ga. 53.

A pledgee was allowed to have an additional lien upon a steamer pledged for advances he was compelled to make or liabilities he assumed to secure its release, it having been libeled, while in pledge for a collision occurring previously. Fagan *v.* Thompson, 38 Fed. Rep. 467.

So the pledgee of an insurance policy could recover for premiums paid by him to keep the policy alive. Raley *v.* Ross, 59 Ga. 862.

Where goods come into the pledgee's possession in an unfinished state, such that a court of equity would order them to be finished by a receiver, and the pledgee does in that respect what the court would have ordered the receiver to do, while the pledgee is probably chargeable with the avails of the finished goods, although finished with his own property and by his means, he is, nevertheless, entitled to have such avails applied in the first place to the payment of his disbursement upon the property, before any application is made upon the debt. Rowan *v.* State Bank, 45 Vt. 160.

Where raw material is pledged, the pledgee has no right to manufacture finished goods therefrom and charge the pledgor with the cost of manufacture, except by virtue of an express contract. Boody *v.* Goddard, 57 Me. 602.

1. Schouler Bailm., § 215; Story Bailm., §§ 306a, 343; Sturrett *v.* Barber, 20 Me. 457; McCalla *v.* Clark, 55 Ga. 53; Blake *v.* Buchanan, 22 Vt. 548, as to question of costs.

2. Story Bailm., § 332; 2 Kent Comm. 578; Jones Bailm., §§ 23, 75; Commercial Bank *v.* Martin, 1 La. Ann. 344; Third Nat. Bank *v.* Boyd, 44 Md. 47; Erie Bank *v.* Smith, 3 Brews. (Pa.) 9; Girard F. & M. Ins. Co. *v.* Marr, 46 Pa. St. 504; Scott *v.* Crews, 2 S. Car. 522; Petty *v.* Overall, 42 Ala. 145; Wells *v.* Wells, 53 Vt. 1; St. Losky *v.* Davidson, 6 Cal. 644; Maury *v.* Coyle, 34 Md. 235; Cooper *v.* Simpson, 41 Minn. 46; Cutting *v.* Marlor, 78 N. Y. 454; Ouderkirk *v.* Central Nat. Bank, 119 N. Y. 263; Hollister *v.* Central Nat. Bank, 119 N. Y. 634; Minneapolis etc. Elevator Co. *v.* Betcher, 42 Minn. 210.

The early rule laid down by Sir Edward Coke, in Southcote's Case, 4 Rep. 83 b, that a pledgee was liable only for such care as he used over his own property was rejected by Sir William Jones, Bailm. 75, who states, practically, the rule in the text with the following comment: "This is expressly holden by Bracton; and when I rely on his authority, I am perfectly aware that he copied Justinian almost word for word." Bract. 99 b.

3. See cases in preceding note.

tent for the parties to stipulate for a different degree of liability than that which the law puts upon them; in such case the express agreement will govern.[1] If the pledgee mixes pledged property with his own he must bear all the inconvenience of confusion; if he cannot distinguish and separate his own, he will lose it; and if damages are given to the plaintiff for the loss of his property, the utmost value will be taken.[2]

b. EMPLOYMENT OF AGENTS.—Where the pledgee employs agents about the pledge, he is liable for their negligence as well as for his own.[3] But where it becomes necessary for a pledgee, in the exercise of the diligence required of him, to employ an agent on account of his particular profession and skill, he will not be responsible for the neglect or misconduct of the latter, where reasonable care was shown in the choice of the agent as to his skill and ability.[4]

c. LIABILITY FOR DAMAGE AND LOSS—(1) *In General.*—For loss, damage or depreciation occurring in regard to the pledged property the pledgee is not responsible, unless it is caused by his negligence.[5]

On demand and tender by the pledgor, a good reason for not returning the pledge in good order must be shown by the pledgee and evidence failing to show lack of ordinary care he cannot be charged.[6] On the other hand, if the pledgee gives no satisfactory explanation, he shall be held liable unless the injury appears due to some other cause.[7] If the evidence in regard to

1. Bank of British Columbia *v.* Marshall, 11 Fed. Rep. 19.

So the liability may be increased. Drake *v.* White, 117 Mass. 10.

Where the pledgor agreed that goods should be stored in a certain warehouse at his risk and expense, the removal by the agent of the pledgee, though without the latter's knowledge, made him responsible for any damage to said goods caused by their removal to an insecure or improper place of storage. St. Losky *v.* Davidson, 6 Cal. 644.

2. Hart *v.* Ten Eyck, 2 Johns. Ch. (N. Y.) 62; Ringgold *v.* Ringgold, 1 Har. & G. (Md.) 11.

See ACCESSION AND CONFUSION OF GOODS, vol. 1, p. 50.

3. St. Losky *v.* Davidson, 6 Cal. 644; Schouler Bailm., § 209.

See AGENCY, vol. 1, p. 331.

This applies also to corporation pledgees.

See Androscoggin R. Co. *v.* Auburn Bank, 48 Me. 335; Third Nat. Bank *v.* Boyd, 44 Md. 47; Dearborn *v.* Union Nat. Bank, 61 Me. 369; Cutting *v.* Marvor, 78 N. Y. 454.

4. Commercial Bank *v.* Martin, 1 La. Ann. 344.

5. Jones on Pledge, § 405; Scott *v.* Crews, 2 S. Car. 522; Erie Bank *v.* Smith, 3 Brews. (Pa.) 9.

For a loss occurring after it is the pledgee's duty to return the property, he holding it without right, he is liable. Coggs *v.* Bernard, 2 Ld. Raym. 909, 917.

If perishable goods are pledged, the pledgee is bound to use ordinary care to preserve them; but if they perish naturally the loss will fall on the pledgor. Thomason *v.* Dill, 30 Ala. 444.

If one of several things pledged be lost with fault of pledgee, the remainder are liable for the whole debt. Ratcliff *v.* Davis, Yel. 178.

6. Story Bailm., § 409; Schouler Bailm., § 338; 2 Kent Comm. 580, 581; Jones on Pledge 409; Winthrop Sav. Bank *v.* Jackson, 67 Me. 570.

Where the pledgor claims the pledge is lost by neglect, he must show the neglect, and that damage resulted to him therefrom. Murphy *v.* Bartsch (Idaho, 1890), 23 Pac. Rep. 82.

7. Stuart *v.* Bigler, 98 Pa. St. 80.

the degree of diligence employed is equally balanced the presumption that the pledgee has done his duty will leave the case with him.[1]

It is, however, a question of fact for the jury to determine from the circumstances as to whether ordinary diligence was used.[2]

Such loss through negligence of the pledgee does not discharge *pro tanto* the debt secured.[3]

(2) *In Case of Theft.*—Theft *per se* establishes neither responsibility nor irresponsibility in the pledgee. If theft is occasioned by ordinary negligence, the pledgee is responsible; if without any or with less than ordinary negligence, he is discharged.[4]

(3) *Measure of Damages for Loss by Negligence.*—This question chiefly arises in regard to securities the value of which is liable to large fluctuations between the time of their loss and the time of the demand for them. In *Maryland*, the value at the time of the loss is assessed,[5] while in other States, the value at the time of demand governs.[6]

5. Right to Assign the Pledge.—The pledgee may deliver over the pledge into the hands of a stranger for safe custody without consideration;[7] he may sell or assign all his interest in the pledge, and the assignee will stand in his place;[8] or he may convey the

1. Mills *v.* Gilbreth, 47 Me. 326; Clark *v.* Spence, 10 Watts (Pa.) 335.

2. Arent *v.* Squire, 1 Daly (N. Y.) 347; Abbett *v.* Frederick, 56 How. Pr. (N. Y.) 68.

The question of what is ordinary diligence is materially affected by the value of the property pledged, the liability to loss or theft, and the precaution taken against these. Third Nat. Bank *v.* Boyd, 44 Md. 47.

The usages generally followed by others pursuing the same line of business in the same locality are to be taken into account, and the latest applications for the protection of property need not be adopted unless it is commonly done by others in the same business. Scott *v.* Crews, 2 S. Car. 522.

3. Cooper *v.* Simpson, 41 Minn. 46.

4. Story Bailm., § 338; 2 Kent Comm. 580; Abbett *v.* Frederick, 156 How. Pr. (N. Y.) 68; Petty *v.* Overall, 42 Ala. 145; Maury *v.* Coyle, 34 Md. 235; Third Nat. Bank *v.* Boyd, 44 Md. 47; Second Nat. Bank *v.* Ocean Nat. Bank, 11 Blatchf. (U. S.) 362; Scott *v.* Crews, 2 S. Car. 522; Jenkins *v.* National Village Bank, 58 Me. 275; Winthrop Sav. Bank *v.* Jackson, 67 Me. 570.

Where the pledgee takes the same care of pledged goods as he does of his own and both are stolen, he is presumed to have used the care of an ordinary man in the same position. Only proof of actual negligence can rebut this presumption. Story Bailm., § 338. But if the pledgee can be shown to have taken less care of the pledged goods than of his own it furnishes strong and in some cases almost decisive proof of negligence. Vere *v.* Smith, 1 Vent. 121; Syred *v.* Carrauthers, El. B. & E. 469; Petty *v.* Overall, 42 Ala. 145.

Sir William Jones held that where the pledged property was taken by robbery the presumption was in favor of the pledgee, but if the property was stolen or taken by stealth, the presumption was against him. Jones Bailm., § 75, 119; but the rule in the text seems the most reasonable and is generally adopted.

It is incumbent on the pledgor to show both the negligence and the damage therefrom. Murphy *v.* Bartsch (Idaho, 1890), 23 Pac. Rep. 82.

5. Third Nat. Bank *v.* Boyd, 44 Md. 47.

6. Second Nat. Bank *v.* Smith, 8 Phila. (Pa.) 68.

Such loss or depreciation in the value of the property pledged does not operate to discharge the debt secured *pro tanto.* Cooper *v.* Simpson, 41 Minn. 46.

7. Ingersoll *v.* Van Vokkelin, 7 Cow. (N. Y.) 670.

8. Warner *v.* Martin, 11 How. (U. S.) 209; Jarvis *v.* Rogers, 15 Mass. 408;

same interest conditionally by the way of pledge to another person.[1]

The pledgee may release a portion of the goods pledged, and such release, if made to the pledgor, or with his consent to his assignee, does not affect the pledgee's lien upon the remainder of the property, or his right of action against the debtor upon the personal obligation.[2]

The lien of a pledge cannot be separated either from the possession of the pledge or from the debt, so that to make an effectual sale both must pass to the assignee.[3]

Whitaker *v.* Sumner, 20 Pick. (Mass.) 399; Thompson *v.* Patrick, 4 Watts (Pa.) 414; Ashton's Appeal, 73 Pa. St. 153; Bullard *v.* Billings, 2 Vt. 309; Bush *v.* Lyon, 9 Cow. (N. Y.) 52; Goss *v.* Emerson, 23 N. H. 38; Bailey *v.* Colby, 34 N. H. 29; Baltimore M. Ins. Co. *v.* Dalrymple, 25 Md. 269; Bulkeley *v.* Welch, 31 Conn. 339; Calkins *v.* Lockwood, 17 Conn. 154; Shelton *v.* French, 33 Conn. 489; Belden *v.* Perkins, 78 Ill. 449; Whitney *v.* Peay, 24 Ark. 22; Macomber *v.* Parker, 14 Pick. (Mass.) 497; Hunt *v.* Holton, 13 Pick. (Mass.) 216; Ferguson *v.* Union Furnace Co., 9 Wend. (N. Y.) 345; Bradley *v.* Parks, 83 Ill. 169; Mores *v.* Conham, Owen 123; Johnson *v.* Stear, 15 C. B., N. S. 330; Donald *v.* Suckling, L. R., 1 Q. B. 585; Ratcliffe *v.* Davies, Yel. 178; Demainvray *v.* Metcalfe, 2 Vern. 690; Mann *v.* Shiffner, 2 East 523; McCombie *v.* Davies, 7 East 607; Halliday *v.* Holgate, L. R., 3 Ex. 299. This is the chief distinction between a mere lien and a pledge. Hubbell *v.* Drexel, 21 Am. L. Reg., N. S. 452; Daubigny *v.* Duval, 5 T. R. 604; Legg *v.* Evans, 6 M. & W. 36; McCombie *v.* Davies, 7 East 6.

So of negotiable instruments. Hayes *v.* Riddle, 1 Sandf. (N. Y.) 248; Chapman *v.* Brooks, 31 N. Y. 75; Duncomb *v.* New York etc R. Co., 84 N. Y. 190; 88 N. Y. 1; Gould *v.* Farmers' Loan etc. Co., 23 Hun (N. Y.) 322; Lewis *v.* Mott, 36 N. Y. 395; Baldwin *v.* Ely, 9 How. (U. S.) 580; Fennel *v.* McGowan, 58 Miss. 261; White Mts. etc. R. Co. *v.* Bay State Iron Co., 50 N. H. 57; Merchants' Bank *v.* State Bank, 10 Wall. (U. S.) 604.

The pledgee may assign the pledged property with or without the consent of the pledgor. Curtis *v.* Leavitt, 15 N. Y. 9.

In several States it is made a criminal offense to sell or repledge collateral securities without the consent of the pledgor. *Massachusetts* Pub. St. 1882, chap. 203, § 72, 73.

Such an offense is not indictable as embezzlement, but only under the statute. Com. *v.* Butterick, 100 Mass. 1; *Pennsylvania* Laws 1878, ch. 155, § 200; Act of May 25, 1878. But in 1881, Act of June 10th, Pub. Laws 1881, p. 107, this statute was modified by a proviso that it shall not be construed to prevent brokers from pledging or hypothecating stock or other securities which they have purchased, in whole or in part, with their own money or credit for others, and for which they have not been wholly reimbursed by the parties for whom such stock or other securities have been purchased.

The payee of a negotiable note, holding other notes as collateral security may lawfully transfer the collateral notes to an indorsee of a principal note, although he has given his debtor a written undertaking to redeem the collaterals, and if the indorsee to whom the securities are transferred wrongfully converts them to his own use the original payee is not liable in trover for such conversion. Goss *v.* Emerson, 23 N. H. 38.

1. McCombie *v.* Davies, 7 East 63; Ratcliffe *v.* Davies, Yel. 178; Jarvis *v.* Rogers, 15 Mass. 389; National Bank *v.* Winston, 5 Baxt. (Tenn.) 685; Lewis *v.* Mott, 36 N. Y. 395; Jarvis *v.* Rogers, 15 Mass. 408.

2. Faulkner *v.* Hill, 104 Mass. 188.

3. Whitney *v.* Peay, 24 Ark. 22; Johnson *v.* Smith, 11 Humph. (Tenn.) 396; Bullard *v.* Billings, 2 Vt. 309; and see Lewis *v.* Barnum, 12 Abb. Pr. (N. Y.) 305.

Where therefore the debt secured has been assigned with the pledge, the pledgor cannot maintain an action of trover against the pledgee for con-

The security, however, being a mere incident of the principal debt, an assignment of the debt passes either a legal or equitable interest in the pledge, unless it is otherwise agreed between the parties.[1]

The original contract of pledge is not put an end to by assigning the thing pledged, and therefore the original pledgor can only recover it by first paying or tendering the amount of his debt secured by the pledge.[2]

If the pledgee sells absolutely the pledged property before the debt secured is due, he is guilty of conversion and liable for the difference between the value of the pledged property at the time

version of the property, although the latter's assignee may have converted the property to his own use. Goss *v.* Emerson, 23 N. H. 38; Baily *v.* Colby, 34 N. H. 29; Stiger *v.* Third Nat. Bank, 6 Fed. Rep. 569.

Nor can the pledgor maintain replevin or detinue for the thing pledged in the hands of the assignee without paying or tendering the debt secured by the pledge. Halliday *v.* Colgate, L. R. Ex. 299; Johnson *v.* Stear, 15 C. B., N. S. 330; Evans *v.* Potter, 2 Gall. (U. S.) 13; Lewis *v.* Mott, 36 N. Y. 95; Lane *v.* Bailey, 47 Barb. (N. Y.) 395; but in Neiler *v.* Kelley, 69 Pa. St. 403, and Work *v.* Bennett, 70 Pa. St. 484, trover was maintained for an illegal conversion of the thing pledged by selling or repledging it, though defendant was allowed to recoup from the damages of the conversion the amount due him secured by the pledge. But see Thompson *v.* Patrick, 4 Watts (Pa.) 414.

1. Stearns *v.* Bates, 46 Conn. 313; Belcher *v.* Hartford Bank, 15 Conn. 383; Lewis *v.* De Forest, 20 Conn. 427; Jones *v.* Quinnipiack Bank, 29 Conn. 25; Poe *v.* Bank of Montreal, 39 U. C., Q. B. 54; Esty *v.* Graham, 46 N. H. 169; Stearns *v.* Bates, 46 Conn. 306; Homer *v.* Savings Bank, 7 Conn. 478; *contra*, Johnson *v.* Smith, 11 Humph. (Tenn.) 396, where the court said that delivery or possession was essential to the pledge, the passage of the debt alone could not pass security without the delivery. It seems, however, that the original pledgee might ordinarily be regarded as holding possession of the pledge as the agent of his assignee. Jones on Pledge, § 418, n.

As the pledgee cannot separate his special property in pledge from the debt secured by it, so that the debt shall be owned by one person and the pledge by another, it is, therefore, held that the assignee of the pledge cannot maintain an action or enforce a lien unless he shows that he also owns the debt secured by the pledge. Van Eman *v.* Stanchfield, 13 Minn. 75.

The assignee of a principal debt and the collateral securities holds the latter upon the same terms that the original pledgee held them. Ponce *v.* McElvy, 47 Cal. 154; Dupre *v.* Fall, 10 Cal. 430; Alexandria etc. R. Co. *v.* Burke, 22 Gratt. (Va.) 254; Fant *v.* Miller, 17 Gratt. (Va.) 47.

2. Donald *v.* Suckling, L. R., 1 Q. B. 585; Talty *v.* Freedman's Sav. etc. Co., 93 U. S. 321; Thompson *v.* Patrick, 4 Watts (Pa.) 414; Bradley *v.* Parks, 83 Ill. 169; Belden *v.* Perkins, 78 Ill. 449; Steiger *v.* Third Nat. Bank, 6 Fed. Rep. 569.

Where the pledgee makes a sale or repledge wholly inconsistent with the contract of pledge, the pledgor's proper remedy is an action on the case for the injury done instead of detinue or conversion. Donald *v.* Suckling, L. R., 1 Q. B. 585, 610. Per Blackburn, J.

Trover was also sustained in Merchants' Nat. Bank *v.* Trenholm, 12 Heisk. (Tenn.) 520. In First Nat. Bank *v.* Boyce, 78 Ky. 42, 19 Am. L. Reg., N. S. 503, the pledgor was allowed to maintain an action against a subpledgee without first tendering or paying the original debt, but the subpledgee was allowed a right of set-off against the original pledgor.

So long as nothing is done to deprive the pledgor of his right to redeem on payment of the amount due on the principal debt, he is not injured and cannot complain of the assignment. Chapman *v.* Brooks, 31 N. Y. 75.

of conversion and the amount of the debt secured.[1] There is ordinarily no implication in law that the pledgee shall keep the pledge in his own exclusive possession.[2]

6. Duty to Return Pledge.—When the debt or engagement for which the pledge was given has been performed and the lien of the pledgee discharged, it is the latter's duty to return the pledge to the pledgor.[3]

XII. Rights, Liabilities and Remedies of Pledgee of Corporeal Property After Default—1. In General.—The remedies of the pledgee on the pledgor's default, lie in two general directions: first, by suit on the debt itself; second, by recourse to the property pledged as security.

2. Suit on the Debt Secured—*a.* In General.—The fact that a creditor has taken collateral security for a debt does not in any way preclude his suing on the debt before resorting to the security.[4]

1. Kilpatrick *v.* Dean (City Court), 3 N. Y. Supp. 60.

2. Donald *v.* Suckling, L. R., 1 Q. B. 585; Talty *v.* Freedman's Sav. etc. Co., 93 U. S. 321; Hopper *v.* Smith, 63 How. Pr. (N. Y.) 34; Lewis *v.* Mott, 36 N. Y. 95.

It has been suggested, however, that an obligation on the part of the pledgee to keep the pledge in his own personal care may in some cases be inferred from the nature of the thing pledged, as in the case of a valuable work of art, which it is to be supposed that the pledgor would not desire to give to the care of strangers. Per Cockburn, J., in Donald *v.* Suckling, L. R., 1 Q. B. 585.

3. Story on Bailm. § 450; Lyle *v.* Barker, 5 Binn. (Pa.) 457; Pomeroy *v.* Smith, 17 Pick. (Mass.) 86; Dean *v.* Lawhan, 7 Oregon 423.

But he need not do this until demand made, or he is notified that his debt has been paid. Dewart *v.* Masser, 40 Pa. St. 302.

Where claims are received, to be collected and applied to the payment of debts, an offer to return them is sufficient, unless some are lost through negligence in proceeding thereon. Mullen *v.* Morris, 2 Pa. St. 85.

4. Butterworth *v.* Kennedy, 5 Bosw. (N. Y.) 143; Langdon *v.* Buell, 9 Wend. (N. Y.) 80; Elder *v.* Rouse, 15 Wend. (N. Y.) 218; Queen's Co. Bank *v.* Leavitt (Supreme Ct.), 10 N. Y. Supp. 194; Beckwith *v.* Sibley, 11 Pick. (Mass.) 482; Whitwell *v.* Brigham, 19 Pick. (Mass.) 117; Cornwall *v.* Gould, 4 Pick. (Mass.) 444; Whitaker *v.* Sumner, 20 Pick. (Mass.) 399; Bank of Rutland *v.* Woodruff, 34 Vt. 89; Darst *v.* Bates, 95 Ill. 493; Wilhelm *v.* Schmidt, 84 Ill. 189; Cushman *v.* Hayes, 46 Ill. 145; Archibald *v.* Argall, 53 Ill. 307; Rozet *v.* McClellan, 48 Ill. 345; Robinson *v.* Hurley, 11 Iowa 410; Jones *v.* Scott, 10 Kan. 33; Dugan *v.* Sprague, 2 Ind. 600; Sonoma Valley Bank *v.* Hill, 59 Cal. 107; Kemmil *v.* Wilson, 4 Wash. (U. S.) 308.

South Sea Co. *v.* Duncomb, 2 Str. 919; Ewes *v.* Widdowson, 4 Car. & P. 151; Anonymous, 12 Mod. 564.

Nothing in the *California* statutes precludes a pledgee from suing for the debt without first resorting to the pledge. Ehrlich *v.* Ewald, 66 Cal. 97.

There is no obligation on the part of the pledgee to sell collateral securities before suing on the debt. Queen's Co. Bank *v.* Leavitt (Supreme Ct.), 10 N. Y. Supp. 194.

Suit for Deficiency.—A suit may be maintained by the pledgee for a deficiency arising after the application of the pledged property to the debt. Mauge *v.* Heringhi, 26 Cal. 577.

Presenting Claim to Personal Representatives of Deceased Pledgor.—Unless the pledgee seeks recourse against other property of the pledgor besides that held in pledge, he need not present his claim. *In re* Kibbe, 57 Cal. 407; Huyler *v.* Dahoney, 48 Tex. 234.

But where collateral security for a debt is uncollectible in *Texas*, the pledgee may be compelled to present his claim in the probate court. Huyler *v.* Dahoney, 48 Tex. 234.

In *Arkansas*, by statute, if the re-

Nothing short of the recovery of the amount of the debt itself will release the security.[1] Even the recovery of judgment,[2] taking out execution or attachment against other property of the debtor,[3] and committing the debtor's body to prison on execution for the debt,[4] do not impair the right to hold the security.

Even refusal of tender of the amount of the debt at maturity, while it discharges the lien, leaves still the right to sue on the debt.[5]

b. RETURN OF SECURITY.—The return of the security in general is not a condition precedent to the recovery by suit on the debt, for the pledgee can hold it until after his debt is satisfied,[6] and if the pledged property is not then returned, the pledgee is liable in trover.[7] In some States by statute the creditor must produce the security or account for its absence as a preliminary to recovery.[8] And he cannot escape this obligation by showing

demption of the pledge is for the benefit of the estate, the executor may be compelled to redeem it. *Arkansas* Dig. 1874, § 183.

1. Where, after suit was brought upon a note, the plaintiff sold collateral security for more than enough to pay the balance due on the note, held, that this was equivalent to payment *pendente lite* and discharged the cause of action, but that the surplus could not be recovered in set-off. Lewis *v.* Jewett, 51 Vt. 378.

2. Smith *v.* Strout, 63 Me. 205; Jones *v.* Scott, 10 Kan. 33; Sonoma Valley Bank *v.* Hill, 59 Cal. 107; Charles *v.* Coker, 2 S. Car. 122.

3. Taylor *v.* Cheever, 6 Gray (Mass.) 146; Whitwell *v.* Brigham, 19 Pick. (Mass.) 117.

4. Morse *v.* Woods, 5 N. H. 297; Chapman *v.* Clough, 6 Vt. 123; Trotter *v.* Crockett, 2 Port. (Ala.) 401; Smith *v.* Strout, 63 Me. 205; South Sea Co. *v.* Duncomb, 2 Str. 919.

But see Cleverly *v.* Brackett, 8 Mass. 150; Sellick *v.* Munson, 2 Aik. (Vt.) 50; 2 Vt. 13.

5. Jones on Pledges, §§ 542, 592; Mitchell *v.* Roberts, 17 Fed. Rep. 776.

Where the stock and other assets of one bank had been transferred to another bank, to secure it against existing liabilities, and such transfer was set aside as fraudulent, it was held that the debt was not thereby rendered void; it lost the benefit of the security, but was entitled to the privileges of other creditors. Johnston *v.* Southwestern Bank, 3 Strobh. Eq. (S. Car.) 263.

6. Taylor *v.* Cheever, 6 Gray (Mass.) 146; Chapman *v.* Clough, 6 Vt. 123; Morse *v.* Woods, 5 N. H. 297; Scott *v.* Parker, 1 Q. B. 809; Lawton *v.* Newland, 2 Stark. 72.

Even where an agreement was made that on payment of a part of the debt a proportionate part of the shares pledged was to be returned, it was held that the shares were to be returned after the money was paid. Scott *v.* Parker, 1 Q. B. 809.

By statute in *Minnesota* one who has taken security for a debt as therein provided, may bring his action on the original claim, in the first instance, holding himself ready to prove that in fact he had no security, and will not be put to a useless expense and delay simply for the purpose of demonstrating this by a judicial decision; but by their admission of the assignment to them of such security, they put themselves out of court, until they either show that it was exhausted before bringing the suit, or that it was valueless. Schalck *v.* Harmon, 6 Minn. 265.

Offer to Return.—In *Louisiana* a creditor who has obtained possession of property of an insolvent debtor held in pledge by another creditor, by paying the debt due the latter, cannot afterwards sue to recover the money paid by him without offering to restore the pledged property. Byrne *v.* Hibernia Nat. Bank, 31 La. Ann. 81.

7. Scott *v.* Parker, 1 Q. B. 809.

8. Ocean Nat. Bank *v.* Faub, 50 N. Y. 474; Smith *v.* Rockwell, 2 Hill (N. Y.) 482; Stuart *v.* Bigler, 98 Pa. St. 80; Spaulding *v.* Bank of Susquehanna Co., 9 Pa. St. 28; Bank of U. S. *v.* Peabody, 20 Pa. St. 454.

that the security, subsequent to its deposit, became worthless, since it does not follow but that he may have disposed of it to advantage while it was still of value.[1]

c. DEFENSES.—The debt being a transaction independent of the pledge contract, as a rule the value of the pledged property cannot be set-off or recouped against the debt sued on,[2] nor is it a good defense that the property pledged has greatly depreciated in value between the time of default and the bringing of the suit.[3] The fact that the debtor gave security for the debt does not preclude him from setting up an antecedent defense.[4] For the giving of security in no way affects the antecedent rights of the parties.[5] But by statute in several States, the pledgor may set up as a defense the conversion of the pledge.[6]

It is no defense to a suit on the debt that the pledgee has failed to sell or otherwise realize on the security pledged, as he has the power to do.[7] Of course, when the debtor has realized on the security, that is a defense *pro tanto* to the suit on the debt secured.[8] A covenant not to sue until the return of the security

The failure or refusal to give an account of the application of goods received as collateral security for a debt, will operate as a bar to the recovery of the debt itself. Simes *v.* Zane, 1 Phila. (Pa.) 501.

Where a creditor holds collaterals in pledge to secure his claim, he is properly required to account therefor before sharing in the proceeds of a receiver's sale of the debtor's property. Bryan etc. Shoe Co. *v.* Block, 52 Ark. 458.

1. Stuart *v.* Bigler, 98 Pa. St. 80.

2. Winthrop Sav. Bank *v.* Jackson, 67 Me. 570.

3. Rozet *v.* McClellan, 48 Ill. 345.

The failure of a pledgee of stock to sell it on request of the pledgor at the maturity of the debt secured, cannot be set up as a bar to a suit on the debt, but the loss occasioned by the failure may be in that case set-off. Taggard *v.* Curtenius, 15 Wend. (N. Y.) 155.

4. Hancock *v.* Palmer, 17 Abb. Pr. (N. Y.) 335.

5. Gahn *v.* Niemcewicz, 11 Wend. (N. Y.) 321; Elwood *v.* Diefendorf, 5 Barb. (N. Y.) 409; Wagaman *v.* Hoag, 14 Barb. (N. Y.) 239; Taylor *v.* Allen, 36 Barb. (N. Y.) 297; Fox *v.* Parker, 44 Barb. (N. Y.) 541; Darlon *v.* Christie, 39 Barb. (N. Y.) 613; Taggard *v.* Curtenius, 15 Wend. (N. Y.) 157; Pring *v.* Clarkson, 1 Barn. & Cress. 14; Twopenny *v.* Young, 3 Barn. & Cress. 208.

6. Cass *v.* Higenbotam, 27 Hun (N. Y.) 406; Stearns *v.* Marsh, 4 Den. (N. Y.) 227; Bank of British Columbia *v.* Marshall, 11 Fed. Rep. 19; Scott *v.* Crews, 2 S. Car. 522.

Where the pledgee, with the consent of the pledgor, gave the goods pledged to a factor to sell, on a suit on the debt secured, the pledgee was held to account for the value of the goods even though the factor had failed to account to him; for the pledgee, having dealt with the factor, has the right and duty of compelling the latter to account. Bigelow *v.* Walker, 24 Vt. 149.

7. See *infra*, this title, *Obligation to Sell.*

Butterworth *v.* Kennedy, 5 Bosw. (N. Y.) 143; Napier *v.* Central Ga. Bank, 68 Ga. 637; Stover *v.* Flack, 41 Barb. (N. Y.) 162.

That the pledgee has wrongfully sold other securities which he held for the same debt, is no defense. Hayes *v.* Riddle, 1 Sandf. (N. Y.) 248.

8. In an action by a bank on a promissory note, to which the defense was payment by a sale of bonds of a corporation held as collateral security, parol evidence was admitted against the defendant's objection to show that the bank held the bonds also as collateral security for a previous note of which the note in suit was a renewal or was given as security, and that, having a claim against the bankrupt estate of an indorser of the previous note, the bank made an arrangement with the assignee in bankruptcy,

cannot be set up as a bar to the suit on the debt; but there may be a suit for breach of the covenant.[1]

d. ATTACHMENT OF PLEDGED PROPERTY.—The pledgee may, if he likes, waive his lien and have the pledged property levied upon and sold under execution or attachment issued upon judgment recovered on the debt secured.[2]

3. Recourse to Security—*a.* IN GENERAL.—On the failure of the pledgor to redeem, the pledgee does not become the absolute owner of the pledged property, for his right is simply to hold the goods for security.[3] To work a forfeiture of the pledgor's title, a foreclosure of some kind must take place.[4]

Outside of agreement by the parties and the operation of statute law, the right of the pledgee to foreclose the title of the pledgor is enforced by filing a bill in chancery and having a judicial sale under a regular decree in foreclosure or by selling without judicial process upon giving reasonable notice to redeem.[5]

b. ELECTION OF FUNDS.—A creditor having two securities for the same debt may rely on either or both.[6] But when another

by which the bonds were sold by public auction, the bank agreeing to bid a certain amount for them, and to prove the balance of the claim against the estate; that no one else bid any more, and the bank kept the bonds and proved the remainder of its claim. *Held* that this evidence was admissible; also, that the fact that the bank received a dividend from the trustees of the property of the corporation, to whom a mortgage had been given to secure the bonds, was not evidence tending to show that the bonds were actually sold by the bank. Globe Nat. Bank *v.* Ingalls, 126 Mass. 209.

1. Foster *v.* Purdy, 5 Met. (Mass.) 442.

So under a statute in *California*, a creditor of a corporation may sue the stockholders, though he hold security of the corporation for the same debt. Sonoma Valley Bank *v.* Hill, 59 Cal. 107.

2. Sickles *v.* Richardson, 23 Hun (N. Y.) 559; Legg *v.* Willard, 17 Pick. (Mass.) 140; Whitaker *v.* Sumner, 20 Pick. (Mass.) 399; Buck *v.* Ingersoll, 11 Met. (Mass.) 226; Jacobs *v.* Latour, 5 Bing. 130; but see Arendale *v.* Morgan, 5 Sneed (Tenn.) 703.

Exempt Property.—Where property exempt from execution has been pledged, the exemption is waived and the property may be sold under execution issued on judgment recovered on the debt secured. Jones *v.* Scott, 10 Kan. 33.

But where a sheriff holding a note as collateral security for the payment of an execution against the owner of the note, made a void levy under the execution, the lien was not waived. Fisher *v.* Meek, 38 Ill. 92.

3. Unless especially authorized by the terms of the bailment, the pledgee cannot appropriate the security in satisfaction of the debt. Conyngham's Appeal, 57 Pa. St. 474; and even then he may be compelled to account to the pledgor. Kingsbury *v.* Phelps, Wright (Ohio) 370.

In some States such an agreement is of no avail. Lucketts *v.* Townsend, 3 Tex. 119.

4. Brownell *v.* Hawkins, 4 Barb. (N. Y.) 491; Mitchell *v.* Roberts, 17 Fed. Rep. 776.

5. Robinson *v.* Hurley, 11 Iowa 410; Ogden *v.* Lathrop, 1 Sweeny (N. Y.) 643; Lucketts *v.* Townsend, 3 Tex. 119; King *v.* Texas B. & Ins. Co., 58 Tex. 669; Stearns *v.* Marsh, 4 Den. (N. Y.) 227.

6. Buchanan *v.* International Bank, 78 Ill. 500; Prout *v.* Lomer, 79 Ill. 331; Collum *v.* Emanuel, 1 Ala. 23; Taylor's Appeal, 81 Pa. St. 460; Morris *v.* Fales, 43 Hun (N. Y.) 393; Farmers' Loan etc. Co. *v.* Walworth, 1 N. Y. 433.

A subsequent judgment creditor, whose claim is jeopardized by an appropriation of payments to an earlier lien, has no equity which will authorize him to interfere in said distribution, where the security remains which he

party has a lien upon or interest in only one of these funds the creditor will be compelled in equity to resort to the other.[1] But this rule is never enforced to the prejudice of the double-fund creditor,[2] as where the fund to be resorted to is dubious or is one which can be reached only by litigation.[3]

c. SALE AT COMMON LAW—(1) *In General.*—The rule at common law is now well settled that on default of payment of his debt the pledgee,[4] by giving to the pledgor reasonable notice to redeem and of the intended sale, may, without judicial process or decree of foreclosure, sell the pledged property at public auction and give a good title.[5]

had when his judgment was received. Johnson's Appeal, 37 Pa. St. 268.

A creditor may resort to his collateral security, although he has taken and discharged the bail of his principal debtor upon a *capias ad satisfaciendum.* Hartshorne *v.* McIver, 1 Cranch (C. C.) 421.

1. Besley *v.* Lawrence, 11 Paige (N. Y.) 581; Ingalls *v.* Morgan, 10 N. Y. 178; Hawley *v.* Mancins, 7 Johns. Ch. (N. Y.) 174; Geller *v.* Hoyt, 7 How. Pr. (N. Y.) 265; Davis *v.* Walker, 51 Miss. 659; Turner *v.* McCarter, 42 Ga. 491; Breedlove *v.* Stump, 3 Yerg. (Tenn.) 257; White *v.* Dougherty, Mart. & Y. (Tenn.) 309; Glass *v.* Pullen, 6 Bush (Ky.) 346.

This rule is not applicable where a party has merely an election between the two funds and no other liens are involved. Farmers' Loan etc. Co. *v.* Walworth, 1 N. Y. 433.

Security Out of the State.—It makes no difference that the unincumbered property is out of the State. Hays *v.* Ward, 4 Johns. Ch. (N. Y.) 123; but there must be full, clear and distinct evidence that the security beyond the State is substantial, of certain value, and likely to prove available at once for liquidating some considerable part of the creditor's claim. Calloway *v.* People's Bank, 54 Ga. 541. Otherwise the election will not be enforced. Denham *v.* Williams, 39 Ga. 312.

2. Jervis *v.* Smith, 7 Abb. Pr., N. S. (N. Y.) 217; Evertson *v.* Booth, 19 Johns. (N. Y.) 486; Westervelt *v.* Haff, 2 Sandf. Ch. (N. Y.) 98; Wolf *v.* Smith, 36 Iowa 454; Sweet *v.* Redhead, 76 Ill. 374; McArthur *v.* Martin, 23 Minn. 74; Hardy *v.* Overman, 36 Ind. 549; Kendall *v.* New England Carpet Co., 13 Conn. 383.

A creditor who claims a lien on two funds, but abandons his claim on one of the funds with full knowledge that his debt cannot be satisfied out of the other without injury to another creditor who has a subsequent lien on that fund only, will not thereby forfeit his lien on the second fund unless his right to resort to the fund which he chose to abandon was clear and not seriously contested, and the remedies for applying that fund were reasonably prompt and efficient. Kidder *v.* Page, 48 N. H. 380.

3. Walker *v.* Covar, 2 S. Car. 16.

So a creditor, holding security upon different kinds of property, cannot be compelled to select that which is least convenient and available to himself, in order to aid other creditors, not secured, in the collection of their demands. Emmons *v.* Bradley, 56 Me. 333.

Where, under a general assignment made in *New York*, a preferred creditor held collateral security, equity will not interfere to compel such creditor to resort to such collateral, but the mode of distribution laid down by the statute must be followed. Benedict *v.* Benedict, 15 N. J. Eq. 150.

4. The pledgee's assignee has the same right under the same restrictions to sell that the pledgee himself had. Alexandria etc. R. Co. *v.* Burke, 22 Gratt. (Va.) 254.

5. Vaupell *v.* Woodward, 2 Sandf. Ch. (N. Y.) 143; Hart *v.* Ten Eyck, 2 Johns. Ch. (N. Y.) 62; Garlick *v.* James, 12 Johns. Ch. (N. Y.) 146; Patchin *v.* Pierce, 12 Wend. (N. Y.) 61; Parker *v.* Braneker, 22 Pick. (Mass.) 40; Union Trust Co. *v.* Regdon, 93 Ill. 458; Cushman *v.* Hayes, 46 Ill. 145; Mange *v.* Heringhi, 26 Cal. 577; Wilson *v.* Brannan, 27 Cal. 258; Lucketts *v.* Townsend, 3 Tex. 119; Brightman *v.* Reeves, 21 Tex. 70; King *v.* Texas B. & Ins. Co. 58 Tex. 669; Robinson *v.* Hurley, 11 Iowa 410; DeLisle *v.* Priestman, 1 Browne (Pa.) 176; Vest *v.* Green, 3 Mo. 219; Thomason

The right to sell within these limits is implied from the pledge contract.[1]

But the pledgee has only the right to sell the pledgor's interest in the property, and if that interest from its nature, is such that the thing pledged cannot be sold, the pledgee has only the right to hold.[2]

(2) *Obligation to Sell.*—In the absence of express agreement making it the duty of the pledgee to sell the property pledged within a specified time, the pledgor cannot compel the pledgee to sell by requesting or directing him to do so.[3]

But the pledgee, on the other hand, has a right to sell at any time, and is under no obligation to wait until a depressed money market is better.[4]

(3) *Notice of Default and Demand of Payment.*—When the time at which the debt secured will be due is not fixed,[5] depends

v. Dill, 30 Ala. 444; Perry *v.* Craig, 3 Mo. 516; Tucker *v.* Wilson, 1 P. Wms. 261; Lockwood *v.* Ewer, 2 Atk. 303; 9 Mod. 275; Pothonier *v.* Dawson, Holt 385; Kemp *v.* Westbrook, 1 Ves. 278; Pigot *v.* Cubley, 15 C. B., N. S. 701; Martin *v.* Reid, 11 C. B., N. S. 730.

But see, as to the title of purchasers, Arendale *v.* Morgan, 5 Sneed (Tenn.) 703.

"The old rule required a judicial sentence to warrant a sale, unless there was a special agreement to the contrary. But as the law now is the pledgee . . . may sell without judicial process upon giving reasonable notice to the pledgor to redeem, and of the intended sale." Stearns *v.* Marsh, 4 Den. (N. Y.) 227, 230; Cortelyou *v.* Lansing, 2 Cai. Cas. (N. Y.) 200.

In *South Carolina* a pledge may be sold at private sale if more can be realized thereby than at public sale. *Ex parte* Fisher, 20 S. Car. 179.

1. Jerome *v.* McCarter, 94 U. S. 734; Alexandria etc. R. Co. *v.* Burke, 22 Gratt. (Va.) 254; Lockwood *v.* Ewer, 9 Mod. 275.

2. In Robertson *v.* Wilcox, 36 Conn. 426, the court by Park, J. said: "He (the pledgor) may have only an interest for life, or for a term of years, or he may have simply a lien, or a right by a former pledge; still he may pledge the property to the extent of his interest. But the pledgee in all such cases has no right to sell the property on non-fulfillment of the contract, although he may pursue the proper course for the purpose, for the pledgor has no such right to confer. The pledgee must content himself, in such cases, with holding the possession of the property till his debt is paid, or the interest of his pledgor in the property has expired."

3. Cooper *v.* Simpson, 41 Minn. 46; Minneapolis etc. Elevator Co. *v.* Betcher, 42 Minn. 210; Badlam *v.* Tucker, 1 Pick. (Mass.) 400; Robinson *v.* Hurley, 11 Iowa 410; De Cordova *v.* Barnum (Supreme Ct.), 9 N. Y. Supp. 237.

In a case where the pledgor demands that the property pledged be sold at once, the pledgee refusing to sell at that time, afterwards did sell at a much lower price than could have been obtained at the time the request to sell was made, it was held that the pledgee, having exercised honest judgment, was not liable for the loss occasioned by his refusal to sell. Field *v.* Leavitt, 37 N. Y. Super. Ct. 215.

Where a pledgee agreed that the proceeds of the sale of the pledge should be applied in a certain manner, it was held not to impose an obligation to sell, in the absence of a request. Wilkinson *v.* Culver, 33 Fed. Rep. 708.

4. King *v.* Texas B. & Ins. Co., 58 Tex. 669. Where, however, additional time to redeem was given the pledgor, the pledgee cannot sell before the expiration of extension of time. Wadsworth *v.* Thompson, 8 Ill. 423.

Where collateral was given to secure a note for three months it was held that the pledgee need not wait for the expiration of the three days of grace before selling. Rankin *v.* McCullouch, 12 Barb. (N. Y.) 103.

5. If the debt is expressly payable

on an event to occur in the future, or may depend on some future event at the option of the pledgee, the latter must give the pledgor notice of the happening of such event,[1] and demand payment of the debt, or that the pledge be redeemed, before the property pledged can be sold.[2]

This rule has no application where a definite time is fixed for the payment of the debt or where notice and demand have been waived by agreement between the parties.[3]

If the pledgor cannot be found to make a demand on him for the payment of the debt, the pledgee must have recourse to a judicial sale.[4]

(4) *Notice of Time and Place of Sale.*—Reasonable notice of the time and place of sale must be given to the pledgor unless the right to such notice has been expressly waived.[5] Nor is no-

on demand the pledgee cannot sell without first making demand. Wilson *v.* Little, 1 Sandf. (N. Y.) 351.

When no time is stipulated for the payment of debt secured by a pledge of property, the law will, in the absence of something from which a contrary presumption would arise, presume that the payment is to be made on demand. King *v.* Texas B. & Ins. Co., 58 Tex. 669.

Where the stipulated time has been rendered indefinite by a subsequent agreement between the parties, it is not competent to the pledgee to sell without proper demand and notice. Pigot *v.* Cubley, 15 C. B., N. S. 710.

1. National Bank *v.* Baker, 128 Ill. 533; Milliken *v.* Dehon, 27 N. Y. 364.

2. Stearns *v.* Marsh, 4 Den. (N. Y.) 227; Bryan *v.* Baldwin, 52 N. Y. 233; Wheeler *v.* Newbould, 16 N. Y. 392; Haskins *v.* Patterson, 1 Edm. Sel. Cas. (N. Y.) 120; Cortelyou *v.* Lansing, 2 Cai. Cas. (N. Y). 200; Garlick *v.* James, 12 Johns. (N. Y.) 146; Hart *v.* Ten Eyck, 2 Johns. Ch. (N. Y.) 62; Wilson *v.* Little, 1 Sandf. (N. Y.) 351; Milliken *v.* Dehon, 10 Bosw. (N. Y.) 325; Genet *v.* Howland, 45 Barb. (N. Y.) 560; Lewis *v.* Graham, 4 Abb. Pr. (N. Y.) 106; Stevens *v.* Hurlbut Bank, 31 Conn. 146; Hyatt *v.* Argenti, 3 Cal. 151; Gay *v.* Moss, 34 Cal. 125; Bowman *v.* Wood, 15 Mass. 534; Parker *v.* Bancker, 22 Pick. (Mass.) 40; Washburn *v.* Pond, 2 Allen (Mass.) 474; Davis *v.* Funk, 39 Pa. St. 243; Diller *v.* Brubaker, 52. Pa. St. 498; Conynham's Appeal, 57 Pa. St. 474; De Lisle *v.* Priestman, 1 Browne (Pa.) 176. See Martin *v.* Reid, 11 C. B., N. S. 730.

3. Chouteau *v.* Allen, 70 Mo. 291. Waiver of notice of time and place of sale is not waiver of a demand for payment before sale. Mowry *v.* Wood, 12 Wis. 413.

Pledgee executed to pledgor a receipt for property pledged to secure a note, stating that if the note were not promptly met at maturity pledgee reserved the right of selling the property at private sale, the proceeds to be applied to pay the debt and any surplus to be paid to the pledgor. *Held*, that this agreement changed the legal rights of the parties only by dispensing with notice to the debtor to redeem as prior to the creditor's right to sell. Robinson *v.* Hurley, 11 Iowa 410.

While it is well settled that when the time for payment of the debt secured is uncertain, demand of payment and notice to redeem should be given before a sale, there is also a strong tendency, as shown by the cases in the preceding note, to make such a demand and notice necessary in all cases whether the time of payment is fixed or uncertain. To avoid possible difficulties, demand and notice should always be made before a non-judicial sale.

4. Stearns *v.* Marsh, 4 Den. (N. Y.) 227; Wheeler *v.* Newbould, 16 N. Y. 392; Strong *v.* National etc. Banking Assoc., 45 N. Y. 720; Ogden *v.* Lathrop, 1 Sweeny (N. Y.) 643.

5. Garlick *v.* James, 12 Johns. (N. Y.) 146; Hart *v.* Ten Eyck, 2 Johns. Ch. (N. Y.) 62; Stearns *v.* Marsh, 4 Den. (N. Y.) 227; Wheeler *v.* Newbould, 16 N. Y. 392; Bryan *v.* Baldwin, 52 N. Y. 232; Milliken *v.* Dehon, 10 Bosw. (N. Y.) 325; Jaroslauski *v.* Saunderson, 1 Daly (N. Y.) 232;

Lewis *v.* Graham, 4 Abb. Pr. (N. Y.) 106; Brown *v.* Ward, 9 How. Pr. (N. Y.) 497; 3 Duer (N. Y.) 660; Nelson *v.* Edwards, 40 Barb. (N. Y.) 279; Ogden *v.* Lathrop, 65 N. Y. 158; Haskins *v.* Paterson, 1 Edw. Sel. Cas. (N. Y.) 120; Genet *v.* Howland, 45 Barb. (N. Y.) 560; Parker *v.* Brancker, 22 Pick. (Mass.) 40; Washburn *v.* Pond, 2 Allen (Mass.) 474; De Lisle *v.* Priestman, 1 Browne (Pa.) 176; Davis *v.* Funk, 39 Pa. St. 243; Conyngham's Appeal, 57 Pa. St. 474; Diller *v.* Brubaker, 52 Pa. St. 498; Rosenzweig *v.* Frazer, 82 Ind. 342; Evans *v.* Darlington, 5 Blackf. (Ind.) 320; Indiana etc. R. Co. *v.* McKerwan, 24 Ind. 62; Belden *v.* Perkins, 78 Ill. 449; Rozet *v.* McClellan, 48 Ill. 345; Cushman *v.* Hayes, 46 Ill. 145; Gay *v.* Moss, 34 Cal. 125; Dewey *v.* Bowman, 8 Cal. 145; Hyatt *v.* Argenti, 3 Cal. 151; White *v.* Phelps, 14 Minn. 27; Morgan *v.* Dod, 3 Colo. 551; Stevens *v.* Hurlbut Bank, 31 Conn. 146; Chouteau *v.* Allen, 70 Mo. 290; Alexandria etc. R. Co. *v.* Burke, 22 Gratt. (Va.) 254; Mowry *v.* Wood, 12 Wis. 413; Lockwood *v.* Ewer, 2 Atk. 303; Tucker *v.* Wilson, 1 P. Wms. 261.

In Milliken *v.* Dehon, 27 N. Y. 364, the court by Marvin, J., said: "The principal reason assigned for the rule is, that he (the pledgor) may have an opportunity to attend the sale, and see that it is fairly conducted; that he may exert himself in procuring buyers, and thus enhance the price; that he has, in fact, the right to redeem the pledge at any moment before the sale shall be actually made."

If the pledgee could sell without notice of any kind this right to redeem would be valueless. Wilson *v.* Little, 2 N. Y. 443.

Actual Knowledge.—Formal notice of the time and place of sale is unnecessary if the pledgor has actual knowledge. Alexandria etc. R. Co. *v.* Burke, 22 Gratt. (Va.) 254.

"The safest course is to have a formal written notice served upon him (the pledgor), for then the fact of notice can be easily proved. If this safe course be not pursued, the creditor must, at his peril, be prepared to prove otherwise that the debtor was informed of the time and place of sale a reasonable time before the same was to take place." Alexandria etc. R. Co. *v.* Burke, 22 Gratt. (Va.) 264.

In *Louisiana*, a notice of thirty days is necessary before the institution of the hypothecary action. Gentis *v.* Blasco, 15 La. Ann. 104.

Waiver.—This requirement of notice may be waived by agreement of the parties. Mowry *v.* Wood, 12 Wis. 413; Loomis *v.* Stave, 72 Ill. 623; Genet *v.* Howland, 45 Barb. (N. Y.) 560.

This waiver generally takes place when the parties agree that the property may be disposed of at public or private sale, at the option of the pledgee. Robinson *v.* Hurley, 11 Iowa 410. So it was held in a peculiar case in *New York*, where it was considered to be more than an ordinary contract of pledge and was construed according to its language and surrounding circumstances. Milliken *v.* Dehon, 27 N. Y. 364; revg. 10 Bosw. (N. Y.) 325; and see on this point Murdock *v.* Columbus Ins. Co., 59 Miss. 152.

The consent of the pledgor after the contract of pledge has been entered into that the sale may be made without notice, is a waiver. Hamilton *v.* State Bank, 22 Iowa 306.

An agreement that the pledgee shall have the right to determine the time of the sale does not waive notice. Belden *v.* Perkins, 78 Ill. 449.

If the agreement to waive be in writing its sufficiency is a question for the court, not for the jury. Mowry *v.* Wood, 12 Wis. 413.

Sufficiency of Notice.—Either the general owner of the property or his authorized agent must be notified, otherwise it is ineffectual. Washburn *v.* Pond, 2 Allen (Mass.) 474.

Notice to the owner after the sale that he can have a certain time to redeem is of no use, for he may not be able to raise funds, while he might have been able to get bidders to attend the sale. Washburn *v.* Pond, 2 Allen (Mass.) 474.

Notice of the time and place of sale left in the absence of the pledgor at his office with the person in charge is sufficient. Potter *v.* Thompson, 10 R. I. 1; so is a notice properly directed, sent by mail. Worthington *v.* Tormey, 34 Md. 182.

Gilbert, J., in Bryan *v.* Baldwin, 7 Lans. (N. Y.) 174, states the rule of notice, quoting from Shaw, Ch. J., in Granite Bank *v.* Ayers, 16 Pick. (Mass.) 392: "All notices at one's domicile, and all notices respecting transactions of a commercial nature at one's known place of business, are deemed in law to be good constructive notice, and to have the legal effect of actual notice."

tice dispensed with by the fact that the time for payment of the debt secured is fixed; for whether the time of payment be fixed or uncertain, the pledgor has the right to redeem at any time before the sale and to be at the sale to protect his own interests.[1]

d. SALE UNDER POWER OF SALE—(1) *In General.*—The parties in interest may regulate in advance the remedy which the pledgee must resort to in subjecting property pledged to the payment of the debt secured; may fix the time and place of sale, and may agree that the property may be sold without notice and at private sale.[2] The power of sale so given is a power coupled with an interest and passes on the pledgee's death to his representatives.[3] Such a power is not affected by an attachment of the pledgor's interest, nor by making the pledgee a trustee or garnishee.[4] A power of sale, however, is revoked by the discharge of the lien by which the pledgee holds the pledged property.[5] Where the pledgee, being expressly empowered to sell the pledge, sells it in pursuance of the power, the sale is not a conversion.[6]

But Jewett, J., in Stearns *v.* Marsh, 4 Den. (N. Y.) 227, states the rule thus: "Personal notice to the pledgor to redeem, and of the intended sale, must be given . . . in order to authorize a sale by the act of the party. And if the pledgor cannot be found, and notice cannot be given to him, judicial proceedings to authorize a sale must be resorted to." See also, in support of the latter view, Wheeler *v.* Newbould, 16 N. Y. 392; Strong *v.* National etc. Banking Assoc., 45 N. Y. 720; Ogden *v.* Lathrop, 1 Sweeny (N. Y.) 643; Garlick *v.* James, 12 Johns. (N. Y.) 146; Hart *v.* Ten Eyck, 2 Johns. Ch. (N. Y.) 62; De Lisle *v.* Priestman, 1 Browne (Pa.) 176; Bowman *v.* Wood, 15 Mass. 534.

The case of Bryan *v.* Baldwin, 7 Lans. (N. Y.) 174, was a strictly commercial transaction, and may possibly be distinguished from the other cases mentioned on that ground.

A notice without date and without signature left at the pledgor's office was held insufficient. Genet *v.* Howland, 45 Barb. (N. Y.) 560.

So a notice of intention to sell without specifying time or place was bad. Goldsmith *v.* First Meth. Church, 25 Minn. 202; Wheeler *v.* Newbould, 16 N. Y. 392. And a notice by the pledgee that he will sell unless an excessive sum be paid immediately does not justify a sale. Pigot *v.* Cubley, 15 C. B., N. S. 701.

1. In Stearns *v.* Marsh, 4 Den. (N. Y.) 227, the court by Jewett, J., said: "In either case the right to redeem equally exists until the sale; the pledgor is equally interested to see to it that the pledge is sold for a fair price. The time when the sale may take place is as uncertain in the one case as in the other; both depend on the will of the pledgee, after the lapse of the term of credit in the one case, and after a reasonable time in the other, unless indeed the pledgor resorts to a court of equity to quicken a sale."

2. King *v.* Texas B. & Ins. Co., 58 Tex. 669; Stevens *v.* Bell, 6 Mass. 343. The parties may agree that the pledgor shall receive a commission for selling pledged goods. Goodwin *v.* Massachusetts Loan etc. Co., 152 Mass. 189.

3. Chapman *v.* Gale, 32 N. H. 141; Henry *v.* Eddy, 34 Ill. 508.

4. Chapman *v.* Gale, 32 N. H. 141.

5. Mowry *v.* First Nat. Bank, 54 Wis. 38.

6. Cole *v.* Dalziel, 13 Ill. App. 23. If a pledgee makes the sale of the pledge by the direction or express consent of the pledgor, or if the latter knowingly accepts the proceeds of the sale, he cannot object that the sale was not made in accordance with the law regulating the sales of pledged property. Hamilton *v.* State Bank, 22 Iowa 306.

If the pledged property is in its nature divisible, the pledgee should sell no more than is necessary to satisfy his lien; if he does so he may be responsible to the pledgor for the damages sustained

(2) *Purchase by the Pledgee—(a) At Private Sale.*—Unless it is so especially provided in the power of sale, the pledgee cannot, either directly or indirectly, purchase the pledged property at a private sale. Nothing passes by such a sale, and the pledgee still holds under his original lien, leaving the title, as before, in the pledgor.[1]

(b) At Public Sale.—While the title does not pass immediately to the pledgee purchasing at a public sale, still the sale being not void but voidable is not a conversion,[2] and

thereby. Fitzgerald *v.* Blocher, 32 Ark. 742.

Where the evidence shows that a person taking a pledge in writing has authority to sell all the articles in a certain building containing the articles in pledge, mixed with others belonging to the pledgor, the sale of all the articles in the building by the pledgor is valid. Clark *v.* Bouvain, 20 La. Ann. 70.

Where a pledgee with a power of sale exchanges the pledged property for other property, whether such other property is the property of the pledgee and subject to his debts depends upon whether the debtor ratifies or repudiates the exchange. In the absence of any evidence to the contrary the exchange is regarded as ratified if within a reasonable time the pledgor brings an action against an attaching creditor of the pledgee for taking the exchanged property. Strong *v.* Adams, 30 Vt. 221.

The plaintiff stored corn in the defendant's warehouse upon the following agreement by the defendant: "February 9, 1860. We hereby agree to store ear corn for (the plaintiff) till the first of June next, for three cents per bushel; two cents for shelling. If sold before the first of June, we are not to charge for shelling; if not sold by the first of June, we are to charge one-half per cent. per month till it is sold. The corn to be good and merchantable." *Held*, that after the first of June, the relation of the parties became analogous to that of pledgor and pledgee, and that upon giving the proper notice to the plaintiff the defendant might then sell the corn at public auction for the charges upon it. Cushman *v.* Hayes, 46 Ill. 145.

1. Duden *v.* Waitzfelder, 16 Hun (N. Y.) 337; Chicago Art. Well Co. *v.* Corey, 60 Ill. 73; Killian *v.* Hoffman, 6 Ill. App. 200; Stokes *v.* Frazier, 72 Ill. 428; Blood *v.* Hayman, 13 Met. (Mass.) 231; Middlesex Bank *v.* Minot, 4 Met. (Mass.) 325; Hestonville etc. R. Co. *v.* Shields, 3 Brews. (Pa.) 257; Morgan *v.* Dod, 3 Colo. 551; Baltimore M. Ins. Co. *v.* Dalrymple, 25 Md. 269; Maryland F. Ins. Co. *v.* Dalrymple, 25 Md. 242; Indiana etc. R. Co. *v.* McKernan, 24 Ind. 62; Bank of Old Dominion *v.* Dubuque etc. R. Co., 8 Iowa 277; Thornton *v.* Irwin, 43 Mo. 153; Chouteau *v.* Allen, 70 Mo. 290.

2. Bryan *v.* Baldwin, 7 Lans. (N. Y.) 174; Canfield *v.* Minneapolis etc. Assoc., 14 Fed. Rep. 801. In Bryan *v.* Baldwin, 52 N. Y. 232, affg. 7 Lans. (N. Y.) 174, the court by Grover, J. said: "This sale to the plaintiff was not void, but voidable at the election of the defendant. The defendant was at liberty to ratify the sale, and had he done so it would have been valid for all purposes. The ratification would have made it lawful and relieved it from any imputation of being tortious as to him. The title of the plaintiff to the stock would have been thereby made perfect, and the defendant entitled to credit upon the note for the net proceeds of the sale. But the defendant has not done this, but has elected to treat the purchase by the plaintiff as illegal. This avoids the sale, and that being avoided by the defendant, the parties are remitted to their rights the same as though no sale had been attempted. The defendant is liable upon the note, and the plaintiff still holds the stock as pledgee."

In a case where the pledgee had purchased at a sale, he was allowed to show that the sale was made, by agreement between the pledgee and one liable on another debt secured by the same collateral, for the purpose of valuing the security, this valuation being necessary for outside reasons, and that the security had never left his hands. Globe Nat. Bank *v.* Ingalls, 126 Mass. 209.

the pledgor may elect to treat such sale as valid and the title will pass.[1]

e. SALE IN EQUITY OR JUDICIAL SALE.—The pledgee may come into equity and have a decree for a judicial sale;[2] and he should do this where he cannot give the pledgor personal notice to redeem and of the time and place of sale,[3] where the remedy at law is inadequate, or where his rights and powers are in any manner questioned or denied.[4] A provision that collateral may be sold summarily upon default does not exclude a sale under judicial decree.[5] Where the pledgee, though not actively participating in a fraud, is acquainted with circumstances concerning the pledge that should have put him on his guard, equity will not help him foreclose his lien.[6] A pledgee may purchase

1. Chouteau *v.* Allen, 70 Mo. 290; Stokes *v.* Frazier, 72 Ill. 428. But see Fitzgerald *v.* Blocher, 32 Ark. 742.

2. Briggs *v.* Oliver, 68 N. Y. 376; Vaupell *v.* Woodward, 2 Sandf. Ch. (N. Y.) 143; Boynton *v.* Payrow, 67 Me. 587; Sitgreaves *v.* Farmers' etc. Bank, 49 Pa. St. 359; Stokes *v.* Frazier, 72 Ill. 428; Cushman *v.* Hayes, 46 Ill. 145, Arendale *v.* Morgan, 5 Sneed (Tenn.) 703; Robinson *v.* Hurley, 11 Iowa 410, Smith *v.* Coale, 12 Phila. (Pa.) 177

In the earliest common law the only method by which the pledgee could realize on his lien and cut off the pledgor's equity of redemption was by getting in equity authority to sell. Ogden *v.* Lathrop, 1 Sweeny (N. Y.) 643; 2 Story's Eq., § 1008.

It is also the rule of the civil law. Hart *v.* Ten Eyck, 2 Johns. Ch. (N. Y.) 62. And is the only method of disposing of pledged property in *Louisiana.* Brother *v.* Saul, 11 La. Ann. 223.

There can be no decree of strict foreclosure, for the pledgee never had the absolute ownership at law, and his equitable rights cannot exceed his legal title. The remedy is restricted to a sale under decree. Carter *v.* Wake, 4 Ch. D. 605.

A factor may enforce his lien by an equitable suit as a pledgeè, not only for commissions and advances but for a general balance, and may have a judgment for deficiency on the sale. Whitman *v.* Horton, 46 N. Y. Super. Ct. 531.

A judicial sale may be decreed on a default in interest when that interest is by terms or necessary implication a part of the debt. Swasey *v.* North Carolina R. Co., 1 Hughes (U. S.) 17.

3. Stearns *v.* Marsh, 4 Den. (N. Y.) 227; Indiana etc. Cent. R. Co. *v.* McKernan, 24 Ind. 62; Wheeler *v.* Newbould, 16 N. Y. 392. See *supra*, this title, *Sale at Common Law.*

4. This method is more complete than that of sale or notice, for the pledgee relieves himself of all doubt as to the legality of his procedure, and the interests of others in the pledge will be cared for. Homer *v.* Savings Bank, 7 Conn. 478.

Under a peculiar state of facts, a judicial sale was allowed in *Massachusetts*, although the jurisdiction of the court of equity was limited at the time. Merchants' Nat. Bank *v.* Thompson, 133 Mass. 482.

Where the deed of land is pledged, as in *England*, it seems that the only method of sale of the land is by decree in equity, for otherwise the pledgee could only sell the deed itself, which would be of little use. Clark *v.* Gilbert, 2 Bing. N. Cas. 343.

Account.—Even where the jurisdiction in equity is limited to those cases where the remedy by sale or notice is not complete, the court will enforce a sale of the pledged property where an accounting is necessary. Durant *v.* Einstein, 5 Robt. (N. Y.) 423; Conyngham's Appeal, 57 Pa. St. 474. But if the amount is merely a matter of computation, a bill in equity will not be allowed. Dupuy *v.* Gibson, 36 Ill. 197; not even though there is possibility of questions of account arising in the future. Thames Iron Works Co. *v.* Patent Derrick Co., 1 J. & H. 93.

5. Coffin *v.* Chicago etc. Co., 67 Barb. (N. Y.) 537.

6. Williamson *v.* Morton, 2 Md. Ch. 94. But if the plaintiff can make out his case without introducing fraud into it,

at a judicial sale of the pledge on an execution in his favor against the pledgee.[1]

f. SALE UNDER STATUTE.—In most of the States there are statutes regulating in some way the sale of pledged property. Some of these statutes exclude all other modes of sale, while others are simply permissive, allowing the other methods to be used if desired. In some States these provisions apply to pawnbrokers only, while in others there are provisions governing pawnbrokers in addition to the general provisions governing sales of pledged property.[2]

In some States the rate of interest the pawnbroker charges is regulated by statute; and, although the pledgee agrees to pay more than the statute authorizes, he can recover his property by tendering the amount of the debt with the legal rate of interest.[3]

g. ACCOUNTING—(1) *In General.*—The pledgee, after turning the pledge into money, or otherwise disposing of it, must account to the pledgor for his disposition of it.[4]

(2) *Application of Proceeds.*—A creditor who holds security, without special stipulations for its application, for various debts due, some of which are guaranteed and some not, in case of the insolvency of the principal debtor, may apply the proceeds of the pledged property to the unguaranteed debts.[5] But if the security is for the aggregate amount of debts otherwise unsecured, the proceeds must be applied *pro rata.*[6]

the court will not allow the defendant to introduce it. Chaffee *v.* Sprague Mfg. Co., 14 R. I. 168.

1. Adams *v.* Coons, 37 La. Ann. 305.

In *England*, the court may authorize the pledgee to bid at the sale, but he cannot himself conduct the sale. Carter *v.* Wake, 4 Ch. D. 605.

2. Jones on Pledge, § 616. See statutes in the various States.

In *Illinois*, it was held that a city ordinance requiring every licensed pawnbroker to give the superintendent of police each day a written statement of the articles received on the preceding day, with a description of persons from whom they were received, was not unreasonable, unjust or oppressive. Launder *v.* Chicago, 111 Ill. 291.

It was held in *Massachusetts* and *California* that the mode of sale provided for by statute did not affect the common law mode of sale. Covell *v.* Loud, 135 Mass. 41; Mauge *v.* Heringhi, 26 Cal. 577.

3. Jackson *v.* Shawl, 29 Cal. 267.

4. So before sharing in the proceeds of a receiver's sale of the pledgor's property, the pledgee must account for his collateral. Bryan etc. Co. *v.* Block, 52 Ark. 458.

On accounting, a pledgee of cotton is not entitled to get credit for losses occasioned by sales and purchases of futures against such cotton made by him with the knowledge and consent of the pledgor. Goodwin *v.* Massachusetts Loan etc. Co., 152 Mass. 189. Though he may for commissions on sales if agreed to by the pledgor. Goodwin *v.* Massachusetts Loan etc. Co., 152 Mass. 189.

5. Wilcox *v.* Fairhaven Bank, 7 Allen (Mass.) 270.

6. Beach *v.* State Bank, 2 Ind. 488.

Where a creditor had two demands, one secured by pledged property and the other by the note of a third person, it was held that, on the sale of the pledged property, the proceeds must be applied to extinguish both debts. Strong *v.* Wooster, 6 Vt. 536.

Where two notes are secured by a lien on land, and, through the failure of an assignee thereof to use due diligence to collect, the lessor is released from his liability on one, the proceeds of the land should be applied equally

(3) *Surplus Proceeds.*—Whenever the debt secured by the pledged property is satisfied, the pledgor is entitled to the surplus absolutely, and it is held in trust for him by the pledgee.[1]

The pledgor may sue at law for the surplus, but he should make a demand before suing on the theory of assumpsit.[2]

h. ILLEGAL SALE—(1) *In General.*—A sale made without observing the requirements of the law is a conversion,[3] and the right of the pledgor to redeem still exists.[4]

The purchaser at such a sale acquires no higher right than the pledgee possessed.[5]

(2) *Ratification.*—Defects in the sale of a pledge may be cured by after-ratification.[6]

Ratification of the sale may be inferred from an acceptance by the pledgor, with a full knowledge of the facts, of the proceeds of such sale to apply on the debt secured.[7]

to the two notes. Green *v.* Cummins, 14 Bush (Ky.) 174.

1. Earle *v.* New York L. Ins. Co., 7 Daly (N. Y.) 303; Selden *v.* Vermilya, 3 N. Y. 525; *In re* Bonner, 8 Daly (N. Y.) 75; Foster *v.* Berg, 104 Pa. St. 324; Peck *v.* Merrill, 26 Vt. 686; Sparhawk *v.* Drexel, 12 Nat. Bankr. Reg. 450; Stevens *v.* Bell, 6 Mass. 343.

A pledgee who, in replevin for the pledge, recovers judgment for its value in money, which realizes him more than the amount of his demand, holds the balance in trust for the pledgor. Miles *v.* Walther, 3 Mo. App. 96.

2. Loomis *v.* Stave, 72 Ill. 623; Taylor *v.* Turner, 87 Ill. 296; Stephens *v.* Hartley, 2 Mont. 540.

3. Hope *v.* Lawrence, 1 Hun (N. Y.) 317; Ainsworth *v.* Bowen, 9 Wis. 348.

The pledgor's remedies, the measure of damages, etc., in this case, are as enumerated under REDEMPTION.

To avoid a sale of goods by the pledgee, on the ground of fraud, it must be shown that the purchaser participated in the fraud. Cole *v.* Cosgrove, 16 Ill. App. 167.

If the pledgee sells the pledge fairly and publicly, he is not answerable for the loss from its selling for less than its estimated value. Ainsworth *v.* Bowen, 9 Wis. 348.

At an auction of collaterals to enforce payment of a loan due A, A made a bid, which was raised, and then B requested A not to bid again, saying that he wanted to buy the securities, and would collect the debt and pay to A all that could be realized. A refrained from bidding again. *Held*, in a suit by A against his debtor, that there was nothing in A's conduct that was objectionable. Corning *v.* Pond, 29 Hun (N. Y.) 129.

Where railroad bonds were pledged in *Texas* and sold in *New York*, it was held a good sale, as *New York* is the financial center of the country. King *v.* Texas B. & Ins. Co., 58 Tex. 669.

4. Norton *v.* Baxter, 41 Minn. 146; Bryan *v.* Baldwin, 7 Lans. (N. Y.) 175.

But where the debtor delayed bringing his bill to redeem for three years it was held that the claim had become stale, and that he could not recover his property. Gilmer *v.* Morris, 80 Ala. 78.

5. Lucketts *v.* Townsend, 3 Tex. 119.

6. Child *v.* Hugg, 41 Cal. 519.

The fact that the pledgor after the sale bought the goods sold at about the same price for which the pledgee sold them is not a ratification. Ainsworth *v.* Bowen, 9 Wis. 348.

Where it appeared that a pledgor had by parol abandoned the pledge to the pledgee, was present at the sale of the pledge, which had been advertised at "public auction," and with full knowledge made a bid for it, and drank with the pledgee and the purchaser in celebration of the sale, and that the sale took place in a room which, though not usually open to the public, was so open when the sale occurred, it was held that the pledgor thereby ratified the sale. Earle *v.* Grant, 14 R. I. 228.

7. Chouteau *v.* Allen, 70 Mo. 290; Hamilton *v.* State Bank, 22 Iowa 306.

The consent of the pledgor that the pledgee may purchase, passes the title, and such consent is presumed where the facts are open and notorious.[1]

4. Pledgee's Right When Pledgor Is Insolvent or Becomes a Bankrupt.—In the absence of fraud the pledgee's right to hold his security is not affected by the insolvency or bankruptcy of the pledgor,[2] and an assignee in bankruptcy or for the benefit of creditors of such property gets only the right the pledgor had in it.[3]

If the pledge was fraudulent, the assignee has the same right to have it set aside that the general creditors would, but otherwise the pledgee's right to hold is not affected.[4]

After the default in payment of the debt secured, the pledgee has all the right, regarding the disposal of the security that he could have had had the pledgor remained solvent.[5]

Whether or not the pledgee can prove his debt against the estate of the pledgor and share the benefits of it with the general creditors is disputed, some cases holding that he can; though in that case if he receives enough from the estate to make the collateral more than sufficient to pay his debt, the collateral must be disposed of for the benefit of the other creditors.[6]

Where the pledgor, after the sale with full knowledge of the facts, promised to pay a deficiency due the pledgee, it is a waiver of any irregularity in the sale. Child *v.* Hugg, 41 Cal. 512.

It was held that even where it was provided by statute that "a pledgee or pledge-holder cannot purchase the property pledged except by direct dealing with the pledgor," the pledgor could, as the statute was for his benefit, ratify a sale to the pledgee. Child *v.* Hugg, 41 Cal. 512; Hill *v.* Finigan, 62 Cal. 426.

1. Hamilton *v.* State Bank, 22 Iowa 306; Carroll *v.* Mullanphy Sav. Bank, 8 Mo. App. 249.

2. Jerome *v.* McCarter, 94 U. S. 734; Yeatman *v.* New Orleans Sav. Inst., 95 U. S. 764; Dayton Nat. Bank *v.* Merchants' Nat. Bank, 37 Ohio St. 208; Moses *v.* St. Paul, 67 Ala. 168; Dowler *v.* Cush. 27 Md. 355.

Notwithstanding the pledgor's insolvency, the pledgee can sell the pledge as stipulated in the contract; under *Louisiana* Code, arts. 2178, 2182, the ownership of the insolvent's property does not pass to the creditors. Jacquet *v.* Creditors, 38 La. Ann. 863.

3. Mitchell *v.* Winslow, 2 Story (U. S.) 630; Cook *v.* Tullis, 18 Wall. (U. S.) 332; Gibson *v.* Warden, 14 Wall. (U. S.) 244; Partee *v.* Corning, 9 La. Ann. 539; Dowler *v.* Cushwa, 27 Md. 354; Casey *v.* La Societe etc., 2 Wood (U. S.) 77; Com. *v.* Chesapeake etc. Canal Co., 32 Md. 591.

If the assignee realizes on pledged property in the possession of the pledgor for a temporary purpose, he holds the proceeds for the pledgee. *In re* Wiley, 4 Biss. (U. S.) 171.

4. Bank of Alexandria *v.* Herbert, 8 Cranch (U. S.) 36; Casey *v.* Cavaroc, 96 U. S. 467.

So while the pledgor could not have the pledge set aside as fraudulent the assignee might. Bank of Alexandria *v.* Herbert, 8 Cranch (U. S.) 36; Casey *v.* Cavaroc, 96 U. S. 467.

A receiver appointed to take charge of the affairs of an individual or corporation has the same right as an assignee to have fraudulent pledges overthrown and to recover the property pledged. Casey *v.* Cavaroc, 96 U. S. 467; Casey *v.* La Societe etc., 2 Wood (U. S.) 77.

5. Jerome *v.* McCarter, 94 U. S. 734.

After the pledgor's insolvency, his syndic cannot oppose a sale at the pledgee's instance because attended with great sacrifice. There is no alternative but to redeem by paying the debt, or to sell. Rasch *v.* Creditors, 1 La. Ann. 31.

6. Jervis *v.* Smith, 7 Abb. Pr., N. S. (N. Y.) 217; Midgeley *v.* Slocomb,

Other cases hold that the pledgee can put in a claim only for the difference between the value of the security and the debt secured, when the former is less than the latter.[1]

XIII. Rights, Liabilities and Remedies of Pledgee of Negotiable Instruments After Default—1. In General.—The remedies of a pledgee of negotiable instruments are in general the same as those of an ordinary pledgee of corporeal property, viz: suit on the debt secured and recourse to the instruments pledged as security.

2. Suit on the Debt Secured—*a.* In General.—The right of a debtor to enforce payment of a debt is not in general affected by taking negotiable instruments as security for the same, and, on the debt becoming due, the debtor may sue on it as though no collateral had been taken and without surrendering the security.[2] Nor can the debtor compel his creditor to resort to his collateral

32 How. Pr. (N. Y.) 423; Shunk's Appeal, 2 Pa. St. 304; Moses *v.* Ranlet, 2 N. H. 488; Findlay *v.* Hosmer, 2 Conn. 350; Walker *v.* Baxter, 26 Vt., 710; Putnam *v.* Russell, 17 Vt. 54; West *v.* Bank of Rutland, 19 Vt. 403; Van Mater *v.* Ely, 12 N. J. Eq. 271; Logan *v.* Anderson, 18 B. Mon. (Ky.) 114; Wurtz *v.* Hart, 13 Iowa 515; Brough's Estate, 71 Pa. St. 460; Mason *v.* Bogg, 2 M. & C. 443.

If the pledgee collects the security and so reduces his debt, and a *pro rata* dividend is declared by the assignee, that which the pledgee receives will be proportionate to the debt as reduced by the proceeds of the security. Midgeley *v.* Slocomb, 32 How. Pr. (N. Y.) 423.

1. **Under the Bankrupt Act.**—*In re* Brand, 3 Nat. Bankr. Reg. 324; *In re* Newland, 7 Nat. Bankr. Reg. 477; Streeper *v.* McKee, 86 Pa. St. 188; Richardson *v.* Wyman, 4 Gray (Mass.) 553; Middlesex Bank *v.* Minot, 4 Met. (Mass.) 325; Haverhill Loan etc. Assoc. *v.* Cronin, 4 Allen (Mass.) 141; Amory *v.* Francis, 16 Mass. 308; Farnum *v.* Boutelle, 13 Met. (Mass.) 159; *Ex parte* Smith, 2 Rose 63.

Before presenting his claim, the security must be appraised by jury or otherwise. Middlesex Bank *v.* Minot, 4 Met. (Mass.) 325.

After such appraisement the creditor may proceed to enforce the collateral. Streeper *v.* McKee, 86 Pa. St. 188.

2. Clark *v.* Young, 1 Cranch (U. S.) 181; Butterworth *v.* Kennedy, 5 Bosw. (N. Y.) 143; Langdon *v.* Buel, 9 Wend. (N. Y.) 80; Elder *v.* Rouse, 15 Wend. (N. Y.) 218; Case *v.* Boughton, 11 Wend. (N. Y.) 106; Munger *v.* Albany City Nat. Bank, 85 N. Y. 580; Taylor *v.* Cheever, 6 Gray (Mass.) 148; Hale *v.* Rider, 5 Cush. (Mass.) 231; Whitwell *v.* Brigham, 19 Pick. (Mass.) 117; Townsend *v.* Newell, 14 Pick. (Mass.) 332; Beckwith *v.* Sibley, 11 Pick. (Mass.) 482; Royal Bank *v.* Grand Junction R. etc. Co., 100 Mass. 444; Firemen's Ins. Co. *v.* Wilkinson, 35 N. J. Eq. 160; Winthrop Sav. Bank *v.* Jackson, 67 Me. 570; Snow *v.* Thomaston Bank, 19 Me. 269; Comstock *v.* Smith, 23 Me. 202; Bank of Rutland *v.* Woodruff, 34 Vt. 89; Chipman *v.* Clough, 6 Vt. 123; American Bank *v.* Harrison Wire Co., 11 Mo. App. 446; Sonoma Valley Bank *v.* Hill, 59 Cal. 107; Rich *v.* Boyce, 39 Md. 314; Robinson *v.* Hurley, 11 Iowa 410; Dugan *v.* Sprague, 2 Ind. 600; Mills *v.* Gould, 14 Ind. 278; Mendenhall *v.* Lenwell, 5 Blackf. (Ind.) 125; Bank of U. S. *v.* Peabody, 20 Pa. St. 454; Kittera's Estate, 17 Pa. St. 416; Abercrombie *v.* Mosely, 9 Port. (Ala.) 145; Trotter *v.* Crockett, 2 Port. (Ala.) 401; Bank of Woodstock *v.* Kent, 15 N. H. 579.

Where a debtor deposits notes with his creditor as collateral security, to be collected and accounted for, or to be returned within a specified time, and the creditor thereupon covenants or promises not to sue the debtor until the securities shall be given up, such covenant or promise is not a bar to a suit by the creditor, though brought before he has given up the securities. Foster *v.* Purdy, 5 Met. (Mass.) 442.

In Minnesota.—An indorser of a secured note is within the spirit of the act of March, 1860, compelling parties

security before suing on the debt secured.[1] The merger of the principal debt into a judgment does not destroy the pledgee's right to hold the collateral, for nothing but the actual satisfaction of the debt can do that.[2] The taking of collateral security for a precedent debt does not, in the absence of special agreements,[3] suspend the right to sue on the debt when due.[4] A special agreement to suspend such action, however, may be shown by

who hold collateral, to exhaust that before suing on the original indebtedness. Swift *v.* Fletcher, 6 Minn. 550.

1. Lewis *v.* U. S., 92 U. S. 618. Not even if the debtor is the maker of accommodation paper. Lord *v.* Ocean Bank, 20 Pa. St. 384; but see Comstock *v.* Smith, 23 Me. 202.

Where, however, the debtor has died and his estate is not sufficient without selling the real estate to satisfy the debt, if the collateral security is ample, the creditor may be compelled to resort to that. Alexander *v.* Alexander, 64 Ind. 541.

Surety.—A surety cannot compel the creditor to resort to his collateral security before suing the surety, for the surety can at any time get possession of the collateral by paying the debt. Brick *v.* Freehold Nat. Bank Co., 37 N. J. L. 307.

But the creditor might be compelled to apply the proceeds of collateral pledged by the debtor to the debt before suing on collateral given by the surety. Jenkins *v.* Gunnison, 50 Wis. 388.

An indorsee cannot be compelled to resort to securities given by the payee in order to allow the maker to set off against the payee a claim not *in esse* at the time the note was transferred. Munger *v.* Albany City Nat. Bank, 85 N. Y. 580.

2. Duncomb *v.* New York etc. R. Co., 84 N. Y. 193; 88 N. Y. 1; Butler *v.* Miller, 1 N. Y. 496; Whitwell *v.* Brigham, 19 Pick. (Mass.) 117; Beckwith *v.* Sibley, 11 Pick. (Mass.) 483; Fisher *v.* Fisher, 98 Mass. 303; Smith *v.* Strout, 63 Me. 205; Comstock *v.* Smith, 23 Me. 202; Sonoma Valley Bank *v.* Hill, 59 Cal. 107; Waldrom *v.* Zacharie, 54 Tex. 503; Chapman *v.* Lee, 64 Ala. 483; Hale *v.* Rider, 5 Cush. (Mass.) 231.

Nor does the recovery of judgment on the debt and the arresting of the debtor's body on execution destroy the right to hold collateral. Smith *v.* Strout, 63 Me. 205.

So where the pledgee proved for the full amount of his debt in insolvency proceedings against the pledgor, that did not destroy his right to hold the collateral. *In re* Litchfield Bank, 28 Conn. 575.

3. As in Calvo *v.* Davies, 73 N.Y. 211.

4. U. S. *v.* Hodge, 6 How. (U. S.) 279; Peter *v.* Beverley, 10 Pet. (U. S.) 532; Cary *v.* White, 52 N. Y. 138; Tobey *v.* Barber, 5 Johns. (N. Y.) 68; Etten *v.* Troudden, 67 Barb. (N. Y.) 342; Pratt *v.* Coman, 37 N. Y. 440; to the contrary is discredited; Darst *v.* Bates, 95 Ill. 512; Wilhelm *v.* Schmidt, 84 Ill. 183; Firemen's Ins. Co. *v.* Wilkinson, 35 N. J. Eq. 160; McIntyre *v.* Kennedy, 29 Pa. St. 448; Jaffray *v.* Cornish, 10 N. H. 505; Bank of Rutland *v.* Woodruff, 34 Vt. 89; Hawks *v.* Hinchcliff, 17 Barb. (N. Y.) 492; Allen *v.* Clark, 65 Barb. (N. Y.) 563; West *v.* Carolina L. Ins. Co., 31 Ark. 476; Willoughby *v.* Spear, 4 Bibb (Ky.) 397; Neimcewicz *v.* Gahn, 3 Paige (N. Y.) 613; 11 Wend. (N. Y.) 312.

Under certain circumstances, however, taking collateral may seem to suspend the right to sue. Harshaw *v.* McKesson, 65 N. Car. 688.

Acceptance of debtor's own note, though not payment, will extend time for payment. Place *v.* McIlvain, 38 N. Y. 96; Meyers *v.* Welles, 5 Hill (N. Y.) 463; Feldman *v.* Beier, 78 N. Y. 293; Putnam *v.* Lewis, 8 Johns. Ch. (N. Y.) 389; Buswell *v.* Pioneer, 37 N. Y. 312; Muldon *v.* Whitlock, 1 Cow. (N. Y.) 290.

Even though the parties agree that the pledgee's note shall be taken in payment, such an agreement will not be upheld. Cole *v.* Sackett, 1 Hill (N. Y.) 516; Hill *v.* Beebe, 13 N. Y. 556; Rice *v.* Dewey, 54 Barb. (N. Y.) 455; Waydall *v.* Luer, 5 Hill (N. Y.) 448.

Where, after the dissolution of a firm, one of the partners gave a firm creditor his note for the debt, it was held to discharge the other partners. Millerd *v.* Thorn, 56 N. Y. 402;

express contract to that effect or may be inferred from the surrounding circumstances.[1]

b. DEFENSES TO SUIT.—All the usual defenses to a suit on a debt may be set up, and, in addition, some growing out of the pledge relation may be involved. What are and what are not considered good defenses are to be seen in the note.[2]

Arnold *v.* Camp, 12 Johns. (N. Y.) 409.

1. Firemen's Ins. Co. *v.* Wilkinson, 35 N. J. Eq. 169; Wildrick *v.* Swain, 34 N. J. Eq. 167.

The right to recover on the original debt still exists, though negotiable paper given as collateral has been dishonored in the hands of the pledgee. Hunter *v.* Moul, 98 Pa. St. 13.

So under the same circumstances, though the pledgee by indorsing the notes had had them discounted. Small *v.* Franklin Min. Co., 99 Mass. 277.

In *Massachusetts*, where notes are given as collateral for a simple contract debt with the understanding that if they are paid at maturity the original debt shall be satisfied thereby, on their not being so paid, the original debt can be sued on. The Kimball, 3 Wall. (U. S.) 45; Dows *v.* Swett, 134 Mass. 140.

So if discounted at bank and not paid. Alcock *v.* Hopkins, 6 Cush. (Mass.) 484.

The notes may be returned at maturity or suit brought on the debt secured without returning the collateral. Small *v.* Franklin Min. Co., 99 Mass. 277; Comstock *v.* Smith, 23 Me. 202; Whitwell *v.* Brigham, 19 Pick. (Mass.) 117.

2. For the defense that the collateral was taken as payment, see *infra*, this title, *Payment.*

So where a creditor irregularly foreclosed mortgages held as collateral and purchased the property himself, held no defense. Smith *v.* Buntug, 86 Pa. St. 116.

Where the pledgee irregularly sold notes pledged and himself became the purchaser, the pledgor was not allowed to set off the value of the securities at the time of the sale. Killian *v.* Hoffman, 6 Ill. App. 200.

The loss of negotiable security by theft where there was no negligence on the part of the pledgee was not a good defense to a suit on the debt, the duty to keep safely not being a condition precedent to recovery on such suit. Winthrop Sav. Bank *v.* Jackson, 67 Me. 570.

Damages for the conversion of the pledged collateral by the pledgee can be set off in a suit on the debt secured. Cass *v.* Higenbotam, 100 N. Y. 248.

Judgment on Collateral.—Judgment on the instruments given as collateral does not satisfy the principal debt and is not a defense thereto. Hawks *v.* Hinchcliff, 17 Barb. (N. Y.) 492; and where the creditor on receiving part payment of his judgment assigned it to the debtor, the original debt was only discharged *pro tanto.* Burnheimer *v.* Hart, 27 Iowa 19.

Non-Collection of Collateral. — See *infra*, this title, *Diligence in Collection.* In lieu of gross neligence or bad faith on the part of the pledgee, the failure to collect collateral is not a good defense to an action on the debt secured. Marschuetz *v.* Wright, 50 Wis. 175; Kiser *v.* Ruddick, 8 Blackf. (Ind.) 382; May *v.* Sharp, 49 Ala. 140.

So the failure of pledgee to present and collect at maturity notes pledged, is not a good defense. Reeves *v.* Plough, 41 Ind. 204.

Where, however, the pledgee allowed the collateral note to be barred it was a good defense. Fennell *v.* McGowen, 58 Miss. 261.

Non-Production of Collateral.—Non-production of collateral without satisfactorily accounting for its absence is a good defense. See *infra*, this title, *Return of Security or Accounting.*

Where such securities placed in the hands of a third person, not under the control of the pledgee, selected by the pledgor, were lost, the non-production of them by the pledgee was considered no defense. Bank of U. S. *v.* Peabody, 20 Pa. St. 454.

The objection of non-production of collateral raised for the first time in the appellate court was held to be too late. Compton *v.* Blair, 46 Mich. 1.

Non-Surrender of Collateral.—This is not a good defense, for the pledgee has the right to hold until his debt is actually satisfied.

So where, on the protest of the original note given as security, two others were given, and one of these was paid and

3. Recourse to Security—*a.* IN GENERAL.—Recourse to negotiable instruments pledged as security is in general by collection without suit, with suit, and by sale of the collateral.

b. ELECTION OF FUNDS.—The pledgee having several securities for the same debt may, provided he used good faith in so doing,[1] resort to any or all of them to satisfy his debt, holding the surplus, if any, for the benefit of the third persons interested and of the pledgor.[2]

c. COLLECTION OF COLLATERAL—(1) *In General.*—In regard to negotiable instruments pledged as collateral, the pledgee having the legal title stands in the position of trustee, and as such is bound at all times to care for such property with due respect to the right of the pledgor therein.[3]

the other protested, the pledgee was allowed to enforce the note without surrendering the collateral note. Hunter *v.* Moul, 98 Pa. St. 13.

Collection of Collateral.—Of course where the pledgee has collected the value of instruments pledged, he cannot recover on the debt secured. See *infra*, this title, *Collection of Collateral.* Dugan *v.* Sprague, 2 Ind. 600; Reeves *v.* Plough, 41 Ind. 204.

Statute of Limitations.—A payment made to the pledgee by a third person without the authority or consent of the pledgor does not revive the debt secured that has been barred by the statute. Harper *v.* Fairley, 53 N. Y. 443.

Where the pledgor as agent of the pledgee collected money on a collateral note and paid it to the pledgee, it revived the debt barred by the statute. Whipple *v.* Blackington, 97 Mass. 476.

In *Louisiana*, as long as a note or other evidence of debt is secured by collateral, the statute will not run against it. Police Jury *v.* Duralde, 22 La. Ann. 107; Blanc *v.* Hertzog, 23 La. Ann. 199; Citizens' Bank *v.* Knapp, 22 La. Ann. 199.

1. Mowry *v.* First Nat. Bank, 54 Wis. 38.

2. Third Nat. Bank *v.* Harrison, 10 Fed. Rep. 243; Ober *v.* Gallagher, 93 U. S. 199; Union Bank *v.* Laird, 2 Wheat. (U. S.) 390; Buchanan *v.* International Bank, 78 Ill. 500; Chapman *v.* Clough, 6 Vt. 123; Andrews *v.* Scotton, 2 Bland (Md.) 629; *Ex parte* Mure, 2 Cox 63; Kellock's Case, L. R., 3 Ch. 776; Darlow *v.* Cooper, 34 Beav. 281; Andrews *v.* Scotton, 2 Bland (Md.) 629.

But where an indorser on one of two securities was an accommodation indorser and the indorser on the other not, the pledgee was required to resort to the latter first. Goodwin *v.* Massachusetts Loan etc. Co., 152 Mass. 189.

Marshaling.—Where the pledgee holds two securities for the same debt, on one of which another creditor has a lien, the pledgee, unless injustice would be caused him by so doing, is obliged to resort first to the security on which he alone has a lien. Dumont *v.* Fry, 13 Fed. Rep. 423; Hazard *v.* Fiske, 83 N. Y. 287; Door *v.* Shaw, 4 Johns. Ch. (N. Y.) 17; Cheseborough *v.* Millard, 1 Johns. Ch. (N. Y.) 409; Farwell *v.* Importers etc. Nat. Bank, 90 N.Y. 483; Morrison *v.* Kuntz, 15 Ill. 193; Greenwood *v.* Tyler, 1 R. & M. 187; Wiggin *v.* Dorr, 3 Sumn. (U. S.) 410; *In re* International Ins. Co., L. R., 2 Ch. D. 476.

The same rule applies to a subpledgee holding several securities for the same debt. Gould *v.* Central Trust Co., 6 Abb. N. Cas. (N. Y.) 381; Gould *v.* Farmers' Loan etc. Co., 23 Hun (N. Y.) 322.

If the pledgee offers to substitute the other lien holder to his place on payment of his debt, he will not be restricted to one security. Brinkerhoff *v.* Marvin, 5 Johns. Ch. (N. Y.) 320; Woolcocks *v.* Hart, 1 Paige (N. Y.) 185; Evertson *v.* Booth, 19 Johns. (N. Y.) 486.

3. Nelson *v.* Eaton, 26 N. Y. 410; Wheeler *v.* Newbould, 16 N. Y. 392; Hanks *v.* Hinchcliff, 17 Barb. (N. Y.) 492; Knights *v.* Putnam, 3 Pick. (Mass.) 185; Zimpleman *v.* Veeder, 98 Ill. 613; Union Trust Co. *v.* Rigdon, 93 Ill. 458.

(2) *Right and Duty to Collect.*—The purpose of giving collateral security is to place in the creditor's hands the means of re-imbursement of the original indebtedness if default occurs in its payment. Therefore it is the right and duty of the pledgee to collect the full face value of the securities when they fall due.[1]

A person holding property or securities in pledge occupies the relation of trustee for the owner, and as such, in the absence of special power to do otherwise, is bound to proceed as a prudent owner would. Joliet Iron Co. *v.* Scioto etc. Co., 82 Ill. 548.

Especially is this so in *Vermont* and *New Hampshire.* Williams *v.* Little, 11 N. H. 66; Jenness *v.* Bean, 10 N. H. 266; Austin *v.* Curtis, 31 Vt. 72.

1. Farwell *v.* Importer's etc. Nat. Bank, 90 N. Y. 483; Nelson *v.* Wellington, 5 Bosw. (N. Y.) 178; Nelson *v.* Eaton, 26 N. Y. 410; Nelson *v.* Edwards, 40 Barb. (N. Y.) 279; Wheeler *v.* Newbould, 16 N. Y. 392; Flagg *v.* Munger, 9 N. Y. 492; Wilson *v.* Little, 2 N. Y. 443; Bank of Chenango *v.* Osgood, 4 Wend. (N. Y.) 607; City Bank *v.* Perkins, 4 Bosw. (N. Y.) 420; Brookman *v.* Metcalf, 5 Bosw. (N. Y.) 429; Lewis *v.* Varnum, 12 Abb. Pr. (N. Y.) 305; Hancock *v.* Franklin Ins. Co., 114 Mass. 155; Batchellor *v.* Priest, 12 Pick. (Mass.) 399; Bowman *v.* Wood, 15 Mass. 534; Lyon *v.* Huntingdon Bank, 12 S. & R. (Pa.) 61; Beale *v.* Farmers' etc. Bank, 5 Watts (Pa.) 530; Roberts *v.* Thompson, 14 Ohio St. 1; Jennison *v.* Parker, 7 Mich. 355; McLemore *v.* Hawkins, 46 Miss. 715; Comstock *v.* Smith, 23 Me. 202; Androscoggin R. Co. *v.* Auburn Bank, 48 Me. 335; Onerlock *v.* Hills, 8 Me. 383; Dix *v.* Tully, 14 La. Ann. 460; Reeves *v.* Plough, 41 Ind. 204; Jones *v.* Hawkins, 17 Ind. 550; Slevin *v.* Morrow, 4 Ind. 425; Vallette *v.* Mason, 1 Ind. 288; Williams *v.* Norton, 3 Kan. 295; Zimpleman *v.* Veeder, 98 Ill. 613; Loomis *v.* Stave, 72 Ill. 623; Houser *v.* Houser, 43 Ga. 415; May *v.* Sharp, 49 Ala. 140; Hilton *v.* Waring, 7 Wis. 492; Union Nat. Bank *v.* Roberts, 45 Wis. 373; Northwestern Ins. Co. *v.* Germania Ins. Co., 40 Wis. 446; Lazier *v.* Nevin, 3 W. Va. 622; Foote *v.* Brown, 2 McLean (U. S.) 369.

A chose, which is transferred as collateral security, is put under the dominion of the creditor to make his claim out of it, and it is not in the nature, or subject to the incidents, of a pawn or pledge. Chambersbury Ins. Co. *v.* Smith, 11 Pa. St. 120.

Where promissory notes are pledged as security, the transaction, *ex vi termini*, imports authority to collect. Nelson *v.* Wellington, 5 Bosw. (N. Y.) 178.

"By an assignment of collateral security, a privity in contract is established, which invests the assignee with the ownership of the collateral for the purposes of dominion over the debt assigned. He alone is empowered to recieve the money to be paid upon it, and to control it to protect his rights." Hanna *v.* Holton, 78 Pa. St. 334.

The pledgee cannot enforce a separate and independent contract made by a third person with the pledgor to pay the debt secured. Second Nat. Bank *v.* Grand Lodge, 98 U. S. 123.

A power of sale given to the holder of collateral will not limit his right to collect. Nelson *v.* Eaton, 26 N. Y. 410; Nelson *v.* Edwards, 40 Barb. (N. Y.) 279; Nelson *v.* Wellington, 5 Bosw. (N. Y.) 178; Third Nat. Bank *v.* Harrison, 10 Fed. Rep. 243.

Indorsement.—If the securities are made payable "to bearer," even though they are unindorsed, the pledgee can collect. Houser *v.* Houser, 43 Ga. 415; Louisiana State Bank, *v.* Gaienne, 21 La. Ann. 555.

Where statutory enactment gives the right of action to the real party in interest, the pledgee of unindorsed negotiable instruments may collect them. White *v.* Phelps, 14 Minn. 27. So of non-negotiable paper. Hilton *v.* Waring, 7 Wis. 492. Also of unindorsed negotiable paper where the pledgee has power to collect by agreement of the parties. Lobdell *v.* Merchants' etc. Bank, 33 Mich. 408.

Collection of Short Time Notes.—A pledgee holding as collateral paper that matures before the debt secured falls due, has the same right and duty to collect them as in long notes falling due after the debt secured matures. He holds the moneys so collected in place of the collateral notes. Farwell *v.* Importers' etc. Nat. Bank, 90 N. Y. 483; Nelson *v.* Eaton, 26 N. Y. 410; Wheeler *v.* Newbold, 16 N. Y. 362; Garlick *v.* James, 12 Johns. (N. Y.) 146; Jones *v.* Hawkins, 17 Ind. 550.

As to the manner of enforcing payment the pledgee, so long as he acts in good faith and in the exercise of reasonable care and prudence, may use his own judgment.[1] Should the pledgee decline to enforce payment of the security the pledgor, on giving proper indemnity, may enforce it himself.[2]

(3) *Diligence in Collection.*—The pledgee of negotiable instruments is bound to use the reasonable ordinary care of a prudent man in its collection.[3] He is the pledgor's attorney or agent for that purpose, and must use the care that such a person is called upon to exercise.[4]

He cannot apply them to liquidate the debt secured until default in payment thereon has occurred and demand made. Wilson *v.* Little, 2 N. Y. 443; Garlick *v.* James, 12 Johns. (N. Y.) 148; Lewis *v.* Varnum, 12 Abb. Pr. (N. Y.) 305.

1. Bast *v.* First Nat. Bank, 101 U. S. 93; Hayes *v.* Ward, 4 Johns. Ch. (N. Y.) 123; Lamberton *v.* Windom, 12 Minn. 232; Wells *v.* Wells, 53 Vt. 1.

2. Bast *v.* First Nat. Bank, 101 U. S. 93; Lawrence *v.* McCalmont, 2 How. (U. S.) 426; Soule *v.* Union Bank, 45 Barb. (N. Y.) 111; Roberts *v.* Thompson, 14 Ohio St. 1; Lamberton *v.* Windom, 12 Minn. 232; Pickens *v.* Yarborough, 26 Ala. 417; Lee *v.* Baldwin, 10 Ga. 208.

3. Lawrence *v.* McCalmont, 2 How. (U. S.) 426; Childs *v.* Corp, 1 Paine (U. S.) 285; Barrow *v.* Rhinelander, 3 Johns. Ch. (N. Y.) 614; Girard F. & M. Ins. Co. *v.* Marr, 46 Pa. St. 504; Muirhead *v.* Kirkpatrick, 21 Pa. St. 237; Bank of U. S. *v.* Peabody, 20 Pa. St. 454; Sellers *v.* Jones, 22 Pa. St. 423; Lyon *v.* Huntingdon Bank, 12 S. & R. (Pa.) 61; Miller *v.* Gettysburg Bank, 8 Watts (Pa.) 192; Lishy *v.* O'Brien, 4 Watts (Pa.) 141; Roberts *v.* Thompson, 14 Ohio St. 1; Whitin *v.* Paul, 13 R. I. 40; Kiser *v.* Reddick, 8 Blackf. (Ind.) 382; Slevin *v.* Morrow, 4 Ind. 425; Reeves *v.* Plough, 41 Ind. 204; Lamberton *v.* Windom, 12 Minn. 232; Lee *v.* Baldwin, 10 Ga. 208; Colquitt *v.* Stultz, 65 Ga. 305; Blouin *v.* Hart, 30 La. Ann. 714; Wells *v.* Wells, 53 Vt. 1; Powell *v.* Henry, 27 Ala. 612; Jones *v.* Hicks, 52 Miss. 682; McLemore *v.* Hawkins, 46 Miss. 715; Steger *v.* Bush, Smed. & M. Ch. (Miss.) 172; Noland *v.* Clark, 10 B. Mon. (Ky.) 239; Hoffman *v.* Johnson, 1 Bland (Md.) 103; Williams *v.* Price, 1 Sim. & Stu. 581; *Ex parte* Mure, 2 Cox. 63.

In Hazard *v.* Wells, 2 Abb. N. Cas. (N. Y.) 444, the court by Smith, J., said: "A creditor holding negotiable paper as collateral security is required to use a different kind of diligence from that required of one holding merchandise or other corporeal property; and yet the diligence in each case is only such as is appropriate to the nature of the property. If the property be precious stones, safekeeping is all that is required. If it be grain, it must be properly stored and protected from all injury. The diligence required of the holder of promissory notes or other securities for the payment of money has reference to the danger that the parties liable on them may become solvent and unable to pay. A prudent business man will collect such obligations when they are due, or will endeavor to enforce them by suit; if, therefore, a creditor neglects to enforce the collection of such securities held in pledge, and delays till the parties liable become insolvent, he is as much guilty of negligence as if he had suffered grain held in pledge to be destroyed by dampness or heat for lack of proper storage."

Where the pledgee knows that the maker of a pledged note is in embarrassed circumstances, he must use greater diligence than if maker were known to be solvent. Slevin *v.* Morrow, 4 Ind. 425.

If the parties have made an express agreement as to the diligence to be used, they will be bound by that and not by the general law. Lee *v.* Baldwin, 10 Ga. 208.

Where collateral security is deposited with a creditor upon the express condition that it shall not be sued upon or collected until every legal effort has been made to collect the debt owing from the principal debtor, the creditor is bound by such condition. Barr *v.* Kane, 32 Ind. 416.

4. Hazard *v.* Wells, 2 Abb. N. Cas. (N. Y.) 444; Buckingham *v.* Payne, 36

The most important consideration is that the pledgee should act in strict good faith. If he does so the pledgor cannot complain. For fraud or gross negligence only is the pledgee liable.[1]

What constitutes negligence sufficient to charge the pledgee is a question of fact to be determined from the circumstances of the case.[2]

The obligation to collect ceases upon the payment to the pledgee of the principal debt.[3]

(4) *Liability for Negligence.*—The ground of the creditor's liability for a loss to his debtor, occurring through the creditor's negligence in enforcing the collateral security, is said to rest in the privity in contract between the debtor and creditor, established by the debtor's assignment of the collateral, which invests the creditor with the ownership of the collateral for all purposes of dominion over the debt assigned.[4]

The authorities do not agree as to whether the negligence of the pledgee of itself makes the note his and cancels his claim against the pledgor, or whether the pledgee can be allowed to show the actual loss caused by his negligence and be liable for that only.

The supporters of the first view claim that the adoption of their rule makes the relative rights and liabilities secure and ascertainable, avoiding litigation and compelling diligence.[5]

On the other hand, it is held that the true measure of damages is the actual loss suffered by the pledgor by the negligence of the pledgee,[6] and this view seems preferable.

Mere proof of negligence, under this latter view, is not enough

Barb. (N. Y.) 81; Kephart *v.* Butcher, 17 Iowa 240; Lawrence *v.* McCalmont, 2 How. (U. S.) 426; Commercial Bank *v.* Martin, 1 La. Ann. 344.

1. Black River Bank *v.* Page, 44 N. Y. 453.

2. Buckingham *v.* Payne, 36 Barb. (N. Y.) 81; Sellers *v.* Jones, 22 Pa. St. 423; Ward *v.* Morgan, 5 Sneed (Tenn.) 79; Davis *v.* Alston, 61 Ga. 225.

The degree of care required under the circumstances is said to be a question of law. Waterman *v.* Gowdy, 10 Bosw. (N. Y.) 208.

3. Overlock *v.* Hills, 8 Me. 383. If the maker of the collateral note is insolvent, its retention for never so long a period will not authorize the inference of payment of the principal debt. Powell *v.* Henry, 27 Ala. 612.

4. Hanna *v.* Holton, 78 Pa. St. 334.

Negligence in failing to collect can be taken advantage of by the surety of the principal debt as well as the debtor. Hoffman *v.* Johnson, 1 Bland (Md.) 103; but a general creditor of the pledgor cannot. Dyott's Estate, 2 W. & S. (Pa.) 463.

5. Phœnix Ins. Co. *v.* Allen, 11 Mich. 501; Jennison *v.* Parker, 7 Mich. 334; Rose *v.* Lewis, 10 Mich. 483; Whitten *v.* Wright, 34 Mich. 92; Blanchard *v.* Tittabawassee Boom Co., 40 Mich. 566.

In Peacock *v.* Pursell, 14 C. B., N. S. 728, the court by Earle, C. J., said: "The legal effect of taking a bill as collateral security is that if, when the bill arrives at maturity, the holder is guilty of laches, and omits duly to present it and give notice of its dishonor, if not paid the bill becomes money in his hands, as between him and the person from whom he received it."

6. Clark *v.* Young, 1 Cranch (U. S.) 181; Westphal *v.* Ludlow, 6 Fed. Rep. 348; Hunter *v.* Moul, 98 Pa. St. 13; Hanna *v.* Holton, 78 Pa. St. 334; Kephart *v.* Butcher, 17 Iowa 240; Grove *v.* Roberts, 6 La. Ann. 210; Powell *v.* Henry, 27 Ala. 612; Steger *v.* Bush, Smed. & M. Ch. (Miss.) 172; Kennedy *v.* Rosier, 71 Iowa 671. Dissenting opinion in Jennison *v.* Parker, 6 La. Ann. 210.

to make the pledgee liable,[1] but the actual loss must be shown.[2] It would seem that the fact that the maker of the note was solvent at its maturity but afterwards became insolvent, is necessary to a recovery.[3]

The burden of proof is upon the pledgor to establish the negligence of the pledgee and the loss occasioned thereby.[4]

The pledgee may then, if he can, show an excuse for his negligence.

In any event, if through the negligence of the pledgee the security is entirely lost, he is liable for its full value,[5] and in all other cases for at least the actual loss.[6]

Story on Notes, § 405; Chitty on Bills, 441, 498; 2 Parsons on Bills and Notes, 184; Cumber *v.* Wane, 1 Smith's Lead. Cas. (8th Eng. ed.) 357.

1. Aldrich *v.* Goodell, 75 Ill. 452; Gilbert *v.* Marsh, 12 Hun (N. Y.) 519; Steger *v.* Bush, Smed. & M. Ch. (Miss.) 172.

2. So if the debtor held good security himself for the pledged note, he suffers no loss from the failure of the pledgee to protest the note, and cannot charge the pledgee for negligence. Westphal *v.* Ludlow, 6 Fed. Rep. 348; Marschnetz *v.* Wright, 50 Wis. 175.

3. In Lamberton *v.* Windom, 18 Minn. 506, the court by Berry, J. said: "There is a distinction taken between the liability of a creditor to a principal debtor for negligently failing to collect collateral securities pledged by such debtor, and the liability of a creditor to a surety for neglecting to proceed against a principal. We can, however, conceive of no reason why the rule, which in the latter case requires that, in order that the creditor be held liable, the principal debtor should be solvent at the time when the surety requests the creditor to proceed against him, should not apply in principle in the former case. In the case of Herrick *v.* Borst, 4 Hill (N. Y.) 650, it is said: 'The question to be decided, is, whether under our rule for the protection of sureties a jury should be allowed to speculate on the event, and bar a creditor accordingly, as they may guess that the suit against the principal would have been successful or not, I understand the rule to be, not that the jury can appraise the possibility, and relieve the surety in proportion to the value of the chance, but that if the principal was solvent when the notice was given, and the neglect to sue followed by subsequent insolvency, the whole action is barred.' It seems to us that these reasons for making the solvency of the principal necessary to the creditor's responsibility to the surety, apply with equal force in a case like this at bar. There is the same danger and impropriety in the latter as in the former, in permitting a jury to peculate upon the chance of success in collecting a debt of a person who is not solvent; a person, according to the definition given in the case cited, who is not able to pay all his debts from his own means, or whose property is not in such a situation that all his debts may be collected out of it by legal process. To make the liability of the creditor depend upon his ability to collect from a person in this condition would be, it seems to us, to engraft an element upon commercial law altogether inconsistent with its characteristic and necessary certainty."

At any rate where the security was not accounted for and the maker was shown to be solvent at its maturity, the pledgee was charged with the amount. Commercial Bank *v.* Martin, 1 La. Ann. 344.

4. Vose *v.* Yulee, 4 Hun (N. Y.) 628; Sellers *v.* Jones, 22 Pa. St. 423; Girard F. & M. Ins. Co. *v.* Marr, 46 Pa. St. 504; Covely *v.* Fox, 11 Pa. St. 171; Dugan *v.* Sprague, 2 Ind. 600; Kiser *v.* Reddick, 8 Blackf. (Ind.) 382; Charter Oak L.Ins.Co. *v.* Smith, 43 Wis. 329. So to show bad faith on the part of the pledgee. Wells *v.* Wells, 53 Vt. 1.

5. Spaulding *v.* Bank of Susquehanna Co., 9 Pa. St. 28; Lyon *v.* Huntington Bank, 12 S. & R. (Pa.) 61; Stuart *v.* Bigler, 98 Pa. St. 80; Wakeman *v.* Gowdy, 10 Bosw. (N. Y.) 208; Westphal *v.* Ludlow, 2 McCrary (U. S.) 505; Roberts *v.* Thompson, 14 Ohio St. 1; Wood *v.* Matthews, 73 Mo. 481; Powell *v.* Henry, 27 Ala. 612; Cocke *v.* Chaney, 14 Ala. 65; Noland *v.* Clark, 10 B. Mon. (Ky.) 239; Whitteker *v.* Charleston Gas Co., 16 W. Va. 717; Hanna *v.* Holton, 78 Pa. St. 334.

6. Hoard *v.* Garner, 10 N. Y. 261;

(5) *Duty to Demand Payment and Give Notice.*—The first duty of the pledgee under such circumstances is, when the negotiable security falls due, to demand payment of the maker of the instruments and on his refusal so to do to charge the indorsers of such instrument by giving them due notice of the demand and refusal.[1] The reason for thus requiring a pledgee to preserve the

Barrow *v.* Rhinelander, 3 Johns. Ch. (N. Y.) 614; Baker *v.* Briggs, 8 Pick. (Mass.) 129; Grove *v.* Roberts, 6 La. Ann. 210.

1. Brooklyn City etc. R. Co. *v.* National Bank, 102 U. S. 14; Foote *v.* Brown, 2 McLean (U. S.) 369; Allen *v.* King, 4 McLean (U. S.) 128; Childs *v.* Corp, 1 Paine (U. S.) 285; Rice *v.* Benedict, 19 Mich. 132; Whitten *v.* Wright, 34 Mich. 92; Jennison *v.* Parker, 7 Mich. 355; McLughan *v.* Bovard, 4 Watts (Pa.) 308; Ormsby *v.* Fortune, 16 S. & R. (Pa.) 302; Hunter *v.* Moul, 98 Pa. St. 13; Charter Oak. L. Ins. Co. *v.* Smith, 43 Wis. 329; Russell *v.* Hester, 10 Ala. 535; Peacock *v.* Pursell, 14 C. B., N. S. 728; Cutting *v.* Marlor, 78 N. Y. 454; Dayton *v.* Trull, 23 Wend. (N. Y.) 345; Barrow *v.* Rhinelander, 3 Johns. Ch. (N. Y.) 614; Ocean Nat. Bank *v.* Faut, 50 N. Y. 475; Pickens *v.* Yarborough, 26 Ala. 417; Kennedy *v.* Rosier, 71 Iowa 671; McLemore *v.* Hawkins, 46 Miss. 715; Jones *v.* Hicks, 52 Miss. 682; Whitin *v.* Paul, 13 R. I. 40; Phoenix Ins. Co. *v.* Allen, 11 Mich. 501; Blanchard *v.* Tittabawassee Boom Co., 40 Mich. 566.

It is a part of due diligence on the part of the pledgee to produce the collateral when making a demand for payment of the person liable thereon, for it is the latter's right on paying his debt to receive back the evidence of his indebtedness. Ocean Nat. Bank *v.* Faut, 50 N. Y. 474.

Where an officer of the State was negligent in presenting paper held by the State as collateral, for payment, it did not release the debtor. Seymour *v.* Van Slyck, 8 Wend. (N. Y.) 403.

The fact that the maker of a pledged note is insolvent does not excuse failure to demand payment, for the maker may have funds to pay that particular note. Stocking *v.* Conway, 1 Port. (Ala.) 260.

Nor is it an excuse that the maker declares he has a defense to the demand. Wakeman *v.* Gowby, 10 Bosw. (N. Y.) 208.

Delay.—A delay of three days in presenting a draft for payment makes the pledgee liable for a loss occasioned by the insolvency of the drawer occuring shortly after. Smith *v.* Miller, 43 N. Y. 171; Betterton *v.* Roope, 3 Lea (Tenn.) 215.

Notice to Pledgor.—Where the pledgor is not a party to the instrument by indorsement, it is not necessary for the pledgee to give him notice of the refusal of the maker to pay the instrument on demand. Gibson *v.* Toby, 53 Barb. (N. Y.) 191; Hunter *v.* Moul, 98 Pa. St. 13; Williams *v.* National Bank, 70 Md. 343.

The pledgor in this case stands rather in the position of a guarantor, not subject to the duties or benefits of an indorser. He is liable on the original debt to be sure, but unless he has suffered loss by the failure of the pledgee to give him notice of demand and refusal, he cannot complain. Wildes *v.* Savage, 1 Story (U. S.) 22; Douglass *v.* Reynolds, 7 Pet. (U. S.) 125; Hunter *v.* Moul, 98 Pa. St. 13; Gibbs *v.* Cannon, 9 S. & R. (Pa.) 198; Oxford Bank *v.* Haynes, 8 Pick. (Mass.) 423.

"The plaintiffs are not held to strict rules in regard to the presentation at maturity of the note taken as collateral security and notice of non-payment to their debtor. The note was not received, although indorsed by the defendant, upon the condition that they would exercise such diligence. It does not represent the original debt, and to hold the defendant, it is not necessary that the plaintiff should regularly proceed to have the note presented and protested. It was not a satisfaction or extinguishment of the original debt, and a failure to give notice will not necessarily defeat a recovery." Westphal *v.* Ludlow, 2 McCrary (U. S.) 505.

Notice Not Needed.—When an unaccepted bill of exchange is pledged and the drawee never was supplied with funds, the pledgee was held not liable for a loss occurring by reason of not giving the drawee notice, the drawer not having been injured thereby.

legal validity of the pledge is to preserve its pecuniary value. Just as the pledgee of corporeal property is bound to keep it in a good state of preservation and go to expense for that purpose, so the pledgee of negotiable instruments must, so far as is in his power, keep intact the value of the collateral. Especially is this so for the reason that he has the sole power so to do,[1] he alone having the authority to receive the money due thereon.[2]

(6) *Duty to Enforce Payment.*—After the maturity of the pledged collateral, the pledgee must use due diligence to enforce the payment therefor or be liable for a loss arising from his negligence.[3] In the exercise of such diligence the pledgee is authorized to and should use active measures to enforce payment of the collateral.[4] If the pledgor desires the prompt collection of the

Rhett *v.* Poe, 2 How. (U. S.) 457; Compton *v.* Blair, 46 Mich. 1; Sharp *v.* Bailey, 9 B. & C. 44; Clodridge *v.* Dalton, 4 M. & S. 226. So where the residence of the drawer was not to be found by reasonable diligence, the holder of collateral was excused for not giving notice of dishonor. Reynolds *v.* Douglass, 2 Pet. (U. S.) 497. Rhett *v.* Poe, 2 How. (U. S.) 457; Duncan *v.* McCullough, 4 S. & R. (Pa.) 480; Putnam *v.* Sullivan, 4 Mass. 53; Bateman *v.* Joseph, 2 Camp. 462.

1. In Lamberton *v.* Windom, 12 Minn. 232, the court by McMillan, J., said: "In case of an ordinary pledge of tangible personal property, the pledgee is bound to ordinary diligence in the preservation of the property, whether it is perishable or not. What would be ordinary diligence in one case would not be in the other; but the diligence is required whatever may constitute it. The identical property, when it can, must be preserved; but if it cannot, then the value must be preserved. Why will not the same rule apply to bills, notes, bonds, and other choses in action? It is not alone the bill, note, or bond that is pledged, for those are but the evidence of the indebtedness, but the indebtedness itself is the substantial matter of the pledge; it is as capable of protection as the paper or contract which is the evidence of it; the latter may be lost without impairing the former, but if the former is lost the latter is valueless. The indebtedness, then, is the substantial pledge; and as men in the exercise of ordinary care generally preserve property of their own of this character, they may also by the same care, preserve it when it is the subject of a pledge; and as between the parties to a contract of pledge like the one under consideration, we see no reason why the pledgee is not answerable when the pledge is lost through his negligence."

2. Beale *v.* Farmers' etc. Bank, 5 Watts (Pa.) 529; Hanna *v.* Holton, 78 Pa. St. 334.

3. Barrow *v.* Rhinelander, 3 Johns. Ch. (N. Y.) 614; Hall *v.* Green, 14 Ohio 499; May *v.* Sharp, 49 Ala. 140; Pickens *v.* Yarborough, 26 Ala. 417; Cardin *v.* Jones, 23 Ga. 175; Reeves *v.* Plough, 41 Ind. 204; Lile's Succession, 24 La. Ann. 550; Charter Oak L. Ins. Co. *v.* Smith, 43 Wis. 329; Word *v.* Morgan, 5 Sneed (Tenn.) 79; Bonta *v.* Curry, 3 Bush (Ky.) 678; Noland *v.* Clark, 10 B. Mon. (Ky.) 239; Lacroix *v.* Derbigny, 18 La. Ann. 27; Douglass *v.* Mundine, 57 Tex. 344; Semple etc. Mfg. Co. *v.* Detwiler, 30 Kan. 386; Harper *v.* Second Nat. Bank, 13 Lea (Tenn.) 678; Hanna *v.* Holton, 78 Pa. St. 334.

4. Hoard *v.* Garner, 10 N. Y. 261; Wakeman *v.* Gowdy, 10 Bosw. (N. Y.) 208; Lyon *v.* Huntington Bank, 12 S. & R. (Pa.) 61; Whitin *v.* Paul, 13 R. I. 40; Slevin *v.* Morrow, 4 Ind. 425; Williams *v.* Price, 1 S. & St. 581; *Ex parte* Mure, 2 Cox 63.

That the maker of a note is a nonresident is not an excuse for not enforcing the note. Burt *v.* Horner, 5 Barb. (N. Y.) 501; but see Noland *v.* Clark, 10 B. Mon. (Ky.) 239.

Nor that he threatens that he has a defense. Wakeman *v.* Gowdy, 10 Bosw. (N. Y.) 208.

When the maker is notoriously insolvent the pledgee need not bring a useless suit. Clark *v.* Young, 1 Cranch

collateral he should demand this of the pledgee; if the latter uses ordinary diligence and speed he will not be held liable.[1] In case the pledgee fails to use sufficient speed in enforcing the payment of collateral, the pledgor may at any time redeem the collateral by paying the principal debt and enforce payment himself.[2] After the creditor has obtained judgment on the collateral and had an execution returned unsatisfied, he is not bound to do more unless to present the claim in bankruptcy or insolvency proceedings, should they be begun.[3]

The maker of and indorsers on negotiable paper pledged as collateral are liable on the same just as they are on ordinary paper held by a holder for value to whom it has been regularly indorsed in good faith.[4] They have no right to pay it to any one but the

(U. S.) 181; Smith *v.* Felton, 85 Ind. 223; Wood *v.* Mathews, 73 Mo. 479; Holmes *v.* Parker, 125 Ill. 478.

Where the payee of a note indorses it over to a savings bank as collateral, guaranteeing it, and the bank holds it for a year and a half after it matures, no request being made by the payee that it shall be collected, and then the maker becomes insolvent, the payee and not the bank must bear the loss. City Sav. Bank *v.* Hopson, 53 Conn. 453.

If delay in collection, causing a loss, was through the consent of the pledgor, the pledgee is not liable. Lee *v.* Baldwin, 10 Ga. 208; Mitchell *v.* Levi, 28 La. Ann. 946; Runals *v.* Harding, 83 Ill. 75; Brown *v.* Hiatt, 1 Dill. (U. S.) 372.

When the securities are not in the pledgee's hands, he need not collect. Bank of U. S. *v.* Peabody, 20 Pa. St. 454; Noland *v.* Clark, 10 B. Mon. (Ky.) 239.

Interest on Collateral.—The pledgee may collect the interest on interest bearing collateral as it falls due and account to the pledgor for the same on the maturity of the debt secured. Hancock *v.* Franklin Ins. Co., 114 Mass. 155; Whipple *v.* Blackington, 97 Mass. 476; Androscoggin R. Co. *v.* Auburn Bank, 48 Me. 335.

But these collections are deemed payments on the debt secured at the time they are collected, and for that purpose bar the Statute of Limitations. Whipple *v.* Blackington, 97 Mass. 476; Porter *v.* Blood, 5 Pick. (Mass.) 54; Haven *v.* Hatheway, 20 Me. 345.

Negligence of Agents.—Where the pledgee has exercised reasonable discretion in the selection of agents in connection with the collection of collateral, he is not liable for their negligence. Goodale *v.* Richardson, 14 N. H. 56; Exeter Bank *v.* Gordon, 8 N. H. 66; Commercial Bank *v.* Martin, 1 La. Ann. 344.

So if a bank employed to collect notes is negligent, any one interested in the collateral has a right of action against it. Whitney *v.* Merchants Union Express Co., 104 Mass. 153; McKinster *v.* Bank of Utica, 9 Wend. (N. Y.) 46.

Statute of Limitations.—Though the debt secured may be barred by the Statute of Limitations, yet as that affects only the remedy, collateral security held for the same debt may still be enforced. Chouteau *v.* Allen, 70 Mo. 290.

1. Cherry *v.* Miller, 7 Lea (Tenn.) 305; Wells *v.* Wells, 53 Vt. 1.

So where extraordinary diligence was required in collection, no demand being made for it by the debtor, the creditor was held not liable for loss occasioned by failure to collect. Westphal *v.* Ludlow, 6 Fed. Rep. 348; Marschnetz *v.* Wright, 50 Wis. 175.

A delay of five months in the collection of a demand note given as collateral, the maker being supposed to have ample property, and no request to collect being made, did not make the debtor liable for the loss occasioned by the maker's insolvency. Goodall *v.* Richardson, 14 N. H. 567.

2. Kittera's Estate, 17 Pa. St. 424; O'Neil *v.* Whigham, 87 Pa. St. 394; Androscoggin Bank *v.* Auburn Bank, 48 Me. 335.

3. Burnett *v.* Thompson, 1 Ala. 469.

4. Third Nat. Bank *v.* Harrison, 10 Fed. Rep. 243.

pledgee, and, should they do so, are still, if there is no equitable defense, liable to him for the full amount.[1]

(7) *Collection Before Debt Secured Due.*—Money collected from negotiable instruments is held as a substitute therefor by the pledgee as a sort of trustee on the same terms as the original security.[2] If the date of the maturity of the principal debt is definitely fixed, the proceeds of collection cannot be applied to liquidate the debt until the time of maturity arrives; or if the principal debt was payable on demand, not until the demand has been made and refused.[3]

But there is no obligation on the pledgee to collect on short notes until the principal is due and unpaid, unless requested by the pledgor, or bound so to do by express agreement.[4]

On such enforcement of short-time notes, the pledgee need credit on the debt secured only the amounts collected.[5]

d. COMPROMISE.—The pledgee cannot, without the consent of the pledgor, give up the collateral for less than the sum due thereon. If he does so he makes himself liable for the full amount.[6]

1. Williams *v.* Smith, 2 Hill (N. Y.) 301; Mayo *v.* Moore, 28 Ill. 428; City Bank *v.* Taylor, 60 Iowa 66; Valette *v.* Mason, 1 Smith (Ind.) 89; Fennell *v.* McGowan, 58 Miss. 261; Dix *v.* Tuly, 14 La. Ann. 460; Steere *v.* Benson, 2 Ill. App. 560; Richardson *v.* Rice, 9 Tenn. 290.

2. Farwell *v.* Importers etc. Nat. Bank, 90 N. Y. 483; Blydenburgh *v.* Thayer, 3 Keyes (N. Y.) 293; Garlick *v.* James, 12 Johns. (N. Y.) 146; Comstock *v.* Hier, 73 N. Y. 269; Jones *v.* Hawkins, 17 Ind. 550.

So of bonds. Allen *v.* Dallas etc. R. Co., 3 Wood (U. S.) 316.

3. Wilson *v.* Little, 2 N. Y. 443; Lewis *v.* Varnum, 12 Abb. Pr. (N. Y.) 305.

If the pledgee has agreed not to proceed on the collateral unless the principal debt is not paid at its maturity, then suit cannot be maintained until the latter date. Moor *v.* Miller, 7 Oregon 486.

In *Massachusetts*, however, it was held that where collateral security is received for a debt, with power to convert the security into money, and the proceeds of the security equal or exceed the amount of the debt, the debt is *de facto* paid, for the same person being the party to receive and pay, no act applying the money to the debt is necessary, but the law makes the application. Hunt *v.* Nevers, 15 Pick. (Mass.) 500.

4. Jones on Pledge, § 667; Overlock *v.* Hills, 8 Me. 383.

5. Blouin *v.* Hart, 30 La. Ann. 714.

6. Garlick *v.* James, 12 Johns. (N. Y.) 146; Hawks *v.* Hinchcliff, 17 Barb. (N. Y.) 492; Gage *v.* Punchard, 6 Daly (N. Y.) 229; Grant *v.* Holden, 1 E. D. Smith (N. Y.) 545; Zimpleman *v.* Veeder, 98 Ill. 613; Wood *v.* Matthews, 73 Mo. 479; Stevens *v.* Hurlburt Bank, 31 Conn. 147; Union Trust Co. *v.* Rigdon, 93 Ill. 458; Depuy *v.* Clark, 12 Ind. 427; McLemore *v.* Hawkins, 46 Miss. 715.

A compromise takes place whenever any arrangement is made by which the collateral is given up for less than its face value. Union Trust Co. *v.* Rigdon, 93 Ill. 471.

Even where a power of sale was given to the pledgee. Zimpleman *v.* Veeder, 98 Ill. 613.

The pledgee of negotiable collateral is not bound to receive property in payment therefor, nor is he bound to notify the pledgor of the proposition. Rives *v.* M'Losky, 5 Stew. & P. (Ala.) 330.

Nor can the pledgee be compelled to accept a good compromise even by the pledgor. Rhinelander *v.* Barrow, 17 Johns. (N. Y.) 538.

Where, however, the maker was insolvent and nothing could be collected by suit, a compromise was upheld. Exeter Bank *v.* Gordon, 8 N. H. 66.

Surrender.—The pledgee of negotiable instruments pledged as security has no

With the consent of the pledgor, however, a compromise is binding.[1]

Where an illegal compromise has taken place, the pledgor has his election either to sue the maker of the collateral for the balance unpaid or the pledgee for fraudulently disposing of his property recovering the face value of the securities, less the amount of the debt secured.[2]

e. SALE OF COLLATERAL.—The general rule of law is that, without an express agreement to the contrary, negotiable collateral, as it has no market value, cannot be enforced by either public or private sale;[3] though some States, regarding this class of

right to surrender them to the maker without payment, but is bound to return them to the pledgor or be charged with the full amount, less the debt secured. Wood *v.* Matthews, 73 Mo. 477; Depuy *v.* Clark, 12 Ind. 427; Spenser *v.* Morgan, 5 Ind. 146; Cox *v.* Reynolds, 7 Ind. 257.

If the pledgee shows that the maker had a good equitable defense against the pledgor, he may be excused. But he must prove this absolutely, and it is not enough that the pledgor was indebted to the maker of the note for the pledgee cannot set this up. Union Trust Co. *v.* Rigdton, 93 Ill. 458.

Exchange.—The pledgee of negotiable collateral security has the right to exchange the same for others, but he is liable for any loss occurring through lack of diligence in so doing. Hunter *v.* Moul, 98 Pa. St. 13; Girard F. & M. Ins. Co. *v.* Marr, 46 Pa. St. 504; Randolph *v.* Merchants' Bank, 9 Lea (Tenn.) 63; Muirhead *v.* Kirkpatrick, 21 Pa. St. 237.

But the loss must be conclusively shown. Girard F. & M. Ins. Co. *v.* Marr, 46 Pa. St. 504. But see *supra*, this title, *Compromise for Cases of Exchange Held Otherwise.*

Extension of Time.—An extension of the time for the payment of negotiable securities by the pledgee makes them his own. Freeman *v.* Benedict, 37 Conn. 559.

It was on this principle that exchange of the note pledged for part money and a new note, made the pledgee liable. Southwick *v.* Sax, 9 Wend. (N. Y.) 122; Nexsen *v.* Lyell, 5 Hill (N. Y.) 466; Gage *v.* Punchard, 6 Daly (N. Y.) 229; Depuy *v.* Clark, 12 Ind. 427.

So if the pledgee, without a definite agreement for delay, so deals with the collateral as to delay its collection, he is responsible. Smith *v.* Miller, 43 N. Y. 171.

But if the note for which a new one extending the time was exchanged, was without a consideration, the exchange will make a consideration for the second note. Muirhead *v.* Kirkpatrick, 21 Pa. St. 237.

1. Thayer *v.* Putnam, 12 Met. (Mass.) 277; Pence *v.* Gale, 20 Minn. 257; Randolph *v.* Merchants' Bank, 9 Lea (Tenn.) 63.

2. Hawks *v.* Hinchcliffe, 17 Barb. (N. Y.) 492; Garlick *v.* James, 12 Johns. (N. Y.) 146; Union Trust Co. *v.* Rigdon, 93 Ill. 471; Depuy *v.* Clark, 12 Ind. 427.

The pledgee may, on being sued by the pledgor, set up as defense whatever excuse he may have; that the notes were for accommodation, etc. Union Trust Co. *v.* Rigdon, 93 Ill. 471.

Where a sub-pledgee makes such a compromise the first pledgee is not liable. Goss *v.* Emerson, 23 N. H. 38.

3. Nelson *v.* Edwards, 40 Barb. (N. Y.) 279; Garlick *v.* James, 12 Johns. (N. Y.) 146; Brown *v.* Ward, 3 Duer (N. Y.) 660; Brookman *v.* Metcalf, 5 Bosw. (N. Y.) 429; Morris Canal etc. Co. *v.* Lewis, 12 N. J. Eq. 323; Fletcher *v.* Dickinson, 7 Allen (Mass.) 23; Joliet Iron Co. *v.* Scioto etc. Co., 82 Ill. 548; Union Trust Co. *v.* Rigdon, 93 Ill. 458; Zimpleman *v.* Veeder, 98 Ill. 613; White *v.* Phelps, 14 Minn. 27; Nelson *v.* Wellington, 5 Bosw. (N.Y.) 178; Lamberton *v.* Windom, 12 Minn. 232; *In re* Litchfield Bank, 28 Conn. 575; Whitteker *v.* Charleston Gas Co., 16 W. Va. 717; Walker *v.* Carleton, 97 Ill. 582; Wheeler *v.* Newbould, 16 N. Y. 392; Atlantic F. & M. Ins. Co. *v.* Boies, 6 Duer (N. Y.) 583; Brown

securities after its maturity in the same light as an ordinary pledge, allow it at that stage to be sold.[1]

The rule denying right to sale does not apply to long-time negotiable municipal, government, or corporation bonds which can be sold after default in the same manner that stock can.[2]

v. Ward, 3 Duer (N. Y.) 660; Moody *v.* Andrews, 7 Jones & Sp. (N. Y.) 302; affd. 64 N. Y. 641.

When a party to whom a promissory note had been indorsed as collateral by the payee sold and transferred the same without the payee's consent, the measure of damages was held to be the value of the note at the time of sale, or, *prima facie*, the amount of the note and interest; and in a suit against such indorsee by the payee, an instruction that the plaintiff was entitled to recover interest on the balance, if any, found due him from the defendant after deducting advances made by the defendant, with interest, and a compensation for collecting the note, was sufficiently favorable to the defendant. Hazzard *v.* Duke, 64 Ind. 220.

In another case it was held that the pledgor might recover the difference between the face of the note and the sum advanced. Davis *v.* Funk, 39 Pa. St. 243.

1. Potter *v.* Thompson, 10 R. I. 1; Davis *v.* Funk, 39 Pa. St. 243; Richards *v.* Davis, 5 Clark (Pa.) 471; Brightman *v.* Reeves, 21 Tex. 70.

In *California*, it seems to be held that negotiable paper, under a foreclosure in equity may be sold like other pledged property. Especially is this the case where the pledgor is a non-resident. Donohoe *v.* Gamble, 38 Cal. 340.

In *Texas*, on the death of the pledgor, though all lien holders are required to prove their claims before the probate court, the pledgee of negotiable paper is allowed to pay himself from the security he holds; but if he should prove his claim he might be allowed to sell the security. Huyler *v.* Dahoney, 48 Tex. 234.

2. Fraker *v.* Reeve, 36 Wis. 85; Jerome *v.* McCarter, 94 U. S. 734; Brown *v.* Ward, 3 Duer (N. Y.) 660; Union Cattle Co. *v.* International Trust Co., 149 Mass. 492; Hancock *v.* Franklin Ins. Co., 114 Mass. 155; Fletcher *v.* Dickinson, 7 Allen (Mass.) 23; Washburn *v.* Pond, 2 Allen (Mass.) 474; Morris Canal etc. Co. *v.* Lewis, 12 N. J. Eq. 323; Duffield *v.* Miller, 92 Pa. St. 286; Newport etc. Bridge Co. *v.* Douglass, 12 Bush (Ky.) 673; Alexander etc. R. Co. *v.* Burke, 22 Gratt. (Va.) 254.

This class of bonds has a fixed market value, and bad faith on part of pledgee is easily detected; therefore a sale of them is allowed. Chouteau *v.* Allen, 70 Mo. 290; Loomis *v.* Stave, 75 Ill. 623.

Where coupon bonds of a corporation are deposited as collateral to secure notes on short time, it is to be presumed, in the absence of all special agreement, that they are not deposited as choses in action, to be collected by the pledgee, but as a pledge, to be sold after demand and notice, as in the case of a pledge of any article having a market value. Morris Canal etc. Co. *v.* Lewis, 12 N. J. Eq. 323.

Where, however, railroad bonds were payable only on condition, so that their market value could not be ascertained, it was held that there was no implied power of sale. Joliet Iron etc. Co. *v.* Scioto Fire Brick Co., 82 Ill. 548.

A pledgee neglecting to sell negotiable bonds of this class can never have a larger title in them than his pledgee's lien. Hancock *v.* Franklin Ins. Co., 114 Mass. 155; Whipple *v.* Blackington, 97 Mass. 476; *In re* Litchfield Bank, 28 Conn. 575; White Mt. R. Co. *v.* Bay State Iron Co., 50 N. H. 57.

The subsequent insolvency of the pledgor does not bar this right of sale. Jerome *v.* McCarter, 94 U. S. 734.

Where the value of a number of such bonds is largely in excess of the amount of the debt secured, the sale of all of them by the pledgee may be enjoined. Fitzgerald *v.* Blocher, 32 Ark. 742.

Demand and Notice.—Where a pledgee, being unable to make demand or give notice to the pledgor, sold the bonds, the pledgor was allowed either to ratify or to repudiate the sale at his option. Strong *v.* National etc. Bank Assoc., 45 N. Y. 718; Stokes *v.* Frazier, 72 Ill. 428; Middlesex Bank *v.* Minot, 4 Met. (Mass.) 325.

Right to election may be waived.

In *New York*, though there was a well recognized usage permitting the sale of negotiable collateral at private sale at the best price that could be obtained after demand for payment and notice that the sale would be made, it was held that, negotiable securities having no market value, there was no implied right to sell. Perhaps this exception may include notes which do not mature until long after the debt secured becomes payable.[1] The parties to the pledge contract may agree that the negotiable security shall be sold on default in payment of the debt secured and the purchaser will get a good title, though he paid less than the face value.[2] Such a power of sale is not exclusive of, but in addition to, all the other remedies of the pledgee.[3] The same diligence must be exercised in making such a sale as is required in the sale of other kinds of pledged property.[4] The purchaser at a valid

Chouteau *v.* Allen, 70 Mo. 290; City Bank *v.* Babcock, Holmes (U. S.) 180.

On sale of bonds by sub-pledgee, notice of sale must be given to both the original pledgor and original pledgee. Fletcher *v.* Dickenson, 7 Allen (Mass.) 25.

Sale made without the proper formalities makes the pledgee liable for a subsequent enhanced value. Read *v.* Lambert, 10 Abb. Pr. N. S. (N. Y.) 428.

Where the date of the maturity of the principal debt is definitely fixed, demand and notice are not needed, a power of sale having been agreed upon. Chouteau *v.* Allen, 70 Mo. 290.

Whether the notice is sufficient is a question of fact to be decided from the circumstances of each case. Advertising is the proper method. Washburn *v.* Pond, 2 Allen (Mass.) 474.

Actual notice a reasonable time before the sale is sufficient. Stokes *v.* Frazier, 72 Ill. 428.

Notice after the sale, even though the pledgor was known not to be able to redeem, made the sale invalid. Alexandria R. Co. *v.* Burke, 22 Gratt. (Va.) 254.

1. Richards *v.* Davis, 5 Clark (Pa.) 471.

2. Goldsmidt *v.* First Meth. Church, 25 Minn. 202; Brightman *v.* Reeves, 21 Tex. 70; Fraker *v.* Reeve, 36 Wis. 85.

Under a power of sale, where the collateral was not sold in the prescribed manner, the pledgor's equity of redemption was not destroyed. Valley Nat. Bank *v.* Jackaway, 80 Iowa 512; Valley Nat. Bank *v.* Johnson Directory Co., 80 Iowa 772.

A pledgee who has paid a draft accepted by him for the benefit of the pledgor under instructions that he "can relieve himself by raising money on the notes" given as collateral, may lawfully dispose of them. Dortch *v.* Frazier, 1 Head (Tenn.) 243.

3. Nelson *v.* Eaton, 26 N. Y. 410; Nelson *v.* Edwards, 40 Barb. (N. Y.) 279; Brookman *v.* Metcalf, 5 Bosw. (N. Y.) 178; Nelson *v.* Wellington, 5 Bosw. (N.Y.) 178; First Nat. Bank *v.* Kimberlands, 16 W. Va. 555; Whitteker *v.* Charleston Gas Co., 16 W. Va. 717; Third Nat. Bank *v.* Harrison, 3 McCrary (U. S.) 316.

This power of sale, however, does not prevent other creditors from attaching the pledgor's equity, subject to the pledgee's lien. Pickens *v.* Webster, 31 La. Ann. 879.

4. Brightman *v.* Reeves, 21 Tex. 70; Union Trust Co. *v.* Rigdon, 93 Ill. 458; Wilson *v.* Little, 2 N. Y. 443; Sparhawk *v.* Drexel, 12 Nat. Bankr. Reg. 450.

In Goldsmidt *v.* First Meth. Church, 25 Minn. 202, the court by Gilfillan, J., said: "It was competent for the parties to agree how the sale should be made; but without any such agreement, and where the power to sell is merely given, the power will be construed to be such a power as exists in respect to pledges generally, and must be exercised in the same way. In respect to pledges generally, the power can be exercised only upon reasonable notice to the debtor to redeem, and of the time and place of sale." Wheeler *v.* Newbould, 16 N. Y. 392; Fraker *v.* Reeve, 36 Wis. 85.

When the pledgee of negotiable

sale of either negotiable bonds or paper gets the title of the pledgor absolutely, entirely free from the lien of the pledge contract.[1]

f. SUIT ON COLLATERAL.—When negotiable paper has been indorsed to the pledgee, either in full or in blank, he having the legal title, may, whether the principal debt is due or not,[2] recover on the collateral in his own name[3] without making a previous de-

notes, although empowered to sell the same "at public or private sale, without advertising the same, or demanding payment, or giving notice," sold them to the maker for the amount of the debt secured, that being less than their face value, the court decided that such a sale was against the intention of the parties. Union Trust Co. *v.* Rigdon, 93 Ill. 458.

So if the maker was informed of the place of sale, while the pledgor was not, a purchase by the maker for a sum less than the face value was considered a compromise and void. Zimpleman *v.* Veeder, 98 Ill. 613; McLemore *v.* Hawkins, 46 Miss. 715.

The pledgee need not watch for a favorable market. Whitin *v.* Paul, 13 R. I. 40.

1. Duncomb *v.* New York etc. R. Co., 84 N. Y. 190; Lewis *v.* Mott, 36 N. Y. 395; Jerome *v.* McCarter, 94 U. S. 734; Allen *v.* Dallas R. Co., 3 Woods (U. S.) 316; Stokes *v* Frazier, 72 Ill. 428; Union Trust Co. *v.* Rigdon, 93 Ill. 458; White Mts. R. Co. *v.* Bay State Iron Co., 50 N. H. 57; Newport Bridge Co. *v.* Douglass, 12 Bush (Ky.) 673.

Where the purchaser has notice that the sale is fraudulent, he does not get a good title. Goldsmitt *v.* Trustees, 25 Minn. 202.

Purchase by Pledgee.—If the pledgee purchases at a sale made without authority, the pledge relations are not altered in the least, and the pledgor still has the right to redeem. Walker *v.* Castle, 97 Ill. 582; Stokes *v.* Frazier, 72 Ill. 428; Bank *v.* Dubuque R. Co., 8 Iowa 277; Killian *v.* Huffman, 6 Ill. App. 200.

When long-time negotiable bonds were validly sold the pledgee was allowed to purchase. Sickles *v.* Richardson, 23 Hun (N. Y.) 559.

2. Jones *v.* Hawkins, 17 Ind. 550.

The pledgee of collateral paper may enforce its collection even though the pledgor has paid the principal debt in full, unless the maker of the note is thereby deprived of some equitable defense he might have against the payee. Logan *v.* Cassell, 88 Pa. St. 288.

The holder of negotiable bonds as collateral for a debt, is entitled to enforce payment on the coupons, even though the principal debt is not due. Warner *v.* Rising Fawn Iron Co., 3 Woods (U. S.) 514.

3. Third Nat. Bank *v.* Harrison, 10 Fed. Rep. 243; Nelson *v.* Edwards, 40 Barb. (N. Y.) 279; Moody *v.* Andrews, 7 Jones & Sp. (N. Y.) 302; Bowman *v.* Wood, 15 Mass. 534; Tarbell *v.* Sturdevant, 26 Vt. 513; Hilton *v.* Warring, 7 Wis. 492; Kinney *v.* Kruse, 28 Wis. 183; Curtis *v.* Mohr, 18 Wis. 615; Jones *v.* Hawkins, 17 Ind. 550; Houser *v.* Houser, 43 Ga. 415; Moore *v* Hall, 48 Mich. 143; Nelson *v.* Wellington, 5 Bosw. (N. Y.) 178; Brookman *v.* Metcalf, 5 Bosw. (N. Y.) 429; Lindsay *v.* Chase, 104 Mass. 253; Hayne *v.* Furnis, 117 Mass. 290; Boyd *v.* Corbitt, 37 Mich. 52; Ducasse *v.* McKenna, 28 La. Ann. 419; Dix *v.* Tully, 14 La. Ann. 460; Louisiana St. Bank *v.* Gaiennie, 21 La. Ann. 555.

The indorsement may be on a separate piece of paper and still be legal. Crosby *v.* Roub, 16 Wis. 616.

The following indorsement was sufficient to enable the pledgee to sue in his own name: "Pay to A B (the pledgee) for account of C D (the pledgor)." Nelson *v.* Wellington, 5 Bosw. (N. Y.) 178.

The holder in pledge of accommodation paper may enforce without being compelled to resort first to other securities for the same debt, the maker of the note not being entitled to demand that. Cronise *v.* Kellogg, 20 Ill. 11.

By suing on the collateral, the pledgee does not become a surety for the maker. Cardin *v.* Jones, 23 Ga. 175.

If the creditor receives the notes under a special agreement, by which he is not to sue, but to collect in any other mode, he must as to all persons without notice of the extent of his powers, be regarded as the general

mand on the pledgor for payment[1] or showing that the original debt has not been paid.[2] Where the collateral is unnegotiable in form or has not been formally indorsed to him the pledgee may sue in the name of the legal holder; for the pledging of the collateral gives him implied authority to collect.[3]

There is no obligation on the pledgee holding a note given as conditional payment to sue on the note; for if the debtor wishes it sued on he may pay his debt, take up the dishonored note and sue on it himself.[4]

In carrying on the proceedings subsequent to the suit in enforcing the security, the same reasonable care must be used by the pledgee or he will be liable for a loss occasioned by the lack of it.[5]

g. AMOUNT OF RECOVERY.—The holder of negotiable instruments in pledge is, unless they are held subject to equitable defenses, entitled to recover the full face value of the instruments, whatever may be the amount of the debt secured, holding the surplus for the benefit of the pledgor.[6]

holder, and notice to sue may be given to him. Pickens *v.* Yarborough, 26 Ala. 417; McCrary *v.* King, 27 Ga. 26.

1. White *v.* Phelps, 14 Minn. 27.

Where a creditor gave a receipt for a collateral note whereby he agreed to use all legal means to collect the note if so directed by the debtor, it was held that the creditor need not wait for a direction from the debtor. Bay *v.* Gunn, 1 Den. (N. Y.) 108.

So where a bank held collateral from a depositor, it was held that the bank could enforce the collateral without trying to collect its debt from the deposits. Third Nat. Bank *v.* Harrison, 3 McCrary (U. S.) 316.

Bergen *v.* Urbahm, 83 N. Y. 49; Langdon *v.* Buel, 9 Wend. (N. Y.) 80; Lucas *v.* Harris, 20 Ill. 167; Matteson *v.* Matteson, 55 Wis. 452.

Where such evidence has been turned into a judgment, the judgment is sufficient as evidence. Ober *v.* Gallagher, 93 U. S. 206; Connecticut M. L. Ins. Co. *v.* Jones, 8 Fed. Rep. 303; Wayman *v.* Cochrane, 35 Ill. 154.

2. McCarty *v.* Clark, 10 Iowa 588.

So if the maker of the collateral paper pay it to the pledgor, knowing that it has been pledged, the pledgee may still recover on it. Fennell *v.* McGowan, 58 Miss. 261.

3. Jones *v.* Witter, 13 Mass. 304; Whitteker *v.* Charleston Gas Co., 16 W. Va. 717.

4. Rice *v.* Benedict, 19 Mich. 132; Dodge *v.* Stanton, 12 Mich. 408.

Under codes which allow the assignee of a chose in action to sue in his own name, the pledgee of unindorsed negotiable instruments may sue in his own name. White *v.* Phelps, 14 Minn. 27; Ducasse *v.* McKenna, 28 La. Ann. 419; Bank of Lafayette *v.* Bruff, 33 La. Ann. 624.

5. McQueen's Appeal, 104 Pa. St. 595.

So, where after judgment on the collateral note levy was made on land of the maker, which was more valuable than the judgment, notice not being given to the pledgor of the sale, the pledgee was held liable for loss caused by a low price received for the land. McQueen's Appeal, 104 Pa. St. 595.

6. Tooke *v.* Newman, 75 Ill. 215; Thayer *v.* Mann, 19 Pick. (Mass.) 536; Knights *v.* Putnam, 3 Pick. (Mass.) 185; Tarbell *v.* Sturtevant, 26 Vt. 513; Jones *v.* Hicks, 52 Miss. 682; McLemore *v.* Hawkins, 46 Miss. 715; Plants Mfg. Co. *v.* Faevey, 20 Wis. 200; City Bank *v.* Perkins, 4 Bosw. (N. Y.) 420; Reid *v.* Furnivale, 1 Cr. &. M. 538; Rice *v.* Southern Pa. Iron etc. Co., 9 Phila. (Pa.) 294; Union Nat. Bank *v.* Roberts, 45 Wis. 373; Matthews *v.* Rutherford, 7 La. Ann. 225; Dresser *v.* Missouri etc. R. Co., 93 U. S. 92; Hotchkiss *v.* National Banks, 21 Wall. (U. S.) 354; Morris *v.* Preston, 93 Ill. 215; Greenwall *v.* Hayden, 78 Ky. 332; Williams *v.* Smith, 2 Hill (N. Y.) 301; Watson *v.* Cabot Bank, 5 Sandf. Ch. (N. Y.) 423; Case *v.* Me-

If, on the collection of the collateral, less is recovered than the debt secured, the pledgee has his action against the pledgor for the deficiency.[1] But if the pledgee has taken the paper subject to equitable defenses, he can recover in suit upon it no more than is actually due him on the principal debt.[2]

Where accommodation paper given without restrictions has been transferred as collateral security in good faith in the usual course of business, a pledgee holding for value is entitled, under the presumption that he gave full value, to recover the full amount thereof, although he may have had knowledge that it was

chanics' Banking Assoc. 4 N. Y., 166; City Bank *v.* Perkins, 4 Bosw. (N. Y.) 420; Duncombe *v.* New York etc. R. Co., 84 N. Y. 190; Allaire *v.* Hartshorne, 21 N. J. L. 665; Duncan *v.* Gilbert, 29 N. J. L. 521; Jackson *v.* First Nat. Bank, 42 N. J. L. 177; Stoddard *v.* Kimball, 6 Cush. (Mass.) 469; Fisher *v.* Fisher, 98 Mass. 303; Chicopee Bank *v.* Chapin, 8 Met. (Mass.) 40; Belding *v.* Manley, 21 Vt. 551; Collins *v.* Martin, 1 B. & P. 648; Treuttel *v.* Barandon, 8 Taunt. 100; Edwards *v.* Jones, 7 C. & P. 633; Simpson *v.* Clark, 2 C. M. & R. 342; Parish *v.* Stone, 14 Pick. (Mass.) 198; Hubbard *v.* Chapin, 2 Allen (Mass.) 328; Cardwell *v.* Hicks, 37 Barb. (N. Y.) 458; Petti *v.* Hannum, 2 Humph. (Tenn.) 102; Hoeman *v.* Hobson, 8 Humph. (Tenn.) 127; Williams *v.* Cheney, 3 Gray (Mass.) 215; Valette *v.* Mason, 1 Ind. 288; Kerr *v.* Cowen, 2 Dev. Eq. (N. Car.) 350.

That the obligation of the pledgor to the pledgee does not reach the full value of the collateral, does not in any way affect the maker thereof, for he is liable for the full amount. Wilkinson *v.* Jeffers, 30 Ga. 153; Tarbell *v.* Sturtevant, 26 Vt. 513.

The pledgee of negotiable bonds has the same privilege. Cromwell *v.* Sac Co., 96 U. S. 51; Jerome *v.* McCarter, 94 U. S. 739; Hancock *v.* Franklin Ins. Co., 114 Mass. 155; Stoddard *v.* Kimball, 6 Cush. (Mass.) 469; Allaire *v.* Hartshorne, 21 N. J. L. 665; Chicopee Bank *v.* Chapin, 8 Met. (Mass.) 40; Williams *v.* Smith, 2 Hill (N. Y.) 301.

On the pledgor of bills of exchange becoming insolvent, the pledgee may put in a claim for the full face value thereof. *In re* Commersal, L. R., 16 Ch. D. 138; *Ex parte* Newton, L. R., 16 Ch. D. 330; *Ex parte* Phillips, 1 M. & D. 232.

Whether the maker has paid the pledgor or not, he must still pay the pledgee. Williams *v.* National Bank, 72 Md. 441.

Where a promissory note to bearer is surreptitiously passed to a *bona fide* holder as collateral for the past and future advances, and the full amount is advanced before notice, he may recover from the maker, although some advances were made after the note fell due. Bancroft *v.* McKnight, 11 Rich. (S. Car.) 663.

1. Faulkner *v.* Hill, 104 Mass. 188.

2. Farwell *v.* Importers etc. Nat. Bank, 90 N. Y. 483; Youngs *v.* Lee, 12 N. Y. 551; Huff *v.* Wagner, 63 Barb. (N. Y.) 215; Stalker *v.* McDonald, 6 Hill (N. Y.) 93; Williams *v.* Smith, 2 Hill (N. Y.) 301; Stoddard *v.* Kimball, 6 Cush. (Mass.) 469; Roche *v.* Ladd, 1 Allen (Mass.) 436; Williams *v.* Cheney, 3 Gray (Mass.) 215; Chicopee Bank *v.* Chapin, 8 Met. (Mass.) 40; Fisher *v.* Fisher, 98 Mass. 303; Tarbell *v.* Sturtevant, 26 Vt. 513; Mayo *v.* Moore, 28 Ill. 428; Gammon *v.* Huse, 9 Ill. App. 557; Easter *v.* Minard, 26 Ill. 494; Randolph *v.* Merchants' Bank, 9 Lea (Tenn.) 63; Grant *v.* Kidwell, 30 Mo. 455; Valette *v.* Mason, 1 Ind. 288; White *v.* Phelps, 14 Minn. 27; Lobdell *v.* Merchants' etc. Bank, 33 Mich. 408; Allaire *v.* Hartshorne, 21 N. J. L. 665; Louisiana State Bank *v.* Gaiennie, 21 La. Ann. 555; Steere *v.* Benson, 2 Ill. App. 560; Union Nat. Bank *v.* Roberts, 45 Wis. 373.

Where paper was given in the first instance as collateral and then subpledged on a suit by the sub-pledgee against the maker, the latter was allowed to show on the trial, the identity, nature and amounts of the demands for which it was originally pledged. Garton *v.* Union City Bank, 34 Mich. 279.

Where the negotiable collateral was unindorsed to the pledgee, he was al-

accommodation paper.[1] But where the presumption that a pledgee holding accommodation paper as collateral, gave full value is overthrown, only the amount of the debt secured can be recovered by a suit. The consent of the pledgor to the surrender of the paper to the maker on such recovery should be obtained.[2]

In case of its misappropriation, the pledgee who has advanced value thereon in good faith is entitled to recover only the amount of his advances.[3] Also where it is pledged for an antecedent debt.[4]

4. Simultaneous Remedies on Debt Secured and on Collateral.—Though entitled to but one satisfaction of his debt, the pledgee may enforce the negotiable security and at the same time get judgment and issue execution on the debt secured as in other cases of pledge.[5]

lowed to recover only the amount of his advances. *Ex parte* Philips, 1 M. & D. 232.

So if the paper has been taken after maturity only, the amount which the payee himself could recover can be sued for. Kelly *v.* Ferguson, 46 How. Pr. (N. Y.) 411; Logan *v.* Cassell, 88 Pa. St. 288.

Where the bonds of a company are pledged by it as collateral security for its own indebtedness, in a smaller amount than the par value of the bonds, and the pledgee still holds them, he is entitled to recover from the company no more than the amount secured by the pledge. Jesup *v.* City Bank, 14 Wis. 331.

1. First Nat. Bank *v.* Grant, 71 Me. 374; Dunn *v.* Weston, 71 Me. 270; Robbins *v.* Richardson, 2 Bosw. (N. Y.) 253; Brown *v.* Mott, 7 Johns. (N. Y.) 360; Seybel *v.* Nat. Currency Bank, 54 N. Y. 291; Harrington *v.* Dorr, 3 Robt. (N. Y.) 275; Com. *v.* Pittsburgh, 34 Pa. St. 496; Smith *v.* Knox, 3 Esp. 46; Lord *v.* Ocean Bank, 20 Pa. St. 384; Bank of Newbury *v.* Rand, 38 N. H. 166; Maitland *v.* Citizens' Nat. Bank, 40 Md. 540; Stoddard *v.* Kimball, 6 Cush. (Mass.) 469; Fisher *v.* Fisher, 98 Mass. 303; Bowman *v.* Millison, 58 Ill. 36; Louisiana State Bank *v.* Gaienne, 21 La. Ann. 355; Gardner *v.* Maxwell, 27 La. Ann. 561; Cook *v.* Norwood, 106 Ill. 558. In Mechanics' etc. Bank *v.* Barnett, 27 La. Ann. 177, the pledgee was only given the amount of his advances.

2. Teutonia Nat. Bank *v.* Loeb, 2 La. Ann. 110.

3. Jackson *v.* First Nat. Bank, 42 N. J. L. 177; Duncan *v.* Gilbert, 29 N. J. L. 521; American Nat. Bank *v.* Harrison Wire Co., 11 Mo. App. 446; Stoddard *v.* Kimball, 6 Cush. (Mass.) 469; Fisher *v.* Fisher, 98 Mass. 303; Maitland *v.* Citizens' Nat. Bank, 40 Md. 540; Williams *v.* Smith, 2 Hill (N. Y.) 301; Watson *v.* Cabot Bank, 5 Sandf. (N. Y.) 423; Case *v.* Mechanics' Banking Assoc., 4 N. Y. 166; Allaire *v.* Hartshorn, 21 N. J. L. 665; Small *v.* Smith, 1 Den. (N. Y.) 583; Collins *v.* Gilbert, 94 U. S. 753.

4. Cromwell *v.* Sac. Co., 96 U. S. 51; Allaire *v.* Hartshorne, 21 N. J. L. 665; Williams *v.* Smith, 2 Hill (N. Y.) 301; Chicopee Bank *v.* Chapion, 8 Met. (Mass.) 40; Stoddard *v.* Kimball, 6 Cush. (Mass.) 469; Fisher *v.* Fisher, 98 Mass. 303; Atkinson *v.* Brooks, 26 Vt. 569; Tarbell *v.* Sturtevant, 26 Vt. 513; Grocers' Bank *v.* Penfield, 69 N. Y. 502; Maitland *v.* Citizens' Nat. Bank, 40 Md. 570; Grant *v.* Kidwell, 30 Mo. 455; Atlas Bank *v.* Doyle, 9 R. I. 76; Mayo *v.* Moore, 28 Ill. 428; Steere *v.* Benson, 2 Ill. App. 560; Jones *v.* Heffert, 2 Stark. 356; Citizens' Bank *v.* Payne, 18 La. Ann. 222; Grant *v.* Kidwell, 30 Mo. 455.

So where the note is tainted with usury. Taylor *v.* Daniels, 38 Ill. 331.

But in the case of a pledgee, holding paper for a pre-existing debt, who is accountable to some third person for the surplus, the rule is different. Fisher *v.* Fisher, 98 Mass. 303; Stoddard *v.* Kimball, 6 Cush. (Mass.) 469.

Counsel Fees.—Not even the pledgee's attorney or counsel fees can be recovered. Second Nat. Bank *v.* Hemingray, 34 Ohio St. 381.

5. Sickles *v.* Richardson, 23 Hun (N. Y.) 559; Butler *v.* Miller, 1 N. Y. 496; Corn Exch. Ins. Assoc. *v.* Babcock, 57 Barb. (N. Y.) 233; Royal Bank *v.* Grand Junction R. etc. Co.,

5. Return of Security or Accounting—*a.* IN GENERAL.—On the final settlement between the pledgor and pledgee in regard to the debt secured, it is the duty of the latter to either return the collateral[1] or account for its absence.[2]

100 Mass. 444; Chapman *v.* Lee, 64 Ala. 483; Plant's Mfg. Co. *v.* Falvey, 20 Wis. 200.

Suit on the debt may be begun even though the pledgee has attached property of persons liable on a pledged note. Chapman *v.* Clough, 6 Vt. 123.

Where a negotiable security is taken as collateral to an existing debt, the holder may endeavor to make it available by a suit; and, failing of success, he may resort to his original security, without restoring that taken as collateral. Comstock *v.* Smith, 23 Me. 202.

Recovery of judgment on the debt secured does not bar recovery on collateral. See *supra*, this title, *Suit on Debt Secured.* Steel *v.* Lord, 28 Hun (N. Y.) 27; McCullough *v.* Hellman, 8 Oregon 192; White *v.* Smith, 33 Pa. St. 186; Burnheimer *v.* Hart, 27 Iowa 19.

But where the pledgee assigned judgments recovered on the collateral, it will be presumed that the assignment was absolute and that the pledgee has elected to take them to extinguish the debt secured. Hawks *v.* Hinchcliff, 17 Barb. (N. Y.) 422.

Costs in both suits may be recovered. Hilton *v.* Waring, 7 Wis. 492; Plant's Mfg. Co. *v.* Falvey, 20 Wis. 200.

A payee of a note to whom the maker has assigned a larger note as collateral security, and who has therefrom collected more than enough to reimburse himself, retaining the collateral, cannot enforce payment of the smaller note; and a judgment thereon, taken under a power of attorney attached thereto, and without the maker's knowledge or consent, is fraudulent and void. Rea *v.* Forrest, 88 Ill. 275.

1. Hoffman *v.* Johnson, 1 Bland (Md.) 103; Mullen *v.* Morris, 2 Pa. St. 85; Ocean Nat. Bank *v.* Faut, 50 N. Y. 474; Stuart *v.* Bigler, 98 Pa. St. 80; Reavis *v.* Fielden, 18 Ill. 77; Spalding *v.* Bank of Susquehanna Co., 9 Pa. St. 28; Lucas *v.* Harris, 20 Ill. 167; Matteson *v.* Matteson, 55 Wis. 452; Lewis *v.* Mott, 36 N. Y. 402; Whipple *v.* Blackington, 97 Mass. 476; Hale *v.* Rider, 5 Cush. (Mass.) 231; Bank of Rutland *v.* Woodruff, 34 Vt. 89.

That the notes have since become valueless is not a good excuse for their non-production, for it does not exclude the possibility of a transfer by the pledgee before they became of no worth. Stuart *v.* Bigler, 98 Pa. St. 80.

Where a debtor has delivered promissory notes to his creditor, under the agreement that the creditor shall collect the amounts due thereon, and after deducting all expenses, apply the net proceeds to the payment of the debt, and such creditor afterward gets judgment against his debtor for the remainder due on his claim, after applying the collections on the collaterals toward the payment of the debt, the judgment debtor is entitled to receive the collaterals uncollected, upon the payment of the judgment and costs. Under a sufficient answer, setting forth such a state of facts established upon the trial, the court should not require the payment of the judgment and costs, in the absence of the collaterals uncollected, and compel the defendant to recover them in a subsequent proceeding. The surrender of the collaterals and the payment of the judgment ought to be contemporaneous. Semple etc. Mfg. Co. *v.* Debwiler, 30 Kan. 386.

When the pledgee of a note hands it to the maker to be delivered to the payee, the pledgor, he thereby constitutes him his agent, and after an offer by such agent to deliver it to the payee, and a refusal to accept it, the latter cannot maintain an action against the pledgee for its conversion. Norman *v.* Rogers, 29 Ark. 365.

Where, after a note is paid, a city bond given to the holder as security is not returned to the maker, in the absence of any showing that the holder has converted it to his own use, no cause of action accrues to the maker therefor until demand for its return and refusal. Auld *v.* Butcher, 22 Kan. 400.

Return of Identical Bonds.—Where the collateral consists of negotiable bonds having a market value, the identical bonds pledged need not be returned if the pledgee has other bonds of the same kind to take their place. Levy *v* Loeb, 85 N. Y. 365; Gilpin *v.* Howell, 5 Pa. St. 41; Stuart *v.* Bigler, 98 Pa. St. 80.

2. Starrett *v.* Barber 20 Me. 457; Rice *v.* Benedict, 19 Mich. 132

Upon the non-production of the collateral and failure to account for its absence, the pledgee is chargeable with its face value or its actual value, for otherwise if the collateral has been transferred by the pledgee to a *bona fide* holder for value before maturity, the pledgor will be liable for the amount of the collateral as well as for the debt secured thereby.[1] If the pledgee by selling or transferring the security, elects to make it his own,[2] the presumption is to that effect.[3]

b. APPLICATION OF PROCEEDS.—Where the collateral has been pledged to secure a certain debt, the proceeds of collection of such collateral can only be applied to that specific debt.[4]

A creditor holding his debtor's note, and the notes of third persons as collateral security, under an arrangement that, if the debt were not paid at a specified time, the collateral notes should become his, absolutely, sued the principal note, recovered judgment, and collected the full amount thereof. But, pending the suit, he sold the collateral notes, and failed to account in any way for the proceeds, or to credit the amount upon the judgment. *Held*, that he was liable to the debtor for the amount received on the sale of such collaterals. Dorrill *v.* Eaton, 35 Mich. 302.

Notes which had been pledged to secure a claim upon which, afterwards, judgment was recovered, as they became due were paid to the pledgee. *Held*, that the money so received would be treated as having been applied in satisfaction of the judgment, and would not be regarded as a fund to be recovered back by the pledgor, subject to be reduced by the judgment as a set-off. King *v.* Hutchins, 28 N. H. 561.

On paying the debt, the pledgor could recover the note, or, on refusal, would have his action of trover against the pledgee, in which the latter may show in good faith, in reduction of damages, the maker's insolvency. Grove *v* Roberts, 6 La. Ann. 210.

Expenses of Collection.—Expenses of collecting a collateral, may be first deducted from the amount recovered, and the balance only applied to the extinguishment of the principal debt. Griggs *v.* Howe, 2 Abb. App. Dec. (N. Y.) 291; Starrett *v.* Barber, 20 Me. 457.

1. Lucas *v.* Harris, 20 Ill. 167; Spalding *v.* Bank of Susquehanna Co., 9 Pa. St. 28; Carr *v.* Fielden, 18 Ill. 77.

When the maker of a pledged note was shown to have been solvent for some time after the maturity of the note, the pledgee failing to produce the note, was charged with the full face value. Goodall *v.* Richardson, 14 N. H. 567; Commercial Bank *v.* Martin, 1 La. Ann. 344.

A pledgee may relinquish a collateral security given him by a debtor without the consent of other creditors, without jeopardizing his right to resort to the debtor's other property, but he must still account to the debtor for the security lost. Dyott's Estate, 2 W. & S. (Pa.) 463.

2. Harris *v.* Johnson, 3 Cranch (C. C.) 311; Cocke *v.* Chaney, 14 Ala. 65.

3. Hawks *v.* Hinchcliff, 17 Barb. (N. Y.) 492.

4. See *supra*, this title, *Debt or Engagement Secured.* Wyckoff *v.* Anthony, 90 N. Y., 442; Talmage v. Third Nat. Bank, 91 N. Y. 531; Duncan *v.* Brennan, 83 N. Y. 487; Lane *v.* Bailey, 47 Barb. (N. Y.) 395; Robinson *v.* Frost, 14 Barb. (N. Y.) 536; James' Appeal, 89 Pa. St. 54; Selden *v.* National Bank, 69 Pa. St. 424; Buckley *v.* Garrett, 60 Pa. St. 333; Hathaway *v.* Fall River Nat. Bank, 131 Mass. 14; Hancock *v.* Franklin Ins. Co., 114 Mass. 155; Neponset Bank *v.* Leland, 5 Met. (Mass.) 259.

Chester *v.* Wheelwright, 15 Conn. 562; Teutonic Nat. Bank *v.* Loeb, 27 La. Ann. 110.

But where the same pledgor pledged two separate sets of collateral for two separate debts to the same pledgee, after one of the debts was paid and some of the securities for the other were found to be worthless, the pledgee, on the insolvency of the pledgor, was allowed to apply the securities for the debt that had been paid to secure the unpaid one. *In re* McVay, 13 Fed. Rep. 443.

When collateral is given for several debts, the debt of the longest standing can be first liquidated if no directions to the contrary are given by the debtor.[1] Where short-time notes, maturing before the principal debt, are collected, the proceeds cannot be applied to the principal debt until its maturity.[2]

c. SURPLUS OVER DEBT SECURED.—Any surplus recovered by the pledgee on the collateral over the debt secured and reasonable expenses of collection, belongs to the pledgor.[3] If this is not paid over, the pledgor can have his action for it.[4]

XIV. RIGHTS, LIABILITIES AND REMEDIES OF PLEDGEE OF STOCK—1. Before Default—*a.* IN GENERAL.—As has been pointed out elsewhere, confusion has arisen between the relations of the pledgee of stock indorsed to him in blank and those of the pledgee who has had the stock transferred to himself on the books of the company. It will be understood in the decision of the pledgee's rights and liabilities that those of the pledgee having the stock in his own name on the books of the company are in general designated, unless the contrary is expressly stated.

b. RIGHT TO TRANSFER ON THE BOOKS.—The pledgee of stock who holds only the certificate indorsed in blank has the right to compel the transfer to be made to himself on the books of the corporation, and the issue of a new certificate, and this is not a conversion of the stock.[5]

When the debt secured is payable by installments, the proceeds of collateral may be applied to over due installments as the pledgee desires. Saunders *v.* McCarthy, 8 Allen (Mass.) 42.

1. Pattison *v.* Hull, 9 Cow. (N. Y.) 747; Jones *v.* Benedict, 83 N. Y. 79.

But where a debtor gave his creditor collateral security upon the aggregate amount of several separate claims, the proceeds of such collateral security must be applied, *pro rata*, upon each of the claims. Beach *v.* State Bank, 2 Ind. 488.

2. See *supra*, this title, *Collection Before Principal Debt Due.*

3. Hilton *v.* Waring, 7 Wis. 492; Plant's Mfg. Co. *v.* Falvey, 20 Wis. 200; Jones *v.* Hawkins, 17 Ind. 550; Union Nat. Bank *v.* Roberts, 45 Wis. 373; Hawks *v.* Hinchcliffe, 17 Barb. (N. Y.) 492.

Or if the rights of others have attached, the pledgee holds the surplus as trustee for them. Houser *v.* Houser, 43 Ga. 415.

4. *In re* Litchfield Bank, 28 Conn. 575; Hunt *v.* Nevers, 15 Pick. (Mass.) 500; Overstreet *v.* Nunn, 36 Ala. 649.

Where the debtor paid the principal debt without knowing that the creditor had already collected on the collateral and tendered the amount collected with the rest of the collateral, the debtor could not recover back the principal debt paid. Young *v.* Stahelin, 34 N. Y. 258.

On refusal of a pledgee after collecting a note to appropriate the surplus after paying his own debt in the manner directed by the pledgor, he is responsible for any loss occasioned by a depreciation in the currency after such refusal. Knight *v.* Yarborough, 7 Smed. & M. (Miss.) 179.

Interest on Surplus.—Where notes have been pledged to secure a claim upon which judgment has been recovered, interest should be cast on the notes so pledged, to the time of their payment, also upon the judgment to the same time. In an action brought to recover back the surplus, the plaintiff is entitled to interest upon the excess of the proceeds of the notes over the amount received for the judgment, up to the rendition of his judgment. King *v.* Hutchins, 28 N. H. 561.

5. Rich *v.* Boyce, 39 Md. 314; Heath *v.* Griswold, 18 Blatchf. (U. S.) 555; Heath *v.* Silverthorn etc. Co., 39 Wis. 146; Adams *v.* Sturges, 55 Ill. 468; Hubbell *v.* Drexel, 21 Am. L. Reg., N. S. 452.

c. PLEDGEE HAS RIGHTS AND LIABILITIES OF A STOCKHOLDER.—When once the transfer on the books of the company has taken place and a new certificate issued, the pledgee becomes a stockholder subject, unless exempt by statute, to all the liabilities, and in general, having all the rights belonging to one holding the position of a stockholder.[1]

So a sub-pledgee of stock has the same right under the same circumstances. *In re* Tahiti Co., L. R., 17 Eq. 275.

So a transfer to the name of a third person who held for the pledgee was not, in the absence of tender and demand, a conversion. Day *v.* Homes, 103 Mass. 306; Adams *v.* Sturges, 55 Ill. 468.

A corporation reduced its capital stock. *Held*, that a pledgee of some of the shares did not unlawfully convert them by surrendering the certificate to the corporation and accepting a new one. Donnell *v.* Wyckoff, 49 N. J. L. 48.

Corporation stock, held as collateral to secure certain notes, was transferred by the holder to relatives to avoid liability as a stockholder, he taking back the certificates with a power of attorney to him to transfer. *Held*, that there was nothing in the transaction which amounted to a conversion of the stock. Heath *v.* Griswold, 18 Blatchf. (U. S.) 555.

Relief to Pledgor.—Where such a transfer has been made and the pledgee exercises all the rights of legal ownership to the exclusion of the pledgor, in a proper case, the court of equity will declare the proper relationship of the parties, and if necessary order a retransfer and an adjustment of accounts. Brick *v.* Brick, 98 U. S. 514; Gilpin *v.* Howell, 5 Pa. St. 41; McCalla *v.* Clark, 55 Ga. 53; Newton *v.* Fay, 10 Allen (Mass.) 505; Pinkerton *v.* Manchester etc. R. Co., 42 N. H, 424.

Parol evidence is admissible to show the true relationship of the parties. Brick *v.* Brick, 98 U. S. 514; Lathrop *v.* Kneeland, 46 Barb. (N. Y.) 432; McMahone *v.* Macy, 51 N. Y. 155; Burgess *v.* Seligman, 107 U. S. 20; Tonica etc. R. Co. *v.* Stein, 21 Ill. 96; Pittsburgh R. Co. *v.* Stewart, 41 Pa. St. 54; Jones *v.* Portsmouth etc. R. Co., 32 N. H. 554.

1. Germania Nat. Bank *v.* Case, 99 U. S. 628; Cecil Nat. Bank *v.* Watsontown Bank, 105 U. S. 217; Pullman *v.* Upton, 96 U. S. 328; Heath *v.* Griswold, 18 Blatchf. (U. S.) 555; Bowden *v.* Farmers' Bank, 1 Hughes (U. S.) 337; Vail *v.* Hamilton, 85 N. Y. 453; Johnson *v.* Underhill, 52 N. Y. 203; *In re* Empire City Bank, 18 N. Y. 199; Roosevelt *v.* Brown, 11 N. Y. 148; Adderley *v.* Storm, 6 Hill (N. Y.) 624; Wheelock *v.* Kost, 77 Ill. 296; Adams *v.* Sturges, 55 Ill. 428; Kellogg *v.* Stockwell, 75 Ill. 18; Barre Nat. Bank *v.* Hingham Mfg. Co., 127 Mass. 563; Holyoke Bank *v.* Goodman Paper Mfg. Co., 9 Cush. (Mass.) 576; Crease *v.* Babcock, 10 Met. (Mass.) 525; Holyoke Bank *v.* Burnham, 11 Cush. (Mass.) 183; Brewster *v.* Sim, 42 Cal. 139; Magruder *v.* Colston, 44 Md. 349; Albert *v.* Savings Bank, 1 Md. Ch. 407; Hale *v.* Walker, 31 Iowa 344; Pittsburg etc. R. Co. *v.* Stewart, 41 Pa. St. 54; Aultman's Appeal, 98 Pa. St. 516; McCalla *v.* Clark, 55 Ga. 53; Fisher *v.* Seligman, 75 Mo. 13; Griswold *v.* Seligman, 72 Mo. 110; Moore *v.* Jones, 3 Woods (U. S.) 53; Franklin Bank *v.* Commercial Bank, 36 Ohio St. 350; Burgess *v.* Seligman, 107 U. S. 20.

Any secret trust existing between pledgor and pledgee is not a defense to an action against the pledgee by third persons. Aultman's Appeal, 98 Pa. St. 516.

The pledgee of stock, holding the certificate indorsed in blank, was allowed to interfere to protect the property of the corporation from the wrongful acts of its officers. Baldwin *v.* Canfield, 26 Minn. 43.

So where the pledgee's name was registered on the books of the corporation. Vail *v.* Hamilton, 85 N. Y. 453.

In *California*, one whose name is on the books of the company is the stockholder, whether another holds the certificate or not. People *v.* Robinson, 64 Cal. 373.

Where the corporation pledged its own stock, it was held that the pledgee was not liable as a stockholder. Union Sav. Assoc. *v.* Seligman, 92 Mo. 635, overruling Griswold *v.* Seligman, 72 Mo. 110.

Restricting Pledgee's Liability—If it

By the same act the pledgor severs his connection with the corporation and is released from all claims held on him by the company.[1]

In States where statutory enactment provides that the stockholders of the corporation shall be liable for its debts, the pledgee who has the stock transferred to himself on the books of the corporation is liable as a stockholder.[2]

But in many States those who hold stock in a representative capacity or as collateral security are exempt from the usual liabilities of stockholders;[3] but there seems to be a growing inclination to make the person whose name appears on the books of the corporation liable for unpaid subscriptions to the same.[4]

One to whom a corporation has pledged its stock is also within the statutory exemption[5] and the fact that the pledgee has the stock transferred to his name and without authority votes on it, does not estop him from claiming the exemption.[6]

is desired the purpose of the transfer, with its terms, showing debt secured, may be indorsed on the certificate, and this will be notice of pledgee's restricted interest and exempt him from liability. Barre Nat. Bank *v.* Hingham Mfg. Co., 127 Mass. 563.

An indorsement of delivery as being for "collateral security" was held enough. Matthews *v.* Albert, 24 Md. 527.

Where, on the first pledging of a certificate it was indorsed "as collateral" and afterwards redeemed indorsed in blank by pledgee to pledgor, and again pledged, the second pledgee was not put on his notice by the words "as collateral," and first pledgee was liable as stockholder. Matthews *v.* Massachusetts Nat. Bank, Holmes (U. S.) 410.

1. Cecil Nat. Bank *v.* Watsontown Bank, 105 U. S. 217.

2. Blanchard *v.* Dedham Gas Light Co., 12 Gray (Mass.) 213; Fisher *v.* Essex Bank, 5 Gray (Mass.) 373; Agricultural Bank *v.* Burr, 24 Me. 256; Shipman *v.* Ætna Ins. Co., 29 Conn. 251; Dutton *v.* Connecticut Bank, 13 Conn. 498; Oxford Turnpike Co. *v.* Bunnell, 6 Conn. 558; Skohegan Bank *v.* Cutter, 49 Me. 315; Peoples' Bank *v.* Gridley, 91 Ill. 457; People *v.* Devin, 17 Ill. 86; Pittsburgh R. Co. *v.* Clarke, 29 Pa. St. 146; Purlierton *v.* Manchester etc. R. Co.. 42 N. H. 424; Heath *v.* Erie R. Co, 8 Blatchf. (U. S.) 347; Williams *v.* Mechanics' Bank, 5 Blatchf. (U. S.) 59; Wheelock *v.* Kost, 77 Ill. 296; Aultman's Appeal, 98 Pa. St. 505.

Even where the statute declares that not only the person whose name appears upon the books of a corporation as stockholder. but also all equitable owners shall be liable, the pledgor is not an "equitable owner" within the meaning of the statute to make him liable in place of the pledgee.

In re Empire City Bank, 18 N. Y. 199; Richardson *v.* Abendroth, 43 Barb. (N. Y.) 162.

One who received as collateral from a bank, shares of its own stock for money loaned to it, was held liable as a stockholder.

Pullman *v.* Upton, 96 U. S. 328; Wheelock *v.* Kost, 77 Ill. 296; Johnson *v.* Laflin, 5 Dill. (U. S.) 65.

3. *New York*, 2 Rev. Stat. 1881, p. 1548, § 11; *Massachusetts* Pub. Stat. 1882, ch. 105, § 25; *Ohio* Rev. Stat. 1880, § 3259; *Missouri* Rev. Stat. 1879, §§ 934, 935; *Indiana* Stats. 1876, p 371, §§ 8, 9; Rev. Stat. 1881, §§ 3008, 3009; *Wisconsin* Rev. Stat. 1878, p. 532, § 1827; *Maryland* Rev. Code, 1878, p. 323, § 61; *Colorado* G. L. 1877, p. 150, § 210; *Washington* Code, 1881, § 2435; *Dakota* L. 1879, ch. 9, 14; *Wyoming* C. L, 1876, ch. 34, §§ 16, 17.

4. Burgess *v.* Seligman, 107 U. S. 20.

5. The State courts of *Missouri* decided contrary to the rule in the text. Fisher *v.* Seligman, 75 Mo. 13; Griswold *v.* Seligman, 72 Mo. 110; but they were overruled by *United States* Supreme court, in Burgess *v.* Seligman, 107 U. S. 20.

6. Burgess *v.* Seligman, 107 U. S.

d. DURATION OF RIGHTS AND LIABILITIES AS STOCKHOLDER. —The pledgee continues to hold the position of stockholder, with his rights and liabilities, until the re-transfer of the stock on the books takes place, even though the debt secured may have been paid and the pledge lien discharged.[1] Nor can the liability be avoided by a transfer of the stock to an irresponsible third person;[2] but a transfer in the first instance to a third

20; Matthews *v.* Albert, 24 Md. 527; McMahon *v.* Macy, 51 N. Y. 155.

In the case of Griswold *v.* Seligman, 72 Mo. 110, Sherwood, C. J., said: "This is a case where acts speak louder than words; where plausible theories go for nothing when confronted by palpable facts. We cannot impute to the pledgees either ignorance of, or a desire to violate, the law, and so must conclude that they by the act of voting the stock represented themselves to the corporation, and were by the corporation regarded as fully entitled to the privileges they claimed and exercised. This being the case, they certainly cannot be heard to gainsay their heretofore admitted title: to assert that title, if there was a profit, and deny it if there was a loss."

But in the case of Burgess *v.* Seligman, 107 U. S. 20, Bradley, J., said, in reply to the above: "If the law allows stock to be held in trust, or as collateral security, without personal liability, and if, as we suppose, the clear effect of the contract was to create such a holding in this case, we do not see how the doctrine can apply. The only parties to complain would be the other stockholders, who might, perhaps, complain that stock held merely in trust, or as collateral security, is not entitled to participate with them in the privilege of voting. But from them no complaint is heard. Creditors would not complain, for, on the hypothesis that stock may be lawfully held at all in trust, or as collateral security, without incurring liability to them, the act of voting on the stock cannot injure or affect them. In the absence of such a law the case might be different. Undoubtedly it has been held in cases innumerable that acting as a stockholder binds one as such; but that is where the law does not allow stock to be held at all without incurring all the liabilities incident to such holding. The present is an action at law based upon the supposed liability of the defendants under a statute which makes the distinction referred to, and which does not make all stockholders liable indiscriminately. . .. It is by no means clear, however, that the pledgee did not have a right to vote on the stock, even as against the stockholders. . . . But, as before said, if the pledgee in voting on the stock exceeds his right as such pledgee, it cannot have the effect of making the stock his own. No one is injured, and no one can complain except the other stockholders whose rights are invaded."

1. Johnson *v.* Underhill, 52 N. Y. 203; Adderly *v.* Storm, 6 Hill (N.Y.) 624; Kortright *v.* Buffalo Commercial Bank, 20 Wend. (N. Y.) 91; Walker *v.* Bennett, 18 C. B. 845.

In a State where the pledgee as stockholder is exempt from liability, after the debt secured was paid, the stock still remained in the pledgee's name. The corporation became insolvent, and though the pledgee returned the certificate indorsed in blank to the pledgor, still the pledgee was liable to the creditors of the corporation, the statute exemption being of no avail, as the pledge contract had ceased before the insolvency. Erskine *v.* Lowenstein, 11 Mo. App. 595.

But where a pledgee, believing the corporation to be insolvent, sold under a power of sale, his stock, owing to its being but the fulfillment of a past contract, he was allowed thus to relieve himself from liability. Magruder *v.* Colston, 44 Md. 349; Holyoke *v.* Burnham, 11 Cush. (Mass.) 183.

2. Germania Nat. Bank *v.* Case, 99 U. S. 628; Bowden *v.* Johnson, 107 U. S. 215; Davis *v.* Stevens, 17 Blatchf. (U. S.) 259.

"Courts will be sedulous in their endeavors to defeat all schemes and contrivances whereby parties may seek to receive and enjoy the benefit and privileges incident to the position of stockholders, and at the same time be exonerated from the burdens imposed by law." Fisher *v.* Seligman, 75 Mo. 13.

person to hold for the pledgee, relieves the pledgee of liability.[1]

e. RIGHT TO VOTE.—When the stock stands in the pledgee's name on the books of the corporation the pledgee, in the absence of restrictive statutes, has the right to vote thereon; for it is an incident of the pledge contract.[2] If, however, the certificate is only transferred in blank and the stock still stands in the pledgor's name on the books, the pledgor has the right to vote.[3]

f. RIGHT TO DIVIDENDS.—The pledgee of stock, holding the certificate indorsed to him or in blank, is entitled and is bound to collect the dividends and other accretions accruing on the stock, whether it stands in his name on the books of the corporation or

1. Anderson *v.* Philadelphia Warehouse Co., 4 Fed Rep. 130.

2. *In re* Barker, 6 Wend. (N. Y.) 509; *Ex parte* Willcocks, 7 Cow. (N. Y.) 402; *In re* Mohawk etc. R. Co., 19 Wend. (N. Y.) 135; Vail *v.* Hamilton, 85 N. Y. 453; *In re* Empire City Bank, 18 N. Y. 199; Rosevelt *v.* Brown, 11 N. Y. 148; *In re* Long Island R. Co., 19 Wend. (N. Y.) 37; Adderly *v.* Storm, 6 Hill (N. Y.) 624; Heath *v.* Silverthorn etc. Co., 39 Wis. 147; Pittsburgh R. Co. *v.* Stewart, 41 Pa. St. 54; Chase *v.* Merrimack Bank, 19 Pick. (Mass.) 564; Fisher *v.* Seligman, 75 Mo. 13; Griswold *v.* Seligman, 72 Mo. 110; Hoppin *v.* Buffum, 9 R. I. 513; Brewster *v.* Hartley, 37 Cal. 15.

"A person in whose name the stock of the corporation stands on the books of the corporation is, as to the corporation, a stockholder, and has a right to vote upon the stock. . . . Nor could this result follow any the less certainly if the shares of stock were received in pledge only to secure the payment of a debt, providing the shares were transferred on the books of the company to the name of the pledgee." Franklin Bank *v.* Commercial Bank, 36 Ohio St. 350.

Stock owned by the corporation cannot be voted on by anyone, even if it has been transferred to the name of the pledgee. *Ex parte* Desdoity, 1 Wend. (N. Y.) 98; *In re* Barker, 6 Wend. (N. Y.) 509; American Railway Frog Co. *v.* Haven, 101 Mass. 398; State *v.* Smith, 48 Vt. 266; Brewster *v.* Hartley, 37 Cal. 15.

In *California*, they regard the pledgee as a trustee for the pledgor and allow the latter on proof of pledge contract to exercise right of ownership in the stock pledged. Brewster *v.* Hartley, 37 Cal. 15.

In *New York*, a preliminary injunction was granted to distrain a trustee of the pledgee, the stock standing in the trustee's name, from voting. McHenry *v.* Jewett, 26 Hun. (N. Y.) 453; which case was afterwards reversed on technical grounds. McHenry *v.* Jewett, 90 N. Y. 58.

The pledgee voting on the stock is not guilty of conversion. Heath *v.* Silverthorn etc. Co., 39 Wis. 146.

Statutory Restrictions.—In several States it is provided by statute that the pledgor may attend meetings and vote as stockholder even though the stock stands in the name of the pledgee. The proof of the fact that the stock is pledged is also provided for. *New Hampshire*, G. L. 1878, p. 355, § 12; *Maine*, Acts 1872, ch. 69; *Washington*, Code 1881, § 2432; *Nevada*, C. L. 1873, ch. 2. § 3400; *Indiana*, Rev. Stat. 1881, § 3009; *Missouri*, Rev. Stat. 1879, § 714; *Maryland*, R. Code 1878, p. 316, § 13; *Wyoming*, C. S. 1876, ch. 34, § 17; *New Mexico*, G. L. 1880, p. 206, § 12; *New Mexico*, R. L. 1875, p. 622, § 12.

3. Becker *v.* Wells F. M. Co., 1 Fed. Rep. 276; *In re* Barker, 6 Wend. (N. Y.) 409; *Ex parte* Willcocks, 7 Com. (N. Y.) 402; *In re* Cecil, 36 How. Pr. (N. Y.) 477; Strong *v.* Smith, 15 Hun (N. Y.) 222; Merchants' Bank *v.* Cook, 4 Pick. (Mass.) 405; McDaniels *v.* Flower Brick Mfg. Co., 22. Vt. 274.

The pledgee, his name not being on the books, is not entitled to notice of the meetings. McDaniel *v.* Flower Brick Mfg. Co., 29 Vt. 274; and is not chargeable with knowledge of facts in the possession of the corporation or its officers. Baker *v.* Woolston, 27 Kan. 185.

not. He holds these dividends as he does the stock, to secure his debt.[1]

g. LIABILITY TO LIENS OF THE CORPORATION.—The liens allowed by statutory authority to a corporation on its stock, for debts owed to it by one in whose name it stands on the books, are valid against a pledgee of a stock certificate with blank power of transfer, who demands such transfer just as to any holder for value in the same position.[2] But where the corporation has

1. Herran *v.* Maxwel, 47 N. Y. Super. Ct. 347; Hasbrouck *v.* Vandervoort, 4 Sandf. (N. Y.) 74; Butterworth *v.* Kennedy, 5 Bosw. (N. Y.) 143; Hill *v.* Newicahwanick Co., 48 How. Pr. (N. Y.) 429; Fairbanks *v.* Merchants' Nat. Bank, 30 Ill. App. 28; Gaty *v.* Holliday, 8 Mo. App. 118; Merchants' Bank *v.* Richards, 6 Mo. App. 454; March *v.* Eastern R. Co., 43 N. H. 520; Conant *v.* Seneca Co. Bank, 1 Ohio St. 298; Kellogg *v.* Stock-Well, 75 Ill. 71; Isaac *v.* Clark, 2 Bulst. 306.

So a sub-pledgee holding the certificate by proper indorsement can collect the dividends, but he must account therefor. Chamberlain *v.* Greenleaf, 4 Abb. N. Cas. (N. Y.) 178.

The pledgee may sue for the dividends in his own name. Merchants' Bank *v.* Richards, 6 Mo. App. 454; aff. 70 Mo. 77.

So a broker holding the stock on margin must collect and put to the credit of his customer the dividends. Markham *v.* Jaudon, 41 N. Y. 235.

Where misappropriated stock was pledged and the original owner collected the dividends he was compelled to deliver them over to the pledgee. Herrann *v.* Maxwell, 47 N. Y. Super. Ct. 347.

So where the pledgor collected the dividends he was compelled to hand them to the pledgor. Hill *v.* Newichawanick Co. 48 How. Pr. (N.Y.). 429; Gaty *v.* Holliday, 8 Mo. App. 118.

Unless the certificate is properly indorsed to the pledgee, he has no right to the dividends. Dow *v.* Gould etc. Co., 31 Cal. 649.

If bonds issued to stockholders are allowed by the pledgee to be received by the pledgor, the pledgee is liable for damages to third persons, caused thereby. Fitchburg Savings Bank *v.* Torrey, 134 Mass. 239.

A received from B stock in pledge. The stock was owned by C; but A had no notice of this until after default in payment of the loan, when he was requested by C to delay selling the stock. During the delay C collected dividends. *Held*, that he received them as trustee for A. Herrman *v.* Maxwell, 47 N. Y. Super. Ct. 347.

The pledgee cannot be said to acquiesce in payment of dividends to the pledgor when he is ignorant that any have been declared. Fairbanks *v.* Merchants' Nat. Bank, 30 Ill. App. 28.

Whereon the renewal of the note secured the old note and contract of pledge are returned and new ones given, the pledgee has no right to dividends accruing on the pledged stock before the renewal of the note. Fairbanks *v.* Merchants' Nat. Bank, 30 Ill. App. 28.

2. Union Bank *v.* Laird, 2 Wheat. (U. S.) 390; Bank of Commerce's Appeal, 73 Pa. St. 59; Pendergast *v.* Bank of Stockton, 2 Sawy. (U. S.) 108; McDowell *v.* Bank of Wilmington, 1 Harr. (Del.) 27; Lockwood *v.* Mechanics' Nat. Bank, 9 R. I. 308; Walm *v.* Bank of North America, 8 S. & R. (Pa.) 86; Stebbins *v.* Phœnix F. Ins. Co., 3 Paige (N. Y.) 350; McCready *v.* Rumsey, 6 Duer (N. Y.) 574; Leggett *v.* Bank of Sing Sing, 24 N. Y. 283; Tuttle *v.* Walton, 1 Ga. 47; Sabine *v.* Bank of Woodstock, 21 Vt. 353; Cecil Nat. Bank *v.* Watsontown Bank, 105 U. S. 202; Case *v.* Citizens' Bank, 100 U. S. 446; Succession of Rousseau, 23 La. Ann. 3; Hoss *v.* Williams, 24 La. Ann. 568; New Orleans Canal etc. Assoc. *v.* New Orleans, 30 La. Ann. 1971; New London Bank *v.* Brocklebank, L. R., 25 Ch. Div. 302; Childs *v.* Hudson's Bay Co., 2 P. Wms. 207; Mechanics' Bank *v.* New York R. Co., 13 N. Y. 595; McCready *v.* Rumsey, 6 Duer (N. Y.) 574; Stebbins *v.* Phœnix F. Ins. Co., 3 Paige (N.Y.) 350; Arnold *v.* Suffolk Bank, 27 Barb. (N. Y.) 424; James *v.* Woodruff, 10 Paige (N. Y.) 541; Reese *v.* Bank of Commerce, 14 Md. 271; Merrill *v.* Call, 5 Me. 428; Skowehegan Bank *v.* Cutler

notice of such pledging of the stock, it cannot have a lien for indebtedness incurred by the pledgor after the notice has been given.[1] The corporation may waive its lien upon

49 Me. 315; McLean *v.* Lafayette Bank, 3 McLean (U. S.) 587; St. Louis Perpetual Ins. Co. *v.* Goodfellow, 9 Mo. 149; Tuttle *v.* Walton, 1 Ga. 47.

Such lien extends to all the stock of a debtor, although it may greatly exceed the amount of the debt; nor will the lien be barred by the running of the Statute of Limitations against the debt. Geyer *v.* Western Ins. Co., 3 Pittsb. (Pa.) 41.

The statutory lien, the stock standing in the name of a trustee, is good against the *cestui que trust.* New London Bank *v.* Brocklebank, L. R., 21 Ch. Div. 302.

A lien is not defeated by the taking of collateral securities for the payment of any particular debt of a stockholder. Union Bank *v.* Laird, 2 Wheat. (U. S.) 390.

Where a by-law required the special consent of the directors to a transfer of stock while the transferrer was indebted to the company, a lien was good on the stock of one partner for a debt owing by the firm. Mechanics' Bank *v.* Earp, 4 Rawle. (Pa.) 384; Geyer *v.* Western Ins. Co., 3 Pitts. (Pa.) 41.

Under a statute of *Connecticut* (Gen. St. of 1875, tit. 17, ch. 1, § 8) providing that corporations shall at all times have a lien upon all the stock owned by any person therein for all debts due to them from such person, it was held that there existed such a lien in favor of the corporation upon the stock which had previously been pledged to the third person, such pledge being merely by delivery of the certificate of stock and the power of attorney for its transfer with no notice given to the corporation as required by law; so the corporation had a lien upon stock pledged after the passage of the act, though the pledgee took it without notice of the lien. First Nat. Bank *v.* Hartford Ins. Co. 45 Conn. 22.

Misappropriated or Fraudulently Issued Stock Certificates.—Where a certificate of stock fraudulently issued and indorsed in blank by an agent of a corporation came into the hands of an innocent purchaser for value, and he on presentation thereof to the corporation received in return a new certificate standing in his own name, it was held that the corporation was estopped by the issuing of the new certificate from denying the validity of the old. Manhattan Beach Co. *v.* Harned, 27 Fed. Rep. 484.

A certificate of shares, properly issued by a corporation having power to issue stock certificates, is an affirmation by the corporation to all who may innocently purchase the certificate that the person to whom it is issued is the owner of the number of shares of the capital stock of the corporation specified in the instrument. Holbrook *v.* New Jersey Zinc Co., 57 N. Y. 616. The purchaser need not inquire further to ascertain whether there is any infirmity in the title of the person named as owner in the certificate. It is wholly within the power of the agents of the corporation to ascertain whether the person to whom the certificate has been issued has the legal title to the shares, when such title is only transferable upon the books of the corporation; and it is their duty towards every person who may become a purchaser upon the faith of a certificate to exercise due diligence in this behalf. Western Union Tel. Co. *v.* Davenport, 97 U. S. 369. The purchaser may reasonably repose upon the belief that this duty has been faithfully discharged. Hence it follows that if by their negligence, or even by their malfeasance, a certificate has been issued by agents of the corporation while acting within the general scope of their powers, the purchaser has a right to rely upon the truth of the recitals, and to treat them as the formal representation of the corporation, made by those who are entitled to act and speak for it in the particular transaction. Bank of Kentucky *v.* Schuykill Bank, 1 Pars. Eq. Cas. (Pa.) 180; New York etc. R. Co. *v.* Schuyler, 34 N. Y. 30; Hall *v.* Rose Hill etc. Road Co., 70 Ill. 673; Shaw *v.* Port Philip etc. Min. Co., 50 L. T. R., N. S. 685. Those who have acted upon the faith of such an affirmation may insist that it shall not be retracted to their prejudice by the party responsible for it, because it would be a breach of good faith to do so.

1. Bank of America *v.* McNeil, 10

stock, and in such case, the pledgee will take it entirely free.[1]

A lien not given by statutory enactment, or by provision of a charter of a corporation, even though it may be based upon a rule or a by-law, is not good against the pledgee of a stock certificate indorsed in blank, holding for value and without notice.[2]

Where the corporation wrongfully asserting such a lien refuses to make the transfer of the stock on the books to the pledgee, the latter can recover for the damage done to him by the refusal.[3]

If under a statutory lien the company claims more than is due, in order to put it in the wrong, the stockholder must tender what is actually due.[4]

The corporation's lien being only a right to hold, is in no sense a security;[5] it can only be enforced by refusing to make a transfer when requested so to do by one holding the certificate and power of attorney to make the demand.[6]

A purchaser at an execution sale of the stock takes it subject to the company's lien.[7]

Bush (Ky.) 54; Conant *v.* Seneca Co. Bank, 1 Ohio St. 298.

1. Cecil Nat. Bank *v.* Watsontown Bank, 105 U. S. 217; Case *v.* Citizens' Bank, 100 U. S. 446.

2. Case *v.* Citizens' Bank, 100 U. S. 446; Cecil Nat. Bank *v.* Watsontown Bank, 105 U. S. 217; Carroll *v.* Mullanphy Sav. Bank, 8 Mo. App. 247; Driscoll *v.* West Bradley etc. Mfg. Co., 59 N. Y. 96; New Orleans Bank Assoc. *v.* Wiltz, 10 Fed. Rep. 330; Bryon *v.* Carter, 22 La. Ann. 98; Smith *v.* Crescent City Live Stock etc. Co., 30 La. Ann. 1378; Moore *v.* Bank of Commerce, 52 Mo. 379; Union Bank *v.* Laird, 2 Wheat. (U. S.) 390; First Nat. Bank *v.* Lanier, 11 Wall. (U. S.) 369; Willard *v.* National Eagle Bank, 18 Wall. (U. S.) 598; Bank of Attica *v.* Mfg. Bank, 20 N. Y. 505; Rosenback *v.* Bank, 53 Barb. (N. Y.) 495; Massachusetts Iron Co. *v.* Hooper, 7 Cush. (Mass.) 183; Sargent *v.* Franklin Ins. Co., 8 Pick. (Mass.) 90; Nesmith *v.* Washington Bank, 6 Pick. (Mass.) 329; Steamship Dock Co. *v.* Heron, 52 Pa. St. 280; Guyer *v.* Insurance Co., 3 Pittsb. (Pa.) 41; Bank of Holly Springs *v.* Pinson, 58 Miss. 421.

But where the face of the certificate contains a statement of the liability, the lien of the corporation was held to be good. Vasdands *v.* Middlesex Co. Bank, 26 Conn. 144.

A power given by charter provision to pass by-laws for the regulation of transfer of stock certificates will not entitle a company to create a secret lien upon the shares of stocks in the hands of a *bona fide* holder for value without notice of the by-law. Driscoll *v.* West Bradley etc. Mfg. Co., 59 N. Y. 96; Bullard *v.* National Eagle Bank, 18 Wall. (U. S.) 589; U. S. *v.* Vaughan, 3 Binn. (Pa.) 394.

No presumption arises in favor of a company refusing to transfer such shares by reason of any claim of which such holder of value is not chargeable with notice. Bullard *v.* National Eagle Bank, 18 Wall. (U. S.) 589; First Nat. Bank *v.* Lanier, 11 Wall. (U. S.) 369; Carroll *v.* Mullanphy Sav. Bank, 8 Mo. App. 249; Driscoll *v.* West Branley etc. Mfg. Co., 59 N. Y. 96; Massachusetts Iron Co. *v.* Hooper, 7 Cush. (Mass.) 183; Steamship Dock Co. *v.* Heron, 52 Pa. St. 280; Sargent *v.* Franklin Insurance Co., 8 Pick. (Mass.) 90.

3. Case *v.* Citizens' Bank, 100 U. S. 466; Duncan *v.* Hinckley, 2 McN. & G. 30.

4. Pierson *v.* Bank of Washington, 3 Cranch (C. C.) 363.

5. *In re* Dunlop, L. R., 21 Ch. D. 583; Bute *v.* Conyngham, 2 Russ. 275; Averal *v.* Wade, Lloyd & G. 252.

6. Choteau Spring Co. *v.* Harris, 20 Mo. 382; Conant *v.* Seneca Bank, 1 Ohio St. 298; Sabine *v.* Bank of Woodstock, 21 Vt. 353; St. Louis Perpetual Ins. Co. *v.* Goodfellow, 9 Mo. 149.

7. West Branch Bank *v.* Armstrong, 40 Pa. St. 278.

h. RIGHT TO SUB-PLEDGE STOCK.—Ordinarily and in the absence of any agreement or assent by the pledgor, the pledgee has no right to sub-pledge the thing pledged, and such a use of it is illegal. But, under special circumstances, depending somewhat upon the nature of the pledge, and in all cases, with the assent of the pledgor, express or implied, the property pledged may be used by the pledgee in any way consistent with the general ownership, and the ultimate rights of the pledgor.[1]

Authority to sub-pledge stock may be inferred from the circumstance of the pledge contract, and previous transactions between the parties may be brought in to show such authority.[2] It seems to be a general custom among brokers and bankers to allow pledgees of stock to sub-pledge it, and such a custom is valid.[3] Such a contract of sub-pledge, of course, recognizes the right of the original pledgor to get back his stock on payment of the debt due, and the broker must be prepared to return it at his peril.[4] Of course the parties may always agree that the stock may be sub-pledged and no custom will be allowed to vary such contract.[5]

i. RIGHT OF PLEDGEE WHEN HE IS A BROKER.—A broker who, on deposit of a certain percentage of the purchase price, advances the remainder, buys and carries on that margin stock for his customer, holds, unless they agree otherwise the stock, in pledge for his advances.[6] The broker acts as agent for the cus-

1. Lawrence *v.* Maxwell, 53 N. Y. 19.

That is a pledgee cannot sell stock without an express power to do so. Authority to "use, transfer, hypothecate," included power to sell. Ogden *v.* Lathrop, 65 N. Y. 158.

So, where, without authority the pledgee of stock sub-pledged it for his own debt, he was held liable in conversion for the value of the stock at the time of conversion. Fay *v.* Gray, 124 Mass. 500.

But if the pledgee simply makes another a trustee to hold the stock to escape liability on it, or to keep his own credit good by not appearing to own too much of it, it was not a conversion. Heath *v.* Griswold, 5 Fed. Rep. 573; Day *v.* Holmes, 103 Mass. 306.

2. Lawrence *v.* Maxwell, 58 Barb. (N. Y.) 511; 53 N. Y. 19; Chamberlain *v.* Greenleaf, 4 Abb. N. Cas. (N. Y.) 178; Hope *v.* Lawrence, 1 Hun (N. Y.) 317.

Where the pledgee gave a receipt for stock, reciting that he held it as collateral, and that he could sell on "one day's notice," parol evidence could not be introduced to show an agreement that he could sub-pledge. Fay *v.* Gray, 124 Mass. 500.

3. Vanhorn *v.* Gilbough, 21 Am. L. Reg., N. S. 171; Canfield *v.* Minneapolis etc. Assoc., 14 Fed. Rep. 801; Goss *v.* Emerson, 23 N. H. 38; Jarvis *v.* Rogers, 15 Mass. 389; Levy *v.* Loeb, 85 N. Y. 370; Stewart *v.* Drake, 46 N. Y. 449; Frost *v.* Clarkson, 7 Cow. (N. Y.) 24; Allen *v.* Dykers, 3 Hill (N. Y.) 593; Hubbell *v.* Drexel, 11 Fed. Rep. 115; Price *v.* Grover, 40 Md. 102; Donald *v.* Suckling, L. R., 1 Q. B. 385; Langton *v.* Waite, L. R., 6 Eq. 165; France *v.* Clark, L. R., 22 Ch. D. 830; *Ex parte* Sergeant, 17 L. R., 17 Eq. 279.

4. Oregon etc. Co. *v.* Hilmers, 20 Fed. Rep. 717.

But the pledgee cannot recover the stock from the sub-pledgee without paying the debt secured. New York etc. R. Co. *v.* Davies, 38 Hun (N. Y.) 477.

5. Stenton *v.* Jerome, 54 N. Y. 480; Baker *v.* Drake, 66 N. Y. 518; Lawrence *v.* Maxwell, 53 N. Y. 19; Taussig *v.* Hart, 58 N. Y. 425; Levy *v.* Loeb, 85 N. Y. 365; Odgen *v.* Lathrop, 65 N. Y. 158; Hubbell *v.* Drexell, 11 Fed. Rep. 115.

6. Baker *v.* Drake, 66 N. Y. 518; Stenton *v.* Jerome, 54 N. Y. 480; McNeil *v.* Tenth Nat. Bank, 55 Barb. (N.

tomer in purchasing the stock; he becomes the customer's creditor by advancing money on the purchase price, and the customer's pledgee by holding the stock for his advances. While it is true the stock is never actually delivered to the broker by the customer, yet the effect is exactly and in essence the same. The result of this rule is that the broker cannot on default sell the stock for his advances without notifying the customer.[1]

In *Massachusetts,* however, it is held this relation between the broker and his customer to be merely an executory contract by which the broker may, upon default of the customer, sell without notice.[2]

Y.) 59; 46 N. Y. 325; Lawrence *v.* Maxwell, 53 N. Y. 19; Horton *v.* Morgan, 19 N. Y. 170; Markham *v.* Jaudon, 41 N. Y. 235; Vaupell *v.* Woodward, 2 Sandf. Ch. (N. Y.) 143; Brass *v.* Worth, 40 Barb. (N. Y.) 648; Clarke *v.* Meigs, 22 How. Pr. (N. Y.) 340; Gruman *v.* Smith, 81 N. Y. 25; Capron *v.* Thompson, 86 N. Y. 418; Read *v.* Lambert, 10 Abb. Pr., N. S. (N. Y.) 428; Nourse *v.* Prime, 4 Johns. Ch. (N. Y.) 490; Calb *v.* Owen, 90 N. Y. 368; Morgan *v.* Jaudan, 40 How. Pr. (N. Y.) 340; De Cordova *v.* Barnum, (Supreme Ct.), 9 N. Y. Supp. 237; Thompson *v.* Toland, 48 Cal. 99; Wynkoop *v.* Seal, 64 Pa. St. 361; Diller *v.* Brubaker, 52 Pa. St. 498; Esser *v.* Linderman, 71 Pa. St. 76; Gilpin *v.* Howell, 5 Pa. St. 41; Child *v.* Hugg, 41 Cal. 519; Worthington *v.* Tormey, 34 Md. 182; Hatch *v.* Douglas, 48 Conn. 116; Baltimore M. Ins. Co. *v.* Dalrymple, 25 Md. 269; Maryland F. Ins. Co. *v.* Dalrymple, 25 Md. 242.

In Markham *v.* Jaudon, 41 N. Y. 235, the court by Hunt, C. J., said: "Under such a contract the broker undertakes and agrees—1. At once to buy for the customer the stock indicated; 2. To advance all the money required for the purchase, beyond the ten per cent. furnished by customer; 3. To carry or hold such stocks for the benefit of the customer so long as the margin of ten per cent. is left good, or until notice is given by either party that the transaction must be closed—an appreciation in the value of the stocks is the gain of the customer, and not of the broker; 4. At all times to have in his name or under his control, ready for delivery, the shares purchased, or an equal amount of other shares of the same stock; 5. To deliver such shares to the customer when required by him, upon the receipt of the advances and commissions accruing to the broker; or, 6. To sell such shares upon the order of the customer, upon payment of the like sum to him, and account to the customer for the proceeds of such sale. Under this contract the customer undertakes—1. To pay a margin of ten per cent. on the current market value of the shares; 2. To keep good such margin according to the fluctuations of the market; 3. To take the shares so purchased on his order, whenever required by the broker, and to pay the difference between the percentage advanced by him and the amount paid therefor by the broker."

This rule cannot be applied, however, to dealings in cotton, wheat, etc., "on a margin," for then the goods never actually come into the possession of the broker, as does stock. Corbett *v.* Underwood, 83 Ill. 324.

1. Mulsham *v.* Jaudon, 41 N. Y. 235, over-ruling, Sterling *v.* Jaudon, 48 Barb. (N. Y.) 459; Schepeler *v.* Eisnier, 3 Daly (N. Y.) 11; Hanks *v.* Drake, 94 Barb. (N. Y.) 186.

2. Covell *v.* Loud, 135 Mass. 41.

In Covell *v.* Loud, 135 Mass. 41, the court by Devens, J., said: "The relation of the parties existed by force of a mutual and dependent contract, by which the defendant agreed to purchase, and hold or convey for the plaintiff, a certain number of shares of stock, the plaintiff paying a certain sum of money at the time, and agreeing to pay interest on the sums advanced by the defendant, and, in case the stock depreciated, to make what is termed "a margin" of ten dollars per share in the cost of the market price of the stock, as that might change from time to time. When the plaintiff failed to perform his part of the contract, by making the necessary advances upon demand, the stock having rapidly de-

j. DUTY TO RETURN STOCK.—A broker carrying stock on a margin is not bound to keep in his possession the identical stock purchased and held in pledge, but fulfills his duty if he keeps in possession and ready for delivery to his principal on demand, an amount of stock equal to that purchased by him.[1] So if a pledgee rightfully transfers pledged stock, which is without "ear-marks," into his own name on the books of the corporation, having shares of his own in the same corporation, and indiscriminately sells shares but always keeping enough to give back the number pledged, he is not guilty of conversion.[2] The reason that stock differs from ordinary chattels in this respect, is that one share of the same kind of stock is of exactly of the same value as any other, and, therefore, it can make no difference to the pledgor that the identical shares are not returned as long as he gets those of the same value.[3] But the pledgee must always have on hand or under his immediate control, stock of the same kind to return; and the burden is on him to show that he has so kept the stock.[4]

2. After Default—*a.* IN GENERAL.—The remedies of a pledgee of stock after default by the pledgor in paying the debt secured, are substantially the same as those of a pledgee of corporeal property, especially as to his remedy by suit on the debt secured. In regard, however, to his more common remedy by sale of the collateral stock, a body of cases has accumulated, making it necessary to start again here, "recourse to security" in pledges of stock.

b. SALE OF STOCK AT COMMON LAW.—The pledgee of stock

preciated in value, he has no ground of complaint that the defendants ceased to hold and carry it for him, and therefore disposed of it."

Nor can the broker be liable for conversion in selling stock without notice, for the customer has no right to possession until payment. Wood *v.* Hayes, 15 Gray (Mass.) 375.

1. Horton *v.* Morgan, 19 N. Y. 170; Gruman *v.* Smith, 81 N. Y. 25; Allen *v.* Dykers, 3 Hill (N. Y.) 593; Levy *v.* Loeb, 85 N. Y. 370; Hardy *v.* Jaudon, 1 Robt. (N. Y.) 261; Stewart *v.* Drake, 46 N. Y. 449; Taussig *v.* Hart, 58 N. Y. 425; Salters *v.* Genin, 7 Abb. Pr. (N. Y.) 193; Genin *v.* Isaacson, 6 N. Y. Leg. Obs. 213; Chamberlain *v.* Greenleaf, 4 Abb. N. Cas. (N. Y.) 178; Worthington *v.* Tormey, 34 Md. 182; Hubbell *v.* Drexel, 21 Am. L. Reg., N. S. 452; Thompson *v.* Toland, 48 Cal. 99; Haywood *v.* Rogers, 62 Cal. 348.

The same rule holds as to negotiable bonds. Stuart *v.* Bigler, 98 Pa. St. 80.

2. Allen *v.* Dykers, 3 Hill (N. Y.) 593; Nourse *v.* Prime, 7 Johns. Ch. (N. Y.) 490; Neiler *v.* Kelly, 69 Pa. St. 409; Gilpin *v.* Howell, 5 Pa. St. 41; Boylan *v.* Huguet, 8 Nev. 345; Worthington *v.* Tormey, 34 Md. 182; Fay *v.* Gray, 124 Mass. 500; Hubbell *v.* Drexel, 11 Fed. Rep. 115; Berlin *v.* Eddy, 33 Mo. 426.

But the stock must be of exactly the same kind Wilson *v.* Little, 2 N. Y. 443.

So if he sell all the stock held in his own name, but has under his absolute control others, it is enough. Le Croy *v.* Eastman, 10 Mod. 499.

3. Hawley *v.* Brumagim, 33 Cal. 394; Atkins *v.* Gamble, 42 Cal. 86.

4. Allen *v.* Dykers, 3 Hill (N. Y.) 593; Chamberlain *v.* Greenleaf, 4 Abb. N. Cas. (N. Y.) 178; Hardy *v.* Jaudon, 1 Robt. (N. Y.) 261; Taussig *v.* Hart, 58 N. Y. 425; Horton *v.* Morgan, 19 N. Y. 170; Nourse *v.* Prime, 4 Johns. Ch. (N. Y.) 490; 7 Johns. Ch. (N. Y.) 69.

So if the pledgee sells the stock before the debt is due and afterwards purchases other stock of the same kind to return, this is a conversion. Dykers *v.* Allen, 7 Hill (N. Y.) 497; *contra*, Thompson *v.* Toland, 48 Cal. 99.

on the default of the pledgor in payment of his debt cannot, in the absence of agreement to that effect, appropriate the stock to his own use without foreclosing by some process the pledgor's right to redeem.[1]

At common law the pledgee of stock or corporate negotiable bonds has the right on default after demanding payment of the debt secured and giving the pledgor notice of the time and place of sale, to sell the stock or bonds at public auction,[2] for such securities having a market value it is presumed that it was the intention of the parties in making the pledge, that the collateral should be sold on default.[3] After such a sale, of course, the

1. Conyngham's Appeal, 57 Pa. St. 474; Sitgreaves *v.* Farmers' etc. Bank, 49 Pa. St. 359; Davis *v.* Funk, 39 Pa. St. 243; Diller *v.* Brubaker, 52 Pa. St. 498.

An offer to pledge stock, "or if after holding the stock awhile I have no objection to their keeping the stock," and a note and receipt for stock as collateral security, dated twenty-one days later, without such stipulation, give the pledgee no title to the stock other than as security, although eight years elapse without payment after the maturity of the note. Diller *v.* Brubaker, 52 Pa. St. 498.

Where pledgee asks that he be declared the owner of bonds payable to bearer, and the title to which vests by delivery, the pledgor is a necessary party, for he has the right to redeem and has an interest in the surplus over the debt secured. Newcombe *v.* Chicago etc. R. Co. (Supreme Ct.), 8 N.Y. Supp. 366.

Nor can the pledgee for the purpose of so getting the absolute title after default, compel the corporation to transfer the stock to him on its books. Indiana etc. R. Co. *v.* McKernan, 24 Ind. 62.

But where the pledgor gave the pledgee power to sell pledged stock on default and after default had the stock transferred on the books of the corporation to the pledgee, who then canceled the evidence of indebtedness, it was considered an absolute transfer. Small *v.* Saloy, 42 La. Ann., 7 So. Rep. 450.

2. See *supra*, this title, ***Rights**, etc., of **Pledgee of Corporeal Property After Default.***

Canfield *v.* Minneapolis etc. Assoc., 14 Fed. Rep. 801; Wallace *v.* Berdell, 24 Hun (N. Y.) 379; Vaupell *v.* Woodward, 2 Sandf. Ch. (N. Y.) 143; Cortelyow *v.* Lansing, 2 Cai. Cas. (N. Y.) 200; Brown *v.* Ward, 3 Duer (N. Y.) 660; Nabring *v.* Bank of Mobile, 58 Ala. 204; Stevens *v.* Hurlbut Bank, 31 Conn. 146; *Ex parte* Fisher, 20 S. Car. 179; Fletcher *v.* Dickinson, 7 Allen (Mass.) 23; Stokes *v.* Frazier, 72 Ill. 428; Denton *v.* Jackson, 106 Ill. 433; but see Joliet Iron Co. *v.* Scioto etc. Co., 82 Ill. 548; Water Power Co. *v.* Brown, 23 Kan. 676; Indiana etc. R. Co. *v.* McKernan, 24 Ind. 62; Alexandria etc. R. Co. *v.* Burke, 22 Gratt. (Va.) 254; Morris Canal etc. *v.* Lewis, 12 N. J. Eq. 323; Franc *v.* Clark, L. R., 22 Ch. D. 830.

After a proper demand and notice of sale the pledgor cannot, though the stock will be sacrificed, prevent its sale. Rasch *v.* Creditors, 1 La. Ann. 31.

Even if the pledgor becomes bankrupt the pledgee has a right to sell under the Bankrupt Act. *In re* Grinnell, 9 Nat. Bankr. Reg. 29; Jerome *v.* McCarter, 94 U. S. 734.

When the pledgee allowed the consignee in bankruptcy to put an estimated value on the securities as if sold, it is not conclusive evidence of a sale. Globe Nat. Bank *v.* Ingalls, 130 Mass. 8.

Though State courts will not permit a creditor to share in the assets of an insolvent debtor corporation, still the creditor has the right to sell bonds pledged for the debt. Union Cattle Co. *v.* International Trust Co., 149 Mass. 492.

3. Morris Canal etc. Co. *v.* Lewis, 12 N. J. Eq. 323.

A number of persons associated themselves together to purchase of a corporation a large parcel of flats. As part of the consideration, the flats were to be filled by the corporation within seven months. The conveyance was

pledgor's right to redeem is gone.[1] On such a sale the interest of the pledgor should be taken into consideration as well as that of the pledgee, and every reasonable effort should be made to obtain the best price for the securities sold.[2] And the pledgee should sell no more of the securities than are necessary to pay his debt, for, by doing so, he will be responsible to the debtor therefor.[3]

The purchaser *bona fide* and for value, at a sale of stock, gets the title thereto whether the sale was authorized or not.[4]

made to trustees of the associates; and the interests of the latter were divided into shares, and the trustees issued to each associate a certificate of the number of shares belonging to him. Each associate paid to the corporation in money ten per cent. of his proportion of the entire con ideration, and executed to the corporation his personal bond for the payment of the remaining ninety per cent. of his proportion, payable one half in two years and one-half in three years, with interest semi-annually, and transferred to the corporation his certificate of shares, as collateral security for the payment of the bond. The bond also contained a clause, by which it was agreed that the whole or any part of it might be paid, when interest was payable, and that when paid either by advance payments, or by the regular payment of installments, the shares pledged should be released. By the terms of the transfer, the corporation was authorized to receive any dividends which might be made by the trustees, and, on payment of the bond "by said dividends or otherwise," the certificate was to be reassigned to the owner.

Held, on a bill in equity, that the corporation, taking one of these certificates as collateral security for the payment of a bond, was not obliged to hold it until paid by dividends arising from the proceeds of the sale of the land, but was entitled, upon default in payment of the bond, to foreclose the pledge by a sale of the certificate. Merchants' Nat. Bank *v.* Thompson, 133 Mass. 482.

1. Haywood *v.* Eliot National Bank, 96 U. S. 611.

2. Schouler's Bailm. & Carriers (2d ed.) 226. See Newsome *v.* Davis, 133 Mass. 343.

So where several sets of securities were given for several debts they should be sold separately. Mahoney *v.* Caperton, 15 Cal. 313.

But he need not divide the number of shares covered by one certificate into lots to get better prices. Newsome *v.* Davis, 133 Mass. 343.

3. Fitzgerald *v.* Blocker, 32 Ark. 742.

4. Talty *v.* Freedman's Sav. etc. Co., 93 U. S. 321; Little *v.* Barker, Hoffm. Ch. (N. Y.) 487; Wood's Appeal, 92 Pa. St. 379; Conyngham's Appeal, 57 Pa. St. 474; Prall *v.* Tilt, 27 N. J. Eq. 393.

But if he has knowledge of a defect in the sale he gets no title against the pledgor. Weston *v.* Bear River etc. Min. Co., 5 Cal. 186; 6 Cal. 425.

The fact that the power of attorney attached to the certificate does not correspond to the rules of the stock exchange does not affect purchaser's title. Smith *v.* Slavin (Supreme Ct.), 9 N. Y. Supp. 106.

When the pledge is stock of an association, having no other corporate property than real estate, held that the purchaser at the sale, who had succeeded to all the rights of the original pledgor, could recover the land by a suit in equity, on reimbursing the grantees, who obtained their title with notice of his rights and equities, the amount they are actually out of pocket.

To arrive at such sum, an account must be had of rents, profits and income received by such grantees while in possession of the real estate. Canfield *v.* Minneapolis etc. Assoc., 14 Fed. Rep. 801.

Bonds pledged as collateral for a loan, were sold for default on the floor of the stock exchange, the terms of sale being cash on immediate delivery. Some of the bonds were delivered at once and paid for. A day's delay ensued in delivering the rest, and before delivery the buyer was notified that they did not belong to the pledgor. *Held*, that the buyer's rights were not affected by the notice, and a decision to the contrary made by the committee of the exchange to whom disputed questions are referred did not affect the

(1) *Demand and Notice.*—The rules for demand and notice are the same as those governing the sale of corporeal property;[1] but such demand and notice are absolutely necessary, and must be made in good faith.[2] The notice to redeem must give a reasonable time in which to pay the debt.[3]

(2) *Public Sale.*—It is absolutely necessary also that in absence

case. Morris *v.* Grant, 34 Hun (N. Y.) 377.

In an illegal sale of pledged bonds, where the purchaser took in good faith, the debt secured was held to pass with the bonds so that a subsequent purchaser of the pledgee's claim could neither enforce the debt nor get back the security. Whitney *v.* Peay, 24 Ark. 22.

1. See *supra*, this title, *Rights, Liabilities and Remedies of Pledgee of Corporeal Property After Default;* France *v.* Clark, 22 Ch. Div. 830.

2. Lewis *v.* Graham, 4 Abb. Pr. (N. Y.) 106; Genet *v.* Howland, 45 Barb. (N. Y.) 560; Odgen *v.* Lathrop, 65 N. Y. 158; Little *v.* Barker, Hoffm. Ch. (N. Y.) 487; Strong *v.* National Banking Assoc., 45 N. Y. 718; Sitgreaves *v.* Farmers' Bank, 49 Pa. St. 359; Stokes *v.* Frazier, 72 Ill. 428; McNeil *v.* Tenth Nat. Bank, 55 Barb. (N. Y.) 59; Stenton *v.* Jerome, 54 N. Y. 410; Hinckley *v.* Smith, 51 N. Y. 25; Cameron *v.* Durkheim, 55 N. Y. 425; Child *v.* Hugg, 41 Cal. 519; Conyngham's Appeal, 57 Pa. St. 474; Fletcher *v.* Dickinson, 7 Allen (Mass.) 23; Van Horn *v.* Gilbough, 10 W. N. C. (Pa.) 347; Morris Canal etc. Co. *v.* Lewis, 12 N. J. Eq. 323; Stearns *v.* Marsh, 4 Den. (N. Y.) 227; Brown *v.* Ward, 9 How. Pr. (N.Y.) 497; Patchin *v.* Pierce, 12 Wend. (N. Y.) 61; Hyatt *v.* Argenti, 3 Cal. 151.

Demand and Notice to Redeem.—The pledgee must give notice to the pledgor to redeem when the exigency, which gives the right to sell, has occurred. National Bank *v.* Baker, 128 Ill. 533.

Where the pledgee wrote several times to the pledgor after default asking him to pay the debt secured, it was held to be a good demand, although that word was not used in the correspondence. Carson *v.* Iowa etc. Co., 80 Iowa 638.

The notice to be given by the pledgees on the falling of stocks, so that the collaterals did not amount to the margin stipulated, was not a notice to redeem, but a notice to make the security deposited equal to the margin stipulated in the contract or the pledgees would proceed to sell and convert the stock into money, and apply the proceeds to reimburse themselves for the moneys advanced, with the interest and commissions. Brass *v.* Worth, 40 Barb. (N. Y.) 648.

Where the pledgor has himself put it out of the power of the pledgee to give him notice as a corporation by closing its office, ceasing to do business, the pledgee is released from the obligation to give notice. City Bank *v.* Babcock, 1 Holmes (U. S.) 181.

Notice of Time and Place of Sale.—A custom among brokers to sell stock without notice was held invalid.

Wheeler *v.* Newbould, 16 N. Y. 392; Lawrence *v.* Maxwell, 53 N. Y. 19; Markham *v.* Jaudon, 41 N. Y. 235. *Contra*, Covell *v.* Loud, 135 Mass. 41; Worthington *v.* Tormey, 34 Md. 182.

See *supra*, this title, *Rights of Pledgee When He is a Broker.*

The parties may waive the right to notice by express agreement. Taylor *v.* Ketchum, 5 Robt. (N. Y.) 507.

If the pledgor cannot be found to give such demand and notice, there can be no sale except a judicial one. Strong *v.* National etc. Banking Assoc., 45 N. Y. 718.

Notice that unless the debt was paid the stock would be "used," is not sufficient notice. Genet *v.* Howland, 45 Barb. (N. Y.) 560.

3. Genet *v.* Howland, 45 Barb. (N. Y.) 560.

Length of Notice.—Notice of sale given seven days before the sale was sufficient. Maryland F. Ins. Co. *v.* Dalrymple, 25 Md. 247. So of five days. Vose *v.* Florida R. Co., 50 N. Y. 369; and also two days. Bryan *v.* Baldwin, 7 Lans. (N. Y.) 174; Steward *v.* Drake, 46 N. Y. 449; Willoughby *v.* Comstock, 3 Hill (N. Y.) 389.

One day's notice to "put up margin" too short, and sale voided. Colt *v.* Owens, 90 N. Y. 368. *Contra*, Milliken *v.* Dehon, 27 N. Y. 364.

So where notice of less than a day was given it was too short. Burkett *v.* Taylor, 86 N. Y. 618.

of agreement to the contrary, the sale should be public,[1] but the sale of the securities on the floor of the stock exchange or broker's board has been upheld in some States,[2] though it is essentially a private sale, the public not having access thereto, and such a sale without express authority is not countenanced.[3] Where, however, the sale was held at the stock exchange and the pledgor fails to object within a reasonable time, he is said to be estopped by his silence from afterwards objecting.[4]

(3) *Purchase by Pledgee.*—The pledgee has no right to purchase the stock sold on default, and if he does so the pledgor has his election to treat it as a conversion[5] and sue for damages or as a nullity, in which case the pledgee still holds the stock subject to redemption,[6] or to ratify the sale if it is a good one.[7]

It seems that the pledgee himself may purchase at a judicial sale, for then the sale is under the control of an officer of the court,[8] and when stock is sold "under the rule," in the stock ex-

1. Baltimore M. Ins. Co. *v.* Dalrymple, 25 Md. 269; Rankin *v.* McCullough, 12 Barb. (N. Y.) 103.

2. Maryland F. Ins. Co. *v.* Dalrymple, 25 Md. 242; Ravenstock *v.* Torney, 32 Md. 169; Cheever *v.* Meyer, 52 Vt. 75.

3. Brown *v.* Ward, 3 Duer (N. Y.) 660; Markham *v.* Jaudon, 41 N. Y. 235; Dykers *v.* Allen, 7 Hill (N. Y.) 497; Rankin *v.* McCullough, 12 Barb. (N. Y.) 103; Brass *v.* Worth, 40 Barb. (N. Y.) 648; Castello *v.* City Bank, 1 N. Y. Leg. Obs. 25. But see Schepeler *v.* Eisner, 3 Daly (N. Y.) 11.

4. Willoughby *v.* Comstock, 3 Hill (N. Y.) 389.

The burden of proof to show that the place and manner of sale was improper is on the pledgor. Schepeler *v.* Eisner, 3 Daly (N. Y.) 11.

If he does not object within a reasonable time, he is presumed to be satisfied. Vanhorne *v.* Gilbough, 10 W. N. C. (Pa.) 347; Kelsey *v.* Bank of Crawford Co., 69 Pa. St. 426.

5. Canfield *v.* Minneapolis etc. Assoc., 14 Fed. Rep. 801; Marye *v.* Strause, 5 Fed. Rep. 483; Killian *v.* Hoffman, 6 Ill. App. 200; Maryland F. Ins. Co. *v.* Dalrymple, 25 Md. 342; Bank of Old Dominion *v.* Dubuque etc. R. Co., 8 Iowa 277; Middlesex Bank *v.* Minot, 4 Met. (Mass.) 325; Carroll *v.* Mullanphy Sav. Bank, 8 Mo. App. 249; Stokes *v.* Frazier, 72 Ill. 428; Brookman *v.* Rothschild, 3 Sim. 155; Baltimore M. Ins. Co. *v.* Dalrymple, 25 Md. 269; Bryson *v.* Rayner, 25 Md. 424.

6. Canfield *v.* Minneapolis etc. Assoc., 14 Fed. Rep. 801; Bryan *v.* Baldwin, 52 N. Y. 232; Mott *v.* Havana Bank, 22 Hun (N. Y.) 354; Duden *v.* Waitzfelder, 16 Hun (N. Y.) 337; Wright *v.* Ross, 36 Cal. 414; Pickering *v.* Demeritt, 100 Mass. 416; Bryson *v.* Ryner, 25 Md. 424; Hestonville R. Co. *v.* Shields, 3 Brews. (Pa.) 257; Richardson *v.* Mann, 30 La. Ann. 1060; Star F. Ins. Co. *v.* Palmer, 41 N. Y. Super. Ct. 267; Middlesex Bank *v.* Minot, 4 Met.(Mass.) 325; Chicago Art. Well Co. *v.* Corey, 60 Ill. 73. See cases in preceding note.

7. Carroll *v.* Mullauphy Sav. Bank, 8 Mo. App. 249, and cases in preceding notes.

Such a purchase by the pledgee at a private sale without notice, does not affect in any way the relationship between pledgor and pledgee. Sharpe *v.* Nat. Bank, 87 Ala. 644.

8. Newport etc. Bridge Co. *v.* Douglass, 12 Bush (Ky.) 673.

On the same principle, where the pledged stock was sold under garnishee proceedings and the pledgee purchased at the sale, it was held a valid sale. Harrell *v.* Mexico Cattle Co., 73 Tex. 612.

Where bonds, part of an issue, all of which are secured by a fund to be realized by a public sale of real estate upon public notice by a trustee for the bondholders and grantors in a trust deed, are pledged, the pledgee owes no duty to the pledgor of bidding at the sale of the land, and may lawfully bid and become a purchaser of the land himself. Easton *v.* German-American Bank, 24 Fed. Rep. 523.

change, the transaction being between members, the pledgees may purchase.[1]

(4) *Waiver of Irregularities.*—If the pledgor does not, within a reasonable time after the sale, tender the amount of the debt and offer to redeem, or does some affirmative act, acquiescing in the sale, he will be considered to have waived his rights.[2]

(5) *Effect of Illegal Sale.*—When the pledgee has sold the stock given as collateral, without proper demand and notice, or in any other way has made an illegal sale,[3] the pledgor, by tender of the debt due,[4] and offer to redeem within a reasonable

1. Quincy *v.* White, 63 N. Y. 370.

2. See *infra*, this title, *Redemption*. Hayward *v.* Eliot Nat. Bank, 96 U. S. 611; Colket *v.* Ellis, 10 Phila. (Pa.) 375.

What is a reasonable time under the circumstances, is a question for the jury. Bevan *v.* Cullen, 7 Pa. St. 281; Porter *v.* Patterson, 15 Pa. St. 229.

The value of stock varies so rapidly and so much in a short time that a delay not unreasonable in asserting one's rights to other kinds of property would be unreasonable here. So a delay of four months was held to be unreasonable. Colket *v.* Ellis, 10 Phila. (Pa.) 375.

Plaintiff pledged bonds to defendant as collateral. There was a default, and defendant had the bonds put up for sale and bought them himself. Then plaintiff indorsed them so that defendant could sell them. Two years afterwards, the bonds having risen in value, plaintiff brought a suit in equity to recover the increased value. *Held*, that the suit could not be maintained. Lacombe *v.* Forstall, 133 U. S. 562.

Waiver by Delay.—Where a pledgee delayed making his demand eleven years, he was held to have waived his right. Waterman *v.* Brown, 31 Pa. St. 161. So a delay of seven years. Adams *v.* Sturges, 55 Ill. 468. And of nineteen years. Robert *v.* Sykes, 30 Barb. (N. Y.) 173.

Bonds of a corporation, payable to holder, are presumed to belong to the person in possession thereof. Where such bonds had been converted by the pledgor before pleading them, and the pledgee was innocent, and the amount of the pledge insignificant, and the pledgee caused the bonds to be sold, and bought them in himself, through a third party, held, that the title of one claiming under the purchase was sufficiently made out, after the lapse of years and the death of the person who made the purchase, although there was no evidence as to the actual manner of sale. Martin *v.* Somerville Water Power Co., 27 How. Pr. (N. Y.) 161.

Waiver by Acquiescence.—The acceptance by the pledgor of the surplus proceeds of the sale, claimed to have been made with pledgor's consent, ratifies the action of the pledgee in selling. Hamilton *v.* State Bank, 22 Iowa 306.

But where the sale was made illegally by the pledgee, relying on his supposed rights under the contract of pledge, acceptance of the surplus by the pledgor is not acquiescence. Fitzgerald *v.* Blocker, 32 Ark. 742.

A sale of pledged stock will not be set aside where there was no fraud, and where the pledgor accepted a check for the balance due him and delayed four years to proceed to attack the sale. McDowell *v.* Chicago Steel Works, 22 Ill. App. 405.

So a voluntary payment of a deficiency on the debt secured, caused by the collateral selling at a low figure, is a ratification, but not if made by the pledgor in order to secure outside advantages. Stenton *v.* Jerome, 54 N.Y. 480.

It is an acquiescence by the pledgor if he brings an action for money had and received against the pledgee. Hancock *v.* Franklin Ins. Co., 114 Mass. 155. So if the pledgor approves an account and promises to make good a deficiency, it is a wavier. Child *v.* Hugg, 41 Cal. 519.

3. Where the pledgee sold stock without notice and himself purchased at the sale so that he is always able to return it, and then gives notice of his intention to sell, no commission accrues. Perry *v.* Birmingham Nat. Bank (Ala.), 9 So. Rep. 299.

4. See *infra*, this title, *Redemption*.

time, has a cause of action against the pledgee for damages.[1] If the purchaser knew of the illegality, the pledgor may follow and recover the stock, but the burden of proof is in the pledgor to prove knowledge on the part of the purchaser.[2]

(6) *Measure of Damages.*—The general rule of damages for conversion of stock by the pledgee is the value of the stock at the time of its conversion with interest from that time until the time of trial, together with whatever other incidental damage may have occurred.[3]

In *New York* the old rule for the measure of damages for conversion of stock, was the highest market price of the stock between the time of conversion and the time of trial, provided the suit be brought within a reasonable time.[4] But subsequently the

James *v.* Hamilton, 2 Hun (N. Y.) 630; Wilson *v.* Little, 2 N. Y. 443. This tender is necessary, for otherwise the pledgor has no right to possession, and can therefore get no damages for being kept out of it. Holliday *v.* Holgate, L. R., 3 Ex. 299.

Though the sale is illegal the pledgee may enforce payment from the purchaser who, if he buys in good faith, gets a good title. Capron *v.* Thompson, 86 N. Y. 418.

1. Conyngham's Appeal, 57 Pa. St. 474; Little *v.* Barker, Hoffm. Ch. (N. Y.) 487; Read *v.* Lambert, 10 Abb. Pr. N. S. (N. Y.) 428.

If one who holds mining stocks in secret trust for another, pledges the same for his debt, without notice to the pledgee of the interest of the *cestui que trust*, and the pledgee sells the stock without previous demand and notice, the right of action for the conversion is in the pledgor, and not in the *cestui que trust*. If the *cestui que trust* has a cause of action outside of the contract of pledge, he must first pay or tender the money for which the stocks were pledged. Thompson *v.* Toland, 48 Cal. 99.

2. Canfield *v.* Minneapolis etc. Assoc., 14 Fed. Rep. 801; Little *v.* Barker, 1 Hoffm Ch. (N. Y.) 487.

See *supra*, this title, *Title of Pledgee to Stock Evidenced by Fictitious, Fraudulent or Misappropriated Certificates.*

The dividends, etc., also belong to the pledgee. Conyngham's Appeal, 53 Pa. St. 474.

See *infra*, this title, *Redemption.*

3. Sturges *v.* Keith, 57 Ill. 451; Robinson *v.* Hurley, 11 Iowa 410; Boylan *v.* Huguet, 8 Me. 345; Fowler *v.* Ward, 113 Mass. 548; Jarvis *v.* Rogers, 15 Mass. 389; Kennedy *v.* Whitwell, 4 Pick. (Mass.) 466; Bickell *v.* Colton, 41 Miss. 368; Pinkerton *v.* Manchester etc. R. Co., 42 N. H. 424; Frothingham *v.* Morse, 45 N. H. 545; Gray *v.* Portland Bank, 3 Mass. 364; Greenfield Bank *v.* Leavitt, 17 Pick. (Mass.) 1; Loomis *v.* Stave, 72 Ill. 123; Rand *v.* White Mts. R. Co., 40 N. H. 79; Baltimore etc. R. Co. *v.* Sewell, 35 Md. 238; Maryland F. Ins. Co. *v.* Dalrymple, 25 Md. 242; Wyman *v.* American Powder Co., 8 Cush. (Mass.) 168; Hill *v.* Smith, 32 Vt. 433; Orange etc. R. Co. *v.* Fulvey, 17 Gratt. (Va.) 366.

Some cases hold as a modification of the rule in the text that where the illegal sale is unknown to the pledgor at the time it occurs, the measure of damages will be based on the value of the stock at the time the sale is brought home to his knowledge. O'Meara *v.* North America Min. Co., 2 Nev. 133; or when demand for the return of the stock was made.

Pinkerton *v.* Manchester etc. R. Co., 42 N. H. 424; Baltimore etc. R. Co. *v.* Sewell, 35 Md. 238.

Where stock was sold before the maturity of the debt, the pledgor was held entitled to the price received and was not to suffer for a depreciation occurring afterward. Allen *v.* Dykers, 3 Hill (N. Y.) 593.

4. Romanie *v.* Van Allen, 26 N. Y. 309; Markham *v.* Jaudon, 41 N. Y. 235; Anderson *v.* Nicholas, 28 N. Y. 600; Allen *v.* Dykers, 3 Hill (N. Y.) 593; Wilson *v.* Little, 2 N. Y. 443; Burt *v.* Dutcher, 34 N. Y. 493; Morgan *v.* Gregg, 46 Barb. (N. Y.) 183; Wauman *v.* Caldwell, 2 Sweeney (N. Y.) 212; Rankin *v.* McCullough, 12 Barb.

rule was modified, making the measure of damages the difference between the price for which the stock sold and its market price then or within such reasonable time after notice of the sale as would have enabled the pledgor to replace the stock in case such market price exceeded the price realized.[1]

In *Pennsylvania* there was a disposition at first to follow the old *New York* rule;[2] but the present rule for the measure of damage on an illegal sale of stock in the absence of any trust, relationship or duty, on the one converting the stock to deliver it, is the value of the stock at the time of conversion with dividends and interest.[3] When there is a trust relationship or duty to deliver, the old *New York* rule is still followed.[4]

c. OBLIGATION TO SELL.—The pledgor of stock or corporate negotiable bonds, in the absence of special agreement, is under no more obligation to sell the security than the pledgee of any other kind of property on default of payment by the pledgor,[5] and the pledgee, where the sale is not requested by the pledgor, is not liable for any loss occasioned by his failure to sell,[6] for the

(N. Y.) 103; Read *v.* Lambert, 10 Abb. Pr., N. S. (N. Y.) 428; West *v.* Beach, 3 Cow. (N. Y.) 82.

Where shares of stock had been pledged as a security for debt, and wrongfully sold by the pledgee, and the debtor offered to pay the debt, and requested a return of the stock, and the pledgee promised to return the shares, or others of the same kind, and the debtor waited from time to time for him to do so, and in the meantime the stock rose in value, it was held, in an action for wrongfully selling the stock, that the pledgor might recover the enhanced value. Wilson *v.* Little, 2 N. Y. 443.

1. Baker *v.* Drake, 66 N. Y. 518; Gruman *v.* Smith, 81 N. Y. 25; Thayer *v.* Manley, 73 N. Y. 305; Colt *v.* Owens, 90 N. Y. 368; Roberts *v.* Berdell, 61 Barb. (N. Y.) 37.

So in *California*. Page *v.* Fowler, 39 Cal. 412.

What is a reasonable time under the circumstances of the case is a question for the jury. Colt *v.* Owens, 90 N. Y. 368; Baker *v.* Drake, 53 N. Y. 211.

2. Bank of Montgomery *v.* Reese, 26 Pa. St. 143; Musgrave *v.* Beckendorff, 53 Pa. St. 310; Conyngham's Appeal, 57 Pa. St. 474; Phillips' Appeal, 68 Pa. St. 130; Vaughn *v.* Wood, Mylne & K. 403.

3. Huntingdon etc. R. Co. *v.* English, 86 Pa. St. 247; Worth *v.* Philips, 89 Pa. St. 250.

4. Miller *v.* Kelley, 69 Pa. St. 403; Work *v.* Bennett, 70 Pa. St. 484; Worth *v.* Phillips, 89 Pa. St. 250.

5. O'Neill *v.* Whigham, 87 Pa. St. 394; Colquitt *v.* Stultz, 65 Ga. 305; Robinson *v.* Hurley, 11 Iowa 410; Rozet *v.* McClellan, 48 Ill. 345.

A provision in a contract of pledge of bonds as collateral security, authorizing the pledgee, in case of default, to sell the bonds at public auction in Chicago, does not exclude other lawful modes of proceeding for satisfaction of the debt, and in particular does not preclude the creditor from bringing suit in the State where he resides and has the bonds, to foreclose the pledge and have a judicial sale in that State. Coffin *v.* Chicago etc. Co., 67 Barb. (N. Y.) 337.

It makes no difference that the stock stands in the pledgee's name on the books of the corporation, for the pledgor may request him to sell and he will be then liable for loss. Colquitt *v.* Stultz, 65 Ga. 305.

One whom his debtor has promised to pay a certain sum at a specified time, less the amount which pledged collaterals may "realize" is not bound, in absence of special agreement therefor, to take legal steps to enforce payment of the securities. At maturity of his claim he is entitled to judgment, with privilege in the pledged effects, and to a judicial sale to realize their value to apply thereon. Friedlander *v.* Schmallnski, 35 La. Ann. 520

6. O'Neill *v.* Whigham, 87 Pa. St. 394; Howard *v.* Brigham, 98 Mass. 133; Newsome *v.* Davis, 133 Mass. 343; Colquett *v.* Stultz, 65 Ga. 305; Richard-

pledgor may redeem the stock and sell it himself,[1] or he may sell his interest in the stock, and, by payment of the debt secured, the pledgee must deliver the stock to the purchaser.[2]

But it is generally considered enough to make the pledgee liable for loss occasioned by a failure to sell, that he had especially agreed to do so, or that the pledgor had requested him to sell.[3]

The pledgee need not sell immediately on default even at the request of the pledgor, but he may exercise his own judgment, carrying the stock at his own risk.[4] While such request by the pledgor, and failure to sell thereafter does not conclusively show negligence, yet it tends to show it and may be essential to establish it.[5]

d. SALE UNDER POWER OF SALE.—The parties to the contract of pledge always have the power to provide that the pledgee, on default of the pledgor, may sell without notifying the pledgor in any way of the intended sale.[6] Of course, such a power of sale

son *v.* Virginia etc. Ins. Co., 27 Gratt. (Va.) 749.

So if bonds in the pledgee's possession rapidly depreciate in value after the maturity of the debt in the absence of any demand for them, or that they be sold, the pledgee is not liable for the loss. Williamson *v.* McClure, 37 Pa. St. 402.

1. Granite Bank *v.* Richardson, 7 Met. (Mass.) 407; Rozet *v.* McClellan, 48 Ill. 345.

2. Rozet *v.* McClellan, 48 Ill. 345.

3. Colquitt *v.* Stultz, 54 Ga. 305.

But it was held in *Georgia* that even where the pledgor requested the pledgee, he was not bound to sell, even though the pledgee led the pledgor to believe he was trying to sell, Narier *v.* Central Ga. Bank, 68 Ga. 637.

4. O'Neill *v.* Whigham, 87 Pa. St. 394; Franklin Sav. Inst. *v.* Preetorins, 6 Mo. App. 470.

5. Goodall *v.* Richardson, 14 N. H. 567.

6. Loomis *v.* Stave, 72 Ill. 623; Chouteau *v.* Allen, 70 Mo. 290; Milliken *v.* Dehon, 27 N. Y. 364; Bates *v.* Wiles, 1 Handy (Ohio) 532; Baker *v.* Drake, 66 N. Y. 518; Ogden *v.* Lathrop, 65 N. Y. 158; Quincy *v.* White, 63 N. Y. 158; Stenton *v.* Jerome, 54 N. Y. 480; Wicks *v.* Hatch, 62 N. Y. 535; Colket *v.* Ellis, 10 Phila. (Pa.) 375; Clark *v.* Bouvain, 20 La. Ann. 70; Hamilton *v.* State Bank, 22 Iowa 306; Child *v.* Hugg, 41 Cal. 519; Hyatt *v.* Argenti, 3 Cal. 151; Bryson *v.* Rayner, 25 Md. 424; Maryland F. Ins. Co. *v.* Dalrymple, 25 Md. 242; Carson *v.* Iowa City Gas Light Co., 80 Iowa 638.

In the early cases this was thought to be a waiver of right to redeem and discountenance. Wilson *v.* Little, 2 N. Y. 443; Hanks *v.* Drake, 49 Barb. (N. Y.) 186; Campbell *v.* Parker, 9 Bosw. (N. Y.) 322.

An insolvent debtor may authorize his creditor to sell without notice and the debtor's assignee will be bound by the agreement. Sparkawk *v.* Drexel, 12 Nat. Bankr. Reg. 450.

Where a note with days of grace was secured by stock given as collateral under a power to sell when the debt was due, it was held that the pledgee could sell on the exact maturity of the note without waiting for the three days of grace to pass. Rankin *v.* McCullough, 12 Barb. (N. Y.) 103.

An agreement by the pledgor of shares in the capital stock of a corporation, that the pledgee might sell the stock "without further notice," if the loan it was given to secure was not paid on one day's notice according to agreement, dispensed with all notice of sale, and only left upon the pledgee the obligation to sell publicly and fairly for the best price he could obtain. Maryland F. Ins. Co. *v.* Dalrymple, 25 Md. 242; Baltimore M. Ins. Co. *v.* Dalrymple, 25 Md. 269.

Where a pledgee was directed to pay drafts drawn on him from "proceeds of securities in his hands" a power to sell such securities was implied therefrom. Hyatt *v.* Argenti, 3 Cal. 151.

Authority to sell at private sale was

cannot be exercised before default,[1] but it may be immediately thereafter;[2] though if the debt is payable at an indefinite time, a demand for payment, with reasonable time to redeem, must precede the sale.[3] The same rule applies to brokers carrying stock on a margin,[4] unless it is specifically agreed that the broker shall sell at any time when the margin fails.[5]

Where by agreement only the notice of the sale is waived, the pledgee must sell fairly at public sale;[6] and where the parties

inferred from a command to give the security "to any broker to sell." Bryson *v.* Raynor, 25 Md. 424.

A minor on arriving at majority may rescind a waiver of notice previously made by him. Heath *v.* Mahoney, 12 N. Y. Week. Dig. 404.

The sale by a pledgee, on his own account, of a stock note, which he had a general authority to "use, transfer, or hypothecate," before its maturity, is a conversion for which an action will lie. Ogden *v.* Lathrop, 1 Sweeny (N. Y.) 643.

Where additional securities are given a broker to keep the margin good, these are to be sold on the same terms as the original security. Baltimore M. Ins. Co. *v.* Dalrymple, 25 Md. 269.

If the pledgor by his own act has rendered the giving of the notice agreed upon impossible, the pledgee is not bound to give it. City Bank *v.* Babcock, 1 Holmes (U. S.) 180.

A pledgee authorized to sell in the event of the security "depreciating in market value" cannot, on discovery that the stock is spurious, sell. National Bank *v.* Baker, 128 Ill. 533.

1. Allen *v.* Dykers, 3 Hill (N. Y.) 593.

2. Chouteau *v.* Allen, 70 Mo. 290.

Shares of stock were pledged to secure a loan. It was explicitly agreed that they might be sold, on default, without demand of payment or further notice. Long after a default the shares were sold by the pledgee without notice. Afterwards they appreciated in value. *Held*, that the pledgor had no claim to relief, and that it was immaterial that, before the sale, it having been discovered that certain of these shares were spurious, genuine shares had been substituted for them by the corporation whose issue they purported to be. Jeanes' Appeal, 116 Pa. St. 573.

The pledgor delivered to the pledgee two certificates of a number of shares of stock in each of two corporations as collateral security for the payment of a debt, "with authority to sell the same without notice, either at public or private sale, or at brokers" board, at the option of the holder or holders hereof, on the non-performance of this promise, he or they giving me credit for any balance of the net proceeds of such sale remaining after paying all sums due from me to the said holder or holders." *Held*, in action for loss occasioned by the pledgee's negligence in the sale of the stock, that, under the authority given him, the pledgee had the right, on the non-performance of the plaintiff's promise, to sell either certificate of stock, or both if the proceeds of the sale of one did not satisfy the debt, and was not bound to divide either certificate into small lots, or to sell the stock immediately on default, or to postpone the right to sell if the stock was then depreciated in value. Newsome *v.* Davis, 133 Mass. 343.

3. Wilson *v.* Little, 2 N. Y. 443; Porter *v.* Parks, 49 N. Y. 564; Genet *v.* Howland, 45 Barb. (N. Y.) 560; Sitgreaves *v.* Farmers' etc. Bank, 49 Pa. St. 359; France *v.* Clark, 22 Ch. D. 830.

4. See *infra*, this title, ***Right of Pledgee When He is a Broker.***

5. Wicks *v.* Hatch, 62 N. Y. 535.

6. Maryland F. Ins. Co. *v.* Dalrymple, 25 Md. 242; Baltimore M. Ins. Co. *v.* Dalrymple, 25 Md. 269; Bryson *v.* Rayner, 25 Md. 424; Loomis *v.* Stave, 72 Ill. 623.

The fact that the price for which the stock was sold was less than the market price does not of itself, without further evidence of negligence, make the pledgee liable. Durant *v.* Einstein, 5 Robt. (N. Y.) 423.

Two certificates of stock in two corporations, for one thousand shares each, were pledged as collateral security for a debt, the pledgee having the right to sell them, by public or private sale, if the debt was not paid when due. When the debt was payable, and for

have agreed that the pledgee may sell at private sale, he must get the best price he can.[1]

If the power of sale specifies nothing as to the time, manner and place of sale, the pledgee is subjected to the common law rule of reasonable notice of time and place of sale with a previous demand for payment.[2]

e. SALE IN EQUITY OR JUDICIAL SALE.—Where stock has been pledged by mere delivery of the certificate without any power of attorney,[3] or where any other formal detail in carrying out the contract of pledge has been neglected, as in fixing exactly the date of maturity of the debt secured,[4] or where an accounting is asked,[5] the proper remedy of the pledgee is to go into equity and have a judicial sale decreed.[6]

some time after, the shares of one of the corporations were worthless, and the shares in the second corporation had no known or uniform price, and sometimes they could not be sold at any price. The pledgee sold all the shares at private sale for $850. In an action by the pledgor against the pledgee for negligence in the sale, the plaintiff was allowed to put in evidence of a sale of one hundred shares of the second corporation at $1.37½ per share, the day following the sale by the defendant, and a sale of fifty shares of the same stock, three days later, at $1.12½ per share. Newsome *v.* Davis, 133 Mass. 343.

1. Milliken *v.* Dehon, 27 N. Y. 364; Genet *v.* Howland, 45 Barb. (N. Y.) 560; Hamilton *v.* State Bank, 22 Iowa 306; Robinson *v.* Hurley, 11 Iowa 410; Fitzgerald *v.* Blocker, 32 Ark. 742.

Under such a power, the pledgee can sell the stock on the floor of the stock exchange, but he is bound to get the best price possible. Sparhawk *v.* Drexel, 12 Nat. Bankr. Reg. 450; Wicks *v.* Hatch, 38 N. Y. Super. Ct. 95; Castello *v.* City Bank, 1 N. Y. Leg. Obs. 25.

The circumstances must determine whether or not the sale is collusive, but a seemingly inadequate price may be shown to be otherwise. Carson *v.* Iowa etc. Co., 80 Iowa 638.

2. Stearns *v.* Hurlbut Bank, 31 Conn. 146.

A bank held certain stocks as collateral security for the plaintiff's indebtedness, with the right to sell them if the indebtedness was not paid within a reasonable time, but with no arrangement as to the time, place, or manner of sale. Some months after, the bank, without previous notice to the plaintiff, made a conditional sale of the stocks, which was to take effect if the plaintiff did not, on that day pay, or satisfactorily secure his indebtedness, and give notice that unless his indebtedness was paid, or satisfactorily secured on that day, the stocks would be sold. The plaintiff remonstrated, and asked to be allowed one day more for the purpose, and in fact the next day procured the means of paying the greater part of the debt, but the bank closed the sale on that day. *Held*, that the conduct of the bank was unreasonable and wrongful, and that it was liable to the plaintiff in damages. Stevens *v.* Hurlbut Bank, 31 Conn. 146.

3. Johnson *v.* Dexter, 2 McArthur (D. C.) 530.

4. Stokes *v.* Frazier, 72 Ill. 428.

Defendant, in good faith, received from his debtor a stock certificate, as a pledge to secute a *bona fide* debt, without injury to other creditors; but no act was made as required by *Louisiana* Civ. Code, 125. At the same time the debtor gave a power of attorney purporting to be for value and irrevocable, and authorizing defendant to transfer the stock to himself or any third person. *Held*, that the defendant could sell the stock only by judicial order, and that a transfer to himself and the power, even as between the parties, were nullities. Brother *v.* Saul, 11 La. Ann. 223.

5. See *supra*, this title, *Rights, Liabilities and Remedies of Pledgee of Corporeal Property After Default.*

6. Robinson *v.* Hurley, 11 Iowa 410.

Where two separate sets of stock were pleged for two separate debts, an order directing all the stock to be sold in gross and applied to the whole indebtedness was error. Mahoney *v.* Caperton, 15 Cal. 313.

f. Accounting and Application of Proceeds After Sale of Stock.—The pledgee of stock is just as a pledgee of corporeal property obliged to account for the money he receives on the sale, and any surplus belongs to the pledgor or those claiming through him.[1] On a suit to recover the surplus, pledgor must allow to the pledgee the amount he would have been compelled to tender when the debt was due together with interest and expenses.[2]

XV. Redemption—1. Right to Redeem.—From the fundamental difference between a mortgage and a pledge, it follows that the debtor in the first case has no right to redeem except in equity or by the force of statute, while the right of redemption is given to him in the latter by the very contract of pledge itself. The title never having passed from the pledgor, his right to redeem exists, though he has not paid the debt secured or otherwise performed the conditions of his contract, until his right of redemption is foreclosed.

This right is part of the contract of pledge, whether it be express or implied, and the parties can make no valid agreement in that contract that there shall be no redemption after default.[3]

Where a pledgee of shares in a corporation has illegally sold them to himself and has had them transferred on the corporation books so that they stand in his name as legal owner, equity has jurisdiction to afford relief to the pledgor. Bryson *v.* Rayner, 25 Md. 424.

Certain shares of stock standing in the name of a testator, who, in fact, held them merely as collateral security for a note of his son, one of the executors—ordered to be transferred to the son on his paying the note. Squier *v.* Squier, 30 N. J. Eq. 627.

1. Stokes *v.* Frazier, 72 Ill. 428.

Where stock in an insurance company was pledged on which seventy-five per cent. of the face value was paid in and after the death of the pledgor, the insurance company paid up the other twenty-five per cent. on the stock from money due the pledgor on a policy he held in the company, the pledgee on a sale of the stock was allowed to keep only seventy-five per cent. of the proceeds. Myers *v.* Scully, 85 Pa. St. 360.

If the pledgor ratifies an unauthorized sale of pledged stock, he is entitled to credit on his debt for only the proceeds of such sale. Killian *v.* Hoffman, 6 Ill. App. 200.

Where the pledgee of parcels of stock belonging to different persons sub-pledged them for his own debt and the sub-pledgee on default sold them, the latter was not allowed to satisfy his debt out of any one parcel of stock, but was obliged to draw ratable from all. Gould *v.* Central Trust Co., 6 Abb. N. Cas. (N. Y.) 381.

When the pledgee mixed the pledged stock with other of the same kind belonging to himself, and on default sold the number pledged, though not the identical ones, he was charged only with the price received, it not being a conversion. Berlin *v.* Eddy, 33 Mo. 426; Nouse *v.* Prime, 7 Johns. Ch. (N. Y.) 69.

A pledgee who wrongfully sub-pledges stock for his own debt cannot recover from the sub-pledgee the difference between his debt and the amount realized on the sale, but the original pledgor can. Persch *v.* Consolidated Bank, 13 Phila. (Pa.) 157.

2. Van Blarcom *v.* Broadway Bank, 37 N. Y. 540.

3. Hart *v.* Burton, 7 J. J. Marsh. (Ky.) 322; Wadsworth *v.* Thompson, 8 Ill. 423; Marshall *v.* Williams, 2 Hayw. (N. Car.) 405; Luckett *v.* Townsend, 3 Tex. 119; Dorrill *v* Eaton, 35 Mich. 302; Kingsbury *v.* Phelps, Wright (Ohio) 370; Stoker *v.* Cogswell, 25 How. Pr. (N. Y.) 267.

In Hart *v.* Burton, 7 J.J. Marsh. (Ky.) 323, the court by Robertson, C. J., said: "The right of redemption attaches equally to both [mortgage and pledge], and it is as difficult to transmute the one as the other into a sale, by the operation of the original contract. Though

The reason of the rule is because otherwise it would put the borrower too much in the power of the lender, who, being distressed at the time, is generally too much inclined to submit to any terms. Therefore, if it is stipulated by written or oral contract of pledge that the property shall be absolutely the property of the pledgee if the debt be not paid at the time stipulated, the right to redeem exists, in spite of the agreement of the parties. The law recognizes no agreement to prevent a redemption of the pledge.[1]

At any time subsequent to the making of the contract of pledge, the parties may agree that the creditor shall take the pledge in satisfaction of the debt, for then the debtor may be supposed to be freed from the duress of financial embarrassment. So they may agree that the creditor may take the goods at a stipulated price and credit the pledgor with the amount. To shut out the right of redemption, the whole transaction must be free from fraud or duress, the agreement must be clearly proved, and the creditor must actually elect to take the property at the price agreed upon by giving personal notice of such election, or by giving the debtor credit on his books for the amount.[2]

2. Discharge of Lien—*a.* IN GENERAL.—The lien of the pledgee may be discharged by payment of the debt, tender of the amount due, or by waiver on the part of the pledgee.[3]

Upon payment or tender of the amount of the specific debt

anciently at Rome, the creditor and debtor were permitted, by the *lex commissaria*, to make an agreement at the date of the pledge whereby it would, on a prescribed contingency, become the absolute property of the pawnee, such a power was not indulged, even at Rome, since the days of Constantine, who abolished the law by which it had been sanctioned. Every agreement for preventing redemption of pawns is prescribed by the common law as emphatically as are similar agreements in mortgages of real estate."

"By the early Roman law the debtor and creditor might agree that if the debtor did not pay the debt within a time specified, the thing pledged should be forfeited and become the absolute property of the creditor. But a law of Constantine prohibited such contracts, on the ground that they were unjust and oppressive to debtors; and declared that every contract should be null and void which provided that the thing pledged should pass to the creditor without sale or appraisement, or that the debtor should forfeit his right of redemption if he failed to pay at the proper time. The law of Constantine prohibiting such contracts, has been imported into the law of France (Poth. Nantissement, 18), and into the modern law of Continental Europe. The creditor cannot stipulate that if he is not paid at the time appointed, the thing pledged shall become his own property, for such an agreement would be *contra bonos mores;* for the pledge is given to the creditor only as security for the debt, and not to enable him to profit by the indigence of his debtor. Domat, lib. 3, tit. 1, §§ 3, 11:" Falkard's Law of Pawnbrokers, p. 11, n. f.

A stipulation of a mortgagee in the assignment of a mortgage as collateral security, that he shall forfeit all interest in it if he fail to pay his debt at the maturity, does not cut off his right to redeem it afterwards. Hughes *v.* Johnson, 38 Ark. 285.

Where pledgees of negotiable bonds payable to bearer ask that they be declared owners of the bonds, the pledgor is a necessary party, as he has a right to redeem and an interest in the balance remaining over the debt secured. Newcome *v.* Chicago etc. R. Co. (Supreme Ct.), 8 N. Y. Supp. 366.

1. Jones on Bailm., § 553.

2. Beatty *v.* Sylvester, 3 Nev. 228.

3. Payment or tender of the debt due are the only means by which the pledgor by his own act can discharge

secured, the pledgee has no power over the security except to hold it and deliver it on demand.[1] He has no right to retain it as security for any other debt unless it is so expressly agreed.[2]

Upon payment of the debt, or tender of its amount, the pledgor, or any one standing in his place, is entitled to receive the property pledged discharged of the debt.[3]

Where no time is fixed for redeeming a pledge, the pledgor may redeem at any time, and the right of redemption survives on his death to his legal representatives against the pledgee and his representative.[4]

b. PAYMENT—(1) *In General.*—Payment of the debt for which the property is taken as collateral, discharges the pledge,[5] and the pledgor becomes again the absolute owner.[6] Anything that

the lien on his property and revest the right to possession in himself. Henry *v.* Eddy, 34 Ill. 508.

1. See *supra*, this title, *Rights, Liabilities and Remedies of Pledgee of Stock.*

An administrator having assigned to a creditor of the decedent certain claims of the estate, as collateral security, there being then no evidence of insolvency, such creditor is not bound to reassign them except on payment or tender of the whole amount due him. Kittera's Estate, 17 Pa. St. 416.

Where property was pledged to secure a debt and by written instrument, it was agreed that the pledgees should have the right to "terminate" the agreement and that they should "retain their interest and claims" therein till they should be fully paid their said indebtedness "up to such time as they shall terminate this agreement," but they shall, "upon payment of the debt, "re-assign their said interest" in such property to the pledgor, it was held, that on the termination of the agreement by pledgee, the pledgor was entitled to an accounting and upon payment or tender of the amount due, to the re-assignment of the property. Barry *v.* Coville (Supreme Ct.), 7 N. Y. Supp. 36.

2. See *supra*, this title, *Debt or Engagement Secured.* Hathaway *v.* Fall River Nat. Bank, 131 Mass. 14.

But where the agreement to reconvey stock pledged to secure a note recited that the loss on a custom house mortgaged the pledgee "is bound" by the transfer of the stock, the deficiency on the foreclosure sale of the house was held to be secured by the stock pledged. Bartlett *v.* Johnson, 9 Allen (Mass.) 530.

3. Jones on Pledge, § 544; Geron *v.* Geron, 15 Ala. 558; Cressman *v.* Whitall, 15 Neb. 592.

Though in some cases damages in any action of trover by the pledgor may be mitigated, proof that the goods converted have been returned to the owner or the proceeds applied to his use, this does not apply to an assignee in bankruptcy, or for the benefit of creditors, because he represents both creditors and the pledgor. Hathaway *v.* Fall River Nat. Bank, 131 Mass. 14; Stetson *v.* Exchange Bank, 7 Gray (Mass.) 425.

A change in the form of indebtedness, or renewal of the note secured, unless such is the intention of the parties, does not release the collateral security. Fairbanks *v.* Merchants' Nat. Bank, 30 Ill. App. 28; Williams *v.* National Bank, 72 Ind. 441.

4. Cortelyou *v.* Lansing, 2 Cai. Cas. (N. Y.) 200; Perry *v.* Craig, 3 Mo. 516.

Mere lapse of time, without offering to redeem a pledge, but also without circumstances of equitable estoppel does not bar pledgee's right to redeem. Cridge's Appeal (Pa. 1890), 18 Atl. Rep. 1010.

Where a pledgee, who was surety on a promissory note, transferred the pledged property to the payee for the purpose of discharging the debt—held, that the transfer did not change the *status* of the property, and that the pledgor had the right to redeem even after maturity. Morgan *v.* Dod, 3 Colo. 551.

5. Callawan *v.* Smart, 60 Iowa 305.

6. Lapping *v.* Duffy, 65 Ind. 229;

effects the satisfaction of the debt is payment,[1] but the full debt must be paid in order to discharge the lien.[2]

(2) *Accounting for Profits.*—When the pledgee has paid the debt which was secured by the pledge, the pledgee must, in the absence of agreement to the contrary, account for all the income, profits and advantages derived by him from the bailment.[3]

(3) *Application of Payments.*—The payment must be applied strictly to the debt secured.[4] But where property was pledged

Compton *v.* Jones, 65 Ind. 117; Ward *v.* Ward, 37 Mich. 253; Merrifield *v.* Baker, 9 Allen (Mass.) 29; Elliott *v.* Armstrong, 2 Blackf. (Ind.) 198.

A pledge ceases to be operative when its object is effected, and the whole beneficial interest in the security pledged then becomes absolute in the equitable owner. Ward *v.* Ward, 37 Mich. 253.

A firm holding bonds as collateral security for a debt cannot retain them after its payment unless the owner so requests; and upon a subsequent change in the membership of the firm, and a continuation of the owner's account with the new firm, notice of his title to the bonds may be proved by circumstantial evidence. Merchants' etc. Bank *v.* Masonic Hall, 62 Ga. 271.

When stock is held as collateral security for the payment of a note, and the agreement to reconvey it upon the payment of the note recites that the loss on a certain house "is bound" by the transfer of the stock, and the holder of the note has forclosed a mortgage on such house, the value of which is less than the amount of the mortgage and interest, he is not bound to return the stock until he has been paid for the loss or the mortgage including interest, and without being charged with any rent which he did not receive. And it is immaterial that the maker of the note subsequently guaranteed the defendant in a new contract against loss on the house, and the parties at that time computed the amount thereof. Bartlett *v.* Johnson, 9 Allen (Mass.) 530.

1. Bacon *v.* Lamb, 4 Colo. 578; Strong *v.* Wooster, 6 Vt. 536.

Satisfaction must be substantial, and not the effect of a technical rule of law.

Two notes were indorsed over as security for the performance of contracts by the pledgor. The pledgee sued for an accounting on the contracts, and two drafts not stated in his bill of particulars were ruled so that the amount recovered by him was lessened by the amount of these drafts. He was allowed to sue on the notes and recover this sum. Steele *v.* Lord, 28 Hun (N. Y.) 27.

The maker of a mortgage given as additional security for the payment of a purchase-money mortgage is not discharged by the fact that a receiver has been appointed in the suit to foreclose the purchase-money mortgage at the instance of the mortgagee, and with the consent of the purchaser; such an appointment not changing the title to or creating any lien upon the land or giving any advantage or priority to the mortgagee. Pascault *v.* Cochran, 34 Fed. Rep. 358.

A pledged property to the United States to secure the return of B's alcohol to a bonded warehouse in a certain district. The United States permitted the alcohol to be returned to a warehouse in another district. *Held*, that the condition of A's obligation was satisfied and his pledge discharged. Boehm *v.* U. S., 20 Ct. of Cl. 241.

The renewal of a note secured by a pledge does not operate to discharge the lien. Collins *v.* Dewey, 4 Colo. 138; Pinney *v.* Kimpton, 46 Vt. 80; Moses *v.* Trice, 21 Gratt (Va.) 556.

If part of the note secured is paid and a new note given for the remainder of the debt, in the absence of agreement to the contrary, the pledge given as security will stand as security for the new note. Dayton Nat. Bank *v.* Merchants' Nat. Bank, 37 Ohio St. 208.

2. Jones on Pledge, § 540.

So in *Louisiana* it is provided by statute. R. Civ. Code, 1870, p. 376, arts. 3163, 3164.

Where a slave was pledged "to be redeemed at any time by the pledgor paying the amount which may be due," it was held that the slave could only be redeemed by payment of what was due at the time of redemption. Bigelow *v.* Young, 30 Ga. 121.

3. Hunsaker *v.* Sturgis, 29 Cal. 142; Geron *v.* Geron, 15 Ala. 558.

4. See *supra*, this title, *Debt or En-*

to secure several debts contracted at different times, in the absence of power in either debtor or creditor to determine the application, payments should be applied to the debts in the order in which they were contracted.[1] But a general payment may be applied to debts secured according to the discretion of the creditor.[2] A valid agreement that the pledge shall be held to secure only part of a debt can be made, and when the payments made cover that part, the security must be returned.[3]

c. TENDER—(1) *In General.*—Tender of the amount of the debt at the time when it is due is equivalent to payment, and discharges the lien on property pledged to secure it, and revests the absolute title in the pledgor.[4] But the full amount of the debt must be tendered.[5] The debt itself, however, is not discharged by tender, but only the lien,[6] and the pledgee may still have his action for the debt.[7]

gagement Secured. Phillips *v.* Thompson, 2 Johns. Ch. (N. Y.) 418; Geffcken *v.* Slingland, 1 Bosw. (N. Y.) 449; James' Appeal, 89 Pa. St. 54; Marzion *v.* Pioche, 8 Cal. 522.

So where the property was subpledged the pledgee cannot direct his assignee to apply the proceeds to the pledgee's debt. Ware *v.* Otis, 8 Me. 387.

1. Jones *v.* Benedict, 17 Hun (N. Y.) 128; affd. 83 N. Y. 79. See note to Pattison *v.* Hull, 9 Cow. (N. Y.) 747.

2. Wilcox *v.* Fairhaven Bank, 7 Allen (Mass.) 270.

3. Fridley *v.* Bowen, 103 Ill. 633.

4. Haskins *v.* Kelly, 1 Robt. (N. Y.) 160; Ball *v.* Stanley, 5 Yerg. (Tenn.) 199; McCalla *v.* Clark, 55 Ga. 53; Mitchell *v.* Roberts, 17 Fed. Rep. 776; Norton *v.* Baxter, 41 Minn. 146; Ratcliff *v.* Davies, Cro. Jac. 244; Coggs *v.* Bernard, 2 Ld. Raym. 909; Ryall *v.* Rowles, 1 Atk. 165, 167.

The assertion of absolute ownership in the thing pledged by the pledgee relieves the pledgor of the necessity of tendering the amount of the debt secured before suing for conversion. Lucketts *v.* Townsend, 3 Tex. 119.

Where collateral security has been sold to a third party, who has a lien upon it for the payment of the note which it secured, the holder of the security cannot be required to surrender it without a tender of the amount due upon the note. Lewis *v.* Mott, 36 N. Y. 395.

Amount Tendered.—The amount of the debt with interest and costs and expenses up to the time of tender should be offered. Cass *v.* Higenbotam, 100 N. Y. 248; Kennedy *v.* Hammond, 16 Mo. 341.

When a party who has pawned articles under a contract to pay greater interest on the money borrowed than the law allows, tenders to the pawnbroker the principal and lawful interest thereon, he is entitled to the possession of his property, although the statute establishing the rate of interest in such cases only provides a penalty for, and does not prohibit the charging of more than lawful interest. Jackson *v.* Shawl, 29 Cal. 267.

The amount tendered should include charges, assessments rightfully paid by the pledgee. McCalla *v.* Clark, 55 Ga. 53. But see Ponce *v.* McElvy, 47 Cal. 154; Flowers *v.* Sproule, 2 A. K. Marsh. (Ky.) 54.

But if interest was not contracted for and none has accrued by way of damages after a demand, it need not be tendered. Hines *v.* Strong, 56 N. Y. 670, affg. 46 How. Pr. (N. Y.) 97.

After Maturity.—Even if made after maturity of the debt a tender otherwise sufficient, when refused without good reason, discharges the lien of the creditor upon property held in pledge as security for the debt. Norton *v.* Baxter, 41 Minn. 146.

After the commencement of an action on the debt, the amount due with costs, was tendered and held to be good. Cass *v.* Higenbotam, 100 N.Y. 248. But see Butts *v.* Burnett, 6 Abb. Pr., N. S. (N. Y.) 302.

5. Appleton *v.* Donaldson, 3 Pa. St. 381; Bigelow *v.* Young, 30 Ga. 121.

6. Jones on Pledge, § 542.

7. Mitchell *v.* Roberts, 17 Fed. Rep. 776.

The tender should be absolute and conditional as a general rule, but it may be conditioned on the return of the security pledged and still be good.[1] The money should be actually produced unless on the pledgor being ready and offering to pay it, the pledgee expressly states that it need not be produced, for it will not be accepted.[2] As the tender has only the effect of extinguishing the lien and does not discharge the debt, keeping the tender good or bringing the money into court is not required.[3]

1. Cass *v.* Higenbotam, 100 N. Y. 238; overruling same case 27 Hun (N. Y.) 406.

In Cass *v.* Higenbotam, 100 N. Y. 238, the court by Miller, J., said: "If a deposit were made without a delivery of the goods the pledgor might lose his money and afterwards fail to obtain his goods or be left to an action for the recovery of the same.

"A tender of performance may always be restricted by such conditions as by the terms of the contract are conditions precedent, or simultaneous, or proper to be performed by the party to whom tender was made." Wheelock *v.* Tanner, 39 N. Y. 481.

2. Hancock *v.* Franklin Ins. Co., 114 Mass. 155; Thomas *v.* Evans, 10 East 101; Kraus *v.* Arnold, 7 Moore 59.

So where the pledgee, the amount due having been agreed upon, requested that the business be postponed until later, and demanded the full value of the property pledged which was much more than the amount due, the tender, although a check was being drawn for the amount of the debt, was held to be ineffectual. Dunham *v.* Jackson, 6 Wend. (N. Y.) 22.

Offer to Pay.—A mere offer by the original pledgor to pay an assignee of the pledge the amount due thereon, unattended by an actual tender of the original debt secured, is insufficient to extinguish the lien and entitle such pledgor to a return of the securities. Such offer to pay is not equivalent to an actual tender. Lewis *v.* Mott, 36 N. Y. 395.

But where a watch, having been pledged for the payment of a loan made without a specified time for repayment, the creditor subsequently notified his debtor that he must redeem the watch or it would be sold, and an agent of the latter called upon the pledgee a number of times with money sufficient for the purpose, and offered to pay even more than the amount which the creditor claimed to be owing him, but upon one and another pretense the agent was put off for several months, when the creditor declared that he had disposed of the watch in exchange for another and a sum of money, it was held that the debtor could maintain a suit for the conversion of the watch without any formal demand, and without a formal tender of the money due. Rosenzeig *v.* Frazer, 82 Ind. 342.

3. Cass *v.* Highenbotam, 100 N. Y. 248; Mitchell *v.* Roberts, 17 Fed. Rep. 776; Kortright *v.* Cady, 21 N. Y. 343.

In Cass *v.* Higenbotam, 100 N. Y. 248, the court by Miller, J., said: "Being a conditional tender, and depending upon the return of the property which was demanded, there would seem to be no obligation on the part of the defendant (pledgor) to pay the money into court, as in that event the plaintiff (pledgee) would have been entitled to the money absolutely. He had no right to it without the return of the goods, and as that was refused, no reason exists why the defendant should pay the money into court. The plaintiff was fully protected without the defendant so doing, as he retained the property in his possession. The obligations of the pledgor and pledgee are mutual, concurrent and reciprocal. Where either party performs, he is entitled to performance by the other as a condition of his own performance. The refusal of either, where performance is tendered, furnishes ground for an action. Holmes *v.* Holmes, 12 Barb. (N. Y.) 138. Tender is not required in such a case by a deposit in court, for the reason that a payment into court is unconditional, and from that time the money becomes the property of the plaintiff absolutely. Becker *v.* Boon, 61 N. Y. 322."

It seems the provision of the *New York* Code of Civil Procedure (§ 732) in reference to tenders refers only to that class of tenders which satisfy and

(2) *Refusal of Tender*.—By refusing to accept a tender properly made the lien is at an end, and the pledgee suing to recover his debt, the value of the pledge at the time of such refusal, will be deducted from the amount of the debt.[1] The pledgor may maintain trover for the property and recover its full value without deducting the amount of the debt for which it was pledged, the creditor having to bring a separate action for his debt.[2]

If, in such a case, there had been a surety to the debt, he is discharged, for the security to which he is entitled on paying the debt has, by the creditor's own act, been destroyed.[3]

d. WAIVER.—If the pledgee voluntarily surrenders the possession of a pledge with an intention to abandon his right, or if he, by his own voluntary act, places the pledge beyond his own power to restore it, as by agreeing that it may be attached at the suit of a third person, it will amount to a waiver of the pledge.[4]

discharge the debt. Cass *v*. Higenbotam, 100 N. Y. 248.

1. Griswold *v*. Jackson, 2 Edw. Ch. (N. Y.) 461; Hathaway *v*. Fall River Nat. Bank, 131 Mass. 14; Hancock *v*. Franklin Ins. Co., 114 Mass. 155.

By unjustly refusing a tender sufficiently made, the pledgee loses his right to retain the pledge as against another creditor of the pledgor who has subsequent to the making of the pledge, acquired rights in the property, even though the tender has not been kept good. Norton *v*. Baxter, 41 Minn. 146.

2. Ball *v*. Stanley, 5 Yerg. (Tenn.) 199; Mitchell *v*. Roberts, 17 Fed. Rep. 776.

3. Griswold *v*. Jackson, 2 Edw. Ch. (N. Y.) 461.

Upon the tender of the amount of a debt for which an accommodation note is held as security, the maker of the note being in effect a surety, is discharged, and on being sued he need not plead the tender or bring the amount into court. Appleton *v*. Donaldson, 3 Pa. St. 381.

4. Arendale *v*. Morgan, 5 Sneed (Tenn.) 703.

While chattels were in the possession of a pledgee, the pledgor mortgaged them, and they were seized under the mortgage. The pledgee, while claiming ownership and objecting to the seizure, did not assert his lien. *Held*, that he did not waive it by failing to assert it. Gunsel *v*. McDonnell, 67 Iowa 521.

A creditor recovering judgment on a debt, and arresting the body of the debtor thereon, is not thereby precluded from continuing to hold railroad bonds as collateral security, although he has made, without consideration, a promise to the debtor to give them up. Smith *v*. Strout, 65 Me. 205.

R, being the owner of certain musical instruments, pledged them to F, and was afterwards employed to assist in the management, care, and renting of the same; and in the course of his employment rented a piano (part of the pledged property) to D, but instead of making the lease in the name of F, as he was directed, made it in his own name. F notified D that he was the owner, and D agreed to hold the property for him, and at the end of the lease to return it to him. R made a bill of sale of the property to P to satisfy a debt, and at the same time assigned the lease made by him to D, P taking with notice of F's claim. P notified D of the sale, and the latter accepted from the former a lease. In an action by P against D, held, that F had not lost his lien, and that D was entitled to set up the title of F as a defense to the action. Palmtag *v*. Doutrick, 59 Cal. 154; 43 Am. Rep. 245.

But leaving a pledge in the hands of the pledgee, no offer to redeem or demand of payment being made, is not sufficient evidence of abandonment. Cridge's Appeal, 131 Pa. St. 189.

Fraudulent Representations. — A pledgee who, by fraudulent representations, has been induced to release his interest in the property under pledge, is entitled, upon discovering the fraud, to reassert his claim. Easton *v*.

So if the pledgee attaches or issues execution on the goods pledged under a judgment on the debt secured, he waives his lien.[1] But if the goods are taken for another debt owed to the pledgee by the pledgor, and the officer levying is notified of the lien and told to maintain it, the lien is not waived.[2]

3. Enforcement of Right to Redeem—*a.* IN GENERAL.—The discharge of the lien must first be accomplished;[3] then, on refusal of the pledgee to return the security, the pledgor may seek his remedy in equity or at law.[4]

b. REMEDY IN EQUITY—(1) *In General.*—As a rule a bill in equity does not lie to redeem property from a pledge, because the remedy at law is ample.[5] But some special ground of inadequacy of the remedy at law must be shown, as that a discovery is needed, an account wanted, or that there has been an assignment of the pledge.[6]

But if the pledgor comes into a court of equity, he must do equity by first paying the debt secured and allowing for other set-offs.[7]

Hodges, 18 Fed. Rep. 677; Bruley *v.* Rose, 57 Iowa 651.

1. Citizens' Bank *v.* Dows, 68 Iowa 460; Buck *v.* Ingersoll, 11 Met. (Mass.) 226; Legg *v.* Willard, 17 Pick. (Mass.) 140; Jacobs *v.* Latour, 5 Bing. 130.

So if the goods be held by the agent of the pledgee. Swett *v.* Brown, 5 Pick. (Mass.) 178.

Where a pledgee assigned his debt without the lien and allowed the pledged property to be attached by the assignee and other creditors without notifying the officer of the lien, the lien was held to be waived. Whitaker *v.* Sumner, 20 Pick. (Mass.) 399.

2. Whitaker *v.* Sumner, 20 Pick. (Mass.) 399; Townsend *v.* Neivell, 14 Pick. (Mass.) 332.

3. Hendrix *v.* Harman, 19 S. Car. 483. See *supra*, this title, *Discharge of Lien.*

4. The right to redeem cannot be enforced against the administrator of a deceased pledgee unless it is alleged and proved that the pledged property came into the administrator's possession. Angus *v.* Robinson (Vt. 1890), 19 Atl. Rep. 993.

5. Doak *v.* Bank of State, 6 Ired. (N. Car.) 309; Durant *v.* Einstein, 5 Robt. (N. Y.) 423; Genet *v.* Howland, 45 Barb. (N. Y.) 560; Flowers *v.* Sproule, 2 A. K. Marsh. (Ky.) 54; Chapman *v.* Turner, 1 Call (Va.) 280.

On the ground that a pledge is a trust, it has been held that the pledgor may have his bill for specific delivery of the property held in trust, but such a practice seems to violate the fundamental principle of a pledge, which is that the legal title and not an equitable one remains in the pledgor. Brown *v.* Runals, 14 Wis. 693.

In that case the court said: "Where a party obtains possession of chattels through some trust or fiduciary relation to the owner, and then attempts to hold the possession wrongfully, a court of equity may entertain a suit for specific delivery of the thing withheld. The subject of trusts is a matter peculiarly of equitable cognizance, and we suppose a pledge of personal property creates a trust in respect to such property. The pledgee has a right to retain and hold the property pledged until his debt is paid, and then he is bound to restore it to the pledgor. Thus a fiduciary relation is created between the parties in respect to the pledge, from which arise various obligations and duties."

6. Kemp *v.* Westbrooke, 1 Ves. 278; Story Eq., § 1032; Hasbrouck *v.* Vandervoort, 4 Sandf. (N. Y.) 74.

Where the security for a debt was adjudged void at law, chancery decreed a payment of the debt. Little *v.* Fowler, 1 Root (Conn.) 94.

7. Newton *v.* Fay, 10 Allen (Mass.) 505; Hathaway *v.* Fall River Nat. Bank, 131 Mass. 15; Holliday *v.* Holgate, L. R. 3 Ex. 299.

(2) *Accounting.*—So, although the pledgor may have a remedy at law, if an account is wanted he may come into equity.[1] But the account must be a real one, having a series of transactions on both sides, and not merely one item on one side and a number of set-offs on the other.[2] In this case it is not essential that the pledgor should tender the amount of the account before filing a bill to redeem; but if he offers to account with the pawnee and pay whatever is found due on such accounting, and that offer is refused, he may bring his complaint for accounting and redemption at the same time, and if the pledgee has sold the goods, he may have a decree for the balance due him from the proceeds of the sale.[3]

(3) *Redemption of Stock.*—When stock in a corporation is the property pledged, and the shares have been transferred on the books of the company to the pledgee's name, thus giving him the legal title, possession of the shares can only be recovered in equity by an order for redelivery. Though the legal title passes in this case, yet the contract of pledge gives the pledgor this special right of compelling redelivery. So, if the pledgor seeks for an account of receipts and dividends, although the law could afford a remedy equity also has jurisdiction, and especially where the relief at law involves a multiplicity of suits.[4]

c. REMEDY AT LAW—(1) *In General.*—The remedy of a pledgor, where the pledgee refuses to return the pledged property, is in general at law and not by bill.[5] The remedies at law are:

First—To recover the thing itself by replevin.[6]

Second—Where the pledge has been sold to sue on assumpsit for the money received by the pledgee.[7]

1. Kemp. *v.* Westbrook, 1 Ves. 278; Vanderzee *v.* Willis, 3 Bro. Ch. 21; White Mts. R. Co. *v.* Bay State Iron Co., 50 N. H. 57; Hart Ten Eyck, 2 Johns. Ch. (N. Y.) 62.

Where the pledged property had been assigned, and an accounting in equity demanded without making the assignor a party, it was denied. Lewis *v.* Varnum, 12 Abb. Pr. (N. Y.) 305.

2. Durant *v.* Einstein, 35 How. Pr. (N. Y.) 223; 5 Robt. (N. Y.) 423.

3. Beatty *v.* Sylvester, 3 Nev. 228.

4. Jones on Pledge, § 558; Brick *v.* Brick, 98 U. S. 514; Hayward *v.* Eliot Nat. Bank, 96 U. S. 611; Burke's Appeal, 99 Pa. St. 350; Canfield *v.* Minneapolis etc. Assoc., 14 Fed. Rep. 801; Newton *v.* Fay, 10 Allen (Mass.) 505; Hathaway *v.* Fall River Nat. Bank, 131 Mass. 15; Pinkerton *v.* Manchester etc. R. Co., 42 N. H. 424; Bryson *v.* Raynor, 25 Md. 424; Strasburg etc. R. Co. *v.* Echternacht, 21 Pa. St. 220; Fraser *v.* Charleston, 11 S. Car. 486; Hasbrouck *v.* Vandervoort, 4 Sand. (N. Y.) 74.

So equity will compel the corporation to make the transfer back to the pledgor where the pledgee refuses to order it. Cushman *v.* Thayer Mfg. Co., 76 N. Y. 365; Phillips *v.* Berger, 2 Barb. (N. Y.) 608; White *v.* Schuyler, 1 Abb. Pr., N. S. (N. Y.) 300; Middlebrook *v.* Merchants' Bank, 41 Barb. (N. Y.) 481; Treasurer *v.* Commercial Min. Co., 23 Cal. 391.

Where stock was held as collateral for an anticipated loss upon a mortgage of a house not yet foreclosed, upon a bill to redeem the stock, the court, in order to ascertain the amount of such loss, will order the house to be sold, unless the pledgee will accept the decision of a master or referee appointed to ascertain the value. Bartlett *v.* Johnson, 9 Allen (Mass.) 530.

5. Doak *v.* State Bank, 6 Ired. (N. Car.) 309.

6. Stoker *v.* Cogswell, 25 How. Pr. (N. Y.) 267.

7. Read *v.* Lambert, 10 Abb. Pr., N. S. (N. Y.) 428; Cushman *v.* Hayes, 46 Ill. 145.

Third—But the more usual remedy is to sue for damages for conversion, and this is the better remedy where the pledgee refuses to return the pledge or has wilfully disposed of it so as to put it out of his power to return it.[1]

There may be a conversion of incorporeal as well as corporeal property, and trover will lie for such conversion.[2]

(2) *What Constitutes Conversion*—(*a*) *In General.*—As the pledgee comes rightfully into possession of the property pledged, he is not liable for conversion until that element of right has been removed. Therefore, to lay the ground for an action for conversion the lien of the pledge must first be discharged, generally by tender.[3]

1. Luckey *v.* Gannon, 37 How. Pr. (N. Y.) 134; 1 Sweeny (N. Y.) 12; Campbell *v.* Parker, 9 Bosw. (N. Y.) 322; Henry *v.* Martin, 3 E. D. Smith (N. Y.) 71; Flowers *v.* Sproule, 2 A. K. Marsh. (Ky.) 54; Elliott *v.* Armstrong, 2 Blackf. (Ind.) 198.

In Lawrence *v.* Maxwell, 53 N. Y. 19, the court by Allen, J., said: "Whatever rights the pledgee may have during the continuance of his special property, when the obligation is discharged and the property released, the pledgor is entitled to the thing pledged. When the special property of the bailee ceases, the general owner may have his property, and if it has been converted by the bailee, or lost through his default or neglect, trover will lie. The right to use as well as the right to retain the pledge, ceases the instant the lien is discharged by the tender or payment of the debt, or the performance of the covenant or engagement for which the security is given."

2. Campbell *v.* Parker, 9 Bosw. (N. Y.) 322; Luckey *v.* Gannon, 37 How. Pr. (N. Y.) 134; Decker *v.* Mathews, 12 N. Y. 313; Baltimore M. Ins. Co. *v.* Dalrymple, 25 Md. 269.

So, for the conversion of bank bills specially pledged. During the civil war a customer of a bank in South Carolina left four thousand dollars of his own bills with the bank as security for the return of a like sum in Confederate treasury notes, borrowed for a short limited time. Within this time he tendered this sum in treasury notes, and demanded the return of the bank-bills, and upon refusal of the bank to deliver them, brought trover for their conversion. It was held that his right to recover was not taken away by the fact that the property pledged was money, or the bills of the bank itself; but that the same principle was to govern as if the article deposited had been a watch or a jewel. Abrahams *v.* Southwestern etc. Bank, 1 S. Car. 441; Millard, J., dissenting.

3. Talty *v.* Freedman's Sav. etc. Co., 93 U. S. 321; Jarvis *v.* Rogers, 15 Mass. 389; Amos *v.* Sinnott, 5 Ill. 440; Henry *v.* Eddy, 34 Ill. 508; Cooper *v.* Ray, 47 Ill. 53; Kennedy *v.* Hammond, 16 Mo. 341; Doak *v.* Bank of State, 6 Ired. (N. Car.) 309; Donald *v.* Suckling, L. R., Q. B. 585.

See *infra*, this title, *Tender*.

A demand made upon a broker for stock pledged to him as collateral security without tendering him the money due, which demand was refused under a false pretext without objecting to the omission of tender, was held good. Fisher *v.* Brown, 104 Mass. 259.

A pledge obtained by false pretenses vests no title in the pledgee and may be recovered on demand without paying the debt. Mead *v.* Bunn, 32 N. Y. 275.

Where a person had borrowed money at usurious interest, which the contract did not exhibit on its face, and gave a pledge for its repayment, held, that he could not treat such contract as void, and sue for the recovery of the pledge, without a tender of the money actually due, and legal interest thereupon. Causey *v.* Yeates, 8 Humph. (Tenn.) 605.

Sale by Pledgor to Third Person.—If the pawnor sell the property to a third person while it is in the pawnee's hands, and the pawnee refuse to give it up to the vendee on being tendered the amount of the debt for which it was pledged, the vendee may maintain trover against him. Ratcliff *v.* Vance, 2 Mill (S. Car.) 239; S. P. Bush *v.* Lyon, 9 Cow. (N. Y.) 52.

Then a demand for the return of the pledged property must be made, on the refusal of which the action lies.[1]

(*b*) *Unauthorized Sub-pledge or Illegal Sale.*—An unauthorized sub-pledge or an illegal sale is commonly spoken of as a conversion,[2] but the discharge of the lien and demand are equally necessary whether the security is in the hands of the original pledgee or has been re-pledged or sold by him to one who has loaned upon it or purchased it in good faith without notice of the owner's rights.[3] It once was held that when the pledgee had voluntarily put it out of his power to return the pledged property, tender and demand were necessary;[4] though without a demand

1. Luckey *v.* Gannon, 37 How. Pr. (N. Y.) 134; 6 Abb. Pr., N. S. (N. Y.) 209; Cass *v.* Higenbotam, 100 N. Y. 248; Williamson *v.* McClure, 37 Pa. St. 402; Grant *v.* Taylor, 35 N. Y. Super. Ct. 338; Dewart *v.* Masser, 40 Pa. St. 302; Yeatman *v.* New Orleans Sav. Inst., 95 U. S. 764.

But where a pledgee of a note hands it to the maker to be given by him to the payee as pledgor, he thereby constitutes him his agent, and after offer to deliver by such agent to the payer and refusal to accept, the latter has no action for conversion against the pledgee. Norman *v.* Rogers, 29 Ark. 365.

Time of Demand.—It was held in *New York* that to lay the foundation for an action against a pledgee for conversion of a thing pledged as security for a note payable on a fixed day, the debtor's offer and demand must be made on the day of maturity; though it would be otherwise of an action to redeem. Butts *v.* Burnett, 6 Abb. Pr., N. S. (N. Y.) 302. See McCalla *v.* Clark, 55 Ga. 53.

2. Hays *v.* Riddle, 1 Sandf. (N. Y.) 248; Hope *v.* Lawrence, 1 Hun (N. Y.) 317; Cooke *v.* Haddon, 3 F. & F. 229.

Where a railroad company pledged its own coupon bonds for its debts, and the pledgee cut off and presented for payment the coupons, it was held not to be a conversion. Androscoggin R. Co. *v.* Auburn Bank, 48 Me. 335.

Where general authority to "use, transfer, or hypothecate" a stock note was given and the pledgee sold the note on his own account, it was held to be a conversion. Ogden *v.* Lathrop, 1 Sweeny (N. Y.) 643.

3. Lewis *v.* Mott, 36 N. Y. 395; Williamson *v.* McClure, 37 Pa. St. 402.

Nor is the tender excused by the fact that the pledgor's note is in the hands of his pledgee. If the note is matured, its negotiable character is gone and it may safely be paid to the purchaser or second pledgee taking the security in good faith. After making such a tender instead of suing at law the pledgor may bring a bill in equity and have the rights of all parties determined. Talty *v.* Freedman's Sav. etc. Co., 93 U. S. 321.

When bonds were sub-pledged, the original pledgor to recover their value on an unauthorized sale by the sub-pledgee, must show that the latter did not have a valid title or, if it did have it, has lost it by tender of the amount of his lien by the original pledgor. Thompson *v.* St. Nicholas State Nat. Bank, 113 N. Y. 325.

4. Cortelyou *v.* Lansing, 2 Cai. Cas. (N. Y.) 200; Dykers *v.* Allen, 7 Hill (N. Y.) 497; Wilson and Little, 2 N. Y. 443; Lewis *v.* Graham, 4 Abb. Pr. (N. Y.) 106; Lucketts *v.* Townsend, 3 Tex. 119; Reed *v.* Lambert, 10 Abb. Pr., N. S. (N. Y.) 428.

A broker having purchased gold for a customer upon a pledge of bank stock as collateral was ordered by the customer to sell at a stipulated price at which it might have been sold; but the broker, claiming the order to be discretionary, failed to do so, but subsequently sold it for a less price; the customer thereupon tendered the broker a sum sufficient to pay the balance of the account, if the gold had been sold pursuant to his order. After such tender, the broker sold the bank stock. It was held that this was a conversion of the stock, and that the customer was entitled to recover its value after deducting the actual indebtedness for which the stock stood in pledge. Hope *v.* Lawrence, 1 Hun (N. Y.) 317.

Unauthorized Sub-pledge.—If a mechanic pawns a chattel that is put into

on the pledgee or affording him an opportunity to surrender the pledged property, he is not liable to the pledgee for any depreciation in the value of such property during the time they remain in his possession after the time they might have been demanded.[1] But the rule is now that an unauthorized sale of the pledge by the pledgee does not render the pledge contract void *ab initio*,[2] and therefore is not of itself a conversion, unless the pledgor so elects to consider it. His cause of action does not arise until he discharges the lien and demands a return of the pledge, and the pledgee neglects or refuses to return it.[3]

(3) *Defenses.*—Though the pledgee impliedly undertakes to return the pledge to the pledgor, the latter, in the first place, impliedly warranted the property to be his own; and if this warranty turns out to be false the pledgee is absolved from his undertaking to restore the property to the pledgor, but should restore it to the true owner and show in defense to an action for conversion that the pledge was the property of the person to whom he has returned it.[4] The estoppel against the bailee ceases

his possession to be repaired, the owner may maintain trover against the pawnee, without tendering the sum for which it was pawned. Gallaher *v.* Cohen, 1 Browne (Pa.) 43.

So also, in case of a carrier, Kitchell *v.* Vanadar, 1 Blackf. (Ind.) 356.

1. Williamson *v.* McClure, 37 Pa. St. 402.

2. First Nat. Bank *v.* Boyce, 78 Ky. 42; 19 Am. L. Reg., N. S. 503.

3. Hopper *v.* Smith, 63 How. Pr. (N. Y.) 34; Butts *v.* Burnett, 6 Abb. Pr., N. S. (N. Y.) 302; Halliday *v.* Holgate, L. R., 3 Exch. 299; Morgan *v.* Jaudon, 40 How. Pr. (N. Y.) 366.

In Hopper *v.* Smith, 63 How. Pr. (N. Y.) 34, the court by Rumsey, J., said: "Outside of authority, the rule that a sale by the pledgee is not *ipso facto*, a conversion, seems to be good sense. The rights of the parties are based upon the contract. The sale by the pledgee is wrongful. If that sale in and of itself determines the contract without more, then the pledgee by his wrongful act may rescind his contract in spite of the wish of the other party to it. I am not aware of any other case in which this can be done, and I can concieve of no reason for permitting it in this case. It may be for the interest of the pledgor to keep his contracts alive, and, if it is so, I cannot see why he may not do it. The maxim that no one shall take any advantage by his own wrongful act, may fairly apply to this case; and we may hold that, although the unlawful sale does not *per se* operate as a conversion, yet the pledgor may, at his option, so consider it, and that he may regard the contract as at an end, tender or offer to pay his debt and demand his pledge, or may sue for damages for the sale. I think the cases sustain that rule, and that it reconciles the cases which otherwise appear to conflict, but do not in fact. [Strong *v.* National etc. Banking Assoc., 45 N. Y. 718; Bryan *v.* Baldwin, 52 N. Y. 232.] I do not think that the plaintiff was called upon to notify defendant of his disaffirmance of the sale at the time defendant told him of it. There is no pretense of any estoppel. Nothing has occurred to give defendant reason to believe that the contract was waived, and he took no action afterwards in the strength of the plaintiff's silence. As long as the contract was in force both parties were bound by it. The plaintiff might rely upon it, and the defendant must keep ready to perform it. Neither party by his own act simply could free himself from its obligation."

So the pledgor may waive a tortious conversion by the pledgee through an illegal sale of the pledge by presenting a statement showing the amount he claimed to be due, and offering to receive the same in full satisfaction. Butts *v.* Burnett, 6 Abb. Pr., N. S. (N. Y.) 302.

4. The Idaho, 93 U. S. 575; Bates *v.*

when the bailment is determined by what is equivalent to eviction by title paramount.[1] But the pledgee cannot impeach the pledgor's title without setting up title in another,[2] and he cannot set up this title in a third person without that person's express authority,[3] or unless the property has been taken from him by the true owner,[4] or he has been sued by a third person claiming title to the pledged property.[5] That the pledge is retained after the payment of the debt secured to secure another debt due from the pledgor to the pledgee is not a good defense.[6]

(4) *Measure of Damages—(a) In General.*—The measure of damages is the value of the pledged property at the time the action for conversion will first lie;[7] that is, when the tender, demand

Stanton, 1 Duer (N. Y.) 79; Hayden *v.* Davis, 9 Cal. 573; Dodge *v.* Meyer, 10 Pac. Coast L. J. 169; Pitt *v.* Albretton, 12 Ired. (N. Car.) 74; Ogle *v.* Atkinson, 5 Taunt. 759; Wilson *v.* Anderton, 1 B. & Ad. 450; Dixon *v.* Yates, 5 B. & Ad. 313; Watson *v.* Lane, 11 Exch. 769; Sheridan *v.* New Quay Co., 4 C. B., N. S. 618; Thorne *v.* Tilbury, 3 H. & N. 534; Cheesman *v.* Exall, 6 Exch. 341.

Where a part owner of stock pledges it for his individual benefit, with the authority and consent of his co-owner, the pledgee is estopped to set up the co-owner's title as a defense to an action by the pledgor for its conversion. Sharpe *v.* National Bank, 87 Ala. 644.

A sub-pledgee may defend against the owner of the thing pledged by showing that before the owner's offer to redeem he had returned it to his own pledgor. Jarvis *v.* Rogers, 15 Mass. 389.

Burden of Proof. — The burden of proof to show that such third person is the true owner is on pledgee. Biddle *v.* Bond, 6 Best. & S. 225; Cheesman *v.* Exall, 6 Exch. 341; Sheridan *v.* New Quay Co., 4 C. B., N. S. 618.

1. Shelbury *v.* Scotsford, Yelv. 23; Biddle *v.* Bond, 6 Best & S. 225; Palmtag *v.* Doutrick, 59 Cal. 154.

2. Smith *v.* Hall, 67 N. Y. 48.

3. Palmtag *v.* Doutrick, 59 Cal. 154.

4. Godfrey *v.* Pell, 49 N. Y. Super. Ct. 226.

5. Cass *v.* Higenbotam, 27 Hun (N. Y.) 406. In that case the court said: "The pledgor standing in his position as guarantor of the title to the plaintiffs as pledgee, and knowing of the pendency of the action in which he was bound to defend that title, he could not, we think, by a simple demand, put the present plaintiff in the position of a wrongdoer, in converting the property for which the other action was pending."

6. Hardy *v.* Jaudon, 1 Robt. (N. Y.) 261; Luckey *v.* Gannon, 1 Sweeny (N. Y.) 12; 37 How. Pr. (N. Y.) 134.

7. Loomis *v.* Stave, 72 Ill. 623; Eisendiath *v.* Knauer, 64 Ill. 396; First Nat. Bank *v.* Boyce, 78 Ky. 42; Newcomb Buchanan Co. *v.* Baskett, 14 Bush (Ky.) 658; Robinson *v.* Hurley, 11 Iowa 410; Ainsworth *v.* Bowen, 9 Wis. 348. Damages for conversion after default. Cushman *v.* Hayes, 46 Ill. 145; Stearns *v.* Marsh, 4 Den. (N. Y.) 227; Belden *v.* Perkins, 78 Ill. 449.

When the pledgee having sold the pledge, refused to give any information respecting the sale and the owner had to file his bill of discovery, the pledgee was obliged to pay costs. Cake *v.* Shull (N. J. 1888), 13 Atl. Rep. 666.

It was held in Johnson *v.* Stear, 15 C. B., N. S. 330, Williams, J., dissenting, that the actual damage sustained by the pledgor was the true measure of damages, and as there was no intention to redeem, the damage was merely nominal.

The owner of goods converted by a pledgee is not obliged in order to fix the amount of damages, to purchase an equal amount of similar goods. Kilpatrick *v.* Dean (City Ct.), 3 N. Y. Supp. 60.

Where confusion of goods has occurred, the utmost value of the goods lost will be given. Hart *v.* TenEyck, 2 Johns. Ch. (N. Y.) 62; Ringgold *v.* Ringgold, 1 Har. & G. (Ind.) 11.

The plaintiff deposited with the defendant two notes, as collateral security for a note of third persons held by defendant, which plaintiff procured to be discounted; and was obliged to pay at maturity, as well as the two notes

and refusal occur.[1] But if the pledgee, having sold the pledge, the pledgor sues in assumpsit for the money he can recover only the amount actually received by the pledgee.[2]

(*b*) *Mitigation of Damages.*—While the pledgee has no right to hold the pledge for another debt than the one secured, yet when he has sold the pledge, he may, in mitigation of damages, show that he has applied the proceeds to another debt.[3]

(*c*) *Set-off.*—The pledgee is always allowed to set-off against the value of the pledge the debt secured by it.[4] But he cannot set up as counterclaim a debt not secured by the pledge, for the pledgor sues in his original title and not on a promise of the pledgor.[5]

(*d*) *Damages on Sub-Pledge.*—When the pledge has been given by the pledgee as security for his own debt to another without destroying the original contract of the pledge,[6] the original

deposited with defendant, and discounted by him. *Held*, that, upon offering to return the dishonored note received from defendant, plaintiff might, in an action for money had and received, recover the amount of the two notes deposited with the defendant. Mayo *v.* Peterson, 126 Mass. 516.

For amount to be recovered on the wrongful sale of stock, see *supra*, this title, *Sale of Stock.*

1. Reynolds *v.* Witte, 13 S. Car. 5.

2. Read *v.* Lambert, 10 Abb. Pr. N. S. (N. Y.) 428; Cushman *v.* Hayes, 46 Ill. 145.

3. Hathaway *v.* Fall River Nat. Bank, 131 Mass. 14; Loomis *v.* Stave, 72 Ill. 623; Belden *v.* Perkins, 78 Ill. 449; Baldwin *v.* Bradley, 69 Ill. 32; Bailey *v.* Godfrey, 54 Ill. 507.

4. Stearns *v.* Marsh, 4 Den. (N. Y.) 227; Jarvis *v.* Rogers, 15 Mass. 389; Ward *v.* Fellers, 3 Mich. 281; Belden *v.* Perkins, 78 Ill., 449; Rosenzweig *v.* Frazer, 82 Ind. 342; Smith *v.* Hall, 67 N. Y. 48; Shaw *v.* Ferguson, 78 Ind. 547; Baker *v.* Drake, 53 N. Y. 211; 66 N. Y. 518; Baltimore M. Ins. Co. *v.* Dalrymple, 25 Md. 242; Levy *v.* Loeb, 47 N. Y. Super. Ct. 61; Gruman *v.* Smith, 81 N. Y. 25; Vanderslice *v.* Matthews, 79 Cal. 273; Johnson *v.* Stear, 15 C. B. N. S. 330.

In an action for conversion of bags of coffee, it was held that neither the cost of weighing and selling them, nor storage which had been paid by a third person with an understanding that if the owner recovered, it should be paid back, be set-off. Kilpatrick *v.* Dean (City Ct.), 3 N. Y. Supp. 60.

Pledgor's damages and expenses may be set-off against the debt secured. Levy *v.* Loeb, 47 N. Y. Super. Ct. 61.

In an action by a receiver of a bank against M to recover the amount of a loan, held, that the bank was chargeable with negligence, because the trustees left the entire management of the bank to the president, without vigilance; and M was entitled to counter-claim the value of certain collateral securities converted by the president. Cutting *v.* Marlor, 78 N. Y. 454.

When a number of shares of stock of the same kind are given as collateral security for a loan, and are divided by the pledgee into several lots and separately converted, in an action for the conversion of one of those lots the pledgee has a right to set off against plaintiff's claim a portion of the debt bearing the same proportion to the whole thereof as the said claim does to the value of all the shares pledged. New York etc. R. Co. *v.* Davies, 38 Hun (N. Y.) 477.

5. Smith *v.* Hall, 67 N. Y. 48.

Warehousemen with whom a pledge is stored, and who, after subrogation to the rights of pledgees, convert the goods, cannot set off, in tort for the conversion, debts due from the pledgor in independent transactions, though the contract of pledge provided that the pledgees might apply the proceeds of sale to all demands against the pledgor; especially where such warehousemen had assented to a delivery order which specified the advances to which the goods were subject. Kilpatrick *v.* Dean (City Ct.), 3 N. Y. Supp. 60.

6. In Donald *v.* Suckling, L. R., 1 Q.

pledgor can only recover his property from the second pledgee by paying him the amount of the debt due the first pledgee.[1] If he sues the second pledgee in trover, he may recover the value of the property, deducting the amount of the original debt secured.[2]

d. STATUTE OF LIMITATIONS.—After the debt secured has been barred by the Statute of Limitations, the pledgee has no increased right in the pledged property, for the statute affects in no way the pledgee's lien, but only his personal remedy against the pledgor.[3] The pledgor's right to redeem might be barred by a very long lapse of time without any claim to redeem on his part, and the title pass absolutely to the pledgee.[4] But though the

B. 585, the court, by Cockburn, C. J., said: "The question here is whether the transfer of the pledge is not only a breach of the contract on the part of the pawnee, but operates to put an end to the contract altogether, so as to entitle the pawnor to have back the thing pledged without payment of the debt. I am of opinion that the transfer of the pledge does not put an end to the contract, upon which the owner may bring an action for nominal damages, if he has sustained no substantial damages; for substantial damages, if the thing is damaged in the hands of the third party, or the owner is prejudiced by delay in not having the thing delivered to him on tendering the amount for which it was pledged."

Where the pledgee of securities wrongfully pledged them, and the second pledgee took them in good faith—held, that the first pledgor could recover from the second pledgee a surplus arising from a sale of the securities by the second pledgee to satisfy his loan, which was a larger sum than that for which the securities were originally pledged. *In re* Bonner, 8 Daly (N. Y.) 75.

The pledgee of a mortgage note, who violates the contract of pledge by pledging the note to a third person, is responsible to the owner of the note for the full amount of the note, unless he clearly proves that the note was worth less than its face. Whoever actively violates a contract need not be put in default. Laloire *v.* Wiltz, 29 La. Ann. 329.

1. Talty *v.* Freedmans' Sav. etc. Co., 93 U. S. 321; Lewis *v.* Mott, 36 N. Y. 395; Evans *v.* Potter, 2 Gall. (U. S.) 13; Donald *v.* Suckling, L. R., 1 Q. B. 585; Halliday *v.* Holgate, L. R., 3 Ex. 299; Johnson *v.* Stear, 15 C. B., N. S. 330.

2. Work *v.* Bennett, 70 Pa. St. 484; Neiler *v.* Kelley, 69 Pa. St. 403; Maryland F. Ins. Co. *v.* Dalrymple, 25 Md. 242.

But the sub-pledgee must have acted in complete good faith and have taken the pledge for a valuable consideration without knowledge of the original pledge. First Nat. *v.* Boyce, 78 Ky. 42.

3. Hancock *v.* Franklin Ins. Co., 114 Mass. 155; Moses *v.* St. Paul, 67 Ala. 168; Whelan *v.* Kinsley, 26 Ohio St. 131; Kemp *v.* Westbrook, 1 Ves. 278; Waterman *v.* Brown, 31 Pa. St. 161.

Where a surety received from his principal a note as indemnity and passed over the same note to the creditor as collateral security for the principal debt, it was held that the creditor could not recover on such note after the principal debt was barred by the statute, though he might have done so if the note was delivered to the creditor in discharge of the liability of the surety. Russell *v.* La Roque, 13 Ala. 149.

4. Story Bailm., § 298; Jones on Pledge, § 581; Mims *v.* Mims, 3 J. J. Marsh. (Ky.) 103.

So where a pledgee holding stock with power to sell on non-payment of the debt at the end of six years, the stock not being of the value of the debt, kept it as his own, after eleven years had elapsed in which time the stock had advanced in price, a court of equity refused to interfere. Waterman *v.* Brown, 31 Pa. St. 161.

It was held in *New York* that such a case comes within the section of the Revised Statutes relative to bills of relief, in cases of trusts not cognizable at law, etc., and that under the statute, if the action to redeem is not brought within ten years from the time the debt

remedy to enforce his debt against him may be barred, the pledgor can never recover his property without paying his debt.[1]

PLUNDER.—The common meaning of this word is, to take property from persons or places by open force, as in the case of pirates or banditti. Another meaning (in some degree figurative) expresses the idea of taking property from a person or place without just right, but not expressing the nature or quality of the wrong done.[2]

PLY, PLYING.—See note 3.

POINTS.—See note 4.

secured is payable, it will be barred. Roberts *v.* Sykes, 30 Barb. (N. Y.) 173.

In *Louisiana*, the code provides that the right to redeem shall never be barred by prescription or limitation. R. Civ. Code, 1870, art. 3175; Conger *v.* New Orleans, 32 La. Ann. 1250; Citizen's Bank *v.* Knapp, 22 La. Ann. 117; Blanc *v.* Hertzog, 23 La. 293; Citizens' Bank *v.* Johnson, 21 La. Ann. 128; Police Jury *v.* Duralde, 22 La. Ann. 107. So held in *California*. Cross *v.* Eureka Lake etc. Canal Co., 73 Cal. 302.

It seems to be held in some States that after a tender by the pledgor and refusal on the part of the pledgee or some other act showing a determination on the latter's part to put an end to the trust relation, that the statute will begin to run. Whelan *v.* Kinsley, 26 Ohio St. 131; Jones *v.* Thurmond, 5 Tex. 318.

Rights of Pledgee.—In *North Carolina*, four years' possession by a pledgee of the lessee of the property pledged does not confer title on the pledgee so that he can recover it from the true owner, who has peaceably gotten possession of it. Pate *v.* Hazell (N. Car. 1890.), 11 S. E. Rep. 1089.

1. Jones *v.* Merchants' Bank, 6 Robt. (N. Y.) 162; *In re* Oakley, 2 Edw. Ch. (N. Y.) 478; Roots *v.* Mason City etc. Co., 27 W. Va. 483.

2. Carter *v.* Andrews, 16 Pick. (Mass.) 9.

A statute of the *United States* provides for the punishment of "every person who plunders, steals or destroys any money, goods, merchandise, or other effects from or belonging to any vessel in distress, or wrecked," etc. The defendant was indicted for taking and carrying away goods belonging to a wrecked vessel and floating near it. The court, by Hammond, J., said: "If we admit that the facts in this case do not constitute larceny, or that those do not which are mentioned in State *v.* Curran, 18 Mo. 321, where an iron safe belonging to a wrecked vessel was taken from the river and its contents appropriated after notice of their ownership, under circumstances said by the supreme court of Missouri to show that the perpetrators were 'unmindful of the duties of good and honest men,' I am still of opinion that either case falls within the statute, because, if not stealing, in the sense of the common law, it was 'plundering,' as known to this statute; if not in the Conway case, certainly in this, where the distressed vessel was almost in sight, and the goods were confessedly known to belong to her. Mr. Stephen says of this word 'plunder,' that he does not know that it has any special legal signification. Stephen Dig. Crim. Law (St. Louis ed. 1878) 261, 266 m and notes." United States *v.* Stone, 8 Fed. Rep. 232.

See also U. S. *v.* Pitman, 1 Sprague (U. S.) 198.

See generally LARCENY, vol. 12, p. 760.

3. Within the meaning of an *English* license act, a carriage stationed for hire by the public, but never hired, is "plying for hire." Allen *v.* Tunbridge, L. R., 6 C. P. 481. But see Case *v.* Story, L. R., 4 Ex. 319.

Plying Coastwise.—See COAST, vol. 3, p. 288, 3 n.

4. An *Illinois* act authorizes railroad corporations "to cross, intersect, join and unite its railways with any other railway before constructed at any point in its route and upon the grounds of such other railway company." This does not authorize a railway corporation to appropriate a portion of the right of way of another company ex-

POINTS AND AUTHORITIES—(See also BRIEF, vol. 2, p. 565).—The terms "brief" and "points and authorities" are synonymous (as the term "brief" is used in this country), both being a condensed statement of the propositions of law which the counsel desire to establish, and indicating the reasons and authorities which sustain them.[1]

POISONS AND POISONING.—(See also ABORTION, vol. 1, p. 28; DRUGGIST, vol. 6, p. 31; HOMICIDE, vol. 9, p. 548; MEDICAL JURISPRUDENCE, vol. 15, pp. 248–255.)

A poison may be defined as a substance having an inherent, deleterious property which renders it, when taken into the system, capable of destroying life.[2] Again, it may be defined to be that which, when administered, is injurious to health or life.[3]

The treatment given to this subject elsewhere leaves nothing to be said here, save from the standpoint of the law of homicide, as applied where poison is the instrument used, and from the standpoint of the criminal jurisprudence governing the offense of administering or attempting to administer poison.

In many of the States the offense of administering poison is defined by statute, and the punishment thereof regulated thereby. There is, however, no very essential difference between the statutory crime and the crime at common law.[4]

tending longitudinally a distance of ten or eleven miles. The court by Mulkey, J., said: "It will be observed that the crossing intersecting, joining, and uniting therein authorized are limited to a 'point' on the route of the proposed road." Illinois etc. R. Co. *v.* Chicago etc. R. Co., 122 Ill. 473.

Sailors' Point.—A sailor's "point" is not a mathematical point at the end of a promontory; it is the whole of the promontory. "The point begins where a vessel having to go round it, either up or down the river, would, if there were nothing in the way, be obliged to use her steerage power for the purpose of continuing her course, and it ends where the necessity, if there were nothing in the way, of using the steerage in order to go round, ceases." "Rounding" a point "begins from the time when, if there were nothing in the way, a vessel would have to begin to use her steerage to go round, and that the rounding ends at the same place that I before stated, where, if there were nothing in the way, she would cease using her steerage for the purpose of going round, and would then be straight for her opposite course." Per Brett, M. R., The Margaret, 9 P. D. 47.

1. Duncan *v.* Kokler, 37 Minn. 379.

2. Whart. & Stille, Med. Jur., § 493; Taylor on Poisons.

3. Coleridge, C. J., in Reg. *v.* Cramp, 5 Q. B. D. 307.

For the purposes of the English Pharmacy Act, 1868 (31 & 32 Vict. ch. 121), the following are by § 2 and Sch. A, deemed poisons: Arsenic and its preparations; prussic acid; cyanides of potassium, and all metallic cyanides; strychnine and all poisonous vegetable alkaloids and their salts; aconite and its preparations; emetic tartar; corrosive sublimate; cantharides; savin and its oil; ergot of rye and its preparations; oxalic acid; chloroform; belladonna and its preparations; essential oil of almonds, unless deprived of its prussic acid; opium and all preparations of opium or of poppies.

4. The history of the art of poisoning may be read in 1 Beekman's History of Inventions 74, *et seq.*; but with the historical aspect of the subject we are not here concerned.

Administering Poison.—In Rex *v.* Harley, 4 Car. & P. 369, the accused, a servant, in preparing the breakfast of her mistress, put arsenic into the coffee-pot, and told her mistress that she had prepared the coffee for her, upon which the mistress took the coffee for her breakfast, and this was held an administering of poison.

In Rex. *v.* Cabman, Ry. & M. 114, the question was raised whether a cake containing poison and taken into the mouth by the person for whom it was intended, at the instance of the accused, but not swallowed, because of a suspicion of poisoning, constituted the offense of administering poison. And see, as explanatory of this case, Rex. *v.* Harley, 4 Car. & P. 369.

Where it appeared that A accused her servant of stealing, and that the next morning the servant brought up poisoned tea for A's breakfast, and the tea was partaken of by A, there was a finding that the poison was administered. Rex. *v.* Draper, 1 Car. & P. 176.

In Rex. *v.* Cluderoy, 2 Car. & K. 907, a conviction was sustained where poisonous berries (of the *coculus indicus*) were inclosed when administered in a strong shell or pod, which was innoxious and not likely to be broken in its passage through the body.

In Ann *v.* State, 11 Humph. (Tenn.) 159, it was held that a conviction of murder was not sustained where the evidence was that the accused, a young nurse girl, administered the fatal dose of laudanum to the infant under her charge in total ignorance of its deadly properties, and with the intention merely of quieting the child in order that she might absent herself for improper purposes of her own.

In Sumpter *v.* State, 11 Fla. 247, it was held not enough to constitute the crime of administering poison that poison was placed in food intended for certain persons, so long as they did not partake of it.

Under Ohio Statute.—It was said in Robbins *v.* State, 8 Ohio St. 131, that a purpose to kill was an essential ingredient of murder by poison under the *Ohio* statute. In Blackburn *v.* State, 23 Ohio St. 146, it was said neither fraud nor deception was a necessary ingredient in the act of "administering poison," within the statute.

Under Michigan Statute.—In People *v.* Carmichael, 5 Mich. 10, it was adjudged, under the *Michigan* statute providing against the administration of poisons "with intent to kill or injure," that the offense was complete where the poison was administered and operated to derange the healthy organization of the system, temporarily or permanently, whether the injury was great or small, as where morphine was administered in a dose sufficient to cause deep sleep but not death.

When Taken by Person Not Intended.—Even where the person whom it was intended to kill does not take the poison, but another person does take it, death resulting, the crime of murder is complete. Saunders' Case, Plowden's Rep. 473; State *v.* Fulkerson, Phill. (N. Car.) 233. And see Rex *v.* Lewis, 6 Car. & P. 161; Rex *v.* Ryan, 2 Moo. & R. 213.

Attempt to Administer Poison.—To maintain an indictment for an attempt to poison, it must be shown that the accused attempted to administer the poison and that the attempt was unsuccessful. Archbold's Cr. Pr. & Pl. 259.

In Rex *v.* Cabman, Ry. & M. 114, where the poisoning was held not to be completed because the poison was not actually taken into the stomach, the offense (Archbold says) it would seem, would be punishable under the clause of the statute governing attempts, as an attempt to poison. But where A gave poison to B, with directions to administer it to C, and B instead of doing so, handed it over to C, telling him at the same time of the instructions he had received from A, it was held that here was not an attempt on A's part to administer the poison. Rex *v.* Williams, 1 Car. & K. 539.

In Rex *v.* Hanson, 2 Car. & K. 912, where a man gave a woman a quantity of cantharides mixed in rum, which made her very ill, but did not endanger her life, the counsel for the prosecution, seeing that the facts would not sustain an indictment for poisoning or attempting to poison, framed an indictment as for a misdemeanor at common law; but it was held that it was no misdemeanor at common law; and the prisoner was accordingly acquitted.

It is not necessary, under the *English* statute to prove that any bodily injury was effected by the attempt.

Mr. Bishop (Crim. Law § 756) declares the *English* doctrine to be, that an attempt to poison is not committed by administering a substance not poisonous, yet believed to be poisonous; because if it kills, the person killed is not poisoned to death; and cites, as supporting the *English* doctrine, State *v.* Clarissa, 11 Ala. 57, and refers to, as illustrative, Com. *v.* Manley, 12 Pick. (Mass.) 173; Rex *v.* Coe, 6

Car. & P. 403; Reg. *v.* Williams, 1 Den. C. C. 39; Rex. *v.* Hughes, 5 Car. & P. 126; Reg. *v.* Leddington, 9 Car. & P. 79.

"But," says Bishop, "the question lies very near the debatable ground. For, if the substance administered should resemble poison, and appear to ordinary observation to be such, while yet it could be scientifically ascertained not to be, the requirements of the statute would be filled to ordinary apprehension, in a case where the principles of the common law would demand a conviction."

Indictment.—As to the indictment, it may be said generally, that where it is upon a statute, as it usually is, the words of the statute, or at the least their substance, should be followed. La Beau *v.* People, 6 Park. Cr. (N. Y.) 371; Com. *v.* Galavan, 9 Allen (Mass.) 271; Com. *v.* Bearse, 108 Mass. 487; Bishop Cr. Proc., § 644.

In Com. *v.* Galavan, 9 Allen (Mass.) 271, it was held, as in *England*, that an averment that the accused knew the substance administered to be poisonous was unnecessary. In State *v.* Yarborough, 77 N. Car. 524, the court held otherwise, but the *Massachusetts* rule appears to be the better one.

It was held in Hicks *v.* Com. 86 Va. 223, that under the *Virginia* statute, making it a felony to attempt to administer poison in food, drink, etc., with intent to kill, that an indictment which charged the accused with an attempt to poison A, with intent to kill, by buying the poison, and delivering it to B, and soliciting B to administer it in coffee to A, but which failed to aver that B consented to do this or that anything further was done, was defective.

It was held in Collins *v.* State, 3 Heisk. (Tenn.) 14, that an indictment under the *Tennessee* statute for an attempt to poison need not charge an assault. So in Garnet *v.* State, 1 Tex. App. 605.

An allegation of an actual poisoning includes, by necessary implication, an allegation that the substance employed was poison; but an indictment of an attempt to poison must specifically allege that the substance employed in the attempt was a deadly poison. Anthony *v.* State, 29 Ala. 27.

In an indictment for poisoning, where the crime charged is the mingling of poison with food, drink, or medicine, with intent to injure the victim, the statement of the taking of the poison and the consequences thereof, form no part of the crime, and are surplusage. Madden *v.* State, 1 Kan. 340.

Under the *Minnesota* statute, a charge of a wilful and premeditated killing, by giving poison, is sufficient, without charging that the poison was taken into the stomach of the deceased, whereof he at a specified time died. Bilansky *v.* State, 3 Minn. 427.

Evidence.—The questions of evidence arising upon indictments for homicide by poisoning fall, for the most part, within the domain of medical jurisprudence, and are dealt with under that title of this work. See MEDICAL JURISPRUDENCE, vol. 15, pp. 248–255.

It was held in Joe *v.* State, 6 Fla. 591, that, where some imperfect evidence of symptoms of poison was the only testimony to prove the crime, and no analysis had been made of the stomach or bowels, and no motive for the perpetration of the crime appeared, there was not sufficient evidence to authorize a conviction.

In Osborne *v.* State, 64 Miss. 318, where it appeared that the accused gave a powder to a boy, telling him to mix it with a spoon for A, as he hated A and wanted to kill him, and on the boy's refusal, the accused did it himself and members of A's family ate it and became very sick, but did not die, it was held that it did not sufficiently appear that the powder, which the accused called "Rough on Rats," was poisonous.

In La Beau *v.* People, 34 N. Y. 223, it was held competent, on a trial for poisoning, to show that the accused had threatened the deceased with injury from other instruments, as for example, a slung shot, the evidence tending to show intent.

So in Rex *v.* Mogg, 4 Car. & P. 364, it was held on the question of intent that it might be shown that poison was administered to the injured person at other times than that charged in the indictment.

Where, on the trial of an indictment for murder by poisoning A, it appeared that A had procured insurance in his wife's favor; that the wife died after a short illness; that A then made the defendant his beneficiary; that, in a few days, A died from the effects of arsenic, and that the defendant received the insurance money; and evidence was introduced tending to show

POLICE COURTS.—See JUSTICE OF THE PEACE, vol. 12, p. 391; MUNICIPAL COURTS, vol. 15, p. 1202.

POLICE JUSTICE OR MAGISTRATE—(See also JUSTICE OF THE PEACE, vol. 12, p. 393; MUNICIPAL COURTS, vol. 15, p. 1202).—A magistrate charged exclusively with the duties incident to the common law office of a conservator or justice of the peace, and the prefix "police" serves merely to distinguish them from justices having also civil jurisdiction.[1]

POLICE POWER.—See Index of Cross-References in the notes.

I. **DEFINITION.**—Police power, in its broadest acceptation, means

a scheme on the defendant's part to murder the wife as well as the husband, as a part of the plan to get the money. It was held that evidence tending to show that the defendant poisoned the wife was competent. Com. *v.* Robinson, 146 Mass. 571.

And see also, on questions of evidence, State *v.* Hinkle, 6 Iowa 380; People *v.* Robinson, 2 Park. Cr. (N. Y.) 235; People *v.* Hartung, 4 Park. Cr. (N. Y.) 256; Stephens *v.* People, 4 Park. Cr. (N. Y.) 396; Templeton *v.* People, 27 Mich. 501; Com. *v.* Falvey, 108 Mass. 394.

Expert testimony is competent as to the effect of poisons generally, and in the particular case. State *v.* Bowman, 78 N. Car. 509; State *v.* Hinkle, 6 Iowa 380; State *v.* Cook, 17 Kan. 392; People *v.* Williams, 3 Park. Cr. (N. Y.) 84; People *v.* Hartung, 4 Park. Cr. (N. Y.) 256; Rex *v.* Long, 4 Car. & P. 398.

Conviction and Punishment.—On an indictment for murder, perpetrated by means of poison, the jury can find the prisoner guilty of murder in the second degree; and the court, upon such conviction, will inflict the punishment prescribed by law for the latter offense. State *v.* Dowd, 19 Conn. 388.

Jurisdiction.—Where poison is prescribed and delivered to a person in one county, and such person takes the poison to another county, and there swallows it and dies thereof, the criminal act is commenced in one county and consummated in another county, and the latter county has jurisdiction of the offense, though the accused was never in that county. Robbins *v.* State, 8 Ohio St. 131.

Death by Poison Within an Insurance Policy.—It was held in Cole *v.* Accident Ins. Co., 5 T. R. 370, that a death by poison was none the less such, within an exception in a policy, because the poison was taken accidentally and not intentionally.

1. Wenzler *v.* People, 58 N. Y. 530, Allen J.

the general power of a government to preserve and promote the public welfare, even at the expense of private rights.[1] It is difficult, if not impossible, to define the exact scope of the term. The Supreme court of the *United States* has declined to do so, stating that it would only determine each case as it arose.[2]

1. Cooley's Const. Lim. (6th ed.) p. 704; Tiedeman's Limitations of Police Power, § 1; Patterson's Federal Restraints.

Definitions of Police Power.—Probably the best definition is that given in the case of New Orleans Gas Light Co. *v.* Hart, 40 La. Ann 474; 8 Am. St. Rep. 574, where it is said: "Police power is the right of the State functionaries to prescribe regulations for the good order, peace, protection, comfort and convenience of the community which do not encroach on the like power vested in Congress by the Federal Constitution."

Blackstone defines public police and economy to be "The due regulation and domestic order of the kingdom, whereby the individuals of the State, like members of a well-governed family, are bound to conform their general behavior to the rules of propriety, good neighborhood, and good manners; and to be decent, industrious and inoffensive in their respective stations." 4 Blackstone's Com. 162; Cooley's Const. Lim. 4th ed. 570.

In Com. *v.* Alger, 7 Cush. (Mass.) 84, the court by Shaw, C. J., lays down the doctrine clearly: "We think it is a settled principle growing out of the nature of well ordered civil society, that the holder of property, however absolute and unqualified may be his title, holds it under the implied liability that his use of it shall be so regulated that it shall not be injurious to the equal enjoyment of others having an equal right to the enjoyment of their property, nor injurious to the rights of the community. All property in this commonwealth, as well that in the interior as that bordering on tide waters, is derived directly or indirectly from the government, and held subject to those general regulations which are necessary to the common good and general welfare. Rights of property, like all other social and conventional rights, are subject to such reasonable limitations in their enjoyment as shall prevent them from being injurious, and to such reasonable restraints and regulations established by law as the legislature, under the governing and controlling power vested in them by the constitution may think necessary and expedient."

It is also thus defined: "The conservation of private rights is attained by the imposition of wholesome restraint upon their exercise; such a restraint as will prevent the infliction of injury upon others in the enjoyment of them; it involves a provision and means of enforcing the legal maxim which underlies the fundamental rule of both the human and the national law: *sic utere tuo ut alienum non laedas.* The power of the government to impose this restraint is called police power." Tiedeman's Lim. of Police Power, § 1; Broom's Legal Maxim's, 327.

2. **Scope of the Term.**—In Stone *v.* Mississippi, 101 U. S. 814, the court by Waite, C. J., said: "Many attempts have been made in this court and elsewhere to define the police power, but never with entire success. It is always easier to determine whether a particular case comes within the general scope of the power than to give an abstract definition of the power itself which will be in all respects accurate." See also Boston Beer Co. *v.* Massachusetts, 97 U. S. 25; People *v.* King, 110 N. Y. 423.

Shaw, C. J., in the case of Com. *v.* Alger, 7 Cush. (Mass.) 85, uses the following language: "It is much easier to perceive and realize the existence and sources of this power, than to mark its boundaries, or prescribe limits to its exercise. There are many cases in which such a power is exercised by all well ordered governments, and where its fitness is obvious, that all well regulated minds will regard it as reasonable. Such are the laws to prohibit the use of warehouses for the storage of gunpowder near habitations or highways; to restrain the height to which wooden buildings may be erected in populous neighborhoods, and require them to be covered with slate or other incombustible material; to prohibit

This power has an intimate relation to numerous subjects which

buildings from being used for hospitals for contagious diseases, or for the carrying on of noxious or offensive trades; to prohibit the raising of a dam, and causing stagnant water to spread over meadows, near inhabited villages, thereby raising noxious exhalations, injurious to health and dangerous to life." See also Com. *v.* Tewksbury, 11 Met. (Mass.) 57; People *v.* Draper, 25 Barb. (N. Y.) 374; *affirmed* 15 N. Y. 532; Wynehamer *v.* People, 13 N. Y. 378; Hart *v.* Mayor etc. of Albany, 9 Wend. (N. Y.) 571; 24 Am. Dec. 165; License Cases, 5 How. (U. S.) 583; Munn *v.* Illinois, 94 U. S. 113; Indianapolis etc. R. Co. *v.* Kercheval, 16 Ind. 84; New Albany etc. R. Co. *v.* Tilton, 12 Ind. 3; 74 Am. Dec. 195; Mayor etc. of Baltimore *v.* State, 15 Md. 390; Ohio etc. R. Co. *v.* McClelland, 25 Ill. 123; Police Commrs. *v.* Louisville, 3 Bush (Ky.) 597.

Again in Mayor etc. of N. Y. *v.* Miln, 11 Pet. (U. S.) 139, the court by Barbour, J., said: "Every law comes within this description" (of a regulation of police) "which concerns the welfare of the whole people of the State, or any individual within it, whether it relates to their rights or their duties; whether it respects them as men or citizens of the State whether in their public or private relations; whether it relates to the rights of persons or of property of the whole people of the State, or of any individual within it; and whose operation is within the territorial limits of the State, and upon the persons and things within its jurisdiction."

In the case of Thorpe *v.* Rutland etc. R. Co., 27 Vt. 149; 62 Am. Dec. 625, it was thus defined by Redfield, C. J.: "The police power of the State extends to the protection of the life, limbs, health, comfort and quiet of all persons, and protection of all property within the State according to the maxim *sic utere tuo ut alienum non laedas*, which being of universal application, it must, of course, be within the range of legislative action to define the mode and manner in which every person may so use his own as to not injure others. And further, by this general police power of the State, persons and property are subjected to all kinds of restraints and diligence in order to secure general comfort, health, and prosperity of the State. Of the perfect right in the legislature to do which no question ever was, or upon acknowledged principles ever can be, made so far as natural persons are concerned." See also Jefferies *v.* Williams, 5 Exch. 792; Humphries *v.* Brogden, 12 Q. B. 739; Pixley *v.* Clark, 35 N. Y. 520; 91 Am. Dec. 72.

In Hannibal etc. R. Co. *v.* Husen, 95 U. S. 465, it is said: "The police power of a State extends to the protection of the lives, limbs, health, comfort, and quiet of all persons, and to the protection of all property within the State, and hence, to the making of all regulations promotive of domestic order, morals, health, and safety."

Other definitions have been given by courts. Thus in State *v.* Noyes, 47 Me. 211, it is said: "With the legislature the maxim of law *salus populi suprema lex*, should not be disregarded. It is the great principle on which the statutes for the security of the people are based. It is the foundation for criminal law in all governments of civilized countries and of other lands, conducive to safety and consequent happiness of the people. This power has always been exercised by governments and its existence cannot be reasonably denied. How far the provisions of the legislature can extend, is always submitted to its discretion, provided its Acts do not go beyond the great principle of securing the public safety, and its duty to provide for the public safety within well defined limits and with discretion, is imperative. . . All laws for the protection of the lives, limbs, health, and quiet of person, and for the security of all property within the State, fall within this general power of government."

Likewise in Lake View *v.* Rose Hill Cemetery Co., 70 Ill. 192, the court says: "The police power of a State is co-extensive with self-protection and is applicably termed the law of overruling necessity. It is the inherent and plenary power in the State, which enables it to prohibit all things hurtful to the comfort and welfare of society." See also Hale *v.* Lawrence, 21 N. J. L. 714; Tiedeman's Lim. of Police Power, § 1.

are made separate titles in this work, and to avoid duplication of such articles here it need not be treated from its broadest aspect.[1]

1. Police Power Under Different Forms of Government.—Under forms of government where limitations upon executive and legislative power are ill-defined or do not exist at all, the exercise of the police power is subject to no such restrictions as are placed upon it in a constitutional government, like that of the *United States*.[2]

The constitutional provisions which limit the power of the Federal Government to that which is expressly delegated to it, and the State and Federal constitutions, which exclude the State legislatures from the invasion of private and public rights, impose peculiar restraints upon the exercise of police power by either the State or Federal Government.[3]

2. Distinguishable from Power of Eminent Domain.—This power is to be distinguished from the right of eminent domain. Police

1. **Index of Cross-references.**—Police power as conflicting with the power vested in Congress is treated under the subjects: CONSTITUTIONAL LAW, vol. 3, p. 670; DUE PROCESS OF LAW, vol. 6, p. 52; FRANCHISES, vol. 8, p. 620; FREIGHT, vol. 8, p. 906; IMMIGRATION, vol. 9, p. 936; INTOXICATING LIQUORS, vol. 11, p. 587; INTERSTATE COMMERCE, vol. 11, p. 539; NAVIGATION, vol. 12, p. 273; RAILROADS.

Police power as affecting the obligations of contracts is treated under CONSTITUTIONAL LAW, vol. 3, p. 670; CORPORATIONS, vol. 4, p. 212; FOREIGN CORPORATIONS, vol. 8, p. 329; FRANCHISES, vol. 8, p. 620; LICENSE, vol. 13, p. 520; RAILROADS; TRUSTS.

Police power as applied in particular cases is treated in ADULTERATION, vol. 1, p. 207; BOARDS OF HEALTH, vol. 2, p. 431: CONCEALED WEAPONS, vol. 3, p. 408; CORPORATIONS, vol. 4, p. 212; DRAINS AND SEWERS, vol. 6, p. 6; HAWKERS AND PEDDLERS, vol. 9, p. 311; HEALTH, vol. 9, p. 321; HOSPITALS, vol. 9, p. 774; IMMIGRATION, vol. 9, p. 936; IMPOUNDING, vol. 10, p. 187; IMPROVEMENTS, vol. 10, p. 275; INTOXICATING LIQUORS, vol. 11, p. 587; INTERSTATE COMMERCE, vol. 11, p. 539; LICENSE, vol. 13, p. 250; LOTTERIES, vol. 13, p. 1167; MUNICIPAL CORPORATIONS, vol. 15, p. 1166; NAVIGATION, vol. 16, p. 273; NUISANCE, vol. 16, p. 922; ORDINANCES; PHYSICIANS AND SURGEONS; QUARANTINE; RAILROADS; RELIGIOUS SOCIETIES; SUNDAY; THEATRES; TRUSTS; WATER AND WATER COURSES; WEIGHTS AND MEASURES.

2. It is scarcely necessary to say that the form of constitutional government which exists in the *United States* has no exact parallel in other countries. The Magna Charta and other guaranties of the rights of the people in *England* are mere legislative enactments subject to repeal or alteration by the legislature. See 1 Minor's Inst. (3rd ed.), p. 60, 73; 1 Blackstone's Com. 127-8; 4 Minor's Inst. 416. Under such governments, therefore, the proceeding by which the judicial power annuls a statute by declaring it unconstitutional, although passed in an attempted exercise of the police power, is unknown.

"This is the subject of the present work. viz.: Legal limitations upon the police power of American government, National and State. Where can these limitations be found, and in what do they consist? The legislature is clearly the department of the government which can and does exercise the police power, and, consequently, in the limitations upon the legislative power are to be found the limitations of the police power. Whether there be other limitations or not, the most important and the most clearly defined are to be found in the national and State constitutions. Whenever an act of the legislature contravenes a constitutional provision it is void, and it is the duty of the courts so to declare it, and refuse to enforce it." Tiedeman's Limitations of Police Power, § 2.

3. See CONSTITUTIONAL LAW, vol. 3, p. 670, *et seq.*

power is devoted principally to the care and preservation of the public health and morals, and is commonly exercised in restricting the actions of individuals and in regulating their use of property. The right of eminent domain is employed for the advancement of a means of commerce and transportation and for public convenience, and involves always an appropriation of private property. Neither power, however, is confined strictly to such objects.[1]

1. See EMINENT DOMAIN, vol. 6, p. 511, and authorities cited.

To illustrate: A law revoking the charter of a lottery company or prohibiting its continuance, or a law regulating the sale of food or of food products, or forbidding the establishment of fertilizer manufactories within certain limits is an exercise of police power, and might be justifiable on that ground alone. On the other hand, a law granting a certain railway company a right of way, or establishing a new road through the lands of a private person, would be an exercise of the right of eminent domain. In one there is an appropriation of private property for public use, and a compensation for it—in the other, there is neither, but generally instead, only a restriction upon the actions of individuals. See Cooley's Const. Lim. (4th ed.), ch. 15, 16; Stone *v.* Mississippi, 101 U. S. 814; Philadelphia *v.* Scott, 81 Pa. St. 80; 22 Am. Rep. 758; EMINENT DOMAIN, vol. 6, p. 511, *et seq.*

In Com. *v.* Alger, 7 Cush. (Mass.) 84. where a law prohibiting riparian freeholders from building wharves beyond a certain limit was under discussion, the court by Shaw, C. J., said: "This is very different from the right of eminent domain, the right of a government to take and appropriate private property to public use, whenever the public exigency requires it; which can be done only on condition of providing a reasonable compensation therefor. The power we allude to is rather the police power, the power vested in the legislature by the constitution, to make, ordain and establish all manner of wholesome and reasonable laws, statutes and ordinances, either with penalties or without, not repugnant to the constitution, as they shall judge to be for the good and welfare of the commonwealth, and of the subjects of the same."

As was said in the case of Bancroft *v.* Cambridge, 126 Mass. 438, 441, laws passed in the legitimate exercise of the police power of a State cannot be considered as obnoxious to constitutional provisions merely because they do not provide compensation to the individual who is inconvenienced by them. He is presumed to be rewarded by the common benefits secured.

This distinction is again seen in the case of Com. *v.* Tewksbury, 11 Met. (Mass.) 55. It appeared that a statute imposed a penalty on any person who should take, carry away, or remove any stones, gravel, or sand from any of the beaches in the town of Chelsea. Defendant was indicted for a violation of this statute and on the trial pleaded that he was the owner of the land in fee; that no condemnation proceedings had been held to deprive him of his property in it and no compensation rendered to him. It was held, however, that the act was an exercise of police power intended for the protection of the harbor of Boston, and not an exercise of eminent domain. Therefore, no condemnation proceedings were necessary, nor could compensation be claimed.

See generally McElroy *v.* Kansas City, 21 Fed. Rep. 257; Blanchard *v.* Kansas, 16 Fed. Rep. 444; Werth *v.* Springfield, 78 Mo. 107; Johnson *v.* Parkersburg, 16 W. Va. 402; Chambers *v.* Cincinnati R. Co., 69 Ga. 320. *Compare* White *v.* Yazoo City, 27 Miss. 357.

Appropriating Private Property for Public Improvements.—In the case of Hollingsworth *v.* Parish of Tensas, 17 Fed. Rep. 109, it is said that private property can only be taken, appropriated or damaged for public use through the exercise of the single principle of eminent domain, which in all cases carried with it the right of just idemnity. Therefore, under the exercise of its general police power, which extends only to the regulation of the owner's use and dominion of private property, a State cannot for levee or

Where private property is destroyed to prevent the spread of fire, under statutes or ordinances authorizing such destruction, it seems to be the better doctrine that it is a case of the exercise of police power and of eminent domain, and therefore there can be no compensation unless specially provided for by statute.[1]

3. Distinguishable from Power of Taxation.—A law which might be invalid as an exercise of the right to tax for revenue might be sustainable where its purpose was the promotion of the general public health or morals. In exercising the power of taxation, no

other public purposes take, appropriate, or damage private property, so as to deprive the owner of its dominion, use, control and profits, and especially without due compensation being first paid.

But it is doubtful whether this last view of the subject can be sustained. See Bass *v.* State, 34 La. Ann. 499; Com. *v.* Alger, 7 Cush. (Mass.) 84, which latter case has been many times cited with approval. See also Philadelphia *v.* Scott, 81 Pa. St. 80; 22 Am. Rep. 738; Meeker *v.* Van Rensselaer, 15 Wend. (N. Y.) 397. Also MUNICIPAL CORPORATIONS, vol. 15, pp. 1161, 1162.

In the case of Green *v.* Swift, 47 Cal. 536, the legislature had established a board of "city levee commissioners" who were empowered to "turn or straighten" the channel of the American River. It appeared that during a certain season of the year this river was liable to overflow, and that thereby the safety of the city of Sacramento was seriously endangered. The Board in conformity to their instructions, changed the bed of the river to a considerable extent, the doing of which involved a virtual destruction of a portion of plaintiff's premises. Upon his bringing suit for damages the court held that it was within the State's police power to authorize such proceedings since they were necessary for the safety of a large class of people. That although private property had been virtually appropriated, it had been by the exercise of police power, and, therefore, the party was not entitled to compensation. See same principle in Zimmerman *v.* Union Canal Co., 1 W. & S. (Pa.), 346.

These cases would therefore seem to contradict the doctrine stated in the case of Hollingsworth *v.* Parish of Tensas, 17 Fed. Rep. 109, so far as it defines such narrow limits to the exercise of police power.

1. Municipal Liability for Destruction of Private Property to Prevent the Spread of Fire.—There is some conflict of authority upon this question. There are several cases in which the right of one person to destroy the property of another on the ground of urgent necessity, without liability for damages, has been sustained. Mouse's Case, 12 Coke 63; Maleverer *v.* Spinke, 1 Dyer 36b; Respublica *v.* Sparhawk, 1 Dall. (U. S.) 337. The principle of these cases is without application where the person destroying property acts under authority given him from the government by statute or a municipal ordinance. Principle, as well as the great weight of authority, seems to favor the view that such taking of property is an exercise of police power justified by the maxim *salus populi suprema lex* and not of eminent domain and, therefore, there can be no recovery by the party suffering. Keller *v.* Corpus Christi, 50 Tex. 614; Field *v.* Des Moines, 39 Iowa 575; Russell *v.* Mayor etc. of N. Y., 2 Den. (N. Y.) 461; Philadelphia *v.* Scott, 81 Pa. St. 80, 85; Surocco *v.* Geary, 3 Cal. 69; McDonald *v.* Red Wind, 13 Minn. 38; American Print Works *v.* Lawrence, 21 N. J. L. 248; Ruggles *v.* Nantucket, 11 Cush. (Mass.) 433; Dunbar *v.* San Francisco, 1 Cal. 355; Correas *v.* San Francisco, 1 Cal. 452; Hale *v.* Lawrence, 23 N. J. L. 590; Green *v.* Swift, 47 Cal. 536; Bass *v.* State, 34 La. Ann. 499; Bowditch *v.* Boston, 101 U. S. 16, 19; Wynehamer *v.* People, 13 N. Y. 378, 401; White *v.* Charleston, 2 Hill (S. Car.) 571; Taylor *v.* Plymouth, 8 Met. (Mass.) 462; 2 Dillon Mun. Corp., § 955 (757.)

Statutory Compensation for Destroyed Property.—In many States, however, this matter has become to be entirely regulated by statute. The same statute which authorizes the destruction of property in such a case also providing for compensation on certain cases. This portion of the subject is discussed

discriminations are to be made; while in the exercise of police power the State is ordinarily to be governed only by considerations of what is for the public welfare.[1]

II. **WHERE LOCATED.**—In the *United States,* the police power belongs to the several States, and not to the Federal Government, except so far as Congress may exercise it over the Territories and the District of Columbia.[2] This principle is not affected by the Fourteenth Amendment, and Congress cannot, in pursuance of it, exercise control over affairs of police in a State. The amendment only authorized Congress to prohibit an infringement by the States of the rights secured to citizens, and this cannot be construed to justify Congressional interference unless a State has attempted to infringe the rights secured.[3] Neither the legislature of a State

in MUNICIPAL CORPORATIONS, vol. 15 pp. 1161, 1162. See also EMINENT DOMAIN, vol. 6, p. 363.

1. Police Power Distinguished from Power of Taxation.—State *v.* Mayor etc. of Hoboken, 33 N. J. L. 280; License Tax Cases, 5 Wall. (U. S.) 462; Cooley's Const. Lim. (4th ed.) 201, 586; 1 Dillon's Mun. Corp., § 357; LICENSE, vol. 13, p. 532; Ash *v.* People, 11 Mich. 347; 83 Am. Dec. 74; Tenney *v.* Lenz, 16 Wis. 566; Mayor etc. *v.* Miln, 11 Pet. (U. S.) 102. *Compare* Brown *v.* Maryland, 12 Wheat. (U. S.) 419.

An example of this difference is seen in the case of State *v.* Cassidy, 22 Minn. 312; 21 Am. Rep. 765. The State of *Minnesota* had passed an act requiring all persons dealing in spirituous liquors to take out a special license (in addition to the ordinary license already required), paying therefor the sum of ten dollars, and provided for the enforcement of this law by fine and imprisonment. The act also provided that the money so received should be expended in providing an asylum for the inebriate, etc. The defendants in the case contested the validity of the statute on the ground that it provided for taxation that was discriminating and not uniform. But it was held that it was an exercise of police power and therefore within the power of the State. A power to regulate included the power to license or to tax.

2. United States *v.* DeWitt, 9 Wall. (U. S.) 41 (where it is said that this principle is so well fixed as to be beyond all controversy); License Cases, 5 How. (U. S.) 631; Barbier *v.* Connelly, 113 U. S. 27; Passenger Cases, 7 How. (U. S.) 283; License Tax Cases, 5 Wall. (U. S.) 470; United States *v.* Reese, 92 U. S. 214; United States *v.* Cruikshanks, 92 U. S. 542; Gibbons *v.* Ogden, 9 Wheat. (U. S.) 205; Civil Right Cases, 109 U. S. 3; *Ex parte* Yarborough, 110 U. S. 651; Wilkinson *v.* Rahrer, 140 U. S. 545; Tiedeman's Lim. of Police Power, § 202; CONSTITUTIONAL LAW, vol. 3, p. 675.

Therefore, when Congress passed an act prohibiting the sale of certain kinds of oil, or of oil unable to undergo a fire test, it was held that such act was plainly a police regulation relating exclusively to the internal trade of the State, and, therefore, beyond the power of Congress to pass. It could only be operative within the District of Columbia. United States *v.* DeWitt, 9 Wall. (U. S.) 41.

Power of Congress as to police regulations in the District of Columbia, and other places within its jurisdiction, is granted by art. 1, § 8, par. 17 of the Const. of U. S.; also by art. 4, § 3. See also Cooley's Principles of Const. Law 90; Cohens *v.* Virginia, 6 Wheat. (U. S.) 264, 424; Loughborough *v.* Blake, 5 Wheat. (U. S.) 317, 322.

3. For this reason the act known as the "Civil Rights Bill" was declared unconstitutional. Civil Rights Cases, 109 U. S. 3, where the doctrine of the text is fully sustained. See also CONSTITUTIONAL LAW, vol. 3, p. 728; Cooley's Const. Lim. (4th ed.) 742; Slaughter House Cases, 16 Wall. (U. S.) 36.

In United States *v.* Cruikshanks, 92 U. S. 542, the court in its opinion observes that "every republican government is in duty bound to protect its citizens in the enjoyment of an equality of right. That duty was originally assumed by the States and it still re-

nor the State itself can, by contract or otherwise, part irrevocably with its right to exercise the police power.[1]

Police power can only be exercised by legislative enactment, and it rests solely within legislative discretion to determine when public welfare or safety requires its exercise.[2] Courts are authorized to interfere and declare a statute unconstitutional only when it conflicts with the constitution; with the wisdom, policy, or necessity of such an enactment they have nothing to do.[3] But while such are the legislative functions, there must always be a reason for the exercise of the power, and rights guaranteed by Federal or State constitutions cannot be violated by the mere declaration that an occupation or any particular act is injurious to the public

mains there, the only obligation resting upon the United States government is to see that the States do not deny the right."

1. Stone *v.* Mississippi, 101 U. S. 814 (a statute revoking the charter of a lottery company held constitutional); Boston Beer Co. *v.* Massachusetts, 97 U. S. 25; Richmond etc. R. Co. *v.* Richmond, 96 U. S. 521; Butchers' Union etc. Co. *v.* Crescent City etc. Co., 111 U. S. 746; Toledo etc. R. Co. *v.* Jacksonville, 67 Ill. 37; 16 Am. Rep. 611; Dingman *v.* People, 51 Ill. 277; Thorpe *v.* Rutland etc. R. Co., 27 Vt. 140; 62 Am. Dec. 625. In this last case and the one preceding, the question was discussed as to whether a railroad company might be compelled to submit to certain statutory regulations notwithstanding such regulations were a *quasi* violation of their charter, and in both cases the right of the State to exercise this police power was upheld.

This question is also noted at some length in the article FRANCHISES, vol. 8, p. 621, *et seq.*, and the distinction between the principles stated in the text and the principles laid down in the famous Dartmouth College *v.* Woodward, 4 Wheat. (U. S.) 518, *i. e.*, that a corporation's charter is a contract the obligation of which may not be impaired by statute, is there stated. See also CORPORATIONS, vol. 4, p. 212.

2. Tiedeman's Lim. of Police Power, § 2; Lake View *v.* Rose Hill Cemetery Co., 70 Ill. 192; Toledo etc. R. Co. *v.* Jacksonville, 67 Ill. 37; 16 Am. Rep. 611; Munn *v.* Illinois, 94 U. S. 113.

See also *supra*, this title, *Police Power under Different Forms of Government.*

3. **Interference of the Courts.**—In Munn *v.* People, 69 Ill. 93, the court observes: "We have nothing to do with the policy of the enactment; that was a question exclusively within the jurisdiction of the legislative assembly, which under no circumstances has the judicial department a right to question or arraign." And the same view is upheld in many cases. Lake View *v.* Rose Hill Cemetery Co., 70 Ill. 192; Bepley *v.* State, 4 Ind. 264; 58 Am. Dec. 628, note; Goddard *v.* Jacksonville, 15 Ill. 588; 60 Am. Dec. 773; Soon Hing *v.* Crowley, 113 U. S. 703, 710.

It is an established principle in this country that so long as the legislature does not pass the limits fixed by the constitution, the courts have no authority to interfere on the ground that the legislative acts in question violate the natural principles of justice and right. Tiedeman's Lim. Police Power, § 2; State *v.* Wheeler, 25 Conn. 290; People *v.* Toynbee, 2 Park. Cr. (N. Y.) 329; Wynehamer *v.* People, 13 N. Y. 378; Cooley's Const. Lim. (4th ed.) 168; Bertholf *v.* O'Reilly, 74 N. Y. 509; Butler *v.* Palmer, 1 Hill (N. Y.) 324; Doe *v.* Douglass, 8 Blackf. (Ind.) 10; Stein *v.* Mayor etc. of Mobile, 24 Ala. 614; Boston *v.* Cummins, 16 Ga. 102; 60 Am. Dec. 917; Hamilton *v.* St. Louis Co. Ct., 15 Mo. 23; Guilford *v.* Chenango Co., 13 N. Y. 143.

In People *v.* Toynbee, 2 Park. Cr. (N. Y.) 329, the court observes: "The doctrine that there exists in the judiciary, some vague, loose, and undefined power to annul a law because in its judgment it is contrary to natural law and equity, is in conflict with the first principles of government, and can, I think, never be maintained."

Likewise, Black, J., in Sharpless *v.* Mayor etc. of Philadelphia, 21 Pa. St. 147; 59 Am. Dec. 759, observed: "A law if not prohibited is not void because

welfare.[1] In like manner, although power may be delegated to a municipal corporation to control its internal police, and ordinances or by-laws passed in pursuance thereof have the effect of legislative acts,[2] a municipal corporation is equally prohibited from an arbitrary exercise of police power under the pretense that it is essential to the public welfare.[3]

III. **Manner of Exercise.**—The police power of a State may be exercised by the entire or partial prohibition of a particular business regarded as injurious, such as a lottery; but more commonly it is exercised by imposing taxes or penalties to discourage or restrict occupations or practices deemed injurious.[4]

it violates the spirit of our institutions, or impairs any of those objects which it is the object of a free government to protect."

The whole doctrine is thus summed up: "It is the province of the law making power to determine when the exigency exists for calling into exercise the police power of the State; but what are the subjects of this exercise is clearly a judicial question." Lake View *v.* Rose Hill Cemetery Co., 70 Ill. 192.

1. Thus, where the legislature of *New York* passed a statute making it a misdemeanor to manufacture cigars in cities of more than 500,000 inhabitants in any tenement-house occupied by more than three families, except on the first floor of such house on which there is a store for the sale of cigars and tobacco, it was held that the act was an arbitrary exercise of power violative of the rights guaranteed by the constitution and not warranted by the constitution. *In re* Jacobs, 33 Hun (N. Y.) 374; affd. 98 N. Y. 98; 50 Am. Rep. 636.

The facts in the case and not the act of the legislature constitute any property or action a nuisance. Butcher's Union etc. Co. *v.* Crescent City etc. Co., 111 U. S. 746; Wynehamer *v.* People, 13 N. Y. 378; Pumpelly *v.* Green Bay Co., 13 Wall. (U. S.) 166.

For this reason an ordinance of the city council of Stockton forbidding the establishment of public laundries within the city was held unconstitutional. *In re* Tie Loy, 26 Fed. Rep. 611. Similar cases are found in Yates *v.* Milwaukee, 10 Wall. (U. S.) 505; Ward *v.* Maryland, 12 Wall. (U. S.) 430; Bepley *v.* State, 4 Ind. 264; 58 Am. Dec. 628, note.

2. 1 Dillon Mun. Corp., § 141; Com. *v.* Plaisted, 148 Mass. 375; 12 Am. St. Rep. 566; Cranston *v.* Augusta, 61 Ga. 572; Municipal Corporations, vol. 15, p. 1167, *et seq.*

Therefore, the power cannot be delegated or bargained away, nor can the corporation by any contract hamper itself in the exercise of it. Gale *v.* Kalamazoo, 23 Mich. 344; 9 Am. Rep. 80; Pontiac *v.* Carter, 32 Mich. 171; Brimmer *v.* Boston, 102 Mass. 19; State *v.* Cincinnati Gas Light etc. Co., 18 Ohio St. 262; Birdsall *v.* Clark, 73 N. Y. 73; 29 Am. Rep. 105; Brooklyn *v.* Breslin, 57 N. Y. 591. *Compare* Hitchcock *v.* Galveston, 96 U. S. 341.

In the case of Pickles *v.* McLellan Dry Dock Co., 38 La. Ann. 412, it is held that under the police power of the State the legislature may abrogate the powers conferred on one municipality or police-jury and confer them on another. The act under consideration was the *Louisiana* Act, April 27th, 1870, which in effect gave the city of New Orleans control of the right bank of the Mississippi in Algiers, and consequently, exclusive right to the allotment of space therein for a public ferry.

3. Therefore, the city council cannot by an ordinance declaring such acts or property a nuisance make it such. This must be determined by recognized principles, and in cases of doubt it is a matter for the determination of the court. Yates *v.* Milwaukee, 10 Wall. (U. S.) 497; Wreford *v.* People, 14 Mich. 41; State *v.* Street Commrs. of Trenton, 36 N. J. L. 283; Everett *v.* Council Bluffs, 46 Iowa 66; *Ex parte* O'Leary, 65 Miss. 80; Cooley's Const. Lim., 6th ed. 741, note. See also Hawkins Point Light-house Case, 39 Fed. Rep. 87; Yazoo etc. R. Co. *v.* Board of Levee Commrs., 37 Fed. Rep. 24.

4. Examples of the absolute prohibition may be seen in the suppression

IV. Subjects for Its Exercise—1. Preservation of the Public Health.—Health[1] being the *sine qua non* of all personal enjoyment, it is not only the right, but the duty of a State to pass such laws as may be necessary for the preservation of the health of the people. For this purpose a State may forbid or restrict such trades and pursuits, or such uses of private property, as might prove injurious to the health of the community. The following are examples of police regulations for this purpose which have been held valid: Forbidding slaughtering of cattle except within certain limits;[2] forbidding the adulteration of food products,[3] or

of lotteries, the prohibition of the pursuit of any trade or calling on Sunday, and similar instances. See Stone *v.* Mississippi, 101 U. S. 814; *Ex parte* Andrews, 18 Cal. 685; SUNDAY. An example of partial prohibition may be seen in the regulation of the sale of intoxicating liquors. See INTOXICATING LIQUORS, vol. 11, p. 592–634.

License.—Under the article LICENSE, vol. 13, p. 532, the whole subject of restriction of occupations or pursuits by means of taxes or penalties is reviewed. See also Tiedeman's Lim. of Police Power, § 101; Leavenworth *v.* Booth, 15 Kan. 627; Cooley's Const. Lim. (4th ed.) pp. 201, 495, 586; Ash *v.* People, 11 Mich. 347; 83 Am. Dec. 740; Walters *v.* Duke, 31 La. Ann. 668; MUNICIPAL CORPORATIONS, vol. 15, p. 1173.

1. See generally HEALTH, vol. 9, p. 320.

2. Villavaso *v.* Barthet, 39 La. Ann. 247; Butchers' Union etc. Co. *v.* Crescent City etc. Co., 111 U. S. 746; Slaughter House Cases, 16 Wall. (U. S.) 36; New Orleans *v.* Stafford, 27 La. Ann. 417; 21 Am. Rep. 563; Gale *v.* Kalamazoo, 23 Mich. 344; 9 Am. Rep. 80; Watertown *v.* Mayo, 109 Mass. 315; 12 Am. Rep. 694; Gall *v.* Cincinnati, 18 Ohio St. 563; Spaulding *v.* Lowell, 23 Pick. (Mass.) 71; Wartman *v.* Philadelphia, 33 Pa. St. 202; Cooley's Const. Lim. (4th ed.) 596. *Compare* Blydenburg *v.* Miles, 39 Conn. 485. See also MARKETS, vol. 14, p. 459.

It has also the right to change the designated districts for such business, if the slaughter houses established under its previous authority should become nuisances to the surrounding neighborhood. Villavaso *v.* Barthet, 39 La. Ann. 247.

The law which forbids, under a penalty, the keeping of a private market within six squares of a public market, has been held to be neither repealed nor unconstitutional. State *v.* Natal, 39 La. Ann. 439.

Compare, Gale *v.* Kalamazoo, 26 Mich. 344; 9 Am. Rep. 80.

3. ADULTERATION, vol. 1, p. 207, and cases cited. See also State *v.* Campbell, 64 N. H. 492; People *v.* West, 44 Hun (N. Y.) 162; People *v.* Arensberg, 105 N. Y. 123; 59 Am. Rep. 483; Butler *v.* Chambers, 36 Minn. 69; Waterbury *v.* Newton, 50 N. J. L. 534.

Oleomargarine.—The act of *New Hampshire*, 1885, prohibiting the sale of imitation butter, unless colored pink, being intended to prevent fraud on the public in the sale of provisions, is within the police power of the State. State *v.* Marshall, 64 N. H. 549.

Maryland Acts 1884, ch. 213, requiring all oleomargarine sold to be stamped as such, is plainly within the constitutional power of the legislature. Pierce *v.* State, 63 Md. 592.

Pennsylvania Act of 1885, prohibiting the manufacture and sale of oleomargarine or the keeping the same with intent to sell, is a valid exercise of the police power; and the fact that pure oleomargarine may be wholesome is immaterial. Powell *v.* Com., 114 Pa. St. 265; 127 U. S. 679; State *v.* Addington, 12 Mo. App. 214. *Compare*, however, People *v.* Marx, 99 N. Y. 477; 52 Am. Rep. 34, where it is held that a statute prohibiting the manufacture or sale for food of any substitute for butter or cheese produced from pure unadulterated cream or milk is unconstitutional. *Reversing*, 35 Hun (N. Y.) 528; People *v.* Marx, 99 N. Y. 477; 52 Am. Rep. 34. But this case seems itself to have been somewhat modified. People *v.* Arensberg, 105 N. Y. 123; 59 Am. Rep. 483.

The case of Powell *v.* Pennsylvania, 114 Pa. St. 265, must be regarded as a very extreme one. The defendant was engaged in the manufacture and sale

the pollution of the water sources,[1] and requiring every person practicing medicine to obtain a license;[2] regulating the locality of burying grounds,[3] or prohibiting the practice of dangerous or ob-

of oleomargarine. On the trial he offered to prove that this article was made of perfectly pure and wholesome materials and that it was equally wholesome as an article of food as butter made from pure milk; nor was there any attempt to sell the article under a false name or as an adulteration. The case was simply this: that the legislature saw fit to prohibit the manufacture or sale of a pure and wholesome article simply because it was not consonant with their ideas of what was necessary for the public weal. The case of People *v.* Marx, 99 N. Y. 377, decided upon a very similar state of facts, reached a very different conclusion. The latter case is warmly approved in 1 Dillon Munic. Corp., § 142, note.

Watered Milk.—That the sale of milk below a certain standard may be forbidden though it be mixed with pure water is, however, established by several cases. Com. *v.* Waite, 11 Allen (Mass.) 264; 87 Am. Dec. 711; State *v.* Smyth, 14 R. I. 100; 51 Am. Rep. 344; State *v.* Campbell, 64 N. H. 402. See also People *v.* Cipperly, 101 N. Y. 634; *reversing* 34 Hun (N. Y.) 324.

1. **Water Supply.**—An act forbidding the pollution of a reservoir, or of streams which supply it, is an exercise of the police power, and not objectionable as the taking of private property without compensation, although it forbids the introduction of offensive matter into a stream, notwithstanding the water would be purified before reaching the reservoir. State *v.* Wheeler, 44 N. J. L. 88.

The power to provide for the health of citizens, whether in the legislature, or delegated by it to a municipal corporation, authorizes the regulation of the water supply—particularly of cities. And this "power to regulate" includes the power to purchase and maintain water works, or to provide for their establishment otherwise, and in general to pass all ordinances which may be necessary in order to provide a wholesome and abundant supply of pure water. 1 Dillon Mun. Corp., § 146. See also in this connection Livingston *v.* Pippin, 31 Ala. 542; Rome *v.* Cabot, 28 Ga. 50; Hale *v.* Houghton, 8 Mich. 458.

But a municipal corporation owning lands adjacent to a stream may not by virtue of police power so divert the water as to injure other riparian owners; this can only be done by the exercise of the right of eminent domain, which involves the duty to render just compensation. Stein *v.* Burden, 24 Ala. 130; 60 Am. Dec. 453; Fleming's Appeal, 65 Pa. St. 444.

See also Suffield *v.* Hathaway, 44 Conn. 521; 26 Am. Rep. 483; People *v.* McClintock, 45 Cal. 11; MUNICIPAL CORPORATIONS, vol. 15, p. 949. See also HEALTH, vol. 9, p. 322.

2. Orr *v.* Meek, 111 Ind. 40; Dent *v.* West Virginia, 129 U. S. 114.

The State may also prescribe by statute the qualifications of persons wishing to engage in the practice of medicine or surgery. Eastman *v.* State, 109 Ind. 278.

The *Indiana* act of 1887, to regulate the practice of dentistry is a proper exercise of legislative power. Nor is it objectionable in delegating to the Indiana Dental Association the power to name three members of the board of examiners. Wilkins *v.* State, 113 Ind. 514.

A statute requiring physicians to register, and granting registration upon passing a proper examination, or proof of reputable practice of the profession for five years previous to the enactment of the statute, is a valid exercise of the police power of the State. Richardson *v.* State, 47 Ark. 562.

A statute requiring physicians and midwives to report births and deaths, and imposing a penalty of $10 for each omission, is neither unconstitutional nor unreasonable. Robinson *v.* Hamilton, 60 Iowa 134; 46 Am. Rep. 63. See also PHYSICIANS AND SURGEONS.

3. **Cemeteries.** — Sohier *v.* Trinity Church, 109 Mass. 1; Brick Presbyterian Church *v.* Mayor etc. of N. Y., 5 Cow. (N. Y.) 538; Coates *v.* Mayor etc. of N. Y., 7 Cow. (N. Y.) 585; Woodlawn Cemetery *v.* Everett, 118 Mass. 354; City Council of Charleston *v.* Baptist Church, 4 Strobh. (S. Car.) 306; Kincaid's Appeal, 66 Pa. St. 411; 5 Am. Rep. 377; Craig *v.* First Presbyterian Church, 88 Pa. St. 42; 32 Am. Rep. 417; Reg. *v.* Justices, 5 El. & B.

noxious professions;[1] or compelling the clearing and drainage of lands which might otherwise create malarial or other diseases;[2] or providing in any other reasonable way for the preservation of the public health.[3]

2. Preservation of the Public Morals.—The preservation of the public morals is an object of scarcely less importance than that of the public health, and laws for this purpose are a very proper exercise of police power. Under this division would be classed statutes suppressing lotteries,[4] prohibiting or restricting the sale

702. See also CEMETERIES vol. 3, pp. 49–50; HEALTH, vol. 9, p. 323.

But this right is not to be abused. See Lakeview *v.* Rose Hill Cemetery Co., 70 Ill. 191. Thus an act providing that lands held by a city for burial purposes may be devoted to other public uses, when in the opinion of the city council the public good will be served thereby, cannot be upheld as an exercise of the police power of the State to protect the public health, as it confers on the city council general power to divert land from use as a burial ground to any other purpose, without reference to the requirements of the public health. Stockton *v.* Mayor etc. of Newark, 42 N. J. Eq. 531.

Removal of Dead Bodies.—A statute of *California* made it an offense to disinter or remove from the place of burial the remains of any deceased person without a permit, for which a fee of ten dollars must be paid. In the case of *In re* Wang Yung Quy, 6 Sawy. (U. S.) 442, it was held that this statute did not interfere with the right of Congress to control interstate or foreign commerce, and that it did not conflict with the provision of the fourteenth amendment which prohibits any State from denying to any person within its jurisdiction the equal protection of its laws. It was a sanitary measure within the police power of the State, and therefore constitutional and valid.

See generally, DEAD BODY, vol. 5, p. 115.

1. Taylor *v.* State, 35 Wis. 298; Sedg. on Stat. and Const. Law 512; Regents *v.* Williams, 9 Gill & J. (Md.) 365.

The legislature may forbid a person to undertake a dangerous business except at his own risk, and may forbid entirely a hazardous or pernicious business, even though it may affect prior contracts. Kirby *v.* Pennsylvania R. Co., 76 Pa. St. 506; People *v.* Hawley, 3 Mich. 330.

2. DRAINS AND SEWERS, vol 6, p. 7; Winslow *v.* Winslow, 95 N. Car. 25; Donnelly *v.* Decker, 58 Wis. 461; 46 Am. Rep. 637.

3. A statute of a State which provides that "the board of health in each seaport town may at any time cause a vessel arriving in such port, when such vessel or cargo thereof is, in its opinion, foul or infected, so as to endanger the public health, to be removed to the quarantine ground, and thoroughly purified at the expense of the owners, consignees or persons in possession of the same," is within the police power of the State. Train *v.* Boston Disinfecting Co., 144 Mass. 523; 59 Am. Rep. 113. Nor are such laws obnoxious to any constitutional provision, because they do not provide compensation. Train *v.* Boston Disinfecting Co., 144 Mass. 523; 59 Am. Rep. 113.

In granting an exclusive franchise to supply water to one of its cities and its inhabitants, the legislature of the State does not part with the police power and duty of protecting the public health. Stein *v.* Bienville Water Supply Co., 34 Fed. Rep. 145.

See also BOARD OF HEALTH, vol. 2, p. 429; QUARANTINE.

4. Stone *v.* Mississippi, 101 U. S. 814; Moore *v.* State, 48 Miss. 147.

LOTTERIES, vol. 13, pp. 1169, *et seq.* The subject of lotteries is discussed at length in a note to Yellowstone Kit *v.* Alabama, 7 Lawy. Rep. Ann. 599.

As elsewhere stated this power is not to be abused. Thus it is held that a statute of *New York* prohibiting the sale or disposal of any article of food on an inducement that anything else will be delivered to the purchasers as a gift, prize, premium, or reward, is unconstitutional. It is not a valid exercise of the police power nor of the legislative power to enact what shall amount to a crime, and it is violative of

of injurious drugs,[1] or intoxicating liquors,[2] or requiring the suppression or destruction of obscene books and pictures,[3] or of improper games or amusements,[4] or prohibiting polygamous or incestuous marriages,[5] or providing for the observance of Sunday,[6] and all other regulations having for their object the improvement of public morals.[7]

the constitutional provision securing to every person liberty and property unless he is deprived thereof by due process of law. People *v.* Gillson, 109 N. Y. 389.

Gambling.—The police power of the State authorizes its legislature to pass all laws necessary for the suppression of all forms of gambling; not only small games in gaming houses and the like, but larger enterprises, *e. g.*, the dealing in futures, option contracts, etc. See Tiedeman's Lim. of Police Powers, §§ 99, 99*a*. GAMBLING CONTRACTS, vol. 8, p. 992. See also GAMING, vol. 8, p. 1033; GAMING HOUSES, vol. 8, p. 1065.

1. State *v.* Ah Chew, 16 Nev. 50; 40 Am. Rep. 488.

An act to regulate the sale of opium and to suppress opium dens, which forbids its sale or gift, except on a physician's prescription, to any persons other than druggists or physicians, is a proper exercise of police power and therefore constitutional. *Ex parte* Yung Jon, 28 Fed. Rep. 308. See also HEALTH, vol. 9, p. 322.

2. INTOXICATING LIQUORS, vol. 11, pp. 588, 589, where this subject is fully discussed. See also Cooley's Const. Lim. (4th ed.) 725; Tiedeman's Lim. of Police Power, § 103; Leisy *v.* Hardin, 135 U. S. 100, where this right is reviewed as subject to the limitation that it shall not infringe upon the power of Congress to regulate interstate and foreign commerce.

See also a later case, *In re* Rahrer, 43 Fed. Rep. 556.

The legislature of *Kansas* passed an act providing for the prohibition of manufacture within her limits of all intoxicating liquors. It was held in a case arising under it that the statute was a proper exercise of the police power of the State, and was therefore not unconstitutional. The provision of the constitution providing that no person shall be deprived of life, liberty or property without due process of law was considered not to be violated, the court holding that the prohibition simply upon the use of property for purposes that are declared by valid legislation to be injurious to the health, morals, or safety of the community cannot in any just sense be deemed a taking or appropriation of property for a public benefit. The State cannot be prevented from providing for the discontinuance of any manufacture or traffic which is injurious to the public morals by any incidental inconvenience which individuals or corporations may suffer. The State has power to declare that any place kept and maintained for the illegal manufacture and sale of intoxicating liquors shall be deemed a common nuisance and be abated, and at the same time provide for the enjoyment and control of the offender. Mugler *v.* Kansas, 123 U. S. 623; Kansas *v.* Ziebold, 123 U. S. 623; Our House No. 2 *v.* State, 4 Green (Iowa) 172; State *v.* Donehey, 8 Iowa 396; Lincoln *v.* Smith, 27 Vt. 328; State *v.* Robinson, 33 Me. 568; Boston Beer Co. *v.* Massachusetts, 97 U. S. 32; Foster *v.* Kansas, 112 U. S. 201.

3. Cooley's Const. Lim. (4th ed.) 596.

A license tax may be required to be paid for the privilege of selling publications deemed to be immoral in their influence. Thompson *v.* State, 17 Tex. App. 253.

4. Tanner *v.* Trustees of Albion, 5 Hill (N. Y.) 121; 40 Am. Dec. 337; Com. *v.* Colton, 8 Gray (Mass.) 488; State *v.* Hay, 29 Me. 457; State *v.* Freeman, 38 N. H. 426; Wallack *v.* Mayor of N. Y., 3 Hun (N.Y.) 87.

5. Reynolds *v.* United States, 98 U. S. 145.

6. See SUNDAY; Lindenmuller *v.* People, 33 Barb. (N. Y.) 576.

7. Thus the exhibitions of stallions in public places may be prohibited. Nolin *v.* Mayor of Franklin, 4 Yerg. (Tenn.) 163.

It is upon this ground (*i. e.*, the promotion of the public morals) that statutes providing for peculiar respect to divine services, etc., may be sus-

3. **Regulation of Business Enterprises.**—It is a difficult question to determine when police regulations intended to prevent extortion are valid. No satisfactory criterion has been established as yet. At common law, regulations of the charges to be made by ferrymen, common carriers, hackmen, bakers, millers, wharfingers, and perhaps others existed,[1] and the validity of similar regulations, as proper exercises of a State's police power, is not now doubted.[2] The criterion suggested by the leading

tained. See *Ex parte* Andrews, 18 Cal. 678.

Thus the *Illinois* Crim. Code, § 59, makes it an offense to vend refreshments at a camp-meeting without the consent of those in charge thereof, with a proviso that one having a regular place of business there shall not be required to suspend it. Such is a valid police regulation, and not in restraint of trade, nor invalid as authorizing the camp-meeting authorities to license. Meyers *v.* Baker, 120 Ill. 567; 60 Am. Rep. 580.

Massachusetts St. 1867, ch. 59, so far as it prohibits a person, during the time of holding a camp or field meeting for religious purposes, and within one mile of the place thereof, from establishing or maintaining a building for vending provisions or refreshments, without permission from the authorities or officers having the charge or direction of the meeting, provided that a person having a regular, usual, and established place of business within such limits is not required to suspend his business, is constitutional. Com. *v.* Bearse, 132 Mass. 542; 42 Am. Rep. 450. And it is not necessary to the maintenance of an indictment under such statute to show that there was a formal organization of the meeting, or that notice of its existence was given to defendant. Com. *v.* Bearse, 132 Mass. 542; 42 Am. Rep. 450. See also State *v.* Read, 12 R. I. 135.

Obscenity.—See OBSCENITY, vol. 17, p. 5. See also as to obscene language *Ex parte* Slattery, 3 Ark. 484; *Ex parte* Delaney, 43 Cal. 478.

Bawdy-houses. — The legislature may regulate or absolutely suppress all houses of ill fame as tending to subvert the morals of the community. State *v.* Williams, 11 S. Car. 288. See also DISORDERLY HOUSES, vol. 5, p. 695 *et seq.*

1. Munn *v.* Illinois, 94 U. S. 113. See also Chicago etc. R. Co. *v.* Iowa, 94 U. S. 155; Peik *v.* Chicago etc. R. Co., 94 U. S. 164; Chicago etc. R. Co. *v.* Ackley, 94 U. S. 199; Winona etc. R. Co. *v.* Blake, 94 U. S. 180; Stone *v.* Winconsin, 94 U. S. 181.

See generally, Cooley's Const. Lim. (6th ed.) 734; Tiedeman Lim. of Police Power, § 93.

Extortion.—A common instance of the exercise of police power to prevent extortion is seen in laws regulating the rate of interest upon money. These have been known to exist from the earliest times. Cooley's Cons. Lim. (6th ed.) 235. See also INTEREST vol. 11, p. 379; USURY.

2. See FREIGHT, vol. 8, p. 907, *et seq.*; CORPORATIONS, vol. 4, p. 209; FRANCHISES, vol. 8, p. 620; INTERSTATE COMMERCE, vol. 11, p. 553.

This doctrine was first laid down in the leading case of Munn *v.* People, 69 Ill. 80; affd. 94 U. S. 113, and this case has been cited and approved many times since. People *v.* Boston etc. R. Co., 70 N. Y. 569; Bertholf *v.* O'Reilly, 74 N. Y. 509; Buffalo etc. R. Co. *v.* Buffalo etc. R. Co., 111 N. Y. 132; People *v.* King, 110 N. Y. 418; Nash *v.* Paige, 80 Ky. 539; Hockett *v.* State, 105 Ind. 250; Chesapeake Teleph. Co. *v.* Baltimore etc. Tel. Co., 66 Md. 399; Davis *v.* State, 68 Ala. 58; Louisville etc. R. Co. *v.* Railroad Commission, 19 Fed. Rep. 679; FREIGHT, vol. 8, p. 908. The most prominent late case is People *v.* Budd, 117 N. Y. 1, where the same principal was laid down. See also 24 Am. Law Review, 908 for a discussion of these cases.

See further as sustaining the principles stated in the text. Com. *v.* Stodder, 2 Cush. (Mass.) 562; 48 Am. Dec. 609; City Council *v.* Pepper, 1 Rich. (S. Car.) 364; Morrill *v.* State, 38 Wis. 428; 20 Am. Rep. 12; Cooley's Const. Lim. (4th ed.) 743; Arnutt *v.* Inglis, 12 East 577; Bolt *v.* Stennett, 8 T. Rep. 606; Mayor etc. of Mobile *v.* Yuille, 3 Ala. 140; 36 Am. Dec. 441. (In this case the stat-

case[1] is that such regulations are valid when they relate to a business "affected with a public interest;" but it is evidently difficult, if not impossible, to classify the different kinds of business as within or without this rule[2].

It is by virtue of this power that the legislature may limit the hours of labor of women and children in manufacturing establishments, and also provide for the manner in which they are to be paid.[3] It may also authorize municipal corporations to pass ordinances regulating the weight of bread, and in one case it is said even its price.[4]

4. Civil Rights.—The regulation of the civil rights of individuals is unquestionably a proper subject for the exercise of a State's police power, and laws passed to effect such regulation have been uniformly held constitutional and valid, except in extreme cases.[5] The common instances of its exercise in this respect are seen in statutes intended to secure to all persons, regardless of race or color, equal privileges and accommodations at all places of public entertainment or amusement, such as inns, restaurants and

ute regulating the price of bread was upheld). Lord Hale's Treatise *De Portibus Maris*, 1 Harg. Law Tracts, 78.

1. Munn *v.* Illinois, 69 Ill. 80; affirmed 94 U. S. 113.

2. Cooley, J., names the following cases in which property and business may be said to be affected with a public interest:

1. Where the business is one, the following of which is not of right, but is permitted by the State as a privilege or franchise. Under this head would be comprised the business of setting up lotteries, giving shows, of keeping billiard-tables for hire, and of selling intoxicating drinks when a sale by unlicensed parties is forbidden; also the case of toll-bridges, etc.

2. Where the State on public grounds renders to the business special assistance by taxation or otherwise.

3. Where for the accommodation of the business some special use is allowed to be made of public property or of a public easement.

4. Where exclusive privileges are granted in consideration of some special return to be made to the public. Cooley's Const. Lim. (4th ed.) 594. To these may be added:

5. Those employments which are *quasi* public and tend to the business of the country, but of which circumstances give to a few persons a virtual monopoly of each important commercial center, such as those who own elevators for the storage of grain in the city of Chicago. Munn *v.* Illinois, 94 U. S. 113.

6. The case of money loans. This last is an exception difficult to defend on principle, but the power to regulate the rate of interest has been employed from the earliest days and has been too long acquiesced in to be questioned now. Cooley's Principles of Const. Law, 235.

3. Com. *v.* Hamilton Mfg. Co., 120 Mass. 383.

A statute of *Maryland* requiring that the employes of a certain corporation shall not be paid otherwise than in legal tender money of the United States, the whole amount of their wages was upheld in the case of Shaffer *v.* Union Min. Co., 55 Md. 74.

4. Tanner *v.* Trustees of Albion, 5 Hill (N. Y.) 121; 40 Am. Dec. 337; Paige *v.* Fazackerly, 36 Barb. (N. Y.) 392. An ordinance regulating the price of bread was sustained in Mayor etc. of Mobile *v.* Yuille, 3 Ala. 139; 36 Am. Dec. 441.

5. This subject has been reviewed in CONSTITUTIONAL LAW, vol. 3, pp. 713, 729, and nothing more than later decisions, presenting slightly different phases of the same question need be mentioned here. See, as sustaining the doctrine of the text, Cooley's Const. Lim. (6th ed.) 733, 734. Civil Rights Cases, 109 U. S. 3 (where the principle was laid down that the power to regulate civil rights of individuals resided with the States and with them alone;

theatres;[1] also laws providing for separate schools for the different races, and separate accommodations by common carriers.[2]

and that Congress could not interfere or provide for such regulation). Tiedeman's Lim. of Police Power, pp. 194, *et. seq.*; People *v.* King, 110 N. Y. 418.

1. A fair sample of such statutes may be seen in that of *New York*, where it is provided that, "No citizen of this State can, by reason of race, color, or previous condition of servitude, be excluded from the equal enjoyment of any condition, facility, or privilege furnished by inn-keepers, or common carriers, or by owners, managers, or lessees of theaters or other places of amusement, or by teachers and officers of common schools and public institutions of learning, or by cemetery associations." Any violation of this section is made a misdemeanor. *New York* Penal Code, § 383. The constitutionality of this statute is upheld in the case of People *v.* King, 110 N. Y. 418.

In the case of Donnell *v.* State, 48 Miss. 661, 12 Am. Rep. 675, a statute providing that negroes shall have equal privileges at all public places was held constitutional. It appeared that a negro was admitted to a theater, but that the owner refused to give him a seat in a particular part of the building upon the ground that the pecuniary value of the seats adjacent would be materially affected. He offered, however, to give him an equally attractive seat in another portion of the building. Such action on the part of the owner of the theater was considered a violation of the statute. This case is criticized in Tiedeman's Lim. of Police Power, 232.

Mr. Cooley upholds the constitutionality of such laws in the following language: "Theaters and other places of public amusement exist wholly under the authority and protection of the State laws. Their managers are commonly licensed by the State, and in conferring the license it is no doubt competent for the State to impose a condition that the proprietors shall admit and accommodate all persons impartially. Therefore, such regulation corresponding to this established by Congress must be clearly within the competency of the legislature, and might be established as suitable regulations of police. Cooley on Torts, p. 285.

Many other cases uphold the constitutionality of similar acts. See Ferguson *v.* Gies, 82 Mich. 358; Custard *v.* Poston (Ky. 1886), 1 S. W. Rep. 451; Baylies *v.* Curry, 30 Ill. App. 105; affd. 128 Ill. 287; Messenger *v.* State, 25 Neb. 674 (barber-shop); People *v.* Board of Education, 127 Ill. 613; McGuinn *v.* Forbes, 37 Fed. Rep. 639.

But in the case of District of Columbia *v.* Saville, 1 McArthur (D. C.) 581; 29 Am. Rep. 616, a statute forbidding the owner of a theater to reserve particular seats in any portion of his building to any particular individual, or to mark such seats as reserved by the sale of tickets previous to the opening of the exhibition, was held an unconstitutional interference with the rights of private property. But this, it will be observed, was owing to the extreme character of the statute and not to the principle involved.

2. A *Mississippi* statute requiring railway companies to provide separate accommodations in their carriages for white and colored races was upheld so far as it related to railroads transacting business entirely within the State in the case of Louisville etc. R. Co. *v.* State, 66 Miss. 662; affd. 133 U. S. 587; 41 Am. and Eng. R. Cas. 36.

The constitution of *Missouri* requires separate free schools for the education of negro children. Later statutes provided that schools for negro children should be established in any school district where there were fifteen or more ot such children of the required age, and that if in some districts there were less than fifteen, they might attend school in any district in the county where a separate school for negroes was maintained. It was held that this did not conflict with the Fourteenth Amendment of the Federal constitution. Lehew *v.* Brummell (Mo.), 15 S. W. Rep. 765.

A *New York* statute providing for separate schools for white and negro children was upheld in the case of People *v.* Gallagher, 93 N. Y. 438. See also State *v.* McCann, 21 Ohio St. 210; Cory *v.* Carter, 48 Ind. 337; 17 Am. Rep. 738.

An act of *Kentucky* providing for separate schools was upheld in the case of Dawson *v.* Lee, 83 Ky. 49. And such acts have been held valid everywhere. See Roberts *v.* Boston, 5 Cush. (Mass.) 198 (where Shaw, C. J., states the doctrine very clearly).

5. General Welfare.—Under this head may be classed many cases not previously mentioned where the State, for the welfare and safety of its citizens, may authorize the destruction either of animals affected with dangerous diseases, in order to prevent the spread of such diseases,[1] or of such animals as are injurious to the general public, *e. g.*, dogs,[2] or, in certain cases, other domestic ani-

Bertonneau *v.* Directors of City Schools, 3 Wood (U. S.) 177; Ward *v.* Flood, 48 Cal. 36.

The same principle has been upheld in the case of common carriers in West Chester etc. R. Co. *v.* Miles, 55 Pa. St. 209; The Sue, 22 Fed. Rep. 843; Logwood *v.* Memphis etc. R. Co., 23 Fed. Rep. 318; Murphy *v.* Western etc. R. Co., 23 Fed. Rep. 637; Chesapeake etc. R. Co. *v.* Wells, 85 Tenn. 613.

Jurors.—An act of *Maryland* provided that the jurors should be selected from two lists, one made up of the white male taxable inhabitants of the county, and the other of all the names on the poll-books, and that the selection should be made with special reference to intelligence, sobriety and integrity, but with no reference to political opinion. It was held that this act did not discriminate against any persons on account of color, and was, therefore, not contrary to the Fourteenth Amendment. Cooper *v.* State, 64 Md. 40.

Fourteenth Amendment.—It is now well established that this amendment created no new rights whatever, but only extended the operation of existing rights to a certain class of people hitherto excluded, and furnished additional protection to such rights. The power to control and regulate civil rights of citizens is still reserved to the State, except that no distinction may be made between classes on account of race, color, or previous condition of servitude. Barbier *v.* Connelly, 113 U. S. 27; United States *v.* Cruikshanks, 92 U. S. 542; Slaughter-house Cases, 16 Wall. (U. S.) 36; Minor *v.* Happersett, 21 Wall. (U. S.) 162; CONSTITUTIONAL LAW, vol. 3, p. 727.

1. Hannibal etc. R. Co. *v.* Husen, 95 U. S. 465; Salzenstein *v.* Mavis, 91 Ill. 391, both of which cases, while they declare the statutes under question unconstitutional, still admit the right mentioned when properly exercised. See *infra*, this title, *Limitations Upon Its Exercise.*

The *Kansas* statutes of 1881, 1883, and 1884, having for their object the exclusion from the State of cattle having infectious diseases, are a valid exercise of the police power. Missouri Pac. R. Co. *v.* Finley, 38 Kan. 550.

An act of *New Jersey* making animals with contagious and infectious diseases common nuisances, and authorizing their destruction by certain officials under certain conditions, and an act making horses affected by glanders common nuisances, and authorizing their destruction by certain officers, are within the police power of the State. Newark etc. R. Co. *v.* Hunt, 50 N. J. L. 308. See also Yeazel *v.* Alexander, 58 Ill. 254.

A statute which makes one who has in his possession, in Iowa, Texas cattle which have not wintered in the North, liable for damage done by them to other cattle is constitutional and valid. Kimmish *v.* Ball, 129 U. S. 217.

2. Faribault *v.* Wilson, 34 Minn. 254; The Washington *v.* Meigs, 1 McArthur (D. C.) 53; Tenney *v.* Lenz, 16 Wis. 566; Morey *v.* Brown, 42 N. H. 373; Cranston *v.* Augusta, 61 Ga. 572. These last two cases sustain the validity of statutes authorizing the killing of all dogs found without a collar, and the same doctrine is upheld in *Massachusetts*. Tower *v.* Tower, 18 Pick. (Mass.) 262.

A law taxing dogs, and appropriating the proceeds to payment of damage done by dogs to sheep, is a constitutional exercise of police power. Van Horn *v.* People, 46 Mich. 183; 41 Am. Rep. 159; Mitchell *v.* Williams, 27 Ind. 62.

A dog law, as applied to a city, is not unconstitutional in providing for the registration of dogs, and for a fee for keeping, which varies with the sex, and which provides for their summary destruction if found running at large in violation of the law. State *v.* Topeka, 36 Kan. 76; 59 Am. Rep. 529.

In Blair *v.* Forehand, 100 Mass. 136; 1 Am. Rep. 94, it is said that dogs being animals in which the owner has no absolute property, are subject to such regulations as the legislature

mals, even such as are not diseased;[1] or pass laws forbidding houses of inflammable material to be constructed or repaired within certain parts of cities or towns,[2] or the keeping of gunpowder or other explosives in large quantities there,[3] or authorizing the destruction of private property to prevent the spread of a conflagration,[4] of a pestilence or of a hostile army, or other public calamity.[5]

Here also belong statutes or ordinances providing for the regulation of laundries in certain parts of cities;[6] for the abatement

may prescribe, and it is not unconstitutional to authorize their destruction, without previous adjudication, when found at large without being licensed and collared according to the statutory regulation. See also Carter *v.* Dow, 16 Wis. 298; Tiedeman's Lim. of Police Power, § 141 a; *Ex parte* Cooper, 3 Tex. App. 489; Harrington *v.* Miles, 11 Kan. 480. Consult also, in this connection, East Kingston *v.* Towle, 48 N. H. 57; 2 Am. Rep. 174; 97 Am. Dec. 575; State *v.* Lymus, 26 Ohio St. 400; 20 Am. Rep. 772; Ward *v.* State, 48 Ala. 161; 17 Am. Rep. 31.

1. An ordinance prohibiting the keeping of swine within its densely settled portions is not beyond the police power of a city. Com. *v.* Patch, 97 Mass. 221.

As to keeping cows in a city see *In re* Lineham, 72 Cal. 114.

2. The building or repairing of such houses within certain limits may be prohibited, but a house already constructed there cannot be molested. Klingler *v.* Bickel, 117 Pa. St. 326; Salem *v.* Maynes, 123 Mass. 372; Wadleigh *v.* Gilman, 12 Me. 403; 28 Am. Dec. 188; Brady *v.* Northwestern Ins. Co., 11 Mich. 425; Respublica *v.* Duquet, 2 Yeates (Pa.) 493. *Compare* Booth *v.* State, 4 Conn. 65.

It is held, however, that a dwelling house cut up into small apartments, inhabited by a crowd of poor people in a filthy condition calculated to breed disease, is a public nuisance, and may be abated by individuals residing in the neighborhood, by tearing it down, especially during the prevalence of a disease like the Asiatic cholera. Meeker *v.* Van Rensselaer, 15 Wend. (N. Y.) 397.

See also, in this connection as sustaining the text, 7 Dillon's Mun. Corp. § 405; *Ex parte* Fiske, 72 Cal. 125; Fields *v.* Stokley, 99 Pa. St. 306; 44 Am. Rep. 109; MUNICIPAL CORPORATIONS, vol. 15, p. 1176.

3. Foote *v.* Fire Department of N. Y., 5 Hill (N. Y.) 99; Fisher *v.* McGirr, 1 Gray (Mass.) 27; 61 Am. Dec. 381. See also Barnacoat *v.* Six Quarter Casks of Gunpowder, 1 Met. (Mass.) 225; Williams *v.* City Council of Augusta, 4 Ga. 509.

4. Surocco *v.* Geary, 3 Cal. 70; McDonald *v.* Red Wing, 13 Minn. 38; Mayor etc. of N. Y. *v.* Lord, 18 Wend. (N. Y.) 138; 17 Wend. (N. Y.) 285; Stone *v.* Mayor of N. Y., 25 Wend. (N. Y.) 57; Russell *v.* Mayor etc. of N. Y., 2 Den. (N. Y.) 461. This is clearly an exercise of police power, not of eminent domain. Philadelphia *v.* Scott, 81 Pa. St. 80. *Compare*, however, Hale *v.* Lawrence, 21 N. J. L. 715. See *supra*, this title, *Definition.*

5. Cooley's Const. Lim. (4th ed.) 594, 595; Philadelphia *v.* Scott, 81 Pa. St. 80; 22 Am. Rep. 738; Meeker *v.* Van Rensselaer, 15 Wend. (N. Y.) 397; Mitchell *v.* Harmony, 13 How. (U. S.) 115.

6. **Laundries.**—Thus a city, by ordinance, may prohibit washing and ironing in public laundries between the hours of 10 P. M. and 6 A. M. This is a legitimate exercise of the police power, and impairs no constitutional right. Barbier *v.* Connelly, 113 U. S. 27; Soon Hing *v.* Crowley, 113 U. S. 703.

But this power does not extend to a city ordinance that makes it an offense for any person to carry on a laundry where clothes are washed for pay, within the habitable portion of the city, without regard to the character of the structure, or the appliances used or the manner in which the occupation is carried on. Such ordinance is unconstitutional, as being too great an infringement of the rights, privileges and immunities which belong to every citizen. *In re* Tie Loy, 26 Fed. Rep. 611. See also *In re* Sam Kee, 31 Fed. Rep. 680.

A San Francisco ordinance conferred

of nuisances generally;[1] the regulation of public highways;[2] the suppression of obnoxious trades or professions, particularly that in intoxicating liquors,[3] and this, even though such trades were in their origin lawful.

6. **Miscellaneous.**—There are also other instances.[4]

unlimited power on certain officials to grant or refuse leave to carry on public laundries in wooden buildings. The power was exercised wholly against Chinamen, and in favor of all others. It was held an unlawful discrimination. Yick Wo *v.* Hopkins, 118 U. S. 356; decided *contra* in 68 Cal. 294.

1. **Nuisances.**—Cooley's Const. Lim. (4th ed.) 596; Watertown *v.* Mayo, 109 Mass. 315; 12 Am. Rep. 694; Bepley *v.* State, 4 Ind. 264; 58 Am. Dec. 628; Goddard *v.* Jacksonville, 15 Ill. 588; 60 Am. Dec. 773, note; Miller *v.* Craig, 11 N. J. Eq. 175; Pittsburg etc. R. Co. *v.* Brown, 67 Ind. 45; 37 Am. Rep. 73; Chicago etc. R. Co. *v.* Joliet, 79 Ill. 25. See also NUISANCE.

But under snch power the city has not the right to tax a lot owner for the expense of abating a nuisance on his lot which the city itself had created. Weeks *v.* Milwaukee, 10 Wis. 242. See also Smith *v.* Milwaukee, 18 Wis. 63; Pettigrew *v.* Evansville, 25 Wis. 227; 3 Am. Rep. 50.

The ringing of mill-bells at a certain hour having been enjoined as a nuisance, the legislature may authorize the ringing at that hour. Sawyer *v.* Davis, 136 Mass. 239; 49 Am. Rep. 27.

The provisions of the general statutes of *Massachusetts* giving to a board of health the power to forbid within the limits of the State, the exercise of any trade which is a nuisance or is hurtful to the inhabitants, or dangerous to the public health, or the exercise of which is attended with noisome and injurious odors, or is otherwise injurious to their estates, and providing that during the pendency of an appeal to the jury, the trade shall not be exercised, constitute a proper exercise of police power and are, therefore, not unconstitutional. Taunton *v.* Taylor, 116 Mass. 254.

In pursuance of the same principle a State is authorized to pass statutes for the prohibition or suppression of all nuisances, and, also, to declare what shall constitute such nuisances. Com. *v.* Howe, 13 Gray (Mass.) 26; Com. *v.* Owens, 114 Mass. 252; Com. *v.* Intoxicating Liquors, 115 Mass. 153; Com. *v.* Colton, 8 Gray (Mass.) 488.

2. **Use of Public Highways.**—Cooley's Const. Lim. (4th ed.) 588. LAW OF THE ROAD, vol. 12, p. 957.

Thus city ordinances prohibiting swine or other animals from being driven or allowed to stray through the streets are valid and binding. Roberts *v.* Ogle, 30 Ill. 459; 83 Am. Dec. 201; Com. *v.* Curtis, 9 Allen (Mass.) 266; McKee *v.* McKee, 8 B. Mon. (Ky.) 461.

A statute forbidding the use of bicycles on a certain road, unless permitted by the superintendent of the road, is valid exercise of the police power. State *v.* Yopp, 97 N. Car. 477.

Sidewalks.—As to the power of a municipal corporation to require each owner of land abutting on a highway to repair or build his own sidewalks, see HIGHWAYS, vol. 9, p. 362, *et seq.*; James *v.* Pine Bluff, 49 Ark. 199. See also STREETS, SIDEWALKS; EMINENT DOMAIN, vol. 6, p. 548.

3. Boston Beer Co. *v.* Massachusetts, 97 U. S. 25; Mugler *v.* Kansas, 123 U. S. 623; Davenport *v.* Richmond City, 81 Va. 636; 59 Am. Rep. 694; Fertilizing Co. *v.* Hyde Park, 97 U. S. 659. INTOXICATING LIQUORS, vol. 11, p. 583.

Junk Shops and Pawn Brokers.—Dealers in second-hand articles and keepers of junk shops may properly be classed with pawn browkers and keepers of loan offices, and the imposition of a license tax upon such occupations is a proper and valid exercise of police power. Marmut *v.* State (Ohio), 12 N. E. Rep. 1263.

4. **Sale of Cotton by Night.**—*Alabama* Act of 1872–79, p. 206, prohibited the transportation by night, within certain counties of "any cotton in the seed," and made it unlawful for any person to sell or offer for sale, barter, exchange, or buy, within said counties, any cotton in the seed. It was held, that such act was not unconstitutional but was a lawful exercise of the State's police power. Mangan *v.* State, 76 Ala. 60; Davis *v.* State, 68 Ala. 58; 44 Am. Rep. 128.

Public School Books. — Unless restrained by its constitution a State in the exercise of its police power may provide by contract that certain persons shall have exclusive privileges, *e. g.*, that of supplying the common schools of the State with text books of a specific character and price. Bancroft *v.* Thayer, 5 Sawy. (U. S.) 502.

Patent Rights.—A statute requiring vendors of patent rights to file copies with the county clerk and to make affidavit of their genuineness and of the authority to sell and to insert the words: "Given for a patent right" in notes taken, is a valid police regulation, and therefore not unconstitutional. New *v.* Walker, 108 Ind. 365; 58 Am. Rep. 40; S. P. Brechtbill *v.* Randall, 102 Ind. 528; 52 Am. Rep. 695. *Compare* Grover, etc., Sewing Mach. Co. *v.* Butler, 53 Ind. 454.

It is competent for the State to exact a license for the sale of patented articles as well as those not patented. Webber *v.* Virginia, 103 U. S. 347; Vannini *v.* Paine, 1 Harr. (Del.) 65.

The legislature of *Kentucky* passed an act providing that "all oils and fluids which may be used for illuminating purposes should be inspected by an authorized State officer before being sold or offered for sale." The inspectors were required to brand all casts as "standard oil" or as "unsafe for illuminating purposes," according as their inspection should show. The defendant, an assignee of the patentee, claimed that such a law deprived her of constitutional rights; that the power to pass such a law resided in Congress alone. But it was considered by the court that the statute was but a legitimate exercise of police power, and therefore not invalid. Patterson *v.* Kentucky, 97 U. S. 501. See also an interesting case very similar to the above in Jordan *v.* Overseers of Dayton, 4 Ohio 295. Also United States *v.* DeWitt, 9 Wall. (U. S.) 41.

Wharfs.—It is within the police power of the State to establish wharf lines beyond which the riparian owners may not extend their structures, even though their ownership in fee simple may extend much farther out; and to declare every structure which shall be created beyond such line a nuisance. But such a statute could not, save in an extreme case, affect wharfs already established. Com. *v.* Alger, 7 Cush. (Mass.) 53; Yates *v.* Milwaukee, 10 Wall. (U. S.) 497. See also WHARFS AND WHARFAGE.

Dangerous Weapons.—A State may also by authority of its police power regulate or forbid the carrying or sale of arms of certain character. Dabbs *v.* State, 39 Ark. 353; 43 Am. Rep. 275; English *v.* State, 35 Tex. 476. See also this subject more fully treated in CONCEALED WEAPONS, vol. 3, p. 408; ARMS, vol. 1, p. 718. See State *v.* Burgoyne, 7 Lea (Tenn.) 173; 40 Am. Rep. 60, for the construction of a statute forbidding the sale of such weapons.

Hawkers and Peddlers.—Laws regulating and providing for the licensing of what are known as hawkers and peddlers, are within the police power of a State. See HAWKERS and PEDDLERS, vol. 9, p. 307. See also Morrill *v.* State, 38 Wis. 428; 20 Am. Rep. 121; Mount Carmel *v.* Wabash Co., 50 Ill. 69; Graffty *v.* Rushville, 107 Ind. 502; 57 Am. Rep. 128; Com. *v.* Brinton, 132 Pa. St. 69; Com. *v.* Gardner, 133 Pa. St. 284; *In re* Butin 28 Tex. App. 304.

Armed Bodies of Men.—It is also a matter within the regulation and subject to the police power of a State to determine whether bodies of men with military organization or otherwise, under no discipline or command by the United States or the State, shall be permitted to parade with arms in populous communities or public places. Dunne *v.* People, 94 Ill. 120; 34 Am. Rep. 213.

Foreign Corporations.—It is by virtue of its police power that a State may provide laws fixing the conditions upon which a foreign corporation may do business within its limits. Bank of Augusta *v.* Earle, 13 Pet. (U. S.) 519; Paul *v.* Virginia, 8 Wall. (U. S.) 168; Pierce *v.* People, 106 Ill. 11; 46 Am. Rep. 683. See FOREIGN CORPORATIONS, vol. 8, p. 365. See also INTERSTATE COMMERCE, vol. 11, p. 548.

Learned Professions.—In order to provide for the safety and care of a people and to prevent imposition, the State legislature may prescribe the qualifications for the practice of all learned professions, *e. g.*, dentistry, medicine, law, and others.

As to dentistry, see Wilkins *v.* State, 113 Ind. 514; State *v.* Vandersluis, 42 Minn. 129; Gosnell *v.* State, 52 Ark. 228.

As to the practicing of medicine, see State *v.* Dent, 25 W. Va. 1; 129 U. S. 114; Eastman *v.* State, 109 Ind. 278; People *v.* Phippin, 70 Mich. 6; Robinson *v.* Hamilton, 60 Iowa 134; 46 Am. Rep. 63; PHYSICIANS AND SURGEONS.

As to lawyers, see St. Louis *v.* Sternberg, 4 Mo. App. 453; 69 Mo. 289; Lanier *v.* Macon, 59 Ga. 187; LICENSE, vol. 13, p. 538.

But the right to practice such professions cannot be denied until after the applicant has been given an opportunity of being heard. State *v.* State Medical Examining Board, 32 Minn. 324: Gage *v.* Censors, 63 N. H. 92; 56 Am. Rep. 492; *Ex parte* Robinson, 19 Wall. (U. S.) 513; *Ex parte* Bradley, 7 Wall. (U. S.) 364; 4 Minor's Inst. (2nd ed.) 180. See also in this connection, Cooley's Const. Lim. (6th ed.) 744, 75; MUNICIPAL CORPORATIONS, vol. 15, p. 949.

Recovery of Damages.—The legislature of the State may, by virtue of its police power, fix the amount of damages which may be recovered by a party injured by the negligence of a railway company, or prescribe a limit within which a jury, in assessing such damages may exercise their discretion. Damages over and above compensation, by way of punishment to the company for its negligence, may be required, and it is not a valid objection that the sufferer, instead of the State, receives them. The statute upon the validity of which this case was decided, was one providing that where any person was injured by the gross negligence of a railway company, he might recover double the amount of damage received. Missouri Pac. R. Co. *v.* Humes, 82 Mo. 221; *affirmed* 115 U. S. 512.

So a statute in *New Hampshire*, authorizing the recovery of double damages in case of injury from a dog bite, was held to be penal and not unconstitutional. Craig *v.* Gerrish, 58 N. H. 513; Quimby *v.* Woodbury, 63 N. H. 370. See also, sustaining a similar principle, Cairo etc. R. Co. *v.* Warrington, 92 Ill. 157; Missouri Pac. R. Co. *v.* Haley, 25 Kan. 35; Brown *v.* Swineford, 44 Wis. 282; 28 Am. Rep. 582; DAMAGES, vol. 5, p. 27.

Inspection Laws.—There is an express provision in the constitution that a State may lay duties on imports or exports so far as is necessary for executing its inspection laws. Const. of U. S., art. 1, § 10. Therefore a law imposing penalties on merchants who should sell hay without having it first inspected according to law, is not a violation of the Congressional power of control over interstate commerce, but simply a protection to the public against the introduction of commodities unfit for commerce. State *v.* Fosdick, 21 La. Ann. 256. And inspection laws when not too comprehensive, have uniformly been held constitutional. City Council of Charleston *v.* Rogers, 2 McCord (S. Car.) 495; Stokes *v.* New York, 14 Wend. (N. Y.) 87; Hay Inspectors *v.* Pleasants, 23 La. Ann. 349.

Instances in which State inspection laws have been considered so comprehensive as to invade the realm of Congressional jurisdiction are seen in Foster *v.* Master etc. of N. O., 94 U. S. 246; *In re* Barber, 39 Fed. Rep. 641; 136 U. S. 313; Brimmer *v.* Rebman, 41 Fed. Rep. 867; 138 U. S. 78.

Other Cases.—It is by virtue of the police power vested in the government that laws may be passed regulating weights and measures, and providing for uniformity by requiring public scales to be used. Stokes *v.* New York, 14 Wend. (N. Y.) 87; Intendant & Commissioners of Rawley *v.* Sorrel, 1 Jones (N. Car.) 49; Yates *v.* Milwaukee, 12 Wis. 673; Gaines *v.* Coates, 51 Miss. 335. See also WEIGHTS AND MEASURES.

In this country power to fix the standard of weights and measures is vested in Congress. U. S. Const., art. 1, § 8, par. 5. And this power when exercised is exclusive, since otherwise there would be no standard. Cooley's Principles of Const. Law 82.

A law requiring operators of butter and cheese factories on the co-operative plan to give bonds for faithful accounting for property received for manufacture is not unconstitutional. Hawthorn *v.* People, 109 Ill. 302; 50 Am. Rep. 610.

A State law which forbids selling or keeping specific kinds of game during certain months is not invalid as applied to game brought from another State, as a regulation of commerce. State *v.* Randolph, 1 Mo. App. 15.

A statute of *Pennsylvania*, prohibiting the floating of loose logs in the Susquehanna River without being rafted, etc., is a lawful exercise of the police power of the State upon a subject within her rightful jurisdiction, and is, therefore, constitutional and valid. Craig *v.* Kline, 65 Pa. St. 399.

The immigration laws of *Louisiana*, providing that "the master in command

V. Limitations Upon Its Exercise.—While it seems that everything necessary for the promotion and preservation of the public welfare may be done by the legislature in the exercise of the State's police power, it must be remembered that there are two written constitutions fixing the limits which may not be transcended; vis., the Federal constitution and the State constitution.[1]

1. Under the Federal Constitution.—Questions regarding the limitations upon the police power of States have commonly arisen in cases involving the express or implied prohibitions in the Federal constitution of certain kinds of State legislation.

a. State Laws Impairing the Obligation of Contracts.—The Federal constitution provides that "No State shall . . . pass any law impairing the obligation of contracts."[2] This clause has been frequently construed with reference to the contract involved in the grant of a charter to a corporation. While not confined to this class of contracts,[3] the limitations upon this exercise of the police power are elsewhere sufficiently treated.[4]

b. Due Process of Law.—The Federal constitution provides that no person shall be deprived of life, liberty, or property without due process of law.[5] This subject in its application to the police power is likewise elsewhere sufficiently treated.[6]

of any vessel coming from any other State or country than Louisiana must make a report under oath to the commissioners of immigration, etc., of every passenger landed," are a valid police regulation which the State may properly adopt for the protection of its own citizens. Commrs. of Immigration *v.* Brandt, 26 La. Ann. 29.

The statute of *New York* prohibiting, except under certain restrictions, the deposit of offal or dead animals, in certain rivers and bays, is a proper police regulation. Mayor etc. of N. Y. *v.* Furguson, 23 Hun (N. Y.) 594.

1. "Like other powers of government, there are constitutional limitations to the exercise of police power. The legislature cannot, under pretense of exercising this power, enact laws not necessary to the preservation of health and safety of the community that will be oppressive and burdensome upon the citizens. If it should do so, it would be the duty of the court to declare such legislative act void." Toledo etc. R. Co. *v.* Jacksonville, 67 Ill. 37; 16 Am. Rep. 611.

"All-embracing and penetrating as the police power of the State is, and of necessity must be, it is nevertheles subject, like all other legislative powers, to the paramount authority of the State and Federal Constitutions." 1 Dillon Mun. Corp. 142; Cooley's Const. Lim. (6th ed.), ch. 16. See Constitutional Law, vol. 3, pp. 670–760.

2. United States Const., art. 1, § 10; Cooley's Principles of Const. Law, p. 301 *et seq.*

3. Constitutional Law, vol. 3, p. 748.

4. Constitutional Law, vol. 3, p. 741; Corporations, vol. 4, p. 212; Franchise, vol. 8, p. 621. See also Thorpe *v.* Rutland etc. R. Co., 27 Vt. 140; 82 Am. Dec. 625; People *v.* Hawley, 3 Mich. 330; Reynolds *v.* Geary, 26 Conn. 179; Charles River Bridge *v.* Warren Bridge, 11 Pet. (U. S.) 548; New Orleans Gas Light Co. *v.* Louisiana Gas Light etc. Co., 115 U. S. 650; Chandler *v.* Montgomery Co., 31 Ark. 25; Bancroft *v.* Thayer, 5 Sawy. (U. S.) 502.

5. United States Const. Amendments, arts. 5, 14.

6. Due Process of Law, vol. 6, p. 43; Service of Process. In the original Constitution this was a restriction upon the Federal Government only, but by the Fourteenth Amendment the prohibition is extended to the States. See Pennoyer *v.* Neff, 95 U. S. 714, *et seq.*

The provision that private property shall not be taken for public use without just compensation applies only to

c. STATE REGULATIONS OF INTERSTATE COMMERCE.—The Federal constitution provides that Congress shall have power "to regulate commerce with foreign nations and among the several States."[1] This subject, except so far as the law is further settled by late and important decisions and statutes, is dealt with under another title.[2]

the exercise of eminent domain. See EMINENT DOMAIN, vol. 6, p. 515-16.

This whole principle is nothing more than an application of the two well-known maxims: *Salus populi suprema lex*, and *necessitas publica major est quam privata.* See Broom's Legal Maxims. See also *supra*, this title, *Definition; Subjects for Its Exercise.* Philadelphia *v.* Scott, 81 Pa. St. 80; 22 Am. Rep. 738; MUNICIPAL CORPORATIONS, vol. 15; Meeker *v.* Van Rensselaer, 15 Wend. (N. Y.) 397. *Compare* Hollingsworth *v.* Parish of Tensas, 17 Fed. Rep. 109.

1. United States Const., art. 1, § 8, par. 3.

2. See INTERSTATE COMMERCE, vol. 11, p. 552.

State Regulations of Interstate Commerce; Original-Package Decision.—The relation of the police power to interstate commerce is treated elsewhere. (See INTERSTATE COMMERCE, vol. 11, p. 539.) Since the publication of the article referred to, new and important developments of the law on the subject have been made in decisions of the United States Supreme court. The case of Leisy *v.* Hardin, 135 U. S. 100 (popularly known as "The Original-Package Decision"), and involving State statutes passed in pursuance of the police power regulating the sale of intoxicating liquors, raised an issue as to the constitutionality of an *Iowa* statute. The court was divided upon the question, a dissenting opinion having been filed by Gray, J., with whom concurred Harlan and Brewer, JJ. It was held that a statute prohibiting the sale of any intoxicating liquors, except for pharmaceutical, medicinal, chemical or sacramental purposes, and under a license from a county court of the State is, as applied to a sale by the importer, and in the original packages unbroken and unopened, of such liquors manufactured in and brought from another State, unconstitutional and void, as repugnant to the interstate commerce clause of the National Constitution. In the majority opinion the court by Fuller, C. J., said: "The doctrine now firmly established is, as stated by Field, J., in Bowman *v.* Chicago etc. R. Co., 125 U. S. 507, that where the subject upon which Congress can act under its commercial power is local in its nature or sphere of operation, such as harbor pilotage, the improvement of harbors, the establishment of beacons and buoys to guide vessels in and out of port, the construction of bridges over navigable rivers, the erection of wharves, piers and docks, and the like, which can be properly regulated only by special provisions adapted to their localities, the State can act until Congress interferes and supersedes its authority; but where the subject is national in its character, and admits and requires uniformity of regulation, affecting alike all the States, such as transportation between the States, including the importation of goods from one State to another, Congress can alone act upon it and provide the needed regulations. The absence of any law of Congress on the subject is equivalent to its declaration that commerce in that matter shall be free. Thus the absence of regulations as to interstate commerce with reference to any particular subject is taken as a declaration that the importation of that article into the States shall be unrestricted. It is only after the importation is completed, and the property imported has mingled with and become a part of the general property of the State, that its regulations can act upon it, except so far as may be necessary to insure safety in the disposition of the import until thus mingled.

"The conclusion follows that, as the grant of the power to regulate commerce among the States, so far as one system is required, is exclusive, the States cannot exercise that power without the assent of Congress, and, in the absence of legislation, it is left for the courts to determine when State action does or does not amount to such exercise, or, in other words, what is or is not a regulation of such commerce. When that is determined, controversy is at an end. Illustrations exemplifying the general rule are numerous. . .

"These decisions rest upon the undoubted right of the States of the Union to control their purely internal affairs, in doing which they exercise powers not surrendered to the National Government; but whenever the law of the State amounts essentially to a regulation of commerce with foreign nations or among the States, as it does when it inhibits, directly or indirectly, the receipt of an imported commodity or its disposition before it has ceased to become an article of trade between one State and another. or another country and this, it comes in conflict with a power which, in this particular, has been exclusively vested in the general government, and is therefore void." Leisy *v.* Hardin, 135 U. S. 100.

Fuller, C. J., states the effect of this decision in the subsequent case of *In re* Rahrer, 140 U. S. 545, as follows: "The laws, however, under consideration in Bowman *v.* R. Co. 125 U. S. 465 and Leisy *v.* Hardin, 135 U. S. 100, were enacted in the exercise of the police power of the State, and not at all as regulations of commerce with foreign nations and among the States, but as they inhibited the receipt of an imported commodity, or its disposition before it had ceased to become an article of trade between one State and another, or another country and this, they amounted in effect to a regulation of such commerce. Hence it was held that inasmuch as interstate commerce, consisting in the transportation, purchase, sale and exchange of commodities, is national in its character and must be governed by a uniform system, so long as Congress did not pass any law to regulate it specifically, or in such way as to allow the laws of the State to operate upon it, Congress thereby indicated its will that such commerce should be free and untrammeled, and, therefore, that the laws of *Iowa* referred to were inoperative, in so far as they amounted to regulations of foreign or interstate commerce, in inhibiting the reception of such articles within the State. or their sale upon arrival in the form in which they were imported there from a foreign country or another State. It followed as a corollary that when Congress acted at all, the result of its action must be to operate as a restraint upon their perfect freedom which its silence insured."

The Wilson Bill—Act of Congress Regulating Intoxicating Liquor in Original Packages.—Within a short time after the rendering by the United States Supreme court of the Original-Package Decision (Leisy *v.* Hardin, 135 U. S. 100) Congress passed an act known as the Wilson Bill (1890, 26 Statutes 313), which provided as follows:

"That all fermented, distilled or other intoxicating liquors, transported into any State or Territory, or remaining therein for use, consumption, sale, or storage therein, shall upon arrival in such State or Territory be subject to the operation and effect of the laws of such State or Territory enacted in the exercise of its police power, to the same extent and in the same manner as though such articles had been produced in such State or Territory, and shall not be exempt therefrom by reason of being introduced therein in original packages or otherwise."

That the Wilson Bill is constitutional is established by the case of *In re* Rahrer, 140 U. S. 545. It was there urged, in effect, that the act was unconstitutional, because, since the National constitution gave to Congress the power to regulate interstate commerce, this power was intended to be exclusive, and that Congress could not by the act in question so regulate it as to bring any of its subjects within the grasp of the police power of the State; that an act of Congress which simply rendered articles of commerce, otherwise not within the operation of State police laws, subject to those laws, whatever their provisions, because made so by act of Congress, was not a constitutional exercise of the power to regulate commerce. But it was held that in surrendering their own power over external commerce, the States did not secure absolute freedom in such commerce, but only the protection from encroachment afforded by confiding its regulation exclusively to Congress. The ability of several States to act upon the matter solely in accordance with their own will was extinguished, and the legislative will of the general government substituted. No affirmative guaranty was thereby given to any State of the right to demand as between it and the others what it could not have obtained before; while the object was undoubtedly sought to be attained of preventing commercial relations partial in their character, or contrary to the common interests. Congress might

d. PRIVILEGES AND IMMUNITIES OF CITIZENS IN THE SEVERAL STATES.--Other constitutional limitations upon the police power of the State are seen in the clause providing that "citizens of each State shall enjoy all the privileges and immunities of citizens of the several States," and that "no State shall make or enforce any law which shall abridge the privileges or immunities of citizens of the United States."[1]

2. Under State Constitutions.—The constitutions of the several States contain prohibitions and guaranties which act as limitations upon the legislature in the exercise of the police power.

enact the law in question in the exercise of the discretion reposed in it in concluding that the common interests did not require entire freedom in the traffic in ardent spirits. In so doing, Congress had not attempted to delegate the power to regulate commerce, or to exercise any power reserved to the States, or to grant a power not possessed by the States, or to adopt State laws. It had taken its own course and made its own regulation, applying to these subjects of interstate commerce one common rule whose uniformity was not affected by variations in State laws in dealing with such property. The court in an opinion by Fuller, C. J., said: "The differences of opinion which have existed in this tribunal in many leading cases upon this subject, have arisen, not from a denial of the power of Congress, when exercised, but upon the question whether the inaction of Congress was in itself equivalent to the affirmative interposition of a bar to the operation of an undisputed power possessed by the States. We recall no decision giving color to the idea that when Congress acted its action would be less potent than when it sat silent. The framers of the constitution never intended that the legislative power of the nation should find itself incapable of disposing of a subject-matter specifically committed to its charge."

The argument was also urged that since the decision in Leisy *v.* Hardin, 135 U. S. 100, had declared these State laws unconstitutional they became as if never enacted, and could not be given life or brought into existence by means of the act of Congress, but it was held that the decision referred to did not have the effect of annulling such prohibitory laws. While some difference of opinion had developed upon this question in the lower Federal courts, the Supreme court refused to sustain the argument just given. See also *In re* Rahrer, 43 Fed. Rep. 556; *In re* Spickler, 43 Fed. Rep. 653; *In re* Van Vliet, 43 Fed. Rep. 761.

The decision as to the constitutionality of the Wilson Bill was unanimous, although the justices who had dissented from the Original-Package Decision refused to follow the court's opinion in all its reasoning.

1. An example of the first is seen in the case of State *v.* Barber, 39 Fed. Rep. 641; affd. 136 U. S. 313, where the State of *Minnesota* had passed an act providing for the inspection within the State of all animals intended for slaughter within twenty-four hours previous to their being slaughtered, and making it a misdemeanor to sell meat from any animal which had not been so inspected. It was held that this statute operated virtually as an exclusion of citizens of other States from trading in this particular article and was therefore a violation of the constitutional provision. Distinguishing Patterson *v.* Kentucky, 97 U. S. 501.

An example of the second provision mentioned in the text is seen in the Stockton Laundry Case, 26 Fed. Rep. 611, where it was held that an ordinance making it an offense for any person to carry on a laundry, where clothes are washed for pay, within the habitable portions of the city, was unconstitutional as violating the provision quoted from the Fourteenth Amendment.

A similar statute in *Virginia* providing for the inspection of all meat to be sold within the State, unless it had been slaughtered within less than 100 miles from the place where it was offered for sale. Brimmer *v.* Rebman, 41 Fed.Rep. 867; 138 U. S. 78.

These provisions vary in minute particulars, but are substantially the same in all the States.[1]

a. FREEDOM OF SPEECH AND OF THE PRESS.—The constitutional provisions, found in every State, providing for the freedom of speech and the liberty of the press are not to be construed as giving to any one the right to indulge in unrestrained slander or libel, or any disgraceful obscenity in language written or spoken. It is therefore within the police power of the State to set bounds for the exercise of this liberty so as to prevent any injury to the public well-being, particularly with reference to the public morals.[2]

b. RELIGIOUS LIBERTY.—The constitution of every State (there seems to be no exception) contains a guaranty that no law shall be passed in any way affecting or prejudicing any citizen's right of religious freedom.[3] But this guaranty is not to be construed to prevent the legislature of a State from setting apart a certain day in the week as a day of rest, and on which no labor shall be done or business transacted;[4] nor does it render uncon-

1. See DUE PROCESS OF LAW, vol. 6, p. 43. For example, the constitution of *California* provides that no person shall on account of sex be disqualified from entering upon or pursuing any lawful business, vocation, or profession, and the courts have held that by this the legislature is deprived of the power to prohibit the employment of females in drinking cellars and other places where liquors are kept for sale. Matter of Molly Maguire, 57 Cal. 604; 40 Am. Rep. 125. See also *In re* Quong Woo, 13 Fed. Rep. 229.

In *Indiana*, however, under a constitutional provision forbidding the general assembly to grant "to any citizen or class of citizens" privileges or immunities, which upon the same terms shall not equally belong to all citizens, does not preclude the restricting of the license for the sale of intoxicating liquors to males. Blair *v.* Kilpatrick, 40 Ind. 312.

And under this same provision it is held that a law forbidding the pursuit of all trades or business on Sunday, and excepting from the operation of the statute such persons as conscientiously observe another day, is not unconstitutional. Johns *v.* State, 78 Ind. 332; 41 Am. Rep. 577. See also SUNDAY; CONSTITUTIONAL LAW, vol. 3, p. 670.

2. LIBERTY OF THE PRESS, vol. 13, p. 510. See also OBSCENITY, vol. 17, p. 5; Tiedeman's Lim. of Police Power 191.

As said by Parker, C. J., in the case of Commonwealth *v.* Blanding, 3 Pick. (Mass.) 313: "The sixteenth article of the *Massachusetts* constitution declares that 'liberty of the press is essential to the security of freedom in a State, and it ought not, therefore, to be restrained in this commonwealth.' But the liberty of the press not its licentiousness is intended. . . . this is a construction which a just regard to the other parts of that instrument, and to the wisdom of those who founded it requires." See also Story on the Const. § 1889; 2 Kent's Com. 17; Respublica *v.* Dennie, 4 Yeates (Pa.) 267; 2 Am. Dec. 402.

3. For example, see *Virginia* Const. (1869), art. 1, § 18; Bill of Rights of id., art. 5, § 14.

The constitution of *Mississippi* provides that "no preference shall ever be given by law to any religious sect or mode of worship, but the free enjoyment of all religious sentiments and the different modes of worship shall ever be held sacred. The rights hereby secured shall not be construed to justify acts of restriction injurious to morals or dangerous to the peace and safety of the State. Const. of *Mississippi* (1890), § 18.

The first amendment to the Federal constitution contains a guaranty of religious liberty, but that, as has already been seen, is intended only as a restriction upon Congress. "Congress shall pass no law, etc." U. S. Const. Amendt. art. I; CONSTITUTIONAL LAW vol. 3, p. 726; Cooley's Principles of Const. Law 205.

4. State *v.* Judge of Section A, 39

stitutional laws exempting church property from taxation, or encouraging the exercise of religion by similar means.[1] Nor does this guaranty authorize any citizen under pretense of the exercise of his religion to engage in practices subversive of the morals of the community, *e. g.*, polygamy, "free love," cruel sacrifices, etc.[2] And if any practice has manifestly a tendency to disturb the peace or to subvert the morals of any community, it may be prohibited by statute, and no person can excuse himself for the violation of such statute upon the plea that he is engaged in worship according to his religious faith.[3]

POLITICAL.—Pertaining to policy or the administration of government.[4]

POLITICAL QUESTIONS.—Questions of which the courts decline to take cognizance in view of the line of demarkation be-

La. Ann. 132. See also SUNDAY, where the authorities on this subject are all set forth.

1. Since experience has shown that religion has a tendency to improve the moral welfare of every community. See Cooley's Princ. of Const. Law, 208; *In re* Mayor of New York, 11 Johns. (N. Y.) 77; Broadway Baptist Church *v.* McAtee, 8 Bush (Ky.) 508; RELIGIOUS SOCIETIES.

But such laws are mere favors, and are to be strictly construed, and may be repealed at pleasure. See authorities just cited. Christ Church *v.* Philadelphia Co., 23 How. (U. S.) 300.

2. Cooley's Princ. of Const. Law 208, *citing* Spear, Religion and State, 315, 318; Reynolds *v.* United States, 98 U. S. 145. (In which case the constitutionality of the act of Congress, known as the "Edmunds-Tucker Law," forbidding the practice of polygamy in Utah was upheld.) See also United States *v.* Cannon, 4 Utah 122; 116 U. S. 55; Wenner *v.* Smith, 4 Utah 258; United States *v.* Crawford, 6 Mackey (D. C.) 319; Gould & Tucker's Notes on Rev. Sts., § 5352; Const. of *Mississippi* (1890), § 18.

In the case of Reynolds *v.* United States, 98 U. S. 145, the true definition of "religion," as used in our statutes and constitutions, was clearly laid down.

3. In the case of Commonwealth *v.* Plaisted, 148 Mass. 375; 12 Am. St. Rep. 569, an ordinance of the city of Boston was passed to regulate and restrain the playing of itinerant musicians in the streets and other public places of the city. The defendant, a member of the Salvation Army, was indicted for a violation of this ordinance by taking part in a procession of the Salvation Army, and playing upon a cornet. There was no disturbance or breach of the peace. The court held, that the mere fact that he was engaged in religious worship according to the dictates of his conscience, and to his religious creed, could not excuse such a violation of the ordinance. It was also held that the ordinance was a valid and proper exercise of police power, and therefore not unconstitutional.

A similar state of facts existed in the case of State *v.* White, 64 N. H. 48, and the same doctrine was upheld.

The principle was clearly laid down in the case of Reynolds *v.* United States, 98 U. S. 145, where the court observed that "religious freedom can never be accepted as a justification of an overt act made criminal by the law of the land."

4. People *v.* Morgan, 90 Ill. 563.

Political Liberty.—See LIBERTY, vol. 13, p. 508.

Political Corporation.—A political corporation is one which has principally for its object the administration of government, or to which the powers of government or a part of such powers have been delegated. Winspear *v.* Holman, 37 Iowa 544; (quoting Bouvier's L. Dict.); State *v.* Hackensack Improvement Commission, 45 N. J. L. 115. See also MUNICIPAL CORPORATIONS, vol. 15, p. 949.

Political Office.—Political offices are such as are not immediately connected with the administration of justice, or

tween the judicial branch of the government on the one hand, and the executive and legislative branches on the other.[1]

POLITICS, in its original meaning, comprehends everything that concerns the government of the country.[2]

POLL.—See CRIMINAL PROCEDURE, vol. 4, p. 881; DEEDS, vol. 5, p. 453; ELECTIONS, vol. 6, p. 255; MANDAMUS, vol. 14, p. 173; TAXATION.

POLYGAMY.—See BIGAMY, vol. 2, p. 192.

PONDS.—See LAKES AND PONDS, vol. 12, p. 610.

POOL—(See also RAILROAD).—*Stagnum*, in English, a pool, doth consist of water and land; and therefore by the name of *stagnum*, or a pool, the water and land shall pass also.[3]

POOR AND POOR LAWS.

with the execution of the mandates of a superior, as the President or head of a department. Fitzpatrick *v.* United States, 7 Ct. of Cl. 293.

1. For an exhaustive treatment of this subject as viewed from its constitutional aspect, see JURISDICTION, vol. 12, p. 258.

2. Chesterfield *v.* Janssen, 2 Ves. Sr. 156.

3. Co. Litt. 5 b; Johnson *v.* Rayner, 6 Gray (Mass.) 110. See also LAKES AND PONDS, vol. 12, p. 610.

Real Estate Pool.—"Pool in the sense here used ('a real-estate pool') is of modern date, and may not be well understood, but in this case it can mean no more than that certain individuals are engaged in dealing in real estate as a commodity of traffic. Kilbourn *v.* Thompson, 103 U. S. 168. *Compare* Harris *v.* White, 81 N. Y. 541.

Combination of Stakes.—A pool is a combination of stakes, the money derived from which goes to the winner. Commonwealth *v.* Ferry, 146 Mass. 203.

I. **Definition.**—In statutes providing for the relief of the poor, the term is used to describe that class who are entirely destitute and helpless and therefore dependent upon public charity.[1] It may be used synonymously with "poor person," "person in distress," "indigent person" and "pauper."[2] The term pauper does

1. State *v.* Osawkee, 14 Kan. 324; Beardsley *v.* Selectmen, 53 Conn. 492; Sturbridge *v.* Holland, 11 Pick. (Mass.) 459; 11 Pick. (Mass.) 540; Kirk *v* Brazos Co., 72 Wis. 449; Opinion of the Justices, 11 Pick. (Mass.) 539.

The term poor is used in two senses. It is used in one sense simply as opposed to the term rich, and it is used also to describe persons so completely destitute of property as to require assistance from the public. "The dictionaries recognize this two-fold sense. Thus Webster gives this definition: '1st, destitute of property, wanting in material riches or goods, needy, indigent. It is often synonymous with indigent and with necessities denoting extreme want. It is also applied to persons who are not entirely destitute of property, but who are not rich, as a poor man or woman, poor people; 2nd (law), so completely destitute of property as to be entitled to maintenance from the public.'" State *v.* Osawkee, 14 Kan. 324; *In re* Hoffen's Estate (Wis.), 36 N. W. Rep. 409; Sankville *v.* Grafton, 68 Wis. 192.

The word, as used in the statutes, is defined to be a poor person, particularly one so indigent as to depend upon the parish or town for support. Lee Co. *v.* Lackie, 30 Ark. 764.

The casual poor are such poor persons as are suddenly taken sick or meet with some accident when from home, and are thus providentially thrown upon the charity of those among whom they happen to be. Force *v.* Haines, 17 N. J. L. 405.

Sometimes "poor" is used as a term of endearment. Anon., 1 P. Wms. 327; 2 Jarman on Wills, 126, 127.

A trust for the benefit of "the poor" of a locality does not, as a general rule, include those who are receiving parochial relief. Attorney General *v.* Exeter Corp., 3 Russ. 395; Attorney General *v.* Clarke, 1 Amb. 422; Attorney General *v.* Wilkinson, 1 Beav. 370; Attorney General *v.* Gutch, Reg. Lib. A. 1830, fo. 2720; 1 Jarman on Wills 209; Lewin on Trusts 531, 532; Deptford *v.* Sketchley, 17 L. J., M. C. 22, 23. A charity for the benefit of "poor boys" was held not confined to those poor boys who required parish relief, or to the boys of persons requiring such relief. Canterbury Gdns. *v.* Canterbury Corp., 31 L. J. Ch. 810. See Charities, vol. 3, p. 122.

2. Hutchings *v.* Thompson, 10 Cush. (Mass.) 238.

not necessarily imply a person who actually receives support.[1] It may be used indiscriminately to designate poor and indigent persons standing in need of relief, and poor persons likely to become chargeable, as well as such poor persons as have actually received support.[2] The meaning of the word pauper as defined by the courts, depends largely upon circumstances and the statute under which the case arises.[3]

1. Walbridge *v.* Walbridge, 46 Vt. 67. See Holland *v.* Belgium, 66 Wis. 557.

The question whether a person is chargeable to a town as a pauper does not depend merely upon the fact that they have furnished him relief, but likewise upon their legal obligation to do so. Ludlow *v.* Weathersfield, 18 Vt. 39.

The fact that a family of eight persons received municipal aid to the extent of $1.67 in a year does not make them paupers. Port Washington *v.* Saukvile, 62 Wis. 454.

2. Hutchings *v.* Thompson, 10 Cush. (Mass.) 238; Walbridge *v.* Walbridge, 46 Vt. 617; Sand Lake *v.* Berlin, 2 Cow. (N. Y.) 485; Sturbridge *v.* Holland, 11 Pick. (Mass.) 459.

3. Statutes defining paupers are given a reasonable construction. Thus, under a statute providing that "all persons who have not estates sufficient for their support shall be provided for and supported at the expense of the town where they belong," it was held that a man was entitled to help who was partially blind and nearly incapacitated for work and occupied with his wife the basement of a small house with an acre of ground, having a life interest in the land and basement, which interest was not worth over $200, and was all the property he owned, and it was not necessary that his interest in the property should be disposed of and the proceeds expended before he could be regarded as a pauper. Fish *v.* Perkins, 52 Conn. 200; Wallingford *v.* Southington, 16 Conn. 435, was a case where supplies were furnished a person claimed to be a pauper, and to rebut the claim that he was a pauper the defendants claimed and offered to prove that the alleged pauper owned and possessed real estate of the value of more than one hundred dollars, consisting of about three-quarters of an acre of land and a small dwelling-house in which he and his family lived. Waite, J., says: "We cannot think the law upon this subject is so rigid that if a poor man owns a miserable hovel, used as a shelter for himself and family, he must sell it, provided it is of any value whatever, before he can properly call upon the selectmen to assist him in procuring medicine and bread for his sick and famishing children. Such a rule would be harsh and inconvenient."

So in Poplin *v.* Hawke, 8 N. H. 305, it was held that a person who cannot relieve his immediate wants without disposing of property which is essential, and which, if parted with, must be immediately replaced to enable him to live, was to be deemed a pauper.

One who, having no property except growing crops not worth more than $25, and no means of support but his labor, sustains a personal injury rendering him helpless for several weeks, is a pauper during such period. Blodgett *v.* Lowell, 33 Vt. 174.

Though a man had a homestead right in forty acres of land, and was the owner of certain personal property kept on said land, yet if he was aged, infirm, and unable to maintain himself by labor, and his homestead and property were in the control of his wife and children, who, by their cruel treatment, made it impossible for him to live at home, or to control his property without litigation, he was a "poor person." [Adams and Seevers, JJ., dissenting.] Jasper County *v.* Osborn, 59 Iowa 208.

If the money consists of a promissory note, it seems that it should be collected and exhausted before the person can be deemed a pauper. Stewart *v.* Sherman, 4 Conn. 556. *Compare* Sturbridge *v.* Holland, 11 Pick. (Mass.) 459.

But some of the cases hold that a person is not a pauper if he has an estate, whether accessible or not. Or an estate which is not sufficient for his support. Peters *v.* Litchfield, 34 Conn. 264; Stewart *v.* Sherman, 5 Conn. 244.

In Chelsea *v.* Brookfield, 27 Vt. 587, it is held that the wife of a man own-

II. State Control—1. Generally.—By the constitutions of many States, the several counties are required to provide poor-houses for the aged, infirm, and unfortunate,[1] and also asylums for indigent deaf-mutes, blind and insane persons,[2] and indigent lunatics.[3]

2. Disfranchisement.—In a few States there are constitutional provisions disfranchising paupers. Thus, in eight States no pau-

ing an equity of redemption valued at $285 is not a pauper.

Under a statute providing that "every poor person who is blind, lame, old, sick, impotent, or decrepit, or in any way disabled or enfeebled so as to be unable to maintain himself, shall be maintained by the county or town where he may be," it is held that any person is a pauper who is in want of immediate relief by reason of sickness, insanity or in immediate need of food, clothes, or shelter. Charleston *v.* Groveland, 15 Gray (Mass.) 15; Goodale *v.* Lawrence, 88 N. Y. 513; 42 Am. Rep. 259. See East Hartford *v.* Pitkin, 8 Conn. 393; Whiting's Case, 3 Pittsb. (Pa.) 129.

Insane Persons.—Under a statute defining a pauper to be "every person who shall be unable to earn a livelihood in consequence of any bodily infirmity, idiocy, lunacy, or other avoidable cause," the term "pauper" is held to include lunatics who were paupers, although the trouble and expense were increased by reason of their insanity. See County of Macoupin *v.* Edwards, 15 Ill. 197.

Illinois Rev. Stat., ch. 50, § 6, is not to be construed to include insane persons having adequate means of support. Alton *v.* Madison, 21 Ill. 115. See Ludlow *v.* Weathersfield, 18 Vt. 39.

Persons Able to Support Themselves.—In Wood *v.* Simons, 4 N. Y. Supp. 368, it is held that one who has always been able to support himself and family by manual labor, though the wages earned by him were not more than sufficient for that purpose, is not a pauper within the meaning of the *New York* Rev. Stat., pt. 1, § 20, tit. 1. See Wilson *v.* Brooks, 14 Pick. (Mass.) 341; Danville *v.* Wheelock, 47 Vt. 57.

But a family are "poor and unable to support themselves," although the head of the family earns enough for their partial support, and although their poverty is caused by intemperance or improvidence. New Hartford *v.* Canaan, 52 Conn. 158. See Commonwealth *v.* Cambridge, 20 Pick. (Mass.) 267.

So where a man has a wife and children under his immediate care and protection, and with his family is unable to support himself and them, he is to be considered a pauper within the meaning of the act of 1821, ch. 122. Poland *v.* Wilton, 15 Me. 363.

A man was in good health and capable of earning four shillings per day, but that he was wholly destitute of property, had been turned out of his former dwelling-place, and had no other place to go to; and that the woman whom he lived with as his wife, though she was not legally such, and his children by her were sick and in needy circumstances. *Held*, that the man was a pauper. Lyme *v.* Haddam, 14 Conn. 394.

Person Smitten with Contagious Disease.—In the technical sense the word pauper does not apply to a poor person, smitten with a contagious disease, who receives aid from the county under a pauper act. La Salle County *v.* Reynolds, 49 Ill. 186.

Transient Pauper.—A pauper who comes into town intending and desiring to remain and stays for months, able to walk about, is not a "transient pauper," for supporting whom an individual furnishing necessaries can recover reimbursment from the town. Macoon *v.* Berlin, 49 Vt. 13.

Vagrants sent to the house of correction are not "foreign paupers," though they may have no settlement in the commonwealth. Opinion of Justices, 31 Met. (Mass.) 572.

1. Kan. Const., pt. 7, art. 4; Tex. Const, pt. 11, art. 2; pt. 16, art. 8; Nev. Const., pt. 13, art. 3; S. Car. Const., pt. 11, art. 5; Ala. Const., pt. 4, art. 45; Miss. Const., pt. 12, art. 29; Fla. Const., pt. 10. art. 3; La. Const., 163.

2. N. Car. Const., pt. 11, art. 10; Ark. Const., pt. 19, art. 19; Nev. Const., pt. 13, art. 1; Colo. Const., pt. 8, art. 1; S. Car. Const., pt. 10, art. 7; pt. 11, art. 1; Miss. Const., pt. 12, art. 27; Fla. Const., pt. 12, art. 1.

3. Tex. Const., pt. 16, art. 54.

per can vote.[1] So in two no person kept at a poor-house or asylum at the public expense;[2] and in *Texas* no pauper supported by any county can vote. But in *Massachusetts*, these provisions do not apply to any person who has served in the United States army or navy in time of war and been honorably discharged.[3]

III. **Statutes.**—It is clearly within the power of the legislatures of the States to charge upon towns and cities the support of the poor, distributing the burden by general laws applicable alike to all, and based upon benefits derived from previous residence, payment of taxes, occupancy and ownership of land, military and official service, and the like. So statutes have been enacted by the several States providing modes for adapting public charity to those in need of relief. Indeed, the subject is regulated entirely by statute. As the statutes of the different States are dissimilar in many respects, no general rules can be stated concerning the law regulating the management of the poor. But it is frequently found that the statutes of a State have not sufficient scope to govern all cases that may arise, and the courts, in adjudicating these cases have settled many questions not provided for by statute. The decisions that have arisen under other statutes will also aid the practitioner in construing the statutes of his own State.

The increase in pauperism necessitates greater facilities for relieving the poor, consequently frequent changes have been made in the statutes, and a great many cases that have been adjudicated under earlier statutes are practically valueless. These decisions, in so far as they are of no assistance in construing statutes already in force have been rejected.

IV. Powers and Duties of Officers of the Poor—1. Overseers— *a.* Generally.—Where it is by statute made the duty of overseers to relieve the poor in distress, the manner in which this relief shall be administered is left, in the first instance, to the sound discretion of the overseers, who are bound to act reasonably and in good faith.[4] This rule applies not only to such paupers as have gained a legal settlement, but also such as are casual residents.[5] And where it is thus made their duty to relieve those requiring support it is within the scope of their official powers to settle and pay claims made against their town on account

1. N. H. Const., pt. 2, art. 28; Mass. Const. Amdt. 3; Me. Const., pt. 2, art. 1; R. I. Const., pt. 2, art. 4; N. J. Const., pt. 2, art. 1; Del. Const. pt. 4, art. 1; W. Va. Const., pt. 4, art. 1; Tex. Const., pt. 6, art. 1.

2. Mo. Const., pt. 8, art. 8; S. Car. Const., pt. 8, art. 2.

3. Mass. Const. Amdt. 28.

4. Clinton *v.* Benton, 49 Me. 550; City of Albany *v.* McNamara, 117 N. Y. 931.

An overseer, in giving temporary relief to a pauper, is not bound to employ, in case of illness, the physician employed by the county superintendents. Gere *v.* Supervisors of Cayuga, 7 How. (N. Y.) Pr. 255.

5. Cincinnati *v.* Ogden, 5 Ohio 23; Overseers of Roxborough *v.* Bunn, 12 Serg. & R. (Pa.) 293; Board of Commissioners *v.* Wheeldon, 15 Ind. 147; Wolcott *v.* Wolcott, 19 Vt. 37; Mussel *v.* Tama Co., 73 Iowa 101.

It is the duty of an overseer of the poor, under the Vt. Gen. Stat., ch. 20, § 13, to provide for the support of a transient person suddenly taken sick,

of expenses incurred in another town in supporting their paupers.[1] But they cannot incur for the county a liability beyond the sum prescribed by statute for relief in a single case without the consent of the superintendents of the poor.[2]

Overseers of the poor being public agents and trustees of the town in respect to the poor, have, without any express authority from the legislature, a capacity to sue commensurate with their public trusts and duties, and are corporations *sub modo*;[3] so they may sue and be sued for acts done in the time of their predecessors, but after they have ceased to be overseers they are not liable for debts contracted or acts committed by them acting in their official capacity as overseers, and within the scope of their authority, the action should be against their successors.[4] They have no power to discontinue a suit, though commenced in their name, after their term of office has expired; and if they unite with their successors in doing so, they need not be made parties to the suit.[5] So after two overseers of the poor have united in commencing a suit for a breach of the excise laws, one of them has no power to discontinue it without the concurrence of the other.[6] They may waive any objection arising from informality in a

if in need of relief. His knowledge of such person's possession of personal property unavailable as a means of present relief is immaterial, in a suit for the support by his town against the town wherein the person has a legal settlement. Danville *v.* Sheffield, 50 Vt. 243.

1. Harpswell *v.* Phisburg, 29 Me. 313. A person not authorized by law for that purpose, cannot furnish board to one who is on the list of paupers and an inmate of the poor house, and have a claim therefor upon the county, whether he knew the party to be a pauper or not, and the overseers of the poor have no power under the statute to bind the county to the payment of such claim. Commissioners of Knox County *v.* Jones, 7 Ind. 3.

2. Gere *v.* Supervisors of Cayuga, 7 How. (N. Y.) Pr. 255. Selectmen and overseers of the poor cannot bind the town for more than $5, for the support of a pauper, without an order from a justice, according to section 20 of the poor act. Ives *v.* Wallingford, 8 Vt. 224.

3. Pittstown *v.* Plattsburgh, 18 Johns. (N. Y.) 407; Overseers *v.* Kline, 9 Pa. St. 217; Unity *v.* Thorndike, 15 Me. 182. See Superintendents of the Poor *v.* Nelson, 75 Mich. 154. One of two overseers of the poor is authorized to institute and carry on proceedings for the seizure of the property of one who has absconded leaving his wife or child chargeable to the town. Downing *v.* Rugar, 21 Wend. (N.Y.) 178. Where a suit is brought on the application of individuals, but in the name of overseers of the poor, for a violation of the excise law, and an attorney is employed to conduct the proceedings, who obtains judgment against the defendant, but the overseers acknowledge satisfaction thereof, they are liable to the attorney for his costs and counsel fees. Wright *v.* Smith, 13 Barb. (N. Y.) 414.

In Taylor *v.* Green, 12 N. J. L. 124, it is held that overseers of the poor cannot maintain an action in their own name against the defendant, to recover moneys expended by them, as agents of the township, for the benefit of the defendant. It should be brought in the name of the township. Overseers of the poor are not a corporate body, and cannot be sued as such. Gould *v.* Bailey, 2 N. J. L. 6.

To the contrary in Virginia: Chapline *v.* Overseers of the Poor, 7 Leigh (Va.) 231.

4. Grant *v.* Faucher, 5 Cow. (N. Y.) 309; Todd *v.* Birdsall, 1 Cow. (N. Y.) 260; Superintendents of the Poor *v.* Nelson, 75 Mich. 154.

5. Wright *v.* Smith, 13 Barb. (N. Y.) 414.

6. Perry *v.* Lynen, 22 Barb. (N. Y.) 137.

notice or answer, and may receive as legal a verbal, instead of a written, answer to a notice.[1]

Upon the decease of a pauper the overseers may take possession of his effects pursuant to the statute, and if administration is not taken out within the time prescribed by statute, they may sell so much of the property as may be necessary to repay the expenses incurred for him, nothwithstanding the appointment of an administrator before the sale takes place.[2] But it seems that the overseers of the poor have no authority as such to intermeddle with the property of persons who are receiving relief from their towns as paupers, unless the authority is delegated to them by such persons.[3] So it is no part of the duty nor within the powers of the overseers of the poor to bring an action of replevin for property alleged to belong to the town,[4] nor will the warrant of two justices be a justification in trespass against overseers of the poor for seizing the property of a man, leaving his wife and children a charge upon the town, unless it appear that the man had actually left his wife and children to be such charge.[5]

b. EXCLUSIVE CONTROL.—Under a statute providing that "where a city of the first or second class is embraced within the limit of any township, the board of supervisors may appoint an overseer of the poor, who shall have within said city all the powers and duties conferred by this chapter on the township trustees," the overseers' control of the city is exclusive and not concurrent with that of the township trustees.[6] And where overseers have exclusive control, the whole duty of executing the poor laws devolves on them, and it is not necessary that the justice of the peace of the town join in ordering relief.[7] But where the overseers have not exclusive control of the poor, and they receive their authority to provide relief from an order of a justice, and such order is made, they are bound to maintain it, and if it be once voluntarily or expressly abandoned, it cannot be afterwards enforced.[8]

c. CONTRACTS.—A contract by overseers for the support of the poor binds the town.[9] So where each town is required under

1. Unity *v.* Thorndike, 15 Me. 182.
2. Haynes *v.* Wells, 6 Pick. (Mass.) 462.
3. Furbish *v.* Hall, 8 Me. (8 Greenl.) 315. See ARBITRATION, vol. 1, p. 654. *Compare* Briggs *v.* Whipple, 6 Vt. 95.
4. Baldwin *v.* Whittier, 16 Me. 33.
5. Bowman *v.* Russ, 6 Cow. (N. Y.) 234.
6. Hoyt *v.* Black Hawk County, 59 Iowa 184.
7. Clay County *v.* Plant, 42 Ill. 324.
8. Perth Amboy *v.* Piscataway, 19 N. J. L. 173. See Cadwallader *v.* Durham, 46 N. J. L. 53.
9. Washington *v.* Rising, Brayt. (Vt.) 188; Perth Amboy *v.* Smith, 19 N. J. L. 52; Overseers of Roxborough *v.* Bunn, 12 Serg. & R. (Pa.) 293; Saddle River *v.* Colfax, 6 N. J. L. 115; Board *v.* Cronk, 6 N. J. L. 119, Perth Amboy *v.* Smith, 19 N. J. L. 52; Belfast *v.* Leominster, 1 Pick. (Mass.) 123, Kirk *v.* Brazos County, 73 Tex. 56, Tufts *v.* Town of Chester (Vt.), 19 Atl. Rep. 988; Holmes *v.* Brown, 13 Barb. (N. Y.) 599; Waltham *v.* Town of Mullally, 27 Neb. 483; Wilington *v.* West Boylston, 4 Pick. (Mass.) 24.

A physician contracted with the overseers of the town of P that he would render medical services to a pauper, who was then chargeable to P, and

statute to elect an overseer of the poor, and he alone is authorized and required to perform the duties of the office, contracts entered into by him for the support of such poor persons, binds the county, and the agents of the county have no discretion, but must discharge the obligation; nor can the action of the chairman of the board, by notice or otherwise, limit or abridge the powers of the overseer of the poor. But when the overseer of the poor has made an improvident and extravagant contract for the support of a pauper, that body may, no doubt, when it is reported them, reduce the amount, but until such action is had by the board, the contract, if fair and unaffected by fraud, may be binding on the county.[1] So if the overseer does not act in the line of his duty and by legal authority he will not bind the faith of the government to the fulfillment of the contract, but he will be personally liable.[2] No action will lie against the town for the breach of a contract made by him not within the scope of his authority.[3] Where a statute provides that "the overseers of the poor shall have the care and oversight of all such poor and indigent persons so long as they remain at the charge of their respective cities or towns, and shall see that they are suitably relieved, supported, and employed in the work-house or alms-house, or in such other manner as the city or town directs or authorizes at the discretion of such overseers," the overseers have authority to bind the town by a contract for support to be furnished in another town to a pauper

that, if the town of P should, in a contemplated order of removal, succeed in establishing the legal settlement of the pauper to be in the town of S, he should receive from P a reasonable compensation for his services, but if P failed to establish the settlement of the pauper to be in S, he should receive nothing for his services, and it appeared that P did succeed, upon the order of removal, in establishing the settlement to be in S. *Held*, that the contract so made between P and the plaintiff, being a wagering contract, was not invalid, as between them, but that the plaintiff might recover from P the value of his services, notwithstanding it had been adjudged, that, as between the towns of P and S, the contract was against the policy of the law, that no recovery could be had by P for expenses for the services so rendered. Edson *v.* Pawlet, 22 Vt. 291. After the incorporating of a town, no agreement between the towns is binding which differs from the act of incorporation. Norton *v.* Mansfield, 16 Mass. 48.

1. Clay County *v.* Plant, 42 Ill. 324. An overseer of the poor, in deciding whether relief shall be furnished to a pauper, acts with the authority of a principal, not under the restrictions of an agency; his decision to aid is a final adjudication; and persons contracting with him to relieve transient paupers are not bound to inquire whether he exceeds his authority. Holloway *v.* Barton, 53 Vt 300.

2. King *v.* Butler, 15 Johns. (N. Y.) 281; Palmer *v.* Vandenberg, 3 Wend. (N. Y.) 193; Norwich *v.* New Berlin, 18 Johns (N. Y.) 382; Wimer *v.* Worth Poor Overseers, 104 Pa. St. 317; Reed *v.* Lancaster (Mass.), 25 N. E. Rep. 974.

The defendant, being one of the overseers of the poor of the town of A, in Vermont, with the other overseers, contracted in behalf of the town, with the plaintiff, for the support of a poor person who had a settlement in that town, but neglected to procure the requisite order from a justice of the peace for an allowance for the support of such person, so as to render the town liable. *Held*, that the defendant was personally liable in an action of assumpsit. Ives *v.* Hulet, 12 Vt. 314.

3. Flower *v.* Allen, 5 Cow. (N. Y.) 654; Gourley *v.* Allen, 5 Cow. (N. Y.) 644; Everts *v.* Adams, 12 Johns. (N.

whose settlement is in the former town, but he at the time the contract for his support is made is too ill to be removed to the town of his settlement.[1]

An overseer of the poor may contract as to a pauper's labor and support, and make a settlement under the contract binding on the pauper.[2] But an overseer, in apprenticing a pauper child, does not bind the town, by his covenant, for the apprentice's fidelity during his term.[3]

d. AUDITING ACCOUNTS.—The statute requiring superintendents to allow and audit all accounts of overseers of the poor, justices of the peace, and all other persons, for services relating to the support, relief and transportation of county paupers, does not require the audit and allowance of accounts in favor of individuals dealing with the overseers in the several towns. It is the duty of the overseers to adjust such accounts and charge them in their bills against the county.[4]

A charge by the overseers for trouble in procuring a place of abode for a pauper is not a legal charge, and cannot be recovered.[5] Nor can all that was actually paid be recovered, if the charges are exorbitant and unreasonable.[6]

e. NEGLECT OF DUTY.—Where overseers of the poor do not make the provisions required by statute for persons who are poor and stand in need of relief, they are liable for such neglect of official duty.[7] Indictment lies for such neglect.[8] So if a pauper is improperly treated and the overseer upon complaint made neglects to provide suitable support, or to correct the misconduct complained of, an individual is warranted in providing for his relief at the expense of the town.[9] Where a statute makes it the

Y.) 352; Gibson *v.* Plumbereek Poor District (Pa.), 15 Atl. Rep. 926.

Where the overseers of the poor of a town, which was chargeable with the support of certain paupers, had promised to pay such sums as might be expended in their support by the overseers of the poor of another town, *held*, that as the method of ascertaining and collecting such expenses was expressly provided by 1 *New York* Rev. Stat. 622, §§ 31–34, the contract was beyond the scope of their authority, and void. Norwich *v.* Pharsalia, 15 N. Y. 341.

1. Aldrich *v.* Blackstone, 128 Mass. 148.

2. Billings *v.* Kneen, 57 Vt. 428.

3. Baldwin *v.* Rupert, 8 Vt. 257.

4. *Ex parte* Green, 4 Hill (N. Y.) 558.

5. Conway *v.* Deerfield, 11 Mass. 327.

6. Southbridge *v.* Charlton, 15 Mass. 248.

7. Otis *v.* Strafford, 10 N. H. 352.

No action lies against overseers of the poor for omitting to apply to a justice, to obtain an order for the relief of a pauper settled in their town, at the suit of one who, after requiring them to obtain such order, supports the pauper at his own expense and without a request from the overseers. Minklaer *v.* Rockfeller, 6 Cow. (N. Y.) 276.

8. State *v.* Hoit, 23 N. H. 355; State *v.* Hawkins, 77 N. Car. 494.

An indictment charging that the overseers of the poor, though requested to grant relief, did not, nor would grant it, but disregarding their duty as such overseers, neglected and refused so to do, was held bad, because it did not charge a willful and intentional neglect of duty. State *v.* Hoit, 23 N. H. 355.

9. Worden *v.* Leyden, 10 Pick. (Mass.) 24; Shreve *v.* Budd, 7 N. J. L. 431.

duty of an overseer of the poor of a town to render an account to the town officers of such towns of all moneys received and disbursed by him, a willful neglect of such duty is therefore punishable according to the provisions of such statute.[1]

f. LIABILITY FOR MONEY COLLECTED.—Overseers of the poor are not jointly liable for money collected by them severally in their official capacity; but if they are charged jointly by the auditors with a balance, and they acquiesce in that settlement, they become liable to an action for the whole amount of the balance found in their hands.[2]

g. OVERSEER ACTING UNDER COLOR OF LAW.—A person duly elected as overseer of the poor, and acting as such *colore officii*, although he has neglected to take the oath of office as prescribed by the statute, if he has not been superseded by the appointment of another, and especially if he has been recognized by the town committees as an overseer of the poor, may bind the township by his reasonable contracts for the support of paupers, or by any acts by which the township would have been bound if he had been duly sworn, so far at least as respects third persons.[3]

h. INDEMNITY.—A poor person suddenly taken sick and chargeable upon the public may properly indemnify the overseer of the poor as far as possible.[4] Moneys expended by overseers of the poor, for the support of a pauper, cannot be recovered of such pauper without a special contract for repayment.[5] So a bond taken by the overseers of the poor to indemnify against the expenses of supporting such pauper is valid, where relatives are legally obliged to support him, unless the bond be taken by the obligees wrongfully and grounded upon corruption, to which their office is a mere shadow of color.[6]

2. Justice of the Peace.—It is generally made the duty by statute of the justice of the peace, together with the overseers, to inquire into the condition of paupers, and if it shall appear necessary to such officers, the justice gives an order on the overseers for an allowance to the pauper.[7] So an order signed by two justices to an overseer of the poor to provide for the maintenance of a pauper under such statute is valid. Though such order does not recite that the justice and overseer inquired into the state and circumstances of the pauper before giving the order, such inquiry will be intended to have been made and implied from the order.

1. Matter of Pickett, 55 How. (N. Y.) Pr. 491.
2. Hirling *v.* Overseers, 3 Watts & S. (Pa.) 367.
3. Perth Amboy *v.* Smith, 19 N. J. L. 52.
4. Church *v.* Fanning, 44 Hun (N. Y.) 302.
5. Selectmen of Bennington *v.* M'Gennes, 1 D. Chip. (Vt.) 44; Benson *v.* Hitchcock, 37 Vt. 567; City of Albany *v.* McNamara (N. Y.), 22 N. E. Rep. 931.
6. Turner *v.* Hadden, 62 Barb. (N. Y.) 480; Selectmen of Bennington *v.* M'Gennes, 1 D. Chip. (Vt.) 44; Lyndon *v.* Belden, 14 Vt. 423.
7. Ives *v.* Wallingford, 8 Vt. 224; Ives *v.* Hulet, 12 Vt. 314; King *v.* Butler, 15 Johns. (N. Y.) 281; Palmer *v.* Vanderberg, 3 Wend. (N. Y.) 193; Sayres *v.* Springfield, 8 N. J. L.

The justice and overseer need not make the inquiry together for the order is not to be their joint act;[1] so where a magistrate makes an order to maintain a pauper as a non-resident, his adjudication is conclusive upon the supervisors until regularly set aside.[2] The finding of justices, that an alleged pauper is likely to become chargeable, is good, although the complaint sets forth that he is chargeable, and the jury under the complaint necessarily pass upon such finding.[3]

3. Commissioners.—In some States, the charge, disposal and support of county paupers are intrusted by statute to the county commissioners. The determination of the question of the pauper's legal settlement in any town in the State and of the validity of any claim for support against the county is in the first instance the duty of the commissioners.[4] They have in relation to paupers all the powers of the court of general sessions, and their order allowing a town's claim against a county for support, so long as not reversed or modified has the effect of a judgment in favor of the town charging the county therewith.[5] Although the finding of the commissioners upon the question of the pauper's settlements may be conclusive as a judgment until impeached or set aside, it may, however, be set aside for fraud or mistake if justice requires it.[6] If commissioners of the poor inhumanely neglect to supply the poor under their charge with food and shelter, they may also be indicted.[7]

4. Superintendents.—Where the statutes confer upon the county superintendent the power to support and maintain the county poor, it must be exercised according to statute provisions at the

166; Overseers *v.* Baker, 2 Watts (Pa.) 280. See Superintendents of the Poor *v.* Nelson, 75 Mich. 154.

1. Adams *v.* Supervisors of Columbia, 8 Johns. (N. Y.) 323; *Ex parte* Overseers of Gates, 4 Cow. (N. Y.) 137.

But persons who are both overseers of the poor and justices of the peace cannot, in the same case, act in the double capacity of complainants and justices ordering a removal; if they so act, the proceedings will be quashed on motion in the county court. Windham *v.* Wardsboro, 53 Vt. 675.

2. People *v.* Supervisors of Cayuga, 2 Cow. (N. Y.) 530; *Ex parte* Dow, 1 Cow. (N. Y.) 205.

3. Hardwick *v.* Pawlet, 36 Vt. 320.

4. Concord *v.* Merrimack County, 60 N. H. 521.

In *Pennsylvania* there is one statute providing for the maintenance of the poor of the county on the commissioners of a certain estate, and another requiring certain officers of boroughs or townships to maintain the poor within their respective districts, and provide taxation necessary until such poor are committed and delivered to the hospital on such estate. The duty of the commissioners of the estate to care for and maintain the poor of the county does not begin under such statute until they are committed and delivered to the said hospital.

5. Salesbury *v.* Merrimack County, 59 N. H. 359.

An order of the court of county commissioners declaring a certain person a pauper, and allowing her a certain sum, "payable monthly out of any money in the treasury not otherwise appropriated," but not contracting with any one therefor—*held*, not to authorize the probate judge to draw his warrant on the county treasurer in payment of a claim for the support of such pauper at the rate specified, until the claim has been audited and allowed by the commissioners. Boothe *v.* King, 71 Ala. 497.

6. Concord *v.* Merrimack County, 60 N. H. 521.

7. State *v.* West, 14 Lea (Tenn.) 38.

county poor-house, or at such other place as may be provided for that purpose under the direction of the board of supervisors, and no power is given to the superintendents to spend money for the temporary relief of the poor, or to spend any money for their support elsewhere than at the poor-house, or a place provided for their support as a substitute therefor under the direction of the supervisors.[1] So, where the superintendent has full power to provide such temporary relief as he may deem proper, a single member of the board of superintendents possesses the whole power of the board, limited probably by an express assent of the majority in a particular case.[2] The superintendents of the poor may sue for the conversion of personal property belonging to the county, either in their corporate names or individual names with the addition of their name of office.[3]

Under a statute authorizing superintendents of the poor "to audit and settle all accounts . . . for services relating to the support, relief, or transportation of county paupers," they may audit the bill of an attorney employed by them in bastardy proceedings.[4] And he is not liable for not auditing and paying a physician's claim for services to a pauper, not itemized and verified as required by statute.[5]

5. Selectmen.—Where a statute provides that "when a person not an inhabitant of the town in which he resides shall become poor and unable to support himself, the selectmen of such town shall furnish him with necessary support as soon as his condition shall come to their knowledge," it is not necessary that the selectmen should act as a body or upon consultation in such a case, but

1. People *v.* Commrs. of Emigration, 27 Barb. (N. Y.) 562; Gallup *v.* Bell, 20 Hun (N. Y.) 172; Marshall Co. *v.* McLeod, 34 Kan. 306.

Superintendents of the poor have capacity to contract a liability for supplies furnished for the county poor-house, which may be enforced by suit. But where it appears that the credit for supplies thus furnished was given to a fund, in the county treasury, raised by virtue of section 50 of the act for the relief of indigent persons, and not to the superintendents, on the supposition that the goods would be paid for by a draft on the treasurer, no action will lie against the superintendents until after an application has been made to them for an order on the fund, and they have refused to give it. Hayes *v.* Symonds, 9 Barb. (N. Y.) 260.

Where a person sells to the superintendent of the poor, provisions for the poor-house, upon an agreement that it is to be a cash sale, or if an order shall be given, that it shall answer as cash, whereupon the superintendents give him an order upon the treasurer of the county, for the amount, and, upon presentment of such order to the treasurer, payment is refused, for want of funds, the vendor is remitted to his original right of action against the superintendents, and may recover of them the value of the supplies. Paddock *v.* Symonds, 11 Barb. (N. Y.) 117.

2. Hewitt *v.* Superintendents of the Poor, 5 Mich. 166.

3. VanKeuren *v.* Johnston, 3 Den. (N. Y.) 183; Alger *v.* Miller, 56 Barb. (N. Y.) 227.

The office of superintendent of the poor of a county, although invested with corporate powers, is a mere agency of the county, and the relation is that of principal and agent. People *v.* Bennett, 37 N. Y. 117.

4. Neary *v.* Robinson, 27 Hun (N. Y.) 145.

5. Hawley *v.* McIntyre, 24 Hun (N. Y.) 459. See Nason *v.* Directors of Poor, 126 Pa. St. 445.

that any one of them is empowered to furnish the relief needed. The town is therefore liable for necessaries furnished to such a person upon the request of one of the selectmen.[1] So, where supplies are furnished to a pauper, who actually needs relief, by order of one of the selectmen of the town, the assent of the other selectmen may be presumed.[2] If the assent of the other selectmen can be presumed, the presumption is one of fact and not of law, and it is to be made by the jury and not by the court.[3] Selectmen are not empowered, by virtue of their office, to submit to arbitrament a question regarding the settlement of a pauper, which involves the right or liability of the town.[4] So the selectmen of one town have no authority to appoint an overseer over a person in another town.[5]

6. Trustees.—The nature and extent of the relief required by the poor, whether it should be transient or permanent, and whether one should be removed to the county asylum, are, in some States, matters for the exercise of the discretion of the township trustee. While orders issued by him for supplies are not conclusive, they are admissible in evidence in a suit against the county for the supplies furnished.[6] So, the trustees of a township may recover the amount expended for the assistance of a person as a pauper, from any person liable for his support, although they do not remove the pauper to the poor-house, there being one in the county.[7] And where a county has no poor-house they have power to bind it for medical services rendered a person temporarily a pauper, who is a resident of the county and township.[8] But township trustees cannot delegate their duty of deciding who are entitled to relief as paupers by signing a number of blank orders and leaving them with one of their number to be filled out whenever he was called upon by physicians.[9]

V. Settlement—1. Generally.—The word "settlement," used in reference to a pauper, means that such individual has, in case of need, a right of support from the inhabitants of the town where his settlement may be.[10] Continuous residence for a certain length of time, owning real estate and living thereon, paying taxes, hiring and serving for wages, apprenticing, service in the army and navy,

1. Welton *v.* Wolcott, 45 Conn. 329.

2. Lee *v.* Deerfield, 3 N. H. 290.

If one selectman undertakes to make a general and unlimited contract in behalf of his town, for the future support of a person admitted to be a county pauper, residing in the town, but not shown to have been recognized by the selectmen as a pauper, or to have stood in urgent need of immediate assistance, the assent of the other two selectmen to his action cannot be presumed, and the town is not bound by it. Burbank *v.* Piermont, 4 N. H. 43.

3. Burbank *v.* Piermont, 4 N. H. 43.

4. Griswold *v.* N. Stonington, 5 Conn. 367.

5. Stratford *v.* Fairfield, 3 Conn. 588.

6. Posey Co. *v.* Harlem, 108 Ind. 164. See Sloan *v.* Webster County, 61 Iowa 738.

7. Springfield *v.* Demott, 13 Ohio 104.

8. Clay County Commissioners *v.* Renner, 27 Kan. 225.

9. Sloan *v.* Webster County, 61 Iowa 738.

10. Jefferson *v.* Washington, 19 Me. 293.

marriage, etc., are some of the conditions enumerated in the statutes under which a settlement may be claimed. If a settlement is claimed by residence the residence must not only be continuous, but it must also be open and notorious and attended by such circumstances as to lead the authorities of the poor, in the exercise of proper vigilance, to the conclusion that there is an intention to gain a settlement.[1]

2. Intention.—When a person takes up his abode in a certain place without any present intention to remove therefrom, such place of abode becomes his residence, and will continue to be his residence, notwithstanding temporary personal absences, until he shall depart with intention to abandon such residence.[2] In order to break it up there must be an act of removal from the place where it exists,[3] accompanied by an intention of the pauper to remain permanently at the place of removal, or at some other place, or at least the pauper must leave without any present intention of returning to the place from which he removed, and such intention must be simultaneous with the act of removal, or in some way connected with the natural residence in another place.[4] Intentions of a pauper as to change of domicil may be gathered by the jury from his declarations, which are not conclusive evi-

1. Henrietta *v.* Brownhelm, 9 Ohio 76; Windham *v.* Portland, 4 Mass. 384; Billerica *v.* Chelmsford, 10 Mass. 394; Athol *v.* Watertown, 7 Pick. (Mass.) 42; Monson *v.* Chester, 22 Pick. 385.

To acquire a settlement by residence in a particular town, the person must actually have resided there continuously for the requisite number of years, intending to make that his home and place of residence. Occasional absences, however, for short periods during the time, without any intention of abandoning his residence in the place, would not interrupt the running of the term. But if, during any part of the period, he had determined to abandon his residence, and had actually carried his determination into effect for ever so short a period, it would prevent his gaining a settlement. Wayne *v.* Green, 21. Me. 357.

2. Warren *v.* Thomaston, 43 Me. 406.

3. Gorham *v.* Springfield, 21 Me. 58. See Barton *v.* Irasburgh, 33 Vt. 159; Monroe County *v.* Jackson County (Wis.), 40 N. W. Rep. 224.

Where a person, residing in Jamaica, purchased a tract of land in another part of the town, and partly cleared it, and, with the intention of building a house upon the land and residing in it as soon as it should be finished, removed, with his family and all of his effects, except a few articles of furniture of little value or use, to the town of Londonderry, and resided there 29 days, having no intention of again living in the house which he had left in Jamaica, and intending to remain in Londonderry until his house should be finished which he was about building, and then removed again to Jamaica—*held*, that this was a change of domicile, and interrupted his gaining a settlement in Jamaica by residence. Jamaica *v.* Townshend, 19 Vt. 267.

If, at the time of the incorporation of a town, a person, having a legal home there, is resident in another town, at service, with the intention of returning at some future day, which intention is afterwards abandoned, such subsequent abandonment of the purpose of returning does not affect the question of settlement. St. George *v.* Deer Isle, 3 Me. 390.

4. Where a pauper is absent from the place of his domicile, and is temporarily in another town, and while there forms an intention to remove to and reside in a third town, but, instead of doing so, remains for a longer time at his temporary abode, this is not sufficient to break up the continuity of his residence in the place of his domicile. Bangor *v.* Brewer, 47 Me. 97.

dence on that point, nor his acts all taken in connection.[1] So when a pauper leaves a town where he has resided, having no family, leaving no house or place therein to which he has any right to return, and having no effects save the clothes he wears, the law does not presume either that he intends or does not intend a temporary absence, and has a continuing purpose to retain a home in such town, and return to it at some future period; the intent is for the jury to determine.[2]

3. Ways of Acquiring Settlement—*a.* BY ACQUIRING PROPERTY. —A settlement may be acquired by owning an estate of freehold or inheritance and residing thereon. The time of residence is fixed by statute in various States.[3] The property should be held in his own right,[4] but it is sufficient to entitle the owner to a set-

1. Thomaston *v.* St. George, 17 Me. 117; Solon *v.* Embden, 71 Me. 418.

Declarations accompanying the act of leaving the town of one's residence, are admissible on the question of intention. Etna *v.* Brewer, 78 Me. 377.

The pauper's declarations made after 1880, with acts done in pursuance of such declarations, tending to show a disposition on his part to acquire a settlement in V, and avoid one in B, thereby implying that his settlement was not before that time in V, were admissible to show his bias and prejudice, when testifying as a witness in 1887 to his intention between 1860 and 1866 of making his permanent home in V; it being admitted that no new settlement was ever acquired by him after 1866. Inhabitants of Belmont *v.* Inhabitants of Vinalhaven (Me.), 20 Atl. Rep. 89.

Declarations made by a pauper whilst temporarily in a town away from the place of his domcile, indicating an intention to remove to and reside in still another town, not having been carried into execution, are inadmissible in evidence. Bangor *v.* Brewer, 47 Me. 99.

2. Ripley *v.* Hebron, 60 Me. 379.

3. Mount Washington *v.* Clarksburgh, 19 Pick. (Mass.) 294; Worcester *v.* Springfield, 127 Mass. 540; Kirby *v.* Waterforford, 15 Vt. 753; Tewksbury *v.* Readington, 8 N. J. L. 319; Beaver *v.* Hartley, 11 Pa. St. 254; Wakefield *v.* Alton, 3 N. H. 378; Poplin *v.* Hawke, 8 N. H. 124; Oxford *v.* Benton, 36 N. H. 395; Pittsfield *v.* Barnstead, 40 N. H. 477; Wellfleet *v.* Truro, 5 Allen (Mass.) 137.

Paying Rent.—Under section 3 of the act of 1835, a person residing in the same or different tenements in a district for a year, paying rent for the same at or above the rate of $10 per year, acquires a settlement in such district, whether he pays the whole rent or not. Allegheny City *v.* Allegheny Township, 14 Pa. St. 138; Butler *v.* Sugarloaf, 6 Pa. St. 262; Plattekill *v.* New Paltz, 15 Johns. (N. Y.) 305; Fort Ann *v.* Kingsbury, 14 Johns. (N. Y.) 365; Harmony *v.* Forest County, 91 Pa. St. 404.

In order to acquire a settlement "by purchase," a contract for a conveyance on the payment of the consideration money, is not sufficient; a title must be given, and it must appear that a consideration to the amount of $75 has been actually paid. Scaghticoke *v.* Brunswick, 14 Johns. (N. Y.) 199; Augusta *v.* Paris, 16 Johns. (N. Y.) 279. See Bridgewater *v.* Brookfield, 3 Cow. (N. Y.) 299.

But where the consideration of the conveyance to the pauper was a quitclaim by him of lands supposed to be of $700 value, which quitclaim afterwards proved to be of no value, on account of failure of title, it was held that he could not be deemed to have paid the sum of $75, *bona fide*, so as to gain a settlement. Pompey *v.* Laurens, 19 Johns. (N. Y.) 238.

4. Charleston *v.* Acworth, 1 N. H. 62. See Nottingham *v.* Amwell, 21 N. J. L. 27; Newfarre *v.* Somerset, 49 Vt. 411; Oakham *v.* Rutland, 4 Cush. (Mass.) 172; Barkhampstead *v.* Farmington, 2 Conn. 600; Hebron *v.* Center Harbor, 11 N. H. 571.

Real estate held *jure uxoris* is not held in the husband's own right, as our statutes now are, within the meaning of the fourth subdivision of § 1, ch. 19 of the Gen. Stats., which provides that every person of full age, who shall

tlement if the property is seized by an apparent good title and no present right of entry is outstanding in another.[1]

Under a statute, however, which provides that a citizen "having an estate of inheritance or freehold in any town, and living on the same three years successively, shall gain a settlement in such town," he does not gain a settlement by thus living on an estate which he has in remainder, as tenant of the owner of the preceding estate of freehold. The statutes refer to such an estate as the party has a right to occupy, and not to an estate in expectancy where there is a preceding estate of freehold in another.[2]

Where a statute provides that a settlement may be gained by an inhabitant of another town in the State, if he shall have been possessed, in his own right, in fee, of real estate of a certain value "free from any incumbrance," in the town to which he may have removed," etc., the word incumbrance does not include a mortgage which has in fact been satisfied, although it may not have been canceled of record.[3]

If a certain income is required, such income is to be ascertained by deducting all expenses to which it might necessarily and legally be subjected, and must be valued as if the property had been subjected to taxation, when the forbearance to tax it has been on account of the poverty of the occupant.[4]

reside in any town in this State and whose ratable estate held in his own right, the percentage of the value of which, besides his poll, shall be set in the list of such town at the sum of three dollars or upwards, for five years in succession, shall thereby gain a settlement in such town. Baltimore *v.* Chester, 47 Vt. 648.

Persons who reside on lands purchased by or ceded to the United States for navy-yards, forts and arsenals, do not thereby gain a settlement for themselves or their children. Opinion of the Judges, 1 Met. (Mass.) 580.

In Canton *v.* Dorchester, 8 Cush. (Mass.) 525, it is held that a husband, who for three years successively occupies land assigned to his wife as dower, obtains a settlement by virtue of the act of 1821, ch. 94, and *Massachusetts* Rev. Stat., ch. 45, § 1. Windham *v.* Portland, 4 Mass. 384.

Where a person leased a farm to carry on at the halves, and the same was put in the list to himself and the lessor jointly, *held*, that such person did not hold the land in his "own right" so as to give him a settlement under the pauper act of 1817. Newfane *v.* Dummerston, 34 Vt. 184.

1. Brewster *v.* Dennis, 21 Pick. (Mass.) 233; Conway *v.* Deerfield, 11 Mass. 327; Newark *v.* Pompton, 3 N. J. L. 1083.

A settlement may be gained by purchasing and occupying a farm, though the title is only under a bond for a deed. This, in effect, is equivalent to a deed with a mortgage back. Weston *v.* Landgrove, 53 Vt. 375.

It is not necessary to prove that the deed was recorded, under which land was held, in order to establish a settlement under the acts of 1789, ch. 14, § 1, and 1793, ch. 34. Belchertown *v.* Dudley, 6 Allen (Mass.) 477.

But an actual occupation of real estate is necessary in order to acquire a settlement under the statute. Weston *v.* Reading, 5 Conn. 255. *Compare* Grandby *v.* Amherst, 7 Mass. 1; Sherburne *v.* Norwich, 16 Johns. (N. Y.) 188.

2. Ipswich *v.* Topsfield, 5 Met. (Mass.) 350. See Leverett *v.* Deerfield, 6 Allen (Mass.) 431. The interest of a husband in the reversionary estate of the wife is not "real estate" within the statutes relating to the settlement of paupers. Orford *v.* Benton, 36 N. H. 395.

3. Clinton *v.* Westbrook, 38 Conn. 9.

4. Freeport *v.* Sidney, 21 Me. 305; Groton *v.* Boxborough, 6 Mass. 50; Conway *v.* Deerfield, 11 Mass. 327;

1. *Application of Statutes.*—Statutes providing that a person may gain a settlement by having an estate of a certain value, are held, in some cases, to apply to personal estate as well as to real.[1] So where a statute requires that the person shall have "an estate of inheritance or freehold," an equitable is as effectual as a legal estate to give a settlement.[2]

2. *Fraudulent Conveyance.*—The occupation of an estate of freehold by the grantor, after a conveyance thereof which is fraudulent and void as against creditors, is not sufficient to gain a settlement.[3]

3. *Undivided Estate.*—A person entitled to a distributive share of a deceased person's estate of sufficient amount will gain a settlement thereby, though there has been no decree of distribution, the other requirements of the law being complied with.[4]

b. BY PAYMENT OF TAXES.—A person may gain a settlement by payment of taxes,[5] but the taxes must be actually paid by the

Grantby *v.* Amherst, 7 Mass. 1; Western *v.* Leicester, 3 Pick. (Mass.) 198; Boston *v.* Wells, 14 Mass. 384.

In order to give a citizen of the United States, twenty-one years of age, a settlement under the act of 1793, ch. 34, § 2, cl. 4, by having a freehold "of the clear yearly income of three pounds," "and taking the rents and profits thereof three years successively," it is not necessary that he should have actually taken and received that sum yearly free of all charges. Pelham *v.* Middleborough. 4 Gray (Mass.) 57.

1. Boston *v.* Bedham, 4 Met. (Mass.) 178.

Vt. act of 1862 directed listers to set dogs in the grand list at the sum of $1 each. *Held*, that this made dogs "ratable estate," within the meaning of the pauper law declaring how a settlement may be obtained. Marshfield *v.* Middlesex, 55 Vt. 545.

2. Smith *v.* Angell, 14 R. I. 192; Orleans *v.* Chatham, 2 Pick. (Mass.) 29; Randolph *v.* Norton, 16 Gray (Mass.) 395; Conway *v.* Ashfield, 110 Mass. 113.

3. Canton *v.* Dorchester, 8 Cush. (Mass.) 525.

In Boylson *v.* Clinton, 1 Gray (Mass.) 619 it is held a citizen of the United States, living three years in any town within this State, on land conveyed to him by a warranty deed, gains a settlement in such town by virtue of *Massachusetts* Rev. Stat., ch. 45, § 1, cl. 4, although his grantor had in fact no title to the land.

4. Andover *v.* Merrimack County, 37 N. H. 437.

5. See Randolph *v.* Easton, 4 Cush. (Mass.) 557; Boston *v.* Warwick, 132 Mass. 519; Shrewsbury *v.* Salem, 19 Pick. (Mass.) 389; North Stonington *v.* Stonington, 31 Conn. 412; Burton *v.* Wakefield, 4 N. H. 47; Weare *v.* New Boston, 3 N. H. 203; Henniker *v.* Weare, 9 N. H. 573; Derry *v.* Rockingham, 62 N. H. 485.

A man may gain a settlement by residence and paying taxes in a new district, though his abandoned wife is receiving relief as a pauper in the district of his former settlement. Scranton Poor District *v.* Danville, 106 Pa. St. 446.

Where a settlement may be gained in any poor district by payment of "any public taxes or levies for two years, successively," a settlement may be gained by payment of road taxes. Overseers of Poor of Benezette *v.* Overseers of Poor of Huston (Pa.), 19 Atl. Rep. 1060; Haverhill *v.* Orange, 47 N. H. 273.

Compare America *v.* Sanford, 6 Johns. (N. Y.) 92, where it is held assessment and performance of labor on a highway are not the payment of a tax so as to gain a settlement.

One is not prevented from gaining a settlement, if he pays the requisite tax, although the grand list is defective and illegal. Weston *v.* Landgrove, 53 Vt. 375.

The neglect to enforce the collection of a tax will not operate as a payment, upon the question of settlement. Robbins *v.* Townsend, 20 Pick. (Mass.) 345.

Under the act of March 9, 1771, § 17,

pauper or by another at his request.[1] Only those taxes are to be paid which are assessed,[2] and only when taxes have been legally imposed on a person, does a failure to pay them defeat his right to a settlement afterwards.[3] But it is immaterial that the pauper was taxed by a wrong name.[4] It must appear, however, that the tax is assessed against him individually, and that payment is made by him personally, or by some one at his request, in a manner to make it his legal act.[5] A person will not acquire a settlement in a town by voting and paying taxes there under the erroneous belief that his dwelling-house is within the limits of that town.[6] But where a tax has been duly assessed and notice of the assessment given, the party has a right to pay the amount any time before it is abated, and before such abatement a tender to the collector of the amount of such tax is equivalent to the payment of the tax for the purpose of gaining a settlement.[7]

c. BY TIME OF RESIDENCE.—The requisite time of residence for gaining a settlement is also fixed by statute.[8] The residence,

a settlement was gained by paying a county tax only. Bucks *v.* Philadelphia, 1 Serg. & R. (Pa.) 387.

A United States tax is not a public tax that gives a settlement, under the act of 1771. Bucks *v.* Columbia, 10 Serg. & R. (Pa.) 179.

Payment of taxes during seven successive years, without a residence throughout the same entire term, does not establish a settlement. Tamworth *v.* Freedom. 17 N. H. 279.

1. Wallkill *v.* Mamakating, 14 Johns. (N. Y.) 87; Starksboro *v.* Hinesburgh, 13 Vt. 215. See Beaver Poor District *v.* Rose Poor District, 98 Pa. St. 636.

2. Wrentham *v.* Attleborough, 5 Mass. 430; Andover *v.* Chelmsford, 16 Mass. 236; Billerica *v.* Chelmsford, 10 Mass. 394.

Compare Francestown *v.* Deering, 41 N. H. 438; Westbrook *v.* Gorham, 15 Mass. 160; Templeton *v.* Sterling, 15 Mass. 253.

A person gave a promissory note to a town in payment of a tax assessed against him. *Held*, that the note was not payment of the tax, within the meaning of the act of Dec. 16, 1828, so as to give him a settlement in that town according to the eighth mode prescribed by the statute. Jaffrey *v.* Cornish, 10 N. H. 505.

A neglect to pay a highway tax, legally raised, will prevent the gaining of a settlement, although payment has never been demanded. Bradford *v.* Newport, 42 N. H. 338.

3. Beacon Falls *v.* Seymour, 43 Conn. 217; Berlin *v.* Gorham, 34 N. H. 266; Charlemont *v.* Conway, 8 Pick. (Mass.) 408.

4. Canaan *v.* Grafton County (N. H.), 15 Atl. Rep. 18.

5. Springfield *v.* Enfield, 30 N. H. 71; Plymouth *v.* Wareham, 126 Mass. 475; Inhabitants of Berlin *v.* Inhabitants of Bolton, 10 Met. (Mass.) 115; Warren *v.* Wentworth, 45 N. H. 564.

One cannot gain a settlement where his lessor, not he himself, has paid the taxes assessed upon the estate occupied by him as a tenant. Weare *v.* Deering, 58 N. H. 206.

If a person is under guardianship as a lunatic, and has the amount of property required for a settlement, but it is taxed to the guardian and the taxes are paid by him, the ward will gain a settlement at the end of four years. Andover *v.* Merrimack County, 37 N. H. 437.

6. Ellsworth *v.* Gouldsboro, 55 Me. 94.

7. County of Hillsborough *v.* Londonderry, 46 N. H. 11.

8. See Londonderry *v.* Andover, 28 Vt. 416; Standish *v.* Gray, 18 Me. 92; Augusta *v.* Turner, 24 Me. 112; Inhabitants of Marlborough *v.* Inhabitants of Freehold, 50 N. J. L. 509; Fitchburg *v.* Ashby, 132 Mass. 495; Somerville *v.* Boston, 120 Mass. 574; New Hartford *v.* Canaan, 54 Conn. 39; Canton *v.* Simsburg, 54 Conn. 86; Vernon *v.* Ellington, 53 Conn. 330; Washington *v.* Corinth, 55 Vt. 468; Dedham *v.* Milton, 136 Mass. 424; Brouer *v.* Smith, 46 N. J. L. 72; Cambridge *v.*

however, must be continuous.[1] Absence for a short time with the intention of returning will not interrupt the residence required for the purpose of gaining a settlement.[2] Nor does imprisonment or commitment to an insane hospital interrupt the continuity of the residence.[3] But absence with an intention of never returning, though such intention is changed and he in fact

Boston, 137 Mass. 152; Belmont v. Morrill, 73 Me. 231; Detroit v. Palmyra, 72 Me. 256; Bangor v. Wiscasset, 71 Me. 535; Endicott v. Hopkinson, 125 Mass. 521; Athol v. Watertown, 7 Pick. (Mass.) 42; Hopkinton v. Upton, 3 Met. (Mass.) 165; Southborough v. Marlborough, 24 Pick. (Mass.) 166; State v. Shrewsbury, 49 N. J. L. 188; State v. Bridgewater Poor Overseers, 49 N. J. L. 614; Paris v. Hiram, 12 Mass. 263; East Windsor v. Montgomery, 9 N. J. L. 39; Merrimack County v. Grafton County, 63 N. H. 550.

Supplement of April 6, 1886 (P. L. N. J. 208), to the act for the settlement and relief of the poor, enacts "that any person or persons who have or who shall have resided in any township of this State for the period of ten years shall be considered as legally settled in said township." Under this act, when the condition upon which such legal settlement may be acquired exists, an absolute settlement is established, and not one *prima facie* merely. McLorinan v. Overseers of the poor (N. J.), 10 Atl. Rep. 187.

The provision of Mass. Pub. St., ch. 83, § 1, cl. 4, that "any person of the age of twenty-one years, having an estate of inheritance or freehold in any place within the State, and living on the same three years successively, shall thereby gain a settlement in such place," does not apply to a married woman. Spencer v. Leicester, 140 Mass. 224.

1. Henrietta v. Brownhelm, 9 Ohio 76; Beaver Poor District v. Rose Poor District, 98 Pa. St. 636; Monkton v. Panton, 12 Vt. 250; Royalton v. Bethel, 10 Vt. 22; Lincoln v. Warren, 19 Vt. 170; Reading v. Westport, 19 Conn. 561; Salem v. Lynn, 29 Conn. 74.

2. Lee v. Lenox, 15 Gray (Mass.) 496; Barton v. Irasburgh, 33 Vt. 159; Waterford v. Fayston, 29 Vt. 530; Kennebunkport v. Buxton, 26 Me. 61.

An occasional absence for work does not break the continuity necessary to satisfy the law. State v. Shrewsbury, 49 N. J. L. 188.

Absence from a town, without a definite purpose at all events to return to it as a home, will not interrupt the residence requisite to a settlement, until a new domicile is acquired elsewhere. Worcester v. Wilbraham, 13 Gray (Mass.) 586.

"The voluntary and uninterrupted absence" spoken of in Wis. Rev. Stat. 1858, ch. 34, § 2, subd. 7 (by which a previous settlement was lost), does not include an absence during which the town in which the person had a legal settlement supported the absentee as a pauper in some other town in the State. Scott v. Clayton, 51 Wis. 185.

3. Lopsham v. Lewiston, 74 Me. 236; 43 Am. Rep. 584; Baltimore v. Chester, 53 Vt. 315; 38 Am. Rep. 677; Dexter v. Sangarville, 70 Me. 441; Woodstock v. Hartland, 21 Vt. 563; Northfield v. Vershire, 33 Vt. 110; County of Franklin v. County of Henry, 26 Ill. App. 193; Town of Saukville v. Town of Grafton (Wis.), 31 N. W. Rep. 719; Corinna v. Hartland, 70 Me. 355. *Compare* Choate v. Rochester, 13 Gray (Mass.) 92; Reading v. Westport, 19 Conn. 561.

Vt. Gen. Stat., ch. 20, § 40, which provides that "upon the trial of all settlement cases, the time any person shall be a patient at any lunatic asylum, except inhabitants of the town in which such asylum is situated, shall not be computed as part of the time required by law to gain a legal settlement, but shall be deducted therefrom," is mandatory. Town of Peacham v. Weeks, 48 Vt. 73.

In assumpsit for money paid for the support of paupers, it was claimed that the husband and father of the paupers had acquired a settlement by commorancy in the plaintiff town, and the court charged the jury that, if during his residence there he had been sentenced to State prison for four years, and had served the period of his sentence, if during that time he had no property and no domicile in that town, and upon his conviction and sentence his wife returned to live with her parents in that town, and made it her

returns will prevent him from gaining a settlement.[1] So if the pauper is removed to another town, by direction of the overseers of the poor, to prevent his gaining a settlement in the former town, but with the intention to return at the expiration of a few weeks, the removal being for that purpose alone, the removal is of no effect and the residence is not changed thereby.[2]

A settlement by residence under the statute can only be acquired by persons above the age of legal majority. No allowance can be made for any length of residence during infancy, though it may have been after emancipation.[3] And the residence must have been the result of choice.[4]

d. BY HIRING.—A person who goes into a county or town and makes no arrangements for a home, and who has no home or fixed actual residence, but hires out and is employed by one or more persons, and so continues for a sufficient length of time, acquires a settlement at the place of his employment.[5] If he is a person working out from place to place, his settlement will be in the town in which he has taken his clothing, where it does not appear that he had the right by contract, or an intention to return to any other town.[6] But a settlement cannot be gained by merely working without any bargain as to wages or time of serving.[7]

home there, going out to work at various places, and part of the time in the defendant town, his residence in that town was interrupted by his term of imprisonment. *Held*, that such charge was correct. Washington *v.* Kent, 38 Conn. 249.

In Burke County *v.* Buncombe County, 101 N. Car. 520, it was held that confinement under legal process does not constitute such residence as will change the settlement of a poor person.

1. Westbrook *v.* Bowdoinham, 7 Me. 363; Burnham *v.* Pittsfield, 68 Me. 580.

Where a pauper left a town prior to March 21, 1821, without any intention of returning, and did not return, *held*, that he gained no settlement in that town by the settlement act of that date, although he had acquired no home in any other place. Exeter *v.* Brighton, 15 Me. 58.

2. Clinton *v.* York, 26 Me. 167.

3. Hartford *v.* Hartland, 14 Vt. 392; Poultney *v.* Glover, 23 Vt. 328; Marshfield *v.* Tunbridge (Vt.), 20 Atl. Rep. 106.

4. Woodstock *v.* Hartland, 21 Vt. 563.

5. Dorr *v.* Seneca, 74 Ill. 101; Byberry *v.* Oxford, 2 Ashm. (Pa.) 9; County of Franklin *v.* County of Henry, 26 Ill. App. 193; Wood *v.* Simmons, 4 N. Y. Supp. 368. See Bristol *v.* Rutland, 10 Vt. 574; Guilford *v.* Gilmantown, 1 N. H. 194.

Where the pauper had been hired in the manufacture of gunpowder, at a certain sum per 100 pounds, and three months' notice, on each side, of an intended termination of the contract was stipulated for, and it appeared that he had occasionally worked out on his own account during the period of his hiring, *held*, that he had gained a settlement by the hiring. Heidleberg *v.* Lynn, 5 Whart. (Pa.) 430.

6. Berlin *v.* Worcester, 50 Vt. 23.

7. Lewiston *v.* Granville, 5 Pa. St. 283. See Bellingham *v.* West Boylston, 4 Cush. (Mass.) 553.

Under the act of 1836, § 9, it is not necessary that there should have been a contract for service for a year to gain a settlement; it is sufficient if there has been service for a year, under one or more contracts. Heidleberg *v.* Lynn, 5 Whart. (Pa.) 430.

In Tioga *v.* Lawrence, 2 Watts (Pa.) 43; Gregg *v.* Half Moon, 2 Watts (Pa.) 342, it is held, that rendering service under a verbal agreement of hiring gives one a settlement. *Compare* Wynkoop *v.* Overseers of New York, 3 Johns. (N. Y.) 15.

e. BY APPRENTICING.—The binding by indenture and a service under it for the time prescribed by statute, gives the apprentice a settlement in the town in which he serves,[1] but an oral binding and an apprenticeship served under it will not confer a settlement.[2] See APPRENTICE, vol. 1, p. 637.

f. BY SERVICE IN THE ARMY OR NAVY.—In *Massachusetts* a settlement may be gained by service in the army or navy.[3] But the statutes giving a settlement for such service, do not apply "to any person who shall have been guilty of willful desertion."[4] So a soldier discharged for disability, does not thereby acquire a settlement, unless it arises from wounds or diseases contracted in the service, which fact must be proved by the party alleging it.[5] The fact that a person has been enlisted and mustered by a false name does not, however, prevent his acquiring a settlement.[6]

The term "quota in any city or town" includes every person who, during the recent civil war, was enlisted and mustered into the military or naval service of the United States.[7] A soldier credited to the quota of a town in conformity with the terms of the statute gains a settlement, even if he was credited in excess of the proportion due at the time of such credit.[8]

1. 2 Birdseye N. Y. Code, 2259. See Franklin *v.* South Brunswick, 2 N. J. L. 442; Leeds *v.* Freeport, 10 Me. 356; Bloomfield *v.* Acquackannuk, 8 N. J. L. 257. See Hopewell *v* Amwell, 2 N. J. L. 422.

An indented apprentice gains a settlement in the township where he serves his master the time prescribed by statute under the indenture. Upper Alloways Creek *v.* Elsingborough, 1 N. J. L. 389.

Even though the master has no settlement there. South Brunswick *v.* Independence, 14 N. J. L. 549.

But there must be actual service for full time. Jefferson *v.* Pequanack, 13 N. J. L. 187.

Act Pa. June 13, 1836, par. 9, § 6, provides that "a settlement may be gained in any district . . . by any person who shall be duly bound an apprentice by indenture, and shall inhabit in the district with his master or mistress for one whole year." The poor-district of the city of L made an indenture with K for the maintenance of a pauper, to enforce which there was incorporated a clause by which K agreed to indemnify the district against all cost for the pauper's support during the term of her apprenticeship. *Held* that, by reason of the indemnity clause, this was not such an apprenticeship as, under the act, was sufficient to create a new settlement. Poor District of the City of Lock Haven *v.* Poor District of Chapman Tp. (Pa.) 13 Atl. Rep. 742.

2. Niskayuna *v.* Albany, 2 Cow. (N. Y.) 537; North Brunswick *v.* Franklin, 16 N. J. L. 535.

A service may be performed by an apprentice by the consent of his master, with another man, so as to gain a settlement, and a formal assignment of the indenture in writing is not necessary; the assent of the original master is all that the law requires. Kingwood *v.* Bethlehem, 13 N. J. L. 221.

If the master discharge the apprentice, without assigning or turning him over, but lets him go without claiming the benefit of his services, the apprentice gains no settlement by living with another person. Orange *v.* Springfield, 14 N. J. L. 321. See also Kingwood *v.* Bethlehem, 13 N. J. L. 222.

3. Newburyport *v.* Worthington, 132 Mass. 510.

4. Cambridge *v.* Paxton, 144 Mass. 520. *Compare* Lunenburg *v.* Shirley, 132 Mass. 498.

5. Ashland *v.* Marlborough, 106 Mass. 266.

6. Milford *v.* Uxbridge, 130 Mass. 107.

7. Bridgewater *v.* Plymouth, 97 Mass. 382.

8. Wayland *v.* Ware, 104 Mass. 46.

Evidence.— A general order of the governor of the State is competent evidence of a call for troops under an act

4. Who May Acquire a Settlement—*a.* CHILDREN—(1) *Generally.*—The settlement of a legitimate child is where the father's settlement is.[1] If the father has none, the child must go to its mother's settlement.[2] While the child is under age, its settlement accompanies and follows that of its father,[3] although not residing in the father's family at the time he changes the place of

of Congress of the assignment of quotas to the town under the call. Hansom *v.* South Scituate, 115 Mass. 336. The fact that calls for troops were made by the President, and quotas assigned to all the towns in the commonwealth during the civil war, are to be assumed without express evidence. Wayland *v.* Ware, 104 Mass. 46.

On the question of whether one acquired a military settlement in a certain town, from his testimony that he was enlisted, and from the fact that his name was found on the rolls, and that his discharge showed that he had served more than a year, it may be held that he was enlisted and mustered and served more than a year, although neither the enlistment and muster-roll, nor copies of them, are put in evidence. Brockton *v.* Uxbridge, 138 Mass. 292.

1. Gloucester *v.* Smithfield, 2 R. I. 30; Vernon *v.* Smithville, 17 Johns. (N. Y.) 89; Amherst *v.* Shelburne, 13 Gray (Mass.) 341; Sharon *v.* Cabot, 29 Vt. 394; Middleborough *v.* Plympton, 140 Mass. 325; Marlborough *v.* Hebron, 2 Conn. 20; Hebron *v.* Colchester, 5 Day (Conn.) 169; Vernon *v.* Ellington, 53 Conn. 330.

A legitimate child, deriving its settlement from its father, cannot acquire that of its mother. Scituate *v.* Hanover, 7 Pick. (Mass.) 140; Sterling *v.* Plainfield, 4 Conn. 114; Marion *v.* Spring, 50 Pa. St. 308.

Where a father gains a settlement in a town by the payment of taxes for two years, his infant child, though not residing with him, or under his immediate charge or control, has a derivative settlement in the same town with him. Adams *v.* Oaks, 20 Johns. (N. Y.) 282.

Nor can the father, by any deed, release, or act of emancipation, divest the son of such derivative settlement. Adams *v.* Foster, 20 Johns. (N. Y.) 452.

Alexandria *v.* Bethlehem, 16 N. J. L. 119; Lewis *v.* Turbut, 15 Pa. St. 145.

2. Vernon *v.* Smithville, 17 Johns. (N. Y.) 89; Lebanon *v* Hebron, 6 Conn. 45.

See Fitchburg *v.* Westminster, 1 Pick. (Mass.) 144; Burrell *v.* Pittsburgh, 62 Pa. St. 472; Bradford *v.* Lunenburg, 5 Vt. 481; Hebron *v.* Colchester, 5 Day (Conn.) 169; Norwich *v.* Saybrook, 5 Conn. 384; Dedham *v.* Natick, 16 Mass. 135; Great Barrington *v.* Tyrigham, 18 Pick. (Mass.) 264; Little Falls *v.* Bernards, 44 N. J. L. 621; Albany *v.* Derby, 30 Vt. 718; Stillwell *v.* Kennedy, 5 N. Y. Supp. 409.

Legitimate children take the settlement of the mother if the father has no settlement in the State. Nor does it make any difference whether the settlement of the mother is one she acquired in her own right or a derivative settlement from her father, or even one derived through several generations. Nor will it make any difference that the mother was a *feme covert*, and the pauper an infant, when the present statute came in force. Rupert *v.* Winhall, 29 Vt. 245.

The settlement of a widow, acquired after the death of her husband, is communicated to her infant children. Dedham *v.* Natick, 16 Mass. 135; Bradford *v.* Lunenburg, 5 Vt. 481. *Compare* Fairfield *v.* Canaan, 7 Me. 90.

Under the rule that a legitimate infant child takes the settlement of its father, if he has one, in preference to that of its mother, acquired by a subsequent marriage where a pauper was the legitimate child of A, whose settlement was in O, and its mother, before the birth of the child, was married to B, whose settlement was in B, where the child was born,—

Held, 1. That such child took the settlement of its father in O, and not that of its mother acquired by marriage in B.

2. That if the mother, after the death of the father, acquired a settlement in her own right, such settlement is communicated to her child. Oxford *v.* Bethany, 19 Conn. 229.

But legitimate children cannot derive a settlement from their mother, without proving that their father had no settlement within the commonwealth. Amherst *v.* Shelburne, 13 Gray (Mass.) 341.

3. Charlestown *v.* Boston, 13 Mass.

his settlement.[1] When a child arrives at full age the settlement derived from his father remains fixed until a new one is acquired.[2] It ceases to follow the settlement of the parent.[3]

An infant who moves with his father to another town and lives with him, after arriving at full age, the length of time prescribed by statute for gaining a settlement, and supports himself during this period, acquires a settlement in his own right.[4] But a pauper cannot gain a settlement in his own right in the same town in which he derives a settlement from his father, the continued residence giving only a derivative settlement.[5]

The *prima facie* settlement of a pauper is the place of his birth,[6] but the birth of a child does not give it a settlement, except when the settlement of the parents is not known, and then only until it is discovered.[7]

469; Milo *v.* Gardner, 41 Me. 551; Hampden *v.* Brewer, 24 Me. 281; Madison Overseers *v.* Monroe Overseers, 42 N. J. L. 493; Brouer *v.* Smith, 46 N. J. L. 72; Washington *v.* Beaver, 3 Watts & S. (Pa.) 548; Limestone Overseers etc. *v.* Chillisquaque Overseers etc., 87 Pa. St. 294; Bozrah *v.* Stonington, 4 Conn. 373; Hebron *v.* Colchester, 5 Day (Conn.) 169; Lebanon *v.* Hebron, 6 Conn. 45.

Pauper Deriving Settlement from Grandfather.—The pauper's grandfather had removed out of the State during the minority of her father. Her father married and she was born out of the State; then the grandfather removed to the State. Afterwards the pauper and her mother did the same, and after that the father also came to the State and lived there till his death. *Held*, that the pauper had the original settlement of her grandfather before his removal out of the State. Waterford *v.* Fayston, 29 Vt. 530. See Bridgewater *v.* West Bridgewater, 9 Pick. (Mass.) 55.

If one, having a legal settlement in this State, removes to another of the United States, and never returns here, his children, born there, take the settlement of their father upon coming into this State. Westford *v.* Essex, 31 Vt. 459. So if a minor child, deriving his settlement from his mother, resides out of the State, whether as an indented apprentice or not, his settlement changes with that of his mother. Great Barrington *v.* Tyringham, 18 Pick. (Mass.) 264.

1. Charlestown *v.* Boston, 13 Mass. 469; Attleborough *v.* Harwich, 17 Mass. 398; Jefferson *v.* Leetart, 3 Ohio 99; Bern *v.* Knox, 6 Cow. (N. Y.) 433.

2. Milo *v.* Gardiner, 41 Me. 549; Hampden *v.* Brewer, 24 Me. 281.

In *Rhode Island*, the settlement which one derives from his father never ceases till he has acquired one of his own. Paine *v.* Smithfield, 10 R. I. 446.

3. Shirley *v.* Lancaster, 6 Allen (Mass.) 31; Springfield *v.* Wilbraham, 4 Mass. 493.

4. Lebanon *v.* Hebron, 6 Conn. 45.

5. Salem *v.* Ipswich, 10 Cush. (Mass.) 517.

6. Overseers of Northumberland *v.* Overseers of Milton Borough (Pa.), 9 Atl. Rep. 449; Windham *v.* Lebanon, 51 Conn. 319; Shrewsbury Overseers *v.* Holmdel Overseers, 42 N. J. L. 373; Wayne *v.* Jersey Shore, 81 Pa. St. 264; Hebron *v.* Marlborough, 2 Conn. 18; Danburry *v.* New Haven, 5 Conn. 584; Woodstock *v.* Hooker, 6 Conn. 35; Windsor *v.* Hartford, 2 Conn. 355; Sterling *v.* Plainfield, 4 Conn. 114; Alexandria *v.* Kingwood, 8 N. J. L. 370; Redington *v.* Tewksbury, 2 N. J. L. 289; Bern *v.* Knox, 6 Cow. (N. Y.) 433; Niskayuna *v.* Albany, 2 Cow. (N. Y.) 537; Patterson *v.* Bryan, 23 N. J. L. 394; Town of Exeter *v.* Town of Warwick, 1 R. I. 63; Rex *v.* Heaton Norris, 6 T. R. 653.

When the mother is fraudulently removed from the town where she has a settlement, that she may be delivered in another town, the child will be considered as born in the former town. Plymouth *v.* Windsor, 7 Vt. 327.

7. Limestone Overseers etc. *v.* Chillisquaque Overseers etc., 87 Pa. St. 294; Vernon *v.* Smithville, 17 Johns. (N. Y.) 189; Madison Overseers *v.* Monroe Overseers, 42 N. J. L. 493; Reg. *v.* Hendon, 32 L. J., M. C. 19.

2. *Emancipation.*—A child is emancipated by law at the age of twenty-one years.[1] If the child is in fact emancipated before arriving at full age, his settlement is that of his father at the time of emancipation,[2] and he gains no settlement through the settlement of his parent acquired after such emancipation.[3] He may acquire a settlement independent of his parents,[4] but until emancipated he is incapable of gaining a settlement in his own right.[5]

Where a child leaves home for temporary employment, even though she receives the proceeds for her own use, is not so uncommon an occurrence as to authorize an inference of any change in the parental and filial ties. It is the father alone who can emancipate the child. Where there is no relinquishment on his part of the right and control of, or repudiation of his parental obligations to the child, but simply an assent to a particular course of life on her part for the time being, it does not amount to emancipation as defined by the authorities.[6] So the binding out of a minor to service by the selectmen does not emancipate such minor from the control of his father, so as to give him a settlement other than that of his father.[7]

The settlement of a pauper is the place of his birth, until he acquires another derivatively from his parents, or by acts of his own. Toby *v.* Madison, 44 Pa. St. 60.

In Wynkoop *v.* Overseers of New York, 3 Johns. (N. Y.) 15, it is held that if the mother has no settlement in the State, the child is settled when it is born.

An alien born does not take the original settlement, in this State, of a father who, before his birth, removed to Canada and never returned. Lyndon *v.* Danville, 28 Vt. 809.

1. Andover *v.* Merrimack County, 37 N. H. 437. See Alexandria *v.* Bethlehem, 16 N. J. L. 119; Rex *v.* Whitton-cum-Swanbrookes, 3 T. R. 355.

A pauper who, from infirmity of mind or body, is obliged to remain with his parents after he is twenty-one years of age, cannot be considered as emancipated so long as he so remains, and is considered as having the settlement of his father during that time. Oxford *v.* Rumney, 3 N. H. 331.

A daughter is emancipated at the age of twenty-one years, though she remains a member of her father's family, unless she is disabled to take care of herself; and she does not take her father's after-acquired settlement. Andover *v.* Merrimack County, 37 N. H. 437.

The illegitimate *non compos* child of a *non compos* mother is considered as emancipated, for all the purposes of the act concerning the settlement and support of the poor. East Hartford *v.* Middletown, 1 Root (Conn.) 196.

2. Lowell *v.* Newport, 66 Me. 78.

3. Dennysville *v.* Trescot, 30 Me. 470. See Calais *v.* Marshfield, 30 Me. 511; Niskayuna *v.* Albany, 2 Cow. (N. Y.) 537; Toby *v.* Madison, 44 Pa. St. 60; Tunbridge *v.* Eden, 39 Vt. 17.

Under the laws of *Maine*, *New Hampshire* and *Massachusetts*, a minor, after emancipation does not follow the settlement gained by the parent. Lowell *v.* Newport, 66 Me. 78.

A son, who has become emancipated from his father's family, will not follow the settlement of his father. Washington *v.* Beaver, 3 Watts & S. (Pa.) 548.

4. Lubec *v.* Eastport, 3 Me. 220; Wells *v.* Kennebunk, 8 Me. 200.

Children do not take the settlement of their parents, if, by any legal emancipation, they can acquire one of their own. Charlestown *v.* Boston, 13 Mass. 469.

5. Farmington *v.* Jay, 18 Me. 376; Shiley *v.* Watertown, 3 Mass. 322; Somerset *v.* Dighton, 12 Mass. 383; Pittston *v.* Wiscasset, 4 Me. 293.

A male child can gain no settlement in his own right during his minority, although he is married. Taunton *v.* Plymouth, 15 Mass. 203.

6. Searsmont *v.* Thorndike, 77 Me. 504; Lowell *v.* Newport, 66 Me. 89.

7. Oldtown *v.* Falmouth, 40 Me. 106.

Emancipation, such as will affect a settlement under the pauper law, however it may be in other cases, must be an absolute and entire surrender on the part of the parent of all right to the care and custody of the child, as well as to its earnings, with the renunciation of all duties arising from such a position, leaving the child, so far as the parents are concerned, free to act upon its own responsibility and in accordance with its own will, and virtually with the same independence as though it were twenty-one years of age.[1]

3. *Adopted Children.*—Under a statute passed for the legal adoption by one person of the child of another, which provides that "a child or person so adopted shall be deemed for the purpose of inheritance and other legal consequences of the natural relation of parent to child, to be the child of the parent or parents by adoption as if born to them in lawful wedlock except," etc., the child so adopted is adjudged to be the child of the parents by adoption to the full extent, as if born to them in lawful wedlock, and the settlement of such an adopted child follows the settlement of its father by adoption.[2] But no one can become a member of another's family, so as thereby to gain a home within the meaning of the settlement laws, unless vo untar there and with the consent of the head of the family.[3] l ily

4. *Children Separated from Parents.*—Children living separate from their father on account of his poverty, the parental and filial relation in other respects continuing, are still under his care and protection as much as his and their condition permits. So supplies furnished such children living apart from their father are supplies indirectly furnished him, and prevent his gaining a settlement by lapse of time in the town in which he may reside.[4]

5. *Marriage of Parent.*—Minor children having the settlement of their mother, did not by the common law acquire any new one she gained by marriage.[5] But the common law in this respect

1. Lowell *v.* Newport, 66 Me. 78.

In Frankfort *v.* New Vineyard, 48 Me. 565, it is held that a minor child of parents who are paupers bound to service by written indenture until twenty-one years of age is not thereby emancipated.

So in Salisbury *v.* Orange, 5 N. H. 348, it is also held that a child is not emancipated by being given away to its relatives.

But in Portland *v.* Gloucester, 16 Me. 427, it is held that if a father gives away his child to persons living in a different town, with whom he ever afterwards lives as their own child, without interference or assistance on the part of the father, the child is emancipated, and may gain a settlement for himself while a minor.

2. Washburn *v.* White, 140 Mass. 568.

3. Etna *v.* Brewer, 78 Me. 377; Corinth *v.* Lincoln, 34 Me. 310.

4. Garland *v.* Dover, 19 Me. 441.

The fact that the head of the family breaks up her home, and goes about working from town to town, does not change the constructive residence of the family. Rowell, J., dissenting. Town of Rockingham *v.* Town of Springfield (Vt.), 9 Atl. Rep. 241.

5. Freetown *v.* Taunton, 16 Mass. 52; Bloomfield *v.* Chagrin, 5 Ohio 315. See Cumner *v.* Milton, 2 Salk. 528; Spencer *v.* Pleasant, 17 Ohio St. 31.

In Spears *v.* Snell, 74 N. Car 210, it was held that a second marriage of a mother, and her removal to another county, cannot change the settlement

has been altered by statutes in some of the States;[1] minor children follow the settlement which their mother acquires by a second marriage,[2] provided none has been gained from their father;[3] so a minor child having the settlement of its deceased father does not lose it and acquire the settlement of its mother on her gaining a new settlement by a second marriage.[4] But the marriage of a woman, having a settlement, to a man having none, does not extinguish her settlement, or suspend its operation so as to prevent the transmission of it to their child.[5]

6. *Children by Divorced Father.*—If a man having a settlement is divorced *a vinculo*, and is married in another State while his former wife, and children by her, are still living, if the second marriage is valid when contracted, the children by it will be legitimate, and have the settlement of their father.[6]

7. *Illegitimate Children.*—Under a statute providing that "every illegimate child shall be deemed to be settled in the place where the mother was legally settled at the time of the birth of such child," its settlement is the settlement of the mother at the time of its birth.[7] It retains the settlement which its mother had at its birth until it gains one in its own right, notwithstanding that she

of a child born, and who continues to reside in the county of her former residence.

A minor child of a woman by a former husband does not take her mother's settlement acquired by a second marriage, although the child continues with the mother, and becomes a member of the stepfather's family. Overseers of Northumberland Borough *v.* Overseers of Milton Borough (Pa.), 9 Atl. Rep. 449.

1. Parsonsfield *v.* Kennebunkport, 4 Me. 50.

2. Goshen *v.* Richmond, 4 Allen (Mass.) 458.

3. Parsonsfield *v.* Kennebunkport, 4 Me. 47.

4. Walpole *v.* Marblehead, 8 Cush. (Mass.) 528; Fairfield *v.* Canaan, 7 Me. 90.

Under the provision of Conn. Gen. Stat. 618, § 5, that if a woman, having a settlement in that State, marries a man who has not, she shall keep and the minor children shall take her place of settlement, until the husband acquires one—where the wife and children had a settlement, but the husband had none, and supplies were furnished to the whole family—*held*, that the town where the wife had a settlement was liable for the supplies furnished to the wife and her children. Goshen *v.* Canaan, 35 Conn. 186.

5. Newtown *v.* Stratford, 3 Conn. 600; Otsego *v.* Smithfield, 6 Cow. (N. Y.) 760; Rex *v.* St. Botolph, Burr. S. C. 367. See Rex *v.* Cottingham, 1 M. & R. 439.

The settlement of a female inhabitant in *Connecticut* who marries a foreigner having no settlement in the State, is not affected by the marriage. Lebanon *v.* Hebron, 6 Conn. 45.

6. West Cambridge *v.* Lexington, 1 Pick. (Mass.) 506.

7. Lower Augusta *v.* Salmsgrove, 64 Pa. St. 166. See Town of Windham *v.* Town of Lebanon, 51 Conn. 323; Sterling *v.* Plainfield, 4 Conn. 114; Fairfield *v.* Canaan, 7 Me. 90; Fayette *v.* Leeds, 10 Me. 409; Sidney *v.* Winthrop, 5 Me. 123; Hebron *v.* Marlborough, 2 Conn. 18; Biddeford *v.* Saco, 7 Me. 270; South Hampton *v.* Hampton Falls, 11 N. H. 134; Dorchester *v.* Deerfield, 3 N. H. 316; Monson *v.* Palmer, 8 Allen (Mass.) 551; Petersham *v.* Dana, 12 Mass. 429; Boylston *v.* Princeton, 13 Mass. 381; Biddeford *v.* Saco, 7 Me. 272; Sidney *v.* Winthrop, 5 Me. 123; Bow *v.* Nottingham, 1 N. H. 260; Oxford *v.* Bethany, 19 Conn. 229; Cabot *v.* Washington, 41 Vt. 168; Manchester *v.* Springfield, 15 Vt. 385; Canaan *v.* Salisbury, 1 Root (Conn.) 155; Windsor *v.* Hartford, 2 Conn. 355; Woodstock *v.* Hooker, 6 Conn. 35. *Compare* Richardson *v.* Burlington, 33 N. J. L. 190.

subsequently acquires another.[1] An illegitimate child does not lose its original settlement, and gain a new one, until emancipated from the control of the mother, its natural guardian.[2] If the statute provides that "after the birth of an illegitimate child, his parents shall intermarry, and his father shall, after the marriage, acknowledge him as his child, such child shall be considered as legitimate to all intents and purposes," the child thereupon takes the settlement of the father.[3]

An illegitimate female child, born in a town wherein her mother had a legal settlement, was removed at six years of age by the mother to a township of another county, where the mother remained several years without acquiring a legal settlement; the mother and her husband then separating, the child, after living with an aunt, went to service in an adjoining borough where, after a few days' service, she was badly burned, and removed to the township, whose overseers, on an order for relief obtained from two justices, relieved her until she died. In an action of assumpsit against the borough overseers to recover the sum expended—*held*, that the district liable therefor was that wherein the mother had a legal settlement at the birth of the child. Nippenose *v.* Jersey Shore, 48 Pa. St. 402.

Where a bastard was born in the State of New York, in the year 1811, of a mother having a settlement in this State, and in 1814, the mother removed, with such bastard child, into this State, where she had since remained, without having at any time lost her original settlement—*held*, that such bastard child had a settlement by birth in the State of New York; and that, on his coming into this State, he did not take the settlement of his mother. Bethlem *v.* Roxbury, 20 Conn. 298.

So where the mother of a bastard child removes from another State into this, and the child is born here, the county of its birth is liable to be charged with the maintenance of the bastard. State *v.* McQuaig, 63 N. Car. 550.

In *New Jersey* the legal settlement of a bastard child is in the town or township where born, unless the mother then has a legal settlement elsewhere in the State, and the last residence by the mother for twelve months continuously in a township other than where the child was born, does not constitute such a legal settlement of the mother, as that the child could derive from it a settlement different from its place of birth. McCoy *v.* Overseer of Poor, 37 N. J. L. 133.

In *Maine* posthumous children have a derivative settlement from their father if he had any; and in this respect are in the same condition with such as are born in his lifetime. Farmington *v.* Jay, 19 Conn. 376.

So in Oxford *v.* Bethany, 19 Conn. 229, it is held that an illegitimate infant child takes the settlement of its mother acquired by marriage.

1. Hallowell *v.* Augusta, 52 Me. 216; Burlington *v.* Essex, 19 Vt. 91; Nottingham *v.* Amwell, 21 N. J. L. 127.

Under the *Vermont* Rev. St., an illegitimate child does not follow the settlement of the mother derived by marriage after the birth of the child. Newport *v.* Derby, 22 Vt. 553.

In *New York* the common law is altered by a statute declaring "that every bastard child shall be deemed and adjudged to be settled in the city or town of the last legal settlement of the mother." Canajoharie *v.* Johnstown, 17 Johns. (N. Y.) 41.

In *Connecticut*, an illegitimate minor child, born in one town, of a woman who has since acquired a settlement by marriage in another town, takes the settlement of its mother thus acquired. New Haven *v.* Newtown, 12 Conn. 165; Danbury *v.* New Haven, 5 Conn. 584. And see Oxford *v.* Bethany, 19 Conn. 232.

2. Fayette *v.* Leeds, 10 Me. 409.

A minor, illegitimate, and *non compos mentis*, was *held* to be incapable of gaining a settlement in a town by residing therein at the time of its incorporation, under the provisions of the act of 1821, ch. 122, its mother living at the time, and there having been no emancipation. Milo *v.* Kilmarnock, 11 Me. 455.

3. Monson *v.* Palmer, 8 Allen (Mass.) 551; Livermore *v.* Peru, 55 Me. 469; Rockingham *v.* Mt. Holly, 26 Vt. 653.

b. INSANE PERSONS—1. *Generally.*—Idiots or persons *non compos mentis* derive their settlements from their fathers.[1] Like slaves in former times, or a wife or minor child, their settlement changes with that of their fathers.[2] This is the rule, though such insane persons are more than twenty-one years of age.[3] But if the pauper becomes insane after he attains his majority, his settlement does not follow that of his father.[4] So, if insanity occurs after legal residence has been established, it does not interrupt a gaining of settlement in the town where such residence was gained.[5] If he removes, however, to another State, and, after acquiring a legal settlement, returns to his former domicile, where he is declared insane, his settlement will be in the State to which he removed, not in his former domicile, according to the general rule that the settlement of a person continues until he gains a new one.[6]

An insane person sent to the insane hospital as a patient by the authorities of the town in which he has established his residence, as provided by law, does not thereby lose the same, but it continues during his residence in the hospital.[7]

1. Shippen *v.* Gaines, 17 Pa. St. 38; Wiscasset *v.* Waldoborough, 3 Me. 388; Upton *v.* Northbridge, 15 Mass. 237. See Monroe *v.* Jackson, 55 Me. 55; Alexandria *v.* Bethlehem, 16 N. J. L. 119.

Compare Montoursville *v.* Fairfield, 112 Pa. St. 99.

Where one *non compos mentis*, after becoming of age, continues to reside with his father, being dependent on him, there is no emancipation, and the child's settlement, therefore, follows that of the father. Islesborough *v.* Lincolnville, 76 Me. 572.

An idiot, who lives with and is supported by the mother, has the settlement of the mother. East Hartford *v.* Middletown, 1 Root (Conn.) 196.

2. Upton *v.* Northbridge, 15 Mass. 237.

3. Wiscasset *v.* Waldoborough, 3 Me. 388; Upton *v.* Northbridge, 15 Mass. 237; Winterport *v.* Newburgh, 78 Me. 136.

The settlement of a *non compos* follows that of his father, though the former is of age. Upton *v.* Northbridge, 15 Mass. 237.

A person *non compos mentis* from birth and not emancipated, though past the age of twenty-one years, will follow the settlement of the father, and cannot acquire an independent settlement by residence in a town for five successive years. Monroe *v.* Jackson, 55 Me. 55.

A *non compos* or insane person is incapable of acquiring a pauper settlement in his own right. Such a person, who lived in his father's family until the age of forty-eight years, and was then sent to the insane hospital—*held*, to follow the residence of his father acquired while the pauper was an inmate of the hospital. Strong *v.* Farmington, 74 Me. 46.

4. Buckland *v.* Charlemont, 3 Pick. (Mass.) 173; Overseers of Gregg Tp. *v.* Overseers of New Berlin Borough (Pa.), 9 Atl. Rep. 461; Poor District Curwensville Borough *v.* Poor District, 9 Atl. Rep. 463.

5. Topsham *v.* Williamstown (Vt.), 12 Atl. Rep. 112; Washington County *v.* Manhaska County, 47 Iowa 57.

Insanity occurring after a person has become an inhabitant of a town will not prevent his acquiring a settlement under *Massachusetts* Rev. Stat., ch. 45, § 1, cl. 12, by living therein ten years consecutively. Chicopee *v.* Whately, 6 Allen (Mass.) 508.

Insanity, occurring after a residence has been established, will not prevent the acquisition of a settlement, if the residence is continued five years without the receiving of pauper supplies. Machias *v.* East Machias, 33 Me. 427.

6. Juniata County *v.* Delaware Overseers, 107 Pa. St. 68.

7. Pittsfield *v.* Detroit, 53 Me. 442.

The commitment and residence of an insane wife in the insane hospital does

2. *How Acquired.*—An idiot or person *non compos mentis* cannot acquire a residence or settlement in any place by virtue of his own acts. His residence or settlement is fixed either by the acts of his father or those having paramount control over him.[1] A pauper can obtain a settlement if he has a mind capable of having a choice and desire as to his place of abode, and in the exercise of that choice goes to and resides in a town voluntarily for the requisite time.[2]

To disqualify a person from making a choice of a settlement, under the poor law, by insanity, the mental derangement need not amount to complete madness. If the mind is diseased to such an extent as to deprive the person of volition, free will and power of choice, or deprive him of self-control as to matters involved in a choice of settlement, this is enough.[3] Until the contrary appears, it is presumed that a pauper has sufficient intellect to exercise a choice and intention in regard to residence; and where an insane person, after she has attained her majority, continues to reside in her father's house, and he afterwards acquires a residence in another town, if she does not take the settlement of her father, she acquires one in her own right by a residence of more than seven years.[4]

c. HUSBAND AND WIFE—1. *Generally.*—The wife takes her

not affect "the period of the residence" of the husband, necessary to change his settlement. Bangor *v.* Wiscasset, 71 Me. 535.

1. Payne *v.* Duwham, 29 Ill. 125. See Augusta *v.* Turner, 24 Me. 112; Plymouth *v.* Waterbury, 31 Conn. 515. *Compare* New Vineyard *v.* Harpswell, 33 Me. 193.

2. Westmore *v.* Sheffield, 56 Vt. 230; Fayett *v.* Chesterville, 77 Me. 28; Concord *v.* Rumney, 45 N. H. 423; State *v.* Dodge County, 56 Wis. 79; Talbot *v.* Chamberlain, 149 Mass. 58.

Where a child's intellect has become so impaired that she is incapable of exercising any choice or intention in regard to her residence, she is not emancipated, on attaining her majority, if she continues to reside in her father's house, and she takes a derivative settlement afterwards acquired by him. Topsham *v.* Chelsea (Vt.), 13 Atl. Rep. 861.

A person who has been from his birth *non compos mentis*, and whose parents are deceased, may reside in a town (within the meaning of the statute) so as to acquire a legal settlement therein, and if he shall continue to reside in a town for the term of five years together, after he is twenty-one years of age, without receiving any support as a pauper from any town, he will gain a lawful settlement therein in his own right. Gardiner *v.* Farmingdale, 45 Me. 537. See Auburn *v.* Hebron, 48 Me. 332; Corinth *v.* Bradley, 51 Me. 540.

Change of Domicile Pending Proceedings for the Appointment of a Guardian.—If an insane person of sufficient mental capacity to change his domicile in good faith, removes his residence to another State pending proceedings for the appointment of a guardian over him, and if his residence there continues until his death, and is assented to by his guardian, after his appointment, his change of domicile is complete. Talbot *v.* Chamberlain, 149 Mass. 57.

3. Townsend *v.* Pepperell, 99 Mass. 40; Buckland *v.* Charlemont, 3 Pick. (Mass.) 173.

Weakness of intellect, subjecting the person to oversight, influence, and care of friends, but not amounting to idiocy, does not incapacitate such person from making a removal of residence and acquiring a new settlement under the poor laws. Ludlow *v.* Landgrove, 42 Vt. 137.

4. Topsham *v.* Chelsea (Vt.), 13 Atl. Rep. 861.

husband's settlement, if he has one; if he has none, she retains her own,[1] but the marriage must be such as the laws recognize and the parties are competent to contract.[2] So, under a statute providing that "when it appears in a suit between towns involving the settlement of a pauper that the marriage was procured to change it by the agency or collusion of the officers of either town, or any person having charge of such pauper under authority of either town, the settlement is not affected by such marriage," the wife is prevented from taking the husband's settlement. Their children, however, will take his settlement instead of hers.[3] And a marriage unlawful and void, as where the first husband was still living, conveys no settlement to the wife, either by derivation from the second husband or by dwelling and having her home in his house.[4] The husband, if he has no settlement, follows the settlement of his wife.[5] If he has a settlement, it continues to be where the husband was last settled, if he gains no new settlement, although they are abandoned by him.[6] The settlement of the husband is gained, even though the wife is living apart from the husband, and receives assistance as a pauper in another town without her

1. North Bridgewater *v.* East Bridgewater, 13 Pick. (Mass.) 303; Buffalo *v.* Whitedeer, 15 Pa. St. 182; Concord *v.* Goffstown, 2 N. H. 263; *Ex parte* Madbury, 17 N. H. 569; Exeter *v.* Richmond, 6 R. I. 149; Newark *v.* Sutton, 40 Vt. 261; Windom *v.* Lebanon, 51 Conn. 319; Lewiston *v.* N. Yarmouth, 5 Me. 66; Guilford *v.* Oxford, 9 Conn. 321; Monroe County *v.* Jackson County, 72 Wis. 449; Hebron *v.* Colchester, 5 Day (Conn.) 169; Danbury *v.* New Haven, 5 Conn. 584; Alexandria *v.* Kingwood, 8 N. J. L. 370; Sherburne *v.* Norwich, 16 Johns. (N. Y.) 186; Cummington *v.* Belcherton (Mass.), 21 N. E. Rep. 435.

Proof of marriage, followed by cohabitation, makes out a *prima facie* case of the settlement of a wife in the place of her husband's settlement. Harrison *v.* Lincoln, 48 Me. 205.

Where the town of B, to which a portion of the town of O had been annexed, agreed with O to take upon itself, for support, L, a pauper of O, having a settlement on the territory transferred, so long as he should live and need help, binding him upon the town of B, for every liability to which towns are subject on account of paupers, and L afterwards married M, who needed support, *held*, that, though such agreement did not change the settlement of L, yet as L's settlement was in B, by virtue of the annexation, and the agreement was not inconsistent therewith, B had no claim upon O for the support of M. Oxford *v.* Bethany, 15 Conn. 246.

2. Dalton *v.* Bernardston, 9 Mass. 201; Middleborough *v.* Rochester, 12 Mass. 363. See Johnson *v.* Huntington, 1 Day (Conn.) 212.

A marriage celebrated by a justice of the peace, without the consent of the parties, is of no validity to change the settlement of the female. Mount Holly *v.* Andover, 11 Vt. 226.

3. Houlton *v.* Ludlow, 73 Me. 583; Appleton *v.* Belfast, 67 Me. 579; Town of Burnham *v.* Town of Corinth (Me.), 10 Atl. Rep. 454.

Where the authorities of a town in which a woman has a settlement procure her marriage to a man having a settlement elsewhere, for the purpose of relieving the town of her support, she does not lose her settlement, and if the town in which her husband lives supports her as a pauper, it may recover the amount expended from the town of her original settlement. Minot *v.* Bowdoin, 75 Me. 205.

4. Pittston *v.* Wiscasset, 4 Me. 293.

A marriage if declared void on account of insanity at the time of marrying, does not confer upon wife the settlement of her husband. Reading *v.* Ludlow, 43 Vt. 628.

5. East Greenwich *v.* Warwick, 4 R. I. 138.

6. Spencer *v.* Pleasant, 17 Ohio St. 31.

husband's knowledge,[1] but the wife gains no settlement during the coverture where the husband gains none.[2]

2. *Separate Settlement.*—Where the husband has voluntarily and absolutely deserted his wife with the intention to renounce the marital rights and duties, and where he compels her to leave and continue separated from him, she may gain a separate settlement as if she were unmarried.[3] So a married woman, whose husband has no settlement of his own, may acquire a settlement in her own right, by the possession of property, as if she were sole.[4] So a married woman after her husband's death may acquire a settlement by her own act,[5] but the residence of a woman during coverture and the continuance of it after the death of her husband cannot be united in determining the place of her settlement.[6]

A married woman, where a husband has a legal settlement within the State, retains that settlement after divorce *a vinculo*, and is not remitted to her maiden settlement.[7] So it is held that a wife who has been divorced *a mensa et thoro* on account of the cruel and barbarous conduct of her husband, and whose husband has deserted her and moved out of the State, can acquire a settlement in her own right, entitling her to support as a pauper.[8]

1. Berkley *v.* Taunton, 19 Pick. (Mass.) 480; Cambridge *v.* Charlestown, 13 Mass. 501.

2. Jefferson *v.* Litchfield, 1 Me. 196; Pittston *v.* Wiscasset, 4 Me. 293.

3. Washington County *v.* Mahaska County, 47 Iowa 57; Burlington *v.* Swanville, 64 Me. 78.

Compare Augusta *v.* Kingfield, 36 Me. 239.

4. Andover *v.* Merrimack County, 37 N. H. 437.

A wife who has separated from her husband because of his intemperate habits, and his failure to support her and her children, can gain a settlement distinct from that of her husband, by leasing real estate and living upon it, by virtue of *Pennsylvania* act of May 4, 1855, § 2, giving to such a woman the rights of a *femme sole* trader; which settlement so gained, can be communicated to her children who live with her, by virtue of section 3 of said act, making the relation between such a woman and her children the same as that between father and child. Overseers of Parker City *v.* Overseers of Du Bois Borough (Pa.), 9 Atl. Rep. 457.

5. Mifflin *v.* Elizabeth, 18 Pa. St. 17.

Where a husband had been absent at sea more than sixteen years prior to March 21, 1821, without having been heard from, except a rumor that he was impressed on board a British vessel of war, this was held to afford legal ground for the presumption that he was dead; so that the wife was capable of acquiring a new settlement for herself by dwelling on that day in another town, under the act of 1821, ch. 122. Biddeford *v.* Saco, 7 Me. 270.

6. Richmond *v.* Lisbon, 15 Me. 434; Thomaston *v.* St. George, 17 Me. 117.

7. Dalton *v.* Bernardston, 9 Mass. 201; Royalton *v.* West Fairlee, 11 Vt. 438; Ossipee *v.* Carroll County (N. H.), 17 Atl. Rep. 1058.

Where a pauper has been divorced from her husband, her settlement is in the district in which her husband resided at the time of the divorce. Lake District Overseers *v.* South Canaan Overseers, 87 Pa. St. 19.

A, an inhabitant of O, married a woman who had her settlement in G. Upon ascertaining, soon after, that she had been begotten with child previous to his marriage, he prayed the legislature for a divorce, which was granted. In an action by G against O, for the maintenance of the woman subsequent to the divorce—*held*, that the marriage was originally valid, and was not avoided *ab initio* by the act of divorce; and that the woman, therefore, took the settlement of her husband in O, and communicated such settlement to her illegitimate child. Guilford *v.* Oxford, 9 Conn. 321.

8. Overseers of Williamsport *v.* Overseers of Eldred, 84 Pa. St. 429.

d. ALIENS.—In *Vermont* it is held that an alien born takes no right to a settlement by derivation, whether he comes to this country during or subsequent to his minority, and whether his parents return with him or not.[1] But under some statutes a foreigner may gain a settlement by commorancy.[2] See ALIENS, vol. 1, p. 464.

5. Changes in Towns.—Where the territory of which a new town is composed was, before the incorporation an unincorporated place, incorporation *ipso facto* gives every one inhabited there a legal settlement.[3] Where part of a town is set off and incorporated into a new town, paupers are chargeable to the town or that part of the town in which their settlements are at the time of incorporation.[4] If a pauper has a settlement in the old town

1. Elmore *v.* Calais, 33 Vt. 468.

2. Somers *v.* Barkhamstead, 1 Root (Conn.) 398; Commonwealth *v.* Sudbury, 106 Mass. 268.

Where an alien enlisted, in 1775, as a soldier in the revolutionary army, and served the United States, as a soldier in that army, during that war, as one of the quota of the town of P —*held*, that such soldier, by virtue of the act of February, 1781, acquired a settlement in the town of P, and, consequently, a capacity to gain a settlement in any other town by commorancy. Griswold *v.* N. Stonington, 5 Conn. 367. See Cummington *v.* Springfield, 2 Pick. (Mass.) 394; Phipps' Case, 2 Pick. (Mass.) 394.

In *Connecticut*, under the act of 1865, as modified by the acts of 1878 and 1879, a man who was naturalized in 1877 and remained thereafter continuously in a certain town for more than four years, gained a settlement as a citizen. Guilford *v.* New Haven, 56 Conn. 465.

In *New Jersey*, in order to gain a settlement, the foreigner must come directly from Europe into the State. Stillwater *v.* Green, 9 N. J. L. 59; New Barbadoes *v.* Patterson, 27 N. J. L. 544.

In *Massachusetts*, by the St. of 1871, ch. 379, amending the St. of 1868, ch. 328, an alien may acquire a settlement by residence. Endicott *v.* Hopkington, 125 Mass. 522.

3. Bath *v.* Bowdoin, 4 Mass. 452; Sutton *v.* Orange, 6 Met. (Mass.) 484; Buckfield *v.* Gorham, 6 Mass. 445; Walpole *v.* Hopkington, 4 Pick. (Mass.) 357; Berlin *v.* Gorham, 34 N. H. 266.

At the common law, when a place is incorporated as a town all the inhabitants of such place at the time, gain a settlement in the town by the act of incorporation. Salisbury *v.* Orange, 5 N. H. 348.

In the act incorporating a portion of an old town into a new one, it was provided, that those, who should afterwards become chargeable to the town as paupers, should be considered as belonging to that town, "on the territory of which they had their settlement at the time of the passing of this act, and shall in the future be chargeable to that town only;" a pauper had gained a settlement in the old town at its incorporation, by residing therein on that part of it made into the new town, but when the new town was incorporated, had removed into a different part of the old town, and there remained until this territory was incorporated into a third town; the pauper, who had never gained any settlement unless by these acts of incorporation, was held to have a settlement in the second town, under the special provision in the act of incorporation. Bloomfield *v.* Skowhegan, 16 Me. 58.

4. Mount Desert *v.* Seaville, 20 Me. 341; Kirkland *v.* Bradford, 33 Me. 580; Yarmouth *v.* North Yarmouth, 44 Me. 352; Clinton *v.* Benton, 49 Me. 550. New Chester *v.* Bristol, 3 N. H. 71; Braintree *v.* Boylston, 24 Pick. (Mass.) 164; Salem *v.* Ipswich, 10 Cush. (Mass.) 517; Ashland County *v.* Richland County, 7 Ohio St. 65; St. George *v.* Deer Isle, 3 Me. 310.

Compare Westborough *v.* Franklin, 15 Mass. 254; Sutton *v.* Dana, 4 Pick. (Mass.) 117.

Under the special act of 1842, by which the town of Minot was divided, and the new town of Auburn incorporated, a person whose settlement in Minot had been gained by residence in

and actually dwells and has his home in the territory included in the new town, when the act dividing the old town and incorporating the new town takes effect, it gives the pauper a settlement in the new town.[1]

The setting off of a part of a town and annexing it to another, has the same effect as the incorporation of a new town, as regards the legal settlement of persons resident on the territory annexed.[2] So where a part of an existing town is by special statute annexed to another existing town, the inhabitants living upon the part detached will acquire a settlement in the town to which they may be annexed.[3] But an actual dwelling, or having a home, on the part annexed, is necessary to effect a change of settlement.[4]

that part of it incorporated as a new town, has his settlement in Auburn, if he has not gained a settlement elsewhere. Winthrop *v.* Auburn, 31 Me. 465.

Where a new town was created of parts of several towns, and it was provided that the new town should support all such persons as before had been, then were, or thereafter might be, inhabitants of those parts of the former towns then incorporated into such new town, and were or might become chargeable, and who had not a settlement elsewhere—it was holden that the new town was not chargeable with the support of paupers who, at the time of the incorporation, were supported by one of the old towns upon the territory forming part of the new town, but whose settlement was derived from owning and occupying real estate in another part of the old town. Southbridge *v.* Charlton, 15 Mass. 248.

1. Frankfort *v.* Winterport, 51 Me. 445; North Andover *v.* Groveland, 1 Allen (Mass.) 75; Eddington *v.* Brewer, 41 Me. 462; Williamsburg *v.* Jackson, 11 Ohio 37; Overseers of Franklin Tp. *v.* Overseers of Clinton Tp., 51 N. J. L. 93.

Where a part of one town has been annexed to another, a pauper residing on the part annexed with one who had contracted with the town to support him, but whose residence had, prior thereto, been in a part not annexed, is not thereby transferred to the town to which the annexation is made—such residence being merely temporary, and not established in that part of the town to which it is. Smithfield *v.* Belgrade, 19 Me. 387.

By *Maine* Rev. Stat. 1841, ch. 32, § 1, the question of settlement in a new town, formed from two or more, depends upon the fact of an actual home, and not upon a temporary residence within its limits at the time of its incorporation. Brewer *v.* Eddington, 42 Me. 541.

A person who has died prior to the division of a town, a part of which is incorporated into a new town, cannot be considered as "absent at the time" of the division, within Me. Rev. St., ch. 24, § 1, cl. 4; neither can he be considered as having his "home in the new town" within the last clause in that section. Rockland *v.* Morrill, 71 Me. 455.

2. Repley *v.* Levant, 42 Me. 308; Hallowell *v.* Bowdoinham, 1 Me. 129.

3. Great Barrington *v.* Lancaster, 14 Mass. 253; Groton *v.* Shirley, 7 Mass. 156; Fitchburg *v.* Westminster, 1 Pick. (Mass.) 144; Inhabitants of Dana *v.* Inhabitants of Hardwick, 10 Met. (Mass.) 208; Bethany *v.* Oxford, 15 Conn. 550; Hay River *v.* Sherman, 60 Wis. 54; Overseers etc. of Bethlehem *v.* Overseers etc. of Alexandria, 32 N. J. L. 66; La Crosse *v.* Melrose, 22 Wis. 459; Hopewell *v.* Independence, 12 Pa. St. 92; Eddington *v.* Brewer, 41 Me. 462.

4. Southbridge *v.* Charlton, 15 Mass. 248; Fitchburg *v.* Westminster, 1 Pick. (Mass.) 146; New Portland *v.* Rumford, 13 Me. 299; New Portland *v.* New Vineyard, 16 Me. 69; Starks *v.* New Sharon, 39 Me. 368; Wilmington *v.* Somerest, 35 Vt. 232; Woodstock *v.* Bethel, 66 Me. 569; Beetham *v.* Lincoln, 16 Me. 137; Franklin Twp. *v.* Clinton Twp., 51 N. J. L. 93.

Where a man having a family had resided with them more than six years, in the territory annexed, and had thereby acquired a settlement thereon, but, a few months before the time of annexa-

Where a town has been divided, each part becomes liable to support such paupers as may have gained a settlement in that part, provided the legislature on division has not prescribed a different rule, and that question as to settlement of paupers must be determined as if the two towns had always been as they are after being divided, except so far as the legislature may have otherwise provided.[1] So where an old town is divided into two new towns, those who have settlements in the old town will become settled in the towns respectively where they may reside at the time of the incorporation.[2]

A settlement is gained by residence within the jurisdictional limits of a town, although without its charter boundaries.[3] But if a pauper has resided for a sufficient time to gain a settlement upon one of a tier of lots lying between two towns, and over which each town has claimed and exercised jurisdiction, no jurisdictional line having ever been established or acquiesced in between them, his settlement will be deemed to be in that town within the charter limits of which the tier of lots actually lies.[4]

6. How Settlement Prevented—*a.* GENERALLY.—The warning of a person in conformity with the statute, prevents the person warned from gaining a settlement, and all others who derive their

tion, his wife being dead, and his family broken up, he went to reside at the almshouse in another portion of the town, and was there supported by the town at the time of annexation—*held*, that this change of his local habitation did not prevent a transfer of his settlement, with the territory, from the one town to the other. Bethany *v.* Oxford, 15 Conn. 550.

1. Town of Haddam *v.* Town of East Lynne, 54 Conn. 34; Bethany *v.* Oxford, 15 Conn. 550; Waterbury *v.* Bethany, 18 Conn. 424.

An act severing a town does not give a settlement to one as a pauper who had not one before. Gilford *v.* Gilmanton, 20 N. H. 456. West Springfield *v.* Granville, 4 Mass. 486. See Strafford *v.* Strafford, 43 N. H. 606.

If a person having a legal settlement is removed from the town when the division is made he will acquire a settlement in that town in which his last dwelling place in the original town happened to fall, upon such division. Lexington *v.* Burlington, 19 Pick. (Mass.) 426; Sutton *v.* Dana, 4 Pick. (Mass.) 117; Hanson *v.* Pembroke, 16 Pick. (Mass.) 167; Windham *v.* Portland, 4 Mass. 384.

By the act of Dec. 16, 1828, upon any division of a town, the settlement of persons then resident elsewhere, but having a legal settlement in the town divided, followed their former dwelling places; if those were dissevered and annexed to another town, their settlement was thereby transferred to that other town. Barnstead *v.* Alton, 32 N. H. 245.

2. Westport *v.* Dartmouth, 10 Mass. 341; Eastbridgewater *v.* Bridgewater, 2 Pick. (Mass.) 572; Princeton *v.* West Boylston, 15 Mass. 257; West Springfield *v.* Granville, 4 Mass. 486.

3. Corinth *v.* Newbury, 13 Vt. 496.

If a town exercise actual and exclusive jurisdiction over land, the residents thereon will gain a settlement in that town, notwithstanding the land is not within its chartered limits; and evidence that the town has for more than seven years levied and collected taxes of a resident upon such land, caused his children to be returned as belonging to one of its school districts, and allowed him to vote at its town meetings, is competent to show that such jurisdiction has been exercised as will give him a settlement in that town; and upon such evidence, if there is no rebutting testimony, the court will be justified in instructing the jury that the person, who had thus been treated by the town, had a legal settlement therein. Reading *v.* Weathersfield, 30 Vt. 504.

4. Landgrove *v.* Peru, 16 Vt. 422.

settlement from him.[1] If he leaves the place and returns after an absence sufficiently long to acquire a settlement elsewhere, a new warning is necessary to prevent a settlement.[2]

Where the statute requires the service of a warrant on the person in order to prevent him from gaining a settlement in a township by length of residence and that such warrant and return be recorded with the clerk of the township, the statute be strictly complied with, and a failure to record the same is fatal.[3]

Furnishing aid to a pauper in need of relief will prevent him from gaining a settlement,[4] and under some statutes it is

1. Northwood *v.* Durham, 2 N. H. 242. See Chelsea *v.* Malden, 4 Mass. 131; Wheelock *v.* Lundon, 6 Vt. 524; Gilford *v.* Epping, 12 N. H. 498; Exeter *v.* Stratham, 2 N. H. 102; Jaffrey *v.* Mount Vernon, 8 N. H. 436; Hardwick *v.* Raynham, 14 Mass. 363; Reading *v.* Rockingham, 2 Aik. (Vt.) 272; Williamsburg *v.* Jackson, 11 Ohio 37; Shirley *v.* Watertown, 3 Mass. 322.

Compare Salem *v.* Andover, 3 Mass. 436; Springfield *v.* Wilbraham, 4 Mass. 493.

In Wayne *v.* Stock, 3 Ohio 71 it is *held* that a person gains a legal settlement in a township, though warned on first settlement to depart, if the warning is not repeated every year.

A warning of a pauper and his family, without naming the latter, is sufficient to prevent the settlement of his wife and infant. Shirley *v.* Watertown, 3 Mass. 322; Somerset *v.* Dighton, 12 Mass. 383.

Warning-out process against husband and wife, if sufficiently served on the husband, prevents the wife's gaining a settlement. Barnet *v.* Concord, 4 Vt. 564.

Under the act of 1801, a woman living with a man as his wife, under a void marriage, was not included in a warning of the man and his family; she might gain a settlement by residence. Manchester *v.* Springfield, 15 Vt. 385.

A warning to persons to depart from a town, to prevent their gaining a settlement, is void, unless the time of their abode in the town appears either in the warrant itself, or in the return of the officer who served it. Loudon *v.* Deering, 1 N. H. 13; Jaffrey *v.* Mount Vernon, 8 N. H. 436; Hamilton *v.* Ipswich, 10 Mass. 506; Sutton *v.* Uxbridge, 2 Pick. (Mass.) 436; Middleborough *v.* Plympton, 19 Pick. (Mass.) 489; Meredith *v.* Exeter, 8 N. H. 136; Coventry *v.* Boscawen, 9 N. H. 227.

Proceedings for warning a pauper are invalid, if the officer's return thereon is not recorded by the town-clerk within a year from the commencement of the pauper's residence; and a subsequent amendment of the record is not allowable. And it must appear that the officer served the warning on the person named, or left at his usual abode a copy, with his return thereon. New Haven *v.* Vergennes, 3 Vt. 89. Reading *v.* Weathersfield, 3 Vt. 349; Mount Holly *v.* Panton, Brayt. (Vt.) 182.

A warning, under the act of 1801, is not vitiated by omission of the words "of this precept with," in the direction "hereof fail not," etc. It is sufficient to serve a warning against man and wife, on the man. If service is made on one of the name and town mentioned in the warning, it is *prima facie* sufficient, in default of evidence of another person of the same name in the town. Dummerstown *v.* Jamaica, 5 Vt. 399.

Return.—The following return on a warning-out process, "Aug, 22d, 1806. I then served this precept, by leaving a true and attested copy of the same, and return, with the within-named N W, as the law directs," was *held* to be sufficient. Fairlee *v.* Corinth, 9 Vt. 265.

The warning out of a pauper is insufficient. if the return admits of any doubt as to the strict regularity of the service. Townsend *v.* Athens, 1 Vt. 284; Marshfield *v.* Monpelier, 4 Vt. 284; Barre *v.* Morristown, 4 Vt. 574.

Burden of Proof—The *onus* of proving the warning out of an inhabitant of a town, under the settlement act of 1801, falls upon the party claiming the benefit of such proceeding. Fayston *v.* Richmond, 25 Vt. 446; Pawlet *v.* Sandgate, 17 Vt. 619.

2. Chelsea *v.* Malden, 4 Mass. 131; Ira *v.* Clarendon, Brayt. (Vt.) 180.

3. Olive *v.* Manchester, 8 Ohio 113.

4. Worcester *v.* Auburn, 4 Allen (Mass.) 574; Oakham *v.* Sutton, 13 Met. (Mass.) 192; Fayette County *v.*

sufficient to prevent a person's gaining a settlement by residence, if he is in need of immediate relief, which is furnished by the town and accepted, although the pauper does not apply for the relief.[1]

Neither a father nor mother can gain a settlement in a town by residence and payment of taxes while their unemancipated son is supported by another town as a pauper in the family at their request.[2] So the reception of pauper supplies by a man's wife,

Bremer County, 56 Iowa 516; Augusta *v.* Mercer (Me.), 13 Atl. Rep. 401. See Gleason *v.* Boston (Mass.), 10 N. E. Rep. 476.

A settlement cannot be gained by residence and payment of taxes while a person is being supported as a pauper by another town. Croydon *v.* Sullivan, 47 N. H. 179; West Newbury *v.* Bradford, 3 Met. (Mass.) 428.

So a person does not acquire a settlement in a town under *Massachusetts* Rev. Stat., ch. 45, § 1, cl. 4, by having an estate of inheritance or freehold in the town, and living on the same three years successively, if he receive support as a pauper during those three years, from the town in which he had his settlement. Oakham *v.* Sutton, 13 Met. (Mass.) 192.

A pauper, while supported as such, has no "home or dwelling-place" within the meaning of the statute of *Vermont.* Wilmington *v.* Somerset, 35 Vt. 232.

In order to have received supplies as a pauper, constructively, so as to prevent the operation of the act of 1821, ch. 122, they must have been furnished to one under the care and protection of him whose settlement is in question, and for whose support he is by law responsible. Hallowell *v.* Saco, 5 Me. 143.

One's receiving aid, while a prisoner, from the town where the prison is situated, on a previous pledge of sufficient personal property to secure a remuneration, does not prevent his gaining a settlement by seven years' residence in the town from which he is removed to the prison. Montpelier *v.* Calais, 5 Vt. 571.

If a town renders aid to a person in discharge of a duty that it has assumed by way of contract, and not in discharge of a duty imposed by statute, such aid will not prevent the person from acquiring a settlement in the town. Town of Cavendish *v.* Town of Mt. Holly, 48 Vt. 525.

1. Corrinna *v.* Exeter, 13 Me. 321. See Canaan *v.* Bloomfield, 3 Me. 172. *Compare* Veazie *v.* Chester, 53 Me. 29.

Aid furnished a pauper by the town in which he resides, but not at his request in good faith, the aid being required, will have the same effect upon a question of settlement as though furnished upon application by the pauper or at his request. Weston *v.* Wallingford, 52 Vt. 630.

Rev. St. Me, 1883, ch. 24, § 1, entitles any one to a settlement, after residence of five years without receiving supplies as a pauper. Under act 1875 (Laws Me. 1875, ch. 21), a soldier dependent in consequence of injuries sustained during the war shall not be considered a pauper. *Held*, that supplies to a soldier, to prevent him from gaining a new settlement, must be given to relieve distress not occasioned by injuries sustained in the war. Augusta *v.* Mercer (Me.), 13 Atl. Rep. 401.

2. Croydon *v.* Sullivan, 4 N. H. 179; Glenburn *v.* Naples, 69 Me. 68; Inhabitants of Taunton *v.* Inhabitants of Middleborough, 12 Met. (Mass.) 35. See Norwich *v.* Saybrook, 5 Conn. 384; Standish *v.* Windham, 10 Me. 97; Clinton *v.* York, 26 Me. 167.

Where certain advancements were made by the selectmen of a town to a female pauper, to aid her in a prosecution for the maintenance of a bastard child, and for her personal relief, which were afterwards reimbursed to the town from money paid by the putative father of the child on a settlement, it was held that such advancement had no effect to prevent her from gaining a settlement in another town by residence. Lebanon *v.* Hebron, 6 Conn. 45.

Compare Raymond *v.* Harrison, 11 Me. 190; Gleason *v.* Boston, 144 Mass. 25.

So when a father has deliberately abandoned his minor daughter, has renounced all obligation to her, and has destroyed all parental and filial relations between them, it constitutes such an emancipation of the child that pau-

when he knows of her necessities and fails to relieve them, will interrupt the process of his gaining a settlement,[1] and in order to prevent a pauper from gaining a settlement by furnishing supplies it is not necessary that notice be given to the town of his settlement of the furnishing of such supplies.[2]

Supplies are considered as furnished to a man as a pauper when furnished either to himself personally or to some of his family, who reside under his immediate care and protection.[3] So supplies furnished to a family by the overseers of the poor will be considered as furnished to all the members thereof, including those of full age and not subject to the control of any other member of it.[4] So if a town furnish one of its paupers a house in which to live and land on which to work, the house and land may be regarded as pauper supplies, and prevent the pauper from acquiring a settlement by residence as long as he occupies them.[5] But aid furnished and accepted as a mere act of neighborly kindness, although afterwards voluntarily paid for by the town, does not constitute "supplies" within the pauper act.[6]

7. How Lost—*a.* GENERALLY.—A settlement remains where established until one is acquired in some other town,[7] and when once acquired it is presumed to continue until a subsequent change

per supplies furnished her, even with the father's knowledge, cannot be considered as supplies indirectly furnished to him, and will not prevent his gaining a settlement in another town to which he had removed. Town of Liberty *v.* Town of Palermo, 79 Me. 473.

Supplies furnished by a town to a minor child, without the knowledge or consent of the father, while the father is of ability to support the child, will not prevent the father from gaining a settlement by five years' residence, under the *Maine* Rev. Stat., ch. 32, § 1, subd. 6. Bangor *v.* Readfield, 32 Me. 60.

The families of absent soldiers, in the service of the United States, when standing in need of assistance, do not incur the disabilities of pauperism by receiving supplies from the cities or towns where such soldiers resided at the time of their enlistment. Veazie *v.* China, 50 Me. 518; Milford *v.* Orono, 50 Me. 529; Ames *v.* Smith, 51 Me. 602.

The support of a mother by her daughter is not supporting a poor person as a pauper, within the meaning of the Rev. St. Wis., §1500, subd. 4, providing that no person shall gain a residence in a town by being supported therein as a pauper. Monroe County *v.* Jackson County (Wis.), 40 N. W. Rep. 224.

1. Lewiston *v.* Harrison, 69 Me. 504; Charlestown *v.* Groveland, 15 Gray (Mass.) 15; Woodward *v.* Worcester, 15 Gray (Mass.) 19.

2. Corinna *v.* Exeter, 13 Me. 321.

3. Green *v.* Buckfield, 3 Me. 136.

Supplies furnished to a woman as a pauper, without the knowledge of her husband, she living apart from him, are not supplies received by him as a pauper, within the meaning of the act of 1821, ch. 122, § 2. Dixmont *v.* Biddeford, 3 Me. 205.

4. Corinth *v.* Lincoln, 34 Me. 310.

5. Lee *v.* Wrim, 75 Me. 465. See Wiscassett *v.* Waldoborough, 3 Me. 388.

6. Hampden *v.* Bangor, 68 Me. 368.

7. Sitterly *v.* Murray, 63 How. (N. Y.) Pr. 367; Payne *v.* Dunham, 29 Ill. 125. See Crane *v.* Antrim, 12 Ohio St. 430; Mansfield *v.* Grandy, 1 Root (Conn.) 179; Norwich *v.* Windham, 1 Root (Conn.) 232; Colchester *v.* East Lyme, 18 Conn. 480.

Compare Wilbraham *v.* Sturbridge, 6 Cush. (Mass.) 61.

A legal settlement in one place cannot be lost without acquiring a new one in another place. Phillips *v.* Kingfield, 19 Me. 375.

is shown.[1] So a settlement is lost by gaining one elsewhere.[2] A settlement is not lost or gained by changing the domicile from one place to another in the same town.[3]

b. CHANGE OF SETTLEMENT.—Absence for sufficient length of time with an intention of never returning, will change a settlement,[4] but the residence of a pauper with a person who supports him under a contract with the town, his settlement being but temporary, has no effect to change the settlement of the pauper.[5] So an agreement to support stepchildren does not change the legal settlement of the children, although they become a member of the family of the stepfather;[6] nor can the legal settlement of a pauper be changed by the acts or admissions of the overseers of the poor of the town.[7] So no agreement between towns will change the settlement of the inhabitants.[8]

VI. REMOVAL—1. Generally.—When an application is made to the overseers of the poor for relief by or for any person under their charge, certain proceedings are directed by statute for determining his settlement. Justices of the peace are generally empowered to adjudicate and determine the legal settlements of persons asking for relief, and they may summon the pauper and other witnesses, or compel the appearance of the former by warrant, in order that he may be examined and his objections given to such removal.[9] And if his settlement is found to be within the county or township over which the overseers have jurisdiction, an order can be made for relieving the person. If such settlement is found to be in some other county or township, an appropriate order of removal may be directed.[10]

1. Chicopee *v.* Whately, 6 Allen (Mass.) 508. See Sterling *v.* Plainfield, 4 Conn. 114; Newfane *v.* Dummerston, 34 Vt. 184.

2. Bethelem *v.* Roxbury, 20 Conn. 298; Chelsea *v.* Malden, 4 Mass. 131; Dalton *v.* Bernardston, 9 Mass. 201; Canton *v.* Bentley, 11 Mass. 441; Townsend *v.* Billerica, 10 Mass. 411; Poor *v.* Overseers (Pa.), 18 Atl. Rep. 549.

Compare Morris *v.* Plymouth, 64 Conn. 270; Peterborough *v.* Lancaster, 14 N. H. 382; Hanover *v.* Weare, 2 N. H. 131; Landaff *v.* Atkinson, 8 N. H. 532.

A person having a settlement in one State loses it by gaining a settlement in another State, and can regain his former settlement in no other manner than any other inhabitant of another State. Middleton *v.* Lyme, 5 Conn. 95.

3. Princeton *v.* West Boylston, 15 Mass. 257; Overseers Lower Augusta Tp. *v.* Overseers Howard Tp. (Pa.), 9 Atl. Rep. 446; Malden *v.* Melrose, 125 Mass. 304.

4. Burlington *v.* Swanville, 64 Me. 78. See *supra*, this title, *By Time of Residence.*

5. Smithfield *v.* Belgrade, 19 Me. 387. See Turnbridge *v.* Norwich, 17 Vt. 493; Brookfield *v.* Hartland, 10 Vt. 424.

6. Spencer *v.* Pleasant, 17 Ohio St. 31.

7. New Vineyard *v.* Harpswell, 33 Me. 193; Peru *v.* Turner, 10 Me. 185.

8. Brewster *v.* Harwich, 4 Mass. 281.

9. Shirley *v.* Lunenberg, 11 Mass. 382.

10. Patterson *v.* Bryain, 23 N. J. L. 394; Upper Alloways Creek *v.* Elsinborough, 1 N. J. L. 389; Shawanqunk *v.* Mamakating, 1 Johns. (N. Y.) 54; Berlin *v.* Morristown, 20 Vt. 574; State *v.* Jones, 17 Ohio St. 148; Philadelphia *v.* Bristol, 6 Serg. & R. (Pa.) 562; Overseers of Donegal Tp. *v.* Overseers of Sugar Creek Tp.,

2. Order of Removal.—The order for the removal must show, on its face, that all the facts which are requisite by statute actually exist; that the officers making the order acted within their authority, and that the facts necessary to authorize the order were duly proved before the officers who made it.[1] There must be a strong probability at the time of making the order that the person is "likely to become chargeable."[2] He cannot be removed while a freeholder in the town.[3] The justices must make a special direction in the case; so, where paupers are to be sent out of the State, the justices in their order of removal must designate the route by which the pauper is to be transported.[4] But where a pauper has actually become chargeable to a town, there is no necessity to order him to remove to his last legal settlement, previously to issuing a warrant for his removal.[5]

It is not sufficient reason to quash an order to remove a man and his family that they are named, unless it is made to appear that the pauper had a family on whom the order was to operate, and then if such order would not be good as to the family it would only be quashed as to them.[6] So, where the place of settlement of children removed with their parents has been adjudged, their ages need not be set out in the order of removal.[7]

3. Notice.—A town must have notice of an order for removal of a pauper to be concluded by it as to his settlement,[8] and a de-

(Pa.) 11 Atl. Rep. 213; Rockingham *v.* Springfield (Vt.), 9 Atl. Rep. 241.

1. New Barbadoes *v.* Patterson, 27 N. J. L. 544; Princeton *v.* Brunswick, 23 N. J. L. 196; Landgrove *v.* Plymouth, 52 Vt. 503; Newburg *v.* Plattkill, 1 Johns. (N. Y.) 330; Derby *v.* Barre, 38 Vt. 276; Goshen *v.* Hillsborough, 45 N. H. 139; Princeton *v.* Brunswick, 23 N. J. L. 169; Newbury *v.* Brunswick, 2 Vt. 151; Danville *v.* Peacham, 41 Vt. 333.

Orders for the removal of a pauper must state a complaint and adjudication that the pauper was likely to become chargeable. Dromore *v.* West Hanover, 1 Yeates (Pa.) 366. *Compare* Elizabethtown *v.* Springfield, 3 N. J. L. 475.

An order for the removal of one who has never been a public charge, without notice and without an adjudication, and founded only upon the information of the overseers, that he is likely to become chargeable, is void. Gilpin Overseers *v.* Parks Overseers, 118 Pa. St. 84.

2. Londonderry *v.* Action, 3 Vt. 122; Walpole *v.* West Cambridge, 8 Mass. 276; St. Johnsbury *v.* Morristown, 51 Vt. 316; Cornish *v.* Parsonsfield, 22 Me. 433.

3. Middletown *v.* Pawlet, 4 Vt. 202; Walpole *v.* West Cambridge, 8 Mass. 276; Doomore *v.* West Hanover, 1 Yeates (Pa.) 366.

A person in actual possession of a trust estate, and living on the same, with his family, is not subject to removal as a pauper, under the statute, for the rule is the same whether the estate is a legal or equitable freehold. Walden *v.* Cabot, 25 Vt. 522.

That one cannot be removed, as a pauper, from his freehold, applies to tenant in dower; and this may be taken advantage of, on motion to quash the order of removal. Brookfield *v.* Hartland, 6 Vt. 401.

A lunatic, needing support, may be removed to the town where she has a settlement, although she has a reversionary estate in fee, in the town where she resides. Johnson *v.* Huntington, 1 Day (Conn.) 212.

4. Niskayuna *v.* Guilderland, 8 Johns. (N. Y.) 412.

5. Vernon *v.* Smithville, 17 Johns. (N. Y.) 89.

6. Bristol *v.* Braintree, 10 Vt. 203.

7. Elizabethtown *v.* Springfield, 3 N. J. L. 475.

8. Fairfield *v.* St. Albans, Brayt. (Vt.) 176; St. Albans *v.* Georgia, Brayt. 177.

mand by another town for the expense of his support is not notice, for that may be recovered without such order.[1] The notice must state the age of the person, and such facts as may be necessary to be known to the town notified, and a request that he be removed; but no particular form is requisite; and a request of removal may be implied by the statement that the pauper is supported at the expense of the town notified.[2] The notice that the pauper and his family have become chargeable and requesting their removal without stating their names and number is deficient,[3] but a notice which is deficient, if unanswered or not properly objected to, may become sufficient by an acceptance of it by the adverse party, or by waiver of any advantage arising from the deficiency.[4]

Notice relative to a pauper, given to the overseers of a town, becomes wholly inoperative by a lapse of the time prescribed by statute, and cannot in any way vary the rights of the parties, if no judicial decision respecting the settlement has been had, and no action or process is pending between the parties relative to it.[5]

4. **Service.**—Where the statutes designate the officers who may serve the order of removal, all other persons are excluded and it cannot be served by an unauthorized person.[6] The statutory method of service must be followed to bind the town by an order of removal.[7]

5. **Who May be Removed.**—A married woman is not liable to be removed, as a pauper, from her husband, or from the place of his

Compare Bradford *v.* Keating, 27 Pa. St. 275.

1. Fairfield *v.* St. Albans, Brayt. (Vt.) 176.

2. Kennebunkport *v.* Buxton, 26 Me. 61; Uxbridge *v.* Seekonk, 10 Pick. (Mass.) 150; Northfield *v.* Taunton, 4 Met. (Mass.) 433; LaCrosse *v.* Melrose, 22 Wis. 459; Carver *v.* Taunton (Mass.), 25 N. E. Rep. 964; Stillwell *v.* Kennedy, 5 N. Y. Supp. 407; 51 Hun (N. Y.) 114; McKay *v.* Welch, 6 N. Y. Supp. 358.

The statute which provides that the notice given by one town to another shall contain a request to remove the pauper, does not apply where the death and burial of the pauper has occurred before the time allowed to give the notice has elapsed, and the notice has been actually given. Nor is the notice insufficient for the want of the date, if in other respects sufficient; it being proved that it arrived at the post-office in the town chargeable, before the expiration of the three months from the time the supplies were furnished and the funeral expenses paid. Ellsworth *v.* Houlton, 48 Me. 416.

Where the overseers of the poor of a town gave notice to those of another that a certain person, naming him, "has become chargeable in this town, you are hereby notified that we are supporting her at your expense, and shall continue to do so until she is removed, or otherwise provided for"—*held*, that this was sufficient. Kennebunkport *v.* Buxton, 26 Me. 61.

3. Embden *v.* Augusta, 12 Mass. 307; Shutesbury *v.* Oxford, 16 Mass. 102; Bangor *v.* Deer Isle, 1 Me. 329.

If, however, the number is stated, it is sufficient. Orange *v.* Sudbury, 10 Pick. (Mass.) 22.

4. Embden *v.* Augusta, 12 Mass. 307; Paris *v.* Hiram, 12 Mass. 262; Orange *v.* Sudbury, 10 Pick. (Mass.) 22; Shutesbury *v.* Oxford, 16 Mass. 102.

5. Corinna *v.* Exeter, 13 Me. 321.

6. Granville *v.* Hancock, 55 Vt. 323.

7. Whittingham *v.* Wardsboro, 47 Vt. 496; Westminster *v.* Warren, 55 Vt. 522; Georgia *v.* St. Albans, 3 Vt. 42; East Haven *v.* Derby, 38 Vt. 233; Poultney *v.* Sandgate, 35 Vt. 146; Sharon *v.* Strafford, 37 Vt. 74; Barnet *v.* Woodbury, 40 Vt. 266.

actual residence, to the place of her legal settlement, though the husband may have no settlement within the State.[1]

If the husband has abandoned his wife and left the State, the wife, and also their minor children with her, may be removed to the town of his legal settlement, if he has any, and if not, then to the town of her legal settlement at the time of her marriage.[2] But the confinement of the husband in jail by virtue of legal process, cannot be regarded as an abandonment of his family by him, or as breaking up the family relation; and does not justify an order of removal. The family relation still existing cannot be thus invaded.[3]

If a widow acquire a settlement by marriage, the children by the former husband may be removed to their settlement derived from their father; so a pauper of full age may be removed to the place of her settlement, although such removal may separate her from the family of her mother.[4] But children under six years of age, living with their mother, are not to be separated from her, but may be removed with her to her settlement, without inquiring into their settlement.[5]

6. Appeal from Order of Removal.—Where an order of removal has been improperly made an appeal lies.[6] In taking an appeal from an order of removal, all that is necessary is that notice of the appeal be given to the justices, or one of them, and if, after such notice, the justice refuses to certify the appeal *mandamus* will lie;[7] but if the court shall be of the opinion that seasonable notice has not been given, the appeal shall be continued as mandatory.[8] If the order is reversed and quashed, the justices of the peace of the town, to which the pauper was so improperly removed, may make an order for his removal back to the town from which he was removed; or, if it appears that the pauper has no settlement in that town, they may make a new original order for his removal to

1. Northfield *v.* Roxbury, 15 Vt. 622; Hartland *v.* Pomfret, 11 Vt. 440; Danville *v.* Wheelock, 47 Vt. 57; Peacham *v.* Waterford, 46 Vt. 154; Dummerstown *v.* Newfane, 37 Vt. 9.

So a married woman, while the ordinary relation of husband and wife exists, whose husband, residing in the State, has no settlement in the State, cannot be removed to the town of her settlement at the time of her marriage, although by express provision of the statute that settlement is not lost or suspended by the marriage. The reason is, her husband cannot be removed to that town, as he has no settlement there; and to remove her there, would separate her from her husband. Peacham *v.* Waterford, 46 Vt. 154.

2. Wilmington *v.* Jamaica, 42 Vt. 694; Winhall *v.* Landgrove, 45 Vt 376; Bethel *v.* Turnbridge, 13 Vt. 445.

3. Peacham *v.* Waterford, 46 Vt. 154.

4. Randolph *v.* Braintree, 10 Vt. 436.

5. Patterson *v.* Bryam, 23 N. J. L. 394.

6. Marshfield *v.* Calais, 16 Vt. 598; Dorset *v.* Rutland, 16 Vt. 419; Braintree *v.* Westford, 17 Vt. 141; Strafford *v.* Hartland, 2 Vt. 565; Sutton *v.* Cabot, 19 Vt. 522.

7. Town of Orange *v.* Bill, 29 Vt. 244.

On an appeal from an order of removal the burden of proof is on the respondents who must begin *de novo.* Otsego *v.* Smithfield, 6 Cow. (N. Y.) 160.

8. Chester *v.* Londonderry, 51 Vt. 535.

the place of his last legal settlement.[1] Where no appeal is taken from an order of removal made in due form, it is conclusive of the duty enjoined in it and decides the pauper's legal settlement.[2]

No appeal lies from an order of removal which has never been executed in consequence of the death of the pauper.[3] Nor does an appeal lie from an adjudication in favor of a party charged with bastardy.[4] If the appeal is abandoned in consequence of the appellee taking back the pauper, the order though unreversed is not evidence of the pauper's settlement in the appellate town.[5] Abandonment by the appellee of the appeal is not conclusive between the town and the county.[6]

7. When Removal Valid.—An order of removal of a pauper is valid and of binding force upon the adverse town, although no actual removal is made under such order.[7] Justices of the peace are not disqualified from making an order of removal of a pauper, merely because they are rated inhabitants and tax-payers in a town which is a party to the proceedings.[8] So it is not a sufficient ground to quash an order of removal, that the overseer of the poor, who made the complaint, served the same, as constable, when he held both of those offices.[9]

VII. Penalty for Bringing Paupers into Town—1. Generally.—Statutes of the various States impose a penalty for bringing into a State a person having no visible means of support and who has a settlement in another State, or bringing a poor person into a

1. Pittstown *v.* Plattsburg, 18 Johns. (N. Y.) 407.

Pa. act of June 13, 1836, provides that where an appeal from an order for the removal of a pauper is sustained, the court, at the same session, on demand, may award, in addition to costs and charges, a sum to reimburse the appellant for relief furnished the pauper between the time of the removal and the determination of the appeal. *Held,* that the right to make claim subsequently exists when no demand was made at the session. Huntingdon Poor District *v.* New Columbus Borough Poor District, 109 Pa. St. 579.

2. Bradford *v.* Keating, 27 Pa. St. 275; Sugarloaf *v.* Schuylkill, 44 Pa. St. 481; Schuylkill *v.* Montour, 44 Pa. St. 484; Westmoreland *v.* Conemaugh, 34 Pa. St. 231; Elizabeth *v.* Westfield, 7 N. J. L. 439; Renova Overseers *v.* Halfmoon Overseers, 78 Pa. St. 301; Little Falls *v.* Bernard, 44 N. J. L. 621; Rupert *v.* Sandgate, 10 Vt. 278; Dorset *v.* Manchester, 3 Vt. 370; Stowe *v.* Brookfield, 26 Vt. 524; Charleston *v.* Lunenburg, 23 Vt. 525; Sugar Creek *v.* Washington, 62 Pa. St. 479; Southfield *v.* Bloomingrove, 2 Johns. (N. Y.) 105; Chester *v.* Wheelock, 28 Vt. 554.

An order was passed by a magistrate for the removal of a pauper from one town to another, or his place of legal settlement. The latter town appealed, and the overseers of the former took back the pauper, without trying the appeal. *Held,* that the order was not conclusive as to the settlement of the pauper, but the question whether the pauper was not chargeable to the county was still open. People *v.* Cayuga, 2 Cow. (N. Y.) 530.

3. Adams *v.* Foster, 20 Johns. (N. Y.) 452.

4. People *v.* Tompkins General Sessions, 19 Wend. (N. Y.) 154.

5. Vernon *v.* Smithville, 17 Johns. (N. Y.) 89.

6. People *v.* Supervisors of Cayuga County, 2 Cow. (N. Y.) 530.

7. Poultney *v.* Sandgate, 35 Vt. 146.

8. Morristown *v.* Fairfield, 46 Vt. 33; Vernon *v.* Wantage, 2 N. J. L. 311.

9. Bristol *v.* Braintree, 10 Vt. 203.

It is no reason for quashing an order of removal of a pauper, that a warrant was issued by the justice and the pauper

town, with intent to leave him there a charge and burden upon such town.[1] In actions upon these statutes for bringing into and leaving a pauper in a town where he has no legal settlement, the penalty cannot be recovered unless the act appears to have been done with the intention of leaving him a charge and burden upon the town.[2] The intent with which the pauper is removed must be proved to and found by the jury.[3] Under a statute making any one by whose means a person not having a settlement in the State is brought within it, liable for the support of such person if he becomes a pauper, a railroad company, or common carriers of passengers, who, without reason to suspect a person to be a pauper, transport such person into a State, will not be liable for his support;[4] so the penalty of bringing a pauper into a town cannot be recovered against an officer acting under an order from the overseers of the poor;[5] nor can it be recovered against one who carried a poor person into a town with an honest purpose of helping him on his journey;[6] nor for bringing paupers to their place of settlement.[7] The township to which a pauper is im-

was removed, with his own consent, by the constable, before the time for his removing himself, named in the order, had expired. Plymouth *v.* Mendon, 23 Vt. 451.

1. Barnet *v.* Ray, 33 Vt. 205; Luton *v.* Newaygo (Mich.), 38 N. W. Rep. 13; Superintendent of the Poor *v.* Nelson (Mich.), 42 N. W. Rep. 797. See Pittstown *v.* Plattsburg, 15 Johns. (N. Y.) 436; Charlotte *v.* Colchester, 20 Vt. 91; Crouse *v.* Mabbett, 11 Johns. (N. Y.) 167.

The penalty given by the statute for bringing a poor or indigent person, not having a settlement, into any city or town within the State, without legal authority, is incurred as well by bringing such person from one town to another town within the State, as by bringing him from without the State. Thomas *v.* Ross, 8 Wend. (N. Y.) 672.

A penalty imposed by statute—Mass. Gen. Stat., ch. 70, § 20—upon "whoever" brings a pauper into any town, etc., applies to public officers as well as to private individuals. Palmer *v.* Wakefield, 102 Mass. 214.

2. Greenfield *v.* Cushman, 16 Mass. 393; Sanford *v.* Emery, 2 Me. 5; Foster *v.* Conkhite, 35 N. Y. 139. See Coe *v.* Smith, 24 Wend. (N. Y.) 341; Dyer *v.* Hunt, 5 N. H. 401.

Compare Stratford *v.* Sanford, 9 Conn. 275.

3. Wallingford *v.* Gray, 13 Vt. 228; Sanford *v.* Emery, 2 Me. 5; Town of Worcester *v.* Town of East Montpelier, 62 Vt. 139.

1 Rev. St. N. Y., pp. 628, 629, § 58–62, make it a misdemeanor to remove or entice any poor person from any city, town or county, without legal authority, to any other city, town or county, with intent to make the latter chargeable with his support, and provide for the return of such pauper to, and his support by the town or county from which he had been removed, with indemnity to the other county or town for its expenses incurred in the pauper's support and return. Laws N. Y. 1885, ch. 546, applied the above sections to "any pauper . . who shall, of his own accord, come or stray from any city, town or county, into any other city, town or county, not legally chargeable with his support." *Held*, that this amendment did not give a right of action for the support of a pauper, by a county into which he had voluntarily removed, at a time when he was not a pauper, against the county from which he had so removed. Bellows *v.* Courter, 6 N. Y. S. 73.

4. Fitchburg *v.* Cheshire R. Co., 110 Mass. 210.

5. Sturbridge *v.* Winslow, 21 Pick. (Mass.) 83.

Compare Dover *v.* Wheeler, 51 Vt. 160.

6. Deerfield *v.* Delano, 1 Pick. (Mass.) 465.

To subject a party to the penalty, it must be shown that he acted *mala fide.* Thomas *v.* Ross, 8 Wend. (N. Y.) 672.

7. Middleborough *v.* Clark, 2 Pick.

properly removed is to be allowed the expense of maintaining him pending the action by which his settlement is determined.[1]

2. Defenses.—In an action for damages for transporting an indigent person from one town into another, with an intent to make the latter liable for his support, it is no defense to show that the pauper had a settlement in another town in this State, and that his father had property and was able to support him.[2] Nor is it a defense that the pauper had formerly a legal settlement in the place to which he was brought and had not subsequently gained one elsewhere.[3]

VIII. Support—1. Generally.—The place of a pauper's legal settlement is liable for his support.[4] If his settlement is found not to be the place where he resides, then the last place of his legal settlement is liable.[5] If he has no legal settlement in the State, the district in which he resides will be continually liable until such district discovers his place of settlement.[6] This liability is

(Mass.) 28; Canton *v.* Bentley, 11 Mass. 441.

If an order of removal of a pauper be regularly made, persons assisting the pauper to remove voluntarily, within the time prescribed by the order, are not liable to the penalty imposed by statute upon those who bring a poor person into a town, with intent to charge such town with his support. Morgan *v.* Mead, 16 Vt. 644.

So the statute imposing a penalty for bringing into this State a person having no visible means of support, and who has a settlement in another State, does not apply to a case where the person so brought has his domicile and usual place of abode here. State *v.* Benton, 18 N. H. 47.

A pauper came voluntarily to Worcester, and that town allowed him to remain; the town of Montpelier was not liable under R. L. Vt., § 2844, providing for a penalty for bringing a poor person into town with intent to charge the town with his support. Town of Worcester *v.* Town of East Montpelier (Vt.), 17 Atl. Rep. 842.

1. Evesham *v.* Newton, 1 N. J. L. 76.

2. Marshfield *v.* Edwards, 40 Vt. 245.

In an action for bringing a poor person from without the State of New York into any town or county within it, with intent to make such town or county chargeable with his support, contrary to the act of 1831, 346, § 1, it is no defense that the pauper formerly had a legal settlement in the place to which he was brought, and had not subsequently gained one elsewhere, and that the defendants acted, in the removal, as public officers of another State, in conformity with the laws of such State. Winfield *v.* Mapes, 4 Den. (N. Y.) 571.

3. Winfield *v.* Mapes, 4 Den. (N.Y.) 571.

4. Toby *v.* Madison, 44 Pa. St. 60; Park County *v.* Jefferson County (Colo.), 21 Pac. Rep. 912; Saukville *v.* Grafton, 68 Wis. 192; Welcome *v.* Monticello (Minn.) 42 N. W. Rep. 930; Groveland *v.* Medford, 1 Allen (Mass.) 23; Bremen *v.* Brewer, 54 Me. 528.

A pauper having a settlement in the commonwealth cannot be removed to a place out of it, and there supported against his will. Westfield *v.* Southwick, 17 Pick. (Mass.) 68.

5. Loby *v.* Madison, 44 Pa. St. 60; Voorhis *v.* Whippel, 7 Johns. (N. Y.) 89; McCaffreg *v.* Shields, 54 Wis. 645.

6. Harmony *v.* Forest County, 19 Pa. St. 404; Justices' Opinions, 68 Me. 593. See Town of Chittenden *v.* Town of Barnard, 61 Vt. 145; Overseers of the Poor *v.* Overseers of the Poor (Pa.), 18 Atl. Rep. 549.

The district in which a poor person having no legal settlement within the commonwealth first becomes helpless, must provide the relief until the necessity ceases. The fact that he boarded and lodged in another district at the time of the accident, gives him no settlement there, so as to make that district liable. Taylor Overseers *v.* Shenango Overseers, 113 Pa. St. 394.

After coming to this country, an

not defeated by a failure of the supervisors to make a contract for such support, nor by the fact that the town wherein such pauper has a legal settlement is ultimately liable therefor.[1]

Notice that relief is needed should be given to the proper officers of the poor.[2] The notice required to be given of sums expended for the maintenance of paupers should indicate the persons relieved, with sufficient certainty to establish their identity.[3] If notice has been given to the overseers by one furnishing relief to a pauper, and supplies have been furnished by the overseers, believed by them to be sufficient, a new notice is necessary to support an action for supplies furnished afterwards.[4]

2. Order of Relief.—The statutes generally impose the duty of making orders of relief on the justice of the peace.[5] Relief, however, may be extended to one entitled to the benefit of the poor laws, without an order, in cases of emergency, and the overseers or directors are liable to pay for necessary relief furnished by others, provided an order of approval is obtained afterwards.[6] Matters of form and orders for the relief of paupers are not to be overlooked, and the justice has a reasonable discretion as to the nature and extent of the allowance, and if the pauper is sick or wounded, medicines and the attendance of a physician are a reasonable charge, but all the charges in obtaining him must be adjusted and paid in the first instance by the overseers of the poor, who are responsible to the persons rendering the assistance.[7]

Where an attempt is made to impeach an order of relief on the

alien, resided in the town of B, but without gaining a settlement there. He came to want, and applied to the selectmen for relief, who induced him to go to the town of C, promising to pay for his support there, which they did for the first year. After that supplies were furnished him by the town of C, due notice being given to the selectmen of B. Pub. Acts Conn. 1878, ch. 94, § 3, provides that all persons needing relief, who have no settlement in the State, shall be State paupers and be supported by the comptroller for six months; and section 21 that after that time all State paupers shall be sent back to the town where they resided when they first applied for relief. *Held*, that the alien was a State pauper, and that his support was chargeable to the town of B from the end of six months after he first applied to its selectmen for relief. Town of Canton *v.* Town of Burlington, 58 Conn. 277.

1. Davis *v.* Scott, 59 Wis. 604. See Mappes *v.* Iowa County Supervisors, 47 Wis. 31.

2. Merideth *v.* Canterbury, 3 N. H. 80; Salesbury *v.* Orange, 5 N. H. 348.

3. Dalton *v.* Bethlehem, 20 N. H. 505; Chester *v.* Pembroke, 2 N. H. 530; Dover *v.* Paris, 5 Me. 430.

4. Warren *v.* Isleborough, 20 Me. 442.

5. Van Nuis *v.* M'Collister, 3 N. J. L. 805; Cumberland *v.* Jefferson, 25 Pa. St. 463. See *supra*, this title, *Justice of the Peace*.

If the application for an order of maintenance is made to, and the order granted by, the court of sessions, it is no objection to the order that it purports to be made by "county court of sessions," as the word "county" will be rejected as surplusage. Baldwin *v.* McArthur, 17 Barb. (N. Y.) 414.

6. Directors of the Poor *v.* Worthington, 38 Pa. St. 160; Westmoreland *v.* Murry, 32 Pa. St. 178. *Compare* Upshur County *v.* Yeury, 19 Tex. 126.

7. Adams *v.* Supervisors of Columbia, 8 Johns. (N. Y.) 323.

ground of fraud, the pauper's declarations are admissible to show that the officers acted in good faith.[1]

3. By Kindred.—Parents are required to support their children.[2] And it has been held that a grandfather is liable to relieve and maintain his destitute grandchildren when their necessities require it.[3] At common law a child is under no liability to support his parents,[4] but this rule has been changed by statute, and if the child is of sufficient ability, he may be compelled to support his parents on a proper application to the court.[5] So grandchildren are liable for the support of their grandparents.[6] So statutes that require kindred by consanguinity, who are of sufficient ability to contribute to the support of paupers, embraces within these provisions illegitimate children who have become charge-

1. Laporte Overseers *v.* Hillsgrove Overseers, 95 Pa. St. 269.

2. City of New Bedford *v.* Chace, 5 Gray (Mass.) 28; Rowell *v.* Town of Vershire (Vt.), 19 Atl. Rep. 990; Stanton *v.* State, 6 Blackf. (Ind.) 83.

A mother, in poor circumstances, is not bound to support her infant child, when it can be supported out of its own estate, and where she has done so, a just allowance should be made to her for its past maintenance. Stewart *v.* Lewis, 16 Ala. 734.

By section 3 of the *Rhode Island* "act providing for the relief, employment, and removal of the poor," a father is not compelled to pay for the entire support of his son, when by so doing he might be deprived of the means of supporting himself, but to pay in proportion to his ability. East Greenwich *v.* Card, 1 R. I. 409.

On a complaint under Mass. Gen. St., ch. 70, § 5, by a town against a father for the support of his adult pauper daughter, it may properly be found that he is of "sufficient ability" to contribute to her support, where the value of his property, above his debts, is between $5,000 and $6,000, notwithstanding he is in poor health, unable to do hard work, has a wife and child dependent upon him, and his income is less than his expenses. Templeton *v.* Stratton, 128 Mass. 137.

Stepchildren.—A man is under no legal obligation to support his stepchild; and the fact that such child receives aid from a town as a pauper, upon the application of the stepfather, will not make the latter a pauper. Brookfield *v.* Warren, 128 Mass. 287.

3. Duffey *v.* Duffey, 44 Pa. St. 399; Salisbury *v.* Philadelphia, 44 Pa. St. 303; Kiser *v.* Frankford, 3 N. J. L. 410; Buxton *v.* Chesterfield, 60 N. H. 357.

4. Stone *v.* Stone, 32 Conn. 142; Edwards *v.* Davis, 10 Johns. (N. Y.) 281.

5. Commissioners *v.* Dooling, 1 Bailey (S. C.) 73; Speedling *v.* Worth County, 68 Iowa 152; Stone *v.* Stone, 32 Conn. 142; Duel *v.* Lamb, 1 Thomp. & C. (N. Y.) 66; O'Connor's Appeal, 104 Pa. St. 437; Boone *v.* Ruhe, 9 Iowa 276; Tinmouth *v.* Warren, 17 Vt. 606. *In re* O'Donnell (Pa.), 19 Atl. Rep. 42; Jasper County *v.* Osborn, 59 Iowa 208.

The court of sessions ordered that the defendant should support his mother, at his own house; or, in default thereof, that he should pay a certain sum per week. After being supported and well treated at her son's house about a year, she left him without cause. For a while after she left the superintendents of the poor paid for her board, and then removed her to the poorhouse; and, soon after such removal, the son notified the superintendents of his willingness to support his mother at his own house, and that he should not pay for her support out of his family. *Held*, that the defendant had not violated the order. Converse *v.* McArthur, 17 Barb. (N. Y.) 410.

The statute empowering a town, that performs its duty of relieving needy parents, to enforce statutory liability of the children, does not authorize a volunteer to enforce it. Gray *v.* Spalding, 58 N. H. 345.

6. Wethersfield *v.* Montague, 3 Conn. 507; Whiting's Case, 3 Pittsb. (Pa.) 129.

Conn. Rev. Stat., tit. 42, § 31, which provides a mode of compelling the re-

able as paupers.[1] A husband is required to support his wife when she becomes a public charge.[2] But a husband is not liable for the maintenance of the parents of his wife, who are paupers.[3] Nor is a nephew liable for the support of his uncle.[4] A person is bound generally to support his poor relatives only when he can support himself, and his family, and the paupers, from his annual income. The question of ability is to be decided, in each case, upon the state of things then existing.[5] The kindred of a pauper cannot be called upon to pay for his relief, save by the overseers of the town where he is settled, or by some other of his kindred.[6]

4. By Towns.—Where a town is made liable by statute for the support of the poor, it is bound, after notice and request of the proper officers, for necessary expenses incurred by an inhabitant of the town for the relief of a pauper;[7] but if suitable provision

lations of a pauper to contribute to his support, applies only to future support. Stone *v.* Stone, 32 Conn. 142.

1. Willard *v.* Overseers of the Poor, 9 Gratt. (Va.) 139; Lyle *v.* Overseers etc., 8 Gratt. (Va.) 20.

2. Goodale *v.* Lawrence, 88 N. Y. 513; 42 Am. Rep. 259; City of New Bedford *v.* Chace, 5 Gray (Mass.) 28; Bangor *v.* Wiscasset, 71 Me. 535.

A town in which a husband and wife have a settlement, cannot sue the husband for money paid without legal compulsion to another town, for supplies furnished to the wife. Chester *v.* Underhill, 16 N. H. 64.

The superintendent of the poor cannot maintain an action against a husband for necessaries furnished to his insane wife. Goodale *v.* Brocknor, 61 How. (N. Y.) Pr. 451. See HUSBAND AND WIFE, vol. 9, p. 789.

3. Commissioners *v.* Gansett, 2 Bailey (S. C.) 320; Sherman *v.* Nichols, 1 Root (Conn.) 256; Nichols *v.* Sherman, 1 Root (Conn.) 361; Pomeroy *v.* Weils, 8 Paige (N. Y.) 406; O'Keefe *v.* City of Northampton (Mass.), 13 N. E. Rep. 382; Newton *v.* Danbury, 3 Conn. 553; Farr *v.* Flood, 11 Cush. (Mass.) 24.

A wife assisted her husband in caring for a pauper (her husband's father). *Held*, that this gave her no right of action against the town of the pauper's settlement. O'Keefe *v.* Northampton, 145 Mass. 115.

4. Dawson *v.* Dawson, 12 Iowa 512.

5. Colebrook *v.* Stewartstown, 30 N. H. 9.

An individual, who has a small farm, and some personal property, but who has a family, and owes more than he has owing to him, is not of "sufficient ability" to support his poor relations, within the meaning of the statute, unless his property, with his labor, yields sufficient income to maintain his family, pay the interest of his debts, and support such relations. Dover *v.* M'Murphy, 4 N. H. 158.

6. Salem *v.* Andover, 3 Mass. 436; Sayward *v.* Alfred, 5 Mass. 244.

7. Cunningham *v.* Town of Frankfort (Me.), 12 Atl. Rep. 636; Perley *v.* Oldtown, 49 Me. 31; Smith *v.* Inhabitants of Colerain, 9 Met. (Mass.) 492; Knight *v.* Fort Fairfield, 70 Me. 500; Stone *v.* Town of Glover (Vt.), 15 Atl. Rep. 334; Seagraves *v.* City of Alton, 13 Ill. 366; Underwood *v.* Inhabitants of Scituate, 7 Met. (Mass.) 214; Brown *v.* Orland, 36 Me. 376; Gross *v.* Jay, 37 Me. 9; Williams *v.* Braintree, 6 Cush. (Mass.) 399; Wile *v.* Southbury, 43 Conn. 53; Holmes *v.* St. Albans, Brayt. (Vt.) 179.

Compare McCaffrey *v.* Shields, 54 Wis. 645; Beetham *v.* Lincoln, 16 Me. 137; South *v.* Huntington, 1 Watts (Pa.) 527.

A town is liable to one who boards a pauper at his house, if said pauper, when turned away, would not be reasonably able to reach the place provided for him by the town. Knight *v.* Fort Fairfield, 70 Me. 500; Lamson *v.* Newburyport, 14 Allen (Mass.) 30.

A person living in an unincorporated place, who furnishes supplies to a person falling into distress in such place, cannot recover therefor against the inhabitants of the oldest incorporated town adjoining such place, unless

is made by a town for a pauper, and he goes into another town, and there incurs expense, and the fact that the former town provides for him is known to all persons, the person for whom the expense is incurred cannot recover in the former town.[1] A town is not chargeable for the support of a pauper whose settlement is in another town.[2] A town is liable to another town for expenses incurred in furnishing relief to a pauper belonging to the latter if the latter has complied strictly with the requirements of the laws in endeavoring to obtain his removal to the town of his settlement.[3] Expenses incurred by a town in committing a pauper to an insane hospital and supporting him there must be borne by

the pauper has, at the time, his legal settlement in such town. Kennedy *v.* Weston, 65 Me. 596.

An action for relief of a pauper by an individual cannot be sustained against the town of such pauper's settlement, if supported out of that town. Mitchell *v.* Cornville, 12 Mass. 333.

1. New Salem *v.* Wendall, 2 Pick. (Mass.) 341; Shearer *v.* Shelburne, 10 Cush. (Mass.) 3; Norden *v.* Leyden, 10 Pick. (Mass.) 24. See Green *v.* Taunton, 1 Me. 228; Phelps *v.* Westford, 124 Mass. 286.

In *Vermont* it is held that if the overseers contract with one for support of a pauper for a certain time, and he continues the support thereafter, the town is not liable on the ground of the overseers' not taking the pauper away. Aldrich *v.* Londonderry, 5 Vt. 441; Castleton *v.* Miner, 8 Vt. 212; Baldwin *v.* Rupert, 8 Vt. 258; Guilford *v.* Jamaica, 2 D. Chip. (Vt.) 103; Houghton *v.* Danville, 10 Vt. 537; Churchill *v.* West Fairlee. 17 Vt. 447; Thetford *v.* Hubbard, 22 Vt. 440.

2. Peterborough *v.* Lancaster, 14 N. H. 382; Hopkington *v.* Warner, 53 N. H. 468; Townsend *v.* Billerica, 10 Mass. 411; Needham *v.* Newton, 12 Mass. 452; Harwick *v.* Hallowell, 14 Mass. 104; Uxbridge *v.* Seekonk, 10 Pick. (Mass.) 150; Caswell *v.* Hazard, 10 R. I. 490; Salem *v.* Andover, 3 Mass. 436; Sayward *v.* Alfred, 5 Mass. 244; Chittenden *v.* Barnard, 17 Vt. 844.

A town is not liable for the support of the minor child of a father having his settlement therein, to another town that supports such child, unless the latter is actually a pauper; and the child is not a pauper so long as the father has sufficient ability to maintain it. Litchfield *v.* Londonderry, 39 N. H. 247.

A town not chargeable with the support of a pauper agreed with a town by whom the pauper had been maintained, to pay for the future support for a specified time. In an action against the town where the pauper had a settlement—*held*, that such agreement was no answer to the suit. Peterborough *v.* Lancaster, 14 N. H. 382.

3. Mill Creek *v.* Miami, 10 Ohio 375; Wethersfield *v.* Sanford, 1 Root (Conn.) 68; Westfield *v.* Sauk, 18 Wis. 624; Guilford *v.* Abbott, 17 Me. 335; Smith *v.* Inhabitants of Colerain, 9 Met. (Mass.) 492. See Goodell *v.* Mount Holly, 51 Vt. 423; Pawlet *v.* Rutland, Brayt. (Vt.) 175; Bloomfield *v.* French, 17 Vt. 79; Belmont *v.* Pittson, 3 Me. 453; Pawlet *v.* Sandgate, 19 Vt. 621; Essex *v.* Milton, 3 Vt. 17; Templeton *v.* Winchendon, 138 Mass. 109; Dakota *v.* Winneconne, 55 Wis. 522; Voorhis *v.* Whipple, 7 Johns. (N.Y.) 89; Grafton *v.* Grafton, 43 N. H. 382; Hardin County *v.* Wright County, 67 Iowa 127; Overseers of Jenks Tp. *v.* Commissioners of Roads (Pa.), 19 Atl. Rep. 1004.

Where the overseers of the poor of a town bound as an apprentice a poor child whose settlement was in another town, and paid the master a sum of money, it was held that they could not recover it of the other town. Rumney *v.* Ellsworth, 4 N. H. 138.

The liability in *Arkansas* and *Mississippi* is upon the county. See Gunn County *v.* Pulaski County, 3 Pike (Ark.) 427; Colton *v.* Police of Leake County, 27 Miss. 367.

Not only the expenses incurred by a town for the support of a pauper there residing, but also the expenses incurred in burying him at his death, are recoverable of the town in which he had a legal settlement, if the requirements of the statute have been complied with. Ellsworth *v.* Houlton, 48 Me. 416.

the town where he has a settlement.[1] So towns are made conditionally liable for the support of persons committed to a house of correction, jail or county poor house, where they have a legal settlement and the account thereof is audited and certified by the overseers of such house, within the time prescribed by the statutes.[2] Under a statute, which provides that the expense of supporting a pauper in a house of correction "may be recovered of the town wherein he shall have his lawful settlement," the town in which he has a settlement at the time when such expense is incurred, is liable therefor, although he gains a settlement in

S bequeathed a fund to the town of F, the annual interest of which he directed to be applied for the support of his children, grandchildren or great-grandchildren, if any of them should need support; otherwise, for the support of the poor of F; N, a great-grandchild of S, having a legal settlement in the town of M, was supported as a pauper by the town of W. M reimbursed W, and brought a bill in equity against the town of F to obtain the sum thus expended for the support of N. *Held*, that the bill could not be maintained. Marlborough *v.* Framingham, 13 Met. (Mass.) 328.

1. Cummington *v.* Wareham, 9 Cush. (Mass.) 585; St. Johnsbury *v.* Waterford, 15 Vt. 692; Hopkinton *v.* Waite, 6 R. I. 374; *Re* Blewitt, 11 Phila. (Pa.) 652; Danville *v.* Putney, 6 Vt. 512; Manchester *v.* Rupert, 6 Vt. 291; People *v.* Herkimer County Supervisors, 20 Abb., N. Cas. (N. Y.) 123; Board of Supervisors *v.* City of Kingston, 3 N. Y. Supp. 221; 50 Hun (N. Y.) 435; People *v.* Board of Supervisors, 46 Hun (N. Y.) 354; Naples *v.* Raymond, 72 Me. 213; Directors etc. *v.* Toledo, 15 Ohio St. 409; Etna *v.* Brewer, 78 Me. 377; Adams *v.* Ipswich, 116 Mass. 570; Amherst *v.* Shelburne, 11 Gray (Mass.) 107; Smith *v.* Lee, 12 Allen (Mass.) 510; City of Newburyport *v.* Creedon (Mass.), 15 N. E. Rep. 157; West Gardner *v.* Hartland, 62 Me. 246; Township of Franklin *v.* Pennsylvania etc. Hospital, 30 Pa. St. 522; Watson *v.* Charlestown, 5 Met. (Mass.) 54; Merrimack County *v.* Jaffrey, 58 N. H. 426; Nuns of the Order of St. Dominic *v.* Long Island City, 1 N. Y. Supp. 415; Andover *v.* Easthampton, 5 Gray (Mass.) 390; Worcester *v.* Sterling, 5 Gray (Mass.) 393.

Compare Mercer *v.* Warren, 23 N. J. L. 415; Tuerton *v.* Fall River, 7 R. I. 182.

A poor district cannot be made liable for the maintenance of one of its paupers by another district in the State asylum, unless upon notice, in order that it may come in and show that the pauper had some other settlement. Danville etc. District *v.* Montour County, 75 Pa. St. 35.

The expenses legally incurred by a town in committing an insane person to the hospital may be recovered of the town where such person has a settlement; but notice must be given within three months after such expenses are paid, as in ordinary pauper cases. Jay *v.* Carthage, 48 Me. 353.

2. Boston *v.* Amesburg, 4 Met. (Mass.) 278; Freeport *v.* Stephenson County, 41 Ill. 496; South Danvers *v.* Essex, 1 Allen (Mass.) 25; Forest County *v.* House of Refuge, 62 Pa. St. 441; Davidson Tp's Appeal, 68 Pa. St. 312.

In an action against a town by the master of a house of correction, to recover the expenses incurred in support of a pauper therein, *held*, that the certificate "examined and allowed" by the county commissioners, was sufficient to support the master's account. Gilman *v.* Portland, 51 Me. 457.

If a boy is committed to the reform school under void process, and the town from which he was committed pays the charges for his support at that school, such town cannot recover the sums so paid, from the town where the boy had his legal settlement. Lewiston *v.* Fairfield, 47 Me. 481.

A demand for expenses due the master of the house of correction in Boston, for the support of a pauper, must be made by the master, either in person or by letter, or by some person receiving authority from the master or the city. Robbins *v.* Weston, 20 Pick. (Mass.) 112; Boston *v.* Weston, 22 Pick. (Mass.) 211.

another town before the account of such expense is audited and certified by the overseers of such house.[1] It is the duty of the officers of the poor to remove a pauper who may become chargeable in their town, not having a legal settlement therein to the town in which he may have a legal settlement as soon as the state and health of the pauper will admit, and if so removed, the liability attaches to the town to which the removal is made to defray the expense of removal and previous relief furnished.[2]

Under a statute authorizing the municipal officers of a town to provide for a person infected with a dangerous disease, "at his charge, or that of his parents or master, if able, otherwise that of the town to which he belongs,"—the sick person is not chargeable therewith, unless he is able to pay all the expenses thus incurred.[3] So statutes providing for the recovery from a pauper by suit of expense incurred by a town for his support, does not apply to a purely officious payment, which the town was under no legal obligation to make.[4] The right of a town, which has incurred expense for the support of a person as a pauper, to recover the same of such person, may be barred by the Statute of Limitations,[5] and they are not suspended by the ignorance of the

A person in jail on execution, actually destitute, is entitled to relief, although he refuses to make oath that he is able to support himself in jail, and has not property sufficient to furnish security for his support. Norridgewock *v.* Solon, 49 Me. 385.

The illegality of a commitment to jail is no defense to an action for support of the prisoner as a pauper. Taunton *v.* Westport, 12 Mass. 355.

A town having a sufficient almshouse is not liable, under Gen. Sts., ch. 70, § 16, for the rent of a tenement occupied by a pauper able to remove to the almshouse. Rawson *v.* Uxbridge, 113 Mass. 47.

Notice.—A pauper notice is not required, to sustain an action brought by a county against a town, to recover sums paid for the support at the State asylum for the insane, of a person committed to the asylum by the judge of probate. Merrimack County *v.* Concord, 39 N. H. 213.

1. Boston *v.* Amesburg, 4 Met. (Mass.) 278.

Under *Massachusetts* St. 1793, ch. 59, a town where a prison is situated is liable to the jailer for the support of a prisoner confined for debt, after proper application to the overseers of the poor, whether he have a settlement elsewhere or not. Cargill *v.* Wiscasset, 2 Mass. 547; Doggett *v.* Dedham, 2 Mass. 564.

2. Mill Creek *v.* Miami, 10 Ohio 375; Blair County *v.* Clarion, 91 Pa. St. 431.

Compare Londonderry *v.* Windham, 2 Vt. 149.

A constable who executes an order of relief by conveying a pauper from a certain township to the county poor-house is not entitled to the mileage allowed in conveying a pauper from the district where he has become chargeable to the district of his settlement, under an order of removal. Directors of Poor *v.* Shingle, 84 Pa. St. 37.

The town of a pauper's settlement is not liable to another town, in which the pauper becomes furiously insane and falls into distress, for the expenses of his removal to an asylum for the insane in another State, and for his support and medical attendance there, even though a removal to some asylum is necessary to the comfort and relief of the pauper, and as a matter of economy and humanity. Deerfield *v.* Greenfield, 1 Gray (Mass.) 514.

3. Orono *v.* Peavey, 66 Me. 60.

4. City of Newburyport *v.* Creedon (Mass.), 15 N. E. Rep. 157.

5. Kennebunkport *v.* Smith, 22 Me. 445; Adams *v.* Ipswich, 116 Mass. 570.

town furnishing support that the pauper is chargeable upon another county.[1]

a. NOTICE.—Where a town incurs expenses on account of a pauper having a legal settlement in another town, the former is bound to give the notice required by statute to the latter before commencing an action for such expenses.[2] So after a notice from one town to another that a pauper, whose settlement is in the latter town, has become chargeable to the former, if his expenses are paid, and he again stands in need of assistance, a new notice is necessary before an action can be maintained for the new expense.[3] But where a town, on receiving notice that one of its paupers is supported in another town, replies to the notice by denying that his settlement is in the town, and neither removes him nor makes any provision for his support, it is liable without any new notice, for the expenses incurred by the other town for his support, after the notice as well as before, until suit brought.[4] The notice need not be technical. If it gives the necessary information and is a compliance with the statute, it is sufficient.[5] If a notice states what is not true in important particulars, it is not sufficient. The misstatement of material facts—facts so important that they change

1. Washington County *v.* Mahaska County, 47 Iowa 57.

2. Springfield *v.* Worcester, 2 Cush. (Mass.) 52; Rumney *v.* Allenstown, 2 N. H. 470; Poueshiek County *v.* Cass County, 63 Iowa 244; Cooper *v.* Alexander, 33 Me. 453; Camden *v.* Lincolnville, 16 Me. 384; Fox *v.* Kendall, 97 Ill. 72; Cerro Gordo Co. *v.* Wright Co., 50 Iowa 439.

A person who has furnished supplies to a pauper, belonging to one town and residing in another in this State, must give notice to one of the selectmen of the latter town of the condition of such pauper, in order to enable him to maintain an action for such supplies. Kent *v.* Chapin, 6 Conn. 72.

In Westfield *v.* Southwick, 17 Pick. (Mass.) 68, it was held where an individual gave notice to the overseers of the poor that he was supporting a pauper, and should look to the town for his pay, and the overseers thereupon gave notice to the town of the pauper's legal settlement that he had become chargeable, that the first town could maintain an action, though they had paid nothing to such individual.

3. Sidney *v.* Augusta, 12 Mass. 316; Gilford *v.* Newmarket, 7 N. H. 251; Bangor *v.* Fairfield, 46 Me. 558; Medway *v.* Milford, 21 Pick. (Mass.) 349; Inhabitants of Palmer *v.* Inhabitants of Dana, 9 Met. (Mass.) 587; Walpole *v.* Hopkinton, 4 Pick. (Mass.) 357; East Machias *v.* Bradley, 67 Me. 533.

Notice by one town to another of a claim made by the treasurer of a State lunatic hospital for the past and future support of a pauper, is sufficient to support an action for the past expenses (though not actually paid until more than three months after), but not for expenses of the support of the pauper after such notice. Amherst *v.* Shelburne, 11 Gray (Mass.) 107.

4. Topsfield *v.* Middleton, 8 Met. (Mass.) 564.

5. Bethlehem *v.* Watertown, 51 Conn. 490; Lynn *v.* Newburyport, 5 Allen (Mass.) 545; Ware *v.* Williamstown, 8 Pick. (Mass.) 388; Springfield *v.* Worcester, 2 Cush. (Mass.) 52; Newtown *v.* Danbury, 3 Conn. 553; Scott *v.* Clayton, 51 Wis. 185; Worcester *v.* Milford, 18 Pick. (Mass.) 379; East Sudbury *v.* Sudbury, 12 Pick. (Mass.) 1; McKay *v.* Welch, 6 N. Y. Supp. 358; Newbitt *v.* Appleton, 63 Me. 491; Hamden *v.* Bethany, 43 Conn. 212; Petersborough *v.* Lancaster, 14 N. H. 382; Rogers *v.* Newbury, 105 Mass. 533; Hampstead *v.* Plaistow, 49 N. H. 84; Barnstead *v.* Strafford, 8 N. H. 142; New Boston *v.* Dunbarton, 12 N. H. 409; Bangor *v.* Wiscasset, 71 Me. 535; Windham *v.* Lebanon, 51 Conn. 319; Washington *v.* Kent, 38 Conn. 249; Falls *v.* Seymour, 44 Conn. 210; Still-

the settlement of a pauper—will vitiate it.[1] A notice by one town to another, that a certain person has become chargeable as a pauper, is not made insufficient by its being united with one in respect to other paupers, which is so, and it is not proper to instruct the jury in such case that the notice would be bad as to all if they could not distinguish between supplies to the former and to the latter. If they could not ascertain from the testimony that supplies had been furnished to the former, it would be a defect of proof, but would not affect the notice.[2] So a notice *quia timent* from overseers of the poor of a town to those of the town of settlement is not premature, if given after the supplies have been ordered in a case of existing necessity, although none have been furnished or consumed.[3] And where, by a statute, a town furnishing support to a pauper is entitled to recover, against the town in

well *v.* Kennedy, 5 N.Y. S. 407; Fiske *v.* Lincoln, 19 Pick. (Mass.) 473.

Notice to a town of the sums expended for the support of a pauper, signed by two persons as selectmen, will be considered as signed by a majority of the selectmen, until the contrary is shown. Nottingham *v.* Barrington, 6 N. H. 302; Berlin *v.* Gorham, 34 N. H. 266; Ashby *v.* Lunenburg, 8 Pick. (Mass.) 563. Or if signed by one of them purporting to be by order of the whole board, it is sufficient. Westminster *v.* Bernardston, 8 Mass. 104; Quincy *v.* Braintree, 5 Mass. 86; Dover *v.* Deer Isle, 15 Me. 169; Gerland *v.* Brewer, 3 Me. 197.

And a notice signed by the selectmen of a town, who are overseers *virtute officii*, is sufficient. Ashby *v.* Lunenburg, 8 Pick. (Mass.) 563.

If the notice to a town chargeable with the support of paupers is defective in not being signed by the overseers in their official capacity, or in not describing the paupers with sufficient precision, yet, if it is understood and answered without any objections on account of its insufficiency, such objections are thereby waived. York *v.* Penobscot, 2 Me. 1.

Where two letters are sent from the overseers of the plaintiff town, the first one having been answered, and the second one correcting a mistake which occurred in the first one, both letters are to be taken together, and will constitute a good notice. Shelburne *v.* Rochester, 1 Pick. (Mass.) 470.

A notice by one town to another, that "the wife and children of A B" had become chargeable as paupers, is sufficient to entitle the town giving such notice to recover for expenses incurred for the relief of the wife. Sanford *v.* Lebanon, 31 Me. 124.

1. Glenburn *v.* Oldtown, 63 Me. 582; La Crosse *v.* Melrose, 22 Wis. 459.

A notice that a pauper belonging to the town of M was on expense in the town of S, was sent to the selectmen of M in these words: "Mrs Phelps, an inhabitant of M, is on expense in the town of S." *Held*, not sufficient under the statute (Rev. 1866, tit. 50, § 22), which requires that the notice should state the name of the pauper. Salem *v.* Montville, 33 Conn. 141; Auburn *v.* Wilton, 74 Me. 437.

Where a pauper was known by one name in the town of her residence, and by another in the town of her settlement, a notice from the former to the latter, stating only the name by which she was known in the former, was held insufficient. Lanesborough *v.* New Ashford, 5 Pick. (Mass.) 190.

A notice that a pauper, whose settlement is in the defendant town, has become chargeable to the plaintiff, is not notice that his wife and children are also chargeable. Andover *v.* Canton, 13 Mass. 547.

A selectmen's notice under Conn. Gen. St., tit. 15, ch. 2, pt. 1, § 5, that certain persons, "paupers of your town, are here, poor and unable to support themselves"—*held*, to be insufficient, as not showing that the paupers were in fact receiving support from the town sending the notice. Beacon Falls *v.* Seymour, 46 Conn. 281.

2. Sanford *v.* Lebanon, 31 Me. 124.

3. Fayette *v.* Livermore, 62 Me. 229.

which he has his settlement, for expenses incurred before and after notice given, it is immaterial whether the support has been continuous, or only occasional.[1]

b. WAIVER.—Notice may be waived.[2] A refusal on the part of a town to support a pauper, and a denial of their liability to do so, is a waiver of the notice and demand, which would otherwise be necessary previous to an action against them by another town.[3] So a notice may be waived, by returning an answer, denying all liability, on the ground that the pauper has no settlement in the town.[4] But where a town has relieved persons therein, who had fallen into distress, and legal notice thereof has been given to the town in which such persons had a legal settlement, if afterwards, another notice is given, the last notice will be no waiver of any right acquired under that previously given.[5]

c. NOTICE BY MAIL.—Though the putting of a letter into the mail is made, by the statute for the support of paupers, sufficient evidence that notice was given to a town,[6] yet the fact of putting such letter into the mail is to be proved, like any other fact.[7]

d. FAILURE TO ANSWER NOTICE.—A failure of the overseers of the poor of the defendant town to return an answer to the notice sent to them by the overseers of the poor of the plaintiff town estops the defendants to deny that the pauper had a settlement in the defendant town.[8]

e. EARNINGS OF PAUPERS.—Towns are entitled to the avails of the industry of their paupers and are required to contribute only when that industry or means of the pauper fail to afford a com-

1. Attleborough *v.* Mansfield, 15 Pick. (Mass.) 19.

2. Newtown *v.* Danbury, 3 Conn. 553; Strafford *v.* Fairfield, 3 Conn. 588; La Crosse *v.* Melrose, 22 Wis. 459.

An agreement made by the selectmen of a town, before an action is commenced against them, by which they engaged to waive the legal notice required by the statute, of the charges against them for the relief of a pauper, is executory merely, and does not, at the trial of the action, bar the town from objecting to the want of notice in due form. Hanover *v.* Weare, 2 N. H. 131.

3. Newtown *v.* Danbury, 3 Conn. 553.

4. Commonwealth *v.* Dracut, 8 Gray (Mass.) 155. See Easton *v.* Wareham, 131 Mass. 10.

5. New Vineyard *v.* Phillips, 45 Me. 405.

6. Augusta *v.* Vienna, 21 Me. 298; Athens *v.* Brownfield, 21 Me. 443.

Where it appeared that a proper notification to overseers of the poor was deposited in the post-office on a certain day, and actually arrived at the office in the town of the overseers to whom directed, and was actually received by them, but it did not appear on what day, *held*, that the law presumed, in the absence of all other evidence, that it was received in the due course of the mail. Augusta *v.* Vienna, 21 Me. 298.

7. Augusta *v.* Vienna, 21 Me. 298.

8. Leicester *v.* Rehoboth, 4 Mass. 180; Bridgewater *v.* Dartmouth, 4 Mass. 273; Bangor *v.* Madawaska, 72 Me. 203; Stilwell *v.* Coons (N. Y.), 25 N. E. Rep. 316.

Even though he may have no settlement in the commonwealth. Westminster *v.* Bernardston, 8 Mass. 104.

The objection must be in writing, and is sufficient if signed by one of the selectmen. Bridgewater *v.* Dartmouth, 4 Mass. 273.

A town notified another town that James Curtis, his wife and their seven children, naming them all, had fallen into distress and been supplied as paupers. The second town replied, acknowledging receipt of the notice, "touching the Curtis family," and deny-

fortable support.[1] If one is on the town as a pauper, and the value of his labor performed for the town exceeds the amount expended for his relief, he cannot recover for the excess in an action against the town for work and labor.[2] So a town, in stating an account with the commonwealth as to the support of State paupers, is bound to credit the value of the paupers' labor only, and not any share of the profits, if there is any, which the town derives from their labor.[3]

f. CONVICTS.—Towns are not liable to keepers of prisons for the support of their paupers who are in close confinement in such prisons.[4] So a town which has paid money for the support of a criminal in its workhouse cannot maintain an action to recover the same from the town where he had his settlement.[5]

g. DIVISION OF TOWNS.—Where a new town is established out of part of an old one, it is charged with the support of paupers residing within its limits.[6] But acts dividing the territory of towns usually fix the liability of such towns for the support of the poor.[7] The imposition of a liability for the support of a single

ing that James Curtis had a settlement in their town. It was held, that they were not estopped to deny the settlement of the wife and children in their town. Palmyra *v.* Prospect, 30 Me. 211.

A notice from one town to another, given for reimbursement of expenses, while an action is pending, although unanswered, does not operate as an estoppel to prevent the town notified from denying the settlement of the pauper. Newton *v.* Randolph, 16 Mass. 426; Holden *v.* Glenburn, 63 Me. 579; Marshpee *v.* Edgartown, 23 Pick. (Mass.) 156.

1. Clinton *v.* Benton, 49 Me. 550; Commonwealth *v.* Cambridge, 20 Pick. (Mass.) 267.

Where one town is by agreement bound to support the pauper and his wife, and the settlement of his children is in another, the latter may be held to pay for supplies furnished for the children, although the father by his industry is able to support himself and wife, provided he can do no more. Clinton *v.* Benton, 49 Me. 550.

2. Abbot *v.* Fremont, 34 N. H. 432.

A State pauper, duly assigned to an individual to be supported by him, may maintain an action against the assignee for services done for him on a special agreement for certain wages. Church *v.* Wilson, 1 Pick. (Mass.) 23.

3. Commonwealth *v.* Cambridge, 4 Met. (Mass.) 35.

4. Mace *v.* Nottingham West, 1 N. H. 52; City of Boston *v.* Inhabitants of Dedham, 8 Met. (Mass.) 513.

The expense of an infant nursing at the breast of a convict may be recovered of the town by the master of the house of correction; but all expense for particular food of the mother is chargeable to the commonwealth. Watson *v.* Cambridge, 18 Pick. (Mass.) 470.

In Wade *v.* Salem, 7 Pick. (Mass.) 333, it is held that the keeper of a house of correction, after the examination and allowance of his accounts by the court of sessions, may maintain assumpsit for the support of a pauper, against the town where he has a legal settlement. It is no defense for the town that they had no notice of the claim.

5. Worcester *v.* Auburn, 4 Allen (Mass.) 574.

6. Centre *v.* Wills, 7 Ohio, pt. 2, 171; Ashland County *v.* Richland County, 7 Ohio St. 65; Vernon *v.* East Hartford, 3 Conn. 475; Simsbury *v.* Hartford, 14 Conn. 192. See Pike *v.* Union, 5 Ohio 529.

When part of a town is set off and incorporated into a new town, and no provision is made in the act for the support of such paupers in the old town as have no settlement in the State, they must be supported by the town in which they are when the support is given, and no action can be maintained by one of the towns against the other for reimbursement. Winterport *v.* Frankfort, 51 Me. 447.

7. Belmont *v.* Morrill, 69 Me. 314; Calais *v.* Marshfield, 30 Me. 511; Town

specific class of paupers upon the new town, in an act dividing an existing municipality, does not, however, necessarily impose upon the remaining portion the burden of supporting all other paupers not included in such class.[1]

5. By Counties—*a.* GENERALLY.—The obligation of a county to support the poor is statutory, and it is liable in no case except as prescribed by statute.[2] The superintendents of the poor of a county which has adopted the "county system" of pauper support cannot recover from the superintendents of the poor of another county which has adopted the same system the expense of supporting a pauper who had removed from the latter county into the former, unless, at the time of such removal, the pauper had acquired a settlement in some town of the latter county.[3]

b. FUNERAL EXPENSES.—There is no distinction in regard to a county's liability for funeral expenses and its liability for services rendered to the indigent person in his lifetime. In both cases a previous adjudication of poverty by the county court is necessary to fix the liability.[4]

6. Apprenticing.—Statutes giving the officers of the poor the power to bind minors as apprentices, gives them no authority so to do, if the minors' parents are living, or unless the minors are chargeable to the district.[5] If its parents are not living the officers should summon its next friend or the person with whom it resides.[6] See APPRENTICES, vol. 1, p. 637.

7. Medical Services.—Paupers must at all events receive necessary medical attendance at the expense of the town or county in which they belong;[7] so where a physician renders services to a

of Worcester *v.* Town of East Montpelier (Vt.), 17 Atl. Rep. 842.

If a special act, passed since the adoption of the Revised Statutes, and dividing one town into two or more towns, contains provisions at variance from those of the Revised Statutes, relating to the duty of supporting paupers, as between such towns, the provisions of the Revised Statutes, must yield to the latter enactment. Lewiston *v.* Auburn, 32 Me. 492.

1. Holden *v.* Veazie, 73 Me. 312.

2. Cooledge *v.* Mahaska, 24 Iowa 211. See Collins *v.* King County, 1 Wash. 416; King County *v.* Collins, 1 Wash. 469; Clay County *v.* Plant, 42 Ill. 324; Mussel *v.* Tama County, 73 Iowa 101; Perry County *v.* Du Quoin, 99 Ill. 479; Mappes *v.* Iowa County Supervisors, 47 Wis. 31; Lee County *v.* Lackie, 30 Ark. 764; Hamlin County *v.* Clark County (S. Dak.), 45 N. W. Rep. 329.

3. Dane Co. *v.* Sauk Co., 38 Wis. 499.

An action may be sustained by the directors of a county infirmary against the commissioners of another county, for the maintenance of a pauper legally settled in a township thereof, after returning her to the commissioners and requesting them to accept and take care of her. Ashland County *v.* Richland County, 7 Ohio St. 65.

4. Clark County *v.* Hine, 49 Ark. 145.

5. Welborn *v.* Little, 1 Nott & M. (S. C.) 263. See Warner *v.* Swett, 7 Vt. 446.

Overseers of the poor are not authorized to bind out poor children as apprentices, unless their parents are dead or are unable to support them. Demar *v.* Simonson, 4 Blackf. (Ind.) 132.

6. Curry *v.* Jenkins, Hard. (Ky.) 493. See Payne *v.* Long, 2 A. K. Marsh. (Ky.) 158.

7. Morgan Commrs. *v.* Seaton, 90 Ind. 158; Commissioners of Carroll County *v.* Wilson, 1 Ind. 478; Jones *v.* De Soto County Supervisors, 60 Miss. 409; Directors of Poor *v.* Donnelly (Pa.), 7 Atl. Rep. 204; Poor District of Summit Township *v.* Byers (Pa.), 11

pauper by the authority of the proper officers he may recover for such services.[1] If the physician employed by the officers of the poor is too far away to attend a pauper requiring attendance, the physician employed in his absence is entitled to compensation from the county;[2] or if the regular county physician refuses to attend a poor person temporarily in need of medical assistance, the overseers may employ another physician, for the value of those services the county will be liable,[3] but a physician who renders medical services to a pauper with knowledge that other and proper relief had been provided by the officers of the poor, he must be deemed to have rendered them voluntarily and cannot recover therefor in an action against the town.[4] So under a statute mak-

Atl. Rep. 242; Directors of the Poor *v.* Malany, 64 Pa. St. 144; Allegany County Commrs. *v.* McClintock, 60 Md. 559; Montgomery *v.* Le Sueur, 32 Minn. 532; La Salle County *v.* Reynolds, 49 Ill. 186.

A physician rendered a necessary service to a minor, whose property was worth $75, but whose mother was dead and whose father was worthless and irresponsible, *held*, that the physician could charge the county for the service. Christian County *v.* Rockwell, 25 Ill. App. 20.

The law presumes that services by a physician, rendered to a poor person in an emergency, are bestowed in charity. Cantrell *v.* Clark County, 47 Ark. 239.

1. Hamilton County *v.* Myers (Neb.), 37 N. W. Rep. 623; Hamilton County *v.* Raben (Neb.), 37 N. W. Rep. 626; Morgan County *v.* Holman, 34 Ind. 256; Bentley *v.* Chicago County Commrs., 25 Minn. 259; Bucksport *v.* Cushing, 69 Me. 224; French *v.* Benton, 44 N. H. 28; Campbell *v.* Grooms, 101 Pa. St. 481; Cooledge *v.* Mahaska County, 24 Iowa 211; Boothby *v.* Troy, 48 Me. 560; Miller *v.* Somerset, 14 Mass. 396; Kittredge *v.* Newbury, 14 Mass. 448; Underwood *v.* Inhabitants of Scituate, 7 Met. (Mass.) 214; Bay *v.* Cook, 22 N. J. L. 343; Willsinson *v.* Albany, 28 N. H. 9.

Where a physician and surgeon renders professional services, in a case of emergency, on the credit of his patient, who fails to pay the bill, and after several years admits himself to be a pauper, the physician cannot then recover for said services from the directors of the poor. Blakeslee *v.* Chester County Poor Directors, 102 Pa. St. 274.

No action lies by a physician, against overseers of the poor, for services in attending upon a pauper, though upon the most pressing necessity; these services not having been rendered at the request of the overseers, and they not having promised to pay. Nor would they be protected in paying for such services, without a previous order of a justice or justices of the peace. Flower *v.* Allen, 5 Cow. (N. Y.) 654; Gourley *v.* Allen, 5 Cow. (N. Y.) 644; Everts *v.* Adams, 12 Johns. (N. Y.) 352.

2. Morgan County Commrs. *v.* Seaton, 90 Ind. 158; Christian County *v.* Rockwell, 25 Ill. App. 20.

Compare Orange County Commrs. *v.* Ritter, 90 Ind. 362.

3. Gage County *v.* Fulton, 16 Neb. 5.

4. Phelps *v.* Westford, 124 Mass. 286; Gawley *v.* Jones County, 60 Iowa 159; Mansfield *v.* Sac County, 59 Iowa 694; Robbins *v.* Morgan Commrs., 91 Ind. 537; Bartholomew County *v.* Boynton, 30 Ind. 359. See Morgan County *v.* Seaton, 122 Ind. 521.

Where, by the direction of an overseer for the poor, another than the county physician renders medical services to a person not requiring to be wholly supported by the county, and there is a rule of the county board that such a person should resort to the county physician, the county is not liable for said services under Ill. Rev. St. 1874, ch. 107, § 23. De Witt County *v.* Wright, 91 Ill. 529.

To a suit for medical services rendered to a temporary pauper, at the request of a township trustee, an answer that the board had a rule, known to plaintiff, that they would pay for only one visit to a pauper, if he was in a condition to be removed to the county asylum; that the pauper in question was in such condition; and that the plaintiff was the physician of the asylum, was held a good answer.

ing a town liable for "expenses unnecessarily incurred" by a physician against the town for medical attendance upon a pauper, who has a legal settlement in another town, the fact that another person arranges to take care of her will not prevent his recovery, if neither the agent nor the town furnished medical attendance.[1]

To enable a town to charge another town with medical attendance furnished a pauper it is not necessary that the pauper should have known that the physician intended to charge the town.[2]

8. Actions for Support.—Statutes generally provide that paupers must have a legal settlement in the county or town in order to be chargeable to such county or town. So in actions for support, the plaintiff must show that the pauper was legally settled in, and chargeable to the town of the overseer receiving notice to remove him,[3] and the services rendered, moneys expended in behalf of the pauper must be proved. If a pauper is proved to have once had his settlement in the defendant town, the burden is on the town to prove a subsequent settlement gained elsewhere.[4] The party affected should be summoned before the justices, or have reasonable notice of the time and place of hearing. The legal residence of the pauper must first be judicially determined, and an order of removal made out; and the order, or a copy of it, together with the notice required by the statute, should be served by the overseer where the pauper is, upon the overseer of the place where his settlement has been adjudged to be. The justices cannot render judgment and issue execution against the overseer.

Commissioners *v.* Saunders, 16 Ind. 405.

A post mortem examination made by a physician, at the direction of the coroner, is not a service covered by his employment to attend upon the county poor. Gaston *v.* Commissioners of Marion County, 3 Ind. 497.

A physician employed by a town trustee to attend, "during his last illness," a pauper dying from the effects of a tumor, cannot charge the county for making an excision of the tumor after death, so that the body may be encased in an ordinary coffin. Morgan County *v.* Johnson, 29 Ind. 35.

1. Wing *v.* Chesterfield, 116 Mass. 353. See Windham *v.* Portland, 23 Me. 410.

Under a contract between the county commissioners and a physician, by which the latter agreed for a specified sum to "do all the pauper practice in A township, including the county asylum and jail," and "to present no claims or demands for any extra charges," it was held that the physician was bound to treat non-resident paupers within such township, without extra charge, on being requested so to do by the proper officers. Cooper *v.* County Commissioners, 64 Ind. 520.

2. Bridgewater *v.* Roxbuy, 54 Conn. 213.

3. Youngs *v.* Overseers, 14 N. J. L. 517; Mitchell *v.* Cornville, 12 Mass. 333; Miller *v.* Somerset, 14 Mass. 396; Kittredge *v.* Newbury, 14 Mass. 396.

The kindred of a pauper are not liable for his support under St. 1793, ch. 59, § 3, to any town furnishing relief, but only to the town of the pauper's settlement. Salem *v.* Andover, 3 Mass. 436; Saywood *v.* Alfred, 5 Mass. 244.

Massachusetts Rev. Sts. ch. 46, § 18, changed the provision of Sts. of 1793, ch. 59, § 13, and the person who is not an inhabitant of the town where a pauper falls into distress may now recover of such town any expense necessarily incurred by him for the relief of the pauper after notice and request made to the overseers of the poor of the town, and their neglect to provide for the pauper. Underwood *v.* Scituate, 7 Met. (Mass.) 214.

4. Starkes *v.* New Portland, 47 Me. 183.

The warrant directed by the statute ought to set forth the whole proceeding, and show at how much they adjudged the sum necessarily expended.[1]

No person can maintain an action against a town for supplies furnished to a pauper but the one who gave the notice to the overseers.[2] It is not necessary to show that the supplies had been paid for before notice was given to the town chargeable.[3]

POOR DEBTORS.—(See also ARREST, vol. 1, p. 719; FRAUDULENT DEBTOR, vol. 8, p. 780; IMPRISONMENT FOR DEBT, vol. 10, p. 212.)

I. **DEFINITION.**—In several of the *United States,* statutes exist which provide, in substance, that any person arrested or imprisoned for debt, or upon mesne process in an action of contract, desirous to procure his discharge from arrest, may summon his creditor before a magistrate, and there take oath that he has no property with which to pay the debt on which he is detained; and upon this oath, due proceedings being had before the magistrate designated by the law, he may be set at liberty. Persons entitled to the benefit of such laws are called poor debtors; and the law and the oath, respectively, are known as the poor-debtor law and the poor debtor's oath.[4]

II. **IMPRISONMENT.**—In *England,* and generally throughout the *United States,* either by legislative enactment or constitutional provisions, arrest or imprisonment for debt has been abolished,[5] although in most jurisdictions provisions still exist for the arrest of debtors in certain cases of fraud.[6] In those jurisdictions, however, where imprisonment for debt still survives, even where there is no fraud, the poor debtor laws have placed restraints upon the general

1. Youngs *v.* Overseers, 14 N. J. L. 517; Township of Gilpin *v.* Township of Park (Pa.), 11 Atl. Rep. 791.

It is not necessary that an examination should appear upon an order of sessions for the removal of a pauper. Eallowfield *v.* Marlborough, 1 Dall. 28.

2. Warren *v.* Islesborough, 20 Me. 442.

3. Lee *v.* Deerfield, 5 N. H. 290; Northwood *v.* Barrington, 9 N. H. 369.

4. 2 Abbot's Law Dict. 288; 2 Bouvier's Law Dict. (15th ed.) 432.

5. Stat. 32 & 33 Vict., ch. 62; ARREST, vol. 1, p. 719, n. 5.

6. IMPRISONMENT FOR DEBT, vol. 10, p. 213.

power of arrest, and allow an honest but unfortunate debtor to be discharged from arrest upon delivering up his property for the benefit of his creditors, or upon taking the poor debtor's oath.[1]

III. **Proceedings to Obtain a Discharge—1. Preliminary Steps.** —If the debtor desires to obtain his discharge from arrest by taking advantage of the poor debtor laws, he makes application to a magistrate, designated by statute, to be allowed to take the oath for the relief of poor debtors.[2]

1. "The person of a debtor, when there is not strong presumption of fraud, ought not to be continued in prison, after he shall have delivered up his property for the benefit of his creditors, in such manner as shall be prescribed by law." *Rhode Island* Const., art. 1, § 11.

"No person shall be imprisoned for debt, unless upon refusal to deliver up his estate for the benefit of his creditors, in such manner as shall be prescribed by law, or in cases where there is strong presumption of fraud." *Illinois* Const., art. 2, § 12; *Illinois* Rev. Stat., ch. 72, §§ 1-35; *Maine* Rev. Stat., ch. 113; *Massachusetts* Pub. Stat., ch. 162; Genl. Laws *New Hampshire*, ch. 241; *New Jersey* Rev. St., p. 497; Genl. Laws *Oregon*, p. 627; *Pennsylvania*, 1 Brightly's Pur. Dig. p. 66, § 62; *Rhode Island* Pub. Stat., ch. 226.

Genl. Stat. *South Carolina*, §§ 2405 *et seq.;* Code of Civil Proc. *South Carolina*, §§ 199 *et seq.;* Rev. Laws. *Vermont*, §§ 1514-1528; *Virginia* Code (1887), ch. 176; *Wisconsin* Rev. Stat., §§ 4307, 4320.

"Upon taking the oath, the defendant or debtor shall be discharged from arrest or imprisonment, and shall be forever exempt from arrest on the same execution, or on any process founded on the judgment, or on the same cause of action, unless convicted of having willfully sworn falsely on his examination." *Massachusetts* Pub. Stat., ch. 162, § 40.

"It may be stated generally that the object of such statutes . . . is to induce the defendant to pay the debt, give security, or take advantage of the insolvent laws, or of some enactments made especially for the relief of poor debtors. It follows, therefore, that in most of the States a person under arrest for debt may obtain his release in any of these ways. A poor debtor is of course usually compelled to resort to one of the two last mentioned, and although the proceedings differ in the different States, yet, as a rule, he is released upon delivering his property to a trustee or taking oath that he has not more than ten or twenty dollars above the amount exempted by statute in the particular State in which he is confined." 2 Bouvier's Law Dict. 432.

"No crime known to the law brought so many to the jails and prisons (one hundred years ago) as the crime of debt, and the class most likely to get into debt was the most defenseless and dependent, the great body of servants, artisans, or laborers." 1 McMaster's Hist. Peop. U. S. 98.

By the common law, a debtor imprisoned on execution in a civil action could not be discharged without paying the debt, even on taking the poor debtor's oath, if his creditor would pay for his support in prison. 3 Bl. Com, 416; *Massachusetts* Anc. Chart. 650.

The existing statutes do not give the creditor this election, but allow the debtor to obtain his discharge by taking the poor debtor's oath, unless he has been guilty of some fraud or wasteful misuse of his property. Stockwell *v.* Silloway, 100 Mass. 287.

2. Application; Statutory Provisions.— "If the debtor at the appointed time and place, makes a full disclosure of the actual state of his affairs and of all his property, rights and credits, and answers all proper interrogatories in regard to the same, to the satisfaction of said justices, and they are satisfied that the disclosure is true, and do not discover anything therein inconsistent with his taking the oath prescribed in section thirty, they may administer it to him and certify the fact on the writ; and the debtor shall thereupon be discharged from arrest; and no execution issuing on the judgment in the suit, shall run against his body, but against his property only." *Maine* Rev. Stat., ch. 113, § 6. "Any person arrested or committed to jail on execution, or who has given bond as provided by law, may apply to a justice of the supreme

The general practice is for the magistrate[1] to appoint a time and place for the debtor's examination,[2] and to issue notice thereof to the creditor.[3] Then, at the time and place appointed, if the debtor

court, by petition, praying for the appointment of two justices to whom he may apply to be admitted to take the oath for the relief of poor debtors."

"Said debtor may make application to said justices, setting forth that he had not, at the time of his arrest, nor at any time after, estate of the value of twenty dollars, except goods by law exempt from attachment, and praying to be admitted to take said oath." Genl. Laws *New Hampshire*, ch. 241, §§ 1 & 3. And see *Massachusetts* Pub. Stat., ch. 162, § 39.

Application—Requisites of.—The application should be signed. Neal *v.* Payne, 35 Me. 158.

It need not state that the debtor's circumstances are such as to entitle him to the oath. Eaton *v.* Miner, 5 N. H. 542.

It does not matter that the nature of the action in which the judgment was recovered is wrongly stated in the application, where the mistake does not mislead the creditor. Osgood *v.* Hutchins, 6 N. H. 374.

An application is sufficient, if it states the facts necessary to be stated, and contains a petition for the relief provided in intelligible terms, although the word "oath" be omitted. Fernald *v.* Noyes, 30 N. H. 39.

It need not describe the statute, and an erroneous description of it may be rejected as surplusage. Ladd *v.* Deming, 20 N. H. 487.

It need not state the amount of the execution. Allen *v.* Bruce, 12 N. H. 418.

Under the *New Hampshire* statute the application of the debtor must be made, the place of hearing appointed, and the oath administered, within the county in which the arrest was made. Hawley *v.* White, 18 N. H. 67.

Where a person, arrested on civil process, wished to go immediately before the magistrate who signed the writ, who was absent at the time some miles away in another county, it was held that the officer was not bound to comply with the request, the magistrate being out of the county, and that the officer was justified in committing him. Whitcomb *v.* Cook, 38 Vt. 477.

1. Magistrate Must be Disinterested.—Bard *v.* Wood, 30 Me. 155; Baker *v.* Carleton, 32 Me. 335; McGilvery *v.* Staples, 81 Me. 101; Gear *v.* Smith, 9 N. H. 63.

Accordingly a surety on the poor debtor's bond, or a near relative of the debtor is incompetent to act. Winsor *v.* Clark, 36 Me. 110; Gray *v.* Douglas, 81 Me. 427; Bard *v.* Wood, 30 Me. 155; Gear *v.* Smith, 9 N. H. 63. So also where the execution is in favor of the inhabitants of a town, an inhabitant of such town cannot act. Norridgewock *v.* Sawtelle, 72 Me. 484. Nor can the attorney for the debtor act as magistrate. Kane *v.* Learned, 117 Mass. 190. But the fact that the magistrate was a brother of a surety on the debtor's bond, or a creditor of the debtor, does not disqualify him from acting. Downer *v.* Hollister, 14 N. H. 122. Fuller *v.* Davis, 73 Me. 556.

The mere fact that a justice of the peace and of the quorum has issued a citation to the creditor, does not disqualify him from acting in the same case, in the examination of the debtor. Ayer *v.* Woodman, 24 Me. 196; Cummings *v.* York, 54 Me. 386.

The certificate of the administration of the oath need not, however, state the fact of the disinterestedness of the justices. Butler *v.* Fairbanks, 4 Gray (Mass.) 531. *Contra* Scamman *v.* Huff, 51 Me. 194.

2. One desirous of taking the oath for the relief of poor debtors must be examined before magistrates authorized to act in the county in which the arrest was made, and he cannot cite his creditor and be heard with effect before those of any other county. Houghton *v.* Lyford, 39 Me. 267.

3. Notice.—As these proceedings are in the nature of civil proceedings there is no reason why the strict rules which govern criminal cases should be applied to notices, of this kind.

The application of this principle is illustrated by the following cases:

The magistrate issuing the notice need not necessarily be the magistrate who took the recognizance. Elliott *v.* Willis, 1 Allen (Mass.) 461.

The requirement of the *Massachusetts* statute that the notice shall be signed by the magistrate and designate his official capacity, is held not to be satisfied by the mere addition of the word, "magistrate" to the signature. Carter *v.* Clohecy, 100 Mass. 299, nor by the addition of the words, "justice of the peace," although the magistrate is in fact a trial justice. Nash *v.* Coffey, 105 Mass. 341.

A notice to a corporation, which, though not describing it by its true name, was sent to its attorney and acknowledged by him as notice to the corporation, was held sufficient, in Mutual Safety F. Ins. Co. *v.* Woodward, 8 Allen (Mass.) 148.

A notice directed to four only of five joint plaintiffs and served on the attorney of the five has been held sufficient. Dana *v.* Carr, 124 Mass. 397.

So a notice giving only the initial letter of the first name of the creditor. Dwyer *v.* Winters, 126 Mass. 186.

So a notice directed to "A, attorney for B, *et al.*, creditors," where the execution was in favor of B alone. Hill *v.* Bartlett, 124 Mass. 399.

The omission of the debtor's middle name was held not to invalidate a notice in which he was in other ways so described that the creditor could not be misled. Collins *v.* Douglass, 1 Gray (Mass.) 167.

So where the notice gave the debtor's name as "Henry D. Winter," his true name, while the writ, execution, and recognizance described him as "Henry Winters." Dwyer *v.* Winters, 126 Mass. 186. See also Van Kuran *v.* May, 7 Allen (Mass.) 466. And see Peck *v.* Wilson, 14 N. H. 587, in which case the omission of the initial letter of the creditor's middle name was held immaterial, the notice being served on his attorney, and there being no possibilty of a misunderstanding.

If the debtor has been arrested in more than one suit, the notice must specify which suit is referred to.

Merriam *v.* Haskins, 7 Allen (Mass.) 346. But where the debtor had been twice arrested on two executions in favor of the same creditor, it was held that two notices, precisely alike, fixing the same time and place for the examination, and served upon the creditor simultaneously, were sufficient. Way *v.* O'Sullivan, 106 Mass. 118.

A notice describing the execution as issued from the court holden at L., when in fact it was issued from the court holden at B, has been held bad. Shed *v.* Tileston, 8 Gray (Mass.) 244.

A notice making an arrest on execution, when, in fact, the arrest was a *mesne* process, has been held valid. Calnan *v.* Toomey, 129 Mass. 451.

A notice naming seven o'clock P. M. in January does not name an unreasonable hour. May *v.* Foote, 7 Allen (Mass.) 354.

A notice giving the day of the month but omitting the year and the word "next" has been held good. Salmon *v.* Nation, 109 Mass. 216.

A notice designating the place for the examination as the "police court in Lynn" has been held sufficient to designate the place. Danforth *v.* Knowlton, 111 Mass. 76.

A notice to judgment creditors, not residents of the county, addressed to "A, attorney for B and C, creditors," is sufficiently addressed. Pierce *v.* Phillips, 101 Mass. 313.

New Notice.—Under the *Massachusetts* statute providing for a new notice it has been held that, if a poor debtor directs an officer to obtain from a magistrate a notice to the creditor of the desire of the debtor to take the oath for the relief of poor debtors, and to have a time appointed for the hearing not later than a certain day, and the magistrate issues a notice in due form appointing a later day, which notice is duly served upon the creditor, the debtor may repudiate the notice, and give a new notice immediately. Burt *v.* Geary, 128 Mass. 404.

And, the statute providing that no new notice of a poor debtor's application to take the oath shall be given until after seven days from the service of the former notice, unless the former was insufficient, a new notice given the same day by altering a served and sufficient former notice is invalid, although the officer makes return upon the new notice only. Hastings *v.* Partridge, 124 Mass. 401.

And see, further, on the subject of a new notice, under the *Massachusetts* statute, Safford *v.* Clark, 105 Mass. 389; Millett *v.* Lemon, 113 Mass. 355; Skinner *v.* Frost, 6 Allen (Mass.) 285; Grant *v.* Clapp, 106 Mass. 453; McInerny *v.* Samuels, 125 Mass. 425. Browne *v.* Hale, 217 Mass. 158.

Service of Notice.— Service may be waived, and the wavier proved by parol, though the officer's return, showing a defective service, makes no allusion to a waiver. Lord *v.* Skinner, 9 Allen (Mass.) 376; Williams *v.* Kimball, 132 Mass. 214; Goldenberg *v.* Blake, 145 Mass. 354.

The appearance of the creditor's attorney at the time and place mentioned in the notice, for the purpose of examining the notice and return, is not a waiver. Francis *v.* Howard, 115 Mass. 236.

Nor is a special appearance to object. Williams *v.* Kimball, 132 Mass. 214.

An individual gave notice to take the poor debtor's oath, as prescribed in a specified act, which act was repealed. The creditor attended, but did not except to the notice for this cause, and the proper oath was taken. *Held*, that the exception was waived. Bunker *v.* Nutter, 9 N. H. 554.

If, to be good, service should be made before a certain hour of the day, a return showing the day, but not the hour of service, does not sufficiently show a good service. Park *v.* Johnston, 7 Cush. (Mass.) 265. See also Smith *v.* Randall, 1 Allen (Mass.) 456.

The right to his office of the constable *de facto* who served the notice cannot be questioned in a suit to which he is not a party. Elliott *v.* Willis, 1 Allen (Mass.) 461; Petersilea *v.* Stone, 119 Mass. 465.

A sheriff cannot serve the notice outside of his county. Henshaw *v.* Savil, 114 Mass. 74.

The officer's return of service is conclusive, in an action on the recognizance. Niles *v.* Hancock, 3 Met. (Mass.) 568; Collins *v.* Douglass, 1 Gray (Mass.) 167; Henshaw *v.* Savil, 114 Mass. 74; Hall *v.* Tenney, 11 N. H. 517; Woods *v.* Blodgett, 15 N. H. 569.

Facts not appearing in the return may be shown by parol. Taylor *v.* Clarke, 121 Mass. 319.

So, in *Maine*, the certificate of the justices is conclusive as to the fact of notice. Buckley *v.* Page, 1 Cliff. (U. S.) 474; Baker *v.* Holmes, 27 Me. 153; Lowe *v.* Dore, 32 Me. 27; and of the sufficiency of the citation. Gray *v.* Douglass, 81 Me. 427.

But in *New Hampshire*, it has been held to be *prima facie* evidence only. Woods *v.* Blodgett, 15 N. H. 569.

The condition of a recognizance that, within thirty days from the day of the debtor's arrest, he will "deliver himself up for examination before some magistrate authorized to act, giving notice of the time and place thereof," as by law provided, does not require him to have the notice served upon the creditor within the thirty days. Marple *v.* Burton, 144 Mass. 79.

Nor to have the examination commenced within the thirty days. It is sufficient if the notice is issued within that time. Barnes *v.* Ladd, 130 Mass. 557.

Service of the original application to take the oath is sufficient, although the statute requires service of "an attested copy thereof." Callaghan *v.* Whitmarsh, 145 Mass. 340; Eaton *v.* Miner, 5 N. H. 542.

In Young *v.* Capen, 7 Met. (Mass.) 287, it was held insufficient merely to read the notice to the creditor. But, in Goldenberg *v.* Blake, 145 Mass. 354, it was held that the question of waiver was for the jury where the creditor, on the notice being read to him, told the officer that he understood it and would attend the hearing.

In Baldwin *v.* Merrill, 4 Me. 55, it was held that when a seal was upon the citation, when issued, but had accidentally dropped off before service, the service was good. And see Lewis *v.* Brewer, 51 Me. 108.

Under the *Massachusetts* statute a personal delivery to the creditor or his agent or attorney is required; that is, the copy of the notice may not be sent by mail nor handed to a third person. Williams *v.* Kimball, 135 Mass. 411.

Service upon either the creditor's agent or his attorney is good, where both reside in the county. Salmon *v.* Nation, 109 Mass. 216.

Where the creditor resides in the county and his attorney out of it, service upon the latter is sufficient. Harwood *v.* Wiley, 115 Mass 358.

See also Knight *v.* Fifield, 7 Cush. (Mass.) 263.

But service on the creditor, who resides out of the county, instead of on his agent, who resides in the county, will not suffice. Putnam *v.* Williams, 2 Allen (Mass.) 73. This distinction, however, turns upon the wording of the statute.

It has been held that service on the creditor's attorney at his place of business in another county was good, though his place of residence was within the county in which the arrest was made. Carroll *v.* Rogers, 4 Allen (Mass.) 70.

As to the form of notice to be served on the attorney of a non-resident plaintiff, see Pierce *v.* Phillips, 101 Mass. 313.

As to who is an agent of the creditor, see Newcomb *v.* Willcutt, 124 Mass. 178.

is entitled to his discharge under the provisions of the statutes, the magistrate administers to him the oath and discharges him from arrest.[1]

As to the circumstances under which, neither the creditor nor his agent or attorney residing within the county, service may be made on the officer who made the arrest, see Way *v.* Carlisle, 13 Allen (Mass.) 398; Richardson *v.* Smith, 1 Allen (Mass.) 541; Hyatt *v.* Felton, 9 Allen (Mass.) 378; May *v.* Foote, 7 Allen (Mass.) 354; McGurkine *v.* Bates, 113 Mass. 507; Cutler *v.* Boyd, 124 Mass. 181.

1. *Massachusetts* Pub. Stat., ch. 162, § 39.

The procedure is very technical and is governed entirely by statute, but the proceedings are quite similar in the various jurisdictions where such statutes for the relief of poor debtors exist.

As the right to imprison a debtor does not constitute any part of the obligation of the contract, being wholly a matter of remedy, it follows that the States have the right to regulate or abolish imprisonment for debt at their pleasure, even though the debtor may be already imprisoned. Buck *v.* Meserve, 16 N. H. 422; Gooch *v.* Stephenson, 15 Me. 129; Hastings *v.* Lane, 15 Me. 134; Sturges *v.* Crowninshield, 4 Wheat. (U. S.) 122; Sommers *v.* Johnson, 4 Vt. 278; Beers *v.* Haughton, 9 Pet. (U. S.) 329; Mason *v.* Haile, 12 Wheat. (U. S.) 370; Penniman's Case, 103 U. S. 714.

Adjournment of Hearing.—The hearing may be adjourned from time to time. Leach *v.* Pillsbury, 18 N. H. 525; Fales *v.* Goodhue, 25 Me. 423; May *v.* Foote, 7 Allen (Mass.) 354.

After a magistrate has announced his decision not to administer the oath, he has no power to adjourn the case, and the debtor has no right of appeal, and is not bound by his recognizance to appear on any future day to which the case is adjourned. Russell *v.* Goodrich, 8 Allen (Mass.) 150.

As to the legality of adjournments under peculiar states of facts, see Mann *v.* Mirick, 11 Allen (Mass.) 29; Barham *v.* Gomez, 149 Mass. 221.

A mistake made by a magistrate, in giving to a party, who is under recognizance to appear before him for examination, erroneous information of the hour to which the hearing had been adjourned, does not affect the legality of proceedings had in the absence of such party, upon his default, at the time to which the hearing was in fact adjourned. Carlton *v.* Choate, 5 Allen (Mass.) 577.

Under the *Massachusetts* statute, giving a magistrate the discretionary power which courts have in civil actions, as to adjournment and other incidents of a poor debtor's examination, the magistrate may keep open the hearing after the expiration of the hour to which it has been adjourned; and it is immaterial that, without informing the creditor, he had told the debtor that he need not appear till after the expiration of the hour. Lincoln *v.* Cook, 124 Mass. 383.

If the debtor is allowed by the magistrate before whom he is carried, with the consent of the creditor, to go at large from day to day during his examination, and is present at the time and place to which it is adjourned, and waits in readiness to be further examined, and to take the oath, a reasonable time, and until he is informed by the magistrate that the oath will be administered to him, and the creditor does not appear, this is a full performance by the debtor of his duty; and the magistrate, although he does not in fact administer the oath to him, has thereafter no jurisdiction to subject him to further examination, nor has the creditor power to rearrest him. Doane *v.* Bartlett, 4 Allen (Mass.) 74.

Jurisdiction.—The right to the benefit of the poor-debtor laws, being an incident of imprisonment for debt, is a matter of remedy and depends upon the law of the jurisdiction where the action is brought. See ARREST, vol. 1, p. 721, n. 2.

Accordingly it was at one time held that upon processes issuing from the Federal courts, such courts were not bound to observe the poor-debtor laws of the State within which they were sitting, but were to be governed by the rules of such courts and the *United States* statutes. Read *v.* Chapman, Pet. (C. C.) 404; Campbell *v.* Claudius, Pet. (C. C.) 484; Webster *v.* Massey, 2 Wash. (U. S.) 157; McNutt *v.* Bland, 2 How. (U. S.) 9; Offutt *v.* Bowen, 1 Walk. (Miss.) 545; Lockhurst *v.* West, 7 Met. (Mass.) 230.

If the debtor, after being arrested and carried before the magistrate, does not ask to be permitted to take the poor debtor's oath, he may be committed to jail without examination.[1]

2. The Oath.—The oaths are prescribed by statute, but are very similar in the several jurisdictions, and, as a rule, require the debtor to swear that he has not property of the value of twenty dollars above the amount exempted by statute from being taken on execution in the particular state in which he is confined, and that he has not fraudulently disposed of his property.[2]

3. Who May Apply for a Discharge.—Any person imprisoned for debt, whether on mesne process or execution, may apply for his discharge from arrest and take the benefit of the poor-debtor laws;[3] and, in a few jurisdictions, a person imprisoned in an

But by act of Congress the Federal courts are now obliged to adopt the same procedure as is adopted by the State courts. "When any person is arrested or imprisoned in any State, on *mesne* process or execution issued from any court of the United States, in any civil action, he shall be entitled to discharge from such arrest or imprisonment in the same manner as if he were so arrested and imprisoned on like process from the courts of such State. The same oath may be taken, and the same notice thereof shall be required, as may be required by the laws of such State, and the same course of proceedings shall be adopted as may be adopted in the courts thereof. But all such proceedings shall be had before one of the commissioners of the circuit court for the district where the defendant is so held." U. S. Rev. Stat., § 991. And "no person shall be imprisoned for debt in any State on process issuing from a court of the United States where by the laws of such State imprisonment for debt has been or shall be abolished." U. S. Rev. Stat., § 990.

See the Blanche Page, 16 Blatchf. (U. S.) 1.

1. Hart *v.* Adams, 7 Gray (Mass.) 581.

2. *Massachusetts* Pub. Stat., ch. 162, § 39; *Maine* Rev. Stat., ch. 113, § 30; Genl. Laws *New Hampshire*, ch. 241, § 8; *Rhode Island* Pub. Stat., ch. 226, § 11; *Wisconsin* Rev. Stat., § 4312; *Vermont* Rev. Laws, § 1526.

Forms of oaths: "I—, —, solemnly swear" (or "affirm") "that I have no real or personal estate, or interest in any, except what is exempted by statute from attachment and execution, and what I have now disclosed; and that since any part of this debt or cause of action accrued, I have not directly or indirectly, sold, conveyed, or disposed of, or intrusted to any person, any of my real or personal property, to secure it, or to receive any benefit from it to myself or others, with an intent to defraud any of my creditors. So help me God!" (or, "this I do under the pains and penalties of perjury.") *Maine* Rev. Stat., ch. 113, § 30. "I [here repeat the name] do solemnly swear that I have not any estate, real or personal, to the amount of twenty dollars, except the estate, goods and chattels which are by law exempt from being taken on execution, but not excepting intoxicating liquors; and that I have not any other estate now conveyed, concealed, or in any way disposed of, with the design to secure the same to my own use or to defraud my creditors. So help me God!" *Massachusetts* Pub. Stat., ch. 162, § 39.

In *Maine* the justice's certificate of the administration of the oath is conclusive evidence of the fact therein stated. Clement *v.* Wyman, 31 Me. 50. But not in *New Hampshire.* Parker *v.* Staniels, 38 N. H. 251; Banks *v.* Johnson, 12 N. H. 445.

Such certificate may be amended according to the truth of the case. Burnham *v.* Howe, 23 Me. 489; Kimball *v.* Irish, 26 Me. 444; Ayer *v.* Woodman, 24 Me. 196.

In *Rhode Island*, the powers of the clerk of the district court, in the absence of the justice, do not include the administration of the poor debtors' oath. Wilcox *v.* Crowell, 16 R. I. 707.

3. Gen. Laws *New Hampshire*, ch. 241, § 1.

It depends wholly upon the statutes, and the construction placed upon such

action of tort, if there is no fraud, may take the benefit of such laws.[1]

But a person arrested and imprisoned where there has been fraud cannot obtain his discharge by taking the poor debtor's oath.[2]

4. Charges of Fraud—(See also FRAUDULENT DEBTOR).[3]—If the debtor has been guilty of fraud in contracting the indebtedness, or fraudulently conceals his property, or disposes of it with a view of defrauding or delaying his creditors,[4] he will be deprived of the benefit of the poor-debtor statutes, and in some jurisdictions may be sentenced to prison.[5]

statutes by the courts, as to who may take the benefit of such laws. "Any person imprisoned for debt, whether on original writ, *mesne* process or on execution, or for non-payment of a military fine or town or State taxes, or on execution awarded against him as defendant in any action of trespass and ejectment, or trespass *quare clausum fregit*, in which the title to the close was in dispute between the parties. . . . may request to be admitted to take the poor debtor's oath." Pub. Stat. *Rhode Island*, ch. 226, § 1.

A person committed to jail on a judgment for a penalty under the militia law was held entitled to the benefit of the act. Dyer *v.* Hunnewell, 12 Mass. 271; and on an execution for alimony. Shannon's Case, 48 N. H. 407. And in *Massachusetts*, by statute, if imprisoned under the bastardy act, he can take the benefit of the act. Doherty *v.* Clark, 3 Allen (Mass.) 151. But not in *Wisconsin*, where it is held that proceedings under the bastardy act are criminal and not civil in their nature, and therefore the debtor is not imprisoned for a debt in an action of contract or tort, and not entitled to his discharge. Hodgson *v.* Nickell, 69 Wis. 308. For a discussion of the question, whether such proceedings are in their nature civil or criminal, see IMPRISONMENT FOR DEBT, vol. 10, p. 219, n. 1. Persons committed for failure to pay costs or fines may be released under the poor-debtor or insolvent debtor acts. Edwards *v.* State, 22 Ark. 303; State *v.* Williams, 97 N. Car. 414; State *v.* Baker, 9 Rich. Eq. (S. Car.) 521; Thompson *v.* Berry, 5 R. I. 95.

A debtor committed to jail by virtue of an execution issued from the court of chancery to compel the payment of money, is entitled to the benefit of the act. Cannon *v.* Norton, 16 Vt. 334. So is one arrested on a writ of *ne exeat*. Rice *v.* Hale, 5 Cush. (Mass.) 238. But a person taken by an attachment for the non-payment of costs, before he has been committed for contempt, cannot take the benefit of such act, for the process is merely to bring him into court. Jackson *v.* Smith, 5 Johns. (N. Y.) 115. In *Ex parte* Cushman, 4 Mass. 565, it was held that one committed on an attachment for contempt in not paying costs, was not entitled to the benefit of the act.

1. Pub. Stat. *Massachusetts*, 162; Pub. Stat. *Rhode Island*, ch. 227; *In re* Nichols, 8 R. I. 50. In *Maine* a person imprisoned in an action of tort or for costs could not take the benefit of the act. Gooch *v.* Stephenson, 15 Me. 129. In *South Carolina* a person imprisoned in an action of trespass, for an assault and battery, in an action for slander, or in an action of trespass, for shooting the plaintiff's slave, could take the benefit of the insolvent debtor's act. Bampfield *v.* Ellard, 2 McCord (S. Car.) 182; Walling *v.* Jennings, 1 McCord (S. Car.) 10; Braker *v.* Knight, 3 Mc Cord (S. Car.) 80. But in *Illinois* malice being the gist of an action in trespass for an assault, the defendant was held not entitled, under the Insolvent Debtor's Act, to a discharge from imprisonment. *In re* Mullin, 118 Ill. 551; but in an action on the case for seduction, the defendant was held entitled to his discharge. People *v.* Greer, 43 Ill. 213; Hatfield *v.* Boswell, 25 N. J. L. 185.

2. Dennis' Case, 110 Mass. 18; *In re* Payton, 7 R. I. 153.

3. Vol. 8, p. 780.

4. A debtor ran slaves from Mississippi into Texas for the purpose of hindering his creditors, and was held not entitled to the benefit of the prison-bounds' act. Wiley *v.* Lawson, 7 Rich. (S. Car.) 152.

5. "If it appears that such person

The effect, therefore, of a conviction in "cases of fraud" is to deprive the debtor of the benefit of the insolvent or poor-debtor laws, and he must remain in jail until he satisfies the execution or is discharged under a statute limiting the duration of his confinement.[1] And, in some jurisdictions, upon conviction of fraud, he is sentenced by the court to imprisonment for a definite term.[2]

5. The Discharge, Its Validity and Effect.—Discharges are made, sometimes by the magistrate, upon the debtor's taking the oath or complying with certain statutory requirements, or upon the creditor's failure to comply with such requirements;[3] sometimes by the jailer, because of the creditor's failure to provide for the debtor's support in jail,[4] or because the creditor orders the discharge,[5] and sometimes by the passage of an act abolishing or regulating imprisonment for debt.[6]

has been guilty of any fraud, deceit or falsehood in relation to his property, his application shall be refused." Genl. Laws *New Hampshire*, ch. 241, § 6. If the debtor is found guilty of fraud "he shall have no benefit from the proceedings under this chapter, and may be sentenced by the magistrate or court before whom the trial is had to confinement at hard labor in the house of correction for a term not exceeding one year, or to confinement in jail not exceeding six months." *Massachusetts* Pub. Stat., ch. 162, § 52. Under a statute depriving a debtor of the benefit of the poor debtor's oath where it is proved that since the debt was contracted the debtor has hazarded and paid $100 or more in gaming, it is held that such statute does not apply to gaming by a non-resident in another State. Bradley *v.* Burton, 151 Mass. 419.

Under the *Massachusetts* statute, charges of fraud may be filed when the debtor applies to take the oath. Horton *v.* Weiner, 124 Mass. 92. Or at any time before the magistrate announces his decision. Andrews *v.* Cassidy, 142 Mass. 96.

Such charges are in the nature of civil proceedings, and need not be proved beyond a reasonable doubt. Anderson *v.* Edwards, 123 Mass. 273.

Nor need they be stated in a form appropriate to an indictment; it is enough if they are stated with such fullness, clearness, and precision as to inform the debtor of the nature and particulars of the transaction. Stockwell *v.* Silloway, 100 Mass. 287.

And see as to the requirements of such charges, Chamberlain *v.* Hoogs, 1 Gray (Mass.) 172; Clatur *v.* Donegan, 126 Mass. 28; Chapin *v.* Haley, 133 Mass. 127.

1. "In any case where the defendant arrested upon final process shall not be entitled to relief under the provisions of this act, if the plaintiff will advance the jail fees and board in manner hereinbefore provided, the defendant may be imprisoned at $1.50 per day, until the judgment shall be satisfied; provided, however, that no person heretofore or hereafter imprisoned under the provisions of this act shall be imprisoned for a longer period than six months from the date of his arrest." *Illinois* Rev. Stat., ch. 72, § 35. A debtor entitled to a credit of $1.50 for each day's imprisonment may be discharged at any time on payment of the balance between such credit and the amount of the execution. Hanchett *v.* Weber, 17 Ill. App. 114.

2. *Massachusetts* Pub. Stat., ch. 162, § 52.

If the debtor obtains his discharge from liability on the debt under the insolvent law (a separate statute in *Massachusetts*) he cannot afterwards be convicted or imprisoned on "charges of fraud." Everett *v.* Henderson, 150 Mass. 411; overruling, in effect, the contrary doctrine announced in Stockwell *v.* Silloway, 105 Mass. 517.

3. Davis's Case, 111 Mass. 288; Niles *v.* Hancock, 3 Met. (Mass.) 568; Phillips *v.* Gray, 1 Allen (Mass.) 492.

4. Tatem *v.* Potts, 5 Blackf. (Ind.) 534; Richards *v.* Crane, 7 Pick. (Mass.) 216; *Massachusetts* Pub. Stat., ch. 162, § 45.

5. *Massachusetts* Pub. Stat., ch. 162, § 46.

6. Sedgwick *v.* Knibloe, 16 Conn.

If the procedure leading up to the discharge, especially the procedure before the magistrate, is not according to the provisions of the statute, the discharge will be invalid.[1] The discharge exempts the debtor from further arrest in the same cause of action,[2] but does not satisfy the judgment, which remains in full effect, and may be enforced against the estate of the debtor.[3]

IV. Support of Debtor in Jail.—By the early common law neither the jailer nor the creditor was bound to support a debtor imprisoned for debt, but the debtor was obliged to support himself as best he could, either through the aid of his friends or by

219; Baker *v.* Taylor, 1 Cow. (N. Y.) 165; Parker *v.* Sterling, 10 Ohio 357.

1. Thus the discharge will be invalid if the notice of hearing is not properly served upon the creditor. Henshaw *v.* Savil, 114 Mass. 76; or if the debtor is discharged on a holiday. Estes *v.* Mitchell, 14 Allen (Mass.) 156; or if the debtor is discharged, in the absence of the creditor, before the expiration of one hour from the time appointed for the examination. Downer *v.* Hollister, 14 N. H. 122; Hobbs *v.* Fogg, 6 Gray (Mass.) 251. But the creditor may waive compliance with the terms of the statute. Lord *v.* Skinner, 9 Allen (Mass.) 376.

If the examination of a debtor who has been arrested on execution has been begun and then adjourned to a later day, and the creditor appears at the appointed time and remains more than one hour thereafter, without any appearance by or in behalf of the debtor, or continuance or adjournment of the hearing, the magistrate cannot discharge the debtor unless upon a new notice. Sweetser *v.* Eaton, 14 Allen (Mass.) 157.

If a magistrate, before whom a hearing upon the application of a person to take the oath for the relief of poor debtors is appointed, adjudges the creditor in default upon his failure to appear, he has no further jurisdiction except to discharge the debtor, and cannot proceed to administer the oath and to render a judgment upon charges of fraud filed against the debtor. Longley *v.* Cleavland, 133 Mass. 256.

2. Phillips *v.* Wesson, 16 Ga. 137; Willington *v.* Stearns, 1 Pick. (Mass.) 497; State *v.* McNeely, 92 N. Car. 829. "Upon taking the oath, the defendant, or debtor shall be discharged from arrest or imprisonment, and shall be forever exempt from arrest on the same execution or on any process founded on the judgment, or on the same cause of action, unless convicted of having willfully sworn falsely on his examination." *Massachusetts* Pub. Stat., ch., 162 § 40. See Davis' Case, 111 Mass. 288.

Arrest by a Trick.—When an arrest has been procured by means of any trick or fraud, the party so arrested will be discharged on motion. Benninghoff *v.* Oswell, 37 How. Pr. (N. Y.) 235; Metcalf *v.* Clark, 41 Barb. (N. Y.) 45; Carpenter *v.* Spooner, 2 Sandf. (N. Y.) 717; Gaupil *v.* Simonson, 3 Abb. Pr. (N. Y.) 474.

3. The common law concerning the effect of imprisonment upon the judgment debt has been modified by statute in favor of the creditor, as on the other hand, the law of arrest has been modified in favor of the debtor. Imprisonment and discharge under the poor-debtor laws are not a satisfaction of the judgment.

Massachusetts Pub. Stat., ch. 162, § 40; Freeman on Executions, §§ 462, 463; 3 Bl. Com. 416; Phillips *v.* Wesson, 16 Ga. 137; Tatem *v.* Potts, 5 Blackf. (Ind.) 534; Spencer *v.* Garland, 20 Me. 75; Gonnigal *v.* Smith, 6 Johns. (N. Y.) 106; Spencer *v.* Richardson, 7 Johns. (N. Y.) 116; Hunter *v.* U. S., 5 Pet. (U. S.) 173; Tracy *v.* Preble, 117 Mass. 4; Raymond *v.* Butterworth, 139 Mass. 471. "The person of the debtor shall be thereafter forever discharged from arrest or imprisonment on the debt or demand on which he was so arrested or imprisoned; but his estate shall always remain liable therefor and a new execution may at any time issue against such estate." Genl. Laws *New Hampshire*, ch. 241, § 11. Yet now, as at common law, when the debtor is arrested on an execution and is subsequently released by the plaintiff, that is an absolute satisfaction of the judgment. 3 Bl. Com. 515. Freeman on Executions, § 464 and cases cited. To the same effect is Nowell *v.* Waitt, 121 Mass. 554.

private charity.[1] Gradually, however, the law has been changed, so that a creditor is obliged to furnish support for his debtor, if the debtor is unable to support himself and claims support; but in most jurisdictions the expense thus incurred can be recovered from the debtor by the creditor, either as costs on the execution or in a separate action.[2]

V. Recognizance or Bail Bond—1. Nature and Requisites of.— Recognizances or bail bonds[3] are a very common and convenient means for poor debtors, arrested on mesne process or execution, to get a temporary release from arrest or imprisonment. The recognizance or bond is usually conditioned that the debtor shall, within a certain time fixed by statute, take the oath for the relief of poor debtors, or in default thereof, surrender himself to prison.[4]

1. Wadsworth *v.* Wetmore, 6 Ohio 438; McClain *v.* Hayne, 1 Mill. (S. Car.) 212.

In Dive *v.* Manningham, 1 Plowd. 68, Justice Montague says: "A jailer is not bound to find a prisoner meat, but he must live of his own, and if he has no goods of his own, he shall live by the charity of others; and if others will give him nothing, let him die in the name of God."

In *Connecticut*, "until 1810, if the prisoner was unable to pay for his maintenance in prison, he was liable to be sold to service according to the provisions of the 'Delinquent Act,' a species of slavery that disappeared none too soon." Smith *v.* Staples, 49 Conn. 89.

2. *Massachusetts* Pub. Stat., ch. 162, §§ 45, 48; 3 Bl. Com. 416; Smith *v.* Staples, 49 Conn. 87; Field *v.* Putman, 22 Ga. 93; Field *v.* Slaughter, 1 Bibb (Ky.) 160; Howes *v.* Tolman, 63 Me. 258; Spring *v.* Davis, 36 Me, 399; Richards *v.* Crane, 7 Pick. (Mass.) 216; Buttles *v.* Carlton, 1 Ohio 32; Faucet *v.* Adams, 13 Ired. (N. Car.) 235; Commonwealth *v.* Sheriff, 6 Pa. St. 445. But where the prisoner is committed in an action of tort, the county only is liable for his support. Commonwealth *v.* Sheriff, 6 Pa. St. 445. Where the debtor has given bonds for the prison limits, the creditor is not liable for his support. Potter *v.* Robinson, 40 N. J. L. 114; Phillips *v.* Allen, 13 Ired. (N. Car.) 10. But the creditor was held liable in Haas *v.* Bradley, 23 Ga. 345; Buttles *v.* Carlton, 1 Ohio 32; Meredith *v.* Duval, 1 Munf. (Va.) 76.

"When a person confined in close prison on *mesne*, process or execution in a civil action claims support as a pauper, the jailer shall furnish his support at the rate of one dollar and seventy-five cents a week, to be paid by the creditor." *Massachusetts* Pub. Stat., ch. 162, § 45.

It was held in Worcester Co. *v.* Schlesinger, 16 Gray (Mass.) 166, that the creditor was not liable for board furnished to a debtor by the jailer, where the creditor on demand made on him, did not request the detention of the debtor nor that he be boarded, nor promised to pay for his support.

3. A recognizance differs from a bond in being an oral act; and the magistrate's record is merely a memorandum of that act. Accordingly it was held that the magistrate could take the recognizance orally and need not, at the time of taking it, make a written memorandum of the entire recognizance. Townsend *v.* Way, 5 Allen (Mass.) 426.

4. **Requirements of Recognizance.**— The requirements vary in the different jurisdictions. Genl. Laws *New Hampshire*, ch. 240, § 2; *Massachusetts* Pub. Stat., ch. 162, § 28. If the arrest of the debtor was made without authority of law, the recognizance will be void, being given under duress. Gibson *v.* Ethridge, 72 Me. 261; Smith *v.* Bean, 130 Mass. 298; Pindar *v.* Upton, 44 N. H. 358. Whenever there is duress, the bond will be void. Hawes *v.* Marchant, 1 Curt. (U. S.) 136; Thompson *v.* Lockwood, 15 Johns. (N. Y.) 256.

But where a debtor who was privileged from arrest, waived that privilege and was arrested on execution the bond was held valid. Chase *v.* Fish, 16 Me. 132. A bond for the prison bounds, taken before the debtor was committed to prison, is void.

2. Jail Limits—(See also PRISON).—Formerly a debtor imprisoned for debt could give a bond that he would not escape beyond the jail limits or liberties[1] until discharged by due course of law, and he was then permitted to go at large. The abolition of imprisonment for debt in many jurisdictions, and the general use of bail bonds in those jurisdictions where imprisonment for debt still

Northam *v.* Terry, 8 Ired. (N. Car.) 175. But a bond actually executed after commitment, though bearing a date prior to the commitment, is not on that account invalid. Clark *v.* Kidder, 12 Vt. 689. A bond which does not conform to the statutory requirements may be valid as a common law bond. Hathaway *v.* Crosby, 17 Me. 448; Wallace *v.* Carlisle, 20 Me. 374; Hovey *v.* Hamilton, 24 Me. 451; Barker *v.* Ryan, 1 Allen (Mass.) 72. Accordingly a bond voluntarily given, though not given according to any statute, is good. Gibson *v.* Ethridge, 72 Me. 261; likewise a bond to a creditor by a third person only with conditions like an ordinary prison bond under the statute, has been held good at common law. Pratt *v.* Gibbs, 9 Cush. (Mass.) 82. But the debtor is bound to perform no statutory provisions not expressly recited in such bonds. Clark *v.* Metcalf, 38 Me. 122.

As to what magistrate may take a recognizance, see Dike *v.* Story, 7 Allen (Mass.) 349; Gibbs *v.* Taylor, 143 Mass. 187.

After a debtor has had a time and place for his examination fixed by a magistrate, and notice has been given to the creditor, another magistrate is without jurisdiction to take a recognizance, the former application not having been withdrawn. Snelling *v.* Coburn, 10 Allen (Mass.) 344.

The recognizance need not be returned into a court of record. Thacher *v.* Williams, 14 Gray (Mass.) 324; Peck *v.* Emery, 1 Allen (Mass.) 463.

A recognizance is not void, because taken in more than double the amount of the execution. Currier *v.* Poor, 5 Allen (Mass.) 585; Barber *v.* Floyd, 109 Mass. 61. Nor, in an action thereupon, can the defendant object that it was for less than double the amount of the execution. Whittier *v.* Way, 6 Allen (Mass.) 288; Thacher *v.* Williams, 14 Gray (Mass.) 324. Or for less than the *ad damnum* in the writ. As to the rule in *Maine*, see Horn *v.* Nason, 23 Me. 101; Flowers *v.* Flowers, 45 Me. 459; Merchants' Bank *v.* Lord, 49 Me. 99; Ross *v.* Berry, 49 Me. 434; Call *v.* Foster, 49 Me. 452; Gilmore *v.* Edmunds, 7 Allen (Mass.) 360. Nor does it matter that the recognizance does not specify the place fixed for the examination. Whittier *v.* Way, 6 Allen (Mass.) 288; nor the date of the examination. Gilmore *v.* Edmunds, 7 Allen (Mass.) 360.

As to what error in the statement of the amount will vitiate the recognizance, see Adams *v.* Brown, 14 Gray (Mass.) 579.

A recognizance may be conditioned, not only that the debtor shall appear at the examination, but also that he shall abide the order of the magistrate. Adams *v.* Brown, 14 Gray (Mass.) 579.

An execution against two persons, in which the name of one only is erroneously stated, is not void as against the other; and a bond, given by the latter to procure his release from arrest on such execution is valid. Blake *v.* Blanchard, 48 Me. 297.

For additional *Massachusetts* cases involving questions of the validity of recognizances, see Cassidy *v.* Hart, 104 Mass. 221; Underwood *v.* Clements, 16 Gray (Mass.) 169; Cook *v.* Thayer, 121 Mass. 415; Adams *v.* Stone, 13 Gray (Mass.) 396; Com. *v.* Cutter, 98 Mass. 31.

The cases of Hatch *v.* Norris, 36 Me. 419; Smith *v.* Brown, 61 Me. 70; Poor *v.* Knight, 66 Me. 482, deal with the requisites of poor debtor's bonds.

1. 1 Abbott's Law Dict. 649.

"A space of ground in a square, the center of each of whose sides shall be one mile distant from the jail, is declared as the liberties of the jail of each county of the State. The sheriff of each county, where such liberties have not been heretofore so designated, shall, at the expense of the county, designate by visible and permanent marks, the extent and limits of such liberties." *Wisconsin* Rev. Stat., § 4321.

exists, has rendered this branch of the law nearly obsolete, but there are a few states which still retain the procedure.[1]

3. Performance and Breach.—As a rule the surety can only be discharged from liability by a strict performance by the debtor and the surety of the conditions of the recognizance entered into by them,[2] unless that becomes impossible by the act of God, or of the law or of the obligee.[3]

1. *Rhode Island*, Pub. Stat., ch. 225; *Wisconsin* Rev. Stat., §§ 4321, *et seq.; Vermont* Rev. Laws, §§ 1499, *et seq.*

2. **Performance and Breach.**—ABSENCE, vol. 1, p, 39, n. 1. Accordingly there is a breach of the recognizance where the debtor does not appear on the day fixed for the examination. Sanford *v.* Quinn, 147 Mass. 69; or does not take the oath prescribed by statute. Morse *v.* Rice, 21 Me. 53; Wallace *v.* Carlisle, 20 Me. 374; Rider *v.* Thompson, 23 Me. 244; or if the magistrate is absent on the appointed day, Morrill *v.* Norton, 116 Mass. 487; Hills *v.* Jones, 122 Mass. 412; or if no magistrate competent to act is present. Godfrey *v.* Munyan, 120 Mass. 240; or if the debtor does not notify the creditor of the hearing. Gilmore *v.* Edmunds, 9 Allen (Mass.) 379; or if the proceedings are adjourned to a Sunday and the debtor fails to procure a new adjournment. Hooper *v.* Cox, 117 Mass. 1; or if the proceedings intended for the performance of the condition of the bond take place before magistrates having no jurisdiction. Ware *v.* Jackson, 24 Me. 166; or if the magistrate fixes too remote a day for the examination. First Nat. Bank *v.* Gogin, 148 Mass. 448.

If one of the conditions in a poor debtor's bond is, "and further do and perform all that is required in and by the acts in such case made and provided," this imposes the condition that he should abide the order of the justices before whom he should make disclosure. French *v.* M'Alister, 20 Me. 465.

The debtor's appearance before the magistrate, in pursuance of the notice, does not permit a breach of the recognizance, if no proceedings are had under the notice. Millett *v.* Lemon, 113 Mass. 355.

His departure before the examination is completed is a breach of the recognizance. Peck *v.* Emery, 1 Allen (Mass.) 463. So is his departure after the examination is finished, the magistrate having announced his decision to refuse the oath and the certificate not having been completed. Lathrop *v.* Bailey, 14 Allen (Mass.) 514; Knight *v.* Sampson, 99 Mass. 36; though neither the officer nor the execution is present until ten minutes after the completion of the certificate. Fuller *v.* Meehan, 118 Mass. 135. But see Goodall *v.* Myrick, 111 Mass. 484.

3. It is no defense to an action upon the recognizance that performance was impossible because the debtor became a lunatic or was incapacitated by sickness. Anderson's Bail, 2 Chitty's Rep. 104; Cock *v.* Bell, 13 East 355; Newton *v.* Newbegin, 43 Me. 293; Haskell *v.* Green, 15 Me. 33; Symonds *v.* Carleton, 43 N. H. 444; Osborne *v.* Toomer, 6 Jones (N. Car.) 440. But in Fuller *v.* Davis, 1 Gray (Mass.) 612, it was held that the sureties were not liable for a failure to surrender a principal committed to the State lunatic hospital by order of court. But an arrest and imprisonment of a debtor on a criminal charge did not prevent the debtor's default from being a breach. Turner *v.* Bartlett, 109 Mass. 503. The death of the principal discharges his sureties. Lowell *v.* Haskell, 45 Me. 112. The taking of the poor debtor's oath or the debtor's discharge from his debts under the insolvent acts have been held to discharge the sureties. Simms *v.* Slacum, 3 Cranch (U. S.) 300; Kendrick *v.* Gregory, 9 Me. 22; Plummer *v.* Odiorne, 8 Gray (Mass.) 246; Hayden *v.* Palmer, 7 Hill (N. Y.) 385.

A creditor may waive a breach of the bond, but he cannot take advantage of any breach procured to be done by himself. Slocum *v.* Hathaway, 1 Paine (U. S.) 290; Spader *v.* Frost, 4 Blackf. (Ind.) 190; Moore *v.* Bond, 18 Me. 142; Palmer *v.* Everett, 7 Allen (Mass.) 358; Barham *v.* Gomez, 149 Mass. 221.

For facts relied on as constituting a waiver, see Andrews *v.* Knowlton, 121 Mass. 316; Chellis *v.* Leavitt, 124 Mass. 359; Vinal *v.* Tuttle, 144 Mass. 14.

As to the effect of transactions between creditor and debtor, after the

4. Action Upon the Recognizance.—Upon a breach of the recognizance the creditor can bring an action against the sureties and recover the amount of the debt, interest and costs.[1] But where

giving of the recognizance, looking toward a payment of the debt, as bearing upon the question of the discharge of the recognizance, see Bullen *v.* Dresser, 116 Mass. 267; Abbott *v.* Tucker, 4 Allen (Mass.) 72.

The liability of the surety may be discharged by his surrender of the principal. Pacific Mint Ins. Co. *v.* Canterbury, 104 Mass. 433; City Nat. Bank *v.* Williams, 122 Mass. 534; Tucker *v.* Bruce, 121 Mass. 400.

In an action upon a recognizance, it is not a defense that the creditor's affidavit, on which the arrest was founded was willfully false. Everett *v.* Henderson, 146 Mass. 89.

Maine Cases on Recognizances.—The following additional Maine cases involve miscellaneous questions as to the performance or breach of recognizances. Pease *v.* Norton, 6 Me. 229; Williams *v.* McDonald, 18 Me. 120; Granite Bank *v.* Treat, 18 Me. 340; Hill *v.* Knowlton, 19 Me. 449; Wing *v.* Kennedy, 21 Me. 430; Cushman *v.* Waite, 21 Me. 540; Rollins *v.* Dow, 24 Me. 123; Hatch *v.* Lawrence, 29 Me. 480; Bailey *v.* McIntire, 35 Me. 106; Bray *v.* Kelley, 38 Me. 595; Nash *v.* Babb, 40 Me. 126; Warren *v.* Davis, 42 Me. 343; White *v.* Estes, 44 Me. 21; Morrison *v.* Corliss, 44 Me. 97; Jones *v.* Spencer, 47 Me. 182; Hunkins *v.* Palmer, 48 Me. 251; Hathaway *v.* Stone, 33 Me. 500; Randall *v.* Bowden, 48 Me. 37; Jewett *v.* Rines, 39 Me. 9; Farrington *v.* Farrar, 73 Me. 37; Jones *v.* Emerson, 71 Me. 405; Perry *v.* Plunkett. 74 Me. 328; Guilford *v.* Delaney, 57 Me. 589; Stone *v.* Tilson, 19 Me. 265; Sanborn *v.* Keazer, 30 Me. 457; Robinson *v.* Barker, 28 Me. 310; Ayer *v.* Fowler, 30 Me. 347; Horn *v.* Mason, 23 Me. 101.

A breach of the recognizance does not authorize the arrest of the debtor. The creditor has his remedy on the recognizance. Morgan *v.* Curley, 142 Mass. 107.

Jail Limit Bonds.—If the principal escapes from or goes beyond the prison limits there is a breach of the bond. Walker *v.* Riley, 10 Rich. (S. Car.) 87; even though the debtor goes beyond the limits accidentally, as where he was misinformed by the jailor as to the extent of the limits. Farley *v.* Randall, 22 Pick. (Mass.) 146, and a return to the limits or a surrender of the principal before action on the bond does not cure a breach. Spader *v.* Frost, 4 Blackf. (Ind.) 190; Buford *v.* Ganson, 5 Blackf. (Ind.) 585; McGuire *v.* Pierce, 9 Gratt (Va.) 167. Nor is a previous breach cured by the passage of an act abolishing imprisonment for debt. Croom *v.* Travis, 10 Ala. 237; Bowen *v.* Gresham, 6 Blackf. (Ind.) 452. But if no breach, passage of such an act discharges both the debtor and the sureties. Sedgwick *v.* Knibloe, 16 Conn. 219.

1. **Action Upon the Recognizance.** — ***Massachusetts*** Pub. Stat., ch. 162, § 64; Pub. Stat. ***Rhode Island***, ch. 125, § 8; ***Wisconsin*** Rev. Stat., § 4333; McGuire *v.* Pierce, 9 Gratt. (Va.) 167; Knight *v.* Norton, 15 Me. 337; Poor *v.* Beatty, 78 Me. 580. But under the ***Maine*** statute it has been held that only the actual damage is recoverable, although the whole amount can be recovered in the absence of testimony other than that showing a breach. Houghton *v.* Lyford, 39 Me. 267; Clifford *v.* Kimball, 39 Me. 413; Daggett *v.* Bartlett, 22 Me. 227; Smith *v.* Dutton, 74 Me. 468.

In an action on a recognizance, the magistrate's record cannot be impeached or controlled by parol evidence. Sewall *v.* Sullivan, 108 Mass. 355; May *v.* Hammond, 146 Mass. 439. And see Henshaw *v.* Savil, 114 Mass. 74; Lincoln *v.* Cook, 124 Mass. 383.

The recitals in the recognizance are not evidence as to matters not occuring in the presence of the magistrate. For example, it may be shown by the surety that the writ did not authorize the arrest. Learnard *v.* Bailey, 111 Mass. 160.

The production of the recognizance, with proof of the official character of the officer taking it, does not make out a *prima facie* case for the plaintiff. Blake *v.* Mahan, 2 Allen (Mass.) 75.

The declaration, in an action on the recognizance, need not aver affirmatively that the execution had not been paid. Webber *v.* Davis, 5 Allen (Mass.) 393.

For examples of a declaration sufficiently showing the authority of the magistrate to take the recogniz-

the judgment has been paid in full, although by another judgment debtor, the action is defeated.[1]

POOR RELATIONS.—See RELATIONS.

POPULAR.—See note 2.

PORCH—PORTICO.—See note 3.

PORT—(See also MARINE INSURANCE, vol. 15, p. 329, *et seq.;* HAVEN, vol. 9, p. 306; SHIPS AND SHIPPING).—A port, in common sea phrase, may be said to be any safe station for ships; but in law, it is described to be a place for the arriving and lading and unlading of ships in a manner prescribed by law; and near to

ance and of the constable to make the arrest, see Webber *v.* Davis, 5 Allen (Mass.) 393; Com. *v.* Cutter, 98 Mass. 31.

1. Holmes *v.* Day, 108 Mass. 563; National Security Bank *v.* Hunnewell, 124 Mass. 260; Grimes *v.* Turner, 16 Me. 353.

And if there has been a part payment on the debt, the plaintiff can recover only the amount remaining unpaid. Carr *v.* Mason, 44 Me. 77. But it is no defense to the action that the plaintiff is pursuing his remedy also on a bond to dissolve an attachment. Moore *v.* Loring, 106 Mass. 455.

2. **The "popular sense"** of words used in a statute is the sense in which they are understood by persons conversant with the subject-matter. Grenfell *v.* Commissioners of Revenue, L. R., 1 Ex. D. 248.

"**Popular use**" means the occasional and precarious enjoyment of the property by the members of society in their individual capacities — without the power to enforce such enjoyment according to law. Gilmer *v.* Lime Point, 18 Cal. 238.

3. A deed from the commonwealth, of land on a street in Boston stipulated that the front wall of any building erected thereon should be set back twenty-two feet from the street, with the proviso that "porticos and other usual projections, appurtenant to said front wall are to be allowed in this reserved space." It was held that the proviso permitted the erection of a porch within the reserved space. The court, by Holmes, J., said: "Etymologically the words 'porch' and 'portico' are one. Formerly porch was used as synonymous with portico in its classic sense. 'And he made a porch of pillars; the length thereof was fifty cubits.' 1 Kings, vii. 6. The tendency in modern times, no doubt, has been to diminish 'porch' to the shelter in front of the door of a building, and we are very willing to assume that, with the constant growth of distinctions and nice discriminations in the meaning of words, 'portico' retains more of the original suggestion of length and of a roof supported by pillars, among architects and scholarly persons, and that porch is more specially appropriated to a smaller structure, generally with closed sides. But the distinction is not carefully preserved in common speech. With us portico, as well as porch, has shrunk, and usually means a shelter in front of a door. See Dyche & Pardon's Dict. 1754, also Imperial Dict. 1882, Portico. When porticos are cut down to the little structures which we all know, we think that special reference to the mode of support has vanished almost as completely as to the length. The parties to this deed did not mean by portico 'a walk covered with a roof, supported by columns at least on one side.' They meant the shelter to the door of a building, familiar to Massachusetts and to Boston. We are of opinion that they used it as a generic word, including a shelter with closed sides, as well as one with pillars. We agree that in determining the scope of the word we must look at the object of the restrictions and of the exceptions to it. But, as we have said, the permission extends to more serious structures, with closed sides, and therefore there is no reason for excluding porches. Indeed, a portico projecting not more than five feet would, or at least might, obstruct the view of a neighboring house with its pillars almost as completely as if its sides were closed." Attorney General *v.* Ayer, 148 Mass. 584. See also Garrett *v.* Janes, 65 Md. 260.

which is a city or town for the accommodation of mariners and the securing and vending of merchandise. So that in this sense, a public port is a complex subject, consisting of somewhat that is natural, as a convenient access from the sea, a safe situation against winds, and a shore upon which vessels may well unlade; something that is artificial, as keys, wharves and warehouses; and something that is civil, as privileges and regulations given to it by the government.[1]

1. The Wharf Case, 3 Bland Ch. (Md.) 369. See also Nicholson *v.* Williams, L. R., 6 Q. B. 642; Cole *v.* Union Mut. L. Ins. Co., 12 Gray (Mass.) 505; Hunter *v.* Northern Mar. Ins. Co., 13 App. Cas. 723.

The word "port" in a charter-party is to be understood in its popular, or business, or commercial sense; it does not in such a document necessarily mean the port as defined for revenue or pilotage purposes. Sailing-Ship "Garston" Co. *v.* Hickie, 15 Q. B. D. 580, in which case tests for determining the business meaning of "port" were considered. See further Price *v.* Livingstone, 9 Q. B. D. 679.

"Port" is generally a harbor or shelter for vessels from storms. Applied to a place where there is no harbor, may mean only a road or anchorage—a place for loading and unloading cargoes. De Longuemere *v.* New York F. Ins. Co., 10 Johns. (N. Y.) 125. See also De Longuemere *v.* Firemen's Ins. Co., 10 Johns. (N. Y.) 126; Patrick *v.* Commercial Ins. Co., 11 Johns. (N. Y.) 9.

A "port" is a place either on the sea coast or on a river, where ships stop for the purpose of loading or unloading, from whence they depart, and where they finish their voyages. By the Roman law, a port is defined to be *locus conclusus, quo importantur merces, et unde exportantur.* Packwood *v.* Walden, 7 Martin, N. S. (La.) 88.

"Port" of Same Import, as "District."—In the revenue laws, "port" and "district" are often used as words of the same import, in cases where the limits of the port and district are the same. Ayer *v.* Thatcher, 3 Mass. 153, 155.

In an Insurance Policy.—Where a policy contained a clause that insurers take "no risk in port, but sea risk," it was held that the term port was not confined to the port of departure or discharge, but was used in contradistinction to the "high seas," and referred to any port into which the vessel might of neccessity enter during the voyage insured. Patrick *v.* Commercial Ins. Co., 11 Johns. (N. Y.) 9.

Arrive in Port.—A vessel has not arrived in port until she drops anchor or is moored. Gray *v.* Gardner, 17 Mass. 188.

In a United States Statute.—"Port," as used in § 4347 of the Rev. Stat. U. S., providing that merchandise shall not be transported between ports within the United States in foreign bottoms, means any place from which merchandise may be shipped. Petrel Guano Co. *v.* Jarnette, 25 Fed. Rep. 677. See also Rev. Stat. U. S., § 2767.

Port of Delivery.—The phrase port of delivery is sometimes used to distinguish the port of unlading or destination, from any port at which the vessel touches, in the course of the voyage, for other purposes. The Two Catherines, 2 Mason (U. S.) 319, 331.

Port of Destination.—As used in a clause in a time-policy, extending the insurance beyond the term, if at its expiration the ship is at sea, until she reaches her port of destination, means any foreign port to which the vessel may be destined during the voyage, as well as her home port; and includes any usual stopping place for lading or unlading cargo, although not a haven or port, in a legal sense, as a port of entry or clearance. Gookin *v.* New England Mut. Mar. Ins. Co., 12 Gray (Mass.) 501, 516.

Foreign Port.—A port outside of the *United States.* King *v.* Parks, 19 Johns. (N. Y.) 377.

The ports of the States are foreign to each other for some purposes; as, for pledging the credit of the owner for supplies. The Lulu, 10 Wall. (U. S.) 200; Negus *v.* Simpson, 99 Mass. 393. See also MARITIME LIENS, vol. 14, p. 417.

Port Risk.—A risk upon a vessel while lying in port, and before she has taken her departure on another voyage. Nelson *v.* Sun Mut. Ins. Co.,

PORT OF DISCHARGE.—MARINE INSURANCE, vol. 14, p. 346; DISCHARGE, vol. 5, p. 671.

PORT (HOME).—See MARITIME LIENS, vol. 14, p. 417; HOME, vol. 9, p. 422.

PORTICO.—See PORCH.

PORTION—(See also PART, SHARE).—Share, part and portion are frequently synonymous. Applied to property acquired from an ancestor, "portion" is the most comprehensive word that can be used.[1]

PORTRAIT—(See generally PAINTING; PICTURE).—A portrait is the pictorial presentment, taken from life or from "reasonable materials from which a likeness may be framed," of a person (or it may be of more than one person), the chief object of the picture being the preservation of a life-like resemblance of the countenance; and it is not less a "portrait" because accompanied by subordinate accessories more or less of an ideal character.[2]

POSITION.—See note 3.

POSITIVE.—See note 4.

71 N. Y. 459. See also MARINE INSURANCE, vol. 14, p. 347.

1. Lewis' Appeal, 108 Pa. St. 137; Holly *v.* State, 54 Ala. 240; 2 Jarm. 711, 712.

"The words 'her portion' 'her share' are more applicable to a fee than to a life estate." Phelps *v.* Phelps, 55 Conn. 359.

"Portions for Children."—§ 2, Thellusson Act, 39 & 40 Geo. III, ch. 98: "Portions for children are, I think, generally understood to be sums of money secured to them out of property springing from or settled upon their parents; and although there may, no doubt, be cases in which provisions for children out of property in which the parents take no interest may well be called 'portions,' I think that such provisions should only receive that designation where the nature or context of the instrument gives them that character. Where there is a gift to children both of capital and income, and there is nothing in the nature or context of the instrument to impress upon the gift the character of a portion, I do not think it could be called a 'portion' in the ordinary sense of the word, or ought to be so considered within the meaning of this act." Per Turner, V. C., Jones *v.* Maggs, 22 L. J., Ch. 91; s. c., 9 Hare 605. See further the cases there cited; and see also Watson Eq. 8.

2. Leeds *v.* Amherst, 14 L. J., Ch. 73. In that case Lord Lyndhurst, in the course of his judgment, said: "I may be permitted to say this, that if a picture is painted after a man's death, and meant to represent him, if there is nothing affording the materials for the portrait, it is completely an ideal picture, and cannot properly be called a portrait; but if there are reasonable materials from which a likeness may be framed, I do not consider it less a portrait, though painted after the death of an individual than if painted during his lifetime."

3. A *New Jersey* act provided that no person "holding a position" in any city, whose term of office is not fixed by law, and who is an honorably discharged soldier, shall be removed from such position except for good cause shown. *Held*, that, though the provisions of the act are not to be confined to offices *eo nomine*, existing at common law or created by statute, still the word "position" and the language of the act throughout, indicate a purpose to apply it to positions analogous to offices, as distinguished from mere employment, and that a "general workman" was not within the provision, but that a person appointed "bridge tender" was. State *v.* Board of Public Works, 51 N. J. L. 214.

4. **Sale Positive.**—Where an auction sale was announced to be a "sale pos-

POSSE COMITATUS.—See SHERIFF.

POSSESSED—(See also POSSESSION).—"Possessed" is a variable term in the law, and has different meanings as it is used in different circumstances. It sometimes implies a temporary interest in lands; as we say a man is possessed, in contradistinction to being seised. It sometimes implies a corporal having; as we say a man is seised and possessed. But it sometimes implies no more than that one has a property in a thing; that he has it as owner; that it is his.[1]

POSSESSION—(See also EJECTMENT, vol. 6, p. 245m.; ADVERSE POSSESSION, vol. 1, p. 225; FINDER OF PROPERTY, vol. 7, p. 981; FORCIBLE ENTRY, vol. 8, p. 117; LARCENY, vol. 12, p. 766; MINES AND MINING, vol. 15, p. 557; NOTICE, vol. 16, p. 800; OWNERSHIP; OCCUPANCY).—The detention or enjoyment of a thing which a man holds or exercises by himself, or by another who keeps or exercises it in his name. It implies exclusive enjoyment.[2]

itive," it was held that these words are equivalent to "sale without reserve," and therefore it was a fraud on the part of the vendor to employ a bidder to keep up the price on his behalf. Walsh *v.* Barton, 24 Ohio St. 28. See also AUCTIONS AND AUCTIONEERS vol. 1, p. 989.

1. Mayor *v.* Park Commissioners, 44 Mich. 603.

In Wills.—The word "possessed" in a will devising "all my estate both real and personal to me belonging, of which I shall die possessed of" to A, was held to denote ownership and not merely personal or corporal occupation. Hemingway *v.* Hemingway, 22 Conn. 472.

In Noel *v.* Hoy, 5 Mad. 38, a bequest "of all the property of whatever description or sort that I may die possessed of" was held to pass real estate.

And so in Thomas *v.* Phelps, 4 Russ. 348, where the words were "of all that I possess in any way belonging to me," it was held that the real estate passed by these words."

In Pitman *v.* Stevens, 15 East 505, the words were "all that I shall die possessed of, real and personal." *Held*, to pass the realty. In Wilce *v.* Wilce, 5 Moo. & P. 682, 7 Bingh. 664, the words "everything I die possessed of," were held to pass realty. And so of the words, "or whatever I may be possessed of." Evans *v.* Jones, 46 L. J. Exch. 280. See also Day *v.* Daveron, 12 Sim. 200; 10 L. J., Ch. 349.

And so in Davenport *v.* Coltman, 9 M. & W. 481, a bequest "of whatever he may die possessed of" was held to apply to the testator's real estate. But see Monk *v.* Mawdsley, 1 Sim. 286, where it was held that the words "possessed of" were exclusively applicable to personal property, especially when coupled with the words "at the time of my decease," which could not refer to real estate. See also Cook *v.* Jaggard, L. R., 1 Exch. 125, in which case the words were "or whatever I may be possessed of or entitled to," the court distinguished this case from Wilce *v.* Wilce, 5 Moo. & P. 682. And see 1 Jarm. on Wills, 730, 731, 739-742, where these cases are discussed. See also ALL, vol. 1, p. 488, n; Blaisdell *v.* Hight, 69 Me. 309. Cited at length at the end of the note under the title POSSESSION.

2. Redfield *v.* Utica etc. R. Co., 25 Barb. (N. Y.) 54.

Possession means simply the owning or having a thing in one's power. Brown *v.* Volkening, 64 N. Y. 80.

It implies a present right to deal with the property at pleasure and to exclude other persons from meddling with it. Sullivan *v.* Sullivan, 66 N. Y. 41.

Possession (as used in statutes imposing a punishment for "having in possession" burglar's tools or other implements of crime). The meaning cannot be limited to manual touch or personal custody. One who deposits the prohibited articles in a place of concealment may be deemed to have them in his possession. One who leaves them in care of his wife may be deemed to have them in possession jointly with her. State *v.* Potter, 42 Vt. 495.

Possession of Counterfeit Coin.—Secreting the coin within the county and having within one's control is a possession of counterfeit coin, within the meaning of *Iowa* Code, § 2634. State *v.* Washburn, 11 Iowa 245.

New York Factor's Act.—The word possession, in the *New York* factor's act, means such "control of or dominion over merchandise as enables a factor rightfully to take it into actual custody, without the aid of any new authority or document furnished by the owners; in contradistinction to a right derived from documentary evidence furnished by the owners or obtained by factors, by means of their right of possession of the goods." Pegram *v.* Carson, 10 Bosw. (N. Y.) 505.

In a Devise.—A devise was as follows: "Being informed that, by the laws of *New Jersey* concerning a wife's right of dower, the same provide for her the possession of one-third of my personal estate . . . my executors are directed to fulfill the aforesaid provisions of the State of *New Jersey*, and in case of any failure of law, I confirm them to her." It was held that the testator used the word "possession" in the sense of ownership and meant that one-third of his personal estate should be paid to his widow absolutely. Woodford *v.* Woodford, 44 N. J. Eq. 79.

In Possession.—Sometimes "in possession," in relation to an estate, will be construed as "vested." Foley *v.* Burnell, 1 Bro. C. C. 274; 4 Bro. P. C. 319; Martelli *v.* Holloway, L. R., 5 H. L. 532.

But, generally, where an estate or interest in realty is spoken of as being "in possession," that does not, primarily, mean the actual occupation of the property; but means the present right thereto or to the enjoyment thereof, as distinguished from reversion, remainder, or expectancy as illustrated by the old conveyancing phrase—"in possession, reversion, remainder or expectancy." *Re* Morgan, 24 Ch. D. 114; *Re* Atkinson, 31 Ch. D. 577.

In the Mortmain Act (9 Geo. II, ch. 36, § 1), "take effect in possession," means "giving the right to possession." 1 Jarm. on Wills 220, *citing* Fisher *v.* Brierley, 10 H. L. Ca. 159.

See generally ESTATES, vol. 6, p. 896; PERSONAL PROPERTY; REAL PROPERTY; REMAINDERS, REVERSIONS AND EXECUTORY INTERESTS.

Giving Possession.—"Possession" to be given on completion of a purchase does not, of itself, mean "personal occupation;" and, if the property be tenanted, putting the purchaser into the receipt of the rent will be giving him "possession." Lake *v.* Dean, 28 Bea. 607. It is otherwise, however, if the phrase be "actual possession." Royal Bristol Bg. Society *v.* Bomash, 35 Ch. D. 390. "Possession," in this connection, means possession with a good title shown. Tilley *v.* Thomas, 3 Ch. 61.

Possession is one degree of title, although the lowest. It is such an interest in land that one who has only the bare possession may maintain ejectment against a mere wrongdoer who has intruded into the possession. Swift *v.* Agnes, 33 Wis. 240.

Possession of land is denoted by the exercise of acts of dominion over it, in making the ordinary use and taking the ordinary profits, of which it is susceptible in its present state, such acts to be so repeated, so as to show that they were done in the character of owner, and not of an occasional trespasser. Williams *v.* Buchanan, 1 Ired. (N. Car.) 540.

Thus, entering upon, ditching, and making roads in a cypress swamp, cutting down trees and making shingles out of them, denotes a possession of the swamp. Tredwell *v.* Reddick, 1 Ired. (N. Car.) 56. And so in an unnavigable stream, keeping up fish-traps therein, erecting and repairing dams across it, and using it for catching fish every year, constitute an unequivocal possession thereof. Williams *v.* Buchanan, 1 Ired. (N. Car.) 535. So the occupation of pine land, by annually making turpentine on it, is a possession of such land. Bynum *v.* Carter, 4 Ired. (N. Car.) 310.

Possession of land is the holding of and exclusive exercise of dominion over it. Booth *v.* Small, 25 Iowa 177.

The "immediate right of possession" spoken of by the *Michigan* statute relative to the nature and qualities of estates in real property, in defining estates in possession, does not mean the absolute right of possession as against all possible rights or powers given for special purposes, and which have not been, but may or may not be, exerted

POSSIBLE.—Capable of existing or of being conceived or thought of; liable to happen or come to pass; capable of being done; not contrary to the nature of things.[1]

POSSIBILITY—(See also ESTATES, vol. 6, p. 896; EXPECTANCY, vol. 7, p. 489).—The word possibility has a general sense, in which it includes even executory interests, which are the objects of limitation. But in its more specific sense, it is that kind of contingent benefit which is neither the object of a limitation, like an executory interest, nor is founded in any lost, but recoverable seisin, like a right of entry. And what is termed a bare or mere possibility, signifies nothing more than an expectancy, which is specifically applied to a mere hope of succession unfounded in any limitation, provision, trust, or legal act whatever; such as the

or required for the accomplishment of such special purposes. The owner may be said to have an "estate in possession," unless there be some intervening estate in the land, the owner of which has a present paramount right of possession as against him. Campau *v.* Campau, 19 Mich. 116, 123.

Actual Possession. — See ACTUAL, vol. 1, p. 184*g*; ADVERSE POSSESSION, vol. 1, p. 252.

Change of Possession.—See CHANGE, vol. 3, p. 89.

Constructive Possession is that which exists in contemplation of law, without actual personal occupation. Brown *v.* Volkening, 64 N. Y. 80.

Constructive possession is where one claims to hold by virtue of some title, without having the actual occupancy, as when the owner of a tract of land, regularly laid out, is in possession of a part, he is constructively in possession of the whole. Fleming *v.* Maddox, 30 Iowa 241.

Constructive possession, where there is no actual possession, is in him who has the legal title. Norris' Appeal, 64 Pa. St. 275. See also ACTUAL, vol. 1, p. 184 *g*.

Delivery of Possession.—See DELIVERY, vol. 5, p. 520 a.

Naked Possession.—Actual occupation of an estate, without apparent right, or shadow or pretense of right, to hold or continue such possession. Called also bare possession. Gillett *v.* Gaffney, 3 Colo. 360.

Possessions.—A clause in a will was as follows: "I give and devise to my son B . . . all my real estate situate in S aforesaid; and also the residue of my personal estate and possessions of whatever kind or name." Many years after the will was made, a parcel of land not situate in S unexpectedly descended to him from a brother. *Held*, that the latter estate was not devised by the will. The court said: "The word possessions may include real estate if so intended, though such would not be its technical signification. Had the testator intended to include real estate in the word possessions, it strikes us forcibly that he would not have used the prefix personal at all and the language would have been, 'all the residue of my estate and possessions.' The words of whatever kind or name are not naturally descriptive of real estate but usually apply to personal property. Lands are not of various kinds and names." Blaisdell *v.* Hight, 69 Me. 309. See also Chapman *v.* Chick, 81 Me. 109.

As used in an *English* Income Act, *held* to include a trade or business and to denote all property that may be a source of income. Coloquhon *v.* Brooks, 59 L. J., Q. B. 53; 61 L. T. 518.

1. Webster's Dict., *followed* in Topeka City R. Co. *v.* Higgs, 38 Kan. 375; 34 Am. & Eng. R. Cas. 529.

All Possible Foresight—All Possible Skill and Care.—A street railway company carrying passengers for hire, are bound to exercise all "possible skill, foresight and care" in the running of their cars, so that passengers may not be exposed to danger on account of the manner in which the cars are run. "All possible skill and care" implies that every reasonable precaution in the management and operation of street cars be used to prevent injuries to passengers. The phrase means good tracks, safe cars, experienced drivers, careful management, and judicious

hope which an heir, apparent or presumptive, has of succeeding to the ancestor's estate.[1]

An event which may or may not happen; something that is uncertain.[2]

POST.—Means a military establishment where a body of troops is permanently fixed.[3]

POSTAL LAWS.—(See also LETTERS, vol. 13, p. 251; MAIL, vol. 13, p. 1200.)

I. INTRODUCTION.—It is not within purport of this article to detail statutes which have been passed relative to the regulation of the postal system; these statutes are very numerous and voluminous, and it will be sufficient merely to make reference to the volume in which they may be found at length. It is proposed here only to present the law as decided by the courts upon questions which have arisen as to the meaning and extent of the various statutory provisions; only such portions of the statutes being

operation in every respect. "All possible foresight" means anticipation, if not knowledge, that the operation of street cars will result in danger to passengers, and that there must be some action with reference to the future; a provident care to guard against such occurrences; a wise forethought and prudent provision that will avert the threatened evil, if human thought or action can do so. See generally the various titles on NEGLIGENCE. Topeka City R. Co. *v.* Higgs, 38 Kan. 375; 34 Am. & Eng. R. Cas. 529.

As Soon as Possible.—See SOON.

1. Needles *v.* Needles, 7 Ohio St. 443.

2. And. L. Dict., *citing* Bodenhamer *v.* Welch, 89 N. Car. 81; and Stover *v.* Eycleshimer, 46 Barb. (N. Y.) 87. In some of the States it is expressly provided that a mere possibility, such as the expectancy of an heir apparent, is not to be deemed an interest of any kind. Stimpson Stat., § 1350; Col. Code, 1876, 5700; Dak. Civ. C. 192.

3. Caldwell's Case, 19 Wall. (U. S.) 268.

A military "post" is merely synonymous with military "station." In each case it means, not an ordinary residence, having nothing military about it, except that one of its occupants holds a military commission; but a place where military duty is performed, or stores are kept or distributed, or something connected with war or arms is kept or done. United States *v.* Phisterer, 94 U. S. 219.

quoted as may be necessary for a proper understanding of the decisions.

The constitution of the *United States* bestows upon Congress power "to establish post-offices and post-roads." Every law of commerce and every regulation of the executive head of the Post-Office Department concerning the regulation and conduct of the post-offices is comprehended under the title Postal Laws.[1]

The power, therefore, vested in Congress embraces the regulation of the entire postal system of the country, and by virtue of it Congress may designate what shall be carried in the mail, and what shall be excluded, and also may declare what shall constitute an offense against the postal laws and the punishment thereof.[2] A law increasing the rates of postage is not a "law for raising revenue" such as required by the constitution to originate in the House of Representatives, and therefore such a law, though usually termed a revenue law, is only a postal law, and cannot be held unconstitutional because it originated in the Senate.[3]

The power of Congress to provide for the care of mail matter and declare the punishment for offense in relation to it, extends only to mail matter while in the custody on the post-office authorities, therefore before the custody of a letter by the post-office or its agents, and after their voluntary termination of such custody, the rights of the proprietor of the letter are under the protection of local, not the *United States* laws.[4]

While the mail service is the ordinary means of communication between parties at a distance, there is no law of Congress in reference to the postal service which makes it a legal channel of communication which a party may adopt as compulsory upon his correspondent.[5]

1. U. S. Const., art. 1, § 8, par. 7; *Ex parte* Jackson, 96 U. S. 727. Whether this power is exclusive in Congress has never been determined; no State, however, has yet attempted to establish a rival system of mails and post-offices, and it is certain that no State has any power to pass laws regulating in any way the carriage of the mails or conduct of post-offices established by law of Congress.

Exclusive power is vested in Congress under the constitution in three cases, viz:

1. Where it is expressly declared that Congress shall have exclusive power, *e. g.* its power to exercise legislation over the District of Columbia.

2. Where a power is vested in Congress by the constitution and prohibited by it to the States, *e. g.* power to coin money.

3. Where power is vested in Congress and the exercise of the same power by the States would be incompatible with its exercise by Congress, *e. g.* Congress has power to establish a uniform rule of naturalization, therefore the necessary implication is that it has exclusive power to do so, since, if it has not, no uniform rule would be established.

It seems, therefore, that the power of Congress to establish post-offices would be exclusive upon the ground set forth in the third paragraph. See Federalist, No. 30. See also the views of Mr. Calhoun as mentioned in the opinion of the court in *Ex parte* Jackson, 96 U. S. 727.

2. *Ex parte* Jackson, 96 U. S. 727.

3. United States *v.* James, 13 Blatchf. (U. S.) 207.

4. United States *v.* Dauphin, 20 Fed. Rep. 625.

5. Tanner *v.* Hughes, 53 Pa. St. 289.

II. **Powers of Postmaster-General.**—Power is conferred by statute upon the Postmaster-General as the executive head of the Department to make whatever rules and regulations may be necessary for the proper conduct of the mail service not provided for by statute. In the discharge of those duties which are prescribed by law, he is not lawfully subject to the control of the President, and in matters coming properly within his province his decisions are final, and neither a court nor a jury may revise them;[1] he may establish or discontinue post-offices wherever he may deem it necessary for the public convenience, and appoint postmasters of the fourth class;[2] he has also power to

1. United States *v.* Wright, 11 Wall. (U. S.) 648; United States *v.* Kendall, 5 Cranch (C. C.) 163; Reeside *v.* United States, 8 Wall. (U. S.) 38. See also United States *v.* Brown, 9 How. (U. S.) 487.

Thus where a post-office employee invested in real estate, money, stolen from the mails and conveyed the estate to defendant in trust, to sell and to pay the claimants the amount stolen, and the balance remaining, to the grantor, and a bill in equity was filed to enforce the execution of the trust, it was held that the Postmaster-General under the statute of March, 1847, has exclusive jurisdiction in the matter and that the bill should be dismissed. Laws *v.* Burt, 129 Mass. 202.

It rests altogether in the discretion of the Postmaster-General to determine at what hours the mail should leave particular places, and to determine whether it should leave the same place once in a day or more frequently. It is not, therefore, the mere frequency or departure of the carriages carrying mail, that constitutes an abuse of the privilege of the United States mail carriers of traveling on roads without paying the usual toll, but an unnecessary division of the mail bags amongst a number of carriages in order to evade payments of tolls. Neil *v.* State of Ohio, 3 How. (U. S.) 720.

Where the contract for carrying the mails provides that the Postmaster-General may impose certain forfeitures on the contractor for failure to carry the mail within the prescribed time, the exercise of such authority is not subject to review. Allman *v.* United States, 131 U. S. 31.

The Postmaster-General has only power to correct the mistakes in fact of his predecessor; and in cases of rejected claims, on which material testimony has been discovered. United States *v.* Bank of Metropolis, 15 Pet. (U. S.) 378.

The chief clerk and treasurer of the Post-Office Department transferred to the Department a deposit which he had made in his own name, in a bank, which, as he knew, had since become insolvent, and received from the Department, after he had resigned his office, the full value of the deposit, by order of the Postmaster-General. It was held that the adjudication of the Postmaster-General, ordering the money to be paid to him, and entered on the books of the Department accordingly, was not conclusive, and that he was liable under the act of Congress of 1836, ch. 270, § 17. United States *v.* Brown, 9 How. (U. S.) 487.

Chief Clerk of the Department.—It is within the range of the official duties of the chief clerk of the Post-Office Department to superintend all matters relating to finance, and he is not entitled to charge a commission for negotiating loans for the use of the Department. United States *v.* Brown, 9 How. (U. S.) 487.

Railway Clerks.—The Postmaster-General is authorized to appoint clerks for the purpose of assorting and distributing mail in railway post-offices, and the statute provides how they shall be paid. The appointment of these clerks is not for a definite period, and the right to continue a clerk in the service is within the discretion of the Postmaster-General; he may remove him from office or reduce the compensation. The prior rights of postal clerks are not affected by statute of July 1, 1882, which may be referred to as explanatory legislation. Gleeson *v.* United States, 22 Ct. of Cl. 82.

2. He may establish or discontinue post-offices of any class, and the fact

arrange and readjust salaries, to make all contracts necessary for the proper and speedy conveyance of the mails, and for their security.[1]

The constitutionality of the law of Congress authorizing the Postmaster-General to sue in the Federal courts, rests on the ground that the cases arise under some law of the *United States*.[2]

III. **Post-offices—1. Establishment and Discontinuance.** — The Postmaster-General is authorized to establish post-offices at all such places on post-roads established by law as he may deem expedient; which establishment he must promptly refer to the Sixth Auditor. Every person, who, without authority from the Postmaster-General, sets up or professes to keep any business or place of business bearing the sign, name, or title of post-office, is liable for every such offense to a penalty not exceeding $500.[3]

The Postmaster-General may discontinue any post-office where the safety and security of the postal service and revenue are endangered from any cause whatever, or where the efficiency of the service requires such discontinuance; this is also to be promptly certified to the Sixth Auditor.[4]

2. Post-office Building.—Particular provisions are made in the statutes for the renting, furnishing, lighting, and heating of buildings necessary for post-offices of the first, second and third classes, and of the post-office of New York city. In case of post-offices of the first and second classes, and that at the city of New York, it is provided that the expense shall be paid out of the receipts of the office; in case of post-offices of the third class, special appropriation is made. Nothing is said relative to offices of the fourth class.[5]

that he is only empowered to appoint postmasters of the fourth class does not in the least interfere with his power to establish or discontinue post-offices of other classes. Ware *v.* United States, 4 Wall. (U. S.) 617.

1. United States *v.* Vilas, 124 U. S. 86; Gleeson *v.* United States, 22 Ct. of Cl. 82; Fairchild *v.* United States, 12 Ct. of Cl. 226. He may reduce, prospectively, the pay of a railway post-office head clerk. Gleeson *v.* United States, 22 Ct. of Cl. 82. But, in so far as the salaries are governed by law, postmasters may sue in the Court of Claims for the sums due them. Fairchild *v.* United States, 12 Ct. of Cl. 226.

2. Postmaster-General *v.* Early, 12 Wheat. (U. S.) 136.

3. Rev. Stats. U. S., § 3829; Gould & Tucker's Notes on id. 741.

4. Rev. Stats. U. S., § 3864; Gould & Tucker's Notes on id. 741, 745.

The power to discontinue an office and thereby vacate the office, is incident to the power to establish it, unless its exercise is restrained by some provision in the acts of Congress. Ware *v.* United States, 4 Wall. (U. S.) 617, 632; Perkins' Case, 20 Ct. of Cl. 438; Embry *v.* United States, 12 Ct. of Cl. 455.

The fact that a postmaster is appointed by the President with the advice and consent of the Senate, under a statute providing that he is to hold office four years, unless sooner removed by the President, does not interfere with the power of the Postmaster-General to discontinue the office. If he exercises his power and discontinues the office, there can be no longer a postmaster at that place. Ware *v.* United States, 4 Wall. (U. S.) 671.

Where a post-office has been discontinued, the postmaster has lost nothing to which he is entitled. Ware *v.* United States, 4 Wall. (U. S.) 671.

5. Rev. Stats. U. S., § 3860, 3861; Gould & Tucker's Notes on id. 744, 745.

The Postmaster-General has authority to bind the government for rent for an office building only for the fiscal year, not longer.[1]

IV. Postmasters—1. Appointment.—There are four classes of postmasters: those of the first, second and third classes, are appointed by the President by and with the advice and consent of the Senate, and hold their offices for four years unless sooner removed or suspended according to law; while postmasters of the fourth class are appointed by the Postmaster-General, by whom all appointments must be notified to the Auditor for the Post-Office Department.[2]

2. Official Oath—Bond.—The faithful performance of his duties by the postmaster is secured by an oath of office by which he binds himself to the faithful performance of his duties, as set forth in the oath and in the statutes. He is also required before entering upon the duties of his office to give bond with good and full security, and in such penalty as the Postmaster-General may deem sufficient, conditioned for the faithful discharge of all the duties and trusts imposed upon him, either by law or by the rules and regulations of the Department.[3]

In the case of United States *v.* Saylor, 31 Fed. Rep. 543. the postmaster was allowed $1,000 with which to rent an office. He hired an office and received a secret rebate of $300 a year from the proprietor of the building in consideration for his retaining the office on that street; he also sub-let a portion of the office for a news-stand and for a confectionery establishment, thereby virtually obtaining the rent of the office free, while he forwarded to the Post-Office Department at Washington vouchers showing an expenditure of $1,000 for rent. In a suit against him and his sureties on his official bond, it was held that they were liable both for the rebate and for the rent of the news-stand and confectionery stand; that it was no defense that the postmaster had incurred expenses in making repairs for which the government refused to allow him compensation; nor that the special agents of the Department had frequently seen the sub-tenants in possession and had made no claim for rent.

The contracts of the Post-Office Department for the renting of post-office accommodations need not necessarily be in writing. Little *v.* United States, 19 Ct. of Cl. 272.

1. Connecticut Mut. L. Ins. Co. *v.* United States, 21 Ct. of Cl. 195. See also Campbell *v.* James, 18 Blatchf. (U. S.) 96, 2 Fed. Rep. 342.

Therefore where the party sought by bill in equity in U. S. Circuit Court to restrain a postmaster from obeying the Postmaster-General's order to move the post-office to another building, the bill proceeding upon the theory that a former Postmaster-General had executed a four-year lease of the premises, it was held that the bill must be dismissed. Western Star Lodge No. 2 *v.* Schminke, 15 Fed. Rep. 410.

2. Statute of July 12, 1876, ch. 179, §§ 5 & 6; Gould & Tucker's Notes on Rev. Stats. U. S., § 3852.

The postmaster at New York belongs to none of the four classes but stands alone; his salary is fixed at $6,000.

Not a Revenue Officer.—A postmaster is not an "officer of the revenue," within U. S. Rev. St., § 989, which provides for the granting of certificates of probable cause in certain cases. Campbell *v.* James, 18 Blatchf. (U. S.) 196.

3. Rev. Stats. U. S., §§ 3831, 3835; Gould & Tucker's Notes on id. 741.

The course to be pursued when a new bond is required, or when the surety on the bond wished to be relieved, is fully set forth in the U. S. Rev. Stats. to which it is sufficient to refer.

A bond given by a postmaster, with sureties, for the performance of his official duties, does not constitute a binding contract, until approved and accepted by the Postmaster-General. Postmaster-General *v.* Norvell, Gilp. (U. S.) 106.

3. Compensation.—It is provided by statute that the compensation of postmasters shall be a fixed annual salary, for rating which they are divided into four classes—exclusive of the postmaster at New York city, whose salary is fixed at $6,000 per annum.

The salaries of postmasters of the first class is not more than $4,000 nor less than $3,000; of the second class, not more than $3,000 nor less than $2,000; of the third class, not more than $2,000 nor less than $1,000; of the fourth class, less than $1,000.[1]

The salaries of postmasters are to be readjusted by the Postmaster-General once in two years; in special cases, as much oftener as he may deem necessary. The statutes provide specifically the manner in which this readjustment is to be made, according to the amount and character of the business carried on at the office, in order to ascertain which, the Postmaster-General may require the postmaster to state, under oath, the amount of stamps canceled, all box rent received, and all other postage matter sold, etc.[2]

At all newly established offices the Postmaster-General may temporarily fix the salary until the returns of the office may enable him to properly adjust the same.[3]

No postmaster, under any pretense whatever, can receive or retain for himself in the aggregate more than the amount of his salary and his commission on the money order business as pro-

Renewing Bond.—See Rev. Stat. U. S., §§ 3837, 3838.

In the case of Alvord *v.* United States, 13 Blatchf. (U. S.) 279, A was surety for one S, as postmaster, on his official bond. On Sept. 14, 1861, a new bond, with other sureties, was accepted whereby A was, by statute, released from responsibility for all acts or defaults of S committed subsequently. S was afterwards removed from office, and, at that time, was a debtor to the United States. In a suit brought against A, on his bond, to recover such debt, it was not shown by the United States that S had not in his hands on Sept. 14, 1861, ready to be paid or applied, all the moneys of the United States with which he was justly chargeable. It was held that it must be presumed he had such moneys in his hands when the new bond was given; and that A was not liable therefor.

1. Rev. Stats. U. S., § 3852; Gould & Tucker's Notes on id. 743.

A postmaster suspended from office is not entitled to his salary during such suspension, though he is subsequently restored. Embry *v.* United States, 100 U. S. 680.

2. Rev. Stats. U. S., §§ 3854, 3855, 3856; Postmaster's Cases, 12 Ct. of Cl. 226; Gould & Tucker's Notes on Rev. Stats. 743.

In making the biennial readjustment the Postmaster-General has no discretion since it is merely a ministerial act. The statute is mandatory but leaves to the discretion of the Postmaster-General when the first readjustment should be made, with the limitation that it must take place within two years. When the readjustment takes place it only establishes the amount of the salary for two years thereafter, and can only be made where there are quarterly returns for two years preceding on which it can be based. United States *v.* Vilas, 124 U. S. 86.

After the salary of a postmaster has been fixed it cannot be increased until a readjustment of it, based upon his quarterly returns, shall have been made by the Postmaster-General. Such readjustment is an executive act, taking effect in all cases prospectively; and until it is performed the law imposes no obligations upon the government to pay an increased salary. United States *v.* McLean, 95 U. S. 750.

3. But the compensation in such case cannot be fixed at a greater amount than the salary of the officer of the lowest class. U. S. Rev. Stats., § 3853.

vided; and no person employed in the postal service may receive any fees or perquisites on account of the duties to be performed by virtue of his appointment.[1]

Whenever any unusual business accrues at any post-office, the Postmaster-General is required to make a special order allowing reasonable compensation for clerical services and a proportionate increase of salary to the postmaster during the time of such extraordinary business.[2]

4. Powers and Duties.—The general authority to be exercised by a postmaster, and the duties imposed upon him as to the care and custody of the mail, the rendering of his accounts, the keeping of public money, etc., are specifically prescribed by statute, to which it is sufficient to refer.[3] He must, upon application by the proper person, deliver whatever mail may come to his office, and it is made an offense, punishable by fine or imprisonment, or both, for him unlawfully to retain in his office any letter or other mail matter, the posting of which is not prohibited by law, with the intent to prevent the delivery of the same to the person to whom it is addressed.[4] He is forbidden to make any disposition of stamps intrusted to him, except the sale of them at their face

1. U. S. Rev. Stats., §§ 3857, 3858.

2. U. S. Rev. Stats. § 3863; United States *v.* Wright, 11 Wall. (U. S.) 648.

Postmasters, however, are not entitled to an extra allowance for extra labor or for office expenses, unless it is granted by order of the Postmaster-General. United States *v.* Davis, Deady (U. S.) 294.

And in all cases arising under this statute, the Postmaster-General is the sole judge of the exigencies of each case. His decision is not re-examinable by any department of the government. United States *v.* Wright, 11 Wall. (U. S.) 648.

3. Rev. Stats. U. S., §§ 3829-3864; Gould & Tucker's Notes on Id. p. 741.

He is required to keep safely the public money without loaning, using, or exchanging it or depositing it in an unauthorized bank. It is said, however, that he is not bound to keep the moneys received for postage distinct from his own, nor to deposit it specifically in the name of the United States. See Rev. Stats. U. S., § 3846. Trafton *v.* United States, 3 Story (U. S.) 646.

4. Rev. Stats. U. S., § 3890; Gould & Tucker's Notes on id. 752; Nevius *v.* Bank of Lansingburg, 10 Mich. 547.

Any postmaster guilty of a violation of this section is forever after incapacitated from holding the office of postmaster. The Postmaster-General, however, cannot require a postmaster to deliver mail matter in violation of State laws, *e. g.*, insurrectionary papers. 8 A. G. Op. 489.

And the postmaster may properly refuse to deliver mail matter to one who intends to distribute it in opposition to public carriers, or to persons who assume a name in which letters are addressed for the purpose of defrauding the public. 9 A. G. Op. 161-164; United States *v.* Denicke, 35 Fed. Rep. 407.

Remedy.—If a postmaster refuses to deliver valuable letters on which postage has been prepaid, the remedy is by *mandamus* or *replevin*, and not by injunction. Boardman *v.* Thompson, 12 Fed. Rep. 675. See also Commerford *v.* Thompson, 2 Flip. (U. S.) 611.

Indictment.—An indictment against a postmaster under this statute is sufficient if it allege in the words of the statute that the letter was unlawfully detained with intent to prevent its arrival, and it is not necessary to aver that the letter was knowingly and willfully detained; therefore where the indictment alleged that the letter was detained two days "with intent to prevent the arrival and delivery of the same" to the person addressed, the evidence was complete, although at the expiration of the two days there may have been a change of purpose. United States *v.* Holmes, 40 Fed. Rep. 750.

value for cash, to third persons; therefore, where he uses them for the purchase of merchandise or for making change, he is guilty of a violation of the statute, even though no loss may be occasioned thereby, and though he may have been innocent of any intention to commit an offense.[1] He is required to reside within the delivery of the office to which he is appointed, but it is believed that he does not vacate his office by remaining out of the neighborhood of it, until action by the Postmaster-General.[2]

5. Liability.—His bond being conditioned for the faithful discharge of his official duties, a postmaster with his sureties is liable upon it for every breach of duty, whether by negligence or otherwise;[3] but in order to make him liable for negligence, it must appear that the loss or injury sustained by the plaintiff was

1. U. S. Statute, ch. 259; 1 Supp. Rev. Stats. U. S. 359; United States *v.* Douglas, 33 Fed. Rep. 381.

In a prosecution against the postmaster for such an offense it must be shown that the stamps so used were received by him from the Post-Office Department. United States *v.* Williamson, 26 Fed. Rep. 690.

Sale of Stamps on Credit.—A wrote to a postmaster of the fourth class, asking whether, if he (A) would send a quantity of circulars in addressed envelopes, the postmaster would put stamps on them and send out a certain number every day. A promised that if he would do so, he would remit the price of the stamps as soon as the circulars had all been sent out, which would require about twenty-five days. It was held that this was an attempt to induce the postmaster to sell stamps for credit and therefore in violation of the statute providing against the attempt to influence any officer of the United States to a violation of his lawful duties. Rev. Stats. U. S., § 5451; *In re* Palliser, 136 U. S. 257.

2. Rev. Stats. U. S., § 3831; United States *v.* Pearce, 2 McLean (U. S.) 14.

3. Therefore a postmaster, who, after he had placed a sum of money belonging to the government into a mailbag for transportation, intercepted and robbed the carrier of the bag and contents while it was on the way to the steamer, is, with his sureties, liable on his bond for the sum claimed by the government. United States *v.* Jones, 36 Fed. Rep. 759.

After a declaration against a postmaster which alleges that he carelessly and negligently lost a letter of the plaintiff's, any general proof of negligence tending to show that loss was occasioned thereby, and which satisfies the jury that it was so occasioned, is sufficient to sustain the issue of the plaintiff. Cristy *v.* Smith, 23 Vt. 663. See also Danforth *v.* Grant, 14 Vt. 283.

If he assume to charge letter postage on a newspaper because there is an initial letter on the wrapper, he does not act judicially in such a sense as to protect him for an action for improperly detaining such newspaper, although no fraud or malice be alleged or proved. Teall *v.* Felton, 1 N. Y. 537; 9 Am. Dec. 352.

No accident or misadventure will relieve a postmaster and his sureties from liability for property intrusted to the former. The only exceptions are those provided for by the acts of Congress; being losses occasioned by the Confederate forces or guerillas, or by any other armed forces. Hence no surrender of the property of the Post-Office Department to the Confederate government under any other than the coercion of armed force can excuse a postmaster. United States *v.* Morrison, Chase Dec. (U. S.) 521.

A post-office clerk received a letter containing money to be sent as a registered letter, both parties supposing it could be so sent. The clerk on discovering that the letter could not be so sent, by direction of his superior officer, sent the letter by mail unregistered, and it was lost. *Held* that both the clerk and his superior officer were liable for the value of the letter. Fitzgerald *v.* Burrill, 106 Mass. 446.

Where a surety is charged with receipts for postage for part of a quarter only, the return in gross for the full quarter is evidence to show an

in consequence of such negligence.[1] His liability for negligence embraces all losses caused by the carelessness or wrong-doing of the assistants to whom he has intrusted the care and custody of the mail.[2] A deputy postmaster himself, however, is liable on his own bond and is not included in the term "assistants" as just used.[3]

6. Accounts.—Every postmaster is required to render to the Postmaster-General, under oath and in such form as the latter may prescribe, a quarterly account of all moneys received or charged by him at his office, for postage, rent of boxes, or other receptacles for mail matter, or by reason of keeping branch offices or for delivery of the mail matter in any manner whatever; he may be required to accompany such account with a sworn statement of its truth, etc.[4] Upon a failure to render his accounts for

average liability. Lawrence *v.* United States, 2 McLean (U. S.) 581.

See also as to evidence in suits on such bond, United States *v.* Hodge, 13 How. (U. S.) 478.

Suits Against Sureties.—By statute of March 3, 1825, it was required that suits against sureties upon a postmaster's bond must be brought within two years after a default, else the suit would be barred. Postmaster-General *v.* Fennell, 1 McLean (U. S.) 217; United States *v.* Kirshner, 1 Bond (U. S.) 432.

This statute was held not to apply to a default which occurred before the passing of the act. Postmaster-General *v.* Rice, Gilp. (U. S.) 554.

Nor did it operate in cases of balances unpaid at the end of a quarter. which are subsequently liquidated by the receipts of a succeeding one. Postmaster-General *v.* Norvel, Gilp. (U. S.) 106.

As to the law previous to 1825, see Dix *v.* Postmaster-General, 1 Pet. (U. S.) 318, which holds that the obligors on the bond of a postmaster are not discharged by the failure of the Postmaster-General to commence a suit within the time prescribed by law.

At present the suit must be brought within three years from default. Rev. Stat. U. S., § 3838.

In an action by the United States on a postmaster's bond, the defendant may plead a counter-claim, if it appears from such plea that the items thereof have been duly presented to the proper department for allowance, and rejected. United States *v.* Davis, Deady (U. S.) 294. See also Postmaster-General *v.* Cross, 4 Wash. (U. S.) 326.

1. Dunlop *v.* Munroe, 7 Cranch (U. S.) 242. See also Wiggins *v.* Hathaway, 6 Barb. (N. Y.) 632; Coleman *v.* Frazier, 4 Rich. (S. Car.) 146; 53 Am. Dec. 727.

2. Dunlop *v.* Munroe, 7 Cranch (U. S.) 242; Bishop *v.* Williamson, 11 Me. 495. Where it is intended to charge a postmaster for the negligence of his assistants, the pleadings must be made up according to the case, and his liability then will only result from his own neglect in not properly superintending the discharge of their duties in his office. Dunlop *v.* Munroe, 7 Cranch (U. S.) 242.

If the postmaster live out of the neighborhood of his office and it is kept by an assistant, he is still responsible to the department, and to individuals. United States *v.* Pearce, 2 McLean (U. S.) 14.

It has been held, however, in several cases that an action will not lie against the representatives of a deceased postmaster for money feloniously taken out of a letter by one of his clerks. Franklin *v.* Low, 1 Johns. (N. Y.) 396; Schroyer *v.* Lynch, 8 Watts (Pa.) 453; Bolan *v.* Williamson, 2 Bay (S. Car.) 551.

Where issue is taken on the negligence of a postmaster himself, it is not competent to give in evidence to the negligence of his assistants. Dunlop *v.* Munroe, 7 Cranch (U. S.) 242.

3. Maxwell *v.* M'Iloy, 2 Bibb (Ky.) 211; Rev. Stat. U. S., § 3870; United States *v.* Mason, 2 Bond (U. S.) 183.

4. Rev. Stat. U. S., § 3843.

Where an account of the postmaster, regular on its face has been adjusted and allowed by the proper accounting officers and fully paid, such officers

one month after the time, and in the form and manner prescribed, the postmaster and his sureties must forfeit and pay double the amount of the gross receipts at such office during any previous or subsequent equal period of time; and if, at the time of the trial, no account has been rendered, he is liable to a penalty of such sum as the jury shall estimate to be equivalent thereto to be recovered by an action on the bond.[1]

7. Deputies and Assistants.—A distinction is to be noted between a deputy and an assistant in the post-office service; a deputy being considered an officer of the United States, under an official bond to perform his duties faithfully; an assistant being merely a hireling of the postmaster, and, therefore, under no official bond or oath. A deputy is paid out of the United States funds, but a postmaster cannot employ an assistant and pay him out of the government fund without special authority from the Postmaster-General.[2] Every letter carrier being considered a deputy, is required to give bond with sureties, to be approved by the Postmaster-General, for the safe custody and delivery of all mail matter, and the faithful account and payment of all money received by him.[3]

V. MAIL MATTER—CLASSES.—All mailable matter is divided in four classes, viz: 1st. Written matter, which embraces letters, postal cards, and all matter wholly or partly in writing, except as other-

cannot, after the term of office of the postmaster has expired evolve *ex parte* a balance in the government's favor, founded solely upon general and vague allegations of fraud so as to make such balance *prima facie* evidence against the postmaster and his sureties; the allegations must not only be specific but must be sustained by full and competent evidence. United States *v.* Hutcheson, 39 Fed. Rep. 540. As to evidence against a postmaster in a suit by the United States, see United States *v.* Hodge, 13 How. (U. S.) 478.

Where a postmaster's quarterly returns show a balance in his hands, the Postmaster-General may apply such balance to the extinguishment of a previous deficiency. United States *v.* Kershner, 1 Bond (U. S.) 432.

1. Rev. Stats. U. S., § 3845. A postmaster who leaves his office in the middle of the quarter, and who neglects to render an account to the Post-Office Department for one month after the end of the quarter, is liable under the above statute in double that sum, which bears the same proportion to the value of the postages received at the same office in any quarter, as the time for which he has neglected to make a return bears to a quarter. United States *v.* Roberts, 9 How. (U. S.) 501.

2. That an employee in the Post-Office Department is not responsible to parties, unless he is a deputy. See Bolan *v.* Williamson, 1 Brev. (S. Car.) 181; Maxwell *v.* M'Ilroy, 2 Bibb (Ky.) 211.

The postmaster of Syracuse, N. Y., finding it impossible to transact the business of the money order department without assistance, employed two clerks and paid them out of the receipts arising from that department. The Post-Office Department refused to allow this disbursement, on the ground that he had no such authority to employ clerks and pay them out of government funds without special order from the Postmaster-General. United States *v.* Chase, 29 Fed. Rep. 616.

Knowledge of the general postal regulations is imputable to every post-office employee as a matter of law. East Tennessee etc. R. Co. *v.* White, 15 Lea (Tenn.) 340.

3. Rev. Stat. U. S., § 3870.

Liability on Bond.—The sureties upon the official bond of a deputy postmaster are liable for postage stamps re-

wise specially provided;[1] 2nd. Periodical publications, which embraces all newspapers and other periodical publications which are issued at stated intervals and as frequently as four times a year, and are not repugnant to the conditions specified in the statutes;[2] 3rd. Miscellaneous printed matter, which embraces books, transient newspapers and periodicals, circulars and other matter wholly in print, proof-sheets, corrected proof-sheets and manuscript copy accompanying the same;[3] 4th. Merchandise, which class embraces all matter not embraced in the first, second or third classes, which is not in its form or nature liable to destroy or damage the contents of the mail bag or harm the person of anyone engaged

ceived by their principal. United States *v.* Mason, 2 Bond (U. S.) 183. See also, Postmaster-General *v.* Reeder, 4 Wash. (U. S.) 678.

1. For the law relating to letters, see LETTERS, vol. 13, p. 251.

Rates of Postage.—On mail matter of the first class except postal cards and drop letters, postage must be prepaid at the rate of two cents for each half ounce or fraction thereof; postal cards at the rate of one cent each; drop letters at the rate of two cents per ounce or fraction thereof, including delivery at letter-carrier offices, and one cent for each ounce or fraction thereof where free delivery by carrier is not established. The Postmaster-General may, however, provide by regulation for transmitting unpaid and duly certified letters of soldiers, sailors and marines in the service of the United States to their destination, postage to be paid on delivery. Rev. Stats. U. S., § 3875; Gould & Tucker's Notes on id. 748.

What Is Mail Matter.—An order for goods folded and directed as a letter, though not sealed is mailable matter, and, as such, is forbidden by the act of Congress of 1845, ch. 43, § 10, to be carried by any other conveyance than the United States mail, between two places, from one to the other of which there is a mail route. United States *v.* Bromley, 12 How. (U. S.) 88.

2. The conditions upon which a publication is to be admitted to the second class are as follows: 1st. It must be regularly issued at stated intervals as frequently as four times a year and bear the date of issue and be numbered consecutively; 2nd. It must be issued from a known place of publication; 3rd. It must be formed of printed paper sheets without board, cloth, leather or other substantial binding, such as distinguish printed books for preservation from periodical publications; 4th. It must be originated and published for the dissemination and information of a public character, or devoted to literature, the sciences, arts or some special industry, and have a legitimate list of subscribers. It is specially provided, however, that these provisions shall not be construed so as to admit second-class rates to regular publications designed primarily for advertising purposes or for free circulation or for circulation at nominal rates.

Foreign newspapers and periodicals of the same general character as those just mentioned, may under the direction of the Postmaster-General, and on application of the publishers thereof or their agents, be transmitted through the mails at the same rates as if published in the United States.

But any publication which violates any copy-right granted by the United States, cannot be considered as belonging to this class.

Publishers of second-class matter may, without subjecting it to extra postal, fold within their regular issues a supplement; but in all cases the added matter must be germane to the publication which it supplements, and said supplement must in every case be issued with the publication. Rev. Sts. U. S., § 3875; Gould & Tucker's Notes on id. p. 748.

3. U.S. Rev. Stat., § 3878. A "circular" is defined to be a printed letter which, according to internal evidence, is being sent in identical terms. A circular does not lose its character as such when the date and the name of the addressed and of the sender are written therein, nor by the mere correction of typographical errors in writing. 20 U. S. St. 358, § 18.

in the postal service, and not above the weight (four pounds) provided by law.[1]

Where letters remain in a post-office unclaimed and uncalled for, provision is made for their being advertised in a paper of the largest circulation in the place where the post-office is situated; also for the return to the writer of such letter, and in other cases for forwarding them from one office to another.[2]

1. Decoy Letters.—In order to detect and to secure the conviction of persons violating laws relative to the use of the mails, it is allowable to resort to use of decoy letters as a means to that end.[3]

VI. Offenses Against Postal Laws—1. Opening Letters.—Letters and sealed packages subject to letter postage are as fully guarded from examination, except as to their outward form and weight, as if they were retained by the parties forwarding them in their own domiciles; and can, therefore, be opened and examined only under warrants issued under oath or affirmation and particularly describing the thing to be seized. The constitutional guaranty of the right of the people to be secure in their papers against unreasonable searches and seizures, extends to their papers thus closed against inspection wherever they may be.[4] Hence it is considered that the opening of a letter, which had been in a post-office, before delivery to the person to whom it was

1. Printed matter with this provision is defined to be the reproduction upon paper by any process, except that of handwriting, of any words, letters, characters, figures or images or any combination thereof, not having the character of an actual or personal correspondence. Rev. Sts. U. S., § 3875; Gould & Tucker's Notes on id. 749.

A single letter or initial upon the wrapper of a newspaper, is not a writing or memorandum, within the act of Congress of 1825, ch. 64, §§ 13, 30, that will subject the newspaper to letter postage; and the Postmaster-General has no discretionary authority to order letter postage to be charged on newspapers bearing such a mark or sign. Teal *v.* Felton, 12 How. (U. S.) 284.

2. Rev. Stats. U. S., §§ 3930, 3940.

The postmaster is the only judge of the fact as to what paper has the largest circulation as required in the statute; and he is not responsible in any of the State courts for the manner or result of his judgment; even if he acts corruptly and maliciously no common law injury arises; and a special action on the case for damages for the willful refusal to advertise the list of letters in the paper having the largest circulation will not lie. Fosters *v.* McKibbin, 14 Pa. St. 168; 4 Pa. Law Journal, Rep. 303; Strong *v.* Campbell, 11 Barb. (N. Y.) 135.

3. United States *v.* Dorsey, 40 Fed. Rep. 752; United States *v.* Moor, 19 Fed. Rep. 39.

U. S. Rev. Stats., § 5467, makes the embezzlement by a post-office employee, of a letter, "which was intended to be conveyed by mail," an offense, etc., does not embrace a decoy letter, to be withdrawn if (not) stolen by a suspected employee. United States *v.* Matthers, 35 Fed. Rep. 890; United States *v.* Denicke, 35 Fed. Rep. 407.

For a fuller treatment of the subject of decoy letters, see Letters, vol. 13, p. 257.

4. *Ex parte* Jackson, 96 U. S. 727.

No one has authority to open a letter not his own even though it come from a criminal, and is supposed to contain improper information. United States *v.* Eddy, 1 Biss. (U. S.) 227—and in such case the violation by a criminal of an agreement that the sheriff was to inspect all letters written by him before they left the jail—*held*, not to authorize the sheriff to open a

directed, with the intent to pry into his correspondence, even though the letter was not sealed at the time, constitutes an offense against the postal laws.[1]

2. Obstructing the Mail.—The *United States* statutes provide that any person who shall knowingly and willfully obstruct or retard the passage of the mail or any carriage, horse, driver or carrier carrying the same, shall for every such offense be punished by a fine of not more than $100.[2]

letter after it had been deposited in the post-office. U. S. *v.* Eddy, 1 Biss. (U. S.) 227.

1. United States *v.* Pond, 2 Curt. (U. S.) 265. In that case it was said that it was not necessary that the name to which the letter was addressed should be the true name of the person for whom it was intended; also that it made no difference that the letter was written by the defendant himself. See also United States *v.* Parsons, 2 Blatchf. (U. S.) 104; United States *v.* Marselis, 2 Blatchf. (U. S.) 108; Rev. Stat. U. S., §§ 3891, 3892.

A mailable packet of merchandise is included in the statute, though not in terms. United States *v.* Blackman, 17 Fed. Rep. 837.

New York Penal Code, § 642, defines the offense of opening a sealed letter without authority. It was held in the case of McCormack *v.* Perry, 47 Hun (N. Y.) 71, that this section did not apply where the envelope contained nothing but a draft and was opened by one who, by writing on the outside, was directed to open it.

The distinction must be noted between the crime provided against which is mentioned in the text and in Rev. Stat. U. S., §§ 3891, 3892, viz., opening letters, and that provided against by § 5467. It is only where letters containing nothing of value are embezzled that the offense is cognizable under § 3891; if the letters contain any articles of value the offense committed is under § 5467. United States *v.* Lacher, 134 U. S. 624. See also United States *v.* Hartley, 42 Fed. Rep. 835.

The non-existence of anything of value in the letter taken is not an essential characteristic of the offense intended by section 3892, so as to make an indictment under it defective which does not allege that the letter taken contained nothing of value. United States *v.* Davis, 33 Fed. Rep. 865.

But it must be remembered that the writer of a letter has a right to control the use of it, it being his property. Therefore if he authorizes A to take it from the office and read it, though addressed to another, A is guilty of no crime in doing so. United States *v.* Tanner, 6 McLean (U. S.) 128.

In this general connection, see as to evidence necessary to convict, United States *v.* Mulvaney, 4 Park. (N. Y.) Cr. 164.

The right of postmasters, if any, to act as agents of citizens, to open their letters and use the money inclosed, is a very limited one. United States *v.* Bramham, 3 Hughes (U. S.) 557.

Indictment.—Where the indictment charges that the defendant "did secrete, embezzle, and destroy," certain letters, etc., "within the intent and meaning of § 5467, Revised Statutes of the United States," the recital of such section will be considered surplusage, and the indictment, though not good under said section 5467, will be considered sufficient under section 3891, providing against the opening, detaining, secreting, or destroying of any letter, packet, etc. United States *v.* Hartley, 42 Fed. Rep. 835.

2. U. S. Rev. Stats., § 3995.

Under this statute it is a criminal offense to obstruct a mail train even though those guilty were willing to permit the passage of the mail car alone. United States *v.* Clark, 13 Phila. (Pa.) 476.

In the case of United States *v.* Claypoole, 14 Fed. Rep. 127, the defendant being drunk assaulted a post-master in the door of the post-office, from which assault there resulted a delay in the transmission of the mail then in the office. It was held, that an indictment would lie for willfully obstructing or retarding the passage of the mail.

A person who, believing himself to be entitled to transportation on a railway car, resists the conductor's attempt to detach the mail car therefrom and send it on with the mail, commits an

3. Unlawful Use of Mails—*a.* FOR PURPOSE OF FRAUD.—If any person having devised, or is intending to devise, any scheme or artifice to defraud, or to sell, dispose of, or furnish any counterfeit or spurious coin, bank notes, or any security of the United States, or of any State, company, corporation or person, or any scheme or artifice to obtain money by, or through correspondence by what is commonly called the "saw-dust swindle," or "counterfeit money fraud," or by dealing, or pretending to deal in what is called "green articles," "green coin," "paper goods," or similar names, to be effected by opening a correspondence or communication by means of the post-office system of the United States, and in the execution of such scheme or artifice deposits or causes to be deposited any letter, packet, or circular, is guilty of an offense against the postal laws, punishable by a fine of not more than $500, or by imprisonment for not more than eighteen months, or by both.[1] The indictment, information, or complaint may sev-

offense under the statute mentioned. United States *v.* Kane, 19 Fed. Rep. 42.

A person having a lien against horses for their keeping cannot enforce the same in such a manner as to stop the United States mail in the stage coach drawn by such horses. United States *v.* Barney, 3 Hughes (U. S.) 545. No offense, however, is committed by enforcing such lien, unless the mail is *in transitu*, and unless the horses or vehicle taken are actually being used in carrying the mail. United States *v.* McCracken, 3 Hughes (U. S.) 544.

Where the driver of a mail coach was driving through a crowded city at such a rate as to seriously endanger the lives of the inhabitants, it was no offense under the statute of *United States* to stop such driver. United States *v.* Hart, 9 Pet. (C. C.) 390.

The arrest of a mail carrier upon a warrant duly issued from the court of a State upon an indictment for murder cannot be considered an obstruction of the mail within the meaning of the statute. United States *v.* Kirby, 7 Wall. (U. S.) 482.

But a warrant in a civil suit against a mail carrier is no justification for the arrest of such carrier, though the officer may have acted in ignorance of the statute and though the mail carrier was not detained longer than was necessary for the execution of the warrant. United States *v.* Harvey, 8 L. Rep. 77.

The same principle is stated in Penny *v.* Walker, where it is said that a mail carrier although he may not, while in the discharge of his duty, be detained upon any civil suit, is legally liable to arrest upon a charge of any criminal offense; *e. g.*, a violation of the liquor law. Penny *v.* Walker, 64 Me. 430; 16 Am. Rep. 269.

Restricting the speed of trains to six miles an hour by city ordinance does not obstruct the mails within the meaning of the statute. 5 Op. Atty. Gen. 554.

In the case of United States *v.* DeMott (3 Fed. Rep. 478), it was held, that this statute was applicable to a person stopping a train carrying United States mail, although he had obtained a judgment and writ of execution from a State court against the railway company in respect to the lands about to be crossed by such train.

1. The statute as found in the Rev. Stats. U. S., § 5480, has been amended by act of March 2, 1889. The amendment is somewhat lengthy, but the essential part of it is embodied in the text given above. See Gould & Tucker's Note 5 on Rev. Stats. 1033.

An intent to defraud by ordering goods by mail, with the intention of not paying for them, under the false pretense that the persons mailing the orders are merchants, is a "scheme or artifice to defraud"; and to mail a letter or any goods in pursuance of such a scheme is indictable. Evidence of the mailing of similar letters, if set forth in the indictment, is admissible to prove the intent. United States *v.* Watson, 35 Fed. Rep. 358.

To constitute the offense of using the

mail to defraud, the intent not to pay for the goods must exist before credit sought. United States *v.* Wootten, 29 Fed. Rep. 702.

Under the statute mentioned one may be convicted who, in carrying out a fraudulent device which consisted of advertising that agents outfits would be sent to all those sending money and postage stamps by mail, the defendant intending to render no equivalent for the money and stamps sent, takes a letter and packet from the post-office, and deposits a packet in the post-office in pursuance of such fraudulent scheme. United States *v.* Stickle, 15 Fed. Rep. 798.

To constitute the offense it is not necessary that the defendant should be the originator of the fraudulent scheme in which he participates. If the letter is deposited in the post-office under his direction, he may be guilty. United States *v.* Fleming, 18 Fed. Rep. 907.

An attempt to defraud a creditor by inclosing in a letter sent by mail, worthless slips of paper, in place of money stated in the letter to be inclosed therewith, is not an offense under the statute. United States *v.* Owens, 17 Fed. Rep. 72.

Where a party in order to deceive an accident insurance company as to the date of remittance of a sum of money necessary to save his certificate from forfeiture and to promote the allowance of his claim for indemnity, stamped a letter with a false post-mark, dated so as to give it the appearance of having been mailed sooner than it actually was, he does not commit an offense within the statute. United States *v.* Mitchell, 36 Fed. Rep. 492.

Evidence.—Evidence that A devised a scheme to put counterfeit money into circulation by sending through the mail to B a letter calculated to induce B to purchase counterfeit money at a low price for the purpose of circulating it, and that in order to carry such scheme into effect, A placed in the post-office a letter addressed to B for such purpose, is sufficient to establish the offense under the statute, although there is no evidence to show an intention to defraud B or any other particular person. The *corpus delicti* of such offense is the mailing of the letter in execution of the unlawful scheme. United States *v.* Jones, 20 Blatchf. (U. S.) 235.

In the case of United States *v.* Ried, 42 Fed. Rep. 134, defendant was indicted for using the mails in furtherance of a scheme to defraud, by soliciting money, pretending that by an unknown power he was able to answer sealed letters addressed to spirit friends.

The prosecution to show the fraudulent character of the defendant's business, introduced admissions of the defendant that the business was fraudulent. The court held that it was not competent for the defendant to show by the testimony of persons sending him such letters that in any particular instance he had answered them satisfactorily, and that the questions were of such a character that he could not have answered them except by supernatural power. Also that the defendant could not be permitted to give a test or exhibition of his unknown power in open court. The belief of the defendant, however, concerning his power to get answers to questions contained in sealed letters addressed to the spirits of the departed, is a question of fact bearing upon the intent. United States *v.* Ried, 42 Fed. Rep. 134.

The evidence of the intent of the party to defraud must be clear and beyond reasonable doubt. United States *v.* Stickle, 15 Fed. Rep. 798.

See also paragraph immediately following.

Indictment.—To make out an offense under this section of the statutes, three matters of facts must be charged in the indictment and established by proof, viz.: (1) That a scheme or artifice to defraud has been devised by the defendant; (2) that such scheme or artifice to defraud was to be effected by correspondence with another person by means of the post-office establishment of the United States, or by inciting such other person to open communication with the defendant; (3) that for the purpose of executing such a scheme or artifice or attempting to do so, the defendant places a letter or packet in a post-office of the United States, or has taken or received a letter or packet therefrom. United States *v.* Flemming, 18 Fed. Rep. 907; United States *v.* Wootten, 29 Fed. Rep. 702; United States *v.* Hoeflinger, 33 Fed. Rep. 469.

The offense may be charged in the general language of the statute, but the description must be conveyed by a statement of all the particulars essential to constitute the offense or crime and to aqquaint the accused with the nature of the charge; therefore, an in-

erally charge offenses to the number of three, when committed within the same six calendar months, but the court must thereupon give a single sentence, and is to proportion the punishment to the degree in which the abuse of the post-office establishment enters, as an instrument, into such fraudulent scheme or device.[1]

b. DEPOSITING NON-MAILABLE MATTER THEREIN.—Every article or thing designed or intended for the prevention of conception, or for the procuring of abortion; every article or thing intended or adapted for any indecent or immoral use, and every printed or written card, letter, pamphlet, circular, or notice giving information of where such articles or things may be procured, is declared to be non-mailable matter, and a penalty is provided of fine and imprisonment, or both, for depositing such matter in the mail.[2]

dictment is fatally defective if it charge the offense in general language without disclosing the particulars of the scheme or artifice; and it cannot be aided or cured by the verdict. United States *v.* Hess, 124 U. S. 483.

Where certain parties were indicted under the statute for pretending to furnish information that would show certain persons that they were heirs to large fortunes in England, it was sufficient to set forth in the indictment the contents of the letters, *in haec verba*, without alleging that such letters were false. United States *v.* Heeflinger, 33 Fed. Rep. 469.

1. Rev. Stats. U. S., § 5480. This provision does not confine the government to the prosecution of three separate acts alone, nor is it a part of the description of the offense; it relates only to the procedure. It imposes no stricter rule than the common law, and where an indictment charges in different counts, the commission of five separate and distinct offenses, the court may permit the district attorney to enter a *nolle prosequi* as to two of them and proceed as to the others. United States *v.* Martin, 28 Fed. Rep. 812; United States *v.* Nye, 4 Fed. Rep. 888.

Nor does this section prevent the filing of a second indictment charging three offenses after a conviction on a first indictment charging three. *In re* Henry, 123 U. S. 372.

In the case of *In re* Haynes, 30 Fed. Rep. 767, there was a conviction under two indictments, one of which charged two and the other three offenses, all laid within six months; the sentence of six months' imprisonment was pronounced under each conviction, the terms to run concurrently. It was held on appeal that though there could be a conviction for only three offenses in six months, one of the indictments and the conviction thereunder was valid. See also generally Gould & Tucker's Notes on Rev. Stats. pp. 1034, 1035.

2. Rev. Stat. U. S., § 3893; Gould & Tucker's Notes on id. p. 752; OBSCENITY, vol. 17, p. 7.

On the trial upon an indictment for depositing in the mail for mailing or delivery, an article designed or intended to prevent conception or procure abortion, the defendant cannot show in defense that the article deposited would not, in fact, have any tendency to produce such results, and that its harmless character was known to him when he deposited it; it being sufficient that the article, when deposited, was put up in a form and described in a manner calculated to induce its use for the purposes above mentioned, by any one desiring to accomplish that result, and into whose hands it might fall. Likewise where the indictment is for depositing in the mail for mailing or delivery, a notice giving information where or of whom an article designed or intended for the prevention of conception or procuring of abortion may be obtained, if it be shown that such a notice was deposited, it is immaterial whether, in fact, the article was at the place designated. United States *v.* Bott, 11 Blatchf. (U. S.) 346.

A notice, in the form of a letter, inclosed in a sealed envelope, or a written slip of paper, without address or signature, is within the prohibition of the statute, if the prohibited information is by it conveyed. United States *v.* Foote, 13 Blatchf. (U. S.) 418.

Where a publisher knowingly de-

No letter or circular concerning lotteries, so-called gift concerts, or other similar enterprises offering prizes, or concerning schemes and devices intended to deceive and defraud the public for the purpose of obtaining money under false pretenses, is allowed to be carried in the mail. Any person knowingly depositing or sending anything to be conveyed by mail in violation of this provision, is subject to punishment by a fine of not more than $500 nor less than $100, with costs of prosecution.[1]

All matter, upon the envelope or outside cover of which, or any postal card upon which may be written any epithet, or language of a libelous and inflammatory or threatening character, or calculated in any way, and obviously intended to reflect injuriously upon the character or conduct of another, is also declared to be non-mailable matter.[2]

posits in the mail a paper containing a quack medical advertisement giving information prohibited by the statute, he is guilty of the offense, no matter how vaguely the advertisement may be expressed. United States *v.* Kelly, 3 Sawyer (U. S.) 566.

How such a prohibited article or advertisement may be described in an indictment for depositing it in the mails—see United States *v.* Foote, 13 Blatchf. (U. S.) 418; United States *v.* Kelly, 3 Sawyer (U. S.) 566.

1. Rev. Stats. U. S., § 3894; Gould & Tucker's Notes on id. p. 754.

The offense of sending such lottery circulars through the mails is complete, though they be sent in reply to a detective's decoy letter. United States *v.* Moore, 19 Fed. Rep. 39.

The effect of this provision is to declare what is non-mailable matter, and to subject the sender of such by mail to a penalty. It applies to a circular favoring the scheme of the city of Vienna, Austria, to induce purchase of its bonds by prizes to be determined by law. United States *v.* Zeisler, 30 Fed. Rep. 499.

This section does not authorize a postmaster to refuse to deliver letters addressed to the secretary of the lottery company; but if it appears that the letters belong to the company and relate to its business, an injunction to restrain the postmaster from detaining them will not be granted in complainants' favor, since equity will not aid such an enterprise. Commerford *v.* Thompson, 2 Flip. (U. S.) 601.

A letter addresed to a fictitious name and delivered to an officer of the United States, is within the statute prohibiting the depositing in the mail a lottery circular. United States *v.* Duff, 19 Blatchf. (U. S.) 9.

The provision has been held not to embrace one who mails a letter to a lottery dealer and incloses money, nor does it apply to the naked sending to the post-office. United States *v.* Mason, 22 Fed. Rep. 707; United States *v.* Dauphin, 20 Fed. Rep. 625.

Constitutionality.—In *Ex parte* Jackson, 14 Blatchf. (U. S.) 245; 96 U. S. 727, it was held that the provisions of this statute apply to sealed letters, and are not unconstitutional or invalid. See also Dauphin *v.* Keys, 4 McArthur (D. C.) 203.

Under this statute an indictment for sending "five hundred circulars" has been held to charge but one offense. United States *v.* Patty, 9 Biss. (U. S.) 421.

In the same case, however, it was held, that where the indictment charged that on a certain date, and on each date between that and another, certain circulars were mailed, it was bad for duplicity.

2. Rev. Stats. U. S., § 3893, as amended by Act of Sept. 26, 1888. Gould & Tucker's Notes on Rev. Stats. U. S. 752.

In case of United States *v.* Bayle, 40 Fed. Rep. 664, the defendants on three separate occasions sent a postal card to J G containing this or very similar language:

"St. Louis, April 18, 1889.

"You owe us $1.80. We have called several times for same. If not paid at once, we shall place same with our law agency for collection.

"Respectfully,

"St. Louis Pretzel Co."

It was held by the court that such

4. Embezzlement.—The Revised Statutes provide that any person employed in any department of the postal service who shall secrete, embezzle, or destroy any letter or other mail intrusted to him, or which shall come into his possession, and which was intended to be conveyed by the mail, and which shall contain any note, bond, or any other article of value or writing representing the same; and any person who shall steal or take away any of the things out of any letter, packet, etc., which shall come into his possession, either in the regular course of his official duties or in any other manner whatsoever, provided the same has not been delivered to the party to whom it is directed, shall be punished by imprisonment at hard labor for not less than one year nor more than five years.[1] The statute also defines the meaning of the

language was within the statute and prohibited to be written upon postal cards, since it reflected somewhat upon the character of the person addressed.

When a postal card contained these words "please call and settle account which is long past due, and for which our collector has called several times, and oblige," it was not within the prohibition, since such language cannot be said to be threatening or offensive. United States *v.* Bayle, 40 Fed. Rep. 664.

A party is guilty of the offense under the statute where he mails a letter inclosed in an envelope on which the words, "Excelsior Collection Agency" are printed in very large full-face capital letters which occupied more than half the envelope and are so placed as to be entirely separate from the direction to return to the sender. United States *v.* Brown, 43 Fed. Rep. 135.

Before the amendment of September 1888, it was no offense to mail to a party a letter on the envelope of which was printed matter calculated to reflect, by implication, seriously, upon the character of the person addressed, nor a postal card of similar character. See *Ex parte* Doran, 32 Fed. Rep. 76.

1. Rev. Stat. U. S., § 5467; Gould & Tucker's Note on id. p. 1029. It is held that this statute creates two distinct offenses, viz. (1) the embezzlement of a letter carried in the United States mail; and (2) the stealing of its contents; therefore an indictment charging embezzlement only is sufficient, and one may be punished separately for each offense. United States *v.* Taylor, 37 Fed. Rep. 200. See also United States *v.* Harmison, 3 Sawy. (U. S.) 556; United States *v.* Atkinson, 34 Fed Rep. 316.

But an employee cannot be indicted under this statute for an act not within the letter of the statute. United States *v.* Gruver, 35 Fed. Rep. 59.

The fact that an article contained in a letter in course of transmission by mail, is not lawfully "mailable matter," is no defense to an indictment for stealing it. United States *v.* Randall, Deady (U. S.) 524.

The punctuation as found in the Revised Statutes is erroneous; the third line from the last should contain a semicolon after the word "directed," thereby making the statute to describe two separate and distinct offenses, as just mentioned. United States *v.* Lacher, 134 U. S. 624; United States *v.* Atkinson, 34 Fed. Rep. 316.

Evidence of Intent Unnecessary.—The purpose of the statute is to prevent and punish any interference with the contents of a letter in the custody of the mail, therefore a postmaster who takes money out of a registered letter and borrows it with the hope and expectation of returning it and does return it, he commits an offense within the statute. To authorize his conviction it is not necessary to allege or prove a felonious intent or an intent to steal. If the offense is set forth in the language of the statute it is sufficient. United States *v.* Thompson, 29 Fed. Rep. 706; United States *v.* Atkinson, 34 Fed. Rep. 316.

Under this statute it will be noticed that no one can be convicted who is not an employee of the Post-Office Department. United States *v.* Nott, 1 McLean (U. S.) 499; United States *v.* Pearce, 2 McLean (U. S.) 14.

Who Is an Employee.—A mail-carrier is, of course, included within the term "employee." United States *v.* Belew, 2 Brock (U. S.) 280.

Likewise a stage driver employed by a stage company which had a contract for carrying the mails, and who has sworn as a mail-carrier, is an employee within the meaning of the statute, though hired and paid by the stage company. United States *v.* Hanna, 4 N. Mex. 216.

It sufficiently appears that the accused was an employee of the Post-Office Department where it is shown that a demand was made upon him as postmaster for the registered package both by the sender and by the post-office inspectors, that he gave the receipt for the package to a post-office official, and that he claimed to have forwarded the package to another post-office official. United States *v.* Fuller, 4 N. Mex. 358.

A local mail agent employed and paid by a railroad company to carry mail-bags, and who has taken the oath of office.is a post-office employee within the statute, and may be indicted under that section for stealing the contents of a letter handed to him to put upon the train outside of the mail-bag. United States *v.* Hamilton, 11 Biss. (U. S.) 85.

A mail rider in the postal service who steals from the mail-bag money in a registered letter is not the agent or the servant of the person who sent the letter, within the *Alabama* statute against embezzlement. Brewer *v.* State, 83 Ala. 113.

Any Note, Draft, etc.—Under the terms note, draft, etc., "for or relating to the payment of money," a check payable to order and not indorsed is within the statute, and its value need neither be alleged nor proved; it need not be set out *in haec verba;* but the wrongful taking and felonious intent must be averred, although not specified in the statute. Jones *v.* United States, 27 Fed. Rep. 447.

Indictment.—The act establishing a postal money-order system is not a revenue law; therefore, where a party was indicted for embezzling moneys belonging to the money-order office, the indictment must be brought within two years after the offense committed and not within five as provided in case of offenses against the revenue laws. United States *v.* Norton, 91 U. S. 566.

But now (since 1875) by statute such indictment must be brought within three years. See Rev. Stats., U. S. § 1044.

An indictment will lie which charges an employee with having embezzled a letter which was intended to be conveyed by mail and contained an article of value and had been intrusted to him and had come into his possession as such letter-carrier. This section is not confined to the offense of stealing or taking things out of a letter, packet, or book. United States *v.* Pelletreau, 14 Blatchf. (U. S.) 126.

It is not necessary to give a particular description of a letter charged in the indictment to have been secreted and embezzled by a postmaster, nor to describe particularly bank-notes which were inclosed in the letter, but if either are described in the indictment they must be proved as laid. United States *v.* Lancaster, 2 McLean (U. S.) 431.

Where there are several counts and the proof conforms to the affirmance in one of them, in respect to the description of the letters and of the capacity in which the defendant was intrusted with them, a motion to acquit on all counts is properly overruled, though the proof varies from the allegations in the other counts as to those particulars. Walster *v.* United States, 42 Fed. Rep. 891.

If the letter is described according to its direction, which is to some other one than defendant, it is not necessary to allege that the letter or the banknote contained in it was the property of the sender. United States *v.* Laws, 2 How. (U. S.) 115.

In the same case it is said that the indictment need not allege that the clerk obtained the letter by virtue of his employment; that it was enough that, being a clerk he has obtained possession of the letter. Also that it was not necessary to set out the place from and to which the letter was to be carried by post.

But in the case of the United States *v.* Winter, 13 Blatchf. (U. S.) 333, the more proper doctrine is laid down, that the indictment is bad unless it allege that the letter was one intended to be conveyed by mail, that it was deposited in the post-office, or in charge of the defendant, and that it came in his possession in the regular course of his official duties.

Failure to allege that the letter had not been delivered to the person to whom it was directed, is not jurisdictional error that can be taken advantage of in *habeas corpus* proceedings. *In re* Wight, 134 U. S. 136.

words "intended to be conveyed by mail."[1] (See also EMBEZZLEMENT.)[2]

5. **Larceny.**—It is also provided that any person who shall steal the mail, or steal or take out of any mail or post-office, or other

An indictment for theft of a registered letter, may properly allege ownership in the person to whom it was addressed; the sender having no control over it. United States *v.* Jackson, 29 Fed. Rep. 503.

See also EMBEZZLEMENT, vol. 6, pp. 492, 498, n.

See further as to the sufficiency of the description of letters in an indictment, and also as to the proof requisite, United States *v.* Jeuther, 13 Blatchf. (U. S.) 335; Farnam *v.* United States, 1 Colo. 309; United States *v.* McKenzie, 35 Fed. Rep. 826; United States *v.* Sander, 6 McLean (U. S.) 598.

1. **Letters Intended to be Conveyed by Mail.**—Rev. Stats. U.S., § 5468. The case of United States *v.* Matthews, 35 Fed. Rep. 890, defines the meaning further, saying, that it cannot be that a letter is "intended to be conveyed by mail" when the postal authorities acting in operation with the sender intended after the letter is put in the mail to resume possession of it themselves or to permit the sender to do so before it reaches the hands of any carrier, messenger, or other postal employee, for delivery to the proper person. See also United States *v.* Rapp, 30 Fed. Rep. 818.

Letters stamped and postmarked as coming from other post-offices but which are in fact placed upon the distributing table by the postmaster and an inspector addressed to a company in the same town which gets its mail from the office in a pouch of its own, are, if the postmaster and inspector do not intend to intercept them before their delivery to the parties to whom they are addressed, letters "intended to be conveyed by mail." Walster *v.* United States, 42 Fed. Rep. 891.

Where the indictment is made and the defendant convicted, the court will not, on *habeas corpus* proceedings inquire into what the motives with which they were placed in the mail even, though the object was to detect the defendant in his criminal practices. *In re* Wight, 134 U. S. 136.

Where a postmaster received $15 in paper money and $3 in silver which one handed to him, requesting him to send it in a registered letter, and he took the money, put it in an envelope, addressed it, wrote a letter to accompany the remittance, delivered to the sender the usual receipt, received the registration fee, and mentioned that it would be all right, but there was no evidence that the silver money had been exchanged for paper, or that the letter was ever stamped or sealed or put in a special envelope for registered letters, he could not be convicted of embezzling a "letter" under the statute. United States *v.* Taylor, 37 Fed. Rep. 200; Walster *v.* United States, 42 Fed. Rep. 891.

Decoy Letters.—A letter with a fictitious address, which cannot therefore be delivered, is not one "intended to be conveyed by mail." United States *v.* Denicke, 35 Fed. Rep. 407.

The handing of a packet by a post-office inspector to a post-office official to be placed as a decoy in the "nixes basket", is not a mailing of "matter intended to be conveyed by mail." United States *v.* Rapp, 30 Fed. Rep. 818.

But not all decoy letters are excluded from the term "matter intended to be conveyed by mail." Thus the abstracting from a letter in a registered mail package, of a silver certificate, by a railway postal clerk, after he has received it as such, and while in his possession, to be conveyed by him as other registered mail, though placed there to give him opportunity to take it, if he so chooses, is a violation of the statute relating to larceny from the mails. United States *v.* Dorsey, 40 Fed. Rep. 752.

A letter containing money, deposited in the mail, for the purpose of ascertaining whether its contents were stolen on a particular route, and actually sent on a post route, is a letter intended to be sent by post within the meaning of the statute. United States *v.* Foye, 1 Curt. (U. S.) 364.

The purpose for which a letter, from which money was taken, was mailed, is not a question under the act providing for the punishment of the offense. United States *v.* Cottingham, 2 Blatchf. (U. S.) 470.

2. Vol. 6, pp. 493, 498, n.

authorized depository for mail matter, any letter or packet; any person who shall take the mail, or any letter or packet therefrom, or from any post-office, etc., with or without consent of the person having custody thereof, and open, embezzle or destroy any such mail, letter or packet which shall contain any note, bond . . . or any other article of value or writing representing the same; any person who shall by fraud or deception, obtain from any person having custody thereof, any such mail . . . although not employed in the postal service, shall be punishable by imprisonment at hard labor for not less than one year nor more than five years.[1]

6. Robbery.—It is provided that any person who shall rob any carrier, agent, or other person intrusted with the mail, of such mail, or any part thereof, shall be punishable by imprisonment at hard labor for not less than five nor more than ten years; and, if convicted a second time of a like offense, or if in effecting such robbery the first time, the robber shall wound the person having the custody of the mail, or put his life in jeopardy by the use of

1. Rev. Stats. U. S., § 5469; Gould & Tucker's Notes on id. 1031. It will be noticed that this statute punishes any person whether in the employ of the postal service or not, who opens, embezzles, or destroys mail matter containing things of value; notwithstanding the special provisions made for the punishment of postal employees in § 5467. United States *v.* Gruver, 35 Fed. Rep. 59; United States *v.* Marselis, 2 Blatchf. (U. S.) 108, note.

Under this statute any taking or abstracting of articles, or receiving them when so taken, with the object described in the statute, *i. e.* to "open," "secrete," "destroy," "embezzle," or "steal," constitutes the offense. United States *v.* Jolly, 37 Fed. Rep. 108.

To constitute the crime of stealing under this statute, there must be an intent to steal at the time the mail matter was taken; a taking by the authority of the person to whom the letter is addressed, although there is a subsequent embezzlement, or a taking by mistake or with an innocent intent, does not constitute the offense prohibited. United States *v.* Inabnet, 41 Fed. Rep. 130; *In re* Burkhardt, 33 Fed. Rep. 25; United States *v.* Pearce, 2 McLean (U. S.) 14. See also LARCENY, vol. 12, p. 760.

If a letter has been delivered to an authorized agent, there can be no embezzlement of it; nor can there be a convinction for opening a letter not containing an article of value, if he took the letter in the discharge of his duties. United States *v.* Sander, 6 McLean (U. S.) 598; United States *v.* Driscoll, 1 Low. (U. S.) 303; United States *v.* Davis, 33 Fed. Rep. 865.

The penalty of imprisonment prescribed in the last clause of the statute applies also to the preceding clauses, and includes the prohibition of an employee's stealing a letter from a postal car. United States *v.* Falkenhainer, 21 Fed. Rep. 624.

The offense is committed where one buys a land-warrant stolen from the mail, knowing it to have been so stolen. United States *v.* Keene, 5 McLean (U. S.) 509.

Indictment.—An indictment against the carrier of the mail for stealing a letter, is sufficient, without an averment that it contained no article of value, as it is an offense to steal a letter containing no such article; but if the letter contain an article of value, it must be so averred, to subject the defendant to the higher penalty. United States *v.* Fisher, 5 McLean (U. S.) 23.

Evidence—Proof.—See United States *v.* Crow, 1 Bond (U. S.) 51.

That letters were posted at one office and never received at another, is insufficient evidence to charge the first postmaster with stealing them, without calling as witnesses the postmasters of intermediate offices. United States *v.* Emerson, 6 McLean (U. S.) 406.

Where a postmaster is charged with

dangerous weapons, such person shall be punishable by imprisonment at hard labor for the term of his natural life.[1]

Any person who shall attempt to rob the mail by assaulting the person having custody thereof, shooting at him or his horse, or threatening him with dangerous weapons, and shall not effect

stealing a letter from the mail, the other officers through whose hands the letter would pass should be examined, especially if the accused proved an exemplary character. United States *v.* Whitaker, 6 McLean (U. S.) 342.

The record of the conviction of the person charged with stealing a letter is sufficient to establish the fact that it was stolen. United States *v.* Keene, 5 McLean (U. S.) 509.

Where a postal clerk was charged with stealing letters from a postal car and there was testimony tending to show that the letters stolen were taken from a straight package, which he had no right to disturb, it was held that evidence was admissible to show what the contents of the package was when it was received; and that the letters it contained which were not stolen were admissible in evidence for that purpose. United States *v.* Falkenhainer, 21 Fed. Rep. 624.

1. Rev. Stats. U. S., § 5472; Gould & Tucker's Notes on id. p. 1032. See also ROBBERY.

Under this statute, the offense is committed, where the mail, or any part thereof, is taken violently from the possession of the carrier against his will by violence, or putting him in fear. United States *v.* Reeves, 38 Fed. Rep. 404.

The term "mail" as here used means either the whole body of matter transported by the postal agents, or any letter or package forming a component part of it. United States *v.* Inabnet, 41 Fed. Rep. 130.

It is also sufficient to constitute the offense named, if the acts of the offenders created in the mind of the person having the mail in his custody, a well grounded apprehension of danger to his life for refusing to give up the mail. United States *v.* Reeves, 38 Fed. Rep. 404.

The word "rob" is to be taken in its common law meaning, viz: the stealing or taking from the person of another, or in the presence of another, property of any amount, with such a degree of force or terror, as to induce the person to part with it unwillingly. United States *v.* Wilson, 1 Baldw. (U. S.) 78. See also Bishop's Crim. Law, § 553 *et seq.*

If the accused person was present on the occasion of the robbery, aiding and procuring its commission, it is immaterial whether he actually entered the car containing the mail or not; he is to be regarded as a principal and convicted as such. United States *v.* Reeves, 38 Fed. Rep. 404.

As to the allegation of ownership of the property in an indictment against a party for robbing the mails, if it appears in the proof that the contents were sent for the benefit of the person to whom the letter was addressed the proof will be sufficient to support the allegation of ownership. United States *v.* Jones, 31 Fed. Rep. 718; United States *v.* Jackson, 29 Fed. Rep. 503.

Under this section one may be convicted of robbing the postmaster. United States *v.* Bowman, 3 N. Mex. 201.

Dangerous Weapons.—A dangerous weapon within the meaning of this provision is one likely to produce death or great bodily harm. United States *v.* Reeves, 38 Fed. Rep. 404.

Therefore it includes a pistol or dirk, and if an offer or threat is made to shoot with such pistol, the presumption is that it was loaded. United States *v.* Wilson, 1 Baldw. (U. S.) 78; United States *v.* Hare, 2 Wheel. Cr. Cas. (N. Y.) 283.

The sword need not be drawn nor the pistol pointed. United States *v.* Wood, 3 Wash. (U. S.) 440.

Indictment.—It is sufficient to charge in the indictment, a crime in the words of the statute, and the county in which it was committed need not be named; it is sufficient to show that the crime was within the jurisdiction of the court where the indictment is pending. United States *v.* Hare, 2 Wheel. Cr. Cas. (N. Y.) 283.

Presumption of Innocence.—Where one in charge of the mail is on trial for robbing the mail, the presumption that he has done his duty and safely delivered the mail applies in all its force unless there is proof to the contrary.

such robbery, shall be punishable by imprisonment at hard labor for not less than two nor more than ten years.[1]

7. Jurisdiction.—The offense of opening, embezzling, or unlawfully taking a letter under the United States statutes, can only be committed while the letter is in possession of the post-office authorities or their agents; after they have voluntarily abandoned the custody of such letter, any offense committed in regard to it is cognizable only under State laws and by State courts.[2]

Under the provision of the constitution that in all criminal prosecutions the defendant shall have the right to be tried in the State and district where the crime was committed, a petitioner, who mailed a letter improper to be mailed, in a State and district other than the State and district where the letter was received, is triable in the latter district.[3]

The rates of postage to be charged are all fixed by statute, and the circuit court of the *United States* has no jurisdiction to compel a postmaster by *mandamus* to transmit mail matter at a lower rate of postage than that charged.[4]

The United States courts have jurisdiction of suits by and against the Postmaster-General, on the ground that the cases arise under some law of Congress or regulation of the Executive.[5]

VII. Carriage of the Mail.—1. Post-Roads.—By statute of the *United States*, the following are established as post-roads:

United States *v.* Jones, 31 Fed. Rep. 718.

1. Rev. Stats. U. S., § 5473. To constitute an assault under this statute, it is not necessary that serious bodily injury should be inflicted; drawing a gun with a threat to use it, or forcibly ejecting a person in possession of the mails from the mail car, is sufficient. The attempt, under the statute, means an endeavor to accomplish carried beyond mere preparation, but falling short of the ultimate design; the attempt must also be to rob the mail and not merely an attempt to rob the express car or the passengers on the train carrying such mail. United States *v.* Reeves, 38 Fed. Rep. 404.

2. United States *v.* Parsons, 2 Blatchf. (U. S.) 104; United States *v.* Driscoll, 1 Low. (U. S.) 303.

And this doctrine seems to be clearly supported by principle and by the uniform tenor of the decisions as to the relative extent of the jurisdiction of the State and Federal courts. A letter once delivered by the Post-Office Department to a private person authorized to receive it, passes completely out of the jurisdiction of the United States courts. If an offense is committed in regard to such letter, after it passed from the custody of the post-office authorities, such offense is cognizable only in the State courts. Nevertheless it has been held in the case of United States *v.* Hilbury (29 Fed. Rep. 705), by a district court, that where a letter directed to one A, "care of F K" and such letter was delivered by the post-office authorities to said "F K" and the defendant obtained the letter from "F K" and opened it, the defendant was guilty of a violation of the *United States* statutes, § 3892, providing against the opening of letters. The case of United States *v.* Driscoll (1 Low. (U. S.) 303), directly negatives this latter doctrine, and is clearly the better authority.

In this connection see also State *v.* Wells, 2 Hill (S. Car.) 688; State *v.* McBride, 1 Rice (S. Car.) 400.

3. *In re* Palliser, 136 U. S. 257.

4. United States *v.* Pearson, 24 Blatchf. (U. S.) 453.

5. Postmaster-General *v.* Early, 12 Wheat. (U. S.) 136.

In the case of McNamee *v.* United States, 11 Ark. 148, it was said that the United States may sue a postmaster before a justice of the peace if the amount claimed be within his jurisdiction.

All the waters of the United States during the time the mail is carried thereon.

All railroads or parts of railroads which are now, or hereafter may be, in operation.

All canals during the time the mails are carried thereon.

All plank roads during the time the mail is carried thereon.

All letter-carrier routes established in any city or town for the collection and delivery of mail matter.

The road on which the mail is carried to supply any court-house which may be without mail, and the road on which the mail is carried under contract made by the Postmaster-General for extending the line of posts to supply mails to post-offices not on any established route during the time such mail is carried thereon.[1]

2. Mail Contracts.—The Postmaster-General is authorized and directed to contract with carriers for the carriage of the mail between the different post-offices of the country. Specific directions are given in the statutes as to his duty in making such contracts; *e. g.*, as to advertising for bids, etc.[2] Such contracts are to be performed according to the terms expressed in each, and in all cases where money has been paid out from government funds where no service has been rendered therefor or in consequence of the Postmaster-General's having exceeded his authority, suit may be brought for its recovery.[3] Whenever it becomes nec-

1. Rev. Stat. U. S., § 3964; Gould & Tucker's Notes on id. p. 762. See also Searight *v.* Stokes, 3 How. (U. S.) 151; Philadelphia etc. R. Co. *v.* United States, 13 Ct. of Cl. 199.

The streets of New York are post-roads within the meaning of the United States statute and persons delivering letters thereon by express, or otherwise, at regular trips or at stated periods are liable to the penalty imposed by such section. United States *v.* Easson, 18 Fed. Rep. 590.

Letter-carrier routes in cities are post-routes, and the establishing of a private express for the transmission of mailable matter within a city where letter-carrier routes have been established, is unlawful under the statute, and a court of equity will not, at the instance of one pursuing such illegal employment, enjoin the officers of the United States from making searches and seizures as authorized by the statutes in such cases. Blackham *v.* Gresham, 16 Fed. Rep. 609.

2. Rev. Stat. U. S. 3941, *et seq.*

3. Rev. Stat. U. S., § 4057. Money paid out by mistake may be deducted from other money due the payee. United States *v.* Carr, 132 U. S. 644.

But the United States cannot base a claim against a mail contractor on a discrepancy between the contract and its performance, so patent that the Department must have known of it all the while, and must be deemed to have acquiesced in it, and where no fraud appears. Griffith *v.* United States, 22 Ct. of Cl. 165.

Contracts Not Transferable.—By Rev. Stat., § 3737 no contract with the government or any interest therein is transferable, therefore, a contract made by a railroad company with the United States for carrying the mails is annulled under this section upon the foreclosure of a mortgage of all the property of the company; and a company purchasing cannot claim any benefit under the contract. St. Paul etc. R. Co. *v.* United States, 18 Ct. of Cl. 405. See also, Rev. Stat. U. S., § 3963.

Construction of Contracts.—A contracted with the United States to carry through New York city "the mail of the United States." *Held*, that, under his contract, he was bound to carry the "Australian closed mail" sent from England, and forwarded in unopened bags to San Francisco, the cost of transportation of which, under

essary to change the terms of an existing contract for carrying mail or to discontinue any mail route, proper notice must be given.[1] Mail carriers are required to give bond conditioned for the faithful discharge of their duty, and they, with their sureties are liable upon it for any failure to properly discharge their obligations.[2]

a. COMPENSATION OF CONTRACTORS.—The compensation of mail contractors is fixed by contract and by law of Congress. The Postmaster-General may make deduction from the pay of such contractors for failure to perform services according to contract and impose fines upon them for other delinquencies. He may also deduct the price of the trip in all cases where the trip is not

a postal convention, the British government refunds to the United States. Otis *v.* United States, 19 Ct. of Cl. 467.

The Pacific Mail Steamship Company contracted to carry the U. S. mail across the Pacific in certain accepted vessels. In the case of Pacific Mail S. S. Co. *v.* United States (103 U. S. 721), the court in construing this contract held:

1. That the company has no claim to compensation, other than sea postage, for carrying them in vessels which had not been accepted by the Postmaster-General.

2. That it is entitled to recover, under the contract of Aug. 23, 1873, for services performed pursuant to its terms, in vessels which he had, under the contract of Oct. 16, 1866, accepted.

3. That the annulment of the contract by the act of March 3, 1875, ch. 128, does not affect the company's claim for such services on a voyage commenced before that date.

A contract for postal-car facilities, which makes the liability of the United States conditional upon future appropriations, is valid, and becomes operative if appropriations are subsequently made. New York Central etc. R. Co. *v.* United States, 21 Ct. of Cl. 468.

The act incorporating the Union Pacific R. Co., and providing that it shall transport the mails at rates "not to exceed the amounts paid by private parties," constitutes a contract which is not annulled by U. S. Rev. St., § 4001, providing that the Postmaster-General may fix the rate, substantially that provision having existed before the act of incorporation. Union Pac. R. Co. *v.* United States, 104 U. S. 662.

1. Rev. Stat. U. S., § 3958.

Discontinuance of Mail Service.—Under a statute authorizing the Postmaster-General to "discontinue" mail service over certain routes upon allowing one month's pay to the contractor, the Postmaster-General notified a contractor that he would "suspend" the service, but that the contractor must hold himself in readiness to renew it when required. It was held that this was equivalent to a discontinuance in entitling the contractor to extra pay. Reeside *v.* United States, 8 Wall. (U. S.) 38.

Though a postal-route, in 1861, lay within the enemy's lines, the Postmaster-General might have continued it had he chosen, and he having discontinued it, the contractor was entitled to the one month's extra pay assured him by his contract. Campbell *v.* United States, 19 Ct. of Cl. 320.

But where a contractor's route is discontinued before he has rendered any service, he is not entitled to a month's extra pay, as stipulated for in his contract. Mordecai *v.* United States, 19 Ct. of Cl. 11.

If a mail service is in part discontinued, under a contract providing for one month's extra pay therefor, the contractor's right is not forfeited by subsequent misconduct on his part, though the one may be set off against the other. Walsh *v.* United States, 21 Ct. of Cl. 268.

2. Rev. Stat. U. S., § 3945.

The government having assessed, charged, and recovered judgment against a mail contractor and his sureties for a certain sum for failures in carrying the mails, cannot recover against the same defendants, on the mail contractor's bond; because the amount of the former judgment did cover, and was intended to cover, the whole sum due the government on account of the mail carrier's failures. United States *v.* Oliver, 36 Fed. Rep. 758.

performed, and not exceeding three times the price, if the failure be caused by the default of the contractor or carrier.[1]

Compensation for additional services in carrying the mail is not to be in excess of the exact proportion which the original compensation bears to the original services; nor is extra allowance to be made for any increase of expedition in carrying the mails unless thereby the employment of additional stock and carriers is made necessary; and in such case, the additional compensation should bear no greater proportion to the additional stock and carriers necessarily employed, than the compensation in the original contract bears to the stock and carriers necessarily employed in its execution.[2]

1. Rev. Stat. U. S., § 3962.

It is discretionary entirely, with the Postmaster-General to make such reduction from the pay of mail contractors. 14 A. G. Op. 179; 15 A. G. Op. 440.

Where a railroad admits its delay and the reasonableness of the Postmaster-General's reduction therefor, it, of course, cannot be recovered. Jacksonville etc. R. Co. *v.* United States, 21 Ct. of Cl. 155.

If a contractor has been allowed to carry mail under several contracts for many years by a route which is probably a deviation from that fixed by the contracts, the Postmaster-General cannot give the contract a retroactive construction and impose fines upon the contractor nor make retroactive reduction from his pay. Carr *v.* United States, 22 Ct. of Cl. 152.

Sec. 3962, so far as regards railroad companies, was not repealed by Act of March 3, 1879, which provided that the Postmaster-General shall, for every failure of the railroad company to deliver mail on schedule time, deduct not less than one half the price of the trip, and where the trip is not performed, not less than the price of one trip and not exceeding, in either case, the price of three trips. But the latter section merely made an exception to the provisions of section 3962, as to railroad companies, and therefore upon the repeal of that section of the act of 1879, the provisions of section 3962 are again in force. Chicago etc. R. Co. *v.* United States, 127 U. S. 406.

A contractor agreed to carry the mail from A, by B and C, to G and back. For twelve years he carried it back by the direct route, and not through B and C. It was maintained by him in a suit against the United States that since postmasters were required to report delinquencies of contractors to the Postmaster-General (Rev. Stats. U. S. § 3849), the Department must be deemed to have acquiesced in this construction of the contract, and could not charge the contractor with not having fulfilled it. But the court held that such presumption of acquiescence would not exist where it was not shown that the postmasters on the route knew of the terms of the contract, and where it appeared that the Postmaster-General repudiated the contractors' methods as soon as he knew of them. United States *v.* Carr, 132 U. S. 644.

Fines.—A recommendation made by the Postmaster-General to the Secretary of the Navy, that a deduction should be made from the pay of the contractor, on the ground that a portion of the service was performed by a steamer not belonging to the class mentioned in the act, and stipulated for in the contract, is not a fine, within the meaning of the act. United States *v.* Collins, 4 Blatchf. (U. S.) 142.

Proof by a mail contractor that he had been fined for delinquency by the Post-Office Department, it having the right to remit the fines, will not authorize a judgment for their amount against a sub-contractor, through whose fault they were incurred. Riley *v.* Hart, 3 La. Ann. 184.

The Postmaster-General ordered that if judgment should be rendered for the claimants, a fine be imposed in accordance with authority given by the contract. *Held*, that the court could not deduct the amount of the fine from the judgment. Pacific Mail S. S. Co. *v.* United States, 16 Ct. of Cl. 621.

2. Rev. Stats. U. S., §§ 3960, 3961.

By a statute of April, 1880, this proviso was added, "that the Postmaster-

Those railroad companies to which the United States has furnished aid by grant of lands, of a right of way, or otherwise, are required to carry the mail at such price as Congress may provide, and until such price is fixed by law the Postmaster-General may fix the rate of compensation.[1]

General shall not hereafter have the power to expedite a service under any contract either now existing or hereafter given, to a rate of pay exceeding 50 per centum upon the contract as originally levied." Gould & Tucker's Notes on Rev. Stats. p. 761.

Where the number of trips per week to be made by the carrier and the rate of speed are increased, the compensation for the increased speed will be included on the allowance for the services, including the additional trips. Allman *v.* United States, 131 U. S. 31.

A party entered into two contracts for carrying the mail, one for "mail messenger service . . . for carrying the mails between the New York city post-office and the railroad stations and steamboat landings, and between the several stations where transfer service is required;" the other for "mail station service . . . between the New York city post-office and branch offices." Compensation for increased services was provided for in the latter contract, but not in the former. In a suit for extra services, it was held that the services between station E No. 465, 8th Ave. and Hudson River R. Depot, was "mail station service." Also that service between New York city post-office and the Penn. R. Depot in Jersey City, was "mail station service," and that the undertaking contained in the "mail messenger service" contract to perform additional duties without compensation, covered only services in the city of New York.

United States *v.* Otis, 120 U. S. 115. Sec. 4057 of the Rev. Stats. provides that in all cases where money has been paid out of the funds of the Post-Office Department under the pretense that service has been performed therefor, when in fact such service has not been performed . . and in all other cases where money of the Department has been paid to any person in consequence of fraudulent representation or by the mistake of allowance, or loss of any officers or other employee in the postal service, the Postmaster-General shall cause suit to be brought to recover such wrong or fraudulent payment. Under this statute it was held that payments made for expediting mail service under a mistake as to the additional number of men and horses required, and in ignorance that none were employed, could be recovered back by the government, and where such mistake was caused by fraudulent representations by the contractors, it is immaterial whether or not such fraud was participated in by the subordinate officers of the Department. United States *v.* Barlow, 132 U. S. 271.

See also, for the recovery of any excess paid for extra services. United States *v.* Voorhees, 135 U. S. 550.

A verbal contract for expedited and increased services with the order accepting it does not constitute a new contract as authorized by §§ 3960, 3961. Griffith *v.* United States, 22 Ct. of Cl. 165.

1. Rev. Stats. U. S., § 4001.

But while Congress has power to fix the price at which mail service shall be performed by such railroads where it is expressly reserved as a condition of the land-grants, it cannot impose new contracts. The government cannot retain the obligation on the contract as against a company, and at the same time vary its own obligation unless it has reserved the right to do so in the contract itself. Therefore, the performance by a railroad company, of the mail service required by its contract, notwithstanding the notice of the intended reduction of the compensation by the Postmaster-General, cannot be construed as a waiver of its rights or an acquiescence in the new proposals, no matter whether it protested against erroneous constructions of the law or not. Chicago etc. R. Co. *v.* United States, 104 U. S. 680; Chicago etc. R. Co. *v.* United States, 104 U. S. 687; Illinois Central R. Co. *v.* United States, 18 Ct. of Cl. 118; Hannibal etc. R. Co. *v.* United States, 18 Ct. of Cl. 213.

In all these cases just mentioned, the rule was established that the statute quoted in the text did not apply to existing contracts.

A land-grant railroad, after expiration in 1875, of a written contract for

POSTING.—See note 1.

POST-NOTES—(See also BILLS AND NOTES, vol. 2, p. 313).—Post-notes are a species of obligation resorted to by banks when the exchanges of the country, and especially of the banks, have become embarrassed by excessive speculations. They are intended to supply the place of demand notes, which the banks cannot afford to issue or re-issue, to relieve the necessities of commerce or of the banks, or to avoid a compulsory suspension. They are under seal or without seal, at long or short dates, and with or without interest, as the necessities of the bank may require.[2]

POSTERITY.—Embraces not only children, but descendants to the remotest generation.[3]

POSTHUMOUS CHILD.—See LEAVE, vol. 13, p. 5; STATUTES OF DESCENT AND DISTRIBUTION.

carrying the mails, continued to carry them without entering into any new contract. It could not therefore, contest the right of the United States by Act of July 12, 1876, to deduct 10 per cent., and by Act of June 17, 1878, 5 per cent. from the compensation; since a land-grant road by Act of May 17, 1856, is under a perpetual contract to carry the mails at such rates as Congress may by law direct or the Postmaster-General determine. Jacksonville etc. R. Co. *v.* United States, 21 Ct. of Cl. 155; 118 U. S. 626.

While a Federal statute, reducing the rate of compensation for transporting the mails, does not apply to existing contracts, yet, where the contract is implied, a continued performance and acceptance without objection of the reduced rate is equivalent to a consent to a modification of the implied contract. The order of reduction and notice to plaintiff under the act of June 17, 1878, constituted an offer which plaintiff might accept or decline; and receiving the reduced compensation without objection constituted an acceptance. Eastern R. Co. *v.* United States, 129 U. S. 391.

1. General rule 4, adopted by the Florida railroad commission September 23, 1889, and requiring each railroad company to post in a conspicuous place, and keep continuously posted in each of its stations a copy of the schedule of its freight and passenger rates, revised and adopted by the commission for the use of the company, rules and regulations, official classifications and table of distances, means that the publication shall be in placard or bill form, and that the placards shall be so attached to something in a conspicuous place in each station that they can in the position in which they are placed, or without being removed, be read conveniently by the public, and that they shall be kept posted in this manner continuously. Nailing up by one corner in a conspicuous place in a station, and in such manner as to be accessible to every one, a pamphlet of about eleven printed pages, containing the rules and regulations governing the transportation of passengers and freight, or a similar pamphlet containing the classifications, is not a posting within the meaning of the rule, nor is the binding of these pamphlets and the schedules of freight and passenger rates together, and placing them conspicuously upon a conspicuous shelf-desk in the station agent's office, such a posting. It is the duty of railroad companies not only to post, but to keep continuously posted, as provided by general rule 4, whatever falls within its provisions. Furnishing the posters to agents, with instructions to post, does not answer the public duty imposed upon the companies. State *v.* Pensacola etc. R. Co. (Fla.), 9 So. Rep. 89.

2. Hogg's Appeal, 22 Pa. St. 488, 489. Differ from other promissory notes only as to time of payment. *In re* Dyott's Estate, 2 W. & S. (Pa.) 489.

3. Breckenridge *v.* Denny, 8 Bush (Ky.) 523.

POST-NUPTIAL SETTLEMENTS.—See MARRIAGE SETTLEMENTS, vol. 14, p. 552.

POST OBIT CONTRACT—(See also CATCHING BARGAIN, vol. 3, p. 37).—This is an agreement, on the receipt of a sum of money by the obligor, to pay a larger sum, exceeding the legal rate of interest, on the death of a person from whom he has some expectation, if the obligor be then living.[1]

POTENTIALLY means in possibility, not in act, not positively; in efficacy, not in actuality.[2]

POUND—(See also IMPOUND, vol. 10, p. 186).—A pound is a definite quantity of gold, with a mark upon it to determine its weight and fineness.[3]

POWER OF ATTORNEY.—(See also AGENCY, vol. 1, p. 331; POWERS.)

I. DEFINITION.—A power or letter of attorney is the instrument by which the authority of one person to act in the place and stead of another as attorney in fact is set forth.[4]

II. RULES OF INTERPRETATION.—The rules governing the construction of written instruments generally are resorted to in construing powers of attorney. The obvious meaning of terms is not to be extended by implication in the absence of necessity.[5] If that to

1. Boynton *v.* Hubbard, 7 Mass. 119; Chesterfield *v.* Janssen, 2 Ves. Sr. 125*.

Post obit agreements or bonds, are those given by a borrower of money, by which he undertakes to pay a large sum, exceeding the legal rate of interest, on or after the death of a person from whom he has expectations, in case of surviving him. Crawford *v.* Russell, 62 Barb. (N. Y.) 95.

2. Cole *v.* Kerr, 19 Neb. 553.

And in that case, it was held that an unplanted crop was not potentially in existence, *disapproving* the opinion of Hobart, Ch. J., in Grantham *v.* Hawley, Hobart 132.

See also Long *v.* Hines, 40 Kan. 220; MORTGAGES, vol. 15, p. 750, n.

3. Borie *v.* Trott, 5 Phila. (Pa.) 366.

4. Hunt *v.* Rousmanier, 8 Wheat. (U. S.) 174; Porter *v.* Hermann, 8 Cal. 620. In the latter case Field, J., says: "All attorneys in fact are agents, but all agents are not necessarily attorneys in fact; agent is the general term, which includes brokers, factors, consignees, shipmasters and all classes of agents. By attorneys in fact are meant persons who are acting under a special power created by deed. It is true, in loose language, the terms are applied to denote all agents employed in any kind of business except attorneys at law, but in legal language they denote persons having a special authority by deed."

5. Wood *v.* Goodridge, 6 Cush. (Mass.) 117; 52 Am. Dec. 771; Johnston *v.* Wright, 6 Cal. 375; Davidson *v.* Dallas, 8 Cal. 227; Blum *v.* Robertson, 24 Cal. 129; Holladay *v.* Daily, 19 Wall. (U. S.) 606–611; Peckham *v.* Lyon, 4 McLean (U. S.) 45; Billings *v.* Morrow, 7 Cal. 171; 68 Am. Dec. 235; Very *v.* Levy, 13 How. (U. S.) 345; Wright *v.* Ellison, 1 Wall. (U. S.) 16; Nippel *v.* Hammond, 4 Colo. 211; Craighead *v.* Peterson, 72 N. Y. 279; 28 Am. Rep. 150; Howard *v.* Baillie, 2 H. Bl. 618. A power of attorney to act for the owners of a tannery in all matters and business relating to the tannery in that place does not confer power on the attorney to receipt to an officer for horses, etc., used in the tan-

nery, which had been attached as the property of a third person. Weston *v.* Alley, 49 Me. 94. Power to take possession of a mill and manufacture lumber and sell the same does not confer power to purchase fixtures or make improvements in the mill at the expense of the principals. Holmes *v.* Morse, 50 Me. 102; Wilson *v.* Troup, 7 Johns. Ch. (N. Y.) 25; Lawrence *v.* Gebhard, 41 Barb. (N. Y.) 575. Written authority to see a foreign debtor concerning a debt with full authority to act for the principals in the matter gives the agent authority to receive from the debtor personal property in satisfaction of the debt. Oliver *v.* Sterling, 20 Ohio St. 391; Cooley *v.* Willard, 34 Ill. 68; 85 Am. Dec. 296; Merrick *v.* Wagner, 44 Ill. 266; Greve *v.* Coffin, 14 Minn. 345; 100 Am. Dec. 229; Whiting *v.* Western Stage Co., 20 Iowa 554; Wanless *v.* McCandless, 38 Iowa 20; Fuselier *v.* Robin, 4 La. Ann. 61; Long *v.* Long, 5 Ves. 445; 2 Story Eq. Jur., § 1063, 1064; Story on Agency, § 67, note; Hartford F. Ins. Co. *v.* Wilcox, 57 Ill. 180; Bissell *v.* Terry, 69 Ill. 184; Ferreira *v.* Depew, 17 How. Pr. (N. Y.) 418.

A power of attorney must be construed, in the absence of anything to show a different intention, as giving authority to act only in the separate individual business of the principal. Stainback *v.* Read, 11 Gratt. (Va.) 281; 62 Am. Dec. 648.

A direction or authority to do a thing is a reasonable implication of the power necessary to accomplish it, unless there is a special restriction, or unless an intention to the contrary is inferred from other parts of the authority. Laney *v.* Burr, 36 Mo. 85; 88 Am. Dec. 135; Peck *v.* Harriott, 6 S. & R. (Pa.) 146; 9 Am. Dec. 415.

A chairman of a company borrowed money of the company; soon afterward he authorized the secretary of the company by a general power of attorney to execute for him all deeds that might be necessary, and some time afterwards left the country and did not return. After this the secretary executed a mortgage under the power to the company to secure them for the amount borrowed by the chairman. About a month afterward the chairman was adjudged a bankrupt. *Held* that the power of attorney did not authorize the execution of the mortgage, and that it was invalid. *In re* Bowles, 31 L. T., N. S. 365.

In Gilbert *v.* How, 45 Minn. 121, a deed was given in which Bucklin and Clark were named as grantors. The deed was executed by Bucklin in person, and by one Chase as attorney in fact for Clark, but at the time of its execution the land purporting to be conveyed was the sole property of Clark. The attorney in fact (Chase) executed the deed under a written power of attorney given to him by Clark, and Bucklin constituting him "our true and lawful attorney for us and in our names," to enter upon and take possession of all lands "to which we may be in any way entitled or interested, and to grant, bargain and sell the same," etc. It was held that the power of attorney should be strictly construed, and could only authorize a valid conveyance of property in which the agents' principals were joint owners. The court by Collins, J., said: "All powers of attorney receive a strict interpretation, and the authority is never extended by intendment, or construction, beyond that which is given in terms, or is absolutely necessary for carrying the authority into effect, and that authority must be strictly pursued." Rossiter *v.* Rossiter, 8 Wend. (N. Y.) 494; Brantley *v.* Insurance Co., 53 Ala. 554; Bliss *v.* Clark, 16 Gray (Mass.) 60. This rule was applied in Rice *v.* Tavernier, 8 Minn. 248; Greve *v.* Coffin, 14 Minn. 345; Berkey *v.* Judd, 22 Minn. 287. And a party dealing with an agent is chargeable with notice of the contents of the power under which he acts, and must interpret it at his own peril. Sandford *v.* Handy, 23 Wend. (N. Y.) 260; Nixon *v.* Hyserott, 5 Johns. (N. Y.) 58.

"The power under which Chase pretended to convey a tract of land, the sole property of Mary A. Clark, must be construed as authorizing him to convey such lands only as were held and owned by his two constituents jointly, or in common, and not the lands held and owned by either, and separately. By its terms, the attorney was not empowered to convey land held and owned as the undivided property of one and in which the other had no interest, nor was he given authority to transact any business, except that in which the parties were jointly concerned. The authority was special, and the written power joint, in form. No mention was made of the separate property or business of either of the parties who executed it, and it cannot be inferred that they intended to confer upon Chase the power to

be done is not stated specifically, the situation of the parties and the subject-matter and the circumstances of the case may be looked to in aid of the construction.[1]

Where authority to perform specific acts is given and general words are also employed, such words are limited to the particular acts authorized.[2] The intention of the parties as ascertained from the language used, governs.[3]

It should be stated, however, as a rule of interpretation, that, in favor of the rights of persons acting on the faith of a letter of attorney, reasonable intendments are made against the grantor of the power, though not to such an extent as unduly to expand the agency beyond its obvious purpose; or, in other words, ambiguities and terms doubtful in their meaning and susceptible of opposite constructions are rather to be construed so as to protect those acting in good faith upon the one construction.[4]

From one point of view the law governing the construction of powers of attorney is a branch of the law of agency, and the powers of the agent, the liabilities of the principal, and the rights of third parties are similar, whether the authority of the agent is verbal or written, subject to the general rule, that the more formal the instrument, the less latitude of construction is indulged in, and subject to the rules applied to written instruments gener-

convey such property, or to transact such business. Dodge *v.* Hopkins, 14 Wis. 686; Johnston *v.* Wright, 6 Cal. 373. This rule is also recognized in Holliday *v.* Daily, 19 Wall. (N. Y.) 606, although the point was not directly in issue."

1. Maynard *v.* Mercer, 10 Nev. 33; Hitchens *v.* Ricketts, 17 Ind. 625; Merrick *v.* Wagner, 44 Ill. 266; Greve *v.* Coffin, 14 Minn. 345; 100 Am. Dec. 2129; Whiting *v.* Western Stage Co., 20 Iowa 554; Miller *v.* Marmiche, 24 La. Ann. 30; Lamy *v.* Burr, 36 Mo. 85; 88 Am. Dec. 135; McNeil *v.* Shirley, 33 Cal. 202; Taylor *v.* Harlow, 11 Barb. (N. Y.) 232.

2. Billings *v.* Morrow, 7 Cal. 171; Washburn *v.* Alden, 5 Cal. 463; De Rutte *v.* Muldrow, 16 Cal. 505; Jones *v.* Marks, 47 Cal. 242; Wilcoxson *v.* Miller, 49 Cal. 193–195; Dupont *v.* Wertheman, 10 Cal. 354; Taylor *v.* Robinson, 14 Cal. 396; Treat *v.* De Celis, 41 Cal. 202; Dodge *v.* Hopkins, 14 Wis. 686; Long *v.* Fuller, 21 Wis. 121; Gould *v.* Bowen, 26 Iowa 77; Wanless *v.* McCandless, 38 Iowa 20; Rankin *v.* Eakin, 3 Head (Tenn.) 229; Rountree *v.* Denson, 59 Wis. 522; Geiger *v.* Bolles, 1 Thomp. & C. (N. Y.) 129; Blinn *v.* Robertson, 24 Cal. 127; Rountree *v.* Denson, 59 Wis. 522; Gee *v.* Bolton, 17 Wis. 604; Chilton *v.* Wilford, 2 Wis. 1; Atwood *v.* Munnings, 7 B. & C. 278; Perry *v.* Holl, 6 Jur., N. S. 661; 29 L. J., Ch. 677; 8 W. R. 570; 2 De G. F. & J. 38; Harper *v.* Godsell, L. R., 5 Q. B. 422; 18 W. R. 945; 39 L. J., Q. B. 185.

3. Peckham *v.* Lyon, 4 McLean (U. S.) 45; Hartford F. Ins. Co. *v.* Wilcox, 57 Ill. 180; Gould *v.* Bowen, 26 Iowa 77.

The intention of the party giving the power should in all cases govern the construction to be given to and determine the extent of the authority. Laney *v.* Burr, 36 Mo. 85; 88 Am. Dec. 135.

Where the intention fairly appears from the language employed that intention must control. Hemstreet *v.* Burdick, 90 Ill. 444–450.

4. Wharton on Agency, § 223, and cases *cited*, viz.: Blackett *v.* Royal Ins. Co., 2 C. & J. 244; De Tastett *v.* Crousillat, 2 Wash. (U. S.) 132; Brown *v.* M'Gran, 14 Pet. (U. S.) 479; Stall *v.* Meek, 70 Pa. St. 181; Weed *v.* Adams, 37 Conn. 378. See also, for a statement of the principles lying at the foundation of this rule, INTERPRETATION, vol. 11, p. 507.

ally as to varying or controlling, by parol evidence, the obvious meaning of written terms employed.[1]

1. See AGENCY, vol. 1, p. 331.

It is thought desirable here to refer to various cases wherein the courts have been called upon to deal with written letters or powers and to construe them. The list of cases is by no means exhaustive, nor could it be made so without such a duplication of the foregoing article as would be inadmissible. It is designed to be illustrative only.

Though the power of attorney, after particularizing that which is to be done, goes on to say that the attorney is "to transact all business," these words are not to be taken in their general sense, but limited to business connected with the matter in hand. Hay *v.* Goldsmidt, *cited* in 1 Taunt 349; Murray *v.* East India Co., 5 Barn & Ad. 204; Esdaile *v.* La Nauz, 1 Y. &. C. 394; Bengal Bank *v.* McLeod, 7 Moore P. C. 35.

A letter of attorney to receive money, though of the most general nature, has been held not to authorize the attorney to negotiate bills received in payment, or to indorse them in his own name. Hogg *v.* Snaith, 1 Taunt. 347.

A power to compromise, adjust, settle and arrange differences and disputes, and to give and receive discharges in connection therewith is held in Lagow *v.* Patterson, 1 Blackf. (Ind.) 252, not to authorize a confession of judgment by the attorney in the name of the principal.

A power to collect a debt does not authorize the attorney to give a discharge on receipt of the agent's note. Corning *v.* Strong, 1 Ind. 329; Kirk *v.* Hiatt, 2 Ind. 322; Miller *v.* Edmondstone, 8 Blackf. (Ind.) 291. And see Ward *v.* Evans, 2 Ld. Raym. 928; Sykes *v.* Giles, 5 M. & W. 645; Gardner *v.* Baillie, 6 T. R. 591. But see Howard *v.* Baillie, 2 H. Bl. 623.

It was held in Rossiter *v.* Rossiter, 8 Wend. (N. Y.) 494, that a power of attorney to secure, demand and sue for money, to discharge and compound debts, to execute deeds for land, and to accomplish, in the discretion of the attorney a complete adjustment of all the principal's concerns in a certain State, and to do anything in his name which he could do in person did not embrace authority to give a note in the name of a principal. In Story on Agency, § 65 n., this case is thought to stand upon very nice principles of construction, and the editor of the 9th edition cites, a tending to detract from the force of this case, Harper *v.* Godsell, L. R., 5 Q. B. 422; Taylor *v.* Robinson, 14 Cal. 399; Hefferman *v.* Addams, 7 Watts (Pa.) 116; Wood *v.* McCain, 7 Ala. 800: 42 Am. Dec. 612; Pollock *v.* Cohen, 32 Ohio St. 514; City Bank *v.* Kent, 57 Ga. 283.

In Lee *v.* Rogers, 2 Sawy. (U. S.) 550, the power of attorney authorized the collection of judgments by sales under execution, the reception of the money, and the arbitration or composition of the claim, and the employment of counsel. It was held that the attorney had power to authorize counsel to appear in an action and consent to a judgment annulling sales upon terms which enabled the attorney to realize the amount due to the principal.

In Neille *v.* United States, 7 Ct. of Cl. 535, a power of attorney to demand indemnification from a foreign government, and purporting to confer power to do all things necessary, was deemed to authorize the prosecution of the claim by the attorney before a commission.

Treat *v.* Celis, 41 Cal. 212, may be cited to the point that authority to bind the principal by a contract of sale was not conferred by a power of attorney which appeared to contemplate a sale, though not in direct terms authorizing it.

A power "to cite and appear" has been held to embrace the power to prosecute and defend suits. Miller *v.* Marmiche, 24 La. Ann. 30.

It was held in Foster *v.* Paine, 56 Iowa 622, that where a power of attorney authorized the cancellation of a mortgage and the mortgage notes secured thereby, and the taking of new notes and a new mortgage, the cancellation of the old mortgage without taking a new one was unauthorized and did not affect the subsequent mortgagee.

In Posner *v.* Bayless, 59 Md. 56, it was held that the power to sell property or lease it, or "to borrow money and pledge the property by way of mortgage," authorized a conveyance in fee to the lender of the money, and the taking back of a redeemable lease at a rent equal to the interest of the loan.

A power to borrow money and to sign and indorse notes therefor, and give a mortgage, was held in Burnet *v.* Boyd, 60 Miss. 627, to authorize the execution of a mortgage to secure accommodation notes obtained by the attorney from another than the principal, the principal having raised money on these notes and applied it partly in his business and partly to previous liabilities.

A power of attorney, with authority to make a subdivision of land, and acknowledge and record the plat according to law, was held to confer power to dedicate land for street purposes. Wirt *v.* McEnery, 21 Fed. Rep. 233.

In Renwick *v.* Wheeler, 4 McCrary (U. S.) 119, the words "unrestricted power and authority," were held sufficient to authorize the settlement of a mortgage debt by taking the mortgaged property in full satisfaction. See Ward *v.* Thrustin, 40 Ohio St. 347, for a power, which while purporting to give authority to manage land, was held not to confer authority to make a lease.

See Rountree *v.* Denson, 59 Wis. 522, for a statement of the rule that general words in a power of attorney are not to be construed at large, but merely as referring to the special purpose for which the power is given.

In Jernegan *v.* Gray, 14 Lea (Tenn.) 536, it was held that a power of attorney to sign and acknowledge any bond embraced an official bond required of a county officer.

In Alexander *v.* Goodwin, 20 Neb. 216, it was held that a power to sell real estate authorized the attorney to give a quitclaim deed of land, which, possibly, was not owned by the principal.

A power to sell and convey land does not authorize a conveyance without consideration. Randall *v.* Duff, 79 Cal. 115.

In Cooper *v.* Finke, 38 Minn. 2, it was adjudged that a power of attorney "to grant, bargain, sell, and convey any and all personal or real property" conferred authority to sell and convey, by assignment of the certificate of sale, the interest of a purchaser at a mortgage sale, during the period of redemption.

In Horne *v.* Ingraham, 125 Ill. 198, it was held that a power, given by one partner to another, to transact the affairs of the partnership, did not authorize the attorney to admit a new partner into the firm, or to vary the terms of the partnership.

A power of attorney to confess judgment failed to state against whom judgment might be confessed, the blank space after the word "against" being left unfilled. It was held that the power was incomplete and would not support a confession of judgment.

In Hunter *v.* Sacramento Beet Sugar Co., 7 Sawy. (U. S.) 498, it was held that a conveyance of real estate by an attorney was not authorized by a general power to superintend and manage the property.

In Barbour *v.* Skyes (Ky. 1886), 1 S. W. Rep. 600, it appeared that power was given to sell and convey land, to change the mortgages upon it, or, upon payment of certain portions of the mortgage debts, to execute new notes for the residue. The attorney gave a note to one, who as surety on one of the mortgage debts, was compelled to make a payment. It was held that the power of attorney authorized this.

The heirs of a vendee, who had a contract for land, of which he died in possession, after paying the price, executed a power reciting that they were seised of certain land and authorizing their attorney to sell the land whereof they were seised as aforesaid. *Held,* that this power did not authorize the sale of the land held under the contract. Lord *v.* Underdunck, 1 Sandf. Ch. (N. Y.) 46.

Authority to assign a judgment can be conferred by power of attorney. Caley *v.* Morgan, 114 Ind. 350.

A power of attorney given in 1869, authorizing the making and giving of a promissory note, does not authorize a payment of one dollar on the note in 1881, to toll limitation. Miller *v.* Magee (Supreme Ct.), 2 N. Y. Supp. 156.

A power of attorney authorizing the attorneys to "buy, sell or exchange property, to receive and receipt for money, to sell and dispose of property, to give bills of sale thereto, or to sell and transfer real estate, and execute deeds thereto, or to do and perform any lawful act in or about or concerning my (the principal's) business, as fully and completely as if I were personally present," does not authorize the attorneys to execute an assignment of the principal's property for the benefit of his creditors. Gouldy *v.* Metcalf, 75 Tex. 455.

A power of attorney authorizing the donee therein named to collect all mon-

One who deals with an attorney or agent with knowledge that there is a written power of attorney, is bound to take notice of the limitations therein contained, and, failing to do so, must himself bear a resulting loss, rather than the principal giving the power.[1] Such third person, however, is not to be prejudiced by private instructions given to the agent or the principal, and limiting the apparent authority conferred by the power, if the power itself fails to indicate the likelihood of such a limitation.[2]

eys due or to become due his principal on "rents, accounts, bonds and mortgages, or otherwise," and to do all business with a particular bank named in the power, in his principal's name, which the principal could do were he present, gives the attorney no authority to draw money of his principal from another bank. Sims *v.* United States Trust Co., 103 N. Y. 472.

A conveyance of the interest of a deceased partner, in land held by the members of the firm as co-tenants, is not authorized under letters of attorney by his heirs giving power to the surviving partner "to settle all matters growing out of the firm business, to settle up and divide his estate, and to do all acts necessary to accomplish that end." Southern Cotton Oil Co. *v.* Henshaw, 89 Ala. 448.

A power of attorney by which a member of a firm authorizes a co-partner "to bargain and agree for, buy, sell, mortgage, hypothecate, and in any and every way and manner deal in and with, goods, wares and merchandise, choses in action and other property in possession or in action," authorizes such attorney to represent his principal in an assignment of the firm's property for the benefit of its creditors. Paul *v.* Cullum, 132 U. S. 539.

A power of attorney by the owner of land, appointing the attorney to "protect all his interests in and title to the land," is sufficient authority for the attorney to redeem the land for the owner from the purchaser thereof at a sale for delinquent taxes. Townshend *v.* Shaffer, 30 W. Va. 176.

In a power of attorney, authorizing the attorney to "sell, grant, and convey . . all and any land which I may own in," etc., and to "release and discharge forever all mortgages upon all and any real estate which I may have and hold in," etc., the words quoted include not only lands owned and mortgages held by the principal at the time when the power was executed, but also all lands and mortgages subsequently acquired by him before revocation of such power of attorney. Bigelow *v.* Livingston, 28 Minn. 57.

A conveyance of the interest of a deceased partner, in land held by the members of the firm as co-tenants, is not authorized under letters of attorney by his heirs giving power to the surviving partner "to settle all matters growing out of the firm business, to settle up and divide his estate, and to do all acts necessary to accomplish that end." Southern Cotton Oil Co. *v.* Henshaw, 89 Ala. 448.

And see, for additional illustrations of the construction of powers of attorney, Benschoter *v.* Lalk, 24 Neb. 251; Dayton *v.* Nell, 43 Minn. 246.

1. Towle *v.* Leavitt, 23 N. H. 360; 55 Am. Dec. 195; Schimmelpennich *v.* Bayard, 1 Pet. (U. S.) 264; Attwood *v.* Munnings, 7 Barn. & C. 278; De Bouchout *v.* Goldsmid, 5 Ves. 213; Weise's Appeal, 72 Pa. St. 351; Equitable, L. etc. Soc. *v.* Poe, 53 Md. 28; Stagg *v.* Elliott, 12 C. B., N. S. 373; Withington *v.* Herring, 5 Bing. 442; Andrews *v.* Kneeland, 6 Cow. (N. Y.) 354; Rossiter *v.* Rossiter, 8 Wend. (N. Y.) 498. And such was the rule of the civil law. See De Bouchout *v.* Goldsmid, 5 Ves. 213; Schimmelpennich *v.* Bayard, 1 Pet. (U. S.) 264.

2. Fenn *v.* Harrison, 3 T. R. 757; 4 T. R. 177; Whitehead *v.* Tuckett, 15 East 400; Wilson *v.* Hart, 7 Taunt. 295; Bryant *v.* Moore, 26 Me. 84; 45 Am. Dec. 96; Munn *v.* Commission Co., 15 Johns. (N. Y.) 44; 8 Am. Dec. 219; Hildebrant *v.* Crawford, 6 Lans. (N. Y.) 502; Rossiter *v.* Rossiter, 8 Wend. (N. Y.) 498; Rourke *v.* Story, 4 E. D. Smith (N. Y.) 54; Anderson *v.* State, 22 Ohio St. 305; Adams Min. Co. *v.* Senter, 26 Mich. 73; Planters' Bank *v.* Merritt, 7 Heisk. (Tenn.) 177; Johnson *v.* Jones, 4 Barb. (N. Y.) 369; Bryant *v.* Moore, 26 Me. 84; 45 Am. Dec. 96; Earp *v.* Richardson, 81 N. Car. 5; Silliman *v.* Fredericksburg etc. R. Co., 27

While the general rule precluding parol evidence to vary or control the terms of a written instrument is applied to powers of attorney as to other written instruments, this rule is not so to be applied as to exclude evidence tending to show the assent of the principal to an expansion of the authority beyond that apparent from the original terms of the writing.[1]

POWER OF SALE MORTGAGES.—See TRUST DEEDS.

POWERS.—(See also AGENCY, vol. 1, p. 331; POWER OF ATTORNEY.)

Gratt. (Va.) 119; Rafferty *v.* Haldron, 81* Pa. St. 438; Allen *v.* Ogden, 1 Wash. (U. S.) 174; Gibson *v.* Colt, 7 Johns. (N. Y.) 393.

See, however, Peters *v.* Ballistier, 3 Pick. (Mass.) 495, as to the duty of one dealing with an agent to make inquiry in the circumstances. And see Longworth *v.* Conwell, 2 Blackf. (Ind.) 469; Tomlinson *v.* Collett, 3 Blackf. (Ind.) 436; Walker *v.* Skipwith, Meigs. (Tenn.) 502; 33 Am. Dec. 161; Stewart *v.* Woodward, 50 Vt. 78.

A leading case, and one which has been discussed and cited by various courts, is that of North River Bank *v.* Aymar, 3 Hill (N. Y.) 252. Here, the letter of attorney gives authority to draw and indorse notes in the name of his principal and for his benefit. The power was deposited with the bank through which it was supposed that some of the business would be done. Notes and indorsements were made, all of which purported on their face to have been executed for the principal in conformity to and in pursuance of the letter of attorney. In fact, however, the notes had no connection with the business of the principal, but were given for the accommodation of third persons, who indorsed them through the bank, which received them in the legal course of business, without notice and for a valuable consideration. It was held, in the action of the bank against the principal, that he was liable on the notes and indorsements, though as between himself and his attorney they were unauthorized and fraudulent. In this case there was a dissenting opinion, and the decision was reversed by the court of errors, but without an opinion, and, notwithstanding the reversal, the case is deemed of authority both in New York and elsewhere. See Farmers' etc. Bank *v.* Butchers' etc. Bank, 16 N Y. 125; Merchants' Bank *v.* Griswold, 72 N. Y. 472; Westfield Bank *v.* Cornen, 37 N. Y. 320; 93 Am. Dec. 573; Griswold *v.* Haven, 25 N. Y. 595; 82 Am. Dec. 380; Exchange Bank *v.* Monteath, 26 N. Y. 505; New York State Bank *v.* Ohio Bank, 29 N. Y. 619. There is an English case which has been thought to give color to the idea that the appointee must look behind the power; viz. Attwood *v.* Munnings, 1 M. & R. 66; 7 Barn & C. 278. But in this case the power involved was extremely limited, being tied up to the acceptance of bills particularly described, and it is thought by Cowen, J., who delivered the opinion of the court in North River Bank *v.* Aymar, 3 Hill (N. Y.) 252, that the English case is not irreconcilable with the general current of authority.

In New York etc. R. Co. *v.* Schuyler, 34 N. Y. 30, the rule was formulated by the court of appeals as follows: "When the authority of an agent depends upon some fact outside the terms of his power, and which, from its nature, rests peculiarly within his knowledge, the principal is bound by the representations of the agent, although false as to the existence of such fact."

1. In Story on Agency, §§ 79, 80, the

I. DEFINITION—1. In General.—In general, a power is a liberty or authority reserved by or limited to a party to dispose of real or personal property for his own benefit or the benefit of others.[1]

illustration of this principle given is the case of a written power given to buy goods at a limited price, which may be expanded orally so as to authorize a purchase at a greater price, *citing* Hartford F. Ins. Co. *v.* Wilcox, 57 Ill. 182; Williams *v.* Cochran, 7 Rich. (S. Car.) 45.

See PAROL EVIDENCE, vol. 17, p. 419.

1. 1 Chance on Powers 1; Burleigh *v.* Clough, 52 N. H. 267; 15 Am. Rep. 23. See also 1 Perry on Trusts, § 248.

Mr. Wharton defines a power as an authority retained by, or conferred upon, a person to deal with property, so as to affect more or less estates or interests therein, possessed either by himself or others, albeit underived therefrom. Wharton's Conv. 419.

An authority as distinguished from an estate. 1 Steph. Comm. 505.

In its broadest sense it is the authority given to one person by another to act for him.[1]

2. Under Statute of Uses.—In a more limited and technical sense powers are, in effect, future uses.[2] Powers of this class are, strictly speaking, declarations of trust and modifications of future uses. Such a power is an authority to do some act in relation to lands, the creation of estates therein, or of charges thereon, which the owner granting or reserving such power might himself lawfully perform.[3]

An authority expressly reserved to a grantor, or expressly given to another, to be exercised over lands, etc., granted or conveyed at the time of the creation of the power. Watkyns on Conv. 157.

A right to limit a use. 4 Kent's Comm. 316.

A power is, in a general sense of the word, common in jurisprudence, any authority which one gives to another to act for him; as in speaking of the powers of an agent, or of a corporation, of a power of attorney, etc. In a more technical sense, in conveyancing, it signifies an authority vested in one person to dispose of an estate which is vested in another. Abbott's Law Dict.

Anderson defines a power to be an authority conferred upon one person to dispose of an estate vested in another. Anderson's Law Dict.

"A power, in the legal sense of the word, is an authority which enables one person to do an act for another, and it is to be distinguished both from a trust and an interest." 2 Crabbe Real Prop. 678.

A power is an authority which one person gives to another to act for him, or to do certain acts, as to make leases, raise portions or the like; also to modify the use of an estate of which he has the disposal. It is an authority enabling one person to dispose of an interest which is vested in another. Whart. Law Lexicon.

1. Anderson's Law Dict.

Powers are either common law authorities, declarations or directions, operating on the conscience of the person in whom the legal interest is vested, or declarations or directions deriving their effect from the Statute of Uses.

A power given to an executor to sell an estate, where no estate is devised to him, and a power given by legislative act to sell estates, are both common law authorities; so is a power of attorney.

A power to dispose of an estate or sum of money of which the legal estate is vested in another, is a power of the second sort. The legal interest is not divested by the execution of the power, but equity will compel the person seised of it to clothe the estate created with the legal right. Wharton Law Lexicon; Abbott's Law Dict.

See AGENCY, vol. 1, p. 331; POWER OF ATTORNEY.

2. Intr. to Sugden on Powers 13; and the execution of a power confers only a use. Intr. to Sugden on Powers 14; Cornish, Uses 89.

3. 4 Kent's Comm. 315; 1 Chance on Pow. 13; 1 Sugden Pow. 81, 82; Sir Edward Clere's Case, 6 Co. 17 b; Taylor *v.* Horde, 1 Burr. 60; Harrison *v.* Battle, 1 Dev. & B. Eq. (N. Car.) 213.

A provision in a conveyance under the Statute of Uses, giving to the grantor or grantee, or to a stranger, authority to revoke or alter by a subsequent act, the estate first granted. 1 Steph. Comm. 505. Also an authority to revoke a use first limited or to declare a new one. 1 Steph. Comm. 505.

A power, technically speaking, is not an estate, but is a mere authority, enabling a person, through the medium of the Statute of Uses, to dispose of an interest in real property, vested either in himself or in another person. Burleigh *v.* Clough, 52 N. H. 267.

Bouvier defines a power of this class to be an authority enabling a person, through the medium of the Statute of Uses, to dispose of an interest in land, vested either in himself or another person. 2 Bouv. Inst. 335.

Powers are "methods of causing a use with its accompanying estate to spring up at the will of a given person." Bouvier's Law Dict., Powers; Williams' Real Prop. 24; 2 Washb. Real Prop. 300 (4th ed.) 635.

3. Names of Parties.—The party creating or conferring the power is usually called the donor; the party upon whom it is conferred and who is to execute it, the donee or appointor, and the party in whose favor it is executed the appointee.[1]

In the *New York* statute the term "grantor of a power" is used to designate the person by whom a power is created, whether by grant or devise, the term "grantee of a power" to designate the person in whom a power is vested, whether by grant, devise

"The right to designate a person who is to take a use." "A right to limit a use." Bouvier's Law Dict.; 4 Kent's Comm. 316.

"Methods of causing a use, with its accompanying estate, to spring up at the will of a given person." Anderson's Law Dict., *citing* Williams' Real Prop. 245.

"A mere right to limit a use." Anderson's Law Dict., *citing* 4 Kent 334.

The limitation and modifying of estates by virtue of powers came from equity into the common law with the Statute of Uses. The intent of the party who created the power should govern the construction of them. They will not be exceeded nor their conditions evaded, but will be strictly pursued in form and substance. All acts done under a special authority, not in conformity with such authority or warranted by it, are void. Taylor *v.* Howe, 1 Burr. 60.

Mr. Washburne, in his work on Real Property, speaking of shifting and springing uses, says: "Or it might be so limited that the grantor might reserve to himself or a stranger a right, at a future time, to revoke the use which he then declared, and to limit and declare new uses in favor of other persons, which became the origin of the present doctrine of powers." 2 Washb. Real Prop. (4th ed.) 398, 635.

As a power under the Statute of Uses operates not as a conveyance of the land itself, but as a creation or substitution of a use to which the statute annexes the seisin, it is necessary when creating a power to raise or create a seisin in some one which shall be ready to serve the use when created by such appointment; and the seisin must be commensurate with the estates authorized to be created under the power. 2 Washb. Real Prop. *319; Lord *v.* Underdunck, 1 Sandf. Ch. (N. Y.) 46. *Compare* 4 Kent's Comm. *323, *328.

But no seisin is necessary to serve the power conferred on an executor to sell land. Rodgers *v.* Wallace, 5 Jones (N. Car.) 181.

The right to make the designation is termed a "Power of Appointment"; the exercise of it is termed an "Appointment"; and the person in whose favor the appointment is made is termed the "Appointee." 2 Washb. Real Prop. (4th ed.) 637 (*302).

Powers under the Statute of Uses are to be construed as liberally at law as in equity.

Zouch *v.* Woolston, 2 Burr. 1136; 1 Wm. Bl. 281.

Under New York Statute.—Under the statutes of New York, Michigan, Wisconsin, Minnesota and Dakota, a power is defined to be an authority to do some act in relation to lands, or the creation of estates therein, or of charges thereon, which the owner granting or reserving such power might himself lawfully perform.

4 *New York* Rev. Stat., § 74 (Banks' ed.), p. 2446; (1882) p. 2188. Jennings *v.* Conboy, 73 N. Y. 230; Delaney *v.* McCormack, 88 N. Y. 174; Blanchard *v.* Blanchard, 6 Thomp. & C. (N. Y.) 551; 4 Hun (N. Y.) 287; affd. 70 N. Y. 615; Tucker *v.* Tucker, 5 N. Y. 413; Belmont *v.* O'Brien, 12 N. Y. 394; Kinnier *v.* Rogers, 42 N. Y. 534; Smith *v.* Bowen, 35 N. Y. 89; Ocean Bank *v.* Olcott, 46 N. Y. 12; Bailey *v.* Bailey, 28 Hun (N. Y.) 610; Leonard *v.* American Bapt. H. M. Soc., 35 Hun (N. Y.) 293; Fish *v.* Cosler, 28 Hun (N. Y.) 66; Ludlow *v.* Van Ness, 8 Bosw. (N. Y.) 192; Fellows *v.* Heermans, 4 Lans. (N. Y.) 238; Hotchkiss *v.* Elting, 36 Barb. (N. Y.) 46; Hetzell *v.* Easterly, 66 Barb. (N. Y.) 443; Dumpsey *v.* Tylee, 3 Duer (N. Y.) 97; Selden *v.* Vermilyes, 1 Barb. (N. Y.) 62.

See Henly *v.* Fitzgerald, 65 Barb. (N. Y.) 510, for an instance of a power not created within the meaning of the statute.

1. 4 Kent's Comm. *316; 2 Washb. Real. Prop. *302.

or reservation.[1] No person is capable of granting a power who is not capable of aliening some interest in the land to which the power relates.[2]

II. Nature and Origin—1. In General; Under Statute of Uses.—A power is not an estate, and has none of the elements of an estate; it is a mere authority.[3] While powers existed to a limited extent at common law, they owed their importance to, and derived their effect from the equitable doctrine of uses and the Statute of Uses.[4]

Powers, before the Statute of Uses, were mere directions to the trustee of the legal estate how to convey the estate. They were future uses to be designated by the person to whom the power was given. After the statute they still remained as mere rights of designation which bound the conscience of the trustee, and the estates to be created by force of them were still future or contingent uses.[5]

Where the donor makes a direct grant, devise, or gift to one party, subject to a power of appointment by some other party, whether holding a prior estate or having no interest in the property, the grantee or devisee takes a vested interest subject to be devested by the exercise of the power.[6]

1. 4 *New York* Rev. Stat., § 135 (Banks' ed.), p. 2451; (1882) p. 2194; Barber *v.* Carey, 11 N. Y. 397; Van Boskerck *v.* Herrick, 65 Barb. (N. Y.) 258.

2. 4 New York Rev. Stat., § 75 (Banks' ed.), p. 2446; (1882) p. 2188; Ludlow *v.* Van Ness, 8 Bosw. (N. Y.) 192; Dempsey *v.* Tylee, 3 Duer (N. Y.) 97.

Unless executors have power to receive the rents and profits of land, they take no title thereto. Chipman *v.* Montgomery, 4 Hun (N. Y.) 744.

3. 1 Steph. Comm. 229; Goodill *v.* Brigham, 1 Bro. & Pul. 197; Eaton *v.* Straw, 18 N. H. 331; Burleigh *v.* Clough, 52 N. H. 267; 13 Am. Rep. 23; Rodgers *v.* Wallace, 5 Jones (N. Car.) 181.

No seisin is necessary to serve the power, and no adverse possession short of the time fixed by the Statute of Limitations will stand in the way of its execution. Rodgers *v.* Wallace, 5 Jones (N. Car.) 181.

Where a power of sale is given to executors by a will unaccompanied by a devise to them, until the power is executed, the legal title descends to and vests in the heirs. Todd *v.* Wortman, 45 N. J. Eq. 723; Reed *v.* Underhill, 12 Barb. (N. Y.) 113.

4. 4 Kent's Comm. *315; 1 Chance Pow. 5, 13; Intr. to Sugden on Powers 13; 1 Sugden on Powers 73, 81; 3 Washb. Real Prop. *300; Williams, Real Prop. 245; Hunt *v.* Rousmanier, 8 Wheat. (U. S.) 174.

5. 1 Sugd. Pow. (3rd Am. ed.) 82, * 11. "When a power was executed, as the person in whose favor the appointment was made became invested with the use, he instantly gained the legal estate by force of the statute." 1 Sugd. Pow. (3rd Am. ed.) 82, * 11. As stated by Mr. Washburne, it is not that the donee of the power conveys any estate in, or acts directly upon the possession of the land. "His is a mere power, which operates, when exercised in the form prescribed, as a limitation of use in favor of the one he may name; and then the statute at once unites the seisin with the use, the appointee executing it, and thereby perfecting his estate." 2 Washb. Real Prop. (4th ed.) 637.

6. 1 Perry on Trusts, § 250; Carson *v.* Carson, Phil. Eq. (N. Car.) 57; Rhett *v.* Mason, 18 Gratt. (Va.) 541. See Harrison *v.* Battle, 1 Dev. & B. Eq. (N. Car.) 213. And the exercise of the power defeats the inchoate right of dower which has attached. 2 Sugd. Pow. 31; 2 Sugd. Pow. (4th ed.) 479, § 3. But see 2 Sugd. Pow. 480, § 4.

On failure of the power, the grantee or devisee becomes as absolutely en-

A power operates upon an estate or interests vested either in the donee or in some other person.[1] The liberty or authority reserved or limited by the instrument creating the power is not derived out of the estate, but overreaches or supersedes it, either wholly or partially.[2]

While powers sometimes assume the shape of remainders, they have not generally been considered in that light, so as to be subject to the rules relating to contingent remainders.[3]

While a power may possess the qualities of a trust, and will then be considered a trust, ordinarily there is a marked distinction between the two. Powers are not imperative, and may or may not be executed at the will of the donee; if not executed, they fail, and equity will not enforce them. As to trusts the converse is true.[4]

The distinction between an executory use and a power is that, in the former case, the use arises from an event provided for by the deed; in the latter from the act of some agent or person nominated in the deed.[5]

2. Under Local Statutes.—The Revised Statutes of *New York* have dealt with the subject of powers, and the legislation of that State has been followed substantially in *Michigan*, *Wisconsin*, *Minnesota*, and *Dakota*.[6] The changes made by these statutes are not, however, very radical nor considerable, the intention being, in most instances, to simplify and declare the law.[7]

titled to the estate as if the power had never been raised. 1 Perry on Trusts, § 250.

If the donor limits a fund "upon trust for the children of A as B shall appoint, all the children of A take a vested interest,' liable to be divested as to such as are not selected by B. 1 Perry on Trusts, § 250.

It is held in Wickersham *v.* Savage, 58 Pa. St. 365, that the estate could not be divested by the donee, and that his only power was that of apportioning it among the children.

1. 1 Chance Pow. [1.]

2. 1 Chance Pow. [1.]

3. 1 Chance Pow. [20.]

4. 2 Bouv. Inst. 335; 1 Sugden Pow. *158; 2 Washb. Real Prop. 325; 2 Story Eq. Jur., § 1062; 1 Perry on Trusts 250–253; Neves *v.* Scott, 9 How. (U. S.) 196; Sedgwick *v.* Laflin, 10 Allen (Mass.) 432; Gorin *v.* Gordon, 38 Miss. 214.

Powers are never imperative; they leave the act to be done at the will of the party to whom they are given. Trusts are always imperative and are obligatory upon the conscience of the party intrusted. Attorney Gen'l *v.* Downing, Wilm. 1, 23.

In Barnum *v.* Barnum, 26 Md. 172, the court by Weisel, J., said: "If the trust be void, then the power to lease, which is blended with it, as in this case, must be void also. It is not a mere power, distinct from the trust, leaving the act to be done at the will of the party to whom it is given, but it is mixed and blended with the trust, and its execution is as imperative as the trust itself. This distinction is well marked and to be observed. In this case the power is the trust, and the trust is the power. They cannot be separated."

5. 2 Washb. Real Prop. *302, *325; 4 Kent's Comm, *335; Holmes *v.* Coghill, 7 Ves. 506.

6. The substance of this legislation can be seen in Stimson's St. Law, §§ 1650-1659.

7. In relation to the provisions of the New York statutes relating to the execution of powers, Chancellor Kent said: "While many of the provisions are merely declaratory of the existing law, there are others which have rescued this part of the law from much obscurity and uncertainty."

In Dominick *v.* Sayre, 3 Sandf. (N. Y.) 555, Duer, J., says, in reference

Under the statutes of the States aforesaid, a beneficial power is one, whether general or special, in which no person other than the grantee has, by the terms of its creation, any interest in its execution.[1] A power is in trust when a person other than the grantee is entitled to the benefits thereof.[2]

to certain provisions of these statutes: "That they were regarded by the revisers as simply declaratory, we think is fairly to be collected from the language of their notes, and upon a careful examination of the cases, we are satisfied that such is their true character." And see Delaney *v.* McCormack, 88 N. Y. 174.

1. *New York* Rev. Stat. §§ 79–92 (Banks' ed.), p. 2446, 2447; (1882) p. 2189, 2190; Stimson's St. Law, § 1651. See Freeborn *v.* Wagner, 49 Barb. (N. Y.) 54; Bailey *v.* Bailey, 28 Hun (N. Y.) 610; Leonard *v.* American Bapt. H. M. Soc.; 35 Hun (N. Y.) 293; Syracuse Sav. Bank *v.* Porter, 36 Hun (N. Y.) 170; Root *v.* Stuyvesant, 18 Wend. (N. Y.) 270, Jackson *v.* Edwards, 7 Paige (N. Y.) 400, affd. 22 Wend. (N. Y.) 508; Marvin *v.* Smith, 56 Barb. (N. Y.) 606; Barber *v.* Cary, 11 N. Y. 402; Russell *v.* Russell, 36 N. Y. 583; Ackerman *v.* Gorton, 67 N. Y. 96.

By the New York statute it was intended to make the power beneficial both when by its terms the donee was solely interested in its execution, and when it was silent as to the beneficiary. Jennings *v.* Conboy, 73 N. Y. 230; Coleman *v.* Beach, 97 N. Y. 545. Section 92 provides that no beneficial power "other than such as are already enumerated and defined in this article," shall be valid. The word "enumerated" is not to be read literally as limiting beneficial powers to those specifically held in the previous section, but is to be considered as used in the sense of "mentioned," "indicated," "referred to" or "authorized." Cutting *v.* Cutting, 20 Hun (N. Y.) 360. See Salmon *v.* Stuyvesant, 16 Wend. (N. Y.) 324.

A power authorizing a person named to appoint by will to whom real estate the property of the donor of the power should be conveyed, is a general beneficial power within the meaning of this section. Cutting *v.* Cutting, 20 Hun (N. Y.) 360; and on this point the case is affirmed by the court of appeals. The facts of the case were that G, by her will gave certain estate, real and personal, to her executor in trust, to take the rents and profits during the life of F, her son, and apply them to his use, and upon his decease to make over the body of the estate to whomever such son by his will might appoint to receive it. F made an appointment as prescribed. It was held that the will created a valid general and beneficial power within the provisions of the statutes, and that the estate was not chargeable after the death of F, with a judgment obtained against him in his lifetime. Cutting *v.* Cutting, 86 N. Y. 522.

Where the absolute power of disposition is given to executors, no other person has an interest in its execution and it is unaccompanied by a trust; it is a beneficial power in them, and they take an absolute fee. Kinnier *v.* Rogers, 42 N. Y. 534.

The fact that the donee of a mere naked power is entitled to compensation for his services does not give him a beneficial interest. McDonough *v.* Loughlin, 20 Barb. (N. Y.) 244.

2. New York Rev. Stat., §§ 94–5 (Banks' ed.), pp. 2446–7; Jennings *v.* Conboy, 73 N. Y. 230; Delaney *v.* McCormack, 88 N. Y. 174; Kinnier *v.* Rogers, 42 N. Y. 531; Moncrief *v.* Ross, 50 N. Y. 435; Smith *v.* Bowen, 35 N. Y. 89; Bruner *v.* Meigs, 64 N. Y. 506; Hetzel *v.* Barber, 6 Hun (N. Y.) 534; 69 N. Y. 7; Russell *v.* Russell, 36 N. Y. 583; Fish *v.* Coster, 28 Hun (N. Y.) 86; affd. 92 N. Y. 627; Bailey *v.* Bailey, 28 Hun (N. Y.) 611; Syracuse Sav. Bank *v.* Porter, 36 Hun (N. Y.) 170; Fellows *v.* Heermans, 4 Lans. (N. Y.) 230; Hutchings *v.* Baldwin, 7 Bosw. (N. Y.) 241; Arnold *v.* Gilbert, 5 Barb. (N. Y.) 190; Wright *v.* Delafield, 23 Barb. (N. Y.) 517; Smith *v.* Gage, 41 Barb. (N. Y.) 69; Quinn *v.* Skinner, 49 Barb. (N. Y.) 135; Crocheron *v.* Jaques, 3 Edw. Ch. (N. Y.) 207; Dominick *v.* Dayre, 3 Sandf. (N. Y.) 559.

"These provisions show that in all cases of a power in trust, an appointee or beneficiary other than the grantee of the power is contemplated. It is as necessary an ingredient in the case of a power in trust as a *cestui que trust* is in the case of a conveyance or devise in trust." Farmers' L. & T. Co. *v.* Carroll, 5 Barb. (N. Y.) 652.

In Belmont *v.* O'Brien, 12 N. Y. 403, the court by Hand, J., said: "There are powers unconnected with trusts, and powers in the nature of trusts. Most or all of the latter are by statute now denominated powers in trust; between which and a trust, or an estate held in trust, the statute recognizes an obvious distinction; although some of the trusts specified in section 55 are more properly mere powers in trust." And it was held that where a sale is directed in the instrument creating the trust, such sale is not in contravention of the trust.

In Marvin *v.* Smith, 56 Barb. (N. Y.) 600, the court, by Talcott, J., *citing* the Belmont case, makes the following comment: "Although the power in that case was to sell and re-invest upon the same trusts, and in this case there is no specific direction to apply the proceeds of the sale or mortgage to the same trusts, yet the argument of the opinion in that case, I think, satisfactorily shows, if argument were needed, that a trust, and a power to terminate it, contingent or otherwise, may exist together where they are not inconsistent. The decision was approved by the Court of Appeals, 46 N. Y. 571.

In Wainwright *v.* Low, 57 Hun (N. Y.) 386, land was conveyed to a trustee to receive the rents and profits, or to permit the grantor to hold and use the same at her election, and at her death to convey it to such person as she should appoint by deed or will. Though the deed was void as attempting to create a passive trust, which is abrogated by statute (1 New York Rev. St., p. 727, § 45, and p. 728, § 55), it was valid as a power in trust, under section 58, which provides that if a trust, which is void because not enumerated in the preceding section, directs the performance of an act which may be lawfully performed under a power, it shall be valid as a power in trust, since the dormant power to convey might become active under a proper appointment by the grantor.

Section 56 (3 *New York* Rev. St. 7th ed., p. 2181) provides that "a devise of lands to executors or other trustees to be sold or mortgaged, where the trustees are not also empowered to receive the rents and profits, shall vest no estate in the trustees, but the trust shall be valid as a power, and the land shall descend to the heirs or pass to the devisees of the testator, subject to the execution of the power." A testatrix devised all her land to her executors in trust for the "purposes hereinafter named." By a subsequent clause she gave certain parcels to two nieces for life, remainder over. Finally the will empowered the executors to sell the property whenever in their judgment they should deem it best, and invest the proceeds, and pay the income to the two nieces, and "upon the death of either to pay her share of the principal" as "above directed." It was held that under the provisions of the above section, the executors took a power in trust. Delafield *v.* White, 19 Abb. N. Cas. (N. Y.) 104.

If after the termination of the estate legally vested in trustees, by a will, there remain unexecuted valid powers in trust, which would not of themselves have authorized the creation of a trust estate, under the provisions of the Revised Statutes, they may still be executed by the trustees, as powers in trust. Hawley *v.* James, 5 Paige (N. Y.) 318.

A deed between E of the first part and C of the second part, in trust for three infant children of C, "with power to sell and convey or mortgage without the appointment of a guardian," conveyed certain premises to the party of the second part, "their heirs and assigns, forever." There was no other reference to a trust or power than that contained in the first clause. The three infants were held to be the real beneficiaries of the grant, and the land passed to and vested in them (1 New York Rev. St. 728, §§ 47, 49), subject to the execution of the power, which was a general trust power to be executed solely for their benefit. Therefore a mortgage on the land given by C to secure a debt of her husband was not a valid execution of the power and was void. Syracuse Sav. Bank *v.* Holden, 105 N. Y. 415.

The receiver of a bank, of which plaintiff and ten others were trustees, sued them for waste of the bank's funds. In settlement thereof a contract was entered into by which the trustees undertook to pay a percentage of the bank's liabilities, and the receiver transferred to one designated by a majority of them certain real estate of the bank, which they agreed to sell, reimburse themselves out of the proceeds, and return the surplus to the receiver. A conveyance reciting the

III. Classification — 1. Appendant or Collateral.—Powers are either, first, appendant or appurtenant; second, collateral or in gross; or third, simply collateral.[1] Thus, they are either given to a person who has an estate limited to him by the deed creating the power, or who had an estate in the land at the time of the execution of the deed; or to a stranger to whom no estate is given, the power to be exercised for his own benefit; or to a stranger to whom no estate is given, the power being for the benefit of others.[2]

contract was executed to him. Three days thereafter, plaintiff executed an instrument declaring his associates to be equally interested with him in all the benefits from the conveyance. The court of appeals held that the agreement did not create an express trust to sell land for the benefit of creditors, but that, inasmuch as plaintiff's associates joined with him in the contract, and had selected him in the grantee, the conveyance would be deemed a power in trust, within the provision of 1 *New York* Rev. St., p. 729, § 58, that "where an express trust shall be created for any purpose" not thereinbefore enumerated, "no estate shall vest in the trustees, but the trust, if directing or authorizing the performance of any act which may be lawfully performed under a power, shall be valid as a power in trust," and that an exchange of the land for other real estate was not within the purpose of the power taken by plaintiff. Woerz *v.* Rademacher, 120 N. Y. 62.

1. 4 Kent's Comm. *317; 2 Washb. Real Prop. *305; 4 Greenl. Cruise Dig. *134.

This classification is important only with reference to the ability of the donee to suspend, extinguish, or merge the power. 4 Kent's Comm. *317; 1 Sugden Pow. *44 (110); 2 Washb. Real Prop. *307. *Compare* 1 Chance Pow. [26].

2. 1 Sugden Powers (3rd Am. ed.), 106, *40.

The first two classes may be either "appendant or appurtenant," or "collateral or in gross;" the latter class is "in gross," or simply collateral. 1 Sugden Powers (3rd Am. ed.), 107, *40; 1 Chance 25. But Cruise defines a power simply collateral so as to include the second and third classes. 4 Greenl. Cruise Dig. 184, *136.

The last class mentioned by Sugden cannot be extinguished. 1 Chance [26] [3105]; 2 Washb. Real Prop. *307; 4 Kent's Comm. *346; Norris *v.* Thomson, 19 N. J. Eq. 307.

Chance says all powers are either "appendant" or "collateral." 1 Chance [34].

Cruise divides powers into those which relate to the land, and those which are collateral to it, subdividing the former into powers appendant and in gross. 4 Greenl. Cruise Dig. 182, *134.

A power, though appendant to an estate, is not so appendant that it goes with the estate in every transfer made by the trustee, or in every devolution by course of law. 2 Perry on Trusts, § 503, and cases cited in note (3).

Sir Edward Sugden gives the following fuller distinctions: "Powers appendant or appurtenant are so termed because they strictly depend upon the estate limited to the person to whom they are given." 1 Sugden, Pow. 107 (*40). See 1 Chance Pow. 37.

Every power, such as a power to lease, "which enables the party to create an estate which will attach on an interest actually vested in himself," is of this class. 1 Sugden Pow. 107 (*40).

Powers collateral, or in gross, are powers given to a person who

(*a*) Had an interest in the estate at the time of execution of the deed creating the power; or

(*b*) To whom an estate is given by such deed, the deed enabling him to create such estates only as will not attach on the interest limited to him. 1 Sugden, Pow. 107 (*41).

A power may also be given to a mere stranger, who has no estate in the land, and to whom none is given by the deed creating the power. This is simply collateral. 1 Sugden Pow. 107 (*40); 108 (*42).

Wharton defines collateral powers as those which are given to strangers, *i. e.*, to persons who have neither a present nor future estate or interest in the land. He says they are also called "simply collateral," or "powers not coupled

2. General or Special—*a.* INDEPENDENT OF STATUTES.—Powers are also divided into general powers, where the donee may appoint to whom he pleases; and special or particular powers, where the appointment is restricted to specific objects, or among particular objects only.[1]

with an interest," or "powers not being interests," to obviate the confusion arising from the circumstance that powers in gross have been by many called powers collateral. Whart. Law Lexicon; also Abbott's Law Dict.

Where a life interest or the estate is given to the person who is authorized to devise or appoint the property, this is a power in gross. Norris *v.* Thompson, 19 N. J. Eq. 307.

A power which is simply collateral cannot be conferred on a stranger to the consideration, except by a deed which operates as a transmutation of the possession. Taylor *v.* Eatman, 92 N. Car. 601.

A power of appointment annexed to an estate for life is not abridged or withdrawn by a subsequent direction in the will, that, in case the tenant for life, who is the donee of the power, shall marry, she and her husband shall give bond and security for the forthcoming and delivery of the property, at the termination of the life estate, "to be disposed of as before mentioned," there being no disposition before mentioned, other than that which the tenant for life was authorized to make by exercising the power. Neither the marriage of the tenant for life nor failure to give the bond and security after marriage operate to curtail the power. New *v.* Potts, 55 Ga. 420.

An estate in fee may be given to one in remainder and to the same person a power to appoint during the particular estate. Shearman *v.* Hicks, 14 Gratt. (Va.) 96. See also Crooke *v.* Kings Co., 97 N. Y. 421.

A devise to a widow for life with a remainder to her children, with power to dispose by will of the land devised to her children and their survivors, in such shares and in trust or otherwise as she may see fit, creates a power in gross. Thorington *v.* Thorington (Ala.), 1 So. Rep. 716.

A power may be given to executors to sell land which by another clause of the will is devised absolutely. The title vests in the devisee subject to the execution of the power.

Crittenden *v.* Fairchild, 41 N. Y. 289; to like effect, Todd *v.* Wortman, 45 N. J. Eq. 723. See Quin *v.* Skinner, 49 Barb. (N. Y.) 128; Reed *v.* Underhill, 12 Barb. (N. Y.) 113.

The existence of a power given by will does not prevent a limitation over to the heirs after a life estate, from taking effect; but if the power is executed, it defeats the estate given to the heirs.

Ward *v.* Amory, 1 Curt. (U. S.) 430. See Foos *v.* Scarf, 55 Md. 301.

When a mere power of appointment is given to a tenant for life, this gives no estate in the trust, if the power is not executed. Harrison *v.* Battle, 1 Dev. & B. Eq. (N. Car.) 213.

Where a testatrix, who owned an estate in reversion or remainder in certain land, subject to the life estate of her mother, by her will conferred upon her executor "full power to purchase and sell any property he may think necessary and proper," the executor was thereby authorized to sell, and vest in the purchaser, all the estate and interest of the testatrix in said land at the time of her death, but such conveyance would not confer a right of possession until the termination of the life estate. Hairston *v.* Dobbs, 80 Ala. 589.

1. 4 Kent's Comm. * 318; 2 Washb. Real Prop. *307.

Syracuse Sav. Bank *v.* Porter, 36 Hun (N. Y.) 168.

Bouvier states the distinction as follows: A general power of appointment is a power to appoint any person the donee thinks proper. This is a species of ownership. A particular limited or qualified power of appointment is where the donee is limited in the objects of his appointment—where he can appoint only among certain persons, or certain classes of persons. 2 Bouv. Inst. 1922. See also 4 Kent's Comm. * 328.

A general power of appointment is not strictly an ownership until the donee exercises the power in his own favor, especially if in default of the exercise there is a limitation over. 2 Bouv. Inst. 1922. See *infra*, this title, ***Principles Applicable to Powers in General.***

b. UNDER STATUTORY PROVISIONS.—Under the statute of *New York* a power is general which authorizes the alienation in fee by means of a conveyance, will, or charge of the lands embraced in the power to any alienee whatever. It is special where the persons or class of persons to whom the disposition of the lands under the power is to be made are designated; or where the power authorizes the alienation by means of a conveyance, will, or charge of a particular estate or interest less than a fee.[1]

3. Naked or Coupled With an Interest.—Where the right or authority to do the act is connected with or flows from an interest in the subject on which the power is to be exercised, the power is said to be coupled with an interest; but where it is disconnected from any interest of the donee in the subject-matter, it is a naked power.[2]

1. 4 *New York* Rev. Stat. §§ 77-8 (Banks' ed.), p. 2446; (1882) p. 2189; Barber *v.* Cary, 11 N. Y. 397, Jennings *v.* Conboy, 73 N. Y. 230; Delaney *v.* McCormack, 88 N. Y. 174; Coleman *v.* Beach, 97 N.Y. 545; Kinnier *v.* Rogers, 42 N. Y. 534; Russell *v.* Russell, 36 N. Y. 583; Hetzel *v.* Barber, 69 N. Y. 7; Farrar *v.* McCue, 89 N. Y. 139; Fish *v.* Coster, 28 Hun (N. Y.) 66; Bailey *v.* Bailey, 28 Hun (N. Y.) 610; Leonard *v.* American Bapt. H. M. Soc., 35 Hun (N. Y.) 293; Syracuse Sav. Bank *v.* Porter, 36 Hun (N. Y.) 170; *In re* Piffard, 42 Hun (N. Y.) 37; Fellows *v.* Heermans, 4 Lans. (N. Y.) 238; American Bible Soc. *v.* Stark, 45 How. Pr. (N. Y.) 166; Selden *v.* Vermilyea, 1 Barb. (N. Y.) 62; Smith *v.* Gage, 41 Barb. (N. Y.) 69; Jackson *v.* Edwards, 22 Wend. (N. Y.) 508.

A power to be executed absolutely for the donee's own benefit, at his own will, and not for the benefit of any other person whatever, is a general power. Crooke *v.* Kings Co., 97 N. Y. 421; Freeborn *v.* Wagner, 49 Barb. (N. Y.) 54.

"These definitions were established and well understood long before they were substantially adopted by our revised statutes." Talmage *v.* Sill, 21 Barb. (N. Y.) 52.

In a case decided by the superior court of the city of New York, it is said that an instrument did not confer a power within the meaning of these sections, because "no absolute power of disposition was given." Ludlow *v.* Van Ness, 8 Bosw. (N. Y.) 193.

A special power to dispose of by will within the meaning of the *Kentucky* statute, is a power which is specifically expressed, or is clearly and unequivocally manifested, of disposing by will of some particular estate. The following words in a conveyance by husband and wife to a trustee for the use of the wife, do not confer a special power: "To use, sell or exchange, or to re-invest or otherwise dispose of, the whole or any part of such property and effects, and the proceeds thereof in any manner she may see proper." Haris *v.* Harbeson, 9 Bush (Ky.) 397.

2. Washb. Real Prop. *316; 2 Bouv. Inst. 335, 1927; Hunt *v.* Rousmaniere, 2 Mason (U. S.) 244; on appeal, 8 Wheat. (U. S.) 174; Fontain *v.* Ravenel, 17 How. (U. S.) 369; Bloomer *v.* Waldson, 3 Hill (N. Y.) 361; Knapp *v.* Alvord, 10 Paige (N. Y.) 205; De Forest *v.* Bates, 1 Edw. Ch. (N. Y.) 394; Osgood *v.* Franklin, 2 Johns. Ch. (N. Y.) 1; Dorland *v.* Dorland, 2 Barb. (N. Y.) 63; Meakings *v.* Cromwell, 2 Sandf. (N. Y.) 512; Chamberlain *v.* Taylor, 105 N. Y. 185; Clark *v.* Horuthal, 47 Miss. 434; Wilburn *v.* Spofford, 4 Sneed (Tenn.) 698; Hope *v.* Johnson, 2 Yerg. (Tenn.) 123; Palton *v.* Crow, 26 Ala. 426; Stewart *v.* Stokes, 33 Ala. 494; Thompson *v.* Gaillard, 3 Rich. (S. Car.) 418; Haskell *v.* House, 3 Brev. (S. Car.) 242; Doe *v.* Lanius, 3 Ind. 441; Jameson *v.* Smith, 4 Bibb (Ky.) 307; Den *v.* Snowhill, 23 N. J. L. 447; Den *v.* Young, 23 N. J. L. 478; Guyer *v.* Maynard, 6 Gill & J. (Md.) 420; Dexter *v.* Sullivan, 34 N. H. 478; Rankin *v.* Rankin, 36 Ill. 293; 87 Am. Dec. 203; Shelton *v.* Horner, 5 Met. (Mass.) 462; Williams *v.* Veach, 17 Ohio 171; Allen *v.* Davis, 13 Ark. 28. See Huston *v.*

Cantril, 11 Leigh (Va.) 136; Landis *v.* Burk, 41 N. J. Eq. 664.

The interest must be an interest in the thing itself, not in the exercise of the power. Hunt *v.* Rousmaniere, 2 Mason (U. S.) 244; 8 Wheat. (U. S.) 204; Frink *v.* Roe, 70 Cal. 296; Mansfield *v.* Mansfield, 6 Conn. 562; Hartley's Appeal, 53 Pa. St. 212; Wilson *v.* Troup, 2 Cow. (N. Y.) 236; Bergen *v.* Bennett, 1 Cai. Cas. (N. Y.) 15; Coney *v.* Saunders, 28 Ga. 511; Daugherty *v.* Moon, 59 Tex. 397. See Hawley *v.* Smith, 45 Ind. 183. The interest need not be a present one; it may be one to arise in the future. 2 Bouv. Inst. 1927. It is not necessary that it should be a beneficial interest. 2 Bouv. Inst. 1927.

The use of the word "irrevocable" is not of itself evidence that the power is coupled with an interest. As is said by Mr. Justice Story, and quoted in MacGregor *v.* Gardiner, 14 Iowa 340: "The general rule is that the principal may revoke the authority of his agent at his pleasure. But this is open to some exceptions, which, however, are entirely consistent with the reason upon which the general rule is founded. One exception is when the principal has expressly stipulated that the authority shall be irrevocable and the agent has an interest in its execution. Both of these circumstances must concur. For, although in its terms an authority may be expressly declared to be irrevocable, yet if the agent has no interest in its execution, and there is no valid consideration for it, it is treated as a mere nude fact and is deemed in law to be revocable upon the general principle that he alone who has an interest in the execution of an act is also entitled to control it." Story on Agency, § 476. To same effect, Frink *v.* Roe, 70 Cal. 296.

In Hunt *v.* Rousmaniere, 2 Mason (U. S.) 250; the court by Mr. Justice Story, on this question of what constitutes a power coupled with an interest said: "But it is said that this was a power coupled with an interest because upon the face of the instruments the power is said to be given as collateral security for payment of the notes. The power may well be a naked power, and yet be given as collateral security. It is true, in such a case, it may not be effectual if the party die. But the same thing may happen if the property passes to a *bona fide* purchaser without notice before the execution of the power in the lifetime of the party. . . . I do not understand the terms "a power coupled with an interest" exactly in the same broad sense as they seem to be understood in the argument at the bar. The case of Bergen *v.* Bennett, 1 Cai. Cas. (N. Y.) 1, cited at the bar is certainly good law, and it will illustrate the distinction between naked powers and powers coupled with an interest. There the party mortgaged an estate as collateral security, and gave authority to the grantee to sell the estate absolutely. And the court held that this was a power coupled with an interest, and that the grantee might well sell the estate notwithstanding the death of the grantor. But if he did sell, in whose name was the deed to be made? Plainly, not in the name of the grantor, for he was dead; but in the name of the grantee, as his own act, in virtue of his power, and as having an interest in the estate conveyed. But suppose, instead of a mortgage of the estate, there had been a mere power of attorney authorizing the party to sell the land, and apply the proceeds to the payment of the debt, for which such power was given as collateral security. There the power would not be coupled with any estate in the land, but would be a mere naked power to sell, and could not be executed after the death of the grantor of the power. There is a difference between a power coupled with an interest in the property itself, and a mere interest or benefit in the execution of a power. If a man authorizes one as his attorney to sell his ship and apply the proceeds to the payment of a debt due to him, the latter may have an interest that the power should be executed; but the power is not coupled with any interest in the thing conveyed. It would be otherwise in case of a conditional assignment of the ship to one as collateral security with a power to make an absolute sale. Mr. Justice Kent lays down the distinction in very exact terms in the case of Bergen *v.* Bennett, 1 Cai. Cas. (N. Y.) 1 . . . A power, too, may be a naked power, and yet may be executed, nay, by its very terms must be executed, after the death of the party creating it. A power given by a testator in his will to his executors to sell his estate for payment of debts is a naked power; and it can only be executed after the death of the testator; and such execution will then be good, because the act may be done in the name of the executors, and not as the act of the testator. But a devise of the land itself to the executors to sell for a like purpose is a power coupled with an interest, for they have an interest or title in the land itself." See same case on appeal, 8 Wheat. (U. S.) 174. To same effect, Hawley *v.* Smith, 45 Ind. 183.

A power given the mortgagee to sell in case of default is a power coupled with an interest. Wilson *v.* Troup, 2 Cow. (N. Y.) 195; 14 Am. Dec. 458. And may be executed after the mortgagor's death. Varnum *v.* Meserve, 8 Allen (Mass.) 158; Bergh *v.* Bennett, 1 Cai. Cas. (N. Y.) 1.

But the law in *Georgia* is otherwise. Lockett *v.* Hill, 1 Wood (U. S.) 552; as also in *Texas;* Robertson *v.* Paul, 16 Tex. 472; Buchanan *v.* Munroe, 22 Tex. 537.

So a power to sell and convey contained in a mortgage for life is a power coupled with an interest, and is good and effectual to pass the fee. 2 Washb. Real Prop. *324.

See Sedgwick *v.* Laflin, 10 Allen (Mass.) 430; MacGregor *v.* Gardner, 14 Iowa 326.

Where a mortgage given by one to secure the debt of another provides that the holder of the note may extend the time of payment on the maker's executing coupons for interest to accrue during such extension, the power to make such extension is coupled with an interest, and is not revoked by the death of the mortgagor. Benneson *v.* Savage, 130 Ill. 352.

An agent to sell real property has not a power coupled with an interest, unless the instrument containing the power gives him such an interest or estate in the land as will entitle him to execute the power in his own name. Frink *v.* Roe, 70 Cal. 296.

A parcel of land was devised to A and his wife B for life, with the right to sell should they deem proper, and to invest the proceeds in other property, and at their death the land or its proceeds to be divided equally between certain of their children, and such others as might be born. A and B were equally related to the testator, and were his principal and residuary legatees. A was appointed executor and died. B afterwards conveyed for value one half of the land to a son, C, and with the proceeds bought a slave, with whose labor she supported herself and children from the remaining half of the land. After her death her children brought suit against C's grantee for the land sold. *Held*, that, whether B could sell under the joint power to herself and A depends upon whether she had any interest in the land after A's death, with which the power was coupled, and it must be concluded that she had such an interest, whether or not the common law as to estates in entirety prevails in Georgia, and that the sale was valid. Parrott *v.* Edmondson, 64 Ga. 332.

Where land is devised to a woman to hold in trust during the life of her husband, and upon his decease to convey the land to his heirs, the will providing that, if he should request a conveyance to himself or his appointee, she should convey accordingly, the husband takes no estate, but merely a naked power of appointment. Gilman *v.* Bell, 99 Ill. 144.

A verbal authority given to the purchaser of land to fill in the grantee's name in a deed, otherwise complete, confers a power coupled with an interest, and is not revoked by his subsequent sale to another, without having supplied the omission. Threadgill *v.* Butler, 60 Tex. 599.

A naked power does not survive. 2 Bouv. Inst. 1927. See also cases just cited. See also *infra*, this title, *Execution of Powers—By Survivor of Donees.*

A power may be a naked power and yet executed after the death of the party creating it. Hunt *v.* Rousmaniere, 2 Mason (U. S.) 244.

And if the power is coupled with an interest it may be executed notwithstanding the lunacy of the donor. Berry *v.* Skinner, 30 Md. 567.

A contractor borrowed from plaintiff, his foreman on the work, various sums of money to enable him to carry on the contract. Afterwards he executed to plaintiff an assignment of all moneys due, or to become due, "for any work I may perform," the assignment "to remain good and in full force until all notes due, or which are to become due, . . from me are paid." Later he gave plaintiff a power of attorney reciting that "whereas I am now desirous that all moneys that have become or may become due to me by reason of my performance of said contract shall be paid" to plaintiff, which power authorized him to collect such moneys. These instruments were deposited with the other parties to the contract. The contractor died, and the work was finished by his administrator. Plaintiff was held to have such an interest in the moneys due on the completion of the contract as to prevent a revocation of the power by the contractor's death, and to be entitled, as against the administrator, to a warrant therefor. Norton *v.* Whitehead, 84 Cal. 263.

A person who was indebted, upon going abroad, put an agent in possession of his stock in trade, and gave him a written power to sell, etc., any part of the goods, notes, etc., and apply them to the payment of the debts, and to the security or payment of any notes for which such agent might become responsible on his account. The notes of the principal were afterwards renewed, by filling up blank signatures left by the principal for that purpose, which were indorsed by the agent, and afterwards paid by him, after being protested. *Held*, that the power of sale given to the agent was a power coupled with an interest; and that he had power to sell and retain for the amount thus paid by him, notwithstanding the death of the principal. Knapp *v.* Alvord, 10 Paige (N. Y.) 205.

Where, of two partners in raising a crop of corn, one empowers the other to sell his interest in it, and out of the proceeds pay certain expenses, and also to pay himself a debt due to him from the former, it is a power coupled with an interest, and cannot be revoked. Allen *v.* Davis, 13 Ark. 28.

A debtor made to his creditors an instrument in the form of a warranty deed, with a stipulation that the conveyance was intended to operate as provided by an act of the general assembly of *Georgia*, entitled "An act to provide for sales of property to secure loans and other debts" [Acts 1871-72, pp. 44, 45]. It then recited the indebtedness to be secured, and authorized the creditor to sell the property if the debt were not paid at maturity. *Held* that, under the above recited act, the instrument passed title to the creditors; and their power of sale, being coupled with an interest, was not revoked by grantor's death. Roland *v.* Coleman, 76 Ga. 652.

A advanced moneys to pay off the debts of an intestate and prevent a forced sale of his real estate, etc., pay interest on a mortgage, and for repairs. Upon demand for repayment, the guardian of the children of the intestate, at whose request he made the advances, gave him a power of attorney to collect the rents to satisfy his claim, the consideration being stated in the instrument creating the power. *Held*, that this power could not be revoked, and A was entitled to collect the rents until he was reimbursed. James *v.* Lane, 33 N. J. Eq. 30.

Where one borrows money of a bank on certain notes, and agrees to deposit money from time to time to pay them, and authorizes the bank to apply his deposits to the discharge of the notes before maturity, if it so desires, the authority thus given is a naked power, not coupled with an interest, which ceases at the depositor's death, and the bank has no authority, after notice of his death, to make such an application of moneys then standing to his credit. Gardner *v.* First Nat. Bank (Mont. 1890), 25 Pac. Rep. 29.

A devise of land to executors to sell passes an interest: a devise that executors shall sell, or that lands shall be sold by executors gives but a power.

Compton *v.* McMahan, 19 M. A. 494; 4 Kent's Comm. *320; 4 Greenl. Cruise Dig. *133; Wooldridge *v.* Watkins, 3 Bibb (Ky.) 349; Taylor *v.* Galloway, 1 Ohio 232; Mandlebaum *v.* McDonell, 29 Mich. 78; 18 Am. Rep. 61; Clark *v.* Hornthal, 47 Miss. 434; Beadle *v.* Beadle, 2 McCrary (U. S.) 586.

This distinction is first made in Coke; Littleton (§ 16). But its soundness is doubted by Sugden. 1 Sugden Pow. (16th ed.) 128; also 2 Burr. 1031. See Bartlett *v.* Sutherland, 24 Miss. 395.

Where the power of sale is given to executors, but the title is not devised, the legal estate vests in the heir. Downing *v.* Marshall, 23 N. Y. 366; Haskell *v.* House, 3 Brev. (S. Car.) 242.

Property was devised to certain persons "share and share alike," and the will contained the further provision "in case the property cannot be satisfactorily divided, I order and hereby authorize my executors to sell the same, and divide the proceeds," etc. *Held*, the executors took a mere naked power of sale, which became totally extinguished upon the devisees' electing to take without a sale. Chasy *v.* Gowdry, 43 N. J. Eq. 95.

A power given by a will to the

executor to sell, according to the best of his judgment, any of the estate when, and on such terms, as he shall deem expedient, and to reinvest the proceeds or pay debts with them, confers a mere naked power to sell. The executor cannot, therefore, on selling one tract of the land, grant a right to carry a drain through another tract. Atwater *v.* Perkins, 51 Conn. 188.

A testator devised lands and made certain bequests to his wife, and then directed his executor to sell the balance of his property as soon after his death as the executor should deem expedient, and divide the proceeds between his wife and children. *Held* to be simply a direction to the executor to sell property not specifically devised, and not a devise to him with directions to sell, and did not intercept the descent to the heirs. Mitchell *v.* Spence, 62 Ala. 450.

Where the testator devised his real estate to his nephew, and directed his executors to sell such parts as they might think proper and necessary for the payment of debts and legacies, the executors took only a naked power to sell, and until the exercise of that power the estate passed in fee-simple to the devisee, who only was authorized to receive the rents and profits. Therefore an order of the court of chancery appointing one of the executors a trustee to sell the real estate to pay debts and legacies founded upon an allegation of the insufficiency of the personal assets, without any reference to rents and profits, did not affect the devisee's right thereto, nor the accountability of the executor so appointed for such rents and profits if received by him. Guyer *v.* Maynard, 6 Gill & J. (Md.) 420.

A devised and bequeathed to his wife one-half of all his real and personal estate, and the other half to his brothers and sisters, specifying the portion of each. He authorized and empowered his executor to sell the real estate if it should be "necessary for the purpose of distributing" it among the devisees and legatees. *Held* that this conferred only a naked power of sale to be exercised only for the purpose of making distribution among the devisees, if that should be necessary. Hoyt *v.* Day, 32 Ohio St. 101.

Where executors were authorized at their discretion to sell any lands not specifically devised, such a power is a naked power, and can neither be assigned nor executed by a majority of the executors. Shelton *v.* Homer, 5 Met. (Mass.) 462.

A direction to executors to sell and dispose of land, and divide it equally between A and B is a naked power. And though A and B are named as executors, a partition of the land between themselves is not a valid execution of the power. Derr *v.* Young, 23 N. J. L. 478.

Where there is a mere naked power the act is void, if the power is exceeded; but if the power is coupled with an interest, the act is good for so much as is within the power, and void as to the rest only. 2 Bouv. Inst. 335.

In Fontain *v.* Ravenel, 17 How. (U. S.) 369, power was given the executor after the death of the wife to apply the residue of the estate to the benefit of such charitable institutions as he should deem best. The wife survived the executor, and it was held that the latter took a mere naked power, to be executed on conditions that never happened, and therefore became void.

There is a class of cases which clearly show that where the terms made use of in creating the power, detached from the other parts of the will, confer merely a naked power to sell, yet if the other provisions of the will evince a design in the testator that at all events the lands are to be sold in order to satisfy the whole intent of the will, then this is not a mere naked power, but one coupled with other trusts and duties. Franklin *v.* Osgood, 14 Johns. (N. Y.) 554; Peter *v.* Beverly, 10 Pet. (U. S.) 532; Mastin *v.* Barnard, 33 Ga. 520.

Where the testator conferred power upon his executors in the following words: "Giving them full and complete power, as I myself possess, after my decease, to dispose of all my estate, real, personal and mixed, in the way and manner which they may think best calculated to carry into effect all the purposes specified in this my last will and testament, except that no part of my estate shall be sold at public sale," this conferred a power coupled with an interest, and would be so construed, if the other parts of the will seemed to require it, in order to carry out the intention of the testator. Williams *v.* Veach, 17 Ohio 171.

This subject is more fully discussed, and numerous cases are cited *infra*, this title, *Execution of Powers—By Survivor of Donees.*

4. Powers Coupled With a Trust—*a.* DEFINED.—Powers are also distributed into mere powers and powers coupled with a trust, or which imply a trust.[1]

1. 1 Perry on Trusts, 248; Rapalgi & Lawr. Law Dict.; Blanchard *v.* Blanchard, 6 Thomp. & C. (N. Y.) 551; 4 Hun (N. Y.) 287.

This subject is discussed, *infra*, this title, *Execution of Powers—Execution, Discretionary or Imperative.*

In *New York*, where an estate vested in trustees by a will has terminated, and there remain unexecuted valid powers in trust, which would not of themselves have authorized the creation of a trust estate under the Revised Statutes, they may still be executed by the trustees as powers in trust. Hawley *v.* James, 5 Paige (N. Y.) 318.

Where a will devises land to several persons in trust for a child during its natural life, and, after its death, still in trust for other beneficiaries, and confers no power of sale, any contract of sale by one of the trustees is void, and any deed or mortgage executed in pursuance of such sale is inoperative. Lahens *v.* Dupasseur, 56 Barb. (N. Y.) 266.

Where the testator directed that the entire estate should be appraised and divided by his executors into two equal shares, etc., he thereby created a power coupled with a trust. Smith *v.* Winn, 27 S. Car. 591. To the same effect, Delafield *v.* White, 19 Abb. N. Cas. (N. Y.) 104.

The words "the personal property and the use of said farm to be under the exclusive control and management of my wife," occurring in a will, are sufficient to create a valid power in trust. Blanchard *v.* Blanchard, 6 Thomp. & C. (N. Y.) 551; 4 Hun (N. Y.) 287.

A will directing the executor to keep the estate together for ten years, to cultivate the land with slave labor, and then to sell the property not specifically bequeathed, and to divide the proceeds among various legatees, does not create the executor a trustee. Foxworth *v.* White, 72 Ala. 224.

Where an executrix was empowered by the will to sell real estate, as she should deem most expedient, and for the best interest of all the legatees, she took a general power in trust in which she had no interest; and this power was not well executed by a conveyance of real estate to one of the legatees in satisfaction of a debt due from the testator. The power must be executed by a "sale," in the discretion of the executrix, and not by a conveyance. Russell *v.* Russell, 36 N. Y. 581.

A residuary bequest to executors, to be devoted and given by them to such institutions or uses as they in their best judgment may consider the most compatible with the views and instructions which I have given them, creates a trust in the executors to carry out the designs of the testator, so far as they had been confided to them, and does not vest them with the absolute and unlimited power of disposition of the property in their own discretion. McCurdy's Appeal, 124 Pa. St. 99.

In *Michigan* a testator gave his son, a minor, $3,000, when he should attain the age of twenty-one, and $1,000 annually thereafter, until he were twenty-five years old, when he was to have $10,000 more, if in the opinion of the executors named, he had used the amounts received in a judicious, frugal manner; and at the age of thirty-five years, or sooner, if the executors thought best, and on the same conditions, he was to receive the possession of the balance of the estate not otherwise disposed of under the will; but if at twenty-one, and after the receipt of the $10,000, the son had wasted what he then had received, and if in the opinion of the executors he would continue to do so, he then was to receive but the $1,000 annually, and the estate, subject to the other provisions of the will, was to go to the legal issue of the son, and if he died without issue, to testator's legal heirs. It was held that the executors did not take the estate in trust, but only as executors, with certain additional powers, under which, in certain contingencies, the estate might be made to pass from the son to others after the son had arrived at the age of thirty-five years. Perrin *v.* Lepper, 72 Mich. 454.

A by her will devised property to C. She conveyed the same property to B, to convey to A's grandchildren in case C should fail to provide for them, the conveyance to B to be recorded and published only in that

b. PRECATORY WORDS.—Where powers are given to persons, accompanied with such words of recommendation or request, in favor of certain objects as to render them powers in the nature of trusts, the failure of the donees to exercise such powers cannot prejudice the objects thereof, since courts will enforce the trusts.[1]

event. It was held that this was a valid power in trust, not revoked by the will, but ended by the conveyance by C to A's grandchildren, and that after the conveyance to the grandchildren C had no interest in the property which could be attached by his creditors. Bennett *v.* Rosenthal, 11 Daly (N. Y.) 91.

If an instrument contains two provisions, one creating a trust and the other conferring a power to grant or devise, which are so inconsistent and irreconcilable that both cannot stand, the trust must yield to the power. Crooke *v.* King's Co., 97 N. Y. 421. See also Ropp *v.* Minor, 33 Gratt. (Va.) 97.

A testator appointed his wife and one S executors, giving them power to sell any part of his real estate. He also made his wife and another person trustees in relation to certain bequests made in the will. *Held*, that the power of sale was absolute and not dependent on the trusts. Clark *v.* Denton, 36 N. J. Eq. 419.

As to statutory provisions in *New York*, see *supra*, this title, *Nature and Origin—Under Local Statutes.*

1. Harding *v.* Glyn, 1 Atk. 469; Gower *v.* Mainwaring, 2 Ves. 87; Gude *v.* Worthington, 3 De G. & Sm. 389; *In re* Caplin's Will, 34 L. J. Ch., N. S. 578; Izod *v.* Izod, 32 Beav. 242; Doyley *v.* Attorney-Gen., 2 Eq. Cas. Ab. 194.

In Knight *v.* Knight, 3 Beav. 148; 11 Cl. & F. 513, the court by Lord Langdale, M. R., said: "As a general rule, it has been laid down that when property is given absolutely to any person, and the same person is by the giver, who has power to command, recommended or interested or wished to dispose of that property in favor of another, the recommendation, entreaty or wish shall be held to create a a trust: First, if the words are so used that upon the whole they ought to be construed as imperative; Second, if the subject of the recommendation or wish be certain; Third, if the objects or persons intended to have the benefit of the recommendation or wish be also certain."

These three requisites must co-exist. Briggs *v.* Penny, 3 Macu. & G. 554; Moriarty *v.* Martin, 3 Ir. Ch. Rep. 31; Robinson *v.* Allen, 11 Gratt. (Va.) 785; Cook *v.* Ellington, 6 Jones Eq. (N. Car.) 372.

The context may show that words of hope or request or recommendation were not intended to interfere with the discretion of the donee. Williams *v.* Williams, 1 Sim. N. S. 358; Eaton *v.* Watts, 4 L. R., Eq. 151; Haskisson *v.* Bridge, 4 De G. & Sm. 245.

The following words have been held sufficient to raise a trust: "It is my wish," Ward v. Pelonbet, 10 N. J. Eq. 304; "wish and desire," Liddard *v.* Liddard, 28 Beav. 266; Foley *v.* Parry, 2 M. J. & K. 138; "recommend," Tibbits *v.* Tibbits, 19 Ves. 656 (*compare* Meggison *v.* Moore, 2 Ves. Jr. 630); "entreat," Prevost *v.* Clarke, 2 Madd. 458; Pilkington *v.* Boughey, 12 Sim. 114; "desire," Mason *v.* Limbury, cited in Vernon *v.* Vernon, Amb. 4; Lucas *v.* Lockhart, 10 Smed. & M. (Miss.) 466; "dying request," Pierson *v.* Garnet, 2 Bro. C. C., 38, 226; "request," Eade *v.* Eade, 5 Madd. 118; Nowlan *v.* Nelligan, 1 Bro. C. C. 489; "heartily beseech," Meredith *v.* Heneage, 1 Sim. 153; "hope," Paul *v.* Compton, 8 Ves. 375; Harland *v.* Trigg, 1 Bro. C. C. 142; "trusting," Baker *v.* Moseley, 12 Jur. 740; "absolutely trusting," Irvine *v.* Sullivan, 8 L. R., Eq. 673; "well knowing," Briggs *v.* Penny, 3 Macn. & G. 546; "in the utmost confidence," Harrison *v.* Harrison, 2 Gratt. (Va.) 1; Tolson *v.* Tolson, 10 Gill. & J. (Md.) 159; "fullest confidence," Wright *v.* Atkyns, 17 Ves. 255; 19 Ves. 299; "under the firm conviction," Barnes *v.* Grant, 26 L. J., Ch. 92; "confiding," Griffiths *v.* Evan, 5 Beav. 241; *compare* Brook *v.* Brook, 3 Sm. & Giff. 280; Alexander *v.* Alexander, 2 Jur., N. S. 898; "of course he will give," Robinson *v.* Smith, 6 Madd. 194; "having full confidence," Coates' Appeal, 2 Pa. St. 129; Pennock's Estate, 20 Pa. St. 268.

See also Carson *v.* Carson, 1 Ired.

c. SURVIVAL.—Where a power coupled with a trust is not executed before the death of the donee, it is at law held to be extinguished; but in chancery, the trust is held to survive.[1]

IV. PRINCIPLES APPLICABLE TO POWERS IN GENERAL —1. Creation of Powers.—No precise form nor technical words are necessary to the creation of a power. There must be sufficient words to denote the intention.[2] There must be an apt instrument,[3] and there must be a proper object.[4]

The *New York* statute provides that a power may be created by a suitable clause contained in a conveyance of some estate in the lands to which the power relates; or by a devise contained in a last will and testament.[5] A grantor may re-

Eq. (N. Car.) 329; Chase *v.* Chase, 2 Allen (Mass.) 101; Loring *v.* Loring, 100 Mass. 340.

If the gift is absolute in the first instance, it seems that precatory words will not be allowed to reduce it to a mere trust. Eaton *v.* Watts, L. R., 4 Eq. 151; Bouser *v.* Kinnear, 2 Giff. 195; Bernhard *v.* Minshall, Johns. Ch. 287; Sale *v.* Moore, 1 Sim. 504; Ellis *v.* Ellis, 15 Ala. 29; Whipple *v.* Adams, 1 Met. (Mass.) 445; Negroes Chase *v.* Plummer, 17 Md. 166; Alston *v.* Lea, 6 Jones' Eq. (N. Car.) 27; Burt *v.* Herron, 66 Pa. St. 400; Paisley's Appeal, 70 Pa. St. 153; Thompson *v.* McKisick, 3 Humph. (Tenn.) 631; Rhett *v.* Mason, 18 Gratt. (Va.) 541; Van Amee *v.* Jackson, 35 Vt. 173.

1. Fontain *v.* Ravenel, 17 How. (U. S.) 369.

The power of a sheriff to sell land on execution, receive the purchase-money and execute a deed, is a power coupled with a trust which exists after his death, and will be enforced in equity. Stewart *v.* Stokes, 33 Ala. 494.

Where lands are devised to one for life, with power to appoint the remainder to such of the testator's children and grandchildren as the life-tenant may see fit, with a limitation over to the testator's three sons, in default of appointment, the power is not coupled with a trust, and may be released by the life-tenant during her life. Atkinson *v.* Dowling (S. Car. 1890), 12 S. E. Rep. 93.

2. 1 Sugden on Powers, 173 (*117, *118); 4 Kent's Comm. 319; 2 Washb. Real Prop. *315; 4 Greenl. Cruise Dig. *136; Dorland *v.* Dorland, 2 Barb. (N. Y.) 80.

More technicality is required where the power is created by deed than where it is created by will. 2 Washb. Real Prop. *314. But a reservation of a power need not be in the body of the deed. 2 Washburne Real Prop. *314.

3. A power may be created or reserved by deed or by will. 4 Kent's Comm. *319; 2 Washb. Real Prop. *314; 1 Sugden Pow. *118.

Where a power is granted, the instrument should designate the person by whom, as well as the event or circumstances upon which it may be exercised. If a person not named, or distinctly described by his office or character, makes the appointment, or if the circumstances do not warrant it, or there are serious irregularities in executing the power, in all these cases the acts done will be invalid. Clark *v.* Wilson, 53 Miss. 119.

4. 1 Sugd., Pow. *117, 177.

5. 4 New York Rev. Stat., § 106 (Banks' ed.), p. 2448; (1882) p. 2191. Jennings *v.* Conboy, 73 N. Y. 230; Tucker *v.* Tucker, 5 N. Y. 408; Russell *v.* Russell, 36 N. Y. 583; Fish *v.* Coster, 28 Hun (N. Y.) 66; affd. 92 N. Y. 627; Dorland *v.* Dorland, 2 Barb. (N. Y.) 63; Selden *v.* Vermilyea, 2 Sandf. (N. Y.) 580; Fellows *v.* Heermans, 4 Lans. (N. Y.) 238. See Belmont *v.* O'Brien, 12 N. Y. 404.

A power created by deed must be more formal than one created by will. By will a mere naked power may be created, but where the power is created by any other instrument it must be sufficient in form and manner of execution to convey some estate in the land, and then a power relating to the same land may be granted. There is nothing in the statute requiring that the object of the power shall be in terms specified in the instrument creating it, except that every power must be either a beneficial power or a trust power. Jennings *v.* Conboy, 73 N. Y. 231.

serve to himself any power which he might lawfully grant to another.[1]

2. Construction of Powers—*a.* IN GENERAL.—Powers are to be construed in the light of the purpose which the agent or depositary is appointed to accomplish, and the intent of the donor as to the mode of its accomplishment.[2]

1. 4 *New York* Rev. Stat., § 105 (Banks' ed.), p. 2448; (1882) p. 2191; Belmont *v.* O'Brien, 12 N. Y. 404; Genet *v.* Hunt, 113 N. Y. 148.

2. Mayor *v.* Reynolds, 20 Md. 1; 83 Am. Dec. 535; Nevin *v.* Gillespie, 56 Md. 320; Wilson *v.* Troup, 2 Cow. (N. Y.) 195; 14 Am. Dec. 458; Hutchings *v.* Baldwin, 7 Bosw. (N. Y.) 242; Flagg *v.* Munger, 9 N. Y. 488; Capal *v.* M'Millan, 8 Port. (Ala.) 197; Kerr *v.* Verner, 66 Pa. St. 326; Guion *v.* Pickett, 42 Miss. 77; Pomeroy *v.* Partington, 3 T. R. 665; Smith *v.* Doe, 3 Bligh 290; 7 Price, 281; 2 B. & B. 474; Taylor *v.* Horde, 1 Burr. 60.

The general rule of interpretation is that powers must be construed according to the intention of the parties, and, as Lord Kenyon said in Pomeroy *v.* Partington, 3 T. R. 674, "If judges, in construing the particular words of different powers, have appeared to make contradictory decisions at different times, it is not that they have denied the general rule, but because some of them have erred in the application of the general rule to the particular case before them." And see Collins *v.* Foley, 63 Md. 156; 52 Am. Rep. 505.

The extent of the power is to be settled by the language employed in the whole instrument, aided by the situation of the parties and the property, the usages of the country on such subjects, the acts of the parties themselves, and any other circumstance having a legal bearing and throwing light on the question. LeRoy *v.* Beard, 8 How. (U. S.) 466; Carson *v.* Smith, 5 Minn. 78; 77 Am. Dec. 539; Capal *v.* M'Millan, 8 Port. (Ala.) 197.

Such an interpretation must be given to the instrument as to carry out the substantial intention of the party creating the power, not restraining or lessening it by a narrow and rigid construction, nor by a loose and extended interpretation dispensing with the substance of what was to be performed. 2 Hill Real Prop. 559; Hawkins *v.* Kemp, 3 East 441; Right *v.* Thomas, 3 Burr. 1441; Ren *v.* Bulkeley, Doug. 292; Cuthbert *v.* Babcock, 2 Dem. (N. Y.) 96; Jackson *v.* Veeder, 11 Johns. (N. Y.) 169; Pearce *v.* Van Lear, 5 Md. 85; Bartlett *v.* Sutherland, 24 Miss. 395; Goss *v.* Meadors, 78 Ind. 528.

And the general intention must be carried into effect, though it may defeat a particular intent. 4 T. R. 87; Jackson *v.* Veeder, 11 Johns. (N. Y.) 169; Capal *v.* McMillan, 8 Port. (Ala.) 197. *Compare* Wilson *v.* Troup, 7 Johns. Ch. (N.Y.) 25; Bartlett *v.* Sutherland, 24 Miss. 395.

Whether the instrument creates a power or confers an interest upon the grantee, depends on the intention. 1 Sugden Pow. *118. See also, notes to p. 120, ed., of 1856; 1 Chance Pow., ch. 3, § 3; 2 Washb. Real Prop. *315.

And the words used are to be taken in their ordinary and common acceptation, and not according to any legal or technical meaning of them. Griffith *v.* Harrison, 4 T. R. 749.

Naked powers are to be strictly construed. Zouch *v.* Woolston. 1 Wm. Blacks. 281; 2 Burr. 1136.

Where a power of sale is distinctly limited to such lands, the legal and equitable title to which is in the cotenant, a subsequent general description of the law as "fifteen acres or thereabout" will not enlarge the power. Watson *v.* Sutro, 86 Cal. 500.

Powers coupled with property, if merely legal, are to be construed with equal strictness in equity as at law. Zouch *v.* Woolston, 2 Barr. 1136; 1 Wm. Bl. 281.

A power resting on personal confidence in the donee is not to be extended beyond the clear intention of the donor as shown by its express terms. Marks *v.* Tarver, 59 Ala. 335.

Nothing contained in the recital of the instrument as to the consideration moving to the grant of the power will operate as a limitation upon the power. Beatty *v.* Clark, 20 Cal. 11.

And a general power of appointment given by a will is to be construed by itself, and other clauses of the will and other dispositions of property made thereby, cannot be resorted to, to qualify it. Thompson *v.* Garwood, 3 Whart. (Pa.) 287.

Cases in which the words were held to show an intention to create a power. Winston *v.* Jones, 6 Ala. 550; Jones *v.* Jones, 13 N. J. Eq. 236.

Not to create a power. Geroe *v.* Winter, 5 N. J. Eq. 655; Birmingham *v.* Lesan, 76 Me. 482.

An intention will not avail to create an illegal or impossible estate. Burleigh *v.* Clough, 52 N. H. 267; 13 Am. Rep. 23; Smith *v.* Bell, 6 Pet. (U. S.) 68.

Instances of Construction.—A testator devised the residue of what he should die possessed of or in expectancy, of what nature or kind soever, in Jamaica or any other country, to his wife for life, giving her full power to dispose by will of any part of said residue. After her decease he bequeathed to his daughter and her heirs forever whatever of said residue was undisposed of by his wife. *Held*, that the wife had a power of appointment over the whole residuary estate. Cooke *v.* Farrand, 7 Taunt. 122; 2 Marsh. 421.

A testator gave property in trust for his son for life, "and from and after his death, then to the use of such of his children and issue, and in such shares and for such estates as he shall by last will appoint, and, in default of such appointment, then to the use of all his children that may be living at his death." The son died leaving one son only. It was held by the Supreme Court of *Pennsylvania* that the testator's son could not appoint a forfeitable estate to his son, who, therefore, took an absolute estate. Pepper's Appeal, 120 Pa. St. 235.

A deed of trust, after providing for the payment by the trustee of an annuity of $3,000 to A, directed the said trustee to invest for or pay to A the sum of $50,000, for her sole and separate use, the same to be subject to her disposal in any of the ways set forth in the deed. Subsequently A executed a "deed of explanation," to the effect that she understood that said annuity was to be considered as the interest on said sum of $50,000 in the hands of the trustee, and was to be reduced *pro rata* as portions of the principal sum were, from time to time, paid to her. This "deed of explanation" was held to be effectual, and its operation was to reduce the annuity charged upon the lands in the deed of trust in proportion as A reduced the fund charged by her appointment or outlays, so as to make the annuity in each and every year equal to six per cent. interest on so much of said fund as remained unappropriated or unexpended by her in each year. Blake *v.* Hawkins, 98 U. S. 315.

Where a testatrix gives to A the use of property for his life, and provides that if A does not otherwise appoint its use afterwards, B may have it in case she conducts herself toward A during his lifetime in a certain manner, as to which A shall be the sole judge, it is not B's failure to perform the condition but A's judgment in the matter, that is the test in B's right to take in default of an appointment. Krause *v.* Klucken, 135 Mass. 482.

Where a power is expressly given to executors over one portion of the estate and is not expressly given over another portion, the omission manifests an intention that the power shall not be exercised on that portion of the estate over which it is not expressly given, although, in another portion of the will, general words are used, broad enough to justify an implication that the whole estate should be subject to the power. Anderson *v.* Anderson, 31 N. J. Eq. 560.

Power to continue a testator's estate in a mercantile business is not to be inferred from authority given to the executor to manage and convey at discretion for the benefit of devisees. Citizens' Mut. Ins. Co. *v.* Ligon, 59 Miss. 305.

The will of M devised his real estate to his executors in trust, to hold one-third part thereof for the benefit of each of his three daughters during life. It was declared that the executor should stand seised of her third, in case of the death of a daughter, leaving a husband and lawful issue living, "from and immediately after her death, upon trust for the sole use and benefit of such issue;" in case of the death of a daughter single and unmarried, "upon such trust, and for such purpose as she shall or may appoint by her last will;" in default of such appointment "for her sole use and benefit of her next of kin." It was held that the power of appointment related to the remainder in fee; that in each event provided for, the trust in the executors upon the death of the daughter would be purely passive, the remainder vesting in the beneficiaries; that the phrase in the clause giving such power of appointment "upon such trust" meant, not a trust to be created by the daughter, and so limiting the power of disposition, but related to the trust in the executors. Mott *v.* Ackerman, 92 N. Y. 539.

In a case decided by the Supreme Court of Appeals of Virginia, a testator gave property to A in trust for his daughter B, the wife of C for life, and for the use of her heirs after her death, with direction to A, "As soon as convenient and practicable, after having received the said legacy, or proceeds of said devise, to loan out the same at interest, on good and sufficient security, by bond and mortgage on unincumbered real estate, and to apply the interest or income which shall or may arise, accrue, or be derived therefrom, to the payment and discharge of all the expenses and charges necessary, and required for the proper maintenance, support and comfort of my said daughter L; or the said trustee may, if she shall in her discretion deem it proper, pay over the income or interest aforesaid to my said daughter L, semi-annually, in money, on her sole and separate receipt, independent of any interference, hindrance, or control of her husband; and the said interest and income shall not be liable or taken for her husband's debts or contracts, nor be applied to the payment thereof or any part thereof." Upon the division of the estate, L was entitled to one-third of a certain farm, and her husband purchased the other two-thirds and conveyed it to a trustee for the sole and separate use of L for life, and to her heirs after her death, in the same manner and form as the estate left her by the will. A son of the testator, to whom the personal property of his father had been left, conveyed one-third of it to A in trust for L, to be held on the terms of the will. F, a son of L, conveyed his whole interest in the estates aforementioned to L, to her separate use, with power to dispose of it as a *feme sole.* The husband and wife afterwards made a note, and, the trustee under the deed of her husband for his wife's benefit joining, they executed a deed of trust to secure the payment of the note. On a bill filed by the payee of the note to enforce the lien created by the deed of trust, it was held that L had no power to dispose of, charge, or incumber the *corpus* of the estate derived under the will of the father and under the deeds for her benefit (except such, if any, as was acquired under the deed of her son F), nor to anticipate the profits, income, or interest which might arise or be derived from said estate, so far as they might be required for her comfortable support, and the lien of the deed of trust extended and could be enforced only on any excess of profits beyond that necessary for her support, derived from the farm, if any, and the interest, if any, conveyed by the deed of F, the son. Ropp *v.* Minor, 33 Gratt. (Va.) 97.

A husband and wife each purchased a policy of life insurance in favor of the other, or of the representatives of the other. The husband died first, and his wife then died, whereupon the amount of the policy upon her life was paid to the husband's executors. The husband by his will, gave to his wife "all my estate, both real and personal, of whatsoever kind, and wheresoever the same may be at the time of my decease, for and during the time of her natural life, with full power and authority to appropriate to her own use such of the personal property as to her shall seem meet," and after the death of his wife, the residue was given to a person named. As between the husband's residuary legatee and the legatees named in the will of the wife, the former was entitled to the amount of the policy upon the life of the wife, she having only a life estate therein, with no power of appointment. McCauley's Appeal, 93 Pa. St. 102.

A testator devised to his wife property for life, or until re-marriage, with remainder to her children, and also gave her $2,500 "during her natural life or until she may marry," besides $2,500 to be used by her "in the support and education of her children." He made his two nieces residuary legatees. It was held that the wife had a general power of distribution of the money left for the support and education of the children under which she could disburse the whole fund, if necessary for those purposes, and that on her death or marriage the balance did not descend to the residuary legatees but remained for the use of the children. Adams *v.* Mason, 85 Ala. 452.

Where a testator devised the use of all his property to his wife during her life; "that is to say, the personal property to be invested in good securities, and the real estate to be rented, except

b. Power of Revocation and Appointment.[1]—A usual qualification annexed to the execution of a power, is a power to revoke and limit to new uses.[2] If the power be to create a new estate in any one, it is said to be a power of appointment; if to devest or abridge an existing estate, it is called a power of revocation.[3] Powers are either mere powers of revocation, en-

so much as my said wife may elect to occupy herself," the interest and rent to be paid to the wife annually, the occupation by the widow thus authorized was intended to be a personal occupation, and did not give her power to appoint an agent to lease the premises to others. More *v.* More (Supreme Ct.), 4 N. Y. Supp. 927.

A will provided that the "estate shall be kept together as long as practicable, that is to say, as long as it may be profitable or advantageous," and "with this view my executrix shall have full power to manage and control and keep up my farming interest, either upon the tenant or wages system, or both, as she may think best." It was held that a limited power was implied in the executrix to incur debts on the credit of the estate for needful supplies, such as prudent farmers usually do in the management of their own business of like kind. Palmer *v.* Moore, 82 Ga. 177.

Where the persons named in the will as executors are also appointed guardians of the residuary legatee, and the will, in a clause giving plaintiff a monthly allowance during her life, directs the "executors" to expend such further sums for her care and comfort as they deem necessary, the guardians, after their discharge as executors, have power to increase the allowance. Elmer *v.* Gray, 13 Cal. 283.

1. See, as to the revocation of simple powers of attorney, and of powers given to agents generally, Agency, vol. 1, p. 443, *et seq.*

2. 1 Sugd. Pow. (3d Am. ed.) 486, *440; 1 Steph. Comm. 229, 549.

3. 2 Washb. Real Prop. (4th ed.) 641, (*307).

In these cases a power is given which is not exhausted by the first appointment; but the donee may subsequently revoke such appointment, and make a new one when the estate of the first appointee ceases and the new appointee succeeds to it. And it is often the case that the donee is granted the power to make successive appointments and revocations. The power may be to revoke only; or to revoke and make a new appointment. 1 Sugd. Pow. (3d Am. ed.) 458–9; (4th ed.) 382–3. Sheffield *v.* VonDunlop, 7 Hare 42; 17 L. J., Ch. 481; Sanders *v.* Evans, 8 H. L. Cas. 721; 31 L. J., Ch. 233; 7 Jur., N. S. 1292.

At common law a power of revocation in a feoffment or in an ordinary deed, was void; nor could a power of entry for condition broken be reserved to a stranger. By means of powers in connection with uses these difficulties were obviated, and the owner was enabled either to reserve to himself a qualified species of dominion distinct from the legal estate, or to confer that dominion on a stranger, and to withdraw the legal estate out of the trustee and give it a new direction. 2 Washb. Real Prop. *301; 1 Chance. Pow. 278; 4 Kent's Comm. *315, *316.

Powers of revocation are incident to and grow out of the Statute of Uses. 1 Chance. Pow. 278.

A power of revocation differs from a condition. When a condition is broken the estate reverts; but the power of revocation, instead of revesting in the donor the estate, ordinarily vests it in others. And if there is a power to reappoint, the distinction is still more marked. 1 Sugd. Pow. 486, 440.

Even if by revocation the estate is again in the donor it does not get there properly by reversion, or as on condition broken. He is not in as of the old estate, but it returns to him by virtue of the use. 1 Sugd. Pow. 486, *440.

It is not always necessary that the word "revocation" should be used in order to give a power of revocation and new appointment. Thus where a testator gave a bond in a penal sum conditioned to pay after the death of T, £1,000 to such person or persons as T should by deed or will appoint, it was held that such an alternative power to appoint a sum of money, not necessarily working a transmutation of property like an appointment of land, was meant to be ambulatory during the life of the person who was to make the appointment, and therefore that the execution of it by deed, which was retained in the possession of T, may be revoked by cancellation, though it contained no power of revocation. Perrott *v.* Perrott, 14 East 423.

Where the power of revocation is conditional and the conditions are not performed, a deed of revocation is a nullity. Doe *v.* Martin, 4 T. R. 39.

Everything required to be done in the execution of such a power must be strictly complied with, and must be completed in the lifetime of the person by whom it is to be executed. Hawkins *v.* Kemp, 3 East 410.

By a marriage settlement lands were conveyed to trustees to the use of the wife for life, remainder to the use of the husband for life, remainder to the use of all and every children of the marriage, or such of them as the husband and wife should appoint; and in default of such appointment to the use of all the children equally. The deed contained a power enabling the settlors to revoke the use of the settlement, and the trustees to sell the estate and convey it to a purchaser, and that the purchase money should be paid to the trustees, and not to the settlors, and invested in the purchase of other lands to the same use. *Held*, that the remainder to the children was a vested one in fee, liable to be divested by an appointment by the parents; but if no appointment is made, such remainder to the children could not be defeated by a deed of revocation by the parents, and a conveyance by them and the trustees to a purchaser, who paid the consideration money to the settlors, and which was never laid out in the purchase of other lands. Doe *v.* Martin. 4 T. R. 39.

A marriage settlement provided that the settlor might, by deed or instrument in writing attested by three witnesses, and to be enrolled, with the consent in writing of certain trustees, revoke the old and declare new uses. A deed of revocation was executed by the settlor, and all the trustees except one, and the consent of that one was given by means of a general power of attorney before made by him to the settlor to consent to any such deed he might think proper to make. This deed was properly attested and enrolled. Afterwards another deed was properly executed and assented to in person by all the trustees, but was not enrolled till after the settlor's death. *Held*, that the first deed was void, and the defect in it was not caused by the second deed, inasmuch as the latter was not enrolled in the lifetime of the settlor. Hawkins *v.* Kemp, 3 East 410.

The donee executed a deed which expressly confirmed a prior appointment, and which in law amounted to an appointment, and in addition thereto appointed certain other funds. The deed contained a power to revoke the appointment thereby made. *Held*, that the power of revocation applied only to that part of the deed which was expressed in terms of appointment, and not to the part which was expressed in terms of confirmation. Morgan *v.* Gronow, 42 L. J., Ch. 410; 16 L. R., Eq. 1; 28 L. T., N. S. 434.

Where a copy-holder in fee surrendered to the uses of a prior settlement, which latter contained a power to revoke the uses therein declared, and limit new ones, the uses limited in execution of this power were held good, though they had the effect of defeating prior vested estates. Boddington *v.* Abernethy, 5 B. & C. 776; 8 D. & R. 626.

A husband by his will gave all his property to his wife, in trust to apply the income to her own use during her life, and at her death to divide the same among certain persons designated in the will, in such shares as she might by her will appoint, and in default of such appointment, then in the shares fixed by the husband's will. The wife by her will. made a valid appointment of the estate to the objects of the power; but by a codicil she appointed the same to persons not authorized by her will, but did not in terms revoke the appointments made in her will. It was held that the appointments made in her will were not invalidated by the codicil. Austin *v.* Oakes, 117 N. Y. 577.

Seven different estates were devised to a sister, brothers and nephews respectively. one to each stock. As to six of the estates three several lives were included in succession on each estate. The seventh was in the first instance limited only to two persons for life in succession, but there was given to those two a power "to add another life or lives to make three in like manner as after mentioned for other persons to do the same." There then follows this general power: "When and so often as the lives on either of the estates shall be by death reduced to two, then it shall be in the power of the person or persons then enjoying the estate or estates to renew the same, with the person or persons to whom the revenue shall belong,

abling the grantor simply to recall that which he has bestowed, or powers of revocation and new appointment, authorizing the grantor or some other person to alter or make a new disposition of the estate conveyed.[1]

by adding a third life in such estate, and paying such reversioner two years' purchase for such renewal; and also to exchange either of the two lives on payment of one year's purchase," *held*, that this power of renewal only authorized the addition of one life to the three on each estate, and in making one exchange of a life. Doe *v.* Harding, 10 East 549.

A general clause in a will revoking all former wills, revokes a prior testamentary appointment. Thus, a married woman, having a general power of appointment by will over real estate, executed a will appointing the estate. After the death of her husband she made another will revoking all former wills and containing a general devise and bequest of all her real and personal estate. She afterwards made a third will, also revoking all former wills and bequeathing her personal estate, but not devising or appointing her real estate. She had no real estate except that subject to the power. *Held*, that the testamentary appointment under the first will was revoked by the second will, and the second will by the third, and that the real estate went as in default of appointment. Sotheran *v.* Denning, L. R., 20 Ch. Div. 99.

See In the Goods of Merritt, 1 Sw. & Tr. 112; In the Goods of Jois, 4 Sw. & Tr. 214.

In Taylor *v.* Smiley, 14 Phila. (Pa.) 76, it was held that a conveyance in trust with power of revocation may be revoked by will, though the latter contains no reference to the power.

1. 1 Steph. Comm. 505, 547; 2 Washb. Real Prop. (5th ed.) 694.

All powers are, in fact, powers of revocation and appointment, since every power of appointment is strictly a power of revocation, for it always postpones, abridges or defeats, in a greater or less degree, the previous uses and estates, and appoints new ones in their stead. 4 Kent's Comm. 315, 316; 2 Washb. Real Prop. (4th ed.) 642 (*307); 1 Sugd. Pow. (3d Am. ed.) 288, *238; 2 Hilliard's Real Prop. 557.

The power of revocation is usually incident to the power of appointment, though not expressly reserved in the instrument creating the power. To bar the power of revocation it must appear from the instrument that it was intended that there should be but one execution of the power—once for all. 2 Bouv. Inst. 336.

A power to appoint includes in itself a power to revoke. (1 Sugd. Pow. 288, *238). And both may be done by the same instrument. 1 Sugd. Pow. 293, *243.

The power of appointment is a power to "limit to a use." It operates not directly as a conveyance of the land but as a substitution of a new use for the former. It is considered as a species of conveyance. 2 Bouv. Inst. 1921.

In some instruments the power of revocation prior to appointing to new uses is expressly limited, but this is unnecessary. Sand. Uses, 154; 2 Washb. Real Prop. *307.

Where the donee of a power of appointment over personal estate exercised the power and reserved a power of revocation merely, this included the power to limit to new uses. Sheffield *v.* Von Dunlop, 7 Hare 42; 17 L. J., Ch. 481.

Whether a power to revoke simply without giving a power of appointment to new uses confers a power to appoint to new uses, has been questioned. 1 Chance Pow. 288–295. Mr. Sugden answers this question in the negative. 1 Sugd. Pow. 501, 502, *457, *459. But Chancellor Kent lays down the rule otherwise: "A power of revocation," he says, "implies the power of appointment to new uses." 4 Kent Comm. *337.

Mr. Sugden, in remarking on this point, says: "Though in the instrument creating a power there is no express authority to reserve a power of revocation yet the donee may (whether the power be a general or a special one) reserve by the instrument executing the power a power of revocation, or of revocation and new appointment, and such power may be reserved *toties quoties.*" 1 Sugd. Pow. 491, *446.

"Though it was considered incident

c. POWER OF SALE—(1) *In General.*—A power of sale need not be conferred in express words. If, from all the provisions of the instrument, it is clear that the intent was to clothe the donee with the power of disposition, such intent will be effectuated.[1]

to every power that the donee might exercise it with a power of revocation, and so *toties quoties*, yet if he did exercise it without reserving such a power, he could not revoke it; and the reservation in the deed creating the power of a prospective general power of revocation, so that the last execution only might operate, was considered simply void." Intr. to Sugd. and Powers 13.

Effect of Revocation and Limitation of New Uses.—If there is an original power of appointment and then an execution of that power reserving a power only to revoke, followed by a revocation, the original power remains unaffected. Saunders *v.* Evans, 8 H. L. Cas. 721; 7 Jur., N. S. 1292; 31 L. J., Ch. 233.

If in the first instrument executing the original power there is reserved a power of revocation and of new appointment, such instrument does not constitute a new settlement, destructive of the first, nor is the original power thereby exhausted and at an end, but upon the revocation of such instrument exists in full force. Saunders *v.* Evans, 8 H. L. Cas. 721; 7 Jur., N. S. 1292; 31 L. J., Ch. 233.

If there is a power of appointment to be exercised by deed or will, and the first instrument executing the power is a deed, which contains a reservation of the power to revoke and to appoint anew by deed, and then there is a simple revocation of this instrument, the original power of revocation being in full force, there may be a valid execution of it by will as well as by deed. Saunders *v.* Evans, 8 H. L. Cas. 721; 7 Jur., N. S. 1292; 31 L. J., Ch. 233.

"Where trusts are raised with a power of revocation in the settlor, the settlement will not be defeated by the mere act of the trustee reconveying to the settlor. To effectuate a revocation the terms of the power must be complied with. And this is true even though the settlement was voluntary." 1 Sugd. Pow. 366, * 314.

Where an estate was settled to trustees to the use of the settlor for life, with remainder over, and with a power to the settlor, with the consent of the trustees, to revoke all uses in the settlement, if the settlor grants an estate for his own life in the settled estate, a subsequent revocation with the consent of the trustees will not affect the estate so granted by him. Goodright *v.* Cator, 2 Dougl. 477.

Where under a power in a marriage settlement uses are revoked and new uses declared, whereby a younger child, who afterwards becomes the eldest son, takes through the mere bounty of the donor property which, but for such revocation and new appointment, he would have taken as eldest son under the settlement, he does not thereby cease to be entitled to the portion of a younger son under the settlement. Wandesford *v.* Carrick, 5 Ir. Rep. Eq. 486.

Where a donee revokes all the trusts of the deed while the power only extended to the remainder, the party in whose favor the new appointment is made is put to his election. Coutts *v.* Acworth, 9 L. R., Eq. 519.

The donee of a power of appointment validly exercised it by deed in favor of her three sons, and subsequently by will invalidly appointed the same property to her eldest son, giving her younger sons other benefits under the will. *Held*, that the younger sons were not bound to elect between their shares under the deed and the benefits given them by the will. Cooper *v.* Cooper, 39 L. J. Chanc. 525. See also *In re* Swinburne; Swinburne *v.* Pitt, 27 L. R., Ch. Div. 696.

In New York, Indiana, Michigan, Wisconsin, Minnesota, Kansas, Dakota and Alabama the statutes declare that every power is irrevocable unless authority to revoke is granted or reserved in the instrument creating it.

1. Taylor *v.* Harwell, 65 Ala. 1; Harker *v.* Reilly, 4 Del. Ch. 72; Rakestraw *v.* Rakestraw, 70 Ga. 806; Weed *v.* Knox, 77 Ga. 636; Cherry *v.* Greene, 115 Ill. 591; Hamilton *v.* Hamilton, 98 Ill. 254; Putnam Free School *v.* Fisher, 30 Me. 523; Birmingham *v.* Lesan, 76 Me. 482; Hanson *v.* Brewer, 78 Me. 195; Foos *v.* Scarf, 55 Md. 301; Shaw *v.* Silloway, 145 Mass. 503; Baker *v.* Byerly, 40 Minn. 489; Haggerty *v.* Lanterman, 30 N. J. Eq. 37; Belcher *v.* Belcher, 38 N. J. Eq. 126; Holman *v.*

Tiggs, 42 N. J. Eq. 127; Terry *v.* Smith, 42 N. J. Eq. 504; Lindley *v.* O'Reilley (N. J.), 15 Atl. Rep. 379; Livingston *v.* Murray, 39 How. Pr. (N. Y.) 102; Van Winkle *v.* Fowler, 52 Hun (N. Y.) 355; Bradford *v.* Mogk, 55 Hun (N. Y.) 482; Gersen *v.* Rinteln, 2 Dem. (N. Y.) 243; Stewart *v.* Hamilton, 37 Hun (N. Y.) 19; Leonard *v.* American Bapt. H. M. Soc., 35 Hun (N. Y.) 290; Coogan *v.* Ockershausen, 55 N. Y. Super. Ct. 286; *In re* Powers, 11 N. Y. Supp. 396; Vaughan *v.* Farmer, 90 N. Car. 607; Howell *v.* Tyler, 91 N. Car. 207; Coonrod *v.* Coonrod, 6 Ohio 114; Ames *v.* Ames, 15 R. I. 12; Geiger *v.* Kaigler, 15 S. Car. 262; Cooper *v.* Horner, 62 Tex. 356; Faulk *v.* Dashiell, 62 Tex. 642; 50 Am. Rep. 542; Bateman *v.* Bateman, 1 Atk. 421.

Where a testator imposes on his executor trusts or duties which require for their execution or performance an estate in his lands or a power of sale, the executor will take, by implication, such estate or power. Lindley *v.* O'Reilly, 50 N. J. L. 636; 7 Am. St. Rep. 802.

A power in a will to "rent or sell" lands of the testator does not authorize the sale of lands specifically devised. Young *v.* Twigg, 27 Md. 620.

But where the power was to sell any portion of the estate not devised to the testator's children, the executor took a power unrestricted except as to property specifically devised to the children. White *v.* Guthrie (Ky. 1888), 8 S. W. Rep. 174.

Where the will directs and empowers the executor to manage and control the estate as he may think best for the interest of testator's children, power is conferred on him to sell, lease or mortgage the property, if in his opinion necessary to raise money for the objects of the trust. Faulk *v.* Dashill, 62 Tex. 642; 50 Am. Rep. 542; *citing* Orr *v.* O'Brien, 55 Tex. 155; Danish *v.* Disbrow, 51 Tex. 235. *Compare*, McCurdy's Appeal, 124 Pa. St. 99.

A testator gave all his property to trustees, to manage, and to distribute the income under the will. He also gave them power to convey, at public or private sale, in fee-simple, any and all of his land, at their discretion. After providing for several annuities the will contained the following provision: "And I make each and every of the same a first charge upon my estate, into whose hands soever it may come." *Held*, that the trustees had an unrestricted power to sell all of his estate, and that the annuities were not charged on the land so as to form an incumbrance thereon in the hands of a purchaser from the trustees. Bradford *v.* Mogk, 55 Hun (N. Y.) 482.

Where lands are conveyed to a married woman and her trustee, to be sold and conveyed in fee, mortgaged or rented, as she may in writing direct, and in the event of her dying before her husband the estate to vest in her children, her power to convey is absolute and unlimited, and is not affected by the latter provision. Jacko *v.* Tanssig, 45 Mo. 167.

A devise to the executor of "all the balance of the money that" testatrix might receive under a certain will, and also "all the right, title, and interest" which testatrix, as one of the children of a third person, deceased, might be entitled to under such will, "in trust that my said executor will use the same for the purpose of clothing, educating and maintaining her children, confers a power of sale. Van Winkle *v.* Fowler, 52 Hun (N. Y.) 355.

Where a will provided that if the personal estate, and lands at W should not pay the testator's debts, his executors should raise the same out of his copy-hold estate, this language was held to authorize a sale of the copy-hold estate. Bateman *v.* Bateman, 1 Atk. 421.

A general direction in a will that the executors should sell any part of the real estate whenever they should think proper so to do, without any order or decree of the court," there being no clause in the will charging the real estate with the payment of debts, would not authorize the executors to sell the land for that purpose until after the personal estate was exhausted. Graham *v.* Little, 5 Ired. Eq. (N. Car.) 407.

A power to sell certain lots as surveyed, does not authorize the sale of the entire tract by the acre. Rice *v.* Tavernier, 8 Minn. 248; 83 Am. Dec. 778.

In Illinois a testator, by one clause of his will, gave to his wife the entire control of all his property, real and personal, "so long as she lives, for her support and maintenance, in such manner as her situation in life requires." The remainder was devised to a son-in-law of the wife, "in consideration that he take good care of my wife and treat her kindly." He then gave certain real estate to a nephew, and then followed this clause: "All the rest of my estate, real and personal, after the termination of the life estate of my wife, I give to my heirs-at-law." In another clause he gave to his wife full power to sell all his personal and real estate, except the lands willed to the son-in-law and nephew, "should it be necessary for her so to do for her maintenance and support—it being well understood that she is not to waste any property, but I want to give her full power to support herself well, and should she choose to help her daughters or their children, she has full power to do so before the heirs aforesaid take their remainders—hereby giving my wife full power to sell any of the property aforesaid, and give good title to the same, either at public or private sale, using her own judgment as to which shall bring the greatest amount of money." The testator left neither children nor grandchildren. It was held that the wife had power to sell the land, and that her discretion could not be reviewed by the court, and that the purchaser was not bound to see to the application of the purchase-money. Crozier *v.* Hoyt, 97 Ill. 23.

In a Massachusetts case, where a will conferred a power of sale on the executors, and a subsequent deed of the testator to trustees conferred the power of sale on them, and then a codicil confirmed the will, and, after making the codicil, the testator died, and then the trustees conveyed to the executors, it was held that the executors could sell the land. Chesman *v.* Cummings, 142 Mass. 75.

In another Massachusetts case it was held that, where the will empowered the executor to sell "as the proper and convenient settlement of the estate may require," he might not sell for the purpose of making partition and distribution among the devisees. Allen *v.* Dean, 148 Mass. 594.

If the intent not to grant a power of sale is clear, no power will pass, however advantageous it might be. Walker *v.* Walker, 36 N. J. Eq. 376; *In re* Fox's Will, 52 N. Y. 530. Thus where a testatrix devised to her executors real estate which was productive, and also real estate which was unproductive, with power to rent or lease according to their judgment, and invest the income, they took no power of sale as to the unproductive land, though it proved to be an annual drain on the income of that which was productive. Roe *v.* Vingut (Supreme Ct.), N. Y. Supp. 914.

But where authority is given to the executor to sell certain lands, and distribute the proceeds to certain legatees, while by a codicil the same lands are given to various devisees, different from those named as legatees in the will, but the authority to sell is not in express terms revoked, the authority remains and will control. Anderson *v.* Butler, 31 S. Car. 183.

In a *Georgia* case a testator appointed his wife executrix, and directed "that all the rest of my real estate property, including the house and lot I now occupy and a house and lot I own in Lawrenceville, together with my lands be held and controlled by my wife during her lifetime. I would also include whatever money and notes I may own. In short, it is my will that my wife shall have full and entire control of all my effects, of whatever kind." *Held*, that the executrix did not take a power of sale; and that the will created a life estate in the widow, with remainder to the children of the testator; and the life tenant might waive the life estate in the property devised. This would vest the whole estate in the children; and it would be in the power of a court of equity to decree a sale of the whole or a part of the property for the support, education and maintenance of the children and the support of the widow. Rakestraw *v.* Rakestraw, 79 Ga. 806.

Under a devise of real estate to the testator's widow to hold "during her life for her maintenance, but not to sell the same, the said real estate to go to A at her death, if any remains," it was held that the widow took a life-estate by express words of limitation, without any power of disposal annexed, and that the words, "if any remains," being by implication in opposition to the language of the testator, in the same clause by which the widow is expressly prohibited from making sale of the real estate, and apparently inconsistent with every other expression in the will, cannot be held to imply a right of disposal. Birmingham *v.* Lesan, 76 Me. 482.

Where a clause in the will merely provided that the real estate may be sold, if deemed advisable, this is insufficient. Whittemore *v.* Russell, 80 Me. 297. So, too, the facts that property was devised in trust for the support and education of the minor and unmarried children, until the youngest child living should arrive at the age of sixteen

(2) *Power to Convey Fee.*—To enable the donee of a power to convey the fee, it is not necessary, when it appears that the donor intended to authorize such grant, that he should specify the estate to be conveyed as the estate in fee. It is enough if the power be merely a power to sell.[1]

years, at which time the property was to be divided, and that the income was not sufficient for the education and support of the minor children, will not justify a sale of the property by the trustee to supply funds for that purpose. Brome *v.* Pembroke, 66 Md. 193.

The death of one of the objects of the power, or of those for whose benefit the sale was to be made, does not impair the power. Ely *v.* Dix, 118 Ill. 477.

1. 2 Washb. Real. Prop. *314; Wilson *v.* Throup, 7 Johns. Ch. (N. Y.) 34; North *v.* Philbrook, 34 Me. 532.

"Where," says Sir Edward Sugden, "the intention is clear, a power may enable the donee to dispose of the fee, though no words of inheritance be used, as where a testator gives a power to sell lands, the donee may sell the inheritance, because the testator gives the same power he himself had." Quoted in Heinhauser *v.* Decker, 38 N. J. Eq. 430.

Where lands are given to one for life, with remainder over and power is also given to the life tenant to sell or dispose of the lands, the life-tenant takes a power to sell the fee. Hull *v.* Culver, 34 Conn. 403; Lewis *v.* Palmer, 46 Conn. 454; Tolland Co. Ins. Co. *v.* Underwood, 50 Conn. 493; Barnard *v.* Bailey, 2 Harr. (Del.) 56; Jarrof *v.* Vaughn, 7 Ill. 132; Markettie *v.* Ragland, 77 Ill. 98; Crozier *v.* Hoyt, 97 Ill. 23; Henderson *v.* Blackburn, 104 Ill. 227; Clark *v.* Middlesworth, 82 Ind. 240; South *v.* South, 91 Ind. 221; 46 Am. Rep. 591; Downie *v.* Buennagel, 94 Ind. 228; Lillard *v.* Robinson, 3 Litt. (Ky.) 415; Fritsch *v.* Klansing (Ky.) 890; 13 S. W. Rep. 241; Ramsdell *v.* Ramsdell, 21 Me. 288; Shaw *v.* Hussey, 41 Me. 495; Benesch *v.* Clark, 49 Md. 497; Foos *v.* Scarf, 55 Md. 301; Carter *v.* Van Bokkelen (Ind.), 20 Atl. Rep. 781; Dodge *v.* Moore, 100 Mass. 335; Hale *v.* Marsh, 100 Mass. 468; Cummings *v.* Shaw. 108 Mass. 159; Smith *v.* Snow, 123 Mass. 323; Johnson *v.* Batelle, 125 Mass. 453; Norcum *v.* D'Oeuch, 17 Mo. 98; Boger *v.* Allen, 76 Mo. 498; Hazel *v.* Hagan, 47 Mo. 277; Yates *v.* Clark, 56 Miss. 212; Andrews *v.* Brumfield, 32 Miss. 107; Waring *v.* Waring, 17 Barb. (N. Y.) 552; King *v.* King, 12 Ohio 390; Stroud *v.* Morrow, 7 Jones (N. Car.) 463; Bishop *v.* Remple, 11 Ohio St. 277; Nimmons *v.* Westfall, 33 Ohio St. 213; Second Reformed etc. Church *v.* Disbrow, 52 Pa. St. 219; Dillin *v.* Wright, 73 Pa. St. 177; Forsythe *v.* Forsythe, 108 Pa. St. 129; Canedy *v.* Jones, 19 S. Car. 297; McGavock *v.* Pugsley, 1 Tenn. Ch. 410; Bean *v.* Myers, 1 Coldw. (Tenn.) 226; Orr *v.* O'Brien, 55 Tex. 149; White *v.* White, 21 Vt. 250; Hart *v.* White, 26 Vt. 260; Downie *v.* Downie, 9 Biss. (U. S.) 353; Henderson *v.* Cross, 29 Beav. 216; Herring *v.* Barrow, T. R., 13 Ch. Div. 144; 14 Ch. Div. 263; 43 L. T., N. S. 35; Humberstone *v.* Thomas, 3 U. C., Q. B. 516; Anderson *v.* Hamilton, 8 U. C., Q. B. 302; Bergin *v.* Sisters St. Joseph, 22 U. C., Q. B. 204.

Compare Brant *v.* Virginia Coal Co., 93 U. S. 326; Wetter *v.* Walker, 62 Ga. 142; Mulberry *v.* Mulberry, 50 Ill. 67; Frink *v.* Eggleston, 92 Ill. 515; Welch *v.* Belleville Savings Bank, 94 Ill. 191; Kennedy *v.* Kennedy, 105 Ill. 350; Thompson *v.* Vance, 1 Metc. (Ky.) 669; Stuart *v.* Walker, 72 Maine, 145; Dean *v.* Nunnally, 36 Miss. 358; Edwards *v.* Gibbs, 39 Miss. 166; Tatum *v.* McLellan, 50 Miss. 1; Foote *v.* Sanders, 72 Mo. 616; Burleigh *v.* Clough, 52 N. H. 267; Ackerman *v.* Gorton, 67 N. Y. 63; Weed *v.* Aldrich, 5 T. & C. (N. Y.) 105; 2 Hun (N. Y.) 531; Cockrill *v.* Maney, 2 Tenn. Ch. 49; Milhollen *v.* Rice, 13 W. Va. 510; Scott *v.* Josselyn, 26 Beav. 174; Keeler *v.* Collins, 7 U. C., Q. B. 519.

Where real estate is conveyed to a trustee to hold to the separate use, benefit and disposal of a married woman during her natural life, and to such uses as she might by any writing direct and appoint and on her death to such uses as she might by last will direct and appoint, a deed from the trustee and the wife would pass the fee. Pendleton *v.* Bell, 32 Mo. 100.

A testator devised lands to his wife for life, and gave her, "in case she should stand in need, full power to sell his whole estate, real as well as personal for her comfortable support." *Held*, that this was not a devise with power in the devisee in any event to sell at her will and pleasure, but that the power depended upon a particular contingency. Stevens *v.* Winship, 1 Pick. (Mass.) 318; 11 Am. Dec. 178.

Where a testator devised his real estate to his widow for life, with remainder over, and gave to his executor power, if he should see proper, to sell the real estate, and to put out the proceeds, together with all other moneys, at interest, and pay over the interest to the wife every year, the power of sale was limited to the lifetime of the widow. Fidler *v.* Lash, 125 Pa. St. 87; to same effect, Harmon *v.* Smith, 38 Fed. Rep. 482.

A testator gave and devised all his estate, real and personal, to his mother, M, "to hold and enjoy the same during her life, with full power to sell the same or any part thereof, and appropriate the proceeds to her own use and benefit; and all deeds and conveyances of real estate, by her made, shall pass a title in fee to the purchaser, it being my will that she shall enjoy the same as though it were devised to her in fee." The testator further provided that, "after the death of my mother, I devise all of the said estate to my half brother, D." The testator's mother, afterwards by deed, sold, conveyed and warranted a part of the real estate so devised to her to the defendant, who paid her therefor the full consideration and value of the fee simple thereof, and accepted her deed as conveying to and vesting in him the fee of the real estate described therein, and took and held possession thereof, making valuable and lasting improvments thereon. It was held that, in the execution of such warranty deed as aforesaid, the mother, M, manifestly intended to execute the power of disposition conferred on her by the testator's will, and that, by such deed, she conveyed to the defendant, not merely her life-estate, but also the absolute title in fee simple, which she had "full power" to do under the will. Downie *v.* Buennagel, 94 Ind. 228.

A testator gave his widow a life-estate in land, and gave to her as executrix the power, at her discretion, to convey the fee. The will further provided that, in case she declined or resigned the trust, the administrator with the will annexed might execute the power during the widow's lifetime, but only by the license and direction of the probate court. On this state of facts, the widow, as executrix, has power to convey a good title in fee simple, and since she was authorized to expend such portions of all the proceeds as she in her discretion might deem proper for her own support, the purchaser was not bound to attend to the application of the purchase money. Carroll *v.* Shea, 149 Mass. 317.

A testator devised his residuary estate to the husband of his granddaughter, in trust for the granddaughter during her natural life; and in further trust to convey the same, during her natural life, from time to time, to such persons, in such portions, and on such considerations as she might, in writing, request; and to dispose of it upon her decease, as she might by will direct; or, in case of her dying intestate, to hold the same for her next of kin. *Held*, that the trustee was empowered to convey the fee, and not merely an estate for the life of the granddaughter. Weed *v.* Knorr, 77 Ga. 636.

A husband conveyed land in trust for his wife and their children, the deed providing that the land should not be liable for the husband's debts, but that it should be managed, controlled and disposed of by the wife as though she were single, she to have power, the trustee consenting, to incumber or convey the land, her husband to have no interest in the proceeds. Power was also given her to devise the same as though she were single. *Held*, that her conveyance in fee vested a perfect title in the vendee; that the restrictions were meant only to cut off the husband's control; that the interest of the children depended upon their surviving their mother without her having exercised the power of disposition; and that when such power was exercised by her it was binding upon them. Moyston *v.* Bacon, 7 Lea (Tenn.) 236.

Where a testator devised to his wife and daughter his whole estate, they "to be equal and joint heirs, to sell and dispose of the same, and the survivor on the death of either of them," the whole estate to be at the wife's "absolute disposal during the minority of said child" no power to sell was conferred upon the wife for a longer period than during the child's minority. Devereux *v.* Dunn, 2 Ired. Eq. (N. Car.) 206.

Where the testator gives the land on

which he lived to his wife for life; also absolutely all slaves, furniture, etc., on the plantation; "that is, that she enjoy them during her life, and then dispose of them among his lineal descendants as she should think proper," the power of appointment thus given to the wife does not extend to the remainder in the land in which a life-estate was given her, and such remainder vests in the residuary devisees. Mitchells *v.* Johnson, 6 Leigh (Va.) 461.

A testator directed that all his property should be equally divided between his wife and children, his executors to portion the same into as many equal shares as might be necessary to give each beneficiary two shares, and convey one of such shares to each beneficiary in fee, and retain the residue in trust, and pay over the income on the respective shares to each beneficiary during life, the wife's portion remaining in their hands at her death to be divided, etc. The executors were given full power to convey any and all the estate, and invest the proceeds on the same trusts. It was held that the executors could convey at any time the fee in the portion set apart for the use of the wife during her lifetime, and not simply a life-estate. Kortright *v.* Storminger, 49 Hun (N. Y.) 249.

In a recent case in *Kentucky* it was held that, under the circumstances of that case, the life tenant had no power to convey a fee. There the testator by the second clause of his will devised to his wife certain real estate and certain household furniture concluding with the words: "The foregoing mentioned articles are given to my said wife for and during her natural life, and then to return to my estate, except such of it as may be consumed in its use." (The word "articles" in this clause was held to include the realty devised to his wife for life.) The clause concluded as follows: "I give to my wife in addition to the before mentioned property one-third of the proceeds of any personal estate which may remain after paying my debts. This last is an absolute gift."

The third clause of the will directed that after the death of his wife, all of the estate given to her for life "and which may remain, be sold upon a reasonable credit, and the proceeds divided as herein directed."

The sixth clause provided that after the death of the widow all the estate remaining unsold, and the proceeds, should be divided into five equal shares, and pass to his children named.

The seventh clause vested in his executors, or such of them as qualify, full power to sell and convey a good title to any part of his estate, "and the title to my real estate is hereby vested severally in my executors so as to enable them or either of them to pass title thereto to a purchaser or purchasers, but for no other purpose, and to no greater extent." In addition to the land specifically mentioned as devised to the wife for life, the testator owned several other tracts of lands, and such other tracts were also directed to be sold by his executors.

The executors named in the will failed to qualify, and the widow qualified as administratrix with the will annexed, and sold the land devised to her, and placed the purchaser in possession. The land was claimed by the devisees in remainder. *Held*, that the widow acquired only a life interest in the lands devised to her by the second clause of the will, and the power given to the executors to sell by the seventh clause was restricted to a sale after the termination of her life estate; and the widow had no authority to sell any interest greater than her life estate. Dohoney *v.* Taylor, 79 Ky. 124.

Where lands are devised to the testator's widow for life or during her widowhood, and power is given to sell them during widowhood, she can convey the fee. No particular words are necessary provided they show such to be the intention. Thus the Supreme Court of *Missouri* held the following words sufficient for the purpose: "To my wife all my real estate, to do as she shall wish for her own use while she continues my widow; I will that she shall sell one lot (specifying the lot) and apply the proceeds to her own use. Boyer *v.* Allen, 76 Mo. 498. The Supreme Court of *Illinois* held the same way in a case where the testator willed that his wife should take at his decease his whole estate, real and personal, and should manage the same at her discretion and deal with the same as though she were entire and sole owner; that she should pay the debts, etc., out of the estate without any sale of the same except such as she may, in her discretion, voluntarily make;" in the event of his widow's re-marriage, he provided that she was to "be put upon her dower of one-third, and that the fee and ownership of my estate vest in

(3) *Effect Upon Estate.*—A power of sale may override estates in fee.[1]

said heirs, subject to said dower interest." Markillee *v.* Ragland, 77 Ill. 98. In *North Carolina* like effect was given to the following words: "All my property to my beloved wife during her natural life or widowhood, with power to dispose of the same by sale, will or otherwise at her discretion." Stroud *v.* Morrow, 7 Jones (N. Car.) 463. In *Vermont:* "To my beloved wife one-third part of all my real and personal estate to have at her disposal during her natural life or as long as she remains my widow." White *v.* White, 21 Vt. 250, and construing the same will, Hart *v.* White, 26 Vt. 260. In *New Jersey:* "To my beloved wife all my real estate, etc., for her use and benefit for her lifetime and during her remaining widow, with the privilege to sell and dispose of the same at her own free will, but only during her said widowhood." Hemhauser *v.* Decker, 38 N. J. Eq. 426.

And see generally on this point, Giles *v.* Little, 104 U. S. 291; Vaughn *v.* Lovejoy, 34 Ala. 437; Frey *v.* Thompson, 66 Ala. 287; Jenkins *v.* Merritt, 17 Fla. 304; New *v.* Potts, 55 Ga. 420; Green *v.* Hewitt, 97 Ill. 113; Stillwell *v.* Knapper, 69 Ind. 558; Coppage *v.* Alexander, 2 B. Mon. (Ky.) 313; Swope *v.* Swope, 5 Gill (Md.) 225; Gough *v.* Manning, 26 Md. 347; Mandelbaum *v.* McDonnell, 29 Mich. 78; 18 Am. Rep. 61; Dumey *v.* Schoeffler, 24 Mo. 170; Bryant *v.* Christian, 58 Mo. 98; Steger's Estate, 11 Phila. (Pa.) 158; Aaron *v.* Beck, 9 Rich. Eq. (S. Car.) 411; Missionary Soc. *v.* Calvert, 32 Gratt. (Va.) 357; Marples *v.* Bainbridge, 1 Madd. 317; Pickwell *v.* Spencer, L. R., 6 Exch. 190; Evans *v.* Rosser, 2 H. & M. 190; Lloyd *v.* Lloyd, 2 Sim., N. S. 255; Brown *v.* Hammond, Johns. Eng. Rep. 210; Nowlan *v.* Walsh, 4 De G. & Sm. 284; Underhill *v.* Roden, L. R., 2 Ch. Div. 494; Burgess *v.* Burrows, 21 U. C. C. P. 426.

1. Boyce *v.* Hanning, 2 C. & J. 334. See Sugden *v.* Ackerman, 37 N. J. Eq. 442; Crozier *v.* Hoyt, 97 Ill. 23; Proctor *v.* Scharff, 80 Ala. 227.

But if the devisee or legatee have the absolute right of disposal of the property at pleasure, a devise over is inoperative. Ramsdell *v.* Ramsdell, 21 Me. 288; Pickering *v.* Langdon, 22 Me. 413. And a valid executory devise cannot subsist under an absolute power of disposition in the first taker. 4 Kent's Comm. *270; McKenzie's Appeal, 41 Conn. 607; 19 Am. Rep. 525; Burleigh *v.* Clough, 52 N. H. 267; 13 Am. Rep. 23.

It is proper to remark here, in passing, that it has been held repeatedly, both in this country and in *England*, that where a fee is conveyed, any limitation or restriction of the absolute power of the grantee over it is void. Thus, in the case of Mandlebaum *v.* McDonell, 29 Mich. 78; 18 Am. Rep. 61, Christiancy, J., in an elaborate argument on this point, so clearly draws the distinction between the cases where a power would be held valid, and one where it would be void as in restriction of alienation, that it seems proper to make a somewhat extended quotation therefrom. "The estate devised," he says, being an absolute vested estate in fee, the only remaining question is, whether such a restriction of the right of the devisees to sell such an estate is valid. This is the main question in the case and was very properly so treated and discussed by the counsel on both sides. And before proceeding to determine this question, it may, for the sake of clearness, and to avoid the confusion which might arise from confounding questions which might otherwise seem analogous, be as important to point out what the question does not involve, as what it does. It does not, then, involve the question whether a restraint upon the sale of this property for an equal length of time might not have been rendered legally effective by the conveyance of the legal title to trustess, in trust for the benefit of these devisees, according to instructions as to time of sale, which might have been inserted in the will; in which case the validity of the restrictions as to time would depend mainly upon the question whether the period exceeded that allowed by the Rule against Perpetuities. Nor does the question involve an inquiry how far a somewhat similar object might have been accomplished by making this estate in fee in these devisees defeasible, upon the condition of their executing, before a certain period, a conveyance to certain persons, or to any other than certain persons, or to any party what-

d. POWER TO LEASE—(1) *In General.*—The power granted to a life tenant to make leases which shall be effectual, even though the life tenancy may terminate before the end of the term granted, is one of the most useful of powers, and the one which in *England*, is perhaps the most frequently granted.[1]

ever, or of their becoming bankrupt, or allowing a sale upon execution, or permitting a judgment to become a lien, or upon condition of using the property in some particular way, the property being limited over to another, or to be forfeited and revert on breach of the condition. In these cases there would be some party besides these devisees interested in the observance of the condition, with a right to take advantage of the breach, viz: the heirs of the devisor, or the person to whom the property was limited over. It is quite possible that many restrictions or qualifications upon the right of devisees or grantees may be made effectual by making the estate itself dependent upon such condition, to which it could not be subjected if the estate given is absolute, as it is admitted to be here. Nor does the fact that, in the case of an executory devise, or in that of a contingent remainder, or any other interest not vested, a restriction upon the power of the devisees to sell before it shall become vested in interest would be good, in any manner tend to sustain such a restriction upon a vested estate in fee. This devise is not made to trustees for the benefit of the devisees, but directly to the devisees themselves. The estate devised is not a conditional one to be forfeited or to revert to the heirs of the testator, or to go over to others on a breach of the restrictions, nor one which is to vest at some future day, or upon the happening of some future event, but an absolute vested remainder or estate in fee, and though not to come into actual enjoyment until the death of the widow, to whom a life estate is given, it is just as much vested, and the devisees have just as much right to sell the interest or estate devised, as if there had been no intervening estate for life. And the question of the validity of the restriction is, in my view, precisely the same, in all its legal aspects, as if no life estate had been given to the widow, but the whole had been given in fee directly to these devisees, as an absolute estate in fee and in possession, with the same provisions restricting the power of sale. My first difficulty in holding the devisees or their estate bound by the restriction is this: a legal obligation always involves the idea, not only of a party upon whom it rests, but of another party in whose favor, or for whose interest or benefit it is imposed, and who, therefore, has the right to call for its enforcement."

In the case from which the above citation is made, the court held that the restrictions upon the sale were invalid. This case has been followed by the recent English case of Rosher *v.* Rosher, L. Rep., 26 Ch. Div. 801, where a testator devised an estate in fee to his son, provided that if he wished to sell it during the life of testator's wife, she should have an option to purchase it at a sum which was about one-third of its market value. It was held that this proviso amounted to an absolute restraint on alienation during the life of the testator's widow, and was void.

The following cases also hold that a general restriction on alienation after a conveyance in fee, is void. McWilliams *v.* Nisly, 2 S. & R. (Pa.) 507; Hawley *v.* Northampton, 8 Mass. 37; McDowell *v.* Brown, 21 Mo. 57; Kent *v.* Allen, 32 Mo. 87; Wead *v.* Gray, 78 Mo. 59; Chew *v.* Keller, 100 Mo. 362.

This question is fully discussed by Mr. Surrogate Rollins, of the New York Surrogate's Court, *In re* Fernbacher, 17 Abb. N. Cas. (N. Y.) 339, and the cases in New York and elsewhere are reviewed as they are also by the court of appeals in Van Horne *v.* Campbell, 100 N. Y. 287.

See also the note to 57 Am. Dec. 587.

1. 2 Sugd. Pow. (3rd Am. ed.) 275, *305; Taylor *v.* Horde, 1 Burr. 60.

Chancellor Kent says: "It was a clear principle of the common law, that no man could grant a lease to continue beyond the period at which his own estate was to determine; and, therefore, a tenant for life could not, by virtue of his ownership, make a lease to continue after his death. But a lease made under a power may continue notwithstanding the determination of the estate by the death of the person by whom the power is exercised." 4 Kent Comm. *106.

In Taylor *v.* Horde, 1 Burr. 121, Lord Mansfield says: "The plan of this power is for the mutual advantage of possessor and successor. The execution thereof is checked with many conditions, to guard the successor; that the annual revenue shall not be diminished, nor those in succession or remainder at all prejudiced in point of remedy, or other circumstances of full and ample enjoyment." And the same learned judge says that they should be liberally construed. Right *v.* Thomas, 1 Wm. Blacks. 449.

The most important power connected with the making of leases is that given to a tenant for life in modern settlements; and leases made in pursuance of such powers are good against the persons in remainder and reversion. 4 Greenl. Cruise. Dig. *157.

Ordinary trustees, too, have an implied power of leasing where they are charged with the payment of annuities, debts or legacies, and have no power of sale. 2 Perry on Trusts, § 528.

While the power to make leases is one of the most common powers created in *England*, where a large proportion of the lease-holds are held by virtue of the exercise of such powers, they are by no means so frequent in this country. Still they are not unknown. In Collins *v.* Foley, 63 Md. 158; 52 Am. Rep. 505, the court by Miller, J, said: "Powers of leasing are very common in English settlements and wills. In that country every well prepared settlement and will of real estate, unless its value be inconsiderable, or the circumstances of the case do not require it, contains a power of leasing, and as was said by Lord Mansfield in Taylor *v.* Horde, 1 Burr. 120, 'of all kinds of powers this is the most frequent.' The general rule of interpretation which prevails here as in all of the similar cases, is that such powers must be construed according to the intention of the parties."

In this case the testatrix by her will devised the residue of her estate to Daniel J. Foley, his heirs, executors and administrators in trust, to pay an annuity, and to hold "to and for the use and benefit of my son during his life only, and from and after his decease to and for the use and benefit of all and every the children and child of my said son, and their descendants *per stirpes* which should be living at his death, their heirs, executors, administrators and assigns forever." The will also empowered the trustee with the consent of the son during his life, and subject to the approbation of the orphans' court after the son's death, to make such changes of the investments from time to time as he saw fit, "for the which end I hereby authorize and empower my said trustee to do all lawful acts, and execute and deliver all lawful deeds and instruments of writing in the premises, full power to lease being included herein." The testatrix made a codicil in which after providing for certain contingencies she adds: "Lest there be any misunderstanding as to the powers of my said trustee, as to the leasing of the property, I hereby declare it to be my intention, that . . . he shall have full power and authority to make and execute any and all leases whatsoever of my estate which he may deem advantageous and proper."

It was argued that this leasing power was repugnant to the estates created by the will, and therefore void. The court, while admitting that if this were a restraint upon alienation instead of a power to lease it would be void, holds that a power to lease is valid, provided it does not infringe the rule as to perpetuities, and says "this is quite different from clogging a direct devise in fee, with a restriction upon alienation. In fact, one of the principal purposes of interposing the trust seems to have been to enable the testatrix to confer upon the trustee this leasing power, and we think it may be safely affirmed that in all the range of authorities no case can be found in which the validity of such a power, thus conferred and thus limited, has been questioned. Such powers are not only reasonable, but are sometimes necessary, especially in a case like this, where the estate disposed of consists largely of property, the income from which must consist of rent reserved under leases, and where infants are the beneficiaries. At all events the testatrix had the right to dispose of her property as she pleased, and this disposition of it does not, in our opinion, violate any established rule of real estate law." Collins *v.* Foley 63 Md. 158; 52 Am. Rep. 509.

Lands were devised to A for life

with remainder to B for life, with power to A to make leases. A made a lease to C and died during the term. It was held that B could sue upon the covenants. Isherwood *v.* Oldknow, 3 M. & S. 382; Rogers *v.* Humphrey, 4 A. & E. 299.

Rules of Construction of Powers to Lease.—In Kent's Comm. *107, it is said, "Powers to make leases are treated liberally, for the encouragement of agricultural improvement and enterprise, which require some permanent interest." And see Right *v.* Thomas, 3 Burr. 1441; 1 Wm. Bl. 446.

In an early *South Carolina* case the trustees of a charity were prohibited from selling or alienating, and it was adjudged that a power to lease was implied. Black *v.* Ligon, Harper (S. Car.) Eq. 205.

The restrictive portions of a power to make leases are to be strictly construed against the tenant for life and his lessees, and in favor of the remaindermen or reversioners, since the conditions upon which powers of this kind are given are inserted with a view to the interest of the latter. Therefore every circumstance required by the power must be strictly followed, or the lease will be void; and the instruments by which leasing powers are executed are construed more strictly than other deeds of appointment. 4 Greenl. Cruise Dig. *158.

A power to lease lands generally will authorize the leasing of opened mines therein but not of unopened mines. Clegg *v.* Rowland, L. R., 2 Eq. 160. Under a power to executors to lease the testator's real estate, they are authorized to lease the coal in a mine on his estate. Wentz's Appeal, 106 Pa. St. 301. See also cases cited in MINES AND MINING CLAIMS, vol. 15, p. 596.

If an improper covenant is inserted in a lease made under a power, this does not merely render the covenant invalid, but the lease itself is void. 4 Cruise Dig. *158; 2 Perry on Trusts, § 259.

A lease for a longer term than that authorized by the power is bad at law. Sinclair *v.* Jackson, 8 Cow. (N. Y.) 581; but may be held good in equity for the time limited, and void only for the excess. Campbell *v.* Leach, Ambl. 740; Pawcey *v.* Bowen, 1 Ch. Ca. 23; 3 Ch. Rep. 11.

A lease for a less number of years than that prescribed is good. Isherwood *v.* Oldknow, 3 M. & S. 382.

And under a power to lease for twenty-one years, a lease for twenty-one years, determinable at the option of the lessee, is good. Edwards *v.* Millbank, 4 Drew 606.

Where a testator devised an estate to trustees in trust to A for life, with remainder to his children with power in the trustees to make leases not exceeding twenty-one years, and the trustees disclaimed a lease made by the testator's heir at law is void. Robson *v.* Flight, 34 L. J., Ch. 226; 11 L. T., N. S. 725.

A power of leasing was given to A, tenant for life, and after his decease to his son, tenant for life. The son obtained from his father a grant of the latter's life estate (containing no notice of the power), subject to a certain rent, with a power of re-entry for nonpayment. *Held*, that the son couldn't lease under the power during the lifetime of A. Coxe *v.* Day, 13 East 118.

A mortgage contained a provision enabling the mortgagor, till foreclosure, to grant leases. The mortgagor made a lease to one in trust for the mortgagor himself. *Held*, to be a valid exercise of the power. Bevan *v.* Habgood, 7 Jur., N. S. 41; 30 L. J., Ch. 107, 1 Johns & H. 22.

A tenant for life had a power of appointing the estate, by deed or will, among his children or to one of them, but had no power to lease. He granted a lease, and on the day of its date made a will in exercise of the power in favor of a daughter. At the same time the father and daughter gave the lessee a bond of indemnity against the forfeiture of the lease by the death of the appointor during the term. *Held*, that the power was well exercised. Pickles *v.* Pickles, 7 Jur., N. S. 1065; 31 L. J. Ch. 146.

The term of the lease is generally twenty-one years. 2 Washb. Real Prop. *306; 4 Cruise Dig. *170.

By the New York statute, the term may not exceed twenty-one years and must commence during the lifetime of the life tenant on whom the power to lease is conferred. New York Rev. Stat., §§ 87-89 (Banks' ed.), p. 2447; (1882) p. 2190. And see Root *v.* Stuyvesant, 18 Wend. (N. Y.) 257.

A lease for fourteen years is a good exercise of a power to lease for two or three lives, or for the term of twenty-one years. Isherwood *v.* Oldknow, 3

(2) *Following Conditions.*—Where the tenant for life has a power of leasing under certain conditions, the lease must conform strictly to the conditions.[1]

M. & S. 382. See also Whitlock's Case, 8 Coke 69 b; 1 Sugd. Pow. *514; 2 Sugd. Pow. *354.

Under a power of leasing for one, two or three lives, or for any term of years, determinable on one, two or three-lives, the three lives must be certain and co-existing. Doe *v.* Halcomb, 7 T. R. 713.

Where the power is to grant a lease for thirty-one years or for three lives, and the lease was made for three lives and thirty-one years, which ever should last longest, this was a good execution of the power. Commons *v.* Marshall, 6 Bro. P. C. 168.

An estate was settled on several tenants for life in succession, with remainders in tail, with power to each tenant for life, "who should be entitled to the freehold of the premises, or any part thereof, when he should be in the actual possession of the same or any part thereof, from time to time, by indenture, to make leases of all or any part of the lands, whereof he should be in the actual possession as aforesaid, for any term or number of years not exceeding twenty-one, or for the life or lives of any one, two or three person or persons, so as no greater estate than for three lives be at any one time in being in any part of the premises." *Held*, that the power authorized either a chattel lease not exceeding twenty-one years, or a freehold lease not exceeding three lives; that a lease for ninety-nine years, determinable on lives was void, since it might exceed twenty-one years, and that it was not even good *pro tanto* for twenty-one years. Roe *v.* Prideaux, 10 East 158. To same effect, Doe *v.* Hiern, 5 M. & S. 40; Jenner *v.* Morris, 7 Jur., N. S. 385; 9 W. R. 566; 4 L. T., N. S. 347.

In *Maryland*, where property was devised to A, as trustee, and to his representatives, to hold for the use of the son of testator for life, and after his death for the use of the children of said son, with power to A, but not to his representatives, to lease, a lease for ninety-nine years, renewable forever, was held valid. Collins *v.* Foley, 63 Md. 158; 52 Am. Rep. 505. In another case in the same State, power was given to a trustee and his successors "to make such change of investment of my estate . . . as may be in the estimation of my said trustee proper and advantageous, to which end I hereby authorize and empower my said trustee to . . . execute and deliver all needful deeds, leases, and other instruments of writing." It was held that the trustee might make a lease for ninety-nine years. Collins *v.* MacTavish, 63 Md. 166.

A power to lease mines and minerals contained in a gift of a life-estate in the lands under which they lie, though expressed in general terms, does not necessarily imply a power in the life-tenant to make a lease exceeding the term of his own life. Vivian *v.* Jegon, 3 L. R., H. L. Cas. 285; 19 L. T., N. S. 218; 37 L. J., C. P. 313.

Confirmation of Leases.—If the life-tenant grants a lease exceeding his power, such lease is void, and not capable of confirmation by the remainderman. But if, after the death of the life-tenant the remainderman accepts rent as such, this is an admission of the tenancy. Doe *v.* Watts, 7 T. R. 83; 2 Esp. 501. And see Robson *v.* Flight, 34 L. J., Ch. 226; 11 L. T., N. S. 725; Wright *v.* Smith, 5 Esp. 203; Doe *v.* Weller, 7 T. R. 478; Doe *v.* White, 2 D. & R. 716.

1. Caran *v.* Pulteney, 6 Bro. P. C. 175; 5 T. R. 567; 2 Perry on Trusts, § 529.

The statute 12 & 13 Vict., ch. 26 as amended by 13 Vict., ch. 17, providing for relief against defects in leases made under leasing powers, does not apply to leases granted by a mere stranger to a leasing power. *Ex parte* Cooper, 34 L. J., Ch. 373; 11 Jur., N. S. 103.

Before the passage of this act a lease, which varied from the conditions in the interest demised or in the rent reserved could not be supported against the remainderman. Caran *v.* Pulteney, 6 Bro. P. C. 175; 5 T. R. 567.

If a qualification is annexed to a power of leasing which would, if observed, destroy the power or render it nugatory, the law will dispense with it. 4 Cruise Dig. *160; Walker *v.* Wakeman, 1 Vent, 294; Winter *v.* Loveden, 1 Ld. Raym. 267.

Compare Goodlittle *v.* Funucan, 2 Dougl. 565; Pomeroy *v.* Partington, 3 T. R. 365; Doe *v.* Rendle, 3 M. & S. 99.

(3) *In Possession or Reversion.*—A lease in reversion is one that is to commence at a future day. In this sense it is opposed to a lease in possession. But what is usually intended by a lease in reversion, is one which is to commence after the end of a present interest in being.[1] Under powers to lease in

1. 2 Sugd. Pow. *343.

"In legal acceptance a lease for years in reversion and a future interest for years are one and the same; a future lease and a lease in reversion are synonymous." 2 Sugd. Pow. *344.

A lease *in futuro* is one which is granted to take effect from a future date, when there is no prior lease subsisting; or, if there is one, the grant of the new lease is not dependent on it. In this sense a lease *in futuro* may be granted as well of a reversion as of a possession. 2 Sugd. Pow. *343.

As to leases in possession and reversion, Lord C. J. Holt says: "In the most ample lease that is said to be a lease in reversion which hath its commencement at a future day; and then it is opposed to a lease in possession. For every lease that is not a lease in possession, in this sense is said to be a lease in reversion." Winter *v.* Loveday, 1 Com. 37; 1 Freem. 507; 1 Ld. Raym. 267; 2 Salk. 537; 5 Mod. 244, 378.

In determining whether a lease is made to commence *in futuro*, there has been some dispute as to the effect of the word "from." If the lease is to commence "from the day of its date," if the word "from" be held to exclude the day of its date, the lease is manifestly to commence in the future. As will be seen below, this question is now settled by the case of Pugh *v.* Duke of Leeds, Cowp. 714, by which the day of the date is held to be included. And this decision is approved by Mr. Chance. 2 Chance Pow. 286 [2226, 2227].

Mr. Sugden says on this point: "It has long been settled that a lease to hold "from henceforth," "from the making," "from the time of delivery of the indentures" or "from the sealing and delivery of the deed," is a lease in possession, and not *in futuro*." But a lease to hold "from the day of the date" thereof, is a lease *in futuro*. 2 Sugd. Pow. (3rd Am. ed.) 323, *361.

But in Pugh *v.* Duke of Leeds, Cowp. 714, it was decided that "from the day of the date" meant the same as "from the date," including the day of its date, and that the lease was valid under a power to lease in possession only. And this case has been generally followed, and is now the law. 2 Chance Pow. 285. But see Doe *v.* Watton, Cowp. 189.

As the lease takes effect from its execution, and not from its date, it may be shown by extrinsic evidence what was the actual date of its execution, and if not executed till after the time when it was expressed to commence, it will be supported as a lease in possession. 2 Sugd. Pow. (3rd Am. ed.) 325, *363.

It is usual to make the lease take effect "from the day next before the day of the date of the deed." 2 Sugd. Pow. (3d Am. ed.) 325, *363.

If a lease is made to commence only a day after the date of the deed creating it, it is void under a power to grant leases in possession only, as much so as if it were to take effect one hundred years from the time. 2 Sugd. Pow. (3d Am. ed.) 323, *361.

A lease executed in March to the tenant then in possession, *habendum* as to part from the 13th of February preceding, and as to the remainder from the 5th of April then next, under a yearly rent payable quarterly on July 10th, etc., is void, where the power is to lease in possession and not in reversion. Doe *v.* Galvert, 2 East 376.

But though the lease is dated February 17th, *habendum* from March 25th next ensuing, it is good as a lease in possession, if not actually executed and delivered till after March 25th. Doe *v.* Day, 10 East 427.

A lease for twenty-one years to the only daughter of the donee is a good lease, though it is to commence from the day of its date. Pugh *v.* Leeds, Cowp. 714.

And a lease *per verba de præsenti* is not contrary to a power to grant leases in possession, though at the time of granting the lease the estate was held by tenants at will, or from year to year, if at the time they received directions from the grantor of the lease to pay their rent to the lessee. Goodlittle *v.* Funucan, 2 Dougl. 565.

possession, leases in reversion or *in futuro* cannot be granted.[1]

(4) *Lease Relates to Creation of Power.*—A lease granted under a power, like every other estate so raised, takes effect as if it were contained in the instrument creating the power.[2]

(5) *The Rent.*—The questions in regard to rent chiefly concerns the *quantum*, or the mode of reservation.[3] As to the *quantum*, the covenants most generally are "for the usual rent," or for the "ancient rent," or "for the best rent."[4]

1. 2 Chance Pow. 279 [2207]; 4 Greenl. Cruise Dig. *165, *166; 2 Perry on Trusts, § 529; Pollard *v.* Greenville, 1 Ch. Cas. 10; 1 Ch. Rep. 184; Doe *v.* Calvert, 2 East 375; Opey *v.* Thomasius, Raym. 132; Bowes *v.* East London R. Co., 3 Madd. 375; Jacob. 324; Sussex *v.* Weoth, Cro. Eliz. 5; 6 Rep. 33 a; Slocum *v.* Hawkins, Yelv. 222; Doe *v.* Cavan, 5 T. R. 567. And see cases cited in preceding note.

Compare Northampton's Case, 3 Dyer 357 a; Coventry *v.* Coventry, Com. R. 312.

A power to lease generally, without saying anything as to the lease being in possession or reversion, authorizes the creation of a lease to commence at the determination of the former one, and not a mere concurrent lease. 2 Chance Pow. 265 [2173]; Lord C. J. Holt says in Winter *v.* Loveday, 1 Ld. Raym. 267; 2 Salk. 537; 5 Mod. 244, 378, that a power to lease generally empowers the donee to lease only in possession. 2 Chance Pow. 270 [2188]. But the former view was taken in Coventry *v.* Coventry, 1 Com. 312.

But where there is a general power to make leases, the donee may make a concurrent lease to commence immediately, though the lands are already held under an existing lease, made by a former proprietor or by the donee himself. 4 Cruise Dig. *169; Berry *v.* Riebe, Hard. 412; Reed *v.* Nash, 1 Leon. 147; Goodlittle *v.* Funucan, 2 Doug. 565.

Compare Roe *v.* Prideaux, 10 East 184.

Even where there is a power to make leases in reversion it authorizes only the making of a lease to commence at the termination of a lease in possession and not to commence generally at any future period. 4 Cruise Dig. *169.

A power to lease premises for a term not exceeding twenty-one years, and determinable as a former term of ninety-nine years was determinable as the donee should think proper, authorizes only a lease in possession, and not *in futuro.* Shaw *v.* Summers, 3 Moore 196.

An agreement made before the expiration of the term to grant a new lease at the end of the term is not an agreement to grant a reversionary lease, but is within the terms of a power authorizing the making of leases in possession only. Dowell *v.* Dew, 7 Jur. 117; 12 L. J., Ch. 158.

2. 2 Sugd. Pow. (3d Am. ed.) 283, *316.

"Therefore in the common case of a lease by a tenant for life under a power, it precedes, like a common lease, the estate of the person granting it, and he takes the reversion expectant upon it." 2 Sugd. Pow. (3rd Am. ed.) 284, *316; Whitlock's Case, 8 Mod. 69 b; 10 Ves. Jr. 256; Isherwood *v.* Oldknow, 3 M. & S. 382.

3. 2 Sugd. Pow. *386.

4. The best rent means the best rack rent that can reasonably be required by a landlord, taking all the requisites of a good tenant for the permanent benefit of the estate into the account. Doe *v.* Radcliffe, 10 East 278.

Whether the rent reserved is the best rent is always a question for the jury. Doe *v.* Rogers, 2 N. & M. 550; 5 B. & Ad. 755; 2 Sugd. Pow. *386.

Where the special power is to lease lands usually let, or upon the usual rent, it will apply *prima facie* to such lands only as have been generally let, and to the ordinary adequate rent. 2 Perry on Trusts, § 530; Cardigan *v.* Montague, 2 Sugd. Pow., Appendix 14, *339; Osbey *v.* Mohun, 2 Vern. 531; 2 Roll. Abr. 261, pl. 11, 12.

The ancient rent is usually held to mean that which was reserved at the date of the creation of the power. 2 Sugd. Pow. *400.

But the usual rent means the old and uniform custom, and not the rent re-

3. When Power Is Valid.—To render a power valid the purpose for which it is created must be a legal one.[1] A power is not rendered invalid because one of the purposes for which it is

served on a single lease which was executed just before the creation of the power. Doe *v.* Hole, 15 Q. B. 848.

Under a power to demise lands, reserving the ancient rent, a demise of the lands jointly with others at an entire rent is void. Doe *v.* Matthews, 2 N. & M. 264; 5 B. & A. 298

A power to lease, so as the usual rent is reserved or made payable yearly, is well executed, though the usual rent is made payable semi-annually. Fryer *v.* Coombs. 11 A. & E. 403; 4 P. & D. 120, n.

Where the power provides that the lease is to be made for the best rent which can be got, it is not sufficient that the same rent is reserved as in a former lease, where the rent in the former lease was reduced on account of money to be expended by the lessee in improvements. Doe *v.* Lloyd, 3 Esp. 78.

1. Sugd. Pow. *177, *178.

If, by a fair construction of the whole instrument creating a separate estate in a *feme covert*, the *jus disponendi*, and incidental power to encumber and charge the estate, to an extent involving alienation, be inconsistent with the plan and scheme of settlement, and the exercise of these powers would defeat the plain intent pervading the instrument, they must be considered as much forbidden as if expressly denied. Bank of Greensboro *v.* Chambers, 30 Gratt. (Va.) 202; Appman Ropp *v.* Minor, 33 Gratt. (Va.) 97.

A power of sale dependent on a void trust, falls with the trust. Penfield *v.* Tower (N. Dak. 1890), 46 N. W. Rep. 413.

Where a devise in fee to a *feme covert* is accompanied by a power to dispose of the estate without the control of her husband, the power is void. Goodell *v.* Brigham, 1 Bos & Pul. 192.

If the power to be executed is so uncertain as to its objects that a court of equity cannot say what particular person or persons are to take an interest in it, it cannot be carried into effect. 2 Perry on Trusts, § 253.

A power of appointment to give or devise property among such benevolent, religious or charitable institutions as the donee might think proper, is so vague and indefinite as to be void. Morris *v.* Thompson, 19 N. J. Eq. 307.

A power given to executors to purchase a farm in a certain locality and of a certain value, in case the testator had not done so in his lifetime, is too vague and indefinite to be carried into effect and is void. Henly *v.* Fitzgerald, 65 Barb. (N. Y.) 508.

As to effect of indefiniteness in legacies on power of sale, see Denton *v.* Clark, 36 N. J. Eq. 534.

Whether a power, given by a will, to deprive a child of the testator of his share under the will, in case such child should marry without the consent of the donee of the power, is void, if the property would, upon the execution of the power, belong to the donee of such power. Bayeaux *v.* Bayeaux, 8 Paige (N. Y.) 333.

A power of sale upon default given to a mortgagee is valid. Fogarty *v.* Sawyer, 17 Cal. 589, Bradley *v.* Chester Valley R. Co., 36 Pa St. 141, Mitchell *v.* Bogan, 11 Rich. (S. Car.) 686. And it is not necessary that the person to whom the power of sale is given should join in the execution of the mortgage. Leffler *v.* Armstrong, 4 Iowa 482. It must be given in clear and explicit terms. Wing *v.* Cooper, 37 Vt. 169.

Where a will provides that the estate should be sold and the proceeds should remain as a permanent fund for the preservation, adornment and repair of a private monumental structure, as this created a perpetuity for a use not charitable it was void, and the power could not be exercised. Bates *v.* Bates, 134 Mass. 110.

A condition attached to a power of sale in a trust deed that the power should be exercised only with the consent of the grantor does not render it void. Kissam *v.* Dierked, 49 N. Y. 602.

A power to sell real estate for the benefit of creditors is not rendered invalid by reason of the fact that the chief creditor is an alien, incapable of inheriting. Parish *v.* Ward, 28 Barb. (N. Y.) 328.

A testator may delegate to his executor the power to appoint a co-executor; and such appointment made by the executor named in the will, after he

created is void,[1] nor because of circumstances subsequently arising.[2] If based upon a contingency which never happens it becomes void.[3] Where the power applies to an estate in excess of

has qualified, is valid. Hartnett *v.* Wandell, 60 N. Y. 346; 19 Am. Rep. 194.

1. Wilson *v.* Lynt, 30 Barb. (N. Y.) 124, 16 How. Pr. (N. Y.) 348; Haxtun *v.* Corse, 2 Barb. Ch. (N. Y.) 506.

But if the sole purpose for which it is created is void, the power cannot be exercised. Bates *v.* Bates, 134 Mass. 110.

A deed of trust which is void as such, but which contains a direction that the trustee shall convey according to the written appointment of the grantor's wife, confers a valid power, and the trustee would be bound to convey as the wife should direct in writing. Hotchkiss *v.* Elting, 36 Barb. (N. Y.) 38.

If the principal object for which the power is created can be effected, the power is valid, though some comparatively unimportant object, not expressly qualifying the delegated power, may fail. Wilson *v.* Lynt, 30 Barb. (N. Y.) 124.

2. Hitchcock *v.* U. S. Bank, 7 Ala. 386; Wilson *v.* Lynt, 16 How. Pr. (N. Y.) 348; 30 Barb. (N. Y.) 124.

3. Fountain *v.* Ravenel, 17 How. (U. S.) 369; Shrewsbury *v.* Scott, 6 C. B., N. S. 1; 6 Jur., N. S. 452; 29 L. J., C. P. 34.

Testator gave all his property to his wife in trust, to apply the income to her own use during her life, and at her death the estate to be divided among her four sons, a daughter, and the issue of a deceased son, in such shares as she might by will appoint, and, in default of such direction and appointment, the estate to go to such beneficiaries above mentioned, in six equal shares, the issue of the deceased son to take one share. Should either of the beneficiaries die before his or her intended share vested, his or her issue to take such share. By a codicil he directed "that on the death of my said wife the share of my estate to go to our son James and our grandson Charles shall be held by my surviving executors in trust for them during their lives . . . and at their respective deaths the principal shall go to their issue, if any; if none, then the same shall fall into my general estate, or as my said wife shall by will direct." *Held*, that the power of appointment given the wife by the codicil was contingent upon the death of James or Charles after the death of the widow, and did not give her power to appoint the share of either of them who might die in her lifetime to any other than the beneficiaries named in the will. Austin *v.* Oakes, 117 N. Y. 577.

Land purchased with the separate property of a married woman, was conveyed to a trustee, by deed providing that it should be held in trust for the sole use of the wife during her life, and after her death for the use of such person as the husband, "by deed made before or after the death of the wife, but to take effect therefrom," should appoint; and also providing, that in case the wife should survive the husband, the land should be held in trust for her, and her heirs, etc., forever. *Held*, that the power of appointment could only be exercised by the husband in the event of his surviving his wife. McClintock *v.* Cowen, 49 Pa. St. 256.

Where the power is given only upon the happening of a particular contingency, it is essential to the valid exercise of the power that the contingency shall be proved to have happened. And this is a question for the jury. Stevens *v.* Winship, 1 Pick. (Mass.) 318; 11 Am. Dec. 178.

If the sale is made before the contingency happens, it will be void. Gast *v.* Porter, 13 Pa. St. 436. *Compare* Logan *v.* Bell, 1 C. B. 872; 14 L. J., C. P. 276.

Thus where lands were devised to testator's daughter in fee tail, with direction to the executors that in case she died without issue, they should sell the lands, and the daughter died without issue, but leaving a husband entitled to curtesy, a sale by the executors during the life of the husband conveyed no title. Hay *v.* Mayer, 8 Watts (Pa.) 203; 34 Am. Dec. 453.

In a decision by the vice chancellor of Ireland it is held that where the power is executed before the happening of the contingency, it will become valid on the subsequent happening of the event, especially if the contingency is one which cannot be determined till the moment of the donee's death. Wandesforde *v.* Carrick, 5 Ir. Rep., Eq. 486.

that held by the donor it may be good to the extent of his estate.[1]

4. Interest of Donee.—The donee of the power has not, strictly speaking, any interest, right, or title in or to the property. Where the power is for his own benefit, he has the means of acquiring a right, title, and interest.[2]

1. Thus where the devisee of a particular estate with remainder over created a power to dispose of the fee, a conveyance under the power would pass the particular estate. Bowman *v.* Bartlet, 3 A. K. Marsh. (Ky.) 86.

2. 1 Chance Pow. [2]; 2 Bouv. Inst. 1922; Harrison *v.* Battle, 1 Dev. & B. Eq. (N. Car.) 213.

As to distinction between a power and an interest, see 1 Chance Pow. 603, 604.

A general power of appointment is considered a species of ownership. 2 Bouv. Inst. 1922.

Whether the instrument creates a power or confers an interest upon the grantee depends on the intention. 1 Sugd. Pow. 118. See also notes to p. 120, ed. of 1856; 1 Chance Pow. ch. 3, § 3; 2 Washb. Real Prop. 315.

Where powers were conferred by will on one as executor and as trustee, and it was contended that the term "executor" was used in certain instances in the sense of trustee, it was held that the fact that the power given in that connection was one not within the power of an executor as such—as, for instance, to sell land without application to the court—tended to show that the power vested in the donee as trustee and not as executor. Munson *v.* Cole, 98 Ind. 502.

Where land is conveyed to A for life, remainder in fee to B, a power may be given to B to appoint during A's lifetime, notwithstanding the remainder in fee. Shearman *v.* Hicks, 14 Gratt. (Va.) 96.

By means of powers, the right of the owner of the fee to dispose of it may be suspended for any time within the Rule against Perpetuities. Snyder *v.* Ackerman, 37 N. J. Eq. 442; 4 Kent Comm. 328.

Where the power is general to the donee to appoint to whomsoever he may choose either by deed or will, the donee is practically the owner, since he has absolute control, and can appoint as well to himself as to any other person. *In re* Lawrence's Estate (Pa. St. 1890); 11 L. R. A. 85. See Beck's Appeal, 116 Pa. St. 547.

A conveyance to A for life, and then to such persons as A shall appoint, and in default of such appointment by A then to A in fee, vests the absolute estate in A. Bunson *v.* Hunter, 2 Hill Eq. (S. Car.) 483.

Where full liberty of disposition is given, the donee may reserve to himself a life estate, and convey the remainder. Hoxie *v.* Finney, 147 Mass. 616.

If the one to whom the power is given have also an interest in the land which is not to be affected by the exercise of the power, such interest will not be destroyed by any conveyance of the land except by a feoffment. 2 Washb. Real Prop. 306.

If the estate is vested in the donee of the power, upon trust to dispose of it, or with power of appointment, to certain persons or classes of persons, there is no vested estate in the beneficiaries until the exercise of the power. 1 Perry on Trusts, § 250.

Compare Little *v.* Bennett, 5 Jones Eq. (N. Car.) 156.

A power of disposal by will does not, of itself, enlarge a limited interest. Thus a bequest to A for life, and after his death to such person as he may appoint by will to receive the same, gives only a life estate to A, and no one can claim through him save by an execution of the power. *Citing* Craft *v.* Slee, 4 Ves. 60; Nannock *v.* Horton, 7 Ves. 391; Bradley *v.* Westcott, 13 Ves. 445; Ward *v.* Amory, 1 Curt. (U. S.) 425.

Whether a power of disposition annexed to an estate for life enlarges the life estate to a fee, see Burleigh *v.* Clough, 52 N. H. 267, 13 Am. Rep. 23, where the English and American cases are discussed at length.

This is answered in the negative, unless the power is actually executed, in Harrison *v.* Battle, 1 Dev. and B. Eq. (N. Car.) 213.

Under the *New York* statute, if an absolute power of disposition, unaccompanied by a trust, is given to the owner of a particular estate, such estate is changed into a fee, which is absolute as to creditors and purchasers, but subject to any future estates limited thereon in case the power is not executed nor the land taken for debt.[1] If no particular estate is limited to the grantee, he takes a fee subject to any future estates that may be limited

In *Missouri*, it is held that where an express life estate is created by a will, an added power of disposition does not enlarge the estate into a fee. Rubey *v.* Barnett, 12 Mo. 3; Chiles *v.* Bartleson, 21 Mo. 344; Miner *v.* Timberlake, 53 Mo. 378; Wead *v.* Gray, 78 Mo. 59 (where the prior cases are cited); Munro *v.* Collins, 95 Mo. 33; Lewis *v.* Pitman, 101 Mo. 281.

Whether the absolute power of disposal carries the fee generally, turns upon the question whether a life estate is in fact created. See McKenzie's Appeal, 41 Conn. 607; 19 Am. Rep. 525, and Missouri cases cited above.

Chancellor Kent says that the devise of an estate generally or indefinitely, with a power of disposition over it, carries the fee. 4 Kent Comm. *319. Such is the holding of the courts in the following cases: Funk *v.* Eggleston, 92 Ill. 575; Crozier *v.* Hoyt, 97 Ill. 23; Green *v.* Sutton, 50 Mo. 186; Gay *v.* Ihm, 3 Mo. App. 588; Tremmel *v.* Kleiboldt, 6 Mo. App. 549.

It is no objection to a power that the party exercising it has a fee or other interest in the land. Logan *v.* Bell, 1 C. B. 892; 14 L. J., C. P. 276; 2 Washb. Real Prop. *315.

The question whether a power could co-exist with a fee in the same person has been the subject of discussion. On this point Mr. Chance says: "Some years ago the question was much disputed how far a power over the inheritance could co-exist with a fee in the same person. Having regard to the authorities, it is perhaps singular that the point could ever have been doubted. The question now, at least, is perfectly settled." 1 Chance Pow. 43. And he cites the following cases, giving Lord Eldon as an authority in the affirmative: Maundrell *v.* Maundrell, 7 Ves. 567; 10 Ves. 246; Sir E. Cleris' case, 1 Roll. 3, ch. 1; Co. Litt. 111 b, 271 b; Dobbins *v.* Bowman, 3 Atk. 408. He cites some cases in which a power and the fee were directly limited to a person having no prior interest. Cox *v.* Chamberlain, 4 Ves. 631; Road *v.* Wadham, 6 East 288; Moreton *v.* Lees, 2 Sugd. App. 88, *339; Ray *v.* Pring, 5 Mad. 310; 5 B. & A. 561. And persons *sui juris* have had what were considered equitable powers, accompanied by the equitable fee. Abbott *v.* Burton, 11 Mod. 181; Roscommon *v.* Fowke, 6 B. P. C. 158; *cited* in 1 Ves. Sr. 156 and 1 Cowp. 268. Mr. Chance concludes with this language: "The above authorities (and many more might be added) concern freehold estates on which alone the cases where doubts have been expressed arose. Cases, however, might be cited as to other descriptions of property."

Mr. Washburne says: "It was formerly much discussed whether the power was not merged in the fee. It is now settled that it is not, and that a general power of appointment may coexist with the absolute fee in the donee of a power." 2 Washb. Real Prop. *315.

1. 4 *New York* Rev. Stat., § 81 (Banks' ed.), p. 2446; (1882) p. 2189; Ackerman *v.* Gorton, 67 N. Y. 66; Crooke *v.* King's Co., 97 N. Y. 421; Coleman *v.* Beach, 97 N. Y. 545; Freeborn *v.* Wagner, 2 Abb. App. Dec. (N. Y.) 178; American Bible Soc. *v.* Stark, 45 How. Pr. (N. Y.) 166; Jackson *v.* Edwards, 7 Paige (N.Y.) 399; affirmed 22 Wend. (N. Y.) 509; Blanchard *v.* Blanchard, 6 Thomp. & C. (N. Y.) 551; 4 Hun (N. Y.) 290; affd. 70 N. Y. 615; Bailey *v.* Bailey, 28 Hun (N. Y.) 610; Leonard *v.* American Bapt. H. M. Soc., 35 Hun (N. Y.) 293; Rose *v.* Hatch, 55 Hun (N. Y.) 457; Ludlow *v.* Van Ness, 8 Bosw. (N. Y.) 193; *In re* Fernbacher, 17 Abb. N. Cas. (N. Y.) 339; 4 Dem. (N. Y.) 240. See also Van Horne *v.* Campbell, 100 N. Y. 312.

In Terry *v.* Wiggins, 2 Lans. (N. Y.) 276; affd. 47 N. Y. 512, the first devisee took an estate for life, and was at the same time vested with a general and beneficial power to sell the lands devised, the court stated that the above sections (81–85) have "qualified the effect formerly given to powers of disposition in cases like this, by making the estate

thereon, but absolute as to creditors and purchasers.[1] If no remainder is limited, the grantee takes an absolute fee.[2] If a general and beneficial power to devise the inheritance is given to a tenant for life or years, he takes an absolute power of disposition;[3] and every power is deemed absolute by means of which the grantee is enabled in his lifetime to dispose of the entire fee for his own benefit.[4] And such, in substance, is the effect of the statutes of *Michigan, Wisconsin, Minnesota* and *Dakota.*[5]

5. Executor as Donee.—Where a will authorizes the executor to sell lands and invest the proceeds for the benefit of the testator's family, according to directions contained in the will, the

thus created absolute only in respect to the rights of creditors and purchasers, and subject to the limitation over in case the power should not be executed or the land should not be sold for the satisfaction of debts."

And in a later case, the same court says of these sections: "The revisors of our statutes say, 'In reason and good sense there is no distinction between the absolute power of disposition and absolute ownership; it is an affront to common sense to say that a man has no property in that which he may sell when he chooses, and dispose of the proceeds at his pleasure.' And they framed a law which was enacted by the legislature, providing that when the grantee of a power is authorized by the power to dispose of the entire fee of the land for his own benefit, he is entitled to an absolute fee." Kull *v.* Kull, 37 Hun (N. Y.) 476.

Where a testatrix bequeathed certain bonds to her husband, that he might draw and use the income for his life, and gave him power during his life to change the investment or to sell the bonds at pleasure, and to apply the proceeds to his own use forever, this power of absolute disposition would enable him to pledge the bonds as security for a loan. Brown *v.* Farmers' T. & L. Co., 51 Hun (N.Y.) 386.

1. 4 *New York* Rev. Stat., § 82, (Banks' ed.), p. 3446; (1882) p. 2189; Kinnier *v.* Rogers, 42 N. Y. 531: "The will of a testator is always to some extent defeated by the operation of this section. The testator intending to give a fee would never do it by simply giving an absolute power of sale. The statute vests the fee, and to this the will of the testator is made to conform, whatever he actually intended." Crooke *v.* Kings Co., 97 N. Y. 421.

Decisions bearing in sections 82-85 will be found in Blanchard *v.* Blanchard, 6 Thomp. & C. (N. Y.) 551; 4 Hun (N. Y.) 287; American Bible Soc. *v.* Stark, 45 How. Pr. (N. Y.) 160; Hetzel *v.* Barber, 69 N. Y. 7.

2. *New York* Rev. Stat., § 83 (Banks' ed.), p. 2446; (1882) p. 2189, Kinnier *v.* Rogers, 42 N. Y. 534; Freeborn *v.* Wagner, 49 Barb. (N. Y.) 55; American Bible Soc. *v.* Stark, 45 How. Pr. (N. Y.) 166.

3. *New York* Rev. Stat., § 84 (Banks' ed.), p. 2446; (1882) p. 2189; American Bible Soc. *v.* Stark, 45 How. Pr. (N. Y.) 166; Fellows *v.* Heermans, 4 Lans. (N. Y.) 237; Freeborn *v.* Wagner, 49 Barb. (N. Y.) 55.

4. *New York* Rev. Stat., § 85 (Banks' ed.), 1447; (1882) p. 2189; Hetzell *v.* Barber, 69 N. Y. 1; Cooke *v.* King's Co., 97 N. Y. 421; Coleman *v.* Beach, 97 N. Y. 545; Jackson *v.* Edwards, 7 Paige (N. Y.) 400; affd. 22 Wend. (N. Y.) 505; Freeborn *v.* Wagner, 49 Barb. (N. Y.) 55; affirmed, 2 Abb. App. Dec. (N. Y.) 175.

A testatrix devised to her husband all her property for life, giving him full power to dispose of it and use the proceeds for his benefit. The will further provided that if any portion of the estate should be used by him, such use should be restricted to his personal wants and necessities in providing for his support; and that so much of the estate and its profits as he should die possessed of should be disposed of by him for the support and education of orphan children. It was held that as the power of disposition was restricted to the purposes specified, and did not include the right to dispose of the estate by will, it did not become absolute under the provisions of this section. Rose *v.* Hatch, 55 Hun (N. Y.) 457.

5. Stimson's St. Law, § 1656.

executor takes the land, not as executor, but as donee of a power.[1]

6. Powers as Affected by the Rule Against Perpetuities.—A power is void if obnoxious to the Rule against Perpetuities. The question whether a future interest, limited under an appointment in the exercise of a power, is void for remoteness, is determined by

1. Bolton *v.* Jacks, 6 Robt. (N. Y.) 166.

An executor does not take an estate by implication, in the hands of his testator, when the duties enjoined on him can be executed under a power. Tucker *v.* Tucker, 5 N. Y. 408; 5 Barb. (N. Y.) 99; Scott *v.* Monell, 1 Redf. (N. Y.) 431. He may execute the power before probate of the will and the issue of letters testamentary. Bolton *v.* Jacks, 6 Robt. (N. Y.) 166.

The title to lands does not pass to executors under the *New York* statute (1 New York Rev. Stat., § 55) where the purposes of the will do not require it, though the testators may have used words which otherwise would vest the title in them. Chamberlain *v.* Taylor, 105 N. Y. 185.

Where the will gave to the executors all the real and personal estate in trust for the payment of debts and legacies, with power to sell at public or private sale at such time, and upon such terms, and in such manner as they should see fit, no title passed to the executors, and until they exercised the power, the title would vest in the heir or remainderman. Bouton *v.* Thomas, 46 Hun (N. Y.) 6.

But it has been held in *Maine* that a power to executors to sell and make deeds to the real estate, and distribute to the legatees, vests in the executors the title to all the real estate held absolutely, but not to that held in trust by the testator. Richardson *v.* Woodbury, 43 Me. 206.

And in *Massachusetts*, it has been held that where there was a devise to executors in trust for the support of the children of the testator, with power to sell, the executors could make deeds in their own names, and without giving other bonds than as executors. Alley *v.* Lawrence, 12 Gray (Mass.) 373.

The Supreme Court of *Illinois* has held that an administrator who takes a mere power to sell lands to pay debts, cannot in his own name maintain a bill to remove a cloud from the title. Ryan *v.* Duncan, 88 Ill. 144.

Where a testator, after directing the payment of certain debts and legacies, gave to his executor full power of disposal or appropriation of the residue of the estate at the executor's discretion, it was held that the executor was justified in appropriating such residue to himself. Beck's Appeal, 116 Pa. St. 547.

A direction to executors sell the realty and divide it between A and B, conveys no title to A and B, though they are named as executors. Den *v.* Young, 23 N. J. L. 478.

A will which authorizes the executors to sell real estate and pay certain legacies out of the proceeds does not vest title in such executors, especially where by the same instrument the testator bequeaths the "rest and residue" of said real estate to his heirs. Beadle *v.* Beadle, 2 McCrary (U. S.) 586.

A testamentary gift to an executor of all the decedent's interest in a partnership, of which he was then a member, in trust to invest as fast as realized, together with full power to settle with his partners, confers on the executor the fee of the decedent's partnership real estate, with power of sale. Naar *v.* Naar, 41 N. J. Eq. 88.

A testator devised his estate to his wife and children, and gave his executor and executrix full and discretionary power to sell any or all of his estate, and reinvest the same, when they may deem it most conducive to the interest of his wife and children, and for that purpose, vests title to all and every part of the same in them, and in the survivor, if either should die. The wife of the testator was made executrix, and one H executor. The latter died, leaving the wife of testator sole executrix. It was held, that she held the property as trustee, and had power to sell the same, and reinvest, when the interest of the estate demanded, and mere lapse of time would not divest her of this right. Jones *v.* Breed (Ky. 1890), 13 S. W. Rep. 366.

reckoning from the time of the creation of the power, not from the time of its execution.[1]

V. Execution of Powers—1. By What Law Governed.—Where the situs of the property which is the subject of the power and the domicil of the donor are in one jurisdiction, and the domicil of the donee in another, the law of the former jurisdiction controls the mode of execution.[2]

An instrument exercising a special or general power of appointment must be executed and construed according to the rules for the time being applicable to instruments of that kind, although the power may have been created before, but exercised after an alteration of the law as to the construction and mode of execution of such instruments.[3]

2. Good Faith Required.—The power must be executed in good faith to carry out the intention of the donor as expressed in the instrument creating the power.[4]

1. The matter is treated under Perpetuities (Rule against)—*Powers;* as is the distinction between general and special powers as affected by the rule. There also will be found a critical examination of the principle that a limitation made in the exercise of a power must be read as if inserted in the instrument creating the power.

2. Bingham's Appeal, 64 Pa. St. 345; Sewall *v.* Wilmer, 132 Mass. 131.

But it has been decided by the House of Lords, on appeal from Scotland, that a power of appointment reserved by a man residing out of Scotland, in a settlement by him of real estate in Scotland, was well executed by a will in the form required by the law of his domicil. Willock *v.* Ouchterlong, 3 Paton 659; Brack *v.* Johnston, 5 Wils. & Sh. 61. And a like decision was made by Lord Romilly, M. R., in a case of the execution in France of a power created by an English will. D'Huart *v.* Harkness, 34 Beav. 324.

On the other hand, it is held in England that where a power of apppointment by will is given by the will of a person domiciled in England, and is executed abroad by a will in a form required or permitted by the law of England, the will of the donee should be admitted to probate in England, although not executed with the forms required by the law of the donee's domicil. Tatnall *v.* Hankey, 2 Moore, P. C. 342. Alexander's Goods, 1 Sw. & Tr. 454, n.; Barnes *v.* Vincent, 5 Moore P. C. 201; Hallyburton's Goods, L. R., 1 P. & D. 90.

Of this last line of cases it is said by Gray, C. J., in Sewall *v.* Wilmer, 132 Mass. 136, "But it does not distinctly appear whether this is upon the broad ground that the power is well executed; or upon the narrower ground that the will should be formally established as a testamentary instrument in a court of probate, leaving it to a court of construction to determine whether it can have any effect."

3. Freme *v.* Clement, L. R., 18 Ch. Div. 499. See also Banks *v.* Sloat, 69 Ga. 330.

4. Otherwise, the estate of the remainderman is not defeated. Thus, where a power was given for the benefit of the children of the donee, and the donee executed conveyance to one of his children, that the latter might have sufficient property to become bail for the donee, with the understanding that the land was to be reconveyed, such an appointment would not destroy the remainder. Bostick *v.* Winton, 1 Sneed (Tenn.) 524; Cruse *v.* McKee, 2 Head (Tenn.) 1.

An appointment made by a fraudulent combination or collusion, or which is secretly for the benefit of the appointor in fraud of the rights of others, is not a valid exercise of the power, and will be set aside. Hinclimbroke *v.* Seymour, 1 Bro. C. C. 395; *In re* Kirwan's Trusts, 25 Ch. Div. 373; *In re* Turner's Settled Estates, 28 Ch. Div. 205; Shank *v.* Dewitt, 44 Ohio St. 237: See Henty *v.* Wey, 19 Ch. Div. 492; 21 Ch. Div. 332.

A, having mortgaged land to B, gave him a power to sell, and pay the sur-

3. **Execution—When Valid.**—An execution of a power is not void

plus to A's wife. B, under the power, sold the land to C without consideration, and A's wife joined in the deed, for which B paid her $100. C immediately reconveyed to B. *Held*, that the heir of A could maintain a bill to set aside the sale, and to redeem from B. Dobson *v.* Racey, 3 Sandf. Ch. (N.Y.) 60.

But in *California* an execution of the power was held good under the following circumstances: A power of attorney gave the right to sell and convey or to mortgage land which was already incumbered. The attorney, with intent to mortgage it for enough to pay the incumbrance and certain debts of his own, conveyed it to B, upon no consideration other than to cause B to mortgage the land for the requisite sum. B then, at the attorney's request, conveyed the land back to him. *Held*, that the transaction constituted a valid mortgage within the power. Ayres *v.* Palmer, 57 Cal. 309.

The collusive exercise of a limited power as to one-half of certain property, would not render the exercise of an unlimited power as to the other half void. New *v.* Potts, 55 Ga. 420.

Where an appointment has been once set aside as fraudulent, a second appointment by the same donee to the same appointee will not be sustained except on clear proof that such second appointment is entirely free from the taint which attached to the first. Topham *v.* Portland, 39 L. J., Ch. 259; 5 L. R., Ch. 40.

An appointment made under an arrangement which is for the benefit of all the objects of the power, is not invalid because it is also incidentally beneficial to the appointor. *In re* Huish's Charity, 39 L. J., Ch. 499; 10 L. R., Eq. 5; 22 L. T., N. S. 565; 18 W. R. 817; Cooper *v.* Cooper, 39 L. J., Ch. 240; 5 L. R., Ch. 203; 18 W. R. 299; 22 L. T., N. S. 1; Rooch *v.* Trood, 3 L. R., Ch. Div. 429; 24 W. R. 803; 34 L. T., N. S. 105, *reversing* same case, 31 L. T., N. S. 666.

Where a father is by a marriage settlement empowered to divide a fund among his children at discretion, he cannot negotiate or deal with them in executing the power, and a purchase by him of the interest of one of the children will not be upheld. Cunningham *v.* Anstruther, 2 L. R., H. L. Cas. 223.

Where the power of disposition by will is given to a person having no reversionary interest, an attempted execution of the power by a will made in conformity with the terms of an alleged contract, is invalid. The power is not thereby exhausted, and such will is revoked by a subsequent will duly admitted to probate. Wilson *v.* Maryland L. Ins. Co., 60 Md. 64.

A father deeded to his daughter, to whom he was indebted to the amount of the expressed consideration, premises on which they resided together; the deed providing that the father reserved the power to alienate or mortgage the premises during his lifetime, and declaring the intention to be to convey "the remainder" of the premises, provided the father failed to execute the power. *Held*, that a quitclaim by the father to A, who quitclaimed to B, who in turn quitclaimed to the father, the three deeds being executed the same day, without consideration, and for the purpose of defeating the daughter's interest, was fraudulent as to the daughter, and not a valid execution of the power. Harty *v.* Doyle, 49 Hun (N. Y.) 410.

A person having a life interest in a fund, with power to appoint, give, or devise it to others, having made an arrangement with the next of kin of the donor as to the distribution of such fund between herself and them, the arrangement was sustained, it having been validated by an act of the legislature, although some of the appointees under the power were infants, and could not consent to it. Thomson *v.* Norris, 20 N. J. Eq. 489.

A testator gave to his executor "full and unlimited power and authority to appropriate or dispose" of the residue "to such objects, persons, or institutions as in his discretion shall be best and proper." *Held*, that no trust was created, and that the executor might appropriate to himself, "subject to such further uses as he might thereafter by his last will and testament appoint," this being a valid execution of the power. Beck's Appeal, 116 Pa. St. 547.

A deed made in execution of a power is valid as to the remainderman, though made with the intent to defraud creditors. Hanna *v.* Ladewig, 73 Tex. 37.

because it exceeds the power if the part in excess is separable from the part authorized by the power;[1] nor because it falls short of it.[2]

An appointment not good in its creation will not become so by subsequent circumstances.[3]

4. What Constitutes an Execution.—In construing the execution of a power, courts will look to the intent of the party as gathered from the instrument.[4]

1. 2 Sugd. Pow., ch. 9.

Where there is a mere naked power the act is void, if the power is exceeded; but if the power is coupled with an interest, the act is good for so much as is within the power, and void as to the rest only. 2 Bouv. Inst. 335. As in favor of persons who are not objects of the power. 2 Sudg. Pow. *56; 2 Chance Pow. 1521; Seward *v.* Willock, 5 East 198; Somerville *v.* Lethbridge, 6 T. R. 213; Pitt *v.* Jackson, 2 Bro. C. C. 57; Griffith *v.* Harrison, 4 T. R. 737; Routledge *v.* Dorril, 2 Ves. Jr. 364; Kampf *v.* Jones, 2 Inst. 756.

If there is an excess in the quantity of the estate appointed, the execution is good and only the excess void. But if the execution and the excess are not distinguishable, the whole execution will be void. 5 Sugd. Pow. *75; 2 Chance Pow. 1521.

Where conditions are annexed to the appointment which are not authorized by the power, the appointment is good, but the conditions are void. 2 Sugd. Pow. * 84; 2 Chance Pow. 1521; Saddler *v.* Pratt, 6 Sim. 632; Palsgrave *v.* Atkinson, 1 Coll. 190; Roberts *v.* Dixall, 2 Eq. Cas. Ab. 668, pl. 19; Wade *v.* Firmin, 11 Sim. 235.

Compare Hay *v.* Watkins, 2 Bro. & Mar. 339.

Where a restriction or limitation would make the whole exercise of the power void, courts will reject the restriction and leave the rest of the appointment valid. Fry *v.* Capper, Kay 163; 2 W. R. 136; *In re* Teague, 18 W. R. 753; 22 L. T., N. S. 742; Thornton *v.* Bright, 2 My. & Cr. 230.

By a marriage settlement a fund was settled on the husband and wife during their lives, with remainder to the children of the marriage, as the wife, if surviving, should appoint. The wife survived her husband, and appointed a share of the fund to a married daughter for life to her separate use without power of anticipation. *Held*, that as the restraint in anticipation would be bad as violating the Rule against Perpetuities, it would be rejected, and the appointment held good. (*Following* Fry *v.* Capper, Kay 163; 2 W. R. 136.) *In re* Teague, 22 L. T., N. S. 742; 18 W. R. 752.

2. Where a power is given to appoint a fee, a less estate may be appointed, if there are no words of positive restriction. Butler *v.* Huestis, 68 Ill. 594; 18 Am. Rep. 589.

3. Brudenell *v.* Elwes, 1 East 442. See Hitchcock *v.* U. S. Bank, 7 Ala. 386; Wilson *v.* Lynt, 16 How. Pr. (N. Y.) 348; 30 Barb. (N. Y.) 124.

But in a case arising in New Jersey, a testator by his will, gave his estate, real and personal, to his wife for and during her natural life, and after her death to his daughter for life, with power to the daughter to dispose of the same by her last will and testament. The daughter made her will in due form and died in the lifetime of her mother. *Held*, that it was a good execution of the power of appointment. Lindsley *v.* First Christian Soc., 37 N. J. Eq. 277.

Yet it was held in *New York* that, where property was devised to the daughter of the testator with power, in case she should die before her father, to dispose of it by her will, though this power of appointment could not be executed as a power in the lifetime of the father, the father's will would operate to devise the property by its own force in accordance with the provisions of the daughter's will. *In re* Piffard's Estate, 111 N. Y. 410.

4. Benesch *v.* Clark, 49 Md. 497; Meeker *v.* Breintnall, 38 N. J. Eq. 345; Mott *v.* Ackerman, 92 N. Y. 539.

A recital in the instrument that it is executed under a power is no evidence of the power. Hershy *v.* Berman, 45 Ark. 309.

While the intention must be collected from the instrument itself and not from evidence *dehors* the instrument, yet parol evidence is admissible to show the purposes for which the power is exercised, though they may not appear in the deed. Topham *v.* Portland, 32 L. J., Ch. 257.

A, having a power to appoint a trust fund to his children, appointed a portion of the fund upon such trusts as S, one of the children, should appoint, and upon default of appointment, in trust for J during his life, and after his death in trust to his legal representatives as part of his personal estate. The power to S was held void, because accompanied by conditions exceeding the power granted to A. *Held*, that the power to S, being void, the gift over in default of appointment amounted to an absolute appointment to S. Webb *v.* Sadler, 42 L. J., Ch. 498; 8 L. R., Ch. 419.

Where, under a special power, an appointment is made giving a power of appointment which is *ultra vires*, with a gift over in certain courts, the gift over is not invalidated by the invalidity of the power. Stark *v.* Dakyn, 10 L. R., Ch. 35; 44 L. J., Ch. 205.

And where the execution of the power is accompanied by directions and conditions which are *ultra vires*, the appointment will be valid, but the directions and conditions void. McDonald *v.* McDonald, 2 L. R., Sc. App. 482.

But the appointee may, if he choose, give effect to the conditions and directions without invalidating the appointment. McDonald *v.* McDonald, 2 L. R., Sc. App. 482. See also to same effect, Roach *v.* Trood, 3 L. R., Ch. Div. 429; 24 N. R. 803. *Compare* Line *v.* Hall, 43 L. J., Ch. 107.

A power to appoint to children absolutely may be exercised by giving a child an estate for life with power to appoint by will. Starke *v.* Dakyn, 10 L. R., Ch. 35; 44 L. J., Ch. 205; 31 L. T., N. S. 712.

But it is held in *Virginia* that while such an appointment is good, the remainder over is void, and the appointee takes the fee. Hood *v.* Haden, 82 Va. 588.

Says Wood, V. C., in Fry *v.* Capper, Kay 163: "In the case of an appointment under a power, the court looks to the scope and intent of the power; and in appointments by will of real estate as by the doctrine of *cy pres* given effect to that against the very words of the instrument, and has enabled grandchildren, who were not objects of the power, to take under a limitation to a child for life, with the remainder to the children of such child, by treating the first taker as a tenant in tail; and because the words of the appointment would otherwise have been inoperative the court has thus given effect to it in the mode in which it can take effect legally."

Where shares were settled in trust for such person as A might by deed or will appoint, and A took a transfer of the shares in her own name in the usual way, this amounted to an execution of the power in her own favor. Marler *v.* Tommas, 43 L. J., Ch. 73; 17 L. R., Eq. 8.

Where land was devised in trust to such person or persons, use or uses as the devisee should by deed or will appoint, the execution of a mortgage, with a limitation of the surplus after satisfying the debt to the mortgagor and his right heirs, will constitute a complete execution of the power, and will defeat a provision in the will to the effect that, in default of appointment, the property shall be held in trust for certain designated persons. Hicks *v.* Ward, 107 N. Car. 392.

Where a power is conferred upon a tenant for life to appoint by will, a devise for the payment of his own debts is not a valid execution of the power. Balls *v.* Damfman, 69 Md. 390.

Where a conveyance in trust conveyed lands to trustees for the sole and separate use of a married woman and her heirs, with power in her to sell the whole or any part with the consent of the trustees, and either invest the proceeds for the purposes of the trust or dispose of them as she should direct, this gives her the power to charge the estate with the payment of an account contracted for necessaries. Jackson *v.* West, 22 Md. 71. To the same effect, Whiteside *v.* Cannon, 23 Mo. 457; Segond *v.* Garland, 23 Mo. 547; Miller *v.* Brown, 47 Mo. 504.

Executors were empowered to pay and discharge the legacies in money or in real or personal property or both in such manner and at such valuation as should seem to them fair and just. One of the executors made an entry upon the books of the firm, of which such executor was a member, crediting the legatee with a sum in cash equal to the assumed value of certain lands belonging to the testator. *Held*, that this was not sufficient to pass title to the land to such legatee. Ames *v.* Scudder, 83 Mo. 189.

A quitclaim deed by a devisee for life is not an execution of a power given such devisee by the will to sell so much of the land as might be necessary to her support. Grundy *v.* Hadfield, 16 R. I. 579.

Where a power is coupled with an interest the law is satisfied with a substantial compliance with the terms of the power. Rowe *v.* Beckett, 30 Ind. 154; Rowe *v.* Lewis, 30 Ind. 163.

Where an attorney in fact has a power coupled with an interest either in the land itself or the proceeds of a sale thereof, a conveyance by him as such attorney will pass a complete title as showing an election to take his interest in the proceeds of the sale. Little *v.* Weatherford, 63 Tex. 638.

A power to dispose of the proceeds of land may be executed by disposing of the land itself. Boyd *v.* Satterwhite, 10 S. Car. 45.

Where, in pursuance of a power, an executor executes a deed of trust with a power of sale, the fact that he signs and acknowledges the deed as executor makes it none the less an effective execution of the power. Faulk *v.* Dashiell, 62 Tex. 642; 50 Am. Rep. 542.

Instances of Construction.—A testator devised and bequeathed property in trust for the benefit of his son T. The will contained the further provision that "should the said T die, having made a will and testament in due form to be admitted to probate, I direct that the said trust estate shall be handed over and disposed of in such manner as he shall by his said will have directed." The testator's wife by a subsequent will devised property in trust for T and his family, giving T power by an instrument in writing, to order and direct in what manner and to whom and in what proportion the property should be divided between his wife and children after his death. *Held*, that both of these powers were well executed by a will whereby T devised the entire property to his wife and daughter to be divided equally between them when either of them married, and charged the entire estate with the daughter's education during her minority, over and above her interest on a division. Hill *v.* Jones, 56 Ala. 214.

The testator gave to his mother a general testamentary power of appointment over real estate, providing that should his mother die without any will, then the estate was to go to E C. The mother executed a will devising all her real estate, including that over which she had any power of appointment, to trustees in trust for G C, who died in her lifetime. *Held*, that the property belonged to the trustees named, subject to a resulting trust in favor of the heir at law. *In re* Van Hogan; Sperling *v.* Rochfort, L. R., 16 Ch. Div. 18.

A testator gave to his wife the use of his real property for her life; in case its income should be insufficient for her support, the executors were to sell so much thereof as should be necessary therefor. The wife and another were appointed executors. The executor died. The wife as surviving executrix conveyed the land to A in consideration of her past, present, and future support. *Held*, that the execution of the power was invalid. Ferr *v.* American Board, 53 Vt. 162.

A testator devised land to his daughter and her husband to be disposed of as they might think proper. A codicil declared the intention of the testator not to be that the husband, if he survived his wife, should have a fee-simple estate, but a life estate only, the land, upon his decease, to descend to the testator's daughter's children or heirs. A subsequent clause of the codicil gave power to husband and wife, during their joint lives, to dispose of the land by deed jointly executed, proved, and acknowledged. Husband and wife conveyed accordingly, to secure the husband's debt. *Held*, that the estate of the wife's children or heirs was cut off by the conveyance. Shields *v.* Netherland, 5 Lea (Tenn.) 193.

A married woman, by a will to which her husband consented in writing, bequeathed the residue of her property to a trustee, in trust to pay the net income to her husband during his life, and on his death, "provided and on condition" that he made no will directing otherwise, to pay the income to A, until she reached a certain age, and on arriving at that age to pay her the principal, or, in case of her death before attaining such age, to pay the principal to her children. The will further provided that the bequest to A was on the sole and express condition that A should, after the decease of the testatrix, take good care of the husband during his life, "rendering him all the kindly per-

5. Effect of Execution.—By the execution of the power, the possession, right, title, and interest, are altered or devested, and the appointee gains the legal estate.[1] The estate arising from the execution of a power owes its commencement to the deed of appointment, but it takes effect as if it had been created by the deed which raised the power. The appointor is merely an instrument; the appointee is in by the original deed.[2]

sonal attention in her power, tending to make him comfortable and happy, such as a dutiful and affectionate daughter would render; and in case of any ill treatment, neglect or shortcoming in the above-mentioned expected duties and relation," of which the husband was to be "the sole and exclusive judge," he was authorized by will to direct how the residue should go upon his death. At the time the testatrix made her will A was a married woman, living with her husband and children in a neighboring city. She visited the husband of the testatrix on an average once a week, and helped him all she reasonably could. During his illness she visited him daily, did his marketing and took care of his accounts. About a week after his wife's death, the husband urged A to come and live with him, and was angry because she refused, and many times after that was made angry by her refusal of like requests. About a month after his wife's death he made a will, in which he referred to his wife's will and the power of appointment therein given him, reciting that he did it in execution of the power, bequeathed the remainder to a third person. It was held that this will was a sufficient execution of the power given by the will of the wife, and that the court could not find on these facts that he failed to exercise his judgment, or that he acted in bad faith. Krause *v.* Klucken, 135 Mass. 482.

1. 1 Chance Pow. 2; 1 Sugd. Pow. 82; 1 Steph. Comm. 229; Groodill *v.* Brigham, 1 B. & P. 197; Eaton *v.* Straw, 18 N. H. 331; Burleigh *v.* Clough, 52 N. H. 267; 13 Am. Rep. 23; Rodgers *v.* Wallace, 5 Jones (N. Car.) 181.

Where one having a power of appointment exercises the power by devising it to one who dies in her lifetime, this is a valid execution of the power, and the gift over in default of appointment does not take effect. Willoughby Osborne *v.* Holzoake, 22 Ch. Div. 238. *Compare* Hoare *v.* Osborne, 39 L. J., Ch. 586; 12 W. R. 661

2. 4 Cruise Dig. *219; 4 Kent's Comm. *327, *337; 2 Washb. Real Prop. *320; Martin's Law Lexicon; Branzbrook *v.* Attorney Gen., 9 H. L. Cas. 150; Robinson *v.* Hardcastle, 2 T. R. 241; Roach *v.* Nodham, 6 East 289; 2 Smith 376; Isherwood *v.* Oldknow, 3 M. & S. 382; Smith *v.* Garey, 2 Dev. & B. Eq. (N. Car.) 42; Leggett *v.* Doremus, 25 N. J. Eq. 122; Albert *v.* Albert, 68 Md. 352.

Le Blanc, J., says that the instrument derives its force from the person who creates the power. Rogers *v.* Humphrey, 4 A. & E. 299.

The appointer is a mere instrument; the appointee is in by the original deed, and takes in the same manner as if his name had been inserted in the power, or as if the power and the instrument executing the power had been expressed in giving that power. He does not take from the donee as his assignee. 2 Washb. Real Prop. *320; 1 Sugden Pow. (ed. 1856) 242; 2 Sugden Pow. 22; Bradish *v.* Gibbs, 3 Johns. Ch. (N. Y.) 523; Doolittle *v.* Lewis, 7 Johns. Ch. (N. Y.) 45; Burleigh *v.* Clough, 52 N. H. 267; 13 Am. Rep. 23.

But this principle is not extended so as to interfere with intervening rights. 4 Kent's Comm. *338; Jackson *v.* Davenport, 20 Johns. (N. Y.) 537.

One exception is when the person executing the power has granted a lease or any other interest which he may do by virtue of his estate, for then he is not allowed to defeat his own act. But suffering a judgment is not within the exception, as an act done by the party; it is a proceeding *in invitum*, and therefore falls within the general rule. Leggett *v.* Doremus, 25 N. J. Eq. 122.

In Jackson *v.* Davenport, 20 Johns. (N. Y.) 532, the court by Kent, Ch., states this modification of the rule that an estate created by the execution of a power takes effect as if created by the original deed, as follows: "I presume that I may venture upon the strength of the authorities which have been pre-

6. Instrument of Execution.—In the absence of statutory provisions, the creator of the power may provide that it may be executed by any kind of an instrument, even the most informal; even though the subject of the power is real estate, the deed creating the power may provide that it shall be executed by a simple note in writing, or by will unattested or attested by only one witness.[1]

viously mentioned, and upon the reason of the thing to question the universality of the application of this rule, and to insist that it ought to be confined within reasonable limits. If I have not misapprehended the cases on this subject, such a power cannot lie dormant and concealed, and then spring up at any distance of time, and prevail against a conveyance from the person having the legal title to a purchaser for valuable consideration without notice of the power; and especially if the lands lie in a recording county, and the purchaser's deed be recorded before the deed under the power, and without knowledge of that deed."

1. 1 Sugden Pow. (155*); 2 Washb. Real Prop. 317*, 318*; 4 Kent's Com. 330* and note (C); 4 Cruise Dig. 188*; Ladd *v.* Ladd, 8 How. (U. S.) 30; Christy *v.* Pulliam, 17 Ill. 59.

A power given generally may be executed either by deed or by will. 4 Cruise Dig. 194*; (2 Greenl. Cruise 243); 2 Washb. Real Prop. 317*. See 4 Kent's Com. 331*.

A resort to any of the ordinary and usual methods to accomplish the object comes within the scope of such general power. Faulk *v.* Dashiell, 62 Tex. 642; 50 Am. Rep. 542.

Where an appointment is made under a general power of appointment not prescribing the mode, it should be made in such a way as to pass title to the property, if it was owned absolutely by the person making the appointment. Knight *v.* Yarborough, 4 Rand. (Va.) 566.

If it is required that the appointment be made "by will," the will must be a valid one under the statute. 1 Sugden Pow. 215 (*157). See Hill *v.* Jones, 56 Ala. 214; Wright *v.* Wakeford, 17 Ves. 454; Wright *v.* Barlow, 3 Maule & S. 512.

This rule is embodied in the *New York* statute. 3 *New York* Rev. Stat., p. 2192, § 115; American H. M. Soc. *v.* Wadhams, 10 Barb. (N. Y.) 597; Smith *v.* Gage, 41 Barb. (N. Y.) 69.

It is held in *South Carolina* that where land situated in that State was devised by a testatrix who resided in the State, with power of appointment in the devisee, "by her last will and testament duly executed," a will duly executed in another State, but not conforming to the law of *South Carolina*, was not a valid execution of the power. But Simpson, C. J., dissented from this view. Blount *v.* Walker, 28 S. Car. 545.

A power to appoint by will can not be executed by deed, nor *vice versa*. 2 Washb. Real Prop. *317 *318; 1 Perry on Trusts, § 254; Alley *v.* Lawrence, 12 Gray (Mass.) 375; Moore *v.* Dimond, 5 R. I. 121; Bentham *v.* Smith, 1 Chev. (S. Car.) 33.

Where the power is to be executed at death, it must be by will. Porter *v.* Thomas, 23 Ga. 467; Weir *v.* Smith, 62 Tex. 1; Friend *v.* Oliver, 27 Ala. 532. *Compare* Christy *v.* Pulliam, 17 Ill. 59.

But under the *New York* statute if the power is confined to a disposition by grant, it cannot be executed by will, though not intended to take effect till after the death of the donee. 3 *New York* Rev. Stat., p. 2192, § 116 (Rev. of 1889, p. 2449).

In *England*, if the power is to be executed by deed or instrument in writing, it may be executed by will. Taylor *v.* Meads, 4 De G. J. & S. 597; 11 Jur., N. S. 166; 34 L. J., Ch. 303.

And a power to appoint by an instrument in writing with certain formalities may be executed by a will with their formalities. Smith *v.* Adkins, 41 L. J., Ch. 628.

The will applies equally where the power is reserved to the original owner of the estate. 4 Cruise Dig. *189 (2 Greenl. Cruise 237).

The donor may provide that the execution shall be in a manner different from that pointed out by the statute. McDermet *v.* Lorillard, 1 Edw. (N. Y.) 273; *In re* Alexander, 6 Jur., N. S. 354; 29 L. J., C. P. 93.

But the fact that a will is made in ex.

ecution of a power does not exempt it from the general rule that probate cannot be granted of an instrument unless it is duly executed as a will in conformity with the law of the testator's domicil. Crookender *v.* Fuller, 1 S. & T. 441; 5 Jur. N. S. 1222.

Where the deed creating the power requires that it shall be executed by a writing under hand and seal in the nature of a will, and duly attested by two or more witnesses, and the instrument was in writing and attested by two witnesses, but not under seal, it was not a valid execution of the power, except where the devise ultimately inured to charitable uses. *In re* Pepper, 1 Pars. Eq. Cas. (Pa.) 436; Taylor *v.* Meads, 4 De G. J. & S. 597; 11 Jur., N. S. 166; 34 L. J., Ch. 203.

A power of appointment required to be exercised by writing of a testamentary nature under appointor's hand and seal, is validly executed by a will having a *testimonium* clause with the words, "set my hand and seal," no other seal appearing than a dash with the pen one-sixteenth or one-eighth of an inch long at the end of testatrix's name, as such a mark may be assumed as intended for a seal, though similar marks are used in the body of the instrument for punctuation. Hacker's Appeal, 121 Pa. St. 192.

A gave certain lands to B and C, his wife, for the life of B, with reversion in fee to C and her heirs. B covenanted with A and C that the latter should have the privilege, which she might execute during coverture or afterwards, to nominate by last will and testament, or power of appointment, in the presence of two witnesses, such person as she might designate as her heir or heirs to such lands after the death of B. *Held*, that the power was well executed by a holograph will, the provision as to two witnesses applying to methods of appointment other than those by will. Shearman *v.* Hicks, 14 Gratt. (Va.) 96.

Where a mortgage with power of sale authorized the mortgagor, his personal representatives or assigns, to sell, and as the attorney of the mortgagor, to execute a deed to the purchaser, the deed must be in the name of the mortgagor, whether the sale is made by the mortgagor, or an assignee of the mortgagor. A deed by the assignee in his own name would pass no title. Speer *v.* Hadduck, 31 Ill. 439. Where a testator authorizes the executors, if they should consider it advisable, "to sell such number of lots, not exceeding twenty," of twenty-five by one hundred feet, as might be necessary to pay charges and assessments, a sale may be made as well by an executory contract as by a deed of present bargain and sale. Demarest *v.* Ray, 29 Barb. (N. Y.) 563.

A testator gave the residue of his estate to his executors in trust, "with power . . . to sell, dispose of, and convey the same," and invest and apply the proceeds as therein directed. The foreclosure of a mortgage on the realty executed by testator resulted in a large deficiency. In consideration of a small sum of money, the executrix under the will made a bargain and sale deed of the property to the purchaser at the foreclosure sale. *Held*, a valid exercise of the power of sale conferred by the will, it appearing that the estate received adequate consideration for the property, and that it was immaterial that the deed was executed to cure possible defects in the title. Mutual L. Ins. Co. *v.* Woods, 51 Hun (N. Y.) 640; affd. on appeal, 121 N. Y. 302.

Where an instrument capable of operating as an execution of a power recites a past transaction, which was of itself inadequate, this is a sufficient execution of the power. Lees *v.* Lees, 5 Ir. R., Eq. 549.

And where one who was constituted an attorney in fact by two separate and different instruments, one valid and the other invalid executed a deed, such deed passes title, though it purported to be executed under the invalid power, though not referred to in the deed, may be received in evidence in support of it. Link *v.* Page, 72 Tex. 592.

Several Instruments.—A power may be exercised from time to time by several appointments to suit convenience and to promote advantage as exigencies arise, or as expediency may suggest. 1 Sugd. Pow. *341; Cunningham *v.* Anstruther, 2 L. R., H. L. Cas. Sc. App. 223; Zouch *v.* Woolston, 2 Burr. 1136; 1 Wm. Bl. 281.

In one case it was held that two deeds executed at an interval of nine years might be treated as constituting one disposition. Braybrooke *v.* Attorney Genl., 9 H. L. Cas. 150.

But it must appear that the first execution is not intended to be a complete execution, and that the donee in the whole execution does not transgress the limits of the power. Doe *v.* Milborne, 2 T. R. 721; 1 Sugd. Pow. *342.

By Married Woman.—Where a mortgage with power of sale is executed to a married woman, and the power authorizes her to make all necessary conveyances for vesting the premises in the purchaser, she may execute it by her sole deed, with her own seal, and without her husband's consent. Cranston *v.* Crane, 97 Mass. 459.

A power of appointment to a married woman after separate estate may be executed by her signature to a promissory note for a bond. Coats *v.* Robinson, 10 Mo. 757; Whitesides *v.* Cannon, 23 Mo. 457; Segond *v.* Garland, 23 Mo. 547; Schefroth *v.* Ambs, 46 Mo. 114; Metropolitan Bank *v.* Taylor, 62 Mo. 338; Meyers *v.* Van Wagoner, 56 Mo. 115; Burnley *v.* Thomas, 63 Mo. 390; Dyett *v.* North American Coal Co., 20 Wend. (N. Y.) 570; Nanderheyden *v.* Mallory, 1 N. Y. 462; Firemen's Insurance Co. *v.* Bay, 4 Barb. (N. Y.) 407; Yale *v.* Dederer, 21 Barb. (N. Y.) 289; Harris *v.* Harris, 7 Ired. Eq. (N. Car.) 112; Forrest *v.* Robinson, 4 Port. (Ala.) 44; Bell *v.* Kellao, 13 B. Mon. (Ky.) 384; Holme *v.* Tenant, 1 Brown C. C. 16. See 2 Story Eq. Jur., § 1407; and *compare* Ewing *v.* Smith, 3 Desaus. (S. Car.) 417; Reid *v.* Lamar, 1 Strobh. Eq. (S. Car.) 27; Wallace *v.* Coston, 9 Watts (Pa.) 137; Morgan *v.* Elam, 4 Yerg. (Tenn.) 375; Marshall *v.* Stephens, 8 Humph. (Va.) 159; Williamson *v.* Beckham, 8 Leigh (Va.) 20; Montgomery *v.* Agricultural Bank, 10 Smed. & M. (Mass.) 567.

Or even by her indorsement of a promissory note. Claflin *v.* Van Wagoner, 32 Mo. 252.

Attestation.—The English Wills Act (7 Wm. IV, & 1 Vict., ch. 26, § 10) provides that to make an appointment by will valid, the will must be executed and attested in the same manner as a will; and a will so executed and attested shall be a valid execution of the power, though the instrument creating the power may require some other or additional formality.

This act has been held to apply both to powers created after and these created before its enactment. Hubbard *v.* Lee, 4 H. & N. 418; 1 L. R., Exch. 255; 12 Jur., N. S. 435; 35 L. J., Exch. 169.

But it does not apply to a power which is to be exercised by a writing under the hand and seal of the donee. West *v.* Ray, 1 Kay 385; 23 L. J., Ch. 447.

Under a power, created either before or since the Wills Act of 1837, to appoint real estate by deed or will to be respectively signed, sealed and delivered in the presence of, and attested by three witnesses, a will executed in the manner prescribed by that statute is a good execution of the power. Taylor *v.* Meads, 4 De G. J. & S. 597; 11 Jur. N. S. 166; 34 L. J., Ch. 203.

But where the power was created subsequently to that act and was to be executed by any instrument in writing, signed, sealed and delivered in the presence of, and attested by two witnesses, a will duly executed in conformity with the statute, but not sealed, was held not to be a valid execution of the power. Taylor *v.* Meads, 4 De G. J. & S. 597; 11 Jur., N. S. 166; 34 L. J., Ch. 203.

Parol.—An appointment may be by parol unless the power otherwise provides. 1 Perry on Trusts (4th ed.), § 297; Leggett *v.* Grimmett, 36 Ark. 496; Silverthorn *v.* McKinster, 12 Pa. St. 67.

In Leggett *v.* Grimmett, 36 Ark. 500, the court says: "The grantor in the deed empowered the beneficiaries or their agent to substitute a trustee for J. E. B. on his declining to act, etc. No mode of appointment was prescribed; and the cotton being personal property, which may be sold and transferred by delivery without deed, the verbal appointment of appellant was sufficient to authorize him to act as trustee, take possession of the cotton and sell it."

"When power to do any act is conferred on another, and the mode of its execution is defined, the power can be executed only in strict conformity with the terms of the grant. When the power is conferred in general terms, it is an authority to do the act in any mode which the law would sanction or give effect to." Foster *v.* Gorle, 4 Ala. 440.

It is held in *Missouri* also that the execution may be by parol. Miller *v.* Brown, 47 Mo. 504. See State Nat. Bank *v.* Robinson, 57 Mo. 446; M. E. Church *v.* Jaques, 3 Johns. Ch. (N. Y.) 77.

Under a will authorizing the executor to sell real estate to pay debts, a parole sale, not binding on the executor under the Statute of Frauds, passes no estate to the vendee, though

A general power must be executed in a way such as would pass the title if it were owned by the person executing the power.[1]

The *New York* statute requires that powers shall be executed by an instrument in writing. Every instrument except a will shall be deemed a conveyance within the meaning of the statute. If the power is confined to a disposition by will, the will must be duly executed in accordance with the provisions of the Statute on Wills. If the power is to be executed by grant, it cannot be executed by will, though the disposition be not intended to take effect until after the death of the party executing the power.[2]

7. Reference to Power in Instrument of Execution.—It is better that the instrument of execution should recite the power in express terms and state that the execution is in pursuance of the power; but this is not essential, if the instrument shows that the donee had, when executing it, the subject of the power in view.[3]

he has given his note for the price, especially when the debts have all been settled, and there is no necessity for making the sale. Perkins *v.* Presnell, 100 N. Car. 220.

Where a will authorized the executor to sell a chattel purchased by the testator, the price of which remained unpaid, a rescission of the purchase was held to be a due execution of the power. Jones *v.* Loftin, 3 Ired. Eq. (N. Car.) 136.

A devise to testator's wife during her natural life, and also "at her disposal afterward to leave it to whom she pleases," gives only a power to dispose of the property by will, and a disposition by feoffment during her lifetime is void. Doe *v.* Thorley, 10 East 438. *Compare,* Benesch *v.* Clark, 49 Md. 497.

1. Knight *v.* Yarborough, 4 Rand. (Va.) 566.

The *New York* statute makes this rule applicable to every species of power. 3 *New York* Rev. Stat., p. 2192, § 113; Barber *v.* Cary, 11 N. Y. 397; Van Boskerck *v.* Herrick, 65 Barb. (N. Y.) 258.

Where a share of an estate was limited to the use of the child or children forever, without word of inheritance, "subject nevertheless to such divisions, directions, orders and appointments as the husband by will or deed should think fit to direct or appoint, the husband takes a general power to appoint the fee simple, and the power is well executed by indentures of lease and release expressed to be in consideration of money paid, as well as of natural affection." Doe *v.* Jackson, 1 M. & Rob. 553.

A testatrix may, by the same clause in her will, dispose of her own property and that over which she has simply the power of appointment. Lindsley *v.* First Christian Soc., 37 N. J. Eq. 277.

2. 4 *New York* Rev. Stat. (1889), §§ 113–116 (Bank's ed.), p. 2449; (1881) p. 2192; Coleman *v.* Beach, 97 N. Y. 545; Belmont *v.* O'Brien, 12 N. Y. 404; Barber *v.* Carey, 11 N. Y. 397; American H. M. Soc. *v.* Wadhams, 10 Barb. (N. Y.) 607; Van Boskerck *v.* Herrick, 65 Barb. (N. Y.) 258; Bailey *v.* Bailey, 28 Hun (N. Y.) 611.

So far as this applies to the execution by will, it is declaratory of the law as it existed before the passage of the statute. American H. M. Soc. *v.* Wadham, 10 Barb. (N. Y.) 597; Smith *v.* Gage, 41 Barb. (N. Y.) 69.

In Jackson *v.* Edwards, 22 Wend. (N. Y.) 498 (affirming the decree of Chancellor Walworth, which is reported in 7 Paige (N. Y.) 397, where the power was to be executed either by deed or will, it was held that neither the assent of the donee to a sale in her answer to a bill in equity, nor the indorsement in her own handwriting of her approval upon the draft of a decree ordering a sale, could be regarded as a good execution of the power.

3. 1 Sugd. Pow. (ed. 1856) 232; 4 Kent's Comm. *334; 2 Washb. Real Prop. 320; 2 Story Eq. Jur., § 1062 a; 4 Cruise Dig. 197 (2 Greenl. Cruise 246); Jay *v.* Stein, 49 Ala. 523; Mathews *v.* McDade, 72 Ala. 377; Gindrat *v.* Montgomery Gas Light Co., 82 Ala. 596; Terry *v.* Rodahan, 79 Ga. 278; Funk *v.* Eggleston, 92 Ill. 575;

Smith *v.* Smith, 91 Ind. 221; 46 Am. Rep. 591 (reviewing the English and American cases); Silvers *v.* Canary, 109 Ind. 267; Foster *v.* Scarf, 55 Md. 301; Patterson *v.* Wilson, 64 Md. 193; Cooper *v.* Haines, 70 Md. 282; Brown *v.* Smith, 116 Mass. 108; Andrews *v.* Brumfield, 32 Miss. 107; Yates *v.* Clark, 56 Miss. 212; Beard *v.* Baucher, 60 Miss. 26; Reilly *v.* Chouquette, 18 Mo. 220; Campbell *v.* Johnson, 65 Mo. 439; White *v.* Hicks, 33 N. Y. 383; Greeno. *v.* Greeno, 23 Hun (N. Y.) 478; Hutton *v.* Benkard, 92 N. Y. 295; Taylor *v.* Eatman, 92 N. Car. 601; Bishop *v.* Remple, 11 Ohio St. 277; Coryell *v.* Dunton, 7 Pa. St. 530; Jones *v.* Wood, 16 Pa. St. 25; Keefer *v.* Schwartz, 47 Pa. St. 503; Drusadow *v.* Wilde, 63 Pa. St. 170; Weir *v.* Smith, 62 Tex. 1; Hood *v.* Haden, 82 Va. 588; Blake *v.* Hawkins, 98 U. S. 315; Warner *v.* Connecticut Mut. L. Ins. Co., 109 U. S. 357; Lee *v.* Simpson, 134 U. S. 572; Robinson *v.* Hardcastle, 2 T. R. 241; Smith *v.* Adkins, 41 L. J., Ch. 628; 27 L. T., N. S. 90; Doe *v.* Bird, 2 N. & M. 679; 5 Barn & Ad. 695; Wildbone *v.* Gregory, 12 L. R., Eq. 482; *In re* Teape, 16 L. R., Eq. 442; 28 L. T., N. S. 799.

Compare Mines *v.* Gambrill, 71 Ind. 30; Hollister *v.* Shaw, 46 Conn. 248; *In re* Philadelphia Trust Co., 13 Phil. (Pa.) 44; Bassett *v.* Hawk, 114 Pa. St. 502; Johnson *v.* Stanton, 30 Conn. 297.

The tendency of the later decisions is to even further relax the rule, and hold, in harmony with the express statutory provisions of 1 Vict., ch. 26, § 27, that a general devise of real and personal estate shall operate as a general execution of a power, unless a contrary intention should appear in the will. Amory *v.* Meredith, 7 Allen (Mass.) 397; Willard *v.* Ware, 10 Allen (Mass.) 263; Bangs *v.* Smith, 98 Mass. 270; Bolton *v.* DePeyster, 25 Barb. (N. Y.) 539; Collier's Will, 40 Mo. 329; Frink *v.* Eggleston, 92 Ill. 515; 34 Am. Rep. 136, where the English and American cases are reviewed; Russell *v.* Kennedy, 3 Brewst. (Pa.) 438.

The rule, independent of statutory provisions, is that if there be an interest on which the instrument can attach, it will not execute the power. 4 Kent's Comm. *34; 2 Washb. Real Prop. *325; Hay *v.* Mayer, 8 Watts (Pa.) 203; 34 Am. Dec. 453; Birdsell *v.* Richards, 18 Pa. St. 256; Bingham's Appeal, 46 Pa. St. 345; Mory *v.* Michael, 18 Md. 227; Bell *v.* Twilight, 22 N. H. 500; Johnson *v.* Stanton, 30 Conn. 297; Coffing *v.* Taylor, 16 Ill. 457; Dunning *v.* Vandusen, 47 Ind. 423; 17 Am. Rep. 709; Pease *v.* Pilot Knob Iron Co., 49 Mo. 124; Owen *v.* Switzer, 51 Mo. 322.

Compare Miller *v.* Meetch, 8 Pa. St. 417; Bishop *v.* Remple, 11 Ohio St. 277.

But if a will made without referring to the power, cannot have any operation except by virtue of the power, it will be a good execution of the power. 4 Kent's Comm. *335; 2 Washb. Real Prop. *320; Maryland Mut. Ben. Soc. *v.* Clendinen, 44 Md. 429; 22 Am. Rep. 52; Write *v.* Hicks, 33 N. Y. 383; Jones *v.* Wood, 16 Pa. St. 25; Keefer *v.* Schwartz, 47 Pa. St. 503.

And it would seem from what is stated by Cruise that the same is true of a deed. 4 Cruise Dig. *197. See also Write *v.* Williamson, 2 Grant Cas. (Pa.) 249; Jones *v.* Wood, 16 Pa. St. 42; Baird *v.* Boucher, 60 Miss. 326.

But the intent to execute the power must be so clear that no other reasonable intent can be imputed to the will. It must be a case where, to use the language of Cruise, "either the words of the will cannot be satisfied without its operation as an appointment, or where there is some description of, or allusion to, the property which is the subject of the power." 4 Cruise Dig. *200; 4 Kent. Comm. *335; 2 Washb. Real Prop. *320; Blagge *v.* Miles, 1 Story (U. S.) 426, where the English cases are discussed, Doe *v.* Roake, 2 Bing. 497; on error, *sub nom.;* Denn *v.* Roake, 5 Barn. & Cres. 720. In the case as reported in 2 Bingham, Best, Ch. J., reviews all the cases, deducting the conclusion, that the law is as stated by Lord Thurlow in Andrews *v.* Emmott, 2 Brown C. C. 297: "The intent to execute must be so clearly manifest by the will, that it is impossible to impute any other intention to a testator than that of executing it;" and the learned justice's conclusion was that such an intention was shown, and he held the power well executed.

On error the King's Bench, while approving the law as laid down in the Common Bench reversed the judgment on the facts, holding that the intent was not clear. The case was carried to the House of Lords, where the judgment of the King's Bench was affirmed, but the doctrine as announced by the lower courts was clearly settled. Roake *v.* Denn, 1 Dow. & C. 437.

That this strict technical rule was not entirely satisfactory to the English judges, is apparent from the remarks in the closing paragraph of the opinion of Abbott, C. J., in the above case and of Sir Wm. Grant on Jones *v.* Tucker, 2 Meriv. 533. And the law as laid down in Amory *v.* Meredith, 7 Allen (Mass.) 397, and the other American cases above cited is much the more consonant with reason.

Mr. Justice Story states as the result of the authorities, that three classes of cases have been held to be sufficient demonstrations of an intended execution of a power: 1. Where there has been some reference in the will or other instrument to the power; 2. Or a reference to the property which is the subject on which it is to be executed; 3. Or where the provision in the will or other instrument executed by the donee of the power would otherwise be ineffectual, or a mere nullity; in other words, it would have no operation except as an execution of the power. Blagge *v.* Miles, 1 Story (U. S.) 426.

The rule thus stated has been approved by the Supreme Court in Blake *v.* Hawkins, 98 U. S. 326; Warner *v.* Connecticut Mut. L. Ins. Co., 109 U. S. 366; 27 L. Ed. 965; Lee *v.* Simpson, 134 U. S. 572; 33 L. Ed. 1038, and by the Supreme Court of *South Carolina* in Bilderback *v.* Boyce, 14 S. Car. 528.

It is after all a question of intention as shown by the instrument. Pease *v.* Pilot Knob Iron Co., 49 Mo. 124. If such words are used as "all of my estate," or "the balance of my estate," or "property to which I am in any wise entitled," which are sufficient to include the property over which the power extended, this will be sufficient though no direct reference to the power is made. This inference is, of course, strengthened if the will would otherwise be inoperative. Andrews *v.* Brumfield, 32 Miss. 107; Faulk *v.* Dashiell, 62 Tex. 642; 50 Am. Rep. 542; Keefer *v.* Schwartz, 47 Pa. St. 503; Lee *v.* Simpson, 39 Fed. Rep. 235; *on appeal*, 134 U. S. 572; Attorney General *v.* Brackenbury, 1 H. & C. 782; Cooke *v.* Farrand, 2 Marsh. 421; 7 Taunt. 122.

See Cooke *v.* Cunliffe, 17 Q. B. 245; 15 Jur. 1076; 21 L. J., Q. B. 30; Langly *v.* Sneyd, 7 Moore, 165; 2 B. & B. 243.

A will bequeathing exactly the sum the testatrix had a right to dispose of, under a power in her husband's will, to his surviving legatees, if a good execution of the power, although the will contained no direct reference to or express recital of the power. Munson *v.* Berdan, 35 N. J. Eq. 376.

A case decided by a *nisi prius* court in *Pennsylvania* holds that a devise or bequest however unlimited in terms, will not comprehend the subject of a power unless reference is made to the power or to its subject. *In re* Philadelphia Trust Co., 13 Phila. (Pa.) 44.

If there is no express reference to the instrument creating the power, there should be some special reference to the subject on which it is to operate, or some circumstance leading to the conclusion that its execution was intended. Patterson *v.* Wilson, 64 Md. 193.

A testator gave to his wife $14,000, "to be by her used during her natural life at her pleasure, hereby giving her power . . to appoint the same among my legatees, by will, after her decease, according to her judgment and discretion;" otherwise to his legatees "in proportion to the legacies bequeathed by this my will." *Held*, that her will bequeathing exactly the $14,000 among her husband's surviving legatees was a good execution of the power, although the will contained no direct reference to or express recital of the power. Munson *v.* Berdan, 35 N. J. Eq. 376.

If the court can gather from the surrounding circumstances, a clear intention on the part of a settlor to take property comprised in the deed out of a will of prior date, it will not hold the general devise in the will to be an execution of a general power to appoint by deed or will contained in a settlement. *In re* Rudding, 20 W. R. 936.

A will is not a good execution of a power which contains no reference to the power nor to the property that is the subject of the power, nor to anything from which it could be inferred that in framing the will the testator had the power in contemplation. Doe *v.* Johnson, 7 M. & G. 1047; 8 Scott N. R. 761; 14 L. J., C. P. 17.

Under the wills both of the father and mother of M, real and personal property was devised to trustees in trust for the said M during her life, with the power to her of disposing of the same by will. M died leaving a will, in which, with the exception of certain specific bequests of articles of personal property, all the property disposed of is described as "all the rest, residue and remainder of my estate, real, personal and mixed, wheresoever situated and to which I am in any manner whatever entitled." A bill was filed by said trustees, seeking among other things a construction of said will. The bill contained an averment that the said M at the time of her death had, besides that held in trust for her, other property, both real and personal, which she held in her own right absolutely and in fee simple; and no proof was offered tending to show that there was no other property upon which her will could operate, except that subject to the power created by the wills of her father and mother. *Held*, that as there was no reference in the will of M to the power created by the wills of her father and mother, nor to the subject on which the power was to operate; and, it was averred in the bill of complaint and nowhere denied, that she had other property, her will would be operative without the aid of the power, and could not be regarded as an execution of said power. Patterson *v.* Wilson, 64 Md. 193.

See also Myers *v.* McBride, 13 Rich. (S. Car.) 178.

A married woman was the donee of a power of appointment by deed or will over certain policy moneys payable upon her own death, but was unaware of the existence of the power. She concurred with her husband in settling certain family estates by an indenture which treated the policy moneys as the husband's own property, and settled them also. This concurrence was for a purpose entirely unconnected with the policy moneys, and under it she took a life interest in remainder after her husband's death, in the estates, but no interest in the policy moneys. She survived her husband, received in respect to the life interest in the estates a sum exceeding the amount of the policy moneys, and died, leaving a will whereby she gave all her property, over which she had any disposing power, to certain beneficiaries. *Held*, that her concurrence in the deed of settlement for purposes unconnected with the policy moneys subject to the power, and in ignorance of the existence of the power, could not operate as an exercise of the power, though the deed purported to pass the policy moneys, and that the will was a valid exercise of the power. Griffieth-Boscawen *v.* Scott, L. R., 26 Ch. Div. 358.

Where the same person has an interest in land, and a power to sell, and makes a conveyance proper to convey his interest, and also to execute his power, the conveyance shall operate to convey his interest, and not to execute the power. Bell *v.* Twilight, 22 N. H. 500; Jones *v.* Wood, 16 Pa. St. 25

If the party executing the deed has an estate and also a power, and the deed though defective under the power is good at common law, the estate will pass, though it was the intention of the party to execute the power. Doe *v.* Keir, 4 M. & R. 101.

Where an executor, authorized by will to sell real estate, executed a conveyance purporting to be in pursuance of the power, and to pass the testator's estate, and such conveyance was executed by him in his own name, without the addition of his official designation, the estate passed by virtue of the power, although he thereby conveyed his own estate in a part of the premises. Miller *v.* Meetch, 8 Pa. St. 417.

Where executors have plenary power to sell, their deed is conclusive evidence of a sale under the power. White *v.* Williamson, 2 Grant Cas. (Pa.) 249.

The rule as laid down in Sir Edward Clare's Case, 6 Co. Rep. 176, and subsequent cases, is thus stated by Chancellor Kent: "If a will be made without any reference to the power, it operates as an appointment under the power, provided it cannot have operation without the power. If the act can be good in no other way than by virtue of the power, and some part of the will would otherwise be inoperative, and in other intention than that of executing the power can properly be imputed to the testator, the act or will shall be deemed an execution of the power, though there be no reference to the power. Bradish *v.* Gibbs, 3 Johns. Ch. (N. Y.) 551.

Thus where a wife before marriage entered into an agreement with her intended husband that she should have power during the coverture to dispose of her real estate by will, and she, after coverture, made a will devising the whole of her estate to her husband, but without making any reference to the agreement, a court of equity would hold this to be an execution of the power, and her heirs at law would be compelled to convey the legal estate to him. Bradish *v.* Gibbs, 3 Johns. Ch. (N. Y.) 523.

So, if one having only an estate for life, with a power to appoint in fee, devise the property as his own, it is a valid exercise of the power; otherwise, if he had an interest in the reversion. Morgan *v.* Surman, 1 Taunt. 289; Thomas *v.* Snyder, 43 Hun (N. Y.) 14; Towles *v.* Fisher, 77 N. Car. 437. See Maker *v.* Breintnall, 38 N. J. Eq. 345; Bilderback *v.* Boyce, 14 S. Car. 528; Coffing *v.* Taylor, 16 Ill. 457; Mory *v.* Michael, 18 Md. 227. A had an estate of his own in the county of B, and another in the county of C, and had the legal, but no beneficial interest in an estate in the county of D, with power of appointing the latter to either of his sons. He devised all his estates of every nature and kind, in the county of B, and at——in the county of C, or elsewhere in the kingdom of England, to a younger son. *Held*, that the trust estate, over which he had the power, did not pass by the general devise. Roe *v.* Reade, 8 T. R. 118.

Where a party sets up an instrument as an execution of a power, on the ground that the only property upon which it could operate was that subject to the power, the burden is on him to show that the maker was not possessed of other property. Doe *v.* Johnson, 7 M. & G. 1047; 8 Scott N. R. 761; 14 L. J., C. P. 17.

A power acquired after a will has been executed requires a clear manifestation of a new intention to exercise it, and the mere republication of the will by a codicil is not sufficient. Hope *v.* Hope, 5 Giff. 13; Fay's Estate, 11 Phila. (Pa.) 305; See Vaux's Estate, 11 Phila. (Pa.) 57.

And where one, in a deed of trust, reserves the power to appoint by will or otherwise, the power cannot be deemed executed by an instrument made before the trust deed was given. Howard *v.* Carusi, 4 McArthur (D. C.) 260.

Vague and general words of reference to all powers found among words of a general gift and bequest of testator's own property, where the words are justified by the existence of a power as to property in which he had an interest, cannot be extended to operate as an exercise of a special and limited power over property derived from another source. Hope *v.* Hope, 5 Giff. 13.

A recital in the deed of an executor that it was made in pursuance of a written obligation of the testator, is an insufficient reference to a power of sale contained in a will. Hite *v.* Shrader, 3 Litt. (Ky.) 444.

The donee of a power in his deed of appointment "limited and appointed" "not only the lands which were the subject of the power, but those lands belonging to him which were not subject thereto. *Held*, that the words "limited and appointed" operated as a grant of the latter lands. McAndrew *v.* Gallagher, 8 Ir. Rep., Eq. 490.

The mere fact that the bequests in a will exceed the testator's estate will not raise the presumption that it was intended to execute the power. Bingham's Appeal, 64 Pa. St. 345.

Devise of Residue.—A power to appoint by will is not executed by a mere devise of the residue. Buckland *v.* Barton, 2 H. Bl. 136; Doe *v.* Bird, 11 East 49; Powell *v.* Loxdale, 2 B. & A. 291. *Compare*, Attorney Genl. *v.* Brackenbury, 1 H. & C. 782; Cooke *v.* Farrand, 2 Marsh. 421; 7 Taunt. 122.

Though a general residuary devise or bequest, may, unless a contrary intention appears by the will, operate as an execution by the testator of all general powers of appointment, the same rule does not apply to powers of revocation; unless the only power were one of revocation and new appointment. 1 Jarman on Wills, *337.

It is held in *Massachusetts* that a devise of all the rest, residue, and remainder of the estate . . of which testator shall die seised and possessed, or to which he shall be entitled at his decease, passes property of which testator has a power of disposition by his father's will, though he has never owned such property, has other property to which the residuary clause will apply, and does not mention such power of disposition in the residuary clause, but recites it in a previous clause, in which he disposes of a part of the property to which it pertains. Cumston *v.* Bartlett, 149 Mass. 243.

Cases Illustrating the Rule.—Where a widow has a life estate with power of appointment in favor of her children, a bequest of the property to the separate use of a married daughter is a good execution of the power. Friend *v.* Oliver, 27 Ala. 532.

A quitclaim deed by a devisee for life is not a good execution of a power given by the will to sell so much of the land as might be necessary for the support of such devisee. Grundy *v.* Hadfield, 16 R. I. 579.

Property was bequeathed to A in trust to pay the income to the widow of the testator during her life, and on her death to become his absolutely if he survived her; if not, then it was to go to such person as he should by will appoint. A died before the widow, leaving a will by which he gave all his property to his son, but containing no reference to the power. *Held*, not to be an execution of the power. Johnston *v.* Stanton, 30 Conn. 297.

Property was bequeathed in trust to the daughter of the testatrix for life. The will contained a provision "that my daughter Anna is hereby authorized and empowered by her last will and testament, duly executed by her, to dispose of this bequest, . . . as she pleases." The daughter's will contained the following recital: "Whereas, I am entitled to legacies under the last will of my deceased mother, . . . and to a distributive share in the several estates of my deceased sister . . . and my brother," and devised "the entire property and estate to which I am now in any wise entitled, and which I may hereafter acquire, of whatever the same may consist, to my beloved husband." *Held*, to be a valid execution of the power. Lee *v.* Simpson, 39 Fed. Rep. 235; aff'd 134 U. S. 572.

A devisee of a life estate with power to sell for her own support, executed a conveyance in trust of the property whereby she delegated to the trustee named therein her power of sale, and executed to him a quitclaim deed of all the property, said deed containing no reference to the power or the necessity for the sale, excepting a portion which she had formerly conveyed by a deed in which she had recited the power of sale, and which was made for her support. *Held*, that the quitclaim deed was not an execution of the power, and only conveyed her equitable life estate. Phillips *v.* Brown, 16 R. I. 279.

A husband devised property in trust for his wife during life, with power in her to dispose of it by will. By her will she gave her household furniture to W for the use of her grandchildren; and the use of all the residue of her property, of every description, for the maintenance of said children during minority; the residue to be equally divided among them when the youngest should become twenty-one years old. She had substantially no property except the furniture. *Held*, that the will was a good execution of the power of appointment. Hogle *v.* Hogle, 49 Hun (N. Y.) 313.

A tenant in fee of one undivided moiety was tenant for life of the other moiety, with power of appointment as to the latter in fee. By his will he gave and devised all his freehold estates in the city of London, or elsewhere, to his nephew, for his life, on condition that out of the rents he should keep the estates in repair. This was held not to be an execution of the power. Roake *v.* Denn, 4 Bligh, N. S. 3; 1 Dow & C. 437.

A testator devised two tracts of land to his wife for life, with power of disposition by deed or will, and, on failure to appoint, remainder to plaintiffs and others. The first tract was community property of the testator and his wife, while the second was his separate estate. She conveyed both tracts to her son, and as to the first tract her intention to execute the power was apparent. In the second tract she granted all her "right, title, and interest" and, after excepting portions of both tracts previously conveyed, used the following language: "I hereby grant and release all the balance of the said tracts," in fee, followed by a general warranty. *Held*, that the deed executed the power as to the second tract and destroyed the contingent remainder. Hanna *v.* Ladewig, 73 Tex. 37.

By the terms of a will, the widow was vested with a life estate in all the property of the testator, with power to alienate any of it in payment of the debts of the estate, and to defray necessary expenses of the family. The will named her as executor. She was possessed of a small undivided interest in the land in fee simple.

It was held, that in the execution of the power she need not describe herself as executrix, her power to sell arising from the general trust reposed in her, and not simply from her position as executrix; and that a conveyance of land by her which contained no reference to the will or the power of alienation conferred by it, or to anything from which the power might be inferred, would operate to pass only her life estate and her individual interest in the land, and would not execute the power by transferring the fee simple title to the whole land sold, nor would such be the case even if the deed contained covenants of seisin and warranty. Owen *v.* Switzer, 51 Mo. 322.

A, being seised in fee of certain lands, settled them to such uses as he should appoint by deed or will, and in default of appointment to the use of himself for life, with remainder over. He afterwards devised and bequeathed all his real and personal estate whatsoever, and all his estate, right, title and interest therein, and all leasehold premises to which he might be entitled at his death, upon certain trusts. At the time of making the will, and also at the time of his death, A was seised in fee of lands, besides those subject to the power. *Held*, that the devise was not a good execution of the power. Davis *v.* Williams, 1 A. & E. 588; 3 N. & M. 821.

Where a wife has power to convey under a marriage settlement, a deed by the husband and wife, without a valid release of her inheritance, does not convey her title to the land. Myers *v.* McBride, 13 Rich. (S. Car.) 178.

But in *Maryland* it is *held* that where a conveyance was made in trust to allow a wife to hold and enjoy the property, and receive the entire income thereof for her separate use, with power, with the assent of the trustee, to sell, dispose of, convey, and assign, absolutely or otherwise, the whole or any part thereof, and with full power to devise without the trustee's consent, with limitation over of any part not so disposed of. A conveyance absolute by the husband, wife and trustee to a third person, and a reconveyance by him to the husband, vested in the latter a perfect title. Carter *v.* Van Bokkelen (Md. 1890), 20 Atl. Rep. 781.

L and H entered into an ante-nuptial contract, by which she conveyed to one W all her real estate in trust for her separate use during life. H agreed, also, to join with L in all assignments necessary to transfer her personal property to W, upon a similar trust. It was provided that L might give, devise and bequeath all her property, covered by the contract, to H, or to any one or more of her issue, in such shares and proportions as to her should seem meet. L was at the time a minor. The trustee never exercised any control over the property, but it was controlled by L and her husband, she executing annually to W a receipt in full for the amounts she was entitled to. After her marriage L became owner of other real estate. She died in 1855, leaving five children and a will, in which, after referring to the ante-nuptial agreement, and setting forth the provision reserving to her the right to dispose of the property, was contained this provision: "Now, therefore, I . . . give, devise and bequeath unto such child or children as I shall leave or have living at the time of my decease, and to their heirs and assigns forever, all of my real and personal estate of every name and nature, and wheresoever situated, and more particularly described in the instrument herein above referred to; provided, nevertheless, that in case either or any of my children, living at my decease, shall die before he or they shall arrive at the age of twenty-one years and without issue living . . . the share or estate of the child or children so dying shall vest in and belong to, and I give and devise the same to the survivors or survivor." H was appointed executor, and, acting as such after the death of L he took possession of, occupied and controlled the real estate, using its avails, and also the personal property, in his business. N, one of the children, died after the death of his mother before arrival of age, and leaving no issue. H subsequently made a general assignment for the benefit of creditors, preferring his children. The assignees brought an action to determine the amounts to which the children were entitled. *Held*, that the will of L was intended only as an execution of the power of disposition reserved in the contract, and so did not affect property subsequently acquired. Beardsley *v.* Hotchkiss, 96 N. Y. 201; 30 Hun (N. Y.) 605.

There is a recent decision of the Supreme Court of the United States in which the question whether or not the power was intended to be executed, is discussed quite fully. The facts of the case were that Mrs. Clemson had a power given her by the will of Mrs. Calhoun, to dispose by will of certain property. The will of Mrs. Clemson contained the following recital:

"Whereas I am entitled to legacies under the last will of my deceased mother, Floride Calhoun, and to a distributive share in the several estates of my deceased sister, Cornelia Calhoun, and my brother, Patrick Cal-

If the appointor professes in the instrument to act in one capacity he will not be considered as having acted in another, though he also had power to act in such other capacity.[1] A change of the

houn, and, notwithstanding my coverture, have full testamentary power to dispose of the same." It then proceeds as follows: "I will, devise and bequeath the entire property and estate to which I am now in any wise entitled and which I may hereafter acquire, of whatever the same may consist, to my beloved husband, Thomas G. Clemson, absolutely and in fee simple; but should my husband, Thomas G. Clemson, depart this life leaving me his survivor, or should he survive me and then die intestate, in either event I will, devise and bequeath my entire property and estate, as well as that which I may hereafter acquire, of whatever the same may consist, to my granddaughter, Isabella Lee, the child of Gideon Lee, of the State of New York, absolutely and in fee simple."

Mrs. Clemson died before her husband, and he died testate. The last devise and bequest, therefore, to the plaintiff, did not become operative, and the clause containing it is of no effect except so far as its language bears upon the proper construction of the entire instrument. On these facts the court says:

"The view taken by the circuit court was that, as Mrs. Clemson had the right, for her life, to the enjoyment of the property held in trust for her under the will and codicil of Mrs. Calhoun, and the absolute power of disposing of it by will, she treated it by her will as being as much hers as the distributive share, referred to in her will, in the several estates of her sister and brother; that it would be too narrow and technical a construction of the will, under the circumstances, so to limit the language of the devise and bequest as to exclude the exercise of the power; that the mention of the distributive share in the estates of her sister and her brother allowed it to be said that the language of the devise and bequest might have some effect by means of her interest in such distributive share, but that would not be all the effect which the words imported; that if the intention to pass the property held in trust could be discovered, such intention ought to prevail; that the intent to dispose of such property was apparent on the face of the will; that, as it plainly referred to the property covered by the power, its language could not be satisfied unless the instrument should operate as an execution of the power; that the recital in the will that, notwithstanding her coverture, she had 'full testamentary power to dispose of the same' (referring to the legacies under the will of her mother and to a distributive share in the estates of her sister and brother), could not be regarded as merely a reference to the fact that, shortly before that time, married women in South Carolina had, by the constitution of 1868, and the legislation consequent thereon, been enabled to dispose of their property by will, because in that view such statement would have been wholly uncalled for, as she could alienate her own property in any way she chose, while the property held in trust for her for life could be disposed of by her only by will; and that therefore the more reasonable inference was that she referred by the words 'full testamentary power,' to the will of her mother, rather than to her own recently acquired legal capacity, though a married woman, to make a will, as to the property in which she did not have merely a life estate, with a power of appointment."

This reasoning is approved by the Supreme Court. And in commenting upon the words "in any wise entitled," the court says they "are sufficient to cover not only property which she held in her own full right, but also property which she held in a limited right under her mother's will." Lee *v.* Simpson, 134 U. S. 572.

1. Ritchie *v.* Putnam, 13 Wend. (N. Y.) 524; Davenport *v.* Parsons, 10 Mich. 42; 81 Am. Dec. 772.

Where a widow, in assigning a lease, professes to act as administratrix of her husband, she will not be considered as having performed the act as guardian of her children. Ritchie *v.* Putnam, 13 Wend. (N. Y.) 524.

Where the deed of an executor is expressed to be made under an order of the court, such deed cannot be held to be an execution of a power contained in the will, though the order of the court was invalid. Jay *v.* Stein, 49 Ala. 514.

form of personal property cannot be regarded, *per se*, as an execution of a power of disposition over it.[1]

Under the statutes of *New York*, the execution of any instrument conveying an estate or creating a charge, which the donee would have no right to make except by virtue of his power, is a valid execution of the power, though the power is not referred to therein.[2]

So, under the *New York* statute, lands which are the subject of a power of devise shall be held to pass by a will of all the testator's property, unless the intent that the will shall not operate as an execution appears expressly or by implication.[3]

8. Compliance With Conditions.—The conditions attached by the donor to the execution of the power must be complied with strictly, however unessential they may seem.[4]

1. "A change in the precise form of the property, whether it be goods, perishable or otherwise, or money, in order to the practicable and profitable use of the same by the tenant for life, cannot be assumed to be the exercise of absolute dominion over it . . . Any lawful use of the money as tenant for life, is not to be deemed an execution of the power of disposal of it, in the absence of any act evincing that intent . . . As a conveyance of property, by deed or will, will not be regarded as an execution of a power over it, in the absence of any reference to the power or the subject of it evincing an intention to execute it, unless the deed or will must otherwise be inoperative, so here, such an act *in pais* as the use of this money, in the only manner consistent with the profitable enjoyment of it conferred by her husband's will, cannot be regarded as an execution of a power over it." Burleigh *v.* Clough, 52 N. H. 283; 13 Am. Rep. 41.

2. 4 *New York* Rev. Stat., § 124 (Banks' eds.), p. 2450; (1882) p. 2193; Hogle *v.* Hogle, 49 Hun (N. Y.) 313.

It is not essential that the instrument should contain any reference to the power. Brown *v.* Farmers' L. & T. Co., 51 Hun (N. Y.) 386.

By a conveyance in trust, the grantor conveyed all her property, real and personal, in trust for her own use during her life, and to such uses afterwards as she should appoint by will. Her will made no reference in terms to the trust or power, but it being apparent that she intended to devise the trust property. The will was held to be an execution of the power, both as to the real and personal estate; and it was further held that the same result would be attained as to the personalty whether the common law or the statute rule were applied. Hutton *v.* Benkard, 92 N. Y. 295.

Where a widow has a right of dower which is unassigned, and at the same time the power, under her husband's will, to mortgage, for purposes therein expressed, the land to which her right attaches, a mortgage executed by her, without referring to the power, will, under this section, be deemed a mortgage of her dower right, and not an execution of the power. Mutual L. Ins. Co. *v.* Shipman, 119 N. Y. 324.

3. 4 *New York* Rev. Stat., § 126 (Bank's ed.), p. 2450; (1882) p. 2193; *In re* Piffard, 42 Hun (N. Y.) 38; Bolton *v.* DePeyster, 25 Barb. (N. Y.) 564; Mott *v.* Ackerman, 92 N. Y. 539.

A case in which the section was held not applicable, is White *v.* Hicks, 43 Barb. (N. Y.) 91.

The section also applies to personalty. Hutton *v.* Benkard, 92 N. Y. 295.

A will giving the wife certain property for her sole use and benefit during life, contained a provision empowering her to lease, sell, give and devise the whole or any part, with remainder over in case of default. A will in which the wife, after providing for her debts and funeral expenses, gave her property to certain persons in equal shares, was held to be a valid exercise of the power, and passed the property received from her husband. Kibler *v.* Huver, 10 N. Y. Supp. 375.

4. 4 Kent's Comm. *330, and note (c) to 12th ed. *331; 2 Washb. Real Prop. *317 and citations in note (1); Taylor *v.*

By the *New York* statute, when a grantor shall have directed any formality to be observed in the execution of the power, in addition to those which by law would have been sufficient to pass the estate, such additional formality shall not be necessary to the execution of the power. If merely nominal, it may be disregarded wholly. With these exceptions, the intention of the grantor as to the mode, time, and conditions of the execution of a power are to be observed, subject to the power of a court of chancery to aid a defective execution.[1]

9. Execution of Powers of Sale—*a.* POWER, HOW CONSTRUED.—A power of sale given in a will should receive a liberal construction in order to effect the true purposes and intent of the will.[2]

Horde, 1 Burr. 60; Smith *v.* Provin, 4 Allen (Mass.) 516; Richardson *v.* Crooker, 7 Gray (Mass.) 190; Pettis Co. *v.* Gibson, 73 Mo. 502; *In re* Pepper, 1 Pars. Eq. Cas. (Pa.) 436; Loomis *v.* McClintock, 10 Watts (Pa.) 274; Wickersham *v.* Savage, 58 Pa. St. 365; Bakewell *v.* Ogden, 2 Bush (Ky.) 265; Ormsby *v.* Tarascon, 3 Litt. (Ky.) 404; Hall *v.* Towne, 45 Ill. 493; Dellet *v.* Whitner, 1 Chev. (S. Car.) 213; Little *v.* Bennett, 5 Jones Eq. (N. Car.) 156; Riçe *v.* Tavernier, 8 Minn. 248; 83 Am. Dec. 778; Cleveland *v.* Boerum, 27 Barb. (N. Y.) 252; Jaques *v.* Todd, 3 Wend. (N. Y.) 83; Hawkins *v.* Kemp, 3 East 410.

That the power was strictly pursued must appear from evidence *aliunde* the recitals of the instrument whereby it is executed. Pettis Co. *v.* Gibson, 73 Mo. 502; Yankee *v.* Thompson, 51 Mo. 234. Unless the instrument creating the power provides that such recitals shall be evidence of a compliance. Carter *v.* Abshire, 48 Mo. 300; Neilson *v.* Chariton Co., 60 Mo. 386; Hancock *v.* Whybark, 66 Mo. 672.

Where property is devised in trust to be conveyed to such persons as A should appoint, and, in case of A's death without making an appointment, then to such person as his wife should appoint, any appointment by A to be effective to defeat his wife's power must strictly comply with the form pointed out in the will. Haslen *v.* Kean, 2 Term. (N. Car.) 279.

The rule applies to conditions as to time as well as other matters. Booraem *v.* Wells, 19 N. J. Eq. 87. Though it is held in *Pennsylvania* that the condition as to time is not essential. Shalter's Appeal, 43 Pa. St. 83. See Richardson *v.* Sharpe, 29 Barb. (N. Y.) 222; Loomis *v.* McClintock, 10 Watts (Pa.) 274.

See *infra*, this title, *Execution of Powers—Execution of Powers of Sale.*

If the power is coupled with an interest, a substantial compliance with the terms of the power is sufficient. Rowe *v.* Beckett, 30 Ind. 154; Rowe *v.* Lewis, 30 Ind. 163.

In the following cases the rule as to strictness has been relaxed. Richardson *v.* Hayden; 18 B. Mon. (Ky.) 242; Tyson *v.* Mickle, 2 Gill (Md.) 376; Richardson *v.* Sharpe, 29 Barb. (N. Y.) 222; Loomis *v.* McClintock, 10 Watts (Pa.) 274; Sherman *v.* Hicks, 14 Gratt. (Va.) 96.

If the performance of some act is made a condition precedent to the exercise of power, and the performance of the act subsequently becomes impossible by act of the law, it does not follow that the power may be exercised without the performance of the condition. Schrewsbury *v.* Scott, 6 C. B., N. S. 1; 6 Jur., N. S. 452; 29 L. J., C. P. 34. See Aislabee *v.* Rice, 2 Moore 358.

1. 4 *New York* Rev. Stat., §§ 119-21; (Banks' ed.), p. 2450 (1882) p. 2193; Bailey *v.* Bailey, 28 Hun (N. Y.) 611.

While mere formalities may be dispensed with, essential conditions cannot be. Consent is not a mere formality, nor a nominal condition. Kissam *v.* Dierkes, 49 N. Y. 602.

2. 3 Redfield on Wills 137; 4 Cruise Dig. *194; Boyd *v.* Salterwhite, 10 S. Car. 45; Geiger *v.* Kaigler, 15 S. Car. 262; Tower *v.* Hartford, 115 Ind. 186.

The purchaser is bound to ascertain whether the power of sale exists. Harmon *v.* Smith, 38 Fed. Rep. 482.

But where the power exists, to be exercised if the necessity arises, the judgment of the donee as to the necessity is conclusive, if exercised in good faith. Bunner *v.* Storm, 1 Sandf. Ch. (N. Y.) 357. See *infra*, this title, *Execution of Powers—Execution, Discretionary or Imperative.*

Where land was devised to executors in trust for the support of the testator's children, with power to sell any portion, the executors may convey in their own names, and without giving bonds other than as executors. Alley *v.* Lawrence, 12 Gray (Mass.) 373.

Where there was given to the executor discretionary power to sell, and invest the proceeds upon mortgage security or in the purchase of real estate, and upon a sale the executor took back a mortgage for the purchase money, which he afterwards foreclosed and bought in the premises, this was a valid execution of the power. Leggett *v.* Hunter, 19 N. Y. 445.

The sale may be made as well by executory contract as by a deed of present bargain and sale. Demorest *v.* Ray, 29 Barb. (N. Y.) 563.

Where the executor was authorized to sell a chattel which had been purchased by the testator but which had not been paid for, a rescission of the purchase is a due exercise of the power. Jones *v.* Loftin, 3 Ired. Eq. (N. Car.) 136.

A power to sell in fee on ground rent or otherwise is well executed by a sale on ground rent with a clause in the deed allowing a redemption of the rent by the purchaser on payment of a sum of money. *Ex parte* Huff, 2 Pa. St. 227. *Compare* Philadelphia etc. R. Co. *v.* Lehigh Coal etc. Co., 36 Pa. St. 204.

Executors vested with absolute power to sell real estate are authorized to do all that is necessary in the way of insurance, superintendence, repairs and taxes, to preserve the property until sale. Howard *v.* Francis, 30 N. J. Eq. 444. But they are not authorized to give covenants of warranty nor against incumbrances. Ramsey *v.* Wandell, 32 Hun (N. Y.) 482.

Where A has the power to direct trustees to grant and convey the estate in fee, in such parts or shares as A may by will direct, this is an unlimited power, and a direction to the trustee to convey the fee in trust, with a remainder over, is a good execution of it. Appleton's Appeal, 136 Pa. St. 354.

If by the will, the legal estate is expressly vested in the executors, they will not be prevented from selling under the power contained in the will by reason of a mortgage, executed by one having an equitable interest in the estate. Vanderveer *v.* Conover, 40 N. J. Eq. 161.

By a residuary clause of a will the estate was devised to the executors in trust with power to sell, dispose of and convey, and to invest the proceeds as directed by the will. A mortgage which had been placed on the property by the testator, being foreclosed, a large deficit resulted. In consideration of a small sum of money paid, the executor made a deed of bargain and sale of the property to the purchaser under the foreclosure. It appeared that the estate received adequate consideration for the property. *Held*, that this was a valid exercise of the power of sale, and that the validity would not be affected by the fact that the deed was executed to cure possible defects in the title. Mutual L. Ins. Co. *v.* Woods, 51 Hun (N. Y.) 640, *affirmed* on appeal, 121 N. Y. 302.

A owned one tract of land individually, and another in partnership with his brother. The former he empowered his executor to sell. After A's death the deed to the partnership tract was held to be a mortgage only, and, being sold under the mortgage, his executor bought it in. *Held*, that the executor took it with the same power to sell as was given him over the tract owned by A individually. Cummins *v.* Carrick (Ky. 1887), 2 S. W. Rep. 490.

Under a power to sell all the real estate of the testator, the executors are not authorized to sell any other lands than those which the testator owned at the time of the execution of the will. Green *v.* Dikeman, 18 Barb. (N. Y.) 535. But it is otherwise if the direction is to sell all the real estate there might be at the time of the testator's death. In such case, real estate acquired after making the will is subject to the power of sale. Fluke *v.* Fluke, 16 N. J. Eq. 478.

A cemetery lot, in which a former wife of the testator was buried, will not be held to be embraced within a general power of sale of the testator's property. Derby *v.* Derby, 4 R. I. 414.

In *Tennessee*, it has been held that an executor with a power of sale cannot sell lands in the adverse possession of another, though the testator died in possession of them. Peck *v.* Peck, 9 Yerg. (Tenn.) 301.

b. WHAT THE POWER INCLUDES.—An absolute power to dispose of property embraces and includes all powers necessary to effect the disposition.[1]

A power to sell does not confer a power to mortgage;[2] nor to

A sale of part of the lands is good, where the power is a general one. Brewer *v.* Taylor (Pa. St. 1887), 9 Atl. Rep. 515.

Under the *North Carolina* statute (Code, § 1493; Rev. Stat., ch. 46, § 34; Rev. Code, ch. 46, § 40), providing for the sale of lands by the administrator with the will annexed, a good title passes, though the persons entitled to the proceeds may have previously conveyed their interests in the land. Orrender *v.* Call, 101 N. Car. 399.

Land was devised to the widow for life, and at her death the executors were directed to sell it and divide the proceeds among the sons. One of the sons conveyed his interest. *Held,* that this did not affect the power of the executors to sell, but that the grantee of the son would be entitled to the proceeds of one of the shares. Baldwin *v.* Vreeland, 43 N. J. Eq. 446.

Purchase by Donee. — Unless expressly authorized by the will, executors cannot become purchasers at sales under a power given by the will even in cases where the prohibition of the statute against their being interested in sales for payment of debts does not apply. So held in *Wisconsin.* O'Dell *v.* Rogers, 44 Wis. 136.

But it has been held in *New York,* where an executor with power of sale agrees to purchase the land himself from those entitled under the will, and pays a part of the purchase money, and a deed is executed to him and placed in escrow, to be delivered upon payment of the balance of the purchase money, that upon the death of the executor the right of his representatives to the deed will prevail over those of a purchaser from his successor, the agreement not being objected to by those interested under the will. Clark *v.* Jacobs, 56 How. Pr. (N. Y.) 519.

Where an executor with power of sale, upon making the sale, agrees with the purchaser to buy up the widow's right of dower and to pay off incumbrances created by the testator, such agreement binds only the executor personally, and not the estate. Bostwick *v.* Beach, 31 Hun (N. Y.) 343.

Where a sale is merely colorable for the purpose of transmitting the title to the trustee, no title passes. Skillman *v.* Skillman, 2 McCarter (N. J.) 388; Joyner *v.* Conyers, 6 Jones' Eq. (N. Car.) 98. So if the sale is made to relatives for a less price than could have been obtained from others. Oberlin College *v.* Fowler, 10 Allen (Mass.) 545.

1. Kinnan *v.* Guernsey, 64 How. Pr. (N. Y.) 253.

Where the power is to sell real estate, the donee may lawfully dedicate to public use any portion of it which falls within the lines of a proposed street, such dedication being incidental to the sale of the real estate in lots or otherwise on each side of the street. *In re* Sixty-Seventh St., 60 How. Pr. (N. Y.) 264.

A power to sell a mill and other improvements, authorizes the sale of the water rights attached to the mill. McDonald *v.* Bear River etc. W. & Min. Co., 13 Cal. 220.

2. The weight of authority is in accordance with the statement of the text. 1 Sugden Powers (ed. 1856) 513; 2 Perry on Trusts, § 768; Patapsco Guano Co. *v.* Morrison, 2 Wood (U. S.) 395; Butler *v.* Gazzam, 81 Ala. 491; Hubbard *v.* German Catholic Congregation, 34 Iowa 31; Switzer *v.* Wilvers, 24 Kan. 384; 36 Am. Rep. 259; Hirschman *v.* Brashears, 79 Ky. 258; Wilson *v.* Maryland Life Ins. Co., 60 Md. 150; Wood *v.* Goodridge, 6 Cush. (Mass.) 117; Hoyt *v.* Jaques, 129 Mass. 286, and English cases there cited; Morris *v.* Watson, 15 Minn. 212; Stokes *v.* Payne, 58 Miss. 614; 38 Am. Rep. 340; Price *v.* Courtney, 87 Mo. 387; 56 Am. Rep. 453; Ferry *v.* Laible, 31 N. J. Eq. 567; Contant *v.* Servoss, 3 Barb. (N. Y.) 128; Albany F. Ins. Co. *v.* Bay, 4 N. Y. 9; Bloomer *v.* Waldron, 3 Hill (N. Y.) 361; Taylor *v.* Galloway, 1 Ohio 232; Willis *v.* Smith, 66 Tex. 31; Ball *v.* Harris, 4 Myl. & Cr. 264; Haldenby *v.* Spofforth, 1 Beav. 390; Page *v.* Cooper, 16 Beav. 396; Stronghill *v.* Austey, 1 De G. M. & G. 635.

But respectable authorities hold more or less positively the contrary, especially in *England.* Mead *v.*

Orrery, 3 Atk. 239; McLeod *v.* Drummond, 17 Ves. 154; Scott *v.* Tyler, 2 Dickens 725; Andrew *v.* Wrigley, 4 Brown C. C. 125; especially Eden's note to the latter case. Miller *v.* Redwine, 75 Ga. 130; Watson *v.* James, 15 La. Ann. 386; Loebenthal *v.* Raleigh, 36 N. J. Eq. 169; Leavitt *v.* Pell, 25 N. Y. 474; Lancaster *v.* Dolan, 1 Rawle (Pa.) 231; Presbyterian Corporation *v.* Wallace, 3 Rawle (Pa.) 109; Gordon *v.* Preston, 1 Watts (Pa.) 386; Pennsylvania Ins. Co. *v.* Austin, 42 Pa. St. 257; Zane *v.* Kenneday, 73 Pa. St. 182.

As in other questions of construction, this seems to turn largely upon the intent of the donor of the power as shown by the instrument. Says Robinson, J., in Nelson *v.* Maryland L. Ins. Co. (60 Md. 152): "A power of sale, like all other powers, can be exercised only in the mode and upon the terms and conditions prescribed by the instrument creating it. Did the testatrix, then, in authorizing the trustee to sell and dispose of the property devised to him in trust for the purpose of reinvestment, and for this purpose only, mean that he should mortgage it to secure the payment of borrowed money. Or did she mean an out and out sale or conversion of the property and a reinvestment of the proceeds arising from the sale, for the benefit of all parties interested under the will?" After citing Latrobe *v.* Tyson, 42 Md. 325, which was also a case where the property was to be sold and the proceeds reinvested, and where the court held that a sale alone was a proper compliance with the terms of the will, the court continues: "If such, then, be the meaning of the words 'sell and dispose,' as denoting the extent of the power to be exercised by a trustee, is there anything on the face of this will to show that they were used by the testatrix in any other or wider sense? We think not. On the contrary, looking to the nature and objects of the trust, and the character of the property, it is plain she never meant to authorize the trustee to mortgage it for borrowed money. . . . For the purpose of changing the investment, the testatrix authorizes the trustee to sell and dispose of the property; and to say the trustee may do something else, that he may borrow money and mortgage the property, would be giving to the language used in conferring the power, and declaring the purpose for which it was to be exercised, a meaning not warranted by any sound rule of construction." See also Ward *v.* Amory, 1 Curt. (U. S.) 419; Wilson *v.* Troup, 2 Cow. (N. Y.) 195; 14 Am. Dec. 458.

The contrary view is based upon the theory that a power to dispose of or sell would necessarily carry with it the power to incumber or charge, as the greater includes the less. This is the view taken by the Supreme Court of Tennessee in Steifel *v.* Clark, 9 Baxt. (Tenn.) 470, *citing* 4 Kent's Comm. *147.

Some cases go upon the theory that the remaining provisions of the will or other instrument creating a power show an intention in the donor to confer a power of raising money by incumbering the property. See Starr *v.* Moulton, 97 Ill. 525; Faulk *v.* Dashiell, 62 Tex. 642; 50 Am. Rep. 542; Loebenthal *v.* Raleigh, 36 N. J. Eq. 169.

It was held by the same court which decided the case of Steifel *v.* Clark, 9 Baxt. (Tenn.) 466, that a power "to dispose of by last will and testament or by deed of gift," does not include a power to mortgage. Head *v.* Temple, 4 Heisk. (Tenn.) 34.

It has been held that a court may authorize trustees to mortgage the realty for the purpose of raising money to pay debts. Fraser *v.* Fishburn, 4 Rich. (S. Car.) 314. See also Holme *v.* Williams, 8 Sim. 557; Selby *v.* Cooling, 23 Beav. 418; Williamson *v.* Field, 2 Sandf. Ch. (N. Y.) 533; Biles' Estate, 8 Phila. (Pa.) 587. *Compare* Patapsco Guano Co. *v.* Morrison, 2 Wood (U. S.) 395.

And if it appears that the sole object and purpose of the testator in conferring the power to sell was to pay debts or a particular specific charge upon the estate, and the estate itself is devised subject to that charge, the donee may mortgage; but if the intention of the testator was that the estate should be absolutely converted, a mortgage is void. Haldenby *v.* Spofforth, 1 Beav. 390; Ball *v.* Harris, 4 Myln. & Cr. 264; Stronghill *v.* Anstey, 1 De G. M. & G. 635; Hoyt *v.* Jaques, 129 Mass. 288.

A will contained this clause: "If it should seem necessary at any time to dispose of a portion of my real estate for the payment of my debts, I hereby give my executors power to do so, either at public or private sale." The estate included a very large tract of land, which could only be sold to advantage as a whole, and whose value would be greatly depreciated by selling any part or parts of it, and by reason of its character and value a purchaser could only be obtained exceptionally and by effort. On an application by the executors (in which the beneficiaries under the will joined), *held*, that authority to mortgage it to raise sufficient money to pay the debts after applying the personal estate, should be given. Loebenthal *v.* Raleigh, 36 N. J. Eq. 169.

Lands were conveyed to trustees for the sole and separate use of a married woman and her heirs, with power to her to sell the whole or any part thereof with the consent of the trustees, the proceeds to be invested for the purposes of the trust, "or disposed of as she should direct." *Held*, that she had power to charge the estate with the payment of an account contracted for necessaries. Jackson *v.* West, 22 Md. 71.

Where the power is to raise money out of the estate to pay debts, as where the testator charges his real estate with the payment of his debts generally, the trustee has power not only to sell but to mortgage. 2 Story Eq. (13th ed.) 1064b; Ball *v.* Harris, 4 Myln. & Cr. 264.

In Duval's Appeal, 38 Pa. St. 112, it was held that where the testator appointed his wife executrix, and, after giving certain real estate to his children, devised the residue to trustees in trust to sell at public or private sale, apply the proceeds to the payment of his debts and divide the surplus among his children, the trustees had power to convey such residue to the wife as executrix to enable her to mortgage it for the purpose of raising money to pay the debts.

Property was devised to A for life with power to sell and convey the property or any part of it, "the proceeds to be used for the devisee's comfort and otherwise as he may think proper. *Held*, that A might mortgage the property. Kent *v.* Morrison (Mass. 1891), 10 L. R. A. 756.

An estate was devised in trust for such person or persons, and to such use or uses as the devisee should by deed or will appoint. *Held*, that this conferred a general power of appointment, which might well be executed by a mortgage. Hicks *v.* Ward, 107 N. Car. 392.

In Kinney *v.* Mathews, 69 Mo. 520, a conveyance was made to a married woman and her children, which contained an authority to her to sell the land, but provided that the proceeds should be laid out in other land to be secured to her and her children. Upon this state of facts it was held that she was not authorized to mortgage the land to secure a loan of money which was borrowed to pay for land conveyed to a trustee for her use, and such mortgage was held to convey only her title, and to be void as to the children.

In a similar case in the same State, however, where property was devised to the widow, with the right to sell and re-invest as she might desire any part of the same for her separate use and benefit, the will providing that at her death any portion undisposed of should go to the children of the testator, it was held that the widow could make a valid assignment of a note secured by mortgage belonging to the estate, as collateral security for money necessarily borrowed by her for her support. Harbison *v.* James, 90 Mo. 411.

In the orphans' court of Philadelphia we find a similar holding to that of the Missouri court. There the testator devised his property to his wife with the right to dispose of it and to devise it in such portions to their children as she deemed proper, but in case she married again, she was to have only one-third of the estate. Before re-marriage, she executed a mortgage on the estate, one of the minor children joining in the execution. It was held that the mortgage bound only her interest and had no effect on the child's interest in the estate. Steger's Estate, 11 Phila. (Pa.) 158.

It has been decided in *Kentucky* that a power given to a husband and wife to sell the wife's separate estate does not authorize them to mortgage it to secure a debt of the husband. Hirschman *v.* Brashears, 79 Ky. 258.

Where property was conveyed to A in trust to sell and dispose thereof to raise money to pay the grantor's debts, the grantor cannot deny the right of A to mortgage property to redeem from a judicial sale so long as the creditors do not object. This was the holding of the Supreme Court of *Iowa*, but Adams, C. J., dissented therefrom. Waterman *v.* Baldwin, 68 Iowa 255.

It is held by the Supreme Court of *Georgia* that, where a testator devised hotel property to one in trust for the testator's wife and children, clothing him with a power to sell and reinvest at

make a gift of the property or transfer it for any purpose, other than in completion of a sale.[1] But it does confer a power to make a partition.[2]

any time, this included a power to mortgage the property to raise money to carry on the hotel business. Miller *v.* Redwine, 75 Ga. 130.

In *Tennessee* a testator devised to his daughter and her husband certain lands and other property to be disposed of by them as they might see proper. By a codicil he declared that it was not his intention to make the estate of the husband, in the event he survived his wife, a fee simple estate, but that he should hold the same for his natural life only, and upon his decease the lands should descend to the children of the daughter or her heirs. By a subsequent clause in the codicil the testator provided that the husband and wife should have power during their joint lives to dispose of the lands devised to them, by deed executed by them jointly, and proved and acknowledged according to law for disposing of the estates of married women. The husband and wife having joined in a conveyance of the land, in the mode prescribed to secure a debt for money borrowed by the husband, it was held that the conveyance passed the entire estate, and cut off the contingent remainder in favor of the children or heirs of the daughter. Shields *v.* Netherland, 5 Lea (Tenn.) 193.

A statutory power to sell realty to pay debts confers no authority to mortgage. Patapsco Guano Co. *v.* Morrison, 2 Wood (U. S.) 395; Melledge *v.* Bryan, 49 Ga. 397.

Under § 73 of the *New York* Rev. Stat. (2 *New York* Rev. St., pt. 2, ch. 1, tit. 2, art. 3) common law powers are abolished, and it is provided that a power authorizing alienation of the fee to any person in any manner is general, and that when no one but the grantee is interested in its execution, it is beneficial. When an absolute power of disposition, unaccompanied by any trust, is given to the owner of a particular estate for life or years, such estate shall as to creditors and purchasers be a fee, but subject to any future estate limited thereon in case the power shall not be executed. By said article, when the grantee of a power is thereby authorized to dispose of the entire fee for his own benefit during his life, the power is absolute. Under this statute it has been held that a bequest of bonds, the legatee to have the income for life, with power to the legatee during life to charge the investment or to sell the bonds, and apply the proceeds to his own use, conferred a power to hypothecate the bonds as security for money borrowed. Brown *v.* Farmers' L. & T. Co., 51 Hun (N. Y.) 386.

1. Dupont *v.* Wertheman, 10 Cal. 354; Park *v.* American H. M. Soc. (Vt. 1890), 20 Atl. Rep. 107; Mott *v.* Smith, 16 Cal, 533.

To Make Advancements.—Where a testator devised all his property to his wife for life with power to dispose of it by will to their children and also to make advancements to them during her life, discriminating between them in her discretion, and the will contained a further provision that any remainder undisposed of at the death of the widow should be equally divided among the children, it was held that the widow had power to convey a part of the real estate in fee simple to one of the children by way of advancement. Franke *v.* Auerbach, 72 Md. 580.

By a residuary clause of a will the residue of an estate was given to the widow during her widowhood, she being also the executrix. After her death or remarriage the property was to go to the children of the executrix, who was authorized to make advances in her discretion for their support. By another clause of the will she was also appointed guardian of the children with a power to mortgage, lease, sell or dispose of the property embraced in the will. After her second marriage she executed a mortgage upon the property to raise money for the purpose of making advances for the children and for paying advances already made. It was held that the mortgage was valid. New York Mut. L. Ins. Co. *v.* Shipman, 108 N. Y. 19.

2. This is the conclusion reached by the United States Supreme Court in Phelps *v.* Harris, 101 U. S. 370. After reviewing at length the English cases, Mr. Justice Bradley sums up the matter as follows: "It would seem to be finally settled in *England*

c. EFFECT OF EXECUTION.—A power of sale of land, when executed, converts the land into personalty, unless the proceeds are actually re-invested in land, or are stamped with a trust for such re-investment.[1]

d. MODE OF SALE.—Where a general power of sale is given, the time, place, and manner of its execution, as well as the price at which the property is sold, are all discretionary with the donee. He may sell at public or private sale, with or without advertising, as in the exercise of his discretion he may consider most proper;[2]

that a power to sell and exchange does include the power to make partition, and that all doubt on the subject has been removed; and we have not been referred to any decisions in this country which lead to a contrary result." *Compare* 4 Cruise Dig. *179, *180.

The ordinary power of sale and exchange authorizes a partition. Frith *v.* Osborne, 24 W. R. 1061; 3 L. R., Ch. Div. 618; 45 L. J., Ch. Div. 780; 35 L. T., N. S. 146.

A direction in a will that the lands of the testator should be divided in certain proportions among his children, full power being given the executor to sell the whole or any part, on such terms as he may deem best, to carry out the terms of the devise, confers upon the executor power to divide the land in kind or by sale. Anderson *v.* Butler, 31 S. Car. 183.

A will construed by the Supreme Court of Michigan authorized the executors to sell certain lands, at such times and in such manner, as they should deem expedient. The executors effected a partition of some of the lands, which the testator had held in common, by giving a deed to one portion and receiving a release of the balance. It was held that this was within the power of the executors. King *v.* Merritt, 67 Mich. 194.

A will contained a direction to the executrix, to whom an undivided interest in land was devised in trust for the testator's children, "to wind up and liquidate my business interests, either at public or private sale . . . and sell and convert all my property into money and make and execute all necessary or proper transfers thereof." *Held*, that the executrix did not have power to consent to a partition. *In re* Carr, 16 R. I. 645.

Where a will expressly confers a power upon the executors to make partition, and also empowers them to sell at discretion for any of the purposes of the will, they may exercise the power of partition by selling a lot, even during the existence of a life-estate, when such sale becomes necessary to complete the partition. Knapp *v.* Knapp, 46 Hun (N. Y.) 190. See also Hoyt *v.* Day, 32 Ohio St. 101.

Where by a will the realty was directed to be sold by the executors and divided between A and B, a partition of the land by the executors between themselves is not a valid execution of the power, though A and B are themselves the executors. Den *v.* Young, 23 N. J. L. 478. See to same effect, Russell *v.* Russell, 36 N. Y. 581; and *compare* Chesman *v.* Cummings, 142 Mass. 65.

1. Atwell *v.* Atwell, 41 L. J. Ch. 23; 13 L. R. Eq. 23; Mayor *v.* McCune, 59 How. Pr. (N. Y.) 78.

Where a power in trust to executors, to lease the real estate of the testator until it can be sold, would have the effect to suspend the absolute power of alienation in such real estate beyond the time allowed by law, it is void; but the power in trust to sell, in such a case, will still be valid; and the real estate, in equity, will be considered as converted into personalty immediately, where such a conversion is necessary to carry into effect the will of the testator, and to prevent injustice to any of the objects of his intended bounty. Haxtun *v.* Corse, 2 Barb. Ch. (N. Y.) 506.

A sale under a testamentary power for the payment of unscheduled debts, discharges the land from the statutory lien of the testator's debts. Cadbury *v.* Duval, 10 Pa. St. 265.

Where an executor is authorized by the will to sell land, a purchaser from him is, in the absence of fraud, discharged from all liability for the application of the purchase-money by the executor's receipt. Ludlow *v.* Flournoy, 34 Ark. 451.

2. 3 Redfield on Wills, § 135; Coil *v.*

Pitman, 46 Mo. 51; Warden *v.* Richards, 11 Gray (Mass.) 277; Huger *v.* Huger, 9 Rich. Eq. (S. Car.) 217; Tyrrell *v.* Morris, 1 Dev. & B. Eq. (N. Car.) 559; Mead *v.* Byington, 10 Vt. 116; Smith *v.* Hulsey, 62 Ga. 341.

Where a power was given to sell without warranty, a sale with warranty is invalid. Dellet *v.* Whitner, 1 Cheves (S. Car.) 213.

Time of Sale.—The power to sell must in general be strictly construed as to time. Booraen *v.* Wells, 19 N. J. Eq. 87; Richardson *v.* Sharpe, 29 Barb. (N. Y.) 222; Loomis *v.* McClintock, 10 Watts (Pa.) 274.

Where the will directs an immediate sale, such a sale made after a reasonable advertisement and for a fair price will not be disapproved, because there is some evidence that in the future the land would become very valuable for building purposes. Beakly *v.* Beakly, (Md. 1887), 8 Atl. Rep. 658.

Where the power of sale given the executor was for the payment of debts, in case the personal estate should prove insufficient, and the estate was settled in 1836, a sale made in 1878 by the executrix to her daughter reciting the power, was held void. The lapse of over forty years raised a presumption equivalent to affirmative proof that the debts had all been paid. Moores *v.* Moores, 41 N. J. L. 440.

Before the Time.—When the power is given to sell after a certain time a sale before the time named has been held not to be good. Dohoney *v.* Taylor, 79 Ky. 124.

A testator devised his lands to his wife for life, and after her death or remarriage, to be sold, and the proceeds divided among his children. His wife having renounced the will, and dower having been assigned her, the dower of sale could not be executed until after her death or second marriage. Jackson *v.* Logan. 3 Leigh (Va.) 161.

It has been held in *New York* that where a power of sale of land is given in a will, but by other provisions of the will a trust of the rents of the land is created for the benefit of a family "while they continue such," the power of sale cannot be exercised until the family is broken up. *In re* Vandervoort, 1 Redf. (N. Y.) 270. And the same view is taken in a later case, where a testator devised his residuary estate to his executrix, with power to sell, convert into money, and invest the proceeds, which were to be divided into as many parts as he should leave children or descendants of children, to be held for them for life, and after death to go to their children. The testator's dwelling was excepted from this general power of sale, and the executrix was directed to permit the unmarried daughters to occupy it as a home, rent free, during the lives of H and K, two of his daughters, or so long as any of his daughters should remain unmarried. At the death of H and K, or the marriage of all the daughters, the house was to be sold, and the proceeds divided among testator's children or their descendants. The testator left five daughters unmarried. *Held*, that until the death of H and K or the marriage of all the daughters, the executrix had no power to sell the dwelling-house. Kilpatrick *v.* Burrow, 54 Hun (N. Y.) 322.

In another case, in the same State, the will contained a provision that the executors should operate certain factories, which were devised to them in trust, during the period of the trust, or so long within that period as in their discretion could be done without injury to the interests of the estate. *Held*, that this did not imply a power to sell before the expiration of the period limited, but only gave a discretion to suspend business. Downing *v.* Marshall, 1 Abb. App. Dec. (N. Y.) 525.

If the power is to sell after the death of the widow, a sale during her life is not good. Hopkins *v.* Quinn, 93 Ind. 223.

A will contained the following provisions: "I devise to my wife the use of the land and buildings," etc., "during the term of her natural life; and after her death, it is my will that the said land," etc., "be sold by my executors, at their discretion, and the proceeds thereof to be equally divided between my four children, or the survivors of them." During the life of the testator's widow, she and the executor, by a proceeding *ex parte*, obtained an order of court for the immediate sale of the property, and the investment of the proceeds; and the sale was made accordingly, and the price was paid to the master, but never came to the executor. The Supreme Court held that the purchaser took no title, legal or equitable, as against the children of the testator. Davis *v.* Howcott, 1 Dev. & B. Eq. (N. Car.) 460.

But in *New Jersey*, where a testator gave a life estate in certain lands to his wife, with remainder in fee to his executors, with directions that, after her death, they should convert the property into cash and divide the proceeds among his children when the youngest should have attained twenty-five years of age, it was held that the executors could, with the widow's consent, sell the lands in question in her lifetime. Snell *v.* Snell, 38 N. J. Eq. 119.

So, in *Pennsylvania*, a testator devised land in trust for the benefit of his wife for life, to be sold at her decease by his executors, and the proceeds distributed among certain of his children, and appointed his wife an executrix. It was held that a sale during her life, she as executrix joining with the executors in the deed, was a good execution of the power. Gast *v.* Porter, 13 Pa. St. 533.

And even in *New York*, where, as we have seen above, the rule as to time is applied with great strictness, it has been relaxed under circumstances similar to those last mentioned. In Knapp *v.* Knapp, 46 Hun (N. Y.) 190 a testator devised all his property to his wife for life, remainder over. He authorized his executors to sell any or all the land in such manner as they might deem expedient, to pay debts or expenses, to make partition, or for any of the purposes of the will. They were also expressly empowered to make actual partition of land owned by him in common with others. *Held* that, as the only purpose for which sale of the land should be postponed was that the widow might enjoy her life-estate therein, the executors could, with her consent, sell the land in her lifetime.

Where Provision as to Time is Held Directory.---In some cases the provision as to the time of sale has been declared to be directory merely, and a sale after the time has been held valid. Marsh *v.* Love, 42 N. J. Eq. 112; Shalter's Appeal, 43 Pa. St. 83.

Thus in Hale *v.* Hale, 137 Mass. 168, where the will directed that within a year from the time of his death the testator's lands should be sold and the proceeds should remain with his executors for certain specified purposes, it was held that the power of sale could be exercised after the expiration of the year. And in Marsh *v.* Love, 42 N. J. Eq. 112, though the will contained a provision that the sale was to be made in one year, "and sooner if deemed desirable by them," the words "and sooner" did not restrict the time to one year, and the limitation as to time was only directory.

And if the conversion of the land into money for purposes of division is evidently the principal thing contemplated by the testator, a sale made after the time is good. Waldron *v.* Schlang, 47 Hun (N. Y.) 252. And under similar circumstances the same court had previously announced the same rule. Wild *v.* Bergen, 16 Hun (N. Y.) 127. There the will contained a direction by the testator, that "within two years after my decease" the executors sell sufficient lands to pay the debts and legacies. It was held that this did not limit the execution of the power of sale to two years, but its effect was only to compel the payment of the debts and legacies within that time. It was further held that even if this were not so, a creditor could not be deprived of his beneficial interest under the power by the executor's failure to execute it within the time limited.

Even more stringent provisions than the above have been held to be directory merely. In Shalter's Appeal, 43 Pa. St. 83, the testator directed a public sale of his real estate by his executors, "so that it be within one year" after his decease. Yet a sale by the administrator with the will annexed, after the expiration of the year, was held to be as effectual as if it had been made by the executors, who had power to sell after the year, the condition being directory only, and not a condition precedent.

Where the power was to sell within two years from the testator's decease, the power was held to be well executed if the sale is made within the two years, though the conveyance to the purchaser was not executed until after the expiration of that period; and parol evidence was admitted as to the time of the sale. Harlan *v.* Brown, 2 Gill (Md.) 475.

Mode of Sale.—In Coil *v.* Pitman, 46 Mo. 51, where the will provided that the executor should sell the real estate and divide the proceeds, it is held that the manner, time, price, place, etc., of the sale are all matters resting in the sound discretion of the executor.

In Huger *v.* Huger, 9 Rich. Eq. (S. Car.) 217, it is said by the Chancellor: "The executors were not bound to any form or mode of making the sale. Though they had advertised to sell by auction, they were not bound to carry out that plan, and *vice versa*. Their authority was full and complete as that of the testator himself or any other proprietor. They were, as to the matter of that sale, the proprietors."

So in Silverthorn *v.* McKinster, 12 Pa. St. 67, the court by Bell, J., says: "There is no difference between the exercise of a power to sell, unshackled by particular directions for its execution, and a sale made of one's own estate." In this case it was held that the sale might be by parol.

If a public sale is resorted to, all proper advertisements must be made, and everything done to prevent a sacrifice of the property. Lewin, 322; Anonymous, 6 Mad. & Geld. 10.

If the will gives an absolute power of sale, the executor's deed will convey a good title, notwithstanding there has been no advertisement for claims. Wait *v.* Cerqua (Supreme Ct.), 7 N.Y. Supp. 110.

It is held by the *Utah* courts that where the will gives the executor a mere naked power of sale, and contains no direction as to notice, the statutory notice must be given. *In re* Walker's Estate (Utah 1890), 23 Pac. Rep. 930. But where the will points out a different mode, the statutory notice need not be given. So held in *New York.* M'-Dermut *v.* Lorillard, 1 Edw. Ch. (N. Y.) 273.

In *Kentucky* it has been held that in sales of land under a power of sale, the notice must be in pursuance of the power, and the sale in pursuance of the notice. A departure of either from the other renders the sale invalid. Hahn *v.* Pindell, 1 Bush (Ky.) 538.

And the same rule applies in *Missouri*, where it was held that if a deed of trust in the nature of a mortgage provided that in case of default sales should be made "at the east court house door," and there was at the time the deed of trust was executed a court house with an east door, a sale made at the front door of another building, situated in another part of the town, used temporarily as a court house, is not a valid execution of the power, since the sale was not made at the place designated in the deed. Stewart *v.* Brown (Mo. 1891), 16 S. W. Rep. 589.

But *compare* Princeton L. & T. Co. *v.* Munson, 60 Ill. 371.

Public or Private Sale.—Where the will leaves it to the best judgment of the executors as to the mode of sale they have a discretion to sell at public or private sale. Wood *v.* Hammond, 16 R. I. 98.

A will reciting that the testator owned land in partnership with another, and leaving it discretionary with the executrix to sell his half or buy the other half, or to divide, or to sell the lot altogether and divide the money, authorizes a private sale by the executrix jointly with the owner of the other half. Anderson *v.* Holland, 83 Ga. 330.

It necessarily follows that when the will contains a direction to sell at private sale, such course is proper. Gafney *v.* Kenison, 64 N. H. 354.

But where the power is to sell at public auction, a private sale confers no title. McCreery *v.* Hamlin, 7 Pa. St. 87; Griffin *v.* Marine Co., 52 Ill. 130.

As to Order of Court.—If the will so directs, the executor may sell without an order of court. Gafney *v.* Kenison, 64 N. H. 354; Ludlow *v.* Flournoy, 34 Ark. 451. And where the will specifically authorizes and empowers the executors "to grant, bargain, sell, and convey, and, if necessary, to mortgage, any and all real estate, and deeds, releases, and mortgages to make and acknowledge, as fully and amply as I could do were I living," this gives to the executors a power under which they can convey, although no previous authority was obtained from the probate court. Woolworth *v.* Root, 40 Fed. Rep. 723.

Under the statutes of *Texas* in force in 1871, executors authorized by the will to sell, had power to sell lands, without any previous order of court, it not appearing that the estate owed any debts; and such sale would not be void, though not made in strict conformity with the mode prescribed for administration sales, when made under order of court. Wright *v.* Hefner, 57 Tex. 518.

Under the *California* Code (Code Civ. Proc., §§ 1307 and 1561), the former of which provides that children of a testator omitted from the will inherit as in case of intestacy, and the latter that "when property is directed by the will to be sold, or authority is given in the will to sell property, the executor may sell any property of the estate without order of the court," a power of sale in a will does not authorize the sale of the interests of children not mentioned in the will, without the previous sanction of the probate court which is required in ordinary cases, and a subsequent confirmation of the sale

but, as a rule, a general power of sale does not authorize an exchange or barter, but merely a sale for cash.[1]

by the court does not validate it. Smith *v.* Olmstead (Cal. 1890), 22 Pac. Rep. 1143.

Where a conveyance in trust, conferring on the trustee a power of sale, was probated as part of a will, and the trustee, who was also sole executor, obtained an order of sale, which was invalid, but on which he sold the land five years thereafter, and executed a deed as executor, but did not report the sale to the probate court, it was held that to support the conveyance the sale would be referred to the power conferred by the deed, rather than to the order of the court. Matthews *v.* McDade, 72 Ala. 377.

1. Mora *v.* Murphy, 83 Cal. 12; Taylor *v.* Galloway, 1 Ohio 232; Nye *v.* Van Husan, 6 Mich. 329; 74 Am. Dec. 690; Booth *v.* McNair, 14 Mich. 22; Norton *v.* Kearney, 10 Wis. 450; Whipple *v.* Pope, 33 Ill. 336; Powell *v.* Hopkins, 38 Md. 1.

Compare 4 Kent's Com. 331; Ives *v.* Davenport, 3 Hill (N. Y.) 373; Philadelphia etc. R. Co. *v.* Lehigh Coal etc. Co., 36 Pa. St. 204.

Where a legatee of certain bonds with power to sell them, turned them over to one of his creditors as satisfaction of a debt, this is tantamount to a sale. Brown *v.* Farmers' L. & T. Co., 117 N. Y. 266. Yet the same court held in an earlier case that a power to sell generally given to executors is not executed by a conveyance to one of the legatees in satisfaction of a debt from the testator. Russell *v.* Russell, 36 N. Y. 581.

In *Missouri* a trustee under a will with power to pay the legacies in real or personal property in such manner as seemed to him fair, made an entry on the books of the firm of which he was a member crediting one of the legatees with cash equal to the estimated value of certain land belonging to the estate. It was held that this did not constitute a part payment of the legacy, and that no title passed to the land. Ames *v.* Scudder, 83 Mo. 139.

Under a will empowering the executors to settle, adjust, and compromise all debts of the testator, to make settlements with his former partners without authority from any court, and to sell and convey at public or private sale any of testator's land in order to pay his debts, a conveyance by the executors of the testator's interest in a firm whose chief assets were real estate, in consideration of an agreement by the grantee to pay the firm debts, and also certain individual debts of the testator, was held to be a good execution of the power. Valentine *v.* Wysor, 123 Ind. 47.

A testatrix devised all her estate to her children and gave to her executor power to sell any of the land when deemed advisable for the support of the children. The executor conveyed a portion of it for an expressed consideration of a debt owed by testatrix for supplies for her family and the plantation. The children sued to set aside the conveyance, and the husband of the testatrix testified that the debt was a personal one of his. The court nevertheless held that the debt, having been recognized by the testatrix, and the creditor as that of testatrix, and so dealt with by the executor, the latter, in view of the probability of its establishment against the estate, was authorized under the will to discharge it by a deed of the land. Stokes *v.* Stokes, 66 Miss. 456.

Under a power in a will to dispose of the principal for charitable purposes, a widow has no authority to make a gift of a part of it to a private individual "in recognition of kindness, and in testimony of affection and regard," such person not being an object of charity. Park *v.* American H. M. Soc. (Vt. 1890), 20 Atl. Rep. 107.

Sale on Credit.—Where the power is given to sell "for such sum or price and on such terms as to him shall seem meet," the donee of the power may sell on reasonable credit. Carson *v.* Smith, 5 Minn. 78; 77 Am. Dec. 539.

An assignment for the benefit of creditors which authorizes the assignee to "dispose of the property in the ordinary course of business," authorizes a sale on credit. Truitt *v.* Caldwell, 3 Minn. 364; 74 Am. Dec. 764.

A sale on a credit of six months, where the will directed a sale on a credit of twelve months will not render it invalid. Richardson *v.* Hayden, 18 B. Mon. (Ky.) 242.

Exchange.—An authority to sell does not authorize an exchange or barter. Taylor etc. Organ Co. *v.* Starkey, 59

10. Execution of Power to Mortgage.—A power to mortgage generally, without specifying what provisions the deed shall contain, includes the power to insert the usual provisions contained in such instruments in the locality where the land is situated. Thus the instrument may contain a power of sale in case of a default.[1]

N. H. 142; Trudo *v.* Anderson, 10 Mich. 357; 81 Am. Dec. 795; Chamblee *v.* Tarbox, 27 Tex. 139; 84 Am. Dec. 614; Columbus Banking etc. Co. *v.* Humphries, 64 Miss. 1; Hampton *v.* Morhead, 62 Iowa 91.

An undivided moiety of a freehold was vested in trustees with power to sell, dispose of and convey the premises or any part thereof by way of absolute sale, for such a price in money, or by way of exchange for such equivalent or recompense in land and hereditaments, as to them should seem reasonable. The trustees conveyed their undivided moiety to the owners of the other moiety, in exchange for the other moiety. *Held*, a valid execution of the power. Frith *v.* Osborne, 24 W. R. 1061; 3 L. R., Ch. Div. 618; 45 L. J., Ch. Div. 780.

Certain realty was devised to the widow for life or during widowhood, and upon her death or remarriage, in fee to the children. The widow was named as executrix, and full power was given her as such, at any time and upon such terms as she might deem satisfactory, to sell, mortgage or lease the whole or any part of the realty, and to invest the proceeds in good securities, or in the purchase of other real estate, to sell such securities and real estate, and to continue the transfer of the real estate or the proceeds thereof, as long and as often as she might think best; provided, that the proceeds should always be considered real estate. *Held*, that she had power to make a direct exchange of real estate. Mayer *v.* McCune, 59 How. Pr. (N. Y.) 78.

The Purpose.—A general power of sale given to executors authorizes a sale not only for investment, but also for distribution. Manier *v.* Phelps, 15 Abb., N. Cas. (N. Y.) 123. But where the power was to sell personal and real estate, "as the proper and convenient settlement of the estate may require," and the personalty was insufficient to pay debts, legacies, etc., it was held that a sale of the realty could be had, not for the purpose of dividing the proceeds among the devisees, but only for the payment of debts, legacies and charges of administration. Allen *v.* Dean, 148 Mass. 594.

So if the power is given for the purpose of paying debts, or legacies, a sale for any other purpose is not valid. Brome *v.* Pembroke, 66 Md. 193; Wood *v.* Hammond, 16 R. I. 98; Hovey *v.* Chisholm, 56 Hun (N. Y.) 328.

In this last case (Hovey *v.* Chisholm, 56 Hun (N. Y.) 328), it was held that where the executors had power to sell the real estate as they "shall deem most expedient, and for the best interest" of the residuary legatees, they cannot give a good title to one who knows that they have sufficient funds to meet all the legacies referred to in the power of sale.

A testator directed his executors to sell as much of his property as would be sufficient to pay his debts. In a distinct clause in the will he directed them to sell all his property at public auction, on credit, taking notes with approved security, the proceeds to be distributed to his widow and children. *Held*, that a sale to a solvent purchaser, to pay debts, was valid without requiring security. Shelton *v.* Carpenter, 60 Ala. 201.

Power given to an executor to sell and otherwise control the property devised for the support of an imbecile daughter, is unlimited when used for that purpose. Brown *v.* Crittenden, (Ky. 1886), 1 S. W. Rep. 42.

1. Jones on Mortg. 129; Wilson *v.* Troup, 2 Cow. (N. Y.) 195; 14 Am. Dec. 458.

An authority to borrow money to pay debts, and to give a mortgage to secure the money so borrowed, gives the donee of the power the right to give a mortgage directly to the creditors themselves. Magraw *v.* Pennock, 2 Grant Cas. (Pa.) 89.

The owners of certain water lots executed a power of attorney whereby A was authorized to fill up and reclaim the lots, and to raise by mortgage of the premises any money that might be necessary for the pur-

11. By Whom Power May be Executed—*a.* IN GENERAL.—Not only may any person who is competent to dispose of an estate of his own be the donee of and execute a power, but a *feme covert* may, whether the power was given to her while sole or after marriage; and an infant may execute a power which is simply collateral.[1]

pose. A contracted for the filling up of part of the lots, the work to be paid for in cash as it progressed. When the work was completed, there was a balance due to the contractors, and being unable to raise the money by a mortgage of the premises, A mortgaged a part of the premises to the contractors to secure this balance. This was held to be a valid execution of the power. Cumming *v.* Williamson, 1 Sandf. Ch. (N. Y.) 17.

Where lands were devised to the executors to sell at their discretion, and power was also given, in case they could not sell advantageously, to mortgage the lands to pay borrowed money or to keep the property in good condition, the executors were not thereby authorized to pay money borrowed by the testator himself, for which he in his lifetime had executed a mortgage on said lands. The power has sole reference to money borrowed by the executors to keep up the property. Mulford *v.* Mulford, 42 N. J. Eq. 68.

In Ayres *v.* Palmer, 57 Cal. 309, power was given to an attorney to sell or to mortgage land; the land being incumbered, the attorney, with intent to mortgage it for a sum sufficient to pay off the incumbrance and to pay off certain debts of his own, conveyed the land to J B, upon no other consideration than to cause him to mortgage the land for said sum, which was done; and then J B, at the request of the attorney, conveyed the land to the principal. The court held that the transaction was a mode of mortgaging the land within the meaning of the power, and was valid.

A husband having borrowed money, he and his wife joined in a mortgage of her real estate to secure its repayment. Before the debt matured the wife died, and by her will devised all her estate to her husband in trust, to enjoy the income during his life, with remainder to her children. The will also contained a provision that the husband might incumber the estate by way of mortgage, deed of trust or otherwise, and renew the same, for the purpose of raising money "to pay off any and all incumbrances now on said property," and provided that said mortgage or deed of trust should be as valid as though he held an absolute estate in said property. The husband was appointed sole executor without bond. *Held*, that he was empowered to extend the mortgage debt at maturity without notice to the remaindermen, and that the security of the mortgage would not be affected thereby. Warner *v.* Connecticut Mut. L. Ins. Co., 109 U. S. 357.

A power in trustees to raise by mortgage a fixed sum implies a power to raise in addition the incidental costs of the mortgage. Armstrong *v.* Armstrong, 18 L. R., Eq. 541; 43 L. J., Ch. 719.

1. 4 Greenl. Cruise Dig. *139; 2 Washb. Real Prop. *316, *317; 4 Kent's Comm. *324; Thompson *v.* Lyon, 20 Mo. 155.

In re Cardross, 7 L. R., Ch. Div. 728; 38 L. T., N. S. 778; *In re* D'Angiban; Andrews *v.* Andrews, 15 L. R., Ch. Div. 228; *affirming* 49 L. J., Ch. Div. 182.

An infant cannot execute a power unless it is simply collateral, or a naked power, unaccompanied by any interest, and not requiring any discretion. 4 Kent Comm. 324; 1 Perry on Trusts, §§ 52, 296.

Under a will giving the widow of the testator a life estate in his property, subject to division among the children on her death or remarriage, with a further provision that if the widow should wish the executors might sell, the widow does not take a power of sale. Box *v.* Word, 65 Tex. 159.

A trustee under a will, who had also qualified as an administrator *de bonis non* with the will annexed, having in his hands funds belonging to non-resident beneficiaries, who were minors without a guardian and necessitous, instituted proceedings to obtain the authority of the court to pay the income of the share of such children to their father for their support, and upon final settlement to pay over the *corpus* to a duly-qualified guardian.

b. By Married Woman.—Where a married woman is a donee, she may execute the power without the concurrence of her husband.[1]

Under the *New York* statute a general and beneficial power may be given to a married woman to dispose, without the concurrence of her husband, and during the marriage, of land conveyed or devised to her in fee, and of any estate less than a fee

It was held that he did not thereby forfeit the right given him by the will, to make a sale of the testator's real estate without the intervention of the court. Rose *v.* Thornley (S. Car. 1890), 12 S. E. Rep. 11.

Where the power is given to "heirs," without vesting any power in the ancestor, the heirs for the time being can execute. 1 Chance on Powers 689.

1. 4 Kent's Comm. *325, note (a), and the reference to Sugden on Powers therein. Chancellor Kent says that he has examined the leading authorities cited by Mr. Sudgen, and that they bear out the doctrine of the text. 4 Greenl. Cruise Dig. *139; 2 Washb. Real Prop. *316, *317; Cranston *v.* Crane, 97 Mass. 459; Thompson *v.* Lyon, 20 Mo. 155; Claflin *v.* Van Wagoner, 32 Mo. 252; Ladd *v.* Ladd, 8 How. (U. S.) 27; Rush *v.* Lewis, 21 Pa. St. 72; Thompson *v.* Murray, 2 Hill Eq. (S. Car.) 204; Nevin *v.* Gillespie, 56 Mo. 320; Doe *v.* Eyre, 3 C. B. 557; 16 L. J., C. P. 64.

And she may appoint to her husband. Bradish *v.* Gibbs, 3 Johns. Ch. (N. Y.) 523; 2 Sugden Pow. (ed. 1856) 24; Myers *v.* McBride, 13 Rich. (S. Car.) 178; Wood *v.* Wood, 10 L. R., Eq. 220; 39 L. J., Ch. 790; and may also take by appointment from her husband. 4 Cruise Dig. *146; 2 Washb. Real Prop. *320.

The power may be executed by the wife though she is still an infant. *In re* Cardross, 7 L. R., Ch. Div. 728; 38 L. T., N. S. 778.

And an infant wife may appoint in favor of her husband. *In re* D'Angiban, Andrews *v.* Andrews, 15 L. R., Ch. Div. 228; 49 L. J., Ch. Div. 756; 43 L. T., N. S. 135; 28 W. R. 930; *affirming* 49 L. J., Ch. Div. 182; 41 L. T., N. S. 645; 28 W. R. 311.

Cruise lays down the rule as follows: A married woman may without her husband execute a naked authority; another rule is the same where both an interest and an authority pass to the wife, if the authority be collateral to, and does not flow from the interest. 4 Cruise Dig. *142, *143. See also *144.

Perry states the rule thus: Where her own interests or those of her husband are concerned, "she possesses the same legal capacity as if she were *sui juris*. Thus, she may execute any kind of power, whether simply collateral, appendant or in gross; and it is immaterial whether it is given to her while sole or married." 1 Perry on Trusts, § 48. See also § 296; Armstrong *v.* Kerns, 61 Md. 364.

"In equity, the absolute interest in the trust fund is vested in the *cestui que trust*, the trustee is a mere instrument, and any power or authority in the trustee must have the character of a power simply collateral. Therefore, there is nothing, as respects legal capacity, to prevent a married woman from administering a discretionary trust." 1 Perry on Trusts, § 49; Smith *v.* Smith, 21 Beav. 385; Kingham *v.* Lee, 15 Sim. 401; Drummond Tracy, 1 Johns. (N. Y.) 608; People *v.* Webster, 10 Wend. (N. Y.) 554.

In a grant or lease to a married woman, whether the separate use is limited by the deed, or raised by the statute, a power to appoint independently of her husband may be conferred. Armstrong *v.* Kerns, 61 Ind. 364.

Although a trust for a married woman may have been created before the passage of the *Georgia* act of 1866, yet after its enactment she could sell and convey the trust property, and the trust became executed. Thus, where a deed was made to a husband in 1862, as trustee for his wife to secure the property for her use against his contracts and liabilities, with power in him to sell and convey with her written consent, and with power in her "to convey said land to whomsoever she may deem proper by deed or testament," a deed from her is a substantial compliance with the power. Banks *v.* Sloat, 69 Ga. 330.

If the instrument creating the power provides that it may be executed notwithstanding coverture, it

in the lands to which the power relates.[1] She may execute a power during her marriage by grant or devise without the concurrence of her husband, unless, by its terms, the execution during marriage is expressly or impliedly prohibited; but she cannot execute it during infancy.[2] The instrument by which she executes it must be acknowledged in the same manner as a conveyance by a married woman.[3] And when a married woman, entitled to an estate in fee, is authorized by a power to dispose of such estate during her marriage, she may, by virtue of the power, create any estate which she might create if unmarried.[4]

c. BY EXECUTOR.—Where a testator directs his lands to be sold, without designating the person to sell, the executor takes the power by implication.[5] It is not necessary that the fee

may be exercised by the donee while discovert. Doe *v.* Bird, 2 N. & M. 679; Bradish *v.* Gibbs, 3 Johns. Ch. (N. Y.) 523.

1. 4 New York Rev. Stat., §§ 80, 87 (Bank's ed.), pp. 2446–7; (1882) pp. 2189–90; Salmon *v.* Stuyvesant, 16 Wend. (N. Y.) 321; Jackson *v.* Edwards, 7 Paige (N. Y.) 386; on appeal, 22 Wend. (N. Y.) 498; Strong *v.* Wilkin, 1 Barb. Ch. (N.Y.) 9; Frazer *v.* Western, 1 Barb. Ch. (N. Y.) 240; Wright *v.* Tallmadge, 15 N. Y. 313; Bailey *v.* Bailey, 28 Hun (N. Y.) 610.

See Cutting *v.* Cutting, 20 Hun (N. Y.) 360; 86 N. Y. 522.

The above sections do not apply to personal property. Wadhams *v.* American H. M. Soc., 12 N. Y. 415.

2. 4 New York Rev. Stat., §§ 110–11, 117 (Banks' ed.), p. 2449; (1882) p. 2192; Strong *v.* Wilkin, 1 Barb. Ch. (N. Y.) 9; Frazer *v.* Western, 1 Barb. Ch. (N. Y.) 240; American H. M. Soc. *v.* Wadhams, 10 Barb. (N. Y.) 597 (This case was reversed on appeal, but the point involving the construction of this section was not affected. Wadhams *v.* American H. M. Soc., 12 N. Y. 415); Leavitt *v.* Pell, 27 Barb. (N. Y.) 322; on appeal, 25 N. Y. 478; Wright *v.* Tallmadge, 15 N. Y. 307.

Neither of the above sections authorizes the giving to a married woman of a beneficial power to dispose of an estate or interest in lands as a *feme covert*, which interest does not belong to her, and which upon the happening of the contingency or event provided for is limited to some other person. Jackson *v.* Edwards, 7 Paige (N. Y.) 400. See 22 Wend. (N. Y.) 498.

Where the instrument creating the power provides that the wife may appoint "separate and apart from her husband," her disposition in conjunction with her husband is void. Marvin *v.* Smith, 56 Barb. (N. Y.) 600. See same case on appeal, 46 N. Y. 571.

As to necessity that the married woman be of age, see Van Wert *v.* Benedict, 1 Bradf. (N. Y.) 114.

3. 4 *New York* Rev. Stat., § 117, (Banks' ed.), p. 2449; (1882) p. 2192; Van Boskerck *v.* Herrick, 65 Barb. (N. Y.) 258; Firemen's Ins. Co. *v.* Bay, 4 Barb. (N. Y.) 412.

4. 4 *New York* Rev. Stat., § 130 (Banks' ed.), p. 2451; (1882) p. 2194.

And appointment in favor of a husband held void under this section. Dempsey *v.* Tylee, 3 Duer (N. Y.) 73.

5. 1 Sugden Powers 194 (*134); 3 Redfield Wills 138; Blatch *v.* Wilder, 1 Atk. 420; Curtis *v.* Fulbrook, 8 Hare 278; Robinson *v.* Lowater, 5 De G. M. & G. 272; *affirming* 17 Beav. 592; Wrigley *v.* Sykes, 21 Beav. 337; Sabine *v.* Heape, 27 Beav. 553; Bond *v.* Zeigler, 1 Ga. 324; 44 Am. Dec. 656; Rankin *v.* Rankin, 36 Ill. 293; 87 Am. Dec. 205; Davis *v.* Hoover, 112 Ind. 423; Davone *v.* Fanning, 2 Johns. Ch. (N. Y.) 254; Dorland *v.* Dorland, 2 Barb. (N. Y.) 63; Bogert *v.* Hertell, 4 Hill (N. Y.) 492; Meakings *v.* Cromwell, 2 Sandf. (N. Y.) 512; 5 N. Y. 136; Officer *v.* Board of Home Missions, 47 Hun (N. Y.) 352; Coogan *v.* Ockershausen, 55 N. Y. Super. Ct. 286; Young *v.* Twigg, 27 Md. 620; Mandlebaum *v.* McDonell, 29 Mich. 78; 18 Am. Rep. 61; Clark *v.* Hornthal, 47 Miss. 434; Chambers *v.* Tulare, 9 N. J. Eq. 146; Belcher *v.* Belcher, 38 N. J. Eq. 126; Vaughan *v.* Farmer, 90 N. Car. 607; Silverthorn *v.* McKinster, 12 Pa. St. 67; Morriss *v.* Morriss, 33 Gratt. (Va.) 51.

Compare Geroe *v.* Winter, 5 N. J.

Eq. 655; *In re* Fox's Will, 52 N. Y. 530; 11 Am. Rep. 751.

Where the language was "shall be sold at the discretion of my executors," the power of sale was held to be given to the executors by implication. Chambers *v.* Tulane, 9 N. J. Eq. 146; Wood *v.* Hammond, 16 R. I. 98.

Chance says this is certainly true where the proceeds are to be applied to pay debts or legacies (1 Chance Pow. 174); and it is so held in Clark *v.* Hornthal, 47 Miss. 434; and in Wood *v.* Hammond, 16 R. I. 98. But it is not entirely clear where the moneys are to be applied to neither of these purposes. 1 Chance Pow. 183. And see Bentham *v.* Wiltshire, 4 Madd. 14.

Compare Pitt *v.* Pelham, 1 Cha. Ca. 176; Cook *v.* Fountain, 3 Swanst. 592; Drayton *v.* Drayton, 2 Desaus. (S. Car.) 557.

This is in accordance with the rule laid down by the courts of *South Carolina*. Drayton *v.* Drayton, 2 Desaus. (S. Car.) 557.

Under the American system of administering the property of decedents, no power of sale in the executor can be implied from the mere charge of debts upon lands descended or devised. *In re* Fox's Will, 52 N. Y. 530; 11 Am. Rep. 751.

Compare Clark *v.* Hornthal, 47 Miss. 434.

In Lindley *v.* O'Reilly, 50 N. J. L. 636; 7 Am. St. Rep. 802, the court of errors and appeals thus states the law on the subject: "The instances are numerous in which courts of law, as well as courts of equity, in the construction of wills, have implied an estate or power of sale in an executor or trustee from the nature, character and extent of the trusts or duties imposed on him. Mr. Lewin states these propositions as rules of construction adopted by the courts: 1. Whenever a trust is created, a legal estate sufficient for the execution of a trust will, if possible, be implied; 2. The legal estate limited to the trustee will not be carried further than the complete execution of the trust requires. And, in exposition of the first rule, he adds that the court has, in some instances, supplied the estate *in toto*, as where a testator devised to a *feme covert* the issues and profits of certain lands to be paid by his executors, it was held that the land itself was devised to the executors in trust, to receive the rents and profits and apply them to the use of the wife (1 Lewin on Trusts (8th ed.) 212, 213. In further illustration of the rule the author says: 'Thus a trust to sell, even on contingency, conveys a fee simple, as indispensable to the execution of the trust, and the construction is the same in a sale implied, as where the devise is upon a trust out of the rents and profits of an estate to discharge certain legacies made payable at a day inconsistent with the application of the annual profits only.' 1 Lewin on Trusts (8th ed.) 213. Another illustration is given in these words: 'If a testator simply appoints his executor and trustee, it seems the latter word is not so exclusively applied to real estate as to carry by implication a devise of the testator's freehold; but if the testator directs certain acts to be done by the trustee or by the executor, which belong to the owner of the freehold, or which require that the trustee or executor should have dominion over the real estate, such a devise will be implied.' 1 Lewin on Trusts (8 ed.) 214. . . . A power in the executor to sell lands of the testator, where a power of sale is not expressly given, will arise by implication under similar circumstances, the only distinction between the implication of an estate and that of a power being that where the purposes of a trust can be fully accomplished by a sale without an actual estate, the executor will take a power to sell instead of an estate." See, in this connection, Greenland *v.* Waddell, 116 N. Y. 234; 15 Am. St. Rep. 400.

Where land was devised to one as trustee, who was also appointed executor, a deed by him as executor passed no title. Schley *v.* Brown, 70 Ga. 64.

The general rule obtaining in *North Carolina* that executors have no power to sell lands directed to be sold for division among devisees, when no one is designated to make the sale, does not apply where by a proper construction of the will the intent of the testator to vest such power in the executors appears by implication or otherwise. Foster *v.* Craige, 2 Dev. & B. Eq. (N. Car.) 209; Hester *v.* Hester, 2 Ired. Eq. (N. Car.) 330; McDowell *v.* White, 68 N. Car. 65; Vaughan *v.* Farmer, 90 N. Car. 607.

So, where a testator gives all of his property of every description, to his wife for life, and at her death, to be sold and divided among his children, the will, by necessary implication, confers the power of sale on the executor, and a sale, by an administrator with the will annexed, of the realty, made after the death of the life tenant, passes a good title. Council *v.* Averett, 95 N. Car. 131.

In a recent case in *Illinois* the testator appointed his son executor, and, after certain devises, provided that all the rest of his estate should be invested from time to time in safe securities, and that the income should be paid to his son for life, and in event of his death to his wife; after the death of both, the estate was to be divided equally among the son's children. He further provided that his executor should "have full power to convey and release all property conveyed to him in trust by this will." It was held that the executor had express power under the will to convey the real estate, and the purchaser was under no obligation to see to the application of the purchase-money. Bates *v.* Woodruff, 123 Ill. 235.

So in *Iowa*, where certain lands were devised to "my executors in said will named, in trust," with power to sell and convey the land, "whenever they shall think it advisable to do so," the testator's intention to vest in the persons named as executors the power of sale is clearly expressed, and a sale will not be ordered until the persons named renounce the trust. *In re* Van Brocklin's Estate, 74 Iowa 412.

Where an express power of sale is given, an order of the probate court is not necessary. Woolworth *v.* Root, 40 Fed. Rep. 723. But under the code of *Oregon* (Hill's Code, *Oregon*, § 1155), the sale must be reported to the county court, and confirmed. Northrop *v.* Marquam, 16 Oregon 173. An advertisement for claims is not necessary. Nor is an accounting. Wait *v.* Cerqua (Supreme Ct.), 7 N. Y. Supp. 110; Munson *v.* Cole, 98 Ind. 502.

The territorial courts of *Utah* hold that where a mere naked power of sale is given by will, and there is no direction as to notice, a sale without the statutory notice is invalid. (Comp. Laws *Utah*, 1888, § 4145). *In re* Walker's Estate (Utah, 1890), 23 Pac. Rep. 930.

In a case arising under the *Iowa* code (§2396), the facts were as follows: A testatrix directed her executor "to sell my real estate within two years, . . . if such sale can be made without sacrifice, and, if not, then as soon thereafter as possible, that my estate may be settled up and closed with as little delay as cannot be avoided. And this will shall be held a sufficient power and authority to my executor to make such sale of my real estate; and he shall not be required to procure any order of court prior to the making of such sale, nor procure the approval of any court of any sale made under and in pursuance of the provisions of this will." The proceeds of the sale were to be distributed to two legatees. It was held by a majority of the court that when the executor exercised the power by selling the land at private sale for apparently its full value, after giving public notice, the district court had no authority to set aside the sale. But from this view Rothrook, J., dissented. *In re* Bagger's Estate, 78 Iowa 171.

It has been held that, where the will directed land to be sold and its proceeds divided among certain persons named, this was a bequest of money, distributable by the executors, and that they took by implication a power to sell. Rankin *v.* Rankin, 36 Ill. 293; 87 Am. Dec. 205.

But where the estate was bequeathed to the executrix, to be sold after her death, and the will was silent as to who was to make the sale, the executrix cannot sell, nor can she transmit the power to her executor. Waller *v.* Logan, 5 B. Mon. (Ky.) 515. And where the testator gave his estate to his three children, to be divided or sold as two out of the three could agree, and appointed the husbands of two of them executors, the latter had no power to sell or divide the real estate. Geroe *v.* Winter, 5 N. J. Eq. 655.

Certain property, real and personal, was devised and bequeathed to executors in trust, to be paid over to the *cestui que trust* when it should have accumulated to a certain sum. In this case, the executors took a power to sell the realty. Putnam Free School *v.* Fisher, 30 Me. 523.

Where the will directed the residue of the estate to be divided into seven equal shares, one share to be paid to certain trustees, and the other shares to be paid to six children, the executors took a power to sell, for the purpose of making the division. Winston *v.* Jones, 6 Ala. 550.

Under a devise by a testator residing in Massachusetts of the residue of his estate, including lands in Illinois, to trustees and executors, to be kept well and securely invested until the death of the life annuitants, the trustees and executors are not authorized to sell the lands situated in Illinois. Hale *v.* Hale, 125 Ill. 399.

Where property is given to executors in trust, to be equally divided among testator's children, with a direction to pay the sons their shares, and to hold the daughters' shares, and pay them the income thereof in half-yearly payments for life, the executors have power to sell the testator's lands. Belcher *v.* Belcher, 38 N. J. Eq. 126.

Executors to whom a power is given by will to sell lands, but who have renounced the executorship, have yet power to execute a valid deed of the land. Moody *v.* Fulmer, 3 Grant Cas. (Pa.) 17.

A testator directed that his real estate should remain under the control of his wife until his youngest son came of age, and that at any time thereafter, when a majority of the heirs should so direct, the land should be sold, and the proceeds divided between his wife and children. His wife and one of his sons were made executors. The land itself was not devised to any one, and it was not stated who was to make the sale. The power of sale, subject to the restriction named in the will was held to vest by implication in the executors. Potter *v.* Adriance, 44 N. J. Eq. 14.

A testator devised his real estate to his wife for life, remainder to his two daughters and their children. The daughters were permitted, during the minority of their children, to sell the realty and reinvest the proceeds. The will contained a clause providing that the executor should "see that this provision of the will was faithfully carried out." *Held*, that the executor was the proper person to make such deed and a conveyance in fee by the daughter passed only her life-estate. McIlvain *v.* Porter (Ky. 1888), 7 S. W. Rep. 308.

A testator bequeathed to his wife all his property, for her sole use, support, and possession during widowhood, but in case of remarriage only what the law would allow. Power was given the executor to sell, on the request of the wife, the interest on the proceeds to be applied to her support, with remainder over after her death. The executor was authorized to make a deed of the realty the same as the testator "could have done if living." The executor was held to take a general power to convey, subject only to the limitation regarding the wife's right to occupation and possession during her widowhood. Livingood *v.* Heffner (Pa. St. 1888), 13 Atl. Rep. 187.

Executors to whom land has been devised in trust for certain purposes, with authority to sell and re-invest the proceeds upon the same trusts, the duties of which extend far beyond the period of administration, have power to make the sale after their discharge as executors, and their assumption of title as trustees. Scholl *v.* Olmstead, 84 Ga. 693; Keplinger *v.* MacCubbin, 58 Md. 203; Munson *v.* Cole, 98 Ind. 502.

In Cooper *v.* Horner, 62 Tex. 356, the will, which was executed in 1875, bequeathed to executors named therein, all the personal estate, in trust for the payment of the debts of the testator, and provided that no bond should be required of them. It gave to certain legatees all the residue of the estate, real, personal and mixed; required the filing of an inventory of the estate by the executors; and provided that neither the probate nor any other court should have any jurisdiction over the estate, except to probate and register the will. The will, after providing for the education and support of the minor heirs out of the personal property, gave to the executors power, in terms, "to take possession of all of said estate and manage and control and dispose of the same for the interest and benefit of the legatees, under this will, and the payment of debts as hereinbefore specified." *Held*, that the existence of debts authorized a sale of the real estate to pay them, the personal property being insufficient for that purpose, and the purchaser of land from the executors was not bound to follow the money paid by him to see that it was applied to the payment of debts, and the desire expressed that in no event should the estate be subjected to the jurisdiction of the courts in its administration, required a construction of its provisions which would invest the executors with power to sell land to pay debts when such sale was necessary, and when a resort to the courts would result in ordering such sale.

In Munson *v.* Cole, 98 Ind. 502 the testator was the owner, among other property, of a certain town lot. He devised one-fourth of all his property to his widow, one-fourth to his daughter E, and one-half to the children of a deceased daughter, subject to the conditions contained in the fourth clause,

should be in the executor to enable him to sell and convey the lands.[1]

d. CONCURRENCE OF DONEES.—Generally, speaking, all the parties in whom the power is vested must concur in the execution, unless it is expressly stated in the deed creating the power that a part may execute it, or unless there is a statutory provision to that effect.[2]

which was as follows: I hereby constitute and appoint m son-in-law, C, executor of my last will and testament and trustee to manage the property above devised and bequeathed, investing the title in him as such trustee, empowering him and enjoining him, to continue, carry on and manage my business in merchandising and all other business, for the joint interests of his children, my wife and daughter E, for and during the term of five years, and as much longer as shall be mutually agreed upon by my said legatees; investing my said executor with full power under the will to sell and convey all my real estate, or any part thereof, at his own discretion, and without any application to a court of law. . . . I further authorize my said executor to purchase and improve such real estate as he may deem necessary or expedient for the transaction of the mutual and joint business of my said legatees." C qualified as executor, and more than five years afterward, while the settlement of the estate was still pending, he purchased of the widow and daughter their interests in the estate, and to secure the payment of the purchase-money executed to them a mortgage upon all of said real estate. Afterwards he subdivided the town lot above mentioned, and sold the parcels to various persons. There was no agreement that he should act as trustee for a longer period than five years. In a suit to foreclose the mortgage against these purchasers, it was held that the power to sell real estate was conferred upon C as executor, and not as trustee, and that he had power to sell after five years, and that by such sale the title of the devisees was divested, and the mortgage ceased to be a lien upon the land.

1. The legal estate would vest in the heirs at law subject to be divested by the execution of the power. Greenough *v.* Welles, 10 Cush. (Mass.) 571; Downing *v.* Marshall, 23 N. Y. 366; Clark *v.* Hornthal, 47 Miss. 434. Or in the devisee. Braman *v.* Stiles, 2 Pick. (Mass.) 460; Crittenden *v.* Fairchild, 41 N. Y. 289. See Quin *v.* Skinner, 49 Barb. (N. Y.) 128.

2. 1 Chance Pow. 603, 604, 613, 622-626; 1 Sugden Pow. 202 (*142); 3 Redfield on Wills, 227, 229; Marks *v.* Tarver, 59 Ala. 335; Noel *v.* Harvey, 29 Miss. 72; Boston Franklinite Co. *v.* Condit, 19 N. J. Eq. 394; Hertell *v.* Van Buren, 3 Edw. Ch. (N. Y.) 20; Wilder *v.* Ranney, 95 N. Y. 7; Shelton *v.* Homer, 5 Met. (Mass.) 462; Deneale *v.* Morgan, 5 Call (Va.) 407.

Compare First Nat. Bank *v.* Mount Tabor, 52 Vt. 87; 36 Am. Rep. 734.

A power in a will, in case either of two trustees should decline to act, to the survivor of the trustees, to appoint new trustees, authorizes the continuing or active trustee to appoint new ones. But if both decline to act, neither can exercise the power. 1 Sugden Pow. 201, 202 (*142); 1 Perry on Trusts, § 294.

"The number of parties undertaking to execute a power must come within the exact description given of the number of those who are to execute it. Thus, if a power is given to be exercised by a certain specified number, or when they are reduced to a certain number, it cannot be exercised by a less number, and is gone if not exerised before the number is reduced below the number which is named for its execution." 1 Perry on Trusts, (4th ed.), § 294.

It is doubtful whether separate deeds from the several donees of the power would be a valid execution thereof. Chapin *v.* First Universalist Soc., 8 Gray (Mass.) 580; Boston Franklinite Co. *v.* Condit, 19 N. J. Eq. 394.

If the power be given to particular persons by name, it must be exercised jointly. 1 Perry on Trusts, § 294.

A naked power must be executed by all the donees. Wardwell *v.* McDowell, 31 Ill. 364; Osgood *v.* Franklin, 2 Johns. Ch. (N. Y.) 1; Peter *v.*

Beverly, 10 Pet. (U. S.) 532. See 1 How. (U. S.) 134.

Where a testator authorized his executors to sell real estate not specifically devised, at their discretion, the authority is a naked power not coupled with a trust, and cannot be executed by a majority of the executors Shelton *v.* Homer, 5 Met. (Mass.) 462.

A will executed in *Mississippi* contained the following clause: "I do further confer on my executors full power to sell any of my estate, real or personal, for the payment of my debts, should they think it necessary." There were three executors. Two of them sold certain slaves belonging to the estate to the other. *Held*, that the power given being a joint power, the sale was void. Noel *v.* Harvey, 29 Miss. 72.

It was held in *Alabama* under a will appointing the testator's widow, his son and son-in-law executors, and authorizing them to sell if "found necessary in order to effect an equitable division," publicly or privately, "upon such terms as my executrix and executors may deem most advantageous to the devisees and legatees thereof," the conveyance to be "by my executrix and executors, or such of them as may be in office as such," that the power to sell was discretionary, and could be exercised only by the executors jointly. Robinson *v.* Allison, 74 Ala. 254.

A direction to convert land into money is not such an equitable conversion as to authorize two executors out of three to sell. The statute of *Wisconsin* relating to the construction of laws (§ 4971, subd. 3), which provides that words purporting to give a joint authority to three or more confer the power on a majority, unless otherwise provided, is not applicable. §§ 2102 and 2137 expressly provide that a power relating to lands must be executed by all the joint donees. Crowley *v.* Hicks, 72 Wis. 539.

A recent case in *New York* holds that it is immaterial that one of the donees has the right to order the sale to be made. A life estate in land was devised to the wife, with the direction that, if she should deem the income insufficient for her support, she could designate any portion of the property for sale, and the executors, of whom she was one, should sell it, and pay the proceeds over to her absolutely as her own.. It was held that a deed by the wife alone was not sufficient, and that her co-executor must join. Steves *v.* Weaver, 49 Hun (N. Y.) 267.

A power was given to husband and wife jointly, to be exercised by deed or writing. The husband drew up instructions for a solicitor to prepare a deed, the wife consenting thereto; but such consent did not appear on the paper containing the instructions, nor in any other writing. The husband died before the deed was prepared. *Held*, that there must be a joint execution during coverture, and that there was no valid exercise of the power. Hawke *v.* Hawke, 26 W. R. 93.

Certain premises were conveyed to three trustees "in trust for the use of a Sabbath school, to sell or exchange said land and improvements whenever, in the judgment of said trustees, or of their successors, another location would better subserve the objects and purposes of said trusts." It was held that this was a special power, and could not be exercised by two of the trustees, at all events without the consent of the third. Morville *v.* Fowle, 144 Mass. 109.

It seems to make no difference though the sale was made for a valuable consideration and at an adequate price. Daily's Appeal, 87 Pa. St. 487.

In assumpsit by the *bona fide* holder of town bonds, to recover the interest specified in coupons thereof, of which the plaintiff was also the *bona fide* holder, it appeared that the bonds were issued under authority of an act passed to enable the defendant, among other towns, to subscribe for railroad stock in aid of the construction of a railroad, and to issue bonds for that purpose. The act provided that "the assent in writing thereto of a majority of the taxpayers," signed and acknowledged before a justice of the peace by "each person so assenting," should first be had upon an instrument of assent, naming three resident citizens and taxpayers to be commissioners to make such subscription; that when such instrument had been so signed and acknowledged, such commissioners should "append thereto a certificate by them subscribed and sworn to," stating that such assent had been signed and acknowledged, as required by the act, and should cause such instrument and certificate to be recorded in the town clerk's office; and that "such certificate so executed and recorded" should be conclusive evidence

Where a power to sell land is conferred by the will upon several executors, all who qualify and are living must join in the execution.[1]

of the facts stated, and by the act authorized to be stated therein. Defendant offered to prove that the instrument of assent was not signed by a majority of the tax-payers, that but two of the commissioners signed the certificate, and that the third refused to sign because such instrument had not been signed by such majority. *Held*, that at common law, as well as under the Vermont statute, the certificate of the two commissioners, the third having shared in their deliberations but refused to concur in their decision, was a valid certificate in compliance with the act, and conclusive evidence of the facts therein stated; and that the evidence offered by defendant was therefore inadmissible. First Nat. Bank *v.* Mount Tabor, 52 Vt. 87; 36 Am. Rep. 734. *Compare*, Danville *v.* Montpelier etc. R. Co., 43 Vt. 144.

Where a power is given to certain persons, "partners under the style of A and B," having no connection with the ordinary business of the firm, and one partner in the name of the firm attempts to execute the power, such execution is invalid. The power was conferred on the members of the firm individually. Cummings *v.* Parish, 39 Miss. 412.

It was held in *Maine*, in a similar case, that the execution by one member of the firm or both, as individuals, was valid. Purinton *v.* Security L. etc. Ins. Co., 72 Me. 22.

And in *Illinois* where the power to sell was given to "O and J, their survivor and successors in business," they constituting a partnership, the power was held to be vested in the firm, and upon their taking in a new partner, the power was well executed by the new firm. Robbins *v.* Butler, 24 Ill. 387.

1. Osgood *v.* Franklin, 2 Johns. Ch. (N. Y.) 1; on appeal, 14 Johns. (N. Y.) 562; Davoue *v.* Fanning, 2 Johns. Ch. (N. Y.) 254; Bergor *v.* Duff, 4 Johns. Ch. (N. Y.) 368; Niles *v.* Stevens, 4 Den. (N. Y.) 399; Peter *v.* Beverly, 10 Pet. (U. S.) 532; Warden *v.* Richards, 11 Gray (Mass.) 277; Gould *v.* Mather, 104 Mass. 283; McRae *v.* Farrow, 4 Hen. & M. (Va.) 444; Deneale *v.* Morgan, 5 Call (Va.) 407; Floyd *v.* Johnson, 2 Litt. (Ky.) 115; Wooldridge *v.* Watkins, 3 Bibb (Ky.) 350; Coleman *v.* McKinney, 3 J. J. Marsh. (Ky.) 246; Ross *v.* Clore, 3 Dana (Ky.) 189; Wells *v.* Lewis, 4 Metc. (Ky.) 269; Clinefelter *v.* Ayers, 16 Ill. 329; Pahlman *v.* Smith, 23 Ill. 395; Ely *v.* Dix, 118 Ill. 477; Roseboom *v.* Mosher, 2 Den. (N. Y.) 61; McDowell *v.* Gray, 29 Pa. St. 211; Clark *v.* Denton, 36 N. J. Eq. 419; Jennings *v.* Teague, 14 S. Car. 229; *compare* Moody *v.* Fulmer, 3 Grant's Cas. (Pa.) 17; Nelson *v.* Carrington, 4 Munf. (Va.) 332.

If one of several executors refuses to join, the others cannot sell, except the statute so provides, or there is an express or implied power to that effect in the will itself. 1 Sugden, Pow. 202 (*142); Wright *v.* Dunn, 73 Tex. 293. *Compare* 1 Chance Pow. 613, 622, 626.

It has been held that it makes no difference whether the power is discretionary or mandatory. Ely *v.* Dix, 118 Ill. 477. And see Smith *v.* Winn, 27 S. Car. 591. It is also immaterial whether the trustees take as joint tenants or as tenants in common. *In re* Bailey, 15 R. I. 60.

Whether, in case the executors refuse to qualify, they retain the power, is a question not fully settled. Mr. Chance answers it in the affirmative. 1 Chance Pow. 614, 628. See 2 Washb. Real Prop. (4th ed.) 622, § 23.

A sale by two out of three executors, which was ratified by the third, has been held good. Silverthorn *v.* McKinster, 12 Pa. St. 67. See also Niles *v.* Stevens, 4 Den. (N.Y.) 399.

But if made by one without the consent of the other, it is void. Dencale *v.* Morgan, 5 Call (Va.) 407. *Contra*, Nelson *v.* Carrington, 4 Munf. (Va.) 332.

In Noel *v.* Harvey, 29 Miss. 72, it is held that a sale by two of three executors is void; though, in that case, there was an additional reason for the invalidity of the sale, viz: that the executors selling were also the purchasers.

Where the power is to two "or either of three," one may execute alone. Taylor *v.* Dickinson, 15 Iowa 483.

The statute of *Michigan* in this respect is simply confirmatory of the common law. Vernor *v.* Covill, 54 Mich. 281.

Where the power is to be exercised by executors, *virtute officii*, an execution by the one who qualifies is valid. Smith *v.* Winn, 27 S. Car. 591; Weimar *v.* Fath, 43 N. J. L. 1; Denton *v.* Clark, 36 N. J. Eq. 534. And if one is removed from office, the remaining executor may sell. Weimar *v.* Fath, 43 N. J. L. 1.

In *Pennsylvania*, all the executors, whose renunciation is not of record, must join in a conveyance of real estate; and where one executor qualified and alone conveyed real estate belonging to his testator the subsequent renunciation by the other executor did not validate the deed. Neel *v.* Beach, 92 Pa. St. 221. See also Heron *v.* Hoffner, 3 Rawle (Pa.) 396.

In *Massachusetts*, a testator appointed two of his brothers executors of his will, and did "fully authorize them to take upon themselves the trust hereby created, and to do and execute whatever is herein ordered or authorized to be done; and, if necessary for the execution thereof, to sell at public or private sale any part or all my real estate, and make, execute, and deliver deeds to convey the same." One of the brothers declined the trust, and the other undertook the duties of executor. It was held that he had power to sell the estate, if necessary for the payment of debts and legacies, and might do so at private sale, and by a simple warranty deed. Warden *v.* Richards, 11 Gray (Mass.) 277.

In a case arising in *New York*, lands were devised to an executor and executrix, in trust to sell for the payment of debts, and for the division of the surplus among the testator's children, the executor refused to act, and the executrix proved the will, and sold and conveyed a portion of the estate. It was held, that her conveyance passed a valid title. Niles *v.* Stevens, 4 Den. (N. Y.) 399.

In a *South Carolina* case, power was given to executors by a will, executed in 1861, to sell real and personal property "so soon as the value of property shall recover from the depression caused by the existing war." The testator died in 1863, and the sole qualified executor made sale of the lands for confederate money in October, 1863. The court held, that the executor was the proper judge of whether the contingency had happened, and, there being no ground to suspect him of having acted contrary to his honest judgment the sale was declared valid. Jennings *v.* Teague, 14 S. Car. 229. The same court held in an earlier case, where the testator devised a portion of his estate to six persons, named "my executors" in trust to sell, etc., and invest from the proceeds a specified annual sum, etc., for the benefit of his wife; and in a later clause said six persons were appointed executors, and all the six survived him, but only three qualified as executors, that these three had full authority to execute the power. DeSaussure *v.* Lyons, 9 S. Car. 492.

The Supreme Court of *Michigan* declined to adhere to the rule in a recent case growing out of the following rather peculiar state of facts: A testator provided that his minor son should receive $3,000 when he should become of age, and $1,000 annually thereafter until he should attain the age of twenty-five. At that time he was to receive $10,000 more if in the opinion of the executors he had used in a judicious and frugal manner the amounts previously received. At the age of thirty-five he was under the same conditions, and if the executors thought best, to receive the balance of the residue of the estate not otherwise disposed of under the will. If at twenty-five, or if after the receipt of the $10,000, he had wasted what he had received, and if in the opinion of the executors he would continue to do so, in that case he was to receive but $1,000 annually, and the residue was to go to the issue of the son, and in default of such issue, to the testator's legal heirs. Five persons were named as executors, but one of whom qualified. He acted as executor for fifteen years, when he died. He paid the son nothing after the latter was twenty-four years of age; never passed on the son's habits or conduct, and never undertook to exercise the power given him by the will in this regard. The son married and died without issue, leaving his entire estate to his wife. It was held that the power could not be executed by the sole executor, and after the death of the son could not be executed by any one; that upon the testator's death the title to the realty embraced in the residue vested in the son, as did also the personalty, subject to the debts and legacies; and that the whole passed to the son's widow and not to the legal heirs of the testator. Perrin *v.* Lepper, 72 Mich. 454.

Power to several to consent ceases with the death of one.[1]

By the *New York* statute, if the power is vested in several persons, all must unite in its execution; but if, previous to the execution, one or more shall die, the power may be executed by the survivor or survivors.[2]

e. BY SURVIVOR OF DONEES.—The rule of law is that powers do not in themselves survive, unless expressly limited to the survivor. In the case of executors the inclination is to modify the rule, especially if there is more than one survivor, so that the plural number remains.[3]

1. 1 Sugden Pow. *147. See also *infra*, this title, *Execution of Powers—Consent of Third Persons.*

2. *New York* Rev. Stat. § 112 (Banks' ed.), p. 2449; (1882) p. 2192; Van Boskerck *v.* Herrick, 65 Barb. (N. Y.) 258; House *v.* Raymond, 5 Thomp. & C. (N. Y.) 248; 3 Hun (N. Y.) 37; Holtsinger *v.* National Corn Exch. Bank, 6 Abb. Pr., N. S. (N. Y.) 296; 1 Sweeny (N. Y.) 69.

This section does not apply to a case where the consent of two or more third persons is requisite to a valid execution of the power. (§ 122.) Barber *v.* Cary, 11 N. Y. 400.

The section is limited and controlled by section 55, tit. 4, ch. 6 (Banks' ed., p. 2568); Taylor *v.* Morris, 1 N. Y. 341. But where a testator appoints two executors and provides that his real estate may be sold, but one executor is not authorized to sell without the consent and co-operation of the other, and only one accepts and qualifies, he cannot sell and give a valid title, under Code Civil Proc. New York, § 2642, providing that when power to sell is given by will to executors, and all do not qualify, a deed from those who do shall be as valid as if all had joined; the intent of the will being that a single executor, from whatever cause he was such, should have no power to sell. Hyatt *v.* Aguero 1 N. Y. Supp. 339. See *In re* Van Wyck, 1 Barb. Ch. (N. Y.) 565; Ogden *v.* Smith, 2 Paige (N. Y.) 195.

3. 1 Chance Pow. 645, 647, 649, 650; 1 Sugden Pow. 203 (*143); 2 Bouv. Inst. 1927; Gaines *v.* Fender, 82 Mo. 497.

It seems that where the power is given to executors as such, *ratione officii*, as the office survives the power survives. 1 Chance Pow. 606; 1 Sugden Pow. 205 (*146); Dentor *v.* Clark, 36 N. J. Eq. 534; Bradford *v.* Monks, 132 Mass. 405; Smith *v.* Winn, 27 S. Car. 591. Unless the power is expressly a joint one. Davis *v.* Christian, 15 Gratt. (Va.) 11; Philadelphia Trust Co. *v.* Lippincott, 106 Pa. St. 295. See Battelle *v.* Parks, 2 Mich. 531.

In *Illinois* a testator gave all his estate to his widow for her life, and directed that at her death it be disposed of, one-third to the testator's son, one-third to his daughter, A, for her life, the income to be applied, by her and her husband, to her support, and to the support and education of her four children, and at her death her portion to be divided among her said children as they should, respectively, become of age, and the other third to his daughter, B, for her life, the income to be applied in the same manner as with the other daughter. He appointed C, D and E his executors, and authorized them to sell such portions of his real estate as they might think advantageous, and make proper conveyances. E declined to accept and qualify. C and D qualified, and the widow and D died without any sale of real estate having been made. *Held*, that C, the sole surviving executor, had full power to sell. Ely *v.* Dix, 118 Ill. 478.

The Supreme Court of *Vermont* was called upon to construe a deed executed under the following clause of a will: "I give and bequeath to my beloved wife . . . all my personal property, to be at her disposal, and also all my real property, the use of it during her natural life; provided, nevertheless, if the personal property and the use of the real, be not sufficient for her and the support of my well-beloved mother during their natural lives, in such case I order my ex-

Naked powers do not survive, while powers coupled with an interest do.[1]

A mere direction to the executors to sell, there being no devise of an interest, and no trust created, is but a naked power and does not survive. But if anything is directed to be done in which other

ecutors to sell so much of the land as may be necessary for their support while in this life, and after both are deceased, what may be left of my real property I give and bequeath to the American Foreign Missionary Society;" and the wife and brother of the testator were appointed executors. After the decease of her co-executor the executrix deeded the real estate to the plaintiff; the consideration being mainly past and future support. The court held that the deed by one of the two executors was void; and that such a power when so given to two or more, does not survive, and cannot be executed by the survivor, in his own behalf, or interest; also that by the devise a life estate in the farm passed to the widow, and the reversion to the defendant, subject to be defeated, in whole or in part, by the execution of the power, on the happening of the contingency named. But it is a strict rather than a directory power; one to be executed only under the exact circumstances and manner prescribed in the will; that the testator conferred more than a mere power upon the executors; that it was a power coupled with a trust or that implies a trust. Ferre *v.* American Board, 53 Vt. 162.

The testator in a *New York* case gave his property to trustees. In distinct clauses he directed them to "stand seised and possessed of one-third part thereof," upon trust for the use of each of three daughters "during her natural life," and if she "shall be single and unmarried at her death," then, "upon such trust and for such purposes as she shall or may appoint by her last will." The daughters died without issue, two unmarried and one a widow. The widow and another daughter each left a will giving a power of sale to their respective executors. It was held that B, the surviving executor of said daughter, could sell and convey the land. Onderdonk *v.* Ackerman, 62 How. Pr. (N. Y.) 318.

Under the *Kentucky* statute (Rev. Stat. Kentucky, 1867, ch. 37, § 9) a surviving executor or administrator with the will annexed may sell. Shields *v.* Smith, 8 Bush (Ky.) 601.

By virtue of the *Pennsylvania* act of February 24, 1834 (P. L. 73), testamentary powers of sale of real estate vested in two or more executors may be exercised by a surviving executor, unless the testator shall have otherwise provided. This law was construed in the following case. A testator gave a power of sale of real estate to his three executors, whom he nominated in his will. He further directed that "if any of my executors shall die, or decline the executorship, it shall be the duty of the acting executors to appoint another in the place of the executor so dying or declining . . . with the same rights and powers as are given to the executors named in this my will." Vacancies caused by the death of two of said executors were not filled, as directed by the testator. The court held that the direction in the will was not to be construed as such a provision by the testator as would exclude the operation of the above act, so as to prevent the sole surviving executor from exercising the power of sale originally vested in the three executors; that while the orphans' court might, under the act of April 10, 1849, § 2 (P. L. 597), appoint a trustee or trustees in place of those who died, yet it was not necessary that such action should be taken in order that the power of sale might be lawfully exercised; and that the sole surviving executor, in execution of said power of sale, could convey a good title. Philadelphia Trust Co. *v.* Lippincott, 106 Pa. St. 295.

1. Co. Litt. 112b; Robinson *v.* Allison, 74 Ala. 254; Gutman *v.* Buckler, 69 Md. 7; Osgood *v.* Franklin, 2 Johns. Ch. (N. Y.) 1; on appeal, Franklin *v.* Osgood, 14 Johns. (N. Y.) 527; Loring *v.* Marsh, 2 Cliff. (U. S.) 311; Robertson *v.* Gaines, 2 Humph. (Tenn.) 367; Parrott *v.* Edmondson, 64 Ga. 332; Brassey *v.* Chalmers, 16 Beav. 231.

Powers coupled with a trust survive, and will be enforced in equity. Stewart *v.* Stokes, 33 Ala. 494; Robinson *v.* Allison, 74 Ala. 254; Jones *v.* Breed (Ky. 1890), 13 S. W. Rep. 366.

persons are interested, or if others have a right to call on the executors to execute the power, such power survives, even though it is not strictly a power coupled with an interest.[1]

The general principle underlying the decisions is that the power must be executed by him or them in whom the confidence has been reposed. If the confidence is reposed in several, it would seem that a part cannot execute; if in a particular person, his executor or administrator cannot execute.[2] As a summing up of the above principles we have the following rules laid down by Sugden:[3] First. A power given to two or more by their proper names, not made executors, does not survive without express words.[4]

Second. Where a power is given to three or more generally, as "my trustees," "my sons," etc., and not by their proper names, the authority will survive so long as more than one remains.[5]

1. Peter *v.* Beverly, 10 Pet. (U. S.) 532; 1 How. (U. S.) 134; Hunt *v.* Rousmaniere, 2 Mason (U. S.) 244; on appeal, 8 Wheat. (U. S.) 1; Patton *v.* Crow, 26 Ala. 426; Clinefelter *v.* Ayres, 16 Ill. 329; Doe *v.* Lannis, 3 Ind. 441; Jameson *v.* Smith, 4 Bibb (Ky.) 307; Jones *v.* Breed (Ky. 1890), 13 S. W. Rep. 366; Gray *v.* Lynch, 8 Gill (Md.) 403; Druid Park Heights Co., 53 Mo. 46; Battelle *v.* Parks, 2 Mich. 531; Bartlett *v.* Sutherland, 24 Miss. 395; Dexter *v.* Sullivan, 34 N. H. 478; Den *v.* Snowhill, 23 N. J. L. 447; Lippincott *v.* Lippincott, 19 N. J. Eq. 121; Meakings *v.* Cromwell, 2 Sandf. (N. Y.) 512; Franklin *v.* Osgood, 14 Johns. (N. Y.) 527 (for opinion of Chancellor Kent in this case see 2 Johns. Ch. (N. Y.) 1); Dorland *v.* Dorland, 2 Barb. (N. Y.) 63; Bradshaw *v.* Ellis, 2 Dev. & B. Eq. (N. Car.) 20; Foster *v.* Craige, 2 Dev. & B. Eq. (N. Car.) 209; Hester *v.* Hester, 2 Ired. Eq. (N. Car.) 330; Smith *v.* McCrary, 3 Ired. Eq. (N. Car.) 204; Shippen *v.* Clapp, 29 Pa. St. 265; Thornton *v.* Gaillard, 3 Rich. (S. Car.) 418; Hope *v.* Johnson, 2 Yerg. (Tenn.) 123; Robertson *v.* Gaines, 2 Humph. (Tenn.) 367; Williams *v.* Otey, 8 Humph. (Tenn.) 563; Wilburn *v.* Spoffard, 4 Sneed (Tenn.) 698; Garfoot *v.* Garfoot, 1 Ch. Ca. 35; Eyre *v.* Shaftsbury, 2 P. Wms. 102; Hearle *v.* Greenbank, 3 Atk. 714.

Compare Richardson *v.* Woodbury, 43 Me. 206.

2. 2 Story Eq. Jur., § 1062; 2 Washb. Real Prop. *322–323; Shelton *v.* Homer, 5 Met. (Mass.) 462; Tainter *v.* Clark, 13 Met. (Mass.) 220; Bartlett *v.* Sutherland, 24 Miss. 395; Farrar *v.* McCue, 89 N. Y. 139; Cole *v.* Wade, 16 Ves. 27.

Where the language used is, "shall be sold at the discretion of my executors," the power does not survive. Chambers *v.* Tulane, 9 N. J. Eq. 146.

See Proctor *v.* Scharpff, 80 Ala. 227; and *compare* Ely *v.* Dix, 118 Ill. 477; Davis *v.* Christian, 15 Gratt. (Va.) 11.

In *New York* it has been held that where a power of sale is given to executors, if in their judgment it is for the advantage of the estate, the judgment of the surviving partner is conclusive so far as the title of the purchaser is concerned. Carroll *v.* Conley, 56 Hun (N. Y.) 649.

3. 1 Sugd. Pow. 205, 206 (*146); Tainter *v.* Clark, 13 Met. (Mass.) 220.

The rules laid down by Mr. Sugden are quoted with approval by Mr. Washburn (2 Washb. Real Prop. *323), and by Mr. Justice Story (2 Story Eq. Jur., § 1062).

In the note to Greenleaf's addition of Cruise's Digest on Real Property (ed. of 1850) it is stated that in regard to the first two rules, and the first part of the third, the law is the same in *America* as in *England;* but as to the last part of the third rule it would be held by the *American* courts that the power survived. 4 Greenl. Cruise 199, note (1); *citing* Peter *v.* Beverley, 10 Pet. (U. S.) 532; Franklin *v.* Osgood, 14 Johns. (N. Y.) 527; Muldrow *v.* Fox, 2 Dana (Ky.) 74.

4. 1 Perry on Trusts, § 294; Townsend *v.* Wilson, 3 Madd. 261; 1 B. & A. 608.

5. 2 Washb. on Real Prop. *323; 1

Third. Where the power is given to executors and the will does not expressly require a joint exercise of it, even a single surviving executor may execute it; but if given to them *nominatim*, though in the character of executors, it is at least doubtful whether it will survive.[1]

Fourth. Where the power to executors to sell arises by implication, the power will be implied in the survivor.[2]

f. BY PERSONAL REPRESENTATIVE OF DONEE.—The power, by the express language of the instrument creating it, may be extended to the personal representative of the donee.[3]

Perry on Trusts, § 294; Gaines *v.* Fender, 82 Mo. 497.

On this point see 1 Chance on Powers 610. This writer thinks the second rule may apply only to a case where the power is preceded by an estate. 1 Chance Pow. 655, 656.

1. 4 Kent's Comm. *325-26; 1 Perry on Trusts, § 294; Clark *v.* Hornthal, 47 Miss. 434.

Chance says Lord Coke is against this rule (especially the first part of it) and that Coke is sustained by the better authorities (citing them). He further says that the last part of the rule is doubtful. 1 Chance Pow. 657-670.

American authorities supporting the third rule are Warden *v.* Richards, 11 Gray (Mass.) 277; Chandler *v.* Rider, 102 Mass. 268; Gould *v.* Mather, 104 Mass. 283; Davone *v.* Fanning, 2 Johns. Ch. (N. Y.) 252; Jackson *v.* Ferris, 15 Johns. (N. Y.) 346; Mastin *v.* Barnard, 33 Ga. 520; Colsten *v.* Chandet, 4 Bush. (Ky.) 666.

If the power is coupled with a trust, equity will insist upon its execution. 2 Story Eq. Jur,. § 1062.

As to when the power is given *virtute officii*, see Hazel *v.* Hagan, 47 Mo. 277; Anderson *v.* McGowan, 45 Ala. 462.

Where the power is given to the executors *virtute officii*, it none the less survives because it is discretionary. Davis *v.* Christian, 15 Gratt. (Va.) 11; Bradford *v.* Monks, 132 Mass. 405.

2. Where the power to the executors is an implied one, a surviving executor may execute it; but not where it is given by express words. Conklin *v.* Egerton, 21 Wend. (N. Y.) 429; Chambers *v.* Tulane, 9 N. J. Eq. 146.

3. 1 Chance, Pow. 678, 679; 1 Perry on Trusts, § 294.

The principles governing the rule as to survivorship apply in most cases to this and the subject last preceding. The reader is referred, therefore, to the cases under that head, *supra*, this title, *Execution of a Power—by Survivor*.

An authority to a representative will be strictly construed. Thus if the power is extended to the heirs, representatives or administrators of the donee, it cannot be executed by a devisee or assignee. 1 Perry on Trusts, § 294.

If the power is given to several "and their heirs, executors and administrators," the power is limited to the "heirs, executors and administrators" of the survivor. 1 Chance Pow. 696.

Where the deed gave the power of sale to a trustee "or his legal representative," it was held that the power could not be exercised by the administrator of the trustee, but only by his assignee or successor in trust. Warnecke *v.* Lembca, 71 Ill. 91; 22 Am. Rep. 85.

When personal representatives are held competent to execute a power, it is not that a power possesses any descendable or transmissible quality, but because the representatives are expressedly or by implication designated as donees. 1 Chance Pow. 679. Therefore the power cannot be executed by the executor of an executor. 1 Chance, Pow. 683, 686; Walker *v.* Logan, 5 B. Mon. (Ky.) 515. Though the contrary is held in *South Carolina*, where the power is coupled with a trust. Reeves *v.* Tappan, 21 S. Car. 1.

Where the power is an implied one, the executor of the executor may execute it; but not where it is given by express words. Chambers *v.* Tulane, 9 N. J. Eq. 146; Conklin *v.* Egerton, 21 Wend. (N. Y.) 429, and cases there cited.

And where the executor of the executor has the power to sell all the lands, the fact that his own testator by his will conferred the power to sell a part only of the lands, would not restrict the power of the executor's executor. Reeves *v.* Tappan, 21 S. Car. 1.

So, too, the power cannot be executed by the heir of the donee. 1 Chance Pow. 688. Nor by an administrator *de bonis non*. Nicoll *v.* Scott, 99 Ill. 529; nor by the administrator with the will annexed. Comptar *v.* McMahan, 19 Mo. App. 494; Hodgin *v.* Tolis, 70 Iowa 21; Dunning *v.* Ocean Nat. Bank, 61 N. Y. 497; 19 Am. Rep. 293; Dominick *v.* Michael, 4 Sandf. (N. Y.) 374; Cook *v.* Platt, 51 N. Y. Super. Ct. 55; on appeal, 98 N. Y. 35; Paret *v.* Keneally, 30 Hun (N. Y.) 15; *In re* Paton, 41 Hun (N. Y.) 497; Naundorf *v.* Schumann, 41 N. J. Eq. 14.

Compare Hickey *v.* Peterson (Supreme Ct.), 9 N. Y. Supp. 917; Allen *v.* Barnes, 5 Utah 100; and Giberson *v.* Giberson, 43 N. J. Eq. 116.

A distinction is made between cases where the direction to sell is imperative, and those where it is discretionary, holding that in the former case the successor of the executor may sell, and in the latter not. Cook *v.* Platte, 98 N. Y. 35; Bingham *v.* Jones, 25 Hun (N. Y.) 6; Dunn's Estate, 13 Phila. (Pa.) 395; Hinson *v.* Williamson, 74 Ala. 180; Watson *v.* Martin, 75 Ala. 506; Stoutenburgh *v.* Moore, 37 N. J. Eq. 63; Rhode Island Hospital Trust Co. *v.* Pitcher, 16 R. I. 349.

In the *Alabama* case first cited the testator appointed his widow as executrix, and relieved her from giving bond; directed that his estate should be kept together "under her absolute power and control, she having full power to purchase or sell any property she may think proper, so long as she remains a widow; that the annual profits of the estate should be invested by her in making purchases of property at her discretion, to be distributed among the children so as to equalize their distributive shares; and made provision for the immediate distribution of the estate, in the event of her death or marriage. It was held that the will imposed upon the widow a personal trust in the matter of keeping the estate together, which was capable of execution by her alone; and she having refused to accept the trust, or qualify as executrix, the probate court could not confer on administrators *de bonis non* the power to execute it. Hinson *v.* Williamson, 74 Ala. 180.

In Stoutenburgh *v.* Moore, 37 N. J. Eq. 63, the will contained the following clause: "All the rest and residue of my estate, real, personal and mixed, I give, devise and bequeath the income to my two sons, Robert and Edward, to be equally divided between them during their lives, and at their death to be equally divided between my grandchildren, to them, their heirs and assigns." The estate consisted of both real and personal property. He had at the time of making the will only the two sons named, and they were both married, and both survived him. Edward died, leaving a widow and one child; Robert survived and had four children. It was held that the trust created by the will, to invest the residue, to pay over the interest, to sell and convey any or all of the real estate at discretion, and to keep it in repair, was an active one and did not devolve on an administrator with the will annexed.

In a subsequent case in the same State a testator gave all his property for the sole use and benefit of his wife, and in the event of her death "then what shall remain . . . the whole to be disposed of as shall to my executors seem best;" the proceeds to be divided equally among certain specified persons, and the chancellor held that the power to sell the lands, being coupled with a trust or confidence in the executors, did not devolve upon an administrator with the will annexed. Naundorf *v.* Schumann, 41 N. J. Eq. 14.

But in a still later case, a testator devised land to one of his executors for life. His will then contained the following provision: "I order and direct my executors to sell my real estate in such manner as they may think proper, and divide the net proceeds amongst my three sisters." It was held that the power of sale might be executed by an administrator with the will annexed, both the executors having died before the testator. Drummond *v.* Jones, 44 N. J. Eq. 53.

The Supreme Court of *Alabama* recently decided that testamentary provisions authorizing and directing an executor to keep the estate together for the term of ten years, cultivating the lands with the labor of slaves, and at the expiration of that term, to sell all the property not specifically bequeathed and divide the proceeds of sale among the several legatees, construed in the light of the statutory provisions, which in 1863-4 authorized the probate court to confer similar powers on executors, do not impose personal trusts upon the executor, but duties and powers strictly executorial, which he could not exercise without the grant of letters testamentary, and which might be exercised by an administrator with the will annexed. Foxworth *v.* White, 72 Ala. 224.

In Greenland *v.* Haddell, 116 N. Y. 234, the court, by Bradley, J., states the distinction between cases where the power of sale devolves upon the administrator with the will annexed, and those in which it does not, as follows: "The question as to where is located the line between the duties which fall upon an executor, and may be discharged by an administrator with the will annexed, and the powers which must be executed by a trustee, has been involved in some uncertainty, in view of the apparent want of harmony in judicial opinion upon the subject. The theory upon which the distinction seems to have been founded is that the duties of an executor pertain to the office, and those of a trustee to the person, that the character given to a trustee has relation to a personal trust, while that of an executor is official solely. Hence it has, in the more recent case of Mott *v.* Ackerman, 92 N. Y. 553, been said by Judge Finch, in speaking for the court, that 'where the power granted or duty involved implies a personal confidence reposed in the individual over, above and beyond that which is ordinarily implied in the selection of an executor, the power and duty are not those of executors *virtute officii*, and do not pass to the administrator with the will annexed,' and when a discretionary power of sale is given to executors, or when, in the sense as applied to trusts, the duties imposed are active, the executors will be deemed trustees, and such powers cannot be executed by an administrator with the will annexed."

But the Supreme Court of *New York* has held recently that where the testator devises all his real and personal estate in trust for the payment of debts and legacies, "with power to sell and dispose of the same," the court cannot, upon the death of the executrix and trustee, appoint a trustee to execute the power, since the devise is a power in trust, and is inseparably connected with the office of executor. The power will, therefore, pass to the administrator with the will annexed. *In re* Christie, 59 Hun (N. Y.) 153.

Even where the will gives the power to trustees, "and the heirs, executors and administrators of the survivor," yet if it appears that the real and personal estate was to be kept together until the purposes of the trust should be accomplished, and that a personal trust was implied, equity will treat the trust as vacant after the death of the last trustee, and will not permit the power to be executed by either the heirs or personal representatives of the survivor. McKim *v.* Handy, 4 Md. Ch. 228.

Where a power of sale is given to executors for the purpose of paying debts or legacies, and especially where there is an equitable conversion of land into money for the purpose of such payment and for distribution, and the power is imperative and does not grow out of a personal discretion confided to the individual, such power belongs to the office of the executor, and under the statute passes to and may be exercised by an administrator with the will annexed. Mott *v.* Ackerman, 92 N. Y. 539; followed in Greenland *v.* Waddell, 116 N. Y. 234; 15 Am. St. Rep. 400.

A testator, in order to provide a fund to pay his debts, and to preserve a portion of his personalty from sale, authorized his executors to sell his real estate, "for such price as, in their judgment, shall be right." This did not involve such a special trust and reliance in the individuals named as executors as to preclude the exercise of the power by the administrator with the will annexed. Josalemon *v.* Van Riper, 44 N. J. Eq. 299.

The power given to an executrix to keep the estate together as long as practicable, and to manage, and control, and keep up the testator's farming interest either on the tenant or wages system, is not a personal trust, and is exercisable by an administrator with the will annexed. Palmer *v.* Moore, 82 Ga. 177.

A testator, after providing for the payment of debts, directed that his estate, real and personal should remain in the hands of his wife, "to rear and educate his three children, and to remain hers during her lifetime or widowhood," and that, in case of her marriage, his estate, real and personal, should be sold, and the proceeds equally divided between her and his three children. It was held that the power of sale was not a mere personal trust, to be executed only by the executor, but a general power, unattended by any discretionary power, or evidence of personal confidence, which might be exercised, under the statute, by an administrator *de bonis non.* Watson *v.* Martin, 75 Ala. 506.

If the power is given to an individual by name, there is still less reason for his representative acting, without being specially designated, than where the power is given to one *virtute officii.* 1 Chance Pow. 687.

But if the scheme of the will clearly shows that the power was intended to vest in the official representatives of the testator, it may be executed by an administrator *cum testamento annexo,* even though it was given to the executor by name. Fish *v.* Coster, 28 Hun (N. Y.) 64; *affirmed* without opinion, 92 N. Y. 627.

Where executors refuse to qualify, the administrator with the will annexed cannot execute the power, unless the statute so provides. 1 Chance Pow. 621, 683; Tainter *v.* Clark, 13 Met. (Mass.) 220; Anderson *v.* McGowan, 42 Ala. 280 (but this case is overruled on this point in 45 Ala. 462, when the case came again before the Supreme Court); Dohoney *v.* Taylor, 79 Ky. 124.

Under the *Kentucky* statute, which confers upon the administrator with the will annexed all the power and authority of executors, the administrator with the will annexed may sell under a power in the will, notwithstanding a special trust was reposed by the testator in the particular person named as executor. Shields *v.* Smith, 8 Bush (Ky.) 601.

Under the *Missouri* statute, which is similar in its terms (Rev. Stat. *Missouri,* 1889, § 136) it has been held that a sale may be made by the administrator with the will annexed, though the power may be accompanied by and involve the exercise of a discretion, if it does not appear that a special trust or confidence was reposed in the executor named. Dilworth *v.* Rice, 48 Mo. 124; Evans *v.* Blackiston, 66 Mo. 437. In the last case the court held, further, that the administrator *cum testamento annexo* might sell even though the party directed by the will to make the sale was not the executor but a trustee, in case such trustee failed to sell.

The *Alabama* Code (§ 2218) received a construction in the case of Mitchell *v.* Spence, 62 Ala. 450. There the testator bequeathed certain personalty and devised certain realty to his wife. The will contained a direction that "as soon after my death as my executor shall deem expedient, he shall sell all the balance of my property," real and personal, "either at public or private sale, and on a credit or for cash, at his discretion," and that the proceeds should be divided equally between the wife and children. A, a brother of the testator, was appointed executor of the will and guardian of the children, and it was further provided that in case A should die the testator B should be executor. The court held that the will did not confer a mere naked power of sale, within the meaning of the above section, which would pass to the successor in the trust, but a discretionary power, resting in the personal confidence reposed in the executor, constituting a personal trust which could not pass to an administrator with the will annexed.

The *Indiana* statute (2 Rev. St. *Indiana* 1876, p. 529, § 92), provides that when real estate is devised by will to be sold to pay legacies or debts, the executor shall proceed to sell according to the provisions of the will. A testator provided by will that his real estate should be sold, and the proceeds invested for the benefit of his wife. No executor being named in the will, an administrator was appointed. The court held that the administrator with will annexed could sell the real estate without an order of court. Davis *v.* Hoover, 112 Ind. 423.

In 2 *New York* Rev. St., p. 72, § 22, it is provided that administrators *cum testamento annexo,* "shall have the same rights and powers, and be subject to the same duties, as if they had been named executors in such will," where executors are by the will given discretion in the sale of lands, in exercising such discretion they act as trustees; and an administrator *cum testamento annexo* would not be competent to exercise it; but where such executors have made a contract of sale, executing the conveyances is an act of executors merely, which may be done by an administrator with the will annexed. Farmers' L. & T. Co. *v.* Eno, 35 Fed. Rep. 89.

Under the *Delaware* Code (ch. 90, § 17), which provides that "if by any will, real estate be devised to be sold, and no person be authorized to make said sale, the person or persons having the execution of the said will, or the survivor or survivors of them, if several, shall have authority to sell said real estate in execution of said devise," a devise to the widow for life or widowhood, after her death or marriage to the testator's son for life, and after the death of the son the land to be sold and the proceeds to be divided among certain children, was held not to authorize a sale by an administrator *de bonis non* with the will annexed. Chandler *v.* Deleplaine, 4 Del. Ch. 503. But where the will devised lands to the wife, which were to be sold within one year after her death by a person named therein, and in case of his "non-acceptance from any cause which he may deem sufficient, then proper authority shall appoint some suitable person to execute the same," it was held that where the person named died before the testator, and no letters testamentary were applied for by the wife, who was named as executrix, the administratrix with the will annexed had power to make the sale. Curran *v.* Ruth, 4 Del. Ch. 27.

The code of *Maryland* provides (art. 93, § 280) that, when a will directs a sale for any purpose, and the executors decline to act or die, the orphans' court may appoint an administrator *de bonis non* with the will annexed to execute the trusts. By his will, a testator gave the executors a power of sale in a certain contingency, and appointed the same persons executors and trustees of the estate of one of the life tenants. One of them declining and the other dying, a third person was appointed "trustee in the place of L. W., the surviving trustee, with all the power and authority of the original trustee," etc., and afterwards still another was appointed in the place of the latter. The court held that the last-named person had no authority to execute the power of sale, but that an administrator *de bonis non* might do so. Keplinger *v.* Maccubbin, 58 Md. 203.

The statute of *New Jersey* authorizes a sale by the administrator with the will annexed (P. L. N. J. 1888, p. 395); Giberson *v.* Giberson, 43 N. J. Eq. 116; Griggs *v.* Veghte, 47 N. J. Eq. 179.

The statute of *Illinois* authorizing the appointment of an administrator *de bonis non* on the death of the sole or surviving executor, etc., if there "is anything remaining to be performed in the execution of the will," does not authorize such administrator to execute a power of sale in the will. The words, "anything remaining to be performed in the execution of the will," mean only something to be performed as executor, and belonging to the office proper of executor, and do not extend to anything to be done as agent or trustee, under a power to sell land. Nicoll *v.* Scott, 99 Ill. 529.

It was formerly held in *Massachusetts* that where the power of sale is not coupled with an interest, but is united with a trust to dispose of the proceeds in payment of debts and legacies, given in the same clause in which the executor was appointed, and immediately following the mention of his name, an administrator with the will annexed could not exercise the power. Tainter *v.* Clark, 13 Met. (Mass.) 220. See also Greenough *v.* Welles, 10 Cush. (Mass.) 571. These decisions were placed on the ground that the power was given to the executor, *nominatim*, and came within the fourth rule laid down by Sugden. But in two later cases, the *Massachusetts* court clearly departs from the first rule of Sugden. In Chandler *v.* Rider, 102 Mass. 268, the power was sustained, though exercised by a surviving executor; and in Gould *v.* Mather, 104 Mass. 283, it was exercised by one executor after both had qualified, and the co-executor had resigned. These cases are followed in Parker *v.* Sears, 117 Mass. 513. And in Bradford *v.* Monks, 132 Mass. 405, it is held that where the testator intended that a power of sale, given to a trustee or executor, to be exercised by him, *virtute officii*, the power will pass with the office to his successor. To same effect, Nugent *v.* Cloon, 117 Mass. 219.

And where the wife is appointed administratrix, and the will gives her the use of the property for life, and directs that after her death it shall be converted into money, without specifying who shall do so, a power of sale is by necessary implication given to the administrator *de bonis non* with the will annexed. Putnam *v.* Story, 132 Mass. 205.

A direction in a will that all the landed estate be sold and that the proceeds equally divided among all the testator's children, does not confer a power of sale on the administrator with the will annexed. Gay *v.* Grant, 101 N. Car. 206. To same effect, Council *v.* Averett, 95 N. Car. 131.

But where the will empowers the executors "or whoever shall execute this my will," to sell the realty, the

g. DELEGATING POWER.—It follows from the idea of a personal confidence reposed in the donee, that such a power cannot be delegated without an express provision to that effect in the instrument creating it.[1]

sale may be made by an administrator with the will annexed. Royce *v.* Adams, 57 Hun (N. Y.) 415; *affirmed*, 123 N. Y. 402.

A testator bequeathed one-half the income of his real and personal estate to his widow for life, if she remained unmarried. The remainder of the income he gave to his children, to be expended under the directions of his executor, provided that, if any child should die before the youngest child became of age, leaving issue, such issue should take the parent's share. At the death of the wife, and on the arrival of the youngest child at the age of twenty-one, the entire estate was to go to the children equally. A full power of sale was given to the executor. It was held that the children took the fee of the land subject to the power of sale, and a deed by the widow individually, and, as administratrix with the will annexed, would convey a good title. Hickey *v.* Peterson (Supreme Ct.), 9 N. Y. Supp. 917.

In Elmer *v.* Gray, 73 Cal. 283, the executors were empowered to increase an annuity. They settled the estate and were appointed guardians of the annuitant, who was also residuary legatee. It was held that, as guardians, they could execute the power conferred on them as executors.

1. 1 Chance Pow. 699; 1 Sugden Pow. 266 (*214); 2 Washb. Real Prop. *321; 4 Cruise Dig. *211, §§ 74, 77; 1 Perry on Trusts, § 287, 289; Saunders *v.* Webber, 39 Cal. 287; Shelton *v.* Homer, 5 Met. (Mass.) 462; Whittekey *v.* Hughes, 39 Mo. 13; Wood *v.* Haden, 82 Va. 588; Graham *v.* King, 50 Mo. 22; Howard *v.* Thornton, 50 Mo. 291; Bales *v.* Perry, 51 Mo. 449; Brickenkamp *v.* Rees, 3 Mo. App. 585, *affirmed*, 69 Mo. 426; Spurlock *v.* Sproule, 72 Mo. 503; St. Louis *v.* Priest, 14 Mo. App. 575, *affirmed*, 88 Mo. 612; Topham *v.* Portland, 32 L. J. Ch. 257; 1 De G. J. & S. 517.

"The power to sell cannot be executed by attorney when personal trust and confidence are implied, for discretion cannot be delegated. 4 Kent's Comm. *327 (*citing* Combe's Case, 9 Co. 75b; Ingram *v.* Ingram, 2 Atk. 88; Cole *v.* Wade, 16 Ves. 27; Chambers *v.* Tulane, 9 N. J. Eq. 146). Unless as to some particular not requiring the exercise of judgment. Singleton *v.* Scott, 11 Iowa 589. But if the power be given to the donee and his assigns, it will pass by assignment, if the power be annexed to an interest in the donee." Singleton *v.* Scott, 11 Iowa 589 (*citing* How *v.* Whitfield, 1 Vent. 338). See also cases cited under the heads immediately preceding.

If the power be limited to the donee and his assigns, an execution by an assignee is valid; and the term "assignee" includes a devisee. 2 Washb. Real Prop. *322; 1 Sugden, Pow. 215; 4 Cruise Dig. 212; 1 Chance Pow. 721; Purdee *v.* Lindley, 31 Ill. 174; Strother *v.* Law, 54 Ill. 413; Collins *v.* Hopkins, 7 Iowa 463.

Cases may arise where the use of the word "assigns" is not absolutely necessary. Druid Park Heights Co. *v.* Oettinger, 53 Md. 46.

An assignment for the benefit of creditors, after naming the assignees, contained the following language: "Their executors, administrators or assigns, their or each of their true and lawful attorneys, irrevocable, with full power and authority to do and perform all acts, matters or things which can or may be necessary in the premises, as fully and completely as the said assignors might or could do were these presents not executed; and attorney one or more under him to make, nominate and appoint, as they deem necessary, with full power of substitution and revocation." *Held*, that this did not authorize the assignees to delegate their powers. Nye *v.* Van Husan, 6 Mich. 329; 74 Am. Dec. 690.

Sir Edward Sugden expresses the opinion that where the donee of the power has determined on the appointment, the deed of appointment may be executed by attorney. 1 Sugden Pow. 267 (*214–15).

In such a case it would be necessary that the power of attorney should show that the original donee had determined upon the particular appointment. 1 Chance Pow. 705.

But an attorney may perform acts which do not require the exercise of discretion. Thus in a deed of trust to secure a debt, power was given to the trustee to sell upon giving certain notice, and the deed specified the place of sale, the manner thereof, the terms, etc. The notice was published as required, but was not inserted by the trustee, nor did he know that it had been inserted until a day or two before the sale. He was present at the sale, however, and conducted it, and made the deed to the purchaser. It was held that the sale was valid. Singleton *v.* Scott, 11 Iowa 589.

A power of revocation and appointment cannot be delegated to another; but it is said that this doctrine is confined to that part of the execution of the power in which the confidence and discretion are exercised. Cooke *v.* King's County, 97 N. Y. 421. See Guion *v.* Pickett, 42 Miss. 77.

In Cooke *v.* King's Co., 97 N. Y. 421, a married woman, empowered to dispose of the remainder of an estate in which she had a life interest, devised it to her husband for life, in trust to apply the income, in his discretion, to the support of their children, with remainder to them in fee. The husband was empowered to sell and convey "either in fee or lesser estate," and to invest the proceeds on the same trusts. It was held that this was not a delegation of the power, but a complete exercise of it.

If the facts show that no personal trust or confidence was reposed in the donee, a sale by a representative is good. Paul *v.* Fulton, 32 Mo. 110; 82 Am. Dec. 124.

A testator devised all his estate to his widow for life, to use the rents and profits, with power to sell if necessary for her support, remainder over. This power was held to be a personal one, and the grantee in a deed of trust by the widow conveying all the real estate to him, his heirs and assigns forever, in trust to manage and sell as she might do under said power, took only the widow's life-estate. Phillips *v.* Wood, 16 R. I. 274.

A late *Massachusetts* case illustrates the strictness with which courts sometimes adhere to the rule stated in the text. The donor had given a fund to certain trustees "to be by them and their successors held in trust to found and maintain a museum of American archæology and ethnology in connection with Harvard University." A portion of the sum was to be invested, and the income applied to forming and preserving collections of antiquities and objects relating to the earlier races of the American continent; another portion to the establishment and maintenance of a professorship in Harvard University, said professor to be appointed by the university on the nomination of the trustees; and the remainder was to be allowed to accumulate as a building fund, to be used in the erection of a building upon land of the college, and when erected to become the property of the college. The trustees were to keep a record of their proceedings, and to make an annual report to the college authorities. Provisions for filling vacancies followed, as well as for incorporating, for making by-laws, appointing a treasurer, etc., and the trustees were to be at liberty "to enter into any arrangements and agreements with the government of Harvard College, not inconsistent with the terms of this trust, which may in their opinion be expedient." It was proposed to enter into an arrangement whereby the trust funds were to be invested and managed by the college as a part of its general fund, and a proportionate part of the entire income be annually credited to the two funds first mentioned, and be paid to the trustees or their treasurer, and the proportionate share of the remaining fund should be annually added by the college to the third fund until such time as the trustees should demand payment of the whole or any part of the principal or income, upon giving six months' notice. The management of the trust fund was to be held by the college in perpetuity, subject only to the right of the trustees, to demand and receive the income of the two funds first mentioned, and the whole of the third fund; the college to invest the funds as it should see fit, and not to be responsible for any loss. The trustees by a bill in equity asked the instructions of the court as to their right to carry into effect the proposed agreement. *Held*, that as to the two funds first mentioned, the agreement was inconsistent with the terms of the trust, in that it substituted for the trustees selected by the donor new trustees, who were to manage the funds in a manner not intended or contemplated by him. And the fact that the treasurer of the trustees, who had acted without compensation was about to resign, and that the agreement would be beneficial

h. BY SUBSTITUTE.—Courts cannot confer upon trustees appointed by them powers which are merely discretionary, or powers resting on personal trust and confidence. Hence trustees appointed by courts in place of the donees of such powers, cannot execute the powers.[1]

as it would secure the services of efficient treasurers and custodians of the funds without charge, whose services could not otherwise be secured without great expense would not justify the court in altering the scheme of the donor, even as to the objects of the charity, or the agents by whom it is to be administered. It was also held that the last clause of the instrument creating the power, would not warrant the trustees in making the arrangement proposed. Winthrop *v.* Attorney Genl. 128 Mass. 258.

Where the donee appointed by will a life interest to M, who was a proper object of the power, and delegated to said M the right to appoint a life interest to a stranger to the power, and subject thereto appointed the property to the children of M, who were proper objects of the power, the appointment to M for life, remainder to her children, was good, but the delegation of the power was void. Carr *v.* Atkinson, 14 L. R. Eq. 397; 41 L. J. Ch. 785.

A testator appointed T trustee, with certain powers of appointment. T dying before the testator, he by a codicil, named others trustees, "to hold said estate upon the same trusts as the said T." *Held*, that this did not confer upon them the appointing power. Howard *v.* Law, 15 Phila. (Pa.) 341.

The appointment of executors with power to make a division of property is not a delegation of the power to dispose of it. Albert *v.* Albert, 68 Md. 352.

Where one who had a power to appoint among her children by will, devised to her son during his life with remainder to his issue, and provided further that if he died without issue he should appoint to certain classes, such delegation of the power was void. Hood *v.* Haden, 82 Va. 588.

Mr. Washburn says that if there is a general conveyance to A to such uses as he shall appoint, he may delegate the power to B by conveying to such uses as B shall appoint. (*Citing* Watk. Conv. 265; 4 Cruise Dig. 212; 1 Sugd. Pow. 216.) But this does not apply where personal confidence and trust are reposed. 2 Washb. Real Prop. *321.

Sugden says that "where the power is tantamount to an ownership, and does not involve any confidence or personal judgment, and no act personal to the donee is required to be performed, it may be executed by attorney." 1 Sugden Powers (*216); Chance agrees with this [713]. So also does Greenleaf, 4 Cruise *212, § 79.

Where powers are connected with an estate or interest in trustees, it does not follow that if the estate or interest is transferred the power will be so too. 1 Chance Pow. 717.

In cases where the donee is authorized to execute the power through a substitute, proof of the appointment of the substitute is necessary to the validity of his acts. Cheveral *v.* McCormick, 58 Tex. 440.

1. Doe *v.* Ladd, 77 Ala. 223; Hinson *v.* Williamson, 74 Ala. 180; *In re* Bierbaum, 40 Hun (N. Y.) 504; *In re* Christie, 59 Hun (N. Y.) 153; Young *v.* Young, 97 N. Car. 132.

If there is no power to appoint new trustees, and chancery appoints a new one in place of one of the trustees who declines to act, the power is at an end; it cannot be assigned over. 1 Sugden Pow. 211 (*152). See also 1 Perry on Trusts, § 287.

In the case cited above from Alabama, the terms of the power were that the trustee should at all times have the sole and absolute right to sell, and, on giving security, to invest the proceeds according to the terms of the instrument creating the power. It was held that the power attached to the office, and could be exercised by a successor appointed by the court. Doe *v.* Ladd, 77 Ala. 223. In the *North Carolina* case the power given to the trustee was to sell whenever in his opinion best, and to re-invest as he should think best. This was held to be a personal power, which could not be executed by a successor so appointed. Young *v.* Young, 97 N. Car. 132.

A testator in Mississippi devised his entire estate to C, his heirs and assigns, with full power to dispose of the same and apply the proceeds upon specified trusts. By subsequent clauses he

By the *New York* statute power is given to the court to appoint a successor where the surviving donee has died, resigned, or been removed.[1] The statute further provides that every bene-

named C co-executor with two others, limiting the power to sell and convey to C alone; and provided that if C should die or should "refuse to take upon himself the execution of the will," C's power should pass to W. The trust was accepted by C, who qualified as executor and took upon himself the execution of the will. Afterwards he executed a resignation, both as trustee and as executor, and on an *ex parte* application, an orphans' court in Mississippi made an order accepting it, and appointing W his successor. There was no law in that State giving power to any court, upon such an application, to divest a trustee, holding title, of his powers or estate. Soon after C (who did not convey to W) resumed action as trustee, conveyed for value land situated in Ohio to a *bona fide* purchaser; received the purchase-money, and placed it in the hands of the chief executor, who duly applied and accounted for it. W never acted or claimed to act as to the land. The Supreme Court of *Ohio* held that the resignation was not such a "refusal to take upon himself the execution of the will" as transferred title to W; that the action of the orphans' court did not affect C's powers as trustee, and that his deed was valid. Veasie *v.* McGugin, 40 Ohio St. 365.

In a Maryland case, the court of appeals recognized the validity of a sale of land made by a trustee appointed by the circuit court to execute the power, coupled with a trust, conferred by a will on two executors and trustees or the survivor of them, one having renounced and his letters having been revoked, and the other having died, leaving an infant heir. Druid Park Heights Co. *v.* Oeltinger, 53 Md. 46.

1. 4 *New York* Rev. Stat. § 102 (Banks' ed.), p. 2448; (1882) p. 2191. See also Hutchings *v.* Baldwin, 7 Bosw. (N. Y.) 241; Wright *v.* Delafield, 23 Barb. (N. Y.) 517; Leggett *v.* Hunter, 25 Barb. (N. Y.) 81; Quin *v.* Skinner, 49 Barb. (N. Y.) 133; Manier *v.* Phelps, 15 Abb. N. Cas. (N. Y.) 137; Delaney *v.* McCormack, 88 N. Y. 174; Cooke *v.* Platt, 98 N. Y. 39; Greenland *v.* Waddell, 116 N. Y. 234; 15 Am. St. Rep. 400.

M being possessed of a trust estate died without having conveyed the same, but leaving a will, by which she devised all her real estate to her husband during his life, in trust, to receive the rents and profits and apply them, in his discretion, to the support and education of their children, with remainder to them in fee. The trustee, however, was empowered to sell and convey the real estate, "either in fee or lesser estate," the consideration received to be invested and disposed of for the benefit of the children in the same manner as provided for in relation to the original estate. It was held by a divided court that this was not simply a delegation of the power to convey given M by her mother's will, but was a full and complete disposition of the whole estate by will as authorized. Cooke *v.* Kings Co., 97 N. Y. 421.

A power of sale given by a will to the executors is not within the statutory term of express trusts, to execute which the supreme court has power to appoint trustees under sections 69 and 70. The power of sale being vested in executors, such power would be taken by an administrator with the will annexed, and on the acceptance by the supreme court of the resignation of the surviving executor, the power of sale could not be executed by a trustee appointed by the supreme court. Greenland *v.* Waddell, 116 N. Y. 234; 15 Am. St. Rep. 400.

A testator, after making various legacies, gave the residue of his estate to three children specifically named, and directed his executors to invest the same and keep it invested, and to apply the income to the support and education of the said children until they respectively arrived of age; after that to pay to each the income of one-third of the estate, and after the death of two of the children to divide the principal between the survivor and the heirs of the two deceased. The executors were empowered to sell and convey the real estate and to invest the proceeds for the purposes of the will. One of the executors died. The others after paying debts and legacies, and settling the estate in all respects, except as to the sale and distribution of the proceeds of the real estate re-

ficial power, and the interest of any person entitled to compel the execution of a trust power, shall pass to an assignee.[1]

12. In Favor of Whom—*a.* IN GENERAL.—Anyone who is capable of taking lands by a common-law conveyance, may be an appointee.[2] The donee of a power may also exe-

signed. Their resignation was accepted by the supreme court and two more trustees were appointed. At this time the three children were living and all were of age. *Held*, that, conceding the executors were merely donees of a power of sale, it was a general power and imperative, and so subject to the same statutory provisions as to the substitution of new trustees as are applicable to express trusts; that, therefore, the new trustees were lawfully substituted and had power to convey; also that the trust or power was not ended by the payment of debts and legacies and settlement of the executors' accounts, as the principal purpose of the will yet remained to be carried out. Farrar *v.* McCue, 89 N. Y. 139.

1. 4 *New York* Rev. Stat., § 104 (Banks' ed.), p. 2448; (1882) p. 2191, Cooke *v.* King's County, 97 N. Y. 421; Clark *v.* Crego, 47 Barb. (N. Y.) 614; Marvin *v.* Smith, 56 Barb. (N. Y.) 606.

And the assignee may enforce the execution of the power in equity, the same as the one for whose benefit the power was created. Clark *v.* Crego, 47 Barb. (N. Y.) 599.

2. 4 Cruise Dig. *146; 4 Kent's Com. *328; 1 Perry on Trusts, §§ 250, 256.

This rule applies only where the person or classes of persons who are to take under the power, are defined in the instrument creating it. Mr. Jarman states the rule thus: "In the case of appointments, testamentary or otherwise, under powers of selection or distribution in favor of defined classes of objects, the appointees must be persons competent to have taken directly under the deed or will creating the power." 1 Jarman on Wills, 289; Barnum *v.* Barnum, 26 Md. 119. See Robinson *v.* Hardcastle, 2 T. R. 241.

An appointment to take effect at a future period is not void *in toto*, because it may include, or turn out to include, strangers as well as objects of the power. It will fail only as to those appointees who are not objects. *In re* Farncombe, 9 L. R., Ch. Div. 652; 49 L. J., Ch. Div. 328.

A tract of land was purchased in the name of A, for an unorganized church society, to be conveyed by A to the trustees of the society when they should be elected. A executed a deed to the society by name, instead of to the trustees, and this was held to be a valid execution of the power. Centenary M. E. Church *v.* Parker, 43 N. J. Eq. 307.

If a power of appointment has, through mistake, been exercised by the donee, in favor of some who are, and some who are not, the legitimate objects of the appointment, and the donee of the power is dead, it shall not be taken to be good *pro tanto* if the case is one in which, in the absence of an appointment, the fund would be distributed among those persons who are the proper objects of the power, but the appointment is wholly void. Varrell *v.* Wendell, 20 N. H. 431.

A widow who had a power under her husband's to appoint among their children, made a devise to her son during his life, "remainder to the lawful issue of his body forever, and provided that if he died without issue, he should have power to appoint one of the testatrix's children or grandchildren as his devisee. *Held*, that the son took the estate in fee, and that the remainder over was void. Hood *v.* Haden, 82 Va. 588. See Stuyvesant *v.* Neil, 67 How. Pr. (N. Y.) 16.

It was held by a *nisi prius* court in *Ohio* that where a testator devised realty, with a direction to the devisee to divide the fee simple by deed or will, among the heirs of his body, a devise by the latter to one of his heirs to hold for three years, and then distribute among certain parties named in specified proportions, was not a proper exercise of the power. Jennert *v.* Houser, 4 Ohio Circ. Ct. Rep. 353. But in a somewhat similar case in *South Carolina*, where the power was to convey to any of the issue of the testator, a deed to one of the testator's grandsons was valid, though it was intended to be only a means to carry the title to a stranger, and though the grandson, two days afterwards, actually conveyed to such

cute it in favor of himself, or in favor of a husband or wife.[1]

Under the *New York* statute no estate or interest can be given or limited to any person by the exercise of a power which such person could not have taken under the instrument creating the power.[2] The donee must be capable of holding lands, and also, except in the case of married women, of aliening them.[3]

b. CLASSES.—Where power is given to appoint to a class, if it is to such members of the class as the donee shall see fit, he may give all to one and may omit such as he sees fit; but if it be among the members of a class, each one must have a substantial share, though not necessarily an equal share.[4]

stranger. Glenn *v.* Glenn, 21 S. Car. 308.

Where a mixed estate consisting of real and personal property is the subject of appointment, it is not necessary that each of the objects have some of each kind. Morgan *v.* Surman, 1 Taunt. 289.

Where one having a power of appointment among certain persons, dies without having fully executed it, those appointees who have received any thing can claim a share of the residue only by bringing what they have received into the *collatio bonorum.* Knight *v.* Yarborough, Gilm. (Va.) 27.

1. 2 Washb. Real Prop. *310, *321; Williams Real Prop. *220; 2 Cruise Dig. *146.

This grows out of the principle that the execution of the power relates back to the original instrument creating the power, and the estate passes directly from the grantor of the power to the appointee.

A power of disposition in the testator's widow, wholly unlimited as to beneficiaries, may be exercised in favor of her second husband. New *v.* Potts, 55 Ga. 420.

But this rule will be governed by the express terms of the instrument creating the power. Thus where a testator gave his widow his real estate for life, and authorized her to dispose thereof to his heirs as she thought best, she could not so appoint as to secure to herself a substantial pecuniary benefit, as by conveyances in consideration of money paid to her. Shank *v.* Dewitt, 44 Ohio St. 237.

2. 4 *New York* Rev. Stat., § 109, 129 (Banks' ed.), pp. 2449, 2451; (1882) p. 2193; Dempsey *v.* Tyler, 3 Duer (N. Y.) 73; Salmon *v.* Stuyvesant, 16 Wend. (N. Y.) 321; American H. M. Soc. *v.* Wadhams, 10 Barb. (N. Y.) 604.

The prohibition of this section does not refer merely to estates void by reason of an illegal suspension of the power of alienation (Perpetuities, § 128), but to estates which may be lawfully created, but which the appointee is incompetent to take by deed directly from the person creating or reserving the power. Dempsey *v.* Tyler, 3 Duer (N. Y.) 98.

3. 4 *New York* Rev. Stat., § 109 (Banks' ed.), p. 2449; (1882) p. 1291, 2193.

As to power of married women to hold and aliene lands, see *passim*, Albany F. Ins. Co. *v.* Bay, 4 N. Y. 9.

4. Bouv. Inst. 1923; Lippincott *v.* Ridgway, 10 N. J. Eq. 164; Rhett *v.* Mason, 18 Gratt. (Va.) 541; *In re* Meredith, 3 L. R., Ch. Div. 757; 25 W. R. 107; Lloyd *v.* Lance, 14 L. J. Ch. 456; *In re* Veale, 4 L. R., Ch. Div. 61; *affirmed* on appeal, 5 L. R., Ch. Div. 622; 46 L. J. Ch. 699.

A general power to appoint a fund among children in such proportions as shall be thought fit, enables the gift of particular interests and the apportionment of such interests at discretion; as, for instance, an interest for life may be given to one child in a particular share, and the capital of the same share may be limited to another child, or a share may even be limited to a child upon a contingency. The distribution need not be made in gross sums. Beardsley *v.* Hotchkiss, 96 N. Y. 201; *affirming*, on this point 30 Hun (N. Y.) 605.

A testator gave all his property to his wife, in trust, to apply the income to her own use during her life, and at her death to divide the same among her four sons, a daughter, and the issue of a deceased son, in such shares as she might by will direct, and, in default of such direction to the beneficiaries above mentioned, in six equal shares, the issue of the deceased son to take one share. Should either beneficiary die before his intended share vested, his issue was to take such share. No disposition was made of the share of any living child in case of his or her death without issue. By a codicil he directed "that on the death of my said wife the share of my estate to go to our son James and our grandson Charles shall be held by my surviving executors in trust for them during their lives; and at their respective deaths the principal shall go to their issue, if any; if none, then the same shall fall into my general estate, or as my said wife shall by will direct." It was held that as to the two shares mentioned in the codicil the wife had power, in case of the death of either before her without issue, to will such share to any person whom she might select, and that she was not confined to the class named in her husband's will. Austin *v.* Oakes, 48 Hun (N. Y.) 492.

A wife having a power to appoint among her issue living at the date of the appointment, appointed by deed to the children of her daughter in equal shares on their attaining twenty-one. At the date of the appointment, the daughter had three children, and three were born afterwards. *Held*, that each of the children living at the date of the appointment would, on attaining the age of twenty-one, take one-sixth of the property, *plus* an accruing share of the sixth purporting to be appointed to any other child who might die under twenty-one. *In re* Farncombe, 9 L. R., Ch. Div. 652.

Where the power is to appoint to the children of the donee, a child born after the making of the will and in the lifetime of the testator, is a proper object of the power. Morgan *v.* Surman, 1 Taunt. 289.

Where a fund was settled upon the death of E for such descendants of X as E should appoint by will, an appointment to the legal personal representatives of descendants who died before E, was in excess of the power. In default of the exercise of the power, the descendants of X living at the death of E would take in equal shares. *In re* Susanni, 26 W. R. 93.

A power under a marriage settlement to appoint to the children of the marriage is strictly confined to those children. Goodtitle *v.* Weal, 2 Wils. 369. See Doe *v.* Nall, 6 Exch. 102; 20 L. J. Exch. 161.

If there was but one child of the marriage, that child takes the whole. Doe *v.* Dunt, 2 Wils. 536.

Where a power was given to charge an estate with portions for younger children varying in amount according to the number, being if there were four or more, £5000, and four younger children were born, two of whom died before the portions were to be raised, an appointment of the full amount of £5000 is valid, notwithstanding the death of the children. Knapp *v.* Knapp, 12 L. R. Eq. 238; 24 L. T., N. S. 540.

Illusory appointments are those where only a nominal share is appointed to any one or more of the objects of the power. That the exercise of a limited power given by will in respect to one-half of the property was illusory or collusive would not make void the exercise of an unlimited power as to the other half, it not appearing that the latter power would have been differently exercised if the former had not been perverted. New *v.* Potts, 55 Ga. 420.

Such appointments are made valid in *England*, in equity as well as at law, by Statute 1 Wm. IV, ch. 47.

It has been held that no appointment was illusory in a court of law. Morgan *v* Surman, 1 Taunt. 289.

See Gainsford *v.* Dunn, 17 L. R. Eq. 405; 30 L. T., N. S. 283; 43 L. J. Ch. 403.

An appointment made since the passage of the Illusory Appointments Acts (11 George IV and 1 William IV, chap. 46), under a non-exclusive power, of an entire fund unto and among the objects of the power, "and the survivors and survivor of them, and if only one should survive then unto that one," is valid. *In re* Capon's Trusts, 10 L. R., Ch. Div. 484; 48 L. J., Ch. Div. 355; 27 W. R. 376.

Exclusive Appointments.—Where a power is given to A to appoint "among" certain persons, and "in such proportions as A may appoint," A has authority to exclude some of such persons. Ingraham *v.* Meade, 3 Wall. Jr. (C. C.) 32.

Where a widow has a power of appointment in favor of children, a bequest to one daughter is a good execution. Friend *v.* Oliver, 27 Ala. 532.

A husband, by his will, provided as follows: "I give and bequeath all my property, both real and personal,' . . . to my wife, Elizabeth, to use or dispose of in any manner that she may think proper during her lifetime, and at her death may by will dispose of the same between my children and grandchildren as she may think proper." It was held that her interest in the property so given was a life estate, with discretionary power of testamentary disposition among testator's children and grandchildren, but without power to entirely exclude any of them. Wright *v.* Wright, 41 N. J. Eq. 382. This is in harmony with the earlier case of Lippincott *v.* Ridgway, 10 N. J. Eq. 164. There an estate was devised to trustees to pay "to such brothers and sisters of my daughter H and their children, and in such proportions, as she shall, by her last will and testament, or other writing in the nature thereof, etc., direct and appoint—my will being that she shall have power to dispose of the same among her said brothers and sisters and their children, as she may think fit, but to no other person whatsoever." It was held that each brother and sister was entitled to some portion of the fund.

But the court of Appeals of *Maryland* has recently decided that where a testator devised all his property to his wife for life, with power to will it to their children, and also to make advancements to them during her life, discriminating between them in her discretion, and that the remainder undisposed of at her death should be equally divided among the children, the wife could convey in fee-simple part of the realty to one of the children by way of advancement. Franke *v.* Auerback, 72 Md. 580.

By 37 and 38 Vict., ch. 37 (passed July 30, 1874), it was provided that no appointment should be invalid at law or in equity on the ground that any object of such power had been altogether excluded. By the express terms of the act it applies only to cases where the instrument making the appointment was executed after its passage. Therefore, where a married woman, having a power to appoint a fund among her children by her will, by a will executed before the act made an exclusive appointment, such appointment was invalid, though she did not die until after the passage of the act. Moynam *v.* Moynam, 1 Ir. L. R., Ch. Div. 382.

Earlier English cases on the subject of exclusive appointments are Smith *v.* Gregson, 1 T. R. 432; Spring *v.* Biles, 1 T. R. 435; Doe *v.* Alchin, 2 B. & A. 122; Robinson *v.* Hardcastle, 2 T. R. 241; Beard *v.* Westcott, 5 Taunt. 393; 5 B. & A. 801 n; Doe *v.* Denny, 1 Ld. Kenyon 280; Bulteet *v.* Plummer, 6 L. R. Ch. 160; *In re* Moredith, 3 L. R. Ch. Div. 757.

To Grandchildren.—A power of appointment among the children of the testator will not authorize either a general or a partial appointment among his grandchildren. Horwitz *v.* Norris, 49 Pa. St. 213; Little *v.* Bennett, 5 Jones' Eq. (N. Car.) 156; Carson *v.* Carson, Phil. Eq. (N. Car.) 57; Jarnagui *v.* Conway, 2 Humph. (Tenn.) 50.

Compare Ingraham *v.* Meade, 3 Wall. Jr. (C. C.) 32; Doe *v.* Cavendish, 4 T. R. 741 n. 1; East 450; 3 Dougl. 48; Fry *v.* Capper, Kay. 163; 2 W. R. 136, in which case it is held that in such cases grandchildren might take under a limitation to a child for life, with remainder to the children of such child, by treating the first taken as a tenant in tail.

Where the power is to appoint to children, an appointment in favor of children, with remainder to grandchildren, is void as to the excess only. Doe *v.* Welford, 4 P. & D. 77; 12 Ad. & Ell. 61; 5 Jur. 38. To same effect, Carr *v.* Atkinson, 41 L. J. Ch. 785; 14 L. R. Eq. 397; 26 L. T., N. S. 680. See also Adams *v.* Adams, Cowp. 65.

A power of appointment among children, in terms, may, however, include grandchildren, if, in a general way, grandchildren are manifest objects of the trust. Thus where the issue of children were provided for in default of appointment, in the same clause in which children alone were mentioned as entitled to receive under appointment, it was held that such issue was meant to be included within the power of the appointment. Ingraham *v.* Meade, 3 Wall. Jr. (C. C.) 32.

A somewhat peculiar case arose in *New York*, in which the above view was taken. A testator gave a power of appointment to his adopted daughter, who was generally regarded as his illegitimate child. His sisters and their children did not treat her with affection, at which testator, who was very fond of her, was angry, and, before making his will, he said that he would "make a lady of her, in spite of them." She was younger than most of his sisters' children, and would therefore more probably receive care and attention from the grandchildren than the children of testator's sisters, if she should live to old age. Testator devised to her for life, and after her death to such of her lawful issue as she should appoint. In default of appointment, the estate was limited, after her death, to her lawful issue in fee, in equal shares; but, if such issue should be of unequal degrees of consanguinity, the issue of a deceased parent was to take the share the parent would have taken if living. The ninth clause provided that, if said daughter should die without issue, she should have power to appoint the property devised to any of testator's sisters, "or to all or any of the lawful issue" of them, in such shares as she should deem proper. She died without issue, and by will appointed the property to the grandchildren of testator's sisters; their parents then being alive. It was held that, in view of the facts of the case, and of the context of the will, the "issue" of testator's sisters mentioned in the ninth clause included any of their descendants, and that the appointment was valid. Drake *v.* Drake (Supreme Ct.), 3 N. Y. Supp. 760; *affirmed* 10 N. Y. Supp. 183.

A testator gave power to his son to sell a tract of land "to any of my issue and to make a good fee-simple title to the purchaser." The son conveyed this land in fee to his son, a grandson of testator. It was held that the grandson was embraced in the word "issue," and that he took a good fee-simple title. Glenn *v.* Glenn, 21 S. Car. 308.

In *North Carolina* property was devised to the wife for life, with power to dispose of it by will among all of her children. By her will she disposed of a part of the estate to her grandchildren and other more remote descendants, and a part to some of her children for life only. It was held that the will was not a valid exercise of the power, and that the legal title passed to her children as heirs at law. Little *v.* Bennett, 5 Jones' Eq. (N. Car.) 156.

To the same effect is a decision in *Pennsylvania.* Certain real estate was devised by a testator in that State to his daughter for her sole and separate use, and at her decease to descend in fee to such of the children as she might in writing direct. The daughter by will directed the property to be sold by her executor, and the proceeds to be distributed among certain of her children and grandchildren, whom she designated by name. This was held not to be a valid execution of the power. Stephenson *v.* Richardson, 28 Pa. St. 40.

Next of Kin.—Where a power is given to an unmarried woman to appoint among her own family or next of kin, she is not confined to those who are named in the statute as next of kin; but she may exercise the power in favor of any relative. Snow *v.* Teed, 9 L. R. Eq. 622; 23 L. T., N. S. 303.

But if the distribution be left to a court of equity, such court will confine it to the nearest relative. 1 Perry on Trusts, § 257.

An appointment to an object of the power for life, with remainder to his next of kin, will take effect if at the death of the life-tenant his next of kin are objects of the power. *In re* Coulman. Munby *v.* Ross, 30 Ch. Div. 186.

Appointment by Court.—Where the power of appointment is to children as a class, though the donee might have distributed it unequally among them, yet if he fails to execute the power, and it is one where equity will supply the execution, being coupled with a trust, the court will distribute the fund equally among the objects of it. 1 Perry on Trusts, § 250, and cases cited note (5). And this on the ground that equality is equity. 1 Perry on Trusts, § 255.

The law is thus stated by Lord Cottenham in Burrough *v.* Philcox, 5 My. & Cr. 72: "When there appears a general intention in favor of a class, and a particular intention in favor of particular individuals of a class, to be selected by another person, and the particular intention fails from that selection not being made, the court will carry into effect the general intention in favor of the class."

But if the donor of the power lays down any rule by which the donee is to be governed in his selection of the beneficiaries or in the distribution of the fund, the court will place itself in the position of the donee. 1 Perry on Trusts, § 255; Gower *v.* Mainwaring, 2 Ves. 87. *Compare* McNeilledge *v.* Galbraith, 8 S. & R. (Pa.) 43; Harrison *v.* Harrison, 2 Gratt. (Va.) 1; Withers *v.* Yeadon, 1 Rich. Eq. (S. Car.) 324.

Mr. Perry says that if the donee is to select from the donor's relations, he may select from the whole circle,

The *New York* statute provides that where the disposition is directed to be made to, among, or between several persons, without specifying the share of each, all shall be entitled to an equitable proportion. But if the terms of the power import that the estate or fund is to be distributed between the persons designated in such manner or proportions as the trustees shall think proper, the trustee may allot the whole to any one or more of such persons to the exclusion of the others.[1]

13. Consent of Third Person.—Where the instrument creating the power provides that it is to be executed only with the consent or concurrence of some party other than the donee of the power, such consent is essential to a valid exercise of the power.[2]

whether near or distant, and may exclude whom he pleases; but if the power is to distribute to the relations, then he must confine himself to such as would be entitled under the statute of descent and distribution. But if the power devolves upon the court as a trust, it will adopt the rule of the statute, whether the power be one of selection or distribution, unless the donor has himself established a rule of selection. 1 Perry on Trusts, § 256, and cases cited in notes. See also § 250.

While the rule of the statute is used to determine the persons who are to take, reference will be made to the terms of the gift in order to fix the proportions; and if the proportions cannot be determined from the language used by the donor, the distribution will be made *per capita*. If, however, the gift is to the next of kin, the court will confine it to the nearest relations. 1 Perry on Trusts, § 257.

See DeLisle *v.* Hodges, 43 L. J. Ch. 385; 22 W. R. 363; 30 L. T., N. S. 158.

1. 4 *New York* Rev. Stat. §§ 98–9 (Banks' ed.), p. 2448; (1882) p. 2191.

2. Richardson *v.* Crooker, 7 Gray (Mass.) 190; Haymond *v.* Jones, 33 Gratt. (Va.) 317; Hoyt *v.* Hoyt, 17 Hun (N. Y.) 192; Hamilton *v.* New York Stock Exchange etc. Co., 20 Hun (N. Y.) 88.

Where a conveyance in trust for the benefit of husband and wife, with remainder to their children, contains a grant of power to the trustee to sell and convey with the assent of the husband and wife, a sale by the trustee with such assent, and in the absence of fraud, cuts off the rights of the children. Hamilton *v.* Mound City Mut. L. Ins. Co., 6 Lea (Tenn.) 402.

And where a mere naked trustee has power to sell the land with the assent of the first *cestui que trust*, a life-tenant, a warranty deed by the trustee for a valuable consideration, in which all the *cestuis que trustent* join, carries the title. Gindrat *v.* Montgomery Gas Light Co., 82 Ala. 596.

The mere expression by the testator of a wish or a direction that the heirs should be consulted, does not render their consent requisite to a valid sale. Thus in *New Jersey*, where a testator, after directing all his debts to be paid, gave to each of his six children an equal share of all of his estate, the shares of his two daughters to be invested for their use during life, with remainder to their respective heirs, and appointing his son W his sole executor, concluded his will as follows: "My will and wish is to consult the heirs whether it will be best to sell it or otherwise—the homestead property," it was held that the power of the executor to sell, which was given by implication was not dependent upon the consent of the heirs. Haggarty *v.* Lanterman, 30 N. J. Eq. 37.

In a case arising in *Texas*, a sale without consent was upheld, under the circumstances of the case. There a husband and wife conveyed the wife's land in trust for the benefit of their minor children. The deed provided that the trustee should have power to sell at the request of the minors, made through their legal and natural guardian. In 1871 the trustee, at the request of the parents, sold the land, no guardian having been appointed. At that time in Texas no guardian other than the father could have been appointed. It was held that, as against the minors, the trustee's deed conveyed a good title. Harris *v.* Petty, 66 Tex. 514.

Effect will be given to the instrument

so far as may be without violating the intention of the donor. Thus, in *Alabama*, where a husband conveyed lands to a trustee for the separate use and benefit of the wife for her life, remainder to his heirs, directing that the same be kept free from incumbrance, and authorizing the trustee, on the written request of the wife, to sell and re-invest, a mortgage of the property, signed by the trustee and the wife, while it would not convey the fee, will convey the life estate of the wife. Butler *v.* Gazzam, 81 Ala. 491.

So in *Georgia*, where land was conveyed to A in trust for B for life, with remainder to such children as B might have *in esse* at her death, and in default of children, to grandchildren living at the time of her death, with power to A to sell and reinvest with the consent of the persons for whose use he might at any time hold the property, and A sold the land with consent of the life tenant only, while a usee in remainder was in life, and B survived all her children and died, leaving grandchildren, it was held that while the sale did not devest the grandchildren's title, it did convey the life-estate of B. Augusta *v.* Radcliffe, 66 Ga. 469.

It would seem that the concurrence of a trustee may be required, though not expressly provided for in the instrument creating the power. It was so held by a divided court in *Virginia.* A testator devised his property to his wife for life, and further provided, "after the death of my wife I wish my estate divided among my children. I give to each one of my children one-fifth part of my estate. . . . I wish whatever may be coming to my daughters put into the hands of trustees of their own choosing, requiring them to give ample security for the faithful performance of the trust committed to them." Other clauses of the will read, "I wish the portions coming to my daughters placed in the hands of their respective trustees and used for them as hereinbefore directed. . . . Should any of my children die without an heir of their body, it is my desire that whatever may then be left of what they may have received from my estate revert to the same, to be equally divided among my surviving children, with such restrictions in regard to my daughters that may be entitled to a portion, as hereinbefore provided." A daughter married, and pending the partition of the testator's estate, but before an assignment of any portion to her, united with her husband, who was insolvent, in a conveyance of her interest, under the will of her father, to a trustee to secure certain debts of her husband. The majority of the court held that the executor of the testator had no power, under the will, to pay the daughter's legacy to any one except a trustee chosen and qualified as the will directed, and if the daughter had the right to convey it at all, she could only do so with the concurrence of her trustee, and therefore the deed of trust was a nullity. But from this view Judge Christian dissented. Haymond *v.* Jones, 33 Gratt. (Va.) 317.

Where a homestead was devised to the widow for life, with direction to the executor to sell the same and pay the proceeds to his children, the executor may sell during the widow's lifetime, with her consent, the limitation of the power of sale for her life being solely for her benefit. Hamlin *v.* Thomas, 126 Pa. St. 20.

Where the person whose consent is required is afterwards made the donee, the sale may be made without the consent of any one. Williams *v.* Williams, 1 Duv. (Ky.) 221.

Where a sale can be made only with the consent of the devisees, or a majority of them, the devisees do not lose the power to consent by reason of the execution by them of a mortgage to secure a debt due from the testator. Duryee *v.* Martin, 36 N. J. Eq. 444.

By a marriage settlement a power over a trust fund was given to the husband and wife in favor of their children, and they appointed a portion of the fund upon such trusts as S, one of the children should, with the consent of the trustees named in the father's will, appoint. *Held*, that the requirement as to consent was beyond the power of the parents, and being inseparably connected with the appointment, made the power to S void. Webb *v.* Sadler, 4 L. J. Ch. 498; 8 L. R. Ch. 419.

Evidence of Consent.—Where the power to sell real estate is to arise upon the request of the wife, a simple request in writing is sufficient; no privy examination or other formalities are required. Cardwell *v.* Cheatham, 2 Head (Tenn.) 14.

Under the *Alabama* Code, it is sufficient if the person whose consent is required, join in the execution of the deed. Gindrat *v.* Montgomery Gas-

If the person whose consent is required dies before the execution of the power, the power is extinguished.[1]

The *New York* statute requires that where the consent of a third person is necessary, it shall be expressed in the instrument by which the power is executed, or shall be certified in writing thereon. In the first case the instrument of execution, and in the second the certificate, must be signed by the party consenting, and if it is to be recorded, his acknowledgment must be taken.[2]

Light Co., 82 Ala. 596. Or if a writing be indorsed on the deed after its execution, acknowledging that the sale was made with the consent of the party signing it, and at her written request such acknowledgment being duly certified. March *v.* England, 65 Ala. 275.

Her consent to a decree in equity for the sale is sufficient. Tyson *v.* Mickle, 2 Gill (Md.) 376.

And even an oral assent has been held to be enough, where there is a simple waiver of a right. Hamlin *v.* Thomas, 126 Pa. St. 20.

1. Kissam *v.* Dierkes, 49 N. Y. 602; Powles *v.* Jordan, 62 Md. 499.

And a power to several to consent ceases with the death of one. 1 Sugd. Pow. *147.

Where the consent of a majority of the children living at the time of the execution is required, and all the children die before that time, the execution is valid without any consent. Leeds *v.* Wakefield, 10 Gray (Mass.) 514. If the consent of a majority is required, the consent of the majority of those living at the time, is sufficient. Sohier *v.* Williams, 1 Curt. (U. S.) 479.

Land was devised to B for life, remainder to his heirs, power being given to B to sell and convey the same with the consent of his mother and brother. The mother having died without having given her consent, a sale made by B with the consent of his brother would pass no title. Barber *v.* Cary, 11 N. Y. 397.

The *Maryland* case cited above was as follows: By a deed from L and wife, certain land was conveyed to W C, his heirs and assigns, in trust for the sole and separate use of J, a married woman, with a limitation over of the equitable estate after her death. She had the power, however, to defeat this limitation, by selling, conveying and disposing of the whole of the property; but this power was to be exercised with the approbation and consent of W C, and not otherwise. W C died, and by a decree of the circuit court of Baltimore city, J W J was appointed trustee in his place. J, with the approbation and consent of J W J, executed a deed of the property to P, purporting to be in execution of this power. In an action of ejectment by P to recover the property, he offered in evidence in support of his title, this deed to himself from J and J W J. The deed was excluded, the court holding that the approval and consent required of W C to the execution of the power was entirely personal, and did not belong to the estate which he held as trustee; and that having died before the execution of the power, it was gone; and further, that as the deed to P purported to be made in execution of the power, and derived all its efficacy from it, and as the power was extinct and incapable of being executed, no title was conveyed to him. Powles *v.* Jordan, 62 Md. 499.

Where the exercise of a power depends upon a marriage of the donee with the consent of third parties, and such consent becomes impossible by reason of the death of the parties where consent is required before the marriage of the donee, the donee has the right to exercise the power. Aislabee *v.* Rice, 2 Moore 358.

The consent of four trustees, survivors or survivor, was required to cutting timber. All died. *Held*, that it should be referred to a master to determine what timber should be cut. Hewett *v.* Hewett, 2 Eden's Ch. 332.

2. 4 *New York* Rev. Stat., § 122 (Banks' ed.), p. 2450; (1882) p. 2193; Barber *v.* Carey. 11 N. Y. 397.

Consent is not a mere formality nor

14. Equitable Interposition in Cases of Powers—*a.* To Aid Defective Execution.—A defective execution of a power will be aided frequently by equity, as will also an incomplete attempt at execution; but equity will not interfere where there has been a total non-execution of the power.[1]

a nominal condition. Kissam *v.* Dierkes, 49 N. Y. 602.

If the person whose consent is required, dies before the consent is given, the execution of the power becomes impossible, and this rule has not been changed by the above section. This is so decided in Barber *v.* Cary, 11 N. Y. 397. There one A. C. devised certain lands to A. G. C., during his life, and to his heirs, with power in the said A. G. C. to sell the same by and with the consent of his mother and brother. Before the execution of the power the mother died, and A. G. C. afterwards conveyed the land to the brother in trust to sell the same and out of the proceeds extinguish a judgment which constituted a lien on the land. The brother consented to this conveyance, but his consent was not expressed nor certified in accordance with the statute. Gardner, C. J., comments upon these facts as follows: "The defendant (the grantee) in this case sustained the relation of third person to his brother, the donee of the power, undoubtedly; but he was also the grantee in the conveyance by which it was attempted to be executed. Whether this circumstance is to form an exception from the general language of the statute, is the question to be determined. My conclusion is that it does not. The power itself cannot be executed except by some instrument which would be sufficient in law to pass the estate if the person executing the power were the actual owner (§ 113); and by the section already quoted (§ 122) it was the purpose of the legislature that evidence equally satisfactory of the consent, where that was necessary, should accompany or rather form a part of the instrument or conveyance. This evidence is wanting in the deed from A. G. Cary to the defendant. There is no writing showing the assent of the latter, but this is to be inferred, if at all, from the acceptance of the conveyance, a fact to be established by parol. But beyond the delivery, which is essential to give validity to an instrument executed in conformity with this statute, as in other cases, the legislature have said, that purchasers and all others whose interests may be affected by the execution of the power, shall have a writing authenticated by the signature of the defendant in or upon the deed itself. There is nothing unreasonable in this." And Parker, J., after stating that under the common law, where the consent of third parties is required, that condition, like every other, must be strictly complied with, adds: "There is no provision of the revised statutes that changes this well-established rule of the common law. The counsel for the plaintiff argues that § 112 of the revised statutes is applicable, and that one of the two persons whose consent was requisite having died, it was sufficient that the consent was given by the survivor . . . This section is applicable only to grantees of power, not to the persons by whose consent it is to be executed. The person in whom the power is vested is called the 'grantee of the power.' The person whose consent is required is called 'a third person.' The power is in no respect vested in such third person. He can only consent to another's executing it . . . It follows that by the death of Hannah Cary (the mother), it became impossible to execute the power." See also Farmers' L. & T. Co. *v.* Carroll, 5 Barb. (N. Y.) 652.

1. Story Eq. Jur., § 169; American Freehold Land Mortg. Co. *v.* Walker, 31 Fed. Rep. 103; Fontain *v.* Ravenel, 17 How. (U. S.) 369; McBryde *v.* Wilkinson, 29 Ala. 662; Mitchell *v.* Denson, 29 Ala. 327; Lines *v.* Darden, 5 Fla. 51; Wilkinson *v.* Getty, 13 Iowa 157; 81 Am. Dec. 428; Howard *v.* Carpenter, 11 Md. 259; Lippincott *v.* Stokes, 6 N. J. Eq. 122; Harrison *v.* Battle, 1 Dev. & B. Eq. (N. Car.) 213; Schenck *v.* Ellingwood, 3 Edw. Ch. (N. Y.) 175; French *v.* Davidson, 3 Madd. 396; Walker *v.* Walker, 5 Madd. 424; Brown *v.* Higgs, 5 Ves. 501; 8

Ves. 570; Down *v.* Worrall, 1 My. & K. 561; Tollet *v.* Tollet, 2 P. Wms. 489; Mos. 46; 2 Eq. Cas. Ab. 233, pl. 16; 633 pl. 10; Blockvill *v.* Ascott, 2 Eq. Cas. Ab. 659, n.; Piggott *v.* Penrice, Gilb. Eq. Rep. 138; Buckell *v.* Blenkhorn, 5 Hare 131.

See Sanderlin *v.* Thompson, 2 Dev. Eq. (N. Car.) 539; Speck *v.* Wohlien, 22 Mo. 310; Barr *v.* Hatch, 3 Ohio 527. Much germane to this question will also be found *infra*, this title, *Execution of a Power—Power Discretionary or Imperative.*

In Chapman *v.* Gibson, 3 Bro. C. C. 229, the court by Lord Alvanley, M. R., said: "Whenever a man having power over an estate, whether ownership or not, in discharge of moral or natural obligations, shows an intention to execute such power, the court will operate upon the conscience of the heir, to make him perfect this intention."

Equity cannot confer upon a trustee authority to sell, where the instrument appointing him has not conferred such power. Burroughs *v.* Gaither, 66 Md. 171.

Story says that equity will not universally interpose to supply the defect, but will do so in favor of parties for whom the person intrusted with the execution of the power is under a moral or legal obligation to provide by an execution of the power, unless such aid of the defective execution would under all the circumstances, be inequitable to other persons, or it is repelled by some counter equity. 1 Story Eq. Jur., § 169. And see in this connection, Ferre *v.* American Board, 53 Vt. 162.

Cruise mentions three grounds of interposition in such cases: 1. Where there has been a consideration as for securing a jointure to a wife, or a sum of money to a husband, or making provision for younger children or the payment of debts; and no better equity on the other side. 2. Where there is any fraud, or the party is guilty of any deceit or falsehood, by which the execution is prevented; for the person in remainder shall not take advantage of his own wrong. 3. Where a complete execution is prevented by accident; for it would be unconscionable in the remainderman to take advantage of this, provided the person having the power does all he can towards its execution. 4 Cruise Dig. *222.

In regard to mere naked powers, Mr. Perry says that, if the donee executes them, but executes them in a defective manner, courts may aid the execution and supply the defects, but they cannot exercise nor execute mere naked powers conferred upon a donee. 1 Perry on Trusts, § 248, and cases cited in note (2). Even though the party intended to execute it and was only prevented by sudden death. Pigott *v.* Penirce, Com. 250; Gilb. Eq. 138; Sugd. Pow. 392.

If equity should supply the non-execution of a power, it would overthrow the very intention manifested in the creation of the power by depriving the donee of all discretion as to the exercise of it. "On the contrary, when a party undertakes to execute a power, but by mistake does it imperfectly, equity will interpose to carry his very intention into effect, and that, too, in aid of those who are peculiarly within its protective favor; that is, creditors, purchasers, wives and children." 1 Story Eq. Jur., § 170.

Equity will aid a defective execution, whether the mistake be one of law or fact. Love *v.* Sierra Nevada L. W. & Min. Co., 32 Cal. 653.

But the absolute want of execution cannot be aided by proving that it was the intention of the donee to execute it, and that the failure to execute it was owing to a mistake. Wilkinson *v.* Getty, 13 Iowa 157; 81 Am. Dec. 428.

Courts will not give effect to an intention unless an attempt has been made to conform to the terms of the power. A case illustrating this is found in the *Virginia* reports. There one R willed to his wife E for life certain lands with power of appointment by deed or will among their descendants, so that not more than one-half should be given to any one. If she did not appoint, it was to pass to his children. By a codicil he gave her permission to sell and reinvest in other lands upon the same trusts, and added: "But subject to the following qualification, that is to say—that whatever she shall by will, deed or otherwise give beneficially to any of my descendants, the same shall be not given absolutely to such descendant or descendants so as to be under his or her control, but given in trust to him or her, and in case of a female to her sole and separate use." E by her will gave the property to twenty of her grandchil-

Equity will thus aid purchases for a valuable consideration,[1]

dren, though in very unequal proportions, directed that the land should not be sold for six years; that her executor should hold it in the meantime, and when sold he should divide the proceeds of sale, and invest the portion of each for him and her, and pay it to each one on his or her arrival at the age of twenty-one years. It was held by a divided court that the will and codicil of R required that the provision made by E under the power vested in her, for her grandchildren, should be in trust for the several beneficiaries, and for the separate use of the females; that the power which she gave to her executor by her will, which must terminate as to each one as he or she arrived at the age of twenty-one years, did not constitute him such a trustee for the grandchildren as satisfied the will and codicil of R; and that the appointment was therefore invalid. It was further held by the whole court that this was not a case of the defective execution of the power, which a court of equity would remedy. Morriss *v.* Morriss, 33 Gratt. (Va.) 51.

Where the donee of the power did nothing more than express an intention, which she might at any time retract, to give the property to her daughter, consulted a lawyer as to the necessity of making a will in order to dispose of the property, by whom she was advised that the property vested in her in fee simple, and upon her death would descend to her legal heirs, and relying on this advice she made no disposition of the property, these facts amounted neither to an execution of the power, nor to an attempt to execute it such as chancery would aid. Mitchell *v.* Denson, 29 Ala. 327.

Where the power is to appoint among certain persons, and the donee dies without having fully executed it, equity will not give any share of the residue to those who have already received a portion, unless they bring such portion into the *collatio bonorum.* Knight *v.* Yarborough, Gilm. (Va.) 27.

Where property was devised to a woman for life, with power to sell so much thereof as might be necessary for her support, and she executed a quitclaim deed for the property, which contained no reference to the power of sale under the will, and nothing showing an intention to act under the power, and which in legal effect was only a conveyance of her real estate, a court of equity will not aid such execution on the ground that the deed was intended as a conveyance in fee under the power. Brown *v.* Phillips, 16 R. I. 612.

The donee of a special power to appoint by deed made a will, by the terms of which it appeared that the donee supposed the power to have been extinguished. The will, however, purported to be an execution of the power, and of all other powers enabling in that behalf. The appointment was to strangers, some of whom were strangers to the power. *Held*, to be a defective execution which equity will aid in favor of a child otherwise provided for and to the prejudice of other children entitled in default of appointment. Bruce *v.* Bruce, 40 L. J. Ch. 141; 11 L. R. Eq. 371.

A power expressly directed to be executed by deed will in equity be deemed to be well executed by a will, where it is in favor of a wife. 4 Cruise Dig. *225.

A distinction is sometimes drawn between powers created by a party and those created by law, it being held that equity will aid a defective execution in the former case, but not in the latter. McBride *v.* Wilkinson, 29 Ala. 662; Smith *v.* Bower, 38 Md. 463. See Mayor etc. of Baltimore *v.* Porter, 18 Md. 284.

1. Fothergill *v.* Fothergill, 2 Freem. 257; Sergeson *v.* Sealey, 2 Atk. 214; 9 Mod. Rep. 390; Wade *v.* Paget, 1 Bro. C. C. 363; Jackson *v.* Jackson, 4 Bro. C. C. 462; *In re* Dyke's Estate, 7 L. R. Eq. 337; Schenck *v.* Ellingwood, 3 Edw. (N. Y.) 175; Beatty *v.* Clark, 20 Cal. 11; Love *v.* Sierra Nevada L. W. & Min. Co., 32 Cal. 653; Thorp *v.* McCullum, 6 Ill. 615.

Purchasers for a valuable consideration have always been favored in equity, and equity will in such cases supply any defect in the execution of the power. 4 Cruise Dig. *228. And purchasers will be held to include lessees. Campbell *v.* Leach, Amb. 470; Dowell *v.* Dew, 1 Y. & C. C. C. 345; Doe *v.* Weller, 7 T. R. 478; Willes 176; Shannon *v.* Bradstreet, 1 S. & L. 52; King *v.* Roney, 5 Ir. Ch. Rep. 64.

creditors,[1] charities,[2] a wife and legitimate child.[3] Equity will lend its aid as against the remainderman[4] and the heir at law.[5]

To call for the interposition of a court of equity the defect must be one of form; that is, the intention to execute the power

Equity will grant relief to lessees holding under leases from tenants for life with power to lease against the remainderman, where the leases have been defectively executed under the power. Howard *v.* Carpenter, 11 Md. 259. And mortgages, Taylor *v.* Wheeler, 2 Vern. 564; Jennings *v.* Moore, 2 Vern. 609.

1. Wilkes *v.* Holmes, 9 Mod. Rep. 485; Thompson *v.* Towne, 2 Vern. 319; Fleming *v.* Buchanan, 3 De G. M. & G. 976; Mayor *v.* McCune, 59 How. Pr. (N. Y.) 78; Porter *v.* Turner, 3 S. & R. (Pa.) 108; Beatty *v.* Clark, 20 Cal. 11.

2. Attorney Genl. *v.* Tancred, 1 Eden's Ch. 14; Innes *v.* Sayer, 7 Hare 377; *affirmed* on appeal, 3 M. & G. 606; Pepper's Will, 1 Pars. Sel. Cas. (Pa.) 436.

3. Tollett *v.* Tollet, 2 P. Wms. 489; Mos. 46; Fothergill *v.* Fothergill, 2 Freem. 257; Afleck *v.* Afleck, 3 Sm. & Giff. 394; Proby *v.* Landor, 28 Beav. 504; Porter *v.* Turner, 3 S. & R. (Pa.) 108; Dennison *v.* Goehring, 7 Pa. St. 175. Whether they are volunteers, or claim under a meritorious consideration. Hervey *v.* Hervey, 1 Atk. 567; Barron *v.* Constabile, 7 Ir. Ch. Rep. 467. And though they are already provided for. Hervey *v.* Hervey, 1 Atk. 567; Kettle *v.* Townsend, 1 Salk. 187; Chapman *v.* Gibson, 3 Bro. C. C. 229.

And no distinction will be made between children and grandchildren. Huss *v.* Norris, 63 Pa. St. 372; Porter *v.* Turner, 3 S. & R. (Pa.) 108. See Watts *v.* Bellas, 1 P. Wms. 60, and *compare* Bland *v.* Bland, 2 Cox 349; Perry *v.* Whitehead, 6 Ves. 544.

But equity will not lend its aid in favor of a volunteer. Smith *v.* Ashton, 2 Freem. 309; Sergeson *v.* Sealey, 2 Atk. 415; nor of a husband, Watt *v.* Watt, 3 Ves. 244; Hughes *v.* Wells, 9 Hare 749; nor a mother, brother or sister, Goodwyn *v.* Goodwyn, 1 Ves. 228; Goring *v.* Nash, 3 Atk. 189; nor an illegitimate child, Tudor *v.* Anson, 2 Ves. 582; nor a nephew or niece, Strode *v.* Russell, 2 Vern. 621; nor a cousin, Tudor *v.* Anson, 2 Ves. 582; nor the donee himself, Ellison *v.* Ellison, 6 Ves. 656.

4. Coventry *v.* Coventry, 3 P. Wms. 222.

Equity will give no assistance where both the remainderman and the appointee are volunteers. 4 Cruise Dig. *228; though it seems equity will relieve against accidents, even in favor of volunteers. 4 Cruise Dig. *229. See also 1 Story Eq. Jur. § 176.

5. Smith *v.* Ashton, 1 Ch. Cas. 263. *Compare* Speck *v.* Wohlien, 22 Mo. 310.

But if the heir is otherwise unprovided for, the execution will not be aided. Chapman *v.* Gibson, 3 Bro. C. C. 229; Braddick *v.* Mattock, 6 Madd. 363; Rodgers *v.* Marshall, 17 Ves. 294. *Compare* Hills *v.* Downton, 5 Ves. 564.

Though this exception does not apply to a collateral heir. Fielding *v.* Winwood, 16 Ves, 90; Smith *v.* Baker, 1 Atk. 385.

For a valuable consideration lands were conveyed to C in trust for E, with a provision that C should convey the lands to any one designated by E, either by a writing executed during her lifetime or by a will after her death. C died without having exercised the power, and thereupon E verbally requested C's heir at common law to convey the premises to herself, which was accordingly done. Afterwards, E, for a valuable consideration, conveyed the premises to the complainants' mortgagor, through whom they now claim title. The chancellor held that equity would aid the execution of the power, which was only formally defective, and C's heir-at-law would be perpetually enjoined from prosecuting an ejectment to recover the premises. Mutual L. Ins. Co. *v.* Everett, 40 N. J. Eq. 345.

A person claiming under the due execution of a power created by will cannot come into a court of equity for a comfirmation of his title as against the heir. Sanderlin *v.* Thompson, 2 Dev. Eq. (N. Car.) 539.

must appear by some instrument in writing, which is not sufficient by reason of informality[1] or mistake.[2]

1. Shannon *v.* Bradstreet, 1 S. & L. 63; Baron *v.* Constabile, 7 Ir. Ch. Rep. 467; Love *v.* Sierra Nevada L. W. & Min. Co., 32 Cal. 653; Ford *v.* Russell, 1 Freem. Ch. (Miss.) 42; Wilkinson *v.* Getty, 13 Iowa 157; 81 Am. Dec. 428; Howard *v.* Carpenter, 11 Md. 259; Johnson *v.* Cushing, 15 N. H. 178; Mutual L. Ins. Co. *v.* Everett, 40 N. J. Eq. 345.

If the instrument is an appropriate one to execute the power, but is defectively executed, equity will aid. Wade *v.* Paget, 1 Bro. C. C. 363; Cockerell *v.* Cholmeley, 1 Russ. & My. 424; 1 Cl. & F. 60; Lucena *v.* Lucena, 5 Beav. 146.

Or if the instrument is an inappropriate one, as by deed where a will was required, or *vice versa*. Bruce *v.* Bruce, 11 L. R. Eq. 371; Mills *v.* Mills, 8 Ir. Eq. Rep. 192; Sneed *v.* Sneed, Amb. 64; 4 Cruise Dig. *225.

If the writing constitutes an agreement to execute the power, equity will give it effect. Mortlock *v.* Buller, 10 Ves. 292; Lowry *v.* Dafferin, 1 Ir. Eq. Rep. 281; King *v.* Roney, 5 Ir. Ch. Rep. 64; Dowell *v.* Dew, 1 Y. & C. C. C. 345; *In re* Dyke's Estate, 7 L. R. Eq. 337.

If the appointment is not made within the required time, equity will not lend its aid, if time be of the essence of the power. Cooper *v.* Martin, 3 L. R. Ch. App. 47.

Where one trustee has executed a power conferred on several jointly, equity will aid. Roberts *v.* Stanton, 2 Munf. (Va.) 129.

So a deed signed by an attorney in fact in his own name, as attorney for the grantors, will be aided. Ramage *v.* Ramage, 27 S. Car. 39.

Equity will not aid when the instrument creating the power is defective. Piatt *v.* M'Cullough, 1 McLean (U. S.) 69. Except as to mere matters of form, such as the want of a seal or witnesses, or of signatures. American Freehold Land Mortg. Co. *v.* Walker, 31 Fed. Rep. 103; Schenck *v.* Ellingwood, 3 Edw. Ch. (N. Y.) 175.

By a marriage settlement a power was given to the wife of appointment by deed with two witnesses and with the husband's consent in writing. An attempt was made to exercise the power by an unattested deed, without the husband's consent in writing. *Held*, that equity will not aid. Bennett *v.* Bennett, 1 Vict. L. R. 280.

In consequence of the decisions in Doe *v.* Peach, 2 M. & S. 576; Doe *v.* Pearce, 2 Marsh. 102; 6 Taunt. 402; Wright *v.* Wakeford, 4 Taunt. 213; 17 Ves. 434; Wright *v.* Barlow, 3 M. & S. 512; and Buller *v.* Burt, 6 N. & M. 281; 4 A. & E. 15, the act commonly known as Mr. Preston's act was passed (54 George III, ch. 158).

This act provides that every deed or instrument already made with the intention to exercise any power, authority or trust, or to signify the consent or direction of any person whose consent or direction may be necessary, shall, if duly signed and executed and in other respects duly attested, be of the same validity and effect and provable in like manner as if a memorandum of attestation of signature had been subscribed by the witnesses thereto; and an attestation expressing the fact of sealing, or sealing and delivery, without expressing the fact of signing, shall not exclude the proof or the presumption of signature.

Section 2 of the act enumerates the deeds and instruments to which the act extends.

Under this statute, and explanatory thereof, the following decisions were made.

Newton *v.* Ricketts, 9 H. L. Cas. 262; 31 L. J. Ch. 247; 7 Jur., N. S. 953; Doe *v.* Keir, 4 M. & R. 101; Darlington *v.* Pulteny, Cowp. 260; Moodie *v.* Reid, 7 Taunt. 355; 2 Madd. 156; Curteis *v.* Kenrick, 3 M. & W. 461; 9 Sim. 443; 4 Jur. 934; Burdett *v.* Doe, 6 M. & G. 386; 7 Scott N. R. 66; 10 C. & F. 340; 8 Jur. 1; Perry *v.* Watts, 4 Scott N. R. 366; 3 M. & G. 775; Vincent *v.* Sodor, 5 Exch. 683; 19 L. J. Exch. 366; 15 Jur. 365; 20 L. J. Ch. 433; 8 C. B. 905; Johns *v.* Dickerson, 8 C. B. 934; Freshfield *v.* Reed. 9 M. & W. 404.

By the statute of 22 and 23 Vict., ch. 35, § 12, a deed executed in presence of two or more witnesses in the manner in which deeds are ordinarily executed and attested, constitutes a valid execution of a power, though the instrument creating the power may require some additional or other form of execution or attestation.

2. Garth *v.* Townsend, 7 L. R. Eq. 220.

Under the *New York* statute, if the execution of the power is defective in whole or in part, its proper execution may be decreed by a court of equity in favor of the persons designated as its objects.[1] And purchasers for a valuable consideration are entitled to the same relief in equity as purchasers from an actual owner.[2]

The statute further provides that if the trustee with the right of selection dies leaving the power unexecuted, or if the power is created by will and the testator has omitted to designate by whom it shall be exercised, its exercise will devolve on the court of chancery.[3] And the execution of a trust power may be decreed in equity for the benefit of the creditors or assignees of any object of the trust.[4]

b. WHERE POWER IS EXCEEDED.—Where the power has been exceeded equity will support the power so far as its execution was warranted, and treat the excess only as void, while at law it would be void altogether.[5]

1. 4 *New York* Rev. Stat., § 131 (Banks' ed.), p. 2451; (1882) p. 2194; Allen *v.* DeWitt, 3 N. Y. 276.

2. 4 *New York* Rev. Stat., § 132 (Banks' ed.), p. 2451; (1882) p. 2194; Barber *v.* Carey, 11 N. Y. 397.

3. 4 *New York* Rev. Stat., §§ 100, 101 (Banks' ed.), p. 2448; (1882) p. 2191; Crocheron *v.* Jaques, 3 Edw. Ch. (N. Y.) 207; Dominick *v.* Sayre, 3 Sandf. (N. Y.) 559; Read *v.* Williams, 54 Hun (N. Y.) 636. See Hoey *v.* Kenney, 25 Barb. (N. Y.) 396.

The superior court has declared that the intent of these sections was nothing more than to regulate and fix by law what had been the practice of the courts. Meakings *v.* Cromwell, 2 Sandf. (N .Y.) 576.

They are applicable only to a trust power, with an arbitrary and absolute right of selection. Hawley *v.* James, 5 Paige (N. Y.) 468.

In Meakings *v.* Cromwell, 5 N. Y. 139, the court by Ruggles, Ch. J., says: "This section does not require that the designation should be by express words; a designation by necessary implication excludes the case from the operation of the statute. Such a designation is equivalent to a designation by express words."

4. 4 *New York* Rev. Stat., § 103 (Banks' ed.), p. 2448; (1882) p. 2191; Clark *v.* Crego, 47 Barb. (N. Y.) 614; Marvin *v.* Smith, 56 Barb. (N. Y.) 606; Ford *v.* Belmont, 7 Robt. (N. Y.) 109. See Ludlow *v.* Van Ness, 8 Bosw. (N. Y.) 186.

5. 4 Cruise Dig. *202; 2 Sugd. Pow. (6th ed.) 59–93; Hervey *v.* Hervey, 1 Atk. 561; Barnard, 103; Bowman *v.* Bartlett, 3 A. K. Marsh. (Ky.) 86; Knox Co. *v.* Nichols, 14 Ohio St. 260; Campbell *v.* Leach, Ambl. 740; Pawcey *v.* Bowen, 1 Ch. Ca. 23; 3 Ch. Rep. 11; Barnum *v.* Barnum, 26 Md. 119.

Compare Roe *v.* Prideaux, 10 East 158; Doe *v.* Hiern, 5 M. & S. 40; Jennen *v.* Morris, 7 Jur., N. S. 385; 9 W. R. 566; 4 L. T., N. S. 347.

In Alexander *v.* Alexander, 2 Ves. 644, the M. R. thus states the rule: "Where there is a complete execution of a power, and something *ex abundanti* added which is improper, there the execution shall be good and only the excess void; but where there is not a complete execution of a power, or where the boundaries between the excess and execution are not distinguishable, it will be bad." See also 2 Sugd. Pow. (6th ed.) 80; Attorney-Genl. *v.* Griffeth, 13 Ves. 576; Warner *v.* Howell, 3 Wash. (U. S.) 12.

So where there is a complete execution with a condition added, the condition is void. 2 Bouv. Inst. 1924; Warner *v.* Howell, 3 Wash. (U. S.) 12.

An unrestricted power to make a grant or concession authorizes the donee to make it on conditions. New York etc. R. Co. *v.* New York, 4 Blatch. (U. S.) 193.

If the donee attempts to execute the power in favor of a person or a class outside of those designated by the donor, the attempt will be nugatory

c. WHEN GENERAL POWER IS TREATED AS ASSETS FOR CREDITORS.—Where a person has a general power of appointment over property, and actually exercises such power, whether by deed or will, in favor of volunteers, a court of chancery will consider the property appointed as assets, subject to the claims of his creditors in preference to the claims of the appointees. But this is so only where there has been an execution of the power or an attempt to execute it.[1]

and the trust will remain in favor of those for whom it was designed. 1 Perry on Trusts, § 254; Wickersham *v.* Savage, 58 Pa. St. 365; Little *v.* Bennett, 5 Jones Eq. (N. Car.) 156; Lippincott *v.* Ridgway, 11 N. J. Eq. 526.

Thus a power given by will to appoint to the children of the testator does not authorize either a general or a partial appointment to his grandchildren. Horwitz *v.* Norris, 49 Pa. St. 213; Jarnagin *v.* Conway, 2 Humph. (Tenn.) 50.

See *supra*, this title, *Execution of Powers—In Favor of Whom—Classes.*

1. Chance, Powers, § 1817; 4 Kent's Comm. *339; and cases cited in note (b) to page *340; 2 Sugden Pow. *29, § 7; *173, § 2; Ram on Assets, *148–9; Lassels *v.* Cornwallis, 2 Vern. 465.

Compare, In re Harvey Estate, L. R. 13 Ch. Div. 216.

The power must be a general one. Johnson *v.* Cushing, 15 N. H. 298.

And Mr. Justice Story limits the rule to cases where the power is a general one "to raise money." 1 Story Eq. Jur., §§ 169–176, note (4).

If, however, the donee has not exercised the power at all, equity will not interpose in favor of creditors. Sir William Grant and Lord Erskine admit that there is no good reason or justice in the distinction. (Holmes *v.* Coghill, 7 Ves. 506; on appeal 12 Ves. 206); and Mr. Story says in the note above cited that "the distinction is a nice one, and not very satisfactory." 1 Story Eq. Jur., § 176, note (4).

See also, 4 Kent's Comm. *339; Johnson *v.* Cushing, 15 N. H. 298; Cutting *v.* Cutting, 20 Hun (N. Y.) 360; 86 N. Y. 522.

This doctrine is carried into effect, not by annulling the appointment, or altering the disposition made by the donee of the power, but by holding the appointee or trustee for the creditors. Smith *v.* Garey, 2 Dev. & B. Eq. (N. Car.) 42.

Where a woman, upon her marriage, conveyed her property to her husband in trust for her sole and separate use, reserving a power of appointment by will, and with provisions for the disposition of the property in case she failed to execute the power, and she executed the power of appointment by will, the appointees under the power took subject to debts, which were charges upon her separate estate. Knowles *v.* Dodge, 1 Mackey (D. C.) 66.

But where the donee of the power executes it by a will, the property so disposed of cannot be held for the debts of the donee, unless his remaining assets are insufficient to pay his debts. Patterson *v.* Lawrence, 83 Ga. 703.

An estate was devised in trust for the brother of the testatrix, for his use and occupation during his natural life, and at his death to be conveyed to whom and in the manner he should direct. *Held*, that the property was not, at least as to prior creditors, chargeable with his debts. Wales *v.* Bowdish, 61 Vt. 23.

Where one having a life interest in property and a power of appointment by will, executes the power to confirm title to a person who had previously purchased the property for a valuable consideration from the life tenant and his trustee under an order of court, the property is not liable for the debts of the life tenant. Patterson *v.* Lawrence, 83 Ga. 703.

In a *New York* case, the will directed the payment of the testator's debts, and devised certain realty to the wife for life or during widowhood, and upon her death or remarriage, in fee to his surviving children or their issue. The wife was appointed executrix and full power was given to her as such, at any time and on such terms as she might think satisfactory, to sell, mortgage, or lease the whole or any part of the real estate, and to invest the proceeds in good securities or purchase other real estate, to sell said securities and real estate, and to continue the said transfer

By statute in *New York*, *Michigan*, *Wisconsin*, *Minnesota*, *Dakota* and *Alabama*, every special and beneficial power is liable in equity to the claims of creditors in the same manner as other interests that cannot be reached by execution, and execution of the power may be decreed for the benefit of creditors.[1]

15. Execution, Discretionary or Imperative.—A power is discretionary when it is not imperative; or, if imperative, when the time, manner, or extent of its execution is left to the discretion of the donee.[2]

The execution of a power pure and simple, whether naked or coupled with an interest, is discretionary with the donee.[3] The

of the real estate or the proceeds as long and as often as she might think best; provided, however, that the proceeds should be considered real estate. It was held that this proviso withheld the proceeds from becoming a personal fund accessible to creditors. Such proceeds could be followed only in equity, and, under the circumstances, it would seem that no bar would exist to a judgment creditor's application for a resale of the premises. Equity would not aid an effort to impair the legal remedies of the creditors, or sanction an attempt on the part of the executrix to vest individually in herself, and mingle with her own property, real estate, which, until her testator's debts were paid, was chargeable with a trust. Mayer *v.* McCune, 59 How. Pr. (N. Y.) 78.

A judgment against the party having the power of appointment, with the estate vested in him until and in default of appointment, is defeated by the subsequent execution of the power in favor of a third party. Doe *v.* Jones, 10 B. & C. 459; Tunstall *v.* Trappes, 3 Sim. 300; Brandies *v.* Cochrane, 112 U. S. 344.

Even though the appointee had notice of the judgment, and a portion of the purchase money was set aside as an indemnity against it. Eaton *v.* Sanxter, 6 Sim. 517; Skeeles *v.* Shearly, 8 Sim. 153; on appeal, 3 Myl. & Cr. 112. But whether this rule would apply to a case where the appointee is a volunteer, *quære.* Thompson *v.* Towne, Prec. Ch. 52; 2 Vern. 319; *In re* Harvey's Estate, L R., 13 Ch. Div. 216. It has now been altered in *England* by statute. Holtham *v.* Somerville, 9 Beav. 63.

It was held in Cutting *v.* Cutting, 86 N. Y. 522, reversing, in part, 20 Hun (N. Y.) 360, that the common law rule was abrogated by the statutes of that State.

1. 4 *New York* Rev. Stat., § 93 (Banks' ed.) p. 2447; (1882) p. 2190; Marvin *v.* Smith, 56 Barb. (N. Y.) 605; Ford *v.* Belmont, 7 Robt. (N. Y.) 97.

Mich. Stat. (How. Ann.), § 5610; Wis. Rev. Stat. of 1878, § 2120; Minn. Gen. Stat. (ed. of 1891), § 4041; Dak. Civil Code, § 348; Ala. Code of 1887, § 1866. And see Mervin *v.* Smith, 56 Barb. (N. Y.) 603; Ford *v.* Belmont, 7 Robt. (N. Y.) 97; Alford *v.* Alford, 56 Ala. 350.

2. Doe *v.* Ladd, 77 Ala. 223; Robinson *v.* Allison, 74 Ala. 254.

A power in a will is never imperative. Anderson's Law Dict., p. 795.

When the uses created are imperative a power of sale conferred for their execution is equally imperative, if its exercise is necessary for their consummation. Doe *v.* Ladd, 77 Ala. 223.

A testator directed that his wife should have the homestead and two other tracts "to have the use of in the family until Julia and Clinton have their lands set off to them, then the other two lots during her natural life, then to be divided among the children as she directs." The wife took an estate for life with a discretionary power of appointment among her children. Russell *v.* Kennedy, 3 Brewst. (Pa.) 438.

3. Sugden Pow. (4th ed.) 357; Powell Pow. 160; Farwell Pow. 266, 267; 2 Story. Eq. Jur., § 1061; 1 Perry on Trusts, § 248; Fronty *v.* Fronty, 1 Bailey Eq. (S. Car.) 517.

A discretionary power to renew leases will be construed as imperative. 2 Perry on Trusts, § 532.

Where the executor was directed to sell the land of the testator "for the payment of debts if personal estate be insufficient," he must sell if the personalty was not sufficient to pay the debts, whether he deemed it expedient or not. Coleman *v.* McKinney, 3 J. J. Marsh. (Ky.) 246.

same rule applies at law to powers coupled with a trust, or which imply a trust. But equity holds these latter powers to be imperative, and will enforce their execution.[1]

The court of appeals of *Maryland* holds, where a testator gave his realty and personalty in equal shares to his children, and by a codicil authorized his executors to sell at discretion the whole or any part of the realty, the proceeds to be disposed of under the will, that, after distribution of the personalty has been made, the executors may exercise the power to sell the realty, it not appearing that it had been divided. Hoffman *v.* Hoffman, 66 Md. 568.

The same court, in a majority opinion, has decided that where the power of disposing of property by will is given to one who has no reversionary interest therein, a contract binding him to execute the power in a certain way cannot be enforced. From this view Alvey, J., dissented. Wilks *v.* Burns, 60 Md. 64.

A direction to an executor to dispose of the residue of the testator's estate for A's benefit, "or in such manner as he may think just and proper," requires him to exercise the power for A's benefit. Howell *v.* Tyler, 91 N. Car. 207.

A clause in a will declaring that "it is my further desire, out of the proceeds of my estate, leaving the same to the best judgment and discretion of said executors hereinafter mentioned, to pay" certain sums per month to the testator's mother and aunt, gives to the executors, or an administrator, with the will annexed, authority to determine how much shall be paid such beneficiaries. Allen *v.* Barnes, 5 Utah 100.

Executors were directed by will to divide the estate into eight equal shares, and invest the same separately, each of eight children to have the income of one share for life, the principal sum, upon the death of each child to go to his issue. The executors were also authorized to lease the land, and, after the death of testator's widow, to sell and convey it for such prices and upon such terms as they might deem best for the interests of the estate. It was held that the selection of a proper time for the execution of the trust was not within the discretion of the executors; that the direction to divide, invest, and sell operated an equitable conversion at the time of the death of the widow, and that the executors should on the happening of that event dispose of the land for the best prices possible. Hancox *v.* Meeker, 62 How. Pr. (N. Y.) 336.

A testator empowered his wife, "by her last will to make some provision or portion" to their adopted child, whom he "recommended to her good and generous heart." *Held*, that the execution of the power rested in the discretion of the wife; and that an appointment, by her, of two-thirds of the estate to the child was valid. Fronty *v.* Fronty, 1 Bailey Eq. (S. Car.) 517.

A testatrix gave to her executors power to sell certain lands, the power to be exercised within A's lifetime and with A's concurrence, and "on the death of A, or as soon afterwards as they (the executors) may think advisable . . . and within three years from the proof of this will" to convert the land into money. A lived more than three years after probate of the will. Twelve years afterwards the executors attempted to sell. It was held that they could do so, and that, as the purposes of the will required a sale the power was imperative, and was not lost by a failure to exercise it within the time specified. Mott *v.* Ackerman, 92 N. Y. 539.

When a statute confers a power upon a corporation to be exercised for the public good, the exercise of the power is imperative. Anderson's Law Dict. 795.

1. 2 Cruise Dig. (Greenl. ed.) *231, § 31; 1 Perry on Trusts, § 248; 2 Sto. Eq. Jur., § 1061; Rapalje & Lawr. Law Dict; Barnum *v.* Barnum, 26 Md. 119; Smith *v.* Kearney, 2 Barb. Ch. (N. Y.) 533.

In Attorney Genl. *v.* Downing, Wilm. 23, Lord Ch. Justice Wilmot says that powers are never imperative; they leave the acts to be done at the will of the party to whom they are given; but that trusts are always imperative, and are obligatory upon the conscience of the party intrusted. See also Crabb Real Prop. 678, § 1959.

Mr. Washburn says that every power given in a will is considered in a court of chancery as a trust for the benefit of the person for whose use it is created, and as a devise or bequest to that person. 2 Washb. Real Prop. *323. The authority cited is that of Hunt *v.* Rousmanier. But in that case when heard at circuit Mr. Justice Story does not announce any such doctrine (2 Mason (U. S.) 244). When the case came to the Supreme Court, Chief Justice Marshall does use such language as that given by Mr. Washburn. But the context shows that he did not intend to assert the doctrine that all powers are treated in equity as trusts in the sense that they are all imperative, though the language standing alone might seem to convey that idea. Hunt *v.* Rousmanier, 8 Wheat. (U. S.) 207. Most of the authorities and text writers, while recognizing the imperative nature of such powers, still do not treat them as pure trusts, but class them as powers in the nature of trusts.

Thus Mr. Greenleaf, in his addition to chapter 18, of title 32 of volume 4, of Cruise's Digest, says: "But where the power is in the nature of a trust, which it is the duty of the donee to execute, he is considered by a court of equity as a trustee for the exercise of it; and it will not permit his negligence, accident or other circumstances, to disappoint the interests of those for whose benefit he is called upon to execute." 4 Cruise Dig. *231, § 31. See also Gibbs *v.* Marsh, 2 Met. (Mass.) 243.

Mr. Perry says: "Mere powers are purely discretionary with the donee: he may or may not execute them at his sole will and pleasure, and no court can compel or control his discretion or exercise it in his stead and place, if for any reason he leaves the powers unexecuted. . . . It is different with powers coupled with a trust, or powers which imply a trust. In this class of cases the power is so given that it is considered a trust for the benefit of other parties; and when the form of the gift is such that it can be construed to be a trust, the power becomes imperative, and must be executed. . . . Courts will not allow a trust to fail or be defeated by the refusal or neglect of the trustee to execute a power, if such power is so given that it is reasonably certain that the donor intended that it should be exercised. There are mere powers and mere trusts. There are also powers which the party to whom they are given, is intrusted with and required to execute. Courts consider this last kind of power to partake so much of the character of a trust to be executed, that they will not allow it to fail by the failure of the donee to execute it, but will execute it in the place of the donee." 1 Perry on Trusts (3d ed.), § 248, and notes. See also Druid Park Heights Co. *v.* Oettinger, 53 Md. 46.

It is said by the Supreme Court of *Massachusetts*, Bigelow, J., delivering the opinion: "There is a clear and well-defined distinction between a mere power, where the act is left to the will of the party to whom it is given, and powers in the nature of trusts. In cases of the latter class, the rights and interests of third parties, who are beneficially interested in the trusts which arise and grow out of the execution or the power, come in, and can be enforced as against the party to whom the power is given. Greenough *v.* Weeles, of Cush. (Mass.) 571.

As stated by Lord Eldon in Brown *v.* Higgs, 8 Ves. Jr. 561, adopting the opinion of Lord Kenyon: "This was a power to distribute in such manner as the party thought fit; likewise a power to give that the court would not control. But it was also clear that if he did not give at all, the court would give for him to such descendants as at his death the court should hold entitled." After citing Harding *v.* Glyn (1 Atk. 469), he proceeds: "The principle of that cast and of Richardson *v.* Chapman (5 Bro. P. C. 400), which went to the House of Lords, and all those cases is that, if the power is a power which it is the duty of the party to execute, made his duty by the requisition of the will, put upon him as such by the testator who has given him an interest extensive enough to enable him to discharge it, he is a trustee for the exercise of the power, and not as having a discretion whether he will exercise it or not; and the court adopts the principle as to trusts, and will not permit his negligence, accident or other circumstances to disappoint the interests of those for whose benefit he is called upon to execute it."

In the case of a power coupled with a trust which the donee fails to execute, relief must be sought in equity. The chancellor will "compel the trustees, if living, to execute the power, because coupled with a trust, although it would not compel them to execute a mere naked power, not coupled with a trust. If the trustees should decline or refuse to act at all, the court would appoint other trustees, if necessary, to carry the trust into effect. And if the trustee should die without executing the power, it would hold the trust to survive, and would decree its due execution by a sale of the estate for the specified trust." 2 Sto. Eq. Jur., § 1061.

The rule is thus stated by Mr. Perry: "In all cases where parties have an imperative power or discretion given to them, and they die in the testator's lifetime, or decline the trust or office, or disagree as to the execution of it, or do not execute it before their death, or if from any other circumstance the exercise of the power by the party intrusted with it becomes impossible, the court will imply a trust, and will put itself in the place of the trustee, and will exercise the power by the most equitable rule . . . If the trust or power can by any possibility be exercised by the court, the non-execution by the party intrusted shall not prejudice the party beneficially interested, or the *cestui que trust*." 1 Perry on Trusts, § 249 and notes. See also §§ 251, 252 (and cases reviewed) and 257.

In a *Virginia* case, two vacant lots in the city of Richmond were conveyed to trustees in trust for N. and his wife L. and the survivor of them for life, and at the death of the survivor to be conveyed by the trustees to the children and grandchildren of N. and L., who should be living at the death of the survivor; and upon the further trust that if N. should think it expedient to sell the lots, or any part thereof, the trustees should permit him to do so, the proceeds of sale to be secured and held upon the same trusts. N. died without selling the lots, leaving his wife and several children surviving him. Upon a bill filed by N's widow, individually and as guardian of her children, against the trustees and the children, alleging that the interest of the children required a sale of the lots and the investment of the proceeds, and praying for such sale, the court decreed that the lots be sold. The court of appeals, speaking by its president, says:

"But, at all events, the power conferred on Dr. Norton was a trust power, to be exercised for the benefit, not only of himself, but of all others who were interested in the trusts of the deed; that is of his wife, children and grandchildren. Will a court of chancery suffer this most necessary power to die, merely because Dr. Norton has died? And died, too, almost as soon as the power was given; although the necessity for it might long survive, and has already survived more than a quarter of a century? Is it not a settled rule of that court that a trust shall never fail for the want of a trustee? But it is said that this power was discretionary in Dr. Norton, and now that he is gone cannot be exercised. Is not that too strict and literal a view, and does it not sacrifice substance to form? The trust is that the property shall be sold, if it shall become expedient. Now it is true that the framers of the trust referred the question of expediency to the opinion of Dr. Norton; and so long as he lived he was a safe depository of such a trust. But that was a mere means of accomplishing an end; and a court of chancery will not permit the end to be lost because the means marked out have been lost, but will devise other means to accomplish the end. The fact to be ascertained in order to exercise the power is, that it is expedient to make a sale. And that fact the court of chancery is as competent to ascertain as was Dr. Norton. There are many cases in which discretionary powers are also trust powers, which can and will be enforced by a court of chancery. And, although that court will never interfere with the exercise of a discretion which has been conferred by the author of a trust so long as it is fairly exercised, yet there are many cases in which the court will prevent its improper exercise, and will itself exercise it when the person on whom it is conferred refuses to do so, or is prevented by death or otherwise from doing so. The case in which a husband by his will gives property to his wife during her life in trust for the support of herself and her children, according to her discretion, is a familiar case of this kind . . . I, therefore, think that the deed in this case created a trust power of sale, which it was competent for the court of chancery, after the death of Dr. Norton, to execute." Faulkner *v.* Davis, 18 Gratt. (Va.) 651.

One of the authorities cited by the appellee in the foregoing case is that of Hewett *v.* Hewett, 2 Eden's Ch. 332. There a power was given by will to devisees for life, when in possession, to cut down timber, as four trustees, or the survivors or survivor of them should assign, allow of or direct. All four of the trustees were dead. Lord Chancellor Northington held that the court would execute the trust by referring it to a master to see what timber was fit to be cut down from time to time.

In Druid Park Heights Co. *v.* Oettinger, 53 Md. 46, the court by Irving, J, makes this distinction: "Where the discretionary powers are such as would not belong to the court because of its jurisdiction over the subject-matter of the trust, independent of the authority of the will, as, for instance, where the power is one to select the beneficiaries to enjoy the testator's bounty, the court will not exercise it, and under the rules of law cannot confer such a discretion on a trustee. In such case the court will execute it equitably by equal distribution among those named. [See *infra*, this title, *Execution of a Power—in Favor of Whom—Classes*, subhead 12, subd. (b.)]. But it is otherwise where anybody could properly exercise the discretion about the thing to be done, as, for instance, the felling of timber, etc. (Hill on Trustees 317; Ambler's Rep. 508). When the discretion applies to some ministerial act connected with the estate, such as felling timber, leasing or selling the land, such powers are much more under the control of courts than those depending on the exercise of opinion and judgment. (Perry on Trusts, 454 and cases there cited.)"

In Fordyce *v.* Bridges, 10 Beav. 90, the testator gave his personal estate to three trustees and executors, and directed them to lay it out in the purchase of estates in England or Scotland, the settlements in either case to be different. The trustees invested the bulk of the estate in Scotch lands and only a small part was invested in England. A bill was filed charging that the trusts had not been properly executed, that the trustees had invested a larger part of the estate in Scotland than they ought to have done, and asking the court to declare whether the Scotch estates had been properly purchased and to give directions that what remained uninvested should be used for the purchase of estates in England. Lord Langdale, M. R., declined to interfere, saying that "such a discretionary power as is given by this will is not a power which the court, in the absence or without the assistance of trustees, ought to take upon itself to exercise. I am inclined to think that (except by taking care that the persons whom the testator intended to give the discretion are duly appointed, and that what is done is done upon that discretion fairly exercised) the court ought not to interfere at all. The court itself has no means of ascertaining, in such a case, whether it is more or less in accordance with the will of the settlor, or with the interests of the parties entitled under his dispositions, that the discretion should be exercised in favor of English or Scotch estate. The discretion cannot be subject to a rule of equality or proportion of any sort between the estates. There seems to be no tangible principle upon which the exercise of such a discretion, in one way or other, can be justified or impugned. The testator has given the discretion to private hands, appointed by himself, or according to his own rule, and it seems more fit for the court to leave it in those hands."

Courts will not divest trustees of a power conferred upon them by will because of their non-residence, their poverty or their inability to agree in the settlement of their accounts. Nor can the court transfer the execution of the trust by requiring security for its execution, or by imposing a forfeiture of their estate as a penalty for not executing the bond required. The most the court can do is to compel them to execute the power, where it is imperative. Van Boskerck *v.* Herrick, 65 Barb. (N. Y.) 249.

Where a will directs that land be sold as soon as the executors think proper, a sale will be decreed at the instance of those interested after sixteen years, and upon proof that by a sale the income would be increased. Paschall's Estate, 14 Phila. (Pa.) 242.

The fact that there are difficulties and seeming impracticabilities in the way of the execution of these imperative powers by the court, will not prevent its interposition, nor the exercise of the power and the enforcement of the trust. 1 Perry on Trusts, § 249; *citing* Brown *v.* Higgs, 5 Ves. 505, and Faulkner *v.* Davis, 18 Gratt. (Va.) 651.

Where a power to sell for the benefit of legatees upon the death of the widow, is construed as an imperative power, the land is, in equity, to be considered as converted from the date of the widow's death, so as to give the legatees the same interest in the rents

Under the statute of *New York*, every trust power, unless its execution or non-execution is made expressly to depend on the will of the grantee, is imperative. A trust power does not cease to be imperative where the grantee has the right to select any, and to exclude others, of the designated objects.[1] If a discretionary power is exercised in good faith, and without fraud or collusion, courts will not review nor control the discretion.[2]

and profits, until the estate is actually sold as they would have had in the interest of the proceeds of the sale, if such sale had been made immediately upon the death of the widow. Smith *v.* Kearney, 2 Barb. Ch. (N. Y.) 533.

If the power is so uncertain as to its objects that a court of equity cannot say what particular person or persons or class of persons are to take an interest under it as a trust, or if the subject matter to be affected is too uncertain to be dealt with by a court, it will be considered a mere power, and a trust will not be implied. 1 Perry on Trusts, § 253.

So, too, in case there is an express limitation over in case the power is not executed. 1 Perry on Trusts, § 253.

Where property was bequeathed to A to be sold by him and the proceeds distributed among the testator's next of kin, as A should judge of their deserts, and A died without having made any appointment, the property became distributable as in case of intestacy. Frazier *v.* Frazier, 2 Leigh (Va.) 642.

A power given to an executor to sell any portion of the real estate when "absolutely necessary," refers to some pressing exigency of the estate growing out of deficiency of revenue to meet the demands upon it, and a sale should not be ordered, against the will of those entitled to two-thirds of the property, to swell the revenues, already sufficient for all demands. Moale *v.* Cutting, 59 Md. 510.

In *New York*, a trust and a power in trust may still exist together, notwithstanding the statute, where they are not inconsistent. Thus the same person may hold the estate in trust for one purpose, and at the same time be the grantee of a power in trust to be executed or take effect at some future day for another purpose. Belmont *v.* O'Brien, 12 N. Y. 394.

1. 4 *New York* Rev. Stat., §§ 96-7 (Banks' ed.), p. 2448; (1882), p. 2191; Delaney *v.* McCormack, 88 N. Y. 174; Farrar *v.* McCue, 89 N. Y. 139; Belmont *v.* O'Brien, 12 N. Y. 394; Allen *v.* DeWitt, 3 N. Y. 276; Hetzell *v.* Barber, 6 Hun (N. Y.) 534; 69 N. Y. 1; Mott *v.* Ackerman, 92 N. Y. 551; Coleman *v.* Beach, 97 N. Y. 558; Fellows *v.* Heermans, 4 Lans. (N. Y.) 230; 13 Abb. Pr., N. S. (N.Y.) 1; Hotchkiss *v.* Elting, 36 Barb. (N.Y.) 46; Selden *v.* Vermilyea, 1 Barb. (N. Y.) 62; Arnold *v.* Gilbert, 5 Barb. (N. Y.) 190; Crocheron *v.* Jaques, 3 Edw. Ch. (N. Y.) 207; Stewart *v.* Hamilton, 37 Hun (N. Y.) 22. See Prentice *v.* Janssen, 79 N. Y. 478.

Says Duer, J., in Dominick *v.* Sayre, 3 Sandf. (N. Y.) 561: "A power positive in its terms and limited in its execution to a particular class, is not only sufficient, but it seems to us conclusive evidence of the desire of the grantor that it shall be executed. The desire of its execution can be the only motive for its creation, and if the mere wishes of a testator are to be followed as a law, it is surely immaterial whether they are declared in terms or collected by a necessary implication." And the power was held in that case to be imperative.

A trust power, not expressly stating that its execution shall depend on the will of the grantee, is void if no beneficiary is named. Read *v.* Williams, 54 Hun (N. Y.) 636.

In equity the power will be considered as having been executed, and if the power be one of sale, the land will be regarded as converted into money from the time the sale was directed to be made. Moncrief *v.* Ross, 50 N. Y. 431. To same effect, Van Vechten *v.* Van Veghten, 8 Paige (N. Y.) 104.

Where a power comes within this statute, its immediate execution may be enforced by any of the beneficiaries, though the majority of the beneficiaries desire that its execution should be postponed. Van Boskerck *v.* Herrick, 65 Barb. (N. Y.) 249.

2. 2 Perry on Trusts, §§ 511, 532;

Doe v. Ladd, 77 Ala. 223; Bunner v. Storm, 1 Sandf. Ch. (N. Y.) 357; Fronty v. Fronty, 1 Bail. Eq. (S. Car.) 517.

In cases of mere powers, courts will always uphold the discretionary action of the donee, unless peculiar circumstances showing undue influence or want of fairness are proved. In a case arising in Massachusetts a testator gave the residuum of his estate to trustees in trust to pay the net income to his daughter for life, and on her death the principal to go to her issue; but if she left no issue, then one-half to one of the trustees and the remaining half to the heirs of the testator. Power was given to the trustees to change investments, including the realty, as they might deem most beneficial for the parties in interest, but recommended them to invest in real estate in Boston whenever a good opportunity offered. The residuary estate included a lot in Dorchester which the testator had purchased, worth from $15,000 to $20,000, but unimproved and not yielding income sufficient to pay the taxes and charges on the same. The land had risen in value, so that it could readily have been sold for $25,000, but was likely to continue to increase in value. The daughter, who was a widow and childless, requested the trustees to sell the lot. This they thought inexpedient, on the ground that she did not need any increased income; whereupon she brought an action to compel them to sell the lot. The court refused to interfere with the discretion of the trustees by ordering a sale, though she offered to pay a bonus of $2.000 over any price the land might bring, and notwithstanding the fact that one of the trustees had a contingent interest in the fund. Eldredge v. Heard, 106 Mass. 579.

A case in *Pennsylvania* involved the following facts. A testator gave to his executors power to sell real estate, and directed that they should invest the proceeds until the final division of testator's residuary estate, which was to be equally divided between the heirs of testator's daughter H, who might be living at the time of said division and M, son of J, testator's deceased daughter, each to share alike. The will provided: "I would rather prefer not to have a division made of my estate until the youngest child of H arrives at the age of twenty-one years." It then made provisions for advancements to be made to heirs who should wish to engage in business, and provided that if any of them, at the time of final division, should be incompetent, either in mind or body or from intemperance, to manage their estate, the executors should only pay them the interest on their shares. The executors declared their intention, and commenced to take the necessary steps to make distribution of the estate, but were restrained from doing so at the suit of M, the supreme court holding that the division should be into two equal parts, one of which should go to the heirs of H and one to M.

On this state of facts the court held that the expression of a preference by the testator that the final division be postponed until H's youngest child should be of age was merely precatory, and was addressed to the heirs, and not to the executors, who had no power to postpone peremptorily a final division; and that the application of the executors to make distribution exhausted their discretionary powers, if they had any, to determine the time of distribution. Osburn's Appeal, 130 Pa. St. 359.

It is held in *New York* that a devise of twenty acres of certain specified land, "or such other twenty acres of any land of which I may die seised as may be agreed upon between" the devisee and the executors, leaves it to the option of the executors to agree on other land; and where the land specified has been sold under a mortgage during the lifetime of the testatrix, the executors cannot be compelled to exercise the power. Weber v. Lester (Supreme Ct.), 10 N. Y. Supp. 258.

In Leonard v. American Bapt. H. M. Soc., 35 Hun (N. Y.) 290, it was held that, where a testator devised to his wife his estate for her life, with remainder over, appointed her executrix, and expressed the wish that so much of his real estate should be sold as was needful to furnish her with money to supply her wants, giving her power to carry out all the provisions of the will necessary to be performed during her life, she had power to sell, and that the court would not pass upon the question of the necessity for a sale.

But in Hovey v. Chisholm, 54 Hun (N. Y.) 328, the supreme court held that where executors were authorized to sell the real estate as "they shall deem most expedient, and for the best interest" of the residuary legatees, they cannot give a good title to one who knows that they have sufficient funds to meet all the legacies referred to in the power of sale.

In Brome *v.* Pembroke, 66 Md. 193, the court of appeals of ***Maryland*** did pass upon the necessity of the sale, and held it to be unauthorized, because it did not appear to be necessary for the payment of debts. The will in that case directed the executor, who was also appointed a trustee, to hold the property in trust till a certain time, and then divide it, but also authorized him to sell as much of it as might be necessary to pay the testator's debts. The Supreme Court of ***Connecticut*** has done likewise. There an estate was devised to one" to use and improve during his natural life, and if he should want for his support, to sell any part or the whole of it for his maintenance." It was held that the estate could not be sold except in case of actual necessity, and that the devisee was not the judge of the necessity. Hull *v.* Culver, 34 Conn. 403.

In Crozier *v.* Hoyt, decided by the Supreme Court of *Illinois*, the will contained the following provision: "I will that my wife have the entire control of my personal and real estate, of whatsoever kind or nature or wheresoever situated, after the payment of my debts, so long as she shall live, for her support and maintenance in such a manner as her situation in life requires." The remainder, after the termination of the life estate of the testator's wife, in certain real estate described, was given to Roberts, a son-in-law of the testator's wife, the clause so disposing of such remainder concluding thus: "In consideration that he take good care of my wife and treat her kindly, should she call on him to do so, and should she choose to live with him and her daughter—it being understood that he and his wife treat my wife as becomes a son and daughter." The succeeding clause gave certain described real estate to Crozier, the nephew of the testator, and then follows this provision: "All the rest of my estate, real and personal, after the termination of the life estate of my wife, I give to my heirs at law." . . . A further clause provided: "I hereby give to my wife full power to sell all my personal estate and all my real estate, except the lands willed to Crozier and Roberts, aforesaid, should it be necessary for her so to do for her maintenance and support—it being understood that she is not to waste any property; but I want to give her full power so as to support herself well. And should she choose to help her other daughter, if she should become a widow, or help her said daughter or her children, she has full power to do so before the heirs aforesaid take their remainders—hereby giving my wife full power to sell any of the property aforesaid and give good title to the same, either at public or private sale, using her own judgment as to which shall bring the greatest amount of money." The testator had neither children nor descendants of children. After his death his widow sold and conveyed all the real estate. Upon bill filed by the heirs at law of the testator to vacate such sale for the want of power to make it, it was held that the exercise of the power of sale and conveyance was entirely within the discretion of the widow of the testator, and, in the absence of fraud or collusion, was not subject to review or control by a court of equity. Nor was the power to sell and convey to be limited in its exercise by the necessity for the maintenance and support of the testator's widow—but the power was given for all the purposes mentioned—to "help her other daughter, if she should become a widow, or help her said daughter or her children," if she should choose to do so, as well as to provide for her own maintenance and support. The power to help her daughter was not to be considered as restricted to the proceeds of the life estate of the widow, but extended to the whole estate, or to such part of it as she might choose to devote to such purpose, excluding only the real estate specifically devised. Crozier *v.* Hoyt, 97 Ill. 23.

In *Tennessee* it is held that where land is conveyed to a trustee for the benefit of a husband and wife, with remainder to their children, and the trustees clothed with the power to sell and convey with the assent of the husband and wife, or the survivor of them, their discretion cannot be controlled in the absence of fraud, and the conveyance of the trustee, with the assent of the husband and wife, will defeat the remaindermen. Hamilton *v.* Mound City Mut. L. Ins. Co., 6 Lea (Tenn.) 402.

16. Statutory Powers.—Statutory powers can be constructively enlarged only in conformity with the principles governing legal construction, and because something is imported into the statute by a necessary or reasonable implication. The question is not whether the matter of implication will add to the efficiency of what is conferred in terms, but whether, without such matter, the statute will be wholly or in part inoperative.[1]

VI. Extinguishment, Suspension, and Merger.—1. In General.—As a general rule powers may be suspended or extinguished.[2] Powers appendant may be destroyed by release, bargain and sale, or feoffment; powers in gross, by feoffment or release; but powers simply collateral cannot be destroyed by the act of the person to whom they are given.[3]

1. State *v.* Charleston, 1 S. Car. 30. See Markham *v.* Howell, 33 Ga. 508; Paff *v.* Kinney, 1 Bradf. (N. Y.) 1; Peay *v.* Talbot, 39 Tex. 335.

Where a power created by statute has been fully executed, and something not authorized by the statute has been added, but which is clearly distinguishable from the rightful execution, the execution of the power is good so far as authorized by the statute, and void only as to the excess. Knox Co. *v.* Nichols, 14 Ohio St. 260; State *v.* Perryburg Board of Education, 35 Ohio St. 519.

Though an executor, instead of exercising in the manner prescribed by statute a power of sale of land conferred upon him by the will, negotiates the sale, and procures the deed to be executed by the heirs, and receives the proceeds, he may use such proceeds for the purposes specified in the will and required of him by law. Roberts *v.* Roberts, 71 Md. 1.

If the statutory power to two persons is joint, and they give joint security, an act performed by one, after the other has ceased to act, will not bind the sureties. State *v.* Boone, 44 Mo. 254.

While a court of equity may relieve against the defective execution of a power created by a party, it cannot do so when the power is created by law, nor can it dispense with any of the formalities required for its legal execution. McBryde *v.* Wilkinson, 29 Ala. 662; Mayor etc. of Baltimore *v.* Porter, 18 Md. 284; Smith *v.* Bowes, 38 Md. 463.

Compare First Nat. Bank *v.* Mount Tabor, 52 Vt. 87; 36 Am. Rep. 734.

Where there has been an execution of a statutory power, the record of the proceedings must show affirmatively that every formality has been complied with. Leak *v.* Richmond Co., 64 N. Car. 132.

2. 2 Chance, Powers 3102, 3136; Lampet's Case, 10 Rep. 408.

3. Wharton's Law Lexicon.

Where a power is released by the donee to the one having the freehold in possession, reversion or remainder, this operates to extinguish the power. Chance Powers 3137; Williams' Real Prop. *256; 2 Washb. Real Prop. *308.

Chancellor Kent states that a total alienation of the estate extinguishes the power whether appendant or in gross. Thus, if a tenant for life, with a power to grant leases in possession, conveys away the life estate, the power is gone, since its exercise would be derogatory to his own grant. 4 Kent's Comm. *347. But such is not the generally accepted doctrine as to powers in gross. 2 Washb. Real Prop. *309; Chance, Powers, § 3172, though it is true as to powers appendant. 2 Washb. Real Prop. *310.

If the donee of a power appendant grant a lease out of his interest, the power is so far suspended that it cannot be exercised until the expiration of the lease. 4 Kent's Comm. *346; 2 Washb. Real Prop. *310.

A total alienation of the estate operates as an extinguishment of a power appendant, where it cannot be exercised without defeating the interest granted. Thus, if a tenant for life with a power to grant leases in possession conveyed away his life estate, the power is gone. It is no longer possible for him to execute it, since the execution of the power would be in derogation of his own grant. 1 Sugd. Pow. *56.

Mr. Sugden lays down the following rules: 1. That a tenant for life with a power of leasing may exercise it, although he has conveyed away his whole life estate by way of mortgage or security, provided he has reserved to himself that right as against the incumbrancer. On this the cases are agreed. (See Wilson *v.* Troup, 2 Cow. (N. Y.) 195.) Some cases hold that he may exercise the power as against the incumbrancer, even though he has not reserved the right in his conveyance.

2. That a tenant for life with a power of sale and exchange may exercise it, (a) though he has created an interest out of his life estate (or reserved his reversion so as to remain tenant for life under the settlement), and though he has not reserved to himself any right to exercise the power as against the incumbrancer; but the incumbrancer is not affected thereby; (b) where he has parted with his whole life estate by way of mortgage or security, and though he has not reserved to himself the right to exercise the power as against the incumbrancer. 1 Sugd. Pow. *68.

Though the whole estate of the donee of the power is conveyed by him, yet, if it is by way of resettlement, and the prior uses are relimited, and the prior powers of sale and exchange saved and confirmed, these powers may still be exercised, though the present powers of sale and exchange are reserved by the new settlement to different persons. 1 Sugd. Pow. *75.

Sugden also says that an assignment of the whole estate or other alteration of the estate for life, does not affect a collateral power or a power in gross. 1 Sugd. Pow. *85.

So if the donee be tenant for years, and survive the years, still he may exercise his power, because the power does not fall within the compass of his estate, but takes effect out of an interest not vested in him. 1 Sugd. Pow. *85.

Thus, if a tenant for life assume to pass a fee by a bargain and sale, a covenant to stand seized, or a lease and release, the power will not be destroyed, for the reason that such conveyance passes only what the tenant for life might lawfully convey, to-wit: his life estate. Phitton's Case, cited in Hard. 412; Scrope *v.* Offley, 4 Bro. P. C. 237; Savile *v.* Blacket, 1 P. Wms. 777.

But if the tenant for life, with a power in gross, join in a settlement to new uses, though he is still made the tenant for life, his power is destroyed, where the contrary construction would enable him to defeat his own grant. Savile *v.* Blacket, 1 P. Wms. 777.

As powers in gross are independent of the donee, they are not suspended by a grant of a lease. 1 Sugd. Pow. *55; Edwards *v.* Slater, Hard. 413. In this case the lease was from the death of the tenant for life, and therefore did not arise out of the tenancy for life, but out of the first estate.

A present power not simply collateral may be extinguished by release to any one who has an estate of free-hold in the land in possession, reversion or remainder. 1 Sugd. Pow. *89.

The estates which were already defeasible or chargeable by the power are by such release made absolute. Albany's Case, 1 Rep. 110 b; Coke Litt. 265 b.

If a tenant for life with a power of revocation grant a lease, the rent charge, etc., to take effect out of his interest, he will not be permitted to defeat this interest. 1 Sugd. Pow. *48; Goodright *v.* Cator, Dougl. 460; Noell *v.* Henley, M. & Y. 302.

Compare Anonymous, Mo. 612; Billock *v.* Thorne, Mo. 615; Yelland *v.* Ficlis, Mo. 788; *sub. nom.* Yeoland *v.* Fettis, 1 R. Abr. 473 (K), pl. 3.

The power to consent to a sale where donee of the power is the life-tenant, is not necessarily extinguished by the absolute alienation by him of his life-estate. The rule is that, so long as nothing is done in derogation of the alienee's estate, the alienation has no effect on the power. Leggett *v.* Doremus, 25 N. J. Eq. 122.

The trustees of a settled estate had a power of sale, to be exercised at the request and direction of the tenant for life, who was also entitled to the ultimate reversion in fee. The life-tenant made an absolute conveyance of all his interest for value to A, and the trustees subsequently, at the request of the life-tenant, purported to exercise the power of sale by conveying the estate to A. *Held*, that the life-tenant's power to consent was not extinguished by the absolute alienation of his life-estate, and could still be exercised with the concurrence of the purchaser. Alexander *v.* Mills, 6 L. R. Ch. 124; 40 L. J. Ch. 73; 24 L. T., N. S. 206; 19 W. R. 310.

Where one has, under a will, a life-estate in land and a power to appoint by his own will, and the estate is to go to the heirs of the original testator in

2. Where a duty rests upon the donee to exercise the power,

default of the execution of the power, the life-tenant may release his power of appointment to the testator's heirs, or he and they can convey the land. Grosvenor *v.* Bowen, 15 R. I. 549.

Where lands are devised to the testator's wife for life, with remainder to his sons on her death intestate, and with power to her to appoint and designate by will the shares and proportions in which they shall take, under such safeguards, in trust or otherwise, as she may deem proper, a power in gross is created and the widow may release or extinguish the power of appointment by joining with the adult remaindermen in a bill asking a sale of the lands for partition. Thorington *v.* Thorington, 82 Ala. 489.

An undivided one-fourth interest in certain lots was devised to testator's wife for life, with power to appoint the remainder, and the other three-fourths to his three sons in fee. A certain legacy was made a charge on all the lands devised, and, for the purpose of raising money to pay it, the sons conveyed their interest to the life-tenant, who thereupon, by an instrument of doubtful efficiency, attempted to exercise the power by appointing to one of the sons, and then joined with him in executing a fee simple warranty deed, to a purchaser of the lots. These instruments were held to operate as a release of the power of appointment, and it was adjudged that the purchaser took a good title in fee. Atkinson *v.* Dowling (S. Car. 1890), 12 S. E. Rep. 93.

If a tenant for life, with power to grant leases in possession for twenty-one years at the best rent, mortgages his life-estate to trustees to pay an annuity for his life and the surplus to himself, the power is not thereby extinguished, but he may still grant a lease agreeably to the terms thereof. Roe *v.* Bulkeley, 1 Dougl. 292.

Where trustees under a will have during the lives of the life-tenants, power to work a quarry on the estate and are directed to work it and divide the profits among the persons entitled, a court cannot order a partition and sale as long as the power lasts. Taylor *v.* Grange, L. R., 13 Ch. Div. 223; L. R., 15 Ch. Div. 165.

Where a fund was settled upon the death of E for such descendants of X as E should by will appoint, upon default of appointment, the descendants of X living at the death of E would take in equal shares. *In re* Susanni, 26 W. R. 93.

An equitable power of appointment may be effectually released by the voluntary covenant not to exercise it, entered into by the donee of the power with the trustees of the fund which is subject to the power. Isaac *v.* Hughes, 39 L. J. Ch. 379; 22 L. T., N. S. 11.

Where the power is future and to arise by a contingent event, it may be defeasanced, and thereby annulled in whole or in part. 1 Sugd. Pow. *90.

Collateral powers cannot be destroyed or suspended by any act of the donee. Chance Powers, § 3105; 2 Washb. Real Prop. *308; 4 Kent Comm. *346; Wharton's Law Lexicon.

The donee of a collateral power cannot by any act whatever, either his own or that of any other person postpone or extinguish it. 1 Sugd. Pow. 45-46.

"It is a settled rule that where a life interest or other estate is given to the person who is authorized to devise or appoint the property, the person authorized to appoint can release and extinguish the power. This is called a power in gross. But where the power to appoint is given to one who has no estate or interest in the property to be distributed, which is called a power simply collateral, the person intrusted with the power cannot release or extinguish it, but may exercise it notwithstanding any agreement to the contrary." (*Citing* 4 Kent's Comm. 346; 1 Sugd. Powers, 80, 90, 93, 100; Smith *v.* Death, 5 Madd. 371; Albany's Case, 1 Rep. 111; West *v.* Berney, 1 R. & M. 431; Bickley *v.* Guest, 1 Russ. & M. 440; Horner *v.* Swann, 1 T. & R. 430; Hillyard *v.* Miller, 10 Pa. St. 326; Miles *v.* Knight, 12 Jur. 666.) Norris *v.* Thompson, 19 N. J. Eq. 307.

In Fontain *v.* Ravenel, 17 How. (U. S.) 369, where the testator directed that after the death of his wife his executor should apply the residue of his estate for the benefit of such charitable institutions as he should deem best, and the wife survived the executor, it was held that the executor took a mere naked power, to be exercised on conditions that never happened, and that the clause creating it was therefore void.

whether appendant or collateral, he cannot extinguish it by a release.[1]

3. **Where the purpose is accomplished** for which the power was given, or where it becomes impossible of execution, the power ceases.[2]

1. 2 Chance Powers 584, § 3121; Williams' Real Prop. *256; 2 Washb. Real Prop. *309.

2. Fontain *v.* Ravenel, 17 How. (U. S.) 369; Smith *v.* Taylor, 21 Ill. 296; Deveraux *v.* Dunn, 2 Ired. Eq. (N. Car.) 206; Ward *v.* Barrows, 2 Ohio St. 241.

Where, in a deed executing a power, there are words which show that the party has fully executed his power, or which amounts to a release of it, he cannot execute it further. Hervey *v.* Hervey, 2 Atk. 567.

Where a deed of land was made to the grantor's daughter for life, remainder to her children, or in case she should die without leaving children or their descendants, then to the grantor's heirs on the death of the daughter and her husband. And the deed further provided that, if she and her husband should ever sell the land, the purchase-money should be invested in other land, the title to which should be secured to the daughter in the same manner as was the title to the land originally conveyed, and a sale was made and other lands purchased, the power of sale was exhausted with the sale of the land originally granted, and did not extend to the lands purchased with the proceeds. Fritsch *v.* Klausing (Ky. 1890), 13 S. W. Rep. 241.

In a case arising in *New York*, land was devised to the executors with power of sale for the purpose of distributing the proceeds, one-third each to testatrix's brother and sister, and the income of the other third to another sister, A, while she remained the wife of her then husband. If she survived her husband, she was to take the *corpus* of the fund, and, if she did not, there was a void limitation over. Upon the resignation of the surviving executor, the supreme court appointed A as trustee, to whom testatrix's brother and other sister conveyed and transferred their contingent interest in the property. It was held that, as, in the event that A did not survive her husband, testatrix would die intestate as to such fund, or, in case the power of sale was not exercised by sale of the land during her life, the intestacy would be applicable to it, as it would go to testatrix's only heirs and next of kin, the brother and sister; and that, the brother and sister having conveyed their interest to A, she acquired the entire beneficial interest in the property, making the exercise of the power of sale unnecessary. Greenland *v.* Waddell, 116 N. Y. 234; 15 Am. St. Rep. 400.

A power to sell fails when its objects are unattainable. Sharpsteen *v.* Tillou, 3 Cow. (N. Y.) 651; Hetzell *v.* Barber, 69 N. Y. 1. And this is so, though the purpose is defeated by the voluntary act of the person for whose benefit the power was created, as happened in the case last cited. There land was devised, one-third to testatrix's husband in fee and one-third each to their two daughters, with power to the husband to sell and convey; and he deeded first his third and afterwards the whole. The last deed was held to be inoperative, since by deeding the one-third he had disabled himself from complying with the terms of the power. Hetzell *v.* Barber, 69 N. Y. 1. But the death of one of several for whose benefit the power is given, does not impair the power. Ely *v.* Dix, 118 Ill. 477.

Where property is devised to trustees in trust to convey the same to such person or persons as A shall appoint, and in case of his death, leaving his wife, without making such appointment, then according to the appointment of the wife of A, to defeat the power of appointment by the wife of A, there must have been an actual execution of the power by A in the form required by the power. Haslen *v.* Kean, 2 Murph. (N. Car.) 382.

If in the first instrument executing the original power, there is reserved a power of revocation and of new appointment, such instrument does not constitute a new settlement, destructive of the first; nor is the original power thereby exhausted and at an end, but upon the revocation of such instrument exists in full force. Saunders *v.* Evans, 8 H. L. Cas. 721; 7 Jur., N. S. 1292; 31 L. J. Ch. 233.

Where, in the body of a will, authority is given the executor to sell certain lands, and in codicils to the will the lands are given to different legatees from those first named, without revoking in express terms the authority to sell, that authority remains and must control, unless suspended or vacated for cause by the court. Anderson *v.* Butler, 31 S. Car. 183.

Testator bequeathed a portion of his estate to B, his son, who was insolvent. B's son, H, agreed with B, that if the latter would consent to the substitution of H as legatee, he would dispose of all the property, excepting a certain sum, as B should direct. Testator thereupon revoked said bequest and made a similar one in favor of H. After testator's death, B and H made another agreement, by which H conveyed a part of the property to D, to be held for the use of B. By the last agreement B was to control and dispose of a certain plantation so conveyed to D as he saw fit, but in case of his death without marriage, and further issue, D was to reconvey it to H. It was held that B's power of appointment was extinguished by the last agreement, and that he had no estate in the plantation subject to devise by him, but that on his death without further issue, H was entitled to a reconveyance. Hill *v.* Taylor, 81 Ga. 516.

A contract by a testator to sell land does not revoke a power to sell conferred upon his executors. Douglass *v.* Dickson, 11 Rich. (S. Car.) 417.

Where a trustee under a will is clothed with power to sell, a sale by him is not vacated by reason of the estate being subsequently declared insolvent. But the proceeds of the sale would go to the representative for distribution among the creditors. Hitchcock *v.* U. S. Bank, 7 Ala. 386. See Bentham *v.* Smith, 1 Cheves, Eq. (S. Car.) 33.

A power given to executors to sell land becomes inoperative when the estate is settled, or all claims against it barred by lapse of time, and no object of the testator remains to be attained. Ward *v.* Barrows, 2 Ohio St. 241. And if the power to sell is given for the purpose of paying legacies, it ceases when the legacies are all paid. Chamberlain *v.* Taylor, 36 Hun (N. Y.) 24; Hovey *v.* Chisholm, 56 Hun (N. Y.) 328; Swift's Appeal, 87 Pa. St. 502.

A testatrix devised her estate, both real and personal, to her four children in equal proportions, but no part of it was specifically devised. By a codicil to her will, the testatrix authorized her executors to sell the whole or any part of her real estate, in their discretion, the proceeds of sale or sales to be disposed of by them under the directions contained in the will. A part of the real estate was sold by the executors, but the purchaser declined to accept a deed therefor upon the ground that the executors could not give him a perfect title; that having finally settled the estate of their testatrix and made a final distribution in the orphans' court before the agreement to sell was entered into, they had no power to sell. *Held*, that the power of the executors to sell the real estate would not cease with the settlement of the personal estate, but would continue until the whole of the real estate was divided among the several devisees, either by the act of the parties or by legal proceedings. Hoffman *v.* Hoffman, 66 Md. 568.

A power by an executor to sell for payment of debts under order of court must be exercised within a reasonable time. Recaid *v.* Williams, 7 Wheat. (U. S.) 59; Jackson *v.* Jansen, 6 Johns. (N. Y.) 73; Sharpstee *v.* Tillou, 3 Cow. (N. Y.) 651.

A fund was settled for the husband for life, or until he should become an insolvent debtor, with the remainder to the wife for life, remainder to their children or issue, as the survivor should appoint, and in default of appointment, in trust for the children then living and the issue of deceased children. The husband's interest ceased by his insolvency, and his wife afterwards died. *Held*, that the interests of the children and their issue in default of appointment thereupon became vested, and could no longer be varied by the execution by the surviving husband of his power of appointment. Haswell *v.* Haswell, 2 DeG. F. & J. 456; 6 Jur., N. S. 1223; 3 L. J. Ch. 97.

If the power to sell is limited to a specified time, if not executed within that time it is forever gone. Lockett *v.* Hill, 1 Wood (U. S.) 552.

But it has recently been held in *New York* that a power given to an executor to sell real estate and divide the proceeds at any time within three years, remains in force even after the expiration of the period mentioned. Waldron *v.* Schlang, 47 Hun (N. Y.) 252.

A trustee was empowered to sell land at private sale before November 5th, or, if then unsold, to sell it at public sale on that day. He sold at public sale on November 5th, but the purchaser failed to comply with his bid. Instead of compelling him to take the title, the trustee advertised and sold again to another. It was held that the second sale was void; the first having exhausted the power. Simmons *v.* Baynard, 30 Fed. Rep. 532.

The power may also be limited to the lifetime or majority of the donor, the donee or the party to be benefited. Thus in Hubbard *v.* Gilbert, 25 Hun (N. Y.) 596, where A paid the consideration for land purchased of D, and procured the conveyance to be made to himself, to B, and to C, as joint tenants. B and C contemporaneously executed a sealed instrument agreeing to convey the land as A should appoint. A died without appointing. *Held*, that the fee in the land descended to his heirs. The same effect is Frazier *v.* Frazier, 2 Leigh (Va.) 642. There the testator bequeathed property to his brother, to be by him sold, and the proceeds distributed among the testator's next of kin, as the brother should judge of their deserts. The brother died without having made any appointment. It was held that the property bequeathed was distributable as in case of intestacy.

In a case decided by the Supreme Court of *Pennsylvania*, a testator gave to his wife the income of his personalty, and all his realty, for life. The executors, who were the wife and two of the devisees in remainder, were authorized at any time after his decease to convey any or all of the realty. The proceeds of all such sales were to be held for the purpose declared in relation to the realty, and all investments thereof, as well as of the personalty, were to be made in designated securities. Immediately after the wife's death, the whole of the real and personal estate, including the proceeds of all real estate sold by the executors in the wife's lifetime, were to be distributed as provided in the will. It was held (Judge Mitchell dissenting), that the power of sale could be exercised only in the lifetime of the wife. Wilkinson *v.* Buist, 124 Pa. St. 253; 10 Am. St. Rep. 580, and in a subsequent case, where the testator devised his estate to his widow for life, remainder to plaintiff and others, "and, lastly, if my executor, hereinafter mentioned, see proper to do so, the real estate may be sold by him, and the money accruing therefrom, together with all other moneys, is to be put out to interest, and the interest paid over to my wife every year," it was held by the same court, the same judge dissenting, that the power of sale thus conferred was limited to the lifetime of the widow. Fidler *v.* Lash, 125 Pa. St. 87.

A testator in *Oregon* gave the residue of his estate to his executor and trustee, "with full power to sell and convey any or all of said estate, and convert the same into money," in trust for the use and benefit of H, who was made sole legatee, the proceeds to be paid over to her. It was held the power of sale ceased on the death of H. Harmon *v.* Smith, 38 Fed. Rep. 462.

But in Millspaugh *v.* Van Zandt, 55 Hun (N. Y.) 463, the power was held to survive the death of the wife. The facts were as follows: A testator devised land in trust to his executors, to hold it "for the purposes of the trust herein declared for and during the natural life of my said wife, unless before that time the sum of $90 per acre can be realized therefor, or unless, before, that time, in the judgment of all my executors, . . . it shall be deemed to be for the best interest of my said wife and children that the same be sold at a less price," and in each case the executors were authorized to sell the land and make deeds thereto. The will further directed: "When the farm shall be sold as . . . provided, I direct my executors to convert all my estate into cash, and to divide the proceeds into such parts . . . as will give one share to my wife, if then living." It was held that the executors' title to the land, and power to sell the same, did not cease on the death of the wife.

A will provided that, when the testator's eldest son should become of age, there should be divided between the children "any balance which may remain of my estate after the payment of my debts, and the sale of so much of my estate as shall be sufficient, in the opinion of my executor to support and educate my children." It was held that the executor's authority to sell land to make provision for the support and education of the younger children did not terminate on the majority of the eldest son. Hallum *v.* Silliman (Tex. 1890), 14 S. W. Rep. 797.

The *New York* statute provides that when the purposes of a power are accomplished, the power is at an end.[1] A mortgage by a tenant for life having a power to make leases, or by a married woman by virtue of any beneficial power, does not extinguish or suspend the power, but the power is bound by the mortgage.[2]

4. Merger.—There is nothing incompatible in the co-existence in the same individual of an interest and a power, and the general rule is that there is no merger, even though the interest and the power are created by the same instrument.[3]

Where the power of sale is only to be exercised with the consent of the grantor, the death of the grantor before a sale is made extinguishes the power.. Kissam *v.* Dierkes, 49 N. Y. 602. So, too, where a discretion is lodged with the donee of the power. Thus in a case arising in *Tennessee* a testator authorized his executor by name to sell any of his real estate "if he may think it advisable for the interest and benefit of my children," and vest the proceeds, "or such part thereof as he may think right," in other real estate, for the joint benefit of the testator's wife and children, "the part coming to my wife to revert to my children at her death." It was held that the power was personal and discretionary in the executor named, and, on his refusing to qualify, could never be executed. Jones *v.* Fulghum, 3 Tenn. Ch. 193. And in Sites *v.* Eldredge, 45 N. J. Eq. 632, it was held that where a power of sale annexed to a devise of the fee was to be exercised at the discretion of the devisee, and without designating any particular object for which it should be exercised, it expires at the death of the devisee.

A testator directed his executor, who was his son, to pay his debts out of his property, real and personal, empowered him to sell his land, and directed him to divide the proceeds between his son and daughter, his only heirs. The son and daughter took possession of the land by tenants, and occupied it as tenants in common for nine years after their father's death. A creditor of the deceased laid by and took no proceedings to enforce his right during the same period, his debt being kept alive by payments by the son. At the end of this period a judgment creditor of the son caused execution to be levied upon his interest in the land, and the same brought to sale by the sheriff. After the sheriff's sale, and before delivery of the deed, the son and executor sold the land as executor and with the proceeds paid his father's creditor. It was held that the purchaser at sheriff's sale took a title superior to that of the purchaser at the executor's sale. Hackensack Sav. Bank *v.* Morse, 46 N. J. Eq. 161.

1. 4 *New York* Rev. Stat. (Banks' ed.), ch. 1, §§ 67, 102; pp. 2440, 2448; Hutchings *v.* Baldwin, 7 Bosw. (N. Y.) 241; Selden *v.* Vermilyea, 1 Barb. (N. Y.) 61.

Executors were directed and empowered by the testator to sell all the land of which he should die seised, at such time as they might deem best, and to invest the proceeds, together with the personalty belonging to the estate, and pay the income to his two daughters during their lives, and at the death of either, to pay her share of the principal to her children. It was held that the power of sale would cease, as to the moiety of a daughter dying, at the time of her decease. Harvey *v.* Brisbin, 50 Hun (N. Y.) 376.

2. 4 *New York* Rev. Stat. §§ 90–91 (Banks' ed.), p. 2447; (1882) p. 2190.

These sections, so far as they affect married women, refer only to beneficial powers. Marvin *v.* Smith, 56 Barb. (N. Y.) 600.

3. 2 Chance Powers 623, § 3230; Burleigh *v.* Clough, 52 N. H. 267; 13 Am. Rep. 23; Harrison *v.* Battle, 1 Dev. & B. Eq. (N. Car.) 213.

Where an estate is limited to such uses as A may appoint, and in default of appointment to himself in fee, the power is not merged in the fee. 1 Sugd. Pow. *105; 4 Kent Comm. *348; Sir Edward Clere's Case, 6 Rep. 176; Goodhill *v.* Brigham, 1 B. & P. 192; Cox *v.* Chamberlain, 4 Ves. Jr. 631; Tickner *v.* Tickner, 3 Atk. 742; Maundrell *v.* Maundrell, 10 Ves. Jr. 246. See 7 Ves. Jr. 567.

INDEX.

Lightning Source UK Ltd.
Milton Keynes UK
UKHW010342120219
337137UK00004B/193/P